HANYINGYEJINGONGYE CIDIAN

汉英冶金工业词典

明举新 主编
《汉英冶金工业词典》编审委员会 审定

A COMPREHENSIVE CHINESE-ENGLISH DICTIONARY OF METALLURGICAL INDUSTRY

中南大学出版社

HANYINGYEJINGONGYE CIDIAN

汉英冶金工业词典

邵象华 主编
《汉英冶金工业词典》编审委员会 审定

A COMPREHENSIVE
CHINESE-ENGLISH DICTIONARY OF
METALLURGICAL INDUSTRY

冶金工业出版社

《汉英冶金工业词典》编审委员会

总　顾　问：陈国达　王淀佐　黄培云
　　　　　　张寿荣
主 任 委 员：刘业翔
副主任委员：何继善　古德生　钟　掘
　　　　　　黄伯云　王定武　明举新
委　　　员：吴启常　张喆君　刁传仁
　　　　　　傅菊英　尹志民　高　阳
　　　　　　戴塔根　黄可龙　张永健
　　　　　　杨邦荣　黄尚安　刘石年
　　　　　　秦瑞卿

《汉英冶金工业词典》编审委员会

总 顾 问：褚国成 王致佳 黄学云
           米寿荣

主任委员：刘业琳

副主任委员：何维善 古德生 钟 祥

黄仰云 王实先 明学铎

委　　员：吴良紫 邱语春 丁怡之

           储汉英 代志月 高 明

           蒋繁柱 黄守武 张禾楠

           钱祖荣 黄尚安 刘己年

           秦淑卿

前　　言

随着我国改革开放日益深化，对外交往日渐频繁，冶金及相关行业广大科技人员、管理干部以及外贸工作者深切感到目前书橱中缺少一本有关冶金工业的汉英词典，给工作和学习带来诸多不便。为满足这一需求，编者经多年努力编成本词典。

本词典是我国第一部以冶金工业词汇为主的汉英词典，共收入词汇11万余条，涉及的专业主要包括钢铁冶炼、有色金属冶炼、金属压力加工、粉末冶金、半导体材料、烧结与球团、耐火材料、焦化、金相热处理、铸造、焊接、机械、电气、自动化、计算机、建筑、运输、环保、安全技术、劳动保护、企业经济与管理等。词条与英语释义的素材主要从冶金工业出版社出版的《英汉冶金工业词典》、上海交通大学出版社出版的《汉英大词典》等十余种词典中选取。此外，还从近年出版的专业书刊中收录了部分新出现的词汇。词条按汉语拼音顺序排列。书末列有"计量单位表"和"化学元素表"两个附录（中英文对照）。

本词典编审委员会由陈国达、王淀佐、黄培云、张寿荣、刘业翔、何继善、古德生、钟掘、黄伯云等九位中国科学院或中国工程院院士，王定武、吴启常、张喆君、明举新等教授级高工或高级工程师，以及中南大学部分教授、博士生导师组成。词典编审委员会的教授、专家分别审阅了词典初稿的有关内容并提出极其宝贵的修改意见。为此，中南大学出版社及本词典主编谨致衷心感谢！。

由于本书词典涉及的专业宽，词汇量大，疏漏与差错之处在所难免，恳请读者批评指正。

目 录

凡例 …………………………………………………………… (1)
汉字拼音查字表 ……………………………………………… (3)
汉字部首查字表 ……………………………………………… (14)
汉英冶金工业词典正文（附非汉字开头的词条）…………… (1)
附录一：计量单位表 ………………………………………… (1885)
附录二：化学元素表 ………………………………………… (1891)

目 录

凡例 ··· (1)
汉字拼音查字表 ·· (3)
汉字部首查字表 ·· (14)
冶炼稀金属工业词典正文（按非彼字汉头的顺序） ········ (1)
附录一：计量单位表 ··· (1885)
附录二：化学元素表 ··· (1891)

凡 例

一、词条

1. 词条印成黑体字，其他汉字为宋体。
2. 词条按汉字的拼音字母顺序排列。对于同音字，如位于国际区位码表 16～55 区内，按区位码的顺序排列；对多音字以及不在上述 16～55 区内的同音字，参考《现代汉语词典》的顺序排列。
3. 词条中不属于文字与数字的符号及括号 [ ] 内的文字与数字均不参加排序，西文字母、数字以及括号 ( ) 内的文字与数字参加排序。
4. 数字、西文字母与汉字比较排序时，数字在前，西文字母次之，然后是汉字。
5. 以西文字母或数字开头的词条，附于词典正文最后。

二、释义与例证

1. 一词条有多个英语释义时，释义之间用逗号分隔。
2. 例证用空心菱形号"◇"引出。例证中与词条相同的部分以波浪号"～"代替。一词条有多个例证时，例证之间用逗号分隔。
3. 例证多为复合词，带有例证的词条也可视为用检索这些复合词的中间关键词。例如，词条"超低碳不锈钢"既可以在以"超"字开头的词条序列中查到，也可以在词条"不锈钢"的例证中检索到。对于可能有几种首字的词条，尤其以未规范的译名开头的词条，这种检索方式可能更快捷。

三、符号说明

{ } 号表示化学式。

[ ] 号表示代替前面紧相邻的一或几个字,或表示化学式中的元素组。

( ) 号表示可省略的构词成分、附加说明、缩略语或其说明。

【 】号表示使用该词的专业,本词典的专业缩略语含义如下:

【地】:地质	【采】:采矿
【选】:选矿	【冶】:普通冶金
【团】:团矿、烧结	【铁】:炼铁
【钢】:炼钢	【连铸】:连续铸钢
【色】:有色冶金	【压】:压力加工
【粉】:粉末冶金	【半】:半导体材料
【金】:金相热处理	【焦】:焦化
【耐】:耐火材料	【机】:机械
【铸】:铸造	【焊】:焊接
【电】:电气、自动化	【计】:计算机
【建】:建筑	【环】:环境保护
【运】:运输	【企】:企业经济与管理
【数】:数学	【理】:物理
【化】:化学	

- 号为连字符,用于连接词组、组合词、化合物名称及其前面的符号。

— 号为范围号,用于连接数值范围的上下限;对含金成分,其质量分数中的"%"一律省略,仅标明其数值。

~ 表示代替词条本身。

* 号为星标,标注于例证号◇之后的部分复合词条上角,指明这些词条存在于本书其他部分,其页码可根据复合词或扩展词条的汉语拼音顺序查阅。

汉字拼音查字表

说　　明

1. 本表收录《汉英冶金工业词典》全部词条首字(不包括非汉字),汉字右边的数字指词典正文的页码。
2. 单字排列规则见本词典的《凡例》。

	A		ba	绑	33		ben	扁	58	驳	81
	a	扒	17	棒	33	苯	49	苄	59	薄	81
阿	1	八	17	磅	33	本	49	便	59		bu
锕	4	疤	17	蚌	34		beng	变	60	捕	82
	ai	巴	17	傍	34	崩	50	辫	63	补	82
埃	4	拔	19		bao	绷	50		biao	不	84
矮	6	靶	19	胞	34	泵	50	标	63	布	93
艾	6	把	19	包	34	迸	51	表	67	步	96
碍	7	钯	19	孢	36		bi		bie	坏	96
锿	7	坝	19	剥	36	比	51	别	73	部	97
爱	7		bai	薄	36	吡	53		bin		C
	an	白	20	保	38	笔	53	宾	73		ca
鞍	7	柏	22	饱	41	彼	53		bing	擦	98
氨	7	百	22	宝	42	碧	53	兵	73		cai
安	9	摆	22	抱	42	蓖	53	冰	73	裁	98
铵	11	拜	23	报	42	蔽	53	丙	73	材	98
按	11		ban	鲍	42	毕	53	病	74	财	98
暗	11	斑	23	刨	42	闭	54	并	74	采	99
岸	12	班	24	爆	43	铋	55		bo	彩	99
黯	12	搬	24		bei	滗	56	玻	75	菜	99
胺	12	扳	24	杯	44	必	56	拨	76		can
	ang	板	24	苝	44	箅	56	钵	77	参	99
		钣	27	北	44	壁	56	波	77	残	100
盎	12	拌	27	背	44	臂	56	剥	79		cang
	ao	伴	27	贝	44	避	56	博	79	舱	101
凹	12	瓣	27	钡	46		bian	勃	79	仓	101
鳌	13	半	27	倍	46	鞭	56	铂	79	藏	101
奥	13	办	33	备	46	边	56	箔	80		cao
澳	16		bang	焙	47	编	58	伯	80	操	101
	B	邦	33	被	49	贬	58	泊	81	糙	103

槽	103	**chen**		**chu**		**cou**		胆	223	碘	257
草	105	辰	130	初	154	辏	186	氮	223	点	258
ce		尘	130	出	157	**cu**		淡	224	典	262
侧	106	沉	130	雏	160	粗	186	弹	225	垫	262
测	107	陈	133	除	160	醋	189	蛋	225	电	262
ceng		衬	133	杵	163	簇	189	**dang**		淀	300
层	110	**cheng**		储	163	促	189	当	225	**diao**	
cha		撑	134	触	164	猝	189	挡	225	雕	300
插	111	称	134	处	165	**cui**		**dao**		掉	300
叉	112	城	134	**chuan**		摧	189	刀	226	吊	300
差	112	橙	134	川	165	催	189	捣	227	调	301
茶	114	成	135	氚	165	脆	190	倒	228	**die**	
查	114	乘	139	穿	165	萃	191	岛	229	跌	301
岔	114	程	139	传	167	淬	192	导	229	碟	301
chai		澄	140	船	169	翠	194	到	232	蝶	302
拆	114	承	140	喘	169	**cun**		道	232	迭	302
柴	114	秤	141	串	169	村	194	**de**		叠	302
chan		**chi**		**chuang**		存	194	德	233	**ding**	
觇	114	吃	141	窗	170	寸	195	得	234	丁	303
掺	114	持	141	床	171	**cuo**		**deng**		碇	303
缠	115	匙	142	创	171	搓	195	灯	234	钉	303
铲	115	池	142	**chui**		锉	195	登	235	顶	303
产	116	迟	142	吹	171	错	195	等	235	锭	306
闸	116	弛	142	捶	172	**D**		**di**		定	307
颤	116	齿	142	锤	172	**da**		堤	239	订	311
chang		尺	143	垂	173	搭	197	低	239	**diu**	
场	116	赤	144	**chun**		落	197	滴	248	丢	311
尝	117	翅	144	醇	174	达	197	迪	249	**dong**	
常	117	斥	144	唇	174	打	197	笛	249	东	311
长	118	炽	144	纯	174	大	199	狄	249	冬	311
偿	120	**chong**		**ci**		**dai**		涤	249	氡	311
肠	120	充	144	疵	175	呆	204	抵	249	动	311
厂	120	冲	146	磁	175	戴	204	底	249	冻	314
敞	120	春	149	雌	184	带	204	砥	252	洞	314
畅	121	虫	150	瓷	184	代	211	地	252	**dou**	
chao		重	150	刺	184	贷	212	蒂	254	抖	314
超	121	**chou**		次	184	袋	212	第	255	斗	314
潮	128	抽	151	**cong**		待	212	递	256	陡	314
che		酬	153	枞	185	**dan**		缔	256	豆	315
车	129	畴	153	葱	185	丹	212	碲	256	**du**	
扯	130	稠	154	从	185	单	212	**dian**		痘	315
掣	130	臭	154	丛	185	掸	223	巅	257	毒	315

独	315	垩	351	**fei**		浮	435	高	475	**gu**	
读	315	颚	351	菲	391	福	437	缟	500	箍	525
堵	315	鳄	351	非	392	弗	437	镐	500	估	526
杜	316	**en**		霏	398	辅	438	**ge**		孤	526
镀	317	蒽	351	鲱	398	俯	439	搁	501	鼓	526
度	320	恩	351	飞	398	釜	439	戈	501	古	528
渡	321	**er**		肥	399	腐	439	割	501	骨	528
duan		鲕	351	翡	400	副	441	革	502	谷	529
端	321	耳	351	废	400	覆	442	格	502	钴	529
短	321	铒	352	沸	405	赋	443	蛤	504	股	530
锻	323	二	352	费	405	复	443	隔	504	榖	530
断	326	**F**		**fen**		傅	447	镉	505	故	530
缎	328	**fa**		芬	406	腹	447	铬	506	固	530
煅	328	发	363	酚	406	负	447	个	508	雇	537
dui		筏	366	分	407	富	448	各	508	**gua**	
堆	329	伐	366	焚	417	附	450	**gei**		刮	537
兑	331	乏	366	粉	417	**G**		给	509	挂	538
对	331	阀	366	粪	422	**ga**		**gen**		**guai**	
dun		法	367	**feng**		伽	452	根	509	拐	538
墩	334	砝	368	丰	422	钆	452	跟	509	**guan**	
吨	334	珐	368	封	422	**gai**		**geng**		关	538
镦	334	**fan**		蜂	423	改	452	耕	509	官	538
顿	335	帆	368	峰	423	概	452	更	509	冠	538
钝	335	翻	368	锋	423	钙	452	庚	510	观	538
duo		矾	369	风	423	盖	454	**gong**		管	539
多	336	钒	370	冯	428	**gan**		工	510	罐	542
垛	347	繁	370	缝	428	干	454	攻	517	惯	543
躲	348	凡	370	**fo**		甘	459	功	517	灌	543
舵	348	反	370	佛	428	肝	459	供	518	贯	543
惰	348	返	379	**fu**		坩	459	公	519	**guang**	
E		范	380	夫	428	矸	460	弓	520	光	544
e		饭	380	呋	428	杆	460	觥	520	广	550
峨	350	泛	381	麸	428	感	460	汞	520	**gui**	
鹅	350	**fang**		敷	428	橄	462	拱	521	规	551
俄	350	芳	381	扶	428	**gang**		贡	522	硅	551
额	350	方	381	辐	428	冈	462	共	522	归	556
呃	350	房	383	幅	431	刚	462	**gou**		龟	556
恶	350	防	383	氟	431	钢	463	钩	525	轨	556
厄	350	仿	387	符	434	缸	474	沟	525	鬼	557
苊	351	访	387	伏	435	港	474	狗	525	癸	557
扼	351	纺	387	俘	435	杠	474	构	525	贵	557
轭	351	放	387	服	435	**gao**		购	525	**gun**	

辊	558	荷	597	花	615	货	660	荚	701	浇	732
滚	561	赫	598	华	616	**J**		贾	701	搅	734
棍	563	褐	598	滑	616	**ji**		甲	701	铰	736
guo		鹤	599	画	619	击	661	岬	702	矫	736
锅	563	**hei**		划	619	基	661	钾	702	脚	737
国	563	黑	599	化	619	机	664	假	703	角	737
过	565	**hen**		**huai**		矶	671	价	704	绞	739
H		痕	601	坏	623	奇	671	架	704	校	739
ha		**heng**		**huan**		唧	671	驾	705	醇	740
哈	573	哼	601	环	623	畸	671	**jian**		轿	740
铪	574	亨	601	还	627	积	671	监	705	较	740
蛤	574	珩	601	缓	629	箕	672	坚	706	**jie**	
hai		桁	601	换	630	激	672	尖	706	揭	740
海	574	横	601	幻	632	鸡	674	间	706	接	740
氦	577	衡	604	**huang**		吉	674	兼	709	阶	744
亥	577	恒	604	荒	632	极	674	检	709	截	745
han		**hong**		黄	632	棘	677	碱	711	节	745
韩	577	轰	606	磺	634	集	677	拣	715	杰	746
含	577	烘	606	簧	635	急	679	简	715	捷	746
焓	583	虹	606	**hui**		疾	680	剪	716	洁	746
涵	583	洪	607	灰	635	汲	680	减	718	结	746
函	583	宏	607	挥	636	即	680	鉴	720	解	751
焊	583	红	608	辉	637	级	680	贱	720	姐	752
汗	591	**hou**		徽	638	挤	680	见	720	界	752
汉	591	喉	610	恢	638	几	682	键	720	借	753
hang		厚	610	回	638	脊	683	箭	720	介	753
夯	591	后	611	毁	644	己	683	健	720	**jin**	
行	591	**hu**		惠	644	给	683	剑	720	筋	754
航	591	呼	612	会	644	技	684	渐	720	金	754
hao		葫	612	汇	644	季	685	溅	721	津	767
豪	592	胡	612	绘	645	剂	685	建	721	紧	767
毫	592	蝴	612	彗	645	寄	685	**jiang**		堇	768
好	592	糊	612	**hun**		计	686	僵	722	锦	768
耗	592	湖	613	浑	645	记	689	姜	722	进	768
号	592	弧	613	混	645	继	690	浆	722	禁	770
皓	592	虎	614	**huo**		纪	690	桨	722	近	771
he		琥	614	活	651	**jia**		奖	722	浸	771
核	592	护	614	火	655	夹	690	降	722	尽	775
和	593	互	615	钬	659	痂	692	**jiao**		**jing**	
合	593	户	615	获	659	家	692	焦	727	晶	775
盒	597	戽	615	或	659	镓	692	胶	727	腈	782
河	597	**hua**		霍	659	加	692	交	728	精	782

经	787	绝	802	课	834	阔	860	楞	874		lie
井	788		jun		ken		L	冷	874	列	920
警	788	均	805	肯	834		la		li	裂	920
颈	788	菌	807	坑	834	垃	861	厘	885	烈	922
劲	788	军	807		kong	拉	861	梨	885	劣	922
静	788	竣	807	空	834	喇	867	型	885		lin
镜	791		K	孔	842	蜡	867	离	885	林	922
径	791		ka	控	843	锨	867	理	890	磷	922
竞	791	喀	808		kou		lai	李	891	临	925
净	791	卡	808	口	846	莱	867	里	891	邻	927
	jiu		kai	扣	846	来	868	礼	891	鳞	928
纠	794	开	809		ku	铼	868	锂	891	檩	928
鸠	794	凯	814	枯	846	赖	868	粟	892	淋	928
九	794	铠	814	苦	846		lan	励	892	膦	928
酒	794		kan	库	846	蓝	868	砺	892		ling
救	794	刊	814	裤	847	栏	869	历	892	菱	928
旧	794	勘	814		kua	拦	869	利	892	零	929
臼	794	坎	814	夸	847	篮	869	例	892	龄	930
就	794	砍	815	跨	847	兰	869	立	893	铃	930
	ju	看	815		kuai	镧	869	粒	895	灵	930
居	794		kang	块	847	缆	869	沥	897	领	931
橘	794	康	815	快	848		lang	力	898		liu
菊	795	糠	815		kuan	朗	870		lian	溜	931
局	795	抗	815	宽	850	浪	870	联	899	榴	931
矩	796	钪	818		kuang		lao	连	900	硫	931
举	797		kao	筐	851	捞	870	镰	909	馏	937
聚	797	考	818	框	851	劳	870	帘	909	留	937
拒	799	拷	818	矿	852	牢	871	敛	909	刘	937
巨	799	烤	818		kui	老	871	链	909	流	938
距	799	靠	819	亏	856	酪	871	炼	911	铷	943
锯	799		ke	窥	856		le	练	913	六	944
剧	800	苛	819	奎	856	勒	871		liang	镏	945
	juan	柯	819	馈	856		lei	凉	913		long
涓	800	颗	819	溃	857	雷	871	梁	913	龙	945
镌	800	科	820		kun	镭	872	良	914	笼	946
卷	800	钶	822	昆	857	累	872	两	914	隆	946
绢	802	稞	822	醌	857	垒	872	量	916		lou
	jue	壳	822	捆	857	肋	872	晾	917	楼	946
蕨	802	可	822	困	857	类	873	亮	917	漏	946
掘	802	克	831		kuo	泪	873		liao		lu
决	802	刻	833	括	857		leng	钉	917	卢	947
诀	802	客	834	扩	857	棱	873	料	917	炉	947

卤	959	埋	986	**mi**		莫	1020	铌	1046	诺	1062
鲁	960	麦	987	醚	1006	墨	1021	拟	1047	**O**	
橹	960	迈	987	迷	1006	默	1021	腻	1047	**ou**	
露	960	脉	987	弥	1006	**mu**		逆	1047	欧	1063
路	961	**man**		眯	1006	模	1021	**nian**		偶	1063
录	961	满	989	米	1006	牡	1023	年	1048	藕	1063
陆	961	墁	989	觅	1007	母	1023	黏	1049	**P**	
lü		曼	989	泌	1007	苜	1024	碾	1052	**pa**	
吕	961	镘	990	蜜	1007	幕	1024	捻	1052	爬	1065
铝	961	慢	909	密	1007	木	1024	念	1052	耙	1065
履	967	漫	990	幂	1010	目	1025	廿	1052	帕	1065
缕	967	**mang**		**mian**		钼	1025	**niao**		拍	1066
氯	967	芒	991	棉	1010	穆	1027	鸟	1052	**pai**	
滤	971	盲	991	冕	1010	**N**		脲	1052	排	1066
绿	972	**mao**		免	1010	**na**		尿	1052	牌	1070
luan		猫	991	面	1010	拿	1028	**nie**		迫	1070
孪	973	锚	991	**miao**		镎	1028	捏	1052	派	1070
卵	973	毛	991	苗	1011	钠	1028	啮	1052	**pan**	
乱	973	铆	993	描	1011	纳	1028	镍	1053	攀	1070
lue		冒	993	瞄	1011	**nai**		镍	1053	潘	1070
掠	973	帽	994	**mie**		氖	1029	涅	1057	盘	1070
略	973	贸	994	灭	1011	耐	1029	**ning**		判	1072
lun		**mei**		**ming**		奈	1035	柠	1057	**pang**	
轮	973	玫	994	民	1011	萘	1035	凝	1057	旁	1072
伦	974	梅	994	皿	1011	**nan**		宁	1058	**pao**	
论	975	霉	995	敏	1011	南	1035	拧	1058	抛	1072
luo		煤	995	**min**		难	1035	**niu**		咆	1073
螺	975	媒	999	明	1012	**nang**		牛	1059	炮	1073
罗	979	楣	999	铭	1012	囊	1036	扭	1059	跑	1073
逻	980	镅	999	名	1012	**nao**		钮	1060	泡	1074
锣	980	镁	999	命	1012	挠	1036	纽	1060	**pei**	
裸	980	每	1001	**miu**		硇	1037	**nong**		胚	1074
落	980	美	1001	缪	1012	**nei**		浓	1060	培	1074
洛	981	**men**		**mo**		内	1037	农	1061	赔	1074
络	982	门	1003	蘑	1012	**nen**		**nu**		配	1075
M		闷	1004	模	1013	嫩	1041	努	1062	佩	1077
ma		焖	1004	膜	1015	**neng**		**nü**		**pen**	
麻	983	**meng**		磨	1018	能	1041	女	1062	喷	1077
玛	983	蒙	1004	摩	1018	**ni**		钕	1062	盆	1084
码	983	锰	1004	抹	1019	霓	1043	**nuan**		**peng**	
马	983	猛	1005	末	1020	泥	1043	暖	1062	彭	1084
mai		孟	1005	没	1020	尼	1045	**nuo**		棚	1084

硼	1084	pou		迁	1136	穹	1160	人	1199	赛	1226
膨	1085	剖	1108	签	1136	qiu		韧	1201	san	
碰	1086	pu		钳	1136	丘	1160	任	1201	三	1227
pi		铺	1108	前	1136	球	1160	认	1202	伞	1235
坯	1086	葡	1109	潜	1137	求	1164	刃	1202	散	1235
砒	1087	镤	1109	浅	1138	蚯	1164	ri		戬	1237
批	1087	普	1109	嵌	1138	qu		日	1202	sang	
披	1087	浦	1111	欠	1139	趋	1164	rong		桑	1237
劈	1087	谱	1111	茜	1139	蛆	1164	融	1203	sao	
噼	1087	蹼	1112	qiang		区	1164	熔	1203	骚	1237
毗	1087	曝	1112	枪	1139	曲	1165	溶	1211	扫	1237
疲	1087	瀑	1112	腔	1139	屈	1166	容	1214	se	
皮	1088	Q		墙	1139	驱	1167	绒	1215	瑟	1237
芘	1090	qi		蔷	1140	渠	1167	冗	1215	色	1238
铍	1090	期	1113	强	1140	取	1167	rou		艳	1238
苉	1090	七	1113	抢	1142	去	1168	揉	1215	sen	
匹	1090	漆	1113	羟	1142	quan		柔	1216	森	1238
pian		其	1113	qiao		圈	1170	肉	1216	sha	
偏	1090	棋	1113	敲	1143	权	1170	ru		砂	1238
片	1093	奇	1113	桥	1143	醛	1170	蠕	1216	杀	1240
piao		歧	1113	乔	1144	全	1170	铷	1217	刹	1240
飘	1094	畦	1113	鞘	1144	拳	1174	乳	1217	沙	1241
漂	1094	齐	1113	撬	1144	蜷	1174	入	1218	纱	1241
瓢	1094	旗	1114	翘	1144	犬	1174	ruan		shai	
pie		骑	1114	qie		que		软	1218	筛	1241
撇	1095	鳍	1114	切	1144	缺	1174	阮	1221	晒	1242
pin		起	1114	qing		炔	1175	rui		shan	
拼	1095	企	1117	侵	1148	确	1175	瑞	1221	山	1242
频	1095	启	1117	亲	1148	qun		锐	1221	删	1243
贫	1096	契	1118	琴	1148	裙	1175	run		珊	1243
品	1097	砌	1118	撤	1148	群	1175	润	1222	栅	1243
ping		器	1118	青	1148	R		ruo		钐	1243
苹	1097	气	1118	轻	1149	ran		弱	1223	闪	1243
平	1097	弃	1129	氢	1151	燃	1176	S		扇	1245
瓶	1105	汽	1129	倾	1155	染	1179	sa		缮	1245
评	1105	qia		清	1157	rao		撒	1225	嬗	1245
屏	1105	洽	1130	晴	1159	扰	1179	洒	1225	shang	
po		qian		氰	1159	绕	1179	萨	1225	伤	1245
坡	1106	牵	1130	情	1159	re		sai		商	1245
钷	1106	钎	1131	请	1160	热	1179	腮	1225	熵	1246
破	1106	铅	1131	qiong		ren		塞	1225	上	1246
珀	1108	千	1135	琼	1160	壬	1198	噻	1226	shao	

烧	1250	矢	1294	**shua**		**sui**		燧	1386	铁	1406
勺	1258	使	1294	刷	1317	随	1362	燧	1387	**ting**	
少	1258	始	1294	**shuai**		碎	1363	汤	1387	听	1416
she		示	1295	衰	1317	隧	1364	搪	1387	烃	1416
赊	1258	世	1295	甩	1318	遂	1365	膛	1387	廷	1416
蛇	1258	事	1296	**shuan**		燧	1365	唐	1387	停	1416
舌	1258	势	1296	闩	1318	**sun**		糖	1387	挺	1417
舍	1258	嗜	1296	**shuang**		损	1365	躺	1387	**tong**	
摄	1258	噬	1296	霜	1318	榫	1365	淌	1387	通	1418
射	1259	适	1296	双	1318	**suo**		烫	1387	酮	1420
社	1261	释	1297	**shui**		梭	1365	**tao**		同	1420
设	1261	饰	1297	水	1330	羧	1365	逃	1387	铜	1424
shen		市	1297	**shun**		缩	1366	淘	1387	桶	1430
砷	1262	室	1297	瞬	1344	索	1366	陶	1387	捅	1430
申	1263	视	1298	顺	1345	锁	1367	套	1388	筒	1430
伸	1263	试	1299	**shuo**		所	1368	**te**		统	1431
深	1264	铈	1302	说	1346	**T**		特	1389	**tou**	
神	1266	**shou**		**si**				铽	1393	投	1431
审	1266	收	1302	斯	1346	**ta**		**teng**		头	1432
肾	1266	手	1304	撕	1347	他	1369	滕	1393	透	1432
渗	1266	首	1306	私	1347	铊	1369	腾	1393	**tu**	
sheng		守	1306	司	1347	塌	1369	**ti**		凸	1434
声	1269	寿	1306	丝	1348	塔	1369	梯	1393	秃	1436
生	1270	售	1306	锶	1348	踏	1370	剔	1393	突	1436
升	1275	受	1306	死	1348	**tai**		踢	1393	图	1436
绳	1276	瘦	1308	四	1348	胎	1370	锑	1393	徒	1437
省	1277	**shu**		伺	1353	苔	1370	提	1394	涂	1437
盛	1277	枢	1308	似	1353	抬	1370	题	1396	土	1439
剩	1277	梳	1308	**song**		台	1370	体	1396	吐	1440
shi		殊	1308	松	1353	泰	1371	替	1397	钍	1440
失	1277	输	1308	送	1354	钛	1371	剃	1398	兔	1440
施	1278	叔	1310	宋	1355	酞	1373	**tian**		**tuan**	
湿	1279	舒	1310	**sou**		太	1373	天	1398	湍	1440
十	1282	疏	1311	搜	1355	**tan**		添	1399	团	1441
石	1284	书	1311	**su**		坍	1373	填	1400	**tui**	
拾	1289	熟	1311	苏	1355	摊	1373	**tiao**		推	1441
时	1290	鼠	1312	素	1355	弹	1373	挑	1401	腿	1443
食	1291	术	1312	速	1356	坦	1376	条	1402	蜕	1443
蚀	1292	树	1312	塑	1356	钽	1376	调	1402	褪	1443
实	1292	束	1313	**suan**		碳	1377	跳	1405	退	1443
识	1294	竖	1313	酸	1358	探	1385	**tie**		**tun**	
史	1294	数	1314	算	1362	炭	1386	贴	1406	吞	1445

		帷	1471	物	1503	弦	1529	写	1555	xue	
拖	1445	维	1471	误	1505	嫌	1529	卸	1555	削	1581
托	1445	苇	1472		X	显	1529	泄	1557	靴	1581
脱	1446	委	1472		xi	薛	1531	泻	1557	薛	1581
陀	1451	伟	1472	析	1506	现	1531	谢	1557	学	1581
驼	1451	伪	1472	西	1506	腺	1532	楔	1557	雪	1582
椭	1451	尾	1473	硒	1508	陷	1532		xin	血	1582
拓	1452	纬	1473	铈	1508	限	1532	芯	1557		xun
	W	未	1473	矽	1508	线	1533	锌	1558	熏	1582
	wa	胃	1476	吸	1508		xiang	辛	1561	循	1582
挖	1453	喂	1476	锡	1513	相	1536	新	1561	询	1583
蛙	1453	魏	1476	牺	1515	镶	1540	心	1562	寻	1584
瓦	1453	位	1476	稀	1515	香	1540	信	1562	驯	1584
	wai	卫	1479	希	1517	箱	1540		xing	巡	1584
歪	1454		wen	熄	1517	乡	1541	星	1564	逊	1584
外	1454	温	1479	烯	1517	详	1541	型	1564	迅	1584
	wan	文	1482	席	1517	想	1541	形	1567		Y
豌	1458	纹	1482	习	1517	响	1541	行	1568		ya
弯	1458	稳	1482	铣	1517	项	1541	性	1569	压	1585
剜	1460	紊	1483	洗	1518	橡	1541		xiong	鸭	1597
顽	1460		weng	徙	1520	像	1542	雄	1569	芽	1597
烷	1460	嗡	1483	系	1520	向	1542		xiu	牙	1597
完	1461	瓮	1483	隙	1521	象	1543	休	1569	雅	1597
碗	1462		wo	细	1521		xiao	修	1569	哑	1597
晚	1462	蜗	1483		xia	削	1543	锈	1570	亚	1597
万	1462	涡	1485	匣	1523	硝	1543	袖	1571	氩	1600
	wang	窝	1485	霞	1523	销	1544	溴	1571		yan
汪	1463	卧	1485	辖	1524	消	1545		xu	烟	1600
王	1463	握	1486	狭	1524	小	1547	需	1572	淹	1602
网	1463	肟	1486	瑕	1524	肖	1550	虚	1572	湮	1602
往	1464	沃	1486	下	1524	哮	1550	须	1572	盐	1602
望	1465		wu	夏	1527	啸	1550	徐	1572	严	1603
	wei	钨	1487		xian	效	1550	许	1572	檐	1603
威	1465	乌	1489	掀	1527		xie	蓄	1573	研	1603
微	1465	圬	1489	氙	1527	楔	1550	序	1574	岩	1605
危	1470	污	1489	先	1527	歇	1551	絮	1574	延	1605
煨	1470	屋	1490	仙	1527	蝎	1551		xuan	颜	1606
韦	1470	无	1491	鲜	1527	协	1551	悬	1574	沿	1606
违	1470	五	1502	纤	1527	携	1551	旋	1576	掩	1607
桅	1470	伍	1503	威	1529	斜	1552	玄	1580	眼	1607
围	1470	戊	1503	衔	1529	胁	1555	选	1580	衍	1607
唯	1471	雾	1503	闲	1529	谐	1555	眩	1581	演	1608

堰	1608	仪	1644	涌	1671	院	1705	择	1721	照	1738
燕	1608	已	1645	永	1671	**yue**		泽	1721	罩	1739
厌	1608	乙	1645	用	1672	约	1705	**zeng**		兆	1739
焰	1608	钇	1646	烟	1672	越	1706	增	1721	召	1739
验	1608	艺	1647	**you**		跃	1706	甑	1723	**zhe**	
赝	1608	抑	1647	优	1672	钥	1706	**zha**		遮	1739
yang		易	1647	尤	1674	月	1706	扎	1723	折	1740
杨	1608	逸	1649	铀	1674	阅	1706	渣	1724	辙	1741
扬	1609	疫	1649	油	1675	**yun**		轧	1726	锗	1741
羊	1609	意	1649	游	1678	云	1706	铡	1733	赭	1741
阳	1609	忆	1649	有	1679	匀	1707	闸	1733	褶	1741
氧	1613	溢	1649	铕	1685	陨	1707	栅	1734	柘	1741
仰	1623	译	1650	黝	1685	允	1707	炸	1734	蔗	1741
养	1623	异	1650	右	1685	运	1707	**zhai**		**zhen**	
样	1624	翼	1652	釉	1686	晕	1710	摘	1734	珍	1741
yao		**yin**		诱	1686	孕	1710	窄	1734	真	1741
腰	1624	茵	1652	**yu**		**Z**		债	1734	砧	1747
摇	1624	因	1652	迂	1686	**za**		**zhan**		针	1747
遥	1625	殷	1653	淤	1686	匝	1711	毡	1734	榛	1748
窑	1626	音	1653	于	1686	砸	1711	詹	1734	枕	1748
咬	1626	阴	1653	余	1686	杂	1711	粘	1734	诊	1748
杳	1626	铟	1656	逾	1686	**zai**		沾	1735	震	1748
药	1626	银	1656	鱼	1686	灾	1712	斩	1735	振	1749
要	1627	饮	1658	隅	1687	载	1712	辗	1735	镇	1751
ye		引	1658	雨	1687	再	1713	展	1735	阵	1752
耶	1627	隐	1660	与	1687	在	1716	栈	1735	**zheng**	
野	1627	印	1660	宇	1687	**zan**		占	1735	蒸	1752
冶	1627	**ying**		语	1687	暂	1717	战	1735	争	1756
页	1628	英	1660	羽	1687	錾	1717	**zhang**		整	1756
业	1628	鹰	1662	玉	1688	赞	1717	章	1735	正	1758
叶	1628	应	1662	愈	1688	**zang**		张	1735	政	1762
曳	1629	萤	1665	浴	1688	脏	1717	长	1737	挣	1762
夜	1629	营	1665	裕	1688	**zao**		掌	1737	帧	1762
液	1629	荧	1665	预	1688	凿	1717	涨	1737	证	1762
yi		赢	1666	阈	1693	藻	1717	帐	1737	**zhi**	
一	1637	盈	1666	**yuan**		早	1717	胀	1737	枝	1762
医	1641	影	1666	元	1693	噪	1718	障	1737	支	1763
铱	1641	硬	1666	原	1694	造	1718	**zhao**		知	1765
依	1641	映	1671	圆	1700	皂	1721	招	1737	脂	1765
伊	1642	**yong**		源	1704	灶	1721	爪	1737	之	1765
遗	1642	佣	1671	缘	1704	**ze**		找	1737	织	1765
移	1642	壅	1671	远	1704	责	1721	沼	1737	职	1765

直	1765	**zhong**		逐	1801	转	1816	浊	1831	租	1853
植	1772	中	1781	竹	1802	**zhuang**		**zi**		足	1853
执	1772	钟	1791	烛	1802	桩	1821	咨	1831	族	1853
值	1772	终	1792	煮	1802	装	1822	资	1831	阻	1853
指	1772	种	1793	主	1802	撞	1826	紫	1831	组	1854
止	1774	重	1793	柱	1805	状	1827	籽	1832	**zuan**	
只	1774	仲	1796	助	1806	**zhui**		子	1832	钻	1856
纸	1774	**zhou**		贮	1806	锥	1827	自	1832	**zui**	
致	1775	舟	1796	铸	1807	追	1829	字	1847	嘴	1857
置	1775	周	1796	筑	1813	缀	1829	**zong**		最	1857
制	1776	轴	1798	住	1813	**zhun**		棕	1848	**zuo**	
智	1779	肘	1800	注	1813	准	1829	踪	1848	左	1861
秩	1779	皱	1801	驻	1814	**zhuo**		综	1848	佐	1861
稚	1779	昼	1801	**zhua**		卓	1830	总	1849	做	1861
质	1779	骤	1801	抓	1814	琢	1830	纵	1851	作	1861
滞	1781	**zhu**		**zhuan**		啄	1830	**zou**		坐	1862
治	1781	珠	1801	专	1814	着	1830	走	1853	座	1862
蛭	1781	朱	1801	砖	1815	灼	1830	**zu**			

汉字部首查字表

说　明

本表收录《汉英冶金工业词典》全部词条首字(不包括非汉字),汉字右边的数字指词典正文的页码。

一部		丙	73	电	262	向	1542	习	1517	古	528
		平	1097	史	1294	后	611	乡	1541	考	818
一	1637	东	311	凹	12	兆	1739	尺	143	毕	53
丁	303	丝	1348	出	157	每	1001	巴	17	华	616
七	1113	亚	1597	曳	1629	兵	73	孔	842	协	1551
三	1227	再	1710	曲	1165	龟	556	书	1311	克	831
于	454	百	22	肉	1216	卵	973	司	1347	卓	1830
于	1686	夹	690	串	169	系	1520	民	1011	直	1765
上	1246	严	1600	非	392	垂	173	弗	437	南	1035
下	1524	求	1164	畅	121	质	1779	电	262	真	1741
万	1462	更	509	临	925	周	1796	发	363	索	1366
与	1687	束	1313			拜	23	尽	775	博	79
丰	422	两	914	丿部		重	150	乱	973	韩	577
开	809	来	868				1793	乳	1217	厂部	
井	788	表	67	九	794	复	443	承	140		
夫	428	事	1296	千	1135	乘	139	昼	1801	厂	120
天	1398	歪	1454	川	165	靠	819	癸	557	历	892
元	1693	面	1010	壬	1198					厄	350
无	1491	昼	1798	升	1275	、部		二部		压	1585
专	1814	棘	677	长	118					厌	1608
廿	1052	整	1753		1737	之	1765	二	352	励	892
五	1502	囊	1036	反	370	主	1802	干	454	厘	885
水	1330			乏	366	半	27	亏	856	厚	610
互	615	丨部		丹	212	头	1432	五	1502	原	1694
牙	1597			乌	1489	农	1061	井	788	赝	1608
未	1473	丰	422	生	1270	良	914	元	1693		
末	1020	中	1778	失	1277	举	797	无	1491	匚部	
击	661	内	1037	丘	1160			云	1706		
正	1758	北	44	甩	1318	乙(一				区	1164
甘	459	凸	1434	年	1048	乛乚)部		十部		匹	1090
世	1295	旧	794	朱	1801					巨	799
可	822	申	1263	丢	311	乙	1645	十	1282	匝	1711
		甲	701	乔	1144	飞	398	支	1763		

匚	1523	剧	800	伯	80	八(丷)部		拿	1028	衰	1317
医	1641	副	441	佣	1671			盒	597	高	475
卜部		剩	1277	低	239	八	17	舒	1310	离	885
		割	501	住	1813	分	407	勹部		旁	1072
上	1246	冂部		位	1476	公	519			亳	592
卡	808			伴	27	兰	869	勺	1258	商	1245
占	1735	冈	462	伺	1353	半	27	匀	1707	就	794
外	1454	内	1037	佛	428	只	1774	包	34	豪	592
卢	947	同	1420	供	518	并	74	儿部		赢	1666
卧	1485	网	1463	使	1294	关	538			冫部	
卓	1830	肉	1216	例	892	共	522	元	1693	习	1517
刂部		周	1796	侧	106	兑	331	允	1707	冯	428
		亻部		佩	1077	兵	73	光	544	冲	146
列	920			依	1641	卷	800	先	1527	冰	73
划	619	化	619	便	59	单	212	充	144	次	184
刚	462	代	211	修	1569	典	262	克	831	决	802
创	171	仙	1527	保	38	养	1623	兑	331	冻	314
刘	937	仪	1644	促	189	前	1136	几部		冷	874
别	73	他	1369	俄	350	首	1306			冶	1627
利	892	伟	1472	俘	435	真	1741	几	682	净	791
删	1243	传	167	信	1562	兼	709	凡	370	准	1829
刨	42	休	1569	侵	1148	黄	632	壳	822	凉	913
判	1072	伍	1502	债	1734	普	1109	秃	1436	减	718
刺	184	伏	435	借	753	人(入)部		凯	814	凝	1057
到	232	优	1672	值	1769			亠部		冖部	
制	1776	伐	366	倾	1155	人	1199				
刮	537	仲	1796	倒	228	入	1218	六	944	冗	1215
剎	1240	任	1201		231	个	508	市	1297	写	1555
剂	685	伤	1245	俯	439	介	753	玄	1580	军	807
刻	833	价	704	倍	46	从	185	交	728	冠	538
刷	1317	伦	974	健	720	仓	101	产	116	幂	1024
削	1543	仰	1623	做	1861	丛	185	亥	577	讠部	
	1581	仿	387	偿	120	全	1170	充	144		
剑	720	伪	1472	偶	1063	会	644	亨	601	计	686
前	1136	伊	1641	停	1416	合	593	弃	1129	订	311
剌	1398	似	1353	偏	1090	企	1117	伞	1235	认	1202
剐	1393	估	526	假	703	伞	1235	变	60	记	689
剖	1108	体	1396	傅	447	余	1686	夜	1629	许	1572
剜	1460	佐	1858	储	163	含	577	弯	1458	论	975
剥	36	伸	1263	催	189	舍	1258	亮	917	设	1261
	79	作	1861	像	1542	命	1012				
				僵	722						

汉字部首查字表

访	387	陈	133	分	407	双	1318	坎	814	艹部		
诀	802	阴	1853	召	1739	对	331	均	805			
证	1762	附	450	危	1470	发	363	坑	834	艺	1647	
评	1105	陀	1451	负	447	观	538	块	847	艾	6	
诊	1748	降	722	争	1753	取	1167	坩	459	节	745	
译	1650	限	1532	色	1238	叔	1310	坏	1086	芒	991	
试	1299	陡	314	龟	556	受	1306	坦	1376	莳	1472	
询	1583	陨	1707	免	1010	变	60	垃	861	芘	1090	
详	1541	除	160	初	154	难	1035	坡	1106	茜	1090	
语	1687	院	1705	象	1543	曼	989	型	1564	蘢	53	
误	1505	陶	1387	剪	716	叠	302	垩	351	苊	351	
诱	1686	陷	1532	赖	868	又部		城	134	芽	1597	
说	1346	随	1362	劈	1087			垫	262	花	615	
请	1160	隅	1687	力部		廴部		垛	347	芬	406	
诺	1062	隆	946			廷	1416	垒	872	苄	59	
读	315	隐	1660	力	898	延	1605	埋	986	芳	381	
课	834	隔	504	办	33	建	721	埃	4	芯	1557	
调	301	隙	1521	功	517	工部		堵	315	劳	870	
	1402	障	1737	夯	591			基	661	苏	1355	
谐	1555	隧	1364	加	692	工	510	堆	329	苦	846	
谢	1557	阝(在右)部		动	311	左	1861	培	1074	苯	49	
谱	1111			劣	922	功	517	塔	1369	苛	819	
卩(巳)部		邦	33	励	892	贡	522	堰	1608	苹	1097	
		邻	927	助	1806	汞	520	堤	239	苊	44	
卫	1479	耶	1627	努	1062	攻	517	填	1400	苜	1024	
印	1660	部	97	劲	788	项	1541	塌	1369	苗	1011	
仰	1623	凵部		势	1296	差	112	塑	1356	英	1660	
危	1470			勃	79	巯	1164	塞	1225	范	380	
即	680	击	661	勘	814	土部		墙	1139	苔	1370	
卸	1555	凸	1434	厶部				墁	989	茜	1139	
阝(在左)部		出	157			主	1439	墨	1021	莱	701	
		凹	12	允	1707	去	1168	墩	334	草	105	
队	331	画	619	去	1168	圬	1489	增	1721	茵	1652	
阵	1752	函	583	台	1370	在	1716	壅	1671	茶	114	
阳	1609	凿	1717	参	99	尘	130	壁	56	莱	1006	
阶	744	刀(勹)部		能	1041	地	252	士部		荒	632	
阴	1653			又部		场	116			荧	1665	
防	383	刀	226			坏	623	吉	674	药	1626	
陆	961	刃	1201	叉	112	坚	706	壳	822	莱	867	
阿	1	切	1144	支	1763	坝	19	声	1269	莫	1020	
				反	370	坐	1862	鼓	526	获	659	
						坍	1373			菱	928	

汉字部首查字表

董	768	夯	591	抛	1072	拼	1095	携	1551	口	846
蕊	1035	夸	847	投	1431	挖	1453	搬	24	古	528
菲	391	夹	690	抗	815	按	11	摇	1624	叶	1628
菌	807	尖	706	抖	314	挥	636	搪	1387	右	1685
菜	99	奈	1035	护	614	捞	870	摊	1373	可	822
菊	795	奇	671	扭	1059	捕	82	摧	189	号	592
萃	191		1113	把	19	振	1749	摘	1734	占	1735
萤	1665	契	1118	报	42	捏	1052	撒	1095	只	1774
营	1665	奎	856	拟	1047	捆	857	撕	1347	史	1294
萨	1225	奖	722	抹	1019	损	1365	撑	134	召	1739
萏	1164	美	1001	拓	1452	换	630	撬	1144	加	692
葫	612	牵	1130	拔	19	捣	227	撞	1826	台	1370
葡	1109	套	1388	拣	715	捅	1430	操	101	吉	674
葱	185	奥	13	抽	151	掩	1607	擦	98	吐	1440
蒂	254			拐	538	捷	746			吕	961
落	980	**九部**	拖	1445	排	1066	**寸部**	吊	300
蓝	868			拍	1066	掉	300			吃	141
幕	1024	尤	1674	拆	114	掴	172	寸	195	向	1542
蕙	351	**扌部**	抵	249	推	1441	对	331	后	611
蓖	53			抱	42	掀	1527	寻	1584	合	593
蓄	1573	扎	1723	拉	861	捻	1052	导	229	名	1012
蒙	1004	打	197	拦	869	撩	973	异	1650	各	508
蒸	1752	扒	17	捭	27	接	740	寿	1306	吸	1508
蔷	1140	扣	846	拧	1058	掸	223	封	422	味	428
蔗	1741	托	1445	招	1737	控	843	耐	1029	吞	1445
蕨	802	执	1732	披	1087	探	1385	射	1259	呆	204
薛	1581	扩	857	拨	76	择	1721	**小(⺌)部**	吨	334
薄	36	扫	1237	择	1721	揭	802			吡	53
	81	扬	1608	抬	1370	掺	114	小	1547	听	1416
藏	101	抉	428	挂	538	搭	197	少	1258	吹	171
藓	1531	技	684	持	141	提	1394	尘	130	启	1117
蘑	1012	扰	1179	拷	818	揭	740	尖	706	知	1765
藻	1717	扼	351	拱	521	揪	1148	光	544	和	593
廾部	拒	799	挠	1036	插	111	劣	922	呼	612
		找	1737	挡	225	搜	1355	当	225	咆	1073
异	1650	批	1087	挺	1417	搁	501	肖	1550	哑	1597
弃	1129	扯	130	括	857	搓	195	省	1277	咸	1529
大部	折	1740	拾	1289	搅	734	尝	117	品	1097
		抓	1814	挑	1401	握	1486	常	117	响	1541
		扳	24	指	1772	揉	1215	辉	637	哈	573
大	199	抢	1142	挣	1762	摄	1258	掌	1737	咬	1626
太	1373	抑	1647	挤	660	摆	22	**口部**	咨	1831

哮	1550	布	93	衔	1529	饭	380	阉	860	浊	1831
唇	174	市	1297	循	1582	饮	1658	氵部		洞	314
哼	601	吊	300	微	1465	饰	1297			测	107
唐	1387	帆	368	德	232	饱	41	汇	644	洗	1518
唧	671	帐	1737	衡	604	蚀	1292	汉	591	活	651
营	1665	希	1517	徽	638	馈	856	汗	591	派	1070
啄	1830	帕	1065	彡部		馏	937	污	1489	洽	1130
啃	1052	帘	909			亻部		汲	680	洛	981
唯	1471	带	204	形	1567			池	142	浑	645
售	1306	帧	1762	钐	1243	状	1827	汤	1387	浓	1060
商	1245	常	117	参	99	广部		汪	1463	津	767
啸	1550	帷	1471	须	1572			沥	897	浦	1111
喷	1077	幅	431	彩	99	广	550	沙	1241	酒	794
喇	867	帽	994	彭	1084	床	171	汽	1129	消	1545
喂	1476	幕	1024	影	1666	库	846	沃	1486	涅	1057
喘	169	山部		犭部		应	1662	泛	381	涓	800
喉	601					序	1574	沟	525	涡	1483
喀	808	山	1242	狄	249	底	249	没	1020	海	574
嗜	1296	冈	462	狗	525	庚	510	沉	130	涂	1437
噁	350	岔	114	独	315	废	400	浅	1138	浴	1688
嗡	1483	岛	229	狭	1524	度	320	法	367	浮	435
嘴	1857	岸	12	猫	991	席	1517	泄	1557	涤	249
器	1118	岩	1605	猝	189	座	1862	河	597	流	938
噪	1718	岬	702	猛	1005	唐	1387	沾	1735	润	1222
噎	1296	炭	1386	夕部		康	815	泪	873	浪	870
噻	1226	狭	1524			腐	439	油	1675	浸	771
嚼	1087	峰	423	名	1012	鹰	1662	泊	81	涨	1737
口部		骨	528	多	336	门部		沿	1606	涌	1671
		嵌	1138	罗	979			泡	1074	清	1157
四	1348	彳部		夂部		门	1003	注	1813	添	1399
因	1652					闩	1318	泻	1557	淋	928
团	1441	行	591	处	165	闪	1243	泌	1007	淹	1602
回	638	往	1464	冬	311	闭	54	泥	1043	渐	720
围	1470	彼	53	各	508	闲	1529	沸	405	渠	1167
困	857	径	791	条	1402	间	706	沼	1737	淌	1387
国	563	待	212	备	46	冈	1003	波	77	混	645
固	530	衍	1607	复	443	闸	1733	泽	1721	淘	1387
图	1436	徒	1437	夏	1527	阀	366	治	1781	液	1629
圆	1700	徐	1572	夂部		阅	1706	洁	746	淬	192
圈	1170	徙	1520			阑	1693	洪	607	淤	1686
巾部		得	234			阐	116	洒	1225	淡	224
								浇	732	淀	300

汉字部首查字表

深	1264	快	848	迈	987	归	556	弱	1223	纵	1851
涵	583	怅	1569	过	565	寻	1584	弹	225	纸	1774
渗	1266	恒	604	迁	1136	当	225		1373	纹	1482
港	474	恢	638	迅	1584	灵	930	强	1140	纺	387
滞	1781	情	1159	巡	1584	录	961	**女部**		纽	1060
湖	613	惯	543	进	768	彗	645			线	1533
渣	1724	惰	348	远	1704	**尸部**		女	1062	练	913
湮	1602	慢	990	违	1470			好	592	组	1854
湿	1279	**宀部**		运	1707	尺	143	姐	752	细	1521
温	1479			还	627	尼	1045	委	1472	织	1765
溃	857	宁	1058	连	900	尽	775	始	1294	终	1792
湍	1440	宇	1687	近	771	层	110	要	1627	经	787
溅	721	守	1306	返	379	尿	1052	威	1465	绑	33
滑	616	安	9	迟	142	尾	1473	姜	722	绒	1215
渡	321	字	1847	迪	249	局	795	媒	999	结	746
游	1678	完	1461	迭	302	居	794	嫌	1529	绕	1179
满	989	宋	1355	迫	1070	屈	1165	嫩	1041	绘	645
源	1704	宏	607	选	1580	屋	1490	嬗	1245	给	509
滤	971	牢	871	适	1296	昼	1801	**子部**			683
滗	56	灾	1712	追	1829	习	1517			络	982
溴	1571	宝	42	逃	1387	展	1735	子	1832	绝	802
溜	931	定	307	迸	51	履	967	孔	842	绞	739
滚	561	审	1266	送	1354	**己(巳)部**		孕	1710	统	1431
溢	1649	宫	538	迷	1006			存	194	绢	802
溶	1211	实	1292	逆	1047			孟	1005	继	690
漆	1113	室	1297	退	1443	己	683	孤	526	绳	1276
漂	1094	客	834	逊	1584	已	1645	孢	36	维	1471
漫	990	宽	850	速	1356	巴	17	学	1581	绷	50
滴	248	家	692	逐	1801	包	34	孪	1848	综	1848
演	1608	宾	73	造	1718	异	1650	李	793	绿	972
漏	946	寄	685	透	1432	导	228	**纟部**		绥	1829
潜	1137	密	1007	递	256	**弓部**				缆	869
潮	128	富	448	通	1418			纠	974	锻	328
澳	16	赛	1226	逻	980	弓	520	红	608	缓	629
潘	1070	塞	1225	逸	1649	引	1658	纤	1527	缔	256
澄	140	蜜	1007	遗	1642	弗	437	约	1705	缕	967
激	672	**辶部**		逾	1686	弛	142	级	680	编	58
瀑	1112			道	232	张	1735	纪	690	缘	1704
灌	543	边	56	遥	1625	弧	613	纬	1473	缝	428
忄部		迁	1686	遮	1739	弥	1006	纯	174	缟	500
		达	197	避	56	弦	1529	纱	1241	缠	115
忆	1649			**彐(彑)部**		弯	1458	纳	1028	缩	1366

缪	1012	琥	614	枞	185	检	709	歹部		咸	1529
缮	1245	琼	1160	采	98	梳	1308			威	1465
马部		斑	23	构	525	梯	1393	列	920	载	1712
		瑟	1237	松	1353	渠	1167	死	1348	栽	98
		瑞	1221	枪	1139	梁	913	残	100	截	745
马	983	瑕	1524	杰	746	桶	1430	殊	1308	戴	204
驯	1584	韦部		枕	1748	梭	1365	车部		比部	
驱	1167			标	63	棒	33				
驳	81			栈	1735	棱	873			比	51
驻	1814	韦	1470	枯	846	棋	1113	车	129	毕	53
驼	1451	韧	1201	柯	819	植	1772	轧	1726	毗	1087
驾	705	韩	577	柘	1741	森	1238	轨	556	瓦部	
验	1608	木部		查	114	棍	563	军	807		
骑	1114			相	1536	棘	677	转	1816	瓦	1453
骚	1237			柏	22	集	677	轭	351	瓮	1483
骤	1801	木	1024	栅	1243	棉	1010	斩	1735	瓷	184
幺部		本	49		1734	棚	1084	轮	973	瓶	1105
		未	1473	柱	1805	棕	1848	软	1218	甄	1723
		末	1020	亲	1148	椭	1451	轰	606	止部	
乡	1541	术	1312	栏	869	楔	1550	轴	1798		
幻	632	朱	1801	染	1179	楞	873	轻	1149		
王部		杀	1240	柠	1057	楼	946	晕	1710	止	1774
		机	664	架	704	概	452	轿	740	正	1758
王	1463	杂	1711	树	1312	楣	999	较	740	步	96
玉	1688	权	1170	柔	1216	榛	1748	辅	438	歧	1113
主	1802	杆	460	框	851	模	1013	辉	637	肯	834
全	1170	杠	474	橘	794		1021	辊	558	歪	1454
玛	983	杜	316	栗	892	榫	1365	辇	186	支部	
环	623	材	98	柴	114	榴	931	毂	530		
现	1531	村	194	桥	1143	榻	1557	辐	428		
玫	994	束	1313	桁	601	横	601	输	1308	敲	1143
珐	368	条	1402	桡	1470	槽	103	辖	1524	日部	
珀	1108	极	680	格	502	橡	1541	辙	1735		
珍	1741	床	171	桨	722	橄	462	辘	1741	日	1202
玻	75	杨	1608	桩	1821	橙	134	戈部		旧	794
珠	1801	李	891	校	739	檐	1603			早	1717
珩	601	林	922	核	592	檩	928	戈	501	焊	583
班	24	枝	1762	样	1624	犬部		戊	1503	时	1290
球	1160	杯	44	根	509			划	619	昆	857
理	890	枢	1308	桑	1237	犬	1174	成	135	明	1012
望	1465	杵	163	梨	885	状	1827	或	659	易	1647
琴	1148	析	1506	梅	994	臭	154	战	1735	显	1529
琢	1830	板	24								

映	1671	财	98	**手部**		故	530	月	1706	腿	1443
星	1564	责	1721			致	1775	有	1679	膜	1015
晒	1242	货	660	手	1304	效	1550	肋	871	腔	1387
晕	1710	质	1779	拜	23	救	794	肝	459	膝	1393
匙	142	贫	1096	拿	1028	敏	1011	肟	1486	膨	1085
晚	1462	贬	58	拳	1174	敛	909	肘	1800	膦	928
晴	1159	购	525	掌	1737	散	1235	肖	1550	臂	56
替	1397	贮	1806	掣	130	敞	120	肠	120		
量	916	贯	543	摩	1018	数	1314	肮	1221	**欠部**	
暂	1717	贱	720	攀	1070	敷	428	肯	834		
晶	775	贴	1406	**毛部**		整	1756	胀	1737	欠	1139
智	1779	贷	212			辙	1741	股	530	次	184
晾	917	贸	994	毛	991	镦	334	肥	399	欧	1063
普	1109	费	405	尾	1473			胁	1555	软	1218
暖	1062	贾	701	毡	1734	**片部**		服	435	歇	1551
暗	11	资	1831	毫	592			胡	612		
曝	1112	赊	1258			片	1093	胚	1074	**风部**	
日部		赋	443	**气部**		牌	1070	背	44		
		赔	1074					胆	223	风	423
曳	1629	赖	868	气	1118	**斤部**		胂	1266	飘	1094
冒	993	赛	1226	氖	1029			胃	1476		
曼	989	赞	1717	氡	1440	斤	144	胞	34	**殳部**	
冕	1010	**见部**		氩	1527	所	1368	脉	987		
黝	1685			氢	311	断	326	胎	1370	殷	1653
		见	720	氟	431	斯	1346	脊	683	毂	530
水(氺)部		观	538	氢	1151	新	1561	脆	190	毁	644
		规	551	氩	1600			脂	1765		
水	1330	觅	1007	氙	165	**爪(爫)部**		脏	1717	**文部**	
永	1671	视	1298	氨	577			胶	727		
求	1164	觇	114	氧	1613	爪	1737	朗	870	文	1482
汞	520	**牛(牜牛)部**		氤	7	采	98	胺	12	刘	937
录	961			氰	1159	觅	1007	能	1041	齐	1113
尿	1052			氮	223	受	1306	脚	737	紊	1483
泰	1371	牛	1059	氯	967	爬	1065	望	1465	斑	23
氽	50	牡	316			乳	1217	脱	1446		
浆	722	物	1503	**攵部**		舀	1626	脲	1052	**方部**	
滕	1393	牵	1130			爱	7	腻	1047		
贝部		特	1389	收	1302	彩	99	腰	1624	方	381
		牺	1515	攻	517			腮	1225	放	387
贝	44	犁	885	改	452	**父部**		腹	447	房	383
负	447	犟	819	放	387	釜	439	腺	1532	施	1278
贡	522			政	1762	**月(月)部**		腾	1393	族	1853
										旋	1576
										旗	1114

汉字部首查字表

火部		爆	43	必	56	砣	1747	相	1536	钅部	
		斗部		念	1052	砷	1262	省	1277		
火	655			急	679	砥	252	看	815	钇	1646
灭	1011	斗	314	总	1849	砾	892	眩	1581	钆	452
灰	635	戽	615	恶	350	破	1106	眼	1607	针	1747
灯	234	料	917	恩	351	硅	551	瞄	1011	钉	303
灶	1721	斜	1552	悬	1574	硒	1508	瞬	1344	钌	917
灼	1830			惠	644	硇	1037	田部		钍	1440
灾	1712	灬部		想	1541	硬	1666			钎	1131
灵	930			愈	1688	硝	1543	甲	701	钐	1243
炉	947	杰	746	意	1649	确	1175	申	1262	钒	370
炔	1175	点	258			硫	931	电	262	钬	1062
炭	1665	烈	922	母部		碍	7	备	46	钙	452
炼	911	热	1179			碘	257	毗	1087	钚	96
炽	144	煮	1802	母	1023	硼	1084	胃	1476	钛	1371
炭	1385	焦	723	每	1001	碰	1086	界	752	钝	335
炸	1734	蒸	1752	毒	315	碎	1363	留	937	钟	1791
烟	1672	照	1738	贯	543	碇	303	畦	1113	钡	45
炮	1073	熏	1582			碗	1462	略	973	钠	1028
烃	1416	熟	1311	示部		碧	53	畴	153	钢	463
烤	818	燕	1608			碟	301	累	872	钥	1706
烘	606			示	1295	碱	711	富	448	钣	27
烧	1250	户部		奈	1035	碳	1377	畸	671	钨	1487
烛	1802			禁	770	碲	256			钩	525
烟	1600	户	615			磁	175	罒部		钪	818
烫	1387	启	1117	石部		磅	33			钦	659
焊	583	所	1368			碾	1052	四	1348	钮	1060
烯	1517	房	383	石	1284	磺	634	罗	979	钳	1136
焙	582	戽	615	矶	671	磨	1015	置	1775	钴	529
焖	1004	扁	58	研	460	磷	922	皿部		钵	77
烷	1460	扇	1245	岩	1605	龙部				铜	822
焚	417	雇	537	砂	1508			皿	1011	锤	1106
焰	1608			矾	369	龙	945	孟	1005	钻	1856
焙	47	礻部		矿	852			盆	1084	钼	1025
煤	995			码	983	业部		盈	1666	钽	1376
煨	1470	礼	891	砑	1603			盐	1602	钾	702
煅	328	社	1261	砖	1815	业	1628	监	706	铀	1674
熄	1517	视	1298	砒	1087	凿	1717	盏	12	铁	1406
熔	1203	神	1266	砌	1118			盛	1277	铂	79
熵	1246	福	437	砂	1238	目部		盘	1070	铃	930
燃	1176			泵	50			盒	597	铅	1131
燧	1365	心部		砍	815	目	1025	盖	454	铆	993
		心	1562	砝	368	盲	991				
				砸	1711						

铈	1302	铜	4	矫	736	用	1672	穿	165	老	871
铊	1369	锗	1741	短	321	甩	1318	窄	1734	考	818
铋	55	错	195	矮	6	**鸟部**		容	1214	**耳部**	
铌	1046	锚	991	**禾部**				窑	1626		
铍	1090	锡	1513			鸟	1052	窝	1485	耳	351
铒	352	锣	980	利	892	鸠	794	窗	170	耶	1627
铕	1508	锤	172	秃	1436	鸡	674	窥	856	取	1167
铺	1685	锥	1827	私	1347	鸭	1597	**衤部**		职	1765
铝	961	锦	768	和	593	鹅	350			联	899
铜	1424	锭	306	委	1472	鹤	599	补	82	聚	797
铟	1656	键	720	季	685	鹰	1662	初	154	**臣部**	
铠	814	锯	799	种	1793	**疒部**		衬	133		
铡	1733	锰	1004	科	820			袖	1571	卧	1485
铣	1517	锶	1348	秤	141	疫	1649	被	49	**西(覀)部**	
铪	574	锻	323	乘	139	疤	17	裕	1688		
铭	1012	镀	317	租	1855	病	74	裤	847	西	1506
铬	506	镁	999	积	671	疾	680	裙	1175	要	1627
铯	1238	锢	999	秩	1779	痂	692	裸	980	栗	892
铰	736	锻	1053	稀	1515	疲	1087	褐	598	贾	701
铱	1641	镂	800	称	134	疵	175	褪	1443	覆	442
铲	115	镇	1751	移	1642	痕	601	褶	1741	**页部**	
铵	11	镉	505	程	139	痘	315	**疋(亚)部**			
银	1656	镍	1053	稞	822	瘦	1308			页	1628
铷	1217	镏	1028	稚	1779	**立部**		蛋	225	顶	303
铸	1807	镏	945	稠	154			疏	1311	项	1541
铺	1108	镓	692	稳	1482	立	893	**皮部**		顺	1345
铼	868	镗	1387	穆	1027	产	116			须	1572
铽	1393	馒	990	黏	1049	趋	1164	皮	1088	顽	1460
链	909	镜	791	**白部**		竖	1313	皱	1801	顿	335
销	1544	镁	1109			竞	791	**矛部**		预	1688
锁	1367	镨	960	白	20	章	1735			领	931
锂	891	镦	334	百	22	竣	807	柔	1216	颈	788
锅	563	镧	869	皂	1721	意	1649	**耒部**		频	1095
锆	500	镨	872	皓	592	端	321			颗	819
锈	1570	镰	909	**瓜部**		**穴部**		耕	509	题	1396
锇	350	镱	867					耗	592	颚	351
锉	195	镶	1540	瓢	1094	空	834	耙	1065	颜	1606
锋	423	**矢部**		瓣	27	帘	909	耦	1063	额	350
锌	1558			**用部**		穹	1160	**老部**		颤	116
锍	943	矢	1294			突	1436			**虍部**	
锐	1221	知	1765								
锑	1393	矩	796								

虎	614	竹	1802	舟	1796	糊	612	**赤部**		**里部**	
虚	1572	笔	53	舱	101	糙	103				
虫部		笼	946	航	591	糖	1387	赤	144	里	891
		笛	249	盘	1070	糠	815	赫	598	厘	885
		符	434	船	169	**艮(⻖)部**		赭	1741	重	150
虫	150	第	255	舵	348			**豆部**			1793
虹	606	筐	851	**衣部**		良	914			野	1627
蚌	34	等	235			即	680	豆	315	量	916
萤	1665	筑	1813	表	67	**羽部**		短	321	**足(⻊)部**	
蛇	1258	筛	1241	衰	1317			登	235		
蛋	225	筒	1430	袋	212	羽	1687	豌	1458	足	1853
蛙	1453	筏	366	截	745	翅	144	**西部**		距	799
蛭	1781	筋	754	裂	920	扇	1245			跃	1706
蛤	504	筌	1136	装	1822	翘	1144	酒	794	跌	301
	574	简	715	**羊(⺶⺷)部**		翡	400	配	1075	跑	1073
蜗	1483	箕	672			翠	194	酞	1373	跨	847
蜂	423	箍	525			翼	1652	酚	406	跳	1405
蜕	1443	算	1362	羊	1609	翻	368	酮	1420	路	961
蟋	1174	箅	56	差	112	**糸部**		酪	871	跟	509
蜡	867	箔	80	美	1001			酬	153	踢	1393
蜜	1007	管	539	养	1623	系	1520	醇	740	踏	1370
蝶	302	箱	1540	姜	722	素	1355	酸	1358	踪	1848
蝴	612	箭	720	着	1830	索	1366	醋	189	蹼	1112
蝎	1551	篮	869	盖	454	紧	767	醍	857	**身部**	
鳌	13	簧	635	羟	1142	紊	1483	醇	174		
融	1203	簇	189	群	1175	累	872	醛	1170	射	1259
螺	975	**臼部**		羧	1365	紫	1831	醚	1006	躲	348
蠕	1216			羰	1386	絮	1574	**辰部**		躺	1387
缶部		臼	794	**米部**		繁	370			**采部**	
		舀	1626			**麦部**		辰	130		
缸	474	春	149	米	1006			唇	174	釉	1686
缺	1174	**自部**		类	873	麦	987	**豕部**		释	1297
罐	542			籽	1832	麸	428			**谷部**	
舌部		自	1832	粉	417	**走部**		家	692		
		臭	154	料	917			象	1543	谷	529
舌	1258	**血部**		粘	1734	走	1853	豪	592	**角部**	
乱	973			粗	186	起	1114	**卤部**			
舍	1258	血	1582	粒	895	越	1706			角	737
舒	1310	**舟部**		粪	422	趋	1164	卤	959	觚	520
竹(⺮)部				粱	913	超	121				
				精	782						

触	164	基	661	露	960	金	754	靴	1581	音	1653
解	750	斯	1346	**齿部**		鉴	720	靶	19	章	1735
言部		期	1113			鏊	1717	鞍	7	**麻部**	
		雨(⻗)部		齿	142	**鱼部**		鞘	1144		
詹	1734			啮	1052			鞭	56	麻	983
警	788	雨	1687	龄	930	鱼	1686	**骨部**		摩	1018
辛部		雪	1582	**隹部**		鲁	960			磨	1015
		雷	871			鲍	42	骨	528	**黑部**	
辛	1561	零	929	难	1035	鲖	351	**鬼部**			
辫	63	雾	1503	售	1306	鲜	1527			黑	599
瓣	27	需	1572	集	677	鲱	398	鬼	557	墨	1021
青部		震	1748	雄	1569	鳄	351	魏	1476	默	1021
		霉	995	雅	1597	鳍	1114	**食部**		黝	1685
青	1148	霏	398	焦	723	鳞	928			黯	12
静	788	霓	1043	雇	537	**革部**		食	1291	**鼠部**	
其部		霍	659	雏	160			**音部**			
		霜	1318	雌	184	革	502			鼠	1312
其	1113	霞	1523	雕	300	勒	871				
		霰	1237	**金部**							

A a

阿贝尔极限深冲比与加工硬化指数关系曲线　Arber curve

阿贝尔试剂[侵蚀剂]　Abel's reagent

阿贝聚光镜　Abbe condenser

阿比恩双面包锡铅箔　Albion metal

阿比特法(湿法炼铜)　Arbiter process

阿博特钢轨接头　Abbott rail joint

阿布里科索夫模型　Abrikosov model

阿布劳斯镍铬锰耐蚀合金(88Ni,10Cr,2Mn)　abros

阿达尔铝合金(2Cu,1.5Fe,0.6Ni,余量Al)　Ardal

阿达迈特镍铬耐磨铸铁轧辊　adamite roll

阿达曼特耐磨铬钼钢　Adamant steel

阿达曼特锡基巴比合金　Adamant metal

阿达曼特锡基轴承合金(90Sn,7Sb,3Cu)　Adamant alloy

阿达普提熔模铸造法　Adapti investment casting process

阿德莫斯排溢铸造法　Admos die casting

阿德尼克海军黄铜(29Zn,1Sn,余量Cu)　Adnic

阿尔巴裂痕磁力探测[探伤]器　Alba crack detector

阿尔巴洛伊电解淀积用铜锡锌合金(光亮镀层)　Albaloy

阿尔巴特拉铜合金(60Cu,20Ni,20Zn,有时加入1—2Pb;家具用)　Albatra alloy

阿尔巴银钯合金　Alba alloy

阿尔邦杜尔双面复合纯铝超硬铝板(用作飞机构件)　Albondur

阿尔布拉克高强度铝黄铜(2Al,0.3Si,0.05As,19.15Zn,余量Cu)　Albrac

阿尔达尔铝合金(4Cu,0.5Mn,0.6Si,余量Al)　Aldal

阿尔达里铜合金　Aldary

阿尔德雷导线用铝合金(0.5—0.6Si,0.4Mg,0.3Fe,余量Al)　Aldrey

阿尔德雷高强度铝合金线　Aldrey wire

阿尔德雷铝镁硅合金[无铜硬铝](0.3—0.5Mg,0.4—0.7Si,0.3Fe,余量Al)　Aldray

阿尔迪科低合金高强度钢(≤0.15C,≤0.05S,0.25—1.3Cu,0—2Ni,0.5—1.25Cr,0.08—0.28Mo,余量Fe)　Aldecor

阿尔杜布拉铝黄铜(2Al,22Zn,余量Cu)　Aldurbra

阿尔杜尔铝锌镁合金　Aldur

阿尔杜拉尔包铝硬铝合金　Aldural alloy

阿尔法仪(用于测量拉丝模模孔锥角)【压】alfameter

阿尔费尔铁铝磁致伸缩合金(11—13Al,余量Fe)　Alfer

阿尔费留姆铝合金(2.5Cu,0.6Mg,0.5Mn,0.3Si,余量Al)　Alferium

阿尔费罗铁铝磁致伸缩合金　Alfero

阿尔芬二元铝合金(6—10Sn,余量Al)　Alfin alloy

阿尔芬法　Alfin process

阿尔芬尼德铜锌镍合金(60Cu,30Zn,10Ni)　Alfenide

阿尔芬诺尔铝铁合金(14—18Al,余量Fe)　Alfenol

阿尔芬诺尔铝铁合金粉　Alfenol flakes

阿尔芬(铁芯铝制件热浸镀铝铸型)法　Alfin process

阿尔贡三辊式冷轧管机　Argonne three-roll tube reducer

阿尔及尔锡锑系轴承合金(10Sb,0—0.3Cu,余量Sn)　Alg(i)er metal

阿尔卡克(铝及铝合金)表面防蚀化学处理法　Alkak method

阿尔科阿晶粒细化法(用于镁和镁合金)　Alcoa process

阿尔科阿炼铝烟气干式控制法　【环】Alcoa process

阿尔科阿耐蚀铝合金　Alcoa alloy

阿尔科铝基轴承合金(1—2Ba,0.5—1Ca,余量Al)　Alco metal

阿尔科马克斯铝镍钴铜型永磁合金(8Al,

14—15Ni,24Co,3Cu,余量 Fe) Alcomax alloy

阿尔克拉德纯铝覆面的硬铝合金 Alclad

阿尔克雷斯铁铬铝电阻合金（5—10Al,20Cr,70—75Fe） Alcres(s)

阿尔克罗姆铁铬铝电阻合金（5Al,15.5Cr,79.5Fe） Alchrome

阿尔克罗塔尔电阻合金（14Cr,4.5Al,余量 Fe） Alchrotal

阿尔雷铁铬镍耐热合金（Alray D：35Cr,15Ni,余量 Fe） Alray

阿尔马西林铝镁硅合金（1Mg,2Si,余量 Al） Almasilium

阿尔梅莱克铝基合金（0.7Mg,0.5Si,余量 Al） Almelec

阿尔米纳尔铝硅系耐蚀合金 Alminal

阿尔米特铝焊药[料]（4—4.3Al,4.8—5Cu,<0.6杂质,余量 Zn） Almit

阿尔内昂铝锌铜合金（7—22Zn,2—3Cu,0.5—1Fe+Si 及其他元素,余量 Al） Alneon

阿尔尼可烧结铝镍钴磁铁 Alnico sintered magnet

阿尔尼科铁镍铝钴系永磁合金（12Al,17—28Ni,5Co,3—6Cu,余量 Fe） Alnico,aluminium nickel cobalt,Alnico permanent magnet alloy

阿尔尼克铝镍铁沉淀硬化型永磁合金（25Ni,12Al,余量 Fe） Alnic alloy

阿尔尼铝镍磁铁 Alni magnet

阿尔尼铁镍铝永磁合金（51Fe,32Ni,13Al,4Cu） aluminium nickel (Alni)

阿尔尼西铁镍铝硅合金（52Fe,33Ni,14Al,1Si） Alnisi

阿尔帕卡锌白铜（同"德银"）

阿尔珀姆高导磁率铁铝合金（16Al,余量 Fe） Alperm

阿尔丘迈特金黄色铝青铜（8Al,0—2Fe,1Ni,余量 Cu） Alcumite

阿尔丘奈克耐蚀铝黄铜（16—27Zn,2Al,1Ni,余量 Cu） Alcunic

阿尔斯特罗姆锅炉 Ahlstrom boiler

阿尔瓦乙烯树脂 Alvar

阿尔西弗尔硅铁铝合金（20Al,40Si,40Fe） Alsifer

阿尔西隆耐热耐酸铝硅铸铁（9Al,1Si,余量 Fe） Alsiron

阿尔西明硅铁铝合金（15Al,45Si,余量 Fe） Alsimin

阿尔曾 305 铝铜锌合金（30—40Al,5—10Cu,余量 Zn） Alzen 305

阿尔扎克电解抛光法（铝质反射镜的） Alzak process

阿尔扎克铝制反射镜 Alzak aluminium

阿伐莱特铜铝合金（89.25Cu,9.25Al,0.4Sn,0.5Ni,0.6Fe） Availite

阿夫蒂特铁镍四元合金（66Fe,23Ni,5Cu,4W,余量为任意添加剂和杂质） Aphtit

阿盖佐依德铜镍锌焊剂合金（48.5Cu,31Zn,20.5Ni） Arguzoid alloy

阿戈－邦德易熔合金 Argo-Bond alloy

阿戈菲尔铜锰硅合金（0.25Mn,0.25Si,余量 Cu） Argofil alloy

阿戈－弗洛四元合金 Argo-Flo alloy

阿戈－斯维夫特四元合金 Argo-Swift alloy

阿格莱特银矿物型合金 Arguerite alloy

阿基米德原理 Archimedes principle

阿加索依德铜合金（55.5Cu,23Zn,13.5Ni,4Sn,3.5Pb,余量铁与杂质） Argasoid

阿科洛伊镍铬耐热合金（12—18Cr,36—68Ni,余量 Fe） Accoloy

阿科微型刀片（测定金属面漆膜黏附力用） 【钢】Arco microknife

阿克尔－德博尔碘化物热离解法 Arkel-de Boer process, de Boer and van Arkel process, Van Arkel(-de Boer) iodide process [method]

阿克尔电解槽（熔盐分解用） Acker cell

阿克隆铜硅合金（4Cu,1Si,95Al） Acron

阿克坦尼姆镍铬钴低膨胀合金（40Co,

20Cr,15.5Ni,15Fe,7Mo,2Mn,0.15C, 0.03Be) Actanium

阿库拉德高速精密压铸法 Acurad, accurate rapid dense

阿拉伯钢铁协会 Arab Iron and Steel Union (AISU)

阿拉伯树胶 Arabic gum, gum arabic

阿拉达尔铝硅共晶合金(约含 12Si) Aladar

阿拉德硅铝合金(12Si) Alader

阿拉尔代特环氧树脂 Araldite

阿拉尔铝硅铸造合金(4.5—6Si 或 10—13Si,余量 Al;有时加入少量 Cu 及 Zn) Alar

阿里龙耐蚀高硅铸铁 Ariron

阿利格尼高导磁率镍铁合金 Allegheny electric metal

阿列奈特碳化钨系列 Allenite

阿列纽斯活化[激活]能 Arrhenius energy

阿列纽斯蠕变(扩散)公式 Arrhenius equation

阿卢迪罗姆铁铬铝系电热丝 Aludirome

阿卢杜尔铝镁硅合金(0.8Mg,0.7—1.0Si,余量 Al;抗蚀性及导电性均良好,作导线用) Aludur

阿卢弗尔包铝钢板【压】alufer

阿卢弗莱克斯导电合金(0.75Mg,余量 Al) Aluflex

阿卢马尔铝锰合金(1.25Mn,余量 Al) Alumal

阿卢曼铝锰耐蚀合金(约含 1.5Mn) Aluman

阿卢梅尔镍铬热电偶合金(98Ni,2Cr) Alumel

阿卢梅尔镍合金(94Ni,2.5Mn,2Al,1Si,0.5Fe) Alumel

阿卢明锌铝合金 allumen

阿卢奈兹焊药[焊料](用于焊接铝及其合金)【焊】Alunize

阿卢西尔高硅耐热铝合金(20Si,余量 Al) Alusil

阿鲁邦德铝化学防蚀膜处理法 Alubond method

阿罗伊科镍铬系耐蚀合金 Aloyco (Aloyco 20: 19—21Cr, 28—30Ni, 4—4.5Cu, 2.5—3.0Mo, ≤ 1.5Si, 0.65—0.85Mn, <0.07C, 余量 Fe)

阿洛丁(磷酸－铬酸,铬酸－重铬酸盐)铝表面钝化处理法 Alodine process

阿马克斯公司死烧－鼓风炉熔炼法 A-MAX dead roast/blast furnace smelting

阿马洛格镍铬钨合金(刀具用) Amalog

阿马洛伊耐蚀合金(2.5Sn, 2Sb, 余量 Pb) Amaloy corrosion-resistant alloy

阿米多显影剂 amidol, 2,4-diaminophenol dihydrochloride

阿姆柯 48 软磁性合金(47—50Ni,余量 Fe) Armco 48 alloy

阿姆柯换热[蓄热]式均热炉 Armco soaking pit

阿姆柯软钢[纯铁] Armco steel

阿姆柯渗铝钢 Armco aluminized steel

阿姆柯铁(一种工业纯铁,总杂质量< 0.1%) Armco-iron, ingot iron

阿姆柯稳定化钢 Armco stabilized steel

阿姆柯直接还原法 Armco process

阿姆克龙含铬无氧铜合金 Amcrom chromium copper (alloy)

阿姆萨尔弗无氧铜(合金) Amsulf copper

阿姆斯科合成芳烃油溶剂 Amsco G

阿姆斯勒杯突试验 Amsler cupping test

阿姆斯铝青铜(8—12Al, 2—5Fe, 0.5—2Mn, 0.5—2Ni, 余量 Cu) Arms bronze

阿姆斯特朗(双金属轧制)法 Armstrong process

阿姆特尔含碲无氧铜(合金) Amtel tellurium copper

阿姆西尔银铜合金(热电传导用) Amsil silver copper

阿姆泽克锆铜合金 Amzir(i)c zirconium-copper alloy

阿姆泽克铜锆合金 Amzirc

阿尼恩斯铋铅锡易熔合金(30Pb, 20Sn,

50Bi；熔点92℃) Onions alloy

阿普拉特热镀锌法　Aplataer process

阿萨科连续铸造法（铜及铜合金的）　Asarco method

阿萨科-洛伊镉镍合金（1—1.5Ni，98.5Cd）　Asarco-Loy alloy

阿萨科耐蚀铅合金（0.06Cu，0.02Bi，余量Pb）　Asarco lead

阿萨科竖炉　Asarco furnace

阿塞尔轧管机[辗轧机]　Assel mill[elongator]

阿塞姆电阻炉　Arsem furnace

阿瑟无磁性耐热耐蚀钢（22Ni，8Cr，1.8Si，0.25Mn，0.25C，余量 Fe）　Atha's alloy

阿什贝利锡合金（14Sb，2Cu，1Zn，3Ni，余量 Sn）　Ashbury metal

阿氏土粒分组　Atterberg's scale

阿氏限度（土的特性湿度指标）　Atterberg limits

阿斯卡罗伊铬钼耐热钢（12Cr，0.4—1.0Mo，0.2—0.4V，0.6—1.0Mn，少量Nb）　Ascalloy

阿斯卡尼亚显微镜（测量极细拉丝模孔用）　Askania microscope

阿斯卡尼亚压力调节器　Askania regulator

阿斯科洛伊高温合金　Ascoloy

阿斯曼湿度计　Assmann psychrometer

阿斯曼吸引式温度计　Assmann's aspiration thermometer

阿斯特罗洛伊镍基超耐热合金　Astroloy

阿索丁四氯化碳　asordin

阿特巴斯镍铬钢（22Ni，8Cr，1.8Si，0.25Mn，0.25C，余量 Fe）　Atbas alloy

阿特拉斯可锻铝青铜（9Al，9Pb，余量 Cu）　atlas bronze

阿特赖特铜镍锌合金　aterite

阿维阿尔铝合金（0.5Si，2.5Cu，0.6Mg，1.0Ni，0.7Cr，余量 Al）　Avial

阿维昂纳尔铝合金（4Cu，0.5—1Mg，0.5—0.7Mn，0.3—0.7Si，余量 Al）　Avional

阿维奥尔铝合金（0.7Si，0.6Mg，余量 Al）　Aviol

阿维斯塔碳钢（0.7—1.2C，余量 Fe）　Avesta

阿西雷尔铝基合金（3—6Cu，0.1—1.4Fe，0—1.5Mn，0.5—0.9Mg，0—0.4Si）　acieral

阿兹贝尔-卡奈共振效应　【理】Azbel-Kaner resonance effect

锕　actinium Ac ◇ 放射性～*

锕 A {AcA，钋同位素^{215}Po}　actinium A

锕 B {AcB，铅同位素^{211}Pb}　actinium B

锕 C {AcC，铋同位素^{211}Bi}　actinium C

锕 C′{AcC′，钋同位素^{211}Po}　actinium C′

锕 C″{AcC″，铊同位素^{207}Tl}　actinium C″

锕 D {AcD，铅同位素^{207}Pb}　actinium D, actinium lead

锕 K {AcK，钫同位素^{223}Fr}　actinium K

锕 X {AcX，镭同位素^{223}Ra}　actinium X

锕后元素　transactinium element

锕铅　actinium lead

锕射气（氡的同位素）　An{^{219}Em} actinon

锕系[族]　actinium[actinide] series, actinium family

锕系后元素（同"超锕系元素"）

锕系金属　actinide (series) metal

锕系金属合金　actinide metal alloy

锕系金属屑　actinide metal swarf

锕系元素　actinides, actinide element ◇ 超～*，六价～ hexavalent actinide，三价～ trivalent actinide，四价～ tetravalent actinide

锕铀{AcU，铀的同位素^{235}U}　actinium-uranium, actinouranium AcU, uranium-actinium

埃贝巴赫微压痕硬度计　Eberbach

埃尔法尔电泳涂铝钢带　Elphal

埃尔哈特锌基轴承合金（11Cu，1Pb，0.2Sn，余量 Zn）　Ehrhard's metal

埃尔哈特制管法　Ehrhardt process, push bench process

埃尔吉洛伊非磁性合金（用作钟表弹簧；

40Co,20Cr,15Ni,7Mo,2Mn,0.04Be, 0.15C,余量 Fe) Elgiloy

埃尔卡洛伊铜合金焊条 Elkaloy

埃尔科洛依铁镍钴合金 Elcolloy

埃尔科奈特钨铜烧结合金(74.25W,余量 Cu) Elkonite

埃尔科涅特钨铜合金(焊条用) Elconite

埃尔科纽姆接点合金 Elkonium

埃尔韦莱特耐蚀铸铁 Elverite

埃尔沃太特硬钨合金(<30W) Elwotite

埃弗科-诺思拉普无芯高频感应炉 Efco-Northrup furnace

埃弗科-尤迪莱特光亮镀镍法 Efco-Udylite process

埃弗托尔形变硅青铜(3Si,1Mn,余量 Cu) wrought Everdur

埃格特比色管(用于钢含碳量分析) 【化】Eggert's tube

埃格特快速定碳法 【钢】Eggert's test

埃康诺梅特耐热耐蚀铁镍铬铸造合金 (8—10Cr,29—31Ni,余量 Fe) Economet

埃克利普斯压铸镁基合金(1.25Al,1Mn,余量 Mg) Eclipsalloy

埃克曼渗硅法 Eckman process

埃克诺莫渗碳易削钼钢 Economo (Economo 20: 0.18C,0.15Mo,0.8Mn,余量 Fe)

埃莱马加热电阻器(碳化硅电阻棒; 26.7C,63.9Si,4.8O,4.6 其他) Elema heating resistor

埃勒克斯板式电除尘器 Elex precipitator

埃勒因瓦恒弹性镍铁合金(33—35Ni, 53—61Fe,4—5Cr,1—3W,0.5—2Mn, 0.5—2Si,0.5—2C) Elinvar

埃勒因瓦效应 Elinvar effect

埃克赛尔铝阳极氧化处理 Elexal

埃克特龙 AZF 铸造铝镁合金(4Al,3Zn, 0.2—0.5Mn,0.3Si,余量 Mg) Electron AZF

埃克特龙 V−1 镁合金(10Al,0.3−0.5Mn,余量 Mg) Electron V−1

埃雷克特龙铝镁合金 Electron metal

埃雷克特龙镁合金 Electron

埃雷克特龙镁铝锌合金(<11Al,<4.5Zn,余量 Mg) Elektron alloy

埃雷克特鲁金银合金(40—50Au,余量 Ag) Electrum

埃里德特中间抛光液(电镀用) Eridite

埃里科尔可压锭模(模壁可向内挤压) 【钢】Erical mould

埃里克森(杯突深度)**值** Erichsen number

埃里克森(杯突)**试验** Erichsen (cupping) test,cup-drawing [cupping] test

埃里克森杯突[(钢板]深拉]试验机 Erichsen ductility machine

埃里克森深拉试验 Erichsen deep-drawing test

埃利阿奈特耐蚀高硅铁基合金 Elianite

埃利克型球团竖炉 【团】Eric vertical shaft furnace

埃洛纳反应(金氰化反应) Eloner's reaction

埃马莱特重载高级铸铁 Ermalite

埃马里特硬质合金 Elmarit

埃马塔尔铝表面钝化处理法 Ematal process

埃梅尔铸铁(德国低碳高硅珠光体高级铸铁; 2.3—2.8C, 2.1—2.7Si, 0.8—1.4Mn,0.09—0.15S,余量 Fe) Emmel (cast) iron

埃诺铬钼合金 Inor

埃庞热硬化性环氧树脂 Epon

埃皮科特热硬化性环氧树脂 Epikote

埃塞俄比亚假金(88Cu,11.5Zn,0.5 Au) Abyssinian gold

埃赛尔酸浸树脂交换法(低品位铀矿的) Exer process

埃索脆性温度 Esso brittle temperature

埃索−利特尔流态化床海绵铁生产法 【铁】Esso-Little process

埃索缺口冲击试验 Esso notch impact test

埃廷豪森效应 【理】Ettinghausen effect

埃瓦布赖特耐蚀铜镍合金（60—65Cu, 30Ni, 3—8Fe） Everbrite metal
埃瓦杜尔耐蚀硅青铜（95—97Cu, 3Si, 1Zn, Sn 或 Mn） Everdur copper
埃瓦尔德球 Ewald sphere
埃瓦尔德作图法 Ewald's construction
埃瓦黄铜管（冷凝器用） Ever-brass
埃瓦雷斯特铅基轴承合金（14—16Sb, 5—7Sn, 0.8—1.2Cu, 0.7—1.5Ni, 0.3—0.8As, 0.7—1.5Cd, 余量 Pb） Everest metal
矮(胖)高炉 low-shaft blast furnace, blast furnace with low shaft
矮炉身 short shaft
矮竖炉 short shaft, low-shaft furnace
艾昂尼尔锡青铜（49Cu, 49Sn, 2Hg） Ironier's bronze
艾比珀姆钠回收法 Abiperm process
艾伯蒂炉（从矿石中蒸馏汞用的连续反射炉） Alberti furnace
艾伯特（同向捻）钢丝绳 Albert lay wire rope
艾伯特德西双床电炉炼铁[炼钢]法【冶】Albert de Sy process
艾布拉姆森七辊矫直机（用于管材）【压】seven-roll Abramsen machine
艾布拉姆森式管材矫直机 Abramsen machine
艾布拉姆森式五辊（管材）矫直机 five roll Abramsen machine
艾布拉姆森式斜辊(管棒)矫直机【压】Abramsen straightener
艾布拉姆逊码【计】Abramson code
艾德林熔模铝热离心浇铸法 Adeline steelmaking process
艾德万斯康铜（56—60Cu, 余量 Ni） Advance, Advance metal
艾多尼克铜镍锡合金 Adonic
艾尔德里德镍铁芯镀铜线（玻璃-金属焊封用） Eldred's wire
艾费奈德镍银系耐蚀铸造合金 Afenide
艾弗里布氏硬度计 Avery Brinell tester

艾弗里冲杯[杯突]试验 Avery cupping test
艾杰克斯-怀亚特式感应炉(铁心感应炉) Ajax-Wyatt furnace
艾杰克斯-诺思拉普式(无铁心)高频感应炉 Ajax-Northrup furnace
艾杰克斯标准青铜（77.0Cu, 12Sn, 11Pb） Ajax standard bronze
艾杰克斯感应炉 Ajax induction furnace
艾杰克斯磷青铜（79.3Cu, 10Sn, 10Pb, 0.7P） Ajax phosphor bronze
艾杰克斯平炉吹氧炼钢法【钢】Ajax process
艾杰克斯铅青铜（77Cu, 12Sn, 11Pb） Ajax metal
艾杰克斯铅锑锡轴承合金（76Pb, 17Sb, 7Sn） Ajax bearing alloy
艾杰克斯塑性青铜（65Cu, 29Pb, 5Sn, 1Ni） Ajax plastic bronze
艾杰克斯铜锡铅轴承合金（10.98Sn, 7.27Pb, 0.37As 或 P, 余量 Cu） Ajax
艾杰克斯铸造铜硅锌合金（90Cu, 5Zn, 5Si） Ajax casting alloy
艾克里特钴铬钨镍合金（铸造切削工具用；37.5Co, 30Cr, 16W, 10Ni, 4Mo, 2.5C）Akrit
艾克龙得公式【压】Eklund's formula
艾克斯假金叶（64.8Cu, 32.8Zn, 2Sn, 0.4Pb） Aix gold leaf
艾拉尔铝基合金（3.5Cu, 1.8Mg, 0.6Si, 2.25Cd, 余量 Al） Aeral
艾里环（测定透镜系统分辨能力的基准） Airy disc
艾林瓦效应 Elinvar effect
艾留米奈克铝合金 Aluminac
艾龙铝基合金（4Cu, 1Si, 余量 Al） Aeron
艾卢马格尼斯铝合金 Alumagnese
艾伦高铅青铜[铜铅轴承合金]（55Cu, 40Pb, 5Sn） Allen's metal
艾伦式分级圆锥 Allen cone
艾罗莱特铝基多元合金（0.12Zn, 0.4Si, 0.97Fe, 1.15Cu, 0.38Mg, 余量 Al）

Aerolite
艾罗纳克高硅耐热耐蚀铸铁（13.5Si，2.7C总，0.7P，痕迹Mn，余量Fe） Ironac
艾米克斯胺萃提铀流程图 Amex flow-sheet
艾姆科回转真空过滤机 Eimco-rotary vacuum filter
艾姆斯试验室独居石处理法 Ames monazite process
艾姆斯试验室生产铀钍法 Ames process [procedure]
艾姆斯手提式硬度（试验）仪 Ames portable hardness tester
艾奇逊电阻炉 Acheson electric resistance furnace
艾奇逊炉（生产碳化硅用） Acheson furnace
艾奇逊人造石墨 Acheson AGR graphite
艾萨熔炼法 ISA(SIRO) smelting process
艾氏冲击(试验) Izod impact (test)
艾氏冲击试验机 Izod impact (testing) machine, Izod machine
艾氏冲击试样 Izod test piece
艾氏冲击值 Izod impact value
艾氏抗冲击强度 Izod impact strength
艾氏切口（冲击试样的） Izod notch
艾氏缺口（试样）冲击试验 notched Izot test
艾索弗雷克斯小型钟表发条 Isoflex
艾希六O含铁黄铜（36.58Zn，1.02Sn，1.74Fe，余量Cu） Aich's alloy
碍视曲线 【运】blind curve
镁{I$_O$} ionium(钍-230, ^{230}Th)
爱迪生效应 Edison effect
爱立斯·恰默斯造块直接还原法（同"ACAR直接还原法"）
爱立斯·恰默斯直接还原法 【团】Allis-Chalmers direct reduction process
爱立斯·恰默斯可控气氛直接还原法【团】ACCAR (Allis-Chalmers Controlled Atmosphere Reduction) process
爱立斯·恰默斯型链算机－回转窑 【团】Allis-Chalmers grate-kiln machine
爱姆油 Amoil（酞酸戊酯）◇S-～Amoil-S（癸二酸戊酯）
爱皮松油（油蒸气真空泵用油） Apiezon oil
爱泼斯坦磁滞检验仪 Epstein tester
爱泼斯坦方圈 Epstein frames
爱泼斯坦方圈仪（测硅钢薄板铁损用） Epstein square
爱泼斯坦检验仪 Epstein tester
爱泼斯坦铁损测定装置 Epstein apparatus
爱因斯坦比热公式 Einstein's formula for specific heat
爱因斯坦－德哈斯效应 Einstein-de Hass effect
爱因斯坦(晶格)振动模型 Einstein model
爱因斯坦质能关系 Einstein's mass-energy relation
鞍点（鞍形曲线的） saddle point
鞍式运输机（带斗的） saddle type conveyer
鞍头块 saddle piece
鞍形板 saddle plate
鞍形存放卷座 coil storage saddle
鞍形分支连接（管子） branch tee saddle joint
鞍形键 saddle [hollow] key
鞍形卷座 【压】coil saddle
鞍形连接（管子的） saddle joint
鞍形量规 saddle gauge
鞍形曲线 saddle curve
鞍形物[鞍形座，鞍状构造] saddle
鞍形物填料 saddle packing
鞍(座)形步进梁[动梁] saddle [cradle] type walking beam
氨{NH$_3$} ammonia ◇（分解）成～作用 ammonification, 含～的 ammoniac, 化[加]～（作用） ammonification, 离解～ ammogas, 裂化[分解]～ cracked ammo-

nia,洗~塔*,蒸~器*
氨苯磺胺 suphanilamide
氨处理 ammonia treatment
氨分解器 cracker
氨分解气体 AX gas
氨腐蚀 corrosion by ammonia
氨工段 【焦】ammonia plant
氨化钴溶液 ammoniacal cobalt solution
氨化聚丙烯酸 ammoniacal polyacrylic acid
氨化硫酸铵溶液 ammoniacal ammonium sulphate solution
氨化(作用) ammoniation
氨回收 ammonia recovery
氨基安替比林法 【环】aminoantipyrine method
氨基磺酸{R·NH·SO₃H} sulphamic[sufoamidic] acid
氨基磺酸铵{NH₄OSO₂NH₂} ammonium sulphamate
氨基磺酸镍 nickel sulphamate
氨基磺酸盐{R·NH·SO₃M 或 R·NH·SO₂OR'} sulphamate, sulfamate
氨基磺酸盐电解精炼法(铅的) sulphamate electrolytic process
氨基甲酸烷基酯{NH₂COOR} alkyl carbamate
氨基甲酸乙酯 urethane
氨基硅烷 aminosilane
氨基碱金属 alkali amide
氨基金属{MNH₂} ammonobase
氨基氰{H₂N·CN} cyanamide
氨基塑料 amino-plastics
氨基酸 amino-acid
氨基锌 zinc ammine
氨基亚铜 cuprous ammine
氨基乙醇(同"乙醇胺")
氨碱法 ammonia soda process
氨解(作用) ammonolysis
氨介质 ammoniacal medium
氨浸残渣 ammonia leach residue
氨浸(出)[氨液浸出] ammonia leaching

◇ 常压活化~*
氨浸出化学 ammonia leach chemistry
氨浸出液 ammoniacal leach liquor
氨浸法 ammonia leaching process ◇ 高压~*,红土镍矿还原~*
氨浸供液槽 ammonia leach feed tank
氨浸回路[系统] ammonia leach circuit
氨浸氢还原法 ammonia-leach hydrogen-reduction process
氨浸溶液 ammonia leach solution
氨冷冻剂 ammonia refrigerant
氨冷凝器 ammonia condenser
氨冷却管 ammonia pipe
氨冷却器 ammonia cooler
氨离解 ammonia dissociation
氨离解度 degree of ammonia dissociation
氨离解分离器 ammonia dissociation separator
氨离解器 ammonia dissociator
氨－硫铵法 ammonia-ammonium sulphate process
氨明矾{(NH₄)₂SO₄·Al₂(SO₄)₃·24H₂O,或 NH₄·Al(SO₄)₂·12H₂O} ammonia alum
氨萘塔 【焦】naphthalene scrubber
氨气 ammonia ◇ 合成~ ammonia synthesis gas,燃烧~*
氨气分解速率 dissociation rate of gaseous ammonia
氨气洗涤器 ammonia scrubber
氨气压缩机 ammonia compressor
氨气压缩冷冻机 ammonia compression refrigerating machine
氨溶液 ammine solution
氨水 ammonia water [aqua, spirit], aqueous [aqua] ammo-nia, liquid ammonium ◇ 粗~*,浓~*,弱~*
氨水焦油分离器 【焦】decanter
氨性的 ammoniac
氨压计 ammonia manometer
氨蒸馏加料槽 ammonia distillation feed tank
氨蒸馏器 ammonia distiller

氨蒸(馏)柱　【焦】ammonia still ◇ 固定~ fixed still

氨制冷厂　ammonia cooling plant

安伯罗依德镍银合金（12—18Ni，余量Ag）　Amberoid alloy

安瓿　ampoule,bulb

安布拉克铜镍耐蚀合金（75Cu,20Ni,5Zn; 65Cu,30Ni,5Zn）　Ambrac

安布拉洛伊耐蚀铜合金　Ambraloy (Ambraloy 901：9Al,91Cu; Ambraloy 917：9.5Al,5Ni,2.5Fe,1Mn,82Cu; Ambraloy 927：21.95Zn,2Al,0.05As,76Cu)

安布罗斯铜镍锌耐蚀合金（65—75Cu, 20—30Ni,5Zn,0.5Mn）　Ambrose alloy

安大略自硬高铬模具钢（1.48C,11.58Cr, 0.29V,0.75Mo,0.29Mn,0.34Si,余量Fe）Ontario

安德雷德拉单晶法　Andrade method

安德雷德蠕变　【金】Andrade creep

安德雷德蠕变定律　Andrade's creep law

安德森沉降管　Anderson (sedimentation) pipet

安得逊张拉成形法　Androform process

安蒂沃奇蒸汽处理石膏型法　Antioch process

安放型芯　coring up

安伏欧计　avometer

安卡不锈钢（一种18/8型不锈钢）　Anka

安科海绵铁粉　Ancor iron powder

安纳康达铜合金　Anaconda alloy

安诺石　anosvite

安培度量法　amperometrical method

安培计（同"电流表"）

安培计分流器　ammeter shunt, shunt for ammeter

安普科耐热耐蚀铜合金　Ampco (Ampco 12：8.5—9.3Al,2.5—3.25Fe,余量Cu; Ampco18：10.3—11Al,3.0—4.25Fe,余量Cu)

安奇可罗达耐蚀铝硅镁合金（铸造：4—6Si,0.4—1Mg,0.5—1Mn,余量Al; 可锻：0.5—1.5Si,0.5—1Mg,0.5—1Mn,余量Al）Anticorodal

安全棒（控制核反应堆链锁反应的）【理】safety rod

安全标准　safety criterion

安全玻璃　protective glass

安全不爆炸浓度（气体的）　nonexplosive concentration

安全操作温度　safe working temperature

安全衬层　【冶】safety lining

安全程度　degree of reliability

安全出口　fire escape (F.E.)

安全措施　safety precaution, safeguard

安全带　safety-belt, gird

安全挡板　personnel barrier

安全灯照明　safelight illumination

安全点火装置　safety igniter mechanism

安全垫　【机】safety-cushion

安全度　degree of safety

安全阀　safety [relief, guard] valve

安全范围　safe range

安全防爆装置　safety explosion

安全防护用钢丝绳　guard cable

安全服　safety clothing

安全负载[荷载]　safe(ty) load

安全杆　safety lever

安全工程　safety engineering

安全工作温度　safety service temperature

安全工作应力　safe working stress

安全拱　【建】relieving arch

安全钩　safety hook

安全规程[守则]　safety regulation [specifications, laws]

安全规章　【企】safe practice

安全合格牌照　safety approval plate

安全盒　breaker block

安全荷重　safety weight

安全极限　safe(ty) limit

安全技术　safety control [work], accident prevention,【企】safe practice

安全技术措施　safety provisions

安全技术工程师[安全监督员]　safety

an 安   10

supervisor
安全技术规程 safety procedure [reasons], emergency decree
安全技术条件 safety reasons
安全加热极限 safe heating limit
安全界限 safety margin
安全曰 breaker block, breakers, breaking cap, safety pot ◇ 楔形~*,铸铁~*
安全距离 safe distance
安全开关 safety switch
安全离合器 safety clutch
安全联锁(装置) safety interlock
安全联轴器 safety coupling
安全零件 safety [breaking] piece
安全率[因数] safety factor
安全帽 protection helmet (p.h.), helmet shield ◇ 气瓶~cylinder cap
安全门 emergency exit [door]
安全排气阀 safety exhaust
安全屏 safety screen
安全熔断器 safety fuse
安全设备 safety device, safety appliance, safety provisions
安全设计程序 safety programming
安全设施 safety provisions, safety guard
安全室 safety cage
安全寿命 safe life
安全条例 safety rules
安全通风道 safety funnel
安全通梯(车间内的) ramp
安全网 wire guard
安全系数 safety coefficient [factor], margin (of safety)
安全系统 【计】fail safe system
安全隙 safety gap
安全销 safety pin, guard pin
安全性 safety, reliability, security
安全旋塞 relief cock
安全应力 safe stress
安全渣口 【冶】safety cinder notch
安全渣口塞 safety cinder notch stopper
安全轧头(工具机工作台的) safety dog

安全闸 safety brake
安全栅 safety screen
安全罩 safety cage, fence
安全指标 safety figure
安全指示灯 safety light
安全指数 safety index, reliability indices
安全止动器 safe(ty) lock
安全装置 safety device [gear], safety, preventer, relief mechanism, fool-proof, monitor
安时计 ampere-hour meter
安时容量[定额] ampere-hour capacity
安氏型砂粒度测定仪 Andreasen pipette
安塔西隆耐蚀耐磨铁硅合金(14.5Si,余量 Fe) Antaciron
安西斯特铁镍合金 Anhyster (Anhyster B: 35Ni,余量 Fe; Anhyster D: 45 - 50Ni,余量 Fe)
安息坡 slope of bank
安置 fixation
安置刚性箍筋(在铸件上) stiffening hooping
安置轧辊 roll setting [setup]
安装 installation (inst., instl.), instal(l).ment, erection (erec.), mounting, location, placing, laying, assembling, assemblage, arrangement
安装材料 mounting [installation] material
安装程序 erection sequence
安装地点 infield
安装工[人员] erector, erecting personnel, fitter
安装工程 installation works, field engineering
安装规程 installation instruction
安装焊工 field welder
安装好的模板 【铸】mounted pattern
安装机械师[技术员] installing mechanic
安装件 fabricated section
安装孔 mounting hole
安装连接 erection joint

安装螺栓	erection bolt
安装能力	installed capacity
安装器	erector
安装人员	erecting personnel
安装(设备)费用	installation charges [cost, expenses], fabricating cost
安装设计	erection design
安装台	erecting bed
安装头	built up end
安装图	installation drawing [diagram], erection drawing [diagram]
安装位置	position of assembly (P.A.)
安装误差	installation [erection, alignment] error
安装用夹具	mounting fixture, setting-up fixture
安装用起重机	erecting crane
安装用起重架	gin pole
安装用人字架	bipod
铵矾	aluminium ammonium sulphate, ammonium alum
铵化合物	ammonium compound
铵铁矾 {$(NH_4)_2SO_4 \cdot Fe_2(SO_4)_3 \cdot 24H_2O$，或$(NH_4)Fe \cdot (SO_4)_2 \cdot 12H_2O$}	ammonium ferricalum
铵盐	ammonia [ammonium] salt
铵铀云母 {$NH_4(UO_2)PO_4 \cdot 3H_2O$}	uramphite
铵油炸药	ammonium nitrate fuel oil blasting agents (AN-FO, AN/FO)
按比例扩大穿孔机	multiplying punch
按比例缩小[减少]	scale down
按尺寸加工	finish(ing) to size
按铃	belling
按钮[按键](push)	button, push piece, key
按钮开关(push)	button switch, press-button switch [key]
按钮开关灯	push button switch lamp (PBSL)
按钮控制[操纵](push-)	button control, press-button [touch-button, finger-tip] control
按钮控制卸料(矿仓、料仓的)	push-button outflow
按碳含量出钢	tapping on carbon
按条件付款	payment on terms
暗槽	chase
暗草黄色	dark straw (colour)
暗场(同"暗视场")	
暗橙黄热(加热到暗橙黄色)	dark orange heat
暗电流	dark current
暗电阻(光电池的)	dark resistance
暗丁砖	blind header
暗度	opacity
暗缝	concealed joint
暗敷导线	hidden conductor
暗沟	blind drain, covered conduit [gutter]
暗沟排水	blind drainage
暗光阑显微镜	opaque stop microscope
暗盒	film cassette [magazine]
暗褐煤	dull brown coal
暗红热(加热到暗红色)	dark (red) heat, low-red [dull-red] heat, black hot
暗浸蚀	dark etching
暗亮煤型	duroclarite
暗裂纹	masked crack
暗流	under-current
暗冒口	【铸】blind(er) [closed, dummy] riser, blind feeder, bob, pop-up (俗语) ◇ 上半型 ~ cope bob, 下半型 ~ drag bob
暗煤	attritus, durain
暗煤型	durite
暗面	tarnish
暗镍蛇纹石 {$H_4(Mg,Ni)_2 \cdot (SiO_4)_3 \cdot 4H_2O$}	garnierite
暗配线	【电】concealed wiring
暗渠	covered conduit, blind drain, underdrain, culvert
暗色浸蚀区(应力腐蚀区)	【金】dark etching zone
暗色煤	dull coal
暗色碎片	dark coloured fragment

暗室设备　darkroom equipment
暗室显影法　scotography
暗视场(显微镜的)　dark field
暗视场法　【金】dark field method
暗视场反射(光线)法　dark field reflection method
暗视场反射显微镜　dark field reflection microscope
暗视场观察　【金】dark field observation
暗视场检验　dark field examination
暗视场聚光镜　dark field condenser ◇ 抛物面～*,双曲面～*
暗视场透射光(线)法　【金】dark field transmission method
暗视场显微照片　【金】dark field micrograph
暗视场像　dark field image
暗锁　mortice lock
暗网菌属　Pelodictyon
暗线　【电】concealed wiring ◇ 装在瓷柱上与管内的～knob-and-tube wiring
暗线光谱　dark line spectrum
暗线装置系统　conduit system
暗箱长度　bellows length
暗樱红热[加热到暗樱红色]　dark [dull] cherry(-red) heat
岸崩　caving
岸壁　bulkhead (wall), quay
岸标　beacon
岸砂(黏土含量低于5%)　bank sand
黯表面　matte surface
胺　amine
胺萃(取)　amine extraction ◇ 艾米克斯～提铀流程图*
胺化　amination
胺基　amine group, amido
胺基硫酸氢盐　(同"硫酸氢胺")
胺基硫酸盐　(同"硫酸胺")
胺基乙醇　(同"乙醇胺")
胺浸出(法)　amine leaching
胺类　amines
胺类萃取剂　amine (type) extractant
胺类化合物　amine-group compound
胺(类)溶剂　amine solvent
胺溶液　amine liquid [solution]
胺溶液无机萃取　inorganic extraction by amine liquid
胺酸　amino-acid
胺盐　amine salt
盎司铸造铜合金(84—86Cu,4—6Zn,4—6Sn,4—6Pb,<1Ni)　ounce metal
凹疤　depression
凹边(轧件的)　concave [recessed] edge
凹边方孔型　fluted square pass
凹部　rabbet
凹槽　groove, notch, indent(ation), bay, beard
凹碴床　【运】boxed in ballast
凹处　recess(ion), nick, pocket, pothole
凹底离子交换槽　dished bottom exchanger cell
凹底椭圆(形)孔型　oval-type bastard oval, bastard oval (pass) ◇ 菱形～*
凹度　concavity, concave, 【压】(辊身表面的) concave camber, belly
凹缝(焊接钢管缺陷)　deep seam
凹沟　chase ◇ 带～的 fluted
凹光栅　concave grating ◇ 罗兰～ Rowland concave grating
凹辊环　negative collar, collar hole
凹痕　dent, dint, 【压】(钢板黏结时的) dimples, dimpling ◇ 有～的 【金】pitted
凹坑　pitted surface, steel pit(薄板、带钢的表面缺陷), scallops(轧件表面缺陷), stain(表面缺陷)
凹口　recess, depression, hack ◇ 深～*
凹口试验　notch test
凹帽头　【钢】top hat
凹面　concave (surface), concave edge (轧件的)
凹面承坯架　spur
凹面对焊　concave butt weld
凹面反射器　concave reflector

凹面方钢　fluted bar (iron)
凹面(绕射)光栅摄谱仪　concave grating spectrograph
凹面焊缝　inverted weld
凹面晶体反射器　concave reflector
凹面镜　concave mirror
凹面坯块　concave-shaped compact
凹面(轧)辊　concave roll, concave form of roll
凹模　concave die,【压】cavity of die
凹球面铝阴极　concave spherical aluminium cathode
凹铜(含约6% Cu_2O 的铜)　set [dry] copper ◇ 砖红色~brick red set copper
凹透镜　concave lens
凹凸边　rabbet
凹凸不平　uneven, irregularity, rough(ness), asperity
凹凸冲模　offset die
凹凸透镜　concavo-convex lens, meniscus (lens)
凹陷　gab, handling mark, sag, sink(ing) hole,【冶】dinge, dishing (钢板落料缺陷)
凹陷焊缝　sagged weld
凹线辊型　【压】concave camber
凹形板[带]尾　concave camber
凹形槽　concave groove ◇ 巴尔的摩型~ Baltimore groove
凹形反射面　concave reflecting face
凹形辊身　【压】concave barrel
凹形角焊　concave fillet welding
凹形角焊缝　concave fillet (weld)
凹穴　depression, recess, hollow,【冶】dinge
凹衍射光栅　concave diffraction grating
凹座　recess, dimple
螯合(的)　chelate
螯合滴定(法)　chelatometric titration
螯合剂　chelating agent ◇ 多价~ sequestering agent
螯合物树脂　chelating resin

螯合作用　chelation
螯络合物萃取　chelate complex extraction
螯(型化)合物　chelate compound
奥伯豪森炼钢法【钢】Oberhausen process
奥伯霍弗腐蚀液(浸蚀剂, 浸蚀液)(钢铁显微分析用; 1.0 克 $CuCl_2$, 0.5 克 $SnCl_2$, 30 克 $FeCl_3$, 30 毫升浓 HCl, 500 毫升水, 500 毫升酒精)【金】Oberhoffer('s) solution[etchant, reagent]
奥长石　oligoclase
奥达铜镍耐蚀合金(45—65Cu, 27—45Ni, 1—10Mn, 0.5—3Fe)　Oda metal
奥迪欧洛伊高导磁率铁镍合金(48Ni, 余量 Fe)　Audiolloy
奥地利弯曲试验(用于研究金属可焊性)　Austrian bend test
奥顿测温锥　【耐】Orton cones
奥厄火石[发火]合金(30Fe, 65 稀土金属)　Auer metal
奥尔斯特镍铝钴系析出型磁铁　Oersit (Oersit 100: 19Co, 17.5Ni, 3Ti, 7.5Al, 3Cu, 余量 Fe)
奥尔马格铝基合金(2.5Cu, 0.7Mg, 0.6Si, 余量 Al)　Almag
奥尔马西尔铝基合金(1.0Mg, 2Si, 余量 Al)　Almasil
奥尔森杯突试验　Olsen (cup) test
奥尔森杯突试验机　Olsen cup test machine
奥尔森式万能材料试验机　Olsen universal testing machine
奥尔森延性试验(一种杯突试验方法)　Olsen ductility test
奥尔兹莫洛伊镍银[铜锌镍合金](45Cu, 39Zn, 14Ni, 2Sn)　Oldsmoloy
奥福德(顶底)分层炼镍法　Orford (top-and-bottom) process
奥格多孔轴承合金(85—90Cu, 8.5—10Sn, 0—2 石墨)　Ogalloy
奥卡普直接炼铁法　【铁】Orcarb process
奥卡铸造黄铜(72Cu, 24.5Zn, 2.32Fe, 1.1Pb)　Oker

奥克潘锡（炼锡副产物，用于配制巴比合金；80—90Sn，10—15Sb，2—5Cu，<0.25Sb） Ocpan

奥克萨利包覆铜合金（铜丝外包以不锈钢） Oxally

奥克塔尼厄姆镍铬钴低膨胀合金（40Co，20Cr，15.5Ni，15Fe，7Mo，2Mn，0.15C，0.03Be） Octanium

奥克特油（同"辛基油"）

奥雷德黄铜（装饰用；80.5—90Cu，10—19.5Zn，有时加入少量 Sn 和 Pb） Oreide

奥雷德镍黄铜（63—66.5Cu，30.5—32.75Zn，2—6Ni） nickel Oreide

奥雷德装饰黄铜（82.75Cu，16.40Zn，0.55Sn，0.3Fe） French gold

奥利弗隔膜泵 Oliver diaphragm pump

奥利弗回转真空过滤机 Oliver rotary vacuum filter

奥利弗滤器（同"鼓式真空过滤机"）

奥立恰尔黄铜 Orichalc(h)

奥林匹克高强度耐蚀硅青铜 Olympic bronze（Olympic A：96Cu，1Zn，3Si；OlympicB：97.5Cu，1Zn，1.5Si；Olympic C：94.75Cu，1Zn，4.25Si）

奥罗拉低锡铅巴比合金（5Zn，9—15Sb，80—86Pb，0.5Cu） Aurora babbitt metal

奥罗万脆断理论 Orowan brittle fracture theory

奥罗万效应 【理】Orowan effect

奥罗依德铜锡锌合金（16.5Zn，0.5Sn，0.3Fe，余量 Cu） Oroide

奥梅斯电阻直接加热锻造法 Omes electroforging process

奥米伽高硅耐震钢（0.6C，1.85Si，0.7Mn，0.2V，0.45Mo） Omega steel

奥米伽螺纹 Omega thread

奥姆鲁铜锡锌合金（金色：90.5Cu，3Zn，6.5Sn；金色：94.2Cu，5.8Sn；黄色：58Cu，25.5Zn，16.5Sn） Ormulu

奥内拉表面渗铬法 ONERA process（ONERA 系法国国家航空研究管理局 Office Nationald' Etude et de Recherches A'eronautigue 的缩写）

奥内拉铬化法（用氟化物渗铬剂） Onera method

奥尼亚－诺瓦尔费流态化床海绵铁生产法 Novalfer fluid bed process, ONIA－Noval-fer process

奥萨特(气体)分析法 Orsat analysis

奥萨特气体分析器 Orsat (gas) analyzer, Orsat apparatus

奥萨特气体分析试验 Orsat test

奥萨特气体自动分析器 automatic Orsat

奥氏体 【金】austenite（aust.） ◇残余[残留,剩余]～*，初生[一次]～primary austenite，粗晶～ coarse austenite，过冷～*，含氮～ nitrogen austenite，含镍～ nickel austenite，含碳～ carbon austenite，未经相变的～ unchanged austenite，先共晶～ proeutectic austenite，氧化～ oxyaustenite，原始～original austenite，转变前～preexisting austenite

奥氏体本质晶粒度 inherent austenitic grain size

奥氏体不完全等温淬火 progressive austempering

奥氏体不稳定性 austenite instability

奥氏体不锈钢 austenitic stainless steel ◇F.D.P.含钛～*，杜里米特～*，红狐牌～Red-Fox alloy，克房伯～*，马克西尔赖含铜～*

奥氏体不锈钢表面硬化[强化]法 Scottsonizing

奥氏体成分 austenite composition

奥氏体等温时效(处理) austenageing

奥氏体等温退火 ausannealing

奥氏体等温转变曲线 TTT (time-temperature-transformation) curves, C curve

奥氏体等温转变曲线图 TTT diagram

奥氏体锻造 ausforging

奥氏体范围(相图的) austenitic range

奥氏体分解 decomposition of austenite

奥氏体分裂转变　split transformation of austenite
奥氏体钢　austenite [austenic] steel
奥氏体高锰钢（0.9—1.2C,10—13Mn,余量 Fe）　Hadfield (manganese) steel
奥氏体铬镍合金钢　Krupp austenite steel
奥氏体过冷区加工法　marworking
奥氏体合金钢　austenitic alloy steel
奥氏体化　austenization, austenizing, austenite conditioning ◇ 时间-温度-~(TTA)图*
奥氏体化炉　austenitizing furnace
奥氏体化温度　austenitizing temperature
奥氏体(化温度)退火　austenite annealing
奥氏体灰口铸铁　austenitic grey cast iron
奥氏体回火　austempering
奥氏体回火钢　austempered steel
奥氏体基体[晶体]　austenitic matrix
奥氏体晶界　austenite grain boundary
奥氏体晶粒　austenite grain [crystal] ◇ 麦奎德-埃恩~尺寸*,原始~*
奥氏体晶粒度　austenitic grain size
奥氏体晶粒度分级　austenite grain-size classification
奥氏体晶粒长大　austenite grain growth
奥氏体锰钢　austenitic manganese steel ◇ 介稳~*
奥氏体耐热钢　austenitic heat resistance steel
奥氏体镍铬不锈钢　austenitic Ni-Cr stainless steel
奥氏体强化元素　austenite hardener
奥氏体区(域)　austenitic area [range, region]
奥氏体热模具钢　austenitic hot die steel
奥氏体生铁（含 6.58Ni,1.78Cr 的合金生铁）　austenitic pig iron
奥氏体时效(处理)（残余奥氏体在 700℃左右加热分解）　ausageing
奥氏体时效钢　ausageing steel
奥氏体温度范围　austenitic temperature range
奥氏体稳定化处理　austenite stabilization
奥氏体稳定剂　austenite stabilizer
奥氏体细晶粒　fine austenite grain
奥氏体显微组织　austenite microstructure
奥氏体形变(处理)　ausform, ausforming
奥氏体形变淬火　ausform hardening
奥氏体形变热处理　austenite stressing
奥氏体形变热处理钢　ausform steel
奥氏体形变退火　ausform-annealing
奥氏体形成元素　austenite former
奥氏体轧制　ausrolling
奥氏体再结晶　austenite recrystallization
奥氏体铸铁　【铸】austenitic cast iron ◇ 片状石墨~*,无磁性~*
奥氏体状态　austenitic state [condition]
奥氏体组织　austenite structure
奥氏蒸馏塔　【色】Oldershaw column
奥斯马亚尔铝锰合金(1.8Mn,余量 Al)　Osmayal
奥斯蒙铁　Osmund iron
奥斯熔炼法　Ausmelt process
奥斯特铁镍铝钴系永磁合金　Oersted magnet
奥斯特瓦尔德比重瓶　Ostwald-type pycnometer
奥斯特瓦尔德成熟(现象)(Al-Zn-Mg 合金中的)　Ostwald ripening
奥斯特瓦尔德吸附等温曲线　Ostwald's adsorption isotherm
奥斯特瓦尔德稀释定律　Ostwald dilution law
奥斯特瓦尔德(毛细管)黏度计　Ostwald-type viscometer
奥斯汀式坝　Austin dam
奥索尼克软磁合金(50Ni,50Fe)　Orthonik
奥特曼式联轴器　Ortmann coupling
奥托昆普闪速熔炼法　Outokumpu process
奥托昆普型双浇包 28 模浇铸系统　Outokumpu double pouring 28-mould casting system

奥托昆普一步炼铅法　Outokumpu direct process
奥托式焦炉　Otto oven
奥托铜锡合金{68.5Cu,31.5Sn}　Otto's alloy
澳大利亚金币合金(91.66Au,余量 Ag)　Australian gold
澳大利亚矿冶学会　Australian Institute of Mining and Metallurgy（A.I.of M.& M.）
澳大利亚汽车协会　Australian Automobile Association（AAA）

B b

扒 raking, dig up
扒钉 anti-checking iron, cocking piece ◇ 连结～ crowfoot
扒料[炉](停炉的) 【铁】raking out
扒皮机 peeler ◇ 坯料～ billet peeler
扒平 【冶】setting off
扒渣 slag removal, removal of cinder, slagging(-off), slagging out, skim(ming), flush off ◇ 精炼～*
扒渣棒[钩] damping bar, skimmer bar
扒渣并造渣 【钢】change of slag
扒渣侧 slag-off side
扒渣口 skimming bay
扒渣耙 slag rake
扒渣期 slagging period,【钢】flush off period
扒渣勺 skimmer spoon
扒中(间)渣 【钢】intermediate slag removal
八(层)叠板 double-double iron,【压】eights
八重线[态] 【理】octet
八单位码 【计】eight level code
八垛式炉台 eight-stack base
八价 octavalence, octavalency
八角棒材[型钢] octagon bar
八角[面]的 octal
八角钢 octagon steel
八角[隅]体 octet(te)
八角形钢锭浇注台 octagon ingot area
八进位法 octal notation
八进制计数法 octal notation
八进制数 octal number [numeral]
八流连铸机 eight-strand continuous casting machine
八流连铸设备 eight-strand plant
八面石$\{TiO_2\}$ octahedrite
八面体 octahedra
八面体变形 octahedral strain
八面体粉粒 octahedral particle
八面体滑移 octahedral glide
八面体间[空]隙 octahedral interstices
八面体间隙空位 octahedral interstitial void
八面体晶面反射 octahedron-face reflections
八面体空位[穴] octahedral voids
八面体面 octahedral plane
八面体铁矿$\{Fe_3O_4\}$ octahedral iron ore
八面体座[位置] octahedral sites
八水合砷酸钴$\{Co_3(AsO_4)_2 \cdot 8H_2O\}$ cobalt bloom
八维空间 octuple space
八氧化三铀$\{U_3O_8\}$ urano(us)-uranic oxide
八音度 octave
八圆盘式过滤机 eight-disc filter
八张叠轧(薄板的) roll eights
八字试块(型砂抗拉试验用) 【铸】dog-bone
疤 scabby,【冶】mapping ◇ 有～表面 【钢】scabby surface
疤钢 blister steel
疤痕 seam, scab, scar ◇ 有～的 seamy
疤皮 spilliness, shell
巴比[巴氏]合金(3.5—15Sb, 2—6Cu, 余量 Sn, 有时含<1Cd) babbitt('s) metal (babb., B.m.), white metal alloy, babbitt (alloy) ◇ G 砷铅～*, 衬～的轴承 babbitt lined bearing, 重浇～ rebabbit, 高锡～*, 含钙～*, 浇注～ cast-on white metal, 莫霍克～*, 轻载加铅～*, 软～*, 水下用白色～*, 温斯科英～*, 镶～ babbit-ting, 铸造～ cast babbit metal
巴比合金衬套轴承 babbitt lined bearing
巴比合金离心熔铸机 centrifugal babbiting machine
巴比合金轴承 babbittmetal bearing, white-metal (babbitt) bearing ◇ 铸造～*
巴博蒸汽压定律 Babo's law

巴伯隐丝式光学高温计 【理】Barber pyrometer

巴布科克－威尔科克斯立式连铸法 【连铸】Babcock and Wilcox continuous casting process

巴丁－库珀－施里弗超导理论 【理】Bardeen-Cooper-Schrieffer (BCS) theory

巴丁脱氧铁合金(18—20Si, 8—10Al, 4—6Ti, 余量 Fe) Badin metal

巴恩铅基轴承合金(0.7Ca, 0.6Na, 0.2Al, Si、Ni 等 0.5) Bahnmetal

巴尔－巴德盖特短时蠕变试验 Barr-Bardgett creep test

巴尔巴断裂伸长定律(断裂伸长%/试样截面＝常数) Barba's law

巴尔巴赫卧式电极电解银精炼法 Balbach electrolytic process

巴尔巴相似定律 Barba's law of similarity

巴尔布洛克刺钢丝 Barblok

巴尔的摩凹形槽(阳极挂耳上的) Baltimore groove

巴尔末系列(光谱线的) 【理】Balmer series

巴尔斯特拉加热炉(热挤压坯料无氧化加热用的玻璃浴炉) Balestra furnace

巴格利法(内加热炉硅热炼镁法) Bagley process

巴格纳尔－贝瑟尔(专利)水口 【钢】Bagnall-Bethel (patent) nozzle

巴基管 Bucky tube

巴科尔刚玉锆英石(耐火材料) Bacor

巴科尔[氏]硬度 Barcol hardness

巴科尔[氏]硬度计 Barcol impresser

巴科模压铸造法 【铸】Bacco process

巴克豪森磁性跃迁[磁畴陡变] Barkhausen jump(s)

巴克豪森效应(铁磁物质磁化不连续地变化的现象) Barkhausen effect

巴拉斯金刚石(工业用) ballas

巴雷塔氧化钡吸收定碳法 Baryta process

巴雷特作用(磁致体积变化作用) Barret effect

巴林比重计[浮计] Balling hydrometer

巴林杰湿度计 Ballinger hygrometer

巴伦坦硬度试验机 Ballentine hardness tester

巴罗连续铸钢法 Barrow process

巴罗尼亚耐蚀铜合金(冷凝管用, 82—85Cu, 4Sn, 1Fe, 余量 Zn) Barronia

巴罗斯镍铬耐热合金(90Ni, 10Cr, 示差热膨胀计用中性体金属) Baros metal

巴尼特效应(物体旋转产生磁化) Barnett effect

巴诺克斯钢丝磷酸盐处理法 Banox process

巴萨洛伊安全系统合金(44.5Pb, 55.5Bi) Basalloy

巴塞回转窑铁矿处理法 Basset process

巴塞式上下双动型水压机 Bussman simetag press

巴斯脆性白铜(55Cu, 余量 Zn) Bath metal

巴塔尔布拉铜基合金(22Zn, 2Al, 0.03As, 余量 Cu) Batalbra

巴特尔式换接电极尖 BMI electrode transition tip

巴特尔式抗焊道下裂缝试验 Battelle type cracking test

巴特海军黄铜(37Zn, 1Sn, 余量 Cu) Batnaval

巴特雷斯型螺纹(梯形螺纹) Buttress thread

巴特里姆铜铝镍合金(89Cu, 9Al, 2Ni 和其他元素) Batterium

巴特尼科英铜镍铁合金(5Ni, 1.2Fe, 0.5Mn, 余量 Cu) Batnickoin

巴特斯多叶真空过滤机(间歇式) Butters filter

巴西褐铁矿 chapinha

巴西螺母试验 Brazil-nut-sandwich test

巴西劈裂试验 Brazil splitting test

巴西特生铁法(用回转炉) Basett process

巴西圆盘(裂纹)试验 Brazilian disc test

巴西棕榈蜡(二十四烷酸酯) carnauba

wax, Brazil wax

巴西棕榈酸 carnaubic acid

巴扎尔银镍合金(10Ni,余量 Ag) Bazar

拔棒(铝电解的) spike pulling ◇ 风动－液动～机*,机械～机*,斯内兹柯式风动～机*

拔长 drawing-out

拔长锻造 string forging

拔长锻造比 drawing forging ratio

拔长模槽 swedger

拔长模膛 edger, drawing

拔钉钳 nail claw

拔根机 rooter

拔管 【压】tube-drawing ◇ 长芯棒～bar [rod] drawing,超声波振动～*,倒立式～用卷筒 inverted tube block

拔管机 tube drawing bench

拔管模 tube-drawing die, welding bell

拔管小车 plyer

拔拉阻力 pull-out resistance

拔模 【铸】lift

拔模角 【铸】pattern draft angle

拔模外斜度 outside draught

拔模斜度 【铸】pattern taper, pattern draft angle, draught (angle), draft

拔丝 (同"拉丝")

拔丝包装装置 draw-pack, D-pakers

拔丝工字轮(细丝用) wire-drawing reel

拔丝机 (同"拉丝机") ◇ 倒立卷筒～*, 两层～double-deck machine

拔丝冷却剂 coolant for wire-drawing

拔丝模 wire-drawing die

拔丝模板 wire-drawer's plate

拔丝润滑液 wire-drawing fluid

拔丝原理 drawing wire fundamentals

拔销角 draft angle

拔制 drawing ◇ 棒材～bar drawing,无芯棒[顶头]～*

拔制钢 drawn steel

拔桩机 pile extractor [puller, drawer]

靶 target ◇ 制～材料 target material

靶电极(X 射线管的) target electrode ◇ 可更换～装置*

靶极金属(用于 X 线射管) target metal

靶可换阳极 demountable-target anode

靶面 target face

靶面污染 target contamination

靶平面(X 射线的) target plane

靶心 bull's eye

靶型流量计 target meter

靶原子 target atom

靶至胶片距离 target-to-film distance

靶子部件 target assembly

靶子面积 target area

靶子热耗 dissipation of heat from the target

把柄 handle, helve

把持筒(矿热电炉的) 【冶】supporting [carrying] cylinder

把手 handle, claw, holding device, joke, shank

把手柄 【机】pad

钯铂精矿 palladium-platinum concentrate

钯隔板检漏器 palladium barrier leak detector

钯铬黑 palladium chromium black

钯汞齐 palladium amalgam, potarite

钯黑 palladium black

钯基合金 palladium-base alloy

钯金合金(50Au,50Pd;用于牙科) palladium-gold, palau

钯金矿 porpezite

钯石棉 palladinized [palladium] asbestos

钯酸 palladic acid

钯添加合金 palladium addition

钯铜合金(25Cu,5Ag,1Ni,余量 Pd;用于钟表工业) palladium-copper

钯银(合金) palladium-silver

钯轴承合金 palladium bearing metal

坝 dam ◇ 奥斯汀式～Austin dam,有隔墙的～diaphragm dam,支墩[扶壁]～but-tress dam

坝顶 crest ◇ 设有调节水位的～controlled crest

坝顶栏墙	【建】coping wall
坝基截水墙槽	key trench
坝脚抛石	talus
白斑霞石	lythrodes
白班	day shift
白层	white layer
白炽	incandescence, whiteness, white-glowing
白炽带	incandescent zone
白炽灯	filament lamp
白炽灯泡	incandescent lamp bulb
白炽灯丝	incandescent lamp filament [wire]
白炽电灯	incandescent (electric) lamp
白碲金矿	white tellurium
白点	flakes, white spot, lemon spot（钢内缺陷）◇ 钢中~*，小~*
白点发生倾向性[白点敏感性]	【金】susceptibility to flake
白点钢	spotty steel
白断口	white fracture
白垩	chalk
白垩粉	whiting
白垩灰浆	whitewash
白垩涂层试验（用于检查裂纹）	chalk test
白粉	whitening
白辐射	white radiation
白坩埚	【冶】white pot
白钢车刀	high-speed steel lathe tool
白光	white [colourless] light, white radiation
白光照明	illumination by white light
白硅石	crystobalite ◇ 半安定~*
白合金（刚果的一种钴铳）	white alloy
白黄铜	white brass ◇ 布里斯托尔~*
白金	（同"金钯合金"）◇ 科涅尔代用~*，密斯特里~ mystery
白金钢	（同"高铬镍耐酸耐热不锈钢"）
白金焊料（30—80Au,＜12Ni,＜15Zn,少量 Ag 及 Cu）	white gold solder
白金首饰合金	white gold jewelry alloy
白晶石 $\{H_2Be_4Si_2O_9\}$	bertrandite
白口层	【铸】chill
白口化	【铸】bleaching
白口生铁(锭)	white pig iron
白口铁	white cast iron (WCI) ◇ 含锰~*
白口铁铸件	hard casting
白镴（锡铅合金，锡基合金）	pewter ◇ 荷兰~合金，罗马~*
白磷	white phosphorus
白磷钙矿	zeugite
白榴石	leucite
白铳[冰铜]	【色】white matte
白氯铅矿 $\{PbCl_2 \cdot 2H_2O\}$	muriate of lead
白绿矾	white copperas
白煤	anthracite, smokeless [hard] coal
白煤生铁	anthracite pig
白明胶	gelatin(e)
白膜	（见"白锈"）
白泥	white slimes
白泥浆	clay wash
白泥洗液	【色】whitewash
白黏土	argil
白铍石 $\{(Ca, Na)_2BeSi_2(O, OH, F)_7\}$	leucophane
白铅（锌的俗称）	white lead
白铅矿 $\{PbCO_3\}$	cerus(s)ite
白青铜（54Cu, 4Ni, 余量 Zn）	white bronze
白圈	（同"亮边"）
白热	(white) glow, white [glowing] heat, candescence, whiteness ◇ 焊接~ white welding heat
白热丝	hot filament
白热温度	brightness temperature
白热状态	white-glowing, white-hot
白色代银合金（64.5Cu, 32Sn, 3.5As）	white alloy
白色氮化物层（渗氮工件表面氮化铁层）	white nitride layer
白色光亮金属	lustrous white metal
白色合金（银白色低熔点合金，如巴比合	

金、印刷合金、白鑞等锡、铅、锑基合金） white metal

白色金属轴承合金 white metal bearing alloy

白色金银合金（40—50Au, 余量 Ag） white gold alloy

白色浸蚀区域（轴承钢因滚动疲劳组织发生变化而难于浸蚀的部分）【金】white etching area

白色水泥 non-staining cement

白蛇纹石$\{H_4(Mg,Fe)_3Si_2O_9\}$ white serpentine

白砷石 claudetite, arsenphyllite

白石墨 white graphite

白霜（水玻璃砂过吹后的）【铸】sodium bicarbonate

白水泥 white cement

白丝状石棉 amiant(h)us

白酸洗 white pickling

白铁（镀锌铁总称） galvanized iron, tin plate

白铁矿 white iron pyrite, marc(h)asite $\{FeS_2\}$, white iron ore $\{FeCO_3\}$

白铁皮 galvanized iron sheet

白铜 white copper [brass], copper nickel, cupro-nickel (45—97.5Cu, 2.5—4.5Ni) ◇ 贝尔迪克特~*,帕克顿~Packtong, 普拉廷~*

白透辉石 malacolite

白涂[刷]料 white lime, whitewash, whitening（铝铸件用）

白土 clay ◇ 过滤用~filtering earth

白退火（光亮退火） white annealing

白钨矿$\{CaWO_4\}$ scheelite, sheelite, trimonite

白钨矿分解器 sheelite decomposer

白锡 white tin

白箱模型 white-box model

白锌矿 white zinc ore

白心可锻铸铁 white heart malleable (cast) iron, European malleable iron

白心可锻铸铁（欧洲式）退火法 whiteheart process

白锈 chalky rust（镀锌层表面缺陷，又称"白膜"）wet storage stain, white rust

白锈腐蚀（锌产生的） white rust corrosion

白银炼铜法 Baiyin copper smelting process

白云母$\{K_2O \cdot 3Al_2O_3 \cdot 6SiO_2 \cdot 2H_2O\}$ muscovite

白云石$\{CaCO_3 \cdot MgCO_3\}$ dolomite, bitter spar, magnesium [magnesian] limestone,【耐】pearl spar ◇ 成型~ moulded dolomite, 重烧[两次煅烧]~*, 煅烧~*, 克雷斯皮~打结炉衬~*, 轻烧~*, 烧结~*, 生~*, 熟~*, 竖炉焙烧~ shaft-kiln dolomite, 死烧~*, 一次煅烧~*, 硬烧~ shrunk dolomite, 致密~*

白云石补炉机【钢】dolomitethrowing machine

白云石车间 dolomite shop

白云石煅烧窑 dolomite (calcining) kiln

白云石粉(末) dolomite powder [fines], dolomitic stone screenings

白云石和氧化镁加焦油混合料【冶】dolomagnesia-tar mix

白云石化 dolomitization

白云石化石灰石 dolomitic limestone

白云石灰岩 dolomite limestone

白云石矿 crude dolomite

白云石离心机【耐】dolomite centrifuging machine

白云石脉石 dolomitic gangue

白云石镁砖 dolomite-magnesite brick ◇ 焦油结合~*

白云石耐火材料 dolomitic refractory

白云石喷枪[喷补器]【钢】dolomite gun

白云石砌块 dolomite block

白云石熔剂 dolomite flux

白云石熔剂性球团【团】dolomite (fluxed) pellet

白云石砂 dolomitic sand ◇ 合成镁质

白云石筛屑[筛下产品] dolomitic stone screenings
白云石石灰 dolomitic lime
白云石碳质耐火材料 duplex dolomite-carbone refractory
白云石投射机 【钢】dolomite-throwing machine
白云石型锌精矿 dolomitic-type zinc concentrate
白云石质材料 dolomite-based material
白云石质铬砖 dolomite-chromite brick
白云石砖 dolomite brick
"白"噪声 【理】white noise
白渣 white (lime) slag
白渣熔炼(电炉的) melting under white slag
白铸铁 white cast iron
白棕绳 Manil(l)a rope
柏林蓝 Berlin blue
柏林无光黑漆 Berlin black
柏瑞-奥赛特气体分析器 Burrel-Orsat apparatus
柏油 tar, asphalt
柏油混凝土 tar concrete
柏油毡 tar [pitched] felt
百叶[页]窗 window-shades, shades, window-blinds, blinds ◇ 固定~*,活~louver shutter,斜片~abatjour
百叶[页]窗式除尘机 louver deduster
百叶[页]窗式收尘器 baffle type collector
摆臂堆料机 Slewing-boom stacker ◇ 移动式~*
摆差 run-out tolerance ◇ 无~仪表 dead beat instrument
摆锤 pendulum (hammer)
摆锤刀口 impact knife edge
摆锤式冲击试验机 pendulum-type machine
摆锤式磨机 swing hammer mill
摆锤式黏度计 pendulum viscometer
摆动 swing(ing), wobbling motion, jigging motion, oscillating, hunting, rocking (motion), shake, play, flutter ◇ 猛烈~thrash(ing)
摆动臂式切割机 【焊】swinging arm cutting machine
摆动边杆导轨 swing link guide
摆动齿轮 tumbler [tumbling] gear
摆动齿条式冷床 rocker-type cooling bed
摆动阀瓣止回阀 swing-check valve
摆动幅度不足 underswing
摆动杆 swing(ing) lever
摆动缸 swing cylinder
摆动焊炬[焊条]焊接焊缝 weaving weld
摆动溜槽 swinging spout [chute], oscillating trough
摆动溜槽式布料器 swinging-spout feed system
摆动流嘴 【铁】tilting trough
摆动盘法(测定黏度用)【理】oscillating disk method
摆动球法 oscillating sphere method
摆动曲柄 oscillating crank
摆动曲柄装置 oscillating crank gear
摆动筛 【选】rocking screen
摆动升降台 tilting table ◇ 机后~back tilting table, 机前~front tilting table, 移动式~*
摆动式布料器 oscillating feeder
摆动式储料台[装料设备] tilting magazine
摆动式堆取料机 slewing stack-reclaimer
摆动式给料机[装置] pendulum [jig] feeder
摆动(式)流槽 swinging launder, rocking spout
摆动式炉 tilting furnace
摆动式排烟罩 swinging fume hood, swingable hood
摆动式取样器 oscillating sampler ◇ 弧线
摆动(式)圆锯(机) oscillating circular saw

摆动式运输机　shaking conveyer, swinging [shaking] conveyer
摆动式闸门　swinging gate
摆动台　tilter, wabbler
摆动调节器　pendulum governor
摆动箱式取样器　tilting-box sampler
摆动星轮　lowering sprocket
摆动液压缸　hydraulic cylinder for swing
摆动支座[轴承]　pendulum [tumbler] bearing
摆动值　【理】oscillating quantity
摆动周期　time of swing
摆动轴　oscillating axle
摆度(车床的)　swing
摆锻锤头　forming shoes
摆锻机　【压】swing-forging machine, rocker(-action) swaging machine ◇ 砧式～ anvil forging press
摆锻开坯机　【压】swing-forging machine
摆幅　(oscillation) amplitude, swing
摆杆　swing link
摆架　moving section
摆轮　balance wheel
摆轮式混砂法　【铸】mulling
摆轮式混砂机　centrifugal muller
摆式冲击试验　pendulum impact test
摆式冲击试验机　pendulum impact testing machine
摆式磁强计　pendulum magnetometer
摆式打桩机　pendulum pile-driver
摆式给料机(烧结机的)　【团】swing spout
摆式加热器　swing-away heater
摆式剪　【压】rocking shears
摆(式)锯　pendulum [oscillating, swinging] saw, swing cut-off saw
摆式取样器　pendulum-type sampler
摆式热锯　rocking-type hot saw
摆式塑性计[摆式锤塑度计]　pendulum plastometer
摆式压力块　pendulum pressure piece
摆式硬度试验　pendulum hardness test
摆式硬度试验机　pendulum hardness tester
摆式轧机　pendulum mill, vibratory [oscillating] rolling mill, DSW mill, rocker(-action) swaging machine, swing-forging machine
摆式撞击硬度　pendulum hardness
摆线齿轮　【机】cycloidal gear
摆线式分选机　cycloid cleaner
摆线式旋流器　cycloidal cyclone
摆线质谱仪　cycloidal mass spectrometer
摆振　【理】oscillation of pendulum
摆轴　pivoted [oscillating] axle
摆柱　hinge pedestal
拜耳法(氧化铝生产)　【色】Bayer process [method] ◇ 传统～*, 典型～*, 改良～*, 美国～*, 欧洲～*
拜耳法氢氧化铝　Bayer hydrate
拜耳法溶液　Bayer liquor
拜耳法氧化铝厂　Bayer plant
拜耳－霍尔·赫劳尔特法　Bayer/Hall-Heroult process
拜耳体[石]{βAl$_2$O$_3$·3H$_2$O} bayerite
拜尔培层(金相试样表面检验时须去的一层变形的金属)　【金】Beilby layer
斑　spot, stain, speck(le) ◇ 无～的 stainless
斑疤　scabby, scar
斑点　spot, speck(le), stain, plaque, smudge,【压】flecks (表面缺陷), freckle (或 patch, 镀锡薄板缺陷) ◇ 无～的 speckless, 形成～mottling, 有～的 spotted, spotty, granulated
斑点断口铁　mottled iron
斑(点)腐蚀　spot corrosion
斑点模糊(X－射线照相)　blurring of spots
斑点衍射花样　mottled diffraction pattern
斑点状表皮组织　snake-skin texture
斑点坐标读数　reading of spot coordinates
斑痕　smudge, mark
斑鳞　fleck scale
斑铜矿{Cu$_5$FeS$_4$}　bornite, erubescite,

peacock ore

斑脱岩 {(Ca,Mg)O·SiO$_2$·(Al,Fe)$_2$O$_3$} bentonite

斑纹 mottle, mottling, streak

斑岩铜矿 porphyry copper

斑状的 poikilitic

斑状淀积 spotty deposit

斑状腐蚀 patchy corrosion

斑状裂纹 pitting crack

班 crew (cr.), shift, gang

班报表 【企】turn report

班产量(吨) ton per shift

班布里奇－乔丹质谱仪 Bainbridge-Jordan mass spectrometer

搬运 carry, handle, convey, transport haul, tote ◇ 一端～end hauling, 电动～车 electric truck, 下悬式～车 over-the-load carrier

搬运工 handling labour

搬运机 carrier

搬运孔 【铸】handling hole

搬运箱 tote box

搬运造成的划痕 handling scratch

扳动装置 tripping gear

扳放机构 trigger gear

扳钮开关 toggle switch

扳手[子] spanner, wrench (ing iron), plate die ◇ 叉形～fork wrench, 方形螺帽～spanner for square nut, 管一[钳]alligator wrench, pipe wrench, 开脚[插头]～spanner wrench, 轮毂螺母～hub wrench, 取残极～(自耗电弧炉的构件) stub removing wrench, 双头～double end wrench, 套筒～", 弯头～", 爪形～jaw spanner

扳直辊 deflector [deflecting, debending] roll ◇ 开卷机带材～deeoiler roll

扳直机 【压】coil opener ◇ 带卷端头～", 电磁～"

扳直装置 puller ◇ 成卷带材端头～tail puller

扳子口 mouth of tongs, wrech opening [jaw]

板 plate, sheet, panel, plaque, wafer, 【化】block (蒸馏塔的) ◇ 香农～"

板边加工机床 edge-dressing machine

板材 sheet products, plate

板材刨边机[边棱刨床] plate-edge planer

板材标号 plate marking

板材冲床 plate-punching machine

板材冲压件 sheet stampings

板材倒棱[角]机 plate edge-bevel (l)ing machine

板材度量(144立方英寸, 合0.00236立方米) board measure (B.M.)

板材厚度同轧辊直径之比 thickness ratio

板材剪切机 plate cutting machine, plate shears [shearing machine]

板材矫平机 plate straightening rolls

板材浇铸 cake casting

板材矫正[直]机 【压】plate flattening [level(l)ing] machine, planing machine

板材精整机 【压】plate working machine

板材精整跨 sheet finishing bay

板材拉伸 【压】sheet stretch

板材拉伸矫直[矫平]机 sheet stretcher ◇ 辊式～"

板材连续铸锭轧制法 ◇ 亨特～Hunter process

板材劈[开]裂 through-sheet-thickness crack

板材热矫直机 hot mangle

板材试验(荷载、隔热性等) plate test

板材弯边机 plate flanging machine

板材弯曲试验 flat-bend test

板材弯曲塑性[延性] sheet-bend ductility

板材轧辊 plate roll

板材轧机 plate mill, jobbing sheet (-rolling) mill (薄板单张轧制的)

板材轧制 plate milling

板材粘辊 【压】gathering

板材折叠 doubling of sheets

板材纵切整平机 plate stripping planer

板带 sheet strip

板带材中心部分增厚 【压】crowning
板带材中心凸厚部分 【压】crown
板带式运输机 slat conveyer
板带轧制 plate/strip rolling
板的翘离(点焊、滚焊或凸焊缺陷) 【焊】sheet separation
板叠 【压】pack
板叠翻转机 sheet pack turnover
板叠分开 parting of sheet pack
板垛 sheet pile [piling], straight sheet pile, 【压】pack ◇ 运送～的吊具 sheet [pack] carrier
板垛高度 【压】piling height
板垛运送吊具 sheet [pack] carrier
板垛重量 pack weight
板阀 plate valve
板管比 plate and pipe ratio
板厚度 plate thickness
板簧 cup [leaf, plate] spring
板极 (positive) plate, anode, plate electrode
板极靶 plate target
板极电流 plate current
板极电流峰值 peak plate current
板极电势[位] plate potential
板极电渣焊 electro-slag welding with plate electrode
板极反应 plate reaction
板极检波(的) plate-detection
板极检波器 plate [plate-circuit] detector
板极脉冲调制发射机 plate pulsed transmitter
板极耦合的 plate-coupled
板极振荡回路 plate tank
板夹 plate jig
板件拉延[深冲] 【压】plate drawing
板铰链 plate hinge
板结框架 【建】plank frame (pk. fr.)
板晶钙磷酸石 $\{H_2Ca_5(PO_4)_4 \cdot \frac{1}{2}H_2O\}$ martinite
板晶石 melanocerite
板卷 【压】coiled sheet

板卷擦伤(热轧钢板卷间滑动引起的) coil digs
板卷翻转机 downender ◇ 液压～ hydraulic downender
板卷焊 coil weld
板卷轧机 strip sheet mill
板卷折印(钢板卷表面缺陷) coil wrench mark
板框式反渗透膜 【环】plate and frame type membrane
板框式压滤机 plate and frame filter
板沥青 piauzite
板梁 plain girder
板料展开 blank development
板磷锰矿 bermanite
板磷铁矿 ludlamite
板菱铀矿 schroeckingerite
板硫菌属 Thiopedia
板铝石 taosite
板面 pinacoid, pinakoid
板模 cake mould
板黏土 slate clay
板坯 【压】slab, strip breakdown, block ◇ 薄～ bar strip, 初轧～ bloom slab, 粗轧～ breakdowns, 大～ slab, 多流(连铸)～ multi-slab, 连铸～ continuously cast slab, 无用[废]～ dummy slab, 小～*
板坯剥皮机床[修整机床,铣床] slab milling machine
板坯称量辊道 slab weighing table
板坯成型机 mat-forming machine
板坯秤 slab weigher
板坯初轧机 slab (bing) mill, slabber ◇ 大升程～*,二辊式万能～*
板坯出料机 slab extractor
板坯出料机液压系统 slab extractor hydraulic system
板坯垂直[侧,水平]压下 slabbing action
板坯打印工[机] slab marker
板坯定心辊 slab centring roller
板坯堆垛机 slab piler
板坯堆放[存放]场 slab storage [yard]

板坯垛	slab pile
板坯垛挡板	slab pile damper
板坯翻转吊车	slab turning crane [gantry]
板坯翻转机	slab turnover device
板坯翻转装置	slab turning device
板坯返回辊道	slab reject table
板坯返回小车	slab return car
板坯-方坯初轧机	slabbing-blooming mill
板坯感应加热器	slab induction heater
板坯回转台	slab turn table
板坯加热炉	slab (reheat) furnace, sheet bar (heating) furnace
板坯加热炉工	slab handler
板坯剪切机	slab shears
板坯冷却机	slab cooler
板坯连续加热炉	continuous slab-(re)heating furnace
板坯连铸	slab continuous casting
板坯连铸机	(continuous) slab caster, slab (continuous) casting machine ◇ 超小型~*, 大型超低头~*
板坯连铸设备	slab-producing plant
板坯裂纹	slab crazing
板坯强制冷却器	forced slab cooler
板坯齐边压力机	slab reducer
板坯切头	slab butts
板坯清理机床	slab grinder
板坯清理[修整]间	slab grinding building
板坯升降转盘	slab turner
板坯受料装置	slab receiving device
板坯推进[出]机	slab pusher
板坯下料[冲裁]	flat blanking
板坯修整工段	slab conditioning yard
板坯压力调宽机	slab sizing press
板坯运出轨道	slab delivery tracks
板坯运输机	slab transfer
板坯轧机	plate slab mill
板坯轧制	slabbing
板坯装料机	slab charger
板坯装料间	slab loading cabin
板坯装料台	slab depiler
板坯装料装置	slab charging device
板坯自动出料	automatic slab discharging
板片	flat bar, bar of flat,【压】flat
板铅铀矿	$\{(PbO)_2(UO_3)_5 \cdot 4H_2O\}$ curite
板墙筋	【建】stud
板翘曲	slab warping
板式步进梁运输机	slate-type walking beam conveyer
板式电收尘器	electric plate precipitator ◇ 埃勒克斯~ Elex precipitator
板式过滤器	plate filter
板式换热器	plate heat exchanger
板式基础	bed plate foundation, mat foundation
板式积[集]尘电极	collecting plate electrode, collecting [collector] plate
板式给料机	plate feeder
板式结构	【建】plank frame (pk. fr.)
板式静电收尘器	plate (electrostatic) precipitator, plate-type electrostatic dust-precipitator
板式冷却	stave cooling
板式冷却器	plate cooler, stave cooler
板式滤网	plate-screen
板式无焰燃烧器	flat flameless burner
板式阳极	slab anode
板式运输[输送]机	pallet [slat-type, platform, apron] conveyer
板式蒸发器	plate type evaporator
板式(蒸馏)塔	plate tower
板式钻模	plate jig
板钛矿	$\{TiO_2\}$ brookite
板-碳电压损失(氧化铝电解的)	plate-to-carbon voltage loss
板-碳间电阻(氧化铝电解的)	plate-to-carbon resistance
板碳铀矿	schroeckingerite
板条	lath, slat, batten, plank
板条(式)输送机	slat conveyer
板条箱	crate
板条(状)马氏体	【金】lath (of) marten-

site

板网(薄金属板交替切槽或冲槽后拉张而成的网) perforated [expanded] metal

板形控制 【压】shape control ◇ 应力检测~系统

板形理论 flatness theory

板形平直度自动控制 automatic flatness control

板形-凸度-平直度控制 profile-crown-flatness control (PCFC)

板形综合治理 synthetical control of sheet shape

板牙 tapping [plate] die, screw (cutting) die, chaser, V block

板牙架[铰手] die-stock

板牙头 die head

板岩 slate

板岩煤 slate coal

板闸 plate brake

板砖 【耐】splits

板桩(码头、防波堤、围堰、横堰的) sheet pile [piling], pile plank, sheath pile, piling ◇ Z形(断面)[乙字形]~*, 隔水~ cut-off piling, 拉逊氏~ Larrson pile, 锚定式~*, 软泥基中一排 camp sheathing, 企口~grooved pile

板桩挡土墙码头 【建】camp sheathing

板桩断面[型材] sheet piling section

板桩联系帽梁 【建】cap piece of sheet-pile

板状核燃料 【理】plate-type fuel

板状合金 sheet alloy

板状晶 plate-like crystal

板状镍银 silmet

板状团矿 plate briquet

板状锡锑铋铜合金[锡镴] (86Sn, 8Sb, 3Bi, 3Cu) plate pewter

板座栓 crab [fang] bolt

钣金(冲压)成形 sheet metal forming

钣金工具 plate work tools

拌合 mix and stir, blend ◇ 加水~ blunge, 中心~厂*

拌合槽 mixer tank

拌合机[器] mixing machine ◇ 非倾倒式~*, 螺旋式~crutcher

拌合计数器 batch counter

拌胶器 glue mixer

拌沥青骨料 bituminized aggregate

拌泥转筒 wet pan

拌砂(手工进行) 【铸】cut

拌酸处理 acid cure

拌酸矿石 acid-pugged ore

伴生变形 concurrent deformation

伴生金属 associated metal, driver

伴生矿物 associated mineral, satellite

伴生元素 accompanying element

伴生杂质 accompanying impurity

瓣阀 clack, clap [flap] valve

瓣阀式密封 flap type seal

瓣状晶粒(混铁炉内铁水的) 【冶】lobe

瓣状晶粒主晶 【冶】major lobe

瓣状体 rosette

半V形坡口 【焊】single-bevel groove

半V形坡口丁字对接头焊缝 single-bevel tee-butt weld

半安定白硅石(方英石) meta crystabalite

半奥氏体钢 semi-austenitic steel

半杯形断口 half-cupped fracture

半焙烧 【团】green roasting

半焙烧[焙干]的 half-baked

半比例控制 semi-proportional control

半闭路收尘器 semiclosed circuit deduster

半闭式锭模 semiclosed top (S.C.T.) mould

半编译程序 semi-compiler

半波长 half-wave length

半波电位 half-wave potential

半波元件 half-wave element

半波整流 half-wave rectification

半波整流磁化电流 half-wave rectified magnetizing current

半波整流电路 half-wave rectifying circuit

半波整流器 half-wave rectifier

半波整流元件 half-wave element

半不锈钢 semi-stainless steel

半成品　semi-product, semi-manufactured product [goods, material], half-finished product, intermediary (product), intermediates, semi-finished product [material], semis, work in process, green ware
半成品钢　semi-finished steel
半成品丝材　process wire
半成品压力机　subpress
半成品轧材(如初轧坯、小方坯、板坯等等)　semi-finished metal
半成品轧机　semi-finishing mill
半充满能带　semifilled band
半冲填坝　demi-hydraulic fill dam
半处理的　half-black
半穿式公路　half-sunk roadway
半粗铜　semi-blister
半淬火　semi-hardening
半淬硬的　half-hardened
半搭连接　half-lap joint
半单元　half-cell
半当量溶液　seminormal solution
半导电性　semiconduction
半导体　semiconductor, semicon ◇ 纯[本征]～*, 单质[元素]～*, 多谷～*, 二元化合物～*, 非本征～*, 共价～*, 含杂质～*, 耗尽层～*, 互补[抵偿, 补偿]～*, 简并～*, 离子～*, 有机～*, 窄带隙～*, 直接带隙～*
半导体材料　semiconducting [transistor] material
半导体存储器　semiconductor memory
半导体单晶　semiconductor single crystal
半导体二极管　semiconductor diode
半导体工业　semiconductor industry
半导体合金　semiconducting alloy
半导体激光(器)　semiconductor [junction] laser
半导体集成电路　semiconductor integrated circuit
半导体结　semiconductor junction
半导体晶体　semiconducting crystal
半导体开关元件　thyristor

半导体扭矩测定器　transistor
半导体器件　semiconductor device
半导体区域精炼　zone refining of semiconductors
半导体热电堆　semiconductor thermopile
半导体冶金　semiconductor metallurgy
半低架式机组【连铸】semi-low head machine
半地下式(连铸)设备　semiunderground plant
半地下室【建】partially-exposed basement
半电池　half-cell, half element
半电池电势[电位]　half-cell potential
半电池反应　half-cell reaction
半蝶式孔型　semi-butterfly pass
半定量分析　semi-quantitative analysis
半对称晶体　hemihedral crystal
半对称形　hemihedral form
半对数坐标图　semilogarithmic diagram [graph]
半发光涂层　semigloss coating
半肥型砂【铸】medium-strong moulding sand
半封闭的　semi-enclosed (S.E.)
半峰宽度　half-peak breadth
半风【冶】half blast
半缝　dummy joint
半缝式缩缝　dummy type contraction joint
半浮动芯棒　semi-floating mandrel
半复消色差物镜　semiapochromatic objective
半干(法)成型　semi-dry pressing,【耐】stiff-plastic making
半干法成型机　stiff-plastic brickmaking machine
半干法喷补【钢】semi-dry gunning repair
半干黏土器皿　leather-hard
半干自动喷涂料　semi-dry automatic spraying material
半刚性的　semirigid
半钢　semi-steel (SS, ss), gun iron ◇ 转炉～炼钢工艺*

半钢铸件　semi-steel casting (S.S.C.)
半割阶(位错)　half-jog
半隔焰炉　(同"半马弗炉")
半隔焰隧道窑　semi-muffle tunnel kilns
半工业规模　semi-industrial scale, pilot-scale
半工业生产　pilot-plant production
半工业(生产)装置　semi-industrial plant [installation], half-way unit
半工业试验　pilot-plant test, pilot trial
半工业试验厂规模　pilot-plant scale
半工业试验球团[团]pilot-plant pellet
半工业试验设备[装置]　pilot-plant installation [unit, facilities], pilot installation [plant]
半工业试验塔[柱]　pilot-plant column
半工业性试验厂[(试验)工厂]　semi-commercial plant
半工业性试验阶段　pilot-plant stage
半工业阳离子交换设备　semi-works cation exchanger
半功率射束宽度　half-power beam width
半固定层[床]　semistationary bed
半固态成型　semisolid forming
半固态加工　semisolid processing
半固态浆　semi-solid slurry
半固态物质　semisolid mass
半固体状润滑剂　semisolid lubricant
半光亮[泽]的　semibright
半光亮涂层　demiglosscoating
半硅耐火砖　semi-silica firebrick
半硅酸渣　[色](siliceous) half slag
半硅质耐火材料　(< 93% SiO_2, < 10% $Al_2O_3 + TiO_2$) semi-siliceous [semi-acid] refractory
半硅质耐火黏土　siliceous fireclay
半硅砖　semi-silica brick
半贵金属　semi-precious metal
半黑的　half-black
半桁架　half truss
半厚(使辐射强度减少一半的材料厚度)　half-thickness

半厚砖　one-cut brick
半厚砖砌层　split course
半糊状渣　semi-pasty slag
半环形弯头　return bend
半还原　semi-reduction
半还原矿石的熔炼　smelting of semireduced ore
半挥发药皮(熔化时产生少量气体的)【焊】semivolatile coating
半极性键　semi-polar bond
半加器　【计】half adder, two-input [one-digit] adder ◇ 二进制～ binary half adder
半间歇反应　semibatch reaction
半间歇式反应器　semibatch reactor
半减(法)器　【计】half subtracter, two-input [one-digit] subtracter
半焦　semi-coke, partially carbonized coal, coalite
半焦化　semi-coking
半交叉皮带　half-crossed belt
半截锭　butt ingot
半结点[合]　half-joint
半结晶的　hemicrystalline
半金属　semimetal
半金属粉末　semimetallic powder
半金属型铸造　semipermanent mould casting
半晶体　semicrystal, half-crystal
半晶质的　【金】semicrystalline
半精密电阻合金　semiprecision resistance alloy
半精轧[整]机　semi-finishing mill, semifinisher
半精制料　half-finished material
半精制螺栓　half-bright bolt
半精砖坯　half-finished brick
半经验方程　semi-empirical equation
半经验关系(式)　semi-empirical relation
半经验计算　semi-empirical calculation
半径　radius, semi-diameter ◇ 玻尔～ Bohr radius

半净煤气 semi-cleaned gas, primary cleaned gas
半开角焊接 half-open corner joint
半可锻铸铁 semi-malleable cast iron
半块砖 blind header
半棱锥体 hemipyramid
半冷硬轧辊 part-chill roll
半离心铸造 semi-centrifugal casting
半联合冶金工厂(有炼钢和轧钢车间) semi-integrated works
半联轴节 coupling half
半连续操作 semicontinuous operation
半连续操作法 【冶】semibatch process
半连续碘化物热离解法 semicontinuous iodide process
半连续电解法 semicontinuous electrolytic process
半连续工艺 semicontinuous [semibatch] process
半连续离子交换柱 semicontinuous ion-exchange column ◇ 希金斯～Higgins column
"半连续"连铸法 "semicontinuous" continuous casting practice
半连续生产炉 semicontinuous furnace
半连续式带材热轧机 semicontinuous hot-strip mill
半连续式固结 semicontinuous hardening
半连续式宽带钢轧机 semicontinuous wide strip mill
半连续式球团固结设备 apparatus for semi-continuous hardening of pellets
半连续式酸洗 semicontinuous pickling
半连续式酸洗(作业)线 semicontinuous pickling line
半连续式线材轧机 semicontinuous wire-rod mill
半连续式轧机 semicontinuous mill, combination mill
半连续式轧机组 semicontinuous rolling train
半连续推料 semicontinuous stoking

半连续窑 semicontinuous kiln
半连续运转 semicontinuous running
半连续铸造机 semicontinuous casting machine
半连续铸造熔化 semicontinuous casting melting
半连轧 semi-tandem rolling
半流动性电极糊 semi-fluid electrode paste
半流态化床 semi-fluidized bed
半楼(一层与二层中间的阁楼) entresol
半露柱 pilaster
半马弗炉 semi-muffle type furnace, semi-muffle kiln
半马氏体淬火 semi-hardening
半煤气发生炉式燃烧室[炉] semi-producer-type furnace
半煤气烧成 【耐】semi-gas [half-gas] firing
半米库姆转鼓试验 【团】half-Micum test
半密封钢丝绳 semi-locked coil wire rope
半面晶体 hemihedral crystal
半面晶形 hemihedral form
半面体 hemihedron
半面体类 hemihedral class
半面性晶体 hemimorphic crystal
半模 half-pattern, pattern half ◇ 活动[可拆]～movable die
半凝顶弯 【连铸】liquid center bending
半凝固 semisolidification
半凝轧制钢锭 liquid squeezed ingot
半扭折带 half kink bands
半平面 incomplete plane
半破坏性检验 semidestructive examination
半剖视图 semisectional view
半铅淬火盘条(盘条轧出后,进行近似铅淬火过程的控制冷却) semi-patented rod
半墙 semi-wall
半球 hemishpere
半球面凹槽镗刀(修整铸型用)【铸】but-

ton sleeker
半球头　snap head
半球形杯突工具　hemispherical cupping tool
半球状的　dished
半热锻造(高碳钢在蓝脆温度至再结晶温度之间的锻造)　semi-hot forging
半热加工(室温至再结晶温度区间加工)　semi-hot working
半任意长度(管材的)　half random length
半熔材料　vitrified material
半熔锻造　semi-fusion forging
半熔焊(一种表面熔焊)　semi-fusion welding
半熔化的　semi-fused
半熔融灰　semi-molten ash
半软钢　semi-soft steel
半软回火薄钢板　quarter hard temper sheet
半商品性合金　semi-commercial alloy
半烧结状态　semi-sintered condition
半烧结状态挤压　【粉】extrusion under semi-sintered condition
半生产炉　semi-production furnace
半生次砖　grizzle (brick)
半湿式空气污染控制法　【环】semi-wet air pollution control method
半石墨　semi-graphite
半衰期(放射性元素的)　half-life (period), half-period, half-time, half-value period, period of half change
半双工　【电】half duplex
半双联法　【钢】semi-duplex process
半水合三氧化铀$\{UO_3 \cdot \frac{1}{2}H_2O\}$　uranium trioxide hemihydrate
半水合物　hemihydrate
半水煤气　semi-water gas
半丝质体　semi-fusinite
半塑性成型　semi-plastic making
半塑性轴承青铜(76.5—79.5Cu, 5—7Sn, 14.5—17.5Pb, 0—0.4Fe, 0—0.4Sb, 0—0.4Zn)　semi-plastic bronze

半酸性耐火材料　semi-acid refractory
半酸性耐火砖　ciliceous fireclay brick
半酸性黏土　semi-acidic clay
半弹性的　semielastic
半碳化　partial carbonization
半体双晶[孪晶]　hemitrope (twin)
半透明的　translucent, semi-opaque, semi-transparent
半透气[渗透]性　semi-permeability
半脱氧钢　(同"半镇静钢")
半椭圆孔型　【压】half oval pass, feather edge pass
半椭圆立轧边　【压】half oval edge
半挖半填截面[(横)断面]　cut and fill section, cut-fill section
半微量分析天平　semimicro analytical balance
半位错　half-dislocation
半温度时间　【金】half-temperature time
半稳定白云石　semistabilized dolomite ◇不焙烧～耐火材料
半稳定白云石烧块　semistable dolomite clinker
半稳定白云石砖　semistable dolomite brick
半无容器加工工艺　quasi-containerless processing
半无限长锭料(区域熔炼的)　semi-infinite ingot
半无烟煤　semi-anthracite, carbonaceous coal
半吸收厚度　(同"半值厚度")
半像(立体镜像对的)　half image
半写脉冲　【计】write half-pulse
半芯盒制泥芯　【铸】half-core boxcore
半型　【铸】half mould, mould half
半型砂箱　half-part moulding box
半形晶体　hemimorphic crystal
半形性　hemimorphism
半需氧菌　facultative aerobes
半悬吊式炉顶　semi-suspended roof
半选电流　【计】half current

半烟煤　semibituminous coal
半厌氧菌　facultative anaerobes
半氧化焙烧　half-oxidizing roasting
半氧化矿　semioxidized ore
半遥控　semi-remote manipulation
半液体　semi-liquid, quasi-liquid
半液体润滑　mixed-film lubrication
半（阴）影　penumbra
半隐含[隐式]法　semi-implicit method
半硬（美国形变铜合金处理记号，指厚度压缩率20.7%＜板、带材＞或截面压缩率37.1%＜丝材＞的冷加工处理）half hard
半硬磁合金　semi-hard magnetic alloy
半硬钢（0.3—0.4C, 0.15—0.25Si, 0.4—0.6Mn, ＜0.05S, ＜0.05P）semi-hard steel, half-hard steel（Hf H）
半硬钢板　half hard
半硬化　semi-harden
半硬化物质（结晶时的）　semisolid mass
半硬回火薄钢板（经连续式轧机冷轧和平整的）　half-hard temper sheet
半硬面合金轧辊　alloy grain roll
半硬面轧辊　part-chill roll
半硬线材（铝的）　half-hard wire
半硬质[半燧石]黏土　semi-flint clay
半硬状态板材　【色】half-hard temper sheet
半永磁材料　semi-hard magnetic material
半永久炉衬　semipermanent lining
半永久型铸造　semipermanent mould casting
半油脂型砂（同"半肥型砂"）
半圆槽钢　semi-circular channel
半圆钢　half rounds
半圆弓形体　C segment
半圆拱　semi-circular arch
半圆键　woodruff key, semi-circular key
半圆角度规　protractor
半圆头螺栓　cup-head bolt
半圆形分级溜槽　semi-circular stepped chute
半圆形集料架（冷床的）　【压】cowhorn bins
半圆形聚焦　semi-circular focusing
半圆形屋顶　【建】compass roof
半圆形压印　semi-circular depression
半圆砖　【耐】radius brick
半圆锉　half off file, half round file
半镇静钢　semi-killed [semi-deoxidized, semi-rimming, non-piping] steel, balanced steel ◇ GLX-w 低温可焊接～*
半镇静钢锭　semi-killed ingot, half killed ingot, balanced ingot
半镇静钢熔炼　semi-killed heat
半镇静易切削钢　freecutting semi-killed steel
半直接硫酸铵法　【焦】semidirect sulphate process
半值层　half(-value) layer
半值厚度　half-value thickness [width]
半值周期　half-value period
半致密材料　semidense material
半制品　semi-finished product [material], blank
半中和　half-neutralization
半周期　half-cycle, semiperiod
半轴　semi-axis
半轴承　half-bearing
半轴承衬套　half-bearing bush
半柱面　hemiprism
半铸钢　cast semi-steel（CSS）
半砖（宽为标准砖的一半）　(half-)bat, soap brick,【耐】splits
半锥角　semicone angle
半锥体　hemipyramid
半自动称量机　semi-automatic weighing machine
半自动秤　semi-automatic scale
半自动电镀设备[装置]　semi-automatic plating plant
半自动电焊机　semi-automatic welder
半自动焊　semi-autimatic coelding
半自动焊枪　semi-automatic handgun

半自动弧焊机 semi-automatic arc welding machine[welder]
半自动弧点焊机 semi-automatic arc spot welder
半自动化炉 semi-automatic furnace
半自动拖车 semi-trailer
半自动压滤机 semi-automatic filter press
半自磨机 semi-autogenous mill
半自热熔炼 【色】semi-pyritic smelting, partial pyritic smelting
办公室自动化 office automation
邦杜尔形变[可锻]铝合金（与含 4Cu 的硬铝类似） Bondur alloy
邦杜耐蚀铝合金（2—4Cu,0.3—0.6Mn,0.5—0.9Mg,余量 Al） Bondu
邦克－希尔预烧结法 Bunker-Hill presintering practice
绑接钢丝 border wire
绑线 binding band [wire],lashing wire
绑扎 banding,seizing（钢丝绳的绑扎）
绑扎钢丝 tie wire,binder
棒 stick,staff,rod,bar,slug
棒材 (steel,round) bar,bar (steel rolled) stock,rod（细的）◇ 成分均匀[均质]～homogeneous bar,短尺[尺寸不足]～scanty bar,螺丝用～screw stock,铆钉用～rivet rod
棒材拔制 bar drawing
棒材冲断下料工序 fracture rod operation
棒材打号机 【压】bar tagging machine
棒材倒角[倒棱]机 【机】bar chamfering machine
棒材定尺切割 bar dividing
棒材锻造 【压】bar forging
棒材给进机 rod feeder
棒材挤压机 bar extruder
棒材剪断[切]机 【压】bar shearing machine[shears]
棒材浇铸 billet casting
棒材矫直机 bar straightening machine,bar [rod] straightener ◇ 多辊式～*
棒材精整 bars finishing
棒材拉拔 bar [rod] drawing
棒材拉拔机 bar bench
棒材拉拔模 bar drawing die
棒材料架 【机】bar (storage) rack
棒材抛光机 【压】bar polishing machine
棒材切割机 bar cutting machine,machine for parting-off solid bars
棒材弯曲机 bar bending machine
棒材斜轧 bar cross rolling
棒材轧机 bar [rod] mill ◇ 三线式～*
棒材轧尖 bar pointing
棒材轧尖机 bar pointing machine
棒材轧制线 bar mill line
棒钢 bar steel,rod iron
棒帘式电收尘器 electric rod-curtain precipitator
棒料感应加热器 induction bar heater
棒磨 rod milling
棒磨机 pin crusher,【耐】rod mill
棒坯 rod billet ◇ 铆钉用～rivet bar
棒坯清理[修整]装置 rod shaving unit
棒区电阻（铝电解的） stud-zone resistance
棒式炉栅 grid
棒条筛 bar grizzly [screen,grit] ◇ 活动式～moving-bar grizzly,移动式～*
棒条振动筛 rod deck vibrating screen
棒铜 bar copper
棒线材轧机 bar and wire rod mill
棒形磁石 bar magnet
棒形焊料 【焊】bar solder
棒形试样 rod-shaped specimen,test stick
棒状杆菌属 corynebacterium
棒状核燃料 slug type fuel
棒状结晶[晶体] rod-like crystal
棒状硫 rod sulphur
棒状燃料 slug type fuel
棒状绕组 bar winding
棒状型芯 【铸】stock core
磅秤 weigh scale ◇ 带～的 scale-equipped
磅秤车 scale car

磅秤房　scale room
蚌壳式抓土器　clamshell
蚌线　【数】conchoid
傍轴光线(平行轴的)　paraxial rays
胞状反应　【金】cellular reaction
胞状晶体　【金】cellular crystal
包　package (pkg), pack, packet, bale, bunch, sack,【冶】ladle (又称"桶")
包藏　【金】occlude, occlusion
包藏空洞　occluded void
包层钢　sandwich steel
包层金属　clad metal
包层用青铜 (45Cu, 32Ni, 16Sn, 6Zn, 1Bi)　sheathing bronze
包缠　wrap round
包带　gird, binding band (木杆防腐用)
包到包真空脱[除]气　ladle to ladle degassing
包到模真空脱气　ladle to ingot-mold degassing
包底大块砖　bottom block
包杜拉铝　dural alclad
包镀金属粉末　coated metal powder
包镀铝法　alumicoat process
包覆　cladding ◇ 爆炸 ~ explosive cladding, 单层棉纱 ~的, 挤压 ~ extrusion cladding, 轧制 ~ cladding by rolling
包覆不锈钢　stainless cladding
包覆材料　cladding material
包覆层　clad
包覆层下开裂[裂纹]　underclad cracking
包覆粉粒　coated particle
包覆粉末　【粉】coating powder
包覆钢　cladding steel
包覆[包层]钢丝　clad wire
包覆金属　clad(ding) metal, plating
包覆铝　aluminium cladding, metallized aluminium
包覆铜　copper cladding ◇ 奥克萨利 ~合金 ~
包覆用金针(成色在九开以上)　gold-filled
包覆[包层]轧制　sandwich rolling
包钢　steeling
包钢板的　steel-plated
包钢层压制品　clad-steel laminate
包钢的　steel-clad, steel-armo(u)red
包钢钢丝绳　steel-clad wire rope
包工附加费　prime cost (PC, P.C.)
包裹　package (pkg), pack (Pk., pk.)
包含　containing
包焊(沿周边)　contour welding
包合物　clathrate
包合作用　clathration
包夹轧制　composite rolling
包角　angle of wrap
包金　gilding
包金的　goldplated, gold-cased
包金属的　metal-faced
包金硬币　Billon
包晶　【金】peritectic
包晶成分[组成]　peritectic composition
包晶点　peritectic point
包晶反应　peritectic (reaction), metatectic
包晶(反应)线　peritectic horizontal [line]
包晶合金　peritectic alloy
包晶粒化(作用)　peritectic granulation
包晶凝固　peritectic freezing
包晶平衡　peritectic equilibrium
包晶平台(加热或冷却曲线上的)　peritectic halt
包晶球化　peritectic spheroidizing
包晶体　peritectic, metatectic (美)
包晶细化(作用)　peritectic refining
包晶相　peritectic phase
包晶转变　peritectic transformation [change]
包晶组织　peritectic structure
包壳　incrust(ation)
包壳材料　cladding material
包壳轧制　sheath rolling
包铝层板　plymetal
包铝产品　alclad product
包铝钢板　◇ 阿卢弗尔 ~ alufer

包铝钢带　◇费兰~*
包铝钢丝　aluminium-clad wire
包铝氧化硼复合板　◇博罗泽尔~*
包麻钢丝绳　marline clad wire rope
包内残钢[铁]　【冶】ladle scrap
包内混合　ladle mixing
包内脱氧　【钢】ladle deoxidizing, deoxidation in ladle
包内渣瘤[结壳]　【冶】ladle scull
包内(真空)脱气　【钢】ladle degassing
包镍　nickel coat
包镍耐蚀高强度钢板　◇尼克拉德~ Niclad
包镍铁　nickel-clad iron
包镍铜　nickel-clad copper
包皮　sheathing, wrappage
包皮粉末变性剂　wrappage powdered denaturant
包皮金属焊条电弧　coated electrode metallic arc
包皮线　【电】covered wire
包铅　lead coating [covering], terne
包铅的　lead-coated, lead-plated
包铅钢　ferrolum
包铅铜　◇库普拉姆~Cupralum
包砂　【铸】sand scab, burned-on sand
包砂形成　【铸】scabbing
包丝焊丝明弧自动焊　fusarc welding
包套　【粉】can, bag, capsule, container ◇去除~desheathing
包套抽真空　【粉】evacuation of capsule
包套锻结法　canned forging ◇粉末~*
包套挤压法　canned [sheath] extruding, canned extrusion technique
包套铸坯　canned billet
包体　inclusion
包铜不锈钢丝　(同"镀铜不锈钢丝")
包铜层　copper layer
包铜钢丝　copperweld (wire), copper clad wire, coppered wire, 【压】weld wire
包铜铝(电池组电缆用)　copper-clad aluminium

包铜软钢丝　copper coated mild steel wire
包铜铁粉　copper-coated iron powder
包铜铁镍合金丝　◇杜美~*
包围组织　【金】surrounding structure
包析成分[组成]　【金】peritectoid composition
包析反应　peritectoid (reaction)
包析合金　peritectoid alloy
包析平衡　peritectoid [metatectic] equilibrium
包析(体)　【金】peritectoid
包析相　peritectoid phase
包析转变　peritectoid transformation
包锡　tin (ning), tin-coating
包锡铜　tinned copper (Td Cu)
包锌　zinc (covering), zincification, zincing
包样　【冶】ladle sample
包样成分　【钢】ladle chemistry
包样分析　【钢】ladle analysis
包样试验　ladle test
包银的铜　silver clad copper
包银硬币　Billon
包硬铝　dural alclad
包扎　packing, package, wrap
包渣气孔(缺陷)　【铸】slag blowhole
包中放出渣　【冶】ladled slag
包中脱硫　ladle desulphurization
包中孕育[变质]处理(铸铁的)　ladle inoculation
包中孕育[变质]处理剂　ladle inoculant
包装　pack(ing), package, packaging, wrap up ◇机械化~捆扎作业线*
包装材料　packing [wrapping] material
包装秤　pack scale
包装缓冲[贮放]斗仓　packing surge hopper
包装机　packer, packing [baling] press, pack(ag)ing machine, balepress, 【压】packager (钢丝的) ◇滚筒式~*, 自动~*
包装记数器　wrapping counter
包装跨　packing bay [span]

包装流水作业线　packaging conveyer line
包装设备　packing equipment
包装渗碳　pack carburizing
包装台　bundling table
包装套　packing case
包装系统　【冶】packed system
包装重量　packed weight (P.W.), tare
孢子　spore ◇ 不产生~的 nonspore-forming
孢子暗煤　【焦】exinite-durite
剥过皮的　skinned
剥壳(缺陷)　【铸】peel back
剥离试验(接触点焊的)　Peal test
剥落破坏　pull out type fracture
剥皮　scalping (钢锭的), peeling (管坯的)
剥皮机　peeler, sheller ◇ 钢坯~ billeteer
剥皮机床　scalping machine, rotary peeler
剥皮磨床　【压】snagging grinding machine
剥片机　stripping machine
剥下的乳胶膜　stripped emulsion
薄板　sheet (iron, metal, products), light(-gauge) sheet, thin sheet [plate] ◇ 标准一面光亮精加工~*, 待处理[有缺陷]~mender sheet, 覆层[涂层]~coated sheet, 复合金属~clad metal sheet, 厚度合格~on-gauge sheet, 镜面光亮~*, 抛光~*, 平整冷轧的~temper-rolled sheet, 钎焊~*, 商品~*, 瓦垄形金属~*, 完全酸洗~full pickled sheet
薄板材　sheet stock
薄板材料　sheet material
薄板测厚仪[测厚计,厚度卡规]　sheet thickness gauge [calibrator]
薄板(冲压)成型　sheet metal forming
薄板打捆装置　sheet packing device
薄板打印机　sheet printer
薄板带张力轧制　sheet rolling with tension
薄板电磁分送机构　magnetic sheet handling unit
薄板叠　sheet pack
薄板叠合　【压】sheets matching
薄板镀锌设备　【压】sheet-galvanizing equipment
薄板镀锌作业线　sheet-galvanizing line
薄板方向性　directionality in sheet
薄板分层[起鳞]　exfoliation of sheets
薄板分送机　sheet pickup
薄板分选工　sheet metal grader
薄板分选机　sheet classifier
薄板分选系统　single-sheet classification system
薄板辊式矫直机　roller flattener
薄板和板坯加热炉　sheet and pair furnace
薄板厚度　sheet thickness
薄板厚度卡规　sheet (thickness) gauge
薄板加热炉　sheet(-reheating) furnace
薄板剪　tinner's snips
薄板剪切机　sheet mill shears, sheet-iron shears
薄板矫平　sheet level(l)ing, mangling
薄板矫平机　sheet level(1)er, sheet-level(1)ing [sheet-straightening] machine, sheet rectifier (带支持辊的)
薄板金属焊接　light gauge welding
薄板精整　sheet finishing
薄板精整作业线　sheeting line
薄板卷　coiled sheet
薄板库　【压】sheet building
薄板拉伸压力机　sheet-stretch press
薄板冷轧机　cold sheet mill
薄板连续电镀锌[铜、黄铜]法　◇ 谢拉德~Sherrite process
薄板连铸机　continuous belt thin section casting machine
薄板坯　【压】thin slab, sheet bar [billet], bar strip, flat hot rolled bar ◇ 倍尺~sheet bar multiple, 多倍~multiples
薄板坯垛放机　sheet bar stacker
薄板坯加热炉　pair furnace
薄板坯剪切机　sheet bar shears
薄板坯连铸　thin slab (continuous) casting, thin section continuous casting

薄bao

薄板坯连铸机　thin slab (continuous) caster ◇ 双履带活块循环式~*
薄板坯连铸-连轧　thin-slab casting-process ◇ 紧凑式~生产线*
薄板坯配对[双合]　pairing of sheet bars
薄板坯-小[中]坯轧机[薄板坯和钢坯轧机]　sheet bar and billet mill ◇ 连续式~*
薄板坯轧机　sheet bar mill
薄板平整　sheet level(l)ing
薄板平整机　sheet-temper mill, sheet-skin pass mill
薄板热浸镀锌　hot dip sheet galvanizing
薄板热轧机　hot sheet mill (HSM)
薄板伸张法　stretching process
薄板伸张压力机　stretch(ing) press
薄板升降台　sheet lifter
薄板酸洗设备　sheet pickling machinery
薄板碎边(剪下的)　sheet clippings
薄板弯板机　sheet bending machine
薄板修整　sheet dressing
薄板轧辊　sheet roll
薄板轧机　【压】(thin-)sheet mill, laminating rolling mill (贵金属的) ◇ 计算机控制~ computerized sheet mill
薄板轧机机组　sheet mill train
薄板轧机机座　sheet mill stand
薄板折叠　【压】joggling
薄板折叠机　sheet [plate] doubler, sheet-doubling machine
薄板折印(薄板平整前扭折造成的缺陷)　sheet wrench mark
薄板砖　split brick
薄板自动记数器　automatic sheet counter, automatic sheet counting machine
薄壁槽钢　thin-wall channel
薄壁高炉　thin-walled blast-furnace
薄壁管　thin-wall pipe, thin (-walled) tube, light-wall tubing ◇ 胡克~挤压法【压】Hooker process
薄壁结构(炉身)　thin-wall construction
薄壁结晶器　【连铸】thin-walled mould

薄壁炉衬　thin-skinned lining
薄壁模　thin-walled die, draw mould
薄壁盛料器　thin-walled container
薄壁无缝钢管　light-wall seamless tube
薄壁型[钢]材　thin [slender] section
薄壁铸件　thin-section [thin-walled] casting, frail casting
薄边砖　【耐】feather edge brick
薄标本膜　thin specimen films
薄饼　pancake
薄材硬度计　microdurometer
薄层　thin layer, lamella (复数 lamellae), platelet, shallow case (表面硬化的薄层)
薄层金属层状夹板　thinlayered metal-metal laminates
薄层色谱[层析]法　thin layer chromatography ◇ 高效~*
薄层药皮　【焊】thin coating
薄带板形　thin strip flatness
薄带材[钢,坯]　thin strip
薄带材直接铸轧工艺　direct strip cast process
薄带连铸　thin strip continuous casting ◇ 双辊~*
薄带坯连铸机　thin strip caster
薄镀[覆]层　thin [light, curtain] coating, flash coating (钢丝上的铜或锡镀层)
薄覆[敷]层的　thin-coated
薄钢板　steel [thin, light, black] sheet, sheet steel (sh.s), sheet iron (S.I., s.i.), thin-gauge plate ◇ 单张~mill pack, 发蓝~ blue planished steel, 复层[复合]~ clad sheet steel, 光整冷轧的软回火~*, 精整的~ second steel sheet, 美工~* art metal, 汽车用~ automobile sheet steel, 涂漆~*, 网眼~* expanded sheet metal, 小张镀锡的~*, 乙烯基塑料覆面~ vinyl-coated sheet, 优质[一级]~ prime sheet
薄钢板标准厚度(指镀锡钢板、镀锌钢板)　standard sheet metal gauge
薄钢板分选机　sheet classifier

薄钢板记数堆放工	reckoner
薄钢板矫平机	sheet steel straightening machine [unit]
薄钢板热浸镀锌	hot dip sheet galvanizing
薄钢板退火用固定式炉底[炉台]	sheet-annealing base
薄钢板轧辊	sheet roll
薄钢板轧机	(thin-)sheet mill
薄钢片	stalloy
薄钢纸	fish paper
薄(灰)浆	grout
薄胶泥	grout ◇ 涂~ grouting
薄截面	thin section
薄金镀层(用金汞齐镀的)	fine gilt
薄金属片	foil
薄金属切割	light cutting
薄壳拱	【建】shell arch
薄壳屋顶	【建】shell roof
薄壳铸造	shell moulded casting
薄矿层	delf, thin [ore bed, layer]
薄料层	thin [shallow] bed, 【团】low-pellet layer (薄球团料层)
薄料层冷却机	shallow-bed cooler
薄铝板轧机	aluminium sheet mill
薄膜半导体	film semiconductor
薄膜泵	membrane pump
薄膜材料	thin film material
薄膜电极	film electrode
薄膜基体	film matrix
薄膜金刚石	thin film diamond
薄膜晶体	film crystal
薄内衬	thin wall-type inwalls
薄皮钢锭	thin-skinned ingot
薄片	slice, lamina, lamella (复数 lamellae), thin section disk, disc, platelet, tab ◇ 小~ flakelet
薄片黄铜	latten brass
薄片激冷金属	splat
薄片石棉	flaked asbestos
薄片试样	【钢】napkin
薄片锡	flake tin
薄片(状)的	lamellar, laminated
薄片状粉末	leafy powder
薄剖面	thin section
薄铅板	rolled lead
薄墙的	thin-walled
薄切片	slice, thin section
薄球团料层	【团】low-pellet layer
薄砂浆	grout
薄试样膜	thin specimen films
薄塑料涂层(用于在深冲时保护金属带材表面)	liquid envelope
薄铁板	sheet iron ◇ 滑动面~ slipper plate
薄铁板壳[罩]	sheet-iron shell
薄铜板	sheet copper ◇ 电解~ electro-copper sheet
薄涂层的	thin-coated
薄脱碳层(贴近氧化铁皮的)	【压】bark
薄锡层("焦炼")镀锡薄钢板(平均锡层重量0.45--0.68kg/基准箱)	coke (tin) plate ◇ 标准~*, 肯纳~*, 特制~*, 最优~*[高级镀锡钢板]*
薄型断面	thin section
薄样切片机	【金】microtome
薄样硬度计	microdurometer
保安措施	safety measures [methods, precaution]
保安技术	safety technique [methods]
保持触点	retaining contact
保持电流	hold current
保持电路	holding [retaining, sustain] circuit
保持符号	【计】hold mark
保持继电器	holding relay
保持架(滚动轴承的)	retainer
保持接点	residual contact
保持力	retentivity
保持器	retainer
保持线圈	holding [locking] coil
保持性	retentivity
保持阳极(维持电弧阳极)	holding anode
保持装置	holdback
保持状态	【计】hold [freeze] mode

保存 conservation, holding, reservation, retention
保存指令 【计】hold instructure
保存(周)期 【计】retention period
保干器 desiccator
保铬 【钢】Cr yield
保护 protection, defend, (safe) guard, shielding ◇ 有～的 protected (prot.)
保护板 armour plate ◇ 炉喉～*
保护层 protective layer [cover(ing), envelope], (clear) cover, mat [armour] coat, resist, prevent [stop-off] coating (用于化学热处理)
保护层沉浸涂镀法(板材的) dip process
保护衬里 protective lining
保护衬砖层 【冶】safety lining
保护处理 protective treatment
保护措施 protective measures
保护电抗器 protective reactor
保护电路 guard [protection] circuit
保护镀层 protective coating
保护盖板(用于钢板热处理) cover sheet
保护管 protecting tube
保护焊缝背面用气体 backing gas
保护和装饰涂覆处理(法)(镁和镁合金的) manodyzing
保护环 guard ring
保护剂 protecting [protective] agent, 【选】conserving agent
保护继电器 protective relay
保护键 【计】protection key
保护浇注 【钢】protective casting
保护接地 protecting grounding
保护介质 protective medium, shielding atmosphere, 【金】shielding medium, 【焊】envelope
保护警报系统 protective alarm system
保护壳 protective crust, guard plate
保护面层(道路路面的) armour course
保护面罩 (同"防护面罩")
保护膜 protective film [skin, envelope], safety film, frangible disc

保护平台(砌筑多层炉衬用) 【冶】shock scaffold
保护漆 protective paint
保护器 protector
保护气氛 protective [shielding] atmosphere, blanket, 【金】shielding medium ◇ 放热型～(同"放热式气氛")*, 含碳～*, 机械化焊接用～室*, 离解氨～*, 手工焊接用～室*
保护气氛成分不稳定 atmosphere imbalance
保护气氛回火 protective-atmosphere tempering
保护气氛气体 atmosphere [atmospheric] gas
保护气氛设备 atmosphere equipment
保护气氛室内焊接 dry-box welding
保护气氛退火炉 special atmosphere furnace
保护气体 protective [shield(ing)] gas, protective atmosphere ◇ DX 无氧化加热用～DX gas, 焊接级～welding-grade gas
保护气体储罐 protective atmosphere gas storage
保护气体(供应)站[发生装置] protection [protective] gas plant
保护气体进[入]口 atmosphere entry, gas atmosphere inlet
保护气体净化设备 atmosphere-purifying equipment
保护气体螺柱焊 shielded stud welding
保护气体烧结箱 atmosphere-retaining sinter box
保护气体转化[裂化]器 atmosphere gas converter
保护墙 flash wall
保护润滑脂 protective grease
保护设备 protective equipment
保护手套 protecting gloves
保护套 protective sleeve [envelope, cage], protecting jacket

保护套管 protection [sheath] tube
保护涂[镀]层 protective coat [covering], preservating coat, overcoating, topcoat
保护涂料 protective paint [coating]
保护外壳 protective casing [envelop]
保护外罩 guard plate
保护网 guard net
保护物 shield, (safe)guard
保护信号 【计】guard signal
保护性覆盖层 protective coating
保护性能[特性] protective property
保护性熔剂 【冶】covering flux
保护性涂饰 protective finish
保护眼镜(焊接用) protecting spectacles
保护焰帘 protective flame curtain
保护硬钎焊(在保护气氛下进行) blanket brazing
保护渣 【连铸】mould(ing) [casting] powder, protecting slag ◇ 空心颗粒~*, 双高~*, 预熔型连铸~*
保护栅栏 protective grating
保护罩 protecting jacket, protective shield, boot (cap)
保护钟[锥体](布料器的) 【铁】wearing cone
保护装置 protective device, protecting means
保护作用期限[保护寿命](涂层的) protective life
保护铠装 guard shield
保健 health protection [care]
保健机构 health institution
保健事业 health services
保健项目 【环】health item
保留权利 rights reserved
保留时间控制 retention time control
保留体积 retention volume
保密 maintain secrecy
保全措施 safety control
保热 heat retaining
保热器 heat retainer

保湿剂(型砂的) 【铸】humectant
保湿箱 humidistat
保温 insulation, heat preservation, incubation, holding (热处理的保温)
保温材料 heat insulating substance[material]
保温层 heat [thermal] insulating layer, thermal insulation blanket
保温段 【压】holding [soaking] zone (炉子的), 【团】annealing zone, post-heater, preheat hood
保温管 covered pipe
保温罐 (temperature) holding pot, holding ladle (钢水的)
保温加热器 muff heater
保温坑 soaking pit
保温流槽 insulated launder
保温炉 heat retaining furnace, maintaining furnace, holding [retaining] ves-sel, holding hearth, 【压】holding furnace (热坯料的) ◇ 带卷取机的~ coiler [coiling] furnace, 倾动式~ kettle furnace
保温帽 【钢】hot top [dozzle], feeder (head), headbox, runner bush, shrink [sink] head ◇ 带~的钢锭 hot topped ingot, 带~的钢锭模 hot top (ped) mould, 浮悬式~ floating hot top, "虎型"~制造设备 tiger topping plant, 组合~ composite head
保温帽接合处(钢锭的) hot top junction
保温帽口 hot topping
保温帽外壳 shrink head casing
保温帽砖 hot brick
保温瓶 vacuum flask, thermo-flask
保温期 incubation period
保温器 heat retainer
保温前炉 preheated forehearth
保温时间 holding [soak(ing), incubation] time
保温水套 thermal jacket
保温套 insulating sleeve
保温阴极 heat-shielded cathode

保温毡	thermal insulation blanket
保温罩	soaking hood
保温纸	building paper
保温砖	insulation brick
保险	insurance, safety
保险板	safety guard
保险岔道	【运】deflecting track
保险挡	safety dog
保险垫圈[垫片]	frangible disc, 【机】lock washer
保险阀	relief [escape, lock] valve
保险费	insurance
保险费和运费	cost insurance and freight (C.I.F.)
保险杆	safety lever
保险合金	lock alloy
保险件	safety [breaking] piece
保险开关	safety switch
保险螺栓	safety bolt
保险器	safeguard, catch
保险塞	【焊】fusible plug
保险丝	【电】fuse (wire), safety [wire] fuse ◇ 插塞式～fuse plug, 防潮～*, 封闭式～enclosed fuse (EF), 盒形～box fuse, 可熔～fusible cut out, 细[微型]～micro-fuse
保险丝合金	electric fuse metal
保险锁	safe(ty) lock, spur guard
保险筒	【电】cartridge
保险碗	breakers
保险系数	factor of assurance
保险销	safety [guard] pin
保险闸	safety brake
保险装置	safety [locking] device, 【电】interlock
保压(保持最大正塑压力)	dwell(ing)
保压时间(压铸)	【铸】dwell time
保养	maintenance, maintaining, attention, curing
保养费	maintenance cost
保养工程	maintenance engineering
保养频率	frequency of maintenance
保真度	fidelity
保证	guarantee, assurance, warrant
保证试验	warranty test
保证数值	guarantee value
保证数字	guarantee figure
保证系数	assurance coefficient
饱和	saturating (satg), saturation (satn) ◇ 用氧～oxygenation
饱和层	saturated layer
饱和磁感应	saturation induction
饱和磁化	saturated magnetization
饱和磁矩	saturation magnetic moment
饱和(磁)通量密度	【理】saturation flux density
饱和点	saturation point
饱和电抗器	transductor ◇ 直流～*
饱和电流	saturation current
饱和电子枪	saturated gun
饱和度	saturation (level), degree of saturation, saturability
饱和甘汞电极	saturated calomel electrode
饱和感应(饱和磁感应)	saturation induction
饱和活度	saturation activity
饱和活化	saturation activation
饱和极限	saturation limit
饱和剂	saturator
饱和静电荷	saturation charge
饱和绝热过程	saturation-adiabatic process
饱和空气	saturated air
饱和离子交换柱能力	saturation column capacity
饱和率	saturation ratio
饱和浓度	saturated concentration
饱和器	saturator
饱和器煤气分配伞	saturator bell
饱和气体	saturated gas
饱和曲线	saturation curve
饱和溶解氧量	saturated dissolved oxygen
饱和溶液	saturated solution
饱和室	saturation chamber

饱和酸	saturated acid
饱和塔	saturator tower
饱和特性(曲线)	saturation characteristic
饱和铁心	saturated core
饱和铜	(同"凹铜")
饱和吸收	saturated absorption
饱和系数	saturation coefficient
饱和陷阱	saturating trap
饱和因数	saturation factor
饱和油	saturated oil
饱和蒸汽	saturated steam [vapour]
饱和蒸汽表	saturation steam table
饱和脂肪酸	saturated fatty acid
饱和重量	saturated weight
饱和柱能力(饱和离子交换柱能力)	saturation column capacity
饱和状态	saturation state
饱和组态	saturated configuration
宝石	jewel ◇ 鲁尔兹~合金*，汤卡~合金*
抱辊	snubber roll
抱闸	damping brake
报表	report forms, inventory
报表头[提要]	report heading
报表周期	reporting period
报酬	reward, remuneration, pay, 【企】compensation ◇ 工伤~*
报废	rejection, scrapping ◇ 坯料~检查装置*
报废产品	rejected product
报废带卷	rejected coil
报废的	used-up, rejected, abandoned, condemned, spoiled
报废零件	scrapped parts, menders
报废炉次	(同"炼废炉次")
报废器材废钢	dormant scrap
报废数	rejection number
报废压块	rejected compact
报废铸件	misfit cast
报告会	seminar
报号线路	annunciating circuit
报价	offer, quotation
报价单	quotation (of prices)
报警部件	warning piece
报警触点	warning contact
报警灯	alarm lamp
报警符	【电】bell character (BEL)
报警回路	warning circuit
报警继电器	alarm relay
报警器	alarm, annunciator, alertor, siren, warner ◇ 音响~audible alarm
报警显示	alarm display
报警信号	alerting [alarm] signal
报警压力	alarm pressure
报警指示器	warning indicator
鲍多英铜镍钴合金(72Cu,16.6Ni,1.8Co,2.5Sn,7.1Zn,0.5Al)	Baudoin's alloy
鲍尔-巴尔夫法(使钢铁表面形成光亮Fe_3O_4防腐膜)	Bower-Barff process
鲍尔铅基轴承合金(5Sn,9 或 15Sb,80—86Pb,0.5Cu)	Power
鲍曼硫印	【金】Baumann sulphur print (ing)
鲍曼硫印法	【金】Baumann's method
鲍曼试验	Bauman test
鲍曼-斯坦吕克冲击硬度试验机	Bauman-Steinrueck impact hardness tester
鲍施-龙泊粉尘测定仪	Bausch and Lomb dust counter
鲍氏比重计(用于液体)	Bouyoucos hydrometer
鲍氏反应($CO_2 + C \rightleftharpoons 2CO$)	【铁】Boudouard reaction
鲍氏反应曲线	Boudouard reaction curve
鲍斯曼垫物防溅铸锭法	【钢】Bosment process
鲍辛格效应(材料先后受两个方向相反的应力作用时,弹性极限显著下降)	Bauschinger effect
刨边机	edge planer [shaver], edge planing machine
刨齿机[齿轮刨床]	gear shaper
刨床	planing [facing] machine
刨花	wood shavings [chips] ◇ 点火~

kindling wood
刨花板 chipboard
刨平 planing ◇ 铸模表面~【铸】searing
刨削(槽) gouging
爆发 bursting, outburst
爆发室(高速锤的) 【机】firing chamber
爆发现象(马氏体的) 【金】burst phenomenon
爆管 fuse
爆裂 burst(ing), blow out, decrepitation, 【电】sputter, 【建】popping
爆裂强度 bursting strength
爆裂应力 bursting stress
爆裂指数 【团】decrepitation index
爆烈声 bang
爆鸣气 detonating gas
爆破 outburst
爆破材料 explosive material
爆破工程 blasting
爆破力[负载] explosive load
爆破数据 blast data
爆破压力 bursting pressure
爆破用炸药 blasting powder (blstg pwd)
爆燃 explosive combustion, deflagratation, 【化】outburst
爆燃喷镀[涂] 【金】detonation spraying
爆燃速度 deflagration velocity
爆燃性 deflagrability
爆炸 explosion, blast(ing), blowing, bursting ◇ 粉尘~dust explosion, 可~性 explosibility, 易~的 explosive
爆炸包覆(法) explosive cladding
爆炸表面强化[硬化] explosive surface hardening
爆炸成形 explosive forming [shaping, compaction, pressing, fabrication] ◇ 低速~*, 高效炸药~*, 混合气~*, 遥控高速~*, 直接~*
爆炸成形法[工艺] Aeroform method, dynaforming ◇ 闭模~*, 接触式~*, 开式模~*
爆炸成形装置 explosion forming apparatus
爆炸冲击试验 explosive impact test
爆炸冲孔 explosive perforation
爆炸冲压 explosion punching ◇ 远距离高速~成形*
爆炸捣固[捣实](型砂的) 【铸】explosive ramming
爆炸导火线[信线,引线] detonating fuse
爆炸锻造 explosive forging
爆炸反应 explosive reaction
爆炸复衬[复合衬里] explosive lining
爆炸复合板 explosion [explosive] clad plate
爆炸固结 explosive consolidation
爆炸焊接 explosion welding
爆炸混合物 explosive mixture
爆炸加工法 explosive shaping
爆炸校形 explosive sizing
爆炸校正(爆炸冲压后的) explosive correction
爆炸金属 explosive metal
爆炸喷枪(陶瓷金属涂层用) detonation-gun
爆炸膨胀试验 explosion bulge test
爆炸气体 explosive [detonating] gas
爆炸气压成形 explosive gas forming
爆炸试验 explosion test ◇ 佩利尼~*
爆炸式燃烧 explosive combustion
爆炸丝 explosive wire ◇ 带~(液电)成形(同"线爆成形")
爆炸速度 detonation velocity
爆炸锑(电解制得的不稳定锑,具有爆炸性) explosive antimony
爆炸物质 explosive
爆炸性检验 explosibility test
爆炸性气体分析器 explosive gas analyzer
爆炸性气体混合物 explosive gas mixture
爆炸压力机[压床] explosive press ◇ 单活塞~*, 管式~*, 双活塞~*
爆炸压实粉末法 【粉】method of explosively compacting powder
爆炸压制 explosive pressing [compaction]

爆炸掩蔽室　blast shelter
爆炸液压成形　explosive liquid forming
爆炸硬化法　explosion hardening
爆炸造型机　【铸】explosive force moulding machine
爆炸整形　explosive sizing
爆炸铸造　explosive casting
杯突　【金】cup(ping) ◇半球形～工具*
杯突试验　cupping test, cup-drawing [deep-drawing] test ◇阿姆斯勒～Amsler cupping test, 埃里克森～*, 艾弗里～*, 奥尔森～Olsen (cup) test, 圆锥冲头～conical cup test, 约维诺特～Jovignot test
杯突试验机　cupping machine, cup test machine ◇布赫霍尔茨-埃里克森～*, 延性～cup test machine
杯突压力机　【压】cupping press
杯突延性　cup ductility
杯形浇口　【铸】well gate
杯形绝缘子　【电】cup insulator
杯形喷(射)枪　cup gun
杯形铸型(取试样用)　cup-shaped mould
杯状断口(延性材料拉伸试验的)　cup(py) fracture
杯状炉床(电炉的)　cup-shaped hearth
杯状模(电子轰击炉的)　mould cup
杯状破裂　cuppy fracture
杯状压痕深度　depth of cup
杯锥断口　cup-and-cone fracture
杯锥状断裂　cup-and-cone [cup-cone] fracture, cuppiness
芘{$C_{20}H_{12}$}　perylene
北美钢铁工人联合会　United Steelworkers Union (USW)
北美特殊钢工业协会　The Specialty Steel Industry of North America (SSINA)
背板　sheet backing, rear panel
背表面超声波分辨力(背表面与已知大小的缺陷间最小距离)　back surface resolution
背部　back, dorsum (复数 dorsa)

背材[背贴材料]　backing material
背衬　backer
背齿轮　back gear ◇封闭式～encased back gear
背底金属　backing metal
背底能级　background level
背反射X射线检验　back reflection X-ray examination
背反射法　back reflection method
背反射环　back reflection ring
背反射线　back reflection line, back reflection arc
背反射衍射[绕射]花样　back reflection pattern
背反射照相　back reflection photograph ◇劳厄～*
背反射照相机　back reflection camera
背拱　back arch
背极　backing electrode
背景　(同"本底")
背景亮度　background brightness
背景染色[涂染背景]　background colouration
背面　reverse side, other side (O.S.), 【焊】back side (焊缝的)
背面焊道　back run(ning)
背面焊缝　back weld
背面坡口(焊缝的)　underside groove
背面乳胶(胶片的)　back emulsion
背面照明光源系统　back lighting light source system
背膜　backing film
背散射　back scattering
背散射电子　back scattered electrons
背散射角　back scattering angle
背砂　backing sand
背视图　rear [back] view
背向辐射　backward radiation
背压　counterpressure, back pressure (BP)
背锥　back cone
贝茨电解精炼法(粗铅的)　Betts process
贝得石{$Al_8(Si_4O_{10})_3(OH)_{12} \cdot 12H_2O$}

beidellite
贝蒂理论(关于二元合金有序化点阵的) Bethe's theory
贝蒂-斯莱特曲线 【理】Bethe-Slater curve
贝尔反应(即一氧化碳分解反应 $2CO \rightarrow CO_2 + C$) 【铁】Bell's reaction
贝格勒夫铁矿石直接还原法 Bergloef process
贝壳石灰 oyster-shell lime
贝壳形闸门 clamshell gate
贝壳状断口 conchoidal [shell-like] fracture
贝壳状纹理(出现于疲劳断口上) conchoidal markings
贝可勒尔效应 Becquerel effect
贝克尔-奥罗万滑移理论 Becker-Orowan theory of slip
贝克尔范性理论 Becker theory of plasticity
贝克曼玻璃电极 Beckmann glass electrode
贝克曼顺磁型电子分析器 Beckmann electronic analyser of paramagnetic type
贝克曼温度计 Beckmann thermometer
贝克-纽曼反射板布料器 Baker and Newmann distributor
贝克喷水抽气泵 Baker's water jet pump
贝克撇渣器 【铁】Baker dam
贝克砂坝 【铁】Baker dam
贝克式烘炉汽管 Baker's oven tubes
贝克锌萃取法 Baker process
贝拉洛依铜铍合金(1.9Be,<0.5Co,<0.5Ni,余量 Cu) Beraloy
贝莱维尔式盘形弹簧 Belleville spring
贝利碳阻炉 Baily furnace
贝纳多斯法(碳极电弧焊) Benardos system
贝内迪克特白铜(10Ni,20Zn,10Pb,2Sn,余量 Cu) Benedict metal
贝内迪克特镍银(18Zn,60Cu,16.5Ni,4.5Pb,1Sn) white Benedict metal
贝内特耐蚀耐热铝镁合金(含少量钨) Benet metal
贝诺托式抓斗(锤式取土器) Benoto grab
贝日阿托菌属 Beggiatoa
贝塞尔方程 Bessel equation
贝塞尔函数 Bessel function
贝塞麦经验规则(每吨钢所需转炉容积为 27 英尺^3,即 $0.765m^3$) Bessemer rule of thumb
贝塞麦炼钢法 Bessemer process
贝塞麦转炉 Bessemer converter
贝式弓形屋架 Belfast roof truss
贝氏钢 Bessemer [acid] steel
贝氏硫菌科 Beggiatoaceae
贝氏硫细菌属 Beggiatoa
贝氏生铁 Bessemer pig (iron)
贝氏[贝茵]体 【金】bainite ◇ 上~ upper bainite,中间~ intermediate bainite
贝氏体淬火[淬硬] bainite quenching, bainitic hardening
贝氏体低合金高强度钢 ◇ 三菱~*
贝氏体钢 bainitic steel
贝氏体回火 bainite tempering
贝氏体热处理 bainitic heat treatment
贝氏体显微组织 bainite microstructure
贝氏体形核 bainitic nucleation
贝氏体延性铁 bainite ductile iron
贝氏体硬度(淬成贝氏体状态钢的硬度) bainite [bainitic] hardness
贝氏体转变 bainite transformation
贝氏体转变开始点 bainite start point
贝氏体转变终了点 bainite finish point
贝塔石 uranpyrochlore
贝特顿加钙镁除铋精炼法(铅精炼)【色】Betterton's (kroll) process, Kroll-Betterton process
贝特顿氯气除锌精炼法(铅精炼)【色】Betterton process
贝特法比表面积 B.E.T (Brunauer-Emmett-Teller) area
贝陀立体[贝陀立式化合物] (同"不定比化合物")

贝亚德-阿波特电离压力[真空]计 Bayard-Alpert ionization gauge
贝泽热压硬质合金法 Baeeza method
钡{Ba} barium ◇ 含～合金*
钡玻璃 barium glass
钡长石{BaAl$_2$Si$_2$O$_8$} celsian
钡沉淀物 barium precipitate
钡合金 barium alloy
钡化合物 barium compound
钡灰泥(医院特殊抹灰用) barium plaster
钡基合金 barium-base alloy
钡磷铀石 (同"水钡铀云母")
钡铝合金 barium aluminium alloy
钡络合物 barium complex
钡镍阴极 barium-nickel cathode
钡铁氧体 【理】barium ferrite
钡铁氧体磁铁 bestrite
钡铁氧体永磁材料 ◇ 马格纳杜尔～ Magnadur
钡同位素 barium isotope
钡钨(扩散)阴极 barium-tungsten dispenser cathode
钡吸气剂 barium getter
钡盐 barium salt
钡氧化物 barium oxide
钡铀矿 bauranoite
钡铀云母{Ba(UO$_2$)$_3$·P$_2$O$_8$·8H$_2$O} uranocircite
倍半硅酸盐 sesquisilicate
倍半硫化物 sesquisulphide
倍半氯化物 sesquichloride
倍半氧化物 sesquioxide
倍半氧化物-尖晶石转变 sesquioxide-spinel transition
倍半氧化物{Me$_2$O$_3$}-尖晶石平衡 sesquioxide-spinel equilibrium
倍半氧化物相 【金】sesquioxide phase
倍比定律 【化】law of multiple proportions
倍乘器 multiplier (MULT)
倍尺薄板坯 sheet bar multiple
倍尺(长度) multiple length, double length
倍加器 doubler, 【理】multiplier

倍率 multiplying factor
倍频 octonary
倍频程(八度) octave
倍频带滤波器 octave-band filter
倍频器 frequency doubler, frequency multiplier
倍数 multiple, multiplication [multiplicity] factor
倍数的 multiplex
倍压器 voltage multiplier
倍压整流器 voltage-doubler rectifier
倍增 multiplication
倍增电极 dynode
倍增管 【电】multiplier
倍增器 multiplexer, multiplexor, multiplicator ◇ 霍尔效应～*
倍增时间 doubling time
备份 【计】back-up
备份记录 duplicate record
备好配料 【冶】ready-made mixture
备件[品] spare parts [piece], replacement [reserve, service] parts, repair parts [piece], spare, stock, duplicates, duplicate part ◇ 操作～*
备料 charge [feed] preparation, stock
备料部分 feed preparation section
备料车间 charge preparation plant
备料站 preparation station
备品库 spare stockhouse
备用泵 stand-by pump, reserve [jury] pump ◇ 紧急～ emergency pump
备用部分 spare parts
备用出渣槽 stand-by slag runner
备用措施 backdoor
备用电动机 emergency motor
备用电路 spare circuit
备用电源 emergency power, stand-by power supply
备用锭模 emergency mould
备用堆栈 emergency stockpile, surge pile
备用反应器 spare vessel
备用隔膜泵 supplementary diaphragm

pump
备用功率 stand-by [reserve] power, margin of power, spare capacity
备用供给系统 【冶】stand-by supply
备用机组 stand-by unit, emergency set
备用机座 spare stand
备用寄存器 stand-by register
备用计算机 stand-by computer
备用焦炭料场[堆置场] emergency coke storage
备用空气压缩机 stand-by compressor
备用料槽[矿槽,料仓] emergency [stand-by] bin
备用料堆 emergency pile
备(用零)件[备品] spare [replacement] parts
备用路线 emergency route
备用煤气 emergency gas
备用能量 margin of energy
备用旁通管 emergence by-pass
备用燃料 stand-by fuel
备用容量 stand-by [spare] capacity, reserve power
备用设备 stand-by equipment [facilities, unit], backup, spare unit, optional equipment ◇ 应急~*
备用水 emergency water
备用洗涤器 【环】backup scrubber
备用线路 spare line
备用烟囱 donkey stack
备用轧辊 spare roll
备用轧辊库存量 roll inventory
备用贮焦槽 emergency coke bin
备用转炉 【冶】spare vessel
备用状态 readiness ◇ 处于~ standing ready for use
焙(烘) bake ◇ 后烘 after bake
焙解 calcination, calcine, calcining
焙解炉 calciner, calcining [decomposition] furnace
焙烤减量 loss of weight in baking
焙烤炉 baking furnace ◇ 蓄热式连续~*

焙烤损失 baking loss
焙烤周期 baking cycle
焙烤锥体 baking cone
焙砂 calcine, calcined ore, roasted product [mass] ◇ 热~ hot calcine
焙砂淬冷槽 calcine quench tank
焙砂放出口 roasted ore exit
焙砂浸出 calcine leaching
焙砂浸出系统 calcine leaching circuit
焙砂冷却器 calcine cooler
焙砂(料)仓 calcine bin
焙砂排出口 calcine discharge hole
焙砂熔炼 calcine smelting
焙砂溢流 calcine overflow, overflow calcine
焙砂溢流管 calcine overflow duct
焙烧 roasting, calcination, sintering, firing, baking, torrefy (铜矿的焙烧) ◇ 密封~ close-burning, 不完全[半]~*, 除铅镉~*, 分步[部分]~*, 两相~*, 炉中~ kiln roasting, 逆流~*, 全烧煤气~ all gas firing, 全烧天然气~*【团】all-natural-gas firing, 双重[两次]~ double roasting, 顺流式~*, 死~*, 完全~*, 未~的 green, 易~矿石 free burning ore
焙烧杯试验 pot grate test
焙烧不足 underroasting, insufficient firing
焙烧残渣[残余物] roasting residue
焙烧操作 【色】burning operation
焙烧产物 roasted product, product of roasting
焙烧车间 roasting plant
焙烧程度 degree of roasting
焙烧带 roasting [hot] zone
焙烧的碳块 baked carbon block
焙烧段 firing section, furnace zone,【团】firing zone (带式机的)
焙烧段炉罩 firing zone hood
焙烧法 roasting process [method], firing procedure ◇ 德拉沃~*, 流态化~*
焙烧反应 roasting reaction, roast-reaction

焙烧反应法 【色】roasting reaction method, roast-reaction process
焙烧反应机理 mechanism of roasting reaction
焙烧工段 firing section, indurating area
焙烧固结 【团】thermal hardening
焙烧罐法 pot process
焙烧锅焙烧 【冶】pot roasting
焙烧过程 firing cycle, 【团】firing procedure
焙烧过度 overroasting
焙烧-还原反应 roast-reduction reaction
焙烧黄渣[砷锍,砷渣] 【色】roasted speiss
焙烧机 burning machine, firing furnace [strand, unit], agglomerating machine ◇ 带式~*,环式~*
焙烧机罩 indurating furnace hood
焙烧技术 firing technique
焙烧精矿 roasted concentrate
焙烧壳型 【铸】fired mould
焙烧块 roasted mass
焙烧矿 roasted ore, calcine ◇ 热~熔炼*
焙烧矿出口 roasted ore exit
焙烧矿堆 roast heap
焙烧矿石辊碎机 chat roller
焙烧矿装料反射炉(炼铜用) calcine-fed reverberatory furnace
焙烧炉 roaster (furnace, oven), roasting furnace [apparatus, kiln], firing furnace ◇ 布伦顿转动凸底~*,多膛[多层]~ multihearth roaster,戈德弗雷旋转炉膛~*,回转圆筒~*,搅拌~ rabbling roaster,膛式~ hearth roaster,旋风[湍流]式~*,甄式~*,直线~*
焙烧炉尘 roaster dust
焙烧炉床能率 roaster specific capacity
焙烧炉-反射炉熔炼 roaster-reverberatory smelting
焙烧炉控制室 roaster control room
焙烧炉料 roaster charge [mix], roasting charge
焙烧炉料层[炉床] roaster bed
焙烧炉炉气 roaster gas
焙烧炉膛 roaster [roasting] hearth
焙烧能力 roasting capacity
焙烧黏土 calcined clay
焙烧盘 pan roaster
焙烧气体 roast gas
焙烧球团矿 fired pellet, (hard-) baked pellet, heat hardened pellet ◇ 未~ fresh pellet
焙烧球团强度 fired strength
焙烧球团输送机 burnt pellet conveyer
焙烧球团特性 firepellet property
焙烧热 roasting heat
焙烧熔炼 roasting smelting
焙烧砂型 【铸】roast sand mould
焙烧蛇纹石 furnaced serpentine
焙烧设备 roasting equipment [apparatus, plant], firing equipment [furnace, unit], induration equipment
焙烧失重 roasting loss
焙烧室 roasting chamber
焙烧试验 roasting test [experiment], firing test
焙烧竖炉 roasting shaft furnace
焙烧速度 rate of roasting
焙烧损失[减量] roasting loss, loss by [from] roasting
焙烧台车 fire grate car
焙烧同一性[一致性] 【团】identity on firing
焙烧温度 roast(ing) [firing] temperature
焙烧温度区间 【团】span of induration temperature
焙烧循环 firing cycle
焙烧压块 fired briquette
焙烧阳极 baked anode
焙烧氧化球团 hardened oxide pellet
焙烧窑 roasting [burning, stack] kiln, roaster oven ◇ 单炉体~ single-stack kiln,连续式~ progressive kiln,双井式~

double-stack kiln
焙烧制度　firing regime
焙烧装置　calcining plant
焙烧状况　firing pattern
焙烧作业　roasting operation
被比较字　【计】comparand
被变址地址　【计】indexed address
被测对象[物理量]　measurand
被乘数寄存器　【计】multiplicand register
被滴定液　titrate
被调用程序　【计】called program
被调用过程　【计】invoked procedure
被动的[被动轮]　【机】driven
被动土压力　passive earth pressure
被动吸收　passive absorption
被动元件　passive element
被俘电子　trapped electron
被覆电极　coated electrode
被覆金属粉末　coated metal powder
被覆涂层　covering
被覆线　【电】covered line [wire]
被壳　scurf
被控变量　【电】manipulated variable
被转嫁净租金　imputed net rent
苯{C_6H_6}　benzene, benzol, phene ◇含～油[苯化油]benzolized oil, 脱～塔*, 洗～塔*
苯氨腈{$C_6H_5 \cdot NH \cdot CN$}　cyananilide, phenyl cyanamide
苯胺{$C_6H_5NH_2$}　aniline
苯并芘{$C_{20}H_{12}$}　benzopyrene
苯并呋喃{C_3H_6O}　coumarone
苯二(甲)酸钾　potassium acid phthalate (KAP)
苯酚{C_6H_5OH}　(同"酚")
苯酚还原酸浸法　acid leaching using phenic acid as reducing agent
苯酚磺酸{$OH \cdot C_6H_4 \cdot SO_3H$}　phenolsulphonic acid
苯酚磺酸电镀锡法　phenolsulphonic acid process
苯酚磺酸盐{$HOC_6H_4SO_3M$}　phenolsulfonate
苯酚甲醛树脂　phenol formaldehyde resin
苯酐级萘　phthalic grade naphthalene
苯化油　benzolized oil
苯环氮杂蒽　◇1,2～*
苯回收　benzole [benzene] recovery
苯回收工段　【焦】benzole plant
苯回收塔　【焦】benzole scrubber
苯基{C_6H_5-}　phenyl
苯基甲烷{C_7H_8}　phenylmethane
苯甲醇{$C_6H_5 \cdot CH_2OH$}　benzyl alcohol
苯甲基　(同"苄基")
苯甲醛{$C_6H_5 \cdot CH:O$}　benzaldehyde
苯甲酸{C_6H_5COOH}　benzoic acid
苯(甲)酰{C_6H_5CO-}　benzoyl-
苯硫酚{C_6H_6S}　thiophenol
苯芪　phenylstilbene
苯酰丙酮{$C_6H_5COCH_2COCH_3$}　benzyl acetone
苯酰三氟丙酮{$C_6H_5COCH_2COCF_3$}　bemzoyl trifluoroacetone
苯乙酮　(同"乙酰苯")
苯乙烷　(同"乙苯")
苯乙烯{$C_6H_5CH:CH_2$}　styrene
苯乙烯－二乙烯基苯基体　styrene-divinylbenzene matrix
苯乙烯－二乙烯基苯离子交换树脂　styrene-divinylbenzene (ion exchange) resin
苯蒸馏装置　benzole distillation plant
本厂返回炉料　【冶】home returns
本厂废钢(铁)[废金属]　domestic [home, internal, plant, revert, mill] scrap
本厂粉尘　home dust
本床(鼓风炉的)　【冶】internal crucible
本底　background ◇底影～雾*, 扩散[漫射]～diffuse background
本底变黑　background blackening
本底电流　(同"基准电流")
本底辐射　background radiation
本底监测器　background monitor
本底内摩擦　background internal friction

本底强度	background density [intensity]
本底散射	background scattering
本底污染	background pollution
本底吸收	background absorption
本底信号	background signal
本底荧光	background fluorescence
本底噪声	background noise
本地回路	【计】home loop
本地矿石操作实践	home-ore practice
本地终端	【计】local terminal
本多磁钢	Honda steel
本多高强度铝镁锌合金[本多(锻造用)超硬铝合金]	Honda duralumin
本多镍钴钛系磁钢(15—35Co,10—25Ni,8—25Ti,余量 Fe)	Honda alloy
本多-佐藤式冲击硬度试验机	Honda-Sato pendulum
本恩图表	Bunn chart
本戈腐蚀量测定装置(按吸收的氧气量)	Bengough's apparatus
本戈-斯图尔特轻金属阳极化处理法	Bengough-Stuart process
本戈硬铝阳极处理法	Bengough process
本国废钢	country scrap
本国[本地]矿石	domestic ore
本国资源	national resources
本机电池	local battery
本金	principal
本领	ability,capability,capacity,faculty
本身电容	self-capacitance
本生灯	Bunsen burner
本生漏斗	Bunsen funnel
本生吸收系数	【化】Bunsen absorption coefficient
本体	main body, identity, matrix(复数 matrices)
本体试块	test lug
本性	identity
本影	umbra
本征半导体	intrinsic semiconductor
本征层[面]	intrinsic sheet
本征磁导率	(同"内禀磁导率")
本征导电性	intrinsic conductivity
本征电导	intrinsic conduction
本征函数	eigen-function ◇ 旋转~*
本征辉度	(同"内裹辉度")
本征金属	intrinsic metal
本征模	natural mode
本征黏度	intrinsic viscosity
本征铁电体	proper ferroelectric
本征吸收	intrinsic absorption
本征型	(同"特征型")
本征应力	intrinsic stress
本征元素	eigenelement
本征值	proper [eigen] value
本征籽晶	intrinsic seed
本质	essence, nature, intrinsic quality, principle
本质淬透性	【金】inherent hardenability
本质晶粒度	inherent grain size ◇ 奥氏~*
本质细晶粒	inherent fine grain
本质硬度钢(未经热处理的钢)	natural steel
本质锗	intrinsic germanium
崩解效应	disruptive effect
崩溃	collapse
崩料	【铁】slip(ping),charge downslide,interruption,settling of charge
崩裂	break(ing) up ◇ 耐~性*,耐火材料机械~*
崩裂(性)试验	【耐】spalling test ◇ 镶板法~panel spalling test
崩落[坍]	avalanche
崩塌力	【铸】collapsing force
绷条	【焦】tie[anchor] bolt(炉体的),【采】truss bolt
泵	pump ◇ 抽空压气两用~*,恒定体积~constant volume pump,前支~fore pump,双程[双动]~double acting pump,往复板式~reciprocating pump
泵出	pump-out
泵阀	pump valve
泵房[室]	pump room [chamber], pump-

house, pump(ing) compartment
泵管线　pump piping
泵机组　pump assembly
泵唧罐车　pump wagon
泵唧设备　pumping equipment
泵唧装置　pumping installation [unit]
泵间线（预抽真空泵的）　fore line
泵浇[送]混凝土　pump concrete, pumpcrete
泵壳　pump housing [body]
泵坑　pump sump
泵排出端　outlet side of pump
泵排量[出力,工作能力]　pump capacity [delivery, output], pumpage
泵入溶液　aspirated solution
泵升作用　action of pumping up
泵送　pumping ◇ 低温~cryogenic pumping
泵送混合沉降器　pump-mix mixer-settler
泵送能力　pumpage, pumping power
泵送倾析[倾注]洗涤器　pumper-decanter
泵送系统　pumping system
泵体　pump body
泵吸管　tail pipe
泵-蓄力器站　pump-accumulation station
泵旋塞　pump cock
泵(叶)轮　pump impeller [pulley] ◇ 带套的~pump impeller with housing
泵站　pump room [station], pumphouse
泵轴　pump spindle
泵柱　pump column
泵组　pump set
迸出　squirting
迸流　flush(ing)
比阿隆铜铍合金　Beallon (BeA-20C: 1.9—2.15Be, 0.35—0.65Co, 余量 Cu; BeA-27.5C: 2.5—2.75Be, 0.35—0.65Co, 余量 Cu)
比阿洛伊铜铍中间合金（约含 4Be）　Bealloy
比奥普蒂克斯高温计　bioptix pyrometer
比表面测定　specific surface determination

比表面积　specific area, specific surface (area) ◇ 贝特法~*,布莱恩~*
比表面能　specific surface energy
比表面张力　specific surface tension
比表面直径　specific surface diameter
比表面值　specific surface value
比布拉铅锡铋合金（38—40Pb, 9Sn, 8Bi）　Bibra
比长仪　comparator
比冲击能　specific energy of blow
比磁化强度　specific magnetization
比磁阻　reluctancy
比迪里锌基家具[锌铜铅]合金(88.5Zn, 5.75Pb, 5.75Cu)　Bidery metal
比电离　specific ionization
比电容　specific capacity
比电阻　specific (electrical) resistance, mass resistivity ◇ 层间~测试机*
比尔鲍姆微压痕硬度计　Bierbaum microcharacter [tester]
比尔定律　Beer's law
比放射性　specific activity
比辐射　emissivity
比浮计　areometer, hydrometer
比刚度　specific stiffness
比功率　specific power rating
比贯入阻力　specific penetration resistance
比焓　specific enthalphy
比活度　specific activity
比激磁[激发]功率　specific exciting power
比降　gradient
比较布置方案　alternate layout
比较电路　comparator
比较电位计[分压器]　comparison potentiometer
比较法(确定晶粒度)　comparison method
比较检查程序　comparison post-mortem
比较棱镜（分光镜内的）　comparison prism
比较离子　reference [pilot] ion
比较器　comparator, comparing unit

比较设计	alternate design [layout]
比较试验	comparison test
比较试验块	comparative test block
比较物质	comparison substance
比较线	【运】alternative line
比较信号	comparison signal
比较性能[性质]	comparative property
比较仪	comparator
比较用标准样件	reference standard
比较用试验块	comparative test block
比较字[被比较字]	【计】comparand
比抗张强度	specific tenacity
比朗铜金[铜银合金]	(贵金属＜25%) Billon
比里昂轴承合金[铜铅青铜合金]	(70Cu, 30Pb; 65Cu, 35Pb) Bearium bearing alloy
比利时式线材[盘条]轧机	Belgian (rod, wire) mill ◇ 双列～*
比例	proportion(ality), ratio, rate, relation(ship), scale, scaling ◇ 按～分配 apportionment, 按～扩大 scale-up, 按……的～ at the rate of (a/r), 按～缩小[减少] scale down, 不成～ disproportion, 成～的*
比例乘法器	coefficient multiplier
比例尺	(proportional, graduated) scale, (measuring) rule, measure ◇ 不按～的 not to scale (N.T.S.), 用～画的图 scale drawing, 制图～ draughting scale
比例电动机	proportioning motor
比例定律	law of proportionality
比例定值器	ratio setter
比例放大	scaling-up
比例绘图仪	pantograph
比例积分控制	proportional plus integral control, pi-control
比例积分控制器	proportional integral controller (PIC)
比例积分微分控制器	PID (proportional integral differential) controller
比例极限	proportional limit, limit of proportionality, range of proportionality (弹性比例极限)
比例给料机	proportioning feeder
比例控制[调制]	proportional [proportioning, ratio] control
比例控制阀	proportional control valve
比例控制器	proportional controller
比例流量控制	ratio flow control
比例模型试验	scale test
比例配料装置	proportioning plant
比例区	proportional band
比例弹性极限	proportional elastic limit (pel)
比例调节器	proportional regulator [controller], ratio setter
比例微分控制	proportional-plus-derivative control
比例微分控制器	proportional plus-derivative controller
比例误差	ratio [fractional] error
比例系数	scale factor [coefficient], proportionality coefficient [factor]
比例因子	【计】scale coefficient
比例影响	scale effect
比流量	specific yield
比率表[计]	ratio meter, logometer
比率检验	ratio test
比率控制系统	ratio control system
比率调整器	ratio adjuster
比率误差	ratio error
比能	specific energy
比黏(度)	specific viscosity
比黏计	leptometer
比诺达尔线	binodal line
比破碎能	specific crushing [fracture] energy
比气体常数	specific gas constant
比强度	specific strength, strength-to-weight ratio
比热	specific heat (sp.ht) ◇ 爱因斯坦～公式*, 德拜～公式*
比热测量仪	heat capacity measurement u-

比热峰 specific heat peak
比热曲线 specific heat curve
比容 specific volume (s.v., sp.vol.) ◇ 等张～parachor
比容量 specific capacity
比容－浓度图 V-X diagram
比色－比亮(度)高温计 colour-brightness pyrometer
比色参数 colorimetric parameters
比色法 colour [colorimetric] method, colorimetry ◇ 双色～bicolorimetric method
比色分析 colorimetric analysis
比色高温计 colour [colorimetric, pyroversum] pyrometer
比色管 colorimetric cylinder ◇ 埃格特～*
比色光谱 colorimetric spectrometry
比色光学高温计 Bioptix pyrometer
比色剂量计 colorimetric dosimeter
比色计 colorimeter, chromometer ◇ 分裂视场～*, 氢离子～ionocolorimeter, 赛波特～Saybolt chromometer, 双色～bicolorimeter
比色计测量 colorimetric measurement
比色温度计 2-color thermometer
比熵 specific entropy
比湿度 specific humidity, humidity ratio
比斯曼诺尔永磁合金（微粉烧结；16.55Mn, 余量 Bi) Bismanol, bismanal
比杨氏模数 specific Young's modulus
比应力 specific stress
比质量 【理】specific mass
比重秤 gravity [hydrostatic] balance ◇ 韦斯特法尔～Westphal balance
比重计 gravi(to)meter, hydrometer, picnometer, pycnometer, density meter [sensor], specific gravity bottle ◇ 巴林～[浮计] Balling hydrometer, 鲍氏～*, 布里克斯～[浮计] Brix hydrometer, 测银～argentometer, 吸管式～syringe hydrometer

比重偏析 gravity [gravitational] segregation
比重瓶 pycnometer, gravity bottle, specific gravity bottle [flask] ◇ 奥斯特瓦尔德～*
比重瓶法密度 【粉】pycnometric density
比重曲线 specific gravity curve
比重天平法 specific gravity balance method
比浊法 turbidimetric method, turbidimetry ◇ X 射线～X-ray turbidimetry
比浊计 neph(el)ometer
比阻尼力 [比阴尼容量 比衰减率] specific damping capacity
吡啶{C_5H_5N} pyridine
吡啶(鎓){$C_5H_5NH^+$} pyridinium
吡啶碱 pyuidine base
吡咯{C_4H_5N} pyrrole, azole
吡嗪{NCHCHNCHCH} pyrazine
笔杆浇口 【铸】pencil gate
笔尖合金(Os:Rh:Pt=17:2:1) pen alloy ◇ 锇铱～*, 库珀～*
笔尖黄铜(2Sn, 85Cu, 13Zn) pen metal
笔式自动记录器 pen recorder
笔芯合金(铅铋汞合金) pencil alloy
彼施涅型预焙阳极电解槽 【色】Pechiney prebaked cell
碧矾{$NiSO_4 \cdot 7H_2O$} nickel vitriol, morenosite
碧玉铁质岩 jaspilite
蓖麻(籽)油 castor-oil
蓖麻油石墨胶体溶液 castordag
蔽光罩 lightproof [light-tight] cover
毕奥－萨瓦尔定律 【理】Biot-Savart's law
毕奥数 Biot number
毕比联轴器 【机】Bibby coupling
毕赤酵母属 Pichia
毕他图 Bitter pattern
毕他图法 Bitter pattern method
毕特－阿库罗夫粉纹 magnetic powder pattern
毕特粉纹 [磁畴图象] Bitter pattern

毕特粉纹法　Bitter pattern method
毕特线圈　【理】Bitter coil
闭端式运渣线　dead-end cinder track
闭锻模具钢　closed-die steel
闭管扩散　closed ampoule diffusion
闭合　close, closing-up, closure, gather, making
闭合γ-区域[相区]　【金】closed γ loop, closed gamma field
闭合触点　make-contact
闭合磁畴　【理】closure domain
闭合磁路　closed magnetic circuit
闭合电路　closed [completed] circuit
闭合高度　shut height
闭合轨道　closed orbit
闭合回路　loop [completed] circuit
闭合回路设备　closed-circuit installation
闭合回线[环路]　closed loop
闭合壳层　closed shells
闭合壳层原子　【理】closed-shell atom
闭合力　closing force ◇ 触点～contact closing force
闭合器　closer
闭合铁芯　【电】closed core
闭合弯曲试验(弯曲180°)　close bend test
闭合位置　on-position
闭合误差　closing error
闭合循环　【计】closed loop
闭环功率控制　closed loop power control
闭环控制　closed-loop control, close loop control
闭环控制系统　closed-loop control system
闭环设备　closed-circuit installation
闭环式再循环系统　【连铸】closed-loop re-circulation system
闭环调节　closed-loop regulation
闭环系统　closed loop system
闭环自适应控制　closed-loop adaptive control
闭口端　close end
闭口架　closed head
闭(口)孔　closed pore

闭口孔型　【压】tongue-and-groove pass, closed passes [groove], dead hole ◇ 直轧~*
闭口孔型轧制　tongue-and-groove rolling
闭口梁形轧槽　dead-beam pass
闭口模锻液压机　hydraulic closed-die forging press
闭口气孔　closed pore
闭口切分孔型　【压】unopen slitting pass
闭口式机架　【压】closed-topped housing
闭口式矩形[箱形]孔型　【压】closed box groove [pass]
闭口式孔型轧制法[闭口孔直轧法]　tongue-and-groove method
闭口式翼缘(孔型的)　【压】dead flange
闭口式轧机机架　closed-top(ped) roll housing
闭口腿(孔型的)　【压】closed [dead] flange
闭口轧槽　closed passes, closed [dead] groove
闭路　closed circuit (CC), closed-loop circuit
闭路点　make contact
闭路电解系统　closed electrolysis circuit
闭路电视　closed-circuit television
闭路方式　closed-circuit approach
闭路阀　cut-off valve
闭路供水系统　closed water system
闭路过程控制计算机　closed loop process control computer
闭路磨矿[磨碎]　closed circuit grinding
闭路破碎　closed-circuit crushing
闭路器　【电】circuit closer
闭路球磨机　closed-circuit ball mill
闭路筛　closed-circuit screen
闭路筛分　closed-circuit screening
闭路湿磨　wet closed circuit grinding
闭路收尘器　closed-circuit deduster
闭路系统　closed system
闭路循环除锈剂　closed-circulating rust remover

闭路循环法　closed-cycle process
闭路循环破碎机　closed-circuit crusher
闭路循环系统　【环】closed-circuit circulation system
闭路循环选矿机　【选】closed-system separator
闭路液压(传动)系统　closed-circuit hydraulic system
闭路造球方式　【团】closed-circuit balling mode
闭路作业　closed-loop operation
闭皿(闪点)试验器　closed-cup tester
闭模爆炸成形工艺　closed-die explosive forming technique
闭模成形　closed-die forming
闭模锻造　closed-die forging
闭模锻造力学　mechanics of closed die forging
闭模模锻法　【压】closed-die method [process]
闭模模锻工艺　closed-die technique
闭模时间　dwell
闭气孔率　sealed porosity, ratio of closed pores
闭塞　block(ing), blanking, interlock, lockout
闭塞器　closer
闭塞系统(铁道的)　block system
闭塞信号　【运】block signal
闭塞装置　【运】blocking
闭式冲[锻]模　close(d) die
闭式导轨　closed guide
闭式焊缝　closed weld
闭式机座　【压】closed stand
闭式流槽　enclosed launder
闭式模精压[压印]　closed-die coining
闭式砂型[铸]　closed sand mould
闭式压力机　straight sided press
闭锁　lock, blanking, latching
闭锁电压　blocking voltage
闭锁阀　blocking valve
闭锁继电器　block relay
闭锁料斗系统　【铁】lock-hopper system
闭锁器　dead lock ◇矿槽~bin gate
闭锁装置　fastener, stopper ◇压模~*
闭铁芯[磁路]变压器　closed-iron transformer
闭型程序　closed routine
铋{Bi}　bismuth ◇除~*,含~的bismuthiferous,含~合金*,无~铅bismuth free lead
铋碲化合物　bismuth tellurium compound
铋浮渣　bismuth skimmings
铋钙钒石榴石　Bi-Ca-V garnet
铋汞合金　bismuth amalgam
铋焊料　【焊】bismuth solder
铋合金　bismuth alloy ◇焊封用~*
铋华{$Bi_2O_3 \cdot 3H_2O$}　bismite
铋化物　bismuthide
铋基[系]超导材料　Bi-based superconducting material
铋基低熔合金　◇塞罗~Cerro
铋基合金　bismuth base alloy
铋卷线　bismuth spiral
铋矿床　bismuth deposit
铋矿物　bismuth mineral
铋锰磁铁合金(微粉烧结,16.55Mn,余量Bi)　Bismanol, bismanal
铋铅锡合金　◇洪堡~Homburg's alloy
铋铅锡锑易熔合金　◇塞罗马特里克斯~*
铋铅锡易熔合金　◇阿尼恩斯~*,达尔杰特~*,道尔顿~*,利波维茨~Lipowitz alloy,牛顿~*
铋铅锡镉易熔合金　◇塞罗本德~*
铋铅易熔[共晶]合金　◇塞罗贝斯~*
铋青铜　bismuth bronze
铋酸　bismuthic acid
铋酸盐　bismuthate
铋添加合金　bismuth addition
铋同位素　bismuth isotope
铋土　daubre(e)ite
铋细晶石　bismutomicrolite
铋锡铅易熔合金　dalton metal ◇马洛特

~*,梅洛特~*

铋锡铅镉易熔合金 (同"四元共晶合金")

铋锡易熔[共晶]合金 ◇ 塞罗特鲁~*

铋中毒 bismuthosis, bismuthism, bismuthiasis

滗析 decantation, decanting ◇ 真空~ vacuum decanting

必要条件 requisite, requirement, prerequisite

算式焙烧罐 【团】pot-grate furnace

算式焙烧罐试验 pot grate test

算条 bar grate, breaker bar(单辊破碎机的) ◇ 特制~ special make-up bar

算条保护(措施) grate bar protection

算条间距 clearance between bars

算条间隙 grid spacing

算条筛 grizzly screen

算条上缘 grate bar top edge

算条式冷床 【压】cooling grid

算条寿命 【团】bar life

算条锁块 【团】lock(ing) pin

算条下部负压 【团】suction under grate bar

算条型筛子 grizzly bar type screen

算条运输机 transfer grid

壁 wall ◇ 布洛赫~*,尼尔~ Neel wall

壁板 【团】siding ◇ 多层~【建】sandwich panel

壁衬 wall liner

壁反应(反应堆的) wall reaction

壁厚 wall thickness

壁厚不均(管材) eccentricity

壁厚磁测仪 magnetic wall thickness gauge

壁架 【建】ledge

壁垒 (同"势垒")

壁炉(燃烧室) burning-in hood

壁幕 wall screen

壁热损失参数 【冶】wall loss parameter

壁柱 pilaster ◇ 支承拱的~ respond

壁装起重机 wall crane

臂高 arrow height

臂式搅拌机 arm stirrer

臂式升降机 arm elevator

避电器 discharger

避风港 harbour of refuge

避雷计 discharging rod

避雷器 arrester, arrestor, lightning arrester[conductor], discharger ◇ 干阀~ dry valve arrestor, 圆盘式~ disc arrester

避雷针 lightning rod [arrester]

避湿层 【建】cheek course

鞭毛 flagellum ◇ 有~的 flagellate

边 side, edge, margin, rim, edge fog(底片的), web(角铜的), wing(角钢的)

边帮密封 【团】side seal

边帮效应 side (wall) effect

边部减薄控制技术(热轧板带钢的) edge drop control technology

边部浪(薄板缺陷) kink, coil buckling

边部裂纹(带材的) check, edge crack

边部清晰度 【理】marginal sharpness

边部位置控制(装置) edge position control

边部指示控制 side register control

边部状晶体 fringe crystal

边长(正方形的) side length

边翅 edge fin

边锤(多锤水压机的) side ram

边带 webbing

边管提升搅拌器 edge-lift agitator

边辊环 end collar

边厚(垫子等物的) webbing

边火道 【焦】end flue

边际效应 edge effect

边角(废)料 ◇ 加工~ machine waste

边角料废钢 process scrap, prompt industrial scrap

边角料箱(剪切机旁的) tote box

边角(磨圆)防护 【金】edge retention

边角水管 corner pipe

边界 bound(ary), border

边界层 boundary layer

边界层空吸[吸取] 【理】boundary layer suction
边界层理论 【金】boundary layer theory
边界成分(与单相区边界相应) boundary composition
边界储量 marginal reserves
边界腐蚀 【金】delineate etching
边界回波 boundary echo
边界裂纹 【焊】toe crack(ing)
边界轮廓模糊效应 smearing effect
边界膜 【金】boundary film
边界摩擦 boundary friction
边界能量 boundary energy
边界品位 marginal grade
边界条件 boundary [borderline, edge, terminal] condition
边界线 boundary line
边界效应 boundary effect
边界元(素)法 boundary element method (BEM) ◇ 三维弹塑性～*
边距 edge distance
边距比率 edge distance ratio
边跨 end bay
边棱 bead
边棱方向 edge directions
边料 side trimmings,【冶】rim charge
边炉室结构 【焦】end oven construction
边冒口 side riser
边模(锻模的) edger
边内衬 sidelining
边坡 side slope, highwall ◇ 定～benching
边切 side scrap
边饰 fringe
边饰效应 fringe effect
边位调节器(带材的) side-position regulator
边纹辐射 fringe radiation
边限耕地 【环】marginal land
边缘 border, edge, frigne, margin, rim, selvage, lip, skirt ◇ 坯料未加工～*
边缘场 fringing field
边缘带(沸腾钢锭的) 【钢】rim zone

边缘倒棱机 【压】edge-bevel(1)ing [edge-chamfering] machine
边缘读数式仪表 edgewise instrument
边缘辐射 fringe radiation
边缘腐蚀 edge (point) corrosion,【金】delineate etching
边缘钢筋 edge reinforcement
边缘管道行程(高炉的) 【铁】peripheral channeling
边缘滚花机 【压】edge knurling machine
边缘焊缝 edge weld
边缘荷载[边载] edge load
边缘检测器 edge detector
边缘检验 【电】bias check [test]
边缘校验 【计】marginal check
边缘晶体 fringe crystal
边缘科学 boundary science
边缘控制(带钢行进中的) edge point control
边缘裂纹(带材的) edge checks
边缘煤气流(高炉的) peripheral gas stream
边缘模糊[雾翳](底片的) edge fog
边缘坡口焊缝(V形焊缝) V-weld
边缘清晰度 【理】marginal sharpness
边缘区 fringing field, outer zone
边缘扫描器[自动控制器,位置调整器] edge scanner ◇ 带材～*
边缘伸长 marginal elongation
边缘塑性拉伸变形 marginal plastic strain
边缘调整 【计】justified margin
边缘位置的扫描控制(带材的) scanning edge position control
边缘位置控制(带卷的) edge position control (E.P.C.)
边缘线状裂纹 edge seam
边缘效应 fringe [edge] effect
边缘学科 boundary science [subject]
边缘预整加工(板带材的) edge preparation
边折(带钢缺陷) edge break
边振放大器 edgetone amplifier

边振元件(射流技术的) edgetone amplifier
编成日期 【计】creation date
编程员[器] programmer
编辑 edit, compile, compilation, redaction
编辑程序 【计】editor
编篮式砖格 【冶】basket weave checker
编码 code, coding, encode, enciphering
编码板 code plate
编码程序 【计】code program
编码电路 code circuit
编码方法 【计】(en)coding method
编码继电器 encoder relay
编码控制系统 code control system
编码率 【计】code rate
编码器 coder, encoder, code converter, encipherer ◇ 轴头~shaft encoder, 自动~【计】compiler
编码条 【计】encoding strip
编码效率 【计】code efficiency
编码译码器 【计】codec
编码员 coder, encoder
编码字符集 【计】coded character set
编目(资源)控制 inventory control
编排 arrange, listing
编丝 lacing
编写翻译程序系统 translator writing systems (TWS)
编译 【计】compilation, compiling
编译程序 compiling program [routine], compiler ◇ 交叉~cross compi-ler, 可增[逐句]~incremental compiler, 面向语法的~*, 语法制导的~*, 自编译的~*
编译程序的编译程序 compiler-compiler
编译程序的生成程序 compiler generator
编译程序的诊断程序 compiler diagnostics
编译计算机 compiling computer
编译连接并执行 compile link and go
编译系统 compiling system
编译指示语句 compile directing statement
编织层 braid
编织钢丝绳 braided [selvagee] wire rope
编织钢丝网 woven steel fabric
编织机 braiding machine
编织机带 braided belt
编织金属丝 tie wire
编织线 braided [litz(en)] wire
编织用钢丝 weaving wire
编织针用钢线 knitting needle wire
编址寄存器 【计】addressable register
编址系统 【计】addressing system
编制 organization, work out, draw up
编制骨架 framing
编制计划[图表] scheduling
编制目录 【企】inventory-taking
编组 grouping
编组(场)站(铁路的) 【运】classification yard
编组轨道 【运】classified track
贬值 depreciation
扁板坯 slab billet
扁材 flat (stock)
扁插索针(插接钢丝绳的长针) flat spike
扁长形断面 slab-shaped cross section
扁锭 flat section [shaped] ingot, slab ◇ 下注~*
扁锭锭坯 【色】cake
扁豆形花纹钢板 tear plate
扁锻锤 blacksmith flatter hammer
扁钢 flat bar (steel), flat (steel), steel flat, flat bar ◇ 带筋~ribbed flat, 轧制带钢用~sheet slab, 窄~*
扁钢锭 slab ingot
扁(钢)锭模 (ingot) slab mould
扁钢宽展 【压】spreading of strip
扁钢丝 flat wire
扁钢丝绳 flat wire rope, band rope, flat cable
扁钢围盘 flat repeater
扁钢轧辊 jump roll
扁钢轧机 flat-rolling mill

扁钢纵向弯曲试验	longitudinal flat bend test
扁股钢丝绳	flat strand wire rope
扁环链	flat link chain
扁火焰	flat flame
扁挤压筒	【压】rectangular container
扁率	oblateness
扁坯	slab, flat bloom [blank], block, strip breakdown ◇ 大~ bloom slab, 万能式~初轧机
扁坯连铸	continuous casting of slabs
扁坯再加热炉	slab reheating furnace
扁平板桩	straight sheet pile
扁平棒	bar of flat
扁平产品	flat products
扁平电极	flat (type) electrode
扁平锭	flat shaped ingot
扁平钢桩	straight web piling bar
扁平(高频)感应圈	flat high freqency coil, pancake coil
扁平工件	flat article
扁平股	flattened strand ◇ 同心式~钢丝绳
扁平管	flat tube
扁平挤压筒挤压	flat container extruding
扁平浇口	flat gate
扁平颗粒	flat particle
扁平孔型	【压】flat pass, slab pass（板坯初轧用）
扁平孔型轧制	flat rolling
扁平流 V 形喷口	flat stream V-jet
扁平模样	flat pattern
扁平内浇口	flat gate
扁平线圈	disc [plate] coil ◇ 形成磁脉冲的~ flat (magnetic pulse forming) coil
扁平型芯	【铸】cake core
扁平形状	flat pattern
扁平轧材(带材、扁材、板材、箔材等)	flat (rolled) products
扁平状型材	【压】lenticular section
扁平最大值	flat maximum
扁千斤顶(混凝土路面用)	capsular jack
扁钳式点焊头	plier spot-welding head
扁球体	spheroid
扁试样	flat specimen
扁栓	gib
扁水套	squash jacket
扁铜	flat copper
扁铜棒[条]	flat bar copper
扁铜坯[锭]	copper slab, slab copper
扁头	spindle tongue, spade (end)（轧辊、接轴的）, palm end（轧辊的）
扁头夯	【建】pin rammer
扁头夯砂锤	peen pin
扁头钎	cutting-out bar
扁头砂舂	【铸】pin rammer
扁头式传动辊颈	spade type driven neck
扁线材[钢丝]轧机	flat wire mill
扁销	cotter pin, flat cotter, forelock
扁锌坯[锭]	slab zinc
扁型继电器	flat type relay
扁型磨轮修整装置	flat type grinding wheel truing device
扁形多股线	flat type stranded wire
扁圆的	oblate
扁圆坯(轮箍坯)	【压】cheese
扁铸坯	cast slab
苄基	$C_6H_5CH_2$ benzyl-
苄基氯酚	benzyxhlorophenol(B.C.P.)
便道	detour, makeshift road
便桥	auxiliary [detour, emergency, temporary, makeshift] bridge
便梯	auxiliary stair
便携式超声波测厚仪	audigauge
便携式计算机	portable computer
便携式空气冷却器	package type air cooler
便携式线盘	wire carrier
便携式仪表	portable instrument [apparatus]
变 μ 管	supercontrol tube
变暗	darkening, shadowing, tarnish
变暗浸蚀	mat etching
变白(如白熔渣)	whiten

变薄旋压(板厚变薄旋压) stretch planishing
变钡砷铀云母 {Ba(UO$_2$)$_2$(AsO$_4$)$_2$·nH$_2$O} (n<10) meta-beinrichite
变钡铀云母 (同"偏钡铀云母")
变参数[变感]元件 【计】parametron
变磁性 metamagnetism
变脆 embrittlement, development of brittleness
变电所[站] (transformer, electric, power) substation, transformer station, electric substation ◇ 成套~ unit substation, 牵引~ traction substation, 移动式~ portable substation
变动 changing, variation, fluctuation, swing(信号强度的变动)
变动成本 variable costs
变动负载 varying duty
变断面板材 tapered plate
变断面薄板 tapered sheet
变钒钙铀矿 {Ca(UO$_2$)$_2$V$_2$O$_5$·nH$_2$O} (n=5—7) meta-tyuyamunite
变分原理 【数】variation(al) principle
变风量交错并联送风温度自动控制系统 automatic temperature control system with variable blast volume and staggered-parallel blowing
变符号滑动[移] 【金】to-and-fro slip
变感器 variodencer
变高岭石 meta-kaolin
变锆石 arschinowite
变更转储 【计】change dump
变钴砷铀云母 {Co$_2$(UO$_2$)$_2$(AsO$_4$)$_2$·8H$_2$O} meta-kirschheimerite
变黑 blacking, darkening
变厚 thickening
变化磁场 varying magnetic field
变化范围 range of variation
变化荷载 changing [fluctuating] load
变化检测器 change detector
变化率 rate of change
变化性 variability

变坏 deterioration
变换 change, conversion, alternation, transform(ation), transit(ion), commutation, 【数】map ◇ 傅里叶~*, 拉普拉斯~*
变换比 【电】transformation ratio
变换参数 transformation parameter
变换常数 transformation constant
变换齿轮 change gear
变换传感器 transformative transducer
变换对数分离曲线 log-anamorphosed partition curve
变换逻辑 changing logic
变换码 【计】conversion code
变换器 changer, inverter, transducer, transverter, umformer, variator, 【计】converter, convertor ◇ 带负荷抽头~ 【电】on-load tap changer, 数字-交流(电压)~*
变换曲线 reduced curve
变换式 transform
变换速度 velocity of transformation
变换图表 conversion chart
变换系数 conversion coefficient
变换装置 changer, 【计】mapping device ◇ 有载抽头~*
变价氯化法 chlorination by valency change
变焦聚光镜 variable-focus condenser
变焦镜头 varifocus lens, multifocal lens
变截面 variable cross-section
变截面板簧 variable-section plate spring
变截面挤压型材 tapered extruded shape
变截面梁 【建】non-uniform beam
变截面坯块 multiple-section compact
变截面型材 【压】irregular section
变截面轧机 variable-section mill
变径管 stepped taper tube, reductor
变径式除气[洗涤]器 adjustable orifice scrubber
变距 controllable pitch
变孔模 adjustable die

变量 variable (var.), variant, variation, alternating quantity ◇ 被控[操作]~*, 可调[控]~*
变量器 transformer
变料单 burden sheet
变硫铀钙矿 {(UO$_2$)$_6$(SO$_4$)(OH)$_{10}$·5H$_2$O} meta-uranopilite
变流机 converter, umformer ◇ 分级[旋转]~*, 焊接~ welding converter
变(流)量泵 variable delivery pump
变流器 changer,【电】converter, convertor, current transformer ◇ 感应加热~*
变流仪 rheometer
变镁磷铀云母 (同"偏镁磷铀云母")
变模糊 haze formation
变频发生器 variable-frequency oscillator [generator]
变频管 (frequency) converter tube, frequency changer
变频器 frequency transformer [converter, changer], converter, transverter
变频调速 frequency control of motor speed, motor speed regulation by frequency modulation ◇ 交流~*, 双馈~*
变频振荡器 variable-frequency oscillator
变平 flating
变软 softening ◇ 使~soften
变弱 weaking
变色 discolor, discoloration ◇ 可逆示温~漆
变色示温漆 (同"示温漆")
变式 【数】variant (var.)
变水钒钙石 metarossite
变水锆石 {3(SiO$_2$, Zr, HfO$_2$)·H$_2$O} malacon
变水砷钙铀矿 (同"偏水砷钙铀矿")
变水砷铜铀矿 (同"偏水砷铜铀矿")
变水柱铀矿 (同"偏水柱铀矿")
变送器 transmitter,【机】transducer (射流技术的) ◇ 智能~*
变速比 gear ratio
变速齿轮 change [speed-change, change-speed] gear ◇ 带~的电动机 geared motor, 四级~*
变速齿轮架 change gear bracket
变速齿轮箱 variable-speed wheel gear, change speed gear box
变速齿轮装置 geared system, variable-speed drive
变速电动机 gear motor, variable-speed [change-speed, multi-speed] motor
变速杆 gear [shift, striking] lever
变速控制 variable-speed control
变速轮(传动)装置 variable-speed wheel gear
变速皮带机 variable-speed belt conveyer
变速器 (speed) variator, (speed) transmission ◇ 液压离合~*
变速箱 gear(ing)[wheel] box, speed change box
变速运动 variable motion
变速装置 variable-speed gear
变态 variety, modification, abnormal ◇ δ ~*
变态脆性 transformation embrittlement
变体 modification
变铁砷铀云母 {Fe$_2$(UO$_2$)$_2$(AsO$_4$)$_2$·nH$_2$O}(n<8) meta-kahlerite
变通性 versatility
变铜铀云母 (同"偏铜铀云母")
变位 deflection, displacement, deflexion, dislocation ◇ 绝对~absolute deflection
变位能 displacement energy
变温马氏体 athermal martensite
变细 narrowing, diminution
变向 diversion, reversing
变向闸板 diversion damper
变小 lessening
变型 modification
变形 deformation, deforming, (shape) distortion, strain(ing), transformation, variety, modification, flow (金属的) ◇ 残余[永久]~ off-set, 承压~ bearing strain, 点阵[晶格]不变~*, 经年~ secular

distortion, 抗~(能)力*, 可~性 deformability, 难~锥 dead cone, 纽曼~带*, 未~的 undeformed, 无[抗]~钢 non-shrinking steel

变形比 deformation ratio

变形不精确性(铸型或制品的) distortion inaccuracy

变形不均一[不一致]性 strain mismatch

变形不均匀性 unhomogeneity of deformation

变形测定器 strain gauge, wire resistance strain gauge, tensometer

变形程度 extent of deformation, 【压】degree [amount] of reduction [strain, working]

变形储能 stored energy of deformation

变形促进成核 deformation-assisted nucleation

变形度 degree of deformation

变形粉粒 deforming particle

变形合金 deforming alloy

变形剂 【金】modifier

变形计 deformeter

变形金属组织 【压】wrought structure

变形晶体 deformed crystal

变形抗力 deformation [strain] resistance, resistance to deformation ◇ 低~合金 low resistance alloy, 加载下~strength under load, 均匀面~*

变形抗力数学模型 deformation resistance mathematical model

变形(历史)过程 deformation history

变形力 deformation [deforming] force

变形量 amount of deformation

变形铝合金 (同"形变铝合金") ◇ 1100~*

变形率 strain rate, deformation rate【压】degree of working

变形镁合金 ◇ A.3A~*, P.E.~*, 塞莱克特龙~*

变形模式[形式] 【压】deformation mode

变形模型 【铸】distorted pattern

变形耐热合金 (同"形变耐热合金") ◇ N.155~*

变形能 energy of deformation

变形能力 ability to deform

变形镍基耐热合金 ◇ IN-102~*, 瓦斯帕洛伊~*

变形区出口 exit of deformation zone

变形区(域)[范围] deforming region, deformation zone

变形曲线 deformation curve

变形-时间图表[曲线] deformation-time plot

变形双晶[孪晶] deformation twin

变形速度 deformation velocity, speed of deformation

变形速率 deformation rate

变形特性 deformation characteristics

变形温度[point] deformation temperature

变形线 deformation line, flow line [figure]

变形行为 deformation behaviour

变形性 morphotropy, deformability

变形应力 deforming [deformation] stress

变形诱发马氏体的最高温度(M_d点) martensite deformation point

变形余量 distortion allowance

变形振动 deformation vibrations

变形织构 deformation texture

变形状态 strained condition

变形锥(拉模的) 【压】approach angle

变形总功 total work of deformation

变形阻力 (同"变形抗力")

变性 degeneracy, degeneration

变性奥氏体钢 modified austenitic steel

变性处理 【金】modifying, modification

变性剂 modifying agent, denaturant

变性酒精 denatured alcohol

变性铝合金 ◇ 辛达尔~*

变性耐热铸铁 modified heat-resistant iron

变性铸铁 mechanite (metal), modified

cast iron
变压 transformation, variation of voltage
变压比 transformer [transformation] ratio
变压比试验 ratio test
变压变频 variable-voltage variable-frequence (VVVF)
变压表 variodencer
变压发电机 variable-voltage generator
变压器 transformer (Tr.), voltage changer ◇风冷式~*,干式绝缘~*,鼓风冷却~*,固定变比~*,控制功率~*,无~的 transless,五心柱~*,相间~*,旋转~ rotating transformer
变压器场 transformer yard
变压器辅助装置 transformer auxiliaries
变压器钢 transformer steel [iron] ◇马格奈西尔~*
变压器硅[薄]钢板 transformer sheet (steel), magnetic sheet
变压器可控硅控制盘 thyristor operation transformer panel
变压器耦合 transformer coupling
变压器容量 transformer capacity
变压器室[间] transformer room [compartment, house]
变压器套管 transformer bushing
变压器调节器 transformer regulator
变压器铁心 transformer core
变压器线圈 transformer coil
变压器箱 transformer tank
变压器油 transformer oil
变压器－整流器焊机 【焊】transformer-rectifier welding machine
变压器－整流器装置 transformer-rectifier set
变压器组 transformer bank
变压吸附 pressure swing adsorption (PSA)
变压吸附制氧 oxygen from PSA
变应力蠕变试验 change stress creep test
变硬 hardening

变阈神经元模型 transitron
变元 【数】argument, variable
变月形透镜 meniscus lens
变窄 narrowing
变针钒钙石 metahewettite
变直径管 stepped taper tube
变址 【计】index (ing) ◇被～地址 indexed address
变址寄存器 index [base] register, modifier register, loop box
变址字 index word
变质 deteriorate, degeneration ◇使～【冶】inoculate
变质处理 【铸】(同"孕育处理")
变质硅铝明合金(添加0.1Na) modified silumin
变质合金 modified alloy
变质灰铸铁 modified grey cast iron
变质机理 metamorphic mechanism
变质铝硅合金 modified alpax
变质锰钢 inoculated manganese steel
变质岩型铀矿床 uranium deposit in metamorphic rock
变质(孕育)剂 【铸】(同"孕育剂")
变种 variant, variety
变阻合金 rheostan
变阻器 varistor, varister, rheostat, variable resistance (head) ◇管状~* tubular rheostat, 平滑调节~ continuous rheostat, 调节灯光~ dimmer, 圆盘式[刻度盘式]~ dial-type rheostat
变阻箱 rheostat
变阻整流器 varistor rectifier
辫硫细菌属 thioploca
辫线 litz(en) [braided] wire
标本 specimen, model
标称电压 (同"额定电压")
标称负荷 nominal load
标称功率 【电】nominal power
标称化学组分 nominal chemical composition
标称孔径 nominal pore size

标称压力 nominal pressure
标称直径 (同"公称直径")
标称值 (同"额定值")
标称重量 nominal weight
标尺 scale, dial, staff ◇ 活动~ movable-scale
标尺分度 scale division
标锉硬度 file hardness
标定 calibration, gauging
标定尺寸 intended size
标定粉末法衍射花样指数用图解法【理】graphical method for indexing powder pattern
标定管径(外径) nominal bore
标定金银锭 report bullion bar
标定(金银)精炼炉 report furnace
标定曲线 calibration [rating] curve
标定用金属粉末(X-射线照相的) calibrating-metal powder
标定指数 indexing ◇ 作图法~ graphical indexing
标度 scale, graduate, division ◇ 努普~*
标度读数 scale reading
标度始点值 minimum scale value
标度效应 scale effect
标度装置 indexing device
标杆 (gage) staff, target rod
标高 elevation (elev.), altitude, level ◇ 基准点~ datum mark
标高差 difference of elevation
标号 label, marking, sign, stamp, tab, tag number
标号卡片 aspect card
标绘 plot
标绘板 plotting board
标绘器 plotter
标记 tab, sign, mark, label, notation, indication, indicator, emblem mark (工厂,公司的),【计】sentinel, tag ◇ 打~机*,福格特~法*,刷~用液体 marking-out fluid,未敞露[肉眼观察不到的]~*,作~marking-out

标记线 pop mark
标记元素 label(l)ed element
标记原子 label(l)ed atom
标记直径(拉力试样的) gauge diameter
标件 tender
标晶(X射线光谱分析用) standard crystal
标镜 index glass
标距(长) gauge length
标距点[刻度](拉力试棒上的) datum point, gauge mark, pop mark
标距筒(回转式锻造机的) index drum
标量 scalar, invariant, scalar quantity
标量场 scalar field
标量轴 scalar axis
标牌号 brand
标签 label, tag ◇ 贴~机*
标识X射线 (同"特征X射线")
标识部分 【计】identification division
标识辐射纯度 purity of characteristic radiation
标数 Scalar number ◇ 弗劳德~*
标线 graticule, reticule
标线板[片] graticule
标线测微计[测微目镜] filar micrometer
标线密度 reticular density
标线目镜 【金】filar eyepiece
标线以下的 below grade
标志 mark(ing), identification (mark), brands, index, stamp,【计】sentinel ◇ 打~工具【压】marking punch
标志符 designator
标志卡 identification card
标志孔 【计】designation [function] punch
标志脉冲 marking pulse
标志数 【计】designation number
标志台(板材的) marking table, main mill table
标志信号发生器 【电】notch generator
标志性统计数字 benchmark statistics
标桩 stake, hub, nose pile
标准 standard, code, criterion (复数 crite-

标 biao

ria),ga(u)ge ◇ 低于～的重量 un-der-weight,合乎～的 proof
标准 X 射线胶片 standard (X-ray) film
标准板 on-gauge plate
标准半电池[标准电偶] standard half-cell
标准薄锡层镀锡薄钢板(平均锡层重量 0.61kg/基准箱) standard coke tinplate
标准玻璃纤维 staple glass fiber
标准测量 standard measure
标准测量仪 standard meter
标准测温锥 standard pyrometric cone
标准产品 standard products
标准程序 【计】standard program
标准秤 【冶】reference scale
标准匙 standardized spoon
标准齿轮 master gear
标准尺寸变化 gauge variation
标准尺寸木材 dimension lumber
标准磁导率 normal permeability
标准磁感应曲线 normal induction curve
标准大气条件 standard atmosphere conditions
标准大气压(非法定单位,=101.325kPa) standard [normal] atmosphere (atm)
标准单[一]面光亮精加工薄板 standard one-side bright finish sheet
标准点火器 normal ignition hood
标准电池 standard battery [cell],normal cell ◇ 韦斯顿～*
标准电极 standard [normal] electrode
标准电极电势[位] standard [normal] electrode potential,standard E.P.
标准电容 standard capacitance
标准电势[位] standard [normal] potential
标准电位序 standard potential series
标准电源 reference power supply
标准电阻 standard [measuring] resistance
标准锻造 normal forging
标准断口[断裂] standard fracture
标准二进制 【计】ordinary binary
标准方钢 standard square

标准废钢铁 specification scrap
标准分析 standard analysis
标准粉末(X 射线照相用) 【理】standard powder
标准钢材 standard section
标准钢箍 standard steel strapping
标准钢结构 standard steel construction
标准格 reticle
标准工业铜(>96Cu) standard copper
标准功率 standard duty,reference power
标准拱砖 standard arch
标准管尺寸 standard pipe size (s.p.s.)
标准管径 nominal bore
标准规[计] standard [control,master] gauge
标准规格 nominal rating
标准轨距 (同"标准铁路轨距")
标准轨距铁路 full gauge railway
标准辊道 gauge tables
标准焊缝 normal weld
标准化 standardization,standardizing,normalization,normalizing
标准化数 【计】normalized number
标准化箱(拉伸试验载荷校核用) standardizing box
标准黄铜(70Cu,30Zn) standard brass
标准机械压片机 standard-type mechanical tableting machine
标准技术规范 standard specifications
标准加矿温度范围 normal oreing range
标准间隔[距] standard spacing
标准碱溶液 standard alkali
标准碱性渣 slag of ordinary basicity
标准件 building block
标准胶片(X 射线胶片) standard (X-ray) film
标准结构 standard design
标准金 proof gold (试金用),standard gold (英国:91.66Au,余量 Cu;美国:90Au,余量 Cu)
标准晶粒度显微照片 standard grain-size micrograph

标准晶体 (同"标晶")
标准静压力机试验器 standard deadweight press tester
标准局(美国) Bureau of Standards (B.S.,Bur.St.)
标准块 calibration block
标准块规(校正硬度试验机用的金属块) standard (hardness) blick
标准拉力试验 standard tensile test
标准冷凝管合金(Kunifer 30: 30Ni,少量 Fe、Mn,余量 Cu) standard condenser tube alloy
标准离差[偏差] standard deviation (S.D.),dispersion
标准立方晶格物质 standard cubic material
标准立方米 standard cubic meter
标准两面光亮精加工薄板 standard two-side bright finish sheet
标准量度 standard measure
标准量规 check gauge
标准量具 reference gauge
标准流程 standard lineup
标准煤 equivalent coal
标准密度 basic density
标准模型 【铸】standard pattern
标准耐火砖 scone bricks
标准氢电极 standard hydrogen electrode
标准燃料 reference fuel
标准热处理 standard heat treatment
标准热电偶 standard (thermo) couple ◇第二~*,通用~*
标准热电元件 standard thermoelement
标准熔锥(测量耐火度用) standard cone (Std cone)
标准溶液 standard [set] solution
标准筛 standard screen [sieve] ◇德国~*,美国材料试验协会~*,泰勒~*
标准筛序表 standard sizing scale
标准熵 standard entropy
标准设备 conventional equipment
标准设计 standard [typical,modular] design
标准渗透试验 standard penetration test
标准生成热 standard heat of formation
标准时间 standard time ◇格林尼治~*
标准实验室气氛(温度与相对湿度符合规定值) standard laboratory atmosphere
标准试棒 standard bar ◇末端淬火~*
标准试件 standard test piece
标准(试)块 reference block
标准试样 standard sample [specimen], reference specimen,【电】reference material (差示热分析用) ◇现行[工作]~*
标准试液 testing bath
标准体积(标准状态下每摩尔气体所占的体积) standard volume
标准条件(标准温度和压力) standard [reference] conditions
标准铁轨 standard-ga(u)ge rail
标准铁路轨距(=1.435m) standard railway gauge
标准铜 standard copper
标准铜线 standard copper wire (s.c.w.)
标准投影 standard projection
标准温差电偶 (同"标准热电偶")
标准温度 standard [normal] temperature
标准温度计 normal thermometer
标准物品 standard goods
标准物质 comparison substance
标准误差 standard error [deviation]
标准锡 standard tin
标准系列 standard lineup
标准线规 standard wire gauge (SWG, S.W.G.,s.w.g.) ◇法定~*
标准楔形砖 standard wedge
标准斜键 standard taper key
标准泄漏 standard leak
标准信号 reference [standard] signal
标准信号发生器 reference [standard] generator
标准型 normalized form
标准型材[钢] standard [parent] section(s)

标准型式 standard design ◇ 按~设计的 modular

标准压力 standard pressure (S.P., s.p.), normal pressure (n.p.)

标准样板 master gauge

标准样件 reference specimen ◇ 比较用~ reference standard

标准样品 standard reference material (SRM)

标准仪表 standard [calibration, master, reference] instrument

标准银 proof silver（试金用），standard silver（英国：92.5Ag，余量 Cu；美国：90 Ag，余量 Cu）

标准应变 standard strain

标准硬度块(规)（校正硬度试验机用） standard (hardness) block

标准圆试棒 standard round test bar

标准振幅 reference amplitude

标准直形砖 straight standard brick

标准珠光体 normal pearlite

标准烛光 standard candle

标准砖 standard [gauge, straight] brick, standard square,【耐】square, straight ◇ 三分之一~ two-cut brick

标准砖体积当量（= 228.6mm × 114.3mm × 63.5mm，即 9 英寸 × 4 英寸 × 2 英寸） nine-inch equivalen

标准状态 standard state, normal condition, standard condition（试样的）

标准状态空气 standard air

标准浊度液 standard turbidity solution

标准自由能变化 standard free-energy change

标准组织（钢的正火组织）【金】standard structure

表 ga(u)ge, meter, sheet, table (tab.), form, list, chart ◇ 高阻[兆欧，迈格]~ tramgger

表报 statistical tables and reports, bill

表玻璃 watch glass

表层 skin (layer), surface (layer), superficial coat, veneer, case, callow

表层不密实性（缺陷） shallow discontinuity

表层淬硬性 shallow hardenability

表层断裂 skin fracture

表层料层 bed top

表层流 surface flow

表层溶液 surface solution

表层渗碳炉 case-hardening furnace

表层套管 surface casing

表层脱碳的 superficially decarburized

表层硬度 case hardness

表层指状氧化物 surface finger oxide

表处理程序 【计】list processing program

表处理语言 【计】list processing language

表达式 expression, representation

表格 table, form, tableau ◇ 制成~ tabulate

表格式的 tabular

表格式轧制模型 table model

表观 surface appearance

表观比功率 specific apparent power

表观比重 apparent (specific) gravity

表观纯度 apparent purity

表观磁化力 apparent magnetizing force

表观导磁率 apparent permeability

表观功率 apparent power

表观固态体积 apparent solid volume

表观固体密度 apparent solid density

表观(焊缝)喉部 apparent throat

表观活化能 apparent activation energy

表观检查 visual examination

表观矫顽力 apparent coercive force

表观聚焦面 apparent focal area

表观粒度【铁】apparent particle size

表观亮度 apparent brightness

表观密度 apparent density

表观密度计 volumenometer

表观模数 apparent modulus

表观黏度 apparent viscosity

表观膨胀系数（液体的） coefficient of apparent expansion

表观气孔度　apparent porosity
表观清晰度　apparent resolution
表观热膨胀系数(液体的)　coefficient of apparent expansion
表观蠕变　apparent creep
表观软化开始点　apparent initial softening
表观剩磁[剩余]电感　apparent residual induction
表观弹性极限　apparent elastic limit
表观弹性模量　apparent elastic modulus
表观系数　apparent coefficient
表观应变　apparent strain
表观应力　apparent stress
表观硬度　apparent hardness ◇ 砂型～ apparent mould hardness
表观硬化曲线　apparent hardening curve
表观增量磁化力　incremental apparent magnetizing force
表观最大磁化力　maximum apparent magnetizing force
表壳　surface crust
表壳材料　shell material
表列值　tabulated value
表面　surface, face, face side(焊缝的)
表面保护　surface protection
表面比较仪　surface comparator
表面变暗　surface darkening, tarnishing
表面变形现象(钢渗碳后的)　Brinelling
表面玻璃　watch glass
表面波　surface wave ◇ 瑞利～
表面波速　surface wave velocity
表面波探测器[辐射测试器]　surface wave probe
表面不平度　surface irregularity
表面不稳定性　surface instability
表面擦伤(在高速轧制时润滑剂受热失效所引起)　friction mark
表面测量　surface measure(ment) (S.M.)
表面层　surface coat[layer], superficial layer, outer zone, blanket, capper (多层焊缝的表面层)

表面层氮化法　surface layer nitriding
表面层起鳞　【金】case spalling
表面层形成　skin formation
表面差温加热　differential surface heating
表面超硬耐磨层堆焊处理　merchromizing
表面成核　【金】surface nucleation
表面成形(管材的)　surface forming
表面处理　surfacing, surface treatment, surface-conditioning ◇ 化学～法
表面处理钢板　surface-treated sheet
表面处理磨床(轧件的)　【压】surface conditioning grinding machine
表面疵点　surface defect
表面粗糙[凹凸不平]　surface asperity
表面粗糙的　grained
表面粗糙度　surface roughness[irregularity],【铸】pimple(铸件表面的)
表面粗糙度检查仪　surface roughness tester
表面粗糙度因数　surface roughness factor
表面粗糙化　graining
表面粗度仪　talysurf
表面催化反应　surface-catalyzed reaction
表面淬火[淬硬]　(同"表面硬化")
表面淬火喷焰器[喷枪]　surface hardening torch
表面淬硬钢零件　surface-hardened steel part
表面淬硬性　case hardenability
表面点火　surface priming
表面玷污的膜　surface-contaminant film
表面电导[导电性]　surface conductivity
表面电荷密度　surface charge density
表面电位　surface potential
表面电阻　surface resistance
表面定向　surface orientation
表面镀层　surface coating
表面镀覆　surfacing
表面镀铬　chrome-faced
表面锻打[锤锻]　【压】surface hammering
表面断裂　surface fracture

表面堆焊	surface overlaying [deposit, welding] ◇ 电解法~*,钢~steel facing
表面堆焊用合金	facing alloy
表面钝化技术	surface passivation technique
表面钝化铝	alumite ◇ 硬质~hard alumite
表面钝态[性]	surface passivity
表面钝性的	surface-inactive
表面多孔性	surface porosity
表面发暗	surface staining
表面发裂	minute surface crack
表面发纹	【金】shallow seam
表面反应	surface reaction
表面防护层	protective finish
表面非活性物质	surface-inactive substance
表面非金属夹杂物	surface nonmetallic inclusion
表面分布	surface distribution
表面分层	surface lamellation（材料表面缺陷），【金】case spalling
表面分析	surface analysis
表面风化	surface weathering
表面浮凸	【金】surface relief
表面腐蚀	surface corrosion
表面负载	surface load
表面富集	surface enrichment
表面改性	surface modification
表面干燥（铸型的）	surface drying
表面感应加热淬火	surface induction hardening
表面钢化	acierage
表面钢丝（钢丝绳的）	crown wire
表面钢丝绳（外表由楔形钢丝股组成）	keystone strand wire rope
表面高温计	surface pyrometer
表面各向异性	surface anisotropy
表面工程	surface engineering
表面共轭	surface matching
表面光电效应	surface photoelectric effect
表面光度仪	【压】profilograph, profilometer
表面光洁度	surface finish [smoothness, roughness],【机】cleanliness of surface ◇ 测~的 profilographic,高级~*
表面光洁度测定记录仪	contorograph
表面光洁度测量仪	surface analyzer, topograph, surfagage, talysurf（连续测量表面不平度用）◇ 特林蒂尼~*
表面光洁度检查仪	surface finish indicator
表面光轧	skin finishing, skin pass rolling
表面光轧机	tempering mill
表面硅酸	surface silicic acid
表面龟裂	surface checking
表面滚压	surface rolling
表面含碳量	case carbon
表面核化（表面结晶中心核化）	surface nucleation
表面合金化	surface alloying
表面烘干砂型	【铸】flared mould
表面划痕硬度	surface scratching hardness ◇ 马登斯~*
表面划痕（硬度）试验	surface scratching test
表面划伤（由轧辊表面刻槽或焊纹引起的）	surface tears
表面化学反应	surface chemical reaction
表面回火	surface tempering
表面活化	surface activation
表面活化[性]剂	surface active [acting] agent, surfactant ◇ 提波尔~Teepol
表面活性[度]	surface activity
表面活性分子	surface-active molecule
表面活性化润滑剂	surface-active lubricant, polar lubricant
表面活性离子	surface-active ion
表面活性物质	surface-active substance [material]
表面火焰淬火[淬硬]	shorterizing
表面火焰加热淬火	surface flame hardening
表面火焰清理	surface scarfing

表面火焰清理工艺　scarfing technique
表面积　surface [superficial] area
表面积分法　surface integration method
表面激光改性　laser surface modification
表面激冷的　case-chilled
表面技术　surface technology
表面记录　【计】surface recording
表面夹杂物　skin [exposed] inclusions
表面加工　surfacing, surface working ◇ 大理石样～marbleized finish
表面加工过的挤压用锭　scalped extrusion ingot
表面加热　skin heating
表面加热轧制　skin ausrolling
表面检验　surface checking
表面结　surface junction
表面结构　surface structure
表面结晶花纹（有色合金铸件缺陷）【铸】surface crystal pattern
表面金属化　surface metallization
表面晶粒氧化　surface grain oxidation
表面晶析　frosting
表面精轧　【压】skin finishing
表面精整　surface finish [dressing], deseam ◇ 铸态～as-cast finish
表面开裂　【金】surface rupture
表面抗拉强度　tensile surface strength
表面颗[晶]粒　surface grain
表面壳层　surface crust
表面空位　surface vacancy
表面孔隙度　surface porosity
表面扩散系数　surface diffusion coefficient
表面冷凝器　surface condenser
表面冷却器　surface cooler
表面冷却速度　surface cooling rate
表面冷轧机　skin pass mill
表面理论　surface theory
表面力　surface force
表面亮度　surface brightness
表面裂缝[裂开]　surface splits
表面裂纹　surface crack(ing), external crack ◇ 细微～minute surface crack
表面裂纹形态　surface crack morphology
表面磷化处理　phosphating, phosphatizing, alramenting ◇ 科斯特莱辛～法【冶】Costellising
表面硫化（作用）　superficial sulfidization
表面流　surface flow
表面绿锈处理（铜及铜合金的）　patina finish
表面洛氏硬度计　superficial Rockwell hardness tester
表面密度　surface [areal, superficial] density
表面膜　surface film
表面摩擦　surface [skin] friction
表面摩擦系数　skin-friction coefficient
表面耐磨堆焊　hard-facing
表面能　surface energy
表面能带　surface (energy) band
表面能各向异性　surface energy anisotropy
表面能级　【理】surface level
表面黏合剂　surface cement
表面黏结　surface bonding [cement]
表面黏结条痕（带钢缺陷）　sticker break
表面镍电解沉积处理　nickelizing
表面喷丸处理　（同"喷丸处理"）
表面疲劳破断　surface fatigue failure
表面匹配　surface matching
表面偏折　surface segregation
表面平均直径（根据粉末比表面测定）　surface mean diameter
表面破坏　surface damage
表面破裂　surface crack(ing), skin breakage,【金】surface rupture, shallow seam
表面起伏　【金】surface relief
表面气孔　surface blowhole, pit skin,【钢】skin hole（钢锭表面缺陷）,【焊】exposed porosity（焊缝缺陷）
表面气泡　surface blowhole
表面气体　surface gas
表面迁移率　surface mobility
表面浅洼型缩孔　【铸】blink, shrinkage

表 biao

depression
表面强度　surface strength
表面强化　surface peening
表面切割　【压】gouging
表面切割割炬　gouging gas cutter, gouging tip [torch]
表面切割喷嘴(氧气切割)　gouging nozzle, flame-gouging nozzle
表面切割烧嘴　gouging burner
表面清理　surface cleaning [dressing, conditioning], removing surface
表面清理车间(钢坯的)　chipping shop
表面缺陷　surface defect [blemish, imperfection, irregularity] ◇清理过~的坯料 conditioned billet, 修理~(对锭、坯) deseaming, 氧熔制~烧除器
表面缺陷清除　surface-defect removal
表面缺陷清理　dimpling
表面缺陷清理炬　deseaming torch
表面缺陷清理烧嘴　deseaming nozzle
表面燃烧型烧嘴　surface combustion burner
表面燃烧原理　surface combustion principle
表面热　surface heat
表面热处理　surface heat-treatment, thermolizing
表面热电偶　surface thermocouple
表面热力学　surface thermodynamics
表面(热)膨胀系数　coefficient of superficial expansion
表面热清理(烧化钢锭皮，清除表面缺陷)　【压】wash heat(ing)
表面热阻抗　thermal surface impedance
表面熔焊[熔化焊接]　surface fusion welding, wash welding
表面熔化　surface fusion
表面溶(解)度　surface solubility
表面润滑　surface lubrication
表面润滑性　surface lubricity
表面散热系数　surface coefficient of heat transfer

表面伤痕　surface flaw
表面熵　surface entropy
表面烧剥　surface scrafing
表面设施　surface facilities
表面渗氮硬化法　nitrogen casehardening process
表面渗金属　(同"渗金属处理")
表面渗铝　alitizing
表面渗碳　surface [case] carburizing, surface [superficial] cementation, case-hardening, case carburization
表面渗碳层　carburized case
表面渗碳的　case-hardened, case-hardening
表面渗碳钢　case(-hardening) steel, case-hardened steel
表面渗碳箱　case-hardening box
表面渗碳硬化　case hardening
表面失去光泽　surface staining
表面势垒结　(同"表面阻挡层")
表面势垒探测器　surface-barrier detector
表面疏松　surface porosity
表面水分　surface water [moisture], exteraneous moisture
表面水化(作用)　surface hydration
表面水解(作用)　surface hydrolysis
表面速度　superficial velocity
表面损伤　surface damage
表面缩孔　surface pipe
表面碳氮共渗硬化法　nicarbing process
表面碳化钢　cemented steel
表面探测器线圈　surface probe coil
表面特征　character of surface
表面条件　surface conditions
表面突出物(如泡铜表面的)　surface eruption
表面涂层　surface coating, face coat
表面涂漆　lacquer finish, lacquering
表面涂饰　decorative finish
表面涂碳(镍合金电子管的)　carbonizing
表面退火　skin annealing
表面脱碳　surface [skin] decarburization,

【钢】soft skin
表面脱碳层 carbon-free surface layer
表面网纹 【钢】surface crazing
表面网状裂纹 surface checking
表面位错 surface dislocation
表面温度 surface [skin] temperature
表面温度计 adrometer
表面稳定性 surface stability
表面污染 surface contamination [staining]
表面污染物 surface contaminant
表面无涂覆钢丝绳 black wire rope
表面吸附 surface adsorption
表面细纹(搪瓷件的) crizzling
表面瑕疵 surface flaw
表面下腐蚀 subsurface corrosion
表面下(结构)缺陷[结构不连续性] subsurface discontinuity
表面现象 surface phenomenon
表面镶金刚石刀具 diamond surface set cutter
表面效应 surface effect [action], Kelvin effect
表面形貌(学) surface topography
表面形态(学) (surface) morphology
表面形状 shape of surface, macroshape
表面性质 surface nature [property]
表面修整 surface-conditioning
表面锈层(制品的) surface layer of rust
表面压力 surface [face] pressure
表面压应力 compressive stress at surface
表面氧化 surface [superficial] oxidation ◇ 除去～膜 detarnish
表面氧化发黑处理(钢铁材料的) blakodizing
表面氧化物 surface oxide
表面应力 surface [skin, quadric] stress
表面硬度 surface [case] hardness
表面硬度指数 【焦】hardness factor
表面硬化 surface [face, superficial, shell, case] hardening ◇ 奥氏体不锈钢～法*
表面硬化处理 surface-hardening treatment
表面硬化钢 cement [case-hardened, surface-hardened] steel
表面硬化机理 mechanism of cementation
表面硬化剂 case-hardening compound
表面硬化金属 hard surfaced metal
表面硬化炉 case-hardening furnace
表面硬化能力 capability to surface-harden
表面硬化深度 case depth
表面硬化渗碳剂 case-hardening carburizer
表面硬化铸件 case-hardened casting
表面预先淬火(钢筋的) Tempcore
表面杂质 surface impurity
表面再涂层 recoating
表面轧制 surface rolling
表面张力 surface tension, surface tensional force ◇ 密度-～球*,圆环断开～测定法 anchor-ring method
表面张力测定装置 surface tension apparatus
表面张力毛细管测定法 【理】capillary method of surface tension measurement
表面张力平衡 surface-tension equilibrium
表面张力悬滴测定法(熔体的) 【冶】hanging drop method of surface tension measurement
表面折叠(钢材缺陷) surface folding
表面针孔(缺陷) 【冶】surface pinhole
表面振捣器 external vibrator, 【建】puddler
表面振痕(连铸坯的) oscillation mark on CC strand surface
表面质量 surface quality
表面质量检查仪 surface quality tester
表面状况 surface appearance [conditions]
表面状态 surface state [conditions], topography(金属的表面状态)
表面准备 【理】surface preparation
表面着色(成品零件的) dyed finish
表面自扩散 surface self-diffusion

表面自由能	surface free energy
表面阻挡层	surface barrier junction
表面组织	surface structure
表面组织状态	surface structural state
表盘式测厚仪	dial thickness gauge
表盘式仪表	dial instrument
表皮	skin, case, scurfskin ◇ 合格的~层 sound skin, 清除~层的 skinned
表皮分层(热轧板表面缺陷)	skin lamination
表皮干燥(铸型的)	skin drying
表皮干燥砂型	【铸】skin dried mould
表皮光[冷]轧	skin-pass
表皮凝固	skin solidification
表皮偏析(钢锭的)	skin segregate, rim segregate
表皮外部(钢锭的)	【钢】outer rim
表皮效应	skin effect
表皮形成	skin formation
表皮硬度	skin hardness
表皮硬化处理	skin hardening
表色管	chromoscope
表示(法)	expression, representation
表示器	teller
表头	division testing device, gauge outfit
表土	atteration
表土层	overburden(ing)
表镶金刚石	surface set diamond
表镶金刚石钻头	surface set bit
表压	gauge pressure (g.p.), barometric pressure (BP)
别位焊接	out-of-position welding
宾厄姆电解浸蚀液(用于 Zn-Cu-Al 系合金)	Bingham's etching solution
兵器青铜	arms bronze (AMB)
兵器用钢	weapon steel
冰醋酸	glacial acetic acid
冰点	freezing point (f.p.), ice point
冰点测定器	cryoscope
冰点降低	depression of freezing point
冰点降低测定(术)	cryoscopy
冰点降低的	cryoscopic
冰点曲线	freezing point curve
冰冻深度	frozen depth, depth of frost line
冰冻水	ice-cold water
冰花状组织	【金】ice-flower-like structure
冰晶石 $\{Na_3AlF_6, 3NaF \cdot AlF_3\}$	(sodium) cryolite, ice-spar, ice stone, kryolith ◇ 格陵兰~ Greenland spar, 人造~ cryolith, 熔融~ fused cryolite, 完全脱水~
冰晶石电解液	cryolite bath ◇ 霍尔~ Hall bath
冰晶石腐蚀试验炉	cryolite corrosion test furnace
冰晶石回收流程(图)	cryolite recovery scheme
冰晶石熔体	molten cryolite bath
冰冷淬火	【金】cryogenic quenching
冰冷却捕集器	ice trap
冰冷溶液	ice-cold solution
冰面	glaze
冰模(爆炸冲压)	ice die
冰铜炉	matting furnace
冰铜熔炼	(同"造锍熔炼")
冰箱效应	【环】icebox effect
冰盐	cryohydrate
冰中淬火的	quenched in ice (Qi)
冰洲石	Iceland spar
冰阱	ice trap
丙醇	propyl alcohol
丙二酸 $\{COOH \cdot CH_2 \cdot COOH\}$	malinic acid
丙基 $\{CH_3CH_2CH_2-\}$	pripyl
丙膦二胺 $\{CH_3CH(NH_2)CH_2NH_2\}$	propylene diamine, 1,2-diaminopropane
丙炔 $\{CH_3 \cdot C:CH\}$	propyne
丙三醇	glycerin(e) (glyc.), glycerol
丙酸 $\{CH_3CH_2COOH\}$	prtpionec acid
丙酮 $\{C_3H_6O, CH_3COCH_3\}$	acetone (acet.), propanone
丙酮树脂	aeetone resin
丙烷 $\{C_3H_8\}$	propane
丙烷-丙烯混合气体	propane-propylene gas(PPG)

丙烷-丁烷-戊烷混合气体　propane-butane-pentane gas(PBPG)
丙烷-丁烷混合气　blau gas
丙烷气　propane gas
丙烷燃烧器[烧嘴]　propane burner
丙烯{$CH_3CH:CH_2$}　propene, propylene ◇卢赛特～树脂　Lucite
丙烯(塑料)板　acrylic panel
丙烯酸树脂　acrylic resin
丙烯酸酯　methacrylate
丙烯涂灰　acrylic plastering
病毒　virus
病锡　sick tin
并-串行寄存器　parallel-serial register
并存的　concurrent
并发的　concurrent, concurring
并发反应　concurrent reaction
并发流　concurrent flow
并罐式无钟炉顶(高炉的)　【铁】bell-less top with parallel hoppers
并合律　combination law
并合试样　composite sample
并激电动机　shunt(-wound) motor
并联　paralleling, connection in parallel, parallel connection, shunt (connection), multiple, 【电】in-bridge
并联槽式炉　shunting cell furnace
并联电池组　battery in quantity, banked battery
并联电弧炉　parallel-arc furnace
并联(电解)精炼　parallel refining
并联电路　parallel circuit, bypass channel
并联电容器　shunt capacitor, bridging condenser ◇控制极～
并联电阻　shunt resistance
并联法(电解)　multiple process, (同"并联系统")
并联反馈　parallel[shunt] feedback
并联共振电路　tank circuit
并联门　parallel gate
并联频率　anti-resonance frequency
并联绕组　shunt winding

并联热电偶　parallel-connected thermocouple
并联塞孔　bridging jack
并联式鼓风机　cross-compound blowing engine
并联系统　parallel[multiple] system (电解), walker system (电解槽)
并联谐振　【电】current[inverse] resonance
并列　concatenation, juxtaposition
并列反应　parallel reaction
并列回转式开卷-卷取机　【压】double-swivel(l)ing uncoiler and recoiler
并列回转式重卷机　【压】double-swivel(l)ing recoiler
并列喷吹罐　【铁】parallel injection hopper
并列式布置　【铁】side-by-side
并列运转[运行]　parallel running
并流加料　parallel feed(ing)
并流(流动)　concurrent[parallel] flow
并排断续焊　chain intermittent welding
并排断续焊缝　chain intermittent weld
并排断续角焊　chain intermittent fillet welding
并绕　duplex winding
并行　paralleling, pairing
并行操作　【计】concurrent[parallel] operation
并行操作控制　concurrent operating control
并行程序设计　【计】parallel programming
并行处理　【计】concurrent processing
并行传输　parallel transmission[convey]
并行存取　【计】parallel access
并行存储器　【计】parallel storage
并行读出　【计】parallel reading
并行工作　【计】concurrent working
并行计算机　parallel[concurrent] computer
并行控制系统　concurrent control system
并置　concatenation, juxtaposition, pairs
玻耳兹曼定理　Boltzmann's theorem

玻耳兹曼方程　Boltzmann equation
玻耳兹曼分布(律)　Boltzmann distribution
玻耳兹曼恒量[常数]　Boltzmann's constant
玻耳兹曼－普朗克关系　Boltzmann-Plank relation
玻尔半径　Bohr radius
玻尔磁子　Bohr('s) magneton
玻尔磁子数　Bohr magneton number
玻尔－索默菲尔德量子理论　Bohr-Sommerfeld quantum theory
玻尔－索默菲尔德原子模型　Bohr-Sommerfeld's atom model
玻尔原子结构理论　Bohr's theory of atomic structure
玻尔(原子)模型　Bohr picture, Bohr's (atom) model
玻璃　glass (gls) ◇ 敷[镀]金属～metallized glass, 隔[防]热～*, 林德曼～*, 滤热～heat filter glass, 麻粒～*, 磨砂[毛]～ground glass, 内莎～*, 普通无色～plain glass, 清～料 clear frit, 溶性～soluble glass
玻璃板　glass plate ◇ 厚～heavy sheet glass, 涂覆金属～*
玻璃包套　【粉】glass bag, vitreous container
玻璃布　glass cloth
玻璃沉积容器　glass deposition vessel
玻璃衬里反应容器　glass lined reaction vessel
玻璃衬里钢　glass-lined steel
玻璃吹制　glassblowing
玻璃瓷　opal glass
玻璃带　glass ribbon
玻璃碘化物热离解容器　【色】glass deposition vessel
玻璃电极　glass electrode ◇ 贝克曼～*
玻璃粉(挤压润滑剂)　glass powder
玻璃封接用低熔点合金(重量比 Pb:Sn:Hg = 3:2:2.5)　glass cementing alloy

玻璃封口　glass seal
玻璃封套　glass envelope
玻璃钢　glass fibre reinforced plastics, (fibre)glass epoxy
玻璃管　glass pipe [tube]
玻璃管温度计　glass thermometer
玻璃焊封　glass seal
玻璃焊封的　glass-sealed
玻璃合金　glassy alloy, metallic glass
玻璃化　vitrify, vitrification ◇ 不～黏土 non-vitrifiable clay
玻璃化材料　vitrified material
玻璃化砖　vitrified brick
玻璃化作用　vitrification ◇ 局部～*
玻璃环氧树脂　glass epoxy
玻璃胶　glass cement
玻璃介质电容器　glass condenser
玻璃金属封接合金　glass-metal sealing alloy
玻璃金属焊封[密封]　glass-(to-)metal seal
玻璃金属(块)　vitromet
玻璃绝缘子　glass insulator
玻璃块　glass blocks
玻璃框(仪器的)　bezel, besel
玻璃料钮扣试样熔度试验　【粉】button test
玻璃棉　glass cotton [wool]
玻璃黏滞性　viscosity of glasses
玻璃泡　glass envelope
玻璃泡长度(浸液式温度计的)　bulb length
玻璃泡(汞弧)整流器　glass-bulb rectifier
玻璃喷水抽气泵　glass water-jet pump
玻璃片　glass block, sheet glass ◇ 乳白色～opal glass plate
玻璃片窗孔[观察孔]　plate-glass window
玻璃器皿　glassware
玻璃球　glass bead
玻璃球单向阀　glass-ball non-return valve
玻璃熔剂　glass(-type) flux
玻璃容器　glass envelope, 【粉】vitreous

玻璃绒	glass wool
玻璃润滑(法)	glass lubrication
玻璃润滑(热)挤压法	【压】glass extrusion process [method]
玻璃塞	glass stopper ◇ 磨口～ ground glass stopper
玻璃砂	glass sand
玻璃砂纸	glass paper
玻璃水银扩散泵	bottle pump ◇ 拉格尔斯－库尔吉式两级～*, 兰米尔～*
玻璃丝包覆的	fibreglass covered
玻璃态转变温度	glass transition temperature
玻璃搪瓷薄板	vitreous enamelling sheet
玻璃－搪瓷涂层	vitreous-enamel coating
玻璃陶瓷(学,术)	glass ceramics
玻璃套(挤压无缝管润滑用)	【压】glass sock
玻璃套管	glass sleeve
玻璃体	vitreous body
玻璃填充塔	glass tower
玻璃退火炉	glass oven
玻璃退火窑	leer, lehr
玻璃纤维[玻璃丝]	fibreglass, glass fibre, spun glass
玻璃纤维被覆硅橡胶绝缘线	glass-wool coated silicon-rubber insulated wire
玻璃纤维袋	fibreglass bag
玻璃纤维钢板	fibreglass epoxy
玻璃纤维绝缘	fibreglass insulation
玻璃纤维塞	glass wool plug
玻璃纤维增强复合材料	fibreglass reinforced composite
玻璃纤维增强聚酯树脂	glass-fibre reinforced polyester resin
玻璃纤维[玻璃丝]增强塑料	fiber glass reinforced plastics (FRP), glass fibre reinforced plastics
玻璃相	glass(y) phase
玻璃型熔剂	glass(-type) flux
玻璃窑膛大砖	glass tank block
玻璃硬度	glass hardness ◇ 淬火至～的 glass-hardened
玻璃油扩散真空增压泵	glass booster oil diffusion pump
玻璃浴炉(热挤压坯料无氧化加热用)	glass bath furnace
玻璃载片(显微镜用)	glass slide
玻璃渣	vitreous slag
玻璃罩[帽]	glass cap
玻璃质(富玻璃质)	vitric ◇ 非～耐火材料*, 液态淬火～合金*
玻璃质涂层	vitreous coating
玻璃质渣键[玻璃质渣黏结物]	vitreous slag bond
玻璃质状态	glassy state
玻璃钟罩	glass bell jar
玻璃珠	glass bead
玻璃铸型	glass moulds
玻璃转变温度	glass transition temperature
玻璃状断口	glassy [vitreous] fracture
玻璃状硅质熟料	vitreous silica grog
玻璃状炉渣	vitreous slag
玻璃状熔渣	【冶】glass(-like) [lustrous] slag, scoury slag(对碱性炉而言)
玻璃状石英	vitreous silica
玻密特烧结纯铁	Pomet
玻色－爱因斯坦能量分布	【理】Bose-Einstein distribution
玻色(粒)子	【理】boson, Bose particle
玻色统计法	【理】Bose statistics
拨出杆	【压】throw-off arm
拨顶	topping
拨动杆	poke rod
拨动式开关	toggle switch
拨杆	driving lever
拨管机	【压】push-off ◇ 卷筒～ tube block machine
拨号	【电】dial-up
拨号键	dial key
拨号交换机	dial exchange
拨号盘	dial, dial plate

拨号盘式开关　dial twitch
拨号盘速度指示器　dial indicator
拨号盘式连接　dial connection
拨号[自动电话]系统　dial system
拨火(翻煤及加煤)　poking, raking
拨火棒　【压】furnace rake,【耐】poker, poking bar
拨火孔　poke [rabbling, stirring] hole
拨进(从输入辊道上)　【压】drag on
拨卷机　【压】coil ejector, coiler kick-off
拨款　appropriation, allotment
拨款项目　【企】appropriation line
拨料板　switch-plate
拨料杆　【压】take-off arm, shuffle bars(冷床的)
拨料机[器]　kick-out device, kick-off, ejecting device,【压】push-off, diverter, tripper device ◇ 螺旋~kick-out screws
拨料拖运小车　drag-on carriage
拨料爪　drag-on dog ◇ 起伏~disappearing dog
拨线圈(钢丝绳机牵引轮的)　fleeter ring
拨爪　pusher dog
拨爪移送机　dog transfer, sweep arm transfer ◇ 链式~*
钵　bowl
波　wave ◇ 兰姆~Lamb wave
波包　wave(-) packet
波包群　【理】group of wave packets, wave-packet
波包速度　wave packet velocity
波长　wavelength
波长常数　wavelength constant
波长范围　channel of wavelength
波长计　wavemeter, cymometer
波长谱　wavelength spectrum
波长强度分布　wavelength-intensity distribution
波长修正辐射　modified radiation
波长展开度引起的增宽　broadening due to wave length spread
波程　wave-path ◇ V形~vee path, 水中~water path
波穿透[贯穿]　wave penetration
波传播[传布]　wave propagation
波传播[波程]角　wave angle
波导(管)　(wave) guide ◇ 脊形~ridge waveguide, 可压缩~*
波导管分波器　waveguide branching filter
波导管转换开关　waveguide switch
波道　channel
波道按时划分　time division of channels
波点　wave point
波动　fluctuation, flutter, chatter, ripple, surge, undulation, wandering
波动比　fluctuation ratio
波动点　surge point
波动范围(百分比)　variation range, range-percent
波动方程(式)*　wave equation ◇ 薛定谔~
波动光学成像　wave-optical image formation
波(动)函数　【理】wave function
波动荷载　fluctuating load
波动力学　wave mechanics
波动性　【理】wave nature, waviness
波动原理　fluctuation theory
波动张力　fluctuating tension
波段　(frequency, wavelength) band, range
波段开关　band selector, zoning switch
波段宽度　breadth of wavelength band
波段扩展　band spread
波段转换　band switch(ing)
波尔贝克斯线图(了解腐蚀现象用)【金】Pourbaix diagram
波尔迪轻便型硬度计　Poldi
波尔顿灰口铁浸蚀剂　Bolton's reagent
波尔多尼峰(位错运动引起的内耗峰)　Bordoni peak
波尔曼超声显像探伤法　Pohlman method
波尔南德电炉　【冶】Bornand electric furnace
波尔塔尔复杂铝合金(1.1Si, 0.75Mg,

0.4Mn,0.15Ni,余量 Al） Poltal
波反射　wave reflection
波峰　【电】crest
波峰因数　crest factor
波辐射　wave radiation
波幅　amplitude ◇ 距离－～反应曲线*
波腹　antinode, wave loop
波干扰　wave interference
波高　wave height
波函数的复数共轭　complex conjugate of wave function
波拉克冷(压)室压铸机　Polak machine
波拉里乌姆耐蚀耐热钯金合金（10—40Pd,少量 Pt,余量 Au） Polarium
波浪　wave, waviness,【压】corrugation（钢板缺陷）,ripple mark(ing)s（轻合金轧材矫直缺陷）,distortion（缺陷）◇ 压～弯*
波浪边　rippled [wavy] edge（带材缺陷）,flopper（板、带材缺陷）
波浪边锭模　corrugated mould
波浪形　undulation
波浪形的　wavy, undulant; corrugated
波浪形孔型设计　【压】W-pass design
波浪形缺陷(轧材的)　【压】build(ing) up
波浪运动　undulatory motion, billow wave
波浪状的　undated
波利登一步炼铅法　Boliden direct process
波列　wave train
波列频率　wave-train frequency
波模转换开关　mode switch
波频计　cymometer
波谱　spectrum（复数 spectra）
波谱学　spectroscopy
波奇弗里克斯型传动装置　Bogiflex drive unit
波前　wave front
波群速　【理】group velocity
波声测厚仪　reflectogage
波矢　wave vector
波式离心萃取器　Podbielniak extractor
波束　(wave) beam, wave packet

波束导航　beam
波束控制　beam control
波束曲折　【理】bending
波数(单位长度的)　wave-number
波速　wave velocity
波特低级黄铜(锌锡铜铅合金)　Pot metal
波特钢丝镀锌法(钢丝从熔盐中引出)　Potter process
波特温－勒夏式列效应　【金】Portevin-LeChatelier effect
波廷铜锌锡合金　Potin
波托西银[铜镍锌]合金　Potosi silver
波纹　corrugation, ripple, flute, crimp, buckling, cockles（薄钢板边缘的波纹）,waviness（钢板缺陷）,washmarking（钢锭表面缺陷）,ridge（轧件缺陷）◇ 有～的 fluted
波纹板　corrugated [floor] plate
波纹壁锭模　corrugated mould
波纹壁渣罐　【冶】corrugated slag pot
波纹钢板　corrugated steel
波纹(格子)砖　【铁】corrugated brick
波纹管　(flexible) bellows, corrugated pipe, corrugated metal pipe (C.M.P.)（钢管）
波纹管阀　bellow valve
波纹管涵　corrugated culvert
波纹管连接　bellows joint
波纹管元件　bellows element
波纹焊　ripple welding
波纹面(钢锭表面缺陷)　washmarking
波纹石棉水泥板　【建】corrugated asbestos cement board (C.A.C.B.)
波纹[形]碳砖(高炉炉底用)　(carbon) corrugated block
波纹凸起　buckling
波纹图形　【理】Moire pattern
波纹网状填料　corrugated gauze packing
波纹压力机　crimping press
波纹状(钢锭)模壁　【钢】corrugated [rippled] wall

波型壁钢锭模　【钢】rippled mould
波型变换器　mode transducer
波形　waveform
波形变换　wave transformation
波形滑移线　wavy slip line
波形记录[描绘]器　curve tracer
波形图　oscillogram, oscillograph,【电】scope pattern
波形瓦　pentile ◇ 石棉水泥～fibrotile
波形误差　wave-form error
波形因数　shape [form, crest] factor
波性　wave property
波性质　【理】wave nature
波义耳－查理定律　Boyle-Charle's law
波义耳－马略特定律　Boyle-Mariott's law
波阵面　wave front [surface]
波皱面(钢锭下部缺陷)　【钢】rippled surface
波状重皮[折叠](轧材缺陷)　【压】recurrent [surging] lap
波状[波形]的　wavy, undated, wavelike
波状断口　wavy fracture
波状花边　cyma
波状裂纹　wavy crack
波阻　wave resistance [drag]
波阻抗　wave [surge] impedance
剥夺　deprivation
剥离　peel back, delaminating, delamination, shelling-out ◇ 淬硬层～case spalling, 解理状～cleavage foliation
剥离法　method of stripping
剥离腐蚀　exfoliation corrosion
剥离试验　peel test
剥裂　break away ◇ 小～处 multiple spall
剥裂成片　cleavage foliation
剥落　spall(ing), flaking, gaffing, peeling (off)(涂层的), scale off, shelling-out, slabbing,【耐】exfoliation ◇ 不～阳极*, 抗～*, 易～敏感性*
剥落腐蚀　break away corrosion
剥落块　slabbed piece
剥落片　spalled slab

剥落损坏　spalling damage
剥片　flaking, peeling (off),【色】strip (ping) (电解的)
剥片槽　【色】stripping tank
剥片机　【色】stripper
剥片架　【色】stripping rack
剥片间　stripping room
剥片起重机[吊车]　【色】stripper crane
剥片钳　stripping tongs
剥蚀　denudation, gaffing ◇ 耐～合金*
剥线器　wire skinner
博毕尔高锌黄铜（63Cu, 37Zn）　basis brass, Bobierre's metal
博德温蠕变试验机　Baldwin creep tester
博勒高碳银亮钢　Bohler
博勒连铸连轧法　【冶】Bohler strand reduction (BSR) process
博罗德耐磨焊条合金（60WC, 40Fe）　Borod
博罗托锡铅锑合金　Boroto
博罗西尔硼硅铁合金（40--45Si, 3--4B, 余量 Fe）　Borosil
博罗泽尔包铝氧化硼复合板(Boral 的代用品)　Boroxal
博瑞碳化硼包铝复合板(板心为 30％ B_4C －Al, 反应堆用热屏蔽材料)　Boral
博塔硅硼钛铝锰合金　Bortam
博特杰锌汞合金　Bottger's amalgam
博维尔重载铅基巴比合金（82.5Pb, 15Sb, 1Sn, 1As, 0.5Cu）　Boveall-babbitt
勃姆石　(同"一水软铝石")
勃特雷斯型双密封套管　BSD (Buttress Double Seal) casing
铂{Pt}　platinum ◇ 天然～native platinum, 伪～martino alloy
铂钯热电偶　pallador
铂－饱和甘汞电池　platinum-saturated calomel cell
铂杯　platinum cup
铂－铂铑热电偶　platinum platinum-rhodium (thermo) couple
铂箔　platinum foil

铂触点 platinum contact	铂温标 platinum scale
铂的[含铂的] platiniferous	铂钨电触头合金(5W,余量 Pt) platinum-tungsten alloy
铂电极 platinum electrode	
铂电阻高温计 platinum resistance pyrometer	铂钨碳化物 Pt-W [platinum-tungsten] carbide
铂-甘汞电极对 platinum-calomel electrode couple	铂系金属 platinum metal
	铂纤维金属丝 platinum fibrous wire
铂坩埚 platinum (alloy) crucible, platinic crucible	铂线圈 platinum coil
	铂阳极 platinum anode
铂钴永磁体 Pt-Co permanent magnet	铂铱 platinoiridita
铂管 platinotron	铂铱合金 iridioplatinum, Platiniridium (30—75Ir,余量 Pt), platinum-iridio (5—30Ir,余量 Pt), hard platinum
铂焊料(73Ag,余量 Pt) platinum solder	
铂黑 platinum black	
铂(基)合金 platinum alloy ◇ 伯明翰~*,仿造~*,普拉提奈尔热电偶用~*	铂银合金(30—50Ag,余量 Pt) platinum-silver
	铂云母 mahadevite
铂金合金 ◇ 普拉提诺尔~Platinor	铂质电接触材料 C (contact) platinum
铂金银 platinum-gold-silver (PGS)	铂族合金 platinum metal alloy
铂铑-铂热电偶 platinum-rhodium platinum thermocouple	铂族元素 platinum-group element
	铂族重金属 heavy platinum metal
铂铑高温计 Le Chatelier pyrometer	箔 foil, leaf
铂铑合金 platinium-rhodium alloy, rhodioplatinum (90Pt,10Rh)	箔材 foil ◇ 液压~hydrofoil
	箔材对缝焊 foil butt seam welding
铂铑合金带 platinum rhodium belt	箔材缝焊 foil seam welding
铂铑热电偶 platinum-rhodium thermocouple, PR-thermocouple, Le Chatelier couple	箔材钎[硬]焊 foil brazing
	箔材冶金学 foil metallurgy
	箔材轧机 foil mill
铂钌合金(5—14Ru,余量 Pt) platinum-ruthenium alloy	箔活化法(指金属箔) foil activation
	箔片 chaff, paillon
铂皿 platinum dish	伯胺 primary amine
铂青铜 platinum bronze	伯德图 Bode diagram
铂石棉 platinum [platinized] asbestos	伯尔马鞍形填料 Berl saddles
铂丝 platinum wire ◇ 粉冶[沃拉斯顿法]~Wollaston wire	伯格-巴瑞特 X 射线衍射法 Berg-Barrett method
铂丝温度计 platinum thermometer	伯格哈特还原试验【团】Burghardt test
铂酸 platinic acid	伯格哈特指数 Burghardt index
铂酸盐 platinate	伯格曼系(光谱线的) Bergmann series
铂添加合金 platinum addition	伯格斯回路 【理】Burgers circuit,【金】Burgers contour
铂同位素 platinum isotope	
铂铜 platinoid	伯格斯曼微压痕硬度计 Bergsman
铂铜合金 Mock gold	伯格斯矢量 Burgers vector ◇ 特征~*
铂网电极 netted platinum electrode	伯格斯位错 Burgers dislocation

伯里尔科铜铍合金　Berylco alloy
伯利恒宽缘工字钢梁　Bethlehem beam
伯利恒宽缘工字截面　Bethlehem sections
伯利恒型球团竖炉（矩型竖炉）　Bethlehem designed（type）shaft furnace
伯马布赖特可锻铝镁合金（3—6Mg，0.75—1.5Mn,余量 Al）Birmabright
伯马尔压铸铝合金　Birmal alloy
伯马克斯低锡铅基轴承合金（5Sn,9—15Sb,80—86Pb,0.5Cu）Bermax bearing alloy
伯马莱特铸造铝基合金（9—11Cu,0.1—0.5Mg,1.0Fe,余量 Al）Birmalite
伯马斯蒂克航空用耐热铸造铝合金（12Si,2.5—3.5Ni,少量 Fe、Cu、Mn）Birmastic
伯马西尔硅铝特种合金（10—13Si,2.5—3.5Ni,微量 Cu、Fe、Mn,余量 Al）Birmasil special alloy
伯马西尔航空铸造铝合金（10—13Si,2.5—3.5Ni,＜0.6Fe,＜0.5Mn,Cu、Mg、Zn、Pb、Sn 等＜0.1,余量 Al）Birmasil
伯梅塔尔铝铜锌镁合金（0－4.5Cu,5－6Zn,0.5－3Mg,余量 Al,有时含0.3Cr）Birmetal
伯米迪昂铝合金　Birmidium
伯明翰铂合金（57Zn,43Cu）　Birmingham platinum（alloy）
伯明翰高锌黄铜（25Cu,75Zn）　Birmingham platina
伯纳德焊接法（用 CO2 药芯焊丝）　Bernard process
伯纳耳图表　Bernal chart
伯尼尔窗　Berner's window
伯努利常数　Bernoulli constant
伯努利定律　Bernoulli's law
伯努利方程　Bernoulli's equation
伯努利假定　Bernoulli's hypothesis
伯努利理论　【理】Bernoulli's theorem
伯努利数　Bernoulli's numbers
伯齐利尔斯回转窑烟化法（回收氧化锌）Berzelius process
伯斯特兰选择粉碎法　【焦】Burstlein process
伯特型圆筒压滤机　Burt filter
泊水铁铜矾　poitevinite
泊松比　Poisson's ratio
泊松常数　Poisson's constant
泊松分布　Poisson distribution
泊松系数　Poisson's coefficient [ratio]
泊肃叶流动　Poiseuille flow
驳船　barge,pontoon ◇ 钻探～drilling scow
薄膜　（thin）film,diaphragm,shallow layer,wafer ◇ 唐南～学说·
薄膜存储器　【计】thin film memory
薄膜导热系数　film heat transfer coefficient
薄膜电极（涂薄膜电极）　thin-covered electrode
薄膜电路　thin film circuit
薄膜电容器　film capacitor
薄膜电子显微术　thin-foil microscopy
薄膜电阻　thin film resistor,film type resistor,sheet resistance
薄膜法分离　【理】membrane separation
薄膜沸腾法（改良的碘化物热离解法）　film boiling process
薄膜分级（作用）（按粒度）　【选】film sizing
薄膜离子交换　membrane ion exchange
薄膜离子交换设备　membrane ion-exchange plant
薄膜滤片　membrane filter
薄膜强度　film strength
薄膜润滑　film lubrication
薄膜闪蒸器　flash film concentrator
薄膜式泵　surge pump
薄膜式精馏塔　film type rectifying column
薄膜式调节器　diaphragm regulator
薄膜收缩校正值　correction for film shrinkage
薄膜水　film water

薄膜形成器　film former
薄膜压力表[计]　diaphragm (pressure) gauge, membrane pressure gauge
薄膜照明镜(显微镜的)　pellicle mirror
薄膜蒸发器　film evaporator
薄膜制备技术(指金属薄膜)　thin film technique
薄膜质量传递系数　film mass transfer coefficient
薄膜状急冷(冷却速度10—1000万度/秒,制造非晶质金属用)【理】liquisol [splat] quenching
薄膜状析出(物)【金】filmy precipitate
薄弱部分(炉衬的)　vulnerable area
薄涂层　thin [light, curtain] coating
薄药皮　【焊】light coating
薄药皮焊条　thin-coated [thin-covered] electrode, lightly (flux) coated electrode
捕尘袋　catch pocket
捕尘　dust extractor [trap]
捕尘罩　dust head
捕滴器　spray catcher
捕汞器　mercury trap
捕获　trapping, capture
捕获能级　trapping level
捕获[捕集]通量　flux trapping
捕集　trapping, catching, collection, entrapment
捕集[收]剂　【选】collector (coll.), collecting agent ◇ 精选~ scavenger collector
捕集平衡　collection equilibrium
捕集器　catcher, trap, drip, arrester, arrestor ◇ 静电焦油~, 冷却~ cold trap, 木片[碎屑]~ wood catcher
捕集[捕检]气相色层(分离)法　trapped gas-chromatography
捕集设备[系统]　trapping system
捕集速度(通风罩前的空气流速)　capture velocity
捕集系数　collecting coefficient
捕焦油器　【焦】tar extractor
捕收器　catchpot
捕酸器　acid separator
捕雾器　mist catcher [trap]
捕油器　oil-trap
捕渣器(汤道附加物)　【钢】runner extension
捕捉　catch,【电】nip-up
捕捉辊(离槽镀锡板的)　【压】catcher roll
捕捉器　catch
补偿　compensating, compensation, make up, off-set, buck, equilibration ◇ 资源耗竭的~ depletion allowance
补偿半导体　compensated semiconductor
补偿棒(中子补偿棒)　【理】shim rod
补偿不足　under-compensation
补偿测量仪(速度计算的)　backing off meter
补偿磁极　interpole
补偿导线　compensating lead wires, compensation lead
补偿电池　balancing battery
补偿电流　compensating [equalizing] current
补偿电路　compensating circuit
补偿阀　compensation valve
补偿辊修整　【压】compensate roll dressing
补偿合金　compensator alloy ◇ 热磁~
补偿接头(温度的)　compensation joint
补偿镜　compensator
补偿控制器　compensating controller
补偿联轴器　expansion coupling
补偿(零点)测量法　【机】compensation (metering, measuring) method
补偿贸易　compensation trade
补偿目镜　compensating eyepieces
补偿器　compensator, equalizer, expansion U-bend, expansion piece
补偿绕组　【电】compensating [bucking] winding

补偿施主 【半】compensating donor
补偿弹簧 balancing spring
补偿调节器 compensated regulator
补偿线 make up line
补偿线路 compensating [compensation] line
补偿线圈 compensating [bucking] coil
补偿罩 compensating hood
补偿重块 compensating weights
补偿装置 compensating equipment [unit], compensation apparatus, bucking out system
补充 supplement, complement, make up, replenish, boost(ing)
补充泵 make up pump
补充舂实(震实后的) 【铸】butt off
补充处理 aftertreatment
补充符[代]号 supplementary symbol
补充过滤 after-filtration
补充过滤器 after-filter
补充焊道(多层焊的) excessive [extra] bead
补充回火 post tempering
补充记录 addition(al) record
补充加热 supplementary heat, make up heat, post heating
补充加注 【铸】topping-up
补充浇道 【铸】feeder
补充浸出 post-leaching
补充净化 after-purification
补充空气 supplementary air
补充冷却 supplementary cooling
补充器 replenisher
补充燃烧 after-burning
补充热 additional heat
补充[给]溶剂 make up solvent
补充[给]溶液 make up liquid
补充生产能力 surplus productive capacity
补充试验 complementation test
补充[给]水 make up waer, water make-up
补充水系统 make up water system

补充酸量 make up acid
补充碳 additional carbon
补充添加剂 secondary addition
补充项 addition item
补充阴极应用(电镀的) 【金】shadowing
补充支架 arm brace
补刮 rescrape
补焊 repairing welding, build up welding
补焊场[工作间] job welding shop
补焊气孔 fill up of blowholes
补极 commutating pole
补极绕组 commutating winding
补极线圈 commutating coil
补给 replenish, recharge, supply
补给水处理设备 feed water treatment plant
补加焊丝 additional wire
补加金属 added metal
补加矿石(熔炼过程的) 【钢】feed ore
补加[救]设计 engineering back-up
补焦 booster coke
补浇[注](液体金属) 【铸】afterteeming, back pouring [feeding], topping-up
补筋 【铸】cracking strip
补救 rectify, remedy ◇ 可～的错误 recoverable error
补救维修 remedial maintenance
补炉 reline, relining, daubing, fettling ◇ 冷～cold patching
补炉(材)料 fettling [patching, mending] material, refractory patch material, fettling grades, patching compounds ◇ 出铁场～*
补炉车 reline car
补炉工 fettler, patcher, 【钢】dresser
补炉机 fettling machine ◇ 白云石～*
补炉料槽 【冶】clay storage bin
补炉料斗 fettling hopper
补炉镁砂(粉) 【钢】furnace magnesite
补炉耐火材料 refractory patch material
补炉时间 【钢】fettling time
补炉用铬铁矿 【冶】furnace chrome

补码 【计】complement, supplement, true [zero, base, b's] complement ◇ 十的～ ten's complement
补强垫 reinforcing pad
补强构[杆]件 【建】reinforcing member
补强灌浆 strengthening grouting
补强焊道 【焊】reinforcing bead
补强金属 【焊】reinforcement metal
补强连接 reinforced joint
补砂 【铁】stopping-off
补数 complement, base complement
补算时间 【计】make up time
补缩包 【铸】shrink bob
补缩仓(内浇口的圆球形隆起部) ball gate
补缩横浇口 【铸】runner riser
补缩剂 【冶】feedex
补缩浇口 【铸】feeding gate
补缩金属液 【铸】feed metal
补缩料 【铸】feeding compound
补缩冒口 【铸】feeding head, shrinker
补胎胶 tyre cement
补遗 addendum (复数 addenda)
补余误差 complementary error
补足 replenish
不摆检流计 aperiodic galvanometer
不饱和醇 unsaturated alcohol
不饱和的 unsaturated, nonsaturated
不饱和溶液 unsaturated solution
不饱和酸 unsaturated acid
不饱和脂肪酸 unsaturated fatty acid
不爆炸的 inexplosive, non-explosive
不焙烧半稳定白云石耐火材料 【钢】unfired semi-stable dolomite refractory
不变波 constant wave
不变点反应(自由度为零的平衡相转变) invariant reaction
不变符号极限循环 cycle varying from zero to maximum
不变粒度 constant particle size
不变量 【数】invariant
不变平衡 invariant equilibrium

不变色合金 untarnishable alloy
不变式 【数】invariance, invariant
不变系(统)[体系] invariant [nonvariant] system
不变形的 non-deformable, non-deflecting
不变形钢 non-deforming steel
不变形合金 non-deforming alloy
不变形颗粒 non-deforming particle
不变性 invariance, inalterability, constancy, fixity, unity
不玻璃化黏土 non-vitrifiable clay
不剥落阳极 【色】non-disintegration anode
不测事件 eventuality (event.)
不车丝尾管 plain-end liner
不沉淀[沉降]的 non-settling
不沉淀颗粒 nonsettle able particle
不成比例 disproportion
不成对电子 unpaired electron
不充分曝光 inadequate exposure
不重复装置 non-repeat device
不重合 noncoincidence, misalignment, offset
不传导物质 carrier free material
不垂坠的钨丝 non-sag wire
不纯产物 raw product
不纯(度) impurity (level)
不纯黄金 impure gold
不纯孔雀石 musorin
不纯物质 impurity substance
不纯氧化钴 zaffer, zaffre
不纯皂石 ovenstone
不淬硬 unhardening
不带电粒子 uncharged particle
不导电材料 non-conducting material, electrically non-conductive material
不导电液 dielectric fluid
不等边角钢 L-bar, L-shaped iron, unequal angle (iron), unequal(-sided) angle iron
不等边角焊缝 unequal (leg) fillet weld
不等边四边形的 trapezoid
不等边三角形 scalene (triangle), non-equilateral triangles

不等温韧性　anisothermal ductility
不等缘工字梁　differflange beam
不等轴的　anisometric
不电离溶剂　non-ionizing solvent
不定比化合物〖如 Fe_7O_8 等〗【化】berthollide compound
不定成本　variable costs
不定尺长度　random length
不定积分　【数】indefinite integral
不定膨胀　variable expansion
不定期的　unscheduled, irregularly scheduled
不定向的　non-directional
不定型耐火材料　unshaped refractory
不动产　【企】real property
不动时间校正(计数器的)　dead-time correction
不冻结的　nonfreezing
不对称 X[双 V 字]形坡口　【焊】asymmetric double-vee groove
不对称半扭折带　asymmetric half kink bands
不对称电位　asymmetric potential
不对称断面　non-symmetrical section, unbalanced section(轧材)
不对称方式　asymmetrical mode
不对称分布　asymmetric distibution
不对称分布的焊点(熔核)　misplaced nugget
不对称荷载　unsymmetrical loading
不对称晶格　asymmetrical cell
不对称孔型　【压】unsymmetrical pass
不对称冷轧　asymmetrical cold rolling
不对称梁　【建】unsymmetrical [non-symmetrical] beam
不对称炉嘴(转炉的)　eccentric nose section
不对称形钢材　non-symmetrical section
不对称性[现象]　asymmetry, unsymmetry, dissymmetry
不发光的　non-luminous
不发火　misfire

不繁殖滑移　sterile slip
不放渣熔炼　【钢】single-slag melt
不符合　inconformity, disconformity, diversity
不腐蚀的　non-corrodible
不腐蚀金属　non-corrosive metal
不腐蚀性　non-corrodibility, noncorrosion property, non-corrosiveness
不感受性　immunity
不工作时间　outage [down] time
不共格　【理】incoherence, incoherency
不光滑的　nonspecular, rough
不光整冷轧　non-skin pass
不规则的　irregular, abnormal, anomalous (anom.), inordinate, erratic
不规则点阵[晶格]　lattice irregularity
不规则断口[断裂]　irregular fracture
不规则堆积　irregular accretion
不规则废钢铁　irregular scrap
不规则供料　unregulated feed
不规则结块[堆积]　irregular accretion
不规则裂纹　zigzag cracks
不规则螺型位错　irregular screw dislocation
不规则排列[取向]　disordered orientation
不规则碰撞　random collision
不规则刃型位错　irregular edge dislocation
不规则形状技术　random geometry technique
不规则性　irregularity ◇ 结构～structural irregularity
不规则振荡　hunting
不规则珠光体　【金】irregular pearlite
不归零制记录　【计】non-return to reference recording
不过端限规　【机】no-go gauge
不含金属液　lean liquor
不含水分的　moisture-free
不含碎屑[细粉]的　fines free
不含碳的　carbon-free
不含氧化物的　oxide-free

不含铀的　uranium-free
不含铀石墨　dead graphite
不焊合性　nonwelding characteristic
不合标准的　off-standard
不合标准废钢铁　【冶】off-grade scrap
不合标准化学成分的废钢铁　【冶】off-analysis scrap
不合尺寸废钢铁　【冶】off-size scrap
不合格　below grade [proof], off-grade, off-gauge, off-specification, substan-dard, unsoundness
不合格板　off-gauge plate [sheet]
不合格产品　sub-quality [off-grade, off-test, subquality] product
不合格带卷　rejected coil
不合格钢　unsound steel, off-grade metal
不合格海绵金属　off-grade sponge
不合格炉次　【钢】off-grade, off-heat, 【冶】missed heat
不合格批量(产品的)　faulty lot
不合格球团　undersize pellet
不合格熔炼　off smelting, off-melt(ing), lost heat
不合格溶液　not good liquor, NOK (Not OK) liquor
不合格生球　【团】sub-quality ball
不合格铁　(同"号外铁")
不合格锌　off-grade zinc
不合格阳极　rejected anode
不合格氧化铝　off-grade alumina
不合规定的条件　counter condition
不合规格　fall short of specifications
不合规格的长度　off-size length
不烘焙自硬化黏结剂　no-bake self-curing binder
不滑动位错　sessile dislocation
不挥发残渣　fixed residue
不挥发成分　non-volatile element
不挥发氯化物　non-volatile chloride
不挥发性　non-volatility
不挥发性碳氢化合物　non-volatile hydro-carbon

不挥发组分(混和料的)　non-volatile constituents
不混溶金属　immiscible metal
不混溶液相　immiscible liquid phase
不活动滑移系统　(同"静止滑移系统")
不活泼金属　sluggish metal
不活泼气体　inactive gas
不加固的　unreinforced
不加厚(的)(管壁)　non upsetting
不加厚油管　non-upset tubing
不加热炉　black furnace
不加压铝热焊　nonpressure thermit welding (NTW)
不加压烧结　pressureless sintering
不加盐的　no salt added (NSA)
不间断浇注　uninterrupted casting
不间断性　continuity
不健全的　unsound
不接地的　【电】ungrounded, earth-free
不洁钢(含非金属夹杂物)　dirty steel
不结焦的煤　yolk coal
不结晶的　non-crystallizable
不紧密金属(离子半径与原子半径差极大的碱金属)　open metal
不紧张的　unstrained
不精密的　inaccurate
不精确　imprecision
不精确性　inaccuracy ◇几何学上的～
不经济[不节省]的　uneconomic(al)
不均衡　disproportion
不均厚度　uneven gauge
不均匀X射线　heterogeneous X-rays
不均匀变形　inhomogeneous deformation
不均匀布料　unregulated feed
不均匀场　non-uniform field, 【理】inhomogeneous field
不均匀沉淀　ununiform precipitation
不均匀沉降　differential settlement
不均匀淬火　spotty hardening
不均匀点阵转动　【理】inhomogeneous lattice rotation
不均匀范性流变　【理】inhomogeneous

plastic flow
不均匀非触媒反应　non-catalystic heterogeneous reaction
不均匀分布　nonuniform [heterogeneous, uneven] distribution
不均匀分散粉末　【粉】polydisperse powder
不均匀辐照[照射]　uneven irradiation
不均匀共熔体　【金】eutectoid
不均匀过渡层　heterogeneous junction
不均匀厚度　off-gauge
不均匀滑移　inhomogeneous glide
不均匀混合物　heterogeneous mixture
不均匀加热　non-uniform [uneven, inequal] heating
不均匀间距　uneven space
不均匀结　heterogeneous junction,【半】non-uniform junction
不均匀结构　(同"非均质组织")
不均匀介质　non-uniform [heterogeneous] medium
不均匀进料　uneven feeding
不均匀晶[颗]粒　uneven grain
不均匀粒度原料　multi-granular charge
不均匀流　non-uniform [uneven] flow
不均匀区　non-uniform region
不均匀烧结　(同"多相烧结")
不均匀收缩　non-uniform shrinkage
不均匀析出　ununiform precipitation
不均匀系　heterogeneous system
不均匀性　non-uniformity, unhomogeneity, unevenness, off-set (ting), discontinuity (合金结构的)
不均匀压力　uneven pressure
不均匀压下（沿轧件宽度的）【压】unequal draught
不均匀应变条纹(薄板、带材的)　stretcher strains
不均匀质量[物质]　heterogeneous mass
不均匀状态　inhomogeneous [heterogeneous] condition
不均质导体　dissimilar conductors
不均质性　unhomogeneity
不可变的　unchangeable, inalterable
不可变通性　inalterability
不可辨区　uncertain region
不可测定的损失　undeterminable losses
不可测量性　immeasurability
不可拆卸[分割]的　unsplit
不可撤销信用证　irrevocable letter of credit
不可处理矿石　non-treatable ore
不可穿[渗]透性　impenetrability
不可萃取的　inextractable, nonextractable
不可淬相　unquenchable phase
不可分(解)的　indecomposable, undecomposable
不可焊(接)的　non-weldable, unweldable
不可还原矿　irreducible ore
不可磺化的烃[碳氢化合物]　non-sulphonable hydrocarbon
不可恢复[回收]的　nonrecoverable
不可恢复的应变　unrecovered strain
不可毁的　indestructible
不可毁性　indestructibility
不可计量性　immeasurability
不可见光　black [dark] light
不可见光过滤片　black light filter
不可见光谱　invisible spectrum
不可靠程度　degree of uncertainty
不可靠性　unreliability ◇设备～
不可控制的　incontrollable
不可冷凝[凝结]的　uncondensable
不可逆八辊轧机　E-MKW mill
不可逆变化　irreversible change ◇流变应力的～
不可逆磁性时效　irreversible magnetic ageing
不可逆催化反应　irreversible catalysis
不可逆反应　irreversible [non-reversible] reaction
不可逆凝聚过程　irreversible agglomeration process
不可逆热力学　irreversible thermodynam-

ics
不可逆式轧机　unidirectional mill
不可逆性　inconvertibility, irreversibility, nonreversibility
不可逆转变　irreversible transformation
不可逆转[转换]的　inconvertible
不可逆转[转换]性　inconvertibility
不可燃性　non-ignitibility, incombustibility
不可热处理合金　non-heat treatable alloy
不可溶的　insoluble
不可溶混的　（同"不溶混的"）
不可溶性　insolubility
不可润湿的　nonwettable
不可提取的　inextractable
不可通约数　numeric(al), incommensurable numbers
不可弯曲的　inflexible
不可压缩材料　incompressible material
不可压缩性　incompressibility
不可氧化的　inoxidable, inoxidizable
不可氧化性　inoxidizability, non-oxidizability
不可预测的损失　unknown losses
不可预见费　【企】contingency
不扩散[漫射]的　nondiffusing, indiffusing
不扩展裂纹　non-propagating crack
不老化的　non-ageing
不冷凝的　non-condensing (n.c.)
不离解的　nondissociated
不利影响　adverse effect
不连贯(性)　incoherence, incoherency, incohesion
不连通孔　non-intercommunicating pore
不连续　discontinuity
不连续 SiC 增强铝基复合材料　discontinuous silicon carbide reinforced aluminium composite
不连续 SiC 增强体　discontinuous silicon carbide reinforcement
不连续点　discontinuity point
不连续光谱　discontinuous spectrum
不连续滑移　【理】discontinuous glide

不连续晶粒长大　【金】discontinuous grain growth
不连续膜　discontinuous film
不连续谱线　spotty arc
不连续气孔　【冶】nonconnecting pores
不连续切削　discontinuous chip
不连续屈服　discontinuous yielding
不连续跳变　discontinuous jump
不连续析出[沉淀]　【金】discontinuous precipitation
不连续纤维（复合材料的）　discontinuous fibre
不连续性　discontinuity ◇ 表面下结构 ~ *
不连续预焙阳极　【色】discontinuous pre-baked anode
不连续增强金属基复合材料　discontinuously reinforced metal matrix composite
不连续周期操作[过程]　discrete periodic processes
不连续组织（铸件缺陷）　【铸】discontinuous structure
不良导体　poor [bad] conductor
不良混合　poor mixing
不良条件　adverse conditions
不良压实[成形]性　【粉】poor compactibility
不列颠银[锡锑铜装饰合金](74—91Sn, 6—24Sb, 0.15—3.68Cu, 余量 Pb)　Britannia (metal)
不灵敏的　insensitive
不灵敏区　dead zone, blind area, shadow
不流动试剂　stagnant reagent
不流动性　non-flowing character
不漏的　leak-proof, leak-free
不漏光线的封套　light-tight envelope
不漏气的(气密的)　air-tight, gas-tight, gas-proof, leak-tight, vapourtight
不漏气容器　（同"气密容器"）
不漏水的　water-tight, fluid tight
不漏烟的　smokeproof, smoketight
不漏真空的　vacuum-tight

不漏蒸汽的 vapourproof
不满带 【半】partially occupied band
不密致焊缝 【焊】leaky seam
不灭性 (同"不可毁性")
不敏感的 insensitive, dull ◇ 对裂纹~ noncrack-sensitive
不敏感性 insensitiveness, immunity ◇ 结构~*
不明显的 unsharp, indistinct
不命中 overshoot
不耐热的 thermolabile
不挠曲的 non-deflecting
不能操作[工作]的 unworkable
不能机械加工的 unmachinable
不能确定[明确规定]的 undefinable
不能实行的 unworkable
不能行驶的车辆 disabled vehicle
不能冶炼[熔炼]的 unsmeltable
不能运转的 unworkable
不能皂化的 unsaponifiable
不黏合特性 nonsticking characteristic
不黏结性 incoherence, incoherency, incohesion
不凝结的 noncondensing, uncoagulated
不凝气体 noncondensable gas
不凝气屋面材料 【建】non-condensing roofing
不配套工厂[设备] inadequate plant
不膨胀钢(36Ni,余量 Fe) non-expansion steel, Invar (alloy) ◇ 超级~*
不匹配 mismatching, maladjustment
不匹配位错 misfit dislocation
不平的 ragged, uneven
不平度 inequality, unevenness, 【铸】pimple
不平度测量 non-planeness measurement
不平度试验(对钢板,包括波浪度和瓢曲度) flatness test
不平度仪[不平整度测定仪] roughometer
不平断口 splintery fracture
不平衡 unbalance, imbalance, out-of-balance, nonequilibrium
不平衡电流 out-of-balance current
不平衡分布 nonequilibrium partition
不平衡继电器 unbalanced relay
不平衡力 unbalanced force
不平衡凝固 nonequilibrium freezing [solidification]
不平衡压力 uneven pressure
不平衡组织 nonequilibrium structure
不平坦的 rugged
不平行 unparallel, disalignment
不平整断口 uneven fracture, irregular break
不平整性 unevenness
不破坏的 nondestructive
不破损检验 bulk inspection
不起尘的 nondusty
不起反应的 reactionless
不起反应的塔板 physical plate
不起皮钢(高温下) scale-resisting [oxidation-resisting] steel
不起皮合金 non-scaling alloy
不起作用的 inactive, inoperative
不翘曲钢板 warp-free plate
不切实际的 unworkable, unpractical
不清晰 unsharpness
不清晰的 unsharp, indistinct
不清晰像 blurred image
不确定度 uncertainty, indeterminacy
不燃的 non-flammable, incombustible
不燃物 incombustible (matter)
不燃性 incombustibility, noninflammability
不燃性混合物 incombustible mixture
不熔的 infusible, nonfusible
不熔电极(电弧炉的) permanent electrode
不熔合处(铸件缺陷) cold-shut
不熔化焊接(指基体金属不熔化) nonfusion welding
不熔石灰渣(碱度过高而不熔融的高炉渣) lime set

不熔性	infusibility
不溶层	insoluble layer
不溶氮	insoluble nitrogen
不溶混性	immiscibility
不溶混液体	immiscible liquid
不溶碱性氟化物	insoluble basic fluoride
不溶解的	insoluble, indissoluble
不溶解电极	insoluble electrode
不溶(解物)质	nonsolute
不溶解性	insolubility, indissolubility
不溶解杂质	insoluble impurity
不溶相	undissolved phase
不溶(性)残渣[滤渣]	insoluble residue (I.R.)
不溶性单分子层	insoluble monolayer
不溶性肥皂形成(在线材湿拔的润滑液中)	soaping-out
不溶性结垢	insoluble scale
不溶性铅阳极电解槽	insoluble lead-anode tank
不溶性物质	insolubles, insoluble matter [substance]
不溶(性)阳极	insoluble anode
不溶阳极电解	insoluble anode electrolysis
不溶阳极电解槽	insoluble anode tank
不溶阳极电解法	insoluble anode method
不溶于水的	water-insoluble
不溶于水的溶剂	water-immiscible solvent
不烧焦油白云石砖	unburnt tar-dolomite brick
不烧结真空挤压球团矿【团】	unfired vacuum extruded pellet
不烧砖	unburned [unburnt, bonded] brick
不渗水的	water-tight
不渗透层	impermeable bed [layer]
不渗透性	impermeability
不渗透性覆层	impermeable deposit
不渗透(性)石墨	impermeable [impervious] graphite
不渗透性碳	impervious carbon
不生火花合金(指冲击时不生火花)	non-sparking alloy
不生锈[失泽]合金	untarnishable alloy
不生锈金属	unstainable metal
不生氧化皮合金	non-scaling alloy
不湿的	moisture-free
不适当曝光	inadequate exposure
不适合[宜]	unsuitability
不适应	disaccomodation
不适应性	inadaptability
不适用的	not available
不适用性	indaptability, unworthiness
不收缩的	unshrinkable, shrinkproof
不收缩钢	unshrinkable [non-deforming] steel
不守恒凝固	【理】nonconservative freezing
不受控制的波动	uncontrolled fluctuations
不受限制展宽	(同"自由展宽")
不熟练的	unskilled
不衰减波	maintained waves
不顺行	【铁】instable running, aberration ◇ 高炉~*
不顺行高炉	tight blast furnace
不松散钢丝绳	preformed [trulay] wire rope
不随温度变化的常数	temperature-independent constant
不调压式多辊矫直机	non-pressure regulating roller leveller
不跳击弹簧锤	dead-stroke hammer
不停产检修	on line maintenance
不通过量规	not-go gauge
不通孔	unfair hole
不同步的	【电】free running, out of sync, out-sync
不同材料连接	(同"异质材料连接")
不同厚度	dissimilar thickness
不同种类金属【金】	dissimilar metals
不透辐射[射线]的	radiopaque
不透过液体的	fluid tight
不透红外线性	adiathermancy
不透明的	opaque, non-transparent
不透明度	opacity
不透明火焰	opaque flame

不透明剂(搪瓷)	opacifier
不透明性	opaqueness, opacity
不透气的	air-proof, airtight, gas-tight
不透气石墨	impermeable graphite
不透气性	gas-proofness, gas tightness, impermeability to gas, imporosity
不透热的	athermanous
不透声的	soundproof
不透水层	impermeable layer
不透水地层	impervious stratum
不透水地基	impervious foundation
不透水焊接的	water-proof welded
不透水混凝土	watertight concrete
不透水容器	watertight vessel
不透水性	water impermeability
不透水纸	craft paper
不透油焊接的	oil-tight welded
不脱氧钢	【钢】open(-poured) steel
不脱氧熔炼	【冶】nondeoxidized heat
不完全焙烧	【团】green roasting
不完全铲凿	half cut
不完全穿透	incomplete penetration
不完全萃取	incomplete extraction
不完全淬火	slack hardening, incomplete quenching
不完全反应	incomplete reaction
不完全焊透	incomplete penetration ◇焊层间~
不完全还原	[incomplete] reduction
不完全混合	incomplete [imperfect] mixing
不完全混合流	incomplete mixing flow
不完全接地	incomplete grounding
不完全结晶的	subcrystalline
不完全解理	imperfect cleavage
不完全浸透	incomplete penetration
不完全凝结	partial condensation
不完全平衡	incomplete equilibrium
不完全燃烧	incomplete [imperfect] combustion, smoulder
不完全熔化[熔合]	incomplete [poor] fusion
不完全熔化区	incomplete fusion zone
不完全熔透焊缝	incomplete-penetration weld
不完全熔透焊接	incomplete-penetration welding
不完全烧结	【团】incomplete sintering
不完全渗透	incomplete penetration
不完全时效	under-ageing
不完全弹性	imperfect elasticity
不完全退火	slack [partial] annealing, under-annealing
不完全退火的	incompletely annealed
不完全位错	incomplete dislocation
不完全位错壁	【理】incomplete wall of dislocations
不完全系数	imperfection value
不完全压缩	malcompression
不完全氧化	incomplete oxidation
不完全再结晶	incomplete recrystallization
不完善	unsoundness
不完善程度	imperfection level
不完整晶面	imperfect face
不完整晶体	imperfect crystal
不完整位错	imperfect dislocation
不完整性理论	imperfection theory
不吻合	misfit, noncoincidence, poor match
不稳定奥氏体	【金】unstable austenite
不稳定电弧	unstable [erratic] arc
不稳定过程	unstable process
不稳定荷载	fluctuating load
不稳定化合物	unstable compound
不稳定火焰	unstable flame
不稳定控制	astatic control
不稳定流	unsteady [jerky] flow
不稳定炉况[冶炼进程]	【冶】rough furnace movement
不稳定平衡	instable [unstable, labile] equilibrium
不稳定燃烧	unstable [rough] combustion, rough burning
不稳定同位素	unstable isotope
不稳定土	detrimental soil

不稳定现象(铁合金电炉的)	wild effect
不稳定效应	unstable effect
不稳定性	instability, unstability, unsteadiness, fugitiveness
不稳定压力	uneven pressure
不稳定元素	unstable element
不稳定(原子)核	【理】unstable nucleus
不稳定运动	【理】unsteady motion
不稳定运转	instable [unsteady] running
不稳定振荡	【理】unstable oscillations
不稳定值	erratic value
不稳(定)状态	unsteady [non-steady, labile, unstable] state
不稳定组织[结构]	【金】unstable structure
不稳分解	spinodal decomposition
不稳固的	unsteady
不稳态力	nonstationary force
不稳态蠕变	transient creep
不吸收的	nonabsorbent
不衔接性	incohesion
不相称	【化】disproportionation
不相称的	inappropriate, disproportioned
不相干电子散射	【理】incoherent electron scattering
不相干散射	【理】non-coherent scattering
不相干性	incohesion, incoherence, incoherency
不相连孔隙	【冶】nonconnected porosity
不相连气孔	【冶】nonconnecting pores
不相容性	incompatibility
不相容原理	exclusion principle ◇ 泡利～
不相似	dissimilarity
不相应的	contrary
不协调的	inharmonious, inharmonic(al), incompatible, discordant
不协调性	incompatibility
不锈的	stainless, unstainable, corrosion-resistant, corrosion-resisting, non-corrodible, non-corroding, rust-free, rustless, rust-proofing, unoxidizable
不锈复合钢	stainless clad steel ◇ 英加克莱德～Ingaclad steel
不锈钢	stainless steel (SS, ss, SST), stainless steel alloy, rustless [non-rusting, non-corrosive] steel, rust resisting steel ◇ 18-8～*, F.D.P.～*, F.S.L. 低碳～*, 安卡～*, 布里阿雷～*, 超低碳～*, 超级阿斯科洛低耐热～*, 超耐热～superduty steel, 多孔～*, 可锻[形变]～*, 可焊接～*, 克罗曼格～Chromang, 无碳～*, 易切削～*, 优质耐蚀～*
不锈钢板	corrosion-resistant plate ◇ 罗斯特奈特～炉衬法*
不锈钢板[扁]坯	stainless steel slab
不锈钢表面渗氮[氮化]处理	malcomizing
不锈钢带材	stainless steel strip
不锈钢带抛光装置	scouring stand
不锈钢对醋酸的抗蚀性	stainless steel resistance to acetic acid
不锈钢粉	stainless steel powder
不锈钢管	stainless steel tube ◇ 挤压～*
不锈钢锅	stainless steel kettle
不锈钢过滤器	stainless steel filter
不锈钢焊接	austenite welding
不锈钢焊条	stainless steel electrode
不锈钢还原弹	stainless steel bomb
不锈钢还原反应器	stainless steel (reduction) reactor
不锈钢精炼炉	stainless steel refining furnace
不锈钢聚氟乙烯轴承(烧结的)	stainless-fluon bearing
不锈钢-铝复合板	◇ 杜拉内尔～Duranel
不锈钢屏	stainless steel screen
不锈钢球	stainless steel ball
不锈钢筛网	stainless steel screen
不锈钢生产	stainless steel manufacture
不锈钢丝	stainless-steel wire ◇ 镀[包]铜～*

不锈钢涂料[不锈钢漆]（含不锈钢细屑） stainless steel paint
不锈钢无缝管 stainless steel seamless pipe
不锈钢冶炼法 rustless process ◇ 哈密尔顿－伊万斯～*
不锈钢阴极 stainless steel cathode
不锈钢运输带 stainless conveyer belt
不锈钢蒸馏罐 stainless steel retort
不锈钢中空线（飞机制造工业防火用） fire wire
不锈钢种板[母板]（电解用） stainless steel (mother) blank
不锈高速钢 stainless high speed steel
不锈合金钢 stainless steel alloy ◇ 抗裂～*
不锈金属 rustless [non-corrosive] metal
不锈金属包覆 stainless cladding
不锈铁 rustless iron
不锈性 rustless property, stainlessness
不锈殷钢[因瓦合金] stainless Invar
不锈铸铁 rustless cast iron ◇ 高镍～*
不旋转钢丝绳 non rotating wire rope
不氧化覆层[涂层] inoxidizing coating
不氧化合金 non-oxidizable alloy
不易处理的(矿石) refractory
不易浸蚀的(结构)组分 slow etching constituent
不易破损[破碎]的 unbreakable
不易燃烧[着火]的 uninflammable, non-flammable
不易引燃[着火]的 nonignitable
不硬化 unhardening
不预热焊接 welding without preheating
不整形晶体 allotriomorphic crystal
不正常工作 malfunction
不正常[不恰当,未调好]火焰 unbalanced flame
不正常现象 abnormality
不正规分布 faulty distribution
不正确安装 【机】out-of-position
不正确操作 misoperation, maloperation, faulty working, mishandling（仪器的）
不正确就位 【焊】out-of-position
不正确轮廓[外形] incorrect contour [profile]
不正确配置[布置] misarrangement
不致密的 leaky
不准率 degree of uncertainty
不准确的 inaccurate
不准确度 （同"不精确性"）
不准确原因 source of error
不着火 misfire
不着火的 non-inflammable
不足 deficiency, shortage, imperfection, scarcity, deficient, insufficient, lack, negative excess
布邦锡铝合金(50Sn,50Al) Bourbon
布袋(收尘用) bag ◇ 涂层～收尘室系统*
布袋过滤器 cloth bag filter
布袋收尘法 bag process
布袋收[集,除,滤]尘器 bag (house) collector, bag-type (dust) collector, bag (type) filter, dedusting [filtering] bag, cloth dust collector ◇ 反吸风～*,防爆型菱形～*,干式～*,哈尔伯格－贝思型～*,脉冲～impulse bag filter
布袋收尘器烟雾 bag filter fume
布袋收尘室 bag (filter) house, bagroom
布登低压真空计 Bourdon pressure vacuum gauge
布登管(气压计弯曲金属管) 【理】Bourdon's tube
布登压力[真空]计 Bourdon gauge
布尔代数 Boolean algebra
布尔库法(竖炉或回转炉－电炉的铁矿石直接还原法) 【铁】Bourcoud process
布尔运算 Boolean operation [calculation]
布尔运算表 Boolean operation table
布福卡斯特铁硅合金 Buffokast
布格定律(均质试样的吸收比与光程中的试样厚度成正比) 【金】Bouguer's law
布辊 cloth roll, dusting roll（镀锡薄钢板

抛光用）

布辊擦拭镀锌（钢丝的） wire cloth galvanizing

布赫霍尔茨－埃里克森杯突试验机 Buchholz Ericksen tester

布赫霍尔茨继电器 Buchholz relay

布基光阑（X射线散射装置） Bucky diaphragm

布居 population ◇ 反向～ inverse population

布矿器 ore distributor

布拉德－邓恩电解酸洗法 Bullard-Dunn process

布拉克尔斯堡球团矿制法（不加黏合剂） Brackelsberg process

布拉塞特炼铁法（铁水罐苏打打脱硫法） Brassert process

布拉塞特铁粉热压法 Brassert process

布喇德雷型照相机X射线光学装置 X-ray optics of Bradley-type camera

布喇菲晶胞 Bravais unit cell

布喇菲-密勒指数 Bravais-Milla indices

布喇菲晶格［点阵］ Bravais lattice

布喇菲晶格符号 Bravais lattice symbol

布喇菲-唐尼-哈克定则 Bravais-Donney-Harker rule

布喇格X射线衍射法 Bragg method

布喇格电离分光［光谱］计 Bragg ionization spectrometer

布喇格定律［条件］ Bragg's law, Bragg condition

布喇格反射 【理】Bragg reflection

布喇格反射定律［布喇格关系(式)］ 【理】Bragg relation

布喇格反射公式（X射线的） Bragg reflection formula

布喇格反射角 Bragg reflection angle

布喇格方程 Bragg equation

布喇格峰［最大值］(X射线照相的) Bragg peak [maximum]

布喇格峰值强度 intensity of Bragg peaks

布喇格角（X射线衍射的） Bragg angle

布喇格散射 Bragg scattering

布喇格－威廉斯理论 Bragg-Williams theory

布喇格衍射 Bragg diffraction

布喇格（衍射）条件偏差［偏离］ deviation from Bragg condition

布喇格衍射圆锥 Bragg (diffraction) cone

布喇格转动晶体法 Bragg rotating crystal method

布喇开系（光谱线的） Brackett series

布莱恩比表面积 Blaine index number

布莱恩比表面积［平均粒度］测定法 Blaine method

布莱姆切边模 Brehm trimming die

布赖特雷耐热镍铬合金（80Ni,20Cr） bright Brightray

布兰特易熔合金（23Pb,23Sn,48Bi,6Hg;熔点38℃） Brant's metal

布朗定律 Braun's law

布朗管示波器 Braun tube oscillograph

布朗溶解度定律 Braun's law

布朗式旋转布料器 Brown distributor

布朗试验（钢丝绳磨损试验） Brown's test

布朗斯登－班尼斯特喷射撞击试验（从水面下向金属表面喷射空气） Brownsdon-Bannister jet test

布朗－夏普线规（美国） Brown and Sharpe wire gauge (B.S.G.), Brown(e) & Sharpe gauge (B. & S.)

布朗运动 【理】Brownian motion [movement]

布劳特－兰电解抛光法 Blaut-Lang process

布勒尔环（测温用特种粘土制环） Buller's rings

布雷德利－杰伊胶片装入法（记录X射线衍射花样用） Bradley-Jay method

布雷德利(型)照相机 Bradley (type) camera, Bradley chamber

布雷尔金刚石圆锥压头（洛氏硬度试验用） Brale (indenter)

布里阿雷不锈钢（12—14Cr, <0.38C）

Brearley steel
布里克斯比重计[浮计] Brix hydrometer
布里奇曼单晶制取法 Bridgman method
布里斯托尔黄铜 Bristol brass
布里斯托尔白黄铜[铜锌锡合金](37Zn, 58Cu, 5Sn) Bristol alloy
布里渊场 Brillouin field
布里渊公式 Brillouin formula
布里渊函数 Brillouin function
布里渊区 Brillouin zone ◇ 重叠~*
布里渊区结构 Brillouin zone structure
布里渊区填充 【理】Brillouin zones filling
布利克尼质谱仪(交叉场质谱仪) Bleakney mass spectrometer
布料 distribution, 【团】depositing on grate, distribution of green ball, feed of raw mix ◇ (程序)控制~*, 双层~ double layer
布料车 charge car
布料点 【团】charging station
布料端 feed end
布料段 feeding zone
布料方式 type of feeding
布料格栅 distribution grid
布料环 【铁】distributing ring
布料机 spreader ◇ 盘式~ distributing disc
布料机构 distributing gear ◇ 钟罩式 ~*
布料技术 bedding technique
布料宽皮带 wide belt
布料宽皮带机 wide transfer belt
布料矿槽 feeding hopper
布料量调节器 feed rate regulator
布料料罐 【铁】distribution bucket
布料溜槽 chute feeder, spill chute ◇ 多环~*
布料漏斗 spillage hopper
布料密度 mix packing density
布料皮带机 distributing conveyer ◇ 链算机~*, 逆流式~*
布料器[装置] charge distributor, feed arrangement, feeding mechanism, spreader, stock distributing gear, 【铁】distributing device, distributor ◇ 摆动式~*, 贝克-纽曼反射板~*, 带式~*, 辊式[多辊]~*, 截头体~*, 溜槽式~ chute feeder, 瓶式~ bottle distributor, 梭式~*, 旋转~ distributor gear, 移动式~*, 圆辊~*
布料器工作程序 【铁】distributor program
布料器工作顺序 【铁】distributor sequence
布料器滑轮道(炉料的) 【铁】distributor rollers
布料器旋转循环 【铁】distributor movement cycle
布料区 bedding area
布料设备 feeding equipment
布料斜槽 distributing chute ◇ 分叉~ bifurcated chute
布料压力控制 feed pressure control
布料钟 【铁】distributing bell
布滤器 cloth filter
布伦达洛伊 32-12 铁镍钴粉末冶金合金 Blendalloy 33-12
布伦顿转动凸底焙烧炉(回收砷用) Brunton furnace
布伦纳(钢轨)正火法 Brunorizing, Brunner's normalizing
布伦纳正火炉 Brunorizing furnace
布伦诺费克斯发黑氧化处理(碱性溶液中进行) Brunofix
布罗卡电流计 Broca galvanometer
布洛赫波 Bloch wave
布洛赫函数 Bloch function
布洛赫能带 Bloch band
布洛赫色度计 Bloch colorimeter
布洛赫(畴)壁(晶体电子能量壁垒) Bloch wall
布面密度 areal density
布纳橡胶 buna
布囊式集尘器 cloth envelope collector
布抛光轮 【压】full disc buff

布棋式轧机组　staggered rolling train
布圈装置　loop layer
布儒斯特定律　Brewster's law
布瑞兰钢丝连续电镀法　Bry(l)anizing
布瑞姆波脱硅操作法(在铁水罐中吹氧脱硅)　Brymbo dessiliconization practice
布筛　cloth screen
布氏比表面积　Blaine specific area (BSA)
布氏常用对数　Brigg's logarithm
布氏漏斗　Buechner funnel
布氏磨损试验　Brinell wear testing
布氏黏度计　【粉】Brookfield viscometer
布氏体　【金】braunite
布氏(维氏)硬度显示仪　briviskop
布氏显微镜(用于测定硬度)　Brinell microscope
布氏硬度　Brinell hardness (HB, B.H., H.Br.), ball hardness ◇ 测～Brinelling, 锤击～测定法*, 携带式～测定仪 telebrineller
布氏硬度标尺　Brinell (hardness) scale
布氏硬度计　Brinell (hardness) tester ◇ 杠杆式～*, 小型～baby brinell
布氏硬度试验　Brinell hardness test(ing), ball (hardness) test, ball indentation test
布氏硬度试验机　Brinell [ball] hardness testing machine, Brinell's machine
布氏硬度试验球　Brinell ball
布氏硬度值　Brinell hardness number (BHN), BHN hardness, Brinell figure, Brinell (hardness) value, ball hardness number
布思－霍尔电炉　【钢】Booth-Hall electric furnace
布线　wiring, cabling
布线电容　wiring capacitance
布线逻辑　wired logic
布线图　wiring diagram [scheme]
布线用电线　hook-up wire
布歇回转炉直接炼铁法　Boucher process
布置　arrangement, layout, lay, collocation, disposition ◇ 不正确～misar-rangement, 加勒特式～*
布置图　layout, arrangement diagram [drawing]
步长　step length, step size
步话机　walkie-talkie, walky-talky
步进电动机　stepmotor, step-up motor
步进计数器　【计】step counter
步进剪　progressive shears
步进梁　【压】walking beam (WB) ◇ 鞍(座)形～*, 固定型～*, 平板架型～*
步进梁框架　walking-beam frame
步进梁式板坯二次加热炉　walking beam type slab reheat furnace
步进梁式输送机　Walking-beam conveyor [transfer] ◇ 板式～*
步进梁式窑　walking-beam kiln
步进扫描　step scan
步进式电动机【马达】　stepping [stepper] motor, step by step motor
步进式顶锻[镦粗, 锻粗]　progressive upsetting
步进式分段抽风烧结生产线　sintering production line with step-by-step exhausting
步进式继电器　stepping relay
步进式(加热)炉　【压】walking-beam (reheating) furnace, rocker bar furnace
步进式冷床[炉底]　walking beam
步进调节器　step-by-step regulator
步进应力试验　step stress test
步距　pace
步行检查　walk-on inspection
步行式挖土机　walker excavator
步骤　procedure (proc.), step, move
钚 β→α 等温转变曲线　plutonium β→α TTT curve
钚氮化物　nitrides of plutonium
钚堆　plutonium reactor
钚含量分析仪　plutonium analyzer
钚合金　plutonium alloy
钚化合物　plutonium compound
钚金属　plutonium metal

钚生产堆 plutonium production reactor
钚添加合金 plutonium additive alloy
钚同位素 plutonium isotope
钚酰化合物 plutonyl compound
钚再循环 plutonium recycle
部分焙烧 partial [fractional] roasting
部分乘积 partial product,【计】intermediate product
部分充满能带 partially filled energy band
部分吹炼 partial converting
部分萃取 partial [fractional] extraction
部分淬火 local quenching, incomplete quench
部分打开[开启](闸板、旋塞等) partial admission
部分分解 partial decomposition
部分分析 partial analysis
部分辐射高温计 partial radiation pyrometer
部分负荷[负载] partial load
部分固溶体 partial solid solution
部分合金化粉 partially alloyed powder
部分互溶性 partial miscibility
部分还原 partial reduction
部分还原团块 partially reduced briquette
部分回流 partial reflux
部分回流稳定态 steady state at partial reflux
部分回流运转 finite reflux operation
部分结晶 fractional crystallization
部分金属化球团 partially metallized pellet
部分浸没(式)温度计 partial immersion thermometer
部分精炼 partial refining
部分冷凝 partial condensation
部分孪晶化马氏体片 partially-twinned martensite plates
部分凝固 fractional solidification
部分剖视图 phantom
部分嵌固梁 partially fixed-end beam
部分燃烧 partial combustion
部分熔化 partial fusion
部分溶解 partly soluble
部分溶解度 partial solubility
部分烧结 partial sintering
部分石墨化铸铁 partly graphitized cast-iron
部分试样 sample increment
部分受拉 part in tension
部分碎裂[崩解] partial disintegration
部分损失 partial loss
部分碳化 partial carbonization
部分提取[提炼] partial extraction
部分填充(布里渊)区 partially filled zone
部分铁素体化 part ferritization
部分脱[除]硫 partial desulphurization, partial elimination of sulphur
部分脱水 partial dehydration [dewatering]
部分位错 partial dislocation ◇ 弗兰克 ~
部分无序 partial disorder
部分误差 fractional error
部分酰胺 【化】partial amide
部分氧化焙烧 partial oxidation roasting
部分氧化重整(焦炉气的) 【焦】partial oxidation reforming
部分氧化熔炼 melting with partial oxidation
部分有序(化) 【理】partial ordering
部分有序结构 【金】partially ordered structure
部分运转 part-time service
部分再生 partial regeneration
部分中和 partial neutralization
部分主元(素) partial pivot
部分组合泥芯 【铸】branch core
部件 component, parts, piece, subassembly, assembly, packages
部件诊断(程序) 【计】unit diagnostics
部件装配图 【机】grouping

C c

擦除器　eraser ◇ 整体~【计】bulk eraser
擦镀　brushing coating,【金】sponge plating
擦干　squeeze, wipe dry
擦光　buffing, buff [abrasive] finishing,【金】mopping
擦光辊　buffing roll
擦光器　burnisher
擦光毡布　bob
擦痕　striation, scoring
擦净　wiping, squeeze
擦亮　brightening, burnish
擦去　erase, wipe off, obliterate
擦伤　scratch, scotch, scoring, gall(ing), chafing, digs, fray, fretting, gaffing, mar, seizing, tear,【压】gouge(带钢缺陷)◇ 表面~*, 带卷平整~coil femper digs, 耐~性 marresistance
擦伤表面　torn surface
擦伤痕迹　abrasion marks, rubmark
擦拭　wiping, scrub
擦拭辊(带材卷取时除油用)　wiper roll
擦拭焊料【药】　wiping solders
擦拭器　wiper ◇ 石棉夹~*, 梳形~comb wiper
擦拭钎焊合金(42—37Sn, 53—63Pb)　wiping solders
擦拭装置　wiping arrangement
擦刷(用钢丝刷)　scratch brushing
擦碎　fray
裁方　square cut
裁方剪　squaring shears
裁切厚钢板　discrete steel plate
材钢比　rolled steel to steel ratio
材料　material (mat., matl), matter, stock, stuff ◇ 重型~*
材料变异　material variability
材料表　bill of materials (B/M), material list
材料打包装置　material packing equipment
材料工程　material engineering
材料环境敏感裂化　environment sensitive cracking of material
材料回收[重新利用]　material recovery
材料加工　material processing
材料检验试验室委员会(美国)　Committee on Material Inspection and Testing Laboratories (CMI)
材料检验与接收报告　materials inspection and receiving report (MIRR)
材料科学　material science
材料科学与工程　material science engineering
材料空间加工　material processing in space
材料库　material depot
材料利用率　(material) stock utilization
材料力学　mechanics of material, material mechanics
材料连续性　material continuity
材料流变学　material rheology
材料试验　material test(ing), testing of material
材料试验反应堆　material testing reactor
材料试验机　material testing machine
材料(塑性)流变　flow of material
材料特性　material behaviour
材料物理学　material physics, physics of material
材料性状　material behaviour
材料压缩性测量计　piezometer
材料与加工工程促进协会(美国)　Society for the Advancement of Materials & Process Engineering (SAMPE)
材料员【企】material-man
材料织构定量分析　quantitative texture analysis of material
材料指数　material index
材质波动　material variability
材质鉴别仪　identometer
财产　property, assets, goods, means

财务管理　financial management [control]
财政　finance
财政年度　fiscal [financial] year
采光　lighting ◇ 地下室窗～area light,顶部～top light,房顶～井【建】comluvium
采掘　exploitation, excavation ◇ 台阶式～*
采矿　mining, win ◇ 溶液～*
采矿方法　system of mining, mining method
采矿工程师　mining engineer, engineer of mines
采矿工程师协会(美国)　Institute of Mining Engineers (IME)
采矿工程师学会(美国)　Society of Mining Engineers (SME)
采矿机械　mining machine
采矿及采石工程　mining and quarrying engineering (MQE)
采矿设备　mining equipment, quarry plant
采料场　borrow area
采料坑　borrow pit
采暖　heating
采暖费用　【企】cost of heating
采区　block
采石　quarrying ◇ 露天矿坑～法*
采石场　quarry, stone pit, delf
采石场斗车　quarry car
采石工程　rock excavation
采石坑　borrow pit
采石设备　quarrying equipment, quarry plant
采收率　recovery
采选公司[联合企业]　mining-beneficiation complex
采样　sampling, sample drawing ◇ 间隔铲取～法*
采样方法　method of sampling, sampling procedure
采样分析　sampling analysis
采样间隔　sampling interval
采样控制器　sampling controller
采样偏差　sampling variance
采样器　sampler ◇ 试料～sampling thief
采样装置　sampling apparatus
采油平台　oil platform
采准矿石　blocked out ore
彩虹色(石英)　iris
彩虹色的　irised
彩钼铅矿{PbMoO$_4$}　wulfenite
彩屏法　mosaic screen process, autochrome process
彩色玻璃料　coloured frit
彩色单张反转胶片　【金】colour monopack reversal film
彩色反转片　colour reversal film
彩色胶片　colour film
彩色监控器　colour monitor
彩色金相学[金相术]　colour metallography
彩色图像　colour image
彩色涂层　colour coating
彩色涂层钢板　colour coated sheet, organically coated steel sheet
彩色涂层作业线　colour coating line
彩色雾翳　coloured fog
彩色显示　colour display
彩色显像管　chromoscope, colour kinescope
菜花冒口　【铸】cauliflower head
菜花头　【钢】cauliflower [rising, spongy] tops, cauliflower (head) (钢锭头部不规则上涨缺陷),【焦】spongy edge (焦炭的)
菜子油(拔丝润滑剂)　rape seed oil, colza (oil)
参比标准(显微照片的)　comparison standard
参比[考]电极　reference electrode
参比接点　reference junction
参比[参考]离子　reference [pilot] ion
参比[参考]溶液　reference solution
参比[参考]试样　reference sample
参比值　reference value

参变管　parametron
参差(不齐)的　ragged, rugged(断口)
参差断口　broken stick fracture
参考标记　reference mark
参考秤　【冶】reference scale
参考磁道　【计】library track
参考点　reference point ◇ 测量的～ witness mark
参考幅值　reference amplitude
参考控制单元　reference control unit
参考模型自适应控制　model reference adaptive control
参考球　【金】reference sphere
参考输入(量)　reference input
参考数据[资料]　reference data
参考数值中央控制单元　central reference control unit
参考图　reference drawing
参考文献　references, bibliography
参考线　reference line, 【计】reference axis
参考信号发生器　reference generator
参考值基准　reference value standard
参考轴　reference axis
参考资料表　reference lists
参数[参量]　parameter ◇ 拉森－米勒～*
参数二极管　parametric diode
参数激励子[参数器]　parametron
参数敏感性　parametric sensitivity
参数语句　【计】parameter statement
参数转换　parametric switch
参阅　refer to, reference, confer (cf.), see, quod vide (Q.V.)
参照条件　reference conditions
残差　residual error
残处理　residue processing
残存　surviving, remaining
残存 p%的疲劳极限　fatigue limit for p percent survival
残存 p%的疲劳寿命　fatigue life for p percent survival
残存 p%的应力－循环次数(S－N)曲线 S－N curve for p percent survival
残存强度　【铸】retained strength
残存生球　surviving ball
残存物　survival
残存元素　【钢】tramp element, residuals
残电极　butt
残锭　stub ingot, ingot stub
残端损失(焊条的)　stub-end losses
残段　stub
残钢凝集　build up of skull
残极　stub, anode scrap ◇ 取～扳手(自耗电弧炉的构件) stub removing wrench
残极放置室(自耗电弧炉内的装置)　well for stubs
残极率　residual anode ratio
残晶的　malcrystalline
残料　residual feed, 【冶】trash, 【压】remainder, waste(切头、切尾、边料等) ◇ 生产～ treatment tailings
残料分离剪　【压】discard separator
残硫　residual sulphur
残留产物　bottom product
残留马氏体显微相　【金】retained martensite microphase
残留强度　retained strength
残留石英　residual quartzite
残留物　bottoms, residue
残留延伸　remnant elongation
残缺晶　malformation-crystal
残缺铸件　misrun
残数系统　【数】residue system
残酸[残余酸液]　residual acid
残损的　damaged, lame
残碳测定法　Conradson method
残碳值　◇ 康拉德森～*
残铁(铁水罐及出铁沟内的)　crude pig iron ～清理 scrap cleanup
残铁铁水沟(排出撇渣器小坑内残留铁水用)　【铁】punch-out runner
残头　butt
残头废料　end-wastage
残尾　waste end

残阳极　anode scrap [remnant, butt], scrap [residual] anode
残液　raffinate, barren solution, still bottoms ◇ 水相～aqueous raffinate
残余　remnants, remains
残余 β 组织　【金】retained β structure
残余[留]奥氏体　remaining [residual, retained] austenite
残余变形　off-set, residual deformation, permanent set
残余变形屈服应力　offset yield (stress)
残余磁感　residual induciton
残余磁性　residual magnetism
残余淬火应力　residual quenching stress
残余电流　residual current, aftercurrent
残余二氧化硅　residual silica
残余钢液（浇道的）　【钢】excess metal
残余焊接应力　【焊】residual welding stress
残余焦油含量　residual tar content
残余静力强度　residual static strength
残余孔隙[疏松]（缺陷）　【冶】residual porosity
残余冷作　residual coldwork
残余硫分　sulphur retention
残余馏分　residual fraction, end [last] cuts
残余浓度　residual concentration
残余膨胀　after-expansion
残余伸长　persisting elongation
残余渗碳体　residual cementite
残余收缩　after-contraction, after shrinkage
残余塑性流变　after flow
残余碳　residual carbon
残余物　residue, residuum, remainder, remaining
残余误差　residual error
残余压缩应力　residual compressive stress
残余阳极　（同"残阳极"）
残余氧化皮层（带材酸洗后的）　drawn-in scale
残余氧化铁　iron oxide residue
残余[留]应变　remanent strain, overstrain
残余应力　residual [remaining] stress ◇ 焊后～*, 机加工～machining stress, 沙赫～测定法 Sach's method
残余杂质　residual impurity
残余值　residue value
残余珠光体　residual pearlite
残渣　residue, residuum, remnant, remainder, remaining (slag), slime, sludge, bottom ash,【冶】trash
残渣层（电解形成的）　slime layer
残渣沉积坑　【焊】residue settling pit
残渣分析　slime analysis
残渣过滤　residue filtration
残渣净化工段　purification residue section
残渣率　residue ratio
残渣微粒　【冶】sludge particles
舱底污水泵　bilge pump
舱口　hatch, manhole
舱位　shipping space ◇ 运货～freight space
仓储　bunkering
仓库　storehouse, warehouse, depository, depot, magazine, storage, store
仓库备用泵　warehouse stand-by pump
仓库存货过多　overstock
仓库管理员　【企】material-man
仓库用吊车　store [stock, warehouse] crane
仓容能力　bunkering capacity
仓式泵　bin-type pump ◇ 上出料～*
仓式挡土墙　bin type retaining wall
仓式给[加]料器　bin feeder
仓式配料　ben burdening
藏金间　gold room
操纵　operating, control, manipulation, governing, guidance, management, run ◇ 单凭仪表～的 blind, 可～性 handleability, 人工～hand control, 易～性 handiness
操纵阀　control valve
操纵杆[柄]　operating lever [handle], control lever [rod, handle, arm], driving

[master] handle, setting [striking, working] lever, handlebar
操纵工 supervisor
操纵机构 control mechanism, operating mechanism [gear], motivator ◇ 渣口塞杆[堵渣机]～*
操纵盘 control board (CB), dash(board)
操纵器 controller, manipulator, positioner ◇ 微型～micromanipulator, 主从～*
操纵室 control room [cabin, center, booth], operating house,【铁】command room
操纵手 operator ◇ 近距离机械～handler
操纵手柄 control crank
操纵台 control console (CC), control board [booth, box, center, desk, panel, platform, post, pulpit, station], controlling board, operator's desk [pulpit]
操纵凸轮(夹板锤的) friction cam
操纵系统 control system
操纵性 controllability
操纵站 control post
操纵装置 control device [assembly], manipulator, effector
操作 operation, operating, handling, manipulation, working, processing, prac-tice, service
操作半径 handling [working] radius
操作备件[更换件] operational replacement part
操作臂(锻锤的) motion arm
操作变动 【铁】process fluctuation
操作变量 【电】manipulated variable
操作步骤 working step
操作参数 operating variable
操作侧 operating [operation, work] side
操作场所 infield
操作成本 operating cost
操作程序 operation(al) program [procedure], schedule of operation
操作程序图 flow diagram, flow sheet
操作次序 operation order

操作错误 operation(al) mistake
操作地带 working area
操作点整定 operating point setting
操作方法 method [mode] of operation, operating [operational] procedure, working method
操作费用 operating [operational] cost, operating [running] expenses, working expenditure
操作费用核算 operational cost accounting
操作分析 operation analysis
操作负荷 operating load
操作工具 operating facilities
操作工序 working operation
操作工艺 workmanship
操作工助手(拉拔机的) dogger
操作故障 operating irregularity, operational disturbance
操作管理员 operation manager
操作惯例 working rule
操作规程 operational [operating, working] instruction, operation regulations [standard], service manual [instruction, regulations], working specification [order]
操作过道 operation gangway
操作机构 operating mechanism
操作技术 handling technique
操作介质 operating media
操作可焊性 operative weldability
操作控制板 operation control panel
操作控制开关 operation control switch
操作控制(器) 【计】operation control
操作控制台 operator's console,【计】utility control console
操作联合性 integration of operation
操作连续性 continuity of operation
操作灵活性 operating flexibility
操作炉形 【铁】furnace wear lines
操作码 【计】operation [command, action, order] code, function digits
操作盘 【电】operating board

操作平台　operating [operator's, service] platform
操作平稳　uniformity of operation
操作期　operating period
操作器　manipulator ◇ 仿效~ *
操作强度　operating density
操作情况　operational detail
操作曲柄(锻锤的)　【压】motion crank
操作人员　operating [attending] personnel, operation crews, process man
操作设备　operating equipment, handling facility
操作时间　operating [manipulation] time, working hours ◇ 人工~【计】handing time
操作适应性　operational versatility
操作室　operation room, operating house, working chamber
操作室空调设备　cab cooler
操作手册　operation manual
操作数据　operating [operational] data
操作数有效地址　【计】effective operand address
操作水平　operating altitude
操作顺序　sequence of operations, operation order
操作说明　operational instruction
操作说明书　operating instruction [manual], operational instruction [manual]
操作速度　operating speed
操作台　operating [operation] desk, operating stand, operator's station, service platform, working cradle
操作特性曲线　operating characteristic curve
操作条件　operating conditions, conditions in operating
操作停止　interruption of service
操作图表　【企】operating schedule
操作位　【计】function digits
操作温度　operating [operational, working] temperature

操作稳定　【铁】smooth operation
操作系统　operating system
操作系统组成部分　【计】operating system component
操作线　operating line, pilot wire
操作线圈　operation coil
操作效率　operating [operational] efficiency
操作协调　operational consistence
操作信号盘　tell-tale board
操作行程　operational stroke
操作性能　operational performances
操作循环　operating cycle, cycle of operation
操作压力　operating [working] pressure
操作研究　operational research, work study
操作要求　operational requirement
操作一体化　integration of operation
操作译码器　【计】operation decoder
操作因素　operation factor
操作原理　operating principle
操作员[者]　operator, manipulator
操作员控制台　operator (control) console
操作员命令　operator command
操作指标　process index
操作指导系统　operation guide system (OGS)
操作指令　operation order (Opn O)
操作指南　operation(al) manual
操作制度　operating duty
操作周期　operation [operating] cycle
操作状态　operating status
操作字段　【计】operation field
糙面镀锡薄钢板　grained tinplate
槽　tank, trough, basin, bath, cell, container, sump, receiver, vat, channel, chute, ark, cradle, ditch, gab, gutter, pocket, pond, slot, tub, liner (收集氧化皮用) ◇ U 形~breeches chute, 带~的 grooved
槽帮　【色】ledge
槽帮结壳(电解槽的)　【色】ridge, ledge

槽壁(电解槽的) cell wall
槽车 (motor) tank truck, tanker
槽池砌块 tank block
槽池寿命 bath life
槽底 tank bottom, cell bottom（电解槽的）
槽底沉积物 bottom sediment
槽底电压降(电解的) bottom voltage drop
槽电流 【色】cell current
槽电流效率 cell (current) efficiency
槽电压(电解的) cell [bath, tank] voltage, cell potential
槽电阻(电解的) cell resistance
槽顶 top of cell
槽法(制碳黑的一种方法) channel process
槽法碳黑 channel (carbon) black, micronex（牌号名, 用天然气制得）, Wyex
槽钢 channel (steel, iron, section), U-bar, U-iron, U-steel, beam [iron] channel, trough [box] iron, girder, steel channel section, channel beam（大型的）, channel bar（小尺寸的）◇ 截面为四分之一圆的柱用～ quater-cirvle channel, 轧制～ rolled steel channel, 组合～*
槽钢孔型 【压】girder pass
槽功率(电解槽功率) power per cell
槽沟 groove ◇ 带～锭模 fluted mould
槽焊 slot welding
槽焊缝 slotted weld
槽架 truss
槽间隔室(浮选机的) 【选】free circulation compartment
槽角 groove angle ◇ 成～ troughing angle
槽浸出 tank [vat] leaching
槽壳 pot shell
槽壳结构(电解槽的) shell construction
槽口 rabbet, slit orifice
槽帘(铝电解槽的) curtain of aluminium reduction cell, cell hood
槽路 circuit of cells, tank circuit, 【色】channeling
槽轮 grooved [scored] pulley
槽螺母 castellated nut
槽面 slotted surface
槽内浸出 【色】confined leaching
槽内静置清洗 still tank cleaning
槽内配线 【电】channel wiring
槽内物料偏析 bin segregation
槽容量(电解槽容量) power per cell
槽舌接合[接头] grooved and tongued joint
槽舌连接 grooving
槽式拌和机 trough mixer
槽式反应器 tank reactor
槽式分级机 tank classifier ◇ 自由沉降～*
槽式干扰沉降分级机 tank-type hindered-settling classifier
槽式感应炉 channel induction furnace
槽式给矿机 chute feeder
槽式冷却器 channel cooler
槽式冷却装置(炉壳用) channel cooling arrangement
槽式(螺旋)混合器 trough mixer
槽式汽车 (同"槽车")
槽式取样器 riffle sampler
槽式输送机 trough conveyer ◇ 返矿用～ fine pan conveyer
槽式洗涤机 tub scouring machine
槽式洗煤机 launder washer
槽式选矿[分选]机 【选】slot-shaped separator
槽式氧化铁(脱硫)法 【焦】oxide box
槽式运输机 pan type conveyer
槽膛(电解槽的) cell cavity
槽膛外壳(铝电解槽的) stack shell
槽体 trough solid
槽铁 trough iron
槽温(电解的) cell temperature
槽纹辊 fluted roller
槽纹轧辊 【压】knurled roll
槽下筛 pre-skip screen

槽下筛分	rescreening under bin, pre-skip screening
槽型翻钢装置	trough-type tilter
槽型感应炉	channel (type) induction furnace
槽型钢梁	U-beam
槽型双轴螺旋搅拌机	trough-type double-shaft pug mill
槽型运输[输送]机	trough [tray] conveyer ◇ 连续~
槽形铲	split shovel
槽形导电板	cup bus bar
槽形导轨	trough-like guide
槽形电车轨	girder rail
槽形(断面)梁	channel section, beam channel
槽形感应器式混铁炉	channel-inductor hot metal mixer
槽形轨	flange rail
槽形机座	gap bed
槽形挤压型材	extruded channel
槽形件	slotted objects
槽形截面	fluted section
槽形孔型	box groove
槽形料斗	trough-shaped hopper
槽形碾砂机	groove muller
槽形皮带	troughed belt
槽形水力分级机	tank-type hydraulic classifier
槽形托辊	trough idler
槽形屋板面	channel roof slab
槽压测量仪	contractometer
槽液面	bath level
槽液面指示器	tank level indicator
槽浴氮化[渗氮] 【金】	bath nitriding
槽錾 【机】	grooving chisel
槽渣(电解槽的)	cell mud
槽轧辊	grooved roller
槽支架	tank support
槽砖	channel brick
槽总电解反应	overall cell reaction
槽总电阻	overall cell resistance
槽组	bank of cells
草黄色	straw-yellow
草黄铁矾	carphosiderite
草拟大纲	block out
草拟图稿	esquisse
草皮 【环】	ground cover
草绳(型芯内部用) 【铸】	hayband
草酸 $\{HO_2CCO_2H\}$	oxalic [ethanedioic] acid
草酸铵 $\{(NH_4)_2C_2O_4\}$	ammonium oxalate
草酸处理法(在钢表面涂珐琅前进行)	Loxal process
草酸铒 $\{Er_2(C_2O_4)_3\}$	erbium oxalate
草酸复盐	double oxalate
草酸钆 $\{Gd_2(C_2O_4)_3\}$	gadolinium oxalate
草酸钬 $\{Ho_2(C_2O_4)_3\}$	holmium oxalate
草酸盐离子	oxalate ion
草酸钾 $\{K_2C_2O_4\}$	potassium oxalate
草酸浸出	oxalic acid leaching
草酸镧 $\{La_2(C_2O_4)_3\}$	lanthanum oxalate
草酸钠 $\{Na_2C_2O_4\}$	sodium oxalate
草酸钕 $\{Nd_2(C_2O_4)_3\}$	neodymium oxalate
草酸镨 $\{Pr_2(C_2O_4)_3\}$	praseodymium oxalate
草酸氢钾 $\{KHC_2O_4\}$	potassium acid oxalate
草酸氢盐[酯]	binoxalate, bioxalate
草酸铯 $\{Cs_2C_2O_4\}$	cesium oxalate
草酸钐 $\{Sm_2(C_2O_4)_3\}$	samaric oxalate
草酸铈 $\{Ce_2(C_2O_4)_3\}$	cerium oxalate
草酸双氧铀[草酸铀酰] $\{UO_2C_2O_4\}$	uranyl oxalate
草酸锶 $\{SrC_2O_4\}$	strontium oxalate
草酸钍 $\{Th(C_2O_4)_2\}$	thorium oxalate
草酸稀土 $\{(RE)_2(C_2O_4)_3\}$	rare earth oxalate
草酸亚铁 $\{FeC_2O_4\}$	ferrous oxalate
草酸盐沉淀(法)	oxalate precipitation
草酸盐分离法	oxalate separation process
草酸盐涂层(拉拔不锈钢时润滑用)	oxalate coating
草酸阳极氧化处理	oxalic acid anodizing

草酸铀 uranium oxalate
草图 sketch (drawing, plan), preliminary sketch, rough drawing [draft], skeleton layout, scheme, diagrammatic drawing ◇ 画～sketch, block out, 目测～eye sketch, 注尺寸的～*
侧板 side-plate, side wall
侧壁 side [jamb] wall
侧壁大砖 side wall block
侧壁喷嘴[烧嘴] side wall burner
侧壁寿命 side wall life
侧壁斜度(孔型的) 【压】angle of sides
侧壁阻力(高炉炉料的) side wall friction
侧边 broadside, side, leg (三角形的侧边), side edge (板、带材的侧边)
侧边打孔机 side punch
侧边大砖 【耐】side block
侧边弯曲(带钢的) side camber
侧边压缩 edge reduction
侧边纵剪作业线(带材的) side trimming line
侧部导辊 side guide roller
侧部[边]加料 side charging
侧部炉瘤 side crust
侧部密封 【团】side seal
侧部偏析 lateral segregation
侧插棒电解槽 【色】horizontal stud pot
侧插棒连续自焙阳极电解槽 【色】 soederberg cell with side studs
侧插(导电)棒 【色】lateral contact rod
侧插阳极镁电解槽 magnesium electrolytic cell with sidemounted anodes
侧出料式 side-discharged type
侧出料式卷线机 pouring reel
侧出料式(连续加热)炉 side-discharged [side-door] furnace
侧吹法(转炉的) 【钢】side-blown process
侧吹碱性转炉钢 side-blown basic Bessemer steel
侧吹酸性转炉 side-blown Bessemer converter
侧刀剪[侧刀式剪切机] 【压】gate shears, guillotine [frame] shears
侧刀式闸板 guillotine damper
侧导板[轨] side guide [guards], flipper guide ◇ 机械化～*
侧导式围盘 side guards-type repeater ◇ 倾斜～*
侧电极 side electrode
侧端 side end
侧端加料 end-feed
侧翻矿斗 side-dumping hopper
侧拱 side arch
侧管 side tube
侧活套挑 【压】side looper
侧夹紧装置 side clamping device
侧加料电解槽 side-feed cell
侧浇口 side gate, side runner
侧阶梯浇口 side step gate
侧晶(瓣状晶粒的) side lobe
侧孔 side opening
侧立板 cant board
侧流换热器 side stream heat exchanger
侧冒口 side riser
侧面 lateral face, edge,【耐】side face (标准砖的),【金】side-wise (渗碳体长大法)
侧面搭接焊缝 side lap weld
侧面卸料[排矿] side discharge
侧面熔化 side fusion
侧面填角焊缝 side fillet weld
侧面斜度(孔型的) taper of sides
侧面装料(真空)闸板 side-feed lock
侧模板 side-plate
侧内衬 sidelining
侧喷(煤气)焦炉 【焦】gunflue battery
侧膨胀 lateral expansion
侧频带谱 side-band spectrum
侧砌弧[扇]形砖 circle brick on edge
侧砌砖 brick (set) on edge, brick laid on edge
侧砌砖层 course on edge, on-edge course
侧墙 side [swing, monkey] wall, jamb (炉子的) ◇ 碳质耐火材料～环*

侧墙寿命 side wall life
侧墙砖 side wall block
侧燃烧式热风炉(二通式热风炉) side combustion stove
侧燃烧室 side combustion chamber
侧燃烧室结构(热风炉的) side combustion design
侧视图 side view [elevation], lateral [end] view
侧塔 side tower
侧弯曲 side bend
侧吸法(电炉除尘) method of side extraction hood
侧限抗压强度 confined compressive strength
侧限压缩试验(土工试验) confined compression test
侧向冲击 lateral impact
侧向冲头 side punch
侧向滑轨 lateral skid way
侧向挤压 lateral extruding
侧向力 lateral [side] force
侧向挠度 lateral deflection
侧向挠曲 lateral flexure
侧向推力 side thrust
侧向弯曲试验 side-bend test
侧向弯曲试样 side-bend specimen
侧斜端砖 end-skew on edge
侧卸车 side-dump(ing) car, side-tip car [wagon], side-tipping dump car
侧卸吊斗 side-discharge container
侧卸矿车 side-discharge car, drop-side car, side-dumping hopper
侧卸式 side-discharged type
侧卸式送锭车 side tilt car
侧压力 side [lateral] pressure, side [lateral] compression
侧压系数 【粉】coefficient of horizontal pressure
侧压下 edge milling, side work, 【压】edging, indirect rolling action (轧制的) ◇ 板坯～*

侧压下(量) 【压】width reduction, edging [indirect] draught
侧烟道 side flue
侧焰炉[窑] cross-fired furnace
侧移车 side shift(ing) car [truck]
侧移式换辊装置 side shifter
侧轧 edging draught
侧振动 lateral vibration
侧柱 jamb
侧柱砖 bullnose brick
侧砖层 course of stretchers
侧装加热法 side-feed firing
侧装料法 method of side charging
侧装料式炉 side-charged furnace
侧装料窑 side-loading kiln
测不准原理 indeterminate [uncertainty] principle ◇ 海森堡～*
测尘仪 dust gauge ◇ 数字～*
测锤 plumb bob
测磁计 permagnag
测磁强术 magnetometry
测地学 geodesy
测电仪 electroscope
测定 determination, gauging, measuring, measurement, measuration, testing, rating, estimation, evaluation, setting out, survey
测定尺寸 sizing
测定点 measuring point
测定(方)法 (同"测量方法")
测定器 analyzer
测定熔融温度用高温计 fusion pyrometer
测定设备 sensing equipment
测定碳量 determination of carbon
测定值 observed value
测风器 anemoscope
测杆 (sight) rod, measuring staff, gad ◇ 用～探地下水 dowse
测高计 altimeter, goniometer
测功计[器] dynamometer ◇ 电动～electrodynamic meter, 普郎尼闸式～ Prony brake, 绳～ rope brake

测厚规 finger gauge
测厚辊 gauging roll
测厚计[仪] gaugemeter, thickness gauge [tester, indicator], pachometer, pachymeter ◇ X 射线~*,β 射线~*,γ 射线~*,超声波[波声,反射]~ reflectoga(u)ge, 度盘式板材~ dial sheet gauge, 放射性元素~*, 非接触式~*, 接触式~*, 同位素~*, 涡流~*, 虚拟~*
测厚装置 gauging device
测绘板 plotting board
测绘仪器 surveying instrument
测绘装置 mapping device
测积仪 planimeter
测极化术 polarimetry
测剂量装置 dose-meter, dosimeter
测角器[镜] goniometer, clinometer, limb
测角器法(晶体的) goniometer method
测角器分度圈 [理]goniometer arc
测角器头 goniometer head
测角术 goniometry
测角网 【理】goniometric net
测角仪[计] goniometer, direction gauge ◇ 单分度圆周~*, 固定底片~*, 接触式~ contact goniometer, 外森贝格~*, 移动底片~*
测径规[器] caliper gauge, calipers, calibration bar
测距 distance measurement
测距计[器] distance gauge [meter], ambulator, distometer
测距仪 stadiometer, apomecometer, range finder, anallatic lens (光学测距仪)
测宽仪 widthmeter
测力环 proving ring
测力计 dynamometer, load [measuring] cell, load(o)meter (用于测量压下螺丝上承受的轧制作用力) ◇ 扭转式~ torquemeter
测力计式仪表 dynamometer-type instrument

测量 measure, measurement, measuring, measuration, metering, (exploratory) survey ◇ 按时~ timely measures, 不正确~ false measurement, 单件~*
测量变压器 measuring transformer
测量传感器 measuring transducer
测量单位 measuring unit
测量导线 traverse
测量参考点 witness mark
测量范围[极限] range of measurement
测量方法 measuring technique [method], measuration
测量放大器 measuring amplifier [magnifier]
测量辊 measuring roll
测量回路 measuring loop
测量接点(热电偶的) measuring junction
测量结 measuring junction
测量精度 accuracy of measuring
测量轮(测管长用) measuring wheel
测量面 measuring surface [face]
测量数据 measured data
测量数值指示滞后 measuring lag
测量台 test desk
测量探头[针] measuring probe
测量头 gauge outfit, tracer, measuring head (测力计的)
测量误差 measuring error
测量系统 measuring system
测量显微镜 measuring microscope
测量楔(X 射线带钢测厚仪部件) measuring wedge
测量仪表 measuring instrumentation, metering equipment
测量仪器[器具] measuring instrument, measurer, meter
测量元件 measurer
测量员 measurer
测量值指示滞后 measuring lag
测量装置[装备] measuring apparatus [gear, installation, means, unit], gauging machine (测尺寸用)

测量准确度　measuring accuracy
测漏　leak hunting
测钠计　natrometer
测偏仪　derivometer
测偏振术　polarimetry
测频　frequency measurement
测平(法)　boning
测平仪　planometer
测热计　calorimeter
测热滞后　thermometric lag
测色计　metrochrome
测深锤　sinker weight
测深辊　gauging depth roll
测深器　fathometer, deep-sounding apparatus(深水的) ◇ 巴索(深海)~ bathometer
测渗仪　lysimeter, lisimeter
测声计[仪]　phon(o)meter, acoustimeter, sound-measuring device
测湿法　hydrometry
测湿计　hygrostat
测时　【企】time study
测时计　time meter
测试　test, checking, checkout, measurement
测试程序　test program
测试点　test point
测试端子　testing terminal
测试蜂鸣[音]器　test buzzer
测试卡　test card
测试灵敏度　test quality level
测试模块　test module
测试频率　test [inspection] frequency
测试器　chequer, checker
测试设备　test set [instrumentation, device, equipment]
测试数据　test data
测试台　test board [desk, bench]
测试探针　test probe
测试头　measuring head
测试图形发生器　test pattern generator
测试仪表　test(ing) instrument(ation)

测试仪表分度头　division testing device
测试运行　【计】test run
测试质量等级　test quality level
测水管　water-gauge glass
测速电动机　tachomotor
测速发电机　tacho-generator, tachometer [speed] generator
测速计[仪]　tachometer, speedometer, velocity meter ◇ 脉冲~ impulse tacho-meter, 频闪~ strobotach
测碳　(同"定碳")
测碳当量用高温计　pyrometric carbon equivalent detector
测铁高温计　ferrotemp pyrometer
测听计　audiometer
测微尺　microgauge, micrometer
测微光度计(用X射线照相测定)　microdensitometer
测微计[表]　micrometer (gauge), micro-caliper ◇ 电接触式~*, 电容式~*, 气动~ air micrometer, 物镜~ object micrometer, 自记~*
测微计测量[测定]　micrometric measurement
测微目镜(带测微尺目镜)　eyepiece [ocular] micrometer, micrometer eyepiece
测微偏振镜　micropolariscope
测微显微镜　micrometer microscope
测微压力计　【理】micromanometer
测微仪　amesdial, minimeter
测微延伸仪　dial extensometer
测微硬度压头　microindenter
测温棒　thermoscope bar ◇ 霍尔德克罗夫特~*
测温比重计　thermometric hydrometer
测温笔　temperature chalk
测温定碳探头　temperature and carbon sensor
测温法　thermometry ◇ 热金属丝[热隐丝]~ hot wire method
测温管　temperature tube
测温计[器]　thermodetector, thermoscope

◇ 带钢表面~*

测温包 carboy
测温漆 thermopaint
测温色笔 colour pencil
测温探针 thermoprobe
测温涂料 thermopaint
测温学[技术] thermometry
测温仪表 thermometric instrument
测温锥 【耐】fusible cone, thermal wedge, (pyrometric) cone ◇ 奥顿~ Orton cones, 西格~ Seger cone
测温锥等值（表示耐火度的） pyrometric cone equivalent (P.C.E.)
测温锥组 sentinel pyrometers
测隙规 feeler (gauge), clearance gauge
测向计[器] goniometer
测向术 goniometry
测斜器[仪,计] declinometer, inclinometer, gradiometer, batter rule, dip (ping) compass
测压法 manometric method
测压管 pressure sensing tube
测压计 piezometer
测压术 manometry
测压头[发送器] pressure cell
测压液 manometric fluid
测压仪 pressure gauge, load [measuring] cell, load(o)meter
测压仪表[设备] pressure instrumentation
测氧仪 oxygen measuring meter ◇ 电磁~*, 氧化锆~*
测银比重计 argentometer
测应力漆膜 stress-varnish
测针 point gauge, brad
测重设备[装置] weight measuring equipment [device]
测周器 circumferentor
层 layer, course, ply, stratum, storey, stratification, tier ◇ 拜尔培~*
层板 laminate, veneer ◇ 包铝[涂金属] ~plymetal
层板材料 sandwiched material

层板蒸馏塔 （同"多层蒸馏塔"）
层次钎焊 step brazing
层次随机取样 stratified random sampling
层错带 【金】fault ribbon
层错断片 【半】faulted segment
层叠 stackup
层叠冲压钢板 【压】imbricated plate
层叠结构（木模） 【铸】laminated construction
层叠现象 stratification
层叠铸造 stack casting
层段（浇灌混凝土每层厚度） 【建】lift
层堆积（原子的） 【理】layer packing
层格 layer lattice
层硅铈钛矿 $\{Na_3Ca_8Ce_2(F,OH)_7(SiO_3)_9\}$ mosandrite
层合云母板 micanite
层化 lamellation
层间电阻 interlamination resistance
层间电阻率[比电阻]测试机 interlaminar resistivity tester
层间间隔[间距] interlamellar spacing
层间绝热[绝缘] interlaminar insulation
层间温度（多层焊的） interpass temperature
层焦 split coke
层离 delaminate, delaminating, delamination, exfoliation
层裂（轧件缺陷） lamination [compacting] crack, lamination
层流 laminar flow [current], static [streamline] flow
层流板 lamella ◇ 加肋~ lamella with reinforcing rib
层流边界 laminar boundary
层流层 laminar flow layer
层流传热 laminar heat transfer
层流净化器 lamella clarifier ◇ 高效~*
层流冷却 laminar flow cooling, stream cooling
层流冷却段 laminar cooling section
层流冷却系统 laminar flow cooling sys-

tem
层铺(原料的) layering
层燃 grate firing
层燃炉膛 grate-fired furnace
层上密封 over-bed seal
层上燃烧带 overbed combustion zone
层蚀 exfoliation corrosion
层式洗涤浓缩机 tray wash thickener
层析 X 射线照相(术) laminography, planigraphy, tomography
层析法(色层分析法) chromatography ◇ 薄层～*
层下烟气流 【团】underbed gas flow
层线(X 射线) layer line
层线图 layer-line diagram
层压 lamination
层压板 veneer sheet, laminated board ◇ 复合材料～composite laminate
层压复合材料 laminate composite ◇ 正交各向异性～*
层压胶布板 textolite
层压胶木轴承 lignum vitae bearing
层压[层状]金属复合材料 laminated-metal composite
层压木板-铝板复合材料 ◇ 普拉依马克思～plymax
层压轴承 laminated bearing
层状断口 lamellar [laminar, foliated] fracture
层状断裂 laminar [laminated] fracture
层状酚塑料绝缘环 Micarta insulating ring
层状腐蚀 layer [laminal] corrosion
层状复合材料 layered composite
层状结构(组织) layer [laminated, schistose, beded] structure
层状点阵[晶格] layer lattice
层状料层 layered bed
层状裂纹 laminar crack
层状流层 laminar flow layer
层状马氏体 lamellar martensite
层状坯块 laminated compact

层状砂岩 band sandstone
层状石墨 foliated graphite
层状试样 stratified sample
层状撕裂 lamellar tearing, lamination crack
层状体 lamina
层状岩石 foliated rock
层状珠光体 lamellar pearlite
层状组合压坯 composite compact
插板 insert plate
插棒 soaking bar
插棒技术 soaking bar technology
插棒区电阻(铝电解的) stud-zone resistance
插棒式铁芯 plunger magnet
插补 【数】interpolation ◇ 圆弧～*
插承接合 faucet joint
插床 slotting [morticing] machine ◇ 冲模～die slotting machine
插钉 【铸】sprigging
插股 【压】splicing
插棍(插入钢水的脱氧剂或合金等) dipstick
插件 【计】plug-in board [unit], package board [card], card
插接(钢丝绳的) splice
插筋(伸出的) protruding, joint bar
插孔 socket, jack, hub, nest, rabbet ◇ 万能～consent
插扣(钢丝绳的) eye splice
插入 insertion, plug in, implantation, bayonet, interpolation
插入槽 insertion slot
插入法 【数】interpolation
插入记号 【计】caret
插入件 inserted piece
插入开关 【电】insertion switch
插入深度 depth of submersion, depth of immersion(如风嘴)
插入式部件 plug-in unit
插入式测量仪器 bayonet gauge
插入式程序系统 building block system

插入式定位销 【铸】loose (moulding box) pin
插入式隔离开关 plug-in type disconnecting switch
插入式计量辊 bayonet gauge stick
插入式加热器 bayonet heater
插入式抗裂试验 implant (crack) test
插入式冷却板 【铁】water-cooled segment, cigar cooler
插入式冷却器 inset cooler, 【铁】cigar cooler (又称雪茄式冷却器)
插入式振捣器 【建】immersion (-type) [internal] vibrator, intravibrator, pervibrator
插入物 interpolation, insert, inlay
插入型芯 【铸】insert core
插入增益 insertion gain
插塞 connector, plug (adapter)
插塞式保险丝 fuse plug
插塞式开关 plug key
插树还原 (铜火法精炼) 【色】poling (down)
插树精炼铜 pole [poling] tough pitch
插闩式接触器 latching contactor
插算 【计】interlude
插索针 marline spike ◇ 匙状~ spoon spike
插锁 mortice lock, latch rod
插锁式结构 locked-in construction
插头 plug (contact), male plug
插头扳手 spanner wrench
插头连接 plug connection, fork connection (叉形接线)
插头软线 plug cord
插头托架 plug bracket
插头装置 plug device
插图 illustration (ill., illus.), figure ◇ 卷头~ (书籍的) frontispiece
插箱 (代替上箱) 【铸】crib
插销 male [inserted] pin, latch
插销板 【电】pinboard
插销系统 plug system

插值 (同"插补")
插值器 digital difference detector
插座 socket, jack, receptacle, bayonet base, consent, bracket, rosette ◇ 弹簧[防震]~ cushion socket, 卡口~ bayonet socket, 嵌入式~ flush plug consent
叉 fork, gab ◇ 佩尔蒂埃~
叉插销 clevis pin
叉车 fork truck, forklift
叉端 fork(ed) end
叉架(自动装卸机的) 【压】fork ◇ 用~提起[提取] fork
叉接 fork(ed) [vee(d)] joint
叉式电动装卸机 electric fork truck
叉式锻焊 fork welding
叉式模 die fork
叉式万能装卸车 fork lifter [tractor, truck]
叉式万能[自动]装卸机 fork (lift) truck
叉丝 cross hair
叉形扳手 fork spanner [wrench]
叉形出钢[铁]槽 forked runner, forked tapping spout, 【钢】bifurcated runner [spout]
叉形端 fork(ed) end
叉形杆 fork(ed) link, yoke lever
叉形焊缝 fish mouth weld
叉形件 Y-piece
叉形浇口 (同"分流浇口")
叉形接头 fork(ed) joint, fish mouth joint
叉形接线 fork connection
叉形十字头 forked crosshead
叉形试棒 (腐蚀试验用) fork test bar
叉形物 prong
叉形线夹 fish mouth clamp
叉形线圈 fork shaped coil
叉(形)轴 fork(ed) axle, yoke (万向联轴节的)
差错 mistake, error ◇ 消除~ debugging
差电子的 betatopic
差动保护继电器 differential protection relay

差动测量 【电】differential measurement
差动齿轮 differential gear
差动电流继电器 differential current relay
差动电路[装置] differentiator
差动法 differential method
差动放大器 differential amplifier
差动滑车 differential block [pulley]
差动激磁 differential excitation
差动继电器 differential [balanced] relay
差动监控器 differential monitor
差动检流计 differential galvanometer
差动连接 differential connection
差动量热法 dynamic differential calorimetry
差动器侧面伞形齿轮 crown gear
差动线圈 differential coils
差动小齿轮 differential pinion
差动压力表[计] (同"差示压力表")
差动压力传送器 (同"压差传感器")
差动制动器[差动闸] differential brake
差动轴 differential axle
差动装置 differential (device, gear)
差额 balance
差分法 method of difference
差分微分方程 differential-difference equation
差厚电镀锡薄钢板的检辨(借助专用标志系统) identification of differentially coated electrolytic tin-plate
差厚镀层 different thickness coating, differential coating
差厚镀层带材 differential coated strip
差厚面标志方法(双面差厚电镀锡薄钢板的) differential marking system
差接 differential connection
差接变压器 differential transformer
差接滤波器 【电】differential filter
差率 rate
差拍 beat
差频 beat [difference] frequency
差频振荡器 beat(ing) frequency oscillator
差绕复激的 differentially compounded

差热分析 differential thermal analysis (DTA)
差热分析器[仪] differential thermal analyzer
差热分析设备 differential thermal (analysis) apparatus
差热重量分析法 differential thermal gravimetry
差式压力计 draught indicator
差示测压术 differential manometry
差示超声频谱学 differential ultrasonic spectroscopy
差示分光光度法 differential spectrophotometry
差示加热曲线 differential heating curve
差示检漏器 differential leak detector
差示热电偶 differential thermocouple
差示热分析 differential thermoanalysis
差示热膨胀计 differential dilatometer ◇ 自记~*
差示溶剂 differentiating solvent
差示溶液 【化】differential solution
差示[动]式测试仪表 differential measuring instrument
差示温度计 differential thermometer
差示吸收光谱 difference absorption spectrum
差示压力表[计] differential pressure gauge [meter], differential manometer
差速辊(碎机) 【耐】differential speed roll
差速器 differential (mechanism)
差速圆盘剪切机 differential speed disk cutter
差温淬火 differential quenching
差温加热 differential heating
差压传感器 differential pressure cell [pickup, transmitter]
差压发送器 differential pressure transmitter ◇ 带法兰的~flanged differen-tial pressure transmitter
差压挤压 differential pressure extruding
差压计 differential gauge

差压警报器 differential pressure alarm ◇过滤器~*
差压静液挤压 (同"液液静液挤压")
差压开关 differential pressure switch
差压流量表[计] differential pressure type flowmeter
差压敏感元件 differential pressure cell
差压自启动阀 differential pressure self actuated type valve
差异 difference, discrepancy, diversity, variance
差异沉降 differential settlement
差异充气电流 differential aeration current
差异充气腐蚀 (同"氧差腐蚀")
差异法 method of difference
茶壶(式浇)包 syphon pour ladle, teapot [lip-pour] ladle
茶铅(包装茶叶用铅箔;2Sn,98Pb) tea lead
查表 [计]table look-up (TLU)
查尔玛斯金属单晶制取法 Chalmers method
查理定律 【理】Charles' law
查米特海军黄铜 Chamet brass
查米特含锡黄铜(60Cu,1Sn,余量 Zn) Chamet brass
查培克氏培养基 Czapek's medium
查佩隆偶数层绕组 Chaperon winding
查普曼液体渗氮法 Chapmanizing
查找故障(故障检修) troubleshoot
查找故障程序 [计]malfunction routine
查找时间 【计】seek [search] time
岔道 shunting track, turnout, branch road ◇保险~*
拆除 disassembly, dismantling, dismounting
拆除模架 【建】decentering
拆除位置 removing position
拆船废钢 ship (breaking) scrap
拆焊 unsolder
拆毁 break away, demolition

拆卷 uncoil(ing), decoiling, unreel, unwind(ing), stripping
拆卷刀 opening blade
拆卷机 pay-off [feed] reel, decoiler, reeler, unwinder, unwinding coiler
拆开 disconnecting, disassembly, dismantling, dismounting, detachment, uncouple, loosening (铸模)
拆炉砖 debricking
拆模 form stripping
拆卸 disassembly, dismantling, dismounting, demolition, stripping
拆卸部件 disassembly of parts
拆卸车 dismantling car
拆卸拱架 【建】decentering
拆卸机 stripper ◇液压~hydraulic stripper
拆卸架 dismantling chair
拆卸起重机(拆建筑物用) breakdown crane
拆卸器[工具] stripper, take-off fitting, knockout
拆卸时间 【计】take-down time
拆卸台架 dismantling chair
拆修 overhaul
拆修人孔 disconnection manhole(d.m.)
拆装 reassembling
柴油 diesel [fuel, heavy] oil
柴油泵 diesel pump
柴油车 diesel carrier
柴油电力移动式电铲 diesel-electric mobile power shovel
柴油发电机 diesel (engine-)generator
柴油机 diesel (engine), crude oil engine
柴油机铲 diesel shovel
柴油机车 diesel loco(motive)
柴油机废烟 【环】diesel smoke
柴油机送锭车 diesel-driven ingot buggy
柴油汽车 Diesel truck
柴油挖泥机 diesel dredge
柴油运货车 diesel truck
觇标[板](测量用) target, beacon

掺和 admixture, blend ◇ 圆筒～机 blunger	
掺和器 blender	
掺和物 admixture, contaminant	
掺合 admix, blend ◇ 加水～blunge, 有～料水泥 additive cement	
掺合器 admixer	
掺合型砂(天然的) 【铸】blended moulding sand	
掺镓锗 【半】gallium doped germanium	
掺金 gold doping	
掺料 doctor	
掺硼 boron-doping	
掺入 admixing, incorporation	
掺入体 【金】inclusion	
掺碳 carbon dosing	
掺钍钨极 thoriated electrode	
掺铟的合金添加剂 indium-doped addition alloy	
掺油(煤料的) 【焦】oil addition	
掺杂 doping, adulteration, inclusion, intermingle ◇ 气相～技术*, 受控～controlled doping, 轻～籽晶 lightly doped seed, 未～的 virgin, 重～籽晶 heavily doped seed	
掺杂半导体 impurity semiconductor	
掺杂超导材料 impure superconducting material	
掺杂单晶 doped single crystal	
掺杂硅 doped silicon	
掺杂剂 【半】dopant, doping agent	
掺杂结 【半】doped junction	
掺杂熔体 doped melt	
掺杂梯度 doping gradient	
掺杂物 adulterant, adulteration, 【半】dopant	
掺杂元素 doping element	
掺杂再熔法(区域熔炼的) remelt with additions	
掺杂锗 doped germanium	
掺杂致密化 sophisticated densification	
掺杂质 (同"掺杂")	
掺杂质补偿 doping compensation	
缠带 taping	
缠辊 【压】wind-up on the roll, cobbling, collar(ing)	
缠结 tangling	
缠(金属)丝软管 armoured hose	
缠卷装置 coiler, take-up unit	
缠绝缘带 tapping	
缠乱 【压】snarl	
缠绕 winding, wrapping ◇ 自身～试验*	
缠绕电极 wrapped electrode	
缠绕机(在钢丝或棒材上缠绕绝缘纸带) lapping [winding] machine	
缠绕计数器 wrap counter	
缠绕卷筒 winding drum	
缠绕试验 coiling test, wrapping (and unwrapping) test, 【压】mandrel test	
缠绕弯曲(试验) wrap-around bend	
缠绕直径 【压】wrapping diameter	
缠线 spooling	
缠住卷筒(指轧件) collar(ing)	
铲 shovel, spade, chip, scoop	
铲臂 bucket arm	
铲边焊缝 bevel (groove) weld ◇ 双面～double-groove weld	
铲车 shovel car, setting elevator, tractor shovel	
铲除(表面缺陷) chipping(-out)	
铲斗 bucket ◇ 牵引～drag bucket	
铲斗齿 bucket teeth	
铲斗链条 【采】bucket chain	
铲斗排矿 scoop discharge	
铲斗式起重机 crane with dipper attachment	
铲斗挖泥船[机] dipper dredger	
铲斗挖土机 scoop shovel	
铲根 【焊】back chipping	
铲泥机(刮板式) scraping dredger	
铲式挖掘机 shovel excavator	
铲式装载机 shovel loader	
铲土机 earth scraper ◇ 轮胎式拖拉～tyred tractor shovel	

铲削用护目镜　chipping goggles
铲运机　loader-hauler-dumper（LHD），carry scraper ◇ 衡重式~*，机动~motorscraper，拖拉~dragscraper
铲凿　chipping ◇ 不完全~half cut
铲凿清理台(锭坯缺陷的)　chipping bed
产尘量[率]　dust yield
产出金属　resultant metal
产出率　specific yield, delivery, fall, yield factor
产出溶液　resultant solution
产地　place of origin [production]
产量　production（capacity），output（quantity, rate），outcome, quantity [volume] of production, yield ◇ 低于估计的~underrun，炉膛面积~output of hearth area，小时~*
产量定额　darg
产量吨数　tonnage output
产量下降　loss of yield
产量下调　turndown of production
产量指标　production output figure
产量指数　output index
产量-质量关系曲线　yield-mass curve
产率　percentage yield
产品　(finished) product, outgo, turnout ◇ 未经检验[未规定条件]的~【企】off-test product
产品标识码　product identification code
产品尺寸　product size
产品纯度　product purity
产品堆放装置　article handling apparatus
产品方案[大纲]　product mix [program]
产品技术鉴定　product technical appraisal
产品计量器　product weigher
产品金属　resultant metal
产品开发　product development
产品馏分　product cut
产品目录　product list
产品排出管　product line
产品品种　range of products, product variety

产品平均质量　average outgoing quality (AOQ)
产品缺陷记录仪　production analyzer
产品溶液浓度　product [resultant] solution concentration
产品筛目　mesh size of product
产品设计　design of products
产品台架　product rack
产品特性　product property
产品销售收入　【企】revenue from sales of products, sales revenue
产品销售税金及附加　sale tax and extra tax
产品质量　product quality
产品质量合格认证和产品质量安全认证　product quality certification for qualification & safety
产品质量认证机构　certification organization for product quality
产品贮槽　product storage tank
产气(杆)菌　aerobacter aerogenes
产水率　specific yield
产物　product, result, outgrowth
产物出口　product exit [outlet]
产物斗仓　product hopper
产物冷却区　product cooling zone
产物母体　precurser
产物排出管[口]　product discharge
产物贮桶　product drum
产业化　industrialization, commercial adoption
产油率　oil production rate
产值　output value
阐明　clarification, elucidation, illumination
颤动　quake, tremble, tremor, flutter, vibration ◇ 空气压缩机~极限*
颤藻属　Oscillatoria
颤振(轧机的)　chatter
颤振射流　dithering jet
场　field, platform
场磁极　field pole
场磁铁　field magnet

场地 (plant) site, yard, dock, floor, space ◇ 可用~ space availability
场地平整图 site levelling drawing
场地[场房]照明 yard lighting
场电子发射显微术 field electron emission microscopy
场分布 field distribution
场(分布)图 field pattern
场合 occasion, situation
场畸变 field distortion
场激励 field excitation
场绝缘 field insulation
场离子显微镜 field-ion microscope (FIM)
场力线 field line
场强 field strength [density, intensity]
场强分布 field intensity distribution
场强计 field strength [intensity] meter
场区(电子束的) field zone
场扫描 field scanning [sweeping]
场深度 depth of field
场所 place, site, room, ground, situation
场梯度 field gradient
场透镜 field lens
场线圈 field coil
场效应晶体管 【电】field effect transistor (FET) ◇ 面结型~ *
场效应器件 field effect device, fieldtron
场指示器 field indicator
场致电离真空规 field ionization gauge
场致发光 electroluminescence ◇ 阴极~ *
场致发射 field [cold] emission
场致发射(电子)显微镜 field emission microscope
场致发射电子显微镜图像 field emission pattern
场致发射电子显微镜像 field emission image
场致发射电子显微镜照片 field emission photograph [micrograph]
场致发射法 field emission method

场致发射显微术 field emission microscopy
场致光学准直仪系统 field optical collimator system
场致离子法 field ion method
场致离子显微镜 field ion microscope
场致离子显微镜观察 【金】field ion microscopic observation
场致离子显微镜像 field ion image
场致离子显微镜学[技术] field ion microscopy
场致离子显微照片 field ion micrograph
尝试法 back and forth method, cut and trial [try] method, trial-and-error method [procedure] ◇ 试验室~ *
尝试试验 trial-and-error testing
常闭触点 【电】normally closed contact
常闭联锁触点 【电】normally closed interlock
常规成形设备 conventional forming equipment
常规分析 routine analysis
常规检查[检验] routine [normal] inspection, routine examination
常规控制 routine control
常规设备 conventional equipment
常规试验 routine test [experiment]
常规铸锭 normal ingot making
常规作业 routine work
常衡制(英国,以16盎司为1磅的衡量制) avoirdupois (av., avdp)
常化 【金】(同"正火") ◇ 在空气中~的 normalized in air (Na), 在线~ *
常价 【化】normal valency
常价化合物 normal valency compound
常开触点 【电】normally open contact
常量电泳法 macro electrophoretic method
常量定量分析 macro qualitative analysis
常数 constant ◇ 阿伏加德罗~ Avogadro constant, 玻耳兹曼~ Boltzmann's constant, 泊松~ Poisson's constant, 格律埃森~【理】Grueneisen constant, 亨利定律

~Henry's law constant, 霍尔~Hall coefficient, 居里~【理】Curie constant, 里德伯~【理】Rydberg constant, 马德隆~Madelung constant, 塔菲尔~Tafel constant, 韦斯~【理】Weiss constant
常数(存储)区 【计】constant storage [area]
常数项 constant term
常态 normal (state)
常态原子 normal atom
常温 normal temperature (N.T.), atmospheric [ambient room, ordinary, moderate] temperature
常温操作 moderate-temperature process
常温常压 normal temperature and pressure (NTP, n.t.p.)
常温常压浸出 cold atmospheric leaching
常温机械性能 mechanical property at normal temperature
常温浸出 cold leach(ing)
常温浸出液 cold-leach liquor
常温抗压强度 ambient compressive strength
常温强度 cold strength
常温时效 cold [natural] ageing
常温试验 cold test
常温压制 cold-press, cold-compacting, cold compression, cold-moulding
常温自硬砂造型法 ◇"西山"~"
常务董事 nanaging director
常压 normal [ordinary, atmospheric] pressure, normal atmosphere ◇在~下工作的 non-pressurized
常压沸点 atmospheric boiling point
常压高炉[鼓风炉] low-blast furnace
常压活化氨浸 atmospheric activating ammonia leaching
常压碱浸出 alkaline atmospheric pressure leaching
常压浸出 【色】atmospheric pressure leaching
常压烧结炉 normal pressure sintering furnace
常压酸浸法 acid atmospheric pressure leaching
常压再蒸馏 atmospheric rerun
常压蒸馏 air-distillation
常压蒸汽灭菌 free flowing steam sterilization
常用对数 common logarithm ◇布氏~ Brigg's logarithm
常用方法 routine [classical] method
常用设备 conventional plant
常驻管理程序 【计】resident executive
长半衰期物质 【理】long-half-life material
长半轴[半径] semi-major axis
长柄锤 long-handled hammer
长柄捣锤[砂舂] 【铸】floor rammer
长柄勺 ladle
长程辐射 long-range radiation
长程相互作用 long-range interaction
长程应变 long-range strain
长程有序参数 long-range order parameter
长程有序点阵[晶格] long-range order lattice
长程有序度 【金】degree of long-range order
长程有序合金 long-range ordered alloy
长程有序理论 theory of long-range order
长程有序铜金单晶体 copper-gold single crystal with long-range order
长导槽锻锤 long-channel hammer
长顶头拔制[拉拔, 拔管](管材的) mandrel drawing
长度测量 linear measurement, measure of length, linear measure longimetry
长度测量[测定]器 length measuring [sensing] device
长度尺寸 length [linear] dimension
长度倒数 reciprocal length
长度公差 tolerance on length, length tolerance
长度量度 measure of length
长短幅旋轮线 【数】trochoid

长耳子(板、带材的端部缺陷) long ears
长方平锤 square set hammer
长方条耐火砖 whelp
长方形 rectangle,oblong (shape)
长方形容器 rectangular container
长风口 【铁】tuyere with elongated outlet port
长弧 long arc
长火焰的 long-flamed
长焦距电子枪 telefocus gun
长焦距透镜 long-focal (length) lens
长焦距物镜 long-focus [long-distance] objective
长晶核 germination
长径(长度-直径)比 length-diameter ratio (L-D,L/D),slenderness ratio
长颈烧瓶 Kjeldahl flask
长距离输电 long-distance transmission
长宽比 length-width ratio,aspect ratio
长链 long chain
长链胺萃取剂 long chain amine extractant
长链醇 long chain alcohol
长链化合物 long-chained compound
长链脂族胺 long chain aliphatic amines
长流程钢厂 integrated mill
长期订单 standing order
长期封炉(封炉至炉料完全冷却) 【铁】 dead banking
长期腐蚀数据 long-term corrosion data
长期负债 【企】long term liabilities
长期规划 long-range planning
长期趋势 long term trend
长期时效 extended ageing
长期时效变化 【金】secular change
长期试验 long duration [run] test
长期运转 long run
长期运转额定功率 continuous rating
长期运转状态 continuous service
长期债权 【企】long term claims
长钳 alligator pliers
长切口搭接 linear slotted lap joint

长绒布(抛光用) selvyt cloth
长石 feldspar,felspar
长时间蠕变强度 long-time creep strength
长时(间)蠕变试验 long-term [long-time] creep test
长时间退火 long-term [prolonged] annealing
长时拉伸试验 long-time tensile test
长手套 gauntlet,gloves
长寿 【铁】long campaign life ◇高炉~*
长寿的 timeproof,long-lived
长寿技术 long campaign technology
长双晶方向 twinning direction
长水口(砖)[长注口砖] 【钢】teeming [extended] nozzle
长条钢产品 long steel product,longs
长条型芯 【铸】stock core
长条砖 soap brick
长筒式取样器 pipe sampler
长筒橡皮手套 rubber gauntlet (glove)
长筒形取样器 gun sampler
长图记录 long chart record
长图记录仪 strip chart recorder
长途运输 long-distance transport
长椭圆形(的) oblong
长细比 ratio of slenderness
长纤维复合材料 continuous fibre composite
长纤维金属基复合材料 continuous fibre metal matrix composite
长线法预应力混凝土(先张法) long-line prestressed concrete
长线路电流(腐蚀的) long-line current
长向拉条 longitudinal tie rod
长斜方形 rhomboidity
长芯棒拔制[拉拔,拔管](管材的) mandrel [bar,rod] drawing
长芯棒坯 long mandrel block
长型产品 long product,longs
长型换辊套筒 【压】roll balance rod, porter bar
长形材 long product

长形出铁口 long taphole
长焰煤 candle [jet] coal, long flame (bituminous) coal
长焰气煤 parabituminous coal
长焰烧嘴 long-flame burner
长硬壳 incrust
长余辉(阴极射线)管 intensifier tube
长凿 【机】jumper
长凿钢 jumper steel
长折钉 spike nail
长直链伯胺 long straight-chain primary amine
长轴 long [major] axis
长轴驱动辊道(集体传动辊道) lineshaft driven roller table
长锥体旋风除尘器 long cone cyclone
偿还 repay, pay back
偿还部分 【企】redemption
肠杆菌属 Enterobacter
厂房 plant [factory, mill, workshop, industrial] building, hall ◇ 全套~ building complex, 无窗~ black out plant, 交叉式~布置 cross-ward housing
厂房除尘 room dedusting
厂房设备[设施] building facilities
厂房设计 building design
厂价指数 producer price indices
厂内尘埃处理 in-plant dust treatment
厂内返回[回炉]料 in-plant returns, inplant-revert material
厂内返回料[返矿]仓 in-plant returns bin
厂内粉尘 in-plant dust, home dust
厂内(废钢)利用(率) plant usage
厂内废钢铁 internal scrap
厂内废料 plant waste, revert
厂内含铁废料 in-plant ferruginous waste, works arisings
厂内含铁粉尘 in-plant ferrous fines
厂内经常费用[杂项开支] factory overhead
厂内退火 mill anneal
厂内物料运输 shop material handling
厂内消耗 domestic consumption
厂内噪音 in-plant noise
厂内(专用)铁路线 【运】intraplant trackage
厂内自用煤气 gas for works' use
厂区 plant site
厂区地形图 (同"区域地形图")
厂区环境除尘器 plant dedusting precipitator
厂区绿化率 afforestation
厂外培训 off-site training
厂长 factory director [manager]
厂址 site [location] of factory
敞车 open wagon [car]
敞顶式给料装置 open-top feeder
敞顶式炉 open-top furnace
敞罐熔化 open-pot melting
敞开加热带卷退火炉 direct-fired coil furnace
敞开加热处理炉 direct-fired furnace
敞开模浇铸 casting in open
敞开式厂房 open type factory building, open-type facilities
敞开式电解槽 open cell
敞开式电炉 open electric furnace
敞开式鼓风炉 open-top blast furnace
敞开式模 opening die
敞开式水平模 open horizontal mould
敞开式预焙阳极电解槽 open prebaked type cell
敞开退火 open [black] annealing
敞开型缩孔 primary pipe
敞开铸造 open cast
敞口电弧炉 open-top arc furnace
敞口反应器 open reactor
敞口坩埚熔化 open-pot melting
敞口钢锭模 open-top mold
敞口管 open joint tube
敞口锅 caldron
敞口浇注钢 【钢】open(-poured) steel
敞口[敞开]炉 open furnace
敞口喷雾萃取塔 open-spray column

敞口盛料器	open-top container
敞口式锭模	open mould ◇ 上小下大~*
敞口式铁水罐	open-top ladle, open type ladle
敞口烟罩	open hood
敞流	uncontrolled flow
敞炉	hearth ◇ 焦炭~【色】devil, 退火~ annealing hearth
敞篷车	runabout, open car
敞篷车皮	gondola
敞熔(法)	air melting
敞熔合金	air-melted alloy
敞箱造型	【铸】open sand mould(ing)
敞焰加热	open-fired
畅通风口[嘴]	free tuyere
超α型钛合金	super-alpha titanium alloy
超锕系元素	transactinide element, superactinides, transatinides
超薄壁	【压】ultra-light-wall, extra-light wall ◇ 1Cr18Ni9Ti~旋压管*
超薄壁管	ultra-thin wall pipe
超薄壁精密管	over-thin wall precision pipe
超薄带钢	ultrathin strip
超薄镀锡板	ultra-thin tinplate
超薄切片机	ultra-microtome
超薄热轧带钢	ultra thin hot strip (UTHS)
超倍显微术(显微镜检查法)	ultramicroscopy
超标准的	overproofed
超钚(元素)	transplutonium
超参数元素	superparametric element
超测微计	ulter micrometer, ultramicrometer
超差	out-of-tolerance, off-gauge, overproof
超长多炉连浇[铸]	super long sequential casting
超超临界压力锅炉钢管	boiler pipe for ultra-supercritical pressure
超程	overtravel, overrun (ning), overstroke, excess of stroke
超出分析	【化】off-analysis
超出额定范围	over range, overranging
超出控制范围	【理】excursion
超纯度	superpurity
超纯金属	superpurity [superpure] metal
超纯煤	superclean coal
超纯试剂	extra pure reagent
超纯水	hyperpure water
超纯铁素体不锈钢	ultra pure ferritic stainless steel
超淬火(在临界区急冷,在危险区缓冷)	super-quench(ing)
超大断面焊缝	oversize weld
超大规模集成电路	super large scale integration (SLSI), grand scale integration (GSI), very large scale integrated circuit (VLSI)
超大型高炉	superlarge blast furnace
超导	superconductivity, superconduction ◇ GLAG~理论*, 巴丁-库珀-施里弗~理论*
超导半导体	superconducting semiconductor
超导薄膜	superconducting film
超导材料	superconducting material
超导材料制备工艺	superconducting material preparation
超导磁[多镍钢]合金	supermumetal
超导磁铁	superconducting magnet
超导存储器	superconducting memory
超导带	superconducting tape
超导电合金	electrically superconducting alloy
超导电缆	superconducting cable
超导电性硬合金	hard superconducting alloy
超导发电机	superconducting generator
超导分子	superconducting molecule
超导辐射热测量计	superconducting bolometer
超导化合物	superconducting compound

超导结　superconducting junction
超导金属　【电】superconducting metal
超导隧道结 X 射线检测器　superconducting tunnel junction X-ray detector
超导隧道效应　superconducting tunnelling effect
超导态　super conducting state
超导体　superconductor ◇第二类~*，第一类~*，多芯复合~*，硬~ hard superconductor
超导体合金　superconductor alloy
超导体混态热导率　mixed-state thermal conductility of superconductor
超导体临界磁场强度　critical magnetic field intensity of superconductor
超导体丝(铌锡合金 Nb_3Sn 丝)　superconductive wire
超导物质　【电】superconducting matter
超导相　superconducting phase
超导性　superconducting property, superconductivity, supraconductivity
超导性合金　superconducting [superconductive] alloy
超导性破坏　break-up of superconductivity
超导元素　superconducting element
超导转变　superconductive transformation
超导转变温度　superconducting transition temperature
超等离子体　epiplasma
超低硫钢　ultra-low sulphur steel
超低碳 IF [无间隙原子] 钢　ULC-IF steel
超低碳不锈钢　ELC (extra low carbon) stainless steel, ultra-low-carbon stainless steel ◇ASV~冶炼法*，维特恩~冶炼法*
超低碳钢　ultra-low-carbon steel (ULCS), ULC steel, dead mild steel
超低碳钢丝　charcoal wire
超低碳铬铁　extra-low carbon ferrochromium
超低碳加磷高强 IF 钢　extra-low-carbon P-added high-strength IF steel

超低碳无间隙原子钢　extra-low-carbon IF (interstitial-free) steel
超低碳荫罩钢带(彩色显像管用)　untralow carbon steel strip used for hidden cover
超低温(度)　ultralow temperature
超低氧钢　ULO (ultra-low oxygen) steel
超点阵　superlattice, superstructure ◇位错的~*
超点阵反射　superlattice reflection
超点阵线　superlattice line
超点阵形成　formation of superlattices
超点阵转变(指无序 - 有序转变等)　superlattice transformation
超电压　overvoltage, supervoltage ◇电极~*，电解~*，气体~ gas overvoltage
超短波　ultra short wave
超钝化区　transpassive region
超额定值　off-rating
超额生产　excess production
超反铁磁性　superantiferromagnetism
超分辨　super-resolution
超负荷 [负载]　overload, overburden, excess load, extra duty, superimposed load
超负荷系数　factor of overcapacity
超负荷运行 [运转]　overload operation
超钢(一种高速钢)　supersteel
超高　【运】banking, superelevation (铁路弯线外轨加高)
超高倍显微镜　ultramicroscope
超高产率　ultra-high production rate
超高纯度　ultra-high purity
超高纯金属　ultra-high purity metal, ultra-pure metal, very-high-purity metal
超(高)导磁率合金($<6Cr, <2Si, <4Sn$, $40-85Ni, 16-60Fe$)　super Permalloy ◇含钼~*，帕明伏~*
超高导磁率镍铁合金($14Fe, 5Cu, 4Mo$, 余量 Ni)　supermumetal alloy
超高(电)压　【电】extra high voltage (EHV), supervoltage, supertension, superhigh tension

超高功率 【电】ultra-high power (UHP)
超高功率电弧炉 ultra-high power electric arc furnace, ultra-power electric arcfurnace
超高利用系数 ultra-high production rate
超高炉顶压力 super-high top pressure
超高密度 super high density
超高频(率) ultra-high frequency, super-frequency
超高频波 hyper frequency wave
超高频(绝缘)瓷料 【电】ultraporcelain
超高频铁氧体 super high frequency ferrite
超高强度凹螺纹钢筋 super high strength dented ribbed bar
超高强度薄板 ultra-high strength thin sheet
超高强度薄钢板 ultra-high strength steel sheet
超高强度钢 ultra-high strength [tensile] steel, super-strength steel, extra-high tensile steel, ultrastrong steel ◇ 马特里克斯~* matrix steel, 斯特拉克斯~Strux
超高强度合金 super-strength alloy
超高强度结构材料 ultra-high strength structural material
超高强度可焊铝合金 ultra-high strength weldable aluminium alloy
超高强度硬铝(7—9Zn, 1.2—1.8Mg, 0.5—2.5Cu, 0.2—1Mn, 0.1—0.4Cr, <0.8Si, <0.6Fe,余量 Al) extra super duralumin
超高曲线 banking curve
超高深冲 super extra deep drawing
超高速 ultrahigh speed (UHS)
超高速存取 zero access
超高速钢 super-high speed steel
超高速切削合金 super-high-speed alloy
超高速硬化水泥 super-rapid hardening cement
超高温(度) ultra-high temperature
超高温合金 super-heat-resisting alloy
超高温耐火材料 extreme temperature refractory
超高温耐火砖 superduty firebrick
超高(温)温度计 hyperthermometer, ultra-thermometer
超高温信号 overtemperature signal
超高温冶金 ultra-high temperature metallurgy
超高效率电炉 ultra-high-efficiency (UHE) electric arc furnace
超高压X射线管 【理】ultra-high pressure X-ray cell
超高压挤压 super high pressure extrusion
超高压(力) ultra-high pressure (u.h.p.), superpressure, hyperpressure
超高压缩量拉拔 【压】over-drawing, hollow drawing
超高压下量轧制 【压】hollow drawing
超高真空 ultra-high vacuum, ultrahard vacuum
超高真空泵 ultrahigh vacuum pump (UVP)
超高真空蠕变特性 ultra-high-vacuum creep behaviour
超镉 epicadmium
超公差(的) off-tolerance, out-of-tolerance
超公差线材 flat rod
超固相线烧结 supersolidus sintering
超光电摄像管 super-emitron
超光泽镀镍法(用格利马克斯电解液) super Gleamax
超硅镁层 ultrasima
超(过)滤 hyperfiltration, ultrafiltration
超过时间 overtime
超过位置 setover
超合金粉末 superalloy powder ◇ 热加工[热作]~*
超恒温器 superthermostat
超灰雾密度(X射线照相) density above fog
超级阿斯科洛伊耐热不锈钢(<0.2C, 17—20Cr, 7—10Ni, 余量 Fe) super-

Ascoloy
超级不膨胀钢[超恒范钢](31.5Ni,5Co,余量Fe) super-non-expansion steel
超级不锈的 superstainless
超级淬火油 super-quench oil
超级导磁钢 super-isoperm
超级多孔铁镍铜含油轴承 super-oilite bearing
超级多孔铁铜合金(75Fe,25Cu) super oilite
超级多孔铁铜机械零件 super-oilite machine parts
超级硅砖 superduty silica brick
超级恒导磁率铁镍合金(33.3Ni,8Co,49.9Fe,8Cu,0.2Al,0.5Mn) super isoperm
超级恒温器 ultra-thermostat
超级铝镁合金(板)(94.35Al,5.5Mg,0.15Mn) supermagaluma
超级铝锌镁合金 superalumag
超级耐火材料 superrefractory,superduty refractory
超级耐火砖 superduty brick
超级耐热合金 superalloy,supertherm(耐1170℃;26Cr,35Ni,余量Co与W) ◇沉淀硬化型~ "
超级耐蚀铜镍合金(70Cu,30Ni) super-nickel
超级镍合金 supernickel alloy
超级坡明伐恒导磁率合金(9Ni,22.8Co,68.2Fe) super-permivar
超级石墨 supergraphite
超级硬铝 super-dural(umin)
超级硬铝合金 ESD(extra super duralumin) alloy
超级制绳钢丝(抗拉强度1.78—1.93GPa) extra special improved plough steel wire
超级专用钢 ultraservice steel
超碱性岩 ultrabasic rock
超交换 superexchange
超交换相互作用 【理】superexchange interaction
超洁净钢 superclean steel
超洁净弹簧钢 superclean spring steel
超结构式超点阵 superstructural superlattice
超结构线 superstructure lines
超结构衍射线 extra (diffraction) lines
超晶格 (同"超点阵")
超晶格结构 superstructure
超精矿 superconcentrate
超精细分裂(能级的) hyperfine splitting
超精细结构光谱 hyperfine spectrum
超精细组分 【金】hyperfine structure component
超精细组织 【金】hyperfine structure
超静定 indeterminate,redundancy
超静定的 hyperstatical,redundant
超静定结构 【建】hyperstatic structure,statically indeterminate structure
超净煤 superclean coal
超锔核素 transcurium nuclide
超空元素 ultraspatial element
超离心机 ultracentrifuge
超临界流态化床 hyper-critical fluidized bed
超临界速度 supercritical speed
超临界性 supercriticality
超临界压力锅炉(钢)管 supercritical pressure boiler pipe
超临界状态 above-critical state,supercriticality
超流动性 【理】super-fluidity
超流态 super-fluidity
超流态化床 hyper-fluidized bed
超滤器 ultrafilter
超耐热不锈钢 superduty steel
超耐热材料 super-heat-resisting material
超耐热合金 (同"超高温合金") ◇ 2907 多元~ ", 3124 ~ "
超配筋的(钢筋混凝土) 【建】heavily reinforced
超坡莫高导磁率合金(D: 78.5Ni,5.1Mo,

2.5Cu,余量 Fe；H：73.65Ni,10.2Cu, 3.2Mo,余量 Fe） Ultraperm

超坡莫合金 （同"超高导磁率合金"）
超前电流 leading current
超前角 angle of lead, advance angle
超前开启 advanced opening
超前控制 lead [advance] control
超前位错 【理】emissionary dislocation
超强度(的) super-strength
超强钢 ultrafort steel
超强铝活塞合金(20Si,5Cu,2Mn,0.7Fe,余量 Al) supra piston alloy
超切削加工[性] super-machining
超轻便的 ultra-portable
超轻合金(镁合金) ultra-light alloy
超热的 superthermal, epithermal, above-thermal
超热中子 epithermal neutron
超热中子放射性 epithermal activity
超热中子吸收 epithermal absorption
超韧性钢 super-tough steel
超三极管 【电】ultra-audion
超深冲 extra-deep [superdeep] drawing
超深冲 IF[无间隙原子]钢 superdeep-drawing interstitial free steel
超深冲钢 extra-deep drawing steel
超深冲级[质量](钢板) extra deep drawing quality (EDDQ)
超深冲冷轧带钢 superdeep-drawing strip
超深冲性 extra-deep-drawing property
超深冲性能冷轧薄板 cold rolled sheets of extra deep drawing quality
超声波 ultrasonic (wave), ultrasound, supersonic wave
超声波拔丝 （同"超声波拉丝"）
超声波测厚仪[计] 【压】ultrasonic [supersonic] thickness gauge, reflectogauge, ultrasonic thickness meter, thickness gauge, sonizon, sonigauge ◇ 便携式~audigauge
超声波测量 ultrasonic measurement
超声波测温 ultrasonic temperature measurement
超声波测温计 sonic temperature device
超声波成像系统 ultrasonic imaging system
超声波处理 ultrasonic processing
超声波穿透 ultrasonic penetration
超声波淬火 [金]ultrasonic quenching
超声波点焊 ultrasonic spot welding
超声波电镀 supersonic electro-plating
超声波镀覆 ultrasonic [supersonic] coating
超声波发射机 sender
超声波发射探测仪 ultrasonic emission detector
超声波发生器 supersonic generator
超声波法(探测,探伤) ultrasonic method
超声波反射探伤仪 supersonic reflectoscope
超声波反应 ultrasonic response
超声波钢轨探伤器 ultrasonic rail tester
超声波固结 ultrasonic bonding
超声波光谱技术 ultrasonic spectroscopy technique
超声波焊机 ultrasonic welding machine
超声波焊机用加工工具 sonotrode
超声波焊接 ultrasonic welding, ultrasonic bonding（用于半导体材料）
超声波挤压 ultrasonic extrusion
超声波加工 supersonic machining [working]
超声波检测装置 supersonic wave detecting device
超声波检漏器 ultrasonic leak detector
超声波检验[检测] ultra-sonic (US) inspection [test(ing), examination, detection], ultrasonic test (UT), supersonic inspection [test(ing)] ◇ 浸没式~,离线~,双换能[转换]器~,在线~
超声波检验法[技术] ultrasonic process [technique]
超声波接收机[器] ultrasonic receiver
超声波金属成形 ultrasonic metal forming

超声(波)金属探伤[检查] ultrasonic metal inspection
超声波料位计 ultrasonic level meter
超声波裂纹检测 ultrasonic crack detection
超声波灵敏度 ultrasonic sensitivity [response]
超声波脉冲系 ultrasonic pulse system
超声波弥散 【理】ultrasonic dispersion
超声波能 【理】ultrasonic energy
超声波黏度计 ultrasonic viscometer
超声波疲劳试验 ultrasonic fatigue testing
超声波频 ultrasonic wave frequency
超声波频闪观测器 ultrasonic stroboscope
超声波气(蚀成)穴试验装置 ultrasonic cavitation test device
超声波气体雾化(法) ultrasonic gas atomization
超声波钎焊 ultrasonic brazing, ultrasonic [supersonic] soldering
超声波钎焊烙铁 ultrasonic soldering iron
超声波切割 ultrasonic cutting
超声波清理机 ultrasonic cleaning machine
超声波清理装置 ultrasonic cleaning plant
超声波清洗[净化] ultrasonic cleaning (USC), supersonic cleaning, soniccleaning
超声波屈服应力 ultrasonic yield stress
超声波全息照相术 ultrasonic holography
超声波软钎焊 ultrasonic soldering
超声波热处理 supersonic heattreatment
超声波设备探伤 ultrasonic equipment flaw-detection
超声波深拉延 supersonic deep drawing
超声波渗氮 supersonic nitriding
超声波时效 supersonic aging
超声波试验 ultrasonic test(ing)
超声波收尘 ultrasonic precipitation
超声波衰减 【理】ultrasonic attenuation
超声(波)速(度) ultrasonic velocity
超声(波)探测(法) supersonic sounding
超声波(探测)仪[探伤仪,探测器] ultrasonic (crack, flaw) detector, supersonic (crack, flaw) detector, ultrasonic analyzer [gauge], ultrasonoscope, (supersonic) reflectoscope ◇脉冲式～ soniscope, 索诺雷～ Sonoray
超声波探伤 ultra-sonic (US) inspection [test(ing)], supersonic test(ing), ultrasonic crack [flaw] detection, supersonic flaw detecting
超声波探伤设备 ultrasonic equipment of flaw-detection
超声波透镜 ultrasonic lens
超声波脱气 ultrasonic degassing
超声波脱脂 ultrasonic degreasing
超声波温度测量 ultrasonic temperature measurement
超声波温度计 ultrasonic thermometer
超声波无损测定 ultrasonic nondestructive measurement
超声(波)雾化 ultrasonic atomization[gas-atomizing] ◇熔融金属～*
超声波响应 ultrasonic response
超声波斜探头探伤 angle testing
超声(波)学 ultrasonics, supersonics
超声波液体渗碳 supersonic liquid carburizing
超声波影像 ultrasonography
超声波杂乱脉冲干扰 ultrasonic hash
超声波噪音级别 ultrasonic noise level
超声波振动 ultrasonic vibration
超声波振动拔管[压] ultrasonic vibration pipe-drawing
超声波(振动)拉拔 【压】ultrasonic drawing
超声波(振动)拉丝 【压】ultrasonic [supersonic] wire drawing
超声波振动模式变换器 ultrasonic mode changer
超声波铸造 supersonic casting
超声波钻孔(用于拔丝模等) ultrasonic drilling
超声波钻孔机 ultrasonic driller
超声厚度计[仪] (同"超声波测厚仪")

| 超声化学 sonochemistry
| 超声检测 （同"超声波检测"）
| 超声黏度计 ultraviscoson
| 超声频录声 ultrasonography
| 超声频谱 supersonic spectrum ◇ 差示～学*
| 超声频振荡器 supersonic generator, ultrasonator
| 超声热压焊 ultrasonic-thermocompression welding
| 超声束 【理】ultrasonic beam
| 超声(速)的 ultrasonic, supersonic ◇ 特[高]～hypersonic
| 超声速(波)射流(超音速喷气发动机的) supersonic jet
| 超声搪锡 ultrasonic soldering
| 超声显像探伤法 visible sound method, sound vision ◇ 波尔曼～Pohlman method
| 超声压铸法 ultrasonic process
| 超声遥焊 ultrasonic remote welding
| 超声冶金 ultrasonic metallurgy
| 超声硬度计[超声波硬度试验机] ultrasonic hardness tester
| 超声运输材料 material for the supersonic transport
| 超顺磁性 super paramagnetism
| 超松弛 overrelaxation
| 超速 over speed, overrun(ning), running away
| 超速继电器 over speed relay
| 超速检测器 over speed detector
| 超速开关 over speed switch
| 超速离合器 overdrive [overrunning, overriding] clutch
| 超速离心机 ultracentrifuge
| 超速装置 over speed device
| 超塑性 superplasticity, superplastic behaviour ◇ 恒温～焊接*, 临界点～*, 普雷斯塔尔～铅铝合金 Prestal
| 超塑性变形 superplastic deformation
| 超塑性锻造 superplastic forging

超塑性合金 superplastic alloy
超塑性结构 superplastic structure
超塑性蠕变 superplastic creep
超塑性效应 superplastic effect
超弹性 super-elasticity
超弹性变形 hyperelastic deformation
超弹性状态(有色金属冷加工状态,相应的带材压缩率为 68.7%,丝材的压缩率为 90.2%) extraspring temper
超碳钢 supercarbon steel
超碳量渗碳法(表面渗碳) 【金】hypercarb process
超碳量渗碳硬化(法)(表面渗碳) 【金】hypercarb hardening
超特大(的) extra outsize (xos)
超铁磁性 superferromagnetism
超同步的 supersynchronous, hypersynchronous
超同步电动机 supersynchronous motor
超透磁合金 supermalloy, Ultraperm
超微粉末 submicron powder
超微技术 ultramicrotechnique
超微晶合金 ultrafine crystalline alloy
超微金属粉($0.1 \sim 0.001 \mu m$) submicron metal
超微粒空气分级器 infrasizer
超微粒(烧结)磁铁 ultramicro magnet
超微粒(硬质)合金 ultramicro alloy
超微法 ultramicromethod
超微量分析 ultramicro-analysis
超微量化学 ultramicrochemistry
超微量化学的 ultramicrochemical
超微量天平 ultramicrobalance
超微细结构 superfine structure
超微细晶 ultramicrocrystal
超微(细)粒 ultramicron
超微型(计算)机 supermicrocomputer
超位错 super-dislocation
超位错宽度[间距] spacing of superdislocation
超文本传送协议 hypertext transfer protocol

超细电解粉末 【粉】ultrafine electrolytic powder	◇HD 锻造用~ HD alloy, 本多(锻造用)~*
超细粉(小于 10μm 的) 【粉】super-fines	超硬(质)合金 super-hard alloy ◇沃格米特~*
超细粉尘 ultra-fine dust	超优等 best-best-best (B.B.B.)
超细粉矿[料] ultra fines	超铀元素 transuranic element, transuranium (element)
超细粉末 superfine [ultrafine, colloidal] powder, ultrafines	超越度 overshoot
超细颗粒 ultrafine particle, superfine fraction	超越函数 transcendental function
超细羰基法粉末 colloidal carbonyl powder	超越离合器 (同"超速离合器")
超显微(的) ultramicroscopic	超载 overload, superload, excess load, supercharge loading, surcharge
超限运动 overrun(ning)	超载测量计[器] overload meter
超小型板坯连铸机 superminiature slab continuous caster	超载荷因素 factor of overcapacity
超小型(计算)机 superminicomputer	超载[超重]制动器 load brake
超小型轧机 microminiature mill	超再生 superregeneration
超行程 (同"超程")	超再生(的) ultra-audion
超压(力) hyperpressure, overpressure	超再生振荡器 superregenerator
超易切削钢 super-machining steel	超张力 overhead tension
超因瓦低膨胀系数合金(31Ni,4—6Co,余量 Fe) super Invar	超重 overweight, excess weight
超音频 supersonic frequency	超重货物 weight-exceeding goods
超音频的(马赫数大于 5) hypersonic	超重介质[悬浮液] 【选】overdense medium
超音速的 (同"超声速的")	超重氢 (同"氚")
超音速驱动挤压机 ultrasonically activated extruder	超重型(的) ultra-heavy duty (UHD)
超音振荡气体雾化粉 ultrasonically gas-atomized powder	超重元素 superheavy element
超应变 superstrain	超装 【冶】overcharge
超应力 【压】supertension	超子 【理】hyperon
超硬材料 superhard [ultra-hard] material	超自熔性烧结矿 super-fluxed [super-fluxing] sinter
超硬度[性] superhardness	潮解 deliquescence, slaking
超硬钢 extra hard steel	潮解性 hygroscopy
超硬工具合金 super-hard tool alloy	潮解(性)的[易潮解的] deliquescent
超硬金属 hard metal	潮流 tidal current
超硬铝 superduralumin (4.25Cu, 0.6Mn, 0.75Si, 0.5Mg, 余量 Al), ultralumin (4 Cu, 0.5Mg, 0.5Mn, 余量 Al) ◇24S~*, SD~*, 阿尔邦杜尔双面复合纯铝~板*	潮湿 dampness, humidity, moistness
	潮湿大气腐蚀 humid atmospheric corrosion
	潮湿腐蚀 wet corrosion
	潮湿空气 humid [wet] atmosphere, moist air
	潮湿气体 humid gas
超硬铝合金 extra super duralumin alloy	潮湿氢气 moist hydrogen

车板　【铸】sweep（template）,sweeping board
车板模　【铸】sweep pattern
车板横臂　sweep finger
车板造型　【铸】sweep moulding
车拌混凝土　transit-mix(ed) concrete
车床　lathe,turning machine ◇ 锻件剥皮～ forge lathe,型芯～ core(-turning) lathe,制模型～ model maker's lathe
车床床身　lathe bed
车床卡盘　lathe chuck
车床校直(管材的)　lathe straightening
车挡　buffer stop,bumping post
车刀　turning [lathe] tool,cutter,gad
车底式分批热处理炉　car-bottom batch-type furnace
车底式加热炉　reheating furnace with movable hearth
车底式炉　bogie (hearth) furnace,car bottom furnace,car(-bottom) hearth furnace,travel(l)ing-hearth furnace
车底式隧道窑　car-type tunnel kiln
车底(式)退火炉　car-bottom annealing furnace ◇ 连续式～*
车底式窑　sliding-bat kiln
车斗　car hopper
车端面　【机】radial facing,squaring,face work
车队　fleet
车工　turner
车工车间[工段]　turning shop
车钩　draw [draught] gear ◇ 摘～【运】out-of-gear,自动～automatic coupling
车光　bright turned
车间　(work)shop,plant,mill,hall,department
车间布置　plant layout [arrangement]
车间地面　shop [mill] floor
车间废料　plant waste,shop sweepings
车间辅助设备　mill auxiliaries
车间管理人员　shop managerial staff
车间焊接　shop welding

车间平面布置图[车间设计图]　shop layout
车间起重机[吊车]　workshop crane
车间砌炉设备　shop lining facilities
车间设计　plant design
车间试验　(work)shop test
车间手册[规程,须知]　【企】shop manual
车间通风机　shop ventilator
车间之间运输　interdepartment transport
车间主任　workshop director,plant [shop] superintendent
车辆　car,carriage,vehicle ◇ 小型～dilly
车辆荷载(单辆货车装载)　carload
车辆衡　weight bridge
车辆衡器　car weigher
车辆牵引机　car haul
车辆式起重机　low truck crane
车辆停放场　stock carriages
车辆轴承青铜　journal bronze
车辆总数(铁路车辆总数)　rolling stock
车轮　(car) wheel,running roller
车轮辐板辗轧辊　web roll
车轮矿{$2PbS \cdot Cu_2S \cdot Sb_2S_2$}　bournonite
车轮轮辐压弯机　dishing press
车轮轮箍　wheel [rail] tyre
车轮轮箍轧机　railway-wheel-and-tyre mill
车轮坯　wheel blank [block]
车轮坯成型模锻压力机　wheel forging press
车轮式压力机　wheel press
车轮锁紧螺钉　wheel screw
车轮凸缘和踏面的辗轧辊　tread roll
车轮轧机　wheel-rolling [railway-wheel] mill,disc mill ◇ 立式～*,整轧～*
车轮轧机立辊　wheel-mill edger
车螺纹[车丝]　threading,screwing(管材的) ◇ 未～管 threadless pipe (TP)
车棚　car [carriage] shed
车皮　railway wagon ◇ 敞篷～gondola,通用～*
车上底注(法)　【钢】uphill casting on car

车上交货　free on truck
车身　car body
车身保险螺栓　body shear bolt
车身装甲材料　body armour material
车式堆垛机　car piler
车式冷却运输机(热轧带卷的)　car-type cooling conveyer
车丝工具　threading tools
车丝管　threaded tube
车丝机　threader, threading [screwing] machine, bolt cutter ◇ 螺栓~*
车胎　tire, tyre
车台　platform
车台面　car deck
车头灯　head lamp
车厢　car(riage) ◇ 底卸式~*, 平底~ gondola car, 有机车设备的~ dummy car
车厢车轴　railroad car axle
车厢式干燥机　wagon (box) drier
车厢式炉　box car design furnace
车厢试样(从车辆上取的试样)　car sample
车削　turning ◇ 横向~ squaring
车削屑　turnings
车削性能　turning ability
车(削)轧辊　roll turning
车芯板　【铸】core strickle (template)
车样分析(分析车上取出的试样)　car sample analysis
车用电瓶[电池组]　automotive battery
车用汽油　motor spirit
车载钢水包　bogie ladle
车载公差　carload tolerance
车载批量　carload lots
车站　station, depot
车站站长[铁道车站站长]　station master
车辙　cart rut
车制螺栓　turned bolt
车制螺栓机　bolt cutter
车轴　axle (shaft)
车轴钢　axle (shaft) steel
车轴销　linch pin

车铸(法)　【钢】bogie [car] casting
车装货物　car load
车锥度　tapering
车锥度机床　tapering machine
扯掉[开]　tearing-off
扯断　splitting fracture
扯裂[扯破]　pull tear, tearing, ripping
扯裂扩展　tear propagation
扯裂应变　tearing strain
扯磨(损耗)　tear-and-wear
掣子　trigger, catch, hook
辰砂 {HgS}　vermillion, sulphide of mercury, cinnabar (ore), mercuric blende, zinnober ◇ 锑~*, 易燃~*
尘(埃)　dust ◇ 成~*, 高[浓]~区【环】high dust area
尘埃控制　dust control
尘暴　dust-laden air, dust storm
尘袋　【冶】dust bag
尘害　dust nuisance
尘浆泵槽　dust slurry pump tank
尘浆过滤机　dust slurry filter
尘浆浓密机　dust slurry thickener
尘降　【环】dust fall
尘粒　dust particle
尘量计　dust counter [meter], konimeter
尘泥捕集器　sludge extractor
尘状的　dustlike
沉出盐粒　salting up
沉淀　precipitating, precipitation, sedimentation, deposit, settle (ment), settling (-down), landing, subsidency, 【选】kill ◇ 不连续~(见"不连续析出"), 可~的 precipitable, 阳极~*
沉淀槽　precipitation tank [vessel], settling [sump] tank, sludge chamber, 【色】clarification tank ◇ 空气搅拌~*
沉淀程度　degree of precipitation
沉淀池　sediment(ation) tank [basin], settling tank [well], flow [sump] tank, sludge chamber, 【建】slimer ◇ 脏物~ dirt pocket

沉淀的锌渣(炉墙上)　philosopher's stone
沉淀动力学　kinetics of precipitation
沉淀法　precipitation process [method] ◇ 接触～*，直接～*
沉淀法粉末　precipitated powder
沉淀法三氧化钨　precipitated tungstic oxide
沉淀反应　precipitation reaction
沉淀分离　precipitate separation, separation by precipitation
沉淀富集(法)　concentration by precipitation
沉淀高压釜　precipitation autoclave
沉淀剂　precipitant, precipitating [precipitation] (re)agent, precipitator ◇ 反～*
沉淀搅拌机　precipitating agitator
沉淀结晶　precipitating crystallization
沉淀金属　deposited metal
沉淀晶体(镇静钢锭中的)　【钢】sedimentary crystal
沉淀离子　precipitating ion
沉淀能力　settling capacity
沉淀器　settler, sludge chamber, precipitator,【选】killer
沉淀器溢流泵　settler overflow pump
沉淀器溢流槽　settler overflow tank
沉淀强化合金　precipitation strengthening alloy
沉淀区[范围]　precipitation range
沉淀热　precipitation heat
沉淀热处理　precipitation heat treatment
沉淀熔炼　precipitation smelting
沉淀时间　settling time
沉淀时效硬度　precipitation age hardness
沉淀室　settling chamber
沉淀试验　precipitation test
沉淀速度　rate of precipitation
沉淀铜　【色】precipitated [cement] copper, copper precipitate
沉淀铜沉淀器　cement copper settler
沉淀铜滤饼　cement copper cake
沉淀污泥　【环】sedimentation sludge

沉淀物　precipitate, precipitation, deposit, bottom settlings, mud ◇ 具有～的合金 alloy with precipitations, 无～带*
沉淀物浮选　precipitate flotation
沉淀物形态学　【金】morphology of deposit
沉淀析出　cement-out
沉淀析出物　precipitated material
沉淀相　precipitate(d) phase
沉淀相微粒　precipitate phase particle
沉淀相与母相[基体]间相互作用　precipitate-matrix interaction
沉淀硬化　precipitation hardening [strengthening] ◇ RR～型铝合金*，科莫尔41～型铁磁合金*
沉淀硬化合金　precipitation-hardening alloy
沉淀硬化镍基合金　precipitation-hardening nickel-base alloy
沉淀硬化(型不锈)钢　PH (precipitaiton hardening) steel
沉淀硬化型超级耐热合金　precipitation-hardening superalloy
沉淀圆锥　precipitation cone
沉淀障　precipitation facies
沉淀置换　cementation ◇ 气体～(法) cementation by gases
沉淀柱　(同"置换柱")
沉淀作用　precipitating action
沉浮分析　float and sink analysis
沉积　deposit(ion), precipitation, sedimentation, settlement, settling ◇ 后期～later deposition, 集结～*, 退火～ annealing deposit
沉积残渣[废料]　vat wastes
沉积槽　depositing tank
沉积层　sediment bed
沉积池　settling basin
沉积池滤器　sump strainer
沉积点　saltation point
沉积电极　receiving electrode
沉积电位法(测定电动电位)　sedimentation potential method

沉积法 sedimentation (process)
沉积反应 deposition reaction
沉积方式 deposition pattern
沉积灰尘 precipitated dust
沉积灰泥 sludge
沉积机 putting-down machine, gravity pouring machine
沉积机理 deposition mechanism
沉积金(从溶液中) 【色】cement gold
沉积金属 deposit(ed) metal, plated metal
沉积金属量 quantity of metal deposited
沉积矿床 sedimentary (mineral) deposit
沉积矿泥 deposited slimes
沉积黏土 sedimentary clay
沉积平衡 sedimentation equilibrium
沉积瓶 deposition bulb
沉积侵蚀 deposit attack
沉积容器 deposition vessel
沉积设备 deposition equipment
沉积速度 speed of deposition
沉积速率 deposition rate
沉积碳 deposited carbon
沉积铜 deposited [cement] copper
沉积物 deposit, sediment, settlings, scurf ◇ 铜锍~【色】copper bottom
沉积物腐蚀 deposition corrosion
沉积物生成 deposit formation
沉积箱 sediment box
沉积效率 deposition efficiency, efficiency of deposition
沉积型赤铁矿床 sedimentary hematite deposit
沉积阳极泥 deposited slimes
沉寂现象 【冶】dead effect
沉降 sedimentation, settling (-down), settlement, subsidence, subsidency ◇ 易~的 free settling, 整体~ bulk settling, 助~剂 sedimentation aid
沉降比 settling ratio, settlement factor
沉降槽 precipitation tank, sedimentation tank [cell], settler (storer), settling bath [ark, trough], 【建】slimer ◇ 单层~*, 分离~ separating thickener, 圆柱形~ cylindrical settler, 重力~ gravitation settler, 锥形~ cone settling tank
沉降差 differential settlement
沉降产物 sink product
沉降常数 sedimentation constant
沉降池 sediment trap, settlerstorer, settling [basin, pit, pond]
沉降法 settling process, sedimentometric method (测量粉末粒度组成)
沉降分级 settling classification
沉降分级法 sedimentation sizing method
沉降分级机 settling classifier ◇ 槽式干扰~*
沉降[积]分析 sedimentation analysis
沉降分析结果 sedimentation result
沉降管法(用于测定粉末粒度) pipet method
沉降锅 settling pot
沉降过滤机 filter thickener
沉降机 putting-down machine
沉降技术 sedimentation technique
沉降介质 settling medium
沉降坑 settling pit
沉降粒级 settled fraction
沉降力 settling capacity
沉降漏斗 settling hopper
沉降面积 settling area
沉降器 settler, sediment trap, precipitator, 【建】slimer ◇ 级联~*, 空气升液混合~*
沉降曲线 sedimentation curve
沉降室 settling chamber ◇ 空冷~*
沉降试验 settlement test
沉降速度 sedimentation velocity, settling rate [velocity]
沉降速率 settling rate ◇ 整体~ bulk settling rate
沉降特性 settling characteristic
沉降天平 sedimentation balance
沉降天平法(测定粉末粒度用) sedimentation balance method

沉降条件　settling conditions
沉降桶[锅]（炼锡的）　float
沉降系数　settlement factor
沉降[沉落]性　settling quality
沉降锥　settling cone
沉浸辊　dunking roll, submerged roll（槽中沉浸辊）
沉浸辊装置　dunking roll unit
沉浸钎焊　dip brazing
沉浸式控制器　dip-type controller
沉浸式取样器　immersion sampler
沉浸压辊（带材的）　dunking roll
沉落　sink
沉没　immersion, submergence, sink
沉泥井　catch-basin
沉泥坑　dirt pocket
沉泥器　mud drum
沉排[沉褥]基础　foundation mattress
沉球式黏度计　fallingball viscometer
沉入的　immersed
沉砂池　sedimentation basin
沉铜装置　copper precipitation unit
沉下　settle, submergence, subsidency
沉陷　sink, settling-down,【建】drawdown ◇ 无~的 unyielding
沉箱　(sinking) caisson ◇ 混凝土~*，箱形~ box caisson, 整体~结构*, 钟形~ bell caisson
沉箱工作室　air working chamber
沉箱基础　caisson [coffered] foundation
沉箱式尾矿浓缩机　cassion-type tailing thickener
沉芯　【铸】core sag
沉渣槽[池]　mud settler
沉渣室　slag [cinder] pocket, skim bob, slag chamber
沉重的　bulky
沉桩　pile-sinking
沉桩承载(能)力　capacity of driven pile
陈化　ageing ◇ 溶液~ ageing of solution, 自然~ natural ageing
陈旧(的)　obsolete, out-of-date

衬板　line-plate, liner, packing plate, back(ing) block, bush ◇ 可更新的~ renewable liner, 增强~ reinforcing pad
衬背带材　backing strip
衬背(钢)板　backing sheet
衬背摩擦材料　backed frictional material
衬差不鲜明图像　soft image
衬底　substrate
衬垫　back(ing) strap, back pad, insert(ion), pad(ding), washer,【焊】backup [backing]strip, interleaving
衬垫材料　gasket [jointing] material
衬垫金属　backing metal
衬垫片　spacer block
衬垫调整　shimming
衬度[衬比]　contrast
衬度分辨能力　contrast perception
衬度系数　【理】contrast ratio
衬度增强　contrast enhancement
衬环　bush(ing), bush ring
衬胶钢槽　rubber-lined steel tank
衬胶空转辊　rubber-lined idler roll
衬金属　lining metal
衬里　liner, lining, bush ◇ 临时防护~ flash lining
衬里材料　liner material
衬里坩埚　lined crucible
衬里厚度　liner [lining] thickness
衬里局部侵蚀　selective lining attack
衬里磨损　lining wear
衬里木　lining wood
衬料　lining (mass), packing
衬钼坩埚　molybdenum-lined crucible
衬镍冷凝器　nickel-lined condenser
衬片　gasket, facing
衬铅　lead coating, lead-lining, lining with lead
衬铅槽　lead-lined vat
衬铅的　lead-lined, terned
衬铅高压釜　lead lined autoclave
衬铅流槽　lead-lined launder
衬墙　【建】chemise

衬圈　bush ring, ring gasket, liner
衬套　bush(ing), sleeve, nave, liner（挤压筒的）
衬套金属[合金]　bush metal
衬套用磷青铜（7.5—9Sn, 0.1—0.4P, 余量Cu）　carobronze
衬筒　liner
衬瓦　bush(ing)
衬锡的　tin-lined
衬橡胶　rubber lining [coating]
衬橡胶空转辊　rubber-lined idlerroll
衬纸机（铝箔的）【色】laminating unit
撑钉　【铸】sprills
撑杆　bracing, brace [stay] rod, strut, raker, web
撑管　stay tube, bracing tube, 【钢】hold-down pipe
撑架　corbel
撑螺栓　staybolt, bolt stay
撑木　【建】distance bar
撑墙　buttress wall
撑套杆　looper arm
撑套器　loop lifter, looper
撑条　stay, batten, tension rod, strut
撑条垫圈　stay washer
撑条螺母　stay nut
撑头　【铸】chaplet
撑系框架结构　braced frame construction
撑子　【铸】chaplet
称量[称重]　weigh(ing) ◇ 分批～秤 batch scale, 校核～check weighing
称量车　weigh(ing) car, weigh larry car, weigh beam, scale car, track scale ◇ 单轨～monorail weight car, 双斗～*
称量斗（卸料槽下的）　weighpocket
称量法　weight method
称量辊道　scale roll table, weight-scale table ◇ 输入～*
称量杆[臂]　weigh beam
称量机　weighing machine ◇ 固定式～*, 台式～*, 移动式～*
称量给料槽　scale feed tank

称量计　weightometer ◇ 皮带～belt balance
称量控制台　scale-car pulpit
称量筐　scale pocket
称量料[矿]槽　weigh bin
称量料斗　weigh(ing) hopper, hopper weigher, weigher feeder, measuring bin ◇ 检查～check weight hopper
称量配料器　weigh batcher
称量皮带　weigh(ing) [scale] belt
称量皮带机　weighing conveyor
称量器　weighing device, weighter ◇ 辊道式～*, 自动记录～weightograph
称量(式)给料器　weigher(-type) feeder, weigh-feeder ◇ 矿仓～bin weigh feeder
称量台　weighing bridge, weight-scale table
称量系统　weigh(ing) system
称量装置　weighing device [mechanism]
称重记录员　weigh point man
称重刻度盘准确度　dial accuracy of weighing
城市布局　city lay-out
城市废物　【环】municipal waste
城市给水　municipal water supply
城市工程　urban engineering
城市公用事业　city-owned utilities
城市供热　city heat supply
城市规划　city planning [lay-out]
城市化　urbanization
城市环境卫生措施　【环】city sanitation measures
城市建设　urban construction
城市居民　city dwellers, urban population
城市煤气　city [town] gas
城市排水　municipal drainage
城市燃气　town gas
城市用水　municipal water
橙汞矿　montroydite
橙红铀矿　masuyite
橙黄铀矿 $\{UO_2·(O, OH)_2\}$　vandendriesscheite

橙色合金(美国浓缩铀的代称)	oralloy
橙(色)铅	orange lead
橙色氧化物	orange oxide
橙水铀铅矿{$UO_2 \cdot (O,OH)_2$}	vandendriesscheite
成本	cost, prime [capitalized] cost, self-cost ◇ 最终～assembling cost
成本单	【企】cost sheet
成本估计	【企】cost estimate
成本核算	【企】cost keeping
成本计算	【企】costing
成本会计	【企】cost accounting
成本流转	flow of costs
成比例的	proportional, commensurable
成材率	rolling yield, rate of finished product ◇ 综合～(锭→材)*
成层	lamellation, layering
成层沉积	layered deposit
成层法(检测铸锭)	【钢】layer method
成层缝	coursing joint
成层作用	stratification
成尘	dusting
成尘性	dustiness, dust-forming quality
成叠[垛]薄板	stacked sheets
成叠退火	pack annealing
成堆浸出	leaching in dumps
成堆煅烧	calcination in heaps
成对	pairing, twinning
成对电极	twinned electrode
成对电极焊接	twin-electrode welding
成对电子	paired [coupled] electrons
成对合轧	pair rolling
成对回转炉	twin rotating furnace
成对交叉	pair cross (PC.)
成对交叉轧机	PC (pair cross) mill
成对全位错	(同"带状位错")
成对碳弧焊	twin carbon arc welding
成对位错	paired dislocation
成分	composition, constitution, formulation, ingredient
成分变化	compositional change [variation]
成分波动	compositional variation
成分不合格(生铁)	【铁】off-analysis
成分出格[不合格]炉次	out-of-limit heat
成分范围	composition range
成分分析仪	analytical instrument
成分均匀棒材	homogeneous bar
成分均匀钢	homogeneous steel
成分敏感性	【金】composition sensitivity
成分命中率	【钢】percentage of composition hits
成分三角形	【金】composition triangle
成分特别精确的钢	precision steel
成分梯度	compositional gradient
成分一致性	consistency of composition
成分组成图	【金】constitution diagram
成拱效应	【粉】bridging
成果	achievement, termination
成行缝	coursing joint
成核	nucleation, coring ◇ 变形促进～*, 晶粒间～位置*, 凝固金属～*
成核点	nucleation point
成核动力学	nucleation kinetics
成核方式	pattern of nucleation
成核功	work of nucleation
成核阶段	nucleation period
成核率	【团】seed formation rate
成核临界温度	threshold of nucleation
成核能	energy for nucleation
成核区	nucleation zone
成核时间	time of nucleation
成核速度[速率]	【团】seed formation rate, 【理】nucleation rate
成核(添加)剂	nucleation additive [agent], nucleator
成环	looping, ring formation
成环干扰[故障]	ring formation trouble
成碱元素	base element
成键	bonding
成键轨道	bond(ing) orbital
成角度	angularity
成卷	coiling
成卷薄板[钢板]	【压】sheets in coils

成卷带材　（同"带卷"）
成卷带钢　coiled steel (strip)
成卷电焊条　coiled electrode
成卷[盘]退火　【压】coil annealing, annealing in coils
成卷轧制　【压】coil rolling
成颗粒的　granulous
成孔　pore-creating, pore-forming
成块　caking, lumping, blocking
成块的　cloddy, clumpy, cobbed
成块文件　【计】blocked file
成矿反应　mineralization reaction
成矿作用　mineralization, mineral formation
成捆　fag(g)ot
成粒　granulating, beading
成粒金属　granulated metal, 【粉】shot(ted) metal
成膜能力　film forming capacity
成盘浇注用底板　【钢】group teeming bottom plate, group teeming stool
成盘条钢　coiled bar
成批　batch(es)
成批处理　【计】batch process(ing) ◇脱机～系统*
成批处理中断　batch processing interrupt
成批处理终端　batch terminal
成批淬火　mass-production hardening
成批生产　batch [lot, serial] production, large-lot manufacture, series manufacturing, repetition work
成批数据处理　【计】batch data processing
成批作业　【计】batched job
成品　(finished, end, final) product, finished goods [material, section]
成品板材　finished plate
成品包装跨　packing bay
成品(仓)库　finished products storage (area), product silo, warehouse
成品槽　product bin
成品车间　finishing room
成品尺寸　finished size

成品出口　product exit
成品储存场　product storage yard
成品处理[加工]　product processing
成品处理设备　product handling equipment
成品磁选精矿　final magnetic concentrate
成品打印轮　stamping wheel
成品道次　finishing pass
成品锭　finished ingot
成品断面　finished section
成品堆栈　product pile
成品发运工段　shipping department [yard], dispatch department
成品发运间　shipping building
成品放置架　stock rack
成品分析[化学成分]　product analysis
成品钢　finished steel
成品钢材　final shape
成品工段　finishing work
成品光谱电极　preform
成品机座　（同"精轧机座"）
成品金属　finished metal
成品精整　final finishing
成品卷筒(拉拔机的)　final capstan
成品孔型　（同"精轧孔型"）
成品筐架[收集筐]　loading cradle
成品拉模　finishing die
成品冷却段　product cooling zone
成品粒度　final product size
成品率　production yield
成品模　finishing die
成品模膛　【压】finishing impression
成品前孔断面　【压】leading pass section
成品前孔(型)　【压】leader [leading, former, penultimate] pass
成品前椭圆孔型　【压】leading oval pass
成品球团　finished [final] pellet
成品筛　final screen
成品上限粒度　product top size
成品烧结饼[块]　product sinter cake
成品烧结矿　sintering product
成品烧结矿皮带机　finished sinter con-

成 cheng

veyer
成品输送[运输]机　product conveyer
成品输送皮带机　product belt
成品台架　product rack
成品特性　product property
成品涂油　【压】oiled finish
成品外部涂层　finishing layer
成品线　product line
成品线卷筒　finishing block
成品形状的　net-shaped
成品运输设备　product handling equipment
成品再前孔型　【压】preparatory [preleader] pass, strand pass
成品轧材　finished rolled stock ◇ 库存~ stocking
成品轧材的标准长度　commercial stock length
成品轧辊　polishing roll
成品轧机　finisher
成品质量检查　quality inspection of finished products
成品贮运设施　product storage and shipment facilities
成球　balling (up) ◇ 粉粒~*, 难~矿石*
成球过程　balling process
成球机　【团】nodulizer
成球率　degree of balling
成球盘　pan-pelletizer ◇ 倾斜式~*
成球烧结　pellet sinter
成球速度　【团】rate of ball formation
成球性　sphericity, ballability
成圈　loop laying
成圈器　laying head（线材散卷冷却用），【色】looper
成色　relative purity of gold [silver], fineness quality
成熟　maturing ◇ 奥斯特瓦尔德~(现象)*
成熟混凝土　matured concrete
成束辐射　beamed radiation

成双　pairs, in pairs, double
成酸矿物　acid-forming mineral
成酸氧化物　acid(ic) oxide
成酸元素　acid-forming element
成套　whole [complete] set, nest
成套变电所　unit substation
成套测试设备　integrated test system
成套工具(箱)　tool outfit
成套焊接附件　welding outfit
成套挤压设备　【压】integrated extrusion press plant
成套拉模[模具]　die set
成套模型　pattern assembly
成套设备　integrated [plant] equipment, complete set, aggregate unit
成套轧辊　set of rolls
成套装备　outfit
成团　clustering ◇ 水泥~balling up of cement
成团筛　【选】agglomerate screen
成团现象　cluster formation
成雾　haze formation
成像　image formation, imaging, imagery
成像平面　image plane
成星剂(炼锑的)　starring mixture
成星渣(炼锑的)　starring slag
成型　shaping, forming, moulding,【粉】compacting, compaction ◇ 吹气鼓胀~*,【压】blow forming, 等静压冷[冷等静压]~*, 电水锤[水中放电]~法*, 电铸~ electroform, 画框式加压~法*, 结冰膨胀~法 ice-forming process, 静液压~hydrostatic forming, 流体静压~*, 排辊~【压】cage forming, 气压~*, 热等静气体加压~*, 液压~*, 一步式~ one step forming, 自耗电极~*
成型白云石　moulded dolomite
成型板(制备电极用)　tamping plate
成型薄钢板　profiled sheet iron
成型刨光　shaping
成型变化　mould change
成型标志　【耐】mould mark

成型车间 【耐】moulding shop, assembly room
成型吹板 contour plate
成型大砖 moulded block
成型度 degree of forming
成型法 forming method ◇ 电磁场无模~*
成型管筒 open joint tube
成型焊管机 welding-and-forming mill
成型火焰切割 shape(-flame) cutting
成型机 forming machine [mill], shaper, shaping mill, forming [moulding] apparatus (金属陶瓷制品用), tamping machine (制备电极用) ◇ O形~*, 半干法[低水分(砖)料]~*, 自动~*
成型机构(阴模或阳模) former block
成型机架(冷弯型材及焊接型材) forming stand ◇ 型钢轧机的~strand mill
成型机械 forming mechanism
成型机组 forming block
成型极限(冷弯的) 【压】forming limit
成型焦 moulded coke
成型焦工艺 formed coke process
成型孔型(管材的) forming pass
成型控制器 mouldability controller
成型力 forming force
成型料 【耐】moulding mass
成型率 degree of forming, preforming percentage(表示钢丝绳股预变形程度)
成型密封 mould seam
成型模 forming die, contoured die, bending die(焊管用) ◇ 箱形~box forming die, 自由~*
成型模膛 forming impression
成型刨光 shaping
成型坯件 moulded blank
成型坯体高度 【耐】moulded blank height
成型器 shaper
成型切割(火焰切割) shape(-flame) cutting
成型缺陷 moulding fault
成型润滑剂 mould lubricant

成型栓 mould plug
成型台 workbench
成型效率 forming efficiency, 【耐】moulding efficiency
成型性 mouldability, briquettability
成型压板 【铸】contoured squeeze board
成型压力 forming [moulding, briquetting] pressure ◇ 单位~(见"单位压制压力"), U形~机【压】U-press
成型压实 【铸】contour squeeze
成型压实造型机 contour squeeze moulding machine
成型砖 mould brick
成型装置 forming appliance
成形 form(ing), shaping, profiling ◇ 常规~conventional forming, 低温[冷冻]~cryogenic forming, 高能~energy-rate forming, 高速~*, 高形变速率~*, 可~性 formability, 流体~模【压】fluid die, 燃料燃烧~*, 热[高温]~arde-forming, 凸缘[翻外缘]~【压】flange forming, 线爆[带爆炸丝(液电)]~*
成形淬火机 quenching press
成形电路 (wave) shaping circuit
成形法 【压】forming process ◇ 低速~(薄板的)*, 混合气~gas mixture process, 可燃气体(爆炸)~*, 通用[一般冲压]~*
成形工具 former
成形工艺[技术] forming technique ◇ 一般[习用]~*
成形辊(带material导入多辊卷取机用) 【压】coiler roll, forming roll(er)
成形[型]过程 forming process
成形机 forming machine [mill] ◇ 电力水压~electroshape
成形机夹紧力 shaper clamping force
成形[型]技术 forming technique
成形件 shaped objects
成形介质(爆炸成形的) 【压】forming medium
成形孔型 shaping pass [groove]

成形力　forming force
成形磨削[磨法]　form grinding
成形能　【压】formation energy
成形设备　former, forming equipment ◇ 常规~*
成形性　forming performance [property], formability ◇ 不良~*
成形压力　【粉】compacting pressure
成形压力机　forming press
成形阳模　【压】forming punch
成形轧辊　forming [contoured, former] roll
成形轧制　roll forming
成形铸件　shaped casting
成形铸造　shape casting
成穴断裂　cavitation fracture
成穴蠕变断裂　cavitation creep failure
成穴(作用)　cavitation ◇ 流动~*, 蠕变~ creep cavitation
成盐　salify(ing)
成盐作用　salification
成渣　slag formation
成渣作用　slagging effect
成长方向　growth direction
成组　grouping, nest
成组传动[驱动, 拖动]　group driving
成组传动辊道　group-driven roller table
成组传动液压系统　group-driven hydraulic system
成组打印　【计】group printing
成组进位　【计】group carry
成组控制　group(ed) control
成组模　gang mould
乘常数(视距的)　multiplication constant
乘法器　multiplier
乘法运算　multiply operation
乘(数)商(数)寄存器　【计】multiplier-quotient register
程差　path difference
程序　【计】program(me), routine
程序包　software [program] package
程序编制器　program generator, routine compiler
程序表　program list
程序错(误)　program error ◇ 特定~(同 "程序敏感错")
程序单元　program unit
程序地址计数器　【计】program address counter
程序调用　program [routine] call
程序动态装入　dynamic (program) loading
程序读入　program read-in
程序段　(program) segment, program unit
程序段长度　segment length
程序方框图　flow chart, flow [process] diagram
程序分析　program analysis
程序焊接　program welding
程序寄存器　【计】program register
程序计时器　time programmer
程序计数器　program counter (PC)
程序加速　programed acceleration
程序间通信　interprogram communication
程序兼容性　【计】program compatibility
程序检验　programmed checking
程序减速　programmed deceleration
程序教学　【计】programmed learning [instruction]
程序开关　program switch
程序开关头　program switching head
程序控制　program [sequence] control
程序控制布料　controlled burden distribution
程序控制还原试验　【铁】program-controlled reduction test, Linder test (程序控制的热转鼓还原试验, 又称"林德试验")
程序控制计数器　sequence control counter (SCC)
程序控制板　program board
程序控制器　program controller
程序控制上料　program-controlled charging

程序控制设备　sequence control equipment
程序控制时序计算机　program-controlled sequential computer
程序控制台(轧制制度的)　schedule board
程序控制系统　program controller system
程序控制装置(轧机的)　pre-setting apparatus, program-control device [unit]
程序控制自动轧机　automatic card-programmed rolling mill
程序库　【计】(program, routine) library
程序库程序　library routine
程序库管理[生成]程序　librarian
程序块　【计】(program) block
程序块结构　block structure
程序块首部　block head
程序框图　flow chart, flow [process] diagram
程序连接　program linking
程序敏感错　program-sensitive error
程序模块　【计】programming module ◇ 覆盖装载的～overlay load module
程序设计　【计】program design, programming ◇ 面向文件的～*
程序设计方法学　programming methodology
程序设计语言　programming language
程序(设计)员　programmer
程序升温气相色谱法　programmed temperature gas chromatography (PTGC)
程序说明　programmed description
程序说明书　program specification
程序调节器　time-schedule controller, timer
程序调节系统　process regulating system
程序调试工具　【计】program debugging tool
程序调整的压下装置　preset screwdown
程序停机　【计】program stop
程序序列　program sequence
程序语句　program statement

程序运行　program run
程序执行　program execution
程序指令　programmed instruction
程序中断　program interrupt
程序转换盘　schedule panel
程序装料自动控制系统　【冶】programmed charging automatic-control system
程序组　【冶】batch, program package
澄泥箱　mud box
澄清　clarification, defecation, levigation ◇ 乳浊～de-emulsification
澄清槽　clarifier, clarifying [decantation, settling] tank, decanter, 【色】clarification tank ◇ 锥形～*
澄清池　clarifying [settling] pond
澄清度　clarity
澄清过滤　clarification filtration
澄清过滤器　clarifying filter
澄清机　clarifier, putting-down machine ◇ 灰泥～slurry clarifier
澄清剂　clarifier, fining agent
澄清排水　【环】clarified [clear] effluent
澄清器　clarifier, settler ◇ 圆锥～conical settler
澄清区　clarifying area
澄清溶液　settled solution
澄清设备　clarification equipment
澄清水　clarified water
澄清条件　settling conditions
澄清絮凝　clariflocculation
澄清絮凝器　clariflocculator
澄清液　clarified solution [liquor], clear liquid ◇ 上层～*
澄清溢流　clear overflow
澄清装置　clarifying system
承包　contract
承包人[商]　contractor
承插管　spigot and socket pipe
承插接合(管端的)　socket [spigot] joint
承插套接[承插式接头]　socket-and-spigot joint, bell and spigot joint

承斗(皮带机的) receiving box
承接槽 receiving tank, catchpot
承口 pipe socket, bellmouth ◇ 管子~bell of pipe
承梁 【建】bolster
承料座 load support
承坯架 stilt ◇ 楔形[三臂无点]~ wedge-stilt
承袭误差 【计】inherited error
承压板 【压】riser block
承压变形 bearing strain
承压垫 【压】pressure pad
承压钢管 pressure-resistant pipe
承压块(模具底部的) pressure block
承压墙 carrying wall
承压强度 bearing resistance
承压容器焊缝 pressure-tight seam
承载部件 carrier
承载连接 strength joint
承载梁 carrier bar
承载螺栓 carrier bolt
承载面积 bearing area
承载能力 carrying [bearing, supporting] capacity
承载容量 load-bearing capacity
承载因数 bearing factor
承载值 bearing value
承载致密焊缝 tight-strong seam
承重 load-bearing, support
承重构[框]架 load bearing frame, supporting frame
承重构件 load-carrying member
承重结构 bearing structure
承重能力 load(-bearing) capacity, (weight-)carrying power, bearing power
承重墙 (load) bearing wall, supporting [carrying] wall
承重筒(矿热电炉的) 【冶】supporting [carrying] cylinder
承重桩 【建】bearing pile ◇ 通用~*
承座 abutment, snug
秤 balance, weigh(er), scale ◇ 带~的 scale-equipped, 杠杆~ beam balance, 哈斯勒~ Hasler scale, 皮带~*
秤杆 balance arm, weight beam
秤盘 scale pan
秤式给料装置 (同"称量式给料器")
吃刀深度 【机】depth of cut
持久断[破]裂强度 【金】long-term rupture strength
持久范围 endurance range
持久荷载[载荷] permanent [long-time] load, load of long duration
持久滑移带 persistent slip band
持久极限 endurance limit [range], fatigue limit
持久破断 endurance failure
持久强度 creep rupture strength, endurance strength, enduring quality
持久强度试验机 stress-rupture testing machine, endurance testing machine, permanent strength testing machine ◇ 反复扭转~*
持久强度试验系列 【金】endurance run
持久强度试样 endurance-test piece
持久强度性能 creep-rupture behaviour
持久润滑 permanent lubrication
持久性能 enduring quality
持久性物质 【环】persistent substance
持久张力试验 endurance tension test
持久振荡[动] 【理】persistent oscillation
持平器 level(l)ing vessel
持续变形 persistent deformation
持续吹炼时间 【钢】duration of blow
持续连铸(连炉的) permanent continuous casting
持续流 permanent flow
持续逆火[逆燃] 【冶】sustained backfire
持续时间 (time of) duration, time length, continuance, endurance, extended period, prolongation, last (炼钢)
持续运转工作制 continuous service
持续振荡[动] 【理】sustained oscillation
持续正常运转 continuous normal opera-

持油性　oil retention
持证人（指持许可证）　【环】permittee
匙状插索针　spoon spike
池炉　tank furnace
池形外浇口　【铸】runner basin
池养护（混凝土的）　【建】curing by ponding
池窑砖　tank block
池注水淬法[炉渣粒化]　【冶】pit granulation
池注水淬渣[粒渣]　【冶】pit-granulated slag
迟钝性　insensitiveness
迟缓　delay, slow, tardy
迟缓传递　slow transport
迟缓沸腾　【钢】simmer
迟滞　delay, sluggish
迟滞层　stagnant film
弛垂　sagging
弛垂点　sagging point
弛度　dip,【压】（带钢的）catenary, catenarian
弛度控制（带钢的）　catenary control
弛豫　relaxation
弛豫长度　relaxation length
弛豫过程　relaxation process
弛豫内耗　relaxation internal friction
弛豫谱　relaxation spectrum
弛豫时间　relaxation time
齿　tooth（复数 teeth）, barb, beard ◇画~规 odontograph
齿槽　gullet, spline
齿侧隙　gear backlash
齿杆　toothed bar, ratch
齿根　dedendum
齿根面　root face
齿冠　tooth annulus, crown
齿轨　rack rail
齿辊　fluted roller, spiked roll（单辊破碎机等的）
齿辊式破碎机　toothed roll crusher,【团】pronged roll breaker
齿节　tooth pitch
齿距　pitch（of teeth）, teeth space
齿链　toothed chain
齿轮　gear（wheel）, wheel gear ◇背[后]倒]~ back gear, 灯笼式~ lantern gear, 反转~ counter gear, 横移~ traversing gear
齿轮泵　gear pump ◇余摆线型~ trochoid pump
齿轮比　gear ratio
齿轮变速　gear change [graduation]
齿轮（变速）电动机　gear(ed) motor (GM), geared electric motor, back geared motor
齿轮传动[驱动]　gearing, gear drive ◇液压~ oilgear drive
齿轮（传动，变速）机构　gear unit ◇中间~ intermediate gearing
齿轮传动装置　gear-drive equipment, pinion unit, toothed gearing
齿轮防护罩　gear guard
齿轮钢　gear [pinion] steel
齿轮冠　gear crown, gear(ed) [pinion] ring
齿轮滑车　geared trolley [block]
齿轮换挡拨叉　gear shift fork
齿轮胶合（因温度升高、润滑不良引起的）　【机】gall(ing)
齿轮接合器　adapter gear
齿轮精研机　gear-lapping machine
齿轮[齿型]离合器　gear [tooth(ed)] clutch
齿轮联轴节　gear coupling
齿轮连接　gearing
齿轮龙门刨（床）　gear planer
齿轮啮合　gearing（mesh）, gear engagement
齿轮（啮合）背隙　gear backlash
齿轮刨床　gear shaper
齿轮切削机床　gear-cutting machine
齿轮青铜（88—91Cu, 12.9Sn, 微量 P）

gearing bronze
齿轮倾翻式浇包 ladle with tipping gear appliance
齿轮圈(压装的) 【机】gear(ed) ring
齿轮润滑 gear lubrication
齿轮系(列) gear train
齿轮箱 gear(ing) [wheel] box, gear case [housing]
齿轮牙 gear tooth
齿轮研磨[抛光]机 gear-lapping machine
齿轮移锭器(自耗电炉构件) 【冶】geared retracter
齿轮油泵 geared oil pump
齿轮轴 gear shaft, gear-type spindle ◇ (人字)齿轮座的~ mill pinion
齿轮装置 【机】geared system
齿轮组 cluster gear, gear cluster, gearset, 【机】nest
齿轮座 pinion stand
齿轮座的齿轮轴 mill pinion
齿轮座机体 pinion housing
齿面轧辊 discaling roll
齿片(破碎机的) breaker arm
齿片厚度 breaker arm width
齿墙 cut-off wall
齿圈 gear ring, tooth annulus
齿速比 gear ratio (G.R.)
齿条 rack (bar), rack rod, gear [toothed] rack, toothed bar, notched bar (冷床的) ◇ 借~进行移动 rack
齿条(齿轮)传动 rack and pinion
齿条齿轮机构 rack-and-pinion gear
齿条齿轮起重器 rack-and-pinion jack
齿条传动起重器 rack-operated jack
齿条式顶管机[推床] 【压】toothed-rack push bench, rack pinion drawbench
齿条式拉拔机[拉床] 【压】rack-type drawbench
齿条式冷床 【压】notch-bar cooling bed, notch-bar hot bed, cooling (conveyer) rack (移送机)
齿条式推钢机 rack-type pusher, 【压】ingot pusher with rack (加热炉用)
齿条式移送机 conveyer rack
齿条式装料机(用于废钢铁) 【冶】rack machine
齿条形刀具 rack-shaped cutter
齿隙 【机】back lash, free play
齿型 tooth shape
齿型接轴[齿(轮)型联接轴] gear-type spindle
齿型挠性联轴节 【机】gearflex coupling
齿形半角 half-angle of thread
齿形零件 profiled parts
齿状物 teeth
尺寸 demension (dim.), size, measurement, bulk ◇ 按~加工 finish to size, 按~修剪 trimming to size, 不够~ fall short, 高斯~【理】Gaussian size, 实足[实物, 总]~ full size, 严格按照~ trueness to gauge
尺寸比 size ratio
尺寸变化 dimensional change, change in dimension [size], size variation ◇ 温度变化引起的~ thermal growth
尺寸变量 dimensional variable
尺寸不合格 off-dimension, off-size, out-of-size
尺寸不足 undersize,【压】undergauge
尺寸不足棒材 scanty bar
尺寸测量仪器 gauging instrument
尺寸测量装置 gauging machine
尺寸超差[不符] off-measurement
尺寸大小范围指数 size range index
尺寸大小分布指数 size distribution index
尺寸分析试验 sizing(-assay) test
尺寸复原法 resizing
尺寸公差 dimensional [size] tolerance, tolerance on size
尺寸合格 on-gauge
尺寸互换性 dimensional interchangeability
尺寸减缩指数 index of size reduction
尺寸精确度 dimensional accuracy, accura-

尺寸控制　dimensional [size] control
尺寸偏差　dimensional variation
尺寸缩减比　ratio of size reduciton
尺寸稳定性(指外形尺寸)　dimensional stability
尺寸稳定性试验　dimensional stability test
尺寸线　dimension line
尺寸效应[影响]　dimensional [size] effect
尺寸自动控制[检验]　automatic size control
尺寸走样(线材的)　non-sizing
尺度　scale, dimension, ga(u)ge, yardstick
赤道　equator ◇ 软片～线*
赤道层线　equatorial layer line
赤道平面(球体投影的)　equatorial plane
赤道圆　equatorial circle
赤金(纯金)　pure [solid] gold ◇ 法国～ French red gold
赤面投影图中心　centre of stereogram
赤泥　red mud
赤泥分离　red-mud separation
赤泥洗涤　red-mud washing
赤泥贮存池　impoundment lake
赤热带　hot zone
赤热带比　hot zone ratio
赤热带面积比　hot zone area ratio (HZR)
赤热(的)　(同"红热(的)")
赤闪锌矿　ruby blende
赤铁矿{Fe_2O_3}　h(a)ematite (ore), bloodstone, red iron ore, red oxide of iron ◇ 粗晶[粒]～*, 高硅～codorous ore, 含水～ hydrated hematite, 假象～martite, 坎沙含水～(巴西) Cansa, 菱形刚玉型～*, 土状～*, 叶[片]状～flag ore
赤铁矿床　hematite deposit ◇ 沉积型 ～*
赤铁矿法　hematite process
赤铁矿粉　hematite fines
赤铁矿键　hematite bond
赤铁矿球团　hematite pellet
赤铁矿生铁(用赤铁矿炼出的低磷生铁) hematite (pig) iron
赤铜　red copper
"赤铜"合金(日本的一种装饰合金;4Au, 2Ag, 余量 Cu)　shakudo
赤铜矿{Cu_2O}　cuprite, red oxide of copper
赤铜铁矿　delafossite
赤血盐　(同"铁氰化钾")
赤榆树脂　ulmin(e)
翅管式金属换热器　fin tube type metallic recuperator
翅裂(钢锭表面的)　fin crack
翅片管　finned tube ◇ 椭圆矩形～*
翅形管　gilled pipe
翅形型芯(使铸件中形成孔眼用)【铸】 wing core
斥力　repulsion, repulsive [expulsive, repelling] force
斥水性混凝土　water-repellent concrete
斥水性液体　water-repellent liquid
斥压力　repulsive pressure
炽白色　dazzling white
炽热　glowing, candescence, red-hot
炽热带　incandescent zone
炽热(发光)体　glower
充氨醋酸盐电解液　ammoniacal acetate electrolyte
充氨电解液　ammoniacal electrolyte
充氨硫酸盐电解液　ammoniacal sulphate electrolyte
充氨氯化物电解液　ammoniacal chloride electrolyte
充斥　overflow
充氮灯　nitrogen-filled lamp
充电　charging, electrification, electrify ◇ 大电流～boosting, 连续补充[涓流]～ trickle charge, 升压[加速]～ boost charge
充电不足　undercharge (u.c., u/c)
充电电流密度　charge current desity
充电电压　charging voltage
充电－放电机　charge-discharge machine

充电过度 overcharge (OC)
充电回路 charging circuit
充电机组 charging set
充电开关 charge (over) switch
充电率 charging rate
充电器 charger
充电容量 charge capacity
充电时间 charging time
充电时间常数 charge time constant
充电特性(曲线) charge characteristic
充电站 charging station
充放电曲线图 charge and discharge characteristics
充分焙烧 thorough roasting
充分干燥 intensive drying
充分混合 perfect [intensive, thorough] mixing
充分脱硫 (同"完全脱硫")
充分氧化 complete oxidation
充氦盒[箱] helium atmosphere box
充料装置 filling device
充满 filling (up), impregnation ◇ 未~(孔型)道次 *
充满气体 gassiness
充气 aeration, aerify, gassing, inflation, gas-filling
充气比重(松散状态型砂的) aerated density
充气不均电池 differential aeration cell
充气槽 aerator tank
充气触发器 trigatron
充气的 gas-filled
充气灯 gas filled lamp
充气电池 aeration [oxygen] cell
充气二极管 gas diode
充气阀 (air) charging valve
充气浮选 【选】air flotation
充气腐蚀 aeration corrosion
充气管 gas tube
充气管整流器 gaseous rectifier, gas-filled (tube) rectifier
充气光电管 gas-filled phototube, gas cell

充气滚圈 air-filled tyre
充气混凝土 (同"加气混凝土")
充气活门 charging valve
充气机 inflator, aerator
充气器 aerator
充气溶液 aerated solution
充气三极管 trigatron, gastriode
充气设备 gas-filling device
充气试验 gassing test
充气塔 aeration tower
充气温度计 gas-filled [vapour-filled] thermometer
充气系数 aeration [gas-filled] coefficient
充气箱 plenum box
充气盐浴炉氮化[渗氮] 【金】aerated salt bath nitriding
充气焰(煤气与空气混合火焰) aerated flames
充气站 【焊】recharging plant
充气整流管 gas-filled tube ◇ 冷阴极~ anotron
充气装置 aeration device, air charging system ◇ 圆筒(式)~ *
充填 fill(ing), stowing, load
充填钢丝(钢绳的) filler wire
充填化合物 filling compound
充填剂 filling mass, loading material ◇ 多孔质~ *
充填孔 filling hole
充填框 【铸】filling frame
充填率 filling [stowing] radio, degree of fill, packing factor
充填深度(塞焊缝的) depth of filling
充填式钢丝绳 filler type wire rope
充填式温度计 filled-system thermometer
充填物质 filling mass
充填因数 packing factor
充填用碎砖块 filling brick
充型 cavity fill
充压阀 【铁】equalizer valve
充盐润滑(挤压润滑法) 【压】filled salt lubrication

充氧 oxygenization, oxygenisation, oxygenizing, oxygenating, oxygenation
充氧水 oxygenated water
充氧压力铸造 oxygenated pressure casting
充液(体)温度计 liquid-filled thermometer
充溢 flush
充油电缆 oil-filled cable
充油套管 【电】oil-filled bushing
充注线 filling mark
冲 punching
冲杯试验 ◇艾弗里~ Avery cupping test
冲裁 blanking, punching out (毛坯的)◇造币板~*
冲裁冲头 【压】slugger punch
冲裁工具 blanking tool
冲裁机 clicker press machine, clicker, gouging machine
冲裁间隙 blode clearance, blanking clearance, die clearance
冲裁力 blanking pressure
冲裁模 blanking [cutting] die
冲裁坯(件) sheared blank
冲程 stroke, travel
冲程表 stroke indicator
冲程控制 stroke control
冲出 outbreak
冲出式落砂装置 kicker-type knock-out
冲床 puncher, punch (press), punching machine, press, piercer, stamping press ◇鹅颈式[S形]支柱~*,分段冲裁~*, 高速~*, 辊式送料~*, 落料~blanking machine, 曲柄~crank press, 双冲头[双动]~*, 卧式~*, 中间工序~subpress
冲锤 block stamp
冲淡 dilute, dilution, attenuation, liquefy,【化】fluxing, fluxion
冲淡剂 (同"稀释剂")
冲淡液 rarefaction
冲点 centre-punch,【机】centre-dot

冲垫 die head
冲动 impulse
冲动式预热烧嘴 preheated impulse burner
冲锻 impact forging
冲杆 punch, plunger
冲杆材料 punch material
冲杆冲程 stroke of punch, punch advance
冲杆连接器 punch adapter
冲杆前进速度 speed of punch advance
冲杆压力 punch [plunger] pressure
冲杆支承板 punch-support plate
冲击 shock, impact, surge, attack, dash, bang, batter, bombardment ◇耐~性试验*
冲击摆(冲击试验机的) impact pendulum
冲击板 impact plate
冲击板式流量计 impact-plate flowmeter
冲击边 striking edge
冲击变形 shock deformation
冲击波 shock [impact] wave ◇发散~*,会聚[收敛]~*
冲击波波前[前沿] shock(-wave) front
冲击波(冲压)成形 【压】shock-wave forming
冲击波反射(爆炸成形的) shock-moving back
冲击成形 impact forming [forging]
冲击处理 impact treatment
冲击脆性 impact brittleness
冲击刀口 impact nife edge
冲击点 impact [surge] point
冲击点焊法 impact spot welding
冲击垫 impact pad
冲击电焊 electropercussive welding
冲击电焊机 percussion welder
冲击电流 dash current
冲击电流计 ballistic galvanometer, quantometer
冲击锻(造) impact forging
冲击断口[断裂] impact fracture [rupture]

冲击法测量 【理】ballistic measurement
冲击腐蚀(在紊流液体作用下) impingement corrosion
冲击腐蚀试验 impingement corrosion test
冲击负荷[荷载] impact load
冲击负荷[加载]装置(高速冲压的) shock loading device
冲击功 absorbed-in-fracture energy ◇ 吸收～*
冲击焊(接)(储能冲击焊接) percussion welding (PEW)
冲击机 impactor, impact [shock] machine, drop breaker, ram engine,【机】vertical drop machine,【金】falling tup machine ◇ 锤头～*
冲击唧筒 striker cylinder
冲击激发 shock excitation
冲击挤压 impact extrusion ◇ 胡克～法*
冲击角 impact angle, angle of shock
冲击静电计 ballistic electrometer
冲击拉力试验 impact tension [pulling] test
冲击拉力(试验)机 impact tension machine
冲击拉伸应力 impact tensile stress
冲击浪 blast
冲击力 impact force
冲击磨损 impact wear
冲击耐久性试验 endurance impact test
冲击能量 impact [striking] energy, energy of blow
冲击能吸收 impact energy absorption
冲击扭力试验 impact torsion test
冲击疲劳强度 impact fatigue strength
冲击疲劳试验 endurance impact test
冲击破裂试验 shock-crushing test
冲击器 impacter, impactor
冲击强度 impact strength, strength of blow, knocking resistance ◇ (生)压坯～*
冲击圈(氧气流对转炉中金属的) impact circle
冲击韧性 impact toughness [ductility], absorbed-in-fracture energy, energy tofracture,【压】resilience, resiliency ◇ 夏氏～试件 Charpy test piece
冲击韧性试验 impact toughness test ◇ 单梁式～Charpy test
冲击韧性与回火温度关系变化曲线 drawing temperature-impact toughness plot
冲击式除尘器 impingement dust collector
冲击式过滤机 impact filter
冲击式磨机 impact (grinding) mill
冲击式破碎机 impact crusher,【选】beater, beating crusher
冲击式压力机 impact press
冲击式压砖机 【耐】stamping press
冲击式震动筛 impact [percussive] screen
冲击式钻机 percussive drill, knock-boring machine ◇ 钢丝绳～churn
冲击试验 impact [percussion] test ◇ 埃索缺口～*, 艾氏～Izodimpact test, 摆式～*, 爆炸～*, 德国标准(U形缺口)～DVMtest, 弗雷蒙～*, 吉勒利～*, 两次～法*, 落锤～【金】drop test, 梅氏～*, 施纳特～Schnadt test, 夏氏～*
冲击试验机 impact [shock] testing machine, impact tester,【机】drop breaker, vertical drop machine,【金】falling tup machine
冲击试样[件] impact test piece
冲击试样梅氏缺口 Mesnager notch
冲击撕裂试验 impact tearing test
冲击速度 impact [striking] velocity, ram speed
冲击速降(轧机咬钢时电动机的) impact speed drop
冲击弹性 impact elasticity
冲击调制器 impact modulator
冲击弯曲试验 impact [shock, blow] bend(ing) test
冲击弯曲试样 shock-bending test piece

冲击弯曲性能 impact bending properties
冲击位置 impact position
冲击消泡器 impact froth breaker
冲击效应 impact effect
冲击性能 impact property
冲击性质 shock feature
冲击性试验 toughness test
冲击穴 impact cavity
冲击压力 shock pressure
冲击压碎法(金属镦粗至出现裂纹的试验) shock-crushing method
冲击压缩试验 impact compression test
冲击液压成形 impact hydraulic forming
冲击应力 impact [shock] stress
冲击硬度 impact [pendulum] hardness
冲击硬度试验 impact hardness test
冲击硬度试验机 impact hardness tester ◇ 鲍曼－斯坦吕克～*,本多－佐藤式～*
冲击载荷 impact [shock] load ◇ 大～ heavy shock loads
冲击值 impact value [number]
冲击阻力 impact resistance
冲击钻 churn [percussive] drill
冲积层 alluvial deposit, alluvion, alluvium, atteration ◇ 河流～
冲积矿床 alluvial ore deposit
冲积黏土 alluvial clay, adobe soil
冲积砂层 blanket sand
冲积土 alluvial soil, alluvium
冲积物 drift deposit
冲挤 【压】cold extrusion
冲坑 centre-punch,【机】centre-dot
冲孔 (hole) punching, piercing, stroke
冲孔板 punch plate
冲孔板筛 punch plate type screen
冲孔标记 centre-punch mark
冲孔冲头 piercing punch,【压】slugger punch
冲孔管 perforated pipe
冲孔机 perforating press, drift chisel, piercing mill

冲孔模 punching [perforating] die,【压】piercing die
冲孔器 hollow punch, nail set, piercer ◇ 锻工用～ smith's drift
冲孔试验 punch(ing) test
冲孔芯棒 【压】piercing mandrel
冲孔阳模 piercing punch
冲孔应力 punching stress
冲孔柱塞 【压】piercer plunger
冲力 impulse [force]
冲力矩 impulsive moment
冲量 impulse, momentum
冲量矩 impulsive moment, moment of impulse [momentum]
冲料压力机 【压】blanking press
冲模 (plunger) die ◇ 闭式～ close(d) die,随动～ follow die,缩口～ reducing die,修边～ ripper die,组合～ sectional die
冲模材料 die material
冲模插床 die slotting machine
冲模堆焊 die set welding
冲模钢 blanking [hubbing] steel
冲模工作面 die face
冲模开度[间隙] die opening
冲模切槽用铣刀 die sinking cutter
冲模－压模用磨床 die-and-mould grinding machine
冲模制作 die making
冲模肘节锁定装置 toggle-locking die fixture
冲破 burst(ing), outburst
冲气流化床 slugging fluidized bed
冲切机 notching press
冲砂 sand blowing,【铸】sand cut [wash](铸造缺陷), embedded grit
冲蚀 ablation, erosion-corrosion
冲蚀腐蚀 erosion-corrosion
冲蚀结巴 erosion scab
冲刷 washout, washing, erosion(河岸等的)
冲刷防治 erosion control
冲刷痕 erosion scar, scour mark

冲天炉　（同"化铁炉"）
冲头　punch [piercing] head, punching pin, formed punch, piercer, force(r), platen, puncheon, ram, wad,【压】drift punch ◇ 打出～*,大孔～【压】quill punch,锯齿形切断～ saw-tooth punch,软［液体］～*,细～ bit punch,自动定心～*
冲头行程　travel of ram
冲头用钢　punching steel
冲头状型芯　【铸】punch-like core
冲头座　punch [stem] holder
冲突　impingement, conflict
冲窝　【机】centre-dot
冲洗　rinse, rinsing, flush(ing), washout, washdown, sluicing ◇ 经～的胶片 processed film
冲洗泵　wash-down [wash-out] pump
冲洗槽　rinse bath, flushing box, flushed channel
冲洗沉淀器　irrigated precipitator
冲洗沟　flume ◇ 衬钢板的～ steel-lined flushing flume
冲洗管　flushing tube, irrigation pipe
冲洗机　washer
冲洗筛　【选】rinsing [spraying] screen
冲洗水　rinse [wash, flush] water
冲洗水泵　flushing water pump
冲洗氧化皮（在沟中）　scale sluicing
冲洗液　flushing liquor
冲洗油　flushing oil
冲型剪（切机）　nibbling machine, nibbling shears
冲压　punch(ing), stamp(ing), pressing ◇ 爆炸～ explosion punching,风动机械～法*,复式～工具*,冷～ cold stamping,平整［矫平］～*,气垫［气动］～*,橡皮阴模反～法 marforming
冲压板材　stamp plate
冲压杯状毛坯　cupping
冲压比　tam ratio
冲压裁剪机　die clicker[cutter, die-cutting machine]
冲压车间　【压】stamping [press] room
冲压成形　drawing, stamping ◇ 冲击波～ shock-wave forming,多工序～*,高速～ rate forming,可控冲击能～*,顺次～ progressive forming
冲压废料　stampings
冲压工　puncher, press operator
冲压工长　【压】master-hub
冲压机　punching machine, stamper, stamping [ram] press, bulldozer ◇ 杠杆式～*,高速～*,后开可倾动式～*,冷弯～ press brake,偏心～ eccentric punch,卧式～*,压缩空气～ compressed air ram,蒸汽～ steam stamp
冲压模　blanking cstamping die ◇ 辊式～ roller stamping die,冷～ cold stamping die,球～膛 ball edger
冲压偏斜　mis-strike
冲压切边　stamping trim
冲压用锌合金　zinc alloy for stamping (ZAS)
冲压用优质冷轧薄板　cold-rolled drawing quality sheet
冲眼　hole punching, centre-punch
冲眼模　perforated die
冲盂　【压】cupping
冲盂（成型）操作　cupping operation
冲盂模　cupping die
冲渣沟　sluiceway
冲制　pressing, punching
冲制工具钢　punching tool steel
冲状型芯　【铸】punch-like core
冲子　puncheon, drift pin [chisel], drift hammer, driver, nail set, pointed (steel) hammer ◇ 划线［打标记］～ prick punch,手动～【压】bear punch,锥形～【压】conical punch
冲钻　churn drill ◇ 电动～*
冲钻法　wash boring
舂入侧型芯　【铸】kiss core
舂入芯　superimposed core
舂入型芯　【铸】rampup core

春砂　【铸】ramming ◇ 风动~器*
虫胶　lac(ca), shellac
虫胶酯　shellac ester
虫漆[脂]　lac(ca)
重车(轧辊)　【压】reconditioning, redressing
重叠　lapping, overlap, duplicate, superpose, superposition, fold (缺陷)
重叠(布里渊)区　overlapping zones
重叠长度(点焊或滚焊的)　contacting overlap
重叠传动　superimposed drive
重叠多膛焙烧炉　super-imposed multi-hearth type roaster
重叠罐式多支管浓相输送煤工艺　【铁】series hoppers multibranch coal injection process with dense-phase transport
重叠力　【压】overlap force
重叠量[部分]　overlap ◇ 剪刃~overlap of knives
重叠偏心轮[器]　superimposing eccentric
重叠通道　【计】overlapped channels
重堵缝　reca(u)lking
重复　repeating, (re)duplicate, duplication, double, iterate, iteration
重复操作　repetitive operation
重复测定　duplicate determination
重复淬火　repeated quenching
重复镀铬　after-chroming
重复观察　duplicate observation
重复加载[加应力]　repeated application of stress
重复校验[检查,检验]　duplication check
重复利用　reuse
重复取样　repeated sampling, replicate sample [sampling], resample
重复时效　【金】reageing
重复试验　repeated [duplicate] test
重复调相记录　【计】redundant phase recording
重复调整　readjustment
重复性误差　repeatability error

重复循环　【冶】recycling, recirculation
重复压痕　repeated indentation
重复应力破裂　repeated stress failure
重复运行时间　【计】rerun time
重复载荷　repeated load
重刮　rescrape
重硅酸钙　(同"硅酸二钙")
重焊　rewelding
重合　coincidence, duplication, registration ◇ 刀片~blade overlap
重合电路(脉冲)　coincidence circuit
重合法　【理】coincidence method
重合检测[检验]器　coincident detector
重合脉冲　coincidence impulses
重合闸　reclosing
重混合　reblending
重剪机(钢板用)　reshears
重建　rebuild, reconstruction, reestablish, renew, restitution
重浇巴比合金　rebabbit
重浇铸　recast(ing)
重结晶带　refined zone
重结晶作用　【金】recrystallization
重卷　recoiling, rewind
重卷机　【压】recoiler, recoiling machine [reel], rewinder, re-reeler, rewind reel
重卷机组作业线　recoiling [rewinding] line
重冷设备　recooling plant
重敛缝　reca(u)lking
重炼金属料　【钢】remelting [second-melt] stock
重炼生铁　remelted iron, double refined iron
重料　duplicated charge
重磨(轧辊)　【压】redressing, reconditioning
重排列　rearrangement
重皮　【钢】(钢锭或钢铸件表面缺陷) curtaining, plaster, ingot shell, (single) lap, cold-laps, 【压】pipe (带钢表面缺陷), (double) skin (轧制缺陷) ◇ 波状

~*,反复~*
重砌 【建】rebricking
重燃弧 restrike
重绕 recoil, rewind
重绕机(导线的) rewinding machine
重绕时间 rewind time
重熔 refusion, resmelting, remelt(ing), reflow, melting down ◇ 电渣~electroslag refining, 电子束~*, 二次~double melting
重熔法 【冶】remelt(ing) process ◇ 自耗电极二次~*
重熔费用 cost of remelting
重熔金属 second-melt stock, remelting stock
重熔精炼 refining remelting
重熔炉 remelt furnace
重入程序 【计】reentrant program [routine]
重入码 【计】reentrant code
重上引锭杆 【连铸】restrand
重烧 resintering, 【耐】reburning
重烧白云石 double-burned dolomite, magdolite
重烧材料 fully fired material
重烧收缩 reheat shrinkage
重算 【计】back-roll, recompute
重碳酸盐 (同"碳酸氢盐")
重调 reset, readjustment ◇ 手动~hand reset
重调时间 reset time
重调装置 resetting device
重现精度 fidelity
重现性 reproducibility ◇ 具有~的 reproducible
重像 double [ghost] image, ghost
重写 rewrite, overwrite ◇ 双缝~头*
重新奥氏体化 【金】reaustenitizing
重新包装 repack
重新闭合 reclose
重新处理 reprocessing
重新吹炼 【冶】reblow

重新磁化 remagnetizing
重新打结 【钢】reramming
重新点火[开炉] relighting
重新电镀 replating
重新定义 redefine
重新回火 retempering
重新计划 replanning
重新加载 reload
重新开炉 relighting
重新排序 【计】restart sorting
重新启动点 restart point
重新砌衬 【冶】relin(ing)
重新砌好的转炉 newly relined vessel
重新清砂 【铸】recleaning
重新取向 reorientation
重新取样 resample
重新熔炼 resmelting
重新设计 redesign
重新调节 readjustment
重新涂覆 recoating
重新退火 reanneal
重新喂料 【压】rethreading
重新修筑 rebricking
重新运行 rerun, roll back, back-roll
重新装配 reassembling
重新组合 recombination, rearrangement
重修表面 resurfacing
重选作业线 reclassifier line
重压 【粉】repressing
重压操作 【粉】repress operation
重验 retest
重蒸馏精炼 refining by redistillation
重整 reform(ing) ◇ 煤气~(法) gas reforming
重整天然气 reformed natural gas
重正火 renormalization
重制 reforming, renovation, remaking
重铸 double teeming
抽磅 random weighing
抽查 random inspection, spot-check, selective examination ◇ 按百分数~percentage inspection, 一次~检验[取样] sin-

gle sampling
抽尘　dust extraction
抽尘风扇　dust-fan
抽尘器　dust exhauster
抽尘系统　dust extraction system
抽尘罩　dust (suppression) hood
抽出　extract (ion), abstraction, draw (ing), pumping-out scavenging, tap-off, withdrawal, withdrawing, stripping (芯棒的抽出)
抽出机　extractor, stripper (芯棒抽出机) ◇ 链式～【压】chain stripper
抽出空气　deflation
抽出式断路器　draw-out (circuit) breaker
抽出通风　extract ventilation
抽出轧辊　roll withdrawal
抽出装置　drawing-out [withdrawing] device
抽除　abstraction, removal by suction
抽锭法（电渣炉）【钢】pulling-down method
抽风　air draught, suction air ◇ 逆～back draught(ing), 下向～*
抽风焙烧　downdraught firing
抽风带式焙烧机　downdraught grate, downdraught travelling grate system
抽风点火　downdraught ignition
抽风段　downdraught zone
抽风风流　downdraught air flow,【团】descending air
抽风风箱　suction windbox
抽风干燥　down-draft drying (DDD), downdraught drying
抽风干燥段（带式球团焙烧机的）【团】downdraught dry(ing) section [zone], downdraught drying stage
抽风干燥段风箱　downdraught drying windbox
抽风干燥段炉罩　downdraught drying hood
抽风干燥段排烟除尘器　downdraught drying exhaust dust collector

抽风柜　draught cupboard
抽风过度　overdraft
抽风环式冷却机[环冷机]　downdraught circular cooler, induced draught circular cooler
抽风环式烧结矿冷却机　induced draught circular sinter cooler
抽风回转换热　downdraught recuperation
抽风机[扇]　drawing [downdraught, exhaust(ing), suction, vacuum] fan, (air) exhauster, (air) exhaustor, air extractor, aspirator, exhaust blower, fan facilities, induced draught fan ◇ 喷射式～ejector fan
抽风冷却　downdraught cooling, induced draught cooling ◇ 机上～*
抽风面积（烧结机的）　suction area ◇ 有效～*
抽风强度　intensity of draught
抽风烧结法　downdraught sintering (process)
抽风烧结机　downdraught sintering machine
抽风设备　draught equipment, draughting (炉子的)
抽风式冷却机　downdraught cooler
抽风式冷却塔　induced draught cooling tower
抽风式链算机　【铁】downdraught grate
抽风式链算机循环　downdraught grate cycle
抽风式煤气发生炉　suction gas producer
抽风室　suction chamber
抽风系统　air suction system, downdraught system
抽风箱　suction box, exhaust chamber, wind chamber
抽风循环　draught recycling
抽风烟道　suction flue
抽风预热段　【团】downdraught preheat stage
抽风罩　draught hood
抽风装置　induced draught plant

抽晶 【半】pulled crystal
抽空 evacuation, exhaust(ion), depression
抽空泵 return pump ◇ 机械初步～
抽空度 degree of exhaustion
抽空脱气 degasification by evacuation
抽空压气两用泵 vacuum and pressure air pump
抽力 draft, draught, suction
抽力调节 draught control
抽力调节挡板 draught-regulating damper
抽力调节器 draught regulator
抽泥泵 slush pump, sludger, mud pump
抽气 exhaustion, air exhaust, evacuation, vacuation
抽气泵 extraction [suction] pump ◇ 初步～ rough pump
抽气管 evacuation tube, pump-out tubulation
抽气机 exhaust unit, air extractor, off-gas pump
抽气式汽轮机[抽气透平] bleed(er) turbine, extraction steam turbine
抽气式通风系统 extraction ventilation system
抽气通风 induced draft
抽气烟道 【冶】draught flue
抽取 extraction, abstraction
抽取样 thief sample, sampling
抽去 draw off
抽入 aspiration, suction
抽试 odd test
抽数 【计】extract, isolate
抽水 pumping, draw [pump] water
抽水点 suction point
抽水机 (water) pump
抽水站 pumping station [plant]
抽屉式烘干炉 【金】drawer-type drying stove
抽头 【电】tap(ping), 【压】wapping off (从每盘钢丝中拉下一圈)
抽头变压器 tap transformer
抽头换接调压器 tap-changing regulator

抽头绕组 tapped [split] winding
抽头位置指示器 tap position indicator
抽头转换 tap changing
抽头转换[切换]开关 tap-changer, tap changing device ◇ 无载～ off-load tapchanger
抽吸 sucking-off, drawing-in, suction
抽吸泵 sucking [sorption] pump
抽吸法 suction method
抽吸浇注 suction casting
抽吸能力 pumping power [capacity]
抽吸器 aspirator
抽吸设备[装置] pumping equipment [unit, installation], aspirator
抽吸作用 pumping action
抽象的 abstract, discrete
抽象符号 【计】abstract symbol
抽烟气机 suction fan, flue gas exhauster
抽烟设备 draught equipment
抽扬喷射器 lifting injector
抽样 sampling, spot-check
抽样检查[检验] (lot) sampling inspection, pick-test
抽样理论 sampling theory
抽样率 sampling rate
抽样数据控制 sampled-data control
抽真空 vacuation, evacuation, deaeration, degasifying, degassing ◇ 初步～ roughing, 预～室 preevacuated chamber
抽真空管道 vacuum lead
抽真空口 vacuum orifice
抽真空容积与真空泵效率之比值 time constant
抽真空设备[系统, 装置] vacuum-pumping equipment, pumping system
抽真空时间 pump-down time
酬金 【企】service fees, compensation
畴 【理】domain
畴壁 【理】domain wall [boundary]
畴壁共振 domain-wall resonance
畴壁矫顽力 domain wall coercivity
畴壁能 domain wall energy

畴壁位移	domain wall displacement, boundary [wall] displacement
畴壁运动	domain wall motion [movement]
畴结构	domain structure [configuration]
畴界	domain boundary
畴理论	domain theory
畴能(量)	domain energy
畴长大[生长]	growth of domains domain growty
畴质点[粒子]	domain particle
畴转动	rotation of domain
畴组态	domain configuration
稠度	consistence, consistency, thickness
稠度计	consistometer
稠度系数	consistency factor
稠汞齐	thickened amalgam
稠厚的	gross
稠化	densification, thickening, fix ◇ 炉渣的～ thickening of slag
稠化电解质	electrolytic paste
稠矿浆	thick pulp
稠密层	dense layer
稠密沉积[沉淀]	compacting settling, dense deposit
稠泥	【焊】lime paste
稠黏土浆	【建】puddle
稠浓剂[器]	densener
稠相流化床	fluidized dense phase bed
稠悬浮液	thick dispersion
稠液喷射器	compact liquid jet
稠液比重计	areopycnometer, areopyknometer
稠渣	【冶】pasty [thick] slag, sticky cinder
臭气极限浓度	【环】odour threshold concentration
臭气浓度	【环】odour concentration
臭气强度指数	【环】odour intensity index
臭气物质	【环】odorant, odorous substance
臭氧{O_3}	ozone
臭氧层[圈]	ozonosphere
臭氧处理	ozonization
臭氧定量的	ozonometric
臭氧定量法	ozonometry
臭氧发生[臭氧化]器	ozonator, ozonizer, ozone generator
臭氧分解	ozonolysis
臭氧化物	ozonide
臭氧化(作用)	ozonization, ozonation, ozonidation
臭氧计	ozonometer
臭氧检验器	ozonoscope
臭氧氧化	【环】ozone oxidation
初步焙烧	preliminary [preparatory] roast(ing), preroast
初步布置	skeleton layout
初步沉淀	(同"预析出")
初步抽气泵	rough pump
初步抽真空	roughing
初步处理	preliminary [first, primary] treatment
初步分馏	prefractionation
初步分馏塔	prefractionator
初步工艺设计	preengineering, preliminary design
初步估计	preliminary estimate
初步还原	preliminary reduction
初步火法精炼	preliminary fire refining
初步计划	sketch [rough] plan
初步加工	initial processing, first finishing, preparative treatment, roughening
初步校准曲线	preliminary calibration curve
初步逼近	first approximation [approach]
初步浸出	preliminary leaching
初步精炼	preliminary refining
初步净化[提纯]	preliminary [rough] purification
初步氯化	preliminary chlorination
初步氯化带	preliminary chlorination zone
初步熔炼	primary smelting
初步设定值[调整点]	preliminary set point
初步设计	preliminary [basic, primary]

design, preliminary design work, preliminary project
初步设计书[文件]　preliminary design document (PDD)
初步试验　preliminary [early, rough] test
初步数据　preliminary data
初步调整　pre-setting, initial readjustment
初步脱硫　preliminary elimination of sulphur
初步蒸馏　predistillation, primary distillation
初测　preliminary survey, reconnaissance
初抽(真空)阀　roughing valve
初抽(真空)管路　roughing line
初吹(转炉的)　【钢】first blow
初次成形断面形状　first shape
初次分析　initial analysis
初次结晶　primary crystallization
初次净化　primary purification
初次拉拔　first draw(ing)
初次冷却剂　primary coolant
初次锍[冰铜]　first matte
初次酸洗　(同"初酸洗")
初次压轧　initial breakdown
初次氧(通过高炉风口的)　primary oxygen
初次氧化皮(加热时形成的)　primary scale
初锻　blocker forging.
初锻模　rough die
初发故障　incipient failure
初沸点　initial boiling point (I.B.P., i.b.p.)
初负载　minor load
初基晶胞　【金】primitive (unit) cell
初基平面　primitive plane
初基(平移)轴　primitive axis
初级泵　rough pump
初级产品　primary product
初级除尘器　【铁】rough cleaner
初级电离　primary ionization
初级电压　primary volt
初级辐射　primary [original] radiation
初级辐射常数　first radiation constant
初级鼓风机　primary injector
初级过滤器　primary filter
初级[初炼]金属(直接从矿石炼出)　primary [virgin] metal
初级粒子　precurser, primary particle
初级绕组[线圈]　primary winding [coil]
初级射线　primary rays
初级消光　primary extinction
初级消光长度　primary extinction distance
初级再结晶　primary recrystallization
初加速度　initial acceleration
初键　initial bond
初阶段蠕变　【理】initial stage creep
初浸残渣　primary leach residue
初晶　primary crystal
初晶温度　primary [initial] crystallization temperature
初冷[初次冷却]器　【焦】primary cooler
初裂(发纹的)　【金】incipient crack
初馏点　【焦】drip point
初馏分　first fraction [cut, runnings], fore runnings, overhead distillate [fraction], 【化】head fraction, light ends (炼油的) ◇ 脱除粗苯~【焦】defronting
初磨机　【选】primary (ball) mill
初凝　initial set, 【建】pre-setting
初凝生成的壳层　【冶】initially formed skin
初期　initial [preliminary] stage, prime
初期变形　initial deformation
初期变形温度　initial deformation temperature
初期沉积[析出]　early deposition
初期反应　initial reaction [action]
初期费用　first cost
初期故障　incipient failure
初期还原　initial reduction
初期冷却作用　initial cooling action
初期黏结力　initial bond
初期偏差　initial deviation

初(期)蠕变　primary [initial] creep
初期烧结　incipient sintering
初熔　incipient fusion [melting]
初熔温度　【冶】incipient fusion temperature
初熔析除铜　【色】primary copper removal
初熔渣　fresh slag
初生奥氏体　primary austenite
初生共析碳化物　primary eutectoid carbide
初生固溶体　(同"一次固溶体")
初生晶胞　primary unit cell
初生晶体　primary crystal
初生渗碳体　primary cementite
初生石墨　primary [kish] graphite
初生索氏体　primary sorbite
初生态　nascent state
初生(态)氢　nascent hydrogen
初生碳化物　primary carbide
初生铁素体　primary ferrite
初生硬度钢　natural steel
初生珠光体　primary pearlite
初始焙烧温度　initial roasting temperature
初始变形　initial distortion [deformation]
初始长度(对焊时的)　initial extension
初始动态磁导率　initial dynamic permeability
初始分离槽　initial separatory cell
初始鼓风(量)　initial blast
初始含碳量　initial carbon content
初始滑移系统　primary slip system
初始化　【计】initializing, initialization
初始阶段蠕变　【理】initial stage creep
初始颗粒　【粉】primary particle
初始粒度　original grain [size]
初始凝固　initial set
初始强度　initial strength
初始切向模量　【理】initial tangent modulus
初始水平[水位,水准,标高]　initial level
初始相位　【理】initial phase
初(始)压力　initial pressure, initial force (电阻焊的)
初始硬度　initial hardness
初始语言　【计】original language
初始直径　starting diameter
初始状态[初态]　initial [original] state
初速度　initial velocity
初酸洗　black [first] pickling
初碎　primary crushing
初碎机　primary crusher [breaker]
初铁　first iron
初退火(钢板的)　first [black] annealing
初退火的　black softened
初析晶体　first yielded crystal
初现裂缝荷载　load at first crack
初相[初生相]　primary [initial, first] phase
初选槽　initial separatory cell
初选机　rougher
初选精矿　preconcentrate
初压　first pressing
初渣　early (stages) slag, primary [preliminary] slag, first (run) slag,
初渣生成　【冶】preliminary slag formation
初渣形成层　【冶】zone of preliminary slag formation
初轧　blooming, breakdown, breaking down, cogging(-down)
初轧板坯　bloom slab, slab (billet) ◇ 大型～large slab
初轧板坯齐边压力机　slab reducer, straightener
初轧车间　blooming mill department
初轧方坯　cogged bloom ◇ 火焰清理～scarfed bloom, 再热～reheat bloom
初轧钢坯　bloom, cogged ingot
初轧机　bloomer, blooming [cogging primary] mill ◇ 可逆式～*, 上辊升程大的～ high lift bloomer, 小型～ baby bloomer
初轧机机架　blooming mill housing
初轧机轧辊　bloom(ing) roll
初轧机组　blooming train

初轧机座　blooming (mill) stand, cogging (-down) stand, breakdown mill
初轧坯　cogged ingot, bloom, half-wrought material ◇ 异形~shaped bloom
初轧－轧坯联合轧机　combination blooming billet mill
出斑点　spotting-out
出版　publication, publish, press
出厂　ex-works, ex-factory
出厂价格　factory price
出错率　【计】error rate [ratio]
出错维修[修复]　【计】corrective [unscheduled] maintenance
出错维修时间　【计】corrective maintenance time
出锭(从炉中)　drawing of ingot
出端电阻　output resistance
出风量　air output
出钢　【钢】tap(ping), pouring ◇ 按碳含量~tap(ping) on carbon, 低温~coldmelt, 猛烈~violent tap, 准备~的炉次 ready-to-tap heat
出钢槽金属爆音　runner shot
出钢槽修理　runner makeup
出钢槽渣　spout slag
出钢侧　pouring side
出钢侧炉衬(转炉的)　tap pad
出钢到出钢时间　【钢】tap-to-tap (period, time)
出钢钢水分析　tapping analysis
出钢化学成分　tapping specification
出钢机　【压】pusher, extractor, billet pull-out machine ◇ 横向~(炉用) cross pusher
出钢技术　tapping technology
出钢间隔　【钢】tapping [casting] interval
出钢口　【钢】(hot metal) taphole, steel-tapping hole, tap(ping) hole ◇ (打)开~", 堵~", 人工堵的~ hand closed taphole
出钢口钎　(同"出铁口钎")
出钢口修补　hole patching
出钢口装置　tap fittings
出钢量　tapping
出钢(流)槽　【钢】tapping [steel] spout, (pouring) spout, runner, (tapping) launder, (hot) metal spout, run-out trough ◇ 叉形~", 分流~", 可拆式~removable runner, 事故备用~emergency launder
出钢平台　【钢】tapping platform
出钢前的最后试验　final tapping test
出钢时间　【钢】tapping time
出钢时间经常相重的炉次　frequently bunched heats
出钢时位置(转炉的)　tapping position
出钢温度　【钢】tapping temperature
出钢(试)样　【钢】tapping sample
出钢用钢包　【钢】tap(ping) ladle
出(钢)渣　tapping slag, slay tap, tap [cinder] off
出钢真空脱气法　tap degassing
出钢周期　tap-to-tap time
出钢作业　hot metal tapping
出格　off-specification, off-quality
出格品　off-size material
出故障　failing, malfunctioning
出轨　excursion
出汗　sweat-out, leaker (水压试验的)
出价　offer, bid
出焦侧　【焦】coke end
出金属熔体槽　【冶】tapping spout
出口　exit (port), outlet, egress, escape orifice, exportation, outcome ◇ 废气~exhaust outlet, 空气出口~air outlet, 燃料~fucl outlet, 喷管~nozzle exit
出口槽　outlet trough
出口侧操纵台(轧机机后的)　outgoing control post
出口带钢温度　temperature of outgoing strip
出口带卷小车　delivery coil car
出口导板　delivery guide
出口导板(装置)　【压】run-off block
出口导板盒　delivery guide box

出口导槽(金属或炉渣的) 【冶】spout guide
出口导卫板 【压】exit [outlet] guide
出口导卫台 【压】delivery guide table
出口导卫装置 【压】stripper
出口端 exit end,【压】delivery end
出口垛板机 【压】exit piler
出口翻钢导板 delivery twist guide
出口分水槽 outlet distribution channel
出口负荷 outlet burden
出口管 exit tube, outlet pipe [tube]
出口辊 outlet roller
出口辊道 outlet [run-off] table
出口含尘量[浓度] outlet dust concentration [loading]
出口活套 【压】delivering looper ◇ 多折式~*
出口活套坑 delivery looping pit
出口活套拉辊 exit loop puller
出口夹持器 exit clamp
出口角 angle of departure
出口节流式电路 meter-out circuit
出口开度 outlet opening
出口孔径 exit aperture
出口联结管 outlet connection
出口流钢砖 【钢】lateral outlet brick
出口流量 outlet discharge
出口密封室 delivery seal chamber
出口浓度 outlet density
出口喷管 exit nozzle
出口喷嘴 discharge jet
出口平面 exit plane, delivery plane(轧件脱离轧辊的)
出口(切面)面积 discharge area
出口气流 jet exit
出口区 taphole area
出口区研磨(拉模的) back relief lap
出口水头损失(输出端损耗) exit loss, discharge losses
出口速度 delivery [exit, outgoing] speed, outlet velocity, muzzle velocity
出口速度压头 outlet velocity head

出口损失 exit loss
出口套管 outlet sleeve
出口推床导板(轧机的) delivery (side) guard
出口弯头 outlet bend
出口围盘 【压】escapement repeater
出口卫板(轧异型钢材用) 【压】flange stripper guide
出口温度 exit [outlet] temperature
出口压力 discharge [exit, outlet] pressure, discharge [outlet] head
出口压头 discharge [outlet] head
出口烟道 exit flue
出口张紧辊 delivery tension roll
出口张紧装置 【压】delivery [exit] bridle, exit tension bridle
出口张力(薄板卷通过轧机的) 【压】outlet tension
出口张力辊(在平整机的卷取机侧) 【压】delivery pullers
出口指令 exit instruction
出口主沟 【铁】taphole runner
出口锥 【压】exit angle, back taper(挤压模的), back relief (angle)(拉模的)
出矿地沟 ore-reclaim tunnel, ore trough
出力不足 undercapacity
出料 discharge
出料槽 outlet trough
出料侧 delivery [exit, outgoing] side ◇ 炉子~*
出料侧设备 equipment at delivery side
出料斗 discharge hopper
出料端 【团】delivery end
出料端砌块 discharge-end block, nosering block(回转窑用)
出料活套塔[坑] 【压】outfeed accumulator
出料机 discharging machine ◇ 吊杆式~*
出料口 discharge gate [hole, opening, port], throat piece
出料区 discharging zone

出料区段(冷床的) 【压】pull-off section
出料推杆(冷床的) 【压】kick-off [kick-out] arm
出料斜槽 discharge spout
出料运送机 outfeed conveyer
出料装置[机构] discharging device [gear, mechanism], drawing mechanism, eduction gear, outloading feeder (贮仓的)
出锍口 taphole for matte
出炉侧 【冶】tapping side
出炉辊道 furnace delivery table
出炉机 furnace discharge conveyer
出炉温度 discharge [exit] temperature, furnace drop out temperature, tappingtemperature (熔融金属、炉渣等的)
出坯 compact extraction, ejection of compact, 【粉】knock-out(下冲杆将坯块顶出模口)◇ 弧形~*, 凸轮驱动~ cam-driven knock-out
出坯冲程 knock-out stroke
出坯冲杆 knock-out punch
出坯杆 ejector pin [rod, punch], stripper punch
出坯压力 ejection pressure
出坯应力 ejection stress
出坯装置[机构] 【粉】knock-out [ejection] mechanism ◇ 液压~*
出气 air-out, gassing
出气道 gas off-take
出气的 gassy
出气管 gas outlet tube
出气口 gas outlet [port], escape hole, gas off-take, 【铸】air gate, riser vent
出气冒口 【铸】pop-off, flow-off, riser runner
出铅口 lead tap(-hole), lead tapping well
出砂 【铸】breaking down, shakeout
出射缝隙(光学仪器的) exit slit
出售 sell, offer ◇ 可~产品 saleable material
出水(处理过的) 【环】product water

出水点 【环】point of origin
出水管 discharging tube
出水口 water out(let), delivery gate [port], drain outlet
出水量 water output
出铁 【铁】(iron) tapping, tapping iron, casting, iron removal ◇ 事故[紧急情况] ~emergency tapping, 连续~操作*
出铁槽 【铁】tapping [iron] spout, (hot) metal spout, iron notch ◇ 叉形~*, 化铁[冲天]炉~cupola spout
出铁槽口 iron-notch opening
出铁槽碳砖衬里 carbonblock runner lining
出铁场 【铁】casthouse, (casting, pig) bed ◇ 环形~circular cast house
出铁场班组 casthouse crew
出铁场补炉材料 casthouse materials
出铁场地面 casthouse [casting] floor
出铁场废铁 casthouse scrap
出铁场控制盘 casthouse control panel
出铁场流槽系统 casthouse runner system
出铁场清理 casthouse cleanup
出铁场栈桥(桥吊) casting bridge
出铁场铸铁工 stocktaker
出铁程序 casting schedule
出铁次数 number of casts
出铁沟 lander, iron tap channel
出铁沟残铁 sow iron [scrap]
出铁技术 tapping technology
出铁间隔 casting interval, tapping interval
出铁口 (hot) metal taphole, (iron) tapping hole, spout (hole), taphole, iron-notch ◇ 长形~long taphole, (打)开[打通]~*, 堵~*, 浅[易打开的]~*, 人工堵的~ hand closed taphole, 烧开~ lancing of taphole, 双~高炉*
出铁口标高 tapping hole level
出铁口冻结[冻结的出铁口] hard tap (hole)
出铁口环形凝铁 dog collar
出铁口流槽 taphole trough

出铁口泥料	（同"堵出铁口泥"）
出铁口泥套	(tapping) breast
出铁口泥套修理小刀	taphole slaker
出铁口钎	tap out bar, tap(ping) bar
出铁[渣]口铁框	taphole plate
出铁口外框	headblock
出铁口装置	tap(hole) fittings
出铁[渣]流槽	tapping launder
出铁平台	tapping platform
出铁前的一次出渣	casting flush
出铁时间	tapping time
出铁时间表	casting schedule
出铁试样	tapping sample
出铁温度	tapping temperature
出铁用铁水罐	tap(ping) ladle
出铁渣	tapping slag
出铁周期[间隔时间]	tap-to-tap time
出铁作业	hot metal tapping
出瑕疵	flawing
出现	appearance, occurrence, emergence
出现率	frequency
出现毛刺[梳刺]	finning
出线盒	outlet box
出锌口	[色]zinc tapping well

出渣 slagging(-off), slagging out, slag tap[removal], flush (slag) practice, tapping,【钢】pouring,【铁】flushing,【冶】running-off ◇ 出铁前的一次~【铁】casting flush, 炉后~ back slagging, 炉前~ front flushin, 铁口~ *

出渣槽	slag launder, scum gutter,【钢】runner-trough
出渣侧	slag-off side
出渣车	drag-out slag car
出渣工	【铁】cindersnapper,【团】teazer

出渣口 slag (tap-)hole [tap, eye], taphole for slag, slag notch (aperture), cinder notch, dross hole, scum hole（美）,【冶】taphole ◇（打）开~ *, 打通~铁棒【铁】tapping pin, 堵~ *, 卢尔曼式~ *

出渣口冷却器大套	【铁】big slag cooler
出渣口铁渣	【铁】cinder-notch slag
出渣流槽	tapping launder
出渣率	slag yield
出渣门	cleanout hole
出渣期	flush off period, run-off period
出渣时间	tapping [flushing] time
出渣速度	flushing velocity
出辙	excursion
雏晶	crystallite, matted crystal
雏形锻模	【压】blocker
雏形锻模式锻造	【压】blocker-type forging
雏形锻造（自由锻）	【压】blocking operation
除氨	【环】ammonia removal

除铋 bismuth removal [elimination], debismuthising ◇ 贝特顿[克罗尔－贝特顿]加钙镁~(精炼)法

除铋剂(炼铅的)	debismuthizing agent
除冰	de-icing
除冰液	de-icing liquid [fluid]

除尘 dedust(ing), dust cleaning [abatement, elimination, exhaust, extraction handling, precipitation, removal, separation] ◇ 环境[厂房,室内]~ room dedusting, 热筛~ *

除尘袋	dedusting bag
除尘段	precipitation treatment zone
除尘风机	dust-fan
除尘风量	dedusting volume
除尘机	deduster ◇ 百页窗式~ louver deduster
除尘孔	dusting door
除尘率	degree of dust precipitation, deduster yield
除尘喷嘴	dust suppression spray

除尘[机]器 precipitator, dust extractor [separator, collector, precipitator], deduster, air strainer,【铁】cleaner ◇ 布袋~ *, 厂区环境~ *, 粗[初级]~ *, 多管(式)~ *, 废气~ waste gas filter, 负压袋式~ *, 干式~ *, 管式~ *, 过滤~ *, 机械~ *, 静电~ *, 离心~ *, 排烟~ *, 湿

除　chu

式~*,室式~chamber collector,水封式~*,文丘里管~Venturi scrubber,旋涡~【铁】whirler,油雾~*,圆筒型~*,织物(纤维)过滤~*,转盘式~*,自动力~*

除尘器内停留时间　precipitator retention time

除尘器泥渣　dust-collector residue

除尘器特性　precipitator performance

除尘容积　dedusting volume

除尘设备[装置]　dust-cleaning apparatus, dust-collecting equipment [plant, unit, installation], dedusting [dust-collection, dust-separation] equipment, dust removing plant, dust arrestment equipment, dust control device, (vacuum) cleaning plant

除尘室　dust (collecting) chamber, dedusting chamber

除尘网　dust gauze

除尘系统　dust extraction [collecting, suppression, catching] system, dedusting [captation] system ◇ 环境~*,液体~*

除尘效率　dust removal efficiency, efficiency of dust collection, dedusting efficiency

除尘旋流器　centrifugal dust collector

除尘罩　dust (suppression) hood

除疵【焊】　deseaming ◇ 火焰~flame deseaming

除法器　divider ◇ 数字~digital divider

除法子程序【计】　division subroutine

除酚设备　dephenolizing plant

除浮渣　scum-off

除镉塔(锌精馏精炼的)　cadmium eliminator column

除铬　(同"脱铬")

除根机　rootdozer, rooter, tree dozer, grubber

除根掘土机　grubber

除汞　removal of mercury

除垢(剂)　antiscale

除垢液　descaling solution

除灰　ash removal, deashing

除灰门　cleaning [cleanout] door

除灰箱　dust-settling tank

除金　degolding

除楞角　rolling off

除磷　(同"脱磷")

除鳞　descaling, removal of scale ◇ 电解~*,干法~dry-scale disposal,感应加热[热爆]~*,高压~喷嘴组*,化学~chemical descaling,机械~*,碱洗~alkaline descaling,浸水~*,喷丸~法dreibrite,喷焰~flame descaling,水力~系统*,无酸~acidless descaling,盐浴~salt bath descaling

除鳞泵　descaling pump

除鳞槽(酸洗法)　descaling bath

除鳞锤　scale hammer ◇ 风动~*

除鳞供水管　descaling supply water pipe

除[破]鳞机　descaling machine [mill], descaler, scale breaker ◇ 二辊式~*,拉过式三次弯曲~*,立式~*,连续酸洗作业线上的精~*,两次弯曲~*,喷砂[喷丸]~blast descaler

除鳞机座　descaling stand

除鳞集管　descaling header

除鳞喷水　descaling sprays

除鳞喷嘴系统　descaling spray system, scale semoval [handling] aystem

除鳞喷嘴组　descaling sprays

除鳞设备　descaling equipment

除鳞系统　descaling system, scale removal [handling] system

除鳞用水　descaling water

除鳞用供水(管道)【压】　scale flushing supply water (SFSW)

除鳞装置(轧件的)【压】　descaling equipment [device, unit] ◇ 风动~*,高压水~*

除硫　(同"脱硫")

除(毛)刺　deburring ◇ 电解~*

除毛刺辊　deburring roll

除毛刺机　flash remover
除铆钉　derivetting
除镁　（同"脱镁"）
除醚槽　de-etherization tank
除沫剂　defoamer [anti-foaming] agent
除沫器　(scum) skimmer float skimming device,【选】forth separator
除泥器　sludge remover,【选】slime separator
除镍　denickeling
除镍程度　degree of nickel elimination
除泡勺　【选】bowl skimmer
除漆器　paint remover
除气　（同"脱气"）◇ 低温热处理~【金】baking, 加热~*, 预先~predegassing
除气槽[池]　degassing bath
除气动力学　degassing kinetics
除气剂　degasifier, degasifying agent, degasser, scavenging additions
除气器　deaerator, degasser ◇ 变径式~*
除气室　gas removal chamber, de-airing [deaerating] chamber
除气塔　deaeration [degassing] tower
除气温度　outgassing temperature
除铅塔（锌精馏精炼的）　lead eliminator column
除铅镉焙烧　lead-cadmium elimination roast
除去　removal, elimination, ablation, abstraction, discard, unload
除去空气　deaerate
除去离子　deionize
除热[除去热量]　heat removal [abstraction]
除热剂　heat removing agent
除色剂　decolorizing agent, decolourant
除砂　desanding
除砂石　degritting
除砷　dearsenifying, dearsenication, removal of arsenic
除湿　dehumidification
除数　【数】divisor, divider

除霜　defrost
除水　（同"脱水"）
除酸　deacidify, disacidifying
除酸器　acid separator
除锑　removal of antimony
除铁　deferrization,【色】iron removal ◇ 净化~*
除铁槽　iron removal tank ◇ 最终~*
除铁鳞机　（同"除鳞机"）
除铜　copper removal [elimination], decoppering, decopperization ◇ 二次~*, 科尔科德加硫~法*
除铜槽　decopperizing tank
除铜粗铅　decopperized lead bullion, dross bullion
除铜反应　copper-stripping reaction
除铜工段　decoppering section
除铜精炼锅（炼铅的）　first over kettle ◇ 加硫~*
除铜锌槽　copper-zinc removal tank
除铜锌系统　copper-zinc removal system
除雾器　demister, mist catcher [eliminator, precipitator]
除锡　detin(ning)
除锡废钢铁　detinned scrap
除锡切边　detinning scrap
除锡装置（报废镀锡钢板和切边的）　detinning apparatus
除芯机【铸】　core breaker ◇ 水力~*, 震动~core vibrator
除锌　dezinc, de-zinc(ing), dezincification, dezincify, dezinking, zinc removal [elimination] ◇ 碱-氯化物法~*, 氯气~*, 氧化(精炼)~法*, 真空~*
除锌处理　zinc removal treatment, dezincing treatment
除锌铅　dezinced lead
除锌炉　dezincing furnace ◇ 连续~*
除锌设备　dezincing equipment
除锈(从金属表面)　rust removal [cleaning], removal of rust, derusting, detarnish ◇ 德肖电解液~法 Deshow process, 电

弧～ arc cleaning,电化学～法 derustit,电解～*,高压水射流～*,碱性～法 alkaline derusting,锈蚀材料火焰～*

除锈锤 rust hammer

除锈剂 deruster,descaler,rust remover ◇ 闭路循环～*,无机盐～*

除锈器 scaler

除锈(溶)液 deruster,descaling solution, rust-removing liquid

除烟 smoke abatement

除盐 salts removal

除盐操作 salts removal operation

除氧 (同"脱氧")

除氧化皮 (同"除鳞")

除氧化皮液 descaling solution

除银 【色】silver removal,deprivation of silver,desilvering,desilverization ◇ 加锌连续～*

除银操作 desilverizing operation

除银法 desilverization process ◇ 卢斯—罗赞蒸汽搅拌铅～*,帕廷森粗铅结晶～*

除银锅 desilverizing kettle [vessel] ◇ 粗铅连续精炼～*

除银铅 desilvered lead

除银设备(铅精炼的) desilverization plant

除银作业 desilverizing operation

除油 deoiling,degreasing,unoil ◇ 镀锡薄钢板的～辊 tampico rolls

除油带钢 degreased strip

除油器 oil eliminator [expeller],degreaser

除油液面 cleaning level

除油脂槽 grease-skimming tank

除藻剂 algaecide

除渣 slag removal [disposal],slagging-off,removal of slag [cinder],deslag(ging),cake blow ◇ 氧枪～法 spear slagging,液态～(法) slag drip

除渣锤 deslagging [slagging] hammer

除渣工具 slag-removal tool

除渣锅 dross(ing) kettle

除渣剂 deslagging agent

除渣期 deslagging period

除渣器 slag separator [trap],skimming chamber

除渣勺 scummer,【冶】skimmer spoon

杵锤 【压】tilt hammer

储备 reservation,conservation,margin,stockpile

储备系数 safety coefficient

储仓卸料装置 bin discharger

储仓闸门 bunker gate

储藏 storage,storing

储藏室 storage room,storeroom

储藏稳定性 storage stability

储槽形 X 射线装置 tank-type X-ray unit

储槽组 group of tanks

储存 stockpile,laid-up,store up ◇ 可～性 storability

储存槽 holding vessel

储存单元 storage element ◇ 数据～【计】data location

储存活套(在活套装置中的) storage loop

储存料斗 holding hopper

储存炉 retaining [holding] vessel,【冶】holding furnace (液态金属用)

储存器 accumulator,reservoir,stilling chamber

储存寿命 storage life

储存台 sloping ramp,storage bed (轧材用) ◇ 带卷[焊管坯]～coil magazine

储存装置[设备] 【计】storage device

储碘器 iodine holder

储集活套坑(带材的) loop-storage [looping] pit

储矿仓 ore storage bin

储矿场 ore yard

储料分送机[储放提升进料台](轧件顺序进炉用) magazine (elevating) depiler

储料进给台[储存式装料台](轧件顺序进炉用) magazine-type charger

储料台 magazine ◇ 摆动式～tilting magazine

储料卸出台(炉用) 【压】depiling equipment
储鳞箱 scale bucket
储能[储存能量] stored [accumulation] energy, motivity
储能电路 tank circuit
储能焊 percussion welding ◇电磁场~机*
储气罐[柜] gas tank [holder] ◇浮罩式~*, 干式~ waterless gasholder, 水封式~*
储气瓶 (gas) bomb
储气桶 gas receiver
储热物质 heat retaining mass
储砂斗(吹芯的) 【铸】magazine
储砂筒(吹砂机的) 【铸】cartridge
储水池[罐] aqua storage tank
储箱闸门 bunker gate
储氧(钢)筒阀 oxygen cylinder valve
储液池 liquid [aqua] storage tank
储运机 accumulating conveyer
储渣料仓 slag bin
触变沉淀 thixotropic precipitate
触变剂 thixotropic agent
触变胶 thixotrope
触变现象[行为] thixotropic behaviour
触变性 thixotrophy (character), thixotropism, rheopexy
触变性质 thixotropic nature
触变淤浆 thixotropic slurry
触点 contact (point), tip ◇断弧~arcing tip, 后[静合]~ back contact, 滑动~ moving contact, 静[开路]~ break (back) contact, 空闲~ disconnected contact, 无~的 contactless, 先断后合~*
触点闭合力 contact closing force
触点电阻 contact resistance
触点合金 contact alloy
触点控制器 contactor controller
触点黏结 contact adhesion [sticking]
触点松动 contact chatter
触点态 pundular state
触点温度计 electric contact thermometer
触点[头]压力 contact pressure
触发电极 igniter, ignitor (electrode), trigger electrode
触发电容放电(光谱的) triggered capacitor discharge
触发电压 trigger voltage
触发法 ignition method
触发管 trigger tube, ignitron (tube)
触发机构 trigger mechanism
触发继电器 trigger relay
触发脉冲 【电】gating pulse, trigger impulse
触发脉冲发生器[触发振荡器] trigger generator
触发门[触发选通脉冲] trigger gate
触发器 trigger, flip flop (multivibrator), igniter, ignitor, toggle ◇D型~【计】D-flip flop, RS[置"0"置"1"]~*, 计数型[T形]~*, 射流逻辑~ fluid logic trigger
触发器存储器 【计】flip flop storage
触发(器)电路 trigger [flip-flop] circuit ◇双稳态~*
触发器寄存器 【计】flip flop register
触发器气封(高速锤的) trigger-gas seal
触发器座架(可控式高速锤的) trigger carrier
触发气(高速锤的) 【压】trigger gas
触发位置 trigger gean [mechaniem], trigger assemlly
触发装置 trigger gear [mechanism], 【机】trigger assembly(可控式高速锤的)
触发作用 trigger action
触轮(抛光用) contact wheel
触媒剂 catalyst, catalytic agent, catalyzer ◇载体~*
触媒燃烧装置 catalytic combustion system
触媒作用 【化】catalysis
触头 contact tip
触头材料 contact material, head material

（钢丝录音带、录像带用高导磁率材料）
触头垫片(用于复合电极点焊) contact point insert
触头金属 contact metal
触线圈(钢绳断线自动停车装置的)【压】lashing ring
触针 feeler [contact] pin
处理 treating, treatment, processing, disposal, disposition, handling (disposal), disposition, usage, conduct, curing ◇ 不易~的(矿石) refractory, 盖扎尔~法*
处理标记[记号] handling mark
处理部件 【计】processing unit
处理槽 treating tank
处理程序 treatment schedule, 【计】processing program, processor, handler
处理费用 handling cost, treatment charges
处理机 【计】processor ◇ 阵列~ array processor, 中央~*
处理机出错中断 processor-error interrupt
处理界限 【企】action limit
处理介质 treatment medium
处理开始阶段 head end treatment
处理量 processing rate, throughput (capacity)
处理能力 handling capability [ability], processing rate
处理炉 treatment furnace
处理溶液 treatment solution
处理设备[装置] processing unit, treater
处理时间滞后 process time lag
处理速率 processing speed, treatment rate
处理条件 treatment conditions
处理制度 treatment schedule
处理周期 treatment eycle ◇ 作业线上~*
处置场(废物的) 【环】disposal site
川崎顶部吹氧(脱气)**法** KTB process
川崎氧气顶吹(技术) Kawasaki top blowing (KTB)
川崎氧气顶吹系统 KTB system
川崎氧气顶吹氧枪 KTB oxygen lance

氚{H_3, T} tritium, hyzone, superheavy hydrogen
氚核 triton
穿插 interpenetration, alternate ◇ 连铸坯~装炉*
穿插双晶 interpenetration twin
穿出(钢带的) threading-out
穿带导卫台 threading guide table
穿带－甩带操作 threading and unthreading operation
穿带台 threading table
穿带自动控制装置 automatic threading control device
穿钉 drift bolt
穿过 threading, passing, infiltrate ◇ 无摩擦~带*
穿接 cross under
穿晶断口 transcrystalline frature
穿晶断裂 intracrystalline failure [rupture], intragranular failure, transcrystalline rupture [frature, crack(ing)], transgranular cracking [failure] ◇ 应力腐蚀~*
穿晶辐射 transgranular radiation
穿晶腐蚀 transgranular corrosion
穿晶结构 transcrytallization structure
穿晶粒的 transcrystalline
穿晶裂纹 transcrystalline crack(ing)
穿晶破坏 transcrystalline [intracrystalline] rupture [failure]
穿孔 piercing, pierce, hole punch(ing), perforation, trepan, boring ◇ 辊式[斜轧]~ rotary piercing, 两次~法*, 斯蒂费尔~轧制法 Stiefel roll process
穿孔导板 【压】piercer guide shoe
穿孔顶头 【压】piercing plug ◇ 水冷~*
穿孔杆(多锤水压机的) 【机】piercing needle
穿孔管 Proforator pipe
穿孔机 punch (press), puncher, bear punch, perforator, 【压】piercer, piercing mill [press, machine], perforating press

◇ 曼内斯曼[辊式]~*,蘑菇式[菌式]~*,盘式~*,斯蒂费尔-曼内斯曼~*,桶形轧辊~*,斜轧~*,压力[推轧]~*,锥形辊~*
穿孔机下模　【压】bed
穿孔机轧辊　【压】piercer roll
穿孔挤压　piercing extrusion ◇ 维特恩~法 Witten's process
穿孔毛管　【压】pierced shell
穿孔毛坯在芯棒上扩径[辗压]　【压】saddling
穿孔模　perforating die
穿孔坯料　pierced billet
穿孔器　punch(eon), punching pin, drift hammer,【压】(drift) punch ◇ 锥形~【压】conical punch,自动定心~*
穿孔器横梁　【压】mandrel crosshead
穿孔器回程横梁　【压】mandrel release crosshead
穿孔温度　【压】piercing temperature
穿孔系统回程缸　【压】mandrel retractor cylinder
穿孔系统主缸　【压】piercer cylinder
穿孔芯棒　【压】piercing mandrel, piercer bar, piercing point bar
穿孔压力机　【压】piercing machine [press] ◇ 水力[液压]~*
穿孔用轧辊　【压】piercer disc
穿孔凿　jumper
穿孔针(多锤水压机的)　piercing needle
穿孔针调位装置　【压】mandrel turner
穿孔装置(水压机的)　mandrel unit
穿料　threading, tracking
穿料装置(机组的)　【压】pull-through machine
穿漏　runout
穿炉(焊管坯的)　【压】furnace threading
穿炉引杆　needle
穿模(拉丝时的)　【压】threading-up
穿模带头机　pulling-in machine
穿模装置　【压】drawing-in device
穿墙布线　knob-and-tube wiring
穿墙绝缘子　through[partition] insulator, wall entrance insulator
穿墙布线　knob-and-tube wiring
穿墙套管　wall bushing
穿入(钢带的)　threading-in
穿梭式送锭车　shuttle car
穿梭运输　shuttle traffic
穿通击穿　【半】punch through breakdown
穿通孔　through[punched] hole, full length bore
穿透　penetration, penetrance, permeation, breakthrough, transmission, escape ◇ 滑移~*
穿透点　breakthrough point
穿透度　(degree of) penetration
穿透辐射　transmitted radiation
穿透腐蚀　through[penetration] corrosion
穿透计(射线的)　penetrometer
穿透粒子　【理】penetrating particle
穿透裂纹　through crack
穿透率　degree of penetration, penetration rate
穿透面　【理】penetration side
穿透能力　penetrating power, penetrativeness, breakthrough capacity (离子交换的)
穿透曲线(气体渗碳程度的)　【金】penetration curve
穿透深度(磁场的)　penetration depth ◇ 磁通量~flux penetration
穿透时间　penetration time
穿透系数　coefficient of transmission, penetrating coefficient
穿透性　penetrability, penetrativity, penetrance
穿透作用　penetrating action
穿线挂车(拔丝开始的)　stringing-up
穿靴筒(钢锭缺陷)　bootlegging
穿引设备　threading device
穿引速度(轧件的)　threading speed
穿轧　piercing(billet), rolling on
穿轧法　roll-piercing process ◇ 压力~*

穿传 chuan

穿轧过孔的坯料 pierced billet
穿轧机 (roll) piercing mill ◇ 三辊联合~*
穿轧性能(金属的) pierceability
传播 propagation, diffusion, diffuseness, dissemination, travel, spread, passage
传播差(光线的) propagation difference
传播长度(裂纹的) propagation length
传播方向 direction of propagation
传播速度 propagation velocity [speed]
传播速率 rate of propagation
传播误差 【计】propagated error
传播系数 propagation coefficient
传导 conduct(ion), conductance, transfer, transmission ◇ 不~物质 carrier free material
传导层 conducting layer, 【半】conducting shell
传导传热 heat transfer by conduction, conduction heat transfer
传导电子 conducting [conductivity] electron
传导功率 conducting power
传导机理 conduction mechanism
传导加热 conduction heating
传导介质 transmission medium
传导冷却 conduction cooling
传导率 conductivity, conduction, specific conductance
传导(能)带 conduction (energy) band
传导能带电子能量 conduction band electron energy
传导热损失 conduction loss
传导系数 coefficient of conductivity, transfer coefficient
传导性 conductibility, conductivity, conduction
传递 transfer, transmission, deliver(ing), conveying, impress, transport
传递比 transfer ratio, transmissibility
传递点 transmission point
传递管 transfer piping

传递函数[机能] 【计】transfer function
传递面 【金】transfer surface
传递速率现象 transport rate phenomena
传递损失 transmission loss
传递系数(结构力学弯矩分配法) transfer coefficient, carry-over factor
传递应力(放松预应力钢筋时的) stress at transfer
传动 drive, transmission, transmitting, actuation ◇ 单独~*,直接[不减速]~direct drive,直流~(装置)DC-drive
传动比 gear ratio (g.r.), drive [transmission] ratio, reduction rate
传动侧 drive side [end]
传动侧辊道架 drive-end table frame
传动侧机架 drive-side housing
传动齿轮 drive(r) [transmission] gear, gearing wheel, pinion
传动齿轮箱 drive box, driving gear box
传动带 drive [driving] belt, transmission strap [belt] ◇ 有接头~ sewn belt
传动带导槽 belt guide
传动电机 drive [driving] motor
传动杆 drive rod [link]
传动功率 drive output, transmission power
传动管(打井用) drive pipe
传动辊(夹板锤的) driving roller ◇ 电机~ motorised roll
传动辊道 live-roller gear [table], live-roller (bed) ◇ 圆锥齿轮~*
传动活塞 drive piston
传动机构 drive [transmission, connecting, running] gear, drive, driving device ◇ 阀控~*,控制杆~*
传动机座 drive stand
传动卷筒式地下卷取机 【压】centre-driven mandrel type downcoiler
传动控制系统 drive control system ◇ 全数字~*
传动链 drive [driving, transmission, gearing] chain

传动链轮 driving sprocket
传动轮 drive pulley, driving wheel ◇ 塔形~drive cone
传动螺杆 drive screw
传动螺栓 drive [driving] bolt
传动皮带 drive [driving] belt ◇ 胶合~balata belt
传动绳[索] driving [transmission] rope
传动头 【机】driving head
传动托辊 back spin rolls
传动星轮 driving sprocket
传动爪 driving claw
传动轴 drive [transmission, power] shaft, driving axle, jack shaft (变速箱的) ◇ 主~*
传动装置 drive (unit), driver, gear, transmission, actuating device, actuator, arranger ◇ 带启动停止控制的~start and stop drive, 挠性[波奇弗里克斯型]~Bogiflex drive unit, 伺服系统动力~servodyne
传感器 sensor, sensing probe [device], (sensing) transducer, pick-off, pick-up, inductive transmitter ◇ 差压~*, 带式~【理】tape probe, 福斯特~Foerster probe, 霍尔效应~*, 角度~angle probe, 碳~【电】carbon pickup, 瓦特~watt transmitter, 位移~displacement pick-up, 无触点~contactless pickup, 有源~active transducer, 远距离~remote-transmitter
传感头 sensing head
传感元件 sensor, detector
传感装置 sensing device
传力杆 dowel bar [steel]
传力轴 live axle
传热 heat transfer, thermal transmission, egress of heat, 【冶】passage of heat
传热表面 heat transfer surface
传热材料 heat transfer [conductive] material
传热分析 heat transfer analysis
传热反问题研究方法 heat transfer anti-problem method
传热过程 heat transfer process, diabatic process
传热回路 heat transfer loop
传热剂 heat transfer agent
传热介质 heat transfer medium
传热率 rate of heat transfer
传热面 heat transfer surface [front]
传热模型 heat transfer model
传热速率 heat transfer rate
传热特性 heat transfer characteristic
传热途径 heat passage
传热系数 heat transfer coefficient (HTC), coefficient of heat passage [transmission]
传热性 thermal conduction [conductivity]
传热性能 heat transfer property [character]
传热盐类 heat transfer salts
传热装置 heat transfer arrangement
传声器 microphone
传声温度计 thermophone
传输 transmission, transfer, transport
传输方式 transmission mode
传输功率 transmitted power
传输过程模拟 transport process simulation (TPS)
传输机理 transport mechanism
传输接口转换器 【计】transmission interface converter
传输理论 transport theory
传输门[选通脉冲] transmission gate
传输能力(指传输电流) transmittability, entrainment capacity
传输频带 transmission band
传输时间 【电】propagation time
传输损耗 transmission loss
传输系统 transmission system
传输现象 transport phenomena
传输线 transmission [transfer] line
传送 conveying, transmitting, driving,

transfer(ence)
传送泵 transfer pump
传送带 conveyer [conveying] belt ◇ 检查～inspection conveyer, 脱水～dewatering conveyer
传送带干燥机 belt dryer
传送带管式炉 tubular conveyer-belt furnace
传送带式钼电阻炉 conveyer-type molybdenum resistor furnace
传送带式烧结炉 conveyer-type sintering furnace
传送带用钢丝帘布 steel cord for belt conveyer
传送方式 move [transmitting] mode, 【计】load mode
传送轨道 transfer track
传送机 conveyer, transfer machine
传送介质 transmission medium
传送控制 【电】transfer control
传送溜槽 transfer chute
传送器 translator, conveyer, 【电】sentinel
传送时间 transfer time
传送式淬火槽 conveyer quench tank
传送脱扣继电器 transferred tripping relay
传送小车 transfer bogie [buggy]
传送延迟 propagation delay, transfer lag
传送运输机 transfer conveyer
传送装置 transfer machine, drag-over skid
传统拜耳法 conventional Bayer process
传统方法 classical method
传统冷却方式 【团】conventional cooling
传压杠杆 pressure transmission lever
传压器 pressure transmitter
传真 facsimile
传真电报 facsimile telegraph [telegram], facsimile transmission, photogram, phototelegram, telephotograph
传真电报机 teleautograph, electrograph
传真度 fidelity
传真发送 facsimile transmission

传真机 facsimile apparatus [equipment], fax
传质 mass transfer [transport], matter [material] transport
传质机理 mass-transfer mechanism
传质控制 mass-transfer control
传质速率 rate of mass transfer
船 ship, vessel, craft ◇ 平底～gondola
船边交货价格 free alongside ship (FAS, F.A.S.)
船舶巴比合金 (同"海军巴比合金")
船货 cargo, shipload, freight
船级社 classification society ◇ 劳氏～*
船面板 deck plate
船期 sailing date
船上交货(价格) free on board (FOB, F.O.B.)
船上交货提单 on deck B/L
船式起重机 pontoon crane, boat derrick
船体钢 hull steel
船体结构钢 hull structural steel
船用 C 级燃料油 bunker "C" fuel oil
船用钢板 shipbuilding section
船用锅炉 marine boiler
船用黄铜 (同"海军黄铜")
船用锰黄铜 turbadium
船用镍青铜(9—12Ni, 1—3Al, 0.5—2Zn, 余量 Cu) naval nickel bronze
船用青铜(含 2Zn) admiralty bronze ◇ 高强度～*
船运矿石 ore shipment
喘振 surge ◇ 防～的 surgeproof
串并罐式无料钟炉顶 【铁】bell-less top with series-parallel hoppers
串并联(接线) parallel-series [series-parallel, multiple-series] connection
串罐无钟炉顶 【铁】serial type bell-less top bell-less top with two coaxial vertical hoppers
串激电动机 series(-wound) motor
串激发电机 series generator ◇ 反接～*
串级 cascade, cascading

串级电动机 (同"级联电动机")
串级叠置焊 cascade welding
串级连接 tandem connection
串级区段(电解槽的) cascade sections
串级式干燥炉 cascade drier
串接 cascade connection
串接线图 boosting coil
串联 series (connection), connection in series, cascade (connection), concatenation, tandem connection
串联布置(酸洗槽的) cascade
串联传动(双电动机的) tandem drive
串联萃取 crosscurrent extraction
串联电弧炉 series arc furnace
串联(电解)精炼 series refining ◇ 铜~*
串联电解精炼系统 series system of refining
串联电路 series circuit
串联电阻器 series resistor ◇ 控制板~ gate series resistor
串联法 series process
串联复式汽轮机 tandem compound machine
串联鼓风机 tandem blower engine
串联集中差速传动系统 tandem centralized differential transmission system
串联加热装置 serial heating device
串联拉管 tandem tube drawing
串联流化床 fluid bed in series
串联绕法[绕组] series winding
串联溶解器(串联电解溶解器) series dissolver
串联水口 (同"巴格纳尔－贝瑟尔水口")
串联调径文氏管洗涤器 【铁】serial slit-adjustable Venturi scrubber
串联系统(酸洗槽的) cascading system
串联谐振 voltage resonance
串联圆筒 tandem-drum
串料污染(合金料的) cross contamination
串列布置 tandem

串列(粗轧)－横列(精轧)联合式轧机 【压】combination mill
串列多弧焊 tandem welding
串列连续式轧机 tandem continuous mill
串列汽轮机[透平] tandem turbine
串列湿拉机 wet tandem drawing machine
串列(式)薄板轧机 tandem sheet mill
串列式布置(轧机机座的) train in train, straight-away setup
串列式带材冷轧机 tandem cold strip mill
串列式镀锡薄钢板轧机 tandem tin-plate mill
串列式(多次)拉拔机 tandem-drawing machine
串列(式)冷轧机 tandem cold (reduction) mill, cold tandem mill ◇ 五机架~*
串列式捻股机 tandem stranding machine
串列式(盘条轧机)机组 straight-away stands
串列式喷嘴气切器 separate nozzle gas cutter
串列式(小型型钢)轧机 straight-away mill
串列式轧机 tandem mill
串列轧机机组 tandem rolling mill train
串扰 【电】crosstalk
串扰电流 crossfire
串箱造型 stack moulding
串行操作 【计】serial operation
串行计算机 serial computer
串行数字计算机 serial digital computer
串行运算 【计】serial arithmetic
串音 【电】crosstalk
串铸(用一铸模同时铸造几个零件) pattern grouping
串注浇口 vertical gate
窗 window ◇ 伯尼尔[大钢]~ Berner's window
窗孔 orifice, iris
窗口 window, aperture, hatch, wicket
窗口材料(X射线管的) window material
窗框钢 casement sections, sash bar, win-

dow sash section
窗台　windowsill, ledge
床(层)　bed
床层高度　bed depth, height of bed
床层空隙率(流态床的)　bed voidage
床层密度　bed density
床层膨胀[增涨]　bed expansion
床层稀释剂　(同"料层稀释剂")
床架防护罩　bed guard
床焦　bed coke
床面　【冶】bed surface,【选】deck(摇床的)
床身　bed, body ◇ 下凹～gap bed
床式电阻炉　resistive-hearth furnace
床式炉　hearth furnace, hearth type (smelting) furnace
床式(配)料场　【冶】bedding type stockyard
床头　【机】headstock
创办投资　【企】initial investment
创设费用　establishment charges
吹氨(法)　ammonia blowing
吹玻璃　glassblowing
吹出　blow out, blow over (流态化技术的)
吹出炉尘　flue dust blowout
吹除喷嘴　blow off nozzle
吹风　air blast [blowing]
吹风管　blow out pipe
吹风冷却　forced air cooling
吹风期　blow-period, change on blast
吹风气　air gas
吹风式干湿球湿度计　aspiration psychrometer
吹风氧化　aerial oxidation
吹干　weather
吹管　blowpipe, (air) lance, burner, torch
吹管分析(鉴定矿物的定性分析)　blow pipe analysis
吹管焊　torch welding
吹管机　bulb-blowing machine
吹管试金[试验]　blow pipe assay
吹管头　blow pipe head,【铁】top of lance

吹管焰　blow pipe flame
吹管硬钎焊(铜焊)　torch brazing (TB)
吹弧　【电】blow
吹弧式断路器　air blast breaker (ABB)
吹灰熔炼　【色】drip melting
吹净(型腔的)　blowing off
吹冷　blast cold
吹炼　blowing, converting, blasting, air refining ◇ 低温～blow cold, 空气～*, 连续～*, 两转炉同时～*, 优先[选择]～(法) selective converting, 氧气～oxygen blowing
吹炼半成品(转炉的)　【钢】blown metal
吹炼车间　【冶】converter mill ◇ 铜～*
吹炼次数　【冶】number of blows
吹炼法　【冶】blowing practice, converting process ◇ 复合～*
吹炼工　blower
吹炼鼓风容量　volume of blast blown
吹炼过程　【冶】blowing [converting] process
吹炼剂(空气、氧气等)　blowing agent
吹炼间歇时间　【冶】time between blows
吹炼角　blowing angle
吹炼金属　blown metal
吹炼金属中的铁收得率　【钢】iron yield to brown metal
吹炼炉　【冶】converting furnace
吹炼炉炉渣　converting furnace slag
吹炼期　blowing period
吹炼燃料(转炉炼钢用的碳化钙、碳化硅等)　in-process fuel
吹炼时间　【冶】blowing [heat] time, time of blowing
吹炼条件　blowing condition
吹炼铁水　blown iron
吹炼铁损　loss of iron by blowing
吹炼脱气　【冶】jet degassing
吹炼位置　【冶】blowing position
吹炼温度　【冶】converting temperature
吹炼终点　blowing end point
吹凉　【冶】blast cold

吹炉 【冶】(blown) converter ◇ 固定式～*,竖式～*,卧式～*
吹炉锍[冰铜] Bessemer matte
吹炉炉衬 converter lining
吹落 blow down [off]
吹落风流 snap blow
吹气 gassing, blowing
吹气法(热镀锌的) jet-process
吹气鼓胀成型 【压】blow forming
吹气沥青 (air-)blown asphalt
吹入 blow in
吹入石灰(向转炉内) lime injection
吹扫(砂尘) 【铸】air lancing
吹扫室 blow off cabinet
吹扫用气体 【焦】purge gas
吹扫装置 blow off device
吹砂 blow sand, sand blowing, aerate (铸工的)
吹砂板(吹砂机的) 【铸】blow plate
吹砂机制泥芯 【铸】core blowing, air-blown core
吹砂造型 【铸】blow moulding
吹砂造型机 blow [blast] gun, mould blower
吹砂装置 sand-aerating apparatus
吹石灰粉氧气顶吹转炉 LD-AC converter
吹刷管 scavenge trunk
吹填土(堤) dredger fill
吹透 【铁】blow through
吹洗[刷] blow(ing)
吹洗[刷]喷嘴 sootblower nozzle
吹洗用空气 purging air
吹洗装置 【机】purger
吹芯板 【铸】blow plate
吹芯机 【铸】core blower, core blowing machine ◇ 热芯盒～ hot box core blower,台式～ bench blower,筒形台式～*
吹芯装置 core-blowing installation
吹氩 argon blowing [injection]
吹氩除气 【钢】argon purge ◇ 多孔塞～法*

吹氩处理(钢液的) argon rinsing
吹氩钢包 argon-stirred ladle
吹氩搅拌 【钢】argon-stirring ◇ 顶渣～ top-slag Ar bubbling
吹氩搅拌熔体 argon-stirred melt
吹氩清扫 argon purge
吹氩设备[装置] 【冶】purger
吹氩站 argon flushing station
吹氧 【冶】blowing [blast] oxygen, oxygen blast [injection], 【钢】(oxygen) lancing, jetting ◇ 炉顶～ roof lancing, 熔池～ bath lancing
吹氧管 (同"氧枪")
吹氧精炼钢 oxygen-refined steel
吹氧开口 oxygen tapping
吹氧炼钢法 oxygen jet steelmaking
吹氧炼钢转炉 oxygen-blown steelmaking vessel
吹氧切割弧 oxyarc
吹氧时间 oxygen-lancing time
吹氧速率 【钢】rate of lancing
吹氧转炉 oxygen-blown converter
吹氧转炉车间 BOF [LD] plant
吹制沥青 blown asphalt [bitumen], air-blown asphalt
捶薄 batter
锤 hammer, beater
锤把 dash
锤锻 hammer (forging, smith)
锤锻机 【压】hammering machine, impact hammer, swager
锤锻硬化的 【压】hammer-hardened
锤锻硬化法 【压】hammer-hardening method [process, technique]
锤锻作用 smithing action
锤击 ramming, hammer blow, bumping
锤击布氏硬度测定法 double impression method
锤击机 ram impact machine, ram(ming) machine
锤击式钻岩机 plugger
锤击试验 hammer [forging] test

锤击效应　peening effect
锤击硬化　【压】over-peening, hardening by hammer
锤击硬化处理(表面的)　hammer peening
锤击硬化法　hammer-hardening method [process, technique]
锤击展薄　beating
锤挤铁渣　【冶】hammer slag
锤架　【压】hammer carrier [frame]
锤面　face of hammer, hammer face
锤磨[碎]　hammer-milling
锤磨机　hammer mill
锤平　beat, 【机】drawdown, 【压】mushroom
锤式破碎机　hammer crusher [breaker, mill]
锤碎机　impact crusher ◇ 单转子~*
锤体　ram, 【压】hammer block
锤头　hammer head [top, ram], striker, nozzling, point tool, 【压】tup ◇ 管端~压力机*
锤头冲击机　【压】hammer impact machine
锤头返回活塞(可控式高速锤的)　ram-retraction piston
锤头烙铁　hammer-headed soldering iron
锤头内架[锤-架]式高速锤　ram-and-inner-frame machine
锤展金属　bossing
锤砧　【压】hammer anvil
垂弛　sag
垂锤　sinker weight
垂度　sag, sagitta, deflection, bilge, dip, 【压】(带钢的)catenary, catenarian ◇ 检验墙身~boning, 绝对~absolute deflection
垂拱　drop [blunt] arch
垂丝状动胶菌　zoogloea filipendula
垂线　(同"垂直线")
垂直摆动取样器　vertical-swing sampler
垂直摆锻锤头　vertical (forming) shoes
垂直磁化(强度)　【理】perpendicular magnetization

垂直电磁浇注　vertical electromagnetic casting (VEMC)
垂直锭料(区域熔炼)　vertical ingot
垂直度　verticality, perpendicularity, squareness
垂直发散[垂直散度]　vertical divergence
垂直发散喷嘴扩散泵　vertical divergent-nozzle pump
垂直分力　【理】vertical component
垂直敷设(电缆的)　vertical run
垂直负荷[荷载]　vertical [normal] load
垂直钢筋[蹬筋]　vertical stirrup
垂直供热的均热炉　vertically fired pit
垂直管道　uptake
垂直合力　vertical resultant
垂直机架　vertical stand
垂直极化波　vertically polarized wave
垂直浇口　【钢】tedge
垂直截面　vertical (cross-)section
垂直可动结晶器[可动模]　【钢】vertically movable mould
垂直拉晶技术　vertical pulling technique
垂直溜槽　straight chute
垂直膨胀　vertical expansion
垂直偏析　vertical segregation
垂直切割　vertical cutting
垂直切削　two dimensional cutting, orthogonal-cutting
垂直区域精炼　vertical zone refining
垂直区域提纯　vertical zone refining
垂直入射　normal [perpendicular] incidence
垂直烧结速度　vertical sintering speed
垂直烧嘴　vertical burner
垂直射束探伤法(用超声波)　straight beam method
垂直-水平(的)　vertical-horizontal(VH)
垂直-水平式料罐上料卷扬机　【铁】vertical and horizontal type charging hoist
垂直速度　vertical velocity
垂直调整(轧辊的)　vertical adjustment
垂直跳动辊　vertical dancer-roll

垂直位错壁　vertical walls of dislocations
垂直位移　vertical displacement [shift]
垂直线　vertical [perpendicular] line, catenary, catenarian
垂直线检测摆动辊　catenary detecting swing roll
垂直压力　vertical pressure [compression]
垂直压力降　vertical pressure drop
垂直压下(轧制的)　direct rolling action ◇板坯的～*
垂直烟道　vertical flue
垂直移动带材备用量(机组作业线上的)　vertical strip storage
垂直应力　normal stress
垂直运动　vertical movement [motion]
垂直照明　vertical illumination
垂直蒸汽喷射煤粉燃烧器　vertical steam aspirated coal burner
垂直轴(线)　vertical [normal] axis
垂重　sinker weight
醇化(作用)　alcoholization
醇醚　alcohol ether
醇醛　alcohol aldehyde, hydroxyaldehyde
醇酸树脂　alkyd resin
醇酸树脂漆　alkyd varnish, alkyd resin coating
醇亚铊{TlOR}　thallium alcoholate
醇盐　alcoholate, alkoxide
唇形浇口　【铸】lip feeder, connor gate
唇注包[桶]　【冶】lip-pour ladle
纯白口冷硬轧辊　【压】clear chill roll
纯半导体　pure [intrinsic] semiconductor
纯冰晶石　pure cryolite
纯产品　straight [net] product
纯赤铁矿　pure hematite
纯磁性相互作用　purely magnetic interaction
纯粹培养　pure culture
纯电池　pure cell
纯电阻　active resistance
纯度　(degree of) purity, fineness, rate of purity, fine(金银的), hallmark(金银的)
纯度等级　order of purity
纯度要求　purity requirement
纯沸腾　【钢】quiescent-boil
纯沸腾期　quiescent period
纯橄榄石　dunite
纯铬钢(铬不锈钢)　straight chromium steel
纯焊锡(Al:Sn=1:2)　fine solder
纯化磁铁　purity magnet
纯化方法　purification method
纯化剂　purifying agent
纯碱{Na$_2$CO$_3$}　sodium carbonate, soda(-ash)
纯碱灰　calcined soda
纯剪切(变形)　【压】pure shear
纯金　fine [refined, virgin] gold, proof gold (试金用)
纯金属　pure [fine, simple] metal
纯金属粉末　pure [elemental] metal powder
纯晶体　pure crystal
纯净萃　absolute extract
纯净钢　purity steel
纯净矿石　clean ore
纯净物料[原材料]　【铸】virgin material
纯酒精[乙醇]　straight alcohol
纯利　net profit
纯硫　bright sulphur
纯硫化物　simple sulphide
纯硫酸钴溶液　pure cobalt sulphate solution
纯硫酸盐电解液　all-sulphate electrolyte
纯铝　pure aluminium
纯铝土矿　wochernite
纯螺型位错　pure screw dislocation
纯煤　pure [super] coal
纯镁质硅酸镍矿　pure true garnierite ore
纯木煤　anthraxylon
纯黏滞流　purely viscous flow
纯黏滞流动　【理】Newtonian flow
纯氢　pure hydrogen
纯砂粒(无黏结剂的)　sharp sand

纯闪锌矿　cleiophane
纯射流放大器　pure fluid amplifier
纯石灰[纯氧化钙]　carbonate free lime
纯石灰石　straight limestone
纯始料法(区域熔炼)　starting-charge-only method
纯收入　net income
纯水　pure water
纯水泥混凝土　straight cement concrete
纯碳化钨-钴[纯钴钨硬质合金]制品　simple tungsten carbide-cobalt composition
纯锑　star antimony
纯体积　true volume
纯铁　pure iron ◇ P2覆铝~板*,阿姆柯~Armco steel,玻密特烧结~Powet,电铸电工~板*
纯铁粉　straight iron powder
纯铁粉烧结材料　pomet
纯铁素体基体(生铁的)　【金】all ferrite matrix
纯铁体　【金】ferroferrite
纯铁铜合金　plain iron-copper alloy
纯铜　pure copper ◇ 电积~薄片*
纯铜点阵[晶格]参数　pure copper lattice parameter
纯铜始极片　pure copper starting sheet
纯铜锡合金　straight copper tin alloy
纯弯曲　pure bend
纯氧吹炼时位置(氧气转炉的)　【钢】refining position
纯氧顶吹转炉　(同"氧气顶吹转炉")
纯氧化铝　pure alumina, pure aluminium oxide
纯氧喷吹　pure oxygen injection
纯益　net profit [gain]
纯银(纯度大于99.9%)　fine silver, proof silver(试金用)
纯应力　pure stress
纯轧时间　time in rolls
纯珠光体基体(生铁的)　【金】all-pearlite matrix

纯组元X射线衍射花样　【理】pure-component pattern
疵(点)　fault, flaw, defect
疵砂(铸件缺陷)　embedded grit
磁棒　bar magnet
磁薄膜　(同"磁膜")
磁饱和　magnetic saturation
磁饱和放大器　regulex
磁饱和曲线　magnetic saturation curve
磁饱和铁心　saturated core
磁爆(吹弧)型断路器　magnetic blast type circuit breaker
磁北　magnetic north (MN)
磁变计　(magnetic) variodencer
磁波　magnetic wave
磁补偿合金　magnetic compensating [shunt] alloy ◇ MS~*
磁测厚计　magnetic thickness ga(u)ge
磁测量　【理】magnetic measurement
磁场　(magnetic) field, magnet space ◇ 合量~*, 环形~*
磁场变阻器　field rheostat
磁场成型　(同"磁场中压制")
磁场成型用插入件　field shaping insert
磁场储能焊接机　(同《磁力焊接机》)
磁场磁极　field pole
磁场磁通密度　field density
磁场电效应　galvanomagnetic effect
磁场(电)源　magnetic field source
磁场发生器　magnetic field generator
磁场反向　field reverse
磁场分布　magnetic field distribution
磁场分量　magnetic field component
磁场关系　magnetic field dependence
磁场焊　magnetic force welding
磁场计　magnetic field meter
磁场接地继电器　field ground relay
磁场经济接触器　field economy contactor
磁场绝缘　field insulation
磁场开关　field switch
磁场控制　field control
磁场扭变　distortion of field

磁场强度　magnetic field intensity [strength], magnetic intensity
磁场(强度)差异探测器　field difference probe
磁场热压(在磁场中加热压制)　heated magnetic field pressing
磁场失效继电器　field failure relay
磁场调节器　field regulator
磁场铁心　field core
磁场退火　magnetic anneal(ing)
磁场消失检测器　field loss detector
磁场形变热处理　thermo magnetic mechanical treatment
磁场蓄能(式)焊接　magnetic energy-storage welding, magnetic discharge welding
磁场造型器　field shaper
磁场指示器　field indicator
磁场中冷却　magnetic field cooling
磁场中退火　magnetic field annealing
磁场(中)压制　【粉】magnetic (field) pressing, pressing in magnetic field
磁常数　magnetic constant
磁弛豫　magnetic relaxation
磁赤铁矿　maghemite
磁斥力　magnetic repulsion
磁畴　【理】(magnetic) domain ◇ 闭合[环状]～ closure domain, 泡状～ bubble domain, 巴克豪森～陡变*, 韦斯～ Weiss domain
磁畴壁[边界]　(magnetic) domain wall, magnetic wall
磁畴壁能　domain wall energy
磁畴壁运动　domain wall motion [movement]
磁畴磁化(强度)　domain magnetization
磁畴结构　(magnetic) domain structure
磁畴理论　(magnetic) domain theory
磁畴图(像)　domain pattern ◇ 毕特～ Bitter pattern
磁畴图形法　magnetic domain pattern method
磁吹空气断路器　magnetic blow-out (air) circuit breaker
磁吹灭弧线圈　blow out coil
磁吹熔断器　magnetic blow-out fuse
磁吹熄弧　magnetic blow(out) [quenching]
磁锤(电磁成形的线圈)　magnetic hammer
磁存储材料　magnetic memory material
磁存储器　magnetic memory [storage]
磁存储因数　magnetic storage factor
磁带　(magnetic) tape ◇ 录音～*, 整盘～ magnetic tape reel
磁带存储(器)　magnetic tape storage ◇ 数字～ digital tape storage
磁带机　magnetic tape handler [station]
磁带录音　magnetic recording
磁带录音机　magnetic [tap] recorder, magnetophone
磁带盘　reel
磁带起始工作点　tape load-point
磁带清除　tape erasure
磁带驱动设备　【计】tape driver
磁带设备　【计】tape unit
磁带文件　【计】magnetic tape file
磁带转接部件　【计】magnetic tape switching unit
磁单元　【计】magnetic cell
磁导(磁阻倒数)　magnetic conductance, permeance
磁导率　(同"导磁率")
磁导(率)计[磁导仪]　【理】permeability meter, magnetic conductance meter, permeameter, ferrometer
磁道　【计】magnetic track ◇ 同位标～组【计】cylinder
磁等离子体动力学的　magnetoplasmadynamic
磁点阵　magnetic lattice
磁电式电流计　D'Arsonval galvanometer
磁电性　magnetoelectricity
磁电子　magnetic electron
磁电子透镜　magnetic electron lens

磁动力学 magnetodynamics
磁动势 magnetomotive force (M.M.F., mmf)
磁动态[磁动力学的] magnetodynamic
磁轭 (magnet) yoke ◇ 分层～laminated yoke
磁轭(磁化)法 yoke magnetizing method
磁阀架 magnet valve stand
磁法 magnetic method
磁法测定 (同"磁测量")
磁防护 magnetic protection
磁放大器 magnetic amplifier, magamp, transductor ◇ 带～的调节器 magnetic amplifier regulator, 自反馈式～amplistat
磁放大器调节器 transductor regulator
磁分流器 magnetic shunt
磁分路合金 magnetic shunt alloy ◇ MS ～*
磁分析法 magnetic analysis
磁粉 magnetic particle [powder]
磁粉法 magnetic powder method
磁粉过滤器 magnetic particle filter
磁粉检验[探伤,检查] MP (magnetic particle) inspection, magnetic powder inspection, magnaflux examination [test(ing), inspection], magnetic flaw detection ◇ 马格纳格罗～用粉末 Magnaglo, 荧光～*
磁粉检验[探伤]法 magnetic particle (inspection) method, magnetic powder method, magnaflux (method, process), magnetic flaw-detection (method), magnetographic inspection, magnetography ◇ 极间～*
磁粉熔剂 magnetic powdered flux
磁粉剩余显示法(磁粉检验的) residual method
磁粉探伤技术 magnetic powder technique
磁粉探伤[探测缺陷]显示 magnetic particle inspection flaw indications
磁粉探伤仪 magnetic crack [flaw] detector

磁粉探伤原理 principle of magnaflux inspection
磁粉特征图像 magnetic character figure
磁粉图样 【理】magnetic powder pattern
磁感循环真空脱气法 【钢】circulation by induction degassing
磁感(应) magnetic induction ◇ 标准～曲线*
磁感应场 magnetic field of induction
磁感应分量 magnetic induction component
磁感应高斯量 【理】gaussage
磁感应流量计 magnetic induction flowmeter
磁感应强度 magnetic flux density ◇ 气隙～gap density
磁感应系数 coefficient of magnetic induction
磁刚性[度] 【理】magnetic rigidity
磁钢 magnet(ic) steel, steel magnet ◇ KS～*, TK～*, 本多～Honda steel, 科斯特尔铁钴钼[钨]～*, 铸造～cast steel magnet
磁各向异性 magnetic anisotropy ◇ 轧制诱致～*
磁各向异性常数 magnetic anisotropy constant
磁功率因数(磁损失角的余弦) magnetic power factor
磁共振 magnetic resonance
磁鼓 【计】magnetic drum (MD)
磁鼓标志 drum mark
磁鼓存储器 (magnetic) drum memory, drum storage
磁鼓等待时间 drum latency time
磁鼓分类器 drum sorter
磁鼓控制器(计算机的) drum controller
磁鼓奇偶校验 drum parity
磁光效应 magnetooptic(al) effect ◇ 克尔～*, 能带间～*
磁光学 magneto-optics
磁辊布料 magnetic rolling feeder system

磁耗因数	magnetic dissipation factor
磁后效(现象)	【理】magnetic aftereffect [creep]
磁化	magnetization, magnetizing ◇ 净[基本]~(强度) net magnetization, 可[能]~的 magnetizable, 可~性*, 难~方向*, 剩余~*, 预(先)~ premagnetization, 最易~方向*
磁化焙烧	magnetic [magnetizing] roast(ing)
磁化场	magnetizing field
磁化电流	magnetizing current ◇ 半波整流~*, 交流~*
磁化方向	direction of magnetization
磁化节油器	magnetizing economizer
磁化力	magnetizing force ◇ 表观增量~*, 空气隙~*
磁化率[系数]	(magnetic) susceptibility ◇ 整体~ bulk susceptibility
磁化能(量)	energy of magnetization
磁化能力	magnetizability
磁化器	magnetizer
磁化强度	magnetic intensity, (intensity of) magnetization
磁化曲线	magnetization curve, curve of magnetization, B-H [H-B] curve ◇ 非滞后~*, 基本~*, 塑性变形过程~*
磁化绕组	magnetizing winding ◇ 辅助~ bias winding
磁化热	heat of magnetization
磁化特性(曲线)	magnetization characteristic
磁化线圈	magnetizing coil
磁化学	magneto chemistry
磁化循环	cycle of magnetization, magnetic cycle
磁化滞后	magnetic lag, lag in magnetization
磁化装置	magnetic charger, magnetizer
磁化状态	magnetized condition
磁化作用	magnetization ◇ 交变[反复]~*, 逆平行~*, 循环~*, 直流~*
磁黄铁矿	magnetic pyrite, magnetopyrite, pyrrhotite ◇ 低镍~精矿*
磁机械效应	magneto-mechanical effect
磁机械阻尼	magneto-mechanical damping
磁极	(magnetic) pole ◇ 随机[偶然]~*
磁极化	magnetic polarization
磁极间隙	magnet gap
磁极片	pole piece
磁极强度	magnetic pole strength
磁极性	magnetic polarity
磁计数器	magnetic counter
磁记录	【计】magnetic recording
磁记录带	magnetic recording tape
磁搅弧热真空精炼炉	【钢】ladle furnace, furnace ladle
磁校准	magnetic alignment
磁接触器	magnetic contactor
磁接触印记	magnetic writing
磁结构	magnetic structure
磁结构分析	magnetic structure analysis ◇ 中子衍射法~*
磁金属铁	magnetic metallic iron
磁晶(体)	magnetocrystalline
磁晶各向异性	magnetocrystalline anisotropy
磁晶粒取向	magnetic grain orientation
磁矩	magnetic moment [torque]
磁聚焦	magnetic focusing
磁卡盘	magnetic holding device
磁卡片	【计】magnetic card
磁卡片存储器	magnetic card memory [storage]
磁卡效应	magnetocaloric effect
磁控(电子)管	magnetron, permatron
磁控溅射(法)	magnetic control sputtering
磁框	magnet frame
磁拉法	magnetic pulling method
磁力	magnetic [electromagnetic] force, magnetism, magnet power
磁力测定	magnetometric measurement, magnetometry ◇ 萨克史密斯~天平

Suck smith's balance
磁力成形　magnetic forming
磁力成形机　magnetic forming machine
磁力(成形)技术　magnetic (forming) technique
磁力成形器　field shaper
磁力吊车式分垛机　magnet-crane depiler
磁力垛板机　magnetic sheet piler [bandler], magnetic positioner
磁力翻(板)坯吊车(修整时用)　magnet [slab-turning] crane
磁力仿形轮(主动机构的)　magnetic tracing wheel
磁力放矿槽　【采】magnetic chute
磁力分离　magnetic separation
磁力分离器　magnetic separator ◇ 辊式～[分选机]*
磁力分析　magnetic analysis
磁力分选机　magnetic grader
磁力跟踪装置(切割用)　【焊】magnetic tracing device
磁力辊　magnet(ic) roll
磁力焊　magnetic welding
磁力焊接机　magnetic welding machine
磁力加料抓手　magnetic loading gripper
磁力检验[探伤]　(同"磁粉检验")
磁力搅拌　magnetic stirring
磁力搅拌效果　magnetic stirring effect
磁力接触器　magnetic contactor ◇ 交流～*, 直流～*
磁力金属比测仪　metal comparater
磁力开关　magnetic switch
磁力拉晶法　magnetic puller technique
磁力离合器　magnetic clutch [gear]
磁力-流体动力分离　【选】magnetic-hydrodynamic separation
磁力启动器　magnetic starter
磁力起重机　(同"电磁起重机")
磁力书写[记录]　magnetic writing
磁力提升装置　magnetic lifting device
磁力天平　magnetic balance
磁力熄弧　arc magnetism

磁力线　magnetic lines of force, lines of magnetic force
磁力线图　magnetic character figure
磁力线图　magnetic character figure
磁力形变热处理　thermo-magnetic-mechanical treatment (T.M.M.T.)
磁力絮凝　magnetic flocculation
磁力悬浮熔炼(用磁场加热和搅拌熔炼金属)　levitation melting
磁力选矿　(同"磁选")
磁力学　magnetomechanics
磁力循环　magnetic circulation
磁力运输(分垛)机　magnetic conveyer
磁力制动(器)　magnetic brake
磁力自卸起重机[吊车]　magnet-clamshell crane
磁量子数　magnetic (quantum) number
磁硫铁矿　pyrrhotite ◇ 含镍～*
磁流　magnetic flow [current, stream]
磁流体动力分选[离]　magnetic-hydrodynamic separation
磁流体动力学　magnetohydrodynamics (MHD)
磁流体(动)力学现象　magnetohydrodynamic phenomena
磁流体动能变换[转换,发电]　magnetohydrodynamic energy conversion
磁流体力学搅拌器　magnetohydrodynamic stirrer
磁漏系数　(magnetic-)leakage coefficient
磁路　magnetic path [circuit], iron circuit (铁心的)
磁路不连续性(有气隙)　magnetic discontinuity
磁路长度　flux path length
磁路中空气间隙　magnet gap
磁轮　magnetic pulley
磁脉冲　magnetic-pulse ◇ 形成～的扁平线圈 flat (magnetic pulse forming) coil
磁脉冲成形　【压】magnetic-pulse forming, electromagnetic forming
磁脉冲(成形)法　【压】magnetic-pulse

磁脉冲模冲压工艺 magneform process
磁锰铁矿 garividite, vredenburgite
磁膜 【计】magnetic (thin) film
磁膜存储器 【计】magnetic film memory
磁墨水 【计】magnetic ink
磁墨水扫描器 magnetic ink scanner
磁墨水字符 magnetic (ink) character
磁墨水字符分类机 magnetic ink character sorter
磁墨水字符识别 magnetic ink character recognition (MICR)
磁能 magnetic energy, magnet power
磁能积 energy product
磁能积曲线 magnetic energy-product curve
磁能级 magnetic (energy) level
磁黏性 magnetic viscosity
磁欧姆(磁阻单位) magnetic ohm
磁耦合 magnetic coupling
磁偶 magnetic couple
磁偶极矩 magnetic dipole moment
磁偶极子 magnetic dipole
磁盘 【计】(magnetic) disk [disc] ◇ 活动臂～moving arm disk
磁盘操作系统 disk operating system (DOS)
磁盘存储模件 disk storage module
磁盘存储(器) disk memory [storage], magnetic disc memory
磁盘存取 disk access
磁盘吊车 (同"电磁起重机")
磁盘分类程序 disk sorting
磁盘文件 disk file
磁盘文件访问 disk file addressing
磁盘文件索引 disk file index
磁盘组 disk pack
磁泡 (magnetic) bubble, 【理】bubble domain
磁泡存储器 【计】bubble memory, magnetic bubble storage
磁偏计 declinometer
磁偏角 (magnetic) declination
磁偏转系统 magnet yoke, magnetic deflection system
磁品质因数 magnetic figure of merit
磁屏 magnetic protection
磁屏蔽 magnetic shield(ing), screen(ing)
磁谱 magnetic spectrum
磁谱学 magnetic spectroscopy
磁铅石(一种高矫顽力材料) magnetoplumbite
磁强(度) magnetic strength, intensity of magnetism ◇ 测～术 magnetometry
磁强计 magnetometer, Gaussmeter ◇ 摆式～*, (飞)机用～*, 平衡～*
磁强(自动)记录仪 magnetograph
磁倾角 (angle of) dip, magnetic angle
磁扰动 magnetic perturbation [disturbance]
磁热效应 magnetothermal [magnetocaloric] effect
磁筛过滤器 magnet screen filter
磁摄谱仪 magnetic spectrograph [spectrometer]
磁声技术 magnetoacoustic technique
磁声效应 magnetoacoustic effect
磁石 magnet ◇ 棒形～bar magnet
磁石发电机 magneto, inductor
磁石扩音器 magnetophone
磁时效 (同"磁性时效")
磁矢量 magnetic vector
磁势[位] magnetic potential
磁势[位]差 magnetic potential difference
磁数 magnetic number
磁松弛 magnetic relaxation
磁损(失) magnetic loss
磁损失角 magnetic loss angle
磁弹性 (同"磁致弹性")
磁探针 magnetic probe
磁体 magnet, magnetic body, 【计】core bank
磁体框架 magnet frame
磁体媒质 magnetic medium

磁 ci

磁体强度　strength of magnet
磁条(会计)计算机　magnetic strip accounting machine
磁条文件　【计】magnetic strip file
磁调准　magnetic alignment
磁铁　magnet (iron), magnetic iron ◇ C形~ C magnet, 粉冶[金属粉末制]~ metal-powder magnet, 复合~*, 各向异性~*, 马蹄形[U形]~*, 烧结~ sintered magnet, 烧结氧化物~ ceramic magnet, 伸长单畴(微粒)[ESD]~*, 树胶~*, 特罗模莱特~ Tromolite (magnet), 天然~*, 新提科纳尔~*, 悬挂[吊]~ suspended magnet, 尤尼科拉姆单向柱状晶粒~ Unicolumn magnet, 铸造~ cast magnet, 组合式~ composite magnet
磁铁[石]电铃　magneto bell
磁铁粉　magnet powder, magnetic iron powder, powder magnet
磁铁钴矿　manaccanite
磁铁矿{Fe_3O_4}　magnetite, magnetic [black, octahedral] iron ore, magnetic ore, 【采】ferriferous [ferous-ferric] oxide ◇ 立方尖晶石型~*
磁铁矿床　magnetite deposit
磁铁矿结圈【团】 magnetite ring
磁铁(矿)精矿　magnetite concentrate
磁铁矿球团[生球]【团】 magnetite ball
磁铁矿砂　magnetite sand
磁铁铅矿　magnetoplumbite
磁铁-树脂制品　magnet-resin composition
磁铁锑矿　magnetostibian
磁铁芯　magnetic core
磁铁制品　magnet(ic) product [systems]
磁铁柱　magnet pillar
磁铁组　magnet bank
磁通　【电】flux, magnetic flow
磁通程长度　flux path length
磁通集中器(电磁成形用)　flux-concentrator
磁通计　fluxmeter, maxwellmeter
磁通检验　magnetic flow test
磁通量　magnetic flux [current], magnaflux
磁通量穿透深度　flux penetration
磁通量贯穿　magnetic flux penetration
磁通量集中　magnetic flux concentration
磁通量量子　fluxoid quantum
磁通(量)密度　(magnetic) flux density
磁通路径　magnetic path
磁通势　(同"磁动势")
磁通线　flux line, line of magnetic flux
磁通匝连数　flux linkage ◇ 互感~ mutual flux linkage
磁头　(magnetic) head ◇ 录声~*
磁头缝隙　head gap
磁头组　【计】head stack
磁透镜　magnetic lens
磁透镜成像　magnetic image
磁位移　magnetic displacement
磁温度系数　magnetic temperature coefficient
磁稳定　maturing
磁稳定性　magnetic stability
磁无序态　magnetic disordered state
磁无序(现象)　magnetic disorder
磁吸引　(同"磁引力")
磁系　magnet(ic) system
磁线存储器　【计】magnetic wire storage
磁相互作用　magnetic interaction
磁像检验　magnetographic inspection
磁效应　magnetic effect
磁谐振　magnetic resonance
磁心　magnetic core
磁心板　core plane
磁心材料　(magnetic) core material
磁心存储(器)　【计】(magnetic) core memory [storage] ◇ 大容量~*
磁心矩阵　【计】core array [matrix]
磁心体　core stack
磁心映像　【计】core image
磁心映像库　【计】core image library

磁性　magnetism, magnetic property [performance] ◇ 电弧~【电】arc magnetism, 无[非]~的 non-magnetic
磁性变化　（同"磁性转变"）◇ A2 转变温度区域内的~*
磁性变形　magnetic deformation
磁性材料　magnetic material [medium], magnetics ◇ 海坡姆~(总称) Hyperm
磁性材料化学　magneto chemistry
磁性测定计　permagnag
磁性淬火试验　magnetic quench test
磁性点火装置　magnetic firing assembly
磁性镀层　magnetic coating
磁性(镀层)测厚仪　magnetic thickness tester
磁性粉末　magnetic powder ◇ 马格纳格罗~Magnaglo
磁性附着　magnetic adherence
磁性钢丝　magnetic wire ◇ 福美克斯~*
磁性膏　【理】magnetic paste
磁性过滤　magnetic filtration
磁性过滤器　magnetic filter
磁性焊剂　magnetic flux
磁性焊剂电弧焊　magnetic flux arc welding ◇ 气体保护~*
磁性焊剂二氧化碳气体保护焊接(法)　Unionarc welding
磁性焊剂焊　magnetic flux welding
磁性焊剂气电焊　magnetic-flux gas-shielded welding
磁性合金　magnetic alloy ◇ MSO 铁镍系~*, 海珀廷~Hipertin
磁性记录[录音]带　magnetic recording tape
磁性检验[探伤]　magnetic inspection [test(ing)] ◇ 圆棒电极~法 prod method
磁性介[媒]质　magnetic medium
磁性金属　magnetic metal
磁性金属玻璃　magnetic metal(lic) glass
磁性金属铁　magnetic metallic iron

磁性矿物　magnetic mineral
磁性颗粒　magnetic particle
磁性粒子探伤法　（同"磁粉探伤法"）
磁性联轴节　magnet coupling
磁性零件　magnetic parts
磁性流槽　magnetic chute
磁性硫化铁　mundic
磁性流体　magnetic liquid [fluid]
磁性-流体动力分选[分离]　【选】magnetic-hydrodynamic separation
磁性录音材料　magnetic sound recording material
磁性气体动力学　magnetogasdynamics
磁性强度　intensity of magnetism
磁性散射　magnetic scattering
磁性时效[退化]　magnetic ageing ◇ 不可逆~*
磁性铁氧体　magnetic ferrite
磁性铜合金(60Cu, 20Ni, 20Fe; 或 50Cu, 21Ni, 29Co)　copper magnet alloy
磁性涂层　magnetic coating
磁性位移传感器　magnetic displacement transducer
磁性物质　magnetic substance
磁性相互作用　magnetic interaction
磁性氧化保护层(钢铁氧化处理后形成的)　black oxide coating
磁性氧化铁{Fe_3O_4}　magnetic iron oxide, magnetic oxide iron
磁性氧化物　magnetic oxide
磁性氧化物压坯　【粉】oxide magnetic compact
磁性液体　magnetic liquid [fluid]
磁性荧光铁粉　Magnalite
磁性有序固体　【理】magnetically ordered solid
磁性有序化力　magnetic ordering force
磁性元件　magnetics, magnetic element
磁性原子　magnetic atom
磁(性)跃迁　magnetic transition ◇ 巴克豪森~Barkhausen jump(s)
磁性振摆　magnetic pendulum

磁性致密维氏体	magnetic dense Wuestite
磁性制品	magnetic product
磁性铸钢	magnetic cast steel (Mag. CS)
磁性铸铁	magnetic cast iron (Mag. CI)
磁性转变	magnetic transformation [change, transition]
磁性转变点	magnetic transformation [change] point, 【理】Curie point
磁性转变温度	magnetic transformation [transition] temperature, 【理】Curie temperature
磁性字符	(同"磁墨水字符")
磁悬法(区域熔炼)	magnetic suspension (method)
磁悬浮系统	magnetic suspension system
磁悬区域熔炼	magnetic suspension zone-melting
磁选	magnetic dressing [separation, concenration], preparation by magnetic separation ◇ 高梯度～*, 弱[低强度]～*
磁选厂	【选】magnetic ore-dressing plant
磁选富矿	magnetically separated ore
磁选机	magnetic separator [cobber], electromagnetic separator
磁选精矿	magnetic concentrate, magnetically separated ore
磁选尾矿	magnetic tailings
磁学	magnetics, magnetism
磁压	magnetic pressrue, flux volts
磁压效应	pinch effect
磁移	magnetic displacement
磁移位寄存器	magnetic shift register
磁引力	magnetic attraction [pull]
磁涌检验法(先强磁化,继用弱磁场借粉状铁磁物质检验)	surge method
磁优值	magnetic figure of merit
磁有序(化)	magnetic ordering
磁针罗盘	magnetic compass
磁振动器	magnetic vibrator
磁致等离子体	magnetoplasma
磁致电阻倍增器	magnetoresistor multiplier
磁致电阻率	magnetoresistivity
磁致机械滞后	magneto-mechanical hysteresis
磁致集[趋]肤效应	magnetic skin effect
磁致冷机	magnetic refrigerator
磁致冷却	magnetic cooling
磁致热效应	magnetocaloric effect
磁致伸长	magnetic elongation
磁致伸缩	magnetostriction, magnetoelasticity, magnetic deformation
磁致伸缩材料	magnetostriction [magnetostrictive] material
磁致伸缩常数	magnetostriction constant
磁致伸缩成穴[空化]试验装置	magnetostrictive cavitation test device
磁致伸缩传感器	magnetostrictive transducer
磁致伸缩合金	magnetostriction alloy ◇ 阿尔费尔铁铝～*
磁致伸缩能	magnetostrictive energy
磁致伸缩体	magnetostrictor
磁致伸缩现象	magnetic striction
磁致伸缩效应	magnetostriction [Wiedemann] effect
磁致伸缩性能	magnetostrictive property
磁致伸缩压力计	magnetostriction pressure gauge
磁致伸缩应变仪	magnetostriction strain gauge
磁致伸缩振荡器[振子]	magnetostrictive oscillator [vibrator], magnetostriction generator
磁致伸缩[弹性]滞后	magnetostriction hysteresis
磁致伸缩滞后回线	magnetostriction hysteresis loop
磁致弹性	magnetoelasticity, magnetoelastisity, magnetostriction
磁致弹性能量	magnetoelastic energy
磁致弹性效应	magnetoelastic effect ◇ 维拉里～ Villari effect
磁滞[磁(性)滞后]	【理】(magnetic) hys-

teresis, magnetic retardation [lag]
磁滞功率损失 【电】hysteresis power loss
磁滞后效光谱 spectrum of magnetic aftereffect
磁滞回路偏移范围 magnetic excursion range
磁滞回线 (magnetic) hysteresis loop, B-H loop ◇ 偏移～bias hysteresis loop
磁滞回线损失 hysteresis (loop) loss
磁滞计[(测定,检验)仪] hysteresimeter, hysteresis meter, hysteresigraph ◇ 爱泼斯坦～Epstein tester
磁滞角 (magnetic) hysteretic angle
磁滞曲线 hysteresis curve, B-H loop, ferrograph
磁滞曲线测定仪 ferrograph
磁滞曲线图 hysteresis graph
磁滞伸缩钢 hysteresis steel
磁滞(损耗)系数 hysteresis coefficient
磁滞特性 hysteresis characteristic
磁滞现象 (magnetic) hysteresis, hysteresis phenomenon
磁轴 magnetic axis
磁转鼓 (同"磁鼓")
磁子 magneton ◇ 玻尔～*
磁子午线 magnetic meridian
磁阻换能器 reluctance transducer
磁阻鉴质仪(钢材用) reluctometer
磁阻率[系数] reluctancy, reluctivity, magnetoresistance coefficient
磁阻尼 magnetic damping
磁阻(效应) magnetic resistance, magnetoresistance, (magnetic) reluctance
雌黄 {As$_2$S$_3$} orpiment, yellow arsenic
雌雄榫接合[接头] grooved and tongued joint
瓷杯 porcelain cup
瓷封合金 ceramic sealing alloy
瓷坩埚 porcelain [ceramic] crucible
瓷管 porcelain tubing
瓷夹配线 cleat wiring
瓷绝缘 ceramic type insulation

瓷瓶 (porcelain) insulator ◇ 蝴蝶～shackle insulator
瓷漆 enamel ◇ 上～enamel plating
瓷漆涂层 enamelled coating
瓷器 porcelain, china-ware
瓷器状断口 porcelanic fracture
瓷球磨机 porcelain ball mill
瓷烧箱 【粉】ceramic sagger
瓷(烧)舟 porcelain boat
瓷土 {Al$_2$O$_3$·2SiO$_2$·2H$_2$O} china-clay, porcelain clay
瓷土熟料 china-clay chamotte
瓷型材料 ceramic moulding material
瓷研钵 porcelain mortar
瓷釉 (porcelain, ceramic) glaze ◇ 快干～cellulose enamel
瓷柱布线 【电】knob wiring
瓷柱瓷管布线 【电】knob-and-tube wiring
瓷砖 porcelain brick, ceramic tile
刺度试验[测定] 【焦】penetration test
刺钢丝 barbed wire ◇ 巴尔布洛克～Barblok, 螺旋圈～*
刺猬状孔隙 hedgehog type porosity
次摆线 trochoid
次层(原子结构的) subshell
次大气压 subatmospheric pressure
次等金刚石 bort(z)
次分试样 subsample
次贵金属 less noble metal
次级X射线 secondary X-rays
次级点阵[晶格]缺陷 【金】secondary lattice defects
次级电离 secondary ionization
次级电路 secondary circuit
次级电子发射 secondary electron emission
次级反射 second order reflection
次级辐射 secondary radiation
次级滑移 secondary slip
次级结构 secondary structure
次级晶粒 sub-grain
次级晶粒间界 sub-grain boundary

次级粒子　【理】secondary particle
次级偏析　(同"微区偏析")
次级品　sub-quality products, ungraded
次级绕组　secondary coil [winding]
次级绕组空载电压　open-circuit secondary voltage
次级射线　secondary rays
次级系统　subsystem
次级消光　secondary extinction
次近邻原子　next nearest neighbour
次晶　paracrystal
次晶的　paracrystalline
次磷酸铈{$Ce_2(H_2PO_2)_3$}　cerous hypophosphite
次磷酸盐　hypophosphite
次膦酸　(同"亚膦酸")
次硫酸酮　ketone-sulphoxylate
次硫酸酮衍生物　ketone-sulphoxylate derivative
次硫酸盐{M_2SO_2}　sulphoxylate
次氯酸钙{$Ca(OCl)_2$}　calcium hypochlorite
次氯酸钠{$NaOCl$}　sodium hypochlorite
次氯酸盐　hypochlorite
次氯酸盐浸出　hypochlorite leaching
次煤　dant
次能带　subband
次能级　sub-level
次品　seconds (secs), inferior, reject, sub-standard products
次品板堆垛机　mender piler
次品堆垛机　reject piler
次生贝氏体　secondary bainite
次生共析碳化物　secondary eutectoid carbide
次生固溶体　secondary [intermediate] solid solution
次生孔隙　secondary porosity
次生矿物　secondary mineral
次生沥青铀矿　secondary uraninite
次生渗碳体　secondary cementite
次(生)相　【金】second(ary) [minor] phase, second constituent
次生相析出　second phase precipitate
次生相质点　【金】second phase particle
次生硬度　secondary hardness
次生组织　secondary structure
次网状晶界　sub-network, sub-boundary
次显微组织　metastructure
次烟煤　subbituminous coal
次要产物　secondary product
次要负载　minor load
次要金属　minor metal
次要缺陷(不降低产品合格率的缺陷)　minor defect
次要因素　minor factor
次要元素　minor element
次液　(同"不合格溶液")
次乙基　(同"乙烯")
枞树状裂纹(挤压件的)　fir tree defect, Christmas-tree type of cracking
枞香胶[脂]　(同"加拿大香胶")
葱层状构造　onion (skin layer) structure
葱形拱　ogee arch
从动齿轮　driven [follower] gear
从动辊　driven roll(er)
从动夹送辊　driven pinch roller
从动空转轮　trailing idler
从动控制　servo-actuated control
从动轮　driven wheel [pulley], following pulley
从动托料辊　driven carrying roller
从动轧辊　【压】idle roll
从动轴　trailing axle,【机】driven shaft
从动装置　slave unit
从属关系　dependance
从(属)计算机　slave computer
从属控制台　slave station
从属系统　【计】slave system
从属组分　dependent component
从优方向　preferred direction
丛接头　cluster joint
丛晶(体)　cluster crystal
丛聚　clustering ◇滑移带～*

丛聚焊　cluster welding
丛聚硬化[原子丛聚硬化]　cluster hardening
丛束模型(破裂现象的)　bundle model
辏力　central force
粗氨水　ammonia liquor, crude ammoniacal liquor, raw ammonia water
粗拔钢丝　coarse wire
粗苯　crude benzol, fore runnings ◇ 单馏 ~ *
粗苯萃取脱酚法　light-oil extraction dephenolation process
粗苯馏分　raw benzol
粗泵　roughing pump
粗铋二段阳极熔盐电解精炼　two-stage anodic electrolytic refining of bismuth in fused salts
粗铂矿　polyxene
粗糙表面　rough surface, 【压】pebbles, open surface (黑钢板的)
粗糙的　rough, crude, coarse ◇ 表面~grained, 做工~rustic
粗糙度　roughness (factor), asperity, coarseness, scallops (轧件表面的)
粗糙度传送　roughness transfer
粗糙度试验计　roughness testing instrument
粗糙度系数　roughness coefficient
粗糙断口　ragged fracture
粗糙分级的(颗粒组成)　gap-graded
粗糙和云状花纹表面(镀锌钢板的)　curtains
粗糙化　coarsenization ◇ 表面~graining
粗糙搅拌　harsh mix
粗糙晶粒的　hackly granular
粗糙破裂面(金属的)　hackly
粗糙切割　ragged cut
粗糙因数　roughness factor
粗柴油　gas oil
粗车　rough turning
粗车圆坯　rough-turned rounds
粗尘　coarse dust

粗除尘　【铁】rough cleaning
粗除尘器　【铁】rough cleaner
粗锉　rubber
粗大晶粒　open grain
粗大物料　coarse material
粗锭　raw ingot
粗读数自整角机　coarse selsyn
粗度　coarseness
粗端　【建】butt end
粗锻　rough forging, dummying, blocking
粗锻模　roughing impression
粗锻模膛　preliminary-preparatory impression
粗蒽　crude anthracene
粗放型　【企】extension pattern
粗放型经营　【企】extensive management
粗粉　meal
粗粉末　coarse powder
粗浮选槽　rougher flotation cell
粗钢(指统计产量的钢)　crude [raw] steel
粗钢筋　bar reinforcement
粗格筛　scalping screen
粗汞华　stupp
粗拱　common [plain] arch
粗钴合金　crude cobalt alloy
粗骨料　coarse aggregates
粗过滤器　roughing filter
粗铪　run-of-the-mill-hafnium
粗滑移　coarse slip
粗化　coarsening, coarsing ◇ 使~coarsening
粗挥发汽油　naphtha
粗挤压　(同"毛坯挤压")
粗加工　roughing operations, coarse finish (ing) (表面的), rough turning, roughening, snag, peel
粗加工薄钢板　raw [unfinished] sheet
粗钾碱　potash black-ash
粗碱灰　black ash
粗焦油碱类　【焦】crude tar bases
粗结晶　coarse-crystallization

粗金属	crude [raw, furnace] metal, primary [virgin] metal
粗金属锭	【色】base bullion
粗金属锭熔体	molten bullion
粗金属丝	heavy gauge wire
粗金(银)锭(在灰皿中精炼后仍留在炉中的)	Dore bullion
粗晶	coarse grain [crystalline], macrocrystalline
粗晶奥氏体	【金】coarse austenite
粗晶[粒]赤铁矿	coarse-crystalline [coarse-grained] hematite
粗晶带	coarse grain banding
粗晶锭	【冶】coarse-grained ingot
粗晶钢锭(由过热引起的)	scorched ingot
粗晶硅酸铁	coarse metal
粗晶金属	coarse-grained metal
粗晶粒	macrograin, coarse grain
粗晶粒带	coarse-grain zone
粗晶粒度(断口)	coarse granulation
粗晶(粒)断口	coarse granular fracture, coarse-grained fracture, fiery fracture
粗晶(粒)钢	coarse-grained [scorched] steel
粗晶粒结晶	coarse crystallization
粗晶(粒)金属	coarse-grained metal
粗晶(粒)生铁	coarse-grained iron
粗晶粒铸铁	open-grained cast iron
粗晶粒状的	macromeritic
粗晶区域[范围]	【金】coarse-grain(ed) region [zone]
粗晶体	coarse crystal, granular-crystalline
粗晶现象(钢锭缺陷)	pattern effect
粗晶盐	lump salt
粗晶皱纹(锻造缺陷)	coarse-grain wrinkles
粗晶状物质	coarse-crystalline material
粗晶组织	【金】coarse-grained structure [texture], coarse [open-grained] structure
粗精矿	raw concentrate
粗精整(表面的)	coarse finish
粗(颗)粒	coarse grain
粗矿尘	coarse ore dust
粗拉拔	first draught drawing
粗拉拉丝机	rough wire drawing machine, breakdown drawing machine
粗拉伸机	roughing block, breakdown drawing machine
粗粒X射线胶片	large-grained X-ray film
粗粒部分	coarse fraction [component]
粗粒产物	coarse product
粗粒度[化]	coarse granulation
粗粒方铅矿	alquifou
粗粒粉尘	coarse dust
粗粒浮选	coarse flotation
粗粒级	coarse fraction
粗粒金	coarse gold
粗(粒)晶种	coarse seed
粗粒筛分	【选】rough sizing
粗粒物料	coarse-grained material
粗粒显影	coarse grain development
粗粒悬浮液	coarse-grained dispersion
粗粒影像	coarse-grained image
粗粒照相乳胶	coarse-grain(ed) photographic emulsion
粗粒状的	coarsely granular
粗粒组分	coarse component
粗料	coarse material
粗硫酸镍	crude nickel sulphate
粗馏	crude distillation
粗馏分[物]	crude fraction, raw distillate
粗铳	【色】raw [crude] matte
粗铝	crude aluminium
粗氯化物	crude [raw] chloride
粗氯化物分隔器[放置隔板]	raw chloride spacer
粗滤池	coarse filter
粗滤器	colander, coarse strainer ◇自清洗～*
粗滤清器	coarse cleaner
粗略读数	rough reading
粗略净化气体	roughly cleaned gas
粗麻屑沥青涂包法	hessian wrapping

粗煤气	crude gas
粗煤气冷凝液	crude gas liquor
粗镁	crude magnesium
粗面锤头	rough die
粗面挤压筒	【压】rough container
粗面容器	rough container
粗面轧辊	rough roll
粗磨	coarse [rough, preparatory] grinding
粗磨光	first finishing
粗磨机	snagging grinding machine
粗萘	crude naphthalene ◇ 经离心机处理的～crude whizzed naphthalene
粗镍	crude nickel
粗镍阳极	(impure) nickel anode
粗盘条	heavy rod
粗泡铜	crude blister copper
粗坯	rough blank
粗皮效应	【压】pebbling
粗片状珠光体	coarse-lamellar pearlite
粗汽油	crude gasoline, naphtha
粗铅	【色】wet lead,(鼓风炉产,含银) lead bullion, work lead ◇ 除铜～,熔融～molten bullion
粗铅产出率	bullion fall
粗铅除银精炼法	pattinsonization
粗铅锭(含贵金属的)	base bullion (lead),(crude) lead bullion, pig lead ◇ 含银的～base lead bullion
粗铅精炼	refining of lead bullion
粗铅连续精炼除银锅	continuous lead desilverizing kettle
粗铅熔体	molten bullion
粗铅提取率	bullion fall
粗切削加工	rough machining
粗砂	coarse [open] sand, hoggin
粗砂浸出	【色】sand leaching
粗砂土	gritty soil
粗砂纸	flint (glass) paper
粗筛	coarse screen [mesh]
粗筛孔的	wide-meshed
粗筛矿石	hurdled ore
粗筛旋流器	scalping cyclone
粗筛选	【选】coarse [rough] sizing
粗石	rubble (stone), quarry rock
粗蚀(晶体)	mass etch
粗实线	heavy line
粗视截面积	macroscopic cross section
粗视磨片	macrosection
粗视条痕裂纹检验	macro streak flaw test
粗视硬度	macrohardness
粗水泥	cement grit
粗丝钢丝绳	coarse-wire rope
粗酸洗	(同"初酸洗")
粗碎	coarse crushing [breaking], preliminary [primary] crushing
粗碎机	coarse [primary] crusher, primary breaker
粗碎圆锥	coarse cone
粗碎圆锥破碎机	coarse cone crusher
粗碳酸钾	potash black-ash
粗锑	needle antimony
粗调(节,整)	coarse regulation [control, adjustment], rough control
粗铁	crude iron, kal
粗铜	raw [crude, Bessemer] copper, blister (copper)(铜锍吹炼产物,也称"泡铜")
粗铜焙烧	blister roasting
粗铜焙烧炼铜法	bottom process
粗铜锭	pig copper, copper bullion (含有贵金属的)
粗铜精炼	blister refining
粗铜块	blister cake
粗铜生成[形成]期	blister forming period
粗铜阳极	blister anode
粗洗	【铁】rough cleaning ◇ 煤气～primary gas cleaning
粗洗煤气	primary cleaned gas
粗线绳	twine
粗锌	【色】crude zinc, spelter
粗锌真空精炼过程	vacuum refining process of crude zinc
粗溴化银晶粒影像	coarse-grained image
粗玄武岩	dolerite

粗选槽　roughing separatory cell
粗选机　【选】rougher (cell)
粗压模　【粉】blocking die
粗压延　【压】roughing-down
粗亚晶粒组织(单晶的)　【金】coarse subgrain structure
粗氧化锌　tutty
粗轧　rough rolling, roughing(-down)
粗轧板坯　roughed slab, breakdowns
粗轧成型机座　shaping stand
粗轧除鳞机　primary scale breaker
粗轧道次　preceding [previous] pass
粗轧方坯　roughed bloom
粗轧机　roughing mill (RM), rougher [big] mill, getting-down mill ◇ 第二架 ~ pony rougher, 可逆式 ~ reversing rougher, 冷 ~ cold roughing mill, 轮箍 ~ *, 万能式 ~ *
粗轧机干油润滑系统　roughing mill grease lubrication system
粗轧机工作辊　rougher work roll
粗轧机工作辊磨床　rougher work roll grinding machine
粗轧机润滑系统　roughing mill lubrication system
粗轧机(氧化)铁皮沉淀池　rougher scale sedimentation basin
粗轧机(氧化)铁皮坑　rougher scale pit
粗轧机仪表室　rougher instrumentation room
粗轧机仪表台　rougher instrument pulpit
粗轧机用(γ)射线测厚仪　gamma-ray thickness gauge for rougher
粗轧机支承辊　rougher back-up roll
粗轧机组　roughing mill group, roughing (mill) train ◇ 冷轧 ~ cold roughing train, 连续式 ~ *
粗轧机座　roughing (-down) stand, rougher, breakdown
粗轧孔型　roughing [preceding, breakdown] pass ◇ 方-椭圆~系统 *
粗轧破鳞辊　RSB (roughing scale breaker) roll
粗轧破鳞机　roughing [primary] scale breaker
粗轧椭圆孔型　pre-oval
粗轧温度　roughing temperature (RT)
粗轧轧辊　roughing [shaping] roll
粗轧轧辊车床　roughing roll lathe
粗折痕　coarse fold
粗真空管路　roughing line
粗整　coarse adjustment
粗直径(线材)　heavy gauge
粗直径金属丝　heavy gauge wire
粗制　rough out, snag
粗制产物　raw product
粗制螺母　rough nut
粗制螺栓　rough [black, unfinished] bolt
粗制毡(建筑用)　rag felt
粗珠光体　【金】coarse pearlite
醋酐　acetic anhydride
醋酸{CH$_3$COOH}　(同"乙酸")
簇射　shower(ing) ◇ 级联~【理】cascade shower
簇形结晶　cluster crystal
簇状构造　cluster formation
簇状金刚石整修工具　cluster-type diamond dressing tool
簇状物　cluster
促发形核　catalysis nucleation
促进剂　accelerant, energising [energizing] agent, promoter, promotor
促凝剂　accelerating agent, setting accelerator
促碎剂　disintegration promoting agent
猝熄　quenching
摧毁　destruction, destroy
催镀液(电化学)　quickening liquid
催干油　【铸】drying oil
催化　catalyze, catalysis ◇ 电~的 electrocatalytic, 接触~ contact-catalysis, 酸碱~作用 acid-base catalysis
催化本领　catalytic power
催化产物　product of catalysis, catalysate

催化促进剂	catalytic promoter
催化毒物	catalytic poison
催化反应	catalytic reaction
催化分解	catalytic decomposition
催化过程	catalytic process
催化还原	catalytic reduction
催化活度[性]	catalytic activity
催化剂	catalytic agent, catalyst, catalyzer, catalyser, contact agent, accelerant, accelerating agent, accelerator ◇ 带走的～entrained catalyst, 废～dead catalyst, 分解～*, 接触～contact catalyst, 拉尼合金～*, 烈性～rugged catalyst, 生物～biocatalyst, 载体～supported catalyst
催化剂变质	catalyst deterioration
催化剂毒(物)	catalyst [catalytic] poison
催化剂炉	catalyst furnace
催化剂再生	catalyst regeneration [reactivation]
催化剂中毒	catalyst poisoning
催化加氢法	【焦】catalytic hydrogenation process
催化交换	catalytic exchange
催化裂化	catalytic cracking ◇ 流态化～装置*
催化炉	catalyst furnace
催化能力	catalytic power
催化氢化(作用)	catalytic hydrogenation
催化去氧法(制取高纯气体用)	deoxo process
催化燃烧	catalytic combustion
催化热钾碱法	【焦】catalytic thermal potassium alkali process
催化现象	catalytic phenomenon
催化氧化	catalytic oxidation
催化硬化涂层	catalyst-cured coating
催化助燃剂	【团】catalysis combustion-supporting agent
催化作用	catalysis, catalytic action [effect] ◇ 自～*
催渗剂(固体渗碳的)	energising [energizing] agent
脆	brittle ◇ 变～embrittlement
脆度	frailty, frangibility
脆断	brittle failure ◇ SOD～试验*, 奥罗万～理论*, 低能冲击～转变试验*, 晶界～*
脆化	embrittlement ◇ 镀锌～*, 抗～合金*
脆化处理	embrittlement operation [treatment]
脆化机理	embrittling mechanism
脆化剂	embrittling agent
脆化作用	embrittling effect
脆环试验	brittle ring test
脆裂	brittle crack [rupture]
脆裂点	brittle point
脆裂防止器(阻止大型焊接结构脆裂蔓延用)	crack arrester
脆硫铋矿	ikunolite
脆硫铋铅矿	sakharovaite
脆硫砷铅矿	$Pb_2As_2S_5$ sartorite
脆硫锑铅矿	jamesonite
脆硫锑铜矿	Cu_3SbS_4 famatinite
脆硫锑银铅矿	owyheeite
脆硫铜铋矿	$3Cu_2S \cdot 2Bi_2S_3$ wittichenite
脆韧(性)转变	brittle-ductile transition
脆弱的	friable
脆弱晶格	brittle lattice
脆弱面	weaker plane, plane of weakness
脆弱区	【焊】weakness zone
脆弱性	vulnerability
脆砷铁矿	angelellite
脆铁矿	friable iron ore
脆性	brittlement, brittleness, brittle behaviour, fragility, frailty, frangibility, friability, shortness ◇ 埃索～温度*, 低温～*, 夹渣～slag shortness, 斯特德～*, 退火～*, 消除～退火*
脆性白铜[高锌黄铜]	brittle white brass ◇ 巴斯～*
脆性边界表面渗碳法	brittle boundary technique
脆性材料	friable material

脆性淀积物　brittle deposit
脆性断裂　brittle [crystalline] fracture ◇ 格里菲思~*
脆性断裂源　brittle fracture initiation
脆性断裂转变温度　null ductility transition (NDT), fracture transition (temperature)
脆性发展　development of brittleness
脆性粉末　fragile powder
脆性腐蚀特性[性质]　brittle erosion behaviour
脆性合金　brittle alloy
脆性金属　brittle [fragile, friable] metal
脆性晶体　brittle crystal
脆性裂口　brittle fracture
脆性裂纹扩展　brittle crack propagation
脆性敏感度比　susceptibility ratio to brittleness
脆性偏析　brittle segregation
脆性破断　（同"脆断"）
脆性漆　brittle lacquer
脆性区　brittle zone
脆性生铁　short iron
脆性-塑性转变　brittle-ductile transition ◇ 受压诱发~*
脆性-塑性[延性]转变温度　brittle-ductile transition temperature
脆性涂层法（应力的）　brittle coating method
脆性行为　brittle behaviour
脆性氧化物　embrittling oxide
脆银矿{Ag$_5$SbS$_4$}　black silver, stephanite
脆铸件　frail casting
萃出能力　extractive power
萃出物　extract (ex.)
萃出液密度　extract density
萃合物　extraction species
萃后异己酮　effluent hexone
萃后有机相　organic effluent
萃铌部分[工段]　columbium extraction section
萃取　extract (ex.), extracting, extraction (ext., extn),【化】draw ◇ 不可~的*, 不完全~*, 部分~*, 多级~*, 多批~*, 分级[段]~*, 分批~*, 共[同时]~coextraction, 固态~法*, 回洗~backwash extraction, 浸出~*, 可~的*, 离子缔合[离子型络合物]~*, 两次[双重]~double extraction, 溶剂~*, 双溶剂~*, 水溶液~aqueous extraction, 相~extraction of phases, 液体~*, 一次~single-extraction, 优先[选择]~selective extraction, 有机磷酸~*
萃取部分[工段]　extraction section
萃取残渣　extraction residue
萃取操作曲线　extraction operating line
萃取车间　extraction plant
萃取-电积法　solvent-extraction-electrowinning process
萃取电积铜　solvent-extraction-electrowinning copper
萃取度　degree of extraction
萃取反应　extraction reaction
萃取方法　method of extraction
萃取分离　extraction [extractive] separation
萃取分离[萃取及洗提]设备　extraction and stripping apparatus
萃取复型　extraction replica
萃取化学　extraction chemistry
萃取机理　extraction mechanism
萃取级数　extraction stage ◇ 顺料前流~*
萃取剂　extraction agent, extractant ◇ 胺类~*, 加酸~浸出*, 磷酸酯-胺类联合~*, 烷基胺~*, 有载~loaded extractant
萃取净化[提纯]　extractive purification
萃取率　extraction yield [coefficient], rate of extraction
萃取能力　extraction power
萃取平衡曲线　extraction equilibrium line
萃取器　extractor, extraction apparatus ◇ 波式离心~*, 分离~separation extrac-

tor,复式～ compound extractor,混合沉降～*,离心式溶剂～*,两级～ two-stage extractor,十级连续分离～*,索格利～*,旋转圆盘～*,一级再生～*

萃取器组 extraction battery
萃取溶剂 extractive solvent
萃取容量 extraction capacity
萃取设备[装置] extraction equipment [plant, apparatus] ◇ 混合沉降器～*,级联～*,逆流～*
萃取数据 extraction data
萃取塔[柱] column (extractor), extraction column [tower] ◇ 敞口喷雾～ open spray column,挡板喷雾～ baffled spray column,多级喷射混合～*,赛贝尔搅拌式～ Scheibel column,圆形回转～*
萃取添加剂 extraction modifier
萃取条件 extraction condition
萃取系数 extraction coefficient
萃取[出]相 extract phase
萃取效率 extraction efficiency [coefficient]
萃取冶金(学) extraction [extractive] metallurgy, lyometallurgy
萃(取)液 extract ◇ 酒精～ alcoholic extract
萃取柱操作 column operation
萃钽部分[工段] tantalum extraction section
萃余液 raffinate
淬钢 quench steel
淬火 【金】quenching, hardening, chilling ◇ 8字形～ figure 8 quenching,表面火焰加热～*,不完全～*,差温～*,成批[大批生产]～*,等离子体～ plasma hardening,电弧加热～ arc hardening,电解～*,电热～*,二次[复式]～*,沸水～*,分级～*,风冷[鼓风]～ air blast quenching,负[软化]～*,干法～ dry quenching,高频加热～*,固溶化～ water toughening,光亮～*,火焰加热～*,急冷～*,加增强剂～ intensifier hardening,间歇[断续]～*,金属浴～ metal-bath hardening,局部～*,空气铅～*,冷冻[冰冷]～ cryogenic quenching,冷介质～*,两段～*,临界直径～*,流态化床～*,末端～法*,喷射～*,喷雾～*,喷液～ spray quenching,气体流～ gas quenching,铅浴～*,欠热～ underhardening,强制空气冷却～ forced air quenching,全部～ total hardening,热介质～ hot quench(ing),热油～ hot oil quenching,韧化～*,软～ mild quench,深度～ depth hardening,湿～ wet quenching,双液～ double quench(ing),水中～ quenching in water,顺序～*,特技～*,梯度(末端)～(法)*,完全～ full hardening,未～的 green,硝酸水溶液～*,旋转～*,选择～*,压力[加压]～*,亚临界温度～*,盐浴～*,液氮～ nitrogen quenching,液态火焰加热～(法)*,一次～ primary quenching,油(中)～*,轧制余热～ mill hardening,直接～*,直线～*,周边～ contour hardening,装入式～*,准乎温～*

淬火变形 quenching [hardening] strain, deformation due to hardening
淬火表面 hardsurface
淬火操作[工序] hardening operation
淬火槽 quench(ing) tank [bath], hardening tank [trough] ◇ 传送式～ conveyer quench tank
淬火车间 hardening shop [plant]
淬火池 quenching bath
淬火处理 quench(ing) treatment ◇ 随后回火的～ hardening with subsequent drawing
淬火磁钢 hardened magnet steel
淬火电炉 electric hardening furnace
淬火(冻结的)空位 quenched-in vacancy
淬火-断裂试验 quench and fracture test
淬火法 quench(ing) [hardening] method, quench(ing) [hardening] process ◇ 等温～ austempering method,电场～

elquench process,电流直接加热~,前进旋转火焰~*,同一位置~*
淬火范围 (同"淬火温度范围")
淬火感受性 response to hardening
淬火钢 hardened [quenched, chilled] steel
淬火工段 hardening room [plant, shop]
淬火过度 overquenching
淬火后原状 as-quenched condition
淬火回火 quench tempering, Q-tempering
淬火回火处理 quench-temper, quench-draw treatment, double treatment
淬火回火连续作业线 continuous quench and temper line
淬火回火软化处理(低碳钢的) tough hardening
淬火机 quenching [hardening] machine
淬火机机头(带喷嘴的) quench head
淬火机理 mechanism of quenching
淬火急冷[强烈]度 severity of quench(ing)
淬火剂 hardening agent [compound, medium], hardener, quenching agent [compound], quenchant, media quench ◇ 熔融金属~*
淬火计[仪](鉴定油淬火性能用) quenchometer
淬火加热 hardening heat
淬火间 hardening room
淬火介质 quenchant, quenching media, hardening medium, media quench
淬火冷却器 quencher
淬火裂纹 quench(ing) crack(ing), hardening flaw [crack], heat treatment crack
淬火炉 quenching [hardening, glowing] furnace ◇ 高速~*,氮气氛~*,回转式~*,整体式~*
淬火炉装置 quenching furnace arrangement
淬火马氏体 quenched martensite
淬火敏感性 【金】quench sensitivity
淬火内应力 internal hardening stress
淬火能力[本领](介质的) quenching power, hardening power [capacity]
淬火喷头 quench head
淬火破裂[损坏] hardening failures
淬火钳 hardening tongs, quench extractor
淬火强度 quenching intensity
淬火屈氏体 quenched troostite
淬火缺陷 quenching defect
淬火软化处理 quench annealing
淬火设备 quenching equipment [facilities], hardening outfit
淬火深度-断面晶粒度曲线 (同"P-F曲线")
淬火时间 quenching period, cool time
淬火时效 quench aging ◇ 直接~ direct quench aging
淬火时效硬化 quench age hardening
淬火室 quenching chamber
淬火试验 quenching test ◇ 磁性~*
淬火水 quenching water
淬火速率 quenching rate ◇ 临界~*
淬火索氏体 quenched sorbite
淬火弹簧钢丝 chilled spring wire
淬火特性 hardening characteristics
淬火提取器 quench extractor
淬火条件 quenching condition
淬火弯曲试验 quench(ed) bend test
淬火温度 quenching [hardening] temperature
淬火(温度)区域[范围] hardening (temperature) region, quenching temperature range
淬火温度与硬度关系(曲线) hardening temperature-hardness relation
淬火小车 quenching car
淬火效应 quenching effect
淬火液 quenchant, quenching [hardening] liquid
淬火应变 quenching [hardening] strain ◇ 反复~*
淬火应力 quenching [hardening] stress
淬火硬度 as-quenched hardness ◇ 钢最大~*

淬火硬化　quench-hardening
淬火硬化钢　（同"淬火钢"）
淬火油　quenching [hardening] oil ◇ 超级～ super-quench oil, 海湾高级～*, 快速～*, 普通［习用］～*
淬火盂　quenching cup
淬火罩　quenching hood
淬火蒸发　vapourization in quenching
淬火周期　quenching period
淬火装置　hardening plant [outfit], quench unit（轧件浸渍的）◇ 自动～*
淬火状态　(as-)quenched condition
淬火状态金属　as-quenched metal
淬火状态组织　quenched [hardened] structure, as-hardened structure
淬火组织　quenched [hardened] structure
淬火作业线　quench line
淬火作业线运送带　quench conveyor
淬火作用　quenching effect
淬冷剂　【金】quenching media
淬冷器　quencher
淬裂　quench(ing) crack(ing)
淬裂敏感性　quenching crack susceptibility
淬透　through quenching [hardening], full hardening ◇ 谢泼德斯口～检验 Sheppard P-F test
淬透(层)深度　depth of quenching
淬透度　hardenability, quenching degree
淬透度测量［淬透性量度］　【金】measure of hardenability
淬透钢　fully hardened steel, through-hardening steel ◇ 浅～*
淬透能力　ability to depth-harden
淬透性　quenching degree, hardenability ◇ H带钢～规范*, 固有［本质］～*, 末端～*, 完全［透深, 深层］～*, 心部～ core hardenability
淬透性带　hardenability band, H band
淬透性极限　hardenability limit
淬透性曲线　hardenability curve, depth-hardness curve
淬透性曲线图　hardenability chart（末端的）◇ 格罗斯曼～*
淬透性试棒　hardenability bar
淬透性试验　hardenability test, surface-to-core test ◇ P-F～法*
淬透性增强剂　hardenability intensifier
淬透性值　hardenability value
淬硬　harden(ing), harden quench, quench-hardening ◇ 感应～机理*, 可～的 hardenable, 深～能力*, 完全～的 hardened throughout
淬硬表层　hardened skin
淬硬表面　hardened surface
淬硬层　hardened layer
淬硬层剥离　case spalling
淬硬层深度　depth of hardening zone
淬硬点［端］　hardened point
淬硬法　（同"淬火法"）
淬硬范围［区］　hardening range, quenched zone
淬硬钢（同"淬火钢"）◇ 低～*, 空气～ air-hardening steel, 未～ nonhardening steel
淬硬钢奥氏体晶粒度显示法　◇ 维莱拉和贝茵～*
淬硬钢轧辊　steel chilled roll
淬硬合金钢　quench alloy steel
淬硬区裂纹　hard zone crack
淬硬深度　hardening [hardness] penetration, depth of hardening
淬硬性　hardenability ◇ 表面～ case hardenability
淬渣法（用水池）　【冶】bank expanding process
翠镍矿｛NiCO$_3$·2Ni(OH)$_2$·4H$_2$O｝　emerald nickel, zaratite
翠砷铜铀矿　zeunerite
村上浸蚀液（鉴别合金钢中碳化物用）　Murakami's reagent
存储　store, storage, memory ◇ 易失［非永久性, 暂时］～*
存储保护　memory guard, storage protection

存储层次　memory hierarchy
存储程序　【计】stored program
存储程序计算机　stored program computer
存储池　holding pond
存储单元　【计】memory cell [location], storage cell, bank, memory element
存储堆栈　【计】storage stack
存储封锁　【计】memory lockout
存储交换　【计】memory exchange [swapping]
存储块　【计】memory [storage] block
存储密度　memory [storage] density
存储模件　memory module
存储瓶　holding bottle
存储器　【计】memory (device), storage, accumulator, memory [storage] unit ◇ 半导体～semiconductor memory, 触发器～flip flop storage, 磁盘～*, 大容量～*, 非易失性～*, 分级～体系 memory hierarchy, 高速～high speed storage, 光～*, 后进先出～nesting storage, 缓冲～buffer (storage), 矩阵～matrix storage, 可擦～erasable storage, 快速存取～*, 立即存取～*, 内～*, 破坏性～destructive storage, 射流～fluid memory, 实～real storage, 随机存取～*, 铁氧体磁心～ferrite core memory, 外(部)～*, 微～microstorage, 相联[按内容访问]～*, 虚拟～virtual memory, 循环～*, 引导～bootstrap memeory, 永久性～*, 暂时～*, 直接访问～*, 只读～*, 中间～*, 中央～central memory, 主～*, 坐标～coordinate storage
存储器板　memory plate
存储器保护组件　memory protection module
存储器地址寄存器　memory address register
存储器访问指令　memory reference instruction
存储器共享【计】　memory Sharing
存储(器)管理【计】　memory (storage) management
存储器奇偶中断　memory parity interrupt
存储器容量　memory capacity, size of memory
存储器周期时间　memory [storage] cycle time
存储区　【计】storage area ◇ 公用～common storage area
存储时间　【计】memory [storage] time
存储线圈　【计】memory coil
存储元件　memory element
存储周期　【计】memory [storage] cycle
存储装置　【计】memory [storage] facilities, memory [storage, storing] device
存档带　【计】grandfather tape
存档期　【计】grandfather cycle
存锭　stock pig
存放跨　storage bay [span]
存放时间　holding time
存放寿命　shelf life
存活生球　surviving ball
存货　(existing) stock
存货清单　stock inventory
存焦量　coke storage capacity
存矿量　ore inventory
存量资产　【企】existed capital
存煤　stocking coal
存取　【计】access (ACS) ◇ 磁盘～disc access
存取臂　access arm
存取电路　access circuit
存取法　access method
存取方式　access mode
存取机构　access mechanism
存取时间　access time
存取周期　access cycle
存入　【计】store, write
存砂斗　sand storage bin
存数　【计】content
存在　presence, occurrence, exist
寸动按钮　【电】inching button

寸动电动机 【电】inching motor
搓捻机 【压】bunching machine, buncher
锉 file ◇ 单向齿[刀形,菱形] ~ hack file, 手[钳工] ~ hand file
锉板 【压】filing board
锉床 filing machine
锉刀钢 file steel
锉刀(检验)硬度 file hardness
锉刀开凿机 【计】nicker-pecker
锉式硬度试验器 Hardnester
锉纹锤 file hammer
锉削 filing
锉削粉末(用于 X 射线照相) filed powder
锉削硬度试验 file (hardness) test
锉屑 filings, raspings, scobs
错缝 【压】mismatch
错缝砌筑(砖的) break(ing) joint
错缝砖 bonder
错弧变形 【连铸】misalignment strain
错检(涡流探伤的) 【压】erroneous flaw signalling
错接缝 【建】breaking
错列 stagger arrangement,【数】alternation
错列接头 【运】alternate [broken] joint
错流 cross current, cross-flow(区域熔炼的)
错流萃取 cross current solvent extraction
错流核晶洗涤器 cross-flow nucleation scrubber
错乱 aberration, in confusion
错排 staggered arrangement
错配 misfit,【金】mismatch
错配度 degree of misfit,【金】mismatch
错配[排]能 misfit energy
错配渗入体 miffitting inclusion
错配位错 misfit dislocation
错配物 tramps
错调 missetting, misadjustment
错位(铸件缺陷) 【铸】ram-away, ram-off (defect)
错位焊点(熔核) 【焊】misplaced nugget
错位角 mismatch angle
错误 error, mistake, bug, bust, slip-up
错误操作 misoperation, mishandling
错误处理 mishandling
错误代码 【计】error code
错误的 incorrect, mistaken, erroneous
错误断面形状 mis-shape
错误计算 miscalculation
错误检测[查]程序 【计】error detecting routine, malfunction routine
错误检查 error check
错误校验码 【计】error checking code
错误校正码 【计】error correcting code
错误取向 misorientation
错误群 【计】error burst
错误信号 false signal
错误信息[报文] 【计】error message
错误中断 【计】error interrupt
错误状态 【计】error condition[status]
错误状态字 【计】error status word
错误猝发 error burst
错箱(缺陷) 【铸】(mould) shift, mismatch, cross-jointing, distortion, obligue setting
错芯(缺陷) 【铸】core shift
错移的 staggered

D d

搭板接合 bridge joint, strapped joint
搭缝[搭接]炉焊钢管 lap welded tube
搭焊法 lap weld process
搭焊管 lap-welded pipe
搭焊焊管法 lapweld process ◇ 辊压~*
搭焊机 lap (seam) welder
搭焊接头 overlapping weld, overlapped (joint) weld
搭架(砌砖用的) 【建】horse
搭架砖 【耐】slabbing
搭角焊 lap fillet welding
搭角接合 lapped corner joint
搭接 (over)lap [shear] joint, lap(ped) butt, lapping, overlap
搭接边 overlapping edge, overlap edge
搭接部分 overlap, overlapping part
搭接长度 lap length, contacting overlap (点焊或滚焊的)
搭接点焊 stitch welding
搭接点焊缝 bridge spot weld
搭接缝焊[滚焊] lap seam welding
搭接滚焊缝 bridge seam weld
搭接滚焊接头[搭接焊缝] lap seam weld
搭(接)焊 overlap(ping) welding, (end) lap welding
搭接接头 overlap joint ◇ 直线~ straight lap joint
搭接量(角焊的) landing
搭接炉焊管机组 lap-welded mill
搭接面 lapped face, 【铸】faying surface
搭接片 strap, bonding jumper
搭接台架 bridging table
搭接填角焊缝 lap fillet weld
搭接压焊 mesh(ed) welding
搭配(物) mating
搭棚 【铁】bridging
搭桥 【钢】bridging
溚(焦油,柏油) tar
达尔杰特铋铅锡易熔合金(50Bi, 25Pb, 25Sn, 熔点 93℃) D'Arget's alloy
达利克刷镀(法) brush plating, Dalic plating, Dalic process
达马克辛高级磷青铜(9.2—11.2Sn, 0.3—1.3P, <7Pb, 余量 Cu;作轴承用) Damaxine(alloy)
达派克斯有机磷萃铀法 Dapex process
达派克斯有机磷萃铀设备 Dapex plant
达塞特易熔合金(60Bi, 10Pb, 30Sn) Darcet's alloy
达什深浸蚀液(显示腐蚀坑用) Dash etching solution
达松伐尔电流计 D'Arsonval galvanometer
打板桩 pile sheathing, sheet piling
打包 baling, bagging, packing ◇ 材料~装置*
打包带钢[钢带] ribbon steel, baling strip [band]
打包带钢轧机 package mill
打包废钢 packed scrap
打包废钢铁 fag(g)oting scrap
打包钢丝 baling wire, bale tie (wire)
打包工 packing operator, baler
打包机 bagging [packaging, banding, wrapping] machine, baling [packing] press, packer, baler, 【钢】binding machine ◇ 废钢~*, 自动~*
打包台 packing table
打包用线材 binder
打包窄带钢 baling strip, bale tie (wire), hoop (厚约2.5毫米, 宽约16—150毫米) ◇ 棉花~*
打包窄带钢轧机 hoop mill
打扁锤 flating hammer
打标记 marking
打标记冲子 prick punch
打标记机 label(l)ing machine, label(l)er
打标记[标志,钢印]工具 【压】marking punch
打出(粒子) 【理】knock-on
打出冲头 【压】backing out punch
打出的电子 knock-on electron

打出的原子(从晶格中) 【理】knock(ed)-on atom
打底颜料 body pigment
打光 glazing, abrasive finishing, polish
打光工 glazer
打光机 glazing [buffing] machine
打夯 ramming, punning, tamping
打夯机 ram impact machine, ramming machine, rammer ◇ 内燃~explosion ram, 蛙式~frog rammer
打号装置 marking unit
打滑 slip(page), dragging(机件的), trackslip
打火花 flashing, sparking
打火石 flint, firestone ◇ 休伯斯~合金*
打击 strike, attack, collision, blow, dash, shock
打击锻(造) impact forging
打击力 striking [hitting] force
打击面 striking face
打击限制行程螺母 stroke limiting nut
打尖 nozzling ◇ 辊式~机*
打浆机 beater
打结 knot
打结材料 jointing material
打结底衬 【冶】rammed bottom lining
打结钢包[盛钢桶] rammed ladle
打结混合料 【冶】rammed mixture
打结机 knotting machine, 【冶】plug ramming machine (锥形炉底)
打结料 stamp(ing) mass [mix]
打结料体积 【铁】volume of ramming mix
打结炉衬 rammed lining
打结炉衬材料 monolithic lining material
打结炉底 rammed bottom [hearth], tamped bottom ◇ 碳质~carbon hearth bottom
打结强度(钢丝绳绳心的) knot strength
打结试验(钢丝的) looping [snarl] test
打结数 tie number
打结阳极 bulk anode

打井机 drill(ing) rig
打壳(铝电解的) (crust) breaking ◇ 风动~装置*, 机械~*, 四周~*, 中部~*
打壳锤 crust breaking hammer
打壳锤架 crust breaking hammer carrier
打壳锤头 crust breaking chisel
打壳机 crust breaker ◇ 自动~*, 自行式[自动推进式]~*
打壳周期 crust breaking cycle
打孔 punch(ing), boring, dock, perforation
打孔机 perforator ◇ 侧边~side punch, 拉模~die driller
打孔眼 eyeleting
打捆 banding, packing, fag(g)oting, fag(g)ot,【冶】baling
打捆车屑 baled turnings
打捆废钢 packed scrap
打捆废钢铁 【冶】fag(g)oting scrap
打捆废铁 baled [bundle(d)] scrap
打捆工 bander
打捆机 bander(线盘或带卷的), bundler, bundling machine, fag(g)oting press, tying machine, trusser ◇ 废钢~*, 盘条~*, 自动~automatic bander
打捆切边 【冶】baled shearings
打捆系统 【冶】packed system
打捆运输机 banding conveyer
打捆站 banding station
打捆装置 packing [strapping] device ◇ 薄板~*, 带卷~*
打梅花桩 staggered piling
打磨 polish, burnish, snagging
打拿负阻管(四极管) dynatron
打泥芯 【铸】decoring
打盘机 【压】coil winding machine
打平锤 planishing hammer
打桥钎(打金属桥钎) bridge breaker
打入阻力(桩的) 【建】driving resistance
打条板桩 batten sheet piling
打铁术 blacksmithery

打通　open up, churning（打通浇注系统中的凝固金属）
打通出铁口　【铁】sledging
打通风口　【冶】punching ◇ 机械～*
打箱　【铸】knock-out
打小孔　eyeleting
打芯机　（同"落芯机"）
打型芯　【铸】core knock-out [shake-out]
打眼　boring, drilling, perforation, trepan
打眼薄板　【压】perforated sheet
打眼工　driller, holer
打印　print(ing), stamp(ing), brand, dump, stencil(l)ing ◇ 成组～【计】group printing, 鼓式～barrel printing
打印标号　identification marking
打印部位　print position
打印工　marker, stamper
打印工具　【压】marking punch
打印鼓　type drum
打印机　stamping machine, stamper（轧件的）, marking machine [apparatus], marker, 【计】printer ◇ 点式～dot printer, 杆[条]式～bar printer, 鼓式～drum printer, 回转～*, 击打式～impact printer, 键盘～*, 矩阵式～matrix printer, 宽行[行式]～line printer, 链式～chain printer, 轮式～flying printer, 针式[线式]～wire printer, 阵列～array printer, 自动～automatic stamper, 字符式～*
打印机机头（带组合活字盒）　marking head
打印器　puncher
打印商标　identification marking
打印速度　printer speed
打印台（板材的）　main mill table
打印头　marking head
打印油墨　stamping ink
打印装置　stamping device
打渣　slag chipping
打轴(钢丝用)　spooling
打轴车间　winding shop
打轴机　winding apparatus, spooling machine ◇ 钢丝～*
打轴设备　spooling equipment
打桩　piling, pile driving, pile-sinking, palification
打桩工程　pilework
打桩机　pile driver [engine], piling machine, ram engine, ram(ming)(impact) machine, drop breaker, falling tup machine, vertical drop machine ◇ 摆式～*, 滑动～skid pile-driver, 落锤～*, 人工～ringing pile engine, 水上～*, 斜导架～*, 自动冲锤～*
打桩架　pile driving frame, lead tower
打桩架拉索　back stay of pile driver
打桩设计　piling design
打桩试验　driving test
打桩图　piling drawing
打桩阻力　pile driving resistance
打字机　typewriter (TW, T/W), typer, marking machine ◇ 输入-输出～*
打字机用铜镍铝型合金(57Cu, 20Ni, 3Al, 20Zn)　typewriter alloy
打钻　drilling
大板坯　(sheet, plate) slab
大比例模型　large-scale model
大扁坯　bloom slab
大布喇格角区域　high angle region [zone]
大布喇格角射线　high angle arcs
大侧压下（量）　heavy width reduction
大产量　large(-volume) output, large-tonnage
大肠埃希氏杆菌　Escherichia coli castellani and chalmers
大肠杆菌　Escherichia coli
大车速度（桥式吊车的）　bridge speed
大齿轮　bull gear
大尺寸　large [jumbo] size, heavy gauge
大尺寸筛　oversize screen
大冲击量处理（法）　high impact-value treatment
大冲击载荷　heavy shock load
大锤　(about-)sledge hammer, mall(et),

mickle hammer ◇加工铸件用～flogging hammer, 双手[炉前]用～*.
大单胞菌属　Macromonas
大地测量学　geodesy
大地电位　earth potential
大地回线　earth return (ER)
大地震　great earthquake, megaseism
大电流　heavy [large] current
大电流充电　【电】boosting
大电流电弧　high current [amperage] arc
大电流焊把　【焊】heavy duty electrode holder
大电流间歇焊　(同"点焊")
大洞穴　【采】glory-hole
大端(连杆的)　big end
大端轴承(曲柄连杆用)　big end bearing
大锻件　heavy forgings
大断面连铸坯　heavy section
大断面铸件　heavy section casting
大吨位设备　high tonnage equipment, large-tonnage plant
大吨位转炉　large vessel
大耳阳极　big-lug anode
大范围屈服　large-scale yielding
大方脚　【建】offset footing
大方坯　bloom, cogged ingot
大放大率　【理】high power
大分子　macromolecule
大风道(烧结机的)　【铁】settling chamber
大盖料斗　large bell cup, 【铁】dish
大坩埚　【色】king pot
大钢窗　Berner's window
大钢坯　cogged bloom
大钢坯剪切机　bloom shears
大钢水包　bull ladle
大功率　heavy duty (HD), high power
大功率等离子炬　high power plasma torch
大功率电动机　heavy duty motor
大功率电子学[设备]　power electronics
大功率拖动(装置)　high power drive
大规模操作　plant(-scale) operation
大规模(的)　large-scale, plant-scale, production-scale, commercial scale, industrial-scale
大规模工业　large-scale industry
大规模集成(化)　【半】large scale integration (LSI)
大规模集成电路　【半】large-scale integrated (LSI) circuit
大规模生产　commercial (scale) production, large-scale manufacture [production], mass-production scale, tonnage production
大规模生产法　commercial scale process
大规模试验　large-scale test [experiment, trial]
大规模挖土　bulk excavation
大规模应用　commercial application
大辊径差轧制　big differential diameter of rolls
大和铅基[锡基]轴承合金　Yamato metal
大厚度(重型钢材、板材)　heavy gauge
大厚度渣层　【冶】thick slag
大糊块　paste chunk
大计　【计】major total
大件造型工　【铸】floor moulder
大浇包　bulk [bull] ladle
大角(度)多边形化间界　large angle polygonization boundary
大角(度)非共格间界　large angle incoherent boundary
大角(度)晶界　large [high] angle boundary
大角度衍射线　high angle diffraction lines
大角反射　high angle reflection
大角间界黏滞性　viscosity of large-angle boundary
大角晶粒界　high angle grain boundary
大角区域　high angle region
大角衍射线偶　(同"大衍射角线对")
大截面锻件　heavy section forging
大截面轧坯　【压】large section
大节距(螺纹)　steep [coarse] pitch
大卷轮(卷取厚板卷的)　spool wheel

大卡规　heavy gauge
大开度射束　beam of wide aperture
大孔[空洞]　macroscopic void
大孔冲头　【压】quill punch
大孔洞　cavitation
大孔径透镜　high aperture lens, wide-aperture lens
大孔筛　griddle
大孔网状结构离子交换树脂　macroreticular structure ion-exchange resin
大孔性土　loess
大口的　wide-mouthed
大口径管材壁厚减薄用轧机　◇罗克内尔式～*
大块　clump, bulk, chunk
大块废钢[料]　heavy scrap
大块高炉焦炭　uncrushed blast-furnace coke
大块固体　bulk solid
大块混凝土　mass concrete
大块焦　large-sized [oversize] coke
大块金属　massive metal
大块矿石　lump ore
大块炉衬砖制造（转炉的）　lining block-making
大块马氏体　massive martensite
大块耐火黏土砖　heavy duty fireclay brick
大块破碎机　chunkbreaker
大块破碎机齿辊轴　【团】chunk-breaker shaft
大块筛　scalping screen
大块烧结矿　coarse [oversize] sinter
大块石墨　heavy graphite block
大块碳砖　【铁】carbon block
大块物料　oversize material
大块氧化皮收集箱　butt box
大块砖制造　blockmaking
大框架式（四立柱式）　【铁】four column pillars
大矿槽　large capacity bin
大理石{$CaCO_3$}　marble
大理石配电板　marble switch board

大理石样表面加工　marbleized finish
大理石渣　chicken grit
大理石状断口（高速钢的）　marble [marmorized] fracture
大理石组织　marble structure
大梁　sommer (beam), girder　◇吊车～ crane girder, 伸悬臂拱式～*
大量　a great quantity, a large number, lump, mass, (in) bulk
大量变形　large deformation
大量减风操作　【铁】fanning
大量降下物　shower
大量喷吹　high rate injection
大量喷吹石灰　high rate of lime injection
大(量)喷煤　high rate injection of pulverized coal, high-rate pulverized coal injection, massive coal injection
大量生产　mass [quantity, tonnage, bulk] production, large-lot production [manufacture], large batch production, high volume production, large(-volume) output　◇优质产品～*
大量生产产品　large-tonnage product, stock commodities
大量生产的钢　tonnage steel
大量生产的氧　tonnage oxygen
大料斗　main hopper,【铁】large bell hopper
大料钟　(同"大钟")
大裂隙　macro crack
大流量交通　heavy traffic
大卵石　talus
大螺栓　king bolt
大马士革钢　Damascus steel, Damask (steel)
大马士革炼钢法　Damask process
大马士革铅锡青铜（13Pb, 10Sn, 77Cu）　Damascus bronze
大面　large face
大面单斜横楔砖　feather-side
大面单斜立楔砖　feather-end
大面积屈服　large-scale yielding

大模板　【机】macrotemplate
大批(的)　large-scale, large quantities [numbers, amounts] of, in bulk (i/B)
大批料　large batch
大批生产　(同"大量生产")
大批生产淬火　mass-production hardening
大片分层(热轧板表面缺陷)　【压】skin lamination
大平板　massive plate
大剖面　heavy gauge
"大瀑布"竖式转炉　Great Falls converter
大气暴露(试验)　atmospheric exposure
大气变化　atmospheric changes
大气(层空气)　atmosphere, atmospheric gas, free air
大气尘埃　aerial [airborne] dust
大气放电　atmospheric discharge
大气腐蚀　atmospheric corrosion ◇ 耐~性[抗~性能]*, 湿~*, 室外~*
大气腐蚀疲劳　atmospheric corrosion fatigue
大气腐蚀试验　atmospheric corrosion test
大气候学　macroclimatology
大气回火炉　atmospheric tempering furnace
大气孔　gross porosity
大气孔率　gross porosity
大气冒口芯　pencil core
大气凝聚　condensation of atmosphere
大气曝露(腐蚀)试验　weather exposure test
大气铅污染(铅害)　air pollution by lead
大气侵蚀　weathering
大气散放物　【环】atmospheric emissions
大气湿度　atmospheric humidity, atmospheric moisture capacity
大气水冷器　atmospheric water cooler
大气条件　atmospheric conditions
大气温度　atmospheric temperature, free air temperature
大气污染　(同"空气污染")
大气污染的减少　reduction of atmosphere pollution
大气污染监测网　air monitoring network
大气污染介质[因素]　air pollution agent
大气污染控制区　air pollution control district
大气污染气象中心　air pollution meteorological centre
大气污染损害　damage by air pollution
大气污染物　air [atmospheric] pollutant, airborne contaminant
大气吸收　atmospheric absorption
大气压　atmosphere (at., atm.), atmosphere [atmospheric] pressure, barometric pressure (BP, b.p.) ◇ 低于~的压力 subatmospheric pressure, 高于~的压力 superatmospheric pressure, 国际标准~*
大气压补缩冒口　atmospheric feeder head
大气压力加料　atmospheric pressure feeding
大气压(力)冒口　【铸】atmosphere [William's] riser, atmospheric riser, atmos-pheric (pressure) head
大气压头　atmospheric (pressure) head
大气烟害　air pollution by smoke
大气烟雾　atmospheric aerosols
大气氧　(同"空气氧")
大气氧化　atmospheric oxidation
大球　oversize ball, 【团】oversize pellet
大球团　large-sized [jumbo] pellet
大区规划　broad planning
大熔埚　(同"大坩埚")
大容积焦炉　large capacity coke oven
大容积矿槽　large capacity bin
大容量磁心存储器　【计】large (capacity) core storage
大容量存储器　【计】bulk memory [storage], mass memory [storage]
大容量存储系统　【计】mass memory [storage] system
大容量空气取样装置　【环】high volume air sampler

大容量炉　large capacity furnace
大升程(上轧辊的)【压】high lift
大升程板坯初轧机　high lift slabbing mill
大升程初轧机　high-lift blooming mill
大事故　major accident, major break down
大苏打　(同"硫代硫酸钠")
大梯度　heavy gradient
大体积混凝土坝　mass concrete dam
大铁锤　sledgehammer, marcus
大铁钳　grampus
大铁水罐[包]　bull ladle
大同式单辊行星轧机　Daido's planetary mill
大同式行星轧制法　Daido's planetary rolling
大桶　vat
大头　【建】butt end
大头桩(爆炸成形的)　pedestal pile
大涡模拟[模型]　large eddy simulation
大小变数　dimensional variable
大小头　increaser, concentric reducer, transition pipe
大星轮(烧结机头部的)　sprocket wheel
大型产业　large-scale industry
大型超低头板坯连铸机　large super-low slab continuous caster
大型(初轧)板坯　large slab
大型电动机　heavy duty motor, high capacity motor
大型电解槽　large-scale electrolytic cell, production-scale cell ◇泽德伯格式～*
大型锻件　large forgings
大型废钢铁件　bulky scrap
大型钢材　large section [shape]
大型钢筋混凝土浮坞　cruiser dock
大型钢坯　【压】bloom
大型高炉　large capacity blast furnace
大型工程　big scale work, heavy construction
大型(工程)计划　major project
大型工业电解槽　large industrial cell
大型焊接钢结构　heavy duty welded steel construction
大型集装箱　van container
大型计算机　large (-scale) computer, maxicomputer
大型搅拌器　high duty agitater
大型可破碎的废钢铁　heavy breakable scrap
大型连续自焙阳极电解槽　large Söderberg cell
大型量规　heavy gauge
大型露天矿　【采】large scale opepit [opencast mine]
大型平土机　bullgrader
大型企业　large enterprise
大型砌块构造[建筑]　block construction
大型墙板　large wall panel
大型区域精炼　large-scale zone-refining
大型热阴极二极管　kenotron
大型热轧机　high duty hot mill
大型设备　large-tonnage plant, large-volume unit
大型石墨块　heavy graphite block
大型隧道窑　large tunnel kiln
大型钛合金部件　large titanium alloy parts
大型条钢轧机　【压】heavy merchant mill
大型卧式金相显微镜　large-type horizontal metallurgical microscope
大型型材[型钢]　heavy [large] section
大型型材[型钢]轧机　【压】heavy section mill
大型阳极　full size anode
大型造球设备　production-scale pelleting system
大型轧钢厂　heavy steel rolling mill
大型轧钢机　heavy (merchant) mill
大型铸锭凝固　large-scale ingot freezing
大型铸件　heavy casting
大型砖　jumbo brick
大(型)转炉　large vessel, mammoth converter
大修工厂　back [system] shop

大修(理)	(major) overhaul, big [capital, heavy, major, permanent] repair, repairs heavy, renewal ◇ 提取～基金*
大循环	major cycle
大压下定径机组(线材轧制)	high reduction sizing mill (HRSM)
大压下量	【压】heavy reduction [draught]
大压下量道次	severe pass
大压下量轧机	high reduction mill (HRM)
大压下量轧制	high reduction rolling
大压下量轧制的	strong rolled (Rs)
大烟囱	smokestack
大烟道	main duct, windmain, large chamber, 【团】collecting main
大烟道放灰阀	windmain dust valve
大烟道集尘斗	windmain hopper
大烟道系统	main waste-gas system
大衍射角线对	high-angle pair of diffraction arcs
大洋多金属结核	ocean polymetallic [manganese] nodules
大洋洲金属学会	Australasian Institute of Metals
大洋洲矿冶学会	Australasian Institute of Mining and Metallurgy
大样板	【机】macrotemplate
大样图	detail drawing
大异形坯	bloom-blank, bloom-block
大圆钢坯	cylindrical bloom
大直径炉缸	large [wide] hearth
大直径无缝钢管	large-sized seamless tube
大钟	【铁】large [lower] bell
大钟操纵钢绳	large bell rope
大钟动作调节器	big bell movement controller
大钟角度	large bell angle
大钟料斗	large bell hopper
大钟平衡杆	large bell beam
大钟突缘高度(料钟突出料斗部分的垂直高度)	bell overhang
大钟下料	large bell dump
大周期	【计】major cycle
呆液酸洗	dead pickling
呆滞损失	stand-by losses
呆滞现象	【冶】dead effect
戴伦轧机(早期万能轧机)	Daelen mill
戴马兹发黑处理法(压铸锌基合金的)	Dymaz
戴纳法金属爆炸成形	Dynaforming
戴纳马克斯高导磁率合金(65Ni, 33Fe, 2Mo)	Dynamax
戴纳帕克高能高速成形法	Dynapak process
戴纳帕克高能高速锻造	Dynapak forging
戴纳帕克高能高速锻造法	Dynapak method
戴纳帕克高能高速锻造机	Dynapak machine
戴纳帕克高能高速挤压	Dynapak extrusion
戴纳帕克高能束压机	Dynapak press
戴纳帕克高速冲压机	Dynapak punch
戴纳帕克型高速成形机	Dynapak high-velocity forming machine
戴纳瓦恒弹性合金	Dynavar
戴诺迪克(金属)防麻点法	【压】Dianodic process
戴维斯(镁合金)晶粒细化法(添加碳化铝)	Davis process
戴维斯镍青铜(65Cu, 30Ni, 4Fe, 1Mn;涡轮叶片及高温阀用)	Davis bronze [metal]
戴维斯试剂(用于显示碳化物和钨化物)	Daeves reagent
戴维-威尔逊照相机	Davy-Wilson camera
戴卫-威尔逊晶体取向测角仪(织构测仪)	Davey-Wilson orientation goniometer
带	band, belt, girdle, ribbon, tape, strip, string, tie, strap, streamer, region, zone ◇ 吕德斯～*
带保温帽(铸造)法	hot top process

带臂夹头[卡盘]　lever chuck
带材　【压】strip, ribbon, flat ◇ 差厚镀层～differential coated strip, 多层～multi-layer strip, 厚～heavy strip, 冷轧～*, 切分的～slit strip, 塑料覆层～plastic-coated strip, 退火～annealed strip, 下垂～flap-ping strip, 窄～*
带材板型　strip profile
带材备用量　strip storage
带材边缘定位仪　scanning recorder
带材边缘控制　strip edge control
带材边缘扫描器[自动控制器, 位置调整器]　strip-edge [edge-strip] scanning equipment, edge (strip) scanner
带材表面涂层印花机　strip printer
带材波纹　ridge buckles
带材擦拭器　strip wiper
带材测厚仪　strip thickness gauge
带材测宽仪　strip width meter
带材弛度　slack of strip
带材除[破]鳞机　strip-processing mechanism
带材粗轧机　strip [band] roughing mill
带材存贮装置　strip-storage device
带材导板　band guide
带材导向挡板　strip deflector
带材的净化脱脂过程　cleaning process
带材定心[对中]装置　strip-centering device
带材端头嵌入　strip end engaging
带材对中调节器　edge (strip) scanner
带材对中控制　strip centering control
带材缝合机　stitcher
带材干燥机　strip dryer
带材和焊管坯轧机(连续式)　strip and skelp mill
带材横剪作业线　sheet-shearing line
带材厚度　strip thickness
带材厚度 X 光测微计　Measuray
带材厚度差　grow-back
带材厚度公差　strip thickness tolerance
带材厚度同轧辊直径之比　thickness ratio
带材厚度压下螺丝控制系统　gaugemeter-screw system
带材厚度张力控制系统　gaugemeter-tension system
带材活套张紧装置(辊式)　strip bridle
带材夹持器　strip holding device
带材检测系统　strip detector system
带材矫平　strip flattening
带材精整　strip processing ◇ 机组作业线上的多条～
带材静电涂油机　electrostatic strip oiler, electrostatic strip-oiling apparatus
带材局部切除机　cut-out shears
带材卷　(同"带卷")
带材卷取成卷　strip reeling
带材卷取机　strip coiler, coiling [ribbon] reel
带材卷取机卷筒　strip coiler mandrel
带材卷取温度　coiling temperature
带材卷取装置　strip coiling apparatus
带材开卷机　strip uncoiler
带材拉断　strip breakage
带材冷却设备　strip cooling equipment
带材冷轧机　cold-strip mill ◇ 串列式～*, 环式～*, 四辊可逆式～*, 四机座连续式～*
带材连续镀锌　continuous strip galvanizing
带材连续式正火炉　continuous-strip normalizing furnace
带材连续涂漆　continuous strip lacquering
带材密度　strip density
带材磨光作业线　strip-grinding line
带材平整机　coil-skin pass mill
带材前端　leading strip end
带材清净机　strip cleaning machine
带材热轧机　band hot mill, hot-strip mill ◇ 半连续式～*, 四辊连续式～*
带材失稳判别模型　criterion model of rolled strip stableness
带材试样　strip specimen
带材送进装置　strip-feeding device

带材酸洗机　band pickling machine
带材酸洗装置　strip pickler ◇ 连续式~*
带材涂漆作业线　strip-lacquering line
带材涂油装置　strip oiling device
带材退火　strip annealing
带材尾部　strip tail end
带材下垂度控制器（活套的）　dip controller
带材预卷机　coil preparatory coiler ◇ 胀缩卷筒式~*
带材轧机　strip mill, band and strip rolling mill
带材轧机生产能力　strip mill capacity
带材轧机组　strip mill train
带材轧制　strip-rolling
带材张紧装置（机组作业线上的）　back tension bridle, drag bridle
带材张力　strip tension
带材张力测量辊　strip tension measuring roll
带材张力测量装置　strip tension measuring equipment [unit]
带材张力电测仪　electrical strip tension detector
带材张力计　strip tension gauge, strip tensionmeter
带材张力控制　strip tension control
带材支承辊　strip backing roll
带材支承装置　strip holding device
带材直头机　(同"带卷直头机")
带材自动定心装置　(同"带材边缘扫描器")
带材自动平整机　automatic strip-straightening machine
带材纵切多刀圆盘剪　rotary gang slitter
带材纵切机组　strip slitting machine
带材纵向成型　linear contouring operation
带材纵向剪切机　metal slitting machine
带材纵切圆盘剪　strip slitting shears, strip slitter
带槽沟锭模　fluted mould

带槽辊　grooved roller ◇ 辊道的~*
带槽滚珠轴承　grooved ball bearing
带槽件　slotted objects
带秤　belt scale
带秤的　scale-equipped
带齿心轴　toothed spindle
带翅钢管　finned steel tube
带翅管　finned tube
带出　carry-over
带出速度　carrying velocity
带电　electrification, electrify
带电操作[作业]　hot-line work
带电导线[电线]　live conductor (wire), live wire
带电离子　charged ion, current-carrying ion
带电粒子　charged particle
带电粒子试验　electrified-particle test
带电体　charged body
带电位错　charged dislocation
带电轴　current-carrying shaft
带电轴承衬套　current-carrying bearing insert
带动锁钮　catch knob
带负荷抽头变换器　on-load tap changer
带钢　【压】strip steel, steel strip, flat hoop iron, band steel (<0.12C), band iron (窄的) ◇ 成卷~ coiled steel (strip), 打包~*, 电缆铠装用~ cable tape steel, 镀锌~ galvanized strip, 黑[热轧]~ black strip, 冷轧~*, 扭曲~*, 凸尾~*, 退火~ annealed strip, 脱脂[除油]~ degreased strip, 未脱脂[未除油]~ non-degreased strip, 中等宽度~*
带钢边缘自动控制　automatic strip edgepath control
带钢表面测温计　strip surface thermometer
带钢淬火法　strip annealing process ◇ 切斯特菲尔德~ chresterfield('s) process
带钢打滑　slippage between strip and roller
带钢打印机　strip marker

带钢单向皱纹　ridges
带钢电解清洗作业线　electrolytic strip cleaning line
带钢电解脱脂作业线　electrolytic strip degreasing line
带钢跟踪装置控制用旋转缸　swivel cylinder for strip tracker control
带钢焊机　strip welding machine
带钢夹持器　strip clamping device
带钢剪切机组[作业线]　strip shearing line
带钢卷　strip coil ◇ 拆～装置 steel strip unwinding device
带钢卷取机　strip coiler, power reels (非传动辊轧机的)
带钢宽度　strip width
带钢拉辊　strip drawer
带钢冷轧机　cold-strip (steel rolling) mill ◇ 森吉米尔～*, 泰勒～ Taylor mill
带钢连续镀锌机组[作业线]　continuous strip line galvanizing
带钢连续酸洗机组　continuous strip pickling line
带钢连续退火炉　continuous strip annealing furnace
带钢连铸　steel strip continuous casting
带钢连铸连轧　in-line strip production
带钢前端检测器　strip front end detector
带钢热轧机　hot strip mill ◇ 可逆式～*
带钢涂油机　strip oiler
带钢退火炉　strip annealing plant
带钢拓宽　strip steel widening
带钢压紧辊(抛光机的)　break roll
带钢压力机　strip press ◇ 机座间～*
带钢压延机　hoop mill
带钢游动　strip walking
带钢轧机　strip (rolling) mill ◇ 多机架～*, 伊万斯～ Evans mill, 周期式～ Kessler mill
带钢张力　strip tension
带钢张力计　(同"带材张力计")
带钢支承台　strip support table

带钩钢筋　bar with hooked ends
带箍桩　capped pile
带荷试车　trial run with load
带接头　belt joint
带筋扁钢　ribbed flat
带筋筋(条)　ribbed bar
带筋砖格　ribbed checker
带进硫量(随炉料)　sulphur input
带锯　band [belt, ribbon] saw ◇ 双金属～ bimetal bandsaws
带锯机　band saw(ing) machine
带卷　【压】strip coil, coil of strip, coiled strip [stock], coil ◇ 报废[不合格]～ rejected coil, 紧卷[难松开]的～*, 经切分的～(用多刀圆盘剪切分) gang-slit strip, 冷轧～*, 平整的～ temper-rolled coil, 齐边～ flush wound coil, 松开的～*, 有涂层～ coil-coated stock, 扎紧的～ strapped coil, 组合[加重]～*
带卷仓库　coil storage
带卷测量装置　coil measuring device
带卷长度(带材展开长度)　coil length
带卷称量系统　coil weighing system
带卷成批退火(在罩式炉内)　gang softening
带卷成形辊　coiler roll
带卷秤[称量装置]　coil weighing scale [machine]
带卷尺寸　coil size
带卷储存台　coil magazine
带卷处理　coil handling
带卷存放鞍座　coil storage saddle
带卷打捆站　coil banding station
带卷打捆装置　coil strapping device
带卷单垛退火　single-stack coil annealing
带卷(定尺)横剪作业线　coil cut-up line
带卷定心　coil centering
带卷镀锡前预整作业线　coil preparation line, coiling line
带卷端头　coil tail, strip end
带卷端头扳直机[装置]　(同"带卷直头机")

带卷端头铆接装置　riveter
带卷端头喂进装置　coil end feeding device
带卷堆场　coil yard
带卷堆垛高度(退火时的)　stacking height
带卷垛　coiled stock
带卷垛存台架　storage rack
带卷翻倒装置　coil overturning device
带卷翻转装置　coil-upender attachment
带卷防撞器　coil bumper
带卷分出装置　coil branching device
带卷分离器圆盘　coil separator disc
带卷焊接(机组)作业线(指端头焊接)　coil welding line (CWL, C.W.L.), coil build-up line, strip welding line for coils
带卷缓冲辊　coil snubber roll
带卷回转装置　coil rotating rig, coil turning device
带卷架　coil frame
带卷检查[检验]室　coil inspection room (C.I.R.)
带卷剪切作业线　coil shearing line (CSL, C.S.L.)
带卷接收器　coil receiver
带卷进料箱　coil box
带卷卷紧法　coil compacting method
带卷开卷　coil unwinding
带卷开卷箱　coil box
带卷控制室　coil control pulpit (C.C.P.)
带卷捆扎带卸除分离盘　band strap removal separating disc
带卷捆扎机　strapping machine, coil banding [binding] machine
带卷拉紧装置　coil tightening device (C.T.D.)
带卷冷却运输机　coil cooling conveyer
带卷裂边检查仪　edge (strip) scanner
带卷平整擦伤　coil temper digs
带卷起重夹钳　coil tongs
带卷圈　strip layer, wrap, lap
带卷圈数的增加　coil build-up

带卷热平整机作业线　coil thermal flat line
带卷人工包装设备　manual coil packing equipment
带卷升降车　coil jack
带卷升降回转台　coil lift-and-turn unit
带卷升降机　coil hoist
带卷升降台　coil lifter ◇ 固定式～*
带卷输出台(卷取机旁的)　coil delivery ramp
带卷输入(储存)台(开卷机旁的)　coil entry ramp
带卷输送装置　coil carrying device
带卷双路运输机　two-strand coil conveyer
带卷送进(区)段　entry section
带卷酸洗作业线　coil pickling line (CPL)
带卷台架　coil skid
带卷套入(卷轴)　coil insertion
带卷推出机　extractor fork
带卷推出器(卷取机的)　coil pusher
带卷推出装置　coil pushing-off device
带卷退火炉　(strip) coil (annealing) furnace ◇ 直接[敞开]加热～*
带卷退火作业线　coil annealing line (CAL)
带卷托台　coil saddle
带卷外径　coil outside diameter
带卷小车　coil car ◇ 出口～delivery coil car, 轧入侧～entry coil car
带卷芯子　coil core
带卷芯子拆除装置　coil core removing device
带卷旋转装置　coil rotating device
带卷移送车　coil transfer car [buggy]
带卷移送机　coil transfer [skid]
带卷移送升降机　coil transfer lifter
带卷引头检测器　coil leading detector
带卷预整装置　coil preparation unit
带卷圆周尺寸　circumference of coil
带卷运输车　coil carriage ◇ 带V型托台的～camel-back car
带卷运输机　coil conveyer

带 dai

带卷运输机电气室　coil conveyor electrical room (C.C.E.R.)
带卷运输机控制台　coil conveyor control pulpit (C.C.C.P.)
带卷运输装置　tong
带卷运送车　coil car [buggy], coil conveying truck, strip handling car
带卷支持器　coil holder
带卷支座卷筒(悬臂式)　coil holder head
带卷直径测量装置　coil diameter measuring device
带卷直径检测器　coil diameter detector
带卷直头机[装置]　coil opener [peeler], strip opener, coil-tailing device, tail stripper [puller], pulling device
带卷直头机(插入)錾　coil opener chisel
带卷直头机摆动装置　coil opener swing
带卷贮存跨　coil stocking [yard] bay
带卷转向辊　coil turning roller
带卷装料台　coil loading skid
带卷装卸车调档　coil buggy-shift
带卷装卸台(开卷机旁的)　coil ramp
带卷装卸装置　coil-handling equipment
带卷准备车　coil preparatory truck ◇ 移动式～*
带卷准备[预整]站　coil preparatory station
带卷准备作业线　coil preparation line (CPL)
带卷自动称量系统　automatic coil weighing system
带卷自动收集装置　auto coil handling equipment
带卷自动输送[处理]装置　automatic coil handling device ◇ 进口端～*
带卷自动卸卷车　(同"卸卷车")
带卷自动[万能]装卸车　coil car [buggy]
带卷座(开卷机的)　coil cradle ◇ V形～vee shaped coil rest
带壳挤压　extruding with shell
带孔回转窑　ported rotary reactor
带扣　belt fastener [hook]

带宽　band [frequency] width
带肋钢筋　ribbed (steel) bar ◇ 冷轧～*
带连接板焊接　tie welding
带轮　band pulley
带棚车　covered car
带坯　【压】strip plate ◇ 煤气管～gas strip
带坯连铸　strip casting
带坯连铸工艺　strip casting technology
带坯连铸机　strip caster
带皮挤压　extruding with shell
带谱　band spectrum
带谱分析　band spectrum analysis
带前张力(冷)轧机(带卷的)　coiler tension rolling mill
带圈(圆柱的)　parallel
带绕铁心　tape(-wound) core
带入污染(如电镀槽被阴极污染)　drag-in
带色薄金属氧化膜电沉积法　electrocolour process
带色雾翳　coloured fog
带筛　【选】belt screen
带梢的　tapered
带式(焙烧)机　travel(l)ing grate (induration) machine, travel(l)ing grate [furnace], travel(l)ing grate (pellet hardening) machine, continuous travelling grate machine, grate furnace, straight grate (induration machine), straight grate pelletizing machine, pellet grate, burning machine, agglomeration [firing, grate, indurating, induration, travelling] strand ◇ DL[德拉沃－鲁奇]型～*, 抽风～*, 德拉沃型～*, 鼓风～*, 鲁奇－德拉沃型～*
带式(焙烧)机法　(straight) grate process
带式(焙烧)机球团厂　straight grate (pelletizing) plant
带式焙烧机球团法　straight grate pelletizing process, travel(l)ing grate pel-letizing, Lurgi pelletizing system
带式焙烧炉　moving grate furnace

带式焙烧系统(球团矿的) travel(l)ing grate system
带式布料机[器] travel(l)ing [conveyer-type] charging machine,(travelling) belt feeder,【团】charging conveyer
带式传动 belt transmission
带式传感器 【理】tape probe
带式传送炉 conveyer-belt furnace
带式磁选机 belt magnetic separator, magnet belt separator, magnetic separating belt
带式电阻加热体 strip heater
带式法(生产铝基钢带) strip-type method
带式分选机 belt separator
带式干燥机 band [ribbon] drier, travel(l)ing grate dryer, drying grate
带式刮板 ribbon flight
带式刮油器 belt type oil skimmer
带式过滤机 【色】band filter
带式过滤器 band filter ◇ 油浸自动~*
带式混合机 belt mixer (unit)
带式机 strand type furnace, moving grate (furnace), continuous grate
带式机布料皮带机 【团】grate feed conveyor
带式机布料点 【团】strand charging station
带式机布料器 【团】strand [grate] feeder
带式机法 grate process
带式机利用系数 【团】grate productivity [factor], grate specific production
带式机面积 grating area
带式机排矿 【团】strand discharge
带式机烧结(法) grate sintering
带式机速度 【团】strand speed
带式机系统(循环) 【团】grate cycle
带式机卸矿点 【团】strand discharging station
带式机中心线 strand centerline
带式给料机 belt [ribbon] feeder, belt extractor ◇ 可调速~*

带式加热炉(输送带式) belt type heating furnace
带式浇铸机 straight-line casting machine
带式冷却机 linear [straight(-line)] cooler ◇ 鼓风~*
带式冷却机台车 cooler grate
带式离合器 band clutch
带式连接[连轴]器 band coupling
带式连铸机 belt caster, belt casting machine
带式炉 conveyer type furnace, band oven ◇ 连续~
带式磨床[磨光机] belt grinder, belt grinding machine
带式磨光 (abrasive) belt grinding
带式抛光 abrasive belt polishing
带式抛光机 belt [band] polishing machine
带式抛丸滚筒 conveyer wheelabrator
带式撇油器 belt [strip] skimmer
带式球团焙烧机 travel(l)ing grate pelletizing machine
带式筛分机 【选】belt screen
带式烧结机 straight-line sintering machine, sinter [agglomeration] strand, continuous (pallet-type) sintering machine, continuous sintering machine [strand], continuous strand sinter machine, sintering belt, sinter chain, horizontal travelling grate, endless chain grate ◇ DL型~*, 鲁奇型~*, 普通~*, 延长型~*
带式烧结机电炉联合直接炼铁法 【铁】D.L.M.(Dwight-Lloyd-McWane) process
带式烧结机规格 strand size
带式烧结机排烟罩 grate hood
带式烧结机上行段 top strand
带式输送[运输]机 belt [ribbon, band] conveyor, conveyer-belt (ing), transport conveyer belt ◇ 水冷~*
带式松砂机 【铸】Royer sand mixer (and aerator)

带式探测器 【理】tape probe
带式提升机 band [belt] elevator
带式卸料器 belt tripper
带式窑 belt kiln
带式油刮子 belt type oil skimmer
带式预热机 travel(l)ing grate type pre-heater
带式真空过滤机 belt vacuum filter
带式制动器 band [strap] brake
带式制砖机 auger brick machine
带式自记仪 strip-chart instrument
带榫口模 lock die
带套阳极 bagged anode
带通 band pass
带通滤波器 【电】band (pass) filter
带头试棒 headed test bar
带头线钳 pul(ling)-in dogs
带凸缘轮对(送锭机的) flanged wheels
带凸缘轮箍 flanged tyre
带尾自动停止装置 automatic coil tail end stopping device
带系列(光谱线的) set of bands
带销螺栓 cotter bolt
带芯股钢丝绳 seal construciton rope
带芯冷拔(用于生产毛细管) core drawing
带芯钎焊条 cored solder
带芯铜线 core wire
带烟气体 fume laden gas
带眼杆 eyebar
带眼(拉丝)模坯 cored [preformed] die
带油切削 oily turning
带载调节接点(电炉的) on-load tap changing
带载隔离开关 on-load disconnecting [isolating] switch
带渣金属 drossy metal
带闸 band [strap] brake
带张力轧制 (同"轧件带张力轧制")
带指手套 fingered glove
带状 banding
带状沉淀 【金】banded precipitation
带状赤铁矿石英岩 banded hematite quartzite
带状垫板滚对焊机 【焊】tape butt-seam welding machine
带状发热元件 ribbon element
带状腐蚀 zonal corrosion
带状光谱 band spectrum
带状焊料 【焊】ribbon solder
带状火焰 ribbon flame
带状火焰型多喷孔烧嘴 line burner
带状夹杂 【冶】lamination ◇ 有方向性的 ~物 directional banding of inclusions
带状结构 banded structure, banding, zonal texture, 【金】zone structure
带状结晶[(晶体)带状生长] zonal growth
带状镍银 silmet
带状排列 banded arrangement, zonation
带状热电偶高温计 strip thermocouple pyrometer
带状位错 zonal dislocation
带状枝晶 ribbon dendrite
带状组织 zone [zonal] structure, banded orientation
带走 carrying off, entrainment, dragging
带走的烟尘 carry-over dust
带走干燥(法)(用热气流) entrained drying
带走气体 entrapped gas
带走溶液 entrained solution
带走水分 entrained moisture
带走损失(电解液的) drag-out losses
带走物 entrainment
带阻滤波器 band elimination filter, band-stop filter
代班班组 【企】relay shift
代表类型 representative type
代表性 representativeness ◇ 有~的尺寸 typical dimensions
代表性部分[馏分] representative fraction
代表性取样 representative sampling

代表性试样	representative [unbiased] sample
代表值	representative value
代氟纶(聚三氟氯乙烯树脂)	Daiflo
代理人	agent (Agt)
代理商	factor ◇ 拿佣金的~ commission representative
代理银行	correspondent bank
代码	code ◇ 恒比~ constant ratio code
代码变换器	code converter
代码道	code track
代码检验	code check
代码扩充字符	code extension character
代码转换	code conversion
代入值	【计】call by value
代数	【数】algebra ◇ 逻辑[布尔]~ Boolean algebra
代数表达式	algebraic expression
代数符号	algebraic sign
代数平均值	algebraic average
代数语言	【计】algebraic language
代替锌的能力(代替黄铜中锌的能力)	zinc-replacement capacity
代位晶格位置	substitutional lattice site
代位式固溶体	substitutional solid solution
代位式溶质原子	substitutional solute atom
代位元素	substitutional element
代谢不全硫杆菌	Thiobacillus perometabolis
代谢能	metabolic energy
代阴极(处理电镀溶液用)	dummy cathode
代用材料[物质]	substitute [alternate] material
代用钢	alternative [emergency] steel
代用合金	substitute alloy ◇ 图朗—伦纳德银~ *，库珀金~ Cooper's gold，沃恩银~ Warne's alloy
代用金属	substitute [emergency] metal
代用黏土	plasticine
代用品	substitute, alternatives
代用燃料	substitute [substitutional, alternative] fuel
代用天然气	substitute natural gas
贷款	loan, credit
袋匙式挖泥船[机]	bag and spoon dredger
袋滤器	bag filter, bag house collector, dedusting bag, bag (filter) house
袋式提金器(混汞法)	【色】pocket amalgamator
袋装水泥	bagged [sacked] cement
待处理薄板	mender sheet
待处理中断	【计】armed interrupt
待定系数法	method of undetermined coefficients
待命中断	armed interrupt
待修时间	unattended time
待选矿石	concentrating ore
待用金属(感应炉内的)	heel
待轧	rolling-delay
丹德利昂铅基轴承合金(18Sb,10Sn,余量Pb)	Dandelion (metal)
丹多钢包用砖	Dando brick
丹佛型搅拌机	Denver agitator
丹尼索夫式出镁真空罐(电解槽用)	Denisov vacuum ladle
丹聂尔电池	Daniell('s) cell
单C形吊钩(带卷吊运用)	single C-hook
单J形连接(管子的)	single J joint
单U形坡口焊缝	single-U groove weld
单U形坡口焊接	single U-groove welding
单V形坡口焊缝	single-V groove weld
单V形对接	single V-butt joint
单板剪切机	veneer clipper
单半径椭圆	single radius oval
单倍尺长度	single lengths
单臂锤	【压】overhanging hammer
单臂钢包炉	single-arm ladle furnace
单臂式锻锤	【压】open side hammer
单臂式堆料机	single wing stacker
单臂式切割机	single cantilever cutting machine

单边卷边角焊接头 corner-flange weld
单变的 monotropic
单变(度)平衡【理】univariant equilibrium
单变(度)[变数]系 univariant system
单变量共晶 monovariant eutectic
单变量平衡 monovariant equilibrium
单变现象 monotropy
单变性 monotropism, monotropy
单步操作 【计】one-step [single-step] operation
单槽电解溶解器 single-cell dissolver
单槽焊缝 single-groove weld
单侧(错位)焊点(熔核) one-sided nugget
单侧焊 one side welding
单侧加热炉 side fired furnace
单侧缺口拉伸试样 single-edge notch tension specimen
单侧上烧嘴均热炉 top one-way-fired (soaking) pit
单侧烧嘴均热炉 one-way-fired pit
单侧楔形砖 one-sided wedge-shaped brick, side feather
单侧卸载运输车 one-side transfercar
单层 monolayer, one [single] layer
单层箅条[筛网] simple grid
单层扁平产品 single-layer flat product
单层沉降槽 one-chamber thickener, single-department thickener
单层传动带 single-ply belt
单层堆焊[单道熔敷层] single-bead deposit
单层粉粒 monolayer of particles
单层焊 single-layer welding
单层焊缝 single-bead deposit, one-pass weld
单层建筑物 single-story building
单层流化床反应器【色】single fluidized bed reactor
单层炉 one story furnace, one-deck oven
单层棉纱包覆的 single cotton covered (s.c.c.)
单层钎焊管 single-wall brazing tube

单层人造丝包覆的 single rayon covered (s.r.c.)
单层烧结(法) single-layer sintering
单层丝包线 single silk-covered wire
单层涂饰 single-coat finish
单层振动筛 single-deck vibrating screen
单层纸包装的 single paper covered (s.p.c.)
单程流程 single process flow
单程热交换器 single-pass heat exchanger
单程烧结法 (同"一次烧结法")
单齿辊破碎机 sinter breaker
单尺寸粉【粉】monosize powder
单冲杆压机 single-punch press
单冲杆压模 single-punch die
单畴磁铁 single domain magnet ◇ 伸长~*
单畴铁磁粒子[质点] single domain ferromagnetic particle
单出铁场高炉 single casthouse blast-furnace
单处理机[器]【计】monoprocessor
单床操作 monobed operation
单床离子交换 monobed ion exchange
单(磁)畴 monodomain
单次电离 single ionization
单次拉拔的钢丝 soft-drawn wire
单次拉丝机 single wire-drawing machine, monoblock [single-block] machine, single-deck [single-spindle] motobloc, bull block (drawing) ◇ 立式~*, 卧式~*, 无滑动~*
单次拉丝卷筒 single-hole wire-drawing block, single-spindle wire block
单次酸洗薄板 single-pickled sheet
单道次轧机 single-pass mill
单道次轧制 one-pass rolling, single-pass [one-pass] operation
单道[程]焊缝 one-pass weld ◇ 全熔透~*
单道[程]焊(接) one-pass [single-pass, single-run] welding

单道拉拔 single-pass drawing
单地址计算机 single address computer
单点焊(接) single(-spot) welding, individual spot welding
单点记录器 single-point recorder
单点载荷 point [single] load
单电动机移动式起重机 one-motor travel(1)ing crane
单电极电弧熔炼炉 live-bottom furnace
单电源式电弧电焊机 single-arc welder
单电子键 one-electron bond
单电子原子 one-electron atom
单丁基磷酸 monobutyl phosphoric acid
单动橡皮冲床 single-action rubber press
单动压机 single-action press
单动压制 single-action compression [pressing]
单动(蒸汽)锤 single-acting hammer
单斗卷扬机 single-skip hoist
单斗提升机 skip
单斗挖泥机 dipper dredger
单独传动 individual driving, unit drive, direct gear drive
单独传动辊道 individually driven (roller) table
单独传动机座 individually driven stand
单独电弧加热 independent arc heating
单独基础 isolated foundation
单独激励 independent excitation
单独试验 single test
单独调整 individual [separate] adjustment
单独拖动(装置) separate drive, singly operated drive
单独影响 separate influence
单端斜侧楔形砖 feather-end on edge
单端蓄热 single end regeneration (SER)
单端源 single-ended source
单段 single-stage, one-step
单段操作 (同"一次完成操作")
单断开关 single-break switch
单堆积模型 (同"单塞积模型")

单对接搭板 single butt strap
单垛式炉台 single-stack base
单垛退火 single-stack annealing ◇ 带卷~*
单垛油退火炉(带钢的) single-stack oil annealing furnace
单垛(罩式)炉 single-stack furnace ◇ 辐射管加热的~*
单反射 single bounce
单反应器熔融还原 single vessel smelting reduction
单方面转让 【企】unilateral transfer
单分度圆周测角仪 one-circle goniometer
单分解 simple decomposition
单分取样器 single-split sampler
单分散系 monodisperse system
单分子薄膜 monofilm
单分子层 monomolecular layer, monofilm, monolayer
单分子反应 monomolecular reaction
单分子膜(层) monomolecular [unimolecular] film
单分子吸附 monomolecular adsorption
单峰分布 【数】unimodal distribution
单峰性 unimodality
单峰(值)的 single-peaked
单峰值分析 single-peak analysis
单风机运转 single fan operation
单风嘴 single orifice
单风嘴炉缸(鼓风炉一个风嘴的有效炉缸面积)
【色】elemental furnace
单坩埚炉 single-crucible furnace
单缸发动机 single cylinder machine [engine]
单缸鼓风机 single cylinder blowing engine
单格刻度值 value of division
单铬 monochrome (一种染料)
单个精矿中央射流喷嘴 single concentrate central jet burner
单个颗粒[粉粒,粒子,质点] individual [single, unit] particle

单个生产 【企】job [piece] production	单行铆接 single-riveted joint
单个试样 individual sample	单耗 unit consumption
单个位错 single dislocation	单弧串列焊 single-arc tandem weld
单个原子 individual atom	单弧法（成品圆孔）【压】single plug method
单个铸件 one-of-a-kind casting, unit casting	单弧自动电焊机 single-arc welder, one head automatic arc welding machine
单根长度 single length	单滑车 single pulley
单根焊条电弧焊 (stick) electrode welding	单滑移 single slip
单工 【电】simplex	单活塞爆炸压力机 single piston explosive press
单股的 simple strand	单活套坑装置 single-looping pit
单股钢绳 single-strand wire	单基 isolated foundation
单股线 solid conductor	单机 single unit, one machine
单管路喷吹 【铁】pulverized coal injection process with a main feed pipe	单机架平整机 single stand skin-pass mill
单管烧嘴 simple pipe-type burner	单机可逆式轧机 single reversing mill
单管提升(真空脱气)法 【钢】vacuum lift degassing ◇多特蒙德～ Dortmund method	单机列(的) in one train
	单机列轧机 single-line mill train
单管氧枪 single-hole lance	单机四流连铸机 single 4-strand casting machine
单硅酸盐{2MO·SiO$_2$} monosilicate	单机轧制的连续式轧机 open continuous mill
单硅酸盐渣 【色】monosilicate [uni-silicate] slag, one-to-one slag（炼铅的）	单机座 single stand
单轨 single-track, monorail（小吊车用）	单机座轧机 single stand mill
单轨称量车 monorail weight car	单箕斗 single-skip
单轨吊包 monorail ladle	单极导电率［性］ unipolar conductivity
单轨起重机［吊车］ monorail crane (truck), monorail hoist	单极电位 single electrode potential
	单极发电机 homopolar generator [dynamo]
单轨桥式起重机 single track hoist bridge	
单轨提升装置 monorail hoist unit	单极晶体管 unipolar transistor
单轨线路 monorail track	单极开关 single-switch, single-pole switch
单轨运输机 monorail conveyer	单极性 unipolarity
单轨装料机 monorail charger	单级玻璃油蒸气真空泵 single-stage glass oil-vapor pump
单癸基 monodecyl	
单癸基磷酸 monodecyl phosphoric acid	单级(的) single-stage, one-stage, one-step
单辊破碎机 (single-)roll crusher, disintegrater	单级反应器 single-stage reactor
	单级分批萃取 【色】single-batch extraction
单辊破碎机算板 crash deck	
单辊行星轧机 single planetary mill	单级鼓风机 single-stage blower
单锅式镀锡机组 single-sweep tinning unit	单级混合沉降器(萃取用) single-stage mixer-settler
单焊缝连接 single joint	单级减速机 single (step) reduction gear

unit
单级接触萃取 【色】single-contact extraction
单级流化床反应器 (同"单层流化床反应器")
单级破碎 single-stage crushing
单级文氏管 single-stage Venturi
单级压缩机 single-stage compressor
单价 unit price [cost],【化】univalence, univalency
单价合同 【企】unit price contract
单价金 monovalent gold
单价金属 monovalent metal
单价离子 monovalent ion
单架式锻锤(悬臂式) single-frame hammer
单键 single-linkage, single bond
单件测定[测量] individual measurement
单件供料 single-piece feeding
单件模 single-piece die
单件生产 【企】(single-)piece [job] production
单件整体模 solid single-piece die
单件重量 weight per unit
单搅拌混合沉降器(萃取用) 【色】simple stirred mixer-settler
单脚高架起重机 one-leg construction gantry crane, cantilever(ed) gantry, semi-portal crane
单脚门式起重机 semigantry crane
单脚泥芯撑 stem [stalk-pipe] chaplet
单脚起重机 one-legged crane
单角弯曲(法) three-point bending
单接触法制硫酸车间 single contact sulphuric acid plant
单阶段熔炼过程(钢的) single-stage refining
单结晶体管 uni-junction transistor (UJT)
单金属粉末 one-metal powder
单金属丝 plain wire
单金属系 monometallic system

单晶 monocrystal, single crystal, unit crystal ◇ 安德雷德拉~法 Andrade method, 布里奇曼~制取法*, 查尔玛斯金属~制取法*, 卡皮查~形成法*, 拉~*, 片状~ flat crystal, 熔体生长的~*, 应变退火生长的~*
单晶棒[条] single crystal bar
单晶粉粒 monocrystalline particle
单晶硅 monocrystalline silicon, single crystal silicon ◇ 中子嬗变掺杂~*
单晶拉制电子控制器 electronic controller for crystal-pulling
单晶炉 single crystal (growing) furnace, mono-crystal furnace
单晶面的 pedial
单晶强化 single-crystal reinforcement
单晶取向 orientation of single crystal
单晶取向研究 【理】single crystal orientation study
单晶生长 single crystal growing ◇ 韦纳伊~法*
单晶生长技术 single crystal growth technique
单晶生长器 single crystal grower
单晶石墨 single crystal graphite
单晶体 single crystal, monocrystal, unit crystal
单晶体X射线衍射仪 single crystal X-ray diffractometer
单晶体变形 deformation of single crystal
单晶体单色仪 monolithic crystal monochromator
单晶体金属 single crystalline metal
单晶体磷光体屏 single crystal phosphor screen
单晶体状态 monocrystalline condition
单晶钨丝 single crystal tungsten wire
单晶形的 monocrystalline
单晶照相机 single crystal camera
单晶状态 monocrystalline condition
单镜辐射高温计 single mirror radiation pyrometer

单卷筒拉丝机　single-block machine
单颗粒　【粉】monosize powder
单壳焊接变流［换流］器　monocarcase [one-body] welding set
单空位　single vacancy
单孔穿孔器　unipunch
单孔拉瓦尔氧枪　single-apertured Laval lance
单孔模　single-hole die ◇ 对称断面型材～挤压*
单孔喷嘴　single-jet [single-hole] nozzle
单跨　【建】single span
单跨车间　single aisle building
单块　【计】monolithic
单块衬底　monolithic substrate
单块集成电路　(同"单片集成电路")
单块轧制　【压】one-piece rolling
单立柱　detached column
单链式拉拔机　single-chain drawbench, single-chain-type bench
单梁(小吊车用)　monorail
单梁起重机　(single-)beam crane
单梁式冲击韧性试验　Charpy test
单梁移动桥式起重机　single-beam travel(l)ing crane
单料斗　single-skip
单列球［滚珠］轴承　single-row ball bearing
单磷酸盐　monophosphate
单馏粗苯　once-run benzol ◇ 酸洗～*
单流道双流氧枪　【钢】single channel double flow oxygen lance
单流连铸机　(single-)strand casting machine, one-strand continuous casting machine
单流设备［连铸］single-strand plant
单流式冷凝器　single-pass condenser
单流式汽轮发动机［涡轮机,透平］　uniflow engine, single flow machine
单炉壳电弧炉　single-hearth electric arc furnace
单炉连铸　batch continuous casting

单炉熔炼法　single-furnace process
单炉容量［生产能力］　individual furnace capacity
单炉体(焙烧)窑　single-stack kiln
单铝酸钙　calcium monoaluminate
单铝酸盐　monoaluminate
单轮滑车　gin block
单脉冲焊　single-impulse welding
单弥散的　monodisperse
单面 J 形坡口对接焊　open-single-J butt weld
单面 T 形焊接　single fillet welded T joint
单面 V 形对接　single V butt joint
单面 V 形角焊接　single V corner joint
单面 V 形坡口焊　open-single-V groove weld
单面铲边焊缝　single-groove weld
单面搭板点焊　bridge spot welding
单面搭焊接　single fillet lap joint
单面点焊　indirect welding
单面镀层　side coating
单面镀锌钢材　one-side galvanized steel, one-side zinc coated steel
单面盖板对接焊　single strap butt welding
单面光亮精轧薄板　one-side bright mill finish sheet
单面焊(接)　one-side welding, welding by one side
单面加垫对接　single glut butt joint
单面加热(式)炉　single-fired reheating furnace, top-fired furnace
单面晶　pedion
单面冷床　single-sided (hot) bed
单面立焊　one-operator vertical welding
单面模板　【建】single-sided pattern plate
单面内角焊缝连接　inside single-fillet corner joint
单面坡口对接焊　open-single-bevel butt weld
单面填角焊缝焊接头　single-filled weld
单面涂乳胶［感光药品］的胶片　single-coated [single-emulsion] film

单面外角焊连接	outside single-fillet corner joint
单面无光泽箔材	matte one-side foil
单面斜对焊接	single-bevel butt joint
单模冲压模	single-punch die
单模孔拉丝机	single-hole wire-drawing machine
单模拉拔机	single-die drawbench
单磨粒切削	single grain cutting
单目显微镜	【金】monocular microscope
单能辐射	monoenergetic radiation
单能慢中子透射	transmission of monoenergetic slow neutron
单能中子	mono-energetic neutron
单排点焊接头	single-row weld
单排风口	single-row tuyere
单排推钢机	single pusher ◇ 液压式～*
单盘离合器	single-disc clutch
单喷管[嘴]	single orifice
单批烧结杯(试验性的)	【铁】batch sinter pot
单片	【计】monolithic, one [single] chip
单片处理机	【计】single chip processor, monolithic processor
单片存储器	monolithic storage [storage]
单片集成电路	【计】monolithic integrated-circuit
单片离合器	single-plate clutch
单凭仪表操纵的	blind
单坡的	【建】lean-to
单坡顶	【建】single pitch roof
单坡顶侧跨[附跨,房屋]	lean-to
单坡屋顶	pent roof, lean-to proof
单歧藻属	Tolypothrix
单汽缸鼓风机	single cylinder blowing engine
单钳口筒式卷取机(炉用)	single-slot mandrel type coiler
单腔模	single-cavity die
单腔式芯盒	single cavity core box
单区电收尘器	single stage precipitator
单曲线齿轮	single-curve gear
单圈感应加热器	single-turn induction heater
单人手浇包	dipper
单熔锭	single-melt ingot
单熔区	single zone
单熔区的浮区熔炼技术	single-zone floating-zone technique
单熔区加热器	single zone heater
单溶剂萃取	【色】single-solvent extraction
单塞积模型(关于断裂机理的)	【理】single pile-up model
单色	monocolor, monochrome
单色 X 射线	monochromatic [homogeneous] X-rays ◇ 聚焦～束*
单色点线记录器	one-colour dotted line recorder
单色电视	(同"黑白电视")
单色辐射	monochromatic [homogeneous] radiation
单色辐射通量	monochromatic flux
单色高温计	single colo(u)r pyrometer
单色光	monochromatic [homogeneous] light
单色光镜	monochromator
单色光谱[分光]计	monochromating spectrometer
单色光强度	monochromatic intensity
单色(光)像	monochromatic image
单色化	monochromatization
单色均匀辐射	monochromatic homogeneous radiation
单色蓝光	ultra-blue-light
单色灵敏度	monochromatic sensitivity
单色滤片	monochromatic filter
单色器	monochromator ◇ 光栅～*,机械～*,晶体～*,科舒瓦式～*,弯晶～*,约翰式～*
单色器焦距	focal distance of monochromator
单色器至焦点距离	monochromator-to-focal point distance
单色射束	monochromatic beam, single

wavelength beam ◇ 晶体反射~*
单色物镜 monochromatic objective
单色显示 monochrome display
单色性 monochromaticity, monochromatism
单色仪 monochromator ◇ 纪尼埃型~*
单色源 monochromatic source
单色针孔 monochromatic-pinhole
单烧(一种燃料燃烧) mono-fuel combustion
单式排铸机用铅字合金(80Pb,15Sb,5Sn) monotype metal
单式自动排铸机用压铸合金(64—78Pb, 7—12Sn, 15—24Sb) monotype die-casting alloy
单室电解槽 single-cell
单室式喷浆枪 single-chamber gun
单室窑 single-chamber [single-compartment] kiln
单室蒸发器 single-effect evaporator
单丝包的(导线) single-silk covered (S.S.C.)
单丝复合材料 monofilament composite
单丝聚丙烯织物 monofilament woven polypropylene cloth
单探头探伤法 single probe testing method
单探头系统(扫描的) single [one] probe system
单探针法(测量半导体材料电阻用) one-probe method
单膛[室]的 【冶】single hearth, single-stage
单套产量[设备能力] single-line capacity
单体 monomer, simplex
单体分离 liberation grind ◇ 脉石[废石]~*
单体分离粒度 liberation size
单体滑车 single pulley
单体化合物 monomeric compound
单体晶粒 separate grain
单体硫 free sulphur

单体烧结 【粉】batch sintering
单体石墨 free graphite
单体碳 free carbon
单体液压支柱钢管 steel pipe for one-piece hydraulic pillar
单条薄带退火用连续热处理炉 continuous strand-type furnace
单条带卷 single coil
单铁口高炉 single taphole blast furnace
单通阀 one-way valve
单通烟道 detached chimney
单筒显微镜 【金】monocular microscope
单投开关 single-throw switch
单头 one-head, single-head
单头扳手 single-end (ed) spanner [wrench]
单头螺纹管 single spirally corrugated tube
单头喷嘴 single jet nozzle
单头自动电弧焊机 【焊】one-head automatic arc-welding machine
单涂层搪瓷器皿 one-coat ware
单烷基磷酸{RO(OH)$_2$PO} monoalkylphosphoric acid
单烷基亚膦酸{R·P(OH)$_2$} monoalkylphosphinous acid
单围盘轧制的 singly repeated
单维布置[阵列] one-dimensional array
单位变形 unit deformation
单位变形功 【压】resilience, resiliency
单位表面含碳量 specific surface carbon content
单位产量 specific production[yield]
单位产量所需工时 【企】man-hour requirement
单位产品劳动成本 【企】labor cost per unit of output
单位产品劳动成本指数 index of labor cost per unit of output
单位产品缺陷数 defects per unit
单位产水量 specific yield
单位产值能耗 energy consumption per u-

nit of output value
单位磁导率　unit permeance
单位电耗　specific energy consumption
单位电荷　unit charge
单位断裂功　【理】unit rupture work
单位负荷　specific load
单位功率　specific power rating, unit power, power density（高频热处理的）
单位后张力　【压】specific back tension
单位活度　unit activity
单位加热表面释热量　heat liberation per unit heating surface
单位阶跃　【理】unit step
单位晶胞　【金】elementary [primitive] cell
单位晶格　unit cell [lattice]
单位矩阵　【数】unit(ary) matrix
单位裂纹传播[扩展]能　unit crack propagation energy
单位炉(子)体(积)释热量　heat liberation per unit furnace volume
单位面积　unit area
单位面积电阻[阻力]　unit-area resistance
单位面积功率　power per unit area
单位面积轧制力　specific rolling force ◇ 最大允许～*
单位能耗　specific [unit] energy consumption
单位前张力　【压】specific front tension
单位强度位错　dislocation of unit strength
单位燃料消耗　specific fuel consumption
单位容积　unit volume
单位生产率[能力]　specific [unit] productivity, specific capacity [duty], throughput rate
单位生铁风量　blast rate
单位生铁耗矿石量　【铁】ore ratio
单位生铁炉尘量　dust rate
单位时间　unit time
单位时间流量　flow ratio
单位时间内熔炼炉数　heat frequency
单位矢量　【理】unit vector
单位体积　specific volume (s.v.), unit volume
单位体积密度　specific bulk weight
单位体积试样　unit-volume sample
单位体积质量　volume-weight, unit [bulk] weight, weight by volume
单位投资　specific capital expense, specific investment cost
单位位错　【理】unit dislocation
单位误差　unit error
单位消耗　unit consumption
单位压力　specific [unit] pressure
单位压制[成型]压力　specific moulding pressure
单位延伸　unit elongation
单位应力　unit stress
单位硬度　unit hardness
单位渣量　【铁】slag ratio
单位轧制压力　specific rolling pressure
单位质量　【理】specific [unit] mass
单位重量　unit weight, weight unit
单位重量电阻率　weight resistivity
单位重量发热值（燃料的）　heating value per unit weight
单位重量热容　heat capacity per unit weight
单位阻力　unit resistance
单稳态触发器　【电】monostable trigger
单稳态多谐振荡器[单稳线路]　【电】monostable [one-shot] multivibrator
单物料焙烧　firing of individual material
单析反应(固态反应)　monotectoid reaction
单系列(的)　in one train, uniserial
单细胞藻　unicellular algae
单纤维　monofilament, single fibre ◇ 碳～ carbon monofilament
单纤维复合材料　monofilament composite, single fibre composite
单纤维强化复合材料　filament reinforced composite
单纤维体系　monofilament system
单线电路图　single-line diagram

单线集中润滑系统	one-way lubrication system
单线皮带机通廊	single conveyer gallery
单线式端头-废料剪切机	single-strand crop and cobble shears
单线(式)拉丝机	single head wire drawing machine, single-die drawbench
单线式(线材)轧机	single-strand mill
单线态(原子的)	single state
单线围盘	single-strand repeater
单线相互作用	singlet interaction
单线移送机	single-strand drag conveyer
单线轧制	one-strand [single-strand] rolling
单相边界层	single-phase boundary layer
单相变压器	monophase [single-phase] transformer ◇ 干式～*
单相成核	homogeneous nucleation
单相催化(作用)	homogeneous catalysis
单相电弧炉	single-phase arc furnace
单相电流	monophase [single-phase] current
单相电炉	single-phase furnace
单相-多相催化作用	homogeneous-heterogeneous catalysis
单相二极电(弧熔炼)炉[单相双电极电炉]	single-phase two-electrode furnace
单相反应	homogeneous reaction
单相负荷	single-phase load
单相合金	one phase alloy, homogeneous [homogenized, single-phase] alloy
单相黄铜	(见"α黄铜")
单相混合物	homogeneous mixture
单相交流发电机	single-phase alternator
单相扩散	single-phase diffusion
单相炉底通电[单相单极]电弧熔炼炉	single-phase live-bottom furnace
单相平衡	homogeneous [monophase] equilibrium
单相区	single-phase region
单相烧结	【粉】homogeneous sintering
单相钛合金	single-phase titanium alloy
单相系	【金】homogeneous system
单相状态(合金)	single-phase(d) [homogeneous] condition
单相组织	single-phase [homogeneous] structure
单向成型	【粉】one-direction [single-action] compacting
单向齿锉	hack file
单向导体	unidirectional conductor
单向电流	unidirectional current
单向多头拉伸机	single draught multi-drawing machine
单向阀	check valve (CV), non-return valve ◇ 玻璃球～*
单向非均质性	【理】unidirectional anisotropy
单向复合材料	unidirectional composite
单向杆阀	non-rising stem valve
单向钢筋	one-way reinforcement
单向挤压	single-ended pressing
单向加热炉	one-way furnace
单向节流阀	choke check
单向进给[进口]	single admission
单向拉伸载荷	uniaxial tensile load
单向离合器	pawl [one-way] clutch
单向流动	uniflow, plug (like) flow (流化床的)
单向脉动电流	unidirectional pulsating current
单向凝固	【金】unidirectional freezing [solidification]
单向取向	【理】uniaxial orientation
单向勺式加料器	【色】one-way scoop feeder
单向通道[信道]	【电】forward [half-duplex, one-way] channel
单向通信	one-way communication, simplex
单向压机	single-action press
单向压力	uniaxial pressure
单向压实	one-direction compacting
单向压缩	unidirectional compression

单向压制　one-direction pressing, single-action compression [compacting, pressing], compaction by single action
单向应力　uniaxial pressure
单向应力状态　simple state of stress
单向轧机　【压】unidirectional mill
单向作用的　unilateral
单效压塑　compaction by single action
单效蒸发器　single-effect evaporator
单斜点阵[晶格]　monoclinic lattice
单斜结构　monoclinic structure
单斜晶胞　monoclinic cell
单斜晶系　monoclinic system
单斜晶系对称　monoclinic symmetry
单斜面楔形砖　end-feather
单斜钠锆石{(Na$_2$,Ca)O·ZrO$_2$·3SiO$_2$·2H$_2$O}　cataplei(i)te
单斜系晶体　monoclinic crystal
单斜相　monoclinic phase
单芯电缆　single(-core) cable
单形　monomorphous, simplex
单行程加工　(同"一次完成操作")
单循环　single cycle
单循环液-液萃取　【色】single-cycle liquid-liquid extraction
单烟道　single flue
单焰割炬[焊枪,燃烧器]　rat-tail burner
单焰焊炬　single-flame blowpipe
单叶轮机　single impeller machine
单叶双曲面轮廓　concave hyperbolic contour
单液淬火(法)　simple quench, single-stage quenching
单一(数)　unity
单一 X 射线图样[照相]　【理】single X-ray pattern
单一标准焊缝[焊]　single standard seam
单一波长射束　(同"单色射束")
单一成分[组分]　individual component
单一成分气体　simple gas
单一的高炉煤气　straight blast furnace gas

单一的焦炉煤气　straight coke oven gas
单一分布　homogeneous distribution
单一固溶体　single solid solution
单一能级　single (energy) level
单一溶剂　single solvent
单一溶质　single solute
单一式缓冲器　single bumper ◇ 炉用~
单一涂层　single-coat finish
单一物料　individual material
单一(型)砂　【铸】system sand
单一型式　unimodality
单一原料组分　individual burden constituent
单一状态　homogeneous state
单一总线　【计】unibus
单乙醇胺　mono-ethanolamine
单因次的　one-dimensional
单用过程　【计】procedure
单元　unit, element, cell
单元操作　unit operation [process]
单元常数　location constants
单元穿孔　unipunch
单元反应　unit reaction [process]
单元过程[作业]　unit process
单元记录　【计】unit record
单元金属系烧结　【粉】sintering of monometallic system
单元炉缸　(同"单风嘴炉缸")
单元煤气[气体]　monogas
单元设备　unit plant
单元生产率　unit productivity
单元系　unary [one-component] system
单元运动　elementary movement
单元运行　unit operation
单原子半导体　monoatomic semiconductor
单原子层　monoatomic layer
单原子层堆垛层错　monolayer stacking fault
单原子层孪晶　monolayer twin
单原子金属　monoatomic metal
单原子晶体　monoatomic crystal

单原子气体　monoatomic gas
单原子液体　monoatomic liquid
单原子液体层　monoatomic layer of liquid
单圆角砖　bullnose brick
单圆筒造球　【团】single-drum balling
单渣操作　single-slag practice
单渣(法)钢　single-slag steel
单渣熔炼　【钢】single-slag melt
单渣熔炼法　single-slag process
单站焊接设备[装置]　【焊】single-operator welding set
单站弧焊机　single operator arc welding machine
单张板(单张轧制的板)　【压】singles
单张板轧机　single-sheet rolling mill
单张薄钢板　mill pack
单张镀锌设备　【压】sheet-galvanizing equipment
单张厚钢板　discrete steel plate
单张轧制板材　single-rolled strip
单折叠　【钢】single lap
单值弹性位移　single-valued elastic displacement
单值转变(不可逆的介稳相变)　monotropic transformation
单质半导体　element [monoatomic] semiconductor
单质结　homojunction
单质晶体　elemental crystal
单钟炉顶　bell and hopper top
单重(指镀锡薄钢板的重量单位：kg/基准箱)　【压】(common) substance
单轴非均质性　【理】uniaxial anisotropy
单轴混合机　single-shaft mixer
单轴晶体　uniaxial crystal
单轴取向　【理】uniaxial orientation
单轴压制　uniaxial pressing
单轴张力　simple uniaxial tension
单肘板颚式破碎机　single-toggle jaw crusher
单柱蒸馏塔　one-column still
单铸　single casting
单铸试件　separate cast test bar
单转子锤碎机　single-rotor hammer mill
单组分团块炉料　single component briquette burden
单嘴端包　one-lip hand ladle
单嘴精炼炉　【钢】single snorkel refining furnace
单作用(汽)缸　single-acting cylinder
单座式均热炉　single-ingot pit, cell-type soaking pit
掸笔　【铸】banister brush
胆矾{$CuSO_4 \cdot 5H_2O$}　bluestone, copper [blue] vitriol, chalcanthite
胆矾试验(检验锌镀层用)　blue vitriol test
氮{N}　nitrogen, azote ◇供～nitrogen supply, (含)～的 nitrogenous
氮(保护气)发生器　nitrogenous generator
氮保护气氛　nitrogen atmosphere
氮传递　nitrogen transfer
氮含量[含氮量]　nitrogen content
氮化　nitration, nitridation, nitriding, nitrify, nitrizing, nitrogenization ◇【金】槽浴～bath nitriding, 充气盐浴炉～*, 离子～*, 气体～【金】gas nitriding, 软～*, 液体～*
氮化表面　nitrided surface
氮化钚　plutonium nitride
氮化层　nitrided layer, nitration case ◇典型～组织*
氮化(层)深[厚]度　depth of nitration
氮化处理　nitrizing treatment ◇不锈钢表面～marcomizing
氮化淬火　nitride hardening
氮化电炉　nitriding electric furnace
氮化法　nitriding [nitration] process, nitrizing
氮化钒{VN}　vanadium nitride
氮化范围　【金】nitriding range
氮化钢　nitrided [nitriding] steel
氮化锆　zirconium nitride
氮化铬{CrN}　chromium nitride

氮(化)铬铁　nitrided [nitrogenated] ferrochrome, nitrided ferro-chromium
氮化硅　silicon nitride
氮化硅黏结碳化硅　silicon nitride-bonded silicon carbide
氮化硅结合碳化硅砖　Si_3N_4-bond SiC brick
氮化硅陶瓷　silicon nitride ceramics
氮化过程　nitration [nitriding] process
氮化铪{HfN}　hafnium nitride
氮化合金　nitro-alloy, nitralloy
氮化合金钢　nitralloy steel
氮化合物　nitrogen compound
氮化剂　nitridizing agent
氮化钪{ScN}　scandium nitride
氮化镓　gallium nitride
氮化镧{LaN}　lanthanum nitride
氮化炉　nitriding furnace
氮化铝{AlN}　aluminium nitride ◇ 热压～
氮化铝弥散强化钢　(同"IN钢")
氮化铝陶瓷　aluminum nitride ceramics
氮化钼{Mo_2N}　molybdenum nitride
氮化铌{NbN}　niobium [columbium] nitride
氮化硼{BN}　boron nitride, borazon, white graphite
氮化硼基高温材料　boron nitride based high temperature material
氮化硼陶瓷　boron nitride ceramics
氮化硼涂层　boron nitride foating
氮化硼纤维　boron nitride fibre
氮化气体　nitriding gas
氮化区　【金】nitriding range
氮化热处理　malcomising
氮化设备[装置]　nitriding equipment
氮化时间　nitriding time
氮化铈{CeN}　cerium nitride
氮化室　nitriding chamber
氮化钛{TiN}　titanium nitride
氮化钛涂层　titanium nitride coating
氮化钽{TaN}　tantalum nitride
氮化钍{Th_3N_4}　thorium nitride
氮化温度　nitriding temperature
氮化物　nitride
氮化物表面层　nitride case
氮化物层　nitride layer
氮化物耐火材料　nitride refractory
氮化物黏结碳化硅　nitride-bonded silicon carbide
氮化物强化合金　nitride-reinforced alloy
氮化物－碳化物夹杂型(化合物)　nitride-carbide inclusion types
氮化物－碳化物型夹杂物　nitride-carbide type inclusions
氮化物析出[离析]　【金】nitride precipitation
氮化铀　uranium nitride
氮化作用　nitrogenization
氮基[质]气氛　nitrogen-base atmosphere
氮基气氛发生炉　nitrogen-base atmosphere generator
氮基三醋酸　nitrilotriacetic acid
氮解吸　nitrogen desorption
氮硫化(用于低碳钢表面硬化处理)　sulphinuzing
氮硫化法　sulphinuz process
氮气表　nitrometer
氮气炉[干燥箱]　nitrogen oven
氮氢混合气体　AX gas
氮－水射流等离子体　nitrogen water jet plasma
氮碳共渗　ammonia carburizing
氮析出　nitrogen desorption
氮吸收　nitrogen absorption
氮－稀土复合孕育剂　N-RE multi-inoculants
氮压力　nitrogen pressure ◇ 当量～
氮氧化物　nitrogen oxide
氮茚{C_8H_7N}　indole
氮源　nitrogen source
氮杂苯{C_5H_5N}　pyridine
氮转移　nitrogen transfer
淡钡钛石{$BaSi_4O_9 \cdot 2Na_2(Ti,Zr)Si_3O_9$}

leucosphenite
淡度　dilution
淡红硅酸钇矿{(Al,Fe,Ti)$_2$Si$_2$O$_7$} thalenite
淡红银矿{Ag$_3$AsS$_3$}　proustite
淡磷钙铁矿　collinsite
淡水　sweet water,【环】fresh water
淡水腐蚀　sweet corrosion
弹板刮土机　buck scraper
弹壁温度　bomb wall temperature
弹壳黄铜　cartridge gilding (7Zn,93Cu), cartridge brass (30Zn,70Cu), bullet envelopes (通常为 85Cu,15Zn) ◇ 普通～*
弹内还原反应　bomb reaction
弹式量热计　bomb calorimeter
弹丸　shot,bullet ◇ 粒化～*
弹着速度　striking velocity
蛋白[蛋长]石{SiO$_2$·nH$_2$O}　opal
蛋白质　protein
蛋级焦炭　egg coke
蛋形绝缘子　egg insulator
蛋形升液器　monte-jus
蛋形盛酸器　acid egg
当量　equivalence,equivalent (weight),valent weight ◇ 吉雷特～*,西格锥～*
当量测温锥[当量温锥号]【耐】pyrometric cone equivalent
当量长度　equivalent length
当量氮压力　equivalent nitrogen pressure
当量电导　equivalent conductance [conductivity]
当量断[截]面　equivalent section
当量极限　equivalent limit
当量离子交换剂　equivalent ion-exchange material
当量轮载　equivalent wheel load (EWL)
当量面　equivalent plane
当量熔剂　【团】equivalent stone
当量溶液　normal solution
当量溶液校准差　titer,titre
当量碳含量　equivalent carbon content
当量压应力　equivalent compressive stress
当量原子　equivalent atoms
当量圆断面(用于测定淬透性)　equivalent round [section]
当量直径　equivalent diameter
当量值　equivalent value
当前行指示字　【计】current line printer
当前文件　【计】current file
挡板　baffle (plate),damper,guard,retainer,apron (plate),arrestor,barrier,bump (er),check plate,curtain,division,dog,flapper,lagging,shield,stop (plate),trap,【机】diaphragm,【冶】splasher ◇ 防油溅～oil-splash guard,沟内防冲～ditch retard,可调整～frog,掀动～(卷取机的) flap gate
挡板孔　baffled port
挡板喷雾萃取塔　baffled spray column
挡板式惯性除尘机　louver deduster
挡板式进料加热器　baffle feed heater
挡板式收尘器　baffle type collector
挡板塔　baffle tower
挡板塔盘(蒸馏塔内的)　【化】baffle pan
挡碴木　【运】ballast curb
挡风板　barge board,wind guard,deep bead
挡火墙　flue [fire] bridge,bag [bridge] wall,【铁】breast wall (热风炉的) ◇ 带高～的炉子 semi-muffle type furnace
挡块　stopper,peg,stop dog ◇ 制活砂块的～false part
挡块安装板　dog plate
挡块板(烧结机的)　striker plate
挡料圈　constrict,dam (回转窑的),【团】retaining ring,obstruction ◇ 窑尾～kiln discharge end dam
挡料装置　closing device
挡轮　thrust roller
挡泥板　mud guard,trash rack,【运】splasher (车辆的),dashboard (车前的)
挡片　flapper
挡墙　retaining wall,parapet

挡圈　locking [check, closing, retainer, shield] ring
挡水坝　retaining [check] dam
挡水板　splash [dash] plate, spray catcher
挡水墙(外墙的防水隔墙)　retention wall, waterwall
挡水圈　water deflector
挡铁(转炉托圈的)　【冶】claw, stop (iron)
挡土墙　【建】retaining [breast] wall, bulkhead (wall), astel ◇ 板桩～码头 camp sheathing, 仓式～*, 扶垛式～*, 格间式～*, 框格式[垛式]～ crib retaining wall, 悬臂式～*
挡烟桥　【冶】bridge
挡油板　coolant guard,【机】oil baffle
挡油盖　coolant guard
挡油环　oil scraper ring
挡油器　oil guard
挡渣　slag stopping
挡渣棒　【铸】skimmer bar
挡渣浇口　【铸】skim(ming) gate, skim bob gate, gate strainer
挡渣内浇口　ball gate
挡渣耙　damping bar
挡渣器　【冶】dirt trap,【钢】slag bridge (钢包零件), mop (坩埚炼钢用)
挡渣墙　hot-metal and slag separator
挡渣芯　【铸】skimmer core
挡渣芯片　【铸】choke
挡爪　catch pawl
刀杆钢　mandrel steel
刀杆支架　bar steadier, arbor support
刀鼓　knife drum
刀痕　incision
刀架　tool carriage [carrier], cutter carriage, blade adapter ◇ 滑动～ blade head, 上滑动～ top knife head
刀架导轨[导槽]　carriage guide
刀架座　【机】bogie
刀尖　tool tip [nose]
刀剑钢　cutlery steel
刀具　cutter, tool ◇ 硬质合金～*, 用～加工 tooling

刀具不锈钢　cutlery (type) stainless steel
刀具导承[导轨]　【机】cutter guide
刀(具)钢　cutlery [shear(ing)] steel
刀具工具磨削　cutter-and-tool grinding
刀具合金　cutting alloy ◇ 雷尼克钨镍～*
刀具滑板　cutter slide ◇ 复式～ compound slide
刀具硬质合金　tool carbide ◇ 海恩斯-斯特莱特6号～*, 卡塔尼特～*
刀具折裂　tool tear
刀具轴　cutter spindle
刀口　knife-edge
刀口承　knife-edge bearing
刀口堆焊　tip welding
刀口支点(天平的)　knife-edge support
刀梁　knife beam
刀瘤　built up edge
刀面角　【机】rake (angle)
刀盘(破碎机的)　impeller, impellor
刀片　blade, knife, tool bit
刀片侧间隙　blade side clearance
刀片定位机构[装置]　knife aligning device
刀片钢带(剃刀片用)　razor-blake strip
刀片钢含碳量　razor temper
刀片滑块　blade [knife] head, knife block (剪切机的)
刀片架　blade holder
刀片开度　knife opening
刀片磨床　knife grinder
刀片配置盘　knife set up base
刀片倾斜度　blade rake
刀片式刮路机　blade drag
刀片相对[相迎]剪断机　【压】opposed-blade shears
刀片镶焊[铜焊]　tip brazing
刀片斜度(侧方剪的)　knife rake
刀片行程　cutting stroke
刀片(用)钢　razor [shear(ing)] steel
刀片重合度　blade overlap

刀片状浇口 【铸】knife gate
刀刃 cutting edge [lip], cutter [tool] edge, knife-edge ◇ 下~bed knife
刀刃[口]材料 knife-edge material
刀刃堆焊 tip welding
刀刃钢 shear steel
刀刃磨床 knife grinder
刀头 tool tip, bit
刀头材料[镶刀头材料] tool tip material
刀形锉 hack file
刀形开关 knife-blade [knife-edge] switch, contact breaker
刀形枢轴 knife-edge pivot
刀闸 【电】knife switch ◇ 隔离~disconnecting knife
捣棒 tamper, beater, bettle ◇ 风动~air tamper
捣锤 stamp [slogging] hammer, pestle, tamping iron, dabber（捣固型砂用）◇ 长柄~【铸】floor rammer, 风动~*
捣锤混汞法 battery amalgamation
捣打 ramming, stamp, tamping ◇ 压缩空气~装置*
捣打锤 rammer
捣打(混合)料[物]（耐火材料）【冶】ramming mix [mass]
捣打机[装置] 【耐】tamping machine ◇ 压缩空气~*
捣打(耐火)材料 rammed material
捣固 tamp(ing), beetle, 【铸】ram ◇ 爆炸~[捣实]*
捣固锤 compactor
捣固电极 tamped electrode
捣固机 tamping machine [tool], beetle
捣固焦炉 stamp-charging coke oven
捣固炼焦技术 stamp-charging coking technology
捣固器 drop breaker
捣结 stamp, ram ◇ 碳素~料*, 整体~炉缸*
捣臼 stamp box
捣矿箱 stamper box

捣磨 stamp milling
捣磨矿浆 stamp pulp
捣实 tamping, 【铸】ram(ming) ◇ 动力法震动[振打]~kinetic ramming
捣实度 【铸】degree of ramming
捣实混凝土 compacted concrete
捣实机(蛤蟆夯) pummel
捣实密度 rammed [packing] density
捣实器 packer
捣实土壤 packed soil
捣碎 stamp (crushing), stamping, crush, comminute, pounding, trituration
捣碎的金属粉末 stamp metal powder
捣碎粉 chopped powder
捣碎辊 smasher
捣碎[矿]机 stamp(ing) mill, stamper ◇ 混凝土~concrete breaker, 蒸汽~steam stamp
捣碎[矿]机组 stamp battery
捣碎能量 size reduction energy
捣碎入炉[装料] stamp charging
捣碎物 stampings
捣碎细锡矿 floran-tin
捣碎箱（用于碳热还原金属氧化物） forging container
捣蹄 stamp shoe
捣砧 stamping die
捣制底衬 【冶】rammed bottom lining
捣制钢包 rammed ladle
捣制料 stamping mass
捣制炉衬 【冶】rammed lining
捣制炉衬用模型 【冶】ramming form
捣制炉底 【冶】rammed bottom [hearth]
捣制炉顶 【冶】castable roof
捣制镁砂炉床[炉缸] rammed magnesite hearth
捣制耐火材料 tamped refractory
捣制耐火混合料 refractory ramming mixture
捣制黏土料 tamping clay
捣制预穿风眼转炉炉底 spiked bottom
捣筑工具 tamper

捣筑炉衬　tamped liner [lining]
捣筑炉底　【冶】tamped bottom
捣筑炉缸　【冶】rammed well
捣筑黏土填料　tamped clay fill
捣筑设备　tamping plant
倒扳开关　tumbler switch
倒包[罐,桶]　ladle-to-ladle, reladling ◇ 浇桶[铸罐]～工段*
倒包脱气法　ladle to ladle degassing
倒闭　bust, close down
倒车　back run(ning), back(ward) motion, backing, astern running
倒车齿轮　reverse gear
倒出法(用于测定液相穴深度)　pour-out method
倒带时间　rewind time
倒拱　【建】invert arch
倒拱底　bottom of invert
倒焊　【半】face down bonding
倒换　reversion
倒极性　reversed polarity
倒角　chamfer(angle), chamfering, (shoulder) fillet, bevelled end ◇ 作～【机】bevelling
倒角边(焊管坯的)　bevel edge
倒角边缘　tapered edge
倒角环　fillet ring
倒卷　back-roll
倒空　loading out
倒棱　chamfer(cut), chamfering, rolling off(锻模的), tailoring(轧辊槽的)
倒棱[角]的　chamfered (chfd)
倒棱[角]机　chamfering machine ◇ 边缘
倒棱机床(焊管坯的)　chamfering machine
倒棱清理机床　chamfering unit
倒冷凝　retrograde condensation
倒冷却速率曲线　inverse-rate cooling curve
倒立卷筒　【压】inverted [gravity] block, vertical inverted block

倒立卷筒拔[拉]丝机　gravity block wire-drawing machine
倒立式拔管用卷筒　【压】inverted tube block
倒流休风　【铁】back draught(ing), draught back ◇ 独立～(不经热风炉的)*
倒流休风系统　back draught system
倒流休风烟囱　back draught stack
倒炉(转炉的)　【钢】turndown
倒炉温度　turndown temperature
倒逆退火(铸铁的)　inverse annealing
倒牛角状浇口　【铸】reverse horn gate
倒穹结构　【建】inverted dome construction
倒数第二风箱　next-to-last windbox
倒数线色散率(光谱的)　reciprocal linear dispersion
倒数值　reciprocal value
倒速率曲线　inverse-rate curve
倒塌　collapse
倒相电路　inverter circuit
倒相放大器　【电】inverter amplifier
倒相级　【电】inverter stage
倒相器　【电】phase inverter [reverser]
倒相器供电电炉　inverter-operated furnace
倒烟(晶体的)　puffing
倒烟炉　downshot-type furnace
倒焰　downdraught, flare back
倒焰炉　downdraught furnace
倒焰窑　downdraught kiln
倒易点阵　reciprocal lattice
倒易点阵层　reciprocal lattice layer [level]
倒易点阵概念　reciprocal lattice concept
倒易点阵结点序列　reciprocal lattice point row
倒易点阵[晶格]平面　reciprocal lattice plane
倒易晶胞　reciprocal cell
倒易晶胞棱边　reciprocal-cell edge
倒易晶格　【理】inverse lattice
倒易律　reciprocity law

倒易矢量　reciprocal vector
倒易投影　【理】reciprocal projection
倒圆　shoulder fillet, tailoring, blending（拉模钻孔后的）
倒圆环　fillet ring
倒圆角　chamfer, fillet
倒运　loading out
倒渣　slag tipping, deslag
倒账　【企】bad debt ◇ 消费者的~ consumer bad debts
倒蒸发　retrograde vaporization
倒置坩埚　inverted crucible
倒转　reverse rotation, reversal, back(ward) motion, backing
倒装　【铁】reversed filling, 【压】upside down charging
倒装法　flip chip
倒装焊接　face down bonding
倒装焊接机　flip chip bonder, face down bonder
倒装料　【铁】reversed filling
倒装站　transfer station
倒锥度　back draught(ing)
岛模型(晶界的)　【理】island model
岛式布置　【铁】echelon-type arrangement
导板　guide (apron, board), guidance, channel, former bar, stripper plate, trough ◇ 出口~delivery guide, 吊挂~*, 固定~resting guide, 可撤~retractable guide, 扭转出口~*
导板根部　【压】guard heel
导板台　guide table, entry guide box, sticker box ◇ 绕枢轴旋转的~ pivotable guide table
导板箱[盒]　【压】guide box [cage]
导爆线[索]　detonating fuse
导槽　channel (guide), guidance, guide (groove), slot guide ◇ 传动带~ belt guide
导层　【半】conducting shell
导出　derivation, leading-out
导出的微分曲线　derived differential curve
导磁合金　permeability alloy ◇ 镍铁钼~*
导磁率　magnetic conductibility [inductivity, permittivity], magnetoconductivity, permeability, magnetic inductive capacity ◇ 表观~*, 绝对~*
导磁率检验　magnetic permeability inspection
导磁体　magnetizer
导磁系数　permeability [permeance] coefficient, (unit) permeance, magnetic (inductive) capacity, magnetic permeability
导磁性　magnetic conductibility [permeability]
导磁性温度系数　temperature coefficient of permeability
导带　conduction (energy) band
导带电子能量　conduction band electron energy
导弹　guided missile
导弹材料冶金(学)　missile metallurgy
导弹工业　missile industry
导电　electric conduction, conduction of electricity, conduction ◇ 阿卢弗莱克斯~合金*, 不~的 non-conducting, dielectrical
导电板　current-conducting [current-carrying] plate
导电棒　contact rod [stub], current-conducting rod, contact spike（铝电解槽的）◇ 新~clean stub, 烛状~*
导电玻璃　conductive glass
导电玻璃纤维　electric conducting glass fiber
导电材料[物质]　conducting material
导电层　【半】conducting shell [layer]
导电电极　current-carrying electrode
导电电子　conduction electron
导电钢板　steel current conducting plate
导电轨　conductor [contact] rail
导电辊　conductor roll

导电合金　electrical conductivity alloy
导电横臂(电弧炉的)　electrode arm
导电计　conductometer
导电夹片　(current) contact jaw, current-carrying jaw
导电接头　current connection [conductive] tab
导电介质　conducting medium
导电零[部]件　live [current-carrying] part
导电流体　electrically conducting fluid
导电炉底(电炉的)　【钢】conducting bottom [hearth]
导电炉底式电炉　conducting-hearth furnace
导电铝合金　Cond aluminium
导电铝线　electrical aluminium wire
导电率　electric(al) conductivity [conduction], conductivity
导电率测量装置　conductivity measuring device
导电膜　conductive film
导电难熔材料　conducting refractory material
导电能力　conducting power
导电气体　gaseous conductor
导电迁移率　conductivity mobility
导电墙　conductive wall
导电熔剂　conducting flux
导电溶液　conducting solution
导电式炉　conductive furnace
导电水　conductivity water
导电塑料　conductive plastics ◇ 马凯特~ Markite
导电陶瓷　conductive ceramics
导电体　(current) conductor, electrical conductor
导(电)条　bus bar, conductive bar
导电铜合金(98.2—99.2Cu, 0.5—1.8Sn, 0.8—1.0Cd)　electrical conductivity alloy
导电涂层　conductive [current-conducting] coating
导电系数　conductivity factor, conduction, electrical conductivity
导电线用青铜[导电青铜合金](99.2—98.2Cu, 0.8—1.0Cd 或 0.5—1.8Sn)　conductivity bronze
导电性　(electric) conductivity, conduction, conductance
导电性指示器　conductivity indicator
导电盐　conducting salt
导电元件[元素]　conducting element
导电嘴　current contact nozzle, electrode nozzle
导洞(隧道的)　pilot tunnel
导阀　pilot valve
导杆　guide (bar, pole, rod), rod guide, leader
导沟(铸型的)　【铸】stria
导管　(guide) conduit, guide tube, pipe line, leader, leading ◇ 炉底~ bottom guide tube
导管灌注混凝土　tremie concrete
导管阻力　duct friction
导轨　guide (rail), guidance, fence, runway, (slide) rail, sliding guide [track] ◇ 后缘~ back guide, 可伸缩~ telescopic guide, 有槽~ grooved rail, 重级~ heavy duty runway
导轨滚轮　guide roller
导辊　deflector roll, guide roll(er), leading sheave, pressure roller, sheave, sink roll ◇ 螺栓固定~ bolted on guide roll
导辊装置　【压】roller (guide) apron
导滚　guide barrel
导函数　【数】derivative
导航　pilot, guidance
导弧环　arc ring
导环　guide [carrier, carrying, lead] ring
导火线　blaster ◇ 爆炸~ detonating fuse
导架　guide bracket, guides, liner
导键　spline key
导焦槽　【焦】coke guide

导抗 【理】immittance, adpedance
导块 guide [leading] block
导料槽 baffle box
导轮 guide pulley [idler, roller, wheel], jockey pulley, leading sheave, pres-sure roller, driving wheel (焊接机的) ◇ 皮带～belt guide pulley, 斜侧面滚动～bevelled wheel
导螺杆 driving [engaging, lead] screw
导螺栓 guide bolt
导螺旋 driving screw
导纳三角形 admittance triangle
导能带 conduction (energy) band
导盘 guide disc ◇ 迪舍尔旋转～*
导频油路 pilot circuit
导圈 guide ring
导热 (heat) [thermal] conduction
导热材料 heat conductive material, thermal conductor
导热法(高炉炉缸内衬设计体系之一) thermal solution concept
导热杆 chill bar
导热管 heat pipe
导热合金 thermal conductor alloy
导热计 diathermometer, conductometer of heat, conductometer
导热介质 heat conducting medium, heat transfer agent
导热率 (heat) conductivity, conductivity for heat, specific conductance, thermal coefficient
导热姆换热剂 Dowtherm
导热片 conducting strip, heat conducting fin
导热系数 heat conductivity, thermal coefficient [conductivity], coefficient of heat passage, conductivity factor
导热性 heat [thermal] conductivity, conductivity for heat
导热性曲线 heat conductivity curve
导热性试验 conductivity test
导入角 lead angle

导数 【数】derivative (der.), differential coefficient
导数吸收光谱(图) derivative absorption spectrum
导数(信号)发生器 rate generator
导水管 aqueduct
导水器 water deflector
导体 (electrical) conductor ◇ 非～non-conductor
导体绞线芯 【电】conductor core
导卫 【压】guide, guard
导卫安装工 guide setter
导卫板 guide piece, guard, guide shoe (穿孔机的), fore plate (轧机下轧辊的) ◇ 借～进行轧制 roll by guide, 借助～在轧机机座间串送轧件 repeating, 悬挂式～flipper, 轧机～rolling mill guides
导卫板串送 repeating
导卫管 guide conduit
导卫划痕(轧材缺陷) guide scores [marks, scratch]
导卫剪伤(轧制缺陷) guide shearing
导卫台 guide table ◇ 出口～*
导卫调整工 guide setter
导卫轧制 guide rolling
导卫轧制圆钢 guide rounds
导卫装置 guide fittings, guides and guards ◇ 辊式～*, 盘条用～wire-rod guide, 下～bottom stripper, 轧机～roll fittings
导卫装置调整工 tackle fettler
导温率[性] temperature conductivity
导温系数 temperature coefficient [diffusivity], temperature transfer coefficient
导线 conducting wire, (current) conductor, wire ◇ 多芯～cable, 哑铃形[8形]～*, 引入～lead-in wire
导线包覆绝缘塑料的装置 plastic extruder
导线测量 traversing
导线重绕机 rewinding machine
导线额定强度 rated strength
导线管 conduit (cnd.), wire conduit

导线环(拉丝卷筒的) 【压】fleeter ring
导线孔(钢丝绳机的) wire guide
导线用合金 alloy for conductor
导向板 guide plate
导向边 guide edge
导向表面 guide surface
导向传动件 driver
导向挡板 deflector (apron, gate) ◇ 下辊～*
导向阀门 deflecting gate, guide valve
导向杆 guide bar [lever, peg], stem guide, sweep arm (大型轧机推床的)
导向隔墙 deflecting wall
导向管 guide tube
导向轨座 sliding base
导向辊 deflecting roller, steering roll
导向辊道 table deflector
导向辊支架 deflector roller bracket
导向横梁[滑块] guide crosshead
导向滑条式冷床 skid-type hot bed
导向环 deflector [guide] ring
导向机 pilot machine
导向架 guide frame, pilot bearing
导向键 feather [guidance] key
导向漏斗 guide cone
导向轮 guide pulley [wheel] ◇ 皮带～ belt guide pulley
导向螺栓 guide bolt
导向螺丝 guide screw
导向面 guide surface
导向台 guide table, table deflector ◇ 折叠式～ folding guide table
导向套管 guide sleeve
导向弯道[管] guided bend
导向弯曲试验 guided-bend test
导向弯曲试验夹具[模胎] guided-bend test jig
导向销 guide pin ◇ 开口～*
导向叶片 guide vane [blade], stator blades
导向圆锥 guide cone
导向轴 guiding axle

导向轴承 guide [direct, pilot] bearing
导向轴套 guide sleeve
导向装置 director, liner, guiding device [mechanics], 【压】guide piece ◇ 球形～ ball guide
导引端(带卷的) 【压】pilot end
导轴 guide shaft [spindle], guiding [leading, pony, steering] axle
导轴衬(套) 【机】guide bush
导轴承 guide [pilot] bearing
导柱 guide column [pin, post, pile], leading pile
导锥 guide cone, starting taper
到达角(电波的) acceptance angle, angle of arrival
道碴 hoggin,【建】ballast ◇ 砾石～ gravel ballast, 烧结黏土～ burnt bal-last, 枕间～*
道碴密度 ballast density
道岔 【运】(railroad) switch, side-track
道岔钢材 switch plate section
道岔轨枕 switch tie
道岔箱 switch box
道次 【压】pass, run, step (拉拔的) ◇ 奇数[道前]～*, 空轧～*, 立轧～ edging (pass), 偶数～*, 轻压[小压下量]～ light pass, 中间轧制～ intermediate pass, 最后～ final pass
道次程序 pass schedule
道次间隔(时间) interpass time, pass interruption time
道次间冷却(拉丝的) interpass cooling
道次间退火 interpass annealing
道次设计 pass design
道次压下量 reduction in pass
道次与中间退火流程图(拉拔的) pass-and-reheating schedule
道钉 (track, rail) spike ◇ 钩头～ cut-spike, brob, 小～ spike nail
道钉型钢 spike rod
道尔顿铋铅锡易熔合金(60Bi, 25Pb, 15Sn; 熔点92℃) Dalton's alloy

道尔顿定律　Dalton's law
道尔顿式化合物[道尔顿体]　Daltonide, Daltonian compound
道尔分级机　Dorr classifier
道尔型搅拌机　Dorr agitator
道节距　【计】track pitch
道克斯 1 强碱性阴离子交换树脂　Dowex 1
道克斯 2 强碱性阴离子交换树脂　Dowex 2
道克斯 3 弱碱性阴离子交换树脂　Dowex 3
道克斯 30 磺酚阳离子交换树脂　Dowex 30
道克斯 50 磺化聚苯乙烯阳离子交换树脂　Dowex 50
道拉斯双二辊式轧机　Dowlais mill
道森轴承青铜(84Cu, 15.9Sn, < 0.1Pb, 0.05As)　Dawson's bronze
道屋 G 高强度铸造镁铝合金(9Al, 2Zn, 0.1Mn, 余量 Mg)　Dowmetal G
道屋法海水炼镁厂　Dow sea-water plant
道屋海水炼镁法　Dow process
道屋镁电解槽　Dow cell
道屋镁铝合金(9Al, 2Zn, 0.1Mn, 余量 Mg)　Dowmetal
德拜比热　Debye specific heat
德拜比热公式　Debye formula for specific heat, Debye's specific heat formula
德拜 T^3 定律　Debye T^3 law
德拜法(X 射线粉末法)　Debye method
德拜方程　Debye equation
德拜粉末法(X 射线)衍射花样　Debye powder (X-ray) pattern
德拜粉末法 X 射线衍射图　Debye powder diagram
德拜环(X 射线衍射的)　Debye ring
德拜环上择优取向最大强度值　preferred orientation maxima on Debye ring
德拜晶格振动模型　Debye model
德拜(晶体衍射)图　Debye crystallogram [film]

德拜频率　Debye frequency
德拜(特征)温度　Debye (characteristic) temperature
德拜-瓦勒温度因数[德拜因数]　【理】Debye-Waller temperature factor, Debye (temperature) factor
德拜-瓦勒因数(X 射线衍射的)　Debye-Waller factor
德拜-谢乐 X 射线分析　Debye-Scherrer X-ray analysis
德拜-谢乐 X 射线粉末衍射检验　Debye-Scherrer diffraction testing
德拜-谢乐 X 射线衍射法　Debye-Scherrer technique
德拜-谢乐反射　Debye-Scherrer reflections
德拜-谢乐粉末法 X 射线谱　Debye-Scherrer spectrum
德拜-谢乐(粉末法)照相　Debye-Scherrer (powder) photograph
德拜-谢乐(粉末衍射)法　(同"X 射线粉末衍射法")
德拜-谢乐环(X 射线衍射的)　Debye-Scherrer ring
德拜-谢乐环(湿度)最大值　maxima of Debye-Scherrer ring
德拜-谢乐试样　Debye-Scherrer specimen
德拜-谢乐(衍射)线轮廓(X 射线照相的)　Debye-Scherrer line profile
德拜-谢乐照相机　Debye-Scherrer camera ◇普通~*
德博尔碘化物热解瓶(用于钛锆等的少量生产)　de Boer bulb
德博尔-冯·阿克尔碘化物热离解法　(同"阿克尔-德博尔碘化物热离解法")
德布兰科尔顺流换向器回转炉　Deblanchol rotary furnace
德布罗意波　de Broglie wave
德布罗意定律　de Broglie law
德布罗意关系(式)　de Broglie relation

[equation]

德尔布鲁克散射　Delbruck scattering

德尔汉姆法(炼铝烟气干式控制法)　【环】Derham process

德尔塔马克斯高导磁率铁镍合金(50Ni,50Fe)　Deltamax

德尔托伊德 $\alpha-\beta$ 黄铜(60Cu,40Zn)　Deltoid

德夫利硬度试验　Devries test

德弗克斯硫化物涂敷法(挤压前的)　Devex process

德古萨氯化钠－氯化铍熔体电解制铍法　Degussa process

德古萨转盘雾化粉末法　Degussa process

德古西特陶瓷刀具　Degussit(以Al2O3为主的刀具)

德国标准(U形缺口)冲击试验　DVM test

德国标准筛　German standard sieve

德国钢铁工程师协会　Verein Deutscher Eisenhuettenleute (VDEh)

德国钢铁协会还原试验法　V.D.E. method

德国工业标准　DIN (Deutche Industrie Normen), DIN standard

德国黄铜　(见"顿巴克黄铜")

德国专利　German Patent (G.P., Ger. pat.)

德哈斯－范阿尔芬效应　【理】de Haas-van Alphen effect

德克尔－阿斯普－哈克法(用衍射法求作极点图)　Decker-Asp-Harker method

德拉贡反应堆(高温气体冷却式)　Dragon reactor

德拉贡实验(确定铀爆炸临界量用)　【理】Dragon experiment

德拉洛特锰黄铜合金(80Cu,18Zn,2Mn)　Delalot's alloy

德拉沃焙烧法　【铁】Dravo process

德拉沃－鲁奇型带式焙烧机　(同"DL型带式焙烧机")

德拉沃型带式焙烧机　【团】Dravo straight-grate pelletizing machine

德莱沃特离心铸管法　De Lavaud process

德莱沃特离心铸管机　De Lavaud casting machine

德赖弗－哈里斯720高强度铜锰镍合金(60Cu,20Mn,20Ni)　Driver Harris 720 alloy

德劳利控制电解粉末粒度法　Drouily's method

德雷克斯尔煤气洗涤瓶　Drexel bottle

德雷珀效应　Draper effect

德鲁德－洛伦茨自由电子理论　Drude-Lorentz free electron theory

德马克－洪堡矮(身)炉炼铁法　DHN (Demag-Humboldt low-shaft) process

德麦勒沉淀脱铣法　De Merre process

德斯科一次有效型芯压铸法　Desco process

德瓦达铜铝锌合金(45Al,50Cu,5Zn)　Devarda's alloy

德维尔－佩奇尼碱石灰烧结法(氧化铝生产用)　Deville-Pechiney process

德沃尔夫(型)照相机　de Wolff(-type) camera

德肖电解液除锈法　Deshow process

德银(52－80Cu, 5－35Ni, 10－35Zn)　German silver, argentan, copper nickel, Alpakka ◇ 斯皮德克斯～*, 韦塞尔～*

德银丝[德国铜镍锌合金线]　German silver wire

德银条[德国铜镍锌合金条]　German silver bar

得克萨公司(煤炭)气化法　Texaco process

灯笼式齿轮　lantern gear

灯笼式小齿轮　lantern pinion

灯泡钨丝[铌钨灯丝合金]　Osram

灯丝　(lamp) filament, glower, ignition wire ◇ 锇钨～合金 Osram, 加钍～*, 盘绕线圈式～coiled-coil filament, 双螺旋～coiled coil, 涂氧化物～*

灯丝电离真空计　hot-filament ionization

gauge
灯丝金属　filamentary metal
灯丝炉　filament furnace
灯罩级硝酸钍　mantle-grade thorium nitrate
登普斯特质谱仪　Dempster mass-spectrometer
等比　【数】analogy, equal ratio
等比均布荷载　equivalent uniform load
等比例的　isometric
等边对称填角焊缝　equal leg fillet weld
等边拱　equilateral arch
等边角钢　equal angle (steel, iron), equal leg angle iron, isosceles angle steel, equal-sided angle iron, angle iron with equal legs
等边三角形　equilateral triangle ◇ 吉布斯～Gibbs triangle
等差级数　arithmetical progression
等长多层绞线　equilay conductor
等沉降比　equal settling ratio
等磁力线分选机　isodynamic separator
等代压力　(同"等效压力")
等待时间　waiting time,【计】latency time
等待修复时间　awaiting repair time
等待状态　【计】waiting state
等电(位)点　isoelectric [equipotential] point
等电位金属化　equipotential metallization
等电位连接　equipotential [cross] connection
等电位透镜(电子等电位透镜)　equipotential lens
等电位温度　isoelectric temperature
等动态样品　isokinetical sample
等断面轧制　straight [parallel] rolling
等分递推法(用于炉膛辐射换热计算)　equi-zoning reciprocity method
等分子的　equimolecular
等幅(的)　zero-decrement
等幅波　continuous [maintained] waves
等幅波振荡器　continuous wave generator
等幅振荡　continuous waves

等腐蚀曲线　isocorrosion curve
等高线　contour (line) ◇ 河底～depth contours, 画～contouring
等高线(地)图　contour map
等光程的　aplanatic
等规聚合物　【化】isotactic polymer
等含碳量曲线(平衡图的)　【金】isocarb
等焓的　isenthalpic
等焓线　isenthalp(ic), constant enthalpy line
等活度　isoactivity
等活度线　isoactivity curve
等级　grade, class, degree, gradation, level, magnitude, order, rank ◇ 提高～upgrading
等级分析　grade analysis
等级名　grade name
等剂量面(放射性辐射的)　【理】isodose surface
等价[值]　equivalence, equivalency
等价问题　【计】equivalence problem
等降分级　classifying by equal falling
等降富集　enriching by equal falling
等角度投影(法)　equiangular projection
等角拱坝　constant-angle arch dam
等角图　isometric drawing
等截面梁　【建】uniform beam
等结构的　isostructural
等晶织构　equigranular texture
等经度点　points of equal longitude
等静压火花烧结　spark isostatic press sintering
等静压技术　isostatic pressing technology
等静压冷成型　cold isostatic compacting
等静压力　isostatic pressure
等静压设备　isostatic pressure apparatus
等静压制　【粉】isostatic pressing, isopressing ◇ 高速～high speed isostatic pressing, 冷～isostatic cold pressing, 自动[机械化]～mechanized isostatic pressing
等静压(制)成型　【粉】isostatic compacting, isopressing compaction

等静压(制)机　isostatic press, isostatic pressing machine ◇ 绕丝～ wire-wound isostatic press
等静压制装置　arrangement for isostatic pressing
等矩形截面结晶器(薄板坯连铸用)　equi-rectangle section mould
等距离的　equidistant, isometric
等距离相邻原子　equidistant neighbors
等离子沉积[淀积]法　plasma deposition process
等离子淬火　plasma quenching
等离子点火器　plasma ignitor
等离子电弧成形　plasma arc forming
等离子电弧敷层　plasma arc coating
等离子(电弧)炉[等离子体加热炉]　plasma arc [heating] furnace, plasmarc furnace
等离子电弧切割　plasma arc cutting
等离子电子束焊接　plasma electron beam welding
等离子反应堆[器]　plasma reactor
等离子腐蚀　plasma etching
等离子复合　plasma recombination
等离子感应炉　plasma induction furnace
等离子钢包炉　plasma ladle furnace
等离子管[等离子流发生器, 等离子体电焊机, 等离子焰喷嘴]　plasmatron
等离子焊　plasma welding
等离子弧堆焊　plasma arc surfacing
等离子弧焊　plasma arc welding
等离子弧焊机　plasma arc welder
等离子弧加热器　plasma arc heater
等离子化学气相沉积(法)　plasma chemical vapour deposition
等离子还原　plasma reduction
等离子炬　plasma torch
等离子流　plasma jet [flow]
等离子流切割　plasma flame [jet] cutting, nontransferred constricted arc cutting (美)
等离子喷镀层　plasma jet [spray(ed)] coating
等离子喷射　plasma injection
等离子喷射[雾]法　plasma spray process
等离子喷涂　plasma spraying
等离子(气)体　plasma (pl.), plasma body [gas] ◇ 磁～动力学的 magnetoplasmodynamic, 磁致～ magnetoplasma, 氮－水射流～*, 环形～ toroidal plasmas, 激光～ laser plasma, 气体放电～ gas-discharge plasma, 完全电离的～ stripped plasma
等离子枪　plasma gun
等离子枪加热器　plasma torch heater
等离子区　(ion) plasma
等离子区平衡　plasma balance
等离子熔炼　plasma melting
等离子束喷注　plasma beam injection
等离子体波长　plasma wavelength
等离子体淬火　plasma hardening
等离子(体电)弧　plasma arc ◇ 气体保护金属极～联焊法*
等离子体电弧枪　plasma torch
等离子体电子　plasma electron
等离子体反应　plasma reaction
等离子体放电　plasma discharge
等离子体钢包炉　plasma ladle furnace
等离子体化学气相沉积　plasma assisted chemical vapo(u)r deposition
等离(子体)激元(物)　【理】plasmon
等离子体挤压　plasma squeezing
等离子体技术　plasma technology
等离子(体)加热　plasma heating ◇ 电弧～ arc plasma heating, 连铸中间包～*
等离子体扩散　plasma diffusion
等离子体密度　plasma density
等离子体刨削[表面切割]　plasma gouging
等离子(体)喷镀[喷涂]　plasma spraying ◇ 电弧～金属*
等离子体漂移　plasma drift
等离子体频率　plasma frequency
等离子体切割　plasma cutting
等离子体色谱法　plasma chromatography

等 deng

等离子体探测器　plasma probe
等离子(体)物理学　plasma physics
等离子体振荡分析仪　plasma oscillation analyzer
等离子体注入器　plasma injector
等离子脱铜法　removal of copper with plasma
等离子旋涡熔炼法　plasma cyclone smelting
等离子冶金　plasma metallurgy
等粒度料　equigranular charge
等量加载(试验)法　equal load increments method
等落比　equal settling ratio
等落颗粒　equal settling particle
等面　iso-surface, equivalent face
等内聚[黏结]温度　equicohesive temperature
等能的　isodynamic
等能反射器　equal-energy dish
等能面　equal-energy surface
等黏度温度　equi-viscous temperature
等浓度扩散　【半】isoconcentration diffusion
等浓度线　isopleth
等偏差值　equal errors size
等强度焊缝(与基本金属的)　full strength weld [joint]
等强度连接(与基本金属的)　full strength joint
等氢离子指示溶液　【化】isohydric [adjusted] indicator solution
等倾角照相机　equi-inclination camera
等倾消光条纹　【理】bend contour
等热线　equipotential line
等容　isometry
等容比热　specific heat at constant volume
等容过程　isometric [isovolumetric] process, constant volume process
等容[等体积]线　isochor(e), isochoric line, isometric, constant volume line
等色花纹　isochromatic pattern
等色温线　isotemperature line
等色线　isochromatic, isochromat
等熵过程　【理】is(o)entropic process
等熵膨胀　isentropic expansion, constant entropy expansion
等熵线　isentrope, isentropic, constant entropy line
等熵压缩　【理】isoentropic compression
等深线　depth contours [curve]
等渗压力　isotonic [isosmotic] pressure
等渗压溶液　isotonic solution
等时加热　isochronal heating
等时退火　【金】isochronal annealing
等式　equation, equality
等势(线)　isopotential
等速剖面线　isovelocity section lines
等速取样　isokinetic sampling
等速蠕变　steady creep
等塑性应变线　equi-plastic strain line
等弹性(的)　isoelastic
等弹性弹簧合金(35—37Ni, 7—7.65Cr, 0.45—0.75Mn, 0.35—0.75Mo, 0.3—0.6Si, 0.008—0.2C, ＜0.2S, ＜0.15Cu, 余量Fe)　ISO-Elastic
等弹性学　isoelastics
等体积萃取　equal-volume extraction
等体积的　isometric, isopyknic
等同速率　equivalent rate
等外板　off-gauge [off-grade] plate
等外级氧化铝　off-grade alumina
等外矿石(手选的)　dradge
等外品　off-grade (product), off-quality, off-specification, wasters, rejects, off-size (钢材的)
等外品的　below proof
等外品锌　off-grade zinc
等外铁　(同"号外铁")
等外轧材(指尺寸)　【压】off-gauge material
等纬度点　points of equal latitude
等位　isopotential
等位变换吸收波长(点)　isosbestic point

等位吸收波长(点)(光谱的) isoabsorptive point
等位线 equipotential line, isopotential
等位直流磁场 equipotential DC magnetic field
等温变化 isothermal change
等温常化 【金】isothermal normalizing
等温处理 isothermal treatment
等温淬火 【金】isothermal hardening [quenching], austemper(ing) ◇ 加载～ austemper stressing, 阶段升温～ step-up austempering, 铅浴～*, 逐级～*
等温淬火表面硬化 austemper case hardening
等温淬火处理 【金】isothermal quenching treatment ◇ 轧制加工～ ausroll tempering
等温淬火法 austempering method
等温淬火钢 austempered steel
等温淬火用带式盐浴槽 belt type austempering salt bath
等温锻造 isothermal forging
等温反应 isothermal reaction
等温分解 isothermal decomposition
等温干燥 isothermal drying
等温回火 【金】isothermal tempering
等温挤压 isothermal extruding [extrusion]
等温截面 isothermal section
等温可逆反应 isothermal reversible reaction
等温离解 isothermal dissociation
等温马氏体 【金】isothermal martensite
等温面 isothermal level, isothermal surface, isothermic surface
等温模 isothermal die
等温凝固 isothermal solidification
等温膨胀 constant temperature expansion, isothermal expansion
等温平衡 isothermal equilibrium
等温区 isothermal region [zone]
等温球压退火 isothermal spheroidizing

等温曲线 isothermal curve
等温热处理 isothermal heat treatment
等温韧性 isothermal ductility
等温烧结 isothermal sintering
等温生长 isothermal growth
等温退火 【金】isothermal annealing
等温吸热 decalescence
等温线 isotherm(al), isothermal [isothermic] line, constant temperature line
等温形变热处理 isoforming ◇ 非～*
等温压缩 isothermal compression
等温应变 isothermal strain
等温正火 【金】isothermal normalizing
等温止裂试验 isothermal crack arrest test
等温质量转移现象 【理】isothermal mass transfer phenomenon
等温转变 【金】isothermal transformation, temperature-time transformation
等温转变表面硬化处理 isothermal transformation case hardening
等温转变产物 isothermal transformation products
等温转变处理 isothermal transformation treatment
等温转变强化处理 isothermal transstressing
等温转变曲线 isothermal transformation (IT) curve, S-shaped curve, temperature-time transformation (TTT) curve, S-curves (奥氏体的) ◇ 钚 $\beta \to \alpha \sim$ *
等温转变图 isothermal transformation diagram
等误差分割点 equal errors cut point
等误差值 equal errors size
等相区 equiphase zone
等响度曲线图[等响线] 【环】loudness (level) contour
等效 equivalence, equivalency
等效的 equivalent
等效[值]电路 equivalent circuit
等效电子 equivalent electrons
等效二进制位 equivalent binary digits

等效负载	equivalent [dummy] load
等效焦距	equivalent focal length
等效均布荷载	equivalent uniform load
等效轮载	equivalent wheel load (EWL)
等效面	equivalent plane
等效弹性模量	equivalent elastic modulus
等效碳	equivalent carbon
等效弯曲力矩	equivalent bending moment
等效吸收	equivalent absorption
等效压力	equivalent compressive force
等效应力	equivalent stress
等效直径	equivalent diameter
等效值	equivalent (value)
等旋干涉纹	neutral line, isogyre
等寻元素(历史上对周期表中尚缺元素的称呼)	eka-element
等压	isopressing
等压过程	isobaric process
等压截面	isobaric section
等压膨胀	constant-pressure expansion
等压曲线	equal pressure curve
等压溶解	isobaric dissolution
等压烧结	isobaric sintering
等压式焊炬	balanced pressure torch
等压吸附线	adsorption isobar
等压线	equal pressure curve, isobaric [constant-pressure] line, isobar, isostatic curve
等压应力状态	equilateral state of stress
等压原则(焊炬的)	balanced pressure principle
等应变曲线	isostrain curve
等应变图	iso-strain diagram
等应力	iso-stress
等硬度曲线	isohardness curve
等硬度线	isosklers
等于	equal (to), equivalent to
等圆断面(异型钢材的)	ruling section
等轧策略	standstill tactics
等张比容	parachor
等值	equivalence
等值功率	equivalent power
等值面	equivalent plane, isosurface
等值面组合[集合]	set of equivalent faces
等值线	contour, isopleth, constant value line
等值因数[系数]	equivalence factor, coefficient of equivalence
等致密压制坯块	【粉】isodense compact
等轴	isometry
等轴对称(结晶)物质	cubic substance
等轴晶(粒)区[带]	equiaxed zone, zone of equiaxial [equi-axed] crystals
等轴晶(体)	equiaxed [equiaxial, isometric] crystal
等轴晶粒	equiaxed grain
等轴(晶体)组织[结构]	equiaxed (crystal, grain) structure
等轴晶系	cubic (system), regular [isometric, tesseral] system
等轴铅钯矿	zvyagintsevite
等轴砷镍矿	krutovite
等轴树枝状组织	equiaxed dendrilie structure
等轴铁素体晶粒	equiaxed ferritic grain
等轴系晶体	regular crystal
堤岸墙	quaternion wall
堤坝	(embankment) dam, dyke-dam
堤防土工	banker
低 Ms 点铁镍碳马氏体	low Ms iron-nickel-carbon martensite
低矮型连铸机	(同"低头式连铸机")
低安培电流	low current
低爆炸成形	low-explosive forming
低爆炸限度(可燃混合物的)	lower explosive limit (L.E.L.)
低倍断口金相学[照相术]	macrofractography
低倍分析试样	macrospecimen
低倍观察术	macroscopy
低倍检验[检查]	(同"宏观检验")
低倍金相浸蚀	macrographic(al) etching
低倍浸蚀	macro-etch(ing) ◇冯泽拉德

~液

低倍浸蚀检验　macro-etch testing
低倍浸蚀磨片　macro-etched slice
低倍磨片　macrosection
低倍偏析　macrosegregation
低倍试样　【金】macrotemplate
低倍[低放大率]物镜　low-power objective
低倍[低放大率]显微镜　【金】low-power(ed) microscope, microscope of low magnification
低倍显微镜像　low-power microscopic(al) image
低倍显微照片　low-power micrograph
低倍照相(术)　macrography, macrophotography
低倍状态　【金】macroscopic state
低倍组织　【金】macroscopic structure, macrostructure
低倍(组织)照片　macrograph, photomacrograph, macrophoto
低本底的　【理】low-background
低变形抗力合金　low resistance alloy
低标号水泥　low-grade cement
低布喇格角衍射线　diffraction lines at low Bragg angle
低层错能　small stacking-fault energy
低层湿源　【环】low moor
低插　under-shoot
低产量[产出率]　low [poor] yield
低产量(乙炔)发生器　low-output (acetylene) generator
低潮透气性　trough permeability
低成本　low cost
低成色黄金　low-karat gold
低成型性　poor-compactibility
低传导性　low-conductivity
低纯度的　low-purity
低磁滞(硅)钢(含2.5—4Si)　low hysteresis steel
低淬透性　low hardenability
低淬透性钢[低淬硬钢]　low [shallow, surface] hardening steel
低氮钢　V.L.N. (very low nitrogen) steel
低氮钢冶炼法　(同"极低含氮量炼钢法")
低档(的)　low-quality
低导磁率合金　low permeability alloy
低导热性炉料　low thermal-conductivity charge
低灯头　【焦】low(er) burner
低电流继电器　undercurrent relay
低电流密度(电解)法　low-density process [method]
低电压　low voltage [tension]
低电压的　under-voltage
低电阻钢丝　low resistance wire, extra best best wire (美国)
低电阻合金　low resistance alloy, alloy of low electrical resistance
低堆位层错能临界切应力(金属的)　critical shear stress in metal of small stacking-fault energy
低堆位层错能在金属中的流变应力　flow stress in metal of small stacking-fault energy
低对称性晶体　low-symmetrical crystal, crystal of low symmetry
低发热值[量]　low heat value (LHV), lower heating value, low caloric value
低发热值煤气　low caloric value gas, low-grade gas, LBTU gas
低发热值燃气　low-BTU fuel gas
低钒铀矿　vanuranylite
低沸点金属氯化物　low boiling metal chloride
低沸点馏分　light cut
低分辨率　low-resolution
低分辨率光谱[分光]计　low-resolution spectrometer
低分辨率织构　low resolution texture
低风量　low wind
低负荷滴滤池　low-rate trickling filter

低 di

低富氧　low oxygen enrichment
低钙辉石　low calcium pyroxene
低钙炉渣　lean cinder
低锆海绵铪　low-zirconium hafnium sponge
低铬(的)　low-chromium
低铬钢　low-chrome steel
低铬合金铸铁　low-chromium alloy cast-iron
低功率　low power
低共熔冰盐结晶　cryohydrate
低共熔点　eutectic point
低共熔混合物　eutectic
低共熔体　eutectic
低共熔体系　eutectic system
低共熔温度　eutectic temperature
低共熔点移动　eutectic shift
低共熔合金　eutectic alloy
低钴氨络合物　cobaltous ammine complex
低固体泥浆　low-solids slurry
低硅操作[作业]　low-silicon operation [practice], low-Si operation
低硅铝土矿　low-silicon bauxite
低硅青铜(97.7Cu, 1.5Si, 余量 Zn)　low-silicon bronze
低硅生铁　dry iron, low-silicon pig iron
低硅生铁生产工艺 【铁】low-silicon practice
低硅铁合金　siliconeisen
低硅铸铁　low-silicon cast iron
低铪锆　low-hafnium zirconium
低含量(贵重组分)试样　low assay
低含量硫(生铁中的)　below average sulphur
低焊接裂纹敏感钢　steel with low sensitivity to welding crack
低焊接烟雾锡青铜[锡铜焊条合金]　(tin-copper) low-fuming bronze
低合金　low-alloy, dilute alloy ◇ 优质~废料*
低合金钢　low-alloy steel, lean alloy steel ◇ 全脱氧~*

低合金钢焊条　low-alloy steel covered arc welding electrode
低合金高强度钢　low-alloy(ed) high strength steel ◇ 阿尔迪科~*, 海图夫~*, 克罗马多尔~*, 曼-腾~Man-Ten steel, 莫德菲~(80 公斤级)Modfiy, 奈克罗姆~Nykrom, 西尔坦~*
低合金高强度钢焊条　low-alloy high-strength steel covered arc welding electrode
低合金工具钢　low-alloy tool steel
低合金马氏体　dilute-alloy martensite
低合金铸钢件[低合金钢铸造]【铸】low-alloy steel casting
低合金铸铁　low-alloy cast iron
低灰分还原物料　low-ash reducing material
低灰分焦炭　low-ash coke, high carbon coke
低挥发分烟煤　low-volatile bituminous coal
低辉铜矿　durleite
低级材料　low-grade material
低级钢　dry steel
低级煤　lean[inferior, low-rank] coal, grizzle (含硫的)
低级耐火黏土砖　low-duty fireclay brick
低级耐火砖　low-grade firebrick
低级燃料　low-grade fuel
低级软煤　dant
低级铜　low-grade copper
低级银合金　vellon
低挤压性粉末　low-compressibility powder
低价化合物　compound of lower valency, subcompound
低价化合物蒸馏法　subcompound method
低价金属盐　protosalt
低价金属氧化物　metal suboxide
低价金属氧化物挥发　metal suboxide volatilization
低价离子　low-valent ion

低价卤化铝　aluminium subhalide
低价卤化钛　titanium subhalide
低价卤化物　subhalide
低价卤化物歧化　disproportionation of lower halide
低价氯化物　lower chloride, subchloride
低价氧化铪　hafnium suboxide
低价氧化物　lower oxide, suboxide
低架筛　low-head screen
低架式连铸机　(同《低头式连铸机》)
低碱度　low basicity
低碱水泥　low-alkali cement
低矫顽磁力的　low-coercivity
低角度式焊接　slant angle shooting
低角法(X射线的)　low angle method
低角区域　low-angle region
低角衍射花样　【理】low-angle pattern
低阶[级]反射　low-order reflection
低阶织构系数　low-order texture coefficient
低结晶对称相　【金】phase of low crystal symmetry
低金合金　low gold-content alloy
低开黄金　low-karat gold
低空发散　low level emission
低孔隙度[率]　low porosity
低矿渣水泥　low-slag cement
低料位指示器　low-level indicator
低料位贮仓　low-level storage bunker
低料线操作(高炉的)　low stockline operation
低料柱　【冶】low column
低料柱作业　【冶】operation with low ore-column
低磷钢　low-phosphorus steel ◇含铅～*, 加硫～*
低磷生铁　hematite [low-phosphorous] pig iron
低磷铁矿石　Bessemer ore
低磷铜　low-residual-phosphorous copper
低硫低杂质泡铜　low sulphur and low impurity blister copper

低硫钢　low-sulphur steel
低硫化物　protosulphide
低硫还原剂　low-sulphur reducing agent
低硫焦　low-sulphur coke
低硫煤　low sulphur coal
低硫燃料　low-sulphur fuel
低硫生铁　low-sulphur iron
低硫酸盐　protosulphate
低硫烟气　【环】weak gas ◇反射炉～*
低硫原油(含硫1.3%以下)　low-sulphur crude oil, low-sulfur crude (LSC)
低卤化物　lower halide
低氯化物　protochloride
低脉石球团　(同"低渣量球团")
低锰(的)　low-manganese
低锰合金　spiegeleisen
低锰合金结构钢　◇杜科尔～Ducol steel
低锰铁　spiegel iron
低密度气体　low-density gas
低密度材料　low-density material
低密度法　low-density process
低密度分离[分选]　【选】low-density cut
低密度粉末　low-density powder
低密度合金　low-density alloy
低密度炉料　low-density charge
低能冲击脆断转变试验　low-blow brittle transition (LBBT)
低能电子衍射[绕射]　【理】low-energy electron diffraction (LEED)
低能(级)电子　low-energy electron (LEE)
低能离子源　low-energy ion source
低能(量)位错　low-energy dislocation, dislocation of lower energy
低能态　lower-energy state
低黏度油　low-viscosity oil
低镍氨络合物　nickelous ammine
低镍磁黄铁矿精矿　low-nickel pyrrhotite concentrate
低镍锍　coarse metal
低凝(固点)液体　low-freezing liquid

低浓缩铀 low-enrichment uranium
低配筋的 under-reinforced
低喷溅氧枪 low spitting lance
低膨胀钢 low-expansion steel
低膨胀合金 low-expansion alloy (LEA)
低膨胀耐蚀高镍铸铁 ◇米诺瓦~*
低膨胀镍铁铬钴合金 ◇尼洛~Nilo
低膨胀系数材料 low-expansion material
低膨胀系数的 low-expansion
低膨胀(系数)高硅铝合金 ◇洛-埃克斯~*
低膨胀(系数)合金 low-expansion alloy ◇超因瓦~*,费尼柯~*,费尼克罗姆~*,尼尔瓦超~*,特尔柯西尔~*,因瓦~*
低膨胀系数合金铸铁 ◇敏瓦尔~*
低膨胀系数镍铁合金 ◇农格罗~*,帕马特~*
低膨胀系数铁镍合金 ◇ADR~ADR alloy
低膨胀系数线材合金 ◇杜美~*
低频(率) low frequency (LF, lf)
低频变压器 low-frequency transformer
低频电磁场 low-frequency electromagnetic field
低频(电)炉 low-frequency (electric) furnace ◇罗恩~Rohn furnace
低频电气熔铁炉 low-frequency electric smelting furnace
低频感应(电)炉 induction low-frequency furnace
低频继电器 under-frequency relay
低频声波 low-frequency sound wave
低频周期 low-frequency cycle
低品位 low grade, poor in quality, inferiority
低品位赤铁矿 low-grade hematite
低品位钴精矿 low grade cobalt ore
低品位金属锑 low-grade antimony metal
低品位精矿 lean concentrate
低品位矿(石) low-grade ore (LGO), poor ore, low-metal content ◇难选~sub-mill-grade ore
低品位锍[冰铜] low-grade matte
低品位铝土矿 low-grade [poor-quality] bauxite
低品位锰矿浸滤提锰法 【冶】dithionate process
低品位耐火黏土 low-heat-duty clay
低品位难选铁矿 low-grade refractory iron ore
低品位铜 low-grade copper
低品位原矿 low-grade run-of-mine
低品位自熔性烧结矿 low-grade fluxed sinter
低气压 subatmospheric pressure, low atmospheric pressure
低铅黄铜(96Cu, 3.5Zn, 0.5Pb) low-leaded brass
低铅锡青铜(<0.5Pb) leaded tin bronze
低强度 low-strength, low-intensity, weak intensity
低强度材料 low-strength material
低强度操作 low-intensity operation
低强度磁选 low-intensity magnetic separation
低强度等级 low-strength level
低强度电流 low current
低强度焊缝 weak weld
低强度合金 low tensile alloy
低强度混凝土 weak concrete
低强度水泥 low-strength cement
低强度线 line of low intensity
低强焦炭 soft [weak] coke
低氢(电)焊条 basic (flux) electrode, low hydrogen electrode
低氢合金焊条 low hydrogen alloy rod
低氢型涂料电弧焊条 low hydrogen type covered electrode
低氢铁 hydrogen-purified iron
低氢型药皮 【焊】hydrogen-controlled coating
低屈服点钢 low yield point steel
低屈服点合金 low yield alloy

低燃料比操作　low fuel-rate operation
低燃烧器　【焦】low(er) burner
低热膨胀系数的　(同"低膨胀系数的")
低热效率　thermal inefficiency
低热值　(同"低发热值")
低热值热量　low-grade heat
低熔点　low temperature fusibility, low-melting
低熔点高电阻合金　◇佐伽克~*
低熔点共晶　low-melting-point eutectic
低熔点固体物质　low-melting solid
低熔点合金　low-melting alloy (LMA), low-melting-point alloy, fusible alloy ◇伍德~*
低熔点化合物　low-melting compound
低熔点金属　low-melting (point) metal
低熔点金属相　low-melting metal phase
低熔点金属组分　low-melting metal ingredient
低熔点炉渣　low-melting-point slag
低熔点铅合金　cerrobase
低熔点铜溶金属　low-melting copper-soluble metal
低熔点物的热熔　sweating out
低熔点重金属　low-melting heavy metal
低熔点组分　low-melting component [constituent]
低熔生铁　eutectic cast iron
低身电炉　low-shaft electric furnace
低身竖炉　low-shaft furnace
低湿度炮泥[堵出铁口泥]　【铁】low-moisture taphole mix
低湿度送风　【铁】dry blast
低湿送风高炉　dry-air blast-furnace
低式　【连铸】low-head
低水分沉淀物　low-moisture precipitate
低水分料成型　【耐】stiff-plastic making
低水分砖料成型机　(同"半干法成型机")
低水位　low water level (L.W.L.), low water ◇锅炉~断流装置*
低速 X 射线胶片　low-speed X-ray film
低速爆炸成形　low-explosive forming
低速成形法(薄板的)　low velocity forming method
低速电子　low velocity electron
低速(度)　low speed
低速搅拌器　low-speed agitator
低速轧制　【压】idling
低塑性钢　low-ductility steel
低塑性合金　low ductile alloy
低塑性黏土　low plastic clay
低缩性混凝土　low-shrinkage concrete
低碳　low-carbon
低碳半硬质冷轧板　low carbon half-hard cold strip
低碳带钢　low-carbon steel strip
低碳低合金钢　low-carbon HSLA steel
低碳钢(0.1—0.25C)　low-carbon steel, mild steel (MS, m.s.), mild carbon steel, soft (carbon) steel, decarbonized steel ◇超~*, 结构用~structural mild steel, 扩散渗硅处理的~*, 铝化~aluminized mild steel, 搪瓷用~*, 完全退火~*, 再加硫再增磷~*
低碳钢板　mildsteel plate ◇涂珐琅~enamelled iron
低碳钢薄板　mildsteel sheet
低碳钢锭　mildsteel ingot
低碳钢(电)焊条　low carbon steel welding electrode
低碳钢焊丝　mild steel welding rod
低碳钢熔炼　low-carbon heat
低碳钢丝　mild steel wire, iron wire
低碳钢线材　mesh grade [quality] wire rod
低碳钢阴极　mildsteel cathode
低碳铬铁　low-carbon ferrochromium
低碳合金　low-carbon alloy
低碳炉次　【钢】low melt
低碳马氏体　【金】low-carbon martensite
低碳锰铁(85Mn, 0.2C, 余量 Fe)　low-carbon ferro-manganese
低碳镍铁　low-carbon ferro-nickel

低 di

低碳深冲钢　low-carbon deep-drawing steel
低碳生铁　low-carbon pig iron, semi-steel
低碳铁素体不锈钢（<0.1C,11—30Cr）stainless iron
低碳铸钢　low-carbon cast steel
低碳铸铁　low-carbon cast iron, gun iron
低铁假板钛矿　ferro-pseudobrookite
低铁菱镁矿　low-iron magnesite
低铁酸性渣　【钢】low-iron acid slag
低铁损材料　low coreloss material
低铁钽矿{(Fe,Mn)Ta$_2$O$_6$}　ferrotantalite
低铜镍硫阳极　low-copper nickel matte anode
低头式连铸机　low-head continuous casting machine
低头型振动筛　low-head screen
低透气性炉料　dense charge
低位能带　low-lying energy band
低位能级　low-lying (energy) level
低位排放　low level emission
低位数位　low order digit
低温　low temperature
低温泵送[泵唧]　cryogenic pumping, cryopumping
低温比热　low temperature specific heat
低温变态　low temperature modification
低温变形　low temperature deformation
低温材料　low temperature material
低温操作　low temperature operation
低温槽　deep freeze tank
低温超导体材料　low temperature superconducting material
低温成形[型]　low temperature form, cryogenic forming, cryoforming
低温冲击　low-temperature impact
低温冲击试验　low temperature impact test
低温出钢　cold melt
低温处理　low temperature treatment, 【金】cold treatment（指零下）
低温吹炼　【冶】blow cold

低温磁性　cryomagnetic property
低温脆性　black brittleness [shortness], brittleness at low temperature, low temperature brittleness [embrittlement], cold brittleness, rheotropic brit-tleness [embrittlement]
低温电解（法）　low-temperature electrolytic processing
低温端　low temperature end
低温段　low-temperature zone
低温断裂　low temperature cracking
低温钝化　low-temperature passivation (LTP)
低温放电渗硫真空炉　low-temperature gas discharge vacuum furnace for sulphurization
低温反应堆[器]　low temperature reactor
低温粉化　low-temperature breakdown (LTB), low-temperature degradation (LTD)
低温干馏气　【焦】low temperature (carbonization) gas
低温干燥器　primary dryer
低温钢　low-temperature steel
低温固结(法)　low temperature hardening
低温固结团块　【团】low-temperature bound briquette
低温管　cryotron
低温焊接　low-temperature welding
低温合金　low temperature alloy
低温恒温器　cryostat
低温烘烤　low baking
低温化学　cryochemistry
低温还原　low temperature reduction
低温还原粉化　low temperature reduction degradation
低温还原粉化率　low temperature reduction degradation index ◇赫施～测定法 Heosch method
低温回复　【金】low temperature recovery
低温回火　low (temperature) tempering ◇特瑞-诺雅～法 Terre-Noire process

低温回火处理(用于高速钢刀具) under-hardening
低温计 cryometer, frigorimeter
低温加工 cryoforming, cryogenic preparation, zero-working
低温加工金属(材料) cryogenically worked metal
低温加热 low temperature heating
低温焦油 low temperature tar
低温浇注 pour [cast] cold
低温阶段[时期] 【冶】low temperature stage
低温结构 low temperature texture
低温金属 cryogenic metal
低温金相学 kyroscopy
低温绝缘 low temperature insulation
低温可熔性 low temperature fusibility
低温控制轧制 low temperature rolling
低温冷凝器 low temperature condenser
低温冷却 low temperature cooling, subcooling
低温炼焦炉 low-temperature carbonizing retort
低温炉 low temperature furnace
低温炉次(钢水) cold heat
低温马氏体 low-temperature martensite
低温破碎 low-temperature breakdown (LTB)
低温钎焊 low temperature brazing ◇西尔布拉洛伊～合金 Silbralloy
低温球团固结法 【团】low temperature pellet hardening process
低温区 low-temperature zone
低温缺口韧性 notch toughness at cryogenic temperature
低温热处理 low temperature heat-treatment
低温热处理除气 【金】baking
低温热解 【焦】low temperature pyrolysis
低温韧性 low temperature toughness, toughness at cryogenic temperature
低温熔炼 low temperature melt, low smelting heat
低温熔炼法 【冶】cold melt process
低温蠕变 low temperature creep
低温烧结 low temperature sintering ◇全磁精矿～ *
低温烧结的复合电触头合金 low-sintered composite contact metal
低温渗氮 low temperature nitriding
低温渗碳法 disco process
低温时效 low temperature ageing
低温使用材料 low temperature material
低温室 cold chamber
低温试验 low temperature test
低温试验法 cryogenics
低温试验室 cold (climate) cell
低温塑性 low temperature ductility
低温塑性[低温热]加工(在再结晶温度以下) blue (heat, temperature) working
低温碎裂[粉化(率)] low temperature disintegration
低温碳化炉 low temperature carbonization furnace
低温碳化气 【焦】low temperature (carbonization) gas
低温搪瓷 low temperature enamel
低温条件 cold condition
低温退火 low temperature annealing, process annealing, lonnealing
低温退火处理 low temperature annealing treatment
低温退火硬化 low temperature annealing hardening
低温位错内耗 low temperature dislocation internal friction
低温物理 cryophysics
低温系数 low-temperature coefficient (LTC)
低温现象(通常低于－100℃) cryogenics
低温相 【金】low temperature phase
低温箱 cryostat, deep freezer, low-temperature cabinet
低温性能 low temperature property, cryo-

genic property
低温学　cryogenics
低温压碎强度　cold crushing strength
低温压制(低于常温的压制)　chill-pressing
低温氧化　low temperature oxidation
低温应用(通常低于-100℃)　low temperature application, cryogenic application
低温硬化　hardening at low-temperature, subcritical hardening
低温用钢　cryogenic steel
低温再结晶退火　low temperature recrystallization anneal
低温照相机　low temperature camera
低温蒸馏　low (temperature) distillation
低温蒸汽　low temperature steam
低温状况　cold condition
低温作业　(同"低温操作")
低钨高速钢(1.5C, 1.03Mn, 0.86Si, 8.01Cr, 3.37V, 2.63W, 1.29Al, 0.09N)　low tungsten high speed steel
低钨工具钢　wortle
低析水性水泥　low-water-loss cement
低吸收能力材料　【理】material of low absorbing power
低锡巴氏合金　hardening babbit
低锡焊料　【焊】poor solder
低锡炉渣　low-tin slag
低锡螺钉青铜(93Cu, 5Zn, 1Sn, 1Pb)　screw bronze
低锡铅巴比合金　◇奥罗拉~*
低锡铅基轴承合金　◇伯马克斯~*, 改进型莫尔-琼斯~*, 莫霍克~*, 温斯科英~*
低锡青铜(88Cu, 8-10Sn, 2-4Zn)　low-tin bronze
低线性极限　lower linearity limit
低效率　poor efficiency, inefficiency
低锌粉尘　low-zinc dust
低锌黄铜(80Cu, 20Zn)　low brass, yellow pewter ◇富铜~*, 普卢姆赖特~*
低锌黄铜合金(85Cu, 15Zn)　red brass alloy
低循环(次数)疲劳　【金】low-cycle fatigue
低循环周期下的疲劳裂纹扩展　low-cycle fatigue crack propagation
低压　low pressure, slight pressure, low tension (低电压)
低压泵　low-pressure [low-lift] pump
低压表　low-pressure gauge
低压差式焦炉　low-differential oven
低压导电母线系统　low-voltage-bus system
低压等离子喷涂　low-pressure plasma spray(ing)
低压电弧　low-voltage arc
低压电路　low-voltage circuit
低压电源　low voltage power supply (L.V.P.S.)
低压发生器(乙炔的)　low-pressure (acetylene) generator
低压割炬　low-pressure (type) cutter
低压鼓风　low-pressure blast
低压锅炉　low-pressure boiler
低压(焊)炬　low-pressure (welding) torch, low-pressure blow-pipe
低压挤压　low-pressure pressing
低压开关设备[装置]　low tension switch gear
低压空气喷雾法　low-pressure air atomization
低压轮胎　balloon tyre
低压母线　secondary busbar
低压配电　low-voltage distribution
低压气体　low-pressure gas
低压汽化冷却　【冶】pressureless type evaporative cooling
低压切割器　low-pressure (type) cutter
低压区　depression
低压燃烧器　low-pressure (type) burner
低压熔化　low-pressure melting
低压省煤器　low-pressure coal economizer
低压水冷系统　【冶】low-pressure-cooling circuit

低压旋流式分离器　low-head cyclonic-type separator
低压压铸机　low-pressure die-casting machine
低压液压站　hydraulic low pressure station
低压乙炔发生器　low-pressure (acetylene) generator
低压蒸馏　low-pressure distillation
低压铸造(法)　【铸】low-pressure casting
低压铸造机　【铸】air injection machine
低氧钢　low-oxygen steel
低氧含量轴承钢　low oxygen bearing steel
低氧化镁熔剂　【冶】low-magnesia stone
低氧化物　protoxide
低氧化银　silver [argentic] oxide
低硬度退火　quarter-hard annealing
低原子量的　low-atomic-weight
低原子序数的　low-atomic-number
低原子序数元素　low-Z element
低杂质废钢　low residual scrap
低渣量球团　pellet with low slag content
低折射率平面　low-index plane
低真空　low [poor, coarse, rough, soft] vacuum
低织构钢　low-texture steel
低指数平面　【理】low-index plane
低质量　poor in quality
低质量燃料　low-quality fuel
低周期疲劳　【金】low-cycle fatigue
低转鼓指数球团　【金】low-tumbler-index pellet
低阻抗玻璃捕油器　low-resistance glass oil-trap
低阻抗金属捕油器　low-resistance metal oil-trap
低组分合金　low [lean] alloy
滴点　dropping point
滴定　titration ◇ 螯合～(法)*,被～液 titrate,回[返]～ back titration,可～酸度 titratable acidity,可控阴极电位还原～*
滴定标准　titrimetric standard
滴定标准溶液　titrant
滴定测定(法)　determination by titration
滴定度[率]　titer, titre
滴定法　titrimetric method, titration ◇ 电导～*
滴定分析　titrimetric analysis
滴定分析的　titrimetric
滴定(分析)计　titrimeter
滴定(分析)器　titrator
滴定管　burette ◇ 量液～ measuring buret(te),乳白刻度～ milk scale buret(te),闪蒸～ flash burette,微量～ microburette
滴定管浮标　burette float
滴定管夹　burette clamp
滴定剂　titrant
滴定液(滴定用液)　volumetric solution
滴汞电极　dropping mercury electrode (DME), dropping electrode
滴汞阴极　dropping mercury cathode
滴管　dropper, dropping tube
滴管式给药机　【选】dropper, dropping bottle
滴(降)栓[旋塞]　dropping cock, drip-cock
滴量器　dropper
滴流脱气法　Bochumer Vevein process
滴漏状断口　hour-glass fracture
滴滤池　trickling filter ◇ 低负荷～*,曝气～*
滴落区[带]　dripping zone
滴落[下]试验　dripping test
滴落[下]性状　dropping behaviour
滴瓶　dropper, drop(ping) bottle
滴熔法　drip melting, auto-crucible method
滴熔设备　(同"悬熔设备")
滴入装置(气体渗碳炉的)　drip feed
滴水(板)　【建】dropper
滴水式(乙炔)发生器　water feed generator
滴铁(高炉内焦炭块的)　tricling iron
滴下开始温度　start-of-dripping [start-of-dropping] temperature (SDT)
滴形截面　drop-shaped section

滴液电极　dropping electrode
滴液漏斗　drop(ping) funnel
滴液吸移管　drop(ping) pipette
滴油圈　drip ring
滴油润滑　drop [drip] lubrication
滴重(测量)法(熔体表面张力的)　【冶】drop weight method
滴重计(表面张力滴重计)　stagonometer, stalagmometer, tensometer
滴注式渗碳法　drop feed carburizing
滴注式渗碳炉　drop-type carburized furnace
滴状金属　dropping metal
滴状凝缩　dropwise condensation
迪奥斯考普硬度计(携带式)　Duoskop
迪德外燃式热风炉　Didier-Dunkerque hot stove
迪迪尔式焦炉　Didier coke oven
迪尔加滕夹杂物评级(图片)　Diergarten inclusion chart
迪尔瓦铁镍合金(54—58Fe,42—46Ni)　Dilver
迪合金　Di-alloy
迪卡尔铜硅合金　dical
迪克挤压法(正向)　【压】Dick extrusion method
迪克索尔青铜　dixoilbronze
迪朗斯轴承合金(33.4Sn, 22.2Cu, 44.4Sb)　Dewrance's alloy
迪-莫尔钼高速钢　di-mol
迪努耶尔二级扩散泵　Dunoyer's two-stage pump
迪帕洛伊银焊料[钎焊]合金　Dimpalloy
迪皮伊固体燃料反应罐炼铁法　【铁】Dupuy process
迪舍尔式轧管法　Diescher process
迪舍尔旋转导盘(迪舍尔轧机的)　Diescher rotary guide shoe
迪舍尔轧(管)机(无缝管延伸机)　Diescher pipe rolling mill, Diescher elongator ◇ 限动芯棒~*
迪氏铝铜锌合金　Devarda('s) alloy
迪斯卡洛伊涡轮叶片用耐热合金(镍铬钼钛钢；55Fe, 25Ni, 13Cr, 3Mo, 2Ti, 0.7Mn, 0.7Si, 0.5Al, 0.05C)　Discaloy
迪斯廷顿连铸设备　Distington-concast plant
迪特壳型吹成法　【铸】Dietert process
迪特[迪塔特式]硬度计　Dietert tester
迪维尔合金　Dilver (alloy)
迪尤兰斯合金　Dewrance's alloy
笛管式取样器　whistle-pipe sampler
笛卡儿坐标系　(同"直角坐标系")
狄菲尔换热剂　Diphyl
狄那莫耐磨铝青铜(9—11Al, 4—6Ni, 4—6Fe, <2Mn, <1Zn, 余量 Cu)　Dynamo bronze
涤纶(滤尘)袋　dacron bag
涤气　(gas) scrub(bing)
涤气器　scrubber ◇ 文丘里多管~*, 溢流盘式~*, 圆锥形~*
涤气水　gas (washing) water
抵偿半导体　compensated semiconductor
抵触　interference, conflict
抵抗　withstand, resist(ance)
抵抗力　resistivity
抵抗墙　【焦】pinion wall
抵消　off-set, neutralization
抵消电压　bucking voltage
抵消税　countervailing duty
底　bottom, base, basis, toe, sole
底板　base plate, bed plate [piece], bottom board, chassis, foot, main base, shoe plate, sole, backing electrode (接触焊机的), foundation frame (砂箱的), plancier (檐或楼梯的), 【钢】bottom plate, stool (钢锭模的), moulding bed, 【机】end plate
底板翻面机　【压】base plate turnover machine
底板支座(罩式炉的)　base plate bed
底板准备工段　stool conditioning area
底板组装　【冶】bottom plate assembly
底板座(罩式炉的)　base plate seat
底部　bottom, subbasement, butt end (钢

锭、坯的)
底部点火　bottom priming
底部断面　【钢】bottom section
底部飞边　bottom fash
底部滑板　bottom slide
底部加热　bottom [base] heating
底部加热的焦炉　sole heated oven
底部截槽　undercutting
底部进料炉　under-feed furnace
底部流槽　【铸】bottom runner
底部炉衬(出铁口处)　【铸】breast
底部面积　floor area
底部内衬　bottom inwalls
底部排水　underdrain, bottom discharge
底部片边　bottom fash
底部区域(转炉的)　bottom section
底部掏槽　undercut
底部卸料车　centre dump car
底侧　bottom side
底层　bottom [lower] layer, bottom course [deck, stratum, zone], filling colour, footing course, underlayer, printing coat (多层涂层的), first layer (双涂层的)
底层废钢　【钢】bottom scrap
底层焊接　backing weld(ing)
底层焊条(封底焊条)　uramami welding electrode
底层金属　underlying metal
底层料透气性　【冶】bed porosity
底层炉衬(转炉的)　backup lining
底层炉料　bed charge, hearth layer
底层炉膛　bottom hearth
底层试样　lower sample
底层涂料　prime paint, subbing
底层涂料泡疤(搪瓷缺陷)　ground-coat boiling
底层油漆　paint primer, roughstuff
底沉积　bottom deposit
底衬　bottom liner [lining]
底吹　【钢】bottom blowing
底吹 CO_2　【钢】CO_2 bottom blowing
底吹碱性转炉钢　Thomas steel

底吹气体　bottom blowing gas ◇ 电弧炉～搅拌技术*
底吹气体电弧炉　bottom blown EAF
底吹式浮选机　subaeration cell
底吹氧气转炉　bottom blowing oxygen converter
底吹蒸汽氧气转炉　VLN 炼钢法 (同"极低含氮量炼钢法")
底吹转炉　bottom blown converter ◇ 菲尼克斯－兰斯[PL]～炼钢法*, 碱性～*
底吹转炉风口[嘴]　【钢】tuyere plug
底刀　bed knife
底导炉(炉底导电的炉)　conducting-hearth furnace
底点　base point
底垫　pad, bearing plate, 【焊】backup [backing] strip (焊缝下面的)
底电极　bottom [lower] electrode
底镀层　ground coat, undercoat
底翻式熄焦车　tilting-type quench car
底反射　bottom echo [reflection]
底反射波信号　bottom echo
底放渣炉　slagging-bottom furnace
底盖　bottom [lower] cap
底辊　foot roll
底焊焊道　backing pass
底火黄铜　primer (gilding) brass
底基　foot bed
底极电弧炉　electrode-hearth arc-furnace
底架　chassis, base [foundation] frame, underframe
底架轧材　chassis sections
底焦　bed (coke)
底浇包　bottom pour ladle
底浇口　【铸】bottom gate
底角　base angle
底开门车　bottom dumping car, wagon with hopper bottom
底开式钢锭模　open bottom mould
底坑　foundation pit
底坑法　drift method

底框架	underframe
底梁	sill beam, collar
底料	basic [bed] charge, bottom stuff,【冶】bed, bed(ding) material
底料层	initial bed
底料[焦]高度	【铁】bed height
底流	underflow, under-current
底流泵	underflow pump
底流产物	underflow product
底流挡板	underflow baffle
底流方向仪	bottom current direction meter
底流矿浆	underflow pulp
底流浓度	underflow concentration
底流液	underflow liquid
底锍[冰铜]	starting [seed] matte
底面	bottom side, underside, basal plane
底面反射	bottom reflection
底面积	base area
底面极射投影图	basal plane pole figure
底面双晶	manehach twin
底模	bottom [bed, counter] die, anvil swage, die bed
底耙	bottom rake
底盘	chassis, undercarriage, underpan,【钢】bottom plate, stool
底盘刮刀	bottom rake
底盘型钢	chassis sections
底喷嘴式炉	underburner-type oven
底片箱(电子显微镜的)	plate chamber
底枪	bottom lance
底切	undercut
底切焊接	undercut welding
底区	bottom zone
底燃烧器式炉	underburner-type oven
底热器	bottom heater
底塞	bottom plug, plug (钢锭模的) ◇ 有～的钢锭模 plug bottom ingot mould
底数	【数】radix, base number
底特律型砂杯状试验	Detroit cup test
底特律摇动电炉(生产高级灰口生铁用)【铁】	Detroit rocking electric furnace
底图	reproducible [based] drawing
底涂层[涂料]	base coat, undercoat, first [ground, primary] coat, grounding,【化】primer
底线	bottom [base] line
底箱	bottom box, undercasing,【铸】mould drag
底卸车	bottom dump(ing) car
底卸法	bottom drop
底卸环冷机	bottom dump type rotary cooler
底卸矿车	drop-bottom car
底卸式(矿车)	bottom dump type
底卸式车厢[铁路车皮]	rail car of bottom-dump design
底卸(式)料罐	bottom discharge bucket,【铁】drop-bottom bucket, hopper charging bucket ◇ 蛤壳式～*
底卸式自动倾卸汽车	bottom dump hauler
底心的(晶体)	end-centered
底心点阵[晶格]	base-centered lattice
底压力	base pressure
底压式造型机	(同"下压式造型机")
底质取样	bottom sampling
底质土	【地】bottom deposit
底轴面体(结晶的)	basal pinacoid
底铸	downcast, subsurface ladling, uphill casting,【钢】bottom [group] cast-(ing) ◇ 加压～*
底铸浇口	【铸】rising pipe
底注	bottom running [teeming], cast uphill, up-running, uphill pouring [teeming],【钢】bottom pour, cast [pour] from bottom, indirect casting [pouring, teeming],【铸】rising pouring
底注法	uphill casting ◇ 车上～(法)*
底注管	【铸】trumpet
底注设备[装置](中注管、底板等)【钢】	holloware
底注(式)钢包[浇包,盛钢桶]	bottom pour(ing) [tap] ladle, Bessemer ladle

底注式浇口　【铸】bottom gate
底(注)铸型　bottom pour mould ◇ 上部无浇冒口的～close-top mould
底座　base (frame), basement, foundation plate, steadier, backing, foot
砥石　whetslate, whetstone
地磅　car weigher, track scales, weight bridge, wagon balance ◇ 过车～truck scales
地磅房　weighhouse
地表复原　【环】surface reclamation
地表[面]浓度　【环】ground level concentration, concentration on the ground (level)
地表[面]水　surface [day] water
地表形状　configuration of earth
地层　stratum, terrain, formation
地磁　earth magnetism, geomagnetism
地磁场　earth magnetic field, geomagnetic field
地磁记录法　magnetography
地磁(强度)记录仪　magnetograph
地磁仪　magnetometer ◇ 平衡～balance magnetometer
地带　area, band, zone
地道　subway, under-pass, gallery,【运】tunnel
地段　dock, a section of an area
地对起重机通讯系统　floor to crane communication system
地方钢铁企业　local iron and steel enterprise
地方国营　state-owned but locally-administered
地沟　trench, gallery, sewer
地沟洗矿　【选】gouging
地沟运输机　trench conveyer
地基　foundation, base, ground, subgrade, bottom, pedestal, substructure
地基强度　【建】base strength
地基稳定　base stabilization
地基系数　foundation modulus, bedding value
地基下沉　ground subsidence, setting of ground
地槛　patand
地脚板　foundation [sole] plate, base (anchor), main base, shoe, bed plate (轧机的)
地脚钢筋　anchoring accessories
地脚框架　foot frame
地脚螺栓　anchor [foundation, barb, hacked, stone, tie, truss] bolt, (foot) holding down bolt
地脚植架　anchor frame
地浸　in-situ leaching
地开石　【耐】dickite
地坑砂　【铸】pit sand
地坑式炉　【压】underground furnace
地坑造型　【铸】floor [hearth, pit, bedded-in] moulding
地坑[地面]铸型　【铸】floor mould
地坑铸造　【铸】pit casting
地蜡　ceresin(e), earth wax
地沥青(结合料)　asphaltic bitumen, asphalt
地沥青柏油　asphalt tar
地沥青砂胶(又称地沥青玛狷脂或乳香沥青)　mastic asphalt
地梁　patand, grade beam
地锚钢　anchor steel
地面　ground, floor level
地面标高　【建】ground elevation [level], floor level
地面波　surface wave
地面测量　surface measure (S.M.)
地面电阻　earth resistance
地面覆盖层　【环】ground cover
地面焊接　floor welding
地面加压站　land booster station
地面浇铸　open (sand) casting
地面排水沟　area drain
地面砂　【铸】floor sand
地面设施　ground-based facility, surface

operations
地面以下　below ground
地面运输车辆　floor conveying trucks
地面造型　【铸】floor moulding [work], hearth moulding, bedding in ◇ 盖箱~*
地面整修　【环】landscaping
地面砖　floor tile
地面作业　floor work
地平　horizon
地平标高　floor elevation, ground level
地平面　floor level
地平线　horizon(tal)
地壳　earth's crust, shell, lithosphere
地壳热流(量)　【理】terrestrial heat flow
地球　the earth, the globe
地球表面形状　configuration of earth
地球磁场　earth magnetic field
地球观测卫星　earth survey satellite
地球化学　geochemistry
地球水面　hydrosphere
地球物理地震调查　【地】geophysical seismic exploration
地球物理勘测　【地】geophysical exploration
地球物理勘探工作者协会　Society of Exploration Geophysicists (S.E.G.)
地球物理学　geophysics
地球资源卫星　earth resource (technology) satellite
地区　area (Ar.), district
地热化学　【地】geothermal chemistry
地上放线架　floor reel
地上卷取机　floor reel, [压]upcoiler ◇ 辊式~roll-type upcoiler
地上脱模机　【钢】floor type stripper machine
地上运输机　floor conveyer
地位　position, rank ◇ 最显著~ fore ground
地下　underground, subsurface
地下避难室　dug-out
地下变电所　underground substation
地下储存　underground storage
地下传送带　underground conveyer
地下电缆　(under)ground [buried] cable
地下电缆隧道　cable subway
地下发电站　underground powerplant
地下腐蚀　underground corrosion
地下管道　underground ducting
地下辊式卷取机　roll-type downcoiler
地下过道　under-pass
地下混凝土　buried concrete
地下建筑　hypogee
地下浸出　【色】underground leaching
地下卷取机　【压】down-coiler (D.C.) ◇ 传动卷筒式~*, 外传动辊式~*
地下卷取机顶部辊道　down-coiler top table
地下卷取机夹送辊　down-coiler pinch roll
地下卷取机冷却系统　down-coiler cooling system
地下开采　underground mining
地下勘探　【地】underground exploration
地下矿仓　underground bin
地下料仓　ground bins [bunker]
地下排水　subdrainage
地下室　cellar, basement, vault
地下室窗采光　area light
地下水　(under) ground [phreatic, subsoil] water ◇ 用测杆探~dowse, 最低~basal water
地下水泵汲控制　【环】control of pumping up of underground water
地下水补给　【环】ground-water recharge, recharge of underground water
地下水降落曲线　draw-down curve
地下水流　subsurface flow
地下水位　ground water level, elevation of ground water ◇ 降低~*, 深~deep water table, 天然~*
地下水文学　geohydrology
地下铁道　subway, underground (railway), tube railway
地下停车场　underground car park

地下盐水	underground brine
地下油库	oil cellar, cellar oil
地下油库排污系统	oil cellar drainage system
地下油库通风系统	oil cellar ventilation, ventilation system for oil cellar
地下运输机	underground conveyer, tunnel conveyer (热轧带卷的)
地下贮槽	ground bunker
地心圈	【地】barysphere
地形	terrain, topography
地形测量	contouring
地形图	topographical [relief] map ◇ 区域[厂区]~*
地行揭盖吊车[起重机](均热炉的)	【压】cover crane
地行式不回转装料机	【钢】nonrotating ground-type charging machine
地行式运输机	floor type carryall
地行式装料机	【钢】floor charging machine
地行万能装卸机	floor truck
地域	district, region
地震	earthquake, earth shock ◇ 大~ megaseism, 地球物理~调查*, 遭受地带 nervous earth
地震等级	earthquake magnitude
地震荷载	seismic load
地震扰动	seismographic disturbance
地震系数	seismic coefficient
地震震源[中]	epicenter of earthquakes
地震中心	seismic centre, epicenter of earthquake
地址部分	【计】address component [part]
地址磁道	【计】address track
地址分配	address assignment [allocation]
地址寄存器	【计】address register
地址计算	【计】address computation
地址开关	【计】address switch
地址空间	【计】address space
地址码	【计】address code
地址线	【计】address wire, A wire
地址写入线	【计】address write wire
地址转换	address conversion [translation]
地址字段	【计】address field
地质测量[调查]	geological survey
地质工程师	geological engineer (G.E.)
地质构造	geologic structure
地质勘测	geological survey
地质剖面	geological section
地质资料[数据]	geological data
地质钻探	geological boring
地质作用	geological action
地中衡	weighbridge
地钻	ground auger
蒂戈铅基轴承合金	(78—83Pb, 15—18Sb, 1—3Sn, 1—2Cu) Tego
蒂科尼姆牙科合金	(32.5Co, 31.4Ni, 27.5Cr, 5.2Mo, 1.6Fe, 0.18C, 0.35Si, 0.7Mn) Ticonium
蒂克纳尔铝镍钴永磁合金	Ticonal (magnet)
蒂莫费夫浸蚀液(锌及锌合金显微组织显示用)	Timofeef's reagent
蒂姆肯 X 耐热合金	(30.7Co, 28.6Ni, 16.8Cr, 11Fe, 10.5Mo, 1.4Mn, 0.75Si, 0.13C) Timken X
蒂姆肯铬镍钼耐热钢	(0.1C, 1.35Mn, 0.7Si, 16.72Cr, 25.23Ni, 6.25Mo, 0.15N) Timken (steel)
蒂尼杜尔耐热合金钢	(30Ni, 15Cr, 1.7Ti, 0.8Mn, 0.5Si, 0.15C, 0.2Al, 余量 Fe) Tinidur
蒂尼特锡基轴承合金	Tinite
蒂森-埃米尔高级铸铁	(2.5—3.0C, 1.8—2.5Si, 0.8—1.2Mn, 0.1—0.2P, 0.1—0.15S) Thysen-Emmel
蒂氏金属脆性转变温度试验	Tipper test
蒂斯科-蒂曼格锰镍耐磨钢	(0.6—0.8C, 13—15Mn, 3Ni, 余量 Fe) Tisco-Timang steel
蒂斯科耐磨锰钢	(12Mn) Tisco Mn steel
蒂斯科耐磨镍锰钢	(15Mn, 35—40Ni) Tisco steel

蒂斯科镍铬硅耐磨耐蚀合金 Tisco alloy (Tisco 150: 2.5—3.5C, 2Si, 1—1.5Ni, 28—32Cr, 余量 Fe)
蒂塔纳尔铝基活塞合金(82Al, 12.2Cu, 4.3Si, 0.8Mg, 0.7Fe) Titanal
蒂塔纳洛伊钛铜锌合金 Titanaloy
蒂塔诺尔钛钢(用作刀具) Titanor metal
蒂坦选矿法(先还原,后磁选) Titan process
蒂特迈杰硅青铜(5—10Al, 2.75Si, 少量 Fe, 余量 Cu) Tetmajer
蒂西尔黄铜(97Cu, 2Zn, 1Sn 或 As;用作五金家具或轴承) Tissier's alloy [metal]
蒂兹特高速钢(40—85W, 3—40Fe, 4—15Ti, 3—5Cr, 1—5Ce, 2—4C) Tizit
第 n 级反射 n th order reflection
第二标准热[温差]电偶 secondary standard thermocouple
第二层中间辊(二十辊轧机的) second intermediate rolls
第二次[级]过滤 second stage filtration
第二道冲压工序 second pressing operation
第二干燥段 【团】secondary drying zone
第二级除尘器(旋风除尘器) 【铁】secondary dust catcher
第二级处理(废物的) secondary treatment
第二级电离 secondary ionization
第二级反射 second order reflection
第二级光谱 secondary spectrum
第二架粗轧机 pony rougher
第二架粗轧机座 pony roughing stand of rolls
第二阶段石墨化 second stage graphitization (SSG)
第二类超导体 【埋】superconductor of the second kind, type Ⅱ superconductor
第二类三相平衡($L+\alpha=\beta+\gamma$) class Ⅱ ternary equilibrium
第二类四相平衡($L+\alpha=\beta+\gamma+\delta$) class Ⅱ quaternary equilibrium
第二类五相平衡($L+\alpha=\beta+\gamma+\delta+\varepsilon$) class Ⅱ quinary equilibrium
第二冷却段 secondary (cooling) zone
第二期[阶段]蠕变 second stage of creep, secondary creep
第二下冲杆[下模冲] second lower punch
第二下压头 secondary lower ram
第二相颗粒 second phase particle
第二最近邻原子 next nearest neighbor
第三次[期]渣 third(-run) slag
第三级处理(废物的) tertiary treatment
第三(级)绕组 tertiary winding
第三纪 【地】tertiary (tert.)
第三阶段回火 【金】third stage tempering
第三类三相平衡($L+\alpha+\beta=\gamma$) class Ⅲ ternary equilibrium
第三类四相平衡($L+\alpha+\beta=\gamma+\delta$) class Ⅲ quaternary equilibrium
第三类五相平衡($L+\alpha+\beta=\gamma+\delta+\varepsilon$) class Ⅲ quinary equilibrium
第三期[阶段]蠕变 third stage creep, tertiary creep
第三相消除剂 third-phase eliminating agent
第三最近邻原子 third nearest neighbor
第四孔加屋顶罩 【钢】fourth hole with canopy hood
第四类四相平衡($L+\alpha+\beta+\gamma=\delta$) class Ⅳ quaternary equilibrium
第四类五相平衡($L+\alpha+\beta+\gamma=\delta+\varepsilon$) class Ⅳ quinary equilibrium
第五类五相平衡($L+\alpha+\beta+\gamma+\delta=\varepsilon$) class Ⅴ quinary equilibrium
第一层中间辊(二十辊轧机的) first intermediate rolls
第一产业 primary industry
第一长列(周期)元素 first long row elements
第一次[级]过滤 first stage filtration
第一次浸出 primary leach
第一代计算机 first generation computer

第一道(多道焊缝的) first layer
第一道拉拔 first draught drawing
第一电子透镜 cathode lens
第一机架辊 first roller
第一级除尘器(重力除尘器) 【铁】primary dustcatcher
第一级电离 primary ionization
第一级反射 first order reflection
第一级[阶段]焊接 first class welding
第一级[类]相变 【理】first order change, first order phase transition
第一阶段微滑移 microslip in stage I
第一孔型[轧制道次] first pass
第一类超导体 【理】superconductor of the first kind, type I superconductor
第一类三相平衡($L=\alpha+\beta+\gamma$) class I ternary equilibrium
第一类四相平衡($L=\alpha+\beta+\gamma+\delta$) class I quaternary equilibrium
第一类五相平衡($L=\alpha+\beta+\gamma+\delta+\varepsilon$) class I quinary equilibrium
第一冷却区[段] primary cooling zone, first stage cooling zone
第一炉前工 【铁】keeper
第一炉熔炼(开炉后) pill heat
第一期工程 first phase
第一下模冲 primary lower punch
第一下压头 primary lower ram
第一助手 【钢】first helper
第一最近邻原子 first nearest neighbor
递变断面型材 tapered section
递钢(机座间) catching ◇ 自动～*
递归[推] 【数】recursion
递归程序设计 recursive programming
递回辊 pass-over roll
递减函数 decreasing function
递降分解(作用) degradation
递阶计划结构 hierarchical system of production plan
递送机(板带的) pinch mill
递送力(板带的) pinch force
递推公式 recurrence formula

递增函数 increasing function
递增挤压 incremental extrusion
递增加载试验 incremental loading test
缔合常数 association constant
缔合平衡 association equilibrium
缔合热 association heat
缔合效应 【化】association effect
碲钯矿 merenskyite
碲铋华 montanite
碲铋矿 tellurobismuthite
碲铋齐 hedleyite
碲铋银矿 volynskite
碲铂矿 moncheite
碲的[正碲的] telluric
碲钙石 carlfriesite
碲镉汞 mercury cadmium telluride
碲汞钯矿 temagamite
碲汞矿{$HgTe$} coloradoite
碲汞石 magnolite
碲硅锡杂庚烷 tellurasilastannaheptane
碲合金 tellurium alloy
碲化铋 bismuth telluride
碲化镉 cadmium telluride
碲化合物 tellurium compound
碲化锰 manganese telluride
碲化铅 lead telluride
碲化氢[氢碲酸] hydrotelluric acid
碲化物 telluride
碲化锌 zinc telluride
碲化银 silver telluride ◇ 天然～*
碲黄铁矿 telaspyrine
碲基合金 tellurium-base alloy
碲金矿{$AuTe_2$, $(Au, Ag)Te_2$} calaverite, tellride gold ore
碲金银矿{$(Ag, Au)_2Te$} petzite, antamokite
碲硫铋矿 cziklovaite, csiklovaite
碲(硫)醇 telluromercaptan
碲络合物 tellurium complex
碲锰铅矿 kuranakhite
碲锰锌石 spiroffite
碲镍矿{$NiTe_2$} tellurnickel, melonite

碲镍青铜(98.3Cu,1Ni,0.2P,0.5Te) Telnic bronze
碲铅　tellurium-lead（或 lead tellurium; 0.02—0.085Te),(同"铅碲合金")
碲铅铋矿　rucklidgeite
碲铅华　dunhamite
碲铅矿{PbTe}　altaite
碲铅石　fairbankite
碲铅铜金矿　bilibinskite
碲铅铜石　khinite
碲铅铀矿　moctezumite
碲青铜(1.5Sn,1Te,余量 Cu)　tellurium bronze
碲艳光电阴极　tellurium-caesium photo-cathode
碲酸　telluric acid, hydrogen tellurate
碲酸铵{(NH$_4$)$_2$TeO$_4$}　ammonium tellurate
碲酸钾{K$_2$TeO$_4$}　potassium tellurate
碲酸钠{Na$_2$TeO$_4$}　sodium tellurate
碲酸盐[酯]　tellurate
碲锑矿　tellurantimony
碲添加合金　tellurium addition
碲铁(天然的)　telluric (native) iron
碲铁矾　poughite
碲铁矿　frohbergite
碲铁石　emmonsite
碲铁铜金矿　bogdanovite
碲酮　telluroketone
碲同位素　tellurium isotope
碲铜(1.：1Te,余量 Cu,改善切削性能用； 2.：50Te,50Cu,用作中间合金)　tellurium copper
碲铜矾[石]　teineite
碲铜金矿　bessmertnovite
碲铜矿{Cu$_4$Te$_3$}　rickardite, vulcanite
碲硒矿　selen-tellurium
碲硒铜矿　bambollaite
碲锌锰石　denningite
碲银钯矿　telargpalite
碲银铋矿　von diestite
碲银矿{Ag$_2$Te}　hessite, botesite, savodinskite
碲铀矿　schmitterite
碲黝铜矿　goldfieldite
巅峰透气性　peak permeability
巅值密度　peak density
碘的[五价碘的,含碘的]　iodic
碘盒[储碘器]　iodine holder
碘化　iodize, iodination, iodate　◇阳极～ anodic iodination
碘化钙{CaI$_2$}　calcium iodide
碘化锆{ZrI$_4$}　zirconium iodide
碘化镉　cadmium iodide
碘化铬　chromium iodide
碘化汞　mercuric iodide
碘化硅　silicon iodide
碘化铪{HfI$_4$}　hafnium iodide
碘化合物　iodo-compound
碘化钪{ScI$_3$}　scandium iodide
碘化镧{LaI$_3$}　lanthanum iodide
碘化锂　lithium iodide
碘化铝　aluminium iodide
碘化镁　magnesium iodide
碘化锰　manganese iodide
碘化钼{MoI$_2$,MoI$_4$}　molybdenum iodide
碘化镍　nickel iodide
碘化钕{NdI$_3$}　neodymium iodide
碘化镨{PrI$_3$}　praseodymium iodide
碘化氢{HI}　hydrogen iodide
碘化区　iodination zone
碘化铷{RbI}　rubidium iodide
碘化铯{CsI}　cesium iodide
碘化铊{TlI,TlI$_2$,TlI$_3$}　thallium iodide
碘化钛　titanium iodide
碘化铁{FeI$_3$}　ferric iodide
碘化钨{WI$_2$,WI$_4$}　tungsten iodide
碘化物　iodide
碘化物沉积法　iodide deposition process
碘化物法　[色]iodide method [process] ◇弧熔～材料*
碘化物法锭坯　iodide-process ingot
碘化物法锆　iodide zirconium
碘化物法铪　iodide (process) hafnium

碘化物法铪结块	iodide hafnium chunk
碘化物法铪晶棒	iodide hafnium bar
碘化物法金属	iodide (process) metal
碘化物法精炼	iodide purification [refining]
碘化物法精炼过程	iodide-refining process
碘化物法钛	iodide process titanium
碘化物晶棒	【色】iodide bar
碘化物晶体（用于锆钛等的生产）	【色】iodide crystal
碘化物离解反应	hot wire reaction
碘化物热离解	【色】iodide decomposition ◇ 玻璃～容器*
碘化物热离解法（钛锆等的生产方法）	iodide (decomposition) process, hot filament process ◇ 阿克尔－德博尔[德博尔－冯·阿克尔*,冯·阿克尔(－德博尔)]～*,半连续～*,连续～*
碘化物热离解反应器	iodide decomposition reactor
碘化物热离解瓶	deposition bulb
碘化物热离解器（碘化物法）	deposition vessel
碘化物热离解设备	iodide decomposition unit
碘化物引爆剂	iodide booster
碘化亚汞	mercurous iodide
碘化亚钐$\{SmI_2\}$	samarium diiodide, samarous iodide
碘化氧铋	bismuthyl iodide
碘化钇$\{YI_3\}$	yttrium iodide
碘化银	silver iodide
碘化铀$\{UI_4;UI_6\}$	uranium iodide
碘化作用	iodination
碘晶体	iodine crystal
碘(量)滴定的	iodometric
碘(量)滴定法	iodometry
碘料斗	iodine hopper
碘气氛	iodine atmosphere
碘气流	current of iodine
碘铅	bustamentite
碘熔剂	iodide flux
碘酸镧$\{La(IO_3)_3\}$	lanthanum iodate
碘酸锂	lithium iodate
碘酸铷$\{RbIO_3\}$	rubidium iodate
碘酸盐	iodate
碘酸银	silver iodate
碘同位素	iodine isotope
碘铜矿	marshite
碘氧化物	oxyiodide
碘银矿	iodyrite
碘引爆剂	iodine booster
碘蒸气	iodine vapour
碘蒸气压	iodine pressure
碘值	iodine number [value]
碘柱栓	iodine plug
点	point,spot,dot ◇ 居里[磁性转变]～Curie point
点变形	point deformation
点测器（如硫化镉）	point detector
点穿孔	unipunch
点滴反应	drop reaction
点滴分析[化验]	drop [spot] analysis, spot test
点动【电】	jogging
点动继电器	inching relay
点对点协议	point-to-point protocol
点方式显示【计】	point-mode display
点－缝焊机	spot-and-seam welding machine ◇ 辊式～*
点辐射源	point source
点腐蚀试验	pitting corrosion test
点腐蚀速率	pitting rate
点腐蚀形成过程	pitting process
点概[估]算	point estimate
点固焊	tack welding
点光源	point (light) source
点焊	spot [point] welding ◇ 搭接[用盖板对接]～焊缝*,单面～ indirect welding,电弧～arc-spot welding,电极强冷却～zero welding,惰性气体保护～*,换向控制～*,加搭板对接～bridge welding,加小直径圆垫板的～（用于厚板）but-

ton welding, 钳式～焊枪 bar welder, 手动焊钳～ poke welding, 双面～*, 围绕铸核的一区*, 压薄～ mash spot welding, 圆搭板～*, 自动～*

点焊的U形试样垂直抗拉强度　U-strength
点焊电极工作端　spot-welding tip
点焊缝电弧焊　spot arc welding
点焊铪晶棒电极　tack-welded hafnium crystal bar electrode
点焊焊点[熔核]　weld nugget
点焊焊枪　spot-welding gun
点焊焊条　point [vertical] electrode, spot-welding electrode
点焊机　【焊】spot [mash] welder, spot [point] welding machine ◇ 电容器(放电)～*, 多点～*, 焊枪式～ gun welding machine, 固定式～*,(夹)钳式～*, 台座式～*, 蓄电池～*, 悬挂式～*, 压力控制式～*, 摇臂式～*, 移动式～ portable spot welder
点焊接　spot [point] welding
点焊接头(用滚焊机施焊的)　roller spot weld, tack-weld, spot-welded joint
点焊连接　tack-weld ◇ 压边～ mash-welded joint
点焊钳　pry-bar gun spot-welding gun, pliers spot welding head ◇ C形～ C-type gun
点焊头　spot-welding head ◇ 扁钳式～*
点焊用密封材料　spot-welding sealer
点焊粘结　weldbonding
点弧　【电】striking
点划线　dash-and-dot line, dot-and-dash line
点火　ignition, light(ing)-up, firing (up), priming, allumage ◇ 底[下]部～ bottom priming, 旋流～ cyclone firing, 自动～ automatic firing
点火不足　inadequate ignition
点火车　【团】ignition car
点火点试验　ignition-point test

点火电极　ignitor electrode
点火电路　ignition [firing] circuit
点火电压　ignition [firing, striking] voltage
点火端　ignition end
点火段(烧结炉的)　【团】ignition zone
点火法　ignition method
点火管　ignitron (tube)
点火后负压(抽风烧结法)　post-ignition suction
点火混合剂[点火料]　ignition [priming] mixture
点火火焰　pilot light
点火剂　igniter, ignitor
点火孔　lighting hole
点火控制　ignition control
点火块　ignition block
点火炉　【冶】fore chamber(炉外点火炉),【团】ignition furnace(带式烧结机的)
点火炉设计[型式]　【团】ignition furnace design
点火煤气供应(设施)　ignition gas service
点火门　fire door
点火木柴[刨花]　kindling wood
点火喷嘴　pilot jet, ignition burner
点火起点　starting of ignition
点火器　igniter, ignitor, ignition block, starting burner, lighter, firing [burner] hood(烧结机的) ◇ 标准～ normal ignition hood, 缝式～ multi-slitignitor, 辐射罩式～*, 锯齿型～ saw-tooth ignitor, 两段式～*, 煤气～ gas-fired ignitor, 喷枪式～ torch type ignitor, 喷嘴式～ nozzle type ignitor, 烧结节能～*, 线式～ linear ignitor
点火起点　starting of ignition
点火器温度　hood temperature
点火气体[煤气]　ignition gas
点火前负压　preignition suction
点火强度　ignition [heat] intensity
点火燃料消耗　ignition fuel consumption

点火塞	light-up plug
点火烧嘴	ignition burner
点火烧嘴助燃风机	combustion fan for pilot burner
点火室	burner house, hot bulb,【冶】priming chamber（铝热法生产铁合金的）
点火试验	hot test, firing run
点火顺序	firing order (FO, fo)
点火损失	ignition loss, loss on ignition
点火条件	【团】ignition condition
点火调节	adjustment of ignition
点火温度	ignition temperature, firing temperature (F.T.)
点火线圈	【电】ignition [spark] coil, bobbin,
点火用煤	ignition coal
点火罩（烧结机的）	【团】ignition [burner] hood
点火罩系统	ignition hood system
点火装置	igniter, ignitor, ignition device [system, unit]
点极检验法	point-pole test
点计数技术	point counting technique
点尖用钢丝（金笔的）	ball point wire
点接触钢丝绳	point contact lay wire rope
点金术	alchemy
点聚焦	point focusing
点聚焦单色器	point focusing monochromator
点聚焦电子枪	point-focused electron gun
点聚焦辐射	point-focused radiation
点连(接)	pendular bond
点连状态	pendular [pundular] state
点炉燃料	starting fuel
点密度	point density
点面法	point-to-plane technique
点能源	point source
点排放	【环】point discharge
点缺陷（金属晶格中的）	point defect [imperfection]
点缺陷扩散	diffusion of point defects
点缺陷熵	entropy of point defect
点缺陷位错	point defects dislocation
点群	point group
点群对称	point-group symmetry
点燃	firing, light (ing-up), ignition, inflammation, kindling ◇ 二次～ reignition, 直接～ straight firing
点燃点	firing point
点燃性能	ignition behavior
点燃药粉	ignition powder
点染照相底片	half-tone negative
点蚀	pitting erosion, point(ed) [tubercular] corrosion, (corrosive) pitting
点蚀防止剂（镀镍槽用）	antipit, antipitting agent
点蚀极限	pitting limit
点蚀试验	pitting test
点蚀速率	pitting rate
点蚀系数	【冶】pitting factor
点式打印机	dot printer
点试样	spot sample
点投影 X 射线显微术	point projection X-ray microscopy
点投影显微镜	point projection [projector] microscope
点污染源	point (pollution) source
点压焊	mash welding
点源	point source
点阵[晶格]	(point) lattice, grating ◇ 底心(布喇菲)～*, 布喇菲～ Bravais lattice, 三斜～ anorthic lattice, 泰勒～*, 锑型～ antimony lattice
点阵变形	lattice strain [deformation]
点阵波	lattice wave
点阵不变变形	lattice invariant deformation
点阵不对称	lattice asymmetry
点阵不规则排列	lattice disarray
点阵不规则性	lattice irregularity
点阵不均匀性[点阵异质]	lattice heterogeneity
点阵参数	lattice parameter ◇ 扩展～*
点阵参数标度	lattice parameter scale

点阵参数测定	lattice parameter determination
点阵参数精确[精密]测定	【金】precision [accurate] lattice parameter measurement
点阵参数轴	lattice parameter axis
点阵场	lattice field
点阵常数	lattice [grating] constant
点阵常数平均值	mean lattice constant
点阵重组	shuttling of lattice
点阵错配[错合,交错]	lattice misfit
点阵点序列	【理】point row of lattice
点阵电导率	lattice conductivity
点阵对称	lattice symmetry
点阵放大	lattice amplification
点阵复合体	lattice complex
点阵行列	lattice row
点阵畸变	lattice distortion
点阵畸变扩展	lattice-distortion widening
点阵间距	interlattice-point distance [spacing], lattice distance [space, spacing], crystal lattice spacing
点阵结点	lattice point
点阵结点矩阵表示(法)	【金】matrix representation of lattice point
点阵结构	lattice structure
点阵晶胞	lattice cell
点阵空位[空缺]	lattice vacancy
点阵空位结点	vacant lattice point
点阵扩散	lattice diffusion
点阵类型	lattice type
点阵离子	lattice ion
点阵理论	lattice theory
点阵力	lattice force ◇ 位错~
点阵连续性	lattice continuity
点阵列	lattice array
点阵密度	reticular density
点阵面	lattice plane [face]
点阵面族	family of lattice planes
点阵模型	lattice model
点阵摩擦力	lattice friction
点阵能	lattice energy
点阵扭曲	lattice distortion
点阵膨胀	lattice dilatation
点阵配位数	lattice coordination number
点阵匹配	lattice matching
点阵匹配平面	matched plane of lattice
点阵平面	lattice [net] plane
点阵平面X射线反射	X-ray reflection from lattice plane
点阵曲率	lattice curvature
点阵取向[方位]	lattice orientation
点阵缺位	lattice vacant site
点阵缺陷	lattice defect [faults, imperfection, irregularity]
点阵扰动	lattice disturbance
点阵热容	lattice heat capacity
点阵散射	lattice scattering
点阵散射迁移率	lattice scattered mobility
点阵矢量	lattice vector
点阵式字符打印	【计】dot-character printing
点阵式打印机	dot matrix printer
点阵损伤	lattice damage
点阵条纹	lattice fringe
点阵图样	lattice pattern
点阵弯曲	lattice bending
点阵位错	lattice dislocation
点阵位移	lattice displacement
点阵位置	lattice position[site]
点阵无序	lattice disorder
点阵吸收	lattice absorption
点阵原子	lattice(-point) atom
点阵振动	lattice vibration
点阵振动光谱	lattice vibrational spectrum
点阵周期性(质)	periodicity of lattice, periodic nature of lattice
点阵转变	lattice transformation
点阵转动	lattice rotation
点阵组	lattice group
点直径	【焊】spot size
点注	【铸】topping up a casting
点状腐蚀	(同"点蚀")
点状腐蚀抗力	resistance to pit corrosion
点状裂纹	pitting crack

点状缺陷团　point defect clusters ◇ 辐射感生~*
点状相(析出的)　【金】dotlike phase
点状自然腐蚀　natural pitting corrosion
典型　typical, representative type
典型拜耳法　【色】typical [classic] Bayer process
典型波动方程　typical wave equation
典型成分　typical composition
典型尺寸　typical dimensions
典型氮化层组织　typical nitrided structure
典型分析　typical analysis
典型功率波动　typical power fluctuation
典型计算操作　【计】representative calculating operation
典型乳胶曲线　characteristic emulsion curve
典型设计　typical [modular] design
典型试验　typical run [test]
典型值　typical value
垫　pad, cushion, pillow
垫板　back(ing) board [plate, block, strap], backup [bearing, packing, fill(er), spacer, stay] plate, tie-plate, pillow, rider strips, rider sheets(直通式炉内板叠的),【焊】(焊缝的) backup [backing] strip, backing (bar),【压】riser block,【铸】bed piece
垫板夹具(垫在焊缝下)　backing jig
垫箔滚对接焊机　foil butt seam welding machine
垫层　bedding course, blinding layer(基础的),【钢】backing layer(砌砖的) ◇ 砖铺~ bedding of brick
垫衬　pallet
垫底层　underlayer
垫底料　【冶】bed(ding) material
垫底料透气性　【冶】bed porosity
垫底物块　ballast
垫缝焊接　stitch-welding
垫环　gasket(ed) [backing, packing, caulking, spacer, sealing] ring, ring gasket,【压】curb
垫块　packing [spacer, cushion] block, peg, chock(楔形的)
垫块焊接　pad welding
垫料　pad(ding), packing
垫盘　【耐】plaque
垫片　shim, pad, backup plate, back(ing) strap, adding liner, distance [filling, spacing] piece, gasket, insert, rider strips
垫片调整　shimming
垫片分离剪　dummy block separator
垫圈　washer, gasket, gasketed [packing, carrier, carrying, caulking, sealing] ring, spacer (ring) ◇ 防松~ check washer
垫砂　setting sand
垫石　bed stone, pinner
垫式填料(洗塔的)　mattress packing
垫箱[芯]砂　bedding sand
垫纸卷取机　paper winder
垫纸卷筒　paper reel
垫纸装置　paper feeder
垫子　mat, pad, cushion
垫座　pedestal, tray, pad
电包镀[包覆]　electrocladding
电爆及击发信管　electric and percussion fuze (epf)
电波干扰　jamming
电捕焦油器　electric tar filter [precipitator]
电(测)功率[电测力]计　electric dynamometer, electrodynamometer, electrodynamic meter
电测厚度仪　electric(al) thickness gauge
电测量　electrical measurement
电测温度计　electrical thermometer
电测学　electrometry
电测仪表　electrical measuring instrument
电测仪器　electric(al) meters
电测应变仪　electric(al) strain
电铲　electric shovel [dipper, excavator] ◇ 柴油电力移动式~*,轮式~*,旋转式~*,渣坑除渣~ slag-pit shovel

电场淬火[淬硬]法 【金】elquench process
电场强度 electric field intensity [strength], intensity of electrical field
电场闪络 field flashover
电厂 power plant (PP)
电车 trolley, tramcar (有轨电车) ◇ 工厂用~ mill tramway car, 小~*
电车道 electric railroad, tramroad
电车吊线分叉 frog
电车(钢)轨 tram [grooved, flange] rail, street car rail ◇ 槽形~ girder rail
电车轨道 tramway
电车架空线 trolley wire
电车缆线 trolley cable
电沉积铬 electrodeposited chromium
电沉积收尘器 electrical precipitation filter
电秤 electric weigher
电池 battery (batt.), cell ◇ 充气~*, 丹聂尔~ Daniell('s) cell, 钝化-活化~*, 伏打~ voltaic cell, 伽伐尼~*, 隔膜~*, 赫尔~ Hull cell, 缓冲~(组) buffer battery, 莱克兰舍~ Leclanche cell, 手电筒~ flash light battery, 碳极~ carbon block cell, 韦斯顿~*, 氧浓差~*, 一次~*, 原~*, 组合~ assembled battery
电池腐蚀 galvanic corrosion
电池盒 battery [cell] box
电池绝缘子 battery insulator
电池壳 battery jar [case]
电池铅板 lead grill
电池容器 battery container
电池寿命 battery life
电池酸度 battery acid
电池箱 battery box [container], cell box
电池效率 battery [cell] efficiency
电池用锰{MnO$_2$} battery manganese
电池组 battery, bank of cells, cell grouping ◇ 浮充~ floating battery
电除尘器 (同"电收尘器")
电除焦油器 electro detarrer
电触点烧毁 burning of contact material

电触点温度计 electric contact thermometer
电触式测微表 electricator
电触头合金 contact alloy ◇ 铂钨~*, 复合~*, 钨铜~*, 银钨~*
电触头金银铂合金(69Au, 25Ag, 6Pt) PGS (platinum-gold-silver) alloy
电触头寿命 contact life
电触头双金属 contact bi-metal
电锤 electric hammer
电磁 electromagnetics, electromagnetism, galvanomagnetism
电磁扳直机 (同"电磁直头机")
电磁抱闸 (同"电磁制动器")
电磁泵 electromagnetic [induction] pump
电磁波 electromagnetic waves
电磁测微计(测定轧件厚度用) electromagnetic micrometer
电磁测氧仪 (magnetic) oxygen recorder
电磁场 electromagnetic field
电磁场储能焊机 【焊】electromagnetic stored-energy machine
电磁场动力学能量 dynamic electromagnetic-field energy
电磁场无模成型(作用) (同"电磁脉冲直接成型")
电磁成形 electromagnetic forming
电磁秤[天平] 【电】balance magnetometer
电磁处理技术 electromagnetic processing technique
电磁传输 electromagnetic transport
电磁单位 electromagnetic unit (emu)
电磁电解模型 electromagnetic cell model
电磁定[测]碳仪 【钢】carbanalyzer
电磁动量 electromagnetic momentum
电磁垛板机 (同"磁力垛板机")
电磁阀 magnet(ic) valve (MV), electromagnetic [solenoid] valve ◇ 多通~*
电磁阀架 magnet valve stand
电磁放射液面测量 radio and electromagnetic bath line surveying
电磁分垛机 magnetic lifting device

电磁分离(法) electromagnetic separation
电磁分离器 electromagnetic separator
电磁辐射 electromagnetic radiation
电磁感应 (electromagnetic) induction
电磁感应搅拌 【钢】induction stirring
电磁感应搅拌器 【钢】induction stirrer
电磁(感应)搅拌装置 induction stirring device
电磁感应流 electromagnetic induction flow
电磁感应强度 induction density
电磁感应圈 electromagnetic coil
电磁钢材分类[鉴别]仪 magnetic comparater
电磁惯量 electromagnetic inertia
电磁继电器 electromagnetic relay
电磁加工 electromagnetic processing
电磁检测 electromagnetic measurement
电磁检验法 magnetographic inspection
电磁鉴别仪 Salford magnetic sorting bridge
电磁浇注 electromagnetic casting (EMC)
电磁搅拌[搅动] electromagnetic stirring [agitation]
电磁搅拌器 (electro)magnetic stirrer
电磁搅拌设备 magnetic stirrer installation
电磁搅拌真空脱气法 【钢】induction stirring degassing
电磁接触器 electromagnetic contactor
电磁结晶器 electromagnetic mould
电磁进料装置 magnetic feeder unit
电磁精炼 electromagnetic refining
电磁聚焦装置 electromagnetic focusing device
电磁开闭器 electromagnetic shutter
电磁开关 electromagnetic switch [contactor]
电磁离合器 electromagnetic clutch
电磁(理)论 electromagnetic theory
电磁力 electromagnetic force
电磁联轴节[器] electromagnetic [electric] coupling
电磁连铸法 continuous electromagnetic casting process
电磁流 electromagnetic flow
电磁流量计 (electro)magnetic [magneto-electric] flowmeter
电磁脉冲直接成型(作用) 【压】direct magnetic pulse forming action
电磁脉冲直接成型法[工艺] direct magnetic pulse forming process [technique]
电磁摩擦联轴装置 magnetic gear
电磁能 electromagnetic energy
电磁耦合 electromagnetic coupling
电磁皮带轮 magnetic pulley
电磁屏蔽 electromagnetic shielding
电磁启炉盖机 【焦】magnetic lid lifter
电磁绕组 magnet winding
电磁熔炼 electromagnetic melting
电磁射线 electromagnetic rays
电磁声转换器 electromagnetic acoustic transducer (EMAT)
电磁式电子光学装置 electromagnetic electron optics
电磁式电子显微镜 electromagnetic electron microscope
电磁式钢分类仪 (同"钢分类仪")
电磁式仪表 electromagnetic instrument [meter]
电磁式造型机 【铸】electromagnetic moulding machine
电磁示波器 electromagnetic oscillograph ◇ 直接记录式~*
电磁输送 electromagnetic transport
电磁探伤[探裂]法 magnetic crack detection, electromagnetic method of crack detection
电磁探伤仪 magnetic crack detector
电磁体 electromagnet
电磁铁 electromagnet (EM) ◇ 悬吊~*
电磁铁合金块 EM briquette
电磁(铁)起重机[吊车] magnetic crane, (lifting) magnet crane, (electro)magnetic

电磁铁 lifter, (electro-)lifting magnet
电磁铁线圈 bobbin of electro-magnet
电磁铁心 limb
电磁透镜 electromagnetic lens
电磁雾化 electromagnetic atomization
电磁吸[卡]盘 electric magnet chuck, magnetic chuck
电磁线圈 magnet coil
电磁效应 galvanomagnetic effect
电磁效应系数 galvanomagnetic coefficient
电磁悬浮 electromagnetic suspension
电磁悬浮连铸 continuous casting with electromagnetic suspension
电磁学 electromagnetics, electromagnetism, magnetoelectricity
电磁压力成形加工法 magneform process
电磁压力机 electromagnetic power press
电磁冶金 electromagnetic metallurgy
电磁应变仪 electromagnetic strain gauge
电磁振荡器 electromagnetic vibrator
电磁振动给料机[给料器,加料机] (electric-) vibrating feeder, vibro-feeder, electromagnetic vibrating feeder
电磁直头机(带材端头的)【压】magnetic lifting device
电磁直头式开卷机 magnet-type uncoiler
电磁制动 electromagnetic braking (EMBR)
电磁制动器 (electro)magnetic brake
电磁质量 【理】electromagnetic mass
电磁铸造 electromagnetic casting (EMC)
电磁装料机构 magnetic feeder unit
电磁装卸机 magnetic charger
电瓷瓶 porcelain insulator
电催化性能 electro-catalytic property
电萃取(法) electroextraction
电单位 electric(al) unit
电导 (electrical) conduction, conductance, conductivity
电导波动 conductivity fluctuation
电(导)滴定法 conductometric titration, electrotitration
电导滴定计 conductometric titrimeter
电导(定量)分析 conductometric analysis
电导(定量)分析法 conductometric method
电导率 conductivity (cond.), conductance, specific conductance [conductivity] ◇ 电子[n型]~ n-type conductivity
电导率平均温度系数 mean temperature coefficient of conductivity
电导试验 conductivity test
电导探示器(料位检测用) conductivity probe
电导调浓器 salinometer
电导系数 specific conductivity
电导仪[计] electric conductivity meter
电淀积 electroposition
电动搬运车 electric truck
电动泵 motor pump
电动测功计 (同"电测功计")
电动冲钻 electrical percussive drill
电动锤 electric rammer
电动打字机 electric typewriter
电动的 motor-operated (mot.op.), power-operated
电动蝶阀 motor-driven butterfly valve (MBV)
电动定时器 electrical timer
电动发电机 dynamomotor, motor-generator
电动-发电机组 motor-generator set
电动阀 motor-operated valve, electrically operated valve
电动钢卷钳 electric coil tongs
电动鼓风机 electric blower
电动焊机 motor-driven welding machine
电动滑车[轮]组 electric (turnable) pulley block
电动换能器 electrodynamic transducer
电动机 (electric) motor ◇ 变速~*,超同步~*,齿轮(变速)[带变速齿轮的]~*,串级[级联]~ concatenated motor,

大功率[大型]～ heavy duty motor,电容启动～ capacitor motor,电阻启动～*,短时工作制～ short-hour motor,多速～ multi-speed motor,防爆型～*,防水～*,分激整流子式～*,分马力～*,封闭式～ enclosed motor,风冷～ ventilated motor,复激～ compound-wound motor,恒定功率～ constant power motor,恒速～ constant speed motor,积复激～*,交流标准～ AC-norm-motor,可调速～*,可潜水式～ submersible motor,裂相～ split-phase motor,脉冲～ pulse motor,屏蔽磁极～ shaded-pole motor,牵引式～ traction motor,绕线式(转子)感应～*,鼠笼式～ squirrel cage motor,双电枢～*,双速～ two-speed motor,水冷式～ water-cooled motor,伺服[辅助]～ servo(motor),通用～ universal motor,推斥启动～ dragging motor,微型～*,小功率～*,液压～ hydro-motor,油压～ oil hydraulic motor,整流子～ commu-tator motor,整体～*,周期减速～*

电动机磁场 motor field
电动机电流载荷 motor load
电动机顶推装置 motor thruster
电动机多齿联轴器 multi-tooth coupling for motor
电动(机)-发电机(组) motor generator (MG, mg, M-G), motor generator set ◇ 恒压～*
电动(机)-发电机组电焊机 motor-generator welder
电动(机)-发电机组弧焊机 motor-generator arc welder
电动机工作状态 motoring
电动机黄铜 (见"发动机黄铜")
电动机联轴节 motor coupling
电动机驱动 motor drive
电动机驱动的 motor-operated, motor-driven
电动机托架 motor bracket
电动机直接驱[传]动 direct motor drive
电动机转矩 torque of motor
电动机座 motor stand
电动记时器[仪] electric chronograph
电动剪(切机) electric shears, power(-driven) shears
电动交流发电机(组) motor-alternator
电动搅拌机 electrical stirrer
电动卷线机 motorized coil stock reel
电动卷扬机[绞车,提升机] electric hoist (E.H., e.h.), motor (driven) hoist
电动开孔机(铁合金电炉的) electrical tapper, electrical tapping machine
电动拉辊 【连铸】power-driven withdrawal rolls
电动缆车 cable telpher
电动力学 electrodynamics
电动力学现象 electrodynamic phenomenon
电动联锁装置 electric interlocking device
电动炉门 electrically operated door
电动螺旋式泥浆输送机 electric sludge conveyer worm
电动泥炮 【铁】electrically-driven mud gun, electric screw clay gun
电动泥炮操纵[控制]室 mud gun (control) room
电动起重机 electric crane, motor driven hoist
电动起重器 electrical jack
电动-气动式变流[换流]器 electropneumatic transducer
电动气压阀门[气动阀] electropneumatic valve
电动气压推料机[推车器] electropneumatic pusher
电动气压制动器[气闸] electropneumatic brake
电动汽车 electromobile
电动桥式起重机 electric overhead crane (EOHC)
电动切削台 【耐】power-operated cutting

电动倾倒电弧炉 electric rocking arc furnace
电动倾翻渣罐车 electrically tipped slag ladle
电动砂盘磨床 electric disc sander
电动升降机 electric elevator
电动式安培计 electrodynamic ammeter
电动式仪表 electrodynamic instrument [meter]
电动势 electromotive force (E.M.F.), electrodynamic force ◇ 接触～contact force, 汤姆逊～*, 西贝克～*
电动势差 electromotive difference of potential
电动势序 electromotive series
电动手剪 electrical hand shears
电动推进器 motor pusher
电动推料炉 electric push furnace ◇ 双层～*
电动拖车 electro-carriage
电动挖泥机 motor-driven sludge excavator
电动铣刀 motor-driven milling cutter
电动小车 electric (industrial) truck, motor driving trolly
电动小吊车[起重机] telpher crane
电动旋臂起重机 electric slewing crane
电动旋转式挖土机 electric revolving shovel
电动压尖机 【压】power pointer
电动压力泵 electrical pressure pump
电动压力机 electrically powered press, power press
电动压下螺丝 motor-operated screw
电动压下装置 【压】motor-operated screwdown, screwdown drive, electric screwdown gear
电动液压阀 electro-hydraulic Value
电动液压控制的可逆滑阀 pilot-controlled hydraulic operated valve
电动液压控制器 electrohydraulic controller
电动移动式起重机 electric (power) travel(l)ing crane
电动运料车 electric freight truck
电动造型机 electric moulding machine
电动闸阀 motor-driven gate valve (MGV)
电动振捣器 electric vibrator
电动直流发电焊接设备 motor-generator welding unit
电动直流发电机 motordynamo
电动制动器[抱闸] electric brake
电动转换器 electrodynamic transducer
电镀 electrogilding electroplating, electrolytic plating, electrodeposition, electrocladding, galvanising, galvanization, galvanizing, galvanoplasty, galvanoplastics, electro[plated] coating ◇ 重新～replating, 复合～*, 光亮～*, 碱性～法*, 接触法～contact plating, 金属薄层大电流快速触击【金】striking, 金属快速～电解液 striking solution, 镜面～*, 局部～partial plating, 篮式～basket plating, 流动电解液～flow plating, 全自动～*, 双重[两次]～duplex electroplate, 无电解液～*, 无光～dull plating, 阳极～anodization, 自动～*
电镀包层(法) electrocladding
电镀表面沉淀能力 throwing power
电镀槽 bath [pot], plating [galvanic, galvanizing] bath, plating [bath] tank ◇ 哈林～*
电镀层 electroplate (e.p.), electroplated coating (layer), electro(deposited)[plated] coating, electrodeposition, galvanizing coat
电镀车间 electroplating (work) shop [plant], plating plant
电镀脆性 plating brittleness
电镀法 electroplating [galvanic] process ◇ 克罗马林～*, 卤素～halogen method
电镀铬钢 electrolytic chromium-coated

steel
电镀工 galvanizer
电镀工业 electroplating industry
电镀工作者 electroplater
电镀后处理 postplating treatment
电镀机 electroplating machine
电镀间 plating room
电镀件支架 plating rack
电镀金 electric [chemical] gilding, electrogilding
电镀金属 plated metal
电镀滤器 electroplating filter
电镀能力(镀槽的) covering power
电镀泥 galvanic sludge
电镀镍 nickel electroplating, electronickelling, nickel-plating, nickeling
电镀前清洗 cleaning for electroplating
电镀区段 plating section
电镀设备 (electro)plating machine, plating equipment [plant]
电镀速度 plating speed
电镀陶瓷 electro-plated pottery
电镀铜 electro-coppering
电镀铜法 electro-coppering
电镀物 electroplate
电镀锡 electrolytic tinning, electrotinning ◇ 苯酚磺酸~法*,硫酸锡在苯酚磺酸异构物水溶液中的~法 Ferrostan process,碱液~法*,卤化~法 halogen process
电镀锡薄钢板(平均锡层重量为 0.113—0.454kg/基准箱) electrolytic tinplate, electro-tinplate ◇ 差厚~的检辨*,普通~*,双面差厚~*
电镀锡的 tin-electroplated
电镀锡钢板[电镀马口铁] ferrostan
电镀锡机 electro(lytic) tinning machine
电镀锡设备[装置] electrolytic tinning plant
电镀锡锌合金板材 tin-zinc electroplate
电镀锡作业线 electrolytic tinning line ◇ 连续~[机组]*

电镀锌 electrogalvanizing, electrolytic zincing, cold galvanizing ◇ 钢丝~法*
电镀锌板卷 electro(lytic)-zincing coil
电镀锌薄钢板 electro-zinc coated sheet
电镀锌层 electrogalvanized coating, zinc deposit
电镀锌的 electrogalvanized, cold-galvanized, cold galvanizing
电镀锌钢丝 electro-galvanized steel wire, bethanized wire
电镀锌阳极 zinc-plating anode
电镀锌作业线 electrogalvanizing line (EGL), electrolytic zinc plating line
电镀阳极 galvanic anode
电镀液 electroplating solution [bath], plating solution [bath] ◇ 格利马克斯~ Gleamax,硝酸硫酸混合的~ackey
电镀液电阻 bath resistance
电镀液过滤器 plating-solution filter
电镀液控制 plating bath control
电镀银 electrosilvering
电镀硬铬(法) durionising
电镀用发电机 electroplating dynamo
电镀用滚筒 plating barrel
电镀浴 (electro)plating bath
电镀装置 electrolytic plater, plating machine
电度表 (kilo)watt-hour meter, electric(al) [electricity, energy] meter
电耳 electric ears
电发火器 electric ignitor
电阀 electro-valve (EV)
电法脱水 electrodewatering, electric dehydration
电分离器 electric separator
电风 electric wind
电腐蚀 electrocorrosion, galvano-cautery, electric rot
电干燥箱 electric drying chamber
电杆 telegraph pole, (electrical) pole, 【电】bearing
电感 induction, inductance

电感导磁率　inductance permeability
电感电桥　inductance [induction] bridge
电感计　inductometer, henry meter
电感耦合　inductive coupling
电感耦合等离子(体)　inductively coupled plasma (ICP)
电感耦合等离子体发射光谱法　inductively coupled plasma emission spectroscopy
电感耦合电路　inductive coupling circuit
电感耦合放大器　induction (coupled) amplifier
电感器　inductor
电感式探伤仪　probolog
电感式应变仪　induction (-type) strain gauge
电感式转速计　inductor-type tachometer
电感温度系数　temperature coefficient of inductance
电感线圈　inductance [inductive] coil, inductor
电感(性)电纳　inductive susceptance
电感性阻抗　inductive impedance
电感应　electric induction, electroinduction
电感应加热　electric induction heating
电感应加热焊管机　induction weld mill
电感应强度　electric induction
电高炉　electric blast furnace
电工　electrical engineering, electrotechnics, electrician (电气工人)
电工材料　electrotechnical material
电工测量仪表　electrical measuring instrument
电工钢　electrotechnical [electric(al)] steel, stalloy
电工钢薄板　electrical (grade) sheet, silicon sheet ◇ 非取向～*晶粒取向～*
电工技师[技术员]　electrician
电工铜　electrical copper
电工学[技术]　electrotechnics, electrotechnology
电工用锡铅焊料(普通:60Pb,40Sn 或 63Sn,37Pb;精密仪表:94.5Sn,5.5Pb)　electrician's solder
电工组长　electrical foreman
电功率计　(同"电测功率计")
电功率曲线　electric(al) power curve
电光材料　electro-optical material
电光度计　electrophotometer
电光热气高温计　electrooptical hot gas pyrometer
电光源质谱学　(同"火花源质谱学")
电硅热(还原)法(生产铁合金)　electrosilicothermic process [method]
电过滤器　electrofilter
电焊　electrowelding, electric(al) welding, electric soldering ◇ 冲击～*,高频～*,直流～DC welding
电焊把[钳]　welding electrode holder ◇ 手工焊～*
电焊变压器　welder transformer, welding transformer
电焊车间　electric welding department
电焊扼流圈　welding choke
电焊发电机　welding generator [dynamo] ◇ 交叉磁场～*
电焊防护面罩　arc-welding helmet
电焊缝　arc-welding seam
电焊工　arc-welding operator, arc welder [weldor], electric welder
电焊管　electric-welded pipe [tube] ◇ 光亮冷轧[光面]～*,宋尼申～法 Soennichsen process
电焊管机　electric weld-pipe mill
电焊机　electric welder, electric welding machine, electro-welding machine, arc welder, arc-welding machine [generator], welding converter ◇ 冲击～percussion welder,单电源式电弧～single-arc welder,电动机－发电机组～*,电容[静电]式～*,多弧～multiple-arc welder,高频交流～*,固定式～stationary welder,恒压电源～*,交叉(焊丝)焊接～cross-wire welder,闪光～*,双点

~duplex spot welder, 拖拉机式~welding tractor, 斜焊~deck welder, 直流~DC welding machine, 自动~automatic welder

电焊机合闸凸轮 timing cam
电焊剂 electric flux
电焊夹头 welding clamp
电焊钳 electrode holders, electric soldering [welding] pliers
电焊枪 electric torch
电焊条 welding electrode [rod], electrode rod ◇ 低氢~*, 盘绕[成卷]~coiled electrode, 水下用~underwater electrode, 药皮~*
电焊条材料 electrode material
电焊条熔剂 electrode flux
电焊条芯材 electrode core wire
电焊条药皮材料 electrode coating material
电焊条药皮成份 electrode coating ingradient
电焊装置 electric welder ◇ 倾斜焊条~deck welder
电夯 electrorammer
电荷 electric(al) charge, charge
电荷(电)势 charging potential
电荷电势差 charging potential difference
电荷分布 charge distribution
电荷尖端效应 point potential effect
电荷密度 charge [electric] density
电荷密度径向分布 radial distribution of electric charge density
电荷耦合器件 charge-coupled device (CCD)
电荷散逸[中和]用电子枪 charge neutralizer gun
电荷数 charge number
电荷图像 charge image
电荷守恒 charge cohservation, conservation of charge
电荷守称 charge conjugationparity, charge parity

电合成 electrosynthesis
电烘箱 electric drying chamber
电葫芦 motor-hoist
电弧 (electrical) arc ◇ 产生~arcing, 高电容~condensed arc, 耐~的 arc-resisting, 小电流~low amperage arc
电弧变压器 arc transformer
电弧表面切割 arc gouging
电弧不稳 arc flare
电弧持续时间 arc duration
电弧重熔 arc remelting ◇ 真空~*
电弧除锈 arc cleaning
电弧触发面 striking surface
电弧穿孔(制造钻石模用) piercing by electric arc
电弧磁性 【电】arc magnetism
电弧等离子法 arc plasma processing
电弧等离子体加热 arc plasma heating
电弧等离子体喷镀金属 arc plasma metallizing
电弧点焊 arc-spot welding ◇ 气体保护金属极~*
电弧点火电压 arc-striking voltage
电弧电路 arc circuit
电弧电压降 arc drop
电弧电阻 arc resistance ◇ 纳苏休斯~炉【冶】Nathusius furnace
电弧对接焊 flash butt weld(ing)
电弧反应 electric arc reaction
电弧防护 arc shielding
电弧放电 arc discharge, arc-over, flashing
电弧放电等离子体 arc discharge plasma
电弧缝焊 arc seam welding
电弧功率 arc power
电弧焊(接) (electric) arc welding, electrode welding ◇ CO_2 保护~*, 磁性焊剂~*, 单根焊条~*, 点焊缝~spot arc welding, 惰性气体(保护)~*, 管状[药芯]焊丝~*, 光焊丝~*, (焊条)接触~contact arc welding, 裸金属极~*, 气体保护~*, 青铜丝~bronze weld(ing), 人工焊条~*, 石墨极~graphite-arc

welding,手工~*,双金属极间接作用~*,双碳素极(间接作用)~*,水蒸气保护~*,碳(质电)极~*,涂药焊条~*,韦斯汀~法*,旋转~ rotating arc welding,氩气保护~ argon arc welding,原子氢~*,支靠式焊条~ touch welding,重力式~*

电弧焊把 arc-welding gun
电弧焊电路 arc-welding circuit
电弧焊防护面罩 arc-welding helmet
电弧焊机 arc welder, arc-welding machine [generator]
电弧焊加热 arc-welding heat
电弧焊接供电源 arc welder
电弧焊接头 arc-welded joint
电弧焊炬 arc torch
电弧焊熔剂 arc flux
电弧焊头 arc-welding head ◇ 自调式~ self-adjusting arc head
电弧焊用焊条 arc-welding electrode
电弧焊用碳极 carbon arc electrode
电弧焊整流器 electronic arc welder
电弧击穿 arc-through
电弧加热 electric arc heating
电弧加热淬火 【金】arc hardening
电弧加热炉 arc heating furnace
电弧加热式电解槽 arc-heated cell
电弧加热真空脱气法 【钢】vacuum arc degassing process, arc heating degassing
电弧间接通焊接(熔滴金属的) dip transfer welding
电弧金属喷镀 arc metal spraying
电弧刻蚀 arc etching
电弧控制 arc control
电弧离解设备(钛锆等生产用) arc dissociation unit
电弧力 arc force
电弧炉 electric arc furnace (E.A.F.), 【冶】arc-furnace ◇ 敞口~ open-top arc furnace, 超高功率~*, 底吹气体~ bottom blown EAF, 电动倾倒~*, 反射~*, 辐射~ radiant arc furnace, 坩埚型

~*,格里弗斯-埃切尔~ Greaves-Etchele's furnace, 格林~ Greene furnace, 固定炉顶式~*, 赫劳尔特[三相]~*, 炼钢~*, 炉底导电式~*, 炉顶旋转式~*, 炉盖可移式~*, 炉身[体,底]移出式~*, 伦纳弗尔特~*, 凝壳式~*, 偏心底~*, 普通直接~*, 深坩埚式~*, 试验用[小型]~*, 水冷锭模~ cold mould arc furnace, 酸性直接~*, 塔格列费里~ Tagliaferri furnace, 卧式~*, 氩~ argon arc furnace, 摇动[可倾]式~ rocking (arc) furnace, 直接(加热)~*, 直流~*, 自耗电极~*

电弧炉处理(即电弧熔炼) electric arc treatment
电弧炉底吹气体搅拌技术 stirring technology of bottom blowing gas in EAF
电弧炉钢 arc-furnace steel
电弧炉炼钢 arc-furnace steelmaking, electric arc steelmaking
电弧炉炼钢厂 arc-furnace plant
电弧炉炼钢车间 arc-furnace plant [department], arc-furnace (melting) shop
电弧炉炼钢法 arc(-furnace) process ◇ 燃料吹氧废钢~*
电弧炉(内)气氛 arc atmosphere
电弧炉冶炼[熔炼] air arc melting
电弧螺柱焊接 arc stud welding
电弧凝壳熔炼 arc skull melting
电弧喷镀 arc spraying
电弧喷气切割法 arc-air process
电弧喷枪 【金】arc pistol
电弧屏蔽 【电】arc shielding
电弧钎焊[钎接] arc brazing
电弧切割 (metal-)arc cutting ◇ 气流~ gas arc cutting
电弧切割法 【焊】arc-cutting process
电弧区 arc zone
电弧区域熔炼 arc zone-melting
电弧燃烧过程 【焊】arcing process
电弧热补缩(冒口的) arc feeding
电弧熔化 arc-melt(ing)

电弧熔化炉　arc-melting furnace
电弧熔化用金属粉末　arc-melting metal powder
电弧熔炼　(electric) arc melting ◇ 惰性气体保护～*
电弧熔炼炉　electric smelting furnace, arc production furnace ◇ 单相炉底通电[单相单极]～*，六极一线排列～*，三极一线排列～*
电弧熔铸　arc-cast
电弧熔铸的金属　arc-cast metal
电弧闪光　arc flash
电弧闪光焊　arc flash welding
电弧烧蚀　arc erosion
电弧脱气器　【钢】arc degasser
电弧稳定化涂料　arc-stabilizing coating
电弧稳定性　arc stability
电弧稳定性测定仪　arconograph
电弧－物料移动[转移]（电弧引起的）　arc-material transfer
电弧氧乙炔焊　arcogen welding
电弧摇闪　arc flare
电弧移动速度　【焊】arc speed
电弧阴极　arc cathode
电弧原子焊电极　arc atom welding electrode
电弧再加热　arc reheating ◇ 气体搅动～*
电弧真空脱气法　【钢】vacuum arc degassing process
电化当量　electrochemical equivalent
电化电压　electrochemical tension
电化法去除毛刺　electrochemical [electrolytic] deburring
电化分析　electrochemical analysis
电化腐蚀　electrochemical corrosion [attack], couple [galvanic] corrosion
电化腐蚀防护（金属材料的）　galvanic protection
电化(腐蚀)加工　（同"电化学加工"）
电化还原　electrochemical reduction
电化磨削　electrochemical grinding(ECG)
电化抛光　electrochemical polishing
电化溶解　electrochemical solution
电化(顺)序(元素的)　electrochemical series
电化特性　electrochemical behaviour
电化性　electrochemical property
电化性化合物　electrochemical compound
电化学　electrochemistry, galvano-chemistry
电化学保护[防护]　electrochemical [electrolytic] protection
电化学测定　electrochemical determination
电化(学)常数　electrochemical constant
电化学除铁鳞[皮]法　electrochemical descaling process
电化学除锈法　derustit
电化学处理　electrochemical treatment
电化学动力学　electrochemical kinetics
电化(学)镀层[镀覆]　electrochemical coating [plating]
电化学钝化处理　electrochemical passivation
电化学钝态[钝性]　electrochemical passivity
电化学法　electrochemical process [method]
电化学法提[除]铜　electrochemical extraction of copper
电化学反应　electrochemical reaction
电化(学)氟化(法)　electrochemical fluorination
电化学腐蚀　（同"电化腐蚀"）
电化学工业　electrochemical industry
电化学极化　electrochemical polarization
电化学加工　electro-chemical machining (ECM), electrochemical processing, electrolytic machining
电化学碱洗　alkaline electrocleaning
电化学理论　electrochemical theory
电化学－力学机理（腐蚀破裂的）　【理】electrochemical mechanical mechanism
电化学平衡　electrochemical equilibrium

电化学清洗[净化] electrochemical cleaning, electrocleaning
电化学势[位] electrochemical potential
电化学试验 electrochemical test
电化(学)系统 electrochemical system
电化学行为 electrochemical behaviour
电化学性质 electrochemical property
电化(学)选择性 electrochemical selectivity
电化(学)氧化(脱硫) electrochemical oxidation
电化(学)因数 electrochemical factor
电化学转变 galvanic conversion
电化(学)装置 electrochemical unit
电化(学)作用 electrochemical action
电话 telephone (ph.) ◇ 对讲～intercom, 内线～inter-phone, 通[打]～call, phone, 载波～carrier-phone
电话听筒 telephone receiver, handset ◇ 手持式～hand receiver
电话通信装置 telephone communication units
电话线路数传设备 telephone line data set
电回火 electric tempering
电活化加压烧结 【粉】electrically activated pressure-sintering
电火花成形 electrical discharge [spark] forming, electro-discharge forming
电火花淬火 spark hardening
电火花电极铸造 EDM electrode manufacturing
电火花腐蚀加工 spark erosion fabrication
电火花高压成形法 spark-pressure working process
电火花焊接 electric discharge welding, electrospark welding
电火花(加工)法 【机】method X
电火花加热硬化(法) (同"火花放电硬化(法)")
电火花磨削 electric discharge [spark] grinding
电火花抛光 electrospark polishing
电火花喷射器 spark injector unit
电火花起弧 【焊】spark starting
电火花切除 electrical disintegration
电火花(切削)加工 electric spark machining [working], electric(al) discharge machining, electromachining, (electro) spark machining, electro-mechanical drilling (金刚石拉模的)
电火花侵蚀加工法 (同"火花放电侵蚀加工法")
电火花韧化处理 electric spark toughening
电火花烧结 (同"放电加压烧结")
电火花烧蚀机 spark eroding machine
电火花射线 rays of sparks
电火花蚀刻 electrospark engraving
电火花线圈探漏器 spark coil leak detector
电火花液压成形 electrohydraulic forming
电火花硬化(法) spark (discharge) hardening
电火花源质谱学 (同"火花源质谱学")
电火花振荡器 spark oscillator
电火花钻孔加工(金刚石拉模的) electro-mechanical drilling
电击穿 voltage breakdown
电机 electric machine, electric machinery ◇ 永磁～magneto
电机厂 electrical machinery plant
电机传动辊 motorised roll
电机放大机[器] motor amplifier, amplidyne (generator)
电机(硅)钢 dynamo steel [iron]
电机硅钢[片] dynamo sheet
电机皮带轮 【机】motor sheave
电机驱动焊接变流[换流]器 motor-driven welding set
电机室 motor room ◇ 轧钢车间～engine-room of mills
电机调节器 regulex
电机拖动阀 motor-driven valve
电机与电子工程师协会(美国) Institute

电机转矩　motor torque
电机转速　motor speed
电机转子试验装置　growler
电积　electro-deposit(ion),(electrolyte) deposition, electrolytic deposit, electrowinning
电积槽　electrodeposition[winning] cell, depositing[electrowinning] tank
电积层　electrodeposited coating
电积纯铜薄片　thin deposited copper sheet
电积合金　plating alloy
电积金属　plated metal, metal deposit ◇ 多层～板 composite plate
电积金属法　electrowinning
电积金属熔凝　consolidation of deposit
电积能力（镀层对基体的附着能力）throwing power
电积镍　electro-deposited nickel
电积速率　deposition rate
电积铜　(electro-)deposited copper
电积铜粉　electrodeposited copper powder
电积钨粉　【粉】electrowinning tungsten powder
电积物　electro-deposit, electrolytic deposit ◇ 脆性～ brittle deposit
电积周期　【冶】period of deposition
电极　electrode, pole,【理】prod（磁化的）◇ 被覆[有涂层]～ coated electrode, 残～ butt, 顶[上]部～ top electrode, 管状～ tubular electrode, 辊式～ seam-welding roller, 浸液式～*, 空气～ air electrode, 空心～ cored electrode, 篮形～ basket electrode, 挠性～（电池筒的）dangler, 赛璐珞被覆～*, 伸缩式[伸缩自由的]～ retractable electrode, 生坯～*, 石墨～*, 碳素～*, 维弧～ keep-alive electrode, 阴离子（极性）可逆～*, 可偏～ deflecting electrode, 装～手套～*, 自身～
电极－溶液界面　electrode-solution interface
电极扳手　electrode wrench
电极板（电炉的）　pole plate [piece]
电极棒　electrode bar
电极臂[把手]　electrode arm, horn ◇ 可升降～*, 下～*
电极表面　electrode surface [face]
电极柄（点焊的）　【焊】electrode shank
电极并联排列　multiple arrangement of electrodes
电极材料　electrode material
电极残头　electrode stub
电极插入深度　depth of electrode insertion
电极厂　electrode factory
电极超[过]电压　electrode overvoltage
电极沉积钨粉　(同"电积钨粉")
电极成型机械　electrode-forming mechanism
电极纯度　purity of electrode
电极电缆　electrode cable
电极电势[位]　electrode potential
电极电位－氢离子浓度线图　(同"波尔贝克斯线图")
电极电压　electrode voltage
电极吊架　electrode suspension
电极冻结　electrode freezing
电极洞效应　【钢】chimneying
电极端　【冶】electrode cone
电极端弧坑　electrode crater
电极煅烧炉　electrode oven
电极对　electrode couple [pair]
电极粉料混合器　electrode mixer
电极工作端磨锐　penciling
电极滚轮　seam-welding (electrode) wheel, welding wheel
电极过程　electrode process
电极过程动力学　electrode kinetics
电极合金　electrode alloy
电极横向摆动（在焊缝上的）　weave
电极烘干　【冶】baking of electrodes
电极糊　electrode [anode, carbon(aceous)] paste ◇ 半流动性～*

电极糊车间 paste plant
电极糊混合料 electrode mix
电极护管 electrode retainer, electrode-retaining tube
电极化率 (electric) susceptibility, susceptiveness
电极化(强度) (electric) polarization
电极环 electrode (retaining) collar
电极火花检漏器 electrode leak detector
电极给进 electrode feed
电极夹[卡] electrode carrier [collar],【冶】electrode clamp
电极夹持环 electrode retaining collar
电极夹持器 electrode jaw,【冶】electrode clamp [holder] ◇ 链式~*
电极夹架 electrode-carrying superstructure
电极夹圈 electrode-holder ring
电极夹头 electrode grip
电极夹支架[电极把手架] electrode prong
电极(加热)炉 electrode furnace [oven]
电极尖 electrode tip ◇ 换接[可拆换]~*
电极间的 interelectrode
电极(间)距 electrode distance [gap, opening, spacing]
电极间隙 electrode clearance, interelectrode gap
电极接触表面烧蚀(点焊的) tipburn
电极接触表面直径(点焊机的) tip size
电极接触电阻 electrode contact resistance
电极接套 electrode nipple
电极接头 electrode nipple [contact],【冶】nipple
电极接线头 electrode connection
电极节省器 electrode economizer
电极金属 electrode metal
电极浸没式电炉(液体渗碳用) immersed electrode furnace
电极浸入深度 electrode penetration
电极浸渍沥青 electrode impregnation pitch
电极壳(自焙电极用) electrode shell
电极孔 bull's eye
电极孔封严盖 electrode gland
电极孔水套(电炉的) economizer
电极孔用砖 electrode ring
电极控制器 electrode controller
电极控制系统 electrode control system
电极冷却环[圈] electrode cooling ring
电极料 electrode compound
电极帽 electrode cap
电极泥下腐蚀 hide-out corrosion
电极排列 arrangement of electrodes
电极钎焊 electrode soldering
电极强冷却点焊 zero welding
电极区域 electrode zone
电极伸出部 electrode extension
电极升降 electrode up-down [positioning]
电极升降机 【冶】electrode positioning mechanism
电极升降卷扬机 electrode-positioning winch
电极升降装置 electrode lowering and raising device
电极式液位计 electrode type (liquid-)level detector
电极寿命 electrode life
电极碎片 crushed electrode
电极台板(凸焊用) 【焊】backup die
电极碳 electrode carbon
电极调节 electrode regulation
电极调节器 electrode regulator
电极调节装置 electrode adjusting gear, electrode control device
电极跳动(电弧炉熔毕前) 【钢】scorching
电极筒 electrode container [shell]
电极头 electrode head [tip]
电极头滑移 【焊】tip [electrode] skidding
电极头面积 【焊】tip area
电极头温度 【焊】tip temperature
电极头修整工具(点焊用) electrode tip

dressing tool
电极头压力(点焊的) tip [point] pressure
电极头压力计(点焊机的) tip pressure gauge
电极头直径(点焊的) tip diameter
电极头至工件距离 【焊】tip-to-work distance
电极尾 【焊】electrode shank
电极位置[升降]控制 electrode position control
电极下放机 【冶】electrode slipping device
电极下滑带(自熔电极用) 【冶】wisdom ribbon
电极下降装置 【冶】electrode slipping device
电极消耗 electrode consumption
电极效率 electrode efficiency
电极效应 electrode effect
电极行程 electrode stroke
电极修整 electrode dressing
电极修整工(点焊机的) electrode-tip dresser
电极悬臂 stick-out
电极悬放机组 【冶】electrode holding and slipping mechanism
电极悬挂下滑机构 【冶】electrode holding and slipping mechanism
电极学 electrodics
电极压坑(接触焊接的) electrode impression
电极压力(焊接的) welding pressure, electrode force(电阻焊的)
电极压力变化循环(接触焊的) pressure cycle
电极压力系统(接触焊机的) electrode-pressure system
电极压型机 electrode press
电极盐浴炉 electrode salt bath furnace
电极移动电动机 electrode-travel motor
电极移动曲柄 crank for electrode
电极移动装置 electrode drive

电极引线 electrode lead, contact conductor
电极用沥青 electrode pitch
电极圆(电炉的) 【冶】electrode [pitch] circle
电极支架 electrode support [jib, prong], electrode-carrying superstructure
电极支柱(电炉的) 【冶】electrode mast
电极智能控制 【钢】intelligent electrode control
电极转动电动机 eletrode-rotation motor
电极装紧 electrode tightening
电极装置 electrode assembly
电极锥 【冶】electrode cone
电极自动升降装置 automatic electrode assembly
电集尘器 (同"电收尘器")
电计时器 electric clock
电记录器 electrograph
电加工法 electroprocessing
电加热 electric heating [firing], electroheating
电加热炉 electrically heated furnace ◇ 井式～*
电价 electrovalence, electro-valency
电价化合物 electrovalent compound
电价键 electrovalent bond [linkage], electrostatic bond
电键 key, switch, tapper(电报机的)
电接触材料[器材] contact material ◇ 铂质～ contact platinum, 多层～*, 多孔～ porous contacts, 复合～*, 钼银～*, 难熔金属～*, 青铜石墨～*, 烧结～*, 钨铜～*, 银钨～*
电接触点 electrical contact
电接触式测微计 electric contact-making micrometer
电接点合金 electrical contact alloy
电结晶 electrocrystallization
电解 electrolyzing, electrolysing, electrolysis ◇ 闭路～系统*, 二次[再次]～ re-electrolysis, 高电流密度～*, 隔膜～*,

鼓风[空气]搅拌~*,碱性溶液~法*,矿浆(直接)~*,熔盐~*,水溶液~ aqueous electrolysis,水银法~*,酸性溶液~法 acid eletrolyte process,脱铜~*

电解剥离法(涂层的) electrolytic stripping method

电解薄铜板 electro-copper sheet

电解保护 electrolytic protection

电解保护气氛 cell atmosphere

电解槽 electrolytic tank [cell, bath, unit, vessel], electrolyzer, bath [cell, electrowinning] tank, electrolysing [plating, reduction, operating] cell, electrolysis bath, electrolysis [electrolyte] pot, tank house cell, cell, battery,【色】pot, electrolytic furnace(熔盐电解用)◇阿克尔~(熔盐分解用)Acker cell,侧插棒~ horizontal stud pot,侧加料~side-feed cell,敞开式~open cell,大型[生产用]~ production-scale cell,电弧加热式~ archeated cell,对开阳极~cell with split anodes,多阳极~multiple anodes cell,钢壳~steel cell,间歇式~batch cell,接近工业规模的~*,卡斯特纳[铁电极]~(钠电解用)Kastner cell,块状阳极簇~*,连续[自焙]阳极~*,笼形阴极~ basket cathode cell,轮斗式~scoop-wheel cell,铅衬混凝土~concrete lead-lined cell,溶解~dissolution cell,石墨~ graphite cell,双极~bipolar cell,双液~ double fluid cell,水平隔膜~*,唐斯~*,透明熔融石英~*,箱形~box cell,制氯~chlorine cell,钟罩型~bell jar cell,纵向排列~end-to-end placed cells

电解槽操作温度 temperature of cell operation

电解槽侧壁 (reduction) cell sidewall

电解槽侧衬 cell sidelining

电解槽衬里[内衬] electrolytic cell lining, cell [tank] lining

电解槽衬里材料 material for cell lining

电解槽电解液 cell bath

电解槽电压 tank voltage, bath potential

电解槽顶 top of cell

电解槽反应 cell reaction

电解槽废气清洗系统 cell exhaust scrubbing system

电解槽沸腾 boiling of cell

电解槽隔膜 cell diaphragm, electrolytic film

电解槽功率 power per cell

电解槽供料 cell feed material

电解槽供液 cell feed

电解槽集气罩 cell hood

电解槽几何形状 cell geometry

电解槽加[进]料 charging of cell, cell feed

电解槽阶梯式排列 cascade arrangement of tanks

电解槽结构[构造,构筑] cell construction, construction of tank

电解槽模型 cell model

电解槽母线[汇流排] cell busbar

电解槽泥浆[泥渣,沉淀] cell sludge

电解槽配置 arrangement of cells

电解槽气氛 cell atmosphere

电解槽气体 cell gas

电解槽熔体 bath of cell

电解槽容器(放置熔盐电解槽的装置) cell container

电解槽设计 electrolytic cell design, pot design

电解槽寿命 cell life

电解槽维护 cell maintenance

电解槽系列 cell line, line of cells, potline

电解槽系列电流 potline current

电解槽装置 electrolytic cell assembly

电解槽作业 cell operation

电解产物 electrolytic product, product of electrolysis, electrolysate

电解厂房 cell house [room], electrolytic cell [tank] house

电解超电压 electrolytic excess voltage

电解车间 electrolytic plant, potroom, electrolytic cell [tank] house, cell house

[room], tank house [room], electrolysis hall

电解沉淀 electrolytic precipitation, precipitation by electrolysis

电解沉积 （同"电积"）

电解成形 electroform

电解成形加工 electrolytic formation machining

电解池 electrolytic vessel ◇ 分离～*

电解除鳞[除氧化皮] electrolytic descaling

电解除锈 electrolytic derusting

电解处理 electrolytic treatment

电解纯铜 （同"阴极铜"）

电解萃取 electrolytic extraction

电解淬火 electrolytic quenching

电解导体 electrolytic conductor

电解电镀 electrolytic plating

电解电流 electrolytic [electrolysis] current

电解电路 electrolytic circuit

电解电位[势] electrolytic potential

电解电压 electrolysing voltage [tension]

电解电子管金属 electrolytic valve metal

电解淀积层 electrodeposited coating

电解淀积器 electrodepositor

电解淀积用铜锡锌合金 ◇ 阿尔巴洛伊*

电解镀层 （同"电镀层"）

电解钝态[钝性] electrolytic passivity

电解法 electrolysis, electrolytic process [method, route] ◇ 莫比斯银～*, 西梅特预浸～*

电解法表面堆焊（耐磨合金的） electrofacing

电解法分离 plating-out, electrolytic separation

电解法碱洗 electrolytic alkaline cleaning

电解（法去）除（毛）刺 electrolytic deburring

电解法提镍 【色】nickel electrowinning

电解反应 electrolytic reaction

电解分解（作用） electrolytic decomposition, electrodecomposition

电解分离 electrolytic dissociation [separation, parting, isolation], electroparting, separation by electrolysis

电解分析 electroanalysis, electrolytic analysis

电解粉末 electrolytic powder ◇ 德劳利控制～粒度法 Drouily's method, 粉碎～*

电解粉状铁 （同"电解铁粉"）

电解腐蚀 (galvano) cautery, 【冶】electrolytic corrosion（外加电流引起腐蚀）

电解钙屑 electrolytic calcium carrot

电解镉 electrolytic cadmium

电解工业 electrolytic industry

电解过程 electrolytic process

电解过度 over-electrolysis

电解合金粉末 electrolytic alloy powder

电解还原 electrolytic reduction, electroreduction

电解还原槽 reduction cell

电解机理 mechanism of electrolysis

电解－机械联合抛光 electro-mechanical polishing

电解极化 electrolytic polarization

电解级氧化铝 electrolytic alumina, reduction grade alumina

电解加工 （同"电化学加工"）

电解加热 electrolytic heating

电解间 【色】tank room

电解碱洗槽 electrolytic alkaline cleaning tank

电解减薄法 electrothinning

电解结构 electrolysis texture

电解结晶 electrocrystallization

电解浸出 electrolytic leaching

电解浸蚀 electrolytic etch(ing), (galvano) cautery ◇ 宾厄姆～液*, 阴极～ cathodic etching

电解晶体 electrolytic crystal

电解精炼 electrorefining, electrolytic refining, electrolytic(al) purification ◇ 并联~parallel refining, 三层式~炉*, 沃威尔粗金~法 Wohlwill process

电解精炼槽 electrolytic refining tank, refining cell

电解精炼车间 electrolytic refining plant

电解精炼电解液 refinery electrolyte

电解精炼法 electrolytic refining process ◇ 贝茨~(粗铅的) Betts process, 硅氟酸盐~(见"氟硅酸盐电解精炼法"), 熔渣~*

电解精炼设备 electrolytic refining unit

电解精炼铜 (同"电解铜")

电解净化 electrolytic purification

电解炼铝 electrolytic production of aluminum ◇ 赫劳尔特~法 Heroult process, 霍尔~法 Hall process

电解炼镁 electrolytic production of magnesium ◇ I.G.无水氯化镁~法 I.G. process, 伊格-梅尔无水氯化镁~法 IG-MEL process

电解炉 electrolytic furnace ◇ 多阳极~ multi-anode furnace

电解铝 electrolytic aluminium

电解氯 electrolytic chlorine

电解镁 electrolytic magnesium ◇ 高纯~*

电解磨光机 electrochemical grinder, electrolytic grinding machine

电解磨削[光] electro-chemical grinding (E.C.G.), electrolytic polish [grinding]

电解泥 electrolytic [electrolyte] slime

电解泥沉淀 slurry sedimentation

电解泥重复利用【色】slurry reuse

电解泥贮槽【色】slurry [surge] sump

电解镍 electrolytic nickel

电解镍精炼 electronickel refining

电解偶金属 coupled metals

电解抛光 electrobrightening, electropolishing, electrolytic brightening [polishing], electrochemical polishing, electrosmoothing ◇ 喷液~jet polishing, 阿尔扎克~法*, 布劳特-兰~法 Blaut-Lang process, 雅凯~法*

电解抛光工作者 electropolisher

电解抛光设备 electropolishing equipment

电解抛光氧化铝制品 illuminite

电解抛光液 solution for electrolytic polishing ◇ 通用~*

电解抛光装置 electrolytic polisher, electropolisher ◇ 莫维波尔~(试样的)【金】Movipol

电解铍 electrolytic beryllium

电解批料 electrolysis batch

电解漂白 electrolytic bleaching

电解平衡 electrolytic equilibrium

电解器 electrolyzer ◇ 篮式~basket dissolver, 小型~bench scale dissolver

电解气体 electrolytic gas

电解迁移[徙动] electrolytic migration

电解切削 electrolytic machining

电解侵蚀 anodic etching, electrolytic etching [attack]

电解氢 electrolytic hydrogen

电解氢氧化钠[苛性钠] electrolytic caustic soda

电解清洗 electrolytic cleaning, direct cleaning, cathode cleaning ◇ 连续~作业线*, 两极~系统*, 直流~direct-current cleaning

电解清洗工段 electrolytic cleaning section

电解清洗箱 electrolytic cleaning tank

电解清洗液 electrolytic cleaner

电解清洗作业线 electrolytic cleaning line

电解氰化法 electrolytic cyaniding

电解去毛刺 (同"电化法去除毛刺")

电解溶解 electrodissolution, electrolytic dissolution

电解溶解操作电压 dissolver operating potential

电解溶解核燃料 dissolving fuel

电解溶解电流【色】dissolver current

电解溶解剂 electrodissolvent

电解溶解器 electrodissolver ◇ 单槽~

dian 电　　　　　　　　　　　　280

single-cell dissolver
电解溶液　electrolytic [electrolysis, electrolyzing] solution
电解设备　electrolysis plant, electrolytic apparatus
电解渗碳　electrolytic carburizing
电解生产氟化铀铵法　◇弗卢莱克斯~ Flurex process
电解蚀刻　cautery
电解势　electrolytic potential
电解室　cell [tank] house, cell room
电解试验　electrolytic test
电解酸洗　electrolytic acid cleaning, electrolytic [anode] pickling ◇布拉德-邓恩~法 Bullard-Dunn process
电解特性　electrolysis characteristic
电解锑　electrolytic antimony
电解锑厂　electrolytic antimony plant
电解提取　electrolysis [electrolytic] extraction
电解条件　electrolytic conditions
电解调质带钢　electrolysis tempering steel strip
电解调质钢　electrolysis tempering steel
电解调质钢板　electrolysis tempering steel plate
电解铁　electrolytic iron, electroiron ◇熔铸~*, 铸造~*
电解铁粉　electrolytic iron powder ◇辛特雷克斯~*
电解铜　electrolytic(al) (refined) copper, electrorefined copper
电解铜箔　electrolytic copper foil, electrosheet copper
电解铜厂　electrolytic copper producer
电解铜粉　(同"电积铜粉")
电解铜盘条　electrolytic copper wire rod
电解铜线锭　electrolytic copper wirebar
电解脱卤　electrolytic dehalogenation
电解脱脂　electrolytic degreasing ◇带钢~作业线*
电解脱脂槽　electrolytic degreasing bath

电解温度　temperature of electrolysis
电解锡　electrolytic tin
电解系统　electrolytic system [circuit] ◇开路~*
电解现场试验　potroom test
电解效率　efficiency of electrolysis
电解效应　electrolytic effect
电解锌　electrolytic zinc
电解锌厂　electrolytic zinc plant
电解锈蚀　electrostaining
电解学(水溶液的)　electrolytics
电解氧化　electrolytic oxidation, electrooxidation
电解冶金法　electrowinning
电解液　electrolyte, (electrolytic, electrolysis) bath ◇充氨~ ammoniacal electrolyte, 电解精炼~*, 镀黄铜用~ brass solution, 二元~ binary electrolyte, 返回~ return electrolyte, 含盐~ saline electrolyte, 基本[主体]~*, 氯化物~*, 势垒型~*, 调匀~*, 输入~ incoming electrolyte, 污~ foul electrolyte, 阳极~*, 阴极~ cathode liquid [liquor], 用过的~ depleted electrolyte
电解液密度计　electrolyte hydrometer
电解液成分　bath composition
电解液成分调整　【色】bath maintenance
电解液出口　electrolyte outlet [exit]
电解液淬火装置[设备]　【金】electrolyte-hardening plant
电解液高位槽　electrolyte head tank
电解液供应箱　electrolyte feed chamber
电解液金属浓度　metal strength of electrolyte
电解液进口　electrolyte inlet [entrance]
电解液[质]**净化**　electrolyte purification [cleaning]
电解液净化工段　electrolyte purification section
电解液控制元件　controlling member for electrolyte
电解液冷却器　electrolyte cooler

电解液母板 【色】electrolyte matrix
电解液浓度 electrolyte concentration
电解液循环 electrolyte circulation
电解液氧化作用 electrolyte oxidation effect
电解液(液)面[电解质水平] electrolyte level, bath line
电解液张力 electrolytic tension
电解液组成 bath composition
电解仪器 electrolytic apparatus
电解铀晶体 electrolytic uranium crystal
电解渣壳 electrolyte shell
电解整流器 electrolytic rectifier, philcotron
电解置换粉 electrolytical replaced [substituted] powder
电解制氟槽 fluorine cell
电解制取 electrolytic preparation, electrowinning
电解质 electrolyte ◇ 稠化～electrolytic paste, 非离子聚合～nonionic polyelectrolyte, 洁净～*, 两性～*, 凝固的～frozen electrolyte, 熔盐～*, 四元[四成分]～*
电解质比 electrolyte [bath] ratio
电解质表面 bath surface
电解质成分[组成] electrolyte composition
电解质导体 electrolytic [ionic] conductor
电解质电容器 electrolytic capacitor, chemical capacitor [condenser]
电解质电阻 electrolytic [bath] resistance
电解质沸腾 boiling of cell
电解质膏 electrolytic paste
电解质活性碳处理 carbon treatment
电解质结壳 electrolyte crust
电解质黏度 bath viscosity
电解质凝聚剂 electrolytic coagulant
电解质溶液 electrolytic solution
电解质试样 【色】bath sample
电解质体积 bath volume
电解质体系 electrolyte system

电解质相 bath phase
电解质消耗 electrolyte [bath] consumption
电解质选择性 selectivity of electrolyte
电解质盐类 electrolyte salt
电解质主体 bulk of electrolyte
电解质组分 bath component
电解装置 electrolytic apparatus
电解着色 electrolytic colouring
电解着色法 electro-colour process
电解钻孔 electrolytic drilling
电解作用 electrolytic action, electrolysis
电介质[体] dielectric(al), non-conductor, insulator
电介质测试器(测定淬火油含水量用)【金】dielectric probe
电介质分选[分离](矿物的)【选】dielectric separation
电介质干燥炉 dielectric drying stove
电介质耗散系数 dielectric dissipation factor
电介质黏度 dielectric viscosity
电介质强度 dielectric strength
电警报器 electric alarm
电锯 electric saw, sawing machine
电绝缘 electrical insulation
电绝缘材料 electric insulating material
电绝缘检验 electrical insulation inspection
电绝缘体 electric insulator
电均热室 electric heating holding chamber
电开关用铜 switch copper
电抗 reactance, reactive resistance
电抗控制 reactor control
电抗器 reactor ◇ 保护～protective reactor, 干式～dry-type reactor, 限流～*, 阳极～anode reactor, 整流～commutating reactor
电抗线圈 reactance coil
电可变只读存储器 electrically alterable read only memory (EAROM)
电控光致发光 electro-photoluminescence
电控调节 electrically controlled regulation

电控制室　electric(al) control room
电扩散　electrodiffusion
电缆　(electric) cable ◇ 多芯～*, 防鼠(咬)～ gopher protected cable, 海底～ submarine cable, 加热用～ heating cord, 室内～ inside cable, 受电～ power receiving cable, 小容量～*, 引入～ leading-in cable, 中继[连接,拉线]～ (inter) connecting cable, 铠装～ belted cable
电缆包皮合金(1—3Sn,余量 Pb)　cable-sheathing alloy
电缆包皮挤压　extrusion of cable-sheathing
电缆包皮压力机　【压】cable-covering [cable-sheathing] press
电缆编号[标志]　cable mark
电缆标志编号　cable designations
电缆表　cable list
电缆槽　cable channel [chute, duct, trough]
电缆电路　cable circuit
电缆吊车　telpher
电缆敷设　cabling, cable laying
电缆杆　cable pole
电缆供电　cable supply
电缆沟　cable channel [chute, duct, trench], duct run, wiring tunnel
电缆股线绞合机　cable stranding machine
电缆故障(点)指示器　cable fault indicator
电缆管道　cable duct [conduit, pipe], culvert, raceway ◇ 整浇～ monolithic conduit
电缆管道管孔　cableway
电缆夹　cable clip [clamp]
电缆夹套　cable gland
电缆架　cable rack
电缆架布置图　cable rack arrangement drawing
电缆交接箱　section box
电缆绞合机　cable stranding machine
电缆接套　cable lug
电缆接头　cable connector [joint, lug, splice], tag, thimble
电缆接头箱[盒]　connecting box, cable-joint protector box
电缆卷筒　cable reel [drum]
电缆绝缘胶　cable compound
电缆铠装挤压机　cable press
电缆铠装用带钢　cable tape steel
电缆拉链　cable drag chain
电缆连接卡头　cable clamp collars
电缆连接器　cable connector, cable clamp collars
电缆盘　cable hank [drum, tray], (cable) reel
电缆铅包皮压力机　lead cable press
电缆铅坯包皮压力机　【压】billet fed lead cable press
电缆铅皮　lead sheath
电缆入口　cable inlet
电缆隧道　cable tunnel
电缆头　cable head, pothead
电缆头用填料　gasket paste for cable heads
电缆托架　cable tray
电缆线路　cabling
电缆箱　cable [feeder] box
电缆芯　cable core [conductor]
电缆悬挂装置(剪切机的)　cable hanging unit
电缆引入箱　draw-in box
电缆支承设备　cable supporting equipment
电缆终端　cable terminal [end, lug]
电缆终端盒　sealing box, cable terminal box
电缆终端套管　pot head, cable shoe, sealing box
电缆走线架　cable trough
电烙铁　electric (soldering) iron
电雷管　electric detonator [cap]
电离　ionizing, ionization, electrolytic ionization [dissociation] ◇ γ 射线引起的～*, 可～的固体物质 ionizable solid, 未

~的 unionized,致~本领[能力]ionizing power
电离层 ionized layer, ionosphere
电离层吸收 ionospheric absorption
电离层吸收计 riometer
电离常数 ionization constant
电离的原子 atomic ion
电离电流 ionization current
电离电势[位] ionization [ionizing] potential
电离度 ionicity, ionizability, degree of ionization
电离法（X射线衍射法） ionization method
电离(法)渗氮 （同"辉光放电渗氮"）
电离反应 ionization reaction
电离分光计[光谱计,分光仪,能谱仪] ionization spectrometer ◇ 布喇格~*
电离辐射[射线] ionizing radiation
电离剂 ionizer
电离计 ionization gauge ◇ 冷阴极~*
电离计数器 ionization counter
电离解作用 electro-dissociation
电离离解 ionic dissociation
电离理论[学说] theory of ionization
电离粒子 ionizing particle
电离密度 specific ionization, density of ionization
电离能 ionization energy
电离能级 ionization level
电离器 ionizer
电离气体 ionized gas
电离气体介质 【理】ionized gaseous medium
电离强度测量计 ionization meter
电离倾向 ionization tendency
电离热 heat of ionization
电离室 ionization chamber ◇ 电流~【理】current chamber,可携式[轻便式]~*
电离速率 ionization rate
电离损失 ionization loss

电离特性[性能] ionization property
电离系数 ionization coefficient
电离压力[压强]计 ionization gauge [manometer] ◇ 贝亚德－阿波特~*, 菲利普~*
电离压力计探测器 ionization ga(u)ge detector
电离元素 ionizing element
电离原子 ionized atom
电离真空计 ionization (vacuum) gauge ◇ α-粒子~ alphatron gauge,放射性~*,盖德~*
电离质 ionogen, electrolyte
电离组分 ionizing constituent
电离作用 electrolytic ionization
电力 (electric) power
电力变压器 power transformer
电力传动 power drive [transmission]
电力传送链 power transmission chain
电力电缆 power cable
电力电容器 power capacitor ◇ 静电~ static power condenser
电力分配 electric power distribution
电力负荷 power load
电力工业 (electric) power industry, electrical industry
电力供应 (electric) power supply, supply of electricity
电力绞盘 electric capstan
电力矩 【理】electric (dipole) moment
电力输入 power input
电力水压成形机 electroshape
电力拖动(装置) electric drive
电力网 power [electric] network
电力网频率 【电】main-frequency
电力线 power line
电力消耗 electrical power consumption
电力移动式起重机 electric travelling crane
电力整流装置 power rectifying equipment
电力转换设备 power conversion equip-

ment
电量 quantity of electricity, electric (al) mass
电量滴定 coulometric titration
电量分析法 coulometry
电量计 voltameter, electricity meter, coulo(mb) meter, coulometer, argentometer
电量计法(测定镀层厚度用) coulometric method
电磁化处理 【压】electro-granodising
电铃 (electric) bell, ringer ◇ 磁石[磁铁]~ magneto bell
电铃信号 bell signal
电铃装置 bell equipment
电流 current ◇ 傅科~ Foucault currents, 谷值[最小]~ valley current, 恒向~ continuous current, 伽伐尼[动电]~ Galvanic current
电流保护装置 galvanic protector
电流比 current ratio
电流表 ammeter, ampere meter, galvanometer ◇ 钳式~ tong-type ammeter
电流波动 current fluctuation
电流不足 under-current
电流测定法 galvanometry
电流重合选取法 【计】coincident-current selection
电流传感器 current sensor (cs)
电流磁化法 current flow method
电流滴定法 amperometric titration ◇ 双金属~【化】dead-stop method
电流滴定仪[计] amperometric titrimeter
电流电离室 【理】current chamber
电流－电压特性(曲线) current-voltage characteristic
电流－电压特性(曲线)图 current-voltage diagram
电流度量法 amperometrical method
电流发生器 current generator
电流反馈 current feedback
电流放大 current amplification
电流放大器 current amplifier

电流分布 current distribution
电流峰值 peak current
电流感应法 current induction method
电流给定值 current set point
电流互感器 current transformer (C.T.) ◇ 母线式~*
电流回路 current circuit [loop]
电流计 galvanometer (G.A.L.V.), current meter, rheometer ◇ 布罗卡~Broca galvanometer, 磁电式[达松伐尔]~ D'Arsonval galvanometer, 动圈式~ moving coil galvanometer, 微量~ micro-galvanometer, 无定向~ astatic galvanometer, 悬圈式~*
电流计示波仪 galvanometer oscillograph
电流继电器 current relay
电流渐增时间 upslope time
电流控制 current control
电流控制电流源 current controlled current source
电流控制电压源 current controlled voltage source
电流控制器 current controller (C.C.), current sensor (c.s.)
电流量 amperage
电流灵敏度 current sensitivity
电流脉冲时间 current impulse time
电流密度[面积电流] current density ◇ 临界~*
电流密度[面积电流]分布 current density distribution
电流密度[面积电流]分量 current density component
电流密度[面积电流]水平分量 horizontal current density component
电流平衡继电器 current balance(d) relay
电流起磁法 magnetization by electric current, current flow method
电流强度 current intensity [strength, rate], amperage
电流绕组 current winding
电流容量 current capacity

电流式色温计 bioptix
电流试验 electric current test
电流输入 current input
电流调节器 current regulator [controller]
电流调整 current setting
电流通路 current path
电流线圈 current coil
电流消耗(量) current consumption
电流效率 current [Faraday, amperage, ampere] efficiency, power yield (电解的) ◇ 加铜稀释法测定～*, 阳极～*
电流效率测定法 current efficiency determination method
电流谐振 current [inverse] resonance
电流循环(接触焊的) current cycle
电流源 current source [supply] ◇ 电流控制～*
电流直接加热淬火法 tension electric process
电流种类 kind of current
电炉 electric(al) furnace, electrically heated furnace ◇ 波尔南德～*, 布思-霍尔～*, 敞开式～open electric furnace, 超高效率[U.H.E]～*, 单相二极～*, 倒相器供电～*, 低身～*, 底特律摇动～*, 电极浸没式～*, 多炉组～*, 菲亚特～Fiat furnace, 感应搅拌～*, 碱性～basic electric furnace, 交直流～*, 莱克特罗麦尔特～*, 林德布莱德～Lindblad furnace, 炉顶移出[活动,可移]式～*, 炉身[体,底]移出式～*, 酸性～acid electric furnace, 碳棒～carbon bar furnace, 碳阻～*, 沃姆-保尔～【冶】Vom-Baur furnace, 西门子-马丁式～*, 小功率～low-powered furnace
电炉变压器 furnace transformer
电炉车间 electric furnace shop
电炉尘 EAF dust
电炉法 【冶】electric process
电炉钢 electric (furnace) steel, electrosteel, arc-furnace steel ◇ 感应～*
电炉硅铁 (同"电热法硅铁")

电炉还原 electric furnace reduction
电炉回火 electric-furnace tempering
电炉精炼 electric furnace refining
电炉炼钢 electric furnace steelmaking, electric steel heat
电炉(炼钢)炉料 electric furnace feed [stock]
电炉炼铁法(瑞典炼铁法) 【铁】elektrometall furnace process ◇ 索雷尔～*
电炉炉次 electric steel heat
电炉炉渣 electric furnace slag
电炉氯化法 electric furnace chlorination process
电炉泡沫渣炼钢工艺 electric furnace slag foaming steelmaking technology
电炉熔炼 electric-furnace smelting, electro-smelting ◇ 炉渣～electric slag smelting
电炉熔炼试验 electric smelting test
电炉熔铸耐火材料 electro-cast refractory
电炉容量 electric furnace capacity
电炉生铁 electric pig iron
电炉退火 electric-furnace annealing
电炉造锍熔炼 【色】electric matte smelting, electric smelting for matte
电炉渣 electro-slag
电炉渣热裂解 disintegration of EAF slag
电路 electric circuit, electrocircuit, circuit(ry) ◇ 多片～multichip circuit
电路测试器 circuit tester
电路磁阻 circuit reluctance
电路分路 【电】leg of circuit
电路图 circuit [cording] diagram, schematic wiring diagram, circuitry
电路系统 circuitry
电路元件 circuit element
电铝热(还原)法 electro-aluminothermic process
电滤器 electrostatic precipitator ◇ 多级～multistage precipitator, 干式～*, 湿式～irrigated precipitator
电滤器组 bank of precipitators

电滤式文丘里收尘组件　Electro filtering venturi modules
电码　code
电脉冲　electric(al) pulse
电毛细(管)运动　electrocapillary motion
电铆(接)　electric riveting
电铆焊　rivet welding
电铆枪　welding gun
电－煤双热源　double thermal energy of electricity and coal, electric-coal double heating resourse
电敏化作用　electrical sensitization
电模拟法　【电】electric (al) analogy method
电木　bakelite
电纳　(electrical) susceptance
电脑　(同"电子计算机")
电内渗现象　electroendosmosis, electric (al) endosmosis
电能　electric energy
电能动力装置　power unit
电能输送　handling of electrical energy
电能消耗　electric power consumption, power (supply) consumption
电能效率　power efficiency
电钮　push-button
电耦合　electric coupling
电偶(异种金属组成的腐蚀电池)　galvanic couple
电偶腐蚀　couple [galvanic] corrosion
电偶极(子力)矩　electric (dipole) moment
电耙　scraper
电抛光　electropolishing ◇阳极－anode brightening
电抛光装置　electropolisher
电炮　(同"电动泥炮")
电喷镀　electrospraying
电喷镀金属　electrometallization
电平衡　electrical equilibrium
电平开关　【电】level switch (LS)
电瓶车　electromobile, battery truck, accumulator car, storage battery car
电瓶单元　battery jar
电屏蔽　electric screening [shield]
电起重机　electrical jack
电气安装　electrical installation [mounting]
电气安装工　wire man
电气触点材料　electric(al) contact material
电气动力式文丘里烟气净化技术　electrodynamic venturi gas cleaning technology
电气工程　electric work [engineering]
电气(工程)材料　electrical (engineering) material
电气工人　electrician
电气规格说明[技术条件]　electrical specification
电气化　electrification, electrify
电气化铁道　electric railroad [railway]
电气机车　electric locomotive
电气控制装置　electrical control gear
电气联锁　electric(al) interlock, electric locking
电气零件　electric parts
电气器材　electrical products
电气设备　electrical equipment (E.E.), electric(al) apparatus [appliance]
电气石　tourmaline
电气室　electrical room (E.R.)
电气数据　electrical data
电气特性　electrical characteristic [specification]
电气网络　electric network
电气维修　electrical maintenance
电气性能　electric property, behaviour of electricity
电气照明　electric lighting
电气自动调节　electrically controlled regulation
电迁移　electric migration, electromigration, electrotransport

电桥　bridge ◇ 惠斯登～Wheatstone bridge, 凯尔文双～Kelvin double bridge
电桥臂　bridge arm
电桥电路[回路]　bridge circuit
电桥图　bridge diagram
电侵蚀　electrical erosion, electro-etching, electroerosion
电侵蚀加工　electroerosion machining
电亲和力[势]　electroaffinity
电倾析　electrode-decantation
电热　electric heating [firing], electroheating
电热板　electric hot plate
电热保温帽【钢】electric hot top
电热焙烧　electric baking
电热处理　electrothermic treatment
电热淬火(接触式)　electrical hardening
电热镦锻　electroforging
电热法　electrothermal [electrothermic] process, diathermy
电热法硅铁　electrothermic ferrosilicon
电热反应　electrothermic reaction
电热敷金属法　electrometallization
电热辐射炉　electric radiation furnace
电热坩埚　electric crucible
电热辊(镀锡前带钢的)　contact roller
电热锅炉　electric boiler
电热合金　electrical heating alloy, electrothermal alloy ◇ 派罗马克斯～*, 特尔康铜～*
电热烘烤　electric baking
电热化学法【化】electrothermics process
电热还原　electrothermal reduction
电热还原炉　electric reduction furnace
电热器　electric(al) heater ◇ 浸入式～*
电热钎焊[铜焊]　electric brazing
电热前床【色】electrically-heated settler
电热热水锅炉　electric hot water boiler
电热热压机　electric hot compacting press
电热熔炼　electrothermal [electric(al)] smelting, electric melting
电热熔炼炉　electric smelting furnace

电热筛分　electroscreen
电热(式加热)炉　electroheating [electrothermal] furnace
电热式均热炉　electrically heated pit furnace, electrically heated soaking pit
电热式空气循环炉　electrically heated air circulation
电热式仪表　electrothermal instrument, hot wire instrument
电热室　electric heating chamber
电热丝　heating wire
电热丝试验(测定淬火能力)　hot wire test
电热碳还原　electrocarbothermic reduction, electrothermic carbon reduction
电热碳还原装置　electrocarbothermic reduction assembly
电热铁合金车间【冶】electrothermic ferroalloy shop
电热退火　electric annealing
电热旋涡熔炼炉　cyclone-electric furnace
电热学　electrothermics, electrothermy
电热压　hot electric pressing
电热盐浴炉　electric salt bath furnace, electrically heated salt bath furnace
电热冶金　electrothermal metallurgy
电热油浴炉　electric oil bath furnace
电热元件　electric(al) heating element
电热蒸汽锅炉　electric steamboiler
电热装置　electric heating device
电熔刚玉【耐】electromelting corundum, electro-corundum, fused alumina
电熔化　electrofusion
电熔炼　electric(al) smelting, electrosmelting, electromelting ◇ 连续～*
电熔炉　electric melting furnace
电熔镁砖　electrically fused magnesite brick
电熔莫来石　fused mullite
电熔石英　electroquartz
电容　capacitance, capacitor, (electric) capacity

电容测量计 capacitometer
电容传感器 capacity pickup
电容单位 unit of capacity
电容电抗 capacity reactance
电容电桥 capacity bridge
电容计 capacitometer
电容量 capacitance, (electric) capacity, condensance
电容率(MKS制中的介电常数) capacitivity, dielectric constant, inductive capacity, permittivity
电容耦合 capacitive coupling
电容启动电动机 capacitor(-start) motor
电容器 capacitor, condensator, (electric) condenser, condensing-apparatus ◇ 玻璃介质~ glass condenser, 电解质~ chemical capacitor, 隔流~*, 联动[同轴]~ gang capacitor, 钮扣式~ button condenser, 旁路~ bypass capacitor, 油浸~*
电容器放电成形 capacitor-discharge forming
电容器(放电)点焊机 capacitor (discharge) spot-welding machine, condenser (discharge) spot-welding machine
电容器式避雷器 condenser lightning arrestor
电容器式焊机 (同"蓄电池式焊机")
电容器用锡箔 (82Sn,15Pb,2Sb) condenser foil
电容器组 capacitor [condenser] bank
电容时滞 capacity (time) lag
电容式测微计 capacitance micrometer
电容式电焊机 【焊】electrostatic welder
电容式应变仪 capacity-type strain gauge
电容温度系数 temperature coefficient of capacity, capacitance temperature factor
电容箱 capacitance box
电容性电流 capacitive [capacity] current
电容性电纳 capacity susceptance
电容性分量 capacitive component
电容性探测器 capacitive probe
电容蓄能式电焊机 condenser discharge welder
电容应变传感器 capacitance strain transducer
电容滞后 capacity lag
电容贮能式焊接 condenser energy-storage welding
电容阻抗 capacitive impedance, condensance
电色层分离法 electrochromatography
电筛分 electroscreen
电渗电积 electrodialytic precipitation
电渗(析) electric osmosis, electro-osmosis, cataphoresis, electrodialysis
电渗现象(作用) electroosmosis, electroosmose
电声换能[转换]器 electroacoustic(al) transducer
电声学 electroacoustics
电湿法冶金 electro-hydrometallurgy
电石灯 acetylene burber [lamp]
电石灯阀 acetylene torch valve
电石加水操作法[电石加水乙炔制取法] 【焊】carbide-to-water process[method]
电石炉 carbide furnace ◇ 埋弧~*
电石清洗剂 【焊】heratol
电石入水式乙炔发生器 【焊】carbide-to-water (acetylene) generator
电石桶 carbide container
电石筒(乙炔发生器的) 【焊】generating chamber
电石消化的石灰泥渣 slaked carbide
电石乙炔发生器 【焊】carbide feed generator
电石渣 carbide slag
电石贮罐 【焊】carbide drum
电蚀加工 electroarcing, arc machining
电蚀刻 electro-etching
电蚀损(放电的) electrical erosion
电视 television (T.V.), radiovision
电视发射机 television [picture, video] transmitter
电视广播 telecasting, videocast

电视监视器[装置] television monitor ◇ 炉顶~*
电视接收机 television set [receiver], televisor
电视金相学 T.V. metallography
电视摄像机 video camera, telecamera
电视设备 television equipment
电视显微镜 television microscope ◇ 定量~*, 飞点扫描~*
电视中继 television relay
电收尘(法) electric(al) (dust) precipitation
电收尘器 electric(al) (dust) precipitator, electro-precipitator, electrical precipitation filter, electric dust collector, electric filter [separator], electrofilter, cottrel(l), cottrell dust precipitator, cottrell treater ◇ 板式~*, 棒帘式~*, 多级~*, 高温~ hot cottrell, 管式~*, 机尾~*, 三沉淀场式~*, 湿式~*, 屋顶~*
电收尘器烟尘 cottrell dust
电收尘器组 bank of precipitators
电收尘室[设备] cottrell plant
电枢 armature ◇ 换~装置*, 盘形~ disc armature
电枢冲片 armature stamping
电枢电抗 armature reactance
电枢端部接线 armature end connection
电枢反应 armature reaction
电枢反应焊接发电机 armature reaction welding generator
电枢辐臂 armature spider
电枢(回路)电阻 armature resistance
电枢检查 armature supervision
电枢绕组[线圈] armature winding·[coil]
电枢绕组用铜 armature copper
电枢铁芯 armature core
电刷 (dynamo, electrical) brush ◇ 整套~ brush set
电刷触点 wiping contact
电刷夹 brush clamp
电刷损失 brush loss

电刷握杆 brush holder rod
电刷引线 brush lead
电刷用紫铜带 brush copper
电刷支架 brush holder bracket
电水锤成型法 hydrospark forming process
电梯 (electric) elevator, (electrical) lift
电梯间[井] elevator hoistway [shaft]
电梯式炉 elevator furnace
电锑 electrolytic antimony
电提取(法) electroextraction
电通(量) electric flux
电铜[阴极铜] cathode copper
电位 potential (Pot.), electric(al) potential ◇ 标准电极~*, 费米~ Fermi potential, 弗拉德~*, 伽伐尼~ Galvani potential, 霍尔~ Hall potential, 阳极~*
电位测定法 potentiometry
电位差 potential difference, difference in potential, difference of potentials ◇ 坐标式~计*
电位滴定(法) potentiometric [electrometric, potentiometer] titration
电位滴定计 potentiometric titrimeter ◇ 可控~*
电位滴定曲线 potentiometric titration curve
电位分析 potentiometric analysis
电位计 potentiometer (Pot.) ◇ A类~*, B类~*, 多点式记录~*, 基准值~*, 平衡式~*, 圆形图表~*
电位计测量 potentiometric measurement
电位计法 potentiometer method
电位计式光学高温计 potentiometric optical pyrometer
电位降 potential drop [fall], fall of potential
电位器 potentiometer ◇ 同轴[多联]~ gang potentiometer
电位器电路 potentiometric circuit
电位器电阻分布特性 taper
电位衰减 potential decay

电位梯度 potential gradient
电位梯度电子枪 gradient gun
电位调节器 potential regulator
电位序(元素的) galvanic [electrochemical] series
电位移 electric displacement
电位跃变 potential jump
电温度计 electrical thermometer
电吸引 electric attraction
电徙动 【电】electric migration
电线 (electric) wire, current lead ◇ 带电～live wire, 康德～铝合金*
电线接头 power lug
电信 telecommunication, electric(al) communication
电信设备 telecommunication equipment
电信线路 telecommunication line
电性价 electrovalence
电性检验 electrical testing
电修车间 electrical workshop
电选机 (同"静电分选机") ◇ 高压～high tension separator
电学 electricity
电讯线材青铜(98.5Cu, 1.5Sn) signal bronze
电压 voltage, (electric) tension ◇ 截止[闭锁]～blocking voltage, 外加～impressed voltage
电压倍增 voltage doubling [multiplying]
电压比 voltage ratio
电压变换器 voltage changer
电压表[计] voltmeter (v.m.) ◇ 多量程～multivoltmeter, 偏压补偿式～slideback voltmeter, 热线式～thermovoltmeter, 数字～digital voltmeter, 直流～*
电压表附加电阻 reductor
电压波[变]动 voltage fluctuation
电压不足的 under-voltage
电压场 electrical pressure field
电压常数 voltage constant
电压冲击[浪涌] voltage surge
电压档间距(变压器的) 【电】tapping interval
电压电流表 voltammeter
电压-电流转换器 voltage-current converter
电压反馈 voltage feedback
电压放大 voltage amplification
电压幅值 voltage amplitude
电压跟随电路 voltage follower circuit
电压互感器 potential transformer (P.T.), voltage transformer ◇ 接地～*, 套筒式～*
电压恢复 voltage recovery
电压回路 volt circuit
电压继电器 voltage relay
电压检测器 voltage detector
电压降 voltage drop, fall of potential ◇ 接触～contact drop, 阳极～anode(potential) drop
电压降测定法 fall of potential method
电压校准[对中](电子显微镜的) voltage alignment
电压控制 voltage control ◇ 恒频～*
电压控制电流源 【计】voltage-controlled current source
电压控制电压源 【计】voltage-controlled voltage source
电压控制器 voltage controller (V.C.)
电压脉动 voltage ripple
电压漂移 voltage drift
电压平衡继电器 voltage balanced relay
电压输出 voltage output
电压损失 voltage loss
电压调节 voltage regulation [control]
电压调节器 voltage regulator (V.R.)
电压突变 voltage jump
电压效率 voltage efficiency
电压谐振 voltage resonance
电压源 voltage source ◇ 电流控制～*
电压增益 voltage gain
电压转换开关 voltage switch
电延迟线 【计】electric delay line
电眼 electric eye (E.E.), magic [tuning]

eye

电冶法 electro-metallurgical method
电冶金家[工作者] electrometallurgist
电冶金(学) electrometallurgy
电冶炼 electric smelting ◇ 连续~*
电冶设备[工厂] electro-metal plant
电液比例换向阀 electro-hydraulic proportional reversal valve
电液比例节流阀 electric-hydraulic-proportional throttle valve
电移 electromigration
电引力 electric attraction
电英岩 tourmaline
电荧 electroluminescence
电硬球 electric-rigid sphere
电泳 electrophoresis, cataphoresis ◇ 埃尔法尔~涂铝钢带 Elphal
电泳(表面处理)溶液 cataphoretic solution
电泳沉积(法) electrophoretic deposition ◇ 阳离子~*
电泳镀层 electrophoretic coating
电泳分析 electrophoretic analysis
电泳力 electrophoretic force
电泳图 electrophoretic pattern, electrophoretogram
电泳(涂)镀 electrophoretic plating [coating], electrophoresis plating
电泳现象 electrophoresis, cataphoresis
电泳仪[装置] electrophoresis [electrophoretic] apparatus
电涌吸收器 surge absorber
电源 (power, current, electric) source, current supply, main power, source of voltage ◇ 恒压~constant voltage source
电源变压器 power [supply] transformer
电源部分 power pack [unit]
电源电缆 power [feed] cable
电源电路 power circuit
电源电压 supply [source] voltage
电源接头 electrical [power] connection
电源开关 power [supply] switch

电源切断 power dump
电源熔丝[保险丝] power fuse
电源线 main lead, [电]feeder
电源中断 power failure
电晕 corona
电晕比电流 specific corona current
电晕闭塞 corona suppression
电晕电流 corona current
电晕放电 corona (discharge)
电晕(放电)屏蔽[防护屏] corona shield
电晕(放电)效应 corona effect
电晕式选矿机[分选器] corona-type separator
电渣 electro-slag
电渣表面堆焊(处理) electroslag surfacing
电渣重熔 electroslag refining (E.S.R.), electroslag re(s)melting
电渣重熔法 electroslag remelting process
电渣重熔钢 electroslag-melted steel
电渣重熔高速钢 high speed steel produced by ESR
电渣重熔炉 electroslag remelting furnace
电渣法[工艺] electroslag process
电渣复合金属法 ◇ 普鲁拉梅尔特~*
电渣焊 (electro)slag welding ◇ 板极~*, 接触~*, 熔化嘴~*, 手工~*, 丝极~*
电渣焊机 electroslag welding machine
电渣加热 electroslag heating
电渣加热补缩(冒口的) electroslag feeding
电渣精炼 electroslag refining
电渣冷硬熔铸(法) electric slag cold-hardening cast
电渣离心铸造 centrifugal electroslag casting (CESC)
电渣炉 electroslag furnace
电(渣炉)渣料 electroslag fluxes
电渣热封顶(法) electroslag hot topping
电渣熔接 electroslag welding (ESW)
电渣熔炼 electroslag melting

电渣(熔炼)法 【冶】electric ingot process ◇ 霍普金斯~*, 凯洛格~*, 连续~*
电渣熔铸 electroslag remelting and casting(ESRC)
电渣冶金 electroslag metallurgy
电渣铸造 electroslag casting
电振给矿机 electro-vibrating feeder
电指示器 electric indicator
电致发光 electroluminescence
电致伸缩[电缩作用] electrostriction
电致伸缩效应 electrostrictional effect
电中和原理 principle of electroneutrality
电中性 electroneutrality
电重力测量(学)[电重量(分析)法] electrogravimetry
电重力测量法 electrogravimetric method
电轴 electric axis
电铸 electroforming, electroform, electromoulding, galvanoplasty, galvanoplastics ◇ 厚层~板 heavy electroplate
电铸板用铅基压铸合金(93Pb, 4Sb, 3Sn) electrotype alloy
电铸槽 electrotyping bath
电铸成型[沉积] electroform
电铸的 galvanoplastic
电铸电工纯铁 electroform electrical pure iron
电铸电工纯铁板 electroform electrical pure iron plate
电铸术 galvanoplasty, galvanoplastics, electrotyping
电铸制版(法)[成型法] electromoulding
电铸制版术 electrotypy, galvanography
电着色(处理) electrocolouring
电子 electron ◇ 3d层~ 3d electron, 被俘~ trapped electron, 不成对~ unpaired electron, 成对~*, 打出的~ knock-on electron, 简并化~ degenerated electrons, 拒[疏]~的 electrophobic, 类波[与波相似的]~ wave-like electron, 能级较低的~*, 亲[吸]~的 electrophilic, 去~作用 deelectronation, 失[差]~的 betatopic, 失~蜕变 betatopic change, 增~反应*
电子半导体 electronic semi-conductor
电子倍增管[器] electron(ic) multiplier
电子本征函数 electronic eigenfunction
电子比 electron ratio
电子比热 electronic specific heat
电子笔 【计】electronic pen [stylus]
电子波 electron wave
电子波动光学 electron (wave) optics
电子波动理论 wave theory of electrons
电子波函数 electron wave function
电子捕集器 electron trap
电子布居数 electron population
电子操作台 electronics console
电子测厚仪 electronic thickness gauge
电子测宽仪(板材的) electronic width gauge
电子测试仪器 electronic instrument
电子测微计 electronic micrometer
电子层 electron orbit ◇ 有空位~ vacant shell
电子称量 electronic weighing
电子成像 electron image
电子秤 electronic weigher, electronic (loadcell) scale ◇ 复式~ double electronic scale
电子传感[发送]器 electronic pickup
电子磁子 【理】electronic magneton
电子词典 electronic dictionary
电子簇射 electronic showering
电子单位 electron unit
电子导电 electron conduction
电子导(电)体 electron conductor
电子导电性 electron conductivity
电子等电位透镜 equipotential lens
电子等离子体 electron plasma
电子电导率[系数] electronic [n-type] conductivity
电子电荷 electron(ic) charge
电子电离 electronic ionization
电子电路 electronic circuit
电子电位计 electronic potentiometer

电子对 electron pair, duplet
电子对耦合 electron-pair linkage
电子发射 electron emission ◇ 自动～autoelectronic emission
电子发射镀层 emissive coating
电子发射器[装置] electron producing device
电子发射体 electron emitter
电子反应 electron reaction
电子放大[倍增] electron(ic) magnification [multiplication]
电子放大镜 hiccough
电子放大率 electron multiplication, electron(ic) magnification (影像的)
电子放大器 electronic amplifier
电子放电 electron-discharge
电子放电管 electron-discharge tube
电子放射变化 betatopic change
电子分布 electron distribution
电子分光计 electron spectrometer ◇ 俄歇～*
电子分级控制器 electronic step controller
电子分类控制装置 electronic classifier control
电子分选机 electronic separator
电子辐射 electron radiation
电子俘获 electron capture, inverse β decay ◇ E层[轨道]～E-capture
电子干涉仪 electron interferometer
电子感应加速器 betatron, rheotron
电子感应加速器射线照相术 betatron radiography
电子工业 electronic industry
电子管 electron, (radio) tube, electron, (radio) valve, tyratron, vacuum tube [valve] ◇ 小型～bantam tube, 阳极射线～canal ray tube, "硬性"～hardtube
电子管变频器 vacuum-tube converter
电子管电压表[伏特计] (electron, vacuum) tube voltmeter, vomax, valve voltmeter
电子管放大器 valve amplifier

电子管金属 valve metal
电子管脉冲发生器 pulse tube oscillator
电子管式高频变换器 vacuum-tube-type high-frequency converter
电子管稳压器 valve (voltage) regulator
电子管振荡器 vacuum tube oscillator [generator], tube-type oscillator, thermionic [valve] oscillator, tube [valve] generator
电子管整流器 valve [vacuum-tube] rectifier
电子光谱 electron(ic) spectrum
电子光学 electron (wave) optics
电子光学棱镜 electron optical prism
电子光学透镜 electron (optical) lens
电子光学物镜 electronic objective
电子光学轴 electron optical axis
电子光学装置[系统] electron optical system ◇ 电磁式～*
电子轨道 electron orbit [trajectory]
电子恒湿器 electronic humidistat
电子恒温器 electronic thermostat
电子轰击 electron bombardment
电子轰击电流 bombarding [bombardment] current
电子轰击法 electron bombardment technique ◇ 悬浮区域～*
电子轰击感生导电性 electron bombardment induced conductivity (ebicon)
电子轰击加工 electron bombardment working
电子轰击炉 【冶】electro-bombardment furnace
电子轰击区域熔化[熔炼] 【半】electrobombardment [electron bombardment] zone melting
电子轰击熔炼 electron bombardment melting
电子轰击熔炼供电 electron bombardment power supply
电子轰击熔炼炉 electron bombardment melting furnace

电子轰击蒸发	electron bombardment evaporation
电子弧焊机	electronic arc welder
电子化	electronization
电子化合物	electron compound ◇ 休姆－罗瑟里~ Hume-Rothery compounds
电子化合物相	Hume-Rothery phase
电子回旋共振	electron cyclotron resonance (ECR)
电子回旋共振等离子溅射(法)	electron cyclotron resonance plasma sputtering
电子回旋加速器	betatron, rheotron, microtron
电子机器人	electronic robot
电子机械积分器	electro-mechanical integrator
电子积分器	electronic integrator
电子激发光(阴极电子激发光)	cathodoluminescence
电子计数器[电路]	electronic counter
电子计算机	electronic computer (E.C.), electronic brain
电子计算器	electronic calculator
电子记录器	electronic recorder, electronic recording equipment
电子继电器	electronic relay
电子加热	electronic heating
电子加速器	electron-accelerating device, electron accelerator ◇ 感应式~*
电子间相互作用	electron-electron interaction
电子焦点	electron focus
电子交换	electron exchange [interchange]
电子交换能	electronic exchange energy
电子交换树脂	electron exchange resin
电子角动量	electronic angular momentum
电子接受体	electron acceptor
电子结构	electronic structure
电子结构因素	electron structure factor
电子金相学	electron metallography
电子聚光镜孔径	condenser aperture
电子聚集	electron collection
电子聚焦	electron focusing
电子开关	electronic [vacuum] switch, switching gate
电子壳层	electron(ic) shell [envelope] ◇ 填满~*, 未填满[有空位]~*
电子壳层结构	electron shell structure
电子空位	electron vacancy
电子空位位置	vacant electron site
电子空穴	electron hole, vacant electron site
电子－空穴对	electron-hole pair
电子－空穴结[过渡层]	electron-hole junction
电子－空穴界面	p-n interface
电子－空穴偶	electron-hole pair
电子－空穴碰撞	electron-hole collison
电子孔径	electron aperture
电子控制仿形轧辊车床	electronically-controlled contour roll lathe
电子控制器	electronic controller ◇ 微型~*
电子控制设备	electronic control equipment
电子控制轧机	electronically operated mill
电子冷冻(法)	electronic freezing
电子冷发射	autoelectronic emission
电子冷却	electronic cooling
电子流	electron(ic) current [flow]
电子流量计	electronic flowmeter
电子脉冲发生器	electronic impulser
电子密度	electron density [concentration]
电子密度径向分布	radial electron denisty distribution
电子敏感乳胶	electron sensitive emulsion
电子能带	electron energy band
电子能级	electron (energy) level
电子能量	electronic energy
电子能量[谱]分布	electron energy distribution
电子(能)谱	(同"电子光谱")
电子能态	electron energy state

电子浓度　electron concentration ◇ 每个原子的~electron-per-atom concentration
电子偶　electron pair, coupled [paired] electrons
电子偶键　electron-pair bond
电子排斥力　electron-repelling power
电子排列　electron(ic) arrangement [configuration]
电子碰撞　electron collision
电子漂移　electron(ic) drift
电子屏蔽　electron screening
电子气　electron gas [atmosphere] ◇ 费米~Fermi gas
电子迁移　electronic transition
电子迁移率　electron(ic) mobility, electron-transfer step
电子枪　electron gun, electronic torch ◇ 点聚焦~*, 电荷中和[散逸]用~charge neutralizer gun, 电位梯度~gradient gun, 电子束熔炼用~*, 二~熔炼炉 two-gun melting furnace, 后加速~post-acceleration gun, 环形~annular gun, 冷阴极~cold-cathode gun, 立式~装置*, 皮尔斯~Pierce gun, 皮尔斯会聚~*, 偏电压~bias gun, 无阳极~work-accelerated gun, 远距~distant gun
电子枪闭锁装置　gun lock
电子枪焦点　gun focus
电子枪冷却系统　gun-cooling lines
电子枪室　gun chamber
电子枪阴极　block cathode
电子枪真空密封装置　electron gun vacuum lock
电子亲和力　electron affinity
电子球面对称分布　spherically symmetric electron distribution
电子扫描　electronic scanning
电子射流　electron jet
电子射束　electron stream
电子射线管　(同"阴极射线管")
电子射线照相术　electron(ic) radiography
电子设备　electron(ic) device [equipment], electronics
电子施主　electron donor
电子时间继电器　electronic timer
电子式仪表　electronic [thermionic] instrument
电子式运动轧件自动测量记录仪　electronic instagraph
电子释出　electron release
电子释放　electron liberation
电子收集　electron collection
电子受体　electron acceptor
电子束　electron [cathode] beam, electron bundle [jet], electronic torch ◇ 圆柱形~cylindrical beam
电子束捕集器[收注栅]　beam catcher
电子束掺杂机　electron beam implantation machine
电子束重熔　electron-beam remelting (E.B.R.)
电子束单晶炉　electron beam single crystal furnace
电子束电流　beam current
电子束电子　beam electrons
电子束发生器[装置]　electron-beam generator [device, apparatus]
电子束管　electron-beam tube [valve], bombarding beam tube
电子束焊接　electron beam welding ◇ 非真空~*
电子束焊接焊缝　electron-beam weld
电子束焊接机　electron-beam welder, electron-beam welding machine
电子束轰击熔炼(法)　electron-beam bombardment melting
电子束轰击引入管　bombarding beam tube
电子束技术　electron-beam technology
电子束剂量测定法[剂量学]　electron-beam dosimetry
电子束加热器　electron-beam heater
电子束精炼　electron-beam refining, electron-beam melting purification

电子束精炼期	electron-beam melting purification cycle
电子束径迹	beam trace
电子束控制	beam control
电子束冷炉膛炉	electron-beam cold-hearth furnace
电子束炉	electron-beam furnace ◇ 凝壳式～*,"阳极－金属滴液"～*
电子束能量	electron-beam energy
电子束切割	electron-beam cutting [slicing]
电子束(切削)加工	electron(ic) beam machining
电子束区域精炼	electron-beam zone refining
电子束区域熔炼	electron-beam zoning
电子束熔锭	electron-beam (melted) ingot
电子束熔炼	electron-beam melting, electronic torch melting ◇ 小型～*,圆穴[钮扣]形～*【冶】button melter
电子束熔炼法	electron-beam process
电子束熔炼炉	electron-beam (melting) furnace
电子束熔炼设备	electron-beam melting system
电子束熔炼用电子枪	electron-beam melting gun
电子束烧结	electron-beam sintering
电子束退火	electron-beam annealing
电子束系统	electron-beam system
电子束显微探测器[探头]【理】	electron-beam microprobe
电子束形成	electron-beam formation
电子束悬浮区	electron-beam float zone
电子束悬浮区域熔炼	electron-beam floating zone-melting (E.B.F.Z.M.)
电子束真空炉	electron-beam vacuum furnace
电子束蒸发沉积	electron-beam vaporation deposition
电子束蒸发法	electron-beam evaporation
电子束蒸发器	electron-beam evaporator
电子束装置	electron-beam device [apparatus]
电子数据处理【计】	electronic data processing (E.D.P.)
电子数据处理系统【计】	electronic data processing system (E.D.P.S.)
电子顺磁共振[谐振]	electron paramagnetic resonance (E.P.R.)
电子弹性散射	elastic electron scatter
电子探伤仪	electron defectoscope
电子探针	electron probe
电子探针 X 射线分析器	electron probe X-ray analyzer
电子探针分析	electron probe [microbeam] analysis
电子探针显微[微量]分析(法)	electron probe microanalysis
电子探针显微分析器[仪]	electron probe microanalyzer (E.P.M.A.)
电子探针研究	electron microprobe study
电子调节器	electronic regulator
电子同步加速器	electron synchrotron
电子透镜	electron (optical) lens
电子透镜极靴缝隙	pole piece spacer
电子图[影]像	electron image, electronic picture
电子图像记录	recording of electron image
电子推斥力	electron-repelling power
电子微探针 X 射线分析仪	electron microprobe X-ray analyzer
电子物镜	electronic objective
电子显微断口照相术	electron microfractography
电子显微复型【金】	electron microscopy impression
电子显微技术[显微镜学]	electron microscopy
电子显微镜	electron(ic) microscope (E.M.S.) ◇ 场致发射～*,电磁式～*,发射式～*,反射式～*,高分辨率～*,高温(载物台)～*,静磁～*,静电式～*,扫描～*,透射式～*,影像～*,

直接观测~*
电子显微镜复型的钨阴影溅射处理 tungsten shadow casting of electron microscopical specimens
电子显微镜观察 electron microscopic observation
电子显微镜检验 electron microscopy test
电子显微镜镜筒 electron microscope column
电子显微镜试样支架 electron microscope (specimen) holder
电子显微镜透射法 electron microscope transmission method
电子显微镜像 electron microscopical image
电子显微镜性能限度 limitations to performance of electron microscope
电子显微镜研究 electron microscope investigation
电子显微(镜)照片 electron micrograph
电子显微(镜)照相 electron microphotograph
电子显微镜振动 vibration on electron microscope
电子显微射线照相术 electronic microradiography
电子显微探针 electron microprobe
电子显微探针数据 electron microbeam probe data
电子显微组织 electron microstructure
电子显象管 kinescope
电子陷阱 electron trap
电子相 electron phase
电子型超导体 n-type superconductor
电子型超导电性 n-type superconductivity
电子选矿 electronic ore sorting
电子学 electronics
电子雪崩 electron avalanche
电子衍射 electron diffraction ◇局部
电子衍射法 electron diffraction technique
电子衍射分析 electron diffraction analysis

电子衍射晶体学 electron diffraction crystallography
电子衍射图[花样] electron diffraction pattern
电子衍射研究 electron diffraction study [investigation]
电子衍射仪 electron diffraction instrument
电子衍射照相 electron diffraction photograph
电子(移动)异构(现象) electromerism, electron isomerism
电子仪表[仪器] electron(ic) instrument [device]
电子逸出 electron liberation
电子异构体 electromer
电子与原子数比率(电子化合物的) electron-atom ratio
电子元件 electronic component
电子－原子核间引力 electron-nuclear attraction
电子跃迁 electron jump [transition]
电子云 electron cloud [atmosphere]
电子窄束 electron pencil
电子占有率 electron occupancy
电子照相机 electrofax
电子照相术 electrophotography
电子质量 electron(ic) mass
电子注 electron beam [bundle], cathode beam
电子注功率管 beam power tube
电子注管 beam tube
电子注阱 beam trap
电子注入[注射] electron injection
电子注四极管 beam tetrode
电子转换开关 switching gate
电子状态 electronic state
电子状态密度 density of electronic states
电子自动调速器 electronic governor
电子自旋 electron spin
电子自旋共振光谱学 electron spin resonance spectroscopy

电子总体 electron population
电子组态 electron(ic) configuration
电子组态模型 electronic configuration model
电阻 resistance (R., res., resis.) ◇ 恩隆~分析法*, 分布~ distributed resistance, 分泄~ bleeder, 集中~ constriction resistnace, 炉用~ furnace resistor
电阻表 ohmmeter, ohm gauge, ohmer
电阻材料 resistance material ◇ 克利普托尔~*
电阻测量[测定] (electrical) resistance measurement
电阻冲击焊 resistance percusion welding
电阻点焊 resistance spot welding
电阻点焊焊缝 resistance spot weld
电阻点焊焊条 resistance spot-welding electrode
电阻点焊机 resistance spot welding machine
电阻电弧炉 resistance arc furnace
电阻-电流转换器 resistance to current converter
电阻电桥 resistance bridge
电阻定碳仪 carbohm
电阻对缝焊管 electric resistance butt welded tube
电阻对焊机 resistance [upset] butt welding machine
电阻对(接)焊 upset butt welding (U.W.), upset welding
电阻对接焊电流 upset current
电阻对接焊缝 upset (butt) weld
电阻对接焊接头 resistance butt weld
电阻对接焊用模具(夹紧模具) upset welding (clamping) die
电阻法研究 resistometric(al) investigation
电阻反射加热炉 resistor type reverberatory furnace
电阻缝焊[滚焊] resistance seam welding
电阻负载 resistive [ohmic] load

电阻高温测定法 resistance pyrometry
电阻高温计 electropyrometer, electric (resistance) pyrometer, resistance pyrometer ◇ 惠普尔~ Whipple indicator, 剑桥~*
电阻高温学 resistance pyrometry
电阻滚动点焊 resistance roller-spot welding
电阻滚焊 resistance seam welding
电阻焊 electric resistant welding (E.R.W.), resistance welding ◇ 螺柱~ resis-tance stud welding, 无线电频率~*, 蓄能~ stored energy welding
电阻焊管 electric resistance welded tube (E.R.W.T.), resistance weld pipe, resis-tance welded tubing
电阻焊管机 (electric) resistance weld mill
电阻焊锅炉管 E.R.W. (electric resistance welded) boiler tube
电阻焊机 resistance welding machine, resistance welder
电阻焊机制造业协会(美国) Resistance Welders Manufacturers Association (R.W.M.A.)
电阻焊接法 resistance welding process
电阻焊控制设备 resistance welding control
电阻焊时间控制器 resistance welding timer
电阻焊套管 E.R.W. (electric resistance welded) casing
电阻焊条 resistance electrode
电阻焊通电时间 resistance welding time
电阻合金 (electric) resistance alloy ◇ 阿尔克罗塔尔~*, 半精密~*, 高欧姆~*, 恒温器~ thermostat alloy*, 克罗马宁~*, 雷西斯托~*, 米纳尔法低温度系数~*, 诺沃康斯坦特铜基~*, 特莫弗莱克斯二元~ Thermoflex, 铜锰~*, 西格蒙德贵金属~ Sigmund, 希罗克斯~*, 伊莎贝林 NCM 精密~*

电阻回复 electrical resistivity recovery
电阻加热 electric resistance heating, resistance [ohmic] heating
电阻加热棒 heating rod
电阻加热锻焊 hammered resistance welding
电阻加热坩埚炉 resistor crucible furnace
电阻加热炉 resistance heating furnace, resistor furnace ◇ 罐式～*, 塔曼石墨～Tammann furnace, 碳管～*
电阻加热器 (electrical) resistance heater ◇ 金属套～*, 浸入式石墨～*
电阻加热切割 resistance cutting
电阻加热式连续退火装置(用于钢丝等) continuous resistance annealer
电阻加热元件 resistance-heating element, resistor element ◇ 碳硅棒～*
电阻接触焊 electric butt welding
电阻炉 resistor furnace, (electric) resistance(-type) furnace, (electric) furnace of resistance type ◇ 阿塞姆～Arsem furnace, 艾奇逊～*, 传送带式钼～*, 床式～*, 辐射～*, 弗里德里希碳料～Friedrich furnace, 高温～*, 可倾式～*, 拼合石墨管～*, 强制空气循环式～*, 塔曼管式～ Tammann Furnace, 碳粒～*, 氧化物～*, 直接加热～*
电阻炉蒸馏 electric resistance furnace distillation
电阻率 resistivity (res.), electrical [mass] resistivity, specific (electrical) resistance ◇ 单位重量～ weight resistivity, 用～测水 resistivity type moisture control
电阻率测试机 resistivity tester ◇ 层间～*
电阻率测水 resistivity type moisture control
电阻率梯度 resistivity gradient
电阻膜 resistive film
电阻耦合的 resistance-coupled
电阻启动电动机 resistance-start motor

电阻(器) resister, resistor ◇ 放电～ discharging resistor, 旁漏～ bleeder resistor, 细磨～ ground resistor, 限流～ current-limiting resister
电阻钎焊 (electric) resistance brazing, resistance soldering
电阻熔炼炉 resistor melting furnace ◇ 石墨棒～*
电阻闪光对焊接头 resistance flash weld
电阻闪光（对接）焊 resistance flash (butt) welding
电阻式测辐射热计 bolometer
电阻式水分控制法 resistivity type moisture control
电阻丝 resistance wire, resistive conductor ◇ 费罗派尔铁铬铝～合金*, 哈尔曼铜锰铝合金～*, 坎塔尔高级～*, 克拉克～*
电阻损耗 resistance [ohmic] loss
电阻碳 resistor carbon
电阻碳粒 resistor carbon granule
电阻体 resistive element ◇ 西利科尼特～*
电阻铜焊 resistance brazing
电阻铜合金 ◇ 雷奥坦～Rheotan
电阻网络 resistance network
电阻温度计 resistance thermometer [pyrometer] ◇ 原标准～*
电阻温度系数 temperature resistance coefficient, thermal resistivity constant, temperature coefficient of electrical resistance
电阻系数 resistance coefficient, resistivity, specific (electrical) resis-tance
电阻箱 resistance box
电阻异常 electrical resistance anomaly
电阻应变计[仪] (electric) resistance strain gauge ◇ 粘贴式～*
电阻应变计检测 resistance strain-gauge test
电阻应变片 strain-gauge resistor
电阻硬钎焊 resistance brazing (R.B.)

电阻元件　resistance [resistor] element
电阻直接加热　direct resistance heating ◇ 奥梅斯～锻造法*
电阻直接加热退火　resistance annealing
电阻制动　resistance braking
电阻制动器[电阻器制动]　resistor brake
电钻开口机　【铁】electric rotary drill
电嘴　candle, sparking plug（火花塞）
淀出物　precipitated material
淀粉　starch (powder)
淀粉溶液　starch solution
淀粉絮凝剂　starch flocculant
淀粉状氧化铝　starchy alumina
淀垢　slime
淀积　deposition ◇ 流态化床～层*，热丝表面[气相]～法【冶】hot wire process, 阳极～*
淀积层形成　deposit formation
淀积池　sediment box
淀积物　deposit(ion)
淀积锥　deposition cone
淀渣　mud
淀渣分析　slime analysis
淀渣干燥炉　mud drier
雕刻用合金板（铅锑合金）　engraving plate
雕刻用铜板　engravers' copper
掉道　derail
掉片　flaking
掉砂（铸造缺陷）　(sand) drop, ram-away, ram-off, clamp-off, push-up 掉下 slump
吊包　【钢】crane [bull] ladle ◇ 单轨～ monorail ladle, 旋转式～【铸】radial ladle
吊包架　【铸】bail
吊臂　floating boom
吊舱　gondola
吊槽　hanging gutter
吊槽式输送机　suspended tray conveyer
吊铲　dragline excavator
吊车　（同"起重机"）
吊车工　craneman
吊车挂钩工　tagman

吊车浇包　【铸】trolley [crane] ladle
吊灯　ceiling [pendant] lamp ◇ 分支～ luster, lustre, 枝形～架 chandelier
吊顶　suspended roof
吊顶式结构（点火器等的）【团】ceiling-slung structure
吊斗　(hand) bucket
吊斗装运机　bucket loader
吊耳　ear, lifting eye
吊耳式坩埚炉　bale out crucible furnace
吊耳装置　lugging attachment
吊杆　hanger rod, boom, suspension arm [rod], gib, gab（吊车的）
吊杆式出料机（坯料出炉用）　unloader boom
吊杆挖土机　boom excavator
吊杆斜角(度)　boom angle
吊杆与戽斗输送法（混凝土的）　boom and bucket delivery
吊拱　【建】hanging arch
吊拱顶　suspended-arch type roof
吊拱砖　suspended arch brick
吊钩　lift hook, cliver, suspender ◇ 单 C 形～*, 砂型～【铸】gagger, 双 C 形～*, 双孔型 C 形～ double eye type C-hook
吊挂导板（上轧辊出口侧的）【压】hanging guide
吊挂工　hooker
吊挂拱　catenary arch
吊挂砌砖[体]　suspended brickwork
吊挂[吊拱]式炉顶（反射炉的）【冶】suspended roof [arch], suspended-arch type roof ◇ 辐射～ suspended radial roof, 镁砖～*, 全～ fully sus-pended roof
吊挂式炉顶砖　suspended arch brick, rib brick
吊挂式炉喉保护板　【铁】hanging armor jacket
吊挂式墙　suspended wall
吊挂卫板　【压】hanging [yield, balanced] guard, top tackle ◇ 弹簧平衡的～ spring balanced guard

吊管钩[器]　tube [pipe] hanger
吊管架　pipe saddle
吊罐　（同"吊包"）
吊环　suspension ring [link], lifting ring, slinger, bail ◇ U 形～shackle, 万向～shackle hook
吊环螺钉孔　【铸】handling hole
吊环螺母　eye nut
吊环螺栓　eyebolt
吊架　cradle, hanger, suspender, rack（电解槽中的），【铸】cross
吊架螺栓　hanger bolt
吊具　slings for lifting loads ◇ 运送板垛的～pack [sheet] carrier
吊筐　basket, crate
吊筐倾翻机构　【焦】tilting-basket mechanism
吊篮　basket ◇ 金属丝～screen wire basket
吊篮式阳极氧化处理　basket anodizing
吊篮装料　【冶】basket charging
吊链　sling (chain), pendant chain
吊笼　suspension cage
吊门　flap shutter, overhang-door
吊门(矿)车　drop-door wagon
吊起　hook(ing)-up
吊钳　tongs ◇ 起重机～crane tongs
吊桥　lifting [suspension] bridge
吊桥索　bridge cable
吊熔法(稀有金属的)　drip melting
吊砂　【铸】coping out
吊扇　ceiling fan
吊索　suspender, sling (rope), slinger, lifting rope, tackle
吊桶　(shaft, hand) bucket, tub,【钢】crane (ball) ladle ◇ 翻转式～tipping bucket
吊线　messenger wire ◇ 悬挂电缆[滑触线]的～*
吊线勾架　wire coil stripper
吊线机　【压】gallows
吊线架　gallows
吊线线夹　suspension clamp

吊楔　lewis (anchors)
吊芯　【铸】suspended [hanging] core
吊运车索道　trolley cable
吊运式钢包　【钢】crane ladle
吊运小车　travel(l)ing jack carriage
吊重索　wire rope sling
吊重装置　sling
吊柱　davit
吊砖　hanger brick ◇ 炉顶～*
调查研究工作　investigation work
调车(铁路的)　【运】shunting
调车场 ◇ 【运】railway marshalling yard, switchyard
调车机车　switcher
调车线[轨道]　【运】shunting track
调车作业　【运】shunting operations [service]
调动(程序)　【计】swap(ping)
调度　dispatching
调度程序　scheduler program, dispatcher
调度电话　dispatcher telephone
调度模拟系统　scheduling simulation system
调度室　scheduling room (S.R.), control center, dispatch(ing) [despatch] room
调度所[站]　dispatch(ing) station [office]
调度优先级[权]　【计】dispatching priority
调罐车装置　ladle car pushing device
调换　exchange, replace, transposition
调头装置　upender
调用[调入]　【计】call ◇ 被～程序 called program, 被～过程 invoked procedure
调用程序块　invoking block
跌差　cascade
跌落(式检查)井　drop manhole
跌水　water fall, (hydraulic) drop ◇ 沟中～设备 ditch check
碟盘给料　disc feeding
碟形　dish ◇ 锻成～dishing
碟形底　dished bottom
碟形底离子交换槽　dished bottom exchanger cell

碟形电极　dished electrode
碟形粉粒　disc-shaped particle, saucer-shape of particle
碟形炉底　dish hearth, saucer-shaped furnace bottom
碟形炉膛　dish hearth
碟形撇渣器　dish skimmer
碟状[形]的　dished
碟状粉末　plate powder
碟状绝缘子　disc insulator
蝶式绝缘子　shackle insulator
蝶式孔型　【压】butterfly pass ◇ 轧制角钢的～butterfly angles pass
蝶式孔型设计　butterfly design
蝶式翼缘　flared out flanges
蝶(形)阀　butterfly valve (B.V.), butterfly (damper), butterfly throttle [gate]
蝶形活套　butterfly loops
蝶形孔型系统设计　flared flange method
蝶形孔型轧制法（角钢的）　butterfly method, bending up method
蝶形螺钉　thumb [winged] screw
蝶形螺母　butterfly [thumb, wign(ed)] nut
蝶形螺栓　butterfly bolt
蝶形轧制法（角钢的）　bending method (of rolling)
蝶形组织（钢轨内的）　【金】butterfly structure
迭代　【数】iteration
迭代法　iteration (method)
迭代公式　【数】iterative [recurrence] formula
迭代过程[运算]　iterative process
迭合　identification
叠板堆垛吊车[起重机]（带吊运托架的）　【压】piling crane
叠板堆垛高度（退火时的）　【压】stacking height
叠板翻转机　pack tilting device, pack tilter
叠板加热炉　(sheet) pack heating furnace
叠板剪切　mill shearing
叠板接触点焊　stack welding
叠板切割　piled plate cutting, stack (flame) cutting
叠板热轧机　hot-pack mill
叠板(弹)簧　laminated [bow-type, leaf] spring
叠板卸垛起重机[吊车]（带托板的）　de-piling crane
叠板轧机　pack mill
叠板轧制　rolling in pack form
叠板制钢包[盛钢桶]用吊钩　laminated hooks for steel ladle
叠层板　laminated plate ◇ 覆铜～，铜箔～copper foil laminate
叠层磁轭　laminated yoke
叠层金属　laminated metal
叠层梁　laminated beam
叠层木板　laminated wood
叠层屋架　lamella truss
叠层因数　lamination [stacking] factor
叠层制品　laminated product
叠加场　【理】superimposed field
叠加电流　applied [superimposed] current
叠加定律（弹性体变形的）　law of superposition
叠加法　method of superposition
叠加交流电流（电镀用）　superimposed AC
叠加原理　principle of superposition
叠架　superpose
叠接　lap joint
叠片　lamination
叠片表面绝缘　lamination surface insulation
叠片磁铁　laminated magnet
叠片硅钢薄板　laminated sheet iron
叠片厚度　lamination thickness
叠片链　laminated chain
叠片铁心　laminated core
叠绕线圈重叠绕法　banked winding
叠箱串注浇口　【铸】vertical gate
叠箱造型　stack moulding

叠箱铸型 【铸】multiple mould
叠型铸造 【铸】stack casting
叠影 ghost (image), foldover
叠轧(薄板的) pack [ply, tight] rolling
叠置 superposition ◇ 串级～焊 cascade welding
叠置(加料)螺旋 overlapping spiral
叠珠焊缝 bead(ing) weld
丁醇 {C_4H_9OH} butanol, ($n-$) butyl alcohol
丁二酸{$(CH_2COOH)_2$} succinic acid
丁二酮肟试验 dimethylglyoxime test
丁二烯{$CH_2:CH\cdot CH:CH_2$} divinyl, butadiene
丁二烯钠聚橡胶 buna
丁基{$CH_3(CH_2)CH_2-$} butyl
丁基卡必醇(二甘醇-丁醚) {$(C_2H_5OCH_2CH_2)_2O$} butyl carbitol
丁基醚{$(C_4H_9)_2O$} butyl ether
丁基亚磷[膦]酸二丁酯 butyldibutylphosphinate(B.D.B.P.)
丁钠橡胶 buna
丁醛 butyl aldehyde
丁酸{$CH_3\cdot(CH_2)_2\cdot COOH$} butyric acid
丁酮 (同"甲基乙基酮")
丁头砌行 header course
丁(头)砖 header
丁(头)砖层 header [heading] course, course bond
丁烷{C_4H_{10}} butane
丁烷-丁烯混合气 butane-butylene gas
丁烷丁烯馏分 butane-butence (fraction) (b.b.)
丁烯二酸 butene dioic acid ◇ 反式～*
丁烯酸 {$CH_3CH\cdot CHCO_2H$} crotonic acid
丁氧基 {$CH_3(CH_2)_2CH_2O-$} butoxy
丁砖与顺砖交叉[隔层]砌合 block bond
丁字对焊 T (tee) butt welding
丁字(对)接头焊缝 T (tee) butt weld ◇ 半 V 形坡口～*
丁字钢 T-section, T-bar, T-beam (girder), tee-profile, T-iron (girder), flange beam ◇ 球头～bulb rail steel
丁字钢帽形断面(型材) top-hat section
丁字管 tee pipe, pipe tee, T-tube
丁字焊 tee welding
丁字接头 T-joint
丁字接头填角焊缝 T-fillet weld
丁字街 T-crossing
丁字梁 T-beam [T-iron] girder
丁字铁 T-iron
丁字头螺栓 T-head bolt
丁字形 tee, T-shape
丁字形材 top-hat section
丁字(形钢)轨 tee [vignoles's] rail
丁字形挤压型材 tee-section extrusions
丁字形筛条 T-shaped rod
碇系离子 anchored ion
钉 nail, tack, peg ◇ U 形～clevis, 造型用～【铸】core iron
钉板 【建】skin plate
钉板刮路器 nail drag
钉棒机 stud pusher
钉厂 nailery
钉碎机 spike mill
钉头切断机 buster
钉扎应力 locking stress
顶板 top [cap, head] plate
顶板锚定件 ceiling anchor
顶板喂进装置 top sheet feeding device
顶壁 hanging wall (H.W.)
顶部部分 【钢】top section
顶部采光 top light
顶部出料 top discharge
顶部吹氧 【钢】oxygen-top blowing
顶部吹氧管 top (blowing) lance
顶部电极 top electrode
顶部飞边 top flash
顶部辊道 top table
顶部加料 top feed [filling]
顶部加料器 top filler
顶部加热 top [overhead] firing
顶部加热镀锌槽 top-heated galvanizing

pot

顶部加热式炉　over-fired furnace
顶部进料式过滤器　top-feed filter
顶部净空　headway
顶部口　top opening
顶部料钟　【铁】top bell
顶部[顶盖]密封　top seal
顶部排出的蒸气　over-the-top vapour
顶部片边(钢锭缺陷)　top flash
顶部砌砖　top brick-work
顶部燃烧　top firing
顶部燃烧均热炉　(同"上烧嘴均热炉")
顶部送风　crown blast
顶部砖格　top checker
顶部装炉系统　top-charging system ◇ 阀封~*
顶层　top [upper] layer, topcoat, top compartment, overstory
顶层试样　upper sample
顶插(导电)棒　(同"上插棒")
顶撑　truss [tie, anchor] bolt, top bracing
顶出力　ejection capacity
顶出销[针](熔模铸造的)　【铸】knock(-out) pin
顶出行程　【粉】ejection stroke
顶出装置　liftout attachment ◇ 模子~die manipulator, 气动~*, 推杆式~ pusher-type knockout
顶吹　top-blowing, top blast
顶吹技术　top blowing technique
顶吹炼钢工艺　top-blowing technique
顶吹喷粉　powder top blowing
顶吹喷枪　top (blowing) lance
顶吹气体搅拌熔体　top gas-stirred melt
顶吹旋转转炉法　top blown rotary coverter process
顶吹氧精炼　top blast refining
顶吹氧气　top oxygen blowing
顶吹氧气炼钢法　top-blown oxygen process
顶吹氧气平炉　roof lance furnace
顶吹氧气石灰粉除磷炼钢法　oxygen lime powder process (O.L.P.)
顶吹氧(气)脱气(法)　top oxygen blowing degassing (method)
顶吹氧气转炉　top-blown oxygen converter, oxygen-blown vessel
顶吹氧气转炉车间　top-blown oxygen vessel plant
顶吹氧气转炉钢　oxygen converter steel
顶吹真空法　【钢】LD-vac process
顶吹转炉(炼铜、镍用)　【色】top blown rotary converter (T.B.R.C.)
顶底复吹法　(同"复吹法")
顶底复吹转炉　(同"复吹转炉")
顶底复合吹氧转炉－真空脱气炼钢法　K-BOP-RH process
顶底铜钨分离法　top and bottom process
顶端淬火(法)　end hardening [quenching]
顶端淬火曲线　Jominy curve
顶端淬火试棒　Jominy bar
顶锻　【压】heading, upset, up-end forging ◇ 步进式~*, 闪光~对焊*
顶锻法　【压】heading [shortening] process
顶锻翻边　joggled lap
顶锻工具　heading tool
顶锻工艺　heading technique
顶锻机　upsetter, upsetting machine [press], header ◇ 钢球~ball header, 螺栓~bolt header
顶锻机构　upset mechanism
顶锻力　upset force
顶锻螺栓　upset bolt, bolt heading
顶锻模　heading die, upsetting die
顶锻时的电流　upset current
顶锻试验[检验]　upset [upending, slug] test, knock down test
顶锻试验机　upset tester
顶锻速度　upset speed
顶锻通电时间　upset current time
顶锻压力　upset pressure
顶锻压力机　heading press
顶锻装置(对焊机的)　upsetting device

顶　ding

顶镦法　【压】heading method
顶镦工序　【压】shortening operation
顶阀(内燃机的)　overhead valve
顶封　【冶】closed-top
顶峰　top batter, top level
顶盖　top cap [cover]
顶盖轴承　top bearing
顶杆　ejector pin, one-piece male punch, push rod, 【压】mandrel, dolly, 【铸】knock(-out) pin (熔模铸造的), 【冶】charging bar (装料机的) ◇ 球形~【压】ball mandrel
顶杆钢　mandrel steel
顶杆框(压力铸造用)　ejector box
顶杆式(起模)造型机　【铸】pin-lift molding machine
顶杆行程限位器　mandrel stroke limiter
顶杆压痕　【铸】ejector marks
顶杆转换装置　【压】plugbar change-over unit
顶钢机　【压】ejector
顶管法　push bench process, cupping [Ehrhardt] process
顶管机　(tube) push bench ◇ 齿条式~ toothed-rack push bench, 辊式模~ roller die push bench, 环式模~ ring die push bench, C.P.E.一组(斜轧、穿孔和延伸机组) C.P.E (cross roll, piercing and elongating) mill
顶管轧制用的毛[荒]管　hollow forging
顶管模(顶管机的)　ring die
顶加热镀锌槽　top-heated galvanizing pot
顶尖　apex, spike ◇ 内装式承受~
顶浇(法)[顶注式浇注系统]　top gating [casting]
顶浇口　top gate
顶角　apex [apical, vertex, point] angle, angularity
顶梁　top beam, headblock
顶铆工具　【机】holding-up tool
顶冒口　【钢】top riser
顶帽(电子管的)　top cap

顶模(铆钉机的)　holder-up
顶模器　die manipulator
顶棚　ceiling, platfond ◇ 安装在~上的 ceiling-mounted
顶棚板面供暖　ceiling-panel heating
顶棚电线头　ceiling outlet
顶棚照明　ceiling lighting
顶篷灯　ceiling light
顶坯杆　ejector rod
顶枪　top (blowing) lance
顶切　top cut
顶区　top zone
顶圈　top ring (casting)
顶燃式热风炉　【铁】top-fired [top-combustion, dome-combustion] stove
顶刃面　heel
顶烧窑　top-fired kiln
顶升楼板　lift-slab
顶升销钉(铸型开箱用)　pin lift
顶室　top compartment
顶视图　top view
顶丝　forcing off screw
顶头　forcer, 【压】(穿孔用) plug, slug ◇ 长~拔制[拉拔]~*, 带~轧制的(用自动轧管机)【压】plug rolled, 断面的~部分 bulb, 无~拔制*, 圆柱形~
顶头螺栓(塞棒的)　【钢】cotter bolt
顶推装置　thruster
顶弯段　【连铸】bending bow
顶弯器　【连铸】curved bender
顶弯式　【连铸】curve bender type
顶弯装置　bending device
顶箱杆　【铸】lifting [stripping] pin
顶箱压实式造型机　【铸】squeeze flask lift machine
顶压式焊机　【焊】press welding machine, press-type machine
顶压式造型机　【铸】top-squeeze moulding machine
顶压系统　【焦】top pressure system
顶渣吹氩搅拌　【钢】top-slag Ar bubbling
顶铸(法)　【冶】top casting, 【钢】direct

casting
顶注 【钢】top [direct] pour(ing), top [downhill, direct] teeming, cast [pour] from top
顶砖 header
顶装锭锁定装置 top ingot lock
顶装料式炉 top-charging furnace
顶装料桶(电炉的) charging bucket [basket]
锭 ingot, pig, butt, stockpile ◇ 成~ingot making, 整~场 conditioning yard
锭边偏析 【钢】L segregates
锭表面 ingot surface
锭长 ingot length
锭车 ingot car
锭秤 ingot weigher
锭底 ingot bottom
锭底裂纹 basal crack
锭浮渣 ingot scum
锭钢 ingot (cast) steel
锭角(部位)偏析 【金】ingot corner segregation
锭角断裂 corner fracture
锭角鬼线 【金】corner ghost
锭壳 【钢】ingot [solidified] shell
锭块 ingot bar
锭筐 cradle
锭料 ingot ◇ 半无限长~*, 环形~*, 凝固~frozen ingot, 修整~*
锭料管(区域熔炼的) ingot tube
锭料冷却室 ingot cooling chamber
锭料夹头 ingot clamp
锭料形状 【色】charge shape
锭料移动(区域熔炼的) ingot moving
锭料转接装置 【压】ingot adapter
锭料装炉机 【压】ingot charger, ingot charging machine
锭料装炉(起重)装置 【压】ingot charging gear
锭模 ingot mould ◇ 埃里科尔可压~*, 半闭式~*, 敞口~open mould, 带槽沟~fluted mould, 废~mould scrap, 瓶口式

~*
锭模安装平台 mould setting platform
锭模壁 ingot mould wall ◇ 皱纹~*
锭模壁斜度 【钢】taper in mould walls
锭模车 mould car [buggy]
锭模吹气[吹氧]铸造法 【冶】quasi-Bessemerizing
锭模底板准备车间(下铸用) bottom plate preparation shop
锭模堆放场 mould storage garage
锭模翻转 mould trunover
锭模分离装置 ingot withdrawing device
锭模工作条件 mould conditions
锭模龟裂痕(钢锭缺陷) 【钢】crazing
锭模浇铸 【钢】direct casting
锭模内垫板 bottom plate
锭模内钢液面控制 mould level control
锭模内脱氧 deoxidation in ingot mould
锭模设计 mould design
锭模台车 mould car
锭模涂料 mould coating material, mould dressing
锭模涂油 mould coating
锭模涂油工段 mould-coating yard
锭模小车 【铸】bogie
锭模振动法 lash
锭模砖(保温帽用) 【钢】mould brick
锭模装置 mould setting
锭模装置平台 mould setting platform
锭模准备工段 mould preparation yard
锭模准备工段跨 mould preparation bay
锭模准备平台 【色】mould preparation stand
锭模准备作业线 mould preparation line
锭凝固 ingot solidification
锭坯 ingot blank, cake slab, 【色】cake ◇ 热轧铜板[铜带]用~copper wedge cake
锭坯感应加热炉 induction-heated billet furnace
锭钳 pig tongs, ingot dogs
锭身(保温帽以下部分) 【钢】chill
锭铁 ingot iron

锭铜 ingot copper
锭头 (ingot) butt, head of ingot, ingot stub,【钢】head ◇ 切除~【压】ingot topping
锭头废料 top discard
锭头切除不足 insufficient cropping
锭尾 butt
锭型偏析 pattern segregation
锭形 ingot shape
锭渣皮 ingot scum
锭子油 spindle oil
锭座(送锭车的) ingot pot (翻斗), ingot chair, cradle
定比 definite proportion
定比定律 【化】law of definite proportion
定比化合物 daltonide (compound)
定比例 scaling
定边坡 benching
定标 scaling, calibration, graduation
定标电路 scaling circuit
定标器 scaler, calibrator
定波 standing [stationary] wave
定尺长度 (specific) cut length, specified [exact] length ◇ 飞剪剪切后的~
定尺挡板 length stop,【压】(剪切机的) gauge stop, measuring gauge ◇ 剪切机活动~, 剪切机移动~辊道【压】shear-gauge table, 移动~
定尺机 (length) shear gauge
定尺机挡板 【压】gauge head
定尺剪切 【压】shear [cut] to length
定尺剪切长度 specific cut length
定尺剪切机 length shear gauge
定尺剪切数字调节 cut-length numeric regulation
定尺剪切作业线(带材的) cut-to-length (shear) line ◇ 热~【机组】hot dividing line
定尺锯 【压】cut-to-length saw
定尺切割 【压】dividing ◇ 棒材~ bar dividing
定尺切削 cutting to length

定尺台 【压】gauge stand [table]
定尺型材 【压】cut-to-length sections
定尺指示器(剪切机的) shear-gauge length indicator
定尺座 【压】gauge stand
定氮仪 azotometer
定点部分 【计】fixed point part
定点计算 【计】fixed point calculation
定点计算机 fixed point computer
定点式火焰淬火法 spot method of flame hardening
定点小数 【计】fractional fixed point
定点运算 【计】fixed point operation [arithmetic]
定额 quota, norm, standard, rate, rating
定额-工时测定员 【企】time-study man
定额流动资金 【企】quota circulating fund
定额消耗 rated consumption
定额制订(劳动定额制订) rate fixing
定额制度 system of rating
定颚 stationary [fixed] jaw
定方等分直径 Martin diameter
定方位 orientation, interception
定公差切割 cut to tolerance
定滑轮 fixed [dead] pulley
定货 order ◇ 紧急~ rush order
定货单 order (form)
定货清单[明细表] customer specification
定货设计的 customed-designed
定货(重)量 ordered weight
定积分 definite integral
定角度内反射元件 fixed angle internal reflection element
定径[管材定径] 【压】sizing
定径淬火 plug quenching
定径带测量仪(拉模的) 【压】zetmeter
定径道次(管材的) sizing pass
定径辊 【压】sizing [size] roll
定径机 【压】sizer, sizing mill [stand] ◇ 回转~ rotary sizer, 脱管~ fine quality sizing (F.Q.S)
定径机组 sizing block

定径区长度(拉模圆柱形部分) 【压】bearing length (of die)
定径区研磨(拉模的) 【压】bearing lap
定径式无漩涡水口 【连铸】calibrated nonswirl nozzle
定径水口 【钢】fixed diameter nozzle, nozzle of constant diameter, sizing nozzle ◇ 锆质~ zircon sizing nozzle
定径压力机 【压】sizing press ◇ 管端~ tube end sizing press
定径轧机 precision mill, sizing rolling mill
定径装置 【压】sizing device
定距(隔)板 distance plate
定距环 distance ring [collar]
定距片 distance [spacing] piece
定理 theorem, dogma, maxim ◇ 玻耳兹曼~ Boltzmann's theorem, 能斯脱~*
定量 quantification, norm, dose
定量泵 constant delivery pump
定量测定 quantitative determination [measurement]
定量沉淀 quantitative precipitation
定量电视显微镜 quantitative television microscope (Q.T.M.), quantimet
定量阀 metering valve
定量反应 quantitative reaction
定量分析 quantitative analysis, quantification
定量给料机 constant(-weight) feeder ◇ 皮带秤式~*
定量给油阀(双线干油润滑系统的) dua-line valve
定量浇铸 constant quantity casting
定量金相学 quantitative metallography
定量滤纸 quantitative (filter) paper
定量器 proportioner
定量试验 quantitative test
定量图像分析仪 quantimet
定量显微分析 quantitative microanalysis
定量型控制器 batch type controller
定量研究 quantitative investigation
定零点 zeroing

定铝传感器[测头] aluminium probe [sensor]
定律 law, principle, rule ◇ 比尔~*, 波义耳-查理~*, 伯努利~ Bernoulli's law, 布拉格~*, 布儒斯特~ Brewster's law, 查理~【理】Charles' law, 杜隆-珀蒂~ Dulong-Pitit's law, 范托夫~*, 菲克~ Fick's (diffusion) law, 费伽~ Vegard's law, 盖-吕萨克~ Gay-Lussac's law, 赫斯~*, 黑格~【金】Haegg's law, 亨利~ Henry's law, 胡克~ Hooke's law, 基尔霍夫~ Kirchhoffs law, 居里~*, 柯诺瓦洛夫~*, 拉乌尔~ Raoult's law, 兰伯特~*, 理查德~*, 莫斯利~ Moseley's law, 诺德海姆~【理】Nordheim's rule, 斯蒂芬-波尔兹曼~*, 斯托克斯~*, 维德曼-弗兰茨~*, 乌里弗-布拉格~ Wulff-Bragg's law, 西韦茨~*
定模(压铸机的) mould cover half, cover die
定模板 【铸】solid plate
定模固定半型(压铸的) 【铸】cover half
定模拟比例因子 【计】analog scaling
定膨胀合金 controlled expansion coefficient alloy
定片 stator
定期付款 payment on terms
定期检查 periodic(al) check [inspection]
定期检修[维修] periodic inspection and repair, regular [routine, periodic, scheduled] maintenance, regular overhauling
定期检修进度表 preventive maintenance schedule
定期试验 routine [periodic] test
定期修理 preventive overhaul, periodic repair
定容量泵(油泵) fixed delivery [displacement] pump
定时 timing ◇ 普通~淬火*
定时错误 【计】timing error
定时电路 timing circuit
定时断路器[定时停车] time cut-out

定时供暖	discontinuous heating
定时机构	timing mechanism
定时继电器	time [timing] relay, definite time relay, timer
定时开关	time switch
定时控制	timing control
定时脉冲发生器	timing pulse generator
定时门电路[定时选通脉冲]	time gate
定时器[装置]	timer, timing device [unit], intervalometer ◇ 减震器[缓冲筒]式~ dashpot-type timer, 控制~ control timer
定时器时钟	【计】time(r) clock
定速加载试验装置	loading pacer
定速应变试验装置	strain pacer
定速装置	pacer
定碳	【钢】carbon determinations ◇ 埃格特快速~法 Eggert's test, 巴雷塔氧化钡吸收~法 Baryta process, 快速硝酸[比色]~法 colour carbon, 燃烧[钢样氧燃]~法 Strohlein method, 索维尔~图*, 液线[凝点,结晶]~*
定碳仪	【钢】carbometer, carbon analyser, carbanalyzer ◇ 电磁~ carba-nalyzer, 电阻~*
定位	location, position, anchor, fix, allocation, spotting
定位板	location-plate, master plate
定位臂	【计】access arm
定位变量	【计】locator variable
定位槽	locating slot
定位槽平台	dowel plate
定位钢筋	spacer bar
定位工序	settling operation
定位焊	fixed position welding, tacking, tack welding
定位焊点	tacked spot
定位焊缝	tack
定位焊机	tack welder
定位焊接	positioned welding
定位焊用夹具	tack-welding jig
定位环	locating [holding, stop(per)] ring
定位环冲子	【压】locating center punch
定位极化	orientation(al) polarization
定位计数器	location counter
定位夹具	positioning fixture
定位键	adjusting [positioning] key
定位孔	location hole
定位控制	constant position control
定位框	【铸】centring frame
定位螺钉	positioning [set, check, fixing] screw
定位螺栓	positioning bolt
定位铆	tack
定位铆钉	tack(ing) rivet ◇ 临时~ dummy rivet
定位器	locator, positioner, retainer ◇ 放射性同位素~ radioisotope posi-tioner, 无线电~ radiolocator
定位停止	constant position stop
定位销	locating [set, guide, retention, steady] pin, pilot pin (薄板冲模上的), adjusting key, 【铸】(砂箱的) fixed (moulding box) pin, dowel ◇ 插入式~*, 带~的砂箱 flask with pin holders, 方榫~*, 合型~(砂箱的)【铸】closing pin
定位销钉	stop dowel, tommy ◇ 模型~ pattern dowel
定位销合模	dowel pin die fixture
定位芯	marking core
定位仪	position indicator ◇ 带材边缘~ scanning recorder
定位轴承	locating bearing
定位桩	【建】guide [nose] pile
定位装置	positioner, positioning [locating] device, aligning guide ◇ 卷材【压】~ coil positioner
定位锥	locating cone
定线(测量)	aligning
定线杆[桩]	setting-out rod
定相(定相位关系)	phasing
定相装置	phasing device
定向	orient(ation) ◇ 不~的 non-direc-

定向波束　direct(ional) beam
定向成核理论　oriented nucleation theory
定向传播　guided propagation
定向反射　direct reflection
定向分布　guided propagation
定向辐射　directional [directed] radiation ◇ 直接~ head on radiation
定向(辐)射线　directed rays
定向继电器　directional relay
定向键　directional bond
定向接地继电器　directional ground relay
定向结合　directional bond
定向结晶　directed crystallization, directional solidification
定向晶体　directional crystals
定向扩展　guided propagation
定向凝固　directional solidification [freezing], controlled freezing ◇ 镍钴~共晶合金
定向凝固方法　directional solidification method
定向凝固原位成形复合材料　directionally solidified in-situ composite
定向凝固设备(熔析精炼用)　apparatus for directional solidification
定向疲劳性能　directional fatigue property
定向提纯　directional purification
定向天线馈电线　beam antenna [aerial] feeder
定向芯头　【铸】core print with register
定向形核理论　oriented nucleation theory
定向氧化　directed oxidation
定向长大理论　【金】oriented growth theory
定向照明配件　directional lighting fittings
定斜度规　batter rule [gauge]
定心　centering, alignment ◇ 用气焰割炬~(用于钢坯) torch centring
定心辊　(同"对中辊")
定心环[圈]　centring ring
定心机(管坯的)　centring machine ◇ 钢坯气动~ air hammer, 液压~*
定心台　centring table
定心弯曲成形(直缝焊管的)　centre bending forming
定心压力机(斜轧穿孔前的)　centre press
定心圆锥式开卷机　cone-type feed [payoff] reel, cone-type uncoiler
定心造型机　【铸】centring moulding machine
定心针　centring pin
定型板　【铸】solid plate, front plate (压铸机的)
定型底板　【铸】fixed plate
定型工具(锤头上的)　fast tool
定型模(锻件的)　fast tool
定型试验　type test
定性测定　qualitative determination [measurement]
定性分析　qualitative analysis
定性检验　qualitative test
定性评价　qualitative evaluation
定性研究　qualitative investigation
定性应变图样　qualitative strain pattern
定序器　【计】sequencer
定压燃烧　(同"恒压燃烧")
定氧　oxygen determination ◇ 直接~技术
定氧测头[传感器]　oxygen probe [sensor]
定氧分析　oxygen analysis
定义　definition (df, def.)
定影　fixation, fixing
定影剂　fixative, fixer, fixing agent
定域电子模型　localized electron model
定员　manning levels, complement, personnel
定则　rule ◇ 布喇菲－唐尼－哈克~*, 洪德~*, 马蒂森~【理】Mattiessen's rule, 休姆－罗瑟里~【理】Hume-Rothery's rule
定值　constant [definite] value, rate
定值监控　set point control (SPC)

定制的 ordered ◇ 按设计尺寸[专门]~ tailor-made
定制的机器(用户定制的) custom-build machine
定中线 alignment
定中心 centring
定子 stator
定子电势定向 stator electromotive force orientation
定子温度指示器 temperature indicator for stator
定做的 purpose made (p.m.)
订合同 contract
丢弃 throw-over, discard
东南亚钢铁协会 Southeast Asia Iron and Steel Institute (SEAISI)
冬季浇灌混凝土 winter concreting
冬季施工 【建】winter construction, cold weather construction ◇ 建筑物~
氡壳电子 radon core electrons
动靶 X 射线发生器 moving-target generator
动靶 X 射线管 moving-target X-ray tube
动臂回转角(起重机的) angle of boom
动臂起重机 gib [swing] crane
动车时间 【铸】track time
动齿条(冷床的) carry-over bar
动磁场 travelling magnetic field
动磁式仪表 moving magnet instrument
动带 moving belt
动带接触器(萃取的) moving-belt contactor
动电电流 galvanic current
动电荷 moving charges
动电势[位] electrokinetic potential
动电位的 potentiodynamic
动电现象 electrokinetic phenomenon
动电学 electrokinetics
动断触点 【电】(normally) closed contact
动颚 movable jaw
动负载 dynamic(al) load(ing)
动刚度 dynamic rigidity [stiffness]
动荷重 brunt, moving load
动荷重塑性 dynamic ductility
动合触点 【电】(normally) open contact, front contact
动滑轮 movable pulley
动畸变 dynamical distortion
动胶菌属 zoogloea
动力 (motive) power, motive [moving] force ◇ 有质~ pondero-motive force
动力苯 motor benzol
动力车间 power plant (P.P.), power room (P.R.), powerhouse
动力冲程 power stroke
动力传感器 dynamic pickup
动力传感器系统 load cell system
动力锤 power hammer ◇ 燃气~
动力电路 power circuit
动力法(震动,振打)捣实 kinetic ramming
动力反应堆 power reactor
动力钢筋弯曲机 power bar bender
动力缸 power cylinder
动力工程 power engineering
动力过滤 dynamic filtration
动力计算 power calculation
动力矩 dynamic torque
动力锯床 power saw
动力流体 power fluid
动(力)黏度 kinetic viscosity
动力平衡叶轮 dynamically balanced impeller
动力驱动的 power-operated, power-driven
动力燃料 energy-producing fuel
动力设备 power equipment
动力生产 power generation
动力师 powerman
动力试验硬度 dynamic hardness
动力水 power water
动力损失 loss in [of] power
动力特性 dynamic behaviour [property]
动力推进 power feed

动力系统	power system
动力限度	margin of power
动力消耗	power (supply) consumption, energy consumption, power expenditure
动力消耗指示器	power consumption indicator
动力需要量	energy requirement
动力学	dynamics, kinetics ◇ 吸附~ adsorption kinetics
动力学分析	kinetic analysis
动力学理论	dynamical [kinetic] theory
动力学模型	kinetic model
动力学强度	dynamic strength
动力学试验	dynamic test(ing)
动力学特性	kinetic characteristics
动力学条件	dynamic conditions
动力学性质	dynamical property
动力学允许的速度场	kinematically admissible velocity field
动力学指数	kinetic index
动力应力	【压】dynamic stress
动力应力-应变曲线	dynamic stress-strain curve
动力应力测量	dynamic stress measurement
动力硬度	dynamic hardness
动力用燃料	power fuel
动力站	power station
动力制动	【电】dynamic braking
动力制动电阻器	dynamic braking resistor
动力制动器	dynamic brake (DB)
动力中断	power break-down
动力中心	power center
动力装置	power set [equipment, installation, pack, unit]
动力资源	energy resources
动梁	movable [walking] beam ◇ 鞍(座)形~ *, 平板架型~ *
动量	momentum ◇ 费米~【理】Fermi momentum
动量变换	momentum transfer
动量传递系数	coefficient of momentum transfer
动量传输	momentum transfer
动量交换	momentum transfer
动量矩	angular momentum, moment of momentum
动量空间	momentum space, k space
动模(压铸机的)	ejector die
动模铸锭机	moving mould casting machine
动模铸造法	moving (mould) casting process
动摩擦	【理】dynamical [kinetic] friction
动能	kinetic energy
动片	moving plate
动片法	moving film method
动平衡	dynamic balancing
动圈(式)	moving coil
动圈式电流[安培]计	moving coil galvanometer [ammeter]
动圈式继电器	moving coil relay
动圈式仪表	moving coil (type) instrument [meter] ◇ 永磁~ *
动圈式转矩电动机	moving coil type torque motor
动态表面电位	dynamic surface potential
动态层	dynamic bed
动态沉降	dynamic settling
动态程序置换	【计】dynamic program relocation
动态处理	【计】dynamic handling
动态传感器	dynamic pickup
动态床	moving bed
动态床反应器	moving-bed reactor
动态床反应器装置	moving-bed reactor system
动态床还原	moving-bed reduction
动态床还原反应器	reduction moving-bed reactor
动态床离子交换设备	moving-bed ion-exchange plant
动态磁导率	dynamic permeability
动态磁滞回线	dynamic hysteresis loop

动态淬火 dynamic quenching [hardening]
动态存储分配 【计】dynamic memory [storage, core] allocation
动态存储器 dynamic memory [storage]
动态存储重新分配 【计】dynamic memory relocation
动态存取【计】 dynamic access
动态错误 【计】dynamic error
动态打印输出 【计】dynamic print-out
动态地址转换器 【计】dynamic address translator
动态电极电势 dynamic E.P.
动态电容 dynamic capacity
动态电容器 dynamic condenser
动态调度 【计】dynamic scheduling
动态断裂韧性 dynamic fracture toughness
动态断裂性能试验 dynamic fracture performance
动态法 dynamic method
动态范围 【计】dynamic range
动态分配程序(内存的) 【计】dynamic allocator
动态腐蚀 dynamic corrosion
动态腐蚀试验 dynamic corrosion test
动态覆盖 【计】dynamic overlay
动态负载 dynamic load, brunt
动态刚性 dynamic rigidity [stiffness]
动态固结 dynamic consolidation
动态规划 【计】dynamic programming (D.P.)
动态规划寻优原理 optimum principle of dynamic programming
动态厚度变换 【压】dynamic gauge changing, gauge change "on the fly"
动态后援系统 【计】dynamic support system (D.S.S.)
动态缓冲 【计】dynamic buffering
动态挤列[挤子] dynamic crowdion
动态校验[检查,检验] dynamic check
动态校准[检定] dynamic calibration
动态介电常数[动态电容率] dynamic dielectric constant
动态控制 dynamic control
动态流程图 【计】dynamic flow diagram
动态漏损[漏泄]测量 dynamic leakage measurement
动态漏泄[漏气]试验 dynamic leak test
动态模数 dynamic modulus
动态模型 dynamic model
动态偏差 dynamic deviation
动态频率特性 dynamic frequency characteristic
动态平衡 dynamic(al) [mobile] equilibrium, dynamic [running] balance, homeostasis(自动调节的)
动态破断应力 dynamic breaking stress
动态强度 dynamic strength
动态屈服应力 dynamic yielding stress
动态蠕变 dynamic creep
动态烧结模型 【团】dynamic sintering model
动态设定型 AGC dynamic setting AGC
动态试验 dynamic test(ing)
动态速降(轧机咬钢时电动机的) impact speed drop
动态弹性 dynamic elasticity
动态弹性极限 dynamic elastic limit
动态特性 dynamic behaviour [charateristics, performance]
动态停机 【计】dynamic stop
动态稳定性 dynamic(al) stability [equilibrium]
动态响应特性 dynamic response
动态效应 dynamic(al) influence
动态寻优搜索方法 search technique for dynamic self-optimization
动态压缩试验 dynamic compression test
动态应变 dynamic strain
动态优先级 【计】dynamic priority
动态指令 【计】dynamic instruction
动态转储 【计】dynamic dump
动态子程序 【计】dynamic subroutine
动铁 moving iron

动铁式安培计	moving iron ammeter
动铁式继电器	moving iron relay
动铁式仪表	moving iron (type) instrument [meter], moving magnet instrument
动位错	moving dislocation
动物胶	animal glue
动物油	animal [tallow] oil
动物脂	tallow
动线	generatrix
动效应	dynamic(al) influence
动型(压铸机的)	【铸】ejector half
动压力	velocity pressure
动载(荷)	dynamic(al) load ◇往复～试验机*
动载应变时效	【金】dynamic strain aging
动作	behaviour, action, actuation, play, work
动作机构	actuating mechanism
动作信号	actuating signal
冻结	freeze, ice, jellification, 【金】frozen in, 【铁】freeze up, gobbed-up (坐料, 高炉炉缸故障)
冻结出铁口	【铁】hard hole
冻结分布(缺陷低温的)	frozen in distribution
冻结炉底	【冶】plated hearth
冻结水银模(精密)铸造法(与蜡模铸造相同, 用凝固汞作模型)	【铸】mercast process, frozen mercury investment casting process, frozen mercury pattern method
冻结温度	solidification point, freezing in temperature
冻结物(炉内或桶内的)	frost
冻结线	freezing curve
冻结周期	freezing cycle
冻结铸造法	【铸】freeze casting
冻结状态	【计】freeze mode
冻解试验	freezing and thawing test
冻融循环	cycle of freezing and thawing
冻熔技术	freeze-melt technique
冻土带	tundra
冻线深度	depth of frost line
冻渣	dross slag
冻胀(道路的)	frost boil
冻住	【金】frozen in
洞	hole, cavity, excavation
洞室[穴]	cave, 【地】grotto
洞隙	miarolitic
抖掉	shake-out
抖动	shake
抖纹(内缺陷)	【压】jarring mark
抖箱	【铸】sand strip, shake-out
斗槽式提升机	paternoster elevator
斗车	hopper car
斗底车	larry
斗链式提升机	girdle pocket elevator
斗轮	bucket wheel
斗轮机	bucket wheel machine
斗轮式堆取料机	wheel-on-boom stacker/reclaimer, combination bucket-wheel stacker-reclaimer ◇支臂～*
斗轮式取料机	wheel-on-boom reclaimer, bucket wheel reclaimer ◇行桥～*
斗轮式挖泥机	wheel dredger
斗轮挖掘机	bucket wheel excavator (B.W.E.)
斗子给料机	skip-type feeder
斗式升降机	elevator bucket, dump skip
斗式输送[运输]机	bucket conveyor
斗式提升机	bucket elevator [hoist, loader], pocket elevator
斗式提升机链条	bucket chain
斗式脱水机	drag dewaterer
斗式挖泥船	bucket dredger
斗式挖泥机	bucket trenching machine, bucket [scoop] dredger
斗式挖土机	bucket excavator
斗式卸料机	bucket unloader
陡变	abrupt change
陡度	steepness
陡度调整	slope control
陡坡	steep slope [pitch], abrupt slope
陡峭曲线	high curve

陡梯度　steep gradient
豆砾石　pea gravel
豆石　pisolite
痘痕(不锈钢退火缺陷)　【金】pockmark
毒度　toxicity
毒害[毒化]　poisoning
毒气[毒性气体]　(toxic, poisonous) gas
毒气防御　gas defense
毒气警报(信号)　gas alarm
毒砂　(同"砷黄铁矿")
毒素　toxin
毒铁矿　cube ore, arsenicated iron ore
毒铁石　pharmacosiderite
毒物　poison, toxic material, 【环】toxicant
毒性　toxicity, toxic property, poisonousness ◇慢性~【环】chronic toxicity
毒性当量　toxic equivalent (TEQ)
毒性硫化氢　toxic hydrogen sulphide
毒性水流　toxic stream
毒性[毒物]危害　toxicity hazard
毒重石{BaCO₃}　witherite
独或元件(射流技术的)　exclusive or amplifier
独居石{(Ce,La,Nd,Th)PO₄}　monazite (roke) ◇艾姆斯试验室~处理法 Ames monazite process
独居石分解　monazite breakdown
独居石硫酸盐溶液　monazite sulphate solution
独居石氯化　chlorination of monazite
独居石砂{(Ce,La,Y,Th)PO₄}　monazite sand
独立操作　independent operation
独立倒流休风(不经热风炉的)　【铁】independent backdraft
独立核算工业企业　independent accounting industrial enterprise
独立立辊轧机[独立轧边机]　detached edger
独立式(炉体钢结构)　【铁】free standing type
独立托圈(转炉的)　【钢】separate ring
独立系统　autonomous system
独立装置　【计】autonomous devices
独立组分　independent component
独联体　Commonwealth of Independent States (CIS)
独石柱　monolith
独通道操作　【计】autonomous channel operation
读出　readout, reading (rdg), 【计】sense
读出电路　sensing [readout] circuit
读出度[能力]　readabity
读出开关　【计】sense switch
读出器　reader
读出时间　read(-out) time
读出式仪表　reading instrument
读出误差　read-out error
读出线　【计】sense wire
读出装置　【计】reader, read out device
读脉冲　read pulse
读入解释器　reader/interpreter
读数　reading (rdg), indication, registration ◇近似(粗略)~rough reading
读数不正确的(指仪表读数)　foul
读数精确度　accuracy of reading
读数灵敏度　sensitiveness of reading
读数偏差　reading variation
读数器　transcribor
读数误差　read(ing) error
读数装置　reading device [unit]
读头　【计】read [playback] head
读图器　【计】graph follower
读写　【计】read-write ◇开始~点 load point, 同时~writing while read
读写磁头　magnetic read/write head
读写记数器　read/write counter
读写校验　read/write check
读写通道　read/write channel
读写头　read/write (combined) head, write read head
堵板　closure plate, stopper plug
堵出钢口　botting
堵(出)铁[渣]口　botting, plugging, stop-

ping-up

堵(出)铁口机 【铁】taphole stopping machine

堵出铁口泥 【铁】taphole mix [loam], ball stuff ◇ 低湿度~·

堵(出)铁口泥炮 【铁】tap(hole) gun

堵出铁[渣]口时间 [plugging period

堵风口 plugging tuyere

堵缝 caulking

堵缝麻絮 【建】caulker's oakum

堵口杆[棒] 【钢】bot(t) stick

堵口料 stopping material

堵口泥 taphole clay [loam, mix], stopping clay [mix], tapping (hole) clay[mix]

堵口钎子 【钢】taphole rammer

堵口塞杆 【铁】taphole plug stick

堵料 plugging

堵塞 blinding, blind plug, blockage, block up, clogging, filling in, obstru-ction, plugging, choke (孔型的) ◇ 筛孔~blinding of screen, 锥形~cut-off conical plug

堵塞处[点] blind spot

堵塞管缝 caulking of tubes

堵塞[头]螺钉 plug screw

堵砂 【铸】hand-up

堵水不良 water shut off not good (W.S.O.N.G)

堵水良好 water shut off okay (W.S.O.O.K.)

堵死 blinding

堵头 【冶】bed plate, tapping pin (铝热剂坩埚放出口的)

堵眼 botting

堵渣机操纵机构 【铁】bott operating mechanism

堵渣口块 cinder block

堵住出铁口 【铁】plugged [stopped] taphole

杜安-亨特极限 Duane-Hunt limit

杜尔赫特抗蠕变钢(1Cr,0.3Mo) Durehete

杜尔柯耐热耐蚀镍铬合金 Durco (Durco D - 10: 57Ni, 23Cr, 8Cu, 4Mo, 2W, 1Mn)

杜尔纳黄铜(40Zn, 0.35Fe, 0.42Mn, 1Sn, 余量 Cu) Durna metal

杜尔西利厄姆铝合金(4Cu, 0.5Mg, 0.5Mn, 余量 Al) Durcilium

杜菲利特液体渗碳渗氮剂(70—80BaCl₂, 25—15NaCN, 5SrCl₂) Duerferrit

杜弗莱克思格子砖系统(热风炉的) Duoflex checker system

杜科尔低锰合金结构钢 Ducol steel

杜拉尔普拉特镁合金双面包覆硬铝板(包层为 1%—3% Mg 的铝镁合金) Duralplat

杜拉弗莱克斯青铜(5Sn, 余量 Cu) Duraflex

杜拉克锌基合金(4.1Al, 1Cu, 0.03 - 0.06Mg, 余量 Zn) Durak alloy

杜拉克锌基压铸合金 Durak (Mazak 5 的代用品)

杜拉铝 (同"硬铝") ◇ 生[铸造]~cast duralumin

杜拉铝镁铜合金 duralum

杜拉洛依耐蚀耐热铬钢 Duraloy (Duraloy A: 27—30Cr, 0.5Mn, 0.2—1C; Duraloy B: 16—18Cr, 0.5Mn, <0.2C)

杜拉纳高强度黄铜 Durana (64.78Cu, 29.5Zn, 2.22Sn, 1.71Fe, 1.7Al), Durana me-tal (65Cu, 30n, 2Sn, 1.5Fe, 1.5Al)

杜拉内尔不锈钢-铝复合板 Duranel

杜拉尼克铝镍锰轻合金(2Mn, 4Ni, 余量 Al) Duranic

杜拉镍合金(0.02Cu, 0.2Fe, 0.2Si, 0.2Mn, 余量 Ni) Z-nickel

杜拉帕姆(硅铝铁)合金(9.5Si, 6Al, 84.5Fe) Duraperm

杜拉钼铬硅合金铸铁(2C, 1.25Si, 3Cr, 5Mo, 余量 Fe) Durachome

杜雷克斯多孔石墨青铜(10Sn, 4—5 石墨, 余量 Cu) Durex bronze

杜雷克斯多孔铁(0—2Cu, 余量 Fe)

杜雷克斯含油轴承(烧结合金;10Sn,4.5石墨,余量Cu) Durex
杜雷克斯含油轴承烧结合金 Durex bearing alloy
杜里龙耐酸铸铁(15Si,0.75C) Duriron
杜里米特奥氏体不锈钢(<0.07C,29Ni,20Cr,2.5Mo,3.5Cu,1Si) Durimet
杜利特 A-40LC 多孔阴离子交换树脂 Duolite A-40LC
杜利特 A-42 强碱性阴离子交换树脂 Duolite A-42
杜利特 C-10 磺酚阳离子交换树脂 Duolite C-10
杜利特 C-20 磺化聚苯乙烯阳离子交换树脂 Duolite C-20
杜利特 C-25 磺化聚苯乙烯阳离子交换树脂 Duolite C-25
杜利特 C-3 磺酚阳离子交换树脂 Duolite C-3
杜利特 CS-100 羧酸阳离子交换树脂 Duolite CS-100
杜利特 S-30 多孔阴离子交换树脂 Duolite S-30
杜利特弱碱性阴离子交换树脂 Duolite (A-2,A-7,A-14 等)
杜龙兹硅青铜(97Cu,1—3Si,0—2Sn) Duronze
杜隆－珀蒂定律 Dulong-Pitit's law
杜罗伊德(碳铬)合金钢(表面堆焊材料) Duroid
杜美包铜铁镍合金丝[杜美(合金)丝,杜美低膨胀系数线材合金](42Ni,58Fe,玻璃－金属封接材料) Dumet wire (alloy), Dumet
杜蒙德聚焦法 【理】Du Mond method of focusing
杜蒙德摄谱仪 Du Mond spectrograph
杜佩伊直接炼铁法 Dupey process
杜普勒镜用合金(80Ag,20Zn) Duppler's alloy
杜瓦(真空)瓶 Dewar (vacuum) flask, Dewar vesse, Dewar's bottle
杜威勒旋转[回转]浇铸法 Durville casting [pouring, process]
杜仲树胶 gutta-percha
镀斑 uncoated spot
镀铂 platinizing, platinization
镀铂碳电极 platinized carbon electrode
镀铂铜 platinum-plated copper
镀槽 coating bath
镀层 coat(ing), plating, cladding, coverage ◇ 薄~*,差厚~ differential coating, 除去~ deplating, 多层~*, 过烧~*, 晶体~ crystalline coating, 局部~*, 熔烧~ fused coating, 无~管 black pipe, 阳极~*, 置换法~*
镀层表面铬酸盐钝化处理 chromate coating treatment
镀层测厚仪 coating thickness gauge [meter]
镀层钢板 clad steel sheet, coated steel
镀层[镀覆]厚度 coating [plating] thickness ◇ 气刀~控制装置*
镀层厚度检验 plating-thickness inspection
镀层黏附力 coating adhesion
镀层软熔塔 melted coat tower
镀层下腐蚀 poultice corrosion
镀层修整 plated finish
镀层阳极溶解法 anodic stripping
镀层重量试验 coating weight test
镀层组分 coating constituent
镀敷浸出(高压优先还原法) plating leach
镀覆 plating, applying ◇ 断续电流~*, 机械~ mechanical plating, 接触法~ contact plating, 两次~ double plating, 热喷~ fused coating, 铁表面~铅锡合金法*, 蒸发~*
镀覆材料 coating material
镀覆脆性 plating brittleness
镀覆合金 plating alloy
镀覆机组作业线(板、带材的) plating

镀覆速率 plating rate
镀覆装置 plater
镀镉 cadmium plating ◇ 滚镀法~*
镀镉钢 cadmium-plated steel
镀铬 chrome-plating, chromium coating [plating], chromalizing, chromalloying, chroming ◇ 电~钢*,二次[重复]~ after-chroming,光亮~ bright chromium plating,豪斯纳高频~法 Hausner process,浸~*,克罗纳克锌[镁]合金表面化学~法 Cronak process,扩散~*,两次~*,磨光~*,热~ hot chromizing,乳白~表面 milky surface,无光泽~ matte chromium plating,装饰性~*
镀铬钢 chromized [chromium-plated] steel
镀铬结晶器(内表面镀铬) chrome-plated mould
镀铬铝 chrome aluminizing
镀铬模 chromium-plated die
镀铬设备[工段] chrome-plating plant
镀铬硬化的 chromium-hardened
镀钴 cobalt plating
镀合金 alloy coating [plating]
镀黑铬 black chromium plating
镀黑镍 black nickel plating
镀黑色层 black plating
镀黄铜 brass plating, brassing, braze over
镀黄铜用电解液 brass plating solution
镀黄铜用黄铜阳极 brass plater
镀金 gold plating, goldplate, gild(ing) ◇ 电~*,火法~ fire gilding,(热)浸[化学置换法]~*
镀金的 gold-cased, goldplated, gilt
镀金工 gilder
镀金黄铜 talmi gold
镀金机 gilding machine
镀金属 metal(lic) coating ◇ 扩散~法*
镀金属玻璃 metallized glass
镀金属的 metal-coated, plated
镀金属晶体 metal-plated crystal
镀金属器 metallizer
镀金用红色[高铜]黄铜合金(85Cu,15Zn) gilding alloy
镀铑(银表面的) rhodanizing
镀铝 aluminizing, aluminising, aluminium coat ◇ 包~法 alumicoat process,浸~dip calorizing,连续~ continuous aluminising,热~层 aluminized coating,热~*
镀铝板 aluminized sheet
镀铝钢 aluminium plated steel
镀铝(镁铍)法 Alplate method
镀铝膜 aluminizer
镀铝生产线 aluminizing line
镀膜机 film plating machine
镀镍 nickelage, nickeling, nickelplate, nickel plating ◇ 超光泽~法*,电~*,非电解[化学]~*,高沉积率~法,光亮~ bright nickel plating,两次~*,磨光~*,尼克雷克斯光泽~法 Nickelex (method),三层~法*
镀镍槽 nickel-plating bath [tank]
镀镍层 nickel coat
镀镍电解液 nickel solution
镀镍钢板 nickel-clad steel plate
镀镍钢丝 nickel-coated steel wire
镀镍钴合金 nickel-cobalt plating
镀镍铁丝 nickel-coated iron wire
镀镍铜 nickel-clad copper
镀铅 lead coating [plating]
镀铅薄钢板 lead-coated sheet, lead-sealed sheet
镀铅槽 lead bath
镀铅钢带 terne-coated strip
镀铅锡合金[镀镴]薄钢板 terne sheet, dull plate ◇ 大张~ long terneplate,经干法擦净的~(用麸糠擦净) dry-finished terneplate,小张~ short terneplate
镀铅锡合金层 terne plating
镀铅锡合金[镀镴]钢板(合金成分: 20Sn,0.2Sb,余量 Pb) terne plate ◇ 油浸过的~ oil finished terneplate

镀 du

镀青铜　bronze plating, bronzing
镀青铜钢　bronze steel
镀钛　titanize, titanizing
镀锑　antimony plating
镀铁　steeling, plating iron
镀铜　copper coating [plating, facing], copper(iz)ing, coppering,【压】(冷加工前的) cuprodine, cuprobond ◇ 渗～copper cementation
镀铜不锈钢丝　copper-coated stainless steel wire
镀铜层　copper facing
镀铜钢板　copper plated steel
镀铜钢丝　coppered wire, copper clad wire, copperweld (wire),【压】weld wire, copperply wire (先镀后拔的)
镀铜设备(钢丝的)　coppering plant
镀铜铁粉　(同"包铜铁粉")
镀铜铁镍合金　dumet
镀铜铁丝　copper coated iron wire
镀铜装置(钢丝的)　coppering plant
镀钍　thoriate
镀钍钨丝　thoriated tungsten wire
镀锡　tinning, tin coating [plating], whiten, blanch(ing) ◇ 带卷～前预整作业线*, 电～*, 接触～(法)*, 冷～cold tinning, 热～hot tin(ning), 未～的 untin-ned
镀锡板斑点(镀锡缺陷)　tinplate patches
镀锡薄板磷酸铬酸盐溶液浸渍保护法　protectatin
镀锡(薄钢)板[薄板,钢板]　tin sheet, tin(ned) plate, tinned steel, tinned sheet iron, taggers tin, canning material ◇ 薄锡层～*, 糙面～grained tinplate, 废～*, 麸痕～*, 厚锡层("炭炼")～*, 花边～scroll tinplate, 极薄～*, 经干法擦净的～(用麸糠擦净) dry-finished plate, 冷轧～cold rolled tin plate, 轻磅～*, 双面～dual-coat plate, 涂漆～*, 无光[毛面]～dull plate, 一级～prime plate, (有)灰斑(缺陷)～dry plate [streak], 有杂斑模纹

的～mottled plate, 罩式退火～*
镀锡薄钢板板坯　tinplate bar
镀锡薄钢板标准面积单位　standard area of tinplate (S.A.T.)
镀锡薄钢板车间　tinplate department
镀锡薄钢板除油辊　tampico rolls
镀锡薄钢板二级品　wasters
镀锡薄钢板精整工段　tin finishing department
镀锡薄钢板切边　tinplate cuttings
镀锡薄钢板轧机　tinplate mill
镀锡薄钢带　tinplate strip
镀锡不锈钢丝　tinned stainless-steel wire
镀锡槽　tin pot, tinning bath [vat]
镀锡槽内的氧化锡　scruff
镀锡层厚度磁性测量计　stannometer
镀锡层黏附(强度)　tin adhesion
镀锡层试验　tin coating test
镀锡车间　tin house, tinning plant
镀锡钢　tin-coated steel
镀锡钢带　tinned strip
镀锡钢丝[导线]　tinned wire
镀锡工　tinner, solderer
镀锡工段　tinning department
镀锡罐　washpot
镀锡辊(板带材的)　tinning roller
镀锡锅　tinning pot
镀锡机　tin machine, tinning unit
镀锡机组　tinning line [stack] ◇ 单锅式～*, 二次～*, 双锅式～*
镀锡金属　tinning metal
镀锡铝线　tinned aluminium wire
镀锡前酸洗(薄板的)　tin pickling
镀锡设备[装置]　tinning stack ◇ 电～*, 自动～*
镀锡铁　tinplate, galvanized iron
镀锡铁板　latten
镀锡铁皮　tinned sheet iron
镀锡铜　tinned copper, tin-coated copper ◇ 乳酪业用～板 dairy copper
镀锡铜丝[线]　tinned copper wire
镀锡线　tinning line

镀锡原板（未镀覆的） uncoated tinplate base

镀锡重量（每箱钢板的） tin coating weight

镀锌 galvanization, galvanizing, galvanising, zinc coat(ing) [plating, cover-ing], zincify, zincing ◇ 布辊擦拭～*,电[冷]～*,非～管 black pipe, 粉末～*,干熔剂～*,厚层～ heavy galva-nizing, 气相～ vapour galvanizing, 热(浸)～*,熔剂～ flux galva-nizing, 砂抹～*,湿法熔剂～ wet galvanizing, 石棉抹～*,西尔弗莱克斯～法*

镀锌板卷 galvanized coil

镀锌薄钢板 galvanized sheet [metal], zinc-coated sheet, galvanized steel (G.S.), galvanized (sheet) iron ◇ 厚锌层～*

镀锌薄钢板厚度号规 galvanized sheet gage (G.S.G.)

镀锌槽 galvanic bath, galvanizing bath [pot], spelter [zinc] bath ◇ 顶部加热～ top-heated galvanizing pot

镀锌槽沉渣 galvanizing dross

镀锌(槽)间 galvanizing(-bath) room

镀锌层 zinc coat ◇ 黄～*

镀锌层测厚仪 zinc coat thickness gauge

镀锌层厚度控制 galvanized coating thick-ness control

镀锌层退火法 galvannealing process

镀锌脆性(脆化) galvanizing (em)brittle-ment

镀锌带钢 galvanized strip

镀锌法[过程] galvanizing process

镀锌钢 galvanized steel

镀锌钢板复合材料 plymetal

镀锌钢材 galvanized iron ◇ 单面～*

镀锌钢管 galvanized (steel) pipe

镀锌钢绞线 galvanized stranded wire

镀锌钢[铁]丝 galvanized (steel) wire, zinc-coated wire, stone wire ◇ 加厚锌层～ double galvanized wire, 可在硫酸溶液中浸渍两分钟的～ two-minute wire, 全～*

镀锌钢丝绳 galvanized steel wire rope (gswr), galvanized wire rope

镀锌工 galvanizer

镀锌工段 galvanizing department

镀锌管 galvanized pipe

镀锌锅 melted zinc bath, zinc pot

镀锌机 galvanizing machine

镀锌机组[装置] galvanizing unit ◇ 带钢连续～*,气刀式～*

镀锌及酸洗的 galvanized and dipped

镀锌炉 galvanizing [zinc-coating] furnace

镀锌熔剂 galvanizing flux

镀锌设备 galvanizing equipment [plant, rig] ◇ 薄板[单张]～*

镀锌铁合金退火薄钢板 Galfan sheet

镀锌铁皮[片] （同"镀锌薄钢板"）

镀锌退火法 galvannealing process

镀锌瓦垄薄(钢)板 galvanized corrugated sheet [steel], corrugated galvanized sheet

镀锌显晶塔 spangle tower

镀锌锌镁合金 zinc magnesium galvaniz-ing alloy

镀锌作业线 galvanizing line ◇ 连续～*

镀银 silvering, silver plating ◇ 电～ elec-trosilvering

镀银槽 silvering bath

镀银层 silver coating

镀银溶液[电解液] silver-plating [silver (ing)] solution

镀银铜 silver plated copper

镀硬铬 hard chrome [chromium] plating, hard plating ◇ 扩散～ hard chromizing

镀硬铬法 merchromizing

镀硬铬活塞杆 hard chromium plated pis-ton rod

度 degree, grade,【数】dimension

度量的 metric

度量分析 measure analysis

度盘 dial, scale ◇ 活动～ movable-scale

度盘刻度 dial scale

度盘式板材测厚仪　dial sheet gauge
度盘式温度计　dial-type thermometer
度谱分析　spectrometric analysis
度数测量　grade measure
渡线　【运】cross over
端板　【机】end plate,【团】(烧结风箱的) dead plate
端包架　【铸】hand shank, bow
端壁　end wall
端部　end, butt, tip
端部加厚管　heavy end tube
端部加料　end charging, end-feed
端部加料正交[纵横]流动区域精炼炉　end-feed cross-flow zone refiner
端部切头(钢锭的)　【钢】top scrap
端部烧焊　boxing
端部烧嘴　end burner
端部卸料[排矿]　end discharge
端部卸载卡车　(同"尾卸卡车")
端部周边焊　boxing
端部周边排料[矿]　end peripheral discharge
端衬板　end-liner
端承口　belingl the ends
端出料(连续加热)炉　end-discharged furnace
端出料加热炉　end pusher furnace, front door furnace
端点效应　end effect
端顶圆周焊缝(压力容器的)　【焊】head seam
端缝螺栓　fox bolt
端盖[罩]　end shield [cap, cover, housing]
端盖衬板　end cover liner
端钩(弹簧的)　end hook
端环　end ring
端际固溶体(多元合金)　【金】terminal solid solution
端际相　terminal phase
端件　tail piece
端接　terminating
端接焊接头　edge joint weld
端接头(焊炬的)　【焊】head tube nipple
端立面　end elevation
端连接　end connection
端梁　end girder
端裂口[纹]　end-splitting
端轮架　end-carriage
端面　end face [surface, plane], abut ◇车~*
端(面,头)淬(火)　end hardening [quenching]
端面滚焊　edge seam welding
端面压力　end pressure
端末插入[砌固]　end built-in
端钮　terminal
端视图　end(-on) view [elevation]
端枢轴承　end (journal) bearing
端填角焊缝　end fillet weld
端头　end, tip, mouthpiece
端头扳直的带卷(送进轧辊前的)　tailed coil
端头车丝试棒　screwed test bar
端头飞剪　flying crop shears ◇转鼓式~*
端头－废料飞剪　【压】crop and cobble flying shears ◇多线式~*
端头－废料剪(切机)　【压】crop and cobble shears ◇单线式~*
端头预加工(管材试验前的)　end conditioning
端隙　end play
端效应　end effect
端卸(的)　end dumping
端卸式送锭车　end-tilt ingot car, end truck front dump type ingot buggy
端支承[支座]　end bearing
端止推轴承　end thrust bearing
端轴承(止推轴承)　dead abutment
端轴颈　(end-)journal
端装料炉　end-charged furnace
端子　terminal, terminating, post, clamp
端子板　terminal board [block, strip]
端子钳间距　electrode opening

短半径[半轴]　semi-minor axis
短棒状石墨　chunky graphite
短柄砂春　【铸】bench rammer, hand rammer
短波　【电】short wave, high frequency wave
短波波长极限　short-wave length limit
短波辐射　short-wave (length) radiation
短程斥力　short-range repulsive force
短程浇铸　short pouring
短程无序　short-range disorder
短程应力　short-range stress
短程有序　short-range order
短程有序参数　short-range order parameter
短程有序点阵[晶格]　short-range order lattice
短程有序度　degree of short-range order
短程有序合金　short-range ordered alloy
短程有序化　short-range ordering
短程有序理论　theory of short-range order
短尺　fall short, off-size,【压】undergauge
短尺板材皮带运输机　【压】short length belt conveyer
短尺棒材　【压】scanty bar
短尺品　【压】short
短尺[等外]轧材　【压】off-gauge material
短冲程控制　short-stroke control
短粗的　blocky
短粗石墨铸铁　vermicular iron
短锭　butt (ingot), ingot butt
短对绞　short pair twist
短钢锭　squat ingot
短钢筋　bar dowl
短钢丝绳　strap
短工　【企】odd man, casual laborer
短工艺流程　simplified process flowsheet
短管　stub, nozzle stub
短弧　short(ing) arc
短弧焊　short arc welding
短划线　dash(ed) line
短环链　pitch chain

短回转炉熔炼　short rotary furnace smelting
短焦距透镜　short-focal(-length) lens
短焦距物镜　short-focus objective
短节距绕组　fractional [short] pitch winding, short-chord winding
短距离移动机构　short shift mechanism
短料　【压】short
短流程　compact processing route, compact process, short route, simplified process flowsheet ◇紧凑式电炉冶金~*
短流程钢厂　mini(-)mill
短流程钢铁生产工艺　short technology process of producing steel manufactures
短流程炼钢工艺　UHP electric furnace-secondary refining-continuous casting process (UHP-CC)
短炉身　short shaft
短路[短接]　short circuit ◇完全~ dead short(-circuit)
短路保护继电器　short circuit relay
短路电弧　short circuiting arc
短路电流　short circuit current
短路方向继电器　directional shortcircuit relay
短路故障　【电】shorts
短路过渡(金属的)　【焊】dip (metal) transfer
短路过渡焊接　dip transfer welding
短路扩散　short circuit diffusion
短路器　short circuiter, plunger, short circuiting switch blade
短路容量　short circuit capacity
短路损耗　short circuit loss
短路线圈测试仪　growler
短期表报　short term reporting
短期非流动债权　【企】short term nonliquid claims
短期工作[职务]　short-time duty
短期蠕变试验(72小时)　time yield
短期生产　short-run production
短期[时间]运转　short-run, short-time

running
短期资产 【企】short term assets
短熔区(区域熔炼的) short (molten) zone
短时出力 intermittent rating
短时工作制电动机 short-hour motor
短时间强照射 acute exposure
短时精确度 short term accuracy
短时拉力试验 short-time tensile test
短时蠕变强度 short-time creep strength
短时蠕变试验 short term creep test ◇巴尔－巴德盖特～*
短时试验特性 【金】short-time properties
短时停车 waiting
短寿命射线 short-lived radiation
短头破碎机 S.H. (short-head) crusher
短头圆锥破碎机 S.H. cone
短途运输 short-distance transport, short haul
短网损失(炼钢电弧炉的) busbar loss
短纤维复合材料 short fibre composite
短纤维金属基复合材料 short fibre metal matrix composite, short fibre MMC
短线产品 undersupplied products, goods in short supply
短线圈无芯感应炉 short-coil coreless induction furnace
短箱档 【铸】chuck
短效黏结剂 fugitive binder
短芯棒拉伸 (同"固定芯棒拉伸")
短型回转窑 short rotary furnace
短行程控制 short-stroke control
短焰煤 short-flame coal
短窑 rotary (smelting) furnace
短窑熔炼 rotary furnace smelting
短应力线轧机 short-stress path mill
短暂负载 short-time duty
短暂浸渍[短时浸洗] brief dipping
短渣(能用水淬裂的渣) 【冶】falling slag
短轴 minor axis, brachydiagonal
短轴半径 minor axis radius
短柱 stub, short column

短柱硫银矿 daleminzite
短铸铁送风管 【铁】penstock
短嘴浇包 top-pour ladle
锻边连接 jump(ed) joint
锻比 ratio of forging reduction
锻扁 malleate, fulling
锻扁锤 stretching hammer
锻长 drawing-out
锻成碟形 dishing
锻锤 forge hammer ◇长导槽～long-channel hammer, 单架式～*, 对击～*, 风动[(压缩)空气]～*, 开坯～cogging hammer, 双锤式～*, 双面～double-faced hammer, 无型[自由]～fore hammer
锻锤锤体 hammer ram
锻锤导轨 hammer guide
锻锤基础 hammer foundation
锻锤夹钳 hammer tongs
锻锤立柱 hammer leg
锻锤汽缸 【机】hammer cylinder
锻点焊 forged spot welding
锻钢 forged steel (F.S.), hammered [tilted, wrought] steel ◇回火～*, 退火～annealed forged steel
锻工 【压】forger, hammerer, hammerman, (hammer) smith, blacksmith
锻工场 smithery
锻工车间 blacksmith shop [house]
锻工冲子 blacksmith punch
锻工锤 (smith's) hammer, mall
锻工工具 blacksmith tool
锻工炉 forge hearth [chimney] ◇铆钉加热用～rivet (heating) forge
锻工钳 smith's [blacksmith] tongs
锻工铁砧 smith's anvil
锻工用尺 hook-and-handle rule
锻工用冲孔器 smith's drift
锻工用穿孔錾 breaking hammer
锻工用甩子 smithing snap
锻工錾[凿] forge [anvil] chisel, breaking down tool

锻焊 forge welding, hammer welding (H.W.), smith-welding, welding by forging ◇ 电阻加热~*,手工~ blacksmith welding
锻焊管 forge welded pipe
锻焊接口操作 scarfing operation
锻焊接头 forge [blacksmith's] weld
锻焊连接 forge welded joint
锻焊熟铁加热炉 fag(g)oting iron furnace
锻焊压力机 fag(g)oting press
锻合金 wrough alloy
锻后余热淬火 forged hardening
锻尖(钢管与棒材端头拉拔前的) tagging, swaging
锻尖机 【压】pointing machine ◇ 回转式~机 pointing swager
锻件 【压】forging, forged piece [product], wrought product, blacksmithing 大[重型]~*,阳模锻出肋条的~ male beaded forging,阴模锻出肋条的~ female beaded forging,中凹~ middle
锻件、轧材和冷拔产品 wrought
锻件剥皮车床 forge lathe
锻件表面凸起部 boss
锻件镦粗 forging upsetting
锻件夹持部分 tong forge
锻件密度 forgings density
锻件刨床(粗加工用) forge planer
锻接 forge [hammer, fire] weld(ing)
锻接焊 forge welding
锻接铝热剂 forging therunit
锻块法(炼镍) 【色】finery [bloomery] process
锻宽锤 peening hammer
锻裂 forging crack
锻裂破断 forge crack failure
锻鳞 forge scale, dross
锻炉 forge furnace
锻铆法 riveting process
锻模 forging die ◇ 闭式[精密]~ close(d) die,挤压~ extrusion-forging die,螺栓~ bolt die,落锤~ drop-forging die

锻模钢 die steel
锻模模座 anvil cap
锻模尾部 die shank
锻模枕 bolster
锻坯 forging stock, half-wrought material
锻坯刨床(粗加工用) forge planer
锻平 fulling, planish
锻伸 forge out
锻铁 wrought iron (W.I.), forge(d) (pig) iron, forge pigs
锻铁炉炉缸 catalan hearth
锻头(拔管前的) cressing
锻透时间 forge [forging] time
锻细 swaging
锻细操作 swaging operation
锻细型锻机 swager
锻压 forge ◇ 多模(腔)[多工位]~*,高能~成形 energy-rate forming,高速~成形 high velocity forming,双动~成形(法) double-action forming
锻压比 ratio of forging reduction
锻压钢轮 wrought-steel wheel
锻压焊 (同"锻焊")
锻压焊缝(焊后锻压的) forged weld
锻压机 forge, forge [forging, hammering] press ◇ 汽动~*
锻压时间 forge time, forge-delay time
锻压试验 forging test
锻压细化(晶粒) hammer refining
锻延 drawing-down
锻冶生铁 forged pig
锻应变 forging strain
锻用钢锭 forging-grade ingot
锻錾 forge [anvil] chisel, hot chisel (热錾用)
锻造 forge, forging, hammering, smithing, blacksmithing, malleate ◇ 拔长~ string forging,爆炸~ explosive forging,闭模~ closed-die forging,标准~ normal forging,雏形~*,多压头~ multiple-ram forging,惰性气体保护~ inert gas forging,工具快速~ fast tool forging,红炉~ smith

forging, 回转～ rotary squeeze, 机械～ mechanical forging, 挤压～ extrusion forging, 精密～*, 空心[中空]～ hollow forging, 扩径～*, becking, 冷态～*, 落锤～ drop forging, 熔融～*, 手工～ hand forging, smith, 无模～ flat die forging, 无斜度～*, 先中部后两端的～ middling(s), 小批量～ short-run forging, 压扁～ flattening forg-ing, 液[水]压～ hydraulic forging, 液体金属～ liquid metal forging, 自由～*.
锻造棒材 bar forging
锻(造,压)比 forge [forging] ratio, forging grade ◇ 起始小～加工(红脆性钢的) nursing, 最低～*
锻造变形 forging strain
锻造操纵[操作]机 forging manipulator
锻造产品 forged product
锻造车间 forge (shop), forging plant [department], smithy
锻造淬火 hammer quenching, ausforging
锻造方法 forging method
锻造废品 forge scrap
锻造工具 forging tool
锻造工具钢 (0.7–1.4C, <0.2Si, <0.35Mn, <0.03P, <0.03S) wrought tool steel
锻造公差 forging [smithing] tolerances ◇ 严格～*
锻造辊 forged roll
锻造焊咀 swaged welding tip
锻造合金 forging alloy ◇ 高强度～*
锻造机 forge, forging machine [press] ◇ 高速～*, 卧式～*, 旋转～(rotary) swager
锻造加工余量 forging envelope
锻造(加热)炉 forging [(drop-) forge] furnace, forge hearth [chimney], smith's hearth ◇ 煤气～ gas forge, 燃煤～ coal forge, 烧油～ oil forge
锻造加热炉温度记录控制器 forge master

锻造开坯 hammer cog(ging)
锻造力 forging force
锻造裂纹 forge crack
锻造流线 forged fibre flow
锻造铝合金 (同"形变铝合金")
锻造毛坯 forging stock, slug, rough forging
锻造密度 forged density
锻造时锻件直径的变化 set down
锻造术 blacksmithery
锻造水压机 forging pump press
锻造铁鳞[氧化(铁)皮] (iron) hammer scale, anvil scale [cinder], forge scale [cinder]
锻造铜硅合金 Herculoy
锻造温度 forging temperature
锻造温度范围 forging temperature region
锻造纤维流线 forged fibre flow
锻造消耗重量 consumed weight
锻造斜度(模锻的) forging draught
锻造形变热处理(过冷奥氏体的) ausforging
锻造行业 blacksmithery
锻造性能 forging property [characteristic]
锻造学 smithing
锻造压力 forging pressure
锻造压缩率 forging reduction
锻造用钢 forging quality steel
锻造用钢锭 forging ingot
锻造用煤 forging coal
锻造用坯 forging stock
锻造用起重机 claw crane
锻造(用)润滑剂 lubricant for forging
锻造用旋臂起重机 smithy slewing crane
锻造用移动式起重机 travel(l)ing forge crane
锻造用自控室状煤气加热炉 gas heating room-form furnace with automatic control used for forging process
锻造余量 forging envelope
锻造轧辊 forging roll

锻造状态	as-forged condition
锻造组织	forged structure
锻渣	blacksmith's slag, anvil dross [cinder]
锻轧半成品	half-wrought material
锻轧机	reduce roll machine, forging rolls
锻制棒材	forged bar
锻制法兰	forged flange
锻制风口	forged tuyere
锻制钢坯	blocking
锻制钢球	forged ball
锻制铁	tilted iron
断背曲线	broken (back) curve
断层	【地】fault, fracture ◇ 下落～ downcast (D.C.)
断层地带	【地】fault zone
断层作用	effect of fault, faulting
断错	dislocation
断点指令	【计】breakpoint instruction [order]
断电	deenergize, deenergise, power failure, interrupt
断电操作	cut-off operation
断电器	breaker, cut-out, disconnector
断电时间	power off-time
断电延迟	off delay
断辊	roll breakage
断合接[触]点	break-make contacts
断弧触点	arcing tip
断键	broken bond
断开	breaking, break away, disconnection, discontinuity, disjunction, interrupt, opening, release, shut, switch(ing) off, throw off, turn-off
断开槽(冒口的)	【铸】break-off notch
断开力	opening [breaking] force
断开时间	off time
断开位置	off-position
断开闸门	cut-off gate
断开值	cut-off value
断开装置	trip
断口	fracture, rupture ◇ 不平～ splintery fracture, 参差～ broken stick fracture, 杰康托莱特～ 标准 Jernkontoret standards, 亮晶[光亮结晶]～*, 小刻面～ facet fracture, 斜面～ angular fracture, 星状[花状]～ rosette fracture, 有黑色～的 black short
断口表面	fracture(d) surface
断口花纹[花样]	fracture texture
断口检验[试验]	fracture test(ing), examination of fracture
断口金相学	fractography
断口金相研究	fractographic investigation
断口金相照片	fractograph
断口晶粒度	fracture grain size, 【金】fracture number
断口类型	fracture mode
断口面	area of fracture
断口收缩率	reduction of area at fracture
断口外貌[形状]	appearance of fracture
断口显微镜研究术	fractography
断口心部	core of fracture
断口形貌	fractography
断口形貌学	fracture topography
断口形状转变温度	fracture appearance transition temperature (F.A.T.T.)
断口样式	fracture mode ◇ 解理～*, 空穴形成的～*
断口组织	fracture structure
断口组织检验	fractography
断离	de-coalescence
断裂	break, breaking off, fracture, disruption, rupture, rupturing, bursting, tear, crack, collapse, disturbance ◇ 巴尔巴～伸长定律*, 混合型～*
断裂产品	disintegration product
断裂带	zone of fracture
断裂点	break(ing) point, point of fracture
断裂发展[扩展]	fracture propagation
断裂方式[类型]	form of fracture
断裂负载	(同"断裂载荷")
断裂机理	fracture mechanism
断裂键	broken bond

断裂角 angle of rupture
断裂开始[形成] fracture initiation
断裂口 broken stick fracture
断裂力学 fracture mechanics
断裂临界应力 critical stress for fracture
断裂路径转变温度 fracture path transition temperature
断裂面 rupture plane, plane of rupture, fracture(d) surface, plane [area] of fracture
断裂能力 【金】rupturing capacity
断裂判据[(判别)标准] failure criteria, criterion of failure
断裂强度 breaking [fracture, rupture] strength, cracking resistance, resistance to rupture, 【压】cheek resistance ◇ 持久~*
断裂强度-密度比 burst strength-density ratio
断裂趋势 tendency to fracture
断裂区(域) fracture(d) zone, region of fracture ◇ 预期~*
断裂曲线 fracture curve
断裂韧性 fracture toughness (characteristic, property)
断裂韧性试验 fracture toughness test
断裂韧性与密度的关系 fracture toughness density relationship
断裂时的面积收缩 contraction of area at fracture
断裂时的延伸率 breaking elongation
断裂时局部延伸(指断口处) local extension at fracture
断裂试验 break(down) [breaking, fracture] test(ing) ◇ 米哈埃利斯~机 Michaelis machine
断裂试验仪 folder
断裂[口]试样 【金】fracture sample
断裂特征 fracture characteristic
断裂特性 fracturing behavour, rupture properties
断裂位置 position of fracture

断裂纹 failure crack
断裂纹扩展速率 fracture speed
断裂习性 fracture habit
断裂系数 breaking factor, coefficient of rupture
断裂线 breaking down line, geosutures
断裂效应 disruptive effect
断裂形式 【金】fracture mode
断裂形态 fracture morphology
断裂行为 fracturing behaviour
断裂延伸度 elongation at rupture
断裂延伸率 breaking elongation
断裂应变 breaking strain
断裂应力 breaking [breakdown, fracture, rupture] stress ◇ 位错~*
断裂载荷 breaking [cracking, fracturing] load, load at failure
断裂制件 【机】product of breakdown
断裂转变能 energy for transitional fracture
断裂转变温度 fracture transition temperature
断裂锥 fracture cone
断流阀 disconnecting [disconnection, cut-off] valve
断流器 【电】interrupter, cutout
断流容量(开关的) 【电】breaking [rupturing] capacity
断流装置 shut-off fitting
断路 broken [open] circuit, beak(age), throw out, turn-off, out-of-gear
断路电势[位] open-circuit potential
断路电压 open-circuit voltage, fritting voltage
断路杆 disconnecting lever
断路开关 【电】disconnecting switch (DS), circuit breaker ◇ 双~ double-break switch
断路开关箱 circuit breaker box
断路器 circuit [current] breaker, break(er), interrupter, chopper, disconnector ◇ 抽出式~*, 磁爆(吹弧)型~*, 多次

重合闸～*,接触式～contact breaker,可熔～fusible cut out,少油～oil-mini-mun breaker,无熔丝～*,直接断弧～plain-break breaker

断路器箱 circuit breaker box
断面 (cross-) section, contour, fracture surface
断面不足的焊缝 undersize weld
断面的顶头部分 bulb
断面的整体变化 overall change of cross-section
断面积 sectional area (S.A.), cross-section(al) area
断面积压缩率 reduction of cross-sectional area
断面可控喷嘴 controllable-area nozzle
断面控制 profile control
断面敏感性 【铸】section sensitivity
断面设计 designing of construction lines, designing of section
断面收缩 cross-section contraction, contraction of (cross sectional) area
断面收缩率 area reduction, (percentage) reduction of area, section shrinkage rate ◇ 冷压～cold reduction percent
断面图 sectional drawing (S.D., s.d.), cross-section(al) drawing [diagram], profile, sectional elevation [view]
断面线 cross hatching
断面形状 cross-sectional shape, form of section
断面走形(缺陷) 【铸】wrong contour
断片 fragment
断热热量表 adiabatic calorimeter
断绳防坠器 safety dog
断水阀 water shut-off valve
断－通比 break-make ratio
断头盘条拉拔的线材卷 split catchweight coil
断线 breakage
断屑 discontinuous chip, chip breaking
断续操作 intermittent operation

断续淬火 (同"间断淬火")
断续灯光 intermitted light
断续电流镀覆 interrupted current plating
断续定位[点固]焊 intermittent tack weld
断续缝滚焊 roller spot welding
断续负载额定出力 intermittent rating
断续滚焊机 stitch welder
断续过程 intermittent process
断续过滤 【环】intermittent filtration
断续焊缝 intermittent weld
断续焊(接) interrupted [intermittent, gap] welding
断续加热 intermittent heating
断续加压 intermittent stressing
断续加载 intermittent loading [stressing]
断续控制 intermittent control
断续裂纹发展 interrupted crack growth
断续器 contact maker, interrupter, interruptor, make-and-break device, chopper, ticker
断续生产 discontinuous running
断续式鼓风焙烧炉 【冶】intermittent-type blast roaster
断续寿命试验 intermittent life test
断续下向过滤 intermittent downward filtration
断续显[指]示 discontinuity indications
断续效应 intermittency effect
断续移动 【压】stick-slip
断续运转 intermittent running
断续作用 discontinuous operation
断续作用调节器 on-off regulator
断续作用蒸罐炉[甑式炉] 【色】intermittent retort

缎面光 satin finish
煅烧 incineration, incinerate calcination, calcining, burning, scorifying ◇ 堆垒～calcination in clumps, 高温～*, 鼓风～【耐】blast roasting, 流态化～*, 摊堆～calcination in heaps, 旋风式～系统*
煅烧白云石 dolime, doloma, calcined

[fired] dolomite
煅烧白云石砖　burnt [fired] dolomite brick
煅烧比　calcination ratio
煅烧不良的　less-well calcined
煅烧不足的　undercalcined
煅烧操作　【色】burning operation
煅烧产出率　calcination ratio
煅烧产物　calcined product
煅烧厂[车间]　calcination [calcining] plant
煅烧程度　degree of calcination
煅烧瓷土　molochite
煅烧带　calcination [calcining] zone
煅烧粉　【冶】calcined powder
煅烧富集　igneous concentration
煅烧高岭土　calcined kaolin
煅烧工　calciner
煅烧硅石　silica refractory grog
煅烧过程　calcination process
煅烧黄铁矿　calcined pyrite
煅烧技术　calcination technique
煅烧矿　calcined ore
煅烧菱镁矿　calcined magnesite
煅烧炉　calciner, calcinator, calcining furnace [oven], incineration furnace, incinerator, calcar ◇ 电极～electrode oven, 反射式～ reverberatory calciner, 回转式～*, 考伯斯～Koppers furnace, 快速～flash calciner, 流态化闪速～fluid flash calciner, 竖式～vertical calciner
煅烧黏土　calcined clay
煅烧区　calcining zone
煅烧熔剂　fired flux
煅烧石灰　burnt lime
煅烧室　calcining compartment
煅烧苏打　calcined soda
煅烧碳酸盐　calcined carbonate
煅烧条件　conditions of calcination
煅烧温度　calcination temperature
煅烧氧化钡　calcined baryta
煅烧氧化铝　calcined alumina

煅烧窑　calcining [burning] kiln ◇ 燃气～*
煅石膏　calcined gypsum
煅制无烟煤　thermoanthracite
堆场　drop
堆存　stockpiling, store up, storage
堆存残渣　stockpiled residue
堆存工　stocker
堆存跨　storage bay
堆存量　stockpiling capacity
堆叠　piling
堆叠退火(板材的)　annealing in stacks, pack annealing
堆叠指数　packing index
堆锭场　ingot storing bay
堆垛　piling, stacking, baling (板材的)
堆垛层错　stacking fault
堆垛层错成核　stacking fault nucleation
堆垛层错带　ribbon
堆垛层错多面体　stacking fault polyhedron
堆垛层错概率　stacking fault probability
堆垛层错宽度　stacking fault width
堆垛层错密度　stacking fault density
堆垛层错能　stacking fault energy (S.F.E.)
堆垛层错缺陷　stacking fault defect
堆垛层错四面体　stacking fault tetrahedron
堆垛层错析出　stacking fault precipitation
堆垛层错形成　stacking fault formation
堆垛车　piling car
堆垛次序　stacking order
堆垛高度　stacking height
堆垛辊道　stacking roller table
堆垛机　stacker, (magazine) piler, piling machine, setting elevator, stacker-reclaimer ◇ 车式～car piler, 机动～mechanical piler, 气垫[空气浮动]～air float piler, 液压提升～hydraulic lift piler, 自动～automatic piler
堆垛跨(钢材的)　piling bay

dui 堆 330

堆垛篦架　piling cradle
堆垛冷却　cooling in packed formation
堆垛冷却台　piling cooling bed
堆垛起重机　stacker crane
堆垛顺序　stacking sequence
堆垛台　piling bed ◇ 坯料升降～billet elevator,提升～elevating piler
堆垛台架　packing bed
堆垛退火　pack annealing
堆垛序　stacking order, order of packing（晶体中原子层的）
堆垛因数　stacking factor
堆垛用隔条　piler bars
堆垛运输带　piling belt
堆垛运输机　stacker-reclaimer
堆垛装置　piling device,【铁】piler
堆放　piling-up, stack, (bulk) storage, stockpile, stockpiling
堆放场　stock place
堆放的材料　lump material
堆放架[台]　piling bin
堆焊　build up welding, deposit [overlay, pile-up] welding, weld(ing) deposit, facing, surfacing ◇ 表面～*,刻痕和～(轧辊表面的) bossing,青铜～bronze surfacing,异形件～shape welding,窄焊道～*,振动电弧～*
堆焊材料　welding material
堆焊层　overlay
堆焊焊条　surfacing (welding) electrode, build up electrode
堆焊金属　deposited (weld) metal, added [all-weld] metal
堆焊速度因数　deposition rate factor
堆焊硬质表面层　hard facing
堆焊原状　as-deposited condition
堆积　building up, piling-up, stackup, heap (ing)
堆积法炼焦　coking in heaps
堆积浸出　dump leaching
堆积密度(炉料的)　packing density
堆积容量　heap capacity

堆积式拉丝机　【压】accumulation type wiredrawing machine
堆积拖送机　stacking trailing conveyer
堆积效应　stack effect
堆积因数　packing factor
堆集　conglomeration, packing, stocking, lumping
堆脊法炼焦　coking in ridges
堆角　angle of rest [repose]
堆浸法　heap [dump] leaching, leaching in heaps [dumps]
堆矿场　ore dock, stock dump
堆矿机(矿石混匀用)　【铁】stacker ◇ 皮带～travel(l)ing stacker
堆垒煅烧　calcination in clumps
堆料　stacking, stockpiling, bedding out,【团】building of pile
堆料场　stocking [stockpiling, storage] area, rickyard
堆料高度　stacking height, burden level
堆料混匀　bedding
堆料机　stacker, stocker, stacking tower, bedding stacker（矿石中和用）◇ 反转支臂式～reversing-boom stacker,悬臂～boom stacker,移动式～travel(l)ing stacker
堆料设备　bedding installation
堆料顺序　stacking sequence
堆料速度　【团】stacking rate
堆料拖运小车　drag-off carriage
堆料装料机　stack loader
堆煤场　coal yard
堆密度　bulk density
堆取料机　stacker-reclaimer ◇ 摆动式～slewing stack-reclaimer,斗轮式～*
堆取样　pile sampling
堆砂　【铸】heap sand
堆烧　【色】heap roasting
堆烧炼焦炉　coke hearth
堆石坝　rock-fill dam
堆石防波堤　rock-mound breakwater
堆摊浸出　leaching in heaps, heap leaching

度盘式板材测厚仪　dial sheet gauge
度盘式温度计　dial-type thermometer
度谱分析　spectrometric analysis
度数测量　grade measure
渡线　【运】cross over
端板　【机】end plate,【团】(烧结风箱的) dead plate
端包架　【铸】hand shank, bow
端壁　end wall
端部　end, butt, tip
端部加厚管　heavy end tube
端部加料　end charging, end-feed
端部加料正交[纵横]流动区域精炼炉　end-feed cross-flow zone refiner
端部切头(钢锭的)　【钢】top scrap
端部烧焊　boxing
端部烧嘴　end burner
端部卸料[排矿]　end discharge
端部卸载卡车　(同"尾卸卡车")
端部周边焊　boxing
端部周边排料[矿]　end peripheral discharge
端衬板　end-liner
端承口　belingl the ends
端出料(连续加热)炉　end-discharged furnace
端出料加热炉　end pusher furnace, front door furnace
端点效应　end effect
端顶圆周焊缝(压力容器的)　【焊】head seam
端缝螺栓　fox bolt
端盖[罩]　end shield [cap, cover, housing]
端盖衬板　end cover liner
端钩(弹簧的)　end hook
端环　end ring
端际固溶体(多元合金)　【金】terminal solid solution
端际相　terminal phase
端件　tail piece
端接　terminating
端接焊接头　edge joint weld

端接头(焊炬的)　【焊】head tube nipple
端立面　end elevation
端连接　end connection
端梁　end girder
端裂口[纹]　end-splitting
端轮架　end-carriage
端面　end face [surface, plane], abut ◇ 车～*
端(面,头)淬(火)　end hardening [quenching]
端面滚焊　edge seam welding
端面压力　end pressure
端末插入[砌固]　end built-in
端钮　terminal
端视图　end(-on) view [elevation]
端枢轴承　end (journal) bearing
端填角焊缝　end fillet weld
端头　end, tip, mouthpiece
端头扳直的带卷(送进轧辊前的)　tailed coil
端头车丝试棒　screwed test bar
端头飞剪　flying crop shears ◇ 转鼓式～*
端头－废料飞剪　【压】crop and cobble flying shears ◇ 多线式～*
端头－废料剪(切机)　【压】crop and cobble shears ◇ 单线式～*
端头预加工(管材试验前的)　end conditioning
端隙　end play
端效应　end effect
端卸(的)　end dumping
端卸式送锭车　end-tilt ingot car, end truck front dump type ingot buggy
端支承[支座]　end bearing
端止推轴承　end thrust bearing
端轴承(止推轴承)　dead abutment
端轴颈　(end-)journal
端装料炉　end-charged furnace
端子　terminal, terminating, post, clamp
端子板　terminal board [block, strip]
端子钳间距　electrode opening

对称轴 symmetry axis ◇ 三次～ trial axis, 左旋～ left-handed screw axis

对称(转动)反演轴 【理】iversion axis of symmetry

对称转炉(形状对称) symmetrical vessel, concentric converter

对冲式放大器 direct impact amplifier

对动螺旋 union screw

对二氮杂苯 pyrazine

对二甲苯 $\{C_8H_{10}\}$ m-dimethyl benzene

对二甲苯酚 $\{C_8H_{10}O\}$ p-xylenol

对分式芯盒 split core box

对分轴瓦 【机】two-part bearing shell

对缝焊管 jump-welded pipe ◇ 电阻～*

对辊 double-roll

对辊破碎机 double crusher, double-roll (crusher), double-roll cutter, crushing rolls, roll crushing mill, roll-type crusher, roll press

对辊压制[制团]机 roll-type briquetting press [machine]

对焊 (同"对接焊")

对焊尺寸检查样板(焊缝检查) butt welding gauge

对焊钢管 butt-welded tube

对焊工具接头 weld-on tool joint

对焊机 (同"对接焊机")

对焊机夹钳 welding jaw

对焊机夹头 butt welding (clamping) die

对焊接头 butt joint ◇ 双边卷边～*

对焊钻杆 butt welded drill pipe

对换 transposition

对击锻锤 counterblow hammer

对击式镦锻机 double swage hammer

对甲苯胺 $\{C_7H_9N\}$ p-methyl-phenylamine

对甲苯腈 $\{C_8H_9N\}$ p-tolunitrile

对甲酚 Paracresol p-cresol

对甲基苯胺 $\{C_7H_9N\}$ p-methylaniline

对甲基联苯 $\{C_{13}H_{12}\}$ p-methyldiphenyl

对讲电话 intercom, intercommunication telephone

对讲电话台[通信站] intercom station

对讲机 inter-phone, intercom

对讲系统 intercom system, paging system

对讲系统放大器 amplifier for handset

对讲系统话筒 phone speaker for handset

对角剪切 diagonal cut

对角孔型 diagonal pass

对角孔型设计 diagonal (pass) design

对角扩散 diagonal diffusion ◇ 非～ off-diagonal diffusion

对角(连)杆 diagonal

对角裂缝[裂纹] diagonal cracking

对角上烧嘴均热炉 【冶】top two-way fired (soaking) pit

对角线 diagonal (diag.), diagonal line ◇ 体～ body diagonal

对角(支)撑 diagonal bracing [strut]

对绞电缆 paired cable

对接 butt, abutment (joint), abutting [butt(ed)] joint ◇ K形坡口～*, 加垫板～ backed butt joint

对接板 【焊】butt cover plate

对接边 【焊】butt(ing) [abutting] edges

对接触点 butt(ing) contact

对接盖板 butt strap

对接滚焊 butt seam welding ◇ 加搭板～ bridge welding

对接滚焊焊缝 butt seam weld(ing) ◇ 用盖板～ bridge seam weld(ing)

对接滚[缝]焊机 butt seam welder, butt seam welding machine

对(接)焊 butt (joint) welding ◇ 凹面～ concave butt weld, 电阻～*, 环缝～*, 开口～接头 open butt weld, 双U形～ double-U butt welding, 微补强～*, 斜线～ scarf welding

对接焊缝 butt weld ◇ K形坡口～ double-bevel butt weld, T字～ double-J tee butt weld, X形坡口～ double-V butt weld, 双U形坡口～ double-U butt weld

对(接)焊机 butt welder, butt welding machine ◇ 垫箔滚～*, 闪光～*

对接接触 butting contacts

对接接头 abutment [abutting] joint, butt joint(ing) ◇ 平焊～downhand butt joint
对接平焊 butt welding in down hand position
对接烧结 butt sintering
对径 diameter
对开径向止推轴承 cup-and-cone bearing
对开联轴节 split coupling
对开连续自焙阳极 split Soederberg anode
对开螺母 split [clasp] nut
对开式轴承 split [two-part] bearing
对开式锥形矿槽 split cone bin
对开阳极 split anode
对开阳极电解槽 【色】cell with split anodes
对抗 counter, oppose
对抗反应 opposing reaction
对立物 antithesis, opposite, counter
对流 convection (current), countercurrent (flow), counterflow, opposite-flow, advection, contraflow
对流层 troposphere
对流传热 convective heat transfer, heat transfer by convection ◇ 自由～
对流传热系数 convective heat-transfer coefficient
对流床 【色】countercurrent bed
对流萃取 counter-current extraction
对流垫板(罩式退火炉的) convector plate
对流风流 countercurrent air flow
对流加热 convection heating
对流浸出 (同"逆流浸出")
对流冷却 convection [convective] cooling
对流炉 convection furnace
对流煤气道 convection pass
对流气－固反应过程 countercurrent gas-solid process
对流气流 convection current
对流热交换器 counterflow [convective] heat exchanger

对流(热)损失 convection losses
对流式干燥机 reversed-current drier
对流式热处理炉 convection-type furnace
对流式散热器 convector radiator
对流温度 convection temperature
对流旋风除尘器 paracyclone dust collector
对流烟道 【冶】convection pass
对流液流 convection current
对流原理 countercurrent principle
对流运动 countercurrent movement
对面 opposite hand (Op.H.)
对偶像 double image
对偶运算 【计】dual operation
对齐 alignment, registration ◇ 向右～【计】right justify
对数 【数】logarithm (lg, log.)
对数表 logarithmic table
对数底 base of logarithm
对数－反对数放大器 log-antilog amplifier
对数放大器 logarithm(ic) amplifier, logafier
对数减量[减缩] log(arithmic) decrement
对数刻[标]度 logarithmic scale
对数律 logarithmic law
对数平均值 logarithmic mean
对数蠕变定律 logarithmic creep law
对数时间律 logarithmic time law
对数型蠕变 logarithmic creep
对数应变 logarithmic strain
对数正态分布 log-normal distribution
对数坐标图 logarithmic graph
对数坐标纸 log paper
对头焊接法(管材的) butt weld process
对外贸易区 foreign trade zone
对位化合物 para compound
对位酸(有机酸) para-acid
对型板 【铸】match plate
对形性 enantiomorphism
对氧敏感[灵敏]的 【金】oxygen-sensitive

对乙基甲苯	p-ethyl toluene
对阴极	anti-cathode, target（X 射线管的）
对阴极（靶）元件	anticathode element
对阴极至底片距离	focus to film distance
对应措施	countermeasure
对应裂纹	reflection crack
对应温度	homologous temperature
对应原理	correspondence principle
对映变形[变态,变种]	enantiomorphic variety
对映晶体	enantiomorphic crystals
对映现象	enantiotropism
对映像（左右对映）	enantiomorphism
对映形类	enantiomorphous class
对映性转变	enantiotropic transformation
对映异构现象	enantiotrop
对照表	balance sheet, table of comparisons
对照取样	check sampling
对照试验	comparison [check] test, comparison [check] experiment
对照样品	check sample
对正挡板[推板]（板带材剪切用）	squaring pusher
对正中心[对中]	centring ◇ 带材～调节器 edge (strip) scanner
对置侧	opposite side
对置曲柄	opposite cranks
对峙反应	opposing reaction
对中辊	centring roll(er)
对中辊道	centring table
对中螺丝	centring screw
对中套筒（带卷开卷的）	centring spool
对中装置	centring device
对重	counterweight (ctwt), counterbalance
对柱	coupled columns
对准	alignment, aim at ◇ 未～*
对准机构	aligning guide
对准末端	endwise
墩	pier, pillar
墩身	dado
墩式基础	pier foundation
吨钢耗新水	make-up water consumption per ton of steel
吨钢可比能耗	comparable energy consumption per ton crude steel
吨钢综合能耗	energy consumption per ton steel, overall energy intensity, specific [equivalent] energy consumption per ton crude steel
吨工时	man hours per ton
吨生产能力	tonnage capacity
吨数	tonnage
吨铁水	ton of hot metal (T.H.M.)
吨位	tonnage (tonn.), burden, deadweight ◇ 大～设备 high tonnage equipment
镦粗【压】	upset(ting), jumping-up, upending ◇ 管端～staving
镦粗比	upsetting ratio
镦粗变形	sinking strain
镦粗对焊	upset butt welding
镦粗法	shortening process
镦粗钢锭	squat ingot
镦粗工序	shortening operation
镦粗机	upsetter, upsetting machine, header, heading machine
镦粗力	upset force
镦粗模	heading [joggling] die
镦粗试验	upset(ting) [jump(ing-up), dump, upending] test
镦粗系数	upsetting factor
镦粗压力	welding pressure
镦粗裕[余]量	upset [push-up] allowance
镦锻【压】	upset(ting), upset(ting) forging ◇ 电热～electroforging
镦锻比	upset(ting) ratio
镦锻操作[作业]	upsetting operation
镦锻对焊接头[连接]	upset butt joint
镦锻机	upsetter, upsetting machine, upset forging machine
镦锻机构	upset mechanism
镦锻金属（料）	upset metal

镦锻模　upsetter die
镦锻坯料　header blank
镦锻[镦粗]时间　upset time
镦锻试验　upset(ting) test
镦锻[粗]试验机　upset tester
镦锻速度　upset speed
镦锻行程　upset travel
镦锻压力　upset pressure
镦锻[粗]压力机　upsetting press
镦锻用圆形坯件　biscuit
镦焊　upset bull welding
镦厚机　upsetter, upsetting machine ◇ 钢管[管端]~*, 腰边~ web edge upsetter
镦头　【压】heading (hdg)
镦头机　heading machine
顿巴克黄铜　Tombac alloy[metal] (3—30Zn, 0—8Sn, 0—0.3As, 余量 Cu), Tombac[Tombak] (67—75Cu, 10—20Zn, 1.75—5Si; 又称德国黄铜), yellow pewter
顿巴希尔耐磨硅黄铜 (67—75Cu, 21—31Zn, 1.75—5Si) Tombasil
钝边　root face
钝边厚度　【焊】thickness of root face
钝齿啮合　pin gearing[toothing]
钝化　immunization, immunizing, passivation, passivity（腐蚀中生成难蚀膜）,【冶】deactivation ◇ 防蚀[表面]~铝 alumite, 过~ transpassivity
钝化处理　passivating (treatment) ◇ 电化学~*, 镀层[涂层]表面铬酸盐~*, 阳极~ anodic passivation
钝化-活化电池　passive-active cell
钝化机理　mechanism of passivity
钝化剂　passivant, passivating agent, passivator, deactivator
钝化金属　passivated[sluggish] metal
钝化铝反光镜片　illuminite
钝化膜　passivating[passive] film
钝化效应　passivation effect
钝化状态　passive state
钝化作用　passivation, deactivation, inactivation ◇ 去~ depassivating effect
钝角　obtuse angle
钝角平分线　obtuse bisectrix
钝金刚石锥体　blunt diamond cone
钝态　passive state[condition], passivity
钝态薄膜理论　film theory of passivity
钝态金属　passive metal
钝态吸附理论　adsorption theory of passivity
钝态硬度　passive hardness
钝性　passivity
钝性的　passive
钝焰　lazy flame
多暗煤组分　durain-rich component
多棒钟形烧结炉　multiple-bar bell-jar
多倍厚板[薄板坯]　multiples, thick iron
多倍精度　multiple precision, multiprecision
多倍精度运算　multiprecision arithmetic
多倍坯料　multiple
多倍字长工作　multiple length working
多倍字长数　【计】multiple length number
多边不锈钢贸易协定(欧美日) Multilateral Stainless Steel Agreement (MSSA)
多边钢铁贸易协定(欧美日) Multi-lateral Steel Agreement (MSA)
多边化 X 射线反射　X-ray reflections of polygonization
多边化程度　【金】degree of polygonization
多边化畴[区域]　polygonized domain
多边形　polygon ◇ 再结晶~化理论*
多边形结构　polygonal structure
多变量　multivariant, multivariable
多变式　multivariant
多变系数[多变系统]　polyvariant system
多变性[现象]　polytropy
多变性的　polytropic
多变压器式多点点焊机　multitransformer spot welder
多播主干网　multicast backbone
多波段(的)　multirange, multiband

多部分组成的　multipart
多槽浮选机　multicompartment cell, multiple cell floatation machine
多槽卷筒　multigrooved capstan
多层　multiple-deck, multilayer, multiple coat, multiple-story, multiwall
多层板式阳极　multiple slab anode
多层薄膜离子交换槽　multiple ion-exchange membrane cell
多层焙烧炉　multihearth roaster
多层布线(大规模集成电路的)　multilayer interconnection [metallization]
多层材料　multilayer material
多层彩色胶片　monopack
多层床　multilayer [multistage, multi-compartment] bed
多层搭接　multiple thickness joint
多层带材　multilayer strip
多层电沉积金属板　composite plate
多层电接触器材　multilayer contact material, multiple-layer contacts
多层镀层[涂层,涂镀]　sandwich coat, multilayer coating
多层堆焊　multiple-bead deposit
多层覆盖层　multilayer coating
多层钢　clad [ply] steel
多层焊缝　multilayer [multiple-layer] weld, multiple-bead deposit
多层焊接　multilayer welding, multiple pass welding ◇阶梯形～*
多层护墙板[多层壁板]　【建】sandwich panel
多层建筑　multi-storied building
多层浇口　side step gate
多层金属化　multiple-layer metallization
多层流(态)化煅烧炉　multistage fluidized calciner
多层炉　multiple-story furnace, multideck oven, multihearth
多层浓缩机[沉降槽]　multitray thickener
多层喷洗塔　multi-wash spray tower
多层切割(用氧炔火焰)　stack (flame) cutting
多层容器　multilayer vessels, compound container
多层烧结(法)　multiple-layer sintering
多层烧结体　【粉】composite sintered compact
多层式窑　multiple-hearth furnace
多层洗涤收尘[集尘]器　multi-wash collector
多层线圈　multilayer coil
多层压机(橡胶的)　multidaylight press
多层银合金　tiers-argent
多层蒸馏塔[柱]　plate (type distillation) column [tower]
多层中心传动式浓缩机　tray thickener
多尘物质　dusty material
多成分球团　composite pellet
多程焊　multirun welding
多程焊缝　multirun weld
多齿联轴节　multi-tooth coupling
多尺寸粉末　【粉】polysize powder
多冲杆压机　multiple-punch press
多重剥离[多重龟裂,多次碎裂]　【金】multiple spalling
多重变址　【计】cumulative indexing
多重处理(系统)　【计】multiprocessing (system) ◇共享～*
多重点缺陷(同"多点缺陷")
多重回归分析(统计学)　multiple regression (analysis)
多重模态分布　【数】multimodal distribution
多重能级　multiplet (energy) level
多重谱线　【理】multiplet ◇宽间距～wide multiplet, 窄间距～*
多重谱线成分　multiplet component
多重特性函数　multiple response function
多重通道　multiplex
多重[次]位错　multiple dislocation
多重线　multiple line
多重线间隔　multiple interval
多重响应函数　multiple response function

多重性 multiplicity
多重性因数 multiplicity factor, multiplication factor（结晶面的）
多重(性)组分 multiplet component
多重(印刷电路)板 multilayer board
多重运算 【计】multiple arithmetic
多重作业操作 【计】multi-job operation
多抽头线圈 tapped coil
多畴(的) 【理】polydomain, multidomain
多处访问 【理】multiple access
多床(层的) multi-bed
多床炉 multiple-hearth furnace
多磁畴 multidomain
多次变压点焊机 multiple transformer spot-welding machine
多次测定 multiple determination
多次重合闸断路器 【电】multiple-reclosing breaker
多次淬火 repeated hardening
多次氮化(处理) multinitriding
多次电离 multiple ionization
多次电离的 multiple-ionized
多次反复 thrash(ing)
多次反射 multiple [zigzag] reflection
多次反射(回)波 multiple (reflection) echoes
多次放[扒]渣 【冶】multiple slagging
多次辐照-退火循环 multiple irradiation-annealing cycles
多次回火 multiple tempering
多次精炼 multiple refining
多次拉拔 【压】continuous drawing
多次拉拔钢丝 dead-drawn wire
多次拉拔机 multidraught machine, multiple station drawing machine
多次拉丝机 multidraught [multidie] machine, multiple station drawing machine, multiple wire-drawing machine, multiplex motobloc, multi-block machine ◇ 滑动式[无蓄力器]~*, 无滑动[积累式]~*
多次脉冲(接触)焊接焊缝 multiple-impulse weld
多次烧结 multiple-sintering
多次深拉压力机 【压】reducing press
多次通过(区域熔炼的) multipass
多次通过分布(区域熔炼的) multipass distribution
多次通过区域精炼 multipass zone refining
多次压痕 repeated indentation
多次压力循环(接触焊的) multipressure cycle
多次折光内孔窥视仪 cave borescope
多次中粗拉丝机 multiple-die medium heavy wire-drawing machine
多带连续式炉 strand type furnace
多单元的 multiunit
多单元法 【计】poly cell approach
多刀刨床(用于修整锭、坯表面) planer-type machine
多刀剪断机 【压】gang shears
多刀圆盘剪纵剪 【压】rotary gang slitting
多刀圆盘(纵)剪机(薄板的) 【压】gang slitting machine, gang slitting shears
多道程序设计(优先权) 【计】multiprogramming priority
多道程序执行系统 【计】executive system of multiprogramming
多道处理 (同"多重处理")
多道次扭转 multi-pass torsion
多道焊缝 multiple-pass [multipass, multi-bead, multirun] weld
多道焊(接) multipass [multirun] welding, multiple pass welding
多道振荡器 【电】multivibrator
多道砖格 multiple-pass checkers
多地址 multiple address, multiaddress
多点点焊机 multielectrode [multipoint] spot welder, multiple-spot welder, multiple-spot welding machine ◇ 多变压器式~*, 水力导向焊条顺序夹持~ hydromatic welder
多点焊接 multiple-spot welded joint, multiple-spot welding

多点连接 【电】multipoint [multidrop] connetction
多点喷吹 multipoint injection
多点缺陷 multiple-point imperfections
多点式记录电位计 multipoint recording potentiometer
多点式记录器 multiple-point recorder
多点式热电偶 multipoint thermocouple
多点凸焊 multiple-projection welding
多点线路 【电】multipoint circuit
多点压射 multipoint injection
多电机拖动(装置) multiple [coordinated] drive
多电极点焊 multiple-electrode spot welding
多电极埋弧焊 multiple-electrode submerged arc welding
多电元素 hyperelectronic element
多电源焊接 (同"多站焊接")
多电源式弧焊机 multiple-arc welder
多电子枪区域精炼 multiple electron gun zone refining
多电子原子 many electron atom
多动压机 multiple(-action) press
多动作粉末成形压机 multiaction powder compaction press
多动作压制(成形) multiaction compaction
多斗提升机 continuous bucket elevator, chain bucket
多斗挖沟机 continuous bucket ditcher
多斗挖掘机 multi-bucket excavator, continuous [chain] bucket excavator
多斗挖泥机 bucket [ladder] dredger
多读馈送 【计】multiread feeding
多段 multi(ple)stage
多段处理 multiple-stage treatment
多段床 (同"多室床")
多段氮化法 multi-nitriding
多段加热 multistage heating
多段结晶 (同"多级结晶")
多段冷却 multistage cooling

多段喷洒洗涤塔 multistage spray tower
多段破碎 multistage crushing
多段绕组 split winding
多段湿式洗涤器 multistaged wet scrubber
多段式加热炉 multi-zone reheating furnace
多段式链箅机 【团】multiple-pass (travelling) grate
多段式链箅循环 multiple-pass grate cycle
多段式中和区 multistage neutralization section
多段洗涤塔 multistage scrubber, stage washer
多段选矿法 multistage ore dressing
多垛罩式退火炉 multiple stack annealing furnace
多耳凸焊接头 multiple-projection weld
多尔合金 Dore metal
多尔科泵 Dorrco pump
多尔流量测量管 Dall tube
多尔型分级机 Dorr classifier
多尔型浮槽分级机 Dorr bowl classifier
多尔型浮槽耙式分级机 Dorr bowl-rake classifier
多尔型搅拌机 Dorr agitator
多尔型流态化焙烧炉 Dorr(co) fluo-solid roaster, Dorrco fluosolids
多尔型浓缩机 Dorr thickener
多尔型圆筒真空过滤机 Dorrco filter
多尔银 Dore silver
多范围(的) multirange
多分散系 polydisperse system
多分散系粉末 【粉】polydisperse powder
多分散相 polydisperse phase
多分子吸附 multimolecular adsorption
多腹板箱形梁 box girder with multiple webs
多坩埚炉 multiple crucible furnace
多钢绳拖运[移送]机 multirope skid gear
多割嘴气割[切割]机 multiple burner, multiple burner [blowpipe, torch] machine

多格洗涤塔　multiple-bay scrubber
多根管材冷拔机　multistrand cold-tube rolling mill
多根连续退火(线材的)　continuous strand annealing
多工件压模　multiple-die set
多工件压制　multiple pressing
多工位锻压　multiple impression forging
多工位焊接发电机　multioperator welding generator
多工位夹具[夹紧装置]　multiple jig
多工位冷镦机　multistage cold former
多工位压力机　transfer press
多工序(冲压)成形　multiplestage forming
多功能团交换剂　polyfunctional exchanger
多谷半导体　many valley semiconductor
多股　multiple strand ◇ 扁形～线 flat type stranded wire
多股钢丝　steel-wire strand
多股钢丝绳　multistrand wire rope
多股绞(导)线　bunch stranded conductor
多管除尘器　multi(cy)clone (dust collector), multi-tube dust collector, multitubular collector, centicell unit
多管反应器　multi-tubular reactor
多管回转式干燥机　multi-tube revolving drier
多管冷却器　multi-tube cooler
多管路浓相输送技术(煤粉的)　multipipe dense phase transport technique
多管路喷吹　【铁】pulverized coal injection process with multibranch feed pipe
多管式冷凝器　multi-tubular condenser
多管式氢还原炉　multiple-tube hydrogen furnace
多管式淘析器　multi-tube elutriator
多管旋风除[集]尘器　multi(cy)clone, multiclone (dust) collector
多管旋风收尘器系统　multiclone system
多管压力计　multi-tube pressure gauge
多管蒸发器　multi-tube evaporator

多光谱摄影术　multispectral photography
多光束干涉测量[量度]法　multiple-beam interferometry
多光子效应　multiphoton effect
多硅钙铀矿　haiweeite
多硅钾铀矿 {$K_2(UO_2)_2(SiO_5)_3 \cdot 4H_2O$}　weeksite
多硅酸盐　polysilicate
多辊布料器　(同"辊式布料器")
多辊矫直机　【压】multi-roll straightening machine, multi-roll straightener, multi-roll flattener (薄板的) ◇ 板材在～上矫直 mangling, 不调压式～*, 二重式～[两排辊子的矫直机]*, 四重式～[四轧辊式矫直机]*, 调压式～*
多辊卷取机的联杆　【压】links
多辊拉矫机　【连铸】multi-roll withdrawal machine
多辊筛　live-roll grizzly
多辊式棒材矫直机　【压】multi-roll bar-straightening machine
多辊式滚焊机　multiwheel seam welder
多辊轧机　multi-roll mill, cluster mill ◇ 可逆式～ reversing multi-roll, 罗恩式～*
多辊轧制　multiroll rolling
多辊张紧装置　multi-roll bridle
多焊道的　【焊】multirun
多焊道熔敷层　multiple-bead deposit
多焊件焊接的焊缝　multiple-joint weld
多焊条电焊　multiple(-electrode) welding
多弧电焊[焊接]机　multiple-arc welder [unit]
多弧焊接　multiarc welding
多弧焊头　multiple-arc head
多弧自动电焊机　multihead automatic arc welding machine
多花键式联轴节　multiple splined type coupling
多环布料(高炉的)　multi-ring burden distribution
多环布料溜槽(高炉的)　【铁】multi-ring

spreader (chute)
多回路系统　multiloop system
多机机组　multiple unit
多机架[座]的　multiplestand, multistand
多机架(连)轧管机　multi-stand pipe mill (M.P.M.)
多机架轧机　【压】multiplestand rolling mill
多机轧制的连续式轧机(英国)　close continuous mill
多极　multipole (M.P.), multi(ple)stage, multistep
多极的　multipolar, heteropolar
多极点焊　multiple-electrode spot welding
多极电炉　multiple-electrode furnace
多极平行弧焊　tangent welding
多级泵　multistage pump
多级处理　multiple-stage treatment, multi-level processing
多级萃取　multistage (solvent) extraction
多级地址　【计】multilevel address
多级递阶控制结构　multi-level (and) hierachical control structure
多级电除尘[电收尘,电滤]器　【冶】multistage precipitator
多级电离　multiple ionization
多级定址　【计】multilevel addressing
多级阀门　multiple valve
多级反应器　multistage reactor
多级放大器　multistage amplifier
多级分离　multistage-separation
多级分馏塔[分离柱]　multiplestage separating column
多级级联萃取装置　multistage extraction cascade
多级接触萃取　multiple-contact extraction
多级[(阶)段]结晶　multistage-crystallization
多级结晶器　multistage crystallizer
多级控制[调节]　multistep control
多级冷却　multistage cooling
多级离心泵　multistage centrifugal pump

◇卧式～
多级流化床氢氟化　multiplestage fluid-bed hydrofluorination
多级逆流萃取装置　【色】multistage countercurrent extraction apparatus
多级逆流倾注洗涤　multistep countercurrent decantation
多级逆流(洗涤)系统　multistage countercurrent system
多级喷射混合萃取塔　multistage jet-mixer extraction column
多级热处理　(同"复合热处理")
多级塔　multistage columns
多级卧式反应器　multiplestage horizontal reactor
多级蒸汽喷射泵　multistage steam ejector pump
多级柱塔　multistage columns
多级座阀　multiple-seated valve
多计算机(系统)　multicomputer (system)
多加热器区域精炼炉　multiheater refiner
多价螯合剂　sequestering agent
多价的　multivalent, quantivalent
多价化合物　multivalent compound
多价元素　multivalent element, polygen
多碱的　polybasic
多碱度烧结矿　different basicity sinter
多件的　multipart
多件可拆模　multiple-segment die
多桨搅拌器　multi-bladed stirrer
多角化　polygonization
多角型砂　【铸】angular-grained sand
多角形　polygon
多角形钢锭模　【钢】polygonal mould
多角形铁素体　polygonal ferrite
多角柱　polygonal [cant] column
多节的　【金】scarred
多结的　nodated
多结结构　multijunction structure
多金刚石整修工具　multiple diamond dressing tool
多金属粉末　polymetallic powder

多金属矿　polymetallic [complex] ore
多金属硫化物精矿　polymetallic sulphide concentrate
多金属系　polymetallic system
多晶衬底　polycrystalline substrate
多晶锭块　polycrystalline ingot
多晶分析法　multiple crystal method
多晶粉末 X 射线分析法　multiple crystal method
多晶固溶体　polycrystalline solid solution
多晶硅　polysilicon, polycrystalline silicon
多晶集合[聚集]体　polycrystalline aggregate
多晶生长　polycrystalline growth
多晶体　polycrystal, polycrystalline unit [aggregate, material, solid]
多晶体极射投影图　polycrystalline pole figure
多晶体加工硬化曲线　polycrystal work-hardening curve
多晶体金属　polycrystalline metal
多晶体散射　polycrystalline scattering
多晶体[形]物质　polycrystalline substance
多晶体衍射花样　【理】polycrystal diffraction pattern
多晶体状态　polycrystalline condition
多晶体组织[结构]　polycrystalline structure
多晶铁素体　polycrystalline ferrite
多晶铜　polycrystalline copper
多晶物质　polycrystalline material
多晶现象　heteromorphism
多晶型　polymorphism, pleomorphism
多晶型的　polymorphic, polymorphous
多晶型物质　polymorphic substance
多晶型(现象)　polymorphism, polymorphy, pleomorphism
多晶型铁　polyiron
多晶型铁粉　【粉】polycrystalline iron
多晶性　polycrystallinity
多晶转变　polymorphic transformation
多镜质组分　vitrinite-rich component

多居里源　multicurie source
多聚形　polymeric form
多卷筒拉丝机　【压】multi-block machine
多开边模　【铸】multiple-part pattern
多刻度电表　unimeter
多孔板　multiorifice, perforated plate
多孔板分馏塔　perforated-plate column
多孔薄膜　porous diaphragm [membrane]
多孔表面　porous surface
多孔不锈钢　porous stainless steel
多孔部位(铸件的)　porous spot
多孔材料　porous [cellular, spongy] material, porosint
多孔沉积物[多孔覆层]　porous deposit
多孔衬背带材　porous backed strip
多孔衬套　porous bush(ing)
多孔带材　porous strip
多孔底　perforated bottom ◇ 烧结玻璃～漏斗 sintered glass funnel
多孔底箱　drain box
多孔电极　porous [perforated] electrode
多孔电接触器材　porous contacts
多孔锭模铸锭　multiple ingot
多孔方铁体　porous wuestite
多孔分流挤压模　porthole extrusion die
多孔分流模挤压　porthole extrusion
多孔粉粒　porous [voluminous] particle
多孔粉末　voluminous powder
多孔粉末烧结零件电解覆层法　etolizing
多孔粉冶材料　porous powder metallurgy material
多孔钢质零件　porous steel parts
多孔格子砖　【铁】cluster-type checker brick
多孔隔板　porous barrier
多孔隔膜　porous diaphragm
多孔隔膜电解槽　porous-diaphragm cell
多孔铬镀层　porous chromium plating
多孔构造　porous structure
多孔固定底式浮选机　mat-type cell
多孔管　perforated [anti-priming] pipe
多孔管道　multiple-duct conduit, void

channel
多孔滚筒　perforated roller
多孔过滤板　porous filter plate, porous disc
多孔过滤器　porous filter
多孔海绵铜　porous copper sponge
多孔焊缝　porous weld
多孔含油轴承　(同"含油轴承")
多孔混凝土　(同"加气混凝土")
多孔基体　porous matrix
多孔焦炭　porous coke
多孔结构　cellular [bubble] structure, honeycomb
多孔金属　porousmetal,【粉】foamed metal
多孔金属过滤板　porous metal plate
多孔金属过滤器　porous [powdered] metal filter
多孔金属零件　porous metal parts
多孔金属元件　porous metallic element
多孔篮　perforated basket
多孔蒙乃尔合金过滤器　porous Monel filter
多孔模　multihole [multicavity, multiple-cavity, multiport, porous] die
多孔模挤压　multihole extrusion
多孔膜　porous membrane
多孔耐磨零件　porous wear-resistant parts
多孔难熔金属　porous refractory metal
多孔黏土　bubbly clay
多孔镍过滤器　porous nickel filter
多孔镍雷汞[镍引爆]杯　porous nickel cup
多孔喷头　multihole nozzle
多孔喷(氧)枪　multihole lance
多孔喷嘴　multiple jet nozzle, multihole nozzle, multijet tip
多孔坯块　【粉】porous compact
多孔撇渣器　perforated skimmer
多孔青铜　porous bronze, oilite bronze (90Cu,10Sn)
多孔青铜分布板　porous bronze distributor
多孔青铜过滤器　bronze (porex) filter, porosint bronze filter
多孔青铜零件　porous bronze parts
多孔青铜轴承　porous bronze bearing
多孔球团　porous pellet
多孔熔渣　perforated slag
多孔塞　porous plug
多孔塞吹氩除气法　【冶】porous plug process
多孔烧结金属　porous sintered metal
多孔烧结碳化钨　porous sintered tungsten carbide
多孔烧结物　porous frit
多孔烧结锡铜轴套(气孔率30%)　oilite bush
多孔烧结氧化铝隔膜　porous sintered alumina diaphragm
多孔烧结制品　porous sintered product
多孔石墨青铜　porous graphite-containing bronze ◇ 杜雷克斯～*
多孔石墨青铜轴承　porous graphite-containing bronze bearing
多孔水口砖　multihole (nozzle) brick
多孔塑料　aerated [foamed] plastics
多孔碳化硅耐火材料　porous silicon-carbide refractory
多孔铁　porous iron, powdiron (0—10Cu, 余量Fe) ◇ 杜雷克斯～*
多孔铁含油轴承金属(100Fe)　iron-oilite
多孔铁基体　porous iron matrix
多孔铁皮(箱式)芯撑　perforated strip-metal chaplet
多孔铁铅石墨轴承　porous iron-lead-graphite bearing
多孔铁铜零件　porous iron-copper parts
多孔铁铜轴承　porous iron-copper bearing
多孔铁轴承　powdiron bearing
多孔铜基体　copper matrix of sufficient porosity
多孔铜铁合金　selfube iron
多孔团块[压块]　【团】porous briquette
多孔维氏体　porous Wuestite

多孔物质　porous mass
多孔卸料[排矿]　multiple (-slot) discharge
多孔型离子交换树脂　porous ion exchange resin
多孔性　porosity, poriness, sponginess
多孔性吸附　persorption
多孔絮凝层　expanded flocbed
多孔岩石　barren rock
多孔阴离子交换剂　porous anion-exchanger
多孔阴离子交换树脂　decolorite ◇ 杜利特 A-40LC~Duolite A-40LC
多孔制品　porous product [article]
多孔质充填剂(乙炔罐的)　filler material
多孔质固体[材料]　porous solid
多孔轴承　porous bearing ◇ 奥格~合金*
多孔铸件　porous casting
多孔铸铁　porous [open-grained] cast iron
多孔砖　perforated [multihole, porous] brick, multiport tile,【耐】cork brick
多孔状物质　spongeous mass
多跨框架[排架]　multiple-bay frame
多跨连续梁　multi-span beam
多莱尔铜基压铸合金(65—83Cu, 34—10Zn, 1—5Si, 有时加 1Al, 1Mn)　Doler brasses
多莱黄铜合金　Doler brass alloy
多莱津克锌基压铸合金(0.1—4.5Cu, 3.5—4.5Al, 0.01—0.08Mg, 余量 Zn)　Dolerzink
多莱锌合金　Doler-zinc
多雷德炼铁法　Dored process
多棱钢锭(带凹边的)　corrugated ingot
多棱圆钢锭　corrugated round ingot
多粒度料　multi-granular charge
多联电位器　(multi-)gang potentiometer
多联结晶器　【连铸】multi-mould
多量程　multirange
多量程电压表　multivoltmeter
多量程仪表　multimeter, multirange instrument [meter]

多列滚柱轴承　multi-row roller bearing
多硫化铵　ammonium polysulphide
多硫化钠{Na$_2$Sx}　sodium polysulphide
多硫化物　polysulphide
多流股(钢)　multistrand
多流(连铸)板坯　multi-slab
多流连铸机　multi(ple)-strand caster, multi(ple)-strand casting machine
多流连铸设备　multistrand plant
多炉连铸　multiple-heat [long-string, uninterrupted] casting, multi-heat continuous casting, series [sequence] continuous casting, back to back casting
多炉系统　multi-furnace system
多炉组电炉　multiple-unit electric furnace
多卤化物　polyhalide
多路　multichannel, multipath, multi-way
多路传输[多路复用, 多工]　【电】multiplex
多路分析仪　multichannel analyzer
多路复用器　multiplexor
多路工作方式　【计】multiplex mode
多路数据终端　multiplex data terminal
多路通道　multiplexer (channel), multiplexor
多路转换[调制, 扫描]器　multiplexer, multiplexor
多路转接器通道　multiplexor channel
多铝红柱{3Al$_2$O$_3$·2SiO$_2$}　mullite
多氯化橡胶漆　multiple chlorinated rubber paint
多脉冲焊接　multiple-impulse welding
多脉冲焊接时间控制器　multiple-impulse weld timer
多媒体技术　multimedia technique
多面角　polyhedral angle
多面棱镜[棱体]　polygon
多面体　polyhedral, polyhedron
多面体的面　face of polyhedron
多面体晶粒　polyhedral grain
多面体晶体　polygonal crystal

多面体网络　polyhedral network
多模锻压　multiple impression forging
多模具模架　multiple-tool adaptor
多模拉丝机　multidie [multihole] wire-drawing machine
多模连续式拉丝机　multidie continuous wire drawing machine
多模(腔)锻压　multiple impression forging
多姆纳费特固体燃料回转窑直接炼铁法　【铁】Domnarfvet process
多目标优化模型　multiple-object program model
多钼酸盐　polymolybdote
多钠锆石{$Na_2O \cdot ZrO_2 \cdot 3SiO_2 \cdot 2H_2O$}　soda-catapleite
多能涡流法检验仪(检验零件用)　multitest
多排(点)焊接头　multiple-row weld
多盘锯　gang saw
多泡的　bubbly
多泡构造[结构]　foamy structure ◇ 有序合金~*
多佩尔杜罗氧乙炔焰表面淬火法　Doppelduro process
多喷口吹管[火嘴]　multijet torch
多喷头喷嘴　multiple jet nozzle
多喷嘴扩散泵　multiple-nozzle pump
多批萃取　multiple batch extraction
多片电路　multichip circuit
多片式离合器　【机】multidisc clutch
多频(率)　multifrequency (M.F.)
多品种精密轧机　versatile precision-rolling mill
多普勒频移　Doppler shift
多普勒效应　Doppler effect
多普洛伊耐蚀铸铁　Dopploy (Dopploy 3：8.5Ni, 2.35Cr, 2.86C, 1Mn, 余量 Fe)
多气锭　gassy ingot
多气孔钢锭　blown ingot
多气泡的　blowy
多气性(孔)　【钢】gassiness
多钳口(炉用)卷取机　multiple-slot coiler

多腔模(压铸)　combination die
多腔式芯盒　multiple core box
多腔造型　【铸】multiple moulding
多腔(组合)铸型　multicavity mould, multiple-cavity die
多羟基羧酸　polyhydroxy-carboxylic acid
多裙式绝缘子　multi-petticoat insulator
多刃圆盘剪纵剪作业线　slitting line
多熔炼炉系统　multi-furnace system
多熔区区域精炼　multiple-zone refining
多柔传动装置　Bogiflex drive unit
多肉　【铸】sticker, rat
多色　multiple-colour, polychrome
多色 X 射线　heterochromatic [heterogeneous] X-rays
多色点线记录器　multi-colour dotted-line recorder
多色辐射　heterochromatic radiation
多色光度计　heterochromatic photometer
多色仪[器]　polychromator ◇ 光栅~*
多砂箱铸型　(同"多箱铸型")
多烧嘴窑　multiburner kiln
多室床　multi-compartment bed
多室式炉　multiple chamber furnace
多室蓄热室　【钢】multiple-pass regenerator
多室窑　multi-chamber kiln
多室蒸发器　(同"多效蒸发器")
多试样试验机　multispecimen testing machine
多数逻辑　【计】majority (logic)
多水高岭土{$Al_2Si_2O_5(OH)_4 \cdot 2H_2O$}　halloysite
多水硅锰矿　vittinkite
多水磷铅铀矿{$PbO \cdot 4UO_3 \cdot P_2O_5 \cdot 9H_2O$}　renardite
多水菱镁矿{$MgO \cdot CO_2 \cdot 5H_2O$}　lansfordite
多水菱铀矿{$6UO_3 \cdot 5CO_2 \cdot 8H_2O$}　sharpite
多水钼铀矿{$UO_2 \cdot 2UO_3 \cdot 5MoO_3 \cdot 12H_2O$}　moluranite

多水偏高岭土 {$Al_2O_3 \cdot 2SiO_2 \cdot 2H_2O$} metahalloysite

多水铜铁矾 guildite

多丝埋弧焊 multiplewire submerged-arc welding

多速电动机 multi-speed motor

多酸(的) polyacid

多探头[针] multiprobe

多探头机构[多头换能器装置] multiple-transducer assembly

多探头式监测器 multiprobe monitor

多膛(焙烧)炉 multiple-hearth (roasting) furnace, multiple-hearth roaster ◇ 重叠～*,赫氏窄轴式～*,机械搅拌～*

多膛式马弗炉 muffled multiple-hearth(-type) furnace

多膛窑 multi-passage kiln

多糖 polysaccharide

多特蒙德单管提升法(真空脱气) 【钢】 Dortmund method

多条带材精整 multiple strip processing

多条连续酸洗作业线 multistrand continuous pickle line

多铁镁质 dofemic difemane

多通道(热)交换器 multipass (heat) exchanger

多通电磁阀 various way-solenoid valve

多通路 【电】multirun, multiple-pass, multipath

多通路射流元件 multi-channel fluid element

多铜绿矾 salvadorite

多筒冷却机 planetary cooler

多头冲模 multiple [gang] die

多头导管 manifold

多头点焊机 multipoint spot welder

多头焊机 multi-head welder

多头[多烧嘴]切割 multiburner [multiple-torch] cutting

多头切割横梁 【焊】header traverse

多头热电偶 split thermocouples

多头焰炬[吹管] multi(ple-)head torch

多头自动电弧焊机 multihead automatic arc-welding machine

多位焊接 (同"多站焊接")

多稳射流装置 multi-stable fluid device

多钨酸盐 poly-tungstate ◇ 碱金属～alkali polytungstate

多硒铜铀矿 derriksite

多锡焊料 【焊】rich solder

多系列造球设备 multi-circuit balling installation

多线拉拔 multihole drawing

多线扭转线材轧机机组 multiple-strand twist block

多线切分轧制 multislit rolling

多线式端头-废料飞剪 multistrand crop and cobble flying shears

多线式拉拔[拉丝]机 multiple drawbench

多线式轧机 multistrand [multiple-strand] mill

多线[条]轧制 multistrand rolling

多相 polyphase, multiphase, heterophase

多相催化作用 heterogeneous catalysis

多相电表 polyphase meter

多相电流 polyphase [multiphase] current

多相反应 heterogeneous reaction

多相反应系统[体系] multiphase reaction system

多相合金 polyphase [multiphase, heterogeneous] alloy, plural phase alloy

多相混合物 heterogeneous mixture

多相结构 (同"非均质组织")

多相流 multiphase flow

多相膜电极 heterogeneous membrance electrode

多相平衡 polyphase [heterogeneous] equilibrium

多相区 【金】polyphase region

多相烧结 【粉】heterogeneous sintering

多相系[体系,系统] polyphase [multiphase, heterogeneous] system

多相系平衡 【金】equilibrium in heterogeneous system

多相性　heterogeneity
多相压制　polyphase compact
多相制　【电】polyphase system
多相状态　heterogeneous [inhomogeneous] condition
多相组织　multiphase [heterogene] structure
多箱铸型　【铸】multiple part mould
多项分布　multinomial distribution
多项开发[研制]　multiple-theme development
多项式　polynomial, polymerization, polynome
多项式回归　polynomial regression
多项式回归分析　polynominal regression analysis
多向马氏体　multidirectional Martensite
多向模锻压力机　multicored forging press
多向应力　multi-axial stress
多向应力模型　multi-directional stress pattern
多效压机　multiple(-action) press
多效真空蒸发器　multi-effect vacuum evaporator
多效蒸发　multiple-effect evaporation
多效蒸发器　multiple(-effect) evaporator
多谐振荡器　multivibrator ◇双稳态~*
多芯电缆[导线]　multiple [multi-core] cable, bank cable
多芯复合超导体　multifilamentary composite superconductor
多芯控制电缆　multi-core control cable
多型铸造　multiple (core) casting
多形的　polymorphic, polymorphous, multiform
多形性　polymorphism, polymorphy
多形性变态　polymorphic modification
多形性转变　polymorphic change
多压头锻造　【压】multiple-ram forging
多焰　【冶】multiflame
多焰焊枪[燃烧器]　multiflame blowpipe, multiple jet [tubed] burner

多焰喷嘴　multiflame tip, multiple jet burner
多焰式吹管[火嘴]　multiflame torch
多焰嘴火焰刨削机　【焊】multiple beam flame planing machine
多焰嘴切割[气割]机　(同"多割嘴气割机")
多阳极电解槽　multiple anodes cell
多阳极电解炉　multi-anode furnace
多样式　multiplicity
多用户访问　【计】multiaccess
多用途　multipurpose, multiple-purpose
多用途反应堆　multipurpose reactor
多用途涂层　multipurpose coating
多用途仪表　multipurpose instrument
多油的　oily
多余电子　excess electron
多余库存　overstock
多余水分　excess moisture
多域　【数】polydomain
多预焙阳极电解槽　【色】cell with prebaked multiple anodes
多元高速钢　complex high-speed steel
多元硅　multielement silicon
多元合金　multicomponent [complex, complicated] alloy ◇弥散型~*, 尼克林~*
多元合金钢　complex alloy steel
多元回归　multi-element regression
多元回归分析　multivariate regression analysis
多元件　multiunit, multicomponent
多元金属系烧结　【粉】sintering of polymetallic system
多元酸　polyatomic acid, polyacid
多元素镀层　multiple-element coating
多元碳化物　multicarbide, multiple-carbide ◇烧结~*
多元碳化物粉末　multiple carbide powder
多元碳化物合金　multiple carbide alloy
多元碳化物硬质合金　【粉】multiple carbide hard metal, cemented multicarbide,

多元碳化物硬质合金刀具　cemented multiple carbide
多元碳化物硬质合金刀具　cemented multicarbide tool
多元系　polynary [multicomponent] system
多原子气体　polyatomic gas
多圆弧曲线　compound curve
多圆盘分移剪切机　【压】gang slitting nibbling machine
多圆盘式剪切机　【压】gang slitting shears
多运算符系统　multiple-operator system
多匝扁平感应加热线圈　pie-plate (heating) coil
多匝感应线圈　multi-turn induction coils
多渣的　drossy
多站焊机[焊接设备]　multioperator welding set
多站焊接　multiple-operator welding
多折式出口活套坑　delivery and loop storage pit
多蒸锅玻璃分馏泵　multiple-boiler glass pump
多蒸气的　vapourous
多支承拱　multiple support arch ◇ 用于~的悬挂砖 M.S. (multiple support) tile
多支承辊颈轴承　【压】multi-part roll neck bearing
多支承墙　multiple support wall
多支承原理　multiple support (M.S.) principle
多值位移　multi-valued displacement
多种粉碎粒度混合物　mixed graded size
多种负荷均衡分配法　harmonious distribution method of multi-load
多种价元素　polygen
多种燃料燃烧　multifuel firing
多种形式　multi-way
多种用途[目的]　multipurpose
多种用途润滑脂　multipurpose grease
多种用途装置　multipurpose plant
多(种)原料　multi-feed

多轴床头　multi-spindle head
多轴应力　multi-axial stress
多主晶的　peroikic
多柱塞泵　multiple-plunger pump
多柱压力机　multidaylight press
多转子式捻股机　【电】multiple rotor stranding machine
多锥式造球机　multiple-cone pelletizer
多锥型混合机　multi-cone mixer
多锥形圆筒造球机　multiple-cone drum
多自由度的　multivariant
多自由度系统　many-degree of freedom system
多组分的　multicomponent, multiple-constituent
多组分化合物　polycompound
多组分混合物蒸馏　multicomponent distillation
多组分炉渣　multicomponent slag
多组分烧结矿　【团】composite agglomerate
多组分系　multicomponent system
多组元混合物　multicomponent mixture
多组元金属系统　【金】multicomponent metallic system
多嘴火焰切割器[多嘴割炬]　multiflame (gas) cutter, multinozzle cutter
垛　pile, stack, bundle
垛板辊道辊子　skew table roll
垛板机　【压】sheet piler, piler (bed), piling device, stacker ◇ 出口~ exit piler,磁力[电磁]~*,真空吸盘~*
垛板升降台　pile lifter
垛板箱　piling box
垛堆层错　【金】stacking fault
垛堆机　clamp forming machine
垛放　stacking, piling
垛放辊道　piling table
垛放机　stacker
垛高　【压】piling height
垛料[板]筐　piling pockets
垛料[堆放,垛放]台　◇ 带板坯~的辊

道 magazine table,炉用~ furnace magazine

垛式挡土墙 crib retaining wall

垛重 stack weight

垛砖机 【耐】setting machine

垛装箱 piling box

躲峰时间 off-peak period

舵枢 gudgeon

惰辊 idler roller,【压】loose roll

惰辊式冷床 dead roller bed

惰轮 idler,idle(r) [free,dead] pulley,idle wheel

惰轮轴 idler shaft

惰钳 lazy tong

惰行冲程 【机】idle stroke

惰性 inertia,inertness,unreactiveness(化学惰性)◇ 非~杂质

惰性材料炉衬 【冶】brasque

惰性尘埃 inert dust

惰性导体 inert conductor

惰性的 inert, reactionless, unreactive, sluggish

惰性电极 inert electrode

惰性电解质 inert electrolyte

惰性固体物质 inert solid

惰性固体载体 inert solid support

惰性硅酸盐 inert silicate

惰性环境 inert environments

惰性混合料 inert mix

惰性加稀气体 inert diluent gas

惰性介质 inert medium

惰性金属 passive metal

惰性气氛 inert (gas) atmosphere

惰性气氛锆电解槽 【色】inert atmosphere zirconium electrolytic cell

惰性气氛退火 inert atmosphere annealing

惰性气体 inert [noble, inactive, indifferent] gas, inerts, noble ◇ 充~的密封室 inert atmosphere room,充~的仓室 inert-gas-filled chamber,充~的料仓 inert-gas-filled hopper,移动式~保护附件 【焊】trailing shield

惰性气体包层 inert gas envelope

惰性气体保护层 inert gas cover

惰性气体保护点焊(法) inert gas spot welding

惰性气体保护(电弧)焊[惰性气体电弧焊] inert gas shielded-arc welding, inert (gas) arc welding

惰性气体保护电弧(焊接)法 inert gas shielded-arc process

惰性气体保护(电弧)焊炬 inert gas shielded-arc torch, inert arc torch

惰性气体保护电弧熔炼 inert gas [atmosphere] arc melting

惰性气体保护锻造 inert gas forging

惰性气体保护(加热)炉 inert atmosphere furnace

惰(性)气(体)保护金属[熔化]极电弧焊 MIG (metal-arc inert-gas) welding, shiel-ded inert-gas metal-arc welding (S.I.G.M.A.), metal inert gas welding

惰性气体保护钎焊 inert atmosphere brazing

惰性气体保护切割 inert-gas shielded-arc cutting

惰性气体保护熔炼法 inert-gas shielded melting

惰性气体(保护)碳极电弧焊 inert gas carbon-arc welding

惰性气体(保护)钨极(电弧)焊 tungsten-arc inert-gas welding (T.I.G., Tig., T.I.G.W.),inert gas tungsten-arc welding

惰性气体(保护)钨极电弧焊焊缝 T.I.G. (tungsten-arc inert-gas) weld

惰性气体(保护)钨极电弧焊炬 inert gas shielded tungsten-arc torch

惰性气体(保护)钨极电弧切割 tungsten-arc inert-gas cutting (T.I.G.C.)

惰性气体(保护)消耗电极焊(接) inert gas consumable-electrode welding

惰性气体保护罩 inert gas shield

惰性气体(保护)自耗电极电弧焊 con-

sumable electrode inert arc welding
惰性气体焊接机　inertia welding machine
惰性气体金属[熔化]极电弧焊接法　metal-arc inert gas welding process
惰性气体起泡　bubbling of inert gas
惰性气体气氛　inert (gas) atmosphere
惰性气体熔化极电弧焊焊缝　metal-arc inert-gas weld
惰性气体洗包　ladle flushing with inert gas
惰性气体原子　inert gas atom
惰性熔体　inert melt
惰性溶剂　inert [passive] solvent ◇ 质子~*
惰性添加剂　【选】inert additive

惰性填料　inert filler
惰性网格　inert grid
惰性物质　inert [dead] matter, inerts
惰性物质含量　inert content
惰性稀释剂　inert diluent
惰性盐类混合物　inert salts mixture
惰性阳极　inert anode
惰性氧化物　indifferent oxide
惰性液体介质　inert liquid medium
惰性运载气体　inert carrier gas
惰性载体　inert support [carrier]
惰性组分　inert component, inerts, 【焦】inertinite (煤岩的)
惰性助熔剂　inert flux

E e

锇笔尖合金　osmium pen alloy
锇黑　osmium black
锇丝　osmium filament
锇丝电灯　osmium electric lamp
锇酸　osmic acid
锇酸酐　osmic acid anhydride, osmium oxide
锇酸盐[酯]　osmate
锇钨灯丝合金　osram
锇钨合金丝灯　osram lamp
锇铱笔尖合金（约含10%天然锇铱的合金）　osmiridium pen alloy
锇铱合金（40Ir，17—45Os，少量 Ru、Pt、Rh）　osmiridium
锇铱矿　[地]osmiridium
锇铑铂笔尖合金（Os:Rh:Pt = 17:2:1）（osmium）pen alloy
鹅颈管　bent pipe,【铁】tuyere stock, swan neck, goose-neck
鹅颈管短截（围管上的一段）【铁】neck
鹅颈进风弯管　【铁】goose-neck
鹅颈式浇口　swan-neck runner
鹅颈式支柱冲床　【压】swan-neck press
鹅颈台　caster table
鹅卵石　grail, cobble(stone)
鹅头床[台]（中厚板剪切机旁的）　caster(transfer)bed, ball stanchion bed
鹅头桩　caster table,【压】goose-neck
俄歇电子分光计　Auger electron spectrometer(AES)
俄歇电子光谱法[能谱学]　Auger electron spectroscopy(AES)
俄歇谱图　Auger spectrogram
俄歇跃迁　Auger transition
额定尺寸　rated size
额定出力　【电】normal rating ◇ 断续[间歇]负载～intermittent rating
额定的　rated, nominal ◇ 低于～[标准的]重量　underweight
额定电流　rated current, current rating
额定电压　rated voltage, voltage rating
额定负载[荷载，载荷]　rated [nominal] load
额定功率　rated [nominal] power, (power)rating, standard duty ◇ 长期运转～【电】continuous rating
额定面积　nominal area
额定能力[容量]　rated [nominal] capacity
额定强度（导线的）　rated strength
额定熔炼量　normal cast weight
额定输出[产量]　rated output
额定输入[处理能力，装入量，产量]　rated input
额定速度　rated speed
额定条件[状态]　rated conditions
额定温度　rated temperature
额定阳极电流密度　nominal anode current density
额定值　rated [nominal] value, (nominal) rating ◇ 低于～under-shoot
额定转矩　rated [nominal] torque
"额外"除渣（转炉的）【钢】"extra" slag removal
额外的　extra, additional(add., addl)
额外反射　extra reflections
额外荷载量　extra-load bearing capacity
额外能量　extra energy
额外烧结现象　【粉】extra-sintering phenomenon
噁唑酮　azolactone
恶臭　【环】offensive odour
恶臭物质　offensive odour substance, malodorous substance
恶果　ill-effects, bad result
恶化　deterioration
恶性膨胀　【团】catastrophic expansion [swelling]
厄尔夫特铝电解槽（德国式）　Erftwerk cell
厄盖尔铝镁锌系合金　Ergal

厄卢明铝合金 (3.5—4.5Cu, 0.4—0.7Mn, 0.4—0.7Mg, 0.4Si, 0.5Fe, 余量 Al) Earlumin aluminium alloy

苊 $\{C_{12}H_{10}\}$ acenaphthere

扼流电阻 choking resistance

扼流控制 reactor control

扼流圈 choke, reactor, reactance coil ◇ 铁心～ iron-core reactor

扼流圈耦合 【电】choke [impedance] coupling

扼流圈输入式整流电路 choke-input type rectifier circuit

扼流线圈 choke [choking] coil

轭 【电】balance beam, 【机】yoke

轭杆 yoke lever

轭铁 yoke(iron), framework ◇ 双倍试件-双倍～法*

轭铁磁化 yoke magnetization

垩状磷酸锌钙铝石 $\{3(Zn, Ca) \cdot 0.2Al_2O_3 \cdot P_2O_5 \cdot 27H_2O\}$ kehoeite

颚板(破碎机的) jaw plate, dog ◇ 破碎机～ crusher jaw

颚口 jaw opening

颚式破碎机 jaw breaker, jaw crusher, alligator ◇ 单肘板～*

颚式破碎机加料口 jaw opening of crusher

颚式破碎机破碎 jaw crushing

颚形离合器 jaw [cheek] clutch

鳄口剪[鳄口式剪切机] (同"杠杆式剪切机")

鳄口效应(轧制的) alligator effect

鳄口形挤渣机 alligator

鳄口状断裂 alligator cracking

鳄皮效应(起珠状皮) alligator effect

鳄式压挤机 crocodile squeezer

鳄鱼皮(钢材缺陷) crocodile skin, crozzling

鳄鱼皮状表面(轧制金属的) alligator skin

鳄鱼嘴(板坯纵向缺陷) fish mouth

鳄嘴裂口(板坯纵向劈裂缺陷) 【压】alligatoring

蒽 $\{C_{14}H_{10}\}$ anthracene

蒽饼 【焦】anthracene cake

蒽糊 anthracene paste

蒽油 anthracene oil, carbolineum

蒽油柱 【焦】anthracene column

恩迪朗斯焊接合金 Endewrance alloy

恩杜龙耐热铸铁 (2.2C, 1.5Si, 1.5Mn, 16.5Cr) Euduron

恩杜罗耐蚀铁基合金 (5—30Cr, 8—20Ni, 0.5—5.0Mo, 0.5—3.0Si, 余量 Fe) Enduro

恩格尔－布鲁尔理论 【金】Engel-Brewer theory

恩格勒黏(滞)度 Engler degree

恩格雷弗斯含铅黄铜 (62.5Cu, 35.75Zn, 1.75Pb) Engravers brass [alloy]

恩格洛伊 255 金镍钎焊合金 (82Au, 18Ni) Engaloy 255

恩隆电阻分析法(分析碳及合金含量) Enlund test [method]

恩氏蒸馏 Engler distillation

恩斯林值 Enslin value

恩斯特轻便硬度试验机 Ernst hardness tester

鲕绿泥石 chamosite

鲕石 oolite

鲕铁矿 【采】clinton ore, oolitic iron ore

鲕状 oolitic

鲕状赤铁矿 kidney ore

鲕(状)褐铁矿 minette(type iron ore)

鲕状结构 oolitic texture

鲕状矿石 flaxseed ore

鲕状铁矿 ballstone

耳孔[环] eye

耳线(轧件的) tramlines

耳轴 trunnion, gudgeon, wrist

耳轴部分(转炉的) journal section

耳轴承 trunnion bearing

耳轴环 trunnion ring

耳轴铜衬 trunnion brass

耳轴销 gudgeon pin

耳轴销钉(转炉的) 【钢】trunion pin
耳轴座　trunnion bed
耳子　【压】fin, ears(板材或带材的端部缺陷), rolling edge(缺陷)
耳子形成　【压】formation of fins
铒添加合金　erbium addition
二氨　【胺】diamine
二氨络合物　diamine complex
二胺基镍　nickel diamine
二倍器　doubler
二苯基　dipeny
二苯醚(氧芴){$C_{12}H_8O$}　dipenylene[biphenylene]oxide, dibenzofuran
二苄基乙二胺　D.B.E.D.(dibenzylethenediamine)
二步淬火　two-stepped quenching
二步冷却段(带式烧结机的)　second stage cooling zone
二冲程煤气机　two-stroke gas engine
二重焙烧　double roasting
二重传动　twin drive
二重淬火　double quenching
二重对称　diad symmetry
二重回火　double tempering
二重螺旋轴　screw diad
二重烧结　double sintering
二重式多辊矫直机　two-high roller leveller
二重双动压机　duplex double-action press
二重性　duality
二重轴　two-fold axis ◇相交~intersecting diads
二重转动[旋转]轴　two-fold rotation axis, rotation diad
二次奥氏体化　【金】reaustenitizing
二次贝氏体　secondary bainite
二次产品　secondary(product)
二次产物　after product
二次称量　second weighing
二次成型　second compacting, secondary fabrication
二次重熔　【钢】double melting ◇自耗电极~法*

二次除尘器　reduster
二次除铜(粗铅的)　secondary copper removal
二次除铜阶段　second copper-removal stage
二次处理　secondary processing[treatment], aftertreatment
二次吹炼　reblow
二次吹氧系统(旋转式转炉的)　【钢】ondary lancing system
二次淬火(渗碳钢的)　regenerating[regenerative, secondary] quenching
二次点火器　post-ignition hood, second ignition furnace, post-heater, preheat hood, secondary ignition furnace
二次电池　secondary battery[cell]
二次电解　secondary electrolysis, re-electrolysis
二次电子发射　secondary electron emission
二次镀铬　after-chroming
二次镀锡锅　red-dipping pot
二次镀锡机组　red-dipping unit
二次煅烧　secondary calcining
二次反应堆　【理】secondary reactor
二次方程式　quadratic(equation)
二次分解　secondary decomposition
二次粉碎机　【耐】secondary breaker
二次风机　secondary air fan
二次风流　secondary air flow
二次风嘴　secondary lance
二次富集(作用)　secondary enrichment
二次共析碳化物　secondary eutectoid carbide
二次固溶体　secondary solid solution
二次光谱　secondary spectrum
二次规划(运筹学)　quadratic programming
二次滚动效应　rerolling effect
二次过滤　after-filtration
二次过滤器　secondary filter, after-filter

二次滑移带　secondary slip band, striae
二次滑移面　secondary slip plane
二次还原　second reduction
二次混合　secondary mixing
二次混合机　secondary [pelletizing] mixer, reroll(ing) drum（圆筒型）, granulation drum
二次混料（烧结的）　【铁】rerolling
二次混料工（烧结机的）　balling operator
二次活套　secondary loop
二次急骤蒸馏（同"二次闪蒸"）
二次挤压　re-extrusion
二次夹杂　secondary inclusions
二次加工　secondary processing, post-processing, re-working, secondary fabrication
二次加焦　secondary coke addition
二次加热　reheat(ing), post[double] heating
二次加水　【团】rewetting
二次浆化　repulping
二次结晶　secondary crystallization
二次金属　secondary metal
二次晶轴　【金】secondary axis ◇ 树枝(状)晶(体)～*
二次精炼　secondary [double] refining, secondary steelmaking
二次精炼技术　secondary steelmaking technology
二次精馏塔　after-fractionating tower
二次精选　【选】recleaning
二次净化　recleaning
二次净化气体　secondary gas
二次聚焦射束　refocused beam
二次颗粒　【粉】secondary particle
二次空气　secondary [auxiliary, supplementary] air ◇ 炉顶～【冶】top air addition
二次拉拔　two holed
二次拉丝机　double draft bull block, double-deck block
二次冷床　secondary cooler
二次冷凝器　secondary condenser, after-condenser ◇ 涡流式～*
二次冷却　secondary cooling, aftercooling ◇ 梁式～*, 喷射法～*
二次冷却带区段　【连铸】section of cooling zone
二次冷却带下部（连铸机的）　lower spray section
二次冷却剂　secondary coolant
二次冷却器　secondary cooler, after-cooler, recooler
二次冷却区　【连铸】secondary (cooling) zone, spray cooling chamber ◇ 弧形～*, 连续喷雾～*
二次冷却室　secondary cooling chamber
二次冷却塔　recooling tower
二次冷轧　double cold reduction (D.C.R.)
二次冷轧钢板　double reduced plate
二次冷轧机　double cold reduction mill
二次离子化原子　doubly ionized atom
二次锂电池　rechargeable lithium battery
二次锂离子电池　rechargeable lithium ion battery
二次硫化物阳极　secondary sulphide anode
二次逆风插值　quadratic upwind interpolation
二次浓缩机　secondary thickener
二次喷水（弧形连铸装置的）　curved sprays
二次平移　secondary translation
二次破碎　secondary crushing, recrushing
二次破碎机　secondary crusher
二次气孔　secondary blow-hole
二次球磨机　secondary ball mill
二次屈氏体　secondary troostite
二次燃烧　secondary [post] combustion, after-burning, secondary burning
二次燃烧率　post-combustion degree (P.C.D.)
二次燃烧氧枪　post-combustion lance
二次燃烧用风[空气]　secondary combus-

tion air
二次热处理的　re-heat-treated
二次熔炼　second melt
二次熔炼的再生金属　second-melt stock, remelting stock
二次蠕变　secondary creep
二次蠕变速率　secondary creep rate
二次筛分　secondary screening, rescreen
二次闪蒸　double-flash evaporation
二次烧结　second sintering
二次射线　secondary rays
二次渗碳体　secondary cementite
二次式　quadratic form
二次收缩　after-contraction
二次送风　【铁】reblow
二次酸洗　double pickling
二次损耗(变压器的)　secondary loss
二次缩孔　secondary pipe [piping]
二次索氏体　secondary [tempered] sorbite
二次添加　secondary addition
二次调浆　repulp, reslurrifying
二次退火　second [double] annealing
二次脱氧产物　【冶】secondary deoxidation product
二次位错　secondary dislocation
二次文氏管　second stage Venturi
二次污染　secondary pollution
二次雾化　secondary atomization
二次细筛　second fine screen
二次线圈　secondary coil
二次消光　secondary extinction
二次压下　double reduction
二次压制　second pressing
二次氧化　reoxidation
二次冶金　secondary metallurgy
二次仪表　secondary instrument [meter]
二次硬度　secondary hardness
二次硬化　【金】secondary hardening
二次硬化材料　secondary hardening meaterial
二次预热　re-preheat
二次原料　secondary raw material
二次圆筒混合机　reroll(ing)drum
二次圆锥破碎机　secondary cone crusher
二次再结晶的抑制　【金】suppression of secondary recrystallization
二次再结晶织构　【金】secondary recrystallization texture
二次再熔炼　【钢】double melting
二次造球　secondary pelletization
二次造球机　secondary pelletizer
二次增亮剂　booster brightener
二次增碳　(同"再增碳")
二次渣　second-run slag
二次轧制　【压】rerolling
二次蒸汽　recovered steam
二次枝晶臂间距　secondary dendrite arm spacing
二次枝晶轴　secondary branch
二次轴　two-fold axis
二次转动轴　two-fold rotation axis
二次转运(材料的)　double-handling
二次自体研磨　secondary autogenous grinding
二次组织　secondary structure
二醋酸乙二醇　ethylene glycol diacedata
二代磷酸锶　(同"磷酸氢锶")
二代酸　secondary acids
二氮化三镁{Mg_3N_2}　magnesium nitride
二氮化三铍{Be_3N_2}　beryllium nitride
二氮杂菲离子(同"试业铁灵")
二挡齿轮　intermediate gear
二等分线　bisecting line, bisector, bisectrix
二等品　seconds
二底图　transparency drawing
二地址　【计】two-address, double-address
二地址码　two-address code
二地址指令　【计】double [two-address] instruction
二地址指令码　two-address code
二碲银锑　silver antimony telluride
二碘化锆{ZrI_2}　zirconium diiodide
二碘化钼{MoI_2}　molybdous iodide
二碘化钐{SmI_2}　samarium diiodide

二碘化铊{TlI₂}　thallium diiodide
二碘化物　diiodide, biniodide
二碘化铟{InI₂}　indium diiodide
二电子枪熔炼炉　two-gun melting furnace
二丁胺{(C₄H₉)₂NH}　di-butylamine, di-n-butylamine
二丁基卡必醇　dibutyl carbitol
二丁基磷酸　dibutyl phosphoric acid (DBP), di-n-butyl phosphoric acid
二丁(基)醚{(C₄H₉)₂O}　(di)butyl ethey
二丁氧基　dibutoxy
二丁氧基二甘醇[二乙二醇]　dibutoxy diethylene glycol
二丁氧基三乙烯甘醇　dibutoxy triethylene glycol
二丁氧基四乙烯甘醇　dibutoxy tetraethlene glycol
二度空间模型　two-dimensional model
二段浸出法　(同"两段浸出法")
二段冷却风机　second stage cooling fan, final cooling supply fan
二段时效　two-steps ageing
二段式链箅机　two-pass grate
二噁烷{(CH₂)₄O₂}　dioxan(e)
二酚　diphenol
二分度圆测角仪　two-circle goniometer
二分之一硬(同"半硬")
二分钟镀锌钢丝　two-minute wire
二氟(化)的　difluorinated
二氟化合物　difluoro compound
二氟化铊{TlF₂}　thallium difluoride
二氟化物　bifluoride, difluoride
二钙　dicalcium
二钙硅酸盐　belite
二甘醇一乙醚　carbitol
二甘醇二乙醚　(同"二丁基长必醇")
二硅化钼{MoSi₂}　molybdenum disilicide
二硅化钼加热元件　molybdenum silicide heating element
二硅化钼陶瓷　molybdenum disilicide ceramics
二硅化物　disilicide

二硅酸钠　sodium disilicate
二硅酸铅　lead disilicate
二硅酸盐　bisilicate, disilicate
二癸胺　di-n-decylamine
二辊粗轧机列　two-high roughing stands in train
二辊可逆式初轧[开坯]机　two-high reversing blooming [cogging] mill
二辊可逆式钢梁轧机　two-high reversing-beam mill
二辊可逆式机座　two-high reversing stand
二辊可逆式精轧机　two-high reversing-finishing mill
二辊可逆式轧机机组　two-high reversing mill train
二辊可逆式中厚板轧机　two-high reversing-plate mill
二辊平整机　two-high dressing mill
二辊式　duo
二辊式薄板轧机　two-high sheet-rolling mill
二辊式齿轮座　two-high pinion stand
二辊式初轧机　two-high cogging mill
二辊式初轧[开坯]机组　two-high cogging mill train
二辊式除[碎]鳞机　two-high scale breaker
二辊式穿孔机　two-roll piercer
二辊式粗轧机座　two-high rougher
二辊式(方坯)初轧机　two-high bloomer, two-high blooming mill
二辊式机座　two-high mill
二辊式矫直机　two-roll reeler
二辊式精轧机　two-high finishing mill
二辊式精轧机组　two-high finishing mill train
二辊式精轧机座　two-high finishing stand
二辊式万能板坯初轧机　2-Hi universal type slabbing mill
二辊式万能轧机　two-high universal mill
二辊式万能轧机组　two-high universal

二辊式斜轧机　2-roller skew-rolling mill
二辊式轧板机(上辊不动的)　balanced mill
二辊(式)轧机　two-high(rolling)mill, duo mill, twin rolling mill, double-high (rolling)mill ◇ 上辊不动的~ jump mill
二辊式轧机机组　two-high mill train
二辊式轧机机座　two-high(rolling)mill stand
二辊式中厚板轧机　two-high plate mill
二辊式中间机组　two-high intermediate roll train
二辊式装置　two-high setup
二辊－四辊联合式轧机　two-high/four-high combination rolling mill
二辊斜轧穿孔机　two-high rotary piercer
二辊轧制(法)　twin roll process
二辊周期式薄板轧机(two-high)　pull-over mill, pass-over[drag-over]mill
二辊周期式轧制　pull-over type rolling
二合络化物[络化剂]　【化】bidentate
二环己基亚硝酸铵　dicyclohexy ammonium
二环戊二烯　cicyclopentadiene
二磺酸　{R·(SO₃H)₂}　disulphonic acid
二磺酸盐[酯]　{R(SO₃M)₂ 或 R(SO₂OR)₂}　disulfonate, disulphonate
二极的(am)　bipolar
二极电(弧熔炼)炉　two-electrode furnace
二极管　diode ◇ 参数~ parametric diode, 充气~ gas diode, 结型~ junction diode, 稳压[齐纳]~Zener diode
二极管函数发生器　diode function generator
二极管矩阵　【计】diode matrix
二极管逻辑　【计】diode logic
二极管逻辑电路　diode-logical circuit
二极管限幅[削波]器　diode clipper
二极管整流器　diode rectifier
二极－三极管　diode-triode

二极－五极管　diode-pentode
二级存储器　secondary memory[storage]
二级反应　second order reaction
二级过滤器　2-stage filter
二级减速传动装置　double reduction gear
二级滤液　second stage filtrate
二级品　second(-rate)
二级品钢轨　second rails
二级时效　two-steps ageing
二级调节器　double-stage regulator
二级[阶]相变　second order phase change [transition]
二级跃迁[转变]　second order transition
二加一地址　【计】two-plus-one address
二甲胺　dimethylamine
二甲苯　{C₆H₄(CH₃)₂}　xylone, dimethyl-benzene
二甲苯胺法(反射炉烟气浓缩法之一)　dimethylaniline process (D.M.A.)
二甲苯基　{(CH₃)₂C₆H₃}　xylyl
二甲基　dimethyl-
二甲基环戊烯　dimethylcyelopentene (D.M.E.P.)
二甲基甲酮连氮　{[CH₃)₂C:N]₂}　dimethyl ketazine
二甲基乙醇胺　dimethyl ethanolanmine
二甲基异酞酸酯　dimethylisophthalate (D.M.I.)
二甲基吡啶　lutidine
二甲基噻吩　{C₆H₈S}　thioxene, dimethylthiophene
二甲基锌　zinc methyl
二价　divalence, divalency, bivalence
二价铱的　osmious
二价镉的　cadmic
二价汞化合物　mercuric compound
二价钴的　cobaltous
二价基　diad
二价碱土金属　bivalent alkaline earth metal
二价金化合物　bivalent gold compound
二价金属　bivalent metal

二价金属硫酸盐	bivalent metallic sulphate

二价离子 bivalent [two-charge] ion
二价锰的 manganous
二价钼的 molybd(en)ous
二价钼化合物 molybdous compound
二价镍(的) nickelous
二价-三价铁氧化物 【化】ferrous ferric oxide, ferriferrous oxide
二价钐的 samarous
二价铈 cerous cerium
二价铁 ferrous [bivalent] iron ◇ 含～和三价铁的化合物 ferroferric compound
二价铁的 ferrous
二价铁化合物 ferrocompound
二价铁离子氧化 ferrous ion oxidation
二价铜 bivalent copper
二价铜的 cupric
二价铜化合物 cupric compound
二价铜离子 double-charge copper ion
二价锡的 stannous
二价元素 bivalent element
二价原子 diad, bivalent atom
二价锗的 germanous
二价锗化合物 germanous compound
二进位换算电路 binary scaler
二进位组 【计】byte
二进制 【数】binary system [base, scale] ◇ 普通～regular binary, 十进制向～的转换*
二进制半加器 【计】binary half adder
二进制编码 binary code
二进制编码的八进制 binary coded octal
二进制编码的十进制 (同"二-十进制")
二进制编码的十进制表示法 binary coded decimal representation
二进制编码地址 binary coded address
二进制编码数字 binary coded digit
二进制编码字符 binary coded character
二进(制)标度 binary scale
二进制布尔运算 binary Boolean operation

二进制单元 【计】binary cell
二进制电路 binary circuit
二进制反码 【计】one's complement, complement of one's
二进制计数器 binary counter
二进制计算机 binary computer
二进制记数法[制] 【计】binary notation [scale]
二进制记数系统 binary notation system
二进制加法计数器 binary up counter
二进制链 【计】binary chain
二进制数码 bit, binary numeral
二进制数字 【计】binary digit
二进制算术运算 【计】binary arithmetic operation
二进制图像数据 【计】binary picture data
二进制位 binary digit [bit] ◇ 等效～*
二进制位密度 【计】bit density
二进制遥测系统 【计】telebit
二进制元素 【计】binary element
二进制装配[装入]程序 binary loader
二聚物 dimer
二聚作用 dimerization
二联炼钢法 【钢】duplex(ing) process
二磷酸烷基酯 alkyl diphosphate
二膦酸烷基酯 alkyl diphosphonate
二膦酸盐[酯] diphosphate, diphosphonate
二硫代磷酸镍锌 nickel zinc dithiophosphate
二硫代磷酸盐 dithiophosphate
二硫化钴{CoS$_2$} cobalt disulphide
二硫化铼{ReS$_2$} rhenium disulfide
二硫化钼{MoS$_2$} molybdenum disulphide
二硫化钠{Na$_2$S$_2$} sodium disulphide [persulphide]
二硫化镨{PrS$_2$} praseodymium disulphide
二硫化铯{Ce$_2$[S$_2$]} cesium disulphide
二硫化钛{TiS$_2$} titanium disulphide
二硫化钽{TaS$_2$} tantalum sulphide
二硫化碳{CS$_2$} carbon disulphide [bisul-

二硫化钍{ThS$_2$} thorium disulphide
二硫化钨{WS$_2$} tungsten disulphide
二硫化物 bisulfide, bisulphide, disulfide, disulphide
二硫化铀{US$_2$} uranous sulphide
二硫酸根络铟 disulphatoindate
二硫酸根络铟铵 (同"硫酸铟铵")
二硫酸根络铟铯 (同"硫酸铟铯")
二流 【连铸】twin-strand
二流雾化 two-fluid atomization
二卤化物 dihalide
二铝化铜 copper auminide
二氯二氟甲烷气 freom gas
二氯二氧化钼{MoO$_2$)Cl$_2$} molybdenum dioxydichloride
二氯二氧化钨{WO$_2$Cl$_2$} tungsten dioxydichloride
二氯二氧化物 dioxydichloride
二氯二氧化铀{UO$_2$Cl$_2$} uranium oxychloride
二氯二乙醚 dichlorodie-ether
二氯化铂 platinum dichloride
二氯化碲 tellurium dichloride
二氯化钒 vanadium dichloride
二氯化锆{ZrCl$_2$} zirconium dichloride
二氯化汞 mercury bichloride
二氯化合物 dichloro compound
二氯化镓{GaCl$_2$} gallium dichloride
二氯化硫 sulphur dichloride
二氯化锰 manganous chloride
二氯化钼{MoCl$_2$} molybdous chloride
二氯化铅{PbCl$_2$} lead dichloride
二氯化三甘醇 triglycol dichloride
二氯化钐{SmCl$_2$} samarium dichloride, samarous chloride
二氯化双氧钼{(MoO$_2$)Cl$_2$} molybdenyl dichloride
二氯化铊{TlCl$_2$} thallium dichloride
二氯化钛{TiCl$_2$} titanium dichloride
二氯化铁 ferrous chloride
二氯化钨{WCl$_2$} tungsten dichloride

二氯化物 bichloride, dichloride
二氯化锡{SnCl$_2$} stannous chloride
二氯化氧锆{ZrOCl$_2$} zirconyl chloride
二氯化铟{InCl$_2$} indium dichloride
二氯化铕{EuCl$_2$} europium dichloride
二氯化锗{GeCl$_2$} germanous chloride
二氯氧化锆{ZrOCl$_2$} zirconium oxychloride
二氯氧化铪{HfOCl$_2$} hafnium oxychloride
二氯氧化铈{CeOCl$_2$} ceric oxychloride
二氯一氧化铪 (同"氯化氧铪")
二氯乙醇 dichloroethanol
二氯溴化物 bromodichloride
二面角 【数】dihedral angle
二面角反射器 dihedral corner reflector
二排风口 bosh tuyere
二硼化物 diboride
二偏硅酸三钙{3CaO·2SiO$_2$} calcium sesquisilicate
二期吹炼(转炉的) second blow
二羟基苯酸{(OH)$_2$·C$_6$H$_3$·COOH} resoreylic acid
二羟基蒽醌 ◇ 1,2-~*
二氢化物 dihydride
二氢化钍{ThH$_2$} thorium dihydride
二氢氧化锰 manganous hydroxide
二取代的 twice-substituted
二熔 second melt
二闪冷却区 【连铸】spray zone
二十二烷{CH$_3$(CH$_2$)$_{20}$CH$_3$} docosane
二十二烷酸{CH$_3$(H$_2$)$_{20}$CO$_2$H} behenic acid, docos(an)oic acid
二十辊(冷)轧机 twenty-high roll mill
二-十进制 binary coded decimal (B.C.D.) ◇ 自然~*
二-十进制数 binary coded decimal number
二十三烷 tricosane
二十四烷 tetracosane
二十四(烷)酸{CH$_3$(CH$_2$)$_{22}$COOH} tetracosanoic[carnaubic]acid

二十烷 {$CH_3(CH_2)_{18}CH_3$} eicosane
二室式链算机循环 two-pass grate cycle
二水合三氧化铀 {$UO_3 \cdot 2H_2O$} uranium trioxide dihydrate
二水合物 dihydrate
二水偏钙铀云母 {$Ca(UO_2)_2P_2O_8 \cdot 2H_2O$} meta-autunite Ⅱ
二素组 diad
二羧酸 dicarboxylic acid
二缩原磷酸 (同"偏磷酸")
二态变量 【计】two-state variable
二钛酸盐 dititanate
二碳化锶 {SrC_2} strontium carbide
二碳化物 dicarbide
二碳化铀 {UC_2} uranium dicarbide
二铁酸钙 calciumdiferrite, hemicalcium ferrite
二烃[烷]基 dialkyl
二烃[烷]基胺 dialkylamine
二烃基磷酸 {HR_2PO_4} dialkyl phosphoric acid
二烃基磷酸萃取剂 dialkyl phosphoric acid extractant
二烃基磷酸钠 {$2NaO \cdot O:P(OR)_2$} sodium dialkylphosphate
二烃基磷酸盐 dialkylphosphate
二烃基氯代甲烷 dialkylmethyl chloride
二烃基亚膦酸 {$R \cdot PO(OH)$} dialkyl phosphinic acid
二烃基亚膦酸烷基酯 {$R_2(RO)PO$} alkyl-dialkylphosphinate
二烃基亚膦酸[酯] dialkylphosphinate
二烃基亚砜 dialkyl sulfoxide
二烃基膦酸烷基酯 {$R(RO)_2PO$} dialkyl alkylphosphonate
二烃[烷]基酯 dialkyl ester
二通式热风炉 【铁】two-pass hot stove
二通蓄热式热风炉 (同"考贝式热风炉")
二维薄膜 two-dimensional film
二维布置 two-dimensional array
二维材料 two-dimensional material
二维层次协调规划模型 two-dimensional hierarchical coordination model
二维场 two-dimensional field
二维超导体 two-dimensional superconductor
二维成核(结晶中心的) two-dimensional nucleation
二维成核动力学 two-dimensional nucleation kinetics
二维点阵[晶格] two-dimensional lattice
二维功率密度函数 two-dimensional power spectral density function
二维光栅 two-dimensional grating
二维金属 two-dimensional metal
二维晶体 two-dimensional crystal
二维空间传热 two-dimensional heat flow
二维空间流 two-dimensional flow
二维模型 two-dimensional model
二维凝固 two-dimensional solidification
二维切削 (同"垂直切削")
二维系 two-dimensional system
二维显示 【电】two-dimensional display
二维衍射光栅 two-dimensional diffraction grating
二维衍射图[花样] two-dimensional diffraction pattern
二维原子网格 【理】two-dimensional network of atoms
二维再结晶 two-dimensional recrystallization
二维正方点阵[晶格] two-dimensional square lattice
二维自相关函数 two-dimensional autocorrelation function
二维走向面 two-dimensional trend surface
二线通道 【电】two wire channel
二线制 two wire system
二相场 two-phase field
二相电流 two-phase current
二相钢 two-phase steel
二相合金 【金】two-phase [duplex] alloy

二相晶粒组织 【金】duplex grain structure
二相流动(气-液相的) 【金】two-phase flow
二相片状结构组分 duplex lamellar constituent
二相平衡 biphase [diphase, two-phase] equilibrium
二相系[制] two-phase [quarter-phase] system
二相显微组织 【金】duplex microstructure
二项式 【数】binomial(expression)
二项式分布 binomial distribution
二项式概率方程 binomial equation of probability
二向压制 (同"双向压制")
二向应力 biaxial stress
二向轴 diad
二象性 duality
二硝基甲苯(炸药) dinitrotoluene(DNT)
二辛胺 dioctylamine
二辛基 dioctyl
二辛基焦磷酸 dioctyl pyrophosphoric acid
二心边心桃尖拱 equilateral arch
二溴化碲 tellurium(di)bromide
二溴化氯 chlorodibromide
二溴化钼{MoBr$_2$} molybdous bromide
二溴化羟氧钼 molybdyl dibromide
二溴化铊{TlBr$_2$} thallium dibromide
二溴化钨{WBr$_2$} tungsten dibromide
二溴化物 bibromide, dibromide
二溴化铟{InBr$_2$} indium dibromide
二溴羟氧化物 oxyhydroxydibromide
二溴羟氧钼{[(MoO)(OH)]Br$_2$} molybdenum oxyhydroxydibromide
二溴氧化锆{ZrOBr$_2$} zirconium oxybromide
二氧化钚 plutonium dioxide
二氧化碲 tellurium dioxide
二氧化钒 vanadium dioxide
二氧化锆{ZrO$_2$} zirconium dioxide [anhydride], zirconia
二氧化锆还原 reduction of zirconium dioxide
二氧化铬 chromium dioxide
二氧化硅{SiO$_2$} silicon dioxide, silica ◇ 蜂窝状～ cellular silica, 活性～ activated silica
二氧化硅残渣 silica residue
二氧化硅测定 silica determination
二氧化硅粉 silica powder
二氧化硅有机复合树脂涂层 silica-organic composite coating
二氧化铪{HfO$_2$} hafnium oxide, hafnia
二氧化铼 rhenium dioxide
二氧化硫{SO$_2$} sulphur [sulfur] dioxide, sulphurous(acid)anhydride
二氧化硫分析记录器 sulphur dioxide analyzer recorder
二氧化锰{MnO$_2$} manganese dioxide [bioxide, peroxide, superoxide], battery manganese, black oxide of manganese ◇ 活性～法
二氧化钼{MoO$_2$} molybdenum dioxide
二氧化铌{NbO$_2$} niobium [columbium] dioxide
二氧化钕{NdO$_2$} neodymium dioxide
二氧化铅{PbO$_2$} lead dioxide [peroxide]
二氧化铯{Cs$_2$O$_2$} cesium dioxide
二氧化铈{CeO$_2$} cerium dioxide, ceric oxide
二氧化钛{TiO$_2$} titanium(di)oxide, titania
二氧化碳{CO$_2$} carbon dioxide, aeric acid (旧名) ◇ 固体～*
二氧化碳(保护)电弧焊 CO$_2$(-shielded) arc welding, carbon-dioxide-shielded arc welding
二氧化碳(保护)粉芯焊丝电弧焊 flux cored CO$_2$ welding
二氧化碳测定计 carbometer
二氧化碳激光(器) carbon dioxide laser
二氧化碳计 anthracometer, carbometer
二氧化碳快干[处理的]型芯 CO$_2$ core
二氧化碳气氛 carbon dioxide atmosphere

二氧化碳气体自动记录仪　carbon dioxide recorder, CO_2 content recorder

二氧化碳－水玻璃砂型硬化［硬化砂造型，制砂型］法　CO_2 process, CO_2 (sodium) silicate process

二氧化碳－水玻璃型砂　【铸】CO_2-sodium silicate sand

二氧化碳吸收器　【铸】carbon dioxide absorber

二氧化碳型砂　carbon dioxide sand

二氧化钍｛ThO_2｝　thorium dioxide [anhydride]

二氧化钍弥散镍　(同"氧化钍弥散镍")

二氧化钨　tungsten dioxide, brown tungsten oxide

二氧化物　dioxide, binoxide

二氧化硒　selenium dioxide

二氧化锡｛SnO_2｝　tin dioxide, stannic oxide

二氧化铀｛UO_2｝　uranium dioxide, uranous oxide ◇ 金属级～*

二氧化铀衬里　uranium dioxide liner

二氧化铀金属陶瓷　uranium-dioxide cermet

二氧化锗｛GeO_2｝　germanium dioxide, germanic oxide

二氧杂环己烷　(同"二噁烷")

二乙撑三胺｛$NH_2C_2H_4NHC_2H_4NH_2$｝　diethylonetriamine

二乙撑三胺碳酸盐　dicthylonctriamine carbonate

二乙醇胺｛$HN(CH_2CH_2OH)_2$｝　diethanolamine

二乙基二硫代氨基甲酸盐　diethyldithiocarbamate

二乙醚｛$C_2H_5OC_2H_5$｝　dicthylether, ethyl oxide

二乙醚萃取　diethyl-ether extraction

二乙烯基｛$CH_2:CH-$｝　divinyl

二乙烯基苯　divinylbenzene

二乙烯三胺溶液　solution of diethylene triamine

二乙铊化氢氧｛$Tl(OH)(C_2H_5)_2$｝　thallium diethyl hydroxide

二异丙醚　diisopropyl ether

二异丙酮｛$[CH_3)_2CH]_2CO$｝　diisopropyl ketone

二异丁基甲酮｛$[(CH_3)_2CH]_2CO$｝　isobutyrone

二异丁基酮　diisobutyl ketone

二异丁烯　diisobutylene

二异戊基　diisoamyl

二异戊甲基膦酸酯｛$(C_5H_{11}O_2)_2POCH_3$｝　diisoamyl methyl-phosphonate

二异戊亚膦酸甲酯　diisoamyl methyl-phosphinate

二异辛基酞酸酯　DIOP (diisooctylphthalate)

二元布尔运算　【计】dyadic Boolean operation

二元电解液[质]　binary electrolyte

二元方程式　binary equation

二元共晶反应　binary eutectic reaction

二元共晶(体)　binary [two-component] eutectic

二元共晶系　binary eutectic system

二元共析(体)　binary eutectoid

二元固溶体　binary solid solution

二元合金　binary [two-component] alloy

二元合金钢　binary [double-alloy] steel

二元化合物　binary compound

二元化合物半导体　binary semiconductor

二元混合物　binary mixture

二元计数器　binary scaler

二元碱度　binary basicity

二元黏度　binary viscosity

二元熔体　binary melt

二元碳化物　double carbide

二元系　binary [two-component] system ◇ 伪[假]～*

二元系平衡图　binary equilibrium diagram

二元系状态图　binary constitutional diagram

二元相图　binary (phase) diagram

二元盐　binary salt
二元运算　【计】binary [dyadic] operation
二原子的　diatomic
二渣　second-run slag
二正丁胺{(C₄H₉)₂NH}　di-n-butylamine
二正丁基磷酸　di-n-butyl phosphoric acid
二正癸胺　di-n-decylamine
二酯　di-n-ester

二酯类　dibasic acid ester
二至十进制转换器　binary to decimal converter
二轴的　biaxial
二轴性　biaxiality
二柱蒸馏塔　two-column still
二组分的　binary

F f

发暗　staining, obfuscation
发暗金属(因腐蚀)　fogged metal
发报机　transmitter
发表　publication (pub., publ.), issue
发车轨路　departure track
发出　issue, send out, delivery, emit, dispatch, evolvement
发出选通脉冲　strobing
发达的　developed, advanced
发电　(electric power) generation ◇ 磁流体动能~*
发电厂[站]　power plant [station], power generating plant, power house, electric power plant, generating plant [station] ◇ 燃气轮机~*, 移动式~*
发电腐蚀　galvanic corrosion
发电机　(electric) generator, generatrix, dynamo ◇ 测速~*, 柴油(机)~*, 磁石~ inductor, 复激~ compound generator, 恒压~*, 弧焊~ arc-welding generator, 降压特性~*, 交叉磁场~ cross field machine, 平复激~ flat compound generator, 牵引~ drag generator, 轻便[可搬式]~ portable generator, 三线式~ Dobrowolsky generator, 外极~ out-pole generator, 涡轮[透平]~ turbogenerator, 永磁~ magne-to-generator, 直流~*
发电机-电动机组(带飞轮的)　flywheel convertor set ◇ 沃德-伦纳德式~*
发电机波动[冲击,喘振]保护装置　generator surge protector
发电机极靴　generator pole piece
发电机间[室,房]　generator compartment [room]
发电机控制[调节]　generator control
发电机特性　generator characteristics
发电设备[机组]　power supply unit (P.S.U.), generating [power] set
发动机　engine, motor ◇ 单缸~ single cylinder machine, 辐射式[星型]~ radial engine, 活塞式~ piston engine, 火花点火~ spark ignition engine, 立式~ vertical engine, 煤气[燃气]~ gas engine, 燃气涡轮~ gas-turbine engine, 铁芯冷却~ core-cooled motor, 组合[复]式~ compound engine
发动机波动[冲击,喘振]保护装置　generator surge protector
发动机房　engine room (ER), enginehouse
发动机黄铜　motor brass (62—65Cu, 31—36Zn, 2—4Pb; 又称电动机黄铜), engine brass (77Cu, 8Sn, 15Pb)
发动机架　engine cradle [bed]
发动机轴　engine shaft
发动机座　engine base [bed]
发端　inception
发光　glow, luminescence, illumination, irradiance, shine
发光壁加热器　luminous wall heater
发光材料　luminous material
发光灯丝高温计　luminous filament pyrometer
发光度　luminosity, radiance, luminous emittance
发光二极管显示器　light-emitting diode display [indicator]
发光分析　luminescent analysis
发光活化[激活]剂　luminescent activator
发光模拟母线　colour mimic buses
发光漆　luminous paint
发光强度　luminous intensity, luminescent (emission) intensity
发光体　luminous body, illuminator, eradiator
发光物质[材料]　luminescent material
发光信号系统　luminous-signal system
发光锥体　luminous cone
发函清单　mailling list
发汗[热析]　sweating, sweat(ing) out
发汗材料　sweating material
发汗冷却　sweat cooling

发黑 blackening, darkening
发黑处理 black finish, blacking ◇ 表面氧化~*,戴马兹~法(压铸锌基合金的)Dymaz,碱液~*,氧化~*,油~*
发黑现象 【金】smut
发红烟硝酸 (同"浓硝酸")
发火 ignition, priming
发火合金 pyrophoric [sparking] alloy ◇ 奥厄~*,孔海姆~*,韦尔斯巴赫~*,休伯斯~*
发火花 sparking, blink, arcing
发夹形钛条 titanium hairpin
发酵 fermentation
发卡钢丝 hairpin wire, bobby pin wire
发蓝薄板钢 blue planished steel, russian iron
发蓝不锈钢 blue stainless steel
发蓝处理 blu(e)ing ◇ 钢的~steel bluing,蒸汽~steam bluing, barffing
发蓝处理的 blue finished
发蓝处理炉 blu(e)ing furnace
发蓝处理用盐 blueing salt
发蓝钢氮化法 nitride process of blueing steel
发蓝钢丝 blue annealed wire
发蓝加热处理 blue heat(ing)
发蓝退火(线材的) blue annealing
发蓝退火薄钢板 blue sheet
发蓝氧化色 blued
发亮光泽 bright [brilliant] luster
发裂 check(ing), craze, craze crack(ing), feather checking, flake, tiny crack, hair(line) crack, micro-flaw,【金】checkmark,【钢】fin crack(钢锭的), flake crack(钢的金相试片上有白点的横断面), shatter-crack(因氢脆引起的), snowflake(由白点引起的),【压】thermal burst, roak(钢材表面的),
发硫菌属 thiothrix
发面冒口 【铸】cauliflower head
发泡的 foaming, bubbly
发泡物质 foaming substance

发票 invoice, bill ◇ 海关~customs invoice
发气压力冒口 【铸】pressure head
发热 heating, warming, calorification ◇ 福塞科~保温剂*
发热本领 thermal value
发热铬铁 chrome X
发热硅铁 silex
发热剂 【钢】thermite, heat generating agent ◇ 非铝~non aluminothermit, 热帽~lunderite
发热量 heat productivity, calori(fi)c capacity [efficiency, power, value], calorimetric value
发热帽 【钢】headbox
发热能力 caloricity, heating [caloric] power
发热器 heater
发热型结晶器保护渣 exothermic mould powder
发热值 calori(fi)c power [value], heat(ing) [thermal, calorie, calorimetric, combustion] value, heat producing value ◇ 单位重量~*
发热装置 warmer
发散 divergence, divergency, transpiration
发散冲击波(爆炸的) diverging shock waves
发散冲击波成形法 diverging shock method
发散度 divergence, divergency ◇ 束~beam divergence
发散角 angle of devergence
发散喷嘴 divergent nozzle ◇ 伞形~*
发散喷嘴扩散泵 divergent-nozzle pump ◇ 垂直~*,水平~*
发散射束 divergent beam
发散透镜 diverging [spread(ing), negative] lens
发散因数 divergence factor
发散锥体 cone of divergence
发闪光(灰吹终了时) fulguration

发 fa

发射 emission, emit(tance), transmission, emanation, firing, launch
发射 X 射线光谱学 emission X-ray spectroscopy
发射电极 emitting electrode
发射镀[涂]层 emissive coating
发射分光计 emission-spectrometer
发射分光镜 emission spectroscope
发射分析 emission analysis
发射功率 transmitted power
发射光 emitted light
发射(光)谱 emission spectrum(ES) ◇ 电感耦合等离子体～法*
发射光谱分析 emission spectral [spectrographic] analysis(ESA)
发射光谱谱线 emission spectral lines
发射光谱学 emission spectroscopy
发射光谱仪 emission spectrograph
发射光谱预燃时间 prearc period
发射光学光谱学 emission optical spectroscopy
发射火焰光度法 emission flame photometry
发射机 transmitter, sender(超声波的)
发射极 emitter
发射极跟随[踪]器 emitter-follower
发射极功能逻辑电路 emitter function logic(EFL)
发射极结 emitter junction
发射极耦合逻辑电路 emitter coupled logic(ECL)
发射率 emissivity, emittance
发射脉冲 transmitted pulse
发射能力[本领] emissive power [ability]
发射频率 emission frequency
发射谱线 emission line
发射器 emitter, ejector
发射强度 emitted intensity
发射式电子显微镜 emission(electron) microscope
发射式(电子)显微镜观察 emission microscope observation

发射式电子显微镜照片 emission micrograph
发射体 emitter
发射物 emission
发射系数 emission factor [ratio]
发射系统 emitting [emission] system
发射显微镜成像 emission image
发射线 emitted line, line of departure
发射阴极 emitting cathode
发射跃迁 emission transition
发声器 acoustic(al) generator ◇ 热致～ thermophone
发声信号 audible signal
发生腐蚀 initiation of corrosion
发生柜 generating chamber
发生量 generating capacity
发生炉(煤气发生炉) producer, generator, generating furnace ◇ 回转炉箅～ revolving grate producer
发生炉房[间，室] generator room
发生炉、高炉与焦炉混合煤气 dreigas
发生炉控制[调节] generator control
发生炉煤气 producer [generator] gas, regenerative producer gas ◇ 西门子～ Siemens gas
发生炉[器]特性 generator characteristics
发生炉压力 generating pressure
发生脉冲 (im)pulsing
发生能力 generating capacity
发生泡沫 foaming
发生器 producer, (re)generator, generatrix ◇ 浮筒式～*, 干式～*, 高产量～*, 霍尔效应～ Hall generator, 基普～ Kipp('s)generator, 接触式～ contact-type generator
发生器房[间，室] generator room [compartment]
发生器控制[调节] generator control
发生室 generating chamber
发生站(煤气、乙炔等的) generating station
发送 transmission, sending, dispatch

(ing),despatch
发送变换器　transmitting transducer
发送机　emitter,transmitter
发送－接收转换装置　transmit-receive transducer assembly
发送跨　delivery bay
发送器　sender,sensing transducer,generator,measuring [load] cell
发送请求　request-send
发送(区)段　delivery section
发送室　dispatch [despatch] room
发送系统　transmission system
发条盒　going barrel
发纹　hair seam [line],tiny crack,stringer (金属缺陷)
发芽　germination
发芽型晶粒长大　germinative grain growth
发烟　fuming
发烟硫酸　fuming sulphuric acid,oleum (acid)
发烟器　smoke gas generator
发烟燃烧　smoulder
发烟酸　fuming acid
发荧光率　fluorescence yield
发荧光期限[寿命]　fluorescent lifetime
发运(产品)　shipping,dispatch
发运跨　dispatch [loading] bay
发展不充分　under-developing
发展区　development area
发展速度　growth velocity,speed of development
发展现状　present day development
发针　hairpin
发状晶体　hair like crystal
发状裂纹[缝]　hairline ◇ 产生～feather checking
筏基　mat foundation
伐斯科洛依－雷曼特碳化钨硬质合金　Vascoloy-Ramet
伐斯科钨钒钢　Vasco steel
伐斯科雾化钨钒钢粉　Vasco powder

乏弹[丸]　spent shot
乏(尔)计　varmeter
乏气　off-gas
乏汽　dead steam
乏液　lean liquor
阀　valve,【机】breather ◇ 凯氏上旋～*,手动～*,遥控[远距离操纵]～remote valve
阀瓣　valve clack [disk]
阀补偿螺栓　valve compensating bolt
阀导承　valve guide
阀垫　valve pad [patch]
阀顶针　valve lift pin
阀封顶部装炉系统　valve seal top-charging system
阀盖　valve cap [cover]
阀杆　valve stem [rod]
阀杆导承　valve rod guide
阀杆密封盖　valve stem gland
阀环　valve collar
阀簧座　valve spring seat [cup]
阀机构　valve gear
阀壳　valve housing [body,casing]
阀控传动机构　control valve actuator
阀帽　bonnet
阀门　valve,flap
阀门挡板[阀行程限制器]　valve guard
阀(门)钢　valve steel
阀门合金(81Cu,3Sn,7Pb,9Zn)　valve metal
阀门控制机构　valve control mechanism
阀门联锁装置[阀闭锁]　valve interlock
阀门螺旋弹簧　valve spiral spring
阀门压力闭合　positive closing
阀膜　membrane for valve
阀盘　valve disc [disk]
阀青铜(2—10Sn,3—9Pb,3—9Zn,余量Cu)　valve bronze
阀球　valve ball ◇ 活塞泵用～*
阀塞　valve plug,vent plug [peg,pin]
阀升程　valve lift
阀栓　valve cock,vent pin [peg]

阀弹簧钢丝	valve spring wire
阀套	valve housing [bush]
阀体	valve body
阀头	valve head
阀销	valve pin
阀心	valve core
阀移动图	valve displacement diagram
阀用红黄铜(合金)(86Cu,8Zn,3.5Sn,2.5Pb)	valve alloy
阀油	valve oil
阀针	valve needle
阀振缓冲器	valve surge damper
阀轴导承	valve spindle guide
阀柱塞	valve plunger
阀装置	valve gear
阀锥	valve cone
阀组	valve block
阀座	valve seat(ing) [holder, stand], clack
阀座垫板	valve seat insert
法布里-珀罗干涉摄谱仪	Fabry-Perot interference spectrograph
法定标准线规(英国的)	Legal standard wire gauge
法方程	normal equation
法国标准	Normes Francaises (NF), French standard
法国赤金	French red gold
法国独立钢材经销商协会	French Association of Independent Steel Stockholders
法国钢铁研究院连续炼钢法	IRSID (Institute de Recherches de la Sid'eurgie Francaise) continuous steelmaking
法国金(82.75Cu, 16.40Zn, 0.55Sn, 0.3Fe)	French gold
法国锡铅合金[锡镴](82Sn, 18Pb)	French pewter
法国专利	French Patent (F.P., Fr.P.)
法克拉洛伊铁铬铝电阻合金(12—13Cr, 4—5Al, 余量 Fe)	Facraloy
法拉第常数	Faraday constant
法拉第电解定律	Faraday's law of electrolysis
法拉第定律	Faraday's law
法拉第效应	Faraday effect
法拉第学会	Faraday's society
法拉计	faradmeter
法拉洛伊耐热铁镍铬铝合金	Fahralloy
法拉姆铅锡合金(60Pb, 40Sn)	Fahlum metal
法兰安装	flange mounting
法兰缝铆接	flanged seam riveting
法兰焊接	flange weld(ing)
法兰径比	ratio of diameters of flange, diametric ratio of flange
法兰接头	flange connection [union], flanged fittings
法兰连接	flanged fittings, flange joint(管材的)
法兰连接管	flanged(joint) pipe
法兰盲板	blind flange
法兰密封	flange seal
法兰(盘)	flange ◇ 管~pipe flange, 红装~shrink flanging, 机械加工~machine flange, 角钢制~steel angle flange, 卷边~beaded flange, 联接~coupling flange, 窄~beaded edge, 装~flanging
法兰盘对接	flanged butt joint
法兰绒	flannel
法兰绒辊	cloth roll
法兰绒抛光辊(镀锡薄板用)	buffing roll
法兰绒抛光轮	flannel disc
法兰绒涂油辊	oiling roller of flannel
法兰式喷管	flanged nozzle
法兰座	flange mounting
法里莫尔镍铬铁锰合金	Firearmor
法里特耐热耐蚀高镍合金	Fahrite(alloy)
法里(锡铜轴承)合金(90Sn, 10Cu)	Fahrig's metal, Fahry'(s) alloy
法伦银亮合金[锡铅宝石装饰合金](29Sn, 19Pb)	Fahlun brilliant alloy
法人	legal person
法人组织的	incorporated(Inc.)
法线	normal

法线入射　perpendicular incidence
法线投影图　pole figure
法线轴　normal axis
法向　normal direction
法向加速度　normal accelaration
法(向)节(距)　normal pitch
法向力　normal force
法向入射　normal incidence
法向应变　normal strain
法向应力　normal stress
法则　law,rule,principle,act,theorem
砝码　weight(Wgt),(counter) poise ◇ 检测灵敏度～*,小～set of weights
珐琅　enamel,glaze ◇ 上透明～vitreous enamelling,涂～(低碳)钢板*
珐琅层　enamelled coating
珐琅质电阻(器)　glassy inorganic enamelled resistor
帆布　canvas duck
帆布带　canvas [woven] belt
帆布隔膜(电解用)　canvas diaphragm, diaphragm of canvas cloth
帆布过滤器　canvas filter
帆布软管　canvas hose
帆布手套　canvas mittens
帆布水罩　canvas hose
帆布鞋罩　canvas spat
翻板机　plate turnorer
翻板输送机　slate-type conveyer
翻边　flanged [raised] edge ◇ 顶锻～joggled lap
翻车工　tipper
翻车机(wagon,car) dumper,(wagon,car) tipper,tippler,dumping plant,rotary car dumper ◇ 回转～drum tripper,活动式～【焦】mobile car tipper,旋转[转动]式～*
翻车机斗料　wagon tipper hopper
翻车设备　dumping plant
翻成侧立状态　uptilt
翻唇垫圈　simmer-ring,simmer gasket
翻倒　roll over

翻锭车(pot-type) ingot buggy,【压】(ingot) tumbler
翻锭机　tipping,tippler,tilting chair(固定式),【压】ingot tilter [tipper, tumbler] ◇ 固定式～*
翻锭座(送锭车的)　dumping cradle
翻锭座框架　ingot chair-tilting frame
翻动　raking
翻斗　skip [tipping] bucket,dump box(壳型用) ◇ 卸料～*
翻斗车　dumping wagon [truck,car],sidedump(ing) car,tilting [tipping] wagon, tilting overturning [skip],skip car,rocker ◇ 前倾～front tipper,普通～conventional skip car
翻斗混合器　skip mixer
翻斗式给料装置　geary feeder
翻斗送锭车　travel(l)ing tumbler
翻斗提升机　【耐】skip elevator
翻斗装料　skip filling
翻斗装料斜槽　skip loading chute
翻钢　【压】manipulation
翻钢次数　number of turns
翻钢次序　sequence of turns
翻钢导板　twist guide ◇ 出口～delivery twist guide,带滚子链的～roller-chain twist guide
翻钢导管　tumbling device
翻钢导卫板　twisting guard
翻钢道次　tilting pass
翻钢斗(连铸装置的)　tilting cradle
翻钢[料]钩　tilting dogs
翻钢辊　tilting roller
翻钢机　tilting gear,tipper,tilter,reverser ◇ 杠杆式～*,钩式～*,辊式～*,移动式～*
翻钢机的翻钢钩　lifting dogs
翻钢夹紧辊　tilting pinch rolls
翻钢冷床　tilting cooling bed
翻钢立轧　turn on edge
翻钢平轧　turn over on side
翻钢套　twister plug

翻钢小车　travel(l)ing-down tilter
翻钢装置　【压】turnover [tumbling] device, tilter ◇ 槽型～trough-type tilter, 夹辊式～grip-type tilter
翻轨机　rail turner
翻滚　tumbling
翻浆　frost boil
翻卷动作　down-end motion
翻卷机　coil downending machine, coil tilter [turner], manipulator mechanism, turnover, downtilter(卷取机旁的), coil down ender(把立放卷翻成卧放), coil u-pender(把卧放卷翻成立放)
翻料车　tilting car, tilting pot buggy
翻料机　turner, turnover gear, upender, 【压】dumper, turnover
翻料孔　stirring hole
翻料装置　turndown rig
翻笼　rotary car dumper, wagon dumper
翻炉浇注　inversion casting
翻路机　scarifier
翻面装置(翻板机的)　turnover rig
翻盘过滤机　revolving-leaf type filter
翻皮(钢锭缺陷)　skull patch
翻平(带卷)　down-tilt
翻倾小车　tipping bogie
翻砂车间设备　foundery machinery
翻砂工　foundery hand, founder
翻砂间　captive foundery
翻砂间起重机　foundery crane
翻砂间移动起重机　foundery travelling crane
翻台式制芯机　core roll-over machine
翻外缘成形法　flange forming
翻箱式造型机　roll-over moulding machine
翻箱铸造　inversion casting
翻卸设备　dumping plant
翻新　revamp, retrofit
翻新轧机　revamped mill
翻译　translation, interpretation ◇ 机器～*，一对一～*
翻译程序　translating program [routine], interpreter, translator ◇ 编写～的系统*
翻译程序书写系统　translator writing systems(TWS)
翻译机[器]　translator, interpreter ◇ 公式～fortran
翻阅背面　turn over(T/O, t.o.)
翻造　reclaim
翻转　overturn, turn(ing), turnover, roll over, tip(ping), turn, tilt(ing) ◇ 可～中段*，用吊车～(钢包) crane tipping
翻转板　【铸】turnover board
翻转导卫板(轧件的)　twisting guard
翻转杆　tilting arm
翻转钩　tilting finger
翻转[料]辊　twist(er) rollers
翻转机　side tilter ◇ 液压～hydraulic tilter
翻转机构　tilting mechanism
翻转箕斗　overturning [self-tipping] skip
翻转开关　tumbler switch
翻转[卸]轮　tipping wheel
翻转式吊桶　tipping bucket
翻转台(盘条的)　tilting chair
翻转位置(转炉的)【钢】inverted position
翻转运动　tilting motion
翻转震击造型机　jar ramming roll-over moulding machine
翻转抓手　tilting finger
翻转装置　tilter, edging device, turner twister, turnover unit, upender ◇ 手控～*
矾　alum ◇ 含～的 aluminous, aluminiferous
矾钙铜矿　tangeit(e)
矾块　alum cake
矾类　vitriol
矾石　aluminite, alley stone ◇ 无水～*
矾土 {Al_2O_3}　alumina ◇ 泥质～argillaceous bauxite, 普通～common alumina
矾土耐火砖　aluminous fire brick
矾土水泥　alumina [aluminous, bauxite]

cement
矾土陶瓷 alumina ceramics [porcelain]
钒钡铜矿 vesignieite
钒钡铀矿 francevillite
钒铋矿 pucherite
钒不锈钢 vanadium stainless steel
钒磁赤铁矿 V-maghemite
钒磁铁矿 coulsonite
钒矾 minasragrite
钒钙铀矿 {CaO(UO$_2$)$_2$V$_2$O$_5$·8H$_2$O} tyuyamunite
钒钢 vanadium steel
钒合金 vanadium alloy
钒合金化 vanadium alloying
钒黄铜 (0.03—0.5V, 29.5—38.5Zn, 0—0.5Mn, 0—1.5Al, 0—1Fe, 余量 Cu) vanadium brass
钒辉石 vanadinaugite
钒灰侵蚀 vanadium attack
钒基合金 vanadium-base alloy
钒钾铀矿 carnotite ◇ 氯化[加盐]焙烧过的~*
钒帘石 mukhinite
钒铝合金(铸造合金) vananum
钒铝铁矿 bokite
钒铝铀矿 vanuralite
钒锰铅矿 pyrobelonite
钒钼铅矿 eosite
钒钠铀矿 strelkinite
钒镍矿 kolovratite
钒镍沥青矿 quisqueite, Peruvian asphaltite
钒铅矿 {(PbCl)Pb$_4$V$_3$O$_{12}$} vanadinite
钒铅铈矿 kusuite
钒铅锌矿 {4(Pb,Zn)O·V$_2$O$_5$·H$_2$O} descloisite, descloizite
钒青铜 vanadium bronze
钒丝 vanadium filament
钒酸 vanadic acid
钒酸铵 ammonium vanadate
钒酸钠 {NaVO$_3$; Na$_3$VO$_4$} sodium vanadate
钒酸铁 ferric vanadate

钒酸盐 vanadate ◇ 溶于碳酸盐的络合~ carbonate-soluble complex vanadate
钒酸铀 uranium vanadate
钒酸铀矿 {UO$_3$·V$_2$O$_5$} ferganite
钒酸铀酰钠 {NaUO$_2$VO$_4$} sodium uranyl vanadate
钒钛磁铁精矿 vanadium-titanium magnetite concentrate
钒钛磁铁矿 V-Ti bearing magnetite ore, vanadic-titanomagnetite
钒钛矿 schreyerite
钒钛铝铁合金 ◇ 格雷纳尔~*
钒钛铁矿 sefstromite
钒锑矿 stibivanite
钒添加合金 vanadium addition
钒铁(中间合金; 50—60V, 1.2—3.5C) ferrovanadium ◇ 高碳~*
钒铁合金 vanadium iron
钒铜铀矿 {Cu$_2$(UO$_2$)$_2$OHV$_2$O$_8$·10H$_2$O} sengierite
钒土 vanadine
钒氧碳 vanadium oxygen carbon (VOC)
钒钇矿 wakefieldite
钒铀矿 {(UO$_2$)$_3$(V$_2$O$_5$)·15H$_2$O} uvanite ◇ 人造~ yellow cake
钒云母 roscoelite
钒渣 【钢】vanadium(-bearing) slag
繁重工作制度 heavy duty
凡士林 vaseline, mineral butter
反 18-8 铬镍钢(18Ni,8Cr) reverse 18-8
反 V 字形导轨 inverted V-guide
反白口(铸件缺陷) inverse [inverted, reverse] chill
反比定律 law of reciprocal proportions
反比(例) inverse ratio [proportion]
反比例的 inversely proportional
反并联桥路 antiparallel bridge
反玻璃化 devitrification
反波(管)**振荡器**(同"回波振荡器")
反补贴税 countervailing duty
反差 contrast

反差比　contrast ratio
反差测量[反衬量度]　measure of contrast
反差区别能力　contrast perception
反差系数　contrast factor [gradient]
反差系数微分值　point gamma
反差性提高　contrast enhancement
反铲(挖土机的)　back acting shovel, back hoe
反铲挖土机　backacter, back digger, hoe shovel
反常贝氏体　inverse bainite
反常晶格电导率　anomalous lattice conductivity
反常晶粒长大　abnormal grain growth
反常警报灯　abnormal alarm lamp
反常快行　【铁】abnormal fast driving
反常炉况　irregular working
反常(炉料)下降指数　abnormal descent index
反常趋肤效应　anomalous skin effect
反常蠕变　abnormal creep
反常性　abnormality, anomalism, anomaly
反常运行　irregular working
反常振幅效应　anomalous amplitude effect
反常组织　abnormal [anomalous] structure
反常(组织的)钢　abnormal steel
反沉淀剂　【选】antiprecipitant
反冲　recoil, kick (-back), kicking-up, backswing ◇ 火焰~back flash
反冲电子　recoil electron
反冲力　recoil force, reactive thrust
反冲能　recoil energy
反冲洗　back wash(ing)
反冲压力机　inverted ram press
反冲原子　recoil atom ◇ 高能~high energy recoil atom
反冲质子　recoil proton
反吹炼　deconverting
反磁化　magnetic reversal, back magnetization
反磁性(同"抗磁性")

反磁性的　diamagnetic, antimagnetic
反磁致伸缩效应　inverse [converse] magnetostrictive effect
反催化剂　anticatalyst, anticatalyzer
反萃剂　back washing agent, stripping [reextracting] agent, strippant
反萃率　stripping efficiency
反萃器　back wash extractor, reextractor
反萃(取)　back(wash) extract(ion), stripping, reextraction, retrograde extra ction, back washing
反萃取塔　stripper column
反萃溶剂　counter solvent
反淬火　inverse chill
反点火　reignition
反电(动)势　back [counter] electromotive force, back e.m.f.
反电动势控制　counter electromotive control
反电极　counter electrode
反电压　back [counter, inverse] voltage
反电晕　back corona
反电子　anti-electron
反对称波函数　antisymmetric wave function
反对称能级　antisymmetrical (energy) level
反对称运算[操作]　antisymmetry operation
反对数　antilog(arithm)
反方向　inverse direction, opposite in direction
反放电　back discharge
反分级作用　【选】film sizing
反辐射　counter-radiation, antiradiation
反复不连续形变　repeated discontinuous yielding
反复冲击拉伸试验　repeated impact tension test
反复冲击弯曲疲劳强度　repeated impact bending strength
反复重皮(轧材缺陷)　recurrent lap

反复磁化(作用) alternating [reversal] magnetization
反复淬火 repeated quenching
反复淬火应变 repeated quenching strain
反复电路 toggle
反复回火 repeated tempering
反复交变应力 repeated alternating stress
反复拉伸试验 repeated tension test, repeated tensile stress test
反复扭转疲劳[持久强度]试验机 endurance testing machine for repeated torsion, reverse torsion fatigue testing machine
反复扭转试验(钢丝的) repeated [reverse] torsion test
反复取样 replicate sample [sampling]
反复热处理 multiplex heat treatment
反复熔炼法 melt-back
反复试验 repeated [repetition] test
反复通过(区域熔炼的) repeated pass, back and forth pass
反复弯曲 reversed [alternating] bending
反复弯曲疲劳强度 repeated bending stress strength
反复弯曲疲劳试验 reversed bending fatigue test
反复弯曲疲劳试验机 reversed bending fatigue machine
反复弯曲试验 reverse [alternating] bending test, ductilimeter test(带钢的) ◇ 詹金斯~ Jenkins' bend test
反复弯曲应力试验 repeated bending stress test
反复应力 repeated [alternate] stress ◇ 交变[替]~*
反复应力试验 repeated [alternate] stress test
反复应力试验机 repeated-stress (fatigue) testing machine
反复应力循环 cycles of stress reversal
反复载荷 repeated load
反感应线圈 bucking coil

反拱度 camber
反共振 anti-resonance
反共振频率 anti-resonance frequency
反光 reflect light, blink, flare, reflection of light
反光电效应 inverse photoelectric effect
反光镜 illuminator, (retro)reflector ◇ 钝化铝~片 illuminite
反光罩 reflection shield
反灰口(可锻铸铁缺陷) inverse greyness
反混合 demixing
反击式破碎机 baffle crusher, impact crusher [breaker]
反极 antipole
反极图 inverse pole figure
反极性 reverse(d) polarity(RP), buck
反极性焊条 reversed polarity electrode
反极性直流(电) reverse(d) polarity direct current(RP – DC)
反挤压(同"反向挤压")
反加压试验(检验密封装置用) back pressurizing testing
反尖晶石型铁氧体 inverse spinel ferrite
反接串激发电机 opposition series generator
反接焊条 reversed polarity electrode
反接间隔(前支泵与扩散泵之间的) backing space
反接绕组 bucking winding
反接线圈 bucking [backing] coil
反结构 antistructure
反结构型缺陷 antistructure defect
反馈 feedback(coupling), back coupling, 【电】back action, regeneration
反馈变量 feedback variable
反馈程度 stage of reaction
反馈电路 feedback circuit
反馈电位计 feedback [follow-up] potentiometer
反馈电压 feedback voltage
反馈放大器 feedback amplifier
反馈环[回]路 feedback loop

反馈控制　feedback control ◇ 自适应～*
反馈控制系统　feedback control system
反馈控制信号　feedback control signal
反馈偏压　back bias
反馈神经网络　feedback neural network
反馈调节　feedback adjustment
反馈系数　feedback factor [ratio]
反馈系统　feedback system
反馈线圈　feedback [tickler] coil
反馈振荡器　feedback oscillator
反扩散　back diffusion, counter-diffusion
反拉力　back pull, backward tension
反拉力拉拔　reactive drawing
反拉力拉[拔]丝　back pull [tension] wire drawing, reactive wire-drawing
反拉力拉丝机　back pull wire drawing machine
反拉装置(带材的)　drag unit
反-(类质)同晶型化合物　anti-isomorphous compound
反冷凝　retrograde condensation
反离子　countra-ion
反粒子　antiparticle
反力　back(ward) [reaction] force
反流　countercurrent, backstreaming
反流态化　defluidization
反码　complement on $N-1$, base-minus-one's complement, (b-1)'s complement
反弥漫　back diffusion
反面　opposite hand (Op.H.), reverse side, counter,【焊】back side(焊缝的)
反面导向弯曲试验(钢管的)　root guided bend test
反面弯曲试样　【焊】root-bend (test) specimen
反挠度　【铸】camber, allowance for camber
反挠曲量　counter-camber
反黏结剂　antiplastering agent
反盘　snarl(成品丝不能成盘), spiral [helical] cast(钢丝盘卷缺陷)
反偏析　reverse [inverse, negative] segregation
反平行加料　antiparallel feed
反芪　trans-stilbene
反气焊法　back hand method
反青铜(90Sn,10Cu)　reverse(d) bronze
反倾销税　anti-dumping duty
反曲线　inverse [counter] curve,【建】cyma
反绕　rewind, back-roll
反绕时间　rewind time
反热电效应　inverse thermoelectric effect
反乳化(作用)　demulsification
反乳化性(能)　demulsibility
反润湿　dewetting
反闪快门　flash back check
反射　reflection, reflectance, bounce, reflexion, reverberation, echo(音响的) ◇ 被～的能量 reflected energy, 布喇格～*, 德拜-谢乐～*, 底(面)～ bottom reflection, 劳厄～ Laue reflections, 正[有规则]～ regular reflection
反射 X 射线显微术　reflection X-ray microscopy
反射 X 射线衍射图　(同"反射照相")
反射板　reflecting board ◇ 自动调节式～*
反射焙烧炉　【冶】reverberatory roaster
反射本领　reflection [reflecting] power
反射表面　echo(ing) area
反射波　reflected wave, reflection, echo
反射波特性　echoing characteristic
反射操作　reflection operation
反射测厚仪　reflectogage
反射测角仪　reflecting [reflection] goniometer
反射电弧炉　arc-image furnace
反射电极　reflecting electrode
反射定律　reflection law
反射对称镜面　mirror plane of reflection symmetry
反射分光光度计　reflectance spectrophotometer

反射干涉仪　reflection interferometer
反射光　reflected light ◇ 暗视场～法*
反射光栅　reflecting [reflection] grating
反射光完全湮没[吸收]　complete annihilation of reflection
反射级　order of reflection
反射计　reflectogauge, reflectometer
反射角　reflection angle
反射介质　reflecting medium
反射晶体　reflecting crystal
反射镜　mirror, reflector, reflectoscope
反射镜照明　mirror illuminator
反射裂纹　reflection crack
反射炉　reverberatory(furnace), reverberating furnace, reverberator, air furnace, flame(contact) furnace ◇ 富尔米纳式～*, 还原～*, 矩形～*, 炼铜～*, 料枪给料～ gun-feed reverberatory, 煤气火焰～*, 热装～*, 圆形～ circular reverberatory furnace, 在～内的处理时间【冶】reverberation time, 铸造用～ foundery air furnace
反射炉焙烧　reverberatory roasting
反射炉处理　reverberatory treatment
反射炉床能率　reverberatory furnace specific capacity
反射炉低硫烟气　weak reverberatory off-gas
反射炉煅烧　reverberatory calcination
反射炉精炼　reverberatory refining
反射炉锍[冰铜]　reverberatory matte
反射炉炉盖　bung
反射炉炉膛　reverberatory hearth
反射炉炉渣　reverberatory(furnace) slag, reverb slag, air furnace slag
反射(炉内处理)时间　reverberation time
反射炉燃烧　reverberatory burning
反射炉熔炼　reverberatory smelting, reverberation
反射炉烟化　reverberatory fuming
反射率　reflectivity, reflectance, index of reflection, reflectance ratio ◇ 混合料～系数*
反射脉冲　reflected impulse [pulse], echo impulse
反射面　reflecting surface [face], reflection plane
反射面积　echo(ing) area
反射面极点　pole of reflecting plane
反射能力　reflection power, reflectivity, reflectance
反射屏　reflection shield, reflecting screen
反射器　reflector, deflector, abatjour, dish, dishpan(探伤用) ◇ 二面角～*, 纪尼埃型～*, 角形～ corner reflector, 两面～ diplane reflector, 筒式晶体单色～ barrel type reflector, 圆筒式～ barrel type reflector, 圆柱形～ cylindrical reflector, 约翰式～ Johann-type reflector
反射器板　reflector sheet
反射器用黄铜　reflector brass
反射强度　reflected intensity
反射球　sphere of reflection
反射区　echo(ing) area
反射热加热　【压】reverberation
反射热渣　reflective slag
反射式电子显微镜　reflection electron microscope
反射式电子显微镜像　reflection-electron microscopical image
反射式电子显微镜照片[显微照相]　reflection electron micrograph
反射式煅烧炉　reverberatory calciner
反射式高温计　reflecting pyrometer
反射式加热炉　reflector oven
反射式摄谱[光谱]仪　reflection-type spectrograph
反射(式)探伤法　reflection method
反射式探伤仪　reflectoscope
反射(式)显微镜　reflecting [reflection, reflexion](type) microscope ◇ 暗视场～*
反射式显微镜照片[显微照相]　reflection micrograph

反射束 reflected beam
反射探测(法) reflection sounding
反射特性 echoing characteristic
反射体 dish, reflector
反射体积 reflecting volume
反射条件 reflection condition
反射投影 reflection projection
反射图 reflectogram
反射系数 reflection coefficient, reflectivity, radiant reflectance
反射系数计 reflection coefficient meter, reflectometer
反射显微镜观察 reflection microscope observation
反射线 reflected rays, reflection arcs
反射线标定 indexing of reflections
反射线轮廓(X射线照相的) reflection profile
反射像(或称反映像) reflection image
反射信号 reflected [echoed] signal, returning echo
反射性 reflectivity
反射衍射图(X射线的) reflection photograph
反射衍射线 reflected diffracted line
反射因数 reflection factor
反射运算(同"反射操作")
反射增宽 broadening of reflection ◇ 竖向发散(度)引起的~*, 水平发散引起的~*
反射照相 reflection photograph
反渗透 reverse osmosis
反渗透膜 reverse osmosis membrane ◇ 板框式~*
反时限延时 inverse-time delay
反时针[时钟]方向 counter-clockwise (CCW), anti-clockwise
反时针(方向)旋转 counter-clockwise rotation
反式 transform, anti-form
反式丁烯二酸{(:CHCO$_2$H)$_2$} fumaric acid

反手焊 backward [backhand] welding
反手焊法 back hand technique
反缩合 retrograde condensation
反锁 counterlock
反弹性曲率 antielastic curvature
反调制 demodulation, countermodulation
反调制器 demodulator
反跳试验(钢丝的) recoil test
反铁磁共[谐]振 antiferromagnetic resonance
反铁磁结构 antiferromagnetic structure
反铁磁晶体 antiferromagnetic crystal
反铁磁居里点 antimagnetic Curie point
反铁磁体 antiferromagnet
反铁磁唯象理论 antiferromagnetism phenomenological theory
反铁磁性[现象] antiferromagnetism
反铁磁性居里温度 antiferromagnetic Curie temperature
反铁磁性物质[材料] antiferromagnetic substance [material]
反铁磁性相互作用 antiferromagnetic interaction
反铁磁性轴 antiferromagnetism axis
反铁电畴[区] antiferroelectric domain
反铁电晶体 antiferroelectric crystal
反铁电体 antiferroelectrics
反铁电性[现象] antiferroelectricity
反团聚 deflocculating
反外延 reverse epitaxy
反弯 back bend
反弯辊 counter bending roller
反围盘 reverse repeater
反吸风袋式除尘器 back air suction bag filter
反洗(液)(离子交换的) back wash(ing)
反相 antiphase
反相(边)界 antiphase boundary (APB)
反相畴 antiphase domain
反相畴界 antiphase domain boundary
反相电流继电器 reversal phase current relay

反相电压继电器　reversal phase voltage relay
反相放大器　inverter [see-saw] amplifier
反相分量　out-of-phase component
反相界　antiphase boundary(APB)
反相界强化　APB (antiphase boundry) strengthening
反相界缺陷　APB faults
反相器　(phase) inverter
反相气体色层(分离)法　inverse gas chromatography
反响　reverberation, echo
反向　backward [opposite] direction, buck, reversion
反向变换[变流]器　inverted converter, inverter
反向变形(焊接前的)　prespringing
反向波　back(ward) wave
反向波动　fluctuation in reverse direction
反向场　reverse field
反向齿轮　reverse gear
反向锄　back hoe
反向穿孔模(挤压筒中的)　inverted piercing die
反向传播神经网络　B.P. (background propagation) neural network
反向带　reverse belt
反向电流　reverse [back(ward)] current
反向电流电解清洗　reverse current cleaning
反向电压　inverse [backward, backswing] voltage
反向电阻　back(ward) resistance
反向光程(金相)显微镜　inverted (metallurgical) microscope
反向换流器　reversing converter
反向击穿　reverse breakdown
反向极性　reverse(d) polarity(RP)
反向挤压　back(ward) [reverse, inverse, inverted, indirect] extrusion
反向挤压金属　back extruded metal
反向夹板(矿热电炉的)　counterclamps
反向夹层生长　【半】inverse sandwich growth
反向加压挤压法　extrusion with front pressure
反向加载　reversed stressing
反向开关　reversing switch
反向控制　reversed control ◇接触式～
反向扩散　reverse diffusion, back-diffusion
反向力　backward force
反向流(变)　inverted [reverse(d)] flow
反向流变应力　flow stress in reverse direction
反向偏析　【金】reverse regregation
反向偏压　reverse bias
反向频率　number of reverse turn cycles
反向器　tension cage, reverse controller
反向清洗　counter-current rinsing
反向蠕变　reverse creep
反向散射　back scattering
反向散射厚度计(用于轧制中的薄板及管壁)　back scattering(thickness) gauges
反向散射角　back scattering angle
反向散射系数　back scattering coefficient [factor]
反向散射系统　back scatter system
反向施压　reversed stressing
反向外延　【半】inverse epitaxy
反向弯曲试验　test-by bending in-opposite direction
反向效应　adverse effect
反向旋压　backward spinning
反向旋转　reverse rotation, counterrotation
反向应变[形变]　reverse strain
反向应力　back stress
反向运动　counter [back(ward), reverse, retrograde] motion, reverse movement
反向再拉伸　reverse redrawing
反向自旋　reversed spins
反向总体[分布]　inverse population
反硝化　denitration, denitrification
反硝化硫杆菌　thiobacillus denitrificans
反硝化细菌　denitrifying bacteria

反肖特基缺陷 anti-Schottky defect
反效应 inverse [converse] effect
反谐振 inverse resonance
反型性 enantiomorphism
反行程 retracting [return] stroke
反行扩散[弥漫] back diffusion
反絮凝 deflocculating, deflocculation
反絮凝剂 deflocculant, deflocculating agent, defloccuator
反絮凝离心机 deflocculator
反絮凝作用 defloccuation
反旋压 backward spinning
反压传送器 back pressure transmitter
反压电效应 inverse [converse] piezoelectric effect
反压辊式矫直机 inverted roller leveller
反压(力) counterpressure, back pressure ◇ 炉内～ furnace back pressure
反压力管 antivacuum pipe
反压(力)铸造 pressure casting with counterpressure, casting under counterpressure
反压式四排辊辊式矫直机 inverted four-high roller leveller
反演 conversion, inverting, inversion ◇ 转动～ rotation-inversion
反演电路 inverter circuit
反演二重轴 inversion diad
反演法 inversion process
反演六重轴 inversion hexad
反演三重轴 inversion triad
反演中心 point [centre] of inversion
反演轴 inversion axis
反焰 back-fire
反焰炉 reverberatory furnace
反氧化剂 antioxidant
反翼缘 counter flange
反翼缘法孔型设计 counterflange method
反阴极 anti-cathode
反应 react(ion),【理】respond ◇ 埃洛纳[金氰化]～ Eloner's reaction, 不起～的 reactionless

反应不足 underaction
反应步骤 reaction step
反应槽 reaction tank, tank reactor
反应产量 reaction yield
反应产物 resultant (of reaction), reaction product
反应常数 reaction constant
反应池 reaction basin
反应带[段] reaction zone,【团】active zone
反应等容线 reaction isochore
反应等温线 reaction isotherm
反应点 reaction point
反应动力学 reaction kinetics, kinetics of reaction
反应度 degree of reaction
反应段长度 reaction length
反应堆 pile, reactor (pile) ◇ 材料试验～*, 德拉贡～*, 低温～ low temperature reactor, 多用途～ multipurpose reactor, 非均匀～ heterogeneous reactor, 沸水型～*, 高温气体冷却式～*, 均匀～ homogeneous reactor, 离子交换～*, 脉冲式～ pulsed reactor, 气体冷却～ gas-cooled reactor, 稀释相型燃料～*, 液体金属燃料～*, 增殖～ breeder (reactor)
反应堆材料 pile [reactor] material
反应堆材料冶金学 reactor metallurgy
反应堆残渣 poison
反应堆辐照合金 pile-irradiated alloy
反应堆级锭料 reactor grade ingot
反应堆级铪 reactor-grade hafnium
反应堆级金属 reactor grade metal
反应堆内蠕变 inreactor creep
反应堆品位级 reactor grade
反应堆燃料 reactor fuel
反应堆用石墨 reactor-grade graphite
反应堆正面 pile face
反应堆周期 reactor period
反应釜 reaction still, agitated reactor
反应副产物 reaction by-product
反应坩埚 reaction crucible

反应钢弹(金属热还原用)　reaction bomb
反应缸　reaction cylinder
反应工程(学)　reaction engineering
反应罐　reaction pot,【铁】retort(直接还原用)
反应罐直接还原法　retort process
反应锅　reaction pot [still]
反应过程热　heat of process
反应焊接　reaction soldering
反应焊药　reaction flux
反应后加热　post-reaction heating
反应后焦炭强度　coke strength after reaction(CSR)
反应化学　reaction chemistry
反应混合物　reaction [reactive] mixture
反应机理[制]　reaction mechanism
反应极限电流　reaction limiting current
反应级数　order of reaction
反应剂　reactant
反应加速器[剂]　reaction accelerator
反应阶段　reaction step, stage of reaction
反应界面　reaction interface
反应空间(转炉的)【钢】reaction space
反应扩散　reactive diffusion
反应力　reaction, reagency
反应量　reacting weight
反应炉　reaction furnace
反应率　reactivity, reaction rate
反应门限电平　response threshold level
反应面　reaction surface
反应模型　reaction model
反应能　reaction energy
反应能力　reactive capability, reactivity
反应平衡　reaction balance [equilibrium]
反应瓶　reaction bulb
反应期　reaction period, stage of reaction
反应器　reactor ◇ 敞口~ open reactor, 多管~ multi-tubular reactor, 多级卧式~*, 分批[间歇]处理~ batch reactor, 管状~ tubular reactor, 连续床~*, 流态化(床)~*, 螺旋搅动床~*, 水平式~ horizontal reactor, 脱水~ dehydration reactor, 有料~ charged reaction vessel, 振动盘~ vibrating tray reactor
反应器壁　reactor wall
反应器堵塞　reactor plugging
反应器进料　reactor feed
反应器壳　reactor shell
反应器理论　reactor theory
反应器中形成沟流　channeling in reactor
反应钎焊　reactive brazing
反应前端　reaction front
反应区(同"反应带")
反应热　reaction heat
反应熔炼　reaction smelting
反应容器　reaction vessel ◇ 装有料的~ charged vessel
反应烧结　reaction [reactive] sintering
反应生成物　resultant of reaction
反应式　equation
反应室　reaction chamber
反应竖炉　reaction shaft
反应顺序　sequence of reactions
反应速度　reaction speed [velocity], rate of reaction
反应速度常数　(reaction) rate constant
反应速度限制阶段　rate-determining step
反应速率　reaction rate ◇ 绝对~理论*
反应速率方程　reaction rate equation
反应速率过程　【化】rate process
反应速率控制因素　rate-controlling factor
反应塔　reaction tower [column] ◇ 填充~ packed reaction tower, 中间~*
反应物扩散　diffusion of reactant
反应物消耗　consumption of reactant
反应物(质)　reactant, reacting [reaction] mass, reacting [reative] substance
反应效率　reaction efficiency
反应性　reactivity, reactiveness, responsiveness
反应性工艺　reactive process
反应性[能力]控制　reactivity control
反应性偏差[扰动]　reactivity disturbance
反应性试验　reactivity test

反应性温度系数 reactivity temperature coeficient
反应液体 reaction liquid
反应研磨 reaction milling
反应指示器[剂] reaction indicator
反应柱 reaction column ◇ 立管式～
反应自由能 free energy of reaction
反应坐标 【理】reaction coordinate
反原子 inverted atom,antiatom
反张力拉拔 back tension drawing,drawing with back tension
反张力装置(带材的) drag unit
反照 reverberation
反照率 albedo
反振荡电路 antihunting circuit
反蒸发 retrograde vaporization
反置电极 counter electrode
反质子 anti-proton
反中微子 antineutrino
反中子 antineutron
反重力浇铸 counter-gravity pouring
反重力铸造 counter-gravity casting
反轴机 rewinder
反骤成巨晶(现象) antigermination
反转 reverse rotation, reversion, back turn, roll back,counter revolution
反转齿轮 counter gear
反转底板(照相的) reversal plate
反转固相线 retrograde solidus
反转胶片 reversal film ◇ 彩色单张～
反转性 reversibility
反转循环(次)数 number of reverse turn cycles
反转照相纸 reversal paper
反转支臂式堆料机 reversing-boom stacker
反自旋取向 opposite spin orientation
反作用 reaction, back action, counteract, bucking
反作用电压 bucking voltage
反作用辊 【压】counter roll
反作用力 reacting [reaction, reactive, back(ward)] force
返尘加入斗 return dust charge hopper
返尘[料]料斗 return dust hopper
返尘送给运输机 return dust feed conveyor
返滴定 back titration
返粉 return fines(R.F.), revert fines, returned dust
返回 return, go [come] back, kick-back, roll in
返回代码 return code
返回道次 return pass
返回地址 return address
返回电解液 return electrolyte
返回法 back run process
返回废钢 return [recirculating] scrap, scrap return, recycled material
返回废料 recirculating scrap
返回管 return pipe
返回管线 return line
返回轨道 retracting rail
返回辊 return roll
返回辊道 return [bypass] table, feedback table roller
返回浸出 recycled leach
返回矿粉烧结矿 return fine sinter
返回料 recycled material,【冶】reverts
返回流槽 return launder
返回双过滤器 return double filter
返回水供应槽 return water supply tank
返回酸 return acid
返回物 returns
返回线 return line
返回阴极液 recycled catholyte
返回运动 retrograde motion
返回运输机 feedback conveyer, discard transfer(送回加热炉用)
返回轧制 roll on return pass
返回指令 link order, breakpoint order(射流技术)
返混 back mixing
返焦 returned coke

返焦贮槽 backing coke bin
返矿 return fines, return (fine) sinter, recycle, sinter dust ◇ 炉前筛下～*,烧结矿筛下～*
返矿比[率] return fine rate [ratio], percentage of returns, proportion of return fines
返矿槽 reclaim hopper, return fines bin, sinter fines bin(烧结的)
返矿(产出)量 return fines output [make], returns-out
返矿产出率 return fines output
返矿粉 sinter fines [dust]
返矿含量 return fines content
返矿皮带机 return fines conveyer
返矿平衡 return fines balance
返矿添加量 return fines content [level], proportion of return fines, returns-in
返矿(循环)系统 return circuit system
返矿用槽式输送机 fine pan conveyer
返矿贮槽 backing ore bin
返力 return force
返料 returns (rets), return product, returning charge,【团】return chat(s),【冶】revert(s)
返料槽 reclaim hopper
返料管 refeed line
返料颗粒 revert particle
返料皮带[运送带] return conveyor
返料运输机 reclaim conveyor
返铅流槽 lead return launder
返砂喷砂机 vacu-blast
返水 rewater
返修焊 rewelding
返渣 return slag
范德瓦尔斯方程 Van der Waals' equation
范德瓦尔斯结晶 Van der Waals' crystal
范德瓦尔斯力 Van der Waals' force
范德瓦尔斯物态方程 Van der Waals' equation of state
范德瓦尔斯引力 Van der Waals' attraction [bond]

范德维恩慢弯曲脆断缺口试样 Van der Veen specimen
范德维恩慢弯曲脆断试验 Van der Veen test
范宁方程式 Fanning equation
范托夫定律 Van't Hoff law
范托夫原理 Van't Hoff principle
范围检查 range check
范围清晰度 range resolution
范型仪表 standard [master] instrument
范性 plasticity, plastic property ◇ 滑移引起的～变形
范性变形抗力 resistance to plastic deformation
范性滑移 plastic slip
范性极限 plastic limit
范性晶体 plastic crystal
范性理论 theory of plasticity ◇ 贝克尔～*
范性连续体理论 continuum theory of plasticity
范性流变[流动] plastic flow ◇ 片层～ laminar plastic flow
范性流变理论 theory of plastic flow
范性流变量 amount of plastic flow
范性流变曲线 flow curve
范性流变速率 rate of plastic flow
范性切变 plastic shear
范性伸长 plastic extension
范性弯曲 plastic bending
范性位移 plastic displacement
范性形变 plastic deformation
范性形变的稳态理论 theory of stability of plastic deformation
范性形变机理 mechanism of plastic deformation
范性形变效应 plastic deformation effect
范性行为 plastic behaviour
范性压痕 plastic indentation
范性应力集中系数 plastic stress concentration factor
"饭高"(铜镍铝)合金(4—6Ni,5—7Al,余

量Cu） Iitaka's metal
泛美采矿工程与地质学会 Pan-American Institute of Mining Engineering and Geology(P.A.I.M.E.G.)*
芳基 aryl (group, radical)
芳基核 aromatic nucleus
芳基化物 arylide
芳基金属（化合物） arylide
芳烃[芳族燃料]油 aromatic naphtha
芳香度[性] aromaticity
芳(香)环缩合 aromatic ring condensation
芳香剂 aromatic
芳(香)族的 aromatic
芳族胺 aromatic amine
芳族化合物 aromatic compound
芳族溶剂 arsol, aromatic solvent
芳(族,香)烃 aromatic hydrocarbon
芳族稀释剂 aromatic diluent
方案 scheme, plan, program, proposal
方案性设计 conceptual design
方柄凿(锻造工具) hardy
方波发生器 square-wave generator
方波极谱法 square-wave polarography
方材 square bar, squares
方差 variance
方差分析 variance analysis
方程(式) equation ◇ 爱因斯坦～ Einstein equation, 贝塞尔～ Bessel equation, 玻耳兹曼～ Boltzmann equation, 伯努利～ Bernoulli's equation, 布喇格～ Bragg's equation, 范德瓦尔斯～*, 格里菲思～ Griffith equation, 吉布斯－亥姆霍兹～*, 加达姆～*, 克拉珀龙－克劳修斯～*, 拉普拉斯～ Laplace equation, 朗之万～ Langevin equation, 劳厄－赫林～*, 努森～ Knudsen equation, 佩奇～ Petch equation, 皮奇－克勒～ Peach-Koehler equation, 谢勒～ Scherrer's equation, 约翰逊－梅尔～*
方程组 combined equations, equation set
方底金刚石棱锥体 square-based diamond pyramid
方沸石｛NaAl(SiO$_3$)$_2$·H$_2$O｝ analcime, analcite
方钙铈锏矿｛Ca$_3$(Ce, La, Di)$_4$Si$_3$O$_{15}$｝ beckelite
方钢 square steel [section, iron], square steel (bar), squares, quadrantiron, four sided section
方镉石 monteponite
方格图 graticule
方格纸 scale [quadrille] paper
方钴矿 skutterudite
方管 square pipe
方辊头 square wobbler
方盒信号 【运】box signal
方黄铜矿 chalmersite
方辉锑银矿 polyargyrite
方键 square key
方角边缘的 square-edged
方解石｛CaCO$_3$｝ calcareous spar, calcite (limestone), calcspar ◇ 双折射透明～ Iceland spar
方解石晶体 calcite crystal
方颈螺栓 carriage bolt
方块 block
方块料 brick
方块料(铺砌)路面 cube pavement
方块[体]试验 cube test ◇ 空气中～*, 水中～*
方块字型组织 Chinese script structure
方框图 block-diagram (BLODI), block scheme [representation], skeleton [functional] diagram
方矿[料]槽 square bin
方棱扁钢 square edge flat
方磷锰矿 tetragophosphite
方硫铁镍矿｛(Ni, Fe)S$_2$｝ bravoite
方镁石｛MgO｝ periclase, periclasite
方镁石尖晶石耐火材料 periclase-spinel refractory
方镁石耐火材料 periclase refractory
方镁石砖 periclase brick ◇ 高强度～*

方锰矿 {MnO}　manganosite
方钠矿 {NaCl·3NaAlSiO$_4$}　sodalite
方铌钽矿 {Fe(Nb,Ta)$_2$O$_6$}　mossite
方硼石　boracite
方硼矿　borate of magnesia
方坯 (square)　billet ◇ 抽出～billet withdrawal, 大～bloom, cogged ingot, 异形～shaped bloom
方坯－板坯初轧机　blooming slabbing mill
方坯抽出　billet withdrawal
方坯打印机　bloom stamping machine
方坯检查　inspecting of billets
方坯连铸机　billet caster
方坯连铸机拉矫机　withdrawal & staightening machine of billet CC
方坯轧辊　bloom roll
方坯轧机机组　billet rolling train
方铅矿 {PbS}　galena, galenite, dice mineral, lead glance ◇ 含银～argentiferous galena
方石　ashlar
方石块(铺砌)路面　cube pavement
方石英　crystobalite
方式选择器　mode selector
方铈矿 {(Ce,Th)O$_2$}　cerianite
方铈铝钛矿　zeraltite
方榫定位销　【铸】cottered pin, slotted (moulding box) pin
方坦－莫罗锌基压铸合金 (90－92Zn, 7－8Cu, Pb+Fe<3)　Fontaine-Moreau alloy
方坦－莫罗锌铁铅青铜　Fontaine-Moreau's bronze
方锑矿 {Sb$_2$O$_3$}　senarmontite
方铁矿　Wuestite
方头　square end
方头螺栓　coach [square-head] bolt
方团矿机 (同"柱塞式团矿机")
方钍矿 {ThO$_2$·U$_3$O$_8$}　thorianite
方－椭圆粗轧[开坯]孔型系统　square oval roughing passes

方位　direction, position, bearing, azimuth
方位计　declinometer
方位角　azimuth, position angle
方位平面　azimuthal plane
方位指示仪　direction gauge
方钨铁矿 {FeWO$_4$}　reinite
方向比较式微波继电器　directional comparison microwave relay
方向比较载波继电器　directional comparison carrier relay
方向角　direction angle
方向控制阀　direction(al) control valve
方向灵敏度[敏感性]　directional sensitivity
方向图(辐射的)　directional pattern
方向性　directivity, directionality, orientation ◇ 有～的带状夹杂物 directional banding of inclusions
方向性函数　directivity function
方向性系数　directivity [space] factor, front to rear ratio
方向性性质　directional property
方向选择性　directional selectivity
方型材　square, four sided section, quadrangular section ◇ 弧边～Go-thic square
方形粗轧孔型　square roughing pass
方形垫圈　square washer
方形断面　square (cross-) section
方形钢芯　square steel core
方形焊管　quadrangular seamed tube
方形孔型 [轧槽]　square pass [groove]
方形偏析　【钢】centre(line) pattern
方形阳极　【色】square anode
方形砖　quarry
方眼　grid
方眼筛　square-mesh screen, square sieve ◇ 金属丝编织～*
方英石 {SiO$_2$}　cristobalite
方铀矿 {UO$_2$, UO$_3$; U$_3$O$_8$}　ulrichite, uraninite
方铀钍石　uranothorianite
方圆标志产品质量认证(中国)　CQM

方圆标志质量体系认证(中国)	CQM system-certification diplomas
方爪离合器 【机】	square-jaw chutch
方正度要求高的	resquared
方柱石{$Ca_4Si_3O_{10}$}	mel(l)ilite
方砖	square brick
方钻杆	kelly bar [stem], square kelly pipe ◇ 凯里～安全配合接头
房顶采光井 【建】	compluvium
房基通风井 【建】	dry area
房基线	building line
房式烟道	chamber flue
房屋	building(bldg.), house ◇ 预制墙板式～panel-type house, 装配式～fabricated building
房屋重建	building reconstruction
房屋构架	building frame
房屋构造	building construction
房屋界线	building line
房屋勘测员	building surveyor
房屋跨度	building span
房屋体积	bulk of building
房屋主要立面	frontispiece
防爆的	explosion-proof, flame-proof (FLP)
防爆阀[管]	explosion stack
防爆罐(气焊的)	flash back tank
防爆剂	antiknock reagent
防爆门	explosion door
防爆盘	explosion [bursting] disc
防爆气氛	nonexplosive atmosphere
防爆式探测器	explosion proof type detector
防爆型电动机	explosion-proof motor
防爆型菱形布袋收尘器	flame-proof and diamond bag collector
防波堤	mole ◇ 堆石[抛石]～rock-mound breakwater, 格构式～cellular break water
防缠槽(导卫板的)	whip channel
防潮保险丝	NH(non-hygroscopic) fuse
防潮层	damp(proof) course(d.p.c.)
防潮的	dampproof, moisture-proof, moistrue-repellent, moisture-tight, water proof
防潮堤	coastal levee
防潮脱硫剂	moisture-proof desulphurizer
防潮纸	building paper
防尘	dust control
防尘的	dust-proof, dust-tight
防尘盖	dust cap
防尘环	dust collar
防尘建筑	dust-tight construction
防尘密封	dust seal
防尘(排烟)系统	hood system
防尘网	dust gauze [screen]
防尘污染法规(空气的)	dust control legislation
防尘罩	dust cap [guard, jar], antipollution control hood
防冲铺砌	downstream apron
防冲芯片 【铸】	splash core
防臭	deodorization
防喘振的	surgeproof
防磁的	antimagnetic
防弹玻璃	armoured [bulletproof] glass
防弹钢板	armour plate
防倒轮(高炉皮带机的)	anti-reverse-rotation device
防滴(漏)的	drip-proof, drip tight ◇ 开启式～open drip-proof
防冻措施	antifreezing precaution [measures]
防冻剂	antifreezer, antifreezing mixture
防冻深度	frost proof depth
防冻添加剂	antifreeze admixture [additive]
防冻(涂)层	antifreezing coat
防冻液	antifreeze solution
防毒的	poison-resistant
防毒面具	gas(proof) mask
防风雨格栅	weather protection grids
防辐射材料	antiradiation material

防辐射的 radiation-proof
防腐 corrosion prevention [protection], corrosion resistant(CRE), antisep-tisis
防腐材料 anticorrosive [antirot] substance
防腐处理(木材的) brush [antiseptic] treatment
防腐底漆 etch primer
防腐剂 anticorrosive(agent), preservative (compounds), antiseptics, aseptic, corrosion preventive, protector
防腐减垢涂料 anticorrosion and lessening encrustation paint
防腐漆 anticorrosive paint, corrosion resistant coating
防腐石材 corrosion resistant stone
防腐蚀 anti-corrosion, inhibit
防腐蚀(保护)颜料 anticorrosive pigment
防腐蚀绝缘层[隔层] anticorrosive [anticorrosion] insulation
防腐蚀作用 inhibition
防腐添加剂 anticorrosive additives
防腐作用 antiseptic effect
防垢剂 anticrustator, antiscaling compound ◇ 锅炉~ boiler compound
防洪(洪水控制) flood control [protection]
防弧药皮 【焊】shielded-arc coating
防护 protection, shield, guard ◇ 加以~的 protected(prot.), 未加~的 unprotected
防护标准 criterion of protection
防护玻璃 protective glass
防护材料 shielding material
防护层 protective covering
防护层处理 protective finish
防护程度 degree of protection
防护垫板 bottom plate
防护方法 protecting means
防护服(装) safety [protective, protection] clothing
防护隔板 shield separator

防护管 guard tube
防护环 ferrule
防护剂 protective agent, protectant, preventive ◇ 阴极~ cathodic protector
防护建筑物 protective structure
防护晶体 protected crystal
防护面具 face guard
防护面罩 helmet (shield), protective mask, face shield(焊工的) ◇ 电(弧)焊~ arc-welding helmet, 喷镀金属~ metal spraying helmet, 喷丸[砂]清理用~, 折翻式~ tilting helmet
防护能力(润滑脂的) protective value
防护屏 protection [protecting, protective, fire] screen, guard shield [board] ◇ γ射线~ gamma shield, 电晕放电~ corona shield, 阳极~ anode shield
防护设备 preventer
防护式电动机 protected(type) motor
防护手套 finger guard, gauntlet
防护套 protecting jacket
防护套管 protective sleeves
防护透镜 protective lens
防护(性)的 preventive
防护眼镜 eye protector safety goggles
防护用具 safety ware
防护用筛盖 protection screen deck
防护罩 protection hood, blimp ◇ 床架~ bed guard, 可移式~ movable guard
防护装置 protector, protective device
防滑 deslicking, anti-skidding
防滑金属 antislip metal
防滑路面 skid-free road surface, anti-skid surface
防滑轮胎 antiskid tyre
防划伤处理 antiscuffing treatment
防划伤膏 antiscuffing paste
防活套折叠 looping
防火 fire prevention [control, protection, safety]
防火安全系统 flame safeguard system
防火的 fire [flame] proof

防火花的	flame-proof(FLP)
防火绝缘线	flame proof wire
防火门	fire(resisting) door
防火幕	safety [fireproof] curtain
防火皮带	flame proof belt
防火栓	fire protection flap
防火用液压流体	fire resistance hydraulic fluid
防碱(蚀)的	anticaustic
防溅板	splasher
防溅槽	save all tank
防溅挡板	splash guard [shield]
防溅垫(加在锭模中)	【钢】bolster
防溅垫板	splash ring disc
防溅护板	antisplash shield
防溅屏	spatter shield
防溅渗外壳(的)	hose-proof
防溅式电动机	splash-proof motor
防溅砖[器](真空脱气时用)	【钢】stream limiter
防晶粒长大	antigermination
防晶粒长大处理	antigermination treatment
防卡塞特性	antiseizure characteristic
防空工程[工作]	air defence work
防空壕	dug-out
防空气污染控制系统	housekeeping air pollution control system
防浪矮墙	parapet
防浪涌的	surgeproof
防老(化)剂	antioxidant
防裂钩	anti-checking iron
防裂环	【铸】breaker ring
防裂筋	【铸】cracking strip, cooling fin
防漏的	leak-proof
防漏剂	leak preventive
防霉的	fungusproof
防磨的	wear-preventive, abrasion-proof
防磨炉衬	wearing lining
防磨蚀	erosion resistance
防磨凸块(芯盒上缘)	elevator bar
防磨涂层	wear resistant coating
防沫剂	anti-foaming agent
防挠材	stiffening band, stiffener
防逆阀	back [retaining] valve
防黏剂	antistick(ing) agent
防黏砂涂料	antipenetration wash
防黏特性	antiseizure characteristic
防黏涂料	paint barrier
防黏着磨损剂	antiseize compound
防鸟格栅	bird protection grid
防凝水内衬	anti-condensation lining
防爬撑	bunton
防爬木撑	transverse brace
防爬器	【运】anti-creeper
防跑偏侧辊	side guide roller
防跑偏控制(带卷的)	eccentricity protection control(EPC)
防跑偏(控制)装置	edge position control
防跑偏装置	anti-meandering equipment
防泡[沫]的	antifoaming
防起泡剂	forth breaker
防热玻璃	glass for protecting against heat
防热屋顶	cricket
防蠕变	anticreep
防闪络环	arc ring
防射线混凝土	radiation-shielding concrete
防射线抹灰(用含钡砂浆)	barium plaster
防渗层	impervious barrier
防渗[增]碳覆层	anticement
防渗碳膏	anticarburizing paste
防渗碳漆[涂料]	carburization-preventing paint, no-carb lacquer, anticar-burizing paint
防湿层	damp(-proof) course(d.p.c.)
防湿的	dampproof, moisture-proof, moisture-repellent
防蚀	corrosion prevention, anticorrosion ◇阳极~法 anodization
防蚀处理	protective treatment, 【金】immunizing
防蚀钝化铝	alumite
防蚀绝缘层	anti-corrosion insulation

防蚀热处理 immunizing
防蚀热喷涂 thermal spraying
防蚀涂层 inhibit coating
防蚀涂料(钢材的) etching primer
防蚀锌 anode zinc ◇ 马齐克-黑膜浸镀法 Mazic zinc black method
防蚀纸 antirust [antitarnish, inhibited] paper
防鼠(咬)电缆 gopher protected cable
防水层 waterproof layer ◇ 沥青~*
防水电动机 submersible motor, deluge proof motor
防水帆布屋面 canvas decking
防水防汽内孔窥视仪 waterproof and vapourproof borescope
防水混凝土 waterproof concrete
防水剂 water-repellent substance, waterproofing agent [admixture]
防水沥青 waterproofing pitch
防水膜 waterproof membrane
防水(喷射)挡板 water guard
防水性 water impermeability
防水锈剂 anticrustator, disincrustant
防水油漆 water-resistant paint
防松机构 lock(ing) gear
防松螺栓 (同"锁紧螺栓")
防酸耐火材料 acid-proof refractory
防酸水泥 (同"耐酸水泥")
防碎裂 anti-degradation
防碎溜槽 anti-degradation chute
防湍流冲击垫【连铸】turbulence proventing pad
防弯辊 anti-buckle roll
防污 antifouling
防污剂 antifouling compound [agent]
防污染 pollution control
防污染措施 measures against pollution
防污染设备 pollution abatement equipment
防污染设施 pollution control facilities
防污染协定 agreement on pollution prevention
防污涂层(防止海生物附着用) antifouling coating
防污油漆 antifouling paint
防雾(化)作用 antifogging action
防锈 antirust, rust-proof, rust protection [prevention, inhibition], rust-preventing, rust-preventive, rust-proofing, rust-resisting ◇ 磷酸盐~处理*,气相抑制剂~*
防锈层 antirust coat
防锈剂 antirust additive, antirusting [rust-preventing] agent, rust-prevent(at)ive, rust protection agent, inhibitor, rust preventer
防锈漆[涂料] antirust(ing) [anticorrosive] paint
防锈清漆 antirust varnish
防锈涂层 antirust coat, rustproofing [rust-inhibiting] coating
防锈氧化膜 rust-resisting oxide film
防锈油 rust-preventative [antirust] oil, rust-preventive
防锈纸 antirust [antitarnish] paper
防焰的 flame proof
防氧化 oxidation protection
防氧化剂 oxidation inhibitor
防氧化切削 cover cutting
防氧化脂 antirust [oxidation-inhibited] grease
防音的 soundproof
防油溅挡板 oil-splash guard
防油器 oil guard
防雨的 raintight
防雨密封装置 rain seal
防雨罩 rain hood
防御柱 fender pile
防折器 loop lifter [holder],【压】looper
防折轧机 anti-fluting mill
防震层 buffer layer
防震插座 cushion socket
防震的 shockproof
防震滚柱 anti-flutter roller
防震基础 vibration proof foundation

防震弹簧	damping spring
防振的	vibration-proof
防治污染	pollution prevention
仿描头	tracing head
仿生材料	biomaterial, bionic material
仿生计算机	bionic computer
仿生纳米复合材料	nano bionic composite
仿生自动机	biorobot
仿效操作器[机械手]	(master-)slave manipulator
仿形	profile modeling, profiling shape, copy(ing)
仿形板	gauge finder, cam
仿形机	imitation machine
仿形机床	contour(ing) [profiling, copying, duplicating] machine
仿形机构	copying mechanism
仿形轮	tracing [contour] wheel
仿形磨头	copy-grinding head
仿形切割机【焊】	profiler ◇ 按比例~ ratio cutting machine
仿形铣床	reproducing pattern milling machine, (die) profiler
仿形装置	duplicator, copying [tracer] unit ◇ 手工~ hand tracing device
仿银(铜镍)合金	imitation silvers
仿造铂合金(60黄铜,37.5Zn,余量杂质;50青铜,32.5Zn,余量杂质)	imitation platinum alloy
仿造锰青铜(55Cu,43Zn,余量Sn及Al)	imitation manganese bronze
仿真	simulation, emulation
仿真程序	emulator, simulated program
仿真负载	artificial [dummy] load
仿真技术	simulation technique
仿真模型	simulation model ◇ 计算机~
仿真器[机]	simulator, emulator
仿真神经网络	artificial neural network (ANN)
仿真实验	emultation test
仿真线	bootstrap
仿真响应	emulation response
访管【计】	supervisor call(SVC)
访管中断	supervisor interrupt
访问	visit, access, addressing ◇ 多处~ multiple access, 快速~道 revolver
访问存储器	reference to storage ◇ 按内容~ content addressable memory(CAM)
访问存储器指令	memory reference instruction
纺织机械	textile machinery
纺织机针用工具钢带	tool steel strip for textile machine needle
放出的电子	ejected electron
放出的热量	heat of evolution, exothermic heat
放出阀	outlet [escape] valve
放出管	outlet pipe, downflow spout
放出金属液	tapped-out [spout] metal, metal tapping
放出金属液试样(从炉内)	tapping sample
放出开关	draw-off cock
放出孔	bleed hole
放出口	tap(ping) [outlet] hole, well
放出口流槽	taphole launder
放出口修补	hole patching
放出炉底积铁(指高炉)	salamander tapping
放出气体	liberation [development] of gas
放出氢气	liberation of hydrogen
放出物	emission, tappings(熔炉的)
放出旋塞	release cock
放出总管	offtake main
放大倍数	magnification(factor)
放大常数[恒量]	amplification constant
放大尺度(超声波检验的)	distance gain size(DGS)
放大发电机	amplidyne generator
放大管	amplifier tube
放大机	amplifier ◇ 电机~ amplidyne generator, 交磁~ amplidyne, 直流~ metadyne

放大级 amplifier [amplification] stage, booster

放大镜 magnifier, magnifying glass ◇ 手动～ hand magnifier

放大率 amplification (ratio), magnification, mu-factor, gain

放大目镜 amplifying eyepiece

放大器 amplifier (ampl), magnifier, expander, enlarger ◇ 电机～ amplidyne, 对冲式～ direct impact amplifier, 对数－反对数～ log-antilog amplifier, 跟踪～ follower amplifier, 缓冲～ buffer amplifier, 汇流式～*, 级联[串级]～ cascade amplifier, 射流～ fluid amplifier, 双弯道～*, 压力～ pressure multiplier, 运算～ operational amplifier

放大器插头 amplifier plug

放大图 enlarged drawing

放大系数 amplification coefficient [factor], enlargement [magnification, multiplying] factor, mu-factor

放大像 magnified [enlarged] image

放大型目镜 amplifying eyepiece ◇ 霍马尔～ Homal eyepiece

放大照相 photomicrogram, macrophotograph

放电 (electric) discharge, discharging, uncharge

放电棒 discharging rod

放电成形 electrical discharge forming, electro-discharge forming

放电电极 discharge [discharging] electrode ◇ 金属丝～*

放电电流 discharge current

放电电路 discharging circuit

放电电势[位] discharge potential

放电电阻器 discharging resistor

放电粉末烧结 electro-spark sintering (ESS)

放电管 discharge tube [lamp], ignitron (tube) ◇ 克鲁克斯～ Crookes tube

放电管漏泄指示器 discharge tube leak indicator

放电管整流器 discharge-tube rectifier

放电焊接 electric discharge welding, electrospark welding

放电辉点 discharge spot

放电加工机 electric discharge machine (EDM)

放电加热的区域熔炼 zone melting by electrical discharge

放电加热硬化 electric discharge hardening

放电(加压)烧结 electric discharge sintering, (electro)spark sintering

放电间隙 discharge gap, striking distance

放电磨削 electric discharge grinding

放电器 discharger, (lightening) arrestor, spark gap

放电(切削)加工 electric(al) discharge machining (EDM)

放电容量 discharge capacity

放电时间常数 discharge time constant

放电系数 discharge coefficient

放电液压成形 electrohydraulic forming

放电真空计 discharge gauge

放风 【铁】snort(en)ing, checking

放风阀 air-pressure release valve, blow down [off] valve, 【铁】snort valve, bleed in damper

放风阀绳轮 【铁】snort wheel

放风坐料 【铁】snort(en)ing

放钢斜坡(炉底的) drainage slope

放灰阀(除尘器的) dust (discharging) valve ◇ 风动～ air-operated dust valve, 配重式～*, 双层～*

放灰管 windleg, 【团】leg, 【铁】dust leg (除尘器的)

放灰漏斗 dust hopper

放金属口 metal notch

放进 admission

放空阀 dump valve

放宽 relaxation

放矿口 discharge lip

放矿口修补　hole patching
放矿装置　eduction gear
放(卸)料　discharge, lowering of charge
放(卸)料仓　discharge bin
放(卸)料量　withdrawal rate
放(卸)料斜槽　discharge chute
放(卸)料装置　discharge deviec
放流槽　down-spout
放流工　tapper
放流口冷却套(鼓风炉的)　【色】tapping breast
放流温度　tapping temperature
放锍口　matte taphole, taphole for matte
放锍流槽　matte tapping launder
放炉料　lowering of charge
放沫旋塞　scum cock
放能反应　exo(en)ergic reaction
放泥口　slime run-off
放气　gassing, (air-) bleeding, (air) exhaust, air-out, deflation, gas release
放气阀　gas bleeder, bleeding [exhaust, snuffle] valve, gas escape [sluice] valve, air relief valve, blow off cock
放气管　gas bleeder, vent pipe ◇ 炉顶气体~ top air bleeder
放气活门　discharge valve, air bleed valve
放气开关　blow out switch
放气孔　vent,【铸】whistler
放气口　air [gas] vent
放气门　air eliminator [relief]
放气喷嘴　blow off nozzle
放气旋塞　air relief cock, release cock
放气装置　release system
放弃　abandon, back out, kicking-up, put away, throw-over
放汽　bleeding of steam
放铅口　lead tap(-hole), lead tapping well ◇ 虹吸~ siphon lead tap
放氢　hydrogen desorption
放热　heat release [liberation, evolution, removal, withdrawal], exothermic, liberation [evolution] of heat, thermic release

放热点　【金】recalescence point
放热法熔炼车间(同"金属热熔炼车间")
放热反应　exothermal [exo(en)ergic] reaction, heat generating reaction
放热分析　exergy analysis
放热副反应　exothermic auxiliary reaction
放热过程　exothermic [exo(en)ergic] process
放热化合物　exothermic compound
放热还原反应　exothermic reducing reaction
放热基气氛　exothermic base atmosphere
放热冒口套　【铸】exothermic riser sleeve
放热能　exothermic energy
放热式气氛[放热型保护气氛]　exothermic atmosphere ◇ DX~*, NX 氮基~*
放热(速)率　heat release [liberation] rate, exothermic rate, rate of heat liberation
放热特性　exothermic character
放热-吸热气氛　exothermic-endothermic atmosphere
放热型气体　exogas, exothermic gas ◇ 高发热值的~*
放热性炉气　exothermic furnace atmosphere
放热性气体发生炉　exothermic gas generator
放入　admission
放散阀　air-escape valve, blow off valve,【铁】bleeder [discharge] valve ◇ 高炉~平台~, 均压~【铁】relief valve, 炉顶~【铁】bleeder door, 炉气~*
放散阀液压传动装置(高炉的)　hydraulic thruster arm
放散管　monkey,【铁】bleeder(煤气的)
放散管煤气压力　【铁】bleeder stack pressure
放射　radiation, emission, emit(tance), emanation
放射安全　radiological safety
放射测厚法　radiographic thickness gaug-

ing
放射产生的铅　radiogenic lead
放射电极　emitting electrode
放射化分析　radioactivation [activation] analysis
放射化学　radiation chemistry, radiochemistry
放射化学分析　radiochemical analysis
放射化学性能　radiochemical behaviour
放射率　emittance
放射能力　radioactivity, emissive ability
放射示踪剂[物]　radiotracer
放射图　curiegram
放射系　radioactive series [family], decay series
放射现象　radioactivity
放射线[放射性射线]　radioactive rays, radiation ◇自动～照相 autoradiograph
放射线病　irradiation sickness
放射线辐照硬化现象　thermal spike
放射线损伤　radiation damage
放射型拉模　radiused [convex-face] die, bell mouth [shaped] die
放射型锥模　radiused conical die
放射性　radioactivity, activity ◇缓发～ delayed activity, 人工～(现象)*
放射性WC微粉渗浸处理(钢表面的)【金】atomic treatment, Atomloy treatment
放射性锕(钍的同位素)　radioactinium
放射性半衰期　(radioactive) half-life
放射性材料容器　needle
放射性测厚计　radioactive thickness gauge
放射性测量仪　radioactivity meter
放射性产物　active product
放射性电离压力[真空]计　radioactive ionization gauge
放射性淀积(物)　active deposit
放射性毒物　radioactive poison
放射性废物　radioactive waste, radwaste
放射性分解　radiolysis
放射性分析　radioanalysis, radioassay
放射性辐射　radioactive radiation

放射性辐照　atomic irradiation
放射性钴　radioactive cobalt, radiocobalt
放射性核素　radionuclide
放射性化　radioactivation
放射性灰尘[尘埃]　radioactive dust [ash]
放射性检测器　radioactive detector
放射性检验　radiographic testing
放射性降落物　radioactive fallout
放射性金　radioactive gold
放射性金属　radioactive metal
放射性矿物　radioactive mineral
放射性料面指示器　radioactive charge level indicator
放射性密度计　radioactive density gauge
放射性母同位素　radioactive parent isotope
放射性气体检验(气密性)　radioactive gas test
放射性强度　radioactive intensity, activity
放射性扫描　radiological scanning
放射性射气[惰性物质]　radioactive emanation
放射性示踪　radioactive tracing
放射性示踪剂　radioactive tracer
放射性示踪元素　radioactive tracer element
放射性衰变　radioactive decay [disintegration]
放射性衰变链　radioactive (decay) chain
放射性碳　radiocarbon, radioactive carbon
放射性同位素　radio(active) isotope
放射性同位素定位器　radioisotope positioner
放射性同位素料面指示器　radioactive charge level indicator
放射性同位素示踪剂[物]　radioactive [radioisotopic] tracer
放射性(同位素)指示剂　radioisotope indicator [tracer], radioactive indicator
放射性微粒掩蔽室　fallout shelter
放射性物质[材料]　radioactive [active, activated] material, radioactive subs

tance, radiomaterial, active mass ◇ 强~研究实验室*

放射性吸收剂 radioactivity absorber

放射性液面[水位]计 radioactive level gauge

放射性元素 radioactive element, radioelement

放射性元素测厚仪 radiation thickness gauge

放射性元素化学 hot chemistry

放射性(元素)族 radioactive family

放射性原子 radioactive atom

放射性照射 radiation exposure, atomic irradiation

放射(性)指示剂 radiothor, radiotracer

放射性指示剂扩散 tracer diffusion

放射性重晶石 radiobaryte

放射性最强点 【理】hot spot

放射学 radiology, radioactivity

放射冶金学 radiometallurgy

放射源 radioactive source

放射源存贮器[放射性物料库] radioactive source store

放射照相 radiography

放射状结构[组织] radiating [radiated] structure

放射族 decay series

放水管 adjustage, offlet, discharging tube, water-drain pipe, bleed(er) line

放水开关[旋塞] drain cock

放水时间 discharge time

放松 relaxation, slacken, loosen, unjamming

放松机构 tripping gear

放下渣 【铁】front slagging

放线 【压】paying-off, unreeling, taking-off

放线车(wire) barrow

放线工 pay-off man

放线机筒 pay-off reel cone

放线机制动器 pay-off reel brake

放线架 feeding reel, flipper(拨丝的) ◇ 地上~floor reels

放线菌亚纲 Actinomycetes

放线设备 pay-off equipment

放线装置 wire flipper, pay-off

放泄阀 drainage [unloading, release] valve

放泄口 escape hole

放泄塞 drain plug

放泄旋塞 relief [drain] cock

放锌口 zinc tapping well

放压孔 pressure tap

放压装置 pressure release device

放样操作[工序] templating operation

放液 tapping, drain ◇ 机械~机*

放液阀 tapping valve

放液孔 tap opening, taphole

放液孔塞 taphole plug

放液流槽 taphole launder

放映 show, project ◇ 普通转速~法 time lapse technique

放渣 slagging(-off), slagging out, tapping slag, slag removal, deslagging, flush off, flushing of slag, run(ning)-off, tap, hot drainage(从炉底)

放渣班(组) slagging crew [team]

放渣板 【色】skimming plate

放渣操作 slagging practice, flush(slag) practice

放渣侧 tapping [slag-off] side

放渣工 【铁】slagger

放渣孔 tap(ping) hole

放渣口 slag tap-hole, slagging door, taphole for slag

放渣平台 slagging platform

放渣期 【钢】flush off period, run-off period

放渣区 slagging area

放渣时间 flushing time

放渣速度 flushing velocity

放真空阀 vacuum relief valve

放置过久 overdone

放置时间 standing time

菲{$C_{14}H_{10}$} phonanthrene

菲奥法直接还原设备[厂] Fior plant
菲奥直接还原法 【铁】Fior process(The Esso fluid iron ore direct reduction process)
菲啶 {C$_{13}$H$_9$N} phenanthridine
菲啶酮 {C$_{13}$H$_9$NO} phenanthridone
菲尔德煤气洗涤机(喷头旋转的) Feld washer
菲酚-[2] 2-phenanthrol
菲克第二定律 Fick's second law
菲克第一定律 Fick's first law
菲克(扩散)定律 Fick's(diffusion) law
菲克扩散方程(式) Feck's diffusion equation
菲里辐射高温计 Fery radiation pyrometer
菲利普电离压力[真空]计 Philips ionization gauge
菲利西姆炮铜(86.25Cu, 7.4Sn, 6.35Zn) Philisim
菲尼克斯-兰斯[PL]底吹转炉炼钢法 Phoenix-Lance(P.L.) process
菲尼克斯软巴比合金(同"软巴比合金")
菲尼特因瓦镍合金(36Ni,余量Fe) Fenit
菲涅耳区域 Fresnel region [zone, range]
菲涅耳透镜 Fresnel lens
菲舍尔筛下粒度分析仪 Fisher subsieve sizer
菲舍尔效应 Fisher effect
菲锑铅矿 fyzelyite
菲亚特电炉 Fiat furnace
"非" NOT, negate, negative
非饱和充电 undercharging
非饱和的 unsaturated
非焙烧球团法 nonfired pellet method
非本形的 alltriomorphic
非本征半导体 extrinsic semiconductor
非本征传导率 extrinsic conductivity
非本征导体 extrinsic conductor
非闭合轨道 open orbit
非标准长度 off-standard length
非标准的 nonstandard, off-standard, un-graded
非标准设备 optional equipment
非玻璃质耐火材料 nonglassy refractory
非传动侧辊道架 light-end table frame
非传动辊式冷床 dead roller bed
非传动式纵剪 pull-type slitter
非磁性材料 non-magnetic material [substance]
非磁性钢(0.4—0.5C, 5Mn, 8—10Ni, 9—12Cr) nonmagnetic steel
非磁性高电阻合金铸铁(9—12Ni, 5—7Mn, 2.0—2.5Si 2.5—3.0C) Nomag
非磁性合金 non-magnetic alloy ◇ 埃尔吉洛伊~*
非磁性金属 non-magnetic metal
非磁性矿石 non-magnetic ore
非磁性耐蚀高强度镍铝合金(4.4Al, 0.5Si, 0.4Ti, 0.35Fe, 0.3Mn, 0.05Cu, 余量Ni) Duranickel
非磁性体 non-magnetic body
非磁性物 non-magnetics
非催化反应 uncatalyzed reaction ◇ 非均匀~*
非单价的 【化】un-univalent
非当量面 nonequivalent planes
非导体 non-conductor, idioelectric
非等熵的 non-isoentropic
非等弹性 anisoelasticity
非等弹性的 nonisoelastic
非等温催化反应 non-isothermal catalytic reaction
非等温的 anisothermal, non-isothermal
非等温分解 anisothermal decomposition
非等温马氏体 (同"变温马氏体")
非等温热重分析 nonisothermal thermo-gravimetric analysis
非等温韧性 anisothermal ductility
非等温退火 anisothermal annealing
非等温形变热处理 anisothermal treatment
非等温转变 anisothermal transformation
非等效面 nonequivalent planes

非点污染源　non point source
非电解的光亮浸液　nonelectrolytic bright dip
非电解淀积　electroless deposition
非电解镀覆[浸镀](法)　nonelectrolysis [electroless] plating
非电解镀镍　nonelectrolytic [electroless] nicket plating
非电解镍镀层　electroless nicket
非电解溶液　electroless solution
非电解质　non-electrolyte, anelectrolyte
非电离络合物　non-ionic complex
非电离性辐射　(同"非致电离辐射")
非电容式交流电弧源　noncapacitive A-C arc source
非定常的　transient, nonsteady
非定常力　nonstationary force
非定常温度　transient temperature
非定期观察　casual observation
非定期检验　casual inspection
非定向键　nondirectional bond
非定重线捆　catchweight coils
非镀锌管　black pipe
非对称方式　asymmetrical mode
非对称交叉轧制　non-pair cross rolling
非对称孔型　asymmetrical pass
非对称脉动电流　nonsymmetrical pulsating current
非对称谱线增宽　asymmetric [unsymmetric(al)] line broadening
非对称束　asymmetrical beam
非对称效应　asymmetrical effect
非对称(衍射)线轮廓(X射线照相的)　asymmetrical line profile
非对角扩散　off-diagonal diffusion
非惰性杂质　non-inert impurity
非发光体　non-luminous body
非法代码　illegal [forbidden, nonexistent] code
非法指令校验　unallowable instruction check
非法字符　illegal [unallowable] character

非反射衰耗　nonreflection attenuation
非放射性污染物　nonradioactive pollutant
非沸腾型冷媒　【压】unebullition cooling medium
非分馏蒸馏　nonfractionating distillation
非浮动开关　floatless switch
非腐蚀性气体　non-corrosive gas
非高炉炼铁　non-blast furnace ironmaking
非各向同性的　nonisotropic
非工作孔型　dead pass
非工作位置　idle position, off-position
非共格的　incoherent, non-coherent
非共格间界　incoherent boundary ◇ 大角(度)～*
非共格晶粒间界　incoherent grain boundary
非共晶易熔合金　non-eutectic fusible alloy
非规定尺寸　off-size
非硅酸盐炉渣　non-silicate slag
非过渡金属　non-transition metal
非合金钢　unalloyed steel
非合金工具钢　unalloyed tool steel
非黑体　non-black body
非胡克定律现象　non-Hookeian
非胡克式相互作用　non-Hookeian interaction
非互溶的　immiscible
非化学活性金属　nonreactive metal
非化学计量(法)　non-stoichiometry
非化学计量化合物　non-stoichiometric compound
非化学计量缺陷　nonstoichiometry defect
非灰段　non-gray zone
非灰段法　non-gray zone method
非灰气体　non-gray gas
非活性焦炭　unreactive coke
非活性金属　nonreactive metal
非活性状态　inactive state
非基面滑移　nonbasal glide
非机动冷床　(同"固定式冷床")
非极化的　nonpolarized
非极化辐射　unpolarized radiation

非极性半导体	nonpolar semiconductor
非极性分子	nonpolar molecule
非极性化合物	nonpolar compound
非极性基	nonpolar group
非极性键	homopolar binding [bond]
非极性键合	nonpolar linkage
非极性结构	nonpolar structure
非极性气体	nonpolar gas
非极性液体	nonpolar liquid
非极性轴	nonpolar axis
非计划停工[风,机,炉]	unscheduled shutdown [delay]
非计划维修时间	nonscheduled maintenance time
非简并半导体	nondegenerate semiconductor
非简并能级	nondegenerate(energy) level
非简并态	nondegenerate state
非简并(性)气体	undegenerate gas
非键轨函数[非键轨道的]	nonbonding orbital
非焦化(的)	non-coking
非焦性煤	dead coal
非胶结硅石	uncemented quartzite
非接触测量	non-contact measurement
非接触端	non-contact end
非接触焊接设备	non-contact welding equipment
非接触冷却法【环】	no-contact process
非接触冷却水【环】	noncontact cooling water
非接触式 X 射线测厚仪	X-ray noncontact thickness gauge
非接触式测厚仪(带材的)	non-contact thickness gauge
非接触式飞测千分尺	gamma gauge
非接触式核磁共振法[核子法]【理】	non-contacting nuclear method
非接触式调整[扫描跟踪]器(带材边缘位置的)	non-contact scanning detector
非接触型测量仪	contactless gauge
非接触型千分尺	non-contact micrometer
非结合水分	mobile moisture, unbound water
非结焦[焦化]煤	non-coking coal
非结晶的	uncrystalline
非结晶体	non-crystal
非结晶性	non-crystalline
非金属	nonmetal
非金属粉末	non-metal powder
非金属覆层	non-metallic coating
非金属光泽	non-metallic lustre
非金属合金元素	non-metallic alloying element
非金属合金组分	non-metallic alloy ingredient
非金属化合物	non-metallic compound
非金属还原剂	non-metallic reduction agent
非金属基复合材料	non-metallic matrix composite
非金属基体	non-metal(lic) matrix
非金属夹杂(物)	non-metallic inclusions [matter],【冶】non-metallics ◇ 固体~*,齐勒~计量法【钢】Zieler process, 外来~*,云状[微粒]~slag clouds
非金属加热元件	non-metallic heating element
非金属加入料[添加剂]	non-metallic additive
非金属键	non-metallic binding [bond, linkage]
非金属晶体	non-metallic crystal
非金属矿石	non-metallic ore
非金属矿物	non-metallic mineral, barren mineral
非金属离子	non-metallic ion
非金属摩擦组分	friction producing non-metallic ingredient
非金属纳米材料	non-metallic nano material(s)
非金属黏结剂	non-metallic binder
非金属球团法	non-metallic pelletizing
非金属润滑剂	non-metallic lubricant

非金属涂层　non-metallic coating
非金属物质　non-metallic matter, non-metallics
非金属相　non-metallic phase
非金属氧化物　non-metallic oxide
非金属元素　non-metallic element
非金属杂质　non-metallic impurity
非金属轴承　non-metallic bearing
非金属组分　non-metallic ingredient
非晶半导体　amorphous semiconductor
非晶超导体　amorphous superconductor
非晶超导材料　amorphous superconducting material
非晶硅　amorphous silicon
非晶区　amorphous region
非晶态材料　amorphous material
非晶态粉尘　amorphous dust
非晶态合金　amorphous alloy
非晶态转变　amorphous [non-crystalline] transition
非晶体金属（含 Si－B 半金属的铁钴镍合金）　amomet, amorphous metal
非晶形结构　amorphous structure
非晶(形)态　amorphous form [state, condition]
非晶形碳[非结晶碳]　（同"无定形碳"）
非晶形[体]物质　（同"无定形物质"）
非晶形相　amorphous phase
非晶性　amorphism
非晶质薄膜　amorphous film
非晶质材料　non-crystalline material
非晶质(的)　amorphous
非晶质合金　non-crystalline alloy
非晶(质)体　amorphous body, non-crystal
非晶状　non-crystalline
非精炼混铁炉　【钢】inactive (hot-metal) mixer
非镜面的　nonspecular
非局部的　nonlocal
非局部化学结构　non-topochemical structure
非绝热精馏　nonadiabatic rectification

非均相反应　heterogeneous reaction
非均相反应操作　heterogeneous reaction operation
非均相反应器　heterogeneous reactor
非均相上浮自由流股　heterogeneous buoyancy plume
非均一组织　heterogene structure
非均匀变形　nonhomogeneous [heterogeneous, non-uniform] deformation
非均匀成分　heterogeneous composition
非均匀成核　heterogeneous nucleation
非均匀反应堆　heterogeneous reactor
非均匀非催化反应　non-catalytic heterogeneous reaction
非均匀辐射　heterogeneous radiation
非均匀介质　non-uniform medium
非均匀静电场　non-uniform electrostatic field
非均匀渗碳[碳化]　inhomogeneous carbonization
非均匀性　heterogeneity
非均质材料　dissimilar material
非均质的　heterogeneous, nonuniform
非均质合金　heterogeneous alloy
非均质晶体　inhomogeneous crystal
非均质性(现象)　anisotropy, heterogeneity
非均质组织　heterogeneous structure
非可逆式轧机　non-reversing (rolling) mill, one-way rolling mill
非空气喷砂处理法　non-air blasting process
非扩散的　nondiffusing, diffusionless
非扩展性裂纹　non-propagating crack
非劳克铝合金　ferrocal
非劳左特铁镍合金　Ferrozoid
非离子化合物　non-ionic compound
非离子聚合电解质　nonionic polyelectrolyte
非离子(型)晶体　non-ionic crystal
非离子型助凝剂　non-ionic coagulant aid
非离子洗净[去垢]剂　non-ionic detergent

非理想材料　imperfect material
非理想气体　imperfect [nonideal] gas
非理想溶液　nonideal solution
非立方系晶体　noncubic crystal
非联合钢铁企业　nonintegrated steel plant [works]
非连续孔隙(缺陷)　nonconnected porosity
非连续炉　batch type furnace
非连续气孔　disconnected pores
非连续式运输机　discontinuous conveyer
非连续式轧机　non-continuous rolling mill
非连续相　discontinuous phase
非连续预焙阳极电解槽　electrolytic cell with discontinuous prebaked anode
非炼焦煤　candle [non-metallurgical, dead] coal
非临界性　noncriticality
非零点测量法　deflection method
非灵敏区　dead band [spot]
非硫化物矿　nonsulphidic ore
非铝发热剂　【钢】non aluminothermit
非孪生的　【金】untwining
"非"逻辑　【计】inversion
非满载容量　undercapacity
"非"门　【计】NOT gate [element], inversion, inverter ◇ A"与"B～", B"或"A～ A implies B gate, 与 A 无关的 B～ negative Bignore A gate
"非"门电路　【计】"Not" circuit
非挠性的　inflexible
非凝聚的　uncoagulated
非黏结性煤　dry-burning coal
非黏土陶瓷体　nonclay body
非黏滞流　non-viscous flow
非牛顿性液体　non-Newtonian liquid
非欧姆电阻(器)　non-ohmic resistor
非偏压电子枪　unbiased gun
非偏振辐射　unpolarized radiation
非偏振光　unpolarized light
非平衡分配　nonequilibrium partition
非平衡凝固　(同"不平衡凝固")

非平衡偏聚　non-equilibrium segregation
非平衡热力学　nonequilibrium [unequilibrium] thermodynamics
非平面　non-planar surface
非平面应变　antiplane strain
非屏蔽源　free source
非破坏读出　nondestructive read(NDR)
非破坏性测量　nondestructive measuring
非破坏性检验　nondestructive examination
非破坏性试验　nondestructive test(ing) (NDT), testing without destruction
非气体反应产物　non-gaseous reaction product
非倾倒式拌和机　bantam mixer
非球形粉粒　non-spherical particle
非球状畸变　non-spherical distortion
非取向电工钢薄板　non-oriented electrical steel(sheet)
非确定范围　uncertain region
非燃性　non-ignitibility
非热处理合金　(同"不可热处理合金")
非热过程　athermal process
非热溶体　【金】athermal solution
非热转变　athermal transformation
非熔剂性球团　unfluxed pellet
非熔练焊剂　ceramics flux
非溶剂　insolvent(insolv.)
非润滑正向挤压　unlubricated forward extrusion
非烧结砖　no-firing brick
非渗透性　impermeability
非生产性的　unproductive
非石墨碳　agraphite carbon
非时效合金　non-ageing alloy
非时序计算机　nonsequential computer
非矢量场　scalar field
非守恒运动　non-conservative motion ◇ 割阶的～"
非受力状态腐蚀　stress-free corrosion
非疏松物质　non-porous mass
非束缚电子　nonbonding electron

非数值[字]项 non-numeric item
非水电解液[质] non-aqueous electrolyte
非水溶剂 non-aqueous solvent
非水溶液 non-aqueous solution
非水溶液萃取法 non-aqueous extraction process
非水溶液电积(法) electrodeposition from non-aqueous solution
非水溶液电解 non-aqueous solution electrolysis
非水溶液镀 non-aqueous solution plating
非水质环境影响 nonwater-quality environmental impact
非税性负担 nontax liability
非税性负担的支付金额 nontax payments
非塑性黏土 non-plastic clay
非塑性物料 non-plastic material
"非"算符 NOT operator
非锁定 【计】non-locking
非弹性 inelasticity, non-elasticity, unelastics
非弹性变形 inelastic deformation
非弹性部分应变 unrecovered strain
非弹性电子散射 inelastic electron scatter
非弹性范围 inelastic range
非弹性碰撞 inelastic [non-elastic] collision
非弹性散射 inelastic scattering
非弹性体 inelastic [non-elastic] body
非弹性衍射 inelastic diffraction
非弹性作用 inelastic action
非特(失效率单位,以 10^{-9}/h 表示) FIT
非填充区域 【半】empty band
非调质微合金钢(Nb - V 钢) unquenched microalloyed steel
非铁材料 non-ferrous material
非铁磁性材料 non-ferromagnetic material
非铁磁性金属 non-ferromagnetic metal
非铁合金 non-ferrous(metal) alloy
非铁素体材料 non-ferritic material
非铁冶金学 non-ferrous metallurgy
非同位素 heterotope

非退化态 nondegenerate state
非完整坐标 quasi coordinate
非位移线(X射线的) undisplaced line
非稳定过程 unstable process
非稳定挤压(过程) non-stationary extrusion
非稳定流动 unsteady flow
非稳定平衡 unstable balance
非稳态 non-steady state [behaviour], unsteady state
非稳态传热 nonstationary state heat transfer
非稳态扩散 unsteady-state diffusion
非稳态流动 unsteady(-state) flow
非稳态行为 non-steady behaviour
非稳态运动 unsteady motion
非稳态振荡 unsteady(-state) oscillations
非吸收介质 nonabsorbing medium
非线性 nonlinearity
非线性电阻 non-linear resistance, varistor, varister
非线性规划 non-linear programming
非线性规划等功率余量计算 calculation of equal-gargin of powers with nonlinear programming
非线性理论 non-linear theory
非线性黏弹性固体 nonlinear viscoelastic solid
非线性失真 harmonic distortion
非线性弹性理论 non-linear elastic(ity) theory
非线性特性(曲线) non-linear characteristics
非线性调节器 dead-zone [dead-band] regulator
非线性应力－应变关系 non-linear stress-strain relation
非线性优化 non-linear optimization
非线性元件 non-linear element
非线性振动 non-linear vibration
非相干辐射 non-coherent radiation
非相干强度 incoherent intensity

非相干散射　incoherent scattering
非相交二重轴　nonintersecting diads
非蓄热式炉　non-regenerative furnace [oven]
非选择性吸收　nonselective [neutral] absorption
非延性的　inductile
非氧化气体　non-oxidizing gas
非氧化退火　bright annealing
非氧化物玻璃半导体　non-oxide glass semiconductor
非冶金用煤　non-metallurgical coal
非易失性存储器　non-volatile memory [storage]
非异构的　anisomeric
非应力腐蚀　stress-free [stressless] corrosion
非永久性存储器　volatile memory [stroage]
非永久性中毒[吸附有害离子](离子交换中的)　nonpermanent poison
非预定维修时间　nonscheduled maintenance time
"非"元件　【计】negation element
非圆截面管　non-circular tube
非再生资源　non-renewable resources
非增感 X 射线胶片　non-sensitized X-ray film
非战略性钢　nonstrategic steels
非真空电子束焊接　non-vacuum electron beam welding
非真空精炼法　non-vacuum refining process
非蒸散型消气剂　non-evaporable getters
非正规物　irregular
非正交系统　non-orthogonal system
非正弦振动　non-sinusoidal oscillation
非直线性　nonlinearity, misalignment
非执行语句　【计】nonexecutable statement
非指令性计划　nondirective plan
非致电离辐射　non-ionizing radiation
非致命错误　【计】nonfatal error

非滞后磁化曲线　anhysteretic magnetization curve
非中心对称晶体　noncentrosymmetri(al) crystal
非周期(大阻尼)检流计　aperiodic galvanometer
非周期的　aperiodic, non-periodical, deadbeat
非周期电路　aperiodic circuit
非周期放电　aperiodic discharge
非周期分量　aperiodic component
非主量元素　non-prime element
非专门技术人员　【企】nonprofessional technical staff
非自耗电极　non-consumable-electrode
非自耗(电极)电弧炉　non-consumable-electrode arc furnace, non-consumable arc-melting furnace
非自耗(电极)电弧熔炼　non-consumable arc-melting
非自耗电极电炉　permanent electrode furnace
非自耗(电极)熔炼　non-consumable(-electrode) melting
非自耗熔锭　non-consumable ingot
非自熔性球团　non-self-fluxing pelle, unfluxed pellet
霏细石　felsite
鲱骨状解理　(同"人字形解理")
飞边(edge)　fin, overfill, burr, rag, 【钢】flash, 【铸】burr flash, feather edge ◇ 顶部～top flash, 切一机【压】deburring machine, 去～*, 热切～【压】hot trim (ming)
飞边槽(锻模的)　(flash) gutter
飞边修除器　flash trimmer
飞测厚度计[千分尺](测量轧件用)　flying micrometer ◇ 非接触式～gamma gauge, 接触式～*
飞车　running away
飞车速度　run away speed
飞尘　flying [airborne] dust, respirable-size

airborne dust(可被吸入的)

飞翅 【钢】flash, spill,【压】rolling edge

飞翅形成 【压】formation of fins

飞船 craft

飞刺 fin,【压】flash

飞刺沟(锻模的) flash pan

飞点扫描电视显微镜 fly(ing spot) television microscope

飞点扫描法 flying spot scanning

飞点扫描显微镜 flying spot microscope

飞渡 transit

飞弧 arc-over, flash over, spark-over ◇ 逆~【焊】back flashover

飞灰 flyash, loose ashes

飞灰沉积 deposition of fly ash

飞机带筋壁板 aircraft wing spar

飞机废金属 aircraft scrap

飞机骨架 air-frame

飞机结构钢 aircraft structural steel

飞机蒙皮构件 aircraft skin components

飞机起落架(底盘) landing gear

飞机起落架轮 landing gear wheel

飞机翼梁 aircraft wing spar

飞机用磁强计 airborne magnetometer

飞机用钢管 aircraft tube

飞机用钢索 (同"航空钢丝绳")

飞机用青铜 (同"航空青铜")

飞剪 flying shear, flying-shear cutter ◇ 端头-废料~*, 滚筒式~*, 快速~*, 气动~*, 汽动~*, 曲柄式~ flying crank shears, 往复式~*, 摇杆式~*

飞剪板 (经飞剪剪得的薄板) fly sheared sheet

飞剪剪切后的定尺长度(板材的) fly sheared length

飞剪控制系统 【压】control system for flying shears

飞剪式碎边剪 flying shear cutter

飞剪作业线 flying shear line ◇ 模式~ flying die shear line

飞溅 splash, sparge, splatter, sputtering, spray, spill,

飞溅冷凝器(竖罐炼锌用) splash condenser

飞溅冷却器 splash cooler

飞溅润滑 splash lubrication

飞溅损失 spatter loss

飞锯 flying cut off saw ◇ 热~flying hot saw

飞轮 flywheel, flier, flyer, balance wheel ◇ 平衡~balance wheel

飞轮传动 fly wheel drive

飞轮盖(壳) fly housing(cover)

飞轮判据 flywheel criteria

飞轮调节[调速]器 flywheel governor

飞轮效率 fly wheel officiency

飞轮止推环 flywheel thrust ring

飞轮装置 flywheel gear

飞球转速计 flyball tachometer

飞碟 (同"圆夯")

飞行 flight, flying

飞行器 air [flight] vehicle

飞行时间质谱仪 time-of-flight mass-spectrometer

飞檐 cornice, overhanging eaves

飞越 transit(ion)

肥料级硫酸铵 fertilizer grade ammonium sulphate

肥煤 bituminous [fat, rich] coal

肥黏土 fat [strong] clay

肥砂 【铸】fat [gummy] sand

肥沃土 mellow soil

肥型砂 (同"强黏力型砂")

肥皂 soap ◇ 不溶性~形成, 像~样的 soapy

肥皂泡法(气密性试验) soap bubble method

肥皂泡模型(晶格结构的) soap bubble model

肥皂溶液法(气密性试验) soap solution method

肥皂润滑剂(拔丝用) soap lubricant

肥皂润滑拉丝 soap drawn wire

肥皂水 soapy water

肥皂水润滑冷轧的光洁度 soap-rolled finish
肥皂质的 soapy
翡翠 jadeite
翡翠绿装饰黄铜（50Cu，49Zn，0.5—1.0Al） emerald brass
废板堆垛[垛堆]机 reject stacker, scrap sheet piler
废板堆垛机转运机 reject piler transfer conveyor
废板坯 dummy slab
废板修整线 reclaiming line
废（薄）板运输机 reject sheet conveyer
废边 scrap[slitter]edge ◇ 卷好的～卷 finished scrap bundle
废边卷取机 scrap coiler, coiler for trimmings
废边链式运输机 scrap chain conveyer
废边印痕（钢带的） scrap mark
废布头 waste cloth
废车 disabled vehicle
废衬砖 salvaged lining
废催化剂 dead catalyst
废带 【计】scratch tape
废带钢卷取机（连续炉焊管的） scrap skelp coiler
废电极 electrode scrap
废电解液 spent[depleted, discarded]electrolyte
废电解质 waste cell melt
废锭 rejected ingot
废锭模 mould scrap
废镀锡薄钢板 waste(r) waste, menders（镀层有缺陷），dry tinplate（有露铁部分）
废风阀（热风炉的） air-escape valve, blow off valve
废矸石 worthless gangue
废钢 steel scrap, scrap(steel, iron, material), recrement ◇ 报废器材～dormant scrap, 本厂～*, 打捆[包]～ packed scrap, 大块[难熔]～ heavy (melting) scrap, 返回～*, 分类[级]～ classified scrap, 过烧～burnt scrap, 合尺寸～sized scrap, 加工厂[边角余料]～ prompt industrial scrap, 经加工[处理]的～processed scrap, 冷却～*, 冷装～法*, 炼钢等级[适合炼钢用]～*, 切碎～ shred scrap, 轻[小块]～ fine[small-sized]scrap, 人造～*, 熔渣回收～slag scrap, 适于作～的 scrappable, 小型～捆bustling, 压缩～ pressed scrap, 铸造～casting scrap
废钢板 plate scrap, reject sheet
废钢比 scrap ratio ◇ 高～炉料 high scrap charge
废钢槽 scrap box
废钢场吊车 scrap yard crane
废钢车 scrap car
废钢重熔 remelting of scrap
废钢处理 conditioning[disposal]of scrap
废钢（处理）场 scrap yard[drop]
废钢处理车间 scrapworks
废钢打包 scrap balling
废钢打包[捆]机 scrap bundler, scrap baling machine
废钢堆置场[平台] scrap pen
废钢法 【钢】scrap practice
废钢返回利用法 method of refusing scrap
废钢分类 segregation
废钢轨 rail scrap
废钢积累 scrap accumulation
废钢剪（切机） scrap shears, scrap shearing machine
废钢件处理 disposal of scrap pieces
废钢焦炭炼钢法 scrap and coke process
废钢跨 scrap bay
废钢冷冻处理 cryogenic preparation of scrap
废钢利用 scrapalurgy ◇ 厂内～（率） plant usage
废钢炉料 scrap charge
废钢盘 scrap pot
废钢切割 scrap cutting

废钢切割器　scrap cutter
废钢切碎机　(scrap) shredder
废钢收集站　scrap collecting station
废钢铁　iron and steel scrap, ferrous waste ◇ 标准[合格]～ specification scrap, 不规则～ irregular scrap, 不合标准～*, 除锡～ detinned scrap, 大型～件*, 回炉～*, 机器～ machinery scrap, 家庭用品～ household scrap, 精整烧结打包～ prolerizing scrap, 经破碎清理的～ macerated scrap, 可利用的～ ferrous salvage, 劣质～ junk scrap, 落锤[砸铁机]破碎的～ drop-broken scrap, 汽车～ automotive scrap, 入炉[装料]～ charge scrap, 商品～ merchantable scrap, 未污染[未掺杂]～ contaminant-free scrap, 压碎[破碎]的【铁】fragmented scrap, 已污染[已掺杂]～ contaminated scrap, 油污染的～ oily scrap, 重型～ heavy scrap
废钢铁堆放场　scrap stockyard
废钢铁价值　scrap value
废钢铁剪切机　scrap shearing machine
废钢铁解体[破碎]　scrap handling
废钢铁利用　scrap usage
废钢铁料桶　scrap charging bucket
废钢铁破碎机　scrap breaker
废钢铁[金属]商品　resalable scrap
废钢铁水炼钢法(平炉的)　scrap and hot metal practice
废钢铁协会(美国)　Institute of Scrap Iron and Steel(ISIS)
废钢铁[金属]重新利用　scrap metal reclamation
废钢铁装运[废金属装运, 废钢批, 废铁批, 废金属批]　scrap shipment
废钢铁准备[废金属解体, 废钢破碎]车间　scrap preparation shop
废钢箱　scrap bucket
废钢消耗(量)　(specific) scrap consumption
废钢与铁水比　scrap-metal ratio
废钢运输线　scrap-delivery track

废钢增碳法(加石油焦)　【钢】scrap-carbon process, scrap-and-coke practice
废钢轧入　rolled-in-scrap
废钢枕　sleeper scrap
废钢装料侧(转炉的)　scrap charging side
废钢装料机　scrap charger ◇ 卡尔德龙～*
废钢装料系统　scrap charging system
废钢装箱跨　scrap box filling bay
废钴粒　discarded cobalt granule
废焊条　electrode scrap
废核燃料　depleted material
废核燃料元件　spent fuel element
废机器　machinery scrap
废甲基异丁酮　depleted MIBK
废碱液　alkali waste liquid ◇ 排弃～ exhausted lye
废浇口　sprue-and-runner scrap
废金属　scrap [waste] metal, old-metal, (metal) scrap ◇ 飞机～ aircraft scrap, 零星堆积～*, 汽车～ automotive scrap, 轻质～ light scrap, 松散[未整理好的]～ loose scrap
废金属打包机　scrap press
废金属堆　baling of scrap
废金属料　scrap charge
废金属料斗　scrap charging bucket
废金属运输　scrap traffic
废金属重熔用熔剂　fluxes in melting scrap
废浸出液　stripped leach liquor
废矿　waste [spent, refuse] ore ◇ 排弃～浆 exhausted pulp
废矿物堆　bing
废料　waste(material), wastage, scrap(material, stock), abatement, (residual) discard, refuse, refuse(d)[rejected, spent, revert] material, sweepings,【压】short,【冶】trash ◇ 厂内[车间]～ plant waste, revert, 大块～ heavy scrap, 含铁～*, 回炉～*, 炉子外廓～*, 市政和工业～*
废料拔除装置　【压】discard-ejecting

means
废料仓 scrap bin [bunker]
废料槽 scrap box [chute], waste bunker
废料出口 waste exit
废料处理 waste disposal [treatment] ◇ 液态~ liquid waste processing
废料处理厂 recycling plant
废料处置[排出] refuse disposal
废料处置用料斗 hopper for rubbish disposal
废料堆 scrap [discard] pile, rubbish heap, waste heap [tip]
废料(堆)场 waste dump, scrap yard, waste storage, scrap stockyard
废料返回利用法 method of refusing scrap
废料分类 conditioning of scrap
废料滑槽 scrap chute
废料加工厂 scrapworks
废料间 refuse compartment, salvage department
废料卷 【压】balled scrap
废料卷取机 scrap reel
废料坑 scrap pit
废料利用[生产废料利用] salvage
废料利用车间 salvage [salvaging] department
废料量 scrappage
废料门 waste gate
废料排除口 waste [reject] gate
废料盘 scrap pot
废料生物处理法 biological waste treatment
废料拾取钳 scrap-handling tongs
废料收集坑 crop disposal bin
废料输送机 scrap conveyer
废料运输车 refuse [scrap-hauling] truck
废料再生利用法 method of refusing scrap
废料值 scrapping value
废锍 matte scrap
废炉衬 used [salvaged] lining
废铝 aluminium scrap
废铝箔 aluminium-foil scrap
废铝合金 scrap aluminium alloy
废滤液 wasted filtrate
废镁 magnesium scrap
废模型(铝生产的) patterns scrap
废品(废旧物品) wastage, scrap, cobble, spoilage, refuse; (不合格品) waste [rejected, return] product, reject(ion), below proof (b.p.), 【耐】cull ◇ 有用~ disposable waste
废品板垛箱 reject box
废品等级[级别] rejection level
废品卷取机 【压】reject tension reel, cobble baller
废品率 defective index, number of rejects, rejection rate, scrap rate, scrappage
废品排除斜道 rejection chute
废品区 cobble area
废品数 rejection number
废品推出机 cobble pusher
废品修整工段 reclamation department
废品指标[指数] defective index
废气 exhaust [exit, effluent, flue, offtake, reject, spent, waste, tail] gas, exhaust (exh.), off-gas, outgoing air [gas], spent atmosphere, waste air, 【环】gaseous effluent [waste]
废气安全阀 exhaust guard valve
废气瓣 damper valve
废气泵 flue gas pump
废气成分[分析] waste-gas [off-gas] analysis
废气抽出机 waste gas exhauster
废气除尘[过滤]器 waste gas filter
废气处理系统 off-gas handling system
废气带走的热损失 waste heat losses
废气导管 waste gas duct
废气阀 exhaust gas valve, flue (gas) valve, chimney valve ◇ 盘式~ disc type waste valve
废气废热加热器 exhaust feed heater
废气分析 analysis of exhaust gas
废气风机 exhaust fan, flue gas fan

废气管道　waste gas duct, off-gas line
废气加热器　exhaust feed heater, waste gas(feed) heater
废气(节流)孔　【团】waste gas orifice
废气净化　waste gas purification [handling]
废气净化器　off gas scrubbing device
废气净化系统　waste gas cleaning system
废气量　amount of flue gas
废气排出道　fume offtakes
废气排出机　waste gas exhauster
废气排出(装置)　waste gas exhaust
废气排放　dirty discharge
废气排放标准　waste gas emission standard
废气排放达标率　up to standard rate of waste gas discharging
废气排放合格率　compliance with waste gases emission limitation
废气燃烧烟道　flare(stack)
废气热损失　waste heat rejection
废气损失　waste gas loss
废气通路　exhaust passage
废气温度　flue(gas) temperature
废气洗涤器　exhaust [vent] scrubber, off gas scrubbing device
废气消音器　exhaust gas silencer
废气循环焦炉　recirculation coke oven
废气循环管道　waste gas recirculating duct
废气烟囱　waste(gas) stack
废气烟道　waste gas flue
废气逸出温度　gas leaving temperature
废气预热器管(锅炉的)　economiser tube
废气再循环装置　【环】exhaust gas recirculation equipment
废气综合利用　multipurpose use of waste gas
废弃　discarding, 【环】abandonment
废弃残液　discard raffinate
废弃金属　discard(ed) metal
废弃矿浆　depleted [barren] pulp

废弃滤液　depleted filtrate
废弃溶液　depleted [discard, outgoing] solution
废弃物　discard ◇ 滤去～reject
废弃物质　depleted material
废汽　waste [discharge, spent] steam
废汽供暖　exhaust steam heating
废汽锅炉　waste-steam boiler
废汽总管　exhaust steam main
废铅　scrap lead
废铅矿石(待选的)　fausted ore
废铅重炼　reclaiming of lead
废(切)头　waste end
废青铜　bronze scrap
废燃料　waste fuel, fuel wastage
废热　waste [used] heat
废热供暖　waste heating
废热锅炉　(同"余热锅炉")
废热过热器　waste heat superheater
废热焦炉　waste heat oven
废热利用　(同"余热利用")
废熔剂　spent flux
废石　barren rock [gangue], burrow, deads, debris, residual discard, waste rock, 【冶】offscourings, 【选】recrement, trash ◇ 含～铁矿 incrustated iron ore, 混有矿石的～boose, 黏土质～argillaceous gangue, 剔出～discard
废石仓　refuse bin
废石槽　dirt chute
废石场　wastedump, waste-rock yard, 【采】recrement
废石单体分离　【选】gang(ue)-grain release
废石堆　burrow, spoilbank, rubbish heap, 【采】recrement, 【环】refuse dump [pile], waste pile
废石分离器　deshaler
废石含量(矿石中的)　gang(ue) content
废石灰　used lime
废石间　refuse compartment
废石拣出器　shale extractor

废石流槽(选矿厂的) slate chute
废石棉 asbestos lumber
废食品罐 food can scrap
废释热元件 spent fuel element
废水 waste [discharge, reject, spent, tail(ing)] water, effluent, water [liquid, aqueous] effluent, liquid waste ◇ 工厂排放的～factory effluent, 含碱～处理装置*, 碱性～alkali(c) waste water, 矿山酸性～acid mine drainage, 排放～waste discharge, 中和过的～neutralised waste water
废水处理[处置] waste water treatment, effluent treatment [disposal] ◇ 综合～*
废水处理站 waste water treatment station
废水处理装置 waste water treatment plant
废水点源 point source of waste water
废水反应池 waste reacting basin
废水分析 tailing water analysis
废水负荷 【环】waste water load(ing)
废水回收利用(率) reclamation of waste water
废水汇集[蓄收] waste water impoundment
废水净化 polishing
废水联合处理设施 joint waste water treating facility
废水流出[排放] waste water effluent, effluent discharge
废水排放许可证 effluent discharge permit
废水注入井 injection well
废水综合处理厂 integrated waste water treatment plant
废水综合利用 multipurpose use of waste water
废塑料喷吹 plastic scrap injection
废酸 spent [waste] acid
废酸回收厂[车间,设备] acid recovery [restoring] plant
废酸回收工段 acid recovery section
废酸溶液 waste pickle liquid
废酸洗液 pickling acid waste, spent pickle liquor, drag-out
废酸洗液槽 drag-out tank
废酸洗液回收 drag-out recovery
废酸再生式带钢连续酸洗机组 continuous strip pickling line including regeneration
废酸渣 acid waste product
废钛 scrap titanium
废铁 scrap [old, grab, broken] iron, (iron) scrap
废铁仓 scrap bin [bunker]
废铁堆 scrap pile
废铁剪 scrap iron shearing machine
废铁盘 scrap pot
废铁批 scrap shipment
废铁压块(压力)机 scrap baling press
废铜 copper scrap [junk], scrap [waste] copper
废头料卷取机(带卷的) heavy-end reel
废物 waste [refuse(d), rejected] material, waste, rubbish, crock, garbage, recrement, 【冶】offscourings ◇ 可用～disposable waste, 生物法～处理*, 遗弃～waste discharge
废物堆 【环】refuse dump [pile], waste pile
废物焚化厂 waste incineration plant
废物负荷 waste load(ing)
废物利用 salvaging, recycling of waste
废物流出[排放] waste effluent
废物排放许可证 waste discharge permit
废物排放准则 waste discharge guidelines
废物全部贮存(法) total impoundment
废物再利用 recycling of waste
废物治理系统 waste abatement system
废物综合利用 multipurpose use of waste
废锡 tin refuse
废锡矿 tin ore refuse
废线材 wire scrap
废线卷取机 scrap baller

废屑　attle, sweeps
废型砂　used sand
废锈铁皮　oxidized steel sheet scrap
废阳极　scrap anode, anode scrap
废阳极层　spent anode layer
废阳极液　spent anolyte
废液　waste [barren, spent] liquor, waste [discard, barren, spent] solution, discharge [used] liquid,【环】liquid waste [effluent, discharge]
废液槽　spent solution tank, waste tank
废液处理　liquid waste processing
废液排出　effluent disposal
废液污染　【环】contamination by effluent
废液再生工段　regenerative section
废阴极内衬　spent cathode lining
废阴极液　spent catholyte, barren catholyte solution
废铀　waste uranium
废油　waste [spent] oil
废油再生器　recuperater, used oil reclaimer [regenerator]
废杂物　lumber, gob
废渣　waste slag, slag muck, throw-away slag(抛弃的)
废渣压块　baling
废渣铸石　tailings glass-ceramics
废蒸汽　waste [bleb, exhaust] steam
废铸件　waste [spoiled, fault] casting, faulty cast, off-cast ◇ 蜂窝状砂眼～ honeycombed casting, 未铸满～ short-run casting
废铸铁　cast iron scrap
废砖　rejected [crushed] brick,【耐】cull, broken piece
沸点　boiling point (BP, b.p.), boiling temperature ◇ 恒～混合物 constant boiling mixture
沸点计　ebullioscopy, ebulliometer
沸点计法[沸点测量术]　ebulliometry
沸点酒精计　ebullioscopy
沸点曲线　boiling point curve, liquidus

沸点升高　boiling point elevation
沸点[沸腾]压力　boiling pressure
沸石　zeolite
沸石软水器　zeolite softener
沸水冷却(方式)　boiling water cooling
沸水型反应堆　boiling water reactor (BWR)
沸水(中)淬火　quenching [hardening] in boiling water
沸腾　boil(ing), ebullience, ebulliency, ebullition, bubbling, effervescence, overswelling ◇ 薄膜～法,轻[弱]～【钢】light-boiling, 脱碳～【钢】carbon boil, 无～熔炼【钢】dead melting, 无矿～ oreless boil
沸腾层[床]　(同"流(态)化床")
沸腾范围　boiling range
沸腾传热　boiling transfer
沸腾钢　rimmed [unkilled, rimming, boiling, effervescent, effervescing] steel, open (-poured) steel ◇ 加盖～ cooler-plated steel, 压盖[封顶]～ capped steel
沸腾钢板　rimmed steel sheet
沸腾钢锭　rimmed ingot
沸腾钢锭剖面图像　section pattern of rimmed steel
沸腾钢熔炼　rimmed heat
沸腾剂　【钢】rimmer
沸腾开始　inception of bubbles
沸腾泡沫　【选】effervescent bubbles
沸腾期　boiling period
沸腾式实验反应堆　boiling reactor experiment(Borax)
沸腾特性[性能]　【钢】rimming property
沸腾硝酸试验(测定晶间腐蚀倾向)　boiling nitric acid test
沸腾型冷媒【压】　ebullition cooling medium
沸腾状态　state of ebullience
沸腾作用　【钢】rimming action
沸涌　overswelling
费布赖特镍铬铁耐热合金(35Ni, 17Cr,

48Fe) Febrite

费德勒尔炉(焙烧还原矿石用) Federal hearth

费尔奈特耐热耐蚀合金 Fernite(Fernite No.2:15—28Cr,20—50Fe,22—65Ni)

费尔普斯-道奇法(一种竖炉直接还原法) Phelps-Dodge process

费尔铁铝合金(25Al,75Fe) Feal

费伽定律 Vegard's law

费克拉洛伊铁铬铝合金(12—13Cr,4—5Al,余量 Fe) Fecraloy alloy

费拉里感应测试仪器 Ferraris instrument

费兰包铝钢带 Feran

费兰包铝钢带轧制法 Feran process

费兰蒂感应炉 Ferranti furnace

费劳克斯立方晶系铁淦氧[铁氧体]软磁材料 Ferrox Cube, Ferroxcube(material)

费劳克斯普兰铁氧体 Ferroxplan

费劳克斯普雷那铁氧体(由 BaMFe$_{16}$O$_{27}$、Ba$_2$MFe$_{12}$O$_{12}$、Ba$_5$MFe$_{24}$O$_{41}$等组成) Ferroxplana

费劳克斯鸠尔永磁材料(钡铁氧体) Ferroxdure

费雷铜镍合金(55Cu,45Ni) Ferry

费里马格铁磁合金 ferrimag

费力工作 forced working

费龙铁镍铬(耐氧化)合金(50Fe,35Ni,15Cr) ferron

费鲁尔铅黄铜(54Cu,40Zn,5Pb,1Al) Ferrule brass [alloy]

费鲁姆制铁粉法 Ferrum process

费罗卡特压粉[高频用]铁心 Ferrocart

费罗派尔铁铬铝电阻丝合金 Ferropyr (Ferrpyr 1:86Fe,7Cr,7Al)

费罗-特克冷固结球团法 Ferro-Tech process

费米-狄喇克统计法 Fermi-Dirac's statistics

费米电势[电位] Fermi potential

费米电子气[费米气体] Fermi gas

费米动量 Fermi momentum

费米分布 Fermi distribution

费米分布曲线 Fermi distribution curve

费米函数 Fermi function

费米极限 Fermi limit

费米粒子 Fermi particle

费米面 Fermi surface

费米面动量 momentum at Fermi surface

费米能 Fermi energy

费米(能)级 Fermi level

费米温度 Fermi temperature

费米中子龄 Fermi age

费米子 fermion

费尼柯低膨胀系数合金(54Fe,28Ni,18Co) Fernico

费尼克罗姆低膨胀系数合金(37Fe,30Ni,25Co,8Cr;玻璃焊封用) Fernichrome

费希尔-哈特-普里硬化 【金】FHP hardening

费用计算程序 accounting routine

芬顿锌基(耐磨)轴承合金(80Zn,14.5Sn,5.5Cu) Fenton's alloy, Fenton's (bearing) metal

芬克尔-莫尔法 【钢】Finkl-Mohr process

芬克尔真空脱气装置 Finkl system

芬克氢气保护热镀铝法 Fink process

芬西德镁屑结压入铁水法 【铸】Finsider process

酚{C$_6$H$_5$OH} phenol, carbolic acid(也称"石炭酸") ◇除-设备 dephenolizing plant, 含~废水 phenolic effluents, 脱-【焦】dephenolization

酚的溶剂萃取 solvent extraction of phenol

酚腐蚀 phenol corrosion

酚基 phenolic group

酚氰污水 phenol-cyanogen waste-water

酚醛 metlbond

酚醛层压板 paxolin

酚醛环氧树脂 bakelite epoxy resin

酚醛胶纸层合板 Micarta

酚醛黏结剂 bakelite cement

酚醛树脂 phenolic resin

酚醛树脂漆　bakelite lacquer
酚醛树脂清漆　bakelite varnish
酚醛塑料　bakelite, pertinax
酚树脂　phenol resin, resinol
酚酞 $\{C_{10}H_4O_4\}$　phenolphthalein
酚酞指示剂　phenolphthalein indicator
酚型树脂衬里　phenol resin lining
酚盐　alkoxide, phenoxide
分板机　◇风动～pneumatic separator
分贝计　decibelmeter
分贝列线图　decibel chart
分辨　resolution ◇可～的 resolvable, 未～峰值 unresolved peak
分辨极限(显微镜的)　resolution limit
分辨率　resolution(res.), resolving power (显微镜的)
分辨率提高　increase in resolution
分辨能力　resolution capacity, resolving power, discrimination, definition
分别成核　separate nucleation
分别加料　separate feed [charging]
分别洗提　differential stripping
分别氧化　selective oxidation
分布　distribution, spread ◇玻耳兹曼～(律) Boltzmann distribution, 泊松～ Poisson distribution
分布板　distribution plate ◇多孔青铜～*
分布不均匀　maldistribution
分布电容　distributed capacitance
分布电阻　distributed resistance
分布定律　law of distribution, partition law
分布放大(频带的)　distributed amplification
分布钢筋　distributing [spacing] bar
分布函数　distribution function
分布荷载[负载]　distributed load
分布角(载重的)　【建】angle of distribution
分布矩　distribution moments
分布密度　distribution [partition] density
分布曲线　distribution curve [pattern]

分布式计算机　distributed computer
分布式控制系统　distributed control system(DCS) ◇计算机～*
分布式数据库技术　distributed database technique
分布式网络　【计】distributed network
分布图[状况]　distribution pattern
分布系数　distribution coefficient [number]
分布因数　distribution factor
分步焙烧　fractional roasting
分步沉淀(同"分级沉淀")
分步沉降法　fractionation sedimentation method
分步重复工序　step and repeat process
分步分离　fractional separation
分步加载的　step-loaded
分步结晶(法)　fractional crystallization
分步结晶顺序　fractional crystallization series
分步解吸　fractional desorption
分步溶剂萃取　fractional solvent extraction
分步升华　fractional sublimation
分步水解　fractional hydrolysis
分步塑型[压制]　fractional moulding
分步同喷　sequenced co-injection
分部程序编制　part programming
分部中和　fractional neutralization
分层　lamination, demixing, exfoliation, lamellation, slabbing, sliver, subcutaneous defect(缺陷),【压】(轧材缺陷) delaminate ◇轧件前端[头部]～*
分层布料　layer-by-layer charging [distribution] ◇透镜状～*
分层部分(缺陷)　slabbed section
分层磁轭　laminated yoke
分层电池　layer-built cell
分层电阻　lamination stack resistance
分层堆叠焊　pile welding
分层放置　layering
分层灌筑混凝土　concreting in lifts

分层加料	separate feed
分层绝缘	lamellar insulation
分层坯块	laminated compact
分层铺底料	bedding of furnace
分层铺料	bedding out ◇炉底～技术 bedding technique, 人字形～【团】chevron layering
分层器	quantizer
分层缺陷	layer-buit defect
分层(缺陷)探测仪	lamination detector
分层摄影法	◇X射线～laminography, 轴向横断面～*
分层[分部]射线照相术	sectional radiography
分层试样	stratified sample
分层缩孔	【钢】pipe seam
分层填土夯实	compaction by layers
分层温度	demixing point
分层装料	layer-by-layer charging, layered charge, layer filling
分叉	branching, bifurcation, forking, furcation, tee-off
分叉布料斜槽	bifurcated chute
分叉点	bifurcation
分叉火焰	split flame
分叉浇口	spray [double-branch] gate
分叉浇口箱	runner box
分叉溜槽	(double) bifurcated chute, bifurcated launder, two-way-chute
分叉式矿槽	twin outlet bin
分厂经理	branch work manager
分车带	dividing strip
分车岛	dividing island
分成几部分	apportionment, merotomy
分成窄馏分	close fractionation
分程序	block
分程序结构	block structure
分程序首部	block head
分程序体	block body
分出	detachment, diversion, segregate, tap-off, drawing (从废有色金属分出黑色金属)
分床操作	split-bed operation
分等(级)	gradation, classifying
分等粉末	classified powder
分度	dividing, (scale) division, graduate, calibration, indexing
分度尺	graduated scale, diagraph
分度工作台	index table
分度规	graduated scale [arc], angle gauge, protractor
分度机	dividing machine
分度镜	graticule
分度盘	index dial [plate], graduated disk, limb
分度器	protractor, graduator
分度头	index [dividing] head, index (centre) ◇测试仪表～*
分度误差	index error
分段	segmentation, batching, fragment
分段奥氏体化	stepped austenitizing
分段程序	segmented program
分段冲裁冲床	nibbling machine
分段处理	stepped treating
分段萃取	(同"分级萃取")
分段淬火	stepped quenching
分段多层焊	block(sequence) welding
分段(多层)钎焊	block brazing(BB)
分段反向焊法	step-back method (of welding)
分段焊接法	progressive method
分段还原	stage [stepwise] reduction
分段加热	multistage heating
分段加载	【金】step stressing
分段精炼	stepped refining
分段冷却法	stage-cooling method
分段硫酸化	stage sulphation
分段磨矿	stage [step] grinding
分段内孔窥视仪	sectionized borescope
分段(疲劳)试验	step test
分段破碎	stage [graded] crushing
分段扫描	step scan
分段时效	progressive aging
分段式加热炉	(见"快速加热炉")

分段水解	graded hydrolysis
分段跳焊	skip block welding, wandering welding
分段退焊	backstep welding
分段退焊法	step-back procedure [sequence]
分段退火	stepped annealing
分段位错	segmented dislocation
分段压制	graded pressing
分段氧化	stepwise oxidation
分段预热	stage preheating
分段装料	stepped filling
分断电流	breaking current
分断容量[能力]	breaking capacity
分垛机	depiler ◇ 磁力吊车式[钢板磁力]～magnet-crane depiler, 电磁～*
分发机	sorter
分发室	despatch room
分风管	【铁】air manifold
分干线	submain
分割	cut apart, division, part(ition),【采】cut-off
分割图	cutaway drawing
分割线	dividing line(DL)
分格槽子	divided bath
分格取样器	riffle sampler
分格砂箱	sectional flask
分隔粉	【铸】parting compound
分隔构件	separating member
分隔器	spacer, divider
分隔式均热炉	cell-type soaking pit
分股退火	strand-annealing
分光比色法	spectrocolorimetry
分光法[技术]	spectroscopic technique
分光光电的	spectrophotoelectric
分光光度分析	spectrophotometric analysis
分光光度计	spectrophotometer, spectralphotometer ◇ 简易型～*, 手提式 hand spectrophotometer
分光光度学[(测定)法, 术]	spectrophotometry
分光化学分析	spectroanalysis
分光计[仪]	spectrometer, spectroscope ◇ 电离～ionization spectrometer, 高透射～*, 棱镜～prism spectrometer, 扫描间歇流体～*, 闪烁～*, 弯晶～*, 吸收～absorption spectrometer, 中子～neutron spectrometer
分光镜	spectroscope
分光镜分析法	spectroscopic(al) method
分光棱镜	spectroscopic prism
分光吸收比	spectral absorptance
分光显微镜	microspectroscope
分光仪[镜]分析	spectroscopic analysis
分光质量	spectroquality
分划板	reticles
分激电动机	shunt(-wound) motor
分激发电机	shunt generator
分激整流子式电动机	shunt commutator motor
分级	gradation, grading, graduation, classification, classifying, fractionating, fractionation, separation, sizing,【选】settle ◇ 等降～*, 逆流～法*
分级变流机	【焊】slip-pole(rotary) converter
分级变压器	step transformer
分级槽	classifier tank
分级沉淀	fractional [fractionation] precipitation
分级池	classifying pool
分级萃取	stage(-wise) extraction
分级淬火	graded [broken, interrupted] hardening, interrupted [time] quenching, martemper, marquenching (高于 Ms 点的) ◇ 特种～*
分级淬火处理	martempering treatment
分级淬火用油	martemp oil
分级存储器体系	memory hierarchy
分级等温淬火	up-quenching, progressive [step-up] austempering
分级等温热处理	progressive austemper
分级电离	fractional ionization, ionization

by step
分级电阻器 sectional resistor
分级反应 step reaction
分级[类]废钢 classified scrap
分级[类]粉末 classified powder
分级浮选 stage flotation
分级格筛 sizing grid, sorting grizzly
分级火焰淬火法 marquench flame hardening
分级机 classier(CL), grader, sizer ◇ 槽式~tank classifier, 沉降~settling classifier, 道尔型~Dorr classifier, 风力~air separator, 浮槽式~bowl classifier, 惯性力~", 虹吸~siphonsizer, 回路~loop classifier, 机械~", 链耙式~drag classifier, 螺旋~", 耙式~rake classifier, 三层式洗涤~", 双螺旋~", 旋风~", 旋流~cyclone classifier, 圆锥~cone classifier, 自由沉降~free falling classifier
分级机溢流 classifier overflow(CO)
分级加热法 【色】bleeding
分级加载 【金】step stressing
分级精炼 stepped refining
分级控制[调节] step control ◇ 电子~器"
分级矿石 sized ore
分级冷凝 fractional condensation
分级冷凝器 fractional condenser
分级冷却法 stage-cooling method
分级连接 step connection
分级料 sized feed
分级料仓 classifying bunker
分级料场 classification yard
分级磨矿 stage grinding
分级破碎 stage reduction
分级溶解 fractional solution
分级筛 classifying [sizing] screen, sorting grizzly
分级烧结矿 sized sinter
分级设备 classifying equipment
分级石灰块 lump-graded lime
分级时效 interrupted [progressive] ageing
分级试验 grading test
分级收尘器 cascade-type deduster
分级顺序淬火 progressive quenching
分级效率 classification [grade] efficiency
分级旋流器 classifying cyclone
分级因数 gradation factor
分级装料 classified charge
分拣员 sorter
分接 tap-off, tapping, shunting
分接变压器 tap transformer
分接头 【电】tap
分接线 extension wire
分阶段退火 stepped annealing
分节铸铁锅炉 sectional cast-iron boiler
分解氨 cracked ammonia
分解氨热镀锌法 Sendzimir(coating, galvanizing) process
分解槽 decomposer, decomposing tank [vessel], breakdown vessel, 【焦】springing tank
分解产物 decomposition product, product of decomposition, breakdown product
分解成氨作用 ammonification
分解程度 extent of decomposition
分解催化剂 decomposition catalyst
分解的奥氏体 decomposed austenite
分解电势[位] decomposition potential
分解电位曲线 decomposition potential curve
分解电压 decomposition voltage ◇ 实际~"
分解电压范围 decomposition voltage level
分解电压曲线 decomposition voltage curve
分解反应 decomposition [breakdown] reaction
分解釜 decomposing pot
分解机理 decomposition mechanism
分解矿糊(用浓酸) breakdown paste
分解炉 decomposition furnace, precalciner
分解能力 capacity of decomposition

分　fen

分解器　decomposer,【计】resolver
分解切应力　resolved shear stress
分解热　decomposition heat
分解容器　breakdown vessel
分解设备　breakdown equipment
分解时间　decomposition [resolving] time
分解试验　decomposition run
分解水　decomposition water
分解速度[速率]　decomposition rate, rate of resolution
分解塔　decomposing tower
分解温度　decomposition temperature
分解系数　decomposition coefficient
分解原理[法则]　resolution principle
分解蒸馏　destructive distillation
分界表面的　interfacial
分界面　division [separation] surface, interface
分界线　dividing line, line of demarcation
分界砖　【焦】distributor
分金　【色】parting ◇ 湿法~法 wet process of parting
分金槽　parting cell
分开　separation, part, dividing, division, split
分开的　separate(sep.)
分控制中心　sub-control-centre
分块模型　【铸】sectional pattern
分类　classify(ing), classification, itenmize, sort, assortment, assorting,【选】settle(按密度)
分类程序　sorter
分类法　classification
分类器[装置]　sorter, grader ◇ 磁鼓~ drum sorter
分类生成程序　sort generator
分类应用　sort application
分类运输机　sorting conveyer
分类轧钢机　section steel rolling mill
分类贮存　component storage
分类作业线　assoring line
分离　separate, separation, segregation, detachment, disconnection, disconti nuity, disjunction, splitting, part(ing), partitioning, unmixing ◇ 精确~【选】sharp separation, 塞曼~', 使~(使离合器分离) throw out, 压余[残料]~【压】discard seperator 分离槽 separation tank [bath], separator tank [bath], segregation sump, decanter, skimming tank(分离废油用)
分离层　separation layer
分离沉降槽　separating thickener
分离成核(现象)　separate nucleation
分离池　segregation sump
分离萃取器　separation extractor
分离的原子　destroyed atom
分离电解池(指阳极阴极电解液分离)　divided cell
分离阀　separating valve ◇ 喷嘴~'
分离分析(非金属夹杂物鉴定用)　isolation analysis
分离粉　【铸】parting powder
分离杆　disconnecting [tripping] lever
分离辊　separating roller
分离环(反应塔中的)　partition ring
分离机　separator, whizzer,【压】distributor
分离技术　separation technology
分离剂　splitting-up agent,【铸】release agent(芯盒的)
分离键　disengaging latch
分离界限粒径　cut diameter
分离介质　separating [parting] medium
分离精(确)度　accuracy of separation, separation sharpness
分离科学　separation science
分离冷却　cooling in spaced formation
分离流量条件(萃取的)　separation flow conditions
分离面　parting(sur)face, separation surface,【铸】division [parting] plane
分离能带　separate energy bands
分离能级　discrete(energy) level
分离能力[本领]　separative [separating] power

分离谱技术(一种超声波探伤技术) discrete spectrum technique
分离器 separator, extractor, splitter, dividing box ◇ 鼓式～ drum separator, 静电～*, 排水～ drain separator, 弯管～ elbow separator, 旋流～*, 锥形～ cone separator
分离气孔(炉衬材料的) disconnected pores
分离熔炼(铜镍锍的) top and bottom smelting
分离设备 separation plant, stripping apparatus
分离双重线 separated doublet
分离塔 separating column
分离同位素的质谱分析法 mass-spectrographic method of isotope separation
分离系数 separation factor
分离系统 separation system [circuit]
分离箱(废油用) skimming tank
分离效率 separation efficiency
分离液 parting liquid
分离圆盘 separating disc
分离装置 disconnecting gear
分立点 discrete spots
分立元件(集成电路的) discrete component
分粒 classification
分粒机 sizer, classifier ◇ 逆流～ counter-current sizer
分料 splitting
分料机 depiler ◇ 提升～*
分料料斗(带格板的) divided hopper
分料溜槽 splitter chute
分料漏斗 separatory [tap] funnel
分裂 splitting (-up), split-up, disintegration, disorganization, cleavage, 【理】fission ◇ 可～的 fissionable
分裂剂 disintegrating agent
分裂(视)场比色计 split-field colorimeter
分裂位错 splitting dislocation
分裂性 fissility

分裂中子 fission neutron
分裂转变 split transformation
分溜槽 split chute
分馏 fractional [differential, progressive] distillation, fractionating, fractionation (by distillation), dephlegmation, distillation separation, selective evaporation ◇ 多蒸锅玻璃～泵*, 非～蒸馏*, 间歇[分批]～ batch fractionating
分馏带 fractionating zone
分馏点[温度] cut point
分馏法 method of fractional distillation
分馏分析 fractional analysis
分馏盘 rectifying plate
分馏器 reflux exchanger
分馏塔[柱] fractional [fractionating, separating] column, fractionating tower, fractional distilling tube, fractionator, dephlegmator ◇ 多孔板～ perforated-plate column
分馏塔底板 bottom plate of column
分馏塔盘 refluxing tray
分馏退吸法气体分析 fractional desorption gas analysis
分馏效率 fractionation efficiency
分馏液体(相对)含量 fractional liquid content
分馏油扩散真空泵 fractionating oil diffusion pump
分馏真空泵 fractionating pump
分馏蒸发气体分析 fractional evaporation gas analysis
分流 bypass (flow), shunt, split-flow, diversion, side stream
分流操纵 shunting operations
分流出钢槽 bifurcated runner (spout)
分流处理 split-stream treatment
分流电路 branch [shunt, divided] circuit
分流电容器 bridging condenser
分流电阻 shunt resistance, diverter
分流阀 flow dividing valve
分流放出槽 forked runner, forked tapping

spout	
分流浇口	bifurcated [split] runner
分流控制	【电】shunting operations
分流块(射流技术的)	divider
分流模挤压	sectional mould extrusion
分流氖灯	tattelite
分流片(射流技术的)	divider
分流器	shunt, diverter, distributor
分流器用锰铜(10Mn,4Ni,余量 Cu)	shunt manganin
分流箱	splitter [slide] box
分流砖(三通砖)	deflecting block ◇ 中心~deflecting block
分炉熔化精炼法	【钢】MR process
分路	diversion of road, bridging, 【电】shunt(circuit)
分路标志	diversion sign
分路传送辊道	bypass carryover table
分路工作线路	【计】way-operated circuit
分路辊道	bypass table
分路送风	【铁】split wind blowing
分马力电动机	fractinal horse power motor(小于 1 马力), subfractional horse-power motor(1/20 马力以下),
分泌	oozing ◇ 水分~weepage
分泌物	ooze
分模线(锻模的)	die [flash, split] line, die parting line
分凝	segregate, segregation, dephlegmation(分馏作用), fractional condensation, liquation
分凝管	fractional condensing tube
分凝器	fractional condenser, segregator
分凝塔	dephlegmator
分凝系数	segregation coefficient
分配	distribution, allocation, assignment, share, assortment ◇ 按比例~apportionment, 集体~法*
分配板(矿槽的)	distributor plate
分配泵	proportion(ing) pump
分配比	distribution [partition] ratio
分配仓	distribution bin
分配槽	distributing [sistributor] tank, splitter(hopper, tank), spreader-ho-pper
分配常数	distribution constant
分配齿轮	distributing gear
分配定律	distribution [partition] law ◇ 能斯脱~*
分配阀[活门]	distributing [distribution] valve
分配方程式	distribution equation
分配辊	distributing roll
分配溜槽	divided chute, two-way-chute
分配漏斗	splitter hopper
分配密度	partition density
分配盘(蒸馏塔的)	distributor tray
分配器	distributor, dispatcher, allotter, divider, dividing box, splitter ◇ 辊式模~roller distributor, 平面槽式~flat ruffle, 体积[粒料]~bulk distributor
分配色层(分离)法	partition chromatography
分配塔[站]	distributor tower
分配系数	distribution coefficient [modulus, number, ratio], partition coefficient [factor, ratio]
分配系统	distributing [distribution] system
分配线路[网络]	distribution network
分配箱	distribution [splitter] box
分配轴	distributing [tappet] shaft
分配轴齿轮	counter gear
分配总管	distributing main
分批操作	batch operation
分批称量	batch weighing
分批称量秤	batch scale
分批称量装置	batch weighing device
分批处理	batch treatment [handling, processing]
分批处理法	batch method (of treatment)
分批处理反应器	batch reactor
分批萃取	batch(wise) extraction ◇ 两级~*
分批供应	batchwise supply

分批过滤	batch filtration
分批过滤器	intermittent filter
分批混合	batch mixing
分批混合器	batch mixer
分批给料	batch feed
分批给料器	batch meter
分批加热器(混凝土骨料用)	batch heater
分批加入	stage addition
分批交货	partial [segment] delivery
分批结晶	batch crystallization
分批浸出	batch leach(ing)
分批精炼锅	batch refining kettle
分批精馏	batch rectification
分批净化	batch purification
分批离子交换	batch ion exchange
分批炉	batch type furnace
分批配料记录器	batch counter
分批配料控制	batch meter control
分批区域精炼[提纯]	batch zone refining
分批区域精炼炉	batch zone refiner
分批取样检查	lot sampling inspection
分批渗滤浸出系统	batch percolation system
分批生产	batch production
分批式炉	batch oven
分批式熔炼炉	batch smelter
分批酸洗(叠板的)	batch pickling ◇摇臂式~机*,柱塞式~装置*
分批提纯	batch purification
分批提取	batchwise extraction
分批退火	batch annealing
分批退火机组作业线	batch type annealing line
分批退火炉	batch annealing furnace
分批研磨	batch grinding
分批运料车	batch truck
分批蒸馏	batch(steam) distillation
分批装出料的室式热处理炉	periodical furnace
分批装料	batch feed, charging by batches
分批(装料)式浴槽	batch bath
分批装模压型法	batch weight method of moulding
分批装运	installment [partial] shipment
分批作业法	batch method of operation
分片式检测辊(BFI辊)	multi-piece type stressmeter(BFI rolls)
分频	frequency division [demultiplication]
分频器	frequency dumultiplier
分期付款	instal(l)ment
分期付款的定金	down payment
分歧	bifurcation, out-of-balance, difference
分歧点	bifurcation, ramification point
分气道	【冶】gas-distribution channel
分切	parting cut
分切锯	dividing [parting] saw
分切应力	component of shear stress
分区	subregion, demarcation, zoning
分区式系统	【建】zone system
分群	【企】grouping
分溶层析法	partition chromatography
分容积	partial volume
分散	dispersal, dispersion, deflocculation, diffuse(ness), dissemination
分散度	dispersion degree (size), degree [scale] of dispersion, dispersity, dispersiveness
分散断裂模型	dispersed fracture model
分散工序[过程,流程]	discrete process
分散剂	dispersing [dispersion] agent, dispersion reagent, disperser, disper-sant (agent), dispersed medium
分散间隔焊	wandering welding
分散浇口注入	multipoint injection
分散介质	dispersion medium
分散器	disperser
分散取样	discrete sampling
分散数据处理	decentralized data processing
分散缩孔	【铸】dispersed shrinkage
分散塔	dispersion tower
分散系	dispersed system
分散系数	dispersion coefficient

分散相	disperse(d) phase
分散效应	dispersion effect
分散硬化	cluster hardening
分散作用	dispersion(effect)
分砂筛	【铸】sand riddle
分时	【计】time sharing
分时(操作)系统	time sharing(operating) system, time shared system
分时分配	【计】time sharing allocation ◇ 硬件资源的～*
分时分配程序	time sharing allocator
分时计算机	time sharing computer
分数	fraction, fractional number ◇ 不变～constant fraction
分数的	fractional
分水	【环】(water) diversion
分水沟	【环】diversion ditch
分水界	divide water shed
分水器	moisture separator, water knock-out trap
分水渠	【环】diversion channel
分水塔	valve tower
分水线	divide line
分送(板垛中的叠板)	destacking
分缩塔	dephlegmator
分体式机壳	split casing
分体制造	split manufacturing
分条小堆造堆法	windrow method
分析	analysis (复数 analyses), breakdown, dissection ◇ 傅里叶［调和］～【数】Fourier analysis, 在线～on-line analysis
分析波长	analytical wavelength
分析纯	analytically pure(A.P.)
分析纯的	analar
分析萃取	analytical extraction
分析法	analytical method
分析方法	analytical [analysis] procedure
分析机	analytical engine
分析极隙	analytical gap
分析技术	analysis technics
分析晶体	analyzing crystal
分析块	【计】analysis block
分析谱线	analytical line
分析器	analyser, analyzer ◇ 连续～*
分析取样	analytical sampling
分析(人)员	analyzer, analyst, assayer
分析试剂	analytical reagent(A.R.)
分析试剂纯度[品级]	analytical reagent quality
分析试验室	analytical [assay] laboratory
分析试样	analysis sample, assay sample (试金的)
分析数值	assay value
分析天平	analytical [assay] balance
分析误差	analytical error
分析线	analysis line
分系统	subsystem
分线盒	cable [branch, distributing, pull] box
分线盘	noseplate, nozzle plate
分线箱	junct(ion) box,【电】connection box
分相器	phase-splitter
分项(列记)	itemize
分泄电阻	bleeder(resistor)
分型板	【铸】match plate
分型剂	【铸】parting agent [medium, compound], release agent
分型面	【铸】division [parting, jointing] plane, parting(face), die [mould] joint, joint face,
分型面浇口	parting [joint] gate
分型模型	part(ed) pattern
分型砂	parting [tap] sand
分型线	【铸】parting line
分选	classifying, separation, grading, graduation, sorting, sizing ◇ 精确～sharp separation, 旋风器气力～*, 重悬浮液～*
分选场[平台]	sorting floor
分选工	classifier, grader
分选工段	assoring room
分选辊	sorting roller

分选辊道	classifying table
分选机	classifier, separator, sorting machine, dividing box ◇ 摆线式～*，槽式～*，磁力～ magnetic grader，带式～ belt separator，挡板式～ baffle separator，风力～ air separator，管式同轴～*，静电～*，螺旋～ spiralcoil separator，上升气流～*，涡形～ snail separator，旋流～ cyclone separator，(圆)锥形～*
分选机系统	classifier system
分选粒度	separation size
分选炉	selector
分选器	classifier ◇ 电晕式～ corona-type separator
分选器挡板	classifier gate
分选筛	separating screen
分选台	classifying [sorting, gauger] table
分选细粒	graded shot
分选柱(水力分级机的)	sorting column
分选装置	sorting unit
分选作业线	assorting line
分压	partial [fractional] pressure
分压定律	【化】law of partial pressure
分压器	potentiometer, voltage divider, divisor
分压装置	bleeder mechanism
分焰炉	split flame furnace
分样器	sample splitter, riffle sampler, dividing box
分液漏斗	separatory [tap] funnel
分银炉	dore furnace
分应变	strain component
分应力	stress component
分油器	oil-trap, oil separator
分枝状[分支]浇口	branch gate
分支管	Y-branch
分支焊接[接头]	branch joint
分支溜槽	bypass chute, chute by-pass
分支(内)浇口	finger [spray] gate
分支排气道	bypass vent
分支套管(电缆)	multiple joint
分支位错	splitting dislocation
分支洗金槽	【选】under-current
分支线	branch wire [line]
分支线夹	tee connector
分支运输系统	bypass conveying system
分支状流槽	【钢】branched runner
分柱法	【建】intercolumniation
分装(炉料的)	separate [split, block] charing, classified charge
分子泵(真空)	molecular pump ◇ 盖德～ Gaede's molecular pump，霍尔韦克～*
分子层	molecular film [layer]
分子场[韦斯]近似法	molecular field approximation, Weiss approximation
分子场理论	molecular field theory
分子导电率	molecular conductivity
分子点阵[晶格]	molecule lattice
分子电子学	molectronics, molecular electronics
分子镀	molecular plating
分子分解	molecular decomposition
分子复型(制备)法	molecular replica
分子附着	molecular adhesion
分子光谱学[分析法]	molecular spectroscopy
分子化合物	molecular compound
分子间距	molecular spacing
分子间力	intermolecular force
分子间引力	inter-molecular attraction
分子键	molecular binding [bond, linkage]
分子结构	molecular structure
分子结构式	structural formula
分子结合热	molecular combining heat
分子晶体	molecular crystal
分子扩散	molecular diffusion
分子类型分析	molecular(-type) analysis
分子离子	molecular ion, molion
分子离子束喷注	molecular ion beam injection
分子力	molecular force
分子量	molecular weight (MW, mol. wt)
分子量子力学	molecular quantum mechanics

分子流动	molecular flow
分子膜	molecular film
分子内部滑移	intramolecular slippage
分子能	molecular energy
分子频率	molecular frequency
分子气体激光(器)	molecular gas laser
分子热	molecular heat(mol. ht.)
分子热容	molecular heat capacity
分子筛	molecular sieve, subsieve ◇ 碳～*
分子筛层析法	molecular sieve chromatography
分子筛干燥剂	molecular sieve desiccant
分子筛净化系统(煤气的)	dry molecular sieve system
分子筛气体发生器	molecular sieve generator
分子筛脱硫	molecular sieve desulphurization [sweetening]
分子束分光计	molecular beam spectrometer
分子束外延	molecular beam epitaxy
分子弹性论	molecular theory of elasticity
分子体积	molecular volume
分子性明显界面	molecularly sharp interface
分子压力	molecular pressure
分子压力计	molecular gauge
分子引力	molecular attraction
分子运动	molecular motion [transport]
分子运动论	kinetic theory
分子真空计	molecular vacuum gauge
分子蒸馏	molecular distillation
分子蒸馏釜	molecular still
分子质量	molecular mass
分子组成	molecular composition
分组开关	cluster switch
焚化	incineration ◇ 废物～厂
焚化炉	incineration furnace, incinerator ◇ 流态化～ fluidized incinerator
粉	powder, dust
粉斑(探伤)	powder blotting
粉尘	(fine) dust ◇ 产生～的设备 dust-generating unit, 含铁～【铁】blue dust, 回收～ returned dust
粉尘爆炸	dust explosion
粉尘比电阻	dust resistivity
粉尘测定仪	dust gauge ◇ 鲍施－龙泊～*
粉尘处理方法	dust disposal method
粉尘处理运输线	dust(-disposal) track
粉尘返回装置	dust return device
粉尘飞扬	flying of dust
粉尘还原设备	dust reducing equipment
粉尘回收(利用)装置	dust-reclaiming mill
粉尘回收率	deduster yield
粉尘颗粒	dust particle
粉尘利用	recycling of waste fines, conditioning of dust
粉尘利用技术	【团】dust-recycling technique
粉尘量	dust volume ◇ 带走的～ dust entrainment
粉尘浓度	dust concentration
粉尘排放[浓度]	dust emission
粉尘烧结	agglomeration of dust
粉尘损失	dust loss ◇ 严重～ heavy dust loss
粉尘污染	dust nuisance
粉尘箱	dirt box
粉尘造块	agglomeration of dust
粉尘状	dust form
粉带	【粉】powder strip ◇ 冷轧～ cold (rolled) strip, 未经烧结[轧制]的～卷 coiled green strip, 轧制～*
粉带轧制	strip-rolling
粉红色假金	pink gold
粉红色玉髓	pink chalcedony
粉红相渗铬	pink-phase chromizing
粉化	atomising, atomizing, atomization, pulverization, pulverizing, powdering, dusting, efflorescence, chalking(镀层表面缺陷)

粉化率　degradation [powder] ratio
粉化器　pulverizator
粉浆　slurry
粉浆浇铸制件　slip-casting
粉浆浇注　slurry [slip] casting
粉焦　pulverized [small(-sized), fine, low-mesh] coke
粉金　powdered [flour] gold
粉块　cake
粉矿　fine ore [material], finely divided ore, pulverized [ground, comminuted, milled] ore, ore fines,【团】direct pellet feed
粉矿比　fine percentage
粉矿仓　fine(ore) bin
粉矿处理　handling of ore fines
粉矿量[率]　rate of fine ores
粉矿炉　fine ore furnace
粉矿团块　fine particle aggregate
粉矿造块　agglomeration of fine ore ◇ 福尔森－法 Follsan process
粉粒　(powder, droplet) particle ◇ 变形～deforming particle, 角状～angular particle, 连生～【粉】locked particle
粉粒边界　particle boundary
粉粒表面引力　particle surface attraction
粉粒成球　balling up of particles
粉粒尺寸　particle dimension
粉粒纯度　particle purity
粉粒构造　particle structure
粉粒结块　particle agglomerate
粉粒孔隙(度,率)　particle porosity
粉粒密度　particle density
粉粒平均值　particle-size average
粉粒塑性　particle plasticity
粉粒外形　contour of particles
粉粒显微构造　microstructure of powder particles
粉粒形状　particle shape [configuration]
粉粒与粉粒间烧结　particle-to-particle sintering
粉粒长大　particle growth

粉料　fine material, powder(lot)
粉料[矿]槽　miscellaneous materials fines bin
粉料混合机　powder mixer
粉料撒布器　powder dispenser
粉料箱　dirt box
粉料贮存室　powder storage room
粉煤　pulverized [powdered, fine] coal, beans
粉煤仓　breeze bunker, (同"粉料槽")
粉煤机　pulverizing mill
粉煤加热炉　pulverized coal furnace, coal powder furnace, coal-dust furnace
粉煤喷吹 (同"煤粉喷吹")
粉煤燃烧　coal-dust firing
粉煤燃烧器　pulverized coal burner
粉煤烧嘴　coal burner
粉煤制备设备　pulverizing machinery
粉面　flour
粉磨机　pulverizing mill ◇ 叶轮式～
粉末　powder, flour, fines breeze, pulvis ◇ 劣质～poor-quality powder, 流动性不好的～non-flowing powder, 磨碎[碾碎]～【粉】milled powder, 疏松～loose powder, 新制～virgin powder
粉末 X 射线衍射试样　specimen for powder work
粉末包套锻结法　canned powder forging
粉末包套挤压法　canned powder extrusion
粉末爆炸成型法　【粉】method of explosively compacting powders
粉末比表面(积)测定　determination of powder specific surface area ◇ 斯佩克～仪 Spekker absorptiometer
粉末层　powder bed
粉末产物　powdered product
粉末车间　powder shop
粉末成型　powder compaction
粉末成型法　【粉】process for powder moulding
粉末成形模具　powder compacting tool set

粉末处理　powder processing [treatment]
粉末处理设备　powder-handling equipment
粉末磁芯　powder core
粉(末)带(材)成型　compacting of powder into strip
粉末镀锌　sherardising galvanizing
粉末镀锌法　sherardising process
粉末锻造　powder forging ◇ HRC~法*
粉末法(X射线衍射分析法)　powder method
粉末法X射线衍射示意图样　diagrammatic powder pattern
粉末法(X射线)衍射图[花样]　powder diagram [pattern] ◇ 德拜~*
粉末法X射线衍射图样　powder (pattern) photograph
粉末法衍射图样的线分辨能力(X射线的)　line resolution of powder pattern
粉末法衍射线强度　intensity of powder line
粉末分布不匀　non-uniform [unequal] powder distribution
粉末分级　powder grading, classification of powder
粉末过滤器　powder filter
粉末焊接法　powder weld process
粉末合金元素　powdered alloying element
粉末化　flouring
粉末还原　powder reduction
粉末混合度测定器　◇ 米克西~Mixee
粉末[料]混合物　【粉】powder mix(ture), mixture of powder ◇ 摩擦类~*
粉末活度　activity of powder
粉末火花试验　powder spark test
粉末级别　powder fraction
粉末挤压　powder extrusion
粉末加工　powder processing
粉末加料斗　powder feed hopper
粉末加料器　powder feeder
粉末结块　agglomerated particle

粉末金属　powdered metal (PM)
粉末金属齿轮　powdered metal gear
粉末金属过滤器　powdered metal filter
粉末金属摩擦元件　powder metal friction element
粉末(金属)气割炬　powder (metal) torch
粉末金相学　powder metallography
粉末晶体X射线衍射花样　powdered-crystal pattern
粉末均匀分布　uniform powder distribution
粉末孔隙度(自由撒放的)　【粉】powder porosity
粉末冷挤压　cold powder extruding
粉末离合器　powder clutch
粉末粒度　powder size
粉末粒度分级　powder fraction
粉末料斗　powder hopper
粉末流　powder flow
粉末流动性　powder flowability, flow rate of powder
粉末流量计　powder flowmeter
粉末流速　【粉】flow rate of powder
粉末铝化　powder calorizing
粉末率　fine percentage, dust [abrasion] index, 【团】chip index, powder [degradation] ratio
粉末落差　powder head
粉末密度　powder density
粉末模压装置　powder press-molding apparatus
粉末钮扣试样熔度试验　【粉】button test
粉末喷镀[喷涂]　powder spraying
粉末喷枪　powder pistol
粉末坯[压]块　powder compact ◇ 羰基法~carbonyl compact
粉末球化　spheroidizing of powder
粉末热处理　thermal powder treatment
粉末热锻　powder hot forging
粉末热挤压机　powder hot extruder
粉末熔凝　powder consolidation
粉末容器　powder container

粉末润滑剂　powder lubricant
粉末撒布器　powder distributing device
粉末渗碳　powder carburizing
粉末松[散]装密度　apparent powder density
粉末松装烧结　sintering of loose [unpressed] powder
粉末碳　powdered carbon
粉末特性　powder characteristic
粉末添加剂　powder additive
粉末调整　powder conditioning
粉末铁芯　powder(iron) core
粉末图像(X射线衍射的)　powder film
粉末外形　powder appearance
粉末物料　powder material
粉末物质　powder mass
粉末洗涤　powder washing
粉末显微构造　powder microstructure
粉末显象　powder-cloud development of image
粉末芯　powder core
粉末性质不均匀　non-uniformity of powder characteristics
粉末压实机　powder compacting press
粉末压塑性　compactibility of a powder
粉末压缩性　compressibility of powder
粉末压头　powder head
粉末压制　powder compaction [compression], pressing of powder
粉末衍射法　powder diffraction method [technique] ◇ 德拜-谢乐~*
粉末衍射光谱　powder diffraction spectrum
粉末衍射环(X射线的)　powder ring
粉末衍射术　powder diffractometry
粉末衍射线(X射线的)　powder line
粉末衍射照相机　powder diffraction camera
粉末氧化物　powdered oxide
粉末氧熔切割(金属粉末氧熔切割)　metal powder oxygen cutting(POC)
粉末冶金　powder metallurgy (PM, P/M), particle metallurgy, cermet ◇ 金属纤维~ fibre metallurgy, 连续~*, 应用~*
粉末冶金材料　powder metallurgical material
粉末冶金产品　powder metallurgy product(s)
粉末冶金超级合金(耐高温、高强度的)　P/M super alloy
粉末冶金成品　finished powder metallurgic(al) product
粉末冶金法　powder metallurgic(al) process [method, practice, approach]
粉末冶金法生产　manufacture by powder metallurgy
粉末冶金法制硬币　coinage by powder metallurgy
粉末冶金高速钢　PM high speed steel
粉末冶金工业　powder metallurgy industry
粉末冶金工艺[技术]　powder metallurgical [metallurgy] technique
粉末冶金工作者　powder metallurgist
粉末冶金含油轴承　powder metallurgy oil-impregnated bearing
粉末冶金合金　powder metallurgical alloy
粉末冶金零件　powder metallurgy parts, sintered metal powder parts ◇ 浸渗~*
粉末冶金零件(压制)成型　P/M parts moulding
粉末冶金马氏体时效钢　PM maraging steel
粉末冶金设备　powder metallurgy equipment
粉末冶金学　powder metallurgy, ceramal(s), ceramet, ceramettalics
粉末冶金制品　PM parts, sintered metal product
粉末荧光屏　powder screen
粉末原料　powder stock
粉末云显示法　powder-cloud method
粉末运搬设备　powder-handling equip-

ment
粉末造型法 （同"粉末成型法"）
粉末轧机 powder rolls
粉末轧制材料 roll-compacted powder material
粉末轧制成型 powder rolling
粉末轧制(成型)的 roll-compacted
粉末轧制法 powder rolling process
粉末轧制技术 powder rolling technique
粉末轧制加料装置 powder roll feed arrangement
粉末照相法 X 射线分析 X-ray analysis by powder photographs
粉末照相机 powder camera
粉末直接轧制 direct powder rolling
粉末制备 powder preparation
粉末制品 pulverulent product
粉末制取 【粉】powder extraction
粉末制取冶金(从矿石直接制成金属粉末或海绵金属) powder extraction metallurgy
粉末装填 powder packing
粉末状的 pulverous, pulverulent, micromeritic
粉末状合金 powdered alloy
粉末状配制合金的元素 powdered alloying element
粉末状态 powder(ed) condition
粉末自燃性 【粉】pyrophorosity of powder
粉坯 powder compact ◇ 轧制~ *
粉球 sphere of powder
粉砂 silt
粉碎 pulverization, pulverizing, crushing, comminution, disintegration, levigation, shattering, size reduction
粉碎拌和工段 【耐】grinding-mixing section
粉碎的烧结矿 broken sinter
粉碎电解粉末 pulverized [disintegrated] electrolytic powder
粉碎粉末 【粉】pulverized [comminuted] powder

粉碎机 disintegrator, pulverizing machinery, pulverizer, comminutor, mill ◇ 二次~【耐】secondary breaker, 环状辊式~ annular roller mill, 机械~ *, 旋转[鼠笼式]~ rotating disintegrator
粉碎能量 size reduction energy
粉碎器 pulverizer, pulverizator, disperser
粉碎指数 【团】degradation index
粉体学 micro-meritics
粉纹 powder pattern ◇ 毕特~ *
粉纹线图(X 射线衍射的) line diagram of powder pattern
粉芯焊丝 flux cored filler rod ◇ 二氧化碳(保护)~电弧焊 *
粉芯焊条 flux core(type) electrode
粉芯焊线 flux cored wire
粉芯(填充)焊条 flux cored filler rod
粉性 mealiness
粉冶铂丝 Wollaston wire
粉冶成品 （同"粉末冶金成品"）
粉冶磁铁 metal-powder magnet
粉冶钼 powder metallurgy molybdenum
粉冶青铜 （同"烧结青铜"）
粉冶钨棒[条] powder metallurgy bar of tungsten ◇ 环锻~ *
粉冶用金属粉末 powder metallurgical metal powder
粉冶用压机 powder metallurgy press
粉冶制铂法 ◇ 沃拉斯顿~ Wollaston process
粉状白云石 dolomitic stone screenings
粉状磁铁 powder magnet
粉状磁铁矿 pulverized magnetite
粉状的 powdery, pulverescent, pulverous, pulverulent, dustlike
粉状电解质 powdered electrolyte
粉状浮渣 powdery dross
粉状腐蚀剂 ground caustic
粉状固体填料化学热处理法 D.A.L. (Diffusion Alloys Ltd.) process
粉状硅岩粉 ground ganister
粉状焊接熔剂 welding powder

粉状金刚砂　powdered carborundum
粉状矿石　dust ore
粉状镁　powdered magnesium
粉状木炭　powdered charcoal
粉状耐火黏土　ground fire clay
粉状钎焊剂　soldering powder
粉状燃料　powdered [pulverized, dust] fuel ◇ 烧～炉　pulverized-fuel(-fired) furnace
粉状熔剂　flux(ing) powder, fine [powdered] flux
粉状烧结矿　soft-dusty sinter
粉状渗碳剂　cementing powder
粉状石墨　plumbago
粉状碳化物药皮焊条　powdered carbide electrode
粉状体　powdered solid
粉状物料　powdery [pulverulent] material
粉状物质　powdered substance
粉状锡　powdered [powdery] tin
粉状锡(残)渣　powdery-tin skimmings
粉状皂(拉丝润滑用)　powdered soap
粪化石硫杆菌　thiobacillus coproliticus
丰富[度]　abundance
封板　shrouding,【采】skin plate
封闭　seal(up), close(down), blockage, blocking, hermetization, locking
封闭 γ 区的元素(相图上的)　loop forming element
封闭 γ - 相区(同"闭合 γ - 相区")
封闭层　seal(ing) coat
封闭畴　closed domain
封闭的孔　blind hole
封闭电弧焊　shield arc welding
封闭含水层　confined aquifer
封闭环　gasketed [sealing] ring
封闭(气)孔　closed pore
封闭 X 射线(发生)管　sealed-off tube generator
封闭式保险丝　enclosed fuse(EF)
封闭式背齿轮　encased back gear
封闭式淬火炉　sealed quench furnace

封闭式电动机　enclosed motor
封闭式滚珠轴承　enclosed ball bearing
封闭式浇注系统　positive-pressure gating system
封闭式金属桶　drum ladle
封闭式跨轮　encased back gear
封闭式溜槽　closed launder
封闭式配电盘　enclosed switch board
封闭式膨胀箱　closed expansion tank
封闭式热水暖气系统　closed hot water heating system
封闭式筛　closed-type screen
封闭式通风系统　closed system of ventilation
封闭式外部冷却　enclosed external cooling
封闭式贮矿仓　enclosed storage bin
封层　seal(ing) coat
封底焊　back run welding, sealing run(焊主焊缝后的)
封底焊道(焊主焊缝前的)　backing bead
封底焊缝　back(up) weld
封顶　【钢】(沸腾钢锭)capping, plugging, 【冶】closed-top
封顶(沸腾)钢　capped [plugged] steel ◇ 化学～chemically capped steel
封顶钢锭(沸腾钢的)　capped ingot
封堵　clogging, plugging
封灌的　imbedded, embedded
封焊　sealing, soldering and sealing
封接　sealing in ◇ 铜玻璃～*
封接合金　sealing alloy
封口焊缝　caulk(ing) weld
封口环　mouth ring
封口胶　sealing compound ◇ 可熔注～*
封炉　【铁】banking ◇ 长期～*
封炉期　banking period
封炉损失　banking losses
封面料(土壤的)　【环】sealant
封泥　lute,【铸】jointing
封气黏胶水泥　air tack cement
封墙　wicket
封入　enclosure

封锁　lockout
封套　envelope, wrappage ◇ 不漏光线的～ light-tight envelope
封头（压力容器的）　closure
封头旋压操作　dishing operation
封檐板（山墙的）　barge board
封装　encapsulation
封装密度　packaging density
蜂巢状烧结块　honeycomb clinker
蜂房式冷却器　beehive cooler
蜂房[巢]式炼焦炉　beehive oven
蜂房式炉　beehive kiln
蜂房式烧结矿冷却机　cellular cooler
蜂房式线圈　honeycomb(ed) coil, lattice wound coil
蜂焦　sponge coke
蜂焦头　spongy end
蜂鸣[音]器　buzzer, hummer, ticker
蜂鸣制动器　buzzer stop
蜂窝（缺陷）　honeycombs (h/comb), caverne, void flute crack ◇ 形成～（混凝土缺陷）blistering
蜂窝夹层板铍铝合金　◇ 洛卡洛伊～
蜂窝焦炭　beehive coke
蜂窝气孔　peripheric blister
蜂窝气泡　rim-hole, honeycomb blister ◇ 皮下～
蜂窝体辐射　thermal radiation in honeycomb ceramics
蜂窝状沉淀　cellular precipitation
蜂窝状[形成蜂窝状](的)　honeycombing
蜂窝状二氧化硅　cellular silica
蜂窝状腐蚀　honeycomb corrosion
蜂窝状构造　honeycomb formation [structure]
蜂窝状夹层板　honeycomb sandwich panels
蜂窝状夹心材料　honeycomb core material
蜂窝状结构　honeycomb structure [construction], areolar [cell(ular)] structure
蜂窝状晶体　cellular crystal

蜂窝状气孔　honeycomb blow holes
蜂窝状砂眼废铸件　honeycombed castings
蜂窝状渣　honeycombed slag
蜂窝状枝晶　cellular dendrite
蜂眼　【铸】knot
峰　peak, apex, hill, hump ◇ 波尔多尼～*，布喇格～Bragg peak，齐纳～*，斯诺克～*
峰墩　land abutment
峰谷形布料方式　【铁】rill and valley pattern
峰间幅值（正负峰间的幅值）　peak-peak value
峰面积　peak area
峰值　peak(value), crest(value)
峰值点　maximum point
峰[值]电位　peak potential
峰值电压表　peak voltmeter
峰值负荷　peak(of) load
峰值功率　peak power
峰值脉冲电压　peak pulse voltage
峰值密度　peak density
峰值强度射线　peak intensity ray
峰值曲线　maximum curve
峰值热处理法　hump process
峰状长大　spike growth
锋钢　high speed steel
风铲　pneumatic digger, pneumatic (chipping) hammer, air chipper [chisel]
风铲工　chipper
风淬钢渣粒化　granulating slag by compressed air
风带（化铁炉的）　air [wind] belt, air box
风挡　air damper [shutter], damper plate（烟筒的）
风挡箱　【焦】damper box
风道　air duct [course, flue], duct, wind channel
风动舂砂器　【铸】pneumatic sand rammer
风动除鳞锤　pneumatic (de) scaling hammer
风动除鳞装置　pneumatic descaling appa-

ratus

风动传送管　pneumatic tube

风动锤　pneumatic rammer, air ram

风动打壳装置　【色】pneumatic crust breaking device

风动打印机　pneumatic marker

风动捣棒[风动夯]　air tamper

风(动)捣锤　hammer impact machine, air ram

风动捣打　air ramming

风动捣[搅]料机　pneumatic poker

风动锻锤　air forging hammer, compressed air(forging) hammer

风动阀　pneumatic [air-operated] valve

风动放灰阀　air-operated dust valve

风动分板机　pneumatic separator

风动缸　pneumatic cylinder

风动工具　air-operated tool

风动管道　pneumatic piping

风动机械(冲压)法　pneumatic-mechanical process

风动机械高速(冲压)成形　pneumatic-mechanical high-velocity forming

风动给料机　pneumatic feeder

风动给[加]料装置　pneumatic feeding device, air assisted feeder

风动夹紧装置　air-clamping fixture, pneumatic pressure device

风动夹具[夹持器]　air-clamping [air-operated] fixture, air jig

风动尖锤　pneumatic peening hammer

风动剪　air shears, pneumatic cutter

风动搅拌器　pneumatic stirrer

风动开出钢[铁,渣]口　pneumatic tapping

风动开口钻　air-operated taphole drill

风动捆带装置　pneumatic operated strapping device

风动炉门　pneumatic firedoor

风动铆(钉)枪[机]　pneumatic [air] gun, air [compression] riveter

风动气体力学　pneumatics

风动升降机　pneumatic lift

风动式滑动阀门　air-operated slide gate

风动输送　pneumatic transport

风动输送机　（同"风力输送机"）

风动输送系统　pneumatic conveying system ◇ 高炉灰[炉顶灰]～

风动提升机　pneumatic elevator

风动填隙[凿密]　pneumatic caulking

风动弯曲模　air bend die

风动卸料装置　pneumatic discharging device

风动型控制器　pneumatic type controller

风动－液动拔棒机（阳极棒的）【色】pneumatic-hydraulic pin puller

风动圆盘闸　pneumatically operated disc brake

风动渣口塞棒　air-operated slag stopper

风动撞击机　air ram

风阀　blast gate, air valve

风干　air-drying, 【耐】seasoning

风干尺寸　air dried size

风干煤　air-dry coal

风干强度　air(-dried) strength

风干砂型　air-dry sand mould

风干失重　【耐】air-drying loss

风干湿度(燃料的)　air dried moisture

风干收缩　【耐】air(-dried) shrinkage

风干砖(坯)　air(dried) brick, adobe

风镐　air rammer [pick]

风沟　【色】channels

风管　air(line) [wind] pipe, air duct [conduit], 【铁】blast pipe, air blast connection pipe

风化　efflorescence, erosion, slacking(煤的), weathering(岩石等的)

风化层[地带]　weathered zone

风化硅土　tripoli

风化矿石　efflorescent ore

风化黏土　aeroclay

风化蛇纹石　weathered serpentine

风化石灰　air slaked lime

风化石油　mineral tar

风化条件　weathering condition

风化土壤　solum
风化岩石　decomposed [decayed] rock
风化渣　sla(c)king slag
风化作用　weathering action [effect], wind abrasion
风机　fan(facilities), bower ◇ 加速~ blow over fan, 离心式［径向］~ radial fan, 喷射~ ejector fan, 双进口~ double inlet fan, 一段冷却式~*
风机电耗　fan power consumption
风机风量　fan delivery [flowrate, volume], blower capacity
风机负压　fan suction
风机工人　blower driver
风机负载　fan duty
风机机壳　fan casing
风机静压力　fan static pressure
风机能力　blower[fan] capacity
风机排气　fan discharge
风机曲线　fan curve
风机入口[进风口]　fan inlet
风机室　fan house [room]
风机效率　fan efficiency
风机叶轮　fan impeller
风机叶片　fan blade ◇ 后弯式~*
风积黏土　air-deposited clay
风积土　aeolic soil
风镜　goggles
风口　air port [vent], blast gate [hole], 【冶】(也称"风嘴") tuyere(gate), twere, twyer(e), blast nozzle, 【铁】tuyere(opening), 【钢】tuyere hole [notch] (转炉的) ◇ 长[出口延长的,突出炉内的]~*, 畅通~ free tuyere, 打通~*, 带~的炉底(转炉的)【钢】tuyere bottom, 底吹转炉~【钢】tuyere plug, 堵塞~ blind tuyere, 高速~ high velocity tuyere, 鼓风[使用]~ blowing tuyere, 挂[涌]渣~【铁】sloppy tuyere, 灌铁~*, 坏~ failed tuyere, 可动~套*, 可调节~ adjustable tuyere, 冷硬铸铁~【铁】chill cast tuyere, 炉腹[二排]~【铁】bosh tuyere, 螺旋[双角]~*, 偏心螺旋~*, 烧坏的~ burnt tuyere, 水冷~ water-cooled tuyere, 陶瓷覆层~*, 捅~*, 文丘里式~ Venturi-type tuyere, 无锥度~ straight-type tuyere, 小~ monkey tuyere, 斜~ angle (flow) tuyere, 预鼓风~ foreblow hole, 远程[维索夫型]~ tuyere remoteness, 制好的~ fabricated tuyere
风口板(底吹转炉炉底的)　【钢】tuyere plate
风口报废(底吹转炉的)　【钢】tuyere blanking
风口比　tuyere ratio
风口标高　tuyere level
风口插套(高炉的)　tuyere insert
风口大套　【铁】tuyere breast, tuyere-cooler casting [holder, housing]
风口大套挂钩　tuyere snatcher
风口带　tuyere area [zone, region], 【铁】tuyere belt ◇ 炉缸~炉墙 tuyere-breast wall, 碳砖砌~*, 外部水冷~*
风口带钢箍[风口区炉壳]　【铁】tuyere belt
风口带加固圈　【钢】tuyere breast
风口带炉(缸外)壳　【铁】breast plate, tuyere jacket
风口挡　draught screen
风口冻结　【铁】tuyere freezing
风口堵塞　tuyere blockage, blinding of tuyere
风口阀　【铁】tuyere valve
风口法兰　breast, 【铁】tuyere cooler holder, tuyere jacket
风口盖　tuyere wicket, 【铁】tuyere [stock] cap, wicket
风口拱　tuyere arch
风口鼓风速度　tuyere velocity
风口观测器　tuyerescope
风口灌渣　blinding of tuyere, flooded tuyere
风口灌渣铁　ironing
风口焦炭取样机　【铁】tuyere coke sam-

feng 风

pler(TCS)
风口截面　tuyere section
风口镜[玻璃](高炉的)　tuyere glass
风口孔　【铁】tuyere opening
风口拉杆　【铁】bridle, tightening bolt
风口拉杆弹簧　tuyere spring
风口冷却板　tuyere cooling plate
风口冷却器　tuyere cooler [block]
风口冷却器拱[风口套拱]　【铁】tuyere jacket ringwall
风口冷却水　tuyere cooling water
风口冷却水套　tuyere arch cooler,【铁】(同"风口大套")
风口煤气(高炉的)　tuyere gas
风口凝结金属　nose
风口配换机　tuyere replacing machine
风口喷吹　tuyere injection
风口喷嘴　tuyere nozzle
风口平面　tuyere plane [level]
风口前端[前沿](突出炉内部分)　【铁】nose of tuyere, tuyere snout
风口前火焰温度　tuyere nose flame temperature
风口前区　front of tuyeres
风口前燃烧带温度　【铁】raceway flame temperature
风口区　tuyere area [zone],【冶】tuyere region
风口区温度　tuyere(-zone) temperature
风口燃烧区　tuyere raceway
风口烧坏　tuyere melting
风口设备弯管　【铁】leg pipe
风口寿命　tuyere life
风口数量(一座高炉的)　tuyering
风口损坏　【钢】boring ◇ 炉底~"
风口损失　tuyere losses
风口弯管　【铁】tuyere offtake, curved pipe
风口弯头　tuyere, stock,【铁】eye-sight elbow, penstock
风口系统　tuyere system
风口弦带　【铁】tuyere ring
风口线　tuyere line

风口箱　tuyere box
风口小弯管　【铁】bootleg
风口型燃烧器(喷吹燃料用)　【铁】tuyere type burner
风口砖(转炉的)　tuyere brick [block]
风口装置　tuyere apparatus
风口装置肘管　【铁】leg pipe
风口总有效截面积　【铁】total tuyere area, total blast nozzle area
风口嘴　【铁】tuyere nose
风冷　air cooling ◇ 炉底~盘"
风冷淬火　air blast quenching
风冷电动机　ventilated motor
风冷机　cooling fan
风冷炉底　【铁】air-cooled bottom
风冷盘条　air-blown rod
风冷式变压器　air-cooled transformer
风冷式换向器　ventilated commutator
风冷阴极　air-cooled cathode
风力分级[分选]　air classification,【选】air sizing
风力分级[分选]机　air separator [classifier]
风力分级系统　air sizing system
风力浮选　air flotation
风力干燥机　pneumatic dryer
风力-机械制动器　pneumatic-mechanical brake
风力给料系统　pneumatic feed system
风力收尘器　pneumatic deduster
风力输送[运输]机　pneumatic conveyer, air(float) conveyer
风力输送系统　pneumatic handling system
风力送料　air-feed
风力摇床　pneumatic table
风力中和　air blending
风力中和仓[槽]　air blending silo
风量　air quantity [output, volume], blowing [air-flow, wind] rate, blast volume [capacity],【铁】weight of blast ◇ 低[弱]~ low wind, 鼓入~ volume of blast blown, 全~【铁】full wind

风量不足　slack wind, deficiency in draught
风量分布仪　wind distribution meter
风量分配[分布]　air[wind] distribution,【铁】distribution of blast
风量计　air volume meter, blast meter ◇ 连续式~*
风量记录　blast volume trace
风量控制[调节]　air(quantity) control, blast volume control
风量控制[调节]器　blast volume controller, air weight controller,【冶】blast (volume) regulator
风量消耗　blast consumption
风流　air-flow, air stream ◇ 恒[稳]定~ constant air flow
风流带走物　air-entrained material
风流控制[调节]　air control
风流[量]控制系统　air control system
风流平衡阀门　flow balance damper
风流调节门　flow control damper
风流循环　air circulation,【团】draught recycling
风帽　blast cap, nozzle button(流态化炉的)
风门　air shutter, blast gate, tuyere gate(炉子的)
风门板　flap shutter
风门操纵杆　throttle lever
风桥　airbridge
风扫(球)磨　air-swept ball mill
风筛　【选】air sizing
风扇　fan, ventilator ◇ 烟道废气~ flue gas fan
风扇冷却器　fan cooler
风扇式喷雾器　fan atomizer
风扇调速器　fan governor
风扇通风机　fan ventilator
风扇罩　fan guard
风蚀　weathering
风蚀作用　wind abrasion
风速　wind[air] speed, wind rate, blast [air, wind] velocity
风速表[计]　anemometer, airmeter, airspeed gauge, wind gauge ◇ 自记~*
风速测定法　anemometry
风速记录仪　anemo(bia)graph
风速气压表　anemobarometer
风损　windage loss
风温　【铁】blast[wind] temperature
风温均衡炉　【铁】equalizer
风险分析　【企】risk analysis
风险评估[价]　risk assessment
风箱　blast box, windbox, wind chamber, wind[air] chest, bellow(pipe), suction box[chamber], air belt[box](化铁炉的) ◇ 交叉[错]式~ alternate windbox, 虚设[虚假]~【团】false windbox
风箱顶峰温度　peak windbox temperature
风箱分岔　windleg
风箱负压[真空度]　windbox vacuum[depression]
风箱负压指示器　windbox suction indicator
风箱盖　blast box cover
风箱回流　windbox recoup
风箱回热风机　windbox recoup fan
风箱面积　windbox area ◇ 有效~*
风箱排烟风机　windbox exhaust fan
风箱式夹持器(矿热铁合金炉的)　bellows type clamping device
风箱式压力计　bellows manometer
风箱台　wind bench
风箱小格　windleg
风向仪　anemoscope
风选　air separation[classification]
风压　blast[wind] pressure
风压表[计,指示器]　blast(pressure) indicator, blast meter[gauge], draught indicator
风檐板　eaves board
风应力　wind stress
风雨防护罩　weather-proof hood
风錾　chipping hammer ◇ 清理缺陷用~

【压】dresser
风凿　air chisel
风闸　air [atmospheric, pneumatic] brake ◇ 快速～quick action air brake
风筝气球　kytoon
风钻　pneumatic drill, air motor drill
风嘴【眼】【冶】(同"风口")
风嘴滑出(底吹特炉)【钢】slipping-down
风嘴口【铁】tuyere snout
风嘴帽(流态化炉的)　tuyere head
风嘴清孔机【冶】tuyere puncher
风嘴伸入度　tuyere penetration
风嘴作用[工作]　tuyere action
冯·阿克尔(-德博尔)碘化物热离解法(同"阿克尔-德博尔碘化物热离解法")
冯米塞斯(塑性)条件　Von Mises criterion
冯泽拉德(铝合金)低倍浸蚀液　Von Zeelader
缝　gap, seam, slot ◇ 小～tiny gaps
缝边裂纹【焊】toe crack(ing)
缝焊　seam(resistance) welding ◇ 箔材～foil seam welding, 电弧～arc seam welding, 双辊～*
缝焊滚轮　seam-welding roller
缝焊焊头　seam-welding head
缝焊机　seam welder, seam-welding machine ◇ 辊式～*, 活动焊头～travel head seam welder, 双层～double seam welder, 万能～universal seam welder
缝焊用(电流)断续器　seam-welding control
缝合　stitching
缝接　seaming
缝式点火器　multi-slit ignitor
缝式给料装置　lip feeder
缝式(加热)炉　slot(-type) furnace
缝隙　gap(ping), crevice, slit, slot, aperture, interstice, rent ◇ 索勒～*
缝隙腐蚀　crevice corrosion
缝隙间距　slit separation

缝隙浇口【铸】slit [slot, connor] gate
缝隙漏泄　clearance leakage
缝隙内浇口【铸】pressure [edge] gate
缝隙筛　slitbar screen
缝隙式探测器(超声波检验用)　gap probe
缝隙系统(X射线缝隙系统)　slit system ◇ 索勒聚焦～*
缝隙系统散射　slit system scattering
缝隙效应　gap [crevice] effect
佛德斯薄壳铸型法　Fordath process
夫琅和费区域　Fraunhofer region
呋喃黏结剂　furan binder
呋喃树脂　furan resin
呋喃树脂砂　furane resin bonded sands
麸痕镀锡薄钢板　dusty tinplate
敷箔　foliation
敷层　blanket
敷镀金属　overlay metallization
敷粉　dusting,【铸】dusting-on, powdering
敷金属玻璃　metallized glass
敷铝　aluminize
敷煤滚筒(生球团的)　coal coating drum
敷设　lay ◇ 电缆～cabling, 干管～mainlaying
敷设导线　wiring
敷设机　placer
敷钍　thoriate
敷钍钨丝　thoriated tungsten(wire), thoriated filament
敷线　wire
扶壁坝　buttress dam
扶垛式挡土墙　buttressed retaining wall
辐板　web
辐板车轮轧机【压】mill for rolling centre disc-type wheels
辐板压弯(车轮的)　dishing
辐亮度　radiance
辐射　radiation, exposure, radio, beaming ◇ 标识[特性]～纯度*, (波长)修正～modified radiation, 成束～beamed radiation, 穿透～transmitted radiation, 定向～

directional radiation, 对~灵敏[敏感]的 radiosensitive, 多色~*, 非致电离[非电离性]~*, 缓发~ delayed radiation, 晶体反射的~*, 滤过~ filtered radiation, 漫散~ diffuse radiation, 耐~的 radioresistant, 气体[煤气]火焰~ gas-fire radiation, 切伦科夫~ Cerenkov radiation, 韧致~ braking radiation, 软性~*, 弱穿透性~ soft radiation, 剩余~ restrahlen, 特征~*, 未滤过~ unfiltered radiation, 吸收~(能) absorption radiation, 荧光~*

辐射安全物理学　health physics
辐射杯(辐射式燃烧器的)　radiant cup
辐射杯烧嘴加热炉　furnace with radiant cup burner
辐射本领　radiating capacity, emissivity
辐射不透明的　radiopaque
辐射测量[度量]的　radiometric
辐射测量(术)　radiometry
辐射测量仪　radiation measuring instrument
辐射测微计　radiomicrometer
辐射测温术　radiation thermometry
辐射场　radiation field
辐射常数　radiation constant ◇初级~*
辐射传热　radiation heat transfer, heat transfer by radiation
辐射脆化　radiation embrittlement
辐射等离子体　radiating plasma
辐射点　radiant
辐射点(分布)密度　radiant density
辐射电弧炉　radiant arc furnace
辐射电阻炉　radiant resistance furnace
辐射吊挂式炉顶　suspended radial roof
辐射对流作用　radivection
辐射发光　radioluminescence
辐射反射比　radiant reflectance
辐射方向特性曲线(天线的)　radiation pattern
辐射防护　radiation shielding [protection]
辐射防护屏[闸]　radiation shield [shutter]

辐射分解　radiolysis, radiolytic breakdown
辐射腐蚀　radiation corrosion
辐射感光　radiation exposure
辐射感生点状缺陷团　radiation induced point defect cluster
辐射感生扩散(或称辐射诱致扩散)【理】radiation induced diffusion
辐射高温计　radiation thermometer [pyrometer], radiant pyrometer, pyroscope, thermoscope, radiation detector(测量轧件温度用) ◇部分~*, 单镜~*, 菲里~*, 全~*, 双镜式~*, 瓦科尔熔池~ Warchol pyrometer
辐射高温计元件　radiation detecting element
辐射高温学[测定法]　radiation pyrometry
辐射功率　radiant power, radiating capacity
辐射拱型点火器　radiant arch igniter
辐射管　pipe eradiator, radiant tube
辐射管加热的单垛(罩式)炉　single-stack radiant tube furnace
辐射管加热的罩式(退火)炉　radiant-tube-fired cover type furnace
辐射管加热式退火　radiant-tube annealing
辐射管加热箱式退火炉　radiant-tube box annealer
辐射管加热罩式炉　cylindrical radiation furnace
辐射管加热钟罩式退火炉　radiant-tube bell-type annealing furnace
辐射管炉　radiating-tube furnace ◇连续式~*
辐射管用黄铜(一般不加铅)　radiation brass
辐射贯穿计【理】penetrameter
辐射光谱[频谱]　radiation [transmitted] spectrum
辐射光谱[分光]计　radiation spectrometer

辐射光栅　radial grating
辐射弧　radiating arc
辐射化学　radiation chemistry
辐射化学反应　radiation chemical reaction
辐射激活[活化]　radioactivation
辐射剂量　radiation dose ◇ 吸收～`, 有害～测定`
辐射剂量计[监测器]　radiation monitor [dosemeter]
辐射计　radiometer, radiation gauge
辐射计测量　radiometric(al) measurement
辐射计法[辐射量分析法]　radiometric method
辐射加热器　radiant heater
辐射加热无氧化辊式热处理炉　radiation-heating scale-free roller-type heat treating furnace
辐射加热元件　radiant heating element
辐射聚焦的区域熔炼　zone melting with focused radiation
辐射冷却　radiation cooling, cooling by radiation
辐射亮度　radiance
辐射流　radiation flow
辐射流盘　radial flow tray
辐射炉　radiation furnace
辐射面　radiating(sur)face]
辐射能　radiating [radiant] energy
辐射能力　radiant power
辐射能量[能值]　quantity of radiant energy
辐射能谱　energy radiation spectrum
辐射频谱学　radio (-frequency) spectroscopy
辐射屏　radiation screen
辐射屏蔽　radiation shielding
辐射器　radiator, exciter
辐射强度　radiation strength [intensity], radiant [ray] intensity ◇ 黑～blackbody intensity
辐射强度比率(试样透过的)　subject contrast

辐射强度测量计　quantorecorder
辐射(强度)指示器　radiation indicator
辐射缺陷团　radiation defect clusters
辐射热　radiant [radiating, radiogenic] heat ◇ 真空电阻测～计　vacuum bolometer
辐射热测量器[电阻式辐射热量测计]　bolometer
辐射热交换[换热]　radiation interchange, heat-exchange by radiation
辐射热流　radiant heat flux
辐射热损失　radiant heat loss
辐射热阻[辐射阻力]　radiative resistance
辐射散射　scattering of radiation
辐射杀伤[伤害]　radiation injury
辐射烧嘴　radiation burner
辐射湿度计　radiation moisture gauge
辐射式发动机　radial engine
辐射式余[废]热锅炉　radiation waste-heat boiler
辐射式分布曲线　radial distribution curve
辐射式煤气炉　radiant gas furnace
辐射式燃烧器　radiant burner, fletcher radial burner
辐射(式)真空计　radiometer gauge ◇ 努森～`
辐射束　beam of radiation
辐射衰减　radiation damping, attenuation
辐射损伤　radiation damage ◇ 耐～性`
辐射损失　radiation loss, loss by radiation
辐射探测器　radiation probe [detector]
辐射体　radiating body, (ir)radiator, radiation emitter ◇ α～ alpha radiator, 缓发 α 粒子～ delyed-alpha emitter, 阳电子～ positron emitter
辐射通量　radiation flux
辐射通量计　radiometer, radiation fluxmeter
辐射头　radiation head
辐射图[理]radiation pattern [diagram]
辐射危险[危害性]　radiohazard, radiation hazard

辐射稳定性　radiation stability
辐射物体　eradiator
辐射吸收　radiation absorption
辐射吸收比　radiant absorptance
辐射系数　radiation coefficient, emissivity (factor)
辐射[照]效应　radiation effect
辐射性标准化　radioactive standardization
辐射性质　radiation quality
辐射冶金学[术]　radiometallurgy
辐射硬度　radiation hardness
辐射原子　radiating atom
辐射源　radiation source [emitter], (ir)radiator, emitter
辐射(源)效率　radiant efficiency
辐射源有限宽度引起的增宽　broadening due to finite source width
辐射源至底片距离　source-to-film distance
辐射源至晶体(单色器)距离　source-to-crystal distance
辐射跃迁　radiative transition
辐射照相术　radiography
辐射罩式点火器(带式烧结机的)　radiant-hood ignition furnace
辐射中毒　radiation poisoning
辐射状收缩　radial shrinkage ◇ 烧结时 ~ *
辐射状态　radiant state
辐射状砖　radial brick
辐射阻抗　radiation impedance
辐条钢丝　spoke wire(车轮的), cycle spoke wire(自行车、摩托车用)
辐条轮毂　【压】spider
辐照　irradiation, irradiance, radiation exposure, (radioactive) bombardment ◇ 多次 ~ 退火循环 *, 经 ~ 金属 irradiated metal, 受 ~ 面积 irradiated area, 未受 ~ 的 nonirradiated, unexposed
辐照脆化[脆性]　irradiation embrittlement
辐照度　irradiance

辐照后组织　radiated structure
辐照剂量计　radiation exposure badge
辐照面积　radiating area
辐照器　irradiator, irradiation machine
辐照燃料模拟合金　fissium(alloy)
辐照燃料模样　fizzium, fissium
辐照蠕变　【理】irradiation creep
辐照损伤　irradiation damage, bombardment damage(射线辐照损伤)
辐照退火作用　radiation annealing effect
辐照性能[状态]　irradiation behaviour
辐照硬化　【金】(ir)radiation hardening ◇ 放射线 ~ 现象 thermal spike
幅(度)　amplitude(amp)
幅度不足(摆动幅度不足)　underswing
幅频　amplitude frequency
氟{F}　fluor(ine) ◇ 含 ~ 气体 *
氟电解槽　fluorine cell
氟发散[放出]　fluorine emission
氟钙镁石　zamboninite
氟钙钠钇石　gagarinite
氟锆酸钾{K_2ZrF_6}　potassium fluorozirconate [fluozirconate], potassium zirconium fluoride salt
氟锆酸盐{$M_2\{ZrF_6\}$}　fluo(ro)zirconate
氟硅钙镁石　silicomagnesiofluorite
氟硅钙钠石　agrellite
氟硅化物　silico-fluoride
氟硅化锌　fluralsil
氟硅铝石　zumgite
氟硅铌钠矿{$RNb_2O_6F_2RSiO_3$}(R = Ce, Na, Zr, Ca)　chalcolamprite
氟硅铈矿{$Na_3Ca_8Ce_2(FOH)_7(SiO_3)_9$}　johnstrupite
氟硅酸{$H_2[SiF_6]$}　fluosilicic acid, hydrofluosilicic acid
氟硅酸铵{$(NH_4)_2[SiF_6]$}　ammonium silicofluoride
氟硅酸钙{$Ca[SiF_6]$}　calcium fluosilicate
氟硅酸钴　cobaltous fluorosilicate
氟硅酸钾{$K_2[SiF_6]$}　potassium fluosilicate [silicofluoride]

氟硅酸镁　magnesium fluosilicate
氟硅酸钠 {Na$_2$[SiF$_6$]}　sodium silicofluoride
氟硅酸铅 {Pb[SiF$_6$]·2H$_2$O}　lead fluosilicate [hexafluorosilicate, silicofluo ride]
氟硅酸铷 {Rb$_2$[SiF$_6$]}　rubidium fluosilicate
氟硅酸铯 {Cs$_2$[SiF$_6$]}　cesium silicofluoride, {Cs[SiF$_6$]}　cesium fluosilicate
氟硅酸盐 {M$_2$[SiF$_6$]}　fluosilicate, silicofluoride
氟硅酸盐电解精炼法（铅的）　silico-fluoride electrolytic process
氟硅酸盐电解质 {M$_2$[SiF$_6$]}　fluorosilicate electrolyte
氟硅酸盐铅精炼法　fluosilicate lead refining process
氟硅酸盐烧结法　silicofluoride sintering method
氟硅酸银　isotachiol
氟硅钛钇石　yftisite
氟硅钇石 {(Y,Ce,La)$_4$Fe(Si$_2$O$_7$)$_2$·F$_2$}　rowlandite
氟铪酸钾 {K$_2$HfF$_6$}　potassium hafnium fluoride, potassium fluorohafnate
氟铪酸钾 {K$_3$[HfF$_7$]}　potassium fluohafnate
氟铪酸盐［氟铪化合物］{M$_2$(HfF$_6$), M$_3$(HfF$_7$)}　hafnifluoride, fluohafnate, fluoro-hafnate
氟化　fluoration, fluorination, fluorization ◇ 电化(学)～*，流态化床～ fluidized fluorination, 阳极～ anodic fluorination
氟化铵 {(NH$_4$)F}　ammonium fluoride ◇ 酸式～*
氟化钡 {BaF$_2$}　barium fluoride
氟化钡锰　barium manganese fluoride
氟化焙烧法　fluoride roasting process
氟化钚　plutonium fluoride
氟化的　fluoric
氟化法　fluoride process, fluorination
氟化(反应)器　fluorination reactor ◇ 塔式～*

氟化分解　fluorination breakdown
氟化钆 {GdF$_3$}　gadolinium fluoride
氟化钙 {CaF$_2$}　calcium fluoride
氟化钙衬里　calcium fluoride liner
氟化钙催化剂　calcium fluoride catalyst
氟化钙涂料　lime fluorspar coating
氟化钙型结构　calcium fluoride structure
氟化钙渣　calcium fluoride slag
氟化锆 {ZrF$_4$}　zirconium fluoride
氟化锆铵［氟锆酸铵］{(NH$_4$)$_2$[ZrF$_6$]}　ammonium zirconium fluoride, ammonium fluo-zirconate
氟化镉　cadmium fluoride
氟化铬　chromium fluoride
氟化硅　silicon fluoride
氟化剂　fluorizating [fluorating, fluorinating] agent
氟化镓　gallium fluoride
氟化钾 {KF}　potassium fluoride
氟化钾复盐　potassium double fluoride
氟化钪 {ScF$_3$}　scandium fluoride
氟化镧 {LaF$_3$}　lanthanum fluoride
氟化锂 {LiF}　lithium fluoride
氟化锂平面晶体单色器　plane lithium-fluoride monochromator
氟化铝 {AlF$_3$}　aluminium fluoride ◇ 游离～ free aluminium fluoride
氟化镁 {MgF$_2$}　magnesium fluoride
氟化镁炉渣　magnesium fluoride slag
氟化锰　manganese fluoride
氟化钼 {MoF$_3$, MoF$_4$, MoF$_6$}　molybdenum fluoride
氟化镎　neptunium fluoride
氟化钠 {NaF}　sodium fluoride
氟化钠-氟化铝熔体　sodium fluoride-aluminium fluoride melt
氟化钕 {NdF$_3$}　neodymium fluoride
氟化铍 {BeF$_2$}　beryllium fluoride
氟化镨 {PrF$_3$}　praseodymium fluoride
氟化氢 {HF}　hydrogen fluoride ◇ 脱～ dehydrofluorination

氟化氢的 fluorhydric
氟化氢回收设备 hydrogen fluoride recovery plant
氟化氢蒸发器 hydrogen fluoride vapourizer
氟化氢铵{(NH$_4$)HF$_2$} ammonium-bifluoride, ammonium hydrogen fluoride
氟化氰{FCN} cyan(ogen) fluoride
氟化热塑塑料 fluorinated thermoplastics
氟化铷{RbF} rubidium fluoride
氟化铯{CsF} cesium fluoride
氟化钐{SmF$_3$} samaric fluoride
氟化铈 cerium fluoride
氟化锶{SrF$_2$} strontium fluoride
氟化铊{TlF, TlF$_2$, TlF$_3$} thallium fluoride
氟化塔 fluorination tower
氟化锑 antimony fluoride
氟化铁 ferric fluoride
氟化铜 cupric [copper] fluoride
氟化钍{ThF$_4$} thorium fluoride
氟化钨{WF$_3$, WF$_6$} tungsten fluoride
氟化物 fluoride, fluorine compound ◇ 不溶碱性~*
氟化物衬里 fluoride liner
氟化物电解 electrolysis of fluorides
氟化物电解法 fluoride electrolysis process
氟化物分解 fluoride breakdown ◇ 锆英石~*
氟化物复盐 double fluoride
氟化物挥发法 fluoride process
氟化物结晶法 fluoride crystallization method
氟化物金属热还原 metallic reduction of fluorides
氟化物离子 fluoride ion
氟化物-氯化物电解槽 fluoride chloride bath
氟化物络合物 fluoride [fluoro] complex
氟化物熔盐电解 fluoride fused salt electrolysis
氟化物溶解 fluoride dissolution
氟化物盐类 fluoride salt

氟化锡 {SnF-2, SnF-4} fin fluoride
氟化效率 fluorine efficiency
氟化亚铜 copper fluoride
氟化亚锡 stannous fluoride
氟化氧铋 bismuthyl fluoride
氟化冶金 fluoridizing metallurgy
氟化钇{YF$_3$} yttrium fluoride
氟化银 silver fluoride
氟化铀{UF$_4$, UF$_6$} uranium fluoride
氟化铀铵{NH$_4$UF$_5$} ammonium uranium (double) fluoride, double fluoride of ammonium and uranium ◇ 弗卢莱克斯电解生产~法 Flurex process
氟化装置 fluorinator system ◇ 流态化床~*
氟化作用 fluoridation, fluoration, fluorination, fluorization
氟回收 fluorine recovery
氟钾云母 chacaltaite
氟金云母 fluorophlogopite
氟钪酸铵{(NH$_4$)$_3$[ScF$_6$]} ammonium fluoscandate
氟钪酸钾{K$_3$[ScF$_6$]} potassium fluoscandate
氟钪酸盐 fluoscandate
氟锂云母 fluor-lepidolite
氟利昂[三氟甲烷] freon
氟利昂 11 (同"一氟三氯甲烷")
氟利昂冷冻挡板 freon refrigerated baffle
氟利昂气 freon gas
氟磷钙石 spodiosite
氟磷灰石[氟磷酸钙]{Ca$_5$(PO$_4$)$_3$F} fluorapatite
氟磷铝石 fluellite
氟磷锰铁矿 zwieselite
氟磷镁石 pleuroclase
氟磷酸盐{M$_2$(PF$_7$)} fluo phosphate
氟磷铁石 zwieselite
氟铝钙石{CaF$_2$·2Al(FOH)$_3$·H$_2$O} prosopite
氟铝石{AlF$_3$·H$_2$O} fluellite
氟氯铅矿 matlockite

氟钠镁铝石{Na₂,Mg)F₂·3Al(F,OH)₃·2H₂O} ralstonite

氟铌酸钾{K₂NbF₇} potassium fluoninbate [fluocolumbate], potassium-niobium [potassium-columbium](double) fluoride

氟铌酸盐{M₂(NbF₇)} fluoniobate, fluo columbate

氟硼酸{H(BF₄)} fluo(r)boric aciol

氟硼酸盐 fluo(r)borate

氟硼酸钠{NaBF₄} Sodium flourborate

氟铍酸铵{(NH₄)₂BeF₄} ammonium fluoberyllate

氟铍酸盐 fluoberyllate

氟镤酸钾{K₂[PaF₇]} potassium fluoprotactinate

氟镤酸盐 fluoprotactinate

氟气 fluorine gas

氟氢化钾{KHF₂} potassium hydrogen fluoride, potassium bifluoride

氟氢化钠{NaHF₂} sodium hydrogen bifluoride

氟氢酸{HF} hydrogen fluoride ◇ 稀～*

氟砷钙镁石 fluoradelite, tilasite

氟石 （同"萤石"）

氟铈(镧)矿 fluocerite

氟钛酸钾{K₂[TiF₆]} potassium fluotitanate

氟钛酸盐 fluotitanate

氟钽酸钾{K₂[TaF₇]} potassium fluotantalate [tantalifluoride], potassium-tantalum double fluoride, tantalum potassium fluoride

氟钽酸盐{M₂(TaF₇)} fluotantalate, tantalifluoride

氟碳钙石 brenkite

氟碳钙铈矿 parisite

氟碳钙钇矿 yttroparisite, yttrosynchysite

氟碳镧[铈]矿 bastnaesite

氟碳钕钡矿 cebaite-(Nd)

氟碳钕矿 bastnaesite-(Nd)

氟碳铈钡矿 cebaite

氟碳酸钡铈矿 cordylite

氟碳铈矿 bastnaesite, buszite

氟碳酸铈矿 hamartite

氟碳钇矿 yttrobastnaesite, bastnaesite-(Y)

氟危害 fluorine damage

氟吸收(反应)器 fluorine clean-up reactor

氟锡酸{H₂(SnF₆)} fluostannic acid

氟锡酸盐{M₂(SnF₆)} fluostannate

氟溴银矿 megabromite

氟亚锡酸{H₂(SnF₄)} fluostannous acid

氟盐 villiaumite

氟焰反应 fluorine flame reaction

氟氧铋矿 zavaritskite

氟氧化铼{ReOF₄,ReO₂F₂} rhenium oxyfluoride

氟氧化钼 molybdenum oxyfluoride

氟氧化铌 niobium [columbium] oxyfluoride

氟氧化铊{TlOF} thallic oxyfluoride

氟氧化物 oxyfluoride

氟氧铌钾{K₂NbOF₅·H₂O} potassium-niobium [potassium-columbium] oxyfluoride

氟氧铌酸钾{K₂[NbOF₅]} potassium fluooxycolumbate

氟氧铌酸盐 fluooxycolumbate

氟乙烯 flouro-othylene

氟钇钙矿 tveitite

氟铀酸铵 （同"氟化铀铵"）

氟铀酸钠{NaF·UF₄} sodium-uranium double fluoride

氟铀酸盐 fluorouranate

符号 character, sign, symbol, mark, code, designation, notation, legend ◇ 改变～ reversal, 赫曼－摩干～*

符号板(装料用) 【冶】symbolic panel

符号编辑器 【计】symbolic editor

符号编[定]址 【计】symbolic addressing

符号变换器 sign changer [reverser]

符号表示法 【计】symbolic notation

符号触发器 【计】sign flip flop

符号串 【计】symbol [sign] string

符号代码 【计】symbolic code
符号地址 【计】symbolic address
符号翻译[转换]程序 【计】symbolic conversion program(SCP)
符号汇编程序 【计】symbolic assembler
符号汇编(语言) 【计】symbolic assembly (language)
符号机器代码 【计】symbolic machine code
符号逻辑 【计】symbolic logic
符号位 【计】sign digit
符号语言 【计】symbolic language
符号指令 【计】symbolic instruction
符号组 【计】set of symbols, field
符合 coincide, fit, correspond, conformity,
符合检出器 coincident detector
符合门 【计】coincidence [coincident, identify] gate
伏安表[计] volt-ampere meter, voltammeter, unimeter
伏安特性(曲线) current-voltage characteristics, voltage-current characteristics, volt-ampere(characteristic) curve
伏打电池 voltaic cell ◇ 光生～*
伏打效应 Volta effect
伏特毫安计 volt-milliampere meter
伏特计附加电阻 reductor
伏特数 voltage
俘获 capture, trapping ◇ 位错的～trapping of dislocation
俘获断面(中子的) capture cross-section
俘获介质 capturing medium
俘获系数 【半】capture coefficient
俘获效率 【环】capture efficiency
俘获中心 trapping centre
俘获中子介质 capturing medium
俘获状态 capturing state
服务中断(指停电、停水等) service interruption
浮标 buoy, float(er) ◇ 铁制～iron float, 土制～debiteuse
浮标式测量仪 float type gauge

浮标液面控制器 float type level regulator
浮(标液)面指示器[液位计] float gauge, float level indicator [meter]
浮槽(分级机的) dish
浮槽(式)分级机 bowl classifier
浮沉分级 float and sink fraction
浮沉模具 floating die(assembly)
浮沉模台 floating die table
浮沉模压机 floating die press
浮沉模座 floating base
浮沉试验 float and sink test, sink-and-float test
浮秤 areometer, hydrometer
浮尺 float meter
浮充电池组 floating battery
浮船 pontoon
浮点表示法 floating point representation
浮点程序包 【计】floating point package
浮点计算机 floating point computer
浮点精度 【数】floating point precision
浮点十进制运算 floating decimal arithmetic
浮点数 【数】floating(point) number
浮点系数[尾数] 【计】floating point coefficient, mantissa
浮点运算 【计】floating point arithmetic [operation]
浮点运算子程序 【计】floating point routine
浮雕抛光(显微磨片的) relief polishing
浮吊 floating [pontoon] crane, boat derrick
浮顶 floating top
浮动 float(ing), flotation
浮动程序 relative [relocatable] program
浮动床洗涤塔 floating bed scrubber ◇ 六级～*
浮动磁头 floating head
浮动地址 【计】floating address
浮动点 floating point
浮动阀 float operated valve
浮动辊 floating roll

浮动汇率 【企】floating rate
浮动活塞(双锤式高速锤的) floating piston
浮动价格 fluctuate price
浮动开关 float switch
浮动密封板 floating seal
浮动区域精炼法(区熔精炼) floating zone process
浮动塞棒 floating plug
浮动式卷取机 shifting winding reel
浮动式轧机(机架可升降的三辊式轧机)【压】jumping mill
浮动调整方式 【理】floating control mode
浮动头 floating head
浮动吸头 float suction
浮动芯棒 floating core rod
浮动芯棒轧制 floating mandrel rolling
浮动信号灯 floating pilot lamp
浮动原[零]点 floating zero
浮动轴承座 【机】floating chock
浮筏基[础] raft foundation, foundation on raft
浮阀 float(operated) valve
浮杆(起重机) floating boom
浮罐效应(高炉喷煤系统的) bunker floating effect
浮集式水口 collector nozzle
浮计 (见"比重计"例证)
浮架[框] floating frame
浮力 buoyancy, buoyant force
浮码头 pontoon
浮膜 offscum
浮桥 floating [bateau, ferry] bridge, pontoon
浮球阀 ball float
浮区熔炼技术 floating zone technique ◇ 单熔区的~*
浮区提纯 floating zone purification
浮上分离法 floatation
浮石 floatstone, pumice(stone)
浮石骨料混凝土 pumice aggregate concrete

浮石混凝土 pumeconcrete, pumecrete
浮石渣 pumice stone slag
浮石渣砖 pumice-slag brick
浮石状熔剂 pumice-like flux
浮石状渣 honeycombed slag
浮体 float(er), floating body
浮筒 float(bowl), hydrofoil
浮筒起重机 floating crane
浮筒式发生器(乙炔的) bell(type) generator
浮筒式汽水阀[回水盒] bucket steam trap
浮筒式液位自动调节器 float level controller
浮凸饰 boss
浮坞 floating dock ◇ 大型钢筋混凝土~ cruiser dock
浮悬式保温帽 【钢】floating hot top
浮选 flotation(flot., flotn), flotation separation, floatation ◇ 充气[风力]~ air flotation, 可~的 floatable, 曝气~(法) dispersed-air flotation, 全~ bulk flotation, 热~法 hot flotation(method), 溶气~(法) dissolved-air flotation, 梯流~法 cascade process, 完全~法 all-flotation, 阴离子~法*
浮选槽 flotation cell, cell
浮选产品[产物] flotation product
浮选厂[车间] flotation concentration plant
浮选处理 flotation treatment
浮选-高压釜处理法 method of flotation-autoclave treatment
浮选高压浸出钛精矿 flotation and autoclave titanium concentrate
浮选活化剂 floatation activator
浮选机 floatation machine [device], flotation machine [cell] ◇ 底吹式~ su-baeration cell, 多槽~ multicompartment cell, 多孔固定底式~ mat-type cell, 气升式~ airlift cell, 再~ aftertreatment cell
浮选精矿 flotation [floatation] concen-

trate
浮选矿泥　flotation slurry
浮选砂　flotation sand
浮选设备　floatation device
浮选水冶设备　floatation leaching plant
浮选尾矿　flotation tailings
浮选线　float line
浮选性　floatability
浮选(药)剂　floatation agent, flotation(re)agent, flotating chemicals
浮选抑制剂　depressing agent
浮选油　flotation oil
浮选柱　flotation column
浮选装置　flotation unit ◇ 逆流～ countercurrent column
浮游球衣菌　Sphaerotilus natans Kuetzing
浮渣　dross(slag), floater, lather, offscourings, scum(ming), skimmings, floss, scruff ◇ 除去～despumation, 含铜～*, 灰色 ～【色】grey scum, 碱性～ caustic dross, 金属～ dross metallics, 氯化物～ chloride dross, 泡沫状～ foam like scum, 撇～勺【色】bowl skimmer, 撇取～ skim, 熔剂池～ flux bath dross, 锑～ antimony skimmings, 铜～*, 细粒～dross fines
浮渣捕集器　dross trap
浮渣操作　dross(ing) operation
浮渣车　dross bogie
浮渣处理　dross handling
浮渣处理设备　scum treatment facility
浮渣(处理)翻车机　dross tippler
浮渣(处理)反射炉　dross reverberatory furnace
浮渣粉　dross fines
浮渣滚筒　【色】dross mill
浮渣锅　dross kettle
浮渣排出口　dross hole
浮渣破碎车间　dross crushing plant
浮渣生成　scum formation
浮渣调料槽　dross conditioner
浮渣调料系统　dross conditioning system
浮渣箱　dross box

浮渣贮仓　dross storage
浮罩式储气罐　floating bell gasholder
浮置充电法　floating charge technique
浮置坩埚技术　floating crucible technique
浮置线圈(磁场中称量金属用)　levitation coil
浮子开关　float switch
浮子黏度计　float viscometer
浮子式流量计　float meter
浮子式液位计　float type level gauge
福蒂亚第快速疲劳试验　Fotiadi test
福尔马落锤深冲法　Formall process
福尔森粉矿造块法　Follsan process
福富米带换热器回转炉　Fofumi furnace
福格特标记法　【理】Voigt's notation
福井式锥形杯冲深试验　Fukui conical cup drawing test
福拉尔铝磷合金(变性剂)　Phoral
福利设施　【企】welfare facilities
福林合金(19.23Bi, 3.84Cu, 76.9Sn, 少量 Hg)　Pholin's alloy
福伦轧管法　Foren process
福美克斯磁性钢丝(录音钢丝)　Formex wire
福诺青铜(1.4Sn, 0—1Si, 微量 Cd, 余量 Cu)　Phono-bronze
福塞科发热保温剂　【铸】Foseco feeding compound
福斯利克含磷镍青铜(5Te, 1.1Ni, 0.22P, 余量 Cu)　Phosnic bronze
福斯普雷磷酸盐浸镀法　Fospray process
福斯特高温计　Foster pyrometer
福斯特探测[传感]器　Foerster probe
弗戈镍铬钨系合金钢(1: 0.24C, 18Cr, 8Ni, 4.4W, 余量 Fe; 2: 0.48C, 13Cr, 14Ni, 2.2W, 0.7Mo, 余量 Fe)　virgo
弗吉尼亚银[铜镍锌]合金　Virginia silver
弗拉德电位　Flade potential
弗拉格曼聚焦照相机　Phragmen focusing camera
弗莱浸蚀剂(软钢用; 90 克 CuCl2, 120 毫升 HCl, 100 毫升水)　Fry's reagent

弗莱史库特夹具钢(1C,4Cr)	Flashkut
弗莱试剂	【金】Fly test reagent
弗莱斯尼尔干燥法	Fleissner drying
弗兰克部分位错	Frank partial dislocation
弗兰克-里德位错增值机理	【理】Frank-Read mechanism
弗兰克-里德(位错)源	F-R(Frank-Read) source
弗兰克-里德源耗竭	exhaustion of Frank-Read sources
弗兰克位错	Frank dislocation
弗劳德标数(水文计算用)	Froude number
弗勒克斯弗劳型余热锅炉	Fluxflow waste heat boiler
弗雷茨-穆恩(焊管)法	(同"连续式炉焊管法")
弗雷里铅-碱土金属轴承合金(<1Ca,<2Ba,余量Pb)	Frary metal
弗雷蒙(冲击,回跳硬度)试验	Fremont (impact) test
弗雷斯内尔(衍射)条纹	Fresnel fringes
弗雷西奈预(加)应力法	Freyssient system of prestressing
弗里德里希碳料电阻炉	Friedrich furnace
弗里克感应电炉	Frik furnace
弗里克浸蚀剂(铝及铝合金用)	Flick's reagent [etch]
弗里克铜锌镍电阻丝合金(50-55Cu,30-31Zn,17-19Ni)	Frick's alloy
弗里曼直接还原法	【理】Freeman process
弗林式炉顶装料装置(超高压炉顶的)	【铁】Freyn charging system
弗卢莱克斯电解生产氟化铀铵法	Flurex process
弗伦克尔模型(位错的)	Frenkel model
弗伦克尔(晶格空位)缺陷	Frenkel defect
弗伦克尔缺陷	(同"填隙-空位偶")
弗罗因德结构钢(0.1—0.15C,0.7—1.3Si,0.3—0.6Mn,少量 Cr)	Freund steel
弗洛不锈钢氮化炉局部渗氮法(英国专利)	Floe nitradation
弗洛丁电炉直接炼钢法	Flodin process
弗洛渗氮法	Floe nitradation, Floe process
弗洛因德里赫吸附方程式	Freundlich adsorption equation
弗洛硬化剂	Fluo-Hard
弗思硬度计	Firth hardometer
辅钩(吊车的)	auxiliary hoist(A.H.)
辅机	auxiliary machinery
辅剪	auxiliary shears
辅量子数	subsidiary quantum number
辅助泵	auxiliary [jury, donkey] pump
辅助闭合触点	auxiliary make contact
辅助变压器	auxiliary transformer(AT)
辅助材料	accessory [auxiliary] material
辅助操作	【计】auxiliary operation
辅助操作人员	janitor labour
辅助车间	auxiliary shop [plant], accessory plant
辅助程序	bootstrap
辅助除尘系统	secondary dedusting system
辅助传动(装置)	auxiliary drive ◇ 直流~DC-auxiliary drive
辅助磁化绕组	bias winding
辅助存储器	【计】auxiliary [secondary] memory
辅助电动机	auxiliary [pilot, pony] motor, servomotor
辅助(电)弧	pilot arc ◇ 用~使焊弧起弧 pilot-arc starting
辅助电弧起弧	pilot-arc starting
辅助电极	auxiliary electrode
辅助电源	auxiliary power [source]
辅助动力[电源]设备	auxiliary power unit
辅助动作	underaction
辅助断开触点	auxiliary break-contact
辅助发电机	pilot generator
辅助反应	auxiliary reaction
辅助风机	additional [secondary] air fan

辅助风流　bypass air
辅助风嘴　auxiliary tuyere
辅助符[代]号　supplementary symbol
辅助干线　submain
辅助钢筋　auxiliary bar
辅助隔膜泵　(同"备用隔膜泵")
辅助拱　【建】relieving arch
辅助管道　subsidiary conduit
辅助辊道　auxiliary roller table
辅助回路　auxiliary circuit, subsidiary loop
辅助机构　auxiliary mechanism
辅助机械设备　accessory machinery
辅助继电器　auxiliary relay(Aux RL)
辅助加热炉　auxiliary oven
辅助加热系统　additional heating system
辅助金属　anxiliary metal ◇ 黏结~*
辅助卷扬　auxiliary hoist
辅助空气　auxiliary air
辅助控制　auxiliary control
辅助控制杆　auxiliary control rod
辅助控制台　auxiliary console
辅助跨　auxiliary bay
辅助冷凝器　auxiliary condenser
辅助例行程序　【计】auxiliary routine
辅助料斗　auxiliary hopper
辅助密封配电盘　auxiliary cubicle (aux.cub.)
辅助汽缸　auxiliary cylinder
辅助驱动装置　auxiliary drive device
辅助燃烧器[辅助烧嘴]　auxiliary [additional, pilot] burner
辅助设备　accessory [additional, ancillary, associated, commissary, peripheral, supplemental] equipment, accessories, auxiliaries, ancillaries, auxiliary apparatus [facilities] ◇ 轧钢车间~*
辅助设施　support facilities
辅助生产设备　auxiliary operating equipment
辅助数据　auxiliary data
辅助添加剂　secondary addition
辅助停止阀　auxiliary stop valve

辅助拖动(装置)　servo drive
辅助洗涤器　【环】backup scrubber
辅助系统　subsystem, accessory system
辅助消弧触点　arcing contact
辅助烟囱　bypass stack
辅助阳极　auxiliary anode(电镀的), supplementary [booster] anode
辅助仪表　auxiliary instrument
辅助油扩散真空泵　booster oil diffusion pump
辅助运输机　auxiliary conveyer
辅助轧辊　【压】helper roll
辅助轧机　supplementary mill
辅助振动装粉法　vibration-assisted filling
辅助证据　contributary evidence
辅助装置　auxiliary assembly
辅助作业　less important work, redundant work
俯焊　downhand(welding)
俯焊焊缝　downhand [underhand, flat] weld
俯瞰图　aerial [aeroplane, air] view, aeroview, bird's eye view
俯视[瞰]　overlook
俯视图　top [vertical] view
釜残渣　stillage residue
釜脚　still bottoms
腐积土壤　cumulose soil
腐烂　perish
腐泥煤　sapropelic coal
腐蚀　corrosion, erosion, fretting, burn-in, rot ◇ 剥落[氧化膜破裂]~ break away corrosion, 不~的 non-corrodible, 差异充气~*, 充气~ aeration corrosion, 大气~*, 电化学[电偶]~ couple corrosion, 发生~ initiation of corrosion, 干[高温气体]~ dry corrosion, 活性~ active corrosion, 可[易]~的*, 留碳[碳化]~*, 起泡~ blister corro-sion, 强烈~*, 区别~*, 缺[厌]氧~ anaerobic corrosion, 燃灰[油灰]~ ash corrosion, 石墨生物~ 软化*, 使用[工作条件下]~ service corro-

sion,受控～controlled etching,水（溶液）～aqueous corrosion,脱（合金）成分～dealloying,析氢［氢去极化］～*,选择～*,严重～heavy corrosion,氧（浓）差～*,抑制～corrosion inhibition,易～路径*,有氧～aerobic corrosion,中度～moderate corrosion

腐蚀斑点 corrosion spot
腐蚀测量［测定］ corrosion measurement
腐蚀测试器 corrosion probe
腐蚀产物（加压水冷反应堆冷却剂的）corrosion products,crude
腐蚀常数 corrosion constant
腐蚀程度 degree of corrosion
腐蚀脆性 corroding brittleness, corrosion embrittlement
腐蚀电池 corrosion cell
腐蚀电流 corrosion current
腐蚀电势［位］ corrosion potential
腐蚀断裂 corrosion cracking [failure]
腐蚀反应产物 product of corrosion reaction
腐蚀沟纹 corrosion grooving
腐蚀(后)寿命降低 corrosion weaking
腐蚀环境 corrosion [corrosive] environment
腐蚀毁坏 ravage of corrosion
腐蚀机理 corrosion mechanism
腐蚀剂 corrosive(agent,chemicals),corrodent,corroding [attack,etching]agent, etching reagent,caustic,etchant
腐蚀加工 ◇化学～（法）chem-milling,湿式～chemical machining
腐蚀开裂 corrosion cracking
腐蚀坑 【金】etch(ing) pit(ting)
腐蚀坑密度 etch pit density
腐蚀空穴［气孔］ corrosion cavity
腐蚀控制 corrosion control
腐蚀块 corrosion piece
腐蚀类型 forms of corrosion
腐蚀量测定装置 ◇本戈～*
腐蚀裂纹 corrosion [etch] crack

腐蚀率 coefficient of corrosion, corrosion index ◇重量～weight corrosion index
腐蚀麻点 corrosion pit(ting)
腐蚀敏感性 corrosion susceptibility
腐蚀能力 corrosive power
腐蚀抛光法 attack polishing method
腐蚀疲劳 corrosion fatigue
腐蚀疲劳持久极限 corrosion fatigue endurance limit
腐蚀疲劳断裂 corrosion fatigue cracking
腐蚀疲劳极限 corrosion fatigue limit [life]
腐蚀疲劳裂纹 corrosion fatigue crack
腐蚀疲劳裂纹扩展 【金】corrosion fatigue crack propagation
腐蚀疲劳强度 corrosion fatigue strength
腐蚀疲劳试验 corrosion fatigue test
腐蚀疲劳试验机 【金】corrosion fatigue testing machine ◇黑格－罗伯逊～Haigh-Robertson machine,肯尼恩～Kenyon machine
腐蚀疲劳寿命 corrosion fatigue life
腐蚀疲劳效应［作用］ corrosion fatigue effect
腐蚀破裂 corrosion failure
腐蚀起层 exfoliation corrosion
腐蚀起鳞 layer corrosion
腐蚀气氛 corrosion [corrosive] atmosphere
腐蚀铅 corroding lead
腐蚀倾向 tendency to corrode
腐蚀深度 corrosion [etch] depth
腐蚀深度（英寸/年） inches penetration per year(IPY,ipy)
腐蚀时间 time of etching
腐蚀试片 etch test cut
腐蚀试验 corrosion [etching] test,【金】corroding proof ◇冰晶石～炉*,自然条件～natural condition test
腐蚀试验台［站］ corrosion testing station
腐蚀试验箱 corrosion cabinet
腐蚀试验装置 corrosion testing apparatus

腐蚀试样[试件] corrosion-test piece,【金】corroding proof	腐蚀因素 corrosion factor

腐蚀试样[试件] corrosion-test piece,【金】corroding proof
腐蚀数据 corrosion data ◇ 长期~*
腐蚀速度 corrosion velocity
腐蚀速率 corrosion [erosion] rate
腐蚀损坏 corrosive wear, ravage of corrosion
腐蚀损失 corrosion losses
腐蚀探测 detection of corrosion ◇ 旋转圆试棒电位降~法*
腐蚀探针[探测器] corrosion probe
腐蚀特性 corrosion performance
腐蚀图[像]【金】corrosion [etching] pattern, corrosion [etch(ing)] figure
腐蚀系数 coefficient of corrosion, corrosion efficiency
腐蚀系统 corroding system
腐蚀性 corrosiveness, corrosivity, corrosive power
腐蚀性冲蚀 corrosion erosion
腐蚀性断裂(晶间的)【金】caustic cracking
腐蚀性焊剂 corrosive flux
腐蚀性化学药剂 corrosive chemicals
腐蚀(性)介质 corrosion [corrosive] environment, corrodent,【金】corrosive medium
腐蚀性介质中使用[工作]【金】corrosive service
腐蚀性硫 corrosive sulphur
腐蚀性能 corrosion performance
腐蚀性气体 corrosive [active, aggressive, subversive] gas
腐蚀性侵蚀 corrosion erosion
腐蚀性溶液 corrosive solution
腐蚀性损坏 corrosion trouble
腐蚀性烟气 corrosive fume
腐蚀性液体 corrosive [subversive] liquid
腐蚀液 corrosive liquor,【金】etching solution ◇ 奥伯霍弗~*, 奈塔尔硝酸乙醇~*
腐蚀抑制剂 corrosion inhibitor

腐蚀因素 corrosion factor
腐蚀裕量 corrosion allowance
腐蚀孕育期 initiation of corrosion
腐蚀增重 surrosion
腐蚀值 corrosion value
腐蚀指数 corrosion index
腐蚀中心 corrosion centre, centre of attack
腐蚀重量指标 weight corrosion index
腐蚀装置 corrosion unit
腐蚀作用 corrosion [corrosive, etching] effect, corrosive action, attack by corrosion
腐殖煤 sapropelic [humic] coal
腐殖质[土] humus
副产氨 by-product ammonia
副产焦 by-product coke
副产矿物 by-product mineral
副产法 by-product process
副产炼焦炉 by-product(coke) oven
副产品[物] by-product, coproduct, subsidiary [after] product
副产煤气 by-product gas
副产品回收工艺 by-product process
副产品回收设备 by-product recovery unit
副产品回收装置 by-product plant
副产物回收 by-product recovery
副产烟气[烟雾] by-product fume
副产银 by-product silver
副反应 auxiliary [secondary, parasitic(al), side] reaction, by-reaction, sub-reaction
副黑钒矿 paramontroseite
副后角【机】front clearance
副晶粒 subgrain
副经理 deputy [assistant] manager
副矿物 accessory [auxiliary] mineral
副磷锌矿 parahopeite
副檩条 subpurlin
副泥芯【铸】branch core
副品 substandard goods
副起重机 auxiliary hoist

副枪技术	sublance technology
副枪系统	sublance system
副砷锑矿	paradocrasite
副砷铁石	parasymplesite
副碳钙铀矿	parawyartite
副铁钒矿	paramontroseite
副系杆	counter-tie, subtie
副研究员	associate researchfellow
副(氧)枪	【冶】sub-lance
副样	duplicate sample
副应力	secondary stress
副轴	backshaft, auxiliary [counter] shaft, layshaft
副轴(线)	【机】secondary axis
副柱铀矿 $[5UO_3 \cdot 9.5H_2O; 3UO_3 \cdot 7H_2O]$	paraschoepite
副总工程师	assistant chief engineer (ACE), deputy chief engineer
副族符号	designation of subgroup
副族元素(周期表中的)	subgroup element ◇ B~B subgroup element
副作用	after-effect, by-effect, side-effect
覆板	cleading, 【建】skin plate
覆层	coat(ing), encasing ◇ 薄~*, 多孔粉末烧结零件电解~法 etolizing, 盖以不透明~ frosting, 无[不生成]中间扩散层的~ alloy-free coating
覆层板	clad plate
覆层薄板	coated sheet
覆层[复合]薄钢板	clad sheet steel
覆层材料	clad material
覆层脆度检验	brittle coating test
覆层钢	clad [ply, composite] steel
覆层管	clad pipe
覆层焊条	coating electrode
覆层厚度测量仪	coating thickness gauge
覆层硬度	coating hardness
覆镀	plating
覆盖	covering, coverage, overlap
覆盖本领[能力]	covering capacity [power]
覆盖材料	clad material
覆盖层	coating, clear cover, coverage, blanket, envelope, garnish ◇ 金属底层的~ metal-backed coating
覆盖焊道	【焊】cover pass
覆盖矿石的脉石	【地】burden
覆盖物	cover, shroud
覆盖装载的程序模块	【计】overlay load module
覆钢板的	steel-plated
覆钢层压制品	clad-steel laminate
覆钢的	steel-clad
覆金	gilding
覆金属的	metal-faced, 【金】plated
覆铝(的)	Al-clad, alclad ◇ P2~纯铁板*, 无缝~管件*
覆铝铁	aluminium coated iron
覆面	covering, 【建】dressing
覆面板	facesheet, 【建】shell [sheathing] plate
覆面材料	facing material
覆面层	surface deposit, chemise ◇ 皮带~ belt cover
覆面的	faced, lined
覆面砂	【铸】facing sand
覆面铜板	roofing copper
覆膜	tectorial membrane, membrane tectoria
覆膜钢板	Himac steel plate
覆膜砂(壳型铸造)	【铸】precoated sand, shell coated sand
覆镍钢	nickel-clad steel
覆铅	lead-plating ◇ 铁板~spot-homogen
覆铅钢	ferrolum
覆铅钢板	fevrolum
覆饰用极薄金箔	rolled gold
覆碳处理(脱碳钢表面的)	carbon restoration
覆铜层	copper layer
覆铜(的)	copper-clad, copper-coating ◇ 苏维内尔单面或双面~钢板 Su Veneer
覆铜(叠层)板(印刷电路用)	CCL (copper clad) plate

覆锌　zinc-plating
覆银　silver-plating ◇谢菲尔德~铜板 Sheffield plate
覆罩(火焰安全灯网上的)　bonnet
覆罩电弧　shielded arc
赋量　◇已~语句 parameter statement
赋值　【计】assignment, bind, call by value, enable
赋值语句　【计】assignment statement
复本　(同"副本")
复变函数　【数】complex function
复变系统　multivariant system
复查　reinspection
复齿轮　compound gears
复吹[复合吹炼]法　【钢】combined [top-bottom] blowing process ◇LD-CB~
复吹转炉　combined blown [blowing] converter, top-bottom converter
复磁导率　complex permeability
复道砖格　multiple-pass checkers
复的　multiplex
复断路器　【电】double break
复对数坐标图　log-log plot
复对数坐标纸　log-log paper
复二辊式平整机　【压】unit-temper mill
复二辊式轧机组　double two-high rolling train
复二重轧机　double duo mill
复钒矿　vanoxite
复分解　metathesis, double-decomposition
复分解反应　metathetical [double-decomposition] reaction
复风　【铁】reblow
复杆　compound lever
复硅酸盐　double silicate
复轨器　rerailer
复核试验　check [proof] test
复合　recombination, compound, complex
复合板　composite [clad] plate, sandwich ◇爆炸~*, 罗斯林耐热~*
复合变形处理(不锈钢丝的)　complex drawing

复合材料　composite(material) ◇定向凝固原位成形~*, 加强热塑~*, 难熔金属~*, 细碎黏弹性~*, 自生~composite in situ
复合材料部件[器件]　composite component
复合材料层压板　composite laminate
复合材料发动机　composite engine
复合材料驱动轴　composite driveshaft
复合材料设计　composite design
复合材料铸造[浇铸, 铸件]　composite material casting
复合层厚度比　clading ratio
复合超导材料　composite superconducting material
复合产品(铝镁的)　clad products
复合齿轮　compound gears
复合触点　composite contact
复合磁铁　compound [built-up, fag(g)ot] magnet
复合磁铁系制品　composite [combined] magnet systems
复合导体[导线]　composite conductor
复合等温处理　combined isothermal treatment
复合电触头合金　composite contact metal ◇低温烧结的~*
复合电镀(法)　composite plating
复合电极　composite [combination] electrode ◇水冷~*
复合电接触材料　composite contact material
复合电缆　composite [compound] cable
复合电路　composite [compound] circuit
复合镀层　composite coating
复合断面　compound section
复合废气箱　combined wind box
复合粉末　composite powder
复合钢　composite [clad, compound, ply] steel ◇康弗雷克斯~*
复合钢板　clad steel plate, steel sandwich, sandwich steel ◇包不锈钢的~* per-

maclad,普鲁拉梅尔特不锈钢～pluramelt,双金属～plymetal
复合钢材　composite steels,bimetal ◇ 农用～agricultrual ply steel
复合杠杆　compound lever
复合管　composite tube
复合焊条　composite electrode
复合核　【理】compound nucleus
复合挤压（同时正、反挤压）　combined extrusion
复合剂　【冶】complexing agent
复合夹杂　【钢】duplex inclusions
复合浇注　composite casting
复合结构　composite structure
复合金属　composite [clad, bonded, bonding] metal ◇ 恒温器用～thermostatmetal,普鲁拉梅尔特～法【钢】Pluramelt process
复合金属板　clad [bonding] metal
复合金属薄板　clad metal sheet
复合金属材料　bonding metal,【金】composite metallic material ◇ 造币～coinage composite
复合金属管　clad tube
复合进风箱　combined wind box
复合控制　compound control
复合矿　complex ore, grandidierite $\{2Na_2 \cdot 4FeO \cdot 8(Fe,Al,B)_2O_3 \cdot 5SiO_2\}$
复合矿物　complex [composite] minerals
复合冷却器（高炉的）　complex plate
复合离子的　complex-ionic
复合力　compound force
复合模　compound [gang, multiple] die, duplex die（挤压用）
复合耐酸涂料　multiple acid-proof paint
复(合)喷(吹)　co-injection ◇ 煤粉和矿粉～*
复合喷吹比　co-injection rate
复(合)喷(吹)技术　co-injection technique
复合坯块　【粉】compound [composite] compact
复合疲劳强度　combined fatigue strength

复合平衡图　complex equilibrium diagram,【金】double diagram
复合强度（应力状态下的）　combined strength
复合青铜（87—89Cu,9.5—10.5Sn,1.5—2.5Zn,0.5—1.5Pb,0.75Ni）　composition bro-nzes
复合球团矿　composite pellet
复合区　composite zone
复合热处理　multiplex heat treatment
复合烧坯［烧结体］　compound sintered compact
复合设备　equipment complex
复合生坯　composite green compact
复合绳股　compound strand
复合水口　composite nozzle
复合碳（材料）　composite carbon, coke/graphite composite
复合碳化物　double carbide, multicarbide
复合碳酸铁铵$\{(NH_4)_2CO_3 \cdot Fe_2(CO_3)_3\}$　complex ammonium-iron carbonate
复合涂层　composite coating
复合团块［矿］【团】composite briquette, composite agglomerate
复合脱硫剂　composite desulphurizer
复合脱碳工艺　combined decarburization process
复合脱氧方法　【钢】complex deoxidization method
复合脱氧剂　【钢】composite [complex, double] deoxidizer, combined deoxidant
复合位错　compound [mixed] dislocation
复合物　composite, complex,（double）compound
复合吸收剂　composite absorber
复合线材　composite [clad] wire
复合小型轧机　compound rod [small-section] mill
复合谐波电压　complex harmonic voltage
复合循环　composite [compound] cycle
复合压块　composite compact [briquette]
复合压模　multiple pressing tool

复合压坯	【粉】composite [compound] green compact
复合氧化铁皮形成	complex scale formation
复合氧化物	complex [double] oxide
复合阴模	sandwich die
复合应力	complex [combined] stress
复合应力函数	combined stress function
复合应力疲劳试验	complex-stress fatigue test
复合应力试验	combined stress test
复合硬质合金电接触材料	composite hard metal base contacts
复合预还原球团	composite prereduced pellet
复合原子核	（同"复合核"）
复合约束型制振钢板	composite damping steel sheet
复合轧辊	composite [compound, duplex] roll
复合轧制法	composite [sandwich] rolling process
复合针状球墨铸铁	acicular spheroidal graphite cast iron
复合制品	composite [laminated] product
复合中心	【半】recombination centre
复合中子吸收材料	composite neutron-absorbing material
复合周期断面钢材	double period section steel
复合轴承	composite bearing
复合铸件	compound [composite] casting
复合铸拉过程	composite cast-drawing process
复合砖	composite brick
复合状态图	【金】double diagram
复合阻燃剂	complex flame retardant
复合组织	【金】duplex structure
复滑车	tackle
复滑移	multiple slip [glide], complex slip
复辉(共析钢的)	recalescence
复辉曲线	recalescence curve
复基	complex radical
复激磁	compound excitation
复激的	compounded, compound-wound ◇差绕~
复激电动机	compound-wound motor
复激发电机	compound generator
复激绕组	【电】compound winding
复极的	bipolar
复极性	bipolarity
复离子	complex ion
复孪晶	compound twin
复平衡状态图	double equilibrium state diagram
复曲线	compound curve
复燃	after-combustion
复燃烧器	after-burner
复绕的	compounded, compound-wound ◇过~ heavily compounded
复绕机(线材的)	re-spooling machine
复绕线圈	compound [coiled] coil
复热(式)焦炉	compound oven ◇双联火道~ *
复热下喷式焦炉	combination fired underjet oven
复溶	re-dissolution, redissolve
复砷镍矿{NiAs$_2$}	chloanthite
复式	double, compound, duplex, multiple
复式簿记	【企】double entry bookkeeping
复式冲压工具	multiple pressing tool
复式萃取器	compound extractor
复式淬火	（同"二次淬火"）
复式刀具滑板	compound slide
复式电子秤	double electronic scale
复式发动机	compound engine
复式弧焊机	multiple operator arc welding machine
复式加热蛇形管	multiple heating coil
复式交叉(多条道路汇合)	【运】compound [multiple] intersection
复式交分道岔	【运】double slip points
复式卷扬机	double-drum winch
复式炉	duplicate furnace

复式麦氏真空计　double McLeod gauge
复式镍-铬-镍热电偶(NiCrNi)　double thermocouple
复式皮带助卷机　double belt wrapper
复式破碎机　duplex breaker
复式气体节省器　dual-gas economizer
复式清洗　multiple cleaning
复式热电偶　compound thermocouple
复式弯压模　compound bending die
复式移动起重机　twin travel(l)ing crane
复式闸门　double lock
复式转线轨道　【运】double crossover
复双晶　compound twin
复田(surface)　reclamation, landfill
复位　reset(ing), replacement ◇ 手动～ hand reset
复位按钮　reset button
复位脉冲　reset pulse
复位[原]时间　reset time
复位调整　reset adjustment
复位置位　reset-set(R-S)
复位装置　resetting device
复硒镍矿　ahlfeldite
复稀金矿　polycrase, polycrasite
复现性　reproducibility, repeatability
复相　multiphase, polyphase ◇ B/M一组织
复相成核　【理】heterogeneous nucleation
复相关系数　【金】rerelationship coefficient
复相晶粒组织　duplex grain structure
复相平衡　heterogeneous equilibrium
复相区　two-phase region
复相赛隆材料　diphase sialon
复相陶瓷　multiphase ceramics
复消色差校正　apochromatic correction
复消色差透镜　apochromat(ic) lens
复消色差物镜　apochromatic objective
复谐式液压柱塞泵　complex harmonic plunger pump
复型　【金】replica ◇ 聚乙烯醇缩甲醛树脂～ Formvar replica, 万能显微～印法*, 阴影溅射处理～ shadow cast replica, 预阴影溅射处理过的～ preshadowed replica, 铸塑～(制备)法 cast replica
复型(制备,制造)法(电子显微镜检验用)　replica technique [method], thin film technique ◇ 两步～*
复型制取法　model(l)ing
复压　【粉】repressing
复压复烧坯　【粉】double pressed and sintered blank
复盐　double salt
复验　retest
复验分析　(re)check analyses
复氧化物　double oxide
复用模板　repetitive form
复用增碳剂　repeating compound
复原　restoration, restore, reclaiming, reset, recovery
复原位置(高速成形机的)【压】　recocking position
复原系数　coefficient of recovery
复杂点阵[晶格]　compound lattice
复杂断面坯块　(同"变截面坯块")
复杂反应　complicated [complex] reaction
复杂硅酸盐夹杂物　complex silicate inclusions
复杂合金　complex alloy
复杂化合　complex combination
复杂还原　complex reduction
复杂精矿　complex concentrates
复杂矿石氯化　chlorination of complex ores
复杂立方结构　complex cubic structure
复杂零件　complex parts [sections]
复杂模具　【压】complicated die set
复杂衰变　complex decay
复杂铁合金　complex ferro-alloy
复杂型材[型钢]　complex sections [shape]
复杂型芯铸造　intricate cored casting
复杂形状　complicated shape
复杂形状模　intricate shape die
复杂性　complexity

复杂(振动)方式 【理】complex modes
复制 duplicating, duplication, replication, reproducing, reproduction, copy, doubling, replica ◇ 可~的 reproducible
复制模造型 reproduced model moulding
复阻抗 complex impedance
傅科电流 Foucault currents
傅里叶积分理论 theory of Fourier integrals
傅里叶级数理论 theory of Fourier series
腹板 web plate
腹杆(桁架或空腹梁的) web member
腹状轨道 【理】belly orbit
负拔模斜度 【连铸】(同"负滑脱")
负催化剂 negative catalyst
负催化(作用) negative catalysis
负淬火 negative quenching
负导线(热电偶的) negative leg [conductor]
负电荷 negative charge
负电荷电子云 negatively charged electron cloud
负电极 negative [cathode] electrode
负电接头 negative contact
负电势[位] electronegative potential
负电位金属 (同"阳极金属")
负电性 electronegativity, electronegative character
负电性金属 electronegative metal
负电性元素 (electro)negative element
负电性杂质 electronegative impurity
负电原子 electronegative atom
负电子 negative(ly)(charged) electron, negatron
负电阻 negative resistance
负反馈 degeneration, inverse [negative] feedback
负复型(制备法) negative replica
负公差 negative allowance [tolerance]
负公差尺寸 undersize
负荷 load, charge, duty ◇ 轻~ light-duty, 重~操作 forced working

负荷触点 operating contact
负荷电阻(器) load resistor
负荷范围 load(ing) range
负荷分布 load distribution [allocation]
负荷还原 reduction under load (R.U.L.)
负荷还原软化性状 【冶】reduction-softening behaviour under load
负荷还原试验 reduction test under load (RTuL), R.U.L. (reduction under-load) test test
负荷继电器 load relay
负荷开关 load switch
负荷密度 density of load
负荷曲线 load(ing) curve
负荷软化(特性) softening under load (SUL)
负荷试验 load trial
负荷体 carrier material
负荷条件 loading condition(s)
负荷图 load diagram [chart]
负荷系数 load(ing) coefficient
负荷下的屈服点 yield point under load
负荷增加 increase in load
负荷周期变化 load cycling
负滑动结晶器 【连铸】mould with negative strip
负滑脱[滑动] 【连铸】negative slip
负滑脱往复移动(结晶器的) reciprocating with negative strip
负滑脱原理 principle of negative strip
负滑脱往复运动结晶器 reciprocated mould with negative strip
负回授 inverse [negative] feedback
负畸变(光栅的) barrel [negative] distortion
负极 (同"阴极")
负价 negative valence [valency]
负尖峰(信号) underswing, negative spike
负交互作用能 negative interaction energy
负晶体 negative crystal
负抗蚀剂 negative resist
负扩散 【理】uphill [negative] diffusion

负离子　（同"阴离子"）
负离子空位　negative-ion vacancy
负逻辑　【计】negative logic
负脉冲　【电】negative(im)pulse
负脉冲信号　under-shoot, underswing
负母线　negative bus-bar
负偏差　negative deviation [allowance], minus tolerance ◇ 理想～*
负偏差控制　【压】minus-deviation control
负偏差轧制　minus-deviation rolling
负偏析　negative [inverse] segregation
负片　negative film(plate, print)
负曲率　negative curvature
负刃型位错　negative edge dislocation
负溶解度系数　negative solubility coefficient
负熵　negentropy
负速铸坯　【连铸】negative strip
负特性　negative characteristic
负透镜　negative [concave] lens
负透镜的目镜　ampliphan eyepiece
负土深度　depth of overburden
负位错　negative dislocation
负温度系数　negative temperature coefficient
负像　negative image
负型目镜　negative [Huygens'] eyepiece
负型杂质　negative-type(N-type) impurity
负压　negative [suction, subatmospheric] pressure, depression, suction, vacuum
负压表　draught gauge
负压测定(值)　suction measurement
负压煅烧　negative pressure calcination
负压袋式除尘器　negative pressure bag precipitator
负压力　negative pressure, underpressure
负压头　negative head
负压值　suction level
负压铸造　vacuum moulding, negative pressure casting
负异性石　{(Na, Ca, Fe)$_6$Zr(OH, Cl)(SiO$_3$)$_6$} eucolite

负阴极液　（同"废阴极液"）
负应力　negative stress
负载　load, duty, burden, inventory ◇ 初～ minor load, 计算[假定]～ assumed-load, 受～作用的 loaded, 在～下 on load, 自动～分配调节器*
负载变化自动控制　loadamatic control
负载变压器　load transformer
负载不足　underload(ing)
负载单元　load cell(LC)
负载电流　load current
负载电阻(器)　loading resistor
负载范围(试验机的)　capacity range
负载感应泵　load induction pump
负载功率　load power
负载过重　surcharge
负载交变频率　frequency of load alternations
负载量　capacity
负载能力　load-carrying ability
负载曲线　load curve [diagram]
负载试验　load test
负载损失　load loss
负载特性(曲线)　load characteristic
负载调节器　load regulator
负载图　load diagram
负载系数　capacity [load] factor
负载线圈　load(ing) coil
负载张力　load tension
负转移　negative transfer
负阻管　negative resistance tube, dynatron ◇ 打拿～dynatron
负阻器件　【半】negative-resistance device
负阻效应　【电】dynatron effect
富丙烷气　enriched propane gas(EPG)
富玻璃质　vitric
富氮碳钛矿　sorbite
富电子合金　electron-rich alloy
富尔米纳式反射炉(铸铁用)　Fulmina furnace
富尔纳钢表面磷酸盐浸镀法　Foolner process

富钙铀云母　calcium autunit
富铬合金　chromium-rich alloy
富铬绿脱石 {(Al, Fe, Cr)₄·(Si₄O₁₀)(OH)₈}　volchonskoite
富铬碳化物　chromium-rich carbide
富钴固溶体　cobalt-rich solid solution
富硅带　silicate-rich zone
富硅高岭石　anauxite, ionite
富化　enrich(ment),【化】prepare
富混合物　rich mixture
富混凝土　fat [rich] concrete
富集　enrich(ment), concentration,【选】beneficiation, prepare ◇ 等降～*, 化学法～*, 筛选～ enriching by screening, 物理法～*, 中间～*, 重悬浮液～*
富集比　ratio [grade] of concentration
富集度　grade of concentration, degree of up-grading
富集矿　enriched ore
富集锍[冰铜]【色】concentrated matte
富集率　grade of concentration
富集铅　enriched lead
富集区[带]　enriching section [zone, region]
富集熔炼　concentrating smelting
富集斜面(矿泥的)　jagging board
富集铀　enriched uranium
富镓熔体　【半】Ga rich melt
富金脉　run of gold
富精矿　rich concentrate
富矿(石)　rich [bucked, valuable, premium] ore, high grade ore, direct smelting ore, direct-shipping ore(块) ◇ 手拣～ rich hand-picked ore
富矿操作实践　rich-ore practice
富矿床　high grade deposit
富矿块　direct-shipping ore
富矿烧结矿　high grade ore ore sinter
富勒氏(级配)曲线　Fuller's curve
富硫铋铅矿　heyrovskyite
富硫化物的　sulphide-rich
富硫酸盐矿渣水泥　super-sulphated metallurgical cement
富硫铀矿　sulphide-rich uranium ore
富锍[冰铜]　rich matte
富铝的　allitic
富铝角　alluninum-rich corner
富铝红柱石　(同"莫来石")
富铝土　allite
富马酸 {(:CHCO₂H)₂}　fumaric acid
富煤气　rich [strong] gas
富煤气分配管　rich gas manifold
富煤气总[主]管　rich gas main
富锰铁矿石　manganiferous iron ore
富铌矿　columbium-rich ore
富镍合金　nickel rich alloy
富普尔硬度试验　Foeppl test
富气　unstripped [rich] gas
富铅矿　bing ore
富石灰　fat lime
富钛角[区]【金】titanium-rich corner
富碳区　carbon-rich area
富特式换接电极尖　Foote electrode transition tip
富铁粉(氧乙炔)切割法　iron-rich powder process
富铁黄土　raw sienna
富铁辉石　ferroaugite
富铁角[区]　iron-rich corner ◇ 合金系～*
富铁晶粒　【金】iron-rich grain
富铁矿　high grade iron ore
富铁球团　【团】iron-rich pellets
富铁钨铁　iron-rich ferrotungsten
富铁锌尖晶石 {(Zn, Fe)(Al, Fe)₂O₄}　Kreittonite
富铜低锌黄铜(82 - 87Cu, 余量 Zn)　rich low brass
富铜浮渣　【色】copper-rich dross
富铜基体　copper-rich matrix
富铜渣　【色】copper-rich dross
富铜中间相　copper-rich intermediate phase
富吸热型气体　rich endogas

富锡固溶体	tin-rich solid solution
富锡母合金	tin-rich master alloy
富锡相	tin-rich phase
富锡渣	tin-rich scale, hardhead
富锌粉尘	zinc-rich dust
富锌壳(冷凝器的)	zinc-rich crust
富锌相	【金】zinc-rich phase
富选	separation, beneficiation ◇ 重悬浮液～float sink separation
富选精矿	upgraded concentrate
富选矿石	upgraded ore
富选铁矿	beneficiated iron ore
富氧	oxygen enrichment ◇ 鼓风～
富氧焙烧	oxygen-enriched air roasting
富氧表层	oxygen-enriched skin layer
富氧操作	oxygen-enrichment operation
富氧吹炼	oxygen-enriched air converting
富氧大喷煤	【铁】high pulverized coal injection with oxygen-enriched blast
富氧带	oxygen-rich area
富氧点火烧结工艺	igniting technology with enriched oxygen for sintering
富氧鼓风	enriched blast, oxygen-enriched (air) blast, air enrichment, oxyge-nized air, oxygen enrichment of blast, 【铁】oxy-enriched [oxy-boosted] blast
富氧(鼓风)焙烧	oxygen enriched air roasting, roasting by oxygen-enriched blast
富氧化剂混合物	oxidant-rich mixture
富氧火焰	flame enrichment
富氧空气	oxygenized [O-enriched] air, 【钢】oxygen-enriched air
富氧率	【铁】oxygen enrichment precentage
富氧喷吹	enriched air injection
富氧喷煤(高炉的)	【铁】oxygen-enriched pulverized coal-injection, pulverized coal injection with enriched oxygen, coal injection with oxygen-enriched blast, O_2 enrichment and PCI (pulverized coal injection) operation
富氧喷煤技术	oxygen-enriched coal injection technology
富氧气氛	oxygen-enriched [rich-oxygen] atmosphere
富氧区	oxygen-rich area
富氧烧结	oxygen enrichment sintering
富液	rich solution, pregnant liquor
富液泵槽	pregnant liquor pump tank
富液槽	pregnant liquor tank
富液预热器	rich solution pre-heater
富银壳	silver-rich crust
富铀钛铀矿	lodoanikite
富油	rich oil
富渣	rich slag
富锗的锗硅合金	germanium-rich germanium-silicon alloy
附壁放大器	wall attachment amplifier
附壁效应(射流技术的)	wall effect
附加变形	additional deformation
附加处理	additional treatment
附加磁极	interpole
附加电阻	additional resistance ◇ 伏特计～reductor
附加反射	extra reflections
附加荷载	additional load, superload
附加极绕组	【电】interpole winding
附加(剪)切变(形)	additional shear
附加接点	trailing contact
附加晶格结点	【金】additional lattice point
附加励磁	biasing
附加料[物]	additional charge, adding material
附加强度	additional strength
附加燃烧器	extra burner
附加热(量)	additional [supplementary] heat
附加设备	additional [auxiliary, optional, peripheral] equipment
附加生产能力	(同"补充生产能力")
附加维修	supplementary maintenance
附加物	addend(um), annex, extra, superaddition

附加阳极	supplementary anode
附加阴极(电镀用)	robber
附加阻力	additional resistance
附晶生长	【半】overgrowth
附聚过程	agglomeration process
附聚物	agglomerate
附聚物分散	dispersion of agglomeration
附聚值	agglomerating value
附聚(作用)	agglomeration
附面层元件(射流技术的)	boundary layer amplifier
附属建筑	annex, adjacent accomodation
附属设备	accessory equipment, auxiliaries, auxiliary facilities
附随应力	contingent stress
附铸试棒	cast-on bar
附铸试样	cast-on test piece
附装设施(水道、照明等)	finishings
附着	adherence, adherency, adhering, adhesion, attachment, sticking
附着的气体粒子	attached gas particle
附着功	work of adhesion
附着机理	【理】adhesion mechanism
附着剂	adhesives
附着力	adhesion, adhesional force, cohesive affinity, traction
附着能	energy of attachment
附着能力	cohesiveness
附着气泡	captive bubble
附着强度	adhesive [bond] strength
附着式振捣器	external [attached] vibrator
附着系数	factor of adhesion
附着性	adhesivity, stickiness
附着性能	adhesive property
附着压力	adhesion pressure
附着应力	adhesive stress
附着作用	adhesive action

G g

伽伐尼电池　Galvanic battery [cell]
伽伐尼电流　Galvanic current
伽伐尼电势[位,压]　Galvani potential
钆合金　gadolinium alloy
钆基合金　gadolinium base alloy
钆镓石榴石　Gd-Ga garnet
钆添加合金　gadolinium addition
钆同位素　gadolinium isotope
改变钢号炉次　diverted heat
改变配料　burden change
改建　rebuild, reconstruct, transform, redevelopment
改进　improve(ment), perfection, retrofit, mend
改进的鲍尔·福格尔法　modified Bauer-Vogel process
改进的轧机　revamped mill
改进剂　improver, modifying addition
改进炮铜　modified gunmetal
改进设计　design modification
改进型莫尔－琼斯低锡铅基轴承合金(5Sn, 9—15Sb, 80—86Pb, 0.5Cu)　More-Jones improved alloy
改良拜耳法　【色】modified Bayer process
改良硅酸盐水泥　modified portland cement
改良克罗尔法　【色】modified Kroll process
改良韦斯廷豪斯换接电极头　modified Westinghouse electrode transition tip
改良型蒙乃尔铸造合金　modified Monel metal (MMM)
改善　improvement, perfect, better, mend
改善工程　betterment work
改善加工性能的退火　machinability annealing
改善切削性添加剂　free machining addition, free cutting additives
改型　retrofit
改造　restructuring, revamp, modernization, transform, conversion, renovation, redevelopment
改正　correction, amendment, rectification
改正因数　correction factor
改正值　correction
改正指数　index of correction
改装　repack, conversion
改组　restructuring
概差　probable deviation [error]
概率　probability
概率不确定度　probable uncertainty
概率的　probable, stochastic
概率方程　probability equation ◇二项式~*
概率分布律　probability distribution law
概率分析　probability analysis
概率分析法　stochastic process
概率化　randomization
概率积分　probability integral
概率解释　probability interpretation
概率密度函数　probability density function
概率曲线　probability curve, probable performance curve
概念流程　conceptual flowsheet
概算　general [financial, budgetary] estimate, approximation, 【企】costings
钙{Ca}　calcium ◇含~的 calcareous, calciferous, 含~合金*, 脱[去]~*
钙冰晶石　yaroslavite
钙长石　cristianite
钙磁铁矿　calciferous magnetite
钙钒石　ettrigite
钙钒华　pintadoite
钙钒铜矿　calciovolborthite tyuyamunite
钙钒铀矿　calciocarnotite; tyuyamunite
钙方铁矿　calciowustite
钙粉　calcium fines
钙沸石　poonahlite, scolecite
钙橄榄石　lime-olivine
钙铬矾　bentorite

钙 gai

钙铬榴石{Ca₃Cr₂(SiO₄)₃} uvarovite, uwarowite
钙硅钡合金(脱氧剂) 【钢】calsibar
钙硅铍钇矿 calciogadolinite
钙硅铈镧矿 lessingite
钙硅铈石 lessingite
钙合金 calcium alloy
钙还原 calcium reduction
钙还原四氟化钍法 thorium tetrafluoride-calcium process
钙还原氧化钍法 thorium oxide-calcium process
钙黄绿素 calcein
钙基合金 calcium-base alloy
钙基膨润土 calcium bentonite, southern bentonite(美国)
钙磷铁矿 calcioferrite
钙铝硅合金(10—14Ca,8—12Al,50—53Si,余量Fe) calcium-aluminium-silicon alloy
钙铝硅铁固溶体 calcium and aluminium silicoferrite (SFCA)
钙铝合金 calcium-aluminium alloy ◇卡洛依~*
钙(铝)黄长石{2CaO·SiO₂·Al₂O₃} gehlenite
钙铝榴石{Ca₃Al₂(SiO₄)₃} grossularite
钙镁电气石 uvite
钙镁方柱石 (同"镁黄长石")
钙镁橄榄石{CaO·MgO·SiO₂} monticellite, shannonite
钙镁合金 calcium-magnesium alloy
钙镁磷肥 calcium magnesium phosphate (fertilizer)
钙锰硅包内脱氧剂 calcium-manganese-silicon ladle deoxidizer
钙锰硅脱氧剂合金(17—19Ca,55—60Si,10—14Fe,10—16Mn) calcium-manganese-silicon alloy
钙钠斜长石 labradorite
钙铌钛矿{7(Ca,Ce,Fe,Na₂)O·6TiO₂·Nb₂O₅} dysanalite, dysanalyte

钙铌钛铀矿{Ca₂(Nb,Ta)₂(Ti,U)₂O₁₁} mendeleeffite, mendeleyevite
钙铌钽矿{(Y,Fe,U,Mn,Ca)(Nb,Ta,Sn)₂O₆} hjelmit
钙铌钇铀矿 calciosamarskite
钙镍华 dudgeonite
钙硼合金(脱氧除气用;61B,39Ca) calcium boride
钙铅合金(含0.025—0.04Ca;蓄电池等用) calcium lead (alloy)
钙热还原(法) 【冶】calcium (thermic) reduction, calciothermic reduction
钙砷铅矿 hedyphane
钙砷铀云母{(UO₂)₂As₂O₈·nH₂O(n=8-12)} uranospinite
钙钛矿 perofskite, perovskite
钙钛矿型结构 perovskite structure
钙钛铀矿{(U,Ca)(Nb,Ta,Ti)₃O₉·nH₂O} betafite
钙添加合金 calcium addition
钙铁橄榄石 kirschstainite
钙铁辉石 hedenbergite
钙铁榴石{Ca₃Fe₂(SiO₄)₃} andradite
钙铁石 brown millerite
钙钍黑稀金矿 lyndochite
钙钍石 calciothorite
钙钨矿 scheelite
钙系易切削钢 calcium series free cutting steel
钙霞石 cancrinite
钙斜长石{CaAl₂Si₂O₈} anorthite
钙屑 calcium chip ◇电解~*
钙盐 calcium salt
钙钇铒矿 kainosite
钙钇铍硼硅矿 calcybeborosillite
钙硬度(水的) calcium hardness
钙铀矿 calciouranoite
钙铀钼酸盐 calcurmolite
钙铀云母 autunite
钙质 calc
钙质材料 【建】limy material
钙质的 calcic

钙质集料　calcareous aggregate
钙质膜　calcareous film
钙(质润滑)皂(拉丝用)　calcium [lime-base] soap
盖　cover, lid, cap ◇ 活[可开]~ detachable head, 用钢板~上 implate
盖板　cover(ing) [cap, top] plate, apron, patch, covering flag (铸型的),【焊】strapping plate
盖板对接点焊焊缝　bridge spot weld
盖板对接滚焊焊缝　bridge seam weld(ing)
盖板焊　bridge welding
盖板焊缝　strap seam
盖板加热元件　top plate heating element
盖保岩　cap rock
盖德电离真空计　Gaede's ionization gauge
盖德分子泵　Gaede's molecular pump
盖德高速金属扩散泵　Gaede's high-speed metal pump
盖德回转式真空泵　Gaede-type pump
盖德回转水银真空泵　Gaede's rotary mercury pump
盖德扩散泵　Gaede's diffusion pump
盖革 X 射线钢样分析仪　Geiger steel analyzer
盖革计数器[管]　Geiger counter
盖革计数器衍射仪　Geiger-counter diffractometer
盖革－弥勒计数管　Geiger-Mueller counter, Geiger-Mueller (counter) tube, Gei-ger-Mueller counting tube
盖格－弥勒计数器　Geiger-Mueller counter (G-M)
盖卡洛伊微粉磁铁[盖克洛磁心合金]　Gecalloy
盖利冷冻法(除鼓风水分)　【铁】Gayley process
盖－吕萨克定律　Gay-Lussac's law
盖螺母　box nut
盖螺栓　cover [cap, bonnet] bolt
盖氏铁柄杆菌　Gallionella

盖斯勒管　【理】Geissler tube
盖碳保护　【铁】coal layer protection
盖屋顶　roofing
盖箱　mould cope, top (moulding) box
盖箱地面造型　covered floor moulding
盖箱地面铸型　covered floor mould
盖芯　cover core
盖扎尔处理法(钢包精炼用)　Gazal process
盖罩　covering hood, housing
干氨　dry ammonia
干拌混凝土　dry-mix concrete
干冰　dry ice, solid carbon dioxide
干冰酒精浴　dry ice alcohol bath
干残渣[残留物]　dry residue
干稠度　dry consistency
干磁粉(探伤用)　dry powder
干磁粉检验法　【金】dry method
干大气腐蚀　dry atmoshperic corrosion
干袋等静压制　dry-bag isostatic pressing
干的　dry, moisture-free ◇ 全~ bone dry
干电池　dry battery [cell] ◇ 碱~ alkaline dry cell
干镀锌法　dry galvanizing
干阀避雷器　dry valve arrestor
干法　dry process [method]
干法成型　dry pressing,【耐】dry-press process
干法除鳞[排除氧化皮]　dry-scale disposal
干法处理　dry processing [treatment]
干法淬火　dry quenching
干法分析　dry analysis
干法搅拌的　dry mixed (d.m.)
干法净化　dry purification (提纯), dry cleaning (烟气或煤气的), 氧气转炉烟气~技术"
干法拉拔[拉制]　dry drawing
干法拉丝　dry wire drawing
干法粒化　【铁】dry granulation method
干法粒渣　dry granulated slag
干法喷补混合料　【冶】dry-gun mix

干法氰化　dry cyaniding
干法筛分　dry screening [sieving]
干法收尘　dry dust collection
干法淘选　dry elutriation
干法涂搪瓷　dry process enameling
干法物理处理　dry physical processing
干法洗气　【冶】dry gas cleaning
干法选矿　dry cleaning
干法烟气洗涤　dry fume scrubbing
干法研磨　dry milling
干法冶金　dry process, pyrometallurgy
干法转化法　【色】dryway conversion process
干放射性照相底板的时间常数　time constant of xeroradiographic plate
干粉尘　dry dust
干粉混合机　dry powder blender
干粉末试样[标本]　dry powder specimens
干浮渣　dry dross
干腐蚀　dry corrosion [etching]
干管　【运】collector
干管敷设　main-laying
干辊冷轧精整[光洁度](板材的)　dry-rolled finish
干氦(气)　dry helium
干灰　dry dust
干混　【冶】dry mixing
干混合料　dry mix
干火泥　dried cement
干基(成分,分析)　【焦】dry basis
干精矿　dry concentrate
干精矿料仓　dry concentrate bin
干净滤液　clear filtrate
干夸特(衡量)　dry quart
干矿仓　dry ore bin
干矿石(不含贵金属的矿石)　dry ore
干酪盒式蒸馏釜　【化】cheese box still
干冷(却)　dry cooling
干料　dry matter
干料熔炼　dry charge smelting
干裂　【耐】drying crack
干馏　dry distillation,【焦】carbonization
干镏炉　shale oven
干炉床熔炼　dry hearth smelting
干炉床熔炼技术(铜反射炉的)　dry-hearth technique
干炉底(底吹转炉的)　【钢】dry bottom
干滤器　dry filter
干密度　dry density ◇ 毛体积～dry bulk density
干模铸件　dry castings
干膜润滑剂　dry film lubricant
干磨　dry grinding [milling]
干磨机　dry grinder, dry grinding mill
干摩擦　dry [solid, unlubricated] friction
干摩擦阻尼减振装置　dry friction dampler
干泥渣　dry mud
干黏结强度(造型材料的)　【铸】dry bond (strength)
干碾机　【耐】chaser mill, dry (pan) mill, dry edge-runner mill
干盘轮碾机　dry pan (mill)
干疲劳　dry fatigue
干贫混凝土　dry-lean concrete
干砌(砖)　dry masonry, dry-brick (building)
干汽　dry steam
干强度(造型材料的)　【铸】dry [baked] strength, dry bond
干氢　dry hydrogen
干球　dried ball, dried green pellet
干球强度　dried strength
干球温度　dry bulb temperature
干球温度计　dry bulb thermometer
干扰"0"输出　【计】disturbed zero output
干扰"1"输出　disturbed one output
干扰沉降[落](微粒的)　【选】hindered sedimentation [falling, settling]
干扰沉降分级　【选】hindered settling classification
干扰源　noise [interference] source
干熔剂　dry flux
干熔剂镀锌(钢丝的)　dry galvanizing

干熔剂镀锌法(钢带的) dry-fluxing process
干润滑皂 dry soap
干润滑轴承 dry lubricated bearing
干砂 dry [dried] sand
干砂器 【铸】sand drier
干砂型 【铸】dry [roast] sand mould
干砂型芯 【铸】dry sand core
干砂造型 【铸】dry (sand) moulding
干砂铸型 【铸】dry (sand) mould
干筛 dry screening [sieving]
干射线照相术 dry radiography
干涉 interference, intrusion ◇ 最高阶~",最大值~"
干涉斑点坐标读数 reading of spot coordinates
干涉(测量)膨胀计 interference [interferometric] dilatometer
干涉测量法[测量术,量度学] interferometry
干涉带 interference band [fringe]
干涉法 【理】interference method
干涉球 【理】interference sphere
干涉条纹(光波的) 【理】interference fringe ◇ 明亮~ bright fringe, 莫阿~"
干涉图 interferogram
干涉图像 interference image [figure]
干涉图样[(条纹)花样] 【理】interference [fringe] pattern
干涉物 interferent
干涉物质 interfering substance
干涉系数 interference coefficient
干涉显微镜 interference microscope
干涉显微术 interference microscopy
干涉显微照片 interference micrograph, interferogram
干涉现象 interference phenomenon
干涉相位 interfering phase
干涉效应 interference effect
干涉序[级] 【理】order of interference
干涉仪[干扰计] interferometer
干涉仪测量[测定] 【理】interferometer measurement
干涉仪显微镜 interferometer microscope
干涉应变仪 interferometer strain gauge
干涉硬化 【金】interference [interfering] hardening
干涉作用 interference [hindered] action
干生球 dried green ball [pellet]
干湿交替腐蚀 wet-and-dry corrosion
干湿球温度计 wet-and-dry-bulb thermometer
干蚀 dry corrosion
干式安全[保险]阀 【焊】dry back-pressure valve
干式保护装置 dry-run-protection
干式变压器 dry-type [air-immersed] transformer
干式布袋滤尘器 dry bag house type collector
干式侧砌 【建】dry-on-edge masonry
干式除尘 【冶】dry gas cleaning, dry dust removal
干式除[收]尘器 dry precipitator, dry-type dust collector
干式储气罐[柜] dry [waterless] gasholder
干式磁选 dry magnetic beneficiation [dressing]
干式单相变压器 single-phase dry-type transformer
干式淬火 dry quenching
干式电抗器 dry-type reactor
干式回火 dry tempering
干式回水蒸汽供暖系统 steam heating system with dry return
干式混合机 dry mixer
干式进[装]料 dry feed
干式静电沉淀[电滤]器 dry electrostatic precipitator
干式静电除尘器 dry electrostatic cleaner, dry conttrell
干式绝缘变压器 dry-insulation transformer

干式连续磁场法(探伤) dry continuous field method
干(式)滤器 dry filter
干式煤气脱硫法 【焦】dry-purification process
干式磨机 dry grinding mill
干式碾磨机 pan (grinding) mill
干式喷砂清理 【金】dry sandblasting
干式破碎 dry crushing
干式氰化[渗氰]法 dry cyaniding process
干式熔炼 【冶】dry smelting
干式润滑 dry lubrication
干式筛分 dry screening
干式试金[金银分析](法) dry assay
干式收尘设备[系统] dry-type dust collection system
干式脱硫法 【焦】dry-purification process
干(式)熄焦 coke dry quenching (CDQ), dry cooling
干式熄焦法 dry quenching process
干式洗气机 dry washer
干式旋风除[收]尘器 dry cyclone (collector), rotoclone dry-type dust collector
干式(乙炔)发生器 dry residue(-type) generator, tray-type (acetylene) generator
干式预涂覆 【压】dry precoating
干式真空泵 dry vacuum pump
干式整流器 dry [metallic, contact] rectifier
干式止回阀 【焊】dry back-pressure valve
干式重力除尘[分离]器 dry inertial collector
干式自冷变压器 dry self-cooled transformer
干式自磨 dry autogenous
干水泥 dried cement
干送风高炉 dry-air blast-furnace
干态强度 【铸】dry strength
干态硬度(如砂型) dry hardness
干淘析 dry elutriation
干套模 【粉】dry bag
干填土 dry placed fill

干铁磁粉显示剂 dry-powder developer
干铁鳞抽出系统 dry scale suck off system
干铜 dry copper
干透气度[率] 【铸】dry permeability
干透气性 【铸】baked permeability, dry permeability
干土密度 dry soil density (D.S.D.)
干雾霭 dry fog
干物镜(显微镜的) dry objective
干熄焦 dry quenched coke (DQC), coke dry quenching (CDQ)
干洗法 dry-scrubbing process
干显示剂(显现渗透液用) 【金】dry [nonaqueous] developer
干型 【铸】fired mould
干型砂 【铸】dry sand
干型铸造 【铸】dry sand casting
干性油 【铸】dry(ing) oil
干选 dry dressing
干选煤 dry-cleaned coal
干压 dry pressing
干氩 dry argon
干养护 dry curing
干乙烯基有机合成物涂层抛光机构 baked vinyl organosol finish mechanism
干硬稠度 dry consistency
干硬性混合料 harsh mix
干硬(性)混凝土 【建】hard [dry, stiff, harsh, no-slump] concrete
干油 consistent grease [fat]
干油泵 grease pump ◇ 机动～motorized grease pump, 脚踏～*
干油和稀油润滑系统 grease and oil system
干油盒 grease box
干油集中润滑系统 centralized grease lubricating system
干油集中压力润滑系统 centralized pressure-grease system
干油润滑 grease lubrication
干油润滑系统 grease lubrication system

◇ 中央强制～*

干油压力润滑系统 pressure grease system

干燥 dry(ing), dry-out, dryness, deliquefaction, exsiccation, desiccating, desiccation,【耐】breaking in ◇ 充分[彻底]～intensive drying, 高频～high frequency drying, 鼓风～blast dehydration, 红外线～infrared drying, 绝对～的 bone dry, 流态化床～fluidized bed drying, 炉子～furnace dry out, 调湿～*, 雾化[闪速]～flash drying, 预先～predry

干燥床 hearth drier

干燥带[区] dry(ing) zone

干燥度 dryness, aridity

干燥段 dry section,【团】drying area ◇ 第二～*

干燥段废气 【团】dry zone off-gas

干燥段炉罩 drying hood

干燥段烟气质量比 【团】drying mass ratio

干燥法 drying procedure, desiccation, exsiccation ◇ 弗莱斯尼尔～*

干燥废品 【耐】drying scrap

干燥过程 drying process, dry run

干燥机 drier, dryer, drying machine [apparatus, unit] ◇ 传送带～belt dryer, 带式～*, 对流式～reversed-current drier, 管式～tube [tubular] dryer, 环式[循环]～ring drier, 接触式～contact drier, 立管式～drying column, 模子表面干燥用轻便～devil, 逆流～counterflowdrier, 汽管式[蒸汽管加热]～steam-tube drier, 热风循环～*, 筛式～screen-type dryer, 室式～cabinet drier, 顺流式[平行流]～parallel flow dryer, 塔式～vertical drier, 涡轮式～turbine dryer, 移动炉箅式～*, 预先～predryer, 圆筒[滚筒]～*, 直接加热～direct-heat drier, 转盘式～rotating disk drier, 转筒式汽热～*, 洗刷～组 brush scrubber

干燥机传送带 dryer belt

干燥剂 drying agent, drier, dryer, desiccant, desiccating agent, desiccative

干燥架 drying rack [hurdle], rack drier

干燥间 drying building

干燥介质 drying medium

干燥抗弯强度 drying transverse strength

干燥坑 pit drying stove, hearth drier,【色】drying pit,【耐】hot floor ◇ 机械搅动式～rabbled-hearth drier

干燥空气 dry air [atmosphere]

干燥炉 drying [dryer] furnace, drying [dry-off, baking, treating] oven, drier, dryer ◇ 串级式～cascade drier, 高频～*, 鼓形～drum furnace, 红外线～*, 间歇[分批]式～*, 盘架～*, 室式～*, 输送机式～*, 双筒～twin-drum dryer, 塔式～* tower-type oven, 灶室～cabinet drier

干燥炉膛 drying [drier] hearth

干燥面 dry face,【耐】hot floor

干燥棚 drying shed

干燥器 drier, dryer, desiccator, baker, baking oven, drying unit, exsiccator, moisture eliminator ◇ 回转窑式～rotary-kiln dryer, 架式～rack drier, 搅拌～agitator drier, 精～fine dryer, 空气～blast dryer, 连续式～*, 喷射式～ejector drier, 热风～hot-air (blast) drier, 闪速[瞬时汽化]～flash drier, 雾化～atomizing drier, 箱式～loft dryer, 旋转式[转筒]～revolving drier

干燥气氛 drying atmosphere

干燥气体滤器 dry gas filter

干燥强度 dried strength

干燥球团 dried pellet

干燥曲线 drying curve

干燥缺陷 drying fault

干燥筛选[筛分]镁砂 dry graded magnesite powder

干燥设备 drying equipment [installation] ◇ 联合～*

干燥生球 (同"干生球")

干燥失重 【耐】drying loss
干燥室 drying chamber [building, room, shed], baking oven, chamber [cabinet] drier, chamber for drying ◇ 格板式~ shelf dryer
干燥收缩 drying shrinkage
干燥送风 【铁】dry blast
干燥速度[速率] drying rate
干燥塔 drying tower, tower dryer
干燥筒 drier drum
干燥退火的 dry-annealed
干燥物料[物质] dry matter
干燥箱 dry box, drying cabinet [case], cabinet [loft] drier
干燥效率 drying efficiency
干燥型砂 【铸】dry moulding sand
干燥型芯 【铸】baked core
干燥窑 dry(ing) kiln, drier, dryer, dry-off oven ◇ 坑式~*, 竖式~ vertical drier, 膛式~*
干燥窑收尘器 dryer dust collector
干燥用运输机 drying [dryer] conveyer
干燥制粒器 dryer-pelletizer
干燥装置 drying unit [machine] ◇ 通用~ all-purpose drying unit
干燥状态 dry state
干燥状态硬度(例如砂型) dry hardness
干燥作用 exsiccation
干轧(板、带材的) dry rolling
干蒸汽 dry steam
干重 dry weight
干轴承 dry bearing
干装料 dry charging
甘醇 glycol
甘汞 (同"氯化亚汞") ◇ 胶态~ calomelol
甘汞半电池 calomel halfcell
甘汞电极 calomel electrode ◇ 饱和~*
甘汞基准电极 calomel reference electrode
甘汞矿 calomel
甘酞树脂 glyptal resin
甘油 glycerin(e) (glyc.), glycerol

甘油测氢(试验)法 glycerine hydrogen test
甘油三硝酸酯 (同"硝化甘油")
甘油三硬脂酸酯 (同"硬脂精")
甘油三油酸酯 {(C$_{17}$H$_{35}$COO)$_3$C$_3$H$_5$} triolein
甘油-水溶液 glycerine-water solution
甘油浴(槽) glycerine bath
肝赤铜矿 hepatinerz
肝锌矿 {ZnO·4ZnS} voltzite
坩埚 crucible, copple, crux, firepot, hearth, 【耐】pot, 【冶】saggar, sagger ◇ 衬里[有衬]~*, 大~ king pot, 试金[化验用]~ assay crucible, 水冷~*, 塔曼管状~ Tammann tube, 圆筒形无底~*, 自成~法*
坩埚壁 crucible wall, side wall of crucible
坩埚衬里[内衬] crucible [mould] lining
坩埚底座 crucible stool [pedestal]
坩埚分隔器 crucible separator
坩埚腹部 crucible belly
坩埚盖 crucible cover [lid]
坩埚钢 crucible [pot] steel
坩埚高度调节 hearth height adjustment
坩埚红热处理 【冶】nailing
坩埚(夹)钳 crucible tongs, hawkbill
坩埚架 crucible stool
坩埚焦饼 【焦】coke button
坩埚焦饼试验 coke button test
坩埚金属喷镀法 mellozing
坩埚颈 crucible neck
坩埚矿物分析 crucible assay
坩埚冷却水套 crucible cooling jacket
坩埚(炼钢)法 crucible process
坩埚漏损 crucible leakage
坩埚炉 crucible [pot] furnace, pot fire, potoven, 【冶】fire [melting] hole, pot-hole ◇ 电阻加热~*, 吊耳式~*, 感应加热~*, 固定式~, 井式~ shaft crucible furnace, 坑式~ pit-type crucible furnace, 拉出式~*, 倾动的~ tilting crucible furnace, 燃焦~ coke-fired crucible furnace,

蓄热(式)~*
坩埚炉底　siege
坩埚熔炼　crucible melting [fusion] ◇自凝~arc skull melting
坩埚熔炼炉　crucible melting furnace
坩埚渗碳[碳化]　crucible carburizing
坩埚升出式炉　lift-out crucible-type furnace
坩埚试验(膨胀试验)　crucible test
坩埚台　【冶】crucible pedestal
坩埚提升杆　crucible lifting bar
坩埚推车　crucible trolley
坩埚型电弧炉　crucible-type [hearth-type] arc furnace
坩埚支持器　crucible holder
坩埚中冷却　pot cooling
坩埚铸钢　crucible-cast steel
坩埚装料　crucible charge
坩埚嘴　lip of crucible
坩埚座　crucible holder [support]
矸石　waste rock, gangue, deads, dirt,【选】recrement, trash
矸石手选带　sorting belt, collecting band
杆臂　lever arm
杆材浇铸　rod casting
杆秤　balance beam
杆阀　stem valve
杆件试验　bar test
杆菌　Bacillus sp.
杆密封盖[活塞杆密封盖]　rod-gland
杆式打印机　(type-)bar printer
杆式多点检验器(试验树脂用)　bar type multipoint tester
杆式泥芯撑　stem [stalk-pipe] chaplet
杆式推钢机　ram-type pusher
杆式推料机　peel [ram] discharger ◇简易~bar peel
杆式制动器　lever brake
杆套　rod cover
杆销　rod pin
杆形细菌　rod-shaped bacteria
杆闸　lever brake

杆柱　【采】anchor [tie, truss] bolt
杆状锡粉　sprill tin
杆状组织　bacillar structure
杆座　bar foot
感测电路　sensing circuit
感触器　feeler
感光乳剂　(photographic) emulsion ◇双面涂~胶片 double coated film
感抗　【电】inductive reactance
感扰性　response
感色计　leucoscope
感色灵敏度　colour [chromatic] sensitivity
感生磁通(量)　【理】induced flux
感生电动势　induced e.m.f
感生电动势法　induced emf method
感生电流支架(区域熔炼的)　induced current support
感生放射性　【理】induced [artificial] radioactivity
感生各向异性　【理】induced anisotropy
感受器　susceptor
感受热处理的能力　【金】response to heat treatment
感受性　responsibility, sensitivity
感受元件　pick-up
感性负载　reactive load
感应泵　induction pump
感应部件　【电】induction block
感应槽(感应电炉的)　induction channel
感应测试仪　◇费拉里~Ferraris instrument
感应敞熔(法)　air induction melting
感应传感器　induction sensor
感应磁强计　induction magnetometer
感应磁通量　magnetic induction flux
感应淬硬机理　mechanism of induction hardening
感应地磁仪　induction magnetometer
感应点焊机　induction spot welder
感应电动机　induction motor (IM) ◇绕线式~*, 鼠笼型~*, 同步化~*, 线性

~ linear induction motor
感应电荷 induced [inducting] charge
感应电弧炉 induction arc furnace
感应电流 induction [faradic] current
感应电流搅动 induced current stirring
感应(电)炉 (electric) induction furnace, induction electric furnace, induc-tance furnace ◇ 艾杰克斯~*，槽型~*，电解~*，费兰蒂~*【冶】Ferranti furnace, 弗里克~Frik furnace, 环形~*，科尔比~Colby furnace, 可倾式~*，克杰林~【冶】Kjellin furnace, 射频~*，水冷坩埚~*，水平环槽~horizontalring furnace, 提升线圈式~*，铁芯[有芯]~*，无芯~*
感应电炉钢 electric induction steel (E.I.S.), induction furnace steel
感应电路 induced [inductive, induction] circuit
感应电桥式流量计 induction-bridge flowmeter
感应电热硬钎焊 induction brazing
感应电压 induced voltage
感应发电机 induction generator
感应焊管机 induction weld mill
感应焊接法 induweld process
感应焊接机 electromagnetic stored-energy welder
感应加热 induction [inductive] heating
感应加热变流器 work heat transformer
感应加热表面淬火【金】induced heat surface hardening
感应加热[热爆]除鳞 descaling by induction heating
感应加热淬火【金】induction hardening [quenching] ◇ 顺序~
感应加热淬火设备 induction hardening equipment [plant]
感应加热电流 inductive heating current
感应加热电路 induction-heating circuit
感应加热坩埚炉 induction crucible furnace

感应加热焊管 induction weld pipe
感应(加热)焊接 induction welding (IW)
感应(加热)回火【金】induction tempering
感应加热机械设备 induction-heating machinery
感应加热炉 induction-heated furnace ◇ 卧式~*
感应加热器 induction heater, induction heating apparatus
感应加热区域精炼 induction-heated zone-refining
感应加热熔炼【冶】induction melting
感应加热熔炼炉 induction melting furnace
感应加热筛分机 induction-heated screen
感应加热烧结 induction sintering
感应加热设备 induction-heating equipment [installation]
感应加热退火【金】induction annealing
感应加热线圈 induction heating coil ◇ 多匝扁平~*，工频电流~line-frequency coil
感应加速器 induction accelerator ◇ 电子~betatron
感应搅拌 (同"电磁感应搅拌")
感应搅拌电炉 induction stirred furnace
感应搅拌熔体 inductively-stirred melt
感应炉 (同"感应电炉")
感应炉明沟【色】open channel
感应炉熔炼的钛 induction melted titanium
感应炉生铁矿石炼钢法 ◇ 坦纳~Tanna process
感应率 inductivity
感应器 inductor ◇ 扫描[可动]~scanning inductor
感应器线圈 inductor coil
感应器组件 inductor blocks
感应钎焊 induction brazing (IB), induction soldering
感应区域熔炼 induction zone melting
感应圈磁强计[地磁仪] coil magnetome-

感应燃烧器　induction burner
感应热处理　induction heat-treatment
感应熔化离心铸造设备　induction melting and centrifugal casting assembly
感应软钎焊　induction soldering
感应软熔处理　induction reflow
感应烧结　induction sintering
感应式传感器　inductosyn, inductive sensor
感应式传感器倾斜计　inductosyn droop meter
感应式传感器倾斜警报　inductosyn droop alarm
感应式电子加速器　【理】induction electron accelerator
感应式位移传感器　inductive displacement transducer
感应式仪表　induction-type instrument, Ferraris instrument
感应探测器[探头]　inductive probe
感应体　【电】induction block, inductor
感应系数　induction coefficient
感应线　line of induction [influence]
感应(线)圈　induction [inductor] coil ◇ 特斯拉～Tesla coil
感应线圈效率　coil efficiency
感应硬钎焊　induction brazing
感应制动器　induction brake
橄榄蛇纹岩　perido-steatite
橄榄石　olivine {(Mg, Fe)SiO$_4$}, peridot (ite){(Mg, Fe)$_2$SiO$_4$}
橄榄石-尖晶石型转变　olivine spinel transition
橄榄石矿砂　olivine sand
橄榄石耐火材料　olivine refractory
橄榄铜矿　olivenite
冈奈特钢性[可锻]铸铁　Gunite
冈奈特K可锻铸铁(2.3C, 1Si, 0.7Mn, 0.15P, 0.08S)　Gunite K
刚度　rigidity, stiffness ◇ 动～dynamic rigidity, 抗弯～bending rigidity

刚度试验机　stiffness tester
刚度系数　specific stiffness
刚化金属(板)　rigidized metal
刚化纹理钢　rigid-tex steel
刚接　rigid connection
刚铝石[玉]{纯 Al$_2$O$_3$}　alundum, aloxite
刚铝石粉　alumdum powder
刚凝固体　just-freezing solid
刚柔性引锭杆　【车铸】rigid and flexible dummy bar
刚砂{Al$_2$O$_3$}　emery
刚砂块　emery brick
刚石　diamond spar, corundum
刚塑性有限元法　rigid-plastic finite element method
刚体　rigid body
刚性　rigidity, stiffness, inflexibility ◇ 轧材～部分
刚性部件　rigid part
刚性材料　rigid material
刚性分子　rigid molecule
刚性钢筋　rigid reinforcement [armouring]
刚性箍筋　stiffening hooping ◇ 安置～
刚性固定　rigid fixing [fastening]
刚性固定结晶器　rigidly mounted mould
刚性辊　rigid roll ◇ 理想～unflattened roll
刚性机座　stiff stand
刚性加固[强]　stiffening
刚性加强筋　rigid reinforcement
刚性剪切模量　rigidity shearing modulus
刚性结点　rigid joint
刚性结构　rigid construction [structure]
刚性结构装料机　【冶】rigi-type charging machine
刚性拘束抗裂试验　rigid restrain cracking test
刚性连接　rigid [fixed] joint
刚性模量[数]　rigidity modulus
刚性能带模型　【金】rigid band model
刚性区域　【压】rigid region

刚性-塑性区界限(变形区的) rigid-plastic boundary
刚性位错 rigid dislocation
刚性位错越过障碍攀移 climb of rigid dislocation over obstacles
刚性位移 rigid displacement
刚性系数 rigidity [stiffness] coefficient, modulus of rigidity
刚性线 rigid line
刚性原子 rigid atom
刚性装配 rigid binding
刚性状态 hard mode
刚玉｛纯 Al_2O_3｝ alundum, corundum, boule, adamantine [diamond] spar, emery ◇ 电熔[熔融]～ fused alumina, 结晶～ crystal corundum, 卢卡洛克斯～[耐] Lucalox, 普通～ common corundum
刚玉粉 pulverized corundum, alundum powder, emery (powder, flour), smergal
刚玉坩锅 corundum crucible
刚玉管炉 alundum furnace
刚玉管马弗炉 alundum tube muffle furnace
刚玉绝缘体 alundum insulator
刚玉管 alundum tube
刚玉马弗炉管 alundum tube muffle
刚玉磨料 aloxite
刚玉-莫莱石制品 [耐] corundum-mullite product
刚玉砂布 emery cloth
刚玉砂带 emery fillet
刚玉砂轮 emery cutter [wheel, disc, stone]
刚玉砂磨床 emery grinder, emery grinding machine
刚玉砂纸 emery paper
刚玉烧舟 alundum boat
刚玉石 emery stone
刚玉砖 corundum brick
钢 steel (st.) ◇ IF～ interstitial-free steel, Z形～*, 奥氏体～*, 半镇静[半脱氧]～*, 贝氏体～ bainitic steel, 超高强度～ extra-high tensile steel, 冲模～ blanking steel, 粗[原]～*, 低级～ dry steel, 底吹碱性转炉[托马斯]～ Thomas steel, 反常(组织的)～ abnormal steel, 沸腾～*, 高硫～ high sulphur steel, 过吹～ overblown steel, 过还原～ over-reduced steel, 过烧～*, 号外～ off-grade metal, 合成～ synthetic steel, (化学)成分特别精确的～ precision steel, 加铅～ leaded steel, 加特种元素的～(如加硼等) treated steel, 金刚石[极硬]～ extra-hard steel, 耐大气腐蚀～*, 耐碱～*, 耐酸～*, 泡面[疤]～ blister steel, 硼强化～ boron intensified steel, 普通[大量生产的]～ tonnage steel, 全～的 all-steel, 烧结～ cemented steel, 渗铝～*, 渗铜～*, 石墨化～ graphitizable steel, 双相～ dual phase steel, 似～的 steely, 特软～*, 特优～ extra-fine steel, 退火～ annealed steel, 脱氧～*, 无气泡～ blister free steel, 压盖[封顶]～ capped steel, 氧气(吹炼的)～ oxygen steel, 液态挤压[加压凝固]～ liquid compressed steel, 易切削[自动机床用]～*, 殷～*, 镇静～*, 直接还原～ direct-process steel
钢安全日 steel pad
钢板 (steel) plate, sheet iron ◇ 镀铜～ copper plated steel, 复合[夹层]～*, 黑～(未镀的), 经磷酸盐处理的～ bonderized sheet, 炉子配件[附件]～[冶] bucking plate, 耐蚀～*, 内衬－砖*, 热浸镀铝～ aludip, 塑料涂层～*, 搪瓷～*, 凸点～ button plate, 涂珐琅～ enamelled iron, 瓦垄[波纹]～ corrugated steel (plate), 网纹～*, 用～盖上 implate, 油浸过的镀铅锡合金的～ oil finished terne-plate
钢板测厚仪 steel plate thickness meter
钢板衬背 sheet backing
钢板衬里 steel plate lining
钢板磁力分垛机 magnet-crane depiler
钢板吊车 plate [sheet-iron] crane

钢板镀覆用铅锡合金　tin terne alloy
钢板厚度　plate thickness
钢板厚度计　rolling mill gange, sheet-iron gange
钢板厚度自动分选机　automatic-gauge classifier
钢板剪切机　plate shears [shearing machine]
钢板精确剪切　【压】resquaring
钢板精整机　(同"板材精整机")
钢板壳体　sheet steel housing
钢板黏结　【压】sticking of sheets
钢板坯　plate slab
钢板平整[矫平]机　(同"板材矫正机")
钢板翘曲(缺陷)　camber of sheet
钢板切边　swarf
钢板热矫正机　hot plate straightening machine
钢板热渗铝　Aludip
钢板深拉试验机　◇埃里克森～*
钢板弹簧　plate spring ◇汽车悬挂～ suspended leaf spring
钢板外壁　outer steel plate wall
钢板弯折　dings
钢板运输机　plate transfer
钢板轧机　plate mill ◇可逆式～ reversing plate mill
钢板轧机机座　plate mill stand
钢板轧机组　【压】plate rolling train
钢板轧辊　plate mill roll
钢板轧制　(steel) plate rolling
钢板闸门　steel plate gate
钢板重量自动分选机　automatic-weight classifier
钢板桩　steel sheet pile, piling beam [bar] ◇Z形(断面)[乙字]～ Z-(type) piling bar, 带锁口的～ lock sheet piling bar, 带正反锁口的～ reverse-lock sheet piling bar, 拉森式～ Larssen's sheet piling, 直股～ straight web piling bar
钢板自动移动装置　automatic plate shifting device

钢棒　steel bar, iron pin (铝电解槽的) ◇光亮～*, 黑～ black bar
钢棒测温法　【钢】rod test for temperature
钢包　(steel, casting, Bessemer) ladle ◇出钢用～ tap(ping)ladle, 大～ bull ladle, 底注～*, 虹吸式～ siphon(-type) ladle, 浇注用～ teeming ladle, 喷补～ gunned ladle, 塞棒－塞座式～*, 砖砌～ brick ladle
钢包壁　ladle wall
钢包操作工　ladle operator
钢包操作平台　ladle operation platform
钢包车　ladle bogie [car, truck], buggy ladle
钢包衬　ladle lining
钢包衬砖　ladle brick ◇通用～ universal ladle brick
钢包处理　ladle treatment
钢包处理设备　ladle treatment facility
钢包处理站　ladle treatment station
钢包翻倒[倾斜]　ladle tipping
钢包翻倾装置　ladle tilter, ladle tilting facility
钢包翻转机　ladle tripper
钢包放出渣　ladled slag
钢包盖　ladle cover [lid]
钢包(钢水)容量　ladle capacity, ladleful
钢包管理系统　ladle management system
钢包合金料添加器　ladle feeder
钢包烘烤装置　ladle dryer, ladle drying system
钢包回转架　【连铸】merry-go-round
钢包回[旋]转台　ladle turret ◇连杆式～ lindage ladle turret
钢包加料槽　ladle additions chute [bunker]
钢包加热设备　ladle heating plant
钢包浇注口[钢包嘴]　ladle spout [lip]
钢包浇注时间　ladle pouring time
钢包精炼　ladle refining
钢包精炼炉　ladle refining furnace
钢包坑　ladle pit

钢 gang

钢包空包时间　ladle emptying time
钢包炉　ladle furnace, furnace ladle ◇ 等离子体～plasma ladle furnace,直流～DC ladle furnace
钢包内衬　ladle liner
钢包内衬修砌工段　hot metal ladle relining shop
钢包内衬修砌台　ladle-lining table
钢包砌衬场　ladle bricking station
钢包砌衬修理　ladle rebricking
钢包倾翻时间　ladle-reversal time
钢包热修衬　hot preparation of ladle
钢包容量　ladle capacity
钢包塞棒　ladle stopper
钢包砂　burning-in
钢包水口[砖]　ladle nozzle
钢包台　teeming ladle stand
钢包添加剂料仓　ladle additions bunker
钢包调整绞车　ladle-positioning winch
钢包停车场　ladle yard
钢包涂料　ladle wash
钢包脱硫　ladle desulphurization
钢包喂线技术　ladle wire-feeding technique
钢包外壳　ladle shell
钢包性能　ladle performance
钢包修理库　ladle-repair shop
钢包冶金　ladle metallurgy (LM)
钢包冶金设备　ladle metallurgy facility
钢包冶金站　ladle metallurgy station
钢包运输[输送]车　casting teeming ladle transfer car, steel transfer car
钢包渣　ladle slag
钢包罩式精炼法　ladle hood refining process
钢包真空处理设备[装置]　ladle degassing plant
钢包支座　ladle stand
钢包砖衬　ladle brickwork
钢包砖衬修理坑　teeming ladle reline pit
钢包准备场　ladle preparation station
钢包座架　ladle support [stool, trestle, chair]
钢背[衬板]　steel backing
钢背板　steel backing plate
钢背铅青铜　◇ 克利瓦特～*
钢背轴承合金　steel-backed bearing alloy [metal]
钢笔型剂量计　pen-type dosimeter
钢表面堆焊　steel facing
钢表面磷酸盐浸镀法　◇ 富尔纳～Foolner process
钢表面清理[修整]　steel conditioning
钢材　rolled steel [products, iron], steel ◇ 复合～bimetal,冷拔～cold-drawn steel,菱形～diamonds,普通～common iron,轻型～*,商品～merchant shape,小截面[薄壁]～light material,小型～light shape,再轧[利废]～*,周期断面～deformed steel bar
钢材打印跨　marking bay
钢材堆垛跨　piling bay
钢材分选装置　grader
钢材合格率　ratio of good rolled steel
钢材加工服务中心协会(美国)　Steel Service Center Institute
钢材均整机　steel straightening and leveling machine
钢材品种　rolling shapes
钢材清理机组　cleaning unit
钢材取样块　test piece
钢材优质值($Q=$抗张强度$\times$延伸率)　merit number
钢材轧后工厂退火　mill anneal
钢材轧机　ferrous rolling mill
钢槽　steel tank ◇ 衬胶[橡胶衬里]～rubber-lined steel tank
钢厂　steel plant [works], steelmaker ◇ 短流程～mini-mill
钢成分　composition of steel
钢匙　steel spoon
钢尺　steel rule(r)
钢带　steel strip [band, tape, strap] ◇ 超低碳罩～*,打包～*,极平～dead flat

strip,搪瓷[涂珐琅]~ enamell(ed) strip

钢带缠绕机 taping machine

钢带打尾(故障) strip tail side shaking

钢带卷吊运工具 【压】hupender

钢带宽展 【压】spreading of strip

钢带裙式运输机 steel belt-apron conveyer

钢带热轧机 (同"带钢热轧机")

钢带运输机 steel-band conveyer

钢带轧机 (同"带钢轧机")

钢带张力测量装置 strip tension measuring unit

钢带张力控制 strip tension control

钢带自动矫直机 (同"带材自动平整机")

钢弹(还原钢弹) bomb ◇ 反应~*,气密还原~【色】gas-tight bomb,密闭~反应器 closed bomb reactor

钢弹还原的金属块 bomb reduced biscuit

钢弹还原法 bomb (reduction) process

钢弹还原炉 bomb furnace ◇ 煤气外热~ gas-fired bomb furnace

钢导电棒 steel collector (bar), steel contact

钢导管弯曲装置 steel conduct bending device

钢的生产(包括加工) steel manufacture

钢的时效 steel ageing

钢的氧化气氛加热 barking

钢的铸造 steel casting (SC)

钢锭 (steel) ingot, ingot (cast) steel ◇ 薄皮~ thin-skinned ingot,带保温帽的~ hot topped ingot,带有框形帽头缺陷的~ box hat ingot,锻造用~ forging ingot,多棱~*,多气孔~ blown ingot,封顶~*,过热~ bony ingot,过烧~ burned ingot,开裂~ clinked ingot,开坯~ broken down ingot,空心~ hollow ingot,漏钢~ bleeding ingot,冒顶~ bleeding ingot,实心~ solid steel ingot,特定规格~ specifi-cation ingot,五层~*,压含~(美) stuck ingot,异型~ shaped ingot,有裂纹的~ dry ingot,有气泡~ bleb ingot

钢锭凹面 ingot flute

钢锭扒皮床 ingot plaing madine

钢锭扒皮[剥皮,修整]机床 peeling [ingot-scalping] machine

钢锭表层组织 subsurface ingot structure

钢锭表层外部 【钢】outer rim

钢锭底部漏钢(下注时) bottom bleeder

钢锭顶部电加热保温法 kellog (hot-top) method

钢锭堆 sheaf

钢锭回转台 turnaround machine

钢锭回转装置 (同"钢锭转盘")

钢锭加热炉 ingot heating furnace

钢锭浇铸平台 ingot casting platform

钢锭结疤 scab

钢锭精整 ingot conditioning

钢锭均热 pit soaking

钢锭开坯法 【压】blocking process

钢锭冷却箱(电子束熔炼的) ingot cooling can

钢锭裂纹 ingot crack

钢锭冒顶 ingot bleeding

钢锭帽 box-hat

钢锭模 (ingot, steel, iron, block) mould ◇ 波型壁~ rippled mould,敞口~ open-top mold,带保温帽的~ hot top (ped) mould,多角形~ polygonal mould,开底式~ open-bottom mould,可抽式~ retractable ingot mould,上大下小~*,上小下大~*,实底~ closed bottom mould,脱锭~ off-loading mould,无底~ open-ended mould,有底塞的~ plug bottom ingot mould,铸铁~ cast iron mould

钢锭模车 ingot mould car, mould buggy [car]

钢锭模底板 ingot mould bottom plate, ingot mould stool

钢锭模涂料 mould coating material, mould dressing

钢锭模涂油 mould coating, casting oiling

钢锭模斜度[锥度] slenderness ratio

钢 gang

钢锭凝固 ingot solidification [freezing]
钢锭剖面图像 ingot pattern
钢锭切槽机 slicer
钢锭切割[分]机 (ingot-)slicing machine
钢锭切头 ingot-crop end, butt ingot
钢锭清理[整修] ingot conditioning
钢锭缺陷 ingot defect
钢锭生产能力 ingot capacity
钢锭头部上涨 overfill in external pipe
钢锭脱模工段 stripping room
钢锭脱模机 ingot puller
钢锭外壳 ingot skin
钢锭外皮 exterior part of ingot
钢锭修整 dressing of steel ingot
钢锭压盖 【钢】ingot cap
钢锭渣皮[浮渣] ingot scum
钢锭折断机(车轮轮辋用) ingot breaker
钢锭折断压力机 ingot-breaker press
钢锭转盘 【压】ingot turner, ingot turning device
钢锭装炉起重机 【压】ingot charging crane
钢锻件 steel forging ◇ "日制钢～热处理法 Niseko Process
钢发蓝处理 steel bluing
钢分类仪(电磁式) steel sorter ◇ 电磁～*
钢粉 comminuted steel shot ◇ 铝热焊接用～*, 破碎～*
钢坩埚 steel crucible
钢格构桁架 steel lattice truss
钢构件 steel member
钢箍 steel hoop [tie], tyre seating (钢锭模的)
钢骨架建筑 steel skeleton building
钢骨架坯块 steel skeleton compact
钢固体渗碳硬化(法) harveyizing
钢管 steel pipe [piping, tube, tubing] ◇ API 标准～*, 承压～ pressure-resistant pipe, 带翅[加肋]～ finned steel tube, 单体液压支柱～*, 镀锌～ galvanized steel pipe, 高(抗拉)强度～ high tensile steel tube, 焊接～*, 挤压～ extruded pipe, 精密～ precision steel pipe, 离心铸造～材*, 双层卷焊～*, 无缝～*, 轴承～ ball bearing tubing
钢管倒角[倒棱]机 pipe chamfering machine
钢管吊架 pipe saddle
钢管定径拉拔法 【压】plug drawing
钢管对焊法 ◇ 林德—Linde welding
钢管镦厚机 tube upsetting machine
钢管翻边[凸缘]机 pipe flanging machine
钢管工艺试验(总称) 【压】manipulation
钢管辊拔法 【压】roller die drawing process for steel pipe
钢管焊接机 pipe-welding machine
钢管减径 【压】tube reducing
钢管矫直机 pipe straightener (machine), tube straightening machine[press] ◇ 旋转式～*
钢管矫直压力机 tube straightening press
钢管结构 steel-pipe construction
钢管空拔 【压】tube sink drawing
钢管扩展压力机 tube expanding press
钢管内壁检查镜 borescope
钢管内径圆棒检查法 rodding
钢管切头机 pipe cropping machine
钢管水银温度计 mercury-in-steel thermometer
钢管托辊 tubular steel idler
钢管压扁机 pipe crushing machine
钢管轧后余热淬火工艺 direct quenching technology of steel
钢管张拉[拉伸]矫直机 tube stretching machine
钢管张力减径机 (同"管材张力减径机")
钢管桩 steel pipe pile ◇ 焊接～*
钢罐 steel can
钢轨 (steel, railroad) rail ◇ Z形～ zee-rail, 电车～ grooved rail, 环形[圆形]～*, 抗磨～ anvil faced rail, 平底～ flat bottom rail, 桥形～ bridge rail, 双头～*,

在线热处理~*

钢轨标志 rail brand

钢轨表面剥落 shelling of rail

钢轨垫板 bearing plate bars, tie-plate bar, sole plate

钢轨垫板轧机 tie-plate mill

钢轨顶面索氏体化法[森德贝格钢轨顶面余热淬火法]【压】Sandberg sorbitized process

钢轨端面铣床 rail-ending machine, rail-end-milling machine

钢轨断面 rail section [profile]

钢轨钢 rail steel

钢轨检验器 rail tester

钢轨矫直－精整机组 rail conditioning unit

钢轨矫直机 rail straightener, rail-straightening machine

钢轨接头 rail joint ◇ 阿博特~ Abbott rail joint

钢轨接头轨枕 joint tie

钢轨锯(切机) rail saw, rail sawing machine

钢轨孔型 rail pass

钢轨扣件 rail fastening

钢轨(落锤试验机) rail breaker

钢轨切分轧机 rail-slitting millting mill

钢轨切头 rail butts

钢轨头 head of rail

钢轨弯曲(压力)机 (同"弯轨机")

钢轨轧机 rail mill

钢轨轧机组 【压】rail mill train

钢轨轧制系统 rail rolling sequence

钢轨枕 steel sleeper [tie]

钢轨正火法 ◇ 布伦纳~*

钢轨支柱 rail upright

钢轨铸焊接头 cast-welded rail joint

钢轨自动埋弧电渣焊 automatic submerged slag welding of rail

钢辊 steel roll ◇ 实心~ solid steel roll

钢焊条 ferrous electrode

钢号 steel grade,【钢】type number ◇ 改变~炉次*, 美国汽车工程师学会~标准*

钢护面机架 steel-armo(u)red housing

钢化玻璃 armoured glass ◇ 赫尔克莱特~ Herculite

钢化学成分 composition of steel

钢化作用 steeling

钢灰色金属 steel-gray metal

钢加蓝 bluing of steel

钢加强铝合金导线 aluminum alloy conductor steel reinforced (AACSR)

钢架坯块 steel skeleton compact

钢鉴别仪 steel sorter

钢件表面贴金法 Damascening

钢绞线 steel strand, strand (wire) ◇ 镀锌~*

钢绞线层(预应力混凝土) layer of strands

钢绞线热处理 strand heat treatment

钢绞线芯(钢丝绳的) strand core

钢洁净度 steel cleanliness

钢结构 steel structure (SS), steel construction, steelwork, structural steel-work

钢结构安装吊车 steel erecting crane

钢结构框架 structural steel frame

钢结硬质合金 steel bonded carbide, steel bond hard alloy

钢结硬质合金刀具 steel bonded carbide tool

钢筋 reinforced [reinforcing] bar, rebar, reinforcement concrete [core] iron, reinforcement metal, ribmet (竹节钢、螺纹钢等),【建】carcase, carcass ◇ 粗~ bar reinforcement, 带钩[弯钩]~ bar with hooked ends, 单向~ one-way reinforcement, 地脚~ anchoring accesso-ries, 分布~ distributing bars, 光面~*, 横向~ lateral reinfor-cement, 加双重~ double armouring, 架立[分布]~ spacing bar, 交替~ alternate bar, 冷轧带肋~ cold rolled ribbed bar, 连接~ connection bar, 螺纹~*, 配力~ distribution rod, 热轧带肋

~*,受力~*,特弯特短~*,弯~*,无节~*,斜(置)[弯起]~*,轧制~的孔型[轧槽] deforming groove,周期断面~ deformed bar,竹节~*

钢筋比率 ratio of reinforcement
钢筋表 bending list [schedule]
钢筋材料 【建】reinforced material
钢筋钢 concrete steel
钢筋箍 stirrup
钢筋混凝土 reinforced concrete (R.C.), steel concrete, ferroconcrete ◇ 环氧覆面~模*
钢筋混凝土墩 reinforced concrete pier
钢筋混凝土工程 reinforced concrete work
钢筋混凝土构造 reinforced concrete construction
钢筋混凝土管 【建】reinforced concrete pipe (R.C.P.)
钢筋混凝土建筑 concrete-steel construction
钢筋混凝土结构 reinforced concrete structure (R.C.S.), concrete-steel construction ◇ 劲性~*,整体式[现浇式]~*
钢筋混凝土梁 【建】concrete beam
钢筋混凝土模(爆炸冲压用) reinforced concrete die
钢筋混凝土托梁 reinforced concrete girder [pier]
钢筋混凝土用钢筋 concrete reinforcement steel
钢筋剪[切]断机 bar cropper [cutter]
钢筋截面面积 area of reinforcement, area of steel
钢筋埋入长度 embedded length of bar
钢筋面积比 steel area ratio
钢筋排列 arrangement of reinforcement
钢筋图 reinforcement drawing
钢筋弯曲机 angle-bender ◇ 动力~ power bar bender
钢筋弯[挠]曲器 bar bender

钢筋网 mesh reinforcement, (bar) mat reinforcement
钢筋网用线材 mesh grade [quality] wire rod
钢筋轧机 reinforcing bar mill
钢筋支座 bar chair
钢筋质量认证局(英国) Certification Authority for Reiforced Steel (CARES)
钢紧固件 steel fastener
钢锯 hack saw
钢卷 coil of strip ◇ 塔形~(卷取缺陷) telescoped coil
钢卷包装机 coiled steel wrapper
钢卷尺 【机】steel tape [strap]
钢卷吊钩 coil grab
钢卷检查站 coil inspection station
钢卷宽度自动对中装置 automatic coil width centering unit
钢卷钳 coil tongs ◇ 电动~ electric coil tongs,自锁~*
钢卷推送装置 coil pusher equipment
钢壳 steel casing [body]
钢壳电解槽 steel cell
钢壳混凝土桩 steel-shelled concrete pile, cased pile
钢框架 steel superstructure
钢框架结构 steel-frame construction
钢盔 helmet
钢缆 wire cable, wirerope, guy
钢冷却壁 steel stave
钢粒(机械粉碎的) comminuted steel shot
钢梁 steel beam, girder steel,【建】girder ◇ L形~ ell-beam, T形~ flange beam, Z形~【压】zee beam,格雷式~ Grey girder,滚轧工字形小~ rolled I-section joist,焊接轻量~*
钢梁剪切机 【压】joist shears
钢梁孔型 【压】girder pass
钢梁轧机 beam (rolling) mill, structural mill ◇ 宽缘~ wide-flange beam mill,普培式万能~ Puppe mill,万能式~ univer-

sal beam mill
钢梁轧机机组 girder mill train
钢梁轧机机座 structural stand
钢流 flow of steel
钢流保护法 【连铸】shielding practice
钢流聚中[调中,瞄心]控制 stream centering control
钢流密封 【连铸】strand seal
钢流脱气设备 stream degassing plant
钢流氩气保护 impact method
钢流(真空)脱气 stream degassing
钢流自动调中控制 automatic stream centering control
钢铝线 steel-aluminium conductor
钢模 steel die
钢坯 billet steel (BTST), steel feed, 【冶】billet ◇ 大～ cogged bloom, 锻制～ blocking, 空心～ hollow billet
钢坯剥皮机 billeteer
钢坯抽取 extraction of billet, billet withdrawal
钢坯感应加热炉 induction-heated billet furnace
钢坯加热炉 billet (re)heating furnace ◇ 推料式～ *
钢坯剪切机 billet [block] shears
钢坯框座 billet cradle
钢坯拉出 【连铸】withdrawal of section
钢坯冷床 billet racks
钢坯气动定心 air hammer
钢坯切口 billet necking
钢坯清理装置 billet chipper
钢坯烧剥器 scarfer
钢坯输出辊道 billet discharge conveyer
钢坯推出机 billet pusher
钢坯-型钢剪切机 billet and bar shears
钢坯修磨机 steel billet conditioning machine
钢坯修整机组 cleaning unit
钢坯轧辊 billet roll
钢坯轧机 billet mill
钢坯连轧机组 billet rolling train

钢坯自动堆垛机 billet unscrambler
钢皮砖 steel-clad brick
钢瓶 steel cylinder
钢瓶运输车 cylinder truck
钢瓶运输小车 cylinder trolley
钢铺层(用钢轨、钢管铺成) metal skid
钢-气相直接反应(转炉的) 【钢】direct metal-gas reactions
钢钎 bull-prick, drill rod ◇ 开炉日用～ tapping rod
钢潜在最大硬度 potential maximum hardness of steel
钢切屑 steel cuttings
钢琴丝 picano wire
钢青铜 steel bronze
钢球 steel ball, ball (硬度试验机用) ◇ 车制的～ turned ball, 滚磨用～ tumb-ling ball
钢球成形压力机 ball forming machine
钢球顶锻机 ball header
钢球内应力 internal stress in steel ball
钢球抛光 ball burnishing
钢球式砂型硬度计 autopunch
钢球轧机 ball rolling mill
钢球轧制 ball rolling
钢圈轧机 ring rolling mill
钢熔池 steel bath
钢软化 softening of steels
钢散热片 steel fins
钢砂 steel shot [grit]
钢生产商协会(美国) Steel Manufacturers Association
钢绳落锤 drop rope hammer
钢绳起重机[绞车] rope hoist
钢绳松弛开关 slack cables switch
钢绳铁 cable iron
钢绳拖斗 cable-drawn scoop
钢水 molten [liquid] steel, liquid [hot] metal ◇ 精炼期～finishing metal
钢水包[罐] (同"钢包")
钢水保温罐 holding ladle
钢水池 steel bath

钢水浇注台 hot metal pouring stand
钢水静压力 ferrostatic pressure
钢水连铸板带材直接轧制法 ◇哈彻莱特~*
钢水面 【冶】heel of metal
钢水凝固 steel solidification
钢水氢化物脱硫法 ◇斯莫里~Smalley process
钢水试样 hot metal sample
钢水脱氧(使钢镇静) 【钢】killing
钢水预处理 hot metal pretreatment
钢水运输车 hot metal transfercar
钢水运输线 hot metal track
钢水再污染 molten steel secondary pollution
钢水真空脱气 steel degassing
钢水最终化学成分 final metal analysis
钢丝 (steel) wire, string wire ◇绑接~*,包层[复层]~ clad wire,包铝~*,表面[外层]~(钢丝绳的) crown wire,表面有摺痕的~ slivery wire,超低碳~ charcoal wire,超级制绳~*,刺~*,粗拔~*,淬火弹簧~ chilled spring wire,打包~*,单次或两次拉拔的~ soft-drawn wire,低电阻~*,低碳~ iron wire,点尖用~*,电镀锌~*,镀锌~*,多次拉拔[强拉]~*,发蓝~*,辐条~*,光亮~*,黑(退火)~*,几股~ply,金属喷镀~ spray wire,矩形~ rectangular wire,开口铆钉用~*,捆扎用~*,冷镦~*,冷拉~*,磷酸盐处理的~ phosphating steel wire,六角~ hexagonal wire,能在硫酸铜溶液中浸渍一分钟的~ one minute wire,铅淬火~ patented steel wire,桥索~ bridge wire,去弹性~*,热浸镀锌~*,软拉~*,渗碳细~(制特殊针用) pin bar,特号~*,退火~ annealed wire,椭圆~ oval wire,外层~(钢丝绳的) cover wire,芯~(钢丝绳的) core wire,形变热处理~ ausformed steel wire,硬拉~*,有刺[花园]~制造机 barbed wire machine,预应力~*,针布~ wire for card clothing,制螺栓用~ bolt wire,制刷用~*,中等电阻~*,中间退火~*
钢丝玻璃 ferroglass
钢丝缠绕机架 wire wrapped frame
钢丝厂 wire works
钢丝成盘性 cast of wire
钢丝床用钢丝 mattress netting steel wire
钢丝打轴机 (wire) spooling machine
钢丝电(解)镀锌法 bethanizing (process)
钢丝镀锌 wire galvanization ◇波特~法*,马林诺~法 Marino process
钢丝放线包装 【压】pay-off-pack
钢丝剪(切机) wire cutter
钢丝交咬角(钢丝绳的) crossing angle of wires
钢丝矫直机 【压】spinner
钢丝进给机 【压】wire-feeding machine
钢丝进给机构 【压】wire-feed mechanism
钢丝进速调节 wire-feed speed control
钢丝锯条用钢丝 fretwork saw blade wire
钢丝开卷机座 pay-off stand
钢丝框形(磁场)指示器 steel-wire indicator
钢丝拉过式连续退火炉 【压】pull-through type furnace
钢丝拉伸机 wire stretcher
钢丝粒(切碎的钢丝) cut wire shot, chopped steel wire
钢丝连续电镀法 【压】baylanizing ◇布瑞兰~*
钢丝帘布[帘线] (all-)steel cord ◇传送带用~*,轮胎~ steel cord for tyre,三角皮带用~ steel cord for V-belt
钢丝磷酸盐处理法 ◇巴诺克斯~*
钢丝录音机 magnetic wire recorder
钢(丝)棉 steel wool
钢丝磨刷机 scratchbrush machine
钢丝盘卷不匀 bad cast
钢丝盘卷均匀 dead cast
钢丝破断拉力总和(钢丝绳内的) aggregate breaking force (A.B.F.)

钢丝热镀锌法 brutonizing ◇ 赫曼~ Herman process, 卡赞尼加~ Cazzaniga process

钢丝绳 (steel-)wire rope, steel [wire] cable ◇ 半密封~*, 包钢~*, 包塑料~ plastic-coated wire rope, 编织~*, 扁~*, 不松散~*, 不旋转~ non rotating wire rope, 充填式~*, 点接触~*, 钢芯~*, 光面~ bright wire rope, 航空~*, 合股~ strand rope, 赫尔克里士~*, 黑[表面无涂覆]~ black wire rope, 簧式捻~ spring lay wire rope, 混合捻~*, 畸变~*, 极软~*, 架空索道用承载~*, 金属螺旋绳芯~(钢芯钢丝绳) metallic spiral core rope, 精密高级[特号]~ plow steel rope(P.S.R.), 空心[管式]~ hollow wire rope, 缆式~ cable lay wire rope, 螺旋状~ spiral wire rope, 麻钢混捻~*, 梅花股芯~*, 密封~*, 面接触~*, 内润滑~*, 帕拉弗雷克斯~*, 平面股~*, 平行捻~*, 普通捻~*, 牵引用~ hauling wire rope, 软~*, 三角股~*, 绳式股芯~*, 双层扁股~*, 松散~ non-preformed wire rope, 特软~*, 特种~ special wire rope, 同向捻[顺捻]~*, 瓦灵顿式~ Warrington wire rope, 西尔式~*, 细丝~ fine wire rope, 线接触~*, 新型带钢丝绳芯的~ N.I.W.R.C.(new independent wire rope core) wire rope, 硬[粗丝]~*, 硬捻~ hard laid wire rope, 右捻~*, 圆~*, 左捻~*

钢丝绳安全系数 factor of safety for wire rope

钢丝绳冲击式钻机 churn (drill)

钢丝绳传动斗 cable-drawn scoop

钢丝绳断线[断丝]测定仪 deflectoscope for wire rope

钢丝绳结构 construction of wire rope

钢丝绳捆 rope coil

钢丝绳偏心度测量仪 cable eccentricity gauge

钢丝绳破断强度试验 rope breaking strength test

钢丝绳破断强度试验机 rope breaking strength tester

钢丝绳普通搓捻法 ordinary lay

钢丝绳牵引车 cable-driven car

钢丝绳牵引送锭车 cable-driven ingot buggy

钢丝绳牵引冷床 rope-driven hot bed, rope-type cooling bed

钢丝绳试验机 wire rope tester

钢丝绳探伤器 rope fault finder

钢丝绳拖运机拨爪 cable-drawn dogs

钢丝绳芯 rope core

钢丝绳移送机 rope transfer

钢丝绳用钢丝 rope wire

钢丝绳有效金属断面 metallic area of wire rope

钢丝绳周长(外接圆周长) circumference of wire rope

钢丝试样 【压】wire specimen

钢丝刷 wire [steel] brush ◇ 用~机械清理 mechanical wire brushing, 用~手工清理 hand wire brushing

钢丝刷清理 brushing

钢丝酸洗设备 wire pickling machinery

钢丝缩径 wire diameter shrinkage

钢丝索 steel rope

钢丝弹簧 wire spring

钢丝涂灰(上石灰) chalking of wire

钢丝弯边压力机 【压】wiring press

钢丝弯曲工具 wire bending tool

钢丝网 mat reinforcement, metal gauze, steel mesh ◇ 编的~ woven steel fabric, 焊接~ welded wire fabric

钢丝网焊接机 (wire) mesh welding machine

钢丝网炉箅 steel mesh grate

钢丝网配筋 wire mesh reinforcement, fabric reinforcement

钢丝网水泥 ferrocement

钢丝网运输带 (wire) mesh belt

钢丝芯(钢丝绳的) wire core
钢丝压扁 wire flattening
钢丝压扁机 【压】wire flattening machine
钢丝压尖机 wire pointer
钢丝预涂熔剂处理 【金】wire prefluxing
钢丝轧扁收线机 take-up of flat steel wire rolling mill
钢丝栅栏 wire fence
钢丝直径 gauge of wire
钢丝制品 (fabricated steel) wire products, merchant wire
钢丝制品用钢丝 manufacturer's wire
钢丝轴(线) wire axis
钢酸洗废液 spent steel pickle liquor
钢索 (同"钢丝绳")
钢索轨道 funicular
钢索滑轮 wire-rope pulley
钢套 steel jacket [bushing]
钢条 steel rod [bar]
钢铁表面蒸黑处理法 ◇ 格斯纳~Gesner process
钢铁表面热浸铝法 mollerizing, mollerising
钢铁材料 ferrous material
钢铁厂 iron and steel plant [works], steel works ◇ 非联合~*, 小(型)~*
钢铁厂废料 steel plant waste
钢铁厂废料球团 【团】steel plant by-product pellet
钢铁厂废料造块(法) 【团】steel plant by-product agglomeration
钢铁厂粉尘 steel plant dust
钢铁厂工业炉 iron-and-steel furnaces
钢铁成分快速响应工艺 steel compositions rapid response process
钢铁废料 ferrous waste
钢铁工程 steelwork
钢铁工程师协会(美国) Association of Iron and Steel Engineers (AISE, A.I.S.E.)
钢铁工业 (iron and) steel industry, ferrous (metal) industry

钢铁加工工业 iron-working industry
钢铁局(英国) Iron and Steel Board (ISB)
钢铁联合企业(完整的) fully integrated steel plant, integrated mill, iron and steel complex
钢铁料消耗 【钢】(specific) pig iron and scrap consumption, specific iron and steel consumption, ferrous charges consumption
钢铁侵蚀剂 ◇ 勒夏特列1号~*
钢铁学会(英国) Iron and Steel Institute (ISI)
钢铁冶金(学) metallurgy of iron and steel, ferrous metallurgy, siderurgy, metallurgy of ferrous metals
钢铁冶金的 siderurgical
钢铁冶金原理 principle of ferrous metallurgy
钢桶炉 (同"钢包炉")
钢脱氧剂 steel deoxidiser
钢瓦挂铅青铜法 ◇ 马歇尔~【铸】Masher process
钢丸 steel shot
钢蜗壳 steel volute chamber
钢系杆 steel tie
钢弦 string wire
钢显微组织 steel microstructure
钢线 steel wire ◇ 编织针用~ knitting needle wire
钢消费量(国家或地区的) apparent steel consumption per capita ◇ 人均~*
钢屑 steel scrap [swarf, cuttings]
钢屑刷 cold wool
钢芯的(电缆) steel cored (sc)
钢芯钢丝绳 I.W.S.C. (independent wire strand core) wire rope, steel-cored wire rope
钢芯铝电缆 aluminum cable steel reinforced (ACSR, A.C.S.R.)
钢芯铝绞线 aluminium cable steel reinforced (A.C.S.R.), steel cored aluminium strand

钢芯铝线　steel-aluminium conductor, steel-cored aluminium

钢型　【铸】matrix

钢性生铁　semi-steel, half steel

钢性铸铁　cast semi-steel (CSS), gun iron, steely iron,【冶】ferrosteel ◇ 冈奈特~Gunite

钢性铸铁件　semi-steel casting (S.S.C.)

钢压板　keeper plate of steel

钢压模　steel die

钢阳极　steel anode

钢样分析仪　steel analyzer ◇ 盖革X射线~

钢样氧燃定碳法　Strohlein method

钢冶金(学)　steel metallurgy, metallurgy of steelmaking

钢液　molten [liquid] steel ◇ 残余~

钢液成分　heat analysis

钢液(成分)调整　adjustment of bath, bath maintenance

钢液分布　steel distribution

钢液流　steel stream

钢液流动　flow of steel

钢液面[位]控制　(liquid) steel level control ◇ 锭模内~mould level control

钢液面自动控制　automatic steel level control

钢液压头　head of molten metal

钢阴极　steel cathode

钢印　brand, embossed stamp, steel seal ◇ 打~工具【压】marking punch

钢印标记　die-stamped marking

钢用光谱仪　steeloscope, styloscope

钢渣　steelmaking slag

钢渣口冻结　【冶】hard tap(hole)

钢轧辊　steel roll ◇ 硬面[淬硬]~steel chilled roll

钢枕　sleeper bar, steel sleeper

钢枕孔型　sleeper pass

钢蒸馏罐　steel retort

钢支柱　steel supporting column, steel upright

钢纸板　presspahn

钢制冷却蛇管　steel cooling coil

钢制品　steelwork

钢制烧杯　steel beaker

钢质量　steel quality

钢质运输带　steel conveyer belt

钢中白点　steel flake

钢中夹杂物　inclusion in steel

钢种　steel grade

钢种数字代号　【钢】type number

钢珠　steel grit [ball]

钢珠火花鉴别法　【钢】pellet test

钢铸件　steel casting

钢铸件的夹杂物　snotter

钢铸块　steel ingot

钢铸模(铸铁机的)　【铁】steel mould

钢铸造　steel foundry

钢注流　steel stream

钢桩　piling bar, piled steel, steel pile

钢锥硬度计　◇ 卢德维克~Ludwick hardness tester

钢组分　steel constituent

钢最大淬火硬度　maximum martensitic hardness of steel

缸径　hearth diameter (HD)

缸体油压探测器　cylinder oil pressure detector

缸筒用高精度冷拔钢管　cold-drawn high-precision steel tube for cylinder bodies

港口门式起重机　quaternion crane

杠杆摆动式铡刀剪　rocker guillotine type shears

杠杆臂　lever arm [bar]

杠杆(臂之)比　lever ratio, leverage

杠杆操纵　lever control

杠杆掣爪锤　lever-trip hammer

杠杆秤[天平]　beam balance

杠杆传动　leverage, lever operation

杠杆传动装置　rod gear

杠杆锤　lever [shaft] hammer

杠杆定律[定理]　【理】lever law [rule]

杠杆关系　lever relation(ship)

杠杆回动机构	lever reversing gear
杠杆机构	lever mechanism, linkage ◇ 偏心凸轮~*
杠杆开关	lever switch
杠杆力臂	lever arm
杠杆式布氏硬度计	【金】lever-type Brinell machine
杠杆式冲压机	lever punch (press)
杠杆式翻钢机	lever-type turn-over device
杠杆式焊钳	pincer gun
杠杆式焊枪	lever gun
杠杆式夹钳	lever-type clamp ◇ C形点焊用~*
杠杆式剪切机	lever [crocodile, alligator] shears, crocodile shearing machine ◇ 立切~*, 下切~ upcut lever shears
杠杆式启动器	lever-type starter
杠杆式倾动锤	helver
杠杆式热锯	hot drop [lever-type] saw
杠杆式试验机	lever testing machine
杠杆式推钢机	lever pusher
杠杆式万能材料试验机	Olsen universal testing machine
杠杆手柄	lever handle
杠杆台座	fulcrum bracket
杠杆系统	compound lever (arrangement), leverage, levers
杠杆压砖机	【耐】lever [toggle] press
杠杆原理	lever principle
杠杆装置	lever assembly
杠杆作用[杠杆率]	leverage
高Q值	high Q, high quality factor
高安培电弧	high amperage arc
高安息角氧化铝	high angle of repose alumina
高倍放大显微镜像	high power microscopic(al) image
高倍物镜	high magnification objective lens, high power objective
高倍显微镜	microscope of high magnification, high power(ed) microscope
高倍显微术	high power microscopy
高倍显微照片	high power micrograph
高比阻铜镍合金	advance metal
高铋易熔焊料	bismuth solder
高标号水泥	high grade [strength] cement
高标准	stringent specification, high standard
高标准检验	tightened inspection
高布喇格角衍射线	diffraction lines at high Bragg angle
高层错晶体	heavily faulted crystal
高层错能	large stacking-fault energy
高差仪[精密高差仪]	cathetometer
高产出率	high yield
高产量	high production [yield]
高产量(乙炔)发生器	heavy duty (acetylene) generator
高产率作业	high productivity performance
高超声学	hypersonics, praetersonics
高超音速的	hypersonic
高尘区	【环】high dust area
高尘染率	heavy concentration of dust
高沉积率镀镍法	Ni-speed
高成色黄金	high karat gold
高程差	difference of elevation
高冲击性	high impact (H.I.)
高重显性热电偶	high reproducible thermocouple
高传导率	high conductivity (HC)
高醇	higher alcohol
高醇黄药捕集剂	high alcohol xanthate collector
高纯电解镁	high purity electrolytic magnesium
高纯度	high purity
高纯度硅铝砖	high purity alumina-silica brick
高纯度氧	high purity oxygen
高纯度氩保护气氛	high grade argon atmosphere
高纯晶体	high purity crystal

高纯铝 high purity aluminium ◇拉弗纳尔～Raffinal (99.99Al)
高纯镍 malleable nickel
高纯钛 high purity titanium
高纯锌 high purity zinc
高磁导率合金 (同"高导磁率合金")
高磁导率铁镍合金 (同"高导磁率铁镍合金")
高磁感 Hi-B 硅钢薄板 orient high B
高磁感晶粒取向硅钢 ◇HI-B～*
高次谐波 high (order) harmonic(s), upper harmonic
高次谐波滤波设备 high harmonic filter equipment
高次衍射束 higher order diffracted beam
高次转变 higher order transition
高淬火性油 【金】fast quenching oil
高淬透性 high hardenability
高淬透性钢 high hardenability steel
高氮(的) high nitrogen
高导磁率 49 合金 (17—50Ni,余量 Fe) high permalloy 49 alloy
高导磁率材料 high permeability material
高导磁率钢 high permeability steel
高导磁率硅钢薄板 ◇海珀西尔～*
高导磁(率)合金 high (magnetic) permeability alloy ◇超坡莫～*,戴纳马克斯～*,海珀科～*,海珀姆～Hyperm,含高钼的坡莫因瓦～(45Ni, 25Co, 22.5Fe,7.5Mo) Mo-perminvar,尼卡洛伊～(49Ni, 51Fe) Nicaloy,无线电用～*
高导磁率镍铁合金 high permeability nickel-iron alloy ◇阿利格尼～Allegheny electric metal,坡莫菲～*
高导磁率软磁合金 ◇海珀洛伊～(50Ni,50Fe) Hiperloy
高导磁率铁钴合金 high permeability Co alloy ◇海珀科～*
高导磁率铁硅合金 high permeability silico alloy
高导磁率铁铝合金 ◇阿尔珀姆～(16Al,余量 Fe) Alperm,海珀马尔～Hypermal
高导磁率铁镍合金 permalloy ◇奥迪欧洛伊～(48Ni,余量 Fe) Audioloy,海珀洛依～Hyperloy,海珀马洛伊～*,海珀尼克～*,罗梅塔尔～*,帕明诺姆～*
高导电率 high conductivity, high conducivity for electricity
高导电率材料 material of high electric conductivity
高导电率锡镉青铜 (99—98Cu, 0.8—1.0Cd, 0.5—1.8Sn) phonoelectric bronze
高导电性金属 high conductivity metal
高导电性铜 high conductivity copper
高导电性无氧铜 oxygen-free high-conductivity copper (OFHC)
高导热耐火砖 high conductivity firebrick
高道 elevated track
高灯头 【焦】high(er) burner
高等级 high grade
高低档瓦特表 high low watt meter
高低(位)调节 high low control
高低限值 【计】high low limits
高低压信号器(锅炉的) high lock alarm
高碘酸{HIO₄} periodic acid
高碘酸铷{RbIO₄} rubidium periodate
高碘酸盐 periodate
高碘酸氧化反应 periodic acid oxidation, Malaprade reaction
高电导率 high conductivity (HC) ◇希坦索～青铜*,科姆巴洛依～银铜*
高电流铝电解槽 high amperage aluminium cell
高电流密度电解 high current density electrolysis
高电流密度电解(炼锌)法 【色】high density method [process], Tainton method
高电容电弧 condensed arc
高电压电子显微镜 high voltage electron microscope

高电压短焦距透镜(电子束熔炼用)　high voltage "einzel" lens
高电压工程　high tension engineering
高电压绕组　high voltage winding
高电压射线照相术　high voltage radiography
高电压试验　high voltage test
高电阻伏特计　high resistance voltmeter
高电阻高硬度超基合金　◇海恩斯～ Haynes alloy
高电阻合金　high resistance alloy, alloy of high electrical resistance
高电阻金属　high resistance metal
高电阻镍铬合金　◇派罗利克～(80Ni, 20Cr) Pyrolic, 皮尔勒斯～
高电阻坡莫合金　resist permalloy
高读数温度计　high reading thermometer
高度电离气体　strongly ionized gas
高度计　altimeter, height gauge
高度记录仪　altigraph
高度精炼法　【钢】superrefining process
高度可调节的　vertically adjustable
高度可调节的堰管　adjustable height weir tube
高度耐火[耐热,耐蚀,耐酸,难熔]的　highly refractory
高度石灰喷射　high rate of lime injection
高度调节板　offset block
高度压下量　【压】reduction in height
高度氧化的　highly oxidized
高度真空(的)　microvac, high vacuum
高度之间应力状态　【压】high triaxiality
高度致密石墨　high density graphite
高堆位层错能的流变应力　flow stress of large stacking-fault energy
高堆位层错能临界切应力　critical shear stress of large stacking-fault energy
高对称性晶体　highly symmetrical crystal, crystal of high symmetry
高发热值　high(er) heating value
高发热值的放热型气体　rich exothermic gas

高发热值煤气[燃气]　high B. Th. U. (British thermal unit) gas, rich gas
高钒钢　high-vandium steel
高钒钾铀型矿　high vanadium carbotite type ore
高反应性煤　highly reactive coal
高放大率　【理】high power [magnification]
高放大率显微镜　(同"高倍显微镜")
高放射性　high activity
高放射性源　multicurie source
高废钢比炉料　high scrap charge
高沸点化合物　higher boiling compound
高沸点金属　high boiling metal
高沸(点)馏分　high boiling fraction, 【化】heavy [last] cut
高沸点杂质　high boiling point impurity
高分辨率　high resolution (HR)
高分辨率电子显微镜　high resolution electron microscope
高分辨率分光[摄谱]仪　high resolution spectrometer
高分辨率核磁共振摄谱仪　【理】high resolution NMR (nuclear magnetic resonance) spectrometer
高分辨率[能力]屏　high definition screen
高分辨率[反差]射线照相术　high definition radiography
高分辨率显微术　high resolution microscopy
高分辨率仪器　high resolution instrument
高分辨率自动射线照相术　high resolution autoradiography
高分子　high molecular
高分子醇　high molecular alcohol, higher alcohol
高分子电解质　polyelectrolyte
高分子聚合物　high molecular weight polymer, high polymer
高风量　high wind
高风温　high blast temperature
高风温高炉操作　blast furnace operation

at higher hot blast temperature
高附加值企业 【企】high added-value enterprise
高钙镁砂 high calcium magnesite
高钙熔剂 high calcium flux [stone]
高钙石灰 high calcium lime
高钙渣 【色】high lime slag, limey slag
高钙质还原渣 【钢】highly calcareous reducing slag
高刚度轧机 high rigidity rolling mill, stiff mill ◇ 连接板型~*
高锆酸钠 sodium perzirconate
高锆酸盐 perzirconate
高铬不锈钢 high chromium-stainless steel
高铬钢 high chromium [chrome] steel ◇ 高碳~*
高铬合金 high chromium [chrome] alloy
高铬金属陶瓷 high chromium content cermet
高铬镍耐酸耐热不锈钢(23—28Cr, 18Ni, 1Mn, 0.2—0.3Mo, 余量 Fe) platinum steel
高铬生铁 high chromium iron
高功率 high power (HP, hp), high activity
高功率大电炉 high power electric arc furnace
高功率管 high power(ed) tube
高功率偏心炉底出钢电炉 (HP + EBT) EAF (同"偏心炉底出钢电炉")
高鼓风温度 high blast temperature
高钴磁钢 ◇ K.S.~ K.S. steel
高钴的 cobaltic
高钴锍[冰铜] 【色】high cobalt matte
高固定碳焦 high carbon coke
高光亮光洁度 best bright finish
高光强物镜 high power objective
高硅表面层 high silicon surface layer
高硅赤铁矿 codorous ore
高硅焊剂 high silica flux
高硅镜面生铁(含10—12Si) glazed pig, glazy pig (iron)
高硅铝合金 silumin
高硅铝土矿 high silicon bauxite, siliceous bauxite, high silica diaspore
高硅蒙乃尔合金 high silicon Monel
高硅耐酸铁(13—16Si) Supiron
高硅黏土砖 Jersey fireclay brick
高硅青铜(96Cu, 3Si, 余量 Pb) high silicon bronze
高硅熔[焊]剂 high silica flux
高硅砂 high silica sand
高硅生铁 high silicon pig iron, (同"银白生铁")
高硅铁矿 high silica iron ore
高硅锡渣 highly siliceous tin slag
高硅珠光体灰口铁(4Si, 2.5Cr, 少量 Mo) loaded iron
高硅铸铁(13—17Si) high silicon cast iron ◇ 阿里龙耐蚀~Arivon, 科罗西龙耐蚀~*, 西拉尔~*
高铪精矿 high hafnium concentrate
高铪酸钠 sodium perhafnate
高铪酸盐 perhafnate
高含尘率[度] heavy concentration of dust
高含量贵重组分试样 high assay
高含碳量 high carbon
高含铁炉渣 high FeO slag
高含铜量 high copper
高合金比合金 concentrated alloy
高合金锻钢 high alloy forged steel
高合金钢 high alloy steel
高合金钢棒轧机 high-alloy steel bar mill
高合金工具钢 high alloy tool steel
高合金焊丝 high alloy welding wire
高合金马氏体 high alloy martensite
高合金铁铸件 high alloy iron casting
高合金铸钢件 high alloy steel casting
高合金铸铁 high alloy iron
高化学活性元素 highly reactive element
高还原度烧结矿 high reducibility sinter, highly reduced sinter
高还原性气氛 highly reducing atmo-

高灰分的 high ash, ash-rich
高灰分焦炭 high ash coke
高灰分煤 high ash coal
高挥发分煤 high volatile coal, fat coal
高挥发分烟煤 high volatile bituminous coal
高挥发分烟煤喷吹系统 【铁】high-volatile bituminous coal injection system
高回火温度材料[金属] high tempering temperature material
高活性[活力] high activity
高活性碳形态 highly active form of carbon
高活性元素 highly reactive element
高级巴比特合金 majestic babbitt alloy
高级表面光洁度 superior surface finish
高级材料 perfect [good, premium-grade] material
高级产品 high grade product
高级镀锡钢板 best coke grade tin plate
高级反射 high order reflection
高级反应 high order reaction
高级合金钢 high-grade alloy steel
高级黄铜 high brass
高级灰口铁 high quality grey iron
高级焦油酸 higher tar acids
高级磷青铜 damaxine ◇ 达马克辛～*
高级煤 top-grade [high-rank] coal
高级醚 higher ether
高级耐火材料 high refractory ◇ 科尔哈特～*
高级耐火砖 high refractory brick
高级强韧铸铁(经电石渣还原精炼而得) sendait metal
高级燃料 high grade fuel
高级熔剂 high grade stone
高级碳素钢 high-grade carbon steel
高级铁素体不锈钢 super ferrite stainless steel
高级酮 higher ketone
高级统计分析程序语言 ASTAP (advanced statistical analysis program)
高级烟煤 high rank bituminous coal, gas coal
高级优质可锻铸铁 high duty malleable (cast) iron
高级优质耐火黏土砖 high-duty fireclay brick
高级优质铸件 high duty casting
高级优质铸铁 high duty [test] cast iron
高级语言 【计】higher (-order) [high-level] language, high order language
高级铸件 premium casting
高级铸铁 high quality [grade] cast iron, up-grade cast iron ◇ 埃马立特重载～Ermalite, 蒂森－埃米尔～*, 米格拉～*
高挤压性粉末 high compressibility powder
高技术热轧带钢 Hi-Tech hot strip
高价硫化物 higher sulphide
高价锌氨络合物 higher zinc ammine complex
高价氧化物 higher oxide
高价氧化铀 higher uranium oxide
高架轨道 elevated track
高架柜 elevated tank
高架矿仓 elevated bin
高架料仓贮斗 high line hopper
高架平台用小车 elevating platform truck
高架起重机 overhead crane (O.H.C.), gantry (crane), portal crane ◇ 单脚～*, 双脚～full gantry crane, 移动式～*, 折臂式～folding jib gantry
高架移动起重机 overhead travelling crane, transfer gantry
高架铸钢平台 【连铸】elevated casting platform
高架装料滑槽(转炉的) 【钢】overhead shoot
高架装料起重机 【冶】charging gantry crane
高架装载机 overhead loader
高间隙缺陷 high interstitial defect

高碱度的 high basic
高碱度精炼渣 white refining slag
高碱度球团 high basicity pellet, super-fluxed pellet
高碱度烧结矿 high basicity sintered ore, highly fluxed sinter, super-fluxed [super-fluxing] sinter, self-fluxing agglomerate
高碱水泥 【建】high alkali cement
高碱性熔剂 high calcium stone
高碱性渣 highly basic slag
高矫顽力的 high coercive, hard magnetic
高矫顽力合金 high coercivity alloy
高矫顽力加铝磁钢 ◇ MT(三岛、牧野)～
高矫顽力特性材料 high coercivity material
高矫顽力永磁合金 ◇ 三岛～Mishima alloy
高角度反射 high angle reflection
高角度区域 high angle region
高阶反射 high order reflection
高阶反应 high order reaction
高阶(曲)线 high order lines
高结晶对称相 【金】phase of high crystal symmetry
高介电材料 high dielectric material
高金含量的 highly auriferous
高金合金 high gold content alloy
高精度比色红外光纤温度计 infrared 2-colour thermometer with high-accuracy
高精度测量 high precision measurement
高精度辊式矫直机 high-precision roller straightener
高精度磨削 seal ground finish
高精度[灵敏]度调节器 superregulator
高精度轧制 high-precision rolling (HPR)
高精度轧制工艺 high-precision rolling process
高精度(轧制)轧机 HPR (high-precision rolling) mill
高经济增长 high economic growth
高聚物 superpolymer

高开黄金 high harat gold
高抗拉强度钢 high tensile steel
高抗拉强度钢管 high tensile steel tube
高抗拉强度焊条 high tensile electrode
高抗拉强度合金 high tensile alloy
高抗拉强度黄铜 (同"高强度黄铜")
高抗拉强度结构钢 high tensile structural steel
高抗拉强度性能 high tensile property
高抗拉强度铸钢 high tension cast steel
高抗拉强度铸铁 high tensile [tension] cast iron
高抗破裂[压溃]套管 high collapse casing
高抗张[拉]强度的 high tensile (HT, H.T.)
高空高压传输线用铝合金 ◇ 康德～(99.5Al) Cond-Al
高跨比 depth-span [rise-span] ratio, pitch ◇ 1/4(屋架)～one-fourth pitch
高拉力 high tension
高拉碳钢 tapped-on-carbon steel
高拉碳牌号钢种 catch-carbon steels
高铼酸{HReO$_4$} perrhenic acid
高铼酸铵 ammonium perrhenate
高铼酸钾{KReO$_4$} potassium perrhenate
高铼酸盐{MReO$_4$} per(r)henate
高利用系数操作 【铁】high productivity performance
高亮度 high light (brightness)
高亮度火花 high intensity spark
高钌酸盐 perruthenate
高料层(烧结的) deeper bed depth
高料位指示器 high level indicator
高料柱 【冶】long column
高磷焦炭 high phosphorus coke
高磷镍铁 high phosphorus ferronickel
高磷生铁 high phosphorus iron, phosphoric (pig) iron, Thomas (pig) iron
高磷铁矿 high phosphorus iron ore
高磷铸铁(15-25P) ferrophosphor, high-phosphorus iron
高菱镁水泥 magnesium oxychloride ce-

ment, magnesia cement
高岭石{Al$_2$O$_3$·2SiO$_2$·2H$_2$O}　kaolinite
高岭土　kaolin (clay), argil ◇ 多水~*，胶状~*，铁质~ ferruginous kaolin(e)，煅烧~ calcined kaolin
高岭土化(作用)　kaolinization
高岭土泥浆[悬浮物]　kaolin(e) slip
高岭土生料　crude kaolin(e)
高岭土悬浮物　kaolin(e) slip
高硫矾沥青　quisqueite
高硫钢　high sulphur steel
高硫号外铁　off-sulphur iron
高硫焦炭　high sulphur coke
高硫煤　sulphur coal, high sulphur content coal
高硫生铁　high-sulfur pig iron
高硫铁矿　high-sulphur iron ore
高硫原油(含硫3%以下)　high-sulfur crude (HSC)
高流动性型砂　【铸】free flowing sand
高流动性渣　【冶】highly fluid slag
高楼架空底层用柱　pilotis
高炉　【铁】blast furnace (B.F.) ◇ 矮(胖)~*，常压~ low-blast furnace，单出铁场~*，高压~*，焦炉型~*，巨型~ jumbo blast furnace, 框架式~*，拉舍特异形~*，料车上料式~ skip-filled furnace, 密封炉顶式~ closed top furnace, 模拟~ pseudoblast furnace, 皮带上料~*，四柱悬挂式~*，土~*，现役~ current blast furnace，原煤~*，自身承重型~*
高炉本体　blast furnace proper
高炉不顺行　irregular blast-furnace performance
高炉操作　blast furnace operation [practice], operating of blast furnace
高炉操作指数　blast furnace operating index
高炉产量　furnace output [productivity]
高炉产量指标　blast furnace productivity index
高炉产量指数　blast furnace output index

(BOI) (100BOI 约等于以炉缸面积计 43t/(m^2·d))
高炉长寿　long campaign of blast furnace
高炉车间　blast furnace plant
高炉车间运输　blast furnace transport
高炉尘　blast furnace (flue) dust
高炉称料工　boxman
高炉出铁　blast furnace tapping [casting]
高炉大修　blast furnace rebuilding [relining]
高炉大砖　blast furnace block
高炉点火　lighting of blast furnace
高炉顶压力　high-top pressure (HTP)
高炉动力学(特性)　furnace dynamics
高炉反应　blast furnace reactions
高炉翻斗绞车　blast furnace skip hoist
高炉放散阀平台　furnace bleeder platform
高炉废料　blast furnace waste
高炉废铁　blast furnace scrap
高炉辅助设备　auxiliary blast-furnace equipment
高炉改造　modernization of blast furnace
高炉工　blast furnace operator [worker, man], pig iron producer
高炉工长　blast furnace foreman
高炉鼓风　blast furnace air
高炉鼓风机　blast furnace blower, blast furnace blowing engine, stove blower
高炉故障　blast furnace trouble
高炉硅酸盐水泥　blast-furnace portland cement
高炉过程控制　blast furnace process control
高炉过程控制系统　blast furnace process control system
高炉横烟囱　furnace bridge
高炉环梁　blast furnace lintel plate
高炉环梁壳　mantle
高炉环状风管　blast furnace bustle pipe
高炉灰　blast furnace (flue) dust
高炉灰产出量　flue dust production
高炉灰尘捕集　flue dust separation

高炉灰风动输送系统　flue dust pneumatic conveying system
高炉灰组分　flue dust constituent
高炉基础　blast furnace foundation
高炉加湿鼓风装置　blast furnace steam blower
高炉焦产率　furnace coke yield
高炉焦炭　blast-furnace [metallurgical] coke ◇ 大块~*
高炉绞车　blast furnace hoist
高炉结构　blast furnace design
高炉进程　driving
高炉精料　high grade blast furnace burden
高炉旧炉衬拆除设备　blast furnace tear down appparatus
高炉开炉　put on the blast, on-stream
高炉控制盘　blast furnace control panel
高炉控制仪表室　blast furnace instrument control house
高炉矿槽　blast furnace bunker
高炉矿焦混装　mixed burden charging in BF
高炉矿渣硅酸盐水泥　portland blast-furnace cement
高炉矿渣水泥　blast furnace slag cement
高炉冷却板　blast furnace cooling plate
高炉冷却壁　blast furnace stave
高炉冷却介质　blast furnace coolant
高炉冷却器　blast furnace copper
高炉冷却系统　blast furnace cooling system
高炉利用系数　furnace productivity, capacity factor of blast furnace, utilization coefficient of blast furnace
高炉粒煤喷吹　blast furnace granular coal injection
高炉炼铁　blast furnace ironmaking [smelting]
高炉炼铁法[工艺]　blast furnace process, blast furnace smelting [melting] operation
高炉料仓[槽]　blast furnace bin
高炉料场　furnace yard
高炉料车卷扬机　furnace hoisting machine
高炉料罐车　blast furnace car
高炉料罐提升机　blast furnace bucket hoist
高炉料面指示器　blast furnace charge level indicator
高炉料线手测　hand sounding
高炉料钟　blast furnace top bell
高炉料钟操作　furnace bell operation
高炉料柱　stock
高炉流槽　sow
高炉炉尘　blast furnace soot, flue dust
高炉炉尘泥　blast furnace top gas mud
高炉炉衬　blast furnace lining
高炉炉底　blast furnace bottom ◇ 敲落的~结块　knock down salamander
高炉炉底冷却系统　underhearth cooling system
高炉炉底砖衬(砌体)　blast furnace bottom lining
高炉炉顶煤气　(total) top gas
高炉炉顶煤气压力　top (gas) pressure
高炉炉腹　blast furnace bosh
高炉炉缸　blast furnace crucible [hearth, well]
高炉炉喉　blast furnace throat [mouth]
高炉炉架　blast furnace frame (work)
高炉炉壳　blast furnace shell [jacket]
高炉炉况　blast furnace conditions, driving, furnace movement
高炉炉况不顺行　(同"高炉不顺行")
高炉炉况失常　upset in blast furnace operation
高炉炉况实时智能预测系统　real time intelligent predicting system for blast furnace process, real time intelligent system for forecasting blast furnace status
高炉炉龄[期]　(同"高炉一代寿命")
高炉炉料　blast furnace burden (material), blast furnace charge [feed, mixture] ◇ 优质~*

高炉炉料结构[组成]　blast furnace burden material
高炉炉身　blast-furnace shaft [stack], in-wall
高炉炉身外壳　blast furnace stack casing
高炉炉头(炉顶锥形部分)　top cone
高炉炉型[内型]　blast furnace profile [lines], inner profile
高炉炉腰　belly of blast furnace
高炉炉渣　(iron) blast furnace slag ◇ 粒状~*, 气冷~*
高炉慢风操作　slack-wind blowing
高炉煤气　blast furnace gas (BFG) ◇ 单一的~*, 剩余[过剩]~*
高炉煤气处理[清洗]　disposal of blast furnace gas
高炉煤气阀　blast furnace gas valve
高炉煤气含尘控制　flue dust control
高炉煤气净化　top gas cleaning
高炉煤气净化器废水　blast furnace gas cleaner effluents
高炉煤气净化装置　blast furnace gas cleaner
高炉煤气燃气轮机　blast furnace gas turbine
高炉煤气燃气轮机发电厂　blast-furnace gas-turbine power plant
高炉煤气燃烧器　◇ 过剩~excess gaqs burner
高炉煤气温度　blast furnace gas [offtake] temperature
高炉煤气总管　blast furnace gas main
高炉模拟[仿真]试验　blast furnace simulation test
高炉模型　blast furnace model
高炉耐火砌体　blast furnace masonry
高炉难行　stiff [tight] furnace operation, tight furnace
高炉泥炮　blast furnace gun
高炉泡沫渣　blast-furnace foamed slag
高炉配料　blast furnace mixture
高炉配料计算　blast furnace burden calculating
高炉喷吹　BF (blast furnace) injection, injection in blast furnace
高炉砌体磨损检查　blast furnace wear check
高炉砌砖　blast furnace brick work
高炉全高　total height
高炉燃料　blast furnace fuel
高炉燃烧控制系统　blast furnace combustion control system
高炉燃油　furnace oil
高炉热化学模型　thermochemical blast-furnace model
高炉热平衡　blast furnace heat balance
高炉热行　thermal performance
高炉熔剂　blast furnace flux
高炉熔炼　blast furnace smelting, operating of blast furnace
高炉熔炼操作　blast furnace melting [smelting] operation
高炉熔炼反应　blast furnace reactions
高炉熔渣　(同"高炉炉渣")
高炉熔渣堵塞物　scaffold
高炉软水密闭循环冷却系统　closed cooling system with soft water for BF
高炉上升管温度　blast furnace offtake temperature
高炉烧结矿　blast furnace sinter
高炉设计　blast furnace design
高炉设计性能[指标]　projected furnace performance
高炉身(高)炉　high shaft furnace
高炉生产率[能力]　pig iron output, furnace output
高炉升降机　blast furnace lift
高炉水冷环管　furnace cooling water circle pipe
高炉水泥　blast-furnace cement
高炉顺行[正常炉况]　regular blast-furnace performance
高炉死铁　bear
高炉提升机　furnace hoisting machine

高炉托[支]圈　blast furnace ring, deck ring

高炉无料钟布料系统　◇考伯斯-沃思式~*

高炉下部(包括炉缸和炉腹)　blast furnace well

高炉下渣　tap cinder

高炉小钟保护罩　blast furnace shroud

高炉型线　blast furnace line

高炉冶金工作者　blast furnace metallurgist

高炉冶炼　blast furnace smelting [operation, process]

高炉冶炼进程　furnace movement

高炉冶炼进程困难　(同"高炉难行")

高炉冶炼趋势预报系统　smelting trend predicting system for blast furnace

高炉一代寿命　blast furnace production campaign, campaign life

高炉余压发电设备　TRT (top recovery turbine) equipment of BF

高炉原料　blast furnace feed

高炉渣　(同"高炉炉渣")

高炉渣产量　blast furnace slag output

高炉渣成分　blast furnace slag analysis

高炉渣和炼钢渣混合设备　blended steel and blast furnace slag plant

高炉渣中的铁粒　buckshot

高炉蒸汽鼓风机　blast furnace steam blower

高炉支承结构　blast furnace supporting structure

高炉铸铁　blast furnace cast iron

高炉专家系统　blast furnace expert system

高炉砖　blast furnace brick

高炉装料设备　(blast) furnace charging [filling] equipment

高炉总容积　total volume

高铝矾土熟料　bauxite chamotte

高铝钢包砖　high alumina ladle brick

高铝红土矿　aluminous laterite

高铝炉渣　aluminous slag

高铝耐火材料　high alumina refractory, aluminous refractory

高铝(耐火)砖　aluminous [alumina] firebrick, high alumina (fire) brick, alumina-rich brick, firebrick rich in Al_2O_3

高铝黏土　high alumina clay

高铝缺陷　high aluminum defect

高铝水泥　high alumina cement, aluminous cement

高铝铁矿石(脉石主要是Al_2O_3)　aluminous ore

高铝渣　high alumina slag

高铝铸铁　aluminium cast iron

高铝砖　high-alumina brick

高氯化物　perchloride

高氯酸{$HClO_4$}　perchloric acid

高氯酸锂　lithium perchlorate

高氯酸镁{$Mg(ClO_4)_2$}　magnesium perchlorate

高氯酸钠{$NaClO_4$}　sodium perchlorate

高氯酸铷{$RbClO_4$}　rubidium perchlorate

高氯酸铯{$CsClO_4$}　cesium perchlorate

高氯酸盐{$MClO_4$}　perchlorate

高氯酸盐分解　perchlorate decomposition

高氯酸盐铅(电解)精炼法　perchlorate lead-refining process

高孪生晶体　highly twinned crystals

高镁方解石　high-magnesiam calcite

高镁(炉)渣　【冶】high magnesium slag

高镁石灰　high magnesium lime

高镁水泥　high-magnesia cement

高锰白云石　mangan-dolomite

高锰钢(0.9—1.2C, 10—13Mn; Mn/C≈10) (high) manganese steel　◇哈德菲尔德[奥氏体]~*, 泰曼~丝 Timang

高锰高氮(奥氏体)不锈钢　◇USS坦尼隆~*

高锰铬耐热钢　◇克罗马杜尔~Chromadur

高锰镍耐磨钢　Tisco steel

高锰酸{$HMnO_4$}　permanganic acid

高锰酸钾{$KMnO_4$}　potassium hyperman-

ganate [permanganate]
高锰酸盐　hypermanganate, permanganate
高锰酸银　silver permanganate
高锰碳钢　high manganese carbon steel
高锰锌合金　high manganese zinc alloy
高锰渣　【钢】manganese-rich slag
高锰铸钢　high manganese cast steel (SCMnH1:: 0.9—1.3C, >11Mn, <0.1P, <0.05S; SCMnH$_2$: 0.9—1.2C, 11—14Mn, <0.4Si, <0.07P, <0.04S)
高密度　high density
高密度材料　high density material
高密度电流　high intensity current
高密度法　high density process [method]
高密度分选[分离]【选】high-density cut
高密度粉末　high density powder
高密度高导热性炉料　high density high conductivity charge
高密度高强度材料　high strength material of higher density
高密度高强度石墨　high-density and high-strength graphite
高密度硅砖　high density silica brick
高密度合金　high-density [heavy] alloy
高密度金属　high density metal
高密度炉衬　super-dense lining
高密度炉料　high density charge
高密度氯化物　high density chloride
高密度耐火材料　monofrax
高密度能量　high density energy
高密度坯块　high density pressing
高密度燃料　high density fuel
高密度石墨　high density graphite
高密度钨合金　high density tungsten alloy
高密度砖　dense brick
高密度装配　high density assembly
高密度组分　high density constituent
高耐腐蚀状态　immunity
高耐火度黏土　high duty fireclay
高耐拉强度的　high tensile
高耐磨性　high wearing feature
高耐蚀性铅合金　Asarco lead
高耐酸性硅铁　ihrigized iron
高内(电)阻电源　high resistance power supply
高能成形　high energy forming, energy-rate forming
高能冲压　high energy impact pressing
高能等离子体　energetic plasma
高能电子　high energy electron, hard electron, energetic electron
高能锻压成形　energy-rate forming
高能反冲原子　high energy recoil atom, energetic recoil atom
高能辐射　high energy radiation
高能高速成形　high energy rate forming (HERF) ◇ 戴纳帕克~法*
高能高速锤　【压】high energy rate machine
高能高速锻造　high-energy-rate forging
高能级(的)　high level
高能离合器　high energy clutch
高能粒子　high energy particle, energetic particle
高能力连续狭缝式烧嘴装置(火焰清理机的)　high capacity continuous slot unit
高能量燃料　high energy fuel
高能(量)位错　dislocation of high energy
高能束冲压　high-energy impact pressing
高能速变形　high energy rate deformation
高能速[率]成形　high energy rate forming
高能速压制　very high rates of pressing
高能态　energetic state
高能韧致辐射　high energy bremsstrahlung
高能永久磁铁　high energy permanent magnet
高泥料浆　high slime feed pulp
高黏度指数　high-viscosity index (HVI)
高黏(结)性煤　strongly coking coal, highly caking coal
高镍(的)　nickelic
高镍钢合金　platinite alloy

高镍铬合金钢 high nickel-chrome steel
高镍合金 high nickel alloy ◇ 哈斯特洛伊 N～*
高镍锍 high (grade) nickel matte
高镍锍浇铸 high nickel matte casting
高镍炉渣 nickel rich slag
高镍锰铜合金(15—20Mn,9—12Ni,余量 Cu) high nickel manganin
高镍耐热[耐蚀,不锈]铸铁 Ni-resist cast iron
高镍耐蚀耐热合金 (同"耐热耐蚀高镍合金")
高镍铁矿 bobrovkite
高镍铜锡合金(50Ni,40Cu,10Sn) high nickel-copper-tin alloy
高镍延性(球墨)铸铁 ductile Ni-resist cast iron
高浓度区 【金】rich zone
高浓缩铀 highly enriched uranium
高欧姆电阻合金 high ohmic resistance alloy
高欧姆铁铬铝电阻合金(20Cr,5—8.8Al,0—5Co,余量 Fe) ohmax
高喷吹比 high rate injection
高喷煤比 high rate injection of pulverized coal, high-rate pulverized coal injection
高喷煤比高炉 blast furnace with high-rate PCI
高喷煤比技术 high PCI technology
高硼钢 high boron steel
高膨胀率膨润土 high swelling type bentonite
高膨胀(系数)钢(12Ni,5Mn,3Cr,0.6C) high expansion steel
高膨胀(系数)合金 high expansion alloy
高膨胀性煤 high expanding coal
高频 high frequency (HF,hf,h.f.)
高频变换器 high-frequency converter ◇ 电子管式～*
高频变压器 high frequency transformer
高频表面淬火 high-frequency surface hardening

高频波 【电】high frequency waves
高频部件 (同"高频装置")
高频磁场 high frequency magnetic field
高频次疲劳 high cycle fatigue
高频淬火 high-frequency hardening [quenching], induction hardening ◇ 托科曲轴表面～法*
高频淬火车间 high frequency hardening plant
高频淬火机[设备,装置] high frequency hardening machine [plant]
高频电磁场 high frequency electromagnetic field
高频电磁感应 high frequency electromagnetic induction
高频电焊 high frequency welding
高频电火花隙振荡器[电火花发生器] high frequency spark gap oscillator
高频电缆 high frequency cable
高频电炉 high frequency (electric) furnace
高频电能 high frequency energy
高频电源 high frequency power source
高频电阻(加热)淬火 high frequency resistance hardening
高频电阻焊 high frequency resistance welding
高频电阻加热 high frequency resistance heating
高频扼流圈 high frequency choke (coil)
高频发电机 high frequency generator
高频发生器 high frequency oscillator
高频放大 high frequency amplification
高频放大器 high frequency amplifier
高频干燥 high frequency drying
高频干燥炉 high frequency drying stove
高频感应 high frequency induction
高频感应(电)炉 high-frequency (induction) furnace, coreless induction furnace ◇ 艾杰克斯－诺思拉普式(无铁心)～ Ajax-Northrup furnace, 无芯～*
高频感应焊接 high frequency induction

高频(感应)加热 high frequency heating, radio-frequency [diathermic] heating
高频感应(加热)淬火 high frequency induction hardening
高频感应加热熔盐电解槽 high frequency induction heated cell
高频感应渗氮 high frequency induction nitriding
高频感应线圈 high frequency induction coil ◇ 扁平～ flat high freqency coil
高频工艺[过程] high frequency process
高频管 high frequency tube
高频焊接 HF (high frequency) welding, induction welding (IW)
高频焊接异型钢管 HF (high frequency) welded shaped tube
高频烘芯法 【铸】dielectric core baking
高频烘芯炉 【铸】dielectric core oven
高频激发 high frequency excitation
高频极谱法 high frequency polarography
高频加热淬火 high frequency hardening [quenching]
高频加热法 【压】dielectric heating
高频交流电焊机 high frequency a-c welding machine
高频炼钢炉 high frequency steel furnace
高频-埋弧双功能螺旋焊管机组 high-frequency/submerged-arc dual-function spiral weld-pipe mill line
高频扭转疲劳试验机 high-frequency torque fatigue tester
高频钎焊 induction brazing (IB), high frequency brazing
高频损失 high frequency loss
高频探伤法 high frequency flaw detection method
高频特性 high frequency characteristic
高频铁芯 high frequency core ◇ 费罗卡特～ Ferrocart
高频线圈 high frequency coil
高频(型芯)烘干炉 【铸】dielectric dryer, high frequency dielectric core oven
高频选矿 high frequency separation
高频引线 high frequency lead
高频振荡起[引]弧 【焊】high frequency starting, spark starting
高频振荡器 【电】high frequency oscillator [generator, alternator]
高频振荡型 high frequency mode
高频振荡压铸法(美国专利) vibrocast
高频振动器 high speed vibrator
高频直缝焊管技术 high frequency straight seam welding technology
高频质谱仪("奥米伽器") mass synchrometer, omegatron
高频装置 【电】HF (high frequency) unit
高品位 high grade
高品位赤铁矿 high grade hematite
高品位铪精矿 high hafnium concentrate
高品位精矿 high grade concentrate
高品位矿(石) high grade ore, valuable [rich] ore
高品位矿石浸出 high grade ore leaching
高品位铝土矿 high quality bauxite
高品位锍 high grade matte
高品位镍锍 (同"镍高锍")
高品位球团 high grade pellet
高品位(铜)锍 high grade (copper) matte
高品质因数 high Q, high quality factor
高起始导磁率合金 high initial permeability alloy
高气压 superatmospheric pressure
高铅(含量)粉尘 high lead-content dust
高铅黄铜(65Cu,33Zn,2Pb) high leaded brass
高铅青铜 high-lead bronze ◇ 艾伦～*, 凯尔美特～轴承合金*
高铅酸盐 plumbate
高铅轴承合金 high lead bearing alloy
高强度 hi(gh)-strength, high-intensity (H.T.), strong intensity
高强度半镇静钢 GLX-W steel
高强度材料 high strength material, strong

material
高强度粗钢筋 high-tensile steel bar
高强度船用青铜(52—59Cu, 36—42Zn, 2—3Mn, 1Al, 1Fe) steel bronze bronze
高强度磁选 high intensity magnetic separation
高强度低合金钢 high strength low alloy (HSLA) steel, high-yield low-alloy steel
高强度低镍铬合金钢 ◇奈克罗姆~Nykrom
高强度电流 high(-intensity) current
高强度锻造合金 high strength forging alloy
高强度方镁石砖 super-strength periclase brick
高强度辐射 high intensity radiation
高强度钢 high tensile steel (HTS), high strength [duty] steel, strengthened steel, Hi-(stren) steel (低合金的)◇A-R~*, N型再渗氮~ steel type N, T-1易焊~T-1 steel, 低合金~*, 含铌~*, 航空用~magnaflux steel, 调质~*, 铁硅基~*, 韦尔康~Welcon
高强度钢管 high tensile steel tube
高强度钢丝 high-tensile steel wire ◇铅淬火~*
高强(度)钢丝缠丝机 high-strength wire-wound machine
高强度高韧性铝镁合金 ◇乌尔马尔~*
高强度管 high strength tube
高强度含钛锌基合金 ◇海德罗~*
高强度焊条 high strength [tensile] electrode
高强(度)合金 high strength [tensile] alloy, hard metal alloy
高强度黄铜(>17Zn, 2Al+Mn+Ni+Fe) high strength [tensile] brass ◇杜拉纳~*, 铝砷~albrac, 麦基奇尼~*, 斯特林~*
高强(度)混凝土 high strength concrete, strong concrete
高强度级 high strength level

高强度焦炭 hard [strong, strength] coke
高强度结构材料 high strength structure material
高强度结构钢 high tensile structural steel
高强度金属 high-duty metal (HDM)
高强度金属合金 high strength metallic alloy
高强度可焊铝合金 high strength weldable aluminium alloy
高强度铝合金 high strength aluminium alloy ◇阿尔德雷~线*, 雷西达尔易切削~Recidal, 尼克拉尔~*, 齐克拉尔~*, 齐休姆~*, 西尔卡姆~*
高强度铝黄铜(含铝锰的七O黄铜: 69Cu, 20Zn, 6.5Al, 2.5Fe, 2Mn) super bronze ◇阿尔布拉克~*
高强度铝镁锌合金 ◇本多~Honda duralumin, 康斯特拉克塔尔~Konstruktal
高强度锰青铜(64Cu, 0.5Sn, 3.5Mn, 5Al, 3Fe, 0.2Pb, 余量 Zn) high strength man-ganese bronze
高强度耐低温钢 high-strength low-allow steel (HSLA steel)
高强度耐磨含镍高锰钢 ◇曼加那尔~*
高强度耐热铁合金 ◇朱厄尔~jewell alloy
高强度耐蚀铬钢 ◇杰瑟特~*
高强度耐蚀铬镍钢 high-strength corrosion-resistance chromium-nickel steel
高强度耐蚀硅青铜 ◇奥林匹克~*
高强度耐蚀黄铜 ◇伊玛迪厄姆~*
高强度耐蚀铝青铜 ◇尼卡留~Nikalium, Superston-40, 苏珀斯通~*
高强度耐蚀锰青铜 ◇帕森~*
高强度耐蚀青铜 ◇鲁贝尔~*
高强度耐蚀铜板 Roean copper
高强度耐蚀铸造黄铜 ◇坦赛莱特~*
高强度青铜(60—68Cu, 2—4Fe, 3—7.5Al, 2.5—5Mn, 余量 Zn) high strength bronze ◇霍尔福斯~离心铸造法 Holfos process

高强度热处理 maraging
高强度热轧钢筋 high strength hot rolled reinforced bar
高强度烧结矿 high strength sinter
高强度双相钢钢丝 high strength dual steel wire
高强(度)水泥 【建】high strength cement ◇ 快硬~*
高强度线 line of high intensity
高强度性能 high tensile property
高强度轴承合金 ◇ 莫塔锡基~*
高强度珠光体铸铁 perlit
高强度铸钢 high tension cast steel
高强度铸铁 high tensile cast iron (HT-CI), high strength [tension] cast iron ◇ 含镍~*, 普罗马尔~Promal
高强度铸造黄铜 ◇ 萨姆~*
高强度铸造镁铝合金 ◇ 道屋 G~*
高强度铸造锰青铜 ◇ 特比斯顿~*
高强度钻探管 high strength drill pipe
高强高导铜合金 high-strength high-conductivity copper alloy
高强高韧合金 high-strength high-ductility alloy
高强高效管材 effective high strength steel pipe
高清晰度 high resolution, fine [high] definition
高屈服点钢 high yield strength steel
高屈服点合金 high yield alloy
高燃烧器 【焦】high(er) burner
高热期 full fired stage
高热效率 high heat efficiency
高热值 high(er) heating value
高热值煤气 high heating value gas
高热值燃料 high-energy fuel (HEF)
高热滞石 irreversible steel
高韧性钢 high toughness steel
高韧性管线钢 high toughness pipeline steel
高韧性合金 high-ductility alloy
高熔点 high melting point

高熔点材料 high(er) melting point material
高熔点合金 high melting point alloy
高熔点化合物 refractory compound
高熔点夹杂物 refractory inclusions
高熔点金属 high melting (point) metal, refractory metal
高熔点金属粉末 refractory powder
高熔点耐火材料 high melting point refractory
高熔点黏结剂 high melting binder
高熔点新金属 refractory newer metal
高熔点硬质合金 refractory hard metal
高熔点重金属 high melting heavy metal
高熔点组分 high melting (point) component, high melting constituent
高熔剂性烧结矿 (同"高碱度烧结矿")
高溶解能力 high solvency
高蠕变强度钢 high creep strength steel
高蠕变强度金属 creep-resistant metal
高蠕变强度钛基合金 ◇ 海莱特 65~*
高声信号器(润滑系统用) (loud) hailer, howler
高生产率 high production (rate), high-duty
高湿度试验 high humidity test
高湿度养护室(混凝土用) damp-storage closet
高铈的 ceric
高铈化合物 ceric compound
高数位 high order digit [position]
高斯尺寸 Gaussian size
高斯分布 Gaussian distribution
高斯分布曲线 Gauss distribution curve
高斯公式 Gauss formula
高斯计 gaussmeter
高斯误差 Gaussian error
高斯误差函数 Gauss error function
高斯形状(光谱线的) Gaussian shape
高速 X 射线胶片 high speed X-ray film
高速泵 high speed pump
高速变形 very high rates of deformation

高速成形机 high speed forming machine ◇ 戴纳帕克型~*
高速齿轮 high speed gear
高速冲击硬化法 velocity impact hardening (V.I.H.)
高速冲剪下料 high speed blanking
高速(冲压)成形 high velocity forming (HVF), rate forming ◇ 风动机械~*
高速冲压机[冲床] high speed ram machine
高速锤磨机 high speed hammer mill
高速锤式粉碎机 high speed hammer mill
高速淬火炉 high speed hardening furnace
高速存储器[装置] 【计】high speed memory [storage]
高速打印机 high speed printer (HSP)
高速等静压制 high speed isostatic pressing ◇ 自动~*
高速电子 high speed electron
高速度 high speed (HS, h.s.)
高速(锻)锤 rapid-action hammer ◇ 锤头内架[锤-架]式~*,双锤式~【压】two-ram machine
高速锻造机 high velocity forging machine ◇ 赫姆斯~Clearing Hermes,佩特罗压缩空气~*
高速断路器 【电】high speed circuit breaker (HSCB)
高速对流燃烧器 high velocity convection burners
高速发电机 high speed generator
高速发动机 high speed engine
高速粉碎机 high speed disintegrator
高速风口 high velocity tuyere
高速感光无屏蔽胶片 fast no-screen film
高速钢 high-speed-steel (HSS, h.s.s.), quick-speed [quick-cutting] steel, rapid (machining) steel ◇ 低钨~*,蒂兹特~*,电渣重熔~*,多元~*,坎农~*,克虏伯~*,特里普尔~*
高速钢镀硬铬法 Lundbye process
高速钢复合轧辊 high speed steel compound roll
高速钢鳞皮 high speed steel scale
高速钢热处理法 ◇ 泰勒-怀特~*
高速钢轧辊 high speed steel roll
高速工具钢 high speed tool steel, rapid tool steel, red-hard steel
高速过滤器 high rate filter
高速合金 ◇ 普雷米乌姆~*
高速环 【计】high speed loop
高速缓冲存储器 【计】cache memory
高速活性污泥处理法 high rate activated sludge process
高速挤压 【压】high velocity [speed, rate] extrusion
高速记忆装置 【计】high speed memory
高速继电器 fast speed relay
高速剪切头尾 high speed cropping
高速搅拌式混合机 high agiting mixer
高速开卷机 【压】biflaker
高速冷轧管机 high-speed cold Pilger mill
高速离心机 high speed centrifuge, supercentrifuge
高速连铸 high speed continuous casting ◇ 圆坯的近终形~*
高速连铸技术 CC technology of high casting speed
高速连铸小方坯结晶器 high speed billet casting mould
高速料仓 track hopper
高速列车 high-speed train
高速流体喷射加工 high velocity liquid jet machining
高速屏蔽 high speed screen
高速气流 high velocity air
高速切削 quick-cutting
高速切削钢 (同"高速钢")
高速切削黄铜 high-speed brass
高速切削金属 high speed cutting metal
高速氰化处理 cyaniding of high speed steel
高速球磨机 high speed ball mill
高速热压机 high speed hot press

高速熔断丝 【电】high speed fuse
高速烧嘴 high speed burner
高速摄影术 high speed photography
高速射流加工 high speed fluid jet working, high velocity liquid jet machining
高速射线照相术 high-speed radiography
高速石灰喷射 【钢】high rate of lime injection
高速铁路 rapid transit [high-speed] railway
高速下料 high speed blanking
高速限流熔丝 【电】high speed current limiting fuse
高速线材轧机 high speed wire rod mill
高速需氧处理 high rate aerobic treatment
高速(旋转)洗气机 【铁】high speed disintegrator
高速压力机 high speed press
高速压力加工 very high rates of deformation
高速压实 【粉】high-speed compaction
高速氧化燃料 high velocity oxidization fuel (HVOF)
高速氧气射流 high velocity oxygen jet
高速液相色谱法 high speed liquid chromatography
高速印刷器 high speed printer
高速应变脆性 rheotropic brittleness
高速轧机 high speed mill, fast mill
高速照相术 high speed photography
高速周期式冷轧管机 high speed cold pilger mill
高速钻机 high speed drill
高塑性钢 high-ductility steel
高塑性黏土 high plastic clay
高酸消耗 high acid consuming
高酸性炉渣 highly acid slag
高钛合金 titanium master alloy
高钛炉渣 high titanium slag
高碳表面层(渗碳钢的) high carbon case
高碳钒铁(83—86V,10.5—13C,2—3Fe)【钢】carvan
高碳钢 high carbon steel (hcs), high steel
高碳钢耐磨(炉顶)衬板 【钢】high carbon steel wearing plate
高碳钢全贝氏体热处理法 ◇ 珀内尔～Purnell process
高碳钢熔炼 high carbon heat
高碳高钒模具钢 high-carbon high-vanadium die steel
高碳高铬钢 high carbon high chromium steel
高碳高合金奥氏体 【金】high carbon high alloy austenite
高碳高合金钢 high carbon high alloy steel
高碳铬 high-carbon chromium
高碳铬钢 carbon chromium steel
高碳铬铁 (high) carbon ferrochrome, charge chrome
高碳铬轴承钢 high carbon chromium bearing steel
高碳合金钢 high carbon alloy steel
高碳焦 high-carbon coke
高碳冷压球团 【金】high carbon content cold-binding pellet
高碳炉次 hard melt
高碳马氏体 high carbon martensite
高碳耐磨铸铁 adamite
高碳生铁 high carbon (pig) iron
高碳铁粉 high carbon iron poweder
高碳铁合金 high carbon iron alloy
高碳铁水 high carbon hot metal
高碳银亮钢 ◇ 博勒～Bohler
高碳直接还原铁 high carbon DRI
高碳铸钢 high carbon cast steel
高碳铸钢轧辊 iron-base roll
高梯度磁选 high gradient magnetic separation
高锑炉渣 antimony-enriched slag, slag high in autimony
高铁比炉料 high iron charge
高铁波特兰水泥 high iron Portland cement
高铁(分)炉渣 high iron slag

高铁钙渣 【色】high iron limey slag
高铁铝土矿 high iron bauxite
高铁钼华 (同"水钼铁矿")
高铁石棉 {(Fe^{2+}, Mg, Al)$_7$(Si, Al)$_8$O$_{22}$(OH)$_2$} amosite
高铁水比熔炼 【钢】high hot metal heat
高铁酸 ferric acid
高铁酸盐 ferrate
高铁钛铁矿 kalkowskite
高铁钛铀矿 {20FeO·8Fe$_2$O$_3$·4(RE)$_2$O$_3$·UO$_2$·74TiO$_2$} ufertite
高铁团块 high iron briquette (HIB)
高铁钨华 {Fe$_2$O$_3$·WO$_3$·6H$_2$O} ferritungstite
高通滤波器 high pass filter
高铜(浮)渣 【色】copper-rich dross
高铜黄铜 (同"红色黄铜")
高铜铸造黄铜 (84-86Cu, 4-6Zn, 4-6Sn, 4-6Pb, <1Ni) composition brass, ounce metal
高透射光谱[分光]计 high transmission spectrometer
高凸度轧机 HC (high crown) mill
高顽磁 【理】high remanence
高位槽 elevated [head] tank
高位储[贮,料]槽 high level tank, overhead [elevated] bunker
高位料仓 overhead bin
高位能级 high lying (energy) level
高位水箱 elevated water tank, headbox
高位显示器 overhead display
高位贮水槽 balance tank
高温 high temperature (HT), elevated [hot] temperature, hi-temperature, high heat
高温 X 射线(照相)技术 high temperature X-ray technique
高温焙烧 high temperature roasting
高温焙烧(过)的 high fired, hard burnt
高温焙烧石灰 hard burned lime
高温变态[变质处理] 【金】high temperature modification

高温变形 high [elevated] temperature deformation
高温变质 pyrometamorphism
高温表 pyrometric scale
高温不起皮钢 oxidation-resisting steel
高温材料 high temperature materail
高温操作 high temperature operation
高温测量学[测定法] pyrometry
高温超导材料 high temperature superconducting material
高温超导体 high temperature superconductor
高温陈化 high temperature ageing
高温成形 high temperature forming, elevated temperature compaction, ardeforming, hot forming
高温持久强度特性 high temperature stress rupture characteristic
高温处理 high temperature [heat] treatment, pyroprocessing, thermal treatment
高温传热介质 high temperature heat transfer medium (HTM)
高温脆性 high-temperature brittleness
高温淬火 quench hot, hot quenching
高温带 high temperature zone, hot zone [space]
高温导电性 pyroconductivity
高温等温退火法 high temperature isothermal annealing process
高温电收尘器 hot cottrell
高温电子显微镜 hot stage electron microscope
高温电阻炉 high temperature resistance furnace
高温短时时效 high temperature short time ageing
高温段(窑、炉的) hot section ◇ 煤焰～ coal-flame hot zone
高温煅烧 high temperature calcination
高温断裂 high temperature fracture
高温反应 high temperature reaction
高温反应堆 high-temperature reactor

高温范围 high temperature region
高温沸腾 high boiling
高温分解 high temperature decomposition, pyrogenic [pyrolytic] decomposition, pyrolysis
高温分解涂层(气体涂层) pyrolytic plating
高温风机 hot fan
高温辐射脆化 high temperature irradiation embrittlement
高温腐蚀 high [elevated] temperature corrosion, hot corrosion
高温负载特性 high temperature characteristics under load
高温坩埚 high temperature crucible
高温钢 high-temperature steel
高温高分辨率金相学 high temperature high resolution metallography
高温高强度合金 superalloy
高温高压技术 high-temperature and high-pressure technique
高温高压设备 high-temperature high-pressure apparatus
高温工艺气体 hot process gas
高温固结 【团】thermal hardening
高温观察法 high temperature method of observation
高温管式电[电热管式]炉 high temperature electric tube furnace
高温光谱仪 spectropyrometer
高温合金 high temperature alloy, heat resisting alloy, refractory alloy ◇ 阿斯科洛伊～ Ascoloy, 格里克阿斯科洛伊～ Greek Ascoloy
高温化学 pyrochemistry
高温还原 high temperature reduction
高温还原浸出 high temperature reducing leach
高温回火 high (temperature) tempering ◇ 马氏体中～组织 troosto-sorbite
高温回火钢 high temper steel
高温火焰 high temperature flame

高温机械性能 mechanical property at elevated temperature
高温级 high temperature level
高温挤压 high temperature extruding
高温计 pyrometer (pyr.) ◇ 比色光学[比奥普蒂克斯]～*, 铂铑[勒夏特里耶]～ Le Chatelier pyrometer, 测碳当量用～*, 电光热气～*, 电阻～ electropyrometer, 发光灯丝～*, 福斯特～*, 光电～*, 光敏元件～*, 光学～*, 红外线辐射～*, 灰楔～ grey wedge pyrometer, 霍尔博恩～ Holborn pyrometer, 监测～ sentinel pyrometer, 浸入式～ immersion pyrometer, 偏光～ polarizing pyrometer, 手动[携带式]～ hand pyrometer, 手枪式～【冶】pistol pyrometer, 水测～ hydropyrometer, 速浸式～*, 微型～ pyromike, 吸色～*, 显微[精测]～ micropyrometer, 响音～ noise thermometer, 隐丝式～*, 真空～ suction pyrometer, 自记～ autographic pyrometer
高温计保护套管 pyrometer protection tube
高温计管 pyrometer tube
高温计记录器 pyrometer recorder
高温记录器(氧割自动机的) pyrograph
高温加工 elevated temperature working, pyroprocessing
高温加热 high temperature heating
高温焦炭 high-temperature coke
高温阶段 hot stage
高温结构 high temperature texture
高温结构材料 high-temperature structural material
高温结构组分 high temperature constituent
高温金相学 high temperature metallography
高温精炼 【冶】fire refining
高温静电除尘[沉淀]器 high temperature electrostatic precipitator
高温静液挤压 high temperature hydro-

static extrusion
高温绝缘 high temperature insulation
高温均匀化 high temperature homogenization
高温抗拉强度 hot tensile strength
高温抗氧化涂层 high-temperature oxidation resistant coating
高温抗[耐]氧化性 oxidation resistance at elevated temperature
高温快速加热炉(分段的) 【压】high speed heating furnace
高温扩散正火 diffusion normalizing
高温拉拔[拉丝] 【压】elevated temperature drawing (ETD)
高温拉伸试验 hot tension test
高温拉伸性能 tensile property at elevated temperature
高温炉 high temperature [heat] furnace
高温炉次 high temperature heat, hot heat
高温炉顶 high top heat
高温氯化 high temperature chlorination
高温氯化法 (同"氯化挥发法")
高温马氏体 high-temperature martensite
高温模具钢 hot-die steel
高温磨削 high temperature grinding
高温耐火材料 high temperature refractory
高温耐氧化钢 (同"热稳定钢")
高温内摩擦(力) high temperature internal friction
高温泥浆 high temperature mortar
高温黏度计 high temperature visco(si)meter
高温扭转试验 hot torsion [twist] test
高温疲劳强度 high temperature fatigue strength
高温疲劳试验 high temperature fatigue test
高温疲劳试验机 high temperature fatigue strength testing machine
高温破裂[裂缝] high temperature cracking
高温曝光 elevated temperature exposure
高温气体 hot [high-temperature] gas
高温气体腐蚀 dry corrosion
高温气体冷却反应堆 high temperature gas-cooled reactor (HTGR)
高温气相色谱法 high temperature gas chromatography
高温钎焊 high temperature brazing
高温强度 elevated [high] temperature strength, hot strength, strength at elevated [high] temperatures
高温强度铁基合金 (同"耐高温铁基合金")
高温切削 high temperature machining
高温氢气保护炉 high temperature hydrogen furnace
高温球团 hot pellet
高温球团层 hot pellet bed
高温区(域) high temperature region [zone], hot space
高温热处理 high-heat treatment
高温热电偶 high temperature thermocouple, thermocouple for high temperature
高温熔炼 high melt, high temperature heat, hot heat
高温熔模 heat disposable pattern
高温溶解 high temperature digestion
高温蠕变 high [elevated] temperature creep
高温蠕变成形 elevated temperature creep forming
高温蠕变动力学 high temperature creep kinetics
高温软化(水的) hot process softening
高温润滑剂 high temperature lubricant
高温烧结 high (temperature) sintering, advanced sintering
高温烧结块 hot agglomerate
高温烧结零件 high sintered parts
高温烧结砖(荷兰式) 【耐】Dutch brick
高温射线照相术 hot radiography
高温设施 high temperature service

高温渗氮　high temperature nitriding
高温渗碳法　high temperature carburizing (process)
高温渗碳钢　high temperature carburized steel
高温湿法冶金　high temperature hydrometallurgy
高温时效　high [elevated] temperature ageing
高温使用　high temperature service
高温试验　high temperature test(ing), hot test
高温衰减[内耗]　high temperature damping
高温双金属　bimetal for high temperature
高温水　high temperature water
高温水解　high temperature hydrolysis, pyrohydrolysis
高温塑性　high temperature plasticity, pyroplasticity
高温碳化　high temperature carbonization
高温碳素还原制镁法　Hansgirg process
高温探测器　pyrometer probe
高温陶瓷　high temperature ceramics, pyroceram
高温特性　high temperature characteristics
高温天平　thermo-balance
高温铁氧体　pyroferrite
高温透气性　high temperature permeability, hot permeability
高温退火　annealing at elevated temperature
高温温度计　high temperature [reading] thermometer
高温稳定性试验(壳型树脂砂的)　thimble test
高温稳态蠕变　high temperature steady state creep
高温物体　hot body
高温细菌　high-temperature bacteria
高温显微镜　high temperature microscope, hot stage microscope, heating microscope ◇ 真空～*
高温显微镜观察　hot stage microscopic observation
高温显微镜(图)像　high temperature microscopic(al) image, hot stage microscopic(al) image
高温显微镜照相　hot stage photomicrograph
高温显微术　high temperature microscopy, hot stage microscopy
高温相　【金】high temperature phase
高温形变热处理　high-temperature ausform
高温形态　high temperature form
高温行为　high temperature behaviour
高温性能　high [elevated] temperature property, high temperature behaviour
高温性状[行为]　high temperature behaviour, thermal behaviour
高温压力浸出　high temperature pressure leach
高温压缩蠕变　high temperature compressive creep
高温压制　elevated temperature compaction, high temperature pressing
高温研磨　(同"高温磨削")
高温氧化　high temperature oxidation (HTO)
高温氧化环境　hot oxidizing environment
高温氧化增重率　rate of weight gain by oxidation at elevated temperature
高温氧化渣　【冶】hot oxidizing slag
高温氧乙炔火焰　high temperature oxygen acetylene flame
高温冶金　thermometallurgy, pyro-metallurgical method
高温冶金学　pyrometallurgy
高温冶金学的　pyrometallurgical (PM)
高温冶炼　pyrolytic smelting
高温应变仪　high temperature strain gauge
高温应力　high temperature stress rupture

高温硬度 hot hardness
高温硬度测定器 hot hardness device
高温硬度曲线 hot hardness curve
高温硬度试验 hot hardness testing ◇ 凯泽~Kayser hardness test
高温硬度试验机 hot hardness tester
高温硬度试验装置 hot hardness assemble
高温硬质合金 high temperature cemented carbide
高温用双金属 bimetal for high temperature
高温载物台(显微镜的) hot stage
高温载物台显微镜 (同"高温显微镜")
高温照相机 high temperature camera
高温照相术 thermal-photography
高温罩式(退火)炉 batch type high temperature furnace
高温真空处理 hot vacuum treatment
高温蒸馏 high-temperature distillation
高温正火处理 high-temperature normalizing treatment
高温轴承钢 high-temperature bearing steel
高温组织 high temperature texture
高温作业 high temperature operation [work]
高钨酸盐{M_2WO_3[O_2]} pertungstate
高吸收能力材料 【理】material of high absorbing power
高锡巴比合金(含83—87Sn) high tin babbit
高锡焊料 【焊】rich solder
高锡耐蚀合金 ◇ 斯坦尼欧尔~*
高锡铅基轴承合金 ◇ L.B.142~*, 霍伊特~*, 卡特拉斯塔~*
高锡青铜 high tin bronze ◇ 诺伊尔~(20Sn,余量Cu) Noil
高锡重载轴承合金 ◇ 斯塔纳姆~*
高锡轴承合金(78—85Sn, 5—11Cu, 9—15Sb) plastic metal
高纤维素型焊条 high cellulose type electrode
高向温差(炉墙的) 【焦】vertical temperature difference
高效薄层色谱 high performance thin layer chromatography (HPTLC)
高效层流净化器 high duty lamellar clarifier
高效矫直法 effective method of straightening
高效矫直机 high performance leveller (HPL)
高效连续狭缝烧嘴组件 high capacity continuous slot unit (HCSU)
高效连铸 high efficient continuous casting, efficient (fully) continuous casting, fastcast system ◇ 罗可普~ROKOP fastcast system
高效率操作[工作,作业] high efficiency operation
高效率冷床 【压】high duty cooling bed
高效率燃烧器[高效烧嘴] high efficiency burner
高效能纯氢保护气氛罩式退火炉 HPH (high performance hydrogen) bell type furnace
高效小方坯连铸机 efficient billet continuous caster
高效液相色谱法 high performance liquid chromatography
高效再生 highly efficient regeneration
高效炸药 high explosive
高效炸药爆炸成形 【压】high explosive operation [forming]
高锌粉尘 high zinc dust
高锌黄铜 white [high] brass, platina ◇ 博毕尔~*, 伯明翰~*, 马莱特~*, 普拉廷~(57Zn,余量Cu) Platine, 瑟斯顿~*
高新技术 high-tech
高形变速率成形 high strain rate forming
高性能合金 high-performance alloy
高性能金属 high performance metal

高序位错 high order dislocation
高悬式矿仓 trestle bin
高循环次数疲劳 high cycle fatigue
高压(力) high pressure (HP, h.p.), heavy pressure
高压(高电压) high voltate, high tension
高压 X 射线管 high voltage X-ray tube
高压氨浸出法 【色】pressure ammonia leaching, ammonia pressure leach process
高压氨水和邻室抽吸法(焦炉装煤除尘) high pressure ammonia liquor me thod with neighbouring chamber extracting
高压拔[拉]丝模 high pressure die
高压拔[拉]丝模座 high pressure die block
高压保护气氛贮罐 high pressure protective atmosphere storing unit
高压保险丝 【电】high voltage fuse
高压泵 high pressure pump
高压变态 high pressure modification ◇ 铈(同素异晶)的～*
高压变压器 【电】high tension transformer
高压表 high pressure gauge
高压操作 【铁】high (top) pressure operation
高压成形 high pressure forming ◇ 电火花～法*
高压除鳞喷嘴组 【压】high pressure descaling [water] sprays
高压处理 pressurization
高压单晶炉 high pressure crystal pulling furnace
高压导线 【电】high tension wire
高压电灯 high voltage lamp
高压电动机 high voltage motor
高压电力供应 high voltage power supply
高压电流 high tension current
高压(电路)断路器 【电】high pressure circuit breaker (HPCB)
高压电选机 high tension separator
高压电源 high voltage supply
高压电子显微镜 high voltage electron microscope
高压二极管阳极 kenotron anode
高压二极整流管 kenotron rectifier
高压发电机 high voltage [tension] generator
高压反应器 high pressure reactor
高压放电电极 high voltage discharge electrode
高压风 high pressure blast
高压釜 (high pressure) autoclave ◇ 衬铅～ lead lining autoclave, 管式～ tube autoclave, 回转～ rotating autoclave, 加压浸出～*, 卧式～*, 新蒸气直接加热式～ live-steam autoclave, 蒸汽搅拌～*, 柱式～ column autoclave
高压釜沉淀(法) autoclave precipitation
高压釜处理 autoclave treatment, autoclaving ◇ 间歇式～*
高压釜分离 autoclave separation
高压釜固结(法) autoclave hardening
高压釜碱[碳酸钠,苏打]浸出法 autoclave-soda process
高压釜浸出 autoclave leach
高压釜球团 autoclave-hardened pellet ◇ 英迪斯科～法 Indesco process
高压釜(球团)硬化车 autoclaving wagon
高压釜溶出 autoclave digestion
高压釜湿法冶金 autoclave hydrometallurgy
高压釜酸浸 【色】acid autoclave leaching
高压釜脱硅 autoclave desiliconizing
高压釜组 battery of autoclaves
高压高炉 high pressure blast furnace
高压隔膜泵 high pressure diaphragm pump
高压工程 high tension engineering
高压鼓风机 (high) pressure blower
高压固体燃料喷吹系统 【冶】high pressure solids injection system
高压管 pressure tube [pipe]
高压管路 pressure line
高压罐 pressurizing tank

高压锅炉　high pressure [duty] boiler
高压锅炉管　boiler tube for high pressure service
高压焊炬　high pressure torch
高压化学　piezochemistry
高压还原　pressure reduction
高压还原法　pressure reduction process
高压还原浸出　reducing pressure leaching
高压汇流排　【电】high tension bus-bar
高压活塞泵　high pressure piston pump
高压机械整流器　mechanical high-voltage rectifier
高压碱浸法　alkaline pressure leaching process
高压交流电动机　high voltage alternate current motor
高压进线馈电(控制)板　high voltage incoming feeder panel
高压浸出　(high, elevated) pressure leaching, autoclaving, pressurized lea-ching ◇ 碳酸盐~carbonate autoclaving
高压浸出系统　pressure leaching train
高压浸出液　pressure-leach liquor
高压绝缘子　【电】high tension (support) insulator
高压开关　high voltage [tension] switch
高压开关站　high voltage switch gear station
高压开关装置　high tension switch gear
高压苛性碱系统　pressure caustic system
高压空气　(high) pressure air
高压空气喷雾法　high pressure air atomization
高压空气喷雾器　high pressure (air) atimizer
高压控制盘　high tension panel
高压冷却管路　high pressure cooling circuit
高压离子交换　pressure ion exchange
高压联合启动器　【电】high tension combination starter
高压流体　high pressure fluid

高压炉　pressure furnace ◇ 石墨~
高压炉顶　【铁】high-top pressure (HTP) ◇ B-I式~Bailey-IHI top
高压炉顶操作　high (top) pressure operation
高压炉顶高炉　high top pressure blast furnace
高压炉顶容量　high top pressure capability
高压炉顶压力　high top pressure
高压煤气发生炉　pressure-gas producer
高压煤气燃烧器　pressure-gas burner, injector gas burner
高压灭菌器　autoclave
高压模塑　high pressure mould(ing)
高压模铸　high pressure die casting
高压母线　【电】high tension bus-bar, primary busbar
高压配电　high voltage distribution
高压喷煤　pressure coal injection
高压喷水清理　hydroblast(ing)
高压喷水连续淬火　high quench
高压喷雾器　high pressure (air) atomizer
高压喷嘴　high pressure nozzle
高压气氛　pressurized atmosphere
高压(气)瓶　(high) pressure bottle [tank]
高压气体　pressure gas
高压气体调节　high pressure gas regulation
高压气筒　gas cylinder
高压汽化冷却　【铁】pressure type evaporative cooling
高压燃烧器　high pressure burner
高压绕组　high-voltage [high-tension] winding
高压热水[热蒸汽]硫化罐　high pressure hot water vulcanizing can
高压溶出　(pressure) digestion
高压溶出器　digester
高压容器　(high) pressure vessel [container]

高 gao

高压容器用钢板　high pressure vessel steel plate
高压湿法冶金　pressure hydrometallurgy
高压室　pressure chamber
高压试验　high voltage test, high pressure test
高压手摇泵　high pressure manual pump
高压水　(high) pressure water
高压水泵站[房]　high pressure water pump stand [room]
高压水除鳞装置　【压】hydraulic jet descaler
高压水除锈　hydroblasting
高压水冷却管路　high pressure cooling circuit
高压水喷射[喷雾]　hydraulic spray
高压水喷雾嘴　hydraulic spray nozzle
高压水射流除锈　high pressure water jet removing-rust
高压酸浸法　acid pressure leach
高压缩性粉末　high compressibility powder
高压缩性晶体　crystal of high compressibility
高压塔　high pressure tower
高压羰化　pressure carbonglation ◇ 因科~法
高压羰基法　high pressure carbonyl process
高压套管　high voltage (H.V.) bushing
高压调节阀　【铁】throttling [septum] valve
高压系统　high pressure system
高压线(路)　【电】high tension line [cable]
高压线圈　【电】high tension coil
高压橡胶软管　high pressure rubber hose
高压信号器(锅炉的)　high lock alarm
高压(挤)铸(造)　high pressure squeeze casting
高压氧化浸出　oxidizing pressure leaching
高压液态成形　high pressure liquid forming

高压乙炔发生器　high pressure acetylene generator
高压引线　【电】high voltage lead
高压用油　extreme pressure oil
高压造型　【铸】pressure moulding
高压蒸汽　high pressure steam
高压蒸汽腐蚀　high pressure steam etching
高压蒸汽套管预热器　jacketed-pipe high-pressure steam preheater
高压整流管　【电】kenotron, high-voltage rectifier tube
高压整流器　【电】high tension [voltage] rectifier
高压铸造　high pressure casting [mould(ing)]
高压装料　high pressure charging
高压自动开关　high tension automatic switch
高烟囱排放　high chimney emission
高延性钢　high ductility steel
高延性合金　high ductile alloy
高延性镉银合金(85Ag,15Cd)　cadmium silver (alloy)
高扬程水泵　high lift pump
高氧化矿石　high oxide ore
高氧化铝耐火材料　high alumina refractory
高氧化铝耐火砖　high alumina firebrick
高氧化铝渣　high alumina slag
高氧化镁打结耐火材料　◇ 莱米克斯~Ramix
高氧化速率　high rate of oxidation
高氧化钛型焊条　high titanium oxide type electrode
高氧化亚铁渣　【铁】high FeO slag
高银含量的　highly argentiferous
高银壳　high silver crust
高银天然金(＞20Ag)　Electrum
高应力结构　highly stressed structure
高硬度　high hardness
高硬度表面层　case of intense hardness

高硬度冷轧钢板　full tempers
高硬度渗碳钢　rose steel
高油　【选】tall oil, talloel
高原子序数金属　metal of high atomic number
高原子序数物质　high Z material
高原子序数元素　high-Z element
高张力　high tension (HT)
高折射率[高指数]面　high index plane
高真空泵　high vacuum pump ◇ 海瓦克～Hyvac pump, 罗茨～roots high vacuum pump
高真空电子管　high vacuum tube, hard tube
高真空(度)　high [perfect, fine] vacuum, microvac
高真空封蜡　high vacuum sealing wax
高真空感应加热炉　high vacuum induction heated furnace
高真空回转油泵　◇ 森科(海瓦克)～Cenco(Hyvac) pump
高真空技术　high vacuum technique
高真空计　high vacuum gauge
高真空炉　high vacuum furnace
高真空熔化　high-vacuum melting
高真空软管　high vacuum hose
高真空烧结　high vacuum sintering
高真空设备　high vacuum apparatus [equipment]
高真空橡胶软管　high vacuum hose
高真空冶炼炉　high vacuum melting furnace
高真空蒸馏　high vacuum distillation
高质量　high-quality (H.Q.)
高质(量)钢　high-quality steel
高质量回炉废料　【冶】high grade melting scrap
高质量金属　high-test metal
高质量黏土　high grade clay
高质量烧结矿　high quality sinter
高质量铸铁　high-duty iron
高中子通量反应堆　high flux reactor

高周波　high frequency (HF, hf), high cycle
高转鼓指数球团　high tumbler index pellet
高桩承台　elevated pile foundation
高自由能相　higher energy phase
高阻表[计]　megameter, megger, tramegger, earthometer
高阻导线　resistive conductor
高阻合金　high-resistance alloy
高阻尼合金　high damping alloy
高阻镍钢　climax
缟纹　【地】stria
缟状排列　banded arrangement
锆{Zr}　zirconium ◇ 低铪～low-hafnium zirconium, 碘化物法～iodide zirconium, 海绵～sponge zirconium, 含铪～*, 无铪～hafnium free zirconium
锆厂[制锆车间]　zirconium plant
锆沉积管(碘化物法)　zirconium deposition tube
锆电极　zirconium electrode
锆电解槽　zirconium electrolysis cell ◇ 惰性气氛～*
锆锭　zirconium ingot
锆矾　zircosulfate
锆氟化钾{K_2ZrF_6}　potassium zirconium fluoride
锆氟酸钾还原　reduction of potassium zirconium fluoride
锆钙钛矿{$3Ca(Ti, Zr)_2O_5 \cdot Al_2TiO_5$}　uhligite
锆钢　zirconium steel
锆硅铁　zirconium ferrosilicon
锆铪分离系统　hafnium zirconium separation (system)
锆铪混合物　zirconium-hafnium mixture
锆合金　zirconium alloy
锆晶棒　zirconium crystal bar
锆矿床　zirconium deposit
锆锂大隅石　sogdianite
锆络合物制备　zirconium complex prepa-

锆锰大隅石　darapiosite
锆铅合金　zirconium lead alloy
锆青铜　zirconium copper
锆溶液　zirconium solution
锆砂{ZrO_2}　zirconia, zircon(ia) sand
锆石　azorite, auerbachite, calypotolite, jacinth, jacynth, diocroma, engelhardite, ostranite
锆始锭　zirconium starter plug
锆酸{H_2ZrO_3, H_4ZrO_4}　zirconic acid
锆酸钡{$BaO·ZrO_2$}　barium zirconate
锆酸钙{$CaO·ZrO_2$}　calcium zirconate
锆酸酐{ZrO_2}　zirconium anhydride
锆酸镁{$MgO·ZrO_2$}　magnesium zirconate
锆酸钠{Na_2ZrO_3}　sodium zirconate
锆酸铅　lead zirconate
锆酸锶{$SrO·ZrO_2$}　strontium zirconate
锆酸钍{$ThO_2·ZrO_2$}　thorium zirconate
锆酸盐{M_2ZrO_3}　zirconate
锆钛钙石　belyankinite
锆钛合金　zirtan
锆钛酸铅　lead zirconate titanate
锆钽矿　lavenite
锆碳化物烧结合金　◇齐尔坦~Zirtan, Zirten
锆添加合金　zirconium addition
锆铁(中间合金；14-40Zr,39-52Si) ferrozirconium ◇西尔卡兹~合金*,西尔瓦克斯~合金*
锆铁矿　zirfesite
锆铜合金　zirconium-copper alloy ◇阿姆泽克~*
锆铜钼合金　◇ATR~*
锆钨电极　zirconiated tungsten
锆锡合金　zircaloy ◇吉尔卡洛伊~Zircaloy
锆盐　zirconium salt
锆英粉　zircon flour
锆英石{$ZrSiO_4$}　zircon(ia) sand, zircon(ite)
锆英石氟化物分解　fluoride breakdown of zircon
锆英石氯化　chlorination of zircon
锆英石耐火材料　zircon refractory ◇巴科尔刚玉~Bacor
锆英石碳化　carburization of zircon
锆铀矿{$ZrSiO_4 + UO_3$}　naegite
锆与硅酸盐的化学键　zirconium-to-silicate bond
锆针钠钙石{$6CaSiC_3·2Na_2ZrO_2F_2Ti(SiO_3)(TiO_3)$}　rosenbuschite
锆质定径水口　zircon sizing nozzle
锆质高级耐火材料　◇吉尔科弗拉克斯~Zircofrax
锆质耐火材料　zirconia refractory
搁架炉　shelf furnace [oven], tile furnace
搁栅　【建】joist
搁栅撑　【建】bridging
搁置不用　laid-up, lie idle
搁置槽 (用于从水相残液中分离出有机相) delay vessel
戈德尔水泥砂造型法　【铸】Godel process
戈德弗雷旋转炉膛焙烧炉　Godfrey roaster [roasting furnace]
戈尔德施密铝热还原(法)　Goldschmidt thermit reduction
戈尔德施密铝热还原焊接法　Goldschmidt('s) process
戈尔丁黄铜代金合金(90Cu,10Zn)　Goldine
戈斯金属连铸法　Goss process for continuous casting of metal
戈斯织构(晶粒取向硅钢组织)　【金】Goss('s) structure, Goss texture
割把　burning tool ◇带小孔烧切装置的~burner with a small hole cutting attachment, 切管用~tube cutting burner, 三软管式~three-hose (gas) cutter
割管炬　tube-cutting torch
割阶　【理】jog ◇填隙式~interstitial jog, 位错~*
割阶非守恒运动　non-conservative motion of jogs

割阶扩散(位错的) jog diffusion
割阶螺型位错 jogged screw dislocation
割阶密度 jog concentration
割阶能量 energy of jogs
割炬 cutting torch [blowpipe, burner], blow torch ◇ 表面切割~*, 煤气-氧气~*, 手工~*, 双焰~*, 氧弧~ arc-oxygen torch, 乙炔焰~*, 铸铁~ cast iron cutting burner
割炬附件 cutting attachment
割炬火焰清理 torch deseaming
割炬喷嘴 blow pipe head
割炬切割 torch cutting
割炬烧喷嘴 torch head
割炬嘴 cutting nozzle
割口石墨电阻棒 split-rod graphite resistor
割切口 notching
割切位错 cutting dislocation
割嘴 cutting tip [torch] ◇ 氧熔剂~(喷)孔*
革兰氏阳性细菌 Gram-positive bacteria
革兰氏阴性水处理 Gram-negative
革兰氏阴性细菌 Gram-negative bacteria
革新 updating, renovation, innovation
格板炉顶 checker board roof
格板式干燥室 shelf dryer
格仓 cell bunker
格槽分样[缩样]器 riffle
格床基础 raft foundation
格迪奇合金 Gedge's alloy
格尔特直接炼铁法 Gurlt process
格尔瓦纳姆铝合金 Galvanum
格构 cancellation, lattice, treillage
格构梁 lattice beam [girder]
格构式 【建】lattice
格构式导热率[传热性] lattice heat [thermal] conductivity
格构式防波堤 cellular breakwater
格构式结构 cancelled structure
格架式焙烧炉 roasting shelf furnace
格间式挡土墙 cellular retaining wall

格孔(热风炉砖格子的) checkerwork cell
格孔板(雨水井口的) catch-frame
格孔尺寸 【冶】checker flue dimension
格孔通道面积 checker free-flow area
格框 【建】catch-frame, gridiron
格拉菲道克斯硅钛钙铁合金(48—52Si, 9—11Ti, 5—7Ca, 余量 Fe) Graphidox
格拉弗拉姆石墨-铝混合(炉衬打结)料 【冶】 Graphram
格拉西尔耐摩合金(11.5Sb, 2Sn, 余量 Pb) Glacier anti-friction alloy
格赖纳-克林根施泰因铸铁金相(组织)图 Greiner-Klingenstein's (constitutional) diagram
格兰内耐摩轴承青铜(75—76Cu, 15Pb, 9—10Sn) Graney bronze
格兰尼拉布收尘组件 Granilab module
格兰耶斯冷固球团 Graengcold pellet
格兰耶斯冷固球团法 Graengcold method
格雷茨桥接全波整流器 Gretz rectifier
格雷茨全波桥接电路 Graetz full-wave bridge circuit
格雷夫简式旋转氧气炼钢炉 Graef rotor
格雷-金焦型 Gray King coke type
格雷-金试验 Gray King assay
格雷纳尔钒钛铝铁合金(12—25V, 15—20Ti, 10—20Al, 余量 Fe) Grainal
格雷宁格图表 Greninger chart
格雷式钢梁 Grey girder
格雷式宽缘工字梁 Grey beam
格雷式轧机(宽缘钢梁用) Grey mill
格里菲思脆性断裂 【理】Griffith's crack
格里菲思脆性断裂理论 【理】Griffith theory of cracks
格里菲思方程(式) 【理】Griffith equation
格里菲思公式 Griffith formula
格里菲思临界裂纹长度 【理】Griffith critical crack-length
格里菲思-欧罗万-伊尔文脆性断裂公式 【理】Griffith-Orowan-Irwin formula
格里菲思-欧罗万-伊尔文脆性断裂理论 【理】Griffith-Orowan-Irwin theory

格里芬低压浇注法　Griffin process
格里芬空气预热系统　Griffin system
格里弗斯－埃切尔电弧炉　Greaves-Etchele's furnace
格里柯铅基轴承合金(70Pb,22Sb,8Sn)　Glyco (metal)
格里柯锌基轴承合金(85.3Zn,5.5Sn,4.7Sb,2.5Cu,2Al)　Glyco (metal)
格里克－阿斯科洛伊高温合金　Greek-Ascoloy
格里姆－佐默菲尔德化合物　Grimm-Sommerfeld compounds
格里姆－佐默菲尔德相　【金】Grimm-Sommerfeld's phases
格里诺显微镜　Greenough microscope
格利布耳焊接热循环模拟装置　Gleeble machine
格利马克斯电镀液　Gleamax
格利维尔铅基[锌基]轴承合金(铅基:76.5Pb, 8Sn, 14Sb, 1.5Fe; 锌基:73.3Zn,7Sn,4.2Cu,9Sb,5Pb,1.5Cd)　Gliever bearing metal
格林电弧炉　Greene furnace
格林纳瓦尔特式不连续烧结法　【团】Green(a)walt process
格林纳瓦尔特式烧结盘　【团】Greenawalt
格林威治(标准)时间　Greenwich (standard) time
格林橡胶模(冲压)成形法　Guerin forming, Guerin (rubber forming) process
格陵兰冰晶石{Na_3AlF_6}　Greenland spar
格鲁兹双金属铸造法　Grusz process
格律埃森常数[恒量]　Grueneisen constant
格律埃森关系式　Grueneisen's relation
格伦达尔法压块[团块]　Groendal briquette
格伦达尔矿石直接还原法　【铁】Groendal process
格伦瓦尔炉底导电直接电弧炉　【冶】Groenwall furnace
格伦瓦尔炉底导电直接电弧炉熔炼法　【冶】Groenwall process
格罗斯法(铝精炼)　【色】Gross's process
格罗斯曼淬透性曲线图　【金】Grossmann hardenability chart
格洛拜洛伊耐热铸铁(2C$_{总}$,6Si,0.5Mn,4Cr)　Globeloy
格米诺尔镍铬－镍硅系热电偶　Geminol
格排基础　grillage foundation
格排梁式基础　beam grillage
格排柱基　grillage column base
格奇含铁黄铜(60Cu, 38Zn, 1.5Fe)　Gedge's alloy
格筛　grizzly (griz.), grate, riddle ◇ 轨道式～rail grizzly
格筛条　grizzly bar
格栅　grille, grillage, cascade, catch-frame, crate, grating
格栅排[床]　grillage
格栅盖板　grate covering
格栅间隙　grid spacing
格栅面积　grate (bar) area
格栅式冷床　【压】cooling grid
格栅式清洗　grid cleaning
格栅式运输机　transfer grid
格栅型辐射喷烧器　gird-type radiant burner
格式表　format list
格式大梁　trellis girder
格式结构　cellular structure
格式控制字符　【计】(format) effector
格式语句　【计】FORMAT statement
格斯纳钢铁表面蒸黑处理法　Gesner process
格思里易熔合金　Guthrie's alloy
格型梁　cellular beam
格砖　checker fire-brick
格砖顶部保护层　checker top paving
格砖炉算(热风炉的)　【铁】steel grid
格子　checker, chequer, gird, grate, grill(e), lattice
格子地板　grilled floor
格子法　【理】cellular method

格子房砌砖　checkered brickwork
格子条　grate bar
格子砖　checker (fire-) brick, gitter brick (热风炉用) ◇ 波纹～【铁】corrugated brick, 杜弗莱克思～系统*, 多孔［花砖型］～*, 加热器～heater brick, 莫尔［椭圆］～Moll checker
格子砖室　checkerwork brick chamber
格子砖体(蓄热室的)　checker work
格子砖温度　checker temperature
格子状的　net-shaped
蛤壳式底卸料桶　clamshell-type dump bucket
蛤壳式料桶　clamshell bucket
蛤壳形导板　clamshell guide
隔板　baffle (plate), distance plate [piece], partition, division (plate), separating plate, spacer (plate), clapboard, curtain, spacing piece, semi-wall (镁电解槽的),【机】diaphragm,【团】internal lifter
隔板式圆锥分级机　cone-baffle classifier
隔层　interlayer
隔成小间的　boxed off
隔垫　distance plate
隔断阀(空气预热器、热风炉用)　burner door valve
隔粉　separating medium
隔焦　coke split, buffer coke charge
隔绝　exclusion, isolation
隔绝覆盖层　stop-off coating
隔离变压器　【电】isolating [insulating] transformer
隔离刀闸　disconnecting knife
隔离阀　isolating valve
隔离放大器　【电】isolating amplifier
隔离粉　【铸】parting powder
隔离环　spacing [distance] ring
隔离开关　isolator (switch), isolating switch, disconnecting switch, disconnector, extractor ◇ 带负荷［带载］～on-load disconnecting [isolating] switch, 双投～*

隔离器　isolator
隔离气孔(炉衬材料的)　【冶】disconnected pores
隔离物　insulator, spacer
隔离线路　buffer
隔离箱　shielded box
隔离罩(钢包精炼用)　shielding can
隔离轴环　set collar
隔离轴套　distance sleeve
隔料网[栅]　feed retainer
隔流电容器　isolating capacitor, stopping [bridging] condenser
隔膜　(separating) diaphragm, membrane, curtain, iris ◇ 电解槽～cell diaphragm, 帆布～*, 螺旋卷管型～*, 棉布～袋cloth [muslin] bag, 阳离子～cation membrane, 阴极～*
隔膜包裹式阳极　diaphragm enclosed type of anode
隔膜保持油箱　diaphragm conservator
隔膜泵　diaphragm [membrane, surge] pump ◇ 奥利弗～Oliver diaphragm pump, 备用[辅助]～*, 高压～*, 金属～metallic diaphragm pump, 容量型～*, 橡皮～rubber diaphragm pump
隔膜泵房　diaphragm pump room
隔膜布　diaphragm cloth
隔膜电池　diaphragm (type) cell
隔膜电解　diaphragm electrolysis
隔膜电解槽　diaphragm (electrolytic) cell ◇ 多孔～porous-diaphragm cell
隔膜(电解)法　【色】diaphragm process
隔膜阀[活门]　diaphragm valve
隔膜缸　diaphragm cylinder
隔膜恒量泵　diaphragm constant pump
隔膜框架　diaphragm frame
隔膜扩散系数测定法　【理】diaphragm cell method of diffusion measurement
隔膜面积　membrane area
隔膜泥浆泵　diaphragm slurry pump
隔膜式启动器　diaphragm type actuator
隔膜式压力计　diaphragm type pressure

隔膜体 【机】diaphragm body
隔膜调节阀 diaphragm regulating valve
隔膜烟罩 membrane hood
隔膜阳极 diaphragm enclosed type of anode
隔片 distance plate [pick-up]
隔片销 spacer pin
隔墙 baffle [batter, cut-off, partition] wall, dividing [division, diaphragm, flash, separating] wall,【建】septum ◇ 有～的坝 diaphragm dam
隔墙承重底拱 curtain arch
隔墙大砖 reflecting block
隔圈 spacer ring
隔热 thermal [heat] insulation, lagging
隔热板 (heat) insulating plate, thermal [heat] barrier, heat baffle
隔热玻璃 (同"防热玻璃")
隔热材料 heat insulating material [substance], thermal insulator, thermal insulating material ◇ 外部～*
隔热层 heat insulating layer, thermal insulation blanket
隔热垫砖 insulating pack-up block
隔热炉 insulated furnaces
隔热面砖(电炉的) hot face insulation
隔热耐火材料 (heat) insulating refractory
隔热钢包 thermal ladle
隔热体 insulator
隔热填料 insulating packing
隔热屋面板 (同"绝缘屋面板")
隔热纤维板 insulating fibre-board
隔热砖 (heat) insulating brick, insulation brick
隔砂 【铸】parting (dust)
隔栅 retainer
隔室 compartment, bay
隔室墙 chamber wall
隔水板桩 cut-off piling
隔焰焙烧炉 【冶】muffle roaster

隔焰的 flame proof
隔焰炉 (同"马弗炉")
隔夜试验 overnight test
隔音板 sound panel, dumboard, celotex (用木质纤维毡压制的绝缘板)
隔音材料 noise insulating material, acoustic [damping] material
隔音屏 sound baffle
隔音纸 building paper, deadening felt
隔渣板(高炉的) 【铁】sand dam, dam plate
隔渣板[墙]冲刷 gate washout
隔渣装置 slag filter
隔直流电容器 block [insulating] condenser
镉{Cd} cadmium ◇ 除[脱]～塔*, 电解～ electrolytic cadmium, 镀～钢 cadmium-plated steel, 海绵～ cadmium sponge, 含～的 cadmiferous, 含～烟雾*, 阴极～ cathode cadmium
镉铵溶液 cadoxam
镉棒 stick cadmium
镉棒测试专用电压表 cadmium test voltmeter
镉比率[值] 【理】cadmium ratio (C.R.)
镉铋汞齐 cadmium-bismuth-mercury amalgam
镉标准电池 cadmium standard cell
镉脆化 cadmium embrittlment
镉的(二价镉的) cadmic
镉电池 cadmium cell
镉电解 cadmium electrolysis
镉电解槽 electrolytic cadmium cell
镉锭 cadmium ingot
镉镀层 cadmium coating
镉(镀)层厚度 thickness of cadmium plate
镉汞标准电池合金 cadmium mercury
镉汞电池 cadmium-mercuric oxide cell
镉汞合金[汞齐,汞膏](78.26Hg, 21.74Cd) cadmium(-mercury) amalgam
镉红 cadmium red

镉红色谱线　cadmium red line
镉(灰收集)箱(锌精馏的)　cadmium canister
镉黄　cadmium yellow [lithopone], cadmopone
镉基合金　cadmium base alloy
镉金装饰合金　cadmium gold
镉块　bar cadmium
镉镁合金　cadmium magnesium alloy
镉镍合金(1.0—1.5Ni, 98.5Cd)　cadmium nickel alloy ◇ 阿萨科－洛伊～*
镉镍蓄电池　cadmium-nickel storage battery
镉钎焊合金[镉焊料](82Cd, 18Zn)　cadmium solder
镉铅红　derby red
镉青铜(0.5—1.5Cd, 余量Cu)　cadmium bronze
镉闪锌矿　cadmiferous blende, pr(z)ibramite
镉试剂　cadion
镉丝　cadmium wire
镉酸盐　cadmate
镉塔冷凝器(锌精馏的)　cadmium-column condenser
镉添加合金　cadmium addition
镉条　bar cadmium
镉铜合金(0.5—1Cd, 余量Cu)　cadmium copper
镉团块　cadmium briquette
镉污染　cadmium pollution
镉硒光电池　cadmium-selenium photo-cell
镉硒矿　cadmoselite, kadmoselite
镉锌共晶合金　cadmium-zinc eutectic alloy
镉冶金　cadmium metallurgy
镉易熔合金　cadmium fusible alloy
镉银合金　cadium-silver alloy ◇ 高延性～*
镉银蓄电池　cadmium-silver storage battery
镉蒸气　cadmium vapour

镉中毒　【环】cadmium poisoning
镉轴承合金　cadmium bearing alloy
铬{Cr}　chrome, chromium ◇ 电沉积～*, 镀黑～black chromium plating, 富～合金 chromium-rich alloy, 海绵～chromium sponge, 含～合金*, 加～渗碳 chrome carburizing, 贫～chromium depletion, 渗～*, 脱[除, 去]～*
铬白云石耐火材料　chrome-dolomite refractory
铬白云石砖　chrome-dolomite brick
铬不锈钢　straight-chromium stainless steel ◇ 13～*, 雷迪阿奈特～Radianite, 铁素体～*
铬磁铁矿　ishkulite
铬淀积(层)　chromium deposition
铬镀层　chromium coating [plating] ◇ 多孔～*, 微裂纹～* 无孔～ pore-free chromium, 无裂纹～crack-free chromium
铬矾　chrome alum
铬钒钢　chrome-vanadium steel ◇ 克雷斯达～Crestaloy
铬钙石　chromatite
铬橄榄石砖　chrome-olivine brick
铬钢　chromium [chrome] steel ◇ α化～*, 纯～*, 杜拉洛依耐蚀耐热～*
铬高岭石{(Al, Fe, Cr)₄·(Si₄O₁₀)(OH)₈}　volchonskoite
铬革长手套　chrome leather gauntlet
铬硅镀层　chrome-silicon coating
铬硅钢　chrome-silicon steel
铬硅耐热钢(4Si, 8Cr, 0.4C, 余量Fe)　silchrome
铬硅线石耐火材料　chrome-sillimanite refractory
铬硅质耐火材料　chrome-silica refractory
铬硅砖　chrome-silica brick
铬合金　chrome alloy
铬化　chromaking, chromalloying, iriditing ◇ 水银～merchromizing
铬化处理　chromising, chromizing, chromizing (process)

铬 ge

铬化镀层　iridite
铬化法　chromizing process　◇奥内拉~*
铬黄{PbCrO$_4$}　chrome yellow
铬基合金　chromium base alloy, chrome-base alloy　◇碳化物强化~*
铬钾矿　lopezite
铬尖晶石{(Mg, Fe)(AlCr)$_2$O$_4$}　chrome spinel, picotite
铬尖晶石砖　chrome-spinel brick
铬金金属化　chromium-gold metallizing
铬矿　chrome (ore)　◇含碳~球团*
铬矿床　chrome deposit
铬矿物　chrome mineral
铬鳞镁矿　bouazzer, stichtite
铬铝钢　chromium aluminum steel
铬铝共渗　chrome aluminizing
铬铝钴耐热钢　kanthal
铬铝硅合金钢　sichromal steel
铬铝耐火材料　chrome-alumina refractory
铬铝热电偶　chromel-alumel couple
铬铝石　selwnite
铬铝陶瓷金属　metamic
铬铝英石{(Al, Cr)$_2$O$_3$·2SiO$_2$·2H$_2$O}　miloschite
铬铝砖　chrome-alumina brick
铬绿　chrome green
铬绿帘石　chromium complex
铬镁耐火材料　chrome-magnesia [chrome-mangesite] refratory
铬镁(耐火)砖　chrome-magnesite (fire) brick　◇烧结~*
铬镁水泥　chrome-magnesite cement
铬蒙脱石{(Al, Fe, Cr)$_4$·(Si$_4$O$_{10}$)(OH)$_8$}　volchonskoite
铬锰氮不锈钢　◇特内伦~*
铬锰钢　chromium-manganese [chrome-manganese] steel
铬锰硅(合金结构)钢　chrome-manganese-silicon steel　◇克罗曼西尔~*
铬明矾　chrome alum
铬钼不锈钢　◇希科尔~Hicore
铬钼钒高速钢　◇克房伯~*
铬钼钢　chrome-molybdenum [chromium-molybdenum] steel, Hascrome　阿达曼特耐磨~adamant steel
铬钼合金　chrome molybdenum (CM)
铬钼耐热(合金)钢　croloy　阿斯卡罗伊~*
铬钼铸钢　cast chromium molybdenum steel
铬耐火砖　(同"铬砖")
铬内聚能　cohesive energy of chromium
铬黏土　alexandrolite
铬镍奥氏体不锈钢　chromium-nickel austenite stainless steel
铬镍钴耐热钢　◇H335~*
铬镍焊条　chrome-nickel electrode
铬镍合金　chrome-nickel alloy, uniloy alloy　◇H.H.~*
铬镍(合金)钢　chromium-nickel [chrome-nickel] steel　◇反18-8~*, 科洛尼亚尔耐蚀~*, 耐热~*, 尤尼洛伊~*
铬镍矿　ni(cco)chromite
铬镍钼耐热钢　◇蒂姆肯~*
铬镍钼耐蚀耐热钢　pyrasteel
铬镍特种合金　chronite
铬镍铁合金　inconel
铬镍－铜镍热电偶　chromel-copel thermocouple
铬镍线　chrome-nickel wire
铬硼粉末合金(12—23B, 60—70Cr, 7—15Al)　chromium boride
铬贫化　chromium depletion
铬坡莫合金(78Ni, 3.8Cr, 余量 Fe)　chrome permalloy
铬铅矿{PbCrO$_4$}　crocoite
铬铅锌矿　jossaite
铬青铜(2.5Sn, 2Fe, 1Cr, 余量 Cu)　chromium-bronze
铬酸{H$_2$CrO$_4$}　chromic acid　◇海奈克~处理 Hinac steel plate 派卢明~氧化处理法 Pylumin
铬酸表面处理法　chromic acid process

铬酸废水　chromic acid waste water
铬酸镁{MgO·Cr$_2$O$_3$}　magnesium chromate
铬酸钠　sodium chromate
铬酸铅{PbCrO$_4$}　lead chromate
铬酸铷{Rb$_2$CrO$_4$}　rubidium chromate
铬酸铜　copper [cupric] chromate
铬酸锡　stannic chromate
铬酸锌　zinc chromate
铬酸锌浸镀法(钢的)　zincote process
铬酸亚铁{FeO·Cr$_2$O$_3$}　ferrous chromite
铬酸盐　chromate
铬酸盐薄钢板　chromated sheet
铬酸盐表面浸渍法(镁和镁合金的)　chromating process
铬酸盐表面涂层处理　chromate treatment
铬酸盐处理　chromating
铬酸盐底层涂料　chromate primer
铬酸盐钝化处理　chromatizing ◇ 镀[涂]层表面～*
铬酸盐钢带　chromated strip
铬酸盐还原槽　chromate reduction basin
铬酸盐冷却系统　chromate cooling system
铬酸盐(染色)处理(法)(钢表面的)　chromadizing, chromodizing
铬酸盐酸洗(镁合金的)　chrome pickle
铬酸盐涂层　chromate coating
铬酸阳极化处理(铝合金的)　chromic acid anodizing
铬钛导体　chromium-titanium conductor
铬碳钢　chrome-carbon steel
铬碳共渗　chrome carburizing
铬添加合金　chromium addition
铬铁　chromium iron, ferrochrome, ferrochromium ◇ 超低碳～*,氮(化)[含氮]～*,发热～*,高碳～*,克罗姆索尔易熔～Chromsol,碳素～*,辛普雷克斯低碳低硫～*,铸造用[再炼]～ foundery ferrochrome
铬铁的　chromiferrous
铬铁矿{FeCrO$_4$,FeO·Cr$_2$O$_3$}　chrome-iron ore, chrome ironstone, chromite ◇ 补炉用～*【冶】furnace chrome,含～耐火材料
铬铁矿氯化　chlorination of chromite
铬铁矿砂　chromite sand
铬铁氧体　chromium ferrite
铬铜电导合金　◇ 马洛里3～Mallory 3
铬铜　(同"铜铬合金")
铬铜耐蚀钢　◇ 塞浦里提克～*
铬透磁钢[合金]　chrome-permalloy
铬透辉石　chrome diopside
铬钨钒钢　chromium-tungsten-vanadium steel
铬钨钢　chrome-tungsten steel
铬钨钴焊条合金　Stoody
铬雾　chromium fog
铬盐感光印像装置　photo-chromic
铬－氧化铝金属陶瓷(70Cr,30Al$_2$O$_3$)　metamic
铬叶绿矾　knoxvillite
铬云母　avalite, verdite
铬质火泥浆　chrome mortar
铬质耐火材料　chrome refractory
铬(质耐火)砖　chrome [chromite, chromium] (fire) brick ◇ 白云石质～dolomite-chromite brick
铬砖耐火材料　chromite-containing refractory
个位数位置　【计】unit position
各向不均扩散　anisotropic diffusion
各向同性　isotropy
各向同性磁铁　isotropic magnet
各向同性磁致伸缩　isotropic magnetostriction
各向同性分布　isotropic distribution
各向同性介质　isotropic medium
各向同性晶体　isotropic body, isotrope
各向同性热膨胀　isotropic thermal expansion
各向同性散射　【理】isotropic scattering
各向同性弹性[弹力]　isotropic elasticity
各向同性弹性介质　isotropic elastic medium

各向同性条件　isotropy condition
各向同性现象　isotropism
各向异性　anisotropy, anisotropism, aeolotropism, aeolotropy, anisotropic nature ◇ 感生~【理】induced anisotropy, 横向~*, 力学［机械］性能~ mechanical anisotropy, 能隙~*
各向异性场　anisotropy field
各向异性常数　anisotropy constant
各向异性磁铁（24Co, 14Ni, 8Al, 3Cu, 51Fe）　anisotropic magnet
各向异性磁致伸缩　【理】anisotropic magnetostriction
各向异性的　anisotropic, eolotropic, nonisotropic, aeolotropic
各向异性电介质　anisotropic dielectric
各向异性钢　anisotropic (sheet) steel
各向异性硅钢　directional [anisotropic] silicon steel ◇ 克里斯塔洛伊~带 Crystalloy
各向异性介质［媒质］　unisotropic medium
各向异性晶体　anisotropic crystal
各向异性能　anisotropy energy
各向异性膨胀　anisotropic expansion
各向异性系数　anisotropy factor
各向异性现象　anisotropism
各向异性效应　anisotropic effect
各向异性组织　anisotropic structure
各向异性作用　anisotropisation
给定风量　ordered wind
给定极限　prescribed limit
给定时间　preset time
给定值　given [prescribed] value
给质子［氢离子］溶剂　protogenic solvent
根　【化】radical
根部　【焊】root
根部凹入度（气孔串）　【焊】root concavity
根部焊道（多层焊的）　root pass [bead, layer, run]
根部焊道焊接　root-pass welding
根部焊缝（角钢或槽钢焊接的）　heel weld
根部间距［距离］　【焊】root spacing
根部间隙　【焊】root gap
根部裂纹（焊缝的）　root cracking
根部面厚度　thickness of root face
根部坡口　【焊】root groove
根部缺陷（焊缝的）　root defect
根部熔深　root penetration
根部未焊透［未熔合］（焊缝的）　lack of root penetration
根部形状（螺纹的）　root form
根轨迹　root locus
根号　【数】radical
根距（铆钉离边尺寸）　shifting gauge
根瘤菌科　Rhizobiaceae
根值　【数】radix
跟随器　follower ◇ 阴极~ cathode follower
跟踪　track, follow up
跟踪程序　trace program [routine], tracer
跟踪放大器　follower amplifier
跟踪机构　follower, tracker, tracer
跟踪控制［调节］　tracking [follow-up] control ◇ 无偏~*
跟踪能力　traceability
跟踪探测器［探棒］　tracing probe
跟踪头　tracing [tracer] head
跟踪系统　tracking system, tracker, following up system, servosystem
跟踪仪　tracker
跟踪装置　tracker, tracing device, follow up device, follower
耕地界限　【环】marginal land
更迭　interchange, alternate
更迭过滤机　alternate filter
更换　changing, exchanging, replace(ment), renew(al)
更换（零）件　spare parts, replacement part
更换炉口内衬　【冶】nose reline
更换台车用起重机［吊车］　pallet removal crane
更换转炉炉衬　【冶】vessel reline
更替通路　alternate routing
更新　renew, renovation, updating

更新改造　technical renovation [updating] and transformation
更新状态　【机】renewed state
庚酸 $\{C_6H_{13}COOH\}$　enanthic acid
庚烷 $\{CH_3(CH_2)_5CH_3\}$　heptane
工班产量　output per manshift (oms)
工步　【机】conversion
工场　workshop, shop, yard
工场试验　workshop test
工厂　factory (fact.), plant, mill, works ◇小型～ minimill, miniworks
工厂安全规程[条例]　factory safety laws, plant safety rules
工厂布置　plant layout [arrangement]
工厂厂长[经理,管理人]　works manager
工厂成本　factory cost
工厂废料　factory wastes
工厂附属设备　mill auxiliaries
工厂管理　【企】plant [works] management
工厂利废　plant usage
工厂内的　intrafactory
工厂(排放的)废水　factory effluent
工厂配置方式　plant configuration, plant layout philosophy
工厂清理废钢的铁路网　scrapworks trackage
工厂商标　manufacturer's [trade] mark
工厂设备　plant equipment [facilities], shop equipment
工厂设计　plant engineering [design]
工厂设计依据　basis of plant design
工厂设施　plant facilities
工厂生产污水系统　work's production sewer system
工厂生产指标　plant-performance figure
工厂试验　factory [plant, mill, shop] test
工厂试验室　plant laboratory
工厂条件　plant conditions
工厂用电车　mill tramway car
工厂用设备　plant-scale equipment
工厂预制　prefabrication
工厂照明　factory lighting [illumination]
工厂专用铁路线　factory railway
工厂装配　factory assembling
工厂装配螺栓　workshop bolt
工程报告　engineering report
工程承包单位　engineering contractor
工程处　engineering office
工程地质勘探　engineering geological prospecting
工程地质学　engineering geology
工程服务　engineering service
工程管理　engineering supervision [management]
工程技术人员　engineering staff, engineering technical personnel
工程技术数据[资料]　engineering data
工程计划　engineering project
工程加工车间　engineering shop
工程结构　engineering structure
工程金属　engineering metal
工程经济学　value engineering (VE)
工程经纬仪　engineer's transit
工程控制论　engineering cybernetics
工程内聚强度　technical cohesive strength
工程热力学　engineering thermodynamics
工程蠕变　engineering creep
工程设计　engineering design
工程设施　engineering service, job facilities
工程试验　engineering test
工程数量表　quantity sheet
工程水平　engineering level
工程索引(美国)　Engineering Index (EI)
工程陶瓷　engineering ceramics
工程图　engineering drawing
工程维持费　turnover
工程维护　engineering service
工程项目　construciton project
工程心理学　applied experimental psychology, engineering psychology, humam engineering
工程性能[性质]　engineering property
工程学　engineering

工程研究 engineering study [research]
工程验收 acceptance of work
工程冶金学 engineering metallurgy
工程因素 engineering factor
工程应力 engineering stress
工程应力-应变曲线 engineering stress-strain curve
工程用低碳钢 En steel (英国标准)
工程用钢 engineering steel ◇ 英国~规范 En specifications
工程用抗蠕变合金 engineering creep-resistant alloy
工程蒸汽 engineering steam
工程铸铁 engineering cast iron
工程铸铁件 engineering iron casting
工程准备事项 engineering preliminaries
工地 (building, construction) site
工地焊接 site [field, erection] welding
工地焊接工 field welder
工地架设的贮槽 field erected tank
工地搅拌 mixed-in-place
工地试验 site [field] test
工地运料路 【建】haul road
工地制作厂 on-site plant
工地作业 site work
工段 (workshop) section, aisle, compartment, department, floor, station
工间休息 lie time, coffee break
工件 job, work, working piece, workpiece
工件断面调节 workpiece shape control
工件垛[堆] stack of work
工件夹持装置 work-holding attachment
工件检测样板 work testing gauge
工件精加工 finishing of workpiece
工件热处理 component heat treatment
工具 tool, means, implement (ation), appliance ◇ 手用~ hand tool, 镶有金刚石的~ dia-tool, 用~加工 tool work
工具材料 tool material
工具车 tool wagon (TW)
工具房 tool house
工具钢 tool steel (TS) ◇ 哈尔范铬钒~*, 合金~ alloy tool steel, 冷加工用~*, 帕拉冈不变形~*, 热加工用[热作]~*, 水淬~*, 凿~ chisel tool steel, 轧辊刻网纹用钨~*
工具钢含碳量（一般为 1.25%） tool temper
工具钢护边操作 safe-ending
工具架 tool stand [rack]
工具接头 tool joint
工具快速锻造 fast tool forging
工具磨床 tool-grinding machine
工具磨损 tool wear
工具书 reference book ◇ 资料~ data book
工具箱 tool [cabinet, case, compartment], instrument box
工具作业 tool work
工况 operating mode, working condition
工频 line-frequency, power frequency, main-frequency
工频电流感应加热线圈 line-frequency coil
工频(感应)电炉 main [normal, line] frequency furnace
工频感应加热炉 line-frequency heating furnace
工频焊 industry frequency welding
工频无芯感应炉 mains-frequency coreless induction furnace
工人工资等级 workers' rates
工日率 man-day rate
工伤报酬 compensation for injuries
工伤事故 industrial injury
工商业转让支付额 business transfer payments
工商业组成指数 【企】index of business formation
工时 man-hour
工时标定 【企】time study
工时率 man-hour rate
工时需要[单位产量所需工时] man-hour requirement

工效学　ergonomics
工效学理论　ergonomic theory
工形柱　H-column ◇ 组成～built H-column
工序　process [working] step
工序间备用料　interprocess [in-process] inventory
工序间退火　(inter-)process annealing
工序能力　process capability
工序研究　operational research
工序自动化　process automation
工业安全　industrial safety
工业标准　industrial standard
工业博览会　industries fair
工业操作　commercial operation
工业测量　commercial measurement
工业产品　industrial product
工业纯度　commercial [technical] purity
工业纯铝(99.7Al)　commercially pure aluminium
工业纯毛坯　commercial purity stocks
工业纯品位　technical-pure grade
工业纯钛(平均含 99.2Ti)　commercially pure titanium
工业纯碳酸钠　soda-ash grade of sodium carbonate
工业纯铁　ingot iron ◇ 卡尔鲍姆～
工业纯铜　tough pitch (copper)
工业纯锡　standard tin, Straits tin (99.9%, 马来西亚生产)
工业等级　industrial [engineering] grade
工业等级质量　commercial quality
工业电解槽　industrial cell
工业电视　industrial television (ITV)
工业电视监控器　industry television monitor (ITVM)
工业电视系统　industrial television system (ITVS)
工业电视装置　utiliscope
工业电源　commercial power
工业电子学　industrial electronics
工业发展组织(联合国)　Industrial Development Organization (I.D.O.)
工业放射学　industrial radiology
工业废钢[料]　industrial scrap
工业废料[物]　industrial waste
工业废气　process gas, industrial waste gas
工业废水　【环】industrial effluent [sewage], trade effluent
工业废水的人口当量　【环】population equivalent of industrial waste water
工业分析　industrial [technical] analysis
工业粉末　technical powder
工业粉末分级　fractionation of technical powder
工业辐射学　industrial radiology
工业干扰　industrial [man-made] interference
工业工程　industrial engineering
工业管理　industrial management
工业规模操作　technical scale operation
工业规模(的)　industrial [technical, technological] scale, commercial scale [size] ◇ 接近～near-commercial-scale
工业规模炉子　industrial-scale furnace
工业规模试验　full scale test
工业耗热量　commercial heat consumption
工业合金　industrial [commercial] alloy
工业环境　industrial environment [atmosphere]
工业黄铜　(同"再生黄铜")
工业灰尘　industrial dust
工业回收(矿石中金属的)　【冶】commercial recovery
工业基础[地]　industrial base
工业机器人　industrial robots
工业级　production-grade, technical grade
工业给[供]水　industrial water supply
工业技术　industrial engineering
工业加热协会　Industrial Heating Association (IHA)
工业价值　commercial value
工业建筑　industrial building [architecture]

工业结构钢　commercial structural steel
工业金刚石　industrial diamond, carbonado
工业金属　commercial metal
工业净产值　net industrial output value
工业矿石　pay dirt
工业硫酸　commercial sulphuric acid
工业炉　industrial [commercial, merchant] furnace ◇ 钢铁厂～
工业炉喷枪　furnace gun
工业煤气　industrial gas
工业镁　commercial magnesium
工业镍　commercial nickel
工业频率　(同"工频")
工业品位[级]　industrial [commercial, production, technical] grade ◇ 矿石最低～[矿石边界品位] limiting grade of ore
工业品位四氟化铀　production-grade green salt
工业品位铀　production-grade uranium
工业企业人员　industrial personnel
工业气氛　industrial atmosphere
工业铅　commercial lead
工业青铜　commercial bronze
工业氢　commercial hydrogen
工业球团　commercial pellet
工业熔渣　commercial slag
工业溶剂　industrial [commercial] solvent
工业烧结炉　industrial sintering furnace
工业烧结青铜制品　commercial sintered bronze product
工业烧结制品　commercial sintered product
工业射线照相术　industrial radiography
工业设备　industrial equipment [installation, plant, unit], commercial equipment [installation, plant, unit]
工业(生产)事故　industrial accident
工业生产液流　process stream
工业生产质量管理　industrial quality control
工业生产专用铁路线　industrial track
工业生产装置　industrial installation

工业生铁　commercial iron, merchant pig
工业实验[研究]室　industrial laboratory
工业试生产阶段　commercial prototype stage
工业试验装置　pilot commercial plant
工业数据处理　industrial data processing
工业水重复利用率　industry water reuse rate, reuse of recirculated water
工业钛　commercial titanium
工业钛合金　commercial titanium alloy
工业碳酸钠　commercial sodium carbonate
工业卫生　industrial sanitation [hygiene]
工业卫生规程　industrial sanitation regulations
工业污水　(同"工业废水")
工业锌　commercial zinc
工业型号(钢的)　commercial forms
工业(型回转)窑　commercial size kiln
工业型设备[装置]　【冶】commercial size unit, engineering-scale plant
工业性焙烧　【冶】commercial induration
工业性实验窑　pilot kiln
工业性试验厂　pilot commercial plant
工业氧　commercial [technical, tonnage] oxygen
工业氧化铝　commercial alumina
工业氧气站　tonnage oxygen plant
工业样机　commercial machine
工业仪表[仪器]　industrial [technical] instrument
工业用电频率　commercial frequency
工业用红黄铜(83Cu, 4Sn, 6Pb, 7Zn)　commercial red brass
工业用轧制锌　commercial rolled zinc
工业余热　industrial exhaust heat
工业原型电解槽　industrial prototype cell
工业运行　commercial operation
工业造型　industrial moulding
工业增加值(现价)　industrial value added (at current price)
工业展览会　industries fair
工业蒸汽　process [engineering] steam

gong 工

工业制造 commercial manufacture
工业铸铁件 commercial iron casting
工业装置 industrial installation
工业综合体 【环】industrial complex
工业总产值(XXXX年不变价) gross industrial output value (at XXXX constant price)
工艺泵房 process pump house
工艺变量 process variable
工艺步骤[阶段] processing step
工艺参数 process parameter [variable], technological parameter
工艺残渣[废料] process residue
工艺操作法 processing method
工艺操作条件 process condition
工艺程序 process sequence
工艺带[段] process zone
工艺废水 【环】process effluent
工艺废物 【环】process(ing) waste
工艺方案 process concept
工艺分段 sub-process zone
工艺风机耗电量 process fan power
工艺风流 process air
工艺工程师 process engineer
工艺规程 process specification (Pr. Spec.), technological procedure, operation sheet
工艺规范 【企】technical regime
工艺过程 technical process, technological process [chain], manufacturing [work] process
工艺过程检查 process inspection
工艺过程控制 process monitoring
工艺过程控制装置 process controller
工艺过程信号 process signal
工艺合金(铜基合金) technic metal
工艺化学 process chemistry
工艺加热 process heating
工艺卡片 route sheet
工艺卡头(铸件上的) locating pad
工艺可焊性 operative [operation] weldability

工艺控制回路 process control loop
工艺灵活性 process flexibility
工艺流程 (process) flow, technological process
工艺流程设计 process design
工艺流程图 technological [process] flow sheet, process flow diagram, process chart, flow [route] sheet, flow scheme [chart], schedule drawing ◇发光模拟~*, ◇通用~*
工艺气流 process gas flow [stream], 【团】on-gas
工艺气流平衡 process gas balance
工艺气流洗涤器 process gas scrubber
工艺缺陷 defective workmanship ◇除去~ debugging
工艺燃料(转炉用的碳化钙、碳化硅等) 【钢】(in-)process fuel
工艺热量 process heat
工艺热量损失 process heat loss
工艺热气体 hot process gas
工艺溶液 process liquor
工艺设备 process(ing) equipment [unit] ◇新~*
工艺设计 process [technological] design
工艺设想 process image
工艺师 technologist
工艺时间 process time
工艺适应[多用]性 process versatility
工艺试验 process run, technology testing
工艺水总管 process water main
工艺条件 technological [processing] conditions
工艺图 flow sheet
工艺污染废水 【环】process-contaminated waste water
工艺系列 treatment line
工艺系统温度状况 system temperature profile
工艺线 processing [production] line
工艺性能 processing [fabrication] properties

工艺学家　technologist
工艺烟气　【团】on-gas
工艺研究　technical study
工艺要求　process requirement
工艺冶金学　process metallurgy
工艺用风　【团】process air
工艺用汽　process steam
工艺用水　process water
工艺制度　schedule
工长　headman, foreman ◇ 炼钢[熔炼]~ chief melter
工种　profession, kind of work
工资　wages, salary, labor costs, cost of labour
工资标准[等级]　work [wage] rates, wage scale
工资费用　wage costs
工资率　【企】wage rate
工资指数　【企】wage index
工资制　wage system
工资总额　total pay-roll
工字大梁　I-girder
工字断面(型钢)　I-section
工字钢　(double) I-steel, I-bar, (steel) I-beam (section), I-iron, I-section, H-bar, double tee iron, double (T-) iron, girder steel, joist ◇ 宽(翼)缘~*, 轧制~*
工字钢断面　I-beam section
工字钢腹板　rail web
工字钢轨　bull head rail
工字钢矫直机　beam straightener
工字钢孔型　【压】joist pass
工字钢梁　【建】I-beam [I-iron] girder, steel I-beam ◇ 伯利恒(宽缘)~ Bethlehem beam, 球头~ bulb beam
工字钢轧机　joist (rolling) mill
工字钢桩　H-beam pile
工字钢桁架　【建】I-beam girder
工字梁　H-beam (H.B.), I-beam (I.B.), H-bar, flanged beam, 【压】joist ◇ 不等缘~ differflange beam, 轧制~用的异形坯 beam blank

工字梁用异形坯　beam blank
工字轮　(disc) spool, bobbin ◇ 合绳机~*, 绕在~上的钢丝卷[钢丝绳卷, 带钢卷]【压】bobbin coil
工字轮架(合绳机的)　creel stand
工字轮摇篮(钢丝绳机的)　bobbin cradle [flier]
工字轮张力装置　bobbin tensioning device
工字(型钢)柱　I-column, H-column ◇ 翼缘加板~ H-column with covers
工作班　shift, operating crew, turn
工作板　working plate
工作半径　working radius ◇ 起重机~ crane radius
工作臂　actuating arm
工作标准试样　working standard sample
工作表面　working surface
工作波长　operating [analytical] wavelength
工作参数　operating [working] parameter
工作槽　operating cell
工作侧　drive [work] side
工作层(砌衬的)　working lining [face]
工作场地　working floor [place]
工作程序　【计】working routine [program]
工作程序图　process chart
工作带(拉模的)　reduction zone
工作道次　working pass
工作地点　working place
工作电势[位]　operating potential
工作电压　operating [running, service, working] voltage, working tension
工作段　working zone, 【团】upper [top] strand
工作方式　operating mode
工作方式转换开关　mode switch
工作缝　【建】construction joint
工作服　(work, business, protective) clothing, overalls ◇ 有冷却的~(高温车间用) man-cooling jacket, 专用~ special clothing

工作负荷[负载] work(ing) [service] load

工作杆件[构件] working member

工作功率 operating power

工作辊【压】 work(ing) roll (W.R.) ◇下修整~*

工作辊重磨 work roll redressing

工作辊道【压】 mill table ◇ 机后~*, 机前~* front table, 轧机前后~*, 主要~*（轧机的）main table

工作辊反弯【压】 negative work roll bending

工作辊横移 work roll shift (WRS)

工作辊横移技术【压】 work-roll-shifting technology

工作辊横移式四辊冷轧机 work-roll-shifting 4-high mill

工作辊横移式轧机 work-roll-shifting mill

工作辊换辊装置【压】 work roll changer

工作辊交叉式轧机 work rolling cross mill

工作辊快速更换[换辊]装置 work roll quick changing device [rig]

工作辊磨床 work roll grinding machine

工作辊弯曲[挠度] work roll bending

工作辊弯曲缸 work roll bending cylinder

工作辊弯曲装置 work roll bending system

工作辊预弯方式 work roll bending type

工作辊支撑装置 work roller supporting apparatus

工作辊轴承 work roll bearing

工作辊轴套 work roll cage

工作辊轴座 work roll chock

工作辊自动换辊 automatic work roll changing

工作环境 working environment [atmosphere]

工作机座【压】 working stand

工作极隙【化】 analytical gap

工作计划（表） working scheme [programme]

工作介质 working [actuating] medium, working substance

工作进度[时间]表 operating [work] schedule

工作距离（试样的） working distance

工作空间 work space

工作孔（回转炉的） workhole

工作孔型【压】 working [live] pass

工作量规 working gauge

工作流体 operating fluid, pressure fluid（液压系统的）

工作炉型（高炉的） operating profile

工作帽 helmet shield

工作门 working door

工作面 working face [area], plane of working,【机】operating profile（轮齿的）

工作面积 work area

工作母机 machine tool

工作能力 working [productive] capacity

工作平面 working plane

工作平台 operating platform

工作谱线 analytical line

工作强度 working strength

工作区 working area,【计】working set

工作人员 working personnel, staff member

工作任务 assignment

工作日 workday, working day ◇ 全~ full time

工作日程表 calendar progress chart

工作容积 working volume (WV), displacement（气缸的）

工作设备 working equipment

工作时间 working time [hours, period], running time, on-time（接触焊加热时间）

工作室 working chamber, work space, operating room

工作试验 service test

工作寿命 （同"使用寿命"）

工作台 operating floor, (working) platform, scaffold, table, workbench

工作台护板　table apron
工作台架操纵工　rack operator
工作台手轮(机床的)　【机】table handwheel
工作台造型工　bench moulder
工作台造(铸)型　bench mould
工作特性(曲线)　working [performance, operating] characteristic
工作条件　working [operating, running, service] conditions
工作条件下腐蚀　service corrosion
工作图　working diagram [drawing]
工作图表　【企】operating schedule
工作温度　service temperature
工作细则　working instruction
工作线圈　operating coil
工作效率　operating efficiency
工作行程　working stroke [travel]
工作循环　duty [motive, operating] cycle
工作样板　working gauge
工作仪表　service instrument
工作油罐　fuel service tank
工作域　【数】scope
工作原理　operating principle, principle of operation [work]
工作轧辊　work roll
工作张力　working tension
工作直径　working diameter
工作制度　working regime, character of service, working system [schedule]
工作周期　work [duty] cycle, working period
工作转[扭]矩　working torque
工作阻力　working resistance [strength]
攻丝　tapping, screwing, thread
攻丝机　tapper, threading machine
攻丝设备　threading device
功函数　work function
功率　power, rate of work, capacity (factor), activity
功率变换器　power inverter
功率变压器　【电】power transformaer ◇

控制~*
功率表[计]　power meter, wattmeter, dynamometer
功率补偿装置　compensating equipment
功率不足　undercapacity, underpower
功率超载值　overload power
功率储备　margin of power, operating margin
功率单位　power unit (P.U.)
功率电平　power level
功率额定　power rating
功率(放大)管　power tube
功率放大器　power amplifier
功率记录器　dynamograph
功率均衡器　power equalizer
功率利用系数　power utilization coefficient
功率密度　power density
功率密度函数　power spectral density function ◇二维~*
功率曲线　power curve
功率输出　power output (P.O.)
功率损耗　power [watt] loss
功率调节器　power regulator [governor, controller]
功率系数　power efficiency, specific capacity
功率消耗　watt [energy] consumption, consumption of power
功率因数　power factor (P.F.)
功率因数补偿　power factor compensation
功率因数补偿设备　power factor compensator equipment
功率因数指示器　power factor indicator
功率因数自动调节器　automatic power factor regulator
功能材料　functional material
功能地址指令　【计】functional address instruction
功能方框图　function block
功能合金　function alloy
功能互换性　functional interchangeability

功能积木化 【计】functional modularity
功能监控 functional monitoring
功能检验 functional inspection
功能键(键盘的) function key
功能器件 functional device
功能设计 【计】functional design
功能试验 functional test
功能图 functional diagram
功用 function, usage
功指数 work index
供带(轮)盘(录音的) supply reel
供电 power [electric, current] supply, supply electricity, 【电】feed(ing), delivery
供电部分 power pack
供电次序[方式] 【电】delivery order
供电电缆 power supply cable, service cable
供电干线 【电】feed main, main supply
供电母线 【电】feeder bus-bar
供电设备 power supply unit (P.S.U.), supply unit
供电设施 power service
供电事故 power failure
供电网 supply network
供电系统 power supply system
供电线路 power supply circuit, charging line
供粉装置 powder feeding device
供风 air blowing [charge]
供风不足的火焰 (同"欠氧火焰")
供风道 air supply duct
供风管路 supply air line
供风系统 air supply system, supply air system
供风装置 air supply arrangement
供货者 supplier, shipper
供给 supply, feed, deliver, provision, furnish ◇ 过分~(燃料的) overfeeding
供给泵 feed pump
供给电压 service voltage
供给管 supply pipe [tube], feeder sleeve
供给管线 intake pipeline

供给器 feed device, feeder
供给箱 feed(ing) box
供给源 supply
供给资金 finance
供碱系统 alkali supply system
供卷运输机 entry coil conveyer
供料 feed (material), admission
供料槽 feed vessel
供料次数 delivery frequency
供料带 zone of supply
供料管 feeder sleeve
供料辊道 supply table
供料机 feeder ◇ 混匀~ blending feeder
供料口 feeding gate
供料流量控制 feed rate control
供料能力 feed capacity
供料温度 feed temperature
供料系统 feed system
供料线 supply line
供料支线 delivery track
供料中断 breakdown of feed
供料装置 feed device
供氯 chlorine supply
供煤量 coal input
供暖 heating (htg.) ◇ 顶棚板面~ ceiling-panel heating, 分区式~系统 zone system, 集中~ central heating, 间歇式[定时]~ discontinuous heating, 绝对~效应 absolute heating effect, 隐蔽式~ concealed heating, 再循环~机组 drawn-through heater
供暖能力 heating capacity
供暖器 calorifier
供暖总管 heating main
供暖总站 central heating plant
供坯机(挤压的) billet loader
供坯装置 billet loading unit
供气管线 gas feed [supply] line
供气支管 gas manifold
供汽管道 steam supply line
供热[供给热量] heat supply [addition], thermal input ◇ 上下~的炉子

供热方式　heat pattern
供热管道　heat supply pipeline
供热能力　heating capacity
供热系统　district heating line system ◇ 席式~*
供水　water supply [delivery], feedwater
供水泵　make up pump
供水泵井　feed pump well
供水车[船]　water tender
供水工程　【建】water service
供水管道　water piping, water-supply pipe
供水系统　water system ◇ 闭路~closed water system
供水箱　(water-)supply tank
供酸泵　acid supply pump
供酸系统　acid supply system
供线装置　wire-feeding device
供氧　oxygen supply, delivery of oxygen
供氧管路　oxygen supply line
供液泵　solution feed pump
供液槽　feed [distributing, distributor] tank
供液管　feeder tube
供液流(湿法冶金)　feed stream
供液嘴　feeder nose
供应仓口(炉前用料)　【铁】service hatch
供应槽　supply [filling] tank
供应厂商　supplier
供应船　tender
供应范围　extent [limit] of supply
供应过剩　oversupply
供应距离　supply distance (SD)
供应料仓　live storage
供应能力　deliverability
供应条件　delivery specifications
供应系数　accommodation coefficient
供应线　service track [line]
供应状态　【企】state as received
供油　oil supply
供油泵　oil feed pump
公差　allowable error, allowance, tolerance ◇ 超~(的)*, 小[紧缩]~close tolerance, 允许~admissible tolerance
公差范围　margin of tolerance
公差极限[限度]　tolerance [tolerant] limit
公差值　tolerance value
公称尺寸　nominal [intended, specified] size, nominal dimension
公称管径　nominal bore
公称化学组分　nominal chemical composition
公称面积　nominal area
公称容量　nominal [rated] capacity
公称条件　rated conditions
公称应变　apparent strain
公称直径　nominal diameter (n.d.), basic size
公称值　nominal value
公共场所　public places
公共电子　collective electrons
公共工程　public work
公共[众]关系　public relations
公共广场　public area
公共燃烧空窝(鼓风炉的)　【色】common raceway
公共轴　common axis
公害　【环】environmental pollution, public disaster [menace, hazard]
公害(引起的)疾病　【环】pollution-related disease, disease caused by pollution
公斤　(同"千克") ◇ 百~kintal
公斤净重　kilogram net weight (K.N.)
公式　formula (复数 formulae), expression, equation ◇ 艾克龙得~【压】Eklund's formula, 高斯~【理】Gauss formula, 格里菲思~*, 克拉珀龙-克劳修斯~*, 兰姆~*, 林德曼~*, 曼逊-哈费德~*, 莫特-纳巴罗~*, 能斯脱~*, 斯托克斯~*, 塔菲尔~*, 西门斯~*）
公式翻译程序语言　FORTRAN (formula translator)
公式翻译器　fortran
公式化[表示]　formulation

公式推导 【数】derivation [development] of equation

公司 company (Co.), corporation (Corp.), incorporation (Inc.)

公司利润课税负担额 【企】corporate profitstax liability

公司帐目 【企】company accounts

公盈 【机】interference

公盈压配合 【机】interference fit

公用存储区 【计】common storage area

公用服务事业 utility service

公用福利设施 public welfare

公用可控硅二次配电盘 common thyristor secondary panel

公用块 【计】COMMON block ◇ 空[无标号]~*

公用设施 utility (ut.), utility service(s), general services, utility

公用设施场地 utilities area

公用事业 utility (ut.), utility service 城市～city-owned utilities

公用语句 【计】COMMON statement

公用轴 common axis

公制 (同"米制")

公制单位 metric unit

弓架式集电器 pantograph collector

弓锯床[机] bow [hack] sawing machine

弓弦拱 bowlstring arch

弓形 bow(-shape), arc, arch (form) ◇ 弯成～bowing, 悬臂～架*

弓形拱 segmental [sprung] arch

弓形焊接梁 cambered beam

弓形夹 cramp(ing) frame

弓形梁 cambered [bow] beam, segmental girder

弓形体 segment, toxoplasm

弓形弯(冷轧工作辊的) bow action

弓状集电器 bow collector

觥子(造型工具) 【铸】sleeker, slicker

汞{Hg} mercury (merc.), quick silver, hydrargyrum ◇ 含～烟雾 mercurial fume, 含银～argental mercury, 加～作用 mercuration, 冷凝～condensed mercury, 天然～native mercury

汞钯矿 eugensite, potarite

汞捕集器 mercury trap

汞槽 mercury trough [bath]

汞池阴极 mercury-pool cathode

汞触点 mercury contact

汞灯 mercury (vapour) lamp, mercury(-discharge) lamp (放电式)

汞电池 mercury cell

汞断流器 mercury cut-off ◇ 斯密特低阻抗～*

汞断路器 mercury circuit-breaker

汞弧整流器 mercury (vapour, arc) rectifier, mercury vapour arc retifier, mercury-arc converter

汞化 mercuration, mercurization

汞化产物 mercurate

汞化物 mercuride

汞化铀 uranium mercuride

汞化作用 mercuration

汞基合金 mercury(-base) alloy

汞金矿 amalgam

汞开采 mercury mining

汞控恒温器 mercury thermostat

汞矿 mercury ore, hydrargillite ◇ 斯皮雷克型粉～焙烧炉 Spirek furnace

汞矿床 mercury ore deposit

汞矿物 mercury mineral

汞矿业 mercury mining

汞扩散泵 mercury diffusion [vapour] pump ◇ 通用电气公司(美国)型三级玻璃～*, 瓦兰～Waran's pump

汞冷凝器 mercury condenser

汞膜电极 mercury film electrode

汞喷射泵 mercury ejector pump

汞齐(合金)[汞合金, 汞膏] amalgam (AAA, amal.), mercury amalgam, mercury-(-base) alloy ◇ 贵金属～precious metal amalgam, 基恩迈耶～*, 碱金属～*, 胶泥[涂层]～*, 金～gold amalgam, 麦肯齐～*, 浓[稠]～thickened amalgam,维也纳金属黏结用~*,牙科用~*,液体~liquid amalgam

汞齐板 【色】amalgam(ation) plate

汞齐泵 amalgam pump

汞齐捕集器 amalgam catcher [trap]

汞齐电池 amalgam cell

汞(齐)电极 amalgam electrode

汞齐电解 amalgam electrolysis

汞齐镀覆(用于金、银) amalgam plating

汞齐法 amalgam(ation) process

汞齐分解率 amalgam-decomposition degree

汞齐化 amalgamize, amalgamation ◇ 可~的 amalgamable, 使~quicksilvering, 使~溶液 amalgam solution

汞齐化电极 amalgamated electrode

汞齐还原法 amalgam reduction

汞齐加压[挤压]机 amalgam press

汞齐试验法(铜或镁合金的) 【金】amalgam(ation) test

汞齐形成金属 【金】amalgam-forming metal

汞齐压榨机 amalgam squeezer

汞齐冶金 amalgam metallurgy

汞齐蒸馏罐 amalgam (pot) retort

汞齐蒸馏炉 amalgam distilling furnace

汞气(扩散)泵 (同"汞扩散泵")

汞气计 mercury vapour meter ◇ 灵敏~*

汞渗透法 mercury penetration method

汞酸盐 mercurate

汞添加合金 mercury addition

汞污染 mercury pollution

汞吸收(汞齐化) mercury absorption

汞锡合金 quick silver

汞盐 mercuric salt

汞氧化物 mercury oxide

汞冶金 metallurgy of mercury [quicksilver]

汞液滴定法 mercurimetry

汞阴极 mercury-cathode

汞阴极电解槽 mercury cathode cell

汞银矿 kongsbergite

汞黝铜矿 mercury [mercurial] fahlore, schwartzite, spaniolite

汞真空[蒸气]泵 mercury vacuum pump ◇ 克劳福德~*

汞蒸气 mercurial [mercury] vapor

汞蒸气锅炉 mercury vapour boiler

汞蒸气检测器 mercury-vapour detector

汞中毒 mercury poisoning, hydrargyria, hydrargyrism ◇ 有机~organic mercury poisoning

汞柱 mercury column ◇ 毫米~*,纳米~*

汞注入法(测量毛细孔径用) mercury intrusion method

汞煤 mercurial soot

拱 arch ◇ 平圆~*

拱坝 arch dam ◇ 恒角[等角]~constant-angle arch dam

拱半径 radius of crown

拱背线(拱外缘线) extrados

拱边支柱 buckstay

拱顶 vault, apex [top] of arch, (arched) crown, curved arch, roof arch, top dome, 【冶】curved roof ◇ 加肋~ribbed arch [roof], 可更换~bung toparch

拱顶石 【建】capstone, choke stone, key stone [block]

拱顶形 dome-shape

拱顶支承结构 sprung arch design

拱顶砖 crown brick

拱顶砖衬 roof arched lining

拱度 camber, crown ◇ 路面~camber of paving, 上[反]~camber, 桁架~camber of truss

拱高 arch rise [height], height of camber, bilge, crown

拱基 skewback, chaptrel, abutment, impost

拱架 bow member, arch centre [centering], rider arch ◇ 拆卸~decente-ring

拱肩 spandrel

拱脚 skewback, balance of roof, abutment, impost ◇ 弹簧(加载)式~斜石块*

拱脚砖 skew(back) brick, skew block, edge skew, springer ◇ $\frac{1}{2}$长~half-length skew, 全长~whole-length skew

拱脚砖斜角 angle of skew

拱壳砖 arched roof brick

拱跨 arch span

拱肋 【建】groyne, groin, arch rib

拱梁 arched beam [girder]

拱起 crowning

拱桥构造 arch formation

拱桥效应 bridging effect

拱桥形成 【粉】bridge formation

拱圈 arch ring

拱圈底面 plancier

拱矢 arch camber

拱矢高 kiln crown

拱式压力机 arch-type press

拱推力 arch thrust

拱心砖 bullhead

拱形 arch, arc, arcuation

拱形板桩 arch-type sheet pile, deep-arc piling, arched type piling bar (钢材)

拱形桁架 arch truss

拱形梁 arched beam

拱形[式]炉顶 arch roof, arched (furnace) roof, arched dome, sprung roof ◇ 硅砖~*, 加肋硅砖~*

拱形炉门 arched door

拱形炉膛 arched hearth

拱形汽室 arched dome

拱形栈桥 arch viaduct

拱形蒸汽锤 arch-type steam hammer

拱形砖 radial brick

拱压力 arch pressrure

拱腰 【建】haunch

拱鹰架[装置] 【建】centring

拱应力 arch stress

拱罩 arch cap

拱砖 arch brick ◇ $\frac{1}{2}$长~$\frac{1}{2}$length arch

拱座 abutment (abut.), butment, skewback

拱座石 【建】abutment stone, skewback

贡黄 (同"铬黄")

共变的 covariant

共变式 【数】covariant

共掺杂 codope

共沉淀 coprecipitation

共沉积 codeposition

共萃取 coextraction

共存的 coexistence, concurrent

共存范围[区域](相的) 【金】coexistence region

共轭点 conjugate point

共轭光(平)面 conjugate [conjugation] planes

共轭滑移 【理】conjugate glide [slip]

共轭滑移系 【理】conjugate glide [slip] system

共轭滑移系交叉滑移 【理】conjugate slip system cross slip

共轭孔型 【压】conjugate pass

共轭梁 conjugate beam

共轭面 conjugate surface

共轭平面 conjugate [conjugation] planes

共轭溶液[溶体] 【金】conjugate solution

共轭梯度[斜量]法 【数】conjugate gradient method

共轭线 conjugation line

共轭相 【压】conjugate phase

共轭压力 conjugate pressure

共轭液相 【理】conjugate liquid phase

共轭值 conjugate value

共轭轴 conjugate axis

共发射极 【理】common emitter

共反萃 costrip

共沸混合物 azeotrope, azeotropic mixture

共沸混合物锅炉 azeotrope boiler

共沸混合物贮槽 azeotrope tank

共沸精馏 azeotropic rectification

共沸蒸馏 azeotropic distillation ◇ 选择

性[选择溶剂]~*
共格边界 (同"相干边界")
共格沉淀(物) 【金】coherent precipitate [precipitation]
共格重合点阵[晶格] coherent coincidence lattice
共格点阵理论 coherent lattice theory
共格晶核 coherent nucleus
共格析出(物) coherent precipitate [precipitation]
共格性 (同"相干性")
共格应力 coherency stress
共活化作用 coactivation
共基极 common base
共集电极 common collector
共挤压(双金属型材的) coextrusion
共挤压模 coextruding die
共价 【化】covalence, covalency
共价半导体 covalent (type) semiconductor
共价化合物 covalence [covalent] compound
共价键 covalent binding [bond, link, linkage]
共价键晶体 covalent solid
共价键力 covalent force
共价键型 covalent form of binding
共价结构 covalent structure
共价晶体 (同"原子晶体")
共焦点目镜 parfocal eyepiece
共晶 【金】eutectic crystal
共晶奥氏体 eutectic austenite
共晶白口生铁 eutectic white pig iron
共晶-包晶反应 eutectic-peritectic [eutecto-peritectic] reaction
共晶成分 eutectic composition
共晶点 eutectic point [arrest]
共晶点移动 eutectic shift
共晶反应 eutectic reaction
共晶反应线 eutectic horizontal
共晶分解 eutectic decomposition
共晶粉末 eutectic powder

共晶复合材料 eutectic composite
共晶钢 eutectic steel
共晶焊接 eutectic welding
共晶焊条 eutectrod ◇ 尤特克劳德~*
共晶合金 eutectic alloy ◇ 镉锌~*,镍钴定向凝固~*
共晶混合物 eutectic mixture
共晶集团[群体] (grain) eutectic colony
共晶结构[组织] eutectic structure ◇ 片状~*
共晶结晶 eutectic solidification [crystallization]
共晶晶粒 eutectic grain
共晶扩散 eutectic diffusion
共晶凝固 eutectic freezing [solidification]
共晶平衡 eutectic equilibrium
共晶平台(加热或冷却曲线的) eutectic halt
共晶侵入(晶间偏析) eutectic intrusion
共晶熔化 eutectic melting
共晶溶液 eutectic solution
共晶烧结 eutectic sintering
共晶渗碳体 eutectic cementite
共晶生铁(含4.3C) eutectic pig iron
共晶石墨 eutectic [eutectiform] graphite ◇ S-H高强度高硬度含钛~铸铁 S-H castiron
共晶碳化物 eutectic carbide, carbide of eutectic
共晶体 eutectic crystal, eutectic(um) ◇ 汉字形~ chinese script eutectic,离异~ divorced eutectic
共晶网状组织 eutectic network
共晶温度 eutectic temperature [point]
共晶系统 eutectic system
共晶线 eutectic line
共晶相 eutectic phase
共晶型铝硅合金 ◇ 威尔米尔~*
共晶型凝固 eutectic-type freezing
共晶盐 salt eutectic
共晶易熔合金 eutectic fusible alloy
共晶铸铁 eutectic cast iron

共晶转变	eutectic transformation
共晶状态	eutectic state
共晶组成	eutectic composition
共聚焦面目镜	parfocal eyepiece
共聚物	copolymer
共聚(作用)	copolymerization
共离散	covariance
共面的	coplanar
共面性	coplanarity
共鸣	resonance
共熔 (同"同成分熔化") ◇ 临界－点[温度]*，不均匀～体 eutectoid
共熔焊	eutectic bonding
共生	intergrowth, paragenesis
共生金属	associated metal
共生晶体	intergrowth crystal
共生生金菌	Metallogenium symbioticum
共生体	associate, association
共生现象	mutualism
共态抑制比	【理】common mode rejection ratio
共同还原	coreduction
共同离子	【理】common ion
共析出	coprecipitation
共析带[区]	eutectoid zone
共析点	eutectoid point
共析反应	eutectoid reaction
共析分解	eutectoid decomposition
共析钢(含100%珠光体)	eutectoid [saturated, true] steel
共析合金	eutectoid alloy
共析混合物	eutectoid mixture
共析平衡	eutectoid [dystectic] equilibrium
共析渗碳体	eutectoid cementite
共析石墨	eutectoid graphite
共析碳含量	eutectoid carbon content
共析碳化物	eutectoid carbide ◇ 初生～*，二次[次生]～*
共析体	【金】eutectoid
共析铁素体	eutectoid ferrite
共析温度	eutectoid temperature
共析系	eutectoid system
共析珠光体	eutectoid pearlite
共析转变	eutectoid transformation
共析组成[成分]	eutectoid composition
共析组织	eutectoid structure
共吸附	coadsorption
共享程序	【计】shared routine
共享多重处理	sharing multiprocessing
共用[共享]	share
共用存储器	shared [common] storage
共用底	common base
共用电池	common battery
共用集料皮带(机)	common gathering belt
共用控制器	shared control unit
共振	resonance (oscillation), resonant vibration ◇ 回旋～cyclotron reso-nance
共振(测厚)法	resonance method
共振反应	sympathetic [resonant] reaction
共振分裂	resonance splitting
共振峰	【理】resonance peak [hump]
共振辐射	resonance radiation
共振共价键理论	resonating covalent bond theory
共振技术	resonant technique
共振键(合)	【理】resonance bonding
共振结晶器	resonant mo(u)ld
共振能级	resonance (energy) level
共振频率	resonance frequency
共振器	resonator
共振探伤	resonant frequency inspection
共振条件	resonance condition
共振吸收	【理】resonance absorption
共振吸收器	resonance absorber
共振消音器	resonant silencer
共振效应	resonance effect ◇ 阿兹贝尔－卡奈～*
共重	total weight
共轴	coaxing
共轴传动	tandem drive
共轴的	co-axial
共轴圆筒黏度测定法	(同"同轴圆筒黏

钩　hook, bail, barb, beard, finger, gab
钩杆　tripping lever
钩环　shackle (hook), staple
钩环链　hook link chain, ladder chain
钩接　hook [clasp] joint
钩连接　hooking
钩式翻钢机　【压】hook tilter, hook turnover device, finger tilt mechanism
钩式起重机　hook type crane
钩式运输机　hook [rocker, hook-to-hook] conveyer, hook carrier
钩头道钉　dog(-head) [hook-headed] spike, crooked nail, cut-spike, brob
钩头垫板　hook plate
钩头钉　brob ◇ 三棱～bayonet shaped spike
钩头键　【机】gib-headed key
钩头螺栓　hook bolt
钩形　hook-type, hooked ◇ 弯成～hooking
钩形板手　hook spanner, hookwrench
钩住　hooking, grapple
钩爪　knuckle
钩爪式移送机　dog-bar type conveyor
沟　channel, ditch, dike, gutter, guirk, trough
沟槽　ditch, trench, cannelure, flute
沟槽式孔隙[疏松] (铸锭缺陷) channel porosity
沟槽状裂纹　flute crack
沟道　channel, sluiceway, trench
沟管模板　dod
沟流　【色】channeling, channels ◇ 反应器中形成～channeling in reactor, 填充塔内形成～"
沟流流化床　【色】channeling fluidized bed
沟埋式管道　ditch conduit
沟内防冲挡板　ditch retard
沟渠　conduit, channel
沟铁(铁水罐及出铁沟内的)　sow iron, crude pig iron

沟堰　ditch check
沟中消能槛[跌水设备]　ditch check
沟铸型　groove cast
沟状腐蚀　channel(l)ing corrosion
"狗骨"　【压】dog-bone
构成　constitution, formation, building
构架　frame, (structural) framing, backbone, skeleton, framework
构架工程　framework
构架结构　frame(work) structure
构架梁　frame girder, binder (炉子的)
构架栈道　frame trestle
构件　member, (structural) component, structural member [parts], structure element, unit, building block (射流技术的)
构形　configuration
构形积分　configuration integral
构形熵　configuration entropy
构造　structure, constitution (constr.), makeup, setup, texture, organism, organization
构造变形　structural deformation, tectonic deformation (地质上的)
构造缝　build joint
构造图　constructional drawing
构造详图(机器的)　detail of construction
构筑(物)　structure, construction
构筑物面积　area of structure
购进粉末　incoming powder
箍　clip
箍钢　(flat) hoop iron, banding steel
箍钢带(含＜0.12％C)　hoop steel
箍间绝缘　【电】interturn insulation
箍筋　hooped [lateral, web] reinforcement, hooping (vertical) stirrup
箍梁　【建】gird
箍圈　hoop
箍圈导板　hoop guide
箍圈分离器和折弯器　hoop separator and bender
箍缩效应　pinch effect
箍条拆除器(带卷的)　band stripper

箍铁轧机 【压】hoop mill
箍用角条 boom angle
估定 estimation, evaluation, assessment
估定值 estimated value
估计 estimate, estimating (estg), estimation (estn), appreciation, calcutation ◇ 低于~的产量 under-run
估计不足 underestimation, underrating
估计产量 estimated output
估计过高 overestimate
估计器 estimator
估计值 estimated value, estimate
估价 (account) valuation, evaluate
估算 estimation, (preliminary) estimate
估算费用 estimated cost
估算装置 evaluating unit
孤立的 isolated, discrete
孤立体 free body
孤立(体)系 isolated system
孤立原子 isolated atom
鼓肚[鼓凸成型] bulge, bulging
鼓肚变形(连铸板坯的) bulging deformation [strain]
鼓肚成形 bulge forming
鼓风 air blast (a.b.), air blast supply, air blowing (-in) [injection], airing, blast (air), blasting, blow(ing), up-draft, up-draught, 【铁】on-blast, furnace blast (鼓风炉的) ◇ 除去~中水分 blast dehydration, 大气~【铁】atmospheric blast, 富氧~ air enrichment, 加湿~*, 均衡~ balanced blast, 调节~ conditioned blast, 氧气~ blast oxygen, 预热~ blast heating, 蒸汽~*, 综合~*
鼓风焙烧 blast roasting, up-draught firing
鼓风焙烧炉 blast roaster, roasting blast-furnace ◇ 断续[间歇]式~*
鼓风参数 blast characteristics
鼓风淬火 air blast quenching
鼓风带式焙烧机 【团】up-draught travelling grate
鼓风带式冷却机 【团】straight-line forced draught cooler, up-draught straight-line cooler
鼓风道 air pressure duct
鼓风动能 【铁】blast momentum
鼓风端(回转炉的) lancing end
鼓风煅烧 【耐】blast roasting
鼓风分配指数 blast distribution index
鼓风风口 blowing tuyere
鼓风风流 up-draught air flow
鼓风富氧 oxygenation of blast
鼓风干燥 up-draft drying (UDD), blast dehydration, up-draught drying
鼓风干燥风机 up-draught drying fan
鼓风干燥炉 【团】up-draught drying furnace
鼓风干燥炉风箱 【团】up-draught drying windbox
鼓风干燥炉罩 up-draught drying hood
鼓风干燥区段 up-draught drying zone
鼓风干燥装置 dry-blast plant
鼓风工段 up-draught section
鼓风管 blast pipe, 【铁】blast supply
鼓风管道 air pressure duct
鼓风环式冷却机[环冷机] forced draught circular [rotary] cooler, rotary for-ced-air cooler, updraft [pressure, forced air] circular cooler
鼓风机 blowing machine [engine], (air) blower, blast engine [fan], blower(fan), force [updraught] fan, forced draught fan, fanner ◇ 并联式~*, 单(汽)缸~*, 电动~ electric blower, 罗茨~ Root's blower, 煤气增压~*, 汽动~*, 燃气(驱动)~*, 热风~ hot blower, 升压~ booster blower, 透平~ turboblower, 往复式~ reciprocating blower, 旋转活塞~ rotary piston blower, 压缩空气~ compressed air blower, 轴流式~ axial (flow) blower, 自动同步式~控制系统*
鼓风机间[房,室] blower house, blast [blowing] engine house, blowing room
鼓风机空气室 blower casing

鼓 gu

鼓风机设备　blower installation, blast apparatus
鼓风机司机　blower driver
鼓风机外壳　blower casing
鼓风机站　blowing plant
鼓风集管系统　manifold-blowing system
鼓风搅拌电解　electrolysis with air blowing
鼓风精炼　purifying with air
鼓风口　blast orifice
鼓风冷却　blast [up-draught] cooling ◇ 机上～*
鼓风冷却变压器　air blast transformer (a.b.t.)
鼓风冷却的　air blast cooled (ABC)
鼓风冷却机　pressure cooler
鼓风炼钢(法)　air-blown pneumatic steelmaking
鼓风量　blast [air] volume, blast [blowing] rate ◇ 需要～*, 最低～ critical air blast
鼓风量控制　blast volume control
鼓风量控制[调节]器　blast volume controller [regulator]
鼓风炉　blast furnace (B.F.), shaft(-type) furnace ◇ 常压～ low-blast furnace, 炼铜～*, 炼锌～ zinc blast furnace, 试验性～*
鼓风炉床能率　blast furnace specific capacity
鼓风炉工长　blast furnace foreman
鼓风炉料面指示器　blast furnace charge level indicator
鼓风炉锍[冰铜]　blast furnace matte
鼓风炉炉缸　blast furnace crucible [hearth]
鼓风炉炉架　blast furnace frame(work)
鼓风炉炉气　blast furnace gas
鼓风炉炉渣　shaft-furnace slag
鼓风炉砌砖　blast furnace brick work
鼓风炉前床　blast furnace settler
鼓风炉熔炼　blast furnace treatment, shaft (furnace) smelting
鼓风炉熔炼法　blast furnace method
鼓风炉熔炼作业　blast furnacing
鼓风炉砖　blast furnace brick
鼓风炉装料设备　blast furnace charging equipment
鼓风率　blast rate, rate of blowing,【铁】rate of driving
鼓风能力　blast capacity
鼓风排烟机　positive-pressure exhauster
鼓风期　blowing period, period of blowing
鼓风强度　blast intensity
鼓风去湿装置　dry-blast plant
鼓风熔炼　【冶】blast smelting
鼓风入口　blast hole
鼓风烧成(砖的)　【耐】blast roasting
鼓风烧结　【团】up-draught sintering
鼓风烧结法　up-draught sintering process
鼓风烧结锅　blast roasting pot
鼓风烧结机　up-draught sintering machine
鼓风设备　blast apparatus, blasting [blowing] equipment
鼓风湿度[含水率]　blast moisture, moisture content of air
鼓风湿度调节[调剂,控制]　(air) blast moisture control, blast humidity control
鼓风时间　blowing time, stack time (转炉的)
鼓风室　blowing room
鼓风速度　blast velocity
鼓风速率　blowing rate,【冶】wind rate (WR)
鼓风调剂　【铁】blast conditioning, beneficiation of blast
鼓风调节　blast governing[treatment]
鼓风脱水　blast dehydration
鼓风温度　(air) blast temperature,【铁】wind temperature
鼓风系统　blast system,【冶】up-draught system
鼓风压力　blast pressure (BP) ◇ 全～*
鼓风压力记录仪　blast pressure recorder

鼓风预热　up-draught preheating
鼓风预热器　(同"空气预热器")
鼓风增氧　oxygenation of blast
鼓风制度［状况］　blowing regime
鼓风重量　blast weight
鼓风装置　blowing plant
鼓风自然湿度　natural blast humidity
鼓风作用　action of blast
鼓冷风　cold (air) blast, cold-blast air [inlet]
鼓轮　drum
鼓轮罩　drum shell
鼓泡　bubbling, blistering, barbotage
鼓泡层　bubbling bed
鼓[起]泡的　blistered, blistery, blistering
鼓泡管　【焦】cracker pipe
鼓泡控制　gas bubbling control
鼓泡器　bubbler
鼓氢泡　hydrogen blistering
鼓入　blow in
鼓入风量　volume of blast blown
鼓入还原气体（操作）　reducing blast (practice)
鼓入空气　blast air
鼓入空气重量　blast weight
鼓入气体　blast gas
鼓式打印　barrel printing
鼓式打印机　drum [barrel] printer
鼓式分离器　drum separator
鼓式过滤机　(rotary) drum filter
鼓式拉拔［拉丝］机　drum-type drawbench
鼓式倾料器　drum tripper
鼓式湿度记录器　drum-hygrograph
鼓式真空过滤机［真空滤器］　drum vacuum filter, Oliver filter
鼓凸成型　bulging
"鼓外产品"焦　undersize coke
鼓型给矿器　drum feeder
鼓形电枢　drum armature
鼓形干燥炉　drum furnace
鼓形辊　barrel type roller
鼓形浇包　cylindrical ladle

鼓形绝缘子　drum [knob] insulator
鼓形控制器　drum controller
鼓形炉　rotary furnace
鼓形炉罩　(同"均热段炉罩")
鼓形率　【压】barrel ratio
鼓形启动器　drum starter
鼓形绕组［线圈］　drum winding
鼓形阴极　drum cathode
鼓形闸门　drum gate
鼓形制球机　balling drum
鼓形转换开关　drum [barrel] switch
鼓胀(机座之间的管子)　ballooning
古和氯化焙烧法（用于处理硫酸渣球团矿）　Kowa process
古氏坩埚　Gooch crucible
古塔树胶（绝缘材料）　gutta-percha
古铜辉石{(Mg, Fe)SiO$_3$}　bronzite
古铜辉岩　bronzite, bronzitfels
古铜色的　bronze coloured
骨干　backbone
骨干企业　key enterprise
骨干人员　【企】skeleton staff
骨骼状晶体　skeleton crystal
骨架　skeleton (frame), frame(work), carcase, carcass ◇ 编制 ~ framing
骨架方块示意图　block skeleton diagram
骨架结构　skeleton construction, post and beam construction
骨架晶型　skeleton crystal form
骨架颗粒　【粉】skeleton particle
骨架模造型　skeleton pattern moulding
骨架体　skeleton body
骨架制作　carcasing
骨胶　gelatin(e)
骨科用易熔合金　anatomical alloy
骨料　【建】aggregate ◇ 人工 ~，水泥量与 ~ 孔隙比率
骨料基层　aggregate base course (A.B.C.)
骨料间断级配　gapped aggregate grading
骨料粒径(混凝土的)　aggregate size
骨料配料箱　aggregate batcher

骨煤　bone (coal), bony [slate] coal
骨炭　animal charcoal, bone char [black, coal], charred horn
谷槽砌层　valley course
谷蛋白(型芯用)　gluten
谷类黏结剂　【铸】cereal binder
谷(值)点　valley [minimum, saddle] point
谷值电流　valley current
谷值曲线　minimum curve
钴{Co}　cobalt ◇ 放射性～*, 富～固溶体*, 含～合金*, 粒状～ granulated cobalt, 六方(晶)～ hexagonal cobalt, 阴极～ cathodic cobalt
钴氨络合物　cobalt-ammine complex, cobaltous ammine ◇ 低～*
钴沉淀工段　cobalt precipitation section
钴的　cobaltous, cobaltic
钴电解精炼槽　electrocobalt refining tank
钴矾　bieberite, rhodalose
钴方解石　cobaltocalcite
钴粉　cobalt powder
钴钢　cobalt steel
钴高速钢(14W,4Cr,1V,5Co)　cobalt high speed steel
钴铬钢　cobalt-chromium steel
钴铬(钼)耐热合金　◇ J～*
钴铬镍基形变耐热合金　◇ S.590～*
钴铬铁矿　cochromite
钴铬钨刀具合金　◇ 雷克斯～Rex alloy
钴铬钨合金　cobalt-chromium-tungsten alloy, Stellite ◇ 斯图迪～(焊条) Stoody, 星 J～*
钴铬钨镍合金　◇ 艾克里特～*
钴铬钨镍耐热合金　◇ 海恩斯 25～*
钴铬系耐热合金　◇ 科克罗姆～Cochrome
钴含量　cobalt content
钴合金　cobalt alloy ◇ 粗～ crude cobalt alloy
钴华 {Co₃(AsO₄)₂·8H₂O, Co₃As₂O₈·8H₂O}　cobalt bloom [ocher], crust of cobalt, erythrine, erythrite

钴化合物　cobaltic compound
钴黄铁矿　cobalt pyrite
钴回收工段　cobalt recovery section
钴回收系统　cobalt recovery circuit
钴基合金　cobalt-base alloy ◇ 梅尔科～*
钴基铝青铜[钴铜铝合金](50-60Co,30-40Cu,10Al)　sun bronze
钴基耐热合金　◇ S.816 形变～*
钴(结碳化)钛硬质合金　cobalt-cemented titanium carbide
钴(结碳化)钨硬质合金　cobalt-cemented tungsten carbide ◇ 卡勃洛伊～*
钴浸出车间　cobalt leach plant
钴精矿　cobalt concentrate
钴精矿焙砂　calcined cobalt concentrate
钴壳　crust of cobalt
钴孔雀石　kolwezite
钴矿床　cobalt deposit
钴矿物　cobalt mineral
钴蓝　cobalt blue [ultramarine], zaffer-blue
钴蓝釉　zaffer, zaffre
钴粒　cobalt granule [button], granulated cobalt
钴锍[冰铜]　cobalt matte ◇ 高～ high cobalt matte
钴绿(锌酸钴)　cobalt green
钴镁明矾　kasparite
钴锰土　cobaltiferous wad
钴明矾　masrite
钴钼铬合金　◇ 维塔留姆～*
钴钼铁永磁合金　◇ 科莫尔～*
钴镍合金　cobalt-nickel alloy
钴镍黄铁矿　cobalt-nickel pyrite
钴镍精矿焙砂　calcined cobalt-nickel concentrate
钴镍铸铁　cobalt-nickel cast iron
钴青铜　cobalt bronze
钴砷精矿　cobalt-arsenic concentrate
钴砷矿　cobalt-arsenic ore
钴酸盐　cobaltates
钴添加合金　cobalt addition

钴铁(75—78Co)　ferrocobalt
钴铁黄片合金　◇ 塞门杜尔~*
钴铁镍锰合金　◇ 曼格林瓦~*
钴铁氧体　Co ferrite ◇ 维克托莱特~*
钴铁氧体烧结磁铁　◇ OP—OP magnet
钴铜铝铁合金　◇ 麦塔林~*
钴土矿(锰钴的水合氧化物){CoMn$_2$O$_5$·4H$_2$O}　earthy cobalt, asbolan(e), asbolite
钴钍回收　spent Co and Th recovery
钴钨合金　cobalt tungsten alloy
钴盐　cobalt salt
钴氧化处理　cobalt oxide treatment
钴珠　cobalt button
股　strand
股(角钢的)　web, wing
股份　share, stock
股息　dividend
毂　nave
毂盖　hub cap
毂环　nave collar
故障　fault, trouble, failure, breakdown, accident, bug, malfunction, defect, disruption, disturbance, mischief ◇ 初发~ incipient failure, 检查及排除~ troubleshoot, 消除~ debugging, 有~(的) out of order (OOO)
故障传感器　fault sensor
故障的　defective
故障点测定　fault localization
故障电流　fault current
故障电路　faulted circuit
故障定位问题　【计】trouble-location problem
故障记录　【计】failure logging
故障记录器　fault [trouble] recorder
故障继电器　barrier relay
故障监控系统　fault supervisory system
故障检测　fault detect(ion)
故障检测继电器　fault check relay
故障检验器　flaw detector
故障警告继电器　failure warning relay
故障率　fault [failure] rate ◇ 合格~ acceptable failure rate
故障时间　fault [down] time
故障探测　tracing, fault-finding
故障探测器　fault finder, tracer
故障寻找　trouble hunting
故障诊断　fault diagnosis
故障指示流程图　fault indicating flow chart
故障指示器　fault [obstacle] indicator
固滴法　【冶】sessile drop method
固定氨　fixed ammonia
固定氨蒸柱　fixed still
固定百页[叶]窗　abat-vent, jalousie, louver
固定板　【团】dead plate,【铸】fixed plate
固定保温帽　fixed hot top
固定半阴模　fixed die
固定算条　stationary grate, fixed rod
固定臂　【焊】fixed arm
固定变比变压器　fixed ratio transformer
固定部分　fixed section
固定槽式酸洗　stationary [vat] pickling
固定层　fixed [stationary] bed (也称"固定床"), stationary layer
固定层焙烧　fixed bed roasting
固定层反应器　static bed reactor
固定层还原　【冶】fixed bed (type) reduction ◇ 间歇式~*
固定层还原法　fixed bed reduction process
固定层氯化　fixed bed chlorination
固定层烧结　fixed bed sintering
固定层试验　static bed test
固定长块　【计】fixed length block
固定长字　【计】fixed length word
固定沉降　permanent set
固定成本　fixed [constant] cost
固定成分　fixed composition
固定程序操作[加工]　rigidly programmed operation
固定程序计算机　fixed program computer
固定秤　fixed weighing machine

固定尺寸	fixed [set] dimension
固定触点	fixed contact
固定床	(见"固定层")
固定床交换柱	fixed bed column
固定床气化	fixed bed gasification
固定床气化装置	fixed bed gasifier
固定床设备	fixed bed unit
固定存储器	fixed memory [storage], noneraseable storage
固定单晶	stationary single crystal
固定氮	fixed nitrogen
固定挡板	stationary stop
固定刀杆	fixed plug ◇ 锥形~*
固定刀片	stationary knife
固定导板	fixed [resting] guide, stationary guide shoe
固定导电夹片	solid jaw
固定底片测角仪(用X射线)	stationary-film goniometer
固定底式炉	stationary-hearth furnace
固定点	fixed point
固定点反应(自由度为零的)	【金】invariant reaction
固定电荷	permanent charge
固定电极	fixed electrode
固定电极电位(电镀的)	static E.P.
固定电阻器	fixed [permanent] resistor
固定顶杆	fixed plug
固定颚板	fixed jaw
固定端	fixed [built-in, stiff] end
固定费	fixed [permanent] charge
固定费用	fixed costs, constant expense
固定感应器	static inductor
固定钢架(炉子的)	rigid binding
固定高度	fixed level
固定格筛	fixed bar grizzly screen
固定格式输入	【计】fixed format input
固定隔栅	stationary grate
固定工序	settling operation
固定工字轮的捻股机	fixed bobbin strander
固定拱	fixed [built-in] arch
固定拱脚斜石块	【建】fixed skewback
固定贯穿轴	fixed through shaft
固定辊	fixed roll
固定滑环电阻	fixed slip resistance
固定滑轮	fixed [fast] pulley, fixed block
固定灰分	fixed ash
固定基数记数法	【数】fixed radix notation
固定夹	fixing clamp, bracket, 【铸】binder (砂箱的)
固定夹具	stationary clamp, pick-up
固定夹片	solid jaw, fixed [stationary] jaw (接线柱的)
固定夹钳	fixed claw, stationary clamp
固定加料管	stationary feedpipe
固定架	holding yoke, fixed mount
固定剪刃	【压】fixed blade
固定件	mount(ing)
固定胶片照相机	stationary film [stationary-plate] camera
固定接地	dead earth, solid earthing
固定截面喷嘴	fixed area nozzle
固定结晶器	【连铸】fixed mould
固定介质分选[分离]	【选】static separation
固定卷筒(拉丝机的)	dead block
固定空气	fixed air
固定块	holding piece [block]
固定联接件	rigid part
固定联轴器	permanent [closed] coupling
固定连接	fixed [dead, permanent] joint
固定梁	fixed [built-in] beam, dormant
固定流化床	fixed fluidized bed
固定炉	fixed furnace
固定炉床	stationary hearth
固定炉顶式电弧炉	fixed roof type electric arc furnace
固定炉盖	permanent top
固定炉管	stationary furnace tube
固定炉膛式炉	fixed hearth furnace
固定螺钉	fixing [set, clamping, check] screw
固定螺母	retainer nut

固定螺栓　fixing [set] bolt
固定煤气道　(同"固定烟道")
固定煤气发生炉　simple stationary gas producer
固定美元计算数字　【企】constant dollar estimates
固定面板式配电盘　dead front switchboard
固定模空拔　fixed die drawing process
固定模台压机　nonrotary press
固定模座　stationary die holder
固定喷头洗涤塔　stationary-spray tower
固定疲劳寿命曲线图　constant life fatigue diagram
固定钳　fixing clamp
固定熔点　definite melting point
固定蠕变　【金】stationary creep
固定砂箱　【铸】tight [rigid] flask
固定筛　fixed screen [grizzly]
固定筛框　stationary frame
固定筛条　fixed rod, static grid
固定射束　fixed beam
固定实心主轴　fixed solid spindle
固定式称量机　(同"固定秤")
固定式吹炉[贝氏炉]　【钢】fixed converter
固定式带卷升降台　stationary coil lifter
固定式点焊机　pedestal [fixed] spot welder
固定式电焊机　stationary welder, stationary welding machine
固定式翻锭机　stationary ingot tilting pot, stationary tipping
固定式翻卷辊道　fixed [stationary] tilting table
固定式坩埚炉(有色压铸用)　stationary pot [crucible] furnace, bale-out furnace
固定式钢锭模　【钢】stationary mould
固定式刮刀[燕翅杆]　stationary cutter bar
固定式火焰淬火法　【金】stationary method of flame hardening
固定式卷筒(拔丝用)　【压】stationary [dead] block
固定式筐架　stationary type cradle
固定式冷床　stationary cooling bed
固定式炉底[台]　【压】base, coil base (带卷退火用的) ◇薄钢板退火用～sheet-annealing base
固定式皮带运输机　stationary belt conveyer
固定式起重机　fixed [stationary] crane
固定式前炉　stationary forehearth
固定式热电偶　stationary thermocouple
固定式烧结矿冷却机　stationary sinter cooler
固定式烧结盘　stationary pan
固定式水冷燃烧器　fixed water cooled burner
固定式压模　fixed mould
固定式研磨盘　fixed abrasive lap
固定式乙炔发生器　stationary acetylene generator
固定式转炉　stationary converter
固定术语　fixed term
固定水流(铸件水力清砂用)　【铸】fixed spray
固定水平　fixed [dead] level
固定碳　fixed carbon (F.C.)
固定铁栅筛　fixed bar grizzly screen
固定桶式酸洗　stationary [vat] pickling
固定投资额　【企】fixed investment
固定头　fixed head
固定(污染)源　【环】stationary source
固定下冲杆[模冲]　stationary lower punch
固定线夹　stationary clamp
固定相　stationary phase
固定销　set [steady] pin,【铸】fixed (moulding box) pin (砂箱的)
固定楔形座　stationary wedge bed
固定斜(支承)拱　fixed skewback arch
固定芯棒　【压】fixed mandrel, fixed [stationary] plug, stationary core rod

固定芯棒拔管	fixed plug tube drawing
固定芯棒拉伸	stationary-mandrel drawing
固定芯棒轧制	fixed mandrel rolling
固定心轴	fixed mandrel [plug] ◇ 锥形~
固定型步进梁	settle-type walking beam
固定形式编码	【计】fixed form coding
固定性	fixity, stationarity
固定选通脉冲振荡器	fixed gate generator
固定盐	fixed salt
固定阳极	stationary anode
固定阴极	stationary cathode
固定载荷	fixed [seating] load
固定爪(拖运机的)	stationary dogs
固定支柱	dead abutment, stationary column (炉子的)
固定支座	dead abutment, hold-down support
固定制动器[固定闸]	retaining [holding] brake
固定中心	dead centre
固定周期操作	【计】fixed cycle operation
固定轴	fixed [stationary, dead] axle
固定轴承	fixed [rigid] bearing
固定轴承座	fixed chock
固定轴环	set collar
固定柱	fixed leg
固定铸坑浇铸	【钢】fixed pit casting
固定装料机	rigid charging machine
固定装置	fixing device, fixative, fixer, setting-up fixture, back set
固定状态	stationary state
固定资产	【企】fixed [capital] assets
固定资产净值	net value of fixed assets
固定资产投资	investment in fixed assets
固定资产原值	original value of fixed assets
固定座(型板上的)	fixing pad
固端梁	built-in beam, beam with both ends built in, beam with fixed ends
固-固反应	solid-solid interaction [reaction]
固-固转变	solid-solid transition
固化	solidification, cure
固化炉	curing furnace, curing oven (表面涂层的)
固化时间	cure [setting] time
固件	【计】firmware
固接部件	fastening part
固结	consolidating, consolidation, strengthening, binding, induration
固结材料	cementing material
固结动力学	kinetics of hardening
固结度	degree of consolidation [packing]
固结反应	binding reaction
固结工段	induration section, indurating area
固结灌浆	consolidation grouting
固结过程	bonding [induration] process
固结机	induration machine
固结机理	strengthening mechanism
固结集合体	consolidated aggregate
固结矿槽	hardening bin
固结炉顶	bonded roof
固结球团	【团】hard-baked pellet
固结设备	consolidation device, indurating equipment [unit], induration equip-ment
固结时间	indurating [set(ting), hardening] time
固结相(烧结矿的)	【团】binding phase
固结系数	coefficient of consolidation
固结氧化球团	hardened oxide pellet
固结仪	consolidometer
固结周期	induration cycle
固结状态材料	material in solid bulk form
固结作用	bonding action strengthening effect
固硫	【焦】fixed-sulfur
固硫率	sulfur fixation ratio
固硫作用	sulphur fixation
固-气还原(反应)	solid-gas reduction
固-气转变	solid-gas transition

固溶	solutionize ◇ 双节点~曲线 binodal line
固溶处理	solution treatment, solutionize
固溶处理合金	solution-treated alloy
固溶处理温度	solution treatment temperature
固溶淬火	solution quenching [hardening]
固溶度	【金】solid solubility
固溶度极限	solid solubility limit
固溶度曲线	solubility curve, solvus
固溶度线	solid solubility line, solvus line
固溶化	solutionizing
固溶化淬火	water toughening
固溶极限	solid solubility limit
固溶晶体	solid solution crystal
固溶强化	solid solution strengthening, (solid) solution hardening
固溶强化合金	solid solution strengthened alloy
固溶热处理	(solid) solution heat treatment ◇ 两段~
固溶热处理后人工时效	full heat treatment
固溶热处理状态	solution heat-treated condition
固溶熵	solutioning entropy
固溶体	solid solution (SS), sosoloid, mischcrystal, mix-crystal ◇ 代位式[置换型,替代]~, 分解着的~ decomposing solid solution, 固体中的~, 浓度不均~, 缺位~, 无限[完全]~, 无序~, 稀薄~ dilute solid solution, 液体中的~, 一次[初生]~ primary solid solution, 有缺陷~ defect solid solution
固溶(体)饱和率	solid solution saturation ratio
固溶体材料	solid solution material
固溶体成分	solid solution composition
固溶体分解	breakdown of solid solution
固溶体分解曲线	solvus
固溶体合金	solid solution alloy ◇ 间隙~ interstitial alloy
固溶体结构	structure of solid solution
固溶体金属陶瓷	solid solution cermet (SSC)
固溶体晶格	solid solution lattice
固溶体晶体	solid solution crystal
固溶体连续系列	【金】continuous series of solid solutions
固溶体区[固溶范围]	solid solution range
固溶体型反应	solid solution type reaction
固溶体形成	solid solution formation
固溶体衍射花样(X射线的)	solid solution pattern
固溶退火	solution treatment annealing (STA), solution annealing [treatment]
固溶线	liquidoid
固溶相	solid solution phase
固溶相线	solvus
固溶性	solid solubility
固溶硬化	(solid) solution hardening
固溶状态	solid solution condition
固砂木片	【铸】soldiers
固态	solid state, solidity
固态不混溶范围[区域]	【金】solid immiscibility region
固态稠度渣	【冶】unfluxed slag
"固态"除气剂(液态合金用)	"solid gas"
固态萃取法	【色】solid-extraction method
固态点	solidus point
固态电解法	solid state electrolysis
固态反应	solid state reaction
固态焊	solid-state welding
固态合金	solid alloy
固态化学反应	solid state chemical reaction
固态还原	solid state reduction
固态激光器	solid state laser
固态计算机	solid state computer
固态加工	solid processing
固态键	solid state bonding
固态金属	metallic solid
固态扩散	solid state diffusion
固态理论	solid state theory

固态马氏体	solid state martensite
固态黏合[结]	solid state bonding
固态平衡	solid state equilibrium
固态器件	solid state device, croystron
固态区域精炼	solid zone refining
固态区域(能带)理论	zone theory of solids
固态烧结	solid sintering
固态收缩	solid shrinkage
固态(特性)研究	solid state study
固态图像放大器	solid state image amplifier
固态完全不互溶(性)	complete solid immiscibility
固态完全互溶(性)	complete solid miscibility, complete miscibility in solid state
固态物理学	solid state physics
固态线	solidus
固态相变	solid-solid transition, solid-state phase changes
固态氧	solid oxygen
固态元件	【电】solid state component [element, device]
固态置换方法	solid state cementation process
固体	solid (body, mass) ◇ 刚凝结的～ just-freezing solid, 胡克～ Hookian solid
固体表面能	energy of surface of solid
固体冰晶石	solid cryolite
固体成型机	solid forming machine
固体电解质	solid (-state) electrolyte [bath]
固体电解质测氧仪	solid electrolyte sensor
固体电解质传感器	solid electrolyte sensor
固体电路	solid (state) circuit
固体二氧化碳	solid carbon dioxide, dry ice
固体非金属夹杂物	sonim
固体非金属杂质	solid nonmetallic impurity
固体废钢脱铜	removal of copper from solid scrap
固体废物	【环】solid waste, waste solid
固体焊剂	solid flux
固体含量	solids content
固体合成渣	solid synthetic slag
固体夹杂物	solid inclusion
固体键[连接桥]	solid bridge
固体件锻造法	【压】solid forging method
固体颗粒	solid particle
固体颗粒冲[撞]击	solid impingement
固体颗粒装入比率	solid(s) loading ratio
固体理论	theory of solid
固体料流	solid flow
固体料运动	solid movement
固体流动	solid flow
固体流态化技术	fluidized solids technique
固体锍[冰铜]	【色】solid matte
固体锍氧气吹炼	solid matte oxygen converting (SMOC)
固体锍氧气吹炼炉	SMOC furnace
固体炉料	solid charge ◇ 煤气与～间的反应【冶】gas-solid reaction
固体弥散	solid dispersion
固体密度	solid density ◇ 表观～ apparent solid density
固体摩擦	solid friction
固体能带论	band theory of solids
固体培养基	solid medium
固体桥接	solid bridging
固体桥形成	solid bridging
固体氰化	solid cyaniding
固体燃料添加量	solid fuel level
固体热载体	solid heat [thermal] carrier
固体熔剂	solid flux, solid fluxing agent
固体溶剂	solid solvent
固体润滑	solid [dry] lubrication
固体渗铬	solid chromizing
固体渗铬钢	IK (Inkromierung) steel
固体渗铝[铝化]	powder [pack] calorizing
固体渗碳[增碳]	solid [box, pack] car-

burizing, box hardening ◇ 哈维～硬化钢 Harvey steel

固体渗碳剂 solid carburizer, carburizing compound [medium], packing agent, case-hardening compound

固体渗碳剂渗碳[增碳] carburizing by solid matters, carburizing with carbonaceous solids

固体渗碳炉 solid-carburizing furnace, pack-hardening furnace

固体石油 petroleum coal

固体收缩 solid contraction

固体探测器 solid probe

固体推进剂 grain

固体托辊 solid idler

固体物理学 solid state physics

固体物料处理系统 solid material handling system

固体物质 solid material [matter] ◇ 可电离的～ ionizable solid

固体氧 solid oxygen

固体炸药爆炸成形 solid explosive forming

固体中的固溶体 solutions of solids in solids

固体中的气溶体 solutions of gases in solids

固线温度 solidus temperature

固线下 sub-solidus

固线下相关系 subsolidus phase relation

固相 solid phase, solidoid

固相点 solidus point

固相电解法 solid state electrolysis

固相反应 solid-phase reaction

固相分解 decomposition of solid phases

固相关系 【金】solid phase relationship

固相焊接法 solid-phase bonding process

固相扩散 solid diffusion

固相面 solidus face

固相区域精炼 solid zoning

固相区域熔炼 solid phase zone melting

固相曲线 solid phase curve

固相烧结 solid (phase, state) sintering

固相析出[沉淀] solid phase precipitation

固相线 solid phase curve, solidus (curve, line)

固相线烧结 solidus sintering

固相线温度 solidus temperature

固相压焊 solid-phase pressure welding, solid-phase welding

固相优先挥发[汽化]分离法(钽铌的) solid-vapour process

固相自由能曲线 solid phase free energy curve

固液比 solid-to-liquid ratio,【冶】S/W ratio

固-液萃取 【色】solid-liquid extraction

固-液混合 solid-liquid mixing

固-液界面 solid-liquid interface

固-液相界面 solidification contour [front]

固-液旋流器 solid liquid cyclone

固液异成分熔点 incongruent melting point

固液异成分熔融化合物 incongruently melting compound

固液异成分熔融相 【金】incongruently melting phase

固-液转变 solid-liquid transition

固有半导电性 intrinsic semiconduction

固有不稳定性 inherent [intrinsic] instability

固有磁场 self-magnetic field

固有淬透性 【金】inherent hardenability

固有导电性 intrinsic conductivity

固有电导 intrinsic conduction

固有电容 self-capacitance, natural capacitance

固有还原性 (同"内禀还原性")

固有灰分 inherent ash

固有夹杂物 【冶】indigenous inclusions

固有晶粒度 inherent grain size

固有孔隙 inherent porosity

固有扩散系数 intrinsic diffusion coeffi-

固有模糊度 inherent unsharpness
固有黏度 intrinsic [inherent] viscosity
固有频率 natural frequency (nat. freq.), free frequency
固有频率振动试验 natural frequency vibration test
固有强度 inherent strength
固有衰耗[衰减] nonreflection attenuation
固有水分 inherent [fixed] moisture
固有酸度 initial acidity
固有损失 inherent loss
固有特性[性能] inherent characteristics, intrinsic property
固有稳定性 inherent [intrinsic] stability
固有误差 inherent [intrinsic] error
固有细晶粒 inherent fine grain
固有延展性 inherent ductility
固有运动 proper motion
固有杂质 inherent impurity, intrinsic contaminant
固有沾染 intrinsic contaminant
固有振荡 natural oscillation
固有振动 natural vibration [oscillation]
固有值 proper value
固有周期(振动的) natural period
固有阻抗 natural [intrinsic] impedance
固着 adherence, adherency
雇员 employee
刮 scraping, raking
刮板 scraper (blade), plough, plow, scalper, skimmer blade, striking plate, 【铸】sweep (template), sweeping board, flight (切边切头运输机的) ◇ 给料~ feed shoe, 皮带~ belt scraper, 手动~ hand scraper
刮板导框 【铸】sweeping guide
刮板搅拌机 【选】agitator with scrapers
刮板拉链(输送)机 drag [drawing] link conveyer ◇ 火烟道排灰~*
刮板链式输送机 drag chain [link] conveyer, drawing link conveyer
刮板马架 【铸】sweeping horse
刮板模型 【铸】sweep pattern
刮板式铲泥机 scraping dredger
刮板式水泥装卸机 cement hog
刮板推土机 rake dozer
刮板脱水机 scraper dewaterer
刮板用具 【铸】sweeping tackle
刮板运输[输送,运送]机 scrape [drag, rake, plough, push-plate, chain-and-flight] conveyer, flight (bar) conveyer,【压】crop skip hoist (收集切头用) ◇ 拉链~*,链式~ chain flight conveyer, 倾斜式~*
刮板造型 【铸】strickle [sweep, template] moulding, strickling, sweeping-up ◇ 控制截面~*
刮板支承 flight support
刮板座 flight support
刮铲 spatule, spatula
刮尺 darby, floating rule
刮刀 scraper (blade, knife, bar), skimmer blade, blade, doctor knife, plough (plate), plow, scraping mechanism, rotating bar (混合机内的),【团】cutter[cut-off] bar, paddle ◇ 底盘~ bottom rake, 固定式~ stationary cutter bar, 毛刺~ shaver, 盘底~【团】bottom scrapper, 旋转式~*
刮刀排料[矿] plough discharge
刮刀前刃[刮料板前缘] 【团】leading edge
刮刀刃 trimming edge
刮刀刃棱 scraper edge
刮刀卸料式冷却机 plough discharge cooler
刮刀钻头 (blade) drag bit
刮垢刀片 clearance blade
刮痕 scratch (Scr., scr.)
刮痕硬度 scratch(ing) hardness
刮净 scrape out
刮料板 striking [plough] plate, scraper bar,【团】cut-off plate, lifting flight, strike off plate ◇ 调压式~*, 弯曲~*

刮料机构　scraping mechanism
刮料器【机】　scraper,【团】cutting-off machine ◇ 移动式~*
刮路机　drag planer ◇ 刀片式~ blade drag, planer
刮路器　drag ◇ 钉板~ nail drag, 链式~ chain drag
刮模板　【铸】sweep template
刮泡勺　【选】bowl skimmer
刮平　blading
刮砂板　【铸】straight edge
刮伤　scratch, scuffing
刮勺　spatule, spatula,【铸】slicker spoon
刮土机　scraper, skimmer shovel ◇ 弹板~ buck scraper
刮削机　skimming machine
刮芯板　【铸】core board
刮油器　oil wiper ◇ 带式~ belt type oil skimmer
刮制铸型　【铸】sweeping mould
刮子　【铸】slick
挂壁　【冶】wall built-up
挂标签　tagging
挂耳　lug, hangers（电解极板上的）, suspension loop
挂耳式阳极　coped-lug type anode
挂钩　tieback, hook hitch, hanger
挂钩拖车　dog trailer
挂环　suspension loop [hook]
挂金属　close plating
挂料　bridging (of charge),【铁】bridging, hanging (of charge), hang(ing)-up, burden suspending, suspend,【铸】hand-up（在砂斗中）
挂炉　【色】magnetite coating
挂轮　lantern gear [pinion]
挂模锭　【钢】catched ingot
挂渣风口　sluggish tuyere,【铁】sloppy tuyere
拐点　【数】inflection [inflexion, break(ing)] point, knee (point)
关闭　closing, closure, shut-off, throw off, turndown
关闭塞棒　【钢】shut-off
关闭位置　off-position
关闭文件　【计】closed file
关闭指令　【计】CLOSE
关断　【电】cut-off, turn-off, shut-off
关断点　cut-off point
关断阀　closing [stop] valve
关键路径　【计】critical path
关键码　【计】key
关键污染物参数　【环】critical pollutant parameter
关键字　keyword ◇ 相联~ associative key
关节杆　articulated arm
关节连接　articulated joint
关节销　knuckle pin
关税　customs, duty, tariffs
关税分类【类别】　tariff classification
关税及贸易总协定　General Agreement on Tariffs and Trade (GATT)
关税率　rate of duty, tariffs, tariff rate
关系操作符　【计】relation operator
关系曲线　dependance, relation curve
关系式　【数】relation, relational expression ◇ 格律埃森~*, 科希~ Cauchy relations, 莫特-纳巴罗~*
官能团　functional group
冠齿轮　crown gear [wheel]
冠丝(钢丝绳的)　crown wire
冠形螺母　horned nut
冠岩　cap rock
观测　observation, observe, viewing
观测报告　observation report
观测方程　observation [observed] equation
观测孔　observation hole [opening, port], loop hole
观测强度　observed intensity
观测数据　observational data
观测误差　observation error
观测仪　visualizer
观测值　observed value
观察　observation, viewing, overview, sur-

vey, watch, overlook ◇ 非定期~ casual observation, 可~的[可~量] observable, 肉眼[宏观]~*
观察窗 (observation) window, (sight) glass, peephole ◇ 进料计量~ feed gauge glass
观察法 【理】method of observation
观察管 sight tube
观察结果 observed results
观察孔 eye hole [split], eye-sight, observation hole [opening, port, window], peep (hole), sight (window), viewing window [port], window, glory-hole, sight-hole, wicket ◇ 石英玻璃~ silica window, 有机玻璃~ perspex window
观察门 observation door
观察数据 observation data (OD)
观察台 observatory
观察误差 error of observation
观探孔 inspection port
管 tube, pipe ◇ 布登~*, 盖斯勒~*, 库里几~ Coolidge tube, 小口径~ fine tubing
管扳手 pipe wrench [grip(per), dog], alligator [dulldog] wrench
管板锻件 tube plate forging
管棒矫直机 【压】bar and tube straightening machine
管壁 tube [pipe, duct] wall, shell of pipe
管壁厚度 shell thickness
管壁(厚度)测量仪 pipe-wall gauge ◇ X射线~ X-ray pipe-wall gauge
管壁厚度电测仪 electric tube caliper
管壁厚度计 tube wall thickness gauge
管壁减薄轧机 trommel roll
管壁增厚控制(连轧管的) stomach-control
管材 tube, tubing, tubular goods ◇ API管线用~ API line pipe
管材车间设备 tubular mill
管材成形机 tube-forming mill
管材成形加工 tubing

管材储备 tubing inventory
管材存放架 tube storage rack
管材定径 【压】sizing
管材公称直径 nominal size of pipes
管材挤压 tube [mandrel] extrusion
管材挤压机 tube extruder
管材减径机 tube-reducing machine [mill]
管材矫直机 tube straightening machine ◇ 艾布拉姆森式~*
管材均整机 reeling mill
管材拉拔 tube-drawing
管材拉拔模 tube-drawing die
管材冷轧 cold reduction of tube
管材连轧 mandrel rolling
管材量规 tube gauge
管材平滑端 plain end
管材清理机 pipe-swabbing machine
管材生产 tube making
管材(水压)试验机 (hydraulic) pipe testing machine
管材斜轧穿孔 tube cross piercing
管材旋压 tube spinning
管材在芯棒上的辗轧 plugging operation
管材轧机 pipe [tube(-rolling)] mill
管材轧制 tube rolling
管材(轧制)孔型设计 grooving of tube
管材张力减径机 tube stretcher, tube stretch reducing mill
管材制品 tubular product
管长测量轮 measuring wheel
管簇 tube nest
管道 pipe-line (P/L), channel, duct, piping, pipe (culvert), pipework, tubing (tbg), conduit (电缆用) ◇ 无接箍~ integral-joint tubing
管道安装[铺设] pipe installation [laying]
管道布置 pipework
管道布置图 piping diagram
管(道长)廊 pipe gallery
管道萃取器 tube extractor
管道吊箍 pipe clip

管道吊架	pipe hanger [bridge]
管道堵塞	pipe clogging
管道工程	pipework, duct-work, plumbing
管道过水能力	carrying capacity of pipe
管道化溶出	pipeline [tube] digestion
管道及仪表布置图	piping and instrumentation diagram (P&ID)
管道路线	duct route
管道配置	pipe arrangement
管道全位置自动焊接	all position pipeline automatic arc welding
管道设施	piped service
管道式干燥机	duct-type drier
管道输送	pipeline transportation, pip(e)age
管道(输送)煤气	piped gas
管道调压器	pipeline regulator
管道通过能力	pipe capacity
管道图	piping plan
管道网	network of pipe lines, pipe arrangement ◇ 连通～
管道系统	pipe [piping] system, ducting, pipage, pipework
管道现象[行程](高炉故障)【铁】	channeling
管道悬挂夹头	pipe hanger
管道压力	tubing pressure (T.P.)
管道支架	duct support
管道装炉【焦】	pipeline charging ◇ 科尔特克预热煤～法 Coaltak method
管道总站	pipeline terminal
管的冷减径	cold reduction of tube
管底	socle, base
管电流(X射线管的)	tube current
管堵(头)[盲板, 密封]	pipe close(r) [caulking]
管端	tube [pipe] end, spigot
管端锤头压力机	tube end swaging press
管端定径压力机	tube end sizing press
管端墩粗	staving
管端墩厚机	tube upsetting press [machine]
管端加厚	end upsetting
管端扩口水压机	tube end belling press
管端扩口压力机	slapping press
管端圆边精整	rounding
管法兰	pipe flange
管钢	tube [pipe] steel
管工	pipeman, pipefitter
管工黄铜(60—71Cu, 1Sn, 3Pb, 25—36Zn)	plumber's brasses
管工用铜锌镍合金(25Zn, 15Ni, 1Pb, 1Fe, 余量Cu)	plumber's white
管工(用锡铅)焊料(67Pb, 余量Sn)	plumber's solder
管工组长	fitter foreman
管沟	pipe canal
管箍	binding band
管焊接	tube welding ◇ 啃口～ bite type tube welding
管环缝焊机	orbital pipe welder
管夹头	pipe grip
管夹头锻制机	tube pointer
管夹头压制机	squeeze pointer
管架	tube holder, pipe clamp [support]
管件	pipe fitting ◇ 挤压～ extruded pipe
管件间V形焊缝	flare-V weld
管脚(电子管的)	base pin
管接地	pipe earth
管接口用稀油	liquid pipe dope
管接螺母	union nut
管接头	union joint [coupling], (tube) union, pipe connection [branch, joint], connecting pipe, pipe coupling, fitting pipe ◇ 烟气阀～
管接头毛坯	pipe connection blank
管结构	tubular construction, tube design
管进给机构	tube feeding crosshead
管径	caliber, calibre, pipe diameter
管径电测器	electric tube caliper
管壳式热交换器	shell-and-tube exchanger
管口盖凸缘[法兰]	blind [blank] flange
管理程序	supervisory program [routine],

manager, supervisor
管理程序调入 supervisor call
管理对策 management games
管理费用 management [overhead] charges
管理水平 【企】control level
管理图表 control chart
管理信息系统 management information system (MIS)
管理性数据处理 administrative data processing
管理严密的 handling tight
管理员 controller, manager
管料 pipestock
管路 pipe line, piping ◇供氧~ oxygen supply line
管路敷设 piping installation, pipe laying
管路过滤器 linear [in-line] filter
管路网式过滤器 line strainer
管路装置 piping installation
管螺纹 pipe thread (P.T.) ◇美国标准协会~ *
管磨机 【选】tube mill
管排 bank [row] of tubes
管坯 tube blank [bloom, rounds, shell, stock], tubular billet ◇焊接前~成型机 tube-forming mill, 空心~ hollow (bloom, shell), 水平连铸圆~*, 预先钻孔~ predrilled billet
管坯剥皮 peel
管坯壁厚 shell thickness
管坯回转定径机 billet sizer
管坯剪切 bloom-shearing
管坯辗轧 rolling off
管钳 pipe tongs [vice, twist, wrench], alligator wrench
管钳工 pipe fitter
管熔切器 tube cutting burner
管塞 pipe plug [close(r), stopper]
管式爆炸压力机 【压】tube-type explosive press
管式电炉 electric tube furnace ◇高温

管式电收尘器[静电收尘器,(静电)除尘器] electric pipe precipitator, pipe-type electric [electrostatic] (dust-) precipitator, tubular (electrostatic) precipitator
管式干燥机 tube [tubular] dryer, tube drier
管式钢丝绳 hollow wire rope
管式高压釜 tube autoclave
管式过滤器[机] tube [tubular] filter
管式合绳机 tubular type closer
管式换热器 tubular heat exchanger
管式给[加]料机 pipe feeder
管式加热炉 tubular oven
管式加热器 tube heater
管式结晶器 【连铸】tube [tubular] mould
管式空间结构 tubular space structure
管式空气冷却器 tubular air cooler
管式空气预热器 tubular air preheater
管式冷凝器 tubular condenser
管式冷却器 pipe [tubular] cooler
管式连续生产炉 continuous tube furnace
管式炉 tube [tubular, pipe] furnace, pipe still ◇传送带~*, 高温电热~(见"高温管式电炉"), 倾斜~ slanted tubular furnace, 碳硅棒~ globar tube furnace, 威尔顿~ Wilton still
管式炉渗碳 tube carburizing
管式螺旋运输机 tubular screw conveyer
管式马弗炉 tubular retort furnace
管式捻股机 【压】tubular stranding machine, tubular [snake] type strander
管式球磨机 ball tube mill
管式取样器 pipe [gun] sampler
管式热电偶 pipe thermocouple
管式热风炉 【铁】pipe stove
管式热交换器 tubular heat exchanger ◇卡尔贝特~*
管式渗碳炉 carburizing tube furnace
管式收尘器 tubular dust collector, tubular deduster
管式台架 tubular skid

管式同轴分选[选矿]机 【选】coaxial tube separator, concurrent separator
管式压力机 pipe [tubular] press
管式阳极 tube anode
管式引杆(焊管坯用) pipe needle
管式预热器 tubular preheater
管式蒸馏釜 pipe still
管束 pipe bundle, tube bundle [bank, nest]
管束筐架 bundling cradle
管丝口扳钳 pipe die
管丝锥 pipe tap
管态 【计】executive [supervisor] mode
管膛 barrel of pipe
管套 pipe socket [box, sleeve]
管套接 bell and plain end joint
管筒 tubular body
管凸缘 pipe flange
管托 pipe clamp
管网 pipe network
管尾三角(缺陷) 【压】tube-end triangular
管线[系] pipe-line (P/L), (line) piping, tubing (tbg), duct, pipe arrangement
管线安装[敷设] pipelining
管线(分布)平面图 piping plan
管线钢 pipeline steel
管线路 route of pipe line
管线系统 pipework
管线系统图 schematic pipe diagram
管线(用)钢 pipeline steel ◇ 高韧性~*
管线增压泵 line booster pump
管型发夹式炉 tubular hair-pin furnace
管形的 tubular
管形熔断器 tube [cartridge] fuse
管形燃烧室 pipe-type (combustion) chamber
管乐器黄铜(81Cu, 17.8Zn, 1.2Sn) trumpet brass [metal]
管轧机 tube mill
管中扩散 pipe diffusion
管轴(线) tube [tubular] axis
管桩 pipe [tubular] pile ◇ PHC~端板

管桩钢 pipe pile steel
管状变阻器 tubular rheostat
管状电极 tubular [hollow] electrode
管状反应器 tubular reactor
管状焊丝电弧焊 flux cored (arc) welding
管状焊条[丝] tube wire, electrode core, cored electrode [bar]
管状加热器 tubular heater
管状截取[分样]器 【选】tubular splitter
管状结晶器 (同"管式结晶器")
管状炉 (同"管式炉") ◇ 卧式~*
管状热风炉 pipe stove ◇ 连续式~*
管状缩孔 【冶】pipe cavity
管状碳(极焊条) cored carbon
管状洗涤器 tubular washer
管状芯骨 【铸】core barrel [spindle]
管状蒸馏罐 tubular retort
管状制品 tubular body
管子承口 bell of pipe
管子底面 bottom of pipe (B.O.P.)
管子脚手架 tubular scaffold
管子弯头 pipe bend
管子斜弯头 pipe mitred bend
管组 nest of tubes, bank of tubes, block
管嘴 adjustage, mouthpiece
管座 socket, tube [valve] socket (电子管座), pipestock, tube stand (X射线管的)
罐 tank (Tk), jar, pot, tin, balloon, cage, can, 【冶】ladle
罐车 tank car, 【冶】ladle car
罐衬里 tank lining
罐耳(渣铁罐的) trunnion
罐壳 【冶】ladle casing [bowl]
罐炉 pot furnace
罐内加料 【冶】ladle addition
罐熔法 pot melting process
罐熔炉 pot melting furnace
罐身 【冶】ladle body
罐式电阻加热炉 resistance heated pot-type furnace
罐式冷却捕集器[罐式冷阱] pot-type cold trap

罐式炉	pot-annealing furnace,【色】pan [pot] furnace(熔炼低熔点合金用)
罐式燃烧室	can-type (combustion) chamber
罐头材料	canning material
罐头工业	canning industry
罐头盒	tin can
罐头盒底	can end
罐头盒体	can body
罐头制造	canning
罐蒸馏法	retort method
罐装气	cylinder gas
惯性功率[测功,测力,拉力]计	inertia dynamometer
惯性焊接	inertial welding
惯性荷载	inertial loading
惯性收尘[集尘,捕尘,除尘]器	inertial dust separator ◇ 挡板式 ~ louver de-duster
惯性矩	inertia moment ◇ 几何 ~*
惯性力	inertial force
惯性力分级机	inertia force classifier
惯性力偶	inertia couple
惯性量	inertia
惯性落砂	【铸】inertia shake-out
惯性误差	inertial error
惯性压力	inertial [mass] pressure
惯性折断(挤压缺陷)	【压】inertia break-off
惯性轴	inertia axis
惯性作用	inertial effect
惯用方法	conventional process
惯用设备	conventional plant
灌封	embed(ment), imbed
灌溉用水	irrigation water
灌溉用污水处理	irrigation sewage disposal
灌浆	grouting ◇ 固结 ~ consolidation grouting
灌浆碎石路	penetration macadam
灌浆造衬护炉技术(高炉的)	grouting repair technology for BF lining protection
灌铅	plumbing
灌输	implantation
灌铁风口(高炉操作事故)【铁】	"ironed-in" tuyere
灌渣铁(风口的)	【铁】ironing
灌筑	placing, pour ◇ 混凝土可~性*
灌(筑)混凝土	【建】concreting, concrete placement ◇ 分层 ~ concreting in lifts, 连续 ~ continuous concreting, 现场 ~ concrete in situ
灌筑机	placer ◇ 自行式混凝土~*
灌筑量	【建】pour
灌筑塔[混凝土灌筑塔]	dump tower
灌注	priming, bottling, flood
灌注机	impregnating machine, bottler placer
灌注桩	filling pile, bored concrete pile
贯穿	penetrating, penetrance, breakthrough, intersect
贯穿辐射	penetrating [hard] radiation
贯穿辐射源	penetrating radiation source
贯穿计(测定辐射用)	penetrameter, penetrometer
贯穿粒子	【理】penetrating particle
贯穿孪晶	penetration twin
贯穿螺栓	through bolt
贯穿面	【理】penetration side
贯穿能力	penetrating power, penetrativeness
贯穿深度	penetration depth
贯穿性	penetrability
贯穿性成分(射线的)	【GJ】hard component
贯穿作用	penetrating action
贯流(离子交换的)	breakthrough
贯流分析池	flow cell
贯流式润滑(冷轧机的)	environmental lubrication
贯入度仪[贯入器]	penetrometer
贯通孔	through [full] hole, full length bore,【粉】communicating pores
贯通式炉	through(-type) furnace

贯眼型(对焊钻杆的连接型式) full hole (FH) style
光 light ◇ 切伦科夫~ Cerenkov light
光 X 射线照相术 photoroentgenography
光拔钢 bright drawn steel
光比色法 photocolorimetry
光笔 light pen [gun]
光笔跟踪 【计】light pen tracking
光笔中断 【计】light pen attention
光变送器(射流技术的) light transducer
光标 cursor
光波干涉 light (wave) interference, optical interference
光波通讯 lightwave communication
光彩 luster, lustre
光彩石 {2Al$_2$O$_3$·P$_2$O$_5$·3H$_2$O} augelite
光测 【理】optic(al) measurement
光测的 photometric
光测读数 photometric [optical] reading
光测高温计 (同"光学高温计")
光测弹性 (同"光弹性")
光测弹性法 photostress [photoelastic, photoelasticity] method
光测弹性研究 photoelastic study
光测弹性应力 photoelastic stress, photostress
光测弹性应力分析用材料 photostress
光测弹性照相 photoelastic photograph
光场照明 lightfield illumination
光程差 optical path difference (OPD), difference in optical path, propagation difference
光触发开关 light activated silicon controlled rectifier (LASCR)
光磁存储器 【计】photo magnetic memory
光磁性 photomagnetism
光瓷 luster, lustre
光存储器 【计】photo [optical] memory
光带 【理】(light) band
光导管 light pipe
光导摄像管 vidicon
光导通讯 guided optical communication
光导图像变换器 photoconductive image transducer
光导纤维 optical fibre
光导纤维束 fibre optic bundle
光导纤维通信 optical fibre communication
光缔合 photoassociation
光电 photoelectricity
光电安培计 photoammeter
光电倍增管 multiplier phototube, photomultiplier tube
光电比色高温计 radiation pyrometer, photocell colorimetric system
光电比色计 optimeter, photocolorimeter, photoelectric colorimeter
光电编码盘 photoelectric coded disc
光电变换器[图像变换管] image converter (tube)
光电材料 photoelectric material
光电成像装置 photoelectric imaging device
光电池 photocell, photoelectric [light, photovoltaic] cell ◇ 阻挡层~
光电传感头 photo head
光电磁 photo-electro-magnetic (PEM)
光电磁效应 PEM effect
光电导 photoconduction
光电导管 photoconductive cell
光电导率 photoelectric conductivity, photoconductivity
光电导衰减 photo-conductivity decay
光电导体 photoconductor
光电导性 photoconductivity
光电动势 photoelectromotive force
光电二极管 photorectifier, photodiode
光电发光 photo-electroluminescence
光电发射率[能力] photoemissivity
光电发射效应 photoemissive effect
光电发射元件 photoemissive element
光电分光光度计 photoelectric spectrophotometer
光电分光计 photoelectric spectrometer

光电高温计　photoelectric pyrometer,photopyrometer,optimatic pyrometer
光电管　photoelectric cell（PEC,p.e.c.）,electric eye,light[photoelectric]cell,photoelectric tube,photoelement,phototube ◇充气～*,孪生～*,韦斯顿～Weston photronic cell,氧化亚铜～*
光电管传感器　photocell pick-off
光电管高温计　photocell pyrometer
光电光度测量(法)　photoelectric photometry
光电光度计　photoelectric photometer
光电计　photoelectrometer
光电计数器　photoelectric counter
光电继电器　light[photoelectric]relay,photoswitch
光电检波管　photorectifier
光电晶体管　phototransistor
光电开关　photoswitch
光电(控制)活套调节器　photo electric loop regulator
光电流　photocurrent,photoelectric[light]current
光电疲劳　photoelectric fatigue
光电扫描器[设备]　photoelectric scanning device,photoscanner
光电摄谱仪　photoelectric spectrograph
光电射线照相术　photoradiography
光电伸长计[引伸仪]　photoelectric extensometer
光电式照度计　photoelectric illuminometer
光电探测器　photodetector
光电探伤仪　photo defectoscope,photoelectric scanner,hole detector
光电吸收　photoelectric absorption
光电显微镜　photoelectric microscope
光电显像密度计　photoelectric densitometer
光电效应　photoelectric[electrooptical,photovoltaic]effect,photoeffect ◇阻挡层～*
光电(效应)阈频率　photoelectric threshold frequency
光电学　photoelectricity
光电压　photovoltage
光电眼　photoelectric eye
光电阴极　photocathode ◇嵌镶～mosaic electrode
光电元件　photocell（pick-off）,（light）cell,photoelectric element[tube],phototube
光电元件疲劳　fatigue of photocell
光电阅读器[光电读出器]【计】photoelectric reader,photoreader
光电浊度计　opacimeter
光电子　photoelectron
光电子传感器　photoelectronic transducer
光电(子)发射　photoelectron emission,photoemission
光电子学　photoelectronics,optoelectronics
光度　luminosity
光度(测定,测量)法　photometric method,photometry
光度滴定(法)　photometric titration
光度读数　photometric reading
光度分析　photometric analysis
光度计　photometer,photometric receiver ◇球形～spherical photometer
光度计测量　photometric(al) measurement
光度曲线　photometer curve
光度系统　photometric system ◇双光束～*
光度学[术]　photometry
光度直线性(光谱的)　photometric linearity
光范性的　photoplastic
光峰　photopeak
光干涉　light（wave）interference
光干涉法　optical interference method
光杠(车床的)　feed shaft
光管(非车丝管)　plain-end tube
光焊丝　bare[uncoated]wire
光焊丝电弧焊　bare wire arc welding

光焊丝焊电弧　bare wire metallic arc
光焊条　bare [uncoated] electrode
光焊条电弧焊　bare metal arc welding
光焊条焊接　bare electrode welding
光核的　photonuclear
光核子　photonucleon
光和氯化焙烧法　Kowa process
光合(成)　photosynthesis
光合细菌　photosynthetic bacteria
光合自养生物　photosynthetic autotrophs
光滑　smoothness
光滑连续矫直　smooth continuous straightening
光滑凝固　smooth freezing
光滑试样拉伸性能　【压】smooth-tensile property
光滑退火的(指轻金属)　slick-annealed
光化电　actinoelectricity
光化还原　photochemical reduction
光化性能[性质]　photochemical property
光化学　photochemistry, actinochemistry
光化学反应　photochemical reaction
光化学感应　Draper effect
光化学空气污染物　【环】photochemical air pollutant
光化(学)效应　photochemical effect
光化学烟雾　photochemical smog
光化(学)氧化还原滴定　photochemical redox titration
光激发光　(同"光致发光")
光激可控硅整流器　light activated silicon controlled rectifier (LASCR)
光激射器　laser (light amplification by stimulated emission of radiation)
光激中子　photoneutron
光继电器　light [optical] relay
光碱度　optical basicity
光洁度　finish, fineness, degree of finish [fineness], roughness ◇ 表面～*, 冷轧钢带经加工的高～边*, 毛面[无光]～*, 研磨～*【机】grinding finish
光解的　photolytic

光警报系统　optical alarm system
光刻　photo-etching
光刻法　photoetching process, photolithography
光刻胶　photo-resist
光控场致发光　photo-electroluminescence
光控继电器　(同"光电继电器")
光阑　(light) diaphragm ◇ 布基～*, 孔径～*
光阑材料　aperture material
光阑狭缝　diphragm slit
光阑作用　iris action
光量计　quantometer
光量子　(同"光子")
光亮贝塞麦钢丝　bright Bessemer wire
光亮常化　bright normalizing
光亮淬火　bright [scale-free] hardening, bright quenching
光亮电镀　bright plating ◇ 周期反向电流～法 PR method
光亮电镀槽　bright plating bath
光亮电镀范围　bright (plating) range
光亮电镀能力　bright throwing power
光亮电镀用电解液　bright solution
光亮镀层　bright coating [deposit]
光亮镀铬　bright chromium plating
光亮镀镍　bright nickel plating ◇ 埃弗科－尤迪莱特～法 Efco-Udylite process, 瓦特～溶液 watt solution
光亮度　radiance, radiancy, luminance
光亮钢板　bright luster sheet
光亮钢棒　bright (steel) bar
光亮钢丝　bright wire ◇ 石灰处理～lime bright wire
光亮黄铜(5－10Zn, 余量 Cu)　gilding brass
光亮回火　bright tempering
光亮加工的　bright machined
光亮结晶断口　(同"亮晶断口")
光亮浸镀[浸渍(处理), 浸洗]　bright dipping
光亮浸镀槽　bright dip bath

光亮浸液　bright dip ◇ 非电解的~*
光亮晶面　facet
光亮精整钢　bright finished steel
光亮拉拔[拉丝]　bright drawing
光亮冷拔棒材　bright (drawn) bar
光亮冷轧电焊管　bright electrically welded tube
光亮磨光[加工](圆钢的)　turned finish ◇ 精密~*
光亮磨光钢丝　bright ground wire
光亮磨光圆钢　turned bar
光亮抛光　bright turned,【金】brilliant polish
光亮清洗　fine cleaning
光亮热处理　bright heat treatment
光亮湿拔的　【压】bright wet drawn
光亮湿拉拔[伸]　wet bright drawing
光亮酸浸　brightening dip
光亮酸洗　bright [white] pickling
光亮酸洗抛光[精整]　bright dipped finish
光亮涂层　bright coating, finishing coat
光亮退火　bright [clean, light, white] annealing
光亮退火的冷轧薄钢板　silver finish sheet
光亮退火钢丝　bright annealed wire
光亮退火炉　bright [clean] anneal(ing) furnace
光亮退火作业线　bright annealing line
光亮研磨的　bright ground
光亮阳极氧化处理　bright anodizing
光亮正火　bright normalizing
光灵敏度　luminous sensitivity
光卤石{KMgCl$_3$·6H$_2$O}　carnallite ◇ 脱水~dehydrated carnallite
光率体(结晶的)　【理】indicatrix
光密度　optical density
光密度比较仪　densitometer comparator
光面车削(热轧材的)　bright turned [turning]
光面电焊管　(同"光亮冷轧电焊管")
光面钢筋　plain bar [reinforcement],【建】unnotched bar
光面钢丝绳　bright wire rope
光面辊破碎机　smooth roll crusher
光面冷硬铸铁轧辊　plain chilled iron roll
光面磨损　smooth wear
光面尾管　plain-end liner
光面线　bright wire
光面轧辊　smooth [plain] roll
光面铸铁轧辊　plain cast iron roll
光敏材料　photosensitizer, photochromic
光敏的　photosensitive, photoactive
光敏电池　photoconductive [light-sensitive] cell
光敏电阻(器)　photoresistor, photoresistance cell, photoconductor, light resistor
光敏度　light [lumen] sensitivity ◇ X射线胶片~*
光敏反应　photosensitized reaction
光敏剂　photosensitizer
光敏乳胶　sensitive emulsion
光敏探测器　light-sensitive detector
光敏性　photosensitivity, light sensitivity
光敏元件高温计　light-sensitive cell pyrometer
光能测定器　actinoscope
光能源　luminous energy source
光盘只读存储　compact disk read only memory
光谱　spectrum (复数 spectra), light spectrum ◇ 比色~*, 不可见~*, 成品~电极*, 精细结构~fine spectrum
光谱背景　spectral background
光谱比较器　spectral comparator
光谱波长　spectral position
光谱不均匀性　spectral inhomogeneity
光谱测定　spectral measurements, spectrographic determination
光谱测量法　spectrometry
光谱纯　spectroscopic pure
光谱纯度　spectrographic [spectroscopical, spectral] purity
光谱纯石英　spectrosil

光谱纯铁（>99.999%Fe） puron
光谱带 spectral band
光谱带头 【半】band head
光谱倒数线色散率 reciprocal linear dispersion
光谱等[同]位变换吸收波长（点） isosbestic point
光谱等[同]位吸收波长（点） isoabsorptive point
光谱短波端 short-wave (length) end of spectrum
光谱发射率 spectral emissivity
光谱反射比 spectral reflectance
光谱反射系数 spectral reflection factor
光谱分辨率 spectral resolution
光谱分布定律 spectral distribution law
光谱分析 spectrum [spectral, spectrographic, spectrometric, dry] analysis, analysis of spectra
光谱（分析）法 spectrographic method
光谱分析线 analysis line
光谱辐(射)出度 spectral radiant exitance
光谱辐射度学[辐射测量（法）] spectroradiometry
光谱辐射计 spectroradiometer
光谱辐射亮度 spectral radiance
光谱辐射能量 spectral radiant energy
光谱辐(射)照度 spectral irradiance
光谱高温计 spectral pyrometer, spectropyrometer
光谱光度直线性 photometric linearity
光谱鬼线 spectral ghost
光谱化学 spectrochemistry
光谱化学分析 spectroanalysis, spectrochemical analysis
光谱化学分析法 spectrochemical method
光谱化学缓冲剂 spectrochemical buffer
光谱化学载体 spectrochemical carrier
光谱级 spectral order, order of spectrum
光谱计 (optical) spectrometer ◇ 高透射~*，计数器~ counter spec-trometer，棱镜~ prism spectrometer，弯晶~*，正比计数器~*
光谱棱镜 spectroscopic prism
光谱灵敏度 spectral sensitivity [response]
光谱能级 spectroscopic energy level
光谱偏光计 spectropolarimeter
光谱强度 spectral intensity
光谱（强度）分布 spectral distribution
光谱锐线系 【理】sharp series
光谱色度学 spectrocolorimetry
光谱闪光灯 spectral flash lamp
光谱投射器 spectro projector
光谱图 spectrogram, spectrum chart ◇ 线状~【理】line pattern
光谱温度 spectroscopic temperature
光谱吸收比 spectral absorptance
光谱线 spectral [spectrum] line
光谱线对 line pair
光谱线分裂 splitting of spectral lines
光谱线漫射系 diffuse series
光谱线系 series of spectral lines ◇ 基本~*
光谱响应 spectral response
光谱序 order of spectrum, spectral sequence
光谱学 (optical, light) spectroscopy ◇ X射线~*，β射线~*，γ射线~*，穆斯堡尔~*
光谱仪 spectrograph, spectrometer, spectroscopic instrumentation ◇ 钢用~ steeloscope, stylyoscope, 阶梯~ echelle spectrometer, 直读~*
光谱照相术 spectrum photography
光谱中出现束 【化】banding
光谱自蚀 self-reversal
光气{O:C:Cl₂} phosgene
光强（度） light intensity, intensity of light
光切 【机】clean cut
光散射法 light scattering method
光散射光度计 light-scattering photometer
光栅 【理】raster, (optical) grating, light barrier, grate ◇ 晶体空间~ crystal space

grating,两维[交叉]～ cross grating	
光栅常数 grating constant	
光栅单色器 grating monochromator	
光栅多色器 grating polychromator	
光栅光谱[分光]学 grating spectroscopy	
光栅间距[绕射光栅间距] grating space, slit separation	
光栅摄谱仪 grating spectrograph	
光扫描法 photo-scanning method	
光渗 irradiation	
光生电压 photovoltage	
光生伏打电池 photovoltaic cell	
光生伏打太阳电池 photovoltaic solar cells	
光生伏打效应 photovoltaic effect	
光生载流子 photon-generated carrier	
光蚀 photo-etching	
光蚀法 photolithography	
光势垒 light barrier	
光束 light beam, luminous flux ◇ 聚集～ pencil	
光束发散度 luminous exitance	
光束截面 beam cross-section	
光塑性的 photoplastic	
光弹性 photoelasticity ◇ 散射光～*	
光弹性材料 photoelastic material	
光弹性分析 photoelastic analysis	
光弹性条纹法 fringe method in photoelasticity	
光弹性条纹花样 photoelastic fringe pattern	
光弹性涂层法(测应力) photoelastic-coating method	
光调谐指示管 magic eye	
光调(制)器 【电】light modulator	
光通量 light [luminous] flux	
光通量密度 density of luminous flux, pharosage	
光瞳间距离 interpupillary distance	
光稳定性 light stability, photostability	
光吸收 light absorption, photoabsorption	
光纤测温仪[温度计] optical fiber measuring temperature instrument ◇ 高精度比色红外～*	
光显示终端 optical display terminal	
光线矿 abichite	
光学比较仪 optimeter, optical comparator	
光学表面光洁度测量仪 surfascope	
光学玻璃 optical glass	
光学玻璃纤维 optical (glass) fibre	
光学测角仪 optical goniometer	
光学测量 optic(al) measurement	
光学测微计 optiminimeter, optical micrometer	
光学长度 optical length	
光学垂准器 optical plummet	
光学单色器 optical monochromator	
光学电子学 optoelectronics	
光学发射摄谱仪 optical emission spectrograph	
光学放大(率) optical magnification [multiplication]	
光学分辨率[能力] optical resolution	
光学分光计 optical spectrometer	
光学干涉 optical interference	
光学干涉仪 optical interferometer	
光学高温计 optical pyrometer, leucoscope, adrometer ◇ 电位计式～*,恒定亮度～*,目测～*,隐丝式～*	
光学高温学[测定法] optical pyrometry	
光学各向异性[非均质性] optical anisotropy	
光学光谱线系 【理】optical series	
光学活化剂[物质] optically active substance	
光学技术 optical technique	
光学记录 optical record [registration]	
光学碱度 optical basicity	
光学焦点 optical focus	
光学介质 【理】optical medium	
光学镜面(真空)涂膜(法) optics filming	
光学孔径 optical aperture	
光学模式 【理】optical mode	
光学全息术 optical holography	

光学摄谱仪 optical spectrograph
光学示差膨胀计 optical differential dilatometer
光学图像 optical image
光学位移传感器 optical displacement sensor
光学文字读出[识别]器 optical character reader (O.C.R.)
光学纤维[光纤] optical fibre
光学纤维[光纤]通讯 optical fibre communication
光学显示报警器[信号] visual alarm
光学显微镜 optical [light, photon] microscope
光学显微镜法 optical microscopy method, light microscopical method
光学显微镜观察 optical [light] microscope observation
光学显微镜像 optic [light] microscopical image
光学显微术 optical [light] microscopy
光学衍射光栅 optical diffraction grating
光学仪器 optical instrument
光学应变仪 optical strain gauge
光学振动模式[方式] optical mode of vibration
光焰辐射 luminous flame radiation
光氧化物 photo-oxide
光阴极 (同"光电阴极")
光应力 photostress
光应力测定法 (同"极化光应力测定法")
光源 light [illuminating, luminous] source, illuminant ◇ 背面照明～系统*
光晕 halation, halo
光泽 luster, lustre, glaze, gloss, burnish ◇ 表面失去 ～ surface staining, 除去 ～ delustring, 失去 ～ 的[发暗]金属*, 使发～ planish, 无～表面 tarnish
光泽镀镍法 ◇ 尼克雷克斯～ Nickelex (method)
光泽计 glossmeter

光泽色微粒[质点] light-colored particles
光泽搪瓷 gloss enamel
光泽稳定性 gloss retention
光泽增强剂 brightening addition
光轧薄板硬度 planished temper
光轧道次 planishing pass
光轧孔型 【压】planisher
光照 illumination
光照(强)度 intensity of illumination, illuminance
光整冷轧 skin (pass) rolling, skin pass, pinch pass rolling ◇ 轻 ～ un-der-skin pass
光整冷轧薄板 skin-passed sheet
光整冷轧的软回火薄钢板 skin-rolled temper sheet
光整冷轧钢板 skin-passed temper
光致电离 photo ionization
光致发光 photoluminescence ◇ 电控～*
光致反应 photoreaction
光致抗蚀剂 photo-resist
光致蜕变阈 photodisintegration threshold
光致氧化 photo-oxidation
光制 finishing, fine cleaning
光制辊颈轧辊 【压】necked roll
光制轧辊 finished roll
光质子 photoproton
光轴 optic(al) axis, bare shaft
光柱 streamer
光子 (quantum) photon, light quantum ◇ 多～效应 multiphoton effect
光子辐射体 photon emitter
光子计数器 quantorecorder, photo counter
光子铅板 Lymar
光子－强子相互作用 photon-hardon interactions
广角目镜 wide-field eyepiece
广角内孔窥视仪 wide-field borescope
广角物镜 【理】wide-angle objective
广视场金相显微镜 large-field metallographic microscope

广义函数　distribution, generalized function
广义流态化　generalized fluidization
广义模型　generalized model
广义膨胀系数　【理】generalized expansion coefficient
广濑行星轧机　【压】Hirose's rolling mill
规　ga(u)ge
规尺黄铜(62.5Cu, 35Zn, 2.5Pb)　rule brass
规尺青铜(62.5Cu, 35Zn, 2.5Pb)　rule bronze
规定尺寸　designated size, fixed [set] dimension ◇ 超过~的 overgauge
规定范围　preset range, prescribed limit, restriction
规定风量　ordered wind
规定负载[装载量]　specified load
规定粒度　【选】designated size
规定浓度　normal concentration, normality
规定溶液　normal [standard] solution
规定时间　set [schedule] time
规定数值　predetermined value
规定条件　rated condition
规定温度　set [rated] temperature
规定压力　authorised pressure
规定值(技术条件)　theoretic value
规定(重)量　ordered weight
规度　normality, normal concentration
规度溶液　normal solution
规范　standard, specification, criterion, regime
规范化　standardization, standardize
规格　specifications (spec.), standards (stds)
规格化　normalization, normalizing, standardizing
规格化数　【计】normalized number
规格石料　dimension stone
规号　◇ 惠氏~*
规划　planning, project, programming
规划设备　mapping device
规律　law, regular pattern
规模　scale ◇ 原~的 full scale
规模适化　rightsizing
规线　gauge line
规则　rule, regulation, ordination, code
规则结构　regular structure
规则晶格位置　regular lattice site
规则内部结构(晶体的)　【金】regular internal structure
规则排列　regular arrangement [array], ordered array
规则锌花(镀锌板表面的)　regular spangle
规则形状　regular shape
规准杆　gauge bar [rod], gauging rod
硅{Si}　silicon, silicium ◇ 掺杂~ doped silicon, 含~的 siliceous, silaceous, codorous(指矿石), 晶体管级~*, 准~(即锗) eka-silicon
硅(p-n)结　(同"硅结")
硅半导体　silicon semiconductor
硅钡铍矿　barylite
硅钡石　sanbornite
硅掺杂　Silicon doping
硅传感器　silicon pickup
硅电流调节器　silicon current regulator
硅堆　silicon stack [dropper]
硅对称开关　silicon symmetrical switch (SSS)
硅二极管整流器　silicon diode rectifier
硅肺病　(同"矽肺病")
硅粉　silicon powder
硅氟酸盐　(同"氟硅酸盐")
硅钙合金　calcium silicon, silicon calcium alloy, silicocalcium
硅钙镁合金　silico-calcium-magnesium alloy
硅钙铅锌矿　esperite
硅钙铅铀钍铈矿　nenadkevite
硅钙钛中间合金　◇ 西尔卡兹~*
硅钙铁铀钍矿　ekanite
硅钙铀矿{$CaU_2Si_2O_{11} \cdot 7H_2O$}　urano-

phane, uranotile, lambertite ◇ β~*

硅钢　silicon [silicium] steel, silicon iron, electric(al) steel (0.5—5Si) ◇ 各向异性~*，石墨化~*

硅钢薄板　silicon sheet, silicon (ized) plate, electric core sheet (铁心用) ◇ 电机用～dynamo sheet, 叠片～laminated sheet iron, 高磁感 Hi-B～orient high B, 晶粒取向~*，罗海斯～（含 2Si) Lohys, 热轧~*，双取向~*，无取向~*

硅钢带　silicon strip

硅钢片　silicon(steel) sheet

硅锆钙钾石 $\{K_2CaZrSi_4O_{12}\}$　wadeite

硅锆钠石　vlasovite

硅锆铁矿 $\{ZrO_2, Fe_2O_3\} \cdot SiO_2 \cdot nH_2O\}$　zirfesite

硅铬（合金）　silicochromium, silicon chromium

硅铬铝耐酸钢　◇ 西克罗马尔~*

硅铬钼系耐蚀耐热合金钢　◇ 西克罗莫~*

硅铬耐蚀钢 (8.25Cr, 3.5Si, 0.45C, 余量 Fe)　silichrome

硅铬铁　ferrochrome silicon ◇ 止碳~*

硅光电管[光电池，光电元件]　silicon photocell

硅光电探测器　silicon photodetector

硅铪锆矿　alvite

硅含量[含硅量]　silicon content ◇ 铁水～预报系统*

硅合金　silicon alloy

硅华　fiorite, geyserite, siliceous sinter

硅化　【钢】siliconising, siliconizing, silication, silicatization, silicifica-tion

硅化钡 $\{Ba_2Si\}$　barium silicide

硅化处理层　siliconized layer

硅化法　siliconising process

硅化覆[涂]层　siliconized coating

硅化钙(钢的脱氧剂; 28—35Ca, 60—65Si, 6Fe)　calcium silicide

硅化铬 $\{Cr_4Si_3\}$　chromium silicide

硅化矿石　siliceous ore

硅化钼　molybdenum silicide

硅化钛　titanium silicide

硅化钽　tantalum silicide

硅化铁　iron silicide

硅化物　silicide

硅化物半导体　silicide semiconductor

硅化物耐火材料　silicide refractory

硅化铀　uranium silicide

硅化作用　silication, silicatization, silicification

硅还原法　【冶】silicothermic process

硅黄铜（1—5Si, 70—95Cu, 4—32Zn, 少量 Mn, Al 或 Fe）　silicon brass ◇ 顿巴希尔耐磨~*

硅灰石 $\{Ca_3Si_3O_9\}$　wollastonite, grammite

硅灰石膏　thaumasite

硅基催化剂　silica-base catalyst

硅钾铀矿 $\{K_2(UO_2)_2(SiO_5)_3 \cdot 4H_2O\}$　weeksite

硅碱钙钇石　ashcroftine

硅碱钇石　monteregianite

硅胶　silica gel ◇ 活化～activated silica gel

硅胶吸附塔　silica gel column

硅结(p-n 结)　【半】silicon junction

硅结合的碳化硅耐火材料　silicon-bonded silicon carbide refractory

硅结砾岩　silcrete

硅晶核孕育剂　silicon inoculant

硅晶体　silicon crystal

硅镜铁　silico-spiegel, silico-spiegeleisen

硅可控整流器　（同"可控硅整流器"）

硅孔雀石 $\{CuO \cdot SiO_2 \cdot 2H_2O\}$　chrysocolla

硅控整流元件　【电】silicon controlled rectifier (SCR)

硅控制　silicon control (SC)

硅砾过滤器　silica gravel filter

硅利用率　silicon efficiency

硅磷酸盐　silicophosphate

硅铝　sial (sphere)

硅铝钡铁合金　silicon-aluminum-barium ferroalloy

硅铝磁钢（1—1.2C，2.5—3.5Cr，1—2.5Al，0.8—1.3Si，余量 Fe） SA (silicon-aluminum) magnet steel

硅铝共晶合金(8—13Si,余量 Al) silumin (alloy)

硅铝合金 silicon-aluminum alloy ◇ M.V.C. 耐蚀铸造～*，阿拉德～(12Si) alader，西卡尔～*，西拉方特～*

硅铝矿物 silica-alumina

硅铝明合金(87Al,13si) alpax ◇ γ～*，变质～*，含锌的～*，库普弗尔～*

硅铝耐火砖 silica-alumina refractory brick，alumina-silica firebrick

硅铝热剂法 silica-thermite method

硅铝酸二钙 gehlenite

硅铝酸钙渣 lime silico-aluminate slag

硅铝酸铁锰 {FeO·MnO·SiO$_2$·Al$_2$O$_3$} ceroxide

硅铝酸盐 silico aluminate

硅铝陶瓷纤维 fibrefrax

硅铝特种合金 ◇ 伯马西尔～*

硅铝铁（中间合金；45—50Al，35—40Si，2—3Ti）ferrosilico-aluminium ◇ 杜ális帕姆～合金*，森达斯特～合金薄板*

硅铝铁率 silica-sesquioxide ratio

硅铝脱氧剂 silico-aluminium deoxidizer

硅铝脱氧转炉钢 ALTO steel

硅－铝型杂质 silica-alumina-type impurity

硅铝砖 alumina-silica firebrick ◇ 高纯度～*

硅镁钙铀矿 （同"水钙镁铀石"）

硅镁铝合金 magnesia-alumina-silica

硅镁铝青铜 ◇ HE－HE alloy

硅镁镍矿 garnierite ore

硅镁石 {Mg$_7$(SiO$_4$)$_3$(OH,F)$_2$} humite ◇ 块状～*，粒状～*

硅镁铀矿 sklowdowskite

硅锰钙合金 calcium-manganesesilicon alloy

硅锰合金 70Mn,20Si,0.5—1C) silico-manganese，silicon-manganese

硅锰合金钢(弹簧钢；1.8—2.5Si，0.7—0.9Mn，0.5—0.7C) silico-manganese alloy

硅锰矿 siliceous manganese ore

硅锰铝铁合金 ◇ 西马纳尔～*

硅锰铁合金（15—20Mn，10Si，4C，余量 Fe) silico-spiegeleisen，ferrosilico-manganese，fero-manganesesilicon

硅钼酸 silicomolybdic acid

硅钼酸盐 silicomolybdate

硅钼(特殊)钢 ◇ 西尔莫～*

硅钠钡钛石 joaquinite

硅钠锶镧石 nordite

硅钠钛矿 {Na$_2$(Ti,Zr)$_4$O$_9$·Na$_2$Si$_4$O$_9$} lorenzenite

硅铌钠矿 {RNb$_2$O$_6$(OH)$_2$CeSiO$_3$}(R=Na$_2$,Ca) endeiolite

硅镍矿 konnarite

硅镍青铜 ◇ 西尔尼克～*

硅硼钛铝锰合金 ◇ 博塔～Bortam

硅硼钽钍稀土矿 karyocerite

硅铍钠石 {Na$_2$Be(SiO$_3$)$_2$} chkalovite

硅铍石 phenacite {Be$_2$SiO$_4$}，bertrandite {H$_2$Be$_4$Si$_2$O$_9$}

硅铍稀土石 semenovite

硅铍钇矿 {Be$_2$FeY$_2$Si$_2$O1$_6$} ytterbite，yttrite，gadolinite

硅片 【半】silicon slice [wafer]，chip of silicon

硅平面结 silicon planar junction

硅铅铀矿 {PbO·UO$_3$·SiO$_2$·H$_2$O} kasolite，woelsendorfite

硅青铜(1—5Si，少量 Mn，Fe，Zn，余量 Cu) silicon bronze ◇ P.M.G.～*，埃弗托尔形变～*，埃瓦杜尔耐蚀～*，蒂特迈杰～*，杜龙兹～*，库西洛伊—合金系*，铸造埃发杜尔～*

硅青铜管 silicon bronze pipe

硅热法炼镁厂 silicothermic magnesium plant

硅热反应 silicothermic reaction

硅热还原　silicothermic reduction ◇ 拉维利～炼镁法,使金蒸罐炉～炼镁法,乌氏～U_3O_8法

硅热(还原)法　【冶】silicon reduction process, silicothermic [ferrosilicon, siliconthermit] process ◇ 电～(生产铁合金)*,马里纳熔渣导电半连续～炼镁*

硅三铁矿　suessite

硅砂　siliceous silt, silica sand, ganisand

硅砂石　dinas silica

硅石{SiO_2}　silica, dinas ◇ 胶态～colloidal silica, 熔凝～fused silica

硅石耐火砖　dinas firebrick

硅石熔剂　silica flux

硅石砖　dinas [ganister] brick

硅铈铒矿　buszite

硅铈铌钡矿　ilimaussite

硅酸{$SiO_2 \cdot nH_2O$}　silicic acid ◇ 表面～surface silicic acid, 凝胶状～gelatinous silicic acid

硅酸钡　barium silicate

硅酸[石]比　silica ratio

硅酸铋　bismuth silicate

硅酸度　silicate degree

硅酸二钙{$2CaO \cdot SiO_2$}　bicalcium [dicalcium] silicate

硅酸方解石{$Ca_3[SiO_4]_2[CO_3]$}　spurrite

硅酸氟铁钇矿{$(Y, Ce, La)_4Fe(Si_2O_7)_2 \cdot F_2$}　rowlandite

硅酸钙　calcium silicate {$CaSiO_3$}, calcic silicate {$Ca_3(SiO_4)_2$}

硅酸钙钠{$Na_2O \cdot CaO \cdot SiO_2$}　sodium calcium silicate

硅酸钙盐　calsil

硅酸锆{$ZrSiO_4$}　zirconium silicate

硅酸铪{$HfSiO_4$}　hafnium silicate

硅酸钾　potassium (meta) silicate, potash water glass

硅酸铝{$Al_2O_3 \cdot 2SiO_2$}　aluminium silicate, aluminosilicate

硅酸铝钠　sodium aluminosilicate

硅酸铝耐火材料　alumina-silica [alumino-silicate] refractory

硅酸铝砖　alumino-silicate brick

硅酸率　【耐】silica modulus

硅酸镁{$MgO \cdot SiO_2$}　magnesium silicate

硅酸镁盐　britesorb

硅酸锰{$2MnO \cdot SiO_2$}　manganese [manganous] silicate

硅酸锰锑铁矿{$Sb_2O_3 \cdot Fe_2O_3 \cdot SiO_2$}　langbanite

硅酸钠{Na_2SiO_3}　sodium silicate, liquid [soluble, water] glass

硅酸钠保温槽　【钢】tiger top

硅酸钠盐　metso

硅酸镍　nickel silicate

硅酸凝聚剂　coagulation of silicic acid

硅酸硼玻璃　borosilicate glass

硅酸铍{$BeSiO_3$}　beryllium silicate

硅酸铅{$PbSiO_3$}　lead (meta) silicate

硅酸铷　rubidium silicate

硅酸三钙{$3CaO \cdot SiO_2$}　tricalcium silicate

硅酸锶{$2SrO \cdot SiO_2$}　strontium silicate

硅酸铁{$FeO \cdot SiO_2$}　iron silicate

硅酸铁(炉)渣　ferruginous [iron] silicate slag

硅酸铜{$Cu_2O \cdot SiO_2$}　copper silicate

硅酸钍矿{$ThSiO_4$}　thorite

硅酸钍钇矿{$(Y, Th)_2O_3 \cdot 2SiO_2$}　yttrialite

硅酸锌{$ZnO \cdot SiO_2$}　zinc silicate

硅酸盐　silicate ◇ 非～炉渣 non-silicate slag, 含水络含镍镁～*, 纤维状～fibrous silicate

硅酸盐玻璃质　silicate glass

硅酸盐夹杂物　silicate inclusions ◇ 复杂～*

硅酸盐键[结合]　silicate bond

硅酸盐结合砖　silicate bonded brick

硅酸盐矿物　silicate mineral

硅酸(盐)炉渣　silicate [siliceous] slag

硅酸盐黏合的烧结镁石　silica-bonded mangesite clinker

硅酸盐水泥　portland cement ◇ 改良

~*,高炉矿渣~*,火山灰~*,矿渣~*

硅酸盐型夹杂物 silicate type inclusions
硅酸盐型蛇纹石矿 silicate type serpentine ore
硅酸盐阳离子交换树脂 Zeo-Dur
硅酸盐铀矿石 silicate uranium ore
硅酸乙酯 ethyl silicate
硅酸渣 siliceous slag ◇ 四分之一~*
硅钛钒锆铁合金 ◇ 西尔瓦克斯~*
硅钛钙铁合金 ◇ 格拉菲道克斯~*
硅钛铌铈矿 tundrite
硅钛钕矿 tundrite-(Nd)
硅钛铈钠石 laplandite
硅钛铈钇矿 techeffkinite
硅酞酸盐 silicotitanate
硅碳棒 silicon carbide rod
硅碳耐火材料 siloxicon
硅碳铁锰矿 spencerite
硅—碳组分图 ◇ 莫勒~*
硅铁(中间合金; 25—95Si,低P,低S) ferrosilicon, silicon iron, silicoferrite, ferrosilicium, siliconeisen (5—15Si) ◇ 电热法[电炉]~*,发热~silex,晶粒取向~oriented silicon iron,粒状~granular ferrosilicon,转炉~Bessemer ferrosilicon
硅铁合金 ferrosilicon [iron-silica] alloy ◇ 高导磁~[铁硅合金]*
硅铁还原法 ferrosilicon reduction process
硅铁炼镁法 ferrosilicon process
硅铁铝合金 ◇ 阿尔西弗尔~*,阿尔西明~*
硅铁锰锆合金 ◇ SMZ~*
硅铁生产工艺 【铁】ferrosilicon practice
硅铁蒸罐炉(炼镁用) ferrosilicon rotort furnace
硅酮{RR'SiO} silicone ◇ 浸渗~silicone impregnation
硅酮漆 silicone lacquer
硅酮树脂 silicone resin
硅酮油 silicone oil [fluid]
硅同位素 silicon isotope

硅铜 copper silicon
硅铜合金(中间合金；10—50Si；其他：1—5Si) silicon-copper
硅铜线 silicon bronze wire
硅铜铀矿{Cu(UO$_2$)$_2$Si$_2$O$_7$} cuprosklovskite,jachymovite
硅脱氧钢 silicon-killed steel
硅烷{Si$_n$H$_{2n+2}$} silane,silicane
硅吸收 silicon pickup
硅线石{Al$_2$O$_3$·SiO$_2$} sillimanite,fibrolite,【耐】ganister
硅线石板 sillimanite plate
硅线石坩埚 sillimanite crucible
硅线石耐火材料 sillimanite refractory
硅橡胶 silastic,silicone rubber ◇ 玻璃纤维被覆~绝缘线*
硅橡胶复合物 silicone-rubber compound
硅效率 silicon efficiency
硅锌(含二氧化硅) galmey
硅锌矿{Zn$_2$SiO$_4$} willemite
硅锈(硅钢薄板的) silicon fur
硅氧化 silicon oxidation
硅氧化期(转炉炼钢的) 【钢】silicon blow
硅氧平衡 silicon-oxygen equilibrium
硅氧烷 siloxane
硅氧烯 siloxen
硅氧系数 【耐】silica modulus
硅镱石 keivyite
硅铀矿{U$_5$Si$_2$O$_{19}$·6H$_2$O} soddyite
硅铀钍铝矿 pilbarite
硅孕育剂 silicon inoculant
硅杂质 siliceous impurityg
硅藻(软)泥 diatom ooze
硅藻石 randanite
硅藻土{SiO$_2$·nH$_2$O} diatom(aceous) earth, diatomite, tripoli(te), mount(ain) meal, mount flour, guhr, fossil (flour), infusorial [siliceous, barbadoes] earth, randanite, kieselgunr, bergmeal, ceyssatite, moler,
硅藻土粉(抛光粉) tripoli powder
硅藻土砖 diatomaceous [diatomite] brick

硅渣	silica slag [residue], white residue [slime]（氧化铝生产的）
硅整流焊机	silicon rectifier welder
硅整流器	silicon rectifier
硅质材料	siliceous material
硅质矿物	silicoide
硅质脉石	siliceous gangue
硅质脉石的铁矿石	siliceous ore
硅质耐火材料	silica [siliceous] refractory ◇ 黏土结合～*，石灰结合～*
硅质耐火黏土	silica [siliceous] fireclay
硅质熔剂	siliceous flux ◇ 含金属的～*
硅质砂	siliceous sand
硅质烧结矿	siliceous sinter
硅质石灰石	siliceous limestone
硅质石灰岩	cherty limestone
硅质水泥	silica cement
硅质添加剂	siliceous additive
硅质涂料	ganister
硅质外壳[皮]	【铸】siliceous skin
硅质岩石	siliceous rock
硅质页岩	siliceous shale
硅质异极矿	siliceous calamine
硅质砖	siliceous brick
硅砖	silica (fire) brick, quartzite [ganister] brick, dinas (brick) ◇ 超级～super-duty silica brick, 雷西斯塔尔耐蚀～Resistal
硅砖衬炉	silica oven
硅砖格子蓄热室	silica-brick checkers regenerator
硅砖拱	silica crown
硅砖拱式炉顶（反射炉的）	silica sprung arch
硅砖炉衬	silica lining
硅砖碱性混砌炉顶	【钢】zebra roof
硅砖炉衬转炉	silica brick-lined furnace, silica-lined vessel
硅砖炉顶	silica (brick) roof
硅砖炉墙	silica brick wall
硅砖炉头	silica end
硅砖膨胀	silica brick growth
硅砖软熔	silica drip
归零	zero, return to zero,【计】clear ◇ 不～制记录*
归零制记录	【计】return-to-zero recording
归纳	conclude, extrapolation,【数】induction
归一化常数[因数]	normalization constant
归约公式	reduction formula
龟裂	alligator, (alligator-hide) crack, crazing, fissure, worming
龟裂表面	checked surface
龟裂耐火材料	shuffs
龟裂趋势（淬火时的）	【金】susceptibility to cracking
龟裂土	adobe soil
轨道	(railroad) track, pathway, rail, runway, orbit, trajectory ◇ 编组～【运】classified track, 存坏车～【运】bad order track, 非闭合～【理】open orbit, 小～【运】baby track, 沿～运行 orbit, 转线～【运】cross over
轨道半径	orbital radius
轨道超高度	【运】cant of track
轨道车	track car, motor-trolley ◇ 内燃机[自动]～trackmobile
轨道撑	bunton
轨道电子	orbital [planetary] electron
轨道电子俘获	E-capture
轨道函数	【理】orbital function
轨道衡	(railroad) track scales, wagon weigher, weight bridge
轨道继电器	track relay
轨道角动量量子数	【理】orbital angular-momentum quantum number
轨道量子数	orbital quantum number
轨道起重机	track [goliath] crane
轨道式格筛	rail grizzly
轨道式矿槽	rail-mounted hopper
轨道试验车	dynagraph car
轨道手推车	rail carriage
轨道挺直器	jim crow

轨道运动　orbital motion
轨道自旋　orbital spin
轨道自旋晶体生长［自旋式拉晶法］　orbital-spin crystal pulling
轨底　rail base [chair, flange, foot]
轨底翼缘(钢轨的)　base flange
轨端淬火机　rail-end-hardening machine
轨端钻孔机床　rail-drilling machine
轨腹板(工字钢的)　rail web
轨函数　orbital
轨迹　locus, trajectory, travel, path
轨距　ga(u)ge (of railway), track gauge, railroad ga(u)ge (铁路的)
轨距尺(铁路用)　gauge rule [bar]
轨距规　track [platelayer's] gauge
轨距连杆　cross-tie
轨扣件　rail fastening
轨梁　【压】beam-and-rail, track beam
轨梁翻转机构(冷床的)　setting-up device
轨梁精轧机　rail finishing mill
轨梁弯曲机　beam-and-rail bender
轨梁轧机　(rail-and-)structural steel mill, rail-beam (and section) mill, girder and rail mill ◇ 万能式～*
轨梁轧机机座　structural stand
轨式冷床　rail-type hot bed
轨条　skid bars
轨条螺栓　track bolt
轨条铺层　rail skid
轨条铺栅　skid bed
轨条筛　bar screen
轨头　rail head
轨头淬火　end hardening
轨下料仓　track hopper
轨线　path, trajectory
轨形件底部宽展　rail stock spread in base
轨形件头部宽展　rail stock spread in head
轨形孔型　rail pass
轨行式堆料机　rail-mounted stacker
轨旋管　orbitron
轨腰　rail web
轨应力迹　stress trajectory

轨枕　(cross-)sleeper ◇ 钢轨接头～joint lie, 金属～sleeper plate, 斜角～*
轨枕槽规　adzing gauge
轨枕钢　sleeper bar
轨座　(fish) chair, rail chair [rest, support], foundation plate, shoe
"鬼"掺入体　ghost inclusion
鬼线(钢的组织缺陷)　phosphorus banding, ghost (bands, lines) ◇ 光谱～spectral ghost
鬼线裂纹　【金】ghost crack
癸胺　{$CH_3(CH_2)_8CH_2NH_2$}　decylamine
癸醇　{$CH_3(CH_2)_8CH_2OH$}　n-decyl alcohol
癸二酸　{$(CH_2)_8(COOCH)_2$}　sebacic acid
癸二酸丁酯　(油蒸气真空泵用油) {$C_8H_{16}(COOC_4H_9)_2$}　butyl sebacate
癸二酸戊酯(油蒸气真空泵用油) {$C_8H_{16}(COOC_5H_{11})_2$}　amyl sebacate
癸二酸盐[酯]　{$C_8H_{16}(COOM)_2$}　sebacate
癸基　{$CH_3(CH_2)_8CH_2$}　decyl
癸酸　{$CH_3(CH_2)_8COOH$}　capric[decylic]acid
贵电势　noble potential
贵橄榄石{$(MgFe)_2SiO_4$}　chrysolite
贵金属　precious [noble] metal ◇ 次～less noble metal, 烧结～sintered precious metal
贵金属捕集剂　precious metal collector
贵金属粉　precious metal powder
贵金属汞齐　precious metal amalgam
贵金属合金　precious [noble-metal] alloy ◇ 沙德克铜基～*
贵金属回收　precious metal recovery
贵金属精炼厂　precious metal refinery
贵金属热电偶　noble-metal thermocouple
贵金属提取　precious metal extraction
贵榴石{$Fe_3Al_2(SiO_4)_3$}　almandine, almandite

贵铅　precious metal containing lead
贵重元素　noble element
辊　roll(er) ◇ 炉内~furnace roll,通电~ power application roll
辊拔力　roller die drawing force
辊边　roll shoulder
辊承弯曲试验　roller bond
辊道　roll(er) table [bed, conveyor, gear, way], roll-way, table roller, table (tab.) ◇ 成组传动~*,分路[绕行,返回]~ bypass table,固定式翻卷~*,弧形~ arc-shaped roller bank,空转[自出]辊~ dead roller table,连接~*,起落式~collapsible table,驼峰~*,延伸~additional roller table,支线~branch roller table,中间~*,贮料~magazine table
辊道秤　roller bed balance
辊道传动侧框架　【压】bed plate
辊道传动装置　roller-table gear
辊道的带槽辊　【压】grooved table roller
辊道电动机　roller table motor
辊道端部挡板　table end stopper
辊道辊子　【压】table rolls
辊道横梁　table beam
辊道护板　table apron
辊道划线台　lay-out table
辊道架　【压】table frame ◇ 传动侧~ drive-end table frame,非传动侧~light-end table frame
辊道炉床[膛]　roller-hearth
辊道炉膛加热炉　roller-hearth furnace
辊道炉膛烧结炉　roller-hearth sintering furnace
辊道炉膛推料炉　roller-hearth push furnace
辊道炉膛退火炉　roller-hearth annealing furnace
辊道炉膛运输带　roller-hearth conveyor
辊道式称量器　table-type scale
辊道输送机　(live-)roller conveyer
辊道台架　roller rack
辊道线　roller line

辊道窑　roller kiln
辊道正置辊　straight table roll
辊道主传动长轴　table lineshaft
辊道主传动轴油槽[箱]　lineshaft trough
辊道座架的非传动侧　table-side girder
辊底式连续热处理炉　roller-hearth continuous furnace
辊底式连续退火炉　roller-hearth continuous annealing furnace
辊底式炉　roller-hearth furnace [kiln], roller-hearth continuous furnace(连续热处理炉)
辊底式送锭车　roller-type ingot buggy
辊端　roller end
辊锻　roll forging
辊锻机　forge rolling machine, roll foging machine
辊缝　roll opening, (roll) gap, clearance between rolls, (roll) bite ◇ 开口~open roll gap
辊缝飞边　【压】roller fin
辊缝控制　roll opening control ◇ 恒定~*,液压~*
辊缝控制装置　roll gap control device
辊缝锁口　roll parting
辊缝调定　roll-gap setting
辊缝调整机构　roll-separating mechanism
辊缝调整器　roll gap setter
辊缝调整系统　gap setting system
辊缝仪　【连铸】roll gap device
辊缝值数字指示器　roll gap value digital indicator
辊缝指示　roll opening indication
辊缝指示器　roll gap [opening] indicator
辊痕裂纹(热轧钢材的)　chill crack
辊环　【压】(roll) collar, roll ring ◇ 中间~inner collar
辊环尺寸　collar dimension
辊环痕　collar mark
辊环斜度　collar taper
辊脊　【压】(roll) collar, (roll) hump
辊架　roller housing

辊肩　roll shoulder
辊颈　(roll) neck, (roll) journal
辊颈部分　journal section
辊颈加工　necking
辊颈量规　roll neck gauge
辊颈铝锡合金轴承　◇摩戈伊尔~*
辊颈折断(事故)　neck break
辊颈支架　neckrest
辊颈轴承　roll neck bearing ◇多支承~*
辊颈轴承衬　journal-bearing bushing
辊颈座　chock
辊距　【压】roll(er) spacing, pitch
辊口(穿孔轧机的)　roll throat
辊口处的摩擦　roll-bite friction, friction in bite
辊轮　running roller
辊轮拉丝模　roller die
辊轮式小车焊缝跟踪装置　carriage roller follower
辊面　roll surface
辊模　【压】roller die, roll-die ◇Y型三辊~　Y type three-roll die
辊模拉拔　roll-die drawing technique
辊磨机　roller mill
辊碾机(智利式)　Chilian mill
辊盘　roll disc
辊圈　ridging ring
辊筛　roll(er) screen, sizing roll
辊上铸造法　roll-casting principle
辊身　body (of roll), (roll) barrel ◇凹形~concave barrel, 凸形~convex barrel
辊身表面压嵌着氧化皮的轧辊　banded roll
辊身长度　barrel [face] length, roll body length, length on face
辊身掉[缺]角　corners broken off main body
辊身对角折断　diagonaly body break
辊身平孔型　bull-head pass
辊身凸度[轮廓]　roll camber
辊身凸度计算　camber design
辊身沿轴线垂直面折断　vertical body break
辊身硬度　barrel hardness
辊身折断　body break
辊身正沿轴线垂直面折断　vertical perpendicular body break
辊身直径　barrel [roll] diameter
辊身做出凸度　barrelling
辊式板材矫直机　mangle
辊式板材拉伸矫直机　roller-stretching machine
辊式板坯堆放台　roller-type slab magazine
辊式布料器　【团】roller conveyor(-screen), live-roll feeder
辊式侧导板　roller side guide
辊式冲压模　roller stamping die
辊式穿孔　rotary piercing
辊式穿孔[穿轧]机　(同"曼内斯曼穿孔机")
辊式磁选机[磁力分选机,磁力分离器]　roll-type magnetic separator
辊式淬火　roll quenching (RQ)
辊式打尖机　pointing rolling machine
辊式导板[导线器]　roller guide
辊式导卫装置　roller (guide) apron, anti-crimp rolls
辊式地上卷取机　roll-type upcoiler
辊式地下卷取机　mandrel down coiler
辊式点-缝焊机　roller spot-and-seam welding machine
辊式电极　roller electrode, seam-welding roller
辊式电极传动　【焊】wheel drive
辊式翻钢机　roller tilter, roller-type turnover device
辊式分级机　roller grader [sizer]
辊式分配器　roller distributor
辊式缝焊[滚焊]机　roller-type seam welding machine
辊式干燥机　roller drier
辊式挤锌装置　wipe
辊式给料机　roll(er) feeder

辊式剪断机　roll shears
辊式矫形法　contour correction rolling
辊式矫正机(型材的)　gagger
辊式矫直(钢管、型钢的)　roll(er) straightening
辊式矫直机　roll(er) straightener, roll(er)-straightening machine, roller flattener(薄板的),(板带材的) roller leveling machine, roller leveller ◇ 带支承辊的～backed up type roller leveller, 反压～*, 支承压力可调整的～*
辊式矫直机矫直　roller flattening [levelling]
辊式结晶器　roll-type mould
辊式卷取机　roll-type coiler, roller reel, coiler gear ◇ 地下～roll-type downcoiler
辊式拉伸矫直机　roller stretcher
辊式冷床　roller(-type) cooling bed [bank], cooling roller bed
辊式冷矫直机(薄板的)　cold mangle
辊式冷弯成形(轧)机　cold roll-forming mill [machine] ◇ 悬臂～*, 自动～*
辊式模顶管机【压】roller die push bench
辊式模拉拔[拉丝]【压】roller die drawing
辊式磨机　ring-roller mill
辊式扭转导板　(mechanical) roller twister, roller twist guide
辊式扭转导板槽　roller twister trough
辊式破碎机　roll crusher [breaker, mill], kibbler roll, roller mill
辊式破碎机破碎　roll crushing
辊式送料冲床(薄板用)　roll feed press, roller press
辊式碎煤机　roll coal crusher
辊式涂镀　roller coating
辊式涂镀设备　roller coater
辊式涂油机　oil roll machine
辊式弯曲机　roll bending machine, channel(l)ing machine
辊式型材矫直机　roller section-straightening [shape-straightening] machine

辊式压力机　roll press
辊式压制[制团]机　(同"对辊压制机")
辊式运输机　roller conveyor ◇ V形～*, 环形～*
辊式张紧装置【压】bridle ◇ 入口～entry tension bridle
辊式支座　roller pedestal
辊式组合拉模　turn head die
辊套　roll ring
辊筒　bowl
辊弯成形　roll-bending formation
辊弯(成形)机　roll-forming machine ◇ 连续式～*, 七机座～*
辊系弹性变形模型　elastic deformation model of rolls
辊隙【压】(roll) gap
辊隙间作用力　forces in roll throat [gap]
辊隙开口度　roll gap opening
辊箱式拉丝卷筒　spinner block
辊楔拉分轧制　pull-separated rolling by roll wedge
辊芯　roll core [heart, mandrel]
辊型【压】roll shape [camber, curve, sweep], camber of rolls ◇ 凹线～concave camber, 凸线～*, 轧辊～roll crown(ing)
辊型计算　camber design
辊型检查仪　profilograph, profilometer
辊型磨制自动装置　cambering mechanism
辊型设计　cambering, designing of construction lines, designing of section ◇ 轧辊～roll contouring
辊形调整　crown adjustment
辊压成形　gauge forming
辊压淬火　rolled hardening
辊压搭焊焊管法　roll lapweld process
辊压对焊焊管法　roll buttweld process
辊压机　rolling press, roll squeezer ◇ 瓦垄板～curving machine
辊腰(穿孔机的)　gorge
辊印(轧件的)　roll [collar, ragging, chatter] marks, (roll) pick-up

辊轧扁钢　float rolled steel
辊轧成形　roll forming
辊轧锻造　gap-mill forging
辊轧冷弯成形　cold roll forming
辊轴　arbor, roll mandrel [shaft, center], shaft centre
辊轴筛　roll(er) screen, rolling axial screen
辊子　(同"辊")
辊子去垢剂　roll detergent
辊子闸门(密封缝隙用)　roll seal
辊子支座　roller saddle
滚边机　【压】edge knurling machine
滚槽机　channel(l)ing machine
滚齿　hobbing
滚齿机　(gear-)hobbing machine
滚打　【压】flop forging
滚刀　hob, hobbing cutter
滚道　rollaway nest
滚点焊　roll(er) spot welding
滚动　rolling, trundle, volution, tumbling action
滚动长度　rolling length
滚动触点　rolling contact
滚动焊剂法　flow solder method
滚动摩擦　rolling friction
滚动偏析　rolling segregation
滚动寿命　rolling life
滚动轴承　rolling bearing ◇耐磨～*
滚动铸型　roll cast
滚动阻力　resistance to rolling
滚动作用　tumbling action
滚镀　tumble-plating ◇转筒～*
滚镀法镀镉　cadmium plating by barrel method
滚镀法镀镉装置　barrel equipment for cadmium plating
滚锻　roll forging ◇楔模～*
滚对焊　butt seam welding ◇带状垫板～机*, 金属箔带式盖板～tape butt-seam welding
滚缝焊　roller seam welding
滚光间　rumbling room

滚焊　roll welding, seam (resistance) welding ◇搭接～接头 lap seam weld, 端面～edge seam welding, 横缝～transverse seam welding, 环形～*, 加搭板对接～bridge welding, 压薄～mash (seam) welding, 压边～连接 mash-welded joint
滚焊焊缝　roller seam weld ◇搭接～bridge seam weld, 连续～continuous seam weld, 用盖板对接～bridge seam weld
滚焊焊头　seam-welding head
滚[缝]焊机　seam welder, rolling [seam] welding machine ◇对接～多辊式～multiwheel seam welder, 辊式～*, 横焊缝～transverse seam welder
滚焊轮　seam-welding (electrode) wheel
滚焊头　electrode wheel head ◇万能～*
滚焊用(电流)断续器　seam-welding control
滚焊用机械(电流)断续器　mechanical seam welding control
滚花　(annular) knurling, ragging ◇边缘～机
滚花螺钉　knurled [milled] screw
滚回　roll back
滚拉轧辊　turks head roll
滚链　block [roller] chain
滚轮点焊焊缝　roller spot weld
滚轮滚焊焊缝　roller seam weld
滚螺纹模　knurling die
滚磨锤　bumping hammer
滚磨机　tumbling mill
滚磨精整[抛光]　rotary finishing
滚磨体　tumbling body
滚磨筒　burnishing barrel
滚磨用钢球　tumbling ball
滚盘铁栅筛　disc-grizzly screen
滚切机(管材的)　roll cutting shearer
滚球式黏度计　rolling-ball viscometer
滚圈　supporting tyre, rolling ring [track] (回转窑的) ◇实心橡胶～solid rubber type
滚圈座　tyre support

滚式焊接头　electrode wheel head
滚式给料机　distributor drum
滚式炉　roll-down furnace
滚水坝　retaining [rolling, weir] dam
滚丝板　thread rolling die
滚丝机[滚轧螺纹机]　roll threading machine, screw rolling machine ◇ 螺栓～bolt screwing machine
滚丝模　thread rolling die
滚桶混汞法　(同"转桶式混汞法")
滚筒　rotary drum, revolver,【机】roller tube ◇ 敷煤～*, 抛光～burnishing barrel, 皮带～belt roller
滚筒干燥机　(同"圆筒干燥机")
滚筒钢管　roller tube
滚筒过滤机　(rotary) drum filter
滚筒混合　barrel mixing
滚筒精整　roller finish
滚筒磨光(锻件的)　rumbling
滚筒[桶]抛光　barrel polishing [finishing, burnishing, tumbling], barrelling
滚筒抛光机　tumbling machine
滚筒清理　tumbling, barrel cleaning [finishing]
滚筒清理间　rumbling room
滚筒清砂　rumbling, drum cleaning ◇ 湿式～法 wet tumbling process
滚筒筛　drum [revolving, rotary, trommel] screen
滚筒筛分机　revolver
滚筒式包装机　drum packager
滚筒式擦洗机　【选】tumbling scrubber
滚筒式飞剪　rotary flying shears, rotating drum shears
滚筒式焊缝清理机　rotary-type flash trimmer
滚筒式给料机　(同"转筒给料机")
滚筒式剪切机　drum(-type) shears
滚筒式料仓闸门[闭锁器]　【铁】roller bin gate
滚筒式路碾[压路机]　drum roller
滚筒式磨机　drum [tumbling] mill

滚筒(式)喷砂机　【铸】sandblast barrel mill, blasting tumbling machine
滚筒式喷丸机　barrel-type shot-blasting machine
滚筒式切分剪　rotary dividing shears
滚筒式切头飞剪　rotary [drum-type] flying crop shears
滚筒式切头剪　rotary crop shears
滚筒式酸洗装置　drum-type pickler
滚筒式洗涤器　tumbling scrubber
滚筒式阳极氧化处理　barrel anodizing
滚筒式真空过滤机　rotary drum vacuum filter
滚筒式振动器　tumbling shaker
滚筒辗轧操作　barrel rolling operation
滚筒罩　drum shell
滚铣　hobbing
滚压　stitching, rolling (depression)
滚压叠层法　Marvibond process
滚压辊　seaming roll
滚压焊　roll-welding
滚压螺纹用模　thread rolling die
滚压模槽　roller
滚压硬化　hard rolling
滚缘工序(硬币的)　edge-rolling [edge-upsetting] operation
滚轧　rolling ◇ 螺纹～roll threading
滚轧工字形小钢梁　rolled I-section joist
滚轧机　roll [reeling] machine
滚辗　fulling
滚针轴承　needle [nail, quill] bearing
滚轴筛　revolving grizzly, roller picker
滚珠滚柱轴承　ball and roller bearing
滚珠轴承　ball bearing ◇ 带槽～grooved ball bearing, 调心[自动定位]～*, 止推[推力]～*
滚珠轴承钢　ball bearing steel
滚珠轴承钢丝[滚珠用钢丝]　ball bearing wire
滚珠轴承圈钢[滚珠座圈钢]　ball race steel
滚珠轴承圈厚壁管　ball bearing tubing

滚珠轴承座圈　ball race
滚柱罩[滚柱盒(轴承)]　roller cage
滚柱止推轴承　roller step bearing
滚柱轴承　roller bearing ◇ 多列～*
滚柱轴承钢　roller-bearing steel
滚柱轴承圈[环]　roller race
滚锥　rolling cone ◇ 平衡式～轴承*
滚子链　roll(er) chain
棍棒石　cordylite
锅　pan, pot, kettle,[冶]ladle
锅垢　boiler scale, scale incrustation, incrustant ◇ 脱除～descale
锅炉　boiler ◇ 分节铸铁～*, 汞蒸气～mercury vapour boiler, 火管式～*, 壳式～shell-type boiler, 水管～water tube boiler
锅炉安全塞合金　boiler plug alloy
锅炉低水位断流装置　low water cut-off device
锅炉房　boiler room (BR), boiler house, steam dome
锅炉防垢剂　boiler compound
锅炉腐蚀　boiler corrosion
锅炉钢　boiler steel [iron]
锅炉钢板　boiler plate
锅炉(钢)管　boiler pipe [tube] ◇ 超临界压力～*, 电阻焊～*, 高压～*
锅炉管割炬　boiler tube cutting torch
锅炉过热器　boiler superheater
锅炉火箱钢　firebox steel
锅炉碱脆[碱裂]　boiler embrittlement
锅炉拉条　boiler brace
锅炉煤　steam coal
锅炉燃烧室　boiler furnace
锅炉(水)垢　boiler scale
锅炉体　boiler drum
锅炉筒[外壳]　boiler shell
锅炉托架　boiler cradle
锅炉烟气　boiler flue gas
锅炉砖衬　boiler brickwork
锅炉砖砌面层　boiler clothing
锅内温度　kettle temperature

锅形底　dome-shaped bottom
国产的　domestic, home-made, indigenous
国产化　nationalization, domesticating
国产设备　domestic plant, home equipment
国际标准大气压　international standard atmosphere (ISA)
国际标准规范[规格]　international standardized specifications
国际标准化协会　International Standardization Association (ISA)
国际标准化组织　International Standardization Organization (ISO), International Organization for Standardization
国际标准化组织标准 V 型缺口冲击试验　ISO V-notch impact test
国际标准退火铜　international standard annealed copper
国际材料试验协会　International Association for Testing Materials (I.A.T.M.)
国际单位　international unit (I.U.)
国际单位制　International System of Units
国际地震工程师协会　International Association of Earthquake Engineering (I.A.E.E.)
国际电报工程委员会　International Electrotechnical Commission (IEC)
国际符号　international symbols
国际度量衡局　International Bureau of Weights and Measures (I.B.W.M.)
国际度量衡委员会　Comite International des Poids et Mesures (CIPM)
国际飞机标准　International Aircraft Standards (IAS)
国际钢铁学会　International Iron and Steel Institute (IISI)
国际钢材贸易协会　International Steel Trade Association
国际钢筋和线材出口商与生产商协会　International Rebar and Rod Exporters and Producers Association
国际焊接学会　International pipe Standard (IPS)

国际还原度指数　international index of reducibility
国际光学委员会　International Commission for Optics (I.C.O.)
国际管材标准　International Pipe Standard (IPS)
国际航空器标准　International Aircraft Standards (IAS)
国际互联网　internet, INTERNET
国际货币基金组织　International Monetary Fund (IMF)
国际货币基金组织的黄金部分头寸　gold tranche position in IMF
国际计算中心　International Computation Center
国际间收支往来　international transactions
国际建筑师联合会　International Union of Architects (IUA)
国际金属工人联合会　International Metal-Worker's Federation (IMF)
国际金相学会　International Metallographic Society (IMS)
国际晶体生长委员会　International Commission of Crystal Growth (I.C.C.G.)
国际矿冶学会　Institution of Mining and Metallurgy
国际理论和应用化学协会　International Union of Pure and Applied Chemistry (IUPAC)
国际理论和应用物理学协会　International Union of Pure and Applied Physics (IUPAP)
国际理论力学和应用力学协会　International Union of Theoretical and Applied Mechanics (IUTAM)
国际铝土矿、铝土与铝研究委员会　International Committee for Studies of Bauxites, Alumina and Aluminum (ICSOBA)
国际铝土矿、氧化铝与氢氧化铝研究委员会　International Committee for Studies of Bauxites, Oxides and Hydroxides of Aluminium (ICSOBA)
国际能源机构　International Energy Agency (I.E.A.)
国际能源署　International Energy Agency (I.E.A.)
国际镍公司　International Nickel Corporation (INCO)
国际镍公司高压羰基法　INCO pressure carbonyl process (IPC)
国际镍公司铜镍锍冶炼法　INCO (International Nickel Company) process
国际镍公司型闪速熔炼炉　INCO flash smelting furnace Engineering (I.A.B.S.E.)
国际铅-锌研究组织　International Lead-Zinc Research Organization (ILZRO)
国际桥梁与结构工程协会　International Association for Bridge and Structural
国际韧铜标准　International Annealed Copper Standard (IACS, I.A.C.S.)
国际筛规　international sieve unit
国际深冲研究组　International Deep-Drawing Research Group (IDDRG)
国际实用温标　International Practical Temperature Scale (IPTS)
国际市场　international market
国际通用科技常数手册　International Critical Tables (I.C.T.)
国际铜研究协会　International Copper Research Association (INCRA)
国际退火铜标准　International Annealed Copper Standard (IACS)
国际温标　International Temperature Scale
国际物理化学和工艺常数表汇编　International Critical Tables (I.C.T.)
国际锡业理事会　International Tin Council (I.T.C.)
国际先进水平标准　world advanced standard
国际冶金工作者联合会　International Union of Metallurgists

国际原子量 international (atomic) weight (I.Wt)
国际质量协会 International Association for Quality (IAQ)
国际专利文献中心 International Patent Documentation Center (INPADOC)
国家标准局(美国) National Bureau of Standards (NBS)
国家标准局标准(美国) NBS (National Bureau of Standards) standards
国家标准总局(中国) State Bureau of Standardization
国家标准线规(美国) national wire gauge (NWG)
国家航空航天局(美国) National Aeronautics and Space Administration (NASA)
国家计划委员会 State Planning Commission
国家鉴定 state verification
国家经济委员会 National Economy Commission
国家科学技术委员会 State Scientific and Technological Commission
国家煤炭局(英国) National Coal Board (NCB)
国家熔炼公司(英国) National Smelting Company (N.S.Co.)
国家统计局 State Statistical Bureau
国家物理研究所(英国) National Physical Laboratory (NPL)
国家冶金研究中心法还原指数(比利时) C.N.R.M. (Centre National de Recherches M′etallurgiques) index
国家冶金研究中心还原试验法(比利时) C.N.R.M. test (method)
国立橡树岭实验研究所(美国) Oak Ridge National Laboratory (ORNL)
国民生产总值 gross national product (GNP)
国民收入 gross national income ◇ 人均~*

国内的 internal (intern.), domestic, home
国内生产总值[国内总产值] gross domestic product (GDP)
国内私人(总)投资 gross private domestic investment
国内消耗 domestic consumption
国务院 the State Council
国营的 state-operated, state-run
国有工业企业 state-owned industrial enterprise
过磅工 weigher, weigh point man, weighman
过饱和 oversaturation, supersaturation
过饱和 β 相 supersaturated beta
过饱和奥氏体 supersaturated austenite
过饱和(程)度 (degree of) supersaturation
过饱和固溶体 supersaturated solid solution
过饱和固溶体状态 supersaturated solid solution state
过饱和合金 supersaturated alloy
过饱和极限 supersaturation limit
过饱和溶液 supersaturated solution [liquor]
过饱和铁素体 supersaturated ferrite
过饱和相 supersaturated phase
过焙烧 overroasting
过补偿 over compensation
过车地磅 truck scales
过程 process (proc.), procedure, course, run ◇ 随时间变化的~history
过程操作系统 process operating system (POS)
过程仿真 process simulation
过程废水 process effluent
过程废物 process(ing) waste
过程分析 process [procedure] analysis
过程计算机网络系统 process computer network system
过程监控 process monitoring
过程控制 process control

过程控制辊　process control roller
过程控制技术　process control technique
过程控制计算机　process (control) computer
过程控制计算机系统　process control computer system (PCCS)
过程控制系统　process control system
过程模拟　process simulation [modeling]
过程模型　process model
过程平衡　process balance
过程柔性　process flexibility
过程识别　process identification
过程输入/输出设备　process input/output equipment
过程物理冶金学　process physical metallurgy
过程信号转换器　process signal converter (PSC)
过程优化　process optimization
过程中的控制　【环】in-process control
过程终端控制　【环】end-of-process control
过充电　surcharge (s/c), overcharge
过充满孔型　overfull groove, overfilled pass
过冲　overshoot
过吹(转炉的)　overblow(ing)
过吹钢　overblown steel
过吹炉次　overblown melt
过粗粉粒　oversize particle
过粗粉末　oversize powder
过醋酸{CH_3CO_3H}　peracetic acid
过淬火　overquenching
过大尺寸[粒度]　oversize
过道　gangway aisle
过电流　over-current, excess current
过电流保护　over-current protection
过电流继电器　over-current relay (OCR)
过电流接地继电器　over-current ground relay
过电流切断器　over-current cut-out
过电流跳闸指示器　overcurrent trip indicator
过电流跳闸[脱扣]装置　over-current trip
过电位[势]　overpotential ◇ 活化～*
过电压　excess voltage, overhead tension, supertension ◇ 电极～electrode overvoltage, 阳极～*, 阴极～cathodic overvoltage
过电压保护　over-voltage [rise-in-voltage, surge] protection
过电压继电器　overvoltage relay
过电压检测器　overvoltage detector
过电压释放　overvoltage release
过电压吸收器　surge absorber
过顶火道　【焦】crossover flue
过顶烟道　overhead flue
过陡坡度　excessive grade
过度变质　overmodification
过度沉降　excessive settlement
过度处理　【环】overtreatment
过度淬火　overquenching
过度的　excessive, overdone, undue
过度辐照　overexposure, overirradiation
过度还原渣　over-reduced slag
过度挥发　excessive volatilization
过度回火状态　overtempered condition
过度混合　excessive mixing
过度剂量　overdose
过度搅拌　excessive agitation, overagitation
过度冷却　(同"过冷")
过度膨胀　overexpansion, overswelling
过度曝光[照射]　overexposure
过度曝光的劳厄图像　overexposed Laue film
过度熔化　excessive [undue] fusion
过度熔炼　overmelt
过度伸长　overstretch, excess elongation
过度渗碳　excess [over] carburizing
过度施加应力　overstressing
过度使用　overuse
过度松弛　overrelaxation
过度酸化　overacidification
过度酸性　superacidity

过度退火　overannealing, superannealing
过度压入　excessive indentation
过度研磨　overground, overmastication
过度应变晶体　overstrained crystal
过度应变状态　overstrained condition
过度应力　overstress
过度长大　excessive growth
过度中和　over-neutralization
过渡　transit(ion)
过渡层　transition [depletion] layer
过渡层理论（晶界的）　transition layer theory
过渡点　point of transition
过渡点阵[晶格]理论　transition lattice theory
过渡辊　pass-over roll
过渡过程　transient (process)
过渡过程恢复特性（曲线）　recovery characteristic
过渡过程时间　transient [response] time
过渡阶段　transition stage [step]
过渡结构　transition structure
过渡金属　transition-metal ◇ 有机～化学*
过渡金属合金　transition-metal alloy ◇ 锰的～*
过渡金属合金的拓扑密堆积结构　topologically close-packet structure of transition metal alloy
过渡(金属)族　transition group
过渡流　transition flow
过渡配合　transition(al) fit
过渡配合接头　crossover sub
过渡区　transition zone [region]
过渡曲线　transition curve
过渡蠕变　Andrade [transition] creep
过渡时间　transit time
过渡(时)期　transition stage [duration], 【冶】transient period
过渡锁接头　crossover sub
过渡台架　bridging table
过渡特性　transient characteristic [behaviour]
过渡特性曲线　transient characteristic
过渡温度梯度　transient temperature gradient
过渡相　transition phase
过渡型氧化铝　amorphous alumina, amorphous aluminium oxide, transition alumina
过渡形结晶的　malcrystalline
过渡形态　transition form
过渡性流动状态　transition flow
过渡液相　transitory liquid phase
过渡元素　transition element
过渡状态　transition state [condition]
过渡组织　transition(al) structure
过渡组织区　transition zone
过钝化　transpassivation
过分粉碎　excessive comminution
过分供给　overfeeding
过分疏松（缺陷）　excessive porosity
过分长大　overgrowth
过粉碎　overcrushing
过辐射(光子的)　overshoot
过复激(磁)　over-compound excitation
过复激的　over-compounded
过复绕的　heavily compounded
过负荷　overload ◇ 装料～【冶】overburden(ing)
过负荷保护　overload protection
过负荷警报　overload warning
过负荷开关　overload switch
过负荷控制　control of overload
过负荷系数　factor of overcapacity
过高焊道　excessive bead
过高温退火黄铜　overannealed brass
过锆酸盐　peroxyzirconate
过共晶合金　hypereutectic alloy
过共晶铁　hypereutectic iron
过共晶组织　hypereutectic structure
过共析钢(0.85—1.7C)　hypereutectoid steel
过共析合金　hypereutectoid alloy
过共析区　hypereutectoid zone

过共析组织　hypereutectoid structure
过焊　overwelding
过耗的　outworn
过和低控制器　over-and-under controller
过烘　overbaking
过烘干铸型　dead burned mould
过还原　overreduction
过还原钢　over-reduced steel
过回火　overtempering
过加料　overcharge
过街沟　cross drainage
过界　overline
过精炼[净化]　overrefinement
过拉　over-drawing, hollow drawing
过拉(拔)的　overdrawn (o.d.)
过拉伸　overstretch
过拉线　overdraw wire
过冷　overcool(ing), supercooling, undercooling, excessive cooling ◇ 组成[组分]～*
过冷奥氏体　overcolling [sub-cooling] austenite
过冷奥氏体等温热处理　austenaging
过冷奥氏体轧制形变热处理[温轧制]　ausrolling
过冷奥氏体亚稳定区均热淬火　aus-bay quenching
过冷淬火　overquenching
过冷度　degree of supercooling [undercooling]
过冷合金　supercooled alloy
过冷炉缸　undercooled hearth
过冷炉缸底　under-cooled hearth bottom
过冷能力　undercooling capacity
过冷却度　degree of undercooling
过冷溶液　supercooled solution
过冷现象　surfusion, superfusion
过冷蒸汽　supercooled [steam] vapour
过冷状态　supercooled state
过梁　breast-summer, bressummer, lintel (门窗的)
过两次筛的　double screened

过量　excess (ex.), overbalance, overdose
过量氨　excess of ammonia
过量反应性　excess reactivity
过量加料[充电]　overcharge
过量碱　excess alkali
过量金属　excess metal
过量空气　excess air
过量卸料[排放]　overdischarge
过钌酸盐　perruthenate
过磷酸　peroxyphoric [perphosphoric]acid
过磷酸钙　superphosphate ◇ 三元～*
过硫化钠{Na_2S_2}　sodium persulphide
过硫化物　persulphide
过硫酸铷{$Rb_2S_2O_6[O_2]$}　rubidium persulfate
过硫酸盐　persulphate, peroxysulphate
过硫碳酸{$H_2CS_2[S_2]$或H_2CS_4}　perthiocarbonic acid
过流脱扣(器)　over-current release
过氯酸铯　cesium perchlorate
过氯酸水溶液　aqueous perchlonic acid
过滤　filtering, filtration, straining, colation ◇ 澄清～*, 断续下向～*, 间歇式[分批]～batch filtration, 接触～contact filtration, 精致～[环]polishing
过滤板　filter plate
过滤杯　filter cup ◇ 烧结多孔镍～*
过滤泵　filter pump
过滤比　filter(ing) ratio
过滤槽　filter tank
过滤层　filter bed [blanket], filtering layer
过滤除尘器　filter dust separator
过滤袋　filter bag
过滤底　filter bottom
过滤斗　filter cone
过滤额　filterability
过滤法　filtration process ◇ 生物～biofiltration process
过滤方程式　filtration equation
过滤房　filter house
过滤坩埚　filter crucible ◇ 烧结[多孔]玻璃～*

过滤工段 filtering section, filtration area, 【冶】dewatering section
过滤管 filter tube
过滤机 filter (Fil., flt) ◇ 沉降～filter thickener, 带式～″, 更迭～alternate filter, 鼓式[滚筒]～″, 回转圆筒～″, 间歇式～batch filter, 拉线排料～″, 篮式～″, 压力～pressure filter, 叶片式～leaf (type) filter, 预涂助滤剂的～precoat filter, 圆盘(式)～″, 蒸发～″, 转盘～″, 撞击式～impinge-ment type filter
过滤机给料槽 filter feed tank
过滤机架 filter rack
过滤机组 filter bank
过滤剂 filtering agent
过滤间 filter house
过滤介质 filter(ing) medium
过滤浸出 filter leaching
过滤空气供给 filtered air supply
过滤漏斗 filter(ing) funnel
过滤率 filterability
过滤滤饼[渣]【色】 filtered product
过滤面(积) filter(ing) surface [area], filtration area
过滤能力[过滤机生产率] filter capacity
过滤浓缩机[槽] filter thickener
过滤盘 filter disk
过滤片 filter disk ◇ 不可见光～black light filter
过滤瓶 filter flask
过滤器 filter (Fil., flt), filtrator ◇ 补充～after-filter, 布袋～cloth bag filter, 澄清～clarifying filter, 磁筛～magnet screen filter, (多孔)金属～″, 二次～″, 返回双～return double filter, 分批[间歇]～intermittent filter, 管路～″, 硅砾～silica gravel filter, 霍夫曼～Hoffman filter, 机械～mechanical filter, 铰链带式～hinged belt filter, 精细～fine [polishing] filter, 静电～electrostatic filter, 框式～frame filter, 砾石～[池] gravel filter, 流线型～stream filter, 罗斯～Ross filter, 内表面～internal-surface filter, 旁通～bypass filter, 平行孔～parallel pore filter, 汽套式～steam-jacketed filter, 倾动盘式～tilting pan filter, 软管～hose filter, 筛网[网式]～″, 烧结金属～″, 石墨～graphite filter, 筒式～cartridge filter, 吸收～absor-bent filter, 洗涤式[涤气, 气体净化]～″, 线网～wire mesh filter, 向心～″, 压力带～pressure belt filter, 织物(纤维)～fabric filter, 重力～″, 自动～″
过滤器差压警报器 filter differential pressure alarm
过滤设备 filter plant, filtration equipment
过滤式离心机 (同"离心脱水机")
过滤式文丘里收尘组件 filtering venturi module
过滤速度[速率] filtering [filtration] rate, rate of filtration
过滤损失 filter loss
过滤特性 filtration characteristic
过滤桶 filter tank
过滤网浇口 filter gate
过滤洗涤 filtration washing
过滤系数 filtration coefficient
过滤箱 filter box
过滤效率 filter efficiency, efficiency of filtration, filtering effectiveness
过滤性 filt(e)rability
过滤性指数 index of filtrability
过滤用白土 filtering earth
过滤用焦炭 filter coke
过滤用黏土 filtering clay
过滤用无烟煤 Anthrafilt
过滤圆筒 filter drum
过滤圆锥 filter cone
过滤织物 filtration fabric
过滤装置 filter unit, filtering apparatus
过满的 overfull
过磨铁粉 heavily milled iron powder
过钼酸 {$H_2MoO_3[O_2]$, $H_2MoO_2[O_2]$} permolybdic acid

过钼酸盐 {xR$_2$O·yMoO$_2$[O$_2$]} permolybdate	过熔(透)焊道 excessive penetration bead
过凝固(现象) supersolidification	过溶度 super-solubility
过平衡 overbalance	过三氧化二锆 (同"过氧化锆")
过(破)碎 overcrushing	过筛 screening, sieving
过曝 burn-up	过筛焦(炭) screened [sized] coke
过期的 overdue	过筛矿石 sized ore
过桥 【冶】bridge wall	过筛煤 sized coal ◇ 中块~ middle-grade coal
过桥 footwalk, gangway	过筛筛网筛目 mesh size of scalping screen
过切削现象 【机】overcutting	
过氢化物 perhydride	过筛烧结矿 screened sinter
过热 overheat (ovht), excess heat, overfire, superheat, super-heating	过筛碎石 hoggin
	过筛型砂 riddled sand
过热保护(装置) overheating [overtemperature] protection	过烧 (over)burning, overfire, over-firing, 【压】burnt
过热点 hot point [spot]	过烧部分[区域] burnt place
过热度 degree of superheat	过烧的 overburnt ◇ 严重~ hard burned, overfired
过热钢 overheated [perished] steel	
过热钢锭 bony ingot	过烧镀层(电流密度过大造成) burnt deposit
过热钢液[钢水] superheated molten steel	
过热后冷却 desuperheat	过烧废钢[废料] burnt scrap
过热继电器 overtemperature relay, thermally operated device	过烧钢 burned [burned, fiery] steel, burnt iron
过热警报(器) heat [temperature] alarm	过烧钢锭 burned ingot
过热控制 overheat control	过烧黄铜 burnt brass
过热炉 superheater	过烧结 oversintering, excessive sintering
过热敏感性 overheating sensitivity	过烧金属 burnt metal
过热器 superheater ◇ 锅炉~ boiler superheater, 无水氟化氢~ A.H.F. superheater, 稀氟氢酸~ D.H.F. superheater	过烧面 crozzled surface
	过烧砂 burned sand
	过烧石灰 over-burned lime
过热器钢管 superheater tube	过烧砖 over-burned brick
过热器烟道钢管 superheater flue tube	过烧组织 burned [burnt] structure
过热区 overheated zone	过深桩 overdriven pile
过热热量 (heat of) superheat	过渗碳 over-carburization
过热寿命试验 overheating life test	过渗碳钢 perished steel
过热调节器 attemperator	过剩 excess, surplus
过热信号 temperature alarm	过剩变形 redundant deformation
过热信号(器) temperature alarm	过剩反应性 excess reactivity
过热蒸汽 superheated steam (SS), supercharged [gaseous] steam, superheated [hot] vapour	过剩(高炉)煤气燃烧器 excess gas burner
	过剩还原剂 excess reducing agent
过热组织 overheated structure	过剩金属 excess metal

过剩空气　excess(ive) air, air excess	过钨酸{$H_2WO_3[O_2]$, $H_2WO_2[O_2]$}　pertungstic acid
过剩空气流(量)　excess air flow	过细　overground
过剩空气率[系数]　excess air rate [ratio, coefficient]	过线　overline
过剩空穴　excessive hole	过压　over-roll, overdrive, overpressure
过剩能　excess energy	过压缩[压下]　excessive rolling
过剩气体放散阀　excess gas bleeder	过氧化　overoxidation, peroxidation
过剩渗碳体　excess cementite	过氧化钡　barium peroxide
过剩施主浓度　excess donor concentration	过氧化苯酰催化剂　benzoyl peroxide catalyst
过剩酸　excess acid	
过剩碳　extra carbon	过氧化反应　peroxidization, peroxidation
过剩相　excess phase	过氧化铪　hafnium peroxide
过剩压力　excess pressure	过氧化铼　rhenium peroxide
过剩氧火焰　excess oxygen flame	过氧化锰　(同"二氧化锰")
过剩乙炔火焰　excess acetylene flame	过氧化镁　peromag
过剩重量　excess weight	过氧化钠{Na_2O_2}　sodium dioxide [peroxide]
过失致死　【环】involuntary manslanghter	
过湿　overmoistening, overwetting	过氧化镨{Pr_2O_3}　praseodymium peroxide
过湿带[段]　over-wet stage, overmoistened [overwetting] zone	过氧化铅{PbO_2}　lead peroxide
	过氧化氢{H_2O_2}　hydrogen peroxide [superoxide], peroxide of hydrogen
过时的　out-of-date, obsolete	
过时效　overageing	过氧化熔炼[炉次]　over-oxidized heat
过时效合金　over-aged alloy	过氧化铷{Rb_2O_4}　rubidium peroxide
过时效状态　overaged condition	过氧化铯{Cs_2O_4}　cesium peroxide
过水合物　perhydrate	过氧化锶{SrO_2}　strontium peroxide [superoxide]
过水能力　discharge capacity ◇ 道管～ carrying capacity of pipe	
	过氧化铊　(同"五氧化二铊")
过四氧化二钾{$K_2[O_4]$}　potassium peroxide	过氧化钛　(同"三氧化钛")
过四氧化二铷{Rb_2O_4}　rubidium peroxide	过氧化铁　peroxide of iron
过四氧化二铯　(同"四氧化铯")	过氧化铜　copper dioxide [peroxide]
过速检测器　over speed detector (OSD)	过氧化物　peroxide, superoxide, hyperoxide
过速装置　over speed device (osd)	过氧化物沉淀(法)　peroxide precipitation
过酸洗　overpickling	过氧化锌　zinc peroxide
过碎　overcrushing	过氧化钇{Y_4O_9}　yttrium peroxide [superoxide]
过碳酸{$H_2C_2O_6$}　percarbonic acid	
过碳酸盐{$M_2C_2O_6$}　percarbonate	过夜试验　overnight test
过调节[过调量]　overshoot, overregulation	过应变　overstrain
过退火　(同"过度退火")	过应变时效　overstrain aging
过退火黄铜　overannealed brass	过应变状态　overstrained condition
过弯曲　overbending	过硬(化)的　overhardening
	过铀酸{$H_2UO_5 \cdot H_2O$}　peroxyuranic acid

过载 overload(ing) (OL, ovld), overburden(ing), supercharge loading
过载保护 overload [overcurrent] protection
过载断路器 overload (circuit) breaker
过载防护装置[安全设备,保险器] overload safeguard
过载极限 overload margin
过载继电器 overload [over-current] relay
过载离合器 overriding clutch
过载能力[容量] overload capacity
过载试验 overload test
过载探测器 overload detector
过载脱扣[释放](器) overload release
过载系数 overload factor
过载指示器 overload indicator
过早熔化 premature fusion
过早烧结 premature sintering
过早硬化 premature hardening
过致密介质 overdense medium
过重 overbalance, excess(ive) weight, overweight
过珠光体钢 hyperpearlitic steel
过装 surcharge (s/c), overcharge

H h

哈彻莱特钢水连铸板带材直接轧制法 Hazelette (strip casting) process

哈彻莱特双带浇铸机 【色】Hazelette twin-belt caster

哈达斯(硬质)氧化铝膜处理法 Hardas process

哈代特耐热镍铬硅合金(35—93Ni,10—18Cr,1—2Mn,2—7Si) Hardite

哈德菲尔德高锰钢(0.9—1.2C,10—13Mn,余量Fe) Hadfield (manganese) steel

哈德菲尔德热帽铸锭法 【钢】Hadfield ingot process

哈丁回转干燥炉 Hardinge drier

哈丁式回路分级机 Hardinge type loop classifier

哈丁圆锥式球磨机 Hardinge ball [conical] mill

哈尔伯格－贝思型袋式滤尘器 Halberger-Beth type filter

哈尔范铬钒工具钢(0.4C,0.7Mn,1Cr,0.2V,余量Fe) Halvan tool steel

哈尔基恩铅精矿熔盐电解法 Halkyn molten salt electrolysis

哈尔科姆合金钢 Halcomb (热加工用; Halcomb 218: 0.4C,1Si,5Cr,0.35V,1.35Mo; Halcomb 236: 0.3C,0.5Si,0.35Mn,12W,12Cr,1V)

哈尔曼铜锰铝合金电阻丝 Halman (Halman No.1: 10.46Mn,3.95Al,0.04Fe,0.02Si,余量Cu; Halman No.2: 11.56Mn,4.93Al,0.24Fe,0.04Si,余量Cu)

哈菲尔德快速蠕变[时间－屈服]试验 Hatfield time-yield test

哈里森熔融态下铸造和随后模锻制造零件法 Harrison process

哈里斯表层渗碳深度公式 Harris formula for case depth in carburizing

哈里斯粗铅碱性精炼法 Harris process

哈里斯粗铅碱性精炼设备 Harris plant

哈里斯渗碳深度公式 Harris equation

哈林电镀槽(测定用) Haring cell

哈林顿耐摩轴承青铜(55.73Cu,42.67Zn,0.97Sn) Harrington bronze

哈林顿喷水抽气泵 Harrinton's water-jet pump

哈曼铁矿石直接还原法 Harman process

哈梅塔格旋磨法 Hametag process

哈梅塔格旋磨粉末 Hametag powder

哈梅塔格旋涡冲击式磨机 Hametag impact mill

哈梅塔格旋涡磨机 Hametag (eddy) mill

哈梅特加压铸锭法 【钢】Harmet process

哈密尔顿－伊万斯不锈钢冶炼法 Hamilton-Evans process

哈密尔顿密度 Hamiltonian density

哈密尔顿锌基轴承合金(3Cr,1.5Sb,3Pb,余量Zn) Hamilton metal

哈诺瓦锡基轴承合金(8Sb,5Cu,余量Sn) Hanover metal

哈钦森热电偶合金(10Sn,90Bi) Hutchinson alloy

哈斯克洛姆耐热耐磨铬锰钢(10—14Cr,0.8—1.2C,3—5Mn) Hascrome

哈斯勒秤 Hasler scale

哈斯特莱特钻具钢 Hastellite

哈斯特洛伊 B 耐盐酸镍钼合金(62Ni,28Mo,5Fe;65Ni,30Mo,5Fe) Hastelloy B

哈斯特洛伊 C 耐氧化耐酸镍钼铬钨合金(54Ni,17Mo,15Cr,5Fe,4W; 17Mo,14Cr,5W,5Fe,余量Ni) Hastelloy C

哈斯特洛伊 D 镍硅铜耐蚀合金(85Ni,10Si,3Cu;9Si,余量Ni) Hastelloy D

哈斯特洛伊 N 高镍合金(6.0—8.8Cr,15—18Mo,5Fe,0.5Si,0.8Mn,0.04—0.08C,0.01B,0.03S,0.5Al＋Ti,67—72Ni) Hastelloy N

哈斯特洛伊镍基耐蚀耐热合金 Hastelloy

哈斯特洛伊陶质耐蚀耐热镍基合金 ceramic Hastelloy

哈特菲钢　Hadfield steel

哈特里-福克自动匹配场法　Hartree-Fock's mehtod

哈特里自洽(力)[自协]场　Hartree self-consistent field

哈特曼线[形变带]　Hartman(n) lines

哈维固体渗碳硬化钢　Harvey steel

哈兹莱特连铸机　Hazelett continuous caster

铪{Hf}　hafnium, celtium (旧名) ◇碘化物法～*, 反应堆级～*, reactor-grade hafnium, 海绵～ hafnium sponge (metal), 含～矿物*

铪板　hafnium plate

铪带　hafnium strip

铪的谐振构造　hafnium resonance structure

铪的中子吸收截面　hafnium cross section

铪锭　hafnium ingot

铪废料　hafnium scrap

铪分离设备　hafnium separation plant

铪锆石　hafniun zircon

铪焊丝　hafnium welding wire

铪合金　hafnium alloy

铪基合金　hafnium base alloy

铪晶棒　hafnium crystal (bar) ◇点焊～电极*

铪精矿　hafnium concentrate ◇高(品位)～*

铪块　hafnium regulus

铪络合物　hafnium complex

铪丝　hafnium filament

铪酸钙{CaO·HfO₂}　calcium hafnate

铪酸盐{MO·HfO₂}　hafnate

铪钛合金　hafnium titanium alloy

铪添加合金　hafnium addition alloy

铪条　hafnium ban ◇U字形～hairpin of hafnium

铪锌合金块　hafnium zinc alloy biscuit

铪氧基　hafnyl

蛤蟆夯　frog rammer, ram(ming) machine

海岸线状纹理　beach markings

海拔　elevation, altitude

海拔高(度)　height above sea level, sea level elevation, altitude

海波(定影剂硫代硫酸钠)　hypo

海布拉姆铝镁硅合金　Hyblum

海布尼克尔含铝18-8不锈钢(<3Al)　Hybnickel

海德拉挤压模具钢(0.26—0.30C, 3.0—3.5Cr, 9—10W, 0—0.5Mo, 0—2.5Ni)　Hydra metal

海德拉热作模具钢(E型:0.3C, 3.5Cr, 9-10W; Z型:0.26C, 3Cr, 9-10W, 0.5Mo, 2.5 Ni)　Hydra steel

海德雷克斯镍铬耐热不锈钢(65Ni, 15Cr, 0.75—1.25Mn, 0.2C, 0.5Si, 余量Fe)　Hydrex

海德隆铅钠合金(66Pb, 34Na)　Hydrone

海德罗高强度含钛锌基合金(0.08—0.16Ti, 0.4—0.7C, 0.002—0.01Mn, 0.003—0.02Cr, 余量Zn)　Hydro-T-metal, Hydro titanium metal

海德罗合金(挤压模用; type E: 0.3C, 3.5Cr, 9—10W; type Z: 0.26C, 3Cr, 9—10W, 0.5Mo, 2.5Ni)　Hydro metal

海德罗纳留姆耐蚀铝镁合金(2—10Mg, 0.2—1.5Si, 0.2—1.0Mn, 余量Al)　Hydronalium

海底沉积　benthal deposits

海底电缆　submarine cable

海底管道[线]　submarine pipline

海底矿物资源　suibmarine mineral resources

海底生物　benthos

海恩浸蚀法　Heyn's etching method

海恩浸蚀剂(钢铁用)　Heyn's reagent

海恩晶粒度测定法　Heyn method

海恩斯-斯特莱特6号刀具用硬质合金(<55Co, >33Cr, <6W)　Haynes-stellite No.6

海恩斯-斯特莱特耐铁耐热合金(2—15W, 20—65Co, 11—32Cr, 0.5—2.5C,

有时尚含 Fe、Ni、Mo、V、Mn、Si 等) Haynes stellite

海恩斯 25 钴铬钨镍耐热合金(蚀级：50Co, 25Cr, 15W, 10Ni, 0.1C, 2Fe, 1.5Mn) Haynes 25 alloy

海恩斯 713C 真空熔炼[惰性气氛熔炼]镍基合金 Haynes alloy 713 C

海恩斯高电阻高硬度超基合金 Haynes alloy

海恩应力(金属晶粒间的) Heyn [textural] stress

海尔矿石直接还原反应罐海绵铁生产法 HyL (Hajalata Y Lamina) process

海金沙 spora lygodii

海军巴比合金(65—75Sn, 12—15Sb, 10—18Pb, 2—3Cu) marine babbitt

海军黄铜 admiralty brass [metal] (29Zn, 1Si, 70Cu), naval brass (60Cu, 39Zn, 1Sn) ◇ 阿德尼克~ *, 巴特~ *, 查米特~ Chamet brass, 耐蚀~ *, 托宾~ *

海军混合黄铜 admiralty mixture brass

海军科学研究实验所(美国) Naval Research Laboratory (NRL)

海军镍 admiralty nickel

海军炮铜(87—89Cu, 9.5—10.5Sn, 1.5—2.5Zn) government bronze, admiralty gun metal

海军炮筒 naval gun barrel

海军青铜 navy bronze (86—90Cu, 5.5—6.5Sn, 1—2Pb, 余量 Zn), admiralty bronze(含 2Zn)

海科马克斯铝镍钴系永久磁铁(21Ni, 20Co, 9Al, 2Cu, 余量 Fe) Hycomax

海莱特 65 高蠕变强度钛基合金(6Sn, 5Zr, 3Al, 0.5Mo, 0.5Si, 余量 Ti) Hylite 65

海利亚克法焊接(TIG 焊接的专利名) Heliarc welding

海绿石{K, Mg(Mn, Fe)$_3$Si$_6$O$_{18}$·3H$_2$O} glauconite, tere veate

海绿云母细砂岩 gaize

海马克斯永磁合金 Hymax alloy

海曼铝合金(3Cu, 0.8Si, 0.5Mg, 0.5Ni, 余量 Al) Hyman

海梅特碳化钛硬质合金 Hinet

海绵铂 platinum sponge

海绵锆 sponge zirconium, zirc (onium) sponge ◇ 克罗尔法~ *, 洗过的~ wetted zirconium sponge

海绵锆料 feed-sponge zirconium

海绵锆蒸馏炉 zirconium sponge distillation furnace

海绵镉 sponge cadmium, cadmium sponge

海绵铬 chromium sponge

海绵铪 hafnium sponge (metal) ◇ 低锆~ *, 镁还原的~ *

海绵挤水器 bulb sponge

"海绵"焦头 spongy end

海绵金属 sponge (metal), metallic sponge, biscuit ◇ 弧熔~ arc melted sponge, 混合~ blended sponge, 湿[洗过的]~ wet sponge

海绵金属层 sponge bed

海绵金属淀积 treeing

海绵金属料 feed-sponge

海绵面(板坯的) spongy surface

海绵镍 sponge nickel ◇ 泥状~ *

海绵铍 beryllium sponge

海绵塑料 aerated plastics

海绵钛 sponge [spongy] titanium, titanium sponge

海绵钛[锆]金属 ◇ 克罗尔~ *

海绵钛反应器 titanium sponge reactor

海绵钛蒸馏罐 titanium sponge distillation retort

海绵体 sponge mass [structure], cavernous body

海绵铁 sponge iron ◇ 米德雷克斯法~ Midrex sponge iron

海绵铁饼 sponge iron cake

海绵铁粉 sponge iron powder, iron sponge powder ◇ 安科~ Ancor iron powder, 霍加内斯~ Hoeganas powder, 林茨~ Linz powder, 派伦~ Pyron iron powder, 瑞典

海绵铁生产[制取,还原]法 sponge iron process ◇ SL-RN~还原法 SL-RN reduction process,埃索-利特尔流态化床~*,奥尼亚-诺瓦尔费流态化床~*,海尔矿石直接还原反应罐~*,霍格-普罗发~ Hoag-Purofer process,霍耶拉塔和拉米纳~*,纽-流态化床~ Nu-iron process,切诺特~ Chenot process,普罗费竖炉~ Purofer process,维伯格~ Wieberg process
海绵铜 spongy copper, copper sponge
海绵铜镍合金 copper-nickel sponge
海绵锌 zinc sponge
海绵铀 uranium sponge
海绵铸铁 spongy cast iron
海绵状 sponginess, spongy
海绵状材料 spongy material
海绵状赤铁矿 iron froth
海绵状粉粒 spongy particle
海绵状粉末 sponge [spongy] powder
海绵状腐蚀 spongious corrosion
海绵状覆盖层 spongy coating
海绵状焦 sponge coke
海绵状金属块 sponge cake
海绵状孔隙 sponge-type porosity
海绵状溃蚀(金属的) sponge-like decay
海绵状铅 spongy [mossy] lead, lead sponge
海绵状涂层 spongy coating
海绵状物 sponge
海绵状物质 spongeous mass
海绵状橡皮 sponge rubber
海绵状锌 mossy zinc
海绵状阳极泥[海绵泥渣] slime sponge
海绵状银 sponge silver
海绵状组织 sponge structure
海穆80软磁合金(79Ni,4Mo,余量Fe) Hymu 80
海纳克耐蚀钢板 Hynack steel plate
海奈克(铬酸处理覆膜)钢板 Hinac steel plate

海尼卡尔铁铝镍磁性合金(32Ni,12Al,余量Fe) Hynical
海尼柯铁镍钴磁性合金(20Ni,10Al,6Cu,13Co,余量Fe) Hynico
海帕伦 Hypalon
海帕伦橡胶 Hypalon rubber
海珀科高导磁合金(由钴、铬和铁组成) Hyperco
海珀科高导磁率铁钴合金(36Co,1—2其他金属元素,余量Fe) Hiperco alloy
海珀洛依高导磁率铁镍合金 Hyperloy
海珀洛伊高导磁率软磁合金(50Ni,50Fe) Hiperloy
海珀马尔高导磁率铁铝合金 Hypermal
海珀马洛伊高导磁率铁镍合金(40—50Ni,余量Fe) Hypermalloy
海珀姆高导磁率合金(系) Hyperm
海珀尼克高导磁率铁镍合金(40—50Ni,余量Fe) Hypernic, Hipernik
海珀廷磁性合金 Hipertin
海珀瓦克超真空回转油泵 Hypervac rotary oil pump
海珀西尔高导磁(率)硅钢薄板[铁硅合金](0.03C,0.02S,0.02P,0.1Mn,3—3.5Si,余量Fe) Hipersil
海森堡测不准原理 Heisenberg principle of indeterminancy
海上试验 marine test ◇ 浸渍~ sea water dip test
海上污染源 maritime source of pollution
海上装船码头 offshore shiploading berth
海上钻井结构 off-shore drilling structure
海上钻探 off-shore boring
海蚀 (marine) abrasion, marine corrosion
海事工程 maritime work
海水淡化工厂 desalination plant, seawater desalting plant
海水腐蚀 sea water corrosion, marine corrosion, corrosion in marine environments ◇ KS高弹性耐~青铜*,耐~青铜
海水镁砂 sea water magnesia
海水镁砂白云石耐火材料 seawater mag-

nesia-dolomite refractories
海水镁砂烧结块 sea water magnesia clinker
海水氢氧化镁 seawater magnesium hydroxide
海水提铀 extraction of uranium from seawater
海斯真空渗碳处理法 Hayes process
海特勒-伦敦理论(氢分子结构的) Heithler-London's theory
海滕西尔黄铜(23Zn,3Mn,3Fe,4Al,余量Cu) Hytensyl bronze
海图夫低合金高强度钢(0.25C,1.3Mn,1.5Si,1.8Ni,0.4Mo,余量Fe) Hy-Tuf steel
海瓦克高真空泵 Hyvac pump
海湾高级淬火油 Gulf super-quenching oil
海洋沉积土 marine deposit
海洋处置 ocean disposal
海洋港口 ocean port
海洋环境下腐蚀 corrosion in marine environments
海洋开发技术 oceanology
海洋矿业 ocean(ic) mining
海洋锰结核 ocean manganese nodule
海洋倾倒 ocean dumping
海洋情况 oceanographic condition
海洋生态系(统) 【环】marine ecosystem
海洋水文情况 oceanographic condition
海洋水文学 marine hydrography
海洋学 oceanology
海洋用金属 sea metal
海运包装 seaworthy packing
海藻 alga (复数 algae)
海中排放口 submarine outfall
氦{He} helium ◇ 充~盒[箱] helium atmosphere box, 焊接级[用]~ welding-grade helium, 通~·, 液~ liquid helium
氦保护电弧焊 helium arc welding
氦出口 helium out
氦弹加压抽真空试验 (同"反加压试验")

氦低温恒温器 helium cryostat ◇ 柯林斯式~·
氦(电)弧焊 heliarc welding
氦轰击法(检漏方法) helium bombing
氦弧焊炬 heliarc torch
氦检漏器 helium leak detector
氦检漏器动态灵敏度 dynamic sensitivity of helium leak detector
氦壳电子 helium core electrons
氦氖激光(器) helium-neon laser
氦漂移 helium drift
氦气保护焊接 heliwelding
氦气氛 helium atmosphere
氦气氛淬火炉 helium atmosphere quenching furnace
氦气柜[瓶] helium tank
氦气驱气 helium purge
氦入口 helium in
氦温度计 helium thermometer
氦循环 helium cycle
氦-氩比 helium-argon ratio
氦液化机[器] helium liquefier
氦溢流(检漏试验) helium drift
氦照相机 helium camera ◇ 简易~·
亥姆霍兹自由能 Helmholtz free energy
韩国钢铁协会 Kerean Iron and Steel Association (KISA)
含钯硬钎焊料 palladium containing brazing alloy
含钡合金 barium containing alloy
含苯油 benzolized oil
含铋合金 bismuth containing alloy
含尘空气 dusty [dust-laden] air
含尘量[浓度] dust content [burden, load(ing), concentration], dustiness ◇ 出口~·, 入口[进气]~·
含尘率 dust index ◇ 高~·
含尘气体[炉气,煤气] dust-laden [ash-laden] gas, dust borne gas
含尘洗涤器水 【环】dust-laden scrubber water
含尘指数 dust index

含氮奥氏体	nitrogen austenite
含氮铬铁	nitrided [nitrogenated] ferrochrome
含氮合金	nitrogen-containing alloy
含氮锰铁(含 4N)	manganese-nitride
含二价铁和三价铁的化合物	ferroferric compound
含废石铁矿	incrustated iron ore
含酚废水	phenolic effluents, phenol wastewater
含氟气体	fluoride bearing gas, fluorine containing gas
含氟水	fluoridic water
含氟烟尘	fluorine containing dust
含氟阴离子	fluo anion
含钆合金	gadolinium-containing alloy
含钙巴比合金(1.35Cu,1.75Ca,0.1Na, 0.1Sr,1.0Ba,余量 Pb)	calcium metal
含钙材料[物质]	calcareous material
含钙合金	calcium containing alloy
含钙水泥	calcareous cement
含锆残液	zirconium raffinate
含镉废水	cadmium wastewater
含镉烟雾	cadmium (laden) fume
含铬合金	chrome-bearing [chromium-containing] alloy
含铬铁矿耐火材料	chromite-containing refractory
含汞合金	mercury containing alloy
含汞烟雾	mercurial fume
含钴合金	cobalt containing alloy, cobalt-bearing alloy
含钴化合物	cobaltiferous compound
含钴黄铁矿	cobalt-bearing [cobaltiferous] pyrite
含钴黄渣	cobalt (containing) speiss
含钴精矿	cobalt-bearing concentrate
含钴镍铁	cobalt-bearing ferronickel
含钴溶液	cobalt-carrying solution
含钴烟雾	cobalt containing fume
含硅合金	silicon-containing alloy
含硅矿石	siliceous ore
含硅蒙乃尔合金(62—65Ni,<0.35Fe, 0.5—1.5Mn,<0.25C,3.5—5Si,余量 Cu)	S Monel
含硅蒙乃尔铸造合金(63Ni,30Cu,4Si)	silicon Monel
含硅耐蚀青铜(75—85Cu,10—20Zn, 4.5—5.5Si)	silzin (bronze)
含硅膨润土	distribond
含硅烧结矿	siliceous sinter
含硅无氧铜	silicon deoxidized copper
含硅烟雾	silica fume
含硅页岩	siliceous shale
含硅铸铁	silicon-containing brass ◇ 西莱尔～
含铪残液	hafnium raffinate
含铪锆	hafnium containing zirconium
含铪合金	hafnium containing alloy
含铪矿物	hafnium containing mineral
含铪离子	hafnium carrying ion
含铪溶剂	hafnium laden solvent
含铪阳离子	hafnium containing cation
含铪阴离子	hafnium containing anion
含灰量	ash [dirt] content
含机油废水	machine oily waste water
含镓合金	gallium-containing alloy
含镓矿物	gallium-bearing mineral
含镓物料	gallium-bearing material
含碱废水处理装置	alkali containing waste water treatment plant
含碱介质	alkali containing medium
含碱量	alkali content
含焦量	coke content
含金的银块	doré metal
含金合金	gold containing alloy
含金黄铁矿	auriferous pyrite
含金矿(石)	gold-bearing ore, auriferous ore
含金量[率]	gold content
含金母液	pregnant gold solution
含金泥	gold-bearing slimes
含金溶液	gold-bearing solution
含金石英	goldquartz

含 han

含金石英砂　gold-bearing quartz sand
含金属的　metalliferous, metal-bearing
含金属的硅质熔剂　siliceous metal-bearing flux
含金属的硫化物　metal-bearing sulphide
含金属废水　metallic wastewater
含金属矿物　metal-bearing mineral
含金属溶液　pregnant solution
含金银锭　doré silver
含镧合金　lanthanum-containing alloy
含锂合金　lithium-containing alloy ◇雷达利思~Redulith
含锂烧结气氛　lithium-containing sintering atmosphere
含量　content (cont.)
含磷合金　phosphorus-containing alloy
含磷量　phosphorus content
含磷(炉)渣　【钢】phosphatic [phosphorus-bearing] slag
含磷镍青铜　◇福斯利克~*
含磷酸盐矿物　phosphate-containing mineral
含硫百分数　percentage sulphur
含硫钢　sulphur bearing steel
含硫根　sulphur-bearing group
含硫合金　sulphur-containing alloy
含硫量　sulphur content
含硫量允差　sulphur tolerance
含硫镍阳极　sulphur-bearing nickel anode
含硫气体　sulphur-bearing [sulphur-laden, sulphurous] gas
含硫燃料　sulphur-bearing fuel
含硫石油腐蚀　sour corrosion
含硫铜　sulphur copper
含硫物　sulphur carrier
含硫易切削钢（SUMIA；<0.15C, <0.04Si, 0.4—0.8Mn, 0.05—0.15P, 0.1—0.25S）　sulphur free-cutting steel, sulphur bearing steel
含铝18-8不锈钢　◇海布尼克尔~（<3Al）Hybnickel
含铝合金　aluminium bearing [containing] alloy
含铝矿物　aluminium bearing mineral
含铝六七黄铜　◇普罗米修~*
含铝镍铜合金　kunial
含铝铁　alferric
含铝涂模浆　【钢】hydropaste
含铝土的　aluminous, aluminiferous
含铝铸铁　aluminium cast iron
含氯中间产品　chlorine-bearing secondary
含镁合金　magnesium bearing [containing] alloy
含镁矿物　magnesium bearing mineral
含镁石灰　dolomitic lime
含镁石灰岩　magnesian limestone
含锰白口(铸)铁　manganese [manganiferous] white cast iron
含锰合金　manganese containing alloy
含锰矿石　manganiferous ore
含锰矿物　manganiferous mineral
含锰生铁(含14Mn)　manganese iron
含锰铁　manganous iron
含锰铁矿石　manganiferous iron ore
含钼超导磁率[超坡莫]合金（79Ni, 5Mo, 15Fe, 0.5Mn）　Supermalloy
含钼合金　molybdenum containing alloy
含钠铅合金　natrium lead
含铌高强度钢（含<0.05Nb）　columbium [niobium] bearing high strength steel
含铌合金　columbium containing alloy
含铌水相　columbium-bearing water phase
含泥精矿　（同"黏土质精矿"）
含泥量　clay content
含泥砂的河流　burdened stream
含黏土的砂　argillaceous sand
含黏土多的砂　gummy sand
含镍奥氏体　nickel austenite
含镍白口硬铸铁（3C, 4Ni, 2Cr, 0.5Mn, 0.4Si, 余量Fe）　Ni-hard
含镍磁硫铁矿　nickel-containing pyrrhotite
含镍返回料　nickel-bearing revert
含镍高强度铸铁（含1—4Ni）　Ni-ten-

silorin, Ni-tensyl iron
含镍红土矿 nickeliferous [nickel-bearing] laterite, lateritic nickeliferous iron ore
含镍基性岩 nickel-bearing basic rock
含镍矿物 nickel-bearing mineral
含镍溶液 nickel-bearing solution
含镍蛇纹石 nickeliferous [nickel-containing] serpentine
含镍蛇纹石矿 serpentine nickel ore
含镍铁合金 nickel-containing iron alloy
含镍铁矿 nickeliferous iron ore
含镍铸钢(2.25—3.5Ni, 0.15—0.25C, 0.5—0.75Mn, 0.25—0.45Si) nickel cast steel
含硼合金 boron bearing [containing] alloy
含硼马氏体钢 boron martensitic steel
含硼铁合金 needling agent
含硼铁精矿 boronic iron concentrate
含铍合金 beryllium containing alloy
含气量偏高的炉次 bleeding heat
含气量试验 air-content test
含气率 air voids, entrainment ratio (加气水泥的)
含气三极管 trigatron
含铅60黄铜(含1-3Pb) yellow metal
含铅低磷钢(易切削钢) leaded low-phosphorus steel
含铅钢(含0.2Pb) lead bearing steel
含铅合金 lead containing alloy
含铅黄铜 lead-containing brass ◇ 恩格雷弗斯~*, 轮用~*, 尼阿格~*, 弯头螺钉用~*, 威恩~*
含铅量 lead content ◇ 容许~lead tolerance
含铅锍[冰铜] leady matte
含铅硬焊料 leady spelter
含铅轴承合金 lead bearing alloy
含氢合金 hydrogen-containing alloy
含氢马氏体 hydrogen martensite
含氢气体 hydrogen-bearing gas
含热量 heat content

含铯合金 cesium-containing alloy
含砂水垢[氧化铁皮] gritty scale
含砷合金 arsenic containing alloy
含砷化合物 arsenic compound
含砷黄渣 【色】arsenical speiss
含砷混凝土 arsenic concrete
含湿量 moisture content (mc), moisture(-holding) [moisture-retention] capacity
含石灰球团 limecontaining pellet
含石灰熔剂 lime-bearing flux
含石墨青铜 graphited bronze
含石墨轴承 graphite-containing bearing
含时破裂 time-dependent collapse
含铈合金 cerium containing alloy
含铈混合稀土合金 mischmetal(l)
含铈绿帘石 cerium epidote
含水材料 hydrous material
含水层 water-bearing bed [stratum], aquifer ◇ 封闭~*, 弱~*
含水赤铁矿 hydrated hematite
含水分空气 moisture-laden air
含水硅酸盐 hydrosilicate
含水量 water [moisture] content, water [moisture (-holding), moisture-retention] capacity
含水量测定计 drimeter, moisture gauge
含水硫酸镁矿{$MgSO_4 \cdot 7H_2O$} epsomite, Epsom salt
含水馏分 watery distillate
含水率 water ratio, percentage of moisture, dampness
含水络合镍镁硅酸盐 complex hydrated nickel-magnesium silicate
含水能力[性能] moisture-retaining capacity, ability to retain moisture
含水凝胶 aqueous gel
含水土壤 aqueous soil
含水霞石 nepheline hydrate
含水性 moisture-retaining capacity
含水岩层 water-bearing formation
含水针铁矿 hydrogoethite
含酸萃取剂 acid-bearing extractant

含酸废水处理装置　acid-containing waste water treatment plant
含酸量　acidic content, acid content
含酸阳极液　acid-containing anolyte
含钛磁铁矿矿床　titaniferous magnetite deposit
含钛锰铁　titaniferous ferromanganese
含钛碳质复合耐火材料　TiC containing carbon composite refractory
含钛铁矿石　titanium-containing iron ore
含钛渣　titaniferous slag
含钛铸铁（0.1—0.5Ti）　titanium cast iron
含钽残液　tantalum raffinate
含钽萃液　tantalum extract
含钽青铜（10Al, 0.2Ta, 1.2Mo, 余量Cu）　tantalum bronze
含钽液流　tantalum-bearing stream
含碳奥氏体　carbon austenite
含碳保护气氛　carbonaceous atmosphere
含碳材料　carbonaceous [carboniferous] material
含碳铬矿球团　carbon-bearing chromite pellet
含碳合金　carbon-bearing [carbon-containing] alloy
含碳合金钢　carbon-containing alloy steel
含碳合金马氏体　alloy carbon martensite
含碳化合物　carbon-containing compound
含碳量　carbon content, temper ◇单位表面~*, 等~曲线（平衡图的）isocarb, 高~high carbon, 錾具钢~*
含碳马氏体　carbon martensite
含碳耐火材料　carbon-bearing refractory
含碳气体　carbonaceous gas
含碳涂料　carbonaceous dressing
含碳团矿　carbon-containing pellet
含碳物质　carbonaceous material [matter]
含碳蒸气　carbon-bearing vapour
含炭沫渣　kish slag
含锑合金　antimony containing alloy
含锑炉渣　antimony-bearing slag
含锑母液　pregnant antimony solution
含锑铅　antimonial lead
含锑铅阳极　antimonial lead anode
含锑铅阴极　antimonial lead cathode
含锑溶液　antimony solution
含锑烟雾　antimony fume
含锑银　antimonial silver
含锑黝铜矿{Cu$_{12}$Sb$_4$S$_{12}$}　antimonial gray copper ore
含铁波特兰水泥　ferroportland cement
含铁废料　iron-bearing [ferruginous, iron-containing] waste ◇厂内~works arisings, 细粒~fine waste material
含铁粉尘　iron-bearing [ferrous] fines, fine waste material, 【铁】blue dust
含铁粉尘球团　dust pellet
含铁浮渣　ferruginous dross
含铁硅质岩　iron-bearing siliceous rock
含铁和镁的　ferromagnesian
含铁合金　iron-containing [iron-bearing] alloy
含铁黄铜　Sterro metal [alloy] ◇格奇~*, 马赫特~*
含铁颗粒　iron-bearing particle
含铁矿石　iron-bearing ore
含铁量　iron content
含铁（炉）料　ferric charge, iron-bearing burden material, ferruginous burden
含铁炉渣　【铁】ferriferous slag
含铁铝的　alferric
含铁滤饼　【色】ferric [iron] cake
含铁黏土　ferruginous clay
含铁铅丹[含铁氧化铅]　iron minium
含铁熔剂　ferruginous flux
含铁砂　ferruginous sand
含铁石灰　ferruginous lime
含铁石英岩　jaspilite
含铁水泥　iron cement
含铁燧石　ferruginous flint
含铁物料　iron-bearing material
含铁细屑　iron-bearing fines
含铁锌镀层　protectorite

含铁氧和铝氧的　alferric
含铜的硅铝明合金（12.5Si，0.8Cu，0.4Mn，余量 Al）　copper silumin
含铜浮渣　copper-bearing [cupriferous] dross
含铜钢　（同"铜钢"）
含铜高的　high copper
含铜合金　copper-bearing [copper-containing] alloy
含铜黄铁矿　copper [cupriferous] pyrite
含铜金(矿)　copper gold
含铜金属废料　copper-containing scrap
含铜量　copper content
含铜铅　copperized lead
含铜溶液　copper solution [liquor]
含铜铁矿　cupreous iron ore
含铜物　aerose
含铜硬铝　copper silumin
含铜铸铁　copper iron
含钨钢　tungsten-bearing steel
含钨原料　tungsten-containing raw material
含锡残渣　tin residue
含锡合金　tin bearing alloy
含锡黄铜　tin bearing brass ◇ 查米特 ~*，西米勒 ~*
含锡(六 O)黄铜(38Zn，1Sn，61Cu)　One-ton brass ◇ 罗曼 ~*
含锌的硅铝明合金(5Si，<15Zn，余量 Al)　zinc silumin
含锌合金　zinc bearing alloy
含锌黄铜　Tombak
含锌炉渣　zincy slag
含锌铅　zincy lead
含锌硬铝　zink dural(umin)
含盐电解质　saline electrolyte
含盐度　brinishness，salinity，saltness
含盐量　salt content [loading]，【环】salinity
含盐水　saline water
含盐洗提液　salt-containing strip solution
含氧奥氏体　oxy-austenite
含氧合金　oxygen-containing alloy
含氧化锆合金　zirconium oxide-containing alloy
含氧化铪合金　hafium oxide-containing alloy
含氧化铝合金　aluminium oxide-containing alloy
含氧化镁合金　magnesium oxide-containing alloy
含氧化钍合金　thorium oxide-containing alloy
含氧化合物　oxygen-containing compound
含氧化物矿石　oxide-bearing ore
含氧化物杂质　oxide-containing impurity
含氧化学药品　oxychemicals
含氧化钇合金　yttrium oxide-containing alloy
含氧夹杂物　oxygen bearing inclusions (OBI)
含氧离子　oxygen-bearing [oxygen-carrying] ion
含氧量　oxygen content
含氧硫酸铜　copper-oxysulfate
含氧硫酸盐　oxysulphate
含氧汽油　oxygasoline，oxybenzine
含氧溶剂　oxygen-containing solvent
含氧酸　oxy-acid，oxacid，oxygen acid
含氧酸盐　oxy-salt
含氧铁素体　oxy-ferrite
含氧铜　oxygen-bearing copper
含氧硝酸盐　oxynitrate
含氧盐　oxy-salt
含氧阴离子　oxygen-containing anions
含氧杂质　oxygen-containing impurity
含一价铜和二价铜的化合物　cupro-cupric compound
含铱合金　iridium containing alloy
含铟合金　indium-containing alloy
含银粗铅锭　base lead bullion
含银方铅矿　argentiferous galena
含银汞　argental mercury
含银铅　silver-bearing [argentiferous] lead

含银铜　silverized [silver-bearing] copper
含银黝铜矿　argentiferous tetrahedrite
含铀材料　uranium-bearing material
含铀多金属矿石　uraniferous polymetallic ore
含铀废石　uraniferous waste rock
含铀褐煤　uraniferous lignite
含铀矿水　uraniferous mine water
含铀砾岩　uraniferous conglomerate
含铀磷矿石　uraniferous phosphate rock
含铀煤质页岩　uraniferous coal-containing shale
含铀泥炭　uraniferous peat
含铀砂岩　uraniferous sandstone
含铀石墨　live graphite
含铀铁矿石　uraniferous iron ore
含油废水　oily waste water
含油量　oil content
含油气　olefiant gas
含油性　lubricity
含油轴承　oilless [oiliness, oil-retaining, oil-impregnated, selfoiling] bearing ◇ 多孔铁～金属(100Fe) iron-oilite, 杜雷斯～*, 渗硫铁系～ferroporit bearing
含油轴承金属　◇ 多孔铁～(100Fe) iron-oilite
含有　contain
含杂质半导体　impure [impurity, extrinsic] semiconductor
含杂质晶体　impure crystal
含杂质熔剂　impure flux [stone]
含锗合金　germanium-containing alloy
焓　enthalpy, heat content
涵洞　culvert ◇ 筒形～barrel culvert
涵管[筒]　pipe culvert ◇ 黑铁～black culvert
函件分发器　mail exploder
函数　function ◇ 贝塞尔～Bessel function, 布里渊～Brillouin function, 布洛赫～Bloch function, 费米～Fermi function, 吉布斯～Gibbs function, 数组元素后继～*, 直接插入～in-line function

函数表　function table
函数发生器[生成程序]　function(al) generator ◇ 任意～*
函数开关　function switch
函数(求值)子程序　【计】function evaluation routines
焊疤　burr
焊把　electrode holder [carrier, adapter] ◇ 大电流～*
焊把钳口　electrode holder jaw
焊棒　metal pencil
焊边　pass, toe
焊边间距　distance between toes of a weld
焊边间隙　welding gap
焊波表面　rippled surface
焊补　weld repair, doctoring ◇ 铝热法～铸型 thermit mould
焊蚤　(stringer) bead
焊蚤形成　bead forming
焊层　layer of weld ◇ 最后[最上面]～*
焊层间不完全焊透(多层焊缝的)　incomplete inter-run penetration
焊层施焊顺序(多层焊的)　joint welding sequence, build up sequence
焊池　welding bath, (weld) pool, molten crater
焊池深度　molten crater depth
焊穿　through penetration
焊刺　burr ◇ 去除～装置 deburring unit
焊刺清理机　deseaming machine
焊道　(weld) run, pass, weld bead ◇ 板上～试验 bead on plate lest; 背面～back-run(ning), 补充～(多层焊的)extra bead, 封底～*, 加宽～spreading bead, 凸(形)～convex bead
焊道间熔合　interrun fusion
焊道清理机　weld bead conditioning machine
焊道下裂纹　underbead crack
焊道下裂纹敏感性　underbead crack susceptibility
焊道形成　bead forming

焊灯　soldering lamp [torch], blowtorch
焊滴（仰焊的）　warts
焊点　weld spot, soldered dot, fusion [cast] nugget
焊点间距[距离]　spot spacing, longitudinal [back] pitch
焊点熔核间界面　interface of weld nugget
焊点直径　spot size
焊点纵向间距　longitudinal pitch
焊粉　welding powder, powdered flux
焊封　solder(ing) seal ◇ 玻璃金属～ glass-to-metal seal, 普拉提奈特玻璃～合金～, 铜玻璃～copper-glass seal
焊封用铋合金　seal alloy
焊缝　weld, welding [soldering] seam, juncture ◇ J形槽焊[坡口]～*, V形[边缘坡口]～*, X形～*, 凹陷～ sagged weld, 闭式～closed weld, 并排断续～chain intermittent weld, 不坚固～weak weld, 不致密～leaky seam, 从上到下施焊～vertical-down weld, 从下到上施焊～vertical-up weld, 单一标准～single standard seam, 等强度～*, 低强度[不坚固]～weak weld, 断面不足的～undersize weld, 封口[填隙]～*, 根部[沿棱]～*, 角[圆根]～beaded joint, 漏泄～sagged weld, 内角(接头)～inside cornerweld, 坡口[铲边]～bevel (groove) weld, 全熔透～*, 十字交叉焊丝～cross-wire weld, 手工～hand weld, 受张力～tension weld, 疏松[有气孔]～porous weld, 凸形[加强]～convex weld, 削平补强[无凸面]～flush weld, 斜角～bevel weld, 压力焊[加压]～pressure weld, 有裂缝的～cracked weld, 有缺陷[毛病]～defective [faulty, poor] weld, falling seam, 窄[叠珠]～bead(ing) weld, 周围～around weld
焊缝背[反，里]面　back [underside] of weld ◇ 保护～用气体 backing gas
焊缝背面坡口　backing groove
焊缝长度　weld length
焊缝尺寸　weld size
焊缝尺寸检查样板　welding gauge
焊缝底缘　root edge
焊缝垫(板)　weld backing [back-up]
焊缝反面加强代号[符号]　melt-thru (weld) symbol
焊缝反面弯曲[根部外弯]　root [back] bend
焊缝反面弯曲试验　root-bend test
焊缝跟踪装置　weld tracker ◇ 辊轮式小车～
焊缝滚压　weld seam rolling
焊缝焊后退火　post annealing
焊缝焊透[熔焊]　weld penetration
焊缝喉部　weld throat ◇ 表观～apparent throat
焊缝喉深　throat thickness
焊缝厚度　throat depth
焊缝计算厚度　effective throat thickness
焊缝记号　weld marking
焊缝加厚　reinforcement of weld
焊缝间隔　weld interval
焊缝间隔时间控制器　weld interval timer
焊缝间距　pitch of weld
焊缝检测　weld seam detection
焊缝检验　weld inspection
焊缝界面　weld interface
焊缝金属　weld metal [material]
焊缝(金属)裂纹　weld-metal crack
焊缝(金属)破裂　weld-metal cracking
焊缝(金属)区　weld metal area
焊缝金属试样　weld-metal specimen
焊缝金属组织　weld structure
焊缝开裂　weld failure
焊缝开裂试验　bead weld cracking test
焊缝孔隙[气孔]　weld porosity
焊缝宽度　distance between the toes of a weld, weld width
焊缝量规　weld gauge
焊缝凝固　weld freezing
焊缝起点　weld starting
焊缝强度　weld strength

焊缝强度与基本金属强度比 design efficiency
焊缝倾角 weld slope, angle of slope
焊缝清理 weld cleaning
焊缝清理机 deseaming machine, (weld) trimmer ◇ 滚筒式~*, 火焰~ hot deseamer, 拉切式~ draw-cut trimmer
焊缝区 weld (metal) area, weld zone
焊缝熔敷金属 weld(ing) deposit
焊缝熔合线 weld-fusion line
焊缝实际厚度 actual throat
焊缝试样 button
焊缝塑性 weld ductility
焊缝（外）表面 face of weld
焊缝外形[观] weld contour [appearance]
焊缝型式代号[符号] weld symbol
焊缝形状 form of weld, weld shape
焊缝形状符号[代号] contour symbol
焊缝修整 weld dressing
焊缝修整机 deseamer
焊缝硬化 weld hardening
焊缝匀整性 evenness of weld
焊缝增强部分 reinforcement metal
焊缝中心距 pitch of weld
焊膏 soldering paste, paste flux, butter
焊割两用气焊枪[烧嘴，(焰)炬] combined welding and cutting burner [blowpipe], combined torch, welding and cutting torch
焊根 root (of weld) ◇ 不留间隙的~ closed root, 有间隙~ open root
焊根裂纹 basal crack, root crack
焊工 welder, solderer
焊工保护面罩 face mask
焊工护目镜 welder's goggles
焊工台 Welding table[bench]
焊管 welded tube [pipe] ◇ 对缝~ jump-welded pipe, 弧~ arc-welded pipe, 冷拔~ cold drawn welded tube, 连续式炉[弗雷茨－穆恩]~法*, 螺旋~ spiral welded pipe, 液压~法*, 直缝~ butt welded pipe[tube]

焊管成形机 skelper
焊管钢 skelp steel
焊管机 pipe welder, pipe welding machine, tube welding machine [mill], welding mill, welded tube mill ◇ 成型~*, 电感应加热~ induction weld mill, 电阻~*, 隐弧~ submerged-arc weld mill, 约德式连续~*
焊管拉模 welding gutter
焊管坯 tube skelp [strip], skelp (feed), tube strip ◇ 带材和~轧机*, 热轧宽幅~ broad hot strip, 斜边~ bevelled edge skelp
焊管坯储存台 coil magazine
焊管坯穿炉装置 threading machine
焊管坯加热炉 skelp heating furnace, welding furnace, butt welding furnace (连续式)
焊管坯斜边成形轧辊 scarfing roll
焊管坯轧机 skelp mill
焊管坯装炉机 skelp threading machine
焊管坯装炉装置 furnace (skelp) threading machine
焊管坯作蛇形直立放置（利用振动器进行） "Christmas candy" shape
焊管平头机 welded pipe end-facing machine
焊管用磁环 magnetic welding girdle
焊合 welding-on, filling in, sticking, seaming
焊合裂缝 welded fissure
焊合点 bonding point
焊合断口[断裂处] welded fracture
焊合温度 welding-on temperature
焊喉厚度 throat thickness
焊后残余应力 residual welding stress
焊后处理 postweld treatment
焊后顶锻 post-weld upsetting
焊后机械加工 subsequent machining
焊后加热电流 postheating current
焊后加热焊接 welding with postheating
焊后冷却时间 post-weld interval

焊后清理(焊件的)	post-weld cleaning
焊后热处理	post-weld [subsequent] heat treatment
焊后热处理电流调节	postheat control
焊后热处理工艺	postheat technique
焊后热处理加压时间	postheat(ing) pressure time
焊后热处理区	postheating zone
焊后热处理时间	postheat(ing) time
焊后退火	post annealing
焊后状态	as-welded (condition)
焊糊	paste flux
焊弧电压	welding arc voltage
焊弧间隙	arc space
焊机	welding machine [unit, outfit], welder, weldor ◇ 电(弧)~*, 顶压式~*, 多头~ multi-head welder, 蓄电池[电容器]式~*, 旋转式~ rotary welding machine, 整流器式~*
焊机启动控制装置	welder controls
焊机压力调节器	welding outfit pressure regulator
焊剂	(welding, soldering) flux, fluxing compound ◇ 粉状~ welding powder, 熔融~ fused melt
焊剂残渣(工件的)	flux residue
焊剂层下熔焊	submerged melt welding
焊剂处理温度	fluxing temperature
焊剂垫	welding cartridge
焊剂垫焊	welding with flux backing
焊剂粉	flux(ing) powder
焊剂回收装置	flux reclaiming device, flux recovery unit
焊剂芯(管状焊条的)	flux core
焊件	weldment
焊件间隔	welding gap
焊件间隙	joint clearance
焊件检查员	welding inspector
焊件接触面积	weld contact area
焊件设计	weldment design
焊脚(角焊缝的)	leg
焊角长度(角焊缝的)	leg length
焊接	welding, weld(ed) joint, soldering ◇ K形坡口 T形~ double-bevel T, X形坡口~*, 保护气氛室内~ dry-box welding, 不便位置上~ out-of-position welding, 不透水~的 water-proof welded, 磁场蓄能式~*, 底层~*, 地面~ floor welding, 电容贮能式~*, 短路过渡[电弧间接通]~*, 分支~ branch joint, 光[无药]焊条~ bare electrode welding, 海利亚克法~*, 恒压~*, 间歇式~ wood pecker welding, 可控气氛室中~*, 坑内~ bell hole welding, 链节式药皮包丝~ cover chain welding, 气电(联合)~ gas-arc welding, 强制成形~ enclosed welding, 全方位~*, 熔敷金属~ deposit welding, 手工~*, 受控金属过渡~*, 未~的 unwelded, 削平补强~ flush joint, 小电流[小熔透]~ cold running, 液动压~ hydrodynamic welding, 原子氢~*, 窄焊道~ beaded joint, 自耗电极~*
焊接白热	white welding heat
焊接算条	welded rod
焊接边	weld edge
焊接变流机[器]	welding converter ◇ 电机驱动~*
焊接变形	welding deformation [distorsion]
焊接变压器	welding transformer
焊接波纹管	welded bellow
焊接补强	weld reinforcement
焊接部位	weld area
焊接材料	weld(ing) material
焊接材料供应仓库	welding supply house
焊接残余应力	welding residual stress ◇ 十字形~试验 cruciform test
焊接侧	welding side
焊接测微计[焊件尺寸检验规]	welding micrometer
焊接车间	welding shop [plant, department]
焊接程序[工序]	welding procedure ◇ 平

衡~*
焊接程序表 welding procedure sheet (WPS)
焊接脆性 solder embrittlement
焊接衬垫 welding backing
焊接带 arc zone
焊接道次[次数] weld pass
焊接道次顺序(多层焊缝的) pass sequence
焊接地线 welding ground
焊接点 weld spot, welding [soldering] point
焊接垫板 backup
焊接电弧电压 welding-arc voltage
焊接电极 welding electrode
焊接电流 welding current
焊接电流调整范围 welding range
焊接电路 welding circuit
焊接电压 welding voltage
焊接电源 welding current supply, welding source [set] ◇ 恒电压[硬外特性]~*
焊接电源电压 welding load voltage
焊接段 welding zone
焊接断裂处 welded break
焊接断面 welding section
焊接发电机 welding generator ◇ 电枢反应~*, 多工位~*
焊接法 welding process [operation] ◇ 伯纳德~*, 对头~*, 阶梯形多层~ cascade process, 碳(极电)弧~ carbon-electrode process, 无间隙接头~ closed joint method, 有间隙~ open joint method
焊接法兰盘 welded flange
焊接方法 welding method
焊接防护镜 welding lens
焊接飞溅 weld spatter
焊接符号 welding symbol
焊接腐蚀 corrosion due to welding, weld decay
焊接钢 weld(able) [welding] steel
焊接钢管 welded steel pipe
焊接钢管桩 welded steel pipe pile
焊接钢结构 welded steel structure ◇ 大型~*
焊接钢筋网 weld steel fabric
焊接钢丝网 welded wire fabric
焊接膏 welding paste
焊接隔墙 welded-in partition
焊接工长 welding foreman
焊接工程 welding engineering [practice]
焊接工段检验员 welding inspector
焊接工艺 joint welding procedure, welding practice, bonding technology
焊接工艺参数 welding condition, welding parameter
焊接工艺[序]卡片 welding procedure sheet
焊接工艺图 welding procedure drawing
焊接管 (同"焊管")
焊接规范 welding code [conditions]
焊接规范参数 welding variables
焊接辊 welding rolls
焊接和切割两用烧嘴 (同"焊割两用烧嘴")
焊接合金 welding alloy ◇ 恩迪朗斯~ Endewrance alloy
焊接护目镜 welding goggles
焊接滑轮 welding wheel
焊接机 (同"焊机") ◇ 电子束~ electron-beam welder, 多弧~ multiple-arc unit, 钢丝网[线网, 金属筛]~*, 脚踏~*, 内燃机驱动~组*, 窄搭缝~ narrow lap welder
焊接级保护气体 welding-grade gas
焊接级[用]氦 welding-grade helium
焊接级[用]氩 welding-grade argon
焊接技术 welding technique ◇ T形钢~*
焊接剂 solder
焊接夹具 welding jig [fixture]
焊接夹钳 welding tangs
焊接加工 welding fabrication
焊接加压辊 welding pressure roll
焊接加压时间 weld pressure time

焊接间隔(时间)控制器　weld interval timer
焊接件　weldment, weld(ed) assembly
焊接溅渣　welding dribble
焊接接触面　weld interface
焊接接合面　welding side
焊接接头　weld(ed) joint [junction], welding joint
焊接接头晶间腐蚀　weld decay
焊接接头弯曲试验　welding bent test
焊接结构　welded structure [construction, assembly], weldment
焊接结构型钢　welded structural shape
焊接金属　weld(ed) metal
焊接颈法兰盘　welding neck flange
焊接力　welding force
焊接链　welded chain
焊接梁板　welded plate girder
焊接裂纹　welding crack(ing)
焊接裂纹敏感性　susceptity to weld crack
焊接面　face of weld
焊接面罩　welding [face] mask, face mask ◇ 手持~(welding) hand shield
焊接配件(焊管连接用)　welding fittings
焊接平台　jig
焊接坡口　welding groove
焊接起点　weld starting
焊接气氛　welding atmosphere
焊接前处理[加工]　preweld treatment
焊接前管坯成型机　tube-forming mill
焊接强度　weld strength
焊接轻量钢梁　welded light weigh beam
焊接区　welding zone
焊接区[熔池]保护　weld shielding
焊接缺陷　weld(ing) defect
焊接热　welding heat
焊接热输入　weld heat input
焊接热循环　weld thermal cycle, coelding thermal cycle
焊接热循环模拟装置　◇ 格利布耳~ Gleeble machine

焊接熔池　molten weld pool, weldpool, weld puddle
焊接熔敷金属　weld deposit metal
焊接熔剂　(同"焊剂")
焊接熔渣　welding cinder
焊接软管　welding hose
焊接筛条　welded rod
焊接设备[装置]　welding equipment [device, apparatus, outfit, set] ◇ 电动直流发电~*, 交直流两用~*
焊接设备变压器　welder transformer
焊接深度　depth of weld
焊接时间　weld(ing) time [period]
焊接时间间隔　weld interval
焊接时间率　arcing time factor
焊接式[焊接结构]钢包　ladle of welded construction
焊接试验　weld(ing) [bond] test ◇ 约束下~restrained weld test
焊接试样　welded specimen, welded test sample
焊接顺序　welding sequence
焊接顺序和规范　welding schedule
焊接速度　welding speed
焊接速率[生产率]　weld(ing) rate
焊接胎具　welding positioner
焊接台[室]　welding station
焊接特性　welding characteristic
焊接头　welding head
焊接凸轮　welding cam
焊接涂料　welding paste
焊接温度　welding temperature
焊接线　weld line
焊接效率[系数]　welding factor, welding coefficient
焊接性　weldability, weldableness, welding property
焊接性能　welding performance
焊接性(能)不良的　hard [difficult] to weld
焊接循环　weld(ing) cycle
焊接循环周期　welding period

| 焊han

焊接循环记录装置　cycle recorder
焊接压力机　welding press
焊接压力头　welding pressure head
焊接烟雾[气]　welding fume ◇ 少~锡铜焊条合金*
焊接焰　welding flame
焊接冶金(学)　weld(ing) metallurgy, welding consumables and metallurgy
焊接阴极　welded cathode
焊接应变　welding strain
焊接应力　welding stress ◇ 残余~residual welding stress
焊接用铝热剂　welding thermit
焊接用输电线　welding power lead
焊接用碳极　welding carbon
焊接预防措施　welding precaution
焊接整流器　welding rectifier
焊接质量　weld quality
焊接中的夹渣　slag inclusions in welds
焊接周期　weld(ing) cycle [period], weld(ing) (cycle) time
焊接准备　weld preparation
焊接姿势　welding position
焊接助熔剂　welding flux
焊接作业线　welding line
焊颈接头　weld neck connection
焊炬　(welding, blow) torch, (welding) blowpipe ◇ 等压式~balanced pressure torch, 电弧~arc torch, 惰性气体保护(电弧)~inert arc torch, 厚金属切割~heavy cutting torch, 手工~hand torch, 碳弧~carbon arc torch, 氩弧~argon arc torch
焊炬臂　torch arm
焊炬尺寸　torch size
焊炬点火器　torch lighter
焊炬横向摆动　weaving
焊炬火焰　torch flame
焊炬喷嘴[烧嘴]　torch [welding] tip, blow pipe head
焊炬(手)把[手柄]　torch [welding] handle, blow pipe handle

焊开　unsolder
焊口　crater ◇ 形成~cratering
焊料　solder, welding [soldering] flux ◇ 阿卢奈兹~*, 棒形[条状]~bar solder, 对半~*, 库珀铅基~*, 普拉提诺依德镍铜锌~*, 气焊~blow pipe solder, 枪式~槽 gun hopper, 塞弗特铝用~*, 苏珀洛依管装~合金*, 廷曼~合金*, 涂抹~pasting, 铸铁~合金 castolin
焊料黄铜　brazing brass
焊料熔化炉　plumber's furnace
焊料熔注钎焊　flow brazing
焊料细棒[条]　solder stick
焊瘤　burr, cold-laps, flash (管材对缝焊的) ◇ 去除~装置 deburring unit
焊瘤清除[修除]器　deseamer, flash trimmer
焊漏　through penetration
焊炉　soldering furnace, brazier
焊轮调节器　weld wheel conditioner
焊帽　weld cap
焊面　face of weld
焊钳　pinch welder gun, welding gun, electrode holder [adapter, wrench] ◇ 杠杆式~pincer gun, 手动~poke gun
焊前处理[加工]　preweld treatment
焊前清理　preweld cleaning
焊前预热时间　preweld interval
焊枪　welding gun [torch, blowpipe], torch tube ◇ 多焰~multiflame blowpipe, 杠杆式~lever gun, 焊嘴可换式~variable-head torch, 横振式~*, 喷射式~injector torch, 钳式~*, 携带式~portable welding gun, 液压~hydraulic welding gun, 乙炔~acetylene burber
焊枪联结螺母　torch head fitting
焊枪喷嘴　torch neck
焊枪式点焊机　gun welding machine
焊枪手柄　welding handle
焊枪套帽　torch head fitting
焊枪施焊焊点　push weld
焊丝　electrode [welding, soldering] wire

han 焊

◇ 补加～ additional wire, 填充～*, 自动焊接～*
焊丝导向装置 wire guide
焊丝进给[供给]机构 wire-feed mechanism
焊丝进给自动弧焊机 stick feeder (welding) machine
焊丝冷态送进 cold wire feed
焊丝送进[进给] wire feed (WF)
焊丝送进机 wire-feeding machine
焊态 as-welded
焊条 welding rod [stick], (welding) electrode (电焊条) ◇ 埃尔卡洛伊铜合金～ Elkaloy, 薄药皮～*, 带涂层～ covered filler rod, 粉芯～*, 高强度～*, 高纤维素型～*, 管状～*, 光[裸, 无药皮]～*, 焊药壳装～ flux encased electrode, 厚药皮～*, 碱性[低氢]～*, 绞合～[焊丝] strand electrode, 双层药皮～ double coated electrode, 涂药～*, 网状包丝药皮～ braided electrode, 压制～ pressed elec-trode, 有机物被覆[带有机物药皮]的 organic coated electrode, 铸铁用铜镍系～合金*
焊条残端[头] stub end, stub (-end) wastage
焊条导线 lead [electrode] cable
焊条钢丝 welding [electrode] wire
焊条工作端 welding tip
焊条焊着率 manipulation ratio
焊条横向摆动 weaving
焊条烘烤[干燥] baking of electrodes
焊条夹持机构 welding electrode assembly
焊条夹持器 electrode holder ◇ 悬挂式～*
焊条夹钳 bolster
焊条接触电弧焊 contact arc welding
焊条金属 welding base metal
焊条进给装置 rod feeder
焊条利用率 stub efficiency
焊条钎焊 electrode soldering
焊条[丝]熔化速率 wire burn-off rate
焊条容器 welding rod container
焊条送进 electrode feed
焊条送进机 (同"送丝机")
焊条头垂落时间 head lowering time
焊条头抬起时间 head lift time
焊条涂层相对重量 flux/wire ratio
焊条涂药 electrode compound
焊条外伸长度 stick-out distance
焊条往复移动 flagging
焊条芯 electrode core, core wire, filler rod
焊条芯矫直机 core wire straightening machine
焊条压涂机 welding rod extrusion press
焊条药皮 electrode coating
焊铁 (pointed) soldering iron
焊铜 bit copper
焊头 welding head ◇ 自备能源～*
焊透 penetration ◇ 完全～ good penetration
焊透侧 penetration side
焊透连接 joint penetration
焊透率 penetration rate
焊纹面 rippled surface
焊锡 (tin) solder, soldering tin ◇ 纯～*, 普龙布索尔～*
焊锡粉 solder powder
焊芯 core welding-wire
焊芯直径 core diameter, electrode size
焊须 warts
焊盐 soldering salt
焊眼 welded eye
焊药 solder, soldering paste, welding agent [compound], fluxing agent [com-pound] ◇ 阿卢奈兹～*, 镉～*, 气焊～ blow pipe solder, 廷史密斯～*, 铜锌～*, 涂抹～ pasting
焊药垫 bed of flux, melt backing
焊药[锡]膏 solder paint
焊药壳装焊条 flux encased electrode
焊液 welding [soldering] fluid
焊引弧板 tab weld
焊油 soldering paste

焊渣　welding slag
焊渣清理　slag cleaning
焊珠　bead, weld(ing) deposit
焊珠清理机　bead scarfer
焊住　soldering up
焊着金属　weld(ing) deposit, all-weld metal
焊着效率　deposition efficiency
焊嘴　tip
焊嘴尺寸(氧焊机的)　tip size
焊嘴可换式焊枪　variable-head torch
汗珠(铸件表面的)　sweat ball
汉弗莱浸蚀剂　Humphrey's reagent
汉明码　Hamming code
汉斯加格碳热还原炼镁法　Hansgirg process
汉字发生器　chinese character generator
汉字形共晶体　chinese script eutectic
夯　rammer, tamper, pummel ◇ 风动～air tamper
夯具　compactor, tamper ◇ 手工～bishop
夯实　tamp, ramming, breaking in, bettle ◇ 分层填土～*, 人工～的 hand tamped, 素土～packed soil, 未～土吸水能力*
夯实度　【铸】degree of ramming
夯实回填土　tamped [compacted] back fill
夯实机　beater, puddler ◇ 凸轮～cam-ram machine
夯实黏土　puddle
夯实黏土层　bed puddle clay
夯实器　tramper ◇ 混凝土～concrete rammer
夯实土基　rammed soil type of foundation
夯实造型机　ramming molding machine
夯土机　earth rammer
夯土建筑　beaten cob construction
行　line, row ◇ 终［结束, END］～End line
行(编)号　line number
行会　gild
行距　array [row] pitch

行列　ranks
行情(表)　quotation
行式打印装置　line printer
行式数据集　line data set
行业　trade, profession, industry
航海和渔业用钢丝绳　wire rope shipping and fishery
航空材料　air material (AM), aeronautical material
航空材料技术条件　aeronautical material specification (AMS)
航空测量　aerial survey(ing)
航空测图　aerial mapping
航空灯塔　aerial light house, beacon
航空发动机　aircraft engine, aeromotor
航空钢丝　aircraft cord wire
航空钢丝绳　aircraft cable [cord], aircraft wire rope
航空航天　aerospace
航空合金　aerometal
航空铝合金(0.2—4Cu, 0.3—1.3Fe, 0—0.2Mn, 0—3Mg, 0—3Zn, 0.1—1Si)　aerometal
航空器　(air)craft
航空青铜(4.5Al, 4.5Ni, 0.2Ti, 1.0Zn, 余量Cu)　aero-bronze
航空摄影　aerial photography
航空细钢丝绳　aircraft cord
航空线　airline
航空用高强度钢　magnaflux steel
航空(用)金属　aerial metal
航空用耐热铸造铝合金　◇ 伯马斯蒂克～*
航空用优质钢　aircraft quality steel
航空用铸造铝合金　◇ 伯马西尔～*
航空站　spaceport, space station, depot
航天电源系统　space power system
航天电子设备　space electronics
航天飞机　(space) shuttle
航天工程技术　space technology
航天技术　space technique
航天金属　space metal

航天器 spacecraft, space vehicle
航天时代 space age
航天时代材料 space age material
航天速度 space velocity
航线(航空的) airline
航行 navigate by air, navigate by water, logging
航运包装 seaworthy packing
豪斯纳高频镀铬法 Hausner process
豪斯纳系数(密度比) Hausner ratio (TD/AD)
豪泽尔铅铋镉易熔合金(50Pb,33.3Bi,余量 Cd) Hauser's alloy
毫(10^{-3}) m (milli-)
毫安(培) mill ampere, milliampere (mA)
毫安表[计] milliammeter
好气(杆)菌 aerobacter aerogenes
好气菌 aerobic bacteria
耗电(量) (electrical) power consumption, power expenditure
耗费 consumption
耗费时间的 time-killing
耗风量 rate of blowing, blast consumption
耗碱量 alkali consumption
耗竭 exhaustion ◇ 弗兰克-里德源~*, 资源~的补偿 depletion allowance
耗竭蠕变理论 theory of exhaustion creep
耗尽 depletion, exhaustion
耗尽层 depletion layer
耗尽层半导体 depleting-layer semiconductor
耗尽型 depletion mode
耗尽型曲线 depletion-type curve
耗能元件 absorption cell
耗热量 heat consumption ◇ 工业~*
耗散材料 dissipative material
耗散力 dispersion force
耗散能量材料 dissipative material
耗时的 time-consuming
耗水量 water consumption
耗水率 water rate
耗酸矿物 acid-consuming mineral
耗酸组分 acid-consuming constituent
耗损 consumption, expenditure, detrition
耗碳系数 carbon factor
耗铁细菌 iron-consuming becteria
耗渣量 slag input
号码 number (No.) ◇ 回转~机 annunciator
号码装订 【计】identification
号外钢 off-grade metal
号外炉次 【钢】off-heat, off-grade
号外铁 off(-grade) [off-analysis, ungraded] iron ◇ 高硫~ off-sulphur iron
皓矾 {$ZnSO_4 \cdot 7H_2O$} goslarite, zinc sulphate [vitriol]
核 core, kernel,【理】nucleus (复数 nuclei) ◇ 有~的 nuclear
核半径(原子的) nuclear radius
核胞沸腾 nucleate boiling
核爆炸 nuclear blasting
核磁共振 nuclear magnetic resonance (NMR) ◇ 非接触式~法*
核磁共振带 NMR band
核磁共振谱分辨率 NMR spectral resolution
核磁共振谱学 NMR spectroscopy
核磁共振摄谱仪 NMR spectrometer ◇ 高分辨率~*
核磁共振射频磁场 NMR radiofrequency field
核磁体 nucleus magnet
核磁子 nuclear [proton] magneton
核电站[核动力发电厂] nuclear power station [plant]
核定投资额 capitalized cost
核定投资总额 capitalized total cost
核堆 nuclear pile
核对 check(ing), verification, verify, identification
核对卡 identification card
核对器 verifier, checker
核对取样 check sampling
核对试验 check test

核对样品　check sample
核对员　verifier
核反应　nuclear [nucleus] reaction
核反应堆　nuclear reactor [pile], atomic pile [furnace, reactor]
核反应堆材料　nuclear reactor material
核反应堆压力容器　nuclear reactor pressure vessel
核反应堆用陶瓷　nuclear reactor ceramics
核范围　atomic field
核沸腾　nuclear boiling
核分裂　nuclear fission [division]
核分析仪　nuclear analyzer
核辐射屏蔽　nuclear shielding
核工艺学　nuclear technology, atomics
核化　nucleation, coring ◇ 凝固金属～*
核化催化剂　nucleation catalyst
核化[晶]浸出(高压优先还原法)　nucleation leach
核化学　nuclear chemistry
核化学方法　chemonuclear method
核化组织　cored structure
核化最后溶液　nucleation end solution
核间距　nuclear spacing [separation]
核截[断]面　nuclear cross section
核晶还原(高压优先还原法)　nucleation reduction
核-壳结构　core-shell structure
核矩　nuclear moment
核聚变　nuclear fusion ◇ 受控～*
核科技范围　atomic field
核力　nuclear force
核裂变　nuclear fission
核磷(酸)铝石{2AlPO_4·4Al(OH)_3·12H_2O}　evansite
核能　nuclear [atomic] energy
核能工程　nuclear engineering
核能金属　nuclear energy metal
核平衡间距　equilibrium internuclear distance
核燃料　nuclear [atomic, fission, reactor] fuel, fuel material ◇ 板状～ plate-type fuel, 棒状～ slug type fuel, 电解溶解的～ dissolving fuel, 废[用过的]～ depleted material, 含～的单位格子 fuel cell, 陶瓷～ceramic fuel, 增殖性[可裂变]～*
核燃料棒束　cluster of nuclear fuel rods
核燃料级品位　fuel grade
核燃料阳极　fuel anode
核燃料氧化物　nuclear fuel oxide
核燃料元件　(nuclear) fuel element ◇ 废～spent fuel element
核乳胶　nuclear emulsion
核嬗变　(nuclear) transmutation
核实　check, nuclear frame
核素　nuclein, nuclide
核算　checking calculation, calculating, business accounting, rechoning ◇ 操作费用～*
核桃焦　coke nuts
核外电子　extranuclear electron
核物理(学)　nuclear [atomic] physics
核吸收　nuclear absorption
核心　core, heart, kernel, center, centre, nucleus,【理】nucleation centre, nuclear centre（结晶的）
核心程序　nucleus, kernel programe
核心态　【计】kernel mode
核心硬件　hardcore
核心组织　core structure
核冶金(学)　nuclear metallurgy
核质量　nuclear mass
核转变　event
核子　nucleon ◇ 非接触式～法*, 焦炭水分～测定仪*
核子爆炸挖土(法)　nuclear excavation
核子间距离　internuclear distance
核子学　nucleonics
和声学　harmonics
和数校验　sum check
和数校验位　sum check digit
和应反应　sympathetic reaction
合板　jointing, package（叠轧时的）
合并　merge, combine, coalesce, incorpora-

tion

合成 synthesis, synthetize, composition, compound, combination, resultant
合成氨气 ammonia synthesis gas
合成保护渣 synthetic shielding slag
合成冰晶石 synthetic cryolite
合成地址 generated address
合成芳烃油溶剂 ◇阿姆斯科~Amsco G
合成刚玉 synthetic corundum
合成钢 synthetic steel
合成拱 compound arch
合成硅酸铝钠 synthetic sodium aluminium silicate
合成金云母 synthetic phlogopite
合成晶体 synthetic crystal
合成绝缘带 synthetic insulating tape
合成力 composite force
合成镁砂 synthetic magnesite
合成镁质白云石砂 synthetic magnesite dolomite clinker
合成莫来石砂 synthetic mullite clinker
合成气体 synthesis [synthetic] gas
合成区 composite zone
合成热塑树脂 synthetic thermoplastic resin
合成熔剂 synthetic flux
合成溶液 synthetic solution
合成赛隆材料 synthetic sialon
合成石蜡 synthetic wax
合成试剂 synthetic reagent
合成树脂 synthetic resin
合成树脂胶泥 synthetic resin cement
合成树脂黏结剂 synthetic resin adhesive, araldite
合成树脂黏结铁氧钴磁铁 ◇卡斯罗克斯~*
合成树脂涂料 keratex paint
合成树脂轴承 synthetic resin bearing
合成物 synthetic, composition, compound
合成误差 composite error
合成洗涤[去垢]剂 synthetic detergent
合成纤维 synthetic fibre ◇绝缘用~板 pressboard
合成纤维隔膜 synthetic-fibre diaphragm
合成纤维绳芯 synthetic fibre core
合成橡胶 synthetic rubber, elastomer
合成型砂 synthetic moulding sand
合成絮凝剂 synthetic flocculating agent
合成阳离子交换剂 synthetic cation exchanger
合成氧化铝 Borolon
合成氧化物 synthetic oxide
合成云母 synthetic mica
合成渣 synthetic flux
合成渣浇注 【连铸】synthetic casting
合成脂肪酸酯 Acrawax
合成铸铁 synthetic cast iron
合成铸铁合金(含15—21Ti) synthetic cast-iron alloy
合尺寸废钢[铁] sized scrap
合钉 dowel
合格 qualified, acceptable, on-size
合格板 on-gauge plate
合格标志 mark of conformity
合格表皮层 sound skin
合格产品目录 qualified products list (QPL)
合格程度 soundness
合格废钢铁 specification scrap
合格钢材 qualified steel
合格故障率 acceptable failure rate
合格矿 shipping ore
合格粒度 target size, on-size
合格粒度范围 target size range
合格率 percent of pass, roundness, soundness
合格品 qualified product, non-defective, on-size
合格球团 specification [on-size] pellet
合格认证 conformity certification
合格溶液槽 OK liquor tank
合格烧结矿 acceptable [bell] sinter
合格生球 on-size ball

合 he

合格试验　qualification test
合格数　acceptance munber
合格水　quality water
合格证书　certificate
合格质量标准　acceptable quality level (AQL)
合格铸件　sound casting
合股　【压】stranding
合股钢丝绳　stranded rope
合股机　stranding [bunching, twinning] machine, strander, buncher
合好的砂型　closed sand mould
合乎标准的　proof
合伙经营收入　partnership income
合计　total, amount to, summation
合金　alloy, compound metal, rafting, alligation ◇ R 蒙乃尔～*, α 相～ alpha alloy, β 相～ beta phase alloy, γ 相～ gamma phase alloy, 巴萨洛伊安全系统～*, 不能成～的金属 nonalloyable metal, 敞熔 [空气中熔炼的]～ air-melted alloy, 带有溶质原子聚集区的[具有 G-P 区的]～ clustered alloy, G-P zone alloy, 低～ dilute alloy, 杜拉帕姆～*, 杜美～丝*, 镀～*, 多元[复杂]～ complex alloy, 福林～*, 高合金（比）～ concentrated alloy, 海德罗～*, 减[抗]摩～*, 有沉淀物～ alloy with precipitations, 科尔莫诺伊～*, 科瓦～*, 可成～的 alloyable, 扩散烧结～*, 尼瓦洛克斯～ Nivarox, 配～*, 坡莫～ permalloy, 全 α-相～*, 时效～*, 坦德姆～*, 特种化学性能～*, 通用～ general-purpose alloy, 涡流式～分检仪*, 无偏析～ nonsegregation alloy, 无序～ disordered alloy, 形成～ alloy building, 易切削～ free machining alloy, 宇航～ aerospace alloy, 再熔～ secondary alloy
合金奥氏体　alloy(ed) austenite
合金板(材)　sheet alloy ◇ 雕刻用～*
合金薄板　latten
合金槽（电解淀积用）　alloy bath
合金层　alloy layer

合金成分　alloy composition, component metal
合金成分偏析　alloy segregation
合金处理　alloy treatment
合金带打印机　alloy belt printer
合金的交滑移受阻　cross slip hindering in alloy
合金镀层　alloy coating [plating]
合金法　alloyage
合金废料　alloy scrap
合金分解　decomposition of alloy
合金分析　alloy analysis
合金粉(末)　alloy powder [dust, filings], powdered alloy ◇ 电解～*, 金属上包覆陶瓷时黏接用～ metallizer, 铁镍[坡莫]～ permalloy powder, 维塔～ Vitallium powder
合金粉坯　【粉】alloy powder compact ◇ 扩散烧结的～*, 热压～*
合金钢　alloy(-treated) steel, steel alloy ◇ CA-FA20 耐蚀～*, 奥氏体～ austenitic alloy steel, 淬硬～ quench alloy steel, 杜罗伊德～(表面堆焊材料) Duroid, 多元～ complex alloy steel, 二元～*, 哈尔科姆～*, 三元～ ternary steet, 烧结～ sintered alloy steel, 时效硬化～*, 无偏析～*, 无碳～ carbon-free alloy steel, 凿具用～ alloy chisel steel
合金钢比　alloy steel ratio
合金钢车间　alloyed-steel department
合金钢粉(末)　alloy-steel powder, powdered alloy steel
合金钢管　alloy-steel tube
合金钢和碳钢混合浇铸法　Stroh steel hardening process
合金钢级别　alloy-steel class
合金钢轧辊　alloy(ed) steel roll
合金钢种类　alloy-steel class
合金钢铸件　alloy-steel casting
合金工具钢　alloy(ed) tool steel
合金汞齐　alloy amalgam
合金焊条　alloy electrode

合金化 alloying, alloyage, alloy building ◇ 金属不恰当～*, 局部～localized alloying, 扩散～diffusion alloying, 完全～粉末*, 直接～direct alloying
合金化处理 alloying
合金化粉末 alloying powder
合金化金属 alloying metal
合金化时间 alloying time
合金化效应[作用] alloying effect
合金级铌(Nb+Ta>95) alloy grade niobium
合金剂 alloying agent ◇韦伯特炼钢～*
合金加成剂 alloy(ing) addition
合金浇合铸造 reinforcement of alloy
合金结 【半】alloy-junction (AJ), alloy(ed) junction ◇脉冲～pulse alloyed junction
合金结构钢 structural [constructional] alloy steel
合金金属 alloying metal
合金近程序破坏 destruction of short-range order in alloy
合金精整[修整] alloy dressing
合金精整场地[工段] alloy-dressing floor
合金块 alloy biscuit
合金扩散技术 alloy diffusion technique
合金料堆放处 alloy storage area
合金料筐 alloying basket
合金料消耗 (specific) alloy additive consumption
合金炉管 alloy furnace tube
合金马弗炉膛 alloy muffle
合金马氏体 alloy martensite
合金名称 alloy nomenclature
合金热力学 thermodynamics of alloy
合金齐纳结 alloy zener junction
合金氢含量测定仪 ◇兰斯莱～Ransley apparatus
合金生铁 alloy iron [pig]
合金时效 alloy ageing
合金术 alliage

合金碎裂[风化] alloy disintegration
合金天平 alloy balance
合金添加剂 alloy additive, alloy(ing) addition, alloying agent, 【钢】(最终的) finishings, finishing additions
合金脱氧剂 reduction alloy
合金系 alloy system
合金系富铁角[区] iron-rich corner of system
合金相 alloy [internal] phase
合金相能带理论 zone theory of alloy phases
合金相平衡图 alloy phase equilibrium diagram
合金屑 alloy filings
合金型晶体管 alloy type transistor
合金形状记忆效应 shape memory effect in alloy
合金硬化 alloy hardening
合金硬[强]化剂 alloy hardener
合金有序化 alloy ordering
合金有序－无序转变 order-disorder change in alloy
合金元素 alloying element [metal] ◇加～alloyage, 形成碳化物的～stabi-lizer
合金元素转移效率 alloy transfer efficiency
合金杂质 alloy contamination
合金再生长结 alloy-regrowth junction
合金整流器[管] alloyed rectifier
合金中间物 alloy-intermediate
合金铸钢 alloy cast steel
合金铸铁 alloy cast iron, cast alloy iron, cast iron alloy ◇考萨尔耐蚀～Causal metal
合金铸铁件 alloy iron casting
合金铸铁轧辊 alloy iron roll ◇麻口细晶粒～*
合金铸造[铸件] alloy casting
合金铸造研究所(美国) Alloy Casting Institute (ACI)
合金组成 alloying constituent [ingredi-

ent]. constitution of alloy
合金组织 alloy structure
合晶 (同"聚晶")
合理半径(弯曲半径) reasonable radius
合理经济规模 rational production scale
合理磨蚀速率 rationalized erosion rate
合理性 rationality
合理性检查 reasonableness check
合理轧制制度 rational rolling schedule
合力 composite [compound] force, resultant (of force)
合力场 resultant field
合力矩 resulting moment
合量磁场 resultant magnetic field
合拢 healing up
合模错位 misalignment of dies
合批 【粉】blending
合批粉 blended powder
合上开关 switch on
合绳机 (crank) closer, closing [laying-up] machine ◇ 筐篮式~·, 雪茄式[管式]~ tubular type closer
合绳机工字轮 closer [laying-up] reel
合适的 suitable, appropriate, fitting
合同 contract, agreement, stipulation ◇ 统包式[启钥,监督]~ turn-key con-tract
合同报价价格 quoted contract price
合同工厂 contract plant
合同终止 termination of contract
合箱 fastening down,【铸】(mould) closing, mould assembling
合箱夹具 mould closer
合型[箱] (mould) closing
合型定位销(砂箱的) closing pin
合型缸 closing cylinder
合型柱塞 closing plunger
合页盖 hinged cover
合营企业[合资] joint venture
合闸 switch on [in], occlude
合闸电流 inrush current
合闸继电器 closing relay
合闸率 time-on in percent

合闸线圈 closing coil
合铸的 cast-on
合资公司 joint venture
合作散射 cooperative scattering
合作现象 cooperative phenomenon
合作制造 split manufacturing
合作作用 cooperative action
盒 box, case, cell, chamber, container, chest, enclosure, packet
盒式磁带 cassette (tape), (tape) cartridge
盒式磁盘 cartridge (disk), cassette cartridge
盒式密封 cassette seal
盒形保险丝 box fuse
河边矿 kobeite
河槽整治工程 channel regulation works
河成层 river deposit
河川图像[河流状图](金属脆断显微组织的) river pattern
河道缓变平衡 regime
河底等高线 depth contours
河分流 diversion of river
河砾(石) river gravel
河(流) river ◇ 含泥砂的 ~ burdened stream
河流沉积 river deposit
河流冲积层 burden of river drift
河流改向[改道] diversion of river
河流挟砂 burden of river drift
河流学 fluviology, rheology
河流状花纹(断口的) river
河砂 river [fluvial] sand
河态[性] regime
荷兰白色钎焊料[白镴合金](81Sn, 10Cu, 9Sb) Dutch pewter, Dutch white metal
荷兰金漆 Dutch gilding
荷兰式砌合 Dutch bond
荷兰(饰)金[荷兰黄铜](含 12—20Zn 的黄铜箔) Dutch metal (gold)
荷特－德里菲尔乳剂校准曲线 (同"密度曝光曲线")

荷载 load ◇ 初现裂缝~ load at first crack,带~的 on load,渐加~ gradually applied load,圆周切向线~*
荷载幅度 load range
荷载-挠度曲线 load-deflection curve
荷载循环 cycle of loads
荷载-应变曲线 load-strain curve
荷载作用点 load point
荷重 loading
荷重能力 loading capacity
荷重软化试验 load test
荷重软化温度[荷重软化点,荷重下耐火度] refractoriness under load (R.U.L.), softening point under load ◇ 最后~*
荷重损坏 load failure
赫伯特摆式[赫氏]硬度 Herbert pendulum hardness
赫伯特摆式硬度试验机 Herbert pendulum hardness tester
赫伯特喷丸试验 Herbert cloud burst test
赫茨应力区 Hertzian field of stress
赫蒂炉渣黏度计 Herty viscosimeter
赫尔-戴维晶格指数表 Hull-Davey charts
赫尔电池 Hull cell
赫尔法（X射线晶体分析法） Hull method
赫尔克莱特钢化玻璃 Herculite
赫尔克里士钢丝绳 Hercules wire rope
赫尔克里士铝黄铜(61Cu,37.5Zn,1.5Al) Hercules (metal)
赫尔克里士耐蚀青铜 (2.5Al, 2Zn, 85.5Cu, 10Sn) Hercules bronze
赫尔克洛伊耐蚀铜硅合金(96—98Cu, 1.75—3Si, 0.25—1Mn) Herculoy
赫加纳克斯制铁粉法 Hoeganacs process
赫克努姆铜镍电阻合金(55Cu,45Ni) Hecnum
赫肯哈姆铜镍电阻合金(56Cu,44Ni) Heckenham
赫劳尔特电弧炉 Heroult (electric) arc furnace
赫劳尔特电解炼铝法 Heroult process
赫硫镍矿 heazlewoodite
赫伦施米特直井焙烧炉（低品位硫化锑矿用） Herrenschmidt furnace
赫洛特锡铅锑轴承合金 Hulot's alloy
赫曼钢丝热镀锌法 Herman process
赫曼-摩干符号 Hermann-Mauguin's symbol
赫姆斯高速锻造机 Clearing Hermes
赫施低温还原粉化率测定法 Heosch method
赫施双联炼钢法 Hoesch process
赫氏圆盘充气混砂机 【铸】Herbert's duplex sand mixer
赫氏窄轴式多膛焙烧炉 Herreshoff furnace [roaster]
赫氏直接还原炉 Herreshof furnace
赫斯定律（化学反应热计算有关） Hess's law
赫斯加费尔铁矿石竖炉低温直接还原法 Husgafvel's process
赫斯曼锡基轴承合金(11Sb, 4.5Cu, 10Pb, 0.4Zn, 余量Sn) Husman's metal
褐赤铁矿 brown hematite
褐硅钠钛矿 {$Na_2Ti_2Si_2O_9$} ramsayite
褐硅铈矿 {$Na_3Ca_8Ce_2(F,OH)_7(SiO_3)_9$} mosandrite
褐金贵重合金(Au:Cu=5:1) brown gold
褐帘石 orthite, allanite, cerepidote
褐硫锰矿 hauerite
褐硫砷铅矿 baumauerite
褐硫铁铜矿 mooithoekite
褐氯汞矿 eglestonite, egrestonite
褐绿泥石 {$MgO·Fe_2O_3·3SiO_2·4H_2O$} iddingsite, chlorophaeite
褐煤 lignite (coal), brown [hydrogeneous, wood] coal ◇ 含铀~ uraniferous lignite
褐煤焦油 lignite tar oil
褐锰矿 {$3Mn_2O_3·MnSiO_3$} braunite, brachytypous manganese ore

褐钕铌矿　fergusonite-(Nb)
褐色黄铜(85Cu,15Zn)　brown metal
褐色氧化处理(钢表面的)　browning
褐色氧化钨　brown tungsten oxide
褐砂岩　brownstone
褐砷铁矿　kerstenine
褐铈铌矿　fergusonite-(Ce)
褐铊矿　(同"铁铊矿")
褐钛石　fulvite
褐炭　hydrogeneous coal
褐锑　black antimony
褐铁矾　castanite,hohmannite
褐铁华　yellow [brown] ocher
褐铁矿{$2Fe_2O_3 \cdot 3H_2O$}　brown (iron) ore,brown ironstone,bog (iron) ore,anhydroferrite, meadow [marsh, morass, swamp] ore ◇ 巴西~chapinha,黏土质[泥质]~(brown) clay iron ore,萨尔茨吉特鱼子状~(德国) Salzgitter ore
褐稀土矿　caryocerite,karyocerite
褐锌锰矿　hodgkinsonite
褐铀钍矿　jiningite
褐钇铌矿{$(Y,Er,Ce,Sc,U,Th)(Nb,Ta)O_4$}　fergusonite
褐钇钽矿{$RE,Ca,Fe,U)(Ta,Nb)O_4$} bragite
鹤嘴锄　pick hammer,hack iron
黑暗适应性　dark adaptation, darkness adaption
黑白群　【金】black white groups
黑白鲜明图像　hard image
黑白云石粉　black dolomite powder
黑斑　carbon stain,black dot (显微镜下金属缺陷),blackening scab (由涂料引起的)
黑斑点　black smudge,black patches (板、带材的)
黑板用搪瓷　blackboard enamel
黑薄板[黑钢板](镀锡用)　black sheet [plate, iron], black tin steel, iron black sheet ◇ 精轧~*,冷轧~*,连续退火~*,退火~annealed sheet iron

黑边　black edge
黑边钢板　black edged plate, smoky-edged plate
黑玻璃紫外灯　black glass ultraviolet lamp
黑辰砂　(同"黑硫化汞")
黑辰砂矿　metacinnabarite
黑赤铁矿　black hematite
黑脆(性)的　black short
黑带钢　black strip
黑点　black spot (锡层表面的),black dot (显微镜下金属缺陷)
黑镀　black plating
黑度　blackness ◇ 火焰~flame emissivity
黑度测量　blackening measurement
黑度差(X 射线的)　density difference
黑度曲线　blackening curve,densograph
黑钒矿　montroseite
黑辐射强度　blackbody intensity
黑复铝钛石　hibonite
黑富铀矿　nivenite
黑钙土　black earth,chernozem
黑刚玉　black corundum
黑钢棒　black bars
黑钢丝　black (drawn) wire
黑钢丝绳　black wire rope
黑高岭土{$Fe_2O_3 \cdot MgO \cdot FeO \cdot SiO_2 \cdot H_2O$} hisingerite
黑格－罗伯逊腐蚀疲劳试验机　Haigh-Robertson machine
黑格定律　【金】Haegg's law
黑格碳化铁{$Fe_{20}C_9$}　Haegg (iron) carbide
黑格型疲劳试验机　Haigh machine
黑光灯　black glass ultraviolet lamp, black light lamp
"黑盒子"　【计】black box
黑褐煤　black lignite [coal]
黑化(处理)(不锈钢的)　blackening
黑灰　black ash
黑火焰温度　blackbody flame temperature
黑火药　black powder
黑(加)热　black heat

黑胶布带	black (friction) tape
黑金刚石	black diamond, carbonado
黑精整(表面的)	black finish
黑沥青	abbertite, albertite
黑料结疤	blacking scab
黑硫化汞{HgS}	black mercuric sulphide
黑铝钙石	hibonite
黑铝镁铁矿	hoegbomite
黑氏体	(同"回火马氏体")
黑煤	black coal
黑镁铁锰矿	jacobsite
黑镁铁钛矿	kennedyite
黑锰矿{Mn$_3$O$_4$}	black manganese, hausmannite
黑钼钴矿{CoMoO$_4$}	pateraite
黑钼铀矿	moluranite
黑泥(汞生产的)	black mud
黑皮	casting skin
黑铅粉(石墨粉)	black lead
黑铅铜矿	murdochite
黑铅铀矿{UO$_3$·2H$_2$O+PbO}	richetite
黑色断口	black fracture ◇ 有~的 black short
黑色封层(沥青路面的)	black seal
黑色金刚石	carbonado
黑色金属	ferrous metal
黑色金属材料	ferrous material
黑色金属废料	iron and steel scrap ◇ 可利用的~ ferrous salvage
黑色金属合金	ferrous alloy
黑色金属矿床	ferrous metal deposit
黑色金属冶金	ferrous metallurgy
黑色金属铸件	ferrous casting
黑色铝热剂	black thermit
黑色铅	black-lead
黑色氢氧化镍	black nickel hydroxide
黑色清漆	black varnish
黑色碎石	coated macadam
黑色退火	black annealing
黑色氧化物	black oxide
黑色冶金工业	ferrous (metal) industry
黑色冶金原理	principle of ferrous metallurgy
黑色冶金学	ferrous metallurgy
黑砂	【铸】black [old] sand
黑蛇纹石	black serpentine
黑石碳酸	black carbolic acid
黑水晶	morion
黑酸洗	black pickling
黑钛石	anosvite
黑钛铁钠矿	freudenbergite
黑钛铀矿	djalmaite
黑体	blackbody
黑体辐射	blackbody radiation
黑体辐射温度	blackbody radiating temperature
黑体辐射系数	blackbody coefficient
黑铁涵管	black culvert
黑铁矿{Fe$_3$O$_4$}	black iron ore, magnetic (iron) ore
黑铜	black copper
黑铜矿{CuO}	tenorite
黑铜熔炼(氧化铜矿石还原熔炼)	black copper smelting
黑涂料	【铸】blacking wash
黑土	black earth
黑退火	black [open, scaled] annealing, blue annealing (热轧钢板的)
黑退火的	black softened (指不锈钢)
黑退火钢丝	black annealed wire
黑钨矿{(Fe, Mn)WO$_4$}	wolframite, megabasite
黑钨矿氯化	chlorination of wolframite
黑锡(黑色锡石)	black tin
黑稀金矿{(Y, Ca, Ce, U, Th)(Nb, Ta, Ti)$_2$O$_6$}	euxenite
黑稀土矿	melanocerite
黑线	black line
黑锌锰矿{(Mn, Zn)O·2MnO$_2$·2H$_2$O}	chalcophanite
黑心(缺陷)	【耐】black core, blackheart
黑心可锻化[韧化]处理	black heart process
黑心可锻铸铁	black heart [cored] mal-

leable (cast) iron, American malleable (cast) iron
黑心可锻铸铁件 black heart malleable casting
黑心铸铁 blackheart
黑氧化物覆层 black oxide coating
黑曜岩 obsidian
黑银矿{Ag_5SbS_4} black silver
黑铀矿 uranotemnite
黑铀钍矿{$UO_2·3ThO_2·3SiO_2·3H_2O$} mackintoshite
黑铀钇铌矿 klopinite
黑云母{$H_4K_2(Mg,Fe)_6Al_2Si_6O_{24}, K(Mg,Fe)_3(Si_3Al)O_{10}(OH)_2$} black mica, biotite
黑渣 black slag
黑𨭎{Hs} hassium
痕迹 trace (tr.), track
痕迹含量 trace content
痕量 trace (amount)
痕量分析 trace analysis
痕量级 trace level
痕量金属 trace of metal
痕量浓度 trace concentration
痕量元素 trace [minor] element
痕量[迹]杂质 trace impurity, trace of impurity
痕量组分 trace component
哼鸣电压 hum voltage
亨利定律 Henry's law
亨利定律常数 Henry's law constant
亨利活度系数 Henrian activity coefficient
亨利计 henry [inductance] meter
亨利特性 Henrian behavio(u)r
亨利效应 Henrian effect [behavio(u)r]
亨特板材连续铸锭轧制法 Hunter process
亨特真空还原钛精炼法 Hunter process
珩磨 honing ◇ **气喷磨料~** vapour honing
桁腹 【建】belly
桁架 truss (frame), framing, girder ◇ A 形~ A-truss, 吊车~ crane girder, 钢格构~ steel lattice truss, 空腹~ vierendeel truss, 拼接~ joggle truss, 三铰构架式~ barn truss, 上承~ deck truss, 梯形~ parallel chord truse, 月牙~ crescent truss
桁架分析 analysis of truss
桁架腹杆构件 webbing
桁架腹杆体系 cancellation
桁架腹系 network
桁架拱度 camber of truss
桁架跨度 truss span
桁架梁 girder truss, truss(ed) beam
桁架形拱 (spandrel) braced arch
桁条 joist, stringer
桁弦 chord
横臂 cross arm, top bridge
横臂结晶器[连结模] (同"横梁结晶器")
横波 transverse wave
横波探测器[探头] transverse wave probe
横撑 cross strut, bunton
横穿通行 T-crossing
横带【铸】cleat
横挡 cross strut
横的 lateral (lat.), transversal
横动缸 traversing cylinder
横动装置 traversing gear
横度 bilge
横断 intersect(ion), traverse
横断面 cross-section (CS, c.s.), transverse section
横断面积 area of (cross) section
横断面图 cross-sectional drawing [view]
横断面硬度 cross-sectional hardness
横断强度 (同"横向断裂强度")
横缝 cross [transverse] joint
横缝滚焊 transverse seam welding
横杆 cross bar, bunton
横管冷凝器 horizontal tube condenser
横管冷却器 horizontal water-tube cooler
横贯炉组的焦炉机械连锁系统 crossbattery interlocking system (CBI)

横过　traverse
横焊　horizontal position welding
横焊缝　horizontal weld
横焊缝滚焊机　transverse seam welder
横-立焊位置　horizontal-vertical welding position
横挤压　lateral [cross] extrusion
横剪刀片　squaring shears
横剪机　crosscut shears ◇ 液压～*
横剪机组　crosscut shear(ing) line
横剪作业线(带材的)　cut-up line ◇ 带材～*, 带卷(定尺)～coil cut-up line, 冷轧带钢～*
横浇道　【铸】cross gate
横浇口　【铸】cross [runner] gate, gate runner ◇ 补缩～runner riser
横浇口延伸端　runner extension
横截的　transverse
横截面　cross section (c.s.), crosscut, lateral section
横截面积　sectional area
横截面形状　cross-section shape
横锯　crosscut saw
横坑
横跨梁　drifting
横连杆　cross tranversing
横连杆　cross link
横连接　cross linkage [linking]
横梁　crossbeam, cross girder [member], lateral girder, adjustage, boom, dormant, gird, top bridge, transverse beam, (机座的) cross spreader, 【压】cross [cramp, rest] bar (轧机牌坊的), 【采】beam,【建】girder ◇ 机座下～bottom-mill separator
横梁结晶器[连结模]　mould coupled with crossbars
横梁式装料机(坯料用)　loader boom
横梁支承　transverse bearing
横列式轧机　open-train [Belgian] mill
横裂　transverse [transversal] crack, hanger crack (钢锭的)
横裂缝　cross crack

横裂纹带(冷拔线材的)　cracked back
横面长度　lateral length
横木　cross-tie
横剖面　crosscut, cross [transverse, lateral] section
横墙　cross wall
横墙温度分布　temperature distribution in heating wall
横切剪　crosscut shears
横切锯　crosscut saw
横切(面)　crosscut
横声速　speed of transverse sound
横式起重器　sliding [swing] jack
横竖焊接焊缝　horizontal-vertical (fillet) weld
横水平线布置(出铁场铁路)　【铁】through track arrangement
横缩率　lateral contraction ratio
横条　skid bars (滑道或台架的), rail
横弯强度　cross-bending strength
横纹(冷拔管的)　【压】jarring mark
横巷　crosscut (X-cut)
横向　cross [transverse] direction,【金】side-wise
横向摆动(焊接)法　cross-weave procedure, weaving technique
横(向)变形　lateral deformation [flow, strain]
横向表面裂纹　transverse facial crack
横向侧切楔形砖　side skew
横向场　transverse field
横向长度　lateral length
横向超高　baking
横向车削　squaring
横向冲击　lateral impact
横向出钢机　cross pusher
横向磁场　transverse (magnetic) field
横向磁化(强度)　transverse magnetization
横向挡墙　【连铸】transverse bulkhead
横向导轨[导向装置]　transverse slides
横向断裂　cross breaking, transverse failure

横(向)断(裂)强度 cross-breaking strength, transverse rupture strength
横(向)断(裂)试验 cross-breaking test, transverse rupture test
横向分布 lateral distribution
横向钢筋 lateral [transverse, web] reinforcement
横向各向同性 transverse isotropy ◇弹性~.
横向各向异性 transversal anisotropy
横向构架 transverse frame, bent
横向固定位置 horizontal fixed position
横向滚动位置 horizontal rolled position
横向焊接 horizontal (position) welding
横向厚度波动值 lateral gauge variation
横向挤压 lateral extruding [extrusion]
横向挤压杆 traversable extrusion ram
横向剪切机 (同"横剪机")
横向剪切试验 transverse shear test
横向剪切作业线 crosscut shear(ing) line
横向角焊缝(剪切)试样 transverse fillet weld (shearing) specimen
横向结晶 transcrystallizaton
横向结晶的 transcrystalline
横向进刀 cross-feed
横向进刀螺杆 cross-feed screw
横向开裂 horizontal split
横向抗弯强度 traverse bending strength
横向扩散 lateral diffusion
横向拉杆 cross-tie, transverse tie rod
横向力 lateral [transverse] force
横向力系数(汽车的) cornering ratio
横向连接 cross-jointing
横向裂纹 transverse [transversal] crack
横向流动 lateral flow, crossflow
横向螺旋轧机 helical rolling mill
横向螺旋轧制 cross helical [spiral] rolling, helical rolling
横向模数 transverse [shear] modulus
横向挠曲 cross flexure
横向黏结 lateral bond
横向浓度梯度 lateral concentration gradient
横向排列[配置] side-to-side setup
横向排水(沟) cross drainage
横向膨胀 lateral expansion
横向膨胀缝 transverse expansion joint (TEJ)
横向偏析 lateral segregation
横向偏斜 transverse deflection
横向坡(度) cross-fall
横向奇偶校验 horizontal parity check
横向强化 transverse reinforcement
横向(取样)检验 transverse test
横向生长 lateral growth
横向试验 transverse test
横向试样 transverse test-piece
横向收缩 lateral [transverse] contraction, necking effect (轧件的)
横向送进 cross-feed
横向速度 transverse velocity
横向缩减(由于纵向拉伸引起) constrained
横向弹性 transverse elasticity
横向填角焊缝 transverse fillet weld
横向推力 lateral thrust
横向弯曲试验 transverse bend(ing) test
横向弯曲试验机 transverse bending testing machine
横向弯曲试样 transverse bend specimen
横向位移 transverse displacement
横向系杆 transverse tie rod
横向斜撑 lateral diagonal
横向压力 horizontal pressure
横向压力分布测定 traversing
横向压缩 lateral constraint
横向延[塑]性 transverse ductility
横向移动 lateral movement, square transfer motion (轧材的)
横向应变 transversal strain
横向应变电阻比 transverse sensitivity
横向应力 lateral [transversal, transverse] stress
横向约束 lateral constraint

横向运输机　cross transfer conveyer, drag-over unit
横向窄焊道法　horizontal string procedure
横向折叠　transverse lap
横向振荡　lateral [transverse] oscillation
横向振荡模式　transverse modes
横向振动　transverse vibration, lateral [transverse] oscillation
横向支撑　lateral braching, transverse brace
横向自动对中　(同"卷宽自动对中")
横向阻力　traverse resistance
横斜度　cross-fall
横压力　lateral pressure
横烟道　cross flue
横移　traversing, sideway
横移齿轮　traversing gear
横移坑　traversing pit
横移装置　traversing facility
横越　crossing
横轧(板坯的)【压】cross [transverse, spread] rolling ◇ 楔模～*
横轧宽展(板坯、板材的)　widening
横折　cross break, coil break (带卷开卷的)
横振动　lateral vibration
横振式焊枪　lateral-drive tip
横轴　lateral [abscissa] axis, cross axle, transverse shaft
横坐标　(scale of) abscissa, horizontal ordinate ◇ 沿～X-direction
横坐标轴　X-axis, axis of abscissa
衡器　weigher, weighing machine [apparatus] ◇ 车辆～car weigher
衡消法　null [zero] method
衡重式铲运机　counterweight scraper
恒比代码　constant ratio code
恒导磁率[磁导率]合金　constant permeability [magneto-conductivity] alloy ◇ 帕明瓦～*, 森珀姆～*
恒导磁率铁镍合金(17.8Ni, 11Cu, 余量 Fe; 38.4Ni, 4Al, 余量 Fe) isoperm ◇

超级～*
恒等距离[行程, 期间] identity distance
恒等(式) identity, identical equation
恒等条件 identical conditions
恒等周期 identity period
恒电位极化曲线 constantisostatic [potentiostatic] polarization curve
恒电位仪 potentiostat
恒电压焊接电源 constant-potential welding source
恒定操作速度 constant operating speed
恒定点 invariant point
恒定电势[位] constant (electric) potential
恒定分解切应力 constant resolved shear stress
恒定风流 constant air flow
恒定负压 constant suction
恒定功率电动机 constant power motor
恒定功率焊接电源 constant-power welding source
恒定功率因数 constant power factor
恒定辊缝控制 constant roll gap control
恒定辊缝轧机 constant-gap mill
恒定励磁器 constant exciter
恒定粒度 constant particle size
恒定亮度光学高温计 constant intensity pyrometer
恒定流量[流速] constant flow rate, constant rate of flow, fixed rate (flow)
恒定煤气[气体]组成 constant gas composition
恒定蠕变【金】steady [stationary] creep
恒定体积泵 constant volume pump
恒定通路 constant path
恒定性 constance, constancy
恒定压力挤压 steady pressure extrusion
恒定应变法 constant-strain method
恒定应变试验 constant strain test
恒定应力拉伸蠕变 constant-stress tensile creep
恒定载荷法 constant-load method

恒定值　constant value (Cv)
恒范钢　(同"不膨胀钢")
恒沸(点)混合物　constant boiling mixture
恒辊缝法　constant-gap system
恒角定律　law of constancy of angles
恒角拱坝　constant-angle arch dam
恒量　constant ◇ 玻耳兹曼～Boltzmann's constant,格律埃森～*,里德伯～【理】Rydberg constant
恒量供油(蒸馏柱的)　【焦】constant oil feed
恒流充电　constant-current charge
恒流焊接电源　constant-current welding source
恒(流)量泵　constant delivery pump ◇ 隔膜～*
恒流调节器　constant-current regulator
恒挠曲试验(应力腐蚀的)　constant delection test
恒频电压控制　constant frequency voltage control
恒热箱　thermostat
恒容燃烧　constant-volume burning
恒容热容量　heat capacity at constant volume
恒湿器　humidistat,hygrostat
恒湿箱　constant humidity cabinet
恒速　constant rate
恒速电动机　constant speed motor
恒速流变　constant rate of flow
恒速流动　fixed rate flow
恒速轧制　constant speed rolling
恒速蒸发　constant-rate evaporation
恒速蒸馏　constant-rate distillation
恒弹性(模量)合金　constant modulus alloy ◇ 戴纳瓦～Dynavar,科贝纽姆～Co-benium
恒弹性(模量)铁镍合金　constant-modulus nickel-iron alloy ◇ 埃勒因瓦～*
恒温　constant temperature (const. temp.)
恒温槽　constant temperature bath,thermostatic [thermostatted] bath,thermostat ◇ 冷却剂～coolant thermostat
恒温超塑性焊接　isothermal superplastic welding
恒温挤压　isothermal extruding [extrusion]
恒温加压焊接(塑态的)　constant-temperature pressure welding
恒温金属　thermostat metal
恒温开关　thermostatic switch
恒温控制器　thermostatic control
恒温炉　constant temperature furnace,thermostat oven
恒温膨胀　constant temperature expansion
恒温器　thermostat (thermo.),calorstat,pilotherm(双金属片控温) ◇ 超级～ultra-thermostat,低温～cryostat,电子～electronic thermostat,接触～contact thermostat
恒温器电阻合金　thermostat alloy
恒温器合金　◇ 威尔科～Wilco alloy
恒温器用复合金属　thermostat metal
恒温室　thermostatic chamber,constant heat cabinet
恒温水浴　aqueous thermostat
恒温调节器　thermostatic regulator
恒温退火　cycle annealing
恒温箱　thermostat,constant temperature cabinet [oven],thermostated container ◇ 晶体～crystal oven
恒温浴　constant temperature bath,thermostatic [thermostatted] bath
恒温(装置用)双金属　thermostatic bimetal
恒温压力焊　constant-temperature pressure welding
恒向电流　continuous current
恒星齿轮　sun gear
恒压　constant pressure (C.P.)
恒压槽　steady head tank
恒压充电　constant voltage charge
恒压电动机-发电机组　constant-voltage

motorgenerator set
恒压电源 constant voltage source
恒压电源电焊机(电弧焊) constant-voltage welder
恒压发电机 constant-voltage [constant-potential] generator
恒压焊接 constant-pressure welding
恒压器 barostat, manostat
恒压燃烧 constant-pressure burning [combustion]
恒压热容量 heat capacity at constant pressure
恒压缩载荷 constant compressive load
恒压调节 constant pressure regulation
恒压直流辅助电动机 constant voltage DC auxiliary motor
恒应力 constant stress
恒载(荷) dead load (d.l.), constant load
恒载拉伸蠕变 constant load tensile creep
恒载试验 constant load test
恒值 constant value
恒重 constant weight
轰击 bombardment, bombing ◇ 电子束～引入管 bombarding beam tube
轰击粒子 bombarding particle
轰击能 bombardment energy
轰击损伤 bombardment damage
轰击阴极 bombarding cathode
烘包器[装置] ladle dryer, ladle drying system
烘(焙) bake ◇ 未～电极[焊条] unbaked electrode
烘焙过度 overbaking
烘干 dry, heat [furnace, oven, thermal] drying, baking, desiccation, stoving(线材的)
烘干工段 bake oven department
烘干后粒度(砂样的) 【铸】dry fineness
烘干机 drying machinery ◇ 转底式～rotating disk drier
烘干炉 drier, drying furnace [oven, stove], curing furnace ◇ 抽屉式～*, 隧道式～drying tunnel, 转向架式～*
烘干煤 heat dried coal
烘干器 baker, drying apparatus
烘干区 baking zone
烘干设备 drying plant
烘干室[房] drying room
烘干型芯 baked core
烘干用焦炭 heating coke
烘架(浇包的) burning-in stand
烘烤 bake out, firing
烘烤过程 baking process
烘烤炉 hot oven
烘烤硬化钢板 bake-hardening steel sheet
烘烤搪瓷 baking enamel
烘烤涂层 baking coating
烘烤硬化 bake-hardening
烘烤硬化钢 BH (bake-hardening) steel
烘炉 baker, baking furnace, drying stove ◇ 携带式～knock down salamander
烘炉(作业) furnace dry out, heating up, 【铁】drying out,【冶】burn-in, initial heating ◇ 焦炉组～*, 热风炉～*
烘炉孔塞砖 heating up hole plug
烘炉汽管 oven tube ◇ 贝克式～Baker's oven tube
烘炉[烘热]时间 warm-up period
烘炉温度 heating up temperature
烘炉用炉外临时小炉 Dutch oven
烘砂炉[器] sand-drying oven, sand drier
烘酥铸型 dead burned mould
烘箱 (bake, baking, dry) oven, baking box ◇ 晶体～crystal oven
烘芯 core baking ◇ 高频～法 dielectric core baking
烘芯板 core plate
烘芯架 core rack
烘芯炉 core drier [oven, stove] ◇ 架式～*
烘芯炉运输车 core oven truck
烘芯托板 core carrier [drier]
烘芯托架 core(-drying) cradle
虹吸 siphon(ing), syphonage ◇ 桶底～

池【色】 ladle well
虹吸放铅口 siphon lead tap
虹吸分离器 siphon separator
虹吸管 siphon (pipe, tube), syphon
虹吸管颈 siphon neck
虹吸管通道 syphon passage
虹吸涵洞 siphon culvert
虹吸能力 siphonage
虹吸器 crane
虹吸气压[压力]计 siphon barometer [gauge]
虹吸式钢[浇]包 syphon pour ladle, siphon(-type) ladle
虹吸式转炉 siphon converter
虹吸脱泥[分级]机 siphonsizer
虹吸弯管 siphon bend
虹吸溢洪道 siphon spillway
虹吸阱[闸门] siphon trap
洪堡铋铅锡合金 Homburg's alloy
洪德定则(电子结构的) Hund's rule
洪峰流量 flood peak rate, peak discharge
洪水过程线图 flood hydrograph
洪水位 flood level
宏程序 macroprogram
宏调用 macro call
宏定义 macro definition
宏观不均匀[不均质]性 macroheterogeneity
宏观尺寸[尺度] macroscopic scale
宏观磁化(强度) macroscopic magnetization
宏观地球化学 macrogeochemistry
宏观断口分析 macroscope fractography
宏观断口金相学 macrofractography
宏观断裂力学 macrofractography mechanics
宏观对称 macroscopic symmetry
宏观反应 macroreaction
宏观范性切变 macroscopic plastic shear
宏观范性弯曲 macroscopic plastic bending
宏观分析 macro-analysis, macro check
宏观分析试样 macrospecimen
宏观腐蚀 macrocorrosion
宏观固体 macroscopic solid
宏观观察 (同"肉眼观察")
宏观过程 macroprocess
宏观滑移面 macroscopic slip surface
宏观化学 macrochemistry
宏观检验[检查] macro check, macro-examination, macrographic [macroscopic] examination, macrography
宏观浸蚀 macro-etch(ing) ◇ 丘克拉尔斯基~剂*
宏观浸蚀检验 macro-etch testing
宏观浸蚀磨片 macro-etched slice
宏观晶粒 macrograin
宏观(晶粒)间界滑移 macroscopic boundary slip
宏观孔隙(率) macro porosity
宏观力 macroscopical forces
宏观裂纹 macro crack
宏观磨片 macrosection
宏观浓度 macroscopic concentration
宏观偏析 macrosegregation
宏观气候学 macroclimatology
宏观气孔 macro pore
宏观切变 macroscopic shear
宏观屈服应力 macroscopic yield stress
宏观蠕变 macro creep
宏观世界 macrocosm
宏观试样 macrotemplate
宏观塑性弯曲 macroscopic plastic bending
宏观缩孔[收缩(量)] macroshrinkage
宏观弹性模量 macroscopic elastic modulus
宏观图 macrograph
宏观效应 macroeffect
宏观形变 macroscopic deformation
宏观性质 macroscopic property
宏观应变[胁变] macrostrain
宏观应力[胁强] macro(scopic) stress
宏观硬度 macrohardness

宏观宇宙	macrocosm
宏观照片	macrograph, photomacrograph
宏观照相	macrography, macrophoto
宏观照相检验	macrography test
宏观照相术	macro(photo)graphy
宏观状态	macro(scopic) state
宏观组织[结构]	macro(scopic) structure
宏观组织照片	macrophoto
宏晶(的)	macrocrystalline
宏量元素	macroelement
宏系统	macrosystem
宏指令	macro instruction ◇ 调试～debug macroinstruction
宏指令定义	macro definition
宏(指令)扩展	macro expansion
红铵铁盐	$\{2KCl \cdot 2NH_4Cl \cdot 2FeCl_3 \cdot 3H_2O\}$ kremersite
红包运转	【钢】hot ladle turn round
红宝石	ruby
红宝石光	ruby light
红宝石激光(器)	ruby laser
红宝石模(拔制金银丝用)	ruby die
红边(光谱的)	red edge
红饼	$\{V_2O_5\}$ red cake
红玻璃滤色镜	red glass filter
红脆	red short
红脆区	【钢】red-shortness zone
红脆性	red brittleness [shortness]
红锭	hot ingot
红钒钙铀矿	rauvite
红钒铅矿	dechenite
红锆(英)石	hyacinth, hyazinth, jacynth
红铬铅矿	phoenicochroite
红汞	mercurochrome
红钴	red cobalt
红(硅)钇石	$\{(Al,Fe,Ti)_2Si_2O_7\}$ thalenite
红合金(刚果的一种钴铣)	red alloy
红接	fire welding
红矿	laterite type iron ore, lateritic ore
红利	dividend
红榴石	(同"镁铝石榴子石")
红铳[冰铜]	red matte
红炉锻造	smith forging
红泥	red mud
红黏土	adamic earth
红铅(粉)	$\{Pb_3O_4\}$ red-lead
红铅铀矿	$\{Pb_2U_2O_4Si_2O_8 \cdot H_2O\}$ (同"硅铝铀矿")
红热	redness, glowing red
红热(的)	red-heat, red-hot
红热坯件	red-hot bar
红热(温度)范围	red heat range
红热硬度	red hardness
红热折断试验	red heat test
红色光焦点	red focus
红(色)黄铜(含铜高于80)	red brass [metal] ◇ 镀金用～合金*,阀用～(合金)*,工业用～*,加铅～*,普卢姆赖特～*
红色黄铜合金	(同"低锌黄铜合金")
红色铝热剂	red thermit
红色滤光镜	red filter
红砷镍矿	$\{NiAs\}$ niccolite, kupfernickel, copper nickel
红砷酸锰矿	$\{8MnO \cdot (Al,Mn)_2O_3 \cdot As_2O_5 \cdot 8H_2O\}$ hematolite
红石榴子石	$\{3(Mg,Fe)O \cdot Al_2O_3 \cdot 3SiO_2\}$ rhodolite
红铊矿	$\{TlAsS_2\}$ lorandite
红铊铅矿	(同"硫砷铊铅矿")
红钛锰矿	$\{MnTiO_3\}$ pyrophanite
红锑粉	kermes mineral
红锑矿	$\{Sb_2O_3 \cdot 2SbS_3\}$ antimony [purple] blende, red antimony, kermesite
红锑镍矿	$\{NiSb\}$ breithauptite
红锑铊矿	urbaite
红铁矾	amarantite
红铜	pure copper, red metal
红铜矿	(同"赤铜矿")
红土	laterite, lateritic clay
红土化(作用)	laterization
红土矿	laterite, lateritic ore ◇ 含镍～*
红土镍矿还原氨浸法[尼加罗炼镍法](古巴)	Nicaro process

红土型铁矿石　laterite type iron ore
红外测温仪　infrared radiation thermometer
红外成像　infrared photography
红外分光光度计　infrared spectrophotometer
红外分光光度学[测定法]　infrared spectrophotometry
红外光电光栅摄谱仪　quantometer
红外光电摄象管电视系统　infrared vidicon television system
红外光谱　infrared spectrum
红外(光谱)分析　infrared analysis
红外光谱学　infrared spectroscopy
红外光谱仪　infrared spectrometer
红外光线　infrared light
红外节能涂料　infrared coating with energy saving
红外区(域)　infrared region
红外(热)辐射　infrared (heat) radiation
红外双色测温　infrared bicolor pyrometer
红外吸收湿度计　infrared absorption hygrometer
红外线　infrared [ultrared] rays ◇ 不透～性 adiathermancy
红外线测径仪　infra-ray diameter gauge
红外线测宽仪　infra-ray width gauge
红外线灯　infrared (ray) lamp
红外线电子学　infranics
红外线定量分析　infrared quantitative analysis
红外线分析系统　infra-red analyzing system
红外线分析仪　infrared analyzer
红外(线)辐射　infrared radiation
红外线(辐射)[红外]高温计　infrared (radiation) pyrometer
红外线干燥　infrared drying
红外线干燥器[机]　infrared drier
红外线技术　infra-red technology
红外线加热　infrared heating
红外线(加热)干燥炉　infrared(-ray) drying oven [stove], infrared oven
红外线(加热)炉　infrared (heating) furnace, infrared oven
红外线加热器　infrared heater
红外线检验　infrared test
红外(线)镜　melanoscope
红外线控制　infrared control
红外线气体分析仪　infrared gas analyzer
红外线钎焊　infrared brazing
红外线热像仪　infra-red thermal image system
红外线扫描　infrared scanning
红外线扫描技术　infrared scanning technique
红外线涂层　infrared coating
红外线无损检验　infrared nondestructive testing
红外线物镜　infrared objective
红外线显微镜　infrared microscope
红外线显微镜观察　infrared microscope observation
红外线显微术　infrared microscopy
红外线显微照片　infrared micrograph
红外线影像　infrared image
红外线照明　infrared lighting [illumination]
红外线照相术　infrared photography
红外线针孔缺陷探伤仪　infrared pinhole detector
红外线蒸发照相(测定仪)　evaporograph
红锡(红色锡石)　ruby tin
红锌矿{ZnO}　zincite
红锈　blood (钢件接触面的) red rust
红烟尘　red fume
红药水　mercurochrome
红页岩(耐酸材料)　red shale
红液渗透探伤　red check
红硬钢　red-hard steel
红硬性　red hardness
红铀矿{(PbO·4UO$_3$·nH$_2$O)(n=4—7)}　fourmarierite
红柱石{Al$_2$O$_3$·SiO$_2$}　andalusite

红装法兰盘　shrink flanging
喉　throat ◇ 护~板【铁】wearing plate
喉口　throat opening
厚板　thick [heavy, massive] plate ◇ 多倍~*，异形~(切断的) sketch plate
厚板冲裁[切断]冲头　quill punch
厚板焊接　plate welding
厚板划线区段　marking-out section
厚板剪切机　heavy plate shears, heavy plate shearing [cutting] machine
厚板矫正机　heavy plate straightener [straightening machine]
厚板轧机　heavy plate mill
厚板桩　plank pile
厚薄不均引起的裂纹　bull crack
厚薄规　feeler, thickness gauge [indicator]
厚壁管　thick-walled tube, heavy wall pipe [tube] ◇ 滚珠轴承圈~ ball bearing tubing
厚壁管材　hollow bar
厚壁管线管　heavy wall line pipe
厚壁还原钢弹　heavy walled bomb
厚壁黄铜毛管(拉拔用)　brass shell
厚壁结构　thick-wall construction
厚壁结晶器　【连铸】thick-walled mould
厚壁容器　heavy vessels
厚壁套筒　thick-walled cup
厚壁铸件　thick-section [thick-walled] casting, heavy section casting
厚玻璃板　heavy sheet glass
厚层电镀品[电铸板]　heavy electroplate
厚层镀锌　heavy galvanizing
厚层干燥　volume drying
厚层泥岩　argillite
厚层阳极化处理　thick anodizing
厚大断面球铁钢锭模　large section mold from nodular cast iron
厚带材　heavy strip
厚度　thickness, depth, gauge ◇ 不均匀~ off-gauge, 不同~ dissimilar thickness, 带材~差 grow-back, 动态~变换*, 小~*

厚度变形　thickness strain
厚度变值　gauge variation
厚度不合格带材　off-gauge strip
厚度不均性　grow-back
厚度的T控制法(张力变动法)　T-method of gauge control
厚度改变　gauge changing
厚度公差　gauge tolerance, thickness deviation
厚度合格薄板　on-gauge sheet
厚度计[仪]　thickness tester [gauge] ◇ β射线~ β-ray thickness gauge, γ射线~ γ-ray thickness gauge, 超声~ sonigauge, sonizon, 反向散射~*
厚度记录器　thickness recorder
厚度减薄　thickness reduction
厚度精调器自动控制(带材的)　vernier gauge control
厚度控制　gauge control ◇ 可变刚度~ variable rigidity AGC, 微米级~系统 micro-level AGC system, 质量流量~ mass flow gage control, 自动~(同"厚度自动控制")
厚度上限　over-gauge (limit)(薄板的)
厚度同轧辊直径之比　thickness ratio
厚度系列号(管材的)　schedule number
厚度下限(薄板的)　undergauge limit
厚度压减　gauge reduction
厚度压下量　reduction in thickness
厚度增加　increase in thickness
厚度指示器　thickness indicator
厚度自动控制　automatic gauge control (AGC), automatic thickness control, "course" gauge control(轧带材的)
厚度自动调整[控制]器　automatic gauge controller
厚钢板　heavy [coarse, iron] plate
厚金属切割　heavy cutting
厚金属切割焊炬　heavy cutting torch
厚金属切割烧嘴　heavy cutting burner
厚金属切口　heavy cut
厚料层　thick bed,【团】deep-bed

厚料层操作	deep [high] bed operation

厚料层操作 deep [high] bed operation
厚料层加压过滤 deep-bed pressure filtration
厚料层冷却机 【团】deep-bed cooler
厚料层烧结法 high bed sintering
厚料层烧结技术 deep-bed sintering process
厚铝板 aluminium plate
厚膜 thick [heavy] film
厚膜电路 thick-film circuit
厚膜覆[涂]层 thick-film coating
厚膜润滑 thick-film lubrication, full film lubrication
厚膜微电子学 thick-film microelectronics
厚内衬 thick wall-type inwalls
厚墙式(高炉的) thick-walled type
厚渗碳层(＞1.5mm) heavy case
厚实涂层 strong coating
厚铁皮生成 heavy scale formation
厚锡层("碳炼")镀锡薄钢板 charcoal (tin)-plate ◇ 普通～*，一般～*，一等～*，最优～*
厚锌层(镀锌薄)钢板 heavy iron
厚氧化铁皮 heavy scale
厚药皮焊条 heavily coated [covered] electrode, heavy-coated [covered] electrode
厚油膜静液挤压法 thick-film hydrostatic extrusion process
厚渣 thick slag
厚(棕榈)油的热镀锡薄钢板 grease plate
后板 back [backboard] plate
后背 back
后备电源 backup power [source]
后壁 back wall
后变形器(钢丝绳的) post-former
后步工序 subsequent operation
后部 backside, heel
后部工程 follow engineering
后部工艺[后加工] post-processing
后产物 after product
后撤机构 pullback mechanism

后沉淀(作用) post-precipitation
后触点 back contact
后处理 aftertreatment, post-treatment, afterprocessing
后吹(转炉的) afterblow, reblow
后吹期 afterblowing period
后倒齿轮 back gear
后导板 back guide
后端 trailing end, after end (板卷的)
后端墙 rear end wall, gable
后端装料和前端出料的加热炉 end-charged end-discharged furnace
后扶架 back rest
后辐照加热 postirradiation heating
后辐照蠕变 postirradiation creep
后辐照射线照相学 postirradiation radiography
后隔离板 back screen
后光阑 rear diaphragm
后滑(轧件的) backward slip [creep, flow], deceleration
后滑区 zone of slippage on entry side
后回火 post tempering
后脊 backedge, backfin
后加热焊接 welding with postheating
后加速电子枪 post-acceleration gun
后加应力 post-stressing
后角(刀具的) angle of backing off
后进先出存储器 nesting storage
后净化 after-purification
后开可倾动式冲压机 O.B.I.P (open-back-inclinable) press
后开式压力机 open-back press
后跨轮外套 quill gear guard
后拉力 back tension [pull]
后拉力拔丝 (同"反拉力拔丝")
后冷却器 after-cooler
后路 backdoor
后喷(吹) post-injection
后喷工艺 post-injection process
后膨胀 after-expansion
后屏蔽 back screen

后期处理	post-processing
后期渣	tap slag, top cinder
后墙	back wall
后墙衬里	rear lining
后墙拱座	back wall skew back
后桥(汽车的)	rear axle
后侵蚀	after-etching
后倾焊	angle backwards welding
后燃效应	afterfiring effect
后热	afterheat
后热处理电流调节	postheat control
后热器	afterheater
后乳化法(渗透检验)	post-emulsification method
后乳化荧光探伤法	post-emulsification fluorescent process
后乳化(作用)	post-emulsification
后散射角	back scattering angle
后烧段(带式烧结机的)	afterfiring zone
后生泡疤表面(晶界腐蚀的)	service blister
后生矿床	epigenetic deposit
后视图	back [rear] view
后收缩	after-shrinkage
后退火	post annealing
后拖量	【焊】drag
后拖线(气割的)	drag lines
后挖前卸式挖装机	back hoe front end loader
后弯式风机叶片	backward inclined fan blade
后向	backward direction
后向条片	back sliver
后效(应)	after-effect, drift, after-working
后卸车	rear dump wagon
后卸卡车	(同"尾卸卡车")
后行程	back action
后续工程	(同"后部工程")
后续工序	downstream process, downstream processing step
后续加工	downstream processing
后续作业	downflow operation
后遗症	sequelae, after effect of disease
后移间隙(高炉风嘴的)	back lash
后缘导轨	back guide
后增稠器	post-thicknener
后张法(预应力)混凝土	poststressed [post-tensioned] concrete
后张法预应力	post-tensioned prestressing
后张钢丝绳	post-tensioned cable
后张力	back(ward) tension [pull], decoiler tension
后张力拉拔	(同"反张力拉拔")
后张力拉丝	(同"反拉力拉丝")
后折叠(行星轧制的)	back fin
后支承环	subbolster
后轴	back [rear] axle, semi-axis, backshaft
后缀	suffix postfix
后座(带式抛光机的)	back stand [seat]
呼叫继电器	call relay
呼叫开关	challenge switch
呼叫系统	paging system
呼叫信号	call signal
呼吸器(电缆的)	breather
呼吸性粉尘	respirable dust
葫芦状断口(脆性材料的)	hour-glass fracture
胡根贝格尔伸长计	Huggenberger (ex)tensometer
胡克薄壁管[药筒]挤压法	Hooker process
胡克冲击挤压法	Hooker extrusion method
胡克定律	Hooke's law ◇ 非[无]~现象
胡克(弹性)固体	Hookian solid
胡克弹性体	hookean elastic body
胡普斯(三层液)铝电解精炼法	Hoopes (three layer) process
胡桃块烧结矿	"nut" sinter
胡桃木钉	hickory peg
蝴蝶瓷瓶	shackle insulator
糊膏挤压成型法	paste process

糊膏挤压机	paste extruder
糊精	flour paste, 【铸】 dextrin {$(C_6H_{10}O_5)_n$}
糊块	paste brick, pasty mass, paste chunk (阳极)
糊态成形	mashy-state forming
糊态锻造	mashy-state forging
糊态混合	mashy-state mixing
糊态挤压	mashy-state extrusion
糊态加工	mashy-state processing
糊态轧制	mashy-state rolling
糊状(熔融材料的)	pasty state
糊状浮渣	pasty [mushy] dross
糊状焊剂	paste flux
糊状混合物[料]	mashy mixture
糊状阶段	mushy stage
糊状金属	pasty [mashy] metal
糊状泥浆[渣]	pasty sludge
糊状捏和物	pasty pug mixture
糊状润滑剂	paste lubricant
糊状渗碳	paste carburizing
糊状铁	pasty iron
糊状物质	pasty mass
湖铜(自然铜矿炼出的)	lake copper
弧边槽钢孔型	Gothic channel pass
弧边锭模	cambered mould
弧边方型材[弧边四方形]	Gothic square
弧边方形孔型	Gothic square pass
弧边角钢孔型	Gothic angle pass
弧边矩形断面钢锭	rectangular ingot with arch edge
弧边菱形粗轧孔型	Gothic roughing pass
弧边菱形孔型	Gothic groove [pass]
弧边形型材	Gothic section
弧边轧扁线材	flattened wire
弧齿联轴节	curved tooth coupling
弧度	radian (rad.), arc, curvature
弧拱	circular arch
弧光	arc ◇ 被~刺伤的眼睛 flashed eyes
弧光灯	arc lamp [light]
弧光电流	arc current
弧光分光计	arc spectrometer
弧光辐射[射线]	arc rays
弧焊	arc welding ◇ 熔剂下~法 submerged arc process
弧焊电极	arc metal
弧焊电源	arc-welding set
弧焊发电机	arc-welding generator
弧焊缝	arc weld, arc-welding seam
弧焊管	arc-welded pipe
弧焊机	arc welder, arc-welding set ◇ 电动(机)-发电机组~*, 电子~ electronic arc welder, 多电源式~ multiple-arc welder
弧焊设备[装置]	arc-welding plant, arc-welding set
弧炬	arc torch
弧菌	Vibrio
弧坑	【焊】(arc) crater ◇ 电极端~ electrode crater, 未满~ unfilled crater, 形成~ cratering
弧坑裂纹	crater crack
弧坑清理器	crater eliminator
弧坑填充料	crater filler
弧菱形孔型曲率半径(轧辊的)	curvature of Gothic pass
弧面辊身	crowned barrel
弧偏吹	arc blow
弧熔碘化物法材料	arc melted iodide process material
弧熔锭	arc-melted ingot ◇ 自耗~*
弧熔海绵金属	arc melted sponge
弧熔金属锭	arc-cast metal
弧熔晶棒	arc-melted crystal bar
弧熔炉	arc-melting furnace
弧熔钼	arc-melting molybdenum
弧熔钼锭	arc-cast molybdenum ingot
弧熔凝固	arc-melting consolidation ◇ 钼~(法)*
弧熔铸锭	arc-cast ◇ 直接~ direct arc-cast (ingot)
弧隙	【焊】arc space [gap]
弧线摆动式取样器	swinging arc-path sampler

弧线运动取样器	arc-path sampler
弧形	arc, curve, progressive bending type（连铸机）
弧形壁	cambered wall
弧形齿轮离合器	curved tooth clutch
弧形出坯	curved discharge
弧形顶弯器	curved bender
弧形顶弯式	curve bender type
弧形二次冷却区	curved secondary cooling zone
弧形二次喷水	curved spray
弧形钢锭模壁	cambered wall
弧形辊	bowed roller
弧形辊道	arc-shaped roller bank
弧形浇注半径	casting radius
弧形结晶器	curved mould
弧形结晶器连铸机[装置]	curved-mould continuous-casting machine
弧形拉模(砌拱用)	soffit scaffolding
弧形连铸机	bow type continuous casting machine, curved continuous casting machine, curved mould horizontal run-out plant, circular arc type plant, S-type machine
弧形(连铸)机组	arc-type plant
弧形连铸装置喷水冷却区	curved spray cooling zone
弧形链节	curved link
弧形炉底	arched hearth
弧形螺旋夹钳	C-clamp
弧形模壁	cambered wall
弧形筛	curved deck screen, sieve bend
弧形砖	circle [radius] brick ◇ 侧砌~ circle brick on edge
弧焰	arc-flame
弧柱	【焊】arc stream [core], arc (gaseous) column（气体弧柱）, acr fan（原子氢焊的）
弧柱电压	arc stream voltage
弧阻加热	arc resistance heating
弧阻炉	arc resistance furnace
虎钳	vice (clamp), jaw vice, pincers
虎钳开度[开口]	clamp opening
"虎型"保温帽制造设备	【钢】tiger topping plant
琥珀蛇纹石	amber serpentine
琥珀酸	（同"丁二酸"）
护岸	revetment
护坝	check dam
护板	back [apron, baffle, guard] plate, armouring, trash rack,【采】skin plate
护壁板	cleading,【建】dado
护壁钢板	siding steel
护壁镶板	wainscot
护壁楔形板	clapboard
护臂	armlet, barcer
护边操作(工具钢的)	safe-ending
护道	【运】berm
护轨	guard [check] rail, counter-rail
护喉板	【铁】wearing plate
护喉钢砖	【铁】throat-armo(u)r (segment)
护环	binding band
护角条	angle bead
护壳式热电偶	sheathed thermocouple [thermoelement]
护栏	guard [side] rail ◇ 梁式~*
护链	chain guard
护炉技术	furnace maintenance technique
护轮(钢)轨	guard [growed, edge] rail
护面(水工的)	protective covering
护木	guard timber ◇ 枕距~ bond timber
护目镜	(protective, safety) goggles, eye protector ◇ 铲削用~ chipping goggles, 防闪光用~ flash goggles, 焊工[焊接]~*
护坡	revetment
护坡道	bankette
护墙	traverse, parapet wall
护墙板	wainscot, clapboard, wall panel,【建】sheeting ◇ 多层~【建】sandwich panel
护圈	retainer, guard ring
护栅	grate

护栅棒　grate bar
护套　sheath(ing)
护套挤压　(同"包套挤压")
护舷桩　fender pile
护销　guard pin
护油环　oil ring
护罩　shield, hooding ◇ 加～压力机 hooded press, 皮带～belt guard
护罩系统　hood system
护桩　fender pile,【建】guard pile
互变　interconversion
互变现象　enantiotropism
互补半导体　compensated semiconductor
互补对称金属氧化物半导体阵列　complementary symmetry MOS array
互补晶体管逻辑电路　complementary transistor logic (CTL)
互不溶(解)的　mutually insoluble
互成直角四辊矫直器　truks head
互斥力　repulsive interaction
互垂轴　quadrature axes
互搭接头　butt and lap joint
互导　mutual conductance, transconductance
互反律　reciprocity law
互感　mutual induction [inductance]
互感磁通匝连数　mutual flux linkage
互感器　mutual inductor
互感系数　mutual inductance coefficient, mutual induction
互换　interchange, counterchange, exchange, interconversion ◇ 可～性
互换机　commutator
互换流　interchange current
互换能(有序合金的)　interchange energy
互换式多片磁盘系统　removable disk carbridge system
互换体系　displacement system
互换性　interchangeability, compatibility
互换作用　exchange interaction
互混性　intermiscibility
互扩散　mutual diffusion, interdiffusion
互联孔　intercommunicating pores [porosity]
互联网络　【计】interconnection network
互连　interconnection
互连函数　interconnection function
互连孔　interconnected [interconnecting] pores
互联系统　【计】interconnected system
互燃　reverse combustion
互熔　interfuse, interfusion
互溶度[性]　mutual solubility, (inter)miscibility
互调　intermodulation
互推斥　repulsive interaction
互相关　cross-correlation
互相关函数　cross-correlation function
互相连结　interlinking
互相吸引　mutual attraction
互压痕硬度试验　mutual indentation hardness test
互压痕硬度　hardness by mutual indentation
互压硬度试验机　mutual indentation hardness apparatus
互易点阵　reciprocal lattice
互易定理　reciprocal theory
互易矢量　reciprocal vector
互撞　collide
户外管道(系统)　house-to curb piping
户外绝缘子　outdoor insulator
户外照明　outdoor lighting
戽斗　bail, bucket ◇ 吊杆与～输送法*, 提升机～轮【选】basket wheel
戽斗牙　bucket teeth
花边　◇ 形成～(板材深冲时) earing
花边镀锡薄钢板　scroll tinplate
花边(镀锡薄钢板)剪切作业线　scroll shear line
花顶燃烧室炉　over-fired furnace
花杆　sight rod, bearing picket
花钢板　checker(ed) plate
花岗片麻岩　granite gneiss

花岗石	grano
花岗岩	granite
花格砖	sole flue port brick
花辊辊道	disc-type roller table
花键(轴)	spline
花键件	splined objects
花括号	brace
花螺母	horned nut
花盘卡爪	face plate chucking jaws
花墙	tracery wall ◇ 带~的炉子 semi-muffle type furnace
花纹	decorative pattern, motif ◇ 描绘~【建】patterning
花纹钢	(同"网纹钢")
花纹钢板	(同"网纹钢板") ◇ 扁豆形~ tear plate
花纹漆	pattern varnish
花纹软钢板	mild steel checkered plate
花纹氧化皮	scalepattern
花样	pattern, motif ◇ 考塞尔~*, 描绘~【建】patterning
花样对称衍射线	symmetrical arcs of pattern
花样记录(衍射的)	pattern recording
花园钢丝制造机	barbed wire machine
花砧(延伸锻造用)	swage block
花砖型格子砖	(同"多孔格子砖")
花状断口	rosette [star] fracture
华	bloom【化】flower
华氏温标	Fahrenheit (thermometric) scale
华氏温度	Fahrenheit (Fahr.), Fahrenheit degree
华氏温度计	Fahrenheit thermometer
滑板	slide (board), slide [sliding] plate, bearing segment
滑板输送式造型机	pallet conveyer mould machine
滑板闸阀	plate-type gate valve
滑槽	chute, spout ◇ 重级~ heavy duty runway
滑槽运输	chuting
滑车	block (sheave), pulley, rope block, tackle ◇ 带钩~ hook block, 三孔~ deadeye, 双轮~ double block
滑车组	pulley [sheave] block
滑尺	slide gauge [calliper, rule], slider
滑触轨	contact rail
滑触集车杆	trolley-pole
滑触线的吊线	catenary, catenarian
滑导承	slide guide
滑道	skidway, slide (way), glide, chute, runway, runner ◇ 吊车梁~ crane runway, 炉底~ skid, 台车风箱间 T 形~密封*
滑道导线	runway conductor
滑道黑印(加热炉的)	skid mark
滑道水管(炉底的)	wet skid
滑动	slide, sliding, glide, gliding, slip (page), slipping (motion)
滑动摆架	slide frame
滑动板	sliding plate
滑动比	【金】slip ratio, ratio of slip
滑(动)臂	sliding arm
滑动部分	slipper
滑动层叠	cluster of lamellae
滑动成型压砖机	sliding mould-type press
滑动齿轮	sliding [slip] gear
滑动触点	sliding [moving] contact
滑动触点材料	sliding contact material
滑动触头	slider, slipper, wiping contact
滑动打桩机	skid pile-driver
滑动挡块	sliding stopper
滑动刀架	blade head, knife block [head]
滑动垫木	skidder
滑动电接头	sliding contact
滑动阀门	sliding valve ◇ 风动式~*
滑动杆	sliding bar
滑动横梁(水压机的)	slide*
滑动集电器	slipper collector
滑动夹层	glide lamella
滑动角	angle of slide
滑动接触	slide contact
滑动接触电极	sliding contact electrode

滑动接头　sliding joint
滑动拉丝机　slip wire-drawing machine
滑动量　slip height, slippage
滑动轮　movable pulley
滑动门　sliding door
滑动密封(装置)　sliding seal
滑动面　sliding surface
滑动面薄铁板　slipper plate
滑动模板　sliding form [formwork, shuttering], slip form
滑动摩擦　sliding [slipping] friction
滑动配合　sliding [slip] fit
滑动皮带　slide belt
滑动区　slipping area
滑动蠕变　creep at sliding
滑动上升模板　【建】climbing form
滑动式多次拉丝机　nonaccumulator multidraft machine
滑动式拉伸机　slip drawing machine
滑动式拉丝机　slipping wire drawing machine, slip(-type) drawing machine
滑动式起重机　skid derrik
滑动束　glide packet
滑动[滑阀式]水口　【钢】sliding gate (nozzle, valve), sliding nozzle, sliding stopper, ladle valve
滑动水口空砖　sliding gate well block
滑动水口系统　sliding gate system
滑动水口下空砖　support block
滑动速度控制机构　rate-controlling mechanism of slip
滑动速率　rate of slip
滑动位错　glissile dislocation
滑动下刀架　lower knife slide
滑动线夹[夹具]　sliding clamp
滑动小件　glide packet
滑动型芯　sliding core
滑动与滚珠组合轴承　plain-and-ball bearing
滑动闸板[阀,门]　slide [sliding] damper
滑动真空密封　sliding vacuum seal
滑动轴承　journal [sleeve] bearing, sliding bearing(平面运动的)
滑动爪　sliding jaw
滑动阻力　resistance to sliding
滑动座架　saddle
滑斗　skid hopper
滑阀　slide [sliding, spool, shuttle] valve, slide box ◇ 电动液压控制的可逆～*, 气动～air slide, 闸门式～gate-type slide valve
滑阀杆　slide valve rod
滑阀控制杆　lap-and-lead lever
滑阀式水口　sliding gate valve
滑轨　slide (rail), skid rail(加热炉内的), skid(重物移送用), sledge ◇ 炉内～furnace skid
滑轨移送机　skid transfer
滑痕(带钢的)　slip mark
滑环　slide [sliding, collector] ring
滑环电动机　slip-ring motor ◇ 带减速齿轮的～slip ring geared motor
滑环密封　slide ring sealing
滑架　carriage, skid transfer, sledge, slide block, bogie, sliding mechanism(烧结机尾的) ◇ 移动挡板的～【压】gauge carriage
滑架返回(打印的)　carriage return
滑架横动　carriage transverse
滑键　sliding [slip] key, feather (key)
滑块　slide (r), slide shoe, slipper, slide bracket(钢包升降机构的), slide block(剪切机的), bearing segment ◇ 刀片～blade head
滑块退回系统　block retracting system
滑块制动器　blocking [slipper] brake
滑料　slip
滑裂　slip crack
滑轮　pulley, (block) sheave, glidewheel, rope block ◇ 握柄[手动]～lever block, 主～head pulley
滑轮架[轭]　pulley [sheave] fork
滑轮托架　pulley bracket
滑轮组　pulley [sheave] block, block pul-

ley, block and falls [tackle]
滑门阀　gate valve
滑面　sliding surface
滑模(施工法)　slip form
滑木　skid
滑坡　landslide, slump,【采】downslide
滑撬　sled
滑石$\{H_2Mg_3(SiO_3)_4\}$　talc (stone), french chalk, soap-stone
滑石粉　talcum powder ◇ 涂～talcing
滑石棉　asbestine
滑台　skid platform [table], sled(ge)
滑坍(岩土的)　creeping
滑条　slide bar
滑脱式砂箱　slip [easy-off] flask
滑瓦　slide shoe
滑线(导电用)　contact [slide] wire
滑线变阻器　rheochord, slide wire rheostat
滑线电位计　slide-wire potentiometer
滑线电阻(器)　sliding resistor, slide wire resistor
滑箱式给料机　sliding-box feeder
滑行螺母　sliding nut
滑行坡度　coasting grade
滑行装置　skid, runners ◇ 重物转移[升降]～skid
滑移　(同"滑动") ◇ 不连续～discontinuous glide, 宏观(晶粒)间界～*, 棱锥面～*, 吕德斯～Lueders slip, 无效～(见"无效蠕变"), 协调～cooperative slip
滑移崩　slip avalanches
滑移层弯曲　bending of glide lamellae
滑移成核　nucleation of slip
滑移穿透　breakthrough of glide
滑移带　glide [slip] band ◇ 二次～*, 交叉～*
滑移带丛聚　clustering of slip bands
滑移带簇　clusters of slip bands
滑移带碎化　fragmentation of glide [slip] bands
滑移带形成　glide-band formation, formation of slip bands

滑移动力学　dynamic of glide
滑移断裂(口)　gliding fracture
滑移繁殖　multiplication of glide
滑移反射面　glide reflection plane
滑移-干扰(加工硬化)理论　slip-interference theory
滑移核　nucleus of slip
滑移痕迹　slip traces
滑移几何　geometry of glide
滑移阶　glide steps ◇ 往～深处生长(晶体的) growth in depth of glide steps
滑移晶体学　crystallography of glide
滑移局部化　localization of slip
滑移扩展　propagation of glide
滑移理论　theory of slip ◇ 贝克尔-奥罗万～*
滑移量　amount of slip
滑移裂纹　slip [pressing] crack
滑移流动　(gliding) flow
滑移面　slip [sliding, glide, gliding] plane, slip surface ◇ 相交～inter-secting slip plane
滑移面沉淀　slip plane precipitate
滑移面法线　normal of slip plane
滑移面析出　slip plane precipitate
滑移判据　criterion for slip
滑移区(域)　slip(ped) area [region], slip zone (金属轧制的), zone of slippage
滑移韧性断裂(口)　gliding fracture
滑移矢量　glide vector
滑移(示意)图　scheme of slip
滑移松弛　glide relaxation
滑移速率　rate of slip
滑移途径　slip path
滑移位错　glide [slip] dislocation
滑移位错理论　dislocation theory of slip
滑移系数　ratio of slip
滑移系(统)　glide [slip] system ◇ 静止[不活动]～*, 主动～active slip system
滑移现象　slip phenomenon
滑移线　slip line, worms,【金】Hartman(n) [Lueders] line, flow line ◇ 激活的～长

度*,交叉～ cross slip line,皮奥伯特～ Piobert lines
滑移线法 slip-line method [technique]
滑移线范围 slip-line field
滑移线痕(轧材矫直时的) stretcher strain markings
滑移线集聚 grouping of slip lines ◇ 强～*
滑移线扩展 propagation of slip lines
滑移线扇形化 fanning of slip lines
滑移线图样 slip-line pattern
滑移形变 slip deformation
滑移穴 slip pocket
滑移要素(晶体的) slip element
滑移引起的范性变形 plastic deformation by slip
滑移应变 glide [slip] strain
滑移硬[强]化 slip hardening
滑移运动 glide movement [motion]
滑移障碍 obstacle to slip
滑移阻力 slip resistance, resistance to slip
滑枕导轨 ram guide
滑座 slide guide [carriage]
滑座锯 (同"往复式锯")
滑座式换辊小车 sledge-type roll changer
画草图 block out, sketch
画齿规 odontograph
画法 draughting
画框式加压成形法(核反应堆燃料的) picture frame process
画图案 patterning
画线针 marking awl
画圆器 cyclograph
划分 division, partition, zoning
划分区域 demarcation
划痕 scratch, score, scoring, mar,【压】 scratch marks(钢板表面缺陷) ◇ 搬运造成的～ handling scratch,切割机～ cutting machine scratch
划痕器(抹灰用) scratcher
划痕试验 scoring test
划痕硬度 scratch hardness

划痕硬度刻度 scratch hardness scale
划痕硬度试验 scratch (hardness) test
划痕硬度试验机 scratch hardness tester
划痕硬度值 scratch (hardness) number
划痕阻力 scratch resistance
划伤 tear ◇ 热轧带～ hot strip scratches
划线 marking (off), marking-out, lining-out, sketch (钢板剪切前的)
划线板 ruler, marking-off
划线冲子 prick punch
划线规 marking [shifting] gauge
划线辊道 marking table, main mill table
划线机(厚板用) measuring machine, ruling engine
划线平板[台] faceplate, layout block, tracing-up plate
划线器 scriber, marker
划线区段 marking-out section
划线针 scriber, marking-off pin
化氨(作用) ammonification
化成电压 formation voltage
化肥级硫酸 fertilizer-grade sulfuric acid
化工厂 chemical plant
化工法 chemical engineering method
化工技术 chemical engineering technique
化工设备 chemical processing equipment
化合 (chemical) combination, (chemical) bonding ◇ 未～的 uncombined
化合氮 fixed nitrogen
化合反应 combination reaction
化合灰分 combined ash
化合价 valence, valency, adicity ◇ 潜～ latent valency,有效～*
化合价的 valent
化合量 combining weight
化合氰化物 combined cyanide
化合热 combination heat
化合水 combined [combination, constitution, hydrate] water, chemically bound water, chemically combined water [moisture], inherent [fixed] moisture
化合碳 combined carbon (CC), carbide

carbon（碳化物的）

化合物 compound (comp., cpd), chemical compound ◇贝陀立式~*, 定比[道尔顿式]~Daltonide(compound), 格里姆-佐默菲尔德~*, 加成~additive compound, 一致[相符, 同成分, 同熔点]~【金】congruent compound

化合物半导体 compound semiconductor ◇Ⅲ-Ⅴ族~*, 金属间~*

化合物分解 compound decomposition

化合物粉末 compound powder

化合物离解 compound dissociation

化合物生成 compound formation

化合形态[状态] combined form

化合作用 chemical combination

化石矿 fossil ore

化石燃料 fossil fuel

化铁炉 cupola (furnace), blast cupola, (iron) melting furnace

化铁炉半开式炉顶 cupola semiclosed top

化铁炉拆炉底机 cupola drag

化铁炉敞开式炉顶 cupola open top

化铁炉出铁槽 cupola spout

化铁炉出铁口黏土泥塞 bod, bot

化铁炉点火烧嘴 cupola torch

化铁炉可锻铸铁 cupola malleable iron

化铁炉前炉 cupola forehearth [receiver]

化铁炉支柱 cupola leg

化锡电炉 electric tin furnace

化学剥离法（涂层的） chemical stripping method

化学变化 chemical change

化学标准 chemical standard

化学表面处理法 chemical surface treating process

化学表面硬化 chemical surface hardening

化学不均匀性 chemical inhomogeneity

化学测定仪 determinator

化学掺杂剂 chemical dopant

化学常数 chemical constant

化学沉淀法 chemical precipitation method

化学沉淀金属粉末 chemically precipitated metal powder

化学沉积 chemical deposition [plating] ◇全~allochem

化学成分 chemical composition [component, constituent], elemental composition, analysis ◇出钢~tapping specification, 炉料~*, 配料~burden chemistry, 物料~material analysis, 一炉钢的~heat chemistry, 烧结矿~控制*

化学成分特别精确的钢 precision steel

化学除垢 chemical cleaning

化学除鳞 chemical descaling

化学触媒反应镍合金镀覆法 ◇卡尼津~Kanigen plating

化学处理 chemical treatment [processing] ◇阿尔卡尼（吕及铝合金）表面防蚀~法 Alkak method

化学处理段 chemical treatment section

化学处理钢（经钝化处理） chemically treated steel

化学纯（的） chemically pure (C.P.), chemical-pure

化学纯度 chemical purity

化学纯品位 chemical-pure grade

化学纯铅（杂质小于0.1%） chemical lead

化学纯锡 chempure tin

化学促进剂 chemical promotor

化学催化还原法镀镍 nickel coating by chemical catalystic reduction

化学催化剂 chemical catalyst

化学当量 chemical equivalent

化学底影（底片的） chemical fog

化学电离质谱测定法 chemical ionization mass spectrometry

化学淀积（物） chemical deposition

化学定量分析 quantitative chemical analysis

化学定性分析 qualitative chemical analysis

化学动力学 chemical kinetics

化学镀覆　chemical plating
化学镀金　chemigold plating
化学镀镍　(同"非电解镀镍")
化学钝性　chemical passivity, inactivity
化学惰性　chemical inertness, unreactivenes
化学发光　chemiluminescene
化学法富集　enrichment by chemical processes
化学反应　chemical reaction ◇ 局部～波峰 topochemical front, 起～attack, 无～渣 nonreactive slag
化学反应工程(学)　chemical reaction engineering
化学反应能力[(活)性]　chemical reactivity
化学反应器　chemical reactor
化学反应式　chemical equation
化学反应效率　chemical efficiency
化学方程式　chemical equation
化学方法　chemical method
化学防护法　chemical protective method
化学分解　chemical decomposition
化学分离　chemical separation
化学分析　chemical analysis ◇ 一般～*
化学分析试样　chemical analysis sample
化学粉碎　chemical disintegration
化学粉碎粉末　chemically disintegrated powder
化学封顶钢　chemically capped steel
化学腐蚀　chemical corrosion [attack] ◇ 抗～钢*, 耐～性 chemical resistance
化学腐蚀加工(法)　chem-milling, chemical-corrosive machining
化学覆层　chemical deposit
化(学)工厂　chemical plant
化学工程　chemical engineering
化学共沉淀　chemical coprecipitation
化学固定　chemical fixation, chem fix
化学固定法　chemfix process
化学固结　chemical induration
化学官能团　electrical functional group

化学灌浆系统(隧道掘进用)　chemical grouting system
化学过程　chemical performance
化学焊　chemical welding
化学合成　chemical synthesis
化学还原　chemical reduction
化学还原法镀镍　nickel plating by chemical reduction
化学还原法制造金属粉末　chemicometal process
化学回收　chemical reclaiming
化学活度　chemical activity
化学活性　chemical activity, chemism ◇ 非～金属 nonreactive metal, 无～渣 nonreactive slag
化学活性膜生成元素　chemically active film former
化学活性渣　reactive slag
化学活性状态　chemically reactive state
化学火焰沉积(法)　chemical flame deposition
化学机理　chemism
化学机械焊(接)　chemino-mechanical welding
化学激励剂　chemical energizer
化学剂黏结型砂　chemically bonded sand
化学剂稳定土壤　chemical soil stabilization
化学计量比　stoichiometric ratio
化学计量的　stoichiometric
化学计量点　stoichiometric point
化学计量[计算]法　stoichiometry
化学计量方程式　stoichiometric equation
化学计量化合物　stoichiometric compound
化学计量混合物　stoichiometric mixture
化学计量组成　stoichiometric composition
化学计算　stoichiometric calculation
化学计算比例　stoichiometric proportion
化学计算需要量　stoichiometric requirement
化学计算重量　stoichiometric weight

化学加工　chemical processing, chemical machining（金属的）
化学加热　chemical heating
化学键　chemical bond(ing) [link]
化学键合　chemical linkage
化学交换　chemical exchange
化学搅拌[搅动]　chemical agitation
化学结构　chemical structure
化学结合　chemical linkage, chemically-bond
化学结合耐火泥　chemically bonded refractory cement
化学结合砖　chemically bonded brick, chemical hardening brick
化学浸镀　electroless plating
化学浸液钎焊　reactive brazing
化学精整　chemical finishing
化学净化厂（自来水的）　chemical purification plant
化学净化　chemical purification
化学可混溶性　chemical compatibility
化学-矿物学组成　chemico-mineralogical composition
化学冷却　chemical cooling
化学历程　chemism
化学能　chemical energy [power]
化学凝集处理　chemical coagulation
化学凝聚剂　chemical coagulant
化学抛光　chemical polishing [brightening]
化学抛光剂　chemical polish (CP), chemical polishing agent
化学偏析　chemical segregation
化学平衡　chemical equilibrium
化学气相沉积　chemical vopour deposition
化学侵蚀　chemical erosion [etching, attack, wear]
化学亲合力[性]　chemical affinity
化学清理　chemical refining
化学清理与加工作业线　chemical-treating line
化学清洗　chemical cleaning [rinse, scrubbing]
化学缺陷　chemical defect [imperfection]
化学热　chemical heat
化学热处理　chemical heat treatment ◇粉状固体填料～法*，卡斯尔表面～法*
化学热的　chemico-thermal
化学热力学　chemical thermodynamics
化学熔剂　chemical flux
化学溶解　chemical dissolution
化学湿选法　wet chemical method
化学蚀刻　chemical milling [etching]
化学蚀损　chemical wear
化学式　chemical formula
化学示踪剂　chemical tracer
化学势[位]　chemical potential
化学试剂　chemical (re)agent
化学试剂区域精炼　zone refining of chemicals
化学数据　chemical data
化学损失　chemical loss
化学探测器　chemical detector
化学特性　chemical characteristics
化学提纯[精炼]　chemical refining
化学提取法　chemical extraction process
化学条件　chemical conditions
化学涂层　chemical coating
化学脱氧　【钢】chemical deoxidation
化学位梯度　chemical potential gredient
化学位移　chemical shift
化学文摘　Chemical Abstract (CHEMABS)
化学稳定（法）　【环】chemical stabilization
化学稳定土壤　chemical soil stabilization
化学稳定性　chemical stability
化学污泥　【环】chemical sludge
化学雾翳（底片的）　chemical fog
化学吸附的氧　chemisorbed oxygen
化学吸附色层（分离）法　chemisorption chromatography
化学吸附（作用）　chemical adsorption, chemisorption

化学吸收	chemical absorption
化学吸收膜	chemisorbed film
化学吸着	chemisorption
化学铣削	chemical milling
化学相容性	chemical compatibility
化学消泡剂	chemical froth breaker
化学效率	chemical efficiency
化学效应	chemical effect
化学行为	chemical behaviour
化学性缺陷	chemical imperfection
化学性质	chemical property [behaviour]
化学需氧量	【环】chemical oxygen demand (COD)
化学研磨	chemical milling
化学药品[药剂]	chemicals ◇ 含氧~ oxychemicals, 精细~ fine chemicals
化学药物溶解装置	chemical dissolving facilities
化学冶金学	chemical metallurgy
化学移动	chemical shift
化学因数	chemical factor
化学引爆[引发]剂	chemical booster
化学硬化(型砂的)	chemical hardening
化学硬化型砂	chemically solidifying moulding sand
化学硬化型芯	chemical-set core
化学浴槽	chemical bath
化学元素	chemical element
化学原理	(principle of) chemistry
化学匀质炉料	chemically uniform burden
化学杂质	chemical impurity
化学蒸发凝聚(法)	chemical vapour condensation
化学蒸气涂覆	chemical vapour plating
化学置换	chemical replacement
化学置换法镀金	(同"热浸镀金")
化学置换法粉末	replaced powder
化学质量	chemical mass
化学转化涂层	chemical conversion coating
化学着色	chemical tinting
化学族	chemical group
化学组成	chemical [elemental] composition
化学组分	chemical constituent ◇ 标称[公称]~*
化学作用	chemical action [attack]
化学镏金	chemigold plating
化验	assay(ing), analysis, chemical examination
化验单	test sheet, laboratory test report
化验结果	laboratory report
化验室	(control) laboratory ◇ 快速~ express laboratory
化验室设备	laboratory equipment
化验用坩埚	assay crucible
化验员	analyst, assayer
化油器	carburet(t)or
化渣操作	slagging operation
化整误差	rounding [round-off] error
坏风口	failed tuyere
环	loop, ring, annulus ◇ 艾里~*, 布勒尔~*, 成~looping, 德拜~*
环秤	ring balance
环磁场	circular field
环带式离子交换设备	endless belt ion-exchange plant
环带运输机	endless (belt) conveyer
环刀	cutting ring
环道	endless track, rotary road
环动仪	gyroscope (GYRO)
环锻	swage, swaging, ring rolling
环锻粉冶[粉末冶金]钨棒	swaged powder metallurgy tungsten rod
环锻机	(rotary) swaging machine
环锻金属条	swage bar
环锻钼条	swaged molybdenum bar
环风管	【铁】bostle pipe
环缝对接焊	circular [circumferential] seam welding
环辐式排列的钢筋	mushroom reinforcement
环箍	ring, strap ◇ 组合~built-up rim
环管	circle pipe

环规　ring gauge ◇ 基准校对～*
环辊破碎机　ring-roll crusher
环辊压(力)机　ring-roll press
环辊研磨机　ring-roll mill
环焊　girth welding ◇ 周圈～ contour welding
环焊试验　ring test
环己向二烯{C_6H_6}　1,3-cyclohexadiene
环己烷　cyclohexane
环己烯二醇四酮(玫棕酸)　rhodizonic acid
环接　ring joint
环境　environmental, circumstance, atmosphere
环境保护　environmental protection [control], house keeping
环境保护[环保]措施　antipollution measure, environmental measurement
环境保护法规　environmental protection legislation
环境保护[环保]局　environmental protection bureau, Environment Protection Administration (EPA) (美国)
环境保护[环保,环境污染防护]设备　environmental control equipment
环境大气　environmental atmosphere
环境除尘　room dedusting, general cleanup, housekeeping dust collection
环境除尘系统　room dedusting system
环境调查　environmental survey
环境复原　environmental reclamation
环境工程学　human engineering
环境管理　environmental control [management]
环境规划　environmental planning
环境化学　environment chemistry
环境监测　environmental monitoring
环境科学学会(美)　Institute of Enviromental Sciences (I.E.S.)
环境空气　ambient air
环境空气质量标准　ambient air quality standard

环境控制表　environment control table
环境评价　environmental evaluation
环境容限　acceptable environmental limit
环境受纳能力　environmental receptivity
环境特性　environmental behaviour
环境条件[状态]　environmental condition
环境微生物学　environmental microbiology
环境危害　environmental hazard, public menace
环境卫生　environmental sanitation, sanitation (sanit.) ◇ 城市～措施*
环境温度　ambient [environmental] temperature
环境污染　environmental pollution [contamination]
环境污染控制措施　environmental pollution control measure
环境污染罪　crime relating to environmental pollution
环境吸收能力　environmental assimilating capacity
环境效应　environmental effect
环境压力　environmental pressure
环境遥控系统　human remote control system
环境因素　environmental factor
环境应力　environmental stress
环境应力裂纹　environmental stress cracking
环境影响　environmental impact [effect] ◇ 非水质～*
环境噪声　environmental [ambient] noise
环境质量标准　environmental quality standard
环境作用　environment effect
环孔锥　annular bit
环冷机　【团】annular [rotary, circular] cooler ◇ 抽风～*, 底卸～*, 鼓风～*, 两段式～*, 深槽式～*
环冷机台车　cooler trough
环链　endless [calibrated] chain ◇ 链轮～

sprocket chain

环链式炉 link belt conveyer furnace

环梁 【铁】mantle (plate, ring), lintel girder, lintel [deck] ring

环梁柱 mantle pillar

环流 circulation, (re) circulating current [flow], circulation, circuiting

环流泵 circulating pump

环流量 circulating rate

环流模型 circulation flow model

环流系统 recirculating flow system

环六亚甲基四胺 (同"六甲撑四胺")

环切 circular [circle] cutting

环球法(测沥青软化点) ring and ball test

环圈 girdle

环绕捆扎 circumferential banding

环式焙烧机 circular grate, circular grate pelletizing machine [system], annular grate kiln

环式焙烧机(球团)法 circular grate pelletizing system, circular grate process

环式带材(三辊)冷轧机 ring type cold-strip mill

环式干燥机 ring drier

环式机 rotary machine [grate]

环式冷却机 (同"环冷机")

环式链箅机 circular grate

环式炉 (同"环形炉")

环式模顶管机 ring die push bench

环式破碎机 ring crusher

环式球团焙烧机 circular grate pelletizing machine

环式烧结机 circular-travel (l) ing grate machine

环式系统 toroidal system

环式窑 【团】annular kiln

环室型标准孔 ring-chamber standard orifice

环首螺栓 eyebolt, ring bolt

环套 bush(ing)

环套塔 【压】tower-type looper

环天平 ring balance

环头杆 eyebar, loop bar

环烷基 naphthenic base

环烷基铅极耐压油 naphthenic lead extremepressure resistance oil

环烷(属烃){CnH_2n} naphthene

环(烷)酸 naphthenic acid

环烷酸盐 naphthenate

环位移(X射线的) ring displacement

环戊二烯{C_5H_6} cyclonpentane, cyclopentadiene

环线示波器 loop oscillograph

环型孔板 ring-type orifice plate

环形槽 annular groove

环形槽试样(用于确定裂纹形成趋势) circular path specimen

环形衬垫[环形垫(板,圈)] back(ing) ring

环形衬砖(炉顶的) ring lining

环形出铁场 circular cast house

环形吹管 ring torch

环形磁场 circular (magnetic) field

环形磁铁 ring-shaped magnet

环形导轨 【团】circular guide

环形导气管 gas ring duct

环形等离子体 toroidal plasmas

环形垫片 ring gasket

环形电磁型X射线管 toroidal electromagnetic type X-ray tube

环形电子枪 annular [toroidal] gun

环形锭料 circular charge

环形断裂[裂缝] ring crack

环形耳轴 ring trunnion

环形风[围]管 bustle pipe

环形风管吊挂锚栓 bustle main anchor

环形风管接头 bustle main junction

环形风管系统 bustle pipe system

环形风管压力 bustle pipe pressure

环形缝隙 annular slit

环形腐蚀 ring worm corrosion

环形干线[管路] ring main

环形感应电炉 ring-shaped induction furnace

环形钢轨　circular rail
环形格筛　ring grizzly
环形轨道　circular track
环形辊式运输机　endless roller carrousel
环形滚焊　circumferential seam welding
环形焊道　circular bead
环形焊缝　circular [circumferential, girth] weld, circumferential [girth] seam
环形(焊缝)滚焊[环形缝焊]机　circular [circumferential] seam-welding machine, circular [circumferential] seam welder, girth welder
环形焊缝焊接　(同"环焊")
环形焊炬　ring torch
环形计数器　ring counter
环形加热炉　rotating hearth furnace
环形加热喷嘴　annular heating nozzle
环形件锻造　ring forging
环形焦点　annular focus
环形浇口　ring gate
环形接头　circular joint
环形阶式轴承　collar step bearing
环形孔板　annular orifice
环形扩散　ring diffusion
环形链　stud chain
环形梁　【铁】ring girder
环形料层　annular layer
环形裂纹　circumferential crack, halo
环形炉　annular [circular, doughnut, ring] furnace, rotary (hearth) furnace ◇ 深室式～*
环形炉缸[坩埚]　ring (shaped) crucible, annular crucible
环形炉膛　annular hearth
环形[状]冒口　ring riser
环形排列机理(原子的)　ring mechanism
环形排水槽　garland
环形配水管网　ring distribution system
环形皮带运输机　endless belt
环形取样器　ring sampler
环形燃烧器　circular [ring] burner
环形试样　ring-shaped specimen

环形水冷通道　【连铸】annular water-cooling passage
环形套筒　annulus
环形天线　ring [loop] antenna, box loop
环形天线塔　loop tower
环形弯曲　rotational bending
环形位移　ring displacement
环形系统　loop [toroidal] system
环形镶块(约束)抗裂试验　circular-patch (restraint) test
环形型芯　ring core
环形压力计　ring manometer
环(形)窑　ring kiln ◇ 霍夫曼～Hoffmann kiln, 室式～transverse-arch kiln
环形轧材　annular [circular] shape
环形止推轴承　collar (thrust) bearing
环形铸铁场　circular cast house
环形转底炉[环形旋转炉底加热炉]　(circular) rotary hearth furnace
环行辊道　run-around table, encircling roller table
环行铁道　circuit railroad
环行运输机　circus
环氧覆面钢筋混凝土模　epoxy-faced concrete die
环氧树脂　epoxy (resin) ◇ 阿拉尔代特～Araldite, 埃庞热硬性～Epon, 埃皮科特热硬性～Epikote
环氧树脂胶　epoxide-resin glue
环氧树脂类及无机黏合剂　metlbond
环氧树脂模型　epoxy pattern
环氧树脂涂层　epoxy coating
环轧　ring rolling
环转窑　【团】annular kiln
环状齿囊　tooth annulus
环状抽风(烧结)冷却机　(同"抽风环冷机")
环状磁畴　closure domain
环状发散喷嘴　annular divergent nozzle
环状构造　ring-shaped structure, ring formation
环状辊式粉碎机　annular roller mill

环状焊瘤(管子对焊的) liver
环状化合物 ring compound
环状夹(头)[夹持器] ring clamp
环状胶片剂量计 film ring
环状炉 (同"环形炉")
环状磨损(拉模的) ringing
环状平台(转炉用) circular platform
环状生长阶 growth loop
环状填料塔 ring-packed tower
环状通路 annulus
环状凸缘 collar flange
环状芽孢杆菌 Bacillus circulans
环状衍射花样 halo
环状圆穹顶 circular domical vault
环状(振动)方式 annular modes
环状钻头 annular bit
还原 reducing, reduction, deoxidation, deoxidization, deacidizing, regeneration, restitution, recovery, restore ◇ 催化～ catalytic reduction, 电解～ electrolytic reduction, 电热～ electrothermal reduction, 钙热～(法)*, 汞齐～ amalgam reduction, 金属热～*, 经～的 reduced, 空气～(炼铅) air reduction, 两段～ two-stage reduction, 流态化床～*, 铝热～*, 难[不可]～矿 irreducible ore, 气体[态]～*, 熔融～*, 使～ hydrogenize, 碳热～*, 未～的 unreduced, 用原子氢～ reduction by atomic hydrogen, 有选择的～ preferential reduction, 增浓～*, 振动盘～*

还原焙砂 reduced calcine
还原焙烧 reduction [reducing] roast(ing)
还原焙烧法 roasting reduction method
还原焙烧炉 reduction roaster
还原本领 reducing power
还原比 reduction ratio
还原不足 insufficient reduction
还原操作 reduction run
还原槽 reducing bath ◇ 铬酸盐～*
还原产物 reduction product
还原厂[车间] reduction plant

还原成分 reducing component
还原成核动力学 reduction nucleation kinetics
还原程度 degree of reduction
还原处理 reducing [reduction] treatment
还原萃取 reduction [reductive] extraction
还原带 reduced [reducing] zone, zone of reduction
还原弹 reduction bomb [vessel] ◇ 厚壁～ heavy walled bomb, 耐火材料衬里的～ refractory-lined bomb, 石灰衬里的～ lime-lined bomb, 直熔锭～ dingot bomb
还原弹壁温度 bomb wall temperature
还原弹产出率[产量] bomb yield
还原弹衬里 bomb liner
还原弹坩埚 bomb crucible
还原弹料 bomb charge
还原弹料组成 bomb charge constituent
还原弹炉 bomb furnace
还原弹内腔 bomb cavity
还原弹预热 bomb preheat
还原弹轴耳 bomb's trunnion
还原弹装料机 bomb filling machine
还原递降 degradation on reduction
还原电极 reducing electrode
还原电位 reduction potential
还原动力学 reduction kinetics
还原度 reducibility (index), reduction-degree
还原(度)指数 reducibility index ◇ V.D.E.法～ V.D.E. index, 林德～*
还原法 reduction process [method] ◇ 钢弹～*, 交替～双金属～*, 碳～*, 自热钙粉～*
还原反射炉 reduction reverberatory furnace
还原反应 reducing [electronation] reaction ◇ 弹内[金属热]～ bomb reaction
还原反应器 reduction reactor ◇ 不锈钢～*, 动态床～*, 连续～*
还原反应器[还原弹(外)]壳 reduction shell

还原反应式	equation for reduction
还原粉化	【团】reduction disintegration, degradation by [on] reduction, breakdown during reduction
还原粉化率[指数]	reduction degradation index (RDI)
还原粉粒	reduced particle
还原粉末	reduced powder
还原副产物	reduction byproduct
还原坩埚	reduction crucible [mould]
还原钢弹	(同"还原弹")
还原钢弹装置	reduction bomb assembly
还原钢罐	bomb crucible
还原高压釜	reduction autoclave
还原隔板	reduction baffle
还原罐[锅]	reduction pot
还原过程	reduction process
还原后(抗压)强度	resistance after reduction (RAR)
还原后冷抗压强度	【团】cold compression strength after reduction
还原后强度	strength after reduction (SAR)
还原后溶液	reduction end solution
还原环境	reducing environment
还原活化剂	reduction activator
还原机理	reduction mechanism
还原剂	reductant, reducing (re) agent [material, matter, medium], reductive [electronating, hydrogenant] agent, reducer, reductor, reduced substance, deoxidant, deoxidizer ◇ 铝－硅热法～*, 内加～ internal reactant, 弱～ mild reducing agent, 铈热～ cerium-thermic reducer, 碳质～*, 外加～ external reactant
还原剂氟化物	reductant fluoride
还原剂氯化物	reductant chloride
还原剂氧化物	reductant oxide
还原阶段[时期]	reduction stage
还原介质	reducing medium
还原金属	reducing metal
还原浸出	reduction leaching, reducing leach ◇ 高温～*
还原矿石	reduced ore
还原炼铁法	reduction ironmaking method
还原料	reduction charge
还原料混合物	reduction charge mixture
还原料液	reduction feed solution
还原炉管	reduction (furnace) tube
还原炉料透气性	reduced-burden permeability
还原炉渣	reducing slag
还原炉装置	assembly of reduction furnace
还原氯化联合法	combined reduction-chlorination process
还原氯化联合炉	combined reduction-chlorination furnace
还原率	percent reduction, reducibility index, ratio of reduction, reduction-degree
还原能力	reducibility, reducing capacity [ability, power], reduction power, deoxidation power
还原膨胀曲线	swelling-reduction curve
还原期	reduction period [cycle], deoxidation period
还原器	reducer
还原气氛	reducing (gas) atmosphere
还原(气氛)炉	reducing [reduction] furnace ◇ 连续加料～*, 竖式～*
还原气体[煤气]	reducing gas
还原气体组成	reducing gas composition
还原前净化	prereduction purification
还原强度	reduction strength
还原氢气	hydrogen reducing gas
还原区	(同"还原带")
还原热	reduction heat
还原热力学	reduction thermodynamics
还原熔炼	reduction smelting [melting]
还原熔炼法	reducing smelting (process)
还原熔炼坩埚	reduction smelting crucible
还原容器	reduction container [vessel]
还原软化性状	reduction-softening behaviour
还原烧结(法)	reduce sintering

还原设备　reduction plant [apparatus, facilities], reducing unit
还原时间　reduction time
还原势　reduction [reducing] potential
还原试验　reduction test ◇ C.N.R.M. (国家冶金研究中心)～法(比利时)*, 伯格哈特～Burghardt test, 程序控制～*, 德国钢铁协会～法 V.D.E. method, 负荷～*, 林德回转炉～法*, 千叶～(法)*, "学振"～法*
还原试验装置　reduction test apparatus
还原收缩孔　reduction shrinkage hole
还原竖炉　vertical reduction furnace
还原速率　reduction rate
还原碎裂　(同"还原粉化")
还原塔　reduction tower
还原态金属　as-reduced metal
还原特性　behaviour under reducing conditions
还原条件　reducing condition [environment], reduction condition
还原铁　reduced [reduction] iron ◇ 粒状～【铁】iron ball
还原退火(粉末的)　reduced anneal(ing)
还原钨粉　reduced tungsten powder
还原物质　reduced substance, reducing matter
还原系数　coefficient of reduction
还原系统　reduction system
还原箱　reduction sagger
还原效率　reduction efficiency
还原性　reducibility, reducing character [capacity] ◇ 内禀[本征,固有,真实]～intrinsic reducibility
还原(性火)焰　reduction [reducing] flame, carbonizing [carburizing] flame
还原(性)气氛　reducing (gas) atmosphere
还原(性)气体　reducing [reduction] gas
还原性燃料喷吹　injection reducing fuel
还原性熔化[熔接]　reducing fusion
还原性数据[指标]　reducibility data
还原性质　reducing property
还原性状[行为]　reduction behaviour, behaviour during reduction, behaviour under reducing conditions
还原-亚硫酸(处理)焙烧　reducing-sulphiding roasting
还原-氧化　reduction oxidation (red.ox.)
还原窑　kiln reducer
还原再熔铸锭法　reduction-casting process
还原渣　deoxidizing slag
还原蒸馏　reduction distillation
还原蒸馏罐　reduction retort
还原中心　reduction center
还原终结溶液　reduction end solution
还原舟皿　reduction boat
还原装置　set-up for reduction
还原状态　reduced state
还原作用　reducing action
缓冲　buff(er), cushion, damping, redemption, amortization ◇ 消息～message buffer
缓冲板　baffle (plate)
缓冲仓　surge bin
缓冲槽　buffer vessel, surge tank
缓冲层　buffer layer, cushion
缓冲存储器　buffer (storage)
缓冲垫　cushion(ing), bumper
缓冲电池(组)　buffer battery
缓冲电路　buffer circuit
缓冲斗仓　surge hopper ◇ 包装～packing surge hopper
缓冲放大器　buffer amplifier (BA)
缓冲辊　snubber roll ◇ 带卷～coil snubber roll
缓冲辊道　retaining rller table
缓冲混合液　buffer mixture
缓冲剂　buffer, buffer (re)agent, depressor
缓冲块(摇床的)　bumping block
缓冲矿仓　feed surge bin
缓冲矿槽　surge hopper
缓冲联轴节　resilient coupling

缓冲梁　buffer beam
缓冲料仓[槽]　buffer bin
缓冲轮　buffer wheel
缓冲能力　buffer capacity, buffering power
缓冲器　buffer (stop), bumper, bumping post, cataract, cushion, damper, dashpot, shock damper [absorber, insulator], snubber ◇接点输入～contact input buffer, 炉内双联式～double furnace bumper, 气垫～*, 人工操作～*, 数据～data buffer
缓冲气体　buffer gas
缓冲区　buffer zone
缓冲溶液　buffered solution
缓冲容量　buffer capacity
缓冲筒式定时器　dashpot-type timer
缓冲圆筒(浓缩槽的)　central well
缓冲桩　cushion piles
缓冲装置　buffer unit, cushioning device
缓冲作用　buffer action
缓动继电器　slow-acting [slow-operating] relay
缓动区(高炉炉缸的)　low-motion zone
缓断开关　slow-break switch
缓发 α-粒子辐射体　delyed-alpha emitter
缓发放射性　delayed activity
缓发辐射　delayed radiation
缓发屈服(现象)　delayed yield(ing)
缓发相变　delayed transformation
缓发形变　delayed deformation
缓发中子　delayed neutron
缓发中子辐射体　delayed neutron emitter
缓和　moderating, mitigation, modification, modulation
缓和剂　moderating material, moderator
缓和热应力材料　thermal stress relaxing material
缓和渗碳剂　milder carburizer
缓化剂　negative catalyst
缓化(作用)　negative catalysis
缓冷　retarded cooling
缓冷工段　slow cool zone
缓冷坑　burial pit, slow cooling pit furnace (钢材的)
缓冷坑盖　slow cooling pit cover
缓冷区段　slow cool section
缓冷室　slow cooling chamber
缓冷箱　slow cooling box
缓冷状态　slow-cooled condition
缓慢反应　deferred reaction
缓慢放出(铁水、钢水)　sluggish tap
缓慢沸腾　【钢】simmer
缓慢燃烧　retarded combustion
缓凝剂　inhibiting agent, retarder ◇水泥～cement retarder, 外加～*
缓凝水泥　retarded cement
缓蚀　corrosion inhibition
缓蚀剂　(pickling, rust) inhibitor ◇酸洗～restrainer, 吸附型～*, 阳极～anodic inhibitor, 乙炔～*, 阴极～cathodic inhibitor, 有机～organic inhibitors
缓蚀纸　inhibited paper
缓释继电器　slow-releasing relay
换班　crew change, change shifts
换标　scale
换衬台(转炉的)　【钢】relining stand
换出　【计】swap-out, swap(ping)
换挡机构　shifter
换挡装置　shifting device
换道　【压】conversion
换电枢装置　armature change-over system
换杆器　rod changer
换辊　roll change [changing] ◇C形～钩 C-hood (roll changer)
换辊班[组]　roll change crew
换辊侧　changing side, off side ◇轧机机座～roll change side
换辊车　roll changing carriage [truck], changing car
换辊工　roll changer
换辊滑车　roll changing sledge
换辊机构　roll change mechanism, roll changing device
换辊设备　roll changing equipment
换辊套筒　roll changing sleeve ◇长型～

porter bar

换小车 roll change buggy ◇ 滑座式～*

换辊用[换辊装置安设]坑 roll change pit

换辊装置 roll change over device, roll changer, roll changing device [gear, rig], roll exchange device, changing rig, shifter ◇ 侧移式～side shifter,立辊对重～*,支承辊～*,自动～*

换极开关 pole-changing switch

换接 changing-over, throw-over, transition

换接触点 break-make contact

换接电极尖[点] (electrode) transition tip ◇ 巴特尔式～*,富特式～*,改良韦斯廷豪斯～*

换进[入] 【计】swap-in, swap(ping)

换镜旋座(显微镜的) (revolving) nosepiece

换孔 【压】conversion

换流器 convector,【电】transverter, converter, convertor, inverter

换炉(热风炉的) changing over stove

换炉衬 relin(ing)

换炉信号 【铁】switchover signal

换炉周期(热风炉的) cycle time

换模 die changing

换模器[装置] die changer [shifter]

换能器 transducer, transverter, changer ◇ 双镶嵌式～twin mosaic transducer, 有源～active transducer,多头～装置 multiple-transducer assembly

换频管[器] frequency changer

换气 air interchange [renewal], gaseous exchange ◇ 小时～次数 air change per hour

换热 heat interchange [transfer] ◇ 抽风回转～*,导热姆～剂,狄菲尔～剂

换热炉 recuperative oven

换热器 (heat) exchanger, (heat) interchanger, recuperator (同流式) ◇ 板式～plate heat exchanger, 管式～tubular heat exchanger, 壳管式～*, 热管～heat pipe exchanger, 油对油～*

换热器砌块 recuperator block

换热器(砖)管 recuperator tube

换热式均热炉 recuperative soaking pit ◇ 阿姆柯～Armco soaking pit

换热式空气加热器 recuperative air heater

换热式空气预热器 recuperative air preheater

换热式冷却器 recuperative cooler

换热式热风炉 ◇ 惠特威尔～Whitwell stove

换热室(同流式) recuperator

换热砖管 recuperator tube

换数字档 figure shift

换算 conversion, convert, scale, scaling, translation, transform

换算表 (inter)conversion table

换算操作 scale operation

换算单位 exchangeable bases

换算电路 scaler, scale [scaling] unit ◇ 二进制～binary scaler,十进位～decade scaler

换算面积 exchange area

换算器 scaler

换算曲线 adjusted curve

换算图表 conversion chart

换算系数 conversion coefficient, scaling [reduction] factor

换算因子 conversion factor

换位 transposition, change of positions

换位连接 cross connection

换位型缺陷 (同"反结构型缺陷")

换相器 phase changer [converter]

换向 change-over, commutation, reversal, reversing, switch(ing), throw-over ◇ 可～的 switchable

换向阀 reversing [change-over] valve ◇ 空气～air-reversing valve

换向机 reversing winch,【焦】reversing machine

换向机构 reversing mechanism

换向极 commutating pole	黄饼(人造钒铀矿) yellow cake
换向开关 change-over [reversing, commutator] switch, reverser	黄长石{Ca$_{12}$Al$_4$Si$_9$O$_{36}$, Ca$_4$Si$_3$O$_{10}$} mel(l)ilite
换向控制点焊 commutator-controlled welding	黄丹{PbO} yellow lead, (yellow) lead oxide
换向器 direction change device, change gear bracket, reverser, switchboard,【电】commutator, collector ◇ 风冷式～*	黄碲矿{TeO$_2$} tellurite
	黄碘银矿 miersite
	黄镀锌层 yellow galvanized coat
换向器辐 【电】commutator spider	黄钙铀矿 becquerelite
换向器环 commutator ring	黄干油 grease
换向器紧缩环 commutator shrink ring	黄锆(英)石 【地】jargoon
换向器片 commutator segment	黄钴土 【地】tuvite, hovaxite
换向器竖片 commutator riser	黄硅钙铌矿 niocalite
换向器铜条 commutator bar	黄硅钾铀矿 boltwoodite
换向区 commutating zone	黄化 【压】rusting, sull(ing)(钢丝的) ◇ 快速～*
换向绕组 commutating winding	
换向时间 change-over [turnaround] time	黄化处理(钢丝的) sull-coating
换向式燃烧 combustion with cycling reversing	黄钾铁矾 jarosite
	黄钾铁矾除铁法 jarosite process
换向台 change-over station	黄钾铀矿 compreignacite
换向线圈 commutating coil	黄金 gold, aurum ◇ 不纯～impure gold, 低开[低成色]～low-karat gold, 高开[高成色]～high harat gold, 首饰～jewellery gold
换向旋塞 reversing [change-over] cock	
换向循环加热 reversing cycle heating	
换向装置 direction change device, reversing arrangement ◇ 小～tumbling gear	
	黄金头寸 【企】gold tranche
换新 renewal	黄晶{M$_2$SiO$_4$(F,OH)$_2$} topaz
换用(的)转炉 alternate vessel	黄蜡布绝缘 cambric insulation
换渣 change of slag	黄蜡绸带 varnished silk tape
幻数 magic number	黄磷 yellow phosphorus, phosphor
幻线 phantom line	黄磷铅铀矿 (同"多水磷铅铀矿")
幻像 ghost (image)	黄磷铁钙矿 xanthoxenite
幻影 ghost	黄菱钡铈矿 khannesite
幻影信号 ghost signal	黄绿色(的) green-yellow (yel-grn)
荒锻 dummying	黄绿色金合金 greenish-yellow gold alloy
荒管 pierced billet, hollow forging ◇ 热轧小直径～*	黄绿石{CaNb$_2$O$_6$·NaF} pyrochlore
	黄绿渣 【铁】bottle green slag
荒煤气 raw coke oven gas,【铁】raw [crude] gas	黄麻包皮(电缆的) jute
	黄麻绳芯 jute core
荒坯 half-finished brick	黄钼铀矿{UO$_3$·2MoO$_3$·4H$_2$O} iriginite
黄白色(回火色) yellow-white	黄镍铁矿 heazlewoodite
黄斑 yellow design (钢板上脂肪酸氧化膜), copperhead (金属板镀层缺陷)	黄曲霉素中毒 【环保】aflatoxicosis
	黄色黄铜 yellow brass ◇ 铸造～*

黄 huang

黄色金合金 (同"22开黄金")
黄色铝青铜(H 型:10Al,90Cu;M 型:5Al, 95Cu;S 型:3Al,97Cu) oranium bronze
黄色条纹(钢板的) yellow treak
黄色氧化钨 yellow tungsten oxide
黄闪锌矿{ZnS} rosin jack
黄砷锰矿 xanth(o)arsenite
黄砷镍矿 xanthiosite
黄砷铀铁矿{Fe$_2$(UO$_2$)$_2$(AsO$_4$)$_2$·8H$_2$O} kahlerite
黄蓍胶 tragacanth (gum)
黄水钼铀矿{UO$_3$·2MoO$_3$·4H$_2$O} iriginite
黄酸钾 (同"黄原酸钾")
黄碳锶钠石 burbankite
黄锑华{H$_2$Sb$_2$O$_5$} stibiconite
黄锑矿{2Sb$_2$O$_4$ 或 Sb$_2$O$_3$·Sb$_2$O$_5$} cervantite
黄铁矾 ihleite
黄铁矿{FeS$_2$} pyrite, pyritic ore, iron pyrite (ore), xanthopyrite, mundic, brassi, brazil, fools gold ◇ 钴镍～ cobalt-nickel pyrite, 含～的煤 pyritic [dross(y)] coal, 含钴～*, 含铜～*
黄铁矿粉焙烧炉 pyrite dust roaster [furnace]
黄铁矿还原 pyritic reduction of ore
黄铁矿精矿 pyrite concentrate
黄铁矿硫 pyritic sulphur
黄铁矿烧渣 pyrite cinder [residue], pyritic calcines [residue],【铁】purple ore
黄铁矿烧渣低温氯化浸出法 ◇ 朗梅德－亨德森～*
黄铁矿烧渣浸出 leaching of pyritic cinders
黄铁矿渣 pyrite dross, pyritic slag
黄铁矿渣焙烧 roasting of pyrite residues
黄铁矿渣烧结矿 pyrite sinter
黄铁矿渣直接炼制铁水法 ◇ 施图策尔伯格～ Sturzelberg process
黄铜 brass, yellow brass, copper-zinc alloy ◇ α[单相]～*, α-β型[双相,热压印]

～*,β～*,γ～*,δ～*,奥雷德～*,奥立恰尔～ Orichalc (h), 薄片～ latten brass, 标准～*, 低铅～*, 低锌～*, 蒂西尔～*, 杜尔纳～*, 镀～*, 顿巴克[德国]～*, 发动机[电动机]～*, 废～ brass scrap, 高(抗拉)强度～*, 高铅～*, 高铜～*, 高锌～ platina, 管乐器～*, 光亮～*, 规尺～*, 过(高温)退火～ overannealed brass, 过烧～*, 海军[船用]～*, 海滕西尔～*, 焊料～ brazing brass, 荷兰～*, 褐色～*, 红色～*, 加铅～*, 较易切削～ semifree cutting brass, 金霍恩～*, 兰菲夏～*, 类～ brassy, (冷却)辐射管用～*, 两相～ duplex brass, 六 O～*, 罗尼阿～ Ronia, 耐蚀～*, 平奇贝克八五～*, 普通～*, 七 O [三七] ～*, 浅红 [中锌] ～(8—17Zn) semi-red brass, 热压～*, 日本～(66.5Cu, 33.4Zn) Sinchu, 深冲用～ deep-drawing brass, 蚀刻用[铸版] ～ etching brass, 首饰～*, 熟[可锻] ～ wrought brass, 特高铅～*, 特种～ special brass, 图尔南～*, 无铅～ nonleaded brass, 西尔卡洛伊～ Silcalloy, 牙科～ wiegold, 易锻造～*, 优质[高级] ～ high brass, 再生[工业] ～*, 针用～*, 中铅～*, 铸造～*, 装饰～*, 字模～ matrix brass

黄铜板(宽>500毫米,厚0.75—4.5毫米) sheet brass, brass sheet ◇ 金色～带*, 中厚～ brass plate
黄铜棒(材) brass rod
黄铜薄板 sheet brass
黄铜箔 brass foil, shim brass(垫片用), flitter gold
黄铜厂 brass works
黄铜衬套 brass bushing
黄铜带 brass strip
黄铜代金合金 ◇ 戈尔丁～(90Cu, 10Zn) Goldine
黄铜电焊条 brass electrode
黄铜镀层 brass coating

黄铜废料　brass scrap
黄铜粉　brass powder ◇ 扩散合金化~*,预制~*
黄铜粉取样器　brass thief
黄铜盖板　brass lid
黄铜工　brazier
黄铜管　brass pipe ◇ 埃瓦~(冷凝器用) Ever-brass
黄铜焊料(40—60Cu,余量 Zn)　brass [strong] solder, brass brazing alloy ◇ 希夫~合金*
黄铜焊料钎焊缝　brazed seam
黄铜焊条　brass welding rod
黄铜合金　brass alloy (80—95Cu,余量 Zn) ◇ δ~系*,EX-B~*,低锌[红色]~*,徽章用~*,克里索林~*,钟壳~*
黄铜接头　braze joint
黄铜矿{$CuFeS_2$}　【地】chalcopyrite, copper pyrite, yellow copper ore
黄铜模　brass pattern
黄铜抛光剂　brass polishes
黄铜配制的铸铁阀　brass fitted cast iron valve
黄铜坯　brass billet ◇ 烧结~块 sintered brass compact, 小直径~*
黄铜片　latten [shim] brass ◇ 深拉用~ eyelet brass
黄铜钎料　brazing spelter
黄铜熔铸炉　brass furnace
黄铜色的　brassy, brazen
黄铜丝　brass wire ◇ 制针用~ pin wire brass
黄铜丝网　brass net
黄铜细工(厂)　brazied
黄铜型(铜合金)　brass type
黄铜型假金　◇ 莫塞克~*
黄铜阳极(镀黄铜用)　brass plater
黄铜轧材　brass mill product
黄铜轧机　brass mill machine
黄铜质　brassiness
黄铜制品　brass (product) ◇ 烧结~ sintered brass product
黄铜制造　[银钎、镀]braze
黄铜中毒热　brass shakes, brass founder's
黄铜制品精整　brass finishing
黄铜铸工(锌烟尘中毒)病[黄铜中毒热]　brass shakes, brass founder's ague, metal fume fever
黄铜轴承　brass bearing
黄铜铸件　brassing
黄铜铸件清整工　brassing dresser
黄铜铸造(厂)　brass foundry
黄土　loess
黄雾翳　yellow fog
黄锡　【地】rosin tin
黄锡矿　【地】tin pyrite
黄榍石　【地】xanthotitanite
黄血盐　(同"亚铁氰化钾")
黄药　【选】xanthate, xanthogenate
黄钇钽矿{(Y,Er,Ce,Sc,U,Th)(Ta,Nb)O_4}　formanite
黄银矿　xanthoconite
黄油　grease, fat, solid lubricant
黄油杯[盅]　grease cup, lubricator
黄油盒　grease chamber
黄油枪　grease gun, lubricating screw
黄油润滑　grease lubrication
黄油箱　grease tank
黄玉{$M_2SiO_4(F,OH)_2$}　topaz
黄原酸钾{$KS_2COC_2H_5$}　potassium xanthate
黄原酸钠{RO·CS·SNa}　sodium xanthate [xanthogenate]
黄渣　speiss ◇ 焙烧~ roasted speiss, 含钴~*, 含砷~ arsenical speiss, 锑~ antimonial speiss
黄渣处理　speiss treatment
黄渣放出口　speiss tap-hole
黄渣浸出　speiss leaching
黄针铁矿{Fe_2O_3}　xanthosiderite
黄棕色(回火色)　yellow-brown
磺胺　sulphanilamide, sulphanilic amide
磺胺噻唑　sulphathiazole

磺酚树脂胺　sulphonated phenolic resin
磺酚阳离子交换树脂　sulphonated phenolic cation exchange resin ◇ 215～*，道克斯 30～Dowex 30，杜利特 C-10～*，卢泰特 DN～*，沃法泰特 KS～*
磺化　sulphonating, sulfonating, sulphonation, sulfonation ◇ 不可～的烃*
磺化焙烧　sulphonating roast
磺化处理　sulphonating treatment
磺化反应　sulphonation reaction
磺化剂　sulphonating agent
磺化交联苯乙烯共聚物　sulphonated cross-linked styrene copolymer
磺化聚苯乙烯　sulphonated polystyrene
磺化聚苯乙烯树脂　sulphonated polystyrene resin
磺化聚苯乙烯阳离子交换树脂　polystyrene-sulphonic acid type cationite ◇ 225～Zeo-Karb 225, HCR～*，道克斯 50～Dowex 50，杜利特 C-20～*，卢泰特 KSN～Lewatit KSN，珀缪泰特 Q～Permutit Q，切姆普罗 C-20～Chempro C-20
磺化煤　sulphonated coal
磺化煤阳离子(HI)交换剂　Zeo-Karb HI
磺化煤阳离子(Na)交换剂　Zeo-Karb Na
磺化天然有机物(即磺化煤)　sulphonated natural organic product
磺化阳离子交换树脂　sulphonated cation resin
磺基　sulphonic acid group, sulfo group
磺基丁二酸盐[酯]　sulphosuccinate
磺基水杨酸　{HO₃SC₆H₃(OH)CO₂H} sulphosalicylic acid
磺基琥珀酸盐[酯]　sulphosuccinate
磺酸{RSO₃H}　sulphonic acid, sulpho-acid
磺酸基{HSO₃⁻}　sulphonic acid group
磺酸树脂　sulphonic acid resin
磺酸盐[酯]　sulphonate, sulfonate
簧板　spring plank
簧环　circlip
簧片　reed, leaf, striking blade

簧片阀　leaf-valve
簧片黄铜(69Cu,30Zn,1Sn)　reed brass
簧式捻钢丝绳　spring lay wire rope
簧丝芯撑　jammer
簧托　spring bracket
灰斑(钢板的)　greyness
灰斑镀锡薄板　dry plate [streak]
灰板墙筋(材料)　studding
灰尘　dust
灰尘负载　dust load
灰尘凝聚　dust conglomeration
灰吹　【色】cupel(late)
灰吹法　cupelling, cupellation (process, method)
灰吹炉　cupel(lation) [cupelling] furnace
灰吹炉渣　cupel slag
灰吹盘　cupel, bone ash disc
灰点　【金】grey spots
灰分　ash (constituent), ash [dirt] content ◇ 含～的 cindery
灰分测定　ash determination
灰分单位曲线　ash-unit curve
灰分分布曲线　ash distribution curve
灰分分析　ash analysis
灰分高的　high ash
灰分含量　ash content
灰分扩散控制　ash-diffusion control
灰分浓度　ash concentration
灰分软化温度　ash-softening temperature
灰分试验　ash test
灰分特性曲线　characteristic ash curve
灰分误差　ash error
灰分杂质　ash-forming impurities
灰缝　mortar joint
灰腐[侵]蚀　ash attack
灰化　ashing, incineration,【压】chalking（上石灰）
灰黄铜合金　ash metal
灰浆　mortar
灰浆返料　solution return
灰浆搅拌机　mortar mixer
灰浆接缝　dipped joint

灰浆砌合　mortar bond
灰胶纸柏板　gypsum
灰金[灰黄铁铜合金]（83Cu,17Fe）　grey gold
灰镜铁　grey spiegel
灰坑　ash-pit,ashcan
灰口　greyness ◇ 反～
灰口化（铸铁的）　greying
灰口(生)铁[灰生铁]　graphitic (pig) iron,grey (pig) iron ◇ 波尔顿～浸蚀剂*
灰口铁铸件　grey iron casting
灰口与球墨铸铁铸造师学会　Gray and Ductile Iron Founder's Society (GDIFS)
灰(口)铸铁　grey [gray] cast iron ◇ 奥氏体～*,变质～*,加硅处理的～*,片状石墨～*,铁素体～*,杂料回炉～*
灰口铸铁粉　grey cast-iron powder
灰冷　ash cooling
灰硫砷铅矿　jordanite,reniforite
灰锰矿　grey manganese ore
灰锰氧　（同"高锰酸钾"）
灰皿　【色】cupelling furnace,cupel
灰皿试金法　cupellation
灰泥　marl,plaster,parget
灰泥板　gypsum
灰泥捕集器　【铁】sludge trap
灰泥厂　plaster plant
灰泥澄清　slurry clarification
灰泥分离器　【选】slime separator
灰泥浓缩池[澄清机]　slurry clarifier
灰耙　hoe
灰盘　ash-pan
灰铅矿　tinyte
灰熔聚流化床（粉煤气化用）　ash melted agglomeration fluidized bed
灰鞣槽　liming tub
灰色次砖　grizzle
灰色浮渣　【色】grey scum
灰色系统理论　grey system theory
灰色锌糊　grey zinc mush
灰色预测　grey prediction

灰砂砖　sand-lime [limesand] brick
灰砷锰矿　elfstorpite
灰石比　【铁】stone rate
灰水比　cement-water ratio (c/w)
灰锑矿　gray antimony
灰体　greybody
灰铁锰矿　partridgeite
灰瓦克　graywacke,greywacke
灰雾密度　fog density ◇ 底片～ fog density of film
灰锡　grey tin,tin pest
灰锡变态[同素异性体]　grey tin modification
灰霞石　cancrinite
灰箱模型　grey-box model
灰楔高温计　grey wedge pyrometer
灰渣　ash,clinker
灰渣混凝土　ash concrete
灰渣石灰铺面　lime-ash flooring
灰锗矿　briartite
灰汁　lixivium
灰质黏土　adobe,adobe soil
灰中冷却　ash cooling
灰铸铁　（同"灰口铸铁"）◇ 轻度麻口～
灰铸铁研究学会　Gray Iron Research Institute (GIRI)
灰组分　ash component
挥发　volatilizing (volat.),volatilization, evaporization,flashing ◇ 不～残渣 fixed residue,氯化～*
挥发焙烧[煅烧]　【色】volatilizing [volatilization] roast(ing)
挥发成分[挥发性组分]　volatile component [constituent],light constituent
挥发带　subliming zone
挥发碘化物　volatile iodide
挥发度　volatility
挥发度测定　volatilization test
挥发度积　volatility product
挥发度计　vapourimeter
挥发法　volatility process,volatilization method

挥发分[挥发性化合物] volatile compound ◇ 脱~(作用) devolatilization
挥发氟化物 volatile fluoride
挥发硫 volatile sulphur
挥发卤化物 volatile halide
挥发卤化物萃取 volatile halide extraction
挥发氯化焙烧 volatilizing chlorinating roasting
挥发氯化物 volatile chloride
挥发率 volatilization rate
挥发器 volatilizer
挥发溶质 volatile solute
挥发损失 volatilization loss
挥发温度 volatilization temperature
挥发物 volatile matter (V.M.), volatile, volatimatter, sublimation product
挥发物含量 volatile(-matter) content
挥发物回收率 volatile-matter yield
挥发性 volatileness, volatility, evaporativity, evaporability, vapourability, vapourizability, fugacity ◇ 不~fixity, 易~fugitiveness
挥发性产物 volatile product
挥发性二碘化物 volatile diiodide
挥发性防锈[缓蚀]剂 volatile errosion inhibitor
挥发性固体 evaporative solid
挥发性金属 volatile metal
挥发性馏分 volatile distillates
挥发性轻油 volatile light oil
挥发性氢化物 volatile hydride
挥发性熔剂 volatile flux
挥发性溶剂 volatile solvent
挥发性润滑剂 volatilizing lubricant
挥发性四氟化硅{SiF_4} volatile silicon tetrafluoride
挥发性碳氢化(合)物 volatile hydrocarbon (V.H.C.)
挥发性羰基镍 volatile nickel carbonyl
挥发性涂层 volatile coating
挥发性压制润滑剂 volatile pressing lubricant

挥发盐 free salt
挥发冶金学 vapometallurgy
挥发油 benzin(e), naphtha
挥发杂质 volatile impurities
挥发增孔剂 volatile spacing agent
挥发柱 【焦】free leg
挥发作用 volatilization
辉铋矿{Bi_2S_3} bismithine, bismuthine
辉铋锑矿 horobetsuite
辉铋铜矿 cuprobismutite
辉长岩 gabbro
辉碲铋矿{$Bi_2Ti_3S_3$} tetradymite, tellur(o)bismuthite
辉点 bright spot ◇ 阳极~anode spot
辉度 brilliance, brilliancy, brightness
辉钴矿{CoAsS} cobaltite, cobalt glance
辉光 glow(ing)
辉光灯丝[加热器] glow heater
辉光放电 glow-discharge
辉光(放电)灯 glow(-discharge) lamp
辉光放电管 glow-discharge tube [lamp]
辉光放电加热 glow discharge heating
辉光放电渗氮[放电氮化,离子氮化] glow discharge nitriding, ionitriding
辉光放电探测器 glow discharge detector
辉光放电整流管[器] glow-discharge rectifier
辉光(离子)炉 glowing furnace
辉光启动器 glow starter
辉矿类 glance
辉绿岩 diabase, dolerite
辉煤 glance coal
辉钼矿{MoS_2} molybdenite ◇ 液体~ (见"液体钼精矿")
辉钼矿焙烧炉 molybdenite roaster
辉钼矿精矿 molybdenite concentrate
辉镍矿 polydymite, beyrichite
辉(砷)钴矿{CoAsS} cobaltite
辉砷镍矿{NiAsS} amoibite, gersdorffite, nickel glance
辉石{$Ca(Mg,Fe,Al)(Si,Al)_2O_6$} pyroxene, pyroxenite, pyroxines, augite

辉石－钛铁矿转变	pyroxene-ilmenite transition
辉铊矿	carlinite
辉锑矿 $\{Sb_2S_3\}$	antimony glance, stibnite, grey antimony (ore), antimonite
辉锑铅矿 $\{Pb_4Sb_{14}S_{27}\}$	zinkenite
辉锑锡铅矿 $\{5PbS·2SnS_2·Sb_2S_3\}$	franckeite
辉锑银矿	miargyrite
辉锑银铅矿	fyzelyite
辉铁矿	iron glance
辉铁锑矿	(同"硫铁锑矿")
辉铜矿 $\{Cu_2S\}$	chalcocite, copper glance, cyprite
辉铜锑矿	(同"硫铜锑矿")
辉纹	striation
辉纹边界	striation boundary
辉钨矿	tungstenite
辉硒银矿	aguilarite
辉银矿 $\{Ag_2S\}$	argentite, argyrite, argyrose
辉银铅锑锗矿 $\{28(Pb,Fe)S·11(Ag,Cu)_2S·3GeS_2·2Sb_2S_3\}$	ultrabasite
徽章用黄铜合金 (86Cu, 14Zn)	medal alloy
恢复	recover(y), restoration, restore, rehabilitation, restitution ◇ 不可～的 non-recoverable, 可～的错误 recoverable error
恢复打印码	【计】print restore (PR)
恢复电压	recovery [restoration] voltage
恢复规划	rehabilitation program
恢复时间	recovery [restoring] time
恢复特性	recovery characteristic
恢复系数	recovery coefficient [ratio], coefficient of restitution
回摆	oscillation (osc.), backswing
回摆单晶	(同"振荡单晶")
回摆晶体	oscillating crystal
回摆晶体(X射线)衍射花样	oscillating-crystal (X-ray) pattern
回摆(晶体)X射线衍射图	oscillation X-ray diagram
回摆晶体法	oscillating crystal method
回摆盘法	(同"摆动盘法")
回摆球法	oscillating sphere method
回摆现象	(同"振荡现象")
回爆	【焊】popping
回波	echo (wave), return waves, anacamptic sound, bounce ◇ 炉底～ bottom bounce
回波法	echo method
回波脉冲	echo (im)pulse
回波区	echo(ing) area
回波探测法	echo sounding
回波探伤器波形图	reflectogram
回波图像	double image
回波效应	echo effect
回波信号	echo (signal)
回波振荡器	backward wave oscillator
回波作用	doubling effect
回采	ditch, recovery ◇ 矿石～ ore extraction
回采率	rate of extraction, recovery (ratio)
回车(打印时的)	(carriage) return
回程	back [return, retracting] stroke, return trip
回程缸	return [drawback, pullback] cylinder
回程皮带	return belt
回程室[缸]	pullback chamber
回程速度	return speed
回程运动	back(ward) motion, return motion [movement]
回冲程	back stroke
回磁比	gyromagnetic ratio, g-factor
回萃器	back wash extractor
回滴定	back titration
回递(通过上轧辊)	drag-over
回动杆	reverse lever
回动机构	reverser, reversing mechanism
回动拉杆	reversing linkage
回动装置	reverse gear, tension cage (试验机的)

回复 reversion, revert, restoration,【金】recovery
回复动力学 【金】recovery kinetics
回复过程 recovery process
回复扩散理论 diffusion theory of recovery
回复理论 theory of recovery
回复期 rest period
回复蠕变 recovery creep
回复时间 recovery [turnaround] time
回复速率 recovery rate
回复现象 recovery phenomena
回复形态理论 formal theory of recovery
回复原位(指仪表) home
回归(合金的) reversion
回归分析 【数】regression analysis ◇ 多重~*
回归设计 regression design ◇ 混料~*
回归时效(沉淀硬化合金系的) 【金】retrogression
回归系数 regression coefficient
回归线 tropic
回归正交试验 regressive normal test
回混 back mixing
回火 【金】tempering (drawing), flare back,【钢】(美国用语) drawing(-back),【焊】(气焊火焰的) back-fire, popping ◇ 保护气氛~*, 贝氏体~bainite tempering, 弹簧油~blazing off, 第三阶段~third stage tempering, 电~electric tempering, 电炉~*, 多次~multiple tempering, 二重[两次]~double tempering, 光亮~bright tempering, 过度~overtempering, 即速~*, 加载[应力]~*, 局部[选择]~*, 抗~性[能力]*, 蓝色~的 blue finished, 铅浴~lead tempering, 消除应力~strain-relief tempering, 在油中~的 tempered in oil (Tpo), 中温~*, 自~self-tempering
回火薄钢板 temper sheet ◇ 半硬~*, 光整冷轧的软~*, 特软~*
回火保险罐 【焊】flash back tank
回火保险器 【焊】flash (back) arrester
回火贝氏体 tempered bainite
回火槽 【金】tempering tank [bath]
回火处理 【金】tempering treatment ◇ 低温~*, 硬化~drawing treatment
回火脆性 temper brittleness [embrittlement]
回火脆性状态 temper brittle condition
回火电炉 electric tempering furnace
回火度 degree of temper
回火锻钢 tempered forged steel (TFS)
回火钢 tempered steel ◇ 奥氏体~austempered steel
回火介质 tempering medium
回火冷轧 temper rolling
回火裂纹 tempering crack
回火炉 temper(ing) [draw(ing)] furnace
回火炉装料 tempering charge
回火马氏体 tempered [black] martensite, β-martensite
回火马氏体脆化[脆性] tempered martensite embrittlement
回火母曲线 master tempering curve
回火铅槽 lead tempering bath
回火铅基轴承合金 tempered lead alloy
回火强化 temper stressing
回火曲线 tempering curve
回火屈氏体 temper [secondary] troostite
回火色 temper(ing) colour, temper drawing colour, temper, heat [letting, oxidation] tint, hot tinting
回火砂 tempering sand
回火石墨 temper graphite
回火时间 temper [tempering] time
回火时效 temper ageing
回火索氏体 tempered [secondary] sorbite, full tempered sorbite
回火碳 temper carbon [graphite]
回火温度 tempering [draw(back), drawing] temperature
回火(温度)范围 tempering range
回火温度与冲击韧性关系图 (同"冲击

韧性与回火温度关系变化曲线")
回火效应　drawing effect
回火性　drawability
回火性能　tempering property
回火性能曲线　tempering curve
回火氧化皮　temper scale
回火硬度　tempered [tempering] hardness
回火硬度值　temper number
回火硬化　temper hardening
回火硬化镍铝黄铜　temper hardening brass
回火油　tempering oil
回火质量　tempering quality
回火状态硬度　tempering hardness
回火着色　colouring by tempering
回火着色法　temper tinting method
回火组织　tempered structure
回拉　reverse drawing
回廊　(winding) corridor
回廊拱　cloister arch
回力(接触焊的)　return force
回磷　rephosphor(iz)ation, phosphorus kickback
回磷钢　rephosphorized steel ◇ MC 型
回磷现象　phosphorus reversion
回硫　resulfurization, resulphurized
回流　return [inverse] flow, back-flow, reflux(ing), spill-back,【团】recoup ◇ 在部分～之下运转(指蒸馏塔) finite reflux operation
回流泵　reflex [reflux] pump
回流比(精馏塔的)　reflux ratio
回流部分　refluxing portion
回流槽　return launder
回流萃取　reflux extraction
回流阀　reflux [return] valve
回流干管　return main
回流供应　reflux supply
回流管道[路]　reflux [recirculation] line, return piping
回流换热段　recuperation section

回流集气管　recuperated air header
回流交换器　reflux exchanger
回流空气　return air
回流冷凝器　reflux [return] condenser
回流量　quantity of reflux
回流热烟气　【团】hot recuperation gas
回流蛇形管　reflux coil
回流设备　refluxing unit
回流水　return water
回流塔　reflux tower [column], refluxing unit
回流塔盘　refluxing tray
回流(系统)热量　recoup system heat
回流蓄热法　(同"逆流蓄热法")
回流烟道　recuperated air header
回流烟气　recoup gas
回流蒸馏　reflux distillation, cohobation
回流柱　reflux column
回流装置　reflux unit
回炉废钢铁　recycled [return] scrap
回炉废料　scrap return ◇ 高质量～
回炉金属　recirculated metal
回炉炉渣　return slag
回炉铁　recirculated iron
回炉物料　revert
回路　(return) circuit, return, chain, contour ◇ 伯格斯～*, 无电～ dead circuit
回路电阻　loop resistance
回路分级机　loop classifier ◇ 哈丁式～*
回路控制　loop control
回路水槽　circuit water tank
回路图　contour map
回能　resilience, resiliency
回能模量　modulus of resilience
回汽管道　steam return line
回热　back heating, post heating (钢丝焊接后的)
回热段　recuperation section
回热[回流换热]方法　method of heat recuperation
回热[回流换热]方式　recoup mode ◇ 旁通管～bypass mode

| 回热风机 (heat) recuperation fan
| 回热管道 (heat) recoup duct
| 回热炉罩 circulating hood
| 回热器 heat regenerator ◇ 金属套管~ metal-shiethed heater
| 回热气流 recoup gas (flow), recoup system gas
| 回热气流调节闸板 recoup flow damper
| 回热系统 (heat) recoup system
| 回热系统烟气 recoup system gas
| 回熔 melt-back
| 回熔扩散法 melt-back diffusion method
| 回熔型晶体管 melt-back transistor
| 回烧 【焊】burning-back
| 回声 echo, bounce (back), anacamptic sound ◇ 炉底~ bottom bounce
| 回声法 echo method
| 回声面积法 echo area method
| 回声探测法 echo [reflection] sounding
| 回声效应 echo effect
| 回声作用 doubling effect
| 回收 recover(y), reclaim, regain ◇ 不可~的 nonrecoverable, 从矿石~金属 depletion, 副产物~ by-product recovery
| 回收百分数 recovery per cent
| 回收泵 recovery pump
| 回收槽 reclaiming tank
| 回收厂[车间,设备] recovery plant ◇ 废酸~
| 回收方法 recovery method
| 回收废钢 return [revert, reclaimed] scrap
| 回收废料 recovered [reclaimed] scrap
| 回收粉尘 returned [reclaimed, reprocessed] dust
| 回收工段 recovery section
| 回收硫酸 reclaimed sulfuric acid
| 回收率 recovery (ratio), coefficient [rate] of recovery, recovery efficiency [factor], percentage recovery, rate of return,【采】rate of extraction
| 回收率误差 yield error
| 回收设备 recovery plant [system], reclaimer ◇ 副产品~
| 回收酸 restored acid
| 回收系数 coefficient of recovery
| 回收系统 recovery system
| 回收液泵 recovered liquor pump
| 回收液槽 recovered liquor tank
| 回收油 return oil
| 回收蒸汽 recovered steam
| 回收装置 reclaiming unit [machine], regeneration plant
| 回授 (同"反馈")
| 回授栅极检波器 ultra-audion
| 回水 return (ing) [reclaimed] water, backwater, damming ◇ 浮筒式~盒 bucket steam trap
| 回水干管 return main
| 回水供应槽 return water supply tank
| 回松装置 unjamming gear
| 回送辊 stripper rolls
| 回送辊道 pullback roll table
| 回送检查 loopback test
| 回弹 spring-back, resilience, resiliency, rebound ◇ 去除~(现象) spring-back elimination
| 回弹力 resilience, resiliency
| 回弹(能)模量 modulus of resilience
| 回弹吸收能量 resilience absorbed energy
| 回弹性 rebound elasticity
| 回弹仪 resiliometer
| 回弹应变 rebound strain
| 回提 back extract(ion)
| 回填 【建】backfill(ing), refilling ◇ 夯实~土
| 回跳 (re)bound, bounce, knock-on, recoil, kick-back
| 回跳硬度 (同"肖氏硬度") ◇ 弗雷蒙~试验 Fremont (impact) test
| 回跳硬度计 scleroscope, durometer (钢轨用) ◇ α(钢轨)~ alpha durometer, 携带式~ duroscope, duroskope
| 回头曲线 hairpin curve
| 回退键 【计】backspace key

回洗　back scrubbing [flush]
回洗萃取　back wash extraction
回洗水　back (wash) water
回线　loop (line, wire), return cable ◇ γ~【金】gamma loop
回线测试仪　loop tester
回线示波器　loop [galvanometer] oscillograph
回行段　return strand
回行轨道　【团】return rail
回行机构　reverser
回行皮带　return belt
回行台车　【团】returning pallet
回性水　tempering water
回旋　convolution
回旋层　whirling bed
回旋共振　cyclotron resonance
回旋加速器　cyclotron, circular accelerator ◇ 电子~betatron
回旋加速器运动　cyclotron motion
回旋破碎　vortex crushing
回旋破碎机　gyratory (gyr.)
回旋区　raceway (zone)
回旋曲线　clothoid
回旋质谱仪　omegatron
回压　back [return] pressure (BP)
回压阀　back pressure valve
回音　echo, anacamptic sound
回折点　inflexion point
回转　gyration, rotation, revolution (rev.), rotary motion, slew, swing, turn (over)
回转360°　swivel round
回转半径　radius of gyration
回转泵　rotary pump
回转不锈钢笼(浸出用)　rotating stainless steel cage
回转车　【耐】carrousel
回转萃取塔　rotary column
回转打印机　rotary stamping machine
回转定径机　rotary sizer ◇ 管坯~billet sizer

回转短窑　(同"短窑")
回转锻造　swage forging, rotary squeeze
回转锻造机(管头的)　tube-swaging machine
回转阀　rotary valve
回转翻车机　revolving tipper, drum tripper
回转干燥炉　rotary drier, rotary drying furnace ◇ 哈丁~Hardinge drier
回转钢桶(磨光用)　rotating steel drum
回转高压釜　rotating autoclave ◇ 卧式~*
回转鼓风机　rotary blower
回转辊　turn-roll
回转过滤机　rotary filter
回转号码机　annunciator
回转滑阀　rotary slide valve
回转混合器　rotary blender
回转机构　rotation [turning, slew(ing), swivel] gear, swiveling mechanism
回转机械真空泵　rotary mechanical pump
回转夹紧装置　rotary jig
回转加热炉　rotary heating furnace
回转架　swing bracket
回转晶体法(X射线分析)　revolving-crystal method
回转精炼炉　rotary refining furnace
回转冷却器　rotary cooler
回转炉　rotary [rotating, revolving] furnace, rotary converter, revolver ◇ 成对~twin rotating furnace, 福富米带换热器~Fofumi furnace, 圆筒形~*
回转炉底　revolving bed, rotary hearth, rotating hearth (环形加热炉的)
回转炉法　rotating hearth process
回转炉箅　rotary [revolving] grate
回转炉箅发生炉　revolving grate producer
回转炉箅煤气发生炉　rotary grate gas producer
回转罗盘　gyro(-compass)
回转能力　slewability
回转器　gyrator, gyroscope (GYRO)
回转热交换器　rotary heat-exchanger

回 hui

回转筛 rotary [revolving] screen, rotating sieve	回转星状加料器 rotary star feeder

回转筛筒破碎机 rotary breaker
回转烧结炉 rotary sintering furnace
回转式棒材加热炉 rotating billet heating furnace
回转式淬火炉 rotary hardening furnace
回转式锻尖机 pointing swager
回转式锻造机 rotary forging machine
回转式煅烧炉 rotary calciner, rotary calcining furnace
回转式煅烧窑 rotary calcining kiln
回转式飞剪 rotary flying shears
回转式干燥机 rotary dryer ◇ 多管~*
回转式火焰刨切机 rotary flame planing machine
回转式剪切机作业线 rotary-shear line
回转式铰链[折叶] rotating hinge
回转式锯 rotary saw
回转式冷却机 rotary-type cooler
回(转)式漏斗 swivelling tundish
回转式模座 rotary die carrier
回转式起重机 (同"旋臂起重机")
回转式球团炉 rotating nodulizing kiln
回转式热飞锯 rotary flying hot saw
回转式烧嘴 swivelling burner
回转式送锭车 rocking buggy
回转式洗气机 【铁】rotary disintegrator
回转式压砖机 revolver press
回转式阳极炉 anode casting barrel
回转式运输机 rotary conveyor
回转(式)真空泵 rotary vacuum pump ◇ 盖德~*
回转式中间包[回转(式)漏斗] swivelling tundish
回转塔 swing tower
回转塔式冲头 turret punch
回转台 turn table, turnaround (machine) ◇ 线卷~*
回转筒 rotary [revolving] drum
回转弯头(180°) return bend
回转洗涤篮 tumbling basket

回转窑 rotary [rotation] kiln (furnace), rotary unit, rotating cylindrical kiln, rotating furnace ◇ 带孔~ ported rotary reactor, 短型~ shortrotary furnace, 工业型~*, 间歇式~ batch kiln, 立波尔~ Lepol system [furnace], 粒铁~ nodulizing kiln, 烧焦炉煤气~ coke oven gas-fired rotary kiln, 烧煤气的[煤气加热]~ gas-fired rotary kiln, 实验型~ laboratory type kiln, 水泥~ cement (rotary) kiln, 卧式~ horizontal rotary kiln, 圆筒~ cylindrical rotary kiln

回转窑焙烧 kiln firing
回转窑操作 kiln performance
回转窑衬里 kiln lining
回转窑衬砖 rotary-kiln block
回转窑点火器 kiln firing hood
回转窑二次风 kiln secondary air
回转窑反应器 rotating kiln reactor
回转窑辅助烧嘴风机 auxiliary kiln burner fan
回转窑滚圈 kiln riding ring
回转窑还原法 kiln(-reduction) process
回转窑还原粒铁冶炼法 ◇ 克房伯-雷恩~ Krupp-Renn process
回转窑结圈 kiln ringing
回转窑进料口 kiln entrance
回转窑炉料 kiln feed
回转窑内半径 inner kiln radius
回转窑内腔 kiln interior
回转窑排料(端) (rotary-)kiln discharge
回转窑排料流 kiln discharge stream
回转窑-气流干燥系统 combination rotary/flash dryer
回转窑热烟气流 hot kiln gas flow
回转窑烧结球球 lump
回转窑烧结球团矿法 Follsan process
回转窑烧嘴 rotary-kiln burner
回转窑生铁生产法 ◇ 卡尔多型~*
回转窑式干燥器 rotary-kiln dryer
回转窑铁矿处理法 ◇ 巴塞~*

回转窑托辊　kiln support roller
回转窑外半径　outer kiln radius
回转窑尾气温度　kiln offgas temperature
回转窑温度曲线　kiln temperature profile
回转窑窑头　exit end of kiln
回转窑窑头罩　kiln firing hood
回转窑运行[运转]状况　kiln behaviour [performance]
回转窑主烧嘴风机　kiln burner fan
回转液压缸　rotary hydraulic cylinder
回转油真空泵　rotary oil pump ◇快速～*
回转圆筒焙烧炉　revolving cylinder roaster
回转圆筒过滤机　rotating cylinder filter
回转圆筒筛　revolving (screen) trommel
回转运动　rotary motion, gyration, revolution
回转载气泵　rotary gas ballast pump
回转真空过滤　rotary vacuum filtration
回转真空过滤机　rotary vacuum filter ◇艾姆科～*,奥利弗～*,线排料～*
回转轴　revolution axis, rotating shaft
回转装置　turning device [arrangement], turner, turnover gear (检查轧件用) ◇带卷～*
回转座　revolving bed
毁坏　destroy, damage, break (age), destruction, injure, demolition
毁损　damage, impair, breakage
惠更斯目镜　Huygens' eyepiece
惠龙橡皮模成型法　Wheelon forming process
惠普尔电阻高温计　Whipple indicator
惠氏规号(薄板厚度或钢丝直径的)　Whitworth gauge
惠斯登电桥　Wheatstone bridge
惠斯勒液压成型法　Whistler hydro-dynamic process
惠特威尔换热式热风炉　Whitwell stove
会话方式　conversational mode
会话式分时　conversational time-sharing
会话式远程作业输入　conversational remote job entry (CRJE)
会话语言　conversational language
会话终端　conversational terminal
会聚　convergence, convergency, converging, condensation ◇射线束的～beam convergence
会聚冲击波　converging shock waves
会聚冲击波成形法　converging shock method
会聚法　convergence method
会聚角　angle of convergence ◇射束～beam convergence angle
会聚射束　convergent beam
会聚透镜　converging lens
会刊[会议论文集]　proceedings (proc., procs), journal of association [society]
会切点　cusp, spinode
会议呼叫　conference call
会议录　proceedings (Pr.)
汇编程序　assembler, assembly program ◇交叉～cross assembler,绝对地址～absolute assembler,一对一～one-to-one assembler
汇编控制语句　assembly-control statement
汇编命令　assembler directive [command]
汇编系统　assemble [assembly] system
汇编语言　assembler language
汇编语言编码　assembly language coding
汇编语言加工程序　assembly language processor
汇编语言输出　assembly language output
汇编指令　assembler instruction
汇合　converge, join, merge
汇集　converge, assemble, collect, compile, influx
汇集时间　【计】binding time
汇接室　junct(ion) box
汇流管道　bus duct
汇流环　collector [slip] ring, collector-shoe gear
汇流排　busbar (wire), omnibus bar ◇电

解槽~【色】cell busbar, 阳极~ anode busbar

汇流式放大器(射流技术的) focused jet amplifier

汇流条 bus-bar ◇ 热挤压~extruded bus bar

汇票 【企】bill (of exchange), draft, draught ◇ 远期~time draught

汇水面积 catchment area

绘图 drawing (drg, drw., dwg), plotting

绘图板 drawing [plotting] board

绘图比例尺 drawing scale

绘图笔 drawing [plot] pen

绘图机 plotter, drawing [draught] machine ◇ 全值~控制~

绘图器 (curve) plotter ◇ 扩大~diagraph

绘图室 drawing chamber [room]

绘图仪 graphic plotter, plotting instrument ◇ XY坐标~XY plotter

绘图仪器 drawing apparatus ◇ 全套~draughting set

绘图圆规 drawing compass

绘图纸 drawing paper

绘制 mapping

彗星尾状构造 comet tails

彗星状枝晶晶粒头部 head of comet grain

彗形像差 coma [comatic] aberration

浑浊度 opacity, turbidity

浑浊度计 opacity meter

混成 hybridization, blend [mix] together

混沌理论 chaos theory

混粉仓 miscellaneous materials fines bin

混汞 【色】amalgamate, amalgamation, amalgamize, quick(en)ing, quicksilvering ◇ 佩蒂奥~提银法

混汞表面 amalgamating surface

混汞槽 amalgamating barrel

混汞车间 amalgamating plant

混汞电精炼 amalgam electrorefining

混汞法 amalgamation, amalgam(ation) process ◇ 捣锤~battery amalgamation, 盘内~pan amalgamation, 转桶式[滚桶]~barrel amalgamation

混汞金属 amalgamated metal

混汞溜槽 plate amalgamator

混汞器[机] amalgamator, amalgamating barrel

混汞溶液 amalgam solution

混汞桶[滚筒,提金器] amalgamation [amalgamating] barrel

混合 mix(ing), mixture, admix(ing), admixture, blend(ing), compound(ing), intermingle, intermix ◇ 充分~intensive mixing, 人工~hand mixing

混合比(例) mixing-ratio, mixture [blending] ratio

混合不足 undermixing

混合槽 mixer [mixing] blending tank, mixing vessel [ark]

混合车间 mixing plant

混合沉淀装置 mixer-settler apparatus

混合沉降级 mixer-settler stage

混合沉降[沉淀]器 mixer settler ◇ 泵送~pump-mix mixer-settler, 单搅拌~*, 两相均上升的~(萃取的) mixer-settler with both phases lifted, 螺旋升液~*, 四级~*, 一列式~in-line mixer-settler, 重相上升的~*

混合沉降器萃取设备 mixer-settler type plant

混合沉降箱接触器 mixer-settler box contactor

混合沉降装置 mixer-settler system

混合沉降萃取器 mixer-settler extractor ◇ 霍利莫特搅拌式~Holley Mott extractor

混合程度 degree of mixing

混合澄清萃取槽 mixed settler extractor

混合床 mix bed

混合床(过)滤器 mixed-bed filter

混合床离子交换 mixed-bed ion exchange

混合床离子交换设备 mixed-bed ion exchanger unit

混合床树脂交换器　mixed-bed exchanger
混合点火　combination firing
混合电缆　compound cable
混合电路　composite circuit
混合阀　mixing valve
混合法　method of mixture, alliage
混合反应　mixed reaction
混合放大器　mixed amplifier
混合废钢　mixed scrap
混合粉矿球团　blended ore pellet
混合粉末　mixed-powder, composite powder
混合辐射　mixed radiation
混合复合材料　hybrid composite
混合钢　mixed steel
混合工段　【团】mixing section
混合构造　mixed construction
混合管　mixing tube, mixing head（喷焊器的）
混合过程　mixing process
混合海绵金属　blended sponge
混合焊接梁　hydrid beam
混合还原料　reduction charge mixture
混合机　mixer blender, conditioner, fluffer, melangeur ◇（皮带）轮式～ belt shredder, 带式～ belt mixer (unit), 单轴～ single-shaft mixer, 多锥型～ multi-cone mixer, 二次～ granulation drum, 干式～ dry mixer, 集中～ central mixer, 间歇式[分批]～ batch mixer, 桨叶[叶轮]式～*, 快速～ positive mixer, 立式～ vertical blender, 六角[边]桶～ hexagonal barrel mixer, 螺旋～*, 碾磨式～ muller-type blender, 盘式～ pan mixer, 三次～ tertiary mixer, 双筒～*, 双轴～*, 循环～ circulating mixer, 圆筒～*, 重力～ gravity mixer, 转臂式～ revolving arm mixer, 转筒[转鼓式]～*, 锥形～*
混合集成电路　hybrid integrated circuit
混合挤压　coextrusion
混合剂　intermixture
混合计算机（模拟数字混合）　hybrid computer
混合继电器　mixing relay
混合搅拌器　mixing agitator
混合结构　combination construction, composite [mixed] structure
混合金属焊接梁　hydrid beam
混合金属硫化物　mixed metal sulphides
混合金属坯块　compound compact
混合金属热还原　mixed metal thermo-reduction
混合金属涂层　miscellaneous metal coating
混合晶　mix(ed)-crystal
混合晶粒　mix granule
混合晶粒度　mixed [duplex] grain size
混合晶种　mixed seed
混合精矿　mixed [blended, bulk] concentrate, concentrate blend
混合孔板　mixing panel
混合控制　mixed control ◇ 基于知识的～系统 knowledge based hybrid control system
混合矿球团　mixed ore pellet
混合矿(石)　mixed ore, ore mix
混合矿石料　ore mixture
混合矿组分　blended composition
混合垃圾　mixed garbage
混合冷凝器　mixing condenser
混合炼钢法　cocktail process
混合料　blended [conditioned] mix, (inter)mixture, mix [pugged] material
混合料布料器　raw mix feeder
混合料仓　【铁】blending bin
混合料槽　raw mix [material] hopper, mixing bin, roll feeder surge bin, mix container, surge hopper,【团】mixed material hopper
混合料处理[运输]　mix handling
混合料堆　mixing heap
混合料反射率系数　blend reflectance index(BRI)
混合料过湿机理　mechanism of mix over-

wetting	
混合料化学成分	mix chemistry, mixture analysis
混合料计算	mix calculation
混合料结构	mix texture
混合料结构组成	mixture structure
混合料均匀性	raw mix consistency
混合料粒度	(raw) mix granulometry
混合料粒度分布	mix-size distribution
混合料粒化	granular batching
混合料配比	mix (material) proportioning
混合料配比调整	mixture adjustment
混合料配料系统	raw mix proportioning system
混合料燃料含量	fuel content of raw mix
混合料烧结透气性	raw mix sintering permeability
混合料水分控制	mix moisture control
混合料系统	mix circuit
混合料压块	batch briquetting
混合料压实	mix compaction [consolidation]
混合料压实密度	mix packing density
混合料真密度	true density of mix
混合料制备设备	mix preparation equipment
混合料准备	mix preparation
混合料组成	blend composition
混合料组分[成分]	mix component,【耐】batch component
混合料组分比率	ratio of mixture
混合硫化矿	mixed sulphide ore
混合硫化物	mixed sulphides
混合流	mixing flow, mixed flow
混合锍	mixed matte
混合炉	holding hearth [furnace]
混合炉料	mix-charge, burden mix (高炉的)
混合煤	duff [duft] coal, coal blend
混合煤气	(同"混合气体") ◇ 发生炉、高炉与焦炉～dreigas, 焦炉 - 高炉 -～*
混合煤气发生炉	mixed gas producer
混合煤气管道	piping for mix-gas
混合模拟	hybridsimulation, hybrid analog-digital simulation
混合膜润滑	mixed-film lubrication
混合磨矿	mix grinding
混合摩擦	mixed friction
混合耐火材料	composite refractories
混合能消耗	mixing power input
混合黏土	compounded clay
混合碾	mixing pan mill
混(合)捻钢丝绳	alternate lay wire rope ◇ 麻钢～combi-rope
混合喷射器	injector mixer
混合喷嘴	mixing [combining, composite] nozzle, injector mixer
混合器	mixer, blender, admixer, commingler,【冶】mixing machine ◇ V形～vee-blender, 级联～cascade of mixers, 耙式～rake mixer, 竖式[轴式]～shaft mixer, 双螺旋～*, 辛普森型～Sympson type mixer, 循环～circulating mixer, 锥形～cone blender
混合气爆炸成形	gas (mixture) forming
混合气管道	piping for mix-gas
混合气体	mix(ed) [mixture, combination, complex] gas, gas mixture
混合气体保护焊	mixed gas arc welding
混合气体成形法	gas mixture process
混合气体气氛	mixed gas atmosphere
混合气体装置	mixture gas system
混合区	composite region
混合燃料	fuel mixture, fuel combination, burning mixture
混合燃料烧结	mixed firing
混合燃烧	combination [mixed] firing, mixed combustion
混合燃烧系统	【团】dual-burning system
混合热	mixing [(ad)mixture] heat
混合溶剂(萃取)法	mixed-solvent process
混合溶液	mixed solution [liquor]
混合容器	blending container
混合入炉	mix-charge

混合熵　mixing entropy
混合烧渣给料机　blended cinder feeder
混合设备　mixing equipment [device], mix preparation equipment, conditioning equipment
混合设计　mix design
混合时间　time of mixing, conditioning time
混合式钢丝绳　◇西尔瓦灵顿～
混合室　mixing compartment [chamber],【焊】mixing section（气焊枪的）
混合室瓣阀　flap of mixing chamber
混合叔胺　mixed tertiary amines
混合树脂离子交换　mixed-bed [dual-bed, monobed] ion exchange
混合树脂离子交换装置　mixed-bed [monobed] ion exchange system
混合水　mixing water
混合水泥　blended cement
混合酸　mixed acid
混合酸浸蚀剂　【金】mixed acid
混合碳酸碱　mixed-alkali carbonate
混合桶　mixing ark
混合涂料　compost
混合挖泥机（虹吸与链斗式）　compound dreager
混合无机镀[涂]层　miscellaneous ingorganic coating
混合物　mix(ture), intermixture, compound, alligation ◇大小不同颗粒的～ mixture of particle sizes
混合物成分控制[调剂]　mixture control
混合物辐射　impurity radiation
混合(物)喷吹　mono-injection
混合物性能相加性　mixture additivity
混合物状态　impurity state
混合物组分　ingredient of mixture
混合稀土　mixed rare earths
混合稀土钴永磁材料　mixed rare earth cobalt permanent magnet
混合稀土合金(含铈的)　mischmetal(l)
混合系统　hybrid [pugmill] system

混合纤维层压材料　multi-fiber laminates
混合相(萃取的)　mixed phase
混合效率　mixing efficiency
混合芯砂　core sand mixture
混合型断裂　mixture cracking
混合型砂　moulding sand mixture
混合(型)位错　(同"复合位错")
混合液　intermixture
混合液贮槽　mixing liquid receiver
混合圆筒　mixing barrel
混合蒸汽　vapour mixture
混合制粒机　mixer-granulator ◇双锥式～
混合智能控制系统　hybrid intelligent control system
混合转鼓　mixing drum
混合装料　mix-charge
混合装置　mixing device [plant, arrangement]
混合组织　mixed [mixture] structure
混合作用　mixing action, immixture
混浇坯　compound casting billet
混晶　mixed crystal, mischcrystal
混晶组织　mixed grain structure
混联(接线)　multiple-series [parallel-series, series-parallel] connection, parallel-series
混练水量　(同"调和水量")
混料　mixing, bed blending, bedding out
混料仓[混合贮仓]　mixing bunker
混料槽　mixture storing bin
混料场　bedding field
混料斗　blending bunker
混料工序　blending procedure
混料回归设计　mixture regression design
混料机　mixer, blender, reclaiming machine
混料圆筒　conditioner drum
混料运输机　blending conveyer
混乱　turbulence, confusion, disorder, disorganization
混乱的　turbid
混乱取向　disorientation

混磨 mix grinding, attrition mixing
混磨机 mix muller, muller (mixer), muller-type blender, mixer-mill
混磨系统 pugmill system
混碾 mulling
混碾机 mixing mill,【耐】tempering mill,【铸】mulling machine
混捏 pugging,【耐】temper（黏土的）
混捏和造粒工段 kneading and balling section
混捏机 kneader, kneading machine ◇ 桨式~*
混凝法 coagulating process
混凝搅拌汽车 motomixer
混凝土 concrete (conc.), beton ◇ 柏油~ tar concrete, 拌好的~ mixed concrete, 不透水[水密性]~ watertight concrete, 车拌[运送拌合]~ transit-mix(ed) concrete, 成熟~*, 斥水性~*, 纯水泥~*, 大块[大体积]~ mass concrete, 富~*, 干硬性~ dry concrete, 高强~ strong concrete, 加气[充气,多孔]~*, 间隙级配~ gap-grade concrete, 可泵送的~ pumpable concrete, 快硬~*, 矿渣~*, 离析的~ segregating concrete, 沥青~ asphalt concrete, 劣质~ poor[faulty] concrete, 流态~*, 路拌~*, 煤[焦]渣~ breeze concrete, 抹平的~ floated concrete, 膨胀炉渣~ expanded slag concrete, 去气~*, 洒水养护的~ water cured concrete, 受钉[可钉钉的]~ nailable concrete, 水渣[湿碾矿渣]~ foamed slag concrete, 塑性[水灰比高的]~ wet concrete, 陶粒~ ceramsite concrete, 纤维性~*, 现场搅拌~ job mixed concrete, 现浇~*, 有和易性~ workable concrete, 预拌[已搅拌]~ ready-mix concrete, 重~ heavy concrete
混凝土按体积配合法 volume method of concrete mix design
混凝土板 concrete bay
混凝土板护坡 concrete slab work
混凝土板桩 concrete sheet piling
混凝土拌合机 concrete mixer ◇ 小型~*, 斜筒式~*
混凝土拌合机预热装置 concrete mixer heating attachment
混凝土包钢梁 steel beam enclosed in concrete
混凝土薄层 concrete lift
混凝土保护层 concrete cover
混凝土标号 concrete grade
混凝土表面磨光 block finish
混凝土沉箱[井] concrete caisson [monolith]
混凝土衬物 concrete casing
混凝土稠度试验 consistency test of concrete
混凝土大孔洞 cavitation
混凝土单块[空心大方块] concrete monolith
混凝土捣碎机 concrete breaker
混凝土导管 tremie
混凝土底部结构 concrete substructure
混凝土底座 concrete bed
混凝土电热养护 electric curing of concrete
混凝土分布机[分配器] concrete distributor
混凝土钢筋 round for reinforced concrete
混凝土-钢筋凝结力[联合作用] cooperation of concrete and steel
混凝土钢筋用刻痕钢丝 deformed steel wire for reinforcement
混凝土隔板 concrete diaphram
混凝土工厂 ready-mix plant
混凝土构造 concrete construction
混凝土管 concrete pipe ◇ 离心浇注~*
混凝土规范 concrete specification
混凝土夯实器 concrete rammer
混凝土和钢筋的握裹力 grip between concrete and steel
混凝土基础 concrete foundation [bed] ◇ 炉体与~间接触面*

混凝土集料　concrete aggregate
混凝土级配比设计　concrete design
混凝土架电抗器　cast-in-concrete reactor
混凝土建筑　concrete construction
混凝土浆　concrete grout
混凝土浇灌[注]机　concrete placer ◇ 压气~*
混凝土搅拌船　floating concrete-mixing plant
混凝土搅拌机　concrete mixer ◇ 斜鼓形~*,转筒式~*
混凝土搅拌(汽)车　concrete mixer truck, truck mixer
混凝土聚合体　concrete aggregate
混凝土可灌筑性　placeability of concrete
混凝土空心砌块[空心砖]　concrete hollow block
混凝土冷却塔　concrete cooling tower
混凝土立方块强度试验　concrete cube test
混凝土梁　concrete beam ◇ 双重配筋~ double reinforced beam
混凝土流动性　flowability of concrete
混凝土流动性试验　flow test of concrete, slumping
混凝土流态稠度　mushy consistency of concrete
混凝土路面　concrete pavement [paving] ◇ 沥青~*
混凝土路面摊铺机[铺路机]　concrete paver
混凝土模板　concrete form
混凝土内部振捣器　internal concrete vibrator
混凝土凝固　concrete setting
混凝土排基　concrete raft
混凝土配合比　proportioning of concrete
混凝土配筋　concrete reinforcement
混凝土配筋钢丝　concrete reinforcement wire
混凝土配筋用钢筋　(concrete-) reinforcing steel [bar]

混凝土龄期　age of concrete
混凝土圈梁　concrete collar
混凝土施工性能　concrete workability
混凝土饰面　concrete casing
混凝土试块　concrete test specimen ◇ 立方体~*
混凝土受料槽　concrete load-out bin
混凝土(输送)泵　concrete pump
混凝土速凝剂　concrete accelerator
混凝土碎块　broken concrete
混凝土摊铺斗　concrete placing skip
混凝土摊铺机　concrete paver [placer], concrete distributor
混凝土心墙的毛石砌体　opus incertum
混凝土徐变　creep of concrete
混凝土养护　concrete curing
混凝土预应力钢(筋)　concrete-prestressing steel
混凝土运送拌和机车　transit concrete-mixer
混凝土运送搅拌车　truck-transit mixer
混凝土振捣机　concrete vibrator
混凝土振动样板　concrete vibrating screed
混凝土整修机　concrete finisher
混凝土支架[支柱]　concrete support
混凝土支柱栈桥　concrete-pier trestle
混凝土制品　concrete product
混凝土中心搅拌站　centralized concrete mixing plant
混凝土柱　concrete column ◇ 配螺旋钢箍的~ spirally reinforced column
混凝土桩　concrete pile ◇ 钢壳~*,雷蒙式~*,外壳可抽出式~ peerless pile,有套管的~ shell concrete pile
混频管　mixer [mixed] tube, mixing tube [unit], mixer ◇ 六极~ mixing hexode
混频器　frequency mixer, mixing unit
混气阀　mixing valve
混砂　(sand) mulling ◇ 碾轮[摆轮]式~法 mulling
混砂机　sand mixer [muller], mixing ma-

chine, puddle mixer, sand mill（辗压式）◇ 赫氏圆盘充气~*，快速~ speed mixer，碾轮式~ roller mixer，叶片式~*

混烧 multi-fuel combustion

混铁罐[包] metal mixer, reservoir ladle ◇ 炉前~ forehearth mixing ladle

混铁炉 mixer (furnace), hot metal mixer, pig iron mixer ◇ 搓揉~ kneading mixer，非精炼~*，可倾式~*，浅熔池~ shallow mixer，筒式~ barrel mixer，预炼~*

混铁炉工 lever mixer, mixer (lever) man

混铁炉间 mixer building

混铁炉内生铁残留状况 drain-out condition

混铁炉式铁水罐[盛铁桶,铁水桶] mixer [submarine, torpedo, Pug-type] ladle

混铁炉式铁水罐车 mixer type iron ladle car

混铁炉铁水 mixer metal

混铁炉渣 mixer slag

混铁桶 mixing ladle

混辛癸烷胺萃取剂 （同"三脂肪胺萃取剂"）

混性 miscibility

混匀 bed blending ◇ 堆料~ bedding，矿石~[中和]*

混匀操作 bedding practice

混匀矿石 【铁】blended [bedded] ore

混匀度 homogenization degree

混匀法 mode of averaging,【选】averaging method

混匀供料机 blending feeder

混匀矿仓 blending [sweetener] bunker, mixing bin

混匀矿槽[料槽] homogenizing silo

混匀料仓 blending hopper, nonsegregating bin

混匀料场 blending yard [field], homogenization plant

混匀料堆 blending stack [pile]

混匀器(混料机) blending machine

混杂铬酸盐 heterochromate

混杂切屑 commingled turnings

混杂铁块（原矿中的） tramp iron

混杂物料 tramp material

混渣 slag entrapment

混装(料) mixed charging [filling]

混浊的 turbid, muddy

混浊点 cloud point

混浊度[性] turbidity, cloudiness

活百页窗 louver shutter

活扳手 adjustable spanner [wrench], shifting spanner, monkey wrench, universal screw-key

活瓣 flap

活底 removable [drop, false] bottom,【冶】removable base, loose bottom（转炉的）

活底槽 false bottom tank

活底车 larry car

活底炉 bogie (hearth) furnace, car-bottom (hearth) furnace, moving-hearth [live-bottom, travel (l) ing-hearth] furnace, car hearth furnace, drawplate[travel (l)ing] oven

活底炉床 car-bottom hearth

活底容器 bottom opening container

活底式电炉 mobile-hearth (furnace)

活底式化铁炉 drop-bottom cupola

活底式窑 sliding-bat kiln

活底摇床 car deck

活底窑 bogie kiln

活地板 false [raised] floor, (free) access floor

活顶尖 running [live] centre

活顶炉 bung type roof furnace ◇ 门式~ gantry-type furnace

活顶汽车 convertible car

活顶式窑 【耐】top change furnace

活动鞍座 free saddle

活动板 shuffle bar

活动板夹头（对焊机的） movable clamping die

活动半径　radius of action (R/A)
活动半模　movable die
活动算条　mobile grizzly
活动臂磁盘　moving arm disk
活动边界法　moving boundary method
活动侧导板(轧件用)　floating side guards
活动程序　active program
活动秤　trolley scale
活动齿轮装置　movable gearing
活动挡板　removal [sliding] stop
活动导板　movable guard
活动吊车　walking crane
活动顶尖　movable centre
活动顶式电弧炉　removable-roof arc furnace
活动定位销　【铸】loose (moulding box) pin
活动度盘[标尺]　movable-scale
活动法兰　loose flange
活动房屋　quonset, movable dwellings
活动盖板　movable covering plate, removable deck, roll top
活动杆　shuffle bar
活动格筛　travel(l)ing grizzly
活动焊头缝焊机　travel head seam welder
活动荷载　movable load
活动横梁　cross head, moving crosshead, plunger crosshead (压力机的)
活动环形区　【铁】active annulus
活动机架面板　moving platen
活动夹具　movable clamp, floating holder
活动架　moving section
活动胶片测量法　moving film method
活动脚手架　jenny scaffold
活动空间(机组周围的)　working clearance
活动孔　mobile hole
活动联轴节　movable coupling
活动梁　movable beam
活动流[斜]槽　movable chute
活动炉底　removable bottom
活动炉顶　removable roof [arch], hung (反射炉的)
活动炉喉布料调节板　【铁】adjustable-diameter stockline armor
活动炉栅　moving grid
活动率　activity ratio [rating]
活动门　removable door
活动模　moving die
活动模板　movable [collapsible] form
活动挠性带间连铸　casting between moving flexible belts
活动墙焦炉　movable wall coke oven
活动桥　movable [draw, traversing] bridge
活动缺陷　mobile defect
活动筛框　live frame
活动烧嘴　tiltable burner
活动式棒条筛　moving-bar grizzly
活动(式)出钢槽　removable runner, handle spouts
活动式翻车机　【焦】mobile car tipper
活动式夹持机构(对焊机的)　moving clamping block
活动式炉床　movable hearth
活动式炉前　mobile forehearth
活动台面深拉压力机　slide drawing press
活动凸缘　loose flange
活动位错密度　mobile dislocation density
活动线夹　movable clamp
活动芯棒[顶杆]　movable mandrel
活动芯棒拉拔　moving-mandrel drawing
活动型板　【铸】movable plate
活动型芯(压力铸造的)　moving core
活动性　avidity, mobility ◇减少～immobilization
活动烟道　movable flue, 【钢】movable offtake
活动烟罩　plate hood, 【钢】(转炉的) (enveloping) skirt, movable hood, apron
活动载荷　moving [live, mobile] load
活动支架[支座]　【建】travel(l)ing support
活动支柱　mobile column
活动主铁沟　removable trough

活动座板　free saddle
活度　(degree of) activity ◇ 绝对～absolute activity, 阳极～anode activity
活度积　activity product
活度计算　activity calculation
活度系数　activity coefficient
活度相互作用系数　activity interaction coefficient
活盖　detachable cap
活隔渣板　【铁】removable dam
活化　activation, radioactivation ◇ 减～(作用)*
活化不足的　under-active
活化槽　activated bath
活化处理　activating treatment
活化法　activation method
活化反应蒸除　activated reactive evaporation
活化分析　activation analysis ◇ γ射线～*
活化分子　activated [trigger] molecule
活化复合体　activated complex
活化硅胶　activated silica gel
活化过电位　activation overpotential
活化核　active nucleus
活化机理　mechanism of activation
活化极化　activation polarization
活化剂　activating [active] agent, activator, activated material, energiser, energizer ◇ 光学～*
活化剂喷洒瓶　activator spray bottle
活化截面　activation cross-section
活化浸出体系　active leaching system
活化控制　activation control
活化扩散　activated diffusion
活化力　activating force
活化硫酸浸出　activating sulfuric acid leaching
活化炉　activation furnace
活化[激活]能　activation energy ◇ 阿列纽斯～Arrhenius energy, 交叉滑移～*, 空位形成～*, 自扩散～*

活化切应力　activating shear stress
活化热　activation heat
活化熵　activation entropy
活化烧结　activated sintering
活化时间　activation time
活化水　activated water
活化物质　activating agent, activated material
活化吸附　activation adsorption
活化效应　activating effect
活化(性)氰化　activated cyaniding
活化应力　activation stress
活化值　activation number
活化中心　activation centre, active nucleus
活化自由能　activation free energy
活化阻止剂　anti-activator
活化作用　activation ◇ 共～coactivation
活节　movable [eye] joint
活节杆　knuckle rod
活节连接器　cardan joint
活节螺栓　eyelet [dog, drop, hinged, link, swing] bolt
活节式构造　articulated construction
活镜水准仪　Y-level
活块(木模或型芯盒的)　loose part [piece], die insert
活块造型　loose pattern moulding
活络阀座　detachable seat
活门　(flap) shutter, clack, trap
活泼金属　(re)active metal
活泼杂质　non-inert impurity
活球接头　ball and socket hinge
活圈(推力轴承的)　housing washer
活塞　plunger, stop, ram, 【机】piston
活塞泵　piston (type) pump, displacement pump ◇ 双动[双程]～*
活塞泵用阀球　valve ball for piston pump
活塞衬套　piston bush
活塞阀衬　piston valve liner
活塞杆　piston [connecting] rod ◇ 镀硬铬的～*
活塞(杆)导筒[管]　piston (rod) guide

活塞杆密封盖　rod-gland
活塞工作面　piston face
活塞合金　piston alloy ◇ 铝～ aluminium piston alloy, 马勒铝硅～*, 潘塞利铝硅～*
活塞环[胀圈]　piston ring, bule
活塞环铸坯　piston ring casting
活塞铝合金(4Cu, 0.5Mg, 2Ni, 余量 Al) piston alloy
活塞式发动机　piston [reciprocating] engine
活塞式挤泥器　piston type applicator
活塞式流动　plug (like) flow
活塞体　piston body
活塞筒　piston cylinder
活塞销　wrist [gudgeon] pin
活砂芯　false core
活砂造型　drawback
活水　flow(ing) [running] water
活套　loop ◇ U形～ U-loop, 储存～*, 二次～ secondary loop, 人工～ hand [manual] looping, 调整～ loop control, 形成～ looping, 形成侧～ side looping, 一次～ primary loop, 自由悬挂～*
活套槽(围盘的)　looping channel ◇ 倾斜式～ sloping loop channel, 围盘～ looping trough
活套长度的磁力调整　magnetic loop control
活套车　loop(ing) car
活套成形器　vibrator
活套程序控制　loop preset control
活套(垂度)调节器　loop regulator ◇ 光电(控制)～*
活套光电管控制　photo-thyratron loop control
活套段铺板(在轧机旁)　looping floor
活套高度调节　loop height regulation
活套辊　looper roll, loop back roll
活套精轧机组　looping finishing train
活套坑　loop pit, bin ◇ 出口～*, 储集～*, 单～装置 single-looping pit, 进料～*, 双～装置 double-looping pit
活套坑塔　looping pit tower
活套控制　loop control ◇ 自动～ automatic loop control
活套控制器　loop controller
活套拉辊　loop puller ◇ 双端～ end-dual loop puller
活套(式)线材[盘条]轧机　rod repeater mill ◇ 加勒特式～*, 连续式～机组*
活套式型钢轧机　looping merchant mill
活套(式)轧机　looping mill
活套塔　looping tower ◇ 出料～*, 机械～*
活套台　loop(ing) table [bed]
活套挑　looper (gear), loop lifter, vibrator ◇ 进口～*, 立式～ uplooper, 下出套的～*, 液压传动～ hydraulic looper
活套挑撑杆　looper arm
活套位置检测器　loop position detector
活套系统　looper system
活套轧机机座　repeater
活套轧机组　looping mill train
活套轧制　loop-mill rolling
活套轧制生产的轧材　loop
活套张力调节　loop tension regulation
活套支持器　looper gear
活套装置　looper ◇ 入口～ entry looper (EL), 塔式～ tower-type looper, 腰板～系统*
活箱带　【铸】cleat
活芯造型　drawback
活性　activity ◇ 无～渣 nonreactive slag
活性层　active layer
活性氮　active nitrogen
活性淀积　active deposit
活性二氧化硅　activated [reactive] silica
活性二氧化锰法　【环】activated manganese dioxide method
活性二氧化物　reactive dioxide
活性反应　active reaction
活性分子　trigger molecule
活性腐蚀　active corrosion

活性硅酸	【环】active silica
活性焊剂	activated rosin flux
活性化	activation
活性基	active group
活性焦	reactive coke
活性金属	(re)active metal ◇ 非～nonreactive metal
活性金属的金属包壳	canning
活性氯	active chlorine
活性铝土	activated alumina
活性络合物	activated complex
活性黏土	activated [active] clay
活性镍	active nickel
活性曝气	activated aeration
活性气体	reactive gas
活性气体保护金属极(电弧)焊接	MAG (metal active gas) welding
活性迁移	active transport
活性氢	active hydrogen
活性区(反应堆的)	fuel core
活性溶剂	active solvent
活性烧结	reactive sintering
活性渗碳	activated carburizing
活性石灰	active lime
活性石油焦	activated petroleum coke
活性碳化	activated carburizing
活性炭	activated [absorbent] charcoal, activated [absorbent] carbon
活性炭处理	【环】activated carbon treatment ◇ 电解质～carbon treatment
活性炭滤器[池]	activated charcoal [carbon] filter
活性炭脱硫	active carbon desulfurization
活性炭吸附法(苯类的)	【焦】active carbon adsorption process
活性炭吸附作用	adsorption on active carbon
活性炭吸收	【环】activated charcoal absorption
活性铁铝氧石	activated bauxite
活性涂层	active coating
活性土	activated clay
活性污泥	【环】activated sludge ◇ 高速～处理法*
活性污泥法	activated sludge process ◇ 完全氧化～*
活性物质	active material [substance] ◇ 光学～*
活性纤维	activated cellulose
活性氧	active oxygen
活性氧化法	active oxygen method
活性氧化铝	activated alumina
活性氧化镁	active magnesia
活性氧化物	active oxide
活性氧化锌	active zinc oxide
活性阴极合金	active cathode alloy
活性渣	reactive slag
活性状态	active state
活性组分	active component [constituent]
活字(合)金(50—90Pb, 2—30Sb, 余量 Sn, 有时加入 Bi)	type metal
火表	watt-hour meter
火铲	firing shovel, 【压】firing scoop
火成晶石 $\{Pb_5Cl(PO_4)_3\}$	pyromorphite
火成矿物	pyrogenic [igneous] mineral
火成物	igneous material
火成岩	igneous [pyrogenetic, eruptive] rock, pyrolith
火床	fire bed, hearth
火道	flue
火法	pyrogenic process
火法处理	pyrogenic attack, fire process (ing) [treatment], pyro-metallurgical treatment
火法镀金	fire gilding
火法技术[工艺, 加工技术]	pyro-processing art
火法精炼	fire [furnace] refining, pyrometallurgical refining, pyro-refining ◇ 预先[初步]～*
火法精炼法	fire refining process [method]
火法精炼金属	fire refined metal
火法精炼镍	fire refined nickel

火法精炼期	fire refining cycle
火法精炼铜	fire refined copper
火法精炼铜车间	fire copper refining plant
火法精炼铜阳极	fire refined copper anode
火法熔炼	fuel fired smelting ◇旋涡式~法
火法提取	pyro-metallurgical extraction
火法冶金法	pyro-metallurgical method [extraction]
火法冶金厂[设备]	pyro-metallurgical plant
火法冶金(学)	pyrometallurgy, thermometallurgy, dry [fire, fusion, igneous] metallurgy
火封软熔热镀锌法	flame seal (galvanizing) process
火管	smoke pipe
火管锅炉	fire [smoke] tube boiler, shell boiler, open-fire kettle
火花	spark(ing) ◇不生~合金", 打~flashing, 发~blink, 凯勒~检验 Keller's spark
火花捕集器	spark trap [arrester]
火花点火发动机	spark ignition engine
火花点火器	spark lighter
火花发生器	spark oscillator
火花放电	spark [disruptive] discharge
火花放电成形	spark discharge forming
火花放电法	spark discharge method
火花放电器	spark discharger
火花放电侵蚀加工法	electroerosion spark discharge process
火花放电硬化(法)	electric discharge hardening, electrospark hardening, spark (discharge) hardening
火花击穿	spark breakdown, spark-over
火花鉴别法(钢的成分)	spark testing
火花喷射器[喷嘴]	spark injector unit
火花切割器	spark cutter
火花塞	spark(ing) [light-up] plug, candle
火花塞电极	spark plug
火花烧坏	sparkwear
火花烧结机	spark sintering machine
火花室	spark chamber
火花隙	spark gap, discharger, 【焊】air gap
火花隙变流器供电炉	spark-gap converter furnace
火花现象	【铁】pyrophoric behaviour
火花源质谱法	spark source mass spectrometry
火花源质谱学	spark source mass spectroscopy
火花障	spark trap
火花罩	spark trap [catcher]
火箭	rocket
火箭喷嘴[管]	rocket nozzle
火箭弹材料	rocket bomb material
火箭炮材料	rocket missile material
火箭燃料	rocket fuel
火箭液体燃料	rocket water
火箭装药	propellant powder charge
火箭追踪器	monitor
火精铜	pole tough pitch, tough pitch (copper), tough cake
火精铜线锭	tough-pitch wirebar
火精铜制结晶器	tough-pitch copper mould
火警传感器	fire perceiving device
火警系统	fire alarm system
火炬	torch (light), flambeau
火坑	hot floor
火口	【焊】crater ◇形成~cratering
火口裂纹	crater crack
火口缩孔	crater cavity
火口枝状裂纹	star crater crack
火力发电工程	heat power engineering
火力发电站	heat [steam] power station
火裂	fire crack
火棉	guncotton, pyroxylin
火棉胶	collodion
火棉胶溶液	collodion solution
火苗	flame head [envelope] ◇燃料~[火舌]长度 fuel spray penetration

火泥	fire [sagger, seat] clay,【耐】mortar		
火泥衬里	fireclay lining		
火泥罐	clay pot		
火泥炉衬	fireclay lining		
火泥密封	luting		
火泥熟料	fireclay grog		
火泥砖	chamber brick		
火泥镘刀	mortar trowel		
火耙	【压】furnace rake		
火钳	(fire) poker, (fire-) tongs		
火墙	fire wall [bridge]		
火桥	fire [flame] bridge,【冶】bridge		
火桥后墙	back bridge wall		
火桥护顶	bridge cover		
火桥炉坡	bridge bank		
火色	heat colour		
火色硫锑银矿	fire blende		
火色温标	colour scale		
火山爆发	volcanic eruption		
火山灰	volcanic [lava] ash		
火山灰硅酸盐水泥	portland-pozzolana cement		
火山灰水泥	pozzolanic [puzzuolanic, trass] cement		
火山口	crater, caldera		
火山喷出物	volcanic ejecta [products]		
火山岩渣	dross, cinder, slag		
火舌	flame (jet), body of flame		
火舌层	flare bed		
火舌管烧嘴	flare stack tips		
火石合金	(同"发火合金")		
火试(金)法	fire assay		
火试金预富集－火花法[技术]	fire assay preconcentration spark technique		
火膛	fire bed		
火箱	firebox, firing box		
火箱底	floor		
火星障	spark catcher		
火烟道排灰刮板拉链输送机	【团】dust drag link conveye		
火焰	flame, fire, torch ◇ 不正常[不恰当, 未调好]～*, 富氧～ flame enrichment, 过剩乙炔～*, 劲(吹)～ harsh blowing flame, 空气过剩～ overventilated flame, 明亮～ clear flame, 欠氧[供风不足的]～ underventilated flame, 调好的～ balanced flame, 嗡鸣～ singing flame, 无光[不透明]～ opaque flame, 无力的～ lazy flame		
火焰表面处理	flame machining		
火焰表面切割	flame machining		
火焰表面清理	scarfing (钢坯的),【铸】flame gouging		
火焰布置	flame arrangement		
火焰常化	(同"火焰正火")		
火焰长度	flame length		
火焰冲击	flame impingement		
火焰除疵	【焊】flame deseaming		
火焰除锈燃烧器	flame cleaning burner for removing rust		
火焰除油[净化]器	flame cleaner		
火焰处理	flame treating		
火焰穿孔	flame drilling [boring]		
火焰传播速度	flame velocity, rate of flame propagation		
火焰淬火	torch hardening		
火焰淬火法	airco process ◇ 定点式～*, 固定式～*		
火焰电离检测器	flame ionization detector		
火焰镀	flame coating		
火焰镀金	fire gilding		
火焰发射率	flame emissivity		
火焰反冲	blowback, back flash		
火焰反应	flame reaction		
火焰辐射能力	flame radiating power		
火焰氟化	flame fluorination		
火焰割炬	flame cutting torch		
火焰割嘴	flame cutting nozzle		
火焰故障警报器	flame failure device		
火焰光度计	flame photometer		
火焰光度学[术]	flame photometry		
火焰光谱	flame spectrum [spectra]		
火焰焊缝清理机	hot deseamer		
火焰焊接的	torch-brazed		

火焰黑度 flame emissivity, flame radiating power

火焰回火 flame tempering,【焊】flame flash back

火焰加热 flame heating

火焰加热淬火 flame hardening ◇ 顺序旋转~*, 依次~*

火焰加热蒸馏 fire distillation

火焰加热装置 flame heating unit

火焰检测器 flame (photometric) detector

火焰降落期 【钢】period of flame drop

火焰校平[直] flame straightening

火焰金属喷涂 flame metal spraying

火焰绝热温度计算机 adiabatic flame temperature computer (AFTCOM)

火焰可调式燃烧器 variable-flame burner

火焰口 【钢】knuckle

火焰离子化鉴定器 flame ionization detector

火焰流 flame jet

火焰炉 flame furnace ◇ 煤气~gas-fired air furnace

火焰炉炉渣 air furnace slag

火焰密封 flame sealing

火焰刨切机 flame planing machine ◇ 回转式~*

火焰刨削 flame milling, flame gouging ◇ 气体~【机】flame milling, 多焰嘴~机*

火焰刨嘴 flame gouging torch, gouging tip

火焰喷补 flame gunning (repair)

火焰喷补层 flame gunned layer

火焰喷补技术 flame gunning technology

火焰喷补料 flame gunning material

火焰喷出 【钢】flame shoot out

火焰喷镀[涂] flame (sprayed) coating, flame spraying, flame plating

火焰喷镀用青铜 flame metallized bronze

火焰喷射金属覆层模 flame spray die

火焰喷射 flame jet

火焰喷涂涂层 flame sprayed coating

火焰喷柱 flame envelope

火焰喷嘴 flame head orifices

火焰钎焊 flame brazing

火焰前锋区 flame front zone

火焰前锋[缘]线 line of flame front

火焰前缘 flame front

火焰前缘速度 flame front speed

火焰强度 flame intensity

火焰强化 flame strengthening

火焰切割 flame [torch, thermal] cutting, flame cut (off), gas cut, torch cut-off

火焰切割工 flame cutting (torch) operator

火焰切割工段(连铸坯的) torch-cutting station

火焰切割机 flame cutting machine [tractor], flame cut off machine, torch cutter, torch cutting machine (连铸坯的) ◇ 异形轮廓~*

火焰切割喷嘴 flame cutting nozzle

火焰切割器 flame cutter, cutting blowpipe [burner] ◇ 多嘴~*

火焰切割设备 flame cutting equipment

火焰切割速度 flame cutting speed

火焰切割用气体 cutting gas

火焰侵蚀试验 flame etch test

火焰清理(表面的) flame cleaning [blasting, descaling], (de)scarfing, (de)flame priming (表面涂漆前的),【焊】flame deseaming ◇ 喷铁粉~*, 热轧件~hot scarfing, 人工~【压】hand scarfing, 锈蚀材料~*, 氧乙炔~oxyacetylene scarfing, 逐点~spot-scarf, 自动~automatic scarfing

火焰清理操作 scarfing operation

火焰清理初轧方坯 scarfed bloom

火焰清理法 scarfing process

火焰清理工段 scarfing yard

火焰清理工艺 scarfing technique

火焰清理机 (hot) scarfing machine, deseamer ◇ 冷态~cold scarfing machine

火焰清理炬 flame cleaning [spalling] torch, scarfing torch

火焰清理棱边	scarfed edge
火焰清理器	flame cleaner, (flame) scarfer
火焰清理台	scarfing bed
火焰热处理	flame heat treatment
火焰烧剥	(de)scarfing, flame blasting
火焰烧除铆钉	flame derivetting
火焰衰减	flame attenuation
火焰四面清理机(板坯的)	four sided scarfer, four sided scrafing machine
火焰缩短	drop of flame
火焰特性	flame characteristics
火焰退火	torch annealing
火焰脱硝	flame denitration
火焰温度	flame temperature
火焰温度分析器	flame temperature analyzers
火焰稳定(化)	flame holding
火焰稳定传布	steady state flame propagation
火焰稳定性	flame stability [stabilization]
火焰形状	flame profile
火焰行程	flame travel
火焰性质[状态]	flame condition
火焰旋涡熔炼	flame cyclone smelting
火焰压头	force of flame
火焰移动式窑	moving fire kiln
火焰逸出	back lighting
火焰异形切割[加工]	flame shaping [profiling]
火焰荧光光谱测定法	flame spectrofluorimetry
火焰预热氧	preheating oxygen
火焰正火	flame normalizing
火焰(直接加热)退火	flame annealing
火焰中心	flame core [kernel]
火焰钻孔	flame boring
火药	gunpowder, powder (powd.)
火冶金属	furnace metal
火冶水冶联合法	pyro-hydro-metallurgical method
火印	hot stamp
火灾	fire (risk), conflagration
火灾危险	fire hazard
火灾保险	fire insurance
火灾警报[信号(装置)]	fire alarm
火砖	firebrick
钬合金	holmium alloy
钬基合金	holmium base alloy
钬添加合金	holmium addition
获得电子(作用)	electronation
或然的	probable, stochastic
或然率	probability
霍博肯虹吸式转炉	Hoboken siphon converter
霍博肯转炉	Hoboken converter
霍恩塞多段回转窑低温直接还原法	Hornsey process
霍恩塞-威尔斯三回转炉直接炼铁法	Hornsey-Wills process
霍尔-阿德林铝热铸造法	Hall-Adeline process
霍尔冰晶石电解质	Hall bath
霍尔博恩高温计	Holborn pyrometer
霍尔常数	Hall coefficient [constant]
霍尔德克罗夫测温棒	Holdcroft thermoscope bar
霍尔电解炼铝法	Hall process
霍尔电势[位]	Hall potential
霍尔福斯高强度青铜离心铸造法	Holfos process
霍尔福斯离心铸造高强度青铜铸件	Holfos bronze
霍尔福斯青铜合金(75—88.3Cu, 5—11.5Sn, 0.7—1.3P, 2Zn, 10—20Pb)	Holfos alloy
霍尔-赫劳尔特电解炼铝法	Hall-Heroult process
霍尔检波器测头	Hall detector probe
霍尔流动性测试仪	Hall tester
霍尔流量[流速]计	Hall flowmeter
霍尔迁移率	Hall mobility
霍尔球磨制粉法	Hall process
霍尔探测器测头	Hall detector probe
霍尔韦克分子泵	Holweck's molecular

pump
霍尔系数 Hall coefficient
霍尔效应 Hall effect
霍尔效应倍增器 Hall effect multiplier
霍尔效应传感器 Hall effect transducer
霍尔效应发生器 Hall (effect) generator
霍尔元件(测定磁场强度用) Hall element
霍夫曼过滤器 Hoffmann filter
霍夫曼环窑 Hoffmann kiln
霍弗斯夹渣计数(法) Hofors slag inclusion count
霍格-普罗发海绵铁生产法 Hoag-Purofer process
霍华德压力机(铅精炼用) Howard press
霍加内斯海绵铁粉 Hoeganas powder
霍利莫特搅拌式混合沉降萃取器 Holley Mott extractor
霍马尔放大型目镜 Homal eyepiece
霍姆伯格烧结系统 Holmberg system
霍普金森效应 Hopkinson effect
霍普金斯电渣法 【钢】Hopkins process
霍氏七喷嘴扩散泵 Ho's 7-nozzle pump
霍斯福尔油淬火铅回火法(琴钢丝的) Horsefall process
霍斯金斯耐热耐蚀高镍[高镍耐蚀耐热]合金(34—68Ni, 10—19Cu, 余量 Fe) Hoskin's metal [alloy]
霍斯金碳质电阻炉 Hoskin's furnace
霍耶拉塔和拉米纳海绵铁生产法 Hojalata y Lamina (HyL) process
霍伊尔铅锡锑轴承合金(42Pb, 46Sn, 12Sb) Hoyle's alloy
霍伊特 11 号锡基轴承合金(2.5Cu, 7Sb, 余量 Sn) Hoyt No. 11

霍伊特 C.B. 铅锑轴承合金 Hoyt's C.B. alloy
霍伊特 I.C.E. 汽油发动机轴承合金 Hoyt's I.C.E. metal
霍伊特纯 A [白色软巴比] 合金(91Sn, 4.5Sb, 4.5Cu) Hoyt's genuine A alloy
霍伊特高锡铅基轴承合金(10—20Sn, 12.5—15Sb, 63—75Pb, 0.2—1.5Cu) Hoyt's reliance alloy
霍伊特锡基轴承[锡锑铜]合金(91Sn, 6.8Sb, 2.2Cu) Hoyt's alloy [metal]
货-客两用升降机 good-passenger lift
货币合金 coinage alloy [metal] ◇ A5 法国~(90Al, 5Ag, 5Cu) A5
货币合金带材 coinage strip
货币金 coinage gold ◇ 斯特林~(合金)*
货币青铜(95Cu, 4Sn, 1Zn) coinage bronze
货车 truck (Tk), freight car [train], wagon ◇ 车门放落的~ drop-door wagon, 无盖~ gondola car
货车交货价格(铁路的) FOR (free on rail)
货到付款[付现] cash on delivery (C.O.D.)
货棚 freight shed
货物 goods, cargo, commodity
货物税 commodity tax
货物提升机 goods lift
货物托运 invoice
货物转移 cargo shifting
货样 sale sample, sample goods
货栈 warehouse, store

J j

击穿 breakdown, breakage, arc-over, flash over, spark-over, disruption, puncture
击穿点 breakdown point
击穿电流 breakdown [striking] current
击穿电压 breakdown [disruptive, puncture] voltage, flash over voltage
击穿放电 disruptive discharge
击穿强度 breakdown [disruptive] strength
击穿试验 breakdown [disruptive, flash] test
击打式打印机 impact printer
击锻 impact forging
击平锤 set hammer
击芯机 core knockout [breaker]
基 base, foundation,【化】group, radical
基本变形 basic deformation
基本材料 parent material, stock
基本磁化(强度) net magnetization
基本磁化曲线 fundamental magnetic curve
基本代码 basic code
基本单位 base unit (BU), fundamental unit
基本电解液[质] (back) ground electrolyte
基本电子排列 ground electron configuration
基本定律 fundamental law
基本反射 fundamental reflection
基本反应 fundamental reaction
基本方程 fundamental equation
基本费用 major costs
基本符号 【计】basic symbol
基本负载 basic [major] load
基本工资 basic [regular] wages
基本光谱线系 fundamental series
基本汇编程序 basic assembler program (BAP)
基本技术[基础工艺] fundamental technique
基本加工硬化 basic work hardening
基本间隔 fundamental interval
基本剪切长度 basic cutting length
基本建设 capital [fundamental] construction
基本建设投资 investment in capital construction, capital charges, capital investment [expenditure]
基本金属 basic metal ◇ 受热影响的～(焊件的) heat affected base metal
基本晶型 fundamental crystal form
基本粒子 fundamental [elementary, ultimate] particle
基本连接 【计】basic linkage
基本流程图 basic flow sheet
基本轮廓 basic outline
基本模式 principal mode
基本模数 basic module
基本频率 fundamental [base] frequency
基本缺陷 major defect
基本人员 【企】skeleton staff
基本设备 essential equipment
基本设计 basic design
基本矢量 basic vector
基本试验 fundamental test
基本数据 【计】master data
基本图[外形] basic outline
基本图表 basical schedule
基本温度 basic temperature
基本(光谱线)系 fundamental series
基本箱 (同"基准箱")
基本项 fundamental term,【计】elementary item
基本形式 fundamental mode
基本因素 fundamental [pacing] factor
基本有序性 basic orderliness
基本语句 basic statement
基本原理 fundamental [cardinal, ultimate] principle, theoretical fundamental, fundament

基波　first [fundamental] harmonic, fundamental wave
基波[基本]振荡　fundamental oscillation
基部平面　basal plane
基部轴面体(结晶的)　basal pinacoid
基槽　ditch for foundation
基层　bottom [footing] course, base course (铺砌的)
基础　foundation (fdn, fndn, found.), base, basis, basement, bottom, subbasement, substructure,【建】bed ◇ 格排梁式~ beam grillage, 踏步式~【建】offset footing
基础板　soleplate, lobe plate, shoe
基础材料　underpinning
基础沉陷　foundation settlement, yielding of foundation
基础底板　foundation [sole] plate
基础垫层　foundation bed
基础电解液　base electrolyte
基础工业　basic industry
基础化学　basic chemistry
基础减震垫　foundation buffer
基础结构　infrastructure, underpinning
基础金属骨架　foundation framing metal
基础晶体学　basic crystallography
基础拉杆(焦炉的)　foundation tie rod
基础理论　basic theory, fundamental
基础理论研究　basic study, fundamental research
基础梁　foundation [footing] beam
基础螺栓　anchor [barb, bay, rag] bolt
基础模量[模数]　foundation modulus
基础物理化学　basic physical chemistry
基础训练　grounding
基础应力　foundation stress
基础月份　basic month
基础整平层　key floating
基床　foundation bed ◇ 砖铺~ bedding of brick
基床系数　bedding value
基带　base band,【半】normal band

基底　base(ment), ground, substrate
基底材料　substrate material,【半】base meterial
基底防蚀剂　substrate inhibitor
基底金属(合金中主要金属)　base [underlying] metal
基底金属试样　base metal test specimen
基底元素　background element
基地　base, home
基地平面图　drawing of site
基地址　base [reference] address
基地址寄存器　base (address) register
基点　base [basic] point (BP), datum (mark)
基恩迈耶汞合金 ($25Zn, 25Sn, 50Hg$) Kienmayer's amalgam
基恩铜基合金 ($75Cu, 16Ni, 2.8Sb, 2.3Zn, 2Co, 0.5Al$) Keen's alloy
基尔霍夫定律　Kirchhoff's law
基尔施硬度试验　Kirsch test
基尔试块　Keel block
基夫赛特旋涡熔炼法　KIVCET-CS process, KIVCET cyclone smelting process
基极　【电】base (electrode)
基极电流　base current
基极回路　base circuit
基建费用　construction cost, capital cost [expenditure]
基建投资　(同"基本建设投资")
基脚　basement,【建】footing
基角　base angle
基晶体　host crystal
基克塑性变形定律　Kick's law
基坑　foundation pit, ditch for foundation
基孔制配合　hole-basis system of fits
基块　base block,【冶】matrix
基林撇渣器　Killeen skimmer
基零点　($-260℃$) fundamental zero
基律纳型铁矿石　Kiruna type iron ore
基罗波罗斯拉单晶法　Kyropoulos crystal pulling technique
基面　cardinal plane, datum, basal plane

(晶体＜001＞面)
基面滑移　basal slip
基面轴承　base bearing
基片　substrate, base tab
基片装置　【半】base wafer assembly
基频　base [fundamental] frequency
基普(气体)发生器　Kipp's apparatus, Kipp('s) generator
基普线收缩试验(铸件的)　Keep's shrinkage test
基石　footing [foundation] stone, sommer
基矢量　basic [base] vector
基数　cardinal [base] number, base, basis, radix
基数数　radix number
基态　fundamental mode, 【理】ground state
基态波函数　ground-state wave function
基态分裂　ground-state splitting
基态能(量)　ground state energy
基特尔塔盘　【焦】Kittel plate
基锑矾　klebelsbergite
基体　matrix (复数 matrices), generatrix, groundmass, 【化】mer, monomeric unit ◇ 铁素体[α铁]~【金】α-Fe matrix
基体材料　basis material
基体钢　matrix steel
基体过饱和　matrix supersaturation
基体合金　matrix alloy
基体化学状态　matrix chemical state
基体金属　matrix [base] metal, principal metal (合金的) ◇ 未受热影响的~【焊】unaffected base metal
基体金属不熔化焊接　nonfusion welding
基体晶格　matrix lattice
基体膜　matrix film
基体贫化　matrix depletion
基体强度　matrix strength
基体收缩　matrix shrinkage
基体效应　effect of matrix
基体析出[沉淀]　matrix precipitation
基体硬度　matrix hardness
基体与沉淀物间界面　matrix-precipitate interface
基体原子　base atom
基体再结晶　matrix recrystallization
基体组织　matrix structure
基铁矾　butlerite
基铜矾　ktenasite
基线　base line (BL), base, bottom [ground] line, datum
基线波动效应　base relief effect
基谐波　fundamental [first] harmonic
基谐模式　fundamental mode
基型　primary [fundamental] form
基性岩　basic rock, basite
基岩　mother-rock, bed rock
基圆　basic circle (投影的), primitive circle (极平射影的)
基址　plot
基址寄存器　base register
基址图　plot plan
基质　matrix (mass), groundmass, host, 【地】matrix
基质晶体原子　host crystal atom
基柱　(显微镜的) pillar
基桩　foundation pile
基桩荷载试验　pile loading test
基锥(伞齿轮的)　generating cone
基准　base, reference, datum, basic standard
基准比重　basic specific gravity
基准边(磁带的)　reference edge
基准标高以下的　below grade
基准程序　bench mark program
基准尺寸　reference size [dimension]
基准地址　reference [base] address
基准点　reference [datum] point, bench mark (B.M.), datum [gauge, pop] mark
基准点标高　datum mark
基准电流　background current
基准电平　reference level
基准电压　reference voltage [potential]
基准黄铜　basic brass
基准校对环规　reference master ring

基准校对塞规 reference master plug gauge
基准结 reference junction
基准面 datum (plane), reference plane [surface], base [reference] level
基准偏差[漂移] datum drift
基准燃料 reference fuel
基准热[温差]电偶 primary standard thermocouple
基准输入(量) reference input
基准水位 datum level
基准速度 (同"参考速度")
基准线 base line (BL), zero line (ZL), datum [reference, fiducial] line,【计】reference axis
基准箱 (镀锡薄板的商业单位; base box (B.B.)
基准箱重量 base weight
基准液面 datum level
基准值电位计 reference value potentiometer
基准轴 (同"参考轴")
基座 seat(ing), foundation bed [support], pedestal
基座拉晶技术 pedestal technique
基珀斯-托切克煤炭气化法 Kippers-Totzek process
机侧 【焦】pusher [machine, ram] side, pusher end
机铲 power shovel, spader ◇ 履带式~ traxcavator
机车 loco(mobile), engine ◇ 双头~ double-ender, 轻便~*, 窄轨~*
机车库 depot, engine house
机车起重机[吊车] locomotive [rail] crane, grass-hopper
机车牵引车 loco-hauled bogie
机车轴承(84Sn,10Sb,6Cu) locomotive bearing
机床 machine tool ◇ 车锥度~ tapering machine, 倒棱清理~ chamfering unit, 计算机控制~*, 金属切削~*, 精密~ precision machine tool, 数控~*, 重型~ heavy machinery
机床工作台 platen
机电偏差 electro-mechanical variation
机床切削 machining
机床生产率 mill production output
机电修配厂[车间] engineering workshops
机电学 electro-mechanics
机电装置 electro-mechanical device
机动铲运机 motorscraper, power scraper machine
机动车 motor-driven truck, motor [automotive] vehicle
机动锤 machine [power, mechanical] hammer
机动堆垛机 mechanical piler
机动阀 motorized valve
机动干油泵 motorized grease pump
机动化 motorization
机动卷线机 motorized coil stock reel
机动冷床 mechanical cooling bed, hot (bed) transfer
机动抹灰板 mechanical float
机动切刀 machine knife
机动倾翻渣罐车 power-tipped slag ladle
机动输送机 powered conveyer
机动台架 transfer bed
机动提升料车 power lift(ing) truck
机动铁水罐 mechanized [power-driven] ladle
机动性 mobility, maneuverability
机动造型机 power-operating moulding machine
机动贮量 live storage
机房 machine room
机工 machinist, mechanist, equipment operator
机工车间 machine shop, mechanical department
机构 mechanism, organ, organization

机构内部设备	in-house facility
机构行程速度	running speed
机构学	mechanism
机柜	frame,【计】rack
机后摆动升降台	back tilting table
机后侧	exit side, upside
机后辅助工作[往复,延伸]辊道	back auxiliary table
机后工作辊道	back live table
机后输出辊道	mill run-out table
机后轧钢工(活套轧机的)	catcher
机后主要工作辊道	back main table
机加工残余应力	machining stress
机加开裂	machining crack
机加工硬化	bench hardening
机加工余量	machining allowance
机架	frame (assembly), framework,【压】stand, (stand, mill) housing (又称牌坊), body ◇ 闭口式~*,开口式~*, 可掀翻顶盖的~ tilting cap housing, 主~(轧机的) main housing
机架变形	stand stretch
机架窗口(轧机的)	housing window
机架窗口衬垫	housing window lining
机架底板[轨座]	housing shoe
机架底座	carriage
机架地脚板	housing feet
机架盖	top housing,【压】housing cap (top)
机架拐角应力	stress around corner of stand
机架辊	breast roll
机架横梁	frame crosshead,【压】beam (of) housing, housing crosshead [separator, traverse]
机架间铺板	sheet between stands
机架拉力计	tens(i)ometer, tension meter
机键轮	Switch wheel
机键(转换)级	Switching stage
机键塞孔	switch jack
机键室	switch room
机件	(machine) parts, work, organ
机焦	coke from machinery [modern] oven
机壳	shell, chassis, envelope
机框	machine frame [portal]
机理	mechanism
机理模型	mechanism model
机力筛	power screen
机力制动器[机动闸,机力闸]	mechanical [power] brake
机列	train
机密的	secret, confidential, classifed
机内校准[检定]器	built-in calibrator
机内脱气	【连铸】on-machine degassing
机内仪表	self-contained [built-in] instrument
机旁台架	local stand
机旁仪表	local instrument
机器	machine, machinery, engine, apparatus ◇ 定制的~*,与~无关的【计】machine independent,与~有关的【计】machine dependent, 重型~ heavy duty machine
机器操作员	machine operator [man]
机器错误	machine error
机器代码	machine code
机器地址	machine [absolute] address
机器翻译	machine [automatic, mechanical] translation
机器房	machine room [shop, house], machinery hall
机器废钢铁	machinery scrap
机器构件	mechanical component
机器光制	machine finish
机器焊接	machine welding
机器间	machinery compartment [hall]
机器检查[校验]	machine check
机器可读的	machinable
机器可读媒体	machine readable medium
机器可读数据	machine readable data
机器可识别的	machine recognizable
机器可用时间	available machine time, machine available time
机器零件	machine components [part(s)]

机器配置 machine configuration
机器切割器筒体 machine torch barrel
机器人 robot
机器人技术 robotics
机器人系统 robotized system
机器人学 robotics
机器识别 machine recognition
机器学习 machine learning
机器油 machine(ry) [lubricating] oil
机器语言 machine [computer] language
机器语言代码 machine language code
机器运行 machine run
机器造型 machine moulding
机器验证 【计】mechanical theorem proving
机器指令 【计】machine instruction
机器制造 machine building [construction, manufacturing], machinery
机器制造厂商 machine builder, machine-building plant
机器(制造)用钢 (同"机械零件用钢")
机器制造用铸铁 engineering cast iron
机器制造者 machine builder
机器智能 machine intelligence
机器周期 machine cycle
机前摆动升降台 front tilting table
机前操纵台 ingoing control post
机前侧 front [entry] side, down side
机前辅助工作辊道 front auxiliary table
机前工作辊道 front table
机前输入辊道 mill run-in table, ingot receiving table
机前推床导板 front side guard
机前主要工作辊道 front main table
机上抽风冷却 【团】downdraught strand cooling
机上鼓风冷却 【团】up-draught strand cooling
机上冷却 bed cooling,【团】on-strand [in-situ] cooling, cooling on (sinter) strand
机上冷却烧结法 on-strand cooled sintering
机上冷却烧结矿 strand-cooled sinter
机上冷却时间 on-strandstrand cooling time
机上冷却式烧结机 extended sinter machine,【团】"in-situ" cooling strand
机身 main body,【机】bed piece
机身漏风 【团】machine leakage
机速 conveyer [grate, machine] speed
机碎材料[碎石] crusher-run materail
机体 body, housing
机体窗口 housing window
机头 drive end [side]【团】charging [feed] side, charge [feed] end, loading end, (strand) charging station
机头除尘点 first dedusting station
机头端板 feed end dead-plate
机头罩 feed hood
机外脱气 【连铸】off-machine degassing
机外脱气工艺 off-machine degassing procedure
机尾 【团】discharge side [station, end], (strand) discharge, strand discharging station, end of strand
机尾算板 discharge end crush deck
机尾摆架 discharge end frame, moving section of discharge end
机尾除尘点 second dedusting station
机尾导轨 discharge end guide
机尾电除尘器 machine discharge end precipitator
机尾端板 discharge end dead-plate
机尾机罩 discharge end hood
机尾框架 discharge end frame
机尾洗涤器 machine discharge scrubber
机尾罩 discharge hood
机械 machine(ry) ◇ 轻型[小功率]~ light-duty machine, 重型~ heavy machinery
机械安装工 millwright
机械拔棒机 【色】mechanical contact extractor
机械焙烧炉 mechanical roaster, mechani-

cal roasting [calcining] oven, mechanical roasting furnace
机械闭锁　mechanical interlock(ing)
机械变形　mechanical deformation
机械操作阀　mechanically operated valve
机械插入式氧枪　mechanically inserted lance
机械铲　mechanical shovel [digger]
机械沉降　mechanical settling
机械称量杠杆系统　mechanical weigharm system
机械冲击　mechanical shock
机械冲击器　mechanical impactor
机械冲压　mechanical stamping
机械初步抽空泵　mechanical roughing pump
机械除尘器　mechanical (dust) collector
机械除鳞　mechanical descaling
机械处理　mechanical treatment
机械传动　mechanical drive
机械传动的活套挑　mechanical looper
机械粗加工　mechanical roughening
机械打出钢[铁]口　mechanical tapping
机械打壳【色】mechanical crust breaking
机械打孔　mechanical drilling
机械打通风口【色】mechanical tuyere punching
机械打印装置　mechanical stamping device
机械单色器　mechanical monochromator
机械(电流)断续器　mechanical interrupter ◇ 滚焊用~*
机械定时信管　mechanical time fuse (MTF)
机械镀覆　mechanical plating
机械锻造　mechanical [machine] forging
机械煅烧炉　mechanical roasting [calcining] oven
机械对流　mechanical convection
机械对中(电子显微镜的)　mechanical alignment
机械放液机　mechanical tapping machine

机械分级机　mechanical(-type) classifier
机械分离[选]　mechanical separation
机械分析　mechanical analysis
机械粉碎　mechanical pulverization [comminution]
机械粉碎机　mechanical disintegrator
机械封顶钢　mechanically capped steel
机械辅助压下装置　mechanical auxiliary screwdown
机械杠杆组装件　mechanical lever assembly
机械工程(学)　mechanical engineering
机械工程师　mechanical engineer (M.E.), machine engineer
机械工程用钢管　mechanical tube
机械功　mechanical work
机械构件　mechanical component
机械故障　mechanical failure
机械过滤器　mechanical filter
机械合金化　mechanical alloying (MA)
机械合金化粉末　mechanically alloyed powder
机械化　mechanization, motorization
机械化包装捆扎作业线　bundling line
机械化剥皮[修整](坯料的)　mechanical peeling
机械化侧导板　mechanical side guides
机械化程度　degree of mechanization
机械化等静压制【粉】mechanized isostatic pressing
机械化割炬　machine cutting torch [blowpipe]
机械化割炬[切割器]筒体　machine cutting (blowpipe) barrel
机械化焊接[机械焊]　mechanized [machine] welding
机械化焊接用保护气氛室　dry box for machine welding
机械化清理　mechanical chipping
机械化清理装置(板坯等的)　chipper
机械化深孔凿岩　mechanized longhole drilling (MLD)

机械化运输机　mechanized conveyer
机械化造型　mechanical [mechanization] moulding
机械化铸造(法)　machine casting
机械化铸造车间　mechanized foundry
机械化装料　machine loading
机械混合物　mechanical (ad)mixture
机械活套塔　mechanical looping tower
机械积分仪[器]　mechanical integrator
机械技术员　mechanical technician
机械记录　mechanical record(ing) [registration]
机械夹杂物　mechanical inclusions
机械加工　machining, mechanical processing [treatment, working] ◇ 经~的边（板、带材的）machine edge, 可~的 machinable
机械加工法兰[凸缘]　machine flange
机械加工废料　machine waste
机械加工焊缝　finished weld
机械加工流程图　machine flow sheet
机械加工图　finished machine drawing, machining drawing
机械加工性能　machinability
机械加工性能指数　machinability index
机械加工应变　machining strain
机械加工(用)润滑剂　lubricant for machining
机械加工余量　machining allowance, machine finish allowance, allowance for machining
机械加料　mechanical feed(ing)
机械加料器　mechanical feeder [charger]
机械加煤　mechanical stoking
机械加煤炉　stoker fired furnace
机械搅拌[搅动]　mechanical agitation [stirring]
机械搅拌槽　mechanically agitated tank
机械搅拌多膛焙烧炉　mechanical multiple-hearth revolving-rabble type roaster
机械搅拌高压釜　【色】mechanically-agitated autoclave

机械搅拌炉　mechanically rabbled furnace
机械搅拌耙　mechanical rabble
机械搅拌器　mechanical agitator [stirrer]
机械搅动式干燥坑　rabbled-hearth drier
机械搅动膛式干燥窑　rabbled-hearth drier
机械矫直　mechanical [machine] straightening
机械校准　mechanical alignment
机械结构用钢　machine construction steel
机械结合　mechanical bonding
机械结晶机　mechanical crystallier
机械进料　positive feed
机械精加工　machine finish
机械控制　mechanical control
机械扩管机　mechanical expander
机械拉深模　stretch mechanical die
机械离心式泡沫渣生产法　slag-expansion machine process
机械联锁　mechanical interlock(ing)
机械零件　machine (ry) [structural] parts, machine element
机械零件用钢(0.2—0.3C)　machine [machinery] steel (MS)
机械螺旋混合器　mechanical screw mixer
机械脉冲　mechanical pulsing
机械密封　mechanical seal
机械密封块　mechanical seal bar
机械模型　mechanical model
机械磨损[磨耗]　mechanical wear
机械能　mechanical energy
机械能力　machine capability
机械拧接　powertight makeup
机械拧紧度(管材的)　machine tight
机械耙　mechanical rake
机械耙动系统　mechanical raking system
机械抛光　mechanical polishing, satin finish (用刷或软布轮) ◇ 锌基压铸件~法 fadgenising
机械喷镀　mechanical plating
机械膨胀　mechanical swelling
机械疲劳　mechanical fatigue

机械平台	【连铸】machinery platform
机械平整	mechanical leveling
机械强度	mechanical strength [ruggedness]
机械强度值	strength value
机械强化	mechanical hardening
机械切割	machine cutting
机械切口	machine cut
机械切削试验	machining test
机械切削台	【耐】mechanical cutting table
机械清灰煤气发生炉	mechanical ashed producer
机械清理	mechanical cleaning, machine scarfing ◇ 用钢丝刷~ mechanical wire brushing
机械取样	mechanical sampling
机械取样器	machine sampler
机械取样设备	mechanical sample taking equipment
机械缺陷	mechanical defect
机械燃煤退火炉	coal-heated annealing furnace with machinery grates
机械筛	power screen
机械设备	mechanical equipment [outfit], machinery, plant equipment
机械升降平台	mechanical lifting platform
机械师	mechanic(ian), mechanist, machinist ◇ 安装~ installing mechanic
机械湿选法	wet mechanical method
机械时效	mechanical [hardness] ageing
机械式分级机	mechanical(-type) classifier
机械式塞棒	【钢】mechanical stopper
机械式制动联动机构	brake linkage
机械试验设备	mechanical test installation
机械试验室	mechanical-testing hall
机械收尘	mechanical separation
机械手	manipulator, mechanical [iron] hand ◇ 仿效~*, 倾斜~ tilting finger, 微型~ micromanipulator
机械手转动机构	manipulator turning gear
机械衰减	mechanical damping
机械双晶	mechanical twin
机械松弛	mechanical relaxation
机械损伤	mechanical damage [abuse]
机械损失	mechanical loss
机械缩孔	【压】mechanical pipe
机械调整台	mechanical stage
机械调准	mechanical alignment
机械跳汰选	machine jigging
机械通风	mechanical ventilation [draught], forced draught
机械通风冷却塔	mechanical-draft cooling tower
机械通风眼	【色】mechanical tuyere punching
机械同步装置	mechanical synchronizing device
机械推料	mechanical stoking
机械推料机	mechanical pusher ram
机械推料器	mechanical pusher
机械雾化[喷雾]器	mechanical atomizer
机械雾化燃烧器	mechanical atomizer burner
机械误差	machine error
机械洗涤器	mechanical scrubber
机械效率	mechanical efficiency
机械效应	mechanical effect
机械形变真空计	mechanical deformation vacuum gauge
机械性剥落[散裂]	mechanical spalling
机械性能[特性]	mechanical behaviour [characteristic, property] ◇ 设计的主要~*
机械性能各向异性	mechanical anisotropy
机械性能试验	mechanical test(ing)
机械(性能)稳定性	mechanical stability
机械修整	mechanical cleaning, machine finish
机械选矿	mechanical beneficiation
机械学	mechanics, mechanology
机械学的	mechanical
机械压板	mechanical hold-down

机械压力 mechanical pressure
机械压力表 mechanical pressure gauge
机械压力机 mechanical press, mechanically operated press
机械压实作用 mechanical packing
机械压下系统 mechanical screwdown system
机械压砖机 mechanical press
机械冶金学 mechanical metallurgy
机械应力 mechanical stress
机械硬度 mechanical hardness
机械用钢 (同"机械零件用钢")
机械用铸铁件 engineering iron castings
机械预抽真空泵 mechanical forepump
机械杂质 mechanical admixture [impurity]
机械黏附[着] mechanical adhesion
机械黏砂 【铸】burned-on sand, metal penetration (铸件上的金属渗透)
机械张弛 mechanical relaxation
机械真空泵 mechanical (vacuum) pump ◇ 金尼型~Kinney pump
机械振打装置 mechanical shaker
机械振荡 mechanical oscillations
机械振荡器 mechanical oscillator
机械振动 mechanical vibration
机械振(动)筛 moto-vibro screen, power riddler, vanning jig
机械蒸发器 mechanical evaporator
机械整流器 mechanical [commutator] rectifier
机械直接控制型控制器 mechanical direct control type controller
机械制动器 mechanical brake
机械制图 mechanical [machine] drawing
机械滞后 mechanical hysteresis
机械滞后理论 theory of mechanical hysteresis
机械滞后损失 mechanical hysteresis loss
机械转矩比率 mechanical torque rate
机械装料 machine loading, mechanical filling

机械装填 mechanical filling
机械装置 mechanical [labor-saving] device, mechanical outfit, mechanism
机械自动控制[自动化] mechanical automation
机械作用 mechanical action [effect]
机修厂 maintenance shop, machine repair shop
机修厂修配间 repair workshop
机修车间 maintenance shop, mechanical [repair] workshop, overhaul shop
机修工 mechanic
机用磁强计 airborne magnetometer
机用青铜 machinery bronze
机油 machine(ry) [engine] oil
机罩 hood, bonnet
机罩抽风[排烟]机 hood exhaust fan
机罩回热[回流]风机 hood recup(eration) fan
机罩密封风机 hood seal fan
机制的 machine-processed, machine-made
机制性 machinability
机轴 boss rod
机铸生铁 machine [chill] cast pig
机铸铁 machine cast iron
机组 (machine) set, assembling unit, bank, complex, train, unit (assembly) ◇ 轧机~mill [roll] train
机组保养 bank maintenance
机组开卷机 processing uncoiler
机组排列 unit arrangement
机组生产能力 capacity of unit
机组维护 bank maintenance
机组作业线除鳞机 flexing unit
机组作业线上的多条带材精整 multiple strip processing
机组作业线停顿 line stoppage
机座 support
机座底架 bed frame, sole plate frame
机座横梁 mill separator
机座间带钢压力机 interstand strip press
机座间递钢 interstand, catching

机座间张力	【压】interstand tension
机座上横梁	top-housing [top-mill] separator
机座弹跳	springing of stand
机座下横梁	bottom-mill separator
矶田铅基轴承合金(10—20Sb,5—20Sn,余量 Pb)	Isoda metal
奇 A 同位素	odd-A isotope
奇 N 同位素	odd-N isotope
奇 Z 同位素	odd-Z isotope
奇级[阶]反射	odd-order reflections
奇偶错误	parity error
奇偶校验	odd-even [even-odd, parity] check ◇ 磁鼓～drum parity check
奇偶校验位	parity bit
奇偶性	parity
奇数	odd number
奇数奇偶校验	odd parity
奇数(轧制)道次	forward pass, odd numbered pass
奇同位素	odd isotope
奇项	odd term
奇质量数	odd mass
奇质量数同位素	odd-mass isotope
唧筒	cylinder ◇ 冲击～striker cylinder
畸变	distortion, aberration,【电】deformation ◇ 非球状～", 负[桶形]～", 生谐～harmonic distortion, 正[枕形]～pincushion distortion
畸变波法	【理】method of distorted waves
畸变度	degree of distortion
畸变钢丝绳	distorted wire rope
畸变晶格	distorted [perturbed] lattice
畸变能理论	distortion-energy theory
畸变石墨	degenerated graphite
畸变试样	distortion specimen
畸变误差	distortion inaccuracy
畸变像	fault image
畸变因数[系数]	distortion factor
畸变张量	distortion tensor
畸形	deformity, malformation
畸形漏磁	zigzag leakage
畸形鱼	【环】malformed fish
积尘	dust deposit(ion)
积尘板电极	(同"板式积尘电极")
积分	integral, integrate, integration ◇ 傅里叶～Fourier's integral
积分变数	integral [integration] variable
积分单元	integrating block
积分电路	integrating circuit, integrator
积分电路网	integrating network
积分电路组件	integrating circuit module
积分反应器	integral reactor
积分方程	integral equation
积分放大器	integrating amplifier, integrator-amplifier
积分负载仪	integrating load-meter
积分剂量	(同"总剂量")
积分[积算]器	integrator ◇ 电子～electronic integrator
积分曲线	integral curve
积分时间	integrating time
积分吸收剂量	(同"总吸收剂量")
积分仪	integrating instrument, integrator ◇ 机械～mechanical integrator
积分原理	integrated theory
积分值	integral value [quantity]
积分转速计[表]	integrating tachometer
积分作用	integral action
积复激电动机	cumulative compound motor
积复激绕组	cumulative compound winding
积垢	(sediment) incrustation, scale deposition, scaling
积灰载重(收尘器的)	dust load
积矩阵	product matrix
积聚	accumulation, build up, balling up (氧化皮)
积累	accumulation, collect, integration
积累式多次拉丝机	accumulator multidraft machine
积料	material deposit
积留	entrapment

积木化	modularization ◇ 功能~*
积木化设计	modular design
积木式的	【计】modular
积木式系统	building block system (BBS)
积木式原理	building block principle
积木式组件	building unit, cordwood module
积木性	modularity
积热	gain of heat
积算式仪表	summation instrument
积碳	carbon deposit(ion) [build-up] (带钢热处理缺陷), sooting ◇ 局部~ patch of carbon
积铁	magnetite iron build-up, 【铁】dead man ◇ 炉底~ (高炉的) shadrach, 炉缸~ bear, old-horse
积铁放出口(炉中的)	bear taphole
积阵	product matrix
箕斗	skip (bucket) ◇ 翻转~ overturning skip
箕斗卷扬机	skip hoist
激变	violent change, surge
激波	shock wave, maser
激波压力	shock pressure
激磁	excitation, initiation, field, magnetization ◇ 差动~*, 极限~ ceiling excitation, 切断~ deenergize, deenergise
激磁电流	exciting [field] current
激磁电路	exciting circuit
激磁[激发]电压	exciting [excitation] voltage
激磁[激发]功率	exciting [excitation] power ◇ 有效[均方根]~ RMS exciting power
激磁机	exciter
激磁机组	exciter set
激磁绕组	field
激磁绕组用铜	field copper
激磁系统	excitation system
激磁指数	excitation index
激动	excitation, actuation, stir
激动式热风供暖	central fan heating
激发	excitation, activating ◇ 未~原子 nonexcited atom
激发带	excitation band
激发电势[位]	excitation potential
激发罐	motivating container
激发光	exciting light ◇ 阴极[电子]~ cathodoluminescence
激发量子	excitation quantum
激发能级	excitation (energy) level ◇ 一次~*
激发频率	excitation [stimulating] frequency
激发器	exciter, promoter, promotor
激发原子	excited atom
激发源	excitation source
激发指数	excitation index
激发子	exciton
激光	laser (light amplification by stimulated emission of radiation) ◇ 二氧化碳~(器) carbon dioxide laser, 氩离子~(器) argon ion laser
激光饱和光谱学	laser saturation spectroscopy
激光表面修整(术)	laser surface modification
激光材料	laser material
激光测距	laser rangefinding
激光测距仪	laser detector, laser range finder
激光差拍系统	laser heterodyne system
激光穿孔	laser drilling
激光传感技术	laser sensing technology
激光传感器	laser sensor
激光淬火	laser quenching
激光打孔	laser drilling [boring]
激光等离子体	laser plasma
激光点焊机	laser spot weler
激光点火器	laser ignitor
激光多普勒速度计	laser Doppler velocimeter
激光发送器	laser transmitter
激光干涉测量法	laser interferometry

激 ji

激光干涉仪	laser interferometer
激光(光)束	laser beam
激光光谱法	laser spectrometry
激光焊机	laser beam welder
激光焊接头	laser welding head
激光加工	laser (material) processing, laser machining (指切削加工)
激光加热	laser heating
激光加热煤粉	laser-heated pulverized coal
激光雷达	(optical) laser radar
激光粒度计	laser granulometer
激光流量计	laser flowmeter
激光毛化	【压】laser roughing
激光毛化技术	laser-textured technology
激光毛化轧辊	laser-textured roll
激光毛面钢板	laser-textured steel sheet
激光熔炼	laser melting
激光偏转板[器]	laser deflector
激光器	laser ◇ 半导体[注入型]～junction laser, 固态～solid state laser, 扫描～scanned-laser
激光切割	laser cutting
激光切削加工	laser machining
激光熔敷合金层	laser remelted alloy coating
激光施照器	laser illuminator
激光矢量速度计	laser vector velocimeter
激光(束)焊接	laser(-beam) welding
激光束技术	laser-beam technique
激光束偏转传感器	laser-beam deflection sensor
激光(束)切割机	laser-beam cutter
激光束烧结	【粉】sintering with laser beam
激光头	laser head
激光显微镜	laser microscope
激光延伸计	laser extensometer
激光应变计	laser strainmeter
激光诱导化学气相沉积(法)	laser-induced chemical vapour deposition
激光质谱法	laser mass spectrometry
激光作用	laser action

激活	activation, sensitization ◇ 加热～heat activation
激活的滑移线长度	active slip line length
激活电势[位]	activation [active] potential
激活法	(同"活化法")
激活面积	activation area
激活能	activation energy
激活能函数	activation energy function
激活能谱	spectrum of activation energies
激活器	actuator
激活熵	(同"活化熵")
激活体积	activated volume
激活系数	activity coefficient
激活原子	activated atom
激活中心	(同"活化中心")
激冷	chill(ing), shock chilling ◇ 包中～ladle chill, 控制～controlled chilling,
激冷材料	chill material, 【铸】densener
激冷层	chill zone, 【金】chilled layer
激冷(层)深度	chill depth, depth of chill
激冷程度	chill depth, severity of quenching
激冷钉	【铸】chill nail
激冷和风冷盘管式冷却系统	chiller and fan-coil type cooling system
激冷激热效应	spalling effect
激冷件涂层[涂料]	chill coating
激冷介质	shock chilling medium
激冷金属	chills
激冷晶体	chill crystal
激冷气体	shock gas
激冷强化	chill strengthening
激冷圈	condensing ring
激冷室	shock chamber
激冷试块	chill block
激冷试验	chill test
激冷铁环	【铸】chill ring
激冷完全淬火	dead-cold chiling
激冷效应	chilling effect
激冷硬化	chill hardening [strengthening], chin-chin hardening

激冷油 【铸】chill oil	吉雷特当量(黄铜的) Guillet equivalent
激冷轧辊 chilled roll	吉雷特图(镍钢的) Guillet diagram
激励 excitation, drive, energize, magnetize	吉曼尼阿锌基轴承合金(10Sn, 4.5Cu, 5Pb, 0.8Fe, 余量 Zn) Germania bearing alloy
激励带 excitation band	
激励灯 exciter lamp	
激励电极 exciting electrode	吉纳科轴承合金(89Sn, 7.5Sb, 3.5Cu) Genarco alloy
激励电流 exciting [field] current	
激励电路 drive(r) [energizing] circuit	吉纳洛依耐热高镍铬合金钢(31—40Ni, 12—21Cr, 0.5C, 余量 Fe) Genalloy
激励功率 driving [excitation] power	
激励管 driver [driving] tube	吉内莱特无润滑烧结青铜轴承合金 (70Cu, 13—14Sn, 5—6Pb, 5—6 石墨) Genelite
激励级 driver stage	
激励剂 energiser, energizer ◇ 化学~ chemical energizer	
	吉塞勒塑性计 Gieseler plastometer
激励器 exciter, activator, actuator	极安全的 foolproof
激励线圈 excitation [drive] coil	极板 polar plate ◇ 涂浆~ grid plate
激励振荡器 driving oscillator	极板间距 plate clearance
激烈增殖 mushrooming	极板面积(电除尘器的) plate area
激子 exciton, (激发核子) baryon, barion ◇ 束缚~态 bound exciton state	极板振打机构 plate shaking mechanism
	极薄镀锡薄钢板(厚度在 0.18mm 以下) tagger plate, taggers
激子超导体 excitonic superconductor	
鸡冠石 {As_2S_2} realgar	极薄药皮焊条 wash-coated electrode
吉布斯(等边)三角形 Gibbs triangle	极磁铁矿 leading stone, lodestone
	极粗晶生铁 very-open-grained pig iron
吉布斯-杜亨方程 Gibbs-Duhem equation	极大极小逼近 minimax approximation
	极大极小策略[战略] minimax strategy
吉布斯函数 Gibbs function	极大极小判据[准则] maxi-mim criterion
吉布斯函数判据 Gibbs function criterion	极大极小原理 minimax principle
吉布斯-亥姆霍兹方程 Gibbs-Helmholtz's equation	极大值 maximum (max), maximum value ◇ 从零到~变化的循环 cycle varying from zero to maximum
吉布斯吸附等温式 Gibbs absorption isotherm	
	极低含氮量炼钢法 very low nitrogen (VLN) process
吉布斯吸附方程 Gibbs adsorption equation	
	极低氢量钢 very low hydrogen steel
吉布斯相律 Gibbs (phase) rule	极低碳 extra-low carbon (ECL)
吉布斯自由能 Gibbs free energy	极低碳素钢 extra-low carbon steel
吉尔卡洛伊锆锡合金 Zircaloy	极点 top, acme, meridian, pole, vertex, culmination
吉尔科弗拉克斯锆质高级耐火材料 Zircofrax	
	极端情况 extreme case
吉尔科纳尔锌基铸造合金(15Cu, 8Mn, 0.5Si, 余量 Zn) Zirkonal	极高纯金属 very-high-purity metal
	极高压 very high tension (VHT), extra-high tension (EHT), extra-high voltage (EHV)
吉赫 【电】gigahertz (GHz)	
吉勒利冲击试验 Guillery	

极高真空（$< 1.33 \times 10^{-10}$ Pa） extreme high vacuum (XHV)

极化 polarization, polarity ◇ 测～术 polarimetry, 活化[激活]～ activation polarization, 阳极～*, 阴极～*

极化电池 polarization cell

极化电流 polarization [polarizing] current

极化电势[位] polarization potential ◇ 阳离子～*

极化电压 polarization voltage

极化度 polarizability

极化方向 direction of polarization ◇ 择优～*

极化光应力测定法 photostress [photoelastic, photoelasticity] method

极化计 polarimeter

极化继电器 polar(ized) [directional] relay

极化(平)面 polarization plane, plane of polarization

极化曲线 polarization curve ◇ 恒电位～*

极化式转矩电动机 polarized torque motor

极化效应 polarizing [polarization] effect

极化行为 polarization behaviour

极化性 polarizability

极化子 polaron

极化作用 polarized action, polarization

极尖 pole tip

极间磁粉探伤法 yoke magnetizing method

极间电容 interelectrode capacitance

极间短路 interelectrode short-circuit

极间极 interpole

极间间隙[空隙] interpolar [pole] gap

极间距(离)[极距] interelectrode distance [space], interpolar distance, anode-cathode distance [separation], electrode distance [spacing], interelectrode space, pole [polar] pitch

极间漏电 interelectrode leakage

极间绕组 interpole winding

极毛菌 Pscubomonas sp.

极泥沉淀 【色】slurry sedimentation

极泥下腐蚀 hide-out corrosion

极泥重复利用 【色】slurry reuse

极泥贮槽 【色】slurry [surge] sump

极片材料 pole piece material

极贫矿石 halvans

极平钢带 dead flat strip

极谱 polarogram, polarograph

极谱测定[测量] polarographic determination [measurement]

极谱法 polarography ◇ 方波～*

极谱分析 polarographic analysis

极谱图 polarogram

极谱仪 polarograph ◇ 矩形波～*

极软 dead-softness

极软钢（< 0.15C） dead soft [mild] steel

极软钢丝绳 extra flexible wire rope

极少填隙式固溶元素 extra-low interstitial (ELI)

极射赤面投影 stereographic projection

极射赤面投影测量 measurements on stereogram

极射赤面投影极点 stereographic pole

极射(赤面投影)三角形 stereographic triangle

极射赤面投影图 (construction on) stereogram

极射图中心 centre of stereogram

极深冲钢 (同"超深冲钢")

极隧射线 canal rays

极图 pole figure

极图直接记录 direct registration of pole-diagrams

极图中心 centre of pole figure

极网(图) polar [pole] net

极微强度 infinitesimal strength

极微丝 hair

极位错 pole dislocation

极隙 pole clearance ◇ 分析[工作]～【化】analytical gap

极细的　extra fine (XF), superfine
极细粉末　superfine powder, powder fines
极细拉丝　superfine [very-fine] drawing
极细粒度　extreme fineness
极细丝　hairline
极细铁粉　finely divided iron powder
极细微粒　submicron solids
极细珠光体　troostite pearlite
极限　limit (LIM, lim.), limitation, ultimate (ult.) ◇ 杜安-亨特～ Duane-Hunt limit, 费米～ Fermi limit, 给定～ prescribed limit
极限半径　limiting radius
极限产量[出力]　ultimate output
极限成分　limiting composition
极限承载能力　ultimate bearing capacity
极限电流密度　limiting current density
极限电压　limit voltage
极限分布　ultimate distribution
极限风量　limiting wind rate
极限负载[荷载, 载荷]　limit(ing) load, ultimate [collapse] load
极限功率　ultimate output, power limit
极限洪水　maximum possible flood
极限回弹能力　ultimate resilience
极限混合物　borderline mixture
极限激磁　ceiling excitation
极限剪(切)应力　ultimate shearing stress (U.S.S.)
极限开关　limit switch (LS), limit stop
极限抗剪强度　ultimate shearing strength
极限抗拉强度　ultimate tensile strength (UTS, uts)
极限抗压强度　ultimate compressive strength
极限颗粒(最小的)　ultimate particle
极限拉伸应力　ultimate tensile stress
极限量　ultimate quantity [capacity]
极限量规　limit gauge
极限密度　peak [ultimate] density
极限浓度　limiting concentration
极限频率　limit(ing) frequency

极限曝光　limiting exposure
极限强度　ultimate strength
极限强度法　ultimate strength method
极限曲线　limit curve
极限屈服点　limiting yield point (LYP)
极限屈服应力　limiting yield stress (LYS)
极限蠕变应力　limiting creep stress
极限塞规　limit plug (gauge)
极限深冲比　limiting drawing ratio ◇ 阿贝尔～与加工硬化指数关系曲线 Arber curve
极限生产能力　limiting capacity
极限试验　ultimate test
极限寿命　ultimate life
极限输出　ultimate output
极限速度　limit(ing) speed [velocity]
极限弹力　ultimate resilience
极限条件[状态]　limiting condition
极限弯(曲力)矩　ultimate bending moment
极限弯曲强度　ultimate bending strength
极限位置　extreme [limiting, end] position
极限温度　limiting temperature
极限误差　limit(ing) error
极限压力　extreme pressure (EP), limit [ultimate] pressure
极限压缩　limiting draft
极限压下量　limiting draft [draught]
极限延伸　ultimate elongation
极限氧化　marginal oxidation
极限应变　limiting [ultimate] strain
极限应力　limiting [critical, ultimate] stress
极限(元素)组成　ultimate composition
极限允许含量　prohibitive amount
极限真空　highest [ultimate] vacuum
极限值　limit(ing) [ultimate, nonoperate] value
极限(状态)设计　limit [ultimate] design
极小值　minimum (value)
极性　polarity
极性半导体　polar semiconductor

极性标志[符号]　polarity mark
极性触点　pole contact
极性反应　polar reaction
极性分子　(hetero)polar molecule
极性化合物　(hetero)polar compound
极性基　polar group
极性键　heteropolar binding [bond], polar bond
极性键合　polar linkage
极性晶体　polar crystal
极性溶剂　polar solvent
极性润滑剂　polar [surface-active] lubricant
极性散射　polar scattering
极性位错　pole dislocation
极性相关　polarity correlation
极性指示器　polar(ity) indicator
极靴　pole piece [shoe, terminal, extension] ◇ 电子透镜～缝隙*
极靴边　pole tip
极靴材料　pole piece material
极延伸部分　pole extension
极硬钢　extra-hard [dead-hard] steel
极值　peak, extreme (value), crest value
极值原理　extremum principle
极轴(线)　polar axis
极坐标　polar coordinates
极坐标图　polar diagram [plot]
棘轮　ratchet (wheel), notch [star] wheel
棘轮扳手　ratchet wrench [spanner]
棘轮柄[杆]　ratchet lever
棘轮机构　ratchet [pawl] mechanism, ratchet(-wheel) gear
棘轮离合器　ratchet [pawl] clutch
棘轮联轴器　ratchet coupling
棘轮与棘爪　ratchet-and-pawl
棘轮装置　ratchet gear [arrangement]
棘(头)螺栓　barb [bat, hacked, jag, lewis, rag, stone] bolt
棘爪　(cam) pawl, pall
棘爪钢　pawl steel
棘爪型压紧装置　ratchet type holdback device

集尘　(同"收尘")
集尘电极　(dust-) collecting [precipitation] electrode ◇ 板式～*
集尘电极管　collecting electrode pipe
集尘斗　dust hopper
集尘风扇　dust-collecting fan
集尘管　【铁】dust leg
集尘极　precipitation electrode
集尘极板　(dust-) collecting plate, collecting plate electrode, collector plate
集尘漏斗　dust-collecting hopper
集尘器　dust-collector ◇ 多层洗涤～multi-wash collector
集尘装置　dust-collecting [dust-catching] plant
集尘作用　dust agglutination
集成　integration
集成电路　integrated circuit (IC) ◇ 超大规模～*, 大规模～*, 纳瓦～*, 小规模～*, 中规模～*
集成电路块　integrated circuit block
集成光学　integrated optics
集成化分布式过程自动控制系统　integrated and distributed automatic process control system
集成系统　integrated system
集电板　collector plates
集电轨　collector rail
集电环　collector [bus] ring, commutator
集电机构　collector-shoe gear
集电极　collector
集电极衬底结　collector-substrate junction
集电极电流　collector current
集电极结　collector junction
集电极损耗　collector dissipation
集电器　(current) collector ◇ 弓架式～*
集电刷　(current-) collector brush, collecting brush, (brush) collector
集风管　collecting pipe, windmain
集肤效应　(同"趋肤效应")
集肤作用　surface action

集管	header, manifold ◇ 进汽~*
集合	assemble, assembling, gather
集合火道	【焦】collecting flue
集合论	set theory
集合体	aggregate, aggregation
集结沉淀[沉积]	consolidation settling
集聚	grouping, collect, assemble
集聚层[区]	cluston
集聚体	conglomerate, congeries
集卷器	(loop) collector, collecting mandrel
集卷室	【压】collecting chamber
集卷筒	collecting [reform] tub
集料	【建】aggregate
集料槽	collecting launder
集料厂	aggregate plant
集料辊道	collecting roller table
集料架	bin ◇ 半圆形~*
集料盲沟	aggregate drain
集料配备厂	aggregate preparation plant
集料配备器	aggregate batcher
集料皮带(机)	collecting conveyer, collector belt, gathering conveyer [belt] ◇ 共用~ common gathering belt
集料平均粒径的测定	aggregate averaging
集料输送机	gathering conveyer
集料系统	gathering system
集流管	collecting pipe ◇ 直接回热~*
集流管调节器	manifold regulator
集流环	collector (ring), slip ring
集流器	current collector
集宁石	jiningite
集气槽	gas-collecting channel [vessel]
集气管	collecting pipe, main dust, 【机】header
集气管道	gas-collecting duct
集气管放灰阀	windmain dust valve
集气管灰斗	windmain hopper
集气管系统	main waste-gas system
集气罐[瓶]	gas-collecting vessel
集气环	gas-collecting ring
集气(检漏)试验	accumulation test
集气帽	gas-collecting cap
集气器	air [gas] collector
集气室	gas-collector chamber
集气套管	gas collection sleeve
集气通道	gas-collecting channel
集气系统	captation system, gas gathering system
集气罩	gas-collecting hood [channel], gas (collecting) skirt ◇ 电解槽~【色】cell hood
集气主管	collecting main ◇ 与~断开的装炉【焦】off-main charging, 与~接通的装炉【焦】on-main charging
集气主管压力	【焦】pressure of dry main
集气总管	collecting [collector] main
集气总管压力	collecting main pressure
集汽鼓(锅炉的)	steam drum
集散式控制系统	distribution control system (DCS)
集散系统	integrated and distributed system
集散型微机控制系统	computerized common-decentralized control system
集砂炉膛(飘悬焙烧炉的)	collecting hearth
集水槽	water (collecting) trough
集水池	【环】impoundment bassin [lake]
集水沟	collection ditch
集水井	collecting well
集水坑	catch pit, water collecting pit, collecting sump
集水坑泵	sump pump
集水器【建】	catchpot
集水箱	water-storage tank
集酸槽的酸	head acid
集体传动	group [collective] drive ◇ 主轴~的(轧机)辊道*
集体电子	collective electrons
集体电子模型	collective electron model
集体分配法(结构力学的)	block distribution

集体相互作用	collective interaction
集线器	【计】concentrator
集烟罩	fume collecting hood（氧气转炉的），【焦】gas chamber
集盐器	salt box [drum]
集液槽	collecting tank, drag-out tank（电解液用）
集液池	collecting basin
集液孔	gathering hole
集油槽	oil sump, oil-trap
集油器	oil receiver
集油箱	oil collecting tank
集油罩	oil-collecting hood
集约方式	intensive way
集运辊道	gathering table
集渣槽[包]	【铸】skim bob, scum riser ◇ 锯齿形~ saw-tooth crossgate
集渣口	skimming gate
集渣冒口	scum riser
集渣器	slag [dirt] trap ◇ 离心（式）~ spinner [whirl] gate
集中	concentrate, centralize, centring, focus, lumping
集中差速传动系统	centralized differential transmission system ◇ 串联~*
集中沉淀池	common sump
集中电阻	constriction [lumped] resistance
集中干油润滑	centralized grease lubrication
集中供暖	central heating
集中管理制	centralized control system
集中混合机	central mixer
集中加热	central heating
集中搅拌厂	central mixing plant
集中控制	centralized control, centralization of control, common control system
集中矿浆池	central collecting sump
集中力	concentrated force
集中排烟烟囱	concentrated [centralized] smoke stacks
集中润滑	centralized lubrication
集中润滑系统	centralized lubricating system ◇ 单线~*, 干油~*, 稀油~*, 自动干油~*
集中（式）数据处理	centralized [integrated] data processing
集中式网络	centralized network
集中性缩孔	gross shrinkage
集中压力润滑	centralized force-feed lubrication
集中载荷[荷载]	concentrated [point, single] load
集中载重	concentrated weight
集中总管	【运】collector
集柱	clustered column
集装	assembling
集装箱	container ◇ 大型~ van container
集总	lumping
集总常数[恒量]	lumped constant
急变试验	（温、压的）shock-testing
急件	urgent document, despatch, dispatch
急冷	chilling, rapid [shock, splat] cooling ◇ 耐~能力 chilling resistance
急冷淬火	hardening by sudden cooling
急冷度	quenching degree
急冷工段	fast cool zone
急冷急热	heat [thermal] shock
急冷晶体	chill crystal
急冷裂纹	chill crack
急冷凝固	rapid solidification, splat cooling
急冷退火	quench annealing
急冷硬化	hardening by sudden cooling
急冷作用	shock chilling function
急流	jerky flow, rapid stream
急热	rapid heating ◇ 冷处理~法 subzero rapid heating
急热急冷淬火	dynamic quenching
急速加热烧结	flash heating sintering
急弯接头	sharp bend
急弯曲线	sharp [abrupt, steep, sweeping] curve
急骤蒸发	flash vaporization
急骤蒸发器	flash type evaporator

急骤蒸馏　flash distillation ◇二次~*
急骤蒸馏塔　flash tower
疾病　disease, sickness ◇公害引起的~*
汲器　dipper
即刻孕育处理　【铸】instant inoculation
即时的　instant, immediate, summary
即时复合材料　in-situ composite
即速回火(淬火后的)　prompt tempering
级　class, order, grade, cascade, stage, step
级别　class, grade, quality ◇要求磨的~【选】milling-grade
级高(离子交换及萃取的)　stage height
级进式冷镦机　progressive header
级联　cascade (casc.), cascading, cascade connection, concatenation, tandem connection
级联操作法　cascade process
级联沉降器　cascade of settlers
级联簇射　cascade shower
级联萃取设备　extraction cascade
级联电动机　cascade [concatenated] motor
级联多级萃取设备　multistage extraction cascade
级联法　cascade method
级联放大器　cascade amplifier
级联过程(宇宙线的)　cascade process
级联混合器　cascade of mixers
级联控制　cascade control
级联三重收回熔区传输精炼炉　【色】cascade of triple-withdrawal zone-transport refiner
级联循环　circulation cascade
级轮　stepcone, stepped pulley
级配　grading, graduation, gradation ◇骨料间断~*, 全部~骨料 fully graded aggregate
级配骨料　graded aggregate
级配曲线(颗粒的)　grading curve ◇富勒氏~Fuller's curve, 累计~*
级数　progression, series, stage number, number of stages ◇傅里叶~Fourier series
级数(发)散度　divergence of series
级温(多级流化床反应器的)　stage temperature
级增应力试验　step stress test
挤拔　extrusion drawing ◇静液力~*
挤出　extrusion, squeeze out, expel
挤干　squeeze, wiping
挤干辊　drying [squeezer, wring(er)] roll, squeezing [wringing] roller ◇洗涤~cleaning wring roll, 橡胶覆面~squeegee roll, squeeze
挤干辊装置　wringer roll unit
挤干辊装置导向辊　wringer steering roll
挤干装置　wiping arrangement
挤光(螺钉冷镦前的)　extrusion finish
挤辊(高频焊管的)　squeeze roll
挤焊　push weld
挤合聚乙烯表面涂层　squeezed-polyoxyethylene surface-coating
挤浆砌筑　buttered masonry
挤浆砌砖法　shove joint brickwork
挤开效应(挤压特硬金属时的)　effect of ploughing
挤列　crowdion
挤泥机　pug ◇螺旋~*, 脱气~【耐】de-airing auger
挤泥器　applicator ◇活塞式~piston type applicator
挤水器(起模用)　moulder's bulb
挤箱　【铸】clamp-off
挤芯机　core extruder, core extruding [extrusion] machine, plunger core machine ◇螺旋式~sausage machine, core extrusion machine
挤锌辊　【压】wipe
挤压　extrusion (extn., extr.), extrusion pressing, bulldoze, pressing, squeezing ◇半烧结状态~*, 包套[护套]~*, 扁挤压筒~*, 差压[带反压力的]~*, 侧向塑流的~side-ways extruding, 带壳[带皮]~extruding with shell, 带芯棒

mandrel extrusion, 低压～ low-pressure pressing, 多孔模～ multihole extrusion, 反(向)[逆向]～*, 非稳定～(过程)*, 复合～*, 高速[快速]～ high velocity extrusion, 高温～*, 共～*, 横[正交]～ cross extrusion, 恒定压力～*, 阶段式～ stepped extrusion, 静液力～*, 可一性 extrudability, 冷冲～ cold impact extrusion, 冷～*, 冷黏结～*, 连续静液～*, 螺旋～ helical extrusion, 毛坯[粗]～ breakdown extrusion, 模压淬火～ die-quenched extruding, 难一合金～*, 坯料接续～*, 切割～ cut extrusion, 软芯锭～*, 水封～ extrusion into water, 稳定～(过程) stationary extrusion, 无黏结剂～*, 有黏结剂～(粉末挤压) extrusion with binder, 再[二次]～ re-extrusion, 真空～ extrusion under vacuum, 正向[直接]～*, 轴线对称～ axisymmetric extrusion

挤压棒材 extruded bar [rod]
挤压包覆(法) extrusion cladding
挤压包套(粉末的) extrusion container
挤压比 extrusion ratio
挤压不锈钢管 extruded stainless steel tube
挤压残料分离机 butt separator
挤压残料滑槽 butt chute
挤压残料-挤压垫分离装置 butt dummy block separator
挤压残料剪切机 butt shears
挤压残料提升装置 butt end lifter
挤压残料卸料装置 butt discharger
挤压产品直径 extruded diameter, diameter of extrusion
挤压常数 extrution constant
挤压车间 extrusion plant
挤压成型 extrusion forming [moulding], extruded shape, 【粉】extrusion compacting, compacting by extrusion ◇ 糊膏～法 paste process, 连续～*, 颗粒金属～ pellet extrusion, 有孔件～*

挤压冲程 extrusion stroke
挤压垫(片) extrusion [pressure] disc, dummy block, pusher [follower] pad ◇ 球腔～ spherical pressure pad
挤压锭 extrusion ingot ◇ 表面加工过的～ scalped extrusion ingot, 有钻孔的～ drilled extrusion ingot
挤压锻造 extrusion forging
挤压锻造模 extrusion-forging die
挤压多孔零件 extruded porous sections
挤压法 extrusion method ◇ 玻璃润滑(热)～*, 迪克～*, 胡克药筒～ Hooker process, 芯棒～*, 于仁玻璃润滑钢材～*
挤压法包套 sheathing by extrusion
挤压坩埚 mycrodyne crucible
挤压杆[冲头] extrusion ram [stem] ◇ 横向～*
挤压杆速度 ram speed
挤压杆芯头 ram nose
挤压杆行程 travel of ram
挤压杆支承 stem holder
挤压钢棒 extruded rod
挤压钢管[管件] extruded pipe
挤压工具 extrusion toolage
挤压工艺 extrusion process
挤压管材用空心锭 cored extrusion ingot
挤压管切头 extrusion discard
挤压辊 extrusion [squeeze] roll, squeezing roller
挤压烘干台 squeezer and dryer table
挤压黄铜(55Cu,45Zn) extrusion brass
挤压机 extruder, extruding machine, extrusion press, squeezer ◇ 超音速驱动～*, 电缆铠装～ cable press, 液压～*
挤压件方向性 directionality in extrusions
挤压结构钢管[结构管件] extruded structural pipe [tube]
挤压结构(钢)型材 extruded structural shape
挤压金属 extrusion metal
挤压开坯 extrusion breakdown

挤压空心棒材　extruded hollow bar
挤压力　extruding [extrusion] force
挤压零件　extrusion sections
挤压铝合金　extrusion aluminium alloy ◇西姆盖尔～*
挤压螺丝　squeezing-screw
挤压模　extrusion die, squeezing die ◇共～*, 空心型材～hollow die, 平～flat extrusion die
挤压模具钢　extrusion die steel ◇海德拉～*
挤压模塑　extrusion moulding
挤压母模　【压】hob
挤压坯　extruded stock [billet]
挤压强度　Crushing strength
挤压曲线　extrusion graph
挤压缺陷　extrusion defect
挤压润滑剂　bonderlube
挤压设备　extrusion plant ◇成套～*
挤压试验　extrusion test
挤压速度　extrusion speed
挤压缩孔(缺陷)　back end (extrusion) defect
挤压筒[缸]　extrusion chamber, (passage of) container ◇平模～*, 锥形端头～conical-ended container
挤压筒背垫　container band
挤压筒壁　container wall
挤压筒内套　container liner
挤压筒外套　container outer barrel
挤压筒座　container holder
挤压凸模　extrusion ram
挤压涂敷　extrusion coating
挤压温度　extrusion temperature
挤压无缝管　extruded seamless pipe
挤压无缝圆管　extruded seamless round tube
挤压系数　extrusion ratio
挤压线材　extruded wire
挤压效应　extrusion [squeeze] effect
挤压型材[型钢]　extruded profile [section, shape], extrudate ◇槽形～extruded channel, 礼帽形～extruded hat-section, 箱形～extruded box, 锥形[变截面]～tapered extruded shape
挤压性　compressibility ◇低～粉末*, 高～粉末*
挤压压力机　squeezing press
挤压压塑　compacting by extrusion
挤压应力　extrusion stress
挤压用润滑剂　extrusion lubricant, lubricant for extrusion
挤压余料　extrusion discard
挤压原理　principle of extrusion
挤压圆形钢材[型材]　extruded rounds
挤压直径　extruded diameter
挤压造型　extrusion moulding
挤压制品　extruded product
挤压铸造　extrusion casting
挤压状态　as-extruded condition
挤压作用　squeezing action
挤渣　shingling ◇鳄口形～机 alligator
挤渣压力机　shingler, shingling press
挤渣轧辊　shingling roll
挤子(晶格的)　crowdion
几何非线性　geometrical non-linearity
几何惯性矩　geometrical moment of inertia
几何横断面　geometrical cross section
几何焦散点[线,面]　geometric caustics
几何结构因子　geometrical structure factor
几何晶体[结晶]学　geometrical crystallography
几何晶型　geometric crystalline form
几何密排相　GCP (geometrically close-packed) phase
几何模型　geometrical model
几何排列　geometrical arrangement ◇原子～*
几何平均直径　geometric mean diameter
几何谱线宽度　geometric(al) arc breadth
几何散射因数　geomtrical scattering factor
几何投影　geometric projection

几何图形[形状] geometric shpae [form], geometry
几何图形软化 geometrical softening
几何相似模型 geometrically similar model
几何像差 geometrical aberration
几何学 geometry ◇ 加热～ heating geometry
几何学上的不精确性[不准确度] geometric(al) unsharpness
几何轴 geometrical axis
几率 (见"概率")
脊 ridge crest
脊面压痕[硬度脊面压痕] ridging indentation
己醇 {C$_6$H$_{13}$OH} hexyl alcohol, hexanol
己二酸二乙酯 dihexy adipate
己二酸盐【酯】adipate
己基磷酸酯 n-hexylphosphaonate
己酸 {CH$_3$(CH$_2$)$_4$CO$_2$H} caproic acid
己酮-[2] {CH$_3$COC$_4$H$_9$} hexanone-[2]
己烷 {CH$_3$(CH$_2$)$_4$CH$_3$} hexane
给出量 delivered weight
给电 power on
给矿操作 charging practice
给矿机[器] (同"给料机[器]")
给矿口 mouth, jaw opening (破碎机的)
给料[矿] feed(ing), feed material, delivering, delivery, input ◇ 分批～ batch feed
给料仓 feed hopper
给料槽 feed trough [bin, tank, chute], feeder channel, feeding hopper, 【选】charging spout
给料称量器 extractor-weigher
给料带 feed zone
给料点 feed point
给料斗 hopper ◇ 闸板式～ gate feed hopper
给料端 feed end [side]
给料段 feeding zone
给料法 method of feeding
给料刮板 feed shoe
给料管 feed(er) tube
给料辊道 feed (roller) table
给料和受料辊道 feeding and catching table
给料环 feed collar
给料化学成分 feed analysis
给料机[器] feeder ◇ 摆(动)式～", 板式～ plate feeder, 比例～ proportioning feeder, 仓式～ bin feeder, 称量[秤]式～", 带式～", 电磁振动[电振]～", 定量～", 斗式～", 风动～ pneumatic feeder, 鼓型[圆筒]～ drum feeder, 管式～ pipe feeder, 滑箱式～ sliding-box feeder, 计量～", 链式～ chain feeder, 螺旋～ screw [scroll] feeder, 盘式～", 配合～ proportioner, 皮带秤式～", 裙板～ apron feeder, 容积式～ volumetric feeder, 筛式～ screen feeder, 扇形～ fan gate, 勺式～ scoop feeder, 湿式～ wet feeder, 双螺旋～ double-screw feeder, 梭式～ reciprocal feeder, 往复板式～", 星式[旋叶, 回转星状]～", 旋桨式～ rotary-paddle feeder, 叶轮式～ vanefeeder, 圆盘～", 圆筒筛～", 振动[脉动]～", 重力～", 柱塞推进式～ plunger feeder, 转筒[滚筒式, 转鼓式]～", 自动～ autofeeder, 自动称[计]量～", 自动润滑～ self-oil feeder, 自动振动～"
给料机构 feed gear(ing)
给料机械 feed mechanism
给料机嘴 feeder nose
给料集储器 supply header
给料井[孔] feed well
给料控制杆 feed control lever
给料粒度级 feed fraction
给料量 feed rate, delivered weight
给料量调节器 feed rate regulator
给料盘 feed tray [table]
给料皮带(机) feed belt [conveyer]
给料平衡仓 feed surge bin
给料区 feed zone
给料上限粒度 feed top size
给料设备 feeding equipment [facilities,

给料室	feed chamber [compartment]
给料速度	feed [delivery] rate
给料酸度	feed acidity
给料台	feed floor
给料体积数	feed volume
给料系统	feed system [circuit]
给料限制器	feed stop
给料箱	feed-box ◇ 振动～vibrating feed-box
给料斜槽	feeder spout
给料卸料车	feeder tripper
给料压力控制	feed pressure control
给料圆盘	feeder table
给料运输机	infeed conveyor
给料中断	breakdown of feed
给料装置	feeder, feed arrangement, discharge device ◇ 缝式～lip feeder, 流动～flow feeder, 重力压差式～gravity-head feeder
给煤	coal input
给煤量	coal rate [input]
给泥器	mud feeding device
给排水设备	plumbing equipment
给水	water supply, feedwater ◇ 补～处理设备*, 毛细管～capillary water
给水[油,料]泵	feed pump (f.p.)
给水槽	water-supply tank
给水干管	down main, service pipe
给水工程	water service
给水管(锅炉的)	feed pipe
给水控制	feed water control
给水系统	water supply system
给水旋塞	feed cock
给水站	【建】pumping plant
给药机	reagent feeder ◇ 滴管式～*
给油	oil supply [feed] ◇ 毛细管～capillary feed
给油指示器	sight feed gauge
给予体	donor, donator
技工	skilled worker, mechanic
技能	technical ability, skill, knack
技巧	skill, technique, craft (smanship), technic, workmanship
技师	artificer, technician, mechanic
技术	technology, technique, skill, art ◇ CCD～*
技术保安	safety work
技术标准	technical [engineering] standard
技术操作规程	regulations for technical operations
技术测量	technical [commercial] measurement
技术厂长	technical superintendent
技术处	engineering office
技术等级	technical grade
技术定额标定[制定]	technical rate setting
技术发展管理局	Directorate of Technical Development (D.T.D.)
技术分类	technical classification
技术改造	technical reconstruction [transformation]
技术革命	technological revolution
技术革新	(technical, technological) innovation, technical improvement
技术管理	technical administration
技术规程	technical regulations [routine, order]
技术规范	technical code [specification, regime]
技术规格	technical specifications [standard], specifications of quality
技术基础[依据]	technical base
技术监督	technical supervision
技术检验报告	technical inspection report
技术鉴定	technical appraisal [appraisement, expertise] ◇ 产品～*
技术建议书	technical proposal
技术经济评价[论证]	techno-economic appraisal
技术经济指标	technical-and-economic indexes [indicators]

技术诀窍	(technical) know-how
技术开发	technological development, development of technology
技术科	engineering department
技术科学	engineering science
技术可行性	technical feasibility
技术考察组	technical studying group
技术秘密	know-how
技术名词	technical terms, technics
技术(人)员	technician, technical staff [personnel] ◇ 安装～installing mechanic, 仪表～instrument technician
技术设计	technical design
技术手册	technical manual (T.M.)
技术数据[特性,性能]	technical data
技术水平	engineering level
技术说明	technical note
技术说明书	technical instruction [specification]
技术套管	protector string, intermediate casing
技术条件	technical conditions [provisions], engineering factor, specification (spec.)
技术维护规程	maintenance instruction [regulation]
技术文件	technological document
技术文献	technical literature
技术细节	ins and outs, technicality
技术性	technicality
技术性能[特性]	technical data
技术研究	technical study
技术要求	technical requirements
技术优越性	technical advantage
技术札记	technical notes (T.N.)
技术指令	technical order
技术主任	technical superintendent
技术助理	technical assistant
技术转让	technologh [technical] transfer
技术资料	technical information [literature, data]
季铵	quaternary ammonium
季铵化合物	{R₄·H·x} quaternary ammonium compound chemene
季铵聚苯乙烯树脂	quaternary ammonium polystyrene resin
季铵强碱型树脂	quaternary ammonium strong base type resin
季铵(型)树脂	quaternary ammonium (-type) resin
季铵	quaternary amine
季胺阴离子交换剂	quaternary amine anion exchanger
季胺阴离子交换树脂	quaternary amine anion exchange resin
季节性开裂	season cracking
季戊四醇四硝酸酯	pentaerythrite tetranitrate (P.E.T.N.)
剂量	dose, dosage, dosis
剂量测[计]量(法)	dosimetry, dose metering
剂量计	dose-meter, dosimeter, radiacmeter ◇ 钢笔型～pen-type dosimeter, 胶片～dosifilm, 袖珍～pocket dosimeter
剂量率	dosage [dose] rate
剂量率计	dose-rate meter
剂量探测器	dosimetry probe
剂量学	dosimetry, dosiology
寄存单元	【计】load cell (LC)
寄存器	register, tell-tale, temporary storage ◇ 编址[可按地址访问的]～addressable register, 变址～*, 并-串行～*, 磁移位～magnetic shift register, 基地址～base register, 界限～limit register, 静态～static register, 控制～control register, 扩充～extension register, 内部操作[状态字]～*, 通用～general register, 校验～check register, 移位～shift register, 中间～distributor
寄存器长度	register length
寄存器传送语言	register transfer language (RTL)
寄存器指示位[字]	register pointer
寄生磁化(强度)	【理】parasitic magneti-

zation
寄生电容 parasitic capacitance
寄生电阻 parasitic resistance
寄生脉冲 ghost [spurious] pulses
寄生铁磁性 parasitic ferromagnetism
寄生误差 parasitic error
寄售 consignment
计策 stratagem, plan
计测 gauging
计测控制 measuring control
计尘器 dust counter
计尘仪 coniscope
计光的 photometric
计划 plan(ning), schedule, project, program, scheme, design
计划产量 scheduled production, designed output
计划检修 preventive maintenance (PM, P.M.), proposed [schedule] repair
计划(任务)书 prospectus
计划维修 planned maintenance
计划休[停]风 【铁】scheduled delay
计划休风时间 scheduled downtime
计划预修进度表 preventive maintenance schedule
计件工资 【企】piece rate [wages]
计件工资制 【企】piece(-rate) system, piece wage rate
计件工作 【企】piece work (job)
计件契约 【企】agreement by piece
计件生产 piece production, piecework
计件制 【企】piece(work) system
计量 metering, measuring, dosing, batching
计量泵 metering [proportioning] pump ◇ 可调～adjustable dosing pump, 燃料～fuel metering pump
计量表 indicator
计量槽 gauge [scale] tank
计量长度 gauge length
计量称量装置 dosing weighing device
计量单位 measuring unit
计量断面(异型钢材的) ruling section
计量工具 metering outfit
计量杆 gauge [gauging] rod
计量给料炉 dosing furnace
计量给料器 dosing tank, batching plant, feed control device, charger-reader device
计量给料装置[机构] 【冶】dosing mechanism
计量精度 accuracy of measuring
计量孔 metering hole
计量矿仓 measuring bin
计量料仓 measuring pocket
计量(料)斗[漏斗,斗仓] measuring [weigh(ing)] hopper
计量螺旋给矿机 metering screw feeder
计量皿 counting cup
计量器 batching plant, batcher (给料用), dose-meter, dosimeter, dosing tank, proportioning device
计量设备 metering equipment
计量试验室 measuring laboratory
计量套 【焦】measuring sleeve
计量箱 dose-meter, dosimeter, dosing [measuring] tank, batch meter
计量学 metrology
计量仪表[装置] metering device ◇ 接触式～contact-type gauge
计量运送带 belt scales
计器 ga(u)ge
计权误差 weighted error
计时 timing
计时测量 timely measures
计时电路 timing circuit
计时电势[位](测定)法 chronopotentiometry ◇ 循环～*
计时范围 timing range
计时工资 【企】time wage
计时工资制 time rate
计时奖励(工资)制 time-premium system
计时开关 time switch
计时起点 time zero
计时器 timer, time-meter, timing unit,

keyer
计时仪 chronograph, calculagraph
计时员 timekeeper, timist
计示压力 gauge pressure
计数 count(ing), tally（镀锡薄钢板包装时的）
计数表 indicator, count table
计数电路 scaling circuit
计数法 counting method
计数管 counter (tube), counting tube ◇切伦科夫～Cerenkov counter, 十进～dekatron, 自猝灭～self-quenched counter
计数管室 counter chamber
计数继电器 counting [metering] relay
计数器 counter (ctr), counting indicator [device], scaler, tally register ◇程序控制～sequence control counter, 二进制～*, 二元～binary scaler, 盖革～[管]*, 库尔特～法Coulter counter method, 十进位～decimal scaler, 数字～digit counter, 双向[可逆]～forward backward counter, 正向～forward counter, 指令～【计】sequence register
计数器齿轮 counter gear
计数器光谱计 counter spectrometer
计数器衍射计法 counter diffractometer method
计数器指针 counter arm
计数损失误差 counting-loss error
计数型触发器 toggle flip flop
计算 calculating, calcutation, computing, count(ing), operation, reckoning
计算常数 design constant
计算长度 effective length
计算尺 computing [calculating] scale, slide rule
计算错误 miscount
计算地址 【计】calculated address
计算法 calculus, calculation [computational] method, numeration
计算复杂性 computational complexity
计算负荷[负载] calculated [assumed] load
计算格式 pattern of calculation
计算功能 computational function
计算公式 design formula (des. form.)
计算机 computer, computing machine, computator, brain ◇并行～*, 程序控制时序～*, 串行数字～serial digital computer, 从(属)～slave computer, 电子～electronic computer, 非时序～nonsequential computer, 分布式～distributed computer, 分时～time sharing computer, 浮点～floating point computer, 固定程序～fixed program computer, 固态～solid state computer, 过程控制～*, 混合～*, 监控～*, 联动～*, 逻辑控制时序～*, 面向～的 computer-oriented, 目标[执行]～object-computer, 全值～absolute-value computer, 热模拟～*, 容错～fault tolerant computer, 实时复合～*, 伺服模拟～servo-analog computer, 台式～desk [table] computer, 通用～general purpose computer, 微型～*, 小型～minicomputer, 虚拟～virtual computer, 源～*, 增量～incremental computer, 阵列～array computer, 直接数字～direct digital computer, 主-从～系统*, 专用～*, 自动时序～*
计算机程序 computer program
计算机程序接口系统 computer process interface system
计算机程序设计[编制] computer programming
计算机代[发展阶段] computer generations
计算机代码 computer code
计算机仿真[模拟] computer simulation
计算机仿真模型 computer aided simulation model
计算机辅助层析X射线摄影[照相]法 computer-assisted tomography (CAT)
计算机辅助层析照相扫描装置 CAT (computer assisted tomography) scanners

计算机辅助教学 computer-aided instruction (CAI), programmed learning
计算机辅助孔型设计 computer aided roll-pass design (CARD)
计算机辅助炼钢 computer-assisted steelmaking
计算机辅助设计 computer-aided design (CAD)
计算机辅助实验 computer-aided experiment
计算机辅助系统 computer subsystem
计算机辅助学习 computer-assisted learning (CAL)
计算机辅助制造[加工] computer-aided manufacturing (CAM)
计算机辅助质量管理系统 computer-aided quality control system
计算机辅助质量控制[管理] computer-aided quality control (CAQC)
计算机跟踪系统 computer tracking system
计算机功能结构 computer architecture
计算机化 computerization
计算机化编目系统 computerized cataloging system
计算机化采集系统 computerized acquisition system
计算机化期刊编目系统 computerized serial system
计算机集成制造系统 computer integrated manufacture system (CIMS)
计算机集散[分布式]控制系统 distributed computer control system (DCS)
计算机监控 supervisory computer control (SCC)
计算机监控系统 computer supervisory control system
计算机监视控制 supervisory computer control (SCC)
计算机接口部件 computer interface unit (CIU)
计算机结构 computer architecture

计算机科学 computer science
计算机控制 computer control
计算机控制方式 computer control mode
计算机控制焊接 computer-controlled welding
计算机控制化铁炉 computerized cupola
计算机控制机床 computer controlled machine
计算机控制系统 computer control system
计算机控制轧机 computer controlled mill, computerized mill
计算机模拟 computer simulation
计算机配置 computer configuration
计算机器[机械] calculating machine
计算机软件程序报告(书) program report for computer software
计算机软件系统 computer software system
计算机视觉 computer vision
计算机数字控制 computer numerical control (CNC)
计算机室 computer room (C.R.)
计算机台 computer desk
计算机体系结构 computer architecture
计算机通信 intercomputer communication
计算机网(络) computer network
计算机系统 computer [computing] system ◇ 颗粒测量~*, 中央处理~*
计算机系统仿真[模拟] computer system simulation
计算机系统硬件 computer system hardware
计算机效率 computer efficiency
计算机学习 computer learning
计算机应用 computer application
计算机硬件系统 computer hardware system
计算机语言 computer language
计算机预测[报] computer prediction
计算机安装(站) computer installation
计算机指令 computer instruction
计算机子系统 computer subsystem

计算技术　computing technique [technology], computation
计算记录器　computing logger
计算结果检验　hi-lo-check
计算跨径　effective span
计算流体力学　computational fluid dynamics (CFD)
计算流体(动)力学语言　computational fluid dynamics language
计算密度　bulk density
计算难度　computational complexity
计算能力　computing power
计算器　calculator, counter
计算强度　calculated strength
计算曲线　calculated curve
计算速率　counting rate
计算速率测定器　count(ing)-rate meter
计算图　nomogram, nomograph, pattern of calculation
计算图表学　nomography
计算图形　pattern of calculation
计算误差　calcutation error
计算员　calculator, teller
计算站　【计】installation
计算值　calculated [computed, estimated] value
计算中心　computation [computing] center
计算重量　calculated weight
计算装置　calculator, calculating [accounting] device
记波器　kymograph
记发机　sender
记号　(identification) mark, symbol(ism), sign
记录　record, log(ging), registration, writing
记录(一览)表　data sheet
记录笔带动机构　pen-driving mechanism
记录笔驱动电机　pen motor
记录表　log [fact] sheet
记录长度　【计】record length

记录打字机　logging type-writer
记录分隔符　【计】record separator (RS)
记录高温计　recording pyrometer
记录管理　record management
记录光谱计　recording spectrometer
记录机构　recording mechanism, charting machine (检测仪器的)
记录间隔　【计】interrecord gap
记录键　【计】recorded key
记录介质　recording medium
记录密度　【计】recording density
记录器　recorder, recording device, logger, register ◇ 可调～controllable register, 双笔～double-pen recorder
记录强度　recorded intensity
记录失真　misregistration
记录式流量计　recording flowmeter
记录式瓦特计　recording wattmeter
记录式微量光度计　recording microphotometer
记录式压力计　pressure recording gauge, recording manometer
记录式应变仪　recording strain gauge
记录首标　【计】record header
记录天平(自动式)　recording balance
记录头　【计】record(ing) head
记录系统　recording [register, paging] system
记录显像密度计　recording densitometer
记录仪　recording [memorizing] meter
记录员　recorder, table man
记录纸　record [log] sheet, record paper [chart], chart
记录纸传动机构　chart-drive mechanism
记录终止符　end of record [EOR]
记录装置　recording gear [device, mechanism]
记入　【计】post, log
记时机构　timing mechanism
记时器　chronograph, timer, calculagraph (钟内的计时卡片)
记时式转速计　chronometric tachometer

记事表　fact sheet
记数法　notation, number scale ◇ 二进制 ~ *
记数器　register
记数式应变仪　counting strain gauge
记数系统　notation system,【计】number representation system, numeration system
记忆　memory ◇ 形状 ~ 合金 shape memory alloy (SMA)
记忆设备　storage device
记忆线圈　memory coil
记忆元件　memory element, storage element [cell]
记忆装置　【计】memory unit, storage device, accumulator
记忆组件　【计】memory module
记载　record
继承　inheritance, heredity
继电保护　relay protection
继电器　relay ◇ 保护 ~ protective relay, 扁型 ~ flat type relay, 布赫霍尔茨 ~ Buchholz relay, 差动电流 ~ *, 定向 ~ *, 短路方向 ~ *, 高速 ~ fast speed relay, 合闸 ~ closing relay, 极化 ~ *, 计数 ~ counting relay, 接地 ~ grounding relay, 距离 ~ distance relay, 闪光［继续］~ flashing relay, 闪烁 ~ flicker relay, 舌簧 ~ reed relay, 失磁 ~ excitation-loss relay, 双线圈 ~ double-coiled relay, 限流 ~ current limiting relay, 选择式接地 ~ selective ground relay, 远程 ~ distant relay, 转发［中继］~ repeater relay
继电器测试器　relay tester
继电器箱　relay box [cabinet]
纪尼埃 - 普雷斯顿区（铝铜合金的）【金】G-P (Guinier-Preston) zone [aggregate, cluster]
纪尼埃 - 普雷斯顿区强化　zone hardening
纪尼埃 - 普雷斯顿条纹　Guinier-Preston streak
纪尼埃型单色仪　Guinier-type monochromator
纪尼埃型反射器　Guinier-type reflector
纪尼埃型非对称聚焦　Guinier-type asymmetrical focusing
纪尼埃型聚焦照相机　Guinier-type focusing camera
纪尼埃照相机　Guinier camera
纪尧姆铁镍低膨胀系数合金　Guillaume alloy
纪尧姆铜铋合金（35—36Bi）　Guillaume's metal
夹　cramp, clip ◇ U 形 ~ clevis
夹板　clamp, clamping [contact] plate, cleat, cleet, dog, hold-down
夹板（落）锤　jump [trip] hammer, board (drop) hammer, drop board hammer
夹板搭接　strap(ped) joint
夹壁墙　bay wall
夹布胶木　textolite
夹布胶木轴承　textolite [fabric, laminated] bearing
夹层　sandwiching, interlayer, lamellation, entresol, interlacing,【压】backedge,【粉】compacting crack
夹层板　sandwich (plate)
夹层材料　sandwiched material
夹层钢板　steel sandwich
夹层胶片　sandwich film
夹层结构　sandwich structure [construction]
夹层钎焊　sandwich braze
夹层双金属离合器盘　sandwich-type bimetallic clutch disc
夹层温度　【冶】demixing point
夹持长度　clamping [grip] length
夹持淬火　fixture [die-press] quenching
夹持端（焊条的）　bare terminal end
夹持工具（锻件的）　【压】porter bar
夹持机构　【焊】clamp assembly
夹持力　clamping force
夹持器　clamper, grip [clamp] holder, collet ◇ 风动 ~ air-operated fixture, 风箱式

夹持时间	clamp holding time
夹持试验	【压】cramp test
夹持装置	clamping fixture, holding device
夹带	entrapment
夹带的空气	(en)trapped air
夹带泥渣	slime entrainment
夹带渣	slag carry-over
夹锭钳	【压】ingot tongs, pincher
夹附	occlusion
夹附物	occlusions
夹附杂质	occluded foreign matter
夹杆	clamp [clip] bar
夹钢锭的操作杆	porter bar
夹辊对	pinch roll pair
夹辊区	【连铸】roller (guide) apron
夹辊式翻钢推床	grip type tilting manipulator, gripper-tilter manipulator
夹辊式翻钢装置	grip-type tilter
夹痕(板材的)	catcher marks
夹灰(缺陷)	【冶】dirt
夹接板	joint bar
夹金属胶合板	plymetal
夹紧	fastening, gripping, jawing, clamp(ing), pinch(off), jig
夹紧表面	gripping surface
夹紧缝(卷筒上的)	clamping slot
夹紧箍	bail
夹紧机构	clamping [gripping] mechanism, clamp system
夹紧螺钉	clamp(ing) screw
夹紧螺母	clamp [grip, binding, retainer] nut
夹紧螺栓	clamping bolt
夹紧模	clamping [grip(per)] die
夹紧气缸	clamping cylinder
夹紧速度	clamping speed
夹紧套	collet
夹紧头(回转锻造机的)	chucking head
夹紧效应	pinch effect
夹紧楔	gripping wedges
夹紧压力	【焊】clamping pressure
夹紧爪	【焊】clamping die
夹紧装置[夹具]	chucking (device), clamp, clamping device, grip (device, jaws), gripping unit, (holding) fixture, work-holding attachment (锻模的), jig ◇ 安装用~ setting-up fixture, 垫板~*, 多工位~ multiple jig, 风动~ air-clamping fixture, 切割黏土用~ chuck-hold, 周边焊接用~*, 装配[组装]~*
夹具钢	◇ 弗莱史库特~ (1C, 4Cr) Flashkut
夹卡爪痕	grip marks
夹壳联轴器	clamp coupling
夹料钳	dogs, pull(ing)-in dogs (拉拔用)
夹模器	【压】die head block, die slide, plate die ◇ 旋转式~ rotary die head
夹模器回转头	die turret head
夹盘	(clamping) chuck
夹片	clamping piece, jaw
夹钎器	chuck
夹钳	tongs, grab, pliers, holdfast, clamp, clamping fixture, grip(per), cramp ◇ 弧形螺旋~ C-clamp, 圆嘴~*, 轧辊运输~ roll tongs
夹钳工	tongsman
夹钳夹持行程	tong holding stroke
夹钳开口度	tongs opening
夹钳起重机(吊车)	(同"钳式起重机")
夹钳升降行程	tong lifting stroke
夹钳式点焊机	(同"钳式点焊机")
夹钳小车	plyer
夹圈	clamping ring [collar], chuck [binding] ring
夹入颗粒	interlocking particle
夹入元素	【钢】tramp element
夹砂	sand inclusion, sandmark, sandbuckle, inclusion of moulding sand
夹砂水	sediment laden
夹生料	【团】unburned material
夹生烧结	(同"不完全烧结")
夹生烧结矿	(同"欠烧烧结矿")
夹石(矿体的)	horse

夹送导辊　eflector pinch roll
夹送辊　pinch [withdrawal] roll ◇ 从动~ driven pinch roller,地下卷取机~ down-coiler pinch roll,下空转~ *
夹条　gib
夹头　tong hold, clamping head, cartridge, chuck, collet, keeper,【压】grip head（拉拔机的）,bar hold（锻造钢材的）◇ 带臂~ lever chuck
夹头锻制机　bar pointer
夹心钢　sandwich steel
夹心钢锭　three-ply ingot
夹心焊接　sandwich braze
夹心结构　(同"夹层结构")
夹心轧制　sandwich rolling
夹心状坯块　sandwich like compact
夹压应力　grip stresses
夹杂计量　inclusion count
夹杂区　extrinsic zone,【金】impurity zone
夹杂熔渣　slag inclusion
夹杂(物)　inclusion, occlusion, occluded foreign substance, impurity, encrusting matter ◇ 迪尔加膝~评级 *,钢铸件~ snotter,固有[原生]~ *,杰康托莱特~级别 *,里斯特~检测法 Rist technique,内在[原有]~ *,尼斯纳渣印~检查法 *,琼－里斯特~检测法 *,司米洛可基~检测仪 Smialowski apparatus,条[线]状~ inclusion line,脱氧型~ *,沿形变方向伸长的~ directional banding of inclusions,氧化物型~ oxide type inclusions
夹杂物多的铸件　dirty casting
夹杂物过滤　inclusion
夹杂物含量　inclusion content
夹杂物模型　inclusion model
夹杂相　【金】impurity phases
夹杂性裂纹（锻件的）　inner crack
夹杂氧化物　included [occluded] oxide
夹杂元素　incidental element
夹渣　slag inclusion [enclosure, entrapment, occlusion, patch, spot], cinder [dross] inclusion, included [enclosed, entrapped] slag ◇ 霍弗斯~计数（法）*,拉长状~物 *,林曼~标准[指数]【钢】Rinman scale
夹渣脆性　slag shortness
夹渣孔　【冶】dirt hole
夹渣铁　slag iron
夹渣线　slag stringer
夹渣针孔（缺陷）　【铸】slag pin hole
夹置(的)　interleaving
夹住　clamp(ing), clip, grip, jam, nip-up, nip(ping), grasping ◇ 坯件~器 blank holder
夹爪　grip [clamping] jaw ◇ 自动夹紧的~ self-gripping jaws
夹爪痕　grip marks
夹砖　【钢】brick inclusion
夹子　clamp, clip, folder, gripper, holding device, keeper
痂状断口　scabbed fracture
家具用钉　coat nail
家庭废物　【环】household refuse
家庭污水　【环】household sewage
家庭用品废钢铁　household scrap
家庭用水　home water
镓{Ga}　gallium ◇ 掺~锗 *,富~熔体 Ga rich melt,含~合金 *
镓的(三价镓)　gallic
镓基合金　gallium-base alloy
镓钾矾{K$_2$SO$_4$·Ga$_2$(SO$_4$)$_3$·24H$_2$O 或 KGa(SO$_4$)$_2$·12H$_2$O}　gallium potassium alum
镓铝砷　gallium aluminum arsenide
镓砷磷　gallium arsenic phosphide
镓酸　gallic acid
镓酸锂　lithium gallium oxide
镓酸钠{Na$_2$GaO$_2$}　sodium gallate
镓酸盐　gallate
镓铟锡合金　gallium-indium-tin alloy
镓族　gallium family
镓族元素　gallium family element
加氢(作用)　ammonification

加氨渗碳　ammonia carburizing
加白　whitening
加摆晶体照相机　oscillating crystal camera
加班费　overtime allowance [pay]
加班工资　【企】wage penalty payment
加班工作　【企】overwork
加班后补休　【企】compensation days for overtime
加班时间　【企】overtime, overhours
加倍(的)　double (dbl, dble), doubling, duplicate, duplication, duplex
加衬　lining
加成反应　addition reaction
加成化合物　additive compound ◇ 卤化物～*
加成剂　addition agent, dope
加成聚合　addition polymerization
加搭板对接点焊[滚焊]　bridge welding
加达姆方程(计算散射能力)　Gardam equation
加大芯头　【铸】augmented core print
加垫板对接　backed butt joint
加垫板焊　welding with backing
加垫板连接　reinforced joint
加垫防溅法　【钢】Bosment process
加电感条件　conditions of loading
加尔石英枪　【色】Garr gun
加法电路　add(ing) [adder, added] circuit, adder
加法机　adding machine
加法器　adder, adding machine, summator, summer ◇ 三输入端～ three input adder, 十进制～ decade adder
加法群　【数】module, additive group
加法运算　【计】add operation
加粉器　powder feeder
加风　【铁】restoring the wind
加复筋　【建】double armouring
加负荷　load up
加盖　【钢】capping, plugging
加盖端　capped end

加盖沸腾钢　cooler-plated steel
加盖钢　plugged [capped] steel
加盖起重机　【钢】capping crane
加感条件　conditions of loading
加感线圈　loading coil
加铬渗碳　chrome carburizing
加工　process(ing), machining, work(ing), handling, treating, treatment, fabrication,【焊】prepare (坡口的) ◇ 二次[再]～ re-working, 可～性 deformability, 手工～ handwork, 未～的 green, coarse, 在～材料 in-process material
加工边脚料　machine waste
加工标准　working standard, processing criterion
加工草图　schedule drawing
加工厂　processing plant [factory]
加工厂废钢　prompt industrial scrap
加工成本　processing [fabrication] cost
加工尺寸　finish size
加工脆性试验　work-brittleness test
加工单　working order
加工导槽(旋锻机的)　working channel
加工范围　working range
加工方法　processing [fabricating] method
加工废钢　shredded scrap
加工费　【企】processing [fabrication] cost, cost of operating
加工符号[代号]　finish mark, finish symbol (焊缝的)
加工工业　processing industries
加工规范　process specification (Pr. Spec.)
加工过程模拟　process modeling
加工过程效率　efficiency of working process
加工过度　overwork
加工后组织　【压】wrought structure
加工技术　process technology
加工金属组织　structure of worked metal
加工精度　working [machining] accurancy, machining precision

加工孔型　roll dressing
加工牢固的　handling tight
加工率　working rate
加工潜力　operating margin
加工熔炼厂　custom smelter
加工软化　work softening
加工设计　fabrication design
加工时效硬化　strain age hardening
加工损失　treatment losses
加工条件　working condition
加工铜　worked copper
加工温度　processing temperature
加工系列　treatment line
加工性　malleability, deformability
加工性能　fabricating characteristic
加工硬度　work-hardness
加工硬化　work harden(ing), strain-hardening ◇ 基本～basic work hardening, 潜在～latent work hardening
加工硬化参数　work-hardening parameter
加工硬化程度　work-hardening capacity
加工硬化范围[区]　work-hardening range
加工硬化粉末　work-hardened powder
加工硬化耗竭假说　exhaustion hypothesis of workhardening
加工硬化合金　work-hardening alloy
加工硬化率　rate of work hardening
加工硬化青铜　work-hardened bronze
加工硬化曲线　work-hardening curve
加工硬化曲线取向关系　orientation dependence of work-hardening curve
加工硬化曲线第Ⅲ阶段 β 蠕变　β-creep of stage Ⅲ of work-hardening curve
加工硬化特性　work-hardening characteristics [behaviour]
加工硬化速率　work hardening rate
加工硬化系数　coefficient of work-hardening ◇ 潜在～*
加工硬化效应　work-hardening effect
加工硬化性能　strain-hardened property
加工硬化指数　work-hardening exponent
加工硬化状态　work-hardened condition

加工余[裕]量　(machining, finish) allowance
加工再结晶　work recrystallization
加工制度　【企】working regime
加工制品　fabricated product
加工制造厂　fabrication plant
加工周期　processing cycle ◇ 作业线上～in-line treatment cycle
加工铸件用大锤　flogging hammer
加工装置　processor
加工作业线　treatment line
加汞作用　mercuration
加固　reinforce, strengthening, consolidate, stiffening, up-grading ◇ 用水泥～consolidation grouting
加固[劲]板　(同"加强板")
加固层　extra layer (多层焊接的), backup coat (熔模的)
加固钢板　stiffener plate
加固筋　dabber
加固连接　strength joint
加固橡胶保护层(管道的)　national coating
加硅处理的灰口铸铁　silicium-treated gray cast iron
加硅脱氧熔炼　silicium killed heat
加荷　loading, stressing
加荷重时间　duration of load application
加和定律　additivity law
加和定则　additivity principle
加和性　additivity
加和性函数　additive function
加合金元素　alloyage
加合物　adducts
加合作用　adduction
加厚　thickening, intensification (底片的) ◇ 不～(管壁) non upsetting
加厚边　beaded edge
加厚部分　bulb
加厚端　thickends
加厚锌层镀锌钢丝　double galvanized wire

加 jia

加护套　sheathing
加护罩压力机　hooded press
加环箍[筋]　hooping
加碱　alkalify, alkalization
加减　plus-minus
加减(法)器　adder-subtractor
加焦量　rate of coke (RC), coke addition [ratio]
加焦球团　ore-coke pellet
加筋铁壳砖　ferroclad brick
加筋铸件　reinforced casting
加筋砖砌筑　reinforced brick masonry (RBM)
加劲板　stiffening plate
加劲杆　stiffener
加剧　intensification
加快处理　speeding treatment
加宽　broadening, widening, spread
加宽台车　extended pallet
加宽焊道　spreading bead
加宽式交叉　flared crossing
加宽线　broadened line
加勒特活套式线材轧机　Garrett looping rod mill
加勒特式布置　Garret type layout
加勒特式卷取机　【压】Garret coiler
加勒特式线材卷取机　pouring [Garrett] reel
加勒特式线材轧机　Garrett mill
加勒特式小型型钢卷取机　Garrett reel
加肋层流板　lamella with reinforcing rib
加肋钢管　finned steel tube
加肋拱(顶)　ribbed arch [roof]
加肋管　ribbed pipe [tube], gilled pipe
加肋硅砖拱式炉顶(反射炉的)　silica ribbed arch
加肋砌层　rib course
加肋铸件　ribbed casting
加里莫尔镍铜锌耐蚀合金　(45Ni, 28Cu, 25Zn, 余量 Fe + Si + Mn 等) Gallimore metal
加力　stressing, loading

加料　feed, charge, batch ◇ 大气压力~*, 反平行~ antiparallel feed, 机械~ power feed, 重力~ gravity loading, 自动~ automatic stoking
加料泵　charge pump
加料部分　feed(ing) section
加料仓　bin feeder, additive bin
加料槽　feed [charging] chute, feed trough, additive bin ◇ 钢包~*
加料槽口　hopper opening
加料侧[厂房]　【冶】charging side
加料秤　charging scale
加料次数　charging frequency
加料斗　(feeder, charge) hopper, feed(er) funnel, addition bunker, additive bin
加料阀　feed valve
加料管　feed [charge, charging, entry] pipe
加料过多　overfeeding
加料机　charger, charging machine, (同"给料机") ◇ 落地式~ mobile ground charger
加料机操作工　【钢】charging machine operator
加料机平台　feeder floor
加料计　poidometer
加料孔　charge hole, charging aperture, feed [receiving] opening
加料控制室　charge control room
加料口　charge door, feed port, jaw opening
加料流槽　feed launder
加料漏斗　charging hopper ◇ 配合~ proportioner
加料率　rate of charge
加料盘　feed tray
加料皮带　feed belt
加料频率　charging frequency
加料平台　charging platform
加料器　(同"给料器"), loader
加料枪　feed(ing) gun
加料设备　charging installation

加料顺序　charging sequence
加料速度　charging rate
加料台　charging deck, table feeder, feed floor, ramp,【钢】charging stage
加料提升导架塔　charge hoist guide tower
加料桶　【钢】charging basket
加料温度　charge temperature (CH. Temp.)
加料系统　feeding [charging] system
加料箱　addition bunker
加料钟　【铁】charging bell
加料钟机构　charging bell gear
加料贮槽　feed storage tank
加料装置　feed device [mechanism], feeder head, charging gear ◇ 风动～, 炉子～furnace charging gear
加硫除铜精炼锅　sulphur treatment kettle
加硫处理　sulphur treatment
加硫低磷钢　resulphurized lowphosphorus steel
加硫钢　resulfurized [resulphurized] steel
加硫酸钠分解　decomposition with sodium sulphate
加硫碳钢　resulfurized carbon steel
加硫增磷低碳钢　resulphurized rephosphorized lowcarbon steel
加鲁塞尔天然气感应电炉直接炼铁法　Galluser process
加铝　aluminium feeding
加煤　stoking
加煤机　stoker ◇ 带～的炉子 stoker fired furnace, 链板式～chain grate stoker
加煤口　【焦】charging hole
加煤量　coal rate
加镁处理的球墨铸铁　magnesium-treated cast iron
加锰　【钢】manganese addition
加拿大标准协会　Canadian Standards Association (CSA)
加拿大标准协会标准　CSA standard
加拿大采矿学会　Canadian Mining Institute (CMI)

加拿大钢铁公司　Steel Company of Canada (Stelco)
加拿大化学学会　Canadian Institute of Chemistry (C.I.C.)
加拿大矿冶学会　Canadian Institute of Mining and Metallurgy (CIMM)
加拿大矿业资源部　Canadian Department of Mines & Resources (CDMR)
加拿大铝业公司　Aluminium Company of Canada (ALCAN)
加拿大香胶[脂]　Canada [Canadian] balsam
加拿大专利　Canadian Patent (Can.P.)
加钠除砷处理　【色】sodium treatment
加铌稳定钢　(同"铌稳定钢")
加黏合剂冷挤压　cold binder extruding
加镍冷硬铸铁轧辊　(同"冷硬镍铸铁轧辊")
加镍麻口铸铁轧辊　【压】nickel (alloy) grain roll
加镍镁冷硬铸铁轧辊　【压】nickel-magnesium chilled iron roll
加镍钼冷硬铸铁轧辊　【压】nickel-molybdenum chilled iron roll
加镍铸铁轧辊　【压】nickel iron roll
加硼易淬硬钢　needle steel
加偏压　biasing
加偏压使截止　【电】bias off
加气灰渣混凝土　gas-ash concrete
加气混凝土　aerocrete, aerated [cellular, gas] concrete, blown out concrete
加气剂　air-entraining agent, air-retaining substance
加气水泥　air-entrained cement
加铅钢(0.15—0.35Pb)　leaded steel, lead treated steel
加铅合金　leaded alloy
加铅红色黄铜　leaded red brass
加铅黄铜　lead(ed) brass (2Pb, 38Zn, 60Cu), binding brass (63 − 64Cu, 35Zn, 1 − 2 Pb)
加铅类红色黄铜　leaded semi-red brass

加铅镍黄铜	leaded nickel brass
加铅镍锡青铜(即耐酸青铜)	leaded nickel tin bronze
加铅镍银	leaded nickel silver
加铅炮铜	leaded gun metal
加铅青铜	(60—70Cu,<2Ni,<15Sn,余量 Pb；用作轴承) lead(ed)-bronze
加铅燃料	leaded fuel
加铅双相黄铜	leaded duplex brass
加铅锡青铜	leaded tin bronze
加强	strengthening, enhance, augmentation, reinforce, energize, upgrade
加强板	stiffening [reinforcing] plate
加强边	beaded edge
加强材料	reinforced material
加强构[杆]件	【建】reinforcing member
加强焊缝	reinforced seam, convex [strapped] weld
加强环	strengthening ring
加强件	reinforcement
加强金属	reinforcement metal
加强筋	stiffener, stiffening band, dabber, strengthening rib, bracing, 【建】tie, 【铸】arbor ◇ 铸件～bracket
加强热塑复合材料	reinforced thermoplastic
加强条钢	stiffening band
加氢	hydrogenation, hydrogenize ◇ 催化～法*
加氢裂化	【化】hydrogen crack(ing)
加氢容器	hydrogenation vessel
加氢设备[装置]	hydrogenation plant
加氢提炼(粗苯)	hydrorefining
加权	weighting, weighing
加权函数	weighting function
加权码	【计】weighted code
加权平均	weighted average (wtd av.)
加权平均分析	weighted average analysis
加权平均压力	average weighted pressure (awp)
加权平均值	weighted mean (value)
加权误差	weighted error
加权系数	coefficient of weight, weighting coefficient
加燃料	fueling
加燃料量	charge of fuel
加燃料器	fuel feeder
加热	heating (htg.), warm(ing), warm up, firing, heat addition, hot conditioning (浮选前矿浆的) ◇ 不～炉 black furnace, 二次[再]～reheat(ing), 黑～*, 集中～central heating, 局部～法*, 套式～jacketing, 直接～straight firing
加热板(回火的)	hot plate
加热棒(电阻式)	heating rod
加热保温坑(锭、坯的)	dead soaking pit
加热表面	heating surface (HS, h.s.)
加热表面积	heating surface area
加热不足	underheating, shortage of heat
加热槽	heating tank
加热层	heated floor
加热程度	degree of heating
加热除气(真空系统的)	bake out
加热带	furnace zone
加热电流	heating current
加热电阻	heating resistor, furnace resistor (炉用) ◇ 埃莱马～*
加热段	heat up section, heating (up) zone, hot area, fire room (加热炉的), tonnage zone (决定加热炉产量的)
加热方法	heat means
加热费	【企】cost of heating
加热干燥	thermal drying
加热工	heater
加热焊料用轻便炉	devil
加热后气孔率	porosity after heating
加热火道	heating flue
加热火道温度	heating flue temperature
加热火焰喷口	heating flame orifice
加热火嘴[火炬, 喷灯]	heating torch
加热激活	heat activation
加热几何学	heating geometry
加热技术	heating technique
加热剂	heating agent

加热介质 heating medium

加热控制 heating control

加热-冷却式深冲模 heating-cooling draw die

加热裂纹[缝] fire check

加热炉 (re)heating [mill] furnace, reheater (rhr) ◇ 巴尔斯特拉~*,步进式~*,车底式~*,带式~*,单侧~ side fired furnace,单面~*,单向~ one-way furnace,电弧~ arc heating furnace,电极~ electrode furnace,电阻反射~*,端出料~*,多段式~*,惰性气体保护~*,反射式~ reflector oven,缝式[窄口]~ slot furnace,辐射杯烧嘴~*,高温快速~*,高真空感应~*,管式~ tubular oven,辊道炉膛~ roller-hearth furnace,红外线~*,后端装料和前端出料的~*,环形旋转炉底~*,回转式棒材~*,间歇[分批]式~*,浸入式烧嘴~*,均匀~ equiflux heater,控制~（见"控温炉"）,快 f furnace,塞拉斯~*,三段式~*,双面~*,碳管短路~*,碳粒短路~*,无氧化~*,悬垂式~ catenary type oven,摇杆推料~*,再~ mill furnace,罩式~*,直接~ direct-heating furnace,钟形~*,周期作业[分批装出料]~*

加热炉炉渣 heating furnace cinder

加热炉推钢机 furnace pusher

加热炉用γ射线板坯探测器 gamma-ray slab detector for reheating furnace

加热面积 area of heating surface

加热面效率 efficiency of heating surface

加热能力 heating capacity [power]

加热喷嘴 heating nozzle

加热喷嘴孔 heating nozzle bore

加热破裂 decrepitation

加热期 period of heating, heat on period, heating up period

加热器 heater (HR,HTR), calorifier, reheater (rhr), warmer,【焦】reboiler (蒸柱下部加热液体的) ◇ 摆式~ swing-away heater,拼合钨管~*,插入式~ bayonet heater,分批[配料]~*,管状~ tubular heater,红外线~ infrared heater,接触~ contact heater,汽套~ jacket heater,闪速~（液体的） flash heater,筒形~ cartridge heater,移动~ moving heater

加热器电路 heater circuit

加热器格子砖 heater brick

加热器管(道) heater tube

加热器恒定运动 constancy of heater motion

加热器能量 heater energy

加热器套管 heater well

加热器往复移动 reciprocating heater motion

加热器移动 heater moving

加热器元件 heater element

加热器组 heating battery

加热区 hot area, zone of heating

加热区段 furnace section, heat up section

加热曲线 heating curve

加热燃气 heating gas

加热燃气消耗(量) heating gas consumption

加热溶出[溶解] hot digestion, high temperature digestion

加热烧结 heat agglomerating

加热蛇管 heat(ing) coil (hc)

加热设备 heating equipment [plant, facility, installation], heater assembly

加热深度 heating depth

加热时间 heating [warm(ing)-up] time, length of heat

加热室 heating chamber

加热试验 heat(ing) test

加热速率[速度] heating [firing] rate, heating speed [velocity]

加热碎裂 degradation by heating

加热塔 heater tower

加热套 heating [hot] jacket

加热体 heater unit

加热调节　heat(ing) regulation [control]
加热筒　cartridge heater
加热温度　heating (up) temperature
加热系统　heating system
加热线圈　heating coil ◇ 内表面~"
加热焰道　heating flue
加热硬度　heating hardness
加热用电缆[软线]　heating cord
加热(用)蒸汽　heating steam
加热元件　heating [furnace] element, heater [heating] unit, hot wire ◇ U字形~"，非金属~"，铅密封~"
加热再生法　【焦】hot-actification process
加热蒸发段(精馏塔的)　boiler portion
加热至赤热形成裂纹　【压】red searing
加热至可见红热温度[开始发光温度]　just visible red heat
加热制度　heat schedule
加热周期　heat cycle
加热主管　heating main
加热装置　heater (assembly), heat(ing) installation [unit, system]
加熔剂的　fluxed
加熔剂人造矿块　flux bearing agglomerate
加熔剂氧炔焰焊接　powdered oxyacetylen welding
加入的氧化物　input oxide
加入合金元素　addition element
加三推焦法　three-addition method
加深钻进　later drilled deeper (L.D.D.)
加湿鼓风　wet blasting, steam addition to blast ◇ 高炉~装置
加湿氧气鼓风　oxygen-steam blast
加石灰　lime feed
加石灰过量的　【冶】overlimed
加石灰球团　limecontaining pellet
加铈孕育[变质]处理的铸铁　cerium-treated cast iron
加水　watering, wetting, moisture addition, imbibition ◇ 二次~[团]rewetting
加水拌[掺]合　blunge
加水分解　hydrolysis

加水量　moisture addition
加水稀释　watering
加斯佩捅风眼机　Gaspe' tuyere puncher
加四氢萘　tetrahydronaphthalene
加速　accelerate, speed-up, quicken, boost(ing)
加速表　accelerometer
加速充电　boost charge
加速处理　speeding treatment
加速淬火油　accelerated quenching oil
加速(电)场　accelerating field
加速电极　accelerating electrode
加速(电)势[位](差)　accelerating potential
加速度　acceleration (acc.), accelerated speed [velocity]
加速(度)表[计]　accelerometer
加速度轧制　zoom rolling
加速风机　blow over fan
加速腐蚀　accelerated corrosion
加速功　work of acceleration
加速管　accelerating tube
加速环流　accelerated circulation
加速激磁　forced excitation
加速剂　accelerant, accelerator, energiser, energizer
加速剂试验　accelerator test
加速继电器　accelerating relay
加速阶段　acceleration phase
加速浸出　accelerated leaching
加速浸蚀液　accelerated solution
加速力　accelerating force
加速力矩　accelerating moment
加速流变　accelerating flow
加速器　accelerator (accel.), booster, speeder
加速燃烧　accelerated combustion
加速溶解　solutize
加速蠕变　accelerated creep
加速栅极　accelerating grid [electrode]
加速时效　accelerated ageing
加速寿命试验　accelerated life test

加速循环	accelerated circulation
加速阳极	acceleration anode
加速养护的	rapid-curing
加速载荷试验	accelerated load test
加酸萃取剂浸出	acid-in-extractant leaching ◇ 溶剂～法 acid-in-solvent process
加酸分解	decomposition with acid, acid splitting
加酸器	acid feeder
加酸溶剂浸出	acid-in-solvent leaching
加酸水解	acid hydrolysis
加算时间	【计】add time
加钛稳定钢	titanium-stabilized steel
加碳酸钠[苏打]焙烧	soda roasting
加碳酸钠[苏打]熔炼	soda smelting
加套的	jacketed
加套桩	lag pile
加特种元素的钢	treated steel
加填料	dopping
加铁粉切割(法)	iron powder cutting
加铁粉氧乙炔切割法	iron-powder process
加铜稀释法	copper dilution method
加铜稀释法测定电流效率	current efficiency determination by copper-dilution
加涂料	doping
加钍钨丝[灯丝]	(同"敷钍钨丝")
加脱氧剂	【钢】killing
加温生球	prewarmed green ball
加硒钢	selenium steel
加锌	zincification, zincing
加锌连续除银	continuous removal of silver by adding zinc
加锌提[除]银(法)(铅精炼)	zinc desilverization ◇ 帕克～*
加锌提[除]银设备	【色】zinc-desilverization plant
加压	pressurization, pressurizing, compression, press, forcing
加压不足	underpressing
加压抽空试验	pressure evacuation test
加压粗流喷水	coarse pressure spray
加压淬火	(同"压力淬火")
加压底[下]铸	bottom pressure casting
加压反应器	pressure bottle
加压杆	compression head
加压罐	pressurizing tank
加压过滤	pressure filtration ◇ 厚料层～*
加压焊缝	pressure weld
加压焊接	pressure welding [bonding], welding with pressure ◇ 恒温～*, 预热～ hot pressure welding
加压焊接接头	pressure welded junction
加压烘干	pressure drying
加压(矫直)回火	press tempering
加压集尘	pressure dust collection
加压结晶	piezocrystallization
加压浸出	pressurized leaching, pressure leach
加压浸出法[过程]	pressure leaching process
加压浸出高压釜	pressure leach autoclave
加压浸出镍钴铜粉法	◇ 谢里特－高尔顿～*
加压浸出系统	pressure leaching train
加压馏出物	pressure distillate
加压流体	pressurized fluid
加压冷焊	press cold welding
加压铝热剂焊(接)	pressure thermit welding (PTW)
加压凝固钢	liquid compressed steel
加压喷射	pressure jet
加压喷雾	pressure atomization
加压气焊	pressure-gas welding (PGW), gas-pressure welding ◇ 氧乙炔～*
加压热剂焊	pressure thermit welding (PTW), thermit pressure welding
加压溶出	【色】pressure digestion
加压润滑	pressure [forced] lubrication
加压烧结	pressure [compression] sintering, applied pressure sintering, sintering under pressure ◇ 电活化～*
加压－烧结－熔化	pressing-sintering-

加荚贾甲　jia

melting (PSM)
加压设备[装置]　pressure device
加压渗氮　pressure nitriding
加压室　plenum chamber
加压水　pressurized water
加压水解　pressure hydrolysis
加压铁(砂箱上部的)　weighting
加压氧化　pressure oxidation
加压液体渗氮(法)　liquid pressure nitriding
加压站　booster station ◇ 地面～land booster station
加压蒸发器　pressure evaporator
加压蒸馏　pressure distillation
加压滞留时间 [焊]　forge delay time
加压铸焊　combined thermit welding, pressure thermit welding
加压铸造　pressurized [injection] casting, die-casting
加盐焙烧　(同"食盐氯化焙烧")
加盐焙烧的钾钒铀矿浸出　salt-roast carnotite-type leach
加盐焙烧过的钾钒铀矿　salt-roasted carnotite ore
加盐处理　brine
加氧化钍　thoriate
加氧气化　oxygen gasification
加腋　angle-table
加应力　stress application
加油　oiling, oil addition
加油器　oiler
加油站　(gasoline) filling station, fueling [petrol] station
加油脂　greasing
加载　loading, load-on, stressing ◇ 重力～gravity loading
加载变形抗力　strength under load
加载等温淬火　austemper stressing
加载后应变孕育期[潜伏时间]　incubation time of strain after load
加载回火　stress tempering (S.T.)
加载类型　kind of stressing

加载强度　intensity of loading
加载速率[度]　loading rate [speed], rate of load application
加载条件　conditions of loading
加载相变法　transformation stressing
加载卸载鉴定试验　back test
加载装置　loading plant
加罩　hooding, encapsulating, jacketing
加重　weighting
加重带卷　(同"组合带卷")
加重的　weighted, heavily reinforced
加注套节　filling socket
加籽晶　seeding
荚硫细菌属　thiocapsa
贾格硬度试验机　Jagger hardness tester
贾卡马铅基轴承合金(71Pb, 10Sn, 余量Sb)　Jacama metal
贾克斯效应　Jaques effect
贾宁摩损检测法　Jannin method
甲板装载提单　on deck B/L (bin of lading)
甲苯{$CH_3C_6H_5$}　methylbenzene, toluene, toluol
甲苯胺　toluidine
甲苯基酸　cresylic acid
甲苄基{$CH_3C_6H_4CH_2-$}　methylbenzyl
甲醇{CH_3OH}　methanol, methyl-alcohol (Me. alc.), wood alcohol
甲醇溶液　methanol solution
甲硅烷　silicane
甲基{CH_3-}　methyl
甲基苯酚　methylphenol
甲基苯基酮{$CH_3COC_6H_5$}　methyl phenyl ketone
甲基吡啶　picoline
甲基丙烯酸{$CH_2:C(CH_3)COOH$}　methacrylic [methylacrylic] acid
甲基丙烯酸甲酯{$C_3H_5CO_2CH_3$}　methyl methacrylate
甲基橙{$(CH_3)_2NC_6H_4N:NC_6H_4SO_3Na$}　methyl orange, tropeolin-D

甲基丁基酮 {CH₃COC₄H₉} methyl-n-butyl ketone, hexanone-[2]
甲基丁烷 2-methyl-butane ◇ 2-~*
甲基二辛基胺 methyldioctylamine
甲基红 methyl red
甲基化酒精 methylated spirit
甲基化物 {M(CH₃)ₙ} methide
甲基膦酸 {CH₃·PO(OH)₂} methyl-phosphonic acid
甲基膦酸脂 methyl-phosphonate
甲基氯 {CH₃Cl} methyl chloride, chloromethane
甲基氯硅烷 methyl chlorsilane
甲基氯甲基酸 methyl chloromethyl ether
甲基乙基酮 {CH₃COC₂H₅} butanone, methyl ethyl ketone
甲基噻吩 {C₅H₆S} methylthiophene
甲基异丙酮 {CH₃COCH(CH₃)₂} methyl isopropyl ketone
甲基异丁基甲醇 methyl iso-butyl carbinol (MIBC)
甲基异丁基甲酮连氮 methyl isobutyl ketazine
甲基异丁丁酮 {(CH₃)₂CHCH₂COCH₃} methyl isobutyl ketone (M.I.K.) ◇ 洗提过的~*
甲基异丁酮贫液 barren methyl isobutyl ketone
甲基异戊酮 {CH₃COC₄H₉} methyl isoamyl ketone
甲基锗 {Ge(CH₃)₂, Ge(CH₃)₄} germanium methide
甲醛 {HCHO} formaldehyde, methyl aldehyde
甲醛浸出 formaldehyde leaching
甲醛树脂 (聚乙烯醇缩甲醛树脂的简称)【金】Formvar
甲酸 {HCOOH} methanoic [formic] acid
甲酸的 formic
甲酸钾 {HCO₂K} potassium formate
甲酸钠 {H·COONa} sodium formate
甲酸镍 nickel formate
甲酸铅 {Pb(CHO₂)₂} lead formate
甲酸双氧铀[甲酸铀酰] {UO₂(HCO₂)₂} uranyl formate [formiate]
甲酸铁 iron(ic) [ferric] formate
甲酸钍 thoroxyl
甲酸亚铊 {TlHCO₂} thallium formate [formiate]
甲酸盐[酯] {HCOOM} formate, formiate
甲酮连氮 {R₂C:N·N:CR₂} ketazine
甲烷 {CH₄} methane, marsh [sludge] gas, fire damp
甲烷八叠球菌 Sarcina methanica
甲烷化 methanation
甲烷裂化法 (用于制热原子碳黑及氢) thermatomic process
甲义[撑] {CH₂=} methylene
岬扁尖凿 cape chisel
钾 {K} potassium (Pot., potass.), kalium
钾铵铁盐 {2KCl·2NH₄Cl·2FeCl₃·3H₂O} kremersite
钾冰晶石 {3KF·AlF₃} potassium cryolite
钾钒铀矿 {K₂O·2U₂O₃·V₂O₅·3H₂O} carnotite ◇ 加盐焙烧的~浸出*
钾钙板锆石 {K₂CaZrSi₄O₁₂} wadeite
钾杆沸石 ashcroftine
钾汞齐 [液态合金] potassium amalgam
钾合金 potassium alloy
钾基合金 potassium-base alloy
钾碱 (同"碳酸钾",俗称)
钾碱矿 wyomingite
钾碱液 caustic potash lye
钾矿物 potassium mineral
钾镁矾 leonite
钾锰盐 chlormanganokalite
钾(明)矾 {K₂SO₄·Al₂(SO₄)₃·24H₂O} potassium [potash] alum
钾钠镁矾 chile-loeweite
钾水玻璃 potash water glass
钾钽铌合金 potassium tantalate niobate alloy
钾铁矾 krausite
钾微斜长石 {KNaAlSi₃O₈} microcline

钾假 jia

钾霞石 {(K,Na)(Al,Si)$_2$O$_4$} kaliophilite
钾硝 {KNO$_3$} saltpeter, saltpetre
钾盐 {KCl} sylvite, potash [kali] salt
钾盐镁矾 {MgSO$_4$·KCl·3H$_2$O} kainite
钾铀矿 {(K,Na)2(UO$_2$)(Si$_2$O$_5$)$_4$·8H$_2$O} gastunite
假表面变形 false brinelling
假沉淀 pseudo-precipitation
假撑(罩式炉的) dummy spacer
假催化(作用) pseudocatalysis
假单变性 pseudomonotropy
假单胞菌属 Pseudomonas
假底 false bottom
假底槽 false bottom tank
假地板 【计】false floor
假定(同"假设") ◇伯努利～Bernoulli's hypothesis
假定负载 assumed load
假定(公)式 assumption formula
假二元合金 quasi-binary alloy
假二元系 pseudobinary (system), quasibinary system
假二元系状态图 pseudobinary diagram
假沸腾层 pseudoliquid layer
假风箱 【团】false windbox
假复型(制备)法 pseudoreplica
假负载 dummy [false] load
假负载电阻器 dummy resistor (DR)
假钢 pseudo-steel
假拱 blank [dumb] arch
假共沸蒸馏(用于粗苯脱非芳香族) pseudo-azeotropic distillati
假共晶(的) pseudo-eutectic, quasi-eutectic
假共晶合金 quasi-eutectic alloy
假共晶体 quasi-eutectic crystal
假共析(的) pseudo-eutectoid, quasi-eutectoid
假共析合金 quasi-eutectoid alloy
假共析体(的) pseudo-eutectoid, quasi-eutectoid
假固体 pseudosolid (body)

假固体构造 pseudosolid body formation
假硅灰石 pseudo-wollastonite
假合金 pseudo-alloy
假化合物 pseudocompound
假回波[声] false echo return
假回波信号 false echo
假碱 pseudo-base
假金 (装饰用铜铝合金;5—10Al,余量Cu) imitation gold ◇埃塞俄比亚～*, 粉红色～pink gold, 克雷格～*, 马尼拉～*, 蒙大拿～*, 纽伦堡～*, 塔尔米～*, 牙科～(Cu:Zn=2:1) wiegold
假金箔 leaf brass
假金叶 ◇艾克斯～*
假晶 pseudomorph, pseudocrystal
假晶的 pseudocrystalline, pseudomorphic, pseudomorphous
假晶现象 pseudomorphism
假考塞耳线 pseudo-Kossel lines
假蓝宝石 {Mg$_5$Al$_{12}$Si$_2$O$_{27}$} sapphirine
假立方晶形 pseudomorphic cubic form
假粒度 (同"表观粒度")
假裂纹 false crack
假密度 bulk density
假摩擦侵蚀 false brinelling
假平衡 false equilibrium
假漆 varnish
假曲率模型(用于补偿铸件翘曲) faked pattern
假缺陷(无损检验的) artefact, artefact
假溶液 pseudo solution
假三元系 quasi-ternary system
假上箱 【铸】false cope
假设 assumption, hypothesis, supposition, presumption ◇可供选择的～alternate hypothesis
假渗氮 pseudo [blank] nitriding
假渗碳 pseudocarburizing, blank carburizing
假数 【数】mantissa
假说 presupposition, hypothesis
假塑性 pseudo-plasticity

假塑性体	pseudoplastic
假酸性	pseudoacidity
假同晶	pseudomorphy
假同晶生长	pseudomorphic growth
假腿	counter flange, temporary flange（孔型的）
假脱机	【计】simultaneous peripheral operations on-line（SPOOL）
假析出	pseudo-precipitation
假相	【金】pseudophase
假箱	【铸】oddside, pattern match
假箱型板	follow board
假想平衡状态图	tentative constitution diagram
假想轴	imaginary axis
假象	false image, pseudomorphism, pseudomorphy
假象赤铁矿{Fe$_2$O$_3$}	martite
假象毒砂	crucite, crucilite
假象牙	celluloid
假斜方晶的	pseudo orthorhombic (pseudo orthor.)
假芯头	【铸】false part
假信号	false [spurious, ghost, dummy] signal, spurious response
假型	oddside, match ◇ 湿砂~ green-sand match
假型板	odd-side [match] board
假型板造型	match-plate moulding
假型芯	【铸】false core
假形晶体	pseudomorphic crystal
假液化层	pseudoliquid layer
假异常（物探中的）	tramps
假翼缘法孔型设计	（同"反翼缘法孔型设计"）
假银	◇ 莫克~ *
假银星石	pseudo-wollastonite
假正方晶的	pseudo tetragonal (pseudo tetrag.)
假中间砂箱	false cheek
假珠光体	pseudopearlite
价	【化】valence, valency

价电荷	valency charge
价电子	valence [valency] electron
价电子层	valence shell
价(电子)带	valence band
价电子带电子	valence band electron
价电子结构	valence electron structure
价电子排列[组态]	valence electron configuration
价电子群	valency group
价电子总数	total valence population
价定律	【化】valency laws
价格	price, cost ◇ 出厂~ factory price
价格表	price list
价格波动	fluctuation in prices
价格补助方案	price support program
价格单	【企】cost sheet
价格分析	analysis of prices
价格加运费	cost and freight (C. & F.)
价格因素	【企】cost factor
价格指数	【企】price index ◇ 生产厂~ *, 原料与产品~ *
价键	valence bond [link(age)], valency bond [binding]
价键带	valence-bound band
价键化合物	valency compound
价键晶体	valence crystal
价键晶体光谱	valence-crystal spectrum
价力（原子价力）	valence force
价数	valence number
价数改变	valency change
价态（化合价态）	valent [valence] state
价效应	valency effect
价值	value (val.), worth, goodness, merit ◇ 韦尔齐费尔有效~常数 *
价值低落	depreciation
价值分析	value analysis (VA)
价值工程(学)	value engineering (VE)
架	frame, rack, shelf, stand, keeper, trestle
架接	bridge joint
架空传输铝线	aluminum overhead transmission line
架空导线	aerial conductor, overhead wire

架空电缆[缆索] overhead [aerial] cable
架空电缆铜镉合金(0.9Cd,余量 Cu) tree wire
架空电力索道 telpher line
架空电线 hook-up wire, overhead conductor
架空管 crossover pipe
架空管道 overhead pipeline
架空管用加热器 heater for cross over pipe
架空冷凝器 overhead condenser
架空料斗 overhead hopper
架空式板坯回转-装料机 overhead revolving slab charging machine
架空式钢锭回转-称量机 overhead ingot turning and weighing machine
架空式输送机 overhead conveyer
架空式装料机 【钢】overhead charging machine
架空输电线 overhead transmission line
架空索道 aerial cableway [ropeway], cableway
架空索道用承载钢丝绳 carrying [track] wire rope for aerial tramway
架空索道用牵引钢丝绳 traction wire rope for aerial tramway
架空铁道 aerial railroad [railway]
架空线路 overhead line
架空烟道 overhead flue
架空运输机[设备] aerial transporter [conveyer]
架立钢筋 spacing bar
架桥现象 【粉】bridge [arch] formation
架桥效应 bridging effect
架设 erection (erec.)
架设图 erection diagram
架式干燥器 rack drier
架式烘芯炉 rack-type core-drying stove
架砖 seating block
架座 frame foundation
驾驶杆 control crank [column, stick]
驾驶间(起重机的) operators cab
驾驶考试 driving test
驾驶室 operator cabin, driver's cab
驾驶室空调设备 cab cooler
驾驶室控制 cab control (C.C.)
驾驶员 driver, pilot
监测 monitoring
监测车 monitoring car ◇ 空气污染~·
监测高温计 sentinel pyrometer
监测网 monitoring net ◇ 大气污染~·
监测仪表 monitor
监督 supervision, monitoring, viewing
监督部件 【计】monitor unit
监督程序 【计】monitor, monitor program [routine]
监督工作(技术的) supervising work
监督系统 【计】monitor system
监工员 inspector, watch master
监控 supervisory control, monitor
监控计算机 supervisory control computer (SCC)
监控继电器 supervisory control relay
监控开关 monitor switch
监控器 monitor unit ◇ 差动~ differential monitor
监控设备 monitoring equipment, watchdog
监控台 【计】master console
监控系统 monitored control system
监控[监视]仪表 supervisory instruments
监控(仪表)盘 supervisory panel
监控元件 monitoring element, supervising member
监视 monitoring, observation, surveillance
监视窗[孔] besel, judas (window)
监视[控]灯 supervisory [pilot] lamp
监视[监听]键 【电】monitoring key
监视器 monitor, invigilator, watch-dog
监视设备 supervisory equipment, supervising device
监视设施 monitoring facility
监视时钟 【计】watch-dog timer
监视室 supervision room

监视(信号)盘　supervision panel
坚固表面(电镀的)　reguline
坚固的　firm, tight, solid, sturdy, hardy, rugged, strong
坚固接头　robust joint
坚固结构　rugged construction
坚固炉结[瘤]　【冶】tight scaffold
坚固涂层　strong coating
坚固性　sturdiness, ruggedness, fastness
坚固致密焊缝　【焊】tight-strong seam
坚壳带(沸腾钢锭的)　【钢】rim zone
坚实表层　reguline
坚实的　solid
坚实度　compactness, degree of solidity
坚实性　solidity
尖齿锹　round-point shovel
尖底淘金盘　batea
尖点　cusp, cuspidal point
尖点最大值　sharp [acute] maximum
尖顶　aiguille, pinnacle
尖端　tip, pointed end
尖端材料　advanced material
尖端的　ultra-modern, most advanced
尖端放电　point [marginal] discharge
尖端计数技术　point counting technique
尖端科学[学科]　top [advanced] sciences
尖端螺丝　pointed screw
尖端效应　point effect
尖拱　cusped [pointed] arch
尖角(度)间界可动性　mobility of large-angle boundaries
尖角磨料　angular abrasive
尖晶石{$MgAl_2O_4$}　spinel ◇ 铬～chrome spinel
尖晶石结构　spinel structure
尖晶石矿物　spinel mineral
尖晶石耐火材料　spinel refractory
尖晶石型铁氧体　spinel (type) ferrite
尖晶石砖　spinel brick ◇ 铬～chrome-spinel brick
尖晶石族　spinellide
尖口钳　clipper

尖裂纹　sharp crack
尖面　spiky surface
尖木桩　picket
尖缺口　sharp notch
尖锐度[性]　acuity ◇ 缺口～notch acuity
尖锐界面模型　sharp interface model
尖头　pointed [sharp] end, beak, nib, spike, peen (锤的), nose (芯棒工作锥的)
尖头(钢)锤　pointed (steel) hammer
尖头螺栓　nibbed [pointed] bolt
尖头物　prong, peg
尖头信号　pip, blip
尖楔　glut, wedge
尖轴铰链　pivot hinge
尖锥形[体]　taper
尖嘴铁砧　beak iron
间氨苯酰胺基脲　cryogenin(e)
间苯二酚{$C_6H_4(OH)_2$}　yesorcin(ol)
间壁　dividing wall, partition,【建】septum
间段杀菌　fractional sterilization
间断　intermittence, interruption, pulsation
间断操作　discontinuous operation
间断操作中和池　discontinuously operating neutralisation basin
间断冲洗　intermittent flushing
间断淬火　interrupted hardening [quenching]
间断淬火热处理　interrupted quenching-hot working
间断点　discontinuity [discontinuous] point
间断供应　batchwise supply
间断焊　intermittent welding
间断(换热)式热风炉　intermittent stove
间断浸入　intermittent immersion
间断控制　discontinuous [intermittent] control
间断切割　skip cutting
间断烧结法　(同"间歇式烧结法")
间断时间　interruption period, length of discontinuity, break time

间断时效　interrupted ageing
间断式烧结机　batch type machine
间断跳变　discontinuous jump
间断相　discontinuous phase
间断性啸声　surging
间二甲苯{C_8H_{10}}　p-dimethylbenzene
间二甲苯酚{$C_8H_{10}O$}　m-xylenol
间发错误［故障］　intermittent error [fault]
间格式贮仓　organ-pipe bunker
间格(式)贮槽　organ-pipe bin, compartment(ed) bin
间隔　interval (int.), space, spacing, distance, gap,【计】blank
间隔槽　compartment tank
间隔测试　interval test
间隔铲取采样法　alternate shovel method
间隔垫圈　spacing washer
间隔分级的　gap-graded
间隔符　blank [space] character
间隔焊　space welding ◇ 分散～wandering welding
间隔架　distance frame, space-stop rack
间隔脉冲　spacing [interval] pulse
间隔磨蚀速率　interval erosion rate
间隔施工(法)　alternate bay construction
间隔时间　spacing interval, interlude
间隔调整器　intervalometer
间甲酚　m-cresol
间接测量　indirect measurement
间接传动　indirect drive
间接地址　indirect address
间接点焊　indirect spot welding
间接电弧焊接　indirect electric arc welding
间接电弧加热　indirect arc heating
间接电弧炉　indirect (electric) arc furnace
间接定址　indirect addressing
间接法　indirect process [method]
间接法还原金属　【色】gas-reduced metal
间接费用　overhead charges [cost, expenses]

间接工商业税　indirect bussiness tax
间接观察［测］　indirect observation
间接还原(法)　【冶】indirect reduction (I.R.), reduction by CO
间接还原度　degree [percentage] of indirect reduction
间接还原率　percentage of indirect reduction
间接回收　indirect recovery ◇ 硫酸盐～*
间接火加热炉　indirect-fired furnace
间接加热　indirect heat(ing)
间接加热电弧炉　indirect-heating arc furnace
间接加热式热处理炉　indirectly fired furnace, convection-type furnace (对流式)
间接加热竖炉　indirect heated shaft
间接加热蒸馏　distillation by indirect firing
间接浇注　【钢】indirect casting [pouring, teeming]
间接控制　indirect [off-line] control
间接拉力试验　Brazil splitting test
间接冷凝器　indirect condenser
间接冷却　indirect cooling
间接冷却法　【环】no-contact process
间接冷却器　indirect cooler
间接冷却水　noncontact cooling water
间接炼钢法　indirect steel making process
间接试验　off-line test
间接输出　【计】indirect output
间接输入　【计】indirect input
间接碳弧焊　twin carbon-arc welding (TCAW) ◇ 泽雷纳～*
间接碳弧硬钎焊(铜焊)　twin carbon-arc brazing (TCAB)
间接氧化　indirect oxidation
间接冶炼法　indirect process
间接照明　indirect illumination [lighting]
间接证据　circumstantial evidence
间接证明　indirect proof
间界　boundary

间界层　interlayer
间界迁移理论　theory of boundary migration
间界移动　boundary movement
间距　interval, spacing, pitch, bay
间距估计(量)　interval estimate
间距误差　interval error
间绕线圈　space-wound coil
间位化合物　meta-compound
间位衍生物　meta-derivative
间隙　clearance (space), interval, gap (ping), play, space, interstice, 【压】clear opening
间隙脆化敏感材料　interstitial embrittlement-sensitive material
间隙法(超声波探伤)　gap method
间隙固溶体　interstitial solid solution
间隙(固溶体)合金　interstitial alloy
间隙固溶原子　interstitial dissolved atom
间隙合金元素　interstitial alloying element
间隙化合物　interstitial compound
间隙级配混凝土　gap-grade concrete
间隙宽　gap width
间隙孔　mesopore
间隙碳原子　interstitial carbon atom
间隙扩散　interstitial diffusion
间隙扩散机理　interstitial diffusion mechanism
间隙离子　interstitial ion
间隙漏泄　clearance leakage
间隙缺陷　interstitial defect
间隙扫描　gap scanning
间隙深度　gap depth
间隙式固溶元素稀少的　extra-low-interstitial (E.L.I.)
间隙式迁移[徙动]　【金】interstitial migration
间隙调整装置　clearance adjusting device
间隙位置　interstitial position [site]
间隙形成(铸坯与铸模间的)　【钢】gap formation
间隙阳离子　interstitial cation
间隙阴离子　interstitial anion
间隙元素　interstitial element
间隙原子　interstitial atom, interstitialcy
间隙原子气团　interstitial atmosphere
间隙原子团　interstitial cluster
间隙原子-位错间相互作用　interstitial-dislocation interaction
间隙杂质　interstitial impurities
间隙杂质原子　interstitial impurity atoms
间隙值　gap width
间歇　intermittence, intermission, interim, interlude, dwell, pause ◇ 马尔泰～机构 Maltese cross
间歇操作　intermittent operation [duty], batch operation
间歇操作法　batch method of operation, batch process(ing)
间歇操作式熔炼炉　batch smelter
间歇冲击荷载　intermittent shock load
间歇处理　batch treatment
间歇淬火　【金】martemper
间歇淬火介质试验　interval quenching-medium test
间歇反应器　batch reactor
间歇放电　intermittent discharge
间歇分馏　batch fractionating
间歇分馏塔　batch fractionating tower
间歇负载　intermittent load [duty]
间歇负载额定出力　intermittent rating
间歇干燥器　intermittent drier
间歇工作　intermittent duty [operation, service]
间歇过程　(同"断续过程")
间歇过滤器　intermittent filter
间歇混合器　batch blender
间歇给料　intermittent feed
间歇加压　(同"断续加压")
间歇浸出　batch leach(ing)
间歇浸入　intermittent immersion
间歇净化　batch purification
间歇离子交换　batch ion exchange
间歇(粒子)流　batch flux

间歇流化床	batch fluidized bed
间歇浓缩机	intermittent thickener
间歇排渣	intermittent flushing
间歇疲劳试验	interrupted fatigue test
间歇取样	intermittent sampling
间歇生产	batch production
间歇生产炉	batch [semi-production] furnace
间歇时间	pause time, time out of rolls（轧制道次间的）, cool time（接触焊的）
间歇式干燥炉	batch type drying stove, batch dryer
间歇式高压釜法[处理]	discontinuous autoclaving
间歇式固定床还原	batch bed reduction
间歇(式)过滤	batch filtration,【环】intermittent filtration
间歇式过滤机	batch filter
间歇式焊接	wood pecker welding
间歇式回转窑	batch kiln
间歇式混合机	batch mixer
间歇式加热炉	batch type heating furnace
间歇式焦化	batch coking
间歇式搅拌器	batch agitator
间歇式精馏塔	batch fractionating column
间歇(式)炉	batch oven [kiln]
间歇式逆流浸出	batch type countercurrent leaching
间歇式烧结法	batch sintering process
间歇式烧结机[设备]	batch sintering machine
间歇式退火炉	periodic annealing furnace [oven]
间歇式小车窑	envelope kiln
间歇(式)窑	intermittent [periodic] kiln, batch (type) kiln
间歇(式)造球	batch balling, pelletizing in batches
间歇式真空过滤机	intermittent vacuum filter
间歇碳化	【焦】intermittent carbonization
间歇性	intermittence
间歇研磨	batch grinding
间歇运转	（同"断续运转"）
间歇蒸馏	interrupted [batch] distillation
间歇蒸馏釜[罐]	batch still
间歇装料	intermittent charging
间歇作业坑式炉	pit-type batch furnace
间乙基甲苯{C_9H_{12}}	m-ethyltoluene
间直混合加热连续式直产炉	【焦】continuous vertical retort with indirectly and directly mixed heating
间柱	stud
兼容软件	compatible software
兼容性	compatibility
兼容硬件	compatible hardware
兼性需氧微生物	facultative aerobes
兼性厌氧微生物	facultative anaerobes
兼性自养生物	facultative autotrophs
检波	detecting, detection, rectification, rectifying, demodulation ◇阳极～*
检波能力	detectability
检波器	demodulator, detection instrument, detector, rectifier, cymoscope ◇晶体～crystal rectifier, 霍尔～测头*
检波头	detecting head, demodulator probe
检波效率	efficiency of rectification
检测	detecting, detection, check, test, gauging, sensing, measureing
检测部件	detecting unit
检测点	check [monitoring] point
检测极限	detection limit
检测灵敏度砝码（天平的）	sensitivity weight
检测能力	detectability
检测器	detector
检测水平	inspection level
检测头(检测器的)	detector head
检测仪表	instrumentation ◇生产过程用～process instrumentation
检测仪器	detection [detecting] instrument, tester
检测用槽液	testing bath
检测用热[温差]电偶	test thermocouple

[thermoelement]
检测元件 detecting element
检查 inspection, checkout, checking, detection, examination, look-up, supervision, audit ◇ 按月～(设备的) monthly inspection, 经探伤仪仔细～的 scanned, 目视～ hand inspection, 未经～的 uninspected
检查报告 inspection report
检查称量料斗 check weight hopper
检查程序 checking program [routine], test routine, audit program
检查传送带 inspection belt [conveyer]
检查窗口 inspection window
检查点 【计】checkpoint
检查分类工序 inspection-assorting process
检查高架平台 inspection platform
检查跟踪 【计】audit
检查工段 inspection station, inspecting yard (锭、坯的)
检查工序 inspection operation
检查工作台架 inspection table
检查和分类作业线 inspection and assorting line
检查合格证 inspection certificate
检查滑道台 inspection skid
检查及排除故障 troubleshoot
检查技工[技师] inspecting operator [mechanic]
检查进度表 inspection schedule
检查井 inspection shaft [well] ◇ 跌落式～ drop manhole
检查孔 inspection hole [port, eye], access eye, manhole
检查孔盖 inspection cover
检查口 inspection opening [door], access hatch
检查量规 test gauge
检查批量 inspection lot
检查平台 inspection platform
检查人孔 inspection manhole

检查筛 scalping [protective] screen
检查筛分 control screening
检查筛分粒度[尺寸] mesh size of scalping screen
检查台 inspection bed [bench], inspecting stand
检查台面辊 inspection bed roller table
检查线 check line
检查一览表 inspection schedule
检查员 inspector, checker, chequer, examiner
检查员印章 inspector's stamp
检查站 inspection station, checkpoint
检查证明书 inspection certificate
检潮标 foot gauge
检定 verification, calibration, detection
检定产品一览表 qualified products list (QPL)
检定器 (同"校准器")
检定用标准[基准] (同"校准用标准")
检定中心 verification centre
检晶器 crystallographer, crystallometer
检孔镜 boroscope ◇ 用～目视检查(管子内壁) boroscope examination
检流计 galvanometer ◇ 镜(反射)式～ mirror galvanometer, 指针式～ needle galvanometer
检漏 leak(age) detection [hunting]
检漏喷嘴 spray probe
检漏器 leak detector [tester]
检漏试验 leak test ◇ 密闭爆发器～ bomb test
检漏试验灵敏度 sensitivity of leak test
检漏头 sniffer
检漏仪 leakage indicator
检漏装置 leakage detecting device
检湿计 hydroscope, hygroscope
检索 search(ing), retrieval, retrieve ◇ 按"或"～ disjunctive search, 区域～ area search
检索比 recall ratio
检修 overhaul, repair (work), service, re-

condition ◇ 不停产～on line maintenance, 无～作业期 maintenance free period

检修盖 access cover

检修孔 access hole [door]

检修门 access door

检修区 repairing area

检修设备 repair facility

检修作业 jobbing work

检验 check (out), test(ing), examination, inspection (insp.), assay, verift ◇ 常规[正常]～normal inspection, 非定期[临时]～casual inspection, 未经～的 uninspected

检验标记 check mark, hallmark

检验程序 checking program [routine], test program [routine]

检验尺寸 checking size

检验单 inspection [test] sheet

检验电路 checking [test] circuit

检验方法 test(ing) method

检验杆 proof [trial] bar

检验钢印 【压】acceptance stamp

检验工具 inspection tools

检验工作 test work

检验焊缝 test weld

检验和 【计】check sum

检验合格证书 test certificate

检验机 checking machine

检验局 inspection bureau

检验粒度 【选】checking size

检验量规 inspection gauge

检验器 tester, checker, detector, scanner, prover

检验墙身垂度 boning

检验设备 test equipment, testing plant, inspection machine [unit]

检验室 (control, testing) laboratory, inspection [test] room

检验试件 check test piece

检验顺序 test sequence

检验头 sampling probe

检验仪 check meter, tester, prover ◇ 爱泼斯坦～Epstein tester

检验用块规 reference block

检验用样品 check sample

检验员 checker, surveyor, controller

碱 alkali, alcali, base, soda ◇ 不溶于～的 alkali-insoluble, 成～元素 base element, 发面～fluffy doda, 加～alkalify, alkalization, 强～的*, 无～物料 alkali-free material, 用～熔解[助熔] fluxing with alkali

碱槽 alkali tank, alkaline bath

碱沉降器 caustic settler

碱处理 alkali [caustic] treatment

碱脆 caustic (em)brittlement [cracking], alkali brittleness ◇ 锅炉～boiler embrittlement

碱脆性 caustic brittleness

碱度 alkalinity (alky), degree of alkalinity, causticity(苛性), basic capacity, basicity (level, ratio), degree of basicity (碱性溶液内氢氧离子的浓度),【冶】(炉渣的) acid-to-base ratio, ratio of base to acid, base/acid (B/A), oxides/acid oxides (B/A), lime/silica (L/S) ◇ 游离～free alkalinity

碱度过高(指炉渣) lime setting

碱度计 alkalimeter

碱度平衡 basicity balance

碱度指数 basicity index

碱法 alkaline process [system]

碱法氯化 【环】alkaline chlorination

碱法脱脂 alkaline degreasing

碱废水 alkali waste water

碱分解 alkali breakdown

碱腐蚀法 alkaline etching

碱干电池 alkaline dry cell [battery]

碱耗 alkali consumption

碱化 alkalify, basify, alkalization, basification

碱化作用 alkalization

碱灰 soda-ash ◇ 粗～black ash

碱集料反应　alkali(ne)-aggregate reaction
碱交换(作用)　base exchange
碱金属　basic [base, alkali] metal, alkalis ◇ 氨基~alkali amide, 烃[烷]基~alkali alkyl
碱金属捕汞器　alkali metal mercury trap
碱金属多钨酸盐　alkali polytungstate
碱金属钒酸铀酰{MUO$_2$VO$_4$}　alkali uranyl vanadate
碱金属氟硅化物[硅酸盐]　alkali silicofluoride
碱金属氟化物复盐　double alkali fluoride
碱金属汞齐　alkali amalgam, amalgam of alkali-metal
碱金属硅酸盐　alkali silicate
碱金属含量　alkali metal content
碱金属合金　alkali metal alloy
碱金属化合物　base metal compound
碱金属硫氢化物　alkali hydrosulfide
碱金属卤化物　alkali halide
碱金属氯锆酸盐{M$_2$(ZrCl$_6$)}　alkali chlorozirconate
碱金属氯铪酸盐残渣　alkali chlorohafnate residue
碱金属氯化物　alkali chloride
碱金属铌酸盐　alkali niobate
碱金属硼酸盐　alkali borate
碱金属钽酸盐　alkali tantalate
碱金属碳酸盐　alkali carbonate
碱金属碳酸盐电解液　alkali carbonate electrolyte
碱金属碳酸盐浸出　alkali carbonate leaching
碱金属温差电偶　base metal couple
碱金属钨青铜{M$_2$O·WO$_2$·nWO$_3$}　alkali tungsten bronze
碱金属盐　alkali (metal) salt
碱金属氧化物　alkali oxide
碱金属蒸气　alkali metal vapour
碱浸　alkali [caustic] dip
碱浸出　alkali(ne) leaching ◇ 常压~*, 高压~法*

碱浸出(提取)率　alkaline leach extraction
碱浸洗液　caustic dip
碱离子　basic ion
碱量滴定试验　alkalimetric test
碱裂　【钢】caustic cracking ◇ 锅炉~boiler embrittlement
碱氯电解槽　alkali chlorine cell
碱-氯化物法除锌　dezincing by alkali-chloride fusion
碱浓度　soda concentration
碱侵蚀　alkaline etching, alkaline attack (碱溶液中),【铁】alkali attack (炉衬受钾钠侵蚀) ◇ 耐~合金 alkali resistance metal
碱清洗槽　alkali cleaning tank
碱熔(法)　alkaline [caustic] fusion
碱溶解[出]　alkaline digestion
碱溶液　aqueous alkali
碱溶液分解法　alkali solution attack process
碱烧结　alkaline sintering
碱石灰　soda lime ◇ 德维尔·佩奇尼~烧结法*, 勒夏特列-莫林~烧结法*
碱蚀脆性　caustic embrittlement
碱式化合物　basic compound
碱式铬酸铅　basic lead chromate
碱式铬酸锌　zinc tetroxychromate
碱式硫酸锆　basic zirconium sulphate
碱式硫酸铝　basic aluminium sulphate
碱式硫酸铅　basic lead sulphate
碱式硫酸铁　basic iron sulphate
碱式硫酸锌　basic zinc sulphate
碱式硫酸亚铜　basic cuprous sulphate
碱式硫酸盐　basic sulphate (salt), subsulphate
碱式硫酸盐沉淀　basic sulphate precipitation
碱式氯化物　basic chloride
碱式碳酸镍{NiCO$_3$·2Ni(OH)$_2$·4H$_2$O}　basic nickel carbonate
碱式碳酸铅{2PbCO$_3$·Pb(OH)$_2$}　basic lead carbonate, white lead, lead white

碱式碳酸铜 {CuCO$_3$·Cu(OH)$_2$ 或 Cu$_2$(OH)$_2$CO$_3$} basic cupric carbonate, verdigris
碱式碳酸锌 basic zinc carbonate
碱式碳酸盐 basic carbonate, subcarbonate
碱式碳酸盐白 basic carbonate white lead
碱式铁盐 basic iron salt
碱式铜盐 basic copper salt
碱式硝酸铋 basic bismuth nitrate, bismuth submitrate
碱式硝酸钪 {Sc(OH)(NO$_3$)$_2$} scandium hydroxynitrate
碱式硝酸盐 hydroxynitrate
碱式锌盐 basic zinc salt
碱式盐 basic salt, subsalt
碱水解 basic hydrolysis
碱铁矾 ungemachite
碱铜矾 euchlorine
碱土 alkaline earth
碱土金属 alkaline [alcaline] earth metal ◇ 二价~ *
碱土金属合金 alkaline earth alloy
碱土金属化合物 alkali-earth compound, alkaline earth metal compound
碱土金属氧化物 alkali-earth oxide, alkaline earth
碱土金属元素 earthy element
碱土族元素 alkaline earth element
碱误差 alkaline error
碱洗(去油,脱脂) alkaline cleaning [washing] ◇ 电化学~ *, 电解法~ *, 立式~ *, 卧式~ *
碱洗斑 caustic stain
碱洗除鳞[氧化皮] alkaline descaling
碱洗机[液,装置] alkaline cleaner ◇ 室温~ *
碱洗塔 alkali scrubber, alkali scrubbing tower
碱性 basicity, causticity, alkalinity, basic character ◇ 微~的 alkalescent
碱性胺化合物 basic amine compound
碱性薄膜 alkaline film

碱性(贝塞麦)炼钢转炉 basic Bessemer steel converter
碱性贝塞麦转炉 basic Bessemer furnace [vessel]
碱性贝塞麦转炉钢 basic Bessemer steel
碱性材料 basic material
碱性除垢剂 alkaline detergents
碱性除锈法 alkaline derusting
碱性底吹氧气转炉炼钢法 quality basic oxygen process (QBOP)
碱性底吹转炉 bottom-blown basic converter
碱性底吹转炉炼钢法 Thomas process
碱性电镀法 alkaline plating process
碱性电弧炉 basic electric arc furnace (BEA)
碱性电弧炉炼钢厂[车间] basic arc furnace plant
碱性电解液 alkaline electrlyte
碱性电炉钢 basic electric furnace steel
碱性反应 alkaline reaction
碱性废水 alkalic waste water
碱性浮渣 caustic dross
碱性钢 basic steel
碱性高岭土 alkaline kaolin(e)
碱性硅酸盐 alkaline silicate
碱性硅质高岭土 alkaline silicon kaoline
碱性焊条 basic (flux, covered) electrode
碱性化合物 basic compound
碱性还原 alkaline reduction
碱性回路 alkali circuit
碱性基 【化】basic group
碱性集料反应 alkali(ne)-aggregate reaction
碱性介质 alkaline medium
碱性浸出 (同"碱浸出")
碱性浸出回路 alkaline leach circuit
碱性浸出溶液 alkaline leach solution
碱性浸出设备 alkaline leach plant
碱性精炼 basic refining
碱性精炼法(粗铅的) alkali chloride improving ◇ 哈里斯粗铅~ *

碱性苦味酸钠溶液 【金】alkaline sodium picrate
碱性离解 basic dissociation
碱性离子交换树脂 base exchange resin
碱性炼钢法 basic steelmaking, basic (steel) process [practice] ◇ 托马斯－吉尔克里斯特～*
碱性磷酸盐 alkaline phosphate
碱性炉 basic furnace
碱性炉衬[衬里] basic lining
碱性炉衬转炉 (同"碱性转炉")
碱性炉床 basic hearth
碱性炉底 basic bottom
碱性炉顶 basic roof
碱性炉料 basic charge [stock]
碱性炉头 basic end
碱性炉渣 basic slag [cinder], caustic slag
碱性炉渣冶炼 working with an basic slag
碱性炉渣砖 basic slag brick
碱性铝酸盐 basic aluminate
碱性氯化物 alkalinous chloride
碱性脉石 basic gangue
碱性耐火材料 basic refractory (material)
碱性耐火制品 basic refractory product ◇ 洛维奈特～lovinit, 马格多洛～Magdolo, 马格多尼特～Magdonit, 马格尼特～Magnit, 麦克罗斯～Macros
碱性耐火砖 basic (refractory) brick, basic firebrick
碱性硼铍石 {Be$_2$(OH)BO$_3$} hambergite
碱性平炉 basic open-hearth (B.O.H.), basic open hearth furnace
碱性平炉钢 basic open hearth steel
碱性氢氧化物 basic hydroxide
碱性清洁[清洗]剂 alkali(ne) cleaner
碱性清洗 (熔模铸件的) caustic dip
碱性球团 basic pellet
碱性染料 basic dye
碱性熔剂 basic [alkaline] flux
碱性熔剂[药皮,涂药]焊条 (同"碱性焊条")
碱性熔体 alkaline melt
碱性溶剂 alkaline [basic] solvent
碱性溶液 alkaline [base] solution
碱性溶液电解法 alkaline electrolyte process
碱性烧结矿 basic sinter
碱性生铁 basic pig (iron)
碱性试剂 alkaline reagent
碱性水解 basic hydrolysis
碱性碳酸高铈 {Ce$_2$(OH)$_2$(CO$_3$)$_3$ 或 Ce(CO$_3$)$_2$·CeCO$_3$(OH)$_2$} ceric basic carbonate
碱性碳酸铜矿 molochite
碱性碳酸盐溶液 alkaline carbonate solution
碱性添加剂 basic addition
碱性铁 basic iron
碱性托马斯转炉法 basic Thomas process
碱性物含量 alkali content
碱性锡酸钠电解槽 alkaline sodium-stannate baths
碱性系统 alkali circuit
碱性锌空气电池 alkaline zinc-air battery
碱性锌锰电池 alkaline zinc-manganese dioxide cell
碱性蓄电池 alkali battery, alkaline accumulator, alkaline storage battery
碱性烟尘 basic smoke
碱性盐 basic salt
碱性阳极液 alkaline [basic] anolyte
碱性氧化铁 basic iron-oxide
碱性氧化物 basic oxide
碱性氧气(顶吹)转炉 【钢】basic oxygen furnace (B.O.F.)
碱性氧气(顶吹)转炉炼钢法 basic oxygen process (B.O.P.), basic oxygen furnace process, basic oxygen steelmaking (process) LD-AC (Linz Donawitz alkaline converter) process
碱性氧气转炉尘 basic oxygen furnace dust
碱性氧气转炉车间 B.O.F. plant
碱性氧气转炉钢 basic oxygen steel

(B.O.S.)
碱性氧气转炉炉嘴 basic oxygen furnace nose
碱性氧气转炉用废钢 basic oxygen furnace scrap
碱性药皮(焊条的) basic coating, lime fluorspar coating
碱性硬度 alkaline hardness
碱性油 basic oil
碱性元素 alkaline element
碱性原子团 【化】basic group
碱性渣 basic slag [clinker], short [soda] slag ◇ 标准~*
碱性渣操作法 basic slag practice
碱性渣磨碎装置 【钢】basic slag grinding plant
碱性砖 basic brick ◇ 浸沥青~ pitch impregnated basic brick, 直接结合~*
碱性转炉 basic (lined) converter, converter of basic lining, basic Bessemer furnace [vessel], Thomas converter [vessel]
碱性转炉低磷低氮钢 H.P.N. steel
碱性转炉低磷低氮钢吹炼法 H.P.N. process
碱性转炉法 【钢】basic converter process
碱性转炉钢 basic converter [Bessemer] steel
碱性转炉炼钢 basic converter steelmaking
碱性转炉生铁 Thomas (pig) iron
碱性转炉渣 Thomas slag
碱(性)组分 basic constituents
碱性组试剂 basic group reagent
碱压浸出 caustic pressure leaching
碱液 alkali liquor, soda solution,【化】lye
碱液泵 lye pump
碱液处理 alkali lye treatment
碱液电镀锡法(薄钢板的) alkaline process
碱液发黑处理 alkali black colouring
碱液浸镀防锈黑氧化膜法 ◇ 切莫伊~*

碱液浸洗 alkaline immersion cleaning
碱液喷洗 alkaline spray cleaning
碱液烧蓝处理 chemag
碱硬锰矿 hollandite
碱硬性 alkaline hardness
碱渣 caustic dross [sludge], soda slag
碱汁 lixivium
碱值 base number
碱致脆性 (同"碱脆")
碱中侵蚀 alkaline etching
拣出 culling
拣矸槽 dirt chute
拣矸带 【选】collecting band
拣矸运输机 picking conveyor
拣选 pick, sorting, hand dressing (矿石的) ◇ 人工[手工]~*
拣选场 sorting yard
拣选车间 sorting plant
拣选皮带 picking belt
简并 degenerate, degeneration ◇ n倍~*
简并半导体 degenerate semiconductor
简并度 degeneracy
简并多重性 degeneracy [degeneration] multiplicity
简并方式 【理】degenerate mode
简并化电子 degenerated electrons
简并结 【半】degenerate junction
简并能级 degenerate (energy) level
简并气体 degenerate gas
简并态 degenerate state [condition] ◇ 四度~*
简并系 degenerate system
简并项 degenerate term
简并性[度] degeneracy
简并样品 degenerate specimen
简并振动 degenerate vibration
简单铵盐 simple ammonium salt
简单反应 simple reaction
简单淬火 simple hardening
简单断面型钢 simple shape
简单固结式套管 solid bushing

简单滑移 simple glide
简单化合物 simple compound
简单机架 simple housing
简单晶胞 simple (unit) cell, primitive cell
简单晶型 simple crystal form
简单立方点阵[晶格] simple cubic lattice
简单立方晶体 simple cubic crystal
简单区域熔炼 simple zone melting
简单绕组 banked [simplex] winding
简单示意图 simplified schematic drawing
简单沃特拉位错 simple Volterra dislocation
简单液体 simple liquid
简单应力状态 simple state of stress
简单圆筒形转炉 simple cylindrical vessel
简单轧制过程 simple rolling process
简单蒸馏 simple distillation
简单支架 simple support
简化 simplifying, simplification, reducing, reduction, shortcutting
简化法 short-cut method, method of reduction
简化方程 reduced equation
简化分析法 shortened analysis
简化分型面型芯 stop-off core
简化公式 reduction formula
简化工艺流程 simplified process flowsheet
简化检验 reduced inspection
简化流程图 simplified flowsheet
简化型 reduced form
简化压应变试验 plain-strain compression test
简化(造型用)型芯 core lightener, lightener core
简述 resume, sketch, indicating
简图 diagrammatic drawing [sketch], sketch (drawing), schematic (diagram, drawing, model), skeleton [elementary] diagram, abbreviated drawing [draft]
简要的 schematic, brief
简易出钢[铁]口 simple taphole
简易杆式推料机 bar peel
简易氦照相机 simplified helium camera
简易焦 coke from simple ovens, simple coke
简易[化]模型 simplified model
简易冷却机 simplified cooler
简易模样 【铸】temporary pattern
简易型分光光度计 abridged spectrophotometer
简易噪音计 simplified sound meter
简支(承) free end bearing
简支的 simply [free] supported
简支梁 simple beam, simply supported beam, beam with simple supported ends
剪板机 plate shearing machine ◇ 铡刀式～ guillotine shears
剪边 trim(ming) ◇ 未～的热轧钢板 black edged plate
剪边工序(板、带材的) trimming operation
剪边机 (同"切边剪")
剪边碎料 chopped trimmings
剪侧边 edge [side] trimming
剪床 (同"剪切机")
剪刀 shears, clipper, scissors
剪刀保险销 shear pin
剪刀撑 diagonal bracing, bridging
剪刀钢 shear(ing) steel
剪刀剪切力 knife pressure
剪刀开角 angle of shear blades
剪断 shear off, cut off, detrusion
剪断机 shearing [clipping] machine, guillotine ◇ 带压紧装置的～ squeezer shears, 刀片相迎[相对]～*, 多刀～【压】gang shears, 辊式～ roll shears
剪口 【压】shears mouth
剪力 shear(ing) (force) ◇ 受～钢筋 shearing bar
剪力强度 shear strength
剪模 shear die
剪钳 cutting nipper
剪切 shear(ing), cutting ◇ 紧急事故～

emergency shearing
剪切安全销　shearing pin
剪切边界法　sheared boundary method
剪切变形　detrusion, shearing deformation ◇ 附加～additional shear
剪切冲头　shearing punch
剪切唇　shear lip
剪切唇部分　shear lip fraction
剪切唇区　shear lip zone
剪切带　shear zone
剪切断裂　【压】shear rupture [fracture] ◇ 韧窝状～dimpled shear rupture
剪切钢　shear steel
剪切钢板　【压】resquaring
剪切工　shearer
剪切工序　cutting operation
剪切(过的)边　sheared edge
剪切厚钢板　discrete steel plate
剪切-焊接机组　shearwelder
剪切荷载　shear(ing) load
剪切和重卷联合作业线　【压】combination shear and recoiling line
剪切和捏和作用　shearing-kneading action
剪切和掀板　shear and opened
剪切机　shears, shearer, shearing machine [press], clipping machine, cutting mechanism, guillotine（铡刀式）, cropper（钢锭、大钢坯的）◇ 不减速式～direct-driven shears, 电动～*, 定尺～length shear gauge, 多圆盘式～gang slitting shears, 杠杆[鳄口]式～*, 滚筒式～drum(-type) shears, 横向～*, 开式～*, 脉冲～impulse cutting machine, 曲柄式～crank shears, 上切式～*, 事故～emergency shears, 双动～down-and-up cut unit, 双刃～double-cut shears, 四轴式回转～*, 碎边～scrap chopper, 万能～*, 下切式～up-cut shears, 斜口～*, 液压～*, 圆盘(式)～*, 轧制线上的～mill shears, 铡刀式～*, 蒸汽-液压～steam hydraulic shears, 直接传动式～*, 中厚板双边修边～*, 重型～heavy du-ty shears
剪切机操纵工　shear operator
剪切机挡板　end gauge, shear gauge
剪切机刀片　shear blade [knife]
剪切机定尺机[工]　gauger
剪切机构　cutting mechanism
剪切机后辊道　after-shear table
剪切机回送辊道　shear pull-back table
剪切机活动定尺挡板　shear (stop and) measuring gear
剪切机机架　shear housing
剪切机机座　shear frame
剪切机开角　angle of backing off
剪切机输出辊道　shear delivery table
剪切机输入辊道　shear entry [approach] table
剪切机移动定尺挡板辊道　shear-gauge table
剪切机用移动槽　shear trough
剪切(机)作业线[剪切机组]　shear [cutting(-up)] line, shearing train, cut-up unit ◇ 回转式～rotary shear line, 联合～*, 轻型～light shear line, 双剪切机～*
剪切间隙　cutting gap
剪(切)角　【压】shear angle
剪切抗力　resistance to shear
剪切跨　shear bay
剪切力　blade force [load] ◇ 剪刀～*
剪切毛边试验　cutting burr test
剪切面　shearing surface, plane of shear
剪切面积　shearing area
剪切模量[数]　shear(ing) modulus
剪切疲劳试验　shear fatigue test
剪切破坏　shear rupture [breakdown, failure] ◇ 韧窝状～dimpled shear rupture
剪切强度　shear(ing) strength
剪切区　shear zone
剪切设备　shearing equipment
剪切试验　shear(ing) test
剪切试验机　shearing test machine
剪切弹性　shear elasticity

剪切弹性极限 elastic limit under shear (E.L.S.)	减径 tube reducing, sink(ing) (管材的), closing (在芯棒上锻造空心零件) ◇ 管子冷～ cold reduction of tube, 空拔～*
剪切头 cropping	
剪切弯曲(轧件的) shear bow	减径定径机 reducing [sinking] sizing mill ◇ 跨鞍式～*
剪切形变 shear deformation	
剪切行程 cutting stroke [travel]	减径定径机组 reducing-sizing block
剪切应变 shearing strain	减径机 reducing [sinking] mill, reducer ◇ 管材～*, 张[拉]力～*
剪(切)应力 shear(ing) stress ◇ 摩擦诱致～*	
	减径孔型 reducing [sinking] pass
剪切应力强度 intensity of shearing stress	减径拉伸 hollow sinking
剪切应力-应变图 shearing stress-strain diagram	减径(量) sizing reduction
	减聚力 decohesion
剪切装置 cutting mechanism	减粒 sizing reduction
剪切作用 shearing action	减量装药 reduced charge (RCh, r-chg)
剪刃 cutting edge ◇ 可移～ moving blade	减慢[缓] retard(ation), slowdown
剪刃粗磨 glazing	减面率 area reduction, reduction of area (RA), draft (拉拔的), draught ◇ 名义～*
剪刃间隙 blade clearance	
剪刃重叠量 overlap of knives	
剪塌(钢坯或钢材端部的) shear distortion	减面率计算法 draughting calculation
	减面率梯度(拔丝的) taper draughting
剪头机 end [crop] shears	减敏感(作用) desedensitization
剪斜的 oblique	减摩材料 antifriction material
剪应力线 shear stress trajectory	减摩镀[涂]层 friction coat
减薄 thinning, burn back (炉衬的), reduction ◇ 电解～法 electrothinning	减摩合金 antifriction alloy [metal]
	减摩剂 antifriction
减薄金属的型芯 【铸】metal saver	减摩金属 antifriction metal
减薄拉延模 【压】ironing die	减摩金属用锌基合金(4Al, 1Cu, 微量 Mg, 余量 Zn) zinc alloy for antifriction metal (ZAM)
减产 loss of yield	
减尘剂 dust palliative	
减低 reducing, cut, lowering	减摩青铜 journal bronze
减法器 subtracter, subtractor ◇ 十进制 ～ decade subtracter	减摩润滑脂 antifriction grease
	减摩元件 antifriction element
减风 slow wind, 【铁】checking, pulling the wind, reduced wind ◇ 大量～ fanning	减摩制品 antifriction composition
	减摩轴承 antifriction bearing
减风操作 【铁】reducing blast operation	减摩铸造青铜学会(美国) Cast Bronze Bearing Institute (CBBI)
减幅波 damped [decadent, decaying] wave	
	减频效应 bathochromic effect
减幅因数 damping factor	减轻 lighten, mitigation, relief, slacking, abatement
减光器 dimmer, diminisher	
减耗 comminution	减去 subtraction, deduction
减活化(作用)(常指去氧) deactivation	减热 heat reduction, abstracted heat
减活化剂 deactivator	减弱 weaking, weakening, slacking, abate

(ment), damp
减弱相（矿热炉生产中的） dead phase
减少 reducing, reduction, decreasing, lessening, abate(ment), diminution ◇ 按（某种）比例～[缩小] scale down
减少活动性 immobilization
减声 noise reduction
减湿剂 dehumidizer
减湿器 dehumidifier, dehumidizer
减湿(作用) dehumidifying
减数 subtractor
减水(外加)剂（混凝土用） water-reducing admixture [agent]
减速 deceleration, retard, speed-down, slow down, slow-up, moderate
减速比 reduction ratio [rate, factor], 【理】moderating ratio
减速齿轮[装置] reducing [reduction] gear, speed reducer gear ◇ 带～的电动机（back) geared motor
减速电动机 speed reducing motor ◇ 周期～ cyclo-reduction motor
减速机 reducer, reducor, reducing unit, speed-reduction unit ◇ 带飞轮的～ flywheel assisted reduction gear unit, flywheel reduction gear, 两段～*, 球面蜗轮～ cone-worm unit, 蜗轮～*, 小型～ packaged reducer, 行星式～*, 正齿轮～*
减速机构 speed-reducing mechanism, reducing gear
减速剂 moderating material, moderator, retarder
减速计 decelerometer
减速阶段 deceleration phase
减速力[转]矩 retarding torque
减速流变 decelerating flow
减速率 【机】reduction rate
减速器 decelerator, reducing [reduction] gear, gearbox (GBX), reducor, speed reducer (gear)
减速系数 【理】moderating ratio

减速箱 gear [reduction] box, reducer casing
减速效应 retardation effect
减速星轮 retarding sprocket
减速行程 slowing-down path
减速运输机 decelerating conveyer
减损 disable
减缩 reducing, shrink ◇ 名义截面～比*
减缩量[率] decrement
减缩曲线 reduced curve
减退 decay, decrease
减小 decrease, downsize, abate, diminution, lessening
减压 decompression, pressure reducing [relief], reduced pressure
减压带 reducing zone
减压阀 pressure reducer, pressure reducing [relief] valve, compression release valve, reducing valve, reducing regulator（煤气的）
减压孔 pressure relief vent
减压门 release cock
减压器 (pressure) reducer, reductor
减压容器 pressure reducing vessel
减压闪馏装置 vacuum flash unit
减压水汽蒸馏法 pressure reduction steam distillation
减压碳酸盐溶液脱硫法 【焦】vacuum carbonate process
减压(洗油)脱苯设备 vacuum debenzolizing plant
减压蒸馏 reduced-pressure distillation
减压装置 pressure release device, decompressor
减音材料 sound absorber
减音器 sound damper
减载拱 【建】relieving arch
减震 shock absorbing, damp(ing), amortization
减震衬垫 damping washer
减震垫 shock pad ◇ 基础～*
减震辊 snubber roll

减震能力 damping [shock-absorbing, cushioning] capacity, buffering power
减震能力试验 damping capacity test
减震器 shock damper [insulator, reducer], buffer, bumper, (shock) absorber, dashpot, snubber, vibration damper, shock eliminator (液压系统的) ◇ 空气～ air bumper, 平衡～ balancing bumper
减震器式定时器 dashpot-type timer
减震试验 damping capacity test
减震弹簧 damping spring
减震托辊 impact idler
减震装置 damping [shock-absorbing] device
减振钢板 anti-vibrational sheet
减至最少 minimizing
减重 weight reduction, saving in weight
减重孔(零件的) lightening hole
减阻 drag reduction, anti-drag
鉴别 discrimination, distinguish
鉴别培养基 differential medium
鉴别器 discriminator
鉴定 appraisal, assay, assessment
鉴定费用 appraisal costs
鉴定器 assessor ◇ 氩离子化～
鉴定试验 approval test, qualification test (质量的)
鉴定细菌学 determinative bacteriolog
鉴定证明书 assay certificate, surveyor's report
鉴频电路 frequency discriminating circuit
鉴频管 discriminator tube
鉴频器 frequency detector [discriminator], discriminator
鉴相器 phase detector [discriminator], discriminator
贱金属 base metal
贱金属化合物 base metal compound
见解 view, opinion, idea, understanding
键 key, gad, 【化】bond, binding, link ◇ 马尔可夫～(概率模型) Markov chain, 黏结[连接]～ bonding bridge

键柄 catch [clasp] handle
键槽 key bed [seat], keyway, slot groove
键槽面 splined surface
键长(度) 【化】bond length [distance]
键传动 key driver
键杆 latch rod
键轨函数 bond(ing) orbital
键轨函数重叠 overlap of bonding orbitals
键合 bonding, linkage, linking
键合强度 cohesive strength
键合热 heat of linkage
键合退化机理 bond degradation mechanisms
键角 【化】bond angle
键校对 【计】key verify
键接施工缝 keyed construction joint
键接组合梁 keyed compound beam
键矩 【化】bond [binding] moment
键控电路 keying circuit
键控器 keyer, manipulator
键类型 【化】form of binding
键联 【化】binding
键螺栓 key bolt
键能 【化】bond energy
键盘 keyboard (KB), key panel
键盘打印机 keyboard printer (KBPr.)
键盘封锁 【计】keyboard lockout
键盘询问 【计】keyboard inquiry
键起子 key driver
键销子 key pin, stud
键轴衬 keyed bush
箭头标志方向 arrow side
箭头(号) arrow ◇ 图中标尺寸的～ crowfoot
箭头形断口(钢脆断的) chevrons
健康保护 health protection
健康普查 【环】health measurement
剑钢 cutlery steel
剑桥电阻高温计 Cambridge pyrometer
渐变 gradation (change), glide
渐变断面型材 tapered section
渐变加载 tapered loading

渐加荷载　gradually applied load
渐进传动　progressive transmission
渐进传动装置(换辊定心用)　inching drive device
渐进电动机　inching motor
渐进断裂　progressive fracture
渐进破裂　progressive failure
渐进延伸　progress elongation
渐近法　【数】approximation method,【理】iteration method
渐近居里点　asymptotic Curie point
渐近曲线　asymptotic curve
渐近线　【数】asymptote
渐开线　【数】involute,evolute
渐开线齿轮　involute gear
渐屈线　evolute
渐缩管　reducing pipe, pipe reducer
渐增　gather
渐增时间　upslope time
溅　spatter, splash
溅疤　splash scale(金属的),【钢】patch scab
溅疤[麻]面(钢锭的)　shelliness, spilliness
溅出溶液　spillage solution
溅出物　spatters
溅底(钢锭的)　curtaining, bottom splash
溅点　flash
溅镀(金属)　sputtering
溅模　【钢】curtaining
溅沫　splatter, splash
溅皮(钢锭的)　shell
溅散　spurting
溅射　sputter(ing) ◇ 阴极~cathode sputtering,致密金属氧化膜~处理*
溅射沉积　sputter(ing) deposition
溅射沉积障碍覆盖层　sputter deposited barrier coating
溅射覆盖层　sputtered coating
溅射扩散障碍覆盖层　sputter diffusion barrier coating
溅射膜　sputtered film

溅射系统　sputtering system
溅射障碍层　sputtered barrier
溅蚀　sputter
溅污　spatter
溅油环　splash ring
溅油润滑　oil-splash lubrication
溅渣　slag splashing, slag ejeculation(转炉的)
溅渣层　slag splashing layer
溅渣护炉　【钢】slag-splashing for protection of converter ◇ 转炉~技术*
建厂周期　construction period
建立　build, set up, establish, erection, install
建立时间　rise time
建立同步交换　【电】hand shaking
建模　【数】modelling
建设[建造]　construction (constr.) ◇ 就地~on-site construction,在~中 under construction (u.c., u/c)
建设费用　【企】cost of construction, establishment charges
建设期利息　interest during construction
建设周期　construction [building] period
建议流程　proposed flowsheet
建造者　constructer, builder
建造质量　construction quality
建筑　architecture, building (bldg.)
建筑薄板[钢板]　building sheet
建筑布局　architectural composition
建筑材料　construction(al) [building] material
建筑采光　architectural lighting
建筑场地　building [builder's] yard
建筑单元　building unit
建筑地址　building site
建筑法规　building code [law]
建筑钢　building iron, structural steel
建筑钢材　building steel
建筑钢筋　fixture wire
建筑工程学　construction [architectural] engineering

建筑工地	construction site, building ground
建筑工人	build labourer
建筑工业	construction industry
建筑规程	building regulation
建筑规范	building code [standards]
建筑黄铜(58Cu,39Zn,3Pb)	architectural brass
建筑结构焊接	structural welding
建筑框架	building frame
建筑立面图	elevation of a building
建筑面积	building area, floor area of building, area of structure
建筑青铜(57Cu,40Zn,3Pb)	architectural bronze
建筑设备	building equipment
建筑设计	building [architectural] design
建筑施工	building operation
建筑施工图	architectural working drawing
建筑条例	building code [bylaws, ordinance]
建筑透视图	architectural perspective
建筑图	construction [architectural] drawing
建筑物	building (bldg.), construction (constr.)
建筑物冬季施工	winter building construction
建筑物跨度	building span
建筑细节	construction details
建筑线	building line
建筑型钢	structural shape
建筑型钢轧机机座	structural stand
建筑学	architecture
建筑学的	architectural (arch.)
建筑业	construction industry
建筑用钢	constructional steel
建筑用具	building implement [appliance]
建筑用砖	building brick
建筑造价[费用]	fabricating [housing, construction] cost
建筑照明	architectural lighting
僵烧的	dead burnt
姜黄试纸	curcuma (test) paper, turmeric paper
浆化	pulp ◇二次[再]~ repulping
浆化车间	slurrying plant
浆化阶段	【色】pulping stage
浆料	pulp
浆砌	grouting
浆式进料	slurry feeding
浆体铸造法[工艺]	slurry casting process
浆状	slurry form, paste
浆状运输	handling in slurry form
浆状炸药爆炸成形	liquid-charge forming
桨架	row-lock
桨轮式提升机	paddle wheel elevator
桨式混合机	compulsory mixer ◇直臂~*
桨式混捏机	paddle-type kneading machine
桨叶	paddle
桨叶耙	rake with blade
桨叶式混合机	【团】paddle (blade type) mixer
桨叶式搅拌机	paddle stirrer, blade [arm, compulsory] mixer, paddle wheel agitator ◇双动~*
桨叶式搅拌器	paddle agitator
奖金	money award, premium
奖励	award, reward
奖励费	【企】incentive payment
降尘管	main duct, windmain (总降尘管)
降尘管系统	main waste-gas system
降尘喷嘴	dust suppression spray
降尘器	dust-settling tank
降尘室	dedusting [dust] chamber, drop out chamber, dust-settling compartment
降尘总管	【团】collecting main
降低	reducing, reduction, decreasing, depression, diminution, fall, lowering, 【半】build down
降低地下水位	lowering of ground water

降焦 jiang—jiao

level ◇ 井点～法 well-point method
降低含量 impoverish
降低金损失 reduction in gold loss
降低水位的井点系统 well-point de-watering system
降级 degradation, degrading, downgrade
降解 degradation
降落 falling, descend, drop-down,【半】build down
降落速度 falling velocity
降落速率 falling rate
降坡 descending grade
降气管 【冶】down-take, downcomer
降速 speed-down
降速蒸发 falling rate evaporation
降碳 【钢】carbon drop, fall of temperature ◇ 停止～*, 尤恰蒂厄斯铁水～法*
降碳速度 rate of carbon drop
降温 reduced temperature, fall of temperature ◇ 桶中～ladle chill
降温工作服 man-cooling jacket
降温速率 detemperature rate
降温转炉(吹炼铜镍锍的) cooling converter
降下 falling away ◇ 大量～物 shower
降压 depressurization, pressure relief, reduction voltage ◇ 两段式～泵*
降压变压器 reduction [step-down] transformer, economizer
降压电阻(器) voltage dropping resistor
降压启动器 reduced voltage starter
降压器 【电】negative booster
降压试验 【电】drop test
降压特性发电机 dropping voltage generator, dropping-characteristic generator [machine]
降雨量 rainfall (volume)
降至最小 minimizing
焦斑 focal spot [area]
焦斑缩小管 reduced focal-spot tube
焦梧 (同"焦炭")
焦桔酸[酚]{(HO)$_3$C$_6$H$_3$} pyrogallol, py-rogallic acid
焦比 coke rate [ratio],【铁】coke-to-metal ratio ◇ 入炉～*, 折算[校正]～*, 综合～*
焦饼 【焦】coke button [mass] ◇ 坩埚～*
焦饼中心缝 【焦】parting
焦饼中心裂缝 【焦】centre cleavage
焦饼中心线[中心焦油层] tar seam
焦饼焖炉 soaking of charge
焦仓 【铁】coke bin
焦侧 【焦】coke end [side]
焦床 coke bed
焦点 focal point, focal spot, focus (复数 foci) ◇ 在～上的 focal
焦点尺寸调节 control of focus size
焦点的 focal
焦点碰撞 focussed collision
焦点至底[软]片距离 focus to film distance
焦丁 nut coke, coke nut
焦恩松应变仪 CEJ strain gauge
焦耳定律 【理】Joule's law
焦耳能 Joule energy
焦耳热 Joule heat [energy]
焦耳热加热 Joule heating
焦耳热区域熔炼 Joule heat zone-melting
焦耳汤姆森膨胀 Joule-Thomson expansion
焦耳效应 Joule effect
焦矾 burnt [dried] alum
焦钒酸盐 divanadate
焦粉 pulverized coke, coke breeze [fines], fine coke dust, ground coke (细磨的) ◇ 筛除～ breeze extraction, 筛下～ coke screenings, 外裹～的 coke-coated, 细碎～*
焦粉槽 coke breeze bin
焦粉后加 late coke addition
焦粉灰浆(炉缸焦结用) blacking
焦(花)头 【焦】cauliflower
焦化 coking, carbonizing, carbonisation,

carbonization, chark(ing), cokemaking ◇ 液态~ fluid coking

焦化厂[车间] coke plant
焦化过程 coking process
焦化机理 mechanism of coking
焦化气体 coking gas
焦化室 coking chamber
焦化性 cokability
焦化作用 carbonification, carbonisation, carbonization
焦结团块 coke briquette
焦距 focal distance [length], focus ◇ 等效~ equivalent focal length, 平均~ midfocal length, 同~的 parfocal
焦块 lump coke
焦磷酸 pyrophosphoric acid
焦磷酸高铈 {CeP$_2$O$_7$} cerium pyrophosphate
焦磷酸氢镧 {LaHP$_2$O$_7$} lanthanum hydropyrophosphate
焦磷酸氢钐 {SmHP$_2$O$_7$} samaric hydropyrophosphate
焦磷酸氢盐 hydropyrophosphate
焦磷酸氢钇 yttrium hydropyrophosphate
焦磷酸铈 {Ce$_4$(P$_2$O$_7$)$_3$} cerous pyrophosphate
焦磷酸四乙酯 tetraethylpyrophosphate
焦磷酸钍 thorium pyrophosphate
焦磷酸辛基酯 octyl pyrophosphate
焦磷酸盐 pyrophosphate
焦磷酸乙四酯 TEPP (tetraethylpyrophosphate)
焦磷酸酯 {[RO(HO)PO]$_2$O} pyrophosphoric ester, pyrophosphate
焦硫酸 {H$_2$S$_2$O$_7$} pyrosulfuric acid
焦硫酸盐 {M$_2$S$_2$O$_7$} pyrosulphate, disulfate, disulphate
焦硫酸盐熔化 pyrosulphate fusion
焦炉 coke oven [furnace], coker(y), coking still, battery ◇ 奥托式~ Otto oven, 侧喷(煤气)~ gunflue battery, 大容积~*, 捣固~ stamp-charging coke oven, 低压差式~ low-differential oven, 迪迪尔式~ Didier coke oven, 底部加热的~ sole heated oven, (废气)循环~ recirculation coke oven, 复热式~*, 活动墙~ movable wall coke oven, 交错蓄热式~ cross-regenerative oven, 跨顶火道式~ crossover oven, 两分式~*, 塞美-索威式~ Semet-Solvay oven, 水平式~ slot-type oven, 威尔浦式~ Wilputte oven, 无回收~ non-recovery coke oven, 下喷式~*, 蓄热~*, 直立火道式~ vertical-flue oven
焦炉布置 layout of battery
焦炉废水 coke oven effluent
焦炉-高炉混合煤气 mixed coke-oven and blast-furnace gas, combination of coke-oven and blast-furnace gas
焦炉工 coke oven operator
焦炉机械联锁装置 interlocking of coke oven machines ◇ 横贯炉组的~*
焦炉焦炭 coke oven coke
焦炉炉顶 battery top
焦炉炉门(coke) oven door
焦炉煤气 【焦】coke oven gas (COG), C-gas ◇ 单一的~ straight coke oven gas, 烧~回转窑【团】coke oven gas-fired rotary kiln, 未脱硫的~ unpurified gas
焦炉煤气闪焰 coke oven gas flare
焦炉煤气压缩站 C.O.G. compress station
焦炉煤气组分 coke oven gas constituent
焦炉气催化重整 【焦】catalytic reforming of coke oven gas
焦炉生产率 coker specific capacity
焦炉碳化室顶面砖 paving on battery top
焦炉型高炉(用焦煤在高炉上部变成焦炭) ferric blast furnace
焦炉用煤 oven coal
焦炉砖 【耐】coke oven shape
焦炉组 coke oven battery
焦炉组烘炉 heating-up of coke oven battery

焦煤　coking [crozzling] coal
焦末　coke braize [breeze,dross], peacoke
焦木素　pyroxylin(e)
焦铌酸盐　pyroniobate
焦批　charge coke, coke (per) charge
焦批重　coke charge weight
焦散线　【理】caustic curve
焦砂层　【铸】sand skin
焦砷酸　pyroarsenic acid
焦深　depth of focus
焦台　【焦】(coke) wharf
焦台衬砖　wharf brickwork
焦台放焦闸　coke wharf gate
焦台排水　【焦】wharf draining
焦(炭)　coke, charred coal ◇ 低灰分~ high carbon coke, 低强~ soft [weak] coke, 蜂窝~ beehive coke, 高灰分~ high ash coke, 高硫~ high sulphur coke, 过滤用~ filter coke, 过筛~ screened [sized] coke, 加热[烘干]用~ heating coke, 接力[补]~ booster coke, 块度均匀~ closely graded coke, 热压~ form coke, 水煤气用~ water-gas coke, 天然~ dandered coal, 未煅烧~ uncalcined coke, 无灰~ ash-free coke, 无氢~ hydrogen-free coke, 小块[蛋级]~ egg coke, 冶金~*, 液态~ fluid coke, 由煤变~的转化 coal-to-coke conversion, 铸造用~ foundery coke
焦炭仓　coke bunker [bin]
焦炭层　coke layer
焦炭产率　coke yield
焦炭敞炉　【色】devil
焦炭称量漏斗　coke-weighing hopper
焦炭处理　coke handling
焦炭床层　coke bed
焦炭的碳　coke carbon
焦炭反应性[能力]　coke reactivity
焦炭分析　coke analysis
焦炭粉　powdered coke
焦炭粉化　coke degradation
焦炭粉化机理　coke degradation mechanism

焦炭负荷　ore/coke (O/C), burden (ratio), ratio of ore-to-coke
焦炭负荷过重　overburden(ing)
焦炭高炉　coke blast-furnace
焦炭供应槽　big coke bin
焦炭含氢量波动　coke hydrogen fluctuation
焦炭含碳量　coke carbon
焦炭化学成分　coke analysis
焦炭还原　coke reduction
焦炭灰分　coke ash
焦炭孔隙率　coke porosity
焦炭块　lump coke ◇ 小~ coke nuts
焦炭块度减小　degradation of coke
焦炭料筐　coke basket
焦炭料批　【铁】coke charge
焦炭落下强度　coke shatter strength
焦炭煤气化　coke gasification
焦炭末　coke fines
焦炭破块机　coke broker
焦炭破碎　coke crushing
焦炭破碎辊　coke cutting wheel
焦炭气化　coke gasification
焦炭气孔结构图象定量分析系统　image quantitative analyzing system for coke pore texture
焦炭燃料　coke fuel
焦炭燃烧速度　coke velocity
焦炭燃烧性　coke combustibility
焦炭熔渣　coke slag
焦炭筛出物　undersize coke
焦炭筛(分机)　coke screen, coke-screening arrangement
焦炭生铁　coke iron, coke pig (iron)
焦炭试验转鼓　drum of coke test
焦炭石墨复合物　coke/graphite composite
焦炭水分核子测定仪　nuclear coke moisture gauge
焦炭碎块　coke cutting
焦炭填充塔　coke(-packed) tower
焦炭脱硫　desulphurization of coke
焦炭稳定性　coke stability factor

焦炭洗涤器　coke scrubber
焦炭细磨　coke grinding
焦炭消耗　coke consumption
焦炭消火机　（同"熄焦机"）
焦炭循环区渣　【铁】raceway slag
焦炭研磨　coke grinding
焦炭预热器　coke preheater
焦炭运输机　coke conveyer
焦炭运输皮带　coke supply belt
焦炭渣垫层　bed of coke breeze
焦炭整粒　coke grain adjustment
焦炭置换比　【铁】coke replacement ratio
焦炭质炉瘤　coke-tree
焦炭中氢含量的波动　coke hydrogen fluctuation
焦炭柱　coke column
焦炭贮仓[贮存场]　coke storage
焦炭抓斗　coke bucket
焦炭砖　coalite
焦炭装料系统　coke charging system
焦糖　caramel
焦锑酸　pyroantimonic acid
焦锑酸盐　pyroantimonate
焦头　（同"焦花头"）
焦屑　coke braize [breeze, dross, screenings], fine coke, gleeds, 【焦】peacoke
焦屑回收料斗　（同"碎焦回收漏斗"）
焦型　coke type ◇ 格雷-金~"
焦性煤　coking [cindery] coal ◇ 非~ dead coal
焦亚磷酸{$H_4P_2O_5$}　pyrophosphorous acid
焦亚磷酸盐[酯]{$M_4P_2O_5$}　pyrophosphite
焦亚砷酸　pyroarsenous acid
焦亚砷酸盐　pyroarsenite
焦油　(coke) tar, tar oil, goudron ◇ 粗~ 碱类【焦】crude tar bases, 粗黑~ black jack, 浸~砖", 矿质~ mineral tar, 喷~ 操作法", 涂~ tarring, 脱水~ dehydrated tar
焦油白云石　tarred dolomite
焦油白云石打结　tar-dolomite rammming
焦油白云石打结[捣结]（混合）料　tar-dolomite rammed mixture, tar-dolomite stamping
焦油白云石混合物　tar-dolomite mix
焦油白云石料　tar-dolomite material ◇ 稳定的~ tar-stabilized dolomite material
焦油白云石炉衬　tar-dolomite lining
焦油白云石泥料　tar-dolomite mass
焦油白云石砖　tar-dolomite brick, tar (red) dolomite block ◇ 不烧~"
焦油残渣　tarry residue
焦油沉积　tar deposit
焦油分离器　tar separator [precipitator]
焦油环氧树脂涂料　tar epoxy paint(ing)
焦油混凝土　bitumen concrete
焦油碱类　【焦】tar bases
焦油结合白云石　tar-bonded dolomite
焦油结合白云石镁砖　tar-bonded dolomite-magnesite brick
焦油结合层　tar-bonded zone
焦油结合捣固混合碱性耐火材料　tar bearing basic ramming mix
焦油结合镁砂　tar-bonded magnesite
焦油结合镁质耐火材料　tar-bonded magnesite refractory
焦油结合砖　tar-bonded brick
焦油沥青　tar pitch [asphalt] ◇ 浸~炉衬 tar-impregnated lining
焦油镁砂　tarred magnesite
焦油镁砖　tar magnesite brick
焦油耐火泥料　tar-refractory mass
焦油黏结剂　tar bond
焦油黏结球团　tar-bonded pellet
焦油酸　tar acid
焦油刷　tar swab
焦油涂抹装置　tar swab
焦油脱除器　【焦】detarrer
焦油雾　【焦】tar fog [mist]
焦油吸收率　degree of tar absorption
焦油毡　tar felt (t.f.)
焦油状物料　tarry material
焦渣混凝土　breeze concrete

焦胶 jiao

焦值　coking value, coke number
胶　glue, gum ◇ 贴[上,涂(橡)]～rubberize, rubberizing
胶硅锰矿　penwithite
胶合　glue,【机】gall(ing)(齿轮的)
胶合板　plywood, laminated [veneer] wood ◇ 夹金属～plymetal, 石棉夹心～asbestos-veneer plywood, 装饰用镶铝～Plymax
胶合传动皮带　balata belt
胶合剂　cement, cemedin
胶合接头　cemented joint
胶合金属板　blymetal
胶合铺料　mastic ◇ 沥青－石棉～*
胶化剂　gelatining [gelling] agent
胶化作用　gelling action
胶结(材料)　cement
胶结(产)物　adglutinate
胶结的　cemented ◇ 以黏土～clay-bonded
胶结剂　cementing [plastering] agent
胶结石英岩　cemented quartzite
胶结填料糊　glue gasket paste
胶结性加入物　【耐】adhesive admixture
胶结指数　cementation index
胶卷(暗)盒　(film) cassette
胶粒　idiozome, idiosome, colloidal particles, micell(a)e
胶磷铝矿{3Ca(Ti, Zr)$_2$O$_5$·Al$_2$TiO$_5$} uholigite
胶铝矿　kliachite, alunogel
胶棉　collodion
胶棉复型(制备)法　collodion replica
胶棉溶液　collodion solution
胶木　bakelite, micarta, ebonite
胶木衬垫　bakelite lining
胶木台[架]　bakelite skid
胶囊　micell(a)e, cachet
胶囊结构　micellar structure
胶泥　daub, mastic cement,【建】puddle,【耐】mortar ◇ 沥青～asphalt grout
胶泥衬里的　mastic-lined

胶泥汞合金(33.3Sn, 33.3Bi, 余量 Hg)　plaster amalgam
胶黏糊　gluing paste
胶黏剂　adhesion agent, adhesives, mastic (gum)
胶黏计　adhesivemeter
胶黏接缝　cement joint
胶黏水泥　mastic (cement)
胶黏铁矿　ehrenwerthite
胶黏性　adhesiveness, glueyness
胶镍硅铈钛矿　hibinite
胶凝　gelate, gelatinize, jellification
胶凝剂　gelatin(iz)ing agent
胶凝物质　gelatinous substance
胶凝作用　gelatification, gelatination, gelatinization, gelation
胶皮管　gum hose
胶片　(摄影用)film ◇ 布雷德利－杰伊～装入法*, 单面涂乳胶[感光药品]的～*, 高速感光无屏蔽～fast no-screen film, 夹层～sandwich film, 经冲洗的～processed film, 慢速～(感光胶片) slower film, 乳胶层可剥～stripping film, 未曝光～raw film
胶片(暗)盒　film cassette [holder]
胶片被 X 射线感光　film darkening by X-rays
胶片测量　film measurement
胶片测量尺　film measuring rule
胶片衬度[反差性]　film contrast
胶片冲洗　film rinsing
胶片处理[加工]溶液　processing solution
胶片感光[曝光]　exposure of film
胶片基底　base of film
胶片剂量计　film meter [packet, badge], dosifilm
胶片均质[连续]性　continuity of film
胶片乳胶　film emulsion
胶片收缩　film shrinkage
胶片速度[感速,感光速率]　film speed
胶片双面感光乳剂层[双面涂感光乳剂]　double coating of film

| 胶片特性曲线 | characteristic curve of (photographic) film
| 胶片与屏幕接触 | film screen contact
| 胶片照相记录 | photographic film record
| 胶片自动处理装置 | automatic film-processing unit
| 胶圈托辊 | rubber-disc idler
| 胶溶剂 | peptizing agent, peptizer
| 胶乳 | latex (复数 latices)
| 胶水 | glue(water), gum water
| 胶态 | colloid, colloidal state
| 胶态材料 | colloid
| 胶态沉淀 | colloidal precipitate
| 胶态粉末 | colloidal powder
| 胶态甘汞 | calomelol
| 胶态汞 | colloidal mercury, hygrol
| 胶态硅石 | colloidal silica
| 胶态金 | colloidal gold, aurosol
| 胶态金属 | colloidal metal
| 胶态离子细胞膜 | micell(a)e
| 胶态磷酸盐沉淀 | gelatinous phosphate precipitate
| 胶态[状]溶液 | colloidal solution
| 胶态物系 | colloid(al) system
| 胶态硒 | seleniol
| 胶态絮状沉淀物 | colloidal flocculent precipitate
| 胶态氧化硅 | colloidal silica, cabosil
| 胶态氧化铝 | colloidal alumina
| 胶态质点 | colloidal particles
| 胶态羰基法粉末 | colloidal carbonyl powder
| 胶钛矿 | doelterite
| 胶体 | colloid, colloidal substance
| 胶体复型(品) | colloidal replica
| 胶体化学 | colloid chemistry
| 胶体混凝土 | colloidal concrete
| 胶体金 | collaurum
| 胶体矿物 | colloid mineral
| 胶体锰酸银 | armanite
| 胶体[态]磨 | colloid(al) mill
| 胶体黏土 | 【铸】colloidal clay

胶体燃料 colloidal fuel
胶体溶液 pseudo solution
胶体溶液稳定剂 deflocculant
胶体渗透压 colloid-osmotic pressure, oncotic pressure
胶体石墨(拔丝用) aquadag, colloidal graphite, oildag
胶体石墨罐 aquadag pot
胶体[态]碳 colloidal carbon
胶体添加剂 colloidal additive
胶体脱水 dehydration of colloid
胶体微粒 colloidal particles
胶体物质 colloidal material
胶体性质 colloidal property [nature]
胶铁矿 siderogel
胶硒雄黄 jeromite
胶纤锌矿 brunvkiyr
胶须藻属 Rivularia
胶压纸板 paprey
胶纸板 pertinax, paxolin, turbonit ◇ 米卡塔～Micarta
胶质 colloid(matter), gelatinoid
胶质层 【焦】plastic zone
胶质衬里 gum lining
胶质(体) colloidal matter
胶状高岭土{$3Al_2O_3 \cdot SiO_2 \cdot nH_2O$} schroetterite
胶状金反应 colloidal gold reaction
胶状硫 sulphidal
胶状氢氧化物 gelatinous hydroxide
胶状物质 gelatinoid
交变冲击 alternating impact
交变冲击试验机 alternating impact machine
交变磁场 alternating field
交变磁化(作用) alternating [reversal] magnetization
交变磁通 alternating flux
交变电动势 alternating e.m.f. (electromotive force)
交变反复应力 alternating repetition of stress

交变负载　alternating [reversal] load
交变加载　alternate stressing
交变力　alternating force
交变扭转疲劳试验　alternating torsion fatigue test
交变扭转疲劳试验机　fatigue testing machine for alternating torsion
交变频率发生器　cycle generator
交变缺口弯曲试验　alternating notch bending test
交变受力材料　cycled material
交变弯曲应力疲劳极限　alternating bending stress fatigue limit
交变应变　alternating strain
交变应力　alternating stress ◇ 最低~*
交变应力可变分量　variable component of stress
交变应力强度　【压】resistance to alternative stresses, alternating stress intensity
交变应力试验　alternate stress test
交变应力(振幅)-循环次数关系曲线 (同"S-N曲线")
交变载荷　alternating [cyclic] load
交变值　fluent
交变周期　period of alternation
交叉　crossing, intercept, intersect(ion), transposition(线路的)
交叉编译程序　cross compiler
交叉标线　cross hair
交叉并联操作(热风炉的)　staggered parallel operation
交叉并联送风　staggered parallel blowing
交叉场　【理】cross(ed) field
交叉场质谱仪　Bleakney mass spectrometer
交叉磁场电焊发电机　cross field welding generator
交叉磁场发电机　cross field machine
交叉垛放　cross piling
交叉方向　cross direction
交叉缝砌筑　herringbone masonry
交叉缝砌砖　herringbone brickwork

交叉杆　cross member
交叉拱　【建】groyne, groin
交叉光栅　cross grating
交叉焊接　welding crosswise
交叉(焊丝)焊接电焊机　cross-wire welder
交叉焊条式压薄点焊　mash welding
交(叉)滑移　cross slip ◇ 共轭滑移系~*, 合金的~受阻, 螺型位错~*, 双重~double cross-slip
交叉滑移带　intersecting slip bands
交叉滑移机理　cross slip mechanism
交叉滑移激活能　activation energy for cross-slip
交叉滑移系统　cross slip system
交叉滑移线　cross slip line
交叉汇编程序　【计】cross assembler
交叉火力　cross fire
交叉间隙　cross gap
交叉检验[查]　cross-checking
交叉连接　cross connection [joint(ing), linking]
交叉流　cross current, cross-flow
交叉皮带　cross [halved] belt
交叉砌合(砌砖)　【建】cross bond ◇ 丁砖与顺砖~block bond
交叉式厂房布置　cross-ward housing
交叉衰减　cross-attenuation
交叉调制　【电】cross modulation, intermodulation
交叉弯曲试验　crossbend test
交叉位错　intersecting dislocation
交叉线圈　【电】cross coil
交叉学科　interdisciplinary science [subject]
交叉右捻　right-hand ordinary lay
交叉轧制　cross [tandem] rolling ◇ 非对称~non-pair cross rolling, 异步~*
交叉轴　concurrent axes, intersecting axis
交叉左捻　【压】left-hand ordinary lay
交磁放大机　amplidyne, cross connected generator

交错(的)　interlacing, alternate, intersect, interleaving, stagger
交错点阵　【理】interleaved lattices
交错点焊　staggered spot-welding
交错断续填角焊　staggered intermittent fillet welding
交错焊　zigzag welding
交错焊缝　staggered seam
交错结构　interlaced structure
交错(排列的)铆接　zigzag riveting
交错切料机构　【压】stagger blanking mechanism
交错塞焊　staggered plug welding
交错[交叉]式风箱　alternate windbox
交错下料装置　【压】stagger blanking mechanism
交错蓄热式焦炉　cross-regenerative oven
交搭　bracing
交道叉　【运】crossing
交点　intersection point, (point of) intersection, cusp（双切线的）
交叠能带　overlapping band
交付　delivery, consignment
交付使用　commissioning
交割过程　intersection process
交互连接吊挂砖　interlocking bricks
交互[叉]捻（钢丝绳的）（同"普通捻"）
交互耦合　cross-coupling
交互生长　intergrowth
交互式控制　interactive control
交互系统　【计】interactive system
交互作用　interaction, cross-correlation
交互作用常数　interaction constant
交互作用定律　interaction law
交互作用力　interacting [interaction] force
交互作用能　interaction energy
交互作用势　interaction potential ◇ 晶格原子～*
交互作用系数　interaction coefficient
交互作用状态　interacting state
交换　exchange, interchange, swapping, commutation ◇ 建立同步～hand shaking, 可～性 exchangeability
交换场　exchange field
交换磁矩　exchange magnetic moment
交换电势[位]　exchange potential
交换反应　exchange reaction
交换缓冲　【计】exchange buffering
交换机　commutator, exchange board, switchboard, interchanger
交换机电键　rocking key
交换剂　exchanger
交换离子　exchange ion
交换力　exchange force
交换面积　exchange area
交换能　exchange energy
交换耦合强度　intensity of exchange coupling
交换平衡　exchange equilibrium
交换器　exchanger, interchanger, converter
交换时间　【计】swap time
交换树脂　exchange(r) resin
交换台　switchboard
交换吸附　exchange adsorption
交换线路　【电】switched line
交换因子　interchange factor
交换站　switching station, exchange plant
交换柱　column ◇ 下流～downstream column
交换柱流出液浓度　concentration in column effluent
交货　delivery ◇ 铁路～delivery by rail
交货尺寸（轧材的）　delivery gauge
交货长度　delivery length
交货单　【企】delivery order
交货条件　delivery specifications, terms of delivery
交货轧材的标准长度　commercial stock length
交货状态　delivery state, state as received, as-received condition, condition of delivery
交键　【化】cross link(age)
交接班　crew change

交接点　take-over point, intersection
交截割阶　intersection jog
交截曲率　cross curvature
交界面　interface
交聚接头　cluster joint
交联　【化】cross linkage [linking]
交联反应　cross-linking reaction
交联剂　cross-linking agent
交联聚苯乙烯树脂　cross-linked polystyrene resin
交联聚合物　cross-linked polymer
交连硅可控整流器　cross connected thyristor
交链　interlinkage
交梁结构　(同"主次梁式结构")
交流　exchange, swap(ping), interflow, interchange, alternating current (电流)
交流变频调速　AC frequency modulation for motor speed regulation
交流标准电动机　AC-norm-motor
交流擦除　【计】ac erasing
交流超高功率电弧炉　ultra-high power AC electric arc furnace (UHP ACEAF)
交流磁化电流　AC magnetizing current
交流磁力接触器　AC magnetic contactor
交流等离子加热　AC plasma heating
交流等离子加热系统　AC plasma heating system
交流等离子炬　AC plasma torch
交流电磁铸造　AC electromagnetic casting
交流电　alternating current (AC, ac)
交流电动机　AC motor
交流电动机直流发电机变流机组　motor-generator set
交流电焊机　A.C. welder
交流电弧　alternating current arc ◇非电容式～源*
交流电弧炉　AC electric arc furnace (ACEAF)
交流电力网　alternating current mains
交流电炉　alternating current furnace
交流电路　alternating current circuit
交流电桥　alternating current bridge
交流电压　alternating voltage
交流电阻　alternating current resistance
交流发电机　AC generator, alternator ◇射频～*
交流换热管道　regenerating pipe line
交流换热器　regenerator
交流换热原理　regenerative principle
交流激励电流　AC exciting current
交流开关(传动)装置　AC-switch gear
交流起磁电流　AC magnetizing current
交流清洗　【计】ac erasing
交流声　ripple, hum (noise)
交流同步器　【电】autosyn
交流无触点自整角机　telegon
交流-直流变换器　AC-to-DC converter
交替　alternation, supersede, replace, cycling, interchange
交替布置辊系　staggered rolls
交替二辊横列式线材轧机　Belgian wire mill
交替反复应力　(同"交变反复应力")
交替钢筋　alternate bar
交替还原法　alternate reduction process
交替换位[使用]　trade-off
交替浸渍试验　alternate immersion test
交替精炼法　alternate refining process
交替排列　alternating arrangement
交替养护　alternating curing
交替载荷　alternate load
交通　traffic, communication ◇大流量～heavy traffic, 禁止～closed to traffic
交通工具　communication facilities, means of transportation
交通量　traffic (amount, volume)
交通条件　traffic conditions
交通线　communication line
交通运输　traffic
交线　intersection line
交咬作用(钢丝绳的)　nip [nick] action
交易　exchange, swap(ping), 【企】business, transaction, trade

"交钥匙"工程　turn-key project
"交钥匙"工程承包合同　turn-key contract
交织(的)　interlacing, interleaving, interweaving
交织点阵　interleaved lattices
交织结构蛇纹石　interlaced serpentine
交织组织　interlaced structure
交直流电炉　double current furnace
交直流两用焊接装置　transformer-rectifier welding machine
交轴次暂态电抗　quadrature-axis subtransient reactance
交轴电路　quadrature circuit
浇包[浇铸桶]　(pouring, teeming, tap) ladle, pouring [ladle] pot, 【铸】casting [foundery] ladle ◇ 茶壶式～【铸】teapot ladle, 齿轮倾翻式～*, 大～bulk [bull] ladle, 底注式～bottom tap ladle, 吊运式～【钢】crane ladle, 短嘴～top-pour ladle, 普通起重机式～*, 小～pony ladle
浇包把[柄]　bewel
浇包车　truck [buggy] ladle
浇包耳轴[轴颈]　ladle trunnion
浇包结瘤　ladle heel
浇包内衬修理　repatching
浇包涂料　ladle wash
浇包嘴　ladle spout [lip]
浇补(缺陷的)　casting-on
浇不满[不足]　【铸】misrun, bleeder, short-run
浇槽(金属浇槽)　【铸】pouring slot
浇道　【钢】gate runner(亦称"汤道"), 【冶】funnel, running channel, 【铸】runner (pipe, gate), geat, git ◇ 补充～【铸】feeder, 横～【铸】cross gate
浇道修理　【铸】runner makeup
浇钢　【钢】teeming
浇钢水口　pouring nozzle
浇钢水口和塞棒装置　pouring nozzle and stopper rod mechanism
浇钢砖　firebrick for teeming

浇灌　【建】pour
浇灌混凝土　【建】cast concrete
浇灌金属(握绳器用)　capping metal
浇灌孔(混凝土的)　pouring slot
浇灌炉顶　【冶】castable roof
浇焊　flow welding (FLOW), flow soldering
浇合　【铸】draining, merge
浇合的　cast-in
浇后掘松　【铸】slaking
浇口　runner (gate, opening), (pouring) gate, sprue (opening), 【铸】down-spout, geat, git ◇ 笔杆～pencil gate, 扁平～flat gate, 补缩～feeding gate, 侧阶梯(多层)～side step gate, 垂直～【钢】tedge, 唇形～lip feeder, connor gate, 带撇渣暗冒口的～riser gate, 挡渣～gate strainer, 倒牛角状～reverse horn gate, 底(注式)～bottom gate, 鹅颈式～swan-neck runner, 分叉～*, 分流[叉形]～*, 分枝状[分支]～*, 缝隙[压边]～connor gate, 横～cross gate, 可缩～collapsible sprue, 离心集渣～wheel gate, 内～cast gate, 萨克管状～saxophone gate, 挖～铁片 gate cutter, 雨淋～*, 直接～drop gate, 铸型补助～dozzle
浇口拔塞　runner plug [stopper]
浇口棒　【铸】gate pin [stick] ◇ 水冷～water-cooled stopper
浇口杯　【铸】sprue cup, (flood) basin, funnel, pouring cup [basin], runner bush, well gate, riser
浇口布置法　【铸】heading
浇口材料　runner material
浇口残铁　【铸】runner scrap, sprue-and-runner scrap
浇口尺寸　runner size
浇口端　【铸】gate end
浇口管　【铸】runner pipe
浇口技术　technique of gating
浇口金属爆音　【铸】runner shot
浇口滤网[滤渣器]　filter core

浇 jiao

浇口滤渣芯片 gate strainer
浇口锓刀[砂刀,修平刀] runner slaker
浇口模棒 【铸】gate pin
浇口切除管[器] sprue cutter
浇口切割机 【铸】gate cutter
浇口圈 【铸】runner bush
浇口砂 【铸】runner sand ◇ 碳质~*
浇口碳块衬里 carbonblock runner lining
浇口套管[钢]runner pipe
浇口退火 mouth annealing
浇口位置 【铸】gate location
浇口(型)芯 【铸】gate [runner] core
浇口溢流 runner overflow
浇口砖 【钢】gate brick [tile] ◇ 中心~ centre brick
浇流涂镀 flow coating
浇冒口 【铸】flowoff, gating-and-risering, deadhead ◇ 打掉~ spruing, flogging, 冷除~ cold spruing, 上部无~的底铸型 close-top mould
浇冒口废料 deadhead
浇冒口清理滚筒 sprue mill
浇冒口系统 gating-and-risering, running and feeding system
浇冒口铸模 gating pattern
浇瓢 【铸】socket cup
浇钎焊 flow brazing (FLB)
浇入 pouring-in
浇砂光滑铬板 grit blasted smooth chrome plate
浇水 watering, dowse
浇桶倒罐工段 reladling station
浇桶浇铸法 【铸】ladle practice
浇涂 flow coating
浇余金属(浇包底的) 【铸】heel
浇铸 casting, pouring, tapping, founding ◇ 敞开模~ casting in open, 地面~ open (sand) casting, 杜威勒翻转~法*, 金属分段~*, 近程[距离]~ short pouring, 离心~ centre die casting, 流动性试样~ fluidity test casting, 小车~ buggy casting, 修补[整]~(缺陷) casting-on, 渣[凝]壳内~ skull casting, 渣液保护~ fluid mould casting, 直接[锭模]~*, 中间和顶层联合~*
浇铸板 【铸】moulding plate
浇铸吊车[起重车] casting [pouring(-side), teeming] crane, (bail) ladle crane
浇铸钢锭 teeming
浇铸工 caster, teemer
浇铸管口 sprue [runner] opening
浇铸机 caster ◇ 离心~*, 水平~*
浇铸口 【铸】filling opening
浇铸漏斗 trumpet bell, sprue cup
浇铸塞座孔 nozzle opening
浇铸收缩 【冶】casting shrinkage
浇铸台 pouring platform ◇ 事故~ emergency casting stand
浇(铸)桶[浇注包] (同"浇包")
浇铸涡流 ragged pouring stream
浇铸系统 running gate system ◇ 去掉~的铸件 fettled casting
浇铸小车 casting bogie
浇铸药包 cast explosive charge
浇铸轧辊 roll casting
浇注 casting, pouring, teeming, filling, founding, ladling ◇ 保护~*, 成盘~用底板*, 抽吸~ suction casting, 翻炉~ inversion casting, 连炉~*, 裂纹[缝]~ 【铸】crack pouring, 破记录~*, 瀑布[台阶]式~ cascade teeming, 气流~法*, 实验~ pilot casting, 手工~ hand ladling, 双棒~装置*, 烫模~*, 无氧化~*, 下潜~*, 直接~ direct chill casting, 自动~ automatic ladling
浇注巴比合金 cast-on white metal
浇注板 【铸】casting plate
浇注半径(连铸机的) casting radius ◇ 弧形~*
浇注槽 charging launder [spout] ◇ 中间~【冶】bakie, tundish
浇注场地 casting [pouring] floor
浇注车 pouring truck
浇注车间 pouring hall

浇注成锭 ingoting
浇注成品率 casting yield
浇注重皮 【钢】teeming [single] lap
浇注底板 【钢】casting bottom
浇注法 pouring procedure ◇ 格里芬低压~Griffin process,卡斯帕松中间罐多流~*,压力~*
浇注粉剂 【连铸】casting powder
浇注钢水分析 cast [pit] analysis
浇注高度 pour(ing) height [elevation]
浇注工 【钢】pourer, ladle stopper man
浇注(工)班 pouring gang [crew]
浇注工段 pouring station, teeming department [floor]
浇注工艺 【钢】teeming practice
浇注管 【钢】tedge, gate spool [tile]
浇注管废钢 sprue-and-runner scrap
浇注辊 casting roll
浇注过程 【冶】run
浇注焊 pour-welding
浇注混凝土 placing [depositing] concrete
浇注机 casting machine ◇ 混凝土~concrete placer
浇注间侧 【铸】pit side
浇注浆 【粉】casting slip
浇注金属与锭模的接触 cast metal/mould contact
浇注坑 pouring [teeming] pit
浇注孔 pouring hole,【钢】green hole
浇注口 sprue gate, cast tuyere,【冶】lip
浇注跨 casting [teeming] bay ◇ 预留~future teeming bay
浇注跨地面 casting bay floor
浇注跨钢包[盛钢桶]吊车 teeming bay ladle crane
浇注跨间 【钢】pouring side
浇注漏斗 sprue cup
浇注密度 poured density
浇注(耐火材)料 castable
浇注披缝 【铸】casting fin
浇注平台 casting platform, pouring [casting] stand, teeming stage

浇注钎焊 flow soldering
浇注缺陷 pouring defect
浇注勺 【铸】socket cup
浇注时间 casting [pouring] time, duration of pouring
浇注试验 pouring test
浇注速度 casting speed, teeming rate [speed]
浇注速率 casting [pouring] rate ◇ 可控[调节]~controlled pouring rate
浇注台 【钢】casting [pouring] stand, teeming table
浇注套箱(无箱浇注用) pouring jacket
浇注桶 (同"浇包")
浇注位置 pouring position
浇注温度 casting temperature, pour(ing) temperature [point] ◇ 熔融金属[铁水]~*
浇注系统 【铸】gating (system), runner (gate) system ◇ 带节流口的~choked runner system, 旋涡式~(集渣用) spinner gate
浇注线 teeming line [track]
浇注眼(底注包的) casting nozzle
浇注用耐火材料 pouring [casting-pit] refractory
浇注用钢包[盛钢桶] teeming ladle
浇注栈桥 【钢】casting bridge
浇注折叠 teeming lap
浇注中间包 pouring tundish
浇注轴承合金 cast-on white metal
浇注组 pouring crew [gang]
浇注嘴 pouring lip [nozzle]
浇注作业 【钢】pouring (pit) practice
搅拌 stirring, agitating, agitation, churning, (inter)mix, rabbling ◇ 过度~overagitation
搅拌棒 rabble, stirrer bar
搅拌焙烧炉 rabbling roaster
搅拌臂 mixing arm
搅拌槽 agitation tank [vat], agitator tank [bath], agitated bath, conditioning tank,

搅 jiao

conditioner cell ◇ 喷汽～steam jet agitator, 气升～airlift tank, 酸性浸出空气～acid pachuca
搅拌厂 batching [mixing] plant
搅拌程度 degree of agitation
搅拌槽式微生物反应器 stiired tank bioreactor
搅拌萃取器 stirring extractor
搅拌淬火 agitation quenching
搅拌(动)效应 stirring [agitation] effect
搅拌反应槽 stirred tank reactor
搅拌干燥器 agitator drier [dryer]
搅拌工序 blending procedure
搅拌混合槽 mixer-agitator tank
搅拌机 agitator, (puddle) mixer, blender, stirrer, stirring machine ◇ 臂式～arm stirrer, 沉淀～precipitating agitator, 丹佛型～Denver agitator, 电动～electrical stirrer, 多尔型～Dorr agitator, 刮板～*, 浆(叶)式～*, 立式～vertical blender, 连续～continuous mixer, 连续式小型～*, 螺旋～*, 锚式～*, 双轴～*, 圆盘～circular pan mixer, 真空～de-airing mixer, 直臂～straight-arm stirrer, 重力～gravity mixer, 转盘式～roller pan mixer
搅拌机械 rabbling machanism
搅拌桨叶 stirrer paddle [arm], stirring blade, mixing paddle [arm]
搅拌浸出 agitation [agitator] leach, leaching by agitation
搅拌浸出高压釜 agitated leaching autoclave
搅拌孔 rabbling hole
搅拌量 amount of agitation
搅拌炉 (焙烧用) rabbling furnace
搅拌耙 rabbling hoe, rake stirrer
搅拌器 agitator, stir(r)er, agitating [stirring] device, rabbler, beater, blending machine ◇ 边管提升[四周气升]～edge-lift agitator, 大型～high duty agitater, 多浆～multi-bladed stirrer, 风动～pneumatic stirrer, 间歇式～batch agitator, 浸入式～submerged agitator, 空气～air (lift) agitator, 空心～hollow stirrer, 框架式～gate (type) stirrer, 连枷状～flail stirrer, 螺条～ribbon stirrer, 密闭～closed agitator, 气升式～airlift agitator, 调整～correction agitator, 弯棒式～bent rod type stirrer, 行星式～*, 叶片式～blade type agitator, 有罩～cage-contained stirrer, agitator with shroud, 蒸汽喷射～steam jet agitator, 中管提升[中央气升]～central lift agitator, 锥底气体弥散～*
搅拌枪 【钢】stirring lance
搅拌强度 amount of agitation
搅拌[搅动]时间 time [duration] of agitation
搅拌室 【建】mixing section
搅拌送料器 agitator conveyer ◇ 搅动床～*
搅拌速度 rate of agitation
搅拌条件 stirring condition
搅拌筒 churn
搅拌卧式高压釜 agitated horizontal autoclave
搅拌系统 pugmill system
搅拌圆盘真空过滤机 Agidisc filter
搅拌质量 quality of agitation
搅拌铸造 stirring casting
搅拌装置 agitating device, stirring device [apparatus] ◇ 带～的汽车 agitator truck
搅拌作用 stirring action
搅棒 stirrer, stirring rod
搅打(机) beetle
搅动 agitation, stirring
搅动臂 agitator arm
搅动冲洗 agitated rinse
搅动床 vibrated bed
搅动床反应器 stirred-bed reactor
搅动床搅拌送料器 stirred-bed agitator-conveyer
搅动床设备 stirred-bed plant

搅动结晶器　agitated crystallizer
搅动流化床反应器　agitated fluid bed reactor
搅动流化床氢氟化反应器　agitated fluid bed hydrofluorination reactor
搅动黏滞性(悬浮粒的)　dilatancy
搅动器　agitator
搅动区　agitation [stirring] section
搅动酸洗　agitator pickling
搅动挖掘[挖泥](法)　agitation dredging
搅动装置　agitating equipment
搅动作用(感应炉的)　stirring
搅孔　poke hole
搅炼钢　puddle steel
搅炼炉炼铁法　puddling furnace process
搅炼炉用生铁　puddled pig iron
搅炼炉渣　puddle [puddling] cinder, floss
搅炼(熟)铁　puddle, puddling iron
搅拌机[器,杆] 【冶】poker ◇ 风动～　pneumatic poker
搅土机　pug mill ◇ 真空～ *
铰床[刀]　reamer
铰接　hinging ◇ 接轴的～叉口　jaw of coupling head
铰接板　hinged panel
铰接导轨　joint guide
铰接翻转式造型机　hinged roll-over machine
铰接盖　hinged cover
铰接杆　articulated arm
铰接拱　hinged arch
铰接夹　toggle clamp
铰接金属模板　shuttering
铰接力矩　hinge moment
铰接链　articulated link chain
铰接式(对开)铸型　【铸】book mould
铰接式防护装置　hinged guard
铰接头　link
铰接下部端板　hinged bottom end plate
铰接支座　articulated support, knuckle [free] bearing
铰接轴　articulated [jointed] shaft, articulation
铰接主轴　articulated spindle
铰孔　reaming, scan
铰孔机　broach(ing) machine
铰孔钻[锥]　reaming
铰链　hinge, link, coupling head (万向接轴的) ◇ 工字～ H-hinge, 有～的门 flapper
铰链扁头　spindle tongue
铰链带式过滤器　hinged belt filter
铰链联轴节　hinge coupling
铰链连接[接合]　hinge(d) joint, articulated joint [juncture]
铰链门　hinged door
铰链式砂箱　【铸】pop-off flask
铰链式升降辊道　hinge-type disappearing table
铰链转动　hinging
铰式斗车　hinged hopper
铰式支座　tumbler bearing
铰栓　link [drop] bolt
铰折板　hinged plate
铰支门形架　articulated portal frame
铰柱脚　hinge pedestal
矫平　flattening (板材的), level(l)ing, iron out ◇ 金属带～metal strip flattening, 瓢曲～curve flattening
矫平冲压　flattening stamping
矫平锤　flat hammer ◇ 圆头～ rounded flatter
矫平机　plate-straightening machine ◇ 薄板～ *
矫平压力　flattening pressure
矫齐　true up
矫顽(磁)场　coercive field
矫顽(磁)力　coerci(ti)ve force, coercive intensity ◇ 表观～ *
矫顽(磁)力计　coercimeter, coercive force meter
矫顽磁性　coercivity
矫顽磁性测量仪　coercivemeter
矫形[正]锤　straightening hammer

矫形锻压 【压】restriking

矫正 level(l)ing, rectification, improvement, correct, mend, gagging, 【压】dressing ◇ 局部加热急冷变形～法*, 手工～ hand dressing

矫正操作工 level(l)ing operator

矫正机 arbor press, flattener, flattening machine [unit], straightening machine ◇ 板材～ planing machine, 辊式～（型材的）gagger, 厚板～*, 拉伸～

矫正-破鳞机 processor leveller

矫正速度 straightening speed

矫正信号 【计】correcting signal

矫正压力机（厚板的）bulldozer

矫直 straightening, aligning, dress(ing), flatten(ing), level(l)ing, gagging, 【压】iron down, true up (初轧坯的), reeling (圆钢的), gag (钢轨的),【铸】coining ◇ 机械～ machine straightening, 冷～*, 连续～*, 翘曲～ curve flattening, 三段曲线～法*, 在拉伸矫直机上～（薄板）stretcher flattening

矫直-破鳞联合机组 combination processor and straightener

矫直车间 straightening shop

矫直辊 flattener [level(l)er, level(l)ing, straightening] roll, mangles (板材的)

矫直辊装置 level(l)ing roller set

矫直机 flattener (unit), flattening [level(l)ing] machine, level(l)er, straightener, straightening machine, rectifier, reeler, unbender (unit) ◇ 艾布拉姆森式斜管棒～*, 多辊～*, 二辊式～ two-roll reeler, 辊式～*, 精密～ precision leveller, 拉伸[张力]～*, 履带给料式～ caterpillar, 梅达尔特型～*, 轻型～ light leveller, 热板材～*, 双曲线辊～*, 四轧辊式[四重式多辊]～*, 腿部～*, 斜辊～*, 压力～*, 腰板～（型材用）web leveller, 张拉辊～ pinch roll leveller

矫直机构 straightening gear

矫直机夹送辊 level(l)er pinch roll

矫直剪切联合机组 combined leveller and shears

矫直切割机 straightening and cutting machine

矫直作用 level(l)ing action

脚手架 scaffold (bridging), rigger, falsework, foot blank ◇ 管子～ tubular scaffold, 活动～ jenny scaffold, 木～ timber scaffold, 梯式～ ladder scaffold, 挑出式～*, 悬臂式～走道 cantilever (ed) gantry, 悬挂式～ suspended scaffolding, 移动～*

脚手架板 gang board

脚手架车 scaffold carriage

脚手架护网 fan guard

脚手架用材料 scaffold-forming material

脚手架用钢管 scaffolding tube

脚手桥 【建】scaffold bridging

脚踏板 foot plate, footboard, foot-treadle

脚踏板拉杆 pedal pull rod

脚踏垫板 pedal pad

脚踏干油泵 foot operated grease pump

脚踏杠杆式压力机 foot lever press

脚踏焊接机 foot operated welding machine

脚踏剪 pedal shears

脚踏（控制）开关 foot operated switch, foot [pedal] switch

脚踏压力机 foot [kick] press

脚踏制动器[脚踏闸] foot brake

脚注 foot note, subscript

角 angle (ang.), corner ◇ 布喇格～*, 成槽～ troughing angle

角板 corner [angle] plate

角变形（焊接接头的） angular destortion

角部纵裂（连铸板坯缺陷） longitudinal corner crack

角材成型作业 angle-forming operation

角撑 angle brace [tie], corner brace, crippling

角撑架 angle bracket, angle-table, console

角撑连接 bracket joint

角撑铁	corner plate
角尺	angle square
角椽[角钢椽条]	angle rafter
角钉	brad (nail)
角动量	【理】angular momentum
角度	angle (ang.) ◇ 成~angularity
角度(数据)传感器	angle probe, angular transducer
角度探测器	angle probe
角度因素	angularity factor
角分辨率[能力]	angular resolution
角钢	(rolled) angle, angle bar [iron, section, steel], L-beam, L-iron ◇ 不等边~L-bar, 等边~*, 球头~*, 翼椽~boom angle
角钢背距离	back to back angles
角钢构架	angle iron frame
角钢剪切机	angle shears, angle (-iron) shearing machine
角钢矫直机	angle straightener, angle straightening machine
角钢孔型	angle pass
角钢框架	angle iron frame
角钢弯曲机	angle bending machine
角钢鱼尾[接合]板	angle fishplate [spider]
角钢制法兰盘	steel angle flange
角汞矿[Hg$_2$Cl$_2$]	mercurial horn ore
角光子	【铸】cornerslick
角规	angle gauge
角焊	fillet [corner] welding ◇ 凹形~concave fillet welding, 并排断续~*, 深熔~deep-fillet welding
角焊导轨	fillet weld guide
角焊缝	fillet weld ◇ 凹形~concave fillet (weld), 横向~剪切试样*, 平顶~*, 凸形~convex fillet
角焊缝槽	fillet welded slot
角焊缝尺寸	fillet (weld) size
角焊缝尺寸样板	fillet welding gauge
角焊缝厚度	throat depth [thickness] of fillet weld
角焊缝连接[接头]	fillet joint
角焊缝破裂试样	fillet weld break specimen
角焊缝延长	fillet weld extension
角焊接头	corner weld ◇ 单边卷边~corner-flange weld
角焊接头抗剪试验	shearing test for fillet welded joint
角焊破裂试验	fillet weld break test
角横裂	transversal corner crack
角滑移	angular slip
角加速度	angular acceleration
角接焊缝	corner weld
角接平焊	fillet welding in flat position
角接(头)	angle [corner] joint
角距离	angular distance
角开度	angular width ◇ 天线~【电】angular aperture
角孔径	【理】angular aperture
角宽	angular width [breadth]
角砾岩	【地】breccia
角砾云母橄榄石	kimberlite
角量子数	angular [azimuthal] quantum number
角裂	corner crack, broken corners
角檩[角钢檩条]	angle purlin
角落	corner
角墁刀	angle sleeker, cornerslick
角煤	horn coal
角锰矿	photicite
角偏差	angular deviation
角偏向	angular divergence
角偏转	angular deflection
角频(率)	angular [radian, circular] frequency, pulsation
角平分线	(angular) bisectrix
角砌砖	edge brick
角钎焊	fillet brazing
角铅矿	phosgenite, matlockite, hornlead
角闪石	amphibole {(Mg,Fe)SiO$_3$}, hornblende {(OH)$_2$·Ca$_2$(Mg,Fe)$_4$·(Si$_6$Al$_2$)O$_{22}$}

角闪岩	amphibolite, irestone
角视野	angular field
角速度	angular speed [velocity]
角塔	turret
角条	angle bead ◇ 籀用～ boom angle
角铁撑	angle brace
角铁切割机	angle cutter
角铜矿	copper horn ore
角位移	angle [angular] displacement
角铣刀	angle cutter
角线规	angular wire gauge
角型联结	angular type coupling
角型鱼尾板	fish plate angle
角形反射器	angle [corner] reflector
角形剖面	angle section
角形托座[角块托]	angle bracket
角形系数(型砂颗粒的)	coefficient of angularity
角旋塞	angle cock
角岩	irestone
角因数	angle factor
角因素的测定	angularity measurement
角阴极	angle cathode
角银矿{AgCl}	cerargyrite, kerargyrite
角轧	angular [diagonal, corner] rolling
角质体(煤岩)	cutinite
角质岩泥[粉料]	horn meal
角砖	angle [edge] brick
角状粉粒	angular particle
角状粉末	horn powder
角状细粉	angular fines
角坐标	angular coordinates
绞车	(hoisting) winch, hoist(er), windlass, (hoist) reel, haulage gear ◇ 缆索～ cable hoist, 立轴～ capstan, 施工～ builder's winch, 手动～ hand winch
绞车房	hoist house
绞车卷筒	winch drum, niggerhead
绞车桥	hoist bridge
绞车移动传动装置	crab travelling drive
绞刀	drift, reamer, rimer ◇ 扩张式[可调(径)]～ expansion reamer
绞合焊丝[条]	strand electrode
绞合线	stranded [twisted, bunched, litz(en)] wire
绞盘	capstan (winch), winch, windlass ◇ 汽力～ steam capstan, 手摇～ hand capstan, 塔式～ cone capstan, 运送车～ buggy winching
绞升料车	hoist carriage
绞线	twisted line, stranded conductor ◇ 导体～芯 conductor core, 等长多层～ equilay conductor, 多股～*
绞线股数	wire strands
绞线机	wire twisting machine
校对	revision, check, proof(read), inspection
校对规	reference [standard] gauge
校对环规	master ring gauge
校对机	checking machine
校对块规	reference block
校对量规	test [master] gauge
校对塞规	master plug gauge
校改	【计】updating
校核测定	check [duplicate] determination
校核分析	check analysis [determination]
校核结果	check result
校核试棒	check bar
校核试验	aptitude test
校核线	check line
校扭	detwisting
校扭机	detwister
校配器	batch bin
校平	level(l)ing
校验	verification, check(ing), calibration, proof (test), testing, inspection
校验环	proving ring
校验寄存器	check register
校验位	【计】check bit
校验问题	【计】check problem
校验指示器	check indicator
校验装置	calibrating apparatus [equipment]
校验总线	【计】check trunk [bus]

校正 check, correction (corr.), correcting, revision, calibration, amendment, rectifying, rectification, updating
校正测定[测量] check measurement
校正电路 correcting [compensating] circuit
校正焦比 【铁】specific coke rate
校正接点 reference junction
校正流变应力比 corrected flow stress ratio
校正曲线 calibration curve [plot]
校正式 correction formula
校正系数 correction coefficient [factor, index]
校正仪表 check gauge
校正元件 correcting element
校正值 corrected value, correction
校直机 (同"矫直机")
校准 calibration, correct, align, aline, graduation, standardizing, collimating ◇ 未~的 uncollimated
校准表 calibration table [scale]
校准材料 calibrating material
校准秤 (同"标准秤")
校准点 calibration point [spot]
校准方程式 calibration equation
校准规 control gauge
校准环 calibrating ring
校准块 (同"标准块")
校准链 calibrated [tested, pitch] chain
校准脉冲 calibration (im)pulse
校准模 sizing die
校准器 calibrator ◇ 机内~ built-in calibrator
校准曲线 calibration curve [plot]
校准试验 calibration test
校准试样 standard sample
校准温度 verification temperature
校准物质 calibrating material (X-射线检验用), comparison substance
校准吸收剂 calibrated absorber
校准仪[校准用仪器] calibration instrument [apparatus], grading instrument, prover
校准因数[系数] calibration factor
校准用标准[基准] calibration standard
校准用金属粉末(X-射线照相的) calibrating-metal powder
校准装置 calibrating apparatus [device, equipment]
酵母菌 Saccharomycete
轿车 (sedan) car ◇ 活顶~ convertible sedan
较低能态 lower-energy state
较低水平(面) lower level (LL)
较高能态 higher energy state
较软钢 (0.08—0.12C, <0.05Si, 0.3—0.5Mn, <0.05P, <0.05S) softer steel
较易切削黄铜 semifree cutting brass
揭盖机 cover carriage
揭露 expose, opening-up
接班组 【企】relay shift
接板(焊缝机的) contact bar
接插头 【电】patchplug
接长 joining, long splice (钢丝绳的)
接触 contact(ing), touch ◇ 非~型测量仪 contactless gauge
接触板 contact plate, welding die (对接焊机的)
接触保护 contact protection
接触表面 contact surface
接触材料 contact material
接触长度 contact length
接触沉淀法 【环】contact sedimentation method
接触重叠[搭接] 【焊】contacting overlap
接触磁化 【理】touch
接触催化 contact-catalysis
接触催化剂 contact catalyst
接触导线 contact conductor
接触点 contact point
接触点焊 resistance spot welding ◇ 叠板~ stack welding

接触点焊机 resistance spot welding machine
接触垫(电极的) contact pad
接触电动势 contact (electromotive) force, contact emf
接触电弧 contact arc ◇ 抛物线形~ parabolic contact arc
接触电弧焊[焊条接触电弧焊] contact arc welding
接触电极 contact electrode
接触电加热退火 resistance annealing
接触电流 pick-up current
接触电势[位] contact potential
接触电位差 contact potential difference
接触电压降 contact drop
接触电渣焊 resistance electro-slag welding
接触电阻 contact resistance
接触镀锡(法) contact tinning, contact tin plating
接触端头 contact end
接触对焊法 Thomson process
接触对焊机 (同"电阻对焊机")
接触法(污水处理) contact method
接触法电镀[镀覆] contact plating
接触法硫酸 contact acid
接触法引[起]弧 【焊】touch starting
接触法制酸厂 contact plant
接触腐蚀 contact [meeting] corrosion ◇ 异种金属~*
接触缸(四辊轧机的) contact cylinder
接触轨 conductor rail
接触辊 【焊】contact roller
接触过程 catalytic process
接触过滤 contact filtration
接触焊 contact [resistance] welding ◇ 螺柱~ resistance stud welding
接触焊机 resistance welding machine
接触焊接时间控制器 resistance welding timer
接触焊控制设备 resistance welding control

接触焊突出部 welding projection
接触恒温器 contact thermostat
接触弧 【压】contact arc, arc of contact ◇ 轧辊~ rolling arc of contact
接触弧长投影 projected contact length
接触还原法 (process of) contact reduction
接触混合 contact blending
接触剂 contact agent, catalyst
接触夹板(矿热电炉的) contact clamp
接触夹具钳口(对焊机的) jaw contact
接触夹片 contact jaw
接触加热器 contact heater
接触检验 contact inspection
接触键 contact bonding
接触焦化 contact coking
接触角 angle of contact [rolling] (轧件同轧辊的), contact angle ◇ 静置气泡~测定仪*
接触界面 contact interface
接触开关 【电】contact switch
接触扩散 contact diffusion
接触冷凝 condensation by contact
接触冷凝器 contact condenser
接触冷却水 (同"直接冷却水")
接触力 contact force
接触炉 catalyst furnace
接触面 contact surface [face, facing]
接触面积 contact area
接触面平直化 contact flattening
接触面压力 contact area pressure
接触摩擦(力) contact friction
接触黏合 contact bonding,【铸】contact cement
接触疲劳 contact fatigue
接触疲劳裂纹 contact fatigue crack
接触疲劳强度 contact fatigue strength
接触片 contact chip [piece]
接触曝气法 【环】contact aeration method
接触器 contact apparatus,【电】contactor (switch, unit) ◇ 插片式~ latching contactor, 动带→*, 文丘里~ Venturi con-

tactor,重负载～ heavy duty contacts
接触器地下室 contactor basement
接触强度 contact strength
接触曲线 contact curve
接触熔炼 【冶】contact melting
接触扫描 contact scanning
接触渗透 contact infiltration
接触时间 touch time
接触式爆炸成型法 contact-type operation of explosive forming ◇ 直接～*
接触式操作(爆炸成形的) contact operation
接触式测厚仪[飞测厚度计,飞测千分尺](轧带材用) electrolimit gauge
接触式测角仪 contact goniometer
接触式电气飞测仪(测冷轧带钢厚度) flying mike continuous gauge
接触式断路器 contact breaker
接触式反向控制 contactor type reversing control
接触式干燥机 contact drier
接触式高温计 contact pyrometer
接触式焊条 touch(-type) electrode
接触式检测仪(测厚仪) contacting gauge
接触式量规[计量仪表] contact-type gauge
接触式起[引]弧 【焊】contact-type start
接触式启动控制 【电】contactor type starting control
接触式热交换器 contact heat exchanger
接触式压力表 contact manometer
接触式(乙炔)发生器 contact-type generator, contact system ◇ 排水～*
接触特性 contact performance
接触头 contact head
接触[接点]温度计 contact thermometer
接触显微射线照相术 contactmicroradiography
接触线 line of contact
接触性能 contact performance [quality]
接触压板 contact bar
接触压焊 pressure contact welding

接触压力 contact pressure
接触印相法 contact printing
接触指示杆 contact indicator rod
接触中毒 contact poison
接触阻化剂 contact inhibitor
接触阻抗法 contact impedance method
接地 ground(ing)(connection), earth (connection) ◇ 不～的 earth-free
接地棒 ground bar, earthing rod
接地保护操作 ground protective operation
接地(保护)过电压继电器 overvoltage ground relay
接地测量仪 earthometer
接地导体 grounding conductor
接地导线 grounding wire, ground [earth] lead, earth(ing) conductor
接地灯 earth lamp
接地电缆[缆线] earthing [ground] cable
接地电压互感器 grounding potential transformer (GPT)
接地电阻 grounding [earth] resistance
接地端 earth-therminal
接地故障保护 earth fault protection
接地辊 earth roll
接地回路 grounded [earth] circuit
接地极 grounding electrode
接地继电器 grounding relay
接地检测(指示)器 ground detector
接地连接 ground joint
接地漏电断路器 earth leakage breaker (ELB)
接地漏泄线圈 earth leakage coil
接地漏泄指示器 earth leakage indicator
接地母线 earth bus [strap]
接地屏蔽 ground(ed) [earth(ed)] screen, grounded [earth] shield
接地线(工程) earth connection
接地线夹 ground clamp
接地阳极 grounded anode
接地装置 grounding [earthing] device
接点 contact ◇ 带载调节～*

接点板　gusset (joint) plate
接点合金　contact alloy ◇ 埃尔科纽姆～ Elkonium
接点输入缓冲器　contact input buffer
接电极橡皮手套(真空电弧炉构件)　rubber glove for bar joining
接法　connection
接缝　seaming, joint ◇ 有～的 seamy
接缝发纹　seam
接缝焊用电极　seam-welding electrode
接缝棱边　joint edges
接钢侧(活套轧机)　catcher's side
接高(烟囱的)　heightening
接轨夹板　foot fishing
接合　joining, joint(ing), juncture, junction, bonding, connection, engagement ◇ 使～(使离合器接合) throw in, 有隙～ open joint
接合板　junction plate
接合点　bonding point, junction (point), juncture
接合端　abutting end
接合杆　engaging lever
接合机理　encounter mechanism
接合螺栓　coupling bolt
接合面　joint face, composition face [surface, plane]
接合泥　jointing cement
接合器　adapter, adaptor, connector, shifting coupling
接合区　composite region
接合榫砖　bonding brick
接合凸缘　coupling flange
接合效率(焊接或铆接的)　joint efficiency
接合状态　coherent state
接火　fire welding
接近　approach, near, approximation
接近成品形状(的)　near net shape
接近传感器　proximity transducer
接近工业规模的电解槽　near-commercial scale cell
接近角　acceptance angle

接近开关　approach [proximity] switch
接近(目标)速度　velocity of approach
接口　calked seam, interface ◇ 计算机程序～系统*
接口部件设计　interface design
接口管　mouthpiece
接口挤压　mouth-piece pressing
接力焦　booster coke
接目镜　eye lens, eyepiece
接入　insertion, switch(ing) in, turn-on,
接绳　【压】splicing
接收　receiving, reception, acceptance, adoption
接收槽　receiver tank
接收架　receiving bracket
接收检验　acceptance inspection
接收器　receptor, acceptor, receiver ◇ 带卷～【压】coil receiver
接收数　acceptance munber
接收站　receiving platform, accepting station
接收中断　receive interruption
接受槽　receiving bin
接受蛋　receiving egg
接受机　【理】receiver
接受盘　catch-plate
接受器　receiver, receiving box, acceptor, receptacle, udell (冷凝水汽的)
接受设施　receiving facilities
接受体分子　acceptor molecule
接受站　take-over point
接通　switching [throw] in, switch on, turn-on, making, key on, occlude, cut-in
接通(电流)时间　【电】on-time
接通电路　make contact
接通位置　on-position
接通与断开机构　on-off mechanism
接头　connect(ion), join, joint (connection), juncture, adaptor, terminal ◇ 电缆～箱 connecting box, 分支～ branch joint, 没有～的 jointless
接头轨枕　joint lie

接头焊接　joint weld(ing)
接头机　【压】splicer
接头连结　【电】bond
接头拧接机　coupling screw-on machine
接头熔深　joint penetration
接头润滑脂　joint grease
接头托架　die block
接头泄漏　joint leakage
接头准备　【焊】joint preparation
接头座　connector
接线　wiring (scheme), connection ◇ 克纳普扎克～法＊
接线板　terminal [distribution] block, wiring board, clamper
接线布置图　wiring layout
接线盒　junct(ion) [terminal, connecting, connection, fishing, joint] box, connection head
接线盒浇注绝缘胶　joint-box compound
接线盘　patch board
接线条　terminal strip
接线头　(connector) lug
接线图　(inter) connection [connecting] diagram, cording diagram, (inter-connecting) wiring diagram
接线箱　joint [junction, connection] box
接线原理图　elementary diagram
接线柱[端子]　terminal, binding post, fastener, clip, stud, connector
接线装置　connection head
接续反应　trailing reaction
接缘线　match line
接渣器　slag catcher
接种　inoculate, inoculation
接种技术　subculturing technique
接种物(体)　inoculum (复数 inocula)
接轴　spindle ◇ 齿型～gear-type spindle
接轴扁头　spade half coupling
接轴架　spindle support
接轴铰接叉口　jaw of coupling head
接轴铰接叉头　spindle jaw half coupling
接轴壳　coupling shaft housing

接轴平衡锤　spindle counterweight
接轴器　coupler
接轴倾斜角　spindle angle
接轴托[支]架　spindle carrier ◇ 弹簧平衡式～＊, 重锤平衡式～＊
接砖　closer (brick)
接转中心　【电】relay center
接桩　pile extension, spliced pile
接着强度(喷补层对残衬的)　bond strength
阶　steps, stairs,【数】order, exponent
阶层　stratum
阶差　jump
阶次　order
阶段　stage, step, phase, period
阶段分析　stage analysis
阶段曝气法　【环】step aeration method
阶段升温等温淬火　step-up austempering
阶段时效　stepped ageing
阶段式处理　stepped treating
阶段式挤压(法)　stepped extrusion
阶段式加载　stepwise loading
阶段退火　step annealing
阶码溢出　【计】characteristic overflow
阶式区段(电解槽的)　cascade sections
阶式收尘器　cascade-type deduster
阶式调节器　step-by-step regulator
阶式循环　circulation cascade
阶式运输机　cascade conveyer
阶式蒸发器　【化】cascade (casc.)
阶数　module
阶梯断面型材　stepped section
阶梯光谱仪　echelle spectrometer
阶梯浇口　【铸】step gate, side step gate
阶梯炉箅　step grate
阶梯式布置　stagger, Garret type layout
阶梯式翻钢机　stepped turnover device
阶梯式迷宫[曲径][密封]　stepped labyrinth
阶梯形齿砌接(圬工)　racking
阶梯形多层焊　cascade welding
阶梯形多层焊接法　cascade process [se-

阶梯形分型面(铸型的) stepped joint
阶梯形分型面制造 parting-down
阶梯形轧制 stepped rolling
阶梯形状 stepped form
阶梯轧辊 step [squabbing] roll
阶梯爪(翻钢钩的) stepped ledge
阶梯状滑移 pencil glide
阶梯状浇口 stepped runner
阶梯状螺型位错 jogged screw dislocation
阶梯状[阶形]曲线 stepped curve
阶跃电压调节器 step voltage regulator
阶跃脉冲 step pulse
阶跃输入时间响应 time response to step input
阶跃响应 step response
截齿具 【机】hob
截顶的 truncated
截断 cut off, parting cut
截断桩 cut-off piling
截获 【电】nip-up
截角锥 truncated cone
截距[段] intercept
截料棒 【团】cut-off bar
截流坝 cut-off dam
截流井 catch pit [basin]
截流塞 cut-off plug ◇ 锥形～ cut-off conical plug
截面 (cross) section, crossover, scarf ◇ 全[整]～试样 full section specimen
截面尺寸效应 section (size) effect
截面积 cross-section area ◇ 粗视～*, 钢筋～*
截面可调[控]喷嘴 controllable-area nozzle
截面流量仪[计] area flow type meter, area flowmeter
截面模数[量] section modulus
截面图 cutaway section
截面形状 cross-sectional shape
截取 cut out, reclaiming (原料), 【采】cut-off ◇ 连续～器*

截去 cut-off
截水沟 catch-drain, crown ditch (路堑坡顶的)
截头锯 deck saw
截头体 frustum
截头体布料器 【铁】frustum
截头圆锥体 truncated cone
截线法 intercept method
截项 cross term
截止 cut-off, pick-off, blockage, abort, closure, stoppage
截止点 cut-off point
截止电流 cut-off current
截止电压 cut-off [blocking] voltage
截止阀(门) shutoff [closing, stop] valve, cut-off gate ◇ 闸门式蒸汽～*
截止滑阀 shut-off slide valve
截止偏压 cut-off bias
截止频率 cut-off frequency ◇ 上限～*
截止品位 cut-off grade
截止期 deadline
截止条件 【半】cut-off condition
截止值 cut-off value
截止状态 cut-off state [condition]
截锥 truncated cone
节 joint, knob, node, nubs, segment, paragraph (文章的), 【运】knot (只用于航行的速度法定单位, 1kn = (1852/3600) m/s) ◇ 有～的 nodated
节材型建筑用钢材 material-saving constructional steel
节点 nodal point, joint, node
节电 power economy
节杆(细)菌属 arthrobacter
节径(齿轮的) pitch diamete
节距 pitch ◇ 大～(螺纹) steep pitch
节链 pitch chain
节流 throttle, throttling ◇ 出口～式电路 meter-out circuit, 入口～式电路 meter-in circuit
节流板 throttle [orifice, damper] plate
节流阀 throttle, throttle [throttling]

valve, butterfly valve [gate, throttle], flow controlling gate, flow control valve ◇ 单向～ choke check, 电液比例～ *

节流阀操纵杆 throttle lever
节流阀曲柄(锻锤的) throttle crank
节流阀组 multiple-valve septum, throttle unit(高炉煤气清洗系统的)
节流阀组件 throttle-valve aggregate
节流孔 orifice
节流门 gate throttle, choker
节流面积 choke area
节流内浇口[铸] choke
节流器 throttler, restrictor, restriction choke, reducer
节流曲线 isenthalp
节流系数 throttling coefficient
节流旋塞 throttling cock
节流止回阀 throttling non-return valve
节煤[节热]器 economizer
节能 energy saving [conservation], power economy
节能降耗 energy conservation and decrease in material consumption, energy saving and consumption reducing
节拍脉冲 clock pulse
节气 throttling
节气板 damper plate
节气阀 throttle (valve), damper
节气阀组 multiple-valve septum
节气关闭阀 gas-saving shutoff valve
节气门 butterfly (valve, damper, gate, throttle), choker
节伸式阀座 detachable seat
节省人工(的) labour-saving
节省试剂 reagent economy
节省投资[资金] saving in capital
节省重量 saving in weight
节水 【环】water-saving
节水器 water saver (equipment)
节涌流化床 slugging fluidized bed
节油杯 simmer-ring
节油器 economizer ◇ 磁化～ magnetizing economizer
节圆(齿轮的) pitch circle (PC), nodal circle
节约 economy, saving ◇ 炉子操作～措施 furnace operating economy
节约装置 economizer
节制坝 check dam
节制活门 regulating valve
节锥(伞齿轮的) pitch cone
杰弗里斯乘数 Jeffries' multiplier
杰弗里斯晶粒度测定法 Jeffries' method
杰弗洛伊－德洛尔热镀锡法 Geoffroy-Delore process
杰康托莱特断口标准 Jernkontoret standards
杰康托莱特夹杂级别 【钢】Jernkontoret's slag inclusions scales
杰克逊锡黄铜(65Cu,30Zn,5Sn) Jackson's alloy
杰利夫镍铬电阻合金 Jellif (Jellif 800：—20Cr,—80Ni,少量 Mn、Mo)
杰罗模顶真空处理法 【钢】Gero process
杰诺莱特磷酸盐除锈液 Jenolite
杰瑟特高强度耐蚀铬钢(10—12Cr,0.1C,少量 Mo、V、Nb、Ni,余量 Fe) Jethete
杰索普 H40 铁素体耐热钢(0.25C, 0.4Mn, 0.4Si, 3Cr, 0.5N, 0.5Mo, 0.75V) Jessop H40
杰塔尔氧化处理法 Jetal
杰特－麦克哈格－威廉斯轧制板材反转极点图求作法 Jetter-McHargue-Williams method
杰伊雷克斯振动筛 Gyrex screen
捷径 bee line, shortcut
洁净的 clean, pure, uncontaminated
洁净度 cleanliness
洁净电解质 uncontaminated electrolyte
洁净度检验 cleanness test
洁净钢 clean steel
洁净剂 cleansing agent
洁净铁 clean iron
结 knot, node, tie ◇ 多～的 nodated

结疤 scab(by), scabbiness, blister, chink(ing), scale formation, dog's ears (轧件的), lap (钢锭的), shell, 【铸】blind scab, expansion scab, veining ◇ 黑料~【铸】blacking scab

结疤的 【金】scarred
结冰膨胀成型法 ice-forming process
结饼 caking
结存 【企】inventory, remnant
结点 joint, kink, node, void, site (晶格的)
结点板 gusset
结点间距 interlattice-point distance [spacing] ◇ 最近~*
结点间碳原子扩散 diffusion of interstitial carbon
结点间原子 interstitial atom
结电阻 【半】junction resistance
结垢 scale formation, fouling, 【铸】build(ing) up (壳型的)
结垢影响 scale effect
结构 structure, constitution, formation, fabric, organism, architecture ◇ α相~*, 布里渊区~*
结构崩裂 structural spalling
结构边界线 structural limits
结构变化 structural change [alteration], change in [of] structure, structure change alteration ◇ 引起~的 structurizing
结构不规则性 structural irregularity
结构不均匀性 structure heterogeneity [inhomogeneity]
结构不连续性 structural discontinuity
结构不敏感性 structure insensitive property
结构不稳定性 structure instability
结构部分 structural portion
结构材料 structural [construction(al)] material
结构测定 structure determination
结构成分 structural constitution
结构重排[重新排列] structure rearrangement

结构粗糙的砖 rusticated brick
结构单元 unit of structure
结构对称(性) structure symmetry
结构分析 structural analysis, structure analysis [determination]
结构腐蚀 structural corrosion
结构复原 【金】restoration of structure
结构改进 structural development, structure modification
结构钢 structural steel (str. st.), structural iron, constructional steel ◇ skhl 低合金~*, 飞机~ aircraft structural steel, 弗罗因德~*, 高(抗拉)强度~*, 工业~*, 克罗曼西尔低合金~*, 马蒂内尔~*, 热镀锌~*
结构钢薄板 structural steel sheet
结构工作状况 behaviour of structure
结构构架 structural framing
结构合金 structural [constructional] alloy
结构化的细滑移 structurized fine slip
结构化系统分析 【计】structured system analysis (SSA)
结构件 construction part
结构浇制 structural casting
结构金属 structural metal
结构晶体学 structural crystallography
结构精细度 fineness of structure
结构镜质体(煤岩) telinite
结构可靠性 structural [built-in] reliability
结构理论 structural theory
结构力学 structural mechanics
结构零件 structural parts [component]
结构敏感性 structure sensitivity
结构模型 structural model
结构内聚力 structure cohesion
结构能(晶体的) structural energy
结构疲劳破断 structural fatigue failure
结构破坏 structural failure
结构破[断]裂 structure-breaking
结构破裂性质 structure-breaking property

结构强度　structural [structure] strength
结构取向[定位]　structural orientation
结构缺陷　structural defect [imperfection], fault of construction
结构设计　structural design
结构设计语言　structural design language (STRUDL)
结构伸长(钢丝绳的)　structural [constructional] stretch
结构(施工)一般说明　general description of construction
结构式(分子的)　structural [constitutional] formula
结构受力构件　bearing carrier
结构损伤　fault of construction
结构特点　structural [design] feature
结构特性　structure property
结构图　structural diagram, structure drawing
结构完整性　structural integrity,【金】perfection of structure
结构稳定性　structural stability
结构相变　structural phase transition
结构型材　structural shape ◇ 挤压~
结构型钢　structural section [shape] ◇ 焊接~ welded structural shape
结构形成　structure formation
结构形态[式,状]　structural form [shape], form of construction
结构修改　structure modification
结构研究　structural study, structure investigation
结构因数[因素]　structural [structure] factor
结构用低碳钢　structural mild steel
结构用(钢)管　structural [mechanical] tube
结构预制件　structural casting
结构元件　structure [structural] element
结构振幅　structure amplitude
结构振幅方程　structure-amplitude equation

结构质量　structural quality
结构转变　structural transformation
结构状态　structural condition
结构族分析　structural group analysis
结构组成[组分]　structural composition [constituent]
结果　result, outcome, consequence
结果程序　object program [routine]
结果代码　【计】object code
结果地址　【计】result address
结果模块　【计】object module
结果输出值　【计】readout
结果语言　【计】object language
结核(矿)　nodule ◇ 大洋多金属~, 锰~ manganese nodule
结核状腐蚀　tubercular corrosion, tubeculation
结核状耐火黏土　nodular fire clay
结合　combine, combination, unite, integrate, bind(ing), bond(ing), incorporation, interlinkage, join, union ◇ 未~的 uncombined
结合点(热电偶的)　junction [bonding] point, binding site
结合电子　bonding electron
结合灰分　combined ash
结合剂(炉衬的)　【冶】martix
结合角　bond angle
结合角钢　connecting angle
结合梁　bond beam
结合硫　fault sulphur
结合面　faying (sur)face
结合耐火材料　bound refractory
结合能　binding [bond, bound] energy, energy of attachment ◇ 双空位~
结合黏土　binding [bond] clay, bond fireclay
结合强度　bond(ing) strength
结合热　heat of linkage
结合石灰　【耐】combined lime
结合水(分)　bound moisture [water], combined [combination, attached, hy-

drate, hydration] water, comnined [attached] moisture
结合碳 combined [bound] carbon
结合物 bonder, ligature
结合性能 binding ability
结合砖 bonded brick
结痂 incrustation
结焦 coking ◇ 不~的煤 yolk coal
结焦饼指数 coke button index (CBI)
结焦率 coking yield ratio, coke yield
结焦素 anthraxylon
结焦性[能力] cokeability
结焦性差的煤 inferior coking coal
结焦性煤 baking coal
结焦性能(煤的) coking characteristics
结焦压力 coking pressure
结焦周期 coking time ◇ 净~ net coking time, 总~ "
结节 nodule
结节状反应 nodular reaction
结晶 crystal (cr.), crystallization, crystallizing, crystallisation, crystallising ◇ 簇形~. cluster crystal, 范德瓦尔斯~ *, 分批~ batch crystallization, 搅动~ agitated crystallizer, 可~性 *, 水合~ crystal hydrate, (树)枝状~【金】 branched dendrite, 细粒~ crystal fines, 延迟[强过冷]~ delayed crystallization
结晶表面 crystal surface
结晶槽 crystallization [crystallizer, crystallizing] tank
结晶层 crystallizing layer
结晶产物 crystallized product
结晶程度 degree of crystallization
结晶赤铁矿 oligist
结晶出来 crystallizing-out
结晶次数 number of crystallization
结晶的 crystalline (cry.), crystallizing, grained ◇ 不~ non-crystallizable, 不完全~ subcrystalline, 过渡形~ malcrystalline
结晶点 crystal point, point of crystallization
结晶定碳 (同"液线定碳")
结晶度 crystallinity, degree of crystallization
结晶发光 crystallo-luminescence
结晶法 crystallization process
结晶范围 crystalline [crystallization] region
结晶分离 separation by crystallization
结晶粉末 crystalline powder
结晶刚玉 crystal corundum
结晶构造学 crystallology
结晶固体 crystalline solid
结晶锅 crystallizer pan
结晶过程 crystallization (process)
结晶核(心) crystallizing nucleus, host crystal, nuclear centre
结晶化学 crystal chemistry
结晶回复 crystal recovery
结晶剂 crystallizing agent
结晶架 crystalline concretion
结晶间隔 crystallization interval
结晶键 crystal bridge
结晶浆液 crystal(line) slurry
结晶角 crystal angle
结晶净化 purification by crystallization
结晶粒度 crystal size
结晶力 crystalline force
结晶良好的 well-crystallized
结晶硫酸锆 $\{Zr(SO_4)_2 \cdot 4H_2O\}$ crystalline zirconium sulphate
结晶面 crystalline face, crystallographic plane
结晶模型 crystalline pattern
结晶盘 crystallizer pan, crystallizing disc
结晶片 crystal plate
结晶器 crystallizer, cristalliser, 【连铸】 mo(u)ld, ingot-forming equipment, casting shell ◇ 薄壁~ thin-walled mould, 带锥度的~ tapered mould, 等矩形截面~ *, 镀铬~ *, 多联~ multi-mould, 负滑动[有负拔模斜度的]~ *, 刚性固定~

jie 结

rigidly mounted mould, 固定式～fixed mould (machine), 管式[状]～tube [tubular] mould, 横梁[横臂]～*, 弧形～curved mould, 开口～open mould, 可拆卸式～separate mould, 可换～interchangeable mould, 宽度可变～variable width mould, 冷却～cooler crystallizer, 立式～*, 连续～continuous crystalizer, 漏斗形～*, 抛物线型～parabolic mold, 喷淋(冷却)～*, 普通水缝式～*, 容克式～Junker's mould, 上大下小～*, 水冷式～water-cooled mould, 四片组合式～four plate mould, 弹簧固定式～spring mounted mould, (往复)振动式～oscillating mould, 无底～open-ended mould, 楔形～*, 直～straight mould, 转筒式多级～*, 装配式～*, 组合式～composite mould

结晶器安装[装配] mounting of mould
结晶器保护渣 mo(u)ld powder [flux]
结晶器保护渣膜 mo(u)ld flux film
结晶器壁 mould wall
结晶器壁面 mould face
结晶器操作工 mould operator
结晶器侧壁斜度 taper in mould walls
结晶器传热监控 mould thermal monitoring
结晶器电磁搅拌(法) in-mould electromagnetic stirring
结晶器非正弦式振动 non-sinusoidal mould oscillation
结晶器负滑脱往复移动 reciprocating with negative strip
结晶器高效润滑 efficient mould lubrication
结晶器管 mould tube
结晶器(截面)形状 shape of mould
结晶器冷却水 mould cooling water
结晶器冷却水套 mould cooling jacket
结晶器膜 mould film
结晶器内钢液面[位] mould level
结晶器润滑 mould lubrication

结晶器润滑剂 mould lubricant
结晶器润滑站 mould lubricating station
结晶器上孔 top of mould
结晶器寿命 mould life
结晶器台 mould table
结晶器往复[运]动 mould reciprocation
结晶器往复移[运]动法 technique of mould reciprocation
结晶器往复移[运]动机构 mould-reciprocating mechanism
结晶器新表面 fresh mould surface
结晶器移动机构 mould-moving mechanism
结晶器运动 mould movement
结晶器振动 mould oscillation [reciprocation] ◇ 正弦式～*
结晶器振动台 mould (oscillation) table
结晶器(振动)行程 mould stroke
结晶器振动装置 mould drive ◇ 弹簧减震式～*
结晶潜热 latent heat of crystallization
结晶区(域) crystalline field [region], crystallization region
结晶取向[位向] crystallographic orientation
结晶全对称现象 pantomorphism
结晶缺陷 crystalline imperfection, imperfection in crystal
结晶热 crystallization heat
结晶失水 efflorescence
结晶水 crystal water, water of crystallization [hydration]
结晶水合物 crystal(line) hydrate
结晶顺序 order of crystallization
结晶速度 crystallization rate [velocity]
结晶碳 crystalline carbon
结晶碳化硅 crystalline carborundum
结晶体沉淀 crystalline precipitate
结晶铜绿 verdigris
结晶桶 crystallizer [crystallizing] tank, crystallization vat
结晶图样 crystalline pattern

结晶温度 crystalline temperature [point], crystallizing temperature [point]

结晶物质 crystalline matter ◇ 等轴对称～cubic substance, 羽毛状～*

结晶析出 crystallizing-out, seed out, separation by crystallization

结晶系(统) crystallizing system, system of crystallization

结晶相 crystal(line) [crystallization] phase

结晶型硫酸钠{Na$_2$SO$_4$·10H$_2$O} Glauber's salt

结晶形石墨 crystalline graphite

结晶形态[状] crystalline [crystallized, crystallographic] form

结晶性 crystallinity

结晶性质 crystalline nature

结晶学 crystallography (crystal.)

结晶学方向 crystallographic direction

结晶学关系 crystallographic relationship

结晶学极 crystallographic pole

结晶学一致[共同]性 crystallographic identity

结晶学原理 fundamentals of crystallography

结晶衍射图 crystallogram

结晶氧化铝 crystal alumina

结晶蒸发器 crystallizing evaporator

结晶蒸煮器 crystallizing boiler

结晶质金属 crystalline metal

结晶中心 crystallization centre

结晶轴 crystallographic axis

结晶转变 (同"晶形转变")

结晶状态 crystalline [crystallized] state

结晶组分 crystallographic component

结晶组织 crystal(line) structure

结晶作用 crystallization

结壳 crust(ing), encrustation, incrustation, shelling,【钢】curtaining, ingot shell, plaster, bridging, accretion, scull, skull(ing) ◇ 薄而易碎的～【色】thin fragile crust, 槽帮～(电解槽的)【色】ridge, 炉子～*,"自给式"～"self-feeding" crust

结壳形成【冶】skull formation

结块 caking, packing, salamander, agglomeration,【冶】accretion, clotting (焙烧矿的), kidneys (转炉的),【色】nubs,【团】conglomerate ◇ 粉末～agglomerated particle, 去除～decaking

结块粉末 agglomerated particle

结块颗粒 agglomerated grain

结料层【冶】coating

结瘤 furnace sow, fused lump, formation of agglomerated ball, salamander,【冶】accretion,【铁】scaffolding,【钢】make up (水口的) ◇ 水口～【钢】nozzle blocking

结瘤物【铁】scaffold-forming material

结膜测温[试验]【钢】film test

结皮(钢锭底的) curtaining, plaster

结圈 ring-forming,【团】ringing, accretion formation, build up of ring, development of ring ◇ 磁铁矿～【团】magnetite ring, 回转窑～kiln ringing, 熟料～clinker ring, 最大～点*

结束 finish, end(-up), terminate, closing

结束标志【计】end mark

结束符 terminating symbol, end mark, terminator ◇ 信息块传送～*

结束行【计】End line

结四面体 tie tetrahedron

结网 netting

结型二极管 junction diode

结型晶体管 junction transistor

结型晶体三极管 junction triode

结硬皮 crusting

结渣 slag-bonding,【铸】build(ing) up,【钢】shadrach (转炉炉嘴的)

解除 relieve, remove, release

解除联锁 release

解除中断 disarmed interrupt

解冻 thawing, unfreezing

解冻熔炼 green smelt

解冻周期　thawing cycle
解毒(作用)　【环】detoxification
解(法)　【数】solution, resolution
解聚合(作用)　depolymerization
解决　solution (sol.), (re)solving
解开(缠绕物)　untwining
解捆　uncoiling
解理　cleavage, cleat ◇ 可～的 cleavable, 人字形[鲱骨状]～ herringbone cleavage
解理程度　cleavage step
解理脆性　cleavage brittleness
解理断口样式　fracture mode by cleavage
解理断裂[断口]　cleavage fracture
解理断裂面　cleavage face
解理晶体　cleaved crystal
解理裂纹　cleavage crack
解理面　cleavage (sur)face [plane]
解理台阶　cleavage step
解理-纤维转变　cleavage-fibrous transition
解理小平面　cleavage facets
解理状剥离　cleavage foliation
解理组织　cleavage structure
解码器　decoder
解磨机　disintegrator ◇ 气体洗涤～*
解剖　dissection
解剖程序[方法]　dissection procedure
解剖分析　dissection analysis [examination]
解释　explain, illumination, interpretation, explanation (xpln)
解释程序　【计】interpreter, interpretive program
解说　comment, illustration, definition
解酸　disacidifying
解算器　【计】resolver
解算时间　resolving time
解算装置　resolver (RSVR), calculator, solver
解题　resolution
解体　decomposition, disassembly, disintegrating

解调　【电】demodulation
解调器　【电】demodulator
解脱机构　release [arming] mechanism
解析法　【数】analytical method
解析曲线　analytical curve
解吸　desorbing, (adsorption) stripping, desorption
解吸剂　desorbent, strippant, stripping agent
解吸溶液　strip(ping) solution
解吸设备　stripping apparatus
解吸(速)率　desorption rate
解吸塔　desorption tower, stripper [stripping] column
解吸条件　desorption condition
解吸液　stripping liquid,【色】strip liquor
解吸圆锥　stripping cone
解吸作用　desorption
解压　decompression
解轴　【压】unreeling
姐妹金属　sister metal
界　boundary
界壁　(同"畴壁")
界标　terminus
界面　interface, border, boundary (surface), interphase ◇ 晶体～状况*, 凸向液体的～*, 液-液[两种非互溶液体间]～ liquid-liquid interface
界面层　boundary layer
界面电效应　electrical effect at interface
界面动力学　interface [interfacial] kinetics
界面断裂　interfacial failure
界面反应　interface [interfacial] reaction
界面反应层　interfacial reaction layer
界面反应动力学　interfacial reaction kinetics
界面高度　interface height
界面滑动　interfacial sliding
界面回波信号　boundary echo
界面活性　interfacial activity
界面活性剂　interfacial agent

界面间层　interfacial layer
界面间电阻[阻力]　interfacial resistance
界面(间)膜　interfacial film
界面间摩擦　interfacial friction
界面间能量　interfacial energy
界面间偏析　interfacial segregation
界面间势能　interfacial potential
界面间吸附　interfacial adsorption
界面剪切强度　interfacial shear strength
界面接触　interfacial contact
界面晶粒　boundary grain
界面控制的(晶粒)生长　interface controlled growth
界面裂纹　interfacial crack
界面面积　interfacial area
界面能　interfacial energy
界面黏结　interfacial bonding
界面黏结强度　interfacial bond strength
界面排出　interface expulsion
界面区　interface region, interfacial [boundary] zone
界面迁移率　interface migration rate, interface mobility
界面势　interfacial potential
界面速度指数　【理】interface speed index
界面脱黏　interfacial debonding
界面位错　【理】interface dislocations
界面温度　interfacial temperature
界面现象　interfacial phenomenon
界面形态学　【金】interface morphology
界面形状　interface shape
界面压缩载荷　bearing load
界面油膜润滑　boundary (film) lubrication
界面张力　interfacial tension
界面逐出　interface expulsion
界偶　【数】bound pair
界偶表　【计】bound pair list
界砂　【铸】tap sand
界石　terminus
界限　limit(ation), bounds, boundary, border, margin, threshold ◇ 较低～法 lower bound method
界限分明的　well-defined
界限寄存器　【计】limit register
界限量规　limit [difference] gauge
界限强度　threshold intensity
界限塞规　limit plug gauge
界限应力　threshold stress
界限应力强度因子幅度　threshold stress intensity factor range
界线　boundary (bndy), boundary line
借土开挖　borrow excavation
借土坑　borrow
借土填方　borrow fill
借土挖方　borrow cut
借位　【数】borrow
介电常数　dielectric constant [coefficient], inductive capacity, inductivity, permittivity(相对的) ◇ 绝对～absolute permittivity
介电常数测定器　dielectric constant meter [detector]
介电体[质]　dielectrics, dielectric substance
介电涂层　dielectric coating
介电吸收常数　dielectric absorption constant
介电系数　dielectric coefficient
介电性能[性质]　dielectric property
介观　mesoscopy
介观体系　mesoscopic system
介晶　mesomorphism
介晶态　【金】mesomorphic state
介晶相　mesomorphic phase
介孔　mesopore
介孔复合体　mesoporous composite
介孔固体　mesoporous solid
介轮　idle wheel [pulley]
介木　【建】cap-sill
介稳奥氏体　【金】metastable austenite
介稳奥氏体锰钢　metastable austenitic manganese steel
介稳定结构状态　metastable structural

介稳(定)系(统)　metastable system
介稳定性　metastability
介稳定状态图　metastable diagram
介稳定组织　metastable structure
介稳过渡相　metastable transition phase
介稳平衡　metastable equilibrium
介稳态　metastable state
介稳相　metastable phase
介稳状态　metastable condition
介原子　mes(on)ic atom
介质　medium（复数 media 或 dediums）, agency, dielectric (diel)
介质电导　dielectric conductance
介质电流　dielectric current
介质电阻　dielectric resistance
介质加热法【压】dielectric heating
介质流量　media flow
介质疲劳【电】dielectric fatigue
介质损耗系数　dielectric loss coefficient
介质相角　dielectric phase angle
介质滞后　dielectric hysteresis
介子【理】meson, mesotron
筋条　rib, fillet
筋状凸焊　ridge welding
金{Au}　gold ◇ 18 开～*, 包～的*, 标准～*, 藏～间 gold room, 掺～gold doping, 沉积～*, 除[去, 脱]～degolding, 纯～refined [virgin] gold, 电镀～chemical gilding, 法国～*, 高～含量的 highly auriferous, 含～合金*, 荷兰～*, 灰～*, 假[仿]～*, 绿～*, 热压～[粉] hot pressed gold, 天然～金钯铂合金 pallas
金钯合金　(75—90Au, 0—10Pt, 余量 Pd) white gold
金币　gold (coin), species
金铂合金　coinage gold ◇ 澳大利亚～*, 普拉蒂纳～(10—12Pt) platina
金铂合金　gold-platinum alloy
金箔　goldfoil, gold leaf, aurum foliatum ◇ 覆饰用极薄～*
金箔工人　goldbeater
金箔轧机　gold rolling machine
金伯利岩　kimberlite
金产地　goldfield
金的　golden, auriferous
金碲合金　gold-tellurium alloy ◇ 西尔瓦奈特～*
金锭　gold bullion ◇ 粗～*
金镀层　gold plating ◇ 薄～*
金锇矿　aurosmirid
金钒(电阻)合金　(1V, 99Au; 标准电阻材料) gold-vanadium alloy
金粉　gold dust
金刚砂　carborundum{SiC}, corundum（氧化铝磨料）◇ 人造～*, 天然～*
金刚砂布　carborundum cloth
金刚砂粉　powdered carborundum, pulverized corundum
金刚砂坩埚　silicon carbide sagger
金刚砂轮　carborundum wheel ◇ 金属黏结的～*
金刚砂抛光　diamond polishing
金刚砂蒸馏罐　carborundum retort
金刚砂纸　carborundum [emery] paper
金刚砂砖　refrax
金刚石　diamond, adamas ◇ 巴拉斯～(工业用) ballas, 次等～bort(z), 簇状～整修工具*, 钝～锥体 blunt diamond cone, 多～整修工具*, 三～整修工具*, 深灰[黑色]～(切削工具) carbonado, 镶嵌有～的硬质合金工具 diamond-impregnated hard metal tool, 镶一粒～的整修工具 single (point) diamond dressing tool, 镶有～的工具 dia-tool, 镶有～的岩心钻头 diamond-impregnated core drill bit
金刚石测量头　diamond-measuring head
金刚石(衬底)电路　diamond circuit
金刚石顶锤　diamond-pointed hammer
金刚石粉　diamond powder [dust], bortz powder
金刚石粉抛光　diamond burnishing
金刚石复合物[片]　diamond composite

金 jin

金刚石钢　extra-hard steel
金刚石工[刀]具　diamond tool, dia-tool
金刚石夹(加工金刚石用)　dop
金刚石尖锥体　pointed diamond cone
金刚石结构　diamond (lattice) structure
金刚石聚晶　polycrystalline diamond
金刚石颗粒　diamond grain
金刚石拉丝模抛光机　【压】diamond die polishing machine
金刚石棱锥体　diamond pyramid ◇ 方底～*
金刚石棱锥体压头硬度　(同"维氏硬度")
金刚石立方结构　diamond cubic structure
金刚石模　diamond die
金刚石磨[砂]轮　diamond-impregnated (grinding) wheel, diamond (grinding) wheel
金刚石抛光粉　diamond polishing powder
金刚石切割机　【耐】diamond cutting machine
金刚石切割轮　diamond cut-off wheel
金刚石(切削)刀具　diamond cutter
金刚石球状压头(硬度试验用)　diamond ball impressor
金刚石砂轮修整器　【机】diamond dresser
金刚石显微硬度试验　◇ 努普～Knoop hardness test
金刚石型点阵[晶格]　【金】diamond (type) lattice
金刚石型立方点阵　diamond cubic lattice
金刚石压头(硬度试验机的)　diamond-measuring head, diamond penetrator ◇ 棱锥形～*, 球形～*
金刚石研磨膏　diamond paste
金刚石岩心钻头　diamond-impregnated core drill bit
金刚石圆锥压头　diamond spheroconical penetrator, diamond cone ◇ 布雷尔～*
金刚石整修工具　diamond dressing tool
金刚石整修工具头　diamond-impregnated head

金刚石正四棱锥体　square-based diamond pyramid
金刚石制品　diamond article [composition] ◇ 金属黏结的～*
金刚石撞针　hammer deamond
金刚状石蜡晶体　diamond-shaped paraffin crystal
金刚石钻进　diamond boring
金刚石钻孔　diamond boring
金刚石钻头　diamond drill (D.D.), diamond-impregnated drill, cast-set diamond bit
金刚石钻岩机　diamond drill
金刚钻　diamond
金工车间　machine shop
金工用锯　metal saw
金汞齐[汞膏]　gold amalgam
金钴热电偶合金(2.1Co, 余量 Au)　gold cobalt alloy
金焊料(5.8—3Au, 1.15Ag, 1.86Cu, 1.15Cd)　gold solder
金焊料合金(5.8—6.5Au, 1.2—2.2Ag, 1.2—2.2Cu)　gold soldering alloy
金合金　gold alloy, billon ◇ 高～high gold content alloy, 黄色～(同"22 开黄金")*, 索夫林～*
金衡盎司[英两]　ounce troy (oz. t.), troy ounce
金衡制　troy ◇ 英国～重量 troy weight
金红石{TiO_2}　rutile, titanic schorl
金红石氯化　chlorination of rutile
金红石型结构　rutile type structure
金红钛铁岩　urbainite
金化合物　gold compound ◇ 二价～divalent gold compound
金黄钡铀矿{$BaO \cdot 6UO_3 \cdot 11H_2O$}　billietite
金黄色断口　golden-yellow fracture
金辉铋矿　aurobismuthimite
金辉砷镍矿　sommarugaite
金霍恩黄铜(含 1Fe, 1Sn 的六 O 黄铜)　Kinghorn metal

金基合金 gold base alloy
金精炼(法) gold-refining ◇ 氰化物~*
金库 gold room
金块 gold bullion
金矿床 gold deposit
金矿区 goldfield
金矿(石) gold(-bearing) [auriferous] ore ◇ 含铜~copper gold
金矿物 gold mineral
金扩散 gold doping
金铑合金 gold-rhodium alloy ◇ 罗塔尼乌姆~*，天然~*
金莲橙-D (同"甲基橙")
金铝合金(78Au,22Al) violet gold
金绿宝石{BeO·Al$_2$O$_3$} chrysoberyl, alumoberyl
金末 gold dust
金泥 gold mud
金泥熔炼 gold-slime smelting
金尼-奥斯本法(制造膨胀渣)【铁】 Kinney-Osbourne process
金尼型机械真空泵 Kinney pump
金镍低熔点合金 nioro
金纽南法 kinnunen method
金漆 gold lacquer ◇ 荷兰~*
金融 finance
金色黄铜 ◇ 里奇~*
金色黄铜板带(7Zn,93Cu) cartridge gilding
金色铝青铜(3—5Al,余量 Cu) gold bronze
金色涂层 gilt
金氏电炉【钢】 Gin furnace
金属 metal (Me.,met.) ◇ 补加~added metal, 不含~液 lean liquor, 不活泼[钝化]~*，初级[初炼,原,未用过的]~*，次要~ minor metal, 粗~*，脆性[易碎]~ friable metal, 大块~ massive metal, 带渣~ drossy metal, 多孔~*，非晶体~*，废弃~ discard(ed) metal, 覆[包]~的 metal-faced, 复合~*，高性能~ high performance metal, 海绵~metallic sponge, 含~的*，黑色~ ferrous metal, 活泼[活性]~ active metal, 火冶~furnace metal, 紧密~*，泡沫状~【粉】foamed metal, 气敏[气脆]~*，烧结~synthetic metal, 双晶型~ dimorphous metal, (酸碱)两性~ amphoteric metal, 同规格~*，原样[未加涂饰的]~ bare metal, 无气~*，纤维强化~*，阳极[负电位]~ anode [anodic] metal, 一炉(次)~ heat of metal, 易熔~ fusible metal, 异种~ heterogeneous metal, 游离~ free metal, 有色~ nonferrous metal, 与氧素和力大的~ oxygen hungry metal, 直接~*，致密~dense metal, 中间~*，助熔~ flux metal
金属 X 射线照相术 metal radiography
金属螯合物 metal shelate (compound)
金属板 metal plate
金属板材圆盘[纵切]剪 metal slitting cutter
金属板护罩 sheet metal lagging
金属板网 perforated metal
金属板延性试验仪 sheet metal ductility testing instrument
金属板余料 scissel
金属半成品 melter product
金属-半导体过渡层 metal-semiconductor junction
金属-半导体接触 metal-semiconductor contact
金属半固态铸造成型技术【铸】 semi-solid metal casting
金属棒材 bar metal
金属包覆(层) metal cladding, cladding of metal, clad(ding)
金属包壳 (活性金属的)canning
金属包皮 metal casing, metallic sheath
金属包套铸坯 canned billet
金属包头 ferrule
金属薄板 sheet metal, latten ◇ 瓦垄形~corrugated sheet
金属薄板加工 sheet metal working

金属薄层大电流快速触击电镀　striking
金属保护　metal protection
金属保护层　coat of metal
金属爆炸差厚成形法　metal gathering
金属爆炸成形　explosive metal forming ◇ 戴纳法～Dynaforming
金属爆炸成形法　propellant powered metal forming method
金属爆炸冲压装置【压】metal-explosive system
金属比较仪　metal comparator
金属编织物　laces
金属变形　flow of metal
金属表面保护　metal surface protection
金属表面显微照相　metallograph
金属表面氧化　tarnishing
金属玻璃(含P-B半金属的Fe、FeNi合金)　metglass
金属波纹管　metal bellows
金属箔　metal foil [leaf, paper], metallic foil
金属箔带式盖板滚对焊　tape butt-seam welding
金属箔冶金学　foil metallurgy
金属不恰当合金化　faulty alloying of metal
金属部件　metal component
金属材料　metal(lic) material
金属残料　【冶】leftover metal
金属层(压木)板　metal wood
金属层压制品　metal laminate
金属产出率　metal yield [fall]
金属产物流(萃取的)　metal product stream
金属超电压　metal overvoltage
金属沉积量　amount of metal deposited
金属沉积物　metal deposit
金属衬垫　metal gasket [insert]
金属衬里的　metal-lined
金属成分　component metal
金属成品率　metal yield
金属成形　metal forming

金属成形法　metal-forming process
金属成形模　metal-forming die
金属处理学会(美国)　Metal Treating Institute (MTI)
金属穿轧性能　pierceability
金属传递　metal transfer
金属纯度　metal purity
金属纯度试样　refining assay
金属催化剂　metallic catalyst
金属脆性转变温度试验　◇蒂氏～*
金属带矫平　metal strip flattening
金属带镶边　implate
金属氮化物氧化物半导体　metal nitride oxide-semiconductor (MNOS)
金属－氮化物－氧化物－硅　metal-ni-tride-oxide-silicon (MNOS)
金属－氮化物－氧化物－硅半导体　MNOS semiconductor
金属导体　metallic conductor
金属导(线)管　metal conduit
金属的　metallic, metalline, metalliferous
金属滴液　【冶】dropping metal
金属底层的覆盖层　metal-backed coating
金属点阵　metal lattice
金属电导率　metallic conductivity
金属电弧表面切割　metal-arc gouging
金属电极[焊条]　metal electrode
金属电极电位　metal electrode potential
金属电位　metal potential
金属电阻　metallic resistance [resistor]
金属锭　ingot (metal), metal ingot, pig [crude] metal, block ◇弧熔～arc-cast metal, 直熔～dingot metal
金属锭生产法　ingot production process
金属锭生锈[锈蚀]　ingot staining
金属镀层　metal coat(ing), metallic coating, coat of metal ◇除去～demetallization
金属镀层保护　protection by metallic coating
金属镀层孔隙度电图检查　electrographic test

金属镀层孔隙度电图显示法 electrography

金属镀覆 coat of metal

金属对 metal pair

金属对轧辊单位压力 specific rolling pressure

金属对轧辊平均单位压力 mean specific roll pressure

金属对轧辊压力 【压】rolling pressure

金属对轧辊总压力 total rolling pressure

金属对轧辊作用合力(轧制时的) resultant roll force

金属飞溅 【冶】metal splashing

金属-非金属制品 metal-nonmetal combination

金属废料 waste [scrap] metal, metal rejects ◇ 含铜~*

金属废料利用 【冶】metal salvage

金属分布 metal distribution

金属分段浇铸 combined intermediate-and-top pouring

金属分馏真空泵 metal fractionating pump

金属分配比 metal distribution ratio

金属分选系统 (同"金属回收系统")

金属粉粒 metal-powder grain, metal particle

金属粉末 metal powder, powdered metal (PM), finely divided metal ◇ 被覆[包镀]~ coated metal powder, 电弧熔化用~*, 粉冶用~*, 化学沉淀~热挤压~坯*, 铜溶~*, 雾化~ atomized metal powder

金属粉末成品 finished metal powder

金属粉末成形 metal-powder forming, shaping of metal powder, moulding of metal powder

金属粉末成形法 method of metal powder formation

金属粉末磁力密实 magnetical consolidating of metal powder

金属粉末工业 metal-powder industry

金属粉末工业联合会(美国) Metal Powder Industries Federation (M.P.I.F.)

金属粉末工业联合会标准 M.P.I.F. standard

金属粉末刮机 carding machine

金属粉末混合 mixing of metal powder

金属粉末计量装置 metal-powder metering apparatus

金属粉末流动性测定仪 metal-powder flow meter

金属粉末喷镀 metal-powder spraying

金属粉末喷[注]射成型[形] metal powder injection moulding (MIM)

金属粉末生产 metal-powder production

金属粉末特性 characteristic of metal powder

金属粉末协会(美国) Metal Powder Association (M.P.A.)

金属粉末协会标准 M.P.A. standard

金属粉末压坯 【粉】metal-powder compact

金属粉末压实[压力]机 powder metal press

金属粉末氧熔切割 metal powder oxygen cutting (POC)

金属粉末轧机 metal-powder rolling mill

金属粉末轧制 metal-powder rolling

金属粉末轧制带材 powder strip

金属粉末制的磁铁 metal-powder magnet

金属粉末制品 metal body from powder

金属粉末制取 formation of metal powder ◇ 曼内斯曼~法*

金属粉末装料室 metal-powder charging chamber

金属粉末自燃性 pyrophoricity of metal powder

金属封油环 grummet, grommet

金属缝缀钢丝 metal-stitching wire

金属辐射屏 metal radiation screen

金属浮渣 metal dross, dross metallics

金属腐蚀 metallic corrosion

金属腐蚀剂 mordant

金属覆层　metal coating, ironclad
金属复合材料　metal composite
金属隔膜泵　metallic diaphragm pump
金属铬　metallic chromium
金属工艺　smithcraft
金属工艺学　technology of metals
金属构件　hardware
金属箍　ferrule, aglet
金属骨架　metallic skeleton ◇基础~*
金属固定　metal fixation
金属固体　metallic solid
金属管　metal tube ◇复合~clad tube
金属光学　【理】metal optics
金属光泽　metallic lustre [luster]
金属光泽的　metalescent
金属硅（＞98Si，＜0.3C，＜0.05P，＜0.05S，＜0.8Fe）　metallic silicon
金属轨枕　sleeper plate
金属过渡特性　【焊】metal transfer characteristic
金属过滤器　metal [metallic] filter
金属焊接　metal welding ◇大断面[厚件]~heavy welding
金属焊条　metal electrode
金属焊条弧焊法　metallic arc-welding method
金属和铸型反应[相互作用]　【铸】metal-mould reaction
金属合金　metal alloy
金属合金元素　metallic alloying element
金属弧焊定位　metal-arc-weld tack
金属弧焊法　metallic arc-welding method
金属护皮电极　sheathed electrode
金属互化物　(同"金属间化合物") ◇铝的~aluminide
金属花边　laces
金属滑动框架（滑动水口的）　metallic slider housing
金属化　metallization, metallizing ◇球团~(率)*
金属化百分率　percentage metallization
金属化产品　metallized product

金属化度　degree of metallization
金属化过程　metallisation process
金属化合物　metal(lic) compound
金属(化)锍　metallic matte
金属化率　【团】percent metallization, degree of metallization
金属化球团(矿)　【团】metallized pellet
金属化球团法　metallized pelletizing
金属化烧结矿　metallized sinter
金属化铁　metallized iron
金属化团块　metallized briquette
金属化温度　metallizing temperature
金属化物　【金】metallide
金属化学　metallochemistry
金属化学损失　chemical metal loss
金属化造块　metallized agglomerate
金属化作用　metalation
金属环　becket(t), ferrule
金属还原(法)　metallothermic [metallic] reduction
金属还原剂　metallic reducing agent
金属换热器　metallic recuperator ◇翅管式~*
金属回收设备　metal recovery unit
金属回收系统　metal recovery system, metal-reclaiming system
金属混合物　metallic mixture
金属基复合材料　metal matrix composite (MMC)
金属基复合材料发动机　MMC engine
金属基体（合金的）　metal(lic) matrix, groundmass
金属基体复合物[材料]　metal matrix composite
金属机械损失　mechanical metal loss
金属极电弧　【焊】metal arc
金属极电弧焊　metal(lic) arc welding ◇气体保护~*
金属极电弧焊条　metal-arc electrode
金属极电弧(切)割　metal-arc cutting (MAC)
金属极惰性气体保护焊　(同"惰性气体

保护金属极电弧焊")
金属极氩弧焊接 argon metal-arc welding
金属级二氧化铀 metal grade uranium dioxide
金属级品位纯度 metal-grade (purity)
金属挤压 metal extrusion
金属夹杂(物) metallic inclusions
金属加工 metal-working, metal finishing
金属加工工业 metal-working [metal-processing] industry
金属加工工艺 metal working process
金属加工机械 metal-working machinery
金属加工润滑剂 metal-processing lubricant
金属加工设备 metal-working equipment
金属加热元件 metallic heating element
金属加入料 added metal
金属架 metal stock
金属间化合物 intermetallic compound, intermetallics, metallide
金属间化合物半导体 intermetallic compound semiconductor
金属间化合物材料 intermetallic material
金属间化合物合金 intermetallic alloy
金属间化合物夹杂 intermetallic inclusions
金属间相 【金】intermetallic phase
金属间相颗粒 intermetallic phase particle
金属间相离析 intermetallic phases isolation
金属检出器 metal detector
金属鉴别仪 【冶】metalsorter
金属键 metallic bind(ing) [bond, linkage]
金属键半径 metallic radius
金属键力 metallic forces
金属键型 metallic form of binding
金属溅镀 sputtering of metal
金属胶合板 metal wood
金属浇槽 【铸】pouring slot
金属浇注温度 metal pouring temperature
金属矫直 metal straightening
金属接触传递 metal transfer

金属结构 metallic structure
金属结构材料 structural metallic material
金属结合力 metallic cohesion
金属浸出率 metal extraction
金属晶格 metal lattice
金属晶体 metal(lic) crystal
金属晶体生长 metal-crystal growth
金属晶须 metal whisker
金属精炼 metal purification [purifying], refining of metal
金属精炼法 (metal-)purifying process
金属精整 metal finishing
金属静力学的 metallostatic
金属聚集槽 metal-collecting trough
金属-绝缘体-半导体器件 metal-insulator-semiconductor device
金属开槽[缝]机 metal slitting machine
金属开槽锯 metal slitting saw
金属壳 metal casing, metallic shell
金属空气换热器 metallic air recuperator
金属孔眼 grummet, grommet
金属块 metal berby [block, biscuit], derby (metal), prill, regulus (复数 reguli) ◇ 制取试样的~ test piece
金属块生产 derby metal production
金属快速触击电镀 【金】striking
金属快速电镀电解液 striking solution
金属框铅锡合金(45Pb, 40Sn, 15Cu) conffin metal
金属矿 metallic ore
金属矿床 metallic mineral deposit, metal deposit, metalliferous ore deposit
金属矿物 metallic mineral
金属矿相学 mineragraphy
金属拉制 metal drawing
金属累计总压下量(多道次轧制的) cumulative reduction
金属冷态静液压成型(法) hydrostatic cold metal forming
金属离子 metal(lic) ion
金属离子浓度 metal ion concentration
金属粒 granulated [grained] metal,

(metallic) shot, clipped wire（用冷拔钢丝切碎的）
金属粒化(制粉法)　shotting
金属粒子　metallic granule, metallics
金属量测定器　metallometer
金属料　metal charge [stock], metallics
金属料头　leftover metal
金属料消耗　specific metal consumption
金属料与消耗焦炭重量比　metallic charge-to-coke ratio
金属磷化物　metal phosphide
金属磷酸膜被覆法　rovalising
金属硫化物　metallic sulphide
金属硫化物氧化细菌　metallic-sulphide-oxidizing bacteria
金属硫酸盐　metallic sulphate
金属流变　flow of metal
金属流长度　metal stream length
金属流出(焊接熔池的)　metal runout
金属流出口　metal notch
金属流动(轧制时的)　metal(lic) flow
金属炉壳　metal shell
金属炉料　【冶】metallics of charge
金属卤化物　metal halide
金属卤化物添加剂　metal halide additive
金属铝　metallic aluminium
金属铝氧化物半导体　metal-alumina-oxide semiconductor（MAOS）
金属氯化物　metallic chloride ◇ 低沸点~
金属氯化物溶液　metal chloride solution
金属滤网　delay screen
金属螺旋绳芯钢丝绳　metallic spiral core wire rope
金属络合物　metal complex
金属毛坯【压】metal block
金属镁　magnesium metal
金属棉　metal wool
金属模　metallic die,【铸】chilled mould
金属模铸造试样　【铸】chill cast sample
金属膜　metal(lic) film, metallic membrane

金属膜电阻(器)　metal film resistor, metalster
金属膜盒　metal bellows
金属磨料　metal abrasive
金属磨蚀　metal fretting
金属磨损　metallic wear, galling
金属摩擦　metallic friction
金属纳米材料　metallic nano material
金属内衬　metal lining
金属铌粉　niobium metal powder
金属黏合(工艺)　metallic bind(ing), metlbond
金属黏结的金刚砂轮　metal bonded diamond wheel
金属黏结的金刚石制品　metal-bonded diamond article
金属黏结剂　metal binder, binder metal
金属黏结钻探用金刚石　metal-bond(ed) drilling diamond
金属偶　metal pair
金属抛光　metal polish
金属喷镀[涂]　metal(lic) spray(ing), (spray) metallizing, metallization, metallising, sprayed metal coating, metalling, metalikon ◇ 电弧~arc metal spraying
金属喷镀层　sprayed metal coating, sprayed-on [metallized] coating
金属喷镀法　metallization process, metallikon ◇ 坩埚~mellozing, 梅塔莱厄~ Metalayer process
金属喷镀钢丝　spray wire
金属喷镀[涂]器　pistol, gas metallizator
金属喷镀枪　metal spray(ing) gun, metallizing gun, metal pulverizer
金属喷镀头　metallizing head
金属喷溅损失　【焊】scatter
金属喷射覆层法　metallikon
金属喷涂(法)　metallikon
金属喷涂线材　metallizing wire
金属喷雾法　spray gun process
金属喷嘴　metal orifice
金属坯块　metal compact

金属疲劳　metal fatigue
金属片　sheet metal ◇ 薄～foil
金属平衡　metal balance, balance of metal
金属屏蔽线　metal-shielded wire
金属破碎机　metal disintegrating machine, metal disintegrator
金属漆　metallic paint
金属器皿　metalware
金属铅　metallic [blue] lead
金属前滑(轧制的)　forward creep
金属强度降低　weakening of metal
金属切除率　metal removal [loss] rate
金属切割　metal cutting
金属切割器　metal cutter
金属切削(加工)　metal (removally) cutting, machining of metal
金属切削机床用钢　machine tool steel
金属氢　hydrogenium, metallic hydrogen
金属氢化物　metal hydride
金属氢氧化物　metal hydroxide
金属清理机　metal-cleaning machinery
金属清理用粉　【金】permag
金属球团连续加料熔炼法　◇ SLPM 电弧炉内～【钢】SLPM process
金属区域精炼　zone-refining of metal
金属取代　metallation
金属染色　dyeing of metal, metallochromy
金属染色探裂法　met-L-chek
金属热处理有关术语定义联合委员会　Joint Committee on Definitions of Terms Relating to Heat treatment of Metals (JHT)
金属热电偶　metallic thermocouple
金属热法坩埚　thermit crucible
金属热反应　metallothermic reaciton
金属热还原　metallothermic [metallic] reduction, thermit(e) reduction, reduction with metal ◇ 氟化物～", 氧化物～"
金属热还原法　metallothermic process [method], thermit(e) process, bomb (reduction) process, metallothermics
金属热还原反应　thermit(e) [bomb] reaction

金属热还原炉料　metal reduction charge
金属热还原熔炼　metallothermic smelting
金属热熔炼车间　exothermic smelter shop
金属熔池　metal(lic) bath, molten bath, pool of (molten) metal, molten metal well (冲天炉的), puddle ◇ 氧枪喷头至～距离　lance-tip metal distance
金属熔炼设备　metal-melting equipment
金属熔体　metallic bath ◇ 出～槽　tapping spout, 放出[倾出]～metal tapping
金属－熔渣反应　metal-slag reactions
金属－(熔)渣乳化物　metal-slag emulsion
金属溶解　metal dissolution
金属溶质　solute metal
金属容器　pot, canister
金属软管　flexible metal tubing, metallic hose
金属筛焊接机　(同"钢丝网焊接机")
金属烧损　【铁】iron loss
金属烧箱　metal sagger
金属烧舟　metal boat
金属伸缩软管　metal bellows
金属渗镀法　cementation metallization
金属渗入砂型　burning-in
金属渗碳　metallic cementation
金属渗透　metal penetration
金属渗渍碳　metallized carbon
金属石墨材料　metal-graphite material
金属石墨电刷　metal-graphite brush
金属石墨复合物　metal-graphite composite
金属石墨制品　metal-graphite combinations
金属饰面材料　metal finishing material
金属饰[砌]面的　【建】metal-lined
金属试验器　metallometer
金属试样　metal sample [specimen]
金属试珠(试金用)　test button
金属收得率　metallic yield, metal efficiency
金属收[捕]集坑(水力除灰系统的)

【冶】catch pit
金属丝 wire, metal(lic) filament ◇ 粗（直径）~ heavy gauge wire, 切断用~【耐】cutting wire, 热拉~ hot drawing wire, 涡流法~检验仪 wiretester, 硬拉~ hard drawn wire
金属丝编织层软管 braided metallic flexible pipe
金属丝编织方眼筛 woven-wire square-mesh screen
金属丝布 wire cloth
金属丝电阻应变仪 wire gauge
金属丝吊篮 screen wire basket
金属丝法(校正热电偶) wire method
金属丝放电电极 wire discharge electrode
金属丝喷射枪 wire pistol
金属丝检验仪(涡流法的) wiretester
金属丝伸长计 wire strain gauge
金属(丝)刷 wire brush
金属丝网 wire mesh [cloth], (metal) gauze ◇ 平纹~ plain
金属丝网隔膜 wire gauze diaphragm
金属丝网筛[金属丝方孔筛] wire screen
金属丝细筛 wire sieve
金属丝应变计[张力计,发送器] wire strain gauge
金属丝振打机构 wire rapping mechanism
金属丝制品 wirework
金属丝竹节状脱裂 off-setting
金属丝铠装的 wire-armored (W.A.)
金属塑料复合物 【冶】plastimets
金属塑性 metal ductility
金属碎屑 sludge
金属损耗 lost metal
金属损失 metal loss
金属损失率 metal loss rate
金属钛 metallic titanium, titanium metal
金属碳化物 metal(lic) carbide ◇ 难熔~ refractory carbide
金属探测器 metal detector ◇ γ射线~ *
金属探伤器 stethoscope, flaw detector
金属羰基化合物 metal carbonyl

金属陶瓷 metal-ceramics, metalloceramics, cermet, ceramal(s), ceramet, ceramatallics, sintered-metal ◇ 高铬~ *, 铬-氧化铝~ *, 摩擦~ friction cermet, 热压~ hot press cermet, 碳化物基~ *, 氧化物-金属型~ *
金属陶瓷材料 cermet material ◇ 弥散硬化型~ *
金属陶瓷电沉积涂层 cermet electrodeposited coating
金属陶瓷电阻 cermet resistance
金属陶瓷复合材料 metal-ceramic(s) composite
金属陶瓷合金 ceramic metal
金属陶瓷化合物 cermet compound
金属陶瓷混成物 metal-ceramic composition
金属陶瓷混合物 cermet mixture
金属-陶瓷间封接 metat-to-ceramic seal
金属陶瓷接触器 cermet contactor
金属陶瓷模 cermet mould
金属陶瓷喷涂 metal-ceramic spraying
金属陶瓷烧结制品 metal-ceramic agglomerate
金属陶瓷涂层 (metal-)cermet coating
金属陶瓷学[术] metal-ceramics
金属陶瓷制品 ceramic-metal combinations, metal-ceramic ◇ 烧结~ sinterings
金属套电阻加热器 metal sheathed electrical resistance heater
金属套管 metallic sheath, metal sleeve
金属套管加热器 metal-sheathed heater
金属特性 metallic character, metallicity
金属锑 metallic [regulus] antimony ◇ 低品位~ *
金属提纯 metal purifying
金属添加剂 metallic addition
金属填料 metallic packing
金属条材 bar metal
金属铁 metallic iron ◇ 磁(性)~ magnetic metallic iron, 局部化学~层 *, 纤维状~生成 *

金属铁(含量)测定	determination of metallic iron
金属同流换热器	metallic recuperator
金属铜	metallic copper
金属涂层	metal coat(ing)
金属涂层保护	protection by metallic coating
金属涂底	metal primer
金属涂覆温度	metallizing temperature
金属湍流	metal turbulence
金属外壳	metal shell [jacket]
金属外套	metal jacket
金属弯月面	metal meniscus
金属弯制	metal bending
金属丸	(metallic) shot
金属丸粒制作与喷镀综合处理法	◇米德兰德－罗斯～*
金属网	wire net(ting)
金属网带输送机	woven-wire-mesh belt conveyor
金属网电极	wire gauze electrode
金属网焊接电极	cross-wire welding die
金属网络	metallic network
金属网筛	wire-mesh screen
金属网(运输)带	wire netting belt
金属网用钢丝	netting [weaving] wire
金属温度计	metallic thermometer
金属污染	metallic pollutant
金属无名损失	unknown metal loss
金属雾	metal fog, pyrosol
金属雾层	metal mist layer
金属物返料	revert metallics
金属物理损失	physical metal loss
金属物理(学)	metal physics, physics of metals
金属物料	metalliferous material
金属物质	metallics ◇炉料～*
金属析出量	amount of metal deposited
金属细粉	metal fines
金属细丝	metallic filament
金属纤维	metal-fibre, metal-fiber
金属纤维粉末冶金	fibre metallurgy
金属线	metal wire, wire (line)
金属线材卷取装置	reeling facility
金属相	metallic phase
金属小粒	metallic granule
金属小珠[球]	prill, button
金属屑	(metal) filings, metal chill, grit, sweeping(s)
金属屑黏覆(冷轧带钢的)	sludge build-up
金属屑压块机	【冶】swarf baling [briquetting] machine
金属锌	metallic zinc
金属型	【铸】cast iron mould, (gravity) die, metal mold
金属型材	(metal) shape
金属型离心铸造	die spinning
金属型涂料	die coating
金属型芯	【铸】metal core, inserts
金属型铸造	gravity [non-pressure] die casting, chill casting, permanent mo(u)ld casting ◇气压～*
金属性的变化	metallic transition
金属性能[性质]	metallic property, metallicity
金属性能变坏	deterioration of metallic properties
金属须	(metal) whisker
金属旋压法	metal spining method
金属学	metallography
金属学会(英国)	Institute of Metals, Metals Society (MS, Met. Soc.)
金属压力加工方法	metal-forming process
金属压制材料	metal forming product
金属烟雾病	metal fume fever
金属盐	metal-salt, saline
金属延性	metal ductility
金属颜料	metallic pigment
金属阳极	metal anode
金属氧化动力学	kinetics of metal oxidation
金属氧化铝半导体	metal-alumina-semiconductor (MAS)

金属－氧化铝－氧化物－硅（结构） metal-alumina-oxide-silicon（MAOS）
金属氧化物 metal(lic) oxide
金属－氧化物－半导体 metal-oxide-semiconductor（MOS）
金属－氧化物－半导体场效应晶体管 metal-oxide-semiconductor field-effect-transistor（MOS FET, MOST）
金属－氧化物－半导体二极管 MOS(metal-oxide-semiconductor) diode
金属－氧化物－半导体电容器 MOS(metal-oxide-semiconductor) capacitor
金属－氧化物－半导体晶体管 MOS(metal-oxide-semiconductor) transistor
金属－氧化物－硅 metal-oxide-silicon（MOS）
金属氧化物还原 reduction of metal oxide
金属氧化物弥散强化复合材料 metal-oxide dispersion composite
金属氧化物研磨纸 crocus paper
金属氧化锡浮渣 scruff
金属冶炼厂 metal smelting [production] plant, smelter(y), smelting works
金属液 molten metal ◇ 补缩～【铸】feed metal, 放出的～【冶】spout metal
金属液层 metal pad
金属液池 metal reservoir
金属液滴 dripping
金属液放出装置 tapping arrangement
金属液含气试验 【铸】settling test
金属液流动性 molten metal fluidity
金属液面 metal bath surface, 【冶】hot metal line
金属液面高度 metal level
金属液面以下距离(结晶器中的) 【连铸】depth below casting level
金属液容器 【冶】metallic reservoir
金属液深度 depth of bath
金属一氧化物 metal monoxide
金属移变作用 metallotrophy
金属异物检出器 tramp metal detector
金属异型材 metal special shape

金属银 argent
金属硬脂酸盐 metal stearate
金属铀 metallic uranium
金属油扩散泵 ◇ 三级～ three-stage metal pump
金属有机化合物 organo-metal
金属有机物的 metallorganic
金属与金属黏合压力 【粉】pressure of metal-to-metal sticking
金属与药包间界面(爆炸成形) metal-explosive interface
金属浴 metal bath
金属浴处理 metal bath treatment
金属浴淬火 metal-bath hardening
金属浴钎焊 metal dip brazing
金属元素 metallic element
金属元素粉末 elemental metal powder
金属原料 raw metal
金属原子 metal atom
金属原子排列 metal atom arrangement
金属跃迁(现象) 【理】metallic transition
金属杂质 metal(lic) impurity, foreign metal impurity
金属载热剂 heat transfer metal
金属皂 metal(lic) soap
金属渣 scoria
金属渣的 scoriaceous
金属－渣平衡 metal-slag equilibrium
金属轧件断面积压缩率 reduction of cross-sectional area
金属轧制 metal rolling
金属毡 metal felt
金属蒸气 metallic vapour
金属蒸气压 metal vapour pressure
金属蒸气中毒 metal fume fever
金属整流器 metal(lic) [dry] rectifier
金属支承架 metal back-up
金属置换 metal replacement
金属置换精炼法 metal substitution refining process
金属制垃圾箱 trash can
金属制品 metal product [work], metal-

jīn 金

金属制品用青铜 hardware bronze
金属制漆器 metal-made lacquer-ware
金属制设备 metal unit
金属质量 metal quality
金属中电子抗磁性 metal electron diamagnetism
金属珠 metallic bead, regulus
金属着色剂 metallochrome
金属总回收率 overall metal recovery
金属铸锭 cast metal
金属铸件 metal(lic) casting
金属铸件变形致密化 consolidation of cast metal by deformation
金属铸块 pig metal
金属-铸模界面 metal-mould interface
金属铸型 【铸】metal [chill] mould
金属铸造 metalcasting, metallic casting
金属装料 metal charge
金属状态 metallic state
金属准静态裂纹增长 quasi-static crack growth in metal
金属总压下量(多道次轧制的) overall reduction
金属组分 component metal, metallic constituent
金属组织 metal structure ◇ 加工~*
金斯顿锡铜轴承合金(88Sn, 6Cu, 6Hg) Kingston's alloy
金丝垫圈 gold wire gasket
金丝垫圈密封 gold gasket seal
金丝环 gold wire gasket
金条 gold bullion [bar]
金铁合金 blue gold
金铜斑 bronzing
金铜焊料 gold-copper brazing alloy
金铜合金 gold copper ◇ 18开~18K gold-copper alloy, 以铜固溶强化的~ copper-hardened gold
金铜矿 auricupride, cuproauride
金铜齐 cuproauride
金锡钎焊合金 gold-tin alloy

金相 metallurgical phase
金相变化 metallurgical phase change
金相分析 metallographic examination
金相观察 metallographic(al) observation
金相技术 metallographic technique [technology]
金相检验 metallographic(al) examination [test(ing)]
金相浸蚀 metallographic etching
金相浸蚀剂 metallographic etchant
金相抛光 metallographic polishing
金相切片 microsection
金相切片机 microtome
金相试片抛光机 metallographic(al) polisher
金相试验[实验]室 metallography laboratory
金相试样 metallographic specimen
金相(试样)制备 metallographic preparation
金相显微构造[组织] metallurgical microstructure
金相显微镜 metallographic [metallurgical] microscope, metalloscope ◇ 广视场~*, 洽特里亚型立式~*
金相显微镜检验术 metalloscopy
金相学 metallography, chalkography ◇ 电子~ electron metallography, 断口~*, 高温高分辨率~*
金相学的 metallographic(al)
金相研究 metallographic study, metallurgical survey
金相研究室 metallurgy cell
金相研究装置 metallographic facilities
金相研磨机 metallographic grinder
金相照片 metallograph, photomicrograph
金相照相机[照相显微镜,显微照相仪] metallograph
金相组织 metallographic [metallurgical] structure
金屑 gold dust
金旋光 bright turned

金叶　gold leaf
金银　gold-silver ◇ GS～触点合金*, 标定～精炼炉*, 干式～分析法 dry assay, 溴氰化提～法 bromocyanide process
金银铂　platinum-gold-silver（PGS）
金银铂合金　◇ 电触头～*
金银（粗金属,合金）锭　bullion（bar）, dore bullion（bar）
金银合金　gold-silver alloy, dor'e metal ◇ 埃雷克特鲁～*, 白色～*
金银合金镀覆［覆层］　gold silver alloy plating
金银精矿　gold-silver concentrate
金银块　dor'e metal
金银矿　kuestelite
金银炉　dor'e furnace
金银首饰　jewel
金银丝首饰　filigree
金银铜镍合金　pink gold
金银铸模　skillet
金云母｛$H_4K_2Mg_6Al_2Si_6O_{24}$｝　phlogopite, bronze mica
金泽尔缺口弯曲试验　Kinzel test
金制的　gold
金制接合线　gold bonding wire
金制容器　goldplate
津卡利厄姆铝合金　（12Zn,3Cu,余量 Al）Zinkalium
津纳尔双面包锡双金属轧制耐蚀铝板　Zinnal
津贴(费)　subsidy, allownce, bounty ◇ 政府～*
紧凑拉伸试样　CT（compact tension）specimen
紧凑式薄板坯连铸连轧生产线　compact strip production（CSP）
紧凑式电炉冶金短流程　compact EAF route flowsheet
紧凑式钢轨生产　compact rail production（CRP）
紧凑式钢轨生产工艺　CRP process
紧凑式钢梁生产　compact beam production（CBP）
紧凑式钢梁生产工艺　CBP process
紧凑式连铸连轧设备　compact continuous casting and rolling equipment
紧凑式轧机　compact rolling mill
紧凑式带钢厂　compact strip plant（CSP）
紧凑型带钢生产线　compact strip production line
紧凑型钢厂　（compact）mini(-)mill, mini steel plant
紧凑型工厂　mini(-)mill, miniplant, miniworks
紧凑型工艺流程　compact process flow, compact processing route
紧凑型一体化钢厂　integrated compact mill
紧带器　belt tightener
紧叠轧制　tight pack rolling
紧固　fastening, fixture, fastening down（铸型的）◇ 手工～的 hand tight
紧固材料　fastening material
紧固件　fastener, fastening（part, piece）◇ 钢～*
紧固螺钉　fastening［holding, forcing］screw
紧固螺栓　fastening［binding］bolt
紧固强度　fastening strength
紧急备用泵　emergency pump
紧急备用管道　emergency pipe line
紧急备用烟囱　emergency stack
紧急操作［紧急状态工作］　emergency operation
紧急措施　emergency（counter）measure, crash program
紧急定货　rush order
紧急控制装置　emergency control
紧急情况出铁　emergency tapping
紧急刹车、　emergency brake［stop］
紧急事故剪切　emergency shearing
紧急释放［脱扣］　emergency release
紧急停车　abort
紧急危险情况　critical emergency

紧急信号 urgent signal
紧急修理 emergency repair, rush repair job
紧急制动器[紧急闸] emergency brake
紧急状况 emergency
紧键 tightening key
紧卷 tight coil, tightly wound coil ◇ 线卷～装置*
紧卷台 压 tight coiling table
紧卷退火 tight coil annealing
紧密 closeness, tightness
紧密包装 dense packing
紧密对接(头) close [tight] butt
紧密接合 tight joint [connection]
紧密结合 tight bond
紧密金属 full metal
紧密排列 close-packing
紧密性 closeness, compactness
紧配合 tight [close] fit
紧塞 obturation
紧塞件 obturator
紧缩 striction, retrench, tighten, contract
紧缩公差 close tolerance
紧握 grip, grasp, anchor-hold
紧线 stay wire
紧线滑轮 snatch block
紧线螺丝 turnbuckle srew
紧线器 wire stretcher, 【机】turnbuckle
紧线钳 toggle, drawtongs
紧张的 intense
堇青石 {(Mg, Fe, Mn)$_2$(Al, Fe)$_4$Si$_5$O$_{18}$·H$_2$O} cordierite
堇青石陶器[陶瓷学] cordierite ceramics
锦生铁 silky pig iron
进场速度 velocity of approach
进厂粉矿 incoming ore fines
进厂粉末 incoming powder
进厂原料 incoming material
进厂原状 as-received condition
进厂状态 state as received
进出站信号 home and starting signal
进刀 (cutting) feed, advancement ◇ 横向～【机】cross-feed
进刀-分度机构 【机】feed-index mechanism
进刀杆 feed spindle
进刀机构 delivering gear
进刀控制杆 feed control lever
进刀调节 feed control
进刀装置 feed gear
进度 rate of progress [advance], schedule
进度表 (time-)schedule
进方孔型的椭圆 oval into square pass
进风口 air slot [intake], blast [air] inlet
进风量 intake
进风温度 incoming air temperature
进风消音器 suction silencer
进户线 fixture wire, 【电】house-service wire
进货价格 prime cost
进给 feed(ing) ◇ 储动～台*
进给齿条 feed(ing) rack
进给法 method of feeding
进给杆 feed shaft [spindle]
进给辊 feed [push] rolls
进给机座 push mill
进给料 incoming feed stock
进给螺杆[丝杆] feed screw
进给速度 feed speed
进给系统 feed system
进给限制器 feed stop
进口 inlet (IN), entrance, entry, admission (hole, opening), inlet (opening), import(ation)
进口导板 entry [entering, inlet, receiving] guide, entry guards ◇ 自动定心～*
进口导板盒 entry guide box, entry box guide ◇ 带调整螺钉的～screw box entry guide
进口端 entrance end [point]
进口端带卷自动输送装置 entry automatic coil handling device
进口段张紧辊装置 entry bridle roller unit

进 jin

进口阀门　inlet [suction] valve
进口法兰　inlet flange
进口风门　inlet damper
进口管　inlet pipe
进口管道　inlet ductwork
进口辊道(轧机的)　run-in table
进口过滤器　inlet strainer
进口和出口护板　entry and delivery aprons
进口缓冲辊　entry snubber roll
进口活套坑　entry-looping pit
进口活套挑　entry looper
进口夹送辊　entry pinch roll
进口绝对压力　inlet absolute pressure (IAP)
进口料槽　inlet trough
进口密封室　entry seal chamber
进口浓度　inlet density
进口平面　entry plane
进口区研磨(拉模的)　approach lap
进口水温　water inlet temperature
进口速度　inlet [entrance] velocity
进口速头[速位差]　inlet velocity head
进口台肩(阴模的)　lead-in shoulder
进口压力　entrance pressure
进口运输机　entry conveyer
进口闸板　inlet damper
进口张紧辊　entry tension roll
进口张力　【压】inlet tension
进口直径　inlet diameter
进矿总站　ore reception terminal
进料　feed (stock), feeding, charge-in, charging, incoming material ◇干式～ dry feed,强制[机械]～ positive feed,双面～(的) dual-feed,梭动式～ shuttle-type feed
进料拨杆(冷床的)　kick-in arm
进料不稳定性　flow instability
进料不足　underfeed
进料槽　charging launder [spout, chute], feed spout
进料侧　entry [front, ingoing] side
进料侧设备　equipment at entry side
进料挡板　feed apron
进料斗　feed hopper, boot
进料斗料槽　boot tank
进料端　feed end [side], entry end
进料端大砖　feed end block
进料端自动上卷装置　automatic entry coil handling equipment
进料阀　feed valve
进料分析　feed analysis
进料管　feed [entry] tube
进料辊　feed roll(er) (FR), push roll, draw roller, charged roller (热卷取机的)
进料辊道　feed(ing) (roller) table
进料辊压下装置　feed rolls screwdown
进料滑槽　feeding chute
进料活套塔[坑]　【压】infeed accumulator
进料机[器]　feeder ◇螺旋～*,振动～ shaking feeder
进料机组　entry group
进料计量观察窗　feed gauge glass
进料计量器　feed gauge
进料加热器　feed heater ◇挡板式～ baffle feed heater·
进料口　feed inlet [opening, nozzle], feeding head
进料矿浆　feed pulp
进料溜槽　inlet chute
进料流槽　feed launder
进料密封装置　entrance lock
进料浓度　feed [input] concentration
进料皮带运输机　entry belt
进料频率　delivery frequency
进料平台　feeder floor
进料枪　feed gun
进料区段　pull-on section
进料设施　receiving facilities
进料室　feed chamber [compartment, space]
进料输送机[带]　receiving [feed, entry] conveyer
进料速度　feed speed [rate], charging rate

进料台　input desk ◇ 储放提升～
进料调节器　feed regulator
进料温度　input temperature
进料堰　【冶】feed sill
进料圆盘　feeding disc
进料重量　charged weight
进料装置　feeder unit, feeding arrangement, admission gear
进料准备　preparation of feed material
进炉辊道　furnace entry table
进路　access, admission passage
进气　air-feed, (air) intake, air-in, gas in, inlet (gas), (air) inflow
进气瓣　inlet clack
进气程度　degree of admission
进气窗孔　inlet louver
进气道　gas intake, air inlet, inlet channel, airscoop
进气阀　inlet [intake, gas] valve, inlet clack
进气风扇　inlet fan
进气管　air inlet pipe [tube], air intake, admitting pipe, gas inlet pipe,
进气管路[管线]　admission line, intake pipeline
进气含尘量　(同"入口含尘量")
进气孔　air intake opening, admission hole, air slot
进气口　air inlet [intake, opening, port], airscoop, gas inlet [intake, entry], access of gas, admission intake
进气流　air inflow
进气歧管　inlet [intake] manifold, suction mainfold
进气室　inlet chamber, air inlet housing
进气速度　【冶】speed of entering
进气压力　intake air pressure
进气支管　inlet branch
进汽集管　suction mainfold
进汽口　steam inlet
进入　entering, entry, entrance, incoming, ingress, inlet
进入的气体　ingoing gas
进入盖　access cover
进入管　admitting [admission, inlet] pipe
进入角(度)　entering [inlet, acceptance] angle
进入口　inlet hole [port]
进入热量　incoming heat
进入水　inlet water
进入线材　inlet wire
进水　influent water, intake (water), water in
进水管　admitting pipe, feed pipe (锅炉的)
进水口　water inlet, water in
进水量　water intake
进酸量　admission of acid
进位　【计】carry(-over), carry bit ◇ 先行～carry lookahead, 小组[成组]～group carry
进位存储　【计】carry storage
进位时间　carry time
进线　inlet wire, incoming line
进线绝缘套管　lead-in bushing
进线绝缘子　terminal insulator, wall entrance insulator
进线配电盘　incoming panel
进向　heading
进油管路(液压系统的)　in(-)line
进油口　oil inlet
进展　progress (prog.), headway
禁带[禁戒能带]　forbidden (energy) band, forbidden zone, exclusion band
禁带能级　forbidden (energy) level
禁带[戒]跃迁　forbidden transition
禁戒值　forbidden value
禁能量区[范围]　forbidden energy range
禁区　forbidden zone [range]
禁线　forbidden line
禁值　forbidden [prohibited] value
禁止　prohibit, forbid,【计】disable, inhibit
禁止车辆通行[禁止交通]　closed to traffic

禁止打印	【计】suppression, non-print
禁止电流脉冲	【计】inhibit current pulse
禁止电路	【计】inhibit circuit
禁止脉冲	inhibit [disabling] pulse
禁止门	【计】A AND NOT B gate, B AND NOT A gate, A expect B gate, except [inhibit] gate
禁止器	【计】inhibitor
禁止输入	inhibiting [inhibitory] input
禁止线	【计】inhibit wire
禁止信号	【计】inhibit signal
禁止中断	【计】disabled interrupt, interrupt disable
禁止[禁戒]状态	forbidden state
近成品型连铸	near-to-shape casting
近程[近距离]浇铸	【铸】short pouring
近程相互作用	close-range interaction
近程有序降低	short-range order decrease
近代物理学	contemporary physics
近端	near end
近共晶合金	near eutectic alloy
近距离机械操纵手	handler
近距离运输	(同"短途运输")
近矿位置	location on ore
近理想结晶	mearly perfect crystal
近煤位置	location on coal
近期建筑	priority construction
近区	near region [zone, field]
近视图	close-up view
近似	approximation, approximateness
近似成分	approximate composition
近似读数	approximate [rough] reading
近似法	approximate [approximation, crude] method, method of approximating, approach ◇ 分子场[韦斯]~*, 逐次~*
近似分析	(ap)proximate analysis
近似(公)式	approximate [approximation] formula
近似估值	approximate evaluation
近似函数	approximation function
近似理论	approximate theory
近似模型	approximate model
近似球形的	near-spherical
近似式	approximation expression, approximants
近似算法	approximate calculation, nearness algorithm
近似显示[示度]	rough indication
近似值	approximate value, approximation, approach
近完美晶体	mearly perfect crystal
近位感应开关	inductive proximity switch
近无渣操作	nearly slagless operation
近因	occasion
近终形成型	near net shape forming
近终[净]形(的)	near net shape (NNS)
近终形加工	near net shape process [fabrication]
近终形加工工艺	near net shape, process
近终形连铸	near net shape continuous casting (NNSCC), continuous casting of similar product
近终形制品	near net shape product
近终形铸造[浇注]法	near net shape casting method
近轴光线(平行轴的)	paraxial rays
浸	soak, steep, immerse
浸沉深度	dipping depth
浸出	leach(ing), lixiviation ◇ 氨液~ ammonia leach, 槽内~*, 常温常压~*, 初次[第一次]~ primary leach, 堆积[矿堆]~ dump leaching, 高压~*, 间歇[分批]~ batch leach(ing), 碱压~*, 搅拌~*, 坑内[就地]~【色】stop leaching, 逆流[对流]~*, 顺流[同流]~*, 稀酸~*, 直接~ straight leaching
浸出部分[工段]	leaching section
浸出残渣[滤渣]	leach(ing) [leached] residue
浸出残渣处理	leach residues processing
浸出操作[作业]	leaching operation
浸出槽	leach(ing) tank [vessel], lixiviating tank ◇ 密闭~ enclosed leaching

jin 浸

tank,帕丘卡[帕氏]空气搅拌~*,转鼓式~ drum-type leaching vat
浸出产物　leaching product
浸出车间　leaching plant [department]
浸出沉淀法　LP (leaching precipitation) method
浸出沉淀浮选法　LPF (leach precipitation floatation) process
浸出沉淀浮选系统　leach-precipitate-float system
浸出处理　leaching treatment
浸出萃取　extraction by leaching
浸出-萃取-电积(技术)　leach-SX-EW
浸出电解法　LE (leaching electrolysis) method
浸出法　leaching process [method], lixiviation process ◇ 两[二]段~*,溶池~ dump pond method,溶剂加酸萃取~*,酸(性)~ acid leach process
浸出反应　leaching reaction, reaction in leaching
浸出浮选联合法　leaching-flotation process
浸出过程　leaching process
浸出后(阶段)　post-leaching
浸出后处理　post-leaching operation [treatment]
浸出化学　leach chemistry
浸出回路　leach circuit
浸出剂　leach(ing) agent, leaching reagent [solvent], lixiviant ◇ 盐水~ brine lixiviant
浸出阶段　leaching stage
浸出介质　leaching medium
浸出矿浆　leach pulp [slurry] ◇ 倾析过(的)~ decanted leach pulp
浸出料　leach feed
浸出流程图　leaching scheme
浸出笼　leaching cage
浸出率　leaching rate
浸出滤饼　leaching cake
浸出木桶　wooden leach tank

浸出泥浆　slimy leach liquor
浸出泥渣　leached mud
浸出前处理　pre-leaching operation [treatment]
浸出前溶液　head solution
浸出溶剂　leaching solvent
浸出溶液　leach(ing) solution
浸出溶液配制　make up of leach solution
浸出溶液再生　leach-solution regeneration
浸出设备　leaching equipment [plant, installation]
浸出时间　leaching time [period]
浸出试剂循环　recycling of leaching reagent
浸出试验　leaching test [experiment]
浸出速率　leaching rate
浸出酸度　leaching acidity
浸出碳化物氯化　chlorination of leached carbides
浸出特性　leaching characteristic, leach behavior
浸出条件　leaching conditions
浸出桶　leaching barrel [vessel]
浸出温度　leaching temperature
浸出系统　leach(ing) system [circuit] ◇ 分批渗滤~*
浸出效率　leaching efficiency
浸出性能　leach(ing) behavior
浸出压力　leaching pressure
浸出液　leach [vat] liquor, leachate, lixiviant, lixivium ◇ 常温~ cold-leach liquor,泥浆状~ slimy leach liquor,弱~ weak leaching liquid
浸出渣　leached mud
浸出渣率　residue ratio
浸出周期　leaching cycle
浸出柱　leaching column
浸出贮液槽　leaching storage tank
浸镀　dip plating [coating], immersion plating [coating], hot dip ◇ 光亮~ bright dipping, 化学[非电解]~ electroless plating, 静止~ dead dipping, 马齐克

浸　jin

防蚀锌黑膜~*,氢气保护~法*,熔融 ~melt dipping
浸镀槽　dipping tank
浸镀铬　iriditing
浸镀铬法　iridite [iriditing] process
浸镀铬溶液　iridite solution
浸镀铬酸盐法　◇派卢明~(铝合金的) Pylumin
浸镀汞[水银]　quicking
浸镀金　(同"热浸镀金")
浸镀铝　dip calorizing
浸挂涂料　【铸】dip-coat material
浸过油的　oil-impregnated
浸焊　dip soldering, solder dipping
浸碱清洗　soak cleaning
浸焦油沥青炉衬　tar-impregnated lining
浸焦油砖　tar-impregnated [pitch-contain] brick
浸金贫液　poor gold-bearing liquor
浸矿　ore [mineral] leaching
浸冷箱　【铸】dip tank
浸铝处理　dip calorizing ◇烧结金属~*
浸滤　lixiviation ◇低品位锰矿~提锰法*
浸没　immersion
浸没电极式盐浴槽　immersed electrode salt bath
浸没法　immersion method
浸没法显微术　(同"油浸法显微术")
浸没管式冷凝器　submerged-tube condenser
浸没管式蒸发器　submerged-tube evaporator
浸没极板　immersion plate
浸没加热(法)　immersion heating
浸没角　angle of immersion
浸没冷却　submerged quenching
浸没墙　submerged wall
浸没清洗　immersion cleaning
浸没燃烧　submerged combustion
浸没燃烧蒸发　immersion burning evaporation

浸没烧结(法)　immersion sintering
浸没深度　depth of immersion [submersion], submergence
浸没式超声波检验[探伤]　immersed ultrasonic inspection
浸没式超声波探伤仪　Immerscope
浸没式鹅颈管压铸机　(同"热压室压铸机")
浸没式"热顶"模　submerged "hot top" mould
浸没式运输皮带　【选】immersed belt
浸没试验　immersion test(ing)
浸没透镜　immersion [immersed] lens
浸没物镜　immersion objective (lens)
浸没装置　immersion fittings [system]
浸泡　dip, soak, bath
浸漂池　dip rinsing cell
浸漆布带　varnish tape
浸漆(绝缘)绸带　varnished silk tape
浸染矿床　【地】impregnation (deposit)
浸染(贫)矿　deaf ore
浸染状矿石　disseminated ore
浸入　immersion, infiltrate, infusion
浸入成形法(铜棒拉制的)　dip-forming process
浸入管　immersion tube, dipleg
浸入剂　intrusion agent
浸入深度　immersion [dipping] depth
浸入式泵　submerged pump
浸入式电热器　electric immersion heater
浸入式高温计　immersion pyrometer
浸入式搅拌器　submerged agitator
浸入式喷吹　submerged injection
浸入式喷吹法　submerged injection process (SIP)
浸入式喷吹风口　submerged injection tuyere
浸入式喷吹技术　submerged injection technique
浸入式喷吹煤　submerged injection of coal
浸入式喷嘴　submerged orifice
浸入式烧嘴　immersion burner

浸入式烧嘴加热炉 immersion(-burner) furnace
浸入式射流 submerged jet
浸入式石墨电阻加热器 graphite resistance immersion heater
浸入式水口 【连铸】submerged nozzle [tube], immersed nozzle, pouring tube
浸入式碳-碳化硅热电高温计 【冶】fitterer pyrometer
浸软 macerate
浸润 soak, bucking,【铸】watering（型砂的）
浸润化 【铸】tempering
浸润性 wettability, wetting property
浸渗 infiltration ◇ 毛细~*
浸渗粉末冶金零件 impregnating P/M (powder metallurgy) parts
浸渗硅酮 silicone impregnation
浸渗后密度 wet density
浸渗剂 infiltrant ◇ 铜基合金~ copper-base infiltrant
浸渗介质 permeating medium
浸渗烧结 infiltration sintering
浸渗石蜡的 paraffin-impregnated
浸湿 soak(ing), moisten, wet,【铸】(型砂的) watering, tempering
浸湿[浸润]角 wetting angle
浸湿净化[清理] soak cleaning
浸湿热法 heat of immersion method
浸蚀 etching ◇ 变暗[无光]~ mat etching, 不易~的结构组分 slow etching constituent, 电解~ cautery, 离子~*, 深(度)~ deep etch(ing), 阳极~ anode pickling
浸蚀操作[工序] 【金】etching operation
浸蚀槽 etching bath
浸蚀处理 etching treatment
浸蚀工段 etching room
浸蚀剂 etchant, etching (re)agent [medium] ◇ 奥伯霍弗法~*, 弗莱~*, 弗里克~*, 海恩~*, 汉弗莱~*, 混合酸~*, 卡拉佩拉~*, 卡勒~*, 卡林~*, 凯勒~*, 坎菲尔德检磷~*, 柯兰~*, 克罗尔~*, 罗森海因*, 马布尔~*, 梅氏~*, 渗碳体~*, 施拉姆~*, 斯特德~*, 斯特劳斯~*, 索维尔~*, 维莱拉~*

浸蚀间 etching room
浸蚀净化 etch cleaning
浸蚀裂纹 etch crack
浸蚀磨片 etched slice
浸蚀磨损 erosion wear
浸蚀试片 etch test cut
浸蚀试验 etch test ◇ 硫酸铜~*
浸蚀特性[指数, 度] etching characteristic
浸蚀图 etch(ing) figure [patterns]
浸蚀性能 etch quality
浸蚀盐酸（钎焊用） killed hydrochloric [muriatic] acid
浸蚀液 【金】etching solution ◇ 村上~*, 达什深*, 蒂莫费夫~*, 加速~ accelerated solution, 克雷姆~*, 梅里卡~*, 梅耶-艾希霍尔茨~*, 图卡~*
浸蚀质量 etch quality
浸蚀作用 etching effect
浸水除鳞（热薄板坯的） boshing
浸水清洗 dunk rinsing
浸酸 pickle
浸酸退火 acid annealing
浸提 digestion
浸提器 diffuser, diffusor, diffusion cell
浸透 soak, saturation, impregnating
浸透法探伤仪 impregnating crack detector
浸透时间 soak time
浸透探伤机 penetrating inspection machine
浸涂 【铸】dip coat(ing) ◇ 离心~(合金)法*
浸涂层 dip coat
浸涂法 dipping method
浸析 leach, lixiviation
浸析反应 leaching reaction

浸洗 (dip) rinsing, immersion (cleaning), dipping ◇ 光亮~*, 经~的 bitten into, 褪光~ dead dipping, matte dip

浸洗槽 dipping tank [cell, tub]

浸焰式燃烧器 submerged flame burner

浸液 immersion ◇ 蓝色汞~(镀银前的) blue dip

浸液(式)电极 dipped [dipping] electrode, immersion-type electrode

浸液式热电偶 immersion(-type) thermocouple

浸油 oil impregnation

浸油处理(线材的) oiled finish

浸油合金 oil-impregnated alloy [metal]

浸油润滑 submerged [flood] lubrication

浸罩深度 【钢】depth of sinking snorkel

浸煮器 digester ◇ 旋转式~ rotary digester

浸渍 soak(ing), immersion, dip(ping), impregnation, infusion, bucking, infiltration ◇ 短暂~*, 铬酸盐表面~法*

浸渍包覆 dip cladding

浸渍槽 immersion [dipping] tank

浸渍管 up-leg

浸渍过程 dipping process

浸渍海水耐蚀试验 sea water dip test

浸渍合金 infiltrating alloy

浸渍机 impregnator

浸渍剂 impregnant, saturant, infiltrant

浸渍绝缘 mass-impregnated insulation

浸渍绝缘胶 impregnating compound

浸渍坑 soaking pit

浸渍冷却 submerged quenching

浸渍毛细渗补 【铸】capillary dip infiltration

浸渍抛光 dip(ping) polish(ing)

浸渍漂洗 dip rinsing

浸渍器 impregnator, infuser

浸渍钎焊 dip brazing (DB) ◇ 化学~ chemical dip brazing

浸渍清漆 dipping [impregnating] varnish

浸渍(溶)液 immersion [dipping] solution, immersion liquid

浸渍软钎焊 dip soldering

浸渍式(乙炔)发生器 dipping(-type) generator

浸渍酸 dipping acid ◇ 死[用过的]~*

浸渍铁粉 【粉】infiltrated iron powder

浸渍涂层材料 【铸】dip-coat material

尽头侧线 dead-end siding

尽头线 【运】dead-end track

尽头线布置 【铁】dead-end track arrangement

晶 crystal ◇ 残缺~ malformation-crystal

晶疤(电镀时金属硫化物的) crystal spots

晶棒 crystal-bar ◇ 弧熔~*

晶棒锆 crystal-bar zirconium

晶胞 【金】(structure, unit) cell, per unit cell, unit of structure ◇ 密排原子~*

晶胞边【棱】 cell [unit(-cell)] edge

晶胞参数 unit-cell parameter

晶胞测定法 method of cell determination

晶胞常数 unit-cell constant

晶胞尺寸【大小】 cell size [dimension], unit-cell dimension

晶胞对称 cell symmetry

晶胞几何学 cell geometry

晶胞间界 cell boundary

晶胞间界距离 spacing of cell boundaries

晶胞结点原子数 number of lattice-point atoms per cell

晶胞结构 cell structure

晶胞面 (unit-)cell face

晶胞矢量 unit-cell vector

晶胞体积 cell volume

晶胞形成 cell formation

晶胞形状 cell shape

晶胞中心 centre of cell

晶簇 druse, vug(g), voog, vugh ◇ 树枝状~ cluster of dendrites, 针状~ cluster of needles

晶带 (crystal) zone

晶带结构(金属的) zone configuration

晶带(平)面 zone plane

晶带曲线 (crystal) zonal curve
晶带轴(线) crystal(lographic) zone axis, zonal [zone] axis
晶锭 【半】crystal ingot
晶洞状(结构) miarolitic
晶格 crystal lattice,(同"点阵") ◇ 不对称～asymmetrical cell,布喇菲～符号*,倒易～inverse lattice,有缺陷～defect lattice
晶格变形 (同"点阵变形")
晶格参数 lattice parameter, parameter in crystal, crystal (lattice) parameter, dimensions of lattice ◇ X 射线测定～*
晶格参数测定 (同"点阵参数测定")
晶格参数观测曲线 observed lattice parameter curve
晶格单位 unit of structure
晶格电导率 lattice conductivity ◇ 反常～*
晶格基底 crystal lattice base
晶格畸变 lattice disturbance ◇ 消除～的退火 annealing of lattice disturbance
晶格间原子 interstitialcy
晶格减聚力 lattice decohesion
晶格结点 lattice point ◇ 附加～*
晶格结点原子 lattice-point atom
晶格局部变乱(金属的) 【金】spike
晶格聚合力 lattice cohesion
晶格空位迁移[徙动] migration of lattice vacancies
晶格空[缺]位(位置) 【金】(lattice) vacancy, vacant (lattice) site, lattice vacant site,
晶格内的 intracell
晶格排列 lattice array
晶格平面系列 【金】set of lattice planes
晶格平移矢量 lattice translation vector
晶格塑性[范性]变形 plastic deformation of lattice
晶格完整性 perfection of lattice
晶格位置[状态] lattice position
晶格稳定性 lattice stability

晶格衍射 (同"晶体衍射")
晶格原子间隙位置 interstitial lattice site
晶格原子交互作用势 interaction potential of lattice atoms
晶格原子排列密度 【半】compactness of crystal lattice
晶格再取向 reorientation of crystal-lattice
晶格振动 (crystal) lattice vibration ◇ 爱因斯坦～模型 Einstein model,德拜～模型 Debye model
晶格指数表 ◇ 赫尔－戴维～Hull-Davey charts
晶格转变点 lattice transformation point
晶格自扩散 lattice self-diffusion
晶核 crystal nucleus, nucleus (of crystallization), host ◇ 新～形成 formation of new nucleus
晶核催化剂 nucleation catalyst
晶核化 germination
晶核形成 nucleation
晶核形成方式 pattern of nucleation
晶核形成机理 nucleation mechanism
晶核形成剂 nucleator
晶核中心 germ nucleus
晶核自发形成 spontaneous nucleation
晶间边界 grain-to-grain boundary
晶间穿透 intergranular penetration
晶间脆化 intercrystalline [intergranular] embrittlement
晶间脆性 intercrystalline brittleness,(同"晶间脆化")
晶间断口 intercrystalline [intergranular] fracture
晶间断裂[破裂] intercrystalline failure [fracture, rupture], intergranular failure [fracture, rupture]
晶间腐蚀 【金】intercrystalline [intergranular, grain-boundary] corrosion ◇ 焊接接头～weld decay, 耐～性*, 时间－温度－－敏化图*, 无～钢*
晶间腐蚀试验 intergranular corrosion test ◇ 斯特劳斯～Strauss test, 休伊～Huey

晶间[晶界]腐蚀性破坏　intergranular corrosive attack
晶间间距　intergranular space
晶间结构　【金】intercrystalline structure
晶间结合破坏　breakdown of intercrystalline cohesion
晶间浸蚀　intergranular attack
晶间扩散　intercrystal(line) diffusion
晶间裂纹　intercrystalline [intergranular] crack(ing), cleavage crack
晶间内聚力破坏　breakdown of intercrystalline cohesion
晶间偏析　intercrystalline segregation
晶间偏析流　intergranular river
晶间溶胀　intercrystalline swelling
晶间收缩裂纹　intercrystalline shrinkage crack
晶间缩孔　micro pipe
晶间位置　intergranular position
晶间[界]氧化　intercrystalline [intergranular] oxidation
晶间氧化膜　intergranular oxide film
晶间组织　intergranular structure
晶键　crystal bond
晶角　crystal angle
晶界变形　grain boundary flow
晶界沉淀　【金】grain boundary precipitation
晶界脆断　boundary brittle fracture
晶界脆化[脆性]　intergranular embrittlement
晶界断口　intergranular fracture
晶界断裂　intergranular failure [fracture], grain boundary fracture, intercry-stalline failure ◇ 蠕变时沿～*
晶界反应　grain boundary reaction
晶界峰　grain boundary peak
晶界腐蚀　crystal boundary corrosion, grain-boundary corrosion [attack]
晶界共晶体　grain boundary eutectics
晶界滑移　grain boundary sliding [slip]

晶界角　grain-boundary angle
晶界阶梯　ledge
晶界结构　structure of crystal boundaries
晶界结构组分　boundary constituent
晶界浸蚀　crystal boundary etching, intergranular attack
晶界扩散　grain boundary diffusion
晶界裂纹　intergranular crack(ing)
晶界流变[流动]　grain boundary flow
晶界膜　boundary film
晶界摩擦力　boundary friction
晶界能(量)　grain-boundary energy, energy of crystal boundary
晶界黏滞性　viscosity of grain boundary
晶界偏析　grain boundary segregation
晶界迁移　(crystal, grain) boundary migration
晶界强度　grain boundary strength
晶界区　grain boundary area
晶界蠕变裂纹　boundary creep crack
晶界松弛　grain boundary relaxation
晶界塑性断裂　boundary plastic fracture
晶界位错　boundary dislocation
晶界位移　grain boundary displacement
晶界无沉淀[析出]物带　precipitate free zone
晶界析出　grain boundary precipitation
晶界线　grain junction line
晶界相交　boundary intersection
晶界效应　boundary effect
晶界移动　movement of crystal boundaries
晶界杂质浓度　grain boundary impurity concentration
晶界再结晶反应　grain boundary recrystallization reaction
晶界张弛　grain boundary relaxation
晶界自扩散　(grain) boundary self diffusion, boundary autodiffusion
晶界组织　crystal boundary structure
晶块　crystal block
晶块间界　crystal block boundary
晶类　crystal class

晶棱　crystal edge, cell corner
晶粒　crystal(line) grain [particle], grain (of crystal) ◇ 经热处理的～heat treated grain, 细～的 close-grained, 铸态～as-cast grain
晶粒边界　grain boundary
晶粒变形　grain deformation
晶粒层　granular bed
晶粒衬度　grain contrast
晶粒尺寸增大　increase in grain size
晶粒重新取向　reorientation of crystallites
晶粒丛　cluster of grains
晶粒粗度　coarseness of grain
晶粒粗化　grain [particle] coarsening, coarsening (of grain), coarsing
晶粒粗化温度　grain coarsening temperature
晶粒大小　grain size
晶粒大小比较目镜　（同"颗粒大小比较目镜"）
晶粒大小测定法　method of grain-size testing
晶粒大小均匀的　even-grained
晶粒度　grain fineness (G.F.), grain size (number), coarseness of grain ◇ ASTM～值*, 奥氏体～分级*, 氧化法测～oxidation grain size
晶粒度测定法　method of grain-size testing ◇ 海恩～Heyn method, 杰弗里斯～Jeffries' method
晶粒度号　grain fineness number
晶粒度效应　grain size effect
晶粒度衍射斑点　grain-size mottling
晶粒反差　grain contrast
晶粒反常长大　exaggerated grain growth
晶粒回复　【金】grain reocvery
晶粒基体界面　particle / matrix interface
晶粒集合体　aggregate of crystal grains
晶粒间(结构)　interparticle structure
晶粒间成核位置　intergranular nucleation site
晶(粒)间辐射　intergranular radiation
晶(粒)间腐蚀抗力　intercrystalline [intergranular] corrosion resistance, resistance to intergranular corrosion
晶(粒间)界　crystal [intercrystalline, intergranular, grain] boundary, boundary (of grain) ◇ 小角～low angle boundary
晶粒间界处内应力　internal stresses at grain boundaries
晶粒间界迁移理论　theory of grain boundary migration
晶粒间距　interparticle distance
晶粒间空隙　grain boundary cavities
晶粒间黏结　interparticle bonding
晶粒接合线　grain junction line
晶粒结构　grain structure
晶粒结构的重原子测定法　heavy atom method of crystal structure determination
晶粒界面　grain boundary interface
晶粒拉长　extension of crystal grains
晶粒粒度分布　grain size distribution
晶粒粒度分析　grain size analysis
晶粒粒度分析器　grain size analyzer
晶粒(粒)度控制　grain size control
晶粒流变　grain flow
晶粒密度　closeness of grain
晶粒模型　grain model
晶粒内结构　intragranular structure
晶粒平均直径　average grain diameter
晶粒取向　grain orientation
晶粒取向电工钢薄板　oriented electrical steel sheet
晶粒取向钢　grain oriented steel
晶粒取向硅钢薄板　grain oriented silicon steel (GOSS), grain-oriented silicon iron
晶粒取向硅铁　oriented silicon iron
晶粒生成　grain formation
晶粒数目　number of grains
晶粒双取向硅钢薄板　（同"双取向硅钢薄板"）
晶粒碎裂　grain fragmentation
晶粒未取向钢　non-grain oriented steel
晶粒位向　grain orientation

晶粒徙动　grain migration
晶粒细化　(crystalline, grain) refinement, (grain) refining ◇ 阿尔科阿~法*, 科芬钢轴~热处理 coffin axle process, 脱氧及~中间合金*
晶粒细化处理　grain-refinement treatment ◇ 心部~*
晶粒细化剂　(grain) refiner
晶粒细化区　grain refined zone
晶粒细化温度　grain refining temperature
晶粒线向　grain flow
晶粒形成　graining
晶粒形状　grain shape
晶粒亚晶界　grain sub-boundary
晶粒延伸　extension of crystal grains
晶粒硬化　grain size hardening
晶粒长大　grain growth ◇ 奥氏体~*, 不连续~*, 发芽型~*, 反常[异常]~ abnormal grain growth, 防~处理*, 临界~ critical grain growth, 临界应变~*, 热处理引起的~*
晶粒长大度　degree of grain growth
晶粒长大键　grain growth bonding
晶粒长大倾向　grain-growth tendency
晶粒长大区域[范围]　grain-growth region
晶粒长大速度　crystalline growth velocity
晶粒长大现象　growth phenomena
晶粒状的　granular, grainy
晶粒自发长大　spontaneous grain growth
晶粒总长大　overall growth
晶粒组织　grain structure ◇ 粗亚~*, 致密~*
晶冕　crown (of crystal)
晶面　crystal plane [face], crystallographic plane, plane of crystal
晶面极点　pole of crystal face
晶面间角　interplanar angle
晶面间距　spacing between lattice planes, planar spacing, grating space, interplanar (crystal) spacing
晶面间距测量[测定]　crystal-spacing measurement
晶面间距　interplanar distance
晶面截距倒数　reciprocal intercepts of plane
晶面与轴的截距　axial intercepts of face
晶面指数　(crystal) face index, face indices, indices of crystal faces, indices [index] of crystallographic plane
晶面中心　centre of cell face
晶面族　family of crystal planes
晶内断裂　(同"穿晶断裂")
晶内核状偏析　coring
晶内偏析组织　cored [coring] structure
晶内铁素体　intragranular ferrite (IGF)
晶内铁素体片　intragranular ferrite plate (IFP)
晶胚　【金】embryo
晶坯　incipient crystal
晶片　chip, crystal plate, wafer ◇ 四分之一波长~ quarter wave plate
晶群　crystal group
晶石　spar
晶态　crystallized form [state]
晶体　crystal (body), crystalline solid, crystalloid ◇ 胞[细胞, 蜂窝]状~ cellular crystal, 不整形~ alltriomorphic crystal, 低对称性~ crystal of low symmetry, 高对称性~*, 高压缩性~*, 各向异性~ anisotropic crystal, 共价[原子, 无极]~*, 含杂质~ impure crystal, 急冷~*, 立方系~*, 连续位错~*, 片状~ crystal plate, 生长良好~ well-developed crystal, 树枝状~ arborescent crystal, 双曲~*, 双折射~*, 四方系~*, 弯曲~ curved crystal, 小~*, 楔形~ cumeat, 沿~扩散 short circuit diffusion, 一定尺寸~ crystal of finite size, 游离[自由生长的]~ free crystal, 圆柱形~ cylindrical crystal, 长大~ grown crystal
晶体 X 射线衍射仪　【金】retigraph
晶体 X 轴　electric axis
晶体 Y 轴　mechanical axis

晶体埃	crystal Angstroem, Siegbahn Angstroem
晶体变态	crystal(line) modification
晶体表面	crystal surface
晶体波函数	crystal wave function
晶体测角仪	crystal goniometer
晶体测试设备	crystal test set
晶体尺寸	crystal-size dimension
晶体磁(性)各向异性	magnetic crystal anisotropy, crystalline magnetic anisotropy
晶体大小	crystal size
晶体单色化 X 射线	crystal monochromatized X-rays
晶体单色镜	reflector
晶体单色器	crystal monochromator, monochromator crystal, reflector ◇ 平面~*, 岩盐~*
晶体单色器照相机	monochromator camera
晶体单色器至焦点距离	crystal-to-focus distance
晶体点阵	crystal lattice
晶体点阵参数	crystal (lattice) parameter
晶体点阵再取向	reorientation of crystal-lattice
晶体垫板	crystal backing
晶体电离度【化】	crystalline ionicity
晶体电势[位]	crystalline potential
晶体镀层	crystalline coating
晶体断口[断裂]	fracture of crystal
晶体对称类	class of crystal symmetry
晶体对称(性)	crystal symmetry
晶体二极管	crystal diode
晶体反射单色射束	crystal-reflected monochromatic beam
晶体反射的辐射	crystal-reflected radiation
晶体范性	plasticity of crystal
晶体范性动力学	dynamic of crystal plasticity
晶体范性理论	theory of crystal plasticity
晶体分光计	crystal spectrometer
晶体分类	crystal class, classification of crystals
晶体分析(法)	crystal analysis
晶体粉末	crystal(line) powder
晶体各向同性	crystal isotrope
晶体各向异性	crystal(line) anisotropy
晶体各向异性能量	crystal anisotropy energy
晶体管	transistor ◇ 单结~*, 合金型~ alloy type transistor, 回熔型~ melt-back transistor, 结型~*, 台面式~ mesa transistor
晶体管放大器	transistor amplifier
晶体管化	transistorization, transistorizing
晶体管级硅	transistor-grade silicon
晶体管－晶体管逻辑电路	transistor-transistor logic (TTL)
晶体管逻辑(电路)	transistor logic (circuit), transilog ◇ 互补~*, 直接耦合~*
晶体管门电路	transistor gate
晶体管整流器	crystal rectifier
晶体惯态	crystal habit
晶体光谱学	crystal spectroscopy
晶体光栅	crystal grating
晶体光学	crystal optics
晶体光轴	crystal optic axis
晶体烘[恒温]箱	crystal oven
晶体滑移	crystal slip [gliding], glide of crystal
晶体回摆	(同"晶体振荡")
晶体回复	crystal recovery
晶体活度[性]	crystal activity
晶体(机械)加载	crystal loading
晶体集合体	crystalline aggregate
晶体几何学	crystal geometry
晶体夹持器	crystal holder
晶体间架	crystal skeleton
晶体检波器	crystal rectifier
晶体检测器	crystallographer
晶体(减震)垫板	crystal backing

晶体键 crystalline binding	晶体生长［长大］ crystal(line) growth [growing]
晶体键合 crystal bonding	晶体生长机理 crystal growth mechanism
晶体接合线 crystal junction line	晶体生长理论 theory of crystal growth
晶体结构 crystal(line) structure, crystallography	晶体生长炉 【半】crystal-growing furnace
晶体结构X射线分析 X-ray analysis of crystal structure	晶体生长器 【半】crystal grower
晶体结构测定法 method of crystal-structure determination	晶体生长速度 rate of crystal growth
晶体结构起源 【理】genesis of crystalline structure	晶体生长现象 【理】growth phenomena
晶体解理 cleavage of crystal	晶体试样固定 crystal mounting
晶体界面状况 boundary conditions of crystal	晶体数量 amount of crystals
晶体金属 crystalline metal	晶体数学 crystal mathematics
晶体开裂 cleavage of crystal	晶体探头 crystal probe
晶体颗粒 crystal(line) particle	晶体投影 crystal projection
晶体空间光栅 crystal space grating	晶体退火 crystal annealing
晶体拉制机 【半】crystal-pulling machine	晶体外形 external form [shape] of crystal
晶体棱边 crystal edge	晶体完整(性) crystal perfection
晶体滤波器 crystal filter	晶体位错 crystal dislocation
晶体脉泽 【半】crystal maser	晶体物理(学) crystal physics, crystallophysics
晶体密度 crystal density	晶体物质 crystalline material [matter, substance]
晶体内的 intracrystalline	晶体习性 crystal habit
晶体内界面 crystal interface	晶体小面 crystal facet
晶体内铁素片技术 intragranular ferrite plate (IFP) technology	晶体形［生］成 crystal formation, crystallization
晶体平面 crystal plane, facet	晶体形态学 crystal morphology
晶体平面系列 【金】set of crystal planes	晶体形状 crystal shape
晶体嵌镶块 crystal mosaic	晶体旋转法 crystal rotation method
晶体切割机 crystal cutting machine	晶体学 crystallography, crystallology ◇ 滑移～
晶体取向［位向］ crystal orientation ◇ 戴卫-威尔逊-测角仪	晶体学关系 （同"结晶学关系"）
晶体取向分布情况 spread of crystal orientation	晶体学极 （同"结晶学极"）
晶体缺陷 crystal defect, crystal(line) imperfection ◇ 变形引起的～ deformation-induced crystal imperfections	晶体压电轴 piezoelectric axis
	晶体衍射 crystal(line) diffraction
	晶体衍射图 crystallogram ◇ 德拜～Debye crystallogram, 劳厄～Laue film
晶体溶体 crystalline solution	晶体一次光轴 ray axis of crystal
晶体三极管 crystal [semiconductor] triode	晶体长大法 crystal-growing processes
	晶体长大机理 crystal growth mechanism
晶体(摄)谱仪 crystal spectrometer	晶体振荡 【理】oscillation of crystal
	晶体-蒸气界面 crystal-vapour interface
	晶体直径 crystal diameter

晶体质量　crystal mass
晶体中原子迁移机理　mechanism of atomic migration in crystals
晶体钟　crystal clock
晶(体)轴　crystal(line) [crystallographic] axis
晶体主要方向　important directions of crystal
晶体转动　crystal rotation
晶体组织　structure of crystal
晶条　crystal-bar
晶系　crystal(lographic) system, syngony
晶隙氢化物　interstitial hydride
晶相检查　examination of crystalline phase
晶向　crystallographic direction, crystal orientation ◇ <111>~˚
晶向指数　【理】index of crystal orientation, orientation index
晶形　crystal (lographic) [crystalline] form, crystalliform, crystal shape ◇ 基本~˚, 具有三种~的元素[金属] trimorphous element
晶形转变[变化]　crystalline [crystallographic] transformation
晶须　(crystal) whisker
晶须生长　【理】growth of whiskers
晶须增强复合材料　whisker reinforced composite
晶须增强金属基复合材料　whisker reinforced MMC
晶铀矿　uranniobite
晶质　crystalline substance ◇ 似~crystalloid
晶质材料　crystalline material
晶质的　crystalline, crystalloid
晶质断口　crystalline fracture
晶质粉末　crystal dust
晶质涂层　(同"晶体镀层")
晶质铀矿　(同"沥青铀矿")
晶种　crystal seed, seed crystal [particle], inoculating crystal [seed], nucleator,【半】seed ◇ 粗(粒)~ coarse seed, 氢氧化铝~˚, 未加~的 unseeded
晶种表面　seed surface
晶种槽　seed tank
晶种粉　seed powder
晶种加入量　seed charge
晶种粒度　seed size
晶种粒度范围　limit of seed size
晶种量　seed quantity, amount of seed
晶轴常数　axial constant
晶状的　crystalline
晶蛭石{H₁₀Al₂Si₃O₁₄}　leverrierite
腈化钛　(同"碳氮化钛")
精拔　(同"精拉(拔)")
精拔钢　bright drawn steel
精测高温计　micropyrometer
精冲　【粉】coining
精冲裁　【压】fine blanking
精吹炼　final blow, further blowing
精读数自整角机　fine selsyn
精度　precision, (degree of) accuracy ◇ 多倍~ multiple precision
精度测量　measure of accuracy
精度等级　accuracy class [rate]; grade [order] of accuracy, precision class
精度系数　modulus of precision
精锻　finish forge [forging], net-size forging
精锻模　finisher
精干燥器　fine dryer
精过滤器　fine filter
精华　goodness
精机加工　finish machining
精加工　fine machining [finishing], finish(ing), precision work, smoothing
精加工锤　(同"精整锤")
精加工法　【机】refining process
精加工滚筒　finishing drum
精加工球磨机　ball mill refiner
精简牵引传动　cord-and-drum drive
精剪机　reshears
精矿　(mineral, ore, preparation) concentrate ◇ 粒状~ granular concentrate, 难

分解~*,黏土质[含泥]~*,生[未焙烧]~*,死烧[全脱硫]~*,酸浸出类~*,造块~*

精矿仓 concentrate storage (bin)
精矿槽 concentrate hopper
精矿堆栈 preconcentrate stockpile
精矿干燥机 concentrate drier
精矿给矿机 concentrate feeder
精矿混合料 concentrate mixture
精矿加料[装入]机 concentrate-charging machine
精矿浆 concentrate pulp
精矿粒 concentrate particle
精矿粒度 concentrate grind
精矿浓缩机 concentrate thickener (conc. thick.)
精矿品位 concentrate grade
精矿氰化残渣[尾矿] concentrate cyanidation residue [tails]
精矿取样 【选】concentrate sampling
精矿-熔剂比 【冶】concentrate-flux ratio
精矿烧嘴[燃烧器] concentrate burner
精矿石 upgraded ore
精矿试样 concentrate sample
精矿贮仓 concentrate storage (bin)
精拉(拔) finish(ing) draw(ing) ◇ 湿法~*
精拉模 finishing die
精炼 refining (fusion, practice), refinement, purifying, purification, affinage, fining, fluxing, final melting, softening (粗铅除砷等的),【钢】finishing ◇ RH多功能~*,电渣~ electroslag refining,电子束~*,化学~ chemical refining,混汞电~ amalgam electrorefining,火法~ fire[furnace] refining,炉内~ furnace refining,热态金属~【冶】hot metal refining,双重~方式(RH+KIP)*,未~的 unrefined,在还原渣下~【冶】refining under deoxidizing slag,罩式升温~技术*,最后~ frenching
精炼扒渣 【冶】finish flush-off
精炼不足 underrefining
精炼厂 refinery, melting finery
精炼厂废水 refinery effluent
精炼厂浮渣 refinery dross
精炼厂副产物 refinery by-product
精炼厂煤气 refinery gas
精炼车间 refining plant
精炼程序 refining procedure
精炼处理 refining treatment
精炼带 refined zone
精炼法 purifying method [process], (re)fining method [process] ◇ 交替~*,热线分解~*
精炼反应 purifying reaction
精炼浮渣 refinery scum, refining skimming
精炼钢 purified [refined, refining, washed, virgin] steel
精炼锅 refining kettle ◇ 分批~ batch refining kettle
精炼锅浮渣 kettle dross
精炼级别 refined grade
精炼金属 refined [fine, finished] metal
精炼炉 refiner [refining, refinery] furnace, (re)finer, purifying [purification, affinage, fining, melting, improving] furnace ◇ 标定~ report furnace,单嘴~*,回转~ rotary refining furnace,熔区传输~*,预备~*,预~操作*
精炼炉床[缸] refinery hearth
精炼炉浮渣 refining furnace dross
精炼炉工人[工长] finer
精炼(炉)渣 refining slag, refinery cinder
精(炼)铝 refined aluminium
精炼镁 refined magnesium
精炼锰铁 refined ferromanganese
精炼泡沫渣 refining foam
精炼期 refining [fining, finishing] period, refining stage
精炼期钢水 finishing metal
精炼器 refiner
精炼铅 refined lead

精炼热　refining heat
精炼设备　refining unit
精炼生铁　【钢】washed metal
精炼时位置　【钢】refining position
精炼损失　treatment losses
精炼锑　（同"精锑"）
精炼添加剂　curative agent, refiner
精炼条件　refining conditions
精炼铜　refined copper ◇ 电解～*
精炼铜生产　refined copper production
精炼铜阳极(电解)法　refined anode process
精炼温度　refining temperature
精炼锌　refined zinc, high grade zinc
精炼用离心机　affination centrifuge
精炼铸铁　refined cast iron
精炼作用　refining action
精料　【冶】prepared burden, 【铁】beneficiated (burden) material ◇ 高炉～*
精馏　rectifying, rectification, (fractional, refinery) distillation, fractionating, redistill(ation), selective evaporation ◇ 分批～batch rectification, 共沸～*, 真空～*
精馏法　【化】refining process
精馏釜　【化】rectifying still
精馏煤气　【化】refining gas
精馏盘　rectifying plate [tray]
精馏期[时间]　【化】refining period
精馏器　【化】rectifier
精馏塔[柱]　rectification tower [column], rectifying tower [column], fractional tower [column], fractionating tower [column] ◇ 薄膜式～*, 二次～*, 间歇式～*
精馏塔汽化段　exhausting section of column
精馏塔生产率　rectification column specific capacity
精馏效率　rectifier efficiency, efficiency of rectification
精馏作用　rectifying action
精煤　cleaned coal

精密保险丝　precision fuse
精密比较仪　precision comparator
精密测量　accurate [precise, precision] measurement
精密称量　precision weighing
精密冲压[下料]　finish blanking
精密单色器　precision monochromator
精密定径　precision sizing
精密定径块　precision sizing block
精密度　precision, accuracy, exactness
精密度指数　index of precision
精密锻件　close tolerance forging, net-size forging
精密锻模　closed die ◇ 组合式～*
精密锻造　precision [net] forging, close tolerance forging
精密方法　exact method
精密分割锚分　（同"窄馏分"）
精密分级　precise fractionation
精密分馏　【化】precise fractionation, precision fractional distillation
精密钢管　precision steel pipe
精密高差仪　cathetometer
精密管　precision tube
精密光亮磨光　precision ground
精密合金　precious alloy ◇ 休伊特～*
精密给料　inching
精密记时计　chronometer
精密矫直机　【压】precision leveller
精密控制　accuracy [fine, close] control
精密临界控制　close critical control
精密扭转试验　precision torsion test
精密配合　exact fit
精密熔丝　precision fuse
精密调整　accurate adjustment
精密温度控制　precise [close] temperature control
精密型材轧机　precise bar mill ◇ 带快速换辊装置的～precise bar mill with rapid roll change
精密压铸　microdiecast ◇ 阿库拉德高速～法*

精密仪表[仪器] precision instrument
精密仪器用钢 precision steel
精密硬度试验计 metalometer
精密轧机 precision-rolling mill ◇ 多品种～*
精密照相机 precision camera
精密轴承 precise bearing
精密铸件 precision casting
精密铸造 precision casting, hot investment casting ◇ 冻结[冷冻]水银～法*, 克娄宁壳型～法 C(Croning) process, 难[不能]机械加工合金～法 microcast process, 熔模[蜡型]～*, 石膏型～法*
精磨 finish [accurate, fine, precision] grinding, debugging, dressing
精萘 refined naphthalene
精抛光 【金】finishing [brilliant] polish ◇ 镁氧膏～(法) skid polishing
精抛光机(拉模孔的) finish polishing bench
精切削 【机】clean cut
精切削加工 finish machining
精确(X射线)图像 precision film
精确测量 (同"精密测量")
精确分选[分离](矿物的)【选】sharp [clean-cut] separation
精确极限 exacting limits
精确剪板机 resquaring shears
精确剪切 [压]resquaring
精确配料 accurate proportioning
精确熔点 【冶】sharp melting point
精确裕度 precision tolerance
精砂 washed sand
精神迟缓 【环】mental retardation
精蚀(晶体) 【半】close etching
精碎矿 fine crushed ore
精锑 (antimony) regulus, star antimony [metal], antimony star, French metal
精锑块 star bowl
精调 fine adjustment [regulation], delicate [precision, minute] adjustment
精调螺丝 fine setting screw

精调系统 fine regulation system
精调整盘 vernier panel
精洗机(煤气的) fine filter
精细粉 【粉】fine powder
精细过滤器 polishing filter
精细化学药品 fine chemicals
精细混合 intimate mixing
精细混合物 intimate mixture
精细结构 fine structure [texture]
精细结构常数 fine structure constant
精细结构光谱 fine spectrum
精细结构研究 fine structural investigation
精细结构组分[谱线] fine structure component
精细研磨 thorough grinding
精细窑炉混合料 intimate oven mix
精细作业 precision work
精下料 fine blanking
精选 concentration (conc.), preparative treatment, beneficiation ◇ 铁矿石～*, 中间～*
精选比(率) concentration ratio
精选捕集[收]剂 scavenger collector
精选槽 cleaner cell
精选度 degree of up-grading
精选段 cleaner section
精选矿 finished [washed] ore
精选煤 cleaned [fancy] coal
精选铁矿 beneficiated iron ore
精选物 concentrate
精选摇床 concentrating table
精压 【粉】coining, (pressure-)sizing, imprinting ◇ 闭式模～closed-die coining, 立体～full coining, 平面～flat coining
精压操作 coining [(pressure-)sizing] opreation
精压操作程序 sizing procedure
精压冲杆 coining press ram, sizing punch
精压出坯[脱模]杆 sizing knockout [stripper]
精压机 coining press [mill]
精压零件 coined parts

精压模 coining [finishing, sizing, calipering] die

精压模冲 sizing punch

精压坯块 coining compact

精研(磨) lapping-out ◇ 齿轮～机 gear-lapping machine

精轧【压】 finish [precision] rolling, (mill) finishing, planishing

精轧板材 finished plate

精轧薄板 planished sheet, finished plate ◇ 单面光亮～*

精轧除鳞泵 finishing descaling pump

精轧除[破]鳞机 finishing scale breaker

精轧道次 finishing pass, final polishing pass

精轧工作辊装配设备 finishing working roll assembly device

精轧黑薄[钢]板【压】 finished black plate

精轧机 finishing mill (FM), finishing rolling mill, finisher ◇ 可逆式～ reversing finisher, 热～*, 四辊～*, 优质～*

精轧机工作辊 finisher work roll

精轧机辊道 finishing roller table

精轧(机)控制盘 finisher control panel

精轧机控制台 finisher control pulpit

精轧机列 finishing roll line

精轧机鳞皮[氧化铁皮]坑 finisher scale pit, finishing mill scale pit

精轧机调整 finishing mill setup

精轧机支承辊 finisher back-up roll

精轧机主硅可控整流器室 finisher main thyristor room

精轧机组 finishing (mill) train, finishing mill group ◇ 活套～*

精轧机座 finishing [finisher] stand, finisher ◇ 冷轧机～ cold finisher, 万能式～*

精轧孔型 finish(ing) pass [groove], final pass, last groove [pass]

精轧控制室 finishing control room

精轧菱形孔型 finishing diamond pass

精轧破鳞辊 finishing scale breaker roll

精轧前孔型 leader pass

精轧速度 finishing speed

精轧椭圆孔型 finishing oval pass

精轧温度 finish rolling temperature

精轧氧化铁皮沉淀池 finishing sedimentation basin

精轧仪表室 finishing instrumentation room

精轧轧辊 finishing roll

精整【压】 finish(ing), dress(ing),【钢】conditioning (钢锭的),【铸】fettle ◇ 黑～(表面的) black finish, 化学～ chemical finishing, 快速～用钢 fast finishing steel, 毛面[无光]～*

精整薄板 trimmed sheet, processing sheet

精整薄钢板 second steel sheet

精整操作 sizing operation

精整成卷带材 strip processing

精整处理 finishing treatment ◇ 空气发蓝～ air-blued finish

精整锤 polishing [sleeking] hammer

精整度 degree of finish

精整费用 cost of cleaning

精整工段 finishing department [floor, work]

精整工段剪切机 finishing department shears

精整工序 finishing operation

精整辊 processing roll(er)

精整机 dressing machine

精整机座 planishing stand

精整跨 finishing bay

精整模 burnishing [calipering] die

精整烧结打包废钢铁 prolerizing scrap

精整设备 finishing equipment [facilities], adjustage

精整速度 finishing speed

精整涂层 finishing layer

精整压力机 sizing press

精整余量 clean-up allowance

精整轧机 leader mill

精整铸件 fettled casting

精整作业线	finishing line
精整作业线除[破]鳞机	processing scale breaker, flexing unit
精致过滤	【环】polishing
精制	refining, refinement, purifying, refinishing, clear up
精制苯	rectified benzol
精制槽	refining tank
精制钙	redistilled calcium
精制钢	finished steel
精制级	refined grade
精制焦油	refined tar
精制焦油碱类	【焦】refined tar bases
精制胶	gelatin(e)
精制矿物油	refined mineral oil
精制硫酸镍{NiSO$_2$·6H$_2$O}	refined nickel sulphate
精制螺母	finished [bright] nut
精制螺栓	burnished bolt
精制萘	refined naphthalene
精制溶剂	refining solvent
精制石灰粉	whiting
精制石墨	washed graphite
精制用溶液	treatment solution
精制油的汽提	oil stripping
精制铸铁	refined iron
经常保养	constant maintenance
经常费用	overhead, standing expenses ◇ 厂内～ factory overhead
经常开支	overhead cost
经常维修	constant maintenance
经常项目平衡	【企】balance on current account
经典电子半径	【理】classical electron radius
经典理论	classical theory
经典力学	classical mechanics
经典流态化	classical fluidization
经典能量分布	classical energy distribution
经典值	classical value
经典自由电子	classical free electron
经度	longitude ◇ 等～点*
经费	funds, running funds, outlay
经费开支	outlay
经济	economy, economics
经济比较	economic comparisons
经济电路	economy circuit
经济断面异型角钢	【压】special-shaped angle steel of economical profile
经济负担	economic burden
经济管理体制	economic management system
经济核算	economic [bussiness] accounting
经济环境	economic environment
经济计算模型	econometric model
经济可行最佳控制技术	best available control technology economically achievable(BATEA)
经济跨度	economic span
经济配筋率	economical ratio of reinforcement
经济评定	economic rating
经济评价	economic assessments [evaluation]
经济情况	economics, economic conditions
经济上可实现的最佳可行控制技术	【环】best available control technology economically achievable (BATEA)
经济时间数列	【企】economic time series
经济衰退	trade recession
经济效率	commercial efficiency
经济型材	economical section
经济学	economics
经济优势	economic advantage
经济运距	economic haul(ing) distance
经纪人	broker
经理	manager, managing director ◇ 分厂～*
经理工程师	manager-engineer
经年变形	secular distortion
经纬仪	theodolite, (surveyor's) transit, altometer

经线	meridian
经线仪	chronometer
经验	experience
经验程序	empirical procedure
经验法则	empirical rule, rule of thumb
经验方程(式)	empirical [observed] equation
经验方法	empirical method [procedure]
经验公式	empiric(al) formula
经验结果	empiric(al) result
经验数据	empiric(al) data
经验数字	arbitrary number
经验系数	experimental constant
经验值	empiric(al) value
经营	management, operation, run, administration
经营成本	operational [operating] cost
经营成本核算	operational cost accounting
经营费	operating expenses [cost], working expenditure
经营模式	operation mode
经营失败	bankruptcy
井壁	side wall (S.W.)
井壁管	cashing pipe [tube]
井的出水量	well yield
井点降低地下水位法	well-point method
井点降低水位系统	well-point de-watering system
井点排水	drainage by well points
井点排水系统	well-point de-watering system
井口车场	bracket
井式电加热炉	electric pit-type heating furnace
井式坩埚炉	shaft crucible furnace
井式连铸设备	sunken-type plant
井式炉	pit (batch-type) furnace, vertical pit-type furnace
井筒	(rock)shaft, pitshaft, tub
井下	underground (U.G.), under shaft
警报	warning, alarm, alert ◇ 反常~灯 abnormal alarm lamp, 事故~ disaster warning, 提前[预先]~*
警报器	warning device, alarm, alertor
警报显示	alarm display
警报信号系统	alarm signal system
警报信号(装置)	alarm
警报压力计	alarm manometer
警报装置	alarm box, alarming apparatus
警笛	alarm whistle
警告标记	warning sign
警告信号	warning [caution] signal ◇ 前置~ advance warning signal
警告[警报]信号灯	warning [danger] light
警铃[钟]	alarm bell
颈	neck ◇ 开一口 necking
颈长率	neck growth rate
颈缩	neck(ing) ◇ 局部形成~【压】localized necking, 形成~ necking-down
颈缩点[位置]	necking point
颈缘过渡处(钢梁的)	junction
颈状物	neck
劲吹火焰	harsh blowing flame
劲度	stiffness
劲火焰	harsh flame
劲性钢筋	rigid reinforcement
劲性钢筋混凝土结构	steel composite construction
静触点	break (back) contact, stationary [fixed] contact
静磁电子显微镜	magnetostatic electron microscope
静磁化曲线	static magnetization curve
静磁能	magnetostatic energy
静磁透镜	magnetostatic lens
静磁学	magnetostatics
静带	dead band
静点	dead point
静电	static electricity
静电场	electrostatic field
静电除尘[集尘,收尘,沉淀]器	electrostatic dust collector, electrostatic precipitator, electrostatic cleaning plant, electro-

static cleaner, cottrell dust catcher ◇ 板式~*,干式~*,高温~*,管式~*,科特雷尔~*,湿式~wet electric cleaner
静电磁力检验[探伤] statiflux
静电单位 electrostatic unit
静电电力电容器 static power condenser
静电镀层[镀覆] electrostatic coating
静电分离[选矿] electrostatic separation
静电分离器[分选机] electrostatic separator
静电复印机 xerographic printer, electrostatic copier
静电感应 (electro)static induction
静电过滤器 electrostatic filter
静电荷 (electro)static charge ◇ 饱和~saturation charge
静电计 electrometer ◇ 毛细管~capillary electrometer, 石英丝~*
静电计电子管 electrometer tube
静电焦油捕集器 electrostatic detarrer
静电浸没透镜 electrostatic immersion lens
静电聚焦 electrostatic forcusing
静电聚焦装置 electrostatic focusing device
静电力相互作用 Coulomb interaction
静电能 electrostatic energy
静电耦合 electrostatic linkage
静电抛光 electrostatic finishing
静电喷镀 electrostatic spraying
静电喷漆[涂] electrostatic paint spraying
静电屏蔽 electrostatic shield(ing)[screen(ing)], electric shielding
静电式电焊机 electrostatic welder
静电式电子显微镜 electrostatic electron microscope
静电透镜 electrostatic [electric] lens
静电透镜成像 electrostatic [charge] image
静电涂镀[敷,漆] electrostatic painting, electropainting
静电涂油机 electrostatic oiler ◇ 带材~*
静电吸引 electrostatic attraction
静电效应 electrostatic effect
静电蓄能焊机 electrostatic stored energy welder
静电学 electrostatics
静电烟气[煤气]除尘 electrostatic gas cleaning
静电引力 electrostatic attraction
静电印刷术 xerography, zerography, electronography
静电影像射线照相术 xeroradiography
静电硬球 static-rigid sphere
静电硬球模型 static-rigid sphere model
静电照相术 electrostatic photography, zerography
静电转速计 capacitor tachometer
静定结构 (statically) determinate structure
静海石 tranquillityite
静荷载[负荷,负载] dead load (d.l.), quiescent [static] load
静荷重塑性 static ductility
静合触点 back contact
静弧 silent arc
静挤压 static extrusion
静寂时间校正(计数器的) dead-time correction
静加负荷 dead-weight loading
静拉力试验机 quiet tensile testing machine
静冷却区 static cooling zone
静力 static force
静力(挤压)法捣实 【铸】static ramming
静力计算 static calculation
静力加工硬化曲线 static work-hardening curve
静力矩 static torque
静力平衡 static(al) equilibrium [balance]
静力试验 static test [trial], slow test ◇ 蒙特-卡罗~法 Monte-Carlo method

静力试验机	funicular machine
静力学变形[静畸变]	static distortion
静流	static flow, stationary stream
静摩擦	static(al) friction
静疲劳(破坏)【金】	static fatigue
静片	stator
静强度	static strength
静区	dead [silent] zone, blind spot
静熔【钢】	dead melt(ing)
静烧结料层	static sinter bed
静升力	static lift, uplift
静绳	standing rope
静水压力系数	hydrostatic pressure ratio
静水压试验	hydrostatic (pressure) test
静水压状态	equilateral state of stress
静态补偿器	static compensator
静态层	static bed
静态存储器	static memory [storage]
静态法	static method
静态分布	static distribution
静态腐蚀	static corrosion
静态还原	static reduction
静(态)挤压	static extrusion
静态寄存器	static register
静态记忆装置	static memory device
静态浇铸	static casting
静态校验【计】	static check
静(态)接点	static contact
静态控制【钢】	static control
静态拉[张]力试验	static tension test
静态模型	static model, steady state model
静态平衡	static [standing] balance, static equilibrium
静态强度	static strength
静态倾析	static decantation
静态屈服应力	static yield stress
静态溶质分布	steady state solute distribution
静态软化	static softening
静态酸洗(无搅拌的)	still pickling
静态特性(曲线)	static characteristic
静态调节器	static regulator
静态脱水	static dewatering
静态稳定性	statical stability
静态误差	static error
静态硬度	static hardness
静态再结晶	static recrystallization
静推力	static thrust (s.t.)
静型(压铸的)	cover half
静型原子位移	static atomic displacements
静压力	static pressure ◇ 标准~机试验器*
静压头	static (pressure) head, head pressure (液体的)
静液力挤拔	hydrostatic extrusion drawing
静液(力)挤压	hydrostatic [ramless] extruding ◇ 高温~*, 厚油膜~法*, 连续~*, 液体-空气~*, 液液~*
静液(力)挤压机	hydrostatic extrusion machine [press]
静液压成型	hydrostatic forming ◇ 金属冷态~(法)*
静液压传动	hydrostatic drive
静液压传动装置	hydrostatic power transmission
静液压挤压材料	fluid extruded material
静液压力计	hydrostatic (pressure) gauge
静液压模压	hydrostatic moulding
静液压平衡	hydrostatic equilibrium
静液压润滑	hydrostatic lubrication
静液压润滑装置	hydrostatic lubricating unit
静液[水]压设备	hydrostatic pressure apparatus
静液压头	hydrostatic head
静液压系统	hydrostatic system
静液压应力	hydrostatic stress
静液压造型	hydrostatic moulding
静液压张力	hydrostatic tension
静液压制	hydrostatic pressing
静应力	static(al) stress
静载试验	static test
静载(重)	(同"静荷载")
静止床反应器	static bed reactor

静止床高度　static bed depth
静止床氯化　static bed chlorination
静止风冷　cooling in still air
静止焊机　【焊】static welding machine
静止滑移系统　inactive slip system
静止角　static angle of repose, angle of rest [repose]
静止浸镀　dead dipping
静止空气　still [dead] air
静止气流　still current of gas
静止时间　quiescent [waiting] time
静止填充塔　static packed column
静止位错　stationary dislocation
静止相　stationary phase
静止液流　still current of liquid
静止质量　【理】rest mass
静止状态　quiescent conditions, inactive state
静置　standing, stewing
静置槽　still bath
静置气泡(接触角)测定仪　captive-bubble apparatus
静滞后　static hysteresis
静重　deadweight (D.W.), dead load (DL)
静子　stator
镜　mirror ◇马顿斯～*
镜赤铁矿　specular hematite
镜－惰煤型　vitrinertite
镜(反射)式检流计　mirror galvanometer
镜观测　mirror viewing
镜剂合金　tin amalgam
镜－亮煤　vitroclarite
镜煤　vitrain, anthraxylon, vitrite
镜煤化(作用)　vitrinization
镜煤类　vitrinoid
镜煤型　vitrite
镜面电镀　speculum plating
镜面对称　mirror-inverted
镜面反射　mirror [specular] reflection
镜面反射装置[反射式伸长计]　mirror apparatus
镜面光洁度　mirror finish
镜面光亮薄板　bright luster sheet
镜面光亮涂镀　high lustre coating
镜面光亮优质薄板　high mirror finished sheet
镜面光亮优质冷轧薄板　cold-rolled lustre finish sheet
镜面精抛光　mirror-finish polishing
镜面空气清理　air cleaning of mirror
镜面抛光　mirror [high] polishing, mirror finishing
镜面抛光薄板　bright polished sheet
镜面青铜(30—45Sn,余量 Cu)　speculum alloy
镜面转动轴　rotoflection axis
镜片　glass (block), optic
镜齐(67Cu,33Sn)　speculum metal
镜青铜(10—30Sn)　mirror bronze [alloy]
镜式棱柱光学伸长计　mirror-prism optical-type extensometer
镜丝煤　vitrofusite, vitrain-fusain, vitri-fusain
镜锑　regulus mirror
镜铁(15—30Mn,5C,余量 Fe)　spiegel (iron), spiegeleisen, mirror [specular] iron
镜铁化铁炉　spiegel cupola
镜铁矿(赤铁矿类)　specular iron ore, specularite, shining ore, iron glance
镜筒设计　column design
镜头　camera lens,【电】frame
镜透光度　specular transmittance
镜系统　mirror system
镜像　mirror image
镜像效应　image [mirror] effect
镜延伸仪　mirror extensometer
镜用合金　mirror alloy ◇杜普勒～*,库珀～*,索利特高度光亮～*
镜质丝煤　vitrofusinite
镜质组　vitrinite, vitrite
镜质组(煤岩)　vitrinite
镜质组反射率　vitrinite reflectance

径迹 track
径迹侵蚀法 【理】track-etch method
径迹照相 track photography
径节 diametral [diametric] pitch
径流 drainage
径流式扇风机 radial flow fan
径流式洗涤器 radial flow scrubber
径流系数 coefficient of runoff
径向 radial direction
径向场 radial field
径向斥力 radial repulsion
径向对称 radial symmetry
径向分布 radial distribution
径向分布[分配]法 radial distribution method
径向分布函数 radial distribution function
径向分布曲线 radial distribution curve
径向分量 radial component
径向风机 radial fan
径向钢筋 radial bar
径向滚珠轴承 annular ball bearing
径向活塞泵 radial piston pump
径向挤压 radial extruding
径向铰链式切割机 【焊】radial articulated-arm cutting machine
径向捆扎机 【压】radial bander
径向拉伸 radial draw
径向拉伸成形 radial-draw forming
径向裂缝 radial crack
径向流 radial flow
径向模式 【理】radial modes
径向切变干涉仪 radial shearing interferometer
径向(取样)检验 radial test
径向散布 radial scatter
径向流 radial flow
径向位移 radial displacement
径向压溃强度 radial crushing strength
径向压溃强度试验 radial crushing strength test
径向压溃强度系数 radial crushing strength constant
径向压溃载荷 radial crushing load
径向压力 radial pressure, radial (unit) roll pressure (径向单位轧制压力)
径向压缩试验 diametral compression test
径向压缩应力 【压】radial compressive stress
径向应变 radial strain
径向应力 radial stress
径向载荷 radial load
径向轴承 radial [supporting, transverse] bearing
径向/轴向收缩比 radial/axial shrinkage ratio
径向柱状的 【金】radial-columnar
竞标 【企】competitive bidding
竞争 contention, compete, competition
竞争长大 【金】competitive growth
净长 net length
净冲击能量 net energy of blow
净磁化(强度) 【理】net magnetization
净电荷 net charge
净度 cleanliness
净吨数 net ton (N.T.)
净费用 net charge
净高 clear height [headway]
净耗碳 net carbon consumption
净荷载[负载] net load
净化 purifying, purification, cleaning, cleanse, depuration, epuration, cleanup ◇ 初步～*, 粗略～气体 roughly cleaned gas, 干式～ dry cleaning, 间歇[分批]～ batch purification, 熔盐～*, 湿法～ wet purification, 未～气体*, 蒸馏～*, 氩气～ argon purification
净化比 purification ratio
净化操作 purification run
净化槽 purification [purifying, cleaning, clarifying] tank ◇ 脱脂～ cleaning tank
净化厂[车间] purification [clarification] plant
净化程度 degree [extent] of purification
净化除铁 【色】iron purification

净 jing

净化的空气　pure air (p.a.)
净化的炉顶煤气　【铁】clean top gas
净化电解液　purified electrolyte
净化段　cleaner section
净化法　purifying [purification] method, refining process
净化反应　purifying reaction
净化工段　purification section
净化罐　purification can
净化罐提升杆　purification can lifting bar
净化过程　cleaning process
净化还原联合操作　【色】combination purification-reduction run
净化还原联合法　combination [combined] purification-reduction process
净化还原联合炉　(combined) purification-reduction furnace
净化回路　purification circuit
净化剂　scavenger, cleaner, purifying [decontaminating] agent, detergent
净化炉　purifying [purification] furnace
净化炉装置　assembly of purification furnace
净化煤气　cleaned [refining] gas
净化母液　purged mother liquor
净化器　purifier, clarifier ◇层流~lamella clarifier, 锯末~sawdust purifier, 喷气~cleansing blower, 塔式~tower purifier
净化气体　cleaned [neat] gas
净化氢　purified hydrogen
净化区　cleaner section
净化溶液　purified solution
净化上水道　washing circuit
净化设备　purification plant, cleaning unit, purifier
净化塔　purifying [cleaning] tower, purifying column
净化脱脂槽　predunk tank
净化脱脂过程　cleaning process
净化系数　【冶】decontamination factor (d.f.)
净化系统　purification system [circuit], cleaning system, clarification system (油的)
净化循环　purification [decontamination] cycle
净化液　purged liquor
净化与还原　purification and reduction (P&R)
净化蒸馏罐　purification retort
净化蒸馏塔　purification column
净化柱　decontaminating column
净化装置　purifying [decontamination, cleaning] plant, clarifying system ◇卧式~horizontal cleaner
净化作用　defecation
净回收　net recovery
净价格　net price (n.p.)
净间距　clear spacing
净焦　【铁】coke blank
净结焦周期　【焦】net coking time
净距　clear distance
净空　clearance, free board, headway (顶部的), clear headway (桥下的), daylight (锻锤锤头与砧座间距离)
净空高度　clearance [free] height, head room (拱、梁等下面的)
净空(界)限　【运】clearance limit
净空图　clearance diagram
净跨　clear span
净宽　clear width
净矿石料　straight ore burden
净拉[牵引]力　net drag force
净煤　pure [super] coal
净煤气　purified [clean] gas
净煤气放出阀　clean gas bleeder
净密度　net density
净气器　air washer, gas cleaner
净热量　net heat
净热值　net calorific value
净熔剂　barren flux
净水　pure water (p.w.), 【环】product water (处理过的)
净水槽　clean water tank

净水器　water clarifier
净水设备　water purification unit
净吸入高度(泵的)　net positive suction head (NPSH)
净现值　net present value [worth]
净现值法　net present value method
净效率　net efficiency
净效应　net effect
净油器　oil purifier
净占地面积　net site area
净正吸引压头　net positive suction head (NPSH)
净制水　clarified water
净重　net weight (nt wt, N.wt.)
纠错码　error correcting code, self-correcting code
纠错时间　【计】make up time
纠错系统　error-correction system
纠正　correcting, rectification
鸠尾(榫)　dovetail
鸠尾榫槽　【建】dovetailed slot
鸠胸拱　【建】ogee arch
九氧化四钇　(同"过氧化钇")
酒精萃液　alcoholic extract
酒精汽油燃料　agrol fluid
酒精燃料　alky gas
酒精水准仪　spirit level
酒精温度计　alcohol [spirit] thermometer
酒石酸镧 $\{La_2(C_4H_4O_6)_3\}$　lanthanum tartrate
酒石酸钾钠　sodium-potassium tartrate
酒石酸钠钾 $\{KNaC_4H_4O_6\}$　potassium sodium tartrate
酒石酸氢钠　sodium bitartrate
酒石酸氢锶 $\{Sr(HC_4H_4O_6)_2\}$　strontium bitartrate
酒石酸氢盐[酯]　bitartrate
酒石酸铷 $\{Rb_2C_4H_4O_6\}$　rubidium tartrate
酒石酸铈 $\{Ce_2(C_4H_4O_6)_3\}$　cerous tartrate
酒石酸锑钾 $\{K(SbO)C_4H_4O_5 \cdot \frac{1}{2}H_2O\}$　potassium antimony tartrate
酒石酸盐[酯]　tartrate

救护车[船,机]　ambulance
救护人员　first aid attendant
救火队　fire fighting crew
救急箱　first aid cabinet
救生用具　buoy
旧轨回轧机　rail-rerolling mill
旧轨再轧钢材　rail steel products
旧井　old well (o.w.)
旧炉衬清除装置　【冶】knocking-out station
旧砂　【铸】old [black] sand
旧式　old style (O.S.)
旧式无底钢轨　edge rail
旧式乙醚萃取法　obsolete ether process
旧酸储存池　old acid storage tank
旧型砂　【铸】used sand
臼形轴承　footstep bearing, dead abutment
就地化验　in-situ analysis
就地建造　on-site construction
就地浇筑　【建】pour-in-place
就地浸出　【色】leaching in place [situ], spot [stop] leaching
就地再结晶　recrystallization in site
就位　into position ◇ 离位和～*
就业机会　job opportunity
居里常数　【理】Curie constant
居里点　【理】Curie point, magnetic change [transformation] point ◇ 渐近～*, 顺磁性～*
居里定律　【理】Curie's law
居里-韦斯定律　【理】Curie-Weiss law
居里温度　【理】Curie temperature
居民分布不均(匀性)　【环】habital segregation
居中　intermediary, intermediate
居住　living, dwelling ◇ 可～性【环】habitability
居住区　dwelling district
橘黄色加热温度　orange heat
橘皮表面[现象]　【压】orange peel (surface), alligator skin, pebbles
橘皮效应　【压】pebble [orange-peel] ef-

fect, pebbling
橘皮状表面缺陷　orange-peel defect
橘色　orange
"菊池"带　【金】Kikuchi bands
"菊池"线　【金】Kikuchi lines
局部变化　local variation [change]
局部表面粗糙度[性]　【金】local surface roughness
局部表面切割　spot gouging
局部玻璃化作用　partial vitrification
局部场　local field
局部脆性区　local [partial] brittle zone
局部淬火[淬硬]　local [partial] quenching, local(ized) [point, spot, decremental] hardening, selective hardening [quenching], differential hardening [quenching]
局部存储器　【计】local storage
局部点阵平移　local lattice translation
局部电池　local battery (L.B., l.b.), local (action) cell
局部电镀[局部镀层]　parcel plating
局部电流　local current
局部电子模型　localized electron model
局部电子衍射　limited area electron diffraction
局部镀金的　parcel-gilt
局部短路　partial short-circuit
局部断电　local power failure
局部断裂延伸　local extension at fracture
局部反射　partial reflection
局部反应　local reaction
局部沸腾　local boiling
局部分布　local distribution
局部分析　partial analysis
局部风机　secondary air fan
局部腐蚀　local(ized) [location-action, regional, selective] corrosion, local corrosive attack
局部干燥铸型　partially dried mould
局部感应加热淬火　selective induction hardening
局部各向异性　local anisotropy

局部供电事故　local power failure
局部固结　partial hardening
局部过热　local overheating
局部合金化　localized alloying
局部滑移　local(ized) slip
局部化　localization
局部化滑移　localized slip
局部化学反应　topochemical reaction
局部化学反应波峰　topochemical front
局部化学还原　topochemical reduction
局部化学还原结构　topochemical reduction structure
局部化学金属铁层　topochemical metallic-iron layer
局部回火　localized [selective] tempering
局部积碳　patch of carbon
局部加热　selective [local(ized), differential, district, spot] heating
局部加热法（消除应力集中用）　heat spotting
局部加热急冷变形矫正法（用于钣金件）　spot quenching
局部晶粒粗化　local grain coarsening
局部颈缩　localized necking
局部均质合金法　spot homogen process
局部控制　local control
局部冷铁[激冷]　local chilling
局部密封剂　selective sealant
局部磨损部位（炉衬的）　localized areas of wear
局部能级　localized energy level
局部凝结　partial condensation
局部扭转　local torsion
局部浓度　local concentration
局部偏析　spot segregation
局部破坏[断裂]　local rupture
局部迁移[徙动]　local migration
局部侵蚀　localized attack
局部清理　partial conditioning
局部取向　local orientation
局部燃烧　partial [zonal] combustion
局部热处理　localized [differential, case]

heat treatment
局部熔化　local [partial] fusion, localized melting
局部熔体　partly fused mass
局部烧结　partial sintering
局部伸长　local elongation [extension]
局部渗氮　selective nitriding ◇ 弗洛不锈钢氮化炉~法*
局部渗碳　local carburization, selective carburizing
局部失稳破坏　crippling
局部收缩　local contraction
局部塑性　【压】local plasticity
局部缩细成颈状[形成局部收缩]　neck(ing)-down
局部填缝料　selective sealant
局部退火　local [differential, partial, selective, spot] annealing
局部徙动　local migration
局部形成颈缩　【压】localized necking
局部性　locality
局部性电偶腐蚀(作用)　【化】local action
局部修磨　partial conditioning
局部压力　localized pressure
局部延伸　local extension ◇ 断裂时~*
局部异构反应　topotactic reaction
局部应变　local strain
局部应力集中　local(ized) stress concentration
局部硬化　partial [point] hardening
局部硬化组织　【金】partially hardened structure
局部有序　【理】local order
局部有序(化)　partial ordering
局部有序结构　(同"部分有序结构")
局部真空　partial vacuum
局部作用　local action
局外原子　stranger atom
矩尺　try square
矩-方孔型系统轧制法　box pass method
矩心　centroid, centre of moment
矩心轴线　centroid axis

矩形　rectangle
矩形棒[杆,条钢]　rectangular bar
矩形比　squareness ratio
矩形波　rectangular [square] wave
矩形波发生器　square-wave generator
矩形波极谱仪　square-wave polarograph
矩形槽　rectangular tank
矩形(磁滞)回线　rectangular (hysteresis) loop
矩形磁滞回线材料　square-loop material
矩形(磁滞)回线铁氧体　square-loop ferrite
矩形电极　rectangular electrode
矩形断面(钢材)[矩形钢材]　rectangular section
矩形(断面)梁　bar rectangular section
矩形断面坯块　briquette of rectangular section
矩形反射炉　rectangular reverberatory furnace
矩形分布　rectangular distribution
矩形钢丝　rectangular wire
矩形管　rectangular tube
矩形涵洞　box culvert
矩形焦点　rectangular focus
矩形孔径　rectangular aperture
矩形孔型　(同"箱形孔型")
矩形孔砖格子　rectangular checkerwork
矩形炉　rectangular furnace
矩形脉冲发生器　rectangular pulse generator
矩形坯　rectangular bloom
矩形图　【数】histogram
矩形窑　rectangular kiln
矩形砖　straight brick
矩形砖格　rectangular-type checker work
矩阵　【数】matrix, array
矩阵表示(法)　matrix representation
矩阵乘法　matrix multiplication
矩阵存储器　matrix memory [storage]
矩阵分析　matrix analysis
矩阵式打印机　matrix printer

矩阵型滤布　matrix cloth
矩阵元(件)　matrix element
举力　lifting [raising] force
举升油缸　lifting cylinder
聚氨基甲酸乙脂衬层　polyurethane lining
聚胺　polyamine
聚胺交联聚苯乙烯树脂　polyamine cross-linked polystyrene resin
聚苯乙烯　polystyrene
聚苯乙烯合金　polystyrene alloy
聚苯乙烯磺酸型阳离子交换剂　(同"磺化聚苯乙烯阳离子交换树脂")
聚苯乙烯基体　polystyrene matrix
聚苯乙烯树脂　polystyrene resin ◇ 交联～*
聚变　【理】(atomic, nuclear) fusion ◇ 可控～controlled fusion, 临界～频率*
聚丙烯腈　polyacrylonitrile
聚丙烯腈钠盐　sodium salt of polyacrylonitrile
聚丙烯塑料　polypropylene plastics, acrylic plastering
聚丙烯酸　polyacrylic acid
聚丙烯酸铵　ammonium polyacrylate
聚丙烯酸盐[酯]　polyacrylate
聚丙烯涂层　polypropylene coating
聚丙烯涂层钢　polypropylene coated steel
聚丙烯酰胺　polyacrylate
聚丁烯　polybutene
聚丁烯润滑油　polybutene oil
聚氟乙烯　polyvinyl fluoride ◇ 青铜～轴承*
聚光灯　focus lamp, spot light
聚光镜　condenser, collecting mirror ◇ 阿贝～Abbe condenser, 暗场～dark field condenser, 明(视)场～bright field condenser
聚光镜孔径　condenser aperture
聚光器　condensator, condenser, condensing-apparatus
聚光透镜　condensing [collector] lens
聚合　polymerization, condensation ◇ 解～作用 depolymerization, 使～converge
聚合的　polymeric
聚合电解质　polyelectrolyte ◇ 阳离子～*
聚合度　degree of polymerization
聚(合)硅　polymerized silica
聚合颗粒　aggregated particle
聚合力　cohesion, aggregation force
聚合黏结剂　【耐】polymer bonding
聚合树脂　polymer resin
聚合体　polymer (pol.), paradigm
聚合体崩解[碎裂]　disintegration of aggregates
聚合物　polymer (pol.), polymeric compound, polymeride ◇ 交联～cross-linked polymer, 协[异分子]～copolymer, 枝型～branched polymer
聚合物(彩色)涂层钢板　polymer-coated steel sheet
聚合物超导材料　polymer superconducting material
聚合物(分子)系　polymer system
聚合物絮凝剂　polymer flocculant
聚合现象　polymerism
聚合作用　polymerization
聚积　accumulating, pile-up
聚积池　accumulating pool
聚集　gather(ing), collection, accumulation, build(ing) up, coalescence, coalescing, conglomeration, aggregation
聚集的游离渗碳体　free coalesced cementite
聚集光束　pencil
聚集盘　collecting disc
聚集皮下气泡　pepper blister
聚集体　aggregate, aggregation
聚集状态　state of aggregate, coherent conditon
聚集组织(珠光体中片状铁素体和渗碳体相互重叠)　colony
聚集作用　aggregation
聚甲丙烯酸树脂　◇ 帕斯派克斯～Per-

聚甲基丙烯酸 polymethacrylic acid
聚甲基丙烯酸甲酯 polymethyl methacrylate
聚甲基丙烯酸树脂 polymethacrylic resin
聚甲基丙烯酸酯 polymethacrylate
聚焦 focusing, concentrating ◇ 纪尼埃型非对称~*, 偏转[致偏]~deflection focusing
聚焦 X 射线 focusing X-rays
聚焦板 focusing plate
聚焦补偿 focusing compensation
聚焦场 focusing field
聚焦单色 X 射线束 focused monochromatic X-ray beam
聚焦单色器 focusing monochromator
聚焦法 focusing method
聚焦反射 focused reflection
聚焦反射器 focusing [concentrating] reflector
聚焦放大镜 focusing magnifier, focuser
聚焦管 focusing tube
聚焦力 focusing force
聚焦面 focal area ◇ X射线管~tube focal area, 表观~apparent focal area, 共~目镜 parfocal eyepiece
聚焦碰撞 focussed collision
聚焦平面 focusing [focal] plane
聚焦屏 focusing screen ◇ 透明玻璃~*
聚焦器 focalizer ◇ 筒型单色点~*
聚焦区 focusing field, focal zone
聚焦圈[环] focus(ing) ring
聚焦摄谱仪 focusing spectrograph ◇ 科舒瓦式~*, 约翰逊式~*
聚焦(射)束[光束] focused beam ◇ 二次~*
聚焦设备 focusing unit, focus set
聚焦深度 depth of focus
聚焦条件 focusing condition
聚焦透镜 focusing lens [glass]
聚焦位置 focusing arrangement
聚焦线圈 focus(ing) coil

聚焦效率 focusing efficiency
聚焦性能 focal property
聚焦衍射束 focused diffracted beam
聚焦影像 focused image
聚焦圆 focal circle
聚焦照相机(用 X 射线) focusing (X-rays) camera ◇ 弗拉格曼~*, 纪尼埃型~*
聚焦罩(阴极) focusing hood
聚焦正透镜 positive lens
聚焦装置 focusing device [unit, arrangement] ◇ 阴极~*
聚结 coalescence, coalescing ◇ 生球~长大*
聚结法(挤压小型无氧铜零件) coalescence process
聚结剂 coalescer
聚结铜 coalesced copper
聚结长大机理 coalescence mechanism
聚晶 polycrystal, crystal combination
聚两性电解质 polyampholyte, polyamphoteric electrolyte
聚氯三氟乙烯 polychlorotrifluoethylene
聚氯乙烯 polyvinyl chloride (PVC, P.V.C.) ◇ 塑化~*, 填料-~片*, 维涅托帕涂~钢板 Vynitop
聚氯乙烯冲杆 polyvinyl plunger
聚氯乙烯合成橡胶 vinyl chloride rubber
聚氯乙烯树脂涂层钢板 vynitop ◇ 太阳牌~Sun-metal, Sun steel
聚氯乙烯塑料薄板 polyvinyl chloride sheet
聚氯乙烯塑料网 polyvinyl chloride wire mesh
聚氯乙烯引下线 polyvinyl chloride drop wire
聚醚 polyehter
聚醚树脂(可作混凝土、钢等的防护层) esserbetol, polyether resin
聚能弹 【铁】cumulative shell
聚氢氰酸 polymerized hydrocyanic acid
聚醛树脂 aldehyde resin

聚三氟氯乙烯〔C_2F_3Cl〕 fluorothene ◇ 凯尔 F～树脂 Kel-F
聚三氟-氯乙烯 polytrifluoromonochlorethylene
聚式流化床 aggregative fluidized bed
聚式流态化 aggregative fluidization
聚束 beaming,〔半〕bunching
聚束系统 beam forming system
聚四氟乙烯板 teflon disc
聚四氟乙烯衬里设备 teflon lined plant
聚四氟乙烯绝缘线 teflon insulated wire
聚四氟乙烯膜盒 teflon bellows
聚四氟乙烯膜盒脉冲发生器 teflon bellows pulse generator
聚四氟乙烯石棉 teflon asbestos
聚酰胺 polyamide, eurelon
聚酰胺树脂 polyamide resin
聚酰胺纤维 nylon, suturamid
聚盐罐 salt-catcher can
聚二醇〔聚乙烯甘醇〕 polyethylene glycol ◇ 卡博瓦克斯÷Carbowax
聚乙烯 polythene, polyethylene ◇ 氯磺酰化～合成橡胶 Hypalon
聚乙烯胺 polyvinyl amine
聚乙烯槽〔桶〕 polyethylene tank
聚乙烯衬里 polyethylene-lined
聚乙烯冲杆 polyvinyl plunger
聚乙烯醇 polyvinyl alcohol, poval
PHTH〕聚乙烯醇淬火 【金】polyvinyl alcohol quenching
聚乙烯醇水溶液淬火 【金】plastic quenching
聚乙烯醇缩甲醛树脂 Formvar
聚乙烯醇缩甲醛树脂复型 【金】Formvar replica
聚乙烯袋 polyethylene bag
聚乙烯对苯二酸酯薄膜 Mylar
聚乙烯隔膜 polythene diaphragm
聚乙烯设备 polythene equipment
聚乙烯石棉塑料 asbovinyl
聚乙烯桶 polyethylene tank
聚酯胶片 prepreg

聚酯树脂 polyester resin ◇ 玻璃纤维增强～*,拉['] 纳克～Laminac
拒电子的 electrophobic
拒绝 refuse, reject, turn down, negate
拒绝中断 【计】disarmed interrupt
拒收 rejection
拒水性液体 water-repellent liquid
巨分子 macromolecule
巨晶 macrocrystalline ◇ 反骤成～（现象）antigermination
巨晶现象 pattern effect
巨砾 bowlder, boulder
巨鼠型掘进机 giant mole
巨位错 giant [large] dislocation
巨型高炉 【铁】jumbo blast furnace
巨型混凝土空心方块 monolith
巨型炼焦反应器 jumbo coking reactor
巨型起重机 goliath crane
距离 distance (dist.), range, space, spacing
距离-波幅反应曲线 distance-amplitude response curve
距离测量 distance measurement
距离继电器 distance relay
距离清晰度 【理】range resolution
距离系数 distance coefficient
距离硬度 distance hardness
距离增益 distance gain size（DGS）
距离振幅校正 distance amplitude correction（DAC）
距离指示 distance indication
距离转换开关 zoning [range] switch
锯 saw ◇ 多盘～gang saw, 盘〔回转式〕～rotary saw, 往复式〔滑座〕～*
锯槽〔痕〕 saw cut
锯齿 sawtooth, serration
锯齿底炉 notched furnace
锯齿钢丝 burr wire
锯齿（式）冷床 【压】rack(ing)-type cooling bed
锯齿型点火器 saw-tooth ignitor
锯齿形 indent(ation), zigzag, sawtooth

锯齿形波　zigzag wave
锯齿形(断裂)花纹　chevron pattern
锯齿形焊缝　crimp seal
锯齿形集渣槽　saw-tooth crossgate
锯齿形破碎机　saw-tooth crusher
锯齿形切变波[超声波]检验　zigzag shear wave inspection
锯齿形切断冲头　saw-tooth punch
锯齿形切割　ragged cut
锯齿形碳化物　saw-tooth carbide
锯齿状凹口　beard
锯齿状断口　ragged [saw-toothed, hackly] fracture
锯齿状晶粒的(断口)　hackly granular
锯齿状晶体　fern-leaf crystal
锯床[机]　saw bench, saw(ing) machine ◇动力~ power saw, 热金属~
锯床挡板　saw guard
锯钢　saw steel
锯口　kerf, saw bite
锯末　sawdust, saw powder, serrago, wood shavings
锯末净化器　sawdust purifier
锯木厂　saw [lumber] mill
锯木架　sawhorse
锯片　saw blade
锯切　saw cutting ◇冷态~(金属的) cold sawing, 摩熔[摩擦]~ fusion sawing
锯切[断]性　【机】sawability
锯条　saw blade, hack saw
锯条夹　blade holder [vice]
锯屑　sawdust, scobs, filing
锯屑铜　saw chips
锯屑炸药　carbonite
锯座　saw carriage
剧烈的　intense, violent, severe
剧烈流出(金属液的)　violent tap
剧烈氧化　vigorous oxidation
涓流充电　trickle charge
镌版黄铜　etching brass
卷边　curling(板材的), crimping, bead(ing), flanged edge, flaring, raised edge ◇单边~角焊接头 corner-flange weld
卷边板材　flanged plate
卷边端头　beaded end
卷边法兰[凸缘]　beaded flange
卷边工具　beader, bead tool
卷边辊　【压】seaming roll
卷边焊　flange edge welding
卷边焊缝　flange weld, flanged seam
卷边机　crimping machine, folder
卷边角　angle of flange
卷边接缝[接合]　seaming
卷边连接　flanged edge joint
卷边模　curling die
卷边试验　flange [flanging] test
卷材　【压】coil, coiled material
卷材边缘　coil edge
卷材定位装置　coil positioner
卷材端头　coil end
卷材矫直机　coil straightener
卷材捆扎　coil strapping
卷材捆扎机　coil strapping machine
卷材平整机　coil-skin pass mill, coil-temper mill
卷层计数器　wrapping counter
卷尺　measuring tape [reel], tape (measure), band tape ◇用~量 taping
卷带磨光　【压】coil grinding
卷带盘(磁带的)　【计】take-up reel
卷高自动对中　【压】automatic coil height centering
卷焊管　brazed tube ◇三层~ triple wall brazed tube
卷好的废边卷　【压】finished scrap bundle
卷簧　spiral spring
卷混现象　entrapment phenomena
卷解试验　【压】wrapping (and unwrapping) test, crack [mandrel] test
卷宽(横向)自动对中　【压】automatic width [transversal] centering
卷铺屋面材　roll roofing
卷曲　curling
卷曲作用　curling action

卷 juan

卷取 【压】coiling, balling up（切边）
卷取车间 winding shop
卷取导管 reel [run] pipe
卷取工段 coiling section, wind-up station
卷取机 coiling [reeling] machine, (re)coiler, recoiling machine [reel], reel(er), strip coiling apparatus, coiling [winder, take-up] reel, (re)winder ◇ 带材~*, 地下~*, 多钳口（炉用）~ multiple-slot coiler, 浮动式~*, 辊式~*, 加勒特式~ Garret coiler, 可涨缩~ collapsible reel, 立式~ vertical coiler, 炉用~ furnace coiler, 平线圈~ pancake oiler, 切边~*, 双位~ duplicate recoiler, 双锥式~ double cone coiler, 筒式~*, 未轧完品~ cobble baller, 卧式~ horizontal reel, 叶片式~*, 张力~*, 胀缩卷筒式~*]
卷取机操纵工 coiler operator
卷取机操纵台 coiler pulpit
卷取机构 spooler
卷取机卷筒 coiler head, reel block
卷取机卷筒夹紧爪 reel gripper jaws
卷取机张力 coiler tension
卷取机张力调节器 reel tension regulator
卷取机支座 coiler stand
卷取计数器 wrap counter
卷取炉 coiling [coiler, reeling] furnace
卷取设备 coiling facilities, taking-up equipment
卷取速度 coiling speed
卷取弯折 reel kinks
卷取尾部控制技术 coiler's strip tail side control technique
卷取温度 coiling temperature（CT）, winding temperature
卷取温度控制 coiling temperature control（CTC）
卷取箱 coiling box
卷取张力 coiling tension
卷取装置 coiling device [apparatus, unit], take-up ◇ 双滚筒~ double take-up
卷绕 coiling, winding, taking-up

卷绕弹簧 coiling spring
卷绕摩擦 wrapping friction
卷绕温度 winding temperature
卷识码 【计】convolutional code
卷筒 coiling drum [block], (wind-up, winding) drum, barrel, capstan, mandrel, cone（拉丝用）◇ 带卷支座~*, 倒立~*, 固定~（拉丝机的）dead block, 拉丝~ capstan, 上出线式~*, 收缩状态的~*, 双层[上下]~ double block, 四扇形块式~*, 张开状态~*
卷筒拔管机 tube block machine
卷筒活动弓形块 flap
卷筒（卷取）张力 reel tension
卷筒冷拔机 bull block (drawing)
卷筒式开卷机 drum-type decoiler, mandrel payoff reel, mandrel uncoiler
卷筒式拉丝机 rotary bench
卷筒收缩（卸卷时的） mandrel collapse
卷筒心轴 mandrel arbor
卷筒胀大 mandrel expand
卷筒中心 mandrel
卷筒组座 winding frame
卷线 wire coiling
卷线机 wire reel, 【电】coil winder ◇ 侧出料式~ pouring reel, 驱动~*, 瓦里~ Vari-coil, 中心出料式[铺卷式]~ laying reel, 轴心进线的~ deadhead coiler
卷线盘 coiling block
卷线筒 wind-up drum, spool(er) ◇ 卧式~ horizontal block
卷线筒支柱 【电】drum stand
卷线圆筒 take-up reel
卷线轴 take-up reel ◇ 十字形~ spider reel
卷线装置 take-up unit
卷芯 coil core
卷芯拆除装置 coil core removing device
卷芯夹出钳 【压】coil core removing tongs
卷扬 hoisting
卷扬程序 hoisting sequence
卷扬电动机 winding motor

卷扬吨位　hoisting tonnage
卷扬(钢丝)绳[钢索]　hoist(ing) rope, winding cable
卷扬高度　hoisting height
卷扬工序　hoisting sequence
卷扬滑车　hoisting tackle
卷扬机　(cable) hoist, (hoisting) crab, hoisting machine, winch, winding engine, windlass ◇ 单斗～single-skip hoist, 电动～", 复式～double-drum winch, 箕斗[料车]～skip hoist, 链式～chain winch, 气动～air hoist, 升降～lift winch, 手动～hand hoist [winch], 双电动机式～", 双料斗～double-track skip hoist, 双筒～", 水力～hydraulic hoist, 斜桥～inclined hoist
卷扬机构　hoisting [lifting] mechanism
卷扬机卷筒　hoisting drum
卷扬机室　hoist(ing) house [compartment, room]
卷扬机手[司机]　hoistman
卷扬机械　hoisting machinery
卷扬绞筒　hoisting barrel
卷扬料罐　【铁】hoisting bucket
卷扬能力　hoisting capacity
卷扬起重机　hoisting crane
卷扬(起重)设备　hoisting equipment [apparatus]
卷扬速度　hoisting speed
卷扬系统　hoisting system
卷扬斜桥(高炉的)　hoist incline [bridge]
卷扬型桥式起重机[(走行)吊车]　hoist type overhead travelling crane
卷扬装置　hoisting unit ◇ 料罐～bucket carriage track
卷折飞边　flash folding
卷折角　furled down corner
卷重　coil weight ◇ 平均～average coil weight
卷轴　reel, former (带、箔、材等的)
卷轴装置　spooling device
卷状薄板切边　coiled shearings

卷座车　cradle car
卷座升程　cradle lift
绢云母　sericite
绢针铁矿　przibramite
蕨叶状　fernlike
掘进机　development machine, tunneller ◇ 巨鼠型～"
掘进装载机　front end loader
掘开效应(挤压特硬金属时发生)　effect of ploughing
掘土机　excavator, rootdozer, power shovel ◇ 除根～grubber
决策　decision
决定　decide, decision, determination
决定性因素　determinative [pacing, decisive] factor, determinant
决算　【企】actual budget, final cost
决议　resolution, decision
诀窍　know-how
绝对埃　absolute Angstroem
绝对编码　【计】direct [specific] coding
绝对测量[测定](法)　absolute measurement
绝对程序设计　absolute programming
绝对垂度[变位]　absolute deflection
绝对纯净　net absolutely (NA, n.a.)
绝对大气压　absolute atmosphere
绝对大小　absolute magnitude
绝对代码　【计】absolute [basic, direct] code
绝对单位　absolute unit, absolute system of units
绝对导磁[磁导]率　absolute permeability
绝对地址　【计】absolute address
绝对地址汇编程序　absolute assembler
绝对电磁单位　absolute electromagnetic unit (aemu)
绝对电磁单位制　CGSM (centimetre gramme second-electro-magnetic) system
绝对反应速率理论　absolute reaction rate theory
绝对沸点　absolute boiling point

绝对干燥的 bone [theoretically] dry
绝对高度 absolute altitude
绝对含水量 absolute water content
绝对黑体 absolute black body
绝对活度 absolute activity
绝对价 absolute valency
绝对介电常数 absolute permittivity, absolute dielectric constant
绝对静电单位 absolute electrostatic unit (aesu)
绝对孔径 absolute pore size
绝对宽展 absolute spread
绝对粒度值 absolute size value
绝对零度 absolute zero (-273℃)
绝对目标程序 absolute object program
绝对黏度 absolute viscosity (abs. visc.)
绝对膨胀 absolute expansion
绝对偏差 absolute deviation
绝对热效率 absolute thermal efficiency
绝对热[供暖]效应 absolute heating effect
绝对渗透性[渗透率,透气性] absolute permeability
绝对生产率 specific efficiency
绝对湿度 absolute humidity
绝对衰变[蜕变]速率 absolute disintegration rate
绝对速率理论 absolute rate theory
绝对弯曲度 absolute deflection
绝对温标[开氏绝对温标] absolute temperature scale, Kelvin('s) (absolute) scale ◇ 开氏~度数 Kelvin (K)
绝对温度 absolute temperature (abs. t.), Kelvin (K)
绝对温度计 absolute thermometer
绝对稳定性 absolute stability
绝对误差 absolute error (AE)
绝对线圈 absolute coil
绝对信号 absolute signal
绝对压力 absolute pressure
绝对压力计[表] absolute manometer, absolute pressre gauge

绝对压力真空计 absolute pressure vacuum gauge
绝对压下量 absolute draught
绝对硬度 absolute hardness
绝对责任 absolute liability [responsibility]
绝对值 absolute value [magnitude]
绝对(最)优化法 method of unconditional optimization
绝密(的) top secret (TS, t.s.)
绝汽冲程 【机】idle stroke
绝热 (heat, thermal) insulation, isolation ◇ 非~精馏*
绝热板 (heat) insulating plate ◇ 镁橄榄石~*
绝热变化 adiabatic change
绝热变形 adiabatic deformation
绝热材料 (同"隔热材料")
绝热衬里 insulating lining
绝热递减率 adiabatic lapse rate, adiabatic gradient
绝热管 covered pipe
绝热过程 adiabatic process
绝热火焰温度 adiabatic flame temperature ◇ 燃烧带~*
绝热混凝土 insulcrete
绝热挤压 adiabatic extrusion
绝热加热 adiabatic heating
绝热精馏 adiabatic rectification
绝热冷却 insulated cooling
绝热量热器 adiabatic calorimeter
绝热流槽 insulated launder
绝热帽 【钢】headbox
绝热耐火砖 insulating firebrick
绝热能力 insulating ability
绝热膨胀 adiabatic expansion
绝热片[件] insulation piece
绝热瓶 Dewar's bottle
绝热曲线 adiabatic curve
绝热去磁[退磁] 【理】adiabatic demagnetization
绝热软化 adiabatic softening

绝热扫描量热计	adiabatic scanning calorimeter
绝热体	insulator, (thermal) isolator, heat guard
绝热系数	adiabatic coefficient
绝热线	adiabatic line, adiabat
绝热效果	heat insulating effect
绝热性能	insulating ability, adiathermancy
绝热压缩	adiabatic compression
绝热毡	thermal insulation blanket
绝热蒸发	adiabatic evaporation
绝热砖	insulbrix
绝热作用	heat insulating function
绝湿的	water-repellent, water-proof
绝微子(直径<5nm 的粒子)	amicron
绝氧的	(同"厌氧的")
绝氧条件	anoxic condition
绝缘	insulation, isolation ◇ 分层~ lamellar insulation, 匝间~ interturn insulation, 热~ heat insulation
绝缘板	insulating plate [board]
绝缘棒	insulating rod
绝缘布带	tape
绝缘材料	insulant, (electrical) insulating material, dielectric(al) ◇ 可铸~ insulating castable
绝缘层	insulating layer [course] ◇ 防(腐)蚀~*
绝缘衬里	insulating lining
绝缘带	insulating strip [tape] ◇ 缠~ tapping
绝缘等级	insulation class
绝缘底电炉	non-conducting hearth furnace
绝缘底座	insulating base
绝缘垫	insulation spacer
绝缘垫圈	insulating washer, grummet, grommet
绝缘电缆	insulated cable ◇ 空气纸~ dry-core cable
绝缘电阻	insulation [dielectric] resistance
绝缘电阻测试器	insulation resistance tester
绝缘电阻压降	IR (insulation resistance) drop
绝缘覆层	insulation coating
绝缘胶处理的	compounded
绝缘管	insulating tube
绝缘环	insulating ring ◇ 层状酚塑料~*, 米卡塔~*, 塔夫诺尔~*
绝缘剂	insulating compound
绝缘夹层	insulating sandwich
绝缘件	insulation piece
绝缘胶	insulation paste, filling compound ◇ 接线盒浇注~【电】joint-box compound, 注~的 compound-filled
绝缘胶布带	friction tape
绝缘距离	insulation distance
绝缘块	insulating block
绝缘漏电	insulation leakage
绝缘铝线	insulated aluminum wire
绝缘密封垫	insulating gasket
绝缘膜	insulating [insulation] film
绝缘模	insulator die
绝缘母线	isolated bus
绝缘能力	insulating ability [power]
绝缘片	insulating strip
绝缘漆	insulating lacuqer [varnish], insullac
绝缘强度	insulating [dielectric] strength
绝缘强度测试设备	dielectric strength test set
绝缘水泥	insulating cement
绝缘塑料	ambroin ◇ 导线包覆~的装置 plastic extruder
绝缘陶瓷涂层	insulating ceramic coatings
绝缘套	insulating sleeve
绝缘套管	insulating bush, empire tube ◇ 进线~ lead-in bushing
绝缘体	insulator, isolator, non-conductor, dielectric body ◇ 热~ heat barrier
绝缘填料	insulating packing
绝缘条	insulating strip
绝缘涂层	inusulation coating ◇ 最终退火

和~作业线*
绝缘屋面板　insulating roof deck plate
绝缘物质　insulating compound
绝缘纤维板　masonite
绝缘线　covered line [wire], insulated wire
绝缘芯棒　insulator mandrel
绝缘性能　insulating property [ability]
绝缘氧化物膜　insulating oxide film
绝缘用合成纤维板　pressboard
绝缘油布　empire cloth
绝缘油纸　empire paper
绝缘纸　insulating [dielectric, felt] paper
绝缘子　(electrical) insulator, arc ring ◇ 杯形~cup insulator, 穿墙~*, 蛋形[拉线]~egg insulator, 电池~battery insulator, 碟状~*, 多裙式~*, 进线~wall entrance insulator, 拉线~guy [egg] insulator, 耐拉~dead-end insulator, 耐雾~fog type insulator, 裙状~petticoal insulator, 悬式~suspension insulator, 直螺脚[卡口]~bracket insulator, 柱桩~anchor insulator
绝缘子串　chain insulator, insulator chain
均布动荷载　moving uniform load
均布荷载　even [uniform] load ◇ 等比[等效]~equivalent uniform load
均称光谱线　homologous lines
均等　parity, equal
均方根　root mean square (RMS), mean square root
均方根激发功率　RMS exciting power
均方根偏差　mean square root deviation, root mean square deviation
均方根值　R.M.S. (root mean square) value
均方偏差　standard deviation (S.D.), mean square deviation
均方位移　mean square displacement
均方误差　mean square error
均方值　mean square value
均分　divide equally, share out equally, equipartition

均衡　balancing, equalization, proportionate ◇ 不~disproportion
均衡的　isostatic
均衡电流　equalizing current
均衡[补偿]电路　equalizer circuit
均衡鼓风　balanced [equilibrium] blast
均衡梁　balance arm
均衡器　equalizer, balancer, (配重) cross-beam, balance beam
均衡送风冲天炉(化铁炉)　equiblast cupola
均衡运转　balanced running
均衡状态　equiponderant state, equipoderation
均厚板坯　【压】uniform gauge slab
均化黏土装置　【耐】device for homogenizing clay
均化器　homogenizer
均化区　conditioning zone
均化溶剂　level(l)ing solvent
均化设备　homogenization installation
均聚合(作用)　【化】homopolymerization
均热　soak (age), soaking, heat soak, blistering ◇ 过冷奥氏体亚稳定区~淬火 aus-bay quenching
均热段　soaking zone [unit], heat soak section, annealing [holding, afterfiring] zone, retention area
均热段炉罩　【团】dog-house
均热加热　soaking heat
均热坑(锭、坯的)　dead soaking pit
均热炉　soaking furnace [pit], soaking pit furnace, soaker, (ingot) pit, pit (heating) furnace, underground furnace ◇ 垂直供热的[中心供热式]~vertically fired pit, 单侧烧嘴~one-way-fired pit, 单座式~*, 电热式~*, 坑式~cell pit furnace, 炉底加热式~*, 煤气加热~gas-heated pit furnace, 切向烧嘴~*, 上部单烧嘴长坑~*, 上烧嘴[顶部燃烧]~*, 蓄热式~*, 圆形~*, 中心燃烧式~*
均热炉床　soaking hearth

均热炉操作　soaking practice
均热炉厂房　soaking pit building
均热炉坑[眼]　【压】hole
均热炉跨　soaking pit bay
均热炉跨间　soaking pit building
均热炉炉盖　soaking pit furnace cover
均热炉(钳式)起重机[吊车]　【压】(soaking, ingot) pit crane
均热炉用伸缩式吊车　【压】telescopic-type soaking pit crane
均热炉渣　soaking pit slag, hearth [flue] cinder, mill (furnace) cinder
均热炉中加热　pit soaking
均热期　【压】soaking [holding] period
均热时间　soak(ing) time, duration of soaking
均热室　soaking unit
均热温度　soaking temperature
均热箱　soaking pot
均相反应　homogeneous reaction
均相反应器　homogeneous reactor
均相[均匀]烧结　(同"单相烧结")
均压　isopressing,【电】dressing, valtage-sharing ◇炉顶～设备
均压阀　【铁】equalizer valve
均压放散阀　【铁】relief valve
均压环　【电】equalizing ring
均压接线　equipotential connection
均压开关　equalizing switch
均压孔　pressure equalizing vent
均压母线　equalizing bar
均压器　pressure equalizer, voltage balancer
均压线　equalizing cable, equalizer
均压箱　surge tank
均压用气体　【铁】equalizing gas
均一　even, uniform, homogeneous, unity
均一粒度原料　equigranular charge
均一系　【金】homogeneous system
均匀X射线　homogeneous X-rays
均匀α固溶体　homogeneous α solid solution
均匀变形　uniform [homogeneous] deformation, uniform straining
均匀场　uniform [homogeneous] field
均匀沉积　uniform deposition
均匀成核　homogeneous nucleation
均匀充填　uniform fill
均匀淬火　uniform hardening
均匀点火　uniform ignition
均匀镀层　homogeneous coating
均匀度　evenness, homogenization degree, degree of consistency
均匀断面梁　【建】uniform beam
均匀反应堆[器]　homogeneous reactor
均匀分布　even [uniform, homogeneous, level] distribution
均匀分布定律　equipartition law
均匀分布载荷　uniformly distributed load
均匀辐射　homogeneous radiation
均匀腐蚀　uniform corrosion [attack]
均匀厚度　uniform gauge
均匀滑移　homogeneous glide
均匀化　homogenizing, homogenization, leveling, level(l)ing action (使镀层)
均匀化料场　homogenization plant
均匀化料堆　homogenization pile
均匀化(热)处理　homogenizing treatment
均匀化设备　homogenization installation
均匀化作用　level(l)ing effect
均匀混合　uniform [homogeneous, intimate, thorough] mixing
均匀混合物　uniform [homogeneous, intimate] mixture
均匀级配砂　【建】uniformly graded sand
均匀给[布]料　regulated feed
均匀加热　uniform heating
均匀加热炉　equiflux heater
均匀结[过渡层]　homogeneous junction
均匀结构　uniform [homogeneous] structure
均匀介质　homogeneous medium
均匀静电场　uniform electrostatic field
均匀颗粒　uniform grain
均匀颗粒度　uniform particle size

均匀力场　uniform field of force
均匀流　uniform flow
均匀面变形抗力[阻力]　resistance to plane homogeneous
均匀磨损　even wear
均匀扭力[扭转]　uniform torsion
均匀膨胀　uniform expansion
均匀频谱噪声　【理】white noise
均匀切变　homogeneous shear
均匀曲线　smooth curve
均匀溶液　homogeneous solution
均匀渗碳(法)　homogeneous carbonizing
均匀涂层　homogeneous coating
均匀退火　homogenizing (annealing)
均匀无序固溶体　uniform random solid solution
均匀雾化　uniform atomizing
均匀系数　uniformity coefficient
均匀下料　smooth descent
均匀相　homogeneous phase
均匀性　uniformity, uniform quality, homogeneity, consistent quality
均匀延伸(量,率)　uniform [proprotional] elongation
均匀应变　uniform straining, homogeneous strain
均匀应力　homogeneous stress
均匀载荷　uniform load
均匀状态　homogeneous state [condition]
均整　【压】expansion, reeling
均整机　reeler, reeling machine [mill]
均质　isotrope, homogeneity ◇ 不～导体 dissimilar conductors, 非～材料 dissimilar material
均质棒材　homogeneous bar
均质成核　homogeneous nucleation
均质钢　homogeneous steel ◇ HOC～铸锭法 (同"均质铸锭法")
均质化　【金】homogenization
均质(化)合金　homogeneous [homogenized] alloy
均质晶体　homogeneous crystal
均质气体　uniform gas
均质砂　【铸】cut sand
均质(特)性　【金】uniform [consistent] quality, homogeneity
均质系　homogeneous system
均质系数　uniformity coefficient
均质蒸汽处理　homo-treatment
均质铸锭　homogeneous casting (HOC)
均质铸锭法　HOC (homogeneous casting) process
均重块　compensating weights
菌式(轧辊)穿孔机　【压】cone mill, cone-roll piercing mill
军械[军用器材]　ordnance
军械[军用]合金　ordnance alloy
军用标准(美国)　military standard (MIL-STD)
军用规格(美国)　military specification (MILSPEC)
竣工　completion
竣工焊缝　completed weld

K k

喀斯特 karst

卡 calorie (cal.)(热量非法定单位,= 4.1868J)

卡/秒(功率非法定单位,= 4.1868W) calorie per second (cal/s)

卡邦德尔镍银(66Cu,18Ni,16Zn) Carbondale silver

卡表 pincers,【电】dogs

卡波弗拉克斯碳化硅耐火材料(含 SiC≥85%) carbofrax

卡博瓦克斯聚乙二醇 Carbowax

卡勃洛伊碳化钨硬质合金 carboloy metal

卡勃洛伊钴钨硬质合金 Carboloy

卡车 (auto)truck,lorry ◇ 通用~general utility truck,尾卸[后卸,端部卸载]~,自动卸货~dump truck

卡车司机 teamster

卡尺 (sliding) cal(l)ipers

卡钉 staple (bolt)

卡恩抗裂试验(美国海军实验室的) Kahn tear test

卡尔鲍姆工业纯铁(总杂质< 0.025;0.001Mn,0.015Si,0.0014Cu,0.004Ni,痕量 S) Kahlbaum iron

卡尔贝特不透性石墨(在高压下不渗漏液体) Karbate graphite

卡尔贝特管式热交换器 Karbate tubular heat exchanger

卡尔贝特无孔碳衬里的设备 Karbate lined plant

卡尔德龙废钢装料机 Calderon (scrap) charger

卡尔德龙装料机 【钢】Calderon charging machine

卡尔多炼钢法 Kaldo process, Kalling-Domnarfvet (KALDO)

卡尔多型回转窑生铁生产法 Kaldo pig iron process

卡尔多转炉 【钢】Kaldo converter [vessel]

卡尔柯茨铜锡铅锌三元合金 Kalchoids

卡尔马什锡基轴承合金(1:12.5Cu, 1.2Pb,余量 Sn;2:7.5Sb,3.7Cu,余量 Sn) Karmash alloy

卡尔曼滤波(法) 【数】Kalman filtering

卡尔梅斯法(轧制无缝管) Calmes process

卡尔梅斯轧辊 Calmes roll

卡尔梅特奥氏体镍铬铝耐热钢(含 25Cr,12Ni) Calmet

卡规 cal(l)ipers, caliber, calibre, gap [snap] gauge ◇ 大~heavy gauge

卡环 【机】circlip, clasp

卡计弹 【理】bomb

卡津施泰因铅基轴承合金(7.5Sn, 16.5Sb,0.5Cu,余量 Pb) Katzenstein alloy

卡津锌镉共晶合金(17.4Zn,余量 Cd;用作钢缆焊料) Cazin

卡紧 clamping

卡克塞特锌合金(模具用;4Al,3Cu, 93Zn) Kirksite

卡肯达尔效应(金属间原子扩散引起标记物质移动的现象) Kirkendall effect

卡口 bayonet

卡口插座 bayonet socket

卡口灯座 bayonet holder [base], swan base

卡口绝缘子 bracket insulator

卡拉坎铅青铜(钟铜)(60—70Cu,14—25Sn,0—14Pb,0—9Zn) Karakane

卡拉佩拉浸蚀剂(不锈钢及铜基合金浸蚀用) Carapella's reagent

卡勒浸蚀剂(钢铁的) Kaller's reagent

卡利特耐热镍铬合金钢(35—68Ni,12—20Cr,0.55C,余量 Fe) Calite

卡林-多姆纳费特回转窑直接还原及脱硫法 【铁】Kalling-Domnarfvet process

卡林浸蚀剂(显示铬钢显微组织用) Kalling's reagent

卡洛米克镍铬铁电热(丝)合金(65Ni,

15Cr,20Fe) Calomic
卡洛依钙铝合金（8—12Ca 或 24—26Ca，余量 Al） Calloy
卡马高电阻镍合金（20Cr, 3Fe, 3Al, 余量 Ni） Karma (alloy)
卡马施锡基装饰合金（85Sn, 5Sb, 3.5Cu, 1.5Zn, 1.5Bi） Karmarsch's alloy
卡梅利亚轴承合金（70.2Cu, 14.75Pb, 10.2Zn, 4.25Sn, 0.05Fe） Camelia
卡姆洛依耐蚀耐热钢（50Fe, 10—20Cr, 25—35Ni） comloy
卡姆帕尼尔石灰质铁矿 Campanil
卡姆普贝尔平炉双联法 【钢】Campbell process
卡纳利斯加铝热剂铸锭法 【钢】Canaris method
卡瑙利巴蜡 （同"巴西棕榈蜡"）
卡尼津化学触媒反应镍合金镀覆法 Kanigen plating
卡诺图 【数】Karnaugh map
卡诺循环 【理】Carnot cycle
卡帕科石膏型铸造法 Capaco process
卡帕碳化物{(FeMo)$_{23}$C$_2$} Kappa carbide
卡盘 【机】cartridge ◇ 带臂～ lever chuck
卡喷特 49 软磁合金（47—50Ni, 余量 Fe） Carpenter 49
卡喷特离心脱水器 【铁】Carpenter centrifuge
卡皮查单晶形成法 Kapitza method
卡片 card, fiche ◇ 卡片叠 deck
卡片抽出器 card draw-out instrument
卡片穿孔 【计】card punch
卡普苏尔铅锡合金（92Pb, 8Sn） Capsule metal
卡钳 cal(1)ipers, caliber, calibre, calibration bar
卡钳开口 clamp opening
卡圈 closing [locking] ring
卡热单位 caloric heat unit (CHU, C.H.U.)
卡斯尔表面化学热处理法（提高钢质零件耐磨性） Cassel process
卡斯罗克斯合成树脂黏结铁氧钴磁铁（17Co, 56Fe, 27O） Caslox
卡斯帕松中间罐多流浇注法 Caspersson's method
卡斯特纳电解槽 Kastner cell
卡塔尼特刀具[碳化物]硬质合金（英国产） Cutanit (alloy)
卡特拉斯塔高锡铅基轴承合金（10—20Sn, 12.5—15Sb, 63.5—75Pb, 0.2—1.5Cu） Cutlasta
卡头 【机】grip head
卡瓦 【机】pipe slips
卡瓦诺活动炉算直接炼铁法 Cavanaugh process, O.R.F. travelling grate process
卡韦基氟硅酸钾分解锆矿石法 Kawecki process
卡欣－贝克病 【环】Kaschin-Beck's diesease
卡赞尼加钢丝热镀锌法 Cazzaniga process
卡爪 claw, jack catch
卡值 （同"发热值"）
卡纸板 card-board
卡住 seizing, jam(ing), freeze, stick-slip
开 carat（含金率）,Kelvin (K)（开尔文，热力学温度单位）
开凹口 hack, notching
开闭阀 on-off valve
开采 mining ◇ 可～的 minable
开采出 tap-off
开采料 borrow
开槽 fluting, grooving, hack, notching, nicking, recessing
开槽边 recessed edge
开槽锤 acute [horning] hammer
开槽焊 slot welding
开槽机 channel(l)ing machine, groover
开槽连接 slotted joint
开槽梁 notched beam
开槽石墨管 slotted graphite tube
开槽铣刀 grooving cutter
开槽錾子 grooving chisel

开坯 bursting
开出钢[铁,渣]口 open tapping, opening of taphole ◇ 风动～ pneumatic tapping, 机械～ mechanical tapping
开出钢[铁]口设备[装置] tapping apparatus [arrangement]
开出铁口 open tapping, opening of taphole, iron-notch opening, sledging, notch breaking ◇ 用氧气～ oxygen tapping, 钻～ drill tapping
开(出铁)口机[器] iron notch opening machine, iron-notch tapper, tapping machine [drill], taphole opener [drill], taphole drilling machine ◇ 电钻～ electric rotary drill, 风动～*, 全液压～*, 液压～*, 撞击式风动～*, 自动～ automatic taphole drill
开锉机 【机】nicker-pecker
开底容器 bottom opening container
开底式锭模
开底式(钢)锭模 open-bottom mould ◇ 上大下小～*
开动 start(-up) ◇ 频繁～(指发动机) jogging
开动能力 startability
开动期 breaking in period
开度 opening, breadth, ◇ 冲模～ die opening, 出口～ outlet opening, 辊隙～ roll gap opening, 轧辊有效[工作]～*
开端 beginning, commencement
开发 developing, exploitation, opening-up
开发区 development area
开发援助机构 development assistance agency
开方 【数】extracting
开方器 square root extractor
开放的γ相区 【金】open [expanded] γ-field, open gamma field
开放式辐射管 open radiation tube
开缝管 open joint tube
开缝隙浇口 【铸】touching
开杆式水压机 open rod hydrodynamic press
开工 start(-up), onset ◇ 全线～ allwork
开工计划 start-up program
开工率 operating [working] rate
开工日期 commissioning [start-up] date
开工投产 commissioning
开沟型[建] side scraper
开沟器 share
开关 switch (sw.), circuit closer, contactor, (current) breaker, cock ◇ 超速～ over speed switch, 非浮动～ floatless switch, 浮动[浮子]～ float switch, 射流～ fluid switch, 手动操作～*
开-关【电】 on-off
开关板 key board, panel
开关冲击[浪涌] switching surge
开关磁心 【电】switch(ing) core
开关阀 switch [on-off] valve
开关杆 switch lever
开关管 switch(ing) tube
开关柜 switch cubicle [box]
开关盒 switch box [case], switchgear cabinet
开关机构 switching [on-off] mechanism
开关控制系统 on-off control system
开关配电板 switch panel
开关器件 switching device,【半】binistor
开关熔丝[保险丝] switch-fuse
开关设备[装置] switchgear, switching device
开关时间 【电】switch(ing) time
开关速度 switching speed
开关台 switch desk
开-关调节器 switching regulator, on-off controller
开关箱 switch box [cupboard]
开关元件 switch(ing) [on-off] element, switching member
开关闸刀 switch blade, knife of switch
开关站 switchgear [switching] station
开管汽相生长法 open-tube vapo(u)r growth method

开 kai

开管式外延生长　open-tube epitaxial growth
开轨道　【理】open orbit
开焊　snap, break
开合螺母　slit [clasp] nut
开合桥　movable [folding, draw] bridge
开弧　free burning arc, open arc
开环　open loop [cycle], ring opening
开环控制　【计】open loop control
开环控制系统　open loop (control) system
开簧器　spring opener
开浇口　cut
开浇口操作　【铸】gating practice
开浇口方法　【铸】gating method
开脚扳手　spanner wrench
开颈口　necking
开卷　uncoil(ing), decoiling, unwind(ing), open coil, unreel, taking-off, paying-off, draw-off (从卷筒上) ◇ 带卷～【压】coil unwinding
开卷工　pay-off man
开卷工段(带卷的)　pay-off station
开卷后张力　decoiling back-tension
开卷机　【压】uncoiler, uncoiling machine [unit, reel], decoiler, decoiling machine, unwinder, unwinding coiler, feed [unwind] reel, reeler, feed [pay-off] coil [strip] opener, coil opening machine, swift (拉丝机的) ◇ 电磁直头式～*, 定心圆锥式～*, 高速～biflaker, 机组～*, 卷筒式～*, 盘式 [线轴式] ～ disc-type decoiler, 三臂～ three-arm payoff reel, 双卷位～*, 双头～ twin-head pay-off reel, 双胀缩式 [双胀缩卷筒式] ～*, 套锥式卷筒～*, 悬垂锥式～*, 圆锥式～cone-type payoff reel, 轧入侧～ entry reel, 胀缩芯轴式～*
开卷机带材扳直辊　decoiler roll
开卷机机架　pay-off housing
开卷机卷筒　pay-off drum
开卷机筒　pay-off reel cone
开卷机油量警报器　pay-off reel oil amount alarm
开卷机张力　decoiler tension
开卷机制动器　pay-off reel brake
开卷机装料台　coil ramp
开卷机座　pay-off stand
开卷－矫直机　【压】uncoiler leveller
开卷卷筒　take-off drum
开卷设备　pay-off equipment
开卷退火装置　open coil annealing plant
开卷箱　pay-off cradle ◇ 带卷～coil box
开卷心轴　winging-off spindle
开卷凿　opening chisel
开卷轴　pay-off shaft
开卷装置　【压】uncoiling device, decoiling equipment
开卷座　pay-off cradle
开孔　piercing, tapping, opening ◇ 电动～机*
开孔结构物料　open-textured material
开孔铆焊焊缝　filled plug weld
开孔面积(筛网的)　open area
开孔器　tapper
开口　opening, open tapping [taphole], broach(ing), aperture, 【压】gorge
开口扳手　open-ended spanner
开口槽　open groove
开口粗轧孔型　open roughing pass
开口导缆钳　open chock
开口导向销　slotted (moulding box) pin
开口锭　open head ingot ◇ 小型～*
开口端　open end
开口对接　open butt joint
开口对接焊接头　open butt weld
开口方形直通[不翻转]孔型系统　open-square strand passes
开口钢钎　tapping rod
开口高度　open height
开口管　open-end tube
开口管筒　open joint tube
开口辊缝　open roll gap
开口焊缝　open weld
开口簧环　【机】circlip

开口机[钻] 【铁】(同"开出铁口机")
开口接头 open joint
开口结晶器 open mould
开口矩形[箱形]孔型 open box pass
开口开坯孔型 open breakdown pass
开口孔型 open pass
开口连接(锻接) split joint
开口梁形轧槽 【压】live beam pass
开口铆钉用钢丝 bifurcated rivet wire, split-rivet wire
开口模锻液[水]压机 【压】hydraulic open-die forging press
开口器 tapper
开口切分孔型 【压】open slitting pass
开口钎 【冶】tap out bar, tap(ping) [taphole] bar
开口腔 open cavity
开口三角形接线 open delta, open-delta connection
开口式机架 open-topped housing, open-top roll housing
开口式剪切机 【压】open-gap shears
开口式模 opening die
开口式芯头 【铸】open core print
开口式翼缘 【压】live flange
开口式轧机 open-top mill
开口缩孔 【钢】major [exterior] shrinkage, open pipe
开口铁棒 tapping pin
开口套管 split coupling
开口铁心(式) open core (type)
开口腿 【压】live [open] flange
开口销 cotter [split] pin, split cotter
开口销敲出工具 nail punch
开口[尾]螺栓 split bolt
开口轧槽 open groove
开口爪扳手 open-jawed spanner
开捆(钢丝的) uncoiling
开扩结构 open structure
开裂 dehiscence, cracking, fissuring ◇ 很小的~缝 narrow open joints
开裂负载 cracking load, load at first crack
开裂钢锭 clinked ingot
开裂试验 split test
开裂循环次数 cycle tocrack
开炉 blow in [on], starting-up ◇ 高炉~ on-stream
开炉锍 【色】starting matte
开炉操作 start-up of furnace
开炉法(高炉的) blow in method
开炉口用钢钎 tapping rod
开炉配料 blown in burden
开炉强化冶炼(高炉的) 【铁】blow-in with intensifying smelting process
开炉烧嘴 start-up burner
开炉用风机 start-up fan
开路 open [broken] circuit, open loop, no-load (operation), 【电】free play
开路触点 break [dead] contact
开路电解系统 open electrolytic circuit
开路电势 open-circuit potential
开路电压 open-circuit voltage
开路接点 circuit-opening contact, break (back) contact
开路磨矿 open circuit grind(ing)
开路破碎 open circuit crushing
开路线圈 【电】open coil
开路循环 open cycle
开坯 【压】blooming, cogging (-down), knobbling, breaking down, breakdown ◇ 钢锭~法 blocking process
开坯-初轧机 blooming mill
开坯道次 bloom(ing) [cogging-down] pass
开坯锻锤 cogging hammer
开坯钢锭 broken down ingot
开坯机 bloomer, blooming [cogging, getting-down] mill, breaking down mill ◇ 摆锻~ swing-forging machine, 机架回转式~ Lamberton mill, 热轧~ hot breaking-down mill, 柔性~ flexible slab mill
开坯机组[列] cogging (roll) train, breakdown train, breaking down train
开坯机座 cogging(-down) stand, break-

开 kai

开坯孔型 break(ing) down pass, break-down [first, reducing, cogging(-down), pinch] pass ◇ 方-椭圆～系统*, 开口～ open breakdown pass

开坯轧槽 bloom(ing) pass

开平方 【数】extract

开坡口 【焊】bevel cutting, bevelling, grooving, veeing

开坡口的 grooved, chamfered (chfd)

开坡口焊 bevel welding

开启工具 opener

开启式防滴 open drip-proof

开气孔 open pore, open porosity

开气孔率 open porosity, open-pore volume, ratio of open pores

开气孔容量 open-pore volume

开缺口 notching

开缺口的宽板试验 notched wide-plate test

开始 begin, start, initiation, commencement

开始产出的晶体 first yielded crystal

开始单元 【计】start element

开始的电镀膜 striking film

开始滴落温度 start-of-dropping temperature

开始读点 【计】load point

开始火焰清理线 start mark

开始馏分 first fraction [cut]

开始软化温度 start-of-softening temperature

开始烧结温度 temperature of sintering start

开始时间 zero time

开始送风 【铁】put on blast, starting-up

开始位 【计】start bit

开始冶炼 on-stream

开始直径 starting diameter

开式边冒口 【铸】open side feeder

开式锻锤 【压】open side hammer

开式锻模 open die

开式对接气压焊 open butt gas pressure welding

开式工形对接坡口 open-square butt groove

开式工形坡口对接焊缝 open-square butt weld

开式剪切机 gap shears, open throat shears, open-sided hot shears, open-side vertical shears, single-sided shears

开式浇注 open cast(ing)

开式结构[组织] open texture

开式流槽 pen launder

开式模爆炸成形工艺 open-die explosive forming technique

开式模锻造 open-die forging

开式模(立体)压印 open-die coining

开式模(模锻)法[模锻工艺] 【压】open-die process [technique]

开式铁水罐 open-type ladle

开式通风系统 open ventilation system

开式退火 open annealing

开式循环 open circulation [cycle]

开[凯]氏绝对温标 Kelvin absolute scale (K)

开氏绝对温标度数 Kelvin (K)

开氏温标 K. scale, Kelvin scale (K)

开氏温度 Kelvin (K) (degree)

开闩汽缸 【机】latch-release cylinder

开锁(信号开锁) 【电】unblanking

开膛炉 【色】open-hearth furnace

开铁口钢钎 tapping iron

开铁口机 (同"开出铁口机")

开通 unjamming

开头 begin, start, outset

开头机 【压】tail opening device

开拓 exploitation, 【采】developing, opening-up (矿山的)

开拓道路 development road

开拓矿量 【采】developed ore

开挖 excavation, cutting ◇ 借土～borrow excavation, 全面～*

开挖的水道 canalized waterway

开挖隧道　tunneling ◇ 压缩空气～法
开尾螺栓　fox bolt
开尾销　split cotter [pin],[铸](砂箱的) cottered pin, slotted (moulding box) pin
开尾销敲出工具　nail punch
开线卷装置　【压】coil holder
开箱　【铸】knock-out
开销　expense, outgo, overhead
开压边浇口　【铸】kissing
开凿者　excavator
开支　expenditure
凯尔 F 聚三氟氯乙烯树脂　Kel-F
凯尔卡洛依熔炼法(熔炼高级合金钢) Kelcaloy (method)
凯尔梅特铜镍铅轴承合金(60—70Cu, 2Ni, 余量 Pb) Kermet
凯尔美特高铅青铜轴承合金(25—35Pb, 0.5—1Sn, 1—2Ni 或 Ag, 余量 Cu) Kelmet
凯尔美特铅青铜(70Cu, 6Sn, 余量 Pb) Kelmet bronze
凯尔纳目镜　【金】Kellner eyepiece
凯尔文热电效应　Kelvin effect
凯尔文双电桥　Kelvin double bridge
凯尔火花检验　Keller's spark
凯勒浸蚀剂(轻金属合金浸蚀用) Keller s etchant [reagent]
凯勒克斯萃取剂　Kelex
凯勒直接电弧炉　【冶】Keller furnace
凯里方钻杆安全配合接头　Kelly saver sub
凯里方钻杆锁接头　Kelly sub
凯里方钻杆套规　Kelly sleeve gage
凯利型压滤机[凯利叶片式压滤机]　Kelley filter (press)
凯洛格电渣法　【钢】Kellog (electric fusion) process
凯洛格热帽电渣法　【钢】Kellog hot-top process
凯梅特钡镁合金消气剂　Kemet
凯米多尔石灰(由白云石制得) Kemidol
凯姆勒锌铝铜合金(76Zn, 15Al, 9Cu) Kemler metal
凯普-布拉塞特直接炼铁法　【铁】Cape-Brassert process
凯氏上旋阀　upper Kelly cock
凯斯勒轧机　【压】Kessler mill
凯斯特尼希耐蚀试验　Kesternich test
凯泽高温硬度试验　Kayser hardness test
凯泽津锡基装饰合金(93Sn, 5.5Sb, 1.5Cu) Kaiserzinn
铠板　armor, armour
铠甲夹(电缆的)　armour clamp
铠装　armouring, shield, armature, sheath, inhibitor (火药的) ◇ 电缆～挤压机 cable press, 金属丝～的 wire-armored (W.A.)
铠装玻璃　armoured glass
铠装材料　【电】reinforced material
铠装电极　sheathed electrode
铠装电缆　armoured [belted, sheathed] cable ◇ 双层～ double-armoured cable
铠装电缆用钢丝　armouring wire
铠装钢带　armouring tape
铠装胶管钢丝　hose armouring wire
铠装热电偶　shielded thermocouple [thermoelement], sheathed thermocouple
铠装热电偶丝　shielded thermocouple wire
刊物　pubiccation (pub., publ.), journal
勘测　survey, investigation, prospecting ◇ 房屋～员 building surveyer
勘探　【地】prospecting, exploration
勘探[察]研究　exploratory research
勘误表　index of correction (IC), corrigenda
坎(德拉)(发光强度)　candela (cd)
坎菲尔德检磷浸蚀剂(检查钢中磷偏析用)　Canfield reagent
坎格罗电解制铁粉法　Kangro process
坎农高速钢(16W, 3.5Cr, 1.0V, 0.70C) Cannon
坎沙含水赤铁矿(巴西)　Cansa
坎塔尔 DR 精密电阻丝(75Fe, 20Cr, 4.5Al, 0.5Co)　Kanthal DR

坎塔尔高级电阻丝　Kanthal Super
坎塔尔铁铬铝系高电阻合金(67Fe,25Cr,5Al,3Co)　Kanthal (alloy)
砍刀　sword
砍口　undercutting
砍平　scraping
看火孔　[冶]sight-hole, glory-hole
看火门　observation door
看水工　[铁]pipe fitter
康德电线铝合金(0.43Fe, 0.32Mg, 0.10Si,余量 Al)　Cond aluminium
康德高空高压传输线用铝合金(99.5Al)　Cond-Al
康登－莫尔斯曲线　[理]Condon-Morse curve
康多合金　Kondo alloy
康弗雷克斯复合钢　conflex
康卡斯特连续矫直曲线　continuous straightening curve of CONCAST
康卡斯特－罗西连续铸钢设备　Concast-Rossi plant
康拉德森残碳值　Conradson carbon value
康洛铜铝合金　conloy
康默莱尔弯曲试验(研究金属材料可焊性)　Kommerell bend test, Austrian test
康姆斯托克热压硬质合金法　Comstock process
康涅尔铁镍铬合金　Conel
康普顿电子　Compton electron
康普顿散射　Compton scattering
康普顿吸收　Compton absorption
康普顿吸收系数　Compton absorption coefficient
康普顿效应　Compton effect
康斯特拉克塔尔高强度铝镁锌合金　Konstruktal
康坦明铜锰镍电阻合金(27Mn, 5Ni,余量 Cu)　Contamin
康特拉铜镍合金丝(约 55Cu,约 45Ni)　Contra wire
康铜(60Cu, 40Ni;用作热电偶)　constantan, konstantan ◇ 艾德万斯～*,拉拉～(45Cu, 55Ni) Lala
康铜[莫尔]热电偶　Moll thermopile
康珀尼克铁镍基软磁合金(约 50%Ni)　Conpernik
糠醇　furfuryl alcohol
糠醛　[$C_4H_3O \cdot CHO$]　furfural(dehyde)
糠醛树脂　furural resin
抗剥落　spall-resistant
抗剥落能力　spalling resistance
抗变色的　tarnish-resistant
抗变色性　tarnish resistance
抗变形钢　non-shrinking steel
抗变形(能)力　resistance to deformation
抗扯裂的　tear-proof
抗尘(性的)　antidusting
抗冲击能力　shock resistance, resistance to shock
抗冲击强度　shock strength, resistance to impact
抗冲击托辊　impact idler
抗冲蚀砖　erosion-resistant brick
抗穿入[穿透]性　resistance to penetration
抗磁磁化率　diamagnetic susceptibility
抗磁合金　diamagnetic alloy
抗磁极性　diamagnetic polarity
抗磁计　diamagnetometer
抗磁体　diamagnet, diamagnetic body [substance]
抗磁物质　diamagnetic substance
抗磁性[现象]　diamagnetism ◇ 金属中电子～*,朗道～Landau diamagnetism
抗磁(性)材料　diamagnetic material
抗磁(性)效应　diamagnetic effect
抗磁(性)作用　diamagnetic contribution
抗脆化合金　embrittlement resistant alloy
抗大气腐蚀性能　(同"耐大气腐蚀性")
抗地震结构　antiseismic structure
抗冻性　cold resisting property, frost-resistance
抗毒的　poison-resistant
抗断强度　breaking [fracture] strength
抗断应力　break(ing) stress

抗反射涂[镀]层　antireflection coating
抗风构架　wind frame
抗风化层　weather-resisting layer
抗风支撑[屋架间抗风剪力撑]　wind brac(ing)
抗风桁架　wind (resisting) truss
抗腐蚀层　corrosion-resistant layer
抗腐蚀的　corrosion-resistant (CRE), incorrodible
抗腐蚀性[能力]　(同"耐腐蚀性")
抗干扰的　anti-interference, antijam(ming), jamproof
抗干扰度　【电】noise immunity
抗高温氧化性[力]　high temperature oxidation resistance
抗焊道下裂缝试验　◇ 巴特尔式～*
抗化学腐蚀钢　chemical-resistant steel
抗坏血酸　ascorbic acid
抗回复性　resistance to recovery
抗回火性[能力]　resistance to tempering
抗碱的　alkaline resistant
抗碱性　alkali resistance [fastness]
抗碱液砖　lye-resisting brick
抗剪钢筋　shear [web] reinforcement
抗剪劲度　shear stiffness
抗剪[切]强度　shearing-strength, resistance to shear ◇ 生坯～试验*
抗溅剂　antispattering agent
抗拒　resisting, withstanding
抗菌剂　antiseptics
抗菌素　antibiotics
抗拉冲击试验　tensile impact test
抗拉构件　tension member
抗拉模量　tensile modulus
抗拉强度　tensile strength (TS, t.s.)
抗拉强度试验　tensile strength test
抗拉性能　tensile property
抗拉应力　tensile stress ◇ 临界～*
抗拉值　tensile figure
抗老化性能　ageing resistance
抗冷性　cold resistance
抗力　resistance (force), persistence

抗裂不锈合金钢　crack resistant stainless steel alloy
抗裂能力　crack resistance
抗裂试验　crack test ◇ CTS～*, T形～ T cracking test, 插入式～ implant (crack) test, 卡恩～*, 利海～*, 铁研式～*, 圆棒(试样)～ round bar cracking test, 圆形槽口～*, 枕形～ pillow test
抗裂纹延伸曲线　resistance curve of crack extension
抗裂性[能力]　crack resistance
抗硫化氢钢　hydrogen sulphide-proof steel
抗硫蚀　resistant to sulfide tarnishing
抗磨材料　(同"耐磨材料")
抗磨的　abrasion resistant, wear-resistant, wearproof
抗磨钢轨　anvil faced rail
抗磨力　abrasion [attrition] resistance
抗磨强度　abrasion strength [index], resistance to abrasion, wear hardness
抗磨蚀的　wear-preventive
抗磨试验　abrasion test
抗磨寿命　wear-life
抗磨损性　wear(ing) resistance
抗磨性　(同"耐磨性")
抗磨指数　abrasion index, resistance to abration
抗磨铸铁　antifriction cast iron
抗摩合金　(同"减摩合金")
抗摩制品　antifriction composition
抗摩轴承　anti-friction bearing (AFB)
抗挠刚度　flexural rigidity
抗挠能力　inflexibility
抗黏着磨损性　antiseize quality
抗扭刚度[性]　torsional rigidity [stiffness]
抗扭构件　torque member
抗扭配筋　torsional reinforcement
抗扭强度　torsional strength [resistance], twisting strength [resistance]
抗扭强度试验机　torsional (strength) tester

抗扭试验　torsion test
抗(疲)劳剂　antifatigue
抗破裂性　resistance to breakage [rupture]
抗侵蚀的　incorrodible
抗侵蚀性　incorrodibility
抗扰　immunization, immunizing, anti-interference
抗热冲击强度　(同"热冲击强度")
抗热力　thermal resistance
抗热损伤强度　pyrolytic stability
抗热震[热急变]性　thermal shock resistance
抗溶剂性　resistance to solvent
抗蠕变材料　creep-resistant material
抗蠕变钢　creep-resistant steel ◇ 杜尔赫特~*
抗蠕变合金　creep-resistant alloy ◇ 工程用~*
抗蠕变金属　creep-resistant metal
抗蠕变强度　(同"蠕变强度")
抗蠕变性　creep resistance
抗乳化剂　demulsifying compound
抗散裂能力　spalling resistance
抗砷素　antiarsenin
抗渗接缝[连结]　impervious joint
抗渗透性　resistance to penetration, anti-permeability
抗生素　antibiotics
抗失泽性　【金】tarnish resistance
抗湿的　moisture-proof, moisture-repellent
抗湿性　resistance to moisture
抗时效钢　ageing-resistant steel
抗时效汽车钢板　ageing-resistant automotive (steel) plate
抗时效性　ageing resistance
抗蚀的　corrosion-proof, non-corrodible, non-corroding
抗蚀剂　resist, anticorrodant ◇ 负~ negative resist
抗蚀金属　(同"耐蚀金属")
抗蚀润滑剂[油脂]　slushing compound
抗蚀性　(同"耐蚀性")
抗蚀性能表　corrosion table
抗收缩的　shrinkproof
抗摔性　drop strength
抗水的　water-resistant, water-repellent, water-proof, hydrostable
抗水化层　weather-resisting layer
抗水性　water resistance, water-resisting property
抗水油漆　water-resistant paint
抗撕裂的　tear-proof
抗撕裂性　【压】resistance to tearing-off
抗酸胶　acid-proof mastic
抗碎裂　anti-degradation
抗碎强度　crushing strength, resistance to crushing
抗铁磁性的　antiferromagnetic
抗弯刚度　bending rigidity, flexural rigidity
抗弯力　contrabending force
抗弯力矩　contrabending moment
抗弯能力　resistance to bending
抗弯强度　bend(ing) [flexural, transverse] strength ◇ 干燥~*
抗弯试验　proof bend test (钢管的), beam test (梁的)
抗锈(的)　rust-resisting (R.R.), rust-proofing
抗锈蚀(的)　tarnish-resistant, resistant to tarnishing [rust]
抗锈蚀法[剂]　rust preventer
抗锈(蚀)性　rust resistance, rust-resisting property
抗锈组分　antirust composition
抗压杆件[构件]　compression member
抗压坏强度　collapse resistance
抗压力　bearing resistance
抗压强度　compression [compressive, pressive] strength, knocking resistance, resistance to compression [impact], 【团】compression rupture value ◇ 侧限~*, 常温[冷]~*

抗压入性　resistance to indentation
抗压试验　compression test ◇ L.K.A.B.～*,圆柱体试件～cylinder test
抗压碎能力　resistance to crushing
抗压缩能力　resistance to compression
抗氧化(的)　oxidation-resisting, oxidation-proof, resistant to oxidation, anti-oxidation
抗氧化镀[涂]层　oxidation-resistant coating
抗氧化钢　oxidation-resisting steel
抗氧化合金　oxidation-resistant [oxidation-resisting] alloy ◇ 马利～*
抗氧化剂　protective agent, antioxidant
抗氧化皮化合物　antiscale compound
抗氧化性[(能)力]　oxidation resistance, resistance to oxidation
抗氧剂　antioxygen
抗应力腐蚀合金　stress corrosion resistant alloy
抗油的　(同"耐油的")
抗再结晶性　resistance to recrystallization
抗再氧化性能[能力]　resistance to reoxidation
抗渣侵蚀性能[能力]　resistance to slag attack
抗渣性　slag resistance, resistance to slag
抗渣性试验炉　slag-test furnace
抗张强度　tensile strength, tenacity ◇ 退火后～*
抗张试验　tensile test
抗张性能　tensile property
抗震建筑　earthquake-proof construction
抗震结构　antiseismic [quake-proof] structure
抗震强度　shock strength
抗震设计　aseismatic design
抗震性　shock resistance, resistance to shock
抗振强度　vibration strength
抗轴向负荷能力　thrust capacity
抗皱性能　wrinkle resistance

抗转运强度　[团]resistance to handling
抗纵弯强度　buckling strength
抗纵弯[抗压曲]系数　safety against buckling
抗纵向弯曲[抗压曲]性　buckling resistance
钪合金　scandium alloy
钪基合金　scandium-base alloy
钪石{ScSi$_2$O$_7$}　befanamite
钪酸盐　scandate
钪添加合金　scandium addition
钪盐　scandium salt
钪钇石{(Sc,Y)$_2$Si$_2$O$_7$}　thortveitite
考贝(式)热风炉　Cowper (blast heater), Cowper stove ◇ 内燃室式～*
考贝式热风炉砖　Cowper brick
考伯式砖格　(同"编筐式砖格")
考伯斯-贝克跨顶火道式焦炉　Koppers-Becker coke oven
考伯斯焦油连续蒸馏装置　Koppers continuous tar plant
考伯斯-沃思式高炉无料钟布料系统　Koppers-Wurth blast furnace filling system
考伯斯蒸汽循环脱酚设备　Koppers vapour dephenolation system
考伯斯煅烧炉　Koppers furnace
考察　exploration
考芬哈尔压力机　couffinhal press
考克斯钢制零件除锈与涂镀法　Cox process
考克斯轧机　[压]Kocks mill
考萨尔耐蚀合金铸铁　Causal metal
考塞尔图样[花样]　[理]Kossel pattern
考塞尔线　[理]Kossel lines
考验　test, trial, ordeal ◇ 经过～的设计 favour time-proved design
拷贝　copy, replica ◇ 硬～hard copy
烤钵　[色]cupelling furnace
烤钵冶金法　[色]cupellation, cupelling
烤干　furnace [oven] drying
烤篮　fire basket

烤漆 baking varnish
靠壁热裂 【耐】skin crack
靠海位置[靠海岸厂址] location on coast
靠矿厂址 location on ore
靠煤厂址 location on coal
靠模 model(ling), profiling, former, template, contour cam
靠模板 【铸】master plate
靠模车床 model maker's lathe, copying lathe
靠模机床 imitation [copying] machine
靠模机构 copying mechanism
靠模铣床 (同"仿形铣床")
靠模线切割 wire-electrode copying cutting
靠重力流动 flow by gravity
苛化 causticizing, causticization ◇ 内部~ inside causticization, 外部~*, 支流~*
苛化反应 causticizing reaction
苛化反应器 causticization reactor
苛化费用 causticization cost
苛化剂 causticizer, causticizing agent
苛化搅拌器 causticizing agitator
苛化器 causticizer
苛化设施 causticizing plant
苛化效率 causticization efficiency
苛化作用 causticization
苛性比(值)(氧化铝生产的) caustic ratio
苛性化 (同"苛化")
苛性钾 (同"氢氧化钾")
苛性碱 caustic alkali
苛性碱槽 caustic soda tank
苛性碱处理 caustic treatment
苛性碱分解法 caustic-opening process
苛性碱粉 ground caustic
苛性碱膏{NaOH·H₂O} cream caustic soda
苛性碱浸出 caustic leach(ing)
苛性碱浸出溶液 caustic leach solution
苛性碱浓度 caustic (soda) concentration
苛性碱熔化 caustic fusion
苛性碱溶出 caustic digestion
苛性碱溶液 caustic (soda) solution
苛性碱洗涤塔 caustic scrubber, caustic scrubbing tower
苛性碱系数 caustic modulus
苛性碱液 caustic liquor [lye], caustic soda liquor, aqueous caustic
苛性镁砂[菱镁矿] caustic magnesite
苛性钠[苛性苏打] (同"氢氧化钠") ◇ 熔融~ fused caustic soda
苛性石灰 caustic lime
苛性苏打灰 {Na₂CO₃ 与 NaOH 的混合物} causticized ash
苛性苏打碱水处理 caustic soda lye treatment
苛性苏打浸出 caustic soda leach
苛性苏打熔化 caustic soda fusion
苛性盐 caustic salt
苛性氧化镁 caustic magnesia
苛性液 caustic liquor
柯安达效应 Coanda effect
柯尔德弗罗冷挤压法 Koldflo process
柯兰浸蚀剂(不锈钢用) Curran's reagent
柯林式脱硫装置 Collin desulphurizing plant
柯林斯式氦低温恒温器[氦液化机] Collins helium cryostat
柯诺瓦洛夫定律 Konowalow's law
柯赛特锌铜铝合金(4Cu, 3.5—5Al, 1Mg, 余量 Zn) Kirsite
柯石英 coesite
柯苏尔镍铬铜合金铸铁(19Ni, 1.5Cr, 4Cu, 2.2—2.8C, 余量 Fe) Causul metal
颗粒 grain, granule, particle ◇ 成~的 granulous, 单个~ single-particle, 夹入~*, 经磨碎分离的~ release grains, 小~ granula, granule
颗粒变形 deformation of particle
颗粒表面积 particle surface area
颗粒材料 granular material
颗粒测定法[术] granulometry
颗粒测量计算机系统 particle measurement computer system

颗粒层 granular bed
颗粒层收尘 gravel bed dust collection
颗粒尺寸[大小] grain [particle] size, grain [particle] dimension
颗粒大小比较目镜 grain size comparison eyepiece
颗粒电极 mosaic electrode
颗粒断口 granular fracture
颗粒分布 granulometric distribution
颗粒分级 volumetrical [granulometric] classification
颗粒分析器 particle analyzer
颗粒粉化 grain disintegration
颗粒覆盖层 particulate coating
颗粒复合材料 particle [particulate] composite
颗粒化 graining ◇ 锡的～graining of tin
颗粒基体界面 particle/matrix interface
颗粒级配 grain size gradation
颗粒级配曲线 grading curve
颗粒计数 grain count
颗粒间接触面积 interparticle contact area
颗粒间距 interparticle distance
颗粒间空隙 interparticle void
颗粒间孔隙 interparticle porosity, macro pore
颗粒间摩擦 interparticle friction
颗粒间黏附 interparticle adhesion
颗粒间黏合力 interparticle cohesion
颗粒间润滑 interparticle lubrication
颗粒间压力【粉】intergranular pressure
颗粒金属挤压成型法 pellet extrusion
颗粒孔隙率 particle porosity
颗粒离析[分离] particle separation
颗粒粒度分布 grain size distribution
颗粒粒度分析 grain size analysis
颗粒粒度分析器 grain size analyzer
颗粒粒度控制 grain size control
颗粒粒级 grading fraction
颗粒料密度计 bulk density meter
颗粒密度 density of particle
颗粒内部开孔率 accessible intraparticle porosity
颗粒内的 intragranular
颗粒黏结 particle bonding
颗粒浓度 particle concentration
颗粒强化 particle reinforcement
颗粒强化复合[包覆]金属 particle reinforced cladding metal
颗粒强化金属 particle reinforced metal (PRM)
颗粒溶解析出长大(机制) Ostward ripening
颗粒烧结 particle-to-particle sintering
颗粒涂层 particulate coating
颗粒团 cluster of grains
颗粒物质 particulate matter
颗粒细度 grain fineness (G.F.), grid (砂轮的)
颗粒显微构造 particle microstructure
颗粒形状 particle shape, grain form, contour of particle
颗粒形状系数 particle-shape factor
颗粒性 granularity, graininess
颗粒压实 particle packing
颗粒冶金 particle metallurgy
颗粒硬度 particle hardness
颗粒云团 swarm of particles
颗粒增强剂 particle reinforcement
颗粒长大 size enlargement
颗粒长大机理 mechanism of granule growth
颗粒真密度 true particle density
颗粒状的 granular, grainy, granulous, granulitic
颗粒状熔剂 granular flux
颗粒组成 grain [size, granulometric] composition, composition of particles
科贝纽姆恒弹性(模量)合金 Cobenium
科比塔留姆耐热铝合金 Cobitalium (Cobitalium 2：1—5Cu, 7—15Si, 0.2—1.0Cr, 0.5—1.5Mg, 0.05—0.13Ti, 余量Al)
科波-卡维基氟硅酸钠分解绿柱石法

Copaux-Kawecki process

科尔比感应炉　Colby furnace

科尔哈特高级耐火材料　【耐】Corhart

科尔科德加硫除[脱]铜法　Colcord process

科尔克拉德耐蚀包层钢材　Colclad

科尔莫诺伊合金　Colmonoy

科尔坦耐大气腐蚀高强度钢（0.1C,0.25Mn,0.75Si,0.15P,0.75Cr,0.4Cu,有时尚含 0.6Ni）Cor-ten

科尔特克预热煤管道装炉法　Coaltek method

科芬钢轴晶粒细化热处理　Coffin axle process

科克罗姆钴铬系耐热合金　Cochrome

科里奥利斯力　Coriolis force

科鲁马克斯铝镍钴铁永磁合金（25Co,8Al,13Ni,1Nb,余量 Fe）Columax (magnet)

科鲁马克斯永久磁铁　Columax permanent magnet

科罗拉多银[铜镍锌合金]（57Cu,25Ni,18Zn）Colorado silver

科罗内尔镍基[镍钼铁耐酸]合金（30Mo,6Fe,余量 Ni；抗无机酸腐蚀合金）coronel

科罗尼尔镍锰铜耐蚀合金（26Cu,4Mn,余量 Ni）Corronil

科罗纽姆铜合金（15Zn,5Sn,余量 Cu）Corronium

科罗西龙耐蚀高硅铸铁（0.8—1C,13.5—14.5Si,余量 Fe）Corrosiron

科洛莫尼镍铬硼合金（耐蚀、耐热、耐磨；68—80Ni,7—19Cr,2—4B,余量 Fe、Si）Colomony

科洛尼亚尔耐蚀铬镍合金钢　Colonial (Colonial 610：16—18Cr,1Ni,<0.12C,余量 Fe）

科莫尔 41 沉淀硬化型铁磁合金（12Co,17Mo,余量 Fe）Comol 41

科莫尔钴钼铁永磁合金（12Co,17Mo,余量 Fe）Comol

科姆巴洛依高电导率银铜（0.1Ag,余量 Cu）Combarloy

科姆索尔银铅焊料　Comsol

科尼克镍锰铜铬合金钢（0.1C,0.35Mn,0.08Si,0.35Ni,0.12Cr,0.25Cu,余量 Fe）Konik

科尼须耐磨轴承青铜（77—83Cu,9.6Sn,12.4Pb,少量 Fe）Cornish bronze

科涅尔代用白金（约 73Ni,约 17Co,8.8Ti,0.55Si,0.26Al,0.16Mn；或者 46Ni,25Co,7.5Fe,2.5Ti,19Cr）Konel [Konal] alloy

科佩尔梅特碳化钨合金　Copelmet

科佩尔铜镍合金　Copel

科普隆铜镍合金　Cupron

科森镍硅青铜[铜镍硅合金]（含 Ni_2Si）Calloy, Corson alloy

科舒瓦式单色器　【理】Cauchois-type monochromator

科舒瓦式聚焦摄谱仪　【理】Cauchois-type focusing spectrograph

科斯特尔铁钴钼[钨]磁钢（12—15Co,Mo 或 10—20W,余量 Fe）Koester alloy, Koester (magnet) steel

科斯特莱京表面磷化处理法　Costellising

科特雷耳-洛默势垒　【金】Cottrell-Lomer barrier

科特雷耳气氛[气团]强化　cottrell hardening

科特雷耳[科氏]气团　【金】Cottrell cloud [atmosphere]

科特雷耳气团锁定　Cottrell locking

科特雷耳气团形成　Cottrell atmosphere formation

科特雷耳势垒　【金】Cottrell barrier

科特雷耳效应　【金】Cottrell effect

科特雷尔静电除尘器　cottrell electrical precipitator

科瓦(铁镍钴)合金（15—19Co,28—30Ni,余量 Fe）Kovar alloy

科维西特熔注制品　【耐】Korvisit

科西亚斯铜锡合金（66Cu,34Sn）Cothias

科希关系(式)　Cauchy relations
科学管理　scientific management
科学技术水平[发展动态]　state of the art(s)
科学领域　universe
科学研究试验室　research laboratory
科学仪器　scientific instruments [apparatus], experiment
科学原理　scientific fundamental
科学院　academy of sciences ◇ 中国～*
科研成果　scientific payoff, result of scientific research
科研设备　experiment
钶合金　columbium alloy
钶铁矿　columbite
稞麦粉(拔丝润滑剂成分)　rye meal
壳层　shell ◇ 初凝生成的～*, 填满～*
壳层材料　shell material
壳层电子　shell electron
壳层结构　shell structure ◇ 满充(电子)～*
壳层空位　shell vacancy
壳层占有　shell occupancy
壳管式换热器　shell-and-tube heat exchanger
壳式锅炉　shell-type boiler
壳体　case, casing, housing, cage, [地]crustobody ◇ 迪威达～设计法　Dywidag system
壳芯吹芯机　【铸】shell core blowing machine
壳型　【铸】shell mould ◇ D～吹成法　D process, α～法　alpha process, 焙烧～　fired mould, 迪特～吹成法　Dietert process
壳型材料　shell mould material
壳型熔模[失蜡]铸造法　shell lost wax process
壳型造型法　shell mould process
壳型铸件　shell (mould) casting
壳型铸造　shell (mould) casting, shell moulding ◇ 克洛宁～法*
壳质体[组]　【焦】exinite

壳状充填　crusted filling
可搬式发电机　portable generator
可报废的　scrappable
可爆炸性　explosibility, explosiveness
可被呼吸的飞尘　respirable-size airborne dust
可泵送混凝土　pumpable concrete
可泵送浇注料　pumpable castable
可比较的　comparable
可编程序计算器　programmable calculator
可编程序控制器连铸控制系统　PLC continuous casting control system
可编程序逻辑控制　programmable logic control (PLC)
可编程序逻辑控制器　programmable logic controller (PLC)
可编程序逻辑阵列　programmable logic array (PLA)
可编程序只读存储器　【计】programmable read only memory (PROM)
可编微程序的　【计】microprogrammable
可变长度　variable length
可变长度指令　variable length instruction
可变长度字　variable length word
可变磁阻　【电】variable reluctance (VR)
可变电抗器　variable reactor
可变电容器　variable [adjustable] capacitor
可变电压　variable voltage (VV) ◇ 伊尔格纳～直流发电机组　Ilgner set
可变电阻　variable resistance (head), varistor, varister
可变电阻器　variable resistor, variohm
可变度　degree of variability
可变放大率目镜　variable power eyepiece
可变放大因数[可变 μ 值]六极管　variable-mu hexode
可变负载　variable load
可变刚度厚度控制　variable rigidity AGC
可变工作制　varying duty
可变光阑　iris (diaphragm)
可变辊型轧机　variable camber mill

可变互导管　supercontrol tube
可变(化合)价　variable valency
可变焦距透镜　variable focus lens, zoom lens
可变角度内反射元件　variable-angle internal reflection element
可变拘束抗热裂试验　【焊】varestraint test, variable restraint test
可变膨胀　variable expansion
可变容量(油)泵　variable displacement pump
可变输出　variable output
可变输入　variable input
可变凸度　variable crown (VC)
可变凸度轧辊　variable crown roll
可变凸度轧机　variable crown mill
可变凸度支承辊　VC back-up roll
可变紊流式热风炉　【铁】variable-turbulence stove
可变形芯棒　deformable mandrel
可变形芯棒拉拔[伸]　deformable-mandrel drawing
可变形性　deformability
可变性　variability, alterability, changeability
可变性钢　transformable steel
可变营运费用　variable operating cost
可变原始成本　variable prime cost
可变周期操作　【计】variable cycle operation
可变主要成本　variable prime cost
可变字长　【计】variable word-length
可变字长计算机　variable word-length computer
可补救错误　recoverable error
可擦存储器　【计】erasable storage
可擦可编程序只读存储器　erasable programmable read only memory (EPROM)
可采矿石　pay dirt
可操纵性　handleability
可测量的　measurable
可测性　measurability

可拆半模　movable die
可拆部分　free [removable] section
可拆除的转炉炉底　【钢】removable plug
可拆换电极尖　(同"换接电极尖")
可拆接插板　【电】removable plugboard
可拆开的　split
可拆连接　demountable, [detachable] joint, releasable connection
可拆模　split(ting) mould [die], split-segment die, segment(al) [collapsible] die ◇ 多件～multiple-segment die
可拆模衬　split die liner
可拆模具　collapsible die assembly
可拆模孔　split die orifice
可拆式 X 射线发生器　demountable (X-ray) generator
可拆式衬垫　【焊】removable backing
可拆式出钢槽　【钢】removable runner
可拆式料车　【铁】detachable skip
可拆式炉顶　removable roof
可拆式炉门坎　strip baffle
可拆(式)砂箱　【铸】snap [pop-off] flask
可拆式芯盒　【铸】collapsible core box, loose frame core box
可拆卸伸缩架　collapsible stripper
可拆卸式结晶器　separate mould
可拆卸性　detachability
可拆型芯　【铸】collapsible core
可拆钟形心轴　detachable bell mandrel
可拆装的直接存取存储器　【计】removable direct access storage
可撤导板　retractable guide
可沉淀的　precipitable
可沉淀性　precipitability
可成合金的　alloyable
可成型耐火材料　mouldable refractory
可成形性　formability, 【粉】compactibility
可重复使用程序　【计】reusable program [routine]
可重复性　repeatability
可抽出的　withdrawable
可抽式钢锭模　retractable ingot mould

可出售产品	saleable material
可除去能力	detachability
可储存性	storability
可触发性	ignitionability
可磁化粉末	magnetizable powder
可磁化熔剂	magnetizable flux
可磁化性	magnetizability
可萃性[度]	extractability ◇ 相对～*
可萃取的	extractable, extractible
可淬相	【金】quenchable phase
可淬性	【金】hardenability
可淬硬的	hardenable ◇ 热处理～*
可淬硬碳钢	hardenable carbon steel
可达性	accessibility
可滴(定)酸度	titratable acidity
可点燃性	ignit(ion)ability
可电解的	electrolyzable
可电离固体物质	ionizable solid
可调换的	replaceable
可钉混凝土	nailable concrete
可动秤	mobile weighing machine
可动触点	movable [pole] contact
可动电极	mobile electrode
可动颚板	movable jaw
可动风口套	【铁】loose-fitting sleeve
可动感应器	scanning inductor
可动夹片	movable jaw
可动胶片照相机	moving-film camera
可动炉床	movable heatrth
可动(炉喉)保护板	movable amour
可动平台	【冶】movable platform
可动倾斜运输机装置	movable inclination conveyer device
可动位错	mobile dislocation
可动线圈	moving coil
可动芯棒	movable core rod
可动支承	movable bearing
可读性	readability
可镀性	platability
可锻不锈钢	wrought stainless steel
可锻合金	wrought alloy
可锻化	malleablizing, malleablization ◇ 黑心～*, 矿石中～ malleablization in ore
可锻化退火	malleablizing annealing
可锻黄铜	wrought brass
可锻金属	malleable [wrought] metal
可锻铝合金	(同"形变铝合金")
可锻锰铸铁(含 14Mn)	manganese iron
可锻耐热合金	(同"形变耐热合金")
可锻镍	malleable nickel
可锻镍银[镍铜锌合金](18Ni)	◇ 西米塔尔斯～Scimitars
可锻轻合金	wrought light alloy
可锻区	【粉】forging corridor
可锻生铁	malleable [forge] pig iron
可锻铁	mitis ◇ 适于制造白口～的生铁 malleable pig iron
可锻铁铸件	malleable (iron) casting
可锻铜铬银合金	◇ 库帕洛依～*
可锻性	forgeability, forging quality, malleability, ductility
可锻性量度[评定准则]	measure of forgeability
可锻性试验	forgeability test
可锻铸铁	malleable iron (M.I., m.i.), malleable cast iron (m.c.i.) ◇ 白心[欧洲]～*, 冈奈特 K～*, 高级优质～*, 黑心[美国]～*, 快速退火～*, 铁素体～*, 硬外层～喷丸处理 permabrasive, 直接还原～*
可锻铸铁废料	malleable (iron) scrap
可锻铸铁管	malleable iron pipe (MIP)
可锻铸铁辊	ductile cast iron roll
可锻铸铁退火	malleable anneal(ing)
可锻铸铁退火炉	malleable annealing furnace
可锻铸铁丸[砂]	malleablized iron shot
可锻铸铁用矿	malleablizing ore
可锻铸铁用生铁	pig iron for malleable cast iron
可锻铸铁铸造协会	Malleable Founder's Society (MFS)
可兑换通货	【企】convertible currencies
可翻转的	tiltable

可 ke

| 可翻转中段 【团】reversible central section
| 可分辨的 resolvable, distinguishable
| 可分解性 decomposability
| 可分开的 detachable
| 可分离[分开]性 separability, detachability ◇ 渣壳[皮]~*
| 可分裂的 fissionable
| 可分模型 【铸】part(ed) pattern
| 可浮选的 floatable
| 可浮选性 floatability
| 可腐蚀的 corrodible, attackable
| 可腐蚀性 corrodibility
| 可复现性 reproducibility
| 可复原性 recoverability
| 可复制图 reproducible drawing
| 可改变的 alterable, convertible
| 可耕地 agricultrual [arable] land
| 可更换靶极装置 interchangeable-target arrangement
| 可更换拱顶 bung top arch
| 可供选择的假设 alternate hypothesis
| 可汞齐化的 amalgamable
| 可共存的 composible
| 可观察的[量] observable
| 可管理性 handleability
| 可焊接不锈钢 joining stainless steel ◇ 克罗马克~*
| 可焊(接)钢 （同"焊接钢"）
| 可焊接头 weldable fittings
| 可焊铝合金 weldable aluminium alloy ◇ 超高强度~*, 高强度~*
| 可焊性 weldability, weldableness, welding property, solderability ◇ 操作[工艺]~ operative weldability, 使用~ overall weldability
| 可焊性试验 weldability test, test for weldability
| 可忽略的 negligible (negl.)
| 可互换盖[帽,头] interchangeable head
| 可互换基础 exchangeable bases
| 可互换性 exchangeability, interchangeability

可互溶的 miscible
可还原变化[变态,变形] reducible variety
可还原性 reducibleness ◇ 两段~试验
可换存储器 【计】changeable storage
可换机座 change stand
可换结晶器 【连铸】interchangeable mould
可换式冷却器 inset cooler
可换式随机存取存储器 【计】movable random access memory
可换铁水沟 replaceable trough, exchangeable runner
可换铁水包流嘴 exchangeable ladle lip
可换向的 switchable
可换轴承合金 interchangeable metal
可换铸型 interchangeable mould
可挥发的 volatilizable, vapourable, vapourizable
可恢复的错误 recoverable error
可恢复性 recoverability, restorability
可回收的 recoverable
可混溶的 miscible
可混溶性 compatibility ◇ 化学~ chemical compatibility
可机械加工的 machinable
可极化的 polarizable
可挤压性 extrudability
可加工的 workable
可加工性 workability, deformability, machinability
可加工性指数 workability index
可检测性 detectability
可见报警信号 visual alarm
可见边 visible edge
可见波长 visible wavelength
可见读数 visible reading
可见辐射 visible raidation
可见光 visible light
可见光谱 visible spectrum
可见光谱域 visible region
可见光起点温度范围（~525℃） black

heat range
可见红热(加热时的) visible redness ◇ 加热至～温度 just visible red heat
可见滑移带 visible slip bands
可见裂缝 visible crack
可见渗透液 visible penetrant
可见信号 visible signal
可见影像 visible image
可见指示控制灯 visually indicating control lamp
可见着色渗透探伤法 visible dye penetrant inspection
可见着色渗透液 visible dye penetrant
可交换性 exchangeability, interchangeability
可浇注性 pourability
可接近性 accessibility, approachability
可结晶的 crystallizable
可结晶性 crystallizability
可解理的 cleavable
可浸出的 leachable
可浸出性 leachability, leaching property
可居住性 【环】habitability
可锯割性 【机】sawability
可开采的 minable
可开盖 detachable head
可靠(程)度 degree of reliability ◇ 不～ degree of uncertainty
可靠的 reliable, fail-safe
可靠性 reliability, dependability, security ◇ 使用～ serviceability
可靠性指数 reliability indices
可控保护气氛 controlled protective atmosphere
可控变量 controllable variable
可控冲击能冲压成形 controlled-energy-rate forming
可控电弧 controlled arc
可控电位滴定计 controlled-potential titrator [titrimeter]
可控硅变流器 thyristor converter [inverter]

可控硅变压器 thyristor transformer
可控硅测试器 thyristor checker
可控硅场电源 thyristor field supply
可控硅传送器 thyristor conveyer
可控硅负极熔断器 thyristor fuse flow out of negative
可控硅控制 silicon control (SC, s.c.)
可控硅励磁系统 thyristor controlled excitation system
可控硅整流电源 thyristor power supply
可控硅(整流器) thyristor-rectifier, silicon controlled rectifier (SCR) ◇ 光激～*, 交连～*, 盘型～ disc-type thyristor
可控硅整流器室 silicon controlled rectifier cubicle (SCRCub.)
可控硅正极熔断器 thyristor fuse flow out of positive
可控硅装置 thyristor equipment [installation]
可控硅组件 thyristor modules
可控浇注速率 controlled pouring rate
可控聚变 【理】controlled fusion
可控孔隙率(缺陷) controlled porosity
可控拉伸矫直 controlled stretcher levelling
可控两段加热法 controlled two-stage heating
可控膨胀(系数)合金 controlled expansion cofficient alloy ◇ 446～*
可控气氛等离子喷涂 controlled atmosphere [air] plasma spraying
可控气氛回转窑[反应炉] 【团】controlled atmosphere furnace (CAF)
可控气氛回转窑直接还原法 【团】CAF system
可控气氛热处理 controlled-atmosphere heat treatment
可控气氛室中焊接 controlled-atmosphere chamber welding
可控切割 controlled cutting
可控热膨胀系数铁镍合金 controlled-expansion nickel-iron alloy

可控温度燃烧器　temperature controlled burner
可控钨极电弧焊　controlled tungsten-arc welding
可控泄漏　controlled leak
可控压力　controlled pressure
可控压力浇注　controlled pressure pouring
可控压屈　controlling buckling
可控阳极电位氧化滴定　controlled anode-potential oxidation titration
可控阴极电位还原滴定　controlled cathode-potential reduction titration
可控制的　controllable
可控制性　controllability, handleability
可扩充性　expandability
可扩充语言　extensible language (EL)
可扩缩性　scalability
可拉拔性　drawability
可拉伸性　tensility, stretchability
可冷加工[冷作]的　cold-workable
可离子化基团　ionogen
可利用的热　available heat
可量度的　measurable
可裂变核燃料　（同"增殖性核燃料"）
可裂变物质　fissile material
可裂变元素　fissile element
可裂变原子　fissionable atom
可裂化性　crackability
可裂性　cleavability
可流动的　fluxible
可流态化粒度　fluidizable particle size
可滤晶体　filterable crystal
可滤性　filterability
可滤性指数　index of filterability
可模锻性　formability
可磨(削)性[可磨度]　grindability
可磨性系数[指标]　grindability index
可磨指数　hardgrove
可挠的　flexible, bendable, springy
可挠管　flexible pipe
可挠引锭杆　flexible dummy bar
可能寿命　life potential

可能误差　possible [probable] error
可能性　probability, feasibility, potentiality, capability
可逆比容量　reversible specific capacity
可逆变化　reversible change
可逆磁导率　reversible permeability
可逆磁化率　reversible susceptibility
可逆电池　reversible cell
可逆电动机　reversible motor
可逆电位　reversible potential
可逆定理　reciprocal theory, law of reciprocity
可逆阀　reversing valve
可逆反应　reversible [reciprocal] reaction
可逆反应温度　reversion temperature
可逆过程　reversing [reversible, quasistatic] process
可逆过程热力学　reversible process thermodynamics
可逆计数器　reversible counter, forward backward counter
可逆膨胀　reversible expansion
可逆式八辊轧机　U-MKW mill
可逆式初轧机　reversing bloomer, reversing blooming mill
可逆式粗轧机　reversing rougher ◇ 万能~
可逆式多辊轧机　reversing multi-roll
可逆式二辊轧机　two-high reversing mill, reversing two-high mill
可逆式二十辊轧机　twenty-high reversing cluster mill
可逆式发动机　reversing engine
可逆式带钢热轧机　reversing hot strip mill
可逆式钢板轧机　reversing plate mill
可逆式钢坯轧机　reversible billet mill
可逆式辊道　reversing roller table
可逆式精轧机　reversing finisher
可逆式冷轧机　reversing cold mill
可逆式皮带(运输)机　reversible belt conveyor, reversible conveyor belt ◇ 倾斜~

sloping reverse belt
可逆式取样器　reversing-type (automatic) sampler
可逆式十二辊轧机　twelve-high reversing cluster mill
可逆式四辊轧机　reversing four-high mill
可逆式轧机　reverse [reversing, reversable] mill ◇ 单机 ~ single reversing mill
可逆式(轧机)机座　reversing mill stand
可逆式轧机轧制厚板　quarto plate
可逆式自动取样器　reversing-type (automatic) sampler
可逆示温变色漆　【冶】reversible thermocolor
可逆性　reversibility
可逆性磁时效　reversible magnetic aging
可逆相变　reversible transition
可逆循环　reversible cycle, reverse circulation
可逆运转状态[工作制]　reversing service
可逆载荷　reversible load
可逆转变　reversible transformation
可凝聚性　condensability
可凝性　coercibility
可凝蒸汽　condensable vapour
可浓缩性　condensability
可判定性　【数】decidability
可喷镀性　sprayability
可膨胀性　expansibility, expandability
可劈性　cleavability
可偏性　deflectivity
可起磁粉末　magnetizable powder
可气化的　gasifiable, vapourable
可汽化的　vapourizable
可钎焊精整(表面的)　solderable finish
可钎焊性　brazability
可迁移的　transportable
可潜水式电动机　submersible motor
可嵌入性　embeddability
可切[可剖开]的　sectile
可切削的　machinable

可切削性　cutting [machining] property, machinability, tooling quality
可切削硬质合金　machinable carbide
可切性　cutability
可侵蚀的　attackable
可倾电炉　tilting electric furnace
可倾动式中间罐　tiltable tundish
可倾料筐　tilting basket
可倾模锭　tilt mould ingot
可倾模锭坯　tilt-mould billet
可倾式电弧炉　rocking (arc) furnace
可倾式电阻炉　rocking resistor furnace
可倾式电阻丝炉　wire-wound tilting furnace
可倾式感应炉　rocking-chair induction furnace
可倾式混铁炉　tipping [tilting-type] mixer
可倾式浇包　【钢】tipping [tilting] ladle
可倾(式)炉　tipping [tilting (-type), tiltable] furnace
可倾式压力机　inclinable press
可倾式真空过滤机　tilting(-type) vacuum filter
可屈服的　yieldable
可燃废物　【环】combustible wastes
可燃混合物　combustible [burning, flammable] mixture
可燃喷吹物　combustible injectant
可燃气体　combustible [fuel, inflammable] gas
可燃气体(爆炸)成形法　【压】combustible gas-forming method
可燃物　combustible (matter), flammable
可燃物料[物质,材料]　combustible material, inflammable material
可燃性　combustibility, flammability, ignitability
可燃性极限　flammability limit
可燃性试验　【焦】combustibility test
可燃液体　flammable liquid
可燃值　combustible value

可染色性	stainability, dyeability
可热处理钢	heat treatable steel
可热处理焊条	heat treatable electrode
可热处理铝合金	◇诺拉尔~Noral
可热处理(强化)合金	heat-treatable alloy
可热加工的	hot workable
可熔保险丝[断路器]	fusible [safety] cut out, electric fuse
可熔炼[熔化]的	smeltable, meltable
可熔模材料	【铸】expendable pattern material
可熔锌芯(铝压铸用)	expendable zinc core
可熔型芯	expendable core(压力铸造的), collapsible core(熔模铸造的)
可熔性	meltableness, meltability, fusibility
可熔注封口胶[密封剂]	castable sealing compound
可溶成分[组分]	soluble component
可溶出的	leachable
可溶出性	(同"可浸出性")
可溶解的	resolvable
可溶极限	soluble end
可溶矿物值	soluble mineral value
可溶物质	soluble material [matter, substance]
可溶性	solubleness, (dis)solubility, dissolvability
可溶性化合物	soluble compound
可溶(性)金属阳极	soluble metal anode
可溶性铝	soluble aluminium
可溶性氯化物	soluble chloride
可溶性陶瓷型芯	leachable ceramic core
可溶阳极	soluble anode
可溶阳极电解	soluble anode electrolysis
可溶阳极电解槽	soluble anode tank
可溶阳极法	soluble anode process
可溶于酸的元素	acid-soluble element
可溶于铜的	copper-soluble
可溶杂质	soluble impurity
可容度	roominess
可乳化能力	emulsibility
可烧结性	sintering property
可伸缩导轨	telescopic guide
可伸缩的	retractable, telescoping
可伸缩橡皮管	flexible rubber
可伸缩橡皮密封	flexible rubber seal
可伸展的	ductile
可伸展性	expansibility
可渗透排水管	permeable drain pipe
可升降电极臂	drop horn
可时效硬化的	age hardenable
可实现性	feasibility, realizability
可使用的	workable
可使用性	workability
可水洗的	water-washable
可塑稠度	stiff-mud consistency
可塑法	stiff-mud process
可塑耐火材料	plastic refractory
可塑性	(potential, latent) plasticity, compliance, malleability, mouldability
可塑性测定	plasticity [mouldable] measurement
可碎性	crushability
可缩浇口	【铸】collapsible sprue
可缩进的	retractable
可碳化的	carbonizable
可探测率	detectivity
可提取的	extractable, extractible, extractive
可提取氧化铝	extractable alumina
可替换的	replaceable
可替换的气垫挡板	air-cushioned shifable stop
可调把手	adjustable grip
可调变量	controllable [regulated] variable
可调变压器	variable (voltage) transformer, variable-ratio transtormer
可调波纹管	adjustable bellows
可调电极	adjustable electrode
可调电阻(器)	adjustable resistor, varistor, varister
可调吊机臂	adjustable jib
可调度盘	adjustable dial

可调阀[活门] adjustable valve
可调封管 【焦】adjustable seal
可调杆 adjustable lever
可调滑车 adjustable pulley
可调机架 【压】adjustable housings
可调计量泵 adjustable dosing pump
可调记录器 controllable register
可调夹头 adjustable grip
可调(截面)喷嘴 variable area nozzle
可调节风口 adjustable tuyere
可调节浇注速率 controlled pouring rate
可调(径)[可调节]铰刀 expansion [adjustable] reamer
可调炉喉直径护板 (同"活动炉喉布料调节板")
可调模 ajustable die
可调排料闸门 adjustable discharge gate
可调偏心螺旋式泵 adjustable eccenter-worm pump
可调气氛 controlled atmosphere
可调入口阀 adjustable port-valve
可调伸缩软管 adjustable bellows
可调速带式给料机 speed adjustable belt feeder
可调速电动机 adjustable-speed motor
可调速螺旋给料机 speed adjustable screw feeder
可调狭缝 adjustable slit
可调限幅器 adjustable limiter
可调性 adjustability
可调闸门料槽 gate controlled hopper
可调整导板 adjustable guide
可调整卷筒张力 adjustable reel tension
可调指示溶液 adjusted indicator solution
可调制动器 adjustable stop
可调轴 adjustable axle
可调轴衬 adjustable bush
可听[闻]度 audibility
可弯的 bendable, springy
可弯度 flexivity
可弯位错 flexible dislocation
可弯位错线 flexible dislocation line

可弯性 bendability, flexibility
可完全混溶的 completely miscible, miscible in all proportion
可维修[维护]性 maintenability, maintainability
可闻度系数 audibility factor
可析出的 precipitable
可吸附的络阴离子 adsorbable complex anion
可洗性 washability
可洗选性试验 【焦】washability test
可掀翻顶盖的机架 tilting cap housing
可镶入性 embedability
可销售产品 saleable product
可携(带)性 portability
可携式电离室 small ionization chamber
可卸炉底(转炉的) detachable bottom
可卸式炉顶 removable arch
可信程度 confidence (level)
可行性 feasibility, practicability
可行性方法 【企】feasibility method
可行性研究 【企】feasibility study
可行性因素 【企】feasibility factor
可选购设备 optional equipment
可选速度 optional speed
可选[寻]址的 addressable
可压度 compressibility
可压实性 【粉】compactibility
可压缩介质 【理】compressible medium
可压缩性 compressibility, coercibility
可压缩性曲线 compressibility curve
可压缩原子 compressible atom
可压印的 coinable
可压印性 coinability
可压制性 pressing characteristic, 【粉】compacting property, compactibility
可研磨性 abradibility
可延伸[展开]性 expandability
可氧化的 oxidizable, oxidable
可氧化性(能) oxidizability, oxidizable nature
可液化的 liquescent, liquefiable

可依赖性	dependability
可移动[运输]的	transportable
可移动的电极	travel(l)ing electrode
可移动性	mobility, shiftability, removability, portability ◇ 熔渣~【钢】removability of slag
可移负载	moving load
可移剪刃	【压】moving blade
可移流槽	rocking spout
可移式防护罩	movable guard
可引爆性	ignitionability
可硬化的	hardenable
可用表面(积)	available surface
可用场地	space availability
可用存储区列表	【计】available storage list
可用废品[物]	utility [disposable] waste
可用频率	allowed [usable] frequency
可用时间	available time
可用性	usability, serviceability
可预测性	predictability
可约簇	reducible variety
可约的	reducible, commensurable
可再现的	reproducible
可再用程序	reusable program [routine]
可增[可逐句]编译程序	incremental compiler
可造化的	【冶】fluxible
可轧(制)性	rollability, aptitude for rolling
可轧制性极限	limit of rollability
可掌握性	handleability
可涨缩卷取机	【压】collapsible reel
可蒸发性	evaporability, vaporability
可蒸馏性	distillability
可支配收入	disposable income ◇ 个人~
可执行指令	【计】executable instruction
可置换的	replaceable
可铸合金	castable alloy
可铸绝缘材料	insulating castable
可铸性试验	castability test
可铸造性	castability
可转化的	convertible
可转换的	switchable
可转换性	reversibility
可转线圈	rotating coil
可着火的	flammable (flam.)
可自燃混合物	self-inflammable mixture
可自乳化的	self-emulsifiable
可钻削性[能力]	【机】drillability
可作废钢用的	scrappable
克/吨	grams/ton (g/t), grams per ton
克尔磁光效应	Kerr magnetooptic effect
克尔效应	Kerr effect
克/分	grams per minute (g/min)
克分子氧平衡	molar oxygen balance
克杰尔达尔烧瓶	Kjeldahl flask
克杰林感应炉	【冶】Kjellin furnace
克拉波热镀锌法	Crapo process
克拉基热压法	Kratky process
克拉克电阻丝	(0.16Si,0.42Mn,10.7Cr, 1.15Al,余量 Fe) Clark resist wire
克拉克铜镍锌合金	(75Cu,14.5Ni,7.5Zn, 1.5Sn,1.5Co) Clark's alloy
克拉克型卧式转盘铸锭机	Clark casting wheel
克拉克值	Clarke number
克拉默铜铅型耐摩合金	(64Cu,30Pb,5Sn, 1Ni) Clamer's alloy
克拉热固性塑料	Kera thermosetting plastic
克拉珀龙方程式	Clapeyron's equation
克拉珀龙-克劳修斯方程式	Clapeyron-Clausius's equation
克拉珀龙-克劳修斯公式	【金】formula of Clapeyron-Clausius
克莱马克斯温差磁补偿合金	(<0.2C,< 0.4Si,<0.1Mn,28.5—31.5,余量 Fe) Climax alloy
克莱森(烧)瓶	Claisen flask
克兰菲尔德射流技术	Cranfield fluidics
克劳福德水银蒸气泵	Crawford pump
克劳氰化提金法	【色】Crowe process
克劳斯往复式板材冷轧机	Krause mill, Krause roll(ing) mill

克劳修斯－克拉珀龙方程 Clausius-Clapeyron equation

克勒锡基合金(10.5Sb,1Cu,1.8Bi,余量Sn) Koeller's alloy

克勒照明 Koehler illumination

克雷格假金(80Cu,10Zn,10Ni) Craig gold

克雷默－萨诺法(即水银法,用于测沥青软化点) Kraemer and Sarnow test

克雷默效应 【理】Kramer effect, exoelectron emission

克雷姆浸蚀液(用于检验钢的回火脆性) Klemm's reagent

克雷姆佩雷尔高速玻璃扩散泵 Klemperer's high-speed glass pump

克雷斯达铬钒钢 crestaloy

克雷斯皮白云石打结炉衬 【钢】Crespi lining

克雷斯塔洛伊各向异性硅钢带 Crystaloy

克里斯托福尔森喷嘴(拉丝用) Christophorsen tube

克里斯托隆人造碳化硅(研磨用) Crystolon

克里索林黄铜合金(66Cu,34Zn) Chrysorin

克里索桥克铜锌铅装饰合金(90.5Cu,7.9Zn,1.6Pb) Chrysochalk

克利尔法 copper leach electrolysis and regeneration (CLEAR)

克利普托尔电阻材料(用于电炉炉衬) Kryptol

克利瓦特钢背铅青铜(70Cu,30Pb; 65Cu,35Pb) steel back Clevite

克利维特铅青铜(70Cu,30Pb; 65Cu,35Pb) Clevite

克利谢锡铅合金(50Sn,32Pb,9Bi,1.05Sb) Cliche, metal

克立奥弌赫超级弹簧钢丝 Cryotech

克/厘米^3 grams per cubic centimeter (g/cm^3)

克林热压法 Koehring process

克灵式铁水罐 Kling type ladle

克流西克(漏损单位,等于10^{2}流西克) clusec

克娄勾牙科合金(45Cu,40Au,1Cr,0.2Pt,余量Ni) Chrogo

克虏伯奥氏体钢焊接法 Krupp welding process

克虏伯奥氏体(镍铬)不锈钢 K.A.(Krupp austenitic) steel

克虏伯法 Krupp process

克虏伯(铬钼钒)高速钢(0.9C,4W,4Cr,2.5Mo,2.5V) Krupp triple steel

克虏伯－雷恩回转窑还原粒铁冶炼法 Krupp-Renn process

克虏伯－普拉策尔行星轧机[克虏伯双重行星辊式轧机] Krupp-Platzer planetary mill

克虏伯锌基轴承合金 Krupp bearing alloy

克虏伯型渗碳钢(4—5Ni,1.5Cr) Krupp-type carburizing steel

克鲁(蠕变速率单位) creep-rate unit (cru, c.r.u.)

克鲁克斯(放电)管 Crookes tube

克鲁司钨钢 Kerus

克罗尔－贝特顿加钙镁除铋法(同"贝特顿加钙镁除铋精炼法")

克罗尔法 Kroll process ◇改良～

克罗尔法海绵锆 Kroll zirconium

克罗尔海绵钛[锆]金属 Kroll reactor product

克罗尔浸蚀剂 Kroll's etchant

克罗尔镁还原法生产海绵钛[锆]金属 【色】Kroll process sponge

克罗尔镁还原卤化物法 【色】Kroll reduction process

克罗尔镁还原四氯化物法 Kroll method

克罗尔镁还原四氯化物反应器 【色】Kroll reactor

克罗里梅特镍铬钼合金(60Ni,18Mo,18Cr,3Fe,C等微量) Chlorimet

克罗洛伊低合金耐热钢(1.2—9.5Cr,

0.08—0.13C, 0.2—0.6Si, 0.5—1.5Mo, 有时尚加入 Al、Ti 等) Croloy
克罗马杜尔高锰铬耐热钢 Chromadur
克罗马多尔低合金高强度钢(＜0.3C,＜0.2Si,0.7－1.0Mn,0.25－0.5Cu,0.7－1.0Cr,余量 Fe) Chromador
克罗马克可焊接不锈钢(16Cr,20Ni,余量 Fe) Kromarc
克罗马克斯含铬铝青铜(67Cu,15Ni,12Zn,3Cr,3Al;作轴承等用) Chromax bronze
克罗马克斯耐热镍铬合金(80Ni,20Cr) Kromax
克罗马克斯镍铬耐热钢(50Fe,35Ni,15Cr;含少量 C) Chromax
克罗马林电镀法(铝及铝合金的) Cromalin
克罗马宁电阻合金(71Ni,21Cr,3Al,5Cu) Chromanin
克罗麦尔镍铬耐热合金(80Ni,20Cr;用作电阻丝及热电偶丝) Chromel (alloy)
克罗麦特铝硅轴承合金(90Al,10Si) Chromet
克罗曼 80/20 型镍铬合金(含 1Mn,0—20Fe) Chroman
克罗曼格不锈钢 Chromang
克罗曼西尔低合金[铬锰硅合金]结构钢(0.1—0.22C, 0.4—0.6Cr, 0.9—1.2Mn,0.6—0.9Si,Cr＋Mn＋Si＝2.5) Chromansil
克罗莫尔镍铬耐热合金(85Ni,15Cr) Kromore
克罗姆索尔易熔铬铁 Chromsol
克罗纳克锌或镁合金表面化学镀铬法 Cronak process
克罗奈特耐蚀耐热合金(Ni/Cr: 55/18 或 38/20 或 20/25 或 12/23,0.75—3W,0.2—0.75C,余量 Fe) Cronite
克罗尼特耐蚀耐热合金(65Ni,20Fe,13Cr,1Mn,0.5Si,0.5Al,作燃烧器配件用) Chronite
克罗斯法 Cross method

克罗托莱特耐热耐蚀铝青铜(耐热铝青铜: 88—90Cu,7Ni,3Al,0.3Mn;耐蚀铝青铜: 88—90Cu,9—9.75Al,0.2—0.6Mn,0.2—2Fe) Crotorite (alloy)
克洛宁壳型铸造法 Cronizing, Croning [Cronic] process
克纳普扎克－格里斯海姆镁连续还原炉 Knapsack-Griesheim furnace
克纳普扎克接线法 Knapsack connection
克奈斯铅镍铜锌轴承合金(42Sn,40Zn,15Pb,13Cu) Kneiss's alloy
克赛石 coesite
克赛特耐热镍铬合金钢[镍铬铁合金] (17—21Cr,37—40Ni,余量 Fe) Xite
克/升 grams per liter (g/L, gpL)
刻槽 carved fillet, nicking
刻度 graduation, mark, scale, division
刻度标记 gauge [graduation] mark(s)
刻度玻璃 index glass
刻度(玻璃)管 graduated tube
刻度长度 length of scale
刻度的工作部分 effective range
刻度读数 scale reading
刻度范围 scale range
刻度分度 scale division
刻度间距 scale spacing
刻度盘 dial gauge [plate], scale (dial), graduated [divided, index] circle ◇ 带～的指示器 dial indicator
刻度盘式变阻器 dial-type rheostat
刻度盘天平 dial balance
刻度盘形变仪 dial extensometer
刻度瓶 graduated bottle
刻度线 graduation line, gauge [scale] mark
刻度仪表 gauge instrument
刻度值 scale value, infinity ◇ 单格～ value of the division
刻格坯块 girdded billet
刻痕 nick(ing), indent, scotch, score, riffling, collaring (轧辊的)
刻痕钢丝 indented steel wire ◇ 混凝土

钢筋用~*，预应力混凝土（结构）用~*
刻痕和堆焊（轧辊表面的） bossing
刻痕硬度值 scratch (hardness) number
刻痕轧辊 ragged rolls
刻模机（床） die sinking machine, diesinker
刻模加工 【铸】die sinking
刻模铣刀 die sinking cutter, engraving cutter
刻纹（轧辊的） ragging
刻线 pop mark
刻线衍射光栅 ruled diffraction grating
客舱 (passenger) cabin
客观的 objective
客户/服务器计算模式 client/server computing mode
客体 object(ive)
课题 assignment, task
肯定 acknowledgement
肯定字符 acknowledge character (ACK)
肯纳薄锡层镀锡薄钢板（锡重0.64kg/基准箱） Kanner's tinplate
肯纳提姆 W_2 重钨合金 Kennertium W_2
肯纳硬质合金 Kennametal
肯尼恩腐蚀疲劳试验机 Kenyon machine
肯塔纽姆硬质合金（K151A: 80TiC, 20Ni; K151B: 70TiC, 30Ni） Kentanium
肯特隆显微（压痕）硬度计 Kentron (tester)
肯尼科特-奥托昆普闪速吹炼法 Kennecott-Outokumpu flash converting process
坑 pit, pocket, hole, sump, well
坑道 mine tunnel, excavation
坑道腐蚀 【采】undermining corrosion
坑道口 adit
坑道台阶式挖掘 【建】chamber bench excavation
坑腐蚀的(金属表面) 【金】pitted
坑盖 pit cover
坑口 bank head

坑面（钢锭缺陷） pitted surface
坑木 mine timber
坑内焙烧 stall roasting
坑内焊接 【焊】bell hole welding
坑内浸出 【色】stop leaching
坑式干燥器 【色】drying pit
坑式干燥窑 pit drying stove
坑式坩埚炉 pit-type crucible furnace
坑式均热炉 cell pit furnace
坑式炉 pit-type furnace, pit fire ◇ 间歇作业~ pit-type batch furnace
坑式(热处理)炉 pit batch-type furnace
坑式设备 sunken-type plant
坑柱 mine timber
坑铸 【钢】(fixed) pit casting
坑注法 pit teeming
空拔 empty sinking ◇ 钢管~ tube sink drawing, 固定模~*
空拔减径 non-plug diameter reducing
空拔圆管 non-mandrel drawn round tube
空白符 【计】blank character
空白溶液 【化】blank solution
空白试验 blank test [assay, determination] ◇ 试剂~*
空白(纸)带 blank tape
空胞 open position
空操作指令 dummy [non-operation, skip] instruction
空层 【理】dead level
空车重翻转 empty retilt
空车停车处 dead parking
空程皮带 return belt
空冲程 【机】idle stroke
空淬合金 air-hardening alloy
空带 empty tape, 【半】empty band
空刀 【机】undercut
空底键 hollow key
空地 opening
空洞 cavity, void ◇ 大~ macroscopic void
空洞缺陷 cavity blemish
空洞率 void raito
空洞型断裂 cavitation fracture

空洞型蠕变断裂 （同"成穴蠕变断裂"）
空洞形成 void formation, cavitation
空斗墙连接砖 bonding brick
空段发生器 void generator
空段体积 void volume
空段移动（区域熔炼的） movement [travel] of void
空风 【冶】vacancy wind
空腹（大）梁 open-web beam [girder]
空腹拱 open-spandrel arch
空腹桁架 vierendeel truss
空公用块 【计】blank common block
空管速度 empty-tube velocity
空辊 idler roller
空盒气压计 aneroid barometer
空化 cavitation ◇ 流动~（现象）*
空化现象 cavitation phenomena
空间 space, void space, enclosure, room, blank, aerospace ◇ 适用于~条件的 space-orien-ted, 适于~应用的 space-rated, 挖空的~gob
空间不足 lack of space
空间布置 spatial arrangement, three-dimensional array
空间磁导率 space permeability
空间点阵[晶格] space lattice
空间点阵[晶格]干涉 space lattice interference
空间点阵[晶格]结点 space-lattice point
空间点阵[晶格]类型 space lattice form
空间电荷密度 space-charge density
空间电荷像差 space charge aberration
空间电荷效应 space charge effect
空间电流 space current
空间电子学 space electronics
空间定位 spatial orientation, spatialization
空间分布 space [spatial] distribution
空间格子 space lattice
空间环境 space environment
空间技术 space technique
空间加热器 space heater
空间结构 space [spatial] structure

空间考察 space exploration
空间科学 space science
空间量子化 space quantization
空间排列 spatial arrangement
空间取向 spatial orientation
空间群 space group
空间群对称 space-group symmetry
空间时代材料 space age material
空间实验室 spacelab
空间受碍现象 【理】stereo-hindrance
空间速度 space velocity [rate]
空间图 space diagram
空间位形[轮廓, 外形] spatial configuration
空间物理学 space physics, spatiography
空间像 space image
空间运动 spatial motion
空间站 space station
空间站时代 space station era
空间坐标系 space [three-dimensional] coordinate system
空间坐标轴 solid axis
空焦 【铁】coke blank
空接点 【电】idle contact
空瞰图 air view
空壳 hollow shell
空壳层 【理】vacant shell
空旷地区道路 exposed road
空拉 【压】(hollow) sinking
空冷沉降室 air-cooled settling chamber
空冷淬火 dry quenching
空冷淬硬钢 self-hardening steel
空冷炉渣 air-cooled slag
空冷韧化处理 air toughening
空冷塞棒 【钢】air-cooled stopper
空冷塞棒芯 【钢】air-cooled stopper rod
空料线 【铁】lowering stockline
空炉时间 【钢】furnace downtime
空路 dead circuit
空能级 【理】empty (energy) level, vacant (energy) level
空能量区 empty energy zone

kong 空

空喷细粉的炉墙密封法 【焦】airborne sealing systems
空气 air, atmosphere, atmospheric gas ◇ 标准状况～standard air, 抽出～deflation, 除去～deaerate, 含水分的～moisture-laden air, 环境[周围]～ambient air, 排出的～outgoing air, 新鲜～live air, 一次～main (combustion) air
空气泵 air pump
空气擦拭器 air wiper
空气层 air layer
空气冲击波 air shock
空气出口 air-outlet
空气储存(期) air storage
空气储存器 air holder
空气吹弧式断路器 air blast breaker (ABB)
空气吹炼 【冶】converting with air
空气吹炼法 【冶】air-refining process [practice]
空气吹炼钢 air-refined steel
空气吹熔装置(焊管坯边的) edge blower
空气锤 air [pneumatic] hammer
空气淬火[空冷淬硬] air quenching [hardening], dry quenching
空气淬火冷拉钢丝 air-patented cold-drawn wire
空气淬硬钢 air-hardening steel
空气导管 antivacuum pipe
空气道 air channel, flue
空气的净化 cleaning of air
空气等离子炬 air plasma torch
空气等离子体 air plasma
空气垫 air-cushion
空气电池 air cell
空气电池组 air cell battery
空气电弧炉 air-arc furnace
空气-电弧切割 air arc cutting
空气电极 air electrode
空气电容器 air capacitor
空气动力天平 aerodynamic balance
空气动力学 aerodynamics

空气动力学反力[反作用] air reaction
空气锻锤 (同"风动锻锤")
空气断路器 【电】air circuit breaker (ACB), air break disconnector, air blast breaker ◇ 磁吹～*
空气对流 air convection
空气发动机 air engine [motor]
空气发蓝精整处理 air-blued finish
空气发生站 air generating source
空气阀(门) air valve [cock, flap, throttle], pressure lock
空气反力[反作用] air reaction
空气分布 air distribution
空气分布板 contractor (contr.), dispersion plate (流态化焙烧炉的)
空气分布器 air distributor
空气分级 air classification [separation]
空气分级机 air classifier
空气分离 air separation
空气分析器 air analyzer
空气浮动堆垛机 air float piler
空气浮选法 【环】air flotation
空气富氧 oxygen enrichment
空气干燥 air-dry(ing), airing
空气干燥器 blast dryer
空气干燥室 air dryer [drier]
空气缸 air cylinder
空气更新 air renewal
空气供给站 air supply station
空气鼓风转炉 air-blown converter
空气管 air tube
空气管道[路] air duct [conduit], piping for air, airline
空气管线图 air piping diagram
空气罐 air cylinder
空气过滤 air filtration
空气过滤器 air filter
空气过剩火焰 overventilated flame
空气过剩率 percentage of excess air
空气过剩系数 air excess coefficient
空气含尘 air-laden dust
空气烘箱 air oven

空气环流炉　air circulating oven
空气还原法(炼铅)　air reduction
空气缓冲器　air damper [dashpot, buffer]
空气换热器　air recuperator ◇ 金属～*，耐火材料制～*
空气换向阀　air-reversing valve
空气回火炉　air tempering furnace
空气活塞　air slide
空气激冷　air chill
空气加热器　air heater ◇ 换热式～*
空气加热器管　air heater tube
空气加热染色法　【金】temper tinting method
空气加湿　air moistening [wetting]
空气减震器　air bumper
空气交换　air interchange
空气搅拌[搅动]　air agitation
空气搅拌沉淀槽　air agitated precipitation tank
空气搅拌电解　(同"鼓风搅拌电解")
空气搅拌器　air(lift) agitator
空气进入　ingress of air
空气进入管　air inlet tube
空气精炼钢　air-refined steel
空气静力学　aerostatics
空气净化　air cleaning [purification]
空气净化器　air cleaner [purifier]
空气净化设备　air cleaning [purge] facility
空气净化装置　air cleaning unit [equipment, installation]
空气绝缘　air insulation
空气开关(器)　air circuit breaker (ACB), air blast breaker, air switch
空气冷凝器　air [aerial, atmospheric] condenser
空气冷却　air cooling
空气冷却淬火　air quenching
空气冷却冷凝器　air-cooled condenser
空气冷却炉墙　air-cooled furnace wall
空气冷却器　air cooler ◇ 便携式～*，管式～tubular air cooler

空气冷却蛇管　air coil
空气冷却塔　atmospheric cooling tower
空气冷却系统　air-cooling system
空气冷却压缩机　air-cooling compressor
空气冷却装置　air-cooling apparatus
空气量　air quantity [volume]
空气量调节器　air volume controller
空气流　air current [stream], airflow
空气流量　air-flow rate
空气流量调节挡板　air-flow regulating damper
空气流量计　air-flow meter
空气流速　air velocity, air-flow rate
空气漏入　air inleakage
空气滤池　aerofilter
空气滤(清)器　air strainer, aerofilter, air filter [cleaner]
空气煤粉混合物　air(-and)-coal mixture
空气煤气　air gas
空气煤气配比调节器　air-gas proportioner
空气密封　air(tight) seal, aeroseal
空气凝固油　air-setting oil
空气泡　air bubble
空气泡黏度计　air bubble viscometer
空气喷口　air jet [end]
空气喷枪　air lance
空气喷砂　air sand blasting ◇ 非～处理法*
空气喷砂机[器]　air-sand blower
空气喷射冷却器　air jet cooler
空气喷射器　air ejector
空气喷雾　air-atomizing ◇ 低压～法*
空气喷嘴　air nozzle [orifice], blow nozzle, skelp blower
空气启动　air start
空气铅淬火　air patenting [palentizing]
空气-氢焊接　air-hydrogen welding
空气清扫　air cleaning
空气取样　air sampling ◇ 大容量～装置*
空气取样法　【环】air sampling method

空气取样瓶　air-sampling vessel
空气燃料比　air-fuel ratio
空气燃料混合物　【冶】air(-and)-fuel mixture
空气-燃气焰加热淬火　air-gas hardening
空气燃烧　air burning
空气染色法　【金】air-tinting method
空气熔炼的　air-melted
空气入[进]口　air inlet [ingress], access of air
空气散放物　【环】air emissions
空气上升道　air uptake
空气蛇管　air coil
空气射流　air jet, air-spray
空气升液泵　airlift pump
空气升液管　airlift pipe [tube]
空气升液管管脚　airlift foot
空气升液混合　airlift mixing
空气升液混合沉降器　airlift mixer-settler
空气升液器　airlift
空气湿度　air humidity [dampness]
空气室　air cell [vessel], blast chamber ◇ 鼓风机~ blower casing
空气收集器　air holder [collector]
空气输送　air transport
空气-水力蓄压器　air-water bottle accumulator
空气水压机　air-hydraulic press
空气速度　air velocity [speed]
空气-碳弧切割　air carbon arc cutting
空气碳酸计　carbometer
空气淘析　elutriation with air
空气淘析器　air elutriator ◇ 罗勒~ Roller air analyzer
空气淘析装置　air elutriation apparatus
空气套冷凝器　air jacketed condenser
空气提升器　airlift
空气调节　air conditioning (A.C.)
空气调节阀　air regulator, air controll valve
空气调节器　air conditioner [regulator], air conditioning unit
空气调节设备[装置]　air conditioning equipment [unit, installation] ◇ 驾驶[司机,操作]室~ cab cooler, 水淋式~*
空气调湿设备　air humidifying equipment
空气通路　air passage, access of air
空气透明度计　diaphanometer
空气脱模装置　air knock-out
空气弯管　air duct bend
空气温度计　air thermometer
空气涡形管　air scroll
空气污染　air [aerial, atmospheric, airborne] pollution, air [aerial, atmospheric] contamination contamination by atmospheric gases ◇ 防~控制系统
空气污染管理协会　Air Pollution Control Association (APCA)
空气污染监测车　air pollution monitoring car
空气污染控制　air pollution control ◇ 半湿式~法*
空气雾化　air atomization
空气雾化喷枪　air atomising lance
空气雾化喷嘴[喷射器]　air atomizer spray nozzle
空气雾化烧嘴　air atomising burner
空气洗涤器　air scrubber [washer]
空气洗涤装置　air-washing plant, impingement scrubber (撞击式)
空气隙　air gap
空气隙磁化力　air gap magnetizing force
空气箱　wind-box, air tank
空气消耗(量)　air consumption, 【冶】rate of blowing
空气心变压器　air-core transformer
空气蓄热室　【冶】air chamber, 【钢】air checker
空气旋流器　air cyclone
空气循环　air cycle [circulation] ◇ 电热式~炉*
空气压力　air pressure
空气压力机　air-pressure mill

空气压力计　air-pressure gauge, air manometer
空气压力释放阀　air-pressure release valve
空气压缩机　air compressor
空气压缩机颤动极限　compressor surge limit
空气压缩机站　compressor station [plant]
空气压缩装置　compressor plant
空气烟气罩　air fume hood
空气氧　aerial [atmospheric] oxygen
空气氧化　air [atmospheric] oxidation
空气养护　air [dry] curing
空气-乙炔焊(接)　air-acetylene welding (AAW)
空气-乙炔炬　air-acetylene torch
空气引出管　air-outlet pipe
空气引入管　air inlet pipe
空气硬化　air-hardening [self-hardening] steel
空气硬化黏结剂　air curing binder
空气硬化型砂　【铸】air-setting sand
空气硬化型芯　【铸】air-set core
空气浴(槽)　air bath
空气预热器　air preheater, blast air heater ◇管式～ tubular air preheater, 换热式～*, 流态化～ fluid air preheater
空气预热器煤气管道　【冶】stove gas main
空气预热室　air-preheating chamber
空气预热温度　air-preheating temperature
空气源　air source
空气增湿器　air humidifier
空气闸板[闸门]　air register
空气蒸汽混合物　air-steam mixture
空气支管　【铁】air manifold
空气直线速度　superficial air velocity
空气纸绝缘电缆　dry-core cable
空气制动器　air [atmospheric] brake
空气中常化的　normalized in air (Na)
空气中淬硬合金　air-hardening alloy
空气中方块试验法　cube-in-air method
空气中固结的　air-bond
空气中熔炼的合金　(同"敞熔合金")
空气中烧结　air sintering
空气中硬化　hardened in air (Ha)
空气轴承　air [pneumatic] bearing
空气转炉钢　【钢】pneumatic steel
空气转炉炼钢法　pneumatic steelmaking process
空气着色法　【金】air-tinting method
空气自动断路器　air circuit breaker ◇消电离～*
空气总管　air main
空气阻力　windage
空气阻尼器　air damper [dashpot]
空气阻尼天平　air damping balance
空腔　cavity (cav.)
空腔型空穴　cavity type void
空腔振荡　(同"空穴振荡")
空切　miscut
空缺位置　【理】vacant [open] position
空燃比寻优　optimal air/fuel ratio
空蚀　(同"空穴腐蚀") ◇耐～钢*
空蚀作用　cavitation
空塔　void column [tower]
空态　empty state
空调　(同"空气调节")
空头　【钢】top hat
空位　【金】vacancy (vac.), vacant site [position], 【计】blank ◇双～ coupled vacancy, 消除～的退火*
空位比　voids ratio
空位丛聚　vacancies clustering
空位错　hollow dislocation
空位堆[累]积　vacancy accumulation
空位对　coupled vacancy, vacancy pair
空位分离　separation of vacancies
空位壑　sink of vacancy
空位环(位错)　vacancy loop
空位机理　vacant site mechanism
空位集合体　vacancy agglomerates
空位集合体退火　annealing of vacancy agglomerates
空位聚集　vacancy condensation, condensation of vacancies

空位扩散	vacancy diffusion
空位(扩散)蠕变	vacancy creep
空位能带	vacant energy band
空位浓度	vacancy concentration
空位流(动)	vacancy flow
空位迁移[移动]	migration of vacant sites, migration of vacancies ◇ 蠕变过程中～*
空位迁移率	vacancy mobility
空位－溶质原子对	vacancy-solute atom pairs
空位式位错割阶	vacancy jog
空位析出[沉淀]	vacancy precipitation
空位线	line of vacant sites
空位消失	vacancy annihilation
空位形成	formation of vacancies
空位形成激活能	activation energy for vacancy
空位形成能	energy of formation of vacancy
空位形成熵	entropy of formation of vacancy
空位湮没	vacancy annihilation
空位源	vacancy source, source of vacancies
空位跃迁	vacancy jump
空位状态	unoccupied state
空吸	suction ◇ 边界层～*
空隙	void, clearance [air] space, interstice, vacancy, gap, 【铸】allowance
空隙百分率	percentage of voids
空隙比	air space ratio, fraction void, void ratio [factor]
空隙度[率]	voidage ◇ 床层～(流化床的) bed voidage
空隙焊	open welding
空隙结合	void coalescence
空隙宽度	gap width
空隙容量	void volume
空隙体积	fractional void volume ◇ 块焦间～*
空闲触点	disconnected [dead] contact
空闲时间	off time
空心板	cored slab
空心棒材	hollow bar ◇ 挤压～*
空心变压器	air-core transformer
空心超导体	hollow superconductor
空心冲头	hollow punch
空心抽油杆	hollowed oil-suction rod
空心磁铁	air-core magnet
空心导线[体]	hollow coductor
空心电极	cored electrode
空心电极炼铁电炉	hollow electrode furnace
空心电抗器	air-core reactor
空心电缆	hollow (core) cable
空心锭	hollow ingot ◇ 挤压管材用～ cored extrusion ingot
空心锻造	hollow forging
空心扼流圈	air(-core) reactor, air choke
空心钢辊	【压】hollow steel roller
空心(钢)坯	hollow billet
空心钢线绳	hollow [tubular] wire rope
空心格子砖	checker tile
空心弓型桩	hollow segmented piling
空心管坯	hollow (bloom, shell)
空心辊	hollow [shell-type] roller
空心焊丝	cored solder wire
空心搅拌器	hollow stirrer
空心结构	hollow structure
空心金属	hollow metal
空心颗粒保护渣	【连铸】hollow grained mould powder
空心粒子	hollow granule
空心楼面砖	floor tile
空心铆钉	hollow [tubular] rivet
空心模型	hollow pattern
空心凝晶框	hollow freezing frame
空心铅阳极	hollow lead anode
空心墙	hollow [cavity] wall
空心十字撑	hollow spacer
空心式离心机	hollow-bowl centrifuge
空心试棒	hollow bar
空心枢	hollow pivot
空心束	【理】hollow beam

空心填料[填充物]	hollow packing
空心铜线	hollow copper wire
空心位错	hollow dislocation
空心纤维隔膜	hollow fibre membrane
空心心轴	hollow mandrel
空心型材	hollow section (profile)
空心型材挤压模	【压】hollow die
空心型芯	【铸】hollow core
空心形状	hollow shape
空心阳极	hollow anode ◇ 水冷~*
空心阴极灯	hollow cathod lamp
空心轧辊	【压】hollow roll ◇ 铸造~hollow cast roll
空心制品	hollow ware
空心轴	hollow shaft [arbor, axle], sleeve (shaft), quill shaft (万向接轴用)
空心轴颈[耳轴]	hollow trunnion
空心铸件	hollow casting
空心铸造	hollow casting, cast hollow
空心铸造合金	slush-casting alloy
空心砖	hollow [air, cavity, cell, perforated] brick
空心钻	core drill
空心钻钢	holsteel
空心钻取样检验	hollow drill testing
空行	free play
空穴	vacancy, pigeon hole (钢锭缩孔缺陷),【电】positive hole ◇ 空腔型~cavity type void, 束缚~bound hole, 重~【半】heavy hole
空穴传导	【半】hole conduction
空穴电导率	hole [p-type] conductivity
空穴电流	hole current
空穴俘获	【半】hole capture [trapping]
空穴腐蚀	cavitation (corrosion, erosion)
空穴扩散	【半】hole diffusion
空穴率	void fraction
空穴脉冲	pulse of holes
空穴迁移率	【半】hole mobility
空穴陷阱	【半】hole trap
空穴效应	void effect
空穴型超导体	hole type superconductor
空穴形成	cavity formation
空穴形成的断口样式	fracture mode by void formation
空穴与粒间相互作用	【半】hole-particle interaction
空穴振荡	【半】cavity oscillation
空穴注入	【半】hole injection
空压机站	compressed-air plant
空圆套(千分尺的)	drum
空运	air transport, air freight
空运单	air way bill
空运转	idle [no-load] operation
空载(的)	idling, no-load
空载电流时间	current off-time
空载电压	no-load voltage, open circuit voltage ◇ 次级绕组~*
空载时间	idle [dead] time, idle period
空载时间损失	dead-time loss
空载试验	no-load test
空载损耗	no-load loss, open circuit loss
空载特性	no-load characteristic
空载运转	no-load [unloaded] running
空轧过的	dummied
空轧机座	dummy stand
空轧孔型[道次]	idle [blind, dead, dummy, false, lost, shallow] pass
空轧通过	dumming
空指令	blank [do-nothing, skip, waste] instruction
空中吊运车轨梁	top-trolley beam
空中放电	air [atmospheric] discharge
空中距离	bee line
空中探测	airborne sound
空中悬浮粒子	airborne particulates
空重	tare [empty] weight
空柱	void column
空转	idle [no-load] running, idling, free play, runfree
空转齿轮	【机】idle(r) gear
空转辊	idle [dummy, drag] roll ◇ 衬胶~rubber-lined idlerroll
空转辊道	idle [dead] roller table

空转机座	【压】idle stand
空转力矩	idling torque
空转轮	idle(r) [free, loose] pulley, idler, idle wheel
空转轮轴	idler shaft
空转时间	idle running time, idle period [hours], dead time
空转试验	running-in test, blank experiment, motoring [racing] test
空转速度[转速]	idling [idle, no-load] speed
空转损失	idling loss
空转位置	idle position
空转压力辊	idle forcing roller
空转轧辊	【压】idle roll
空转轴	pony axle
空字符	【计】null character
孔	hole, opening, aperture, bore, eye, orifice, pore, port (hole), vent ◇ 大~ macroscopic void, 封闭的~blind hole, 墨水池状~*, 收~*, 有~的 meshed
孔板	orifice [aperture, perforated] plate ◇ 环形~annular orifice, 流量~*, 旁通~bypass orifice
孔板流量计	orifice-plate flowmeter, orifice meter, diaphragm (flow) meter
孔槽寿命	groove life
孔槽数目	groove number
孔道	passage, duct ◇ 砖格~*
孔洞	void,【铸】cavity
孔洞率	voidage
孔洞形成	cavity formation
孔洞形核	nucleation of cavity, void nucleation
孔堵塞	blocking of pores
孔海姆发火合金	Kunheim metal
孔焊	eyelet welding
孔喉	gorge
孔环	orifice ring
孔径	aperture, bore (diameter)
孔径尺寸	hole size
孔径分布	pore-size distribution
孔径光阑	aperture diaphragm [plate]
孔径透镜	aperture lens
孔径效应	aperture effect
孔径泄漏	aperture leak
孔径自动控制	automatic aperture control (AAC)
孔口面积	orifice area
孔口圈	orifice ring
孔率计	porosimeter
孔率检验器	porosity tester
孔泡体	【焦】cellular
孔雀石(石绿)	{CuCO$_3$·Cu(OH)$_2$} malachite, molochite
孔雀铜矿	{Cu$_5$FeS$_4$} peacock ore
孔塞	stopple, spout [vent] plug
孔蚀	pitting [hole] corrosion
孔蚀敏感性	pit corrosive sensitivity
孔西戴尔作图法(用于拉伸变形)	Considere's construction
孔隙	pore, aperture gap, void space, freckle (镀锡薄板缺陷),【钢】poriness (缺陷) ◇ 宏观~(率) macro porosity, 连通~* interconnected porosity, 无~膜*, 显[肉眼]~ macro porosity, 有~的 porous, 有~膜 discontinuous film
孔隙比	porosity [void] ratio
孔隙闭合	closing(-up) of porosity
孔隙大小	pore size
孔隙度	porosity, poriness, amount [extent] of porosity, pore space, void content [fraction] ◇ 金属镀层~电图检查*, 可控~(缺陷)*, 受控~材料*, 总~general porosity
孔隙度变化	porosity variation
孔隙度控制	porosity control
孔隙分布	porosity [pore] distribution
孔隙检验	porosity test
孔隙检验仪	poroscope
孔隙结构	porous [cell] structure (焦炭的)
孔隙量	porosity [pore] volume
孔隙率	porosity, air voids, void content

[volume]
孔隙率测定法 porosimetry
孔隙率降低 reduction of porosity
孔隙密度 hole density
孔隙迁移 pore migration
孔隙水 void water
孔隙压力 pore pressure
孔隙直径 pore size [diameter]
孔型 【压】pass, groove ◇ W形~ W-pass, 凹边方~ fluted square pass, 半椭圆~ *, 闭口~ *, 成品前~ *, 成型~（管材的）forming pass, 粗轧~ *, 蝶式~ butterfly pass, 对角[斜置]~ diagonal pass, 非工作~ dead pass, 过充满~ *, 弧菱形~曲率半径 *, 加工~ roll dressing, 精轧[成品]~ *, 开坯~ *, 空轧~ *, 立椭圆~ faux-rond pass, 立轧~ *, 菱形~ *, 平面[平板箱形]~（初轧辊的）bullhead, 切分~ fuller, 双形~ *, 凸起~ former, 喂入~（轧件的）forward journey, 下排~ *, 箱形[矩形]~ *, 斜置~轧制 *, 延伸~ *, 异形~ formingpass, 预轧~ *, 轧制钢筋的~ deforming groove, 中间轧制~ intermediate pass
孔型侧壁 side wall of pass
孔型侧壁斜度 inclination of pass side, slope of groove
孔型出口侧 outlet of pass
孔型顶角（菱形的） pass angularity
孔型断面轮廓 shape of pass
孔型过充满 overfilling of pass, overfill
孔型进口 entrance of pass
孔型开口部分 live hole
孔型宽度 width of groove
孔型轮廓[断面] section of groove [pass], form of groove, pass outline
孔型内圆角 groove fillets
孔型配置 pass positioning
孔型入口侧 inlet of pass
孔型设计 pass [groove] design, roll draughting, grooving ◇带凸缘的直轧~ sfraight flange 反[假]翼缘法~ *, 计算机辅助~ *, 平立[弯折]法~ *, 轧辊~ *, 直轧成品~ *
孔型设计人 roll designer
孔型设计图表 pass schedule
孔型深度 depth of groove
孔型锁口 roll joint, parting of pass
孔型调整 pass setup
孔型凸度 pass convexity
孔型外形 pass contour, contour of groove
孔型系统 pass sequence ◇ 菱-方~ *
孔型详图 pass detail
孔型样板 pass template
孔型圆角半径 groove radius
孔型轧制 rolling in passes
孔型中心线 centre [pitch] line of groove
孔性计 porosimeter
孔穴 void, cavity
孔穴迁移率 【半】hole mobility
孔眼 eyelet ◇ 打~ eyeleting, 有~的 meshed
控冷工艺 controlled cooling technology (CCT)
控冷温度 controlled cooling temperature (CCT)
控温锻造 controlled temperature forging (C.T.F.)
控温[控制加热]炉 temperature control furnace
控温气相色层[分离]法 （同"升温气相色层(分离)法"）
控温热电偶 control thermocouple
控温轧制 temperature-controlled rolling (TCR)
控氧化石墨电极 anti-oxidation graphite electrode
控轧控冷中碳钢 controlled rolled and controlled cooled medium-carbon steel
控制 control, regulating, regulation, governing, manipulation, command, monitoring, guidance ◇ 不加~的 untempered, 不能[难以]~的 incontrollable, 过程中的~【环】in-process control, 可~性 han-

dleability, 人工～ hand control, 无定向[不稳定]～ astatic control

控制按钮 control button (CB)
控制板 control board (CB), control [switch] panel, controlling board
控制棒(核反应堆的) control [absorbing] rod
控制变量 【电】control(led) [manipulated] variable
控制波动[起伏] control fluctuation
控制布料 controlled burden distribution
控制操作 control operation
控制层次 【计】control hierarchy
控制场 controlling field
控制程序功能 【计】function of control program
控制尺寸 control size
控制存储器 control memory [storage]
控制单元 control unit [module]
控制导杆 control-rod guide
控制点 control point [post], point of reference
控制电缆 control cable ◇ 多芯～
控制电流计 control ammeter
控制电路 control [pilot] circuit
控制电压 control voltage
控制电源 control source
控制定时器 control timer
控制阀 control valve (CV), pilot [actuated] valve ◇ 自动输出～
控制阀站 control valve stand
控制范围 controlled area ◇ 超出～【理】excursion
控制方法 control method, controlling means
控制方式 control mode
控制风冷 controlled air cooling
控制改变 【计】control change
控制杆 control rod [lever, arm, stick], regulating rod, 【计】joy stick
控制杆传动机构 control-rod actuator
控制缸 steering cylinder

控制工程 control engineering
控制功率变压器 【电】control power transformaer
控制功能 control function
控制鼓轮 controller drum
控制管 control tube
控制回波[声] control echo
控制回路 control loop [circuit(ry)]
控制机构 control mechanism [gear]
控制激冷 controlled chilling
控制极 control electrode, 【半】gate
控制极并联电容器 gate parallel condenser
控制极触发电路 gate trigger circuit
控制极串联电阻器 gate series resistor
控制极脉冲发生器 gate pulse generator
控制极脉冲放大器 gate pulse amplifier
控制极脉冲抑制 gate pulse suppression
控制级别 【计】control hierarchy
控制寄存器 【计】control register
控制计数器 control counter
控制计算机 control computer
控制继电器 control [pilot, steering] relay
控制继电器盘 control relay panel
控制检验 control test
控制键 【电】control key
控制溅射沉积(法) controlled spray deposition (CSD)
控制截面刮板造型 strickle moulding with gauges
控制界限 control limit
控制介质 control medium, controlling means
控制精度 control precision [accuracy]
控制卷 【计】control volume
控制开关 control switch (CS), pilot switch ◇ 脚踏～ foot operated switch
控制开关盘 control switch-board
控制孔型 【压】control pass
控制块 【计】control block
控制块选择 control block select (CBS)
控制冷却 controlled cooling

控制冷却工艺 controlled cooling technology (CCT)
控制冷却技术 controlled cooling technique (CCT)
控制冷却温度 controlled cooling temperature (CCT)
控制粒度 【选】control size
控制链 control chain
控制论 cybernetics, control theory
控制论分析法 control-theory analysis
控制目标 control goal
控制能力 controllability
控制盘室 control panel room
控制喷雾沉积(法) controlled spray deposition
控制偏心轮 control eccentric
控制屏 control panel
控制器 controller, governor, regulator, manipulator, control box [unit] ◇ 共用 ~ shared control unit, 过和低 ~ *, 机械直接控制型 ~ *, 油压型 ~ *
控制气氛 controlled atmosphere ◇ 通 ~ 的室式炉 curtain-type furnace
控制气氛连续正火(电)炉 continuous controlled-atmosphere (electric) normalizing furnace
控制气氛熔炼 【冶】melting under controlled atmosphere
控制气氛熔炼法 atmosphere melting
控制区段 control section
控制区域 controlled area
控制取样 control sampling
控制绕组 control winding
控制热强度抗裂试验 controlled thermal severity cracking test
控制热强度试验 CTS (controlled thermal severity) test
控制栅极 【电】control grid, guard net
控制筛分 control screening
控制上限 upper control limit (UCL)
控制设备 control equipment [installation], handling facility

控制室 control room (C.R.), control compartment [booth, cabin, cabinet], controlling office, operating house, pulpit
控制手段 control medium
控制数 control number
控制数据 【计】control data
控制数据自动存储器 automatic inspection data accumulator
控制台 control console (CC), console, control desk [platform, pulpit, station, board, booth, post], bench board, operating [operator's, switch] desk, pulpit
控制台打字机 【计】console typewriter (CT/W), console monitor typewriter
控制台调试(程序) console debugging
控制台显示器 console display
控制套 【压】control sleeve
控制特性 control characteristic
控制体系 control architecture
控制通路 control access
控制图 control chart
控制温度 control temperature
控制温度计 control thermometer
控制系数 control coefficient [ratio]
控制系统 control system
控制系统设计 control design
控制线 control line [wire], pilot wire
控制箱 control box [case, casing]
控制项目 control item
控制信号 control [pilot] signal
控制信号盘 tell-tale board
控制旋塞 control cock
控制液压焊接 hydromatic welding
控制液压焊接机 hydromatic welder
控制仪表 control [monitoring, operating] instrument, director
控制因数 controlling [governing] factor
控制元件 control element [component]
控制轧制 control (led) rolling
控制轧制过程 controlled rolling process
控制闸门 control gate
控制站 control station [post]

控制整流器 controlled rectifier
控制只读存储器 【计】control read only memory (CROM)
控制滞后 control hysteresis [lag]
控制中心 control center ◇ 分~ sub-control-centre
控制终端 【计】control terminal
控制轴 control shaft
控制装置 control device [apparatus, assembly, equipment, gear, unit]
控制状态 control state
控制字 【计】control word
控制字段 【计】control field
控制字符 【计】control character
控制总数 control total
控制作用 control action [function]
口径 caliber, calibre, bore
扣齿链 sprocket chain
扣除 deduction, subtraction
扣环 【压】retaining ring
扣紧螺钉 tightening-up screw
扣紧螺母 (同"夹紧螺母")
扣链齿 cocking piece, whelp
扣线滑轮 snatch block
扣箱 fastening down
枯草芽孢杆菌 Bacillus subtilis
苦拔炸药 coopal powder
苦土(氧化镁) magnesia, bitter earth
苦味酸 picronitric [picric] acid
苦味酸浸蚀溶液 【金】picral (etchant)
苦味酸酒精浸蚀液 picric alcohol solution
苦味酸钠 sodium picrate
苦味酸溶液浸蚀 【金】picric etching
苦味酸－硝酸混合浸蚀剂 picric-nitric acid reagent
苦味酸－硝酸酒精溶液浸蚀 【金】picral-nital etch
苦味酸盐 picrate
苦味酸－盐酸混合浸蚀剂 【金】picric-hydrochloric acid reagent
苦盐{$MgSO_4·7H_2O$} bitter salt
库贝克斯(晶粒)双取向硅钢薄板 Cubex

库贝特低温渗硫法 Coubet method
库本德铜焊膏(钢件炉焊用) Cubond
库存 stock, reserve, inventory ◇ 多余~ overstock, 清点[盘查]~【企】inventory-taking
库存材料 stock material
库存成品轧材 【压】stocking
库存程序 【计】library routine
库存量 (stock) inventory, storage
库存量控制 inventory control
库存投资 【企】inventory investment
库尔久莫夫－萨克斯关系 【金】Kurdjumov-Sachs relation
库尔特计数器法 Coulter counter method
库菲尔气焊焊条合金[库菲尔银铜](99Cu,1Ag) Kufil
库里几管 Coolidge tube
库里几钨粉成形法 Coolidge's method
库里几制钨丝法 Coolidge process
库(仑) Coulomb (C)
库仑波函数 Coulomb wave function
库仑滴定 coulometric titration
库仑定律 【理】Coulomb's law
库仑计 (同"电量计")
库仑力 coulombic force
库仑模量 (同"切变模量")
库仑(式)相互作用 Coulomb interaction
库仑势[位] Coulomb's potential
库仑土压力理论 Coulomb's earth pressure theory
库仑楔体(土压)理论 Coulomb's wedge theory
库罗莫尔耐热镍铬合金(85Ni,15Cr) Kuromore
库马纳尔铜锰铝标准电阻合金(88Cu,10Mn,2Al) Kumanal
库米乌姆高导电率铜铬合金(0.5Cr,余量 Cu;作电阻焊的电极用) Kumium
库米亚尔含铝铜镍弹簧合金(1—2.5Al,5.8—13.5Ni,84—92.9Cu) Kumial
库尼阿尔镍铝青铜(8—10Al,3—5.5Ni,3—5.5Fe,1—3Mn,余量 Cu) Cunial

库尼菲尔铜镍铁合金(5 或 10 或 30Ni, 0.5—1Fe, 0.5—1Mn, 余量 Cu) Kunifer alloy
库尼菲尔铜镍铁合金系 Cunifer (Kunifer) alloys
库尼菲铜镍铁永磁合金(20Ni, 20Cu, 余量 Fe) Cunife (alloy), Cunife magnet alloy
库尼科铜镍钴永磁合金(50Cu, 29Co, 21Ni, 余量 Fe) Cunico (alloy)
库尼曼铜镍锰合金(15—20Mn, 9—21Ni, 余量 Cu) Cuniman
库尼西尔铜镍硅高强度合金(1.9Ni, 0.6Si, 余量 Cu) Cunisil
库尼亚尔镍铝铜合金(5—15Ni, 1—2.5Al, 余量 Cu) Kunial
库尼亚尔特种铜镍合金(70Cu, 30Ni) Kunial brasses
库帕洛依可锻铜铬银合金(0.5Cr, 0.1Ag, 99.4Cu) Cupaloy
库珀-休伊特灯 Cooper-Hewitt lamp
库珀笔尖合金(50Pt, 36Ag, 14Cu) Cooper's pen alloy
库珀金代用合金 Cooper's gold
库珀镜用合金(58Cu, 27Sn, 9.5Pt, 3.5Zn, 1.65As) Cooper's mirror alloy
库珀莱特硬质切削合金 Cooperite
库珀偶 【理】Cooper pair
库珀铅基焊料(7—15Sn, 7—9.5Sb, 余量 Pb) Kupper's solder
库普弗尔硅铝明合金(0.8Cu, 13Si, 余量 Al) Kupfersilumin
库普拉利斯铜锂合金(1—10Li) Cupralith
库普拉姆包铅铜 Cupralum
库普拉尼铜镍合金 cupranium
库普龙铜镍合金(45Ni, 55Cu) cupron
库普罗杜尔铜镍硅合金(98.75Cu, 0.75Ni, 0.5Si) Kuprodur
库水硼镁石 kurnakovite
库塔离心萃取器 Coutor extractor
库特恩铜碲合金 Kuttern
库西洛伊硅青铜合金系(1.75—3.0Si, 1—0.3Mn, 余量 Cu) Cusiloy alloys
裤裆管 two legs of breech pipes
夸耳扎尔铝基活塞合金 Quarzal (Quarzal 15: 15Cu, 6Mn, 余量 Al)
夸耳扎尔铝基轴承合金 Quarzal (Quarzal 5: 5Cu, 0—1Fe, 0—1Ni, 0—0.5Ti, 余量 Al)
跨鞍式减径-定径机 straddle type mill
跨步焊法 step-by-step (welding) method
跨导 transconductance, mutual conductance
跨顶火道式焦炉 crossover oven ◇ 考伯斯-贝克~
跨度 span, bay ◇ 高与~比例 depth-span ratio
跨度宽 width of span
跨间 bay, aisle
跨间出渣 rear flushing
跨接 bridge (joint), in-bridge, cross connection
跨接图 bridge diagram
跨接线 【电】jumper (wire, line)
跨界射线 【理】grenz rays
跨径 bay ◇ 计算~effective span
跨距 (width of) span, spacing, track
跨距长度 length of span
跨轮 back gear ◇ 封闭式~encased back gear
跨式齿面淬火 straddle hardening
跨线路的 overline
跨线桥 flyover [dry] bridge, overpass, underbridge, viaduct
跨线栈桥 gantry
跨学科科学 interdisciplinary science
跨学科研究 interdisciplinary study
跨音速流 transonic [mixed] flow
跨越 cross over
跨越桥 flyover bridge
块 block (bk, blk), piece, lump, mass
块标志 【计】blockmark
块度 lumpiness, lump size
块度均匀焦炭 uniformly sized coke,

closely graded coke
块分类 【计】block sort(ing)
块规 block gauge, gauge block ◇ 校对[检验]用~ reference block
块焊接 block welding
块滑石 {$H_2Mg_3Si_4O_{12}$, $3MgO \cdot 4SiO_2 \cdot H_2O$} mica talc, french chalk, steatite
块环链 block chain
块辉锑铅矿 eakinsite
块间空隙 fractional void
块焦 lump coke
块焦间空隙体积 volume of cell space of lump coke
块结构 【金】block structure
块金 nugget
块矿 lump [coarse] ore
块矿炉(炼汞用) 【色】coarse-ore furnace
块磷锂矿 lithiophosphate
块磷铝矿 berlinite
块硫铋银矿 pavonite
块硫锑铅矿 plumosite, yenerite
块煤 lump coal
块名字 【计】block name
块凝物 clot
块钎焊 block brazing
块闪锌矿 schalenblende
块砷铝铜矿 ceruleite
块砷镍矿 aerugite
块石灰 lump lime
块式制动器[块闸] block(ing)[shoe] brake
块体移动 block movement
块铜 copper ingot
块铜矾 stelznerite, arnimite
块铜矿 antlerite, arnimite
块型转变[相变] massive transformation
块渣 lump slag
块状本征锗 bulk intrinsic germanium
块状超导材料 bulk superconducting material
块状带 lump zone
块状的 lumpy, clumpy, massive, cobbed
块状废钢 solid scrap
块状氟铈镧矿 fluocerite
块状硅镁石 {$Mg_3(SiO_4)(OH,F)_2$} norbergite
块状结构的 blocky
块状金属 derby [reguline] metal
块状金属生产 derby metal production
块状炉料 fines free burden
块状马氏体 【金】massive martensite
块状泥料 cake mass
块状氢氧化钠[苛性钠, 烧碱] detached caustic soda
块状熔剂 【冶】lump stone
块状铁合金 briquette ferro alloy
块状铁素体 blocky ferrite
块状物料 lump material
块状物质 cake mass
块状阳极 block anode
块状阳极簇电解槽 【色】cell with packets of block anodes
块状直接还原铁 lump direct reduced iron
块状转变 massive transformation
快动机械压坯[制团]机 quick-acting mechanical briquetting press
快动[快速动作]气力制动器 quick action air brake
快动双效水压机 fast traverse (platen) press
快动水压机 fast cycle hydraulic press
快动油压机 fast cycle oil hydraulic press
快堆 fast reactor
快干瓷釉 cellulose enamel
快干油漆[涂料] quick drying paint
快换模板装置 turn-key pattern equipment
快剪强度 quick shear strength
快剪[快速剪力]试验 quick shear test
快空穴 【半】fast hole
快冷 rapid cooling
快冷槽 quick bath
快冷淬火油 accelerated quenching oil
快冷段[区] fast cool section

快冷室　fast cooling chamber
快料(高炉的)　fast running
快门　shutter, closing device ◇ 照相机~　camera shutter
快凝(的)　quick [fast, rapid] setting, rapid-curing
快凝剂　quick-setting additive
快凝水泥　quick-setting [accelerated, fast-setting, rapid-setting] cement
快凝渣层　fast freezing slag layer
快烧窑　fast-firing kiln
快熟石灰　quick slacking lime
快速安装　quick-setting
快速安装连接管　quick-assembly union
快速保险器　【电】high speed current limiting fuse
快速比色定碳法　【钢】colour carbon
快速测定　rapid determination
快速磁化　flash magnetization
快速淬火　quick-hardening, rapid hardening ◇ 肖塔氧乙炔焰表面~法 shorter process
快速淬火油　【金】fast quenching oil
快速存储器　【计】rapid memory [storage]
快速存取存储器　rapid access memory [storage], quick-access memory [storage]
快速电解除鳞　rapid electrolytic descaling
快速电子　energetic electron
快速镀槽　accelerated bath
快速锻锤　rapid-action hammer
快速煅烧炉　flash calciner
快速断裂　fast fracture, quick break
快速断路[断开]　fast break, quick opening
快速翻译程序　【计】QUICKTRAN
快速反应开关　rapid-respond switch
快速反应停车[机]　rapid response stop
快速访问道　【计】revolver
快速飞剪　snap shears
快速分级淬火用油　fast martempering oils
快速分析　quick [rapid, express] analysis

◇ 熔炼过程~【冶】snap
快速分析法　rapid analysis method
快速风闸　quick action air brake
快速腐蚀　rapid corrosion ◇ RGY~试验法*
快速干燥炉　flash baker
快速公路　express highway
快速过程(脉冲)记录仪　oscillograph
快速焊接　high speed welding, faster welding
快速和慢速连铸法　fast and slow method of casting
快速化学(成分)分析仪　quick chemistry analyzer
快速化验室　express laboratory
快速换辊式精密型材轧机　precise bar mill with rapid roll change
快速换辊装置　【压】roll quick changing rig ◇ 工作辊~*
快速换模　quick die change (QDC)
快速换模压力机　QDC (quick die change) press
快速换型　【铸】quick-change pattern
快速黄化　【压】tigering
快速回转油真空泵　speedivac rotary oil pump
快速混合[搅拌]　flash mixing
快速混合机[器]　positive mixer ◇ 逆流~*
快速混砂机　【铸】speed mixer
快速挤压　high velocity extrusion
快速计数显微镜　flying spot microscope
快速记录示波器　rapid-record oscillograph
快速继电器　high speed relay
快速加热　flash heat
快速加热炉　rapid heating furnace, high speed heating furnace, barrel type furnace (加热管材、焊管坯用, 也称"分段式加热炉") ◇ 无氧化~*
快速加热退火　flash annealing
快速检定　rapid determination
快速搅拌机　speed mixer

快速精整用钢 fast finishing steel
快速开关 【电】high speed switch
快速冷却风机 rapid cooling blower
快速冷却设备［装置］ rapid cooling equipment [installation]
快速磨损 high speed wear
快速凝固 rapid solidification, quick-setting（水泥的）
快速凝固先凝物 rapid solidified precursor
快速疲劳试验 rapid fatigue test ◇ 福蒂亚第～Fotiadi test, 普洛特～Prot test
快速热处理 fast cycle heat treatment
快速热分析 high speed thermal analysis
快速熔解炉 flash calciner
快速烧成 【耐】quick firing
快速烧除 rapid burning-out (RBO), rapid burn-off
快速烧结 flash [rapid] sintering
快速渗氮钢 rapid nitriding steel
快速渗碳法 rapid carburizing [cementation] process ◇ 希默～Shimer process
快速试验［检验］ quick [rapid] test, high speed test
快速探测器 fast detector
快速调整 quick-adjusting, rapid adjustment
快速退火 short(-cycle) annealing
快速退火可锻铸铁 short-cycle malleable iron
快速退火炉 quick anneal oven, short annealing furnace（周期式）
快速显影 high speed development
快速响应 fast [split-second] response ◇ 钢铁成分～工艺*
快速响应热电偶 rapid-response thermocouple
快速响应调节 quick response regulation
快速硝酸定碳法 【钢】colour carbon
快速压力机 fast acting press
快速压缩孔型系统 quick reduction series
快速硬化 （同"快速淬火"）
快速再熔 fast remelt

快速辗砂机 【铸】speed muller
快速蒸发 flash vaporization
快速止动阀 quick action stop valve
快速装配接合 quickfit joint
快速作用的 fast acting
快位错 fast dislocation
快削青铜 free cutting bronze
快行（高炉的） fast running [driving] ◇ 反常～abnormal fast driving
快硬高强度水泥 high early strength cement
快硬混凝土 fast hardening concrete
快硬水泥 quick [rapid] hardening cement, high speed cement
快中子 【理】fast neutron
快中子反应堆 fast neutron reactor
快中子核裂变 fast neutron fission
快中子效应 fast neutron effect
宽板坯 wide slab
宽板试验 wide-plate test ◇ 开缺口的～*
宽板轧机 wide plate mill
宽扁孔型 slabbing pass
宽场目镜 （同"广角目镜"）
宽场内孔窥视仪 （同"广角内孔窥视仪"）
宽带材 wide [board] strip ◇ 连续式～热轧机*
宽带材轧机 wide-strip mill, broad strip mill ◇ 半连续式～*, 中型～medium wide-strip mill
宽带钢 wide flat steel
宽带钢热轧机 hot wide strip mill
宽带式布料器 wide (transfer) belt
宽带式输送机 wide-band conveyer, wide belt coveyer
宽底（钢）轨 wide-bottom flange rail, broad footed rail
宽度 width, breadth
宽度测定 width gauging
宽度计 width gauge
宽度可变结晶器 【钢】variable width

mould
宽度自动检测器 auto-wide detector
宽沸点馏分 wide-boiling cut
宽轨 broad track [gauge], wide gauge
宽轨距 【运】broad gauge
宽轨铁道 wide-gauge track
宽焊道 weave [spreading] bead
宽焊道堆焊 weave beading
宽行打印机 line printer
宽喉的 wide-mouthed
宽厚板轧机 wide plate mill
宽间距多重谱线 【理】wide multiplet
宽角物镜 【理】wide-angle objective
宽口大手套 gauntlet, gloves
宽馏分 long distillate, wide fraction
宽门电路 wide gate
宽面钢齿轮 broad faced steel gear
宽皮带 wide (transfer) belt
宽频带放大器 wide-band amplifier, flat staggered amplifier
宽频带滤波器 wide-band filter
宽射束屏蔽 broad beam shielding
宽台车 extended pallet
宽凸缘的 wide-flanged
宽向摆动法 【焊】cross-weave procedure
宽选通脉冲 wide gate
宽阳极 wide anode
宽腰 T 字钢 high webbed tee iron
宽(翼)缘工字钢(梁)[宽缘工字梁] broad flange (l-) beam, wide-flange beam [girder], wide-flanged joist, wide structural steel I-beam, H beam, H-girder, H-(section) steel, H section, H-iron ◇ 伯利恒 ~ Bethlehem beam, 格雷式 ~ Grey beam
宽音域噪声 broad band noise
宽缘钢梁轧机 wide-flange beam mill
宽缘工字截面(伯利恒宽缘工字截面) Bethlehem section
宽缘梁 broad beam, wide-flange beam
宽缘型钢 universal shape
宽展 【压】(lateral) spread(ing), broadening, broadsiding ◇ 绝对 ~ absolute spread, 强制 ~ restricted spread(ing), 限制 ~ *
宽展比 proportional spread
宽展公式 【压】spread formula
宽展机座 spreading stand, spreader, broadside mill [stand] (用于增大板坯宽度)
宽展量 absolute spread, amount of spread
宽展率 percentage spread
宽展模 spreader die
宽展模型 【压】width-spread model
宽展系数 spread factor, coefficient of spread, spreading coetticient
宽展轧机 broadside mill
宽展轧制 spread [broadside] rolling
宽展作用 spreading effect
筐架 cradle, framework, framing
筐篮式合绳机 planet type closer, planetary closer
筐篮式捻股机 【压】planetary [crank] strander, planetary stranding machine, planet type strander, sun and planet strander, basket type stranding machine
筐篮式捻股机的筐架部分 【压】cage of planetary strander
筐式离心机 basket centrifuge
筐子 【压】basket
框 case, frame, framing, 【计】box
框板 frame [deckle] plate
框盖 frame cover
框格式挡土墙 crib retaining wall
框架 frame (assembly), skeleton frame, chassis, bed plate, stillage
框架结构 skeleton construction [structure], frame construction, 【铁】tower structure ◇ 箱形 ~ *
框架(结构)式压力机 frame ocnstruction press
框架嵌砖建筑 frame and brick veneer construction
框架墙板装配建筑 frame and panel con-

struction
框架式高炉 bracket type blast furnace
框架式搅拌器 gate (type) stirrer
框架[形]水准仪 frame level
框锯 frame [buck] saw
框帽锭(钢锭缺陷) box hat
框式过滤器 frame filter
框式混合[混料,搅拌]器 gate mixer
框式压滤机 frame filter press
框图 block [flow] diagram
框形孔型 flat pass, block scheme
框形帽头缺陷钢锭 box hat ingot
框形芯盒 plain-frame core box, type core box
矿比 【铁】ore ratio
矿仓[槽] ore bin [box], (reef) bin, bunker ◇ 高悬式~ trestle bin, 混匀~ blending bunker, 悬挂式~", 装入~ bunkerage, 锥形~ conical bin
矿仓称量给料器 bin weigh feeder
矿仓系列 bin line
矿仓系统 bin system
矿仓闸门 bin door, ore bin gate
矿仓贮矿 bunkering
矿槽闭锁器 bin gate
矿槽秤 hopper scale
矿槽放矿 bin discharge
矿槽排矿口 bin outlet
矿槽设计[结构] bin design
矿层 ore bed
矿产 mineral product
矿产资源 mineral resources
矿产资源研究中心(美国) Mineral Resources Research Center (M.R.R.C.)
矿巢 【地】nest
矿车 ore wagon, bogie (truck), mine [pit] car, tramcar, tub ◇ 侧卸~ side-dumping hopper, 带棚~ covered car, 底卸~ drop-bottom car, 吊门~ drop-door wagon
矿车翻罐 wagon dumper
矿车轨道 tramway
矿尘 ore [mineral] dust ◇ 悬浮~【采】aerial dust
矿床 (ore) deposit
矿斗 ore bucket
矿堆 stockpile
矿堆浸出 dump leaching, leaching in dumps
矿粉 fine ore, ore [mineral] fines, breeze ◇ 细磨~ ground ore
矿粉仓[槽] breeze bin [bunker]
矿粉产品 ground ore product
矿粉细度 ground ore fineness
矿粉压块 pressing of ore fines
矿工 miner, digger, pitman
矿害 mine pollution
矿化 mineralizing
矿化带 mineralization
矿化度 (degree of) mineralization
矿化剂 mineralizer, mineralizing
矿化系数 coefficient of mineralization
矿化作用 mineralization
矿灰 calx
矿浆 (ore) pulp, slurried ore fines, ore slurry ◇ 稠[浓]~ thickpulp, 稀~ dilute pulp, 载体~ carrier pulp, 自蒸发~ flashing slurry
矿浆槽 pulp cell, slurry tank
矿浆澄清 pulp [slurry, slime] clarification
矿浆池 slurry pond ◇ 集中~"
矿浆处理[输送] slurry handling
矿浆船 slurry transport vessel
矿浆萃取 sludge extraction
矿浆分配器[槽] pulp [slurry] distributor
矿浆分析 pulp-assay
矿浆管道 slurry (pipe)line
矿浆管道总站 pipeline terminal
矿浆回路 slurry circuit
矿浆搅拌槽 raw pulp mixer
矿浆冷却器 slurry cooler
矿浆密度[浓度] pulp density
矿浆密度计 diver
矿浆密度试重法 diver method
矿浆密度指示器 pulp density indicator

矿浆取样　wet pulp sampling
矿浆取样器　pulp samler
矿浆溶剂萃取　【色】solvent extraction in pulp, solvent-in-pulp extraction
矿浆溶剂萃取法　S.I.P. (solvent-in-pulp) extraction [process]
矿浆溶剂萃取设备　solvent-in-pulp apparatus
矿浆输送　slurry transportation
矿浆树脂处理　R.I.P. (resin-in-pulp) treatment
矿浆树脂交换设备　resin-in-pulp apparatus [plant]
矿浆树脂(离子)交换法　resin-in-pulp (process), RIP process
矿浆树脂[矿浆离子交换]提取　resin-in-pulp extraction
矿浆提升机　pulp elevator
矿浆脱水　pulp dewatering
矿浆稀释　pulp dilution
矿浆系统　slurry system [circuit]
矿浆(直接)电解　in-pulp electrolysis
矿浆制备　slurry preparation
矿浆贮槽　pulp holding tank
矿浆状　slurry form
矿焦比　ratio of ore-to-coke, ore/coke (O/C)
矿焦混装　【铁】ore-coke mixed charging, mixed burden charging in BF
矿井　mine, pit, shaft, grube
矿井电缆　shaft [borehole] cable
矿井生产率　shaft efficiency
矿井提升机　mine hoist
矿井瓦斯　damp, mine gas
矿坑　pit
矿坑水　pit water, mine-water
矿坑铁道　mine railway
矿坑通气隔墙　brattice
矿坑照明　mine illumination [lighting]
矿块　nugget, block
矿粒　mineral [ore] particle
矿轮码头　ore-boat wharf

矿脉　【地】vein, lode ore, ledge
矿脉变薄　【地】twitch
矿脉变厚　【地】belly
矿脉断裂　break in lode
矿脉石英　vein quartz
矿棉　mineral cotton [wool], rock wool
矿泥　【选】ore slime [sludge, slurry] ◇ 去~ desludging
矿泥泵　slime pump
矿泥槽　slime [sludge] tank, slack bin
矿泥沉淀　slurry sedimentation
矿泥沉淀池　mud box
矿泥沉淀坑　slime pit
矿泥处理　slime treatment
矿泥处理车间　sludge processing plant
矿泥分离器　slime separator, sludge filtration plant, sludge remover
矿泥分析　slime analysis
矿泥浸出　slime leaching
矿泥流槽　slime launder
矿泥凝固　consolidation of slimes
矿泥排出管道　slime drain line
矿泥筛(分机)　sludge [slurry] screen
矿泥水流程[循环]　washer(y)-water circuit
矿泥提取器　sludge extractor
矿泥絮凝剂　slime flocculant
矿泥摇床　slimer
矿泥再利用　slurry reuse
矿泥重量校正　slurry deduction
矿泥贮槽　slurry [surge] sump
矿桥　【铁】ore (stocking) bridge
矿区　mining area, diggings
矿热电炉　smelting electric furnace, submerged-arc furnace, electric shaft furnace
矿热电炉蒸馏　smelting electric furnace distillation
矿砂　(ore) sand ◇ 未溶解~ undigested sand
矿砂分级机　sand classifier
矿山　mine, diggings, colliery
矿山安全卫生署(美国)　Mine Safety and

Health Administration (MSHA)
矿山安全研究试验所　Safety in Mines Research and Testing Branch (S.M.R.T.B.)
矿山安全研究委员会(英国)　Safety in Mines Research Board (S.M.R.B.)
矿山安全研究院(英国)　Safety in Mines Research Establishment (S.M.R.E.)
矿山工程　mine engineering
矿山公司[企业]　mining venture
矿山机电工程师协会(英国)　Association of Mining Electrical and Mechanical Engineers (AMEME)
矿山机械厂　mining machinery plant
矿山控制站　mine control station (M.C.S.)
矿山平巷　mine tunnel
矿山设备　mining equipment
矿山实验站(美国)　Mines Experiment Station
矿山酸性废水　【环】acid mine drainage (AMD)
矿山铁道　mine railway
矿山污染　mine pollution
矿山用钢丝绳　wire rope for mine
矿山转臂起重机　M.Drk (mine derrick)
矿石　ore　(mass, material)　◇ 拌酸[用酸拌和的]～acid-pugged ore, 不可处理[无使用价值]～ non-treatable ore, 采准～ blocked out ore, 待选～ concentrating ore, 等外～(手选的) dradge, 低品位～ low grade ore (LGO), 高品位～ high grade ore, 工业[可采]～pay dirt, 供冶炼用的～ shipping ore, 含氧化物～ oxide-bearing ore, 混匀～*, 极贫[贫化]～ halvans, 浸染～ dis-seminated ore, 乱～ matrix, 难造[成]球～*, 排出～ ore blowout, 熔剂性～ fluxing ore, 弱磁性～ feebly magnetic (ore), 生[未焙烧]～ unroasted ore, 双合～ binary ore, 新采～ fresh ore, 易选～ free milling ore, 预处理过的～ pretreated ore, 原[未选]～*, 整

粒[分级,过筛]～sized ore
矿石焙烧　ore roasting, calcining of ore
矿石焙烧炉　ore roastor
矿石焙烧窑　ore roasting kiln
矿石焙烧装置　ore-roasting plant
矿石边界品位　limiting grade of ore
矿石衬里梯级溜槽　stone box step type chute
矿石衬料　self-lining
矿石处理　ore-processing, ore dressing
矿石单体分离　【选】ore-grain release
矿石堆(放)场　raw ore stockyard, ore yard, [采]ore-blending plant
矿石法　【钢】ore process
矿石沸腾　【钢】ore boil, oreing
矿石分级　classification [sizing] of ore
矿石分解法　ore breakdown [opening] process
矿石分类　ore conditioning, sizing of ore (按粒度分类)
矿石分配器　ore distributor
矿石分析　ore analysis
矿石富选装置　ore-beneficiation [-dressing] plant
矿石干燥工段　【选】ore-drying plant
矿石化学成分　ore analysis
矿石化验　ore assay(ing)
矿石还原　[冶]ore reduction, reduction of ore
矿石还原难易程度　ease of reduction of ore
矿石回采　ore extraction
矿石混合料　ore mixture
矿石极限等级　limiting grade of ore
矿石加工　ore preparation
矿石加工厂　ore improvement plant
矿石加料机　ore feeder
矿石拣选　ore sorting
矿石浸出　ore leaching
矿石浸出液　ore leach liquor
矿石可选特征　ore preparation character-

矿石料　【冶】ore charge ◇ 净～ straight ore burden
矿石料槽[筐]　ore pocket
矿石料批量　ore charge weight
矿石料上料系统　【铁】iron-bearing system
矿石磨碎　grinding of ores
矿石排出量　ore blowout
矿石配料　ore burden(ing)[proportioning]
矿石批料　batch of ore
矿石品位　ore grade ◇ 入炉～ charge(ore) grade
矿石破碎　ore crushing[reduction]
矿石破碎机　ore crusher
矿石铺底　ore-bedding
矿石铺底烧结法　ore hearth layer sintering
矿石取样　ore sampling
矿石熔炼炉　ore-smelting furnace
矿石溶浸　ore leaching
矿石烧结　ore sintering
矿石烧结机　ore-sintering machine
矿石-食盐混合物　ore-salt mixture
矿石试样　ore sample
矿石手选带　sorting[inspection] belt
矿石碎块　knockings
矿石特性　ore property, character of ore
矿石添加剂[料]　(feed) ore addition
矿石洗选　ore dressing by washing
矿石洗选厂　ore-washing plant
矿石卸船机　ore-boat unloader
矿石预处理　beneficiation
矿石原料　ore material
矿石运出量　ore shipment
矿石整粒　sizing of ore
矿石中和[混匀]　【铁】(ore) blend(ing),(ore-)bedding ◇ 罗宾斯-麦西特～系统*
矿石中和作业　bedding practice
矿石中韧化[可锻化](处理)　malleablization in ore
矿石种类　brand of ore
矿石抓运起重机　【采】ore bucket handling crane
矿石转运机　ore(-handling) bridge
矿石转载机　ore gantry
矿石装卸机线路　ore-bridge track
矿石装卸机支架　【铁】ore bridge pier
矿石准备　ore preparation[conditioning]
矿石准备工段　【选】ore-conditioning plant
矿体　(ore) body, ore[mineral] mass
矿物　mineral (Min., min.) ◇ 成酸～ acid-forming mineral, 副产～ by-product mineral, 耗酸～ acid-consuming mineral, 难熔炼[难处理]～ refractory mineral, 似[类]～ mineralloid, 酸性～ acid mineral, 有用～ ore material
矿物白{$CaSO_4 \cdot 2H_2O$}　mineral white
矿物成分[组成,组分]　mineral(ogical) composition[constituent]
矿物(发光)灯　mineralight lamp
矿物肥料　mineral fertilizer
矿物分类　classification of minerals
矿物分离　minerals separation (M-S)
矿物分析　mineral(ogical) analysis ◇ 坩埚～ crucible assay
矿物刚玉　mineral corundum
矿物共生(体)　mineral association[paragenesis]
矿物含量　mineral content
矿物化学　mineralogical chemistry
矿物夹杂含量(煤的)　dirt content
矿物加工　mineral processing (M.P.)
矿物键　mineral bridging
矿物结构　mineral constitution, mineralogical structure
矿物浸出　mineral leaching
矿物矿石　mineral ore
矿物滤器　mineral filter
矿物燃料　mineral[fossil] fuel
矿物树脂　mineral resin
矿物特性　mineral characteristics, mineralogical character

矿物提取　mineral extraction
矿物添加物　mineral additive
矿物填料　mineral filler
矿物涂料[涂层]　mineral coating
矿物相　mineralogical phase
矿物型焊条　mineral-coated electrode
矿物学　mineralogy
矿物学标度硬度值　mineralogical hardness number
矿物油　mineral oil
矿物值含量　content of mineral value
矿物质　mineral matter [substance] ◇ 去除~ demineralization, 去除~装置 demineralizer
矿物转化　mineral transformation
矿物资源　mineral resources
矿物组成鉴定　mineralogical characterization
矿务局(美国)　Bureau of Mines (B. of M.)
矿相法　mineragraphic method
矿相结构　mineralogical structure
矿相学　mineralography, mineragraphy
矿屑　attle
矿样　ore sample
矿冶学会(英国)　Institution of Mining & Metallurgy (IMM)
矿冶学会会员　Member of the Institute of Mining and Metallurgy (M.I.M.M.)
矿冶学院　Institute of Mining and Metallurgy
矿业　mining industry
矿业研究院(英国)　Mining Research Establishment (M.R.E.)
矿渣　slag, incrustation, mineral waste residue ◇ 水泥用~ cement slag
矿渣分离　slag separation
矿渣骨料　cinder aggregate
矿渣骨料混凝土　clinker concrete
矿渣硅酸盐水泥　portland-slag cement, slag portland cement, clinker-bearing slag cement
矿渣混凝土　slag concrete
矿渣坑　【冶】sludge pit
矿渣硫酸盐水泥　slag-sulphate cement
矿渣密封[封闭]　slag-sealing
矿渣棉　silicate [mineral] cotton, slag [mineral] wool
矿渣砂　【建】slag sand
矿渣生铁　【铁】cinder pig
矿渣石膏隔墙　slag-alabaster partition
矿渣水泥　(portland-) slag [iron-ore, metallic] cement, blast (furnace) cement ◇ 富硫酸盐~*, 石膏~ slag-sulphate cement
矿渣丝[绒]　mineral wool
矿脂　mineral butter [jelly], petrolatum
矿质焦油　mineral tar
矿质污泥　mineral sludge
矿种名称　grade name
矿柱　ore column
亏格　【数】genus (复数 genera)
亏空　deficit
亏料线(高炉的)　stockline
亏损　loss, deficit, decrement ◇ 资本盈余与~*
窥孔砖　sight hole brick
窥视玻璃　observation glass
窥(视)孔　(peep) sight, peep (hole), access [periscope] hole, watch window, sight-hole, wicket
奎因锡锑焊料　Queen's metal
馈电　(power) feed(ing), supply ◇ 并联~ shunt feed
馈电电抗器　feed reactor
馈电电压降　feed drop
馈电电缆　feed(er) [power] cable
馈电点阻抗　feedpoint impedance
馈电干线　feed(er) [supply] main
馈电盘　feeder panel
馈电速度　feed speed
馈电系统　feed [transmission] system
馈电线　feeder (line), transmission [supply] line ◇ 定向天线~ beam aerial feed-

er,铝制~ aluminium feeder
馈电箱　feeder box
馈给控制　feed control
馈给调节器　feed governor
溃决　bursting
溃散　collapse, crumbling
溃散性　（同"压溃性"）
溃通　feed through
昆塔斯绕线机　Quintus wire-winding machine
醌(构)型　quinoid (character)
捆　bale (BL), bind, bunch, package (pkg), tying, truss up ◇ 一~ truss
捆包设备　packing equipment
捆柴排机　choker
捆紧　strapping
捆卷　wrap round
捆卷机　【压】coil strapping machine
捆头(钢丝绳的)　seizing end
捆箱机用软钢丝　box binding wire
捆箱机用硬钢丝　box stapling wire
捆扎　strapping, tie up, tying, seizing, banding ◇ 自动~*
捆扎机　bale tie machine, tying [binding] machine ◇ 径向~(卷材的) radial bander, 盘条[线卷,线盘]~*, 沿周边~(卷材的) circumferential bander
捆扎用带材　【压】tie band
捆扎用(软)钢丝　baling [binding] wire, binders
困料室　【耐】ageing chamber
困泥　【耐】souring, ageing
困泥坑　soak pit
困泥室　sump house
括号　brackets, parenthesis ◇ 大[花]~【数】brace, 方括号 brackets, 圆括号 parenthesis
扩程电阻　swamping resistance
扩程器　【理】multiplier
扩充　enlarge, spread, augmenting, extension
扩充操作码　augmented operation code

扩充寄存器　【计】extension register
扩充率　expansion rate
扩充性　expandability
扩大　expanding, expansion, enlarge(ment), broadening, widening ◇ 按比例~ scale-up
扩大 α 相区　expanded alpha field
扩大部分　【铸】enlargement
扩大的 γ 相区　（同"开放的 γ 相区"）
扩大规模　upscaling, scaling-up
扩大绘图器　diagraph
扩大镜　magnascope, magnifying glass
扩大能力　expanded capacity
扩大器　expander, aggrandizer
扩大生产(能力)　expansion of production capacity, expanded capacity
扩大试验　extended test
扩大再生产　expand reproduction, breeding (核燃料的)
扩底桩　pedestal [club-footed] pile
扩管机　(pipe) expanding mill [machine], (tube) expander ◇ 滚压~ rolary expander, 机械~ mechanical expander, 热~*, 水力~ hydraulic expander, 斜轧式~*
扩管器　tube expander
扩管试验　enlarge [expanding] test ◇ 销钉~*
扩管压力机　tube expanding press
扩建　expanding, expansion, extension ◇ 全面~*【建】general extension
扩建部分　enlargement, addition
扩建计划[规划]　expansion plan [schedule]
扩建系列　expansion line
扩径　expansion, draw(ing) ◇ 穿孔毛坯在芯棒上~【压】saddling
扩径锻造　enlarging forging
扩径对接　bell butt joint
扩径机　【压】expanding [repiercing] mill, expanding machine ◇ 蘑菇形轧辊的管材~ rotary-rolling mill, 斜轧~ plug ex-

扩径芯棒　expanding mandrel
扩径轧制的　rotary rolled
扩孔　reaming, expand, broach 【压】drifting（锻造的）
扩孔冲头　【压】drift
扩孔锻造　enlarging forging, becking
扩孔锻造用心轴　expanding bar
扩孔机　ring-rolling machine
扩孔器　【压】expander, reamer
扩孔试验　bore expand test
扩孔弯边　【压】burring
扩孔钻　expanding auger (driller)
扩口　【压】flaring, bulging
扩口管　flared tube
扩口模　expanding die
扩口试验（管材的）　flaring [expand] test
扩口芯棒　expanding mandrel
扩量程电阻　swamping resistance
扩容改造（高炉的）　technical modernization with capacity expansion
扩散　diffuse, diffusing, diffusion, diffuseness, dispersal, dispersion, dissemination, scattering ◇ 闭管～*, 不[非]～的*, 反（行）～ back diffusion, 各向不均～ anisotropic diffusion, 与缺陷相关的～ defect associated diffusion, 体积～ bulk diffusion, 无～合作运动, 向内～ indiffusion, 沿晶体～ short circuit diffusion, 掩蔽～ masked diffusion
扩散饱和　diffusion saturation
扩散背景[本底]分析　diffuse background analysis
扩散本底　diffuse background
扩散本底分布　（同"散射本底分布"）
扩散泵　diffusion pump ◇ 迪努耶尔两级～*, 多喷嘴～ multiple-nozzle pump, 发散喷嘴～ divergent-nozzle pump, 盖德～*, 汞(气)～ mercury vapour pump, 霍氏七喷嘴～ Ho's 7-nozzle pump, 克雷姆佩雷尔高速玻璃～*, 兰米尔～*, 喷油增压～*, (真空)水银～ mercury diffusion pump
扩散边界层　diffusion boundary layer
扩散标记　diffuse indications
扩散层　diffuse [diffusion] layer
扩散产物　diffusate
扩散场　【环】diffusion field
扩散常化　diffusion normalizing
扩散常数　diffusion constant
扩散长度[范围]　diffusion length
扩散处理　diffusion treatment
扩散传递　diffusional transfer
扩散带　diffusion zone
扩散的统计性质　statistical nature of diffusion
扩散电流　diffusion current
扩散电势[位]　diffusion potential
扩散电阻　diffused resistor
扩散定律　diffusion [scattering] law ◇ 一般～*
扩散镀层[镀覆]　diffusion plating [coating]
扩散镀铬　chromising, chromizing
扩散镀金属法　cementation metallization
扩散镀锌　coronizing
扩散镀锌法　sherardising
扩散镀硬铬　hard chromizing
扩散对　diffusion couple
扩散法　diffusion method
扩散反射　（同"漫反射"）
扩散反射面　（同"漫射反射面"）
扩散反应　diffusion reaction
扩散反应硬化　【金】diffusion-reaction hardening
扩散方程(式)　diffusion equation
扩散分析　diffusion analysis
扩散过程　diffusion process
扩散焊接　diffusion welding
扩散合金粉　diffusion alloyed powder
扩散合金化　diffusion alloying
扩散合金化黄铜粉　diffusion-alloyed brass powder
扩散换位机理　place exchange mechanism

of diffusion
扩散火焰装置　diffusion flame system
扩散机理　diffusion mechanism
扩散极限　limit of diffusion
扩散剂　【半】diffusant
扩散键　diffusion bond
扩散结　【半】diffused [diffusion] junction
扩散结构　diffused structure
扩散结合　【冶】diffusion bonding
扩散介质　diffusion medium
扩散颈缩　【压】diffuse necking
扩散净化　purification by diffusion
扩散距离　diffusion distance [length]
扩散孔隙[疏松]（缺陷）　diffusion porosity
扩散控制生长　【金】diffusion controlled growth
扩散控制转变　【金】diffusion controlled transformation
扩散冷却　diffusion cooling
扩散理论　diffusion theory, theory of diffusion ◇ 回复～
扩散连接[键合]　diffusion bonding
扩散流　diffusion flow
扩散流量　diffusion flux
扩散炉　diffusion [diffusive] furnace
扩散率　diffusivity, diffusion rate, diffusibleness
扩散面积　diffusion area
扩散能力　diffusibility
扩散黏结　【冶】diffusion bonding
扩散喷射泵　diffusion ejector pump
扩散期（渗碳过程的）　diffusion cycle
扩散器　diffuser, diffusor, diffusion cell, bubbler
扩散器叶栅　diffuse grid
扩散氢　diffusible hydrogen
扩散区　diffusion zone [region]
扩散热　diffusion heat
扩散蠕变　diffusion(al) creep
扩散烧结　diffusion sintering
扩散烧结合金　diffusion-sintered alloy

扩散烧结合金粉坯　diffusion-sintered alloy powder
扩散渗氮（用氰化钾盐浴）　tufftride
扩散渗镀　peen plating ◇ 气相～ vapour plating
扩散渗铬　chromium impregnation ◇ 液体介质中～ liquid chromizing, 预先氮化件～ pink-phase chromizing
扩散渗硅（处理法）　siliconizing, ihrigising, ihrigizing ◇ 伊利格～【金】Ihrig method [process]
扩散渗硅处理的低碳钢　ihrigized iron
扩散渗锌　zinc impregnation
扩散渗锌炉　sherardising furnace
扩散势垒　diffusion barrier
扩散速率　diffusion rate, rate of diffusion
扩散特征曲线　【理】indicatrix of diffusion
扩散梯度　diffusion gradient
扩散通量　diffusion flux
扩散途径[途程]　diffusion path
扩散涂层　diffusion coating
扩散退火　diffusion anealing, homogenization, homogenizing (annealing) ◇ 锌镀层～处理 galvannealing
扩散脱氧　【钢】diffusion deoxidation, deoxidation by diffusion
扩散物质　diffusate
扩散系数　diffusion coefficient, diffusion factor, diffusivity (coefficient)
扩散现象　diffusion phenomena
扩散限制凝聚　diffusion limited aggregation
扩散效应　diffusing effect
扩散型　【理】diffusion type ◇ 非～ diffusionless
扩散型烧结矿　【铁】diffusion type sintered ore
扩散（型）相变　diffusion transformation
扩散性　diffusibility, diffusibleness, diffusivity
扩散压力　diffusion pressure
扩散氧化物　subscale

扩散硬化　diffusion hardening
扩散元素　diffusing element
扩散源　diffusion source
扩散杂质　diffusion impurity
扩散障碍层　diffusion barrier
扩散真空泵　diffusion pump
扩散蒸发　diffusive evaporation
扩散正火　diffusion normalizing
扩散致颈缩　【压】diffuse necking
扩散中标志物移动[位移]（克肯达耳效应）　【理】marker shift in diffusion
扩散转移　diffusional transfer
扩散阻力　diffusional resistance [resistivity]
扩砂　【铸】rap(ping)
扩缩性　scalability
扩展　expand, extend, spread, developing, development, propagation, widening
扩展长度　propagation length
扩展点阵参数　expanded lattice parameter
扩展电路　expanded circuit, expander
扩展角　spread angle ◇ 射束~
扩展量　amount of spread
扩展裂纹　running crack
扩展皿　【化】developing dish
扩展能　propagation energy
扩展器　expander
扩展热　spreading heat
扩展时间　developing time
扩展(式)基础　extended [spread] foundation
扩展位错　extended dislocation
扩展线　broadened line
扩张　expand, expansion, extension, enlarge, extend
扩张力　extending force
扩张式绞刀　expansion reamer
扩张(式)离合器　expanding clutch
扩张凸轮　expansion cam
扩张型喷嘴口　diverging nozzle bore
阔边刨(斜口的)　badger

L l

垃圾处理[焚化]厂 【环】destructor plant
垃圾焚化炉 garbage furnace
垃圾填埋(场) 【环】sanitary landfill
拉 draw(ing), pull, haul
拉拔 【压】draw(ing), drag, draft ◇ Y型三辊辊模~*, 超高压缩[压下]量~*, 粗[第一道]~ first draught drawing, 二次~ two holed, 反拉力~ reactive drawing, 反[后]张力~*, 干法~ dry drawing, 高温~*, 光亮~ bright drawing, 辊式模~ roller die drawing, 过~的 overdrawn, 活动芯棒~ moving-mandrel drawing, 可~性 drawability, 可变形芯棒~*, 拉床~ bench drawing, 连续[多次]~ continuous drawing, 毛面~ mat(te) drawing, 强制润滑~*, 湿法~ wet drawing, 细丝~ fine drawing, 一次~ one holed, 再次~ redraw(ing), 皂粉(润滑)~ dry soap drawing
拉拔车间 drawing shop
拉拔成形 draw forming
拉拔次序 drawing sequence
拉拔道次 drawing passes
拉拔道次与中间退火流程图 pass-and-reheating schedule
拉拔工 drawer, draftsman
拉拔工具 drawing tool [device]
拉拔机 (cold) draw(ing) bench, bench, drawing machine, motobloc ◇ 齿条式~*, 串列式(多次)~ tandem-drawing machine, 单链式~*, 单模~ single-die drawbench, 多次~*, 多线式~*, 鼓式~ drum-type drawbench, 链[张力]式~*, 强迫送料的~ push pointer bench, 三列式~ triple drawbench, 双链式~*, 双线式~ double-rod drawbench, 细丝湿~*, 液压~ hydraulic drawbench
拉拔机机头 draw head
拉拔机机座 drawbench bed
拉拔机链条 drawbench chain
拉拔机生产法 drawbench process
拉拔机小车 draw carriage, wagon of drawbench
拉拔机小车车头 carriage head
拉拔机小车返回速度 draw carriage return speed
拉拔机小车夹钳 drawbench jaws
拉拔力 die pull (美), drawing pull (英), block pull, drawing force, pulling capacity, drawing load
拉拔裂纹 draw crack
拉拔模 drawing die ◇ 管材~ tube-drawing die, 组合四辊式异型~ turks head die
拉拔模孔 drawing hole
拉拔钳 drawtongs, drawvice
拉拔润滑脂 drawing grease
拉拔时效硬化 stew(ing)
拉拔速度 drawing speed [velocity]
拉拔头[小车] draw(ing) head, carriage
拉拔小车钩子 draw-head hook
拉拔斜度 【铸】draft, draught
拉拔压力 drawing pressure
拉拔压力机 drawing press ◇ 凸轮式~*
拉拔应力 drawing stress
拉拔用乳剂 (wire-)drawing compounds
拉拔装置 draw-off gear
拉拔总变形量 total drawing deformetion
拉拔作用 drawing effect
拉板[模] drawplate
拉板[活底]炉 drawplate oven
拉槽(孔)压力机 【压】broaching press
拉铲 pull shovel [scraper]
拉铲挖土[挖掘]机 dragline
拉长 elongation, traction
拉长状夹渣物 【金】drawn-out slag streaks
拉出 withdrawal, withdrawing, pull [drag] out
拉出辊 pull-out rolls
拉出机构 pullback mechanism

拉出式坩埚炉　pullout-type crucible furnace
拉出装置　drawing-out device, pull-through machine, puller, 【连铸】withdrawal device [unit]
拉床　broach(ing) machine, broacher, 【压】(cold) draw(ing) bench, drawing mill, bench, motobloc ◇ 绳索式～rope draw-bench
拉床拉拔　bench drawing
拉床拉拔硬化　bench hardening
拉单晶　【半】(single) crystal-pulling
拉单晶法[技术]　single crystal pulling process [technique] ◇ 基罗波罗斯～*, 丘克拉尔斯基～*, 韦纳伊～*
拉单晶机　puller
拉刀　broach ◇ 组合～combined broach, 准削～sizing broach, 整体～solid broach
拉单晶炉　(crystal-)pulling furnace
拉丁锌铜合金　Lattens
拉断　breakage, burst(ing), ingot puller
拉分轧制　pull-separated rolling ◇ 辊楔～*
拉弗里希尔软黄铜(1Sn, 61Cu, 38Zn)　Laveyssiere bronze
拉弗纳尔高纯铝(99.99Al)　Raffinal
拉弗斯相区　Laves phase field
拉杆　draw bar, (pull, nutted) rod, tie-rod, tension bar [rod, member], stay rod (电工用), balance beam (固定绝缘子串用), 【铁】(风口的) shackle [adjust(ing)] bolt, 【机】draft, draught
拉杆机构　drag-link mechanism
拉杆螺栓　staybolt
拉杆牵力　drawbar pull
拉格尔斯－库尔思式两级玻璃水银扩散泵　Ruggles-Kurth two-stage glass pump
拉格朗日密度　Lagrangian density
拉钩　draw(bar) [drag] hook
拉管机　tube drawbench, tube-drawing machine ◇ 三线式～triple tube draw-bench

拉管卷筒　tube block
拉管压力机　tube draw press
拉光　bright drawing
拉光钢　bright-draw steel
拉辊　carry-over pinch roll, 【连铸】withdrawing roll ◇ 电动～*
拉辊操作平台　withdrawal roll platform
拉辊传动　withdrawal-roll drive
拉辊机座　withdrawal-roll set
拉辊矫直装置　withdrawal and straightening unit
拉辊装置　withdrawal-roll facility
拉过连续退火炉(钢丝的)　pull-through type furnace
拉过式三次弯曲除[破]鳞机　(pull-through type) triple scale breaker
拉过式纵剪　pull-type slitter
拉簧　tension [draw, drag] spring
拉剪　draw cut
拉矫　stretcher levelling, stretcher-straightening
拉矫机　tension leveller, withdrawal straightening machine ◇ 自同步连续矫直～*
拉矫机组　【连铸】withdrawal straightening stands
拉紧　straining, tensioning
拉紧杆　spanner bar
拉紧绝缘子　tension insulator
拉紧力　pull-up
拉紧链轮　tensioning sprocket
拉紧螺杆　stretching screw, turnbuckle device
拉紧螺栓　tension [pinch, shackle, tightening, draw-in] bolt, 【铸】drag bolt(下型箱的) ◇ 锥形～wedge bolt
拉紧楔子　tension wedge
拉紧咬送(曳料)辊　drag pinch rolls
拉紧装置　(同"张紧装置")
拉晶　【半】crystal pulling, pulled crystal ◇ 磁力～法*, 轨道自旋式～法*, 水平～技术*, 台基[基座]～法*

拉晶操作　pulling operation
拉晶法　pull(ing) method
拉晶杆[机]　crystal puller
拉晶速率　pulling rate
拉拉康铜(45Cu,55Ni)　Lala
拉力　tension（force, capacity）, draft, draught, draw, pull(-up), pulling(force), tensile force
拉力测力传感器　tensile load cell
拉力测力计　tension dynamometer
拉力脆性　tension brittleness
拉力负载　tension load
拉力杆　tension rod [bar]
拉力钢筋　tension reinforcement
拉力构件　tension rod, tensometer
拉力计　tension gauge [meter], tensile [strain] gauge, tens(i)ometer
拉力减径机　（同"张力减径机"）
拉力强度　intensity of tension
拉力试验　tensile [tension, pull] test ◇ 静态～static tension test, 全焊金属焊缝～*
拉力试验机　tensile [tension] tester, lacerating machine
拉力(试验)试样　tensile test sample [piece], tension test piece
拉力芯棒　pull mandrel
拉力芯棒轧制　pull mandrel rolling
拉力轴　axis of tension
拉链　haulage [hauling] chain, zip fasteners, zipper ◇ 电缆～cable drag chain
拉链刮板输送机　chain scraper bar conveyer
拉链起重机[吊车]　chain hoist
拉料辊　pull-out roll ◇ 炉内～furnace pull out roll
拉料张紧辊　pulling bridle roll
拉裂　【冶】(锭面缺陷) pulling, restriction crack, 【铸】pull crack
拉漏　【连铸】breakout, bleed out
拉漏预报　predicting breaking out
拉马各尔镁铝耐火材料(约含60MgO, 40Al$_2$O$_3$)　Lamagol
拉梅特碳化钽(烧结)硬质合金　Ramet (alloy)
拉门　sliding door [gate] ◇ 同开双～biparting door
拉明纳克聚酯树脂　Laminac
拉模　【压】draw(ing) die (DWDI), draw(ing) block, die ◇ 衬碳化物[硬质合金]的～carbide-lined drawing die, 成套～die set, 放射型～*, 弧形～*, 流线型～radiused die, 磨损～磨光 die ripping
拉模板　draw(ing) [die] plate, draw(ing) [die] block, wire-drawing block, drawing-out frame, block for drawing
拉模材料　die material
拉模重磨　die ripping
拉模出口喇叭口　die relief
拉模打孔机　die driller
拉模定径带直径　bearing diameter of die, throat diameter
拉模定径区长度　land length of die
拉模工作[压缩]带　reduction zone, approach of die
拉模工作锥体锥角　drawing taper
拉模管孔入口　tube entering
拉模盒　die box ◇ 强制加油～pressure die box, 旋转式～rotary die box
拉模划痕　die score [scratch, mark]
拉模加工机　die processing unit
拉模架　drawing-out frame, die stand
拉模孔　drawhole, drawing pass, die hole ◇ 检查钻石～几何形状用显微镜 diamond die microscope, 钻(金刚石)～die drilling
拉模孔壁磨损圈　【压】die drawing ring
拉模孔定径带　die bearing
拉模孔圆柱形部分　die parallel
拉模拉拔　die drawing
拉模坯　die block
拉模嵌入件　die insert
拉模入口锥　die entrance [bell]
拉模压力　die pressure

拉模圆柱部分　drawing cylinder
拉模钻孔　die piercing
拉模座　die stand
拉姆斯登(正型)目镜　Ramsden eyepiece [ocular]
拉尼合金催化剂　Raney catalyser
拉尼铝镍合金(30Ni,余量 Al)　Raney's alloy
拉尼镍合金催化剂(含 42Ni)　Raney nickel catalyst
拉坯　【连铸】billet withdrawal ◇ 连续～过程*
拉坯方向　【连铸】casting direction
拉坯辊　pulling roll
拉坯机构　casting-withdrawal mechanism
拉坯矫直机　withdrawal straightening machine ◇ 六辊～(连铸机的) six-roll set
拉坯曲线　withdrawal curve
拉坯速度　withdrawing [drawing, casting] speed
拉坯系统　withdrawal system
拉坯阻力增大　build up of resistance to stripping
拉普拉斯变换　Laplace('s) transformation
拉普拉斯方程(式)　Laplace('s) equation
拉普拉斯拉应力　Laplace tension stress
拉普拉斯应力　Laplace stress
拉钳　draw vice
拉切　pull-cut, draw cut
拉切式焊缝清理机　draw-cut trimmer
拉森-米勒参数　【理】Larson-Miller parameters
拉森式钢板桩　Larssen's sheet piling
拉舍特异形高炉　Raschette furnace
拉伸　draw(ing), stretch(ing), tensile elongation, tension ◇ 固定[短]芯棒～*,减径[无芯头]～【压】hollow sinking, 可～性*, 小量[轻微]～ shallow draught (ing), 展薄～【压】ironing, 轴对称～ axissymmetric drawing
拉伸比　stretch ratio
拉伸变形　tensile deformation [strain], stretching strain ◇ 临界～critical elongation
拉伸成形　stretch [wrap] forming
拉伸成形机　stretch former [forming machine]
拉伸冲击应力　tensile impact stress
拉伸断裂　tensile fracture [failure, break], tension fracture
拉伸范性变形　tensile plastic strain
拉伸工具　stretching tool
拉伸辊机座　【连铸】set of withdrawal rolls
拉伸滑架(压力机的)　extracting carriage
拉伸加捻机　drawn-twist machine
拉伸机　drawbench, drawing mill ◇ 粗～*, 单向多头～*, 滑动式～ slip drawing machine, 无滑动～*
拉伸剪切试验　tensile shear(ing) test
拉伸剪切试验试样　【焊】tension shear test specimen
拉伸矫平机　stretch flattener ◇ 板材～ sheet stretcher
拉伸矫正机　stretching machine ◇ 型材～*
拉伸矫直　【压】stretcher-straightening, stretch rolling [level-ling], patent level(l)ing ◇ 可控～*
拉伸矫直机　stretcher (machine, leveller), tension straightening machine, stretching machine ◇ 钢管～*, 液压～*, 在～上矫直(薄板) stretcher flattening
拉伸拘束度　tensile restraint
拉伸拘束抗裂试验　tensile restraint cracking test
拉伸力　block pull, die pull(美), drawing pull(英)
拉伸耐久性试验　endurance tension test
拉伸配模计算　drawing (sequence) calculation
拉伸疲劳试验　tensile fatigue test, endurance tension test

拉伸破坏 tensile failure
拉伸强度 tensile strength
拉伸强度试验机 tensile (strength) testing machine
拉伸区域 【压】tensile region
拉伸曲线 tensile curve
拉伸屈服 tensile yield
拉伸屈服点 tensile yield point
拉伸屈服极限 tensile yield limit
拉伸屈服应力 tensile yield stress
拉伸蠕变 tensile creep ◇ 恒定应力～*
拉伸蠕变实验 tensile creep test
拉伸伸长 stretch elongation
拉伸式刮板 【铸】drawing strickle
拉伸试棒 tensile test bar [specimen] ◇ 端头带丝扣的～ specimen with threaded ends, 端头座肩式～ specimen with shouldered end
拉伸试验 tensile [pulling, elongation] test ◇ U形试样点焊～*, 长时～ long-time tensile test
拉伸试验机 tensile (strength) testing machine, tensile machine, pull test machine
拉伸试验夹头(试样的) tension shackle
拉伸(试验)试样 tensile (test) sample [specimen, piece] ◇ 单侧缺口～*, 紧凑～*, 中心缺口板材～*
拉伸试验性能 tension test properties
拉伸速度 tension speed
拉伸速率 rate of stretch
拉伸塑[延]性 tensile ductility
拉伸缩颈 necking in tension
拉伸弹性 tensile elasticity, elasticity of extension
拉伸弹性模量 modulus of elasticity for tension
拉伸图 load-extension diagram
拉伸推出试验 tensioned push-out test
拉伸弯曲矫直机 stretching-bending straightener, tension leveler
拉伸芯棒 drawing mandrel

拉伸形变 tensile deformation
拉伸性 stretchability, extensibility, draftability
拉伸性能 tension test property, drawing property ◇ 光滑试样～*
拉伸压力机 draw(ing) press ◇ 线性～*
拉伸压缩疲劳极限 tension-and-compression fatigue limit
拉伸压缩疲劳试验机 【金】push-pull fatigue-testing machine ◇ 液压～pulsator
拉伸压缩试验 【金】tensile-and-compression test
拉伸压缩试验机 tensile-and-compression testing machine
拉伸压缩载荷 tension-compression loading
拉伸延伸(率) tensile extension
拉伸应变 tensile [stretching] strain
拉伸应变纹 stretcher strain (markings)
拉伸应力 tensile [tension, stretching, pulling] stress, stress in tension
拉伸应力-应变特性(曲线) tensile stress-strain characteristics
拉伸应力-应变图 tensile stress-deformation [stress-strain] diagram
拉伸载荷 tensile load
拉伸状态 as-drawn condition
拉深环 draw ring
拉深模 stretching [cupping, drawing] die ◇ 机械～stretch mechanical die
拉深(延性)系数 cupping (ductility) value
拉绳 hauling cable, stay cord
拉式(送丝) pull out type
拉式应变传感器 strain transducer
拉手 handle, 【机】draft, draught
拉丝 【压】(wire) drawing ◇ 反拉[张]力～ reactive wire-drawing, 肥皂润滑～ soap drawn wire, 干法～ dry wire drawing, 高温～*, 光亮～ bright drawing, 辊式模～ roller die drawing, 普罗佩兹液态

~法 Properzi process,熔铅润滑~法*,湿法~wet wire drawing,泰勒~法*,无模~法*
拉丝板 draw(ing) block, whittle [wire-drawer'] plate
拉丝车间 (wire-)drawing plant
拉丝锭 wire bar
拉丝坩埚 wire-drawing crucible
拉丝工 wiredrawer
拉丝机 (wire-) drawing bench [machine], (draw) bench, cold drawing bench, moto-bloc, block, drawing mill, pull-type drawbench ◇ 粗拉~,单次[单卷筒]~*,单模孔[一次]~*,单线式~ single-die draw-bench,倒立卷筒~*,堆积式[无滑动多次(多级)]~*,多次[多卷筒]~*,多模~*,多线式~*,反拉力~*,鼓式~ drum-type drawbench,滑动(式)~*,卷筒式~ rotary bench,连续~*,两层~ double-deck machine,双线式~ double-rod drawbench,维尔卡格特里克斯辊模~*,无滑动积线式~*,细~*,蓄丝式(多次)~*,张力式[链式]~ pull-type drawbench,直线式~*
拉丝卷筒 (drawing) block, (drawing) capstan, drawing drum ◇ 辊筒式~ spinner block,立式推线~ push-up block,水冷~ water-cooled capstan,塔式[形]~,线轴式~ spooler block
拉丝模 (wire-)drawing die, die ◇ 带眼~坯 cored die,金刚石~ 抛光机*
拉丝模板 whittle [wire-drawer', wortle] plate
拉丝模工作开始时期 bedding in period
拉丝模孔 die channel
拉丝模模孔检查仪 wire-drawing die profilmeter
拉丝模组 die set
拉丝润滑皂 wire-drawing soap
拉丝速度 withdrawing speed
拉丝应力 wire-drawing stress

拉丝用铝棒 aluminium wire bar
拉丝用线材 drawing (grade) quality wire rod
拉丝装置 wire-drawing frame
拉速 【连铸】withdrawal [casting] speed
拉速曲线 withdrawal velocity curve
拉索 dragline, inhaul cable
拉坦斯合金(黄铜旧名) Lattens
拉碳 【钢】catch carbon ◇ 高~牌号钢种 catch-carbon steels,停止~ blocking the heat,一次~ one-go
拉碳操作法 catch carbon method
拉条 brace, bracing, stay, (tension) rod ◇ 炉子~ furnace bracing
拉瓦尔喷嘴[喷管] Laval [contracting-expanding, convergent-divergent] nozzle*
拉瓦尔喷嘴型收缩 Laval constriction
拉瓦尔氧枪 Laval lance ◇ 单孔~*,三孔~*
拉弯 draw bending
拉弯机 draw [stretch] bender
拉维利硅热还原炼镁法(意大利) Ravelli process
拉维特法(用电热盐浴炉退火的) Lavite process
拉钨丝机 tungsten wire drawing machine
拉乌尔定律 Raoult's law
拉乌尔活度系数 Raoultion activity coefficient
拉乌尔线 Raoult's line
拉希格填充瓷圈 Raschig rings
拉细 attenuation, sucking
拉下脱法 withdrawal process
拉下位置 withdrawal position
拉线 backguy, guy (wire), stretching [stay] wire
拉线电缆 connecting cable
拉线杆 stay rod
拉线机 wire stretcher
拉线绝缘子 guy [egg] insulator
拉线开关 pendant (pull) switch, pull(ing) switch

拉线排料过滤机　string discharge type filter
拉线排料装置　string discharge device
拉线用铝锭　aluminium for wire drawing
拉线桩　guy anchor
拉线装置　drawing-ff mechanism
拉削　broach(ing)
拉削模　broaching die
拉逊氏(板)桩　Larrson pile
拉压疲劳试验机　(同"拉伸压缩疲劳试验机")
拉延　【压】mandrelling ◇ 深～法 cupping process
拉延冲头　drawing [cupping] punch, draw-off punch
拉延-反拉延组合模　combination draw-reverse draw die
拉延模　drawing die ◇ 减薄～ironing die
拉延压力机　drawing [stretching] press
拉曳器　barney
拉应变　tension [stretching] strain
拉应力　(同"拉伸应力")
拉轧辊　withdrawal and reducing roll
拉轧机(组)　pull-out and reducing stand
拉直装置　puller
拉制　(wire)drawing ◇ 干法～dry drawing, 金属～metal drawing, 烧结金属的～*, 湿法～wet drawing
拉制的　【压】drawn, holed
拉制端(玻璃熔炉的)　working end
拉制法　drawing process, pull(ing) method (单晶的)
拉制钢　drawn steel
拉制过程　drawing process
拉制件　draw-piece
拉制金属　draw(n) metal
拉制设备　drawing device
拉制(生长)结　【半】pulled junction
拉制温度　draw temperature
拉制无缝管　weldless drawn pipe
拉制线　drawn-wire
拉制性　drawing quality

拉制用油　drawing oil
喇叭　loudspeaker
喇叭管式冷却器　trumpet cooler
喇叭口　bell, flare opening, mouthing, pipe socket, spigot, 【压】trough, bellmouth (导卫装置的) ◇ 拉模出口～【压】die relief, 入口～inlet barrel, 引入～inlet spigot
喇叭口管　faucet pipe
喇叭模　welding bell
喇叭形孔　conical hole
喇叭形坡口焊接　flare (bevel) weld
蜡　wax ◇ 阿克～Acrawax, 巴西棕榈[卡瑙巴]～*, 上～(镀锌钢丝的) waxing, 似～的 waxy-looking
蜡槽　wax bath
蜡衬里的　wax-lined
蜡模　wax pattern
蜡模爆炸成形　explosive wax forming
蜡模铸造　(同"熔模铸造")
蜡泥塑料　plasticine
蜡线　wax string ◇ 逼气～wax vent
蜡线出气孔　【铸】wax-vent
蜡型　(同"熔模")
蜡型精密铸造　(同"熔模精密铸造")
蜡型铸造用耐火材料　investment compound
蜡状芽孢杆菌　Bacillus cereus
镴(锡铅合金)　solder
镴镀层　ternecoating
镴焊法　brazing process
镴焊工艺　joint brazing procedure
镴焊熔剂　brazing mixture
莱昂轴承合金(70～89Sn, 8～3Cu)　Lion bearing alloy
莱德布尔锌基轴承合金(17.5Sn, 5.5Cu, 余量Zn)　Ledebur bearing alloy, Ledebur's bearing metal
莱德尔锌合金(5～6.5Cu, 5～6.5Al, 余量Zn)　Leddel alloy
莱德赖特含铅易切削黄铜(61Cu, 35.6Zn, 3.4Pb)　Ledrite

莱德洛伊含铅易切削钢（加 0.15－0.25Pb） Ledloy
莱登弗罗斯特现象 Leidenfrost phenomenon
莱顿瓶【理】Leyden jar
莱恩蒸气制氢法 Lane process
莱基直接还原法【铁】Leckie process
莱克兰舍电池 Leclanche cell
莱克特罗麦尔特电炉 【冶】Lectromelt furnace
莱马夸恩德耐蚀铜锌合金（39Cu,37Zn,9.8Co,7Ni） Lemarquand
莱马洛伊(铁钼钴)永磁合金（12Co,20Mo,余量 Fe） Remalloy (alloy), Remalloy per-manent magnet alloy
莱米克斯高氧化镁打结耐火材料 Ramix
莱奈特铝铜合金（9—13.5Cu,余量 Al） Lynite
莱切森铜镍合金（60—90Cu,10—40Ni,0.2Al） Lechesne alloy
莱塞 （同"激光"、"激光器"）
莱氏体(4.3C)【金】ledeburite
莱氏体钢 ledeburitic [ledeburite] steel
莱氏体共晶 ledeburite eutectic
莱氏体合金 ledeburite alloy
莱氏体组织 Ledeburite structure
莱辛圈 Lessing rings
莱伊锡铅合金[锡镴]（75—80Sn,20—25Pb） Lay, Ley (pewter)
莱茵铜锡合金 Rhinemetal
来回绕线电阻 go-and-return resistance
来回通过 back and forth pass
来回移动 back and forth movement
来料 incoming material
来料板坯【压】incoming slab
来料厚度【压】incoming thickness
来源 source, origin (orig.)
铼{Re} rhenium ◇ 含～的 rhenium-bearing
铼合金(50—75W,余量 Re) rhenium alloy
铼基合金 rhenium-base alloy

铼酸盐{M_2ReO_4} rhenate
铼添加合金 rhenium addition
铼系元素 rhenides
赖克铝青铜（85.2Cu,7.5Fe,7Al,0.2Pb,0.6Mn） Reich's bronze
赖利铅[锡]基轴承合金（10—16Sb,1—6Cu,余量 Sn 或 Pb） Rely alloy
赖曼系(光谱线的) Lyman series
赖特磨蚀试验装置 Wright's apparatus
蓝 blue ◇ 全～(回火色) full blue
蓝宝石{Al_2O_3} sapphire, leucosapphire, jacut
蓝宝石拉模 sapphire die
蓝边钢 blue edged steel
蓝脆范围 blue brittle range
蓝脆性 blue brittleness [shortness]
蓝脆性温度范围 blue heat range
蓝矾[石] （同"胆矾"）
蓝粉(锌精馏副产物) blue powder [dust, metal]
蓝粉槽[池] blue powder sump
蓝粉泥浆 blue powder slurry
蓝粉筛 blue powder screen
蓝高岭石{$(Al,Cr)_2O_3 \cdot 2SiO_2 \cdot 2H_2O$} miloschite
蓝化(钢) oil blackeite
蓝灰色 bluish grey
蓝辉镍矿 kallilite
蓝辉铜矿 blue [alpha] chalcocite
蓝金(装饰合金;25—33.3Fe,余量 Au) blue gold
蓝晶石{$Al_2O_3 \cdot SiO_2$} cyanite, cianite, kyanite, disthene
蓝晶石砖 cyanite brick
蓝绿色 greenish-blue colour, green-blue, blue-green
蓝绿细菌门 Cyanophyta
蓝绿藻 Blue-green algae
蓝煤气(水煤气) blue [blau] gas
蓝钼矿{$MoO_2 \cdot 4MoO_3$} ilsemannite
蓝黏土 blue clay
蓝(皮)钢 blue [Damask] steel

蓝铅　blue lead
蓝色　blue (BL) ◇ 带～的 bluish (blsh), 暗～oxford-blue
蓝色氨基铜　blue cupric ammine
蓝色汞浸液　blue dip
蓝色回火的　blue finished
蓝色退火　blue annealing
蓝石棉　blue asbestos
蓝水煤气　blue water gas
蓝铁矿{$Fe_3(PO_4)_2·8H_2O$}　blue iron earth, vivianite
蓝铜矿{$2CuCO_3·Cu(OH)_2$}　blue malachite, mineral blue, azurite, blue carbonate of copper
蓝铜锍　blue metal
蓝图　blue print (B/P., b.p.), blue print drawing, heliographic paper ◇ 晒～*
蓝硒铜矿{$CuSeO_3·2H_2O$}　chalcomenite
蓝细菌　Cyanobacteria
蓝线石{$AlB_8Si_3O_{19}(OH)$}　dumortierite
蓝焰　blue flame
蓝氧化铁残渣(约50%铁)　blue billy
蓝氧化钨　blue tungsten oxide
蓝油(无石蜡重油)　blue oil
蓝柱石{$HBeAlSiO_5$}　euclase
蓝锥矿{$BaTiSi_3O_9$}　benitoite
栏板　working plate, side wall
栏杆　rail(ing), balustrade
栏杆钢　hand railing steel
栏墙　cut-off wall
拦板　side-plate
拦板密封　【团】side seal
拦板全高铺边料　【团】full side layer
拦板下段　【团】lower sidewall section
拦洪坝　flooded tention dam, flood-control dam
拦砂(折流)坝　groyne, groin, check dam
拦水坝　retaining [check] dam
拦污栅　trash rack
篮式电镀　basket plating
篮式过滤机　basket filter
篮式离心过滤机　basket centrifuge
篮式溶解[电解]器　basket dissolver
篮网网目　basket mesh
篮形电极　basket electrode
兰伯特定律　【理】Lambert's law
兰加洛伊高镍铸造合金(17Mo, 5W, 5Fe, 0.75Si, 0.75Mn, 余量 Ni)　Langalloy
兰开夏锅炉　Lancashire boiler
兰开夏黄铜(3Cu, 27Zn)　Lancashire brass
兰米尔玻璃水银扩散泵　Langmuir's glass pump
兰米尔金属水银扩散泵　Langmuir's metal pump
兰米尔扩散泵　Langmuir's diffusion pump
兰姆波　Lamb wave
兰姆公式　Lame's formula
兰氏 4R 耐蚀合金(30Mo, 5Fe, 余量 Ni)　Langalloy 4R
兰氏 5R 耐蚀合金(17Mo, 15Cr, 5W, 5Fe, 余量 Ni)　Langalloy 5R
兰氏 X 射线衍射显微镜法　Lang's method
兰氏法(直接还原铁矿石法)　Lang process
兰氏温标　Rankine temperature scale
兰氏温度(°R)　Rankine temperature
兰氏照相机　Lang (type) camera
兰斯莱(合金)氢含量测定仪　Ransley apparatus
兰兹珠光体铸铁　Lanz pearlite iron
兰兹珠光体铸铁浇注法　Lanz-pearlite process
兰兹铸铁　Lanz's cast iron
镧{La}　lanthanum ◇ 含～合金*
镧化物铁氧体　lanthanide ferrite
镧热还原(法)　lanthanothermic reduction
镧热还原剂　lanthanothermic reducer
镧石{$(La,Ce)_2(CO_3)_2·8H_2O$}　lanthanite
镧铈稀土[兰塞安普]合金(约含45—50Ce, >30La, <1Fe 及其它稀土元素)　【冶】Lan--Cer-Amp
镧系[族]元素　lanthanon, lanthanide series [element], lanthanides
镧系元素收缩　lanthanide contraction

镧铀钛铁矿 davidite
缆 cable
缆车 cable [dummy] car, telpher ◇ 电动~cable telpher
缆车运输机 telpher conveyer
缆道 cableway, track cable
缆径测量仪 cable diameter gauge
缆绳 rope ◇ 用~拉紧的铁烟囱 guyed steel stack
缆绳卷筒 cable wheel
缆式钢丝绳 cable lay wire rope
缆索绞车 cable hoist
缆索式起重机 cable crane, telpher conveyer
缆索输送机 cable conveyer
缆索拖铲 cable drag scraper
缆索运输 cable transfer (C.T.)
缆索钻井 cable drilling
朗道抗磁性 Landau diamagnetism
朗道能级 【理】Landau level
朗梅德-亨德森黄铁矿烧渣低温氯化浸出法 Longmaid-Henderson process
朗之万方程式 【理】Langevin equation
浪费 waste, wastage, dissipate
浪费的 uneconomic(al)
浪击式酸洗 surge pickling
浪弯辊压机 crimping machine
浪纹(钢材缺陷) rippling
浪纹线脚 cyma
浪形(薄板带缺陷) shape wave
浪形函数 wave function
浪涌 surge, surging ◇ 防~的 surgeproof
浪涌点 surge point
浪涌电流 surge current
浪涌电压 surge voltage
浪涌发生器 surge generator
浪涌幅度 surging amplitude
浪涌特性 surge characteristic
浪涌调节器 surge regulator
浪涌调配槽 surge tank
浪涌吸收柜 surge absorber cubicle
捞网 dredge, scrape

劳保[劳动保护] labo(u)r protection, job safety
劳保条例 labour insurance regulations
劳动保险 labour insurance
劳动成本 labour cost ◇ 单位产品~*
劳动定额制订 rate fixing
劳动定员 labour requirement
劳动管理 labour management
劳动力 labour [work] force, manpower
劳动密集型产业 labour-intensive industry
劳动强度 labour intensity [strength], intensity of labour
劳动生产率 (labour) productivity, labour capacity ◇ 全员~*
劳动卫生条件 hygienic working conditions
劳动组织 organization of labour, labour management
劳厄X射线衍射法 Laue X-ray diffraction method
劳厄X射线衍射图[花样] Laue X-ray diffraction pattern
劳厄斑标定 【理】indexing of Laue spots
劳厄斑点日晷仪投影(X射线照相的) gnomonic projection of Laue spots
劳厄斑点星芒 asterism of laue spots
劳厄背(反)射照相 Laue back-reflection photograph
劳厄法 Laue method
劳厄反射 Laue reflections
劳厄方程(式) Laue equation
劳厄(晶体衍射)图 Laue diagram [film]
劳厄图像解释 Laue photographs interpretation
劳厄(型)照相机 Laue(-type) camera ◇ 平板~*
劳厄衍射花样 Laue (diffraction) pattern
劳厄衍射花样斑点 Laue-pattern spots
劳厄衍射图 Laue diagram [photograph], Laue (diffraction) pattern
劳厄照片中心 centre of Laue photograph
劳厄照相漫散斑 diffuse spots in Laue

劳厄指数　Laue indices
劳梅特耐蚀镍银合金　Lawmet
劳氏船级　Lloyd's class
劳氏船级社　Lloyd's Register of Shipping
劳塔尔铝硅合金（4.7Cu, 0.5Mn, 1—2Si, 余量 Al）　Lautal alloy
劳特式轧机　【压】Lauth mill
牢固的　firm, solid, fast, fail-safe
牢固性　firmness, fastness
老虎窗　dormer
老虎口　jaw crusher
老虎钳　vise, vice, pincer pliers
老化　ageing, maturing, 【计】burn-in ◇ 不~的 non-ageing
老化界限　ageing boundary
老化时间　ageing time
老化特性　【半】ageing behaviour
老化状态　aged condition
老式车间　obsolete plant
酪朊　casein(ogen)
酪朊胶　casein glue
酪朊酸　caseinic acid
酪朊酸盐　caseinate
烙痕　dent
烙上　burn-in
烙铁　solderer, soldering iron [bit] ◇ 喷灯~*
勒脚底　base course
勒(克斯)计　luxmeter
勒夏特里耶高温计　Le Chatelier pyrometer
勒夏特列－莫林碱石灰烧结法　Le Chatelier-Morin process
勒夏特列1号钢铁侵蚀剂　Le Chatelier No.1 reagent
勒夏特列热电偶　Le Chatelier couple
勒夏特列原理（平衡位移原理）　Le Chatelier principle
雷奥米尔锑铁合金（70Sb, 30Fe）　Reaumur alloy
雷奥坦(电阻铜)合金　Rheo(s)tan

雷宾德尔效应　Rehbinder effect
雷达(台, 设备)　radar, (radio)locator
雷达利思含锂合金　Redulith
雷达天线　gantry, radar antenna
雷德福填料用铅青铜（85.7Cu, 10Sn, 2.5Pb, 1.8Zn）　Redford's alloy
雷德勒型连续流运输机　Redler conveyor
雷德雷镍铬电阻合金（85Ni, 15Cr）　Redray
雷迪阿奈特铬不锈钢　Radianite
雷迪弗洛银焊料（56Ag, 22Cu, 17Zn, 5Sn）　Ready-Flo
雷迪欧姆铁铬铝电阻合金（12—13Cr, 4—5Al, 余量 Fe）　Radiohm
雷格尔锡基轴承合金（83.3Sn, 11Sb, 5.7Cu）　Regel metal
雷古拉斯锑铅合金（4—12Sb, 余量 Pb）　Regulus (metal)
雷管　detonator, detonating cap, capsule
雷管黄铜　cap gilding, brass, primer (gilding) brass
雷管铜(合金)（3—5Zn, 余量 Cu）　cap copper
雷科铁镍钴系永磁合金　Reco
雷克尔铜铝合金（10Al, 1Zn, 1Mn, 余量 Cu）　Rakel's metal
雷克尔铜镍合金（10Ni, 1Zn, 1Mn, 余量 Cu）　Rakel's alloy
雷克斯耐热耐蚀合金钢　Rex steel
雷克斯钴铬钨刀具合金　Rex alloy
雷蒙式混凝土(灌筑)桩　Raymond concrete pile
雷尼克斯压铸铝合金（91.5Al, 4Ni, 4Cu, 0.5Si）　Renyx
雷尼克钨镍刀具合金（94W, 余量 Ni）　Renik's metal
雷诺合金　Reynolds alloy
雷诺判据　Reynolds criterion
雷诺数　Reynolds number (R)
雷诺阻力公式　Reynolds resistance formula
雷齐斯塔尔(耐蚀耐热)镍铬钢（22Ni,

8Cr,1.8Si,1Cu,0.25Mn,0.25C,余量Fe) Rezistal

雷(酸)汞{Hg(CNO)$_2$} mercuric [mercury] fulminate

雷酸盐 fulminate

雷腾滤色镜[器] Wratten filter

雷瓦尔铜银共晶合金 Leval's alloy

雷瓦朗铝黄铜(76Cu,22Zn,2Al;用作冷凝管) Revalon

雷西达尔易切削高强度铝合金 Recidal

雷西斯科铜铝合金(冷凝管用;90.5—91Cu,7—7.5Al,2Ni,0—0.1Mn) Resisco (alloy)

雷西斯塔尔铝青铜(9—10Al,1—2Fe,余量Cu) 【冶】Resistal

雷西斯塔尔耐蚀硅砖 【耐】Resistal

雷西斯塔克耐蚀耐热铝青铜(88Cu,10Al,2Fe) Resistac

雷西斯塔铁基合金(0.2Cu,0.2P,余量Fe) Resista

雷西斯廷铜锰电阻合金(85Cu,12Mn,2Fe) Resistin

雷西斯托电阻合金(69Ni,19Fe,10Cr,1Si,0.4Co,0.5Mn) Resisto

雷约镍铬耐蚀耐热合金(85Ni,15Cr) Rayo

雷兹铜锡铅锑耐蚀合金(75Cu,11.5Sn,9Pb,4.5Sb) Retz

镭{Ra} radium

镭 A(钋-218,^{218}Po) radium A

镭 B(铅-214,^{214}Pb) radium B

镭 C(铋-214,^{214}Bi) radium C

镭 C'(钋-214,^{214}Po) radium C'

镭 C"(铊-210,^{210}Tl) radium C"

镭 D(铅-210,^{210}Pb) radium D,radiolead

镭 E(铋-210,^{210}Bi) radium E

镭 F(钋-210,^{210}Po) radium F

镭 G[镭铅](铅的同位素^{206}Pb,RaG) radium G,radium lead

镭放射[射气] radium emanation

镭检验 radium test

镭-铍中子源 radium-beryllium neutron source

镭同位素{^{228}Ra}(新钍 M$_s$Th$_1$) radium-228

镭系 radium family

镭族 radium series

累积残余应变 accumulated residual strain

累积单分子层 built-up monolayer

累积剂量[辐射量] integrated dose

累积计算器 totalizer

累积膜 built-up film

累积强度 【理】integrated intensity

累积强度测定[测量] integrated intensity measurement

累积曲线 mass curve

累积时间率 cumulative fraction

累积损伤 cumulative damage

累积损伤法则 cumulative damage rule

累积循环次数比 cumulative cycle ratio

累积因素 build up factor

累计产量 【企】ultimate production

累计[积]观测 cumulative observations

累计级配曲线 cumulative grading curve

累计[积](吸收)剂量 integral (absorbed) dose,integrated [accumulated] dose

累计[积]浸蚀 cumulative erosion

累计[积]浸蚀-时间曲线 cumulative erosion-time curve

累计输出量 cumulative shipment

累计通过率 cumulative passing

累计瓦特表 totalizing wattmeter

累计[积]误差 accumulated [cumulative, progressive,aggregated] error

累计重量 cumulative weight

累加寄存器 accumulator register

累加器 【计】accumulator (ACC),totalizer ◇ 数据~ data accumulator

累加器转移指令 【计】accumulator jump instruction

垒砖 brick overlapping

肋 rib,edge fin ◇ 有~的 finned

肋辐结构 【机】rib-and-web

肋骨状吸收剂 rib absorber

肋片板式散热器 finned plated radiator
肋条 rib
肋筒 ribbed tube
肋砖 rib brick
类 class, kind, type, group, family
类包晶反应 peritectoid reaction
类比 analog
类铋 eka-bismuth
类别 class (cls), classification, category, genre
类波电子 wave-like electron
类碲{Po,即"钋"} dvitellurium
类锇 eka-osmium
类汞 eka-mercury
类铪 eka-hafnium
类钬 eka-holmium
类金属(的) metalloid
类金属合金 metalloid alloy
类金属有机化合物 metalloid organic compound
类矿物 mineralloid
类镥 eka-lutetium
类锰{Re,即"铼"} dvimanganese
类钋 eka-polonium
类铅 ekalead
类青铜的 bronzy
类球形颗粒 near-spherical particle
类铯{Fr,即"钫"} dvicesium
类石墨 quasi-graphite (QG)
类水溶剂 waterlike solvent
类似 likenness, analogy (anal.), analog, approach
类似的 similar
类似极 analog poles
类似性 similarity
类铊 eka-thallium
类钽 eka-tantalum
类铜物 aerose
类椭圆型材 oval-like shape
类钨 eka-tungsten
类无向性 【金】quasi-isotropy
类型 type

类铱 eka-iridium
类镱 eka-ytterbium
类质同晶混合物 isomorphous mixture
类质同晶夹杂体 isomorphous inclusion
类质同晶型[同象]的 isomorphic, isomorphous
类质同晶型取代 isomorphous substitution
类质同晶型体 isomorph
类质同晶型系 isomorphous system
类质同晶型置换 isomorphous replacement
泪珠状粉末 tear-drop shaped powder
棱 edge, corner, arris, heel
棱边应力 edge stress
棱角 edge angle
棱角形粉末 angular powder
棱晶 prism
棱镜 (glass, optical) prism ◇ 尼科耳~ Nicol, Nicol('s) prism
棱镜分光 prismatic decomposition
棱镜分光计[光谱计,分光仪] prism spectrometer
棱镜面反射 prism-face reflections
棱镜摄谱仪 prism spectrograph
棱镜照明器 prism illuminator
棱镜折光度 prismoptric
棱形键 prismatic key
棱形砖 feather brick
棱柱 prism
棱柱锰矿{$Mn_2O_3 \cdot H_2O$} prismatic manganese ore
棱柱面 prismatic plane [surface]
棱柱(形)导轨 prismatic guide, vee-guide
棱柱形坯块 prismatic compact
棱柱形位错 prismatic dislocation, R-dislocation
棱柱状滑移 prismatic slip
棱锥面 pyramid(al) plane [surface]
棱锥面滑移 glide on pyramidal planes
棱锥(体) pyramid ◇ 压痕~面积
棱锥体[棱锥状]压痕 pyramid indenta-

tion [imprint]
棱锥形金刚石压头　diamond pyramid indentor [penetrator]
棱锥压痕硬度测定法　pyramid indentation test
楞次定律　【电】Lenz's law
冷疤(表面缺陷)　【钢】cold-shut,【铸】cold shot
冷拔　【压】cold [hard] drawing ◇ 带芯～*,轻度～的 light-drawn
冷拔道次中切管　【压】middling(s)
冷拔镀锡线材　drawn tinned wire
冷拔钢材　cold-drawn steel (CDS) ◇ 光亮～bright drawn bar
冷拔钢管　cold-drawn steel tube [pipe] ◇ 缸筒用高精度～*
冷拔(钢)丝　(hard) drawn steel wire, cold-drawn wire ◇ 空气淬火～*,铅淬火～*
冷拔管　cold drawn tube (C.D.T.), cold-drawn pipe [tubing], (hard) drawn tube ◇ 带芯棒～DOM (drawn-over-mandrel) tubing
冷拔管坯　hollow
冷拔焊管　cold drawn welded tube
冷拔机　cold-drawing machine [bench, mill] ◇ 多根管材～*,卷筒～bull block (drawing)
冷拔加工状态　cold-drawn appearance
冷拔减缩量[率]　cold-drawing reduction
冷拔模　cold drawing die
冷拔设备　cold-draw equipment
冷拔条钢　cold-drawn bar
冷拔无缝管　seamless drawn pipe
冷拔线材　hard-drawn wire (H.D.W.), cold-drawn wire ◇ 加润滑剂～lacquer drawn wire,中硬～medium-hard-drawn wire
冷拔中等硬度(管材)　half hard
冷壁法　cold-wall method
冷变形　cold deformation [work], cold drawing (不锈钢丝的)

冷变形强化　cold deformation strengthening
冷变形硬化　flow harden
冷补炉　【冶】cold patching
冷藏库　cold storage, refrigerator
冷藏室　ice-house, refrigerator
冷藏箱　refrigerator, chill box, freezer
冷层　cold layer
冷成形　cold-forming
冷成形钢　cold-shaping steel
冷成形机　【压】cold former
冷成形金属　cold-shaping metal
冷成形性　cold formability, cold-forming property
冷冲　cold punching
冷冲薄板　stamp plate
冷冲挤压　cold impact extrusion
冷冲压　cold stamping
冷冲压模　cold stamping die
冷冲压优质钢　cold pressing quality steel
冷除浇冒口　【铸】cold spruing
冷处理　【金】subzero cooling [treatment], subzero temperature treatment, cold treatment
冷处理急热法　subzero rapid heating
冷处理强[硬]化　subzero hardening
冷穿孔　【压】cold piercing
冷床　【压】cold [carry-over] bed, cooling table [bank, bed, rack, apparatus], hot bed [bank, rack], transfer, (skid) bank, rack ◇ 摆动齿条式～*,算条式[格栅式]～cooling grid,齿条式～*,带收集装置的～stacking (hot) bed,导向滑条式～skid-type hot bed,二次～secondary cooler,非传动辊式[惰辊式]～dead roller bed,钢丝绳牵引～*,固定式[非机动]～stationary cooling bed,轨式～rail-type hot bed,辊式～*,机动[运输]～*,锯齿式～*,链式～*,螺旋式～*,倾斜式～*,双面～*,一次～primary cooler,爪式～pawl-type cooling bed
冷床堆垛段　packing bed

冷床附近的剪切机　cooling bed shears
冷床冷却　bank cooling
冷床链式移送机　(link-and-)chain cooling bed transfer
冷床熔炼法（熔炼钛、锆、铌等）cold-hearth melting
冷床输出辊道　cooling bed run-out table
冷床输入辊道　cooling bed run-in table
冷床移送机　【压】cooling-bed transfer, hot (bed) transfer
冷吹　cold blow
冷粗轧轧机　cold roughing mill
冷脆　cold brittleness [shortness]
冷脆钢　cold-short steel [iron]
冷脆裂　cold short cracking
冷脆性　cold brittleness [shortness]
冷脆性转折[临界]温度　cold brittle transition temperature
冷淬　cold-quench(ing) ◇ 完全~ dead-cold chilling
冷淬槽　cold-quench tank
冷淬钢　chilled steel
冷等静压（成形）　cold isostatic pressing (CIP), cold isostatic compaction
冷等静压（制）　【粉】cold isostatic pressing, cold isopressing, cool isostatic compression, isostatic cold pressing
冷点（钢锭、钢坯的未热透区）cold spot
冷电阻　cold resistance
冷淀积　cold set(ting)
冷顶锻　【压】cold upsetting [heading]
冷顶锻压力机　cold-heading press
冷冻　freezing, refrigeration ◇ 盖利~法*, 深度~*
冷冻捕集器[冷冻阱]　refrigerated trap
冷冻成形　cryogenic forming
冷冻处理　refrigeration treatment, cryogenic preparation, deep freezing
冷冻淬火　【金】cryogenic quenching
冷冻干燥　freeze drying
冷冻管道　refrig line
冷冻混合物　freezing mixture

冷冻机　refrigerating machine [unit, machinery], cooling machine, refrigerator ◇ 氨气压缩~*
冷冻剂　refrigerant, cryogenin(e), cryogen, freezing mixture
冷冻加工　zero-working
冷冻密封泵　frozen seal pump
冷冻器　freezer (unit), chiller
冷冻蛇管　refrig coil
冷冻设备　refrigerating unit [installation]
冷冻室　freezing compartment, chilling chamber, refrigerating room
冷冻水银模精密铸造（法）（同"冻结水银模精密铸造法"）
冷冻系统　refrigerating system
冷冻液　freezing solution
冷镀锡　cold tinning
冷镀锌　（同"电镀锌"）
冷端　cold side, cold tails (轧制时轧件的), cold junction [end] (热电偶的)
冷端温度补偿　cold-junction compensation
冷端温度校正（热电偶的）　cold junction correction
冷锻　cold forging [hammering, heading, reducing] ◇ 烧结~ sinter cold forging
冷锻件　cold forging, hard-wrought
冷锻模　cold forging die
冷镦　cold-heading
冷镦棒材　cold-heading rod
冷镦成形机　cold former
冷镦粗　cold upset(ting)
冷镦钢　cold forging [heading] steel
冷镦钢丝　cold-heading wire
冷镦工序　cold upsetting operation
冷镦机　cold header, cold heading machine ◇ 级进[连续]式~ progressive header, 铆钉~ riveting press
冷镦模具钢　cold-heading die steel
冷镦压力机　cold-heading press
冷发射　cold [field] emission
冷法贯入　cold-penetration
冷法球团　【团】cold pellet

冷法压块 【团】unfired briquette
冷反应器 cold reactor
冷返矿 【铁】cold return
冷返矿屑 cold recirculating (return) fines
冷范性 cold plasticity
冷范性形变量 amount of cold plastic deformation
冷风 cold air (CA, ca), cold blast ◇ 送~*
冷风白口铁 white cold-blast pig iron
冷风阀 【铁】cold-blast valve ◇ 闸板式~*
冷风阀调节 cold-blast valve control
冷风滑阀 【铁】cold-blast sliding valve
冷风化铁炉 cold-blast cupola
冷风入口 cold-blast inlet
冷风扇 thermantidote
冷风烧结(法) 【团】cool air sintering
冷风总管 【铁】cold-blast main
冷风作业 【冶】blow cold
冷坩埚感应炉 cold-crucible induction furnace
冷隔(钢锭或铸件缺陷) cold-laps, cold-shut(s)
冷鼓风 cold-blast, cold blow
冷固结法[冷法固结] cold hardening
冷固结球团法 nonfired pellet method
冷固结球团(矿) non-fired pellet, cold-bonded Pellet ◇ 费罗－特克~法 Ferro-Tech process, 格兰斯~*
冷固结铁矿球团 (同"铁矿生球团")
冷固结造块 【团】non-fired agglomerate
冷固结造块法 cold agglomeration process
冷灌 cold-penetration
冷灌沥青碎石(路) cold penetration (bituminous) macadam
冷贯入 cold-penetration
冷光 cold light
冷滚螺纹机 cold thread rolling machine
冷焊(合) cold [zero] welding
冷焊条 【焊】cold rod
冷混合料 cold mix

冷挤压 【压】cold extrusion, cold flow pressing ◇ 粉末~ cold powder extruding, 加黏合剂~ cold binder extruding, 柯尔德弗罗~法*
冷挤压力机 cold extrusion press
冷加工 cold-forming, cold work(ing) [deformation, reducing] ◇ 可~的 cold-workable, 少量~(带钢的) killing
冷加工程度 degree of cold work
冷加工处理 cold-working treatment
冷加工脆性 embrittlement by cold work
冷加工感受性 response to cold work
冷加工钢 cold finished steel
冷加工钢材比 cold rolled steel ratio
冷加工金属 cold-worked metal
冷加工晶体 cold-worked crystal
冷加工精整 cold finishing
冷加工精整钢 cold-finished steel
冷加工量 amount of cold work
冷加工能量 energy of cold working
冷加工强化 cold-work strengthening
冷加工铁磁体 cold-worked ferromagnet
冷加工铜 hard copper
冷加工性 cold workability
冷加工性能 cold-working property
冷加工应力 cold-working stress
冷加工硬化 【金】cold hardening, (cold) work hardening, flow harden, mechanical hardening
冷加工用工具钢 tool steel for cold working
冷加工状态硬度 strain hardness
冷加工组织 【金】cold-worked structure
冷加工作业 【压】cold-working practice
冷检(锻件的) cold inspection
冷剪边 cold-trim(ming)
冷剪(机) 【压】cold-shearing machine, cold shears
冷剪机组[作业线] cold shear line
冷剪(切) cold shearing
冷减径机 【压】cold-sinking mill
冷矫直 【压】cold straightening [levelling]

◇ 辊式~机(薄板的) cold mangle
冷接点 cold junction [end]
冷接点温度校正 cold junction correction
冷结 【钢】cold-shut
冷结疤 teeming arrest
冷介质淬火 cold-quench(ing)
冷金属检测器 【压】cold metal detector (CMD)
冷精压 cold-coining
冷精整 cold-trim(ming), cold-finishing
冷阱 cold trap ◇ 人字形~ chevron type cold trap
冷锯(机) 【压】cold saw
冷锯切割[下料]机 cold saw-cutting-off machine
冷卷 cold coiling
冷均压 cold isopressing
冷抗磨试验 cold state abrasion test
冷抗压强度 ambient compressive strength, cold (crushing) strength ◇ 还原后~*
冷空气 cold air (CA, ca)
冷矿筛 【团】cold screen
冷矿渣 cold slag
冷矿振动筛 cold vibro screen
冷拉(拔) (同"冷拔")
冷拉黄铜 hard drawing brass
冷拉金属 cold-drawn metal
冷拉润滑油 drawing oil
冷拉伸 cold stretching
冷拉弹簧钢丝 hard drawn spring wire
冷拉铜丝 hard-drawn copper wire
冷连轧机 tandem cold strip mill ◇ Y型三辊~ Y-type three high mill
冷料 cold charge [burden, mix]
冷料法(转炉炼钢的) cold melt process, stock process
冷料运输机 cold conveyer
冷料转炉 stock converter
冷裂 chill [cold] crack(ing), cooling crack
冷裂缝 cold seaming
冷裂纹 cold crack

冷炉 cold [cool] furnace
冷炉顶(鼓风炉的) cold top
冷炉缸 【铁】chilled hearth
冷炉料 【冶】cold charge [stock]
冷(炉)料熔炼 【冶】cold melting
冷炉膛 cold hearth
冷铆(接) cold riveting
冷媒 refrigerant, 【压】cooling medium ◇ 非沸腾型~*, 沸腾型~*
冷模 chill, chin-chin hardening
冷模淬火 cold die quenching
冷黏合(粉末的) cold bonding
冷黏结挤压(粉末的) cold binder extruding
冷黏结剂【铸】 cold binder, coldbond
冷黏结球团 【团】cold (bond) pellet, COBO-pellet
冷黏结球团[造块]法 cold bond agglomeration process ◇ MTU~*
冷黏结造块 【团】cold-bonded agglomerate
冷凝 condensation, condensing, condensate, freezing ◇ 分级~ fractional condensation, 膜状~ film condensation
冷凝泵 condensate [condenser] pump
冷凝槽 condensate trap
冷凝产物 condensation product, cold finger product
冷凝带 condensing zone
冷凝点 condensation point
冷凝法 condensation process
冷凝废气 condensation exhaust
冷凝粉末 powder by condensation
冷凝工 condenserman
冷凝汞 condensed mercury
冷凝固 cold set
冷凝管 condensate [condensation] tube, cold finger ◇ 标准~合金*, 指形(回流)~*
冷凝管捕集器 cold-finger collector
冷凝罐 condensing pot
冷凝过程 condensation process
冷凝挥发物 condensed volatile

冷凝阱　condensate trap, cryotrap
冷凝毛细管　weeping-out
冷凝膜　condensed film, film of condensate
冷凝排气　condensation exhaust
冷凝排水　condensate drain, condensed water outlet
冷凝盘(旋)管　condenser coil
冷凝瓶　condensing bulb
冷凝屏　condensing shield
冷凝器　condenser (cond.), condensator, condensing vessel, condensing-apparatus ◇衬镍～nickel-lined condenser, 单流式～single-pass condenser, 二次[再]～after-condenser, 分级～fractional condenser, 管式～tubular condenser, 混合～mixing condenser, 架空～overhead condenser, 接触～contactcondenser, 浸没管式～submerged-tube condenser, 空气～*, 逆流～*, 喷射～jet condenser, 气压～barometric condenser, 蛇管～coil condenser, 双流式～two-pass condenser, 水淋式～drip condenser, 套管～double-pipe condenser, 蒸馏～distiller condenser, 中间～intercondenser, 砖砌～brick condenser, 锥形底～cone-bottom condenser
冷凝器出口温度　condenser offtake temperature
冷凝器管　condenser tube
冷凝器灰尘　condenser dust
冷凝器结块　condenser build-up
冷凝器气压管　condenser leg (pipe)
冷凝器系统　condenser system
冷凝器转子　【色】condenser rotor
冷凝气　condensed gas
冷凝曲线　freezing curve
冷凝热　heat of condensation
冷凝容器　condensing vessel
冷凝蛇管　condenser [condensing] coil
冷凝室　condenser [condensing, condensation] chamber
冷凝试验　condensation test
冷凝水　condensate [condensation, condensed, condenser, condensing] water
冷凝水槽　condensed water pot
冷凝水池　condensate tank
冷凝水排除泵　condensate pump
冷凝速率　condensing rate
冷凝塔　condensating [condensation] tower
冷凝套　condenser jacket
冷凝温度　condensation point [temperature]
冷凝物　condensate (ends.)
冷凝物排出孔　condensate drain
冷凝物质　condensed material
冷凝系统　condensation [condensed, condensing] system
冷凝效率　condensation [condensing] efficiency
冷凝锌粉　condensed zinc powder
冷凝锌粉粒　condensed zinc particle
冷凝性　condensability
冷凝液　condensate (liquid) ◇粗煤气～crude gas liquor
冷凝液槽　condensate tank
冷凝液放出装置　condensate discharge device, condensate discharger
冷凝液腐蚀　condensate [rivulet] corrosion
冷凝液管　condensate tube
冷凝液膜　condensate film
冷凝液体　condensed fluid
冷凝蒸汽　condensed vapour
冷喷镀[涂]　cold spraying
冷喷丸处理　cold-peening
冷铺(沥青)路面　cold-laid pavement
冷气管　cold air duct [pipe], 【机】refrigeration pipe
冷气流粉碎法　【粉】coldstream process
冷钎焊　cold soldering
冷切边　cold cropping, cold-trim(ming)
冷切边操作　【压】cold trimming operation
冷切头　cold cropping

冷球 【团】cold pellet
冷却 cooling, chill, burial (在缓冷坑中) ◇ 堆垛~*, 分离~*, 过热后~ desuperheat, 流态化~ fluidized cooling, 洒水式~ water-sprinkled cooling, 水套[冷却套]~ jacket type cooling, 斯太尔摩~*, 随炉~ cooling in furnace, 套式~ jacketing, 未~的 uncooled, 迅速~(的) cooled quickly (Cq), 盐水~(法) brine refrigeration, 在砂中~ cooling by embedding in sand, 在油内~的 cooled in oil (Co)
冷却板 cooling plate, plate cooler, 【铁】water-cooled plate ◇ 插入式~*, 炉腹~*, 罗西~*
冷却棒 【铁】rod-shaped cooler
冷却壁(高炉的) (cooling) stave ◇ 嵌入式~ insert-type stave, 全~*, 铸铁~ cast iron stave
冷却表面 cooling surface
冷却捕集 cold-trapping
冷却捕集器 cold trap ◇ 罐式~ pot-type cold trap, 人字形~*, 液体空气~ liquid air trap
冷却不足 under-cooling
冷却槽 cooling tank [bath, vat]
冷却场地 cooling floor
冷却池 cooling pond
冷却抽风量 【团】cooling draught requirement
冷却带 cooling zone [section]
冷却地道[冷却廊] cooling gallery
冷却段 cooling section [area, zone]
冷却段风箱 【团】cooling windbox
冷却(段)负压 【团】cooling suction
冷却段炉罩 【团】cooling zone hood
冷却堆 【团】cooling pile
冷却堆场 cooling floor
冷却堆栈 cooling wharf
冷却方法 cooling method [means]
冷却方式 type of cooling ◇ 传统~*
冷却废钢 【钢】coolant scrap (转炉降温用), chill scrap (熔池的)

冷却风机 cooling fan ◇ 二段~*
冷却风流 cooling air flow
冷却辐射管用黄铜 radiation brass
冷却杆 chill bar
冷却工段 cooling section [plant]
冷却拱顶 cooling arch
冷却管 cooling tube, 【机】refrigeration pipe ◇ 氨~ ammonia pipe
冷却管道 cooling piping
冷却辊道 【压】cooling [hold(ing)] table
冷却滚筒 cooling drum
冷却过程 cooling process
冷却过度 supercooling
冷却机 chilling unit, 【团】cooler ◇ 薄料层~ shallow-bed cooler, 抽风式~ downdraught cooler, 带式~ straight (-line) cooler, 刮刀卸料式~ plough discharge cooler, 厚料层~ deep-bed cooler, 环式~*, 回转式~ rotary-type coole, 螺旋~ cooling screw, 逆流式~ counterflow cooler, 竖式~ shaft-type cooler, 行星式~ planetary cooler
冷却机槽 cooler trough
冷却机给矿槽[漏斗] cooler feed hopper
冷却机冷却 conventional cooling
冷却机料层 cooler-bed
冷却机入口[装矿口] cooler inlet
冷却机速度控制 cooler speed control
冷却机台车 cooler grate
冷却机尾[排矿端] cooler discharge
冷却集管 cooling manifold
冷却剂 coolant (medium), cooling agent [material, medium, mixture], cooler, cryogen, frigorific [freezing] mixture, heat removing agent
冷却剂出口 coolant out
冷却剂磁力分离器 coolant magnetic separator
冷却剂挡板 coolant guard
冷却剂恒温槽 coolant thermostat
冷却剂喷嘴 coolant jet
冷却剂入口 coolant in

冷却剂通道　coolant passage
冷却剂系统　coolant passage, coolant [cooling] system
冷却架　cooling stack,【钢】cooling rack（钢锭模的）
冷却间隙　cooling gap
冷却结晶器　cooler [cooling] crystallizer
冷却结晶作用　pexitropy
冷却介质　coolant (medium), cooling medium [agent, means], heat elminating medium
冷却介质温度　cooling medium temperature
冷却坑　chilling sump, cooling pit
冷却空气　cooling air, air coolant
冷却控制　cooling control
冷却料场　cooling floor
冷却裂缝[纹]　cooling crack
冷却流槽　cooling launder
冷却面　cooling surface [front], refrigeration surface
冷却面积　cooling area
冷却能力　cooling power [capacity], refrigerating capacity
冷却凝析　cooling liquation
冷却盘　cooler pan, cooling tray [table], table [tray] cooler
冷却喷淋　cooling spray
冷却喷头　cooling spray
冷却喷雾器　cooling sprayer
冷却喷嘴　cooling jet
冷却片(热)损失　cooling-plate loss
冷却期　cooling cycle [stage]
冷却器　cooler, cooling unit, condenser, chiller ◇ 板式～plate cooler, 槽式～channel cooler, 插入[可换]式～*, 蜂房式～beehive cooler, 管式～tubular cooler, 喇叭管式～trumpet cooler, 流态化～*, 炉腹～bosh cooler, 内部～【铁】internal stave, 喷气～gas jet cooler, 平流～horizontal flow cooler, 竖式～shaft cooler, 套管式～shell-and-tube cooler, 外部～【铁】external chill, 箱式～box cooler, 旋转[回转]～【冶】rotary cooler, 雪茄式～*, 圆柱形铸铁～cast iron cigar cooler, 在管线中的～in-line cooler, 直列式～【团】straight cooler, 中间～intercooler
冷却器废气　cooler off-gas
冷却器(热)损失　cooler loss
冷却强度　【金】quenching intensity, intensity of cooling
冷却区　cooling zone [space]
冷却曲线　cooling [freezing] curve
冷却熔析　cooling liquation
冷却容器　cooling vessel
冷却设备　cooling equipment [plant, device, facilities, installation], chilling unit
冷却设备系统　cooling equipment system
冷却石灰石　【钢】coolant stone
冷却时间　cooling time [period], chill time
冷却时间/烧结时间比　【团】cooling/sintering time ratio
冷却式叶片　cooled blade
冷却室　cooling chamber ◇ 氩气保护～argon cooling chamber
冷却室维护平台　【连铸】cooling chamber platform
冷却试验台　cooling rack
冷却水　cooling [jacket, chilled] water, water coolant ◇ 直接[接触]～*
冷却水泵　cooling water pump
冷却水槽　cooling water tank, bosh tank, water bosh
冷却水池　cooling basin
冷却水出口　cooling water outlet
冷却水阀　cooling water valve
冷却水沟渠　cooling water channel
冷却水管　cooling water pipe
冷却水管道　cooling water conduit
冷却水管塞　cooling plug
冷却水过滤器　water filter
冷却水进水口[入口]　cooling water supply [in]
冷却水回路　cooling water circuit

冷却水(连)接头　cooling water connection
冷却水排出口　cooling water outlet [drain]
冷却水排放　cooling water discharge
冷却水塔　cooling stack
冷却水套　cooling (water) jacket, water-cooling jacket
冷却水套挂钩　【铁】cooler snatcher
冷却水套散热损失　jacket loss
冷却水溢流箱　cooling water discharge box
冷却速度　cooling speed [velocity]
冷却速率　cooling rate
冷却速率倒数曲线[倒冷却速率曲线]　inverse cooling curve
冷却隧道　cooling tunnel
冷却塔　cooling tower [stack] ◇ 抽风式~*,二次~ recooling tower,混凝土~ concrete cooling tower,空气~*,喷雾~ spray column,强制通风~*,填充~ packed cooling tower,烟囱式~ chimney cooler
冷却台　cooling table [bench]
冷却套　cooled [cooling] jacket, heat sink
冷却套冷却　jacket type cooling
冷却梯度　cooling gradient
冷却条件　cooling condition
冷却通道　cooling passage
冷却通风机　cooling fan
冷却槽　cooling vat [tank]
冷却筒　tube cooler, quench trommel
冷却物　【铸】chills
冷却系统　cooling system [passage], refrigerating system
冷却系统操作工　cooling system operator
冷却线性收缩　【铸】contraction in length on cooling
冷却箱　cooling box [tank], cooler bin ◇ 炉腹~*,密闭式~*
冷却效率　cooling efficiency
冷却效应　cooling effect
冷却烟道　cooling flue [duct]

冷却液　cooling [coolant] liquid, freezing solution, (liquid) coolant ◇ 切削~【机】cutting fluid,刷式~调合器*
冷却液流　cooling spray
冷却液膜　cooling film
冷却因数　【铸】cooling factor
冷却应变　cooling strain
冷却应力　cooling stress
冷却硬化　hardening by cooling
冷却余热　cooling heat
冷却元件　cooling element
冷却运输机　cooling conveyer ◇ 车式~*
冷却罩　cooling hood, cooling cover
冷却中断　interruption of cooling
冷却周期　cooling cycle, cooling-down period
冷却转变图　【金】C.T. (cooling transformation) diagram
冷却转鼓　cooling [cooler] drum
冷却装置　cooling plant [apparatus, facilities, element, unit] ◇ 槽式~*,洒水~*
冷却状态　cooled condition, state of cooling
冷却锥体　cooling cone
冷却作用　cooling effect
冷蠕变　cold creep
冷筛(分)　【团】cold screen(ing)
冷筛分设备　【团】cold screening facilities
冷筛分系统[循环]　【团】cold-screening circuit
冷烧结矿　cold sinter
冷烧结矿处理系统　【团】cold sinter handling system
冷烧结矿带　cold sinter zone
冷生铁(低硅生铁)　cold pig iron
冷时效　cold ageing
冷室　cold chamber
冷室压力铸造　cold chamber pressure casting
冷室压铸机　cold chamber (die-casting) machine ◇ 波拉克~ Polak machine,水

压~*
冷水冲洗[清洗]槽 cold-water tank
冷水清洗 cold water rinse
冷撕裂 cold tear
冷塑性 cold plasticity
冷塑性变形 cold plastic deformation
冷塑性加工 cold plastic working
冷塑性形变量 amount of cold plastic deformation
冷碎废铁[钢] cold cropping
冷碎强度 cold crushing strength
冷缩配合 shrink [contraction] fit
冷态 cold state [condition, position]
冷态锻造 【压】cold forging
冷态火焰清理机 cold scarfing machine
冷态及热态试验 cold-and-hot test
冷态锯切(金属的) cold sawing
冷态抗磨试验 cold state abrasion test
冷态流变 cold flow
冷态试车[试运转] cold-run trial
冷态延性 cold-ductility
冷铁 【铸】(iron, mould) chill, chill(ing) block, chin-chin hardening ◇ 铸件圆角成形用~ radius chill
冷铁钉 chill nail
冷铁模型 chill pattern
冷铁涂料 chill coating [wash]
冷停堆剩余反应性 【理】cold shut-down (reactivity) margin
冷弯 cold bend(ing)
冷弯边的 cold-flanged
冷弯槽钢 roll-formed channel
冷弯成形(冷弯型材的) cold roll forming ◇ 辊式~*, 线性~*
冷弯冲压机 press brake
冷弯钢 cold-pressing quality steel
冷弯机 forming [shaping] mill, channel (l)ing machine
冷弯试验 cold-bend(ing) test
冷弯型材 moulded section
冷弯型钢 formed section, roll-formed shape, lightweight steel shape, joist webs

◇ 形状复杂~ complex shape
冷弯型钢机 cold shaping
冷陷阱 cold trap
冷芯盒制芯法 【铸】cold box process
冷修补 【冶】cold repair
冷修整 cold-trim(ming)
冷旋压 【压】cold spinning
冷旋转锻造 cold swaging
冷压 cold-compacting, cold compression [pressing], cold-moulding, chill-pressing (低于常温的压制)
冷压冲杆 cold press ram
冷压断面收缩率 cold reduction percent
冷压法 cold-press method
冷压钢 cold-pressed steel
冷压焊 cold (pressure) welding, press cold welding
冷压机 cold press
冷压机座 cold-press bed
冷压块(法) cold briquetting
冷压力加工作业 【压】cold-working practice
冷压铆钉 cold-driven rivet
冷压模 cold stamping die, cold-press die
冷压坯块[团块] cold-pressed compact
冷压球团 cold-binding pellet ◇ 高碳~*
冷压烧结技术 cold-pressing-sintering technique
冷压烧结青铜 cold-pressed and sintered bronze
冷压试验 cold pressing test
冷压缩 cold [compression] reduction
冷压台 cold-press bed
冷压头机 【压】cold heading machine
冷压性能 cold-pressing property
冷压压下百分率 cold reduction percent
冷压折 【压】cold-laps
冷压真空烧结法 cold-pressing vacuum sintering method
冷烟道气 【冶】cold flue gas
冷焰 cool flame
冷阳极 cold anode

冷阳极氧化处理(轻金属合金的) cold anodizing
冷阴极 cold cathode
冷阴极充气整流管 anotron
冷阴极离子(真空)计 cold-cathode ionization gauge
冷阴极电子枪 cold-cathode gun
冷阴极管 cold cathode tube
冷阴极真空计 cold-cathode gauge
冷应变 cold strain(ing)
冷硬 chill,【铸】bleaching
冷硬层 【金】chilled [chilling] layer
冷硬合金铸铁轧辊 alloy chilled iron roll
冷硬钼镁铸铁轧辊 molybdenum-magnesium chilled iron roll
冷硬钼镍镁铸铁轧辊 molybdenum-nickel-magnesium chilled iron roll
冷硬钼铸铁轧辊 molybdenum chilled iron roll
冷硬镍铸铁轧辊 nickel alloy chill roll, nickel chilled roll
冷硬球墨铸铁轧辊 magnesium chilled iron roll
冷硬试验 chill test
冷硬铁 chilled iron
冷硬型芯 【铸】air-set core
冷硬槽铸造轧辊 chill-pass roll
冷硬轧辊 chill(ed) roll ◇ 纯白口~ clear chill roll, 无限~ indefinite chill roll, 有限~ definite chill roll
冷硬铸法试样 【铸】chill cast sample
冷硬铸钢 chilled [hard] cast steel
冷硬铸钢粒 chilled shot
冷硬铸铁 chilled [case-hardened] cast iron
冷硬铸铁风口 【铁】chill cast tuyere
冷硬铸铁砂[粒,丸] chilled iron shot
冷硬铸铁轧辊 chilled (cast) iron roll ◇ 加镍钼~ *
冷硬铸型[模] iron mould
冷硬铸造 chill cast(ing) ◇ 直接~ direct chill casting

冷硬铸造轧辊 chill roll ◇ 双层~ double-pour chill roll
冷渣 【冶】cold slag
冷轧板 cold-rolled plate ◇ 低碳半硬质~ *, 优质~ cold-rolled primes
冷轧板材轧机 reduction mill
冷轧棒材 cold-finished rod
冷轧薄板 (light, flat) cold-rolled sheet, cold-reduced sheet ◇ 1号硬度~ *, 超深冲性能~ *, 冲压用优质~ *, 镜面光亮优质~ *, 四分之一最高硬度~ *
冷轧薄钢板 cold-rolled steel sheet ◇ 光亮退火的~ silver finish sheet
冷轧扁(圆钢丝的) cold flat rolling
冷轧扁钢 flat cold rolled bar
冷轧不锈钢 cold rolled stainless steel
冷轧材[产品] cold-finished product, cold-rolled mill product
冷轧车间 cold-rolling [cold-reducing, cold-reduction] department
冷轧粗轧机组 cold roughing train
冷轧带材 cold (rolled) strip, flat cold rolled strip, cold-rolled band
冷轧带钢 cold rolled steel strip, cold-strip steel
冷轧带钢横剪机组[作业线] cold strip (cross-cut) shearing line
冷轧带钢剪切机组[作业线] cold strip shearing line
冷轧带(钢)卷 cold-rolled coil
冷轧带钢卷筒[卷取机] cold strip reel
冷轧带钢纵剪机组[作业线] cold strip slitting line
冷轧带肋钢筋 cold rolled ribbed (steel) bar
冷轧镀锡板 cold rolled tin plate
冷轧法 cold-rolling practice ◇ 两次~ *
冷轧粉带 cold (rolled) strip
冷轧负荷 cold-rolling load
冷轧钢板 cold-rolled plate ◇ 二次~ *, 高硬度~ full temper, 墙壁用涂搪瓷~ Yodowall, 一次~ single-reduced plate, 最

高硬度~ (full) hard temper
冷轧钢(材) cold-rolled steel (c.r.s., CRST) ◇ 连续退火高强度~*
冷轧钢带的立轧直角边(精度和光洁度低于 No.1 边) No.6 edge
冷轧钢带经加工的高精度或高光洁度的边 No.1 edge
冷轧钢带经圆盘剪剪切的接近直角的边 No.3 edge
冷轧钢带立轧边(圆边) No.4 edge
冷轧钢带去除毛刺的接近直角的边 No.5 edge
冷轧钢带轧制状态的边 No.2 edge
冷轧管 cold-reduced tube ◇ 周期式[皮尔格式]~*
冷轧管法 tube cold-reducing
冷轧管机 cold-reducing [cold-reduction] mill, tube reducer, cold pilger (mill) ◇ 阿尔贡三辊式~*, 高速周期式~*, 行星式~*, 摇摆式[罗克莱特]~ rock-right mill
冷轧光洁度(板材的) cold-rolled finish ◇ 肥皂水润滑~ soap-rolled finish, 煤油润滑的~ kerosene-rolled finish, 乳化液润滑的~ soluble oil-rolled finish
冷轧硅钢 cold rolled silicon steel
冷轧硅钢带 cold rolled silicon steel tape
冷轧辊 cold-roll
冷轧辊道 cold-run table
冷轧黑薄[钢]板 flat cold rolled black sheet
冷轧机 cold(-rolling) mill, cold rolls ◇ 串列[连续]式~*, 二次~*, 可逆式~ reversing cold mill, 克劳斯往复式板材~*, 平整及二次~ temper and DCR mill, 森吉米尔~*, 斯特克尔~*
冷轧机精轧机座[冷轧精轧机] cold finisher
冷轧机跨间 cold mill bay
冷轧结构 【金】cold rolling texture
冷轧金属 cold-rolled metal
冷轧精整 cold-rolled finish ◇ 干辊~*

冷轧宽带钢 wide cold strip
冷轧螺纹钢筋 cold rolled deformed bar
冷轧密闭退火的(钢板) cold-rolled close annealed (C.R.C.A.)
冷轧平整 cold-rolled temper, skin passing
冷轧润滑剂 cold-rolling lubricant
冷轧润滑油 cold-rolling oil
冷轧设计 cold-rolling mill design
冷轧塑性区 plastic zone
冷轧弹簧碳钢 cold-rolled carbon spring steel
冷轧碳钢 cold-rolled carbon steel
冷轧条材 cold-finished bar
冷轧条钢 cold-finished steel bar
冷轧无取向硅钢板 cold rolled non-oriented silicon steel
冷轧型材 cold rolled section
冷轧性能 cold-rolling property
冷轧压缩[压下](量) cold rolling reduction, reduction in cold rolling
冷轧硬化的 temper-rolled
冷轧硬化锌 hardened rolled zinc
冷轧织构的形成 formation of cold rolled texture
冷轧作业 cold-rolling practice
冷胀合金 expanded metal
冷折疤(锻件缺陷) cold-shut
冷折叠 【钢】teeming arrest
冷折痕 【压】cold-laps
冷振筛 cold vibro screen
冷珠 drop, 【铸】cold shot (冷疤)
冷铸 cold cast, cast in chills
冷铸铅青铜 chill-cast leaded bronze, arctic bronze
冷铸(生)铁 chilled cast iron (CCI), chill cast pig
冷铸收缩应变 cast strain
冷铸箱 chill box
冷铸型 chill mould
冷铸轧辊 【压】chilled roll
冷装废钢法 【钢】cold scrap process
冷装料 cold charge [stock]

冷装料炉　cold-charged furnace
冷装炉(钢)锭　cold-charged ingot
冷装炉料[物料]　cold-charged material
冷装熔炼　cold melt
冷子管　cryotron
冷作　(同"冷加工")
冷作钢　cold-working steel
冷作工具钢　coldwork tool steel
冷作时效　hardness [overstrain] ageing
冷作双晶线　Piobert lines
冷作硬化　(同"冷加工硬化") ◇ 消除[清除]~效应*
冷作硬化金属　cold-worked metal, strain-hardening metal
厘米-克-秒单位制　centimeter-gram-second system (CGS)
厘米/秒　centimeters per second (cm/s)
梨形铁水罐　Kling type ladle
梨形转炉　pear-shaped vessel
犁板　earth board
犁钢　plough steel
犁铧　share
犁铧钢　ploughshare section
犁片混合器　plough-blade mixer
犁土机(松土掘根机)　ripper-rooter
离岸价格　free on board (FOB, F.O.B.)
离岗培训　off-site training
离辊时间　time out of rolls
离-合　[电]on-off
离合面　interface
离合片[板]　clutch plate
离合器　【机】clutch ◇ 超速~*, 磁力~ magnetic clutch [gear], 带式~ band clutch, 多片式~ multidisc clutch, 方爪~ square-jaw chutch, 过载~ overriding clutch, 弧形齿轮~ curved tooth clutch, 扩张式~ expanding clutch, 双锥~ double cone clutch, 牙嵌[爪式]~ claw [dog] clutch, 圆盘~ disc clutch, 颚形~ jaw clutch
离合器齿轮　clutch gear
离合器盖　clutch cover [case]
离合器杆　clutch arm
离合器机构　clutch mechanism
离合器面[衬片]　clutch facing [liner]
离合器盘[离合圆盘]　clutch disc [cushion] ◇ 双金属~ bimetallic clutch disc
离合器盘鼓　clutch disc drum
离合器踏板　clutch pedal
离合器套　clutch sleeve
离合器箱　clutch housing
离合器圆锥　clutch cone
离合器制动器[离合器闸]　clutch brake
离合器轴　clutch [engaging] shaft, clutch spindle
离解　dissociation (diss.), disassociating, decomposition, disintegration, segregation, breakdown ◇ 不~的 nondissociated, 电弧~设备*
离解氨　dissociated ammonia, ammogas ◇ 燃烧~*
离解氨(保护)气氛　dissociated ammonia atmosphere, ammogas atmosphere
离解氨保护钎焊　dissociated ammonia brazing
离解氨供应　dissociated ammonia supply
离解氨气体发生器　ammogas atmosphere generator
离解本领[能力]　dissociating power
离解常数　dissociation constant
离解成离子　ionic dissociation
离解度　dissociation degree
离解反应　dissociation reaction
离解化合物　dissociated compound
离解力　dissociating force
离解能　dissociation energy
离解平衡　dissociation equilibrium
离解器　dissociator
离解器蒸罐[曲颈瓶]　dissociator retort
离解热　dissociation heat
离解溶剂　dissociating solvent
离解室　dissociation chamber
离解速率　dissociation [decomposition] rate

离解位错　dissociated dislocations
离解温度　dissociation temperature
离解系数　decomposition coefficient
离解性能[性质]　dissociation property
离解压[力]　dissociation pressure [tension]
离开　leave, turnaway
离散单元法　distinct element method
离散的原子结构　discrete atomic structure
离散点　discrete spots
离散化　discretization
离散微粒　discrete particles
离散(型)规划　discrete programming
离散值　discrete value
离散质点　discrete particles
离位和就位　out of and into position
离析　segregate, liquate, isolation, breakup, emanation, unmixing (混合物的)
离析的混凝土　segregating concrete
离析法　segregation process ◇ 难熔铜矿 ~ *
离析精度　separation sharpness
离析炼铜法　copper segregation process
离析试验(压强上升速率试验)　isolation test
离析铜　segregate copper
离线　off-line
离线备件　off-line spare
离线操作[离线运算, 离机操作]　off-line operation
离线超声波检验　off-line ultrasonic testing
离线试验　off-line test
离心　centrifugation, centrifuge
离心摆式转速计　centrifugal (pendulum-type) tachometer
离心泵　centrifugal pump ◇ 两级 ~ *
离心沉淀机　centrifugal clarifier, bowl centrifuge
离心沉降　centrifugal settling
离心出料提斗机　centrifugal discharge bucket elevator

离心萃取器　【色】centrifugal extractor ◇ 库塔 ~ Coutor extractor, 卢威斯塔 ~ Luwesta extractor
离心淬火　centrifugal quenching
离心法　centrifuge method, centrifuging
离心分级[分选]　centrifugal classifying [classification]
离心分级机　centrifugal classifier
离心分离　centrifugation, centrifugal separation, centrifugalization, whizzing
离心分离机　centrifugal separator, centrifuge
离心分离系数　centrifugal coefficient
离心分离作用　centrifugalization
离心干燥机　centrifugal drier [dryer] ◇ 涡轮式 ~ turbine dryer
离心鼓风机　centrifugal blower
离心过滤产物　product of centrifuge
离心过滤机　centrifugal filter, centrifuge
离心过滤筐　centrifuge basket
离心混汞器　centrifugal amalgamator
离心机　centrifugal machine [apparatus], centrifuge, whizzer ◇ 超速 ~ ultra-centrifuge, 反絮凝 ~ deflocculator, 过滤式 ~ *, 间歇式 ~ batch centrifuge, 精炼用 ~ affination centrifuge, 空心式[无隔板] ~ hollow-bowl centrifuge, 筐式 ~ basket centrifuge, 连续 ~ continuous centrifuge, 螺旋推进式 ~ scroll centrifuge, 脱水 ~ dewatering centrifuge, 振动式 ~ *
离心集渣浇口[集渣器]　【铸】spinner [wheel, whirl] gate
离心继电器　centrifugal relay
离心加速度　centrifugal acceleration
离心浇铸　spun [centrifugal] casting, centre die casting ◇ 艾德林熔模铝热 ~ 法 *
离心浇铸机　centrifugal casting machine
离心浇注混凝土管　centrifugal concrete pipe, centrifugally spun concrete pipe
离心浸涂(合金)法　【铸】centrifugal immersion process

离心净化机　centrifugal clarifier
离心开关　centrifugal switch (cfs)
离心力　centrifugal force (c. f.), centrifugal
离心联轴器　centrifugal coupling
离心轮(喷砂机的)　centrifugal wheel
离心排气风扇　centrifugal exhausting fan
离心排气机　centrifugal exhauster
离心喷[散]布　centrifugal disintegration
离心喷雾　cetrifugal spray
离心喷雾器　centrifugal atomizer
离心皮带运输机　thrower belt conveyer
离心球磨机　centrifugal ball mill ◇ 希斯温～Hyswing ball mill
离心润滑　centrifugal lubrication
离心筛(分机)　centrifugal screen
离心除尘器
离心(式)除[集,收]尘器　centrifugal (dust) collector; centrifugal cleaner, centrifugal dust separator, rotoclone, whirler-type dust catcher
离心式除渣流槽　【冶】whirling runner
离心式风机　radial fan
离心式混砂机　【铸】centrifugal sand mixer
离心式集渣器　whirl gate
离心式搅拌器[机]　centrifugal stirrer [blender]
离心式离合器　centrifugal clutch
离心式磨机　centrifugal mill
离心式泥浆泵　centrifugal slurry pump
离心式抛砂机　【铸】centrifugal sand-throwing machine
离心式喷嘴　swirler
离心式燃料喷嘴　fuel swirler
离心式溶剂萃取器　centrifugal solvent extractor
离心式扇风机　radial flow fan
离心(式)脱水器　dewatering centrifuge ◇ 卡喷特[竖式]～*
离心式洗涤机　centrifugal washer
离心式真空泵　vacuum centrifugal pump
离心式转速表　centrifugal tachometer

离心送风机　fan blower
离心调节[调速]器　centrifugal governor
离心调整器　flyball regulator
离心脱泥机　deslimer centrifuge
离心脱水　centrifugation
离心脱水机　screening [screen-bowl, screen-type] centrifuge, perforated basket centrifuge
离心雾化　【粉】centrifugal atomization
离心洗气机　cyclone gaswasher
离心压坯　【粉】centrifugal compacting
离心压气机　centrifugal booster
离心压塑　compacting by centrifuging
离心叶轮　centrifugal impeller
离心溢流(排放)　centrifuge effluent
离心制动器[离心力闸]　centrifugal brake
离心铸管　centrifugally [spun] cast pipe ◇ 德莱沃特～法*, 莫洛树脂砂衬～法*
离心铸件　centrifugal casting
离心铸型　centrifugal casting mould [die]
离心铸造　(同"离心浇铸")◇ 感应熔化～设备*, 全[水平旋转轴]～*, 斯通～用青铜
离心铸造法　centrifugal casting process ◇ 詹姆斯～*
离心铸造复合球墨铸铁轧辊　centrifugally double poured nodular cast iron roll
离心铸造钢　centrifuge(d) steel
离心铸造钢管材　centrifugally cast steel tubing
离心铸造高强度青铜铸件　◇ 霍尔福斯～Holfos bronze
离心铸造机　(同"离心浇铸机")
离心铸造耐热钢　centrifugal-cast heat-resistant steel
离心铸造轧辊　spun cast roll
离心转动型造球机　【团】centrifugal rolling type pelletizer
离心转鼓　centrifugal drum
离心作用　centrifugal action, centrifugation
离异共晶合金　divorced eutectic alloy

离异共晶体　【金】divorced eutectic
离异渗碳体　divorced cementite
离异珠光体　divorced pearlite
离子　ion ◇ 反[平衡]～【理】counter-ion, 含氧～*, 离解成～ionic dissociation, 配衡[碇系]～ anchored ion, 向外迁移～ outgoing ion
离子半导体　ionic semiconductor
离子半径　ionic radius
离子泵　ion pump ◇ 消气剂～【理】getter-ion pump
离子泵唧系统　ion pumping system
离子层　ionosphere
离子产物　ion(ic) product
离子抽汲系统　ion pumping system
离子氮化(法)　ion nitriding, ionitriding
离子氮硝化动力学　ionitrification kinetics
离子导电率　ionic conductivity
离子导(电)体　ionic conductor
离子缔合萃取　【色】ion association extraction
离子缔合(作用)　【理】ion association
离子点阵[晶格]　ionic [heteropolar] lattice
离子电荷　ionic charge
离子电泳作用　【理】ionophoresis
离子对　【理】ion(ic) pair
离子发射　ion emission
离子反应　ionic reaction
离子分子共存　coexistence of ions and moleculae
离子浮选　ion floatation
离子管　ionic [gas] tube
离子轰击　ion bombardment
离子轰击浸蚀　ion bombardment etching
离子化　ionization, ionizing ◇ 可～基团 ionogen
离子化合物　ionic [ionized] compound
离子化气体　ionized gas
离子化倾向　ionization tendency
离子化受主　【半】ionized acceptor
离子化原子　ionized atom ◇ 二次～doubly ionized atom
离子活度[性]　ion(ic) activity
离子计　ionometer, ionization meter
离子价　【化】ionic valency
离子间距离　interionic distance
离子键　ion(ic) binding [bond, linkage]
离子键力　ionic forces
离子交换　ion exchange (IX), ion interchange, ionic replacement ◇ 间歇[分批]～ batch ion exchange, 连续～*, 阳离子型～*, 液胺～*, 液体～*
离子交换槽　【色】(ion-)exchange cell ◇ 凹底[碟形底]～*, 多层薄膜～*, 平底～*
离子交换处理　ion-exchange treatment
离子交换萃取　ion-exchange extraction
离子交换法　ion-exchange method [route], resin-column process
离子交换反应　ion-exchange reaction
离子交换反应堆　ion-exchange reactor
离子交换分离　ion-exchange separation, separation by ion-exchange
离子交换富集　ion-exchange concentration
离子交换剂　(ion-)exchange material, ionite, ion exchanger ◇ 当量～*, 碳系～*
离子交换接触器　ion-exchange contactor ◇ 摇筛式～*
离子交换介质　ion-exchange medium
离子交换料液　ion-exchange feed
离子交换膜　ion-exchange membrane
离子交换膜电极　ion-exchange membrane electrode
离子交换能力　ion-exchange capacity, exchange capacity for ions
离子交换器　ion exchanger
离子交换情况分析技术　frontal analysis technique
离子交换色谱法　ion-exchange chromatography
离子交换设备　I.E. (ion exchange) plant [unit] ◇ 环带式～*, 流态化床～*
离子交换树脂　exchange (r) [ion-ex-

change] resin, duolite, ionite ◇ 碱性～ base exchange resin, 弱碱性～*

离子交换树脂层 ion-exchange resin bed
离子交换树脂交换容量 ion exchange resin capacity
离子交换树脂解吸 ion exchange resin desorption
离子交换树脂利用率 ion exchange resin efficiency
离子交换树脂吸附 ion-exchange resin adsorption
离子交换树脂选择系数 ion exchange resin selective coefficient
离子交换树脂再生 ion exchange resin regeneration
离子交换提纯[纯化] ion-exchange purification
离子交换提取 ion-exchange extraction, sorption-extraction
离子交换团 ion-exchange group
离子交换吸附(现象) ion-exchange absorption
离子交换系统 ion-exchange system
离子交换性能 ion-exchange property
离子交换柱 ion(-exchange) column, resin column ◇ 全连续～*, 跳汰床[脉动]～*
离子交换(柱处理)法 resin-column process
离子接受体 ion accepter
离子结构 ionic structure
离子浸蚀 ionic etching
离子晶格 ionic lattice
离子晶体 ionic [heteropolar] crystal
离子晶体半径 ionic crystal radius
离子晶体光谱 ionic crystal spectrum
离子晶体烧结动力学 ionic crystals sintering kinetics
离子扩散 ionic diffusion
离子理论 ionic theory
离子流 ion flow
离子密度 ion density [concentration]

离子膜技术 ionic-membrane technique
离子浓度 ion concentration, ionic strength
离子耦合 ion binding
离子偶 ion(ic) pair
离子排斥 ion exclusion
离子排斥理论 theory of ion exclusion
离子结构 ionic structure
离子喷镀 ion plating
离子喷镀法 ion plating process
离子碰撞 ion collision [bombardment]
离子平衡 ionic equilibrium
离子谱线 ion line
离子气氛 ionic atmosphere
离子迁移 ion transfer, ion(ic) migration
离子迁移率 ion(ic) mobility
离子迁移数 transference [transport] number
离子枪 ion gun
离子强度 ionic strength
离子筛 ionic sieve
离子渗氮 (同"离子氮化")
离子渗镀 ion plating
离子渗碳 ion carbonization
离子实 ion core
离子实区 ion-core field
离子受体 ion accepter
离子束 【理】ion beam
离子束测头[探针] ion-(beam) probe
离子束沉淀(法) ion beam deposition
离子束溅射 ion beam dispersion
离子束弥散 ion beam dispersion
离子束蒸发 ion beam evaporation
离子探针谱线图 ion probe spectrum
离子探针质谱仪 ion probe mass spectrometer
离子体系 ionic system
离子微量分析仪 ion microanalyzer
离子微探针分析 ion microprobe analysis
离子微探针质量分析 ion microprobe mass analysis
离子吸附树脂柱 ion-adsorption resin column

离子系　ionic system
离子箱　ion box
离子型络合物萃取　（同"离子缔合萃取"）
离子性[型]晶体　ionic crystal
离子选择电极　ion-selective electrode
离子选择膜　ion-selective membrane
离子雪崩　(ion) avalanche
离子-氧间亲和[互引]力　ion-oxygen attraction
离子移变(作用)　ionotropy
离子移植技术[离子注入]　ion implantation
离子源　ion source [gun]
离子杂质　ionic impurity
离子折射　ionic refraction
离子直径　ionic diameter
离子重量　ionic weight
离子柱　ion column
理查德定律（关于金属熔化熵的经验定律）　Richard's law
理查德耐蚀铝青铜（55Cu,42Zn,2Al,1Fe）　Richard's bronze
理查德图【铁】Reichard's diagram
理查德锡基轴承合金（82Sn,10Sb,8Cu）　Richard's bearing alloy
理查森铜基合金（30Sn,2As,2Ag,0.7Zn,余量 Cu）　Richardson's alloy
理查森效应【理】Richardson effect
理查森浊度计（测定粉末粒度用）　Richardson turbidimeter
理论　theory, rationale ◇贝蒂~", 伯努利~", 布喇格-威谦斯~ Bragg-williams theory, 恩格尔-布鲁尔~", 海特勒-伦敦~"
理论板　theoretical plate [tray], perfect tray
理论边缘　theoretical margin
理论产量[产出率]　theoretical yield
理论成分　theoretical composition
理论电压　theoretical voltage
理论断裂强度　theoretical rupture strength
理论断裂应力　theoretical break-away stress
理论反应热　theoretical heat of reaction
理论方程式　theoretical equation
理论分离系数　theoretical separation coefficient
理论分析　theoretical analysis
理论风[空气]量　theoretical air
理论耗量　theoretical consumption
理论喉部　theoretic(al) throat
理论还原电势[位]　theoretical reducing potential
理论基础　theoretical basis [fundamental, principle], rationale
理论级高　theoretical stage height
理论级高度当量　height quivalent of a theoretical stage (HETS)
理论级数　number of theoretical stages
理论计算　theoretical calculation
理论计算确定的热处理法　PP (paper and pen) heat treatment
理论晶界[边界]　theoretical boundary
理论抗剪强度　theoretical shear strength
理论力学　theoretical [rational] mechanics
理论[理想]流量　ideal flow
理论凝固温度　theoretical solidification temperature
理论切变强度　theoretical shear strength
理论燃烧风量　theoretical combustion air
理论热力学　theoretical thermodynamics
理论塔板数　theoretical [perfect] tray, number of theoretical plates
理论物理学　theoretical physics
理论效率　theoretical efficiency
理论研究　theoretical investigation [research]
理论验证　theoretical examination
理论应力集中系数　theoretical stress-concentration factor (Kt)
理论有效指数　theoretical availability index

理论原理　theoretical principle
理论真空　theoretical vacuum
理论值　theoretic(al) value [amount]
"理想"标准电阻合金(55—60Cu, 40—45Ni)　ideal (alloy)
理想不完整[非完善]晶体　ideally imperfect crystal
理想磁导率　ideal permeability
理想淬火　【金】ideal quench(ing)
理想淬火曲线　ideal quenching curve
理想搭板　perfect plate
理想单色的　perfectly monochromatic
理想负偏差　negative deviation from ideality
理想刚性辊　unflattened roll
理想化晶体　idealized crystal
理想化学成分　ideal chemical compound
理想晶界滑移　ideal grain boundary sliding
理想晶体　ideal crystal
理想晶体切变强度的麦肯齐计算(法)　Mackenzie's computation of shear strenth of ideal crystals
理想临界直径　ideal critical diameter
理想流体　ideal [perfect] fluid
"理想"坡莫合金　Idealoy
理想气体　ideal [perfect] gas
理想气体常数　ideal-gas constant
理想气体定律　ideal gas law
理想溶液　ideal [perfect] solution
理想塑性　ideal [perfect] plasticity
理想塑性材料　ideally plastic material
理想塔板　theoretical plate, theoretically (perfect) plate
理想完整[完美]晶体　ideally perfect crystal
理想效率　ideal efficiency
理想液体　ideal [perfect] liquid
理想轧制过程　simple rolling process
理想直径　ideal diameter
理想值　ideal value
理想周期性　perfect periodicity ◇ 与～的偏差　departure from perfect periodi-city
理想状态　ideal state
理想自由电子模型　【理】ideal free electron model
理想组织　【理】ideal structure
学学士　bachelor of science (BSc)
理由　reason, cause, occasion, argument, consideration ◇ 正当～　justification
李式皮拉尼真空计　LeRossignol's pirani gauge
里衬　lining
里程标　milepost, distance-post
里程表[计]　(h) odometer, velometer, mileage table
里程指示　distance indication
里德伯常数[恒量]　【理】Rydberg constant
里弗拉克托洛依镍基耐热合金(0.03C, 0.7Mn, 0.65Si, 17.9Cr, 37Ni, 20Co, 3.03Mo, 2.99Ti, 0.25Al, 19Fe)　Refractoloy
里弗莱克塔尔形变[锻造]铝合金(0.3—1Mg,余量 Al)　Reflectal
里弗雷克达洛伊镍基耐热合金　Refractaloy
里弗雷克斯碳化硅高级耐火材料　Refrex
里默钢锭用加热防缩孔法　【钢】Riemer process
里奇金色黄铜(90Cu, 10Zn)　Rich gold metal
里斯特夹杂检测法　【冶】Rist technique
里思青铜合金(74.5Cu, 11.6Sn, 9Pb, 4.9Sb)　Reith's alloy
里外螺旋对口平接(管材的)　screwed flush butt and butt
里希腾伯格易熔合金(30Pb, 20Sn, 50Bi)　Lichtenberg metal
礼帽形挤压型材　extruded hat-section
锂{Li}　lithium ◇ 含～合金, 金属～　metallic lithium
锂冰晶石{3LiF·AlF$_6$}　lithium cryolite, cryolithionite

锂电解槽 lithium electrolytic cell
锂汞齐 lithium amalgam
锂合金 lithium alloy
锂辉石{LiAl(SiO$_3$)$_2$} spodumene, spodumenite
锂基合金 lithium-base alloy
锂矿床 lithium deposite
锂矿物 lithium minerals
锂离子电池 lithium ion battery
锂磷铝矿 amblygonite
锂铝矿{LiAl(SiO$_3$)$_2$} kunzite
锂青铜 lithium bronze
锂热还原（法） lithium reduction
锂/石墨电池 Li/graphite cell
锂添加合金 lithium addition
锂霞石{LiAlSiO$_4$} cucryptite
锂盐糊阳极 carbon anode containing lithium salt
锂硬锰矿 oakite
锂云母 lithium [lithia] mica, (lithia micas) lepidolite
锂蒸气 lithium vapour ◇ 利瑟卡伯～保护气氛*
锂蒸气还原 lithium vapour reduction
锂（蒸气）气氛 lithium atmosphere
栗级无烟煤(20—48mm) chestnut
励磁 excitation, exciting ◇ 最大～ ceiling excitation
励磁变压器 exciting transformer
励磁变阻器 field rheostat
励磁不足 underexcitation
励磁电流控制 field current control
励磁电源 field current [power] supply
励磁机[器] exciter ◇ 恒定～ constant exciter
励磁绕组[线圈] exciting winding, field winding [coil, core], magnet(izing) coil
励磁铁心 field [magnet] core
励磁系统 excitation system
砾磨机 pebble [flint] mill
砾砂 【铸】moulding gravel
砾石 gravel, grail, pebble, rounded aggregate ◇ 豆[小]～ pea gravel, 细～ bird's eye gravel
砾石道碴 gravel ballast
砾石骨料混凝土 gravel-aggregated concrete
砾石过滤器[池] gravel filter
砾石混凝土 gravel concrete, gritcrete
砾石行车道 gravel drive
砾岩 【地】conglomerate
砾状铍 pebble of beryllium
砾状效应（金属表面的） pebble effect
历程 course, 【化】mechanism
利波维茨铋铅锡易熔合金 Lipowitz alloy
利废钢材 （同"再轧钢材"）
利废烧结厂 recycling plant
利海抗裂试验 【焊】Lehigh cracking test
利海慢弯曲试验（测定脆断性能用） Lehigh slow-bend test
利硫砷铅矿 liveingite
利润 【企】benefit, profit
利润率 profit rate [margin], earning capacity
利萨茹图形 【理】Lissajous pattern
利瑟卡伯锂蒸气保护气氛 Lithcarb atmosphere
利瑟卡伯锂蒸气保护烧结法 Lithcarb process
利特尔铜锡铅合金(67Cu, 29Sn, 2.45Zn, 1.5As) Little's alloy
利息 interest, dividend
利益 gain, benefit, interest, advantage
利用 use, utilizing, utilization, utility (ut.), recover（废料的）
利用率 availability (coefficient), utilization (factor), use factor
利用系数 productivity (ratio)（高炉）, utilization coefficient（烧结机, 高炉）, utilization factor, specific productivity [production], use factor, percentage yield ◇ 炉子～ furnace availability
例行观察 routine observation
例行检查[检验] （同"常规检查"）

例行维修　routine [scheduled] maintenance
例证　(example) illustration
立标　beacon, day-mark
立波尔法　Lepol system
立波尔(回转)窑　Lepol system [furnace]
立导辊　vertical guide roller
立方八面体　cuboctahedron
立方点阵[晶格]　cubic lattice
立方点阵晶胞　cubic lattice cell
立方对称　cubic symmetry
立方对称相　phase of cubic symmetry
立方根　cube root
立方褐铁矿　devil's dice
立方尖晶石型磁铁矿{γ-Fe$_2$O$_3$}　cubic spinel-like magnetite
立方结构　cube [cubic] structure
立方金属晶体　cubic metal crystal
立方晶[单]胞　cube [cubic] cell
立方(晶格)金属　cubic metal
立方晶棱　cube corner
立方晶面反射　cube-face reflections
立方晶体　cubic [isometric] crystal, cube
立方晶系　cubic [isometric] system
立方晶系物质　cubic substance
立方(晶型)氮化硼　cubic boron nitride (CBN)
立方空间点阵[格子]　cubic space lattice
立方量度生产量　cubic content [capacity]
立方马氏体　【金】cubic martensite
立方强度　cube strength
立方容积　cubage
立方体　cubic (cu., cub.), cube, cube-shaped block, cuboid
立方体对角线　cube diagonal
立方体混凝土试块　cube concrete test specimen
立方体面　cube face
立方体中心　cube centre
立方系　cubic (cu., cub.), isometric system ◇ 非～晶体 noncubic crystal
立方系晶面(即100面)　cubic plane

立方系晶体　crystal of cubic symmetry, regular crystal
立方形包装　cubic packing
立方织构　cube texture
立方织构的　cube-textured
立方轴　cubic axis
立股　stem (T形梁的), web (T形材的)
立管　uprise, riser
立管冷凝器　vertical tube condenser
立管式反应柱　vertical-pipe reaction column
立管式干燥机　drying column
立辊　【压】vertical [edger, edging] roll, vertical mill
立辊对重换装置　counterweighted vertical roll-changing rig
立辊横梁　vertical roll entablature
立辊辊缝　edger opening
立辊开度　edger opening
立辊调宽量　edging reduction
立辊轧边机　vertical edger
立辊轧机　edger, vertical [edger, edging] mill ◇ 独立～*, 与主机座紧配的～ close-coupled edger, 下传动～*
立辊(轧机)机座　vertical roll unit, edger mill
立焊　vertical (position) welding ◇ 从上到下～ vertical-downward welding, 上行[从下到上]～*, 双面～*, 向上～*
立焊焊条　vertical electrode
立活套　vertical looper
立即访问[存取]　【计】instantaneous [immediate, zero] access
立即存取存储器　【计】immediate access storage, instantaneous storage
立交线路　【运】crossover track
立浇　vertical casting
立筋　stud
立克次氏体属　Rickettsiae
立冷板[立式冷却板]　【铁】cooling stave ◇ 铸铁～*
立面图　elevation drawing ◇ 房屋主要～

frontispiece
立母线 vertical bus bar, riser
立-平式 vertical-horizontal (VH)
立剖图 profile in elevation
立砌层 【建】upright course
立砌砖砌体 soldier course
立切杠杆式剪切机 vertical knife lever shears
立式布置[装置] vertical arrangement
立式车床 vertical lathe
立式车轮轧机 vertically wheel rolling mill
立式除[破]鳞机 【压】vertical scale breaker (VSB)
立式单次拉丝机 single vertical block
立(式)导辊 vertical guide roller
立式电磁铸造 vertical electromagnetic casting (VEMC)
立式电子枪装置 vertical gun arrangement
立式放置架(钢包用) 【冶】upright-setting stand
立式混合机 vertical blender
立式活套挑[活套成形器] 【压】uplooper
立式机架 vertical stand
立式挤压机 vertical extruder
立式碱洗(带材用) vertical-type alkaline cleaning
立式搅拌机 vertical blender, vertical paddle mixer
立式结晶器 【钢】vertically supported mould
立式卷取机 vertical coiler
立式冷却机 vertical-type cooler
立式连续干燥炉 continuous vertical drying stove
立式连续炼焦工艺 vertical continuous cokemaking process
立式连铸机 vertical(-type continuous) casting machine
立式炉用升降机 vertical furnace hoist
立式螺旋槽道 vertical spiral chute bunker
立式捻股机 vertical type stranding machine
立式捻绳机 vertical closer, vertical closing machine
立式牛头刨床 vertical shaper
立式皮带助卷机 vertical type belt wrapper
立式清净装置 vertical cleaner
立式水管冷却器 vertical water-tube cooler
立式碳化炉 【焦】vertical retort
立式推线拉丝卷筒 【压】push-up block
立式外延炉 vertical epitaxial furnace
立式-卧式(的) vertical-horizontal (VH)
立式蒸馏釜 cheese box still
立式直结晶器连铸机 vertical straight-mould machine
立式止推轴承 step [toe] bearing
立式柱塞[冷压室]压铸机 【铸】vertical plunger die-casting machine
立式铸造 upright casting
立式装置 vertical arrangement
立式钻床 【机】(upright-)drill press
立视图 elevation
立体测量因素 stereometric factor
立体低倍摄影术 stereomacrography
立体放射线摄影术 stereoradiography
立体观察 stereoscopic viewing
立体化学 space chemistry, stereochemistry
立体几何(学) stereometry, solid geometry
立体交叉 cross over, overhead [flyover] crossing
立体交叉结构 【建】grade separation structure
立体角 stereo angle
立体结构 stereometric structure
立体晶粒度 spatial grain size
立体膨胀 cubic(al) dilatation
立体投影 stereoprojection ◇斜角～cabinet projection

立体投影极点　stereographic pole
立体显示　【电】stereo display
立体显微镜　（同"体视显微镜"）
立体显微照相术　stereomicrography
立体像　space [stereoscopic(al)] image, stereopicture
立体压印[精压]　full coining
立体异构(现象)　alloisomerism, stereoisomerism
立体映像对　double image
立体照片　stereogram, stereograph
立体照相术　（同"体视照相术"）
立体阵列　three-dimensional array
立体坐标轴　solid axis
立椭圆　slug [edge] oval
立椭圆孔型　off-round pass
立弯机组　【连铸】bend discharge machine
立弯式　ordinary bending type, vertical type with bending
立弯式连铸机　bent strand continuous casting machine, continuous casting machine with bending device, vertical-type continuous casting machine with bending of strand, straight mould-bent run-out plant, bend discharge machine, semi-low head machine
立卧(式轧)辊组合装置　VH (vertical-horizontal) roll
立向填角焊接　vertical fillet weld
立窑　vertical[shaft] kiln
立轧　【压】edge finish, rolling on edge ◇ 半椭圆～边 half oval edge, 冷轧钢带一边(圆边)*, 未经过～的边 free edge
立轧道次　edging (pass), upset pass
立轧辊　edging roll
立轧机架　edging mill
立轧机座　vertical mill
立轧孔型　vertical [edging, upset] pass, edging groove ◇ 帽形～(钢轨的) squabbing pass
立轧送料孔型　shallow [dummy] pass
立轧梯形孔型　hat pass

立轧轧槽　edging groove
立轧装置　edging device
立轴　vertical shaft, long axis
立轴承　footstep bearing
立轴绞车　capstan
立柱　upright (column, post), column, fence (水压机的)
立柱和电极装置(电炉的)　mast-and-electrode assembly
立柱母线　riser bus, rising main
立柱用对开式螺母(水压机的)　divided post nut
立铸　vertical casting
粒度　grain (size), granularity, (particle, mesh) size, grading, gradation, fineness ◇ 多～料 multi-granular charge, 烘干后～*
粒度比　fineness ratio
粒度变化　size variation, change in particle
粒度测定　particle-size determination
粒度测定法[术]　granulometry
粒度等级　grain-size scale
粒度范围[上下限]　(particle-)size range, size category ◇ 最大～particle stoppage
粒度范围指数　size range index
粒度分布　grain size distribution, granulometric [size, particle(-size)] distribution, size consist (煤粉的)
粒度分布曲线　size distribution curve
粒度分布指数　size distribution index
粒度分级　size classification [grading]
粒度分析　grain size analysis, grading [granulometric, mechanical, (particle-)size] analysis,【粉】infrasizing ◇ 自动～*
粒度分析器[仪]　grain [particle] size analyzer, particle size indicator
粒度分析法　method of particle-size analysis
粒度分析试验　sizing(-assay) test
粒度函数　function of particle size
粒度号数　grain size number

粒度级(别)　fraction(ation), (particle-) size fraction, size category
粒度级配组成　grading fraction
粒度减小　degradation
粒度控制　grain [particle] size control, size control
粒度累积分布曲线　cumulative size distribution curve
粒度模数　size [fineness] modulus
粒度偏析　size [particle] segregation
粒度频率微分曲线　differential size frequency curve
粒度曲线　particle-size [granulometric] curve
粒度特性　size characteristic
粒度系数　size factor
粒度研究　particle-size study
粒度因数　gradation factor
粒度影响　size effect
粒度值　(particle-)size value ◇绝对~absolute size value
粒度指数　grain fineness (G.F.)
粒度准备　size preparation
粒度组成　grading fraction, granulometric composition, particle (-size) distribution, size analysis [structure, distribution], sieve analysis
粒度组成测定　determination of size distribution
粒度组成值　particle distribution value
粒硅锰矿　alleghanyite
粒核　core particle, seed
粒化　granulating, granulation, pelletizing ◇风淬钢渣~*, 铁水[生铁]水淬~法*
粒化槽　shot(ting) tank
粒化程度　degree of granulation
粒化弹丸　【冶】feather shot
粒化合金　shotted fused alloy
粒化金属　granulated metal
粒化炉渣坑　(同"水渣坑")
粒化能　granulation energy

粒化能力　capacity of granulation
粒化器　【团】nodulizer, pelletizer, granulator
粒化生铁　granulated iron
粒化铁粉　granulated iron powder
粒化渣　grain [granulated] slag
粒化组织　granulated structure
粒级　size fraction, gradation
粒间成核位置　intergranular nucleation site
粒间同化(作用)　interassimilation
粒径　particle [grain, pellet] diameter
粒磷锰矿　fillowite
粒料分配器　bulk distributor
粒煤　granular coal (GC)
粒煤喷吹　GC (granular coal) injection
粒砂　buckshot sand
粒石料　【建】matrix
粒铁　grained iron (g.i.), spherical iron particle, iron shot, luppen, nodule
粒铁[粒化]　【铁】luppen zone
粒铁法　【铁】nodulizing (process)
粒铁回转窑　(rotating) nodulizing kiln
粒析[选]　size separation
粒状斑点　granula, granule
粒状贝氏体　granular bainite (GB)
粒状残渣　granular residue
粒状断口　granular fracture
粒状粉粒　droplet particle
粒状粉末　granular powder
粒状氟化物　particulate fluoride
粒状高炉渣　granulated blast-furnace slag
粒状钴　granulated cobalt
粒状固体层　bed of granular solids
粒状固体反应物　granular solid reactant
粒状硅镁石 $\{Mg_5(SiO_4)_2(OH, F)_2\}$　chondrodite
粒状硅铁　granular ferrosilicon
粒状过滤材料　granular filter material
粒状焊剂　granulated flux
粒状还原铁　iron ball
粒状结构　granular [grain, granulated]

粒状(结构)炉料【冶】 nodular-textured burden
粒状结晶 granular-crystalline
粒状金属 grained [granulated] metal, 【粉】shot(ted) metal
粒状精矿 granular concentrate
粒状矿 acinose ore
粒状矿浆 granular pulp
粒状镁砂[菱镁矿] grain magnesite
粒状耐火材料 refractory bead
粒状镍 granulated nickel
粒状熔剂 granular [granulated] flux
粒状砂 grained sand
粒状渗碳体 granular [spheroidite] cementite
粒状石墨 graphite granule
粒状试样 shotted sample
粒状碳 granular carbon
粒状物料[材料] granular [particulate, bulk, bead] material
粒状锡 granulated tin
粒状相 granular phase
粒状锌 granulated [mossy] zinc
粒状岩石 gruss
粒状渣 grainy slag
粒状珠光体 beaded [granular] pearlite
粒子 particle, corpuscle ◇费米~Fermi particle, 荧光~检验*
粒子场 particle field
粒子大小曲线 particle-size curve
粒子复合材料 particle composite
粒子加速器 【理】particle accelerator
粒子接触面积 particle contact area
粒子流 particle flux ◇间歇~batch flux
粒子速度 particle velocity [rapidity]
粒子特性 particle characteristic
粒子通[流]量 particle flux
粒子增强铝基复合材料 particulate reinforced Al composite
沥滤液 leachate
沥青 pitch, asphalt (asph.), bitumen (bt)
◇吹制[氧化]~*, 粗麻屑~涂包法 hessian wrapping, 含~的 bitumeniferous, 黏质~steep pitch, 轻制[稀释]~*, 溶于石油馏出物中的~asphalt cutback, 弹性~dopplerite, 涂~*, 脱苯~benzol removed pitch, 纤维管~fibre pipe pitch, 液态~liquid pitch, 硬~*, 杂酚油~creosote pitch
沥青泵 pitch pump
沥青表面处理 bituminous surface treatment
沥青槽 pitch tank
沥青产率(焦油的) pitch yield
沥青车间[工段] pitch plant
沥青衬里 asphalt [bitumen] lining
沥青处理基层 bituminous treated base (B.T.B.)
沥青瓷漆涂层 bituminous enamel coating
沥青垫层 bituminous mat
沥青方铀矿 ulrichite uroninite
沥青防水层 asphalt lining
沥青防水膜 bituminous membrane
沥青敷面 bituminous facing
沥青盖层碎石路 coated macadam
沥青膏 bituminized [asphalt] cement
沥青灌碎石路面 asphalt-grouted surfacing
沥青混合物 bituminous compound, moulding mixture (管材接口用)
沥青混凝土 asphalt [bitumen, bituminous] concrete, bitulith (路面用)
沥青混凝土路面 asphalt concrete pavement
沥青基层 black base
沥青浆体燃料 pitch slurry fuel
沥青焦(炭) pitch coke
沥青胶泥 asphalt [bituminous] grout
沥青结合碱性砖 pitch bonded basic brick
沥青浸透法 tar-impregnation
沥青绝缘(层) bituminous coating
沥青矿 asphalite
沥青路面 bituminous pavement ◇冷铺

~ cold-laid pavement, 铺 ~ black top-(ping)
沥青煤　pitch coal
沥青膜　bituminous membrane
沥青磨耗层　bituminous wearing coat
沥青黏结剂　asphalt [pitch] binder
沥青喷洒机　tanker, goudronator
沥青片　bitumen sheet
沥青铺面　asphalt paving
沥青漆　asphalt lac(quer) [paint], bitumastic paint
沥青清漆　bituminous varnish
沥青乳化燃料　bitumen emulsion fuel (BEF)
沥青乳液　emulsified bitumen, asphalt emulsion
沥青软化点　asphalt softening point, ring and ball point
沥青塞缝料　bitumen sealing compound
沥青砂浆　asphalt grout
沥青砂胶[玛琋脂]　asphalt mastic
沥青-石棉胶合铺料　bitomen-asbestos mastic
沥青摊铺机　asphalt-spreader
沥青碳纤维　pitch carbon fiber
沥青搪瓷　bitumen enamel
沥青透层　primary coat
沥青涂层　asphalt [bitumen, bituminous] coating, asphalt [bitumen] sheathing
沥青涂料　asphalt [bituminous, bitumastic] paint, bituminous plastering, carbozite (钢材临时性防蚀涂层)
沥青涂液　bituminous solution
沥青岩　asphalite
沥青页岩　bituminous shale
沥青铀矿{$UO_2 \cdot UO_3, U_3O_8$}　(metamict) uraninite, uranniobite, pitchblende ◇ 原生 ~ primary uraninite
沥青铀钍矿　thucholite
沥青毡　asphalt felt, asphaltic saturated felt, bituminous carpet
沥青纸毡　asphalt sheet

沥青质煤炉　bituminous coal furnace
沥青质石灰石　bituminous limestone
沥青质铁矿石　bituminous ore
沥青质页岩　batt
沥青柱　pitch column
沥青组合屋面　asphalt built-up roof(ing)
力　force, power, strength ◇ 范德瓦尔斯~*, 科里奥利斯~ Coriolis force, 施加的 ~ superposed force
力臂　arm of force
力场　force field, field of force
力场强度　force intensity
力场推斥势　【理】repulsive potential
力的分解　resolution of forces
力方向　force direction
力分布　distribution of forces
力分量　component of force
力矩　force moment, moment (of force), torque ◇ 作用于轧辊的 ~ roll(ing) torque
力矩电动机　torque motor
力矩轴　moment axis
力-距离图　force-distance diagram
力量　power, strength
力能学　energetics
力偶　(force) couple
力偶臂　arm of couple
力偶矩　moment of couple
力强度　force intensity
力-位移关系式　force-displacement relation
力线　force line
力学　mechanics
力学模型　mechanical model
力学试验室　mechanical-testing hall
力学特性[性能]　mechanical behaviour [property]
力学性能各向异性　mechanical anisotropy
力学性能试验　mechanical test(ing)
力学(性能)稳定性　mechanical stability
力学状态方程　mechanical equation of state

力轴 mechanical axis	**联合炉** combined furnace
力作用点 origin of force	**联合企业** 【企】joint venture, complex
联氨 hydrazine, diamide	**联合式压机** combination(-type) press
联邦标准(美国) Federal specifications	**联合碳化物公司**(美国) Union Carbide Corporation (UCAR)
联苯{$C_{12}H_{10}$} biphenyl, diphenyl, phenylbenzene	**联合投资** 【企】joint venture [investment]
联苯酚{$(C_6H_4OH)_2$} diphenol	**联合王国** United Kingdom (UK)
联苯基{$C_6H_5C_6H_4$} xenyl	**联合轧机** combination mill ◇ 串列(粗轧)－横列(精轧)～ combination mill, 二辊－四辊～"
联动 linkage, gear	
联动电容器 gang capacitor	
联动机构 link gear	**联合轧制法** 【压】combination rolling mill practice
联动机组 aggregate unit	
联动计算机 linkage computer	**联合作业** combination process, integration of operation
联动开关 linked [ganged, coupled] switch	
联动控制 gang control	**联机(的)** 【计】on-line
联动叶片泵 combination vane pump	**联机操作** on-line operation
联动装置 linkage, linkwork	**联机工作** on-line working
联斗式挖泥船 ladder dredge	**联机绘图机** on-line plotter
联杆 link rod ◇ 制动～[机械式制动联动机构] brake linkage	**联机计算机** on line computer [machine]
	联机监控 on-line monitoring
联管节 union joint	**联机检验** on-line inspection
联管螺母 union nut	**联机键**(终端的) attention key
联合 join, combination, unite, consolidation, unification	**联机交互系统** on-line interactive system
	联机设备 on-line unit [equipment]
联合采煤机 combine	**联机实时操作** on-line real-time operation
联合传动装置 single driver assembly	**联机实时系统** on-line real-time (OLRT) system
联合法 combination process	
联合干燥设备 combined drier equipment	**联机数据库** on-line data bases
联合铬公司光亮热浸镀锌用浸镀液(美国) Unichrome dip compound	**联机调试** on-line debug(ging)
	联机通信 on-line communication
联合铬公司热浸镀锌法(美国) Unichrome process	**联机预防维修系统** on-line preventive maintenance system
联合工厂 integrated works [plant]	**联机诊断** on-line diagnostics
联合供水系统 amalgamated water works	**联机中断**(终端的) attention interruption
联合公司 integrated corporation	**联机装置** on-line assembly [unit]
联合国 the United Nations (UN, U.N.)	**联接** coupling, bracing, gang, union ◇ 可拆～ detachable joint
联合会 association (Assn, assoc.), union	
联合加料[给矿]器 combination feeder	**联接法兰盘** coupling [attachment] flange
联合剪切(机组)作业线 combination shearing line (CSL)	**联接杆** coupling rod
	联接管 coupler [coupling] tube
联合交错蓄热式焦炉 combination cross-regenerative oven	**联接拉杆** coupling rod
	联接螺母 connecting nut

联接器 couple(r), coupling, adapter, union ◇ 爪形~ jaw coupling

联接线 contact wire, tie

联接轴 coupling spindle ◇ 齿(轮)型~ gear-type spindle

联接轴平衡 spindle balance

联节销 link pin

联结杆 connecting [coupling] link

联结(器)螺栓 coupling bolt

联结销 coupling pin

联结旋塞 coupling cock

联结轴 coupling shaft [axle]

联立程序 coroutines

联立反应 simultaneous reactions

联盟 union

联锁 nterlock ◇ 解除~ release

联锁闭塞区间(铁路的) 【运】interlocking blocks

联锁部件 【电】interlocking blocks

联锁机构 interlocking mechanism

联锁继电器 interlocking [block] relay

联锁接点[接触器] interlock contact

联锁开关 interlock(ing) switch

联锁孔隙 interlocking porosity

联锁连杆 interlocking bar

联锁瓦屋面 【建】interlocking tile roofing

联锁系统 interlock(ing) system

联锁线路 【电】interlock circuit [line]

联锁线圈 【电】locking coil

联锁销 interlocking pin [latch]

联锁圆盘 interlocking disc

联锁装置 interlock(ing) (device) ◇ 焦炉机械的~*

联通孔 interlocking pore

联系 contact, touch, liaison, communication

联系层 binding course

联线(的) 【计】on-line

联线适配器[衔接器] on-line adapter

联运站 【运】union station

联轴节防护器 coupling protection

联轴节连接 muff joint

联轴器[节] (shaft, union) coupling, 【压】coupling box (梅花头型) ◇ 奥特曼式~ Ortmann coupling, 齿轮型~ gear type coupling, 带扁头和滑块的~ palm and slipper coupling, 对开~ split coupling, 固定~*, 弧齿~ curved tooth coupling, 活动~ movable coupling, 夹壳~ clamp coupling, 冕形齿~*, 内齿式~*, 蛇形弹簧[毕比]~ Bibby coupling, 弹性[缓冲]~*, 套筒~*, 外齿式~*, 万向~*, 箱形~ box coupling, 牙嵌~ dog coupling, 液力~ fluid coupling, 硬性~ fast coupling, 永久~ permanent coupling, 圆盘~ disc coupling, 胀缩[补偿]~ expansion coupling, 爪形~*, 锥形~ cone coupling

连包连铸 sequence casting

连苯三酚 (同"焦焙酚")

连串的 consecutive

连串反应 consecutive reaction

连打 beat

连多硫酸 {$H_2S_xO_6$} polythionic acid

连多硫酸盐 {$M_2S_xO_6$} polythionate

连二磷酸盐 {$M_4P_2O_6$} hypophosphate

连二硫酸 {$H_2S_2O_6$} dithionic acid

连二硫酸铷 {$Rb_2S_2O_6$} rubidium ditionate

连二硫酸盐 {$M_2S_2O_6$} hyposulphate, dithionate

连二硫酸盐浸出 dithionate leaching

连杆 connecting rod, link

连杆叉 connecting rod fork

连杆大端 connecting rod big end

连杆端 connecting rod end

连杆盖 connecting rod cap

连杆机构 link gear, link mechanism

连杆(孔)轴承合金 connecting rod metal

连杆式钢包回转台 lindage ladle turret

连杆小端 connecting rod small end

连拱坝 multi-dam

连钩螺栓 sling [shackle] bolt

连管 fitting [connecting] pipe, pipe branch

连环 interlinkage, connecting ring

连枷状搅拌器　flail stirrer ◇ 链式~ chain flail stirrer
连接　connection, connecting, joining, (con)junction, linkage, linking, attachment, couple, interlinkage, bond(ing) ◇ 异质[不同]材料~.
连接板　gusset (joint) plate, gusset, (sticker) patch, tie-plate（铁路钢轨用）,【焊】bond（煤气开闭器的）
连接板型高刚度轧机　connecting plate type of stiff mill (CPSM), stiff mill of connecting plate type
连接板用异型钢材　splice bar
连接编辑程序　【计】link editor
连接程序库　【计】link library
连接点　junction point, point of connection, witness mark
连接电缆　(inter)connecting cable
连接短管　nipple
连接符　【计】connector
连接负荷　connected load
连接杆　tie bar, interconnecting linkage, pitman
连接钢筋　【建】connection bar
连接钩　engaging claw
连接管　connecting [union] pipe, pipe connection
连接辊　spindle
连接辊道　【压】connection roller table
连接焊　joint weld(ing)
连接机构　connection
连接键　bonding bridge
连接件（螺栓、螺钉、螺母等）　attaching parts, adapting [connecting] piece, fastenings
连接件间隙　joint gap
连接接头　connector lug, jointing
连接螺钉[螺丝]　fitting [union] screw
连接螺母　joint [coupling] nut
连接螺栓　connecting [tie, truss] bolt
连接面　joint face
连接母线　【电】connecting bus [bar, bus-bar]
连接皮带机　connecting conveyer
连接器　connector, adapter, coupler, coupling, jointer ◇ 带式~ band coupling, 电缆~ , 活节~ cardan joint
连接软管　connection hose
连接设计　joint design
连接式热风炉　【铁】tie-in stoves
连接套筒　coupling [connecting] sleeve
连接体　connector, interface
连接图　connected graph, connection layout
连接蜗杆　connecting worm
连接线　connecting wire [line], hook-up wire
连接箱　fishing box
连接销　connecting [joint] pin, engaging claw
连接销扣环　bayonet retaining ring
连接轴　engaging shaft, connecting axle
连接装置　connecting gear
连接字　【计】connective word
连接字段　【计】link field
连接作用　【团】bonding action
连结　concatenation
连结扒钉　crowfoot
连结螺栓　binder [binding] bolt
连结体　union body,【冶】interlocking matrix
连结线　tie line
连结支撑　braced strut
连结装置　adaptor
连跨　【建】continuous span
连六硫酸盐 $\{M_2S_6O_6\}$　hexa(poly)thionate
连炉浇注[连桶连铸]　【连铸】continuous-continuous casting
连炉浇注法　"continuous" continuous casting practice
连三甲苯酚 $\{C_9H_{12}O\}$　3,4,5-trimetylphend
连三硫酸铵 $\{(NH_4)_2S_3O_6\}$　ammonium

trithionate
连三硫酸盐 {$M_2S_3O_6$} trithionate
连生粉粒 【粉】locked particle
连生体 intergrowth
连四多硫酸盐 {$M_2S_4O_6$} tetrapolythionate
连四硫酸盐 {$M_2S_4O_6$} tetrathionate
连锁 linkage, chain, concatenation, blocking
连锁反应 chain reaction
连锁机构 blocking mechanism
连锁裂变反应 fission chain reaction
连锁装置 blocking (mechanism)
连通管 communicating pipe [tube], breeches pipe,【钢】snorkel(真空处理的)
连通管道网 interconnecting pipework
连通管线 interconnection piping
连通开关 coupling cock
连通孔 intercommunicating pores [porosity], interconnected [interconnecting pores,【粉】communicating pores
连通孔隙 interconnected [interconnecting] porosity
连通器 connecting vessels
连续 X 辐射 white X radiation
连续 X 射线 continuous X-rays
连续 X 射线谱 continuous X-ray spectrum, white X-rays
连续本底 【理】continuous background
连续表面层 continuous surface film
连续波 continuous wave
连续补充充电 trickle charge
连续彩色涂层作业线 continuous colour coating line
连续操作 continuous [trouble-free] operation
连续槽型运输机 continuous trough conveyer
连续测定[测量] continuous measurement, continuous gauging(成卷带材厚度的)
连续测厚 continuous gauging
连续缠卷装置 【压】continuous coiler
连续沉淀器 continuous precipitator
连续称量 continuous weighing
连续成型 (同"连续压制")
连续成形 progressive forming
连续冲模 progressive [tandem] die
连续出料加热炉 continuous discharge heating furnace
连续出铁操作(高炉的) 【铁】continuous tapping practice
连续除锌炉 continuous dezincing furnace
连续床反应器 continuous bed-type reactor
连续吹炼 【色】continuous converting
连续吹炼法 continuous converting method
连续吹炼机理 mechanism of continuous converting
连续吹炼转炉 continuous converter
连续磁场(检验)法 【理】continuous-field method ◇ 干式~(探伤)*
连续萃取 continuous extraction
连续淬火 【金】continuous hardening [quenching]
连续淬火回火作业线 continuous quench and temper line
连续带式炉 continuous belt furnace
连续带式烧结炉 continuous conveyer-type sintering furnace
连续等温退火 cycle [cyclic] annealing
连续底脚[底座] continuous footing
连续碘化物热离解法 continuous iodide process
连续电磁浇注 continuous electromagnetic casting
连续电磁浇注法 continuous electromagnetic casting process
连续电镀锡机组[作业线] continuous electrolytic tinning line
连续电极 【冶】continuous electrode
连续电解法 continuous electrowinning

process

连续电解清洗作业线(带材的) electrolytic cleaning line

连续电冶[电熔炼]【冶】continuous electric smelting

连续电源 continuous source

连续电渣熔炼法 CESM (continuous electro-slag melting) process

连续顶吹熔炼(法) continuous top blowing process (CONTOP)

连续镀覆 continuous plating [coating]

连续镀铝 continuous aluminising

连续镀锌 continuous galvanizing, continuous zinc coating

连续镀锌机组[作业线] continuous galvanizing line (CGL) ◇ 带钢～*

连续锻造 continuous forging

连续锻造[压]工艺 continuous forging process

连续镦粗 continuous upsetting

连续多点焊 program welding, sequence (resistance) welding

连续法 continuous method

连续反应 continuous reaction

连续反应器 【冶】flow reactor

连续反应系列 continuous reaction series

连续方程 continuity equation

连续分布 continuous distribution

连续分级 continuous grading, series classification

连续分类作业线 continuous assorting line (CAL, CA L)

连续分馏塔 continuous fractionation column

连续分析 continuous [on-stream] analysis

连续分析器 on-stream analyzer, continuous splitter

连续分选作业线(板材的) continuous assorting line

连续粉末取样 continuous powder sampling

连续粉末冶金 continuous powder metallurgy

连续辐射 continuous [white] radiation

连续氟化 continuous fluorination

连续负载 continuous load

连续干燥 flowdrying ◇ 立式～炉*, 隧道式～器*

连续工艺 continuous process

连续工作制 continuous duty

连续供热 progressive feed heating

连续供丝自动电弧焊 continuous feed welding

连续供应 continuous supply

连续鼓风 【冶】continuous blast

连续灌混凝土 continuous concreting

连续光谱 continuous spectrum

连续辊动炉底 continuous roller-hearth

连续辊涂法 ◇ 马威邦德～*

连续滚焊焊缝 continuous seam weld

连续过程 continuous process

连续过程模拟实验 analog simulation

连续焊道施焊 continuous sequence

连续焊缝 continuous weld

连续焊(接) continuous welding ◇ 同时夹持全部焊条多点～commutator-controlled welding

连续焊接机 continuous welder (CW)

连续焊接机组[作业线] continuous welding line (CWL, C.W.L.)

连续桁架 【建】continuous truss

连续行 【计】continuation line

连续荷载 permanent load

连续滑程[滑动(量)] continuous slippage

连续滑移 consecutive slipping

连续还原反应器 continuous reduction reactor

连续回火 continuous tempering

连续回转浓硫酸分解炉 continuous rotating sulphator

连续混合法 【冶】continuous-mixture method

连续混合[搅拌]机 continuous mixer ◇ 刃型～edge-runner mixer

连续混磨机 continuous muller mixer	连续精馏塔 (同"连续分馏塔")
连续基础 continuous foundation	连续精整作业线 【压】continuous processing line
连续基脚 continuous footing	
连续挤压 continuous [straight-through] extrusion	连续静液挤压 continuous hydrostatic extrusion
连续挤压成型(法) continuous extrusion forming	连续可变凸度 continuous (ly) variable crown (CVC)
连续记录 continuous record	连续可变凸度轧机 CVC mill
连续记录黏度计 viscorator	连续孔隙(缺陷) 【冶】continuous porosity
连续加工处理作业线 continuous processing line (CPL)	连续控制 continuous [sequential, stepless] control
连续加料 continuous charging [feed(ing)], consecutive charging	连续跨 【建】continuous span
	连续拉拔 【压】continuous drawing
连续加料还原炉 continuous feed reduction furnace	连续拉杆 continuous draw bar
	连续拉坯过程 【连铸】continuous process of extraction
连续加料式炉 continuous feed type furnace	
连续加热 continuous [stepless] heating	连续拉丝机 【压】continuous drawing machine, multihole wire drawing machine ◇ 上出线~卷筒*, 蓄丝式~*
连续加热炉 continuous (-heating) furnace, pusher-type furnace ◇ 两段式~ two zone furnace, 逆流推进式~*, 三段式~*, 瑟莫式~ Thermo type furnace, 顺流式~*, 五段式~*, 轴向~*	
	连续冷却 continuous cooling (CC)
	连续冷却曲线 continuous cooling curve
	连续冷却转变 【金】continuous cooling transformation (CCT), anisothermal transformation
连续监测[监视] continuous monitoring	
连续监视[检测]器 continuous monitor	
连续检测 continuous detection	连续冷却转变曲线 continuous cooling transformation curve
连续剪切机 【压】continuous shears (CS)	
连续焦化过程 continuous coking process	连续冷却转变曲线图[连续冷却相变图] CCT diagram
连续浇注法 continuous casting process	
连续矫直(连铸坯的) continuous levelling ◇ 光滑~*, 康卡斯特~曲线*	连续冷却转变图 anisothermal diagram
	连续冷轧机 continuous cold mill (CCM)
连续截取(取样机的) continuous splitter	连续离心机 continuous centrifuge
	连续离子交换 continuous ion exchange
连续结晶器 continuous crystallizer	连续离子交换接触器 continuous ion-exchange contactor
连续介质 【理】continuous medium	
连续进料 continuous feed(ing)	连续离子交换装置 continuous ion exchange system
连续进料反应器 continuous-feed reactor	
连续进料炉 continuous charge furnace	连续连铸 continuous-continuous casting
连续浸湿 continuous leaching	连续炼钢 continuous steelmaking, consteel
连续精炼 【冶】continuous refining ◇ 粗铅~除银锅*, 铅~*	连续炼钢法 consteel process
	连续炼铅 continual lead smelting
	连续炼铜 continual copper smelting
连续精炼法 continuous refining process	连续炼型焦法 continuous formed coke

lian 连 904

process
连续梁 【建】continuous beam
连续料层 consecutive layer
连续料流 mass flow
连续流动 continuous flow
连续流化床还原 continuous fluid-bed reduction
连续流化床氢氟化 【色】continuous fluid-bed hydrofluorination
连续流化床直接还原法 ADI process
连续流(态)化床 continuous fluidized bed
连续炉炉况[冶炼进程] 【冶】continuous furnace run
连续膜 continuous film
连续能谱 continuum
连续逆流萃取 continuous counter-current extraction
连续逆流离子交换 continuous counter-current ion-exchange ◇ 三柱～
连续(逆流)倾析洗涤系统 continuous decantation washing system
连续凝固 progressive solidification
连续浓缩机 continuous thickener
连续抛丸清理装置 continuous blasting-and-cleaning plant
连续喷射[喷嘴] continuous jet
连续喷丸清理装置 continuous blasting-and-cleaning plant
连续喷雾二次冷却区 continuous spray cooling zone
连续(频)谱 continuous spectrum
连续气体分析 continuous-gas analysis
连续气体渗碳法 eutectrol process
连续切屑 continuous chip
连续区熔精炼[提纯] 【色】continuous zone refining
连续区(域) continuum
连续区域精炼[区熔]炉 【色】continuous zone refiner
连续区域精炼[提纯]设备 【色】continuous zone-refining apparatus
连续曲线 continuous [full, solid, sweeping] curve
连续取样 continuous sampling [sample]
连续绕射环 (同"连续衍射环")
连续热处理 continuous heat treating ◇ (单条薄带退火用～炉＊，辊底式～炉＊
连续热处理炉 continuous strand-type furnace
连续热镀铝 continuous hot dip aluminizing
连续热浸镀 continuous hot dip coating
连续熔炼 continuous [continual] (s) melting
连续熔炼吹炼法 continuous smelting and converting process
连续熔炼炉 continuous smelter
连续熔炼试验 continuous smelting test
连续溶出 continuous digestion
连续溶出器 continuous digester
连续溶出器组 continuous digester series
连续软化炉 continuous softening furnace
连续润滑 continuous lubrication
连续烧结 continuous sintering, stoking
连续烧结炉 continuous sintering furnace ◇ 推扒式～＊
连续射线谱 continuous arc
连续渗铝 continuous aluminising
连续生产 【企】continuous [in-line, serial] production
连续生长 continuous growth
连续升温时效 progressive aging
连续施焊 (同"连续焊道施焊")
连续式板坯和叠板加热炉 【压】continuous pack-and-pair heating
连续式薄板坯和钢坯轧机 continuous sheet-bar and billet mill
连续式焙烧窑 progressive kiln
连续式车底退火炉 【压】continuous car-bottom furnace
连续式传感器 continuous sensor
连续式粗轧机组 continuous roughing train
连续式带材热轧机 continuous hot-strip

mill

连续式带材酸洗装置 【压】continuous strip pickler

连续式电热浴炉 continuous tank furnace

连续式风量计(转炉用) 【钢】(volume) debitgraphe

连续式反应器 continuous reactor

连续式辐射管炉 continuous radiant-tube furnace

连续式干燥器 continuous drier, flowdryer

连续式干燥窑[炉] continuous drying oven [stove]

连续式钢板测厚计 continuous sheet micrometer

连续式钢坯轧机 continuous billet mill

连续式管状热风炉 continuous-pipe stove

连续式辊弯成形机 continuous roll-forming machine

连续式焊管坯加热炉 continuous butt-weld furnace

连续式活套线材轧机机组 continuous looping rod mill train

连续式活套轧机 continuous repeater mill

连续式加热炉 【压】continuous reheating furnace, continuous-type furnace

连续式宽带材热轧机 continuous wide-strip hot mill

连续式搅拌反应槽 continuous stirred tank reactor

连续式宽带钢冷轧厂 wide continuous cold strip mill plant

连续式冷轧机 (同"串列式冷轧机")

连续式冷镦机 【压】progressive header

连续式炉焊管法 continuous weld process, Fretz-Moon method

连续式炉 strand type furnace

连续式炉焊管机组 continuous butt-weld mill, Fretz-Moon pipe mill

连续式坯料加热炉 【压】continuous billet-heating furnace

连续式气体分析器 continuous gas analyzer

连续式气体渗碳炉 continuous gas carburizer

连续式热处理炉 continuous heat-treating furnace

连续式软化退火(带钢的) line softening

连续式烧结机 【团】continuous sintering machine, travel(1)ing grate type furnace

连续式室窑 continuous chamber kiln

连续式竖罐(蒸馏)法 continuous vertical retort process

连续式酸洗 continuous pickling

连续式退火炉 【压】continuous-type annealing furnace

连续式无缝管轧机 continuous seamless-tube rolling mill

连续式线材[盘条]轧机 continuous wire [rod] mill

连续式线材[盘条]轧机机组 continuous rod mill train

连续式小型搅拌机 continuous flow pug-mill

连续式窑 progressive kiln ◇ 无固定顶盖 ~ archless continous kiln

连续式浴炉 continuous tank furnace

连续(式)轧机 continuous (train) mill, continuous-continuous mill ◇ 串列~*, 非~*, 普罗佩兹式~*, 四机座~*, 自动~*, 综合自动控制~*

连续式轧机机组 continuous mill train

连续试验 long run test

连续试样 continuous sample

连续输送 nonstop handling

连续输送机 continuous conveyer

连续输送式(加热)炉 continuous conveyer-type furnace

连续疏松 【冶】continuous porosity

连续顺序计算机 consecutive sequence computer

连续送丝自动电弧焊 continuous feed welding

连续酸处理 continuous acid treating

连续酸洗 continuous acid-washing

连续酸洗机组　pickle line processor
连续酸洗-冷轧　continuous pickling and cold rolling
连续酸洗作业线　continuous pickling line (CPL) ◇ 多条~*
连续酸洗作业线上的精除[破]鳞机　pickle line processor
连续台车式烧结机　【团】continuous pallet-type sintering machine
连续碳化　【焦】continuous carbonization
连续条件　continuity condition
连续统　【数】continuum
连续涂敷　continuous coating
连续推料式加热炉　continuous pusher-type furnace
连续退火　continuous annealing (CA) ◇ 多根~*，喷焰~*
连续退火高强度冷轧钢　continuously annealed high strength cold rolled steel, CAL-HITEN steel
连续退火黑薄[钢]板(未镀的)　continuously annealed black plate
连续退火炉　continuous annealing furnace [oven] ◇ (钢丝)拉过~*，辊底式~*，塔式~*
连续退火酸洗(作业)线　continuous annealing and pickling line
连续退火装置　【金】continuous annealing plant, annealing-in-line plant ◇ 电阻加热式~*
连续退火作业线　continuous annealing line (CAL, CA L)
连续脱硫(法)　continuous desulphurization
连续脱气　【钢】continuous degassing ◇ 连铸机上~法*
连续脱碳退火机组[作业线]　continuous decarburizing annealing line (CDAL)
连续弯曲点阵　continuously curved lattice
连续位错晶体　continuously dislocated crystal
连续位移　continuous displacement

连续析出[沉淀]　【金】continuous precipitation
连续系统模拟语言　continuous system simulation language (CSSL)
连续系统模型(建立)程序　continuous system modeling program (CSMP)
连续下线坑　continuous coiler
连续纤维　continuous fibre
连续纤维复合材料　continuous fibre composite
连续纤维金属基复合材料　continuous fibre metal matrix composite
连续相　continuous phase
连续相原理　【金】principle of continuous phase
连续性　continuance, continuity
连续性方程(式)　continuity equation
连续性条件　continuity condition
连续压制　【粉】continuous compaction
连续压制的模具[压模装置]　die arrangement for continuous compaction
连续压制法　【粉】continuous compacting process
连续研磨混合机　continuous muller mixer
连续衍射环　continuous diffraction ring
连续阳极　continuous anode ◇ 生糊块~*
连续阳极电解槽　continuous anode cell
连续阳极氧化　continuous anodizing
连续窑　continuous [progressive] kiln
连续冶金设备　continuous metallurgical unit
连续预焙阳极　【色】continuous prebaked anode
连续源　continuous source
连续运动　continuous motion
连续运输器　continuous conveyer
连续运送烧结炉　【粉】continuous-transport furnace
连续运行[运转]　continuous running [operation] ◇ 满载~*
连续轧制　continuous rolling

连续真空过滤机　continuous vacuum filter
连续振荡[振动]　continuous oscillation
连续蒸馏(法)　continuous distillation
连续蒸馏釜　continuous still
连续蒸馏罐　continuous retort ◇ 竖式~*
连续蒸馏设备[装置]　continuous distillation plant ◇ 考伯斯焦油~*
连续蒸馏塔　continuous-distillation column
连续直流电弧电源　continuous D-C arc source
连续中和段　continuous neutralisation section
连续煮沸器　continuous boiling unit
连续铸锭[铸钢]　(同"连铸")
连续铸锭[铸钢]机　(同"连铸机")
连续铸锭跨　continuous casting bay
连续铸钢厂　(steel) continuous casting plant
连续铸钢装置特性　machine conditions
连续铸件　continuous cast shapes
连续铸造　continuous casting
连续铸造法　Asarco method
连续铸造铁棒法　Flocast
连续铸轧　in-line rolling [reduction]
连续铸轧机　continuous casting 82 rolling line
连续装料　continuous charge
连续自焙电极　continuous selfbaking electrode, Söderberg electrode
连续自焙阳极　【色】self-baking continuous anode, Söderberg (continuous) anode ◇ 对开~split Söderberg anode
连续自焙阳极电解槽　cell with self-baking continuous anodes, Söderberg cell, continuous anode cell ◇ 侧插棒~*, 大型~*, 密闭式~*, 上插棒~*
连续自焙阳极糊　Söderberg (electrode) paste
连续作业　continuous operation [flow], continuity of operation
连续作业炉　continuous furnace
连续作用源　continuous source
连轧　continuous rolling (conroll), tandem rolling
连轧管机　continuous tube mill, mandrel (pipe) mill ◇ 限动芯棒~*
连轧机　tandem mill
连轧机轧制厚板　strip mill plate
连轧机组　continuous rolling mill train
连轴器　junct(ion) box ◇ 带式~ band coupling
连铸　continuous casting (CC, concast) ◇ 大断面~坯 heavy section, 薄带~*, 单炉~*, 多炉~*, 高速~*, 高效~*, 活动挠性带间~*, 近终形~*, 拉出小型~坯 billet withdrawal, 连续[连桶]~*, 全~*
连铸板坯　continuously casting slab scarfing machine
连铸板坯火焰清理机　continuous casting slab scarfing machine
连铸保护渣　mold powder for continuous casting
连铸比　continuous casting ratio [rate]
连铸材料　continuously cast material
连铸法　continuous casting process [method] ◇ 阿萨科~*, 巴布科克－威尔科克斯立式~*, 巴罗~* Barrow process, "半连续"~*, 戈斯金属~*, 快速和慢速~*, 罗西振动~ Rossi process, 曼内斯曼~ Mannesmann process, 容沃斯－罗西有色合金振动~*, 停息－拉出~(单炉浇注法)*, 威廉条材~*
连铸钢坯　steel strand, continuously cast steel
连铸管坯　continuous casting billet for pipe-making
连铸过程中钢水连续真空处理　continuous vacuum treatment of steel during continuous casting
连铸机[装置]　continuous casting machine (CCM), continuous caster, conticaster ◇ LGL 轮式~ LGL wheel caster, 带式

~*,单机四流~*,单流~*,低架式[低矮型]~*,多流~*,哈兹莱特~*,弧形~*,立弯式~*,六流~*,倾斜(带)式~*,全弧形圆坯~*,双辊~ twin-roll caster,韦布里奇三联结晶器~*,一机两流浇铸[双浇]~ double-strand plant

连铸结晶器 continuous casting mould

连铸结晶器保护渣 continuous casting mo(u)ld flux

连铸结晶器液位控制 CC mould level control

连铸机上连续脱气法 on-machine continuous degassing procedure

连铸机专用脂 special grease for continuous caster

连铸金属 continuously casting metal

连铸连轧 continuous casting and rolling ◇ 博勒~法*

连铸流 cast strand

连铸坯穿插装炉 charging of continuous casting slab in turn

连铸坯热芯轧制 rolling of continuously casting slabs with liquid-core

连铸坯热装[热送]轧制 hot charge rolling of continuously casting slab, hot charging and rolling technology of continuous casting slab

连铸坯输出辊道 casting discharge conveyer

连铸坯一火成材 continuous casting billet to be rolled as products with one heating

连铸坯直接热装轧制工艺 direct hot charging rolling process on continuous cast billet

连铸坯直接轧制 CC-DHCR, direct strand reduction

连铸热轧法 continuous casting and hot rolling process

连铸－热轧生产过程 CC－HCR (continuous-casting hot-continuous-rolling) process

连铸设备 continuous casting plant ◇ 迪斯廷顿~*,康卡斯特-罗西~*Concast-Rossi plant,塔式~ tower-type plant

连铸阳极 continuous casting anode

连铸氧化铁皮 continuous casting scale

连铸(用)耐火材料 continuous casting refractory

连铸诊断 continuous casting diagnostics

连铸中间包等离子加热 tundish plasma heating technology

镰刀弯 rocker, sweep, camber, side strain

镰刀形(缺陷)带材 bent strip

帘栅极 【电】anode(-screening) grid

帘栅五极管 screen grid pentode

敛缝 calked seam, calking, caulking

敛缝锤 caulking hammer, caulker

敛缝工 calker

敛集因数 packing index

链 chain ◇ 块环[平环,滚]~ block chain

链板式加煤机 chain grate stoker

链板运输机 chain-scraper [chain-and-flight, push-plate] conveyer, scrape(r) [drag] conveyer

链箅焙烧机球团法 【团】grate pelletizing process

链箅机 continuous travelling grate machine, moving grate, travel(l)ing grate (dryer), drying [chain(-type)] grate, horizontal travelling grate, grate [travel(l)ing] furnace, travel(l)ing grate type preheater, band drier, grate-kiln grate (指链箅机-回转窑法的) ◇ 抽风式~*,多段式~*,环式~ circular grate,全抽风干燥式~*,三段式~ three-pass grate,三室式~*

链箅机表面 pellet preheater surface

链箅机布料皮带机 grate feed conveyor

链箅机布料器 grate feeder

链箅机操作工 grate machine operator

链箅机－回转窑 【团】grate kiln (agglomerating machine), firing furnace of grate-kiln type, band drier-kiln ◇ 爱立斯

lian 链

·恰默斯型~·
链算机－回转窑法 grate-kiln process
链算机－回转窑法球团 grate-kiln system pellet
链算机－回转窑法球团机组 grate-kiln type pelletizing unit
链算机－回转窑机组 grate-kiln machine
链算机－回转窑－冷却机机组设计（图） grate-kiln-cooler design
链算机－回转窑－冷却机作业线 grate-kiln-cooler line
链算机－回转窑球团法 grate-kiln pelletizing
链算机－回转窑球团生产线 grate-kiln pelletizing line
链算机－回转窑热回收系统 grate-kiln recuperation system
链算机－回转窑烧结系统生产线 grate-kiln system line
链算机－回转窑式焙烧设备 firing furnace of grate-kiln type
链算机－回转窑中间溜槽 grate-to-kiln transfer
链算机利用系数 grate factor, grate specific production[productivity]
链算机烧结法 grate sintering, grate process
链算机台车速度 grate speed
链算（机）循环 grate cycle ◇ 二室式~ two-pass grate cycle
链算机烟囱 grate stack
链算炉 moving grate furnace
链算烧结机 【团】indurating grate
链算烧结机排烟罩 grate hood
链传动（装置） chain drive
链传动机构 chain gear
链带 chain[link]belt,【化】mer, monomeric unit
链动滑轮 chain block
链动输送机 flight conveyer
链斗式取样器 chain bucket sampler
链斗式挖泥船[机] bucket chain dredge, ladder dredge
链斗式挖土机 chain bucket excavator, elevator-ladder dredger
链斗提升机 paternoster elevator, chain bucket (elevator)
链钢 chain steel
链钩 chain hook, sling
链滑车 chain block
链环[节] chain shackle[link], monomeric unit, mer
链节板 link plate
链节式药皮包丝焊接 cover chain welding
链轮 sprocket (wheel, gear), chain pulley[wheel], star wheel ◇ 头尾~ head and tail sprockets
链轮环链 sprocket chain
链轮台式喷砂机 sandblast sprocket-table machine
链码天平 chain(omatic) balance
链霉菌属 Streptomyces
链耙式分级机 drag classifier
链式拨爪移送机 chain-and-dog type transfer
链式抽出机 【压】chain stripper
链式传送齿条 chain transfer rack
链式打印机 chain printer
链式电极夹持器 chain-type electrode holder
链式砝码 tested[pitch]chain
链式反应 chain reaction
链式反应扩大 autocatalysis
链式刮板运输机 chain flight conveyer
链式刮路器 chain drag
链式给[加]料器 chain feeder
链式绞辘 chain fall
链式卷扬机 chain winch
链式拉拔机[拉丝机, 拉床] 【压】chain [pull-type]drawbench
链式冷床 【压】chain-type cooling bed, chain skid bank（带导向梁的）
链式连枷状搅拌器 chain flail stirrer

链式裂变反应　fission chain reaction
链式炉　travel(l)ing [chain-conveyer] furnace, conveyer-type continuous furnace, travel(l)ing oven
链式码　【计】chain code
链式抛丸[喷丸]机　chain shotblasting machine
链式坯料分配器　chain billet switch
链式起重机　chain hoist
链式筛　chain grit
链式升降机　chain elevator
链式输送机　chain (-linked) conveyer, conveying chain
链式拖运机　chain-type drag
链式芯棒抽出机　chain stripper
链式移送床　chain-type transfer bed
链式移送机　chain transfer, chain-type drag, chain-linked conveyer ◇ 冷床~*
链式移送冷床　【压】chain-conveyer cooling bed
链式运输机　chain (-linked) conveyer, chain-type transfer bed ◇ 四线~*
链式制动器　chain brake
链索铁道　chain railroad
链锁合　chain closure
链条传动　chain transmission
链条导轨[板]　chain guide
链条钢丝　chain wire
链条管扳手　chain pipe wrench, roll grip pipe wrench
链条护罩　chain guard
链条机构　chain mechanism ◇ 带自动升降爪的~chain-and-ducking dog mechanism
链条卷筒　chain drum
链条联轴器　【机】chain coupling
链条落锤　chain-drop hammer
链烷{C_nH_{2n+2}}　alkane
链烷烃　paraffin hydrocarbons
链系　linkage, linkwork, chain
链销　chain pin
链型硫化物　chain-type sulphide [sulfide]
链形绕组[绕法]　【电】chain winding
链闸　chain brake
链状颗粒　【粉】chain like particle
炼丹术　alchemy
炼废炉次　off-melt(ing), aborted heat
炼钢　steelmaking, steel manufacture ◇ 电弧炉~*, 电炉~*, 转炉~*
炼钢操作　steelmaking operation
炼钢生产　steelmaking
炼钢厂　steelworks, steel plant [mill], steelmaker
炼钢车间　steelshop, steel plant, melting house ◇ 碱性电弧炉~*, 全连铸~*
炼钢车间铸锭跨　melting shop teeming bay
炼钢等级[适合炼钢用]废钢　scrap of steelmaking grade, steelmaking scrap
炼钢电弧炉　electric arc steel furnace
炼钢法[过程]　steelmaking process ◇ LWS 底吹氧气转炉~*, OBM 底吹氧气转炉~(德) OBM process, OCP 顶吹氧气和石灰粉的托马斯生铁转炉~*, QEK 底吹氧气转炉~QEK process, 奥伯豪森~Oberhausen process, 顶吹氧气石灰粉除磷~*, 坩埚~crucible process, 混合~*, 极低含氮量[(底吹蒸汽氧气转炉) VLN] ~*, Oberhausen process, 碱性~*, 卡尔多[斜吹氧气]~*, 佩林~Perrin process, 喷射~spray steelmaking, 生铁~pig process, 托马斯~Thomas process, 外加燃料纯氧~*, 氧气顶吹转炉~*, 直接[一步]~*
炼钢废料[品]　steelmaking waste
炼钢工长　chief [head] melter
炼钢工人　steel-worker, steelmaker, steelman, steel smelter, melter
炼钢工艺　steelmaking practice
炼钢工艺流程　steelmaking flowsheet ◇ 直接还原(法)~*
炼钢工作者　steel metallurgist
炼钢流程　steelmaking flowsheet
炼钢炉　steel(making) furnace [vessel] ◇

高频~*,桶式~(同"钢包炉")
炼钢炉尘　steelmaking dust
炼钢炉渣　steelmaking slag
炼钢炉主厂房　main furnace building
炼钢设备　steelmaking equipment [unit], steel facility
炼钢生铁　pig iron for steel-making, conversion pig (iron), steel pig, steel-making) iron ◇ 碱性转炉~ phosphoric (pig) iron
炼钢水淬排渣工艺　technology of removing converter residue by water quench
炼钢平台　steelmaking platform
炼钢物理化学　physical chemistry of steelmaking
炼钢用废钢　steelmaking scrap
炼钢转炉　steelmaking converter ◇ 碱性(贝塞麦)~*
炼锆设备　zirconium plant equipment
炼汞法　(同"提汞法")
炼汞瓦片炉　◇ 斯科特~ Scott furnace
炼焦　coking, cokemaking, coal-to-coke conversion ◇ 捣固~技术*,堆积[堆脊]法~ coking in heaps,副产~法 by-product process,巨型~反应器 Jumbo coking reactor,立式连续~工艺*,配型煤~试验 coking test for blend with briquettes
炼焦产[成]品　resultant coke
炼焦厂[车间]　coke plant
炼焦副产品　coke by-products
炼焦过程　coking process
炼焦精煤　coking coal cleans
炼焦炉　(同"焦炉") ◇ 成排~室 battery of coke ovens,堆烧~*,蜂房式~ beehive oven,有副产品的~ by-product (coke) oven
炼焦炉工　coke oven operator
炼焦炉组　coke oven battery
炼焦煤　coking [metallurgical, cindery, agglomerating, crozzling] coal ◇ 非~ candle [dead] coal,易~ strongly coking coal

炼焦煤气　coke oven gas, C-gas
炼焦气体　coking gas
炼焦速度　coking speed
炼焦烟煤　byerlyte
炼焦用煤　oven coal
炼焦渣　coke residue
炼焦周期　coking cycle
炼金　gold metallurgy
炼锍　【色】matting
炼锍法　matte-making method
炼锍炉　matte smelting furnace, matting furnace
炼铝　aluminum smelting ◇ 阿尔科阿~烟气干式控制法【环】Alcoa process,电解~*,欧洲拜耳~法 European Bayer process,碳热法~*,托思锰还原氧化铝~ Toth process
炼铝厂　aluminium smelter
炼镁　magnesium smelting ◇ 道屋海水~*,电解~*,硅铁~*法,汉斯加格碳热还原~*,碳热法~厂*
炼镁车间　magnesium plant
炼镍　nickel smelting ◇ 奥福德(顶底)分层~法*,毛湾~法*,尼加罗~法*
炼镍厂　nickel smelter [refinery]
炼铅　lead smelting ◇ 奥托昆普~步~*,波利登~步~*
炼铅厂　lead smelter(y)
炼铅厂烟尘　lead-smelting dust
炼铅鼓风炉　lead blast furnace
炼铅鼓风炉炉渣　lead blast-furnace slag
炼铅鼓风炉烟雾　lead blast-furnace fume
炼铅炉　lead-smelting furnace
炼铅炉渣　lead-smelting slag
炼铅膛式炉　lead ore hearth, ore hearth (furnace)
炼锑厂　antimony smelter, producer of antimony
炼锑工业　antimony smelting industry
炼铁　ironmaking, iron-smelting, iron manufacture ◇ 布拉克尔斯堡~回转炉 Brackelsburg furnace,布拉塞特~法*,

炼铁 德马克-洪堡矮(身)炉~*，迪皮伊固体燃料反应罐~ Dupuy process，电炉~法*，高炉~*，流态化~*，卢伯特电热~*，木炭炉~法 charcoal hearth process，韦伯~法*，氧煤~*，直接~法 direct iron process

炼铁厂 iron works (IW, I. Wks), iron-making [iron-smelting] plant, ironplant, iron mill

炼铁电炉 electric iron-making furnace, electric pig iron furnace ◇ 空心电极~*

炼铁工 【铁】pig iron producer

炼铁工程师 blast furnace engineer

炼铁工作者 blast furnace metallurgist

炼铁焦炭 metallurgical coke, skip coke (料车焦)

炼铁炉渣 ironmaking slag

炼铁炉废料 blast furnace waste

炼铁设备 iron-making plant, ironplant

炼铁学 siderology

炼铁原料 ironmaking raw material

炼铜 copper smelting [production], extraction of copper ◇ 粗铜熔烧~法 bottom process，诺兰塔型一步~法*，熔池~bath copper smelting，湿法~*，沃克拉一步~ Worcra process

炼铜厂 copper smelter [smeltory], copper(-smelting) plant, copper works

炼铜反射炉 copper reverberatory furnace, reverberatory copper furnace

炼铜反射炉炉渣 copper reverberatory slag

炼铜工业 copper smelting industry

炼铜鼓风炉 copper(-smelting) blast furnace

炼铜炉 copper (smelting) furnace

炼铜炉渣 copper (smelting) slag

炼铜转炉 copper converter

炼铜转炉烟气 copper-converter gas

炼锡厂 tin smeltery, tin-smelting plant, tinworks

炼锡电炉 tin-smelting electric furnace

炼锡反射炉 reverberatory tin furnace

炼锡炉 tin furnace

炼锡炉渣 tin-smelter slag

炼锌 zinc smelting [metallurgy] ◇ 平罐~*，湿法~*，斯特林电弧炉~法 Sterling process，竖罐~*

炼锌厂 zinc smelter(y) [works], zinc-smelting plant

炼锌电炉 electric zinc furnace

炼锌鼓风炉 zinc blast furnace

炼银厂 silver smeltery

炼油设备用蒸馏管 still tube for refinery service

炼渣 【冶】working slag

练泥机 pug mill ◇ 真空~*

凉焦台 【焦】wharf

凉焦台金属铺板 coke wharf plate

凉水塔[架] 【焦】cooling stack

梁 beam ◇ 部分嵌入~*，基础~footing beam，宽翼缘工字(钢)[H-形]~*，鱼腹式~ fish bellied beam，配受压筋的~ double reinforced beam

梁板结构 beam and slab structure, contignation

梁腹连接盖板 web covers

梁高度 depth of beam

梁架(连续铸钢机的) beam (of) housing

梁间距 case bay

梁间墙 beam filling

梁截面[剖面] 【建】girder section

梁跨度 beam span

梁强度 beam strength

梁式二次冷却 beam type secondary cooling

梁式护栏 【运】beam type guard rail

梁式基础 beam foundation

梁式试样 【金】beam specimen

梁试验 beam test

梁托 【建】beam hanger, corbel

梁形材轧制法 beam method of rolling

梁形孔型[轧槽] beam pass ◇ 斜置~ di-

agonal-beam pass, 开口~ live beam pass
梁形直[正配]孔型　straight beam pass
梁腋　【建】haunch
梁柱结构　【建】post and girder (P.& G.), beam column construction, post and beam construction
梁砖　beam brick
良导体　【电】good conductor
良好再结晶氧化铝　well-recrystallized alumina
良序的　【半】well-ordered
两班操作　two-shift operation
两半模　(同"两片模")
两步法[工艺]　two step process
两步复型制备法　two steps replica process
两步深冲　double-action drawing
两步退火　double annealing
两侧竖焊　two-operator vertical welding
两侧楔形砖　two-sided wedge-shaped brick
两侧卸载运输车　both side transfercar
两层拔[拉]丝机　double-deck machine
两层镀镍法　two-layer nickel plating
两层或三层双金属板　overlay clad plate
两层金属化　double-layer metallization
两叉连管　two legs of breech pipes
两次焙烧　double roasting
两次冲击试验法　double impact testing method
两次出炉间隔　【钢】tap-to-tap time [cycle]
两次穿孔法　double piercing process
两次萃取　double extraction
两次电镀　duplex electroplate
两次电弧熔炼　double arc-melting
两次镀覆　duplex plating
两次镀覆耐蚀处理法　corronising, corronizing
两次镀铬　duplex chromium plating
两次镀镍　dual [duplex] nickel plating
两次煅烧白云石　(同"重烧白云石")
两次过滤　double filtration
两次过筛的细磨耐火材料　double-screened ground refractory material
两次还原　duplex reduction
两次回火　double tempering
两次混合螺旋输送机　double mixing screw
两次混料堆仓　twin mixing-heap bunker
两次拉拔的钢丝　soft-drawn wire
两次冷轧法　two-stage cold rolling method
两次滤液　double filtrate
两次螺旋混合器　double mixing screw
两次铅淬火　double lead patenting
两次铅浴淬火法　double lead (patenting) process
两次烧结　double sintering
两次收缩　【铸】double shrinkage
两次退火　double annealing
两次弯曲破[除]鳞机　two-bend processing scale breaker
两次压缩模　double reduction die
两次压制　double compression, double-pressing
两次压制法　double-press process
两次压制与烧结坯　(同"复压复烧坯")
两次正火[常化]　double normalizing
两端叉形架[夹](支架管子或流槽用)　double-end shank
两端供电(法)　two-sided current supply
两端炉叉　【冶】double-end shank
两端压制　double-ended pressing
两段焙烧操作　【团】two-stage firing operation
两段处理流程图　double-stage treatment flowsheet
两段淬火　two-stepped quenching
两段电解处理　two-stage electrolyte treatment
两段腐蚀　two-stage attack
两段供热的加热炉　double-fired reheating furnace
两段固溶热处理　two steps solid solution treatment

两段还原	duplex [two-stage] reduction
两段混合	two-stage blending
两段减速机	two-stage speed reducer
两段搅拌(浸出)	two-stage agitation
两段浸出法	two-stage [two-cycle, double] leaching (process)
两段可还原性试验	two-stage reducibility test
两段冷却	double-stage cooling
两段磨矿	two-stage grinding
两段疲劳试验	two step test
两段破碎	two-stage crushing
两段破碎机	two-stage crusher
两段熔化法	two-stage melting process
两段[步]熔融还原法	two-stage smelting reduction process
两段烧结	double sintering
两段渗氮	double-stage nitriding
两段时效	【金】double aging
两段式点火器	two zone ignition furnace
两段式环冷机	two zone grate-type annular cooler
两段式降压泵	two-stage pumpdown booster
两段式连续加热炉	two zone furnace
两段式圆盘(造球机)	two-step disc
两段酸浸出	two-stage acid leach
两段退火	two-steps annealing
两段细筛	two-stage fine screen
两分式焦炉(指燃烧室火道两分式)	half-divided oven
两工序深冲	double-action drawing
两股线绳	twine
两极电解清洗系统	bipolar electrolytic cleaning system
两级萃取器	two-stage extractor
两级反应器	two-stage reactor
两级分馏真空泵	two-stage fractionating pump
两级分批萃取	two-stage batch extraction
两级复型	two-stage replica
两级活塞式压缩机	two-stage piston compressor
两级减速机	double reduction unit
两级离心泵	two-stage centrifugal pump
两级疲劳试验	two step test
两级溶出	two-step digestion
两价铁离子	ferrous ion
两脚规	diveder, bow pen, calipers, calliper [bow] compasses
两晶型元素	dimorphous element
两块组合式喷嘴	two-piece nozzle
两面凹的	biconcave
两面锤	double-faced hammer ◇ 手选矿石用～scabbling hammer
两面反射器	diplane reflector
两面凸的	biconvex, lenticular
两面压制	(同"双效压制")
两模造型	【铸】duplex moulding
两片模	【铸】two-piece pattern, cope and drag pattern
两片式液化乙炔气瓶用钢板	hot rolled strip for liquid-acetylene vessel welded from two pieces
两色雾翳	dichroic fog
两砂箱[两开箱]铸型	two-part mould
两探针装置	two-probe arrangement
两通水平式蓄热室	two-pass horizontal regenerator
两头大的锻件	middle
两头燃烧炉	double-end fired furnace
两维光栅	cross grating
两相焙烧(用以回收铼)	two-phase roasting
两相黄铜	duplex brass
两相混合物	two-phase mixture
两相流	two-phase flow
两相铝青铜	duplex aluminium bronze
两相区	two-phase region [field]
两箱造型模	cope and drag pattern
两向加压造型机	bread and butter machine
两向切削	(同"垂直切削")
两性导体	amphoteric conductor

两性电解质　ampholyte, amphoteric electrolyte
两性反应　amphoteric reaction
两性化合物　amphoteric compound
两性金属　amphoteric metal
两性金属污染物　【环】amphoteric metal pollutant
两性离子　amphion, amphoteric ion
两性性质　amphoteric nature
两性盐　amphoteric salt
两性氧化物　amphoteric [intermediate] oxide
两性元素　amphotere
两用铲　convertible shovel
两用车　convertible car
两用燃烧系统　【团】dual-burning system
两用铁(碱性炼钢及酸性炼钢两用)　duplex iron
两用性　compatibility
两圆形件间 V 形焊缝　flare-V weld
两张叠轧　roll doubles, roll in pairs
两指手套　mitten
两转炉同时吹炼　【钢】two-vessel operation
量　quantity, amount
量棒　point gauge, length bar
量杯　measuring [volumetric] glass, counting cup
量变(体)　modification of quantity
量程　(measuring, measurement) range, span
量尺　measuring rule [scale], graduated stick, dipstick
量尺寸　sizing
量电钳　【电】dog
量斗(配料的)　batch box [bin]
量度　measure(ment)
量杆　dipstick, sounding [gauge] rod, measuring bar [rod]
量纲　dimension ◇ 无～的 dimensionless
量纲法　【理】dimensional method
量管　measuring tube, burette
量规　(measuring) gauge, caliber, calibre, 【压, 铸】templet (调整轧辊、检查尺寸用) ◇ 按～加工 finish(ing) to gauge, 大型～ heavy gauge, 检验～ inspection gauge, 接触式～contact-type gauge, 平衡杆式～balanced beam gauge, 消失螺纹～run-out gauge, 轴尖式～point gauge, 组合式～combination gauge
量化器　quantizer, digitizer
量级　order
量角器　angle gauge, graduated arc, protractor
量具　measurer, measuring tool, measuring gauge (精度不高的) ◇ 黏结的组合型芯用～pasting gauge
量具钢　gauge steel, measuring instrument steel
量矿器　measuring pocket
量矿箱　hoppet
量流　quantity flow
量瓶　volumetric [measuring] flask, graduated flask (有刻度的)
量坡规　back sloper
量器　measuring vessel, gauge
量取　measuring off
量热弹　【理】(calorimetric) bomb
量热法　【理】calorimetry, calorimetric method
量热高温计　calorimetric pyrometer
量热计[器]　thermometer, heat meter ◇ 弹式[燃烧弹]～bomb calorimeter
量热计法　calorimeter method
量热器测量　calorimetric measurement
量热器筒　calorimeter vessel
量热试验　calorimetric test
量热学　calorimetry
量热装置　calorimeter assembly
量色计　metrochrome
量筒　(measuring, volumetric) cylinder, graduated cylinder (有刻度的)
量限　range ◇ 不通过～规 not-go gauge
量液杯　measuring glass

| 量液滴定管 | measuring buret(te) |
| 量液移液管 | measuring pipet(te) |

量子 qunatum (复数 quanta) ◇ γ 射线-~ gamma(-ray) quantum, 作用~ quantum of action

量子产额	quantum yield [efficiency]
量子常数	quantum constant
量子发射	quantum emission
量子放大器	maser, quantum amplifier
量子辐射	quantum radiation
量子干涉	quantum interference
量子化	quantization
量子化场	quantized field
量子化角动量	quantized angular momentum
量子化器	quantizer
量子化相互作用	quantized interaction
量子化学	quantum chemistry

量子理论 quantum theory ◇ 玻尔－索默菲尔德~

量子力学	quantum-mechanics
量子力学概念[表示]	quantum-mechanical picture
量子力学理论	quantum-mechanical theory
量子力学原理	quantum-mechanical principle
量子漏泄	quantum leakage
量子能级	quantum (energy) level
量子散射	quantum scattering
量子数	quantum number
量子物理学	quantum physics
量子效率	quantum efficiency
量子效应	quantum effect
量子性质	quantum nature
量子跃变	quantum jump
量子跃迁	quantum transition
量子状态	quantum state
晾干	weather,【耐】seasoning
亮暗煤型	clarodurite
亮斑(缺陷)	【铸】bright spot

亮边(可锻铸铁退火缺陷) picture frame, bright

亮边断口	bright border, picture frame fracture
亮窗	abatjour
亮点	snakes,【铸】bright spot
亮度	brightness, brilliance, brilliancy, luminance
亮度调制	intensity modulation
亮度对比	brightness contrast
亮度反差 [衬比]	luminance difference
亮度高温计	luminance pyrometer
亮度控制	beam control
亮度系数	brightness coefficient
亮度增强剂	brightening addition
亮浮渣(铝生产的)	bright dross
亮光温度	brightness temperature
亮晶断口	bright (crystalline) fracture
亮口(可锻铸铁的)	bright fracture
亮煤	glance [bright] coal, clarain
亮煤型	clarite
钌钯合金	ruthenium-palladium alloy
钌锇铱矿	rustonite
钌合金	ruthenium alloy
钌基合金	ruthenium-base alloy
钌添加合金	ruthenium addition
钌铱锇矿	rutheniridosmine
料棒	charge bar
料饼	resultant cake

料仓 storage bin, silo, bunker, (feed) bin, stock bin [house] ◇ 充有惰性气体的~ inert-gas-filled hopper, 供应~【冶】live storage, 缓冲~ buffer bin, 混合~【铁】blending bin, 移动~ batch truck, 已贮~ bunkerage, 支架式~, 锥形~ conical bin

料仓搬运[起重]小车平台	【冶】lurry car platform
料仓储量	【冶】bin storage
料仓料面[位]计	silometer, bin level controller
料仓料面[位]指示器	silo level indicator
料仓平台(转炉车间的)	【钢】bin

[bunker] platform
料仓系列[一组料仓] bin line
料仓下运输线路 stockhouse track
料仓选择 【铁】bin selection
料仓运输机 bunker conveyer
料仓闸门[闭锁器] bin gate [stopper, fastener] ◇ 滚筒式~【铁】roller bin gate
料仓栈桥 【铁】trestle
料仓中物料分层 bin segregation
料仓贮存 bin storage
料仓组[群] cluster bins
料槽 (batch) bin, hopper ◇ 缓冲~ buffer bin, 进出斗~boot tank
料槽结构 bin design
料槽排料 bin discharge
料槽配料器 measuring pocket
料槽门 bin door
料层 material bed, charge layer, bed layer [charge], mix bed ◇ 散粒~*
料层边缘 edge of bed
料层参数 bed parameter
料层底[下]部 bottom of bed
料层辐射率 pellet-bed emissivity
料层高度 layer height
料层厚度 bed thickness [depth, hight], layer height, mix thickness, depth of charge, charging level
料层厚度控制 bed [charging] level control
料层厚度指示器 bed height indicator
料层交替(高炉的) alternation of beds
料层结块 bed sintering
料层孔隙度[气孔容积] pore space of bed
料层密度 bed packing
料层上部温度 above-the-bed temperature
料层上层[表层料层] bed top
料层烧结 bed sintering
料层收缩 bed shrink [collapse]
料层收缩速度[率] rate of bed collapse
料层水分 【团】charge humidity
料层透气性 bed permeability
料层稀释剂 bed diluent

料层直径 bed diameter
料场 stock [storage] yard, stock ground, stocking area [facilities], stockpiling area, bed blending plant, bedding pile [plant], blending facilities
料场吊车 stock [store, yard] crane
料场跨度 yard span
料场满装面积 full area storage
料场用移动式吊车 mobile yard crane
料场作业 bedding operation
料车 skip (car) ◇ 可拆式~【铁】detachable skip, 装~【冶】charging car
料车臂 tripper boom
料车车体 【铁】skip bucket
料车秤 skip weigher
料车钢绳 skip cable
料车卷扬机 skip hoist [winch] ◇ 高炉~*
料车卷扬机传动 skip hoist drive
料车卷扬机房 skip (hoist) house
料车坑 【铁】skip pit [pocket]
料车列 charging-buggy train
料车容量 skip capacity
料车上料式高炉 skip-filled furnace
料车上料系统 skip charging system
料车绳轮 【铁】sheave
料车式装料机 skip charger
料车提升装料机 skip hoist loader
料车往返周期指示器 skip cycle indicator
料车斜桥 【铁】skip (hoist) incline, skip bridge
料车行程 【铁】skip trip
料车运行程序指示器 skip program indicator ◇ 目视~*
料车运行周期 【铁】skip cycle
料车装料 【铁】skip charging [filling], block charging
料车装料程序 【铁】skip program
料车装料[装载]量(高炉的) skip load [charge, weight]
料秤 stock weigher
料尺 【铁】stock [testing] rod

料 liao

料尺孔 【铁】try hole
料锭 charge bar
料斗 bunker, charging spout,【钢】(charging) box ◇ 大盖～*
料斗车 【钢】pan [box] car
料斗车列 【钢】pan-car train
料斗秤 hopper weigher, bunker scale
料斗[筐]导轨架 container guide bracket
料斗颈 hopper-collar
料斗卷扬电动机 skip hoist motor
料斗－料钟卷扬机 skip-and-bell hoist
料斗－料钟炉顶设计 【铁】cup-and-cone top design
料斗起重机 turnaround charging crane
料斗取样器 【冶】bucket sampler
料斗卸料口 hopper throat
料斗容量 hopper capacity
料斗式的 hopper-shaped
料斗装料 【钢】box charging
料斗装料起重机 trough-charging crane
料堆 (stock) pile, stockpiling, stock heap, material [bedded] pile
料堆参数 bed parameter
料堆端部 pile end
料房 stock house
料封 charge seal
料封管 seal pipe [leg], dipleg
料拱 material bridge
料拱形成 bridging of charge
料罐 【冶】bucket
料罐卷扬装置 bucket carriage track
料罐(上料)卷扬机 【铁】bucket hoist, skip winch ◇ 垂直－水平式～*
料罐式(上料) 【铁】bail type
料罐式炉顶上料 【铁】bucket type top charging
料罐装料式炉顶 ◇ 尼兰德～(高炉)【铁】Neeland top
料浆 feed pulp, slime, slurry
料坑 loading pit
料块尺寸(矿石的) size of feed
料筐 【冶】pocket,【钢】charging basket,【压】bin
料筐倾翻机构 【钢】tilting-basket mechanism
料篮 【钢】(charging) basket
料篮运送小车 【钢】basket transfer bogie
料粒 feed particle
料量调节 feed control
料流 feed influent, feed stock flow
料流分布[形态] flow pattern
料面 charge level
料面探测器[料面探针, 料线探尺] charge level detector, burden profile probe
料面指示器 charge level indicator ◇ 放射性同位素～*, 鼓风炉～*
料末 dead smalls
料内探测器[探针] in-burden probe
料盘温度 tray temperature
料坯 green body ◇ 制～briquetting, 瞬时～能量*
料批 material charge
料批大小 【铁】size of charge
料批重 charge [burden] weight
料批重量调整控制盘 【冶】charge weight selector panel
料批重量选择 charge weight selection
料皮 material deposit
料坡 charge bank
料枪喷管 【色】gun nozzle
料速过快 (同"反常快行")
料桶 【钢】charging basket
料头 crop piece
料位 stock level, level of material
料位计[仪] level gauge, bin level controller ◇ 料仓～*, 同位素～*
料位开关 level switch
料位调节器 (stock-)level controller
料位调整 level adjustment
料位指示器[仪] level gauge (LG), (bin) level indicator, charge gauge, stock-level visualizer
料温 charge temperature (CH. Temp.), feed temperature

料线 【铁】stockline, stock level (SL), charge level ◇ M 形~*

料线保护板 stockline armour

料线测定器 stockline gauge

料线测量[测定] stockline measurement ◇ γ 射线~仪 γ-ray stock gauge

料线高度 stock-level height

料线记录器 stock line recorder

料线控制 stock-level control

料线轮廓[内型] stockline profile

料线探测卷扬机 stockline winch

料线外炉墙 stockline wall

料线直径 stockline diameter

料线指示器[仪] stock (line) indicator, stockline [stock-level] visualizer

料箱 feed(ing) box, cradle,【冶】pocket,【钢】(charging) box,【压】bin

料箱起重机 turnaround charging crane

料箱装料 【钢】box charging

料箱装料起重机 trough-charging crane

料液 feed liquid [liquor, solution]

料液酸度 feed acidity

料液预热器 feed solution preheater

料液贮槽 feed stock tank

料渣 【冶】charge slag

料钟 【铁】(isolation, gas-seal) bell, receiving cone ◇ 顶部~ top bell, 气密~ gas-seal bell, 小~ upper bell, 整体[无焊缝]~ one-piece bell

料钟操纵装置 bell operating rigging

料钟操作机构 bell operating gear

料钟杆 bell rod

料钟钢丝绳 bell cable

料钟和炉料的接触面 charge surface

料钟间的煤气反冲 gas kick between bells

料钟卷扬机 bell hoist [winch] ◇ 气动[气缸式]~ pneumatic bell hoist, 液压~*

料钟开闭气缸 air jack

料钟开闭装置 bell operating rigging

料钟平衡锤 bell counterweight

料钟平衡杆 bell beam, bell fulcrum arm

料钟气密性(能) sealing characteristic of bell

料钟倾角 angle of bell

料钟行程 stroke of bell

料柱 charge [charging, stock, ore] column ◇ 高炉~ stock, 炉缸中心(死)~*【铁】central core, 死[中心]~【铁】pillaring

料柱导风"墙"(竖炉的) 【团】inner column wind guiding "wall"

料柱骨架 【铁】stock column

料柱透气性 bed permeability

料柱阻力 【铁】charge resistance

料嘴 feed nozzle

列车 【运】train, shuttle ◇ 装[载]料~ charging-buggy train

列车调度员 train dispatcher

列举 list, cite

列氏温标 Reaumur scale

列氏温度计 Reaumur thermometer

列线图 (同"诺模图")

裂边 cracked [burst, check, raw] edge ◇ 成卷带材~检查仪 edge(strip) scanner

裂变 fission, split transformation ◇ 可~物质

裂变残渣[毒物] fission poison

裂变产物 fission product

裂变(产物)合金 fissium (alloy), fizzium

裂变气体 fission gas

裂变气体膨胀 fission gas swelling

裂变碎片 fission fragment

裂变物质 fissionable material

裂变元素 fissionable element

裂变原子 fissile [fissioned] atom

裂变中子 fission neutron

裂缝 crack(ing), rupturing, rent, fissure, fissuring, gapping, splits,【金】shake,【压】fin ◇ 有~的焊缝 cracked weld

裂缝充填 filling in of scores

裂缝焊合 【压】(crack-)heal(ing)

裂缝检查器 flaw detector

裂缝浇注 【铸】crack pouring

裂缝扩展能 propagation energy

裂 lie

裂缝连接 split joint
裂缝敏感性组成[成分] cracking sensitivity composition
裂缝前缘形状 crack front shape
裂缝生长 crack growth ◇ 探测～用位移计
裂缝探测仪 crack detector
裂缝效应 crevice effect
裂缝增长 jumps in crack growth
裂缝张开位移 crack opening desplacement (COD)
裂痕 flaw, seam (钢锭缺陷) ◇ 阿尔巴～磁力探测[探伤]器 Alba crack detector
裂后能 【理】postcrack energy
裂化 cracking ◇ 加氢～*, 可～性 crackability
裂化氨气体 cracked ammonia gas
裂化铵 cracking ammonium
裂化剂 cracking agent
裂化馏出物 cracked distillate
裂化气体 cracked gas
裂化气体设备 endogas unit
裂化天然气 cracked natural gas
裂化烃[碳氢化合物] cracked hydrocarbon
裂化温度 cracking temperature
裂化无水氨 cracked anhydrous ammonia
裂化蒸馏 cracking distillation
裂解 dissociation, splitting
裂开 cracking, fissuration, sliver, split-up, breach, bursting
裂口 cleft,【铸】fissure defect (缺陷)
裂口传播[扩展]速率 rate of fracture propagation
裂口焊 cleft welding
裂口扩展特性 fracture propagation characteristic
裂片 shive, splint(er), sliver
裂片断裂[裂片状断口] splintery fracture
裂纹 crack(ing), nick, flaw, split, chink (ing), clink, rupturing (钢锭表面的),【铸】fissure defect (缺陷),【金】shake ◇ 不扩展[非扩展性]～ non-propagating crack, 产生～ flawing, 对～不敏感的 noncrack-sensitive, 厚薄不均引起的～ bull crack, 扩展～ running crack, 格里菲思临界～长度*, 晶界蠕变～ boundary creep crack, 起～【钢】checking, 氢致[诱发]～*, 有～的钢锭 dry ingot
裂纹产生 crack initiation
裂纹产生能 crack initiation energy
裂纹底部 base of crack
裂纹顶端塑性流变 plastic flow at crack tip
裂纹分叉 branching of crack
裂纹分叉角 crack branching angle
裂纹分枝性能 【金】crack branching property
裂纹核化[成核] crack nucleation
裂纹核心 crack nucleus
裂纹缓慢扩展 slow crack growth
裂纹尖端 crack tip
裂纹尖端应力强度 crack tip stress intensity
裂纹检验 crack detection ◇ 粗视条痕～ macro streak flaw test
裂纹扩展[传播] crack propagation [developing, growth] ◇ 由环境引起的～ environmental crack growth
裂纹扩展力 【金】crack extension force
裂纹扩展试验 crack-propagation test
裂纹扩展速度 crack-propagation velocity, crack speed
裂纹扩展[传播]速率 propagation rate of crack, crack growth rate
裂纹扩展抑止温度 crack arrest temperature (CAT)
裂纹路径 crack path
裂纹敏感的 crack-sensitive
裂纹敏感性[形成倾向性] 【金】crack susceptibility ◇ 焊道下～*
裂纹趋势 【金】susceptibility to cracking

裂纹缺陷 seam defect	林德曼公式(关于晶体熔化现象的) Lindemann's formula
裂纹容限 crack tolerance, tolerance of flows	林德试验 (见"程序控制还原试验")
裂纹深度 crack depth	林曼夹渣标准[指数] 【钢】Rinman scale
裂纹始发微观机理 micromechanism in crack initiation	林阴路 avenue (ave.)
裂纹探测 crack detection	磷{P} phosphorus, phosphor ◇ 脱[去]~*
裂纹现象[缺陷] seaminess	磷铵铀矿{NH₄(UO₂)PO₄·3H₂O} uramphite
裂纹形成 crack formaton	磷钡铝矿 gorceixite
裂纹域 slit domain	磷钡铀矿 bergenite
裂纹源 crack initiation	磷带 phosphor [ghost] band, phosphorus banding
裂纹张开 【压】opening of break	磷豆 phosphide pearl
裂纹长大[生长] crack growth	磷反应 phosphorous reaction
裂纹长大速率 crack growth rate	磷分配 phosphorous distribution
裂纹中心 crack nucleus	磷钙钒矿 sincosite
裂隙 crack, fissure, 【铸】fissure defect (缺陷)	磷钙铁矿 borickite, boryckite
裂相电动机 split-phase motor	磷钙土 phosphorite
裂音(钢件加工后发裂产生的) clinking	磷钙土石 brabantite
裂殖菌纲 Schizomycete	磷钢 phosphoretic steel
裂殖藻纲 Schizopycete	磷光屏效率 phosphor screen efficiency
烈性催化剂 rugged catalyst	磷光体 phosphorus, phosphor ◇ 单晶体~,屏*
烈焰 Keen [wild, roaring] flame	磷光体余辉 phosphorescent decay
劣等 inferiority, low-grade	磷光物质疲劳 fatigue of phosphor
劣级砂 badly graded sand	磷光现象 phosphorescence
劣质的 ungraded, inferior	磷硅铝钇钙石 saryarkite
劣质废钢铁 junk scrap	磷硅铈钠石 phosinaite
劣质粉末 poor-quality powder	磷硅钛铌钠石 vuonnemite, wuonnemite
劣质混凝土 faulty [poor] concrete	磷硅钍矿 auerlite
劣质焦煤 inferior coking coal	磷含量回升 【冶】rephosphoration
劣质煤 inferior [low-rank, faulty] coal, bone	磷化 phosphorization ◇ J.A.M. 快速~法*, 辛格~法*
劣质燃料 inferior [low-quality] fuel	磷化处理 phosphate treatment [coating], phosphating, phosphatizing, lithorizing (锌或镀锌、镀镉材料的) ◇ 电~*
林茨海绵铁粉 Linz powder	
林德布莱德电炉 Lindblad furnace	
林德钢管对焊法 Linde welding	
林德还原(度)指数 Linder reducibility index	磷化处理槽 phosphating bath
林德还原反应管 Linder tube	磷化处理法(钢的) Merilising
林德回转炉还原试验法 Linder rotating furnace procedure	磷化处理特性 phosphatability
	磷化钙 calcium phosphide
林德曼玻璃 Lindemann(-type) glass	磷化镓 gallium phosphide

磷化铝　aluminum phosphide
磷化硼　boron phosphide
磷化铅　lead phosphide
磷化铁　iron phosphide
磷化铜　copper phosphide, phosphorized copper
磷化物　phosphide
磷化物共晶(体)　phosphide eutectic
磷化物条痕　phosphide streak
磷化物编[带]状组织　phosphoric banding
磷化锌　zinc phosphide
磷化液　phosphorization
磷化铟　indium phosphide
磷灰石{$Ca_5(PO_4)_3(F, Cl, OH, CO_3)$}　phosphorite, rock phosphate, apatite
磷灰石-霞石岩　apatite-nepheline rock
磷锂矿　Lithiophilite
磷硫酸铅铝矿[磷铅锶矾]{$(Pb, Sr)Al_3[PO_4]SO_4(OH)_6$}　hinsdalite
磷铝石{$2LiF·Al_2O_3·P_2O_5$}　amblygonite
磷铝铈矿　koivinite, koiwinite
磷铝铀矿{$HAl(UO_2)_4(PO_4)_4$}　salengalite
磷氯铅矿{$Pb_5Cl(PO_4)_3$ 或 $PbCl_2·9PbO·3P_2O_5$}　pyromorphite, swamp ore, bog(iron) ore
磷锰矿　reddingite
磷锰铀矿{$Mn(UO_2)_2PO_4·8H_2O$}　fritzcheite
磷钼酸{$H_3PO_4·MoO_4$}　phosphomolybdic [molybdophosphoric] acid
磷钼酸铵　ammonium phosphomolybdate
磷钼酸盐　phosphomolybdate
磷钠铍石{$NaBePO_4$}　beryllonite
磷钠稀土石　vitusite
磷镍合金料(80Ni,20P)　phosphor-nickel
磷铍钙石{$CaBeFPO_4$}　herderite
磷铍锰矿　faheyite
磷偏析　phosphorus segregation
磷平衡　phosphorous equilibrium
磷铅铀矿{$Pb_3(UO_2)_5(OH)_4(PO_4)_4·10H_2O$}　dewindtite

磷青铜(10—14Sn,0.1—0.3P,余量Cu)　phosphor(us) bronze (p.b., ph. bz.), phosphor-tin bronze, high tin bronze ◇艾杰克斯～*,衬套用～*,易切削～*
磷砷铅矿　kampylite, campylite
磷铈镧矿　monazite
磷铈钼矿　(同"独居石")
磷铈钠石　vitusite
磷铈钍石　smirnovskite
磷酸铵　ammonium phosphate
磷酸处理(法)(锌或锌镀层的)　Granodising
磷酸镝{$DyPO_4$}　dysprosium phosphate
磷酸单烷基酯　mono-alkyl phospate
磷酸单亲酯　mono-octyl phosphate
磷酸丁酯　butyl phosphate
磷酸二丁酯　dibutyl phosphate (DBP)
磷酸二氢铵{$NH_4H_2PO_4$}　ammonium dihydrophosphate (ADP)
磷酸二氢锶　(同"一代磷酸锶")
磷酸二辛酯　dioctyl phosphate
磷酸钙{$Ca_3(PO_4)_2$}　calcium phosphate
磷酸钙硅{$5CaO·SiO_2·P_2O_5$}　calcium silicon phosphate
磷酸钙铝石{$3CaO·Al_2O_3·P_2O_5·2H_2O$}　tavistockite
磷酸锆　zirconium (ortho)phosphate
磷酸汞　mercuric phosphate
磷酸铪　hafnium phosphate
磷酸钪{$ScPO_4$}　scandium phosphate
磷酸镧{$LaPO_4$}　lanthanum orthophosphate
磷酸镧钾{$K_3[La_2(PO_4)_3]$}　potassium lanthanum orthophosphate
磷酸镧锆矿{$(Y, Er, La, Di)_2O_3·P_2O_5·2H_2O$}　rhabdophanite
磷酸锂{Li_3PO_4}　lithium phosphate
磷酸铝石{$Al_2O_3·P_2O_5·4H_2O$}　variscite
磷酸镁　magnesium phosphate
磷酸膜被覆法　rovalising
磷酸镍　nickel phosphate
磷酸镨{$PrPO_4$}　praseodymium phosphate

磷酸铅 lead phosphate
磷酸氢二钠 {Na$_2$HPO$_4$} disodium hydrogen phosphate
磷酸氢高铈 {Ce(HPO$_4$)$_2$} ceric hydrophosphate
磷酸氢双氧铀[磷酸氢铀酰] {UO$_2$HPO$_4$} uranyl phosphate
磷酸氢锶 {SrHPO$_4$} strontium monophosphate, secondary strontium phosphate
磷酸氢盐 hydrophosphate, biphosphate
磷酸氢钇 {Y$_2$(HPO$_4$)$_3$} yttrium hydrophosphate
磷酸三丁酯 {(C$_4$H$_9$O)$_3$PO} tributyl phoshate
磷酸三丁酯萃取 TBP extraction
磷酸三丁酯萃取法 TBP process ◇ 新~【色】new TBP process
磷酸三丁酯萃取剂 TBP extractant
磷酸三丁酯分离 TBP separation
磷酸三丁酯-己烷溶剂 TBP-hexane
磷酸三丁酯-硫代氰酸盐萃取法 TBP-thiocyanate process
磷酸三丁酯-煤油溶剂 TBP-kerosene
磷酸三丁酯溶剂 TBP solvent
磷酸三丁酯-硝酸法(萃取) TBP-nitric-acid system
磷酸三丁酯-硝酸分离系统 TBP-nitric-acid separation system
磷酸三丁酯-正己烷法(萃取) TBP-n-hexane system
磷酸三甲酯 {(CH$_3$O)$_3$PO} trimethyl phosphate
磷酸三钠 {Na$_3$PO$_4$} trisodium phosphate
磷酸三烷基酯 trialkyl phosphate
磷酸三氧钼 {(MoO$_3$)PO$_4$} molybdenyl phosphate
磷酸钐 {SmPO$_4$} samaric orthophosphate
磷酸铈 {CePO$_4$} cerous orthophosphate [phosphate]
磷酸锶 {Sr$_3$(PO$_4$)$_2$} strontium (ortho) phosphate, tertiary strontium phosphate
磷酸铁 {FePO$_4$} iron phosphate

磷酸铁被膜防锈法 coslettizing
磷酸钍 thorium phosphate
磷酸稀土 {REPO$_4$} rare earth phosphate
磷酸锌 zinc (ortho) phosphate
磷酸锌表面处理 zinc phosphatizing
磷酸锌处理(钢丝干式拉拔的) granodraw
磷酸锌膜(防大气腐蚀用) lithoform
磷酸亚铈钠 {Na$_3$[Ce$_2$(PO$_4$)$_3$]} sodium cerous orthophosphate
磷酸盐 phosphate ◇ 含~矿物*, 杰诺莱特~除锈液 Jenolite, 熔融~电解液 fused phosphate bath
磷酸盐薄钢板 phosphated sheet
磷酸盐薄膜防锈法 bonderising, bonderizing
磷酸盐(表面)处理 phosphate treatment, phosphating, phosphatizing, phosphate coating ◇ 经~的钢板 bonderized sheel, 蒸汽~*
磷酸盐表面处理法 Merilising
磷酸盐沉淀 phosphate precipitation ◇ 胶态~*
磷酸盐处理槽 phosphating bath
磷酸盐处理的钢丝 phosphating steel wire
磷酸盐处理法 phosphating process, bonderising, bonderizing
磷酸盐处理钢板 bonderized sheet
磷酸盐处理钢丝 phosphating steel wire
磷酸盐处理特性 phosphatability
磷酸盐防锈处理 parkerization, parkerizing, parkerising
磷酸盐防锈处理法 parkerizing process
磷酸盐分离 phosphate fractionation
磷酸盐结合耐火材料 phosphate-bonded refractory
磷酸盐浸镀(处理) walterisation ◇ 福斯普雷~法 Fospray process
磷酸盐抗锈蚀和拉拔用表面处理法 a-trament process
磷酸盐矿粉 ground phosphate

磷酸盐离子　phosphate ion
磷酸盐络合物　phosphate complex
磷酸盐容量　phosphate capacity
磷酸盐配合体活度　phosphate-ligand activity
磷酸盐涂层润滑（法）【压】phosphate coating lubrication
磷酸盐岩石{Ca$_3$(PO$_4$)$_2$}　phosphate rock
磷酸盐云母绝缘化法　micacid insulating process
磷酸盐重量分析法　phosphate gravimetric method
磷酸盐煮沸处理　coslettizing
磷酸钇{YPO$_4$}　yttrium phosphate, phosphate of yttria
磷酸银　silver (ortho)phosphate
磷酸铀络离子　uranium phosphate complex ion
磷酸酯　phosphate ester
磷酸酯－胺类联合萃取剂　combination phosphate-amine extractant
磷酸酯萃取　phosphate extraction
磷酸酯溶剂　phosphate solvent
磷铁　ferrophosphor(us)
磷铁铋石　zairite
磷铁矿　fosfosiderite
磷铁锂矿{LiFePO$_4$}　triphylite
磷铁锰矿　beusite
磷铜（含磷 0.25%）　phosphor-copper, phosphorous copper
磷铜焊料（7—10P,余量 Cu）　phos-copper
磷铜合金　phosphorus-copper alloy
磷铜矿　liebethenite
磷铜铁矿　chalcosiderite
磷钍矿　grayite
磷脱氧铜　phosphorus deoxidized copper
磷钨酸{P$_2$O$_5$·24WO$_3$·nH$_2$O 和 H$_2$[P(W$_2$O$_7$)$_6$]$_7$·nH$_2$O}　phospho-tungstic, [phospho-wolframic] acid, tungstophosphoric acid
磷钨酸铵　ammonium phosphotungstate [phosphowolframate]

磷钨酸钠　sodium phosphotungstate
磷钨酸盐　phosphotungstate, phosphowolframate
磷锡合金　phosphor tin
磷锡青铜（≤20% Sn）　phosphor-tin bronze
磷稀土矿　rhabdophane
磷线　【钢】phosphorus banding, ghost band
磷硝铜矿　likasite
磷锌合金（中间合金；约含 10P）　phosphor zinc
磷锌矿　salmoite, zinkphyllite
磷钇矿　xenotime{(Y, Th, U, Er, Ce)(PO$_4$)}, phosphate of yttria {YPO$_4$}
磷钇铈矿　rhabdophane
磷印　【钢】phosphorus print(ing)
磷铀矿{(UO$_2$)$_3$(PO$_4$)$_2$·6H$_2$O}　phosphuranylite
磷杂质　phosphorus impurity
磷中毒　phophor poisoning ◇ 慢性～ phosphorism
磷珠　phosphide pearl
临界半径　critical radius
临界半径比　critical radius ratio
临界变数　critical variable
临界变形　【压】critical deformation [strain]
临界变形量　critical deformability
临界表面　critical surface
临界参数　critical parameter
临界操作　critical operation
临界常数　critical constant
临界长度　critical length
临界沉淀点　precipitability
临界成分　critical composition
临界尺寸（钢板淬火的）　critical size [dimension]
临界冲击速度（高速成形的）【压】critical impact velocity
临界磁场　【理】critical magnetic field ◇ 超导体～强度*
临界淬火速率　critical quenching rate,

critical rate of hardening
临界淬火温度 critical hardening temperature
临界点 critical point, breakthrough (point), threshold, transformation [arrest(ation), neutral] point, no (n)-slip point, critical temperature ◇ 热～ critical thermal point
临界点超塑性 superplasticity at critical point
临界点法 breakthrough technique
临界点下热处理 subcritical treatment
临界点以下的[低于临界的] subcritical
临界电流密度 critical current density
临界电位[势] critical potential
临界电压 critical voltage
临界法向应力 critical normal stress
临界反应物比 critical reactant ratio
临界范围[区域] critical range ◇ 下[亚]～*
临界方程式 critical equation
临界分切[剪]应力 critical resolved shear stress (CRSS)
临界分应力 critical resolved stress (CRS)
临界风量 critical air blast
临界负荷[荷载] critical [crippling] load
临界功率 critical power
临界共熔点[温度] (critical) consolute point
临界鼓风试验 【焦】critical-air-blast test
临界滑移系 critical slip system
临界减幅 critical damping
临界角 critical [neutral] angle, angle of nonslip point
临界接触曲线 critical contact curves
临界晶粒长大 critical grain growth
临界聚变频率 critical fusion frequency
临界距离 critical distance
临界抗拉[张]应力 critical tensile stress
临界孔隙率 critical void ratio
临界控制 critical control ◇ 精密～ close critical control

临界拉伸变形 critical elongation
临界冷却速度 critical cooling rate [velocity]
临界粒度 critical particle diameter
临界力 critical force
临界流态化空隙度 critical fluidized voidage
临界流态化速度 critical fluidization velocity
临界密度 critical density (dc)
临界面 critical surface,【压】neutral plane
临界能 critical energy
临界凝固速率 critical solidification rate
临界浓度 critical concentration
临界偏压 critical bias
临界频率 critical [threshold] frequency
临界气流 critical current
临界前的 precritical
临界强度 critical intensity
临界切变能理论 critical shear strain energy theory
临界切应变 critical shear strain
临界切应力 critical shear stress ◇ 低堆位层错能～*, 高堆位层错能～*, 施密特～定律*
临界区热处理 intercritical heat treatment
临界曲线 critical curve
临界热 critical heat
临界热流[通]量 critical heat flux
临界溶解[溶液]温度 critical solution temperature (C.S.T.)
临界蠕变速率 critical creep rate
临界散射 critical scattering
临界湿度 critical humidity
临界时效 critical ageing
临界试验 marginal test, critical experiment, breakthrough run
临界衰减 critical damping
临界水分 critical moisture
临界速度 critical speed [velocity], whirling speed
临界塑性变形 critical plastic deformation

临界损失	critical loss
临界条件	critical condition
临界停闪频率	【电】critical fusion frequency (CFF)
临界途径法	critical path method (CPM)
临界温度	critical temperature, thermal critical point
临界温度范围	critical temperature range (CTR)
临界稳定性	marginal stability
临界误差	critical error
临界系数	critical coefficient
临界相变[转变]点	【金】critical transformation point
临界效应	critical [threshold] effect
临界性	criticality
临界性质	critical property
临界压力	critical pressure
临界压力系数	critical pressure coefficient
临界延伸率	critical elongation
临界应变	critical strain
临界应变晶粒长大	critical strain grain growth
临界应力	limiting [critical] stress, crippling stress（纵向弯曲的）
临界应力强度	critical stress intensity
临界应力强度因子	critical stress intensity factor
临界硬度	critical hardness
临界元件	critical element
临界造球速度	【团】critical balling speed
临界增量	critical increment
临界照明度	critical illumination
临界正应力	critical normal stress
临界直径	【理】critical diameter
临界直径淬火	critical diameter quenching
临界值	critical (value), nonoperate [marginal] value, threshold
临界置换比	【铁】critical replacement ratio
临界质量	critical mass
临界转速	【理】critical [whirling] speed
临界状态[状况]	critical state [condition, behaviour], criticality
临界状态工作	critical operation
临界追赶	【计】critical race
临界自由能	【理】critical free energy
临界阻尼	critical damping, dead-beat
临氢重整(的)	【化】hydroforming
临时的	temporary (temp.), occasional
临时点焊点	tacked spot
临时点焊缝	temporary weld
临时定位铆钉	tack(ing) [dummy] rivet
临时堆栈	emergency stockpile
临时防护衬里	flash lining
临时工	outside [odd] man
临时检验	casual inspection
临时料堆	emergency pile
临时铆钉	temporary [dummy] rivet
临时铆接	temporary [dummy] riveting
临时桥	emergency [temporary] bridge
临时燃烧器	extra burner
临时上型箱	【铸】false cope
临时性建筑[房屋]	temporary building [construction]
临时修理	temporary repair
临时应急工具[装置]	doctor
临时有机涂层	temporary organic coating
临时(窄轨)铁路	（同"施工铁路"）
临时支路	diversion
临时装置(夹具)	makeshift
临阈变形	threshold deformation
临阈电势[位]	threshold potential
临阈灵敏度	threshold sensitivity
临阈浓度	threshold concentration
临阈强度	threshold intensity
临阈应力	threshold stress
邻苯二酚	catechol
邻苯二酸铵	ammonium phthalate
邻苯二酸酸	（同"酞酸盐"）
邻丙基苯酚 $\{C_9H_{12}O\}$	mesitol
邻二甲苯 $\{C_8H_{10}\}$	o-dimethyl benzene, o-xylene
邻二甲苯酚 $\{C_8H_{10}\}$	o-xylenol
邻甲苯腈 $\{C_8H_7N\}$	o-tolunitrile

邻甲酚　o-cresol
邻甲基苯胺{C_7H_9N}　o-methylaniline
邻接　adjoin, neighbo(u)r, contiguity, butment
邻接层　adjoining course
邻接[近]偶　【理】close pair
邻近能级　adjacent energy level, nearby (energy) level
邻近效应[邻线影响]　proximity effect
邻乙基甲苯{C_9H_{12}}　o-othyl toluene
邻羟苯亚甲基氨基-乙-苯硫酚　salicylidene-amino-z-thiophenol
鳞板运输机　apron conveyer ◇倾斜式~*
鳞矾铀矿　ferganite
鳞落　scale off
鳞镁铁矿　igelstromite
鳞皮　roll scale, firecoat ◇氧化铬~*，轧制~rolling scale
鳞皮麻面　scale-pitted surface
鳞片　shatter crack, spilliness, snowflake (缺陷)，【钢】flake (缺陷)
鳞片状的　flaky, scalelike, scaly, fish scale
鳞片状裂纹　【金】silver crack
鳞片状组织　flake [scaly] structure
鳞石英{SiO_2}　tridymite, granuline
鳞纹面　【焊】rippled surface
鳞蛭石　vaalite
鳞状沉积　scaly deposit
鳞状焊缝　ripple weld
鳞状结构[组织]　flaser [imbricated] texture
鳞状堆料法　【铁】scalelike stocking method
檩(条)撑　purlin brace
檩(条)屋架　purlin roof
淋水管　spray pipe
淋水冷却器　drip-round cooler
淋洗装置　showering installation
淋下　trickle
淋盐水(腐蚀)试验　water-drip test
淋浴箱　shower-box

膦酸{R·PO(OH)_2}　phosphonic acid
膦酸树脂　phosphonic acid resin
膦酸烷基酯　alkyl-phosphonate
膦酸盐[酯]　phosphonate
膦酸阳离子交换剂　phosphonic type cation exchanger
菱板　quarrel
菱方的　orthorhombic
菱-方孔型系统　rhomb-square groove system, diamond-square sequence [series]
菱-方-菱孔型系统设计[轧制法]　【压】diamond-square-diamond method
菱-方系统孔型　diamond-square pass
菱方锥　orthorhombic pyramid
菱沸石{(CaNa)_2[Al_2Si_4O_{12}]6H_2O}　chabasite
菱钙铀矿　zellerite
菱镉矿　otavite
菱钴矿{CoCO_3}　sphaerocoballite
菱黑稀土矿　steenstrupine
菱角线　【数】cocked hat
菱苦土混合物　magnesite mixture
菱苦土木屑板　xylolite
菱-菱孔型系统　【压】diamond-diamond sequence [series]
菱-菱孔型系统设计[轧制法]　【压】diamond-diamond-diamond method
菱硫铁矿　smythite
菱镁矿{MgCO_3}　magnesite, giobertite ◇低[贫]铁~ low-iron magnesite, 煅烧~ calcined magnesite, 苛性~ caustic magnesite, 粒状~ grain magnesite, 死烧~ dead burnt magnesite
菱(镁)镍矿　gaspeite
菱镁土水泥　magnesia cement
菱镁铀矿{Mg_2UO_2(CO_3)_3·18H_2O}　bayleyite
菱锰矿{MnCO_3}　rhodochrosite
菱锰铅矾　nasledovite
菱锰铁矿　oligonite
菱面体对称　rhombohedral symmetry
菱面体结构　rhombohedral structure

菱面体排列　rhombohedral packing
菱钼铀矿{(UO$_2$)MoO$_4$·4H$_2$O}　umohoite
菱牌氯乙烯覆层金属板　Hishi metal
菱硼硅铈矿　stillwellite
菱水碳铁镁石{6MgO·Fe$_2$O$_3$·CO$_2$·12H$_2$O}　pyroaurite
菱锶矿{SrCO$_3$}　strontianite
菱铁矿{FeCO$_3$}　siderite, chalybite, spathic iron (ore), blackband (ore), sparry iron, white iron ore ◇ 泥[黏土]质~
菱铁镁矿　mesitite, mesitine
菱锌矿{ZnCO$_3$}　smithsonite, zinc spar, szaskaite
菱形　diamond, rhombus
菱形凹底椭圆孔型　diamond-type bastard oval
菱形变形　【铸】rhomboidity
菱形锉　hack file
菱形道岔　【运】diamond turnouts, switch diamond
菱形点阵[晶格]　rhombohedral [trigonal] lattice, R lattice
菱形断面　rhomboidal section, diamond
菱形对称　rhombic symmetry
菱形刚玉型赤铁矿{α-Fe$_2$O$_3$}　rhombohedral corundum type hematite
菱形钢材　【压】diamonds
菱形键　spline key
菱形交叉　diamond crossing
菱形晶(体)　rhombohedral crystal
菱形晶系　rhombic [rhombohedral] system
菱形晶轴　rhombohedral axis
菱形孔型　diamond (pass) ◇ 精轧~
菱形孔型顶角　pass angularity
菱形(六面)晶体　rhombohedral crystal
菱形面　rhombic face
菱形(六面)体[菱面体]　rhombohedron
菱形凸纹钢筋　diamond bar
菱形网纹钢板　checker(ed) [channeled] plate
菱形型材　rhomboidal section

菱形柱　cant column
菱形砖　quarry
菱铀钙石{Ca$_2$U(CO$_3$)$_4$·10H$_2$O}　liebigite, medjidite
菱铀矿{UO$_2$·CO$_3$}　rutherfordite
零次[级]衍射束　zero-order diffracted beam
零地址指令　【计】zero-address instruction
零点　zero (point), null point ◇ 虚~(仪器的) false zero
零点(补偿)测量法　【电】balanced [comparison] method
零点补偿法　zero(-deflection) method
零点电容　zero [minimum] capacity
零点观察　null observation
零点过热　zero superheat
零点校验　check for zero
零点能　zero-point energy
零点漂移　zero drift [creep], wandering of zero
零点屈服强度　zero-point yield strength
零点调整　zero adjustment
零点调整[调准]装置　zero adjuster [adjustment]
零点振动　zero-point vibration
零电势[位]　zero potential
零功率热核装置　【理】zero energy thermonuclear assembly (ZETA)
零活度[零活性, 零放射性]　zero activity
零级　zero order [level]
零级波　zero-order wave
零级反应　zero-order reaction
零价　zero valence
零价的　non-valent, zero valent
零件　part, element, component, fitting, member
零件表　parts list
零件检查　inspection of parts
零件图　detail drawing
零(力)矩　zero moment
零料　batch
零料仓　【冶】batch hopper

零-零跃迁 zero-zero transition
零母线 【电】neutral bar
零能量状态 zero-energy state
零排放 【环】zero discharge [release]
零偏法 zero(-deflection) method
零强度 zero strength [intensity]
零强度温度 zero strength temperature
零韧性 zero ductility
零衰减(量) zero-decrement
零瞬间(仪器读数起点) time zero
零塑性转变温度 null ductility transition (NDT)
零位 zero (position), null (position) ◇中心~仪表*
零位标志 zero mark
零位读数 null reading
零位滑移 zero slip
零位滑移区 【压】zone of zero slip
零位刻度 zero mark
零位偏移 zero drift [offset]
零位漂移 zero shift [drift]
零位平衡电位计 null-balance potentiometer
零位平均应力 zero mean stress
零位调节螺钉 zero adjusting screw
零位调整 zero [null] adjustment, zeroing, zero setting
零位调整值 zero setting
零位调整装置 zero adjuster [adjustment], null-setting device
零位误差 zero error
零位线 zero line, roll parting line (轧辊孔型的)
零位斜线 【铁】zero stock line
零位张力 no pull
零下 minus, subzero (温度)
零下处理 subzero (temperature) treatment
零下冷却 subzero cooling [treatment]
零下速热法 subzero rapid heating
零下温度加工[轧制] subzero working
零下温度试验系列 cryogenic run

零下形变 subzero deformation
零相电流互感器 zero-phase current transformer
零相电压互感器 zero-phase voltage [potential] transformer
零相序电流表 zero-phase-sequence ammeter
零相序电流互感器 zero-phase-sequence current transformer
零相序电压互感器 zero-phase-sequence potential transformer
零相序伏特计 【电】zero phase-sequence voltmeter
零星堆积废金属 【冶】shovel(l)ing scrap
零星修补(道路的) dribbing
零序 zero [null] sequence
零序电抗 zero-sequence reactance
零序分量 zero-sequence component
零延迟 zero lag
零因次[量纲] zero dimension
零值延性过渡[转折]温度 nil-ductility (transition) temperature
零指数 zero index
零滞后 zero lag
零字符 【计】null character
龄期强度关系 age strength relation
铃木锁定(位错的) Suzuki locking
铃木万能显微复型印刷法 Suzuki's universal micro-printing method
铃木效应(合金强化的) 【金】Suzuki effect
灵活性 flexibility, maneuverability ◇使用~*
灵敏 sensitive ◇不~区 blind area
灵敏度 sensitivity, sensi(ti)bility, sensitiveness, responsivity, susceptibility, susceptiveness,【计】sensitivity ratio
灵敏度极限 sensitivity limit
灵敏度控制 sensitivity control
灵敏度调定 sensitivity setting, responsiveness
灵敏度小的 sluggish

灵敏度自动调整[控制]	automatic sensitivity control

灵敏汞气计 sensitive mercury vapour meter

灵敏性 sensitivity, maneuverability, responsiveness

灵敏元件 sensor, sensing [sensitive, detecting] element, feeler

灵敏值 factor [figure] of merit

灵巧 handiness

领圈 supporting tyre, rolling ring [track] (回转窑的)

领示电弧 pilot arc

领先指标 leading indicators

领先位错 lead(ing) dislocation, dislocation head [leading]

领先相(结晶的) 【金】leading phase

领域 domain, field, realm, universe (科学领域)

溜槽 chute(work), flume, sluicing ◇ 半圆形分级～*, 分支[旁通]～ bypass chute

溜槽法(提金) 【色】sluicing

溜槽式布料器 chute feeder

溜槽系统 chuting system

溜道 descent, 【采】downward slope

溜口 chutework, boxhole

榴霰弹合金(94Pb, 6Sb) shrapnel alloy

榴霰弹黄铜(67Cu, 33Zn) shrapnel brass

硫{S} sulphur, sulfur ◇ 带入～量(随炉料) sulphur input [olad], 低含量～*, 腐蚀性～ corrosive sulphur, 含～钢*, 脱[去]～*, 硫化物形态～ sulphide sulfur, 氧化物熔体中的～ sulphur in oxide melts

硫钯矿 vysotskite, vysotskyite, vysozkite

硫棒 rod sulphur

硫铋铅矿 lillianite

硫铋银矿 matildite

硫铂矿{PtS} cooperite

硫捕集指数 sulphur capture index

硫醇 thioalcohol, mercaptan (RSH)

硫代氨基甲酸盐 thiocarbamate

硫代磷酸{H_3PO_3S, $H_3PO_2S_2$, $H_8PO_5S_3$, H_3PS_4} thiophosphoric acid

硫代硫酸铵 ammonium thiosulphate

硫代硫酸钠{$Na_2S_2O_3$} sodium thiosulphate [hyposulphite], hypo(五水合物)

硫代硫酸钠沉淀(法) precipitation with sodium thiosulphate

硫代硫酸钠还原槽 hypo bath

硫代硫酸盐{$M_2S_2O_3$} hyposulphite, thiosulphate

硫代氰酸铪络合物 hafnium thiocyanate complex

硫代氰酸盐萃取 thiocyanate extraction

硫代氰酸盐分离 thiocyanate separation

硫代氰酸盐基团 thiocyanate radical

硫代砷酸盐[酯] thioarsenate

硫代酸{$R\cdot SO_3H$} sulpho-acid

硫代碳酸盐[酯] thiocarbonate

硫代锑酸钠{Na_3SbS_4} sodium thioantimonate

硫代锑酸钠溶液 sodium thioantimonate solution

硫代锑酸盐{M_3SbS_4} thioantimonate

硫代锑酸盐溶液 thioantimonate solution

硫的有害作用 negative value of sulphur

硫碲铋矿 joseite {$Bi_3Te(S,Se)$}, gruenlingite {Bi_4TeS_3}

硫碘化锑 antimony sulfide-iodide

硫碘铊 thallium arsenic sulphide

硫放射性同位素 radioactive sulphur isotope

硫分[含量] sulphur content

硫分配系数 【铁】sulphur partition (ratio)

硫腐蚀 sulphur corrosion [attack]

硫复铁矿 melnikovite

硫负荷 【铁】sulphur load

硫杆菌 thiobacilli ◇ 粪化石～*, 拿波利[拿波氏新多翼]～*, 蚀阴沟～*, 特劳特文～*, 新型～ thiobacillus novellus, 中间型～*

硫杆菌层 thiobacillus

硫杆菌族 thiobacilleae

硫镉矿 {CdS}　cadmium blende, greenockite, xanthochroite
硫汞锑矿 {HgS·2Sb$_2$S$_3$}　livingstonite
硫钴矿 {(Co, Ni)$_3$S$_4$}　cobalt pyrite, linnaeite
硫华　flower of sulphur, sublimed sulfur
硫化　sulphuring, sulphidizing, sulphidization
硫化铵　ammonium sulphide
硫化钡 {BaS}　barium sulphide
硫化处理　sulphidizing, sulphurizing（表面的）
硫化钒　vanadic [vanadium] sulfide
硫化钆 {Gd$_2$S$_3$}　gadolinium sulphide
硫化钙 {CaS}　calcium sulphide, sulphurated lime
硫化锆 {ZrS$_2$}　zirconium sulphide
硫化镉　cadmium sulfide
硫化工　vulcanizer
硫化汞　cinnabar, (black, red) mercury sulfide
硫化汞矿　（同"辰砂"）
硫化罐　vulcanizing boiler, vulcanizer ◇ 高压热水[蒸汽]～*
硫化剂　sulphidizing [vulcanized] agent, curing agent（橡胶用）
硫化金　aurosulfo
硫化精炼　sulphidizing refining
硫化钪 {Sc$_2$S$_3$}　scandium sulphide
硫化矿　sulphide [sulphidic] ore ◇ 生～ green sulphide
硫化矿熔炼的控制现象　controlling phenomena in sulfide smelting
硫化镧 {La$_2$S$_3$}　lanthanum sulphide
硫化裂片菌　Sulfolobus
硫化铝 {Al$_2$S$_3$}　aluminium sulphide
硫化锰　manganese sulphide
硫化钼　molybdenum sulphide
硫化钠 {Na$_2$S}　sodium sulphide
硫化镍 {NiS}　nickel sulphide
硫化镍精矿　nickel sulphide concentrate
硫化镍矿　nickel sulphide ore
硫化镍锍[冰铜]　nickel sulphide matte
硫化钕 {Nd$_2$S$_3$}　neodymium sulphide
硫化镨 {Pr$_2$S$_3$}　praseodymium sulphide
硫化期[时间]　cure time
硫化器　sulfurator, vulcanizer
硫化铅 {PbS}　lead sulphide
硫化铅富集　lead sulphide concentration
硫化铅矿　lead sulphide ore
硫化氢 {H$_2$S}　hydrogen sulphide, hydrosulphuric acid, sulphuretted hydrogen ◇ 毒性～*, 抗～钢*
硫化氢发生　hydrogen sulphide generation
硫化氢气(体)　hydrogen sulphide gas
硫化溶解　sulphidic solubility
硫化铷 {Rb$_2$S}　rubidium sulfide
硫化铯 {Cs$_2$S}　cesium sulphide
硫化钐 {Sm$_2$S$_3$}　samaric sulphide
硫化设备　vulcanizer
硫化砷　arsenones
硫化双氧铀[硫化铀酰] {UO$_2$S}　uranyl sulphide
硫化锶 {SrS}　strontium sulphide
硫化铊　thallium sulphide
硫化铊光电池　thalofide photocell
硫化钛　titanium sulphide
硫化锑(矿)　antimony sulphide [sulfuret] (ore)
硫化铁　ferric sulphide {Fe$_2$S$_3$}, iron sulphide {FeS}
硫化铁夹杂(物)　iron sulphide inclusions
硫化铁矿　sulphide iron ore
硫化铜　copper sulphide
硫化铜矿　sulphide copper ore
硫化钨 {WS$_2$, WS$_3$}　tungsten sulphide
硫化物　sulphide (compound), sulfide ◇ 纯～ simple sulphide, 富～的 sulphide-rich, 高价～ higher sulphide, 含金属的～ metal-bearing sulphide, 链型～*, 细条状～*, 形成～ sulphidizing
硫化物半导体　sulphide semiconductor
硫化物焙砂　sulphide calcine
硫化物焙烧机理　sulphide roasting mech-

anism
硫化物沉淀(法)　sulphide precipitation
硫化物浮渣　sulphide dross
硫化物腐蚀　sulphide corrosion
硫化物夹杂　sulphide inclusion
硫化物结块[炉瘤]　sulphide accretion
硫化(物)精矿　sulphide concentrate
硫化物矿物　sulphide mineral
硫化物矿物浸出　sulphide mineral leaching
硫化物离子　sulphide ion
硫化物凝聚法【环】sulphide coagulation method
硫化物清洗　sulphide washing
硫化物蚀裂[腐蚀破裂]　sulphide corrosion cracking
硫化物损失　sulphidic loss
硫化物涂敷法　◇ 德弗克斯～*
硫化物型夹杂物　sulphide-type inclusions
硫化物(形态)硫　sulphide sulfur
硫化物阳极　sulphide anode
硫化物阳极法　sulphide anode process
硫化物阳极泥　sulphide anode sludge
硫化物氧化　sulphide oxidation
硫化物应力蚀裂　sulphide stress cracking
硫化(物)渣　sulphide slag
硫化硒　selensulfur
硫化锡　tin sulphide {SnS, SnS$_2$}, stannic sulphide {SnS$_2$}
硫化系数　coefficient of vulcanization
硫化细菌　thiobacteria
硫化橡胶　vulcanized rubber
硫化锌{ZnS}　zinc sulphide
硫化锌精矿　zinc sulphide mineral concentrate
硫化亚锑{Sb$_2$S$_3$}　antimonious sulphide
硫化亚铁{FeS}　ferrous sulfide
硫化亚锡　stannous sulphide, tin monosulphide
硫化钇{Y$_2$S$_3$}　yttrium sulphide
硫化铟{In$_2$S$_3$}　indium sulphide
硫化银　silver sulphide
硫化渣法　sulphide slagging
硫化锗{GeS}　germanium sulphide
硫化置换　sulphidizing cementation
硫化作用　sulphuration, sulphidization
硫黄糊　sulphur paste
硫黄石　brimstone
硫镓铜矿{CuGaS$_2$}　gallite
硫金银矿　uytenbogaardtite
硫矿[采]　sulphur ore
硫量不合格生铁　off-sulphur iron
硫螺旋菌属　thiospirillum
硫镁矾{MgSO$_4$·H$_2$O}　kieserite
硫锰矿{MnS}　manganese [glance] blende, alabandite
硫锰锌铁矿　youngite
硫脲{NH$_2$CSNH$_2$}　thiourea, thiocarbamide
硫脲法　thiourea process
硫脲浸出　thiourea leaching
硫脲溶液解吸金　auric-thiourea complex
硫(镍)钯铂矿{(Pt,Pd,Ni)S}　braggite
硫镍钯矿　vysotskyite, vysozkite
硫镍铁矿{(Fe,Ni)S}　pentlandite
硫偏析　sulphur segregation
硫漂浮【金】sulphur flotation
硫平衡　sulphur balance
硫侵蚀　sulphur attack, sulphide tarnishing
硫氰铂酸　thiocyanophlatinic acid
硫氰化处理(零件表面的)　sulphocyaniding
硫氰化汞　mercuric sulphocyanide
硫氰化铅　lead thiocyanate
硫氰钠钴石　julienite
硫氰酸{HSCN}　thiocyanic acid
硫氰酸-乙醚溶液　thicyanic acid-ether solution
硫氰酸铵{NH$_4$SCH}　ammonium thiocyanate [thiocyanide]
硫氰酸[化]钾{KCNS}　potassium thiocyanate
硫氰酸[化]钠　sodium thiocyanate

硫氰酸铷 {RbSCN} rubidium thiocyanate
硫氰酸铁 ferric rhodanate
硫氰酸盐 thiocyanate
硫氰酸盐分离 thiocyanate separation
硫氰酸盐回收 thiocyanate recovery
硫氰酸盐络合物 thiocyanat complex
硫氰铁酸 ferrithiocyanic acid
硫溶解度 sulphur solubility
硫乳 milk of sulphur
硫砷铊铅矿 {(Tl, Ag)$_2$Pb(AsS$_2$)$_4$} hutchinsonite
硫砷锑铊矿 urbaite
硫砷锑铜矿 antimon-luzonite
硫砷铜矿 {Cu$_3$AsS$_4$} enargite
硫砷银矿 {Ag$_3$AsS$_3$} proustite
硫蚀 sulfidation corrosion ◇ 抗～*
硫酸 {H$_2$SO$_4$} sulphuric [brimstone] acid, double oil of vitriol (D.O.V.), vitriol, spirit of alum ◇ 发烟～*, 溶于～ vitriolization, 稀～ dilute sulphuric acid, 棕色～*
硫酸铵 {(NH$_4$)$_2$SO$_4$} ammonium sulphate ◇ 半直接～法*, 肥料级～*
硫酸铵肥料 ammonium sulphate fertilizer
硫酸铵浸出 ammonium sulphate leaching
硫酸铵稀土 rare earth ammonium (double) sulfate
硫酸胺 {(R$_3$NH)$_2$SO$_4$} amine sulphate
硫酸钡 {BaSO$_4$} barium sulphate
硫酸焙烧 【色】sulphuric acid roasting [baking]
硫酸吡啶 pyridium sulphate
硫酸铂 platinic [platinum] sulphate
硫酸钚 plutonium sulphate
硫酸厂 sulphuric acid manufacturer [plant]
硫酸处理 sulphuric acid treatment, vitriolization
硫酸处理焙烧 【色】sulphatizing roasting
硫酸镝 {Dy$_2$(SO$_4$)$_3$} dysprosium sulphate
硫酸铥 {Tu$_3$(SO$_4$)$_3$} thulium sulphate
硫酸铒 {Er$_2$(SO$_4$)$_3$} erbium sulphate

硫酸二氨钴 {Co(NH$_3$)$_2$SO$_4$} cobalt diammine sulphate
硫酸分解 sulphuric acid breakdown
硫酸分金法 sulphuric acid parting
硫酸钙 {CaSO$_4$} calcium sulphate, salt lime ◇ 加有～的糠和锯屑混合粉料(用于清理镀锡薄钢板) pink meal
硫酸高钴 {Co$_2$(SO$_4$)$_3$} cobaltic sulphate
硫酸高铈 {Ce(SO$_4$)$_2$} ceric sulphate
硫酸高铈铵 {(NH$_4$)$_6$[Ce(SO$_4$)$_5$]} ammonium ceric sulphate
硫酸锆 {Zr(SO$_4$)$_2$} zirconium sulphate ◇ 结晶～*
硫酸镉 cadmium sulphate
硫酸根离子 sulphate ion
硫酸根阴离子 sulphate anion
硫酸铬 chromium sulphate
硫酸铬钾 potassium chromium sulphate
硫酸汞 mercuric [mercury] sulphate, mercury persulphate
硫酸钴 {CoSO$_4$} cobalt sulphate
硫酸钴溶液 cobalt sulphate solution
硫酸铪 hafnium sulphate
硫酸合硫酸锆 {H$_2$Zr(SO$_4$)$_3$} zirconium complex sulphate
硫酸(盐)化 sulphatizing, sulfatizing, sulphation ◇ 分段～stage sulphation, 优先～ selective sulphating
硫酸化焙烧 sulphation roasting, sulphating [sulphatizing] roast(ing)
硫酸化焙烧法 vitriolization process
硫酸化焙烧炉 sulphating roaster
硫酸化处理 sulphating, acid cure
硫酸化反应 sulphating reaction
硫酸化剂 sulphatizing agent
硫酸化矿石 sulphatized ore
硫酸化炉膛 【色】sulphatizing hearth
硫酸化气氛 sulphating atmosphere
硫酸化物 {R·H$_2$SO$_4$} hydrosulphate
硫酸镓 {Ga$_2$(SO$_4$)$_3$} gallium sulphate
硫酸镓钾 (同"镓钾矾")
硫酸钾 {K$_2$SO$_4$} potassium sulphate

硫酸钾浸出　potassium sulphate leaching
硫酸浸出　sulphuric acid leach(ing)
硫酸浸出法　sulphuric-acid process
硫酸浸出液　sulphuric acid leach solution [liquor]
硫酸钪 $\{Sc_2(SO_4)_3\}$　scandium sulphate
硫酸钪钾 $\{K_3[Sc(SO_4)_3]\}$　potassium scandium sulphate
硫酸钪钠 $\{Na_3[Sc(SO_4)_3]\}$　sodium scandium sulphate
硫酸镧 $\{La_2(SO_4)_3\}$　lanthanum sulphate
硫酸镭 $\{RaSO_4\}$　radium sulfate
硫酸锂 $\{Li_2SO_4\}$　lithium sulphate
硫酸铝 $\{Al_2(SO_4)_3 \cdot 18H_2O\}$　aluminium sulphate
硫酸铝铵　aluminium ammonium sulphate
硫酸铝钾　alum, aluminum potassium sulphate
硫酸铝钠　aluminum sodium sulphate (ASS)
硫酸铝铷铯 $\{CsRb(SO_4) \cdot Al_2(SO_4)_3 \cdot 24H_2O\}$　cesium rubidium aluminium sulphate, cesium rubidium alum
硫酸铝氯化铁　clairtan
硫酸镁 $\{MgSO_4\}$　magnesium sulphate ◇ 含水～矿*
硫酸锰　manganese sulphate
硫酸钼 $\{Mo(SO_4)_3\}$　molybdenum trisulphate
硫酸钠 $\{Na_2SO_4\}$　sodium sulphate ◇ 结晶型～
硫酸钠分解　decomposition with sodium sulphate
硫酸钠矿 $\{Na_2SO_4 \cdot 10H_2O\}$　mirabilite
硫酸钠稀土复盐　rare earth sodium double-sulfate
硫酸镍 $\{NiSO_4 \cdot 7H_2O\}$　nickel sulphate [vitriol] ◇ 粗～crude nickel sulphate
硫酸镍铵　nickel ammonium sulphate
硫酸镍溶液　nickel sulphate solution
硫酸铍 $\{BeSO_4\}$　beryllium sulphate
硫酸镨 $\{Pr_2(SO_4)_3\}$　praseodymium sulphate
硫酸错钕 $\{Di_2(SO_4)_3\}$　didymium sulphate
硫酸铅 $\{PbSO_4\}$　lead sulphate
硫酸铅矿 $\{PbSO_4\}$　lead vitriol, anglesite
硫酸氢胺 $\{(R_3NH)HSO_4\}$　amine bisulphate
硫酸氢钾　potassium hydrosulphate
硫酸氢镧 $\{La(HSO_4)_3\}$　lanthanum hydrosulphate
硫酸氢钠 $\{NaHSO_4\}$　sodium hydrogen sulphate
硫酸氢钕 $\{Nd(HSO_4)_3\}$　neodymium hydrosulphate
硫酸氢镨 $\{Pr(HSO_4)_3\}$　praseodymium hydrosulphate
硫酸氢铷 $\{RbHSO_4\}$　rubidium hydrogen sulfate, rubidium bisulfate
硫酸氢铯 $\{CsHSO_4\}$　cesium bisulphate, cesium hydrogen sulphate
硫酸氢钐 $\{Sm(HSO_4)_3\}$　samaric hydrosulfate
硫酸氢锶 $\{Sr(HPSO_4)_2\}$　strontium bisulphate
硫酸氢盐 $\{MHSO_4\}$　hydrosulphate, disulphate, disulfate
硫酸氢钇 $\{Y(HSO_4)_3\}$　yttrium hydrosulphate
硫酸溶出　sulphuric acid digestion
硫酸溶液　sulphuric acid solution
硫酸铷 $\{Rb_2SO_4\}$　rubidium sulfate
硫酸铯 $\{Cs_2SO_4\}$　cesium sulphate
硫酸铯铝 $\{Cs_2SO_4 \cdot Al_2(SO_4)_3 \cdot 24H_2O$ 或 $CsAl(SO_4)_{22} \cdot 12H_2O\}$　cesium alum, cesium aluminium sulphate
硫酸钐 $\{Sm_2(SO_4)_3\}$　samaric sulphate
硫酸铈 $\{Ce_2(SO_4)_3\}$　cerous sulphate
硫酸铈铵 $\{(NH_4)[Ce(SO_4)_2]\}$　ammonium cerous sulphate
硫酸铈钾 $\{K_4[Ce(SO_4)_4]\}$　potassium ceric sulphate
硫酸双氧　dioxysulphate
硫酸双氧镧 $\{La_2(O_2SO_4)\}$　lanthanum

dioxysulphate
硫酸双氧钼 {(MoO$_2$)SO$_4$} molybdenyl sulphate, molybdenum dioxysulphate
硫酸双氧铀 {UO$_2$SO$_4$} uranyl sulphate
硫酸锶 {SrSO$_4$} strontium sulphate, celestine
硫酸铊 {Tl$_2$(SO$_4$)$_3$} thallic sulphate
硫酸钛 {Ti$_2$(SO$_4$)$_3$} titanium sulphate
硫酸锑 antimony sulphate
硫酸铁 {Fe$_2$(SO$_4$)$_3$} ferric sulphate ◇ 七水(合)~*
硫酸铁铵 ferric ammonium sulphate [alum]
硫酸铁浸出 ferric sulphate leaching
硫酸铁铯 cesium ferric sulphate
硫酸铜 {CuSO$_4$·5H$_2$O} copper [cupric] sulphate, (同"胆矾")
硫酸铜浸蚀试验 copper sulphate (dipping) test ◇ 普里斯(电镀)~Preece test
硫酸铜溶液 copper sulphate solution ◇ 能在~中浸渍一分钟的钢丝 one minute wire
硫酸钍 {Th(SO$_4$)$_2$} thorium sulphate
硫酸脱水 sulphuric acid dehydration
硫酸雾 【环】sulphuric acid mist
硫酸锡在苯酚磺酸异构物水溶液中的电镀锡法 Ferrostan process
硫酸稀土 {(RE)$_2$(SO$_4$)$_3$} rare earth sulfate
硫酸洗涤 sulphuric acid scrubbing
硫酸洗提 sulphuric acid elution (stripping)
硫酸锌 {ZnSO$_4$·7H$_2$O} zinc sulphate [vitriol], white vitriol
硫酸锌矿 {ZnSO$_4$} zinkosite
硫酸锌溶液 zinc sulphate solution
硫酸亚铁 {FeSO$_4$} ferrous sulfate
硫酸亚铁铯 {Cs$_2$SO$_4$·FeSO$_4$·6H$_2$O} cesium ferrous sulphate
硫酸亚铜 {Cu$_2$SO$_4$} cuprous sulphate
硫酸亚锡电解液 stannous sulphate electrolyte

硫酸盐 sulphate, sulfate, vitriol ◇ 含硫酸基最少的~protosulphate, 含氧~oxysulphate, 耐~水泥*
硫酸盐焙烧 sulphate roast
硫酸盐带 sulphate band
硫酸盐电解液 sulphate electrolyte ◇ 充氨~*
硫酸盐淀出物 sulphate-precipitated material
硫酸盐淀出氧化物 sulphate-precipitated oxide
硫酸盐复盐 double sulphate
硫酸盐化 (同"硫酸化")
硫酸盐化温度 sulphation temperature
硫酸盐还原细菌 sulphate reducing bacteria
硫酸盐间接回收 indirect sulphate recovery
硫酸盐离子浓度 sulphate ion concentration
硫酸盐硫的分析 sulphate sulphur analysis
硫酸盐-氯化物电解液 sulphate-chloride electrolyte
硫酸盐络合物 sulphate complex
硫酸盐-硼酸电解液 sulphate-boric acid electrolyte
硫酸盐溶液 sulphate solution [liquor]
硫酸盐烧结 sulphate sintering
硫酸盐洗提 sulphate stripping
硫酸氧钒 vanadic [vanadium] sulphate
硫酸氧铪 {HfOSO$_4$} hafnyl sulphate
硫酸氧锆 {ZrOSO$_4$} zirconyl sulphate
硫酸氧化高铈 {CeOSO$_4$} ceric oxysulphate
硫酸氧化钪 {(Sc$_2$O)(SO$_4$)$_2$} scandium oxysulphate
硫酸氧钛 {(TiO)SO$_4$} titanyl sulphate
硫酸钇 {Y$_2$(SO$_4$)$_3$} yttrium sulphate
硫酸镱 {Yb$_2$(SO$_4$)$_3$} ytterbium sulphate
硫酸铟 {In$_2$(SO$_4$)$_3$} indium sulphate
硫酸铟铵 ammonium disulphatoindate
硫酸铟铯 {Cs$_2$SO$_4$·In$_2$(SO$_4$)$_3$·24H$_2$O} ce-

sium disulphatoindate, cesium indium alum
硫酸银　silver sulphate
硫酸铀 $\{U(SO_4)_2\}$ 　uranous sulphate ◇ α~矿*,β~矿*
硫酸铀络离子　uranium sulfate complex ion
硫酸铀酰　（同"硫酸双氧铀"）
硫酸铀酰阴离子 $\{UO_2(SO_4)^{2-}\}$ 　anion uranyl sulphate, uranyl sulphate anion
硫酸铕 $\{Eu_2(SO_4)_3\}$ 　europium sulphate
硫酸贮存室　sulphuric acid tank room
硫锑铋镍矿　kallilite
硫锑汞精矿　antimony-mercury concentrate
硫锑汞矿　antimony-mercury sulphide ore
硫锑铅矿　boulangerite
硫锑铜矿　antimonial copper glance, luzonite
硫锑铜银矿 $\{9Ag_2S \cdot Sb_2S_3\}$ 　polybasite
硫锑银矿 $\{3Ag_2S \cdot Sb_2S_3, Ag_3SbS_3\}$ 　antimonial silver blende, pyrargyrite
硫铁比　sulphur-iron ratio
硫铁矿 $\{FeS_2\}$ 　pyrite
硫铁(矿烧)渣[硫酸渣]　（同"黄铁矿烧渣"）
硫铁矿渣　pyrite dross
硫铁镍矿　nickel-pyrite, bravoite
硫铁锑矿 $\{FeS \cdot Sb_2S_3\}$ 　berthierite
硫铁铜矿　chalmersite
硫铜　sulphur copper
硫铜铋矿 $\{Cu_2Bi_2S_4\}$ 　emplectite, emplektite
硫铜钴矿 $\{Co_2CuS_4\}$ 　carrollite
硫铜锑矿 $\{CuSbS_2\}$ 　chalcostibite
硫铜银矿　stromeyerite
硫铜锗矿 $\{Cu_3(Fe, Ge, Zn)(As, S)_4\}$ 　renierite
硫钨矿 $\{WS_2\}$ 　tungstenite
硫硒铋铅矿 $\{PbS \cdot Bi_2Se_2\}$ 　platynite
硫硒碲化合物　colcogenide
硫吸收　sulphur absorption

硫锌铅矿　yenerite, huascolite
硫锈蚀　sulphide tarnishing
硫循环　sulphur cycle
硫氧化剂　sulphooxidant, thiooxidant
硫氧化钍 $\{ThOS\}$ 　thorium oxysulphide
硫氧化细菌　sulphur [sulphide] oxidizing bacteria, thiobacillus concretivorus bacteria
硫氧锑矿　（同"红锑矿"）
硫铟铜矿　roquesite
硫银铋矿　peruvite, matildite
硫银锡矿　canfieldite
硫银锗矿 $\{4Ag_2S \cdot GeS_2\}$ 　argyrodite
硫茚 $\{C_8H_6S\}$ 　thionaphthene
硫印　sulphur print ◇ 鲍曼~*
硫印检验(法)　sulphur printing
硫印试验　sulphur print test
硫铀铜矾 $\{CuO \cdot 2UO_3 \cdot 3SO_3 \cdot nH_2O\}$ 　gilpinite
硫杂质　sulphur impurity
硫载体　sulphur carrier
硫锗铜矿 $\{Cu_3(Fe, Ge, Zn)(As, S)_4\}$ 　renierite
硫族化物　chalcogenide
馏板　【化】disk, disc, dish
馏出的　distilled (dist.)
馏出率　distillate rate (DR)
馏出物　distillation product, distillate, distils, overhead product（塔顶的）◇ 炉(内)~furnace distillate
馏分　distillate, (distillation) fraction, cut, distils, runnings ◇ 高沸点[残余]~last cut, 宽沸点[温度范围宽的]~ wide-boiling cut, 狭~【化】clean cut, 窄[精密分割]~*
馏分分析　【焦】densimetric analysis
馏分组成　fractional composition
留碳腐蚀(对灰口铸铁的)　【金】graphitic corrosion
留碳作用　graphitizing
刘易斯锡铋合金　Lewis's alloy
流　flow, current, stream, strand（连铸的）

流变　fluid deformation, flow ◇ 恒速~ constant rate of flow, 减速~ decelerating flow
流变强度　【压】flow strength
流变区　field of flow
流变曲线　flow curve
流变速率　rate of flow
流变特性　rheological property
流变图形　flow figure
流变性[行为]　rheology, rheological behaviour
流变学　rheology ◇ 材料~ material rheology
流变应力　flow [yield] stress ◇ 低堆位层错能在金属中的~*, 反向~*, 高堆位层错能的~*, 预形变材料~*
流变应力比　flow stress ratio
流变应力的不可逆变化　irreversible change of flow stress
流变铸造　rheocasting
流变指数　flow index
流槽　launder, runner, running channel, sluice, spout, alcove（玻璃熔窑的）◇ 放铳~ matte tapping launder, 分支状~ 【钢】branched runner, 开式~ open launder, 伸缩式~ extensible chute, 振动式~ oscillating launder, 转向~ deflecting chute
流槽材料　runner material
流槽尺寸　runner size
流槽废钢　【钢】sprue-and-runner scrap
流槽口　【钢】runner [sprue] opening
流槽式干扰沉降水力分级机　launder-type hindered settling hydraulic classifier
流槽试样　【冶】runner sample
流槽水套　launder jacket
流槽洗选　trough cleaning
流槽系统（出铁场的）　runner system
流槽修理　runner makeup
流层冷却　lamina flow cooling
流畅的　fluent
流程　flowsheet, route, circuit ◇ 建议采用的~ proposed flowsheet
流程设计　flowsheet design
流程图　flow chart [scheme, pattern, plan], flow [process] diagram, scheme ◇ 示意~ schematic flow diagram, 自动画~程序 autochart
流程图符号　flow chart symbol
流程图规则　flow chart convention
流程物料分析　on-stream analysis
流出　outflow, effusion, run-off, runout, flow out, outgo, effluence, ef-fluent, efflux（ion）
流出管　outlet pipe
流出空气　effluent air
流出口　outflow (opening), outlet (nozzle)
流出量　discharge, outflow
流出馏分　effluent fraction
流出曲线　【化】breakthrough curve
流出速度　outlet velocity
流出速率　outflow rate
流出物　effluxion
流出液　effluent liquid
流出嘴　【铸】outlet nozzle
流道　runner, passageway, sprue,【钢】gate runner,【铸】gate
流道结块　runners
流道砂　【铸】runner sand
流滴盛钢桶脱气法　ladle to ladle degassing
流滴脱[除]气法　【钢】stream drop degassing
流滴铸模脱气法　ladle-to-mould degassing
流动　flow (age), flowing, fluxion ◇ 泊肃叶~ Poiseuille flow, 靠重力~ flow by gravity, 可~的 flexible, 努森~【理】Knudsen flow, 易~渣*
流动区[域]　field of flow
流动成穴[空化](现象)　flow cavitation
流动电解液电镀　flow plating
流动度　(degree of) fluidity
流动负债　floating liability
流动极限　flow limit

流动给料装置　flow feeder
流动介质　yielding medium
流动平衡　mobile equilibrium
流动气氛　mobile atmosphere
流动曲线　flow curve
流动水　flow [running] water
流动水分　mobile moisture
流动速度　(同"流速")
流动特性　flow characteristic
流动条件　flow condition
流动温度范围　flow temperature range
流动现象　phenomenon of flow, yield(ing) phenomenon
流动箱(腐蚀介质的)　flow box
流动性　flowability, (degree of) fluidity, fluidness, liquidity, mobility, flow property [characteristic, quality], runnability, running quality, running power (液态的) ◇ 霍尔～测试仪 Hall tester
流动性不好的粉末　non-flowing powder
流动性不良　poor flow quality
流动性测定　flow factor determination
流动性好的铁水　free running iron
流动性极限　liquidity limit
流动性控制　flow control
流动性良好的粉末　free flowing powder
流动性螺旋(试验)　fluidity spiral
流动性螺旋样模　fluidity [saeger] spiral ◇ 塞格尔～saeger spiral
流动性试验　flow [fluidity] test
流动性试验用铸件　fluidity test casting
流动性试样浇铸　fluidity test casting
流动性试样[试验用]铸型　fluidity mould ◇ 螺旋形～cury fluidity mould
流动性碳当量　carbon equivalent value based on fluidity (C.E.F.)
流动性系数　flow factor
流动性质　nature of flow
流动修理车　mobile repair truck
流动压力　flow pressure
流动应力　flow stress
流动增亮法(电镀锡的)　flow brightening process
流动渣　fluid [running] slag
流动质量　flow mass
流动状态　flow behaviour
流动资本　fluid capital
流动资产　【企】current [floating] assets
流动资金　working capital [funds], circulating funds ◇ 定额～˚
流动资金平衡净额　net liquidity balance
流动资金预测　cash flow forecasting
流动阻力　flow resistance
流度　fluidness, fluidity
流度计　fluid gauge, fluidimeter, fluidity meter
流钢槽　【钢】runner
流钢槽[通道]耐火材料　【钢】runner refractory
流钢道　【耐】canal
流钢尾砖　【耐】end runner
流钢砖　【耐】bottom plate brick, runner [lateral] brick, runner ◇ 出口～lateral outlet brick, 末端～end pot, 中心～˚
流焊　fluid welding

流化　fluidization, fluidizing, fluidifying
流化床　(同"流态化床")
流化剂　fluidizing (re) agent, fluidizer
流化柱培烧炉(无分布板)　fluid column roaster
流化(状)态　fluidizing state
流化作用　fluidization
流量　flow rate, (rate of) flow, flow [discharge] capacity, delivery ◇ 按比例控制～ratio flow control
流量比　flow ratio
流量波动性　flow instability
流量测量[测定]　flow measurement ◇ 多尔～管 Dall tube
流量超载值　overload flow
流量传感器　flow (rate) sensor
流量传送器　flow transmitter
流量计[表]　flowmeter, fluid meter, flow

gauge [indicator, instrument], flow rate meter, rate-of-flow meter, flowrator, hydrodynamometer ◇ 冲击板式~ impact-plate flowmeter, 浮子式~ float meter, 感应电桥式~*, 霍尔~*, 激光~ laser flowmeter, 孔板~*, 螺旋桨式~ propeller-flowmeter, 毛细管~ capillary flowmeter, 膜式~*, 容量式~*, 锐孔~*, 文丘里~ Venturi(meter), 液体~ liquid flowmeter

流量计管 flow tube
流量记录器 flow recorder (FR)
流量继电器 flow relay
流量监控器 flow monitor
流量孔板 orifice [aperture] plate
流量控制 flow (rate) control
流量控制阀 flow control valve (FCV)
流量控制孔板 flow control orifice
流量控制器隔膜片 diaphragm for flow controller
流量调节 flow control [regulation]
流量调节器[控制装置] flow control unit, flow controller [regulator, governor] ◇ CO_2 ~ gassing gauge
流量图 flow diagram
流量系数 discharge coefficient
流量-小时计 flow-hour meter
流量仪 flow meter ◇ 截面~ area flow type meter
流量增益 flow gain
流量指示控制器 flow indicated controller (FIC)
流量指示器 flow indicator ◇ 带手动控制器的~ flow indicator with hand controller
流明当量 lumen equivalent
流明计 lumen meter
流明灵敏度 lumen sensitivity
流容 fluid capacitance
流入空气 leaked-in air
流入(量) inflow, influx
流入水 influent water
流入液体 influent
流散(的) flowing
流砂 drift(ing) [quick] sand
流束 streamer
流数 number of strands
流水稀释 effluent dilution
流水中淬火 hardening in running water
流水作业 continuous flow [process], streamlined [in-line] production
流水作业线 flow line
流水作业线上测定(连续测定) on-stream measurement
流水作业线退火工艺过程(连续镀锌用) annealing-in-line process
流水作业原理 【企】flowline principle
流速 flow velocity [rate], current [velocity, speed, rate] ◇ 颜色测~法 colour-velocity method
流速测定 hydrometry
流速计 flow (rate) meter, hydrodynamometer, hydrometer, rhysimeter, rheometer
流速控制 flow rate control
流速控制脉冲 flow rate impulse
流速水头 draught [kinetic] head
流速指示器 rate-of-flow indicator
流塑旋压 flow spinning
流态化 fluidization, fluidizing, fluosolids ◇ 反~ defluidization, 广义~* 聚式~*, 可~粒度*, 散粒~*
流态化焙砂 fluid(ized) calcine
流态化层 fluidized layer
流(态)化床 fluid(ized) bed (FB), fluid(ized) [fluo, air-fluid(ized), boiling] bed ◇ 超临界~*, 串联~ fluid bed in series, 沟流~*, 间歇~ batch fluidized bed, 搅动~反应器, 节涌[冲气]~ slugging fluidized bed, 浓[稠]相~*, 起泡~ bubbling fluidized bed, 松散~*, 温克勒~*, 循环~ circulating fluid bed
流态化(床)焙烧 fluid bed roasting, roasting in fluidized, fluosolid roasting

流态化(床)焙烧车间　fluidized bed plant
流态化(床)焙烧法　fluidization roasting process, fluidized bed roasting (process)
流态化(床)焙烧反应　fluid bed roasting reaction
流态化(床)焙烧炉　fluid bed furnace [reactor], fluidization [fluidizing, fluosolid] reactor, fluidized bed reactor, fluosolid roaster [furnace] ◇ 多尔型～*
流态化(床)焙烧系统　fluidized system
流态化床处理　fluid bed processing
流态化床床底　fluidizing bottom
流态化床淬火　【金】fluidized bed quenching
流态化床淀积层　fluidized bed deposition
流态化床煅烧　fluidized bed calcination
流态化床反应器　fluid(ized) bed reactor, fluosolid reactor ◇ 单级[层]～*
流态化床分布板　fluidized bed support plate
流态化床分级　fluidized bed classification
流态化床分离[分选]　【选】fluid bed separation
流态化床氟化　fluidized fluorination
流态化床氟化装置　fluid bed fluorinator system
流(态)化床干燥　fluidized bed drying
流态化床干燥器　fluidized bed dryer
流态化床高度　fluid bed depth
流态化床(工作)速度　fluidized bed velocity
流态化床烘干炉　fluosolids sizer dryer kiln
流态化床还原　【冶】fluidized bed reduction ◇ 连续～*
流态化床还原焙烧炉　fluid bed reduction reactor
流态化床还原(反应)器　fluidized bed reduction reactor
流态化床还原化合物　fluid bed reduction compound
流态化床技术　fluidized bed technique

流态化床加热脱硝　fluid bed thermal denitration
流态化床焦化[流态化炼焦]　fluid coking
流(态)化床冷却　fluid bed cooling
流态化床冷却器　fluidized (bed) cooler
流(态)化床离析　fluidized-bed segregation
流态化床离子交换设备　fluid bed ion exchange plant
流态化床连续焦化设备　continuous fluid coker
流态化床流量计　fluid bed flowmeter
流态化(床)炉　fluidized bed furnace
流态化床氯化(焙烧)　fluid(izing) chlorination, fluid bed chlorination
流态化床黏度　fluid bed viscosity
流态化床热处理　fluidized bed heat treatment
流(态)化床热传递　fluid bed heat transfer
流态化床熔炼　fluid bed smelting, jet smelting
流态化床设备　fluidized bed plant [apparatus], fluid unit
流态化床试验反应器　fluid bed test reactor
流态化床四氟化铀半工业试验设备　fluidized bed green salt pilot plant
流态化床酸浸出　fluidized bed acid leaching
流态化(床)碳化　fluidized carbonization
流态化床涂覆法　fluidized bed coating
流态化床脱硝炉　fluidized bed denitrator
流(态)化床型预还原炉　fluidized bed type prereducing furnace
流(态)化床盐酸再生法　fluid bed hydrochloric acid regeneration process
流态化床铀矿精炼法　fluid bed uranium ore refining process
流态化床蒸馏　fluidized distillation
流态化床直接炼铁法(用氢还原)　bubble hearth process
流态化床直接炼铁炉　bubble hearth furnace

流(态)化床装置 fluidized unit
流态化催化裂化装置 fluidized catalytic cracker
流态化导电粒子加热炉 fluided particle furnace
流态化点 fluidization [fluidizing] point
流态化电解 fluid bed electrolysis
流态化煅烧炉 fluidized calciner ◇ 多层～*
流态化法 fluidization method
流态化法方案 fluidized bed concept
流态化反应器 fluidization [fluidizing] reactor
流态化焚化炉 fluidized incinerator
流态化干燥 fluidized drying
流态化固定(床)层 fluidized fixed bed
流态化固体 fluidized [fluidizing] solid
流态化还原(矿石的) 【冶】fluidized reduction ◇ 铁矿石～*
流态化技术 fluidization [fluidized] technique ◇ 固体～*
流态化介质 fluidizing agent
流态化浸出 fluidization leaching
流态化颗粒 fluidized particle
流态化空气 fluidizing air
流态化空气预热器 fluid air preheater
流态化空隙度 fluidized voidage ◇ 临界～*
流态化冷却 fluidized cooling
流态化冷却器 fluidization [fluidizing] cooler
流态化炼铁 【铁】fluidized bed production of iron, fluidized bed iron making
流态化能力 fluidizability, fluidizing capacity
流(态)化起点 point of incipient fluidization, point of onset of fluidization
流态化气体 fluidizing gas
流态化气体分布 fluidizing gas distribution
流态化情况 fluidizing details
流态化闪速煅烧炉 fluid flash calciner

流态化设备 fluidizing equipment [apparatus]
流态化速度 fluidization [fluidizing] velocity ◇ 临界～*
流态化填充(床)层 fluidized packed bed
流态化停滞 defluidization
流态化温度范围 fluid temperature range
流态化物料 fluidized material
流态化系统 fluidized system
流态化线速度 space rate
流态化效率 fluidization efficiency
流态化性能 fluidizability
流态化置换槽 fluidizing cementation tank
流态化质量 fluidization quality
流(态)化柱焙烧炉(无分布板) fluid column roaster
流态化装置 fluidization device, fluidized unit
流(态)化(状)态 fluidized state
流态化自硬砂型(制作)法 【铸】FS process, fluid self setting process
流(态)化作用 fluidization
流态混凝土 【建】guss concrete
流态砂型铸件 fluid mould casting
流态因数(流态化床技术) state of flow factor
流态自硬法 【铸】fluid self setting process
流态自硬砂 【铸】liquid self-hardening sand
流态自硬砂制模法 fluid sand process
流体 fluid (body), influent, fluor ◇ 动力[液压]～ power fluid, 牛顿～ New-tonian fluid
流体比 【铁】fluid ratio
流体成形模 【压】fluid die
流体动力膜 hydrodynamic film
流体(动力)润滑(拉拔的) hydrodynamic lubrication
流体动力学 fluid dynamics, hydrodynamics, hydrokinetics
流体动力学流动 hydrodynamical flow
流体动压力[压强] hydrodynamic pres-

流体粉碎法 【粉】coldstream process
流体工作介质 working fluid
流体化涂槽(线材涂塑料用) fluidizing tank
流体剪磨机 fluid shear mill
流体介质[流质] fluid (medium)
流体静分压 hydrostatic component
流体静力平衡 hydrostatic balance [equilibrium]
流体静力学 hydrostatics
流体静力(学)试验 hydrostatic test
流体静压成型 【粉】hydrostatic compacting
流体静压力[压强] hydrostatic pressure ◇ 外来[杂质]原子与位错间的~相互作用*
流体静压缩 hydrostatic compression
流体静压头 hydrostatic pressure head
流体开关 flow switch
流体离子交换 fluid ionic exchange (FIX)
流体力学 fluid mechanics, hydromechanics
流体逻辑部件 fluid logic component
流体密度 fluid density
流体摩擦 fluid friction
流体黏度 fluid viscosity
流体抛光(法)(加工表面的) hydrofinish
流体喷射技术 water jet technique
流体燃料 fluid fuel
流体渗透性 fluid permeability
流体雾化(法) pneumatic atomisation
流体性状[特性] flow behaviour
流体学 fluidics
流体循环 fluid cycle
流体压力 fluid pressure, pressure of fluidity
流体压制法 fluid compression process
流体质量速度 fluid mass velocity
流铁沟 casting runner, 【铁】iron runner
流铁沟系统 【铁】iron runner system
流铁主沟 【铁】main runner
流通(量) circulation
流通式反应器 flow reactor
流线 flow [strain, stream] line, 【金】river
流线过程 streamline process
流线流 streamline flow
流线网 flow line network
流线型 stream line
流线型过滤器 stream filter
流线型拉模 radiused die
流向 flow direction
流星 meteor
流行的 current, popular
流域 watershed, basin, valley
流域迟滞 basin lag
流渣槽 slag spout [launder, trough], cinder spout
流渣沟 slag trough [spout, runner], 【铁】runner
流渣检验法 running slag test
流嘴 flow spoot, spout, nose, drawn-out lip (铁水罐的), 【色】pouring nozzle ◇ 带~的钢包[铁水罐] labiate, 移动式~*
锍 (Cu2S 和 FeS 等的互溶体,也称"冰铜")【色】matte, regulus, sulfonium ◇ 白~ white matte, 初次~ first matte, 粗~ raw [crude] matte, 低品位~ low-grade matte, 底[开炉]~ starting matte, 放~口 matte taphole, 废~ matte scrap, 富集~ concentrated matte, 高品位~ high grade matte, 固体~ solid matte, 含铅~*, 红~ red matte, 混合~ mixed matte, 炼~*, 凝固~ solidified matte, 熔融~ molten matte, 生~ green matte, 苏打~ soda matte, 提~率 matte-fall, 原生~ primary matte, 再生~ secondary matte, 造~*
锍保温炉 【色】matte holding vessel
锍层 matte layer
锍吹炼 bessemerizing of matte
锍的形成 formation of matte
锍分离 separation of matte
锍富集率 matte-fall
锍品位 matte grade

锍溶解损失	dissolved matte loss
锍生成	matting
锍桶	matte ladle
锍悬浮损失	suspended matte loss
锍阳极	matte anode
锍冶炼[熔炼]	matte smelting
锍中金属粒子	matte separation metallics
六氨硫酸铜	copper hexammine sulphate
六氨络高钴盐	hexamminecobalt (Ⅲ) salt
六氨络硫酸钴	cobaltic hexammine sulphate
六氨络物	hexammine
六胺钙	calcium hexamine
六边桶混合机	hexagonal barrel mixer
六边形板	hexagonal plate
六边形对称	hexagonal symmetry
六重[次]轴	six-fold axis, hexad
六次对称轴	hexad axis, axis of hexagonal symmetry
六次螺旋轴	screw hexad
六次区域熔融	sixzone-pass
六次转动轴	rotation hexad
六点电子记录器	six-point electronic recorder
六点温度记录器	six-point temperature recorder
六方钯矿	allopalladium
六方氮化硼	hexagonal boron nitride (HBN)
六方点阵[晶格]	hexagonal lattice ◇ 密排~*
六方晶格变型	hexagonal modification
六方(晶)钴	hexagonal cobalt
六方晶体	hexagonal crystal
六方晶体特征位错	characteristic dislocations in hexagonal crystals
六方晶系	hexagonal (hex.), hexagonal (crystal) system
六方晶系结构	hexagonal structure
六方(晶)金属	hexagonal metal
六方(晶)金属扭折	hexagonal metal kinking
六方晶系指数	hexagonal indices
六方孔螺钉头用扳手	allen wrench
六方棱镜[柱]	hexagonal prism
六方硫镍矿	heazelwoodite
六方砷镍矿	orcelite
六方砷铜矿	koutekite
六方锑银矿	allorgentum
六方硒镉矿	cadmoselite
六方硒钴矿	freboldite
六方硒镍矿	sederholmite
六方硒铜矿	klockmannite
六方相 【金】	hexagonal phase
六方形片状体	hexagonal plate
六氟锆酸铵{(NH4)$_2$ZrF$_6$}	diammonium zirconium hexafluoride
六氟锆酸钾	(同"氟锆酸钾")
六氟硅酸铅	(同"氟硅酸铅")
六氟化碲	tellurium hexafluoride
六氟化铼{ReF$_6$}	rhenium hexafluoride
六氟化钼{MoF$_6$}	molybdenum hexafluoride
六氟化钨{WF$_6$}	tungsten hexafluoride
六氟化物	hexafluoride
六氟化铀{UF$_6$}	uranium hexafluoride, uranic fluoride ◇ 四氟化铀氧化制~法 Fluorox process
六氟铪酸铵{(NH$_4$)$_2$HfF$_6$}	diammonium hafnium hexafluoride
六氟铪(酸)钾{K$_2$HfF$_6$}	potassium hafnium hexafluoride, potassium hexafluohafnate
六氟铪酸盐	hexafluo(ro)hafnate
六氟络硅氢酸	(同"氟硅酸")
六杆式(盘条)收集机	six pronged capstan
六辊拉坯矫直机(连铸机的)	six-roll set
六辊轧机(用于冷轧带材)	six-roller mill, (six-high) cluster mill ◇ 1-2式~*
六极电(弧熔炼)炉	six-electrode furnace
六极管	hexode ◇ 可变 μ 值[放大因数] ~variable-mu hexode
六极混频管	mixing hexode
六极盐浴炉	six-electrode salt-bath fur-

六极一线排列[一线六极]电弧熔炼炉　six-electrode-in-line furnace
六级浮动床洗涤塔　six-stage floating bed scrubber
六级洗涤系统　six-stage washing system
六甲撑[六亚甲基]四胺{(CH$_2$)$_6$N$_4$}　hexamethylene tetramine (H.M.T.), hexamine
六价　sexivalence, sexivalency, hexavalence, hexavalency
六价钢系元素　hexavalent actinide
六价的　hexavalent, hexabasic, hexad, sexavalent, sexivalent
六价钼的　molybdic
六价钼盐　molybdic salt
六价铬酸盐　hexavalent chromation
六价钨的　tungstic
六价物　hexad
六价铀的　uranic
六角扳手　allen wrench, die nut
六角棒材　hexagonal [hexahedral] bar, bar of hexagonal section
六角钢　hexagonal bar [section, steel], hexahedral bar, hexagon iron, hexagous, bar steel
六角钢立轧法　point-down method
六角钢平轧法　flat down (method)
六角钢丝　hexagonal wire
六角晶体孪生　twinning in hexagonal crystal
六角螺钉　hexagonal screw
六角螺母　hex(agonal) nut
六角螺栓　hexagonal (head) bolt
六角桶混合机　hexagonal barrel mixer
六角头　hex(agon) head
六角型材[断面]　hexagonal section
六角形对称　hexagonal symmetry
六角形晶胞　hexagonal cell
六角形平椭圆　hexagon oval
六角形钻杆　hexagon kelly
六角轴　hexagonal axis

六进制的　【数】senary
六孔模　spaghetti die
六O含铁黄铜　◇艾希~*
六O黄铜(35—45Zn,余量Cu)　4:6 brass ◇含锡~*,西尔夫~焊料*
六流底盘[六孔底板]　【钢】sixway plate
六流连铸机　six-strand continuous casting machine
六流中间包[罐]　【连铸】sixway tundish
六氯锆吡啶　pyridinium zirconium hexachloride
六氯锆酸盐{M$_2$ZrCl$_6$}　hexachlorozirconate
六氯铪酸盐{M$_2$HfCl$_6$}　hexachlorohafnate
六氯化钨{WCl$_6$}　tungsten hexachloride
六氯化物　hexachloride
六氯铊酸钾{K$_3$[TlCl$_6$]}　potassium hexachlorothallate
六氯铊酸钠　sodium hexachlorothallate
六氯铊酸盐　hexachlorothallate
六氯铟酸钾{K$_3$[InCl$_6$]}　potassium hexachlorindate
六氯铟酸盐　hexachloroindate
六面体　hexahedron, rhombohedron, cuboid
六面(体)的　hexahedral
六面体形　hexagous
六氰络铁氢酸{H$_3$[Fe(CN)$_6$]}　ferricyanic acid
六水合物　hexahydrate
六水合硝酸铀酰{UO$_2$(NO$_3$)$_2$·6H$_2$O}　uranyl nitrate hexahydrate (UNH)
六水偏钙铀云母{Ca(UO$_2$)$_2$P$_2$O$_8$·6H$_2$O}　meta-autunite Ⅰ
六羰基钼{Mo(CO)$_6$}　molybdenum hexacarbonyl
六羰基钨　tungsten (hexa)carbonyl
镏金　gild, gold-plating
龙沟　【铁】sow channel
龙门刨(床)　planer ◇齿轮~【机】gear planer
龙门吊(车)[起重机]　frame crane, portal

龙门 jib crane, transfer gantry ◇ 移动式～*
龙门剪 frame [gate, guillotine, square] shears
龙门式气割机 gantry cutting machine
龙门式取料机 portal reclaimer
龙门式万能装卸机 straddle truck
龙门式自动气割机 flame planer
龙内矿 longnanite
龙头 tap, cock, faucet ◇ 灭火～fire hydrant, 吸水～suction cock
笼式区域熔化 cage zone melting
笼式区域精炼[提纯] cage zone-refining
笼统的 general
笼形阴极 basket cathode
笼形阴极电解槽 basket cathode cell
隆起 camber, crown, swell(ing), blow ups (由冻胀引起的), ballooning (机座之间的管子), 【钢】protuberance (钢锭缺陷)
隆起线 ridging, roping
楼梯 stairs, staircase ◇ 螺旋形～geometric stairs, 盘旋～cockle stairs, 悬臂式～bracketed stairs
楼梯间 staircase
楼梯井 stair-well, well hole
楼梯平台 【建】landing
漏 leak(age) ◇ 防[不]～的 leak-proof, leak-free
漏出 leaking, leakage, spilling, spillage, outbreak, oozing
漏出率 inleakage rate
漏出溶液 spillage solution
漏磁场 magnetic leakage field
漏磁检查[探伤] flux leakage test
漏磁通(量) (magnetic) leakage flux
漏磁通量探伤(法) magnetic leakage flux test
漏电 electrical [current] leakage, weep(ing)
漏电导 leakage conductance
漏电抗变压器 leakage reactance transformer
漏电流 leakage [drain] current

漏斗 funnel, hopper ◇ 本生[锥形]～Bunsen funnel, 布氏～Buechner funnel, 回转式～swivelling tundish, 加料～charging hopper, 喷嘴～funnel with nozzle, 批料～*, 热过滤用～double-wall funnel, 形成～funnel(l)ing
漏斗车 wagon with hopper bottom, hopper car [wagon]
漏斗出口[下料口] funnel [hopper] outlet
漏斗管 funnel pipe
漏斗架 funnel stand [support]
漏斗孔 hopper opening
漏斗口 pipe socket, chute opening
漏斗式交叉 flared crossing, trumpet intersection
漏斗脱水器 hopper dewaterer
漏斗形底车 larry car
漏斗型结晶器【连铸】funnel-form [funnel-shaped, hopper-type] mould
漏斗砖 【钢】funnel brick, 【耐】(feed) trumpet
漏斗状[形]的 funnel shaped, crateriform
漏斗状[形]晶体 hopper crystal
漏风 air (in) leakage, infiltration, blast breakout, leaked-in [infiltrating] air
漏钢 bleed out, runout, break(ing) out ◇ 钢锭底部～(下注时) bottom bleeder, 黏结～*, 塞棒损坏～running stopper
漏钢钢锭 【钢】bleeding ingot
漏过点(离子交换的) breakthrough point
漏极电流 drain current
漏检(涡流探伤的) 【压】flaw-missing
漏检错误率 【计】undetected [residual] error rate
漏口 【采】engorgement, chute
漏流 leakage flow [current]
漏模板(造型机的) stripping pattern plate
漏模造型机 stripping plate moulding machine, drop plate machine ◇ 震实式～*
漏气 blow by, blowing, air leak(age), false air, gas leakage [escape], off-gas, weep

(ing) ◇ 不~的*,已~的 gassy
漏气风口　leaking tuyere
漏气试验(钢管的)　air test
漏气探测器　gas leakage detecting device
漏热　heat leak(age)
漏入空气　leaked-in air
漏勺　perforated skimmer [ladle]
漏失　leakage,loss
漏失电流　leakage current
漏失[气,损]率　leak(age) rate
漏失水　leakage water
漏失系数　leakage coefficient
漏水　water leakage,escape of water,weep(ing)
漏水探测器　leaked water detector
漏损　leak(age),leaking,ullage ◇ 无~的 leak-tight
漏损点　leak-off point
漏损路线[漏泄路径](气密性试验)　leakage path
漏损位置　leak-off point
漏箱　【铸】runout,metal break out
漏泄　inleakage, untightness, leak-off, dump,weep(ing) ◇ 缝隙[间隙]~clearance leakage
漏泄点　leak-off point
漏泄电流　leakage [stray] current
漏泄电路　leak circuit
漏泄电阻　leak(age) resistance
漏泄焊缝　sagged weld
漏泄检验　leak testing,leakage detection
漏泄速率　inleakage rate
漏泄损失　leakage loss
漏烟　smoke leakage ◇ 无~的 smoke-proof,smoketight
漏油容器　leak oil container
漏渣　slag breakout,cinder outbreak
卢伯特电热炼铁法　Lubatti process
卢布拉尔铝基轴承合金(G—AE 6CN:5.5—7Sn,1.3—1.7Cu,0.7—1.3Ni,<0.5Si,<0.4Fe,<0.1Mg,<0.15Te,余量 Al) Lubral

卢德维克钢锥硬度计　Ludwick hardness tester
卢尔曼式出渣口　【铁】Luermann's slag notch
卢卡洛克斯刚玉　Lucalox
卢肯斯耐热耐蚀钢　Lukens steel
卢门青铜合金(70—85Cu,5—10Sn,5—25Pb;65Cu,35Pb)　Lumen alloy
卢门锌基轴承青铜(85—88Zn,4—10Cu,2—8Al)　Lumen bronze
卢诺里乌姆牙科耐蚀铸造合金(20Mo,15Cr,5Fe,4W,1Co,余量 Ni)　Lunorium
卢赛特(合成)丙烯树脂　Lucite
卢瑟福散射　Rutherford scattering
卢斯－罗赞蒸汽搅拌铅除银法　【色】Luce-Rozan process
卢泰特 C 羧酸阳离子交换树脂　Lewatit C
卢泰特 DN 磺酚阳离子交换树脂　Lewatit DN
卢泰特 KSN 磺化聚苯乙烯阳离子交换树脂　Lewatit KSN
卢泰特 KS 磺酚阳离子交换树脂　Lewatit KS
卢泰特 M1 弱碱性阴离子交换树脂　Lewatit M1
卢泰特 M2 强碱性阴离子交换树脂　Lewatit M2
卢泰特 PN 磺酚阳离子交换树脂　Lewatit PN
卢威斯塔离心萃取器　【色】Luwesta extractor
卢谢诺镍基电阻合金(30Cu,5Mn,余量 Ni)　Lucerno
炉　furnace, stove, oven, kiln ◇ 艾伯蒂~*,罗赛海因~*,塞西旋转式~*,西门子－马丁~*,
炉算　(fire) grate,grating ◇ 格砖~*,倾动式~tipping grate,透气~permeable grate,无极链式~endless chain grate,小烟道~砖*,移动~moving grate

炉箅边缘 grate edge
炉箅表面 grate surface
炉箅更换 grate change
炉箅更换器 grate changer
炉箅面积 grate area (GA, ga), grate bar area, grating area ◇ 有效~ active [open] grate area
炉箅条 (fire) grate bar, grid bar
炉箅条间隙 grate opening
炉箅下鼓风 under grate blast
炉箅下温度 undergrate temperature
炉箅小车 fire grate car
炉箅摇动炉 shaker-grate furnace
炉箅铸件 grate casting
炉箅子筛格 pigeonhole checker
炉壁 (同"炉墙")
炉壁黑度 furnace wall blackness
炉壁结块 【冶】wall built-up
炉壁里衬 inwall lining
炉壁炉结[炉瘤,结瘤] 【冶】wall scaffold, 【铁】wall accretion
炉壁内衬 wall lining
炉壁砌筑 wall up
炉壁热损失参数 wall loss parameter
炉壁温度探测器 wall-temperature probe
炉壁斜面 inwall slope
炉产量 furnace yield [output]
炉尘 furnace [flue] dust ◇ 单位生铁~量 dust rate
炉尘捕集 flue dust separation
炉尘产出量 flue dust production
炉尘吹出量 flue dust blowout [volume], dust carry-over
炉尘损失 flue dust loss
炉衬 (furnace) lining, liner ◇ 底部~*, 惰性材料~【冶】brasque, 防结渣壳~ skull resistant lining, 高炉旧~拆除设备, 碱性~ basic lining, 浸焦油沥青~ tar-impregnated lining, 旧~清除装置*, 耐磨~*, 喷补~*, 全纤维~ entire fibre lining, 酸性~ acid lining, 新~ fresh lining, 修补~*, 永久性~ permanent lining, 原有~ parent lining, 整体~ monolithic (lining), 砖砌~ brick worklining
炉衬材料 liner material
炉衬重砌期间 【冶】furnace reline period
炉衬费用 lining costs
炉衬腐蚀 blowing out of lines
炉衬厚度 liner thickness
炉衬毁坏 destruction of lining
炉衬基础层(转炉的) backup lining
炉衬磨蚀(转炉的) wear on lining
炉衬磨损特征 lining wear pattern
炉衬黏合剂[材料] jointing furnace material
炉衬膨胀 【冶】bloating
炉衬破裂 breaking out
炉衬侵蚀 lining attack [erosion], 【冶】scouring
炉衬侵蚀速率 【冶】rate of attack
炉衬熔蚀[烧损] lining burn-back
炉衬烧穿 breakthrough
炉衬寿命 【冶】lining life [resistance], vessel(-lining) life (转炉), life span of furnace lining
炉衬维护 refractory maintenance
炉衬性能 lining performance
炉衬修补 patch(ing)
炉衬修补面[部位] patched spot
炉衬修砌部位 relining position
炉衬选择侵蚀 selective lining attack
炉衬砖 lining firebrick, furnace brick ◇ 大块~制造*
炉床 hearth, furnace hearth [bottom], bed of furnace [hearth], (hearth) bottom ◇ 杯状~*, 捣制镁砂~ rammed magnesite hearth, 碱性~ basic hearth, 可动[活动式]~ movable hearth, 碳质~ carbon hearth, 碗状~(电炉的) bowl hearth
炉床比容量(流态化炉的) specific grate capacity
炉床绝热层 hearth insulation
炉床面 【冶】bed surface
炉床面积 hearth area

炉床耐火底层 subhearth block
炉床内衬 hearth lining
炉床深度 depth of hearth
炉床温度 bed temperature
炉床直径 hearth diameter (HD)
炉床砖 hearth block
炉次 heat, melt, cast ◇ 低温~(钢水)【钢】cold heat, 报废[炼废]~【钢】aborted heat, 不合格~【冶】missed heat, 出钢时间经常相重的~ frequentlyf steel, 过吹~【钢】overblown melt, 准备出钢的~ ready-to-tap heat
炉次报废 【冶】heat losing
炉底 (furnace, hearth) bottom, bed (of furnace), bottom side, end plate, well, hearth floor (高炉的) ◇ 打结[捣制]~*, 带风眼的~(转炉的)【钢】tuyere bottom, 捣筑~【冶】rammed well, 碟形~*, 捣筑~【冶】plated hearth, 风冷~【铁】air-cooled bottom, 固定式~【压】base, 弧形~ arched hearth, 碱性~ basic bottom, 可卸~*, 连续(式)辊动~*, 烧结~ burned bottom, 酸性~ acid bottom, 碳质[碳块]~ carbon hearth (bottom), 移动式~ moving floor, 有效~面积 active furnace area
炉底保温[均热]段 hearth soaking zone
炉底不导电式直接电弧炉 direct-arc nonconducting hearth furnace
炉底出钢 bottom tapping
炉底材料 【冶】bottoming material
炉底出钢 bottom tapping
炉底打结 【钢】daub, bottom making
炉底打结[捣筑]机 【冶】bottom ramming machine
炉底打结用白云石 clolomite for crespi-hearth
炉底打结料 【钢】daub
炉底打结用白云石 dolomite for crespi-hearth
炉底大块砖 bottom block
炉底导电式电弧炉 conductive furnace
炉底导电直接(加热)电弧炉 direct-arc conducting hearth furnace, free-hearth electric furnace ◇ 格伦瓦尔~*
炉底导管 bottom guide tube
炉底底层料 floor
炉底电极 hearth electrode
炉底电极电弧炉 bottom electrode arc furnace
炉底顶升车(底吹转炉用)【钢】bottom-hoist car
炉底沸腾 【钢】bottom boil
炉底分层铺料技术 bedding technique
炉底风冷盘(高炉的) 【铁】plenum
炉底风口损坏 【钢】boring of bottom
炉底辊 hearth roll
炉底辊传动设备 driving equipment for hearth rolls
炉底辊道传动装置 roller-hearth drive
炉底烘烤炉(转炉用) bottom heating furnace
炉底滑道 skid
炉底滑道水管 water-cooled skid
炉底滑管 skid (pipe)
炉底回波[声] bottom bounce
炉底火道 【焦】sole flue
炉底[床]基础 【钢】subhearth
炉底基础台 【焦】oven mat
炉底积铁 shadrach, salamander ◇ 放出~ salamander tapping
炉底加热式均热炉 bottom fired soaking-pit furnace
炉底浇灌 【焦】sole grouting
炉底结构 bottom construction
炉底结块 furnace sow, 【铁】horse (高炉的)
炉底空气冷却 【铁】under-hearth air cooling
炉底冷却器 hearth bottom cooler
炉底磨蚀 wear on bottom
炉底喷枪 bottom lance
炉底砌块 oven sole block, 【钢】plug
炉底砌体温度记录仪 【冶】bottom lining

temperature recorder
炉底砌筑[砌体] 【冶】masonry of well
炉底烧结 burn-in, sintering of bottom
炉底寿命 bottom [hearth] life
炉底双侧烧嘴(对嘴)均热炉 bottom two way fired (soaking) pit
炉底水封式煤气发生炉 wet-bottom gas producer
炉底死金属 metal locked up in furnace bottom, metal in absorption in furnace bottom
炉底死铁 【铁】old-horse
炉底死铁层(材料) fixed bed material
炉底填料 bottom stuff
炉底通电电弧熔炼炉 live-bottom furnace
炉底外壳 end plate
炉底维护 bottom maintenance
炉底修补房(转炉的) bottom house
炉底制造(转炉的) 【钢】bottom making
炉底中心部分 【铁】hearth plug, sow
炉底砖 bottom brick, hearth block, oven sole brick
炉底装料立式蒸馏炉 bottom charged vertical distillation furnace
炉顶 furnace [oven] roof, furnace top (高炉的), (furnace) crown, roof (arch), (shaft) top, summit of furnace ◇ 半悬吊式～ semi-suspended roof, 带支架的～ scaffold top, 捣制[浇灌]～【冶】castable roof, 吊挂式[吊拱式, 悬挂]～*, 拱形[式]～*, 碱性～basic roof, 可卸式～removable arch, 冷～(鼓风炉的) cold top, 炉壳支承的～ shell-supported top, 门式提升～*, 密封～(高炉的) sealed top, 棋盘式烧成铬镁砖和镁砖～*, 砌合[固结]～bonded roof, 倾斜式～【冶】sloped roof, 塔架式～ tower top, 旋转布料器[麦基式]～*, 整一构造 full roof construction, 柱支承～column-supported top
炉顶布料装置 【铁】(furnace) top distributing gear
炉顶操作台 【冶】charging scaffold
炉顶(除尘)风机 roof(-cleaning) fan
炉顶吹氧 roof lancing
炉顶吹氧熔炼 roof lance heat
炉顶大砖 roof block
炉顶电视监视器 furnace top T.V. monitor
炉顶吊砖 【耐】block of suspended arch
炉顶端烧嘴 furnace top end burner
炉顶二次空气 【冶】top air addition
炉顶放散阀 【铁】bleeder door
炉顶废气 top discard
炉顶封闭 【铁】top closure
炉顶风口 roof tuyere
炉顶辐射高温计 【铁】dome radiation pyrometer
炉顶钢圈 【铁】top ring (casting), lip ring
炉顶隔墙 roof baffle
炉顶工 furnace top man
炉顶拱 furnace roof arch
炉顶拱高[拱矢] 【冶】roof rise
炉顶桁架 【铁】tower of furnace top
炉顶灰产出量 【铁】flue dust production
炉顶灰尘捕集 【铁】flue dust separation
炉顶灰风动输送系统 【铁】flue dust pneumatic conveying system
炉顶回转 (同"炉顶旋转")
炉顶加料 top charging [filling]
炉顶加料器 top filler
炉顶加热器 top heater
炉顶铰链连接结构 roof hinging
炉顶结构 (furnace) top construction, roof construction, top structure [design]
炉顶卷扬机 top hoist, bell winch
炉顶均压设备 【铁】top pressure equalization equipment
炉顶空间温度 【焦】gas space temperature
炉顶拉杆 roofstay
炉顶冷却器 roof cooler
炉顶料罐 furnace top hopper, 【铁】cup
炉顶料盖 【铁】throat stopper
炉顶煤气 【铁】top gas [smoke], stock gas ◇ 净化的～ clean top gas, 未处理的 to-

炉顶煤气量　top gas rate
炉顶煤气洗涤用水　top gas-cleaning water
炉顶煤气压力　top pressure (TP), top gas pressure
炉顶煤气压力记录仪　top gas pressure recorder
炉顶煤气压力调节器　furnace top pressure controller
炉顶煤气引出管　【钢】top gas offtake
炉顶密封　top seal
炉顶密封装置　furnace top seal valve,【铁】top closing device
炉顶内衬　roof lining
炉顶排气孔　top gas exhaust port
炉顶喷嘴　roof jet
炉顶平台　(furnace) top platform, throat platform
炉顶砌砖用型胎　roof bricking former
炉顶气体　furnace top gas, top air
炉顶气体放气管　top air bleeder
炉顶气体温度　furnace top temperature
炉顶曲线控制　roof-contour control
炉顶燃烧器　roof burner
炉顶熔[软]化　roof running
炉顶扇形砖衬　roof segment lining
炉顶烧嘴　roof [top] burner
炉顶设计　furnace roof draught
炉顶寿命　rooflife, life of (arched) roof
炉顶调剂　【铁】distribution of stock
炉顶托圈　【铁】supporting top ring
炉顶温度　(furnace) top temperature,【铁】dome temperature (热风炉的)
炉顶温度调节　roof-temperature control
炉顶温度调节器　roof-temperature controller
炉顶下塌[烧蚀]　cave in, caving-in
炉顶下压力　furnace roof draught
炉顶小车　【铁】top trolley
炉顶小吊车(放散阀用)　【铁】portable davit

炉顶斜度　【冶】pitch of roof
炉顶悬拱高度　height of crown of roof
炉顶旋转(电炉的)　【钢】roof slew
炉顶旋转机构(电炉的)　roof swinging mechanism
炉顶旋转(式)电炉　【钢】swing-roof furnace, lift-and-swing-aside roof furnace, electric furnace with swing-out roof
炉顶压力　furnace top pressure, furnace roof draught,【冶】roof pressure,【铁】top pressure (TP)
炉顶烟气　top smoke
炉顶烟罩　roof hood
炉顶氧枪　top (blowing) lance
炉顶移出[活动,可移]式电(弧)炉　electric furnace with removable [retractable] roof, removable-roof arc furnace
炉顶用镁铬砌块　magnesite-chrome roof block
炉顶支撑系统　roof restraining system
炉顶支圈　【铁】supporting top ring
炉顶直径　top diameter
炉顶贮料仓　overhead (storage) bunker
炉顶砖　roof [top, dome] brick, roof tile ◇ 吊挂～ rib brick, 致密～ low porosity roof brick
炉顶砖衬　dome lining
炉顶装料　top charging, basket charging
炉顶装料系统　top-charging system ◇ 麦基式～*
炉顶装料装置　top-charging equipment [system, gear] ◇ 弗林式～*, 球阀式～*
炉顶装置　top arrangement, top appliance [structure]
炉顶作用　arch action
炉段下部结构　substructure of furnace section
炉腹　【铁】bosh, cylinder
炉腹底线　lower bosh line
炉腹顶线　upper bosh line
炉腹风口　bosh tuyere

炉腹钢带	bosh band
炉腹高度	bosh height
炉腹角	bosh angle
炉腹结构	bosh construction
炉腹(冷却)板	bosh (cooling) plate
炉腹冷却器	bosh cooler
炉腹冷却箱	bosh plate [cooling] box
炉腹炉结[瘤]	bosh scaffold
炉腹煤气量	bosh gas volume
炉腹砌体	bosh lining
炉腹砌砖	bosh brickwork
炉腹区	bosh area
炉腹烧穿	bosh breakout
炉腹水平线	bosh line
炉腹外壳	bosh casing [envelope], bosh jacket
炉腹液泛现象	bosh flooding
炉腹直径	bosh diameter
炉腹砖衬	bosh lining [brickwork]
炉腹砖墙	bosh wall(s)
炉盖	furnace cover [lid], (top) cover, 【焦】lid ◇ 固定~ permanent top, 启~机
炉盖卷扬机	bell winch
炉盖可移式(电弧)炉	removable-cover furnace
炉盖圈(电炉的)	【钢】roof ring
炉盖行程	【铁】stroke of bell
炉缸	(furnace) crucible, (furnace) hearth, crucible hearth, well, 【冶】basin ◇ 大直径~ large [wide] hearth, 单风嘴[单元]~*, 捣制镁砂~*, 环形~*, 冷~【铁】chilled hearth, 铆接~ riveting hearth, 陶瓷耐火材料~ ceramic hearth, 下部~【铁】crucible hearth
炉缸壁	hearth wall
炉缸侧壁结构	hearth side-wall construction
炉缸尺寸	hearth dimension
炉缸出铁口侧	breast
炉缸点火烘炉法	【铁】hearth-fire drying
炉缸冻结	gobbed up,【铁】chilled hearth, hearth chill
炉缸风口带炉墙	tuyere-breast wall
炉缸高度	hearth height
炉缸护板	【铁】hearth jacket plate
炉缸积铁	【铁】old-horse, bear
炉缸结瘤[块]	【铁】hearth accretion [sows]
炉缸精炼	hearth refining
炉缸冷却	hearth cooling
炉缸冷却壁[立冷板,立式冷却壁]	【铁】hearth (cooling) stave
炉缸冷行[变冷]	【铁】chill in hearth
炉缸里衬	hearth lining
炉缸面积	hearth area
炉缸侵蚀	hearth erosion
炉缸区	【冶】crucible zone
炉缸热量[热工制度]	hearth heat
炉缸烧蚀情况测定	【冶】hearth erosion measurement
炉缸寿命	hearth life
炉缸水平线(炉缸与炉腹交线)	【铁】hearth line
炉缸堆积	【铁】hearth accumulation
炉缸外壳	hearth jacket [casing] ◇ 风口带~【铁】breast plate
炉缸外壳板	hearth jacket plate
炉缸围板	hearth plate
炉缸维修	hearth maintenance
炉缸吸热反应	【铁】endothermic hearth reaction
炉缸系数	hearth factor
炉缸向凉	【铁】hearth chill
炉缸与铁水间界面	hearth-metal interface
炉缸支柱	【铁】furnace column
炉缸直径	hearth diameter
炉缸中心(死)料柱	【铁】central core
炉工	furnace attendant, melter, furnaceman
炉拱	(furnace) arch
炉拱顶	【冶】crown of roof
炉管	furnace tube
炉焊管	continuous furnace welding of tube

炉 lu

◇ 搭接～机组 lap-welded mill, 连续式～机组*

炉黑 furnace black

炉喉 (furnace, hollow) throat, furnace mouth ◇ 活动～布料调节板 [可调～直径护板]*, 窄～的 narrow-mouthed

炉喉－料钟间高度 【铁】throat-bell height

炉喉(保护)板 【铁】throat-armo(u)r (segment), armouring of throat, stockline armour ◇ 吊挂式～hanging armor jacket

炉喉部分 throat section

炉喉挡料装置 【铁】throat stopper

炉喉防护板 【铁】throat plate

炉喉高度 【铁】height of throat sections

炉喉间隙 【铁】bell clearance, annular space

炉喉截面 【铁】stockline area

炉喉平台 【铁】throat platform

炉喉温度 throat temperature

炉喉直径 throat diameter

炉后 【冶】tapping side

炉后出渣 back [rear] slagging, rear flushing

炉后出渣槽 rear slagging spout

炉后墙 rear wall

炉灰 furnace dust

炉灰尘排出量 flue dust make

炉基 furnace foundation [base]

炉结 (同"炉瘤")

炉卷轧机[四辊可逆式炉卷轧机] Steckel mill

炉壳 furnace shell [mantel, casing, body, jacket] ◇ 风口带～*, 喷水冷却～*, 瓦片式～结构*

炉壳冷却 shell cooling

炉壳破裂 【铁】shell rupture

炉壳支承的炉顶 shell-supported top

炉口 furnace [vessel] mouth, glory [poke] hole, kiln entrance, hollow throat, fire door [hole], (转炉的) nozzle, nose cone ◇ 对称～*, 更换[修理]～内衬【冶】nose reline, 同心～*, 窄～的 narrow-mouthed

炉口部分(转炉的) 【钢】nose [top] section

炉口对称型 LD(氧气顶吹)转炉 symmetric LD furnace

炉口对称转炉 【钢】concentric (-nose) vessel

炉口环形砖 nose-ring block

炉口漏气 door leak

炉口面积 nose area

炉口圈 【钢】topmost hood ring

炉口渣壳 【钢】bug

炉口装料斗 【铁】bell and hopper

炉况 furnace (operating) conditions, conditions in [of] furnace, 【钢】working ◇ 不稳定～*, 高炉～*, 热行～*, 正常～*

炉况不顺 stiff furnace operation, 【铁】blast wandering

炉况不顺的高炉 hard driven furnace

炉况控制盘室 furnace control panel room

炉况控制室 furnace control cabin

炉况失常[反常,失调,紊乱] trouble in furnace condition, 【冶】disruption of operation, 【铁】adverse furnace condition, furnace [operating] irregularity, erratic movement, BF operation disorde, aberration

炉况顺行 【铁】regular working, free driving condition

炉况严重失常 【铁】emergency

炉况预测[报] furnace condition prediction

炉冷 furnace cool(ing) [cooled] (F.C.), cooling in furnace

炉里衬 inwall

炉里衬砖 inwall brick

炉料 (furnace) burden, (furnace) charge, charge [charging, burden, mix] material, charging (stock), mixture, stock, kiln feed, blend ◇ 不含碳酸盐的～ carbonate free burden, 底层～ bed charge, 高密度高导热性～*, 含铁～ ferruginous burden, 化学匀质～*, 碱性～ basic stock, 块状[不含粉末的]～ fines free burden, 酸性～ acid burden, 下降～柱*, 整粒～ closely-sized burden

炉料比 charge ratio
炉料表 charge sheet
炉料仓 furnace bunker
炉料车 furnace carriage
炉料成分 charge [burden] composition
炉料程序控制盘 burden program control panel
炉料尺寸 charge size
炉料储存跨 charge holding bay
炉料带入硫量 【铁】sulphur load
炉料低料线 【铁】low-stockline
炉料堆场 charge materials yard
炉料废钢铁 【钢】charge scrap
炉料分布[配] charge [burden] distribution, distribution of charge, 【铁】distribution of stock
炉料分级 furnace burden sizing
炉料分布控制 burden distribution control
炉料分散性 fractional void volume
炉料分析 burden [mixture] analysis
炉料高度 burden level [depth]
炉料化学成分 burden chemistry [analysis], mixture analysis
炉料混合机 charge-mixing [reclaiming] machine
炉料混合间 charge-mixing department
炉料铬铁 charge chrome
炉料计算 (furnace) charge calculation, calcutation of charge
炉料结构 【铁】burden design
炉料金属组分[物质] metallics of charge
炉料控制盘 burden control panel
炉料料斗 furnace hopper
炉料料位记录器 furnace charge level recorder
炉料硫 charged sulphur

炉料流动 charge flow
炉料满料线 【铁】full stockline
炉料密度 charge density
炉料牌 charge indicator
炉料批数 charge number
炉料热电偶 load couple
炉料熔结 sticking of charge
炉料容量 charge capacity
炉料筛分 furnace burden sizing
炉料设计 burden design
炉料水分 【团】charge humidity
炉料顺利下降[顺行] 【铁】freely movement of burden
炉料特性 burden property, characteristics of burden, character of charge
炉料体积 charge volume
炉料停留时间 【铁】retention [residence] time
炉料停滞[顿] stock standstill
炉料透气性 【铁】burden permeability
炉料下降 drop of charge
炉料下降速度 【铁】speed of material descent
炉料下落条件 falling condition of charge
炉料性状 behaviour of burden
炉料选择 charge selection
炉料压实机 burden squeezer
炉料有害成分 injurious burden constituents
炉料与炉衬的界面 charge-liner interface
炉料预还原 【铁】burden prereduction
炉料重量 charge weight
炉料柱压力 pressure of stock column
炉料准备 charge preparation
炉料阻力系数 burden resistance index
炉料组成 burden mix, mixture making, charge makeup
炉料组分 charge component, burden constituent
炉龄[期] campaign life (CL), furnace life [campaign, age], campaign length, lining life, career

炉馏出物 furnace distillate

炉瘤[结,块] (furnace) accretion, incrustant,【铁】(furnace) clinker, wall accretion, scaffold, scar ◇ 侧部~ side crust, 坚固~ tight scaf-fold, 焦炭质~ coke-tree, 硫化物~ sulphide accretion, 炉壁~ wall scaffold, 上部~ top crust, 疏松~ loose scaffold, 锌质~ cadmia

炉瘤爆破 accretion blasting

炉瘤形成 【冶】scabbing, incrustation

炉帽 furnace crown,【钢】nose ◇ 偏口~ (转炉的)【钢】pear

炉门 furnace [fire] door, oven port ◇ 拱形~ arched door, 配重[带平衡锤的]升降~*, 启[摘]~机, 汽冷~ steam-cooled door

炉门侧壁砖 【钢】jamb brick

炉门侧柱 【冶】door jamb

炉门衬砖 door plug

炉门拱顶 【冶】port roof

炉门槛[坎] (furnace) sill, charging door sill ◇ 可拆式~ strip baffle

炉门框 door frame

炉门漏气 door leak

炉门栓 latch bar

炉门内衬 door lining

炉门砖 door [bullnose] brick

炉内壁温度记录仪 inwall temperature recorder

炉内处理时间 furnace time

炉内反压 furnace back pressure

炉内辊 furnace roll

炉内滑轨 furnace skid

炉内结渣 ash erosion

炉内精炼 furnace refining

炉内拉料辊 furnace pull out roll

炉内冷却 furnace cool(ing)

炉内馏出物 furnace distillate

炉内气氛 furnace atmosphere [air]

炉内气氛分析 furnace atmosphere analysis

炉(内)钎[铜]焊 furnace brazing (FB)

炉内水冷滑道 water-cooled skid

炉内透气性 furnace permeability

炉内退火 furnace annealing

炉内压力 furnace pressure

炉内氧化皮 furnace scale

炉内冶炼进程 furnace drive

炉内止碳[初脱氧] 【钢】furnace block

炉皮 furnace casing, hearth casing [mantle]

炉气 furnace [stock] gas ◇ OG 未燃法~回收系统【钢】OG hood system

炉气成分[组成] furnace gas composition

炉气出口 gas exit

炉气放散阀 furnace dirty gas bleeder

炉气分析仪 off-gas analyzer, combustion gas analyzer

炉气控制 furnace atmosphere control

炉气冷凝器 furnace gas condenser

炉气强制循环热处理炉 forced circulation furnace

炉气收集 【冶】gas containment

炉气洗涤器 furnace gas scrubber

炉前班组[工班] furnace crew,【铁】front side crew, casthouse crew

炉前(操作)工 furnaceman, hearth attendant,【钢】forehearth operator,【铁】blast furnace operator [worker, man] ◇ 第一[负责出铁的]~【铁】keeper

炉前出渣 front slagging

炉前吊车 【铁】casthouse crane

炉前返矿槽 pre-skip returns bin

炉前分析 【钢】on-the-spot sample analysis

炉前工具 【铁】keeper's tools

炉前工助手 【铁】keeper helper

炉前辊道 (同"装料辊道")

炉前混铁罐 forehearth mixing ladle

炉前机械 【铁】machinery in casthouse

炉前看水工组长 【铁】fitter foreman

炉前料斗 furnace bin

炉前筛 furnace screen

炉前筛下返矿 pre-skip returns

炉前筛下粉矿 pre-skip fines

炉前设施管理	【铁】casthouse management
炉前用大锤	【铁】sledge hammer
炉前组长	【铁】foreman
炉墙	furnace [fire, oven] wall, inwall, wall (liner), chamber wall (焦炉的), shaft wall (竖炉的) ◇ 空气冷却~", 空喷细粉的~密封法", 水套~jacket(ed) wall
炉墙丁字砖	【焦】hammer head brick
炉墙附着物	【铁】scaffold
炉墙结厚	【铁】BF wall accretion
炉墙黏结物	【铁】(furnace) clinker
炉墙墙衬	【焦】oven wall liner
炉墙上沉淀的锌渣	【铁】philosopher's stone
炉墙损坏	【焦】oven wall damage
炉墙外层	encasing
炉墙温度	【焦】chamber wall temperature
炉墙砖(碳化室的)	【焦】panel brick
炉区	furnace zone
炉热逸出	furnace (heat) liberation
炉容(积)	furnace volume, internal volume
炉容量	heat size, furnace capacity
炉栅	grid ◇ 活动~moving grid
炉上料斗	furnace hopper
炉身	furnace shaft [stack], 【铁】shaft; stack
炉身衬里[里衬, 内衬]	stack [shaft] lining
炉身衬[砌]砖(鼓风炉的)	stack brickwork
炉身基底	furnace box base
炉身角	【铁】shaft [stack] angle
炉身结厚	【铁】shaft wall accretion
炉身冷却板[壁]	【铁】stack cooler [stave], stack-cooling plate
炉身喷吹(原, 燃料)	【铁】stack injection
炉身水平线(炉身至炉喉交线)	top inwall line
炉身外壳	shaft [stack] casing, stack shell
炉身下部	【铁】lower stack
炉身下水平线	【铁】bottom inwall line
炉身斜度[率]	【铁】inwall slope [batter], stack batter
炉身[体,底]移出式电(弧)炉	electric furnace with run-out body
炉身支柱	【铁】shaft supporting column
炉室	furnace chamber [retort], oven chamber, closet (蒸馏炉的)
炉室高	【焦】chamber height
炉台	furnace stage, coil base
炉台料仓	stage bunker
炉台楼梯	【冶】furnace platform stairs
炉台座(罩式炉)	base stand
炉膛	furnace hearth [crucible, laboratory, cavity], melting chamber, fire room [box], hearth ◇ 拱形~arched hearth, 环形~annular hearth, 集砂[收集]~", 浅~shallow hearth, 酸性~acid hearth
炉膛焙烧	hearth roasting
炉膛尺寸	hearth dimension
炉膛吹刷	furnace purging
炉膛高度调节	hearth height adjustment
炉膛高温带	boshes
炉膛构造	hearth construction
炉膛面积产量	output of hearth area
炉膛侵蚀测定	hearth erosion measurement
炉膛熔渣	hearth cinder
炉膛深度	depth of hearth
炉膛温度	hearth temperature
炉膛座板	hearth plate
炉体	(furnace) body, furnace shaft [stack]
炉体挂渣技术	furnace self lining technique
炉体结构	furnace contruction
炉体寿命	【焦】battery life
炉体与混凝土基础间接触面	【铁】block-concrete interface
炉体锥形部分	vessel cone
炉条	fire(-grate) bar, furnace grate
炉条钢	fire [grate] bar
炉条间距	fire bar spacing

炉头　furnace end,【焦】jamb
炉头钢圈　【铁】top[lip]ring
炉头修补　【焦】jamb patch
炉头砖　【焦】jamb brick
炉外处理　【钢】ladle[secondary]treatment, secondary steelmaking process
炉外点火炉　【冶】fore chamber
炉外钢液处理法　◇石川岛中村～*
炉外精炼　【钢】secondary refining[steelmaking]
炉外精炼技术　secondary refining[steelmaking]technique ◇IR-UT～*
炉外壳　【冶】hearth casing[mantle]
炉外燃烧室　【铁】external[separate]combustion chamber
炉外脱磷　【钢】secondary dephosphorization
炉外脱硫　【铁】external desulfurization ◇马塞尼兹～法*,氢氧化钠铁水～*,
炉温程序控制(罩式炉的)　furnace temperature programming control
炉温控制　furnace temperature control
炉温梯度　furnace temperature gradient
炉下走廊　【焦】tunnel
炉型　(furnace)profile,【铁】line ◇工作～*,停炉～*
炉型设计　【冶】designing of construction lines, designing of section
炉型选择专家系统　furnace type choosing expert system(FTCES)
炉压调节烟囱　furnace pressure adjusting stack
炉压控制　furnace pressure control
炉腰　furnace bosh(furnace)waist,【冶】belly,【铁】barrel, belt, body
炉腰高度　【铁】height of straight section above bosh
炉腰支圈　【铁】blast furnace lintel plate, ring[lintel]girder, lintel[deck]ring
炉腰直径　【铁】belly diameter
炉役　campaign life(CL), campaign, career
炉役中期　mid-campaign

炉用单一式缓冲器　single furnace bumper
炉用电阻　furnace resistor
炉用垛料台　furnace magazine
炉用缓冲器　stationary stop
炉用铺设物　furnace skid
炉用输出辊道　furnace delivery table
炉用输入辊道　furnace entry table
炉用双联式缓冲器　double furnace bumper
炉用推钢机　furnace pusher
炉用真空箱　furnace vacuum tank
炉用装料辊道　furnace charging table
炉渣　(furnace)slag,(furnace)cinder ◇低钙～ lean cinder,高铝～ aluminous slag,高锑～*,含～的 cindery,含铁～*,碱性～*,空冷～ air-cooled slag,粒化～[水渣]坑*,铝酸钙～ calcium aluminate slag,酸性～ acid slag,碎～ crushed slag,铁橄榄石型～ fayalite-type slag,托马斯～【钢】phosphatic slag,易熔～ fusible slag,再炼～*,助熔～ flux slag
炉渣保护底层　slag protective padding
炉渣焙烧　slag roasting
炉渣沉积　slag deposit
炉渣沉降条件　conditions for slag settling
炉渣成分　slag composition[analysis, constituent]
炉渣重炼(炼锡的)　slag smelting
炉渣稠化　thickening of slag
炉渣处理　【冶】disposal of slag
炉渣处理[加工]厂　slag-processing plant
炉渣处理炉　slag treatment furnace, slag hearth
炉渣淬裂　【铁】falling
炉渣带铁　【铁】buckshot
炉渣电炉熔炼　electric slag smelting
炉渣堆积　slag accumulation
炉渣沸腾　slag boil
炉渣分离不良　poor slag separation
炉渣分析　slag analysis[assay, test]
炉渣粉　ground-slag
炉渣钙硅比　slag lime-silica ratio

炉渣隔热层	【建】insulating layer of slag
炉渣硅酸度	slag silicate degree
炉渣骨料	breeze aggregate
炉渣加热器	slag heater
炉渣碱度	slag basicity
炉渣碱度平衡	slag basicity balance
炉渣结构	slag constitution
炉渣结块	furnace clinker
炉渣净化电炉[贫化炉]	slag cleaning furnace
炉渣净化法	slag cleaning process
炉渣块	barrings
炉渣粒化	slag granulation [beading]
炉渣粒化池	granulating pit
炉渣粒化贮槽	【铁】water treatment pit
炉渣量	amount of slag
炉渣硫化挥发	slag sulphurizing volatilization
炉渣硫化物容量	sulphide capacity of slag
炉渣流动性	slag fluidity
炉渣漏出	slag breakout
炉渣磨碎机	cinder mill
炉渣黏度	slag viscosity ◇ 赫蒂～计 Herty viscosimeter
炉渣黏附	adhesion of slag
炉渣喷水粒化	【铁】jet granulation
炉渣品位	slag grade
炉渣破碎	slag crushing [breaking], 【铁】falling
炉渣破碎机	slag crusher [breaker]
炉渣起泡	bloating, slag foaming, 【冶】sponging
炉渣强烈起泡	【冶】heavy sponging
炉渣侵蚀	slag attack [action, corrosion, erosion, penetration]
炉渣侵蚀作用	slag action [corrosion], cutting action [effect] of slag, corrosive action of slag
炉渣熔体	slag melt
炉渣筛分机	slag screen
炉渣筛选装置	slag-screening plant
炉渣渗透表层(炉衬的)	slag-impregnated surface layer
炉渣试验	slag test
炉渣试样	slag sample
炉渣数量	slag volume, quantity of slag
炉渣水淬(法)	【铁】granulation of slag
炉渣水淬槽	slag-granulating tank, slag [water] granulator
炉渣水淬流槽	slag granulation chute
炉渣水淬装置	slag granulating unit
炉渣水泥	slag cement
炉渣特性	slag characteristics
炉渣填成地区	slag-filled area
炉渣填充底	slag fill
炉渣铁钙比	slag iron-lime ratio
炉渣铁硅比	slag iron-silica ratio
炉渣条痕	slag streak
炉渣微晶玻璃	slag glass-ceramics
炉渣系	slag system
炉渣析取	scorifying of cinder
炉渣形成	formation of slag
炉渣性质	slag property
炉渣性状[特性]	slag behaviour
炉渣烟化法	【色】slag fuming process
炉渣烟化炉	slag fuming furnace
炉渣溢出	slag overflow, blowup of charge
炉渣溢流口	slag overflow outlet
炉渣砖	slag brick, cinder brick
炉渣状态	slag condition
炉渣组成	slag composition [constitution, constituent]
炉长	chief furnace man, furnace superintendent
炉罩	furnace hood [enclosure, can] ◇ 均热段[鼓形]～ *, 耐火砖衬里～ brick lined hood
炉罩温度	hood temperature
炉罩压力	hood pressure
炉中焙烧[烧成]	kiln roasting
炉中分析	bath analysis
炉中软钎焊	furnace soldering
炉中时效	oven aging
炉中硬钎焊	hearth brazing

炉柱(加热炉的) furnace stay
炉柱扭曲 【焦】buckstay deflection
炉子 (同"炉") ◇ 用～加热[处理](包括熔炼、焙烧、熔解等操作) furnacing
炉子变[参]数 furnace variables
炉子操纵室 furnace control cabin
炉子操作工 【钢】furnace operator
炉子操作工具 furnace tool
炉子操作指标 furnace operating factors
炉子抽力调节 furnace draught control
炉子出口温度 furnace offtake temperature
炉子出口烟道 furnace offtake
炉子出料侧 furnace delivery side
炉子点火 furnace firing up
炉子冻结 【铁】freeze up
炉子放热速率 furnace liberation rate
炉子附件 furnace fittings
炉子干燥 furnace dry out
炉子管接头(鼓风管等的) stove connections
炉子加料装置 furnace charging gear
炉子接头 【冶】stove connections
炉子结构 furnace structure
炉子结壳(耐火砖表面渣化) furnace encrustation
炉子控制盘室 furnace control panel room
炉子跨 furnace bay [aisle]
炉子拉条 furnace bracing
炉子冷却水 furnace cooling water
炉子冷行 【铁】cold furnace condition, cooling-off condition
炉子利用系数[有效利用率] furnace availability
炉子灵敏度 【冶】furnace sensitivity
炉子密封 furnace sealing
炉子内型 furnace lines
炉子配[附]件钢板 【冶】bucking plate
炉子平台 furnace platform, furnace stage
炉子气氛调节 furnace atmosphere control
炉子区段 furnace section
炉子全长 overall furnace length

炉子全宽 overall furnace width
炉子热效率 furnace thermal efficiency
炉子热行 【铁】hot furnace condition
炉子生产率 furnace production rate, furnace output
炉子生产能力 furnace capacity [output], tonnage of furnace
炉子失常[事故,不顺] (同"炉况失常")
炉子寿命 (同"炉龄")
炉子顺行 (同"炉况顺行")
炉子外廓废料 【冶】furnace size scrap
炉子预吹刷 prepurging
炉子运行 【冶】furnace run
炉子自衬技术(炉体挂渣) furnace self lining technique
炉子组件 furnace component
炉组 oven battery [block]
炉组炼焦 battery coking
炉嘴(转炉的) nose (cone), converter nose ◇ 碱性氧气转炉～*,作～nosing
炉嘴倾动式炉 nose-tilting furnace
{Rf} rutherfordium; kurchatovium
卤化 halogenation ◇ 阳极～作用 anodic halogenation
卤化法 halogen(ation) process (电镀锡)
卤化反应 halogenating reaction
卤化钙 calcium halide
卤化铪{HfX$_4$} hafnium halide
卤化剂 halogenating agent
卤化铝 aluminium halide ◇ 低价～*
卤化氢 hydrogen halide ◇ 脱去～dehydrohalogenation
卤化氰 cyan halide
卤化钛 titanium halide
卤化碳 halocarbon
卤化钍 thorium halide
卤化物 halide (compound), halogenide, haloid ◇ 挥发～萃取～*
卤化物还原 reduction of halogen compound
卤化物加成化合物 halide additive compound

卤化物(热)分解　halide decomposition
卤化酰基　acid halide
卤化铟　indium halide
卤化银　silver halide
卤化铀　uranium halide
卤化作用　halogenation
卤镁基　magnesyl
卤砂　salmiak
卤素　halogen（Hlg, hal., X）◇去掉~ dehalogenate
卤素迁移率法　halogen migration method
卤素电镀法　halogen method
卤素[卤化物]检漏器　halide[halogen] leak detector
卤素[卤化物]敏感检漏器　halogen sensitive leak detector
卤素冶金　halogen metallurgy
卤钨灯　halo-tungsten lamp
卤氧化合物　oxyhalogen compound
卤氧化物　oxyhalide
卤氧盐[卤氧化物盐类]　oxyhalide salt
卤银矿　iodembolite, iodobromite
卤载体　halogen carrier
卤族元素　halogen family element
鲁贝尔高强度耐蚀青铜　Rubel bronze
鲁尔收尘器　Luehr filter
鲁尔兹宝石合金（35—50Cu, 25—30Si, 20—30Ag）　Ruolz alloy
鲁夫洛伊耐蚀铅合金（0.25Sn, 0.02Mg, 0.02Bi,余量 Pb）　Roofloy
鲁福斯铝锌镁合金　Rauffoss alloy
鲁奇-德拉沃型带式焙烧机　Lurgi-Dravo traveling grate
鲁奇-德拉沃型带式焙烧机法　【团】Lurgi-Dravo grate process
鲁奇-蒂森工艺　Lurgi/Thyssen process
鲁奇加压气化器　Lurgi pressure gasifier
鲁奇煤炭气化法　Lurgi coal gasification process
鲁奇铅基轴承合金（96.5Pb, 2.8Ba, 0.4Ca, 0.3Na）　Lurgi-metal
鲁奇球团法　Lurgi pelletizing system
鲁奇铁矿石磁化焙烧法　【铁】Lurgi process
鲁奇型带式烧结机　Lurgi type sinter machine
鲁氏去磺弧菌属　desulfovibrio rubetschickii
鲁泽莱特耐蚀压铸铝合金（94Al, 4Cu, 2Mo + Cr_2）　Ruselite
镥合金　lutetium alloy
镥基合金　lutetium-base alloy
镥添加合金　lutetium addition
露出　disclose, show, reveal
露出点　point of emerqence
露点　dew point (dp)
露点分析器　dew point analyzer ◇气体~dew-cell gas analyzer
露点腐蚀　dew point corrosion
露点记录器　dew point recorder
露点连续指示计　continuous-indicating dew-point meter
露点敏感元件[传感器]　dew point sensor
露点曲线　dew point curve
露点湿度计　dew point hygrometer, cold-spot hygrometer
露点温度　dew point temperature
露点指示器　dew point indicator, dew pointer
露点指针　dew pointer
露光量　amount of exposure
露台　【建】balcony
露天　open air, outdoors, in the open
露天变电所　outdoor substation
露天采掘场[坑]　open[strip] pit
露天堆料场　open storage
露天堆栈　open surge pile, open-air repository
露天开采　open-work (o.w.), opencut, barrow excavation
露天矿　open-work (o.w.), open-pit (mine) ◇大型~glory-hole
露天矿原矿石　run-of-pit ore
露天矿坑采石法　glory-hole method of

quarrying
露天料堆　open surge pile
露天栈桥[装卸台]　open trestle
露头　outcrop, heading (hdg)
露头层　header course
路拌混凝土　concrete mixing "en route"
路(边)缘　【建】curb
路标　guide post, road sign, marking
路程　distance, path, route
路堤　earth bank, embankment, subgrade
路径　way, path, passage, travel
路径长度　path length
路径[由]选择控制　【计】routing control
路面　pavement, road surface ◇ 方块料[石块](铺砌)~ cube pavement, 混凝土~摊铺机　concrete paver, 重级~*
路面拱度　camber of paving
路面横向高差　cross-fall
路面破碎机　pavement [road] breaker
路面洒水车　road-sprinkler
路面修整机　finishing machine
路面总体设计　overall pavement design
路碾　road roller ◇ 滚筒式~ drum roller
路氏硬度　Ludwig hardness (Hl)
路线　route, course
路缘石标高以下　below curb
录波器　【理】oscilloscope, oscillograph
录声磁头　magnetic recording head
录像机　video recorder ◇ 屏幕~ kinescope recorder
录音(用磁带)　sound recording, taing
录音(磁)带　magnetic (recording) tape, (audio) tape
录音带盒　cassette
录音电话机　telegraphone
录音钢丝　magnetic wire ◇ 仙牌镍铜铁~合金 Sen alloy
录音机　recorder ◇ 磁带~*
陆地测量　land surveying
陆界　lithosphere
陆运　【运】land transport(ation)
吕德斯带[线](屈服变形出现)　Lueders lines
吕德斯滑移　Lueders slip
吕德斯应变线　Lueders strain
吕登沙伊特锡基合金(72Sn, 24Sb, 余量 Cu)　Ludenscheidt
铝{Al}　aluminium, aluminum ◇ 包~产品*, 纯~ pure aluminium, 粗~ crude aluminium, 电解~ electrolytic aluminium, 杜拉~*, 镀~ aluminium coat, 废~ aluminium scrap, 高纯(度)~ high purity aluminium, 工业[商品]纯~*, 含~(土)的, 加~ aluminium feeding, 精炼~ refined aluminium, 可溶性~ soluble aluminium, (扩散)渗~ aluminium impregnation, 热镀~ calorising, calorizing, 熔融[液态]~ molten aluminium, 商品~*, 渗~*, 酸溶~ acid-soluble aluminium, 涂敷~ aluminium coat, 退火~ annealed aluminium, 脱~(腐蚀)*, 须晶强化~*, 阴极~*, 原~ primary aluminum, 再生~ secondary aluminium, 铸[生]~ cast aluminium, 准~(即镓) eka-aluminum
铝板　sheet [beaten] aluminium, aluminium sheet [plate] ◇ 厚~ aluminium plate, 硬状态~ hard temper sheet
铝板钛矿　tieillite
铝板轧机　aluminium sheet mill
铝棒　aluminium bar [stick] ◇ 拉丝用~ aluminium wire bar
铝包覆层　aluminium cladding
铝避雷器　aluminium-cell arrester
铝表面钝化处理法　◇ 阿洛丁~*, 埃马塔尔~ Ematal process
铝表面防腐蚀化学处理法　◇ 普罗塔尔~ Protal process, 阿尔卡克~ Alkak method
铝箔　aluminium foil ◇ 废~ aluminium-foil scrap, 涂胶~ tenaplate
铝箔窗口　aluminium-foil window
铝箔分卷机　foil separator
铝箔轧机　aluminium-foil mill
铝材　aluminium product

铝材冷轧机	aluminium-cold mill
铝材热轧机	hot-aluminium mill
铝厂	aluminium manufacturer [plant, producer, works]
铝赤铁矿	alumohematite
铝脆性	aluminium brittleness
铝达尔合金	aldal
铝弹	【钢】aluminium bomb
铝当量	aluminium equivalent
铝导线	aluminium conductor, electrical aluminium wire ◇ 全~*
铝电镀法	cromalin
铝电解	aluminium electrolysis ◇ (胡普斯)三层液~精炼法*
铝电解槽	aluminium(-electrolytic) cell, aluminium smelting [reduction] cell ◇ 厄尔夫特~*, 高电流~*, 预焙阳极~*
铝电解法	aluminium electrolytic [reduction] process
铝电解生产	(同"电解炼铝")
铝电解整流器	aluminium (cell) rectifier
铝锭	aluminium ingot [pig]
铝锭铸造机	aluminium pig casting machine
铝镀层	aluminium coat(ing)
铝矾土	bauxite
铝矾土耐火材料	bauxite refractory
铝矾土熟料	bauxite chamotte
铝矾土水泥	bauxite cement, ciment-fondu
铝粉	aluminium powder [flake, dust], powdered aluminium ◇ 片状~flake aluminum, 烧结~*
铝粉末冶金产品	aluminium powder metallurgy product (APMP)
铝粉末冶金学	aluminium powder metallurgy (APM)
铝粉涂料	aluminium paint
铝浮渣	aluminium dross
铝复合材料	aluminium composite ◇ 石墨增强~*
铝钙合金	Kalzium metal
铝钙铀云母	sabugalite
铝盖	cover of aluminium
铝钢(含铝1%)	aluminium steel
铝锆中间合金	aluminium zirconium hardener
铝铬镀层	aluminium chromium coating
铝铬钢	aluminium chromium
铝铬硅耐热钢	sicromal
铝铬铁矿	alumchromite
铝铬中间合金	aluminium chromium hardener [master alloy]
铝汞齐[汞膏]	aluminium amalgam
铝管	aluminium pipe ◇ 杜拉~duralumin pipe
铝管避雷器	aluminium-cell arrester
铝硅比	aluminium/silicon ratio, Al-Si ratio
铝硅共晶合金	◇ 阿拉达尔~*
铝硅合金	aluminium silicon (alloy), alusil alloy ◇ 劳塔尔~*, 珀迈特耐蚀~*, 特勒克塔尔~*
铝硅合金变性处理	modification of aluminum-silicon alloy
铝硅钾土	zorgite
铝硅镁合金	Alsimag ◇ 安奇可罗达耐蚀~*
铝硅耐蚀合金	◇ 西尔梅雷克~*
铝硅片	alsi-film
铝硅热法还原剂	alsithermic reducing agent
铝硅酸钙	calcium-aluminium silicate
铝硅酸盐	alumo-silicate, aluminosilicate
铝硅陶瓷纤维	alumina-silica ceramic fibre
铝硅铁	ferro-silicon-aluminium, alsifer
铝硅铁合金	Al-Si-Fe alloy
铝硅锡轴承合金	◇ 摩戈伊尔~*
铝硅系耐蚀合金	◇ 阿尔米纳尔~Alminal
铝硅轴承合金	◇ 克罗麦特~(90Al, 10Si) Chromet
铝硅轴承青铜	◇ 特尔梅耶尔~*
铝硅铸造合金	◇ 阿拉尔~*
铝硅砖	alumina-silica brick
铝焊料	aluminium solder ◇ 阿尔米特

~*,穆雷~*,索卢米尼姆~*,韦斯特~*,泽尔科~*

铝合金 aluminium alloy, alufer ◇ 1060~*, A~(铝镁硅合金) A alloy, G~*, Y~*,阿达尔~*,阿尔达尔~*,阿尔德雷导线用~*,阿尔费留姆~*,阿维阿尔~*,阿维昂纳尔~*,阿维奥尔~*,艾留米奈克~Alu-minac,艾卢马格尼斯~Alumagnese,波尔塔尔复杂~*,伯米迪昂~Birmidium,杜尔西利姆~*,厄卢明~*,高强度~*,格尔瓦纳姆~Galvanum,海曼~*,航空~*,赫杜尔~Heddur,活塞~*,津卡利厄姆~*,具有 G.P.(溶质原子)聚集层的~ aluminium G.P. zone alloy, 梅拉尔~*,蒙蒂盖尔~*,涅奥纳留姆~*,纽拉尔~*,帕蒂尼乌姆~Partinium,潘塔尔~*,齐伯林~*,撒拉萨尔~*,斯克雷龙~*,托姆~*,西格马利姆~*,形变[锻造]~*,压铸~*,依瓦尼姆~Ivanium,伊盖杜尔~igedur,伊纳留姆~*,铸造~*

铝合金表面防蚀化学处理法 ◇ 阿尔卡克~Alkak method

铝合金低倍浸蚀液 ◇ 冯泽拉德~Von Zeelader

铝合金电镀法 cromalin

铝合金浮渣 aluminium alloy dross

铝合金焊料 aluminium alloy solder ◇ 斯特林~*

铝合金结构 aluminium alloy structure

铝褐铁矿 alumolimonite

铝红磷铁矿 barrandite

铝化 aluminize, alitization, alitizing, calorising, calorisation, calorization, Aliting ◇ 固体~*

铝化处理 aluminize, calorising

铝化低碳钢 aluminized mild steel

铝化钢 calorizing steel

铝化合物 aluminium compound

铝化物扩散敷层 aluminide diffusion coating

铝化学防蚀膜处理法 ◇ 阿鲁邦德~Alubond method

铝化作用 calorisation, calorization

铝黄铜 aldurbra, aluminium yellow brass (55.25Cu, 41.25Zn, 3Pb, 0.5Al), aluminium brass (76Cu, 22Zn, 2Al) ◇ 阿杜布拉~*,阿尔丘奈克耐蚀~*,高强度~*,赫尔克里士~*,雷瓦朗~*,维阿布拉耐蚀~*,约卡尔布罗~*

铝活度 aluminium activity

铝活塞合金 aluminium piston alloy ◇ K.S.~*,超强~*

铝基多元合金 ◇ 艾罗莱特~*

铝基复合材料 aluminium-based [aluminium matrix] composite

铝基钢带 steel strip of aluminum base

铝基硅镁合金 anticorodal

铝基合金 aluminium base alloy, acieral ◇ 138~*, B.195~*,阿尔梅莱克~*,阿西雷尔~*,艾拉尔~*,艾龙~*,奥尔马格~*,奥尔马西尔~*,罗马尼姆~*,日耳曼~*,斯克雷龙~*,无铜~*,西拉尔~*,伯马莱特铸造~*,英帕尔科~Impalco alloy

铝基活塞合金 aluminium base piston alloy ◇ 蒂塔纳尔~*,夸耳扎尔~*,马格纳莱特[曼格莱特]~*,诺瓦赖特~*

铝基耐蚀合金 ◇ 农科拉利厄姆~*

铝基体 aluminium matrix

铝基铜镍镁合金 magnalite

铝基压铸合金 ◇ 帕克~*,斯特耶~*

铝基中间合金 aluminium base hardener

铝基重载轴承合金 ◇ 帕利乌姆~*

铝基轴承合金 aluminium base bearing alloy, palium ◇ 750~*, Z~*,阿尔科~*,夸耳扎尔~*,卢布拉尔~*

铝钾矾 (同"钾(明)矾")

铝件铸造(车间) aluminium foundry

铝绞(合)线 aluminium strand ◇ 钢芯~*

铝(金属互)化物 aluminide

铝金属雾 aluminium mist
铝金装饰合金(78Au,22Al) aluminium gold
铝精炼 aluminium refining ◇ 三层(液)法~电解槽*
铝壳 aluminium shell
铝块 aluminium pig ◇ 投[扔]~[铝饼](往钢包内) javelin
铝矿(石) aluminium ore
铝粒 aluminium shot ◇ 片状~laminal aluminum particle
铝磷合金 ◇ 福拉尔~(变性剂) Phoral
铝镁硅合金 ◇ 阿尔德雷~*,阿尔马西林~*,阿卢杜尔~*,海布拉姆~Hyblum
铝镁合金 aluminium magnesium alloy, magal(uma), almag ◇ M.G.~*,埃雷克特龙~*,贝内特耐蚀耐热~*,伯马布赖特可锻~*,超级~(板)*,海德罗纳留取耐蚀~*,帕拉鲁曼~*,斯塔拉尼姆耐蚀~*
铝镁耐火材料 Normagal
铝镁锰合金 ◇ 佩拉卢曼~*
铝镁锌合金 ◇ 齐马利厄姆~*
铝镁锌耐蚀合金 ◇ 涅奥马格纳尔~*
铝镁锌系合金 ◇ 厄盖尔~Ergal
铝镁铸造合金 ◇ 马格纳利乌姆~*
铝镁砖 alumina-magnesia brick
铝锰合金 aluminium mangnanese alloy ◇ 3S耐蚀~*,阿卢马尔~*,奥斯马亚尔~*,马戈尔~*
铝锰耐蚀合金 ◇ 阿卢曼~(约含1.5Mn) Aluman
铝锰青铜 manganese aluminium-bronze
铝锰铜合金(系) ◇ 苏西尼~*
铝密封 alumiseal
铝棉 aluminium wool
铝膜 aluminizer
铝母线 aluminium busbar
铝镍沉淀硬化型永磁合金 ◇ 阿尔尼克~*
铝镍钢 aluminium nickel steel
铝镍-铬镍热电偶 alumel chromel thermocouple [thermoelement]
铝镍钴钛型永磁铁 Al-Ni-Co-Ti-Fe permanent magnet
铝镍钴(铁)永磁合金 ◇ 科鲁马克斯~*
铝镍钴铜型永磁合金 ◇ 阿尔科马克斯~*
铝镍钴系永久磁铁 ◇ 海科马克斯~*
铝镍钴永磁合金 ◇ B.A.S.No.233~B.A.S.No.233,蒂克纳尔~Ticonal (magnet)
铝镍合金 aluminium nickel alloy, aluminonickel ◇ 拉尼~*
铝镍锰轻合金 ◇ 杜拉尼克~*
铝镍强磁钢(约含10Al,25Ni) Mishima magnet steel, M.K. steel
铝镍青铜 ◇ 约卡尔尼克~*
铝镍型永磁体 Al-Ni-Fe permanent magnet
铝硼氢 aluminium borohydride, aluminium boron hydride
铝硼中间合金 aluminium boron hardener
铝钎焊 aluminium soldering ◇ 特斯卡尔A~合金 Thesscal A
铝钎料 almit
铝青铜 aluminium-bronze, albronze ◇ KMC高强度~*,阿尔丘迈特金黄色~*,阿姆斯~*,阿特拉斯可锻~*,狄那莫耐磨~*,钴基~*,黄色~*,金色~*,赖克~*,雷西斯塔尔~*,理查德耐蚀~*,两相~*,麦吉尔可铸可锻~*,纳莱特极硬~*,斯克雷坦~*,塔夫-斯塔夫~*,西克里坦~*,西利金~*,希杜拉斯斯多元~*,赞塔尔~*
铝球(脱氧用) 【冶】pill of aluminium
铝热 aluminothermy
铝热法 alumino-thermic process, aluminothermics, thermit(e) method [process], aluminothermy ◇ 电~*
铝热(法焊补)铸型 【焊】thermit mould
铝热反应 alumino-thermic reaction, ther-

铝热管对接焊 thermit pipe welding
铝热焊 thermit(e) [exothermic] welding ◇ 不加压~*, 加压~*, 铜与铜[铜与钢]的~(采用氧化铜的) cadweld
铝热焊接法 thermit welding process
铝热焊接焊缝 thermit weld
铝热焊接用钢粉(0.25—0.35C, 0.4—0.6Mn, 0.09—0.2Si, 0.03—0.04S, 0.04—0.05P, 0.07—0.08Al) termit steel
铝热焊冒口 thermit collar
铝热还原法 alumino-thermic process ◇ 电~*
铝热剂 aluminothermics, thermit(e) (TH.), thermit mixture, plain thermit ◇ 焊接用~ welding thermit, 黑色~*, 红色~*, 卡纳利斯加~铸锭法【钢】Canaris method, 普通~ plainthermit, 烧结~*, 铸铁~*
铝热剂管对接焊 thermit pipe welding
铝热剂焊接 thermit [alumino-thermic] welding
铝热剂焊接法 thermit welding process
铝热(剂)还原 thermit(e) reduction, alumino-thermic reduction ◇ 戈尔德施密~*
铝热剂加热 thermit(e) heating
铝热剂接合 thermit joint
铝热剂金属 【冶】thermit metal
铝热(剂)熔焊 fusion thermit welding, thermit fusion welding
铝热压焊 thermit pressure welding
铝熔炼工作者研究学会(美国) Aluminum Smelters' Research Institute (ASRI)
铝砂 aloxite
铝砷高强度黄铜 albrac
铝水(铝电解槽中) aluminium pad
铝酸{正铝酸 H_3AlO_3, 偏铝酸 $HAlO_2$} aluminic acid
铝酸钙{$CaO \cdot Al_2O_3$, $5CaO \cdot 3Al_2O_3$} calcium aluminate
铝酸钙炉渣 calcium aluminate slag
铝酸钙钠{$3CaO \cdot 2Na_2O \cdot 5Al_2O_3$} calcium sodium aluminate
铝酸钙铁{$4CaO \cdot Fe_2O_3 \cdot Al_2O_3$} calcium ferric aluminate
铝酸钠{$NaAlO_2$, Na_3AlO_3} sodium aluminate
铝酸钠溶液 sodium aluminate solution [liquor]
铝酸三钙 tricalcium aluminate
铝酸锌{$ZnO \cdot Al_2O_3$} zinc aluminate
铝酸亚铁{$FeO \cdot Al_2O_3$} ferrous aluminate
铝酸盐 aluminate
铝酸盐溶液 aluminate liquor
铝酸盐耐火水泥 aluminate refractory cement
铝酸盐水泥 aluminate cement
铝酸一钙 monocalcium aluminate
铝碎片 aluminium chips
铝钛硼中间合金 aluminium titanium boron hardener
铝钛氧化物 tialit
铝碳砖 alumina carbon brick
铝-陶瓷复合材料 aluminium-ceramic composite
铝添加合金 aluminium addition
铝铁高导磁合金 alfenol
铝铁硅钙壳 duricrust
铝铁合金 ferroaluminium, alfer ◇ 阿尔芬诺尔~*
铝铁矿物 alferric mineral
铝铁镍锰高级青铜(9—12.5Al, 2.5—7Ni, 3—7Fe, 1—5Mn, 1—2Zn) higher bronze
铝铁青铜 ampco, siliman bronze
铝铁闪石 crossite
铝铁岩 aluminiferous, alite
铝铁中间合金 aluminium iron hardener
铝铜硅合金 ◇ 阿克隆~*
铝铜合金 aluminium copper (alloy) ◇ 莱奈特~*, 真空吸尘器用~*

铝铜镁合金 ◇ 日本高强度~*
铝铜镍合金 hiduminium, R. R. alloy ◇ 尼克洛伊~*
铝铜铁合金 aluminium copper iron
铝铜锌合金 aluminium-copper-zine alloy ◇ 阿尔曾305~*
铝铜锌镁合金 ◇ 伯梅塔尔~*
铝涂层 aluminium coating
铝涂料 aluminium paint
铝土化(作用) bauxitization
铝土矿 bauxite (ore), alumyte ◇ 低硅~ low-silicon bauxite, 低品位~ low-grade bauxite, 高硅~ siliceous bauxite, 高铁~ high iron bauxite, 三水铝石型~*, 一水铝石型~*
铝土矿粉 bauxite powder
铝土矿溶出 bauxite digestion
铝土矿(溶出)渣 bauxite residue
铝土矿原矿 run-of-mine bauxite
铝土砖 bauxite brick
铝脱氧[镇静]钢 aluminium-killed steel
铝丸 aluminium shot
铝稳定钢 aluminium-stabilized steel
铝雾(金属的) aluminium mist
铝锡20铜-钢双金属板 20Sn-Al steel bimetallic plate
铝锡合金 mock silver, alneon
铝锡(合金)轴承 aluminium-tin bearing, morgoil ◇ 摩戈伊尔~润滑装置*, 烧结~*
铝锡轴承合金 ◇ 诺拉尔~Noral
铝线 aluminium wire ◇ 导电~*, 钢芯~*
铝线锭 aluminium wire bar, aluminium for wire drawing
铝屑 aluminium chips
铝芯电缆 aluminium cable
铝锌合金 aluminium zinc alloy ◇ 齐斯康~Ziscon, 西布利~*
铝锌镁合金 ◇ 阿尔杜尔~Aldur, 超级~superalumag, 鲁福斯~Rauffoss alloy, 乌尼杜尔~Unidur

铝锌铜合金 ◇ 阿尔内昂~*
铝锌铸造合金 ◇ 坦查洛伊~*
铝盐 aluminium salt
铝盐溶液 aluminium salt solution
铝阳极处理[氧化]法 aluminite [eloxal] process
铝阳极氧化处理 eloxation ◇ 埃雷克赛尔~Elexal, 谢帕德~法 Shepherd process
铝氧 alumina ◇ 含有铁氧和~的 alferric, 普通~ common alumina
铝氧粉 alumdum
铝氧石 aluminite
铝冶金 metallurgy of aluminium
铝业协会(美国) Aluminum Association (AA)
铝液 (同"铝水")
铝阴极 aluminium cathode ◇ 凹球面~*, 圆形~*
铝银合金(50Al, 50Ag) Japanese silver
铝英石{$Al_2SiO_5 \cdot nH_2O$} allophane
铝硬阳极氧化层[氧化处理] aluminium hard coating
铝铀云母{$HAl(UO_2)_2(PO_4)_4 \cdot 16H_2O$} sabugalite
铝浴 aluminium bath
铝皂 aluminium soap
铝渣 aluminium slag
铝轧件喂入 aluminium feeding
铝针铁矿 alumogoethite
铝整流器(电解用) aluminium rectifier
铝制馈电线 aluminium feeder
铝制品 aluminium product
铝制品表面钼喷镀法 Sprabond
铝质黏土 bauxite clay
铝轴承合金(5.5—7.3Sn, 0.7—1.3Cu, 0.7—1.8Ni, 0.35—0.85Si, 0.7—12.25Mg, 0.3—0.7 Fe, 余量 Al) aluminium bearing alloy
铝珠 aluminium shot, pill of aluminium ◇ 液态~*
铝铸件 aluminium casting

铝族　aluminium family
履带　track (chain), apron wheel, caterpillar chain, crawler belt
履带车　caterpillar, creeper truck, tracked vehicle
履带齿片　grouser
履带传动　caterpillar drive
履带给料式矫直机　【压】caterpillar
履带式铲土机　crawler shovel
履带式斗轮取料机　crawler-mounted reclaimer with bucket wheel
履带式刮土[铲运]机　crawler scraper
履带式机铲　traxcavator
履带式结晶器　crawler type mould
履带式起重机　caterpillar [crawler] crane, creeper derrick
履带式牵引装置(拔丝机的)　caterpillar haul-off unit
履带式倾卸车　crawler dump wagon
履带式取料机　crawler-mounted reclaimer
履带式推土机　crawler dozer
履带式拖车　crawler trailer
履带式拖拉机　caterpillar [crawler] tractor
履带式挖沟机　【建】gopher ditcher
履带式挖土机　caterpillar excavating machine, crawler-mounted excavator
履带式运输机　caterpillar conveyer
履带式装载机　caterpillar loader
履带运行线　endless track
履带装置　caterpillar device
履行　implementation
缕状蒸汽　steam plume
氯{Cl}　chlorine ◇ 电解～ electrolytic chlorine, 含～中间产品, 气态～ gaseous chlorine, 无[不含]～的 chlorine-free, 制～电解槽 chlorine cell
氯苯{C_6H_6Cl}　chlorobenzene
氯比值　chlorine ratio
氯铋矿　bismoclite
氯铂(氢)酸{$H_2[PtCl_6]$}　chloroplatinic acid
氯铂酸铷{$Rb_2[PtCl_6]$}　rubidium chloroplatinate
氯铂酸盐　chloroplatinate, platinochloride
氯处理法　chlorine process
氯萃取　chlorine extraction
氯代甲烷　(同"甲基氯")
氯氮汞矿　kleinite
氯碘铅矿　schwartzembergite
氯丁(二烯)橡胶　neoprene (rubber), duprene rubber
氯丁橡胶垫片　neoprene gasket
氯丁橡胶垫圈　neoprene washer
氯钒矿　zimapanite
氯仿　(同"三氯甲烷")
氯仿萃液　chloroform extract
氯仿稀释剂　chloroform diluent
氯锆酸盐　chlorozirconate ◇ 碱金属～*
氯汞矿　eglestonite
氯汞银矿　bordosite
氯硅烷　chlorsilane
氯铪酸盐　chlorohafnate (salt), alkali chlorohafnate
氯化　chloridizing, chlorinating, chlorination ◇ 初步[预先]～*, 堆摊～ heap chlorination, 高温～*, 还原～联合法*, 碱法～*, 污水～ sewage chlorination, 阳极～(作用) anodic chlorination, 优先[选择性]～*, 有氢～(法)*, 再～ rechlorination, 直接～ direct chlorination
氯化铵(NH_4Cl)　ammonium chloride, muriate of ammonia, sal ammoniac
氯化钯　palladium (bi)chloride
氯化钡{$BaCl_2$}　barium chloride
氯化焙烧　【色】chlorination [chloridizing] roasting ◇ 流态化床～*, 挥发～*, 食盐～*
氯化焙烧法　chloridizing roasting process ◇ 古和～*
氯化焙烧过的钒钾铀矿　salt-roasted carnotite ore
氯化焙烧炉　chloridizing roaster
氯化铋　bismuth chloride

氯化铂　platinum chloride
氯化钚　plutonium chloride
氯化残渣　chlorination residue
氯化产物　chlorination product, chlorinate
氯化处理　chlorination
氯化催化剂　chlorination catalyst
氯化镝{DyCl$_3$}　dysprosium chloride
氯化电炉　electric chlorinator
氯化铥{TuCl$_3$}　thulium chloride
氯化铒{ErCl$_3$}　erbium chloride
氯化二溴　chloroclibromide
氯化二乙铊{TlCl(C$_2$H$_5$)$_2$}　thallium diethyl chloride
氯化法　chlorination process [route, technique], chloridizing [chloride] process, volatile chloride process ◇ 变价～*，电炉～*，高温～[氯化挥发法]*
氯化钒　vanadium chloride
氯化反应　chlorination reaction
氯化分解　chlorination breakdown
氯化钆{GdCl$_3$}　gadolinium chloride
氯化钙{CaCl$_2$}　calcium [hime] chloride
氯化锆{ZrCl$_4$}　zirconium chloride
氯化锆生产设备　zirconium chloride plant
氯化镉　caddy, cadmium chloride
氯化铬　chromium chloride
氯化汞{HgCl$_2$}　mercuric chloride
氯化汞试纸　mercuric chloride paper
氯化钴　cobalt chloride
氯化硅(类){SiCl$_4$, Si$_2$Cl$_6$}　silicon chloride
氯化挥发法　chloridizing volatilization process
氯化挥发工段　chloridizing volatilization section
氯化钬{HoCl$_3$}　holmium chloride
氯化机理　mechanism of chlorination
氯化技术　chlorination technique
氯化剂　chlorinating [chlorination, chloridizing] agent
氯化镓　gallium chloride
氯化钾{KCl}　potassium [potash] chloride, muriate of potash

氯化金{AuCl$_3$}　auric chloride
氯化精炼　refining by chlorination, chloridizing refining
氯化聚乙醚管　chlorinated polyether pipe
氯化钪{ScCl$_3$}　scandium chloride
氯化镧{LaCl$_3$}　lanthanum chloride
氯化铑　rhodium (tri)chloride
氯化镭{RaCl$_2$}　radium chloride
氯化锂{LiCl}　lithium chloride
氯化钌　ruthenium [ruthenic] chloride
氯化硫{S$_2$Cl$_2$, SCl$_2$}　sulphur chloride
氯化硫氯化(法)　chlorination by sulphur chloride
氯化流程　chlorination route
氯化炉　chlorination furnace, chlorinator ◇ 竖式～shaft-type chlorinator
氯化镥{LuCl$_3$}　lutecium chloride
氯化铝{AlCl$_3$}　aluminium chloride
氯化铝电解　aluminium chloride electrolysis
氯化镁{MgCl$_2$}　magnesium chloride
氯化镁电解　electrolysis of magnesium chloride
氯化镁壳　crust of magnesium chloride
氯化锰{MnCl$_2$}　manganese chloride
氯化钼　molybdenum chloride
氯化镎　neptunium chloride
氯化钠{NaCl}　sodium chloride, muriate of soda, (common, table) salt
氯化钠金　gold salt, gold sodium chloride
氯化钠－氯化铍熔体　sodium chloride-beryllium chloride melt ◇ 德古萨～电解制铍法 Degussa process
氯化钠溶液　sodium chloride solution
氯化钠型结构　【金】sodium chloride (type) structure
氯化钠型相　sodium chloride type phase
氯化镍{NiCl$_2$}　nickel chloride
氯化钕{NdCl$_3$}　neodymium chloride
氯化钕错{DiCl$_3$}　didymium chloride
氯化铍{BeCl$_2$}　beryllium chloride
氯化镨{PrCl$_3$}　praseodymium chloride

氯化器　chlorinator
氯化铅{PbCl$_2$}　lead chloride, muriate of lead
氯化氢{HCl}　hydrogen chloride ◇ 脱～ dehydrochlorination
氯化氢气体　hydrochloric acid gas
氯化氰{CNCl 或 ClCN}　cyan(ogen) chloride
氯化溶剂　chlorinated solvent
氯化铷{RbCl}　rubidium chloride
氯化铯{CsCl}　cesium chloride
氯化铯型结构　【金】cesium chloride (type) structure
氯化钐{SmCl$_3$}　samaric chloride
氯化设备　chlorination apparatus, chlorinator plant [unit]
氯化砷　arsenic chloride
氯化石蜡　chlorinated paraffin
氯化室　chlorination chamber
氯化双氧铀{UO$_2$Cl$_2$}　uranyl chloride
氯化锶{SrCl$_2$}　strontium chloride
氯化速率　chlorination rate
氯化铊　thallium chloride
氯化钛{TiCl$_4$}　titanium chloride
氯化钽{TaCl$_3$, TaCl$_5$}　tantalum chloride
氯化铽{TbCl$_3$}　terbium chloride
氯化锑　antimony chloride
氯化铁{FeCl$_3$}　ferric [ironic] chloride
氯化烃　chlorinated hydrocarbon
氯化铜{CuCl$_2$}　copper [cupric] chloride
氯化铜矿　copper chloride ore
氯化铜溶液　copper chloride solution
氯化钍{ThCl$_4$}　thorium chloride
氯化温度　chlorination temperature
氯化钨　tungsten chloride
氯化物　chloride, muriate (旧名 MCl, 一般专指氯化钾 KCl) ◇ 不挥发～ non-volatile chloride, 粗～ crude chloride, 低价～ subchloride, 冷凝～ condensed chloride, 气态～ gaseous chloride, 轻质～ light chloride, 松散～', 易碎～ fluffy chloride
氯化物电解液　chloride(-bearing) electrolyte [bath] ◇ 充氮～*
氯化物－氟化物电解液　chloride-fluoride bath
氯化物－氟化物熔体　chloride-fluoride melt
氯化物浮渣　chloride dross
氯化物挥发法　(volatile) chloride process
氯化物金属热还原　metallic reduction of chloride
氯化物离子　chloride ion
氯化物料　chloride charge
氯化物料罐　chloride can
氯化物料罐隔板　【色】chloride can divider
氯化物配合物　chloride-complex
氯化物歧化　disproportionation of chlorides
氯化物熔体　bath of chloride
氯化物熔盐电解　chloride fused salt electrolysis
氯化物溶液　chloride solution
氯化物升华（法）　chloride-sublimation
氯化物添加剂　chloride addition
氯化物－铁粉压块　【团】chloride-iron briquette
氯化物冶金学　chloride metallurgy
氯化物杂质　chloride impurity
氯化物蒸气　chloride vapour
氯化锡　tin chloride {SnCl$_2$, SnCl$_4$}, stannic chloride {SnCl$_4$}
氯化稀土　rare earth chloride
氯化酰基　acid chloride, chloride of acid
氯化橡胶　alloprene
氯化橡胶清漆　chlorinated rubber varnish
氯化锌{ZnCl$_2$}　zinc chloride, butter of zinc
氯化亚物　protochloride
氯化亚汞{HgCl, Hg$_2$Cl$_2$}　mercurous chloride, calomel, corneous [horn] mercury
氯化亚钴　cobaltous chloride
氯化亚铊{TlCl}　thallous chloride
氯化亚铁{FeCl$_2$}　ferrous chloride
氯化亚铜{Cu$_2$Cl$_2$}　cuprous chloride, nan-

tokite

氯化亚锡 {$SnCl_2$} stannous chloride, spirit of tin

氯化氧锆 {$ZrOCl_2$} zirconyl chloride

氯化氧铪 {$HfOCl_2$} hafnyl chloride

氯化窑 chloridization kiln

氯化冶金 chlorine metallurgy

氯化钇 {YCl_3} yttrium chloride

氯化乙烯树脂涂层钢板 vinyl chloride coated steel plate

氯化镱 {$YbCl_3$} ytterbium chloride

氯化铟 indium chloride

氯化银晶体 silver chloride crystal

氯化铀 uranium chloride

氯化铕 {$EuCl_3$} europium chloride

氯化原料 chlorination stock

氯化锗 germanium chloride

氯化装置 chloridizing [chlorination] unit

氯化作用 chlorination

氯黄晶 {$Al_8(SiO_4)_3 \cdot (F, Cl, OH)_{12}$} zunyite

氯磺化(引入SO_2Cl) chlorosulphonation

氯磺酸 {SO_2ClOH} chlorosulphonic acid

氯磺酰化聚乙烯合成橡胶 Hypalon

氯甲化(作用) chloromethylation

氯甲基醚 {$ClCH_2 \cdot O \cdot R$} chloromethyl ether

氯甲酸 chloro-formic acid

氯甲酸酯 {$Cl \cdot CO \cdot OR$} chloro-formate, chloro-formic ester

氯离子 chlorion

氯锰矿 s(c)acchite

氯泥石板 chlorite slate

氯气 chlorine (gas), gaseous chlorine

氯气除锌【色】chlorine dezincing ◇贝特顿~精炼法 Betterton process

氯气除锌设备 chlorine dezincing apparatus

氯气氛 chlorine atmosphere

氯气分布板 chlorine distributor

氯气(钢)瓶 chlorine cylinder

氯气缸[罐] chlorine tank

氯气流 chlorine flow [stream]

氯气流量 chlorine flow(-rate)

氯气浓度 chlorine concentration

氯气入口 chlorine inlet

氯气消耗 chlorine wastage

氯气引入管 chlorine inlet tube

氯气预热器 chlorine gas preheater

氯铅钾石 Pseudocotunnite

氯铅芒硝 caracolite

氯氢化法【色】hydrochlorination process

氯氢化反应 hydrochlorination

氯砷铅矿 ecdemite, ekdemite

氯酸钙 calcium chlorate

氯酸钾 {$KClO_3$} potassium [potash] chlorate, potassium oxymuriate

氯酸钠 {$NaClO_3$} sodium chlorate

氯酸铷 {$RbClO_3$} rubidium chlorate

氯酸铯 {$CsClO_3$} cesium chlorate

氯酸锶 {$Sr(ClO_3)_2$} strontium chlorate

氯酸盐 chlorate

氯钛酸铵 {$(NH_4)_2[TiCl_6]$} ammonium chlorotitanate

氯钛酸盐 chlorotitanate

氯铜矿 {$Cu_2(OH)_2Cl$} atacamite, smaragdo-chalcite

氯铜铝矾 spangolite

氯铜铅矾 arzrunite

氯锡酸沉淀法 chloro-stannic acid precipitation method

氯锡酸铷 {$Rb_2[SnCl_6]$} rubidium chlorostanate

氯锡酸盐 chlorostanate

氯锌酸盐 chlorozincate

氯溴代甲烷 chlorobromomethane (C.B.)

氯溴银矿 embolite

氯亚铂酸 chloroplatinous acid

氯亚金酸盐 chloraurite

氯氧比 chlorine-to-oxygen ratio

氯氧铋铅矿 perite

氯氧化铋 bismuth oxychloride, bismoclite

氯氧化镝 {$DyOCl$} dysprosium oxychloride

氯滤 lü

氯氧化铒 {ErOCl} erbium oxychloride
氯氧化钒 vanadium oxychloride
氯氧化钆 {GdOCl} gadolinium oxychloride
氯氧化锆 basic zirconium chloride, zirconium oxychloride
氯氧化硅 {SiOCl₂} silicon oxychloride
氯氧化铪 {HfOCl₂} hafnium oxychloride
氯氧化铼 {ReOCl₄, ReOCl₅} rhenium oxychloride
氯氧化钼 molybdenum oxychloride
氯氧化钕 {NdOCl} neodymium oxychloride
氯氧化镨 {PrOCl} praseodymium oxychloride
氯氧化钐 {SmOCl} samaric oxychloride
氯氧化铊 {TlOCl} thallic oxychloride
氯氧化钛 {TiOCl₂} titanium oxychloride
氯氧化铽 {TbOCl} terbium oxychloride
氯氧化锑 algaroth
氯氧化钨 {WO₂Cl₂, WOCl₄} tungsten oxychloride
氯氧化物 oxychloride, oxymuriate
氯氧化物结晶法 oxychloride crystallization
氯氧化镱 {YbOCl} ytterbium oxychloride
氯氧化铟 {InOCl} indium oxychloride
氯氧化铕 {EuOCl} europium oxychloride
氯氧铅矿 blixite
氯氧铜黏固粉 hubbellite
氯乙烯覆层金属板 ◇菱牌~Hishi metal
氯乙烯橡胶 vinyl chloride rubber
氯银矿 kerat, ostwaldite, chlorargyrite
氯载体 chlorine carrier
氯锗仿 (同"三氯甲锗烷")
滤板 filter board [plate]
滤饼 (filter) cake, filtered dirt, resultant cake, residue ◇沉淀[泥]铜~*,含铁~ ferric[iron] cake, 去除[撤除]~ cake removing
滤饼槽 cake hopper

滤饼吹落 cake [snap] blow
滤饼存储设备 cake storage equipment
滤饼干燥段(圆盘过滤机的) cake drying segment
滤饼刮板 cake scraper [scalper]
滤饼破碎机 cake breaker
滤饼(脱水)过滤 cake filtration
滤饼洗涤 caking washing, filter cake washing
滤饼再浆化槽 cake repulper
滤饼贮藏装置 cake storage equipment
滤波 smoothing, filtering ◇卡尔曼~(法)【数】Kalman filtering
滤波电路 smoothing [trap, filter] circuit
滤波器 【电】electric (wave) filter, (wave) filter, absorber ◇倍频带~ octave-band filter, 差接[桥型]~ differential filter, 带阻~*, 晶体~ crystal filter, 平滑~ smoothing filter
滤波器光度计 filter photometer
滤波线圈 【电】smoothing coil
滤波作用 【电】smoothening action
滤布 filter cloth [media], filtration fabric, press cloth
滤布堵塞 cloth blinding
滤槽(过滤机的) filter cell [pocket]
滤层 filter bed [course], filtering layer
滤(尘)袋 filter(ing) [dust, fibreglass] bag, sock ◇涤纶~ dacron bag
滤尘器 dust filter, filter dust separator, air strainer ◇袋式~*
滤池 filter (chamber) ◇生物~*
滤出[去] filter off
滤出母液 filtered pregnant liquor
滤除[掉] removal by filtration
滤底槽[桶] filter bottom tank
滤垫 filter bed
滤斗 filter(ing) funnel
滤缸 filtering jar
滤鼓 filter drum
滤光片[镜] (colour, light, optical) filter ◇吸收~ absorption filter

滤光器　light filter, absorber ◇ 平衡~*, 吸收~[镜]*
滤光器通过带重叠范围　filter overlap
滤埚　filter crucible
滤过辐射　filtered radiation
滤过粒子检验法　filtered particle method
滤净器　cleaning strainer ◇ 空气~ air strainer
滤净作用　defecation
滤菌器　bacteria filter
滤孔　filter opening
滤框　filter frame
滤篮(带滤布的)　basket with cloth
滤料　filter material [media]
滤泥　(filter) mud
滤片(过滤机的)　filter disk [leaf, element]
滤平　smoothing
滤器　strainer, filter ◇ 奥利弗~*, 干燥气体~ dry gas filter, 矿物~ mineral filter, 折式~ folded filter
滤气器　air strainer, inhaler
滤清　filtration, depuration
滤清射束　filtrated beam
滤清水　filtrated water
滤清性能　filtration characteristic
滤去废弃物　reject
滤热玻璃　heat filter glass
滤热器　heat filter
滤色光度计　abridged spectrophotometer, filter photometer
滤色器[镜]　filter lens, colour filter ◇ 雷腾~ Wratten filter, 吸收~ absorption color filter
滤砂　filter sand
滤栅　grating
滤水机　hydrofilter
滤水井　filter water well
滤水器　water filter [cell], hydrofilter, 【铁】cleanser
滤网　filter screen [gauze], strainer, dross trap (浇注系统的) ◇ 浇口~ filter core

滤雾器　mist precipitator
滤吸管　rose pipe
滤叶　filter leaf
滤叶澄清器　leaf clarifier
滤液　filtrate (water), filter liquor, filtered solution ◇干净[清]~ clear filtrate, 两次~ double filtrate
滤液泵　filtrate pump
滤液槽　filtrate tank
滤液接受槽　filtrate sump
滤液排出沟　filtrate discharge channel
滤液排放泵　filtrate discharge pump
滤液真空接受器　filtrate vacuum receiver
滤油器　oil filter [strainer, screen]
滤油网　oil(-filter) screen
滤渣　(filter) residue, filtered dirt ◇ 排除~ cake blow, 去除[撤除]~ cake removing, 浇口~器 filter core
滤渣芯片　【铸】core strainer, strainer tub
滤纸　filter paper ◇ 无灰~ ashless filter-paper
滤纸分析　filter paper analysis
滤纸检验　filter paper test
滤砖　filter block
绿矾　(同"七水硫酸铁")
绿高岭石[绿脱石]　{(Fe, Al)$_2$[Si$_4$O$_{10}$](OH)$_2$·nH$_2$O}　nontronite
绿锆石　beccarite
绿铬矿　eskolaite
绿铬石　prasochrome
绿硅镧铈矿　toernebohmite
绿硅铁矿　forchhammerite
绿化　【环】afforestation
绿化地带　【环】green belt
绿化率　afforestation
绿金(18开；含少量 Ag、Cd、Cu 等)　green gold
绿菌科　Chlorobiaceae
绿菌属　Chlorobium
绿帘石　epidote, allochite ◇ 含铈~ cerium epidote
绿磷锰矿　dickinsonite

绿榴石 （同"钙铬榴石"）
绿硫钒矿{V_2S_5} patronite
绿硫细菌 green sulphur bacteria
绿镁镍矿 alipite
绿蒙脱石 nepheline hydrate
绿锰铁矾 luckite
绿泥石{$H_4(Mg,Fe)_3Si_2O_9$} chlorite
绿镍矿{NiO} bunsenite
绿盘岩[青盘岩]【地】propylite
绿铅矿 pyromorphite
绿色淤泥[渣]（处理铀矿的） green sludge
绿蛇纹石 green serpentine
绿砷钡铁石 dussertite
绿蚀（含铬镍合金的）【金】green rot
绿松石{$CaO·3Al_2O_3·2P_2O_5·9H_2O$} turquoise
绿锑铅矿 monimolite
绿铁(合金) ferroverdin
绿铁碲矿{$Fe_2(TeO_3)_3·4H_2O$} durdenite
绿铁矿 rock bridgeite
绿铜铅矾 arzrunite
绿铜锌矾 calingastite
绿铜锌矿{$5(Zn,Cu)O·2CO_2·3H_2O$} aurichalcite
绿铜锈 green patina
绿透辉石 alalite, traversellite
绿锌铁矾 sommairite
绿锈 patina ◇ 表面～处理*
绿盐{UF_4} green salt
绿铀矾{$6UO_3·SO_3·nH_2O+(Ca,Cu)$} voglianite
绿铀矿{$CuUO_4·2H_2O$} uranolepidite, vandenbrandeite
绿柱石{$Be_3Al_2(SiO_3)_6$} beryl, aquamarine
孪晶 （同"双晶"）◇ 单原子层～monolayer twin, 调节～accommodation twin, 形变～mechanical twins
孪晶边界 boundary of twin
孪晶关系 twin relationship
孪晶间界 twin boundary
孪晶间界能量 energy of twin boundary
孪晶生成现象 twinning phenomenon
孪晶(型)马氏体 twin(ned) martensite
孪晶形成 twin formation, twinning
孪生 twinning
孪生变形 deformation twinning
孪生带 twin(ning) band ◇ 退火～annealing twin bands
孪生淀积物 twinned deposit
孪生二极管 duodiode
孪生方向 twinning direction
孪生光电管 twin photo-electric tube
孪生和基面滑移的交替【金】alternative of twinning and basal glide
孪生结构 twinned structure
孪生面 twinning plane
孪生能(量) twinning energy
孪生切变 twinning shear
孪生位错 twinning dislocation
孪生物质 twinned material
孪生现象【金】twinning phenomenon
孪生应力 twinning stress
卵硫菌属 Thiovulum
卵片状粉末 oval plates powder
卵石 gravel, pebble
卵形断口 kidney-shaped fracture
乱矿石 matrix
乱真反应 spurious response
乱真影像 spurious image
掠入射 glancing [grazing] incidence
掠入射角 glancing angle of incidence
掠射角 glancing angle ◇ 衍射～*
略图 sketch, outline (sketch), schematic diagram [representation], diagrammatic representation
略语 abbreviations (abb., abbr., abbrev., abbs.)
轮 wheel, bob,【机】block（射流技术的）
轮班制 rotating shift system
轮传动 wheel drive
轮带式铸造机 wheel belt caster
轮斗式电解槽 scoop-wheel cell
轮渡 ferry ◇ 拖挂车～ferry bridge

轮对 wheel set ◇ 带凸缘~*
轮辐 web,(wheel) spoke ◇ 弯曲~*
轮辐厚度(车轮的) web thickness
轮辐轧机 wheel-web-rolling mill
轮箍 (wheel) tyre, tire, wheel [binding] band, strake ◇ 无凸缘~ blind tyre
轮箍粗轧机 becking mill
轮箍钢 tyre [tire] steel, tyre bar
轮箍钢锭 tyre ingot
轮箍滚轧机 tyre rolling mill
轮箍坯 【压】cheese
轮箍[缘]弯曲机 tyre bending machine
轮箍压力机 【压】tyre press
轮箍轧机 tyre [tire, schoen] mill, ring rolling mill
轮箍轧制 tyre [tire] rolling
轮毂 (wheel) hub, (wheel) boss, wheel nave
轮毂成型压力机 hub punch press
轮毂滑键 feather in boss
轮毂轴 boss rod
轮迹 cart rut, wheelmark
轮距 (wheel) tread, ga(u)ge, (wheel) track, wheel centre (distance), wheelspan
轮壳 stock
轮廓 outline, line, contour, profile, skeleton, 【压】boundary (轧槽孔型的)
轮廓不清像 diffuse image
轮廓尺寸 overall dimension (o.a.d.), overall size, external measurement
轮廓尺寸图 dimensions chart
轮廓描绘 contouring
轮廓探测器 contour probe
轮廓图 outline (drawing, sketch), profilogram
轮廓显微术 profile microscopy
轮廓线 contour line, sweep
轮廓造型 【铸】contour moulding
轮廓轧机 contour rolling mill
轮廓轧制 contour rolling
轮流 alternation, rotation
轮碾机 muller (mixer), pan (grinding) mill, wheel mill, chaser ◇ 干盘~ dry pan (mill), 湿式~ wet pan, 双轴式~*
轮碾机工[碾轮] 【耐】runner of edge mill
轮碾盘 muller pan
轮盘齿轮 gear wheel
轮圈 rim, ring, rim section (轧材), disc (筐篮式钢丝绳机的) ◇ 汽车~*, 组合~ built-up rim
轮式打印机 flying printer
轮式电铲 BWE (bucket wheel excavator)
轮式混合机 reel-type blender, belt shredder
轮式皮带混合机 reel-type blender ◇ 皮凯型~*
轮式双晶 cyclical twin
轮式挖泥机 wheel dredger
轮胎 tyre, tire ◇ 低压~ balloon tyre, 实心~ band tyre
轮胎钢丝 tyre [bead] wire
轮胎钢丝帘布[细钢丝绳] steel cord for tyre
轮胎钢丝绳 tyre cord wire
轮胎式拖拉铲土机 tyred tractor shovel
轮体 wheel body
轮心 wheel center [body]
轮形探测装置(超声波探伤用) wheel search unit
轮窑 annular kiln ◇ 室式~ annular chamber kiln
轮叶 (wheel) blade
轮叶泵 wing pump
轮用含铅黄铜(30Zn,<2Pb,余量 Cu) wheel brass
轮缘 (wheel) flange, rim, tyre, tire ◇ 组合~ built-up rim
轮缘表面淬火装置 rim-chilling machine
轮轴 (wheel) axle, wheel shaft
轮爪 grouser
轮状的 annular
轮座 wheel seat
伦丁热镀铝法(钢丝的) lundin process
伦敦超导体 London superconductor

伦敦金属[五金]交易所 London Metal Exchange (LME)
伦敦理论 London theory
伦纳弗尔特电弧炉 Rennerfelt furnace
伦琴当量 roentgen-equivalent
伦琴(辐射,射线)计 radiation [roentgen] meter, roentgenometer
伦琴射线 (同"X射线")
伦琴/时·米 roentgen per hour at one meter (rhm)
论点 argument, claim, contention, statement
论据 argument, evidence, datum
论述 discussion, treatment
论文 thesis, article, paper ◇ 博士～ doctoral thesis, 专题～ disquisition
论文集 proceedings (procs), symposium, memoirs
论证 reasoning, argument, demonstration
螺钉 screw (scr.), nut bolt ◇ 定位～*, 堵头[堵塞]～ plug screw, 滚花～ knurled screw, 扣紧～ tightening-up screw, 木～ wood [grub] screw, 内六角～*, 平头～*, 调节～*, 调整～*, 微调[精调]～ fine setting screw, 无头～ headless [grub] screw, 止动～*, 装配[连接]～ fitting screw
螺钉钢 screw steel
螺钉黄铜(58Cu,40Zn,2Pb) screw(ing) brass
螺钉青铜 screw bronze ◇ 低锡～*
螺钉头 screw head
螺钉型钢(制作紧固件) bolt stock
螺杆 screw (rod, arbor, stem), spiral, worm ◇ 进给～ feed screw, 拉紧～ turnbuckle device, 升降～ elevating screw, 制止～ check bolt
螺杆泵 screw pump
螺杆挤压机 screw extruder
螺杆压缩机 screw [helical-lobe] compressor
螺杆制动器[螺杆闸] screw brake

螺管线圈 solenoid (coil) ◇ 消弧～ arc blow compensator
螺管型加热器 steam coil heater
螺环 threaded ring, volution
螺距 (screw-)pitch, (flight) lead
螺距公差 lead tolerance
螺距规 (screw) pitch gauge
螺距量规 lead gage
螺距误差 pitch error
螺距圆 pitch circle (PC)
螺口连接器 threaded adapter
螺硫银矿 acanthite
螺母[帽] (screw, cover, acorn) nut, screw cap ◇ 槽～ castellated nut, 蝶形[翼形]～*, 对开[拼合]～ clasp [split] nut, 盖[套筒]～*, 花[冠形]～ horned nut, 接头～ tube union, 精制～ finished nut, 联管[管接]～*, 锁紧[防松]～*, 凸缘～ flanged nut, 压下～ screw box, 眼(圈)[吊环]～ eye nut, 有槽～ slotted nut, 圆～ circular nut
螺母[帽]扳手 wrench
螺母保险[锁紧] nut lock
螺母冲床 nut press
螺栓 bolt ◇ U形～ U-bolts, 半精制～ half-bright bolt, 半圆头～ cup-head bolt, 粗制～*, 大～ king bolt, 带销～ cotter bolt, 地脚～*, 丁字头～ T-head bolt, 顶头～*, 端缝～ fox bolt, 方头～ coach bolt, 防松～*, 钩头～ hook bolt, 固定～*, 环首[吊环,有眼]～ ring bolt, eyebolt, 活节～*, 基础～ rag bolt, 棘～*, 夹紧[止动,支撑]～*, 尖头～ nibbed bolt, 接合[联结(器)]～ coupling bolt, 紧固～*, 开尾～ fox bolt, 拉紧～*, 连接～*, 六角～*, 埋头～*, 锚定～*, 摩擦紧固～ friction bolt, 配合～ dowel [template] bolt, 膨胀拉杆～ expansion staybolt, 伸缩～ expansion bolt, 双头～ (threaded) stud, 调位～ positioning bolt, 旋转～ sling [shackle] bolt, 圆头～*, 锥形～*, 直通～ through bolt, 止(推)～

bolt with stop
螺栓顶锻[作头] stud driving
螺栓顶锻[锻造]机 bolt header
螺栓锻模 bolt die
螺栓钢 bolt(ing) steel
螺栓钢条[丝] bolt wire
螺栓固定导辊 bolted on guide roll
螺栓固定阳极 bolt on anode
螺栓滚[车]丝机 bolt screwing machine
螺栓连接[接合] bolted joint, bolting
螺栓头 bolt head
螺栓压力机 【压】bolt press
螺丝 screw ◇ 导向～ guide screw, 尖端～ pointed screw, 紧线～ turnbuckle srew, 门栓大～(焦炉的) latch screw, 压下～*, 制～用棒材 screw stock
螺丝扳手 screw key, monkey spanner
螺丝板牙 tapping [screw] die
螺丝刀[起子] screw driver, turnscrew
螺丝攻 【机】(screw) tap
螺丝攻扳手 tap wrench
螺丝黄铜 screwing brass
螺丝接口 screwed joint
螺丝口 threaded socket
螺丝口灯头 screw chuck
螺丝模钢 tap steel
螺丝用棒材 screw stock
螺丝用钢丝 screw wire
螺丝轴 screw shaft
螺条搅拌器 ribbon stirrer
螺尾锥销 conical bolt
螺纹 thread ◇ 奥米伽[Ω]～ Omega thread, 巴特雷斯型～*, 车～*, 母端开始～*, 无～栓 blank bolt
螺纹半角 half-angle of thread
螺纹插座 threaded socket
螺纹[丝]车床 threading unit, threader, thread-cutting lathe
螺纹顶部 【机】crest
螺纹钢(筋) reinforced [ribbed, deformed] bar, rebar, twisted steel ◇ 超高强度凹～*, 冷轧～*

螺纹高度 thread height
螺纹高度量规 thread-height gauge
螺纹管 screw(ed) [threaded] tube ◇ 单头～*
螺纹管接头 thread coupling
螺纹滚轧 roll threading
螺纹接管 screw union
螺纹冷滚轧机 (同"冷滚螺纹机")
螺纹连接塞棒 【钢】rotolok stopper
螺纹(量)规 screw (thread) gauge, thread gauge
螺纹轮廓显微镜 thread-contour microscope
螺纹千分尺 screw thread micrometer
螺纹软管接头 threaded hose connection
螺纹塞规 screw plug gauge
螺纹梳刀 chaser
螺纹轧机 【压】spiral mill
螺纹轧制 thread rolling
螺纹状腐蚀 thread-line corrosion
螺线 spiral, helical, thread
螺线齿 helical tooth
螺线管 solenoid (coil), screw tube, actuator ◇ 消弧～ arc blow compensator
螺线管场 solenoidal field
螺线管阀 solenoid valve
螺线位错源 spiral source of dislocations
螺线钨丝 tungsten helix, spiral tungsten cable
螺线形铜管感应圈(高频炉的) helical coil of copper tubing
螺型位错 【理】helical [screw (-type), Burgers] dislocation ◇ 不规则～*, 阶梯状～*, 平行～*
螺型位错交叉滑移 cross slipping of screw dislocation
螺型位错交割作用范围 field of intersecting screw dislocations
螺型位错十字格 (crossed) grid of screw dislocations
螺型位错阵列 screw dislocation array
螺旋 screw, spiral, coiling ◇ 叠置加料～

overlapping spiral, 对动～union screw, 立式～槽道, 流动性～fluidity spiral
螺旋泵 screw [spiral, helicoidal] pump
螺旋拨料机 screw-type kick-off, kick-out screws
螺旋成形件 spiral-shaped objects
螺旋齿轮 helical [spiral] gear
螺旋齿条 screw rack
螺旋触点 screw contact
螺旋传动装置 screw gearing
螺旋磁性 【理】helimagnetism
螺旋电极 spiral electrode
螺旋定位 screw orientation
螺旋法则 corkscrew rule
螺旋分级机 spiral [screw-type] classifier
螺旋分离器 spiral separator ◇ 振动式～*
螺旋分选机 spiral-coil separator, spiral picker
螺旋风口 【铁】double angle tuyere
螺旋杆 screw rod, endless screw
螺旋管 helical [helicoidal] tube, spiral
螺旋管透镜 solenoidal lens
螺旋管型加热器 steam coil heater
螺旋滚压成形(法) 【压】thread rolling
螺旋焊 spiral welding
螺旋焊管 spirally-welded tube, spiral welded pipe, helical weld pipe
螺旋焊管材 helical weld tubing
螺旋焊管机 spiral pipe welding machine, spiral weld-pipe mill
螺旋焊管机组 spiral weld-pipe line ◇ 高频－埋弧双功能～*
螺旋焊接钢管 spiral steel pipe
螺旋环 spiral [helical] collar
螺旋还原反应器 reduction screw
螺旋混合机[器] ribbon [typhoon] mixer ◇ 双轴～ double shaft mixer, 两次～ double mixing screw
螺旋混合装置 screw mixer device
螺旋挤泥机 screw extruder, 【耐】auger
螺旋挤泥条机 auger machine

螺旋挤压 helical extrusion
螺旋挤压机 screw extruder, screw extrusion press
螺旋给料[加料, 进料, 给矿]机 screw feeder, feed screw ◇ 计量～ metering screw feeder, 可调速～*, 气密式～ gastight screw feeder
螺旋给料器 scroll feed, screw feeder
螺旋夹钳 screw clamp
螺旋加料机械 screw feed mechanism
螺旋桨 (screw) propeller
螺旋桨搅拌机 helical blade stirrer
螺旋桨搅拌器 propeller-agitator, propeller-type agitator
螺旋桨青铜 propeller bronze
螺旋桨式泵 feathering pump
螺旋桨式流量计 propeller-flowmeter
螺旋桨式扇风[送风]机 propeller(-type) fan
螺旋桨叶式搅拌运输机 compulsory mixer
螺旋桨轴 propeller shaft
螺旋搅拌机[器] spiral stirrer agitator, 【团】pugmill type mixer ◇ 铅液～*, 双轴～*
螺旋搅拌进料(器) screw-agitator feed ◇ 卧式～还原*
螺旋搅动床反应器 screw-agitated bed reactor
螺旋角 【压】spiral angle
螺旋进料机料斗 screw feed hopper
螺旋(进料)氢氟化反应器 hydrofluorination screw (reactor)
螺旋卷管型隔膜(反渗透装置的) 【环】spiral-wound membrane
螺旋卡盘 screw chuck
螺旋冷却机 cooling screw
螺旋联接管 screw union
螺旋联接器 screw coupling
螺旋链系 screw chain
螺旋面 spiral surface, helical, helicoid
螺旋排料环 spiral discharge ring

螺旋排绕	【压】spiral [helical] cast
螺旋破裂面法	spiral method
螺旋起重器[千斤顶]	lifting screw, jackscrew, screw jack
螺旋取向	screw orientation
螺旋取样器	worm tube sampler
螺旋圈刺钢丝	concertina barbed wire
螺旋伞齿轮	spiral bevel gear
螺旋生长(晶体的)	spiral growth
螺旋生长花样	spiral growth pattern
螺旋生长阶	spiral growth steps
螺旋升液混合沉降器	screw lift mixer-settler
螺旋式拌和机	crutcher
螺旋式擦拭器	screw wiper
螺旋式混合器	helical [spiral] mixer
螺旋式挤芯机	【铸】sausage machine
螺旋式加热体	spiral heater
螺旋式搅拌叶轮	screw impeller
螺旋式冷床	screw-type cooling bed [table]
螺旋式摩擦压力机	friction screw press
螺旋式砌砖	spiral bricking
螺旋式扫描微探头	scanning auger microprobe (SAM)
螺旋室	volute (chamber)
螺旋试验	spin test ◇ 流动性～ fluidity spiral
螺旋输送机	conveyer worm, screw [auger, spiral, helical, helicoid, worm] conveyor, feed auger ◇ 管式～ tubular screw conveyer, 两次混合～ double mixing screw, 水冷式～", 脱水～"
螺旋输送器	auger conveyor, fusee
螺旋酸洗	spiral pickling
螺旋弹簧	helical [spiral] spring
螺旋弹簧钢	spiral spring steel
螺旋提升机	screw elevator
螺旋体	helicoid
螺旋体纲	Spirochaetae
螺旋调节	screw adjustment
螺旋头	spiral head
螺旋推进给料	scroll feed
螺旋推进式离心机	scroll centrifuge
螺旋推进式泥炮	【铁】spiral type tap-hole gun
螺旋钨丝	(同"螺线钨丝")
螺旋线	helical (line), helix, cylindrical spiral
螺旋线圈	spiral [helical] coil
螺旋型边界	screw boundary
螺旋型磁结构	helical magnetic structure
螺旋型斜槽	spiral chute
螺旋形	helical, spiral, volution ◇ 将钢丝绳股制成～ forming, 转动～加热器 rotating spiral heater
螺旋形导线	fish line conductor
螺旋形锭料(区域熔炼的)	spiral charge
螺旋形断裂	spiral fracture
螺旋形件	screw-shaped [spiral-shaped] objects
螺旋(形)流槽	spiral launder
螺旋形流动性试验	spiral test
螺旋形流动性试样铸型	cury fluidity mould
螺旋形楼梯	【建】geometric stairs
螺旋形盛料器	spiral-form container, helical form container
螺旋形物	helix
螺旋选矿机	spiral-coil separator, spiral concentrator
螺旋压力机	screw(down) [spindle, fly] press ◇ 高能离合器式～ high energy clutch screw press, 楔形进料～ screw wedge press
螺旋叶片型罗茨鼓风机	spiral-lobe-type Roots blower
螺旋运输机	(同"螺旋输送机")
螺旋运输机槽	screw conveyer trough
螺旋轧制	screw rolling ◇ 横向～"
螺旋振动运输机	spiral vibrating conveyer
螺旋轴(线)	screw axis [shaft, spindle]
螺旋装置	screw
螺旋状(的)	helical, helicoid

螺旋状钢丝绳　spiral wire rope
螺旋状内冷铁　chill coils
螺旋钻　twist drill, auger
螺旋钻(挖土)法　【建】corkscrew auger method
螺柱　(threaded) stud, pillar bolt
螺柱电阻[接触]焊　resistance stud welding
螺柱焊(接)　stud weld(ing) (SW) ◇电弧～arc stud welding, 气体保护～*
螺柱焊接工具　stud welding tool
螺柱接触焊枪　resistance stud welding gun
螺柱自动电弧焊装　cyc-arc welding
螺桩　【机】brad, dowel
螺状晶体　hopper crystal
螺状硫银矿　acanthite
罗宾斯-麦西特矿石混匀系统　【铁】Robbins-Messiter system
罗伯特转炉　【钢】Robert converter
罗伯逊法试验(检验钢材脆性的)　Robertson test
罗茨高真空泵　Roots high vacuum pump
罗茨鼓风机　Roots blower ◇螺旋叶片型～*
罗茨排气机　Roots type gas exhauster
罗顿-洛伦兹铜合金显微组织腐蚀法　Rawdon and Lorentz method [technique]
罗恩低频炉　Rohn furnace
罗恩式多辊轧机(极薄带材的)　Rohn mill
罗海斯硅钢薄板(含2Si)　Lohys
罗加指数　【焦】Roga index
罗杰斯特种发动机合金(10或20Sn, 12.5或15Sb, 63.5或75Pb)　Rogers special engine alloy
罗坎含砷铜板(含0.5%As)　Rocan copper
罗可普高效连铸技术　ROKOP fastcast system
罗克莱特冷轧管机　rockright mill
罗克莱特往复摆动式轧管法　Rockrit process
罗克莱特轧机　rockright mill
罗克内尔式大口径管材壁厚减薄用轧机　Roechner tube rolling mill
罗兰凹光栅　Rowland concave grating
罗勒空气淘析器　Roller air analyzer
罗马尼姆铝基合金(1.7Ni, 0.25Cu, 0.17W, 0.25Sb, 0.15Sn, 余量Al)　Romanium
罗马明矾　Roman alum
罗马铅锡合金[罗马白](30Pb, 70Sn)　Roma pewter
罗曼含锡(六O)黄铜(60Cu, <1Sn, 余量Zn)　Roman brass
罗曼铝合金　romanium
罗曼青铜(1: 58—60Cu, 0—2Mn, 1Fe, 1.1Al, 余量Sn; 2: 90Cu, 10Sn)　Roman bronze
罗曼透明石英管氯化炉　Roman Candle (chlorination) furnace
罗梅塔尔高导磁率铁镍合金(36—45Ni, 2—5Cr, 2—3Si, 余量Fe)　Rhometal
罗尼阿黄铜　Ronia brass
罗盘(仪)　(box) compass
罗森海因-奥伯霍费尔浸蚀液(钢铁材料的)　【金】Rosenhain-Oberhoffer reagent
罗森海因浸蚀剂(钢铁浸蚀剂)　Rosenhain's etchant
罗森海因炉　Rosenhain [gradient] furnace
罗斯过滤器　Ross filter
罗斯科效应(金属表面膜层的)　Roscoe effect
罗斯林耐热复合板(不锈钢-铜-不锈钢复合板)　Rosslyn metal
罗斯特奈特不锈钢板炉衬法　Rostenit lining process
罗斯易熔[软焊料]合金(50Bi, 22Sn, 28Pb)　Rose's alloy [metal]
罗塔尼乌姆金铑合金(10—40Rh, 余量Au)　Rhotanium
罗塔斯铅基[铅锑锡]轴承合金(15Sb, 10Sn, 余量Pb)　Lotus metal

罗托弗特高速旋转氧气顶吹转炉法 【钢】Rotovert process
罗西冷却板 【连铸】Rossi cooling plate
罗西振动连铸法 Rossi process
罗谢尔盐 (同"四水合酒石酸钾钠")
罗泽茵镍基合金(40Ni,30Al,20Sn,10Ag) Rosein (metal)
逻辑 logic ◇ 阵列～array logic
逻辑比较 logic(al) comparison
逻辑部件[单元] logic(al) unit
逻辑操作 logic(al) operation
逻辑常数 logical constant
逻辑乘 logic(al) multiply, intersection
逻辑乘积 logic product
逻辑磁心 logic core
逻辑代数 Boolean [logic] algebra
逻辑单元 logic(al) unit [block]
逻辑电路 logic(al) circuit ◇ 互补晶体管～*,三态～tri-state logic (TSL)
逻辑电平 logic level
逻辑分析 【计】Logic analysis
逻辑和 logic(al) sum, disjunction
逻辑记录 logic record
逻辑加 logic(al) add
逻辑加法 disjunction, logical addition
逻辑控制 logic control
逻辑控制时序计算机 logic-controlled sequential computer
逻辑块 logic block
逻辑连接 logical connective [link]
逻辑流程图 logic chart, logical flow chart
逻辑模拟 logic(al) simulation
逻辑判定 logic decision
逻辑设计 logic(al) design
逻辑算符[算子] logic(al) operator
逻辑图 logic(al) diagram [chart]
逻辑型数据 logical data
逻辑移位 logic(al) shift
逻辑元件 logic(al) element
逻辑运算 logic(al) operation [calculus]
逻辑阵列 logic array ◇ 可编程序～*
逻辑指令 logic instruction
逻辑装置 logic(al) device [unit]
逻辑组织程序 logic(al) organisation program
锣用铜锡合金(80Cu,20Sn) gong metal
裸导线 【冶】bare conductor [wire]
裸电极 【冶】bare electrode
裸焊条 (同"光焊条")
裸金属极电弧焊(接) bare metal-arc welding (BMAW)
裸晶 bare crystal
裸露段[部分] bare spot
裸露金属液[裸体熔融金属] naked molten metal
裸镍堆焊丝 nickel bare welding filler metal
裸区 bare spot
裸铜线 bare copper wire
裸线电极 bare wire electrode
裸线端 bare terminal end
裸原子 stripped atom
裸轧 bare rolling
落棒(式)密封装置 【团】drop-bar type seal
落差 drop (height), (fall) head, height of drop
落锤 drop hammer [breaker, weight], falling weight, lift hammer,【冶】vertical drop machine, falling tup machine (用于碎铁),【钢】drop ball (破碎废金属用),【压】block hammer
落锤冲击试验 drop test ◇ 佩利尼～*
落锤冲压法 【压】drop stamping method
落锤冲压设备 【压】drop stamping plant
落锤锤头 hammer striking head
落锤打桩机 drop hammer pile driver
落锤锻模 drop hammer die, drop-forging die
落锤锻造 drop forging [stamping]
落锤锻造[模锻]车间 drop shop
落锤锻造成形 drop hammer forming
落锤锻造机 falling tup machine
落锤破碎的废钢铁 drop-broken scrap

落锤试验　falling (weight) test (车轮、轮箍的),【金】drop test,【铸】drop weight test (球墨铸铁缺口延性检验法)

落锤试验机　drop hammer tester, drop-testing machine

落锤撕裂(破坏)试验　drop-weighted tear test (DWTT)

落地　landing

落地浓度　【环】ground concentration

落地式加料机　mobile ground charger

落地式支架[接收机]　console

落地式装料机　floor [ground-type, rigid-type] charging machine

落后指标　lagging indicators

落料冲床　blanking machine

落料管(装料车的)　【焦】telescope

落料压力机　【压】blanking press

落料状况　falling condition (of charge)

落球法　falling ball [sphere] method

落球回跳硬度　dynamic ball indentation hardness

落砂　crush (缺陷),【铸】knock-out, ram-away, ram-off, sand strip, shake-out ◇ 冲出式~装置 kicker-type knock-out, 改善~性能添加剂 breakdown additive, 震动打箱~法(熔模铸造的)　knock-out

落砂格栅　shake-out grid

落砂工　knocker-out

落砂后保留在铸件上的型砂　loose sand

落砂机　shake-out table

落砂架　knock-out grid

落砂栅格　knock-out grating

落水管　downcomer pipe, leader

落下　drop-out, falling away, slanting

落下冲击　falling impact

落下次数　【团】drop number, number of drops

落下高度(锤头的)　drop height

落下条件　falling condition

落下溜槽　drop chute

落下强度　【团】shatter index (S.I.), drop number, drop [shatter] strength, resistance to dropping [shatter], dropping resistance ◇ 湿[生]球团~ green impact strength

落下试验　【团】drop test

落下速度　falling velocity

落下速率　falling rate

落下指数　【团】shatter index (S.I.)

落下状况　falling condition

落芯　【铸】core knock-out

落芯机　core knock-out machine, core breaker

落重系数　drop-weight factor

洛－埃克斯低膨胀(系数)高硅铝合金 (12Si, 2.5Ni, 1Mg, 1Cu, 0.75Fe, 0.5Mn,余量 Al)　Lo-Ex

洛德式轧机　Lord mill

洛戈铅字合金　Logotype

洛卡洛伊蜂窝夹层板合金　Lockalloy

洛卡洛伊蜂窝夹层板铍铝合金(62Be, 38Al)　beryllium Lockalloy

洛伦兹变换定律　Lorentz transformation laws

洛伦兹磁场　Lorentz magnetic field

洛伦兹函数　Lorentz function

洛伦兹力　【理】Lorentz's force

洛伦兹偏振因数　Lorentz-polarization factor

洛伦兹收缩　Lorentz contraction

洛伦兹显微镜法　Lorentz microscopic method

洛伦兹因数　Lorentz factor

洛莫位错反应　Lomer's dislocation reaction

洛姆铜镍电阻合金(7—7.5Ni,余量 Cu)　Lohm

洛奇－科垂尔煤气净化系统　Lodge-Cottrell system

洛氏 A 标度硬度　A-scale of Rockwell hardness (HRA)

洛氏 B 标度硬度　B-scale of Rockwell hardness (HRB), Rockwell hardness B (Rb)

洛氏 C 标度硬度　Rockwell hardness C scale (RHC, R.H.C.), C-scale of Rockwell hardness (HRC), Rockwell C (Rc)
洛氏 F 标度硬度　Rockwell F hardness (HRF)
洛氏表面硬度　Rockwell superficial hardness
洛氏表面硬度计　superficial Rockwell hardness tester
洛氏表面硬度试验　Rockwell superficial hardness test, superficial Rockwell hardness test
洛氏表面硬度值　Rockwell superficial hardness number
洛氏硬度　Rockwell hardness (HR), cone hardness
洛氏硬度 A 标度　Rockwell A scale
洛氏硬度 B 标度　Rockwell B hardness
洛氏硬度 B 标度试验计　Rockwell B hardness tester
洛氏硬度 C 标度　Rockwell C hardness, Rockwell hardness C scale
洛氏硬度标度　Rockwell hardness scale
洛氏硬度计　Rockwell apparatus, Rockwell (hardness) tester, Rockwell hardness meter
洛氏硬度试验　Rockwell (hardness) test, cone penetration [indentation, thrust] test ◇ 15—30—45N 载荷级~机*
洛氏硬度试验计[硬度机]　Rockwell machine ◇ A-B-C 标度~*
洛氏硬度值　Rockwell hardness number (R.H.N., Rhn), Rockwell (hardness) figure [number]
洛氏圆锥压头硬度　cone hardness
洛维奈特碱性耐火制品　【耐】lovinit
络分子化合物　complex molecular compound
络合滴定(法)　complexmetry, complexometry, complexometric titration
络合钒酸盐　complex vanadate ◇ 溶于碳酸盐的~carbonate-soluble complex vanadate
络合反应剂　complex binding reactant
络合剂　complexing agent, complexant
络合硫酸盐　complex sulphate
络合氯化物　complex chloride
络合色谱法　complexation chromalography
络合碳酸盐　complex carbonate
络合物　complex ◇ 离子型~萃取, 螯型~萃取 chelate extraction
络合(物形成)剂　complexing agent
络合(性)溶剂　complexing solvent
络合冶金学　complex metallurgy
络合指示剂　complex indicator
络合作用　complexation
络离子　complex ion
络镁盐　phyllin
络酸　complex acid
络盐　complex salt
络阳离子　complex cation, cationic complex
络阴离子　complex anion, anionic complex ◇ 可吸附的~*

M m

麻点 【冶】pit(ting), ripple mark(ing)s(轻合金轧材的矫直缺陷),【钢】pinpling(缺陷),【金】pockmark(不锈钢退火缺陷) ◇ 戴诺迪克防～法【压】Dianodic process, 形成～ mottling, 氧化～【压】scale mark
麻点腐蚀 pitting corrosion
麻钢混捻钢丝绳 combi-rope
麻花钻 twist drill
麻口化 【铸】mottling
麻口铁 mottled iron
麻口细晶粒合金铸铁轧辊 grain [graphitic-type] roll
麻口铸铁 mottled cast iron ◇ 加镍～轧辊*,双层～轧辊 double-pour grain roll
麻口组织 【铁】mottled structure
麻粒玻璃 corning glass
麻面 spongy surface, pitted surface(管材的),【铸】pit(ted) skin(缺陷)
麻面触点 pitted contact
麻面防止剂 (同"点蚀防止剂")
麻省理工学院 (即"马萨诸塞州理工学院")
麻芯钢丝绳 hemp core wire rope
麻芯 hemp core
麻芯真空浸油 vacuum oil penetration for hemp core
麻芯真空浸油器 vacuum oil penetrator for hemp core
麻絮 oakum ◇ 堵缝～【建】caulker's oakum
玛琋脂接缝 mastic joint
玛聂尔－布莱登式千斤顶 Magnel-Blaton jack
玛瑙 agate
玛瑙研体 agate mortar
码尺 yardstick
码头 dock, pier, wharf ◇ 板桩挡土墙～【建】camp sheathing, 顺岸～(平行于岸线) quay
码头房屋 terminal building
码头轨道 【运】apron track
码头护木 pier fender
码头起重机 wharf crane
码砖 【耐】setting
码砖方法 way of setting
码砖高度 setting height
码砖工 setter
码砖机 setting machine, setter
码砖面 setting space
马鞍黄铜 saddlery brass
马鞍形填料 saddle packing ◇ 伯尔～ Berl saddles
马布尔浸蚀剂(渗氮钢及不锈钢浸蚀用) Marble's reagent, Marble corrosive liquid
马达拉斯直接还原法 【铁】Madaras process
马德隆常数 Madelung constant
马登斯表面划痕硬度 Martens (surface scratching) hardness
马登斯表面划痕硬度试验 Martens' test
马登斯表面划痕硬度值 Martens hardness number
马登斯体 (同"马氏体")
马蒂内尔结构钢(0.24C, 0.75Mn, 0.1Si) Martinel steel
马蒂森定则 【理】Mattiessen's rule
马丁炼钢法 Martin process
马丁炉 Martin furnace
马丁诺镍铜锌电阻合金 Martino alloy
马丁(直)径 Martin diameter
马顿斯镜 Martens' mirror
马尔可夫链 Markov chain
马尔可夫算法 【计】Markov algorithms
马尔泰间歇[十字轮]机构 Maltese cross
马弗焙烧炉 【冶】muffle roaster
马弗炉 muffle(type)furnace,(furnace) muffle, muffle(kiln), retort furnace, blind roaster ◇ 多膛式～*, 刚玉[氧化铝]管～*, 管式～ tubular retort fur-

nace,石英~膛 quartz muffle,移动式~*,在~内冷却(的) cooled in muffle (Cm)

马弗炉壁　muffle wall
马弗(炉)材料　muffle material
马弗罩　muffle, ashcan cover
马格多洛碱性耐火制品　【耐】Magdolo
马格多尼特碱性耐火制品　【耐】Magdonit
马格马克斯熔铸制品　【耐】Magmalox
马格纳杜尔钡铁氧体永磁材料　Magnadur
马格纳格罗磁性[磁力探伤用]粉末　Magnaglo
马格纳莱特铝基活塞合金(2—3Cu, 1.5Mg, 1.5Ni,余量 Al)　Magnalite
马格纳利乌姆铝镁铸造合金(1.75Cu, 1.75—10Mg,余量 Al)　Magnalium
马格纳罗(着色)荧光探伤法　Magnalo process
马格纳特斯特涡流法圆柱形零件检查仪　【机】Magnatest
马格奈西尔变压器钢(90Fe, 3Si)　Magnesil
马格尼特碱性耐火制品　【耐】Magnit
马格努米纽乌姆镁铝合金　Magnuminium (alloy) (Magnuminium 155:3.5—5Al, 1Zn, 0.15 - 0.4Mn, 0.05Si, 0.15Cu, 0.05Fe, 0.01Ni,余量 Mg)
马格诺克斯核燃料包覆用镁合金　Magnox (alloy)
马格诺利亚铅基轴承合金(15Sb, 5Sn,余量 Pb)　Magnolia (metal)
马格诺镍锰电阻合金(5Mn,余量 Ni)　Magno
马格诺普拉斯特耐火混凝土　Magnoplast
马赫镁铝合金(5Mg,余量 Al)　Mach's metal
马赫数　【理】Mach number
马赫特含铁黄铜(60Cu, 38—38.5Zn, 1.5—1.8Fe)　Macht's metal
马喀铝镁合金　magaluma
马凯特导电塑料　Markite

马克鲁尔式热风炉(三通式)　Meclure type hot stove
马克赛特含钴 18 - 4 - 1 型高速钢　maxite
马克西尔赖含铜奥氏体不锈钢(0.2—0.5Cu)　Maxilvry
马口铁　(同"镀锡薄钢板")
马口铁器皿　tinware
马莱特高锌黄铜(25.4Cu, 74.6Zn)　Mallet alloy
马来树胶(绝缘材料)　gutta-percha
马勒铝硅活塞合金(83—85Al, 11—13Si, 1Cu, 1.2Mg, 1Ni, 0.5Fe, 0.08Mn)　Mahle alloy
马里纳熔渣导电半连续硅热还原法炼镁(法国)　Magnetherm process
马利抗氧化合金(35Ni, 25 黄铜, 20Sn, 10Fe, 10Zn)　Marlie's alloy
马林诺钢丝镀锌法　Marino process
马硫铜银矿　mckinstryite
马洛里1000钨铜镍粉末烧结合金　Mallory 1000
马洛里100铜铍钴硅电导合金　Mallory 100
马洛里3铬铜电导合金　Mallory 3
马洛里73铍铜电导合金(2Be, 0.1Co,余量 Cu)　Mallory 73
马洛里高强度无锡青铜　Mallory metal (Mallory 100; 2.6Co, 0.4Be,余量 Cu)
马洛里 - 沙顿钛铝锆合金(8Al, 8Zr, 1Ta + Nb,余量 Ti)　Mallory-sharton alloy
马洛里铜基合金系　Mallory alloys
马洛特铋锡铅易熔合金(34Sn, 40Bi, 20Pb;熔点 93℃)　Malott metal
马洛伊迪昂铜镍锌耐蚀合金(60Cu, 22.8Ni, 13.5Zn,余量 Fe)　Malloydium
马尼克铜锰镍合金(15—20Mn, 9—21Ni,余量 Cu)　Manic
马尼拉假金(2Pb, 85Cu, 12Zn)　Manila gold
马尼拉绳　Manil(l)a rope
马普洛登失蜡铸齿法　【铸】Maprodent

马齐克防蚀锌黑膜浸镀法　Mazic zinc black method
马琴外燃式热风炉　M-P hot stove
马萨诸塞州[麻省]理工学院　Massachusetts Institute of Technology (M.I.T.)
马塞尼兹炉外脱硫法　【铁】Massenez process
马瑟休斯铅钙[铅锶]轴承合金(1Ca 或 Sr,余量 Pb)　Mathesius metal
马森内尔阳极清洗法(钢铁材料电镀前的)　Madsenell process
马什试砷法　Marsh test
马氏钢球硬度试验　Matsumura indentation hardness test
马氏体　【金】martensite ◇ α~*,ε~*,板条(状)~ lath(of) martensite,变温[非等温]~*,层状~ lamellar martensite,低 Ms 点铁镍碳~*,高碳~ high carbon martensite,固态~ solid state martensite,含氢~ hydrogen martensite,含碳合金~*,回火[黑]~*,块状~ massive martensite,孪晶(型)~ twin(ned) martensite,片状~ plate-type martensite,细~ hardenite,针状~*
马氏体板条　lath of martensite
马氏体变形加工点　Md (Martensite deformation) point
马氏体不锈钢　martensitic stainless steel
马氏体常温形变处理(主要用于线材)　mar-straining
马氏体淬火　martensite quench(ing)
马氏体等温淬火　martempering
马氏体等温淬火用油　martemp oil
马氏体堆焊面层　marfacing
马氏体分解　martensite decomposition, breakdown of martensite
马氏体分解范围[(温度)区]　martensite decomposition range
马氏体钢　martensitic [martensite] steel ◇ 含硼~*,完全淬火成~的最大硬度*
马氏体铬不锈钢　martensitic chromium stainless steel
马氏体构造　martensite formation
马氏体回火　martensite [martensitic] tempering
马氏体基体　martensitic matrix
马氏体晶格　martensite lattice
马氏体类碳钢　carbon martensite steel
马氏体冷作处理　martensite cold working
马氏体片　martensite plate ◇ 部分孪晶化~*
马氏体区　martensite range [area]
马氏体时效(处理)　martensite [martensitic] ageing, maraging
马氏体时效处理　martensite ageing treatment, maraging treatment
马氏体时效钢　maraging steel ◇ 粉末冶金~ PM maraging steel, 12—2 镍锰~*
马氏体时效型不锈钢　maraging stainless steel
马氏体铁　martensitic iron
马氏体显微相　martensite microphase ◇ 残留~*
马氏体显微组织　martensite microstructure
马氏体形变热处理　Marworking, marforming, marstressing
马氏体形成　martensite formation
马氏体形成温度　martensite temperature, Ms temperature
马氏体形态(学)　morphology of martensite
马氏体循环转变　cyclic martensite transformation
马氏体应力　marstressing
马氏体应力淬火　marstressing
马氏体硬度　martensite hardness
马氏体硬[强]化　martensitic hardening
马氏体中高温回火组织　troosto-sorbite
马氏体铸铁　martensitic cast iron
马氏体转变[相变]　martensite [marten-

sitic] transformation
马氏体转变区　martensite range, martensitic range
马氏体转变开始温度(Ms 点)　martensite starting point
马氏体转变完成点(M_f 点)　martensite finishing point
马氏体状态　martensitic state [condition]
马氏体组织　martensite structure
马坦普整磁用铁镍合金　Mutemp
马特里克斯超高强度钢　matrix steel
马提生定则　Mathiessen's rule
马蹄夹子　mould clamp
马蹄式混合机　horseshoe (type) mixer
马蹄式搅拌机　horseshoe stirrer
马蹄铁　horseshoe [cramp] iron
马蹄形磁铁　horseshoe magnet, U magnet
马蹄形的　horseshoe-shaped, U-shaped, hairpin
马蹄形底炉　horseshoe furnace
马蹄形浇口　【铸】horseshoe gate
马蹄形曲线　horseshoe curve
马蹄形楔　horseshoe-shaped wedge
马威邦德连续辊涂法(塑料涂层钢板)　Marvibond process
马歇尔钢瓦挂铅青铜法　Masher process
马谢特自淬硬钢(6—9W, 2Mn, 2C)　Mushet's steel
马耶斯提克轻载巴比合金(65 或 75Sn, 12 或 15Sb, 10 或 18Pb, 2 或 3Cu)　Majestic babbitt
马依尔-莫科科直接还原法　【铁】Maier-Mococo process
马扎克锌基压铸合金　Mazak alloy (Mazak 3: 3.9—4.3Al, 0.03Cu, 0.03 - 0.06Mg, 0.075Fe, 0.003Pb, 0.003Cd, 0.001Sn, 余量 Zn)
马兹-博伦斯平炉　Maerz-Boelens furnace, pork pie furnace
埋层　【电】buried layer
埋焊　slugging
埋弧　immersed [submerged, buried] arc
埋弧半自动焊　semi-automatic submerged arc welding
埋弧(电)焊机　submerged arc-welding machine, submerged arc welder
埋弧电炉　smothered-arc furnace
埋弧电石炉　submerged-arc carbide furnace
埋弧焊(接)　submerged-arc welding (SAW), submerged melt welding
埋弧焊焊缝　submerged arc weld
埋弧熔炼[焊接]法　submerged arc process
埋弧式电阻炉　submerged arc type resistance furnace
埋弧渣　【钢】arc-covering slag
埋弧自动焊　automatic submerged-arc welding, submerged arc automatic welding
埋弧自动焊接法(美国专利)　unionmelt process
埋入　embedding, imbedding, immersion
埋入键　inserted key
埋入件　inserted piece
埋入式吹氧炼钢法　submerged injection process (SIP), SIP process
埋入式电极　immersed electrode
埋入性　imbedability, embedability
埋砂冷却　cooling by embedding in sand
埋设板　anchor(ing) plate
埋设电缆　buried cable
埋设管　embedded pipe (EP)
埋设件　immersion [built-in] fittings
埋头　countersunk [flush] head
埋头键　sunk [sink] key
埋头螺钉　countersunk-headed screw, sunk screw
埋头螺母　countersunk nut
埋头螺栓　flush headed bolt
埋头铆钉　countersunk rivet
埋头钻　countersunk (drill)
埋渣焊　metal buried welding
埋置　embedding, imbedding

埋置钢件　embedded steel parts
埋置钢筋　embedded steel
麦麸　wheat middlings
麦麸抛光辊(镀锡薄钢板用)　branners
麦麸抛光机　branning machine
麦基奇尼高强度黄铜(57Cu,1Fe,1Sn,0.5Pb,余量 Zn)　McKechnie's bronze
麦基式炉顶　(同"旋转布料器炉顶")
麦基式炉顶装料系统　【铁】McKee type top charging system
麦吉尔可铸可锻铝青铜(8—9Al,1—2Fe,余量 Cu)　McGill alloy [metal]
麦卡达米特铸造铝合金(12—18Zn,3Cu,余量 Al)　Macadamite
麦克金纳 WC – TiC 粉末制造法　McKenna process
麦克利德[麦氏](压力,真空)计(测量高度稀薄气体压力用)　McLeod gauge [manometer]　◇复式~*,缩短型~*
麦克罗斯碱性耐火制品　【耐】Macros
麦克内特镍铬耐热钢　Mackenite metal
麦克斯韦－玻尔兹曼分布　【理】Maxwell-Boltzmann distribution
麦克斯韦电桥　Maxwell bridge
麦克斯韦尔定律　Maxwell's law
麦克斯韦尔气团　Maxwellian atmosphere
麦克斯韦计　【理】Maxwellmeter
麦克斯韦应力　【理】Maxwell stress
麦肯齐汞合金(28.5Bi,57Pb,14.5Hg)　Mackenzie's amalgam
麦奎德－埃恩奥氏体晶粒尺寸　McQuaid-Ehn grain size
麦奎德－埃恩奥氏体晶粒度测定试验　McQuaid-Ehn test
麦塔林钴铜铝铁合金(35Co,30Cu,25Al,余量 Fe)　Mataline
麦特尔银焊料　Mattlsolda
{Mt}　meltnerium
迈格表　megameter,tramegger
迈斯蒂克铅基轴承合金(含 10Sb)　Mystic metal
迈斯纳效应　【理】Meissner effect

迈亚里 R 低合金耐热钢(<0.12C,0.2—1Cr,0.25—0.75Ni,0.5—0.7Cu,0.5—1Mn)　Mayari R
迈因纳线性损伤定律(计算材料疲劳抗力用)　Miner's rule
脉层　streak
脉冲　pulse,impulse,burst,impact　◇发生 ~impulsing,全选~【电】full read pulse,始发~【理】inceptive impulse,窄~bang,置"0"~【计】reset pulse
脉冲变压器　【电】pulse transformer (PTr.)
脉冲测速仪　impulse tachometer
脉冲成形　【压】impulse forming
脉冲冲程　(im)pulse stroke
脉冲重复频率　pulse repetition [recurrence] frequency,pulse-repetition rate
脉冲重复周期　pulse-repetition period [cycle]
脉冲除尘器　pulse dust collector
脉冲传感器　pulse transmitter,impulser
脉冲串[群,链,序列]　pulse train [packet]
脉冲袋式除尘器[脉冲式袋滤器]　impulse bag filter,pulse jet baghouse
脉冲等离子体　impulse plasma
脉冲点钎焊烙铁　pulse dot soldering iron
脉冲电动机　pulse motor
脉冲电弧焊　pulsed arc welding
脉冲电离室　pulse ionization chamber
脉冲电流　(im)pulse current
脉冲电路　(im)pluse [pulsing] circuit
脉冲电压　(im)pulse [surge] voltage
脉冲电压试验　impulse test
脉冲电子管振荡器　pulse tube oscillator
脉冲发射机　pulse transmitter
脉冲发生器　pulse generator (PIG),pulser,pulse-generating means,impulse [surge] generator,impulser,surge injector (unit)(电弧焊用)　◇控制极~*,时钟[时标]~clock pulse generator
脉冲发生装置　【电】pulse-generating

means [unit]
脉冲发送机[器]　impulse transmitter, impulse sending machine, impulse sender
脉冲法　pulse technique [method]
脉冲反射法(超声波探伤用)　impulse reflection method
脉冲放大器　【电】pulse amplifier
脉冲放电　impulsive discharge
脉冲分离器　pulse separator
脉冲分频计数器　impulse scaler
脉冲峰[巅值]　pulse peak
脉冲辐射　pulse radiation
脉冲幅度调制　pulse amplitude modulation
脉冲负载　impulsive load(ing)
脉冲干扰　(im)pulse interference ◇ 杂乱~【电】hash
脉冲光线　pulsed light
脉冲焊　impulse [pulsation] welding
脉冲焊接机　shot welder
脉冲合金结　pulse alloyed junction
脉冲回波(探伤)法　pulse echo method
脉冲激发　(im)pulse [impact] excitation, impulsing
脉冲激光蒸发　pulsed laser vaporization
脉冲计　【理】impulse meter, pulsimeter
脉冲计数器　(im)pulse [electronic] counter, impulse meter
脉冲记录器　【理】impulse recorder
脉冲继电器　(im)pulse relay
脉冲间隔　interpulse interval
脉冲间隔时间　interpulse time
脉冲剪切机　impulse cutting machine
脉冲宽度　pulse width [duration, length]
脉冲类型　impulse-type
脉冲冷却　pulse cooling
脉冲／秒　pulses per second (PPS)
脉冲能量　pulse energy
脉冲频率　(im)pulse frequency
脉冲(频)谱　pulse spectrum
脉冲启动　pulse on
脉冲气蚀试验　pulsed cavitation test
脉冲锐化器[修尖电路]　(pulse) peaker

脉冲上升时间　pulse rise time
脉冲烧结　pulse sintering
脉冲时间　pulse [burst] time, step time (间隔焊的)
脉冲式超声波探伤仪　soniscope
脉冲式反应堆　pulsed reactor
脉冲示波器　【理】impulse [surge] oscillograph, pulse oscilloscope
脉冲试验　impulse test
脉冲室　counter chamber
脉冲输出　pulse output
脉冲衰减时间　pulse decay [fall] time
脉冲速度　impulse velocity
脉冲塔板　pulse-column plate
脉冲调谐　pulse tuning
脉冲调制　【电】(im)pulse modulation
脉冲跳增　overshoot
脉冲退火　pulse annealing
脉冲响应　impulse response
脉冲信号　(im)pulse signal
脉冲型式　type of pulses
脉冲应力下疲劳强度　fatigue strength under pulsating stresses
脉冲源　pulser, (im)pulse source
脉冲振幅　pulse amplitude [height]
脉冲中子源　pulsed neutron source
脉冲转速计　impulse [pulsation] tachometer
脉冲[动]装置　pulsing system [unit], pulser
脉动　pulsating, pulsation, pulsing, ripple, fluctuation
脉动成穴试验　pulsed cavitation test
脉动磁场　pulsating field
脉动磁场磁化(强度)　【理】swinging field magnetization
脉动[冲]萃取塔　pulse extraction column [tower] ◇ 筛板~[交换柱]·
脉动淬火压床　pulse quenching press
脉动电流　pulsating current
脉动负荷试验法(金属的)　burst method
脉动负载　pulsating load

脉动混合沉降器　pulsed mixer-settler
脉动活塞杆　pulsed ejector
脉动给[供]料机　【冶】pulsafeeder
脉动减震器　pulsating damper
脉动流　pulsating flow
脉动频率　pulse [ripple] frequency
脉动器　pulsator
脉动燃烧　【铁】pulsation [pulsating] combustion
脉动筛　pulsating screen
脉动式酸洗装置　surging-type pickling apparatus
脉动收尘器　pulsator deduster
脉动[冲]塔　pulse column
脉动填充塔　pulsed packed column
脉动跳汰机　pulsator jig
脉动退火　pulse annealing
脉动吸附塔[离子交换柱]　jigged-bed adsorption column
脉动系数　coefficient of pulsation, ripple factor
脉动效应　pulsating [pulsation] effect
脉动压机　pulsating press
脉动应力　pulsating [fluctuating] stress
脉动张力　pulsating tension
脉幅调制　pulse amplitude modulation (PAM)
脉激　pulse excitation
脉金矿床　vein gold deposit
脉塞[泽]　maser (microwave amplification by stimulated emission of radiation) ◇晶体~【半】crystal maser
脉石　gangue, barren rock, burrow, debris, rocky impurity, waste [variegated] rock, 【采】matrix ◇覆盖矿石的~【地】burden, 黏土质~argillaceous gangue, 酸溶性~acid-soluble gangue
脉石成分[组成,组分]　gangue component [composition, constituent]
脉石单体分离　gang(ue)-grain release
脉石含量(矿石中的)　gang(ue) content [level], amount of gangue
脉石化合物　gangue compound
脉石颗粒　gangue particle
脉石矿物　gangue mineral [material]
脉石物质　gangue solids
脉铁(高硅全珠光铁)　loded iron
脉锡　lode tin, vein tin
脉锡精矿　lode tin concentrate
脉锡矿　lode tin ore, vein tin
脉状凸起　【铸】veining
脉状矿床　vein deposit
满标测量　full scale measurement
满充带　【理】filled band
满充(电子)壳层结构　【理】closed shell configuration
满充壳层　closed shell
满充壳层原子　closed-shell atom
满充能带　full [filled, occupied] energy band
满充能级　occupied (energy) level
满充状态　filled [occupied] state
满磁场　full field
满带能级　filled (energy) level
满电压　full voltage
满负荷　full load
满负荷操作[满载工作]　full load operation, 【冶】full load run
满负荷[容量]炉　full size furnace
满负荷生产　full scale production
满负荷消耗量　full load need
满负荷[满载]运行　【机】full load run
满负载转矩　full load torque
满能级图　complete energy-level diagram
满溢系统[状态]　flooded system
满载连续运转　continuous full-load run
满载消耗量　full load need
满载重量　all-up weight
墁刀　【铸】slick ◇内角(修型)~inside corner slick
曼戈尔铝锰合金(1.5Mn,余量Al)　Mangol
曼戈尼克镍锰合金(3Mn,余量Ni)　Mangonic

曼格莱特铝基活塞合金(2—3Cu,1.5Mg,1.5Ni,余量 Al) Mangalite
曼格林瓦钴铁镍锰合金(35Co,35Fe,20Ni,10Mn) mangelinvar
曼海姆铜锌锡代金合金(83.1Cu,10Zn,6.9Sn) Mannheim gold
曼加那尔高强度耐磨含镍高锰钢(12Mn,3Ni,0.6—0.9C,余量 Fe) Manganal
曼内斯曼(穿孔)法 【压】Mannesmann (piercing) process
曼内斯曼穿孔机轧辊 【压】Mannesmann piercing roll
曼内斯曼金属粉末制取法 Mannesmann powder process
曼内斯曼(连铸)设备 Mannesmann plant
曼内斯曼(式)穿孔机 Mannesmann piercer, Mannesmann (piercing) mill
曼内斯曼式轧机 barrel type roll piercing mill
曼内斯曼铁粉 Mannesmann iron powder
曼内斯曼斜轧穿孔法 (同"斜轧穿孔法")
曼内斯曼型皮尔格轧管机 Mannesmann-type Pilger mill
曼森－哈夫里德蠕变曲线外推理论 Mannson-Hafred theory of creep curve extrapolation
曼逊－哈费德公式(关于蠕变数据的) Manson-Haferd relationship
曼－腾低合金高强度钢 Man-Ten steel
镘尺(抹灰用) darby
镘刀 trowel, sleeker, slicker ◇ 半球面凹槽～*,火泥～mortar trowel,平圆～*,修整加厚边缘～(铸型的) bead sleeker
慢动压机 slow-acting press
慢反应 slow reaction
慢风 slow [slack] wind, 【冶】half blast, 【铁】reduced wind
慢风操作 【铁】mild blast operation, slow blowing, slow-wind operation, operation on slow wind, fanning ◇ 高炉～slack-wind blowing

慢风操作高炉 low load blast furnace
慢风作业 【铁】slow run, mild blast operation
慢化比 【理】moderating ratio
慢化剂 moderating material, moderator
慢空穴 slow hole
慢冷的 cooled slowly (Cs)
慢凝水泥 slow setting cement
慢时变的 slow time-varying
慢速度[慢动] jogging speed
慢速(感光)胶片 slower film
慢速轧机 low-speed mill
慢弯曲脆断试验 ◇ 范德维恩～*
慢弯曲试验 slow-bend test ◇ 利海～*
慢行 【铁】slow run
慢性毒性 【环】chronic toxicity
慢性镉中毒 chronic cadium poisoning
慢性汞中毒 chronic mercury poisoning
慢性磷中毒 phosphorism
慢性曝光 chronic exposure
慢性砷中毒 chronic arsenic poisoning, arsenicalism
慢性硒中毒 alkali disease
慢性锌中毒 Zinacalism
慢性中毒 chronic poisoning
慢氧化 slow oxidation
慢硬化(水泥的) 【建】slow-setting
慢中子 【理】slow neutron
慢转速拍摄 time lapse technique
漫反射 diffuse [scattered, scattering] reflection
漫反射系数 diffuse-reflection factor, albedo
漫流(的) flowing, sheet flood
漫散辐射 diffuse radiation
漫散射 diffuse scattering
漫散射测量[测定] 【理】diffuse scattering measurement
漫射 diffuse (scattering), diffusion, diffuseness ◇ 不～的 nondiffusing,光谱线～系 diffuse series
漫射本底 diffuse background

漫射反射面 【理】diffusely reflecting surface	锚固[定] anchoring ◇ 位错～*
漫射峰 【理】diffuse peak	锚固力 anchoring force
漫射光 diffuse light	锚固强度 anchoring strength
漫射声 diffused sound	锚固位错 anchor dislocation
漫射系 diffuse series	锚环法 anchor-ring method
漫射现象 diffusion phenomen	锚链 anchor[cable] chain
漫射线条 diffuse line	锚塞 male cone ◇ （圆）锥形～*
漫射像 diffuse image	锚式搅拌机[搅拌器,混合器] anchor mixer
漫射最大值 【理】diffuse peak	
漫透射率 diffuse transmittance	锚栓 anchor, crab[cotter, fang]bolt ◇ 耐火材料～refractory anchor
芒茨合金 malleable brass, Muntz metal	
芒古斯镍银[铜镍锌合金] Mungoose metal	锚栓槽 anchoring channel
	锚栓孔 anchor hole
芒硝（矿）{$Na_2SO_4 \cdot 10H_2O$} mirabilite, salt-cake, Glauber's salt	锚栓系统 system of anchoring
	锚形铁钩 grapnel
盲板 blind flange (BF, bf), blank flange, blind[stop]plate ◇ 法兰～blindflange	锚用钢丝绳 mooring wire rope
	锚桩 anchor pile
盲袋 blind bag	锚着长度（钢筋的） 【建】bond length
盲点 blind spot	毛边 raw edge, flash（切口的）, fraze（模锻件飞刺清理后的） ◇ 清除[去]～(de)frasing, deburring, 去除～装置 deburring unit, 无～挤锻模 extrusion-forging die
盲端 block	
盲沟 catch-drain, blind drain（填碎石或砾石的） ◇ 排水～weeper drains	
盲（孔）芯 【铸】blind (set) core	
盲矿床 blind ore deposit	毛边槽（锻模的） flash gutter
盲矿山 shicer	毛病 trouble, mishap, defect, fault ◇ 有～的 faulty, 有～焊缝 falling seam
猫盐（从盐卤中提出的精盐） cat salt	
猫眼（石） 【地】cat's eye	毛玻璃 etched[clouded, frosted, ground]glass
锚 anchor, grapnel	
锚定板 anchor(ing) plate	毛玻璃聚焦屏 ground-glass focusing screen
锚定材料 anchor(ing) material	
锚定件[部分] anchor(ing) part	毛玻璃（荧光）屏 groundglass screen
锚定件加固钢筋 anchoring accessories	毛翅（缺陷） 【压】list edge
锚定框架 anchor frame	毛刺 barb, arris, fin, rag,【压】flash（缺陷）, spilliness（钢丝表面缺陷）,【铸】feather edge, veining ◇ 出现～ finning, 除～辊 deburring roll, 电化法去除～*, 电解法去除～ electrolytic deburring, 磨～机 burr masher, 去（除）[清除]～*, 热去～【压】hot trim(ming), 无～坯件*, 修除～ trim, 压～辊 bar masher
锚定螺栓 anchor(ing) bolt (A.B.)	
锚定式板桩 anchored sheet piling	
锚定物 dead man	
锚定桩 grouser	
锚杆 stay rod, anchoring bolt, footbolt	
锚钢 anchor steel	
锚钩式走行起重机 grapnel traveling crane	
	毛刺刮刀 shaver
	毛刺清理机 burring machine

毛发湿度计 hair hygrometer
毛管 hollow (billet), (pierced) shell, bush, disc, hollow forging ◇ 厚壁黄铜~(拉拔用) brass shell
毛管料 tube bloom [stock]
毛管坯 disc, disk
毛管铸造法 cast shell process
毛化【压】roughing ◇ 激光~ laser roughing, 喷丸~ shot-blasting roughing, 轧辊~ roll surface roughing
毛口 burr, arris ◇ 去~ burring, 去除~装置 deburring unit
毛矿 dirt
毛利 gross profit
毛面 dull ◇ 做成~ frost
毛面薄板 dull-finish sheet
毛面镀层 dull deposit
毛面镀锡薄钢板 dull plate
毛面钢板 dull-finish steel ◇ 激光~
毛面光洁度 frosted [matte] finish
毛面辊 dull roll
毛面精整（板材、轧辊表面的）mat finishing, butler finish
毛面拉拔 mat(te) drawing
毛坯 blank, clot,【压】stock (material),【冶】billet ◇ 冲压杯状~ cupping, 锻造~ slug
毛坯尺寸图 hot dimension drawing
毛坯感应加热器 induction billet heater
毛坯挤压 breakdown extrusion
毛坯加热装置 billet heater
毛坯轧件 initial breakdown
毛坯至装药距离（爆炸成形的）standoff
毛坯铸件 raw [rough, faint] casting
毛皮绿 nitroso-β-naphthol
毛青钴矿 julienite
毛青铜矿 buttgenbachite
毛石 rubble (stone), quarry rock
毛石骨料 rubble aggregate
毛石混凝土 rubble concrete
毛石砌体 rubble masonry ◇ 混凝土心墙的~【建】opus incertum

毛体积 bulk volume
毛体积干密度 dry bulk density
毛铜矿{Cu₂O} chalcotrichite, erythrocalcite
毛湾炼镍法（古巴）Moa Bay process
毛细常数 capillary [capillarity] constant
毛细电极 capillary electrode
毛细电解 capillary electrolysis
毛细管 capillary tube [tubing, pipe], capillary ◇ 表面张力~测定法
毛细管法 capillary (tube) method
毛细管合金法 capillary alloy method
毛细管给水 capillary water
毛细管给油 capillary feed
毛细管静电计 capillary electrometer
毛细管冷凝 weeping-out
毛细管流量计 capillary flowmeter
毛细管黏度计 capillary viscometer, caplastometer ◇ 奥斯特瓦尔德~ Ostwald-type viscometer
毛细管渗透(作用) capillary penetration
毛细(管)吸引[吸力] capillary attraction
毛细(管)现象 capillary phenomenon, capillarity
毛细管现象的 capillary
毛细管压力计 capillary manometer
毛细(管)效应[作用] capillarity, capillary action [effect]
毛细管作用力 capillary force
毛细浸渗[浸渍毛细渗补]（修补铸件缺陷）【铸】capillary dip infiltration
毛细孔 capillary bore
毛细连接【团】capillary bonding
毛细裂缝 capillary crack
毛细凝聚法 capillary condensation method
毛细凝聚力 capillary cohesive force
毛细水 capillar water
毛细水分 capillary moisture
毛细探测器 capillary detector
毛细下降 capillary depression
毛细压力[压强] capillary pressure

毛细有效物质　capillary active substance
毛细状组织　capillary structure
毛细(作用)上升　capillary rise [ascent, elevation]
毛轧板　【压】moulder
毛毡　felt, blanket
毛毡擦拭器　felt wiper
毛毡辊(镀锡薄钢板抛光用)　dusting roll
毛毡轮抛光　bobbing
毛重　gross weight (GWT), bulk [rough, laden] weight, gross ◇ 按～per gross (pr gr.)
毛状断口　woolly fracture
铆钉　rivet, clinch ◇ 除～derivetting, 冷压～cold-driven rivet, 临时定位～*, 埋头～countersunk rivet, 平头～flush rivet, 热铆～poprivet, 双行～连接 double-riveted joint, 氧弧烧除～oxygen-arc derivetting, 圆头～cup rivet
铆钉棒材[坯]　rivet rod [bar]
铆钉成头　rivet heading
铆钉穿孔用烧嘴　blow pipe for rivet piercing
铆(钉)锤　(stud) riveting hammer, bust [cup-shaped] hammer
铆钉钢　rivet steel [iron]
铆钉钢丝[线材]　rivet wire
铆钉火焰清理　rivet washing
铆钉[接]机　rivet machine [buster, driver], riveter
铆钉(加热用锻工)炉　rivet (heating) forge
铆钉间距　rivet pitch
铆钉孔烧穿器　burner for rivet piercing
铆钉冷镦机　riveting press
铆钉模　riveting snap, set die, dolly, hobby
铆(钉)枪　riveting gun, riveter ◇ 风[气]动～*
铆钉枪冲头　riveting punch
铆钉切割　rivet cutting
铆钉上头　closing head
铆钉试验　rivet test

铆钉头顶锻[铆钉作头]　rivet heading
铆钉(头)熔切器　rivet (head) cutting burner
铆钉型锤　cup-shaped hammer
铆钉压头　riveting snap
铆钉用棒材　rivet rod
铆钉用棒坯　rivet bar
铆钉原头　set head
铆杆支柱　【采】anchor [tie, truss] bolt
铆固作用(位错的)　riveting action
铆焊　rivet welding ◇ 开孔～焊缝 filled plug weld
铆焊并用接头　composite joint
铆焊接头　rivet(ed) weld
铆合　riveting
铆合管　riveted pipe
铆接　rivet(ing), rivet(ed) joint ◇ 成卷带材端头～装置 riveter, 交错排列的～zigzag riveting, 双排钉～的 double riveted (d.r.)
铆接操作[工序]　riveting operation
铆接冲子(铆合钉头用)　riveting [set] punch
铆接法　riveting process
铆接钢　riveted steel (R.S.)
铆接炉缸　riveting hearth
铆接模具　riveting set
铆接用压力机　riveting press
铆头模　cupping tools, snap
冒槽　【铸】overswelling
冒出　puffing-up
冒顶(钢锭的)　【钢】(badly) bleeding, rising (top)
冒顶钢锭　rising steel (ingot), rising [bleeding] ingot
冒口　【铸】casting [riser, rising, shrink (age), sink, feeder] head, riser (vent), head (metal), feeder (top), outgate, sullage pipe, 【焊】collar (铝热焊的) ◇ 暗～*, 补缩～feeding head, shrinker, 菜花[发面]～cauliflower head, 出气[溢流]～pop-off, flow-off, 大气(压力)～*, 捣

～棒 feeding rod, 集渣～ scum riser, 磨掉铸件～(用砂轮) snag, 切除～【钢】topping, 热～ live [hot] riser, 易割～*, 有效补缩～ active feeder

冒口补缩 feeding
冒口补贴 riser contact
冒口布置法 heading (hdg)
冒口部分 lost [discard] head
冒口捣杆 feeding rod
冒口发热剂 riser compound
冒口防缩剂 anti-piping compound
冒口废料(已切割下来的) deadhead
冒口割炬 riser cutting torch
冒口根 riser pad
冒口根部 riser base
冒口金属 【钢】dozzle metal
冒口颈 riser neck
冒口腔 feeder head cavity
冒口熔切器 riser cutting burner
冒口贴边 pad(ding), riser contact
冒口通气芯 puncture core
冒口箱 headbox
冒泡 bubbling
冒泡开始 inception of bubbles
冒泡排放图 bubble emission profile
冒泡气体 effervescing gas
冒气 gassing
冒烟 smoke emission, smoking
冒涨钢 wild steel
冒涨(钢)锭 rising steel (ingot), gassy ingot
冒涨钢水[金属] wild metal
帽 cap, hood, lid, hat, head-piece
帽梁 capping beam
帽木 【建】cap piece
帽容比 head and volume ratio
帽形孔型 【压】hat [trapezoidal] pass
帽形立轧孔型(钢轨的) squabbing pass
帽状淬火 cap-like hardening
帽状物体 derby
帽状感应器 cap-like inductor
贸易 trade

贸易库存 【企】trade inventories
贸易平衡 【企】trade balance
玫瑰花状石墨 【冶】rosette graphite
玫瑰花状图样 【金】rosette pattern
梅达尔特型矫直机 Medart straightener
梅尔科钴基合金 (10Ni, 25—35Cr, 6.0—7.5W, 0.015B, 0.25—0.40C, 13.0Cu, 2—4.0Ta, 0.15Y, 余量 Co) Melco alloy
梅尔尼镍基耐热合金 (13—25Co, 20—25Cr, 1.76—3.5Al, 2—4.64Ti, 4.0Mo, 0.1C, 0.1Zr, 0.01B, 余量 Ni) Melni alloy
梅尔曲线 ash-unit curve
梅格派尔铁铬铝电阻丝合金 Megapyr
梅格珀姆铁镍锰高导磁率合金 (45Fe, 45Ni, 10Mn) Megaperm
梅花股芯钢丝绳 star wire rope
梅花接头 【压】wabbler
梅花接轴 wobbler spindle
梅花套筒 【压】coupling box
梅花头(轧辊的) wobbler (end), tenon end
梅花桩 quincuncial pile ◇ 打～ staggered piling
梅科洛依镍银[铜镍锌合金] (60Cu, 25Ni, 10Zn, 2Pb, 2Fe) Mercoloy
梅拉尔铝合金 (3.2Cu, 0.8Mg, 0.3Mn, 1.0Ni, 余量 Al) Meral (alloy)
梅勒霍特铜镍锌合金 (65—67Cu, 16—20Ni, 13—14Zn, 1—3.5Fe) Maillechort
梅里尔压滤机(氰化法提金用) Merrill filter
梅里卡浸蚀液(镍及镍合金用) 【金】Merica's etching reagent
梅洛特铋锡铅易熔合金 (50Bi, 31Sn, 19Pb; 熔点 99℃) Mellotte's alloy
梅氏缺口(冲击试样的) Mensnager notch
梅氏冲击试验 Mesnager impact test
梅氏冲击试样 Mesnager (impact) test piece

梅氏浸蚀剂（钢铁材料用） Meyer's reagent
梅氏硬度 Meyer hardness
梅氏硬度试验 Meyer hardness test
梅氏硬度值 Meyer hardness number
梅氏指数 Meyer index
梅塔尔－英普勒克斯法（消除铸铁孔隙用） Metal-Imprex process
梅塔拉斯蒂克金属－橡胶黏合法 Metalastik
梅塔莱厄金属喷镀法 Metalayer process
梅塔莱因含油轴承合金（35Co,30Cu,25Al,10Fe） Metalline
梅塔洛克铸件和锻件缺陷冷态修补法 Metalock
梅特锡锑合金（95Sn,5Sb） Meter
梅耶－艾希霍尔茨浸蚀液 【金】Meyer and Eichholz reagent
梅轧克锌合金 Mazak alloy
梅兹洛镁合金（5.8—7.2 或 2.5—3.5Al,0.15 或 0.2—1.2Mn,0.4—1.5 或 0.6—1.4Zn,余量 Mg） Mazlo alloy
霉菌 mycete, mould, fungi
煤 (mineral) coal ◇ 次[低级软]~ dant, 风干~ air-dry coal, 肥[高挥发分]~ fat coal, 含黄铁矿的~ dross(y) coal, 给[供]~ coal input, 结焦性差的~, 精选[上等]~ fancy coal, 贫[低级]~ lean coal, 弱黏结性~ feebly caking coal, 上~线[轨道] coaling track, 外来[外矿送选的]~ foreign coal, 由~变焦的转化 coal-to-coke conversion, 中块~ middle-grade coal
煤比 【铁】coal ratio
煤变质程度 coal rank
煤饼 coal cake
煤仓 coal bunker, coalbin, coal silos（动力厂的）
煤仓自动放煤机构 automatic coal-bunker outlet mechanism
煤层变厚 belly
煤层黏土 coal-formation clay

煤层下黏土 seat earth
煤场 coal yard
煤车 jimmy ◇ 井下~ box
煤的准备 coal preparation
煤斗车 hopper coal car
煤斗落料管 【焦】coal chute from hopper
煤粉 braize, coal duff [dust], pulverized [powdered, coombe] coal, dust fuel ◇ 筛除~ breeze extraction, 外裹~ external carbon
煤粉包层 【团】coal coating
煤粉保护底吹氧枪（转炉的） bottom oxygen nozzle protection with pulverized coal
煤粉槽 breeze bin
煤粉和矿粉复合喷吹 simulaneous of pulverized coal and fine iron ore
煤粉加工[制备] pulverized coal preparation
煤粉加料器 powdered coal feeder
煤粉浓相输送技术 【铁】conveying pulverized coal in dense flow
煤粉喷吹 （同"喷煤"）
煤粉喷吹操作 PCI operation
煤粉喷枪 pulverized coal gun
煤粉燃烧率 【铁】combustion rate of pulverized coal
煤粉－悬浊油喷烧器 coal-oil slurry injector
煤干燥器 coal drier
煤化（作用） coalification
煤灰 coal ash, flyash
煤灰污染 【环】contamination by coal ash
煤基本微观结构 【焦】maceral
煤基直接还原 coal-based direct reduction
煤基直接还原法[工艺] coal-based direct reduction process ◇
煤加工转化 coal conversion
煤浆 【冶】coal-water slurry
煤焦油 coal tar [oil]
煤焦油沥青 coal tar pitch
煤焦油燃料 coal tar fuel

煤焦油研究协会　Coal Tar Research Association (C.T.R.A.)
煤焦置换比　【铁】coal-to-coke replacement ratio, replacement ratio of coke by coal
煤阶　coal rank
煤坑　coal pit
煤矿　coal mine, colliery ◇ 靠近~on coal
煤-矿石混合料　coal-ore blend
煤矿用钢丝绳　colliery wire rope
煤粒　rice coal
煤料　coal charge ◇ 装炉时的~水分 moisture as charged
煤料垂直收缩(炼焦的)　【焦】coal vertical shrinkage
煤料高度(碳化室的)　【焦】coal line
煤料细度　fineness of coal
煤末　slack coal, breeze, conny
煤泥槽　【焦】slack bin
煤泥重量校正　slurry deduction
煤膨胀性　coal expansion
煤气　coal gas (cg), gas ◇ 半净~semi-cleaned gas, 厂内自用~gas for works' use, 粗[荒]~crude [raw] gas, 低(发)热值~*, 动力~power gas, 富~strong gas, 含水[未脱水]的~moisture-laden gas, 贫~poor gas, 人造~manufactured gas, 三混~*, 水[蓝]~water-gas, blue gas, 洗过的~clean gas, 原生~primary gas, 远程供应[管道输送]的~piped gas
煤气安装工　gas fitter
煤气爆炸　gas explosion
煤气泵　gas pump
煤气表　gas meter, gasometer
煤气产出率　gas yield
煤气产量　gas throughput [yield]
煤气厂　gas(-making) plant, gasworks
煤气成分　gas composition
煤气出口　【铁】offtake
煤气除尘　gas cleaning
煤气除尘器　gas cleaner
煤气除尘设备　gas cleaning equipment [installation]

煤气粗[初]洗　primary gas cleaning
煤气道　gas duct, flue
煤气灯罩　(gas) mantle
煤气点火器　gas(-fired) ignitor ◇ 双排~two-row gas ignitor
煤气锻造炉　gas forge
煤气二次除尘[二步清洗]　【铁】secondary gas cleaning
煤气发动机　gas engine
煤气发生炉　(coal) gas producer, generating furnace [set], producer furnace, producer gas generator ◇ 抽风式~suction gas producer, 高压~pressure-gas producer, 固定~*, 回转炉算~*, 机械清灰~mechanical ashed producer, 湿式除灰[炉底水封式]~wet-bottom gas producer
煤气发生炉罐　gas-producer retort, generating chamber
煤气发生炉燃料　producer fuel
煤气发生炉效率　gas producer efficiency
煤气发生器　gas generator
煤气反冲　gas kick ◇ 料钟间的~gas kick between bells
煤气房　gashouse
煤气防御　gas defense
煤气放散管　【铁】bleeder stack
煤气分级[分类]　gas classification
煤气分配管道　gas-distributing pipe
煤气分配器　gas distributor
煤气分析仪　gas analysis meter
煤气封盖(大料斗的)　【铁】gas seal
煤气工(高炉车间的)　gasman
煤气供给[供应]管线　gas feed [supply] line
煤气鼓风机　gas blowing engine
煤气管　gas pipe
煤气管带坯　【压】gas strip
煤气管道　gas pipling [conduit] ◇ 倾斜~【铁】down pass, 下喷~*
煤气管线　gas (pipe)line [path]
煤气含量　gas content

煤气火焰	gas flame
煤气火焰反射炉	gas-fired reverberatory furnace
煤气火焰辐射	gas-fire radiation
煤气火焰炉	gas-fired air furnace
煤气机	gas engine
煤气加热回转窑	gas-fired rotary kiln
煤气加热均热炉	gas-heated pit furnace
煤气加热炉	gas-heated [gas-fired] furnace
煤气加热器	gas(-fired) heater
煤气加热设备	gas-fired heating unit
煤气加热箱式炉	gas-heated box furnace
煤气加热浴槽	gas-fired bath
煤气加热罩式炉	gas-fired bell-type furnace
煤气焦炭	gas coke
煤气焦油	gas tar
煤气节流孔	gas orifice
煤气节省器	gas economizer
煤气精洗	fine gas cleaning
煤气警报器	gas alarmer
煤气净化器	gas purifier
煤气净化上水道	washing circuit
煤气净化设备	gas cleaning equipment [installation]
煤气净化系统	【焦】gas purification system ◇ 洛奇-科垂尔~ Lodge-Cottrell system, 文丘里~*
煤气净化装置	gas cleaning device
煤气-空气按比例自动计量(燃烧器内的)	【冶】automatic gas/air proportioning
煤气-空气焊枪	gas(-and)-air torch
煤气-空气混合物	gas-air mixture
煤气-空气界面	gas-air interface
煤气-空气焰	gas-air flame
煤气控制站	gas-control station
煤气冷凝液	【焦】gas liquor
煤气冷却器	gas cooler
煤气利用率	gas utilization efficiency
煤气量	gas volume
煤气流	gas stream [current] ◇ 边缘~*
煤气流量	gas throughput
煤气流量入口/出口调节器	gas flow inner/outer regulator
煤气流量调节挡板	gas flow regulating damper
煤气炉	gas (burning) furnace, gas oven [stove] ◇ 辐射式~ radiant gas furnace
煤气喷灯	gas torch [blowpipe]
煤气喷灯阀	torch valve
煤气喷灯预热	【冶】torch preheating
煤气喷枪	gas pistol
煤气喷射孔	gas orifice
煤气喷嘴	gas jet, shielding cup (气电焊烧嘴的)
煤气喷嘴火焰清理	torch scarfing
煤气平衡	gas balance
煤气钎焊器	gas blowpipe
煤气切断阀	gas isolating valve ◇ 西格里式~*
煤气清洗机	gas cleaner
煤气取样	gas sampling
煤气燃烧	gas firing
煤气燃烧炉	gas burning furnace
煤气燃烧器[烧嘴]	gas(-fired) burner ◇ 高压~*, 泰尔贝克~*, 正压~ pressure-gas burner
煤气上升道	gas up-take
煤气渗碳烧结	gas carbusintering
煤气生物探测器	biological detector of gas
煤气湿法除尘	【冶】wet gas cleaning
煤气室(烘干装置的)	gas [plenum] chamber
煤气收集系统	gas-collecting system
煤气探测器	gas detector
煤气调节	gas conditioning ◇ 闸门式~阀*
煤气调节器	【铁】gas pilot
煤气通道	gas passage [flue]
煤气通道口底部	port slope
煤气外热钢弹还原炉	gas-fired bomb furnace

煤气涡形管 gas scroll

煤气洗涤器[机,装置] scrubber, gas-washer ◇ 菲尔德~*, 圆锥形~ circular-wedge scrubber, 撞击式~ impingement scrubber

煤气洗涤塔 gas wash(ing) tower ◇ 固定喷头~*, 旋转喷头~*

煤气洗涤用水 gas washing water

煤气系统 【冶】gas system

煤气下降管(高炉的) gas down-take, down pass, downcomer (tube)

煤气下降管放灰闸板 downcomer damper

煤气下降管支腿 downcomer leg

煤气修理工 gas fitter

煤气旋塞 gas cock

煤气压差调节 【铁】gas differential pressure control

煤气压力 gas pressure ◇ 放散管~*

煤气压力计 gas gauge

煤气压送泵 gas compression pump

煤气氧气割炬 gas-oxygen torch

煤气氧气烧嘴 gas-oxygen burner

煤气氧焰加热钎焊 oxygas brazing

煤气氧焰切割 oxy-citygas cutting

煤气与固体炉料间的反应 【冶】gas-solid reaction

煤气预冷器 【铁】precooler

煤气预热器 gas preheater [recuperator]

煤气再生[重整](法) gas reforming

煤气增压鼓风机 gas increasing blower

煤气闸板 【钢】gas damper

煤气蒸汽混合物 gas-vapour mixture

煤气质量色谱图 gas mass chromatogram

煤气中毒 gas poisoning

煤气贮存桶 gas holder

煤气-砖(格子)热转移 gas-brick heat transfer

煤气总管 gas main

煤气组成 gas composition

煤气嘴 gas jet

煤球 briquette, eggette

煤燃烧器 coal burner

煤燃烧速率 coal(-burning) rate

煤-燃油混合物 【冶】coal-fuel oil slurry

煤-燃油混合物喷吹 coal-oil mixture injection

煤筛分分析 coal-sizing analysis

煤筛分试验 coal sieve test

煤生黏土 coal-formation clay

煤水车 (water) tender

煤-水混合物 【冶】coal-water slurry

煤素质 【焦】maceral

煤炭气化 coal gasification ◇ 鲁奇~法*, 得克萨公司~法* Texaco process, 基珀斯-托切克~法 Kippers-Totzek process, 温克勒~法*

煤炭燃料 coal-based fuel

煤田 coal field

煤屑 coal dust [slack], slack (coal), burgey

煤屑仓 slack bin

煤屑及烧结返矿运输机 breeze and sinter fines conveyer

煤压块 【焦】coal briquette

煤烟 soot, coom ◇ 沾染~*

煤烟排放标准 emission standards of smoke and soot

煤烟碳 soot carbon

煤岩显微组分 【焦】maceral, coal petrographic constituent

煤岩学 coal petrography [petrology]

煤焰高温段 coal-flame hot zone

煤-氧-矿喷射造气和熔融还原 【铁】gasification and smelting reduction by coal-oxygen-ore injection

煤氧枪 coal-oxygen burner (煤氧竖炉用), coal-oxygen spray gun (电弧炉炼钢用)

煤氧竖炉 coal-oxygen shaft furnace

煤氧助熔(电弧炉炼钢的) coal-oxygen fluxing

煤样 coal sample ◇ 采~coal sampling

煤油 kerosene, paraffin

煤油酒精稀释剂 kerosene-alcohol diluent

煤油润滑冷轧光洁度 kerosene-rolled finish

煤油－涂白粉试验(检验表面裂纹) oil-and-whiting test

煤油洗提 kerosene wash

煤渣 (coal) cinder, beans

煤渣槽 slagholding bin

煤渣混凝土 breeze concrete

煤渣砖 cinder [clinker] block

煤站 coaling station

煤蒸馏衍生物 coal derivatives

煤质页岩 coal-containing shale ◇ 含铀～*

煤种 coal rank

煤砖 briquet(te), moulded coal

媒剂 mordant

媒介 medium, media, agency, agent

媒介物 agent (Agt), intermediary, intermediate

媒体用毕符 【计】end of medium character (EM)

媒体转换 【计】media conversion

媒液 vehicle

楣砖(煤气发生炉的) lintel brick

镅合金 americium alloy

镅基合金 americium base alloy

镅添加合金 americium additive alloy

镁{Mg} magnesium ◇ 除[脱]～de-magging, 粗～crude magnesium, 电解～electrolytic magnesium, 废～magnesium scrap, 工业[商品]～commercial magnesium, 含～的 magnesian, magnesic, magniferous, 含～合金*, 精炼～refined magnesium, 气态～gaseous magnesium, 熔～炉 furnace for magnesium, 原生～primary magnesium, 真空蒸馏～*

镁白云石 konite, conite ◇ 烧成油浸合成～*

镁产出率 magnesium yield

镁尘 magnesium dust

镁尘糊块(碳热法炼镁的) 【色】goop

镁电解 【色】magnesium electrolysis ◇ 侧插阳极～槽*, 上插阳极～槽*

镁电解生产 (同"电解炼镁")

镁锭 magnesium ingot ◇ 酸洗～*

镁方铁矿 magnesio-wuestite

镁粉 powdered magnesium ◇ 尼科尔斯雾化－法 Hichols process, 补炉～*

镁橄榄石{Mg$_2$SiO$_4$} forsterite, white olivine

镁橄榄石绝热板 【钢】forsterite insulating plate

镁橄榄石耐火材料 forsterite refractory

镁橄榄石型化合物 forsterite type compound

镁锆铸造合金 ◇ 尤雷卡 Rz5～*

镁铬合金 magnesite-chrome

镁铬矿 picrochromite

镁铬耐火材料 magnesite-chrome refractory

镁铬砌块 magnesite-chrome black ◇ 炉顶用～*

镁铬铁矿 magn(esi)ochromite

镁铬砖 【耐】magnesite-chrome brick ◇ 直接结合～*

镁合金 magnesium alloy ◇ 埃雷克特龙 V-1～*, 变形～*, 马格诺克斯核燃料包覆用～Magnox alloy, 梅兹洛～*, 双～板*, 铸造～*

镁合金薄板 magnesium alloy sheet

镁合金表面黑色皮膜处理法 ◇ 萨顿～Sutton process

镁合金晶粒细化法 ◇ 戴维斯～*

镁合金双面包覆硬铝板 ◇ 杜拉尔普拉特～*

镁化物 protactinides

镁还原厂 magnesium reduction plant

镁还原的海绵铪 magnesium reduced hafnium sponge

镁还原电弧炉 magnesium reduction arc furnace

镁还原法 magnesium (reduction) process ◇ 克罗尔～生产海绵钛[锆]金属*

镁黄长石{2CaO·MgO·2SiO$_2$} akermanite

镁基合金　magnesium base alloy ◇ 埃克利普斯压铸~*

镁基合金铸件　magnesium base casting

镁焦　magcoke, magnesium coke

镁火晶石　【地】magnesiospinel

镁结晶圈（硅热法炼镁的）　muff

镁矿床　【地】magnesium deposit

镁矿物　【地】magnesium mineral

镁-镧-钛系统陶瓷　magnesia-lanthana-titania system ceramics

镁连续还原炉　◇ 克纳普扎克-格里斯海姆~*

镁磷钙铝石　bialite

镁磷锰矿　talkriplite, magniotriplite

镁磷铀云母｛$Mg(UO_2)_2P_2O_8 \cdot 10H_2O$｝【地】saleit

镁铝合金　magnesium aluminum (alloy), magnadure ◇ 道屋~*, 高强度铸造~*, 马格努米纽乌姆~*, 马赫~*

镁铝尖晶石　【地】magnesia alumina spinel

镁铝耐火材料　magnesite-alumina refractory ◇ 拉马各尔~*

镁铝榴石｛$Mg_3Al_2(SiO_4)_3$｝【地】pyrope, vogesite

镁铝锌合金　◇ 埃雷克特龙~*

镁铝砖　magnesium-alumina brick

镁锰合金　magnesium manganese alloy

镁明矾　magnesian alum

镁铌铁矿　magn(esi)ocolumbite

镁七水铁矾　yarroshite

镁蔷微辉石　merwinite

镁热还原（法）　magnesiothermal [magnesiothermic, magnesium(-thermic)] reduction

镁熔池　magnesium pool

镁砂　magnesite｛$MgCO_3$｝, magnesia（氧化镁）◇ 补炉-【钢】furnace magnesite, 干燥筛选[筛分]~*, 高钙~ high calcium magnesite, 苛性~ caustic magnesite, 粒状~ grain magnesite, 轻烧~*, 熔融~*, 烧结~*, 死烧~ dead burned magnesite, 英国~ britmag

镁砂衬里[内衬]　magnesite lining

镁砂衬套式铸钢塞座（流钢嘴）　nozzle of magnesite thimble-type

镁砂捣打料[打结泥料]　magnesite ramming mass

镁砂浇注料　magnesia castable

镁砂炉底　magnesite bottom

镁砂消化　souring of magnesite

镁十字石｛$5MgO \cdot Al_2O_3 \cdot 6SiO_2 \cdot 4H_2O$｝zebedassite

镁石棉　magnesia-asbestos

镁实收率　magnesium yield

镁水绿矾　jarosite, yarroshite

镁钛矿｛$MgO \cdot TiO_2$｝geikielite, dauphinite, whitmanite

镁碳砖　magnesia carbon brick, MgO-C brick

镁添加合金　magnesium alloy addition

镁铁矿｛$MgFe_2O_4$｝magnesioferrite

镁铁榴石　（同"红石榴子石"）

镁铁氧体｛$MgO \cdot Fe_2O_3$｝magnesium ferrite

镁铁质（的）　mafic

镁稀土锆合金　magnesium rare earth zirconium alloy

镁稀土合金　magnesiu-rare earth

镁屑　magnesium chip

镁屑结压入铁水法　◇ 芬西德~*【铸】Finsider process

镁锌锆合金　◇ ZRE~*

镁盐　magnesium salt

镁阳极　magnesium anode

镁氧　magnesia, magno

镁氧膏精抛光（法）　【金】skid polishing

镁氧水泥　magnesia cement

镁氧陶瓷　magnesia ceramics

镁冶金　metallurgy of magnesium

镁业协会（美国）　Mangesium Association (M.A.)

镁液阀　magnesium valve

镁硬度　magnesium hardness

镁铀云母　saleeite
镁质白云石　magnesitic dolomite, magnesio-dolomite
镁质白云石耐火材料　magnesite-dolomite refractory
镁质白云石砖　magnesite-dolomite brick
镁质捣打混合物　magnesite ramming mix
镁质硅酸镍矿　garnierite ore
镁质火泥　magnesite mortar
镁质耐火材料　magnesite [magnesia] refractory
镁质耐火水泥　magnesia refractory cement
镁质石灰岩　magnesian limestone
镁质制品　【耐】magnesia product
镁珠　magnesium globule
镁砖　【耐】magnesia [magnesite] brick ◇ 烧成~ fired magnesite brick
镁砖吊顶　magnesite suspended arch
镁砖炉衬　magnesite brick lining
镁砖墙板　magnesite panel
镁砖填料　magnetite fill
每班试样　shift sample
每道次延伸量　【压】elongation for each pass
每道压缩量　【压】draught per hole
每道压下量(轧件的)　pass reduction, reduction [draught] per pass, rolling draught
每立方厘米颗粒数(空气的粉尘含量)　particles per cubic centimeter (p.p.c.c.)
每炉操作时间　【冶】tap-to-tap time
每炉熔化炉料(量)　charge smelted per furnace
每批电解料　electrolysis batch
每批料吨数　tons per charge (t/ch.)
每日费用　per diem rate [costs]
每日损失　daily losses
美吨(短吨,合 893kg)　ton short (tn.sh.), short ton
美工薄钢板　art metal
美国安全工程师学会　the American Society of Safety Engineers (ASSE)
美国拜耳法　American Bayer process
美国薄钢板规格　United States Steel Sheet Gauge (USSG)
美国标准　United States Standard (U.S.S.), American Standard (AS)
美国(标准)钢丝规　U.S. Steel Wire Gauge (U.S.S.W.G.)
美国标准管件　American standard pipe
美国标准局　United States Bureau of Standards (USBS), American Bureau of Standards (A.B.S.)
美国标准量规　United States Standard Gauge (USSG)
美国标准筛号　U.S. Standard screen scale
美国标准筛序　U.S. Sieve Series
美国标准试验手册　American standards test manual
美国标准线规　United States standard wire gauge
美国标准协会　American Standard Association (ASA)
美国标准协会管螺纹　ASA pipe threads
美国标准学会　United States of America Standards Institute (USASI)
美国材料试验标准　American standard of testing materials
美国材料试验协会标准　A.S.T.M. standard
美国材料试验协会标准筛　ASTM sieve, standard sieves A.S.T.M.
美国材料试验协会试行标准　A.S.T.M. Tentative Standard
美国材料试验学会　American Society for Testing Materials (ASTM)
美国采矿、冶金、石油工程师学会　American Institute of Mining, Metallurgical & Petroleum Engineers (AIME)
美国采矿工程师学会　American Institute of Mining Engineers (A.I.M.E.)
美国代用钢　NE (national emergency)

美国电化学学会 American Electrochemical Society (AES)
美国电镀工作者学会 American Electroplaters' Society (AES)
美国粉末冶金学会 American Powder Metallurgy Institute (APMI)
美国腐蚀工程师协会 N.A.C.E. (National Association of corrosion Engineer, U.S.A.)
美国钢材规格 United States Steel Gauge (USSG)
美国钢材进口商协会 American Institute for Importers of Steel (AIIS)
美国钢结构学会 American Institute of Steel Construction (AISC)
美国钢铁公司 U.S. Steel Corporation
美国钢铁加工学会 American Society for Steel Treating (A.S.S.T.)
美国钢铁学会 American Iron and Steel Institute (AISI)
美国钢铁制造商协会 Association of American Steel Manufacturers (AASM)
美国工程标准委员会 American Engineering Standards Committee (AESC)
美国工具制造工程师学会 American Society of Tool and Manufacturing Engineers (ASTME)
美国工业卫生协会 American Industrial Hygiene Association (AIHA)
美国供暖、冷藏与空气调节工程师学会 American Society of Heating, Refrigerating and Air-conditioning Engineers (ASHRAE)
美国国际贸易委员会 International Trade Commission
美国国家标准学会 American National Standards Institute
美国海军拉裂试验 U.S. (United States of America) Navy tear test
美国焊接学会 American Welding Society (AWS)
美国航天学会 American Astronautical Society (AAS)
美国化学工程师学会 American Institute of Chemical Engineers (A.I.C.E.)
美国化学学会 American Chemical Society (ACS)
美国机械工程师学会 American Society of Mechanical Engineers (ASME)
美国加仑(=3.785 升) United States gallon (USG), U.S. gallon
美国金(币合金)(90Au, 10Cu) American gold
美国金属熔炼及精炼公司 American Smelting and Refining Company (Asarco)
美国金属统计局 American Bureau of Metal Statistics (ABMS)
美国金属协会 American Institute of Metals (AIM)
美国金属学会 American Society of Metals (ASM)
美国晶体生长协会 American Association for Crystal Growth (AACG)
美国可锻铸铁 (见"黑心可锻铸铁")
美国可锻铸铁铸造师学会 Malleable Iron Founder's Society (MIFS)
美国会计学会 American Accounting Association (AAA)
美国矿物学会 Mineralogical Society of America (M.S.A.)
美国矿冶工程师学会 American Institute of Mining and Metallurgical Engineers (AIMME)
美国矿冶学会 Mining and Metallrugical Society of America (M.M.S.A.)
美国矿业局 United States Bureau of Mines (U.S.B.M.)
美国联邦标准 Federal specifications
美国联邦空气净化法 Federal Clean Air Act
美国铝业公司 Aluminium Company of America (ALCOA)

美国铝业公司铝研究试验室　Aluminium Research Laboratories of the Aluminium Company of America（ALRL）

美国铝业协会　Aluminum Association of America（AAA）

美国锰钢公司　American Manganese Steel Company（AMSCo.）

美国耐火材料学会　American Refractories Institute（ARI）

美国汽车工程师学会钢号标准　SAE（Society of Automobile Engineers）steel standard

美国汽车协会　American Automobile Association（AAA）

美国船级社　American Bureau of Shipping（ABS）

美国润滑工程师学会　American Society of Lubrication Engineers（ASLE）

美国石油学会　American Petroleum Institute（API）

美国式砌砖法　American bond

美国陶瓷学会　American Ceramic Society（A.Cer.S）

美国无损检验学会　American Society of Nondestructive Testing（ASNT）

美国污染控制协会　American Association for Contamination Control（AACC）

美国线规　American wire gauge（A.W.G）

美国线径规　American Steel and Wire gage（AS&WG）

美国线材协会　American Wire Association（AWA）

美国锌学会　American Zinc Institute（AZI）

美国信息交换标准代码　ASCⅡ（American Standard Code for Information Interchange）

美国压力铸造学会　American Die-casting Institute（ADCI）

美国压铸研究基金会　Die Casting Research Foundation（DCRF）

美国原子核学会　American Nuclear Society（ANS）

美国原子能委员会　United States Atomic Energy Commission（U.S.A.E.C.）

美国轧钢机公司　American Rolling Mill Company（ARMCO）

美国铸钢工作者协会　American Steel Foundrymen's Association（ASFA）

美国铸钢业协会　Steel Founders' Society of America（SFSA）

美国铸造工作者协会　American Foundrymens Association（A.F.A.）

美国铸造工作者学会　American Foundrymen's Society（AFS）

美国专利　United States Patent（USP, U.S.P.），American Patent（A.P.）

美国专利局　United States Patent Office（USPO）

美国自动控制委员会　American Automatic Control Council（AACC）

门　door（dr），gate，portal，【机】closing device　◇有铰链的～flapper，与 A 无关的 B～【计】B ingore A gate

门电路　【计】gate circuit　◇晶体管～transistor gate，数字～digital gate circuit

门二极管　【计】gate diode

门拱　door arch

门过梁　door lintel

门槛　sill

门槛应力　（同"界限应力"）

门捷列夫周期律　Mendeleyeev's law

门径　avenue（ave.）

门坎（装料的）　【冶】door bank

门框　door frame［casing］，gate housing

门框清扫机　【焦】jamb cleaner

门螺栓　door bolt

门脉冲　gate［gating］pulse

门脉冲发生器　gate pulse generator（gpg），gate generator

门脉冲放大器　gate pulse amplifier（GPA）

门式吊架　gallows frame

门式刚架结构　portal-framed structure
门式活顶炉　gantry-type furnace
门式起重机　portal crane ◇ 单脚～semi-gantry crane,港口～quaternion crane,双悬臂～*
门式提升炉顶(电弧炉的)　gantry type roof
门栓大螺丝(焦炉的)　latch screw
门栓钩【焦】latch hook
门限能量　threshold energy
门销　door bolt
门心板　door panel
门形架　portal frame,gantry ◇ 铰支～*,起重机～crane gantry
门形起重机(贮矿场的)　ore (stocking) bridge
门形铁塔　gantry tower
门罩　door casing
闷罐车　covered car,boxcar
闷罐卡车　tank truck
闷罐退火(钢板的)　pot annealing
闷炉【铁】banking
焖炉时间【焦】soaking period
蒙次黄铜　Muntz brass [metal]
蒙大拿假金(10Zn,0.5Al,余量 Cu)　Montana gold
蒙德连续铸镍法　Mond nickel continuous casting process
蒙德羰基镍精炼法　Mond carbonyl (refining) process
蒙蒂盖尔铝合金(0.95Mg,0.8Si,余量 Al)　Montegal
蒙乃尔400耐蚀合金　Monel 400
蒙乃尔合金　Monel metal ◇ K.R.～*,R～*,多孔～过滤器 porous Monel filter,高硅～high silicon Monel,含铜～*
蒙乃尔合金衬里的　Monel-lined
蒙乃尔合金管　Monel tube
蒙乃尔合金盘　Monel tray
蒙乃尔镍基合金(26－30Cu,65－75Ni,少量 Fe,Mn)　Monel
蒙乃尔铸造合金　Monel casting alloy ◇ H～H Monel,改良型～*
蒙尼马克斯软磁合金(43Ni,3Mo,余量 Fe)　Monimax
蒙皮用板材(飞机的)【压】sheathing [shell] plate
蒙特－卡罗静力试验法【理】Monte-Carlo method
蒙脱石｛(OH)$_2$Al$_2$[Si$_2$O$_5$]$_2$·nH$_2$O｝　montmorillonite
锰｛Mn｝　manganese (mang.) ◇ 电池用～*,含～合金*,脱[去]～*
锰白铜丝压力计　manganin pressure gauge
锰白云石　manganese dolomite
锰钡矿　hollandite
锰铋磁铁　manganese-bismuth magnet
锰铋化合物　manganese-bismuth compound
锰磁铁矿　sifbergite
锰的过渡金属合金　transition metal alloy of manganese
锰矾｛MnO·SO$_3$·H$_2$O｝　szmikite
锰钒钢　manganese vanadium steel
锰钒工具钢　manganese vanadium tool steel
锰钙辉石　johannsenite
锰橄榄石｛Mn$_2$SiO$_4$｝　tephroite
锰钢(12－14Mn,1C)　manganese steel ◇ 奥氏体～*,蒂斯科耐磨～*,介稳奥氏体～*,耐蚀耐热～*,斯坦托尔～*,瓦尼特易焊～Vanity steel,伊拉耐蚀耐热～Era manganese steel
锰铬钒合金钢　paragon steel
锰硅钢　manganese silicon steel
锰硅合金　manganese-silicon,siliconmanganese
锰硅铝矿｛Mn$_4$Al$_4$H$_5$VSi$_4$O$_{22}$｝　ardennite
锰硅酸盐渣　manganese-silicate slag
锰硅铁(中间合金;20－25Mn,47－54Si)　ferromanganese-silicon
锰(硅)铜低合金钢 ◇ 雅尔坦～*
锰硅锌矿　troostite

锰合金 manganese alloy
锰黄铜(加有 1—4Mn,1—2Sn,1Fe,1—2Al 的六〇黄铜) manganese brass ◇ 德拉洛特~合金*,西尔维尔~*,铸造~*
锰活度 manganese activity
锰基合金 manganese base alloy
锰尖晶石 $\{MnO \cdot Al_2O_3\}$ galaxite, jacobsite
锰结核(矿)[球团矿] manganese nodule, halobolite ◇ 海洋~ ocean manganese nodule
锰矿 manganese ore
锰矿床 manganese ore deposit
锰矿球团厂 manganese ore pellet plant
锰矿物 manganese mineral
锰磷矿 fillowite
锰铝合金 manganese-aluminum, aluflex(电缆电线用)
锰铝青铜 manganese-aluminum-bronze
锰明矾 $\{MnO \cdot Al_2O_3 \cdot 4SO_3 \cdot 22H_2O\}$ apjohnite
锰钠矿 manjiroite
锰铌铁矿 $\{(Mn,Fe)Nb_2O_6\}$ mangano-columbite
锰镍合金(3Mn,余量 Ni) manganese-nickel
锰硼合金(约含 20—25B,60—65Mn) manganese-boron
锰青铜(含锰的六〇黄铜;56—60Cu,38—40Zn,1—3.5Mn,少量 Al,Fe,Sn) manganese bronze (Mang.B.) ◇ 仿造~*,高强度耐蚀~*
锰烧损 manganese loss
锰石榴石 $\{3MnO \cdot Al_2O_3 \cdot 2SiO_2\}$ spessartite
锰酸铷 $\{Rb_2MnO_4\}$ rubidium manganate
锰酸盐 manganate
锰弹簧钢 manganese spring steel
锰钽矿 ixiolite, cassitero tantalite
锰钽铁矿 $\{(Mn,Fe)Ta_2O_6\}$ mangano-tantalite

锰铁(中间合金;76—78Mn,0.6—7C) manganous iron, ferromanganese ◇ 含氮~*,精炼~ refined ferromanganese
锰铁橄榄石 knebelite
锰铁矾铅矿 brackebuschite
锰铁合金(含 14Mn) manganese iron
锰铁尖晶石 magnetostibian
锰铁矿 ferriferous manganese ore
锰铁熔化炉 Fe-Mn furnace
锰铁熔炼 【铁】ferromanganese smelting
锰铁尖晶石 manganetostibian
锰铜(86Cu,12Mn,2Ni) manganin alloy, copper-manganese, manganese copper
锰铜标准电阻丝合金 Minalpha
锰铜低合金钢 Jalten
锰铜合金(50—90Mn,余量 Cu) manganese copper (alloy) ◇ 高镍~*
锰铜矿 crednerite
锰铜镍合金 manganese-copper-nickel
锰铜丝[线] manganin wire
锰土 wad clay, black ocher
锰土微菌 Pedomicrobium manganicum
锰团矿 manganese nodules
锰脱氧[锰镇静]钢 manganese killed steel
锰系元素 manganides
锰纤锌矿 erythrozincite, erythrozinkite
锰锌铁氧体[铁淦氧磁铁](15—45MnO, 7—22ZnO, 45—63Fe$_2$O$_3$, 0—6MgO) manganese-zinc ferrite
锰氧化 manganese oxidation
锰氧平衡 manganese-oxygen equilibrium
锰增量 【钢】manganese addition
锰质结核 manganese concretion
猛烈摆动 thrash(ing)
猛烈出钢 violent tap
猛烈沸腾 【冶】wild(ness),【钢】swirling
猛烈沸腾炉次 【钢】wild heat
孟山都公司动力波湿式气体洗涤器(美) Monsanto Dyna-Wave wet gas scrubber
孟山都公司热回收系统(美) Monsanto heat recovery system

醚化物　etherat
醚化(作用)　etherification
迷宫圈　collar
迷宫式密封　labyrinth (type seal)
迷宫式压盖　labyrinth gland
弥漫　interfuse, interfusion, suffusion ◇ 反(行)~ back diffusion
弥散　dispersion (dpn), dispersal, diffusing, diffusion, deflocculation ◇ 二氧化钍~镍 TD nickel, 水在油中~ water-in-oil dispersion, 油在水中~ oil-in-water dispersion
弥散测量[量度]　measure of dispersion
弥散度　dispersity, dispersiveness, dispersion degree [size], degree [scale] of dispersion
弥散剂　dispersant agent, dispersing agent [medium], dispersion agent [medium]
弥散介质　dispersion [dispersive] medium
弥散力　【理】dispersion force
弥散器　disperser ◇ 旋转式~, 振动挡板式~
弥散气体　dispersing gas
弥散强化　dispersion [precipitation] strengthening, dispersion-hardening
弥散强化材料　dispersion strengthened material, dispersive strengthing material
弥散强化合金　dispersion strengthened alloy ◇ 氧化物~
弥散强化金属　dispersion-strengthened metal
弥散强化铝制品　dispersion strengthened aluminium product
弥散强化铅　dispersion strengthened lead
弥散溶质原子　dispersed solute atom
弥散塔　dispersion tower
弥散添加剂　dispersing additive
弥散涂层　dispersion coating
弥散微粒　【理】dispersion particles
弥散物[体]　dispersoid
弥散物形态学　dispersoid morphology
弥散析出[沉淀]物　dispersed precipitate

弥散系　dispersed system
弥散系数　coefficient of dispersion
弥散现象　dispersion
弥散相　disperse(d) [internal] phase
弥散相硬化　dispersed phase hardening
弥散效应(作用)　dispersion effect
弥散型多元合金　dispersion type complicated alloy
弥散硬化　dispersion-hardening
弥散硬化钢　precipitation-hardening steel
弥散硬化合金　dispersion-hardened alloy
弥散硬化金属　dispersion-hardened metal
弥散硬化铁合金　dispersion hardened iron alloy
弥散硬化型金属陶瓷材料　【粉】dispersion-hardened compact
弥散云　dispersed-cloud
弥散质点　【半】dispersoid, 【理】dispersion particles
弥散质点尺寸[大小]　【粉】dispersoid size
弥散(质点)障碍作用范围　field of dispersed obstacles
弥散状态　state of dispersion
莱　mesitylen, mesitylol
莱基{2,4,6-(CH$_3$)$_3$C$_6$H$_2$-}　mesityl
莱基化氧{(CH$_3$)$_2$C:CHCOCH$_3$}　mesityl oxide
莱酰　mesitoyl
莱氧基{2,4,6-(CH$_3$)$_3$C$_6$H$_2$O-}　mesityloxy
米　meter (m), metre ◇ 按每~计 running meter
米巴赫高效闪光(对)焊机　Miebach high efficiency flash welding machine
米德兰德-罗斯金属丸粒制作与喷镀综合处理法　【金】Midland-Ross process
米德兰德-罗斯竖炉法　【团】Midland-Ross shaft process
米德雷克斯法　【铁】Midrex process
米德雷克斯法海绵铁　Midrex sponge iron
米德雷克斯法直接还原厂　【铁】Midrex plant

米德雷克斯法直接还原炉料 【铁】 Midrex metallized iron material
米德雷克斯法直接还原设备 【铁】 Midrex plant
米德欧姆铜镍电阻合金(22—23Ni,余量Cu) Midohm
米蒂斯铸件(软钢铸件) Mitis casting
米·吨·秒制(单位) metre-ton-second
米格拉高级铸铁 Migra iron
米格式铁合金熔炼炉 Miguet furnace
米哈埃利斯断裂试验机 Michaelis machine
米卡塔胶纸板 Micarta
米卡塔绝缘环 Micarta insulating ring
米克罗利特氧化铝微粒陶瓷切削刀具 Milrolit
米克罗硬度计 Mikro-tester
米克西粉末混合度测定器 Mixee
米库姆转鼓试验 【焦】Micum test ◇ 半~*
米拉耐酸合金 Mira metal
米拉赖特耐蚀铝合金(4.1Ni,0.4Fe,0.3Si,0.04Pb,0.04Na,余量Al) Miralite
米拉耐蚀铜合金[耐酸合金](75Cu,16.3Pb,6.8Sb,0.91Sn,0.62Zn,0.43Fe,0.25Ni)Mira metal
米拉丘洛依耐高压铸造合金(1.5Ni,1.25Mn,0.65Cr,0.4Si,0.35C,0.3Mo,余量Fe) Miraculoy
米拉(铜铅)合金(75Cu,16Pb,7Sb,1Sn,0.4Fe,0.24Ni+Co) Mira
米勒－布喇菲指数 Miller-Bravais indices
米勒指数(晶面的) Miller indices
米纳尔法低温度系数电阻合金(86Cu,12Mn,2Ni) Minalpha
米纳尔法铜锰镍合金(86Cu,12Mn,2Ni) Minalpha
米纳金特铜镍合金(56Cu,40Ni,3W,1Al;银代用品) Minargent
米诺法餐具用锡基合金(17—20Sb,9—10Zn,3—4Cu,余量Sn) Minofar
米诺福尔耐磨轴承合金(66—69Sn,18—20Sb,9—10Zn,3—4Cu,0—1Fe) Minofor
米诺瓦低膨胀耐蚀高镍铸铁(34—36Ni,余量Fe) Minovar
米·千克·秒·安有理单位制(吉奥尔吉制) MKSA (Giorgi) rationalized system of units
米·千克·秒单位制 meter-kilogram-second units (MKS,mks), MKS unit system
米氏合金 pyrophoric alloy
米斯科镍铬铁系耐热耐蚀合金(12—30Cr,30—65Ni,余量Fe) Misco (metal)
米希罗姆铁铬系不锈钢(16—30Cr,0.25—2.5C,余量Fe) Mischrome
米谢效应 Mitsche's effect
米制 metric(al) system
米制测量[量度] metrical measure
米制单位 metric unit
觅数 【计】search
泌浆(混凝土的) 【建】bleeding
泌水 weepage
蜜胺 (同"三聚氰酰胺")
密闭 hermetic closure
密闭爆发器检漏试验 bomb test
密闭槽 closed cell
密闭的 closed,air-proof
密闭度 closeness,leakproofness
密闭钢弹反应器 closed bomb reactor
密闭鼓风炉铅锌熔炼法(英国) Imperial smelting process
密闭罐 pressure-tight retort
密闭搅拌器 closed agitator
密闭金属盒 closed metal box
密闭浸出槽 enclosed leaching tank
密闭内压力成形 pressure-tight forming
密闭(铅锌)鼓风炉(英国) Imperial Smelting Furnace (I.S.F.)
密闭容器 closed container
密闭烧结(的) close-burning
密闭烧舟 closed boat

密闭(式)鼓风炉　closed-top blast furnace
密闭式冷却箱　【铁】closed cooling box
密闭式连续自焙阳极电解槽　enclosed soederberg cell
密闭退火　close annealed (C.A.), box [pot] annealing
密闭退火炉　close annealing furnace
密闭压滤机　closed filter press
密闭烟罩　closed hood
密度　density (den.), specific mass, intensity ◇ 表面[布面]～areal density, 超灰雾～, 哈密尔顿～Hamiltonian density, 真～full density
密度比　density ratio
密度比较仪　densitometer comparator
密度变化　density charge [variation], change in density
密度-表面张力球　density-surface tension bob
密度波动　density fluctuations
密度差　difference in density
密度等级[级别]　density fraction
密度分布　density distribution
密度分布不均　non-uniform density distribution
密度分布函数　density function
密度分离[分选]　density sorting
密度函数　density function
密度计　densi(to)meter, density gauge [meter, sensor] ◇ γ射线～γ-ray density meter, 放射性～*, 记录显像～recording densitometer, 散装物料[颗粒料]～bulk density meter
密度记录器　density recorder
密度检验　density testing
密度降低　density decrease [drop]
密度控制　density control
密度控制[调节]器　denisty controller (DC, D.C.), density-control device
密度瓶　density bottle
密度曝光曲线　H and D (Hurter and Driffield) curve

密度球　density bob
密度曲线　densimetric curve
密度梯度　density gradient
密度增加　density increase
密度值　density value
密度指示器　density indicator
密堆积[堆集]　【理】close(d) packing
密堆积层　close-packed layer
密堆积六方(的)　close-packed hexagonal (cph)
密耳(=0.0254mm, 金属丝直径的测量单位)　mil
密封　seal, packaging, hermetically tight seal, hermetic closure, hermetization, enclosing ◇ 层上～over-bed seal, 挠性不锈钢～盒*
密封瓣阀　flapper seal valve
密封棒　seal [wearing] bar
密封包装　air-tight packing
密封焙烧(的)　close-burning
密封泵　sealed [canned] pump
密封材料　seal(ing) [packing] material, sealant
密封舱　air-lock, sealed cabin
密封槽　seal tank, closed cell
密封层　sealant
密封衬套[套筒]　sealing bush
密封吹氩调整成分(法)　composition adjustment by sealed argon bubbling
密封处理　canning
密封刀边(炉门框的)　【焦】sealing ring [strip], gasketed ring
密封电解槽　sealed elecfrolytic cell
密封垫　(sealing) gasket, air-tight packing
密封垫圈　sealing [joint] washer
密封电解槽　sealed electrolytic cell
密封度　tightness, degree of packing
密封风机　seal fan
密封盖　sealing gland, sealed [sealing] cover
密封钢丝绳　sheathed wire rope, locked coil wire rope

密封辊　seal(ing) roll
密封锅　seal pot
密封焊接　seal welding
密封滑板[块](带式烧结机的)　drop bar
密封环　gasketed [seal(ing), caulking, packing] ring, O-ring seal, joint washer
密封剂　sealant, sealing compound ◇ 可熔注～
密封件　seal(ing) element, packaging, obturator
密封接合　air-tight joint
密封接头　hermetic seal
密封连接　tight connection
密封料斗　seal hopper
密封炉　sealed furnace
密封炉顶(高炉的)　sealed top
密封炉顶式高炉　closed top furnace
密封能力　sealing ability
密封排灰输送机　enclosed dust conveyer
密封气体　sealing gas
密封圈　seal loop [ring], O-ring seal, sealing washer
密封式保险丝[熔断器]　enclosed fuse
密封室　seal chamber ◇ 充惰性气体的～ inert atmosphere room
密封水　seal water
密封缩颈　sealing constriction
密封套　seal housing [cartridge]
密封条　sealing strip ◇ 挠性～【铸】dike, 小～【铸】baby dike
密封涂层　air-tight coating
密封物　densener
密封箱　sealing [stuffing] box
密封箱烧结　sintering in sealed box
密封性　leakproofness
密封压盖　【机】(seal) gland
密封液(体)　sealing [packing, confining] liquid, sealing fluid
密封用铁镍钴合金　◇ 西尔瓦～
密封(装箱)桶　air-tight drum
密封装置　seal, hermetically tight seal, sealing device ◇ 落棒式～【团】drop-bar type seal
密合压扁试验　close-flattening test
密烘铸铁　mechanite (metal)
密化粉末　densified powder
密黄长石　meliphanite {(Ca, Na)₂(Be, Al)[Si₂O₆F]}, meliphane {(Ca, Na)₂Be(Al, Si)₂(O, F)₇}
密积液体　close-packed liquid
密集点阵[晶格]　【理】compact [close-packed] lattice
密集结构　【理】close-packed structure
密集料流　mass flow
密集冷却板　intensified cooling plate
密集取样　close sampling
密级配集料[骨料]　【建】dense-graded aggregate
密接　【粉】closing
密结合　strong [tight] binding
密蜡石　Ca₄Si₃O₁₀, mel(l)ilite
密肋楼板　ribbed slab, rib floor
密排方向　【理】close-packed direction
密排结构　【理】close-packed structure
密排晶格　【理】close-packed lattice, closely spaced lattice
密排(列)　【理】closed packing
密排六方氮化硼　close-packed hexagonal boron nitride
密排六方点阵[晶格]　hexagonal close packed lattice, closed packed hexagon(al) (lattice)
密排六方结构　hexagonal close packed structure, close-packed hexagonal structure
密排六方(结构)金属　hexagonal close-packed metal, close-packed hexagonal metal
密排六方(晶格)变型　【金】hexagonal close packed modification
密排六方(晶格)的　closed packed hexagonal, hexagonal close packed (HCP)
密排六方晶体　close-packed hexagonal crystal

密排六方晶系 close-packed hexagonal system (lattice)
密排六方相 【金】hexagonal close packed phase
密排[集]面 close-packed plane
密排(面心)立方点阵[晶格] close-packed (face-centred) cubic lattice
密排原子晶胞 close-packed atomic cell
密实层 【地】close bed
密实充填 close-packing, dense packing
密实度 consistency ◇ 用贯入法测土～ needle density
密实焊缝 【焊】tight seam, caulking weld
密实化 consolidating
密实混凝土 dense [air-free] concrete
密实系数 (同"致密系数")
密实性 solidity
密实压力 compacting pressure
密斯特里白金[锡铜合金] mystery
密致材料 dense material
密致絮凝层 dense flocbed
幂 【数】power, index, exponent
幂级 power level
幂数 exponent(ial) quantity
棉布带 cotton belt
棉布(隔膜)袋 muslin bag
棉护臂 cotton armlet
棉花打包用窄带钢 cotton tie
棉织品 cotton fabrics [goods]
棉织物 baf(fe)ta
棉籽油 cotton seed oil
冕形齿顶 【机】crowned tooth tip
冕形齿联轴节 crowned tooth [gear] coupling
冕状齿轮 crown gear
免除 immunization, immunizing, remitting
免费 without charge (W.C., w.c.), free of charge, cost free
免维修的 maintenance-free
免疫抗体 immunity resistant
面 surface, face, plane, side ◇ 费米～ Fermi surface

面板 faceplate, panel ◇ 不露带电部分的～ dead front
面板不露带电部分的配电盘 dead front switchboard
面板用仪表 surface type meter
面部纵裂(连铸板坯缺陷) longitudinal facial crack
面层 (mat) coat, topcoat, surface course
面吹(转炉的) surface-blowing, blowup of charge
面吹转炉 surface-blown converter
面瓷砖 furring tile
面对称 face symmetry
面对面撞击 face-to-face impact
面粉状氧化铝 floury alumina
面光源 plane light source, area source
面积 area ◇ 测～法 planimetric method
面积测定器 planimeter
面积测量[量度] square measure, measure of area, planimetering
面积法分析 area analysis
面积分 surface integral
面积计算法(测定晶粒度用) planimetric method
面积收缩[缩减] 【压】reduction of [in] area, contraction of area ◇ 断裂时的～*
面积系数 area coefficient [factor]
面际区 interfacial zone
面间间距 interplanar spacing
面间角 interfacial angle
面角 face [facial] angle
面接触钢丝绳 plane contact lay wire rope, facial-contracted wire rope
面结型场效应晶体管 junction field effect transistor
面筋(可做型芯胶用) gluten
面料 facing
面料层 precoat
面缺陷 【金】plane [planar] defect
面砂 【铸】facing sand
面饰 facing

面缩率　reduction of area (RA)
面下腐蚀　layer corrosion
面向计算机的　computer-oriented
面向空间的　space-oriented
面向人的语言　【计】humam-oriented language
面向商业的通用语言　(同"COBOL 语言")
面向文件的程序设计　【计】file oriented programming
面向信息的语言　【计】information-oriented language (INFOL)
面向语法的编译程序　【计】syntax-oriented compiler
面向制表系统的语言　【计】tabular systems oriented language (TABSOL)
面心点阵[晶格]　【金】face-centered lattice, F lattice
面心立方(晶格)　【金】face-centered cubic (FCC)
面心立方变态(晶型)　face-centered cubic modification
面心立方点阵[晶格]　face-centered cube lattice
面心立方点阵原子密排面堆砌次序　face-centered sequence of layers
面心立方合金　face-centered cubic alloy
面心立方结构　face-centered cubic structure
面心立方金属　face-centered cubic metal
面心立方晶胞　face-centered cubic cell
面心立方晶体　face-centered cubic crystal
面心立方晶系　face-centered cubic lattice system
面心立方晶型　face-centered cubic form
面心立方相　face-centered cubic phase
面心立方铜金合金　face-centered cubic copper-gold alloy
面心四方点阵　face-centered tetragonal lattice
面心位置　【金】face-centered position
面心正交点阵[晶格]　face-centered ortho-rhombic lattice
面罩　(face) mask ◇ 防护[保护]～,焊工～
苗木石　(同"锆铀矿")
描绘　tracing
描绘板　plotting board
描绘花纹[花样]　【建】patterning
描绘器[仪,装置]　tracing device ◇ BH 曲线～BH curve tracer
描迹带　tracing tape
描图仪　tracer, tracing instrument
描图纸　tracing paper ◇ 画详图用的～ detail paper
瞄准　aiming, collimation ◇ 射击前～时间 dead time
瞄准器　sighting device, hairline
瞄准(十字)线　hairline
灭弧　arc extinction [blow-out], quenching
灭弧槽(开关的)　arc chute
灭弧电路　quench [arc-suppression] circuit
灭弧器　spark catcher, extinguisher, quencher
灭弧室　arc-extinquish chamber
灭弧线圈　extinction [arc-suppression] coil ◇ 磁吹～blow out coil
灭火泵　fire pump
灭火剂　fire extinguishing agent
灭火龙头　fire hydrant
灭火器　(fire) extinguisher, (fire) extinguishing apparatus, flame damper
民用建筑　civilian architecture [construction], civil engineering
民用煤气　town gas
皿状的　dish-shaped
敏感层　sensitive layer
敏感度　sensitivity, susceptibility
敏感系数　sensitivity factor
敏感性　sensibility, sensitivity, sensitiveness
敏感性分析　【企】sensitivity analysis
敏感元件　sensing [detecting] element

敏化剂　sensitizer, sensibilizer
敏化温度　sensitizing temperature
敏化状态(不锈钢的)　sensitized condition
敏化(作用)　sensibilization, sensitization
敏热处理　sensitizing (heat) treatment
敏瓦尔低膨胀系数合金铸铁(29 或 36Ni, 2Cr, 余量 Fe)　Minvar
明槽　open groove
明度　lightness
明矾 $\{K \cdot Al(SO_4)_2 \cdot 12H_2O\}$　(white) alum ◇ 烧～burnt alum
明矾凝聚　【环】alum coagulation
明矾石 $\{K_2O \cdot 3Al_2O_3 \cdot 4SO_3 \cdot 6H_2O\}$　alumstone, alunite
明缝　exposed joint, outseam
明沟(感应炉的)　【冶】open channel
明弧焊(接)　open [unshielded] arc welding
明火　open fire [flame, light]
明胶　gelatin(e)
明胶复型　【金】gelatin replica
明浇　open (sand) casting
明浇地面砂型　【铸】open floor mould
明浇砂型　【铸】open sand mould
明接头　exposed joint
明亮干涉条纹　bright fringe
明亮火焰　clear flame
明冒口　【铸】open riser
明排管道　ditch conduit
明配线　open [exposed] wiring
明(视)场(显微镜的)　bright field
明(视)场法　【金】bright field method
明(视)场反射(光线)法　【金】bright field reflection method
明(视)场观察　bright field observation
明(视)场检验　bright field examination
明(视)场聚光镜　bright field condenser
明(视)场透射(光线)法　【金】bright field transmission method
明(视)场显微照片　【金】bright field micrograph
明(视)场像　bright field image

明(视)场衍射反衬[衬映]技术　bright field diffraction contrast technique
明(视)场照明　bright field illumination
明(视)场照明器　bright field illuminator
明缩孔　【铸】open cavity
明挖隧道　open-cut tunnel
明细表　specification, detail list ◇ 电动机～motor list
明显屈服　sharp yield
明显屈服点理论　theory of sharp yield-point
明线　exposed wiring, open wire, aerial conductor ◇ 布设～exposed wiring
明线光谱　bright line spectrum
明芯座　【铸】open core print seat
明焰加热退火　flame annealing
明焰隧道窑　open-flame tunnel kiln
铭牌　name plate (NP), data plate, label
名称　name, designation, nomenclature
名义减面率　【压】nominal percentage reduction of area
名义截面减缩比　【压】nominal unit reduction in area
名义直径　(同"公称直径")
命令　command, order, directive, instruction
命令方式　【计】command mode
命令名称　【计】command name
命令译码程序　【计】command decoder
命令语言　【计】command language
命令字符　【计】command character
命名法[原则]　nomenclature
命题演算　【计】propositional calculus
命中率　hit-rate, hitting accuracy [ratio], percentage of hits ◇ 成分～
缪镍铁铜系高导磁率合金(75Ni, 20Fe, 5Cu)　Mumetal
蘑菇　mushroom ◇ 形成～头(钢线材缺陷) cupping
蘑菇阀　(同"悬钟式阀")
蘑菇式穿孔机　(同"菌式穿孔机")
蘑菇头断裂　cuppiness

蘑菇形轧辊穿孔机[管材扩径机]　rotary-rolling mill
蘑菇状烟云　【理】mushroom
模　mode, modulo
模版印刷　stencil(l)ing
模变换器　mode transducer
模冲固定板　punch plate
模冲接合器　punch adapter
模冲压板　punch clamp
模仿　copy, simulation
模糊　dim, blurring, unsharpness, fuzzy ◇ 斑点～*, 变～haze formation, 曝光致～(底片的) light fog
模糊关系　fuzzy relation
模糊集　fuzzy set
模糊控制　fuzzy control
模糊控制逻辑　fuzzy control logic
模糊控制器　fuzzy controller ◇ 自组织～
模糊理论　fuzzy theory
模糊逻辑　fuzzy logic
模糊逻辑控制　fuzzy logic control
模糊逻辑控制器　fuzzy logic controller
模糊逻辑系统　fuzzy logic system
模糊神经网络　fuzzy neural network
模糊识别理论　fuzzy recognition theory
模糊效应　blurring effect ◇ 边界轮廓～ smearing effect
模糊数学　fuzzy mathematics
模糊学　fuzzlogy
模糊影像　blurred image
模糊诊断　【计】fuzzy diagnosis
模糊专家系统　fuzzy expert system
模架　【粉】adapter, adaptor
模架台　adaptor table
模块　【计】module
模块程序设计　【计】modular programming
模块化　【计】modularity
模块结构　modular construction
模块(件)性　modularity
模量　modulus (mod., 复数 moduli)
模量亏损　modulus defect

模量效应　modulus effect
模内液面　mould level
模内液面控制　mould level control
模拟　analog(ue), analogy, simulation, emulation ◇ 定～比例因子 analogscaling, 人脑[人的]～【计】humam simulation
模拟编译程序系统　analog compiler system
模拟表示法　analog representation
模拟操作台　analogue desk, mimic graphic desk
模拟乘法器　analog multiplier
模拟程序　simulator program [routine]
模拟传输　analog transmission
模拟存储器　analog memory [storage]
模拟电路　analog circuit, simulator
模拟法　analogue method
模拟仿真　analog simulation
模拟放大器　analog amplifier
模拟分析　simulation analysis
模拟高炉　pseudoblast furnace
模拟仿真　analog simulation
模拟分析　simulation analysis
模拟机　analog machine
模拟极　【理】analog poles
模拟技术　analogue [simulation] technique
模拟计数装置　analogue computer
模拟计算机　analog computer, anacom ◇ 区域熔炼～
模拟计算装置　analog computing device, analogue computer
模拟检测器　analogue tester
模拟接口【计】　analog interface
模拟卡片检测器　analogue card checker
模拟开关　analog switch
模拟控制　analog control
模拟控制测量仪　analogue tester
模拟量　analog (quantity)
模拟母线盘　mimic bus panel
模拟盘　mimic diagram board
模拟器　simulator, imitator
模拟热轧机　hot strip simulator

模拟射流　analog fluidic
模拟实验　simulated experiment ◇ 连续过程～analog simulation
模拟试验　simulated [model] test
模拟输出　analog output
模拟输入　analog input
模拟输入操作　analog input operation
模拟输入模件　analog input module
模拟－数字传感　（同"模－数传感"）
模拟－数字计算机　analog-digital computer
模(拟)－数(字)数据互换　【计】analog-digital data interconversion
模(拟)－数(字)转换装置　【计】analog-digital commutater
模拟条件　simulated conditions
模拟通道　analog channel
模拟网络　analog network
模拟系统　analog system, analog(ue)
模拟系统图　mimic diagram, sight-reading chart
模拟显示　analog display
模拟线路图　mimic circuit chart
模拟信号　【电】analog signal
模拟信号发生器　simulated signal generator
模拟研究　analog study
模拟仪　analogue meter
模拟指示器　analogue indicator
模拟装置　analog, analogue device, simulator
模拟组件检测器　analogue module checker
模绕线圈　form wound coil
模式　mode, model, pattern
模式控制　mode control
模式识别　【计】pattern recognition
模式选择器　mode selector
模数　modulus (mod.), module, modulo
模－数传感　analog-to-digital sensing
模数法设计　modular design
模数构造　modular construction

模－数－模转换器　analog-digital-analog converter
模数试验装置　module test unit
模数制　modular system
模－数转换　analog-to-digital conversion
模－数转换器　analog-(to-)digital (A/D, A-D) converter
模态　modality
模型　pattern (patt.), model, mould (matrix) ◇ 玻尔～Bohr picture,成套～pattern assembly,分块～【铸】sectional pattern,弗伦克尔～（位错的）Frenkel model,实物～*,示意～schematic model,一次～【铸】lost pattern,易熔～【铸】fusible pattern,制～车床*,组合～*
模型板　template board [plate]
模型标记　【铸】escutcheon
模型定位销钉　pattern dowel
模型法[化]　model(l)ing
模型黄铜　matrix brass
模型计算　model computation
模型开缝扣榫　【铸】slotted pattern key
模型润滑　mould wash
模型润滑液　【铸】parting liquid
模型上半部　pattern cope
模型设计板　【铸】layout board
模型试验　model test
模型缩尺差错(缺陷)　【铸】wrong pattern allowance
模型托板　follow board
模型系数　mould ratio
模型支架　pattern holder
模型(制作)工　modelmaker,【铸】master
模型组　pattern assembly
模型组合　mould splits, card of patterns
模压　die [mould] pressing, moulding, stamping, blanking, contour forging ◇ 静液压～* hydrostatic moulding
模压成形　die forming ◇ 异形～contour forming
模压淬火　(die-) press quenching, die quenching

模压淬火挤压　die-quenched extruding
模压机　forming [block] press, moulding machine ◇ 浮沉[弹簧]~ floating die press, 液压~*
模压永久磁铁　moulded permanent magnet
模压制模法　【压】cold hobbing
模压铸造　extrusion [squeeze] casting, casting by squeezing ◇ 巴科~法【铸】Bacco process
模制粉末铁淦氧　moulded powdered ferrite
模铸的　moulded-on
模子寿命　life of die
膜　membrane, film ◇ 成~能力 film forming capacity
膜壁烟罩　membrane-walled hood
膜层强度　film strength
膜处置技术　【环】film disposal technique
膜盒　bellows, (diaphragm) capsule
膜盒式流量计　【理】bellows flowmeter
膜盒压力计　bellows gauge
膜盒元件　bellows element
膜片　diaphragm, membrane, capsule, film
膜(渗)平衡　membrane equilibrium
膜渗水解　membrane hydrolysis
膜式流量计　diaphragm (flow) meter
膜式压力计　diaphragm gauge, membrane manometer
膜水解　membrane hydrolysis
膜透过性(指反渗透膜)　membrane flux
膜下腐蚀　underfilm corrosion
膜压式薄壳制型机　diaphragm shell moulding machine
膜压造型　【铸】diaphragm moulding
膜压造型机　【铸】diaphragm moulding machine
膜状冷凝[凝缩]　film condensation
磨剥作用　abrasive action
磨边设备　edger unit
磨擦　gritting, rub
磨成粉　flour,【粉】powdering

磨除铁鳞[氧化皮]　abrasive descaling
磨床　grinding machine, grinder ◇ 冲模-压模用~*, 带式[皮带]~*, 电动砂盘~ electric disc sander, 刚玉砂~*
磨床工　grinding operator
磨掉冒口　snag
磨钝的　dull
磨粉(血滴石粉)　crocus
磨粉浆　abrasive slurry
磨缸机　【机】cylinder grinding machine
磨割机　abrasive cutoff machine
磨工　grinding operator, grinder,【机】mill operator
磨工车间　grindery
磨光　polish(ing), (abrasive) finish(ing), grinding, planish ◇ 带式[用研磨带]~*, 砂带~ linishing, 用灰~ ashing
磨光棒　burnishing stick
磨光表面　grinding surface
磨光镀铬(铜合金的)　buffed chrome finish
磨光镀镍(铜合金的)　buffed nickel finish
磨光粉　polishing [grinding] powder, brilliancy mass, grit
磨光滚轮　burnishing roller
磨光机　polishing device [machine], abrader ◇ 电解~*
磨光剂　grinding materail, buffing compound
磨光聚焦弯晶单色器　curved-and-ground focusing reflector
磨光拉丝机　combined roll grinding and fluting machine
磨光轮　polishing [buffing] wheel
磨光器　polisher, burnisher
磨光砂带　abrasive belt
磨光试样　polished sample
磨光体　tumbling body
磨光弯晶单色器　【理】curved-and-ground crystal
磨光轧辊　【电】ground roll
磨光砖　dressed brick

磨辊 roll grinding
磨辊工 roll dresser
磨耗 wear(ing-away), abrasion, abrasive [attrition] wear, detrition
磨耗层 wearing coat ◇ 沥青~*
磨耗度 degree of wear
磨耗试验 wearing [abrasion, attrition] test
磨耗试验转筒 rattler
磨合性(轴承的) conformability
磨合轴颈 worn-in journal
磨痕(金属表面的) polishing scratch, abrasion marks
磨坏的 worn-out
磨机 grinding machine [mill] ◇ 摆锤式~ swing hammer mill, 冲击~ impact (grinding) mill, 干(式)~ dry grinding mill, 滚筒式~*, 哈梅塔格旋涡冲击式~*, 瀑式~* cascade mill, 实验型~ laboratory mill, 双格式~ two compartment mill, 微粉~*, 智利~ Chilian mill, 周边排矿式~*
磨机装料(量) grinding charges
磨尖 pointing, tagging, slendering
磨角样品 【半】angle lapped specimen
磨具 grinding tool
磨口玻璃塞 ground glass stopper
磨口的 ground-in
磨矿 grinding of ores, milling, bucking ◇ 分段~ step grinding
磨矿操作(工序) grinding operation
磨矿段长度 grinding length
磨矿方式 grinding mode
磨矿工段 grinding section [plant]
磨矿工序 grinding stage
磨矿过细 overgrinding
磨矿机 grinding mill ◇ 湿式~ wet pan mill, 竖筒~【团】vertical mill, 一段~【选】primary mill
磨矿机衬板 mill liner
磨矿粒度 liberation grind
磨矿盘 muller pan

磨矿设备 grinding plant
磨矿系统 grinding system
磨矿系统流程 flow sheet of grinding circuit
磨矿制度 grinding regime
磨粒 (abrasive) grain, abrasive particle
磨料 abrasive (media, grit, material), abradant, abraser, grinding materail, grit ◇ 尖角~ angular abrasive, 软质~ soft abrasives, 用~磨 gritting
磨料粉 abrasive powder
磨料粒度 grit size
磨轮 grinding [abrasive] wheel
磨轮驱动电动机 grinding wheel drive motor
磨轮头 grinding wheel head
磨轮整修工具 wheel dressing tool
磨轮整修装置 grinding wheel truing device
磨轮自动平衡器 grinding wheel auto-balancer
磨毛刺机 burr masher
磨煤 coal grinding
磨煤机 coal pulverizer, coal grinding mill
磨面混凝土 rubbed concrete
磨配工序 matching operation
磨片 (abrasive) disk, (abrasive) disc, polished sample
磨片表面 grinding surface
磨片镜面 grinding face
磨切机 abrasive cutoff machine
磨热发裂 【机】grinding check
磨刃设备 sharpening equipment
磨锐[**快**] whet ◇ 电极工作端~ penciling
磨砂表面 frosting
磨砂玻璃 ground [frosting] glass
磨砂灯泡 frosted lamp
磨伤 abrasive damage, scuffing
磨石 grinding [sharpening] stone, grindstone, whetstone, burrstone ◇ 天然~ grindstone, 细砂质~ buhr

磨石子　terrezzo
磨蚀　erosive [abrasive] wear, abrasion ◇ 易变耐~性*,正常~抗力*
磨蚀试验　abrasion test ◇ 赖特~装置 Wright's apparatus
磨蚀试验机　abrader
磨蚀速率　erosion rate ◇ 合理~*,瞬时~*
磨蚀速率－时间图　erosion rate-time pattern
磨蚀性　abrasive characteristics, abradability, abrasiveness
磨蚀作用　abrasive action
磨碎　grind(ing), comminute, milling, trituration ◇ 闭路~ closed-circuitgrinding, 经~的 ground-down, 矿石~ grinding of ores
磨碎操作(工序)　grinding operation
磨碎段长度　grinding length
磨碎方式　grinding mode [regime]
磨碎费用　grinding cost
磨碎分离颗粒　released grains
磨碎粉末　【粉】milled powder
磨碎工段　grinding section
磨碎工序　grinding stage
磨碎机　grinding mill, grinder, attrition mill, attritor ◇ 黏土~【耐】claymill, 烧渣[炉渣,轧屑]~ cinder mill, 鼠笼式~ squirrel cage mill
磨碎间　grinding chamber
磨碎碱性炉渣　【冶】ground basic slag
磨碎粒度　fineness of gringding
磨碎耐火材料　grog
磨碎设备　grinding equipment [facilities]
磨碎体　grinding element
磨碎作业线　grinding line
磨碎作用　milling action
磨损　abrasive wear [damage], abrasion, attrition (wear), wear (abrasive), wearing-away, chafing, fray, gall(ing), seizing ◇ 使用[运行]~ service wear, 严重~ heavy wear, 原有~*

磨损部分　wear parts
磨损层　wearing coat
磨损衬板　wearing plate
磨损程度　degree of wear
磨损冲击力　abrasive impact energy
磨损的　abrasive, outworn, torn-up, worn-out
磨损度　wearability, wearing capacity
磨损沟(冷拔模的)　worn
磨损机理(炉衬的)　mechanism of wear
磨损极限　wear limit, limit of wear
磨损拉模的磨光　die ripping
磨损量　amount of wear
磨损率　wear rate, specific wearability
磨损面　abrasive surface, wearing face
磨损疲劳　fretting fatigue
磨损期限　wear-life
磨损深度　wearing depth
磨损试验　abrasion [wearing, attrition] test ◇ 布氏~ Brinell wear testing
磨损试验机　abrasion tester, abrasion (testing) machine, wear [attrition] testing machine ◇ 微振~ fretting apparatus
磨损速率　rate of wear
磨损特性　wearing characteristic
磨损系数　coefficient of wear
磨损效应　abrasion effect
磨损性　abrasive characteristics, abradability, abrasiveness, wearing capacity
磨损性(水)射流加工　abrasive water jet processing
磨损性氧化　wear oxidation
磨损性质　abrasive nature
磨损硬度　abrasive hardness
磨损值　attrition value
磨条　abrasive stick
磨头(磨钻模针用)　【压】bistrique
磨细石料　ground stone
磨削　grind(ing) ◇ 高精度~ seal ground finish, 经~的 ground-down, 无心~*
磨削操作(工序)　grinding operation
磨削长度　【机】grinding length

磨削方式	grinding mode [regime]
磨削费用	grinding cost
磨削工段	grinding section
磨削工序	grinding stage
磨削间	grinding chamber
磨削精度	fineness of grinding
磨削冷却油	grinding oil
磨削裂纹	grinding crack
磨削面	grinding face
磨削能力	grinding capacity
磨削热裂敏感性	grinding sensitivity
磨削设备	grinding equipment [facilities]
磨削特性	grinding characteristics
磨削性[可磨削性]	grindability
磨削余量【机】	grinding allowance
磨削作业线	grinding line
磨屑	grinding [abrasive] dust, wheel swarf
磨芯头【铸】	core jigging
磨芯头机	core grinder
磨修工作台	grinding bed
磨渣	slag-grinding
磨渣场[设备]	slag-grinding plant
摩擦	friction, attrition, scouring, chafing ◇ 产生～的粉末 friction producing powder, 未加润滑剂的～ unlubricated friction, 轧机部件内的～ mill friction
摩擦材料	friction material ◇ 衬背～*, 铜基合金～*
摩擦操纵杆(夹板锤的)【机】	friction bar
摩擦层	friction producing layer
摩擦衬片	friction lining [facing]
摩擦触点	wiping contact
摩擦传动(装置、机构)	friction gear(ing) ◇ 锥形～*
摩擦传动辊	friction roll
摩擦锤【压】	friction [jump] hammer
摩擦带【机】	friction band
摩擦导卫板	friction guide
摩擦电	triboelectric, frictional electricity
摩擦电偶	tribocouple
摩擦电偶效应	triboelectric effect
摩擦电序	triboelectric series
摩擦粉	friction producing powder
摩擦粉料	friction type mix
摩擦腐蚀	chafing [fretting] corrosion, cocoa, frettage
摩擦附着	frictional grip
摩擦杆	wearing bar
摩擦工具	rubber
摩擦功	frictional work, work of friction
摩擦辊[滚柱]	friction roller
摩擦滚轮落锤	friction-roll drop hammer
摩擦焊(接)	friction welding [soldering]
摩擦焊机	friction welding machine
摩擦焊接法	friction welding process
摩擦合金法	friction alloying
摩擦痕	friction [abrasion] mark
摩擦滑动	frictional sliding
摩擦混合	attrition mixing
摩擦剂	friction producing material [substance]
摩擦计	tribometer
摩擦夹板锤	friction board hammer
摩擦减震	damping by friction
摩擦减震器	friction shock absorber, friction damper
摩擦鉴别	triboelectric sorting
摩擦角【压】	friction angle
摩擦金属表面发光	smearing
摩擦金属陶瓷	friction cermet
摩擦紧固螺栓	friction bolt
摩擦锯	friction saw
摩擦锯切	friction [fusion] sawing
摩擦类粉末混合物	friction type mix
摩擦离合器	friction clutch
摩擦力	frictional force, friction ◇ 晶界～ boundary friction
摩擦力分布[摩擦峰]【压】	friction hill
摩擦力矩	frictional torque, moment of friction
摩擦联轴器	friction coupling
摩擦零件	friction parts
摩擦流	frictional flow

摩擦轮　friction wheel [gear]
摩擦面　friction facing, surface of friction
摩擦磨损　fretting wear
摩擦盘　friction disc
摩擦抛光机　burnishing machine, burnisher
摩擦疲劳　fretting fatigue
摩擦片　friction disc [wafer, plate]
摩擦起电　tribo-electrification
摩擦(起)电反应　triboelectric reaction
摩擦牵引齿轮　friction draught gear
摩擦热　friction(al) heat
摩擦式推钢机　friction pusher
摩擦式闸门　friction lock
摩擦试验　friction test
摩擦试验机　friction testing machine
摩擦损失　friction loss
摩擦特性　frictional characteristic
摩擦提升器　friction lifter
摩擦条件　friction conditions
摩擦物理学　tribophysics
摩擦系数　friction coefficient [factor]
摩擦效应　friction effect
摩擦性质　frictional property, nature of friction
摩擦锈斑[锈蚀]　cocoa
摩擦学　tribology
摩擦压力机　friction(al) press ◇螺旋式～friction screw press
摩擦氧化　friction(al) oxidation
摩擦应力　friction stress
摩擦硬度　abrasive hardness
摩擦硬化　friction hardening
摩擦诱致剪切应力　friction induced shear stress
摩擦元件　friction element ◇粉末金属～
摩擦制动器[摩擦闸]　friction brake
摩擦制品　friction product
摩擦桩　friction [floating] pile
摩擦桩基　floating pile foundation
摩擦装置　friction assembly

摩擦锥轮　friction cone
摩擦组分　friction producing component [ingredient]
摩擦阻力　frictional resistance [constraint, drag]
摩擦作用　friction ◇产生～的组分 friction producing component [ingredient]
摩电鉴别法　triboelectric sorting
摩电鉴别器[头]　tribosorter
摩电线　runway conductor
摩电线路(桥式吊车的)　contact line circuit
摩电序　triboelectric series
摩尔比热　mole specific heat
摩尔臭度　molar olfactory
摩尔导电率　molar (electrical) conductivity
摩尔等张体积　parachor
摩尔热　molar heat
摩尔热容(量)　molar heat capacity
摩尔溶液　molar [molal] solution
摩尔体积[容积]　molar volume
摩尔吸收率[系数]　molar absorptivity
摩尔选择性(离子交换的)　molal selectivity
摩尔选择性系数　molal selectivity coefficient
摩尔折射　molar refraction
摩戈伊尔辊颈铝锡合金轴承　Morgoil roll neck bearing
摩戈伊尔铝硅锡轴承合金(6.5Sn, 2.5Si, 1Cu,余量 Al)　Morgoil
摩戈伊尔铝锡合金轴承润滑装置　Morgoil lubrication system
摩戈伊尔液体摩擦轴承　Morgoil bearing
摩根式小型轧机　Morgan mill
摩熔锯切　friction [fusion] sawing
摩蚀疲劳　chafing-fatigue
摩损检测法　◇贾宁～Jannin method
摩托化　motorization
摩压焊　friction welding
抹　smearing

抹灰	plastering, troweling
抹灰底层	【建】key floating
抹灰工具	plastering tools
抹灰机[机动抹灰板]	mechanical float
抹平的混凝土	floated concrete
末次渣	【铁】casting flush
末端	terminal, end
末端淬火	end quench, edge quenching
末端淬火标准试棒	standard end-quench test bar
末端淬火法	end quenching process
末端淬火距离	Jominy distance
末端淬火[淬透性试验]曲线	Jominy (end-quench) curve
末端淬火[淬透性]试棒	end-quenched [Jominy] bar
末端淬火[淬硬]试样	end-quench(-test) piece
末端淬火[淬透]性试验	end-quench hardenability test, Jominy test
末端淬透性	Jominy hardenability
末端淬透性曲线图	Jominy diagram
末端打印	【计】end printing
末端电池	end cell
末端跨	end bay
末端冷却	end cooling
末端流钢砖	【钢】end pot
末端屏蔽	end shield
末端向前	endwise
末端效应	end effect
末端治理	【环】end treatment
末端轴承	tail bearing
末期蠕变	(同"第三期蠕变")
末期渣化学成分	final chemical composition of slag
末速度	final [terminal] velocity, end speed
末渣	final slag, top cinder,【冶】tap slag
没食子酸	gallic acid
莫阿干涉法	【理】Moire method
莫阿干涉条纹	【理】Moire fringe
莫阿干涉图样	【理】Moire pattern
莫阿条纹[图形]	【理】Moire
莫比斯银电解法	Moebius process
莫德菲低合金高强度钢	Modfiy
莫尔 – 德马格平炉	【钢】Moll-Demag open-hearth furnace
莫尔格子砖	Moll checker
莫尔[康铜]热电偶	Moll thermopile
莫尔 – 琼斯 – 胡 – 胡软巴比轴承合金(91Sn, 4.5Sb, 4.5Cu)	More-Jones-Hoo-Hoo-alloy
莫尔 – 琼斯轴承合金(10或20Sn, 12.5或15Sb, 63.5或75Pb, 0.2或1.5Cu)	More-Jones alloy
莫尔三钟式(炉顶)装料装置	【铁】Mohr three bell charging system
莫尔斯竖炉直接还原法	【铁】Morse process
莫尔圆	Mohr's circle
莫霍克巴比[低锡铅基轴承]合金(5Sn, 9或15Sb, 80—86Pb, 0.5Cu)	Mohawk babbitt
莫克假银(55Zn, 45Cu; 90Al, 5Ag, 5Cu; 10Sn, 5Cu, 85Al)	Mock silver
莫克铜铂合金(35Pt, 4Zn, 余量Cu; 64Ni, 12Cu, 12Pt, 12Ag)	Mock gold
莫克装饰用合金(1.84Al, 10Sn, 余量Cu; 2.55Zn, 45Cu)	Mock platinum
莫来石{3Al$_2$O$_3$·2SiO$_2$}	【耐】mullite ◇合成~砂*, 人工~ artificial mullite, 熔融[电熔]~ fused mullite, 烧结~ sintered mullite
莫来石耐火材料	mullite refractory
莫来石熟料	mullite chamotte
莫来石砖	mullite brick
莫勒硅 – 碳组分图	Maurer constitution diagram
莫勒铁 – 硅组分图	Maurer's diagram
莫勒铸铁组织图	【金】Maurer constitution diagram, Maurer's diagram
莫里森展性青铜(91Cu, 9Sn)	Morrison bronze
莫洛树脂砂衬离心铸管法	【铸】Monocast

Process
莫诺硬度(压痕硬度)　Monotron hardness
莫诺硬度计　Monotron hardness tester
莫诺硬度试验　Monotron hardness test
莫塞克黄铜型假金(65Cu,35Zn)　Mosaic gold
莫塞特铜银合金(59.5Cu,27.5Ag,9.5Zn,3.5Ni)　Mousset's silver
莫氏天平　Mohr's balance
莫氏硬度　Moh's hardness,【金】scratch resistance
莫氏硬度标(度)[刻度]　Moh's (hardness) scale,【金】scratch hardness scale
莫氏硬度值　Moh's (hardness) number, Moh's scale number
莫斯利定律　Moseley's law
莫塔洛伊粒状锡基合金　Motaloy
莫塔锡基高强度轴承合金(85—87Sn,4—6Cu,8.5—9.5Sb)　Mota metal
莫特-纳巴罗公式　【理】Mott-Nabarro formula
莫特-纳巴罗关系式　Mott and Nabarro's relation
莫特-纳巴罗效应　【金】Mott-Nabarro effect
莫特金属应变硬化理论　theory of Mott
莫特碎化参数　【金】Mott fragmentation parameters
莫特位错攀移[上升运动]模型　【理】Mott's dislocation climb model
莫维波尔电解抛光装置(试样的)　【金】Movipol
墨水池状孔　ink-well pore
墨水瓶状孔隙　ink-bottle pore
墨铜矿　vallerite
墨鱼骨模铸造法(贵金属首饰用)　cuttle-fish process
默尔薄层[连续]炼钢法　【钢】Merle film refining process
默硅镁钙石[牟文橄榄石]　merwinite
默柯铅青铜(88Cu,10Sn,2Pb)　Merco bronze

模　mo(u)ld, die ◇ 敞口式水平~ open horizontal mould, 带榫口~lock die, 两箱造型~*
模板　template (temp.), pattern board [plate], die [match] plate,【团】shuttering,【压】platen,【铸】plate pattern, follow board (砂箱的),【建】casting box (浇灌混凝土用) ◇ 安装好的~【铸】mounted pattern, 大~【机】macrotemplate, 反复使用的~ repetitive form, 滑动上升~【建】climbing form, 活动~ movable form, 双面~*,(阴)沟管~dod, 组合~*
模板法铸造　planchet casting
模板工程　formwork
模板设计　template tayout
模板图　formwork drawing
模板型铸(件)　template casting
模板造型　pattern plate moulding
模壁　die wall ◇ 弧形~ cambered wall
模壁光洁度　die wall finish
模壁面　die wall surface
模壁摩擦　die wall friction
模壁润滑　die wall lubrication
模壁寿命　die wall life
模槽　cavity of die,【压】impression
模槽宽展　【压】spreading of groove
模衬　die liner [bush, insert]
模冲　plunger
模冲压　die stamping ◇ 磁脉冲~工艺 magneform process
模冲压操作[工序]　die-stamping operation
模底　mould bottom
模底板　die shoe
模垫　die backer [bush], backup piece
模锻　drop forge,【压】(die-)forging, stamp [contour] forging, stamping, die forming, swage ◇ 闭模~法*, 可~性 formability, 喷丸~法 shot die forming, 限量~*, 旋转~ circular forging, 液态~*
模锻锤　die [drop] hammer, block stamp

◇无底座式～*

模锻工　press operator
模锻工长　master-hub
模锻焊　die welding (DW)
模锻件　die forgings
模锻炉　drop-forge furnace
模锻丸　stamp shot
模锻压力机　drop press ◇车轮坯成型～wheel forging press
模锻研究协会(英国)　Drop Forging Research Association (D.F.R.A.)
模锻液压机　hydraulic forging press ◇闭口～*,开口～*
模轭　die yoke
模缝　die slot, burr
模焊　mould welding
模盒　die block (电缆包铅机的), mould carrier (等静压制的), 【铸】mould box
模架　die carrier [set], die-holder ◇拆除～【建】decentering
模具　die arrangement [assembly, equipment] ◇成套～die set, 可拆～*, 连续压制的～*
模具凹槽　【压】recess of die
模具不同轴　【压】misalignment of dies
模具测量显微镜　die measuring microscope
模具成形机床　die shaping machine
模具尺寸　die dimension
模具重磨[精加工]机床　die ripping machine
模具定位装置　die set arrangement
模具钢　die steel ◇闭锻～closed-die steel, 挤压～extrusion die steel, 普拉斯蒂隆渗碳～plastiron, 普拉斯塔洛依塑料～*, 热作～*
模具钢含碳量(一般为0.75%)　die temper
模具钢韧度　die temper
模具夹持器　sowblock
模具夹紧力(薄板冲压的)　【压】die hold-down pressure

模具夹紧压力(对焊机夹紧钳口用)【焊】die-clamping pressure
模具加热炉　die oven
模具间距　【压】die spacing
模具磨床　die grinding machine
模具抛光机　die polishing machine
模具气垫　die cushion
模具韧度　die temper
模具润滑剂　die lubricant
模具损坏　die failure
模具缩口法　【压】die shrinking process
模具维修工段　die maintenance area
模具未对准[模具错位]　【压】mismatch [misalignment] of dies, poor match
模具镶块　die insert
模具旋压法　【压】die spinning process [method]
模具圆角半径　【压】die radius
模具制造工段　die fabrication area
模壳(灌混凝土用)　【团】shuttering
模壳断路器　moulded case circuit breaker
模孔　【压】die orifice [bore, mouth, opening], nib
模孔变形锥(模孔第二部分)　die approach angle
模孔出口锥(模孔最后部分)　(die) exit angle, die relief angle, die back
模孔间距　bridge width
模孔喇叭角　generating angle
模孔入口锥　die entrance angle
模孔形状　die profile
模孔修磨(拉丝模的)　reconditioning
模孔压缩锥　die reduction angle
模孔针磨机　needle die polishing machine, needle grinding machine
模裂纹(锭面缺陷)　【钢】surface crazing
模裂纹带(钢丝的)　【压】broken back
模面　die (sur)face
模面黑色涂料　【铸】blacking carbon
模内表面　inner die surface
模坯(拉丝模的)　【压】pellet, nib ◇带眼～cored [preformed] die

模腔　die cavity [chamber], cavity (of die), moulding chamber
模腔边缘　die cavity lips ◇ 润湿～用刷 water brush
模腔轮廓[形状]　die configuration
模切　die cutting
模式剥皮(棒材的)　die scalping
模式飞剪机作业线　flying die shear line
模式剪　die shears
模塑　moulding ◇ 热～ hot moulding, 液压～机
模塑压力　moulding pressure
模台　die table ◇ 浮沉[弹簧]～ floating die table
模台旋转式压机　rotary press
模膛(锻模的)　die impression ◇ 拔长～ drawing, 成型～ forming impression, 球～ ball edger
模套　die sleeve [body, case, mounting], mould shell ◇ 带舌心的～ spider die cap
模体　die body, mould shell [matrix]
模头　die head
模芯　mould core, bush
模样托板　【铸】moulding board
模支承　die support
模制盒式断路器　moulded case circuit breaker
模制混凝土　moulded concrete
模制试块　briquette
模铸　die cast ◇ 高压～*, 普通～*
模铸钢锭　static ingot
模子　mould ◇ 大于坯块尺寸的～ oversize mould, 带锥度的～ tapered mould, 无吸收性的～ non-absorbent mould
模子表面干燥用轻便干燥机　devil
模子顶出装置　die manipulator
模子寿命　die life, life of die
模子咬口　die lock
模组　die set, mould train, 【铸】card of patterns
模座　die seat [bed, mounting, support, holder], bolster, master block, plate die, 【压】die head block, die slide
模座侧送料压力机　muzzle-loading press
牡蛎壳状断口　【金】oyster-shell fracture
牡蛎石灰　oyster-shell lime
母板　(同"种板") ◇ 电解液～ electrolyte matrix
母材试验样　【焊】base metal test specimen
母点　generatrix
母端开始螺纹　box entrance thread
母端螺纹　box thread
母核　parent nucleus
母合金　mother [master, process (ing), rich, tempering] alloy, hardener ◇ V铁铬～*
母合金粉末　master alloy powder
母金属　mother metal
母晶体　parent crystal
母(矿)浆　pregnant pulp
母面　generatrix
母模　offset die, 【铸】master [double-shrink] pattern, master model, double contraction pattern
母模型的原模型　【铸】grand-master pattern
母片[板]法　【色】master slice method
母球　【团】seed (pellet)
母球长大区　nuclei growth region
母球形成速度　seed formation rate
母体　generatrix, parent body
母体材料　parent material
母体金属[母材]　parent metal
母体金属裂纹　base metal crack(ing)
母体金属试样　parent [base] metal test specimen
母体离子　parent ion
母体物质　parent substance
母体元素　parent element
母线　bus-bar, busbar (wire), omnibus bar, trunk, generatrix ◇ 电解槽～【色】cell busbar, 发光模拟～ colour mimic buses, 立～(铝电解的)【色】riser, 立柱～ rising main, 零～【电】neutral bar, 阴

极～ cathode bus(bar)
母线槽　busbar assembly, bus duct
母线电压损失　bus voltage loss
母线架　busbar assembly [frame]
母线配置　busbar arrangement
母线式电流互感器　bar type current transformer
母线通廊　bus gallery
母线弯曲装置　bending device for busbars
母线支架　busbar support
母相　parent phase
母相奥氏体　parent austenite
母相点阵[晶格]　parent lattice
母相奥氏体　parent austenite
母相与沉淀相间界面　matrix-precipitate interface
母型　parent form, 【压】master [female] mould
母岩　mother [parent] rock, 【采】matrix
母液　mother liquid [liquor, solution], master solution, liquor, pregnant solution [liquor] ◇ 酸性～*
母液泵槽　pregnant liquor pump tank
母液槽　mother [pregnant] liquor tank
母液浓度　liquor concentration
母液蒸发器　mother liquor evaporator
母液贮槽　pregnant solution storage tank
母钟　master [primary] clock
苜蓿叶式交叉　【运】cover-leaf crossing
幕墙(柱间非承重墙)　curtain [panel] wall
木棒折断形　broken stick fracture
木材　wood, lumber, timber ◇ 标准尺寸～ dimension lumber
木材衬里　timber lining
木材加工　timber-working
木柴　(fire)wood ◇ 点火～ kindling wood, 燃用～ fuel wood
木锤　(wooden) mallet, 【机】dresser
木醇　wood alcohol [spirit]
木钉　dowel, wood nail, peg
木钉起模　【铸】draw peg

木粉　wood flour
木工车床　model [pattern] maker's lathe, wood turning lathe
木夯　beetle
木花板　xylolite
木灰水　lye
木焦油　wood tar, gum
木脚手架　【建】timber scaffold
木结构　wood construction, timber structure
木精　methyl-alcohol, wood spirit
木锯　wood saw ◇ 狭边[钩齿]粗～ whip saw
木块(路面)　wood block
木框架(大型铸型的)　【铸】lumber
木料　lumber, timber
木螺钉[螺丝]　wood [grub] screw
木煤　wood [bituminous] coal, xylinite
木模　wooden pattern [model]
木模车间　pattern-shop
木模工　wood-pattern maker
木耙　wood rabble, wooden roke
木排　raft
木片捕集器　wood catcher
木砂箱　【铸】wood flask, timber moulding box
木石结构　black and white work
木炭　(wood) charcoal ◇ 蒸汽活化～*
木炭粉　finely ground charcoal, powdered charcoal
木炭高炉　charcoal blast-furnace
木炭基气氛　charcoal-base atmosphere
木炭基气氛发生器　charcoal-base atmosphere generator
木炭加热锻坯　charcoal hammered bloom (C.H.B.)
木炭精炼铁　charcoal knobbled iron
木炭块　lump charcoal
木炭扩散层　charcoal diffuser bed
木炭炉　charcoal(-fired) furnace (燃木炭炉)
木炭炉炼铁法　【铁】charcoal hearth pro-

cess
木炭生铁　charcoal pig(-iron) [iron]
木炭熟铁　charcoal knobbled iron
木铜矿　wood copper
木纹状断口　woody fracture
木纹状结构[组织]　woody structure
木锡矿　dnieprovskite
木锡石　wood tin
木纤维　xylon, wood fibre
木纤维板　beaver board
木箱　wooden crate
木楔　glut, wood key
木罩　wooden hood
木制沉淀槽　wooden precipitation barrel
木制模　wood pattern
木质　lignin, xylon
木质褐煤　woody lignite
木质浸出槽　wooden leach tank
木质镜煤　xylovitrain
木质镜丝炭　xylovitrofusinite
木质丝炭　xylofusinite
木质素　lignin
木质组　xylinoid group
木轴　spool
木轴瓦　wooden bearing shell
木桩　timber [wood(en)] pile ◇ 用～标出 pegging-out
目标　target, goal, object(ive)
目标板型　target profile
目标变量　target variable
目标标识系统　target identification system
目标程序　object program [routine], target program
目标程序库　object program library
目标程序模块　object program module
目标代码　object code
目标管理(制度)　management by objective
目标含碳量　aim carbon content
目标函数　objective [target] function ◇ 双参数～*
目标粒度(值)　target size
目标粒度范围　target size range
目标模块　【计】object module
目标视图　【计】target view
目标数据库　【计】target database
目标位置指示器　target position indicator
目标语言　object [target] language
目标语言程序　object-language program
目测　visual examination, visualization
目测草图　eye sketch
目测法　visual method, ocular estimate
目测光学高温计　visual optical pyrometer
目的　object(ive), goal, purpose
目镜　eye piece [lens], ocular (glass, lens) ◇ (带)测微(尺)～ micrometer eyepiece, 附有微细标尺的～【金】filar eyepiece, 共聚焦面～parfocal eyepiece, 惠更斯[负型]～ Huygens' eyepiece, 颗粒[晶粒]大小比较～*, 凯尔纳～【金】Kellner eyepiece, 拉姆斯登(正型)～*, 十字[双]标线～*
目镜测微计　eyepiece [ocular] micrometer
目录　catalogue, list, contents, directory, inventory
目录磁道　【计】library track
目前文件　【计】current file
目视观测[察]　【金】visual observation
目视检查[验]　visual check, hand inspection ◇ 用检孔镜～(管子内壁) boroscope examination
目视控制　sight control
目视料车运行程序指示器　visual skip program indicator
目视物镜　visual objective
目视证据　visual evidence
目视指示控制灯　visually indicating control lamp
钼{Mo}　molybdenum ◇ 粉冶～*, 含～合金*, 弧熔～ arc-melting molybdenum, 无～钢 molybdenum-free steel, 再还原～ re-reduced molybdenum, 真空弧熔～*
钼靶　molybdenum target

钼白钨矿　seyrigite
钼板　molybdenum plate
钼棒　molybdenum bar
钼棒阴极　molybdenum rod cathode
钼铋矿 $\{Bi_2O_3 \cdot MoO_3\}$　koechlinite
钼箔薄膜压力计　molybdenum foil diaphragm gauge
钼衬里　molybdenum liner
钼承料网　molybdenum supporting grid
钼的　molybdenic, molybdic
钼垫板　molybdenum stool
钼电极导电头　molybdenum electrode tip
钼电极伸出部　molybdenum electrode extension
钼电阻加热元件　Stratit element
钼反射器　molybdenum reflector
钼粉　molybdenum powder [filings]
钼粉冶熔凝(法)　consolidation of molybdenum by powder metallurgy practice
钼辐射屏　molybdenum radiation screen
钼坩埚　molybdenum crucible
钼钢　molybdenum steel ◇ 埃克诺莫渗碳易削～*, 石墨化～*
钼高速钢　molybdenum high speed steel
钼隔料网　molybdenum (feed) retainer, molybdenum retaining screen
钼铬钢　molybdenum chromium steel
钼铬硅合金铸铁　◇ 杜拉～*
钼硅酸盐　silicomolybdate
钼合金　molybdenum alloy
钼弧熔凝(法)　consolidation of molybdenum by arc-melting
钼华 $\{MoO_3\}$　molybdine, molybdite
钼化合物　molybdic compound
钼基粉末电阻合金　◇ 苏珀希特～*
钼基合金　molybdenum-base alloy
钼基合金制品　molybdenum-base compositions
钼加热元件　molybdenum (heating) element
钼尖电极　molybdenum electrode tip, electrode with molybdenum tip

钼矿床　molybdenum deposit
钼蓝　molybdenum blue
钼镁铀矿　calcurmolite, calcurmolith
钼－锰导体　molybdenum-manganese conductor
钼镍铁(高导磁)合金　Monimax
钼屏[帘,网]　molybdenum screen
钼坡莫合金　(同"镍铁钼导磁合金") ◇ 4－79～*
钼铅矿　yellow lead ore, wulfenite
钼绕组　molybdenum winding
钼丝　molybdenum filament ◇ 支承～*
钼丝电(阻加热)炉　molybdenum resistor [electric] furnace
钼丝管状炉　molybdenum wound tube furnace
钼丝加热元件　molybdenum wire element
钼丝炉　molybdenum-wound furnace
钼酸铵 $\{(NH_4)_2MoO_4, 5(NH_4)_2O \cdot 12MoO_3 \cdot 7H_2O\}$　ammonium molybdate
钼酸钆　gadolinium molybdate
钼酸钙 $\{CaMoO_4\}$　calcium molybdate, molyte
钼酸钾 $\{K_2MoO_4\}$　potassium molybdate
钼酸镧 $\{La_2(MoO_4)_3\}$　lanthanum molybdate
钼酸钠 $\{Na_2MoO_4\}$　sodium molybdate
钼酸钕 $\{Nd_2(MoO_4)_3\}$　neodymium molybdate
钼酸镨 $\{Pr_2(MoO_4)_3\}$　praseodymium molybdate
钼酸铅　lead molybdate
钼酸铜　copper molybdate
钼酸盐　molybdate, molybdenate
钼酸银 $\{Ag_2MoO_4\}$　silver molybdate
钼酸铀　uranmolybdate
钼钛合金　molybdenum titanium alloy
钼碳钢　carbon molybdenum steel
钼添加合金　molybdenum addition
钼条　molybdenum bar ◇ 旋[环]锻～*
钼铁(中间合金；70－75Mo, 0.1－2Si, 0.6－3.6C)　molybdenum iron, ferro-

molybdenum
钼铜合金　molybdenum-copper
钼铜矿　lindgrenite
钼钍氧金属陶瓷　thorium oxide-molybdenum
钼钍氧陶瓷金属　thoria-molybdenum
钼钨钙矿{Ca(Mo,W)O$_4$}　powellite
钼钨铅矿{3PbWO$_4$·PbMoO$_4$}　chillagite, lyonite
钼钨铁(中间合金；43Mo,10W,1.8C)　ferromolybdenum-tungsten
钼系高速工具钢　molybdenum series high speed tool steel
钼屑　molybdenum filings
钼阴极　molybdenum cathode
钼银电接触器材　molybdenum-silver contact material
钼银合金　molybdenum-silver
钼铀矿　umohoite

钼质接受[收集]盘　molybdenum catch-plate
钼质热反射器　molybdenum reflector
钼质支承丝　molybdenum support wire
钼中毒　molybdenosis
穆磁铁矿　mushketovite
穆尔伯莱合金　Mulberry alloy
穆尔叶片式真空过滤机　Moore filter
穆雷铝焊料(6—12Al,3—8Cu,80—91Zn)　Mouray's solder
穆列克斯热裂试验　murex hot-crack(ing) test
穆斯堡尔光谱学　Moessbauer spectroscopy
穆斯堡尔效应　Moessbauer effect
穆索回转反应罐直接还原法　【铁】Musso process
穆西利特殊型锡铋汞合金(40Sn,40Bi,20Hg)　Musily silver

N n

拿波利硫杆菌[拿波氏新多翼硫化杆菌] thiobacillus neopolitanus
镎含量分析仪 neptunium analyzer
镎合金 neptunium alloy
镎基合金 neptunium base alloy
镎添加合金 neptunium additive alloy
钠{Na} sodium (sod.), natrium ◇ 艾比珀姆-回收法 Abiperm process, 无~的 sodium-free, 无氧~ oxygen-free sodium
钠泵 sodium pump
钠冰晶石 (同"冰晶石")
钠长石{$Na_2O \cdot Al_2O_3 \cdot 6SiO_2$} albite, cryptoclase
钠长石化 albitization
钠矾{$Na_2SO_4 \cdot Al_2(SO_4)_3 \cdot 24H_2O$ 或 $NaAl(SO_4)_2 \cdot 12H_2O$} soda alum
钠沸石{$Na_2O \cdot Al_2O_3 \cdot 3SiO_2 \cdot 2H_2O$} natrolite, epinatrolite
钠钙长石 oligoclase
钠钙锆石 lavenite
钠钙硅酸盐 (同"硅酸钙钠")
钠锆矿 laevenite
钠管道(输送熔融钠的) sodium line
钠合金 sodium alloy
钠还原法 sodium reduction process, Na-reduction
钠基合金 sodium-base alloy
钠基膨润土 western bentonite
钠钾共晶合金[纳克钠钾共晶合金](56Na, 44K; 反应堆冷却介质) Natrium-Kalium alloy, Nak, Na-K
钠钾水玻璃 double water glass
钠冷却 sodium cooling
钠冷却剂 sodium coolant
钠量计 natrometer
钠铝硅酸盐 sodium aluminosilicate
钠铝硅酸盐离子交换剂 sodium aluminium silicate exchanger
钠明矾石 niatroalumite
钠膜 sodium film ◇ 易燃~ *
钠青铜{Na_xWO_3} sodium bronze
钠热还原 sodiothermic reduction, sodium thermoreduction
钠热(还原)法 sodiothermic reduction [process]
钠闪石 riebeckite {$4Na_2SiO_3 \cdot 5FeSiO_3 \cdot 5Fe_2Si_3O_9$}, crocidolite {$NaFe(SiO_3)_2 \cdot FeSiO_3$}
钠添加合金 sodium additive alloy
钠钨青铜{$Na_2W_2O_6$ 或 $Na_2O \cdot WO_2 \cdot WO_3$} sodium tungsten bronze
钠硝石{$NaNO_3$} soda nitre, nitratine, nitratite, Chile saltpeter [nitre]
钠斜微长石{$(Na, K)AlSi_3O_8$} anothoclase
钠盐(专指氯化钠 NaCl) sodium salt
钠铀矿 clarkeite
钠铀云母{$Na_2(UO_2)_2(PO_4)_2 \cdot 8H_2O$} sodium autunite, natroautunite
钠蒸气 sodium vapor
钠质[基]皂土 sodium bentonite
纳安 nanoampere
纳安计 nanoammeter
纳巴罗-赫林方程式(空位引起蠕变的) Nabarro-Herring equation
纳达铜基合金(3.5-4Ni+Sn, 0.7-1Pb, 余量 Cu) Nada
纳法(拉) nanofarad, millimicrofarad
纳莱特极硬铝青铜(15Al, 5Fe, 1Ni, 余量 Cu) Narite
纳米(10^{-9}m) nanometre (nm), milli(mi)cron, micromillimeter
纳米半导体 nano semiconductor
纳米材料 nano material
纳米材料工程 nano material engineering
纳米材料科学 nano material science
纳米仿生材料学 nano biomaterial
纳米非晶态材料 nano amorphous material
纳米复合涂层材料 nano composite coating material

纳米复合物[材料] nano composite (material)
纳米复相材料 nanomultiphase material
纳米复杂体系 nano complex system
纳米固体 nano solid
纳米管 nano tube
纳米合成 nano synthesis
纳米机器人 nanorobot
纳米结构 nanostructure
纳米晶体(材料) nanocrysalline
纳米晶体材料 nanometer-sized crystalline material
纳米颗粒膜 nano particle film
纳米科学技术 nano science and technology (NST), Nano-ST
纳米空间 nanospace
纳米粒子 nano particle
纳米生物部件 nano bioparts
纳米生物机器 nano miomachine
纳米生物学 nano-biology
纳米丝 nano wire
纳米态 nano state
纳米碳管 Bucky tube
纳米陶瓷 nano ceramics
纳米陶瓷材料 nano ceramic material
纳米体系 nano system
纳米微电子学 nano-microelectronics
纳米微晶 nano-crystal
纳米微粒 nano particle
纳米相 nanophase
纳米相材料 nanophase material
纳苏休斯电弧电阻炉 Nathusius furnace
纳特基锡基轴承合金(18Sb,75Sn,9Cu) Natke's alloy
纳瓦集成电路 nanowatt integrated circuit
纳逊萘尔 A 耐蚀铝合金(0—4Cu, 0—4Mg, 0—7.5Si, 0—0.6Mn, 0—1.5Ni, 余量 Al) National A alloy
氖{Ne} neon ◇ 分流～灯
氖管 neon tube
氖光灯 neon glim lamp
氖壳电子 neon core electrons

耐剥裂性 【耐】resistance to peeling
耐剥蚀合金 exfoliation resistant alloy
耐崩裂性 spalling property
耐崩裂砖 spalling resistant brick
耐变色性 tarnish resistance
耐擦伤性 marresistance
耐冲击钢 shock-resisting steel, notch ductile steel
耐冲击工具钢 shock-resisting tool steel
耐冲击强度 impact strength
耐冲击性试验 impact endurance test
耐冲蚀镀层[涂层] erosion-resistant coating
耐冲蚀性 erosion resistance
耐大气腐蚀钢 atmosphere corrosion resisting steel, antiweathering steel, weathering [weather-resisting] steel
耐大气腐蚀高强度钢 ◇ 科尔坦～
耐大气腐蚀性 resistance to atmospheric corrosion, weather resistance
耐电弧的 arc-resisting
耐电击的 shockproof
耐辐射的 radioresistant
耐辐射损伤性 radiation damage stability
耐辐照合金 radiation resistant alloy
耐腐蚀材料 corrosion-resistant [corrosion-resisting] material
耐腐蚀泵 noncorrosive pump
耐腐蚀合金 corrosion-resisting alloy
耐腐蚀试验 corrosion resistance test ◇ 海水中～marine test, 乡村大气中～rural atmosphere test
耐腐蚀性 corrosion-resisting property, corrosion stability, corrosion resistance, rotproofness, stain-resistance, resistance to corrosion, incorrodibility, immunity to corrosion
耐腐蚀轴承钢 corrosion-resistant bearing steel
耐腐蚀阳极 corrosion-resistant anode
耐高温材料 high temperature resistant material, heat resisting material

耐高温分解性　pyrolytic stability
耐高温坩埚　high temperature crucible
耐高温钢　high-temperature steel
耐高温金属　(high temperature) refractory metal
耐高温黏土砖　high heat duty fireclay brick
耐高温陶瓷材料　heat resistant ceramic material
耐高温铁基合金　hot strength iron-base alloy
耐高温涂层　refractory coating
耐高温性　fire resisting quality
耐高温硬质合金　high temperature cemented carbide
耐高压铸造合金　◇米拉丘洛依~*
耐海水腐蚀青铜　(45Cu, 32.5Ni, 16Sn, 5.5Zn, 1Bi) sea water bronze
耐海水腐蚀性　resistance to sea-water corrosion
耐候钢　(同"耐大气腐蚀钢")
耐化学腐蚀性　chemical resistance
耐火玻璃　refractory glass
耐火补炉料　refractory repairing mass
耐火材料　refractory (material), fireproof material ◇包铁皮~metal-cased refractory, 超级~superrefractory, 高铝~aluminous refractory, 隔热~insulating refractory, 混合~composite refractories, 碱性~*, 浇注用~casting-pit refractory, 结合~bound refractory, 可成型~mouldable refractory, 耐[防]酸~acid-proof refractory, 熔铸~*, 酸性~*, 西门塞特~*, 整体结构用~*, 铸造用~foundery refractory
耐火材料崩裂　spalling of refractories
耐火材料衬里　refractory liner [lining]
耐火材料衬里还原钢弹　refractory-lined bomb
耐火材料成分　refractory constituent
耐火材料法(高炉炉缸内衬设计体系之一)　refractory solution (concept)
耐火材料坩埚　refractory crucible
耐火材料工业　refractory industry
耐火材料机械崩裂　mechanical spalling of refractories
耐火材料绝缘　refractory insulation
耐火材料库　refractory storage [store]
耐火材料粒　refractory bead
耐火材料锚栓　refractory anchor
耐火材料黏结剂　fire bond
耐火材料喷补器　refractory gun
耐火材料喷涂　refractory gunning
耐火材料穹顶　refractory dome
耐火材料热崩裂　thermal spalling of refractories
耐火材料实验室　refractory laboratory
耐火材料损蚀　refractory wear
耐火材料特性[性能]　refractory performance
耐火材料预制块　refractory modular shape
耐火材料渣化　slagging of refractories
耐火材料制空气换热器　refractory air recuperator
耐火侧墙(喷口的)　cheeks
耐火衬里维修　refractory maintenance
耐火层　infusible blanket, flame retardant coating, 【耐】deck(推出式炉底车的)
耐火衬圈(铸锭底板孔的)　brick cup
耐火挡渣墙(连铸中间包的)　refractory bridge
耐火堵泥　brasque ◇碳质~carbonaceous brasque
耐火度　refractoriness, fireproofness ◇荷重~*
耐火盖板　refractory cover
耐火合金　refractory alloy
耐火混合料　refractory mixture
耐火混凝土　refractory concrete, firecrete, fire resisting concrete, castable refractory ◇马格诺普拉斯特~*
耐火浆料　【铸】castable [plastic] refractory

耐火炉衬	refractory (furnace) lining

耐火炉衬 refractory (furnace) lining
耐火炉衬维护 refractory maintenance
耐火炉门 fire screen
耐火门 fire resisting door
耐火面 refractory surface
耐火泥 fire clay, refractory mud
耐火泥[砂]浆 refractory mortar, heat resistant mortar ◇ 气硬(性)~*,中等~*
耐火黏土 fire [refractory, seat] clay, fire stone ◇ 细粒塑性高级~*
耐火黏土大块砖 refractory fireclay block
耐火(黏土)坩埚 fireclay crucible [sagger],【冶】white pot
耐火黏土管 fireclay pipe
耐火黏土罐 clay pot
耐火黏土火泥 fireclay mortar
耐火黏土矿物 fireclay mineral
耐火黏土熟料 fireclay chamotte [grog]
耐火黏土陶瓷 chamotte ceramics
耐火黏土型 fireclay mould
耐火黏土砖 fireclay brick [tile] ◇ 大块~*,低级~*,中级~*
耐火黏土砖衬 firebrick lining
耐火砂 fire [refractory] sand
耐火石 ovenstone
耐火水泥 refractory [fire (proof)] cement, thermolith ◇ 水硬性~*
耐火陶瓷(制品) refractory ceramics
耐火涂层[涂料] refractory dressing [wash], fireproof coating [dope]
耐火土 fireclay
耐火性 fire resistance, fire resisting property, fireproofness, refractability, refractoriness, refractory property [quality, nature, behaviour]
耐火岩石 fire stone
耐火氧化物 refractory oxide
耐火闸门 fire screen
耐火制品 refractory product
耐火舟皿 debiteuse
耐火砖 refractory [furnace, chamotte] brick, fire resistant brick, firebrick(tile), fireproofing tile ◇ 标准~ scone bricks, 衬砌~的 firebrick lined, 绝热~ insulating firebrick, 企口型~ groove type refractory, 碎~ bat, 致密~ dense firebrick
耐火砖壁 refractory wall
耐火砖衬里 firebrick lining (f.b.l.)
耐火砖衬里炉罩[点火器](烧结机的) brick lined hood
耐火砖盖 firebrick lid
耐火砖格子 fireclay brick checkers
耐火砖块 refractory block
耐火砖炉衬侵蚀 refractory wear
耐火砖片 refractory tile
耐火砖墙 refractory wall
耐火砖碎屑 refractory brick debris
耐火砖套 shroud
耐急冷急热性 spalling resistance
耐急冷能力 chilling resistance
耐碱钢 alkali resistant [proof] steel
耐碱清漆 alkali proof varnish
耐碱蚀合金 alkali resistance metal
耐碱性 alkali fastness
耐碱铸铁 alkali-resisting cast iron
耐晶间腐蚀性 (同"晶间腐蚀抗力")
耐久 lasting long, durable
耐久比 endurance ratio
耐久试验 durability test
耐久特性 endurance characteristic
耐久涂层 resistant [long-lived] coating
耐久性 durability, endurance, lasting quality, permanent stability
耐空蚀[耐气穴]钢 cavitation-resistant steel
耐拉绝缘子 dead-end insulator
耐劳极限 fatigue endurance limit
耐硫酸盐水泥 sulphate-resistant cement
耐磨板 wear-resisting plate
耐磨保护层 abrasion resistant coating
耐磨表面 hard wearing surface
耐磨材料 abrasive [wear] resistant material, antifriction material

耐磨衬板　wear liner
耐磨瓷料　wear resistant porcelain
耐磨镀[覆]层　abrasion [wear] resistant coating
耐磨度　abrasion resistance, passive hardness
耐磨钢　abrasion resistant steel, wear-resistant [wear-resisting] steel ◇ 蒂斯科—蒂曼格锰镍~*, 微合金~*
耐磨滚动轴承　antifriction roller bearings
耐磨焊条合金　◇ 博罗德~(60WC, 40Fe) Borod
耐磨合金　abrasion resistant alloy, hard wearing alloy, wear-resisting [antifriction] alloy, wear-resistant alloy (8—9Al, 2.5—3.5Fe, 余量 Cu) ◇ 格拉西尔~*
耐磨合金钢　wear-resisting alloy steel
耐磨金属　antifriction [wear-resistant] metal
耐磨炉衬　abrasion resistant lining, wearing lining
耐磨试验　abrasion (resistance) test, wear test
耐磨试验机　abrasion (testing) machine
耐磨无缝钢管　wear-resistant seamless steel pipe
耐磨性　abradability, abrasion [abrasive, attrition, wear] resistance, abrasion resistant quality, resistance to wear, wear(-resisting) property, wearability, wearlessness, frictional property, wearing quality
耐磨硬度　abrasion [wear] hardness
耐磨铸铁　abrasion resistant cast iron, wear-resisting cast iron
耐磨砖　abrasive brick
耐摩擦性　nongalling property
耐疲劳　antifatigue
耐起鳞能力　resistance to scaling
耐侵蚀的　erosion-resistant, unattackable
耐侵蚀砖　erosion-resistant brick
耐氢钢　hydrogen resistant steel
耐热薄钢板　high temperature sheet steel

耐热玻璃　hard (borosilicate) glass, pyroceram, heat resistant glass ◇ 派列克斯~*, 瓦科尔~电解槽*
耐热不起皮钢　(同"热稳定钢")
耐热不起皮合金　scale-resistant alloy
耐热材料　heat resisting material
耐热冲击性　thermal shock resistance
耐热垫板[垫圈]　heat resisting gasket
耐热电缆　heat resistant cable
耐热度　refractoriness, thermal stability, heat resistance
耐热风机　hot fan
耐热坩埚　heat resistant crucible
耐热钢　heat resistant [resisting] steel, high temperature steel, refractory steel ◇ 奥氏体~*, 克罗洛伊低合金~*, 离心铸造~*, 镍铬~*
耐热高镍铬合金钢　◇ 吉纳洛依~*
耐热铬镍钢　heat resisting CrNi-steel
耐热合金　heat resistant [resisting] alloy, refractory alloy, calorite ◇ C.M.469~*, FID~*, S.816形变钴基~*, α铬基和钼基~α alloy, 超级~*, 蒂姆肯 X~*, 特巴德烧结~*, 西尔弗拉姆~*, 形变[可锻]~*, 因科内尔 X 析出硬化型~Inconel "X", 铸造~*
耐热合金钢　heat resistant alloy steel ◇ TAF 铁素体~*, 蒂尼杜尔~*, 尤尼滕普 212~*
耐热合金模　heat resisting alloy die
耐热滑道(炉内的)　heat resisting skid
耐热混凝土　refractory concrete
耐热胶[皮]带　heat resisting (rubber) belt
耐热金属　heat(ing) resisting metal
耐热聚合物　heat resistant polymer
耐热铝合金　◇ 科比塔留姆~*
耐热耐磨铬锰钢　◇ 哈斯克洛姆~*
耐热耐蚀钢　◇ 卢肯斯~Lukens steel
耐热耐蚀高镍合金　◇ 法里特~Fahrite (alloy), 霍恩金斯~*
耐热耐蚀合金　◇ 费尔奈特~*

耐热耐蚀合金钢 ◇ 雷克斯～Rex steel
耐热耐蚀铝青铜 ◇ 克罗托莱特～*
耐热耐蚀镍铬硅合金 ◇ 尼克洛西～*
耐热耐蚀镍铬合金 ◇ 杜尔柯～*
耐热耐蚀铜合金 ◇ 伊留姆～*
耐热耐蚀镍铁合金 ◇ 尼克罗伊～(50Ni,50Fe)Nikeloy
耐热耐蚀铁镍铬铸造合金 ◇ 埃康诺梅特～*
耐热耐蚀铁镍合金 ◇ 萨马洛依～Thermally
耐热耐蚀铜合金 ◇ 安普科～*
耐热耐酸铝硅铸铁 ◇ 阿尔西隆～*
耐热耐酸砖 heat and acidproof brick (HAB)
耐热镍铬钢 ◇ 尤塔罗伊～*
耐热镍铬钴多元合金 ◇ MT17～*
耐热镍铬钴合金 ◇ K42B～K42B alloy
耐热镍铬硅合金 ◇ 哈代特～*
耐热镍铬合金 ◇ Q～*, 布赖特雷～*, 克罗马克斯～(80Ni,20Cr)Kromax, 库罗莫尔～(85Ni,15Cr)Kuromore, 皮尔克～Pirck's metal
耐热镍铬合金钢 ◇ 卡利特～*, 克赛特～*, 维克洛～*
耐热镍基铸造合金 ◇ 尼莫～Nimocast
耐热皮带 heat resistant belt
耐热漆 heat resistant [proof] paint, Berlin black
耐热渗铝法 【压】alumincoat
耐热试验 heat resistant test, 【半】oven test
耐热塑料 heat resistant plastic
耐热搪瓷 heat resisting enamel
耐热填料 heat resisting gasket
耐热铁镍铬铝合金 ◇ 法伦洛伊～Fahralloy
耐热涂料 heat proof paint, refractory coating
耐热微生物 thermophilic microorganism
耐热稳定性 refractability
耐热细菌 thermophilic bacteria

耐热性 heat resistance [resistivity], resistance to heat, hot-resistance, fire resisting property, fire resisting [proof] quality, thermal resistance [stability], thermotolerance
耐热铸铁 heat proof cast iron, heat resistant iron, heat resisting (cast) iron ◇ 阿尔西隆高铝～Alusiron, 变性～*, 恩杜龙～*, 高镍～*, 格洛拜洛伊～*
耐熔度[性] refractoriness
耐散裂性 spalling property
耐烧的 flame resisting
耐失泽性 【金】tarnish resistance
耐湿性 moisture resistance, moisture-proof, wet fastness
耐时效性 ageing stability
耐蚀泵 acid-proof pump
耐蚀包层钢材 ◇ 科尔克拉德～*
耐蚀材料 corrosion-resisting material
耐蚀层 corrosion-resistant layer
耐蚀阀座合金 ◇ 普拉特纳姆～*
耐蚀钢 corrosion-resistant [corrosion-resisting] steel (CRES) ◇ 硅铬～*
耐蚀钢板 corrosion-resistant plate ◇ 海纳克～*
耐蚀高硅铁基合金 ◇ 埃利阿奈特～Elianite
耐蚀高镍合金钢 ◇ 斯威塔洛伊～*
耐蚀高镍铸铁(14—22 或 28—32Ni；例：3C,14Ni,6Cu,2Cr,1.5Si,余量 Fe) Ni-resist ◇ 尼莫尔～*
耐蚀硅铜 ◇ SM～*
耐蚀海军黄铜 inhibited admiralty brass
耐蚀含钨铝合金(97.6Al,1.4Sb,0.3Cu,0.2Fe,0.1Sn,0.4W) wolframium, wolframinium
耐蚀合金 corrosion-resistant [corrosion-resisting, non-corrosive, anticorrosion] alloy ◇ A.M.F.～*, CA 铜铝镍硅～*, 阿马洛伊～*, 兰氏 4R～*, 蒙乃尔 400～Monel 400, 塞德拉菲特～*, 斯特利特～*, 维里莱特～*

耐蚀黄铜 inhibited [corrosion-resistant] brass ◇ 滕冈姆~*
耐蚀极限 corrosion-resistance boundary
耐蚀金属 (corrosion-)resistant metal
耐蚀铝合金 corrosion-resistant aluminium alloy ◇ 阿尔科阿[美国铝业公司制]~Alcoa alloy,邦杜~*,米拉赖特~*,纳逊萘尔 A~*
耐蚀耐磨铁硅合金 ◇ 安塔西隆~*
耐蚀耐磨铜锰镍合金 ◇ 温德洛伊~*
耐蚀耐热钯金合金 ◇ 波拉里乌姆~*
耐蚀耐热钢 ◇ 卡姆洛依~*
耐蚀耐热合金 ◇ 克罗奈特~*,克罗尼特~*
耐蚀耐热合金钢 ◇ 西里乌斯~*,伊拉~Era
耐蚀耐酸耐热钢 corrosion acid and heat-proof steel
耐蚀镍铝青铜 ◇ 尼克拉~*
耐蚀镍铜系合金 ◇ CA-MM~*
耐蚀镍银合金 ◇ 劳梅特~Lawmet
耐蚀强度 corrosion strength
耐蚀青铜 corrosion-resistant brone ◇ 含硅~*,赫尔克里士~*
耐蚀试验 corrosion-resisting test ◇ 凯斯特尼希~Kesternich test
耐蚀铜合金 corrosion-resisting copper alloy ◇ CAZ~*,安布拉洛伊~*,巴罗尼亚~*,米拉~*,沃尔坎~*
耐蚀铜镍合金 corrosion-resisting copper-nickel alloy ◇ KK~KK metal,埃瓦布赖特~*,超级~*,坦帕洛伊~*
耐蚀铜镍锌合金 ◇ 西摩赖特~*
耐蚀性 corrosion-resisting property, corrosion [corrosive] resistance, corrosion stability [strength, resistance], anti-corrosion, non-corrodibility, non-corrosiveness
耐蚀压铸铝合金 ◇ 鲁泽莱特~*
耐蚀铸铁 corrosion-resistant cast iron ◇ 埃尔韦莱特~Elverite,多普洛伊~*
耐受度 tolerance
耐水的 water-repellent, water-proof, water-resisting
耐水化砖 slaking resistant brick
耐水浸蚀铅青铜(82—83.75Cu,3.25—4.25Sn,5—7Pb,5—8Zn) hydraulic bronze
耐水性 (同"抗水性")
耐酸玻璃蛇管 acid-resisting glass coil
耐酸材料 acid-proof [acid-resisting] material
耐酸槽 acid-resisting vessel
耐酸衬里 acid-proof lining
耐酸风扇 acid-proof fan
耐酸钢 acid-proof [acid-resisting] steel
耐酸缸[陶器] acid-proof stoneware
耐酸合金 acid-proof [acid-resistant] alloy
耐酸混凝土 acid-resisting concrete
耐酸接头 acid-resisting fittings
耐酸灵敏元件 acid-proof feeler
耐酸滤器 acid-proof filter
耐酸密封 acid proof sealing ◇ 轴用~*
耐酸耐火材料 acid-proof refractory
耐酸配件 acid-resisting fittings
耐酸青铜(8—10Sn,2—17Pb,0—2Zn,0—2Ni,余量 Cu) acid bronze [metal]
耐酸清漆 acid-proof varnish
耐酸试验 acid resistance test
耐酸水泥 acid-resisting [acid-proof] cement
耐酸搪瓷 acid-proof enamel
耐酸陶瓷衬 acid-proof ceramic lining
耐酸铁(13—16Si) acid-proof iron
耐酸铜合金(3Si,1Sn,0.1Cd,余量 Cu) AR alloy
耐酸铜铅合金 acid lead
耐酸涂料[漆] acid-resistant paint, acid-proof paint [coating] ◇ 复合~*
耐酸锡青铜(10Sn,2Pb,88Cu) acid metal
耐酸细菌 acid-fast bacteria
耐酸性 acid resistance, resistance to acid, acid fastness, acid resistivity
耐酸烟囱 acid-proof chimney
耐酸铸铁 acid-proof cast iron ◇ 杜里龙

耐酸砖 acid-proof brick (AB) ◇普通~*

耐铁耐热合金 ◇海恩斯-斯特莱特~*

耐雾绝缘子 fog type insulator
耐锈 antirust
耐锈蚀性 rust resistance, stain-resistance
耐压 withstand voltage (耐电压)
耐压管线 pressure line
耐压环 pressure ring
耐压力[性] resistance to pressure
耐压强度 compressive strength
耐压试验 breakdown test, 【电】withstand voltage test, disruptive test
耐盐水腐蚀性 resistance to salt-water corrosion
耐盐酸合金 hydrochloric acid-proof alloy
耐盐酸镍钼合金 ◇哈斯特洛伊 B~*
耐盐雾腐蚀性 salt-fog resistance, salt spray resistance
耐氧化的 (同"抗氧化的")
耐氧化耐酸镍钼铬钨合金 ◇哈斯特洛伊 C~*
耐氧化起鳞能力 resistance to scaling
耐氧化性 (同"抗氧化性")
耐用品 durable goods ◇非~ nondurable goods
耐用设备 durable equipment
耐油的 oil-resistant, oil-proof
耐渣砖 slag resistant brick ◇烧成~*
耐震工具钢 shock resisting tool steel
耐震性 shock resistance, resistance to vibration
耐蒸汽腐蚀合金 steam corrosion-resistant alloy
耐脂肪酸的 fatty acid resistant
奈耳点[温度] antimagnetic Curie point, Neel point [temperature]
奈克罗姆低(镍铬)合金高强度钢 Nykrom
奈培(衰耗单位,=8.686分贝) neper (Np)
奈塔尔硝酸乙醇腐蚀液(钢铁材料用) 【金】Nital (etchant)
奈特移动 【理】Knight shift
萘{$C_{10}H_8$} naphthalene, naphthaline, naphthene (旧名)
萘饼 naphthalene cake
萘撑次萘基-{$C_{10}H_6-$} naphthylene
萘醇 naphthylalcohol
萘堵塞 naphthalene blockage
萘二甲酸{$C_{10}H_6(COOH)_2$} naphthalic acid
萘酚{$C_{10}H_7OH$} naphthol
萘磺酸{$C_{10}H_7SO_3H$} naphthalenesulfonic acid
萘基{$C_{10}H_7$} naphthyl
萘浆 【焦】naphthalene slurry
萘结晶器 naphthalene crystallizer
萘浓度 naphthalene concentration
萘[羧,甲]酸 {$C_{10}H_7 \cdot COOH$} naphtha-lene-car-boxylic acid
萘烷 deca hydronaphthalene
萘油 naphthalene oil
南非钢铁学会 South African Iron and Steel Institute
南非化学冶金及采矿学会 Chemical Metallurgical and Mining Society of South Africa (CMMSSA)
南非全国五金工会 National Union of Metalworkers of South Africa (NUMSA)
难变形钢和合金 less-deformable steel and alloy
难变形金属 【压】difficult-to-form metal
难变形区 stagnant zone
难变形锥 dead cone
难辨认的 indistinct
难成球矿石 (同"难造球矿石")
难成形金属 difficult-to-form metal
难除杂质 troublesome impurity
难处理[熔炼]矿物 refractory mineral
难处理物料 difficult-to-dump material
难磁化方向 direction of hard magnetiza-

tion
难分解精矿 hard to open concentrate
难浮(起)的 difficult-to-float
难关[题] bottleneck
难回收金属 difficult-to-recover metal
难焊(接)的 difficult-to-weld, hard to weld
难还原矿 irreducible ore
难机械加工合金精密铸造法 microcast process
难挤压合金 difficult-to-extrude alloy
难加工钢 low machinability steel
难控制的 incontrollable
难排除的渣 【冶】hard to remove slag
难熔玻璃 high melting glass
难熔材料 (同"高熔点材料")
难熔层 infusible blanket
难熔废钢 heavy (melting) scrap
难熔分散(亚微)颗粒 【粉】submicron refractory dispersiods
难熔粉末 refractory powder
难熔粉末冶金材料[难熔金属陶瓷材料] powdered refractory material
难熔合金 high melting point alloy, refractory alloy
难熔化合物 refractory compound
难熔金属 (同"高熔点金属")
难熔金属电接触器材 refractory metal contacts
难熔金属复合材料 refractory metal base composite material
难熔金属加热元件 refractory metal heating element
难熔金属热[温差]电偶 refractory metal thermocouple
难熔金属熔凝 consolidation of refractory metal
难熔(金属)碳化物 refractory carbide
难熔耐火砖 high heat duty firebrick
难熔(炼)矿物[石] refractory mineral [ore]
难熔硫化矿 refractory sulfide ore

难熔黏合剂 high melting binder
难熔黏土 refractory clay
难熔碳化物回收 reclaiming of refractory carbides
难熔铜矿处理[离析]法 【色】Torco (treatment of refractory copper ore) process
难熔涂层 refractory coating
难熔物夹杂 refractory inclusions
难熔新金属 (同"高熔点新金属")
难熔性 refractory behaviour, infusibility
难熔性渣 refractory slag
难熔氧化物 refractory oxide
难熔砖 high heat duty firebrick
难松开的带卷 (同"紧卷的带卷")
难闻的 smell unpleasant [bad] ◇ 气味~ 气体*
难洗煤 difficult coal
难行 【铁】sticky ◇ 高炉~*
难行高炉 tight blast furnace
难选低品位矿石 sub-mill-grade ore
难选矿石 rebellious [refractory] ore
难选铁矿 refractory iron ore ◇ 低品位~*
难运转[实行,操作,工作]的 unworkable
难造球矿石 【铁】more-difficult-to-ball ore
囊状物 bladder
挠度 (amount of) deflection, bend(ing) (deflection), buckling, flexibility, flexivity, sagging ◇ 反~【铸】camber, 上~ height of camber
挠度计[仪] deflectometer, deflectoscope, flexometer
挠度指示计 deflection indicator
挠矩 (同"弯曲力矩")
挠曲 bending (flexure), deflection, flexure, flexing, flexion ◇ 恒~试验*
挠曲变形[应变] flexural strain, strain of flexure
挠曲断裂 flexure fracture
挠曲力 deflecting force
挠曲模量 flexure [flexural] modulus

挠曲模样 【铸】wraped pattern
挠曲能力 deflectivity
挠曲器 (同"弯曲器")
挠曲强度 flexural [transverse] strength
挠曲试验 deflection [flexibility, flexure, softness] test
挠曲性 deflectivity
挠曲应力 【压】flexural stress
挠性 flexibility, flexivity, flexibleness ◇ 非～的 inflexible
挠性不锈钢密封盒(高压高炉的) flexible stainless steel bellows
挠性磁铁 flexible magnet
挠性导管 flexible conduit
挠性电极 dangler
挠性电缆 flexible cable
挠性电缆磁化(作用) 【理】flexible cable magnetization
挠性钢丝绳 flexible steel wire rope (FSWR)
挠性管 flexible tube, pliable pipe
挠性滚柱轴承 flexible roller bearing
挠性接头[连接] flexible joint [connection]
挠性金属导管 flexible metallic conduit
挠性金属膜盒[软管] flexible metal bellows
挠性联轴节 elastic [flexible] coupling ◇ 齿型～【机】gearflex coupling
挠性密封 flexible seal
挠性密封条 【铸】dike
挠性皮带(传动)落锤 flexible belt drop hammer
挠性软管 flexible hose
挠性软管接头 flexible hose connection
挠性试验 flexion [flexure] test
挠性套筒 flexible skirt
挠性涂层 flexible coating
挠性位错 (同"可弯位错")
挠性压模 flexible mould
挠性油管 flexible oil piping
挠性轴 flexible axle [shaft]

挠性锥 flexible cone
硇砂 sal ammoniac
内拔模斜度 【钢】inside draught
内半径 internal [inside] radius
内剥层法 【压】inside stripping layer method
内保护环(丝扣的) nipple
内壁 inwall, inside wall ◇ 钢管～检查镜 borescope, 镗孔～检验器 bore wall tester
内壁灰带缺陷(不锈钢旋压管的) defective inner surface grey band
内壁砖 inwall brick
内变形损耗 inner deforming loss
内标谱线 internal standard line
内标温度计 enclosed-scale thermometer
内表层预应力处理 autofrettage
内表层预应力处理法 autofrettage process
内表面过滤器 internal-surface filter
内表面加热线圈 ID (inside diameter) heating coil
内表面检查仪(铸件的) endoscope
内禀磁导率 intrinsic permeability
内禀磁化(强度) intrinsic magnetization
内禀磁矩 intrinsic magnetic moment
内禀磁滞[滞后]回线 intrinsic hysteresis loop
内禀感应 intrinsic induction
内禀光电导效应 【理】intrinsic photoconductive effect
内禀还原性 intrinsic reducibility
内禀辉度 intrinsic brilliance
内禀矫顽力 intrinsic coercive force
内禀角动量 intrinsic angular momentum
内禀扩散系数 intrinsic diffusion coefficient
内禀亮度 intrinsic brightness
内禀能态 internal energy state
内禀特性[性能] intrinsic property
内禀亚铁电感 intrinsic (ferric) inductance
内禀(亚铁)感应曲线 intrinsic (ferric)

induction curve
内禀增宽(度)　intrinsic broadening
内禀自旋力矩　【理】intrinsic spin moment
内部变形　internal deformation
内部标准　internal standard
内部不连续性　internal discontinuity
内部不完整性　internal unsoundness
内部参考　internal reference
内部操作寄存器　internal function register
内部测定[测量]　internal measurement
内部尺寸　inside measure, internal dimension
内部抽空　internal evacuation
内部地址　【计】home address
内部电动势　internal e.m.f.
内部洞穴　internal cavity
内部对称(性)　internal symmetry
内部工作容积高度(转炉的)　internal height
内部函数　【计】in-line [intrinsic] function
内部耗散能(量)　internal dissipation energy
内部活动　internal action
内部机构　interior mechanism
内部加热　internal heating
内部校验　built-in check
内部接线图　interconnection diagram
内部结构　internal structure
内部苛(性)化　inside causticization
内部孔隙　internal porosity [voil]
内部宽度　internal width
内部扩散　internal diffusion
内部冷却　internal cooling
内部冷却壁　internal stave
内部冷却器　【铁】internal stave
内部裂纹　internal crack [fissure]
内部轮廓　inside profile
内部磨损[损耗]　internal wear
内部能量　internal energy
内部偏析　internal segregation
内部排放[排水]　interior drainage
内部气孔　internal porosity, deep-seated blowhole
内部气压　internal gas pressure
内部强度　internal strength
内部缺陷　internal defect [unsoundness], interior defect
内部缺陷检测　interior defect detection
内部容积　inner volume
内部散失　internal dissipation
内部设备　inner equipment, internal unit, in-house facility (指机构内部的设备)
内部收缩　interior [internal] shrinkage
内部撕裂　internal tearing
内部缩孔　【钢】interior [minor] shrinkage, internal shrinkage cavity
内部探头[探针]　(同"内探头")
内部体积　interior volume
内部通话装置　intercommunication unit
内部通信　intercommunication, intercom
内部通信联络系统　intercom system
内部通信装置　intercom
内部完整性　internal soundness
内部消耗　internal dissipation
内部信息　in-house information
内部修整　interior trim
内部循环　internal recycling
内部氧化　internal oxidation
内部氧化物　subscale
内部运算　【计】internal arithmetic
内部振捣(混凝土)　pervibration
内部振捣器　pervibrator ◇ 混凝土～'
内部质量　internal quality [soundness]
内部专用车辆　internal wagon
内部装饰　interior trim
内部自动校验　【计】built-in automatic check
内部自行调节[调整]　inherent regulation
内部组织　internal [interior] structure
内部作用　internal action
内藏能量　intrinsic energy
内藏热量　intrinsic heat
内测头　(同"内探头")
内层　first layer, inlayer, subcoat

内层电子　inner electron
内层韧致辐射　inner bremsstrahlung
内插法　【数】interpolation
内插系数　interpolation coefficient
内场　【理】internal field
内衬　(inner) lining, liner ◇ 带～的 inner-cased, 底部～ bottom inwalls, 砌筑～作业 lining work
内衬钢板砖(炉顶砖)　【钢】internally plating brick
内衬里　inside liner
内衬套　inner liner, neck bush
内衬修理(浇包的)　repatching
内齿轮　internal [annular] gear, annular wheel, annulus
内齿圈　【机】inner rim, annular gear
内齿式联轴节套　【机】inner toothed sleeve coupling
内传力法预应力　prestress with bond
内重叠　inside laps
内存储器　internal memory [storage]
内底　inner bottom (I.B.)
内电阻　internal [source] resistance
内镀层　inner coat
内镦厚　【压】internal upsetting
内发裂　【钢】internal seam
内反射光谱　【理】internal reflection spectrum
内反射光谱学[分析法]　【理】internal reflection spectroscopy (IRS)
内反射元件[元素]　internal reflection element (IRE) ◇ 定角度～*, 可变角度～*, 双程～*
内根丁七 O 黄铜(70Cu, 28Zn, 2Pb)　Nergandin
内光电效应　【压】internal photoelectric effect
内光电效应光电管　photoresistance cell
内辊挤压　internal roll extruding
内过程　【计】internal procedure
内含碳　internal carbon
内函数　【计】in-line [intrinsic, inner] function
内函特性　intensive property
内焊缝　inside weld
内耗　(同"内摩擦")
内耗峰值　【理】damping peak
内河运输　inland water transport
内弧半径　internal radius
内华达银[铜镍锌合金]　Nevada silver
内环　【机】inner ring
内火焰炉　internally fired furnace
内加厚(钢管)　internal upset (IU)
内加还原剂　internal reactant
内加还原剂球团　self-reduced pellet
内加热器　internal heater
内加热式盐浴炉　internally heated salt bath furnace
内加热转筒干燥机　internally heated rotary drier
内浇口　flow [cast] gate, gate runner, in(-)gate ◇ 扁平～ flat gate, 节流～ choke
内浇口芯　gate core
内角(接头)焊缝　inside corner weld, inside fillet
内角(修型)墁刀　【铸】inside corner slick
内角圆半径　fillet radius
内接的　built-in
内接缝[接口]　internal seam
内接头连接(电极的)　nipple joint
内结晶　intercrystalline
内径　inside diameter (ID, i.d.), internal diameter, bore (size)
内径测微计[千分尺]　inside micrometer
内径卡规　inside calliper (gauge), internal (caliper) gauge
内径量规　male gauge
内聚键　cohesional bond
内聚力　cohesive force, coherence, coherency, cohesion ◇ 晶间～破坏*
内聚连接　cohesional bond
内聚能　cohesive energy
内聚能力　cohesiveness
内聚强度　cohesive strength

内聚亲和力 cohesive affinity
内聚现象 coherence, coherency, cohesion
内聚性 cohesive property, cohesiveness
内孔窥视仪[检视仪,检查镜,探测镜] borescope, boroscope, intfoscope ◇ 标定式~calibrated borescope, 多次折光~cave borescope, 防水防汽~*, 分段~sectionized borescope, 广角[宽场]~*, 挠性~flexible borescope, 气冷~*, 微型~microborescope
内孔周圆窥视仪 panoramic borescope
内拉力[拉伸] internal tension
内雷宾德尔效应(金属强度的) internal Rehbinder effect
内冷隔 【铸】internal seam
内冷凝管 inner condensing tube
内冷凝器 inner condenser
内冷铁 【铸】internal chill, insert, densener ◇ 螺旋状~chill coils
内力 internal force, stress
内联网 intranet
内连(接) interconnection
内裂 internal crack [break], burst, 【铸】reed
内裂纹 【铸】internal tearing
内流变 internal flow
内六角螺钉 (socket head) cap screw
内漏模板(造型机的) internal stripping plate
内炉缸 【冶】internal crucible
内炉型 【冶】inner profile
内轮缘 【机】inner rim
内螺纹 【机】inside screw, internal thread
内螺纹管 inner spiral pipe [tube]
内螺纹梳刀 【机】inside chaser
内螺纹异型管 internal-thread shaped tube
内螺纹锥度规 internal-thread taper gauge
内螺旋凸筋管 rifled tube
内面 inner face
内模板 internal template
内摩擦 internal friction ◇ 本底~*

内摩擦法 internal friction method
内摩擦特性 internal friction characteristic
内摩擦-温度关系 temperature dependence of internal friction
内摩擦系数 coefficient of internal friction
内摩擦现象 internal friction phenomenon
内摩擦锥 male friction cone
内能级 inner (energy) level
内能态 internal energy state
内啮合 【机】inside [internal, inner] gearing
内配煤球团 iron ore/coal mixed pellet
内平接型(钻杆) internal-flush style, IF style
内坡 back slope
内气孔 internal pore
内气压 internal gas pressure
内迁移离子 【理】ingoing ion
内腔 intracavity, cavity
内墙 interior wall ◇ 从~砌砖 overhand
内燃 internal combustion (IC)
内燃打夯机 explosion ram
内燃机 (internal) combustion engine, explosion engine ◇ 汽油~gasoline engine
内燃机轨道车 trackmobile
内燃机驱动焊接机组 gas-engine-driven welder
内燃式热风炉 internal combustion hot stove
内燃室式考贝热风炉 Cowper with internal combustion
内绕组 【电】inside coil
内容积 inner [internal, interior] volume
内润滑钢丝绳 internally lubricated wire rope
内塞雾化铁粉生产法 Naeser process
内散射 scattering-in, inscattering
内莎玻璃 Nesa glass
内蛇管 inner [inside] coil
内渗透 endosmose, endosmosis
内渗现象 endosmosis, endosmose
内生夹渣 endogenous slag inclusion

内生凝固	【铸】endogenous freezing
内视镜	endoscope
内探头[探针]	inside [internal] probe
内特性(曲线)	internal characteristic
内调制	intermodulation, internal modulation
内涂层	inner coat
内推法	【数】interpolation
内外加厚(钢管)	internal external upset (IEU)
内外卡钳	scribing [double] caliper
内外水冷穿孔顶头	externally/internally water-cooled piercing plug
内外四心桃尖拱	【建】ogee arch
内外座圈表面硬化(轴承的)	out and inner race case-hardening
内务操作	【计】housekeeping operation
内务处理程序	housekeeping routine
内线电话	inter-phone, housephone
内线圈	inside coil
内向扩散	inward diffusion
内向流	indraft, indraught
内斜斜度(炉腹的)	【铁】inward batter
内锌矿{ZnS}	sphalerite
内心白口	(同"反白口")
内型芯	belly core
内形	【冶】inner [inside] profile
内压力	internal pressure ◇ 密闭~成形*
内焰心	inner flame core
内氧化法	internal oxidation method
内氧化合金	internally oxidized alloy
内应变	internal strain
内应变状态	state of internal strain
内应力	inner [internal, residual] stress ◇ 钢球~*, 消除~*
内应力扩展	internal stress widening
内应力系	system of internal stress
内余面	inside laps
内圆磨削	【机】internal grinding
内圆直径	small circle diameter
内蕴场	【理】intrinsic field
内在不稳定性	(同"固有不稳定性")
内在夹杂	natural [native] inclusions
内在素质	intrinsic quality
内在压力	intrinsic pressure
内在应力	inherent stress
内在杂质	(同"固有杂质")
内站	【计】inside plant
内张力	internal tension
内胀型全金属刹车片	internal expanding-type all-metal brake lining
内胀制动器	internal expanding brake
内罩	inner cover
内指示剂	internal indicator
内轴	internal axle
内注口	【连铸】inner nozzle
内装可靠性	built-in reliability
内装式承受顶尖	build in receiving centre
内子程序	【计】in-line subroutine
内阻力	internal resistance
内座圈(轴承的)	【拉】inner race
嫩绿色	bright green (colour)
能	energy, power ◇ 费米~Fermi energy
能程	energy interval
能带	(energy) band ◇ 布洛赫~Bloch band, 满充~full energy band
能带边缘	【理】band edge
能带间磁光效应	【理】interband magneto-optical effect
能带间距	band separation
能带间隙	band gap
能带结构	band [zone] structure
能带宽度	energy band width
能带理论	band theory
能带面	energy surface of band
能带模型	band model
能带上限	top of band
能带图	【理】(energy) band diagram
能带图像	band picture
能带下限	bottom of band
能谷	energy-valley
能含量	energy content
能耗	(同"能量消耗")

能耗总量 gross energy consumption
能壑 【理】energy sink
能积 energy product
能积曲线 energy-product curve
能级 【理】energy level ◇ 费米～ Fermi level, 朗道～*, 塔姆～ Tamm (energy) level, 最高～ topmost (energy) level
能级充填 filling of energy levels
能级分裂 energy-level splitting
能级个数[填满数] level population, population of level
能级简并 degeneracy of energy levels
能级较低的电子 lower lying electron
能级密度 level density, density of level
能级图 energy(-level) diagram
能级退化 degeneracy of energy levels
能级位置 level position
能级移动[位移] level shift
能级跃迁 energy level transition
能级[阶]占有率 level occupancy
能级最低的电子 lowest energy electron
能脊 energy ridge
能见度 visibility
能垒[能量势垒] energy barrier
能(垒)峰 energy hump [hill]
能垒效应 barrier action
能力 ability, capability, capacity, power ◇ 原有～ existing capacity
能力标定 capacity rating
能力范围 capacity range
能力利用 utilization of capacity
能量 (amount of) energy ◇ 被反射的～ reflected energy
能量标度[级别] energy scale
能量储备 margin of energy
能量传递 (同"能量转移")
能量传递介质 【理】energy transmission medium
能量传递系数 energy transfer coefficient
能量单位 energy unit (E.U.)
能量单位消耗 unit energy consumption
能量等值线 【理】energy contour
能量法 energy method
能量范围 energy range [interval]
能量分辨率[能力] energy resolution
能量分布 energy distribution ◇ 玻色－爱因斯坦～*
能量分布函数 distribution function of energy
能量分配 【理】partition of energy
能量辐射率 rate of radiation of energy
能量恢复 energy recovery
能量回收 recovery of energy
能量极限 energy limit
能量级 energy level
能量计 energy meter
能量间隙 energy gap
能量交换 energy exchange
能量节约 power economy
能量禁区 forbidden energy range
能量均分 equipartition of energy
能量均分定律 law of equipartition of energy
能量利用 utilization [recovery] of energy
能量密度 energy density
能量频谱 energy distribution
能量平衡(表) energy balance
能量平衡直接分析法 【理】direct energy balance method
能量区 energy range [zone]
能量释出 energy release
能量释放 energy liberation
能量守恒 energy conservation, conservation of energy
能量守恒定律 【理】law of conservation of energy
能量受控旋压法 【压】controlled energy flow forming method
能量输出速率 rate of delivery of energy
能量输入 energy input [import]
能量输入速度 rate of energy input
能量输送 energy transport
能量损失[损耗] energy loss [waste], loss in [of] energy

能量特性(曲线) energy response
能量突变 energy jump [discontinuity]
能量稳定组态 energetically stable configuration
能量吸收 energy absorption [deposition]
能量吸收能力 energy absorption capability, capacity for energy absorption
能量吸收器 energy sink
能量消耗 energy [power] consumption, consumed power, dissipation of energy
能量蓄积 energy storage
能量硬度 energy hardness
能量阈值[临界值] threshold amount of energy
能量优化炉 energy optimizing furnace
能量跃变 energy jump
能量增量 energy increment
能量中心 energy centre
能量转换[变换] energy conversion
能量转移 energy transfer ◇ 弹性碰撞~*
能量转移系数 energy transfer coefficient
能量子 energy quantum
能流 energy flow [current]
能谱 energy spectrum, spectrum (复数 spectra)
能谱 X 射线定量分析 quantitative energy-dispersive X-ray analysis
能谱不连续(性) energy discontinuity
能谱测量(法)[测定(法),测量学] spectrometry ◇ γ射线~*
能谱分析 EDAX analysis
能谱仪 spectrometer
能斯脱定理 Nernst's theorem
能斯脱灯泡 Nernst lamp
能斯脱分配定律 Nernst distribution law
能斯脱公式 Nernst's equation
能斯脱-普朗克定理 Nernst-Planck's theorem
能斯脱效应 Nernst effect
能态 energy state, eigenstate ◇ 较高~ higher energy state

能通量 energy flux
能隙 energy gap
能隙的低能范围[界限] low-energy side of energy gap
能隙的高能范围[界限] high energy side of energy gap
能隙各向异性 anisotropy of energy gap
能阈 energy threshold
能源 energy [power] source, energy resources
能源产生 energy generation
能源介质分配 energy media distribution
能值模型 energy value model
霓虹灯 neon lamp (NL), neon tube
霓虹灯泡 neon glim lamp
泥板 darby
泥板岩 slate clay
泥泵 sludger, dredge pump
泥刀 slice
泥斗 bagger
泥封放出口 clay luted taphole
泥缸 【铁】clay barrel
泥疙瘩 clot
泥灰石[岩] marlstone
泥灰土 marl
泥浆 slurry, mud, slime (pulp), offscum, ooze
泥浆泵 slurry [mud, sludge, slush] pump, sludger, bailer ◇ 隔膜~ diaphragm slurry pump, 再浆化铅~*
泥浆产物 product slurry
泥浆沉淀池 mud settler
泥浆池 slime basin, mud pit
泥浆处理 sludge treatment
泥浆返料 【建】solution return
泥浆分离 slime-separation
泥浆过滤机 sludge filtration plant
泥浆刮除器 sludge scraper
泥浆化 sliming
泥浆浇注(法) slurry casting
泥浆搅拌机 mud [clay, slurry] mixer
泥浆浸出 slime leaching

泥浆喷补机 【耐】air mortar gun
泥浆喷枪 slurry gun
泥浆清除装置 sludge clearance device
泥浆收集设备 sludge gathering equipment
泥浆输送泵 sludge conveyer pump
泥浆填料(砌炉用) 【铁】chicken feed
泥浆脱水 sludge dewatering
泥浆悬浮物 floating sludge element
泥浆运输 slurry transportation
泥浆制备 slurry preparation
泥浆贮槽 sludge bunker
泥浆状浸出液 slimy leach liquor
泥浆自动排出装置 automatic sludge discharger
泥料 pug
泥料加工 tempering
泥煤 peat (coal), boghead coal
泥煤砖 peat briquette
泥(泞)路 dirt road
泥炮 【铁】tap(hole)[notch, mud, clay] gun, taphole stopping machine ◇ 电动~*, 堵铁口~ tap(hole) gun, 螺旋推进式~*, 全液压驱动』~*, 双筒~*, 蒸汽~*, 柱塞式[气缸式]~*
泥炮操纵[控制] mud gun control
泥炮操纵台 mud gun control console
泥炮控制站 mud gun control centre
泥炮筒 clay barrel
泥炮嘴 gun nozzle
泥片岩 fissile shale
泥塞 bod, bot(t), clay plug ◇ 黏土~*
泥砂 (argillaceous) silt, atteration ◇ 含~的河流 burdened stream
泥砂泵 sand pump
泥砂地 argillo-arenaceous ground
泥水筒 mud drum
泥炭 peat (coal), turf
泥炭[煤]粉(渗碳剂) peat powder
泥炭沼泽 peat bog
泥铁矿 clay ironstone, egrubbin, gubbin
泥铜 (同"沉淀铜")

泥土 earth, soil, dirt, clay
泥土层 dirt-bed, dirty bed
泥土状物质 earthy material
泥土状氧化铁 earthy iron oxide
泥瓦工 mason, bricklayer
泥污 dirt, mire
泥箱 mud box [collector]
泥箱土 sagger clay
泥芯 【铸】(loam) core ◇ 吹砂机制~*, 打~ decoring, 副[部分组合]~ branch core, 有~铸造 cored casting, 主体~ body core
泥芯撑 chaplet ◇ 单脚[杆式]~ stalkpipe chaplet
泥芯堵头 core plug
泥芯干燥器 core-drying stove
泥芯骨 arbor, core iron
泥芯骨架 lantern
泥芯盒 core magazine
泥芯烘烤 core baking
泥芯上漂 core floating
泥型 【铸】loam mould
泥型铸造 loam casting
泥岩 mudstone ◇ 厚层~ argillite
泥渣 mud, slime, sludge, residue, offscum
泥渣捕集器 mud collector
泥渣槽 slime tank
泥渣层 slime blanket
泥渣沉淀池 mud lake
泥渣多级洗涤系统 multistage mud washing system
泥渣放出口 slime run-off
泥渣干燥炉 mud drier
泥渣流槽 slime launder
泥渣倾析 slime decantation
泥渣输送泵 sludge transfer pump
泥渣微粒 【冶】sludge particles
泥渣洗涤系统 mud washing system
泥渣下腐蚀 hide-out corrosion
泥沼地 bog
泥沼土 peat soil
泥质板岩 argillite

泥质矾土　argillaceous bauxite
泥质褐铁矿　(同"黏土质褐铁矿")
泥质矿　argillaceous ore
泥质菱铁矿　argillaceous siderite
泥质黏土　bat
泥质砂子　argillaceous silt
泥质石灰石　argillaceous limestone
泥质氧化物　earth oxide
泥质页岩　argillaceous shale
泥状海绵镍　【色】nickel dust sludge
尼阿格含铅黄铜(9Ni,3Pb,40Zn,余量Cu)　Niag
尼达拔制用锡磷青铜(91—92Cu,8—9Sn,少量P)　Nida
尼厄罗铜金镍合金　Nioro
尼尔壁　Neel wall
尼尔镍铝铁永磁合金(12Al,25Ni,余量Fe)　Nial
尼尔森(清洁度)试验　Nielson test
尼尔斯坦镍铬不锈钢(18—20Cr,8—10Ni,<0.2C,<2Mn,余量Fe)　Nilstain
尼尔瓦超低膨胀系数[超恒范]合金(31Ni,4—6Co,余量Fe)　Supernilvar
尼尔瓦铁镍低膨胀系数[恒范]合金(36Ni,余量Fe)　Nilvar
尼尔质谱仪　Nier mass-spectrometer
尼弗柯镍钴合金系　Nivco alloys
尼加罗炼镍法(古巴)　Nicaro process
尼卡留姆高强度耐蚀铝青铜　Nikalium, Superston-40
尼卡洛伊高导磁率合金(49Ni,51Fe)　Nicaloy
尼凯莱克斯光泽镀镍法　Neckelex
尼科耳棱镜　Nicol('s) prism, Nicol
尼科尔斯雾化镁粉法　Hichols process
尼科林铜镍合金(20Ni,余量Cu)　Nickoline
尼科罗洛依镍铬铁电热合金　Nichroloy
尼科耐蚀铜镍合金(90Cu,10Ni)　Nico alloy [metal]
尼科镍铁　nicofer

尼科镍铜钢(0.2C,0.8Ni,0.5Cu,余量Fe)　Nico alloy [metal]
尼科铅锑合金　Nico
尼克尔廷镍锡合金(50Ni,50Sn)　Nickeltin
尼克拉德包镍耐蚀高强度钢板　Nielad
尼克拉尔高强度铝合金(0.25—0.5Cu,0.25—1Cu,0.5—1Ni,0.25—0.5Mg,余量Al)　Nicral
尼克拉耐蚀镍铝黄铜(39.41Zn,40—46Cu,12—15Ni,1.75—2.5Pb,其余Al)　Nicla(brass)
尼克莱特镍铬耐热合金(80Ni,20Cr)　Nicrite
尼克雷克斯光泽镀镍法　Nickelex method
尼克林多元合金(银的代用合金;55Cu,12.5Ni,20.5Zn,10Pb,2Sn)　Nickelene
尼克林铜镍电阻合金(55—75Cu,18—32Ni,0.2Zn)　Nickeline
尼克林铜镍锰合金(67Cu,30—31Ni,2—3Mn)　Nickelin
尼克林铜镍锌合金(54Cu,26Ni,20Zn)　Nickelin
尼克林锡基合金(85.4Sn,8.8Sb,4.75Cu,0.43Sb,0.28Zn,少量Fe及As)　Nickeline
尼克罗姆镍铬－康铜热电偶　Nichrome-constantan thermocouple
尼克罗姆镍铬电阻丝　Nichrome wire
尼克罗姆镍铬合金粉末　Nichrome powder
尼克罗姆镍铬合金烧舟　Nichrome boat
尼克罗姆镍铬丝电阻　Nichrome resistor
尼克罗姆镍铬丝电阻炉　Nichrome-wound furnace
尼克罗姆镍铬丝加热器　Nichrome heater
尼克罗姆镍铬丝加热元件　Nichrome heating element
尼克罗塔尔L镍铬合金(精密电阻丝材料;75Ni,17Cr,余量Si及Mn)　Nikrothal L
尼克罗伊耐热耐蚀镍铁合金(50Ni,50Fe)

Nikeloy

尼克洛姆镍铬耐热合金　Nichrome(Nichrome: 65Ni, 20Fe, 15Cr; Nichromev: 80Ni, 20Cr)

尼克洛镍铬钎焊料(65—70Ni, 13—20Cr, 约10B)　Nicrobraz(e)

尼克洛西拉尔镍铬耐热耐蚀合金铸铁(18Ni, 6Si, 2C, 1.5Cr, 1Mn, 0.1S, 0.05P, 余量Fe)　Nicrosilal

尼克洛西耐热耐蚀镍铬硅合金(15—30Cr, 16—18Si, 余量Ni)　Nichrosi

尼克洛伊德铜镍耐蚀合金(55—60Cu, 余量Ni)　nickeloid

尼克洛伊铝铜镍合金(94Al, 4.5Cu, 1.5Ni)　Nickeloy

尼克洛伊耐蚀耐热镍铬合金(50Ni, 50Cr)　Nickeloy

尼克洛伊耐蚀铁镍合金(3.5或5或9Ni, 余量Fe)　Nicloy

尼奎斯特判据　Nyquist criterion

尼奎斯特稳定判据[稳定度准则]　Nyquist stability criterion

尼奎斯特线图　Nyquist diagram

尼拉纽姆牙科用钴铬铸造合金(64.2Co, 28.8Cr, 4.3Ni, 2W, 0.2C, 0.1Si, 0.7Al)　Niranium

尼兰德料罐装料式炉顶(高炉)　【铁】Neeland top

尼雷克斯铁镍恒范合金(36Ni, 0.4Mn, 0.1C, 余量Fe)　Nilex

尼龙[纶]　nylon

尼龙覆面金属　nylon-coated metal

尼龙隔垫　nylon spacer

尼龙轮辐　nylon web

尼龙筛网　nylon screen

尼龙手套　nylon glove

尼龙刷　nylon brush

尼龙涂层　nylon coating

尼洛低膨胀镍铁铬钴合金　Nilo

尼洛马格镍铁合金　Nilomag alloy

尼莫尔耐蚀高镍铸铁(12—15Ni, 5—7Cu, 1.5—4Cr, 2.75—3.1C, 1.25—2Si, 1—1.5Mn)　Nimol

尼莫耐热镍基铸造合金　Nimocast

尼莫尼克镍铬系耐热合金　Nimonic

尼帕马格铁镍铝钛系永磁合金(30Ni, 12Al, 0.4Ti, 余量Fe)　Nipermag

尼斯纳渣印夹杂检查法　【钢】Niessner slag-print process

尼斯潘C镍铬钛恒弹性合金(42Ni, 5—6Cr, 2—3Ti, 余量Fe)　Ni-span C

尼斯潘镍铬钛恒弹性合金(40Ni, 5Cr, 2Ti, 余量Fe)　Ni-span (alloy)

尼特拉洛伊渗氮用钢　Nitralloy steel

尼特拉洛伊石墨化渗氮钢(1.35—1.50Al, 1.2—1.3C, 0.5Mn, 0.2—0.4Cr, 0.25Mo, 余量Fe)　graphitic Nitralloy

尼瓦弗莱克斯发条合金(15Ni, 20Cr, 40Co, 7Mo, 2Mn, 0.04Be, 0.15C, 余量Fe)　Nivaflex

尼瓦洛克斯合金　Nivarox

尼维镍青铜　Ni-Vee bronze

铌{Nb}　niobium, columbium ◇含~合金, 合金级~*

铌钇矿　sipylite

铌粉　niobium metal powder

铌钙矿{(Ca, Ce, Na)(Nb, Ti, Fe, Al)$_2$(O, OH, F)$_6$}　fersmite

铌酐{Nb$_2$O$_5$}　niobic [columbic] anhydride

铌合金　niobium alloy

铌基合金　niobium [columbium] base alloy

铌粒(>99.3Nb, <0.16Ta)　columbium pellet

铌氯化炉　niobium chlorinator

铌镁矿　magn(esi)ocolumbite

铌钠矿{NaNbO$_3$}　lueshite

铌士坦　niostan

铌铈钇钙矿　polymignite

铌铈钇矿　zirkoneuxenite

铌酸{HNbO$_3$, H$_3$NbO$_4$, H$_4$Nb$_2$O$_7$}　niobic [columbic] acid

铌酸钙 calcium niobate
铌酸钾 {KNbO₃} potassium niobate
铌酸钠 {NaNbO₃, Na₃NbO₄} sodium niobate
铌酸盐 {MNbO₃, M₃NbO₄, M₄Nb₂O₇} niobate, columbate ◇ 碱金属～alkali niobate
铌钛合金 Nb-Ti alloy
铌钛铁铀矿 {(Y, Re, U, Ca, Th)₂(Nb, Ta, Fe, Ti)₇O₁₈} ampangabeite
铌钛铀矿 uranpyrochlore
铌钛铀铅矿 samiresite
铌钽金属 earth acid metal
铌钽矿床 niobium-tantalum deposit
铌钽矿物 niobium-tantalum mineral
铌钽铁铀矿 {(Mn, Fe, UO)(Nb, Ta)₂O₆} toddite
铌钽钇铀矿 obruchevite
铌添加合金 niobium addition
铌铁(中间合金；50—60Nb, 6Ta) ferroniobium, ferrocolumbium
铌铁矿 {(Fe, Mn)(Nb, Ta)₂O₆} niobite, columbite, ferrocolumbite
铌铁氯化 chlorination of ferroniobium
铌稳定钢 columbium stabilized steel
铌型材 columbium shape
铌氧基 nioboxy (group), columboxy (group)
铌钇矿 samarskite, nuevite, uranniobite
铌钇铁矿 {(Y, Fe)Nb₂O₆} nuevite
铌钇铀矿 nohlite, annerodite
铌易解石 niobo-aeschynite
拟合坐标 fit coordinate
拟抛物面规则 rule of quasi-paraboloid
拟坐标 quasi coordinate
腻料 lute ◇ 修芯～*
腻芯泥料 core mud
腻子 【建】luting, mastic, putty
逆β衰变 (同"电子俘获")
逆抽风 back draught(ing)
逆地址解析协议 reverse address resolution protocol

逆电动势 counter electromotive force (c.e.m.f.)
逆电流 【电】reverse [counter] current, opposite-flow
逆电流继电器 reverse-current relay
逆电流脱扣装置 reverse-current trip
逆电压 back [inverse] voltage
逆动 reversal
逆反应 counter [reverse, back] reaction
逆反应产物 back reaction product
逆飞弧[逆跳火] 【焊】back flashover
逆功率保护装置 reverse power protection
逆弧 【电】arc(ing) back, reignition
逆火 back-fire, flare back, flash back (烧嘴的) ◇ 持续～*
逆尖晶型(铁素体) 【金】inverse spinel
逆浸出 【色】reverse leach
逆扩散 reverse [counter] diffusion
逆扩散长度 inverse diffusion length
逆流 contraflow, backflow, counterstream, countercurrent (flow), counterflow, inverted flow, opposite-flow, reflux
逆流焙烧 【团】countercurrent firing
逆流操作[作业] countercurrent operation
逆流萃取 countercurrent extraction ◇ 酸乙醚～法*
逆流萃取设备 countercurrent extraction plant ◇ 多级～*
逆流分级法 countercurrent classifying
逆流分级[分粒]机 countercurrent sizer
逆流浮选柱 countercurrent column
逆流浮选装置 countercurrent column
逆流干燥机 counterflow drier
逆流还原 countercurrent reduction
逆流级联 countercurrent cascade
逆流交换柱 upstream column
逆流搅拌 countercurrent agitation
逆流浸出 countercurrent leaching ◇ 间歇式～*
逆流浸出试验 countercurrent leaching test
逆流快速拌和机[混合器] counterflow

rapid action mixer
逆流冷凝[凝汽]器 counterflow [countercurrent] condenser
逆流离子交换 countercurrent ion exchange ◇ 连续～*
逆流流动 countercurrent flow
逆流炉 counterflow [countercurrent] furnace
逆流气流 countercurrent gas flow
逆流倾析设备 CCD equipment
逆流倾析[倾注]洗涤 counter-current decantation (CCD)
逆流倾析洗涤法 CCD method
逆流倾析洗涤系统 CCD system
逆流清洗 counter-current rinsing
逆流热交换器 countercurrent heat-exchanger
逆流渗滤(浸出)系统 countercurrent percolation system
逆流式布料皮带机 reverse-flow feed conveyor
逆流式加热 countercurrent firing
逆流式回转窑 counter flow rotary kiln
逆流式冷却机 counterflow cooler
逆流水洗涤 countercurrent water scrubbing
逆流推料式连续加热炉 counterflow push-type furnace
逆流洗涤 countercurrent washing, back flush
逆流蓄热法 【冶】counterflow [upflow] regeneration
逆流循环 countercurrent circulation
逆流原理 countercurrent principle
逆流装置 countercurrent device [arrangement], counterflow apparatus
逆捻(钢丝绳的) (同"普通捻")
逆偏析 negative segregation
逆平行畴 antiparallel domain
逆平行磁化作用 【理】antiparallel magnetization
逆平行桥路 antiparallel bridge

逆燃 backfire, flashback ◇ 持续～*
逆时针方向 counter-clockwise direction
逆时针(方向)旋转 counter-clockwise rotation
逆铁素体 inverse ferrite
逆维德曼效应(磁致伸缩逆效应) inverse wiedemann effect
逆向风流 countercurrent air flow
逆向挤压 (同"反向挤压")
逆向控制 reversing control
逆向拉伸 reverse drawing
逆向运动 reverse motion [movement], counter [retrograde] motion
逆效应 converse effect
逆行 reversal, backing
逆行程缸 (同"回程缸")
逆序 reverse order, inverted sequence
逆序操作 back out
逆压袋式除尘器[逆压式袋滤器] bottom entry reverse flow baghouse
逆止 back stop
逆止阀 check [non-return] valve
逆转 back turn, reversal rotation, reversal, inversion
逆转变 reverse change
逆转固相线 【金】retrograde solidus
逆转机构 reverser
逆转时间(轧机的) reversal time
年报 annual report (Ann. Rep.)
年产量 yearly output (YO), annual output [production, capacity, rate, yield], yearly production [capacity]
年度保养[维修] yearly maintenance
年度检查 annual inspection
年度检修 annual overhaul
年鉴 yearbook (Y.B)
年平均降水量 mean annual precipitation
年平均气压 mean annual pressure
年平均温度 mean annual temperature
年平均相对湿度 mean annual relative humidity
年生产力分解 breakdown of annual ca-

年生产能力　yearly capacity
黏稠焦油　thick tar
黏稠性　vicidity
黏度　viscosity (visc.), ◇ 恩格勒～Engler degree, 绝对～absolute viscosity, 流态化床～fluid bed viscosity, 赛波特通用～*, 体积～bulk viscosity
黏度测定(法)　viscometry, viscosimetry ◇ 同轴[共轴]圆筒～*
黏度等值图　isopleth viscosity diagram
黏度计　viscometer, viscosimeter, fluid meter, fluidimeter ◇ 摆锤[悬摆]式～pendulum viscometer, 布氏～*, 浮子～float viscometer, 滚球式～*, 空气泡～air bubble viscometer, 连续记录～viscorator, 毛细管～capillary viscometer, 球窝～*, 赛波特重油～*, 通用赛波特一秒数*, 旋转式～rotational viscometer, 振动片式～*
黏度控制器　viscosity controller
黏度系数　viscosity index, modulus of viscosity
黏度纤维测定法　fibre method of viscosity measurement
黏度指数　viscosity index (VI)
黏附　adherence, adherency, adhesion, sticking
黏附层　adhering layer
黏附沉积　adherent deposit
黏附剂　adhesive
黏附计　adherometer, adhesiometer
黏附牢固的氧化皮　tight scale
黏附力　adhesional [stick] force, adhesion
黏附摩擦　sticking friction
黏附能力　adhesive capacity
黏附强度　adhesion [adhesive] strength
黏附桥　adhering bridge
黏附损耗　loss by adhesion
黏附体　adherend
黏附系数　coefficient of adhesion
黏附现象　adhesion
黏附性　adhesivity, adhesiveness
黏附压力　adhesion pressure
黏附应力　adhesive stress
黏附状态　coherent condition
黏附作用　adhesive action
黏钢(因烧熔所致)　dead burning
黏合　bind(ing), bonding, cohere
黏合剂　adhesive, binder (material), binding agent, bond, 【冶】matrix (炉衬的)
黏合接头　adhint
黏合力　binding force [power], cohesion
黏合料　binder (material)
黏合强度　bonding [cohesive] strength
黏合试验　bond test
黏合性　binding property
黏痕(薄板缺陷)　sticker mark
黏－滑失稳(静液挤压制品的)　stick-slip instability
黏胶　viscose
黏结　cohere, (adhesive) bonding, cement(ing), sticking, welding (轧件与导卫板的) ◇ 退火～板 annealing sticker
黏结层　binding course
黏结(层)剥离试验　debond test
黏结的组合型芯用量具　pasting gauge
黏结点　bond(ing) point
黏结反应　binding reaction
黏结粉末　bonded particles
黏结辅助金属　cementing auxiliary metal
黏结钢板　【压】sticker
黏结过程　bonding process
黏结焊剂　bond flux
黏结剂　bond(er), bonding agent, binder, agglomerant, binding agent [admixture, element, material], cement, cementing agent [material, medium], plastering agent ◇ 短效～fugitive binder, 金属～binder metal, 气体(硬化)～【铸】gas bond, 热固性～thermosetting adhesive, 热塑性～thermoplastic adhesive, 无～球团～, 暂时～temporary binder, 自硬～cold-setting binder

黏结剂金属　cementing metal
黏结剂去除　binder removal
黏结加入物　binding admixture
黏结键　cement bond, bonding bridge
黏结介质　cementing medium
黏结块破碎机　chunkbreaker
黏结[着]力　bonding [cohesive, clinging] force, cementing bond, binding power
黏结漏钢　【连铸】breakout by sticking
黏结煤　caking [binding, baking] coal
黏结能力　caking capacity, cementing power
黏结强度　bond(ing) [cohesive, caking] strength
黏结区　region of adhesion
黏结熔剂　bond flux
黏结水膜　coherent water layer
黏结土　binding clay
黏结温度　sticking temperature
黏结线（造球制粒的）　tack line
黏结相　binding [binder] phase
黏结性　cohesiveness, adhesivity, caking capacity [quality], cementation, agglomerating capacity
黏结性拉漏　sticking type break-out
黏结性煤　caking [binding] coal ◇ 非～ dry-burning coal, 高～ strongly coking coal, 中～ medium caking coal
黏结性能　bonding property
黏结性指数(煤的)　【焦】caking index
黏结(印)痕(叠板的)　sticker
黏结应力　bond stress
黏结值　cementing value
黏结作用　bonding [cementing] action, cementation
黏块　gob
黏料(形成)　forming of adhesives
黏模(钢)　sticker
黏模(钢)锭　catched ingot, sticker
黏砂(缺陷)　【铸】sand burning, burning-on (sand), burnt sand, sandmark, burning (-on) into sand, gathering-up ◇ 防～涂料(砂型的) antipenetration wash, 机械～ burned-on sand, 型芯～ burning-on into cores
黏砂层　burning sand
黏砂皮(铸件表面缺陷)　gritty scale
黏塑弹性体　visco-plasto-elastomer
黏塑性　visco-plasticity
黏塑性法　viscoplasticity method
黏塑性片　viscoplastic disc
黏弹性变形　viscoelastic deformation
黏弹性材料　viscoelastic material
黏弹性(力学)　viscoelasticity
黏弹性(能)　viscoelastic behaviour
黏土　clay ◇ 煅烧[烧过的]～ calcined clay, 过滤用～ filtering clay, 含～的 clay-bearing, 含铁～ ferruginous clay, 结合～ binding clay, 均化～装置*, 煤层下～ seat earth, 强黏性[软质,肥]～ strong [fat] clay, 轻敷－槽*, 烧过的～ calcined clay, 瘦[弱黏性]～ lean clay, 脱水～*, 以～胶结的 clay-bonded, 硬化～ clunch, 有孔～ keramzite, 制砖～ brick clay, 重～(烧砖用) gault
黏土板岩　clay slate
黏土保温帽　【钢】clay hot top
黏土层　binding course, clay plane, 【地】clay bed ◇ 夯实～ bed puddle clay
黏土搞实　【建】clay tamping
黏土地基　clay bed
黏土多的砂　clayey sand
黏土坩埚　clay crucible
黏土隔膜　clay membrane
黏土夯实　【建】clay tamping
黏土灰浆[火泥]　loam mortar
黏土混合物　loam mixture
黏土基质　clay matrix
黏土加工机械　clay-working machine
黏土浆　clay-grog mortar
黏土胶结的　clay-bonded
黏土焦炭混合物　clay-coke mixture
黏土搅拌机　clay [mud] mixer
黏土结合硅质耐火材料　clay-bonded sili-

黏 nian

黏土结合碳化硅耐火材料　clay-bonded silicon carbide refractory
黏土坑　clay pit
黏土矿床　clay deposit
黏土矿井　clay pit
黏土矿开采　clay mining
黏土脉　【比】clay vein
黏土磨碎机　【耐】clay mill
黏土耐火砖　clay firebrick, fireclay brick
黏土泥灰岩　clay marl
黏土泥浆　clay wash
黏土泥塞　bot(t)
黏土黏结剂　【铸】clay bond [binder]
黏土捏和机　loam kneader masticator
黏土坯体　【耐】clay body
黏土片岩　clay schist
黏土破碎机　clay shredder
黏土切割机　clay cutter
黏土切削机　【耐】clay carving machine
黏土塞头砖　【冶】clay plug
黏土砂浆　clay mortar
黏土烧失　burnt sand
黏土石墨坩埚　clay-graphite crucible
黏土石墨搪料　clay-graphite mixture
黏土石墨制品　clay-graphite product
黏土熟料　【耐】chamotte, burned fire-clay ◇ 硬质～*
黏土熟料粉　chamotte powder
黏土熟料灰浆　clay-grog mortar
黏土熟料砂　chamotte sand
黏土熟料细粉　finely ground fire clay
黏土熟料砖　grog-clay brick
黏土水口砖　clay nozzle
黏土水泥砂浆　clay-cement mortar
黏土似的砂　clayey sand
黏土填塞　clay tamping
黏土吸水能力测定值　Enslin value
黏土洗选　clay washing
黏土型　【铸】loam mould
黏土型芯　【铸】clay [loam] core
黏土袖砖　fireclay sleeve

黏土悬浮剂　deflocculant, deflocculating agent
黏土岩　clay rock, claystone
黏土页岩　bury
黏土造型　【铸】clay moulding
黏土制备机　clay preparation machine
黏土制品　clay ware ◇ 未烧成干燥～ white-hard
黏土质的　clayey
黏土质隔热耐火材料　fireclay insulating refractory
黏土质褐铁矿　(brown) clay iron ore
黏土质精矿　clay-bearing concentrate
黏土质矿石　argillaceous ore
黏土质矿物　clay mineral
黏土质菱铁矿　argillaceous siderite
黏土质脉石[废石]　argillaceous gangue
黏土质耐火材料（30％—47％ Al_2O_3） fireclay refractory
黏土质砂　clayey sand
黏土质塑性耐火材料　fireclay plastic refractory
黏土质碳酸铁矿　clayband ironstone
黏土砖　clay [loam, chamotte] brick, firebrick
黏土砖绝缘　clay brick insulation
黏土砖坯　dobie, adobe
黏土状物质　clay-like material
黏细菌纲　Myxobacteriae
黏吸作用　adhesive attraction
黏性　viscosity (vis., visc.), stickiness
黏性胶体　viscoloid
黏性金属　viscous metal
黏性矿(石)　sticky [gougy] ore
黏性流(动)　viscous [frictional] flow
黏(性炉)渣　【冶】viscous [sticky, pasty, heavy, dry] slag, soft clinker
黏性[黏滞]摩擦　viscous friction
黏性泡沫渣形成　【冶】sponging
黏性熔化带　zone of sticky fusion
黏性砂　clay sand
黏液丝　viscose

黏质沥青 steep pitch
黏滞的 viscous (vis), pasty, tenacious
黏滞度 viscosity ◇ 恩格勒～Engler degree
黏滞计 viscometer
黏滞系数 coefficient of viscosity
黏滞性 viscosity ◇ 微～microviscosity
黏滞性蠕变 viscous creep
黏着层 adhering layer
黏着度[黏着(力)值] bond value
黏着力计 adhesivemeter
黏着磨损 adhesive wear ◇ 防～剂 antiseize compound, 抗～性 antiseize quality
黏着能力 stickability
黏着区 stick [no-slip] region, region of adhesion, 【压】(金属的) stick zone, zone of zero slip, dead-metal (zone)
碾槽(轮碾机的) dish
碾轮式混砂法 【铸】mulling
碾轮式混砂机 【铸】roller mixer, sand roller mill
碾磨 (pan) milling ◇ 湿式～wet pan grinding
碾磨机 end runner mill, attrition [roller] mill ◇ 干式～pan (grinding) mill, 盘式～*, 双轴式～*, 圆筒～cylinder mill, 周边卸料～rim discharge mill
碾磨机加工(铁合金生产中的) pan mill processing
碾磨烧焦 【机】scorching
碾磨式混合机 muller-type blender
碾磨性(磨成粉末) milling quality
碾泥机 loam kneader masticator, pug
碾盘 grinding pan, dish
碾平 planish, malleate
碾砂机 【铸】sand muller, mulling machine, rubbing mill ◇ 槽形～groove muller, 快速～speed muller
碾碎粉末 【粉】milled powder
碾碎辊 cracker
碾碎机 muller (mixer), 【耐】chaser mill
碾压 roller compaction ◇ 压缩[首次]～breakdown rolling
碾压机 rubbing mill
碾子 runner, roller
捻(钢丝绳) 【压】lay
捻比系数 ratio of lay
捻股 【压】stranding
捻股机 stranding [laying-up] machine, strander ◇ 串列式～*, 多转子式～*, 固定工字轮的～fixed bobbin strander, 管式～*, 筐篮式～*, 立式～*, 三级串联～triple tandem strander, 蛇型～snake type strander, 行星式钢丝绳～*, 雪茄式～tubular type strander
捻股模 stranding die
捻角(钢丝绳的) spiral angle
捻距[长](钢丝绳的) pitch, length of lay
捻距范围 【压】range of lay
捻曲椭圆 【压】strained oval
捻绳机 closing machine, (crank) closer
捻向 direction of lay
捻型(钢丝绳的) type of lay
捻旋作用(钢丝绳的) screw action
念球藻属 Nostoc
廿辊轧机 ◇ 1-2-3-4 式～*
鸟瞰图 (同"俯瞰图")
脲微球菌 Micrococcus ureae
尿素[脲] {NH$_2$CONH$_2$} carbamde, urea
尿素甲醛[脲醛]树脂 urea (-formaldehyde) resin
尿烷 urethane
捏和 kneading, pugging ◇ 剪切和～作用*
捏和机 kneading machine [mill], kneader ◇ 黏土～*
捏和试验 pugging test
啮合 engagement, mesh, falling-in, bonding ◇ 使～(使齿轮啮合) engage, throw in
啮合程度 fitness
啮合杆 engaging lever
啮合焊接焊缝 mesh(ed) weld

啮合梁　joggle beam
啮口管焊接　bite type tube welding
镊子　tweezers, forceps
镍{Ni}　nickel ◇ D~(含 4—5Mn) D-nickel, 除~*, 纯~ pure nickel, 粗~ crude nickel, 电积~*, 电解~ electrolytic nickel, 镀黑~ black nickel plating, 高~炉渣 nickel rich slag, 工业[商品]~ commercial nickel, 海军~ admiralty nickel, 含~矿物, 火法精炼~ fire refined nickel, 粒状~ granulated nickel, 片状~ flake nickel, 烧结~ sintered nickel, 羰基~ carbonyl nickel, 铁磁性~*, 脱~(作用) denickelefication, 阳极~ anode nickel, 氧化[二氧化]钍弥散[T.D., TD]~*, 因科~*, 阴极~ cathode nickel
镍氨配合物　nickel ammine
镍白铜(50Cu, 25Zn, 25Ni)　Alpaka
镍饱和溶液　nickel-saturated liquor
镍铋银合金　◇ 普罗普拉提纳~(装饰用) Proplatina
镍币　nickel coin
镍箔　nickel foil
镍产物　nickel product
镍吹炼(法)　【冶】nickel converting
镍吹炼车间　【冶】nickel-converting plant
镍磁铁矿　trevorite
镍催化剂　nickel catalyst
镍萃取　【冶】nickel extraction
镍的　nickeliferous, nickelous (正镍的)
镍电解　【冶】nickel electrowinning
镍电解槽　electrolytic nickel cell
镍电解淀积处理　nickelizing
镍电解精炼槽　nickel electrorefining tank
镍电解液　nickel electrolyte ◇ 无钴高~*
镍电解液净化　nickel electrolyte purification
镍镀层　nickel-plate ◇ 化学[非电解]~ electroless nickel
镍钒钢　nickel-vanadium steel
镍粉　nickel powder, powdered nickel ◇ 羰基法~*
镍粉泥　【冶】nickel dust sludge
镍辐射屏　nickel radiation screen
镍浮渣　【冶】puddle cinder
镍坩埚　nickel crucible
镍钢　nickel steel (N.S.)
镍高锍　【冶】high (grade) nickel matte
镍镉电池　nickel-cadmium battery [cell]
镍铬奥氏体不锈钢　chromium-nickel austenitic stainless steel
镍铬不锈钢　chromium-nickel stainless steel ◇ 奥氏体~*, 尼尔斯坦~*, 派拉~*, 伊诺格扎让~*, 因科~*
镍铬超级铸造合金　◇ 因科内尔 713LC~*
镍铬电热合金　◇ 瓦克-梅尔特~*
镍铬电阻　nichrome resistance ◇ 杰利夫~合金*, 雷德雷~合金(85Ni, 15Cr) Redray, 尼克罗姆~丝*, 伊万欧姆~合金*
镍铬钢　nickel chromium steel ◇ 阿特巴斯~*, 雷齐斯塔尔(耐蚀耐热)~*, 赛克尔 L~*, 威帕拉~Wipla
镍铬钢蒸馏罐　nickel-chrome steel retort
镍铬钴低膨胀合金　◇ 阿尔坦尼姆~*, 奥尔塔尼厄姆~*
镍铬硅耐磨耐蚀合金　◇ 蒂斯科~*
镍铬焊料合金　Nicrobrraz
镍铬合金　nickel chromium alloy, chromium-nickel alloy, nickel-chrome (80Ni, 20Cr) ◇ MM~(96Ni, 4Cr) MM alloy, 克罗曼 80/20 型~*, 尼克罗塔尔 L~*, 帕尔耐蚀~*, 派奥尼尔耐蚀~*
镍铬黄铜　◇ 帕克~*
镍铬-康铜热电偶　chromel-constantan thermocuple
镍铬铝耐热钢　◇ 卡尔梅特奥氏体~*
镍铬锰耐蚀合金　◇ 阿布劳斯~*
镍铬钼不锈钢　◇ 沃思特~*
镍铬钼合金　埃诺~* Inor, 克罗里梅特~*
镍铬钼耐热钢　◇ 特里普尔 H~ Triple H

镍铬钼钢 nickel chromium molybdenum steel

镍铬耐磨铸铁轧辊 ◇阿达迈特~ adamite roll

镍铬耐热不锈钢 ◇海德雷克斯~*

镍铬耐热钢 nichrome steel ◇克罗马克斯~*,麦克内特~Mackenite metal

镍铬耐热合金 ◇F.1260~*,T.E.~*,阿科洛伊~*,巴斯斯~*,克罗麦尔~*,克罗莫尔~(85Ni,15Cr) Kromore,尼克莱特~(80Ni,20Cr) Nicrite,尼克洛姆~*,因科~Inco chrome nickel

镍铬耐热耐蚀钢 ◇因科内尔~ Inconel steel

镍铬耐热耐蚀合金铸铁 ◇尼克洛西拉尔~*

镍铬耐蚀可锻钢 staybrite

镍铬耐蚀耐热合金 ◇雷约~(85Ni,15Cr) Rayo

镍铬耐酸钢 utiloy

镍铬-镍硅系热电偶 ◇格米诺尔~ Geminol

镍铬-镍铝(热电偶用)合金(80Ni,20Cr合金;94Ni,2Al,1Si,2.5Mn,余量Fe合金) chromel-alumel

镍铬-镍铝热电偶(90Ni—10Cr/94.5Ni—2Al 热电偶) chromel/alumel thermocouple,chromel-alumel couple

镍铬硼合金 ◇科洛莫尼~*

镍铬钎焊料 ◇尼克洛~*

镍铬丝 nickel chrome wire,chromel-filament

镍铬钛恒弹性合金 ◇尼斯潘~*

镍铬铁电热(丝)合金 ◇卡洛米克~*,尼科罗洛依~Nichroloy,派罗米克~*,托弗特~*,因科800~Incoloy 800

镍铬铁合金 nickel-chromium-iron, Economent

镍铬铁锰合金 ◇法里莫尔~Firearmor

镍铬铁耐热合金 ◇A~*,费布赖特~*,乔佛~*,韦斯蒂科~*

镍铬铁耐热耐蚀合金 ◇米斯科~*,因科内尔~*

镍铬铁耐蚀合金 ◇尤蒂洛伊~*

镍铬铜合金铸铁 ◇柯苏尔~*

镍铬-铜镍热电偶 chromel copel thermocuple

镍铬钨钢 nickel chromium tungsten steel

镍铬钨合金 ◇BTG~*,阿马洛格~*

镍铬钨系合金钢 弗戈~*

镍铬系耐热合金 尼莫尼克~Nimonic

镍汞合金(99Hg,1Ni) nickel amalgam

镍钴比 nickel-to-cobalt ratio

镍钴定向凝固共晶合金 directionally solidified eutectic nickel and cobalt alloy

镍钴合金 nickel-cobalt ◇尼弗柯~系*

镍钴锍 【色】nickel-cobalt matte

镍钴钛系磁钢 ◇本多~*

镍钴铁锍 【色】nickel-cobalt-iron matte

镍硅合金 nickel-silicon alloy ◇W5~*

镍硅青铜 ◇科森~*

镍硅熔剂 nickel-silicon flux

镍硅铜耐蚀合金 ◇哈斯特洛伊D~*

镍焊丝 nickel bare welding filler metal

镍焊条 nickel electrode

镍合金 nickel alloy ◇AT耐蚀~*,M.C.102~*,阿卢梅尔~*,杜拉[Z硬]~*,菲尼特因瓦~(36Ni,余量Fe) Fenit,富~ nickel rich alloy,高~ high nickel alloy,拉尼~催化剂*,因科内尔~料罐 Inconel(charge) can

镍合金选择腐蚀 denickelefication

镍褐煤 kerzinte

镍华 nickel bloom [ocher], annabergite {3NiO·As$_2$O$_5$·8H$_2$O}, nickel green {Ni$_3$(AsO$_4$)$_2$·8H$_2$O}

镍还原 nickel reduction

镍还原高压釜 nickel reduction autoclave

镍黄铁矿 nickel-pyrite, pentlandite {(Fe,Ni)S}, bravoite {(Ni,Fe)S$_2$}

镍黄铜(含2—14Ni的铜锌合金) nickel brass ◇奥雷德~*,加铅~leaded nickel brass

镍黄渣 【色】nickel speiss

镍回收 【色】nickel recovery

镍活化的钨烧结 nickel-activated sintering of tungsten

镍基超级铸造合金 ◇ M.A.R.M.200~*

镍基超耐热合金 nickel-base heat resisting superalloy ◇ 阿斯特罗伊~Astroloy

镍基磁性合金 ◇ 1040~*

镍基电阻合金 ◇ 卢谢诺~*

镍基合金 nickel base alloy ◇ 沉淀硬化~*,海恩斯 713C 真空熔炼~ Haynes alloy 713 C,科罗内尔~*,罗泽茵~*,蒙乃尔~*

镍基合金焊条 nickel-base alloy covered electrode

镍基耐热合金 ◇ P.E.10~P.E.10 alloy,P.E.K.~P.E.K. alloy,里弗拉克托洛依~*,梅尔尼~*,派罗梅特~Pyromet,派罗斯~*,尤迪梅特~*,尤尼滕普 1753~*

镍基耐蚀合金 abros

镍基耐蚀耐热合金 ◇ 哈斯特洛伊~*

镍结碳化钛硬质合金 （同"镍钛硬质合金"）

镍结碳化钽硬质合金 （同"镍钽硬质合金"）

镍结碳化钨硬质合金 （同"镍钨硬质合金"）

镍-金属陶瓷镀层 nickel cermet coating

镍浸镀 nickel dipping

镍精矿 nickel concentrate

镍精炼 nickel refining ◇ 蒙德羰基~法*

镍矿 nickel ore

镍矿床 【地】nickel deposit

镍矿物 nickel mineral

镍铑合金 nickel rhodium

镍粒 nickel pellet [shot], grain [shot, granulated] nickel

镍硫铁矿 |(Fe,Ni)₂S₃| harbachite

镍锍 【色】nickel [mis] matte ◇ 低~coarse metal,低铜~阳极*,高品位~*

镍锍沉积物 nickel bottom

镍锍吹炼 nickel matte converting

镍锍精炼 nickel matte refining, matte refining of nickel

镍铝覆面铁箔 PN iron

镍铝钴系析出型磁铁 ◇ 奥尔斯特~*

镍铝锰合金 alumel

镍铝-镍铬合金 alumel-chromel

镍铝-镍铬热电偶 alumel-chromel thermocouple

镍铝青铜 (4.5—5.5Ni, 9.0—10.3Al, 0.5—1.0Mn, 5.5Fe, 0.01Pb 余量 Cu) nickel-aluminium bronze ◇ 库尼阿尔~*

镍铝铁永磁合金 ◇ 尼~*

镍铝铜合金 ◇ 库尼亚尔~*

镍铝铸造磁铁 ◇ 阿尔尼~ Alni magnet

镍铝锌铜合金 Aluneon

镍绿泥石 |3(Ni, Mg)·2SiO₂·2H₂O| nepolite

镍锰电阻合金 ◇ 马格诺~(5Mn, 余量 Ni) Magno

镍锰钢 konik(e)

镍锰钴土 nickel asbolan(e)

镍锰铬钢 N.M.C. (nickel-manganese-chromium) steel

镍锰合金 nickel-manganese alloy ◇ D~(含 4—5Mn) D-nickel,曼戈尼克~*

镍锰铜铬合金钢 ◇ 科尼克~*

镍锰铜耐蚀合金 ◇ 科罗尼尔~*

镍钼钢 nickel-molybdenum steel

镍钼热电偶 nickel-molybdenum thermocouple

镍钼铁 nickel-molybdenum iron ◇ 科罗内尔~耐酸合金*

镍钼铁合金 dynamax

镍盘 nickel tray

镍喷镀 nickel flashing

镍硼共晶(体) nickel-boron eutectic

镍片 flake nickel

镍屏 nickel screen

镍氢电池　nickel-hydrogen battery
镍青铜（5—8Ni,5—8Sn,1—2Zn,少量P,余量Cu）　nickel bronze ◇ NM高强度~NM bronze,船用~*,戴维斯~*,尼维~Ni-Vee bronze,涅奥根~*,纽~*
镍熔炼　nickel smelting
镍烧舟　nickel boat
镍试剂　nickel reagent
镍水蛇纹石（水硅镁镍矿）[2NiO·2MgO·3SiO$_2$·6H$_2$O]　genthite
镍酸盐　nickelate
镍钛钢　nickel-titanium steel
镍钛铝合金　durinvar
镍钛硬质合金[金属陶瓷]　nickel-cemented titanium carbide
镍钽硬质合金　nickel-cemented tantalum carbide
镍碳热电偶　nickel-carbon couple
镍锑铅轴承青铜（8Ni,1Sb,10Pb,1Zn,余量Cu）　nickel-antimony-lead bronze
镍提炼　nickel recovery
镍提取　nickel extraction
镍添加合金　nickel addition
镍铁　nickel iron, nickelferrite ◇ 高磷~*,含钴~*,尼科~nicofer
镍铁磁合金　Rhometal
镍铁电池　nickel iron cell
镍铁锭　ferronickel ingot
镍铁钴钒合金　◇ 维林瓦尔~Velinvar
镍铁钴高导磁率合金　permivar
镍铁合金　ferronickel (alloy) ◇ 超高导磁率~*,高导磁率~*,尼洛马格~Nilomag alloy,特级无线电用~*,天然~（见于陨石中）kamacite
镍铁矿　josephinite
镍铁硫[冰铜]　【色】nickel iron matte
镍铁钼超导磁合金　supermalloy
镍铁钼导磁合金（78.5Ni,17.7Fe,3.8Mo）　molybdenum-permalloy, Mo-permalloy
镍铁熔炼　ferronickel smelting
镍铁软磁性合金　nickel iron alloy
镍铁弹簧合金　vibralloy

镍铁铜系高导磁率合金　◇ 缪~*
镍铁芯镀铜线　◇ 艾尔德里德~*
镍铁蓄电池　Nife accumulator
镍铁蓄电池组　nickel iron storage battery
镍铜比　nickel-copper ratio
镍铜钢　◇ 尼科~*
镍铜铬耐蚀铸铁　ni-resist
镍铜合金　nickel-copper (alloy), konstantan ◇ J.A.E.~*,维维安~*
镍铜时效钢　Ni-Cu age steel
镍铜铁热磁补偿合金（69Ni,29Cu,2Fe）　calmalloy, calorie magnetic alloy
镍铜铁氧体　nickel-copper ferrite
镍铜线　contra [Enreka] wire
镍铜锌电阻合金　◇ 马丁诺~Martino alloy
镍铜锌合金　platinoide, nickel brass
镍铜锌耐蚀合金　◇ 加里莫尔~*
镍丸　nickel shot [rondelle]
镍丸分解器　nickel pellet decomposer
镍纹石　nickel iron
镍钨硬质合金[金属陶瓷]　nickel-cemented tungsten carbide
镍锡合金　nickel-tin alloy ◇ 尼克尔廷~*
镍锌铁氧体　nickel zinc ferrite
镍盐　nickel salt
镍阳极　nickel anode ◇ 粗~impure nickel anode,含硫~*
镍冶金　metallurgy of nickel
镍阴极　nickel cathode
镍银　（见"铜镍锌合金"、"铜锌镍合金"）◇ 安伯罗依德~合金*,贝内迪克特~*,加铅~leaded nickel silver,卡邦德尔~*,斯利德克斯~合金 Slidex alloy,图坦纳格~*,西尔弗莱特~合金 Silverite,中国~*
镍银铋合金　proplatinum
镍银系耐蚀铸造合金　◇ 艾费奈德~Afenide
镍印　【金】nickel prints
镍优先还原　nickel preferential reduction

镍质连枷状搅拌器 nickel flail stirrer
镍珠 nickel shot
镍铸铁 nihard, Ni-tensilorin, nickel cast iron
涅奥根镍青铜（58Cu, 27Zn, 12Ni, 2Sn, 0.5Al, 0.5Bi） Neogen
涅奥马格纳尔铝镁锌耐蚀合金（5Mg, 5Zn, 余量 Al） Neomagnal
涅奥纳留姆铝合金（6—14Cu, 0.4—1Fe 及 Si 等, 余量 Al） Neonalium
柠檬酸铵 [(NH$_4$)$_3$C$_6$H$_5$O$_7$] ammonium citrate
柠檬酸锆 zirconium citrate
柠檬酸铪 hafnium citrate
柠檬酸铁 [FeC$_6$H$_5$O$_7$] ferric citrate
柠檬酸盐 citrate (salt)
凝点定碳 （同"液线定碳"）
凝点记录仪 eutectometer
凝锭装置 【连铸】 ingot-forming equipment
凝堵（水口的） 【钢】 make up
凝固 solidification, congealing, consolidation, (hard) setting, freezing ◇ 表皮～ skin solidification, 定向［受控］～*, 有向～ directional freezing
凝固表皮 【铸】 solidified skin
凝固层 frozen layer
凝固成型 solidification moulding
凝固处理 solidification processing
凝固常数 solidification constant
凝固传热 solidification heat transfer
凝固点 freezing point (f.p.), set(ting) point (set.pt.), solidifying [solidification, condensation, congealing] point
凝固点测定法 kryoscopy
凝固点曲线 freezing point curve
凝固电解质 frozen electrolyte
凝固锭料 frozen ingot
凝固反应 solidification [coagulation] reaction, coaguloreaction
凝固范围 freezing range, solidification region

凝固固体 freezing solid
凝固机理 freezing [solidification] mechanism
凝固剂 coagulator, coagulant
凝固加工 solidification processing
凝固界面 freezing interface, solidification contour [front]
凝固金属 frozen metal
凝固金属成核［核化］ 【金】nucleation of solidifying metal
凝固晶体 frozen crystal
凝固壳 solidified shell [skin]
凝固壳厚度 solidifying shell thickness ◇ 三维～分布*
凝固裂纹［开裂］ solidification cracking
凝固模型 solidification model
凝固锍［色］ solidified matte
凝固前沿 solidification [solidifying] front
凝固潜热 solidification latent heat, latent heat of freezing
凝固曲线 solidification curve
凝固热 solidification heat
凝固时间 set(ting) time
凝固试验 setting test
凝固收缩 （同"凝缩"）
凝固收缩凹槽 shrinkage groove
凝固收缩裂纹 solidification shrinkage crack
凝固收缩率 fluid contraction
凝固收缩作用 solidification shrinkage effect
凝固速率 freezing [solidification] rate
凝固温度 solidification [freezing, setting] temperature, point of solidification
凝固（温度）范围［区域］ solidification range [region]
凝固系数 coefficient of solidification
凝固现象 solidification phenomena
凝固线 freeze line, line of solidification
凝固相 solidification phase
凝固渣 solidified [frozen] slag
凝固周期 freezing cycle

凝固组织	solidification structure
凝固[凝结]状态	solidified state
凝灰岩	tufa, tuff
凝灰岩混凝土	tufa cement
凝灰岩水泥混凝土	tuffcrete
凝集	agglutinate, agglutination ◇ 渣[残钢]的～ build up of skull, 强制～沉淀装置
凝集剂	agglutinant
凝胶化(作用)	gela(tina)tion, gelatinization, vitrinization
凝胶(体)	gel, gelatin(e)
凝胶状硅酸	gelatinous silicic acid
凝胶作用	gelling action, gelation
凝结	condensing, coagulation, congealing, concretion, consolidating, freeze, solidification, jellification ◇ 刚～的固体 just-freezing solid
凝结出	freezing out
凝结处理	coagulation treatment
凝结点	set(ting) point (set. pt.), congealing point
凝结法	hardening method
凝结机	hardening machine
凝结剂	agglomerating [coagulating] agent, coagulant
凝结剂沉淀池	coagulant sedimentation basin
凝结块	coagulum
凝结力	coagulability, coagulating power ◇ 混凝土－钢筋～
凝结器	condensator, coagulator
凝结水	condensation water, condensate
凝结温度	condensation [setting] temperature
凝结物	coagulum, concrete, concretion
凝结物质	condensed material
凝结性	condensability, coagulability
凝结指数	agglomerating index
凝聚	condensation, cohesion, coagulation, flocculation ◇ 毛细～
凝聚槽	coagulation tank
凝聚沉淀法	coagulating sedimentation
凝聚核	【理】condensation nucleus
凝聚剂	flocculant (floc.), flocculating [flocculation, coagulating] agent, coagulant, agglomerant
凝聚介质	condensed medium
凝聚力	cohesive force [strength], cohesion
凝聚滤网	【化】agglomerate screen
凝聚能	flocculation energy
凝聚气体	condensed gas
凝聚态物理(学)	condensed state physics
凝聚系统	(同"冷凝系统")
凝聚相	condensed phase
凝聚状态	condensed state
凝壳	skull, scull, bridging,【冶】kish, frost (炉内或桶内的)
凝壳(保护)电子束熔炼炉	skull electron beam melting furnace
凝壳炉膛	【冶】skull lined crucible
凝壳内浇铸	skull casting
凝壳熔炼	skull melting ◇ 电弧～ arc skull melting
凝壳式电弧炉	skull type arc melting furnace
凝壳式电子束炉	electron-beam skull furnace
凝壳(式)炉	skull furnace [crucible]
凝壳铸造	slush casting
凝块	coagulum, clot
凝裂	cold cracking
凝气瓣	gas trap
凝汽罐	moisture trap, steam separator
凝入	freezing in
凝缩	solidification [freezing] shrinkage ◇ 膜状～ film condensation
凝铁线(高炉缸内)	iron freeze line
凝渣	【冶】crust blocks
宁静石	tranquillityite
拧	twist
拧绞(线材或轧件的)	coil buckling, kink
拧接机	screw-on machine

拧接头　coupling screw-up
拧紧　tighten, stall, buck-up
拧松　back out, screw-off, unscrew
拧装机(管接头的)　coupling machine
牛顿铋铅锡易熔合金(28.8Pb, 16.1Sn, 56.1Bi; 熔点95℃)　Newton's metal
牛顿流　【理】Newtonian flow
牛顿流体　Newtonian fluid
牛顿铈铅锡易熔合金(18.8Sn, 50Bi, 31.2Pb; 熔点97.96℃)　Newton's alloy
牛顿(性)液体　simple liquid ◇ 非~ non-Newtonian liquid
牛头刨床　shaping machine, shaper ◇ 立式~ vertical shaper
牛腿　bracket,【建】corbel, angle-table,【金】bull's eye
牛眼形拱　bull's eye arch
牛脂　tallow
扭杆　torsion [twist] bar
扭簧　torsion spring
扭簧式应变仪　CEJ strain gauge, mikrokator
扭绞　twisting, intorsion,【压】(线材或轧件的) coil buckling, kink
扭结变形带　kink band
扭结带生长　【理】growth of kink bands
扭矩电动机　torque motor
扭矩计[测定器]　torsionmeter
扭矩平衡[扭力天平]　torsion balance
扭矩限度　torque limitation
扭力　torsion, torsional [torque, twisting] force
扭力臂　toggle
扭力功率计　torsional dynamometer
扭力计　torsionmeter, torsiograph, torsion balance, torque pickup
扭(力)矩　torsion, torque, torque [torsional, twisting] moment
扭力偶　torsional [twisting] couple
扭力振动　torsional vibration
扭曲　twist (ing), angulation, buckling, cobble, contortion, distortion, kinking, curling (轧材缺陷),【金】skellering (淬火时的)
扭曲带钢　twisted strip
扭曲度(制品的)　degree of distorsion
扭曲面　twist [kink] plane,【压】warped [skew] surface
扭曲塑[延]性　torsion ductility
扭曲型间界　twist boundary
扭曲因数　tortuosity factor
扭曲应力-应变图　torsional stress-strain diagram
扭应变　torsional strain
扭应力　torsional stress
扭应力强度　intensity of torsional stress
扭折　kinking ◇ 六方(晶系)金属~
扭折带　kink band
扭折带密度　kink band density
扭折晶体　kinked crystal
扭折面　kink plane, plane of kinking
扭振　torsional vibration
扭转　torsion, twist(ing) (轧件的)
扭(转)摆　torsion pendulum
扭转变形　torsional deformation [deflection],【压】twisting strain
扭转持久极限　torsional endurance limit
扭转冲击试验　torsion impact test
扭转出口导板(轧件的)　delivery twist guide
扭转导板　twist guide [box, trough], twister ◇ 辊式~
扭转断口试验　split torsion test
扭转断裂　torsional fracture [failure]
扭转断裂模量[系数]　modulus of rupture in torsion
扭转法　torsion technique
扭转方式[模式]　torsional mode
扭转负载　torsional load
扭转钢筋　twisted steel
扭转辊　barrel twister
扭转键　twist key
扭转件　twisted object
扭转矫正机　【压】torsion stretcher

扭转角　torsion angle, angle of twist
扭转开关　twist switch
扭转抗力　torsional [twisting] resistance
扭转孔型　twisting pass
扭转力矩　(同"扭力矩")
扭转流变硬化行为　torsional flow hardening behaviour
扭转面　twist plane
扭转模量[模数]　torsion modulus
扭转挠性　torsional flexibility
扭转疲劳　torsional fatigue
扭转疲劳断裂　torsional fatigue fracture
扭转疲劳极限　torsional fatigue limit
扭转疲劳强度　torsional fatigue strength
扭转疲劳[耐久性]试验　endurance torsion test
扭转疲劳载荷　torsional fatigue loading
扭转频率　torsional frequency
扭转蠕变　torsional creep
扭转式测力计　torquemeter
扭转试验　torsion [twisting] test
扭转试验方法　torsion test method
扭转试验机　torsion testing machine ◇舍佛纳尔德微~*
扭转试样　torsion test piece
扭转寿命　torsion failure life (TFL)
扭转弹性　torsional elasticity
扭转弹性极限　torsional elastic limit
扭转性能[特性]　torsion(al) property
扭转因素　tortuosity factor
扭转应变　【压】twisting strain
扭(转)应力　torsional [twisting, distorting] stress
扭转轧机　twist-block mill
扭转振荡　【理】torsional oscillation
扭转振动　torsional [twisting] vibration
扭转指示器　torsion indicator
钮扣　button ◇玻璃料[粉末]~试样熔度试验【粉】button test
钮扣式电容器　button condenser
钮扣试样熔度试验　【粉】button test
钮扣形电子束熔炼　【冶】button melter

纽-流态化床海绵铁制取法　Nu-iron process
纽拉尔铝合金(含 Mg、Fe、Mn、Si 等的铝合金)　Nural
纽伦堡假金(金色饰品；2.5Au, 7.5Al, 90Cu)　Nurembourg gold
纽洛伊铜镍耐蚀合金(35Ni, 1Sn, 余量 Cu)　Newloy
纽曼(变形,孪晶)带[纽曼(变形)线,纽曼变形双晶]　【金】Neumann band [lamellae, lines]
纽纳姆矿石炼铅炉　Newnam ore hearth
纽-镍青铜(95.8Cu, 3.25Ni, 0.25Mn, 0.73Si)　Nu-bronze
纽-装饰黄铜(13Zn, 97Cu)　Nu-gild
浓氨水　rich ammonia water, strong ammoniacal liquor
浓差电池　concentration cell
浓差电池腐蚀　concentration cell corrosion
浓差电势[位]　concentration potential
浓差极化　concentration polarization
浓差扩散　concentration diffusion
浓差压力　osmotic pressure
浓尘区　【环】high dust area
浓度　concentration (concn.), density, consistence, consistency, strength, enrichment, depth(着色的)
浓度边界层　concentration boundary layer
浓度比　ratio of concentration
浓度波动　concentration fluctuation, fluctuation in concentration
浓度不均固溶体　coring solid solution
浓(度)差　concentration difference, differential concentration, difference in concentration
浓度范围　concentration range
浓度关系　concentration relationship [dependence]
浓度计　concentration meter, densimeter
浓度均匀区(区域熔炼的)　level region
浓度控制　concentration [density] control
浓度控制阀　density control valve

浓度起伏[脉动]　concentration fluctuation, fluctuation in concentration
浓度曲线　concentration curve
浓度扰动(区域熔炼的)　concentration perturbation
浓度三角形　concentration triangle
浓度-深度曲线(合金的)　concentration-depth curve
浓度梯度　concentration [density] gradient
浓度调节器　density controller
浓度系数　concentration factor
浓度指数　concentration index
浓汞齐　thickened amalgam
浓红银矿{Ag_3SbS_3}　pyrargyrite
浓混合物　rich mixture
浓集　concentration
浓浆　thick pulp, underflow product
浓浆泵　underflow pump
浓浸出液　strong leaching liquid
浓料[矿]浆　thick slurry [pulp]
浓硫酸　concentrated [strong] sulphuric acid, brown [concentrated] oil of vitriol (C.O.V.), oil of vitriol (O.V.)
浓硫酸焙烧　sulphuric acid baking
浓硫酸分解炉　sulphator ◇ 连续回转～*
浓煤气冷凝氨水　strong gas liquor
浓密　dense, thick
浓泥　thickened slurry,【焊】lime paste
浓溶剂槽　tight flux bath
浓溶液　concentrated [strong] solution
浓酸　concentrated acid
浓酸分解　concentrated acid breakdown, opening by concentrated acid
浓缩　concentrating, concentration, thickening, graduation, enrich(ment), inspissate, inspissation ◇ 酸性～ acid thickening, 蒸发～ graduate
浓缩氨水　concentrated ammoniacal liquor
浓缩比　【化】concentration ratio
浓缩槽　thickening tank

浓缩产物　thickened product
浓缩池　thickener (tank) ◇ 灰泥～ slurry clarifier
浓缩等离子源　concentrated plasma source
浓缩底流　thickened underflow
浓缩法　concentration process [method]
浓缩分级机　thickener-sizer
浓缩锅　concentrating pan
浓缩[密]机　thickener ◇ 多尔型～ Dorr thickener, 过滤～ filter thickener, 特大型～ superthickener, 洗涤～ washing thickener, 悬轴式～*, 置换～ displacement thickener, 中心传动式～*, 周边传动式～*
浓缩剂　concentrating [inspissating] agent, thickener
浓缩矿浆　thickened pulp
浓缩矿泥　【选】concentrated sludge, thickened slurry
浓缩器　concentrator ◇ 污泥～ sludge concentrator
浓缩溶液　concentrated solution
浓缩物(质)　【理】enriched material
浓缩系数[因数]　enrichment factor
浓缩铀　enriched uranium
浓缩柱　evaporating column
浓缩锥　thickening cone
浓相　dense [concentrated] phase
浓相流化床　dense-phase fluidized bed
浓相流态化　dense-phase fluidization
浓相输送　dense-phase transport [transfer] ◇ 重叠罐式多支管～煤工艺*, 多管路～技术*, 煤粉～技术*
浓相输送系统　dense-phase transport system
浓硝酸　red fuming nitric acid (R.F.N.A.), aquafortis
农格兰含锌锡青铜(87Cu, 11Sn, 2Zn)　Non-gran
农格罗低膨胀系数镍铁合金(36Ni,余量 Fe)　Nongro
农科拉利厄姆铝基耐蚀合金(16Sb, 0.7—

2.5Zn,1.5—3.5Mg,余量 Al) Noncoralium
农业机械　agricultrual machinery
农业生物气候学　【环】agricultrual bioclimatology
农业用地　【环】agricultrual land
农业用水　agricultrual water
农用复合钢材　agricultrual ply steel
努普(金刚石)显微硬度试验　Knoop hardness test
努普显微压痕硬度试验仪　Knoop
努普(硬度)标度　Knoop (hardness) scale
努普硬度值[努氏(显微)硬度]　Knoop hardness (number)
努奇框式真空过滤机　Nutsch filter
努塞尔数　Nusselt number
努森方程　【理】Knudsen equation
努森辐射真空计　Knudsen's (radiometer) gauge
努森流动　【理】Knudsen flow
努森真空计　Knudsen vacuum gauge
女儿墙(防浪矮墙)　parapet
钕合金　neodymium alloy
钕基合金　neodymium-base alloy
钕铌易解石　niobo-aeschynite-(Nd)
钕镨　didymium
钕镨混合物　didymium
钕添加合金　neodymium addition
钕铁硼合金　neodymium iron boron alloy
钕铁硼硬磁合金　neodymium-iron-boron hard magnetic alloy
钕易解石　aeschynite-(Nd)
暖气　central heating
暖气管　heating pipe
暖气片　radiator
诺德海姆定律　【理】Nordheim's rule
诺尔斯克－斯塔尔竖炉直接制取海绵铁法　Norsk-staal process
诺卡氏菌属　Nocardia
诺拉尔铝锡轴承合金[可热处理铝合金]　Noral
诺兰达法　Noranda process
诺兰达反应炉[器]　Noranda process reactor
诺兰达转炉　Noranda converter
诺兰塔型一步炼铜法　Norantas' continuous copper smelting process
诺曼一氧化碳转化　Naumann reversion
诺模图　nomogram, nomograph, nomographic chart, abac, abas
诺模图算法[列线图解法]　nomography
诺三水铝石　nordstrandite
诺瓦赖特铝基活塞合金(85Al,12.5Cu,1.4Mn,0.8Fe,0.3Mg)　Novalite
诺沃康斯坦特铜基电阻合金(82.5Cu,12Mn,4Al,1.5Fe)　Novokonstant
诺伊尔高锡青铜(20Sn,余量 Cu)　Noil
诺伊特铅基耐磨轴承合金(0.11Sb,1.3Na,0.08S,余量 Pb)　Noheet

O o

欧共体政府补贴法规　European Community State Aid Code (EISA)
欧拉柱公式　Euler column formula
欧玛尔铜锰镍电阻合金(87.5Cu,3.5Ni,9Mn)　ohmal
欧姆表　ohmmeter,ohm gauge
欧姆电压降　ohmic drop
欧姆电阻　ohmic resistance
欧姆定律　ohm's law
欧姆接触[接点]　ohmic contact
欧氏体　【金】osmondite
欧洲独立(经营)钢铁生产商协会　European Independent Steelmakers Association
欧洲钢材经销商协会　European Steel Stockholders Federation
欧洲钢管生产商协会　European Steel Tubemakers Association (ESTA)
欧洲钢铁工业联盟　European Confederation of Iron and Steel Industries (Eurofer)
欧洲货币单位　European currency unit (ecu)
欧洲拜耳(炼铝)法　European Bayer process
欧洲经济共同体　European Economic Community (EEC.)
欧洲可锻铸铁　(同"白心可锻铸铁")
欧洲煤钢联营(组织)　European Coal and Steel Community (ECSC)
欧洲美元　Eurodollar
偶　pair,couple,even
偶A同位素　even-A isotope
偶N同位素　even-N isotope
偶存夹杂　accident inclusion
偶存元素　【冶】incidental [tramp] element
偶存杂质　unintentional impurity
偶氮　【化】azo
偶发故障　random failure
偶合　couple
偶合反应　coupled [coupling] reaction
偶合剂　coupler,coupling agent
偶合氧化　coupled oxidation
偶极　dipole
偶极层　dipole layer
偶极点阵[晶格]　dipole lattice
偶极电极　bipolar electrode
偶极分子　dipole molecule
偶极矩　dipole moment
偶极-偶极相互作用　【理】dipole-dipole interaction
偶极天线　dipole,doublet (antenna)
偶极位错　【理】dipole dislocation
偶极形成　dipole formation
偶极子　dipole,doublet ◇ 位错～dislocation dipole,寻向～director,有排列缺陷的～faulted dipoles
偶极(子)极化　dipole polarization
偶极子能级　double (energy) level
偶级[序]反射　even-order reflections
偶联反应　coupling reaction
偶然磁极　(同"随机磁极")
偶然的　occasional,accidental,incidental,random
偶然曝光　accidental exposure
偶然误差　accidental error
偶然性　contingency,fortuity,chance,occasionality
偶数　even number
偶数层绕组　◇ 查佩隆～Chaperon winding
偶数奇偶校验　【计】even parity (check)
偶数同位校验　even parity (check)
偶数(轧制)道次　【压】even-numbered pass,backward pass (可逆式机座中的)
偶项　even term
偶有物料　tramp material
偶质量数　【理】even mass
耦合　coupling,bonding,binding ◇ 疏松～weak bond
耦合变压器　coupling transformer
耦合参数　coupling parameter

耦合间隙 coupling clearance
耦合金属 【电】coupled metals
耦合器 coupler
耦合系数 coupling coefficient
耦合线圈 coupling [pick-up] coil
耦合因数 coupling factor
耦合阻抗 【电】coupling [coupled] impedance

P p

爬高　climb
爬速　crawl speed
爬铁　climbing iron
爬芯　【铸】drop [wing] core
爬行速度　crawl speed, inching speed（轧机的）
耙臂　spider, rabble arm（多膛焙烧炉的）
耙柄[杆]　rabble arm
耙齿（多膛焙烧炉的）　rabble blade
耙动机构　raking mechanism
耙集　raking
耙架（浓缩机的）　arm brace
耙焦机　【焦】coke-drawing machine
耙矿装置（浓缩机的）　【选】revolving arms
耙料机[器]　harrow ◇ 移动～ travel(l)ing plough
耙式分级机　rake classifier
耙式混合器　rake mixer
耙提升装置　rake lifting device
耙渣口[门]　【冶】skim(mer) gate
耙子　rake, rabble
帕蒂尼乌姆铝合金　Partinium
帕尔耐蚀镍铬合金（A：80Ni, 15Cr, 5Cu; B：66Ni, 18Cr, 8.5Cu, 1Mn, 3.5W, 2Al, 0.2 Ti, 0.2B）Parr metal
帕芬德系（光谱线的）　【理】Pfund series
帕克顿（锌）白铜　Paktong, Packtong
帕克方锌白铜　Pakfong, Packfong
帕克加锌除银法（铅精炼）　【色】Parke's method of desilverization
帕克铝基压铸合金（4Cu, 4Ni, 1.5Si, 余量 Al）Pack alloy
帕克镍铬黄铜（60Cu, 20Zn, 10Ni, 10Cr）Parker's (chrome) alloy
帕克特龙铁碳磷母合金　Pacteron
帕拉弗雷克斯钢丝绳　Paraflex wire rope
帕拉冈不变形工具钢（1.6Mn, 0.75Cr, 0.25V）Paragon steel
帕拉鲁曼铝镁合金（变形合金：0.5—1.5Mg, 0.5—1Mn, 余量 Al；铸造合金：2—4Mg, 0.3Mn, 余量 Al）Paraluman
帕里斯疲劳裂纹[缝]形成律　Paris fatigue crack growth law
帕里斯铜镍耐蚀合金（5—15Ni, 5Fe, 5Zn, 1Co, 余量 Cu）Paris metal
帕里西昂铜镍锌合金（69Cu, 19.5Ni, 6.5Zn, 5Cd）Parisian alloy
帕利乌姆铅基重载轴承合金（4.5Cu, 4Pb, 2.6Sn, 0.6Mg, 0.3Mn, 0.3Zn, 余量 Al）Pallium
帕立德铅基轴承合金（82—90Pb, 5—11Sb, 4—7As）Palid
帕马特低膨胀系数镍铁合金（36Ni, 余量 Fe）Permant
帕米特铜镍钴永磁合金（45Cu, 25Ni, 30Co）Permet
帕明杜尔铁钴系高磁导率合金（50Co, 1.8—2.1V, 余量 Fe;）Permendure
帕明伏超导磁性合金（9Ni, 22.8Co, 68.2Fe）super Perminvow
帕明诺姆高导磁率铁镍合金（50Fe, 50Ni;）Permenorm
帕明瓦恒导磁率合金（45Ni, 25Co, 30Fe）Perminvar ◇ 超级～·
帕丘卡串联空气搅拌浸出槽　Pachuca tank cascade
帕丘卡[帕氏]空气搅拌浸出槽　【色】Pachuca (agitator, tank), leaching Pachuca
帕丘卡中性浸出空气搅拌槽　【色】neutral Pachuca
帕森-邓肯法（铸锭）　【钢】Parson's Duncan process
帕森高强度耐蚀锰青铜（可锻：57—60Cu, 0.2—1Mn, 0.6—1.2Fe, 1—1.5Sn, 0—1Al, 余量 Zn；铸造：56—58Cu, 0.2—0.4Mn, 0.8—1.1Fe, 0.7—1.1Sn, 0.2-0.4Al, 余量 Zn）Parson's bronze [alloy]
帕森-莫塔锡锑铜轴承合金（4.5—9Sb,

3—5Cu,余量 Sn) Parson's Mota metal
帕森锡基白金属轴承合金 Parson's whitemetal star alloy
帕森锡基轴承合金(74—76Sn,3—4.5Cu, 14—15Pb,7—8Sb) Parson's brass
帕斯派克斯聚甲丙烯酸树脂[介电有机玻璃] Perspex
帕特克斯油浸探伤法 Partex pentrant process
帕廷森粗铅结晶除银法 Pattinson process
帕廷森铅白 Pattinson's white lead
拍动(拍平) flapping
拍频 beat frequency
拍摄 shoot ◇ 慢转速～time lapse technique
排尘 dust emission [exhaust]
排尘量 dust emission
排尘器 dust exhauster
排尘设备 dust-exhausting equipment
排成线的气孔 line of pores
排斥 repulsion, expulsion, exclusion
排斥场 repulsion [repulsive] field
排斥结 【金】repulsive junction
排斥力 repulsion [repulsive] force
排斥能 repulsive energy
排斥区场 repulsive field
排出 discharge, exhaust, squeeze, bleed off, eject(ing), ejection, discard(ing), effluxion, effusion, evacuation, outflow, pumping-out
排出泵 discharge pump
排出阀 discharge [drainage] valve
排出管 outlet [eduction, tap(ping)] pipe, blow off [out] pipe, downflow spout, bleed(er) line
排出管道[路] discharge (pipe)line
排出金属残渣 hot drainage
排出空气 outgoing air
排出孔 tap, tap(ping) hole
排出口 portal, outcome, outlet, escape hole, (blow off) nozzle

排出矿石 ore blowout
排出炉尘记录仪 【铁】dust recorder
排出门 outgate
排出喷嘴 discharge nozzle
排出歧管 exhaust (outlet) manifold
排出气体 effluent air, exhaust [effluent, evolved, exit, outgoing, vent] gas, release of gas,【冶】off-gas
排出水 drainage [outlet] water, outfall, bleed off water,【环】decanted water, water effluent ◇ 无沉淀物～*
排出速度 exhaust velocity, velocity of discharge,【环】bleed-off rate
排出速率 delivery rate,【冶】outflow rate
排出物 discharge, blowoff, effluent, ejections
排出物限度准则 【环】effluent limitation guidelines
排出压力 discharge [driving] pressure
排出蒸汽总管 exhaust steam main
排出支管 outlet [exhaust] manifold
排出总管 offtake main
排除 removing, removal, reject, draw off, exclusion
排除故障程序 【计】debugging routine
排除滤渣 cake removing [blow]
排除器 eliminator, excluder
排除湿气 moisture removal
排除时间 clean-up time
排除水分 moisture removal
排代(次)序 displacement series
排代反应 displacement reaction, reaction of substitution
排代式乙炔发生器 recession gas generator
排队论 【数】queuing theory, waiting line theory
排队论模型 queuing theory model
排放 discharge, blowoff, blow down, emission, tap
排放池 【环】disposal lake
排放点 【环】point of origin, discharger

排 pai

(废水的)
排放废水 【环】effluent water, waste discharge
排放管 eductor
排放口 taphole ◇ 海中~ submarine outfall
排放浓度 discharge concentration
排放速度 exhaust velocity, velocity of discharge, 【环】bleed-off rate
排放污水流 bleed-off stream
排放物 emission(s)
排放斜坡 drainage slope
排放许可证 【环】discharge permit
排放旋塞[龙头] discharging cock
排放烟囱 bleed off stack
排放装置 eductor, bleeder
排放准则 【环】discharge guidelines
排风机 exhaust(ing) [vent] fan, exhaust blower
排风扇 fan air ejector
排浮渣 scum-off
排管 calandria, block (电缆的)
排辊成型 【压】cage forming
排灰阀 【铁】dust discharging valve (除尘器的) ◇ 闸式~*
排灰渣孔 poke hole
排架 (framed) bent
排架桩桥 trestle bridge
排锯 gang [frame] saw, gang-sawing machine
排矿 ore discharge, discharge material ◇ 烧结机[带式机]~ strand discharge
排矿槽 【团】discharge hopper
排矿口 discharge opening [outlet], throat, ◇ 矿槽~ bin outlet
排矿流槽 discharge launder
排量 displacement, delivery, output volume
排料 discharge (material), blow down
排料仓 discharge bin
排料槽 discharge duct
排料次数 frequency of discharging

排料[矿]点 discharge station [area]
排料[矿]斗 discharge hopper [funnel], discharge cone (圆锥)
排料[矿]端 discharge [delivery] end
排料端分选 【团】kiln discharge separation
排料端尾罩 discharge end housing
排料段 discharge zone
排料阀 dump valve
排料管 discharging [dump] tube
排料间隙(出口的) outlet gap
排料孔 discharge opening
排料口 discharge gate [hole, lip], hopper [bin] outlet, 【团】discharge mouth
排料[矿]量 discharge [withdrawal] rate
排料斜槽 discharge chute
排料闸门 【团】cut-off gate ◇ 可调~*
排料装置 discharge device [aid] ◇ 自动~*
排列 arrange(ment), rank, array, collocation, permutation ◇ 晶格原子~密度*, 佩尔托~图*
排列不当 misarrangement
排列成行 alignment
排列规律(性) regularity of arrangement
排硫杆菌 thiobacillus thioparus
排泥泵 slurry pump
排泥阀 sludge cock, mud valve
排泥管道 slime drain line
排气 (air) exhaust, air-out, deaerate, exhaust fume, gas out
排气安全阀 exhaust guard valve
排气板 exhaustion plate
排气瓣阀 exhaust clack
排气泵 extraction [off-gas, exhaust] pump
排气冲程 ejection [exhaust] stroke, outstroke
排气抽风机 exhaust gas suction fan
排气道 exhaust passage, gas off-take ◇ 旁通[分支]~ bypass vent
排气端 exhaust [flue] end
排气阀 (air) exhaust valve, vent(ilation)

[air-outlet] valve, exhaust flap, air releaser
排气风机[风扇] exhaust air fan, discharge fan, air ejector fan
排气管 air-outlet pipe, blow off [out] pipe, evacuation tube, exhaust stack, gas outlet tube, offtake pipe
排气管道 exhaust air duct, exhaust (pipe) line, discharge duct
排气管线 blow off pipe line
排气机 (air, gas) exhauster, exhaustor, exhaust blower ◇ 罗茨~*, 叶轮式~*, 正压~*
排气及进气支管 exhaust and intake manifold
排气孔 air drain [vent], exhaust window, vent
排气口 exhaust port [orifice, window], gas port [off-take], air-outlet
排气门 air eliminator, exhaust valve
排气能力 exhaust capacity
排气喷嘴 exhaust [exit] nozzle, discharge burner
排气容量 delivery volume
排气设备 exhaust equipment, air exhausting device
排气式清理滚筒 exhaust tumbling mill
排气室 exhaust [discharge] chamber
排气栓 blow off cock
排气凸轮 exhaust cam
排气脱硫 exhaust gas desulfurization
排气尾管 tail [exhaust] pipe
排气污染物 【环】exhaust contaminant
排气系统 exhaust [gas-withdrawal] system
排气箱 exhaust chamber [box]
排气旋塞 air cock, air relief cock
排气烟囱 exhaust [vent] stack, blow off stack
排气烟道 offtake [gas-outlet] flue, 【冶】discharge [draught, exit] flue
排气烟罩 ventilation hood

排气罩 hood, canopy ◇ 带~的清理台 【铸】exhaust bench
排气支[歧]管 exhaust [outlet] manifold
排气装置 exhaust unit, air exhausting device
排气总管 exhaust mains
排气嘴 delivery nozzle
排弃 disposal
排弃场 【环】disposal site
排弃废碱液 exhausted lye
排弃废矿浆 exhausted pulp
排弃废溶液 exhausted solution
排弃废水 exhausted water
排弃废液 exhausted liquid
排汽系统 vapour-exhaust system
排汽装置 vapour exhaust
排热 heat withdrawal [extraction, rejection]
排砂(分级机的) spigot product
排射器 discharge jet
排刷 【铸】blacking brush
排水 drain off [away, discharge] water, dewatering (dewat.), discharging, drain (age), draining, effluent, unwater, water-discharge ◇ 底部~ underdrain, 地下~ subdrainage, 钻井~【环】well dewatering
排水泵 discharge [drain(age), draining, wet-pit] pump
排水槽 drain trough, drainage channel [chute], water (collecting) trough
排水储气罐 water displacement gasholder
排水处理 【环】effluent treatment
排水道 drainage channel
排水垫层 【环】drainage blanket
排水阀 draw off valve, 【机】drain valve
排水分离器 drain separator
排水干管[渠] arterial drainage
排水工程 drainage work, sewerage
排水沟 discharge [drain] ditch, drainage catchment chute, drainage channel, water channel(冲洗氧化皮的)◇ 地面~ area drain

排水管 drain(age) (pipe), water-discharge tube, offtake [water-drain] pipe ◇ 可渗透~ permeable drain pipe
排水管道[线] drainage [discharge] pipeline, (water) drainage line
排水管道清洗器 badger
排水接触式(乙炔)发生器 water displacement contact-type generator
排水井 drain(age) well, 【建】catch pit
排水坑 water-discharge well, drain
排水孔 drain [weep] hole
排水口 drain outlet, spout hole
排水漏斗 draining funnel [hopper]
排水路线 drainage route
排水盲沟 weeper drains
排水渠 drain, conduit
排水塞 drain plug
排水设施 drainage
排水式(乙炔)发生器 water recession generator
排水限值 effluent limitation
排水限值准则 effluent limitation guidelines
排水斜沟 valley
排水闸 outlet [drainage] sluice
排水质量限值 【环】effluent quality limitation
排水装置 drainage facility
排酸槽 acid drain tank
排污 drain contamination, pollution discharge, blow down
排污开关 sludge [scum] cock
排污溶液 【环】bleed solution
排污水系统 sewage system
排污系统 drainage ◇ 地下油库~*
排雾鼓风机 fume blower
排线架 creel stand
排泄 drain(ing), excretion, drop-out, escape
排泄泵 drain(age) [sewage, wet-pit] pump
排泄槽 drain tank, drainage catchment chute
排泄阀 bleed [outlet] valve
排泄干线系统 drainage trunk system
排泄沟道 exhausting duct
排泄管 discharge [drain(age), eduction, tap(ping)] pipe, runback
排泄开关 drain cock
排泄孔 drain hole
排泄口流量 outlet discharge
排泄水 drainage water
排烟 exhaust fume, fume extraction, smoke emission, eject smoke
排烟除尘器 exhaust dust collector ◇ 抽风干燥段~*
排烟道 discharge flue, 【钢】fume offtakes
排烟端 flue end
排烟管余热锅炉 hood waste heat boiler
排烟柜 fume cupboard
排烟机 exhaust fan, flue gas exhauster ◇ 双级~*, 透平式~ turboexhauster
排烟弥散 stack emission dispersion
排烟设备 fume exhaust [removal] equipment
排烟室 fume chamber
排烟损失 loss on stack
排烟系统 fume exhaust [extraction] system, exhaust system
排烟烟囱 draught stack
排烟余热 off-gas heat
排烟罩 fume extraction hood, exhaust hood, canopy ◇ 摆动式~*
排烟装置 fume exhaust facilities [unit] ◇ 涂层机~ coater fume exhaust
排液槽 displacement tank
排液孔 solution-drain hole
排溢铸造法 ◇ 阿德莫斯~ Admos die casting
排油 oil extraction, 【机】overspill(润滑) ◇ 油箱底~泵 bilge pump, 中心~孔 【机】centre drain
排渣 slag tipping, deslagging, 【冶】slag disposal, flush off, slag draining (从浇包)

◇ 炼钢水淬～工艺*
排渣不良 【冶】poor flush
排渣槽 scum gutter
排渣锤 slagging hammer
排渣地沟 trunk sewer
排渣机械 residue extraction mechanism
排渣口 slagging door
排渣炉 slag-tap furnace
排(小)沟 【铁】slag drain
排柱 fence
排阻色层[层析,色谱](法) exclusion-chromatography
牌坊 【压】(见"机架")
牌坊轨座 housing base
牌坊立柱(轧机的) housing post
牌坊立柱凹槽 housing post recess
牌坊上盖 housing top
牌坊下横梁 housing rocker plate
牌号 brand (br),label,trademark (商标)
迫击炮钢管 trench mortar steel tube
派奥尼尔耐蚀镍铬合金(35—38Ni,20—25Cr,35Fe,3Mo,0—4Si) Pioneer metal
派拉镍铬不锈钢(35Ni,20Cr,余量 Fe) Pyrasteel
派朗海绵铁 Pyron iron powder
派列克斯耐热玻璃管 Pyrex tubing
派列克斯耐热[硬质]玻璃瓶 Pyrex bulb
派列克斯耐热(硼)玻璃[派列克斯硬质玻璃] Pyrex (glass)
派卢明铬酸氧化处理法[派卢明浸镀铬酸盐法](用于铝合金) Pylumin
派伦海绵铁粉 Pyron iron powder
派伦制铁粉法(用氢还原铁鳞制铁粉) Pyron process
派罗卡斯特铁铬耐热合金(22—30Cr,余量 Fe) Pyrocast
派罗利克高电阻镍铬合金(80Ni,20Cr) Pyrolic
派罗马克斯电热合金(8—12Al,25—35Cr,<3Ti,余量 Fe) Pyromax
派罗梅特镍基耐热合金 Pyromet
派罗米克镍铬(铁)电热合金(1:80Ni,20Cr; 2:65Ni,15Cr,20Fe) Pyromic
派罗斯镍基耐热合金(82Ni,7Cr,5W,3Mn,3Fe) Pyros
派遣 dispatch(ing),despatch(ing)
攀移 climb(ing) ◇ 刚性位错越过障碍～*,位错～力*
攀移高度 climbing height
攀移速度 velocity of climbing
攀移速率 climbing rate
攀缘式起重机 climbing crane
潘塞利铝硅活塞合金(82—83Al,11.5Si,4.5Ni,0.4Mg,余量 Cu) Panseri alloy
潘塔尔铝合金(<5Si,<1.4Mn,<0.8Mg,余量 Al) Pantal
盘 tray, pan, panel, plate, dish, board, bunch (线材的),bundle (线材的),【化】block (蒸馏塔的) ◇ 一～(盘条) tier
盘板 board
盘焙烧炉 tray roaster furnace
盘边(圆盘造球机等的) peripheral wall
盘边高度 【团】disc edge height
盘边刮刀 【团】side scraper
盘查库存 【企】inventory-taking
盘秤 pan scale
盘底刮刀 【团】bottom scraper
盘段(配电盘的) 【电】block
盘阀碳黑 disc black
盘管 coil (pipe),coiler,coiling,pipe coil,worm pipe ◇ 激冷和风冷～式冷却系统*
盘黑 disc black
盘簧 coil(ing) [spiral] spring
盘簧机 coiling machine
盘架干燥炉 tray oven ◇ 煤气加热～ gas-fired tray oven
盘架干燥器 tray drier
盘角刮刀 【团】corner scraper
盘锯 rotary saw
盘滤机 disc filter
盘轮装压机 disc wheel press
盘磨 disc grind (DG)

盘磨机　disc grinder [crusher, mill], pan mill
盘碾机　pan (grinding) mill
盘绕电焊条　coiled electrode
盘绕线圈式灯丝　coiled-coil filament, double coil filament
盘式布料机　distributing disc
盘式穿孔机　【压】disc piercer ◇ 斯蒂费尔~*
盘式磁选机　disc-type magnetic separator
盘式阀　disc valve
盘式废气阀　disc type waste valve
盘式辊　disc-type roller
盘式过滤机　disk filter
盘式混合机　pan mixer
盘式给矿[料]机　tray [pan] feeder, delivery [distributing] plate, discharge disc, rotary disk
盘式开关(拨号型)　dial switch
盘式开卷机　disc-type decoiler
盘式可调给料机　【团】rariable speed table feeder,【选】baffle pan
盘式冷却机　tray [table] cooler
盘式炉　rotating table furnace,【色】pan [pot] furnace (熔炼低熔点合金用)
盘式碾磨机　pan grinding [mill], rim discharge mill
盘式气体洗涤器　tray-type gas scrubber
盘式取样器　fan plate sampler
盘式烧结法　pan sintering
盘式烧结机　batch type (sintering) machine, A.I.B. (Almaenns Ingenioers Biyaen) type sintering machine (多盘间歇式)
盘式送料机　table feeder,【焊】feed plate (乙炔发生器的)
盘式洗涤器　tray scrubber
盘式运输[输送]机　pan (type) conveyer
盘式运输给料机　pan-conveyer feeder
盘式造粒机　pan nodulizer
盘式造球混料机　disc-pelletizer mixer
盘式造球机　flying saucer,【铁】disc-type pelletizing machines
盘式轧碎机　disc crusher
盘式真空过滤机　vacuum pan filter
盘式振动给矿机　oscillating pan feeder
盘丝(成盘的成品钢丝)　parcel
盘弹簧机　coiling machine
盘条　【压】wire rod, coil (rod), rod coil [bundle, iron, stock], bull rod (供拉拔用的) ◇ 粗~*,风冷~ air-blown rod,热轧~*, 水冷~*, 有辊裂印痕的~ fire cracked rod,紫铜~*
盘条仓库　rod storage dock
盘条打包机　wire brushing machine
盘条打捆机　revolving bundle holder
盘条堆场　rod storage dock
盘条挂钩机　tilting chair
盘条挂送装置　bundle buster
盘条紧捆机　coil [rod] compressor
盘条卷取导管　reel pipe
盘条卷取机　rod coiling machine ◇ 卧式~*
盘条捆扎机　coil compactor
盘条拉拔机　rod drawing machine
盘条切头机　rod cropping apparatus
盘条收集机　capstan ◇ 六杆式~ six pronged capstan
盘条用导卫装置　wire-rod guide
盘条圆钢　rod
盘条轧机　rod mill ◇ 活套式~ rod repeater mill,串列式~机组 straight-away stands,连续式~机组*
盘条轧制散卷[松卷]冷却法　◇ 斯太尔摩~ Stelmor process
盘条支持器　coil holder
盘线　wire in coils
盘型辊　【压】disc roller
盘型可控硅整流器　disc-type thyristor
盘形板(锻造用)　【压】dished plate
盘形底槽　dish bottom tank
盘形电枢　disc armature
盘形辊　disc-shaped roll
盘形活塞　disc piston

盘形炉底炉　dished-bottom furnace
盘形弹簧　disc spring ◇ 贝莱维尔式~ Belleville spring
盘形凸轮　disc cam
盘形外浇口　【铸】pouring disc
盘形线圈　disc coil
盘形闸　plate brake
盘形(转底式)炉　rotating-table furnace
盘旋(楼)梯　circular (geometrical) stairs, cockle stairs
盘旋橡皮管　convoluted rubber tubing
盘圆　coiled bar, rod stock
盘状滑片　disc-shaped patch of slip
判别　cognition
判定标准寄存器　【计】criterion register
判定电路　【计】decision circuit
判定框(图)　【计】decision box
判读　interpretation
判断　decision, judge
判据　criterion (复数 criteria) ◇ 雷诺~ Reynold's criterion, 尼奎斯特~ Ny-quist criterion
旁插棒　【色】side contact spike, side (contact) stud
旁浇口　side gate
旁漏电阻(器)　bleeder resistor
旁路　bypass (channel), byway, branch, bypath, in-bridge
旁路电容器　bypass capacitor
旁路开关　bypass switch
旁路溶液　bypass solution
旁频带谱　side-band spectrum
旁曲柄　side crank
旁通道　by-pass (b.p.), bypass route, bypath
旁通阀　bypass valve,【铁】(热风炉的) air-escape valve, blow off valve
旁通风流　bypass air
旁通管　bypass (main, pipe), side tube ◇ 备用~ emergence by-pass
旁通管道　bypass line
旁通管回热方式　bypass mode

旁通过滤器　bypass filter
旁通孔(板)　bypass orifice
旁通控制　bypass governing
旁通溜槽　bypass chute, chute by-pass
旁通排气道　bypass vent
旁通塞孔　bypass plug hole
旁通旋塞　bypass cock
旁通烟道　bypass flue
抛出装置　lift-out attachment
抛钢机　【压】knock-out, out punch
抛光　polish (ing), burnish (ing), buff (ing), (buff) finishing, glazing, brightening, lapping, scouring (金属表面的),【金】mopping, shaping-up ◇ 带式 [用研磨带]~", 腐蚀~法", 滚筒 [滚桶, 转筒式]~", 化学~", 机械~", 皮革 [毛毡] 轮~ bobbing, 砂带~ belt polishing, 施照喷射~法", 湿法~ wet tumbling, 特亮~", 五金器皿精锑~ hardware finish, 液体磨料~ liquid honing, 用光面带~(混凝土路面的) belting, 着色~ colour buffing
抛光棒　burnishing stick
抛光薄板　polished blue sheet, lustre sheet
抛光布(金相试样的)　polishing cloth
抛光布轮　buff,【金】mop
抛光槽　polishing [burnishing] bath
抛光层　polish layer
抛光带材　polishing strip
抛光粉　polishing [burnishing] powder ◇ 氧化铁~【金】rouge
抛光膏　polishing [antiscuffing] paste
抛光辊　polishing roll ◇ 法兰绒~"
抛光滚轮　burnishing roller
抛光滚筒　burnishing barrel
抛光和漫蚀法　polish-and-etch technique
抛光机　polisher, polishing machine [device], glazing machine, glazer branner, buffing [burnishing] machine,【压】skimming machine (线材的) ◇ 麦麸~", 摩擦~ burnishing machine, 自动~"
抛光剂　brightener, polishing agent, buff-

ing compound
抛光阶段 【金】shaping-up period
抛光轮 buffing [burnishing] wheel, polishing wheel [disc], glazer ◇ 布~【压】full disc buff, 软~【机】dolly, 刷式~brush wheel
抛光面 polished surface
抛光模 polished [burnishing] die
抛光磨片(金相用) polished section
抛光呢 flannel
抛光侵蚀 polish attack
抛光砂纸 polishing paper
抛光铁丹 polishing rouge
抛光头 buffing [rubbing] head
抛光液 polishing solution [fluid] ◇ 埃里德特中间~(电镀用) Eridite
抛光用长绒布 selvyt cloth
抛光用丸粒 burnishing ball
抛光轧辊 polishing roll
抛光装置 planishing device, buffing attachment
抛(巨)石体 enrockment
抛料机 thrower, extractor, kick-out, knock(-out) pin, slinger,【压】out punch
抛锚 breakdown
抛喷清理机 【铸】abrator
抛弃 throw off
抛砂机 【铸】(sand) slinger, sand thrower, shooter
抛砂(丸)机抛头 shot blast impeller
抛砂(丸)装置 shot blast(ing) installation
抛射体 projectile body
抛石 drop-fill rock, riprap
抛石防波堤 riprap [rock-mound] breakwater
抛头 throwing wheel, ramming head (抛砂机的)
抛丸机 shotblasting machine ◇ 链式~*
抛丸机投掷轮 throwing wheel
抛丸清理 impact cleaning ◇ 连续~装置*
抛丸清理机 abrator, shot blast machine,【铸】wheelabrator
抛物面 paraboloid ◇ 拟~规则*
抛物面暗场聚光镜 dark field paraboloid condenser
抛物线 【数】para-curve, parabola, parabolic curve
抛物线型结晶器 【连铸】parabolic mold
抛物线型蠕变 parabolic creep
抛物线型应力-应变曲线 parabolic stress-strain curve
抛物线形接触电弧 parabolic contact arc
抛物线氧化 【冶】parabolic oxidation
抛物柱面 parabolic cyllinder
抛油环 ring oiler, flinger
抛掷器 slinger
咆哮焰(转炉口的) roaring flame
炮钢 gun-steel
炮泥 【铁】taphole clay [loam], tapping hole clay [mix], tapping clay [mix], stopping clay [mix], ball stuff ◇ 低湿度~*,碳质~*,无水~ waterless taphole mix
炮铜(合金) (7—10Sn,2—5Zn,0—5Pb,余量Cu) gun metal [brass] ◇ 菲利西姆~*, 改进~ modified gunmetal, 海军~*, 加铅~ leaded gun metal
炮筒钢 gun barrels steel
跑棒 【钢】running stopper
跑槽 【冶】overflow
跑钢 break(ing) [bleed] out, (badly) bleeding, runout
跑过 overrun(ning)
跑号(拉拔钢丝时的) running out, nonsizing
跑火 【铸】runout ◇ 防~沟(模板的) crush strip, 抬箱~ bleeder, 铸型~ bleeding of mould
跑偏 snaking, meandering,【压】pass outside ◇ 防~装置*, 皮带~ belt slip [tracking]
跑偏带材 【压】running off strip
跑铁 breaking out

跑线　non-sizing
泡　bubble ◇ 鼓[有,起]～的,刮[除]～勺【选】bowl skimmer
泡疤　【压】blow（锻件的）◇ 底层涂料～*,后生～表面*,细小～【冶】pinhead blister,轧制～表面【压】process blister
泡铋矿｛(BiO)₂CO₃·H₂O｝　(baso)bismutite
泡筏　bubble raft
泡筏模型　bubble raft model
泡筏排列烧结　bubble raft sintering
泡筏切变强度　shear strength of bubble raft
泡沸涂料　intumescent coating
泡痕　【压】dimples
泡碱　【化】natron(ite)
泡利不相容原理　Pauli's exclusion principle
泡(面,沫)钢　blister steel
泡面钢棒　blister bar ◇ 脱碳～aired bar
泡沫　foam,froth,lather,offscum,scum
泡沫层　froth layer
泡沫除尘[收尘]器　bubble dust collector, foam deduster
泡沫产品回收（浮选的）【选】froth recovery
泡沫分离（法）　foam fractionation
泡沫浮选精矿　【选】froth floated slurry
泡沫硅砖　foamed silica brick
泡沫管　bubble tube
泡沫含量　foam content
泡沫化倾向（炉渣的）　liable to sponge
泡沫混凝土　foam(ed) concrete ◇ 烧结矿渣～*
泡沫剂　frother,frothing [foam(ing)] agent
泡沫计　froth meter
泡沫结构　foamy [foaming] structure
泡沫聚苯乙烯模型　polystyrene foam pattern
泡沫炉渣生产设备　slag-expanding plant
泡沫铝　foamed aluminium

泡沫黏土　foamed clay
泡沫水泥砖　cementitious brick
泡沫塑料　foamed plastics,polyfoam
泡沫塑料模型　【铸】foam (plastic) pattern
泡沫线　foam line
泡沫消除剂　froth killer
泡沫氧化铝　foamed alumina
泡沫溢流槽　froth overflow channel
泡沫渣　foamed [foaming,expanded] slag, foaming（高炉）◇ 黏性～形成sponging,电炉～炼钢工艺*,机械离心式～生产法*
泡沫状的　foamy,frothy
泡沫状浮渣　【冶】foam like scum
泡沫状金属　【粉】foamed metal
泡沫状铅　（见"海绵铅"）
泡塔　bubble column
泡铜　（见"粗铜"）
泡渣砖　【耐】foamed slag brick
泡胀　macerate
泡胀指数　swelling index
泡罩　bubble cap,bubbling hood
泡罩板　bubble (cap) plate
泡罩(板)塔　bubble cap (plate) column, bubble cap tower,bubble (plate) column
泡罩洗涤器[塔]　bubble cap washer
泡罩蒸馏塔　bubble cap tower
泡状磁畴　【理】bubble domain
胚芽（期）　embryo
培训　training
培训计划[大纲]　training program
培训期　training time
培养（细菌的）　culture
培养基　(culture) medium ◇ 鉴别～differential medium
培养液　culture solution
培育器　grower
培育箱　incubator
培植　inoculate,inoculation
赔偿　compensation for, penalty, reparation, remuneration, restitution ◇ 损害

赔配 pei

~*
赔偿责任 liability to pay compensation ◇ 无辜~*
配备 fitting out
配比 blending ratio, proportioning
配比燃烧器 proportional burner
配比装置 proportioning equipment
配电 distributing, (electric power) distribution, power [current] distribution
配电板 distribution panel [block], distributing [power] board, switchboard ◇ 整体刚性~*
配电变压器 distribution transformer
配电干线 distributing main
配电柜 switch cupboard
配电盘 switchboard (panel), distribution board [panel, switchboard], board, panel, distributor ◇ 表面引出导线的~ live-front switchboard, 固定面板式~*, 台式~ bench board
配电盘室 switchboard gallery
配电屏 switchboard, distribution (switch) board
配电室 distribution building
配电所 distribution substation
配电网 distributing net(work), (electrical power) distribution network
配电系统 distributing system, distribution (system)
配电线 distribution wire
配电线路 distribution line [net], distributing line
配电箱[盒] distributing [distribution, switch] box
配电装置 switchgear, distribution apparatus
配对 pairing
配对操作 matching operation
配风管 【铁】air manifold
配风系统 blast distribution system
配箍筋混凝土 【建】hooped concrete
配管车间 pipe-fitting shop
配管工 pipe fitter
配辊技术 【压】pass positioning
配合 matching, coordination, 【机】fit(ting), fitting in (基孔制的), fitting on (基轴制的), 【化】complexing
配合泵 proportion(ing) pump
配合比 mixing proportion, mixture ratio
配合标记[记号] matchmark
配合单位 【机】unit of fit
配合等级 【机】grade of fit
配合度 fitness
配合公差 fit tolerance, tolerance on fit
配合基[体] ligand
配合给料器[加料器,加料漏斗] proportioner
配合金 alloying
配合金的组分 alloying ingredient
配合螺栓 template [dowel] bolt
配合面 matching face, seating
配合余隙 mating stand off
配衡离子 anchored ion
配衡重 tare weight
配件 fittings, accessories, (spare) parts ◇ 维克托~青铜*
配筋 【建】reinforcing bars, reinforcement ◇ 超~的*, 钢丝网~ fabric reinforcement, 混凝土~用钢筋*
配筋(百分)率 ratio of reinforcement, steel ratio
配筋不足的 under-reinforced
配筋图 reinforcement drawing
配矿 ore blend(ing)
配力钢筋 distribution rod, lacing
配量阀 metering valve
配量阀组 metering block
配量装置 proportioning equipment
配料 charge mixture [makeup], batch(ing), burden(ing), blend, dosage, dosing, (feed, mix) proportioning, mixing, mix material (proportioning), mixture (making) ◇ 按重量~(混凝土搅拌) weigh batching, 开炉~ blown in burden,

手工特制的~ hand-tailored burden,新酸~容器*,中心~厂*,自动~*

配料比 mixing-ratio, mixture ratio,【冶】charge ratio,【铁】burden ratio

配料仓 distribution [batch] bin, mixture (storing) bin, proportioning bin [bunker, hopper]

配料槽 distributing chute, primary [dosage] bunker, surge bin

配料场 bedding area ◇ 床式~

配料车 burden charging carriage, batch truck

配料车间 proportioning plant

配料秤 proportion [batcher] scale, batch weigher, weigh-feeder

配料称量 proportioning weighing

配料成分 charge component

配料单[表] burden sheet

配料分析 mixture analysis

配料化学成分 burden chemistry

配料机 feed control device

配料机构 【冶】dispensing mechanism

配料计 proportioning meter

配料计算 charge [burden, mix(ture)] calculation,【铁】burdening

配料记录器 batch counter

配料加热器 (同"分批加热器")

配料间 charge-mixing department

配料焦炭(比) charge coke

配料阶段 proportioning stage

配料精确度 proportioning accuracy

配料控制 proportion control

配料控制盘 【冶】burden control panel

配料跨 stockyard bay

配料硫 【冶】charged sulphur

配料漏斗 proportioning hopper

配料盘 batching table

配料皮带 proportioning belt

配料皮带秤 dosing belt weigher

配料器 batcher, batching plant, feed control device ◇ 料槽~ measuring pocket

配料设备 proportioning device,【耐】dosing device

配料设计(混凝土的) design mix

配料台 table distributor

配料系统 (material, feed) proportioning system

配料箱 proportioning tank, distribution box

配料有害成分 injurious burden constituent

配料闸板 proportioning gate

配料蒸锅 feed make-up boiler

配料指示器 distributing indicator

配料柱压力 pressure of stock column

配料贮槽 mixture storing bin

配料装置 batching set up, proportioning plant, proportioner,【冶】dispensing mechanism,【耐】dosing device

配料组成 burden [batch] composition

配料组分 burden constituent

配料组分重量比 burden weight ratio

配炉计算 furnace charge calculation

配炉料 furnace burdening

配煤 【焦】mixing coal, mixture making, blending

配煤比 burden constituents

配煤仓 coal blending bin

配模计算 draught calculation

配气器 gas distributor

配气罩 air distributor cap

配入水 make up water

配上 fitting on, cover with

配水 (water) distribution

配水槽 distributing trough

配水干管 【建】distributing main

配水管[器] 【铁】water manifold

配水管网 distributing net

配水系统 distributing system, distribution

配碳量 coke [fuel] addition, fuel content of raw mix, solid fuel level

配套 complement match(ing), mating ◇ 不~工厂[设备] inadequate plant

配套总重 gross combination weight

(gcw)

配位催化剂　complex catalyst

配位滴定(法)　complexometry, complexometric titration

配位度　complex formability

配位多面体　coordinating polyhedron

配位反应　complexation [complexing] reaction

配位化合物　coordination compound [complex], complex compound

配位剂　complexant, coordination agent

配(位)价　【化】coordinate [coordination, coordinative] valence

配位(价)键　coordination [coordinate] bond

配位熵　【理】configurational entropy

配位数　coordinating number ◇ 权重～*

配位作用　coordination

配线　wiring, distribution, conductor arrangement

配线暗沟　wiring tunnel

配线架　wiring shelf, distribution frame

配线图　wiring diagram

配渣计算　slag calculation

配置　configuration, setup, allocation, arrangement, collocation, disposal, distribution ◇ 不正确～ misarrangement, 示意～图*

配置图　arrangement diagram [drawing]

配制　preparation, make up, dosing ◇ 按比例～的试样 proportioning probe, 新～的溶液 freshly prepared liquor

配制合金　alloyage ◇ 用熔化法～ fusion alloying

配制混合料　prepared mix

配制浸出溶液　make up of leach solution

配制品　preparation

配制溶液　make up solution

配重　counterweight, counterbalance, balancer, bob(-weight) ◇ 重锤式蓄势器用～*

配重平衡导板　【压】guard balanced by counterweight

配重升降炉门　counterweighted door lift-type

配重式放灰阀　counterweighted dust valve

配准(图像对准)　【计】registration

配准不良　misregistration

佩德森法(铝酸钙炉渣法生产 Al_2O_3)　Pedersen process

佩蒂奥混汞提银法　Patio process

佩尔蒂埃叉(测温和测热流用)　Peltier cross

佩尔蒂埃热　Peltier heat

佩尔蒂埃系数(热电偶接点的)　Peltier coefficient

佩尔蒂埃效应　Peltier effect

佩尔斯－纳巴罗位错　Peierls-Nabarro dislocation

佩尔斯－纳巴罗应力　Peierls-Nabarro stress

佩尔斯刃型位错　Peierls [Peierls-Nabarro] dislocation

佩尔托排列图(分析废品频数用)　Pareto chart [diagram]

佩弗洛添加剂(用于半光泽镀镍)　Perflow

佩格洛添加剂(用于光泽镀镍)　Perglow

佩拉卢曼铝镁锰合金(锻造: 1.5—6Mg, 0－1Mn, 余量 Al; 铸造: 2—6Mg, 0.3Mn, 余量 Al)　Peraluman

佩利尼爆炸试验　Pellini explosion test

佩利尼落锤冲击试验　Pellini drop-weight test

佩林炼钢法　【钢】Perrin process

佩罗夫斯基组织　Perovskite sturcture

佩奇方程　Petch equation

佩特罗压缩空气高速锻造机　Petro-forge machine

喷补　spray [gunned] repair, mortar injection, patching (焦炉的) ◇ 半干法～*, 火焰～技术, 耐火材料～器 refractory gun, 泥浆～机【耐】air mortar gun, 热态遥控～技术*, 熔射～机*

喷补材料 【建】gunned material
喷补层(高炉的) gunning layer
喷补法 spraying method, torkret process
喷补钢水包 gunned ladle
喷补混合料 gun(ning) mix ◇ 干法～ dry-gun mix
喷补技术 mortar injection technique
喷补料 gunning refractory [material], gun mix
喷补料颗粒 gunning mixture particle
喷补炉[内]衬 gunned lining [repair], sprayed lining, gunning
喷补耐火材料 gunning refractory
喷布器 sprinkler
喷出 blowout, ejection, ejaculation, expulsion, puffing-up
喷出(物) eruption, ejecta, blowoff
喷吹 jetting, blowing, 【铁】injection ◇ FTG～法", 并列～罐", 单管路～", 多管路～", 复合～", 高炉～", 还原性燃料～", 炉身～(原、燃料)【铁】stack injection, 煤粉[粉煤]～", 燃(料)油～fuel oil injection, 碳氢化合物～", 铁口～", 重油煤粉(混合浆)～"
喷吹废塑料 injecting of plastic scrap
喷吹管系 injection piping
喷吹极限 【铁】injection limit
喷吹精炼 injection [spray] refining
喷吹率 injection rate
喷吹煤粉 【铁】pulverized coal injection
喷吹燃料 fuel injection, injected fuel
喷吹燃料风口 fuel injection tuyere
喷吹燃油 oil injection
喷吹石灰 lime injection
喷吹时间 injection time
喷吹脱硫 blowing desulfurization
喷吹系统(燃料的) injection system ◇ 高挥发分烟煤～", 高压固体燃料～"
喷吹效率 【铁】injection efficiency
喷吹冶金(学) injection metallurgy
喷吹元件 【钢】gas supply element
喷吹蒸汽 steam injection

喷吹装置 injection equipment [facilities], injecting device
喷弹 cloudbursting
喷灯 blowlamp, blast [air, Bunsen, brazing] burner, blast lamp, (blow) torch, soldering lamp [torch], burner, blowpipe ◇ 煤气～ gas blowpipe
喷灯焊 torch weld
喷灯烙铁 blow lamp soldering iron
喷灯喷嘴 torch neck
喷镀 spraying, sparge, (spray) metallizing, metallising, splatter, sputter ◇ 爆燃～", 电弧～ arc spraying, 金属～", 可～性 sprayability, 冷～ cold spraying, 铝制品表面钼～ Sprabond, 熔化～ sprayfusing, 熔融金属～ molten metal spraying
喷镀薄膜 sputtered film
喷镀法 spraying method
喷镀钢丝 spray wire
喷镀金属 metalling, metallization ◇ 电弧等离子体～ arc plasma metallizing
喷镀金属的塑料 metallized plastics
喷镀金属法 metallizing process, spray metal coating ◇ 斯库普粉末～ Schoop process
喷镀金属防护面罩 metal spraying helmet
喷镀金属转移 spray metal transfer
喷镀器 sprayer
喷镀枪 spray torch
喷镀渗铝 spray calorizing
喷镀速度 spraying speed
喷镀涂层 sputtered coating
喷发 eruption
喷粉 powder injection ◇ 铁水～脱硫"
喷粉火焰清理 powder scarfing
喷粉法 【钢】dispensing process
喷粉熔镀[喷焊] spray welding
喷粉熔镀法 sprayweld process
喷粉时间 injection time
喷敷(层) spray(ed-on) coating
喷覆塑料膜法 cocoon process
喷管 (injection) lance, spray [jet] tube,

| 喷 pen |

jet (nozzle), nozzle
喷管喉道 (exit) nozzle throat
喷管孔基础台 【焦】nozzle deck
喷管口 nozzle [jet-pipe] mouth
喷焊法 spray weld process
喷焊器 blow pipe, spray welding unit
喷火穿孔 flame drilling
喷加白云石 dolomite injection
喷碱槽 alkali spray tank
喷溅 splash, spatter, sparge, splatter, spray, sputter, spitting, 【钢】(转炉的) slopping, sloppy
喷溅长度(结晶器的) spray length
喷溅防护罩 spray guard covering
喷溅炉次 【钢】sloppy heat (转炉的)
喷溅损失 loss by splashing
喷溅物 splashings (铸造缺陷), spitting, 【钢】ejection (转炉的)
喷浆 mortar injection, guniting
喷浆补炉法 【冶】torkret process
喷浆衬砌[衬里,炉衬] gunite lining ◇ 压力~gunite lining
喷浆工程 gunite work
喷浆机 patching machine (修炉用)
喷浆面层 gunite covering
喷浆耐火材料 sprayed refractories
喷浆枪 pneumatic [refractory] gun ◇ 单室式~ single-chamber gun, 双室式~ double chamber gun
喷浆修补 gunned repair
喷焦油操作法 【团】tar injection practice
喷金属 metallizing
喷口 (nozzle) orifice, throat (转炉的) ◇ 扁平流 V 形~flat stream V-jet
喷口烧蚀 muzzle erosion
喷口速度 nozzle velocity (NV)
喷粒 blasting grit
喷淋冷却法 spray cooling, shower method
喷淋(冷却)结晶器 【连铸】spray-cooled [spray-type, spraying] mold
喷淋冷却器 shower cooler, surface spray cooler

喷淋器 spray head [thrower]
喷淋清洗 spray cleaning [rinse]
喷淋水 spray water
喷淋水套 spray jacket
喷淋塔 spray [splash] tower, spray column
喷淋洗涤 spray washing
喷淋洗涤器 spray tower [washer]
喷流 jet flow
喷流换热器 spraying exchanger ◇ 套管式~*, 箱式~*
喷流模样[形状] spray pattern
喷煤 【铁】pulverized coal injection (PCI), coal (powder) injection ◇ 大~*, 富氧~*, 高压~*, 远距离~*
喷煤操作 PCI operation
喷煤极限 coal injection limit
喷煤总量自动控制 automatic control of coal mass flow rate
喷模 jet mould
喷磨机 aeropulverizer, jet pulverizer [mill]
喷漆 spray painting, paint spray
喷漆标记 paint stenciled making
喷漆器 paint sprayer
喷漆机 paint spraying machine ◇ 无气~*
喷漆枪 painting nozzle, paint-spraying pistol
喷器 spray box
喷气 air lancing [injection] ◇ 电弧~切割法 arc-air process
喷气发动机 jet engine
喷气发动机零件 jet-engine parts
喷气机合金高温高转速试验 ◇ 西屋~*
喷气净化器 cleansing blower
喷气孔(坑) fumarole
喷气口 gas port
喷气冷却器 gas jet cooler
喷气推进发动机 jet-propulsion engine
喷气循环真空脱气法 (同"循环真空脱

气法")
喷气压缩机 【机】gas-jet compressor
喷汽搅拌槽 steam jet agitator
喷汽冷却系统 steam-jet cooling system
喷枪 spray [blast, blow] gun, gun(ite), 【钢】(injection) lance ◇ 爆炸~*, 表面淬火~*, 电弧~【金】arc pistol, 工业炉~furnace gun, 空气雾化~*, 氩弧~argon arc torch
喷枪喷嘴 lance nozzle
喷枪更换装置 【钢】lance changing facility
喷枪式点火器 torch type ignitor
喷枪式燃烧器【烧嘴】 gun-type burner, 【铁】lance type burner
喷枪头 top of lance
喷泉床(流态化技术) spouted bed
喷入燃料[物料]【铁】injectant
喷洒器 sprayer, sprinkler
喷洒水 sparge water
喷洒洗涤塔 spray scrubber ◇ 无填料~*
喷洒液 flushing liquor ◇ 铸模~槽
喷洒装置 spraying apparatus
喷砂 (sand) blast(ing), spray [blow] sand, grit blast ◇ 无损[软粒]~*
喷砂除鳞机 blast descaler
喷砂滚筒 【铸】sandblast barrel mill
喷砂机 (sand) blaster, sand-blast(ing) machine [apparatus], sand blower, sander, peening [blowing] machine ◇ 返砂~vacu-blast, 滚筒~*, 空气~air-sand blower, 链轮台式~*, 软管式~*, 轧辊~强化 mill roll etching, 蒸汽~*
喷砂加工(轧辊的) shot blasting
喷砂加工轧辊 shot blasted roll
喷砂器 sand blower [blast], cleansing blower
喷砂清理 sand [grit] blast(ing), abrasive [grit] blast cleaning, sanding, blasting [sand], cleaning, sandblast finish, shot blast(ing)(轧件的) ◇ 干式~【金】dry sandblasting, 水力~*, 无空气的~airless blast cleaning, 雾状[蒸汽, 液体]~vapour blast(ing)
喷砂清理滚筒 sandblast rolling barrel, shot blasting barrel
喷砂清理机 sandblast cleaning machine, shot blasting machine
喷砂清理间 sandblast cleaning room
喷砂(清理)室 sandblast cabinet, sandblasting [shot-blasting] chamber, shot blast cabinet
喷砂清理系统 shot blast cleaning system
喷砂清理用砂 【铸】sand-blasting sand
喷砂(清理)装置 sandblaster, sand-blast(ing) installation [unit], sanding apparatus [gear], sand-spraying device, shot blast(ing) plant [unit, installation]
喷砂设备 sandblast equipment
喷砂试验 grit-blasting test
喷砂修整 sandblast finish
喷砂造型 blowing
喷砂嘴 sandblast nozzle
喷烧器 pulverizing jet ◇ 格栅型辐射~*, 煤粉-悬浊油~*, 燃料~fuel injector
喷射 spray(ing), jet, injection (inj.), ejecting, guniting, spouting ◇ B.N.F~检验*, 杯形-枪 cup gun, 布郎斯登-班尼斯特-撞击试验*, 细金属~过渡*
喷射泵 injection [eject, jet, spray] pump, ejector (jet) pump ◇ 水流~water-jet injector, 蒸气产物~*
喷射材料 【建】gunned material
喷射层[床] spouting bed
喷射[雾]沉积 spray deposition
喷射[雾]沉积法 spray deposition process
喷射成形 spray forming
喷射充填【采】jet fill
喷射冲击 jet impact
喷射冲击式磨机 jet impact mill
喷射抽气泵 jet pump
喷射淬火 jet quenching
喷射带 sprayed band

| 喷射道 【焦】gun flue
| 喷射电镀 jet electro-plating
| 喷射顶角 jet apex angle
| 喷射法 gunite
| 喷射法二次冷却 jet-type secondary cooling
| 喷射风机 ejector fan
| 喷射管 jet tube, jet-pipe, playpipe ◇ 热水～*
| 喷射管段[节] jet segment
| 喷射灌浆 guniting
| 喷射混合料 【建】gun mix
| 喷射混合器 jet mixer
| 喷射混凝土 gunite concrete, shotcrete
| 喷射混凝土[水泥]覆盖的 gunited
| 喷射浇注 spray casting
| 喷射加料器 splash feeder
| 喷射角 spraying angle
| 喷射精炼 injection refining
| 喷射浸出 jet leaching
| 喷射孔 spray hole
| 喷射扩散泵 jet-diffusion pump
| 喷射冷凝器 injector [ejector, jet] condenser
| 喷射冷却 jet [spray, effusion] cooling
| 喷射力 ejection force
| 喷射炼钢法 spray steelmaking
| 喷射流 injector jet
| 喷射器 injector, ejector, jet, sprayer, spray head [unit] ◇ 抽扬[引吸]～lifting injector, 稠液～compact liquid jet, 混合～injector mixer, 空气雾化～*, 吸引～sucking injector, 旋流式～swirl injector, 支架～stand sprayer
| 喷射汽化器 spray carburettor
| 喷射燃烧器 spray [inspirator] burner
| 喷射熔炼 jet smelting
| 喷射熔炼炉直接还原法 【铁】jet-smelter process
| 喷射式抽风机 ejector fan
| 喷射式干燥器 ejector drier
| 喷射式焊枪 injector torch
| 喷射式气割嘴 injector-type cutter
| 喷射式微粉磨机 jet-O-Mizer
| 喷射室 jet chamber
| 喷射试验 spray test, jet test
| 喷射水泥 jet cement, gunite
| 喷射水泥砂浆 shotcrete, guniting
| 喷射速度 jet [spouting] velocity, jet [spraying] speed
| 喷射速率 injection rate
| 喷射塑模 jet mould
| 喷射特性 spray characteristic
| 喷射洗涤器 jet scrubber
| 喷射系统 injection system
| 喷射效率 injection efficiency
| 喷射压力 jet pressure
| 喷射压力机 ejecting press
| 喷射研磨 jet milling
| 喷射冶金 injection [jet] metallurgy
| 喷射蒸汽 jet steam
| 喷射蒸汽泵 steam-jet pump
| 喷射铸造 spray casting
| 喷射柱塞 injection plunger
| 喷射装置 injection equipment, jet apparatus, spray-off device
| 喷湿 dabble
| 喷石灰粉氧气顶吹转炉 LDAC converter, OLP (oxygen-lime-powder) converter
| 喷石灰粉氧气顶吹转炉炼钢法 LD-AC process
| 喷室 spray box
| 喷水 injecting water, sprinkling, water spraying ◇ 弧形连铸装置～区*, 加压粗流～*
| 喷水槽 spray tank
| 喷水抽气泵 water-jet pump, water ejector pump ◇ 贝克～Baker's water jet pump, 玻璃～glass water-jet pump, 哈林顿～*
| 喷水淬火 spray [stream] hardening, (water) spray quenching
| 喷水分布系统 spray water distributing system

喷水管	spray pipe, water jet, water spray beam
喷水孔	water spray nozzle
喷水口	water jet
喷水冷却	water spray cooling
喷水(冷却)池	spray pond, sprinkling basin
喷水冷却炉壳	spray cooled hearth jacket
喷水冷却器	water spray cooler, drip-round cooler
喷水冷却装置	showering installation
喷水流	water spray beam
喷水泥	gunite
喷水凝固	【连铸】wash(ing) water solidification
喷水器	water spray(er) [eductor], fresh water spray, rinser
喷水区	spray zone
喷水水淬法(炉渣的)	【铁】jet granulation
喷水水淬渣	【铁】jet-granulated slag
喷水水淬渣法	【冶】jet-expanding process
喷水雾	water spray mist
喷水贮槽	water spray tank
喷水装置	moistener
喷水嘴	spray nozzle, water spray nozzle [beam]
喷丝枪	wire pistol
喷铁粉火焰清理(板坯的)	powder scarfing
喷铁粉氧焰清理	powder washing
喷头	spray [sprinkler, blow] head, (shower) nozzle
喷涂	spray coating, flame plating, spatter ◇ 半干自动~料*, 爆燃~*, 金属~metalikon, 消气剂~ getter sputtering, 转筒~barrelling
喷涂层	spray coating, gunned layer
喷涂成形	spray forming
喷涂法	spraying method
喷涂工程	gunite work
喷涂胶片	sputtered film
喷涂金属	metal coating
喷涂金属器	metallizer
喷涂耐火材料	sprayed refractory
喷涂器	sprayer, spray-off device ◇ 石墨浆~black wash sprayer
喷涂射流	spray jet
喷涂速度	spraying speed
喷丸	shot blasting, cloudbursting
喷丸除鳞法	dreibrite
喷丸除鳞机	blast descaler
喷丸除锈	shot peening
喷丸处理	(shot, ball) peening, cloudburst treatment [process], ballizing ◇ 冷~cold-peening, 热~hot peening
喷丸钢板	shot-blasted steel sheet
喷丸钢丸	peening shot
喷丸机	peening machine, compressed air shotblasting machine,【铸】wheelabrator ◇ 链式~*
喷丸加工(清理)	shot blasting
喷丸加工处理法(金属表面的)	blast working process
喷丸加工轧辊	shot blasted roll
喷丸检验法(渗碳钢用)	cloud burst(ing) test
喷丸毛化	【压】shot-blasting roughing
喷丸模夹淬火	shot die quenching
喷丸清理	blast(ing) cleaning, shot blast(ing)(轧件的), rotoblasting, grit blast
喷丸清理滚筒	shot blasting barrel
喷丸清理机	(pneumatic) shot blasting machine
喷丸(清理)室	(shot) blast cabinet, shot blasting chamber
喷丸清理系统	shot blast cleaning system
喷丸清理用防护面罩	(同"喷砂清理用防护面罩")
喷丸清理装置	shot blast(ing) installation, shot cleaning unit ◇ 连续~*
喷丸清理作业	rotoblast operation
喷丸热成形[喷丸模锻]法	【压】shot die forming
喷丸室(轮式)	wheelabrator cabinet

喷丸硬化(处理) (同"喷丸处理")
喷丸硬化设备　shot peening installation
喷丸硬化试验　cloud burst(ing) test
喷丸增强器　shot intensifier
喷丸装置　shot blast(ing) installation, shot blast plant [unit]
喷雾　atomizing, atomisation, (mist) spray, pulverization, spraying, sparge
喷雾焙烧技术　spray-roasting technique
喷雾吹炼　spray converting
喷雾淬火　fog quenching, hardening by sprinkling
喷雾代铅浴(韧化)　fog-cooling-patenting
喷雾阀　spray valve
喷雾法　spray-on process ◇ 金属～spray gun process, 压缩空气～*
喷雾法铁粉　RZ (Roheisen Zunder) powder
喷雾干燥　spray drying
喷雾干燥器　spray dryer, ejector drier
喷雾管喉口　Venturi throat
喷雾冷凝器　spray condenser
喷雾冷却　fog-cooling, mist cooling
喷雾冷却器　spray cooler
喷雾[二次]冷却区　spray zone
喷雾(冷却)塔　spray tower [column]
喷雾连续炼钢法　spray refining process
喷雾器　sprayer, atomizer, atomiser, spray jet [gun, producer, unit], spray (can), projector, disperser, pulverizer, rinser, sprinkler ◇ 风扇式～fan atomizer, 冷却～cooling sprayer, 手动～hand-powder bulb
喷雾器喷嘴(莲蓬式)　rose
喷雾清洗　fog rinse
喷雾燃烧器　(同"雾化燃烧器")
喷雾润滑　atomized [fog, mist] lubrication
喷雾润滑系统　mist lubrication
喷雾式喷嘴　atomized-spray injector
喷雾室(混凝土养护用)　【建】fog room
喷雾收集塔　sprayed collection tower
喷雾酸洗　【压】spray acid cleaning

喷雾涂层　spray painting
喷雾轧制　spray rolling
喷雾蒸发器　spray evaporator
喷雾蒸汽　atomizing steam
喷雾柱　spray column
喷雾装置　spray unit ◇ 无压缩空气～*
喷雾锥　atomizer cone
喷雾嘴　spray [atomizing, mist, disintegrating] nozzle, spray [atomizing] jet, atomizer aperture
喷洗　spray cleaning
喷洗池　spray cell
喷洗筛　【选】rinsing [spraying] screen
喷洗室(气体喷洗室)　spray chamber
喷洗塔　splash tower ◇ 多层～*, 无填料～unpacked spray tower
喷烟　smoke emission
喷盐腐蚀试验箱　salt spray box
喷焰除鳞　flame descaling
喷焰连续退火(线材的)　flame strand annealing
喷焰清理　flame scarfing
喷焰烧槽　jet channel(l)ing
喷氧　【钢】jetting
喷液淬火　spray quenching
喷液电解抛光　jet polishing
喷油器　oil atomizer
喷油润滑　oil spray lubrication, splash lubrication
喷油润滑器　oil spray lubricator
喷油雾润滑　atomized lubrication
喷油系统　oil injection system
喷油增压扩散泵　oil-jet booster-diffusion pump
喷油真空泵　oil-jet type of pump
喷油嘴　oil nozzle
喷渣口　【铁】blowing on monkey
喷渣试验　【耐】slag spray test
喷铸　spray casting
喷注器　inspirator
喷注装置　jet apparatus
喷嘴　spray nozzle [head, apparatus, unit],

nipple, jet nozzle [orifice], injector (nozzle, cone), (injecting, burner) nozzle, jet, atomizer (cone) ◇ 表面切割用～", 出口～ discharge jet, 多焰～ multiflame tip, 放气[吹除]～ blow off nozzle, 焊矩[割矩]～ blow pipe head, 环形加热～", 混合～", 截面可调[控]～", 克里斯托福尔森～", 空气雾化～", 拉瓦尔[收敛发散形, 收缩-扩张]～", 两块组合式～ two-piece nozzle, 排气～", 入口～ inlet nozzle, 限制式～ confined type nozzle, 旋流式～ swirl injector, 直射式～ direct-type gun, 自由降落式～ free fall type nozzle

喷嘴衬 nozzle liner
喷嘴尺寸 [大小] jet size
喷嘴堵塞 nozzle fouling
喷嘴分离阀 (空气预热器、热风炉用) burner door valve
喷嘴管道 nozzle line
喷嘴护栅 nozzle grate
喷嘴[喷雾头]集管 spray header
喷嘴结垢 nozzle fouling
喷嘴孔 nozzle bore
喷嘴口 nozzle mouth [opening, orifice], jet-pipe mouth
喷嘴拉模 (液压拉丝用) nozzle die
喷嘴漏斗 funnel with nozzle
喷嘴喷镀[喷溅] nozzle spatter
喷嘴清整工具 nozzle-cleaning tool
喷嘴燃烧器 jet burner
喷嘴式点火器 nozzle type ignitor
喷嘴调整范围 【冶】turndown range
喷嘴通条 nozzle cleaner
喷嘴型式 burner design
喷嘴圆孔 parallel nozzle bore
喷嘴直径 【焦】jet diameter
喷嘴阻力 nozzle friction
喷嘴组 injector set
喷嘴座砖 【焦】nozzle seating block
盆式辊磨机 bowl mill
彭宁真空计 Penning (vacuum) gauge

棚架车 shelf [rack-type] car, stillage truck
棚架炉 shelf oven
棚料 【冶】arching, 【钢】bridging (电炉的), 【铁】build up of scab and scar (高炉的)
棚下贮存 under-cover storage
硼{B} boron ◇ 含～合金", 准～ eka-boron
硼钢 boron steel
硼(硅)玻璃 borate [borosilicate, borax] glass ◇ 硬质～"
硼硅钡钇矿 cappelenite
硼硅化[硼硅处理] borosiliconizing
硼硅酸钠硬质玻璃 ◇ 瓦科尔～ Vycor
硼硅铈矿 tritomite
硼硅铁合金 ◇ 博罗西尔～"
硼硅钇钙石 hellandite
硼硅钇矿 tritomite-(Y)
硼合金 boron alloy ◇ 硬化性增强～【钢】needling agent
硼合金增强剂 【钢】intensifiers
硼化[硼处理] boronizing, boriding, boronation
硼化钙{Ca₃B₂} calcium boride
硼化锆 zirconium (di)boride
硼化铪 hafnium boride
硼化镧陶瓷 lanthanum boride ceramics
硼化铝 aluminium boride
硼化塑料 boron plastics (BP)
硼化钛{TiB₂} titanium boride
硼化铜 boronised copper
硼化钨 tungsten boride
硼化物 boride
硼(金属)陶瓷 boride cermet
硼化物试验电解槽 boride test cell
硼铝铁 ferroboral
硼镁铁矿 ludwigite
硼泥 boro-sludge
硼铍铝艳石 rhodizite
硼铍石 hambergite
硼强化钢 boron intensified steel

硼砂 {Na$_2$B$_4$O$_7$·10H$_2$O} borax, sodium borate, tinkal(ite), tincal
硼砂玻璃 borax glass
硼砂球[珠] borax bead
硼砷酸盐 boroarsenate
硼铈钙石 braitschite
硼锶石 strontioborite
硼酸 {H$_3$BO$_3$} boric acid
硼烷[硼化氢] {BH$_3$, H$_n$H$_m$} borane
硼酸铵 ammonium borate
硼酸钙 lime borate
硼酸镁 antifungin
硼酸锰 manganese borate
硼酸钠 Boratex
硼酸铅 lead borate
硼酸锌 zinc borate
硼酸锌水泥 zinc borate cement
硼酸铈钍铍矿 cerhomilite
硼酸盐 borate
硼钽石 behierite
硼提取率 efficiency of extracted boron (EEB)
硼铁 iron boron, ferroboron
硼钨酸 {B$_2$O$_3$·24WO$_3$·9H$_2$O} borotungstic acid
硼锡钙矿 nordenskioldine
硼钇铜石 agardite
硼硬化剂 【钢】needlers
硼铸钢 boron cast steel
膨润土 {(Ca,Mg)O·SiO$_2$·(Al,Fe)$_2$O$_3$} bentonite, alta-mud ◇ 钙基~ calcium bentonite, 含硅~ distribond, 无~球团 *
膨润土基体 bentonite matrix
膨润土黏合[结]剂 bentonite binder
膨润土润滑脂 bentone grease
膨润土添加比[量] bentonite/ore ratio
膨润土添加(剂) bentonite addition
膨润土添加剂 bentonite additive
膨胀 expanding, expansion, swell(ing), dilatation, dilation, inflation, bloating, broadening, bulge ◇ 恶性~ *, 突发性~ 【团】dramatic expansion, 逐渐~ gradual expansion
膨胀变化 dilatometric change
膨胀补偿器 expansion bend
膨胀测定法 dilatometry, dilatometric method
膨胀测定法研究 dilatometric study
膨胀测定热处理 dilatometric heat treatment
膨胀测定仪 expansion gauge
膨胀床 expanded bed
膨胀度 dilation, dilatation, 【团】degree of expansion [swelling]
膨胀阀 expansion valve
膨胀缝 expansion [dilatation] joint
膨胀缸 expanding cylinder
膨胀功 expansion work
膨胀管 expansion vessel
膨胀辊 inflatable roll
膨胀合金 expanding alloy [metal]
膨胀剂 expansion [expanding, swelling] agent
膨胀计[仪] expansion meter, dilatometer ◇ 干涉(测量)~ *, 自记式~ autographic dilatometer
膨胀计测定 dilatometer measurement
膨胀计研究 dilatometer investigation
膨胀间隙 play for expansion
膨胀拉杆螺栓 expansion staybolt
膨胀力 expansive force
膨胀裂纹 expansion crack
膨胀炉渣 【冶】expanded slag
膨胀炉渣混凝土 expanded slag concrete
膨胀率 expansion ratio, expansibility, percent swelling, swelling index [number], 【团】degree of swelling
膨胀率标准 【团】swelling specification
膨胀煤 swelling coal
膨胀能力 swelling power
膨胀黏土 expanded clay
膨胀曲线记录 dilatation curve registration
膨胀伸缩缝 expansion gap

膨胀试验	expansion test
膨胀水泥	expanding cement
膨胀速率	rate of expansion
膨胀特性	expanding [swelling] property, swelling characteristics
膨胀凸轮	expansion cam
膨胀涂料	intumescent coating
膨胀温度计	expansion [dilatometric] thermometer
膨胀现象	swelling phenomenon
膨胀系数	expansion coefficient [factor], expansivity, swelling factor, 【理】modulus of dilatation ◇ 表观~(液体的)*, 表面(热)~*, 广义~*, 体(积)~*, 线~*
膨胀线	expansion line
膨胀箱	expansion tank ◇ 封闭式~ closed expansion tank
膨胀效应	dilatometric effect
膨胀性	expandability, expansivity, dilatability, swelling characteristics ◇ 可~expansibility
膨胀性钢包砖	expansion ladle brick
膨胀性能	expansion character ◇ 特殊~金属*
膨胀性土壤	dilative soil
膨胀性状[行为]	swelling behaviour
膨胀絮凝层	dilated flocbed
膨胀旋管(冷却机的)	expansion coil
膨胀压力	swelling pressure
膨胀页岩骨料	expanded slate aggregate
膨胀珍珠岩骨料	expanded perlite aggregate
膨胀指数	swelling index [number]
膨胀砖	expansion brick
碰焊	butt-joint
碰痕	bruise mark
碰伤【钢】	bruising, dog marks
碰撞	collision, colliding, impact, impingement, bombardment, recoil (反冲粒子)
碰撞电离	collision [impact] ionization
碰撞断面[截面]	collision cross section
碰撞辐射	collision radiation
碰撞理论	collision theory
碰撞粒子	colliding [impingement] particle
碰撞密度	collision density
碰撞面	striking face
碰撞模型	collision model
碰撞能沿原子密集排列方向传播的现象【理】	focuson
碰撞频率	collision frequency
碰撞伞【理】	impingement umbrella
碰撞时间	time of impact
碰撞式摇床【选】	percussion table
碰撞游离	impact ionization
坯	blank, butt, cog, semi-finished metal ◇ 整~场 conditioning yard
坯板	blanket ◇ 造币~ coin blank
坯锭	billet ◇ 填充~法*
坯锭加热炉	billet furnace
坯件	blank
坯件夹住器	blank holder
坯壳【连铸】	solidified shell
坯块	briquet, compact ◇ 凹面~ concave-shaped compact, 变截面[复杂断面]~*, 复合[混合金属]~*, 精压~ coining compact, 矩形断面~*, 刻格~*, 冷压~ cold-pressed compact, 曲面~*, 条形~【粉】cored bar, 凸面~*, 柱状~ cylindrical compact
坯块膨胀	compact expansion
坯料【压】	billet, blank, shell, stock (material), web (箍材的) ◇ 穿轧过孔的~ pierced billet, 空心~ hollow billet, 清理过表面缺陷的~ conditioned billet, 锥形端头的~ conical-ended billet
坯料扒[剥]皮机(床)	(billet) peeler
坯料剥皮[修整,清理]	peeling
坯料剥皮车床	rotary peeler
坯料报废检查装置	billet discard unit
坯料仓库	billet storage [yard]
坯料打印机[打印工]	billet marker
坯料带卷	reroll
坯料堆垛机	billet piler

坯料分配器 billet switch ◇ 链式~ chain billet switch, 四线~*, 转鼓式~*

坯料机械分送台 mechanical billet separating skid

坯料机械化剥皮[修整] mechanical peeling

坯料检查修整工段 scarfing dock

坯料接续挤压 billet upon billet extruding

坯料库 stock bank

坯料清理机组 billet cleaning unit

坯料入口 billet entering

坯料未加工边缘(靠近夹持器) no-draw edge

坯料升降堆垛台 billet elevator

坯料试样 blank sample

坯料楔形前端 【压】billet nose

坯料轧机 billet mill

坯体制备 【耐】body preparation

坯条 rod billet, 【粉】cored bar

坯缘压牢器 blank holder

砒霜[As_2O_3] arsenic (trioxide), arsenic white, white arsenic

砒酸 (同"砷酸")

批发价格 wholesale price

批发销售商 merchant wholesaler

批号 lot number (LN), batch number

批量 batch, lot size, consignment ◇ 不合格[有缺陷的]~(指产品) faulty lot, ◇ 脱机~处理系统*

批量给料计 batch meter

批料 batch, consignment

批料成分 batch composition

批料漏斗 (同"零料仓")

披铂碳电极 (同"镀铂碳电极")

披缝(缺陷) 【铸】(burr) flash ◇ 浇注~ casting fin

劈尖角 angle of wedge

劈开的 cleavable

劈开面 cleavage plane

劈开黏结的热轧叠板 【压】parting

劈理(晶体的) cleavage

劈裂 split, cleavage, crocodiling, split crack [end] (轧材缺陷)

劈裂试验 split [cleavage] test ◇ 巴西~ Brazil splitting test

劈裂丝 spelly wire

劈面构造 【金】cleavage structure

劈头(轧件的) 【压】pulling-down

劈形电解槽 electrolytic wedge tank

噼啪声响(电弧的) 【电】sputter

毗邻 neighbo(u)r

疲劳 fatigue ◇ 低周期[低循环次数]~【金】low-cycle fatigue, 接触~ contact fatigue, 耐~[抗~]剂 antifatigue, 新月形~痕 fatigue crescents

疲劳比 fatigue [endurance] ratio

疲劳变形 fatigue deformation

疲劳程度 degree of fatigue

疲劳持久极限 fatigue endurance limit

疲劳点 fatigue point

疲劳电磁测定法 induflux method

疲劳断口 fatigue fracture

疲劳断裂 fatigue failure [fracture, breakdown], fracture in fatigue, repeated stress failure, endurance crack

疲劳断裂的循环次数 cycles-to-failure

疲劳断裂[破坏]面 surface of fatigue break

疲劳范围 fatigue range

疲劳腐蚀 fatigue corrosion

疲劳机理 mechanism of fatigue

疲劳极限 fatigue [endurance] limit, fatigue [point] endurance ◇ 残存的*, 低于~反复加载处理 understressing, 交变弯曲应力~*

疲劳极限值 fatigue value

疲劳抗力 fatigue resistance

疲劳理论 fatigue theory

疲劳裂纹 fatigue [endurance] crack, crack in fatigue ◇ 低循环周期~扩展*, 帕里斯~形成律*

疲劳裂纹扩展界限[门槛] threshold in fatigue crack propagation

疲劳耐力[耐久性] fatigue endurance, endurance in fatigue

疲劳破坏 fatigue breakdown, endurance failure

疲劳破坏应力 punishing stress

疲劳破裂 crack in fatigue, fracture by fatigue ◇ 氢致～*

疲劳起因 causes of fatigue

疲劳强度 fatigue strength [endurance, resistance, value], endurance strength ◇ N 次循环[循环次数为 N 条件下]的平均～*, 复合～*, 脉冲应力下～*

疲劳强度折算系数 fatigue strength reduction factor

疲劳缺口敏感性[灵敏度] fatigue notch sensitivity

疲劳缺口因数[因子] fatigue notch factor

疲劳容许范围 tolerance interval

疲劳蠕变 【金】exhaustion creep

疲劳试验 fatigue [durability] test(ing), repeated stress test ◇ 复合应力～*, 交变扭转～*, 两段[级]～ two step test, 普洛比特统计～ Probit test, 韦勒～ Woehler fatigue test

疲劳试验方法 fatigue test method

疲劳试验机 fatigue tester, fatigue testing machine [rig], repeated-stress (fatigue) testing machine ◇ 反复扭转～*, 黑格型～ Haigh machine, 申尼克～ Schenick machine, 旋转悬臂梁式～*, 直接应力～*, 轴向载荷～ axial fatigue machine

疲劳试验设备 fatigue rig

疲劳试验装置 fatigue test installation

疲劳试样 fatigue test piece [specimen]

疲劳寿命 fatigue life (time) ◇ 残存 p% 的～*, 固定～曲线图

疲劳损伤 fatigue damage ◇ 早期～*

疲劳特性 fatigue [endurance] characteristic, fatigue behaviour [property]

疲劳条痕的形成 formation of fatigue striations

疲劳现象 fatigue phenomenon

疲劳行为 fatigue behaviour

疲劳性能 fatigue property ◇ 定向～*

疲劳应力 fatigue stress

疲劳硬化 fatigue hardening

疲劳预裂纹 fatigue precracking

皮奥伯特滑移线 Piobert lines

皮奥伯特效应(冷轧、冷拉的) Piobert effect

皮尺 tape measure

皮带 belt (blt), strap ◇ 三角[V 形]～ wedge belt, 上料[装料]～【冶】charging belt

皮带称量计 belt balance

皮带秤 belt (extractor) weigher, weigh(ing) [scale] belt, belt conveyer scale, conveyer weightometer [scale], weighing conveyor ◇ 配料用～ dosing belt weigher

皮带秤式定量给料机 belt scale type constant feeder

皮带秤式给料机 belt weigh feeder

皮带传动 belt drive ◇ 塔形～轮 drive cone

皮带锤 belt [strap] hammer

皮带磁选机 【选】magnetic belt separator

皮带导(向)轮 belt guide pulley

皮带堆矿机 travel(l)ing stacker

皮带覆面层 belt cover

皮带刮板 belt scraper

皮带滚筒 belt roller

皮带护罩 belt guard

皮带滑动 creep

皮带滑移 belt slip

皮带机 (同"皮带运输机")

皮带机除尘器 belt cleaner

皮带机清理器 belt plow

皮带(机)通廊 conveyer gallery ◇ 单线～*, 双线～*

皮带机尾轮 conveyer tail drum

皮带机卸料刮刀 belt plow

皮带机转运站 conveyer transfer point

皮带扣 belt fastener [hook], buckle, alligator

皮带轮 pulley, belt pulley [wheel, sheave]

◇ 拼合 ~ split pulley, 平面 ~ flat faced pulley, 三角[Ｖ形] ~ V-pulley, 实心[整体] ~ solid belt pulley, 直辐 ~ straight-armed pulley, 锥形 ~ cone pulley

皮带轮式混合机 belt shredder
皮带落锤 belt drop hammer
皮带磨床 (同"带式磨床")
皮带跑偏 belt slip [tracking]
皮带清理器 belt scraper
皮带清扫器[清理装置] belt cleaning device
皮带上料高炉 belt charged blast furnace
皮带式取样器 conveyer-type sampler
皮带输送机尾轮 conveyer tail drum
皮带速度 conveyer speed
皮带研磨机 belt lapper
皮带(运输,输送)机 belt (conveyer), belt type conveyer, band conveyer, conveyer belt ◇ 带卸料小车的 ~ tripper conveyer, 固定式 ~ *, 环形 ~ endless belt, 集料 ~ *, 进料 ~ entry belt, 可逆式 ~ *, 离心 ~ thrower belt conveyer, 连接[转接] ~ connecting conveyer, 铺料[布料] ~ distributing conveyer, 倾斜 ~ inclined belt conveyer, 取料 ~ reclaim belt, 散料 ~ spillage conveyer, 上料 ~【团】charging conveyer, 上行 ~ *, 枢轴式 ~ pivoted conveyer, 梭式 ~ *, 下吸式单板 ~ *, 装车 ~ loading conveyer
皮带运输机上料 conveyer belt charging
皮带张紧轮 belt stretching roller, tension pulley
皮带张紧装置 belt tightener
皮带助卷机 belt wrapper, wrapping machine ◇ 复式 ~ double belt wrapper, 立式 ~ *, 伸缩式 ~ *, 悬臂式 ~ *
皮带助卷机胶带 belt wrapper rubber belt
皮带装料式炉 belt filled furnace
皮垫圈[垫片] leather gasket, leather packing washer
皮尔格式冷轧管 cold pilgered pipe
皮尔格式无缝管轧机 Pilger seamless-tube mill
皮尔格缩管法【压】Pilger tube-reducing process
皮尔格头【压】Pilger bell end
皮尔格轧机 step-rolled mill
皮尔格周期式轧管 Pilgrim rolling
皮尔格周期式轧管法 Pilger process, Pilgrim rolling process
皮尔格周期式轧管机 Pilgrim mill
皮尔格周期式轧管机轧辊 Pilger roll
皮尔克耐热镍铬合金 Pirck's metal
皮尔勒斯高电阻镍铬合金 (78.5Ni, 16.5Cr, 3Fe, 2Mn) Peerless alloy
皮尔斯电子枪 Pierce gun
皮尔斯会聚电子枪 convergent Pierce gun
皮革轮抛光 bobbing
皮胶 hide glue
皮金蒸罐炉硅热还原炼镁法[皮金法] Pidgeon [ferrosilicon, silicothermic] process
皮凯型轮式皮带混合机【团】Pekay conveyor belt mixer, Pekay fluffer
皮考啉 picoline
皮拉尼差压[差示真空]计 differential Pirani gauge
皮拉尼真空计 Pirani (vacuum) gauge
皮罗特锌基轴承合金 (7.6Sn, 2.3Cu, 3.8Sb, 3Pb, 余量 Zn) Pierott's metal
皮密封垫[圈] leather packing washer
皮奇－克勒方程 Peach-Koehler equation
皮手风箱[皮老虎] (moulder's) bellows
皮托(流量)管 Pitot tube
皮托(压差)计 Pitometer
皮托压力计 Pitot pressure gauge
皮碗 (packing, seal) cup, leather packing (member), cup-type packing
皮下蜂窝气泡(钢锭的) peripheral blowhole
皮下裂纹【连铸】subsurface crack
皮下气孔 subsurface porosity
皮下气泡【钢】skin blowhole, subcutaneous blow holes ◇ 聚集 ~ pepper blister

皮下疏松	subsurface porosity
皮下针孔	【铸】subsurface pinholes
皮下注射(用)管材	hypodermic tubing
皮尤式铁水罐	Pug-type ladle
皮胀圈(填密件)	leather packing (member)
皮重	tare (weight)
皮兹	pieze (pz)
芘 $\{C_{16}H_{10}\}$	pyrene
芘醇	pyreno
芘基 $\{C_{16}H_9-\}$	pyrenyl
铍 $\{Be\}$	beryllium, berillium ◇ 电解～ electrolytic beryllium, 海绵～ beryllium sponge, 含～合金*
铍窗口(X-射线照相用)	beryllium window
铍肺病	berylliosis
铍粉	beryllium powder
铍钢	beryllium steel
铍合金	beryllium alloy
铍化物	beryllide
铍基合金	beryllium base alloy
铍金合金(0.5—5.0Be,余量 Au)	beryllium gold
铍金属	beryllium metal
铍金属间化合物	beryllides
铍矿	beryllium ore
铍矿床	beryllium deposit
铍矿物	beryllium mineral
铍砾	pebble of beryllium
铍榴石 $\{(Be, Mn, Fe, Zn)_7Si_3O_{12}S\}$	danalite
铍铝合金	beryllium aluminium alloy
铍镁晶石 $\{BeMgAl_4O_8\}$	taaffeite
铍密黄石 $\{Ca_8Be_3AlSi_8O_{28}(OH)_4H_2O\}$	aminoffite
铍镍合金(含 2.5Be)	beryllium nickel (alloy)
铍青铜(95.5Cu, 2.5Be)	beryllium bronze, Be-bronze ◇ 特罗达洛伊～*
铍石 $\{BeO\}$	bromellite
铍水碳钙钇矿	beryllium tengerite
铍酸钾 $\{K_2BeO_2\}$	potassium beryllate
铍酸钠 $\{Na_2BeO_2\}$	sodium beryllate
铍酸盐	beryllate
铍钽铌矿	arrhenite
铍添加合金	beryllium addition
铍铜电导合金	◇ 马洛里 73～*
铍铜(合金) (0.4—0.7 或 2—2.8Be)	beryllium copper (alloy)
铍微斜长石 $\{BeKAlSi_3O_8\}$	beryllium feldspar
铍盐	beryllium salt
铍银合金(0.41—0.9Be,余量 Ag)	beryllium silver
铍中毒	beryllium hazard
铍柱石	harstigite
苉 $\{C_{22}H_{14}\}$	picene
匹配	【电】matching, coupling ◇ 不～maladjustment
匹配放大器	matching amplifier
匹配线	match(ed) line
匹配相	coherency, coherent
匹配运算	matching operation
偏八辊轧机	M.K.W mill
偏钡铀云母 $\{Ba(UO_2)_2(PO_4)\cdot 8H_2O\}$	meta-uranocircite
偏铋酸	metabismuthic acid
偏差	deviation, offset, deflection, variance, variation, error, inaccuracy, out-of-balance ◇ 剩余～off-set
偏差放大器	error amplifier
偏差角	deviation angle
偏差调整楔(X射线测厚仪的)	deviation wedge
偏差源	aberrent source
偏差值	amount of deflection, deviate
偏磁化力	biasing magnetizing force
偏电压电子枪	bias gun
偏度计	deflectometer, deflection indicator
偏钒钙铀矿 $\{Ca(UO_2)V_2O_5\cdot n\ H_2O\}$ (n=5—7)	meta-tyuyamunite
偏钒酸	metavanadic acid
偏钒酸钠	sodium metavanadate

偏钒酸双氧铀[偏钒酸铀酰]｛UO$_2$(VO$_3$)$_2$｝ uranyl meta-vanadate
偏方三八面体 trapezohedron
偏感应 bias induction
偏高岭土 metakaolin
偏共晶反应 monotecto-eutectic reaction
偏共晶合金 monotectic alloy
偏共晶平衡图 monotectic equilibrium diagram
偏光 （同"偏振光"）
偏光高温计 polarizing pyrometer
偏光光度计 polarization photometer
偏光镜 Nicol('s) prism, polariscope
偏光性 polarity
偏光仪 polariscope
偏硅酸钠｛Na$_2$SiO$_3$｝ sodium metasilicate
偏硅酸盐 metasilicate, bisilicate
偏航计 yawmeter
偏极性 deflection polarity
偏角 deflection, declination, drift angle, angle off（等边角钢的）
偏角仪 declinometer
偏晶 monotectic (crystal)
偏晶点 monotectic point
偏晶反应 monotectic (reaction)
偏晶合金 monotectic alloy
偏晶平衡 monotectic equilibrium
偏晶体 monotectic (crystal)
偏晶温度 monotectic temperature [point]
偏聚 segregation ◇ 溶质原子向位错～, 原子～clustering
偏聚硬化 cluster hardening
偏口炉帽（转炉的）【钢】pear
偏口转炉 eccentric converter [vessel]
偏离 deviation, divergence, deflection, departure, off-setting
偏离定长 off-length
偏离分析 【化】off-analysis
偏离设计值 off-design
偏离轴心 disalignment
偏磷酸｛HPO$_3$｝ metaphosphoric acid
偏磷酸镧｛La(PO$_3$)$_3$｝ lanthanum metaphosphate
偏磷酸钐｛Sm(PO$_3$)$_3$｝ samaric metaphosphate
偏磷酸铈｛Ce(PO$_3$)$_3$｝ cerous metaphosphate
偏磷酸镱｛Yb$_2$(PO$_3$)$_3$｝ ytterbium metaphosphate
偏菱形 rhomboid(ity)
偏流 bias (current)
偏流计 bias meter, yawmeter
偏铝酸｛HAlO$_2$｝ meta-aluminic acid
偏铝酸钙｛Ca(AlO$_2$)$_2$, CaO·Al$_2$O$_3$｝ calcium metaaluminate
偏铝酸钠｛Na$_2$O·Al$_2$O$_3$｝ sodium metaaluminate
偏铝酸盐｛MAlO$_2$｝ meta-aluminate
偏镁磷铀云母｛Mg(UO$_2$)$_2$P$_2$O$_8$·8H$_2$O｝ meta-saleeite
偏摩尔溶解热焓 partial molar dissolution enthalpy change
偏铌酸盐 metaniobate
偏绕角 fleet angle
偏三角面体 scalenohedron
偏砷钡铀矿｛Ba(UO$_2$)$_2$(AsO$_4$)$_2$·n H$_2$O｝(n＜10) metaheinrichite
偏砷钴铀矿｛Co(UO$_2$)$_2$(AsO$_4$)$_2$·8H$_2$O｝ metakirschheimerite
偏砷酸 arsenic acid
偏砷酸铜 Air-Flo green
偏(水)砷钙铀矿｛Ca(UO$_2$)$_2$As$_2$O$_8$·n H$_2$O｝(n＜8) metauranospinite
偏水砷铜铀矿｛Cu(UO$_2$)$_2$As$_2$O$_8$·8H$_2$O｝ metazeunerite
偏水砷铀矿｛Fe$_2$(UO$_2$)$_2$(AsO$_4$)$_2$·n H$_2$O｝(n＜8) metakahlerite
偏水锡石 souxite
偏水柱铀矿｛UO$_3$·2H$_2$O｝ metaschoepite
偏钛酸钙｛CaTiO$_3$｝ calcium metatitanate
偏钛酸盐 metatitanate
偏铜铀云母｛Cu(UO$_2$)$_2$P$_2$O$_8$·8H$_2$O｝ metatorbernite
偏微分方程 partial differential equation

偏钨酸铵〔(NH$_4$)$_2$W$_4$O$_{13}$〕 ammonium metatungstate [metawolframate]

偏钨酸盐 metatungstate, metawolframate

偏析 segregation, macrosegregation, aliquation, liquate, liquation ◇ 表面～ surface segregation, 脆性～*, 锭边～【钢】L segregates, 方形～*, 滚动～ rolling segregation, 合金成分～【金】alloy segregation, 晶内～组织*, 气泡～ blow hole segregation, 外皮[表皮]～ skin segregate, 微区[次级]～*

偏析布料[上料] segregation feeding, (SF) segregated feed

偏析常数 segregation constant

偏析(程)度 【钢】degree of segregation

偏析带 segregated band, segregation band [streamer, zone], line of segregation, 【金】ghost band, phosphorus banding

偏析点 segregation spot

偏析反应(固态反应) monotectoid (reaction)

偏析区 segregation zone [spot], segregated spot, line of segregation

偏析曲线 segregation curve

偏析色痕 【金】ghost

偏析式烧结箱 segregated sinter box

偏析体 monotectoid

偏析物 【金】segregate

偏析系数 segregation coefficient

偏析线 segregation line

偏析抑制剂 segregation inhibiting agent

偏析指数 segregation index

偏析装料 segregation feeding

偏锡酸 metastannic acid

偏向 deviation, deflection, deflecting

偏向角 deviation angle

偏向力 deflecting force

偏向(频率)不稳定 swing

偏斜 deflection, inclination, tilt(ing)

偏心 eccentricity, off-center, running out

偏心齿轮 eccentric gear

偏心冲压机 eccentric punch

偏心传动 eccentric drive [gearing]

偏心底电弧炉 electric arc furnace with eccentric bottom tapping (EBT-EAF)

偏心度测量仪 eccentricity gauge ◇ 钢丝绳～*

偏心缸回转油泵 eccentric-cylinder rotary oil pump

偏心距 eccentricity

偏心(炉)底出钢 eccentric bottom tapping (EBT)

偏心炉底出钢电炉 【钢】eccentric bottom tapping electric furnace ◇ 高功率～(HP+EBT) EAF

偏心炉嘴(转炉的) eccentric nose section

偏心率[性] eccentricity

偏心率误差 eccentricity error

偏心轮 wobbler, eccentric wheel [sheave], camshaft gear

偏心轮杆 eccentric rod

偏心轮机构 eccentric gear

偏心轮轴 eccentric pivot

偏心螺旋[蜗杆]泵 eccenter-worm pump

偏心螺旋风口 【铁】eccentric spiral tuyere

偏心盘 eccentric disc

偏心皮带轮 eccentric sheave

偏心式泵 eccentric pump

偏心式电极 offset electrode

偏心式风口 【铁】eccentric tuyere

偏心(式)压(力)机 eccentric-type press, eccenter [cam] press

偏心受拉 eccentric tension

偏心受压 eccentric compression

偏心套筒 eccentric sleeve

偏心调节器 eccentric governor

偏心凸轮杠杆机构 【连铸】cam-and-lever mechanism

偏心异径管节 eccentric reducer (ER)

偏心载荷柱 eccentrically loaded column

偏心振动筛 eccentric vibrating screen

偏心轴 eccentric shaft

偏心轴衬 eccentric bush

偏心轴压砖机 eccentric-shaft press

偏压 bias (voltage) ◇ 加~使截止*，截止~ cut-off bias
偏压补偿式电压表 slide-back voltmeter
偏压场 biasing field
偏压电极 bias electrode
偏压检验试样 bias check sample
偏压控制电路 bias control circuit
偏压绕组 bias winding
偏压下(沿轧件宽度的) unequal draught
偏压整流放大器 bias rectifier amplifier (BRA)
偏压装置(射流技术的) bias device
偏亚锑酸 metaantimonous acid
偏亚砷酸 metaarsenous acid
偏移 shifting, off-set (branch), bias, drift
偏移场 biasing field
偏移磁通－电流回线 【理】incremental (biased) flux-current loop
偏移磁滞[滞后]回线 bias hysteresis loop
偏移频率 off-set [deviation] frequency
偏移误差 offset error
偏振 polarization ◇ 测~术 polarimetry, 消~镜 depolarizer, 锥光~仪 conoscope
偏振分光光度计 polarizing spectrophotometer
偏振辐射 polarized radiation
偏振光 polarized light ◇ 圆~*
偏振光反射法 polarized light reflection method
偏振光观察 polarized light observation
偏振(光)镜 polariscope, polaroscope, polarizer ◇ 测微~ micropolariscope, 平面~ plane polariscope
偏振光透射法 polarized light transmission method
偏振光显微镜 polarized light microscope, micropolariscope, polarization [polarizing] microscope
偏振光显微术 polarized light microscopy
偏振光显微照片[照相] polarized light micrograph
偏振光像 polarized light image

偏振光应力测定法 (同"极化光应力测定法")
偏振光照明 polarized (light) illumination
偏振光照明的 illuminated by polarized light
偏振计 polarimeter
偏振角 angle of polarization
偏振片 polarizer, polaroid
偏振(平)面 polarization plane, plane of polarization
偏振因数 polarization factor
偏振元件 polarizing element
偏振子 polaron
偏置 polarization, skewing, off-set, bias(ing), setover
偏置温度 bias temperature
偏轴伞齿轮 hypoid gear
偏柱轴矿{$UO_3 \cdot 2H_2O$} meta-schoepite
偏转 deflection, deviation, diversion, runout, diffraction (光线的), swing (指针的)
偏转阀门 deflecting gate
偏转法 deflection [deflecting] method
偏转极 deflecting electrode, deflector
偏转角 deflection angle
偏转聚焦 deflection focusing
偏转力 deflecting force
偏转散焦(作用) deflection defocusing
偏转矢量 deflection vector
偏转系统 deflection system
偏转线圈 deflection [deflecting] coil
偏最小二乘法 partial least square method
片 thin piece, slice, flake, leaf, sheet, table
片边(钢锭缺陷) fash ◇ 顶部~ top flash
片层范性流变 laminar plastic flow
片段 fragment
片阀 plate valve
片簧 leaf [flat] spring
片簧支架 spring leg
片间距离 lamellar spacing
片金 flake gold
片晶 platelet

片流 laminar current [flow], lamellar [streamline] flow
片落 scale off,【耐】exfoliation
片麻岩 gneiss
片数计数器 sheet counter
片岩 schist
片砖 split brick
片状 laminar, laminal, splinter form
片状边界层 laminar boundary layer
片状赤铁矿{Fe$_2$O$_3$} flag ore
片状单晶 flat crystal, platy monocrystal
片状断口 lamellar [flaky] fracture
片状粉粒 flake particle
片状粉末 flake(like) [lamellar] powder
片状共晶结构 lamellar eutectic structure
片状滑移 laminar slip
片状夹杂 flake inclusion
片状结构 flaky [laminated, schistose] structure
片状结晶[晶粒,晶体] tabular [plate-like] crystal, crystal plate
片状冷却器 stave cooler
片状铝粉 flake aluminum
片状铝粒 laminal aluminum particle
片状马氏体 【金】plate-type martensite
片状镍 flake nickel
片状缺陷 laminal defect
片状烧碱 caustic in flake
片状石墨 flaky [flake(d)] graphite, graphite flake,【钢】kish（自铁水析出的）
片状石墨奥氏体铸铁 flake graphite autenitic iron
片状石墨灰口铸铁 flake graphite gray iron
片状石墨铸铁 flaky graphite cast iron ◇准～*
片状石墨组织 flake graphite structure
片状试样 【钢】napkin
片状铁粉 flake iron powder
片状铁素体 lamellar ferrite
片状铜粉 flake copper

片状析出(物) 【金】lamellar precipitate
片状锡 flake tin
片状悬垂物 flapper
片状氧化物（金属内的缺陷） oxide platelet
片状炸药爆炸成形 sheet-charge forming
片状珠光体钢退火 lamellar annealing
片状组织 lamellar structure
片状组织组分 lamella constituent
片楣石 guarinite {3CaSiO$_3$[Ca(F,OH)]NaZrO$_3$}, hiortdahlite {4Ca(Si,Zr)·Na$_2$ZrOF}

飘尘 flyash, floating dust
飘悬焙烧 shower roasting
飘悬焙烧法 suspension roasting process, flash roast
飘悬焙烧炉 suspension [flash] roaster
漂白土 fuller's earth
漂白黏土 bleaching clay
漂动 wandering
漂浮 float, buoy
漂浮试验（沥青稠度测定法） float test
漂石 boulder, bowlder
漂铜 drift copper
漂洗 rinse, rinsing
漂洗槽 rinse tank [box, vat]
漂洗辊装置 dunking roll unit
漂洗器 rinse box
漂洗水 rinsing water
漂洗作业线 rinsing line
漂芯 【铸】core floating [raise], floating core
漂移 drift, shift(ing), swing, wandering
漂移电流 【半】drift current
漂移电子 wandering electron
漂移功率 drift power
漂移基线 drifting baseline
漂移流动 drift flow
漂移迁移率 drift mobility
漂移速度 drift velocity
漂移作用 drift action
瓢曲 buckling, cobble,【压】（板材缺陷）

bulge,buckle ◇ 热～hot wave
瓢曲矫平　curve flattening
瓢曲试验机(钢板的)　bulging test machine
瓢曲试验试样　【压】bulging test specimen
撇除(浮渣)　【冶】rake-off
撇除滤饼[渣]　cake removing
撇浮渣勺　【色】bowl skimmer
撇沫装置　float skimming device
撇取浮渣　skim
撇油器　oil skimmer ◇ 带式～belt [strip] skimmer
撇渣　drossing, scumming, skim, (slag) skimming,slagging off [out] ◇ 锑～antimony skimmings
撇渣暗冒口浇注系统　【铸】riser-gating
撇渣板　【冶】beater,【色】skimming plate
撇渣棒　slag skimmer
撇渣操作　【色】dross operation
撇渣挡板　skimming gate
撇渣端　skimming end
撇渣工具　skimming tool
撇渣辊　【铸】skimmer bar
撇渣锅　dross(ing) kettle
撇渣口　【冶】skim(mer) gate, skimming bay
撇渣炉　dross furnace
撇渣门　drossing [skimming] door, skim(mer) gate
撇渣器　slag separator [skimmer], dross extractor,skimmer,skimming chamber ◇ 贝克～【铁】Baker dam, 碟形～dish skimmer, 多孔～perforated skimmer, 基林～*
撇渣器沙坝　【铁】level weir
撇渣器小坝　【铁】dam
撇渣桶　skimming ladle
撇渣凸块　【铸】skim bob
撇渣装置　skimmer arrangement, skimming device
拼合齿轮　split gear
拼合管　split tube

拼合截面(铆接或焊接)　fabricated section
拼合轮　parting pulley
拼合螺母　split nut
拼合模　split [composite] die
拼合母模　split master die
拼合坯料　composite billet
拼合皮带轮　split pulley
拼合砂箱　bolted moulding box
拼合石墨管　split graphite-pipe [tube]
拼合石墨管电阻炉　split cylinder type graphite resistor furnace
拼合石墨管顶部加热器　split graphite-pipe top heater
拼合钨管加热器　split tungsten (tube) heater
拼合芯棒　split core rod
拼合型芯　【铸】sectional die
拼合压模　segment die
拼接板　joint lie, splice plate
拼接桁架　【建】joggle truss
拼接梁　joggle beam
拼卷作业线　【压】coil build-up line
拼写　transliterate
拼装结构　section(al) construction
频带　frequency band [range],band (pass)
频带宽度　frequency bandwidth, band [frequency] width,breadth of wavelength band
频带能量面　【理】energy surface of band
频带展宽[扩展]　band spread
频道　frequency channel
频繁开动　jogging
频分多路传输　【电】frequency division multiplexing (FDM)
频率　frequency, periodicity ◇ 工业用电～commercial frequency
频率倍减　frequency demultiplication
频率表　frequency meter
频率波动[起伏]　frequency fluctuation
频率测定　frequency measurement
频率传感器　frequency transmitter [sen-

sor]

频率多边形 【数】frequency polygon
频率范围 frequency range
频率分布 frequency distribution
频率分布表 【企】frequency table
频率计 frequency meter (freq.m.), cymometer, cycle counter
频率继电器 frequency relay
频率控制 frequency control
频率偏移 frequency drift [shift, deviation],【半】creep
频率曲线 frequency curve
频率扫描 frequency scanning [sweeping]
频率失真 frequency distortion
频率特性 frequency characteristic, (frequency) response
频率特性观测仪[描绘器] frequency character viewer, genescope
频率特性曲线 frequency characteristic (curve)
频率调节器 frequency regulator
频率调制 frequency modulation (FM)
频率跳动 wobbulation
频率稳定(性) frequency stabilization
频率响应 frequency response
频率响应特性(曲线) frequency response characteristic
频率因数 frequency factor
频率振动器 frequency vibrator
频率－直流电压变换器 frequency-DC voltage converter
频率指示器 frequency indicator
频率滞后 frequency hysteresis
频率转子转换器 frequency rotor converter
频率装置 frequency device
频率组分 frequency component
频率组合 group frequency
频谱 frequency spectrum, spectrum (复数 spectra)
频谱发射率 spectral emissivity
频谱反射系数 spectral reflection factor
频谱分析 spectrum [frequency] analysis
频谱分析器 (frequency) spectrum analyser
频谱灵敏度 spectral sensitivity
频谱响应 spectral response
频谱仪 frequency spectrograph, spectrometer
频散 (frequency) dispersion
频闪 stroboflash
频闪测速器[仪] strobotach
频闪观测仪[器] strobo(scope)
频闪效应 stroboscopic effect
频闪照明 strobe illumination
频移 frequency shift [deviation] ◇ 多普勒～ Doppler shift
频域分析器 frequency domain analyser
频振器 frequency vibrator
贫放热型气体 lean exogas
贫铬 chromium depletion
贫铬的 impoverished in chromium
贫化 dilution, depletion, impoverishment, degrading ◇ 使～ impoverish
贫化层(矿床的) depletion layer
贫化极限 lean limit
贫化剂 leaning agent
贫化浸染矿 deaf ore
贫化矿(经处理的) barren ore
贫化矿浆 depleted [barren] pulp
贫化矿石 halvans
贫化区 depletion region, depleted [denuded] zone (固体溶液的)
贫化燃料 depleted fuel
贫化物质 depleted [leaning] material
贫(化)铀 depleted uranium
贫混合燃料 lean mixture
贫混合物 lean [weak] mixture
贫混凝土 lean concrete
贫精矿 lean concentrate
贫矿 low-grade ore (LGO), poor [lean] ore, dradge ◇ 含大量废石的～ halvings
贫矿床 low-grade deposit
贫矿带 【采】depleted zone

贫矿炉料　lean ore burden
贫煤　lean [meagre, carbonaceous] coal
贫煤气　poor gas
贫煤气主[总]管　lean gas main
贫铅矿石　keckle-meckle
贫铅银矿石　dry ore
贫燃料混合物　lean mixture
贫溶液　【色】lean solution
贫石灰　lean [meagre] lime
贫铁晶粒　iron-deficient grain
贫铁矿还原法　◇ 约翰森～Johansen's process
贫铁菱镁矿　low-iron magnesite
贫吸热型气体　lean endogas
贫锡焊料　【焊】poor solder
贫锌　zinc depletion
贫(型)砂　【铸】weak sand
贫焰　lean flame
贫氧化矿　oxide-bearing lower-grade iron ore（指铁矿）
贫液　depleted [lean, barren] solution, lean [barren] liquor
贫溢流　【色】barren discharge
贫铀残渣　U-depleted residue
贫油(脱除粗苯的洗油)　lean oil
贫渣　lean slag
贫(装)料　【冶】lean burden
品位　grade, tenor ◇ 截止～ cut-off grade, 提高～ grading up, up-grading, 最低可获利～ minimum payable grade
品位降低　downgrading
品位下限　cut-off grade
品质　quality
品质系数　factor of merit
品质因数　quality factor (QF), Q-value
品质因素　【电】Q-factor
品种　variety, assortment
苹果酸　｛$HO_2CCHOHCH_2CO_2H$｝　malic acid
苹绿泥石　amesite
平凹透镜　plano-concave lens
平板玻璃　plate [sheet] glass
平板车　platform wagon [trailer], dilly, flatcar, flatbed, lorry（铁路的）
平板冲孔机　plate-punching machine
平板焊接　plate welding
平板荷载试验(地基用)　plate-load test
平板架型步进梁[动梁]　【压】pallet-type walking beam
平板劳厄相机　flat film Laue type camera
平板链　flat link chain
平板式加热电炉　【电】hot plate
平板条　flat bar
平板凸轮　plate cam
平板箱形孔型　(同"平面孔型")
平板运输机　crocodile ◇ 倾斜式～*
平板运输机齿　crocodile's teeth
平板(照)相机　flat cassette [film, plate] camera, flat [film] camera ◇ 带测角头的～ flat plate goniometer camera
平板振捣器　vibrating board
平板振动器　plate vibrator
平板砖　bearer block, quarry
平板桩　flat type piling bar
平板状氧化铝　tabular alumina
平背模型　flat back (pattern)
平玻璃照明器　plane glass illuminator
平铲　plain-back shovel
平锤　planing [planishing, plane-bottom, polishing, slogging] hammer, flatter (hammer)（锻造用）
平锤头　flat die
平捣锤　【铸】flat rammer
平底杯突(深冲试验的)　flat bottomed cup (FBC)
平底车箱　gondola car
平底船　gondola, flat-bottomed vessel
平底锤　plane-bottom hammer
平底坩埚　flat bottomed crucible
平底钢轨　flat bottom rail, flange rail
平底孔型　flat pass
平底矿仓　flat bottom bin
平底扩孔钻头　counterbored nozzle bore
平底离子交换槽　flat bottom exchanger

cell
平底料仓　flat bottom bin
平底炉　flat bottom(ed) furnace, hearth furnace
平底烧瓶　flat bottomed flask
平底塔盘　flat bottomed tray
平底铜坩埚　flat copper hearth
平地机　blade machine, grader
平顶　flat roof, flattop
平顶角焊缝　mitre (fillet) weld, flat [faced] fillet weld
平顶特性(曲线的)　flat characteristic
平动　(同"平移运动")
平动滑移　translational slip
平动周期　translation period
平硐　adit
平硐口　adit opening
平锻　【压】flattening
平锻锤　blacksmith flatter hammer
平断口　flat [plane, platy] fracture
平方法则　square rule
平方反比定律　inverse-square law, law of inverse squares
平方反比引力　inverse square attraction
平方律检波器　square-law detector
平房　single-story building
平放锭料(区域熔炼的)　horizontal charge
平放石墨管热压炉　(同"卧式石墨管热压炉")
平分面　bisector, bisectrix
平分线[物]　bisector, bisection
平复激的　flat compounded
平复激发电机　flat compound generator
平拱　flat [jack] arch
平箍钢　flat hoop iron
平罐(炼锌的)　【色】horizontal retort
平罐炼锌　zinc horizontal retorting
平罐炼锌蒸馏炉　zinc horizontal retort furnace
平光锤　smoothing hammer
平辊　【压】flat [plain(-barrelled)] roll
平辊身　straight barrel

平辊型(圆柱形轧辊辊身)　parallel roll profile
平辊轧制　flat
平焊　downhand (welding), flat (position) welding ◇ 对接~",斜头~"
平焊道工艺　flat bead technique
平焊对接接头　downhand butt joint
平焊焊缝　downhand [flat, underhand] weld
平焊焊条　downhand electrode
平焊位置　downhand [flat] position
平夯　【建】flat rammer
平衡　balance (bal.), equilibrium, equibalance, counterbalance, poise ◇ CO~(高炉煤气的)CO balance, 不[失去]~out-of-balance
平衡半径　equilibrium radius
平衡饱和度　equilibrium saturation
平衡比率　equilibrium ratio
平衡臂　balance [balancing] arm
平衡边界法　balanced boundary method
平衡表　balance sheet (B.S., B/S, b.s.)
平衡仓　surge bin ◇ 给料~feed surge bin
平衡测量　balance measurement
平衡产出[产额]　equilibrium yield
平衡常数　equilibrium constant
平衡成分(相的)　equilibrium composition
平衡锤　counterbalance, counterweight, balancing bob (料钟的) ◇ 带~的升降炉门 counterweighted door lift-type
平衡锤固定装置　【压】counterweight lathe
平衡锤坑　counterweight pits
平衡磁强计[地磁仪]　【理】balance magnetometer
平衡次序　【电】equilibrium order
平衡催化剂　equilibrium catalyst
平衡单元　equilibrium [balancing] unit
平衡点　equilibrium [break-even] point, point of equilibrium
平衡电池　balancing battery
平衡电解液　balanced electrolyte solution

平衡电流	balanced [circulating] current
平衡电路	balanced [balancing] circuit
平衡电桥	balanced bridge
平衡电位[势]	equilibrium potential
平衡阀	balanced (gate) valve
平衡砝码	balance weight
平衡法	【电】balanced method
平衡反应	equilibrium [balanced] reaction
平衡方程	equilibrium equation
平衡分布	equilibrium distribution
平衡负载	balanced load
平衡杆	balance beam, balancing arm, crossbeam, equalizing bar
平衡杆式量规	balanced beam gauge
平衡钢锭	balanced ingot
平衡杠杆	counterbalance lever
平衡固溶度	equilibrium solid solubility
平衡罐	surge tank, compensator
平衡过程	equilibrium process
平衡焊接程序	balanced welding (sequence)
平衡环	gimbal
平衡混合物	equilibrium mixture
平衡机	balance [balancing] machine, equilibrator
平衡级	【电】equilibrium order [stage]
平衡剂(氧化还原反应的缓冲剂)	poiser, poising agent
平衡继电器	balanced relay
平衡间距	equilibrium spacing
平衡减震器	balancing bumper
平衡界面层	equilibrium boundary layer
平衡距离	equilibrium distance
平衡离子	【理】counter-ion
平衡力	balance force, counter poise
平衡力偶	balancing couple
平衡料仓	feed surge bin
平衡流动	equilibrium flow
平衡滤波[滤光]器(X射线的)	(X-rays) balanced filter
平衡门	balance gate
平衡能级	equilibrium (energy) level
平衡凝固	equilibrium freezing
平衡浓度	equilibrium concentration (eq. concn), steady state concentration
平衡配筋率	【建】balanced steel ratio
平衡偏析	equilibrium segregation
平衡起重机	balance crane
平衡器	balancer, equalizer, neutralizer, balance beam
平衡曲线	equilibrium (curve, line), equilibria, profile of equilibrium
平衡溶液	balance solution, poising solution (氧化还原缓冲溶液)
平衡绳	balance rope
平衡湿度[水分]	equilibrium moisture, equilibrium water content
平衡试验	balanced test
平衡式电位[势]计	balance type potentiometer
平衡式滚锥轴承	balanced taper roller bearing
平衡试验机	balance [balancing] machine, balancer
平衡数据	equilibrium data
平衡速率	【金】equilibrium rate
平衡弹簧	balancing spring
平衡碳	available carbon
平衡条件	equilibrium condition
平衡调整	balance control [adjustment], 【企】equilibrium order
平衡图	equilibrium (diagram), phase [state, stable, structural] diagram, equilibria, 【金】metallurgical equilibrium diagram ◇复合~【金】double diagram
平衡网络	balanced [balacing] network
平衡位置	equilibrium position
平衡卫板	balanced guard
平衡温度	equilibrium [reversion] temperature
平衡线圈	balancing coil
平衡相	equilibrium phase
平衡相间连线	tie line
平衡相图	equilibrium phase diagram

平衡相组织　equilibrium phase structure
平衡型芯　【铸】balanced core
平衡压力　equilibrium pressure, counter-pressure
平衡压力吹管　balanced pressure torch
平衡有序度　equilibrium degree of order
平衡运转(无跳动,无颤动)　balanced running
平衡闸阀　balanced gate valve
平衡蒸汽压　equilibrium vapour pressrue
平衡直径　equilibrium diameter
平衡值　equilibrium value
平衡重锤[重量]　balance [balancing, counter] weight
平衡重锤式蓄势[蓄力]器　balance weight type accumulator
平衡装置　balancing device [equipment], equilibrium unit, balancer
平衡状态　equilibrium state [conditions], equibalance, balanced [poised] state
平衡状态图　equilibrium state diagram ◇ 假想～*
平衡状态下有序化曲线　curve of equilibrium order
平衡组织　equilibrium structure
平衡作用　balancing [poising] action
平滑　smoothing, smoothness
平滑表面　smooth surface
平滑电路　smoothing circuit
平滑端(管材的)　plain end
平滑断口　smooth fracture
平滑辊式破碎机　【耐】smooth roll crusher
平滑晶面　smooth crystal face
平滑连续曲线　smooth continuous line
平滑流　smooth flow
平滑滤波器　smoothing filter
平滑面砌砖工程　fairfaced brickwork
平滑凝固　smooth freezing
平滑曲线　smooth curve
平滑调节变阻器　【电】continuous rheostat
平滑线圈　smoothing coil
平环链　flat link chain, block chain

平缓的　gradual
平缓梯度　flat gradient
平活套　horizontal looper
平基斯铜合金　Pinkus metal
平挤压模　flat extrusion die
平键　flat key
平铰链　flat [plate] hinge
平角焊　flat fillet welding
平接　flat junction, butted joint
平接盖板　butt strap
平接头　flat junction
平截面　plane section
平界面　planar interface
平晶　(同"平面晶体")
平静凝固　【钢】smooth solidification
平均半衰期　【理】mean half life
平均比表面积　mean specific surface
平均比热　mean [average] specific heat
平均产量　average production [make]
平均长度　average length (av.l.), length average (L.A.)
平均成分　average analysis [assay, composition], mean composition
平均尺寸[大小]　mean size
平均抽力　mean drought
平均初次出故障时间　mean-time-to-failure
平均传输率　【电】average transmission rate
平均单位(轧制)压力　mean unit (rou) pressure ◇ 金属对轧辊～*
平均点阵参数(由 X 射线确定)　average X-ray lattice parameter
平均电压降　average potential drop
平均端面积法　average end area method
平均法　averaging [statistical] method
平均分配　equipartition
平均粉粒密度　average particle density
平均风量　average wind
平均概差[或然误差]　mean probable error
平均故障间隔[平均稳定]时间　【计】

mean time between failures (MTBF)
平均故障率 failure rate (FR)
平均海平面 mean sea level (MSL)
平均含尘浓度 average dust concentration
平均厚度[高度](轧件的) mean height of material
平均化合价 average valence
平均火道温度 average flue temperature
平均焦距 mid-focal length
平均卷重 average coil weight
平均孔径 average pore size
平均离子活度系数 mean ionic activity coefficient
平均粒度 average (particle) size, mean particle size, average grading ◇布莱恩~测定法 Blaine method
平均粒径[粒度] average [mean] particle diameter, particle-size average
平均流变应力 mean flow stress
平均流量 average flow
平均每日交通量 average daily traffic (A.D.T.)
平均磨蚀深度 mean depth of erosion
平均摩尔比热 mean molal specific heat
平均能级 mean (energy) level
平均疲劳寿命 median fatigue life
平均疲劳应力 mean fatigue stress
平均偏差 mean deviation
平均侵蚀率 average erosion rate
平均取数时间 average access time
平均热容 mean heat capacity
平均日产量 【企】average daily production
平均溶质浓度 mean solute concentration
平均蠕变速率 【金】average rate of creep
平均深度 average depth (a.d.), depth average (DA.)
平均渗透率 W-index
平均渗[穿]透深度 mean depth of penetration
平均生产率 average output, efficiency average
平均试车行程 average-test-car run
平均试样 average sample
平均寿命 average life (period), average lifetime, mean life
平均数 average, mean, media
平均水平面 mean level (ML.)
平均速度 average [mean] velocity, moderate speed (m.s.)
平均塑性阻力 mean plastic resistance
平均梯度 average gradient
平均体膨胀系数 average coefficient of cubical expansion
平均调节[调整] average adjustment (av.adj.)
平均停机[故障,休风]时间 mean down time (M.D.T.)
平均温差 average [mean] temperature difference
平均无故障[时间] mean time to failure (MTTF), mean free error time
平均误差 average [mean] error
平均吸收系数 mean absorption coefficient [factor]
平均系数 mid-coefficient
平均线 average [mean] line
平均线膨胀系数 average coefficient of linear expansion
平均相对偏差 mean relative deviation
平均相对位移 mean relative displacement
平均小时工资 average-earned rate, average hourly earnings
平均效果[效应] average effect
平均效率 average efficiency (av.eff.)
平均修复时间 mean time to repair (MT-TR), mean repair time
平均延伸量 mean elongation
平均延伸系数 mean coefficient of elongation
平均应变 mean strain
平均应力 mean stress
平均有效压力 mean effective pressure (m.e.p.)
平均有效值 root mean square value

(R.M.S.), mean effective value
平均有效指示压力　indicated mean effective pressure
平均原子序(数)　effective atomic number
平均原子序数为Z的元素　average-Z element
平均运距　average haul (distance)
平均运算时间　【计】average calculating operation time
平均轧制压力　average roll pressure
平均振动能　mean energy of vibration
平均直径　mean diameter
平均值　average (value), mean (value), general average (GA) ◇ 对时间的～ time-average
平均指示压力　mean indicated pressure (M.I.P., m.i.p.)
平均致命剂量　median lethal dose (MLD)
平均质量水平标准　average quality level (aql)
平均轴　mean axis
平均昼夜产量　【企】average daily production
平均转折点　break-even point
平均自由程　mean free path
平孔型　[压]plain barrel pass
平立法孔型设计　(同"弯折法孔型设计")
平-立辊万能[平-立式]轧机　【压】HV (horizontal vertical) mill
平-立轧制法　flat and edge method
平料板　[团]cut-off plate [bar], striking plate, strike off plate
平流层　stratosphere
平流冷却器　horizontal flow cooler
平流热效　advection
平炉　【钢】open hearth (OH), OH (open-hearth) furnace, (Siemens-) Martin furnace ◇ 塔尔伯特～连续炼钢法
平炉车间　open-hearth shop [plant], Siemens-Martin plant
平炉钢　open-hearth (furnace) steel, martin (siemens) steel, SM (Siemens-Martin) steel
平炉精炼　open-hearth refining
平炉炼钢法　open-hearth (furnace) process, open-hearth (steelmaking) process, S.M. (Siemens-Martin) Process, Siemens process
平炉生铁　open-hearth pig iron
平路机　blader, (road) grader, bullgrader
平螺旋　flat spiral objects
平煤　【焦】setting off
平煤杆　level(l)er, level(l)ing bar
平煤机　level(l)ing machine
平煤器　level(l)er
平煤小门(焦炉的)　level(l)er door
平面　plane (surface), flat, large face (砖的)
平面边界　plane boundary
平面变形　plane deformation
平面标高　mean level (ML., M.L.)
平面波　plane wave
平面布置　plane layout [array]
平面布置图　lay-out plan
平面布置总图　floor [key] plan
平面槽式分配器　【冶】flat ruffle
平面层流射流　plane laminar jet
平面齿轮　face gear
平面导板　flat [level] guide
平面导轨　flat rail [guide]
平面电子束　sheet beam
平面度　flatness, planeness
平面反射器　planar [plane] reflector
平面隔板　plane baffle
平面股钢丝绳　flattened strand wire rope
平面规　planometer
平面滚圈　plain tyre
平面极化[偏振]　【理】plane polarization
平面间距　interplane distance, planar spacing
平面交叉　grade [level] crossing
平面晶体　plane crystal
平面晶体单色器　plane-crystal [flat-crys-

tal] monochromator, plane monochromator crystal
平面晶体管　planar (type) transistor
平面孔型(初轧辊的)　【压】bullhead
平面溜槽　plain chute
平面流　two-dimensional flow
平面炉栅　flat grate
平面模型　two-dimensional model
平面磨床　surface grinder
平面磨削　【机】(flat) surface grinding
平面排列　plane array
平面皮带轮　flat faced pulley
平面偏振辐射　plane-polarized radiation
平面偏振光　plane-polarized light
平面偏振光镜　plane polariscope
平面生长　planar growth
平面视图　plan view
平面试样　test plate
平面束(电子束)　sheet beam
平面双导轨　flat double guides
平面体系　two-dimensional system
平面图　plan (view), plane figure ◇施工组织设计～【建】construction plan
平面弯曲度试验(钢板的)　camber test
平面形变区　field of plane deformation
平面形状　plan view pattern
平面形状控制　plan view pattern control
平面压印[精压]　flat coining
平面压应变试验　plain-strain compression test
平面衍射光栅　plane diffraction grating
平面应变　plane strain
平面-应变断裂韧性　plane-strain fracture toughness
平面应变条件[状态]　plane-strain condition
平面应变应力状态　plane strain stress state
平面应力　biaxial stress
平面应力理论　theory of plane stress
平面应力状态　plane stress state
平面阵列　two-dimensional array

平面指数　indices of plane
平面族　family of planes
平模　flat (faced) die, (flat-) face die
平模浇铸　horizontal mould casting
平模挤压筒　【压】flat ended container, square-end container
平盘蛇管　plate coil
平皮带　flat [straight] belt
平剖图　profile in plan
平铺　layering
平铺矿堆　bedding pile
平铺料　bedding
平铺直[斜]取　【铁】stacking and reclaiming
平奇贝克八五黄铜(含5—15Zn的α黄铜)　Pinchbeck
平齐装料[装粉](指装模)　flush level powder fill, flush filling
平砌层　flat course
平砌砖　brick laid on flat
平砌砖层　course on flat
平锹　plain-back shovel
平切口　square end
平曲线　horizontal curve
平色调照相底片(负片)　【理】flat (faint) negative
平式炉顶　flat arch
平锁板　parallel lock plate
平台　platform, dock, floor, stage, terrace (高炉料面的)
平台式屋顶　deck roof
平台拖车　flat platform trailer
平坦　even, flat, smooth ◇不～的 rugged
平坦部分　flat
平坦范围[区域]　flat region
平坦拱　depressed arch
平填角焊缝　smooth fillet weld
平头　flat head, plain end
平头搭接　plain lap joint
平头大铁钉　holdfast
平头捣锤　【铸】flask rammer
平头倒棱机(钢管用)　end-facing/cham-

fering machine
平头电极(接触焊的) pad electrode
平头钉 flat headed nail, clout nail
平头端 【焊】butt end
平头对(焊)接 plain butt joint
平头机 end-facing machine ◇ 焊管~*
平头剪 【机】snips
平头接合 flush joint
平头连接 square joint
平头螺钉[螺丝] flat head screw, grub screw
平头螺栓[插销] flush bolt
平头铆钉 flat head rivet, flush rivet
平头砂舂 【铸】flat [butt, flask] rammer
平凸透镜 plano-convex lens
平椭圆 flat oval
平纹金属丝网 plain
平稳流化床 quiescent fluidized bed
平稳凝固 【钢】smooth solidification
平稳性 smoothness
平线圈卷取机 pancake oiler
平巷 mine tunnel, gallery (Gal)
平斜端砖 end-skew on flat
平行 parallel ◇ 使~parallelizing
平行柏氏矢量 parallel Burgers vector
平行磁化(强度) parallel magnetization
平行导轨 parallel guides
平行度 parallelism
平行段(拉模或冲模的) parallel land
平行反应 parallel reaction
平行缝焊 parallel seam welding
平行缝焊机 parallel seam sealing machine
平行缝隙系统 ◇ 索勒~*
平行辐射 parallel radiation
平行光管 collimater, collimator, tube diaphragm
平行滑移面 parallel slip plane
平行加料纵横[正交]流动区域精炼炉 parallel feed cross-flow refiner
平行剪(切机) parallel shears
平行剪切 flat cut
平行进料 parallel feed(ing)
平行卷筒式牵引轮 parallel drum type capstan
平行孔过滤器 parallel pore filter
平行粒子流 parallel flux
平行流 parallel flux, cocurrent flow
平行流干燥机 parallel flow dryer
平行螺型位错 parallel screw dislocation
平行面 parallel plane
平行捻钢丝绳 parallel [equal] laid wire rope
平行排列[配置] parallel arrangement
平行刃型位错 parallel edge dislocation
平行射束 parallel beam ◇ 准直~*
平行生长 parallel growth
平行四边形 parallelogram
平行四边形氧气切割机 【焊】oxygraph
平行位错 parallel dislocation
平行弦桁架 trussed beam
平行线 parallel (lines)
平行线布置(出铁场铁路的) parallel track arrangement
平行线族 family of mutually parallel lines
平行性 parallelism
平行轴 parallel axes
平行轴承 parallel bearing
平行自旋取向 【理】parallel spin orientation
平行作业 parallel operation
平叶片 flat blade
平液容器 level(l)ing vessel
平移 translation, advection
平移点阵[晶格] translational lattice
平移对称 translational symmetry
平移晶格群 translation group
平移(位)能 translational energy
平移要素 element of translation
平移运动 translational [translatory] movement, translation
平移周期 translation period
平移轴 translational axis
平圆拱 diminished [hance] arch
平圆镘子 【铸】slicker spoon

平圆镘刀 【铸】heart and square trowel
平轧道次 flat pass
平轧法 beam roughing method
平轧－立轧孔型 slab and edging pass
平整(板、带材的) 【压】level(l)ing, flattening, pinch (pass) rolling, skin (pass) rolling, temper (pass) rolling, temper (强化钢板表层), killing (小压下量轧制), iron out ◇ 冷轧～cold rolled temper
平整薄板 planished sheet
平整冲压 flattening stamping
平整道次 planishing [temper, skin, pinch] pass
平整的成卷带材 temper-rolled coil
平整度 flatness, temper grade, planeness
平整度测量装置 temper grade measuring device
平整[直]度检验 flatness inspection
平整断口 even fracture
平整－防折轧机(带钢的) temper and anti-fluting-mill
平整和二次冷轧机 temper and DCR mill
平整机(板或带材的) level(1)ing machine, level(1)er, planishing [temper] mill, planisher, skin (pass) mill, pinch pass mill ◇ 复[双]二辊式～unit-temper mill, 热～hot leveller, 双机架～组 twin stand temper mill
平整机座 planishing [dressing] stand, temper mill, planisher
平整冷轧的薄板 temper-rolled sheet
平整压下量调节 skin pass rolling degree regulation
平整轧辊 smooth roll
平整轧制 temper-rolling, skin pass rolling ◇ 湿式～装置*
平整作用 level(1)ing action
平直 straightness ◇ 使～flatten
平直度 flatness, straightness
平直度测量与控制 flatness measurement and control (FMC)
平直度试验 flatness test
平直度测量与控制系统 flatness measurement and control system
平直钢板(矫直后的) flat sheet
平直模壁(指钢锭模) flat wall
平嘴夹钳(锻工用) straight-tip tongs
瓶 bottle (bot.), jar, flask ◇ 莱顿～【理】Leyden jar
瓶颈(地区) bottleneck
瓶颈式路 bottleneck road
瓶口(式)锭模 bottle top mould, semi-closed top (S.C.T.) mould
瓶式布料器 bottle distributor
瓶装气 bottled [cylinder] gas
评定 evaluation, assessment, judge, appraisal
评定试棒 【铸】arbitration bar
评估 estimation
评价 appreciation, valuation, survey, assess, estimate
评价过低 undervaluation
评论 comment, review (rev.)
评述 review (rev.), commentary
屏 screen (scr.), panel, curtain, board
屏板电池(组) anode battery
屏蔽 shield(ing), screen, mask, curtain ◇ γ射线～gamma shield, 电晕放电～corona shield, 非～源 free source
屏蔽材料 shielding material
屏蔽磁极电动机 shaded-pole motor
屏蔽导线 shielded conductor [wire]
屏蔽电弧 shielded arc
屏蔽电缆 shielded [screened] cable ◇ H型～H-type cable, 双芯～
屏蔽度 degree of shielding
屏蔽隔板 shield separator
屏蔽盒 shielded box
屏蔽胶片 screen film
屏蔽介质 shielding medium
屏蔽膜 screen film [plate]
屏蔽能力 screening capacity
屏蔽透镜 screen lens
屏蔽线 shielded wire [line]

屏蔽型 X 射线胶片	screen(-type) X-ray film
屏蔽(原子)核	shielded nucleus
屏蔽作用	shielding [screening] action
屏极	plate (electrode), anode
屏极功率输入	plate power input
屏极过热	target overheating
屏极输出器	anode follower
屏极效率	plate efficiency
屏幕	screen
屏幕录像机	kinescope recorder
屏色调	screen tint
屏余辉时间	screen afterglow time
屏障	barrier
坡道	ramp(way), descent, gradient, slope, sloping skid, 【压】downward slope
坡顶屋架	pitched truss
坡度	(falling) gradient, slope, inclination, batter ◇ 填挖平衡的～balanced grade
坡度变更点	【运】break in grade
坡度差	difference in gradients
坡度角	slope [gradient] angle
坡度仪	grading instrument, gradiometer
坡口	【焊】groove, bevelled ends ◇ J形～, K形～, U形～预加工 U-preparation, X形～double V groove, 焊缝背面～backing groove, 开～, 施焊部位～修整 welding V, 未填满～
坡口高度	groove depth
坡口焊(接)	groove welding ◇ 喇叭形～flare (bevel) welding
坡口焊(接)缝	bevel (groove) weld, groove-welded joint
坡口焊接头	bevel groove joint
坡口加工	chamfering
坡口加工面	prepared edge
坡口加工用双头割炬	double head burner [blowpipe] for edge preparation
坡口角度	groove angle, angle of preparation [vee]
坡口面	groove [bevel, fusion] face
坡缕石	mountain cork
坡面	batter, dome (结晶的)
坡莫菲高导磁(镍铁)合金(20Fe,80Ni)	Permafy
坡莫合金	permalloy, permeability alloy ◇ 高电阻～resist permalloy, 理想～Idealoy
坡莫合金薄膜	thin permalloy film
坡莫合金粉	permalloy powder ◇ 压制～
钷合金	promethium alloy
钷基合金	promethium base alloy
钷添加合金	promethium addition
破边(薄板或带钢缺陷)	edge damage
破产	bankruptcy
破断	fracture, rupture
破断机理	fracture mechanism
破断极限	rupture limit
破断抗力	resistance to breakage
破断裂纹	failure crack
破断临界应力	critical stress for fracture
破断强度	rupture strength
破断试验	rupture test
破断试验机	breaking machine
破断试验用带缺口试样	notch-break specimen
破断寿命	rupture life
破断位置	position of fracture
破断因素	breaking factor
破断应力	fracture stress
破断应力密度比	fracture stress/density ratio
破断载荷	rupturing load
破坏	destroy, damage, destruction, disruption, failure, breakage, breakdown, breakup, collapse
破坏电压	breakdown [disintegration] voltage
破坏[裂]面	rupture plane, plane of fracture
破坏强度	collapsing strength, cracking [cheek] resistance
破坏试验载荷	test-failure load
破坏性存储器	【计】destructive storage

破坏性读出	【计】destructive read
破坏性检验	destruction test, destructive examination
破坏性检验法	destructive testing method
破坏(性)试验	destructive [breakdown] test, testing to destruction
破坏应力	(同"断裂应力")
破坏载荷[荷载]	breaking [failure, crippling, collapse] load
破坏中心	centre of attack
破记录浇注	(指连铸时间) record cast
破浪堤	wave breaker
破裂	fracture, rupture, cracking, disruption, break (away), breakage, burst(ing), collapse, shivering, clink (钢锭缺陷),【金】puffing ◇ 氢致~*,易~的 cracky, 与时间有关的~ time-dependent collapse
破裂点	point of fracture [rupture]
破裂负载	crushing load
破裂角	angle of rupture
破裂敏感的	crack-sensitive
破裂敏感性	crack sensitivity
破裂模数	modulus of rupture
破裂强度	rupture [disruptive] strength ◇ 持久~*
破裂趋势	tendency to crack(ing) [fracture]
破裂试验	collapse [burst] test ◇ H形切槽拘束~*
破裂速率	(腐蚀破裂的) cracking rate
破裂特性	fracturing behavior
破裂危险(率)	risk-of-failure
破裂位置	point of rupture
破裂形式	【金】fracture mode
破裂延伸	(蠕变试样的) creep ductility
破裂应力	collapsing stress
破裂作用	disruptive action
破鳞	scale breaking
破鳞辊	descaler [breaker, crimping, descaling, scale-breaking] roll ◇ 粗轧~*,精轧~*
破鳞机	(同"除鳞机")
破鳞轧制	spellerizing, roll knobbling
破碎	break(ing), crush(ing), size reduction, spalling (矿石的),【冶】scrape out (熔渣的) ◇ 闭路~*,不易~的 unbreakable, 二次~*,干式~ dry crushing, 手工~ hand crushing, 四次~ quaternary crushing, 循环式~ cycle crushing, 预先~ preliminary crushing
破碎比	reduction ratio (Rr), ratio of crushing
破碎锤	breaking [granulating] hammer
破碎多孔质材料	crushed porous solids
破碎方法	method of size reduction
破碎废钢铁	【铁】fragmented scrap
破碎负荷	(磨矿机的) tumbling charge
破碎钢粉	crushed steels, crushed steel particle
破碎工段	crushing area [section]
破碎工序	crushing operation
破碎辊	crushing roll ◇ 焦炭~ coke cutting wheel
破碎辊齿数	number of breaker teeth
破碎机	crushing machine [mill], crusher (mill), breaker (bkr), breaking machine, cracker, knapping machine, shredder ◇ 齿辊式~ toothed roll crusher, 冲击式~*,锤式~*,粗碎圆锥~ coarse cone crusher, 大块~ chunkbreaker, 单辊~*,短头~*,对辊~*,鳄式~ alligator, 反击式~ baffle crusher, 复式~ duplex breaker, 辊式~*,环辊~ ring-roll crusher, 回转筛筒~ rotary breaker, 锯齿形~ saw-tooth crusher, 两段~ two-stage crusher, 平滑辊式~*,三段~ tertiary crusher, 湿式~ wet crusher, 手摇~ hand-crusher, 双辊~ double crusher, 特尔史密斯~(偏旋式) Telsmith crusher, 西门式~ Symons crusher, 细碎~ fine crusher, 旋回(圆锥)~*,叶轮式~*,一段~ single crusher, 圆锥(锥形)~*,中间~ intermediate crusher, 重力~ gravity

crusher,撞击式～impact breaker
破碎机齿辊轴 【团】disintegrator [crusher] shaft
破碎机齿片 crushing disc
破碎机颚板 crusher jaw
破碎机房 crusher house
破碎机颊板 cheek plate
破碎机斜槽 crusher chute
破碎机站 crusher station
破碎间 【选】crushing room
破碎块度 breaking size
破碎力学 crushing mechanics
破碎面(圆锥破碎机的) crushing concaves
破碎能力 crushing capacity
破碎排出物 crusher discharge
破碎熔渣 crushed slag
破碎筛分厂 crushing-screening facilities
破碎筛分机[设备] crushing-screening facilities,crusher-screen
破碎筛分室 crushing and screening house
破碎烧结矿 crushed sinter
破碎设备 crushing equipment [appliance, facilities]
破碎特性[性状] crushing behaviour
破碎铁粉 crushed irons
破碎头 crushing [breaking] head
破碎物 broken piece
破碎系数 size ratio,ratio of size reduction
破碎效率 crushing efficiency
破碎压力机 crushing press
破碎指数 breakdown index
破碎铸铁粉 crushed cast irons
破碎装置 crushing device
破碎锥(圆锥破碎机的) crushing cone
破碎作用 crushing effect
破损 damage, failure ◇ 不～检验 bulk inspection,不易～的 unbreakable
破损浓度 damage concentration
破损应变 damage strain
破土 break ground
破屑机 chip breaker

破渣凿[錾]子 slag chipper
珀金锡青铜(76—80Cu,20—24Sn) Perking brass
珀罗克斯焦炉气催化氧化脱硫法 Perox process
珀迈特耐蚀铝硅合金(0—5Cu,1.5—7.5Si,0—1Fe,0—0.4Mg,余量 Al) Permite Aluminium alloy
珀内尔高碳钢全贝氏体热处理法 Purnell process
珀诺特平炉 【钢】Pernot furnace
珀缪泰特 A 强碱性阴离子交换树脂 Permutit A
珀缪泰特 B 强碱性阴离子交换树脂 Permutit B
珀缪泰特 H-70 羧酸阳离子交换树脂 Permutit H-70
珀缪泰特 Q 磺化聚苯乙烯阳离子交换树脂 Permutit Q
珀缪泰特 S-1 强碱性阴离子交换树脂 Permutit S-1
珀缪泰特 W 弱碱性阴离子交换树脂 Permutit W
剖面 section,profile,cut(away),section(al) plane
剖面测试 cross-sectional testing
剖面射线照相术 sectional radiography
剖面图 section(al) drawing [view], section, sectional elevation, cutaway (section,view)
剖面系数 modulus of section
剖面线 cross hatching
剖切铁心 C(cut) core
剖视图 cross-section [cut-open] view, cutaway drawing [view]
剖视组织 phantom structure
铺板 floor plates,pallet,apron ◇ 机架间～sheet between stands
铺板托梁 fish plate
铺边料 【团】side layer (material), side wall layer ◇ 拦板全高～full side layer
铺边料槽 side layer container

铺边料溜槽 side layer chute
铺草地面 【建】grassed surface
铺底 bedding, relayering ◇ 石块～ bottoming
铺底料 bottom [bed(ding)] layer, hearth layer material,【团】bed ◇ 分层～ bedding of furnace, 天然～
铺底料部分[粒级度] hearth layer fraction
铺底料[矿]槽 bedding bin, bedding layer container, hearth layer hopper
铺底料层 hearth layer
铺底料给料皮带机 hearth layer feed belt
铺底料给料器 hearth layer feeder
铺底料给料系统 hearth layer feed(ing) system
铺底料给料闸门 hearth layer gate
铺底料溜槽闸门 hearth layer chute gate
铺底料透气性(带式烧结机的) bed porosity
铺底料准备 hearth layer preparation
铺底铺边料布料器 hearth and side layer feeder
铺底铺边料槽 hearth and side layer bin
铺轨机[工] track layer
铺矿机 【铁】stacker
铺沥青(路面) black top(ping)
铺料 bedding, laying ◇ 分层～ bedding out, 悬臂～机 boom stacker, 移动式～机 travel(l)ing stacker
铺料皮带机 distributing conveyer
铺料器 laying head
铺料式卷线机 laying reel
铺路机 paver, pavior ◇ 混凝土～ concrete paver
铺路块木 wood block
铺面 pavement, revetment
铺面材料 paving
铺砌 paving ◇ 防冲～ downstream apron
铺砌层 pavement
铺砌工 paver
铺砂 sanding, gritting

铺设 lay(ing), placing ◇ 炉用～物 furnace skid
铺设梁(冷床的) fish plate
铺瓦圬工 【建】tile masonry
铺屋面 roofing
铺展(火焰的) spread-out
葡萄糖 $|C_5H_{11}O_5CHO|$ glucose, dextrose
葡萄碲矿 xocomecatlite
葡萄状的 botryoidal
镤合金 protactinium alloy
镤基合金 protactinium base alloy
镤添加合金 protactinium additive alloy
普遍沉淀[析出] general precipitation
普遍化状态方程 【数】generalized equation of state
普遍模糊(底片的) general fog
普遍性 universality
普遍优惠 general(ized) preferences
普遍优惠制 Generalized System of Preferences (GSP)
普查 general investigation, (general) survey, reconnaissance
普拉蒂纳金铂合金(10—12Pt) platina
普拉斯蒂隆渗碳模具钢 Plastiron
普拉斯塔洛依塑料模具钢(0.1C) Plastalloy
普拉斯特阳极黄铜(80—90Cu,余量 Zn;电镀用) Plaster's brass
普拉特-洛伊热浸镀用铅基合金(2.5Sn,2Sb,余量 Pb) Plate-Loy
普拉特纳姆耐蚀阀座合金(55Ni,10—12Sn,余量 Cu) Platnam, Platnum
普拉提奈尔热电偶用铂合金 Platinel
普拉提奈特玻璃焊封合金(49Ni,51Fe;) Platinite
普拉提诺金铂合金(11Pt,余量 Au) Platino
普拉提诺依德铜锌镍电阻合金 Platinoid (Platinoid M; 60Cu, 24Zn, 14Ni, 2W)
普拉提诺依德铜锌镍焊料(47Cu, 42Zn, 11Ni) Platinoid solder
普拉廷白铜[高锌黄铜](57Zn,余量 Cu)

Platine

普拉依马克斯层压木板－铝板复合材料 Plymax

普莱克希丙烯[耐热]有机玻璃 Plexiglas(s)

普朗克常数 Planck's constant

普朗克定律 Planck's law

普朗尼闸式测功器 Prony brake

普雷米乌姆高速合金 Premium high speed alloy

普雷斯塔尔超塑性铅铝合金 Prestal

普里斯(电镀)硫酸铜浸液试验 Preece test

普利铁 perlit

普龙布索尔焊锡[银锡软钎料](3Ag,余量 Sn) Plumbsol

普卢姆赖特低锌[红(色)]黄铜(85Cu, 15Zn) Plumrite

普鲁拉梅尔特不锈钢复合钢板 pluramelt

普鲁拉梅尔特(电渣)复合金属法 【钢】 pluramelt process

普罗费竖炉生产海绵铁法 Purofer process

普罗利特钨钛硬质合金(3—15Co,3—15TiC,余量 WC 及少量其他碳化物) Prolite

普罗马尔高强度铸铁 Promal

普罗米修含铝六七黄铜(67Cu,30Zn,3Al) Promethium alloy

普罗佩兹式(线材)连续轧机 Properzi continuous casting and rolling mill

普罗佩兹液态拉丝法 Properzi process

普罗普拉提纳镍铋银合金(装饰用) Proplatina

普罗塔尔铝表面防腐蚀化学处理法 Protal process

普洛比统计疲劳试验 Probit test

普洛特快速疲劳试验 Prot test

普培式万能钢梁轧机 【压】 Puppe mill

普适气体常数 【理】 universal gas constant

普碳钢 (同"普通碳素钢")

普通操作法 conventional operation

普通敞口式格砖砌筑 conventional open checkerwork setting

普通淬火油 conventional quenching oil

普通带式烧结机 【团】 conventional strand

普通弹壳黄铜(63—70Cu,余量 Zn) basic quality brass

普通导板 conventional guide

普通德拜－谢乐照相机 conventional Debye-Scherrer camera

普通等级 ordinary quality, common grade

普通低碳钢 ordinary low-carbon steel

普通电镀锡薄钢板 straight electrolytic plate

普通定时淬火 simple time quenching

普通锻造 normal forging

普通二进制 【计】 ordinary [normal, regular] binary

普通翻斗料车 conventional skip car

普通刚玉 common corundum

普通钢 common [ordinary, tonnage, unalloyed] steel, commercial metal

普通钢锭模铸锭 【钢】 normal ingot making

普通钢丝绳 bright [black] wire rope

普通高铜黄铜(66Cu,34Zn) common high brass

普通工程 general engineering

普通工具钢 ordinary tool steel

普通公路 average highway

普通管轧机 tubular mill

普通光辊轧制 plain rolling

普通光亮光洁度 regular bright finish

普通光学显微镜 ordinary light [optical] microscope

普通焊料[焊药] common solder

普通焊条 plain-type electrode

普通合金钢 ordinary alloyed steel

普通厚锡层镀锡薄钢板(平均锡层重量为 0.91kg/基准箱) common charcoal tinplate

普通化合物 simple compound

普通化学 general chemistry

普通黄铁矿{FeS$_2$}　common iron pyrite
普通黄铜　plain brass, basis brass (61.5—64Cu, 余量 Zn), common [market] brass (65Cu)
普通灰口铁　ordinary quality gray iron
普通混凝土　【建】normal concrete
普通碱性钢　plain basic steel
普通角闪石{(OH)$_2$·Ca$_2$(Mg, Fe)$_4$·(Si$_6$Al$_2$)O$_{22}$}　hornblende
普通结构　conventional construction
普通(结构)轧机　conventional mill
普通金属　common metal
普通控制轧制　common control rolling (CCR)
普通框式芯盒　plain frame core box
普通铝热剂　plain thermit
普通铝氧[矾土]　common alumina
普通模铸　【钢】conventional ingot teeming, orthodox casting
普通耐酸砖　acid-proof normal brick
普通黏结剂　common bond
普通捻(钢丝绳的逆捻、交互捻、交叉捻)　ordinary [regular, cross] lay, crossing
普通捻钢丝绳　regular lay wire rope, non spinning wire rope, reverse laid rope
普通起重机式浇包　plain crane truck ladle
普通切削钢　ordinary cutting steel
普通切应变增量　increment of ordinary shear strain
普通青铜　commercial bronze
普通球团　normal pellet
普通热(浸)镀锌　conventional galvanizing
普通热轧板卷　dry hot rolled coil
普通软钎焊合金(50Sn, 50Pb)　common solder
普通烧结法　conventional sintering
普通生丝微菌　Hyphomicrobium vulgare
普通生铁　common iron, regular pig
普通十字形辊模头　plain turks head
普通四辊轧机　plain four-high rolling mill
普通水　ordinary [light] water
普通水缝式结晶器　【连铸】normal water cooling type mold
普通酸洗　plain pickle finish
普通酸性转炉铁　standard Bessemer iron
普通弹性力学　ordinary elasticity
普(通)碳(素)钢　plain (carbon) steel, simple steel, straight carbon steel
普通碳素钢铸造[铸件]　normal steel casting
普通碳素工具钢　plain carbon tool steel
普通天平　ordinary balance
普通铁矿石　conventional-grade iron ore
普通无色玻璃　plain glass
普通显微镜　ordinary microscope
普通型(钢包)　orthodox type
普通研磨　conventional grinding
普通阳极结构　conventional anode structure
普通冶金(学)　general metallurgy (GM)
普通元素　common element
普通圆钢　smooth bar
普通直接电弧炉　air-type directric-arc electric furnace
普通中空氧矛切割　plain tube lancing
普通轴承　plain [journal] bearing
普通铸钢　normal steel casting
普通砖　common [stock] brick
普通转炉　common converter
普通转速放映法　time lapse technique
浦项钢铁公司(韩国)　Pohang Iron and Steel Corp. (POSCO)
谱　spectrum (复数 spectra)
谱带宽度　spectral band width
谱缝[隙]宽度　spectral slit width
谱级　【理】order of spectrum, spectrum level
谱级分离器　order-sorter
谱片放大机　spectro-projector
谱强度　spectral intensity
谱图　spectrogram
谱线　spectrum [spectral] line
谱线对　line pair
谱线对称增宽　symmetrical line broaden-

谱线分叉 doubling of line
谱线畸变 (arc) line distortion
谱线宽度 spectral line [arc] breadth, line breadth
谱线轮廓[形状] spectral line profile
谱线密度 spectral density
谱线强度 spectral line intensity
谱线位移[移动] spectral line displacement [shift], line shift
谱线展宽[增宽,加宽] line broadening ◇ 对~的影响 contribution to line broadening, 非对称~*
谱线总增宽(度) total line broadening
谱仪管(质谱仪检漏器的) spectrometer tube
蹼状晶体 web crystal ◇ 枝状生长的~*
曝光 exposure, bombardment ◇ 不适当[不充分]~ inadequate exposure, 慢性~ chronic exposure, 轻微~ light exposure, 通过劈~ wedged exposure, 未~胶片 raw film, 无屏蔽~ no-screen exposure, 照相乳胶的~时限*
曝光表[计] exposuremeter, exposure scale, actinometer
曝光不足 underexposure, inadequate exposure
曝光不足照相底片(负片) faint negative
曝光范围 exposure range
曝光过度 overexposure, burn-up
曝光过度的 burned-up
曝光角 angle of exposure
曝光量 (amount of) exposure

曝光[露]时间 exposure time [period], length of exposure
曝光调节器 intervalometer
曝光系数 exposure factor
曝光源 source of exposure
曝光指数 exposure index
曝光致模糊[雾翳](底片的) light fog
曝露 exposure
曝露站[台](大气腐蚀试验用) exposure station
曝气 【环】aeration ◇ 活性~ activated aeration, 阶段~法 step aeration method, 完全混合~系统*, 循环~槽*
曝气池 aeration basin [tank], aerotank, aerated lagoon
曝气滴滤池 aerated trickling filter
曝气浮选(法) dispersed-air flotation
曝气器 【焦】air-blast-apparatus ◇ 浅盘型焦炭~ coke tray aerator
曝气浅塘 aerated lagoon
曝气头 【焦】air-blast-head
曝气系数 aeration coefficient
曝气装置 aeration device, aerator ◇ 瀑布式~ waterfall aerator, 强制通风式~ forced-draught aerator, 叶轮式~ impeller aerator
曝晒蒸发 solar evaporation
曝晒蒸发器 solar evaporator
瀑布式浇注 cascade teeming
瀑布式铸锭法 【冶】cascade method for pouring ingot
瀑流速度 cascading speed
瀑落式(自)磨机 cascade mill
瀑落(运动) cascading

Q q

期货 futures, forward
期刊 journal, magazine, periodical
期望值 expected value
期限 time limit, allotted [due] time, duration
七氟锆酸铵 {(NH$_4$)$_3$ZrF$_7$} triammonium zirconium heptafluoride
七氟铪酸铵 {(NH$_4$)$_3$HfF$_7$} triammonium hafnium heptafluoride
七氟化物 heptaflouride
七氟络钽酸钾 （同"氟钽酸钾"）
七氟铌酸钾 {K$_2$NbF$_7$} potassium fluocolumbate [heptafluoniobate]
七氟铌酸盐 heptafluoniobate
七氟锆酸钾 （同"氟锆酸钾"）
七氟三铵盐 triammonium heptafluo-salt
七氟钽酸钾 {K$_2$[TaF$_7$]} potassium fluotantalate
七辊冷轧机 Y-mill
七机座成形[辊弯]机 seven-stand forming mill
七极管 heptode
七价的 heptavalent, septivalent
七O[七三,三七]黄铜（25—35Zn, 余量 Cu） standard [3:7, blue] brass ◇ 内根丁~*
七硫化二铼 {Re$_2$S$_7$} rhenium heptasulfide
七水胆矾 boothite
七水(合)硫酸亚铁（又称"绿矾"）{FeSO$_4$·7H$_2$O} green vitriol, copperas
七水(合)硫酸锌 （同"锌矾"）
七水铀矿 {2UO$_2$·7H$_2$O} lanthinite
七氧化二铼 {Re$_2$O$_7$} rhenium heptoxide
七氧化物蒸馏 heptoxide distillation
漆 paint, lacquer, varnish ◇ 示温~ heat indicating paint
漆包铝线 enamel insulated aluminium wire
漆包锰线 enamel manganin
漆包铜线 enamelled copper wire
漆包线 enamelled [lacquered, varnished] wire ◇ 纱包~*
漆布 varnished cloth
漆层 lacquer coating
漆层厚度计 painting film thickness meter
漆封 stop-off lacquer
漆面 lacquer finish
漆器 lacquer-ware
漆涂层 varnish coating, lacquer coat
其他损失 miscellaneous [unaccounted] losses
其余部分 balance
棋盘式荷载布置 checkerboard loading
棋盘式炉顶 checker board roof
棋盘式排列 checker, chequer
棋盘式排列的 checkered
棋盘式烧成铬镁砖和镁砖炉顶【钢】 fired chrome-magnesite/magnesite checkerboard roof
棋盘形图案 checkered pattern
棋式布置的 staggered
奇异贝日阿托氏菌 Beggiatoa mirabilis
奇(异)点【数】 singular point
奇异面 singular surface
奇异石 wonderstone
奇(异)线 line of singularity
歧管 manifold (branch) ◇ 进气~*, 吸气~ suction mainfold
歧管调节器 manifold regulator
歧化(作用) disproportionation ◇ 低价卤化物~*
歧化动力学 disproportion kinetics
歧化反应 disproportionation (reaction)
畦状位能场 furrowed field of potential energy
齐边带卷 flush wound coil
齐边钢板 universal steel plate
齐边控制 side register control ◇ 自动
齐边压力机（板坯的） (edge, slab) squeezer ◇ 初轧板坯~*

齐边轧制 【压】edging
齐边中厚钢板（万能轧机轧制的） universal (mill) plate
齐伯林铝合金 (7.8Zn, 0.45Fe, 0.37Si, 0.72Cu, 0.11Sn, 0.27Mn, 余量 Al) Zeppelin
齐布林向上堆积铸型铸造法 【铸】Zueblin process
齐恩锡基轴承合金 (99Sn, 0.7Pb, 0.3Cu) Zinn
齐尔坦锆碳化物烧结合金 Zirtan, Zirten
齐格罗荧光探伤器 Zyglo
齐格罗油浸荧光（物质）探伤法 Zyglo penetrant method
齐克拉尔高强度铝合金 (7—9Zn, 1.5—3Mg, 1—2Cu, <0.4Cr, 0.1—0.7Mn, 0.7Si, 余量 Al) Zicral
齐拉里特熔铸制品 【耐】Zilarit
齐勒非金属夹杂计量法 【钢】Zieler process
齐洛伊锻造用锌基合金 (0.75—1.25Cu, 0.007—0.02Mg, 0.05—0.12Pb, ≤0.015Fe, 0.005 Cd, 余量 Zn) Zilloy alloy
齐洛伊锌基合金瓦垄板 (1Cu, 0—0.025Mn, 0—0.8Cd, <0.1Mg, 少量 Pb, 余量 Zn) Zilloy
齐马尔锌基压铸合金 (4—4.3Al, 2.5—3.3Cu, <0.15Mn, <0.01Cd, <0.2Pb, 余量 Zn) Zimal
齐马利厄姆铝镁锌合金 (70—93Al, 4—11Mg, 3—20Zn) Zimalium
齐明镜 aplanat
齐纳（二极）管 Zener diode
齐纳峰 【金】Zener peak
齐纳结 zener junction ◇ 合金～*
齐斯康锌铝合金 (25—33Al, 67—75Zn) Ziskon, Ziscon
齐他相（ζ相） 【金】zeta phase
齐休姆高强度铝合金 (15Zn, 1—3Cu, 0—1Sn, 82—83Al) Zisium
齐整轧制（最初几道次的） squaring-up

旗(形)开关 (mechanical) flag switch, flag
旗形装置（行程开关的） flag arrangement
骑墙砖 carry-over sill
鳍片[状]管 finned tube
鳍式热交换器 finned type heat exchanger
起爆 detonation, initiation, ignition, firing, priming
起爆剂 primer, detonator, initiator
起爆检测器 priming detector
起爆器 exploder, initiator, blaster
起爆药 priming
起草 draughting
起层 aliquation
起尘的 dusty ◇ 不～nondusty
起尘性 dustiness
起初加热 initial heating
起唇钢轨 lipped rail
起磁（同"磁化"）◇ 电流～法 current flow method
起点 origin, starting point, zero
起点电容 zero capacity
起点读数 zero [null] reading
起点温度 temperature of start
起电 electrification
起电弧 electroarcing
起动 start-up, switch on, firing, initiation, priming（虹吸管）【计】enable ◇ 全电压～full voltage starting, 接触式～控制, 直接～line start, 自动～的 self running
起动按钮 start [initiate] button
起动变阻器 starting rheostat, rheostatic starter
起动柄 starting handle
起动电动机 starting [pony] motor
起动电流 starting [pick-up] current
起动电阻器 starting resistor
起动杆 starting [actuating] lever
起动工 【企】start-up man
起动功率 start power, starting duty
起动火苗 pilot flame

起 qi

起动开关　starting switch
起动控制　start-up control
起动力　motive [propelling] power
起动脉冲　drive [driving] pulse
起动能力　startability
起动器　starter, starting device ◇ 电动机～motor starter, 隔模式～*, 杠杆式～lever-type starter, 鼓形～drum starter, 手动～【电】hand starter
起动器箱　【电】starting box
起动绕组　starting winding
起动热损失　start-up thermal losses
起动烧嘴[起动喷嘴,起火燃烧器]　starting [start-up] burner
起动室　【机】priming chamber
起动液压缸（液压装置的）　hydraulic kicker cylinder
起动轴　actuation shaft
起动转[力]矩　starting torque
起动装置　starter, starting device [arrangement, gear, unit], actuating device
起阀器　valve lifter
起伏　fluctuation, undulation
起伏比　fluctuation ratio
起伏拨料爪　（同"送料爪"）
起伏原理　fluctuation theory
起伏运动　undulatory motion
起拱　arch camber, arching, rise of span
起拱层　springing course
起拱点　【建】impost, spring
起弧　arcing, flare up, 【焊】arc start（氩弧焊的）◇ 接触法[式]～*, 熔化式～*, 用辅助弧使焊弧～pilot-arc starting
起弧电流　arc [striking] current
起弧电压　arcing [arc-burning, (arc-)striking] voltage
起火　flaming
起火粉末　【粉】pyrophoric powder
起货桅杆　derrick
起痂　【铸】blind [expansion] scab
起裂纹　【钢】checking
起鳞　scaling, slabbing ◇ 表面层～【金】case spalling, 耐～能力 resistance to scaling

起鳞片　spalled slab
起鳞现象（氧化时的）【金】break away phenomenon
起鳞速率　scaling rate
起落架　(alighting) gear, undercarriage（飞机的）
起落式辊道　【压】collapsible table
起模　【铸】pattern draw, lift(ing of pattern) ◇ 木钉～draw peg
起模扳手　lifting key
起模板　draw [lifting] plate
起模棒　loosening bar
起模不良　poor draw
起模锤　rapping hammer
起模钉　draw nail
起模杆　lifting pin, lifter iron, jemmy
起模钩　lifting handle
起模机　pattern draw machine
起模螺钉　draw screw
起模器　ejector ◇ 手动杠杆式～hand lever pattern lift
起模胀砂　rappage
起模针　draw spike [bar], lifter iron, picker
起沫　frothing
起沫剂　frothing [sponging] agent
起沫性[能力]　frothing quality
起沫油　frothing oil
起沫装置　frothing unit
起泡　blistering, bubble (formation), foaming, frothing ◇ 防～剂 froth breaker
起泡层　bubbling bed
起泡点　bubble point
起泡度　frothability, foaminess
起泡法　【耐】foaming method
起泡腐蚀　blister corrosion
起泡剂　frothing [foaming, sponging] agent, foamer, frother
起泡金属　sparkle metal
起泡流化床　bubbling fluidized bed

起泡器 bubbler
起泡气体 effervescing gas
起泡熔炼 foam smelting
起泡试验（检查漏气用） bubble test
起泡涂层 blister coating
起泡温度 bubble point
起泡压力 bubble point pressure
起皮 【铸】crusting（浇铸时），sandbuckle（铸件缺陷）◇ 不～的 non-scaling, 涂料 ～ blacking scab
起偏振片 polaroid, polarizing plate
起氢气泡 hydrogen blistering
起始变形温度 initial deformation temperature
起始操作条件 initial operation conditions
起始地址 【计】initial address, origin
起始点 initial point（IP, i.p.）
起始垫块（电渣焊的） starting block
起始电流 starting [initial] current
起始电压 starting [initial, pick-up] voltage
起始反应 initial reaction
起始方位 initial orientation
起始化合物 starting compound
起始还原 initial reduction
起始记录 【计】home [initial] record
起始脉冲信号 【理】initial pulse indication
起始面积 original area
起始坯料 starting stock
起始偏差 initial deviation
起始倾斜 initial slope
起始燃烧温度 temperature of initial combustion（TIC）
起始蠕变 initial [primary] creep
起始蠕变速率 initial creep rate
起始烧结温度 temperature of beginning sintering, point of incipient sintering
起始条件 starting condition
起始小锻造比加工（红脆性钢的） nursing
起始斜度 initial slope
起始信号 initial signal

起始阴极电流密度 initial cathode current density
起始蒸发温度 initial vaporization temperature（i.v.t.）
起霜 frosting
起雾 haze formation
起型板 【铸】rapping plate
起焰 flare up
起源 origin, source, genesis
起重臂 jib (loading) boom, erector [gib] arm, cathead, outrigger
起重臂提升钢绳 boom hoist cable
起重车 carriage hoist, crane car, lift truck, mobile crane
起重磁盘 lifting magnet
起重吊钩 load hook, crampon
起重杆 mast
起重轨梁（机架旁的） overhead rail
起重横梁（安装机座） lifting beam
起重滑车 hoist block, hoisting tackle
起重机 crane (Cr.), elevator, lift(ing machine), lift, hoist ◇ 铲斗式～*, 磁力自卸～ magnet-clamshell crane, 船式［水上］～*, 单轨～*, 单梁～（single-）beam crane, 地行揭盖～*, 电磁(铁)［磁力，磁盘］～*, 电动～*, 兑铁水用～*, 浮筒～ floating crane, 钢绳～ rope hoist, 高架～*, 更换台车用～ pallet removal crane, 钩式～ hook type cran, 固定式～*, 轨道～ track [goliath] crane, 滑动式～ skid derrik, 机车～*, 加盖～【钢】capping crane, 巨型［强力，移动式大型］～ goliath crane, 卷扬～ hoisting crane, 缆索式～ cable crane, 链式［拉链］chain hoist, 料箱［料斗］～*, 龙门～*, 履带式～ caterpillar crane, 锚钩式走行～ grapnel traveling crane, 门式～ portal crane, 攀缘式～*, 平衡～ balance crane, 气动～ air hoist, 钳式［夹钳，带钳式抓取装置的］～*, 墙装［墙上］～ wall crane, 桥式～*, 轻便落地～ canton crane, 取料［～*, 人字～ derrick, 三脚～ gin, 输出

~*,双钩~ twin hook crane,双梁~ two-girder crane,双腿式~ bipod,水力~ water crane,水平~*,水压~ water lift,塔式~*,台座~ abutment crane,挺杆[动臂]~*,万能~ universal crane,桅杆式~ mast crane,小~ donkey crane,斜座~ angle crane,行走~ moving crane,悬臂(式)~*,旋臂[回转式]~*,旋转式~*,移动式~*,用~翻转(钢水包) crane tipping,运输~ transfer crane,蒸汽~*,重型~ heavy (duty) crane,爪式~ claw crane,crab,抓斗~*,转臂~ bracket swing crane,转柱(式)~*,装在汽车上的~ truck-mounted crane,自卸~ clamshell car

起重机大梁 crane [runway] girder
起重机大桥 crane bridge
起重机吊杆 crane mast
起重机吊钳 crane tongs
起重机钢丝绳 crane rope
起重机(工作)半径 crane radius
起重机工作极限 crane reach
起重机钩 crane hook
起重机轨(道) crane runway [rail, track]
起重机轨面标高 crane rail level
起重机缓冲器 crane buffer
起重机架 crane carriage
起重机驾驶室 operator's cage
起重机链 jack chain
起重机链拖索(拖木材用) jack chain
起重机梁 crane beam ◇ 重级~ heavy duty runway
起重机梁滑道 crane runway
起重机门形架 crane gantry
起重机能力 crane capacity
起重机起重高度 stroke of crane
起重机起重量 crane load
起重机起重能力 carrying [lifting] capacity of crane
起重机司机 crane driver [operator, runner], hoistman
起重机索 elevator rope
起重机索道 tramway
起重机小车 crane carb
起重机小车电动机 trolley motor
起重机行尽线 crane approach
起重机行走机构 crane travel(l)ing gear
起重机柱 crane column
起重机桁架 crane girder
起重(夹)钳 hoisting tongs ◇ 带卷~【压】coil tongs
起重架 elevator frame ◇ 安装用~ gin pole
起重绞车 lifting winch, crab
起重链 crane [elevating] chain
起重量 elevating capacity, crane load
起重螺杆 jack screw
起重能力 elevating [lifting] capacity, lifting power, crane output, carry
起重器 (lifting) jack ◇ 齿条传动~ rack-operated jack,电动~ electrical jack,横式~ sliding jack,螺旋~ lifting screw,气动~ air jack,手动~ hand jack,水力~ hydraulic jack
起重器轴 jack shaft
起重汽车 truck crane, crane truck
起重设备 lifter, lifting apparatus
起重索 load [sling] rope
起重桅杆 gin pole, pole derrick
起重箱 skip
起重小车 crab, trolley ◇ 料仓~平台*
起重爪 lewis
起重装置 lifting unit, derrick ◇ 锭料装炉~*
起铸 start-of-casting
起铸温度 start-of-casting temperature
企口板桩 grooved pile
企口槽【建】ribbet
企口接合[接头] grooved-and-tongued [tongued-and-grooved] joint, match joint
企口连接 grooving
企口型耐火砖 groove type refractory
企业 enterprise, venture
启动键 start [initiate] key

启动信号　start signal,[计]signal enabling
启炉盖机　[焦]lid lifter ◇ 电磁～ magnetic lid lifter
启(炉)门机　[焦]door-extracting machine,door extractor
启示　message
启通　[电]unblanking
启钥合同　turn-key contract
契约　contract,agreement,indent(ure)
砌衬材料　[冶]lining [facing] material
砌衬块体[物料]　[冶]lining mass
砌衬转炉　lined vessel
砌衬作业　lining work
砌道　causeway
砌拱垫块　camber slip
砌拱用楔形砖　end arch
砌拱支架　soffit scaffolding
砌合　[建]bond(ing) ◇ 丁砖与顺砖隔层～block bond,荷兰式～Dutch bond,犬牙式～dog tooth bond,英国式～English bond
砌合构造　bonded construction
砌合炉顶　bonded roof
砌合泥浆　bonding mortar
砌块　[建]block ◇ 大型～构造 block construction
砌炉　wall(ing) up,lay bricks ◇ 塔架式～机[钢]reline tower
砌炉衬　lining-up
砌炉衬砖　lay bricks
砌炉工　furnace builder
砌炉设备　lining facilities ◇ 车间～*
砌炉体　walling-up
砌面　[建]dressing
砌面板　shell [sheathing] plate
砌面石　ashlar masonry
砌面砖　facing brick
砌墙　walling
砌墙石　bonder
砌体　masonry work [envelope] ◇ 高炉～磨损检查*,填充～backfill(ing)
砌筑　[建]masonry

砌筑内衬作业　lining work
砌砖　bricking up,lay(ing) brick,masonry [neat] work,walling-up,brick overlapping ◇ 从内墙～overhand,挤浆～法 shove joint brickwork,炉腹～*,美国式～法 American bond,咬合～*,一层～bed
砌砖衬的钢包　brick lined ladle
砌砖工　bricklayer
砌砖工程　brick work (BWK),brick masonry ◇ 平滑面～fairfaced brickwork
砌砖工具　bricklaying tool
砌砖厚度　brickwork thickness
砌砖结构　brick construction
砌砖体[作业]　brickwork
器壁衬里　wall lining
器壁厚度　wall thickness
器材　facilities,apparatus,fittings,kit,material ◇ 重型～*
器具　implement(ation),furniture,ware
器械　implement,apparatus,tool,unit
气刨　scarfing,air-gouging,(gas) gouging
气刨边　scarfed edge
气泵　air pump
气泵机组　pump assembly
气波　air shock,wave
气操纵系统　air control system
气秤　pneumatic weigh cells
气窗　louver
气吹真空除气法(钢水内吹氩等)　[钢]purging gas degassing
气锤　air rammer [hammer],pneumatic hammer [gun]
气脆金属　(同"气敏金属")
气单胞菌属　Aeromonas
气弹(固定保温帽、发气冒口用)　[铸]gas producing charge
气刀(热镀锌的)　air knife
气刀调节行程　nozzle adjusting path
气刀镀层厚度控制装置　vapour die coating thickness control unit
气刀缝隙　nozzle gap

气 qi

气刀梁　nozzle beam
气刀式镀锌装置　nozzle-type galvanizing unit
气捣　pneumatic tamping
气道　air flue [passage] ◇ 砖格～ checker flue
气垫　air-cushion, air spring, gas cushion ◇ 可替换的～挡板
气垫车　air-cushion car
气垫冲压法　【压】air-pressure method
气垫船　air-cushion craft
气垫堆垛机　air float piler
气垫缝　air-cushion joint
气垫滑轮　hover pulley
气垫缓冲器　air-cushion shock absorber
气垫输送[运输]　air slide transport
气垫轴承　air-cushion bearing
气垫装置　air-cushioning device
气电（联合）焊接　arcogen, electrogas welding ◇ 磁性焊剂～*
气动泵　airlift pump
气动不接触式仪表　pneumatic noncontact gauge
气动测微计　air micrometer
气动冲压法　air-pressure method
气动传动装置　pneumatic actuator
气动－电动控制装置　pneumatic-electrical control device
气动顶出器（制品的）　air-operated kicker
气动顶料器　air-pusher ejector
气动垛板装置　air-operated stop
气动翻转造型机　air turn-over moulding machine
气动飞剪　air-operated flying shears
气动分选器　air-operated classifier
气动缸　（同"风动缸"）
气动滑阀　air slide
气动机械　pneumatic machinery
气动挤压法　process for pneumatic extrusion
气动夹钳[夹紧器]　pneumatic gripping
气动卷扬机　air hoist

气动控制器　pneumatic [air-operated] controller
气动控制系统　pneumatic control system
气动控制仪表　pneumatic control instrument
气动快速开启机构　air-operated quick opening mechanism
气动[气缸式]料钟卷扬机　【铁】pneumatic bell hoist
气动脉冲　air pulsing
气动铆枪　（同"风动铆枪"）
气动起重机　air hoist, pneumatic crane
气动起重器　air jack
气动倾卸车　air-dump car
气动式探测器　air-operated detector
气动推出机　air-actuated stripper
气动推料机　air cylinder pusher
气动压板　air-operated hold-down
气动圆盘闸　（同"风动圆盘闸"）
气动造型机　pneumatic moulding machine
气动震实式造型机　air jarring moulding machine
气动装置　pneumatically operated device
气动錾　pneumatic chisel
气阀　air [gas] valve, gas damper
气阀弹簧门　valve surge damper
气氛　atmosphere ◇ 科特雷耳～强化, 炉内～分析, 预制～ prepared atmosphere
气氛气体　atmosphere [atmospheric] gas
气氛调节[控制]　atmosphere control ◇ 炉子～
气粉射流　gas-particle jet
气封　gas [vapour] seal, 【铁】gas damper（大、小盖间空间的外壳）
气封风机　seal-air fan
气缸　(air) cylinder ◇ 夹紧～ clamping cylinder
气缸衬套　cylinder bushing [cup]
气缸垫　air cylinder cushion
气缸阀　cylinder valve
气缸盖　cylinder cover [cap, head]
气缸歧管　cylinder manifold

气缸塞 cylinder plug
气缸式泥炮 （同"柱塞式泥炮"）
气缸套 cylinder jacket
气缸体 cylinder block
气缸推力 cylinder force
气缸铸铁 cylinder iron
气缸组 cylinder block
气割 【焊】flame [gas] cut(ting), flame cut off, autogenous fusing（用乙炔）◇喷射式～嘴 injector-type cutter
气割穿孔 piercing by thermal cutting
气割工 flame cutting (torch) operator
气割机 gas cutter, gas cutting machine ◇多割[焰]嘴～*，龙门[桥架]式～ gantry cutting machine, 双柱～*, 异形轮廓～*
气割炬 gas(-cutting) torch
气割炬预热 torch preheating
气割器 gas cutter
气割区 【连铸】gas cutoff zone
气割烧把 gas cutter
气割速度 gas-cutting speed
气沟 air channel, channeling
气－固反应 gas-solid reaction
气－固反应过程 gas-solid process
气－固接触 gas-to-solid [gas/solid] contact
气－固接触效果 effectiveness of gas/solid contact
气－固传热［热传导］ gas-solid heat transfer
气－固相分界膜[面] gas-solid film
气－固（相）界面反应 gas-solid [solid-gas] interface reaction
气柜 air reservoir [collector], aerator tank, gas receiver
气焊 flame [acetylene, torch] welding, gas-welding, autogenous soldering ◇加压～*，全熔～*
气焊工 gas welder [solder], gas welding operator
气焊管 gas-welded pipe
气焊焊缝 gas weld

气焊焊料[焊药] blow pipe solder
气焊焊条 gas-welding rod ◇库菲尔～合金（99Cu,1Ag）Kufil
气焊火焰 gas-welding flame
气焊机 gas-welding machine ◇乙炔～ acetylene welding set
气焊机组 gas-welding outfit
气焊剂 gas welding flux
气焊接头[连接] gas-welded joint
气焊枪[炬] air torch, gas (welding) torch, gas jet ◇焊割两用～*
气焊枪阀 torch valve
气焊枪火焰检验 flame torch test
气焊枪气体压力 torch pressure
气焊枪预热 torch preheating
气焊热（量） gas-welding heat
气焊设备 gas-welding equipment
气黑 gas [carbon] black, micronex, Wyex
气候 climate, weather
气候条件 weather [climatic] conditions
气化（法） gasification, gasifying ◇加氧～ oxygen gasification, 悬浮状态下～ suspension gasification
气化冷却器 vapour cooler
气化率 rate of gasification
气化煤 gasified coal
气化模 【铸】gasifiable [gasified] pattern
气化器 gasificator, gasifier ◇鲁奇加气～*
气化渗镀 vapour plating
气化渗锌 vapour sherardizing
气化速率 gasification rate
气化脱硫 gasificating desulphurization
气化（物） vapo(u)r
气化冶金方法 vapometallurgical process
气化冶金(学) vapometallurgy
气化装置 gasifier
气化作用 gasification
气溅金属 wild metal
气焦（煤气厂副产） gas coke
气阱 gas pocket
气孔 gas (blow) hole [cavity, pocket],

(air) blowhole, air pocket [hole], bubble, pinhole, porosity, bleb (材料缺陷), clowhole (美), gas pore (小的),【冶】abscess (缺陷),【钢】skin hole,【铸】blows ◇ 包渣~˙, 大~ gross porosity, 宏观[颗粒间]~ macro pore, 排成线的~ line of pores, 形成~ bubbling,【冶】blistering (缺陷), 一次~˙

气孔度[率] porosity ◇ 表观~ apparent porosity, 隐~ closed porosity
气孔度测验器 porosity tester
气孔链 line of pores
气孔缺陷 gas unsoundness
气孔(缺陷)填焊 welding-up of blowholes
气孔烧合(高温下) sintering-out of cavities
气孔疏松(缺陷)【钢】gassiness
气孔数 pore number
气孔体积 volume of pores
气孔针 【铸】breather, prod
气孔直径 pore diameter
气控阀 air-operated valve
气控仪表 pneumatic control instrument
气浪 air shock [billow]
气冷钢 air cooled steel
气冷高炉炉渣 air-cooled blast furnace slag
气冷内孔窥视仪 【冶】gas-cooled borescope
气冷式引燃管 air-cooled ignitron
气力送样器 air slide conveyer
气量计 gas meter [gauge], gasometer, gassing gauge
气量瓶 gasometer flask
气流 gas flow [stream, current], air flow [current], fluent, (air) stream, jet ◇ 冷~粉碎法˙, 入窑[窑内]~ furnace air flow
气流冲击区 impact area of jet
气流床快速热解装置 airflow bed rapid pyrolytic system
气流电弧切割 gas arc cutting, electric arc-gas jet cutting
气流分布图(高炉的) air-flow distribution pattern
气流干燥系统 combination rotary/flash dryer
气流计 airometer
气流浇注法(熔模铸造) flowing gas casting process
气流强度 current rate
气流上升周期 up-stream cycle
气流输送 pneumatic conveying
气流输送的粉状石灰 airborne lime powder
气流紊乱 turbulence of stream
气流下降期 downstream cycle
气流中心 core of jet
气流阻力系数 flow resistance coefficient
气路 gas circuit
气轮机 (gas) turbine
气煤 gas [fiery, bottle, gas-making, gas-producer] coal
气门 air door, cock
气门导管 valve guide
气门管 vent pipe
气门螺钉 vent screw
气密 air seal, air raid protection, pressurization
气密封接[口] hermetic [air-tight] seal
气密封装 air-tight packing, hermetric sealing
气密焊 pressure-tight welding
气密焊缝 seal [tight] weld
气密还原钢弹 【色】gas-tight bomb
气密加料机构 【冶】gas-tight feeding mechanism
气密结构 air-tight construction
气密壳 gastight shell
气密连接[接头] air-tight [gastight] joint
气密料钟 【铁】gas-seal bell
气密密封 air-tight seal [packing], hermetic seal
气密容器[罐] air-tight [sealed, gastight]

container
气密式螺旋加料器 gas-tight screw feeder
气密室 air-lock, sealed chamber
气密套 gastight shell
气密涂层 air-tight coating
气密性 gastightness, air impermeability, leakproofness
气密性试验 air(-tight) [gas-tight] test
气密压盖[栓塞,封套] gas-tight gland
气密罩 gastight shell
气密轴封 air-tight shaft seal
气密铸件 pressure-tight casting
气密装置 air-tight assembly, obturator
气敏金属 gas-sensitive metal
气膜 gas [air] film
气沫橡胶 air-foam rubber
气幕 gas curtain
气幕风扇 seal-air fan
气幕式炉 curtain-type furnace
气囊 gas envelope
气凝胶 aerogel
气泡 (air) bubble, pinhole, blow hole, (gas) blister, gas envelope, bleb ◇ 产生 ~gassing, 多~的 blowy, 附着~captive bubble, 静着~(接触角)测定仪*, 皮下~【钢】skin blowhole, 无~钢 not blistering steel, 有~钢锭 bleb ingot
气泡边界层 bubble boundary layer
气泡表面 gassy surface
气泡层 blanket of air bubbles
气泡动力学 bubble dynamics
气泡法 bubble method,【粉】pressure [gas] bubble method
气泡控制 gas bubbling control
气泡矿物黏附 【选】bubble mineral attachment
气泡弥散 bubble dispersion
气泡模型 bubble model
气泡黏度测定法 bubble method of viscosity measurement
气泡黏着 bubble addhesion
气泡偏析 blow hole segregation

气泡水准仪 air (bubble) level, spirit level
气泡状结构 bubble structure
气泡群 swarm of bubbles
气泡形成 bubble formation
气喷磨料搪磨[珩磨] vapour honing
气瓶 cylinder, air bottle [collector], gas cylinder
气瓶安全帽 cylinder cap
气瓶钢 gas vessel steel
气瓶配件 gas bottle fittings
气枪 air gun
气切 flame cut off
气切器 gas cutter ◇ 串列式喷嘴~*, 伸缩式比例~pantograph cutter
气切器操纵台 burner (cut off) control desk
气球探测 【环】balloon sounding
气球形烟道 balloon flue
气熔焊 gas fusion welding
气溶胶 【化】aerosol
气溶胶漆 aerosol lacquer
气溶胶谱仪 aerosol spectrometer
气溶胶雾化 aerosol spraying
气溶体 gaseous solution ◇ 固体中的~*
气塞 gas lock
气升混合浸出 airlift mixing leaching
气升搅拌槽 airlift tank
气升式浮选机 airlift cell, airlift flotation machine
气升式搅拌器 airlift agitator
气升运输机 gas lift conveyor
气升装置 gas-lift unit
气蚀试验 cavitation (erosion) test
气蚀数 cavitation number
气蚀云 cavitation cloud
气室 air chamber [space], gas cell [chamber],【机】firing chamber (高速锤的)
气水罐 air-hydraulic cylinder
气水蓄力器 hydropneumatic accumulator
气送 air transport
气碎锤 pneumatic chipping hammer
气锁[栓] air-lock

气态　gas(eous) state, gaseousness, gassiness

气态氨　gaseous ammonia

气态废物　【环】gaseous waste

气态氟化物　gaseous fluoride

气态化合物　gaseous compound

气态还原　gaseous reduction

气态金属　gaseous metal

气态金属冷凝(法)　condensation of gaseous metal

气态流体　gaseous fluid

气态氯化物　gaseous chloride

气态氢　gaseous hydrogen

气态散放物　【环】gaseous emissions

气态烃　gaseous hydrocarbon, hydrocarbon gas

气态污染物　【环】gaseous pollutant

气态物质　gaseous substance

气态氧　gaseous oxygen (GOX)

气态氧吸收　gaseous oxygen absorption

气态杂质　gaseous impurity

气碳黑　(同"气黑")

气套　air jacket [casing], vapour blanket, 【金】vapour barrier(淬火时形成的)

气体　gas, gaseous fluid ◇ 不凝~noncondensable gas, 充有~的 gas-filled, 带烟~fume laden gas, 单一成分~simple gas, 燃烧产生的~fire gases, 无~的 gas-free, 析出[放出]~liberation of gas

气体保护　gas shield(ing), 【焊】gas backup (焊缝背面的), 【金】gaseous protection(熔化金属或加热金属的)

气体保护层(熔池的)　【焊】gas coverage

气体(保护)磁性焊剂电弧焊　magnetic-flux gas-shielded welding

气体保护电焊条　gas-shielded electrode

气体保护电弧焊　(gas-)shielded arc welding

气体保护电弧切割　gas shielded arc cutting

气体保护焊机　gas-shielded welding machine

气体保护焊(接)　gas-shielded welding ◇ 磁性焊剂二氧化碳~Unionarc welding

气体保护金属电极电弧切割　gas shielded metal-arc cutting

气体保护金属极等离子弧　gas metal plasma-arc (GMPA)

气体保护金属极等离子弧联焊法　GMPA (gas metal plasma-arc) process

气体保护金属极电弧　gas metal arc (GMA)

气体保护金属极电弧点焊　gas metal arc spot welding

气体保护金属极电弧缝焊　gas metal arc seam welding

气体保护金属极电弧焊　gas metal-arc welding (GMAW), GMA welding, metal-arc gas-shielded (MAGS) welding, shielded metal-arc welding (SMAW)

气体保护螺柱焊接　gas-shielded stud welding (GSSW)

气体保护气氛　gas atmosphere

气体保护区　gas coverage

气体保护碳(极电)弧焊　gas carbon-arc welding (GCAW), shielded carbon arc welding (SCAW)

气体保护钨极电弧点焊　gas tungsten arc spot welding

气体保护钨极电弧焊　gas tungsten arc welding (GTAW)

气体饱和度　gas pickup

气体饱和熔体　【冶】gassy melt

气体泵　gas pump

气体比率控制　gas ratio control

气体比重测定法　aerometry

气体比重计　aerometer

气体捕集器　gas trap

气体测量【地】gasmetry

气体产量[产出率]　gas yield

气体产物　gas(eous) product

气体常数　gas constant

气体超电压　gas overvoltage

气体沉淀(法)　gaseous precipitation

气体沉淀置换(法)　cementation by gases
气体成分　gas composition
气体冲击　gas shot
气体出口　gas outlet [exit]
气体吹出　gas blow-out
气体吹洗(使金属中气体及夹杂物浮出)　gas purging
气体氮化　【金】gas nitriding
气体导电率(等离子状态的)　【理】gaseous conduction
气体导管　gas conduit
气体等离子喷涂　air plasma spray(ing)
气体点火器　gas lighter
气体电极　gas(eous) electrode
气体电离　【理】gas ionization
气体电离计数管　gaseous ionization counter
气体定律　【理】gas law
气体动力平衡　aerodynamic balance
气体动力学　gas dynamics, aerodynamics
气体动力学理论　kinetic theory of gases
气体发生　gas generation [development] ◇放热性~炉*,水套式~装置*,吸热性~炉*
气体发生瓶[器]　gas-generating bottle
气体发生器　gas generator [producer], gasifier ◇分子筛~*,基普~*,离解氨~*
气体发生器罐　gas-producer retort
气体反(行)扩散法　gas back-diffusion method
气体反应　gas reaction
气体反应剂　gaseous reactant
气体放电测量[测定]　gas-discharge measurement
气体放电灯　discharge lamp
气体放电等离子体　gas-discharge plasma
气体放电真空计　gas-discharge gauge
气体放电装置　gas-discharge device
气体分配[分布]　gas distribution ◇金属制~板(小烟道顶上) metal nozzle plate
气体分散隔膜　gas dispersing diaphragm

气体分析　gas analysis, gasometry ◇分馏退吸法~*,连续~*
气体分析记录仪　gas analysis recorder
气体分析器　gas analyzer [detector], gas analytical apparatus ◇奥萨特~*,柏瑞-奥赛特~*,自动~*
气体分析仪　gas analysis meter ◇红外线~ infrared gas analyzer,热导式~*
气体分子运动论　kinetic theory of gases
气体腐蚀　gas corrosion [attack]
气体鼓泡　gas bubbling
气体管道　gas piping
气体管线　gas (pipe)line [manifold]
气体过滤器　gas filter
气体含量　gas content
气体焊剂　gas flux
气体合金化处理　gas alloying
气体还原　gaseous reduction ◇直接~*
气体还原度　extent of gaseous reduction
气体还原剂　gaseous reducing agent, gaseous reductant(s)
气体还原(剂还原)法　gas(eous) reduction technique [process]
气体还原金属　【色】gas-reduced metal
气体缓冲器　gas cushion
气体回收利用　gas recycle
气体回收系统　gas recovery system
气体混合器　gas mixer ◇引火烧嘴用~*
气体混合物　gas(eous) mixture
气体火焰　gas flame
气体火焰刨削　【机】flame milling
气体火焰辐射　gas-fire radiation
气体火焰硬钎焊　gas brazing
气体计量瓶　gasometer flask
气体夹杂　gaseous inclusion, included gas
气体检测　gas test
气体检测器　gas tester
气体鉴定器　gas detector
气体搅拌[动]　gas stirring [agitation]
气体搅拌冶金反应器　gas stirred metallurgical reactor

气体交换	gaseous exchange
气体搅动电弧再加热	【冶】gas stirring arc reheating
气体节省器	gas economizer ◇ 复式～*
气体介质	【理】gaseous medium
气体介质淬火	gas quenching
气体金属相互作用	gas-metal interaction
气体浸蚀	gas pickling
气体净化	gas purification [cleansing]
气体净化处理	gas cleaning treatment
气体净化费用	gas cleaning cost
气体净化风扇	gas-purifier fan
气体净化过程	gas cleaning process
气体净化过滤器	(同"洗涤式过滤器")
气体净化器	gas purifier [cleaner]
气体净化设备	gas purifying equipment
气体净化效率	gas cleaning efficiency
气体净化装置	gas cleaning plant, gas-purifying device, gas cleaner
气体空截面速度（流化技术中的）	superficial gas velocity
气体控制	gas control
气体扩散	gas(eous) diffusion
气体扩散计	effusiometer
气体扩散设备（提炼铀用）	(gaseous-)diffusion plant
气体冷却	gas cooling
气体冷却反应堆	gas-cooled reactor
气体冷却剂	gaseous coolant
气体冷却器	gas cooler, cooler for gas
气体冷却塔	gas cooling tower
气体冷却系统	gas cooling system
气体离子	gas ion
气体利用效率	gas utilization efficiency
气体量	gas volume, quantity of gas
气体裂化器	gas converter
气体流淬火	【金】gas quenching
气体流量	gas flow (rate)
气体流量计	gas flowmeter
气体流量记录器	gas flow recorder
气体流量控制器	gas flow controller
气体流速	gas velocity [travel], gas flow rate
气体漏出	blow by
气体露点分析器	dew-cell gas analyzer
气体弥散	gas dispersion ◇ 锥底～搅拌器*
气体密度	gas density
气体密度(测量)计	gas density meter, elaterometer
气体密度记录仪	gas-density recorder
气体密封	air seal
气体密封度	gas containment
气体密封装置	gas lock system
气体黏结剂	【铸】gas binder
气体浓度	gas strength
气体排出	gas expelling
气体喷出	gas blow-out
气体喷吹	gas injection
气体喷射搅拌	gas injection stirring
气体喷射压缩机	gas-jet compressor
气体喷洗室	spray chamber
气体屏蔽	【金】gas shield(ing)
气体屏蔽(热处理)炉	gas curtain furnace
气体切向出口	tangential gas outlet
气体清洗	gas cleansing
气体氰化	gas(y) cyaniding
气体区域提纯[精炼]	gas zone refining
气体取样	gas sampling
气体取样孔	gas sampling hole
气体取样器	gas sampler, gas-sampling probe
气体缺陷	gas unsoundness
气体燃料	gas(-type) [gaseous] fuel
气体燃烧器	gas burner,【团】gas-fired ignitor
气体容积	gas containment
气体容量	gas capacity
气体容器	gas container [containment]
气体容器钟罩	gas (holder) bell
气体软氮化过程	gas nitrocarburizing process
气体入口	gas inlet
气体色层[谱](分离)法	【理】gas chro-

matography, gas chromatographic method ◇ 反相～*
气体射流　gas jet
气体渗氮　(同"气体氮化")
气体渗铬　gas chromizing
气体渗漏法(测孔隙度)【粉】gas leakage method
气体渗碳(法)　gas carburization, gas (eous) carburizing, cementation by gases ◇ 连续～eutectrol process
气体渗碳剂　gas carburizer
气体渗碳炉　gas carburizer, gas carburizing furnace
气体渗碳装置　gas carburizing plant
气体渗透　gas percolation
气体渗透速度　gas percolation velocity
气体渗透性[率,度]　gas permeability
气体生成　gassing
气体生物探测器　biological detector of gas
气体升液装置　gas-lift unit
气体释出　gas liberation
气体试剂　gaseous reagent
气体试验　gas test
气体试样　gas sample
气体试样采集器　gas sample collector
气体收集系统　gas-collecting system
气体数据　gas data
气体碳　gaseous carbon
气体碳氮共渗　gas carbonitriding, dry cyaniding
气体探测试验　probe test
气体提纯　gas purification
气体提纯系统　gas purification system [train]
气体体积　gas volume
气体体积计　volumescope
气体调节　gas conditioning [control]
气体调节器　gas conditioner [pilot]
气体通道　gas passage
气体温度计　gas thermometer, pyrometer, gas temperature gauge
气体污染　【环】gaseous contamination, contamination of gases
气体雾化(法)　gas atomization
气体析出　gas liberation, gaseous evolution, deposition of gas
气体析出速率(钢中的)　rate of gas evolution
气体析出物　gaseous educt
气体吸附　gas(eous) adsorption, adsorption of gases, gas pickup
气体吸收法　gas absorption method
气体吸收反应器　clean-up reactor
气体吸收器　gas absorber
气体吸收塔　gas absorption tower
气体吸收系统　gas absorption system
气体稀释剂　gaseous fluxing agent
气体洗涤　(gas) scrubbing
气体洗涤车间　gas washing plant
气体洗涤法　gas cleaning process
气体洗涤机　disintegrator ◇ 泰森式～*
气体洗涤解磨机　gas washing disintegrator
气体洗涤器　gas scrubber, gas-washer ◇ 盘式～*, 筛板式～*, 湿法～ wet gas scrubber
气体洗涤设备[装置]　gas washing equipment [installation]
气体洗涤塔　scrubber wash tower, scrubbing tower, gas scrubber ◇ 栅格式～ hurdle-type scrubber
气体洗涤系统　gas scrubbing system
气体洗涤用水　gas washing water
气体下推力　gas underthrust
气体行程　gas travel
气体旋塞　gas cock
气体循环风扇　circulating fan
气体循环式炉　recirculating furnace
气体循环式热处理炉　cyclone furnace
气体压焊　gas-pressure welding
气体压力　gas pressure
气体压力计　gas manometer, gassing gauge
气体压缩机　compressed gas machine

气体氧化　gaseous oxidation
气体一次冷却　primary gas cooling
气体逸出　gas escape [evolution, liberation]
气体硬化黏结剂　【铸】gas binder
气体预热器　gas preheater
气体杂质　gas(eous) impurity
气体再吸收　reabsorption of gases
气体再循环　gas recycle [recirculation]
气体再循环通道　gas-recirculation flue
气体张力　gaseous tension
气体蒸发法　gas evaporation method
气体整流器　(同"充气管整流器")
气体钟罩　gas (holder) bell
气体转化器　gas converter
气体自动分析器　◇ 奥萨特～ automatic Orsat
气体自动析出　spontaneous gas evolution
气体总管　gas main
气体组成　gas composition
气体组分　gas component
气田【地】　gas field
气铜钢　copper steel
气铜焊的　torch-brazed
气团　air mass ◇ 间隙原子～*，科特雷耳[科氏]～*，位错～*
气团凝聚　(同"大气凝聚")
气味难闻的气体　disagreeable smelling gas
气雾快速冷却　【压】air-vapor high-speed cooling
气析装置　air elutriation apparatus
气隙　air gap [space, breather], gas gap
气隙磁感应强度　gap density
气隙线　【铸】air gap line
气相　gas(eous) [vapour] phase
气相掺杂技术　【半】gas doping technique
气相处理　vapour phase treatment
气相沉积　gaseous [vapour] deposition ◇ 化学～*
气相淀积法　vapour-deposition technique, 【冶】hot wire process
气相镀覆　gas phase plating

气相镀锌　vapour galvanizing
气相法　【金】vapour-phase process
气相反应　gas [vapour] phase reaction
气相防锈剂　vapor phase inhibitor (VPI)
气相腐蚀　gaseous corrosion, vapour phase corrosion
气相罐　vapour phase can
气相还原　vapour phase reduction
气相还原粉末　【冶】fumed powder
气相缓蚀剂[腐蚀抑制剂]　vapour phase (corrosion) inhibitor
气相精炼　vapour phase refining
气相扩散渗镀　gas [vapour] plating
气相流(态)化　gas phase fluidization
气相浓度　gas phase concentration
气相迁移　vapour transport
气相热分解　vapour decomposition
气相色层[色谱,层析](分离)法　gas chromatography, vapour phase chromatography ◇ 高温～*，前流[前沿]～*，控温[升温]～*
气相色谱图　gas chromatogram
气相色谱仪　gas chromatograph
气相渗镀(法)　vapour plating
气相生长(晶体)　growth from vapour phase
气相脱氯　vapour phase dechlorination
气相脱脂[除油]装置　vapour degreasing unit
气相氧化　gaseous [gas-phase] oxidation, vapour phase oxidation
气相－液相分界面　(同"气－液界面")
气相抑制剂　vapor phase inhibitor (VPI)
气相抑制剂防锈　rust prevention by vapour phase inhibitors
气相优先还原分离法(钽铌分离用)　vapour-vapour process
气相阻力　gas phase resistance
气箱脉冲袋式收尘[粉]器　gas tank type pulse bag house dust collector
气象测验　meteorological test
气象台　observatory

气象图 weather chart
气旋 cyclone
气穴 cavitation,【铸】blows ◇ 耐~钢*
气穴腐蚀 cavitation corrosion
气穴腐蚀试验 cavitation erosion test
气穴蚀损[损伤] cavitation damage
气穴数 cavitation number
气穴云 cavitation cloud
气压操纵系统 air control system
气压测定法 barometry
气压沉箱 【建】compressed air caisson, pneumatic caisson
气压成形 【粉】gas-pressure compacting [compaction] ◇ 爆炸~*
气压缸 pneumatic pressure cylinder
气压固结 gas-pressure consolidation
气压焊 gas-pressure [pressure-gas] welding ◇ 开式对接~*,氧乙炔~*
气压计[表] barometer (bar., brm.), barometer [air] gauge, gas manometer, gas-pressure meter ◇ 风速~ anemobarometer, 虹吸~ siphon barometer, 空盒[无液]~ aneroid barometer, 热电偶~ thermocouple gauge
气压计杯 barometer cistern
气压计高度 barometric height
气压计管 barometer tube
气压计盒 aneroid chamber
气压记录器 barograph, barometrograph
气压继电器 gas-pressure relay
气压减震器 pneumatic bumper
气压浇注混凝土 air placed concrete
气压金属型铸造 die-casting with pressurized gas
气压冷凝器 barometric condenser
气压黏合[黏结] (gas) pressure bonding
气压平衡管 barometric pipe
气压烧结 gas pressure sintering
气压式压铸机 air injection machine
气压式研磨机 air-pressure mill
气压水幕 air-pressure water guard
气压调节器 gas-pressure regulator

气压温度计 vapour-pressure thermometer, barothermograph（自记式）
气压温度湿度计 barothermohydrograph
气压蓄力器 pneumatic [air-loaded] accumulator ◇ 无活塞~*
气压真空管 barometric pipe
气压直接推动式压铸机 direct air injection die-casting machine
气压指示器 gas-pressure indicator
气压柱 barometric column [leg]
气眼 air pocket, cavitation,【铸】gas pocket（缺陷）
气焰 gas flame ◇ 用~割炬定心（对钢坯）torch centring
气焰切割 gas-flame cutting ◇ 带金属粉末的~ metal-powder cutting, 带有导向装置的手动~[手动氧气切割] free hand guided (flame) cutting
气焰硬钎焊 gas (flame) brazing
气液混合物 solution-air mixture
气液接触 gas-liquid contacting
气液界面反应 gas-liquid interface reaction
气液流 gas-liquid flow
气-液耦合 gas-liquid coupling
气液色层(分离)法 gas-liquid chromatography (GLC)
气液(相)界面 gas-liquid [gas-solution] interface, liquid-gas surface
气硬 self-hardening
气硬钢 air-hardening steel
气硬耐火砂浆[水泥] air-setting [air-hardening] refractory cement
气硬性砂浆 air-setting mortar
气硬性水泥 air-setting cement
气-油密封系统 gas-oil sealed system
气源部件 air set (A.S.)
气载散放物 【环】airborne emissions
气载污染物 【环】airborne contaminant
气錾 air chisel [chipper], chipping hammer
气闸 air [atmospheric] brake, air-lock

气胀棒坯　【粉】puffed bar
气胀压坯　puffed compact
气枕装置　air-cushioning device
气震台　pneumatic table
气振器　pneumatic vibrator
气柱　air column
气筑　pneumatic tamping
气嘴　air tap [cock]
弃土　spoil
弃土堆　banket(te)
弃渣　waste slag
弃渣场　slag pit
汽包　steam header [dome]
汽泵　steam pump
汽车　automobile, motor vehicle, car ◇ 槽式～*, 电动～ electromobile, 混凝土搅拌～ concrete mixer truck, 活顶～ convertible car
汽车板　automobile steel plate ◇ 微碳～*
汽车薄钢板轧机　autobody sheet mill
汽车车身钢板[薄板]　automobile [motorcar] body sheet, autobody sheet
汽车吊(车)[汽车式起重机]　mobile [truck(-mounted), lorry-mounted] crane
汽车阀门弹簧丝　car valve-spring wire
汽车翻卸矿槽　truck dump pocket
汽车房(库)　garage
汽车废钢铁[金属]　automotive scrap
汽车高速公路　automobile expressway
汽车工程师协会（美国）　Society of Automotive Engineer (SAE)
汽车(结构)用钢　automotive [automobile] steel
汽车离合器　automobile clutch
汽车零件　automobile parts
汽车轮圈　automotive rim
汽车排出废气　automotive exhaust (gas)
汽车式装料机　【钢】mobile charger, mobile-charging machine
汽车修理厂　garage
汽车悬挂钢板弹簧　suspended leaf spring
汽车用薄钢板　automobile sheet steel
汽车载运　truck haulage
汽锤　steam hammer
汽笛　steam whistle, siren, (loud) hailer
汽动锻压机　steam power forging press
汽动飞剪　steam-operated flying shears
汽动鼓风机　steam-driven blower, steam(-driven) blowing engine
汽动(活塞式)推钢机　steam ram
汽动水压机　steam hydraulic press
汽阀青铜　(88Cu, 6Sn, 4Zn, 1.5Pb) steam bronze
汽封　steam [vapour] locking, gland sealing
汽缸　cylinder, drum ◇ 开口～*
汽－固过程　vapour-solid process
汽管式干燥机　steam-tube drier
汽锅　boiler
汽化　vapourization, vapourizing, evaporation, evaporization ◇ 止～(作用) devaporation
汽化点[温度]　vapourization point
汽化镀锌　vapour galvanizing
汽化计　atm(id)ometer, evaporimeter
汽化冷却　evaporative [hot] cooling ◇ 低压[自然循环]～*, 高压[强制循环]～*
汽化冷却器　evaporate cooler,【铁】blister cooler
汽化冷却系统　evaporated cooling system
汽化器　vapourizer,【机】carburet(t)or
汽化潜热　latent heat of vaporization
汽化热　heat of evaporation [vaporization]
汽化室　vapourizing chamber
汽化室阀门　vapourizing chamber valve
汽化损失　vapourization [evaporation] losses
汽化性　vapourability, vapourizability
汽化蒸发　steam raising
汽冷炉门　steam-cooled door
汽力绞盘　steam capstan
汽馏釜　steam-heated still

汽轮发电机组　turbo-unit
汽轮机　(steam) turbine ◇ 单流式～ uniflow engine, 抽气式～ bleeder burbine, 串联[纵联]复式～ tandem compound machine
汽轮机转子钢　turbine rotor steel
汽门　port, valve
汽密性　steamtightness
汽塞　steam[vapour] locking
汽室　steam pocket[dome]
汽水阀　trap seat ◇ 浮筒式～ bucket steam trap
汽水分离器　(steam-) water separator, drip pot, mist eliminator,【冶】expansion tank
汽水隔离管　anti-priming pipe
汽套　steam jacket[casing], jacket(ed) wall
汽套加热器　jacket heater
汽套式过滤器　steam-jacketed filter
汽套蒸发器　steam-jacketed evaporator
汽提　steam stripping ◇ 精制油的～ oil stripping
汽提盘（蒸馏塔的）　stripping tray
汽提试验　stripping test
汽提塔　stripping tower[column]
汽提圆锥　stripping cone
汽提蒸馏器　stripping still
汽雾冷却　evaporated cooling
汽液比　vapour-liquid ratio
汽液对流　countercurrent vapour-liquid flow
汽液分离器　drip pot
汽-液-固　vapour-liquid-solid (V-L-S)
汽-液-固生长　V-L-S growth
汽液交换　vapour-liquid exchange
汽液交换过程　vapour-liquid process
汽液平衡　vapour-liquid equilibrium
汽液转移　vapour-liquid transfer
汽油　gasoline (ga.), gasolene, petrol(eum spirit), benzin(e) ◇ 含氧～*

汽油动力车　gasoline-powered vehicle
汽油发动机轴承合金　◇ 霍伊特 I.C.E.～ Hoyt's I.C.E. metal
汽油（内燃）机　gasoline engine (G.E.)
汽状的　vapourous
沏特里亚型立式金相显微镜　Chatelier-type microscope
牵钢　pull-iron
牵螺栓　drag bolt
牵索　guy (rope)
牵引　draw(ing), drag, draft, draught, haul(ing), traction ◇ 精简～传动 cord-and-drum drive
牵引棒　drawing bar
牵引变电所　traction substation
牵引铲斗　drag bucket
牵引车　drafter, haulage vehicle ◇ 钢丝绳～ cable-driven car
牵引穿模机（钢丝的）　pulling-in machine
牵引发电机　drag[traction] generator
牵引杆　draw bar
牵引钢(丝)绳　traction rope, hauling wire rope ◇ 架空索道用～*
牵引功率　pulling[draw-bar] power
牵引钩　draw(bar)[towing] hook
牵引辊　carry-over pinch rolls, capstan
牵引辊装置　pinch roll unit
牵引簧　drawing[extension] spring
牵引机　traction engine, dragger, tractor ◇ 车辆～ car haul, 小型～ tug
牵引机构　traction mechanism
牵引挤压　drawing extrusion
牵引力　tractive force[effort], thrust, drag force, hauling capacity
牵引链　pull[tension, haulage, hauling] chain
牵引链钳　pul(ling)-in dogs
牵引轮　capstan, traction wheel ◇ 平行卷筒式～*, 双盘式自滑型～*
牵引能力　hauling capacity
牵引盘　capstan, sheave
牵引绳　hauling rope

牵引(式)电动机 traction motor
牵引式钢包 trailer(-mounted) ladle
牵引索 traction [pull] rope, pulling cable
牵引挖斗 drag bucket
牵引系数 traction coefficient
牵引效应 capstan [pulling] effect
牵引装置 draught [draw] gear, drawing unit
钎焊 brazing, hard-soldering, brass soldering ◇ 层次～ step brazing, 电极[焊条]～*, 电阻～*, 惰性气体保护～*, 反应[化学浸液]～ reactive brazing, 分段多层～ block brazing, 高频～*, 高温～*, 焊料熔注～ flow brazing, 红外线～ infrared brazing, 火焰～ flame brazing, 夹层～ sandwich braze, 浇注～*, 金属浴～ metal dip brazing, (化学)浸液～*, 可～性 brazability, 离解氨保护～*, 炉中～ furnace brazing, 煤气氧气焰加热～ oxygas brazing, 热板～ hot plate soldering, 熔波～ wave soldering, 碳弧～ carbon arc brazing, 盐槽～*, 硬焊料～的*
钎焊板材 【压】brazing sheet
钎焊薄板(金属的) close plating
钎焊层 solderable coating
钎焊灯 blow [soldering] torch, blowlamp, blast lamp, brazing burner
钎焊法 brazing process
钎焊工 solderer
钎焊工艺 joint brazing procedure
钎焊管 brazed tube ◇ 单层～*
钎焊合金 brazing alloy ◇ 擦拭～*, 恩格洛依 255 金镍～*, 镉～*, 荷兰白色～*, 普通软～*, 西尔金色耐蚀～*, 硬～*
钎焊机 brazing machine
钎焊剂 soldering powder, soldering flux
钎焊加热 brazing heat
钎焊接头 soldered fitting
钎焊金属 brazing metal
钎焊烙铁 (pointed) soldering copper, soldering tool

钎焊连接 braze (welding) joint
钎焊炉 brazing furnace ◇ 烧煤气的～*
钎焊器 (pointed) soldering copper, soldering tool, solderer ◇ 煤气～ gas blowpipe
钎焊钳 soldering tongs
钎焊熔剂 brazing flux [mixture]
钎焊软膏 brazing paste
钎焊丝 brazing wire
钎焊酸 soldering acid, spirit of salt
钎焊铜烙铁头 soldering copper
钎焊性[能力] solderability
钎焊液(态熔剂) soldering liquid [fluid]
钎焊用喷灯[喷嘴] brazing torch
钎接脆化 solder embrittlement
钎接管 brazed tubing
钎料 brazing filler metal ◇ 黄铜～ brazing spelter
钎料片 brazing sheet
钎子 tap-hole rod, tap-out bar, bot pick, pricker, (hammer) drill ◇ 手工～【机】jumper
钎(子)钢 drill steel, (同"中空钢")
铅{Pb} lead, plumbum ◇ 除锌～ dezinced lead, 除[脱]银～ desilvered lead, 镀[衬, 包]～ terning, 放射产生的～ radiogenic lead, 腐蚀～ corroding lead, 覆[包]～钢*, 工业～ commercial lead, 灌～ plumbing, 海绵(状)～*, 含～的 leady, lead bearing, plumbiferous, 含～钢*, 含银～*, 化学纯～*, 加～钢*, 金属[蓝]～ metallic [blue] lead, 精炼～ refined lead, 弥散强化～*, 软(化)～*, 泡沫状～*, 试～*, 树枝状～ lead tree, 似～的 leady, 塑性～*, 退[去]～*, 无铋～ bismuth free lead, 硬[含锑]～ antimonial lead, 再生～ secondary lead, 渣～ slag lead
铅-210 {^{210}Pb} radiolead
铅巴比合金 (65—75Sn, 12—15Sb, 10—18Pb, 2—3Cu) leaded babbitt
铅白 (同"碱式碳酸铅")
铅白粉 basic lead carbonate

铅板　lead plate, sheet lead, grid (plate)(蓄电池的) ◇ 薄～rolled lead
铅板合金　grid metal
铅板始极片　sheet lead starting sheet
铅版合金(13Sb, 4.5Sn, 82.5Pb)　stereotype alloy [metal]
铅包不锈钢丝　lead-coated stainless-steel wire
铅包皮压力机　lead cable press
铅包线　lead covered wire
铅泵　lead pump
铅笔　pencil
铅笔式热电偶　pencil-type thermocouple
铅笔状滑移　pencil glide
铅铋汞笔芯合金　pencil alloy
铅铋合金　lead bismuth alloy
铅铋合金密封　bismuth lead alloy seal
铅铋镉易熔合金　◇ 豪泽尔～*
铅铋锡易熔合金　Rose metal
铅玻璃　lead glass
铅箔　lead foil [paper] ◇ 阿比恩双面包锡～Albion metal
铅箔(增光)屏　lead-foil screen
铅槽　lead vessel ◇ 回火～lead tempering bath
铅层　lead layer
铅产出量　lead yield
铅衬　leadwork
铅衬混凝土电解槽　concrete lead-lined cell
铅衬里　lead lining
铅衬(里)电解槽　lead-lined electrolytic tank
铅锤　plumb (bob), lead hammer
铅锤测量　plumbing
铅锤位置　【理】gravity position
铅垂线　perpendicular, vertical, 【建】plumb line
铅淬火　(lead) patenting, patentizing ◇ 半～盘条*, 两次～double lead patenting, 熔融盐中～[处理]*
铅淬火槽　lead bath

铅淬火车间　patenting shop
铅淬火钢丝　patented steel wire
铅淬火高强度钢丝(抗拉强度 1.5-1.7GPa) (best) plough steel wire
铅淬火高强度钢丝绳　plough steel wire rope
铅淬火冷拉钢丝　lead-patented cold-drawn wire ◇ 特号～*
铅淬火炉(线材的)　patent(zi)ing furnace
铅淬火炉卷取装置　patenting frame
铅淬火状态　patented condition
铅淬硬化　hardening in lead bath
铅丹{Pb_3O_4}　minium(天然), red-lead, red lead oxide ◇ 含铁～iron minium
铅丹底漆　red coating
铅丹炉　colour oven
铅弹合金(0.9As, 余量 Pb)　shot alloy
铅当量　lead equivalent
铅挡板　lead plate
铅滴　(同"铅雨")
铅碲合金(<1Te, <6Sb, 余量 Pb)　tellurium-lead alloy ◇ 特雷迪姆～*
铅垫料(用于转炉炉底风口密封)　lead washer
铅电解精炼法　lead electrolytic refining process ◇ 氟硅酸盐～*, 高氯酸盐～*
铅电解液　lead electrolyte
铅锭　lead ingot [pig] ◇ 软(化)～*
铅镀层　lead-coat
铅矾{$PbSO_4$}　lead vitriol, sardinianite, anglesite
铅防护板　lead apron
铅防护屏　lead screen
铅防护套　lead sheath
铅废料　scrap lead
铅粉　lead powder, plumbum dust ◇ 雾化～atomized lead
铅封　lead seal(ing), plumbing
铅封带　lead-seal zone
铅封的　lead-tight
铅浮渣　lead dross [skim]
铅钙铀矿　eoracite

铅 qian

铅钙轴承合金 ◇ 马瑟休斯~*
铅钢 leaded steel
铅工业协会(美) Lead Industries Association (L.I.A.)
铅汞合金 lead amalgam
铅鼓风炉 lead blast furnace
铅管 lead pipe
铅焊 lead welding [burning]
铅焊料[药] lead [kupper] solder
铅焊条 burning bar of lead
铅汗 【铸】lead sweat
铅合金 lead alloy, cobitalium (alloy) ◇ DS抗蠕变~DS lead, 阿萨科耐蚀~*, 鲁夫洛伊[耐烛]~*, 含钠~natrium lead, 易熔~fusible lead alloy, 因阿~inalium
铅合金密封 lead alloy seal
铅黑铜 Ledrit
铅护板 lead plate
铅黄 massicot, lead ocher
铅黄铜 leaded brass, ledrite ◇ 费鲁尔~*, 斯特林~*, 制管用~tube brass
铅黄铜板 lead brass plate
铅黄铜带 lead brass band
铅黄铜丝 lead-brass wire
铅黄渣 lead speiss
铅灰 lead ash
铅回流塔 lead reflux column
铅回收 reclaiming of lead
铅回收系统 lead recovery circuit
铅基巴比[巴氏]合金 lead babbit alloy, lead-base babbit (metal), lead-base white metal ◇ F.23高负荷~*, S重载~*, 博维尔重载~*
铅基白合金 lead-base white metal
铅基合金 lead-base alloy ◇ DW热浸镀用~*, 普拉特—洛伊热浸镀用~*
铅基减摩[抗摩擦]合金 lead base antifriction alloy
铅基耐磨合金 ◇ 伊尔牌~*
铅基耐磨轴承合金 ◇ 诺伊特~*
铅基软钎焊料 lead-base solder alloy

铅基轴承合金 lead-base bearing alloy [metal], lead babbit alloy, lead base antifriction alloy, lead-base babbit (metal), graphite metal (68Pb,15Sn,17Sb) ◇ 埃瓦雷斯特~*, 巴恩~*, 鲍尔~*, 大和~Yamato metal, 丹德利昂~*, 蒂戈~*, 格里柯~*, 格利维尔~*, 回火~tempered lead alloy, 矶田~*, 贾卡马~*, 卡津施泰因~*, 赖利~*, 鲁奇~[铅基钙钡轴承合金], 罗塔斯~*, 马格诺利亚~*, 迈斯蒂克~(含10Sb) Mystic metal, 帕立德~*, 萨特科~*, 斯佩里~*, 特米特~*, 乌尔科~*, 西米特~*, 星芒[羽状]~*, 休斯~*, 雅各比~*, 尤尼欧思~*
铅-碱金属合金 lead alkali metal alloy, Mathesius metal
铅-碱土金属轴承合金 ◇ 弗雷里~*
铅浸覆法 lead dip process
铅精矿 lead concentrate, balland ◇ 哈尔基恩~熔盐电解法*
铅精炼厂 【色】lead refinery
铅精炼法 lead refining process ◇ 氟硅酸盐~*, 高氯酸盐~*, 乔利维尔-佩纳罗亚~
铅精炼锅 kettle for refining lead, lead improving kettle
铅精炼锅用搅拌器 lead stirrer
铅块 regulus lead
铅矿(石) lead ore ◇ 废~(待选的) fausted ore, 富~bing ore, 未精选的~ bonze
铅矿焙烧 lead ore roasting
铅矿物 lead mineral
铅粒 lead shot [button]
铅连续精炼 continuous lead refining
铅敛缝 plumbing
铅铳 【色】lead (copper) matte
铅冒口 lead riser
铅锰钛铁矿 {(Fe,Pb)O·2(Ti,Mn)O_2} senaite
铅锰土 wachenrodite, wackenrodite

铅密封的	lead-tight
铅密封加热元件	lead-seal heating element
铅棉密封(转炉底风嘴的)	leadwool seal
铅钼磁钢	comol
铅钠合金(2Na,余量 Pb;用作脱氧剂)	sodium-lead ◇ 海德隆~*
铅内衬	lead lining
铅铌铁矿	plumboniobite
铅泥混合槽	lead slurry mixing tank
铅盆	lead dish
铅皮	lead sheet [covering], rolled lead
铅皮始极片	sheet lead starting sheet
铅皮线	lead covered wire
铅片	lead sheet
铅钎焊合金(2.5Ag, 0.25Cu, 余量 Pb)	lead solder
铅枪(冶炼含铅钢用)	lead gun
铅青铜(合金)(65—70Cu, 35—30Pb)	lead [tin-free, tinless] bronze, copper-lead-bronze alloy ◇ 艾杰克斯~*, 卡拉坎~(系)*, 凯尔美特~*, 克尔维特~*, 雷德福填料用~*, 冷铸~*, 默柯~*, 耐水浸蚀~*, 萨尔瓦克泵叶~*
铅氢化作用	hydroplumbation
铅熔接	lead-burn
铅熔炼	lead smelting
铅熔渣	【色】grey slag
铅容器	lead housing [vessel]
铅绒	spongy lead
铅塞	lead plug
铅色的	gray, grey, plumbeous
铅色氧化锰{Mn₂O₃·H₂O}	grey oxide of manganese
铅烧绿石	plumbopyrochlore
铅生产车间	lead-producing plant
铅石墨含油合金	ledaloyl
铅实收率	lead yield
铅始极片[板]	lead starting sheet
铅始极片制备	lead starting sheet preparation
铅室(制硫酸的)	lead [vitriol] chamber
铅室酸	【化】chamber (plant) acid
铅锶轴承合金	◇ 马瑟休斯~*
铅丝	lead wire, galvanized wire (镀锌铁丝)
铅酸盐	plumbite
铅酸铀	uranium plumbite
铅塔(锌精馏的)	【色】lead column
铅塔冷凝器	lead-column condenser
铅钛矿	macedonite
铅糖	(见"乙酸铅")
铅套	lead housing
铅锑合金	lead-antimony alloy, regulus metal ◇ 尼科~ Nico
铅锑合金密封	lead-antimony seal
铅锑锡(轴承)合金	lead-antimony-tin alloy ◇ 艾杰克斯~*, 罗塔斯~*
铅锑轴承合金	◇ 霍伊特 C.B.~ Hoyt's C.B. alloy, 斯特里特 4 号~*, 休伊特~*
铅提取	lead extraction
铅添加合金	lead addition
铅铜合金	cupro-lead
铅铜矿选厂	lead-copper ore beneficiation plant
铅涂料	lead paint
铅丸合金	shot metal
铅析(金银)法	scorification
铅析渣(铅氧化除精炼的)	lead scoria
铅锡	slicker solder ◇ 大马士革~青*
铅锡铋合金	◇ 比布拉~*
铅锡铂钯矿	zvyagintsevite
铅锡共晶(合金)软焊料(62Sn,38Pb;熔点 183℃)	eutectic solder
铅锡焊料	plumber's solder ◇ 特塔里姆
铅锡合金	Terne alloy (10—15Sn, 85—90Pb), terne (20Sn, 0.2Sb, 余量 Pb), terne metal (80—80.5Pb, 1.5—2Sb, 18Sn) ◇ 法拉姆~*, 钢板镀覆用~ tin terne alloy, 金属框~*, 卡普苏尔~*, 罗马~*, 铁表面镀覆~法 spot homogen process

铅锡合金镀层(薄钢板的) ternecoating
铅锡合金熔池 terne pot
铅锡软焊料(2/3Sn,1/3Pb) quick solder
铅锡锑轴承合金 ◇ 霍伊尔～*
铅锡铁各半软钎料 half-and-half solder
铅锡铜锌轴承合金 ◇ 克奈斯～*
铅锌分离 lead-zinc separation
铅锌混合熔炼 simultaneous zinc-lead smelting
铅锌矿 lead-zinc ore
铅锌矿床 lead-zinc deposit
铅锌矿烧结炉 blowing up furnace
铅锌密闭鼓风炉 imperial smelting furnace
铅锌密闭鼓风炉熔炼 closed blast furnace smelting
铅锌硫化矿 sulphide lead-zinc ore
铅锌装饰合金 ◇ 廷塞尔～*
铅蓄电池 lead storage battery, lead accumulator
铅蓄电池合金(7—12Sb, 0.1—0.5Sn, 余量 Pb) lead battery metal
铅阳极 lead anode, corroding lead ◇ 空心～hollow lead anode, 硬[含锑]～antimonial lead anode
铅冶金 lead metallurgy
铅液 molten lead
铅液泵 lead pump
铅液泵池 lead pump sump
铅液层 lead layer
铅液池 lead pool
铅液冷却溜槽 lead cooling launder
铅液螺旋搅拌器 lead rotor
铅液循环泵 lead circulating pump
铅阴极 lead cathode ◇ 含锑～*
铅银巴氏合金 lead-silver babbitt
铅银合金阳极 lead-silver anode
铅印 【钢】lead [letterpress] printing
铅铀矿{UO₃·2H₂O + PbO} masuyite, richetite
铅铀烧绿石 samiresite
铅雨(鼓风炉炼锌的) 【色】splash-lead, shower of lead droplets, shower of molten lead, lead droplet
铅雨飞溅 lead splashing
铅雨冷凝器 lead-splash condenser
铅浴 lead bath ◇ 喷雾代～*
铅浴淬火 patenting, lead(-bath) quenching, molten lead quenching, lead hardening ◇ 两次～法*
铅浴淬火的 quenched in lead bath (QPb)
铅浴(淬火)炉 lead-bath furnace, lead pot furnace
铅浴等温淬火 molten lead austempering
铅浴回火 lead tempering, tempering in lead bath
铅浴加热 lead-bath heating
铅浴加热后淬火 quenching after heated in lead
铅浴炉内退火钢丝 lead-annealed wire
铅浴热处理 molten lead heat treating [treatment]
铅浴退火 lead(-bath) annealing
铅渣 lead dross [skim, ash]
铅质垫片[垫圈] lead gasket
铅中毒 lead poisoning, plumbism, saturnism
铅珠 lead shot, 【铸】lead sweat
铅铸法(检查锻模尺寸用) lead cast
铅字合金(50—90Pb, 2—30Sb, 余量 Sn, 有时加入 Bi) type-metal, type metal alloy, printing alloy, stereotype metal ◇ 洛戈～Logotype, 铸造～*
千X单位(X射线波长单位, = 10^{-10}m) KX unit
千波特(信息传输率) 【电】kilo baud
千分表 dial gauge, (dial) indicator, amesdial
千分尺 microcaliper, micrometer (gauge) ◇ 飞测～*
千分率 permillage, parts per mille
千伏计 kilovoltmeter
千斤顶 (hoisting) jack, lifting jack

[screw] ◇ 扁~*,玛聂尔－布莱登式~*,施工~ builder's jack,手动~ hand jack,液压~ hydraulic jack,用~升或下降 jacking,用~张拉钢筋【建】jacking,油压~ oil jack
千斤顶操纵杆　jack handle
千斤顶螺杆　jack screw
千枚岩骨料　phyllite aggregate
千瓦(小)时电度表[千瓦时计]　kilowatt-hour meter
千位(二进制)　kilobit
千叶还原试验(法)　chiba reduction test
千字节　kilobyte
迁移　migration, shift, transfer (ence), transport ◇ 向外~离子 outgoing ion
迁移常数　mobility constant
迁移长度　migration length
迁移方法　transportation method
迁移反应　transport reaction
迁移方程　transport equation
迁移方向　direction of migration [translation]
迁移过程　transport process
迁移机理　【金】transport mechanism
迁移理论　transport theory
迁移率　mobility ◇ 霍尔~ Hall mobility
迁移率比　mobility ratio
迁移溶剂　travel(l)ing solvent
迁移数(离子的)　transference [transport, migration] number
迁移速度　migration rate [velocity]
迁移现象　transport phenomena
迁移效率　transport efficiency
迁移杂质　migrating impurity
签到处　clockhouse
钳　pincers, pliers, tongs
钳柄料(锻件的)　tonghold
钳工　benchwork, locksmith, fitter, machinist
钳工车间　locksmith's shop
钳工小锤　fitter's [bench, machinist's] hammer
钳工组长　fitter foreman
钳工锉　hand file
钳工凿[凿]　fitter's [bench, hand] chisel
钳口　jaw (opening), bite, mouth of tongs
钳取机构　grip
钳式安培计[电流表]　tong-type [clampon] ammeter
钳式带卷吊具【压】lifting grab
钳式点焊焊枪　bar welder
钳式点焊机　pincer spot-welding machine
钳式焊枪　pinch welder gun
钳式起重机[钳式吊车,带钳式抓取装置的吊车]　crab [tong] crane, crampo(o)n,【钢】dogging crane ◇ 均热炉~ soaking pit crane
钳式脱模起重机[吊车]　stripping crane
钳位[压]电路　clamping [clip] circuit, clamper
钳位电阻　clamp resistance
钳位器　clamper
钳型焊条夹持器　tongs-type electrode holder
钳形电流表　tongs tester
钳住(用虎钳)　vice
钳子　nippers
前板(轧机下轧辊的)　fore plate
前泵　roughing pump
前表面镜　front surface mirror
前部工序　upstream process, upflow operation
前部工艺[前段过程]设备　upstream process equipment
前触点　front contact
前处理　【金】conditioning
前床　【冶】forehearth, furnace vessel, settler, fore well, external settler [reservoir, crucible], (色)【铸】(iron) receiver (化铁炉、冲天炉的) ◇ 电热~*,熔融金属~*,水冷~*
前床排空　forehearth draining
前床台　front bed
前吹　【冶】foreblow

| 前端 front [head] end, nose
| 前端处理机 【计】front end (processor)
| 前端反应 front reaction
| 前端墙 front end wall
| 前端装载机 front end loader
| 前隔离板 front screen
| 前横梁(机床的) breast beam
| 前后关系 context
| 前后设备(作业线的) terminal equipment
| 前滑 forward flow, speed gain, 【压】(轧制时金属的) forward slip, slip forward in advance ◇ 金属~·
| 前滑角 【压】advance angle
| 前滑区 【压】zone of slippage on delivery side
| 前滑速率 front slip rate
| 前机架 front platen
| 前级泵 fore [rough] pump, prepump
| 前级真空 primary vacuum, backing space
| 前角 anterior angle, rake (angle)
| 前进波 travel(l)ing [advancing, forward] wave
| 前进法(气焊的) forehand technique
| 前进焊 forward welding
| 前进声波 travel(l)ing sound wave
| 前进旋转火焰淬火法 【金】combination progressive-spinning method of flame hardening
| 前坑 fore well
| 前空气擦拭器 front air wiper equipment
| 前馈 feedforward
| 前馈反馈 AGC feed forward and feed back AGC
| 前馈控制 feedforward control
| 前馈自适应系统 feedforward adaptive system
| 前流气相色层(分离)法 gas frontal chromatography (GFC)
| 前炉 forehearth, (iron) receiver (冲天炉的), casting shoe ◇ 固定式~stationary forehearth, 活动式~mobile forehearth
| 前屏蔽 front screen

前期降水{指标} antecedent precipitation (index)
前期渣 【钢】pre-slag
前墙 front wall
前倾翻斗车 front tipper
前倾焊 angle forwards welding
前散射角 forward scattering angle
前伸量(穿孔顶头的) lead
前室 antechamber
前视图 front view (FV)
前送料压力机 front loading press
前台 【计】foreground
前台处理 【计】foreground processing
前向力 forward force
前向散射 forward scattering
前压力挤压法 (同"反向加压挤压法")
前沿分析(离子交换带的) frontal analysis
前沿面 front face
前沿气相色层(分离)法 (同"前流气相色层法")
前一道次[孔型] previous pass
前移区 advance zone
前余角 【机】front clearance
前张力 forward pull, front tension [pull],【压】coiler [outlet] tension
前支泵 backing [holding] pump
前置出发信号 【运】advance starting signal
前置放大器 preamplifier
前置警告信号 advance warning signal
前轴 front axle
前缀表示法 【计】prefix notation
潜磁化率[强度] latent magnetization
潜伏期[时间] incubation (period), latent time
潜弧电炉 submerged arc (electric) furnace
潜弧焊 hidden arc welding
潜弧自动焊 quasi-arc welding
潜(化合)价 latent valency
潜浸扫描 immersed scanning

潜晶　crypto-crystal
潜晶磷酸铝石 {Al$_2$O$_3$·P$_2$O$_5$·6H$_2$O} zepharovichite, bialite, bialite
潜晶质石英　(同"隐晶石英")
潜孔钻机　down-hole drill (DHD)
潜力　potential(ity), latent capacity ◇ 加工~ operating margin
潜流　underflow, under-current, under-run, subsurface flow
潜流放电　creeping discharge
潜热　latent heat (lat.ht, l.h.), potential [submerged] heat
潜溶剂　【化】latent solvent, cosolvent
潜视孔　periscope hole
潜水泵　submersible [submerged] pump
潜水式电动机　submersible motor
潜水箱　cofferdam
潜像　sub-image, latent image
潜像形成　latent-image formation
潜行(物)　under-run
潜在核心　potential nucleus
潜在滑移系统　latent glide [slip] system
潜在机械强度　potential physical strength
潜在加工硬化　latent work hardening
潜在加工硬化系数　work-hardening coefficient of latent
潜在污染物　【环】latent [potential] pollutant
潜在硬化　latent hardening
潜在资源　potential sources
浅杯突试验(薄钢板的)　bulge test
浅草黄色　pale straw yellow
浅层不连续[不密实]性　shallow discontinuity
浅层裂纹　shallow carck
浅(出)铁口(堵泥量不足的)　short hole, short [weak] taphole
浅床　shallow bed
浅淬火　shallow hardening
浅淬透[淬硬]钢　surface hardening steel, shallow-hardening steel
浅底片　faint negative
浅度淬透性　shallow hardenability
浅海【地】　epeiric [shelf] sea
浅红黄铜(8—17Zn)　semi-red brass
浅基础　shallow foundation
浅扩散结　shallow diffused junction
浅蓝白色光亮金属　lustrous bluish-white metal
浅梁　shallow beam
浅裂纹　shallow crack
浅炉膛　shallow hearth
浅盘水淬法(转炉渣处理用)　【钢】tray quenching process
浅盘型焦炭曝气器　coke tray aerator
浅(熔)池　shallow pool, shallow basin [bath] (反射炉的)
浅熔池混铁炉　【钢】shallow mixer
浅熔焊焊缝　shallow weld
浅室型自由沉降分级机　shallow-pocket free-settling classifier
浅塘【环】　lagoon
浅眼　short hole
嵌板　insert plate
嵌布构造　mosaic structure
嵌齿效应　【电】cogging
嵌缝　caulked seam [joint], filleting
嵌缝集料　key aggregate
嵌缝石　choke stone, keystone
嵌接　notch grafting, scarfing
嵌接法　【建】notch grafting, scarf joint method, scarfing method
嵌晶结构　poikilitic texture
嵌平层(油漆的)　filling colour
嵌入　embedding, imbedding, insertion, built-in, implant(ation) ◇ 带材端头~ strip end engaging
嵌入表面的氧化皮(拔丝时的)　drawn-in scale
嵌入槽　insertion slot
嵌入端　built-in end
嵌入格子砖　【铁】insert for checker
嵌入件　inserted piece
嵌入式插座　flush plug consent

嵌入式冷却壁 【铁】insert-type stave
嵌入式仪表 flush type instrument
嵌入式永久型芯 loose core
嵌入性 embedability, imbedability
嵌丝玻璃 wire glass
嵌填膏泥（用于木石孔隙） badigeon
嵌条 fillet
嵌镶光电阴极 mosaic electrode
嵌镶间界 mosaic boundary
嵌镶结构 mosaic structure
嵌镶晶体 mosaic crystal
嵌镶块 mosaic (block)
嵌镶细工 mosaic
嵌镶应力（夹杂物产生的） tesselated stress
嵌置的 built-in
嵌铸物 【铸】cast-in insert
嵌砖混凝土墙 opus latericium
嵌装 flush mounted
嵌装式 built-in (type)
嵌锒块界 lineage boundary
欠焙烧 underroasting
欠补偿 under-compensation
欠产 shortfall in output
欠吹（转炉的） 【钢】young blow, turn-down young
欠吹炉次 young-blown heat
欠电流继电器 undercurrent relay
欠电流脱扣装置 under current trip
欠电压的 under-voltage
欠复励激磁 undercompound excitation
欠火次砖 under-burned [grizzle] brick
欠火的 underburnt, underfired, underheating
欠火球团 【团】underfired pellet
欠精炼 underrefining
欠励磁 underexcitation
欠热 underheating
欠热淬火 【金】underhardening
欠烧 underfiring, insufficient firing, undersintering
欠烧的 undercalcined
欠烧结的 undersintered
欠烧烧结矿 unfired sinter [agglomerate]
欠速淬火 slack quenching [hardening]
欠速淬火的贝氏体组织 slack-quenched bainitic structure
欠酸洗 【压】underpickling
欠压继电器 undervoltage relay
欠压释放【断路】 under-voltage release
欠压跳闸【脱扣】 undervoltage tripping
欠氧火焰 underventilated flame
欠载 underload(ing)
欠载断路器 underload circuit-breaker
欠载运行 under-run
欠轧 【压】under-roll
欠整流 【电】undercommutation
欠重(的) underweight
欠阻尼 underdamp
欠装法 【粉】underfill system
茜素 $\{C_6H_4(CO)_2C_6H_2(OH)_2\}$ alizarin
枪管（石油油井用） barrel
枪管钢 gun barrels steel
枪晶石 cuspidine
枪炮黄铜 gun brass
枪炮青铜 gun bronze
枪炮用钢 gun steel
枪身烧蚀 barrel erosion
枪式焊料槽 gun hopper
枪式喷燃器 gun burner
枪嘴 gun nozzle
腔口速度 muzzle velocity (MV, mv)
腔内 intracavity
墙板 wallboard, 【团】siding
墙壁锚栓件 wall anchor
墙壁锚栓系统 wall anchoring system
墙壁内涂搪瓷冷轧钢板 Yodowall
墙承重结构 wall bearing construction
墙粉 【建】calcimine, kalsomine
墙拱 wall arch
墙角护条 corner head ◇ 异丁(烯)橡胶 ~ butyl rubber beading
墙结合木 【运】bond timber
墙面格间 wall panel

墙内散热器　built-in radiator
墙裙　【建】wainscot, dado
墙上[墙装]起重机　wall crane
墙上悬臂吊车[墙装挺杆起重机]　wall jib crane
墙垣干[无浆]砌　dry walling
蔷薇辉石{MnSiO₃}　rhodonite, manganolite
蔷薇钙铝榴石　xalostocite
蔷薇状共晶组织　【金】rosette
强磁场　intense magnetic field (IMF)
强磁场材料　high-intensity magnetic material
强磁场超导材料　high-intensity magnetic field superconducting material
强磁合金　strong magnetic alloy
强磁性体模型　◇伊星～Ising model
强磁性物料　strongly magnetic material
强磁性物质　ferromagnetic substance
强磁选(法)　high-intensity magnetic separation (HIMS) ◇湿式～*
强电解质　strong electrolyte
强电流　strong [heavy] current
强度　strength (str), degree of strength, intensity, degree of firmness ◇等～连接*, 热处理后～(等级)*, 瞬时～instantaneous strength
强度比　strength [intensity] ratio
强度变化　variation in strength, drift in intensity
强度变量　intensive variable
强度测定　intensity measurement ◇照相法～*
强度测定转鼓　【铁】tumbler
强度常数　strength constant
强度等级　strength level
强度点(反应堆高中子通量的)　hot spot
强度范围　strength range
强度－刚度比　strength to rigidity ratio
强度广延变量　intensive variable
强度极限　maximum strength, break limit, resistance to rupture

强度减半厚度　half-value thickness
强度减低[下降]　deterioration in strength, fall-off in intensity, loss of strength
强度降低系数　strength reduction factor
强度理论　strength theory
强度量　intensive quantity
强度试验　strength test
强度试验机　strength testing machine
强度损失　loss of strength
强度调制　intensity modulation
强度无限小的弹性位错　elastic dislocation of infinitesimal strengths
强度系数　strength coefficient [constant], specific strength
强度性能[特性]　strength property [characteristic], intensive property
强度因数　strength factor
强度值(机械强度)　strength value
强度指标　strength index
强度指数　strength index, stability factor (焦炭的)
强度－重量比　strength-to-weight ratio
强反差图像　hard [contrast, harsh] image
强反差性负片　hard negative
强反差照明　hard lighting
强放射性材料　"hot" material
强放射性试验　hot test
强放射性物质研究实验室　hot laboratory
强风量　high wind
强辐射　【理】intense radiation
强负电性金属　strongly electronegative metal
强固铺板(轧机周围的)　solid apron
强固致密连接　firm and impervious joint
强光部　high light(s)
强光泽涂料　high gross paint
强过冷结晶　(同"延迟结晶")
强滑移线集聚　【金】grouping of prominent slip lines
强化　strengthening, intensification, reinforcement, consolidating, hardening ◇机

械[形变]~ mechanical hardening, 纪尼埃－普雷斯顿区~*, 弥散~*, 碳化物晶须~金属*, 纤维~金属*
强化钢 strengthened steel
强化机理[机制] strengthening mechanism
强化剂 strengthening [intensifying] agent, strengthener
强化颗粒 reinforcing particle
强化流态剂 fluidizer
强化燃烧 intensifying combustion, intensified firing
强化熔炼 positive fusion
强化筛分式布料器 intensified sifting feeder (ISF)
强化物 reinforcement
强化系数 strength coefficient, intensifying factor
强化相 strengthening phase
强化冶炼 strengthening smelting, 【铁】sharp working ◇ 开炉~*
强化因数 intensification factor
强化元素 strengthening element ◇ 奥氏体~ austenite hardener
强化状态 strengthened condition
强化作用 strengthening effect
强还原性气氛 strongly reducing atmosphere
强碱 alkali, alcali
强碱废水 strong alkali waste water
强碱性 alkalinity
强碱性胺 strong base amine
强碱性阴离子交换剂 strong base anion exchanger
强碱性阴离子交换树脂 strong base anion resin ◇ SAR~ Nalcite SAR, 道克斯 1~*, 杜利特 A－42~ Duolite A－42, 卢泰特 M_2~Lewatit M_2, 珀缪泰特 A~
强碱性阴离子交换树脂 FF De-Acidite FF
强键 strong [tight] bond
强结合 strong [tight] binding

强浸出液 strong leaching liquid
强聚焦 strong focusing
强拉钢丝 dead-drawn wire
强拉力[拉伸]的 high tensile
强力场 strong field
强力起重机 goliath crane
强力旋压(减厚) power spinning
强力圆筒混合造球机 strong drum pelletizer
强烈沸腾[搅拌] violent agitation
强烈沸腾炉次 【钢】wild heat
强烈沸腾效应 【冶】wild effect
强烈腐蚀 heavy [active] corrosion
强烈火焰 Keen flame
强烈流态化状态 intensive fluidization condition
强烈起泡 violent bubbling
强烈燃烧 high-intensity combustion
强黏力型砂 【铸】strong (moulding) sand
强黏性黏土 fat clay
强耦合超导体 strong coupling superconductor
强耦合理论 strong coupling theory
强迫润滑－拉模组合装置 nozzle die unit
强迫送料的拉拔机 push pointer bench
强迫展宽 【压】induced spread
强迫振荡[振动] constrained oscillation
强谱线 【理】intense spectrum line
强曝光 acute exposure
强韧化处理 strengthening and toughening
强韧化机制 strengthening and toughening mechanism
强溶剂 strong solvent
强溶性废水(管道) strong soluble waste water (SSWW)
强渗碳气氛 strongly carburizing atmosphere
强势场 strong [high] field
强双氧水(含30%过氧化氢) perhydrol
强酸 strong-acid
强酸废水(管道) strong acid waste water (SAWW)

强酸浸出 strong-acid leach
强酸性溶液 strongly acidic solution
强酸性阳离子交换剂 strongly acidic cation exchanger
强铁磁性铜锰合金 ◇休斯勒~*
强脱硫渣 【钢】strongly desulphurizing slag
强线(X射线衍射线中的) strong line
强相互作用 strong interaction
强氧化矿石 high oxide ore
强氧化(性)渣 【冶】strongly [highly] oxidizing slag
强应力场 high field
强轧的 strong rolled (Rs)
强制 forcing, coercing, constraining
强制沉淀 forced precipitation
强制成形焊接 enclosed welding
强制磁致伸缩 forced magnetostriction
强制点火 forced ignition
强制对流 forced convection (flow)
强制对流式烧结矿冷却机 forced convection sinter cooler
强制风冷式 force ventilated
强制给[进]料 forced [positive] feed
强制鼓风 forced air blast [injection]
强制换向 forced reversing [commutation]
强制激磁 forced excitation
强制加油拉模盒 【压】pressure die box
强制加油器 forced feed oiler
强制搅拌[混合] positive mixing
强制结晶 forced crystallization
强制空气冷却淬火 forced air quenching
强制空气循环炉 forced air circulation furnace
强制空气循环式电阻炉 forced air circulation resistance furnace
强制扩散 forced diffusion
强制冷却 forced [positive] cooling
强制流通贮仓 positive throughflow bunker
强制凝集沉淀装置 【环】compelled coagulation sedimentation equipment
强制润滑(法) forced (feed) lubrication
强制润滑拉拔 【压】drawing with forced lubrication
强制通风 forced [blast, positive] draught, forced ventilation
强制通风风机 forced ventilation fan
强制通风管道 forced draught duct
强制通风冷却 forced air [draught] cooling
强制通风冷却塔 forced draught cooling tower
强制通风式曝气装置 【环】forced-draught aerator
强制通风式直流电动机 force ventilated DC motor
强制脱硫(电渣冶金的) forced desulphurizing
强制脱氧 【钢】forced deoxidation, chemical deoxidation
强制[强行]显示 【计】forced display
强制性 coercibility
强制循环 forced circulation
强制循环冷却 forced circulation cooling
强制循环汽化冷却 (同"高压汽化冷却")
强制循环冷却 forced circulation cooling
强制循环蒸发器(液体的) forced circulation evaporator
强制压尖(盘条拉模时的) push pointing
强制展宽 forced spread
强制振动 【理】constrained vibration
强制着火 forced ignition
强烛光 【电】high candle power
强子 【理】hardon
抢运 【运】rush transport
羟胺 hydroxylamine
羟碲铜石 xocomecatlite
羟碘铜矿 iod-atacamite, salesite
羟钒铜铅石{5(Cu,Pb)O·V$_2$O$_5$·2H$_2$O} mottramite
羟钴矿 transvaalite
羟硅铍钇矿 yberisilite

羟硅铍钇铈矿　yttroceberysite
羟硅铈矿　toernebohmite
羟硅稀土石　tombarthite
羟硅钇石　iimoraite
羟基　hydroxy(1)(group)
羟基丁二酸｛$HO_2CCHOHCH_2CO_2H$｝　malic acid
羟基方钠石　hydroxysodalite
羟基化(作用)　hydroxylation
羟基氯化镁｛$Mg·OHCl$｝　magnesium hydroxychloride
羟基氯化物　hydroxychloride
羟基醛　hydroxyaldehyde
羟基脂肪酸　hydroxy fatty acid
羟离子　(同"氢氧离子")
羟砷钇锰石　retzian
羟碳(钙)铈矿　hydroxyl-bastnaesite
羟钍石　thorogummite｛$(Pb,Th)UO_3·nH_2O$｝,mackintoshite｛$UO_2·3ThO_2·3SiO_2·3H_2O$｝
羟锡矿　hydroromarchite
羟锡锰石　wickmanite
羟锌矿　sauconite,zinkmontorillonite
羟氧钼根(有二价的 $MoO(OH)=$ 和三价的 $MoO(OH)≡$)　molybdyl
羟氧铜矿　botallackite
羟铟石　dzahlindite
羟铀矿　epiianthinite
羟锗铅矾　itoite
敲(打)　knock,beat,strike,rap,tap,percuss ◇ 氧化铁皮～锤 scaling hammer
敲击器　knocker
敲击铁鳞　scale knocking
敲(模)棒　【铸】rapping iron
敲模杆　loosening bar
敲松(模型)　【铸】rapping
敲响检验　aural test
桥　bridge ◇ 打～钎·
桥墩　(bridge)pier ◇ 圆柱形～cylindrical pier
桥墩护栏　pier fender
桥管　bridge pipe,【焦】crossover main, goose-neck
桥管清扫器　【焦】gooseneck cleaner
桥基[桥梁基础]　bridge foundation
桥架式气割机　gantry cutting machine
桥键　【化】bridging
桥接传输　bridge transfer
桥接电路　bridge circuit ◇ 格雷茨全波～·
桥接法　bridge method
桥接塞孔　bridging jack
桥跨[桥梁跨度]　bridge span
桥跨结构拱度　rise of span
桥栏杆　bridge railing
桥梁钢板　bridge steel plate
桥路　bridge circuit[connection]
桥路桥臂　leg of circuit
桥面　bridge floor,deck
桥墙　【冶】bridge wall
桥墙顶砌块　bridge wall cover block
桥式吊包[罐]起重机　【钢】overhead ladle crane
桥式法(测量)　bridge method
桥式放大器　bridge amplifier
桥式接线　full wave connection
桥式联接　bridge connection
桥式起重机[吊车]　overhead crane(O.H.C.),bridge[gantry,travel(l)ing]crane,overhead level(l)ing[travel(l)ing]crane,ore(stocking)bridge (贮矿场的) ◇ 单轨～·,单梁移动～·,电动～·,卷扬型～[走行吊车],装料～ loading bridge
桥式取料机　bridge type reclaimer
桥式输送机　traverser
桥式四端网络　X-quadripole
桥式运输带　conveyer gantry
桥式整流器　bridge rectifier
桥式制动器　【机】bridge brake
桥索钢丝　bridge wire
桥台　land[bridge]abutment,butment
桥头挖方　approach cutting
桥下净高　clear headway of bridge

桥下净空 under-clearance
桥型滤波器 differential filter
桥形触点 bridge type contact, double-break contact
桥形钢轨 bridge rail
乔佛镍铬铁耐热合金〔60Ni,20Cr,余量Fe〕 Jofo
乔利维特－佩纳罗亚铅精炼法（用于除铋） Jollivet-Penarroya debismuthizing process
鞘硫细菌属 thiothece
撬棍〔杆〕 crowbar, crowfoot, wrenching iron, jimmy〔短的〕◇ 铁～ grab iron
翘角 rake angle
翘扭变形 warp
翘起 upwarping, warpage
翘曲 buckle, buckling warp(age), warping, camber, curling,【金】skellering（淬火时的）◇ 不～钢板 warp-free plate, 钢板～（缺陷） camber of sheet, 向上～ upwarping, 消除～【压】iron out
翘曲矫直 curve flattening
翘曲面 【压】warped surface
切 cutting, slicing, chipping, chopping
切板机 plate cutter, plate cutting machine
切边 side crops〔trimmings〕, scrap〔cut〕edge, side shearing, slit selvage, trimming(cut), trash ◇ 卷状薄板～ coiled shearings
切边冲头 cropping〔trimming〕punch
切边刀片 trimming knife
切边剪〔机〕 (edge, side) trimmer, (edge-)trimming machine, side-cut shears, (end) trimming shears, side (trimming) shears ◇ 圆盘(式)～〔切边圆盘剪〕
切边卷取机 【压】balling machine, (scrap) baller
切边模 cropping die ◇ 布莱姆～ Brehm trimming die
切边清理 【压】crop handling
切边－碎边剪 side trimmer and scrap cutter
切边圆盘剪 (同"圆盘(式)切边剪")
切边中厚板轧机 sheared plate mill
切边中厚钢板 sheared plate
切边作业线 side shear line（板材的）, trimming line（带材的）
切变 shear, shearing (strain) ◇ 附加～ additional shear, 孪生～ twinning shear, 远程～ far reaching shear
切变波 shear-wave
切变波双折射技术 shear wave birefringence technique
切变波速度 shear wave velocity
切变波探测器 shear wave probe
切变断口〔断裂〕 shear fracture
切变点阵〔晶格〕 sheared lattice
切变力 shear(ing) force
切变裂纹〔裂缝〕 shear crack
切变模量〔模数〕(G＝剪应力/剪应变) shear(ing) modulus, modulus of shear, Coulomb's modulus, transverse modulus*
切变强度 shear strenth ◇ 理想晶体～的麦肯齐计算(法)*
切变速度 speed of shear waves
切变速率 rate of shear
切变弹性 shear elasticity
切变弹性模量〔模数〕 modulus of elasticity for〔in〕shear
切变探测装置 shear wave search unit
切变位移 shear displacement
切变形式〔模式〕 shear mode
切变硬化 shear hardening
切变增量 increment of shear
切变值 slip height
切变转变 shear transformation
切变组 set of shears
切变组合 combination of shears
切槽 grooving, carved fillet, fluting, nicking ◇ 深-〔机〕heavy cut
切槽填焊焊缝 filled slot weld
切侧边（板带材的） edge〔side〕trimming
切(成)定尺 【压】cut-to-length

切除锭头 【压】ingot topping
切除端部(板、带材的) end trimming
切除冒口 【钢】topping
切除直浇口 sprue cutting
切穿 cut-through
切刀 cutter, gad, 【金】breaking knife (摆锤冲击机的) ◇ 手动~ hand-powered cutter
切点 point of tangency (P.T.), point of contact
切掉 cutaway
切顶(螺纹) crest truncation
切锭机(床) parting [ingot-slicing] machine, slicing lathe
切锭锯 ingot saw
切定尺作业线 cut-to-length (shear) line
切断 cut(ting)-off, shut-off, switch off, throw off [out], turn-off, key off, deenergizing, deenergising, disconnecting
切断操纵杆 disconnecting lever
切断冲头 cutting punch
切断电弧 break arc
切断电源 power cut, dump
切断阀 isolating [stop, septum] valve
切断机 cut-off machine ◇ 钢筋~ bar cutter, 熔化~*
切断激磁 deenergize, deenergise
切断开关 【电】disconnecting switch (DS), cut-off [cut-out] switch
切断轮 cutting-off wheel
切断器 disjunctor, 【压】distributor ◇ 带~的组合模 (bolted) bridge die
切断砂轮 cutting-off wheel
切断旋塞 shut-off [cut-off] cock
切断压力机 cutting-out press
切断用金属丝 【耐】cutting wire
切飞边机 【压】deburring machine
切废 cutting scrap, miscut, chopping
切分 segmentation
切分带材 slit strip
切分剪 (sub)dividing shears ◇ 滚筒式~ rotary dividing sheaar

切分孔型 【压】slitting pass, fuller ◇ 闭口~ unopen slitting pass, 开口~ open slitting pass
切割 cut(ting), slicing, dissection, incision, tranverse, 【铸】coping out (不平分型面的) ◇ 水冷~ cutting with water quench, 随后加热的~ cutting with postheating, 氧气~*, 预热后~*
切割不足 【机】undercut
切割电极 cutting electrode
切割阀 【焊】cutting valve
切割废料 cuttings
切割工序 cut-off operation
切割供氧管 cutting oxygen tube
切割火焰 cutting flame
切割机 cutting machine ◇ 摆动臂式~*, 单臂式~*, 多焰嘴~*, 径向铰链式~*, 冷锯~*, 熔化~*, 手动~*, 双梁~*, 双悬臂~*, 圆盘~*
切割机划痕 cutting machine scratch
切割挤压 cut extrusion
切割间隙 cutting gap
切割金属极限厚度 【焊】cutting capacity
切割力 cutting force
切割流 【焊】cutting jet
切割黏土用夹具 chuck-hold
切割器 cutter, torch ◇ 火焰~*, 同心喷嘴~*, 小孔~*
切割区 【连铸】cut-off station
切割砂轮 【机】(abrasive) cutting wheel
切割烧嘴 cutting burner [blowpipe, head] ◇ 厚金属~*
切割速度 cutting speed
切割速率 cutting rate
切割台 cutting-off table
切割拖后量 cutting drag
切割效率 cutting efficiency
切割焰(气割的) cutting flame
切割甲电极 cutting electrode
切割用氧气 cutting oxygen
切割装置 cut-off unit, cutting apparatus
切管机 pipe cutter, pipe cutting machine,

tube cutting-off machine ◇ 自动～*
切管用割把　tube cutting burner
切过的边　trimmed edge
切换　changing-over, throw-over, switch(ing) over ◇ 抽头～开关 tap-changer
切换机构　shifter
切换继电器　transfer relay
切开　cutting-off, cutting-out, cut apart, slice,
切开带边　slit edge
切口　cut, notch, slot ◇ 割～ notching, 无～的 cutless, 氧乙炔焰切割的～ oxy-acetylene cut
切口边　cutting shoulder
切口脆性　notch-brittle, notch brittleness
切口冲击强度　notch impact strength
切口冲击试验　notch impact (shock) test
切口冲击值　notch bar impact strength
切口底部　base of notch
切口搭接焊　slotted lap welding
切口焊缝　slot weld
切口拉伸试样　notched tensile specimen
切口灵敏度　notch sensitivity
切口韧性　notch toughness
切口试样　notch specimen [test bar]
切口试验　【金】notch test
切口延性　notch ductility
切口形状　notch geometry
切口效应　notch effect
切力面　【压】plane of shear
切料机　【压】blanking machine
切伦科夫辐射　Cerenkov radiation
切伦科夫光　【理】Cerenkov light
切伦科夫计数管　Cerenkov counter
切螺纹　chasing
切面　tangent paane
切莫伊碱液浸镀防锈黑氧化膜法　Chemoy process
切姆普罗 C-20 磺化聚苯乙烯阳离子交换树脂　Chempro C-20
切诺特海绵铁制取法　Chenot process
切坯机　(blank) cutter,【耐】cutting(-off) table

切坯机床　parting machine
切片　cut film, sectioning, skiving
切片机　section cutter, slicer ◇ 超薄～ ultra-microtome, 金相[薄样]～ microtome, 自动晶体～*
切取(铁矿石混匀步骤)　reclaiming
切去头部(暴露钢坯内部缺陷)　ending
切入[深](孔型的)　【压】cutting-in
切深孔型　【压】knifing pass
切深轧制　knifing
切斯特菲尔德带钢淬火法　Chesterfield's process
切四边(裁方)　square cut
切碎废钢　shred scrap
切碎机　shredder, shredding machine, chopper, knife mill,【机】devil ◇ 废钢～【冶】scrap shredder
切头　crop(ping), crop end [piece], croppage, end trimming, ending, front end crops, lost head, scrap end, top crop [cut], discard (head), waste head, trash,【铸】head metal
切头飞剪　【压】flying crop shears (FCS) ◇ 滚筒式～*
切头飞剪进口导板　flying crop shear entry side guide
切头废料　top scrap
切头滑槽　【压】crop chute
切头剪[机]　【压】cropping machine, crop(ping) [end] shears ◇ 盘条～*, 曲柄式～*, 双刃～*, 移动式～*
切头剪侧导板　crop shear side guide
切头剪前辊道　crop shear approach table
切头锯　crop(ping) saw
切头排除　【压】crop handling
切头抛出辊道　【压】crop kick-off table
切头切边收集坑　【压】crop disposal bin
切头清除　crop removal ◇ 轧入侧～辊道*
切头收集站　scrap collecting station
切头尾损失　crop end loss, cropping loss,

切 qie

scrap down
切头推出机 【压】crop end pusher
切头推出机推料杆 【压】crop end-pusher arm
切头箱[桶] 【压】crop [scrap] bucket, crop end bucket
切头箱车 scrap bucket car
切头用翻斗提升机 crop skip hoist
切头优化 crop optimization
切头运输机 【压】crop conveyer
切土机 clay cutter
切挖(不平分型面) 【铸】parting-down
切尾 back end crop, cropping of tail end
切沃里诺夫定则 【铸】Chvorinov's rule
切下 cut-off
切线 【数】tangency, tangent, tangent(ial) line
切线法则 tangent rule
切线逼近法 tangential approximation
切线模数 tangent modulus
切线入射 grazing incidence
切线速度 tangential velocity
切线弯板机 tangent bender
切线应力 tangenttal stress
切向 tangential direction
切向布置烧嘴 tangentially arranged burner
切向成形 tangent forming
切向分量 tangential component
切向检验 tangential test
切向键 tangential key
切向浇口 tangential runner
切向抗拉强度 tangential tensile strength
切向力 tangential force
切向切割 tangential cutting
切向取样检验 tangential test
切向烧嘴均热炉 tangentially fired soaking pit
切向梯度传感器 tangential gradient probe
切向弯曲 tangent bending
切向应变 tangential strain

切向应力 tangential stress
切向铸造 tangential casting
切削 【机】cutting ◇ 垂直[两向,二维]～*,带油的～oily turning,电动～台*,防氧化～cover cutting,可～的 machinable,易～的 free cutting
切削刀具 cutter, cutting-tool
切削刀具材料 cutting tool material
切削刀具用钢 machine tool steel
切削合金 cutting alloy ◇ 库珀莱特硬质～Cooperite
切削机 cutting machine ◇ 黏土～*
切削加工 machining
切削加工特性 machine conditions
切削(加工)性能 machining property, machining [tooling] quality, machinability
切削加工性能指数(机床的) machinability index
切削金属(制造切削刀具用) cutting metal
切削冷却液 【机】cutting [machining] fluid, cutting coolant
切削力 【机】cutting force [power]
切削面 cut surface, cutting face
切削能力 【机】cutting ability [capacity, quality]
切削刃 cutting edge [lip]
切削润滑剂 【机】cutting compound
切削试验 【机】cutting test
切削速度 【机】cutting speed [rate]
切削误差 cutting error
切削屑 cuttings, shavings, turnings
切削性 cutability ◇ 改善～添加剂*
切削液 cutting [machining] fluid
切削硬度 cutting hardness
切削用矿物油 mineral cutting oil
切削油(润滑、冷却用) 【机】cutting oil
切削余量 machining [finish] allowance
切斜 shear drag
切屑 cutting scrap, turnings, scarfings, swarf ◇ 去油[脱脂]～deoiled turnings, 紊乱～tangled turnings, 无～加工 chip-

less machining, 重～ heavy cut
切屑废钢　turnings scrap
切屑防护器　chip guard
切屑篮　chip basket
切屑瘤　built up edge
切屑压块机　【冶】swarf baling [briquetting] machine
切压制模(法)　hubbing
切样器　sample cutter
切伊斯720铜锰镍合金(60Cu, 20Mn, 20Ni)　Chace 720
切应力　shearing stress ◇ 恒定分解～*
切应力-应变图　shearing stress-strain diagram
切应力定律　shear stress law
切应力分量　component of shear stress
切砖　【耐】(brick) cutting
切砖机　brick cutter, brick cutting saw, masonry saw ◇ 移动式电动～*
侵犯[害]　infringement
侵蚀　corrosion, (impingement) attack, eating, erosion ◇ 灰～ ash attack, 抗～性 incorrodibility, 可～的 attackable, 炉衬【冶】scouring, 未受～部分 unattacked area, 阳极[电解]～ anodic etching, 阻止～的涂层*
侵蚀带　attack zone
侵蚀过程　attack process
侵蚀痕　erosion scar [mark]
侵蚀机理　attack mechanism
侵蚀剂　etching (re)agent, etchant, attack agent ◇ 阿贝尔～ Abel's reagent
侵蚀坑　corrosion pit(ting) ◇ 位错～*
侵蚀炉形　【铁】furnace wear lines
侵蚀能力　corrosive power
侵蚀速率[度]　attack rate
侵蚀性　corrosive power, aggressiveness, aggressivity
侵蚀性腐蚀　erosion corrosion
侵蚀性接触　corrosive contact
侵蚀性介质　aggressive medium
侵蚀性气体　aggressive gas

侵蚀性水　aggressive water
侵蚀渣　【冶】scouring cinder
侵蚀作用　corrosion effect, corrosive attack [effect], erosion (effect) ◇ 炉渣～*
亲电子的　electrophilic
亲和[合]力　affinity ◇ 内聚～ cohesive affinity, 选择性～ elective affinity
亲和能[亲和势,亲合性]　affinity
亲气的　air-adherent
亲气元素　atmophile element
亲水胶体　hydrophilic colloid, hydrophile
亲水物　hydrophile
亲水性　hydrophilicity, water affinity, wettability
亲水性粉末　lyophilic powder
亲液胶体　lyophile, lyophilic colloid
亲液物　lyophile
亲质子性溶剂　protophilic solvent
琴钢丝直径标号　music wire gauge
琴(弦)钢丝(0.8—0.95C)　music wire
揿钉　drawing pin
青壳纸　fish paper
青霉菌　Penicillium
青泥　blue mud
青泥灰岩　blue marl
青铅矿　cuprous anglesite
青石棉(钠闪石)　{NaFe(SiO$_3$)$_2$·FeSiO$_3$} crocidolite
青特耳相　【理】Zintl phases
青铜(铜锡合金)　bronze (br, Bz) ◇ α～ alpha bronze, δ～*, 艾杰克斯标准～*, 包层用～*, 兵器～ Arms Bronze (AMB), 导电线用～*, 低硅～*, 低锡～*, 电讯线材～*, 杜拉弗莱克斯～*, 镀[包]～钢～*, 多孔～*, 福诺～*, 复合～*, 高硅～*, 高强度～*, 高锡～ high tin bronze, 工业[普通]～ commercial bronze, 规尺～*, 海军～*, 含钽～*, 火焰喷镀用～*, 货币～*, 加工硬化～ work-hardened bronze, 加铅～*, 减摩～ journal bronze, 建筑～*, 金属制品用～ hardware bronze, 镜～*, 类～的 bronzy,

冷压烧结～*,铝铁镍锰高级～*,螺旋桨～propeller bronze,罗曼～*,耐海水腐蚀～*,耐酸～*,汽阀～*,石墨～*,塑像用～*,碳～*,托宾～*,脱氧～deoxidized bronze,无锡～tinless bronze,易切削铸造铅锰～*,银色～*,硬钎焊～*,致密～dense bronze,中国[钟用]～*,轴承～*,贮乳器～*,铸造～*,装饰用～*

青铜黄铜铸造工作者协会 Association of Bronze and Brass Founders (ABBF)
青铜(表面)堆焊 bronze surfacing
青铜衬里 bronze liner
青铜导板 bronze guide
青铜的 bronzy
青铜废料 bronze scrap
青铜粉 bronze powder
青铜过滤管 sintered bronze filter tube
青铜过滤片 sintered bronze filter disc
青铜焊 bronze weld(ing)[brazing]
青铜焊条 【焊】bronze welding rod
青铜合金(70—90Cu,1—18Sn,1—25Zn,余量 Ni,P,Mn,Al,Pb 等) bronze alloy (B.A.) ◇ 霍尔福斯～*,卢门～*,铅～*
青铜化 bronzing
青铜聚氟乙烯轴承 bronze fluon bearing
青铜坯块 bronze compact ◇ 热压～*
青铜器 bronze ware
青铜(钎)焊料(45Zn,3—5Sn,余量 Cu) spelter bronze
青铜色 bronzine ◇ 着～bronzing
青铜色的 bronze coloured
青铜石墨电接触器材 bronze graphite contact material
青铜石墨电刷 bronze graphite brush
青铜石墨轴承 tin-copper-graphite bearing
青铜丝 bronze wire
青铜丝电弧焊 bronze weld(ing)
青铜填充金属 【焊】bronze filler metal
青铜洗滤器 sintered bronze filter washer
青铜型(铜合金) bronze type

青铜制的 bronzine
青铜轴承 bronze bearing ◇ 烧结[粉冶]～*,塑性高锡～合金,沃尔维特～合金(91Cu,9Sn) Volvit
青铜轴套 bronze bush
青铜铸件[铸造] bronze casting
轻磅镀锡薄钢板 light plate(厚度 0.20—0.28mm), lights(厚度在 0.18mm 以下)
轻便点焊机 portable spot welder
轻便吊杆 【铁】portable davit
轻便发电机 portable generator
轻便高温计 portable pyrometer
轻便机车 dinkey engine[locomotive](运土、石用)
轻便落地起重机[吊车] canton crane
轻便起重机 portable crane
轻便式 X 射线应力测量仪 portable X-ray stress-measuring apparatus
轻便式电离室 small ionization chamber
轻便式模型干燥炉 portable mould drier
轻便手工割炬 manual cutting torch
轻便梯 calwalk
轻便铁道 light railway
轻便(型)炉 portable furnace ◇ 加热焊料用～devil
轻便性 portability
轻便研磨机 portable grinder
轻便硬度试验机 portable hardness tester ◇ 恩斯特～
轻便栈桥 calwalk
轻便罩式炉 portable cover furnace
轻掺杂籽晶 lightly doped seed
轻萃液 light extract
轻捣固[实] 【铸】soft ramming
轻捣实铸型 soft-rammed mould
轻度电离化气体 slightly ionized gas
轻度冷拔的 light-drawn
轻度麻口灰铸铁 lightly mottled gray cast iron
轻度酸洗 【金】mild pickle
轻度凸面轧辊 full roll

轻度氧化	mild oxidation
轻度中毒[吸附有害离子]	mild poison
轻废钢	fine scrap
轻沸腾	【钢】light-boiling
轻敷黏土槽	【冶】dabbed (clay) spout
轻负荷	light-load, light-duty
轻盖	【钢】light cap
轻汞膏	arguerite
轻骨料	light(weight) aggregate
轻骨料混凝土	lightweight aggregate concrete
轻光整冷轧	【压】under-skin pass
轻轨(每m重小于30kg)	light rail
轻混凝土	lightweight concrete
轻击	【铸】rapping
轻击锤	rapping hammer, tapper
轻捷构造	balloon construction
轻捷骨架	balloon framing
轻金属	light metal (L.M.), light nonferrous metal, light-weight metal ◇ 易切削~
轻金属粉末	light metal powder
轻(金属)合金	light alloy (L.A.), light weight alloy
轻金属矿	light metal ore
轻金属冶金(学)	metallurgy of light metals, light-weight metal metallurgy
轻金属元素	light metal element
轻(精)冷轧	pinch pass
轻空穴	light hole
轻空穴带	light hole band
轻冷拔	light-drawing
轻馏分	light distillate [fraction, ends], 【化】head
轻馏分蒸馏设备	【色】topping plant
轻溶剂	light solvent
轻润滑油	light lubricant
轻三合土	lightweight lime concrete
轻烧	light roasting, 【耐】light burning
轻烧白云石	lightly fired dolomite, caustic-burned dolomite
轻烧镁砂	caustic-burned magnesite
轻烧耐火制品	light-burned refractory ware
轻烧石灰	soft burned lime
轻烧熟料	light-burned grog
轻石	pumice (stone)
轻石灰三合土	lightweight lime concrete
轻水	light water
轻水反应堆	light water reactor
轻苏打	light ash
轻贴角焊	light fillet welding
轻烃	light hydrocarbon
轻同位素	light isotope
轻微拉伸	shallow draught(ing)
轻微曝光	light exposure
轻微事故	light accident
轻微压力	light [slight] pressure
轻稀土	light rare earth
轻稀有金属	light rare metal, less common light metal
轻相(常指有机相)	lighter phase
轻相[液]出口(萃取的)	light (phase) out, light liquid outlet
轻相[液]入口(萃取的)	light (phase) in, light liquid inlet
轻型	light-duty, light gauge (钢材), light (-weight)
轻型槽钢	thin-wall channel
轻型钢材	light (gauge) section, lightweight steel shape
轻型钢结构	light section steel structure
轻型工字钢	lightweight I-beam
轻型合金铸件	light alloy casting
轻型化	weight reduction
轻型机械	light-duty machinery
轻型剪切机作业线	light shear line
轻型矫直机	light leveller
轻型角钢	light weight angle steel
轻型型材[型钢]	lightweight section
轻型铸件	light casting
轻型装载机	low loader
轻型钻管	light weight drill pipe (lwdp)
轻压道次	【压】light pass

轻压盖 【钢】light cap
轻压实铸型 【铸】soft-rammed mould
轻压缩 light draft
轻压下 soft reduction
轻压下机构 soft reduction device
轻压轧制(初轧头道的) saddening
轻摇 joggle
轻液 light liquid
轻油 light oil
轻油馏分 light distillate
轻油制气 gasmaking with light oil
轻有色金属 light non-ferrous metal
轻元素 light element
轻原子 light atom
轻载加铅巴氏合金[马耶斯提克轻载巴比合金,塞维斯 D 轻载巴比合金] (同"硬质纯巴氏合金")
轻载的 low-duty
轻载运行 light running
轻制焦油沥青 cutback tar
轻制沥青 cutback bitumen [asphalt]
轻质产物 light-end product
轻质废金属 【色】light scrap
轻质高铝砖 light weight alumina brick
轻质混凝土结构 light concrete structure
轻质炉渣(经泡沫化处理的) lightweight slag
轻质氯化物 light chloride
轻质耐火材料 lightweight refractory
轻质耐火混凝土 light weight fire resisting concrete
轻质耐火浇注料 light weight castable refractory
轻质耐火砖 light fire brick
轻质凝聚渣 lightweight-aggregate slag
轻质膨胀黏土骨料 【耐】lightweight expanded clay aggregate
轻质陶粒骨料 light expanded clay aggregate (L.E.C.A.)
轻质氧化铝砖 light weight oxide alumina brick
轻质砖 light(weight) brick

轻装料 【冶】light burden [charge]
轻组分馏出 flashing off
氢{H} hydrogen ◇ 电解～ electrolytic hydrogen,鼓～泡 hydrogen blistering,含～的 hydrogen-containing, hydrogen-bearing, hydrogenous, 含～气体*,加～*,送－泵 hydrogen blower,脱[去]～*,无[不含]～的 hydrogen-free,析～腐蚀*,吸～ hydrogen pick-up,新生态～*
氢保护气氛 protective hydrogen atmosphere ◇ 高效能纯～罩式退火炉*
氢保护烧结炉 hydrogen sintering furnace, sintering hydrogen furnace
氢爆皮 hydrogen blistering
氢(标准)电极 hydrogen electrode
氢超电压 hydrogen overvoltage
氢触媒吸附 hydrogen-catalyst adsorption
氢脆粉末 hydrogen-embrittled powder
氢脆(性) hydrogen brittleness [embrittlement, shortness], acid brittleness
氢碲酸 hydrotelluric acid
氢电极电位 hydrogen electrode potential
氢电位 hydrogen potential
氢动力学 kinetics of hydrogen
氢分压 hydrogen partial pressure
氢氟化 hydrofluorination ◇ 多级流化床～*,连续流化床～*,氧化物～*
氢氟化反应器 hydrofluorination reactor ◇ 搅动流化床～*,螺旋(进料)～*
氢氟化设备 hydrofluorination equipment
氢氟化温度 hydrofluorination temperature
氢氟化作用 hydrofluorination
氢氟酸 hydrofluoric acid
氢氟酸处理 hydrofluoric acid treatment
氢氟酸浸出 hydrofluoric acid leach
氢氟焰 hydrogen-fluorine flame [torch]
氢腐蚀 hydrogen(-type) corrosion, hydrogen attack
氢臌(罐头的) hydrogen swell
氢过电位(腐蚀) hydrogen [overpoten-

tial] overvoltage

氢含量　hydrogen content ◇ 焦炭中~的波动*, 兰斯莱~测定仪 Ransley apparatus

氢焊(接)　hydrogen-welding, hydrogen brazing ◇ 空气-~ air-hydrogen welding

氢弧焊　hydrogen arc welding

氢化　hydrogenation, hydrogenating, hydrogenizing, hydriding ◇ 催化~*

氢化催化剂　hydrogenation catalyst

氢化钙{CaH_2}　calcium hydride

氢化锆　zirconium hydride

氢化剂　hydrogenant agent

氢化钾{KH}　potassium hydride

氢化锂　lithium hydride

氢化铝锂　lithium aluminium hydride

氢化铝锂还原　lithium aluminium hydride reduction

氢化铝硼　aluminium boron hydride

氢化镁　magnesium hydride

氢化钠{NaH}　sodium hydride

氢化钠碱洗法　sodium hydride process

氢化钕{NdH_3}　neodymium hydride

氢化硼锂　lithium borohydride

氢化硼钠　sodium borohydride

氢化镨{PrH_3}　praseodymium hydride

氢化器　hydrogenator

氢化容器　hydrogenation vessel

氢化铷{RbH}　rubidium hydride

氢化铯{CsH}　cesium hydride

氢化钐{SmH_3}　samaric hydride

氢化设备　hydrogenation plant

氢化钛　titanium hydride

氢化锑　antimony hydride

氢化物　hydride, hydrogenate ◇ 斯莫里铁[钢]水~脱硫法 Smalley process, 稳定六方晶系~*

氢化物除鳞[锈](法)　hydride descaling

氢化物还原　hydride reduction

氢化物还原法　hydride process

氢化物相　【金】hydride phase

氢化锡　tin hydride

氢化铀{UH_3}　uranium hydride

氢化铀汞齐　uranium-hydride amalgam

氢化锗{Ge_nHm}　germanium hydride, germane

氢化装置　hydrogenation plant

氢化作用　hydrogenation

氢还原　hydrogen reduction, reduction by hydrogen (rh) ◇ 多管式~炉*

氢还原法　hydrogen reduction method [process] ◇ 氨浸-~*

氢还原粉末　hydrogen-reduced powder

氢还原高压釜　hydrogen reduction autoclave

氢还原工艺方法　hydrogen reduction technique

氢还原减重　hydrogen loss, loss of weight in hydrogen

氢还原铁粉　hydrogen-reduced iron, H-iron

氢基退火　hydrogen-based annealing

氢减量百分数　hydrogen-loss percentage

氢键　【化】hydrogen bond

氢炬　hydrogen torch

氢醌{$C_6H_4(OH)_2$}　hydroquinone

氢醌(白金或金)半电池　quinhydrone half cell

氢醌催化剂　hydroquinone catalyst

氢醌电极　quinhydrone electrode

氢离子　hydrogen ion ◇ 等~指示溶液*, 给~溶剂 protogenic solvent

氢离子比色计　ionocolorimeter

氢离子浓度　hydrogen ion concentration

氢离子浓度指数　potential of hydrogen (pH)

氢离子(浓度)计　pH-meter

氢离子浓度指数[pH值]　pH value, hydrogenion expondent

氢离子指数　hydrogen ion exponent

氢利用效率　hydrogen efficiency

氢裂　hydrogen disintegration

氢裂纹　hydrogen crack

氢硫化钠{NaHS}　sodium sulfhydrate
氢硫化物{MSH}　hydrosulphide, sulphhydrate
氢硫化铟{In(HS)₃}　indium hydrosulphide
氢硫基乙酸{HSCH₂CO₂H}（即巯基乙酸）thioglycollic acid
氢硫酸　hydrosulphuric acid
氢卤酸　halogen acid
氢铝氟酸{H₃AlF₆}　hydroalumofluoric acid
氢氯酸（同"盐酸"）
氢能　hydrogen energy
氢硼化锆　zirconium borohydride
氢硼化铪{Hf(BH₄)₄}　hafnium borohydride
氢硼化铝　aluminium borohydride
氢硼化钠{NaBH₄}　sodium borohydride
氢硼化物{MBH₄}　borohydride
氢破裂　【金】hydrogen crack(ing)
氢气　hydrogen (gas), gaseous hydrogen ◇ 起～泡 hydrogen blistering, 析出[放出]～liberation of hydrogen
氢气保护浸镀法（镀铝、镁、铍等）alphate process
氢气保护热处理法　hydrozing
氢气保护碳管炉　hydrogen carbon-tube furnace
氢气处理（防止表面氧化）hydryzing
氢气电阻炉　hydrogen resistance furnace
氢气灯　hydrogen lamp
氢气氛　hydrogen atmosphere
氢气氛铜钎焊　copper-hydrogen brazing
氢气(氛)退火　hydrogen annealing
氢气净化　hydrogen purification
氢气净化器　hydrogen gas cleaner
氢气理论需要量　theoretical hydrogen requirement
氢气流　hydrogen flow [stream]
氢气流量[流速]　hydrogen flow rate
氢气泡　hydrogen bubble
氢气瓶　hydrogen cylinder

氢气烧嘴　hydrogen burner
氢气温度计　hydrogen gas thermometer
氢气压力　hydrogen pressure
氢气中焙烧[加热]　hydrogen firing
氢钎焊　hydrogen brazing
氢钎焊炉　hydrogen brazing furnace
氢侵蚀　hydrogen attack
氢氰酸{HCN}　hydrocyanic [prussic] acid
氢去极化腐蚀（同"析氢腐蚀"）
氢缺陷　【金】hydrogen defect
氢燃烧器　hydrogen burner
氢蚀　hydrogen attack [damage]
氢蚀致脆　hydrogen embrittlement
氢酸　hydracid
氢损法　【粉】hydrogen loss method
氢损分析　hydrogen loss analysis
氢-铁法(制铁粉)　H-iron process
氢-铁法铁粉生产厂　【铁】H-iron plant
氢同位素　hydrogen isotope
氢污染　hydrogen contamination
氢析铜粉法　chemetals process
氢硒基　selenyl
氢吸收　hydrogen pick-up
氢细菌　Hydrogenmonas
氢焰　hydrogen flame
氢氧电池　oxyhydrogen cell
氢氧割炬[吹管]　oxyhydric torch, oxyhydrogen blowpipe
氢氧化铵{NH₄OH}　ammonium hydroxide, aqueous ammonia, volatile caustic
氢氧化钡　baryta hydroxide
氢氧化铋　bismuth hydroxide
氢氧化铂　platinic hydroxide
氢氧化钚　plutonium hydroxide
氢氧化镝{Dy(OH)₃}　dysprosium hydroxide
氢氧化铥{Tu(OH)₃}　thulium hydroxide
氢氧化铒{Er(OH)₃}　erbium hydroxide
氢氧化钆{Gd(OH)₃}　gadolinium hydroxide
氢氧化钙{Ca(OH)₂}　calcium hydroxide, calcium hydrate, caustic lime

氢氧化高钴 {Co(OH)$_3$} cobaltic hydroxide

氢氧化高铈 {Ce(OH)$_4$} ceric hydroxide

氢氧化锆 zirconium hydroxide

氢氧化镉 {Cd(OH)$_2$} cadmium hydroxide

氢氧化铬 chromium hydroxide

氢氧化钴 {Co(OH)$_2$} cobalt hydrate [hydroxide]

氢氧化铪 {Hf(OH)$_4$} hafnium hydroxide

氢氧化钬 {Ho(OH)$_3$} holmium hydroxide

氢氧化镓 {Ga(OH)$_3$} gallium hydroxide

氢氧化钾 {KOH} potassium hydrate [hydroxide], caustic potash, kali

氢氧化钾溶液 potash solution

氢氧化金 gold hydroxide

氢氧化钪 {Sc(OH)$_3$} scandium hydroxide

氢氧化镧 {La(OH)$_3$} lanthanum hydroxide

氢氧化锂 {LiOH} lithium hydroxide

氢氧化铝 {Al$_2$O$_3$·3H$_2$O, Al(OH)$_3$} aluminium hydrate [hydroxide], alumina trihydrate, trihydrate alumina ◇ 拜耳法～ Bayer hydrate

氢氧化铝晶种 alumina trihydrate seed

氢氧化铝洗液 【色】whitewash

氢氧化镁 {Mg(OH)$_2$} magnesium hydroxide, hydrate of magnesia

氢氧化锰(Ⅱ) manganous [manganese] hydroxide

氢氧化锰(Ⅲ) (hydrated) manganic hydroxide

氢氧化钼 {Mo(OH)$_3$, Mo(OH)$_4$, Mo(OH)$_5$} molybdenum [molybdic] hydroxide

氢氧化钠 {NaOH} sodium hydroxide [hydrate], caustic soda ◇ 电解～*

氢氧化钠处理 sodium-hydroxide treatment

氢氧化钠浸出 caustic soda leach

氢氧化钠片 flake caustic

氢氧化钠溶解 caustic soda dissolving

氢氧化钠铁水炉外脱硫法 【铁】sodium-hydroxide desulphurization

氢氧化镍 nickel hydrate ◇ 黑色～*

氢氧化钕 {Nd(OH)$_3$} neodymium hydroxide

氢氧化铍 {Be(OH)$_2$} beryllium hydroxide

氢氧化镨 {Pr(OH)$_3$} praseodymium hydroxide

氢氧化铅 {Pb(OH)$_2$} lead hydroxide

氢氧化铷 {RbOH} rubidium hydroxide

氢氧化铯 {CsOH} cesium hydroxide

氢氧化钐 {Sm(OH)$_3$} samaric hydroxide

氢氧化铈 {Ce(OH)$_3$} cerous hydroxide

氢氧化锶 {Sr(OH)$_2$} strontia hydrate [water], strontium hydroxide

氢氧化双氧铀[氢氧化铀酰] {UO$_2$(OH)$_2$} uranyl hydroxide

氢氧化铊 {Tl(OH)$_3$} thallic hydroxide

氢氧化钛 {Ti(OH)$_4$} titanium hydroxide

氢氧化铽 {Tb(OH)$_3$} terbium hydroxide

氢氧化铁 {Fe(OH)$_3$} ferric [iron] hydroxide

氢氧化铁薄膜(钢丝的) sull

氢氧化铜 {Cu(OH)$_2$} cupric hydroxide

氢氧化钍 {Th(OH)$_4$} thorium hydroxide

氢氧化物 hydrated oxide, hydroxide, oxyhydrate, caustic, oxyhydroxide {氢氧化正物} ◇ 胶状～gelatinous hydroxide

氢氧化物滤饼 hydroxide cake

氢氧化锌 zinc hydroxide

氢氧化亚铂 platinous hydroxide

氢氧化亚钼 {Mo(OH)$_2$} molybdous hydroxide

氢氧化亚铁 ferrous hydroxide

氢氧化亚铜 cuprous hydroxide

氢氧化亚锡 stannous hydroxide

氢氧化钇 {Y(OH)$_3$} yttrium hydroxide

氢氧化镱 {Yb(OH)$_3$} ytterbium hydroxide

氢氧化铟 {In(OH)$_3$} indium hydroxide

氢氧化铀 uranium hydroxide

氢氧化铕 {Eu(OH)$_3$} europium hydroxide

氢氧基　hydroxy(l)
氢氧离子　hydroxide [hydroxyl] ion
氢氧离子浓度　hydroxide ion concentration
氢氧(气)　oxyhydrogen
氢氧焰　oxyhydrogen flame
氢氧焰焊接　oxyhydrogen welding (OHW)
氢氧焰切割　hydrogen [oxyhydrogen] cutting
氢疫(铜合金缺陷)　hydrogen disease
氢原子　hydrogen atom
氢原子焊　atomic-hydrogen welding
氢原子弧焊　(同"氢弧焊")
氢值　hydrogen value
氢指数　hydrogen exponent
氢致疲劳破裂　hydrogen assisted fagigue cracking
氢致破裂[氢致裂纹,氢诱发裂纹]　hydrogen(-induced) crack(ing)
氢致滞后裂纹[延迟开裂]　hydrogen assisted [induced] delayed cracking
氢中失重(金属粉末的)　hydrogen loss
氢中失重法　【粉】hydrogen loss method
倾槽式运输机　tipping tray conveyer
倾侧晶界　tilt boundary
倾出(熔渣)　【冶】pouring off
倾出法(测定液相穴深度用)　pour-out method
倾出金属熔液　metal tapping
倾出式芯盒　【铸】turnout core box
倾倒(抛弃)场　dumping site
倾动杆　tilting arm
倾动机构　tilting mechanism [equipment] ◇ 转炉～*
倾动机械　tilting machinery
倾动筐架　tipping cradle
倾动流铁槽　tilting spout
倾动盘式过滤器　tilting pan filter
倾动式保温炉　kettle furnace
倾动式坩埚炉　tilting crucible furnace
倾动式浇包　tilting [labiate] ladle

倾动(式)炉　tiltable [tilting] furnace
倾动式炉算　tipping grate
倾动式铸型　tilt mould
倾动(铸型)浇注　tilt pouring casting
倾动铸造法　tilting cast process
倾动转炉　tilting [tipping] converter
倾动装置　tilting machinery [arrangement, equipment]
倾动座架　tilting frame
倾度仪　dip(ping) compass
倾兑　decant
倾翻　tip(ping), tip-over, tilt(ing), roll over
倾翻操纵机构　controlled dumping mechanism
倾翻车　tilting wagon
倾翻机构　dumping [tripping] gear, tilting [tipping] mechanism
倾翻角度　tilting angle
倾翻力矩　moment of overturning
倾翻力偶(轧机机架的)　roll couple
倾翻式熄焦车　tilt-bed quenching car
倾翻台　dumping table
倾翻箱　tilting box
倾翻装置　tilting device, tipping device [mechanism] ◇ 自动～*
倾覆　turnover, overturn
倾角　dip (angle), angle of dip, (angle of) inclination, slope [rake] angle, incidence ◇ 磁～angle of dip, 焊缝～angle of slope
倾角计　inclinometer
倾料器　tripper ◇ 鼓式～drum tripper
倾炉　furnace tilting ◇ 停吹～*
倾析　decantation, decanting
倾析浸出矿浆　decanted leach pulp
倾析器　cecanter
倾析溶液　decanted solution
倾析水　【环】decanted water
倾析洗涤　decantation washing ◇ 连续(逆流)～系统*, 逆流～法*
倾析洗涤器　decanter ◇ 泵送～pumper-decanter

倾析液　decant
倾析闸板　decanting weir
倾向　inclination, tendency, trend, gravitation ◇ 主要～mainstream
倾向滑移　preferential slip
倾向性　tendentiousness
倾斜　inclination, declination, slanting, obliqueness, obliquity
倾斜板　inclined plate
倾斜板式运输机设施　inclined pallet conveyer plant
倾斜侧导式围盘　sloping bar-side guard-type repeater
倾斜传送辊道　inclined roller path
倾斜(带)式连铸机　inclined conveyor type machine
倾斜斗式输送机　inclined pocket conveyer
倾斜度　batter, gradient, slope, tilt, shelving, slant ◇ 刀片～blade rake
倾斜断裂　slant fracture
倾斜对接焊　mitre welding
倾斜杠杆　tilting lever
倾斜管式炉　slanted tubular furnace
倾斜罐　inclined retort
倾斜辊道　inclined roller table, inclining table
倾斜滚动炉　roll-down furnace
倾斜滚动炉床　roll-down hearth
倾斜焊接　inclined position welding
倾斜焊条电焊装置　deck welder
倾斜后墙[室]　back inclined wall
倾斜机械手　tilting finger
倾斜计　(in)clinometer, tiltmeter, gradiometer ◇ 感应式传感器～*
倾斜浇注　【铸】tilt pouring casting, inclined casting
倾斜角　bank [draft] angle, (angle of) tilt, (angle of) inclination ◇ 屋顶～angle of roof
倾斜晶界　tilt boundary
倾斜可逆皮带机　sloping reverse belt
倾斜炉　uphill furnace

倾斜炉膛　sloping hearth
倾斜煤气管道　【铁】down pass
倾斜盘式运输机　inclined pan conveyer
倾斜皮带运输机　inclined belt conveyer
倾斜区段(煤气弯管的)　sloping section
倾斜式成球盘　tilted-pan pelletizer
倾斜式副枪　slanted sublance
倾斜式刮板运输机　inclined flight conveyer
倾斜式活套槽　sloping loop channel
倾斜式冷床　rake-type cooling bed [bank]
倾斜式鳞板运输机　inclined flat belt type conveyer
倾斜式炉顶　【冶】sloped roof
倾斜式平板运输机　inclined platform conveyer
倾斜式提升机　inclined elevator
倾斜式造球盘　tilted-pan pelletizer
倾斜式蒸馏罐　inclined retort
倾斜台面　inclining table
倾斜位置　inclined position
倾斜线　parallax
倾斜型铸造　sloping casting
倾斜仪　(in)clinometer, tiltmeter, gradiometer
倾斜圆盘　inclined disc
倾斜圆筒混合机　tilted cylinder mixer
倾斜运动　tilting motion
倾斜照明　oblique illuminaiton
倾斜蒸发(电子显微镜试样用)　oblique evaporation
倾斜蒸馏罐(炼汞用)　side hill retort
倾斜铸造　inclined [sloping] casting
倾斜铸造法　tilting cast process
倾卸　dumping, tipping ◇ 液压～机 hydraulic tilter
倾卸操纵机构　controlled dumping mechanism
倾卸车　dump(ing) wagon [car], tipcar ◇ 气动～air-dump car
倾卸式运料车　dumptor
倾卸小车　tipping bogie, skip car

倾卸运货车	dump truck
倾卸装置	tripper
倾注	decant, transfusion
倾注洗涤	（同"倾析洗涤"）
倾转角度[位置]	tilting position
倾转式芯盒	tilting box
倾转轴	tilting axis
清边机(用火焰)	edge scarfer
清玻璃料	clear frit
清除	cleaning, clear (ance), purge, removal, obliteration, sweep(ing), elimination, equalization（应力的）
清除表层金属(修整时)	desurfacing
清除表皮层的	skinned
清除磁头	【计】erasing head
清除地面	clearing ground
清除钢锭缺陷	scalping
清除垢底	scavenging (scvg)
清除机构	scavenger block
清除剂	scavenger
清除孔	cleaning eye
清除口	cleanout
清除毛边	【压】(de)frasing
清除毛刺	（同"去毛刺"）
清除器	cleaner, scavenger ◇ 整体~【计】bulk eraser, 自动摇摆链式~*
清除器械	disposal facilities
清除切头	【压】crop disposal
清除氧化皮用槽[沟]	cale flume
清除氧化铁皮	removal scale
清除杂质	scavenging
清带刷轮	rotary-brush cleaning device
清点库存	【企】inventory-taking
清灰	ash removal, deashing ◇ 烟道[烟囱]~口 floss hole
清灰孔	cleanout opening
清灰门	soot door
清机	【计】clear
清洁操作	clean operation
清洁垫	【压】cleaning disc
清洁度	cleanness, cleanliness ◇ 尼尔森~试验 Nielson test
清洁钢	high quality clean steel, pure steel
清洁工程	cleaning engineering
清洁能源	clean energy
清洁器	cleanser
清洁器刀片	clearance blade
清洁生产	clean production [operation]
清净机	branner
清净设备	cleaning equipment
清净洗涤工段(带材的)	scrubbing station
清理	cleaning (-up), conditioning (cond.), epuration, hogging, scalp, scarf, chip（用錾子或铲）◇ 机械化~装置*, 用割炬火焰~（焊缝） torch deseaming
清理班(组)	cleanout crew
清理残铁	【铁】scrap cleanup
清理场地	land clearing, place cleaning
清理垫片	【压】cleanout plate
清理方法	cleaning means
清理风口	【冶】punching
清理工	【铸】fettler
清理工段(锭、坯的)	conditioning department [floor, site, yard], cleaning zone（轧件的），【铸】(也称清理间) cleaning room [shop], dressing room [shop], fettling room [shop]
清理工序	cleaning operation
清理工作台	【铸】fettling table
清理沟	flume
清理滚筒	tumbling [rolling, rattle] barrel, rattler, tumble drum, cleansing [tumbling] mill（用于铸件）◇ 排气式~exhaust tumbling mill, 湿式~*
清理过表面缺陷的坯料	conditioned billet
清理焊缝	deseaming, trimming
清理焊缝磨床	lap grinder
清理机	descaling machine, 【铸】cleaning machine
清理机构(挤压筒的)	scavenger block
清理剂	cleaning means [mixture]
清理孔	cleaning hole, cleanout
清理口	cleanout door
清理跨	scalping bay

清理炉底用异形坯 cleanout slab
清理器 cleaning device
清理缺陷用风錾 【压】dresser
清理台 conditioning bed（锭、坯的），dressing table,【铸】cleaning bench, fettling table ◇ 铲凿~*, 带排气罩的~【铸】exhaust bench
清理台车 pallet scrubbing
清理铁沟 【铁】scrap [casthouse] cleanup
清理洗涤作业线 scrubbing line
清理细粒 【铸】blasting shot
清理(型芯)用夹具 rubbing fixture
清理站 cleaning station
清理转炉炉口 vessel-mouth cleaning
清料 dislodging
清炉壁 【钢】chipping-out
清炉渣块 cobbings
清滤液 clear filtrate
清漆 varnish ◇ 沥青~ bituminous varnish
清扫吹气管 scavenge trunk
清扫机 scavenging machine ◇ 门框~【焦】jamb cleaner
清扫孔 cleanout opening, handhole (H.H.)
清扫口[门] cleanout hole, cleaning door
清扫器 cleaning device, scavenger ◇ 皮带~ belt cleaning device, 上升管~*
清砂 【铸】cleaning ◇ 水力~ stream jet blasting
清砂费用 cost of cleaning
清砂工段 cleaning plant [room], dressing [fettling] room
清砂滚筒 cleaning [cleanser, tumble] drum, cleansing [rumbling, tumbling] mill, rattler, rattle barrel
清砂机 sand separator
清砂台 cleaning bench
清砂铸件 fettled casting
清刷－洗涤机 scrubbing machine
清水墙 dry wall
清水砖砌体 fairfaced brickwork

清算帐户 open [clearing] account
清晰 limpid, distinct, clear ◇ 不~像 blurred image
清晰斑点群 cluster of sharp spots
清晰度 definition, readability, resolution (res.), sharpness, articulation（声音的）
清晰分离 clean separation
清晰图像 sharp image
清洗 wash(ing), clean(ing)-up, rinse, rinsing, scouring ◇ 槽内静置~ still tank cleaning, 复式~ multiple cleaning, 未~砂 roughing sand
清洗槽 rinse [rinsing, purge] tank, wash water tank
清洗段 cleaning section
清洗工段 cleaning house, rinsing zone
清洗沟 wash water channel
清洗机 cleaning machine ◇ 煤气~ gas cleaner
清洗剂 cleanser, cleaning [cleansing, rinsing, washing] agent
清洗间 cleaning house
清洗器 cleanser ◇ 排水管道~ badger
清洗熔剂 cleansing flux
清洗水 purge water,【环】cleanup water
清洗(脱脂)作业线（板带材的） cleaning line
清洗液 cleaning liquor, cleaner
清洗装置 cleaner, rinser, rinsing unit
清液 clear liquid [solution]
清液层 supernatant liquid [layer, liquor]
清液溢流 clear (solution) overflow
清渣 slag removal [disposal], removal of cinder
清渣车 【冶】cinder bogie
清渣工 【冶】cinder pitman
清渣器 dross extractor
清渣箱(均热炉的) 【冶】cinder box
清渣修整工序（钢锭的） cleaning-and-dressing operation
清整 cleaning-up, drain-out（炉底的）
清整工 【铸】dresser

清整工段	dressing yard
清整机	conditioning machine
清整坯料	conditioned billet
晴雨计	(weather)glass

氰{NCCN}　cyanogen, dicyanogen
氰胺{RNHCN}　cyanamide
氰铂酸　cyanoplatinic [platinicyanic] acid
氰氮化物　cyanonitride
氰高钴酸盐{Me[Co(CN)$_6$]}　cobalticyanide
氰化　carbonitriding, cyanidation, cyaniding ◇ 干式～dry cyaniding, 活化[性]～activated cyaniding, 精矿～尾矿[残渣]～, 克劳～提金法 Crowe process, 气体～【金】gas cyaniding, 选择～selective cyaniding, 液体～liquid cyaniding
氰化铵　ammonium cyanide
氰化钡　barium cyanide
氰化苯{C$_7$H$_5$N}　benzonitrile
氰化表面层　cyanided case
氰化车间　cyanidation plant [section]
氰化处理　cyaniding ◇ 高速～
氰化法　cyanation,【色】cyaniding process (金、银置换析出的), cyanidation (萃取金属用)
氰化钙　calcium cyanide, cyanogas, black cyanide
氰化钙液体氰化法　aerocasing
氰化钢　cyanided steel
氰化工段　cyanidation section
氰化汞　mercury cyanide
氰化合物　cyanogen compound
氰化化学　cyanidation chemistry
氰化钾{KCN}　potassium cyanide
氰化金属　metallocyanide
氰化钠{NaCN}　sodium cyanide
氰化镍　nickel cyanide
氰化铅　lead cyanide
氰化氢{HCN}　hydrogen cyanide, hydrocyanic acid
氰化试验　cyanidation test
氰化铁　iron cyanide
氰化铜　copper cyanide
氰化温度　cyaniding temperature
氰化物　cyanide, cyanogen compound, prussiate ◇ 化合的～combined cyanide, 自由[游离]～free cyanide
氰化物残渣　【色】cyanide residue
氰化物电解铜　cyanide copper
氰化物淀渣　【色】cyanide slimes
氰化物法　【色】cyanide process
氰化物金精炼法　【色】cyanide gold refining
氰化物浸出法　【色】cyanide leaching process
氰化物矿泥　cyanide pulp
氰化物溶液　cyanide solution
氰化物渗碳　【金】cyanide carburizing
氰化物-石灰溶液（提金的）　【色】cyanide lime solution
氰化物硬层(表面的)　cyanide case
氰化物中毒　cyanide poisoning
氰化锌　zinc cyanide
氰化亚金钾　gold potassium cyanide
氰化亚铁　ferrous cyanide
氰化银　silver cyanide
氰化银钾　silver potassium cyanide
氰化硬化　cyanide (case)-hardening
氰化装置　cyanidation plant
氰基氮化钛　titanium cyanonitride
氰酸{HOCN}　cyanic acid
氰酸盐[酯]　cyanate
氰铁酸{H$_3$[Fe(CN)$_6$]}　ferricyanic acid
氰铁酸盐{M$_3$[Fe(CN)$_6$]}　ferricyanide
氰亚铁酸{H$_4$[Fe(CN)$_6$]}　ferrocyanic acid
氰亚铁酸铵　ammonium ferrocyanide
氰亚铁酸锆　（同"亚铁氰化锆"）
氰亚铁酸铪　（同"亚铁氰化铪"）
氰亚铁酸盐　ferrocyanide
氰盐渗碳　cyanide carburizing
情报存储和检索　（同"信息存储和检索"）
情报中心　information center

情况 circumstance, situation, condition, case, behaviour (工作的)
请求重发系统 【电】request-repeat system
琼-里斯特夹杂检测法 【冶】Jean Rist technique
琼脂(冻) agal-agal, agar
穹顶 【建】dome, vault, 【压】doming (落料缺陷) ◇ 锥形~ conoidical vault
穹顶温度 (热风炉的) dome temperature
穹顶砖 dome brick
穹隆 vault
丘克拉尔斯基宏观浸蚀剂 Czochralski's reagent
丘克拉尔斯基拉单晶法 【半】Czochralski crystal pulling technique, Czochralski process [method]
丘克拉尔斯基拉单晶炉 【半】Czochralski crystal-pulling furnace
丘陵地区 difficult country [ground], knob
丘皮钉钢丝 boot and shoe wire
球扁钢 (flat) bulb steel
球层厚度 pellet-bed depth
球冲压模膛 ball edger
球底杯突(深冲试验的) round bottomed cup (RBC)
球顶(热风炉的) 【铁】(top) dome
球顶盖砖 dome plug
球顶塞头砖 (热风炉的) dom plug
球端心轴 centre pin
球阀 globe valve (GI.V.), globe type valve, globe cock, ball cock [valve]
球阀式(炉顶)装料装置 spherical charging system
球管 bulb
球焊 ball bonding
球核 【团】nucleus of pellet
球核长大区 【团】nuclei growth region
球化 balling, globuling, nodulizing, spheroidizing, beading ◇ 碳化物~
球化处理 【金】globularizing, spheroidized [spheroidizing] treatment, spheroi-dising

球化剂 nodulizer, spheroidizing agent, inoculant
球化率(石墨的) 【金】nodularity
球化热处理 spheroidizing heat-treatment
球化水冷退火 【金】water softening
球化碳化物 spheroidised carbide
球化退火 【金】spheroidal [spheroidizing] anneal(ing)
球化孕育剂 nodularizing inoculant
球化组织 【金】spheroidal structure
球化作用 spheroidisation, spheroidization, spheroidizing
球夹 ball chuck
球铰链 ball and socket hinge
球角角钢 bulb-angle iron [steel]
球节[接头] ball joint
球结(晶界析出物) 【金】nodule
球晶 spherocrystal
球径计 spherometer
球粒 spherical particle, spherolite, spherulite
球粒法 pellet technique
球粒粉末 spherical powder
球粒合金 spherical alloy
球粒烤制皮带 pellet curing belt
球粒贮放斗仓 pellet surge hopper
球菱钴矿 bemmelenite, spherosiderite
球菱铁矿 $\{FeCO_3\}$ white iron ore
球面波 spherical wave
球面对称 spherical symmetry
球面对称概率分布 spherically symmetric probability distribution
球面反射器 spherical reflector
球面滚柱轴承 spherical roller bearing
球面枢轴 footstep pivot
球面投影 spherical [stereographic] projection, button type projection
球面透镜 spherical lens
球面蜗轮 globoidal worm gear, Hindley gear
球面蜗轮减速机 enveloping worm-gear reducer, cone-worm unit

球面像差　spherical aberration
球面轴瓦　spherical bush
球模膛　ball edger
球磨　ball milling ◇ 霍尔~粉法
球磨法　ball milling method
球磨粉末　ball milled powder
球磨机　ball mill (B.M.), ball grinder [crusher], pebble] mill ◇ 闭路~*, 初磨[一次]~ primary ball mill, 二次~ secondary ball mill, 风扫式~ air-swept ball mill, 精加工~ ball mill refiner, 微粉~ micro ball-mill, 行星式~ planetary ball mill, 旋回~ gyratory ball-mill, 溢流式~*, 圆锥~ conical (ball) mill, 振动~*
球磨研磨　ball milling
球磨用液体　ball milling fluid
球墨铸铁　SG (spherulitic graphite) cast iron, ductile cast-iron, spheroidal [nodular] graphite cast iron, nodular (cast) iron, Ductalloy ◇ 复合针状~*, 高镍延性~*, 厚大断面~钢锭模*, 加镁处理的~*, 铈硅钙~ oz cast iron, 铁素体(化)~*, 针状~*, 铸态~*
球墨铸铁件　ductile iron castings
球墨铸铁学会(美国)　Ductile Iron Society (DIS)
球墨铸铁用生铁　pig iron for ductile cast iron
球墨铸铁轧辊　nodular [ductile] iron roll, spheroidal graphite roll ◇ 冷硬~*, 离心铸造复合~*
球墨铸铁铸造车间　ductile foundry
球黏土　ball clay
球腔挤压垫　【压】spherical pressure pad
球石　ballstone
球式热风炉　pebble stove
球特性　balling characteristics
球体　sphere
球体六方最密集排列　【理】hexagonal closest packing of spheres
球头T形钢　T-bulb iron
球头扁钢　flat bulb iron, plain bulb, bulb plate
球头丁字钢　bulb rail steel, T-bulb steel
球头工字钢梁　bulb beam
球头关节　ball and socket hinge
球头轨　bulb rail
球头角钢　bulb angle steel, angle bulb iron
球头螺栓　ball head(ed) bolt
球头式振捣棒　bullet nosed vibrator
球头探针　ball ended probe
球团　pellet, ball ◇ COBO法~ COBO-pellet, 白云石熔剂性[加白云石]~*, 焙烧~ baked pellet, 成品~ final pellet, 低渣量[脉石]~*, 干燥~ dried pellet, 高压釜~*, 高转鼓指数~*, 合格~ specification pellet, 混合粉矿~ blended ore pellet, 加[含]石灰~ limecontaining pellet, 加焦~ ore-coke pellet, 碱性~ basic pellet, 焦油黏结~ tar-bonded pellet, 冷固结~*, 链箅机-回转窑法~*, 内配煤~*, 竖炉~*, 水泥固结~ cement bound pellet, 酸性[氧化]~ acid pellet, 碳酸盐黏结~*, 未还原~ unreduced pellet, 未烧结~ unfired pellet, 无黏结剂~*, 无皂土~*, 旋转式[回转式]~炉*, 预干燥~ predried ball, 预热~ preheated ball, 自还原性[内加还原剂]~ self-reduced pellet, 自熔性[熔剂性]~*
球团焙烧　pellet firing [hardening, roasting, induration]
球团焙烧方法[过程]　pellet firing process
球团焙烧机　pellet firing [hardening] machine, pellet machine ◇ 带式~*, 环式~*
球团焙烧设备　pellet firing equipment [machine], pellet induration facilities, pelletizing machine [unit]
球团焙烧系统[工艺循环]　pelletizing firing cycle
球团焙烧循环　pelletizing circuit
球团焙烧燃料　pelletizing fuel
球团变形区　pellet deformation zone
球团表面钝化法　pellet passivation pro-

cess
球团仓 pellet surge hopper
球团层 pellet bed, bed of pellets
球团层表面 pellet-bed surface
球团层辐射率 pellet-bed emissivity
球团层密度 pellet-bed density
球团层速度 pellet-bed speed
球团产量 pellet output [production, yield], pelletizing capacity
球团产率 pellet yield
球团厂 pellet(izing) [pelletisation, agglomerating] plant, pelletizing complex [facilities, installation]
球团厂工程 pellet plant project
球团厂配置 pellet plant layout
球团厂设计 pellet-plant design [project]
球团车间 pellet plant, pelletizing building
球团成分 pellet composition
球团成品堆栈 pellet stockpile
球团钝化 pellet passivation
球团法 pelletization, pelletizing method ◇ 非金属~*, 链箅焙烧机~*, 鲁奇[带式焙烧机]~*, 铁矿石~原理*
球团粉化 pellet degradation
球团工段 pelletizing area
球团工业 pelletizing industry
球团工艺参数 pelletizing parameter
球团公司 pelletizing complex
球团固结 pellet hardening [induration]
球团固结设备 pellet hardening machine, pellet induration facilities ◇ 半连续式~*
球团核 nucleus of pellet
球团化学成分 pellet chemistry
球团还原度 degree of pellet reduction
球团混合料 pellet charge
球团混合物 pelletable mixture
球团基体 pellet matrix
球团机 pelletizer ◇ 圆锥式~ cone pelletizer
球团机组 pelletizing line
球团技术[工艺] pelletizing technique

球团碱度 pellet basicity
球团金属化(率) metallization of pellet
球团矿 pellet ◇ 布拉克尔斯堡~制法*, 复合[多成分]~ composite pellet, 回转窑烧结~法 Follsan process, 未焙烧~ unifired [fresh] pellet
球团矿焙烧 pellet firing
球团矿物组成 mineralogy of pellet, mineral composition of pellet
球团冷却风机 pellet cooler fan
球团冷却机 pellet cooler ◇ 竖式~*
球团粒 【铁】nodule
球团粒度 pellet size
球团粒度控制 pellet size control
球团粒径 pellet diameter
球团流 pellet flow
球团(炉)料 【铁】pelleted charge, pellet burden, pelletized feed stock
球团密度 density of pellet
球团模型 pelletizing model
球团排料泵 pellet pump
球团坯 green ball ◇ 造~ green balling
球团坯生产 green ball production
球团坯性能 green ball property
球团坯制作方式 green balling mode
球团破碎 pellet break-down
球团气孔率 pellet porosity
球团强度 pellet [ball] strength
球团强度特性 pellet strength property
球团燃料 pelletizing fuel
球团热分布曲线 pellet thermal profile
球团(入炉)比 【铁】pellet blending ratio, pellet proportion [consumption, content], pellet in charge
球团筛分分析[粒度组成] pellet screen analysis
球团筛下碎粉 pellet screenings
球团设备 pelletizing equipment [facilities, installation, unit], pellet-(izing) machine
球团生产 pellet production [making], pelletization, pelletizing operation

球团生产法	pelletizing process ◇ 优质铁精矿还原～AGAP process
球团生产能力	pelletizing capacity
球团试验	pelletizing test
球团竖炉	pellet(izing) furnace ◇ 埃利克型～*,伯利恒型～*
球团碎裂	pellet [ball] degradation, pellet break-down
球团碎末	pellet fines
球团特性	pellet characteristics
球团铁矿	pelletized iron ore
球团脱硫	desulphurization of pellets
球团污染	pellet contamination
球团消耗(量)[用量]	pellet consumption
球团压力机	pelleting press
球团氧化度	degree of pellet oxidation
球团冶炼特性	pellet metallurgical property
球团业[界]	pelletization field
球团预还原	pellet prereduciton
球团预热机表面	pellet preheater surface
球团原料（粉矿）	pellet charge, pellet plant feed, pellet (izing) [pelletization, balling] feed
球团再氧化	reoxidation of pellet
球团增重[质量增加]	pellet weight gain
球团质量指数	(pellet) "Q" index
球团种类	【团】kind of pellets
球窝	ball socket
球窝节[接头]	ball and socket joint
球窝黏度计	cup-and-ball viscometer
球心投影	gnomonic projection
球形	spherical shape ◇ 类[近似]～的 near-spherical
球形柄	knob
球形导向装置	ball guide
球形电极	bulb type electrode
球形顶杆[压]	ball mandrel
球形度	(degree of) sphericity
球形端	ball end
球形[球心]阀	globe (type) valve
球形反射器	spherical reflector
球形坩埚	spherical crucible
球形光度计	spherical photometer
球形化晶胞	sphericized lattice cell
球形件	spherical object
球形金刚石压头	spherically shaped diamond indentor
球形颗[粉]粒	spherical [nodular] particle
球形扩脚桩	bulb pile
球形离子	spherical ion
球形炉底	spherical bottom
球形瓶	aryballos
球形三通	globe T
球形砂舂	ball rammer
球形手柄	ball handle
球形枢轴	ball pivot
球形铁粒	spherical iron particle
球形屋顶	bulbous dome
球形芯棒[心轴]	ball mandrel
球形旋塞	globe cock, ball valve
球形[状]压痕	spherical indentation, ball indentation [impression]
球形压痕面(硬度试验的)	【金】surface spherical indentation
球形[球状]压头(硬度计的)	金 ball [bulb] penetrator, spherical indenter ◇ 金刚石～*
球形压头压痕试验	ball indentation test
球形闸门	ball gate
球形支座	free bearing
球形轴衬	spherical bush
球形撞锤	ball rammer
球压焊	ball bonding
球衣菌属	Sphaerotilus
球映像	spherical image
球轧	ball rolling
球轴承	(同"滚珠轴承")
球状二次气孔	globular blow-hole
球状反应	【金】nodular reaction
球状粉末	spherical [nodular, globular] powder
球状结构	【金】globular structure

球状颗粒合金 spherical alloy
球状冒口 sphere riser
球状气孔 globular [secondary] blow-hole
球状气泡 spherical bubble
球状屈氏体 【金】nodular troostite
球状熔滴金属过渡 globular metal transfer
球状溶质原子 spherical solute atom
球状渗碳体 spheroidal [spheroidized, spheroidizing, nodular, nodulous, globular] cementite, spheroidite
球状石墨(即球墨) spheroidal graphite (SG), globular [nodular] graphite
球状衰减 spherical attenuation
球状碳化物离析[析出] 【金】spheroidal carbide precipitate
球状体 ball, globoid
球状阳极 ball type anode
球状增大部分(断面的) bulb
球状炸药爆炸成形 spherical-charge forming
球状珠光体 【金】spheroidal [globular, nodular] pearlite
球状组织 【金】globular structure
求补 【计】complement, supplement
求补运算 【计】complementary operation
求和校验[检查] 【计】sum check
求积 integration
求积法 (method of) quadrature, measuration
求积器 integrator
求(平方)根 【数】root, extract
求助程序 【计】HELP
巯乙酸 (同"氢硫基乙酸")
趋肤效应 skin [kelvin] effect ◇ 磁致~ magnetic skin effect, 反常~ anomalous skin effect
趋气性 aerotaxis
趋势 trend, tendency, gravitation, tide
趋氧性 aerotaxis, oxygenotaxis
蒀{$C_{18}H_{12}$} chrysene
区 area, district, region, zone ◇ 布里渊~ Brillouin zone, 纪尼埃－普雷斯顿[G-P]~ *
区别腐蚀 【金】differentiate etching
区层取样器 zone sampler
区带划分 zoning arrangement
区段 section, sector
区分 dividing, discrimination
区划 compartment, portion
区划图 block plan
区间 interval, space, region, section
区间开通 【运】unblocking
区截(闭塞) 【运】block
区截信号 block signal
区截运行 block movement
区熔 (同"区域熔炼")
区熔单晶 single crystal by zone melting
区熔法装置 zone melting apparatus
区熔技术 zone-melting technique
区熔均化 zone-leveling
区熔均化单晶 zone-leveled single crystal
区熔匀化[夷平]器 zone-leveler
区熔均化曲线 curve for zone leveling
区熔空段法 【冶】zone-void process
区熔提纯金属 zone-purified metal
区熔一次通过法 single-pass method
区位格式 【计】zoned format
区域 area, district, limit, range, region, zone ◇ 菲涅耳~ Fresnel region, 夫琅和费~ Fraunhofer region, 高角度[大(布喇格)角]~ high angle region
区域变电所[站] regional-substation
区域地形图 regional topographic drawing
区域地址 【计】regional address
区域法分析 area analysis
区域工程 zone engineering
区域规划 regional planning
区域检查 range check
区域检索 area search
区域建造 zoned construction
区域精炼[区熔精炼, 区域提纯, 区熔提纯] 【冶】zone refining [purification], zone melting purification ◇ 垂直~*, 大

型~*,电子束~*,多次通过~*,多熔区~*,感应加热~*,固态[固相]~*,化学试剂~*,笼式~ cage zone-refining,气体~*,水平~*,微量~*,温度梯度~*,无盛料器~*,悬浮~*,液体~liquid zoning,准连续~*

区域精炼法 zone refining [melting] ◇ 浮动~ floating zone process

区域精炼金属 zone refined [melted] metal

区域精炼炉 zone refiner ◇ 多加热器~ multiheater refiner,分批~*,连续~*,三重回收~*,三元系~*,太阳能~*,正交[纵横]流动~*

区域精炼曲线 zone refining curve
区域精炼设备 zone-refining equipment
区域精炼盛料器 container for zone refining
区域精炼锗 zone-refined germanium
区域燃烧 zonal combustion

区域熔炼（即区熔）【冶】 zone [zonal] melting, zoning ◇ 磁悬~*,电弧~ arc zone-melting,电子轰击~*[区域熔化],放电加热的~*,辐射聚焦的~*,焦耳热~*,两种液体~ two liquid zone melting,无坩埚~*

区域熔炼法 zone-melting process, zone recrystallization method [process]
区域熔炼炉 zone (melting) furnace
区域熔炼模拟计算机 zone-melting analog computer
区域烧结 zone sintering
区域提纯器 【半】zoner
区域提纯用无阳极电子枪 work-accelerated zone-refining gun
区域提纯材料 zone-refined material
区域提纯装置 zone purification device
区域通过 zone passage
区域位移[移动(量)] zoning run
区域性道路 district road
区域硬化 zone hardening
区域再结晶 【半】zone recrystallization

区域再结晶法 zone recrystallization method [process]
曲壁效应（射流技术） curved wall effect
曲臂 crank (arm, radius, web)
曲柄 crank (arm), crank(ed) lever ◇ 电极移动~ crank for electrode,对置~ opposite cranks
曲柄冲床 crank press ◇ 台式~ bench press
曲柄传动锤 crank-operated hammer
曲柄传动机构[连杆机构,传动装置] crank gear
曲柄导向装置 crank-guide
曲柄定位装置 crank positioning device
曲柄颈轴承合金 crank metal
曲柄式飞剪 flying crank shears
曲柄式剪切机 crank shears
曲柄式切头剪 crank type crop shears
曲柄式推出机 crank type pusher
曲柄箱 crankcase
曲柄销 crank pin
曲柄压力机[冲床] crank press ◇ 台式~ bench press
曲柄圆盘 crank disc
曲柄轴 crankshaft, crank [bent] axle
曲柄轴承 crank(shaft) bearing
曲柄轴承合金 crank bearing metal
曲柄轴承黄铜 crank brass
曲底 curved bottom
曲度 camber, (degree of) curvature ◇ 预留~*
曲杆 curved [knee] lever
曲拐 【机】crank throw, bend
曲轨 【团】circular guide
曲晶石 $\{Na_2Y_2(Zr, Hf)(SiO_4)_{12}\}$ cyrtolite
曲颈瓶 flask ◇ 离解器~ dissociator retort
曲颈生长 【粉】neck growth
曲颈甑 cornue, cucurbit, retort
曲径(式密封) labyrinth
曲率 curvature ◇ 假~模型*,交截~

cross curvature
曲率半径　curvature radius, radius of curvature
曲率计　curvimeter
曲率中心　centre of curvature
曲面坯块　【粉】curved(-faced) compact
曲面蜗轮　globoidal worm gear, Hindley gear
曲面物体　curve-shaped body
曲头钉　brad
曲线　curve (line) ◇ C[S]~TTT diagram, 贝蒂－斯莱特~*, 富勒氏~ Fuller's curve, 康登－莫尔斯~*
曲线板　curve board
曲线的　curved, curvilinear
曲线顶[峰(值), 最高点]　peak [hump] of curve
曲线规　curve(d-drawing) gauge
曲线轨道　curved track
曲线加宽　curve widening
曲线间断(拐折)　(curve) discontinuity, gap in curve
曲线描绘[绘制]仪　curved-drawing instrument, curve plotter, plotting device
曲线起点　beginning of curve (B.C.), origin of curve
曲线图　curve (diagram), graph, abacus (复数 abaci)
曲线图标出[描绘]的结果　plotted results
曲线下降交叉点(三元相图的)　【金】descending fork point
曲线斜度[率]　slope of curve
曲线性炉顶　【冶】curved roof
曲线摇杆　curved rocker
曲线阅读器　【计】curve [graph] follower
曲线运动　curvilinear motion
曲线折减率　curve compensation
曲折　circuitous, zigzag, detour
曲折变形(往复的)　crippling strain
曲折反射　zigzag reflection
曲折拱　zigzag arch
曲折接线(变压器的)　zigzag (connection)
曲折漏磁　zigzag leakage
曲折形　zigzag
曲折形波　zigzag wave
曲折烟道　zigzag flue
曲折应变(往复的)　crippling strain
曲折应力(往复的)　crippling stress
曲轴　crank shaft (c.s.), crank(ed) axle
曲轴机构　crank mechanism
曲轴颈　crankshaft neck
曲轴式压力机　crank type press
曲轴箱　crankcase
曲轴箱用铝合金{1.4Cu, 5Si, 0.5Mg, 0.8Ni, 0.8Mn, 余量 Al)　crankcase alloy
曲轴压(力)机　crank shaft [machine] press
曲轴轴承　crank(shaft) bearing
曲轴转数　crank shaft revolution
屈服　yield(ing) ◇ 哈菲尔德时间~试验*, 明显~sharp yield
屈服比　yield ratio
屈服点　yield(ing) point (YP), breakdown point, proof stress (ps), ductility limit ◇ 低~钢*, 负荷下的~*, 弯曲~*
屈服点合金　low yield alloy
屈服点伸长　yield point elongation
屈服点时滞(现象)　time delay of yield point
屈服后断裂力学　post-yield fracture mechanics
屈服极限　yield limit [value], flow limit
屈服降低机理　yield drop mechanism
屈服能力　yieldability
屈服判据　yield criterion
屈服前微应变　【金】preyield micro-strain
屈服前应变　preyield strain
屈服强度　yield strength (YS), proof stress (ps), offset stress
屈服强度理论　theory of yield strength
屈服现象　yield(ing) phenomenon

屈服限以下松弛	(同"预屈服松弛")
屈服效应	yield effect
屈服性能	yieldability
屈服应力	yield [proof, flow, offset] stress ◇ 残余变形～offset yield, 条件～*
屈服值	yield value
屈服滞后	delayed yield
屈光度	diopter
屈氏-索氏体	troosto-sorbite
屈氏体	【金】troostite ◇ 球状～nodular troostite, 原生[初生]～primary troostite, 针状～acicular troostite
屈氏体-索氏体淬火	troostite-sorbite quenching
屈氏体网	troostite network
屈氏体显微组织	troostite microstructure
屈氏体形成区[范围]	troostite formation range
屈氏珠光体	troostite pearlite
驱动部件	driving parts
驱动电动机	drive [actuating] motor
驱动电路	drive(r) circuit
驱动杆	drive rod, actuating lever [arm]
驱动功率	driving power
驱动和传动设备	drive and transmission equipment
驱动机构	drive mechanism
驱动级	driving [driver] stage
驱动卷线机	motorized coil stock reel
驱动力	driving [propelling] power
驱动力矩	driving torque
驱动轮	drive [driving] wheel
驱动脉冲	【计】drive pulse
驱动模拟器装置	drive simulator
驱动器	driver ◇ 时钟逻辑～clock logic driver
驱动速率	driving rate
驱动凸轮	actuating cam
驱动轴	driving [power] shaft
驱动装置	drive unit [head], driving [actuating] device
驱气	air elimination, purge
渠道渗漏损失	canal seepage loss
渠底	canal bed
取出盘	take-off tray
取代	replacement, substitution
取代反应	displacement reaction, reaction of substitution
取代离子(离子交换的)	displacing ion
取代碰撞	【化】replacement collision
取代(次)序	displacement series
取锭机构(真空电弧炉的)	withdrawal mechanism
取锭连锁装置	ingot removal lock
取锭器	(ingot) retractor, ingot adapter
取锭装置	ingot withdrawing device
取矿耙	【铁】reclaimer
取料	reclamation
取料[矿]机(矿石混匀用)	【铁】(bedding) reclaimer ◇ 斗轮式～*, 龙门式～portal reclaimer, 履带式～*, 桥式～bridge type reclaimer, 移动支臂式～*
取料机桥架[栈桥]	reclaimer bridge
取料坑	borrow
取料皮带机	reclaim belt
取料起重机[吊车](从炉中取料用)	drawing crane
取料设备	reclaiming installation
取料输送机	reclaiming belt
取料系统	reclaiming system
取料装置	reclaiming unit, extracting device
取暖	heating (htg.)
取数	【计】access (ACS), fetch
取数时间	【计】access [latency] time
取双样	double sampling
取土区	borrow areas
取向	orientation ◇ 混乱～disorientation, 晶粒未～钢*, 未～的 undirected, 无～膜 non-oriented film, 无定向[随意]～chaotic orientation
取向变化	orientation change
取向差	orientation difference
取向错误	misorientation

取向电工钢薄板 oriented electrical steel sheet
取向范围 range of orientations
取向分散 dispersion of orientation
取向附生 (同"外延生长")
取向关系 orientation relationship [dependence] ◇ 加工硬化曲线～*
取向硅铁 oriented silicon iron
取向极化 orientation(al) polarization
取向密度 orientation density
取向膜 oriented film
取向三角形 orientation triangle
取向紊乱[无序(现象)] orientation(al) disorder
取向因数 orientation factor
取向织构 【金】orientation texture
取向织构图样[(衍射)花样] 【理】orientation texture pattern
取消 cancel, abolish, back out, holdback, retraction
取消符 【计】erase [ignore] character
取(岩)心钻头 coring bit, rock core bit
取样 sampling (samp.), sample drawing, sample taking ◇ 手工[人工]～ hand sampling, 缩～ curtailed sampling, 现抓取法～ grab sampling, 循环～ round sampling, 用管～ pipe sampling
取样部位 sampling location
取样车间 sampling mill [plant]
取样点 sample point
取样阀 sampling valve
取样方差 sample variance
取样观察 sampling observation
取样管 sample tube, coupon
取样焊缝 sample weld
取样机 sampler ◇ 风口焦炭～*
取样技术 sampling technique
取样检查 sampling inspection ◇ 分批～*
取样孔 sample hole
取样控制 sampling control
取样流程 sampling flowsheet
取样模 sampling mold
取样(平)台 sampling platform
取样瓶 sampling [sample] bulb ◇ 空气～ air-sampling vessel
取样器 sampler, sampling instrument, dip can, sniffer, thief, trier ◇ 摆动式～*, 槽式～ riffle sampler, 沉浸式～ immersion sampler, 笛管式～ whistle-pipe sampler, 管式[长筒式]～ pipe [gun] sampler, 弧线运动～*, 矿浆～ pulp samler, 链斗式～ chain bucket sampler, 料斗[抓斗]～ bucket sampler, 螺旋～ worm tube sampler, 皮带式～ conveyer-type sampler, 旋转弧型～ rotary-arc sampler, (圆)盘式～ fan plate sampler, 闸板[闸阀]式～ flap type sampler, 振动管～*, 直线运动式～*, 锥形～ cone sampler
取样球 sampling bulb
取样勺 sample spoon
取样设备 sampling plant
取样示波器 samploscope, sampling oscilloscope
取样试验 sampling test, pick-test
取样四分法 quater dividing method
取样速率 sampling rate
取样探针 sampling probe
取样头 sampling head
取样维持电路 sample-and-hold circuit
取样误差 sampling error
取样站 sampling station
取样装置 sampling apparatus, sampler
取液样器[液体取样装置] fluid sampling apparatus
取指令 【计】fetch
取周期 【计】fetch cycle
取准 normalize
去冰 de-icing
去冰零件 de-icing parts
去冰液 de-icing liquid [fluid]
去潮器 moisture eliminator
去臭 【环】deodorization
去除剂 remover

去除毛刺 （同"去毛刺"）
去除器 excluder
去磁 demagnetization, demagnetizing, degaussing
去磁场 demagnetizing [degaussing] field
去磁处理 demagnetization treatment
去磁力 demagnetization [demagnetizing] force
去磁能 demagnetizing energy
去磁器 demagnetizer, magnetic eraser
去磁曲线 demagnetization curve
去磁系数 demagnetization [demagnetizing] coefficient
去磁线圈 demagnetizing [degaussing] coil
去磁象限 demagnetization quadrant
去磁因数 【理】demagnetizing factor
去磁作用 demagnetizing effect
去氮 （同"脱氮"）
去电离电势[位] deionization potential
去电子作用 【理】deelectronation
去钝化作用 depassivating effect
去飞边 deburring
去飞边机 dressing machine
去钙 （同"脱钙"）
去铬 （同"脱铬"）
去垢剂 detergent (remover), abstergent ◇ 非离子～non-ionic detergent, 辊子～roll detergent, 阳离子～cationic detergent
去垢能力 detergency
去磺弧菌属 desulfovibrio ◇ 鲁氏～
去灰分 deashing
去极化 depolarization, depolarizing ◇ 氢～腐蚀
去极化还原 depolarizing reduction
去极（化）剂 depolarizer, depolarizing agent ◇ 阳极～anodic depolarizer
去极化作用 depolarization
去碱作用 lixiviation
去金 （同"除金"）
去矿泥 desliming, desludging
去蜡 （同"脱蜡"）
去磷 （同"脱磷"）
去硫 （同"脱硫"）
去硫铸铁 off-sulphur iron
去氯 （同"脱氯"）
去毛边 deburring, frasing
去毛刺 (de)burring, barb
去毛刺机 deburring [dressing] machine
去毛刺[毛边、毛口、焊瘤、焊刺]装置 deburring unit
去毛刺轧辊焊纹 rag
去毛口 burring
去锰 （同"脱锰"）
去沫 forth breakage, defoaming
去泥渣 desliming, desludging
去耦(合) decoupling, uncoupling
去泡(沫)剂 【选】defoaming agent
去皮 peeling, shelling
去漆剂 paint remover
去气 （同"脱气"）
去气混凝土（用真空法抽去气泡的混凝土） deaerated concrete
去铅 （同"退铅"）
去氢 （同"脱氢"）
去氢铁 （同"低氢铁"）
去热 abstracted heat
去乳化 de-emulsification
去[除]乳化剂 emulsifier-remover
去色 （同"脱色"）
去砂 desanding
去湿 （同"脱湿"）
去水 （同"脱水"）
去酸 deacidify
去酸化 deacidification
去酸洗泥 desmutting
去弹性钢丝(机械处理过的) killed wire
去碳 （同"脱碳"）
去碳弧菌 desulfovibrio desulfurican
去铜 （同"除铜"）
去头 【钢】topping
去凸缘 deflanging
去污 decontaminating (decon.), decontamination

去污剂　degergent, decontaminating agent
去污染　depollute
去污装置　decontamination plant
去污作用　decontamination
去雾器　demister
去像散透镜　anastigmat(ic) lens
去像散物镜　anastigmat(ic) objective
去硝　(同"脱硝")
去锌　(同"除锌")
去盐　(同"脱盐")
去氧　(同"脱氧")
去氧化皮　descaling
去氧化皮集管　descaling header
去应变回火　strain relief tempering
去应力回火　stress tempering
去应力退火　stress relief annealing
去油　deoiling
去油段　cleaning section
去油剂　degreasing compound
去油泥　desludging
去油切屑　deoiled turnings
去杂质系数　【冶】decontamination factor
去杂质(作用)　decontamination (decon.)
去载　unload
去渣锤　deslagging hammer
去渣能力　【焊】slag detachability
去脂剂　degreaser
去脂装置　degreaser
圈　loop, turn, circle, 【压】coil (带卷的), wrap (带卷的), layer (卷材的), wap (线卷的) ◇ 莱辛[填充]~Lessing ring
圈梁　【建】ring beam, gird, collar tie beam
圈数　number of turns
权级　power level
权数分配　weighted apportionment
权系数　coefficient of weight
权重　weighing, weight
权重配位数　【化】coordination weighted number
醛{RCHO}　aldehyde (ald.)
醛基次硫酸盐　aldehyed sulphoxylate
醛基次硫酸盐衍生物　aldehyed sulphoxylate derivative
全α-相合金　【金】all alpha alloy
全β-相合金　【金】all beta alloy
全变形　overall [total] deformation
全波检波　double-wave detection
全波接收机　all-wave receiver
全波接线　full wave connection
全波整流　full wave rectification, biphase rectification
全波整流电路　full wave circuit
全部淬火　total hardening
全(部)电气号志系统　all-electric signalling system
全部过硬(铸件难以加工)　mass hard
全部焊缝检验符[代]号　test-all-around symbol
全部合成　total synthesis
全部回流　total reflux
全部级配骨料　fully graded aggregate
全部交替过程　complete alternation
全部熔化(指铜熔铸)　off-bottom
全部使用期限　entire life
全部析出　overall deposition
全部硬化　through-hardening
全部蒸发冷却法　【环】total evaporation-cooling method
全产量　fully yield
全长　all length (a.l.), total [full, overall] length, length overall (L.o.a)
全长淬火　whole-length [full-length, all-length] quenching
全长拱脚砖　whole-length skew
全长热处理　whole-length quenching
全厂净化　【环】general clean-up
全厂实时信息网络　plant-wide real-time information network
全尺寸测量　full scale measurement
全抽风干燥式链算机　all downdraft drying grate
全抽风式链算机循环　all downdraft grate cycle
全磁精矿低温烧结　low-temperae sinter-

ing process with 100% magnetite concentrates
全淬硬　full hardening
全淬硬钢　full-hardened steel
全电压启动　full voltage starting
全吊挂炉顶　fully suspended roof
全镀锌钢丝(先拔后镀)　fully galvanized wire
全断面渗碳(法)　(同"均匀渗碳")
全对称晶体　holohedral crystal
全对称晶形的　holohedral
全对称晶形　holohedral form
全对称性[现象](结晶的)　pantomorphism
全反射　total reflection ◇ 受抑～*，衰减～*
全反射面　【理】totally reflecting surface
全方位焊接　all-position welding
全方位焊接用焊条　all-position (-type) electrode
全分解　total decomposition
全分析　complete [total, bulk] analysis
全封闭不通风　totally enclosed non-ventilated
全封闭风扇通风　totally enclosed fan cooled
全封闭式输送[运输]机　totally [full] enclosed conveyer
全封闭式贮槽　totally enclosed storage bin
全封闭自冷却　totally enclosed self-cooled
全风(鼓风炉的)　full blast
全风吹炼(转炉的)　【钢】full blow, blow full
全风吹炼炉次　【钢】full-blown heat
全风量　【铁】full wind
全风量操作高炉　driving blast-furnace
全风信号　【铁】full blast signal
全辐射高温计　(pyro-) total radiation pyrometer, rayotube (pyrometer)
全氟化物电解液　all fluoride bath
全浮力模型　plume model
全浮选　bulk flotation

全浮选法　all-flotation
全干的　bone dry
全钢的　all-steel
全高　overall [total] height
全工作日　full time
全鼓风压力　【冶】full wind pressure
全规模生产　full scale production
全国钢材经销商协会(英国)　National Association of Steel Stockholders
全国高炉渣处理业协会(美国)　National Slag Associate (NSA)
全国焊接设备制造业协会(美国)　National Welding Supply Association (NWSA)
全国石油协会(美国)　National Petroleum Association (NPA)
全国铸造协会(美国)　National Foundry Association (NFA)
全过程控制　【环】total process control
全焊焊缝　full sized weld
全焊结构　all-welded construction
全焊金属　【金】all-weld metal
全焊金属焊缝拉力试验　all-weld-metal tension test
全焊金属试样　all-weld(-metal) test piece
全焊透　(同"全熔透")
全合成　total synthesis
全厚熔透[烧穿]　【焊】melt-thru
全弧形圆坯连铸机　bow type continuous caster for bar
全化学沉积　allochem
全回流操作　total reflux operation
全回流稳定态　steady state at total reflux
全奇数指数　indices all odd
全剂量测量　full scale measurement
全加工轧辊　necked-and-rough turned roll
全加器　【计】full [one-position, three-input] adder
全碱性炉衬　all basic lining
全焦　total coke
全焦操作　all-coke operation
全截面　bulk cross-section

全截面试样	full section specimen
全金属离合器衬片	all-metal clutch facing
全金属设备	all-metal plant
全金属制动面[闸衬片]	all-metal brake lining
全浸渗透	full dip infiltration
全浸温度计	complete [total] immersion thermometer
全晶[全晶质](的)	holo-crystalline
全精矿小球团烧结	minipelletized sintering process with 100% concentrate
全景曝光[照明]	panoramic exposure
全景摄影	vitagraphy
全景照相机	cyclograph
全开角焊接	full open corner joint
全矿生铁	all-mine pig iron
全拉伸矫直	【压】pure stretch levelling
全蓝(回火色)	full blue
全冷却壁	【铁】entire cooling staves
全离心铸造	true centrifugal casting
全连续离子交换柱	fully continuous ion exchange column
全连铸	full continuous casting, full CC, sequence [continuous-continuous] casting
全连铸炼钢车间	ingot free melting shop
全硫	total sulphur
全硫酸盐电解	all-sulphate electrolyte
全硫锑酸钠{Na₃SbS₄}	sodium thioantimonate
全硫锑酸盐{M₃SbS₄}	thioantimonate
全硫锡酸	thiostannate
全流体控制(射流技术的)	All-fluid control
全铝导线	all-aluminum conductor (A.A.C.)
全氯化	perchlorinate
全氯化物电解法	all chloride electrolytic route
全氯化物电解液	all chloride bath, all chloride electrolyte
全氯乙烯{CCl₂:CCl₂}	perchloro-ethylene
全马氏体组织	all martensite structure
全貌图	overall [close-up] view
全密封	pan-seal
全密封电动机	canned motor
全面计划方案	overall project
全面检查	complete inspection, overall checkup
全面晶型	holohedral crystal [form]
全面开挖(隧道的)	full face digging
全面扩建	general extension
全面体类	holohedral class
全面质量管理	total quality control (TQC)
全内反射	total internal reflection
全能炉(渗碳、淬火的)	all case furnace
全泥浆化	all sliming
全泥浆(化)提金法	all-sliming process
全年平均气压	mean annual pressure
全年平均相对湿度	mean annual relative humidity
全偶数指数	indices all even
全膨胀计	【金】total dilatometer
全气体反应	all gaseous reaction
全氢退火炉	100% hydrogen annealing furnace
全氢罩式退火炉	all-hydrogen batch annealing furnace, high performance bell type annealing furnace of hydrogen atmosphere
全氢退火炉	100% hydrogen annealing furnace
全球定位系统	global positioning system (GPS)
全屈服	fully yielding
全热期	full fired stage
全熔炼	fine melting
全熔气焊(坡口的)	full fusion welding
全熔透	【焊】full (joint) penetration, complete (joint) penetration
全熔透单道焊缝	full penetration single pass weld
全熔透焊缝	complete-penetration weld
全烧杯铸型	dead burned mould

全视图　full [general] view
全数字传动控制系统　full digital drive control system
全水压机　all hydraulic press
全碳电刷　all carbon brush
全碳(量)　total carbon
全碳砖　full carbon brick
全陶粒混凝土　all haydite concrete
全套备件　complete spare parts
全套厂房　building complex
全套锭模　mould set
全套绘图仪器　draughting set
全套机组　complete set
全套设备　complete unit
全铁的　all-iron (AI)
全铁含量　total iron value
全铁素体基体　(同"纯铁素体基体")
全同门　【计】identity gate
全透射　through transmission
全透系统　through-transmission system
全图　full figure (FF), general view
全退火　full annealing (Af)
全脱硫精矿　(同"死烧精矿")
全脱硫氧化焙烧　sweet roast(ing)
全脱盐水　fully desalted water
全脱氧低合金钢　fully killed low alloy steel
全脱氧钢　fully deoxidized [finished, killed] steel, dead (melted) steel, quiet steel
全微粒化(磨至200筛目以下)　all sliming
全位错　perfect [total, whole] dislocation
全息　holographic ◇ 声学～术 acoustic holography
全息干涉图　holographic interferogram
全息干涉仪　holographic interferometer
全息摄影干涉量度法　holographic interferometry
全息图[照片]　hologram, holograph
全息学[照相术]　holography
全息照相存储器　【计】holographic memory [storage]
全纤维结构炉顶　pure fibre roof
全纤维炉衬　entire fibre lining
全纤维燃气双向运动退火炉　dual moving annealing furnace with all fibre and gas-burning
全线开工　allwork
全镶板构造　all-veneer construction
全项检验　one hundred per cent inspection
全向的　【理】omnidirectional
全象　full figure (FF)
全形性　pantomorphism
全选脉冲　【电】full read pulse
全循环　complete alternation
全氧化球　fully oxidized pellet
全液压制小车　【压】full-hydraulic plyer
全液压开铁口机　taphole driller of full hydraulic drive
全液压驱动泥炮　【铁】clay gun with all-hydraulic drive
全应变理论　total strain theory
全硬化钢　fully hardened steel, through-hardening steel
全硬状态(铝板的)　full hard temper
全域　population
全员劳动生产率　overall labour productivity
全镇静钢　quiet [dead] steel
全值绘图机控制　absolute plotter control
全值计算机　absolute-value computer
全重　full weight (F.W.)
全珠光体基体(生铁的)　【金】all-pearlite matrix
全砖结构　all brick construction
全装配式建筑　total-prefabricated construction
全紫色(的)　full purple
全自动电镀　full automatic plating
全自动电弧焊　full-automatic arc welding
全自动焊接头　full automatic weld
全自动化系统　fully automatic system
全自熔性炉料　fully self-fluxing burden

拳石　boulder
蜷柱位错　spiral prismatic dislocation
犬骨状轨道　【理】dog's bone orbit
犬骨状坯　dog-bone bloom
犬牙式砌合　【建】dog tooth bond
缺镀层斑点　uncoated spot
缺乏　be short of, lack, deficiency, deficient, insufficiency
缺角　【压】unfilled corner
缺口　notch, nick, breach, indentation ◇ 开~notching
缺口半径　radius of notch
缺口槽　notch groove
缺口冲击强度　notch impact strength
缺口冲击值　notched-value, notched-bar value
缺口冲击作用[敏感性]　notch impact effect
缺口(锤击)断裂试验(焊接试样的)　nick break (test)
缺口脆性　notch brittleness [embrittlement]
缺口脆性的　notch-brittle
缺口断裂　notch rupture
缺口断裂延性[缺口试样断面收缩率]　notch rupture ductility
缺口缓和系数　notch alleviation factor
缺口尖锐度　notch acuity
缺口扩展　notch propagation
缺口扩展裂纹　notch extension crack
缺口拉伸强度比　notch tensile ratio
缺口拉伸试样　notched tensile specimen
缺口敏感的　notch sensitive
缺口敏感系数　notch sensitivity factor
缺口敏感性　notch sensitiveness [sensitivity]
缺口破断　notch breaking
缺口强度　notch strength
缺口强度比　notch strength ratio
缺口强化　notch strengthening
缺口屈服强度比　notch yield ratio
缺口韧性　notch toughness ◇ 低温~*

缺口深度　notch depth
缺口试棒　notched (test) bar
缺口试验　【金】notch test
缺口试样　notched specimen, notched test bar [piece] ◇ 破断试验用~notch-break specimen
缺口试样(冲击)断裂试验　nicked fracture test
缺口试样(冲击)韧性(试验值)　notched bar toughness
缺口(试样)冲击韧性(值)　notch(ed bar) impact strength
缺口(试样)冲击试验　notch(ed bar) impact test, notched bar test, nick break test ◇ 艾氏~notched Izot test, 楔击~notch wedge impact
缺口试样冲击弯曲试验　notched-bar impact bending test
缺口试样拉力试验　notched bar tensile test
缺口(试样)拉伸试验　notch(ed) tensile [tension] test(ing)
缺口试样拉伸特性　notch-tensile properties
缺口(试样)慢弯曲试验　notched slow bend test
缺口(试样)疲劳试验　notch-bar fatigue test
缺口(试样)弯曲试验　notch(ed) bend(ing) test, nick bend test ◇ 金泽尔~Kinzel test
缺口收缩比　notch constriciton ratio
缺口弯曲试样　notch bend specimen ◇ 三点加载~*
缺口楔形张开加载试样　notched WOL (wedge opening loaded) specimen
缺口延性　notch ductile
缺口延性钢　notch ductile steel
缺肉(铸件缺陷)　misrun, lean
缺肉铸件　misrun casting
缺少　absence, lack, disappearance, shortage, shortfall

缺位　【理】vacant position, omission
缺位丛聚　【金】vacancies clustering
缺位固溶体　【金】defect [deduction, omission] solid solution
缺陷　default, defect, disadvantage, fault(iness), flaw, imperfection, objection, shortcoming, blemish（金属表面的）◇ 次要～*, 反肖特基～anti-Schottky defect, 弗伦克尔～*, 假[伪]～*, 无～的 non-defective, 肖特基～【理】Schottky defect, 有～deformity, unsoundness, 有～表面（钢锭的）scabby surface, 有～部位 unsound spot, 有～材料【理】defective [imperfect, bad] material, 运动位错产生的～*
缺陷半导体　defective semi-conductor
缺陷表　list of defects
缺陷部分（铸件的）　defective portion
缺陷测记器　defectograph
缺陷分辨能力【本领】　defect resolution
缺陷回波信号[回声]　flaw echo
缺陷检验　defect detecting test, defect [flaw] inspection
缺陷结构[构造]　【金】defect structure
缺陷警报系统　flaw warning system
缺陷理论　imperfection theory
缺陷量级　imperfection level
缺陷密度　defect concentration, density of defects
缺陷平衡数目（点阵的）　equilibrium number of defects
缺陷切除剪　【压】nibbler shears
缺陷清理工　chipper
缺陷区延续长度　length of discontinuity
缺陷烧除器　deseaming burner
缺陷探测　flaw detection
缺陷探测灵敏度　sensitivity of defects perception
缺陷位置标度　【金】flaw location scale
缺陷（位置）测定　flaw location
缺陷相关扩散　defect associated diffusion
缺陷修补　healing of defects
缺陷修整工　chipper
缺陷硬化[强化]（晶格的）　defect hardening
缺陷与位错间相互作用　【金】defect-dislocation interaction
缺陷指示器　fault indicator
缺陷铸件　faulty [defective] casting
缺陷状态　faulty condition
缺氧　oxygen deficiency [deficit]
缺氧腐蚀　anaerobic corrosion
缺氧－好氧法生物脱氮工艺　biological denitrification with anoxic-oxic process
缺铸　【铸】misrun
炔　alkyne
确定准确位置　spotting
确实性检查　【计】validity check
裙板　apron（board）, skirtboard（输送带的）
裙板给[加, 进]料机　apron feeder
裙状绝缘子　petticoal insulator
群聚分类　cybotactic grouping
群控　【电】group(ed) control
群论　【数】group theory
群码　【计】group code
群频(率)　【理】group frequency
群速　【理】group velocity
群像　imagery
群柱　bundle pillar, grouped column
群桩　【建】group of piles
群桩作用　action of pile group

R r

燃点 firing point (FP), firing temperature (F.T.), fire [flame, flammability, ignition] point, kindling point [temperature]

燃耗 【理】burn(ing)-out

燃耗率(核裂变材料的) burn-up (ratio)

燃弧电压 arc-burning voltage

燃弧时间 arc (current) time

燃灰腐蚀 ash corrosion, fuel (ash) corrosion

燃焦坩埚炉 coke-fired crucible furnace

燃焦炉 coke-fired furnace

燃尽 burn-out, after-combustion ◇ 未~的 unburned

燃尽率 burn-out rate

燃料 fuel (material), propellant (火箭用) ◇ 动力用~ power fuel, 废~ fuel wastage, 含硫~ sulphur-bearing fuel, 加铅~, 无灰~ ash-free fuel, 雾化~ atomized fuel

燃料棒 fuel rod

燃料泵 fuel pump [actuator]

燃料比 fuel ratio [consumption]

燃料比率 fuel ratio

燃料补充[给] fuel make up

燃料不足的火焰 lean flame

燃料仓 fuel bin [bunker]

燃料层 fuel bed

燃料层燃烧开始区 early part of fuel bed

燃料吹氧[氧气]废钢(电弧炉)炼钢法 FOS (fuel oxygen scrap) process

燃料单位消耗 fuel rate, specific fuel consumption (SFC)

燃料电池 fuel cell

燃料分析 fuel analysis

燃料腐蚀 fuel erosion

燃料富选[别] preparation of fuel

燃料工程 fuel engineering

燃料供给[进给]调节(器) fuel control package

燃料供给管线 fuel supply line

燃料供给[供应](量) fuel input [supply]

燃料耗量 firing rate

燃料核心 【理】fuel core

燃料合金 fuel alloy

燃料化学 fuel chemistry

燃料化学成分 fuel analysis

燃料灰分 fuel ash

燃料挥发性 fuel volatility

燃料回收工厂 fuel reprocessing plant

燃料混合物 fuel [burning] mixture

燃料计量泵 fuel metering pump

燃料焦 coke fuel

燃料进给速率 fuel rate

燃料空气[燃料成分]比 fuel-air ratio (F/a)

燃料空气比控制 fuel-air ratio control

燃料空气混合物分析器 fuel air mixture analyzer

燃料库 fuel storage [bin, reservoir]

燃料(利用)效率 fuel efficiency

燃料量控制 control of fuel rate

燃料流量计 fuel flow meter

燃料喷吹管系 【铁】injection piping

燃料喷吹率 (fuel) injection rate

燃料喷吹系统 injection system

燃料喷吹装置 injection equipment

燃料喷枪 fuel injector

燃料喷烧器 fuel injector

燃料喷射[火苗,火舌]长度 【冶】fuel spray penetration

燃料喷嘴 fuel nozzle [orifice] ◇ 离心式~ fuel swirler

燃料偏析 fuel segregation

燃料平衡 fuel balance

燃料燃烧(爆炸)成形 fuel combustion forming

燃料燃烧量 capacity of fuel combustion

燃料燃烧器 fuel burner

燃料燃烧装置 fuel firing arrangement

燃料烧尽速率 fuel burning up rate

燃料特性 fuel characteristics

燃料添加剂　fuel additive
燃料添加量　fuel addition
燃料添加器　fuel feeder
燃料雾化器　fuel atomizer
燃料系数　fuel factor [ratio]
燃料系统　fuel system
燃料箱　fuel cell
燃料消耗　fuel rate [consumption]
燃料循环　fuel cycle
燃料铀　fuel uranium
燃料油　fuel oil (F.O.), oil fuel ◇ 芳族 ~ aromatic naphtha
燃料油喷吹　fuel oil injection
燃料元件　fuel element, heat liberating devices
燃料再生　【理】fuel regeneration [reproduction]
燃料再生工厂　fuel reprocessing plant
燃料渣　fuel wastage
燃料值　fuel value
燃料装料管　fuel port tube
燃料准备工段　fuel preparation plant
燃料资源　fuel resources
燃煤锻造炉　coal forge
燃煤炉　coal-fired furnace
燃模　【铸】gasifiable pattern
燃木炭炉　charcoal(-fired) furnace
燃气　fuel gas, (fire) gas, gas-type [gas(eous)] fuel ◇ 低发热值~low-BTU fuel gas, 斯特雷福特~脱硫法*
燃气动力锤　gas(-driven) hammer
燃气煅烧窑　gas-fired calcining kiln
燃气(发动)机　gas engine
燃气发生　gas generation
燃气辐射管加热炉　gas tube furnace
燃气鼓风机　gas(-driven) blowing engine
燃气管道　fuel gas conduit
燃气加热设备　gas-fired heating unit
燃气轮机[燃气透平]　gas-turbine (engine)
燃气轮机发电厂[站]　gas-turbine power station

燃气轮机鼓风机　gas(-driven) engine blower
燃气驱动鼓风机　gas(-driven) blowing engine
燃气软管　fuel gas hose
燃烧　combustion, burn(ing), fire, flame ◇ 不能~的 incombustible, 不易~的 uninflammable, 催化~ catalytic combustion, 二次~ post combustion, 恒容~*, 缓慢~ retarded combustion, 浸没~submerged combustion, 两头~炉*, 强化~*, 迅速~ deflagrate, 未~的 unburned, 易~的 free burning
燃烧氨气(热处理保护用)　【金】burnt ammonia
燃烧比($CO_2/(CO_2+CO)$)　combustion ratio
燃烧层　burning zone, fire blanket
燃烧产生的气体　fire gases
燃烧产物　combustion product
燃烧产物腐蚀　fuel (ash) corrosion
燃烧程度　degree of burning
燃烧充分　completeness of combustion
燃烧带　burning zone, fire blanket, zone of fire (Z/F), combustion zone (风口的) ◇ 层上~*
燃烧带绝热火焰温度(高炉风口前的)　raceway adiabatic flame temperature (RAFT)
燃烧弹(量热计)　combustion bomb
燃烧弹量热计　bomb calorimeter
燃烧定碳法　Strohlein method
燃烧端　fire end
燃烧发热值　heating value as fired
燃烧反应　combustion reaction
燃烧范围　【冶】combustion region
燃烧废气　burned [burnt] gas, 【环】combustion gas effluent
燃烧废气烟囱　flambeau
燃烧分析仪　combustion analyzer
燃烧管　burner [combustion] tube
燃烧过程　combustion process ◇ 电弧~

【焊】arcing process
燃烧合成 combustion synthesis
燃烧机理 combustion mechanism
燃烧计算 combustion calculation
燃烧净热值 net heat of combustion
燃烧空间 combustion space [volume]
燃烧空气 combustion air
燃烧空气管 combustion air pipe
燃烧空气需要量 combustion air requirement
燃烧空窝 raceway ◇ 公共~*
燃烧控制 combustion control ◇ 双交叉限幅~*,自动~*
燃烧口 burner port
燃烧离解氨 burned dissociated ammonia
燃烧理论 combustion [burning] theory
燃烧炉 combustion furnace ◇ 碳阻~*
燃烧率 combustion ratio, rate of burning, intensity of combustion
燃烧面 combustion front
燃烧期 combustion period,【铁】gas period(热风炉的)
燃烧器 burner, combustor, inflamer,【团】firing hood ◇ 低~*【焦】low(er) burner, 多焰~multiflame blowpipe, 辐射式~radiant burners, 辅助~pilot burner, 复[再]~after-burner, 过剩高炉煤气~excess gas burner, 环形~*, 火焰可调式~variable-flame burner, 机械雾化~*, 浸焰式~*, 可控温度~*, 临时[附加]~extra burner, 配比~*, 喷枪式~*, 雾化[喷雾]~*, 旋流式~cyclone burner, 压力喷嘴~pressure jet burner, 蒸汽喷射式~*
燃烧器空气流量 burner air flow
燃烧器喷嘴 burner head [top], torch tube
燃烧器调整范围【冶】turndown range
燃烧器旋孔 burner arch
燃烧器用砖 burner brick
燃烧气体 combustion gas
燃烧强度 combustion intensity

燃烧区(域) zone of fire (Z/F), fire room,【冶】combustion zone [region]
燃烧热 heat of combustion (h.c.)
燃烧容积(炉子的) combustion volume
燃烧生成气体 fire gas
燃烧时间 firing time (F.T., f.t.)
燃烧室 burning chamber, combustion chamber [space], burning compartment, burner house, firing box, furnace (chamber, room), hot bulb, combustion well (热风炉的) ◇ 半煤气发生炉式~*, 壁炉~burning-in hood, 炉外~*, 外伸~external furnace
燃烧室壁温 chamber wall temperature
燃烧室衬墙(可拆换的)【铁】skin wall
燃烧室烘顶 ignition arch
燃烧室几何形状 chamber geometry
燃烧室墙【焦】heating wall
燃烧室头部 burner head
燃烧数据 combustion data
燃烧速度 burning [flame] velocity, combustion rate, speed of combustion
燃烧速率【冶】rate of burning ◇ 煤~coal(-burning) rate
燃烧损失 combustion loss, loss by burning
燃烧条件 combustion condition
燃烧温度 combustion [burning] temperature
燃烧效率 combustion efficiency
燃烧行为 combustion behaviour
燃烧性(能) combustion properties, combustibility
燃烧压力 combustion pressure
燃烧用风 combustion air
燃烧嘴 burner tip
燃碳率【色】carbon burning rate
燃用木柴 fuel wood
燃油 fuel oil, oil-type fuel ◇ 高炉~furnace oil
燃油泵 fuel oil pump
燃油供应罐 fuel service tank
燃油炉 oil(-burning) [oil-fired, oil-heat-

ed,petroleum-fired] furnace
燃油喷吹 fuel oil injection
燃油喷管[嘴] fuel (injection) nozzle
燃油烧嘴 oil lighter
染料 dye, colourant, tincture, pigment ◇ 脂溶性~ fat dye
染色 dyeing, colouration, colouring, staining, tintage ◇ 可~性 stainability, 空气~法*, 热~法*
染色技术 staining technique
染色加压试验 pressure dye test
染色渗透剂(探伤用) dye penetrant
染色渗透检验[探伤] dye penetrant inspection
染色渗透液 visible dye
染色渗透液探伤法 【理】dye-penetrant process
染色探裂[探伤]法 dye-check process, spek-chek, spotchek ◇ 金属~ met-L-chek
染色涂饰 dyed finish
染色吸附 adsorption of dyes
染污 spot
扰动 excitation, turbulence, disturbance, perturbation
扰动的 turbulent
扰动分析 perturbation analysis
扰动浓度(区域熔炼的) perturbing concentration
扰动区(金属进入轧辊前的) disturbance zone
扰动土 disturbed soil
绕道 detour
绕法 winding
绕焊 boxing, end turning
绕流 circulating flow
绕卷机 winding machine
绕卷筒 winding reel
绕射 (同"衍射")
绕枢轴旋转辊 pivotable roller
绕丝等静压机 【粉】wire-wound isostatic press

绕丝高压容器 wire-wound high pressure vessel
绕丝焊条 wrapped electrode
绕线 (wire) coiling, winding, wire wrap ◇ 来回~电阻 go-and-return resistance
绕线车 supply reel
绕线电阻(器) wire-wound resistor
绕线机 coiling [bobbin, reeling] machine, (wire) winding machine ◇ 昆塔斯~*
绕线架 reel
绕线框架 wire-wound frame
绕线盘 winding reel, wire spool
绕线式(转子)感应电动机 wound rotor induction motor, induction motor with wound rotor
绕行辊道 bypass table
绕铸核(的)点焊区 corona
绕组 winding, coil ◇ 积复激~*, 双线[股]~ bifilar winding, 筒形~ cylindrical winding
绕组电感 winding inductance
绕组电阻 winding resistance
绕组间的 interwinding
绕组损失[损耗] winding loss
热 heat ◇ 除[放]~ heat removal, 隔~板 heat baffle [barrier], 绝~砖 heat insulating brick, 佩尔蒂埃~*, 载~体[介质] 【理】heating agency
热拔 【压】hot drawing
热拔(钢)管 hot drawn tube
热板 hot plate
热板材矫直机 【压】hot plate straightening machine
热板钎焊 hot plate soldering
热棒材剪机 hot-bar shears
热包覆[层] hot cladding
热剥落[剥片] thermal spalling
热保护自动开关 thermosnap
热爆炸成形 hot explosive forming
热焙砂[焙烧矿] hot calcine
热焙烧矿熔炼 hot calcine smelting
热本底 thermal background

热比重计　thermo-hydrometer
热壁真空炉　【冶】hot wall vacuum furnace
热变电阻　("《热敏电阻》")
热变化　thermal [heat] change
热变化偏转率　thermal deflection rate
热变色漆　heat sensitive paint
热变试验　hot bend test
热变形　heat [hot, thermal] deformation
热变形控制技术　thermomechanical control process (TMCP)
热变形模具钢　hot work tool steel
热变形温度　heat distortion temperature (HDT)
热变形学　thermomechanics
热补　burning-on, hot patching [repair]
热补偿　thermal compensation
热补偿合金　thermal compensation alloy
热补轮胎　vulcanization
热补压　hot repressing
热不稳定的　thermolabile
热不稳定性　thermal instability
"热"材料　hot material
热参数　thermal parameters ◇ 有效～*
热残渣　hot residue
热操作　hot application
热测量头　heat sensor
热差电偶结　thermal junction
热沉淀　thermal precipitation
热沉降板　heat sink plate
热成品检验　hot inspection
热成像技术　thermal imaging technique
热成形　hot shaping [moulding], ardeforming ◇ 喷丸～法*
热成形性能　hot forming property
热迟延　thermal retardation
热弛豫　thermal relaxation
热冲击　thermal [heat] shock ◇ 耐～性*
热冲击交替次数　number of reversals at thermal shock
热冲击强度　thermal shock resistivity, resistance to thermal shock
热冲击试验　thermal shock test, hot impact test
热冲击性质　thermal shock behaviour
热冲击指数　thermal shock index
热冲压　hot stamping
热抽出　hot pull
热出量　thermal output
热除浇口[汤道]　【钢, 铸】hot spruing
热处理　heat treatment (HT, ht. tr.), heat treating, thermal processing [treatment] ◇ 不可[非]～合金*, 等温形变～*, 二次～的 re-heat-treated, 峰值[相变温度]～法【金】hump process, 复合[多级]～*, 固溶～*, 光亮～bright heat treatment, 经～的 heat treated, 可～钢*, 快速～*, 理论计算确定的～法*, 流态化床～*, 铅浴～*, 无畸变～*, 盐浴～*, 在线～*, 中间～*
热处理保护涂料　heat treatment protective coating
热处理车间　heat treating department
热处理吊架[夹具]　heat treatment jig
热处理感受性[感受热处理的能力]　【金】response to heat treatment
热处理钢　heat-treated steel
热处理工　heat treater
热处理和稳定处理过的　heat treated and stabilized (HTS)
热处理后强度(等级)　heat treated strength level
热处理后硬度　heat treated hardness
热处理后组织　heat treated structure
热处理机械设备　heat treatment machinery
热处理净化　purification by heat treatment
热处理绝热炉　insulated furnace
热处理可淬硬的　hardenable by heat treatment
热处理裂纹　heat treatment crack
热处理炉　heat treating [treatment] furnace, treating oven ◇ 车底式分批～*, 对流式～*, 分批装出料的室式～peri-

odical furnace, 辐射加热无氧化辊式~*, 间接加热式~*, 坑式~*, 连续式~*, 炉气强制循环~*, 气体循环式~ cyclone furnace, 室式装箱~*, 碳底分批~*, 卧式分批~*, 无氧化~*, 直接[敞开]加热~ direct-fired furnace, 自动传送带型~*

热处理气氛 heat treating atmosphere

热处理气氛发生炉 heat treating atmosphere producer

热处理曲线 heat treatment cycle curve, 【耐】tempering curve(焦油砖的)

热处理设备 heat treatment facilities [installation, machinery]

热处理温度 heat treatment temperature

热处理氧化膜 heat treating film

热处理引起的晶粒长大 heat treatment induced grain growth

热处理周期 heat treating cycle

热处理铸件 heat treated casting

热处理装置 heat treatment installation

热处理状态 heat treated state [condition] ◇固溶~*

热处理作业线 heat treatment line

热穿孔[穿轧] hot piercing

热传导 heat [thermal] conduction, conduct [egress] of heat, heat passage, thermal conductance

热传导金属 heat transfer metal

热传导率[性] thermoconductivity

热传导系数 (同"传热系数")

热传递 heat transfer ◇流态化床~*

热传递不良 poor heat transfer

热传递分析 heat transfer analysis

热传递速率 heat transfer rate

热传递装置 heat transfer arrangement

热传动触点 thermally actuated contacts

热传感器 heat sensor

热传输 heat transmission

热传送 heat passage

热传送器 temperature pickup, pyrometer probe

热吹 【钢】hot blow

热吹风器 heat gun

热吹压壳型机(造型用) blow hot press shell moulding machine

热磁(补偿)合金(69Ni,29Cu,2Fe) calorie magnetic alloy, thermomagnetic alloy, Calmalloy (alloy). ◇韦斯汀豪斯[西屋]镍铜~ Westinghouse alloy

热磁处理 thermomagnetic treatment, magnetic anneal(ing)

热磁法 thermomagnetic process

热磁分析 thermomagnetic analysis

热磁红外辐射探测器 pyromagnetic infrared radiation detector

热磁系数 magnetic temperature coefficient

热磁现象 thermomagnetism

热磁效应 thermomagnetic effect

热磁性 thermomagnetion, thermomagnetism, pyromagnetism

热磁滞后 thermomagnetic hysteresis

热粗轧 【压】hot roughing

热脆材料 hot short material

热脆范围 hot short range

热脆钢 hot brittle steel, red short steel

热脆开裂 hot short cracking

热脆区 【钢】hot [red] shortness zone

热脆铁(高硫铁) red short iron

热脆(性) hot [red] brittleness, heat embrittlement, hot [red] shortness,

热萃取气体分析 hot extraction gas analysis

热带地下卷取机 hot downcoiler

热带卷运输机 hot coil conveyer

热带气候 tropical climate ◇使设备适应~条件 tropicalization

热带气旋 tropical cyclone

热单位 (同"热量单位")

热当量 heat [thermal] equivalent

热当量值 thermally equivalent quantity

热导管 heat pipe

热导率真空计 thermal conductivity vacu-

um gauge
热导式气体分析仪 thermal conductivity gas analyser
热导探测器 thermal conductivity detector
热导体 heat [thermal] conductor
热导体合金 thermal conductor alloy
热导元件鉴定[探测]器 thermal conductivity cell detector
热的引出 heat removal
热等静气体加压成型【粉】 hot isostatic compacting with pressurized gas
热等静压 pressure bonding
热等静压(加压)时间 HIP time
热等静压(加压)温度 HIP temperature
热等静压法 hot-isostatic-bonding and pressing process
热等静压力 hot isostatic pressure, HIP pressure
热等静压力机 hot isostatic press (HIP)
热等静压设备 hot isostatic apparatus
热等静压制(法)[热等静加压成型] hot-isostatic pressing (HIP), hot isostatic compaction
热等离子体 hot plasma
热滴定(法) pyrotitration
热滴定分析 pyrotitration analysis
热电 thermoelectricity, pyro-electricity
热电变换[反转] thermoelectric inversion
热电材料 thermoelectric [pyro-electric] material
热电测量仪表 thermal electric meter
热电厂[站] thermal power station, heat and power station, steam power plant
热电池 thermal cell, thermoelectric generator
热电传感器 thermoelectric probe
热电当量 electrothermal equivalent
热电动势 thermal electromotive force, thermo-E.M.F.
热电动势系数 Seebeck coefficient
热电堆 thermopile
热电法 thermoelectric method

热电法铁水快速定硅技术 thermo-electromotive force method for rapid determination of silicon content in molten iron
热电放射效应 Edison effect
热电高温计 themoelectric pyrometer ◇浸入式碳—碳化硅~*
热电高温学[测定法] thermoelectric pyrometry
热电功率 thermoelectric power
热电极 thermode, hot rod
热电鉴别器[头](混合物料用)【冶】 thermosorter
热电金属 thermoelectric metal
热电解法 thermoelectrolytic method
热电晶体 pyro-electric [thermoelectric] crystal
热电流 thermocurrent ◇瞬时~*
热电流量计 thermoelectric flowmeter
热电偶 thermal-couple (TC, tc), (thermo) couple, pyrometer [thermoelectric] couple, thermoelement, thermopair, pyod ◇铂铑[勒夏特列]~*, 差示~*, 多头~ split thermocouples, 复式镍—铬—镍~*, 高重显性~*, 管式~ pipe thermocouple, 护壳式~*, 检测用~*, 浸液式~*, 铠装~*, 控温~ control thermocouple, 莫尔[康铜]~ Moll thermopile, 难熔金属~*, 镍铬-镍铝~*, 铅笔式~*, 石墨-碳化硅~*, 速浸式~*, 碳-碳化硅~*, 铁-康铜~*, 铜-康铜~*, 移动式~*, 针式~ needle thermocouple
热电偶保护套管 thermocouple protection tube
热电偶保护装置 thermocouple protection assembly
热电偶成套组件 thermocouple assembly
热电偶高温计 thermocouple pyrometer ◇带状~*
热电偶管 thermocouple tube
热电偶合金 thermocouple alloy [metal], thermopair alloy ◇阿卢梅尔 镍铬~

(98Ni,2Cr) Alumel,哈钦森~*,金钴~*
热电偶继电器　thermorelay
热电偶接头　thermal [thermocouple,thermoelectric] junction
热电偶井　thermocouple well
热电偶铠装线　sheathed thermocouple wire
热电偶孔　thermocouple hole [well],thermowell
热电偶片　thermo couple sheet
热电偶气压计　thermocouple gauge
热电偶热端　pyrometer fire-end
热电偶式真空计　thermocouple-type gauge,thermocouple vacuum gauge
热电偶丝[热电高温计丝]　thermocouple wire
热电偶套管　thermocouple sheaths
热电偶温度　thermocouple temperature
热电偶温度计　thermocouple [thermoelectric] thermometer
热电偶元件　thermocouple element ◇ 同轴~*
热电偶正导线　positive leg
热电色度计　thermoelectric colorimeter
热电式仪表　thermoelectric instrument,thermal meter
热电势[位]　thermoelectric(al) potential
热电特性　pyro-electric behaviour
热电体　pyro-electrics
热电铁氧体　pyroferrite
热电温度计　thermel
热电系数　thermoelectric coefficient
热电现象　thermoelectric phenomenon,thermoelectricity,pyro-electricity
热电效应　thermoelectric(al) [pyro-electric] effect ◇ 凯尔文~*,同质[汤姆逊]~*,异质[西贝克古典]~ Seebeck effect
热电效应系数　coefficient of thermoelectric effect
热电序　thermoelectric series

热电学　thermoelectricity,pyroelectricity
热电元件　thermoelectric element,thermoelement
热电致冷　thermoelectric refrigeration
热电子　thermal [thermionic] electron,thermoelectron,negative thermion
热电子发射体　thermionic [cathode] emitter
热电子氯化法　thermo-electron chlorination process
热电阻器　thermal [heat] resistor
热电阻线　hot wire
热电作用　thermoelectric action
热叠轧机　【压】hot-pack mill
热叠轧作业　【压】hot-pack rolling
热顶[镦]锻　hot heading,hot upset (forging)
热顶锻[镦头]机　hot heading machine
热顶锻[镦锻,镦головка]试验　hot upset test
热锭　hot ingot
热定尺剪切机组[作业线]　【压】hot dividing line
热定径　【压】hot sizing
热定像装置(探伤用)　heat fixing unit
热镀　dip coating,hot dip (coating)
热镀铬　hot chromizing
热镀金属法　metallic coating by hot-dipping process
热镀铝　hot dip aluminium coating,aluminized coating,calorising,calorizing ◇ 芬克氢气保护~法 Fink process,伦丁~法*
热镀铝层　hot dip aluminium coating,aluminized coating
热镀铝后铸铝法　Aluminibond process
热镀锡　hot tin(ning) ◇ 杰弗洛伊－德洛尔~法*
热镀锡薄钢板(镀锡量为每基准箱板材0.39—0.86kg)　hot dipped tin plate
热镀锡薄钢带　hot tinned strip
热镀锌　hot (dip) galvanizing,pot galvanizing,galvanizing by dipping

热镀锌槽　melted zinc bath
热镀锌法[层]　hot dip galvanized coating ◇ 阿普拉特～*，分解氨[森吉米尔]～*，火封软熔～*，克拉波～Crapo process
热镀锌钢丝　hot dip galvanized steel wire
热镀锌机组　hot galvanizing line
热镀锌结构钢　hot galvanized structural steel
热度　hotness
热度比较仪　thermal comparator
热端　hot junction (HJ), hot end
热锻　hot forging
热锻法[工艺]　hot forging process
热锻分级淬火　hot peening marquenching
热锻件　hot forged component
热锻模具钢　hot-working die steel
热锻破坏(原始组织的)　hot breakdown by forging
热锻设备　hot forging equipment
热锻缩减　hot forging reduction
热锻压机　hot press forge
热锻压接头[配件]　hot stamped fittings
热断裂　hot fracture
热断路装置　thermal trip
热对流　heat [thermal] convection
热镦粗　【压】hot upsetting
热镦锻操作[工序]　hot upsetting operation
热惰性　thermal inertia [lag]
热法软化　hot process softening
热反射器　heat reflector
热反应　thermal reaction
热返矿　hot return [recirculating] fines (H.R.F.), 【色】thermal recovery
热返矿槽　hot return bin, hot fines (storage) bin
热返矿系统　hot return fines circuit
热返矿比[率]　【团】hot returns ratio
热返矿型　【团】hot returns plough
热返矿筛　【团】hot fine screen
热返矿圆盘给料机　hot return fines feeder table
热防护层　thermal shield (Ing)
热防护(装置)　thermal protection
热飞锯　flying hot saw ◇ 回转式～rotary flying hot saw
热分布[配]　heat [thermal] distribution
热分布图　【冶】thermograph
热分布状况试验　thermal-profile test
热分解　thermal [pyrolytic] decomposition, thermal breakdown, thermal separation (热轧时乳液的)
热分解法(制取纯金属)　thermal decomposition method
热分界层　thermal boundary layer
热分析　heat [thermal] analysis, thermo-analysis, thermal study
热(分析)曲线　thermal curve
热分析天平　thermal balance
热分析仪　thermal analyzer
热粉化特性　heat degradation property
热封顶　hot topping
热封顶法　hot top process
热风　heated [hot] air, hot-blast air
热风阀　【铁】hot blast valve ◇ 水冷闸板式～*
热风阀操纵　hot-blast valve control
热风干燥鼓风机　hot air drier blower
热风干燥器　hot-air (blast) drier
热风供暖　warm-air heating ◇ 激动式～*
热风鼓风机　hot blower
热风主管　【铁】hot-blast main
热风管道　hot air duct
热风焊接　hot-gas welding
热风滑阀　【铁】hot-blast slide valve
热风化铁炉　hot-blast cupola
热风混合系统　hot-blast mixer system
热风机　hot air heater
热风加热套　hot air jacket
热风控制[调节]阀　hot-blast (flow) control valve
热风冷风混合　【铁】hot-blast/cold-blast

mixing
热风炼铁 hot-blown iron
热风量 hot-blast volume (HBV, h.b.v.)
热风炉 hot-blast stove (HBS), air stove, air heater (AH), (hot) stove, hot air stove [furnace, heater, oven], blast heater ◇ 侧燃烧式~*, 顶燃式~*, 二通式~ two-pass hot stove, 管式~ pipe stove, 间断(换热)式~ intermittent stove, 考贝式[蓄热式二通, 二通蓄热式]~*, 可变紊流式~*, 连接式~*, 马克鲁尔式~*, 内燃式~*, 三通式[中心燃烧式]~*, 石球式~ pebble stove, 外燃式~*, 蓄热式~*
热风炉操作平台 stove platform
热风炉操作顺序 stove operating sequence
热风炉阀门换向设备 hot-blast stove changing equipment
热风炉工 stoveminder, stove operator, stovetender
热风炉烘炉 heating up of blast heater
热风炉换炉 switchover of stoves
热风炉换向操作 stove-changing operation
热风炉恢复送风 opening out
热风炉炉壳 hot-blast stove casing
热风炉炉身 stove stack
热风炉炉身温度 stove stack temperature
热风炉(煤气)燃烧器 hot-blast stove gas burner
热风炉煤气总管 stove gas main
热风炉燃烧(期) on-gas
热风炉燃烧器风机 air heater burner fan
热风炉燃烧器关闭阀 stove-burner shut-off valve
热风炉燃烧系统 stove combustion system
热风炉烧嘴 hot stove burner
热风炉停止送风 shutting out
热风炉系统 hot stove system
热风炉烟囱 stove chimney
热风炉用燃料 stove fuel
热风炉砖格 stove checker

热风炉砖格系统 stove checker system
热风炉砖格子 hot-blast stove checkerwork
热风炉自动换向 automatic stove changing
热风喷枪 heater blower gun
热风器 (steam) air heater, heat gun
热风热容[加热能量] hot-blast heating capacity
热风熔炼[热风热量] hot-blast heat
热风生铁 hot-blast [hot-blown] pig iron
热风围管 hot-blast circulating duct
热风围管压力 【铁】bustle pipe pressure
热风温度 hot-blast temperature (HBT)
热风温度计 hot-blast temperature indicator
热风温度调节 hot-blast temperature control
热风温度调节器 hot-blast temperature controller
热风循环干燥机 circulating hot-air drier
热风压力表 hot-blast pressure indicator
热风支管 【铁】hot-blast outlet
热风总管 【铁】hot-blast main ◇ 砖砌~*
热辐射 heat [thermal, calori(fi)c, temperature] radiation, emission of heat
热辐射传热 thermal radiation heat transfer
热辐射的 thermal-radiating
热辐射计 bolometer, kampometer
热辐射屏 radiation screen
热浮选法 hot flotation (method)
热腐蚀 hot corrosion
热复压 【粉】hot repressing
热负荷 thermal [heating] load, combustion rate (燃烧室的)
热负荷强度 hot load strength
热负荷试验 hot load test
热负载 heat load
热干燥器 heat drier
热干渣 fresh slag

热感受能力	thermal response
热钢板回火	【压】hot plate tempering
热钢材冷却台架	【压】hot rack
热钢锭剥皮机床	hot ingot peeling machine
热钢锭运送铁路线（进入加热炉跨）	hot steel track
热割穿孔	【焊】piercing by thermal cutting
热割法	thermal cutting process
热工参数	thermal parameters
热工工艺（钢的）	heating regulation
热工计算	heat account
热工条件	thermal condition(s)
热工学	heat engineering [technology], pyrology
热工制度	thermal regime, heat pattern
热工制度控制	heat pattern control
热工制度控制系统	heat pattern control system
热工状态	thermal condition(s)
热功当量	thermal equivalent of work, mechanical equivalent of heat
热功率	heat [thermal] power
热功率定额	thermal rating
热鼓风	hot-blast (air), hot blow
热鼓风出口	【铁】hot-blast outlet
热鼓风冷鼓风混合	（同"热风冷风混合"）
热鼓风炉	hot-blast furnace
热固定	thermal fixing ◇ 转移影像～ thermal fixing of transferred image
热固结(法)	【团】heat [thermal] hardening
热固结球团	heat hardened pellet
热固性材料	thermosetting material
热固性聚合物	thermosetting polymer
热固性黏结剂	hot setting adhesive, thermosetting adhesive
热固(性)树脂	thermosetting resin
热固性塑料	thermosetting plastic ◇ 克拉～*
热固性油漆	thermosetting varnish
热管	heat pipe, heat transfer tube
热管换热器	heat pipe exchanger
热光弹性试验	thermal photoelastic experiment
热辊轧制	【压】hot groove rolling
热过程	thermal process
热过电流继电器的热元件	heater of thermal overcurrent relay
热过负荷[过载]继电器	thermal [thermic] overload relay
热过滤用漏斗	double-wall funnel
热含量	thermal capacity [content], enthalpy
热焓	enthalpy, heat [thermal] content
热焓表	heat content table
热焓增加	enthalpy gain
热焊接	thermal welding
热耗	heat rate
热核等离子体	thermonuclear plasma
热核反应	thermonuclear reaction, thermofusion
热核装置	thermonuclear device ◇ 零功率～*
热合金	thermalloy
热盒型芯	【铸】hot box core
热盒制芯	【铸】hot box coremaking
热壑	heat sink
热壑板	heat sink plate
热化学	heat [hot, thermal] chemistry, thermochemistry
热化学沉积(法)	thermochemical deposition
热化学处理	thermochemical treatment
热化学法	thermochemical process
热化学还原	thermochemical reduction
热化学计算	thermochemical calculation
热化学模型	thermochemical model
热化学平衡	thermochemical equilibrium
热化学侵蚀	thermochemical erosion [etching]
热化学涂覆	thermochemical plating
热环锻	hotswage

热还原　heat [hot, thermal] reduction ◇ 碳～*

热还原法　thermal reduction (process), thermic reduction method ◇ 碳化物～*, 尤基电炉～Udy process

热回路　【理】thermal loop

热回收　heat [thermal] recovery, heat recuperation, reclamation of heat ◇ 蓄热式～*

热回收风机　recuperation fan

热回收系统　heat recovery system ◇ 链算机－回转窑～*

热混合料　【团】hot mix

热活化　thermal activation

热活化变形　thermally activated deformation

热活化过程　thermally activated process

热活化转变　thermally activated transformation

热火焰清理机　【压】hot scarfing machine

热机　heat engine

热机械处理　thermomechanical processing [treatment]

热机械过程　thermomechanical process

热机械恒温器　thermomechanical thermostat

热机械加工　thermal-mechanical working, thermomechanical processing

热机械疲劳裂缝　thermal-mechanical fatigue crack

热机械效应　thermomechanical effect

热机械学　thermomechanics

热畸变　heat distortion (HDT)

热激发　thermal excitation [activation] ◇ 原子～*

热激发电子　thermally excited electron

热激活　(同"热活化")

热急变　thermal shock ◇ 抗～性*

热急变强度值　【焊】thermal severity number

热急变性质　thermal shock behaviour

热挤压　hot (press) extrusion ◇ 赛茹尔内～法*, 斯凯夫～法*

热挤压汇流条　extruded bus bar

热挤压机　heat extruder ◇ 粉末～powder hot extruder

热挤压金属粉末坯　hot extruded powder metal billet

热挤压破坏(原始组织的)　hot breakdown by extrusion

热剂　thermit(e) ◇ 加压～焊 thermite pressure welding

热剂铸焊(不加压力的)　thermite fusion welding

热计算　thermal calculation

热继电器　thermorelay, thermal relay, thermoswitch

热加工　hot [heat] working, working hot

热加工超合金粉末　hot worked superalloy powder

热加工成形法　【压】hot forming process

热加工成形钢　wrought steel

热加工处理　hot working treatment

热加工钢　hot work steel

热加工工具钢　hot work tool steel, tool steel for hot working

热加工工序　hot procedure

热加工量　amount of hot work

热加工性(能)　hot workability, hot working characteristic [property], hot forming property

热加工用钢　hot working steel

热加工组织　【金】hot worked structure

热检波器　thermodetector

热检验　hot inspection

热碱槽　hot caustic bath

热碱处理的　flux calcined

热剪(机)　hot shears, red-shears ◇ 下切式～*

热剪切　【压】hot shearing

热件运输机　hot conveyer

热焦　hot coke

热交换　heat exchange [interchange]

热交换管束　heat exchange tube bundle

热交换空区(高炉的) thermal reserve zone
热交换面 heat exchange surface
热交换器 heat exchanger [interchanger] ◇ 单程~*,对流~*,多通道~*,接触式~*,逆流~*,鳍[鱼翅]式~*,双管式~*,翼管式~*
热交换器泵 heat exchanger pump
热交换器管 heat exchanger tube
热交换器原理 heat exchanger principle
热交换器滞后 heat exchanger lag
热交换区 heat exchange zone
热交换图 heat exchange diagram
热交换系统[装置] heat exchanging system
热交换元件 heat exchange element
热搅拌[动] thermal agitation
热矫直 【压】thermal [hot] straightening, hot levelling
热矫直机 hot leveller ◇ 板材~hot mangle
热接点(热电偶的) hot junction (HJ, h.j.), hot end, thermojunction
热接近点(高炉内的) thermal pinch point
热节 【铸】heat [thermal] centre
热节区 【连铸】hot spot
热结合 thermal bonding
热解 pyrolyzation, pyrolysis, pyrogenic decomposition ◇ 气流床快速~装置*
热解废水 pyrogenic waste-waters
热解石墨 pyrolytic graphite
热解石墨合金 pyrographalloy
热解碳 【化】pyrolytic carbon
热解涂层(气体涂层) pyrolytic coating [plating]
热解重量分析(法) thermal gravimetric analysis (TGA), thermogravimetric analysis, thermogravimetry
热解作用 pyrolysis
热介质淬火 hot quench(ing)
热金属辊道 hot run table
热金属检测器 【压】hot metal detector (HMD)
热金属锯机 hot metal sawing machine
热金属丝测温法 hot wire method
热金属液 hot metal
热浸镀(层,法) (hot) dip coating [plating], dip immersion coating ◇ 连续~*
热浸镀覆 immersion plating
热浸镀金 immersion [water] gilding, gilding by dipping
热浸镀金属法 metallic coating by hot-dipping process
热浸镀铝 (hot dip) aluminizing, hot dip aluminium coating, aludip
热浸镀铝层 hot dip aluminium coating
热浸镀铝带钢 hot dipped aluminium coated steel strip
热浸镀铝法 aludipping, Aldip process
热浸镀铝钢板 aludip
热浸镀锡 hot dip tinning
热浸镀锡板坯 hot dip tinning stack
热浸镀锡车间 hot dip tinning plant
热浸镀锡设备 hot dip tinning installation
热浸镀锡作业线 hot dip tinning line
热浸镀(锌) hot (dip) galvanizing (HDG), dip galvanizing, galvanizing by dipping ◇ 薄(钢)板~*,美国联合铬公司光亮~用浸镀液 Unichrome dip compound, 普通~*
热浸镀锌层[法] hot dip galvanized coating
热浸镀锌钢丝 hot dip galvanized steel wire
热浸合金处理 hot dip alloying
热浸(金属)过渡 dip(metal) transfer
热浸渗铝法(钢铁表面的) mollerising, mollerizing
热浸蚀 【金】thermal [hot, heat] etching
热浸蚀试验 hot etching test
热浸涂(层,法) hot dip painting [coating]
热精炼 【色】thermal [heat] refining
热精压 hot coining

热精轧 hot finishing	热扩孔 （管坯的）【压】lifting
热精轧材 hot finished material	热扩散 thermal [heat] diffusion, thermal dispersion, thermodiffusion
热精轧机 hot finisher, hot finishing mill	热扩散分离 thermal diffusion separation
热精整 hot finishing [trim(ming)]	热扩散分离管 thermal diffusion column
热精整工序 hot trimming operation	热扩散流 thermal diffusion flow
热精整设备 hot finishing plant (H.F.P.)	热扩散率[性] thermal diffusibility [diffusivity], diffusivity of heat
热精整作业线 hot finishing line (HFL)	热扩散系数 thermal diffusion coefficient, thermal [temperature] diffusivity
热经济性 heat economy	热拉拔 【压】hot drawing [pull]
热经济学 thermoeconomics	热拉钢[金属]丝 hot drawing wire
热经济学原理 thermoeconomic principle	热拉裂（铸件冷却时的） hot tear [crack]
热阱 hot trap	热拉伸 hot stretch(ing)
热静力学 thermostatics	热拉伸成形 hot stretch forming
热聚变 thermofusion	热拉丝 【压】hot wire drawing
热锯 【压】hot [warm] saw ◇ 杠杆式~*，水平滑座式~*	热冷处理（热形变冷处理） hot-cold working (H.C.W.)
热锯切 hot sawing	热冷加工 【压】hot cold work(ing), warm working
热卷取机 【压】hot coiler	热离解（法） thermal decomposition [dissociation, deposition]
热卷取炉 hot-coiling furnace	热离解还原 reduction by thermal decomposition
热卷箱 【压】coil box	
热卷箱轧制技术 hot coiling-box rolling technology	热离解设备(碘化物的) deposition equipment [unit] ◇ 小型~*
热绝缘 heat insulation	热离解温度 deposition temperature
热绝缘体 thermal insulator [barrier], heat barrier	热离解作用 thermal dissociation
热开关 heat switch, thermoswitch	热离子 thermion
热抗压强度 hot crushing strength	热离子电流 thermionic current
热可用参数 heat availability parameter	热离子发射 thermionic emission
热刻槽技术 thermal-grooving technique	热离子发射器[体] thermionic emitters
热空气 hot air	热离子发射显微技术[显微镜学] thermionic emission microscopy
热控管 thermistor	
热矿 hot agglomerate	热离子发生器 thermionic generator
热矿给料机 hot feeder	热离子管阴[丝]极 filament of thermionic valve
热矿破碎机 hot crusher	
热矿球团法 【团】HOB (hot-ore briquetting) process	热离子管振荡器 thermionic valve oscillator
热矿振动筛 （同"热振动筛"）	热离子弧 thermionic arc
热矿压块(法) hot-ore briquetting (HOB)	热离子能变换[转换,发电] thermionic energy conversion
热矿压块法 HOB process	
热溃散性 hot-collapsibility	
热扩管机 【压】hot tube expanding machine	

热离子学 thermionics
热离子阴极枪 thermionic cathode gun
热离子整流器 thermionic rectifier
热力变质 pyrometamorphism
热力参数 thermal characteristics
热力干燥 heat [thermal] drying
热力工程 heat (power) engineering, heat technology
热力机 heat engine
热力计算[设计] thermal design
热力稳定强化 Cthermodynamically stable reinforcement
热力学 thermodynamics, thermomechanics ◇ 应用~ *
热力学第二定律 second law of thermodynamics
热力学第三定律 third law of thermodynamics
热力学第一定律 first law of thermodynamics
热力学定律 thermodynamical law
热力学定义 thermodynamic definition
热力学方程 thermodynamic equation
热力学方法 thermodynamic process [method]
热力学分析 thermodynamic analysis
热力学概[几]率 thermodynamic probability
热力学过程 thermodynamic process
热力学函数 thermodynamic function
热力学活度[性] thermodynamic activity
热力学机理 thermal mechanism
热力学计算 thermodynamic calculation
热力学可能性 thermodynamic feasibility
热力学临界磁场 【理】thermodynamical critical field
热力学判据 thermodynamic criterion
热力学平衡 thermodynamic(al) equilibrium
热力学平衡常数 thermodynamic equilibrium constant
热力学平衡数据 thermodynamic equilibria
热力学平衡图 thermodynamic diagram
热力学亲合性 thermodynamic affinity
热力(学)势[位] thermodynamic potential
热力学数据 thermodynamic data
热力学数值 thermodynamic value
热力学温标 thermodynamic scale
热力学温度 thermodynamic temperature
热力学系统[体系] thermodynamic system
热力学因子 thermodynamic factor
热力学原理 thermodynamic principle
热力学涨落理论 theory of thermodynamical fluctuation
热力学状态 thermodynamic state
热力循环 thermal circulation
热力再流动法 thermal reflowing process
热连轧 hot continuous rolling (HCR)
热连轧钢板 hot tandem rolled steel strip
热连轧机 hot tandem mill
热炼方法(制备单晶) soaking method
热量 heat quantity [amount], quantity of heat ◇ 除去~ *, 放出的~ heat of evolution, 消耗的~ heat consuming, 需~ heat demand
热量不足 shortage of heat
热量测定 heat measurement
热量测试[探测]器 thermometer probe
热量传输 heat transfer [transmissuon]
热量传输分析 heat transfer
热量储备 heat conservation
热量单位 thermal unit (TU), heat unit (HU), caloric unit
热量供应 heat supply
热量计 calorimeter, hydropyrometer, thermal flowmeter
热量计容器 calorimeter vessel
热量计算 heat calculation [account]
热量亏损 heat deficit
热量输出[支出] heat output
热量输入 heat input

热量输入速率　heat input rate
热量损失　lost heat
热量图示测定法　thermography
热量-物料平衡　heat and mass balance
热量增加　heat gain
热量-质量平衡　heat and pass balance
热裂　thermal checking [crack(ing)], heat [hot, fire] check(ing), heat [hot] crack(ing),【铸】pull crack,【焊】autocrack ◇ 靠壁～【耐】skin crack, 可变拘束抗～试验*, 磨削-敏感性 grinding sensitivity, 易～度 crack ability
热裂试验　hot crack(ing) test ◇ 穆列克斯～*
热临界点　thermal critical point, critical thermal point
热流　heat flow [flux], thermal flow [current], current of heat
热流槽　heated launder
热流测量仪　heat flow meter
热流测试[探测]器　heat flow probe
热流强度　thermal flow intensity
热流试验　heat run test
热流阻力　resistance to heat flow
热漏失　heat leak(age)
热炉次　【冶】hot heat
热炉顶(鼓风炉的)　hot top
热漫散射　thermal diffuse scattering
热铆(接)　hot rivetting
热铆铆钉　pop-rivet
热冒口　live [hot] riser
热冒口浇注系统　riser gate
热帽电渣法　◇ 凯洛格～*
热帽法　hot top process
热帽发热剂　【冶】lunkerite, feedex
热帽钢　【钢】head metal
热帽钢锭　hot topped ingot
热帽拉裂　【钢】head pull
热帽铸锭法　◇ 哈德菲尔德～*
热煤　hot coal
热煤灰　hot coal ash
热闷罐法(处理转炉渣)　【钢】hot closed pot method
热敏材料　heat sensitive material, thermosensitive material
热敏触点　thermally actuated contact
热敏电阻　【电】thermal resistance
热敏电阻(器)　thermal resistor, thermo sensitive resistor, thermistor, critesistor ◇ 正温度系数～posistor
热敏电阻合金　thermistor alloy
热敏电阻探测[检测]器　thermistor detector
热敏电阻温度计　thermistor thermometer
热敏电阻压力[真空]计　thermistor gauge
热敏(感)漆　heat sensitive paint
热敏感器　temperature sensitization apparatus
热敏感性　temperature [heat] sensitivity
热敏金属　temperature-sensitive metal
热敏开关　thermoswitch
热敏油漆　thermocolour
热敏黏合剂　heat sensitive adhesive
热敏元件　temperature sensing element
热模锻　hot press forge, hot forging
热模锻压力机　hot die forging press
热模精压　【粉】hot sizing
热模具钢　hot working steel ◇ 奥氏体～*
热模拟计算机　thermal analog(ue) computer
热模塑　hot moulding
热模压制法　heated die pressing process
热磨损[蚀]　thermal erosion
热能　heat [thermal] energy
热能产额　thermal (energy) yield
热能节约　heat economy
热能节约指标　heat economy figure
热能利用　heat utilization [salvage]
热能利用经济指标　thermal economics
热能利用率[系数]　heat utilization efficiency
热能流　thermal energy flux
热能输入速率　heat input rate

热能吸收　absorption of thermal energy
热能中心　heat centre
热能中子　【理】thermal (energy) neutron
热黏合　thermal bonding
热凝(砌合)泥浆　heat setting (bonding) mortar
热扭　hot torsion
热扭转试验　heat [hot] torsion test, hot twist test
热偶电池[发电器]　thermogenerator
热偶合金　thermocouple [thermopair] alloy
热喷补修理　【冶】hot-gun repair
热喷镀[涂]　hot spraying
热喷镀[涂]法　thermo-spraying process
热喷镀覆　fused coating
热喷浆[热喷射水泥]处理　hot gunning
热喷射[涂]　thermojet, thermal spray(ing)
热喷射法[工艺]　thermal spray process
热喷丸硬化(处理)　hot peening
热膨胀　thermal [heat] expansion, thermal dila(ta)tion (swelling) ◇差示～计*
热膨胀力　thermal expansion force
热膨胀曲线　thermal expansion curve
热膨胀特性　thermal expansion characteristic
热膨胀系数　thermal [heat] expansion coefficient, thermal coefficient of expansion ◇表观～*,表面～*,可控～铁镍合金*
热膨胀性　thermal expansivity
热坯表面修整　Lin-de-surfacer
热坯直接轧制　direct hot charge rolling (DHCR)
热疲劳　thermal [heat] fatigue
热疲劳抗力　thermal fatigue resistance
热疲劳裂纹的萌生　thermal fatigue crack initiation
热疲劳试验　thermal fatigue test
热疲劳试验方法　thermal fatigue test-method

热疲劳寿命　thermal-fatigue life
热疲劳性能　thermal-fatigue property [behaviour]
热片　spacer
热漂洗槽　hot rinsing cell [tank]
热(量)平衡表　heat [thermal] balance sheet, balance sheet of heat
热平衡　heat [thermal, calorific] balance, thermo-balance, heat [thermal] equilibrium
热平衡条件　heat [thermal] equilibrium condition
热平衡图　thermal equilibrium diagram ◇森基～【冶】Sankey diagram
热平整　【压】hot levelling
热平整机　hot leveller
热平整机组电控室　hot skin-pass line electrical room
热平整机组工作辊　hot skin-pass line work roll
热平整机组支承辊　hot skin-pass line back-up roll
热平整(机)组作业线　hot skinpass line (HSL) ◇带卷～*
热屏蔽　heat shield [baffle], thermal shield(ing), thermo-shield
热屏障　heat barrier
热剖面　【铁】thermal profile
热谱法　pyrography
热气　hot gas
热气焊　hot gas welding
热气烘干器　heat gun
热强度　heat [calorific] intensity,【铸】hot (sand) strength, warm strength
热强度试验　【铸】hot (sand) strength test
热强钢　refractory steel, heat resistance steel
热强性材料　high temperature resistant material
热切刀　【压】hot knife
热切法　thermal cutting process

热切飞边 【压】hot trim(ming)	热伸长 thermal extension
热切飞边工序 hot trimming operation	热深冲 【压】hot deep drawing
热切割 thermal [hot] cutting	热渗透 heat penetration
热切头 【压】hot cropping	热生长 physical growth
热侵入 ingress of heat	热时效 heat [thermal, warm] ageing, warm-hardening
热侵蚀 thermal [heat] etching, heat erosion	
热球 hot bulb	热蚀 【金】heat [thermal] etching
热球团层 hot pellet bed	"热"实验室 hot laboratory
热球团流 hot pellet stream	热势 thermal potential
热区 hot zone	热室式压铸机 hot chamber die-casting machine
热驱动装置 heat actuated device	
热去毛刺 【压】hot trim(ming)	热室压铸(法) hot chamber die casting
热染色法 （同"热着色法"）	热试金珠 gum drop button
热熔 hot melt ◇ 低熔点物的～sweating out	热试验 thermal test
	热收入(热平衡中的) heat gain
热熔焊接 sweat soldering	热收缩 thermal contraction
热熔喷镀法 flame spraying	热受主 thermal acceptor
热熔性模 heat disposable pattern	热输出 thermal output
热容矩阵 thermal capacitance matrix	热输入 thermal input
热容(量) heat [thermal, calorific] capacity	热衰减 heat reduction
	热双金属片 thermostatic bimetal-plate
热容滞后 heat capacity lag	热水 hot water (HW) ◇ 电热～锅炉*，封闭式～暖气系统*
热散射造成的背景[本底]（X射线） background due to thermal scattering	
	热水池[井] hot well
热散逸损失 dissipation heat losses	热水干燥槽 hot water drying tank
热骚动 thermal agitation	热水缓冲槽 hot water cushion tank
热砂 【铸】hot sand	热水解 pyrohydrolysis
热砂强度 hot (sand) strength	热水力学不稳定性 【理】thermohydraulic instability
热砂强度试验 hot (sand) strength test	
热砂碳化室 【焦】hot sand carbonizer	热水喷射冲洗槽 hot water (spray) tank
热筛除尘 hot screen dedusting	热水喷射管 boiled water spray pipe
热筛分设备 hot screening facility	热水清洗 hot water rinse
热筛工艺 hot screen process	热水套 thermal jacket
热筛筛板 hot screen deck	热水循环 hot water circulating (HWC)
热烧结 【粉】thermal sintering	热撕裂倾向(性) hot tearing tendency
热烧结矿 hot sinter [agglomerate]	热撕裂铸件 hot torn casting
热烧结矿带 hot sinter zone	热丝(极) hot filament
热烧结矿筛筛板 【团】hot sinter screen deck	热丝表面淀积法 （同"热线分解精炼法"）
热(烧结矿条)筛 【团】hot screen	热丝反应 hot wire reaction
热烧损 heat waste	热丝分析器(测定渗碳气氛碳量的) hot wire analyzer

热丝风速计　hot wire anemometer
热丝式仪表　thermal meter
热送　hot charging (HCR)
热送热装　【压】hot-charging and hot direct charging [charge] (HCR – HDCR), hot-transporting and hot-changing
热送热装工艺　hot charging and direct hot charging process
热送（热装）轧制　hot charge rolling (HCR) ◇ 连铸坯~*
热塑料板　thermoplastic sheet
热塑塑料　thermoplastic ◇ 氟化~*
热塑塑料绝缘电线　thermoplastic-covered wire
热塑性　hot plasticity [workability], thermoplasticity
热塑性变形　thermoplastic deformation
热塑性加工　【压】hot plastic working
热塑性聚合物　thermoplastic polymer
热塑性流动　thermoplastic flow
热塑性黏结剂　thermoplastic adhesive
热塑性树脂　thermoplastic resin
热塑性塑料　thermoplastic plastics
热酸浸蚀的　hot-acid etched
热损耗　waste of heat
热损耗接缝　heat robbing joint
热损伤　thermal damage
热损失　heat loss [waste, expense], thermal [calorific] loss ◇ 废气带走的~*, waste heat losses, 启动的~*
热缩　pyrocondensation,【粉】thermal shrinkage
热态　thermal state,【理】hot position
热态机械加工　hot machining
热态金属精炼　【冶】hot metal refining
热态均匀加压　hot isopressing
热态可塑[可延展]的　hot ductile
热态可塑[可延展]性　hot ductility
热态喷补（高炉的）　hot spray repair on BF
热态遥控喷补技术（高炉用）　remote hot gunning technology

热态状况　thermal behaviour
热潭　heat sink
热弹性（力学）　thermoelasticity
热弹性波　thermoelastic wave
热弹性松弛　【压】thermoelastic relaxation
热弹性系数　thermoelastic coefficient
热弹性效应　thermoelastic effect
热弹性阻尼[衰减]　thermoelastic damping
热碳层　hot bed of carbon
热套　hot jacket
热特性　thermal characteristics
热梯度　thermal gradient
热梯度变化曲线　thermal gradient diagram
热体　hot body
热天平　thermal balance
热调节　heat regulation
热调质（淬火后高温回火）【金】thermal [heat] refining
热铁水　hot metal
热铁氧体　pyroferrite
热停堆剩余反应性（核燃料的）　hot shut-down (reactivity) margin
热通量　heat [thermal] flux
热图　【冶】thermograph
热团矿法　HOB (hot-ore briquetting) process
热脱扣装置　thermal trip
热弯曲　hot bending
热弯曲率　flexivity
热位　thermal potential
热位差　temperature head
热稳定的　heat stable [proof], hot-resistant, thermostable
热稳定钢　oxidation-resistant steel
热稳定氯化物　thermally stable chloride
热稳定试验　heat stabilization test
热稳定性　thermal stability, thermostability, hot-resistance, resistance to thermal shock ◇ 型砂~*
热稳定性检验交替次数　number of rever-

sals at thermal shock
热稳定性检验炉 【耐】spalling furnace
热稳定性试验 【耐】spalling test
热稳定性砖 thermo-shock resistance brick
热涡流烧嘴 thermal vortex burner
热污染 【环】thermal pollution
热无序 thermal disorder
热物理性质[特性] thermophysical property
热物理学 thermophysics
热物理学模型 thermophysical model
热物理应力 thermophysical stress
热析 sweat-out, sweating, 【粉】exudation
热析出 heat evolution, thermal precipitation
热析浮渣 sweat(er) dross
热析炉 【色】sweat furnace
热析温度(焊料或易熔添加剂的) sweating temperature
热吸收 heat [thermal] absorption
热洗炉(轻负荷洗炉) chipping-out
热系统 thermal system
热隙 hot gap
热线 hot wire
热线分解精炼法(高纯度金属用) hot wire process
热线继电器 hot wire relay
热线检流器 barretter
热线式电压表 thermovoltmeter
热线式受话器 thermophone
热线式仪表 hot wire instrument [meter]
热线探测器 hot wire detector
热线压力计 hot wire gauge
热相法 thermography
热相学 thermography, pyrography
热像测试 infrared thermovision measurement
热像炉 thermal imaging furnace
热像仪 thermal imaging device ◇ 红外线~*
热消耗 heat expense
热消耗值 heat consumption figure

热消荧光探伤法 fluorescent thermography
热效继电器 thermal relay, thermally operated device
热效率 heat [thermal, calorific] efficiency ◇ 绝对~*
热效率低 thermal inefficiency
热效应 heat [thermal, temperature, calorific] effect, fuel factor
热楔效应(摩擦的) thermal wedge effect
热斜轧扩径 hot rotary expansion
热芯盒 【铸】hot box
热芯盒吹芯机 hot box core blower
热芯盒黏结剂 hot box binder
热芯盒树脂 hot box resin
热芯盒制芯法 hot box process
热芯盒制芯机 hot box (cores) machine
热形变冷加工 【压】hot cold work(ing), warm working
热行(高炉的) 【铁】working [run] hot
热行炉况 【铁】high temperature work
热性能[性质] thermal [hot] property
热性研究 thermal study
热修补 【冶】hot repair [patching]
热修构筑的(炉)前墙 【冶】hot front wall
热修时间 【钢】fettling time
热修整 【压】hot trim(ming), 【铸】flame chipping
热需要量 heat [calorific] requirement, heat demand
热旋锻 hot swaging
热选 thermal beneficiation
热学 thermology, heat
热循环 heat cycle, thermal cycle [loop], thermocycling, circulation of heat
热循环模拟装置 thermal cycle simulator
热循环蠕变 thermal cycling creep
热循环效应 thermal cycle effect
热压 hot compression, heat pressing
热压包覆(层) hot press cladding
热压成形 hot compacting ◇ 再~ hot recompaction

热压成形法　hot pressing method
热压氮化铝　hot pressed aluminium nitride
热压锻　hot press forging
热压法　hot pressing method,【粉】hot press approach ◇ 布拉塞特铁粉～Brassert process, 克拉基～Kratky process, 克林～Koehring process
热压焊　thermocompression bond(ing), thermal compression welding
热压合金粉(坯)　【粉】hot pressed alloy powder
热压黄铜　【粉】hot pressed brass
热压机　thermocompressor,【压】hot press ◇ 电热～*, 高速～high speed hot press
热压机座[热压台]　【粉】hot pressed bed
热压焦炭　form coke
热压结合　thermocompression bond(ing)
热压金　【粉】hot pressed gold
热压金属陶瓷　hot press cermet
热压块　hot briquette
热压块法　hot briquetting process
热压块坯　hot-pressed compact
热压块铁　hot briquetted iron (HBI)
热压零件　【粉】hot pressed parts
热压炉　hot pressing furnace ◇ 竖管式～*, 卧管式～*
热压模　hot die
热压模型　hot pressing mould
热压萘　hot pressed naphthalene
热压青铜　【粉】hot pressed bronze
热压青铜坯块　【粉】hot pressed bronze compact
热压烧结法　hot pressing sintering process
热压烧结制品　hot pressed and sintered product
热压设备　【粉】hot press equipment
热压室压铸机　die-casting machine with submerged gooseneck ◇ 直接加压的～*
热压缩　hot reducing [reduction]
热压碳砖　hot pressed carbon bricks
热压碳砖-陶瓷杯技术　【铁】hot-pressed carbon bricks-ceramic cup technology

热压铁坯块　【粉】hot pressed iron compact
热压头　hot press ram
热压型焦　hot briquette formed coke
热压阴模法　【铸】die hobbing
热压印　hot stamping [coining]
热压印黄铜　(见"α-β(型)黄铜")
热压制品　【粉】hot pressed product
热压装置　hot press arrangement
热延展　hot stretch(ing)
热延展成形　hot stretch forming
热样板　【压】hot template
热逸散　heat [thermal] dissipation
热阴极　hot [thermal] cathode ◇ 大型～二极管 kenotron
热阴极 X-射线管　Coolidge tube
热阴极电离(真空)计　hot cathode ionization gauge
热阴极发射的电子　thermionic electron
热阴极管　hot cathode lamp [tube]
热阴极真空计　hot cathode gauge
热阴极整流管　hot cathode rectifier
热引发反应(金属热还原)　thermal booster reaction
热引发剂[器]　thermal booster
热隐丝测温法　hot wire method
热应变　thermal [hot] strain(ing)
热应变脆化　hot strain embrittlement
热应答性　thermal response
热应力　thermal [temperature] stress
热应力裂纹[缝]　thermal stress crack
热影响　heat action ◇ 未受～区(金属的)【焊】unaffected zone
热影响区　【焊】heat affected [action] zone (HAZ), (heat) affected area
热影响区开裂　【焊】heat affected [action] zone cracking
热影响区破裂(焊合金钢时的)　hard cracking
热硬度　hot [red] hardness
热硬度测定器　hot hardness device
热硬度曲线　hot hardness curve

热硬度试验　hot hardness testing
热硬钢　red-hard steel
热硬化　thermohardening, warm hardening [aging], thermosetting
热硬性　thermohardening
热油淬火　【金】hot oil quenching
热浴槽　liquid heating bath
热浴淬火　thermo [hot-bath] quenching
热浴淬火时效　hot-bath quench ageing
热元件　thermal element, heat unit ◇ 热过电流继电器的～*
热原子碳黑　thermatomic (carbon) black, thermax
热源　heat(ing) source, source of heat, heat producer, heater (HR, HTR)
热运动　thermal motion [movement], heat motion
热再压　hot repressing
热渣堆场　【冶】hot dump
热轧　hot-rolling, hot reducing [reduction]
热轧半成品带坯　hot rolled breakdowns semi-finished strip
热轧棒材　hot rolled [finished] rod, hot rolled bar
热轧薄板　hot rolled sheet, latten
热轧扁钢　hot rolled flat bar
热轧材料　hot rolled [reduced] material
热轧产品[轧材]　hot rolled (mill) product
热轧成品薄板　hot rolled finished sheet
热轧成品带材　hot rolled finished strip
热轧带材　hot rolled strip
热轧带钢　hot [black] strip, green strip (未经热处理的)
热轧带钢机　hot-strip mill
热轧带(钢)卷　hot strip coil
热轧带钢卷取机　hot strip reel
热轧带划伤　hot strip scratches
热轧带肋钢筋　hot rolled ribbed steel bar
热轧低碳双相钢盘条　hot rolled dual-phase low carbon steel wire rod
热轧分卷线　hot dividing line (HDL)

热轧复合材料　hot-rolled composite
热轧钢板　hot rolled steel plate ◇ 未剪边～black edged plate
热轧钢(材)　hot-rolled steel (HRS, h.r.s.)
热轧钢材质量系数　quality factor [value]
热轧钢带　hot rolled (steel) strip
热轧钢筋　hot rolled reinforced bar ◇ 高强度～*
热轧钢卷　hot rolled coil
热轧管　hot rolled pipe
热轧光洁度　hot rolled finish
热轧硅钢(薄)板　hot-rolled silicon (steel) sheet, ferrosil
热轧辊　hot roll
热轧辊颈润滑脂　hot roll neck grease
热轧辊退火　hot roll annealing
热轧机　hot mill [rolls], hot-rolling mill ◇ 大型～high duty hot mill, 行星式～planetary hot mill
热轧件火焰清理　hot scarfing
热轧件火焰清理机　hot scarfing machine
热轧件火焰清理金属剥离(量)　hot scarfing metal removal
热轧建筑型钢　structural shape
热轧结构型材　rolled structural shape
热轧金属(材料)　hot rolled metal
热轧精轧机　hot finisher
热轧卷取法　hot rolling and reel
热轧开坯机　hot breaking-down mill
热轧宽带钢轧机　hot wide strip mill
热轧宽带卷　broad hot strip
热轧宽幅焊管坯　broad hot strip
热轧模拟器　hot strip simulator
热轧盘条(未热处理的)　green [hot-finished] rod
热(轧)输出辊道　hot run (-out) table (HRT), hot running table
热轧速度　hot rolling speed
热轧酸洗带卷　hot rolled pickled coil
热轧特薄板(<0.45mm)　extra latten
热轧条材　hot-rolled bar

热轧铜板[铜带]用锭坯　copper wedge cake
热轧铜材　hot rolled copper
热轧无取向硅钢薄板　hot rolled non-oriented silicon steel
热轧线材　hot rolled rod
热轧小直径荒管　hot-rolled small-sized mother tube
热轧(用)轧辊　hot rolling roll
热轧优质板[一级品板材]　hot rolled primes
热轧圆钢　hot rolled rounds, green rod (未经热处理的)
热轧窄带钢　mill coil
热轧中厚板　hot rolled plate
热轧轴承钢　hot rolled bearing steel
热轧装甲板(未热处理的)　green plate
热张弛　thermal relaxation
热长大　thermal growth
热涨落　thermal fluctuation
热胀式眼镜阀　【铁】thermal expansion goggle valve
热胀性试验(球团矿的)　swelling test
热障　thermal barrier
热折断(挤压缺陷)　thermal break-off
热震　heat [temperature] shock ◇ 抗～性*
热振动　thermal [temperature] vibration ◇ 原子～*
热振动给矿机　hot vibro feeder
热振动筛　hot vibro screen
热阵面　thermal front
热蒸馏　thermal distillation
热蒸气捕集器　thermal vapour trap
热整定[装配]　thermal setting
热值　heat [thermal] value, calorific value [capacity, efficiency, power], heating capacity, caloricity
热值测定器　heating effect indicator
热值单位　heat value unit
热致电离　thermal ionization
热致发光　【理】thermo-luminescence

热致发光磷　thermoluminescent phosphor
热致发光射线照相术　thermoluminescent radiography
热致发声器　thermophone
热制备　hot preparation
热制度　【冶】thermal system
热滞　thermal lag [retardation]
热滞后　thermal hysteresis
热中心　thermal centre
热中子　【理】thermal (energy) neutron
热中子反应堆　thermal (neutron) reactor
热中子俘获[吸收]　thermal capture
热中子束　thermal beam
热中子(吸收)断面[截面]　thermal neutron cross-section
热重－差热分析　TG－DTA
热重(量)分析　thermogravimetry (TG)
热周期　thermal cycle
热驻[热转变]点　thermal arrest
热转变　thermal transformation
热装法【钢】　hot charge process
热装反射炉　hot-charge reverberatory furnace
热装(料)　hot charging (HCR)
热装轧制　hot charge rolling (HCR)
热装直接轧制　hot direct charging and rolling
热着色　hot tinting
热着色法　【金】heat tinting method
热纵剪作业线　【压】hot slitting line
热阻　heat [thermal] resistance, thermoresistance
热作超合金粉末　hot worked superalloy powder
热作工具钢　(同"热加工工具钢")
热作模具钢(10W,3Cr,0.3V,0.3C)　hot (working) die steel ◇ 海德拉～*,析出硬化型～*
热作业　hot application
壬醇(通常指壬醇－1)　nonanol
壬醇－1{$C_8H_7CH_2OH$}　nonanol－1
壬醇－2{$C_7H_{15}CHOHCH_3$}　nonanol－2

壬酸{CH$_3$(CH$_2$)$_7$COOH} pelargonic acid
壬烷{CH$_3$(CH$_2$)$_7$CH$_3$} nonane
人的模拟 【计】humam simulation
人工 labour, handwork
人工扒料炉 hand-raked furnace
人工拌砂 sand cutting-over
人工采光 artificial daylight
人工采样 hand sampling
人工操作 manual operation, operation by hand
人工操作薄板轧机 hand sheet mill
人工操作[扒料,耙料]焙烧炉 hand-worked [hand-raked, hand-rabbled] roaster
人工操作轧机 hand mill
人工操作反射炉 hand reverberatory furnace
人工操作缓冲器 manually operated damper
人工操作炉 hand worked furnace
人工操作时间 【计】handing time
人工超结构 artificial superstructure
人工成本[费用] labor cost
人工舂箱 【铸】hand ramming
人工床 artificial bed
人工粗碎 【选】sledging
人工打开出铁[钢]口 hand tapping
人工打壳 【色】manual crust breaking
人工打捆 manual banding
人工打桩机 ringing pile engine
人工登记 manual entry
人工递钢(机座间的) manual catching
人工读入 【计】manual read
人工堵的出铁[钢]口 hand closed taphole
人工放射性(现象) artificial radioactivity
人工负载 artificial load
人工骨料 artificial aggregate
人工焊条电弧焊 manual metal arc welding
人工夯实的 hand tamped
人工合成铸铁 synthetic cast iron
人工呼吸 artificial respiration

人工混合 hand mixing
人工火焰清理 【压】hand scarfing
人工加料 hand [manual] feed(ing)
人工间断 (电磁试验的) artificial discontinuity
人工拣选 hand-sorting, hand-pick(ing)
人工控制[操纵] hand [manual] control, manual manipulation [operation]
人工磨光 manual finishing
人工莫来石 artificial mullite
人工神经(元)网络 artificial neural network (ANN)
人工石墨 electrographite
人工时效 artificial ageing
人工时效状态 artificially aged condition
人工蚀坑 artificial pit
人工识别 artificial cognition [perception]
人工输入键 【计】manual load key
人工输入设备 manual input unit
人工数字发生器 manual number generator
人工送入 【计】manual entry
人工填充 artificial replenishment
人工调节[调整] hand [manual] regulation, manual adjustment, hand setting
人工通风 artificial ventilation [draught], positive draught
人工同位素 man-made isotope
人工线 bootstrap
人工氧化铝 borolon
人工语言 artificial language
人工制品 artifact, artefact
人工制造 handwork
人工智能 artificial intelligence (AI)
人工智能技术 AI technique
人工智能静态控制模型 AI static control model
人工智能理论 artificial intelligence theory
人工智能系统 AI system
人工铸锭[浇注] 【冶】hand teeming
人工筑岛法(深基础施工的) artificial island method

人工转移(程序) 【计】force	人造白钨 artificial scheelite
人工装料 hand charging, manual charge	人造白云石 artificial dolomite
人工坐料(炉料) 【铁】forced settling	人造宝石 synthetic jewel
人机工程学 ergonomics	人造冰晶石 (artificial, synthetic) cryolite
人机对话 man-machine interaction	人造的 synthetic
人机工程学 ergonomics	人造地表(面) man-made surface
人机接口 man machine interface (MMI)	人造地球卫星 artificial earth satellite (AES), earth satellite vehicle (ESV)
人机模拟 man-machine silmulation	
人机通信 man-machine communication	人造钒铀矿{$Na_2O \cdot 2UO_3 \cdot V_2O_5 \cdot n H_2O$} artificial [synthetic] carnotite, yellow cake
人机(通信)系统 man-machine (communication) system	
人均钢消费量 apparent steel consumption per capita	人造放射性同位素 artificial radioactive isotope
人均国民收入 average national income per capita	人造废钢 synthetic scrap
	人造沸石 artificial zeolite, Permutite
人孔(检修用) manhole	人造富[块]矿 agglomeration of iron ore, agglomerated material
人孔盖 manhole [inspection] cover	
人孔盖板 manhole plate	人造富矿入炉比 agglomeration rate [ratio], rate of agglomerates
人孔座 manhole-socket	
人口 population ◇工业废水的~当量*	人造干燥 artificial seasoning
人口和工业过密 【环】excessive concentration of population and industry	人造刚玉{SiC} artificial corundum, synthetic corundum [boule], carborundum
人类工效学 ergonomics	人造光卤石 artificial carnallite
人类工效学理论 ergonomic theory	人造硅砂 artificial silica sand
人力搬动 manhandle	人造硅酸铝沸石 synthetic aluminosilicate zeolite
人脑模拟 humam simulation, brain analogue	
	人造海水 artificial sea water
人身事故 humam element accident	人造金刚砂 artificial corundum
人身事故率 fatality rate	人造金刚砂粉 alumdum powder
人时[人工小时] man-hour (man-hr)	人造金刚石 artificial [man-made] diamond
人事工程(学) human engineering	
人体电容效应 body (capacity) effect	人造金属 artificial metal
人体防护板 personnel barrier	人造金云母 synthetic phlogopite
人为故障 man-made faulf	人造晶体 artificial [synthetic] crystal
人为误差 personal [conscious] error	人造块矿 agglomerate material
人行道 footway, footpath, walkway ◇高于路面的~causeway,悬臂式~*	人造矿块 block ore, artificial rich ore ◇加熔剂~*
人行(过道)桥 passing bridge	人造矿石 synthetic ore
人员配备 manning (levels)	人造矿物 artificial mineral
人员培训 personnel training	人造蜡 synthetic wax
人员一览表 personnel list	人造料层 artificial bed
人员组成 manning	人造料粒 【团】pseudo particle

人造裂纹　artificial crack
人造煤气　manufactured gas
人造磨料　artificial [manufactured] abrasive
人造气体　artificial gas
人造缺陷　artificial discontinuity
人造砂　artificial sand
人造石块　cast stone
人造石墨　artificial [synthetic] graphite ◇ 艾奇逊~*
人造石墨粉　synthetic graphite powder
人造树脂　synthetic resin
人造丝包覆的　rayon covered ◇ 单层~*,双层~*
人造卫星　(artificial) satellite
人造污染物　【环】man-made pollutant
人造纤维　artificial [manmade] fibre
人造小球　【团】pseudo particle
人造阳极（阴极保护用）　corrosion piece
人造氧化物　synthetic oxide
人造云母绝缘石　micanite
人字齿轮　herringbone gear, double-helical gear wheel
人字齿轮箱　pinion stand
人字齿轮座的齿轮轴　mill pinion
人字架　propeller strut ◇ 安装用~bipod
人字螺旋齿轮　double-helical gear
人字起重机　derrick
人字屋顶　ridge [gable] roof
人字形分层铺料　【团】chevron layering
人字形分层造堆法　【团】chevron method
人字形解理　herringbone cleavage
人字形冷阱[冷却捕集器]　【色】chevron type cold trap
人字形裂口　chevroning
人字形砌合　herringbone bond
韧钢　annealed [malleable] steel
韧合金钢　tough alloy steel
韧化（处理）　toughening, malleablization, malleablizing ◇ 电火花~*,黑心~ black heart process, 空冷~*, 矿石中~*,水冷~*

韧化处理炉（铸铁的）　malleablizing furnace
韧化淬火　negative hardening
韧化球化　toughened pellet
韧化热处理　toughening heat treatment
韧化调质　tough hardening
韧矿　malleablizing ore
韧铜　tough pitch (copper), tough copper, annealed copper, flat set copper [cake] ◇ 阴极~tough cathode copper
韧窝　【理】dimples
韧窝状断口　dimpled fracture
韧窝状剪切断裂[破坏]　【压】dimpled shear rupture
韧性[度]　toughness, tenacity, viscosity ◇ 冲击~*, 有~的 malleable
韧性材料　ductile material
韧(性)-脆(性)转化　tough-brittle transition
韧性淬火钢　tough hardening steel
韧性断口　tough [ductile] fracture
韧性断裂　ductile fracture [failure]
韧性钢　ductile steel
韧性化　【金】malleablization
韧性基体　tough matrix
韧性金属　tough [ductile, tenacious] metal
韧性软钢　malleable mild steel
韧性试验机　toughness testing machine
韧性铁　malleable iron (M.I.)
韧性涂层　flexible coating
韧性铸铁　malleable [ductile] cast iron
韧硬度　tough hardness
韧致辐射　bremsstrahlung (radiation), braking radiation ◇ 高能~内层~*
韧致辐射测量仪　bremsstrahlung gauge
韧铸铁矿[可锻铸铁用矿]　malleablizing ore
任务　task, assignment, job, designation
任务队列　【计】task queue
任务管理　task management
任务结束　task termination
任务控制块　task control block (TCB)

任选供应设备　optional equipment
任选项　option
任意常数　arbitrary constant
任意长度　random length (RL)
任意单位　arbitrary unit (A.U.)
任意函数发生器　arbitrary-function generator
任意浓度　arbitrary concentration
任意取样　random sampling
任意试样　random sample
任意数　arbitrary number
任意位向　random orientation
认可　acknowledgement
认证　certification ◇质量～制度*,产品质量～机构*
刃钢　shear-steel
刃具　cutting tool, cutter
刃具钢　cutting tool steel
刃具钢含碳量　razor temper
刃口(刃片的)　cutting edge
刃口[线]腐蚀　knife(-line) corrosion, knife-edge attack
刃口蚀缝　knife-edge attack
刃磨　【机】sharpening
刃型边界　edge boundary
刃型连续混合机　edge-runner mixer
刃型连续湿碾机　edge runner wet mill
刃型连续研磨机　【粉】edge(runner) mill
刃型连续研磨盘　edge runner pan
刃型位错　edge (type) dislocation ◇不规则～*,佩尔斯～*,平行～*,同号～*
刃型位错壁　【理】wall of edge dislocations
刃型位错阵列　array of edge dislocations
刃型支座[支架]　blade bearing, knife-edge support, knife-edge bearing
刃型枢轴　knife-edge pivot
刃状构造　bladed structure
日班　day shift
日班工人[工作者]　dayman
日本材料试验学会　Japan Society for Testing Materials (J.S.T.M.)
日本测量标准　Japanese Measuring Standard (JMS)
日本电工技术委员会　Japanese Electrotechnical Committee (JEC)
日本电机工业协会　Japanese Electrical Machine Industry Association (JEM)
日本电缆标准　Japan Cable Standard (JCS)
日本钢铁公司　Nippon Steel Corporation (NSC)
日本钢铁协会　Iron and Steel Institute of Japan (ISIJ)
日本高强度铝铜镁合金　ND (Nippon duralumin) alloy, Nippon duralumin
日本工程标准　Japanese Engineering Standards (JES)
日本工业标准　Japanese Industrial Standard (JIS)
日本黄铜　Japanese brass (55Cu, 45Zn), Sinchu (66.5Cu, 33.4Zn)
日本金属学会　Japan Institute of Metals (JIM)
日本蓝金[装饰用铜合金] (90—99Cu, 10—1Au)　Japanese blue gold
日本流态自硬水泥砂制模法　【铸】Japan hard-fluid cement-sand process
日本汽车标准协会　Japan Automobile Standard Organization (JASO)
日本轻金属协会　Japan Institute of Light Metals (J.I.L.M.)
日本深黑漆　Japanese laequer
日本式贴金术　Japan gilding
日本透气性单位　Japanese Permeability Unit (J.P.U.)
日本银(50Al,50Ag)　Japanese silver
日本银铜合金　shibuichi
日本硬铝　Nippon duralumin
日本专利　Japanese Patent (Jap.P.)
日产量　daily production [output, capacity], output per day, single day production
日常工作　routine work
日常检查[检验]　process inspection, routine check [examination]

日常生产切边[切头] production scrap
日常维修 routine [ordinary, minor] maintenance
日常修理 regular [routine] maintenance, running maintenance [repair], maintenance work, current repair
日常修理进度表 maintenance schedule
日程表 schedule, agenda
日程控制器 time-schedule controller
日储量贮槽 day tank
日耳曼(铝基)合金 (12Zn, 2Cu, 余量 Al) German alloy
日光 daylight
日光灯 fluorescent [daylight, sun] lamp
日光灯启动器 fluorescent lamp starter, glow starter
日光功率计 actinometer
日光榴石 {(Be, Mn, Fe)$_7$Si$_3$O$_{12}$S} helvite
日耗 daily losses
日历作业图表 calendar progress chart
日晷仪球面投影 gnomospherical projection
日晷仪投影 gnomonogram ◇ 劳厄斑点 ~ *
日晷仪投影面 gnomonic plane
日平均值 daily average value
日需要量 daily requirement
日用柜 supply tank
日用量料槽 day bin
日用品 articles of everyday use ◇ 制~用铜板 braziers' copper "日制钢"钢锻件热处理法 Niseko process
融合 fusing, fusion, interfusion ◇ 不完全~ incomplete fusion
融化 thawing, colliquation
融化剂 thawer
熔毕 smelting-down (矿石的), 【钢】fusing, melting away [down]
熔毕分析 【钢】melt-down analysis
熔毕时间 【钢】melt-down time
熔毕时期 【钢】melting-down period
熔波钎焊 wave soldering

熔池 furnace hearth, molten bath [crater, pool], crucible (hearth), melting [fused] bath, 【钢】pool, 【冶】basin ◇ 焊接~ weldpool [puddle], 深~熔炼*
熔池边部冷凝的金属 feather edge
熔池表面 heel of metal
熔池槽 fused bath channel
熔池测试 in-bath measurements
熔池成分 bath constituent
熔池(成分)调整 【冶】adjustment of bath, 【钢】bath maintenance
熔池吹炼 bath converting
熔池吹氧 bath lancing
熔池底 bath bottom
熔池电弧焊 molten-bath arc welding
熔池分析 bath analysis
熔池搅拌(熔化) 【钢】shaking-down
熔池搅动 agitation of bath
熔池快速凝结施焊 cold running
熔池炼铜 bath copper smelting
熔池猛烈沸腾 【冶】open boil of bath
熔池取样 【钢】bath [spoon] sample
熔池熔炼(液态金属的) bath smelting, smelting in melt, pool melt
熔池熔炼系统 bath smelting system
熔池熔炼现象 bath smelting phenomena
熔池勺样 【钢】spoon sample
熔池深度 depth of bath
熔池寿命 bath life
熔池循环 circulation of bath
熔池液面 bath surface [line]
熔出 melting out
熔出孔 (同"熔化孔")
熔穿 burn(ing)-through, drop-through
熔穿孔 burning hole
熔带 molten zone
熔带转变 【冶】zone transformation
熔滴 molten drop, melt dipping [down]
熔滴(金属)过渡 drop (metal) transfer ◇ 球状~ *
熔滴试验 melt-down test, melting and dripping test

熔点 melting point (M.P., mp), fusion point (fn.p., fu.p.), melting temperature, beginning of fusion ◇ 精确～*, 同成分～*

熔点测定 fusing point test

熔点计 meldometer

熔点降低 melting-point depression

熔点曲线 melting-point curve

熔点图 melting-temperature chart

熔度 fusibility, smelting capacity, meltability, fluxibility ◇ 玻璃料[粉末钮扣试样]～试验【粉】button test

熔度曲线 fusibility curve

熔度图 melting-temperature chart, fusibility diagram

熔断 【电】blow (out), fusing

熔断电流 blow out current

熔断器 fusible cut-out, fuse (box) ◇ 磁吹～*, 管形～*

熔断器板 fuse [cut-out] board

熔断器箱 fuse box

熔断丝 thermal element

熔断丝合金 electric fuse metal

熔敷金属 【焊】deposit(ed) metal

熔敷金属层 deposited-metal zone, pad weld (堆焊的)

熔敷金属焊接 deposit welding

熔敷顺序 【焊】deposition sequence

熔敷速度 【焊】deposition rate

熔敷速度因数 deposition rate factor

熔敷系数 【焊】deposition coefficient

熔锅 saggar, sagger ◇ 铁制～*

熔焊 fusion [melting, fluid, non-pressure] welding, fusion bonding, weld(ing) deposit ◇ 焊剂层下～*, 铝热(剂)～*, 气～ gas fusion welding

熔焊层 【焊】weld pad

熔焊法 fusion welding method ◇ 松装金属粉末～*

熔焊焊缝 fusion weld

熔核 【焊】(fusion, cast) nugget

熔合 fusion, fritting, alloying, alloyage, alligation, 【冶】interfusion ◇ 不～处(铸件缺陷) cold-shut, 焊道间～ interrun fusion

熔合不良 (焊缝的) faulty fusion

熔合电压 fritting voltage

熔合法 fusion process

熔合结 【半】fused junction

熔合面 fusion face

熔合区 (母材的) 【焊】fusion area

熔合物 (fusion) rafting

熔合线 【焊】fusion line, weld junction

熔化 melting (down), smelting, fusion, fusing, fuse off, fluxion ◇ 不完全～ incomplete fusion, 低压～ low-pressure melting, 过度～ excessive fusion, 过早～ premature fusion, 可～的 flexible, 同成分～*, 完全～的 clear-melted, 预先～ premelting

熔化比 【铁】melting ratio

熔化操作 melting operation

熔化层 fluxed zone

熔化产物 fusion product

熔化除气 melt outgassing

熔化电流 fusion [melting] current

熔化度 smelting capacity

熔化端 melting end

熔化法 fusion process [method], melting procedures ◇ 用～配制合金 fusion alloying

熔化法配制合金 fusion alloying

熔化废钢[铁] 【冶】melting scrap

熔化坩埚 melting crucible [cup, hearth]

熔化坩埚装置 (自耗电弧炉构件) melting cup assembly

熔化坩埚装置运送车 cart for removing melting cup assembly

熔化工 melter

熔化工段 melting section

熔化锅 melting pot

熔化还原动力学 melting and reduction kinetics

熔化极电弧焊焊缝 metal-arc weld

熔化极惰气保护焊 consumable electrode

熔　rong

inert-gas arc welding
熔化及保温双用炉　【铸】dipout furnace
熔化空洞　【压】fusion void
熔化孔　【粉】melt-off pore
熔化[熔焊]连接　【焊】joint penetration
熔化料　melting charge
熔化炉　melting [fusion, foundery] furnace, melter ◇ 电弧～ arc-melting furnace
熔化炉膛　melting hearth
熔化能力　melting capacity, melting-down power
熔化凝固合并法　melting consolidation process
熔化喷镀　sprayfusing
熔化器　melter
熔化气氛　melting atmosphere
熔化迁移[徙动]（炉衬的）　flux migration
熔化潜热　latent heat of fusion [melting]
熔化切割[断]机　【焊】fusion cutting off machine
熔化区[带]　fusion [fused, melting, fluxed] zone
熔化曲线　fusion curve
熔化热　melting [fusion] heat
熔化热焓　enthalpy of melting
熔(化)熵(变化)[熔解熵变]　【理】melting entropy, entropy change of fusion
熔化设备　melting unit
熔化时间　melting time
熔化（时）期　melting period [cycle, stage], 【钢】melt(ing-)down period
熔化式起[引]弧　【焊】fuse type start
熔化室　melting [fusion] chamber, melting compartment
熔化速度　speed of melting
熔化速率　melting [melt-off] rate
熔化损失　melting loss
熔化台（真空铸锭炉的）　melting platform
熔化条件　melting condition

熔化脱气　【钢】melt outgassing
熔化温度　metlting [fusion, melt-down] temperature
熔化温度范围　melting range
熔化物　melt, fusant
熔化系数　melting coefficient
熔化效率　efficiency of burn-off（电焊条的），【冶】melting [fusion] efficiency
熔化压　melting pressure
熔化铸焊　fusion thermit welding
熔化自由能　free energy of melting
熔化嘴电渣焊　electroslag welding with consumable nozzle
熔灰炉　ash fusion furnace
熔极式电弧炉熔炼法　consel arc method
熔剂　flux (addition), fluxing compound [material, stone], fusing agent, slagging medium, smelting flux ◇ 保护性～【冶】covering flux, 废金属重熔用～*, 含铁～*, 加～的 fluxed, 碱性～basic flux, 净～*, 陶瓷～ ceramic flux, 无～法*, 转炉～【冶】converter flux
熔剂薄膜　flux film
熔剂保护　flux shielding
熔剂材料　【冶】fluxing material
熔剂残渣清除　【冶】flux removal
熔剂仓[贮斗]　flux hopper
熔剂槽　flux bath [bin, tank], chemical bath
熔剂池　flux bath
熔剂池浮渣　flux bath dross
熔剂储仓　flux material stockyard
熔剂处理　flux treatment
熔剂当量　stone equivalent
熔剂镀锌　flux galvanizing
熔剂法　flux method
熔剂粉[粉状熔剂]　flux fine, fine [ground] flux, flux(ing) powder
熔剂覆盖层　flux cover
熔剂干燥炉　flux drying oven
熔剂供料线路　【冶】flux handling route
熔剂辊　flux roll

熔剂含量 flux content
熔剂/焊丝重量比率 【焊】flux/wire ratio
熔剂加料机 flux feeder
熔剂精炼 【冶】flux refining
熔剂块 flux block
熔剂量 amount of fluxing agent
熔剂流量 flux rate
熔剂流速 flux flow rate
熔剂率 【铁】stone rate
熔剂浓度 flux concentration
熔剂枪 flux gun
熔剂切割 （同"氧熔剂切割"）
熔剂渗入 flux penetration
熔剂石灰石 raw stone
熔剂添加管 flux feed tube
熔剂污染（焊缝的） flux contamination
熔剂下弧焊法 submerged arc process
熔剂箱 flux box
熔剂性混合料 fluxed mixture
熔剂性矿石 fluxing ore
熔剂性球团 fluxed pellet ◇ 石灰石～*
熔剂性烧结矿 flux(ed) sinter [agglomerate], flux bearing agglomerate, prefluxed sinter
熔剂性烧结矿炉料 burden fluxing sinter
熔剂装入[添加]系统 【钢】flux handling system
熔剂准备工段 【冶】flux preparation plant
熔剂总含量 total flux content
熔剂组成[组分] flux constituent [component, ingredient]
熔剂作用 fluxing effect
熔接 fusion bonding, welding, butt fusion, autogenous soldering
熔结 fusion, clinkering, fritting
熔结带 clinkering zone
熔结石英 fused silica [quartz]
熔结石英玻璃 fused quartz glass
熔结石英观察窗 fused quartz sight glass
熔结石英管 fused silica [quartz] tube
熔结石英烧舟 fused silica boat
熔结石英圆筒 fused silica cylinder
熔结石英砖 fused silica brick
熔结物 frit
熔结黏砂（缺陷） 【铸】sand fusion
熔解 fusion, decomposition, melting, fluxing ◇ 用硝饼[硫酸氢钠]～fluxing with nitre cake, 快速～炉 flash calciner
熔解温度 melting temperature, temperature of fusion
熔解压 melting pressure
熔块 clinker, frit, fused block [lump], fusion cake
熔矿炉 ore furnace
熔粒耐火材料 fused grain refractory
熔炼 smelting, melting, fusion (metallurgy) ◇ 不合格～*, 不能～的 unsmeltable, 超重～ heavy weight heat, 初步～ primary smelting, 吹灰～*, 低温～*, 电弧～*, 电炉～ electro-smelting, 电(热)～*, 电渣～ electroslag melting, 电子轰击～*, 电子束～*, 富集～ concentrating smelting, 干炉床～*, 干式～ dry smelting, 坩埚～*, 高铁水比～【钢】hig hot metal heat, 接触～ contact melting, 空气～的 air-melted, 冷(炉)料[冷装]～ cold melt(ing), 流态化床～ fluid bed smelting, 闪速～ flash smelting, 试验性～ blank heat, 旋涡～*, 选择性～ selective smelting, 氩弧～ argon arc melting, 再～ melting down, 镇静[无沸腾]～【钢】dead melting, 舟皿～【色】boat melting, 自耗电极～*, 自热～*
熔炼参数 smelting parameter
熔炼操作 smelting operation [practice], melting practice, operation of melting
熔炼槽 melting tank
熔炼产物 product of smelting, smelted product
熔炼厂 【冶】refinery
熔炼车间 smelter shop ◇ 放热法[金属热]～*
熔炼处理 smelting treatment

熔炼法　smelting process [method] ◇ 凯尔卡洛依~*,控制气氛~*,冷床~*,真空感应~inductrovac process
熔炼反应　smelting reaction
熔炼废品　off smelting
熔炼分析　heat analysis
熔炼坩埚　smelting pot
熔炼工　smelter, melter, furnace tender
熔炼工长　chief melter, melter foreman
熔炼工段　smelting room
熔炼工具　furnace tool
熔炼工助手　【冶】melter's mate
熔炼过程　smelting circuit
熔炼过程快速分析　【冶】snap
熔炼过度　overmelt
熔炼焊剂　fused flux
熔炼记录　【冶】heat record [log]
熔炼进度表　【冶】heat schedule
熔炼量[负荷]　metallurgical load ◇ 额定~normal cast weight
熔炼料柱（鼓风炉的）　melting stock column
熔炼流程(图)　smelter flowsheet
熔炼炉　smelting furnace, smelting vessel, S-furnace, melter, smelter ◇ 电阻式~*,分批式[间歇操作式]~batch smelter,感应加热~*,连续~continuous smelter
熔炼炉料　smelting charge
熔炼炉炉膛　smelter hearth, smelting (furnace) hearth
熔炼炉数　◇ 单位时间内~【冶】heat frequency
熔炼炉烟道　smelter flue
熔炼炉渣　smelting slag
熔炼能力　smelting capacity [power]
熔炼期　smelting period
熔炼铅锌法　◇ 英帝国冶炼有限公司~*
熔炼强度　smelting intensity
熔炼情况不良　poor smelting conditions
熔炼设备　melting facility [unit], smelting equipment [unit]
熔炼室　【冶】smelting [working] chamber, furnace cavity [proper]
熔炼竖炉　smelting shaft
熔炼速度[速率]　smelting rate
熔炼损失　smelting loss
熔炼特性　smelting characteristic
熔炼条件　smelting condition
熔炼温度　smelting temperature [point]
熔炼一炉金属　heat of metal
熔炼装置外壳　melting tank
熔料　melting stock
熔炉　smelter, smelting furnace, melter, calcar（玻璃的）
熔镁炉　furnace for magnesium
熔模　【铸】investment pattern ◇ 一次~disposable pattern
熔模材料　investment material
熔模精密造型(法)　investment mould (ing)
熔模精密铸造　(precision) investment casting
熔模壳型　plycast
熔模壳型铸造法　invest shell casting method
熔模预涂层　investment precoat
熔模造型　lost-wax [investment] mould (ing)
熔模铸型　invested mould
熔模铸造　(hot, lost-wax) investment casting, lost-wax [dewaxing] casting, investing, full form casting
熔模铸造法　investment casting (process), lost wax process, cire perdu(e) method [process], plycast process, aquacast process（有色合金的）◇ 阿达普提~*,冻结水银~*,壳型~*
熔模铸造学会（美国）　Investment Casting Institute (ICI)
熔凝　consolidation ◇ 电积金属~*,难熔金属~*
熔凝硅石　fused silica

熔片管	fuse tube
熔铅锅	(lead melting) kettle, market pot
熔铅精炼	softening
熔铅润滑拉丝法	lead lubrication process
熔切	fusion cutting ◇ 三软管式~器*, 双软管式~器*
熔清	【钢】melting away [down]
熔清时期	melting-down period
熔区(区域熔炼的)	molten zone
熔区长度	zone length
熔区传输	zone-transport
熔区传输法	zone-transport method
熔区传输精炼炉	(zone-)transport refiner ◇ 级联三重收回~*
熔区回流	zonal reflux
熔区回流流动	zonal reflux flow
熔区间间距	interzone spacing
熔区空段	zone-void
熔区空段法	zone-void method
熔区空段精炼炉	zone-void refiner
熔区凝固	zone freezing
熔区偏析	zone-segregation
熔区通过	zone pass(age)
熔区通过效率	efficiency of zone passes
熔区形状	zone shape
熔区液体	zone fluid
熔区移动	zone travel [movement], movement (molten) zone, travel zone
熔区移动方向	direction of zone travel
熔区移动机构	molten zone moving mechanism
熔区移动机理	zone travel mechanism
熔区移动速度[速率]	zone speed, travel rate of zone, rate of zone travel
熔融	fusion, melting
熔融冰晶石	molten [fused] cryolite
熔融冰晶石电解液	(同"冰晶石熔体")
熔融铋冷却(反应堆的)	molten bismuth cooling
熔融产物	molten [fusion] product
熔融尘粒	molten dust particle
熔融粗铅	molten bullion
熔融带	smelting zone
熔融滴下	melt down
熔融电解质	igneous electrolyte
熔融度	fusibility, meltableness, meltability
熔融锻造	forge casting
熔融反应	fusion reaction
熔融范围	fusion range
熔融废钢脱铜	removal of copper from molten scrap
熔融氟化剂	fused fluorinating agent
熔融刚玉	fused corundum
熔融过程	fusion process
熔融光卤石	molten carnallite
熔融过程	fusion process
熔融焊缝	fusion weld
熔融焊剂	【焊】fused melt
熔融焊剂和金属	【焊】burden
熔融还原	smelting reduction, melting reduction ◇ 煤-氧-矿喷射造气和~*
熔融还原反应器	smelt-reduction vessel
熔融还原炉【铁】	smelting reduction furnace
熔融还原炼铁	smelt-reduction ironmaking
熔融还原设备	smelt-reduction unit
熔融还原竖炉	shaft furnace for smelting reduction
熔融灰	molten ash
熔融混合物	molten [fusion] mixture
熔融碱	fused alkali
熔融减摩垫(热挤压的)	molten pad
熔融金属	molten [hot] metal
熔融金属本体	parent melt
熔融金属泵	【冶】molten metal pump
熔融金属超声波雾化	【粉】ultrasonic atomization of molten metal
熔融金属池	pool of (molten) metal
熔融金属淬火剂	molten metal quenchant
熔融金属滴	【冶】dropping metal
熔融金属分析	hot metal analysis
熔融金属腐蚀	corrosion by molten metal
熔融金属罐	ladle

熔融金属浇注温度　hot metal casting temperature
熔融金属料　【钢】hot-metal charge
熔融金属面　【冶】heel of metal
熔融金属喷镀　molten metal spraying
熔融金属喷枪　【金】molten metal pistol
熔融金属前床　【色】hot metal receiver
熔融金属溶媒　menstruum of molten metal
熔融金属渗透法　【金】infiltration process
熔融金属试样　hot metal sample
熔融金属压头　head of molten metal
熔融金属装料　【钢】hot metal charging
熔融-浸出操作　fusion leach operation
熔融浸镀　melt dipping
熔融精炼　smelt-refining
熔融连接键　melting bond
熔融磷酸盐电解液　fused phosphate bath
熔融锍[冰铜]　molten matte
熔融炉料　molten charge
熔融炉渣　molten [fused] slag
熔融铝　molten aluminium
熔融镁砂　fused [melted] magnesite
熔融莫来石　fused mullite
熔融耐火材料　fused (cast) refractory
熔融喷补　flame gunning repair
熔融平衡　fusion [melt] equilibrium
熔融期　meltdown period
熔融气化炉　smelting gasifier
熔融铅虹吸　molten lead siphon
熔融溶液　fused solution
熔融烧碱　molten caustic
熔融石英　fused silica [quartz] ◇ 不透明～opaque fused silica, 透明～电解槽
熔融试验　fusion test
熔融速度　melting speed
熔融水泥　fused cement
熔融损失　melting loss
熔融态熔剂　fused flux
熔融态下铸造和随后模锻制造零件法 ◇ 哈里森～*
熔融添加物　melted addition
熔融铜　molten copper
熔融温度　fusing temperature ◇ 测定～用高温计 fusion pyrometer
熔融钨酸盐电解　electrolysis of fused tungstate
熔融钨酸盐电解液　fused tungstate bath
熔融物　fusant
熔融物电解　electrolysis of molten substances
熔融物料　molten material
熔融物质　molten [fused] mass
熔融相　melt phase
熔融硝酸钠处理　nitralising
熔融效率　【冶】melting efficiency
熔融锌槽　melted zinc bath
熔融型烧结矿　【铁】molten type sintered ore
熔融玄武岩　fused basalt
熔融烟尘　molten flue dust
熔融盐　molten salt
熔融盐中铅处理[淬火]（钢丝的）　salt patenting
熔融氧化硅　（同"熔融石英"）
熔融氧化铝　molten [fused] alumina
熔融液滴　molten dripping
熔融铸模　【耐】fusion casting mould
熔融(状)态　molten state [condition]
熔烧镀层　fused coating
熔射喷补机　【焦】smelting gunning machine
熔深（焊接的）　depth of penetration [fusion], penetration
熔深不足　inadequate penetration
熔蚀　corrosion
熔丝　fuse (wire), wire fuse
熔丝断路器　fuse disconnector [cut-out]
熔丝管　fuse tube, tube [cartridge] fuse
熔丝式温度(指示)计　【理】fuse type temperature meter
熔丝组件　fuse block
熔体　melt, molten mass [bath], fused mass, bath, fusant ◇ 电解槽～bath of

cell, 气体饱和~【冶】gassy melt, 酸性~ acid melt
熔体比热 specific of melt
熔体表面 bath surface
熔体成分[组成, 组分] melt [bath] composition, bath constituent
熔体处理法 melt treatment process
熔体粉碎细化（金属的） melt-fragmentation
熔体覆盖物 【冶】cover for fusions
熔体过滤 melt filtration
熔体晶体生长 crystal growth from melt
熔体拉晶法 melt-pulling method
熔体面调节器 liquid level controller
熔体生长的单晶 melt-grown single crystal
熔体试样 molten test sample
熔体体积 molten [bath] volume
熔体温度 bath temperature
熔体形成 melt formation
熔体运动 bath movement
熔体织构生长 melt-texture growth
熔体质量 melt quality
熔铁炉 iron melting furnace
熔透 【焊】fusion penetration ◇ 全厚~ melt-thru, 完全~ good penetration
熔透焊道 under bead
熔透焊缝 penetration [melt-thru] weld
熔析 liquation, liquating, aliquation, 【色】segregation ◇ 初~除铜*, 冷却~ cooling liquation
熔析残渣 residue from liquation
熔析槽 liquation bath
熔析产物 liquated product
熔析出[分离] liquate out
熔析法 liquation process
熔析锅 liquating pot
熔析精炼 liquation refining, refining by liquation ◇ 锌~炉*
熔析炉 liquation furnace [hearth], sweat furnace
熔析铅 liquated lead
熔析铅锅 liquated-lead kettle
熔析铜 liquated copper
熔析铜渣 【色】slag from liquated copper
熔析锌 liquated zinc
熔析渣 scoria
熔锡炉 tin melting furnace
熔锌设备 【色】zinc melting unit
熔盐 molten [fused] salt
熔盐槽 salt bath
熔盐萃取[提取] fused-salt extraction
熔盐淬火 fused salt quench
熔盐电解 molten [fused] salt electrolysis, fusion electrolysis, electrolysis of molten salts [substances], electrolysis from fused salts ◇ 氟化物~*, 氯化物~*
熔盐电解槽 fused salt bath [cell], molten salt container, electrolytic furnace ◇ 高频感应加热~*
熔盐电解法 fused salt process
熔盐电解还原 reduction of fused salts
熔盐电解精炼 fused salt electrolytic refining, molten [fused] salt electrore-fining ◇ 粗铋二段阳极~*
熔盐电解精炼槽 fused salt electrorefining cell
熔盐电解炉 molten salt electrolytic furnace
熔盐电解试验 molten salt electrolytic test
熔盐电解质 fused (salt) electrolyte, molten electrolyte
熔盐还原 reduction of fused salt
熔盐腐蚀 salt corrosion
熔盐混合物 salt bath mixture
熔盐介质 fused salt medium
熔盐净化 fused salt purification
熔盐氯化 fused salt chlorination
熔盐排出口 molten salt drain
熔盐溶剂 fused salt solvent
熔盐渗碳 （同"盐浴渗碳"）
熔盐洗涤器 fused salt scrubber
熔盐浴(槽) molten [fused] salt bath
熔氧精炼 【钢】molten-oxidizing refining

熔液表面　molten surface
熔液碎化　melt-fragmentation
熔浴　liquid-bath, molten [fused, melting] bath
熔浴烧结　liquid bath sintering
熔浴烧结炉　liquid-bath sintering furnace
熔渣　(molten, smelting, fused) slag, clinker, dross, flux inclusion ◇ 玻璃状～*,工业[商品]～ commercial slag, 破碎～ crushed slag, 液体金属表面～(浇桶中的) sullage, 云状花纹[无光泽断口]～ clouded slag
熔渣保护　slag protetction [coverage], flux shielding [envelope]
熔渣保温层　【冶】insulating layer of slag
熔渣地面　clinker floor
熔渣电解精炼法　molten slag electrolysis refining
熔渣反应性[能力]　【冶】reactivity of slag
熔渣飞溅　slag splashing
熔渣分离　slag separation
熔渣分离器　slag separator
熔渣覆[盖]层　slag [clinker] coating
熔渣罐　receiver
熔渣厚度测量　slag thickness measurement
熔渣回收废钢[铁]　slag scrap
熔渣夹杂(物)　slag inclusions [shot], flux contamination
熔渣壳　flux envelope
熔渣可移动性　【钢】removability of slag
熔渣坑　【冶】sludge pit ◇ 碳化物～*
熔渣面　slag surface
熔渣起泡　(同"炉渣起泡")
熔渣侵蚀反应　slagging reaction
熔渣砂　【建】slag sand
熔渣生成　clinker formation
熔渣脱[去]硫能力　【冶】sulphur-carrying power of slag
熔渣砖　slag brick
熔制锭　melted ingot
熔铸　(fusion) casting, founding ◇ 巴比含金离心～机*,电弧～arc-cast
熔铸成形耐火材料　cast refractory
熔铸电解铁　fused electrolytic iron
熔铸工　【冶】remelter
熔铸工业金属　fused industrial metal
熔铸炉　casting furnace ◇ 黄铜～brass furnace
熔铸[熔制]耐火材料　molten [fusion] cast refractory, cast-fused [cast(able) refractory, refractory castable
熔铸内衬　castable lining
熔铸玄武岩(铸石)　fusion cast basalt
熔铸氧化铝砖　fuse cast alumina
熔铸银　fused silver
熔铸制品　◇ 科维西特～【耐】Korvisit, 马格马洛克斯～【耐】Magmalox, 齐拉里特～【耐】Zilarit, 雅各比～【耐】Jakobit
熔铸[熔制]砖　molten [fusion] cast brick, refractory castable
熔锥　pyrometric cone ◇ 标准～*,试验～ test cone
熔锥鉴定法(耐火度的)　pyrometric cone evaluation (P.C.E.)
溶池浸出法　dump pond method
溶出　digesting, digestion, leach(ing) ◇ 高压～digesting, 加热～ hot digestion, 苛性碱～caustic digestion, 两级～ two-step digestion
溶出残渣　digestion residue [slimes]
溶出槽　digestion tank
溶出处理　digesting treatment
溶出过程　digestion process
溶出阶段　leaching stage
溶出矿[料]浆　digested pulp [slurry]
溶出母液　digestion liquor
溶出器(高压的)　digester ◇ 转筒形烧结块～*,蒸汽加热～steam digester
溶出器组　digester group ◇ 连续～*
溶出设备　digestion equipment
溶出时间　digestion time
溶出条件　digestion condition
溶出温度　digestion temperature

溶出系统[系列] digestion system [series]
溶出压力 leaching pressure
溶出液 digesting liquid
溶除锌镀层镀着量测定 stripping test
溶度积 solubility product
溶度系数 solubility factor
溶化锅 dissolution boiler
溶混间隔[间隙] miscibility gap
溶混性(可溶混性) miscibility
溶剂 solvent (solv.), resolver, dissolvant, dissolvent ◇ 芳族~*, 含氧~*, 给质子[氢离子]~ protogenic solvent, 碱性~ basic solvent, 离解~ dissociating solvent, 无水~ anhydrous solvent, 西纳索尔~*
溶剂层(萃取) solvent layer
溶剂成分[组成] solvent composition
溶剂出口 solvent outlet
溶剂萃取[提取] solvent extract(ion), liquid ion exchange ◇ 矿浆~*, 无水~*, 综合~*
溶剂萃取-电积提取铜镍法 SEC-CCS process
溶剂萃取-电解沉积法 solvent-extraction-electrowinning process
溶剂萃取法 solvent extraction method [route], solvent (extraction) process ◇ 威克斯淤浆~ waxco process
溶剂萃取工段 solvent extraction area
溶剂萃取净化 purification by solvent extraction
溶剂萃取净化法 solvent extraction purification process
溶剂萃取器 solvent extractor ◇ 离心式~*
溶剂萃取设备 solvent extraction plant
溶剂萃取塔 solvent extraction column
溶剂分解 solvolysis
溶剂分析 solvent analysis
溶剂化 solvation
溶剂化络合物 solvated complex
溶剂化数 【化】solvation number

溶剂化物 solvate
溶剂回收 solvent recovery
溶剂回收塔 solvent recovery column
溶剂混合物 solvent mixture
溶剂加酸萃取浸出法 acid-in-solvent process
溶剂晶格 solvent lattice
溶剂净化 solvent refining, cleaning by solvent
溶剂净化剂 solvent cleaner
溶剂浓度 solvent strength
溶剂清洗 solvent cleaning
溶剂清洗剂 solvent remover
溶剂-溶质混合物 solvent-solute mixture
溶剂溶质系统 solvent-solute system
溶剂入口 solvent extraction inlet
溶剂水相比 solvent-to-liquid ratio
溶剂提纯 solvent refining
溶剂脱脂 solvent degreasing
溶剂洗提 solvent stripping
溶剂相 solvent phase
溶剂效应 solvent effect
溶剂型显示剂 solvent developer
溶剂选择性 solvent selectivity
溶剂冶金 lyometallurgy
溶剂阴离子 lyate ion
溶剂油 solvent naphtha
溶剂淤浆萃取 solvent-slurry extraction
溶剂元素 solvent element
溶剂原子 solvent atom
溶胶 (colloidal) sol ◇ 带正电的~ positively charged sol, 阳电[阳性]~ positive sol
溶胶化(作用) solation
溶胶-凝胶法(核反应堆燃料的) sol-gel method
溶解 dissolving, dissolution, solution (sol.), solubilizing, solvation, solu-bilization, digestion ◇ 异族~ heterolysis
溶解槽 dissolving tank [vat], digestion tank
溶解电解槽 dissolution cell

溶解动力学　(dis)solution kinetics, kinetics of dissolution
溶解度　solubility, solubleness, dissolubility, dissolvability, degree of solubility [solution] ◇布朗~定律 Braun's law
溶解度常数　solubility constant
溶解度极限　solubility limit
溶解度曲线　solubility [solvus] curve
溶解度温度曲线　solubility-temperature curve
溶解度温度系数　solubility temperature coefficient
溶(解度)线　solubility line, solvus (line)
溶解法　dissolution process [method]
溶解反应　dissolution reaction
溶解范围　soluble end
溶解鼓　dissolving drum
溶解固体　dissolved solid
溶解过程　dissolution [solution] process, course of dissolution
溶解剂　dissolvent (diss.), thawer
溶解加速剂　solutizer
溶解离子　dissolved ion
溶解力增加　increase in resolution
溶解(能)力　solution [solvent] power, solvency, dissolving capacity [power] ◇无~的 insolvent (insov.), 有~的 solvent
溶解期　breaking in period
溶解器　dissolver, dissolving drum ◇小型~ bench scale dissolver, 药剂~ reagent dissolver
溶解气体　dissolved gas
溶解气体雾化(金属的)　soluble gas atomization
溶解热　(dis)solution [dissolving] heat
溶解设备　digestion equipment
溶解速度　dissolving speed
溶解速率　dissolution rate, rate of solution
溶解损失　solution loss
溶解损失反应　solution loss reaction
溶解碳　【冶】dissolved carbon
溶解温度　digestion temperature

溶解物　solute, dissolved matter
溶解系数　solubility coefficient
溶解性　solubility, solubleness, dissolubility, dissolvability
溶解压(力)　solution pressure
溶解氧(量)　dissolved oxygen (D.O.) ◇饱和~*
溶解杂质[污染物质]　dissolved contaminant
溶解装置　dissolving facilities ◇化学药物~*
溶解作用　solvent action, solubilization, (dis)solution
溶浸　leaching
溶浸采矿　solution mining
溶媒　solvent, dissolvant, dissolvent, menstruum, resolver ◇熔融金属~*
溶媒作用　solvent action
溶气浮选(法)　dissolved-air flotation
溶碳(铸铁中的)　impregnation with carbon
溶体　solution
溶纤剂 $\{C_2H_5O(CH_2)_2OH\}$　cellosolve ◇乙酸~*
溶性玻璃　soluble glass
溶性碳化铁　soluble iron carbide
溶性显示剂　soluble developer
溶性盐　soluble salt
溶性油　soluble oil
溶液　solution (sol.), liquor, aqua (aq)
溶液标准浓度　standard strength of solution
溶液采矿　solution mining
溶液槽[箱]　solution tank
溶液陈化　ageing of solution
溶液成分[组成]　solution composition
溶液电解　electrolysis of solution
溶液电阻　solution resistance
溶液动力学[分子运动]理论　kinetic theory of solution
溶液法　solution technique [method]
溶液分析　liquor analysis, solution assay

溶液管道　solution line
溶液还原　reduction of solution
溶液回流[回收]　solution return
溶液混合器　solution mixer
溶液几何模型　solution geometrical model
溶液净化　solution purification
溶液流量　liquor flow, liquid inventory
溶液浓度　solution concentration [strength]
溶液排出孔　solution-drain hole
溶液容纳量　hold-up of solution
溶液试样　liquor sample
溶液收集器　solution catcher
溶液体积[溶液量]　volume of liquor
溶液循环　solution circulation
溶液压头　solution head
溶液氧化电位　solution oxidation potential
溶液中的金属　solute metal
溶液重量摩尔浓度　solution molality
溶液浊度[颜色深度]计　diaphanometer
溶于水的　water-soluble
溶于酸的　acid-soluble
溶胀能力　swelling power
溶质　solute, soluble material [matter] ◇相反～opposite-type solute
溶质点阵[晶格]　solute lattice
溶质分布　solute distribution
溶质分配器　distributor of solute
溶质扩散　solute diffusion ◇应力引起的～*
溶质浓度　solute concentration
溶质气团　atmosphere of solute
溶质元素　solute element
溶质原子　solute atom ◇代位[替代]式～*, 弥散～dispersed solute atom, 球状～*, 有～聚集层的合金 G-P zone alloy, 有～聚集区的合金 clustered alloy
溶质原子向位错偏聚　segregation of solute atoms to dislocations
溶煮锅　dissolution boiler
容差　tolerance, allowance
容错计算机　fault-tolerant computer

容汉斯-罗西循环(连铸的)　Junghans-Rossi cycle
容汉斯-罗西有色合金振动连续铸造法　Junghans-Rossi process
容汉斯原理(连铸的)　Junghans principle
容积　volume, volumetric [cubic] capacity, bulk, roominess
容积百分数　volume-percent (vol. pct)
容积比　volume ratio, ratio by volume
容积比重　bulk specific gravity
容积不变　constancy of volume
容积测量[量度]　volume [cubic] measure
容积吨($0.906m^3$)　volume ton
容积计量槽　volumetric measuring tank
容积可变性　variability of volume
容积密度　volume density
容积浓度　bulk concentration
容积[量]配料　volume batching, proportioning by volume
容积膨胀　volume expansion
容积热容　volumetric heat capacity
容积升压器　volume booster
容积式给料器　volumetric feeder
容积损失[收缩]　loss of volume
容积系数　volumetric coefficient
容积效率[有效利用率]　volume(tric) efficiency
容积-压力曲线　pressure-volume curve
容积仪　volumetric type meter
容积自扩散　volume autodiffusion
容抗　capacitance, capacitive impedance [reactance], condensance
容克式结晶器[水冷锭模]　Junker's mould
容量　capacity (cap., capy), capability, capacitance, volume, bulk, (cubic) content, roominess, volumetric [cubic] capacity, residence capacity (料仓的), condensance (指电容量)
容量单位　unit of capacity
容量法　volumetric method
容量范围　capacity range

容量分析 volumetric analysis [determination]
容量估计 capacity rating
容量计 volume meter, volumeter, volumometer ◇ 斯科特~*
容量记录器 volume recorder
容量控制 volumetric control
容量摩尔[克分子]浓度 volumetric molar concentration
容量瓶 volumetric [measuring] flask
容量曲线 capacity curve
容量式流量计 volumetric type flowmeter
容量收缩 volumetric contraction
容量探示器（料位检测用） capacity probe
容量型隔膜泵 volumetric type diaphragm pump
容量性质 capacity property
容铝量（炉子或坩埚的） aluminium holding capacity
容模[容积]摩尔溶液 molar solution
容纳 holding, accommodating
容纳量[能力] holding capacity
容器 container, holder, vessel, receptacle, reservoir, can, cell, canister, capsule
容器（钢）板 vessel [tank] plate, high pressure vessel steel plate
容器口 vessel mouth [opening]
容器里[内]衬 container liner, vessel internals
容器容量 vessel capacity
容器填充高度指示器 cut-off level gauge
容器外壳 container jacket
容器形状 shape of vessel
容器运输 container transport
容器座 container holder
容气器 gas container
容忍[容许]的 tolerant
容限 tolerance,【计】margin
容性电抗（同"容抗"）
容许变化 permissible variation
容许带[区] permitted [allowed] band

容许电压 allowable [permissible] voltage
容许范围（疲劳的） tolerance interval
容许负荷[负载] allowable load
容许工作压力 allowable working pressure
容许工作应力 safe working stress
容许过载 admissible overload
容许含量[级位] tolerance level
容许含铅量 lead tolerance
容许间隙 safe clearance
容许能带 permitted energy band, allowed (energy) band, allowed energy zone
容许能级 allowed (energy) level, permitted (energy) level
容许浓度 admissible [acceptable] concentration
容许偏差 allowable variation
容许曝光（程）度 allowable exposure
容许曝露程度[容许接触量] permissible exposure level (PEL)
容许添加少量矿石的温度范围 【冶】"ore with caution" range
容许土压力 allowable soil pressure
容许误差 allowable [admissible, permissible] error
容许限度 allowable [permissible] limit, tolerance limit [level]
容许压力 allowable [authorised] pressure
容许应力 allowable [permissible] stress, proof stress (ps)
容许跃迁 allowed [permitted] transition
容许值 allowable [addmissible] value
容重 weight by volume, volume-weight
绒辊（抛光用） dusting roll
绒毛状网纹（搪瓷表面缺陷） fuzzy texture
冗余 redundancy, redundance
冗余位 【计】redundancy bit
冗余(位数)校验 【计】redundancy check ◇ 循环~*
揉捏 kneading, pugging
揉软泥条 blunging
揉土机 【耐】blunger

柔量	compliance
柔软	softness
柔软度	flexibility, pliability
柔软性试验	pliability test
柔顺性	flexibility
柔性传动装置	flexible gearing
柔性带自动捆扎机	automatic flexible strapping machine
柔性关节	flexible knuckle
柔性加工	flexible manufacturing
柔性开坯机	flexible slab mill
柔性调节剂	flexibility modifier
柔性圆锥体	flexible cone
肉豆蔻酸	（同"十四（烷）酸"）
肉眼观察	macroscope [macroscopic] observation, visual inspection, visualizing
肉眼观察不到的标记（磁粉检验）	not-open indication
肉眼观察术	macroscopy
肉眼检查	visual test [control]
肉眼可见的	macroscopic
肉眼孔隙	macro porosity
肉眼控制	visual control
蠕变	creep(ing), creepage ◇ 第三期[末期]～*, 防～ anticreep, 工程～ engineering creep, 过渡[安德雷德]～*, 回复～ recovery creep, 加工硬化曲线第Ⅲ阶段 β～*, 抗～合金*, 扩散～ diffusion creep, 拉伸～*, 抛物线型～ parabolic creep, 无效～ sterile creep, 压曲～ buckling creep, 压缩～*, 周期应变诱发～*
蠕变变形	creep deformation
蠕变变形材料	creep-strained material
蠕变变形与时间关系曲线	creep strain-time plot
蠕变成形法	【压】creep forming
蠕变成穴	creep cavitation
蠕变定律	creep law ◇ 安德拉德～ Andrade's creep law
蠕变断口	creep fracture
蠕变断裂	creep rupture [fracture], fracture in creep, cavitation creep failure ◇ 成穴[空洞型]～*
蠕变断裂强度	creep-rupture strength
蠕变断裂试验	creep-rupture test
蠕变断裂性能	creep-rupture behaviour
蠕变方程（式）	creep equation
蠕变过程	creep process
蠕变过程中空位迁移	【金】vacancies migration during creep
蠕变耗竭理论	exhaustion theory of creep
蠕变后延性	ductility after creep
蠕变回复	creep recovery
蠕变回复理论	recovery theory of creep
蠕变机理	creep mechanism
蠕变极限	creep limit
蠕变抗力	creep resistance
蠕变（扩散）公式	◇ 阿列纽斯～ Arrhenius equation
蠕变流动	creep flow
蠕变区	creep zone
蠕变破断伸长	extension of creep fracture
蠕变强度	creep strength ◇ 长时间～*, 高～金属 creep-resistant metal, 推算～*
蠕变曲线	creep curve ◇ 曼森－哈夫里德～外推理论*
蠕变时间律	time law of creep
蠕变时间律理论	theory of time law of creep
蠕变时沿晶界断裂	intercrystalline failure during creep
蠕变试验	creep(ing) test, creep experiment ◇ 变应力～*, 短期～（72小时）time yield, 哈菲尔德快速～*, 弯曲～ bending creep test
蠕变试验标准	creep-test criteria
蠕变试验方法	creep test(ing) method
蠕变试验机	creep(testing) machine ◇ 博德温～ Baldwin creep tester
蠕变试验炉	creep-test furnace ◇ 自动式～*
蠕变试验装置	creep-test installation
蠕变寿命	creep life
蠕变数据外推法	extrapolation of creep

蠕变速度 creeping speed
蠕变速率 creep rate ◇ 临界~ critical creep rate, 平均~*, 允许~*
蠕变速率与应力关系曲线 creep rate-stress plot
蠕变特性 creep behaviour
蠕变稳度消失 creep buckling
蠕变形态理论 formal theory of creep
蠕变行为 creep behaviour
蠕变性能 creep property [behaviour] ◇ 循环条件~*
蠕变性能的恢复 【金】recovery of creep properties
蠕变性能方向性 directionality of creep properties
蠕变性能分散性 scatter of creep properties
蠕变压屈 creep buckling
蠕变延性 creep ductility
蠕变应变 creep strain
蠕变应力 creep stress
蠕变中的孕育期 【理】induction periods during creep
蠕变中密度变化 density changes in creep
蠕虫状石墨铸铁 compacted graphite cast iron, vermicular iron
蠕动 creeping, snaking
蠕缓放电 creeping discharge
蠕墨铸铁 vermes shape graphite cast iron ◇ 稀土~*
蠕陶土 anauxite
蠕行速度 creeping speed
铷合金 rubidium alloy
铷基合金 rubidium-base alloy
铷添加合金 rubidium addition
乳白玻璃 opal glass
乳白灯泡 opal [frosted] lamp
乳白镀铬表面 milky surface
乳白刻度滴定管 milk scale buret(te)
乳白色玻璃片 opal glass plate
乳钵 mortar

乳化 emulsifying, emulsionizing, emulsification ◇ 产生[引起]~ emulsion-causing, 可~能力 emulsibility, 可自~的 self-emulsifiable, 去[除]~剂*
乳化沉淀(法) emulsion-causing precipitation
乳化地沥青 emulsified asphalt
乳化法[过程] emulsion process
乳化基油 emulsion base oil
乳化剂 emulsifier, emulsifying agent, emulsor
乳化冷却液 oil-in-water type coolant
乳化沥青 emulsified asphalt [bitumen]
乳化沥青浇灌法 bitumen emulsion injection
乳化器 emulsifier, emulgator, emulsor ◇ 熟石灰~*
乳化(溶)剂喷洗 emulsified solvent soak cleaning
乳化时间 emulsification time
乳化树脂黏结料 resin emulsion cement
乳化性 emulsifying property, emulsibility
乳化冶金 emulsion metallurgy
乳化液 emulsion (emul.), water soluble oil solution (冷轧润滑用), oil water emulsion (乳化油的水溶液)
乳化液分解槽 emulsion decomposing tank
乳化液分裂槽 emulsion split tank
乳化液盘 emulsion pan
乳化液清洗 emulsion cleaning
乳化液润滑冷轧光洁度 soluble oil-rolled finish
乳化液烟雾 emulsion fume
乳化油 emulsified oil, soluble oil
乳化油淬火 emulsified oil quenching
乳化油水溶液 oil water emulsion
乳化重油 emulsified heavy oil
乳化作用 emulsification ◇ 产生~的沉淀 emulsion-causing precipitation
乳剂 emulsion (emul.), milk, cream
乳剂脱脂 emulsion degreasing

乳胶 emulsion (emul.), emulsoid
乳胶层可剥胶片 stripping film
乳胶[乳剂]校准曲线 emulsion calibration curve, characteristic emulsion curve ◇荷特-德里菲尔德~*
乳胶颗粒(照片的) emulsion grain
乳胶凝缩 emulsion shrinkage
乳胶体 emulsion colloid, emulsoid
乳酪业用镀锡铜板 dairy copper
乳(粒)硫 milk of sulphur
乳链球菌 Streptococcus lactis
乳色玻璃 bone glass
乳砷铅铜矿 bayldonite
乳状净化剂 emulsion cleaner
乳状[浊]液 emulsion, latex (复数 latices)
乳浊澄清 de-emulsification
入口 access (ACS), entry, inlet (hole), adit, entrance (ent.)
入口带钢温度 temperature of entering strip
入口断面 inlet section
入口(辊式)张紧装置 entry tension bridle
入口含尘量[浓度] inlet dust loading [concentration], dust inlet burden
入口活套装置 entry looper (EL)
入口夹板 clamp-type entry guide
入口夹持器 entry clamp
入口角度 inlet angle
入口节流式电路 meter-in circuit
入口孔 inlet hole, in(-)gate
入口喇叭口 inlet barrel
入口浓度 inlet density
入口喷嘴 inlet nozzle
入口区段 inlet section
入口速度 entry speed
入口台肩(阴模的) lead-in shoulder
入口条件 【计】entry condition
入口压头 inlet head
入口张力辊 entry pullers
入口直径 inlet diameter
入口指令 【计】entry instruction

入口锥(拔丝模的) 【压】cone, entrance angle
入口自动减速装置 entry automatic slow-down device
入炉比 【冶】charging ratio ◇人造富矿~*
入炉废钢铁 【钢】charge scrap
入炉鼓风(量) final blast
入炉焦 skip coke
入炉焦比 【铁】charge coke ratio, coke consumption (coke ratio)
入炉矿品位 iron content of charged iron ore, charge (ore) grade
入炉烧结矿 chargeable sinter
入射X射线束 incident X-ray beam
入射方向 incidence direction
入射缝隙 entrance slit
入射辐射 incident radiation
入射光 incident [impinging] light
入射光强度 incident light intensity
入射光束发散度 divergence of incident beam
入射角 incidence [incident] angle, angle of arrival
入射能(量) incident energy
入射频率 incident frequency
入射平面 incident plane
入射声波 incident sound wave
入射线 incident ray
入射线发散度 divergence of incident radiation
入水口 water inlet
入选原煤 feed coal
入窑空气温度 incoming air temperature
入窑气流 furnace air flow
软 softness ◇使变~soften
软X射线机 soft X-ray machine
软γ射线检查装置 atomic X-ray machine
软暗盒 flexible cassette
软巴比合金(91Sn, 4.5Sb, 4.5Cu) soft babbitt alloy, Phoenix ◇霍伊特白色~*

软巴比轴承青铜(91Sn,4.5Sb,4.5Cu) soft babbitt bronze
软薄钢板 mild sheet steel
软铋矿 sillenite
软玻璃 soft glass
软超导体 soft super-conductor
软冲击 【金】soft impingement
软冲头 flexible [fluid] punch
软锤 soft hammer, dresser
软磁材料 soft magnetic material, magnetically soft material
软磁钢 soft magnetic steel, magnetically soft steel
软磁合金 soft magnetic alloy, magnetically soft alloy ◇ 奥索尼克~*,海穆80~*,卡喷特49~*,蒙尼马克斯~苏帕门杜尔~*
软磁盘 【计】diskette, floppy disc
软磁铁 soft magnet
软磁铁氧体 soft ferrite
软磁性合金 magnetically soft alloy ◇ 阿姆柯48~*,镍铁~nickel iron alloy
软磁性质 soft magnetic property
软淬火 mild quench
软带材 soft strip
软氮化 soft-nitriding, tufftriding ◇ 气体~过程*
软导管 flexible conduit
软碲铜矿 vulcanite, vulkanite
软点 soft spot
软垫 cushion, bolster
软垫填料[充填物] cushion fill
软电缆 flexible cable ◇ 橡皮绝缘~cab-tyre cable
软电线 cord
软度试验 softness test
软粉末(高熔点金属以外的金属粉末) soft powder
软风管 air hose
软钢(0.12—0.2C, <0.2Si, 0.3—0.5Mn, <0.05P, <0.05S) mild steel (m.s.), mild carbon steel, soft [quiet] steel ◇ 阿姆柯~Armco steel, 极~*, 较~*, 特种~*, 易切削~*
软钢板 (同《低碳钢板》)
软钢模 ductile die
软钢丝 stone (dead) wire ◇ 包铜~*, 捆扎用~*
软钢丝绳 flexible [fine] wire rope, flexible steel cable
软膏 paste
软管 hose (pipe), flexible pipe, hog ◇ 缠丝~*, 金属丝编织层~*, 制动~brake hose
软管冲洗 【环】hose flushing
软管冲洗水 hose-down stream
软管过滤器 hose filter
软管加长部分 hose extension
软管接头 hose union [coupling]
软管卷筒 hosedrum
软管联接套[接头] hose (coupling) nipple
软管连接 hose connection
软管喷砂 hose sandblast
软管式喷砂(清理)机 【铸】hose-type sandblast tank machine
软管线 hose line
软硅铜矿 bisbeeite
软焊料 solder metal, quick [slicken] solder ◇ 铅锡共晶(合金)~*,斯利卡铅锡~*
软焊料合金(70Sn, 30Pb; 63Sn, 37Pb; 50Sn, 50Pb) soft soldering alloy ◇ 罗斯~*
软焊料钎焊 soldering
软焊锡 soft solder
软合金 mild alloy, slush metal
软盒 flexible cassette
软化 softening, demineralization ◇ 表观~开始点*,几何图形~*,加工~work softening, 使~soften, 水的~mitigation, 形变加工~*
软化处理 softening treatment ◇ 焰炬加热~*

软化淬火 （同"负淬火"）
软化带 softening zone
软化点 softening point (soft. pt), sagging point
软化锅 softening kettle
软化回火 soft temper
软化剂 softener, softening agent
软化开始温度[软化起点] start-of-softening temperature (SST)
软化炉（铅精炼用） softening furnace, softener ◇连续～*
软化炉浮渣 softening furnace dross, softener slag
软化孪晶 softening twin
软化铅（脱除杂质的铅） softened lead
软(化)铅锭 softened lead bullion
软化水 demineralized [quality] water ◇未～raw water
软化特性 softening characteristics
软化退火 softening annealing, water toughening ◇连续式～*，中间～*
软化退火处理 mild annealing treatment
软化温度 softening temperature [point]
软化(温度)范围[区域] softening range [region]
软化效应[作用] softening effect
软化性状 softening behaviour
软化焰 soft flame
软化终点[终了温度] end of softening
软黄铜 low brass ◇拉弗里希尔～*
软击穿 soft breakdown
软机器钢 soft machinery steel (S.M.S.)
软件 【计】software ◇运算～operational software
软件包 software package
软件工程 software engineering
软件可靠性 software reliability
软件灵活性 software flexibility
软件适应性 adaptability of software
软件文件编制 software documentation
软结晶器 soft mould
软金属 soft metal

软金属层淀积法 【金】soft-facing
软浸焊 dip soldering
软晶体 soft crystal
软科学 soft science
软矿 gougy ore
软拉钢丝 soft [mild] drawn wire
软拉铜丝 soft-drawn copper wire
软粒喷砂 （同"无损喷砂"）
软沥青 soft pitch, maltha
软练法 【耐】soft-mud process
软煤 soft [easy] coal, minge
软锰矿{MnO_2} pyrolusite, black oxide of manganese
软模 flexible die, soft mode
软木(擦拭)夹（钢丝镀锌擦净用） cork press
软木衬垫 cork gasket
软木锯屑 softwood sawdust
软木(塞) cork (stopper)
软泥基中板桩排 【建】camp sheathing
软泥制坯法 【耐】soft-mud process
软抛光轮 【机】dolly
软片暗盒 cassette
软片赤道线（X射线衍射照相的） film equator
软片卷（照相用） cartridge
软片匣 film holder
软钎焊 soldering ◇浸渍～dip soldering
软钎焊管 soldering pipe
软钎焊合金（70Sn, 30Pb; 63Sn, 37Pb; 50Sn, 50Pb） soft soldering alloy ◇普通～*
软钎焊机 soldering machine
软钎焊接 soldered joint
软钎焊料合金[软钎料] solder(ing) alloy ◇普龙布索尔银锡～*
软铅 soft lead
软铅板 soft lead plate
软青铜 soft bronze
软韧性材料 soft ductile material
软熔 soft melt, low-melt, reflow, flow melting（镀锡），fusing（耐火材料的）◇

感应~处理 induction reflow
软熔操作（镀锡钢板的） reflow melting process
软熔带 softening and melting zone,【铁】cohesive (zone)
软熔法 thermal reflowing process
软熔发[光]亮处理 flash melting, (thermal) reflowing, flow brightening
软熔机组 reflow unit
软熔炉次 【钢】soft heat
软熔塔 reflow tower
软烧 soft burning
软烧石灰 soft burned lime
软砷铜矿 trippkeite
软渗氮 soft-nitriding
软渗氮法 tufftriding [tenifer] precess
软渗碳 【金】mild carburizing
软刷 soft brush
软水 soft(ened) [demineralizing] water
软水闭路强制循环冷却系统 forced close cycled soft water cooling system
软水泵房 soft water pump house
软水高位槽 soft water header tank
软水剂 (water) softener
软水密闭循环冷却系统 closed loop soft water cooling system ◇ 高炉~·
软水砂 ("同人造沸石")
软水系统 soft water circuit
软水站 water softening station
软铁 soft [moving] iron
软铁氧体 soft ferrite
软头锤 soft hammer
软退火 soft-annealing
软外壳 bladder
软纤维芯（钢丝绳的） soft fibre core
软线 cord, flexible wire [cord, conductor] ◇ 加热用~ heating cord, 橡皮绝缘~ cab-tyre cord
软像 soft image
软芯棒 (同"可变形芯棒")
软芯锭挤压（钨粉的） ductile-core extrusion

软性部分（如 X 射线、γ 射线、宇宙射线等） soft component
软性电缆 flexible cable
软性辐射 soft [low-energy] radiation
软性钢索 flexible wire cable
软页岩 coaly rashings
软玉 greenstone, kidney stone
软照相底片[负片] 【理】soft negative
软脂酸 （同"棕榈酸"）
软制处理 cutback treatment
软质磨料 soft [mild] abrasives
软质黏土 fat clay
软轴 flexible shaft [axle]
软轴套 flexible shaft protecting hose
软轴用钢丝 flexible shaft wire
软铸铁 soft cast iron (SCI)
软铸轧辊 【压】sand roll
软撞击 【金】soft impingement
朊 protein
瑞典(海绵)铁粉 Swedish Hoeganas powder, Swedish (iron) powder
瑞典还原海绵铁粉 Vogt powder
瑞典(木炭)生铁 Swedish pig iron
瑞典式竖炉 【团】Swedish-type shaft furnace
瑞典自动轧管机 Swedish mill
瑞利表面波 Rayleigh surface wave
瑞利散射截面 Rayleigh cross section
锐边孔板 sharp edged orifice plate
锐边衍射 knife-edge diffraction
锐度 sharpness
锐方向性射束 pencil beam
锐角 acute angle
锐角平分线 acute bisectrix
锐角切口薄板试样 sharp edge notched sheet specimen
锐角切口拉伸强度 sharp edge notch tensile strength
锐角效应 【金】corner effect
锐聚焦反射 sharply focused reflections
锐孔板 orifice plate
锐孔流量[流速]计 orifice meter

锐孔洗涤机[器]　orifice washer
锐面　spiky surface
锐曲线　sharp [steep] curve
锐钛矿{TiO$_2$}　octahedrite, anatase, xanthitane, xanthotitanite
锐线 X 射线图样[照相]　【理】sharp-line (X-ray) pattern
锐线系　【理】sharp series
锐转接头　sharp bend
锐最大值　sharp [acute] maximum
润滑　lubrication, oiling ◇ 集中～*，加工～的 oily
润滑材料　lubricant
润滑残渣　lubricating residuals
润滑处理（锻模的）　swabbing
润滑点　oil site
润滑垫　【压】cleaning plate
润滑工　greaser, oiler
润滑供油　lubricant feed
润滑(沟)槽　lubricating groove
润滑管线图　lubricating oil piping diagram
润滑规程　lubrication instruction
润滑环　drip ring
润滑挤压　lubrication extrusion
润滑剂　lubricant, oil, fat, antifriction material,【钢】coating mixture（钢锭模的）◇ 半固体状～ semisolid lubricant, 挤压～【压】bonderlube, 切削～ cutting compound, 湿拉拔用复合～ wet-drawing compound, 压力铸造用～ die-casting lubricant
润滑剂给进指示器　sight feed gauge
润滑剂碳黑（退火带材的）　carbon smut
润滑膜　lubricating film
润滑能力　lubricating ability, lubricity
润滑器　lubricator, greaser
润滑套管　【机】lubrication quill
润滑系统　lubrication [lubricating] system
润滑系统地下室　oil cellar
润滑性　lubricating property, lubricity, oiliness
润滑液　lubricating fluid

润滑引带剂（拔丝的）　lubricant carrier
润滑油　lubricating [lube, smoothing] oil, lubricant ◇ 冷轧～ rolling oil, 制砖用～ brick oil, 中央～系统*
润滑油垫　oiling pad
润滑油分类　grading of lubricating oils
润滑油管道　supply line
润滑油管路　lubrication piping
润滑油环[圈]　lubricating [oil(ing)] ring
润滑油冷却系统　oil cooling system
润滑油膜　lubricant film
润滑油箱[润滑剂贮存箱]　lubricant container
润滑油压入器　lubricating press
润滑油氧化　oil ageing
润滑油再生系统　oil reclamation [recovery] system
润滑油站　oil station
润滑油脂　fat
润滑油渍（钢板上的）　lubricant residue
润滑皂（金属拉拔用）　soft soap
润滑轧制　tribology
润滑站　lubrication station
润滑脂　(lubricating) grease, consistent grease [fat] ◇ 减摩～ antifriction grease, 重载荷～*
润滑脂槽　grease tank
润滑脂盒　grease box
润滑脂量控制器　grease quantity controller
润滑脂流路图　lubricant-flow scheme
润滑脂润滑　grease lubrication
润滑脂－石墨混合物　grease-graphite mixture
润滑脂箱　grease pocket
润滑脂注嘴　grease nipple
润滑锥（模孔分）　【压】die entrance angle
润滑作用　lubrication (action), smearing effect
润磨机　damp mill
润湿　moisten(ing), wetting, humidification, spreading（液体对固体的），【铸】

watering	(型砂的)
润湿带	wet zone
润湿等温线	wetting isotherm
润湿剂	wetting agent
润湿能力	wetting power, wettability
润湿器	moistener, damper
润湿热法	heat of wetting method
润湿室	moisture chamber
润湿性	water affinity, wettability
润湿作用	wetting action
弱氨水	poor ammonia water, weak ammoniacal liquor
弱场	weak [feeble] field
弱穿透性辐射	soft radiation
弱磁材料[物料]	weakly [feebly] magnetic material
弱磁场	weak magnetic field, low-intensity magnetic field
弱磁性矿石	feebly magnetic (ore)
弱磁选	low-intensity magnetic separation
弱电解质	weak electrolyte
弱度	weakness
弱反差图像	soft image
弱反射镀[涂]层	low-reflecting coating
弱沸腾	【钢】light-boiling
弱风(量)	slack [low] wind
弱功率电路	dry circuit
弱含水层	low water-bearing formation
弱还原剂	mild reducing agent
弱还原气氛	slightly [weakly] reducing atmosphere
弱还原条件	slightly reducing conditions
弱碱	weak base
弱碱废水	weak alkali waste water
弱碱性反应	faintly alkaline reaction
弱碱性离子交换树脂	weak-base ion-exchange resin
弱碱性树脂	weakly basic resin
弱碱性阴离子交换剂	weak base anion exchanger
弱碱性阴离子交换树脂	weak (base) anion-exchange resin ◇ WBR ~ Nalcite WBR, 道克斯 3(弱碱性)~Dowex 3, 杜利特~*, 卢泰特 M_1~Lewatit M_1, 沃法泰特 M~Wofatit M, 珀缪泰特 W~Permutit W
弱碱性阴离子交换树脂 E	De-Acidite E
弱碱性阴离子交换树脂 G	De-Acidite G
弱键	weak bond
弱结合	weak binding
弱浸出液	weak leaching liquid
弱聚焦	weak focusing
弱煤气	weak gas
弱煤气冷凝氨水	【焦】weak gas liquor
弱面	weaker plane, plane of weakness
弱黏结性煤	weak [feebly] caking coal
弱黏性黏土	lean clay
弱耦合	loose coupling
弱强度	weak intensity
弱溶[弱乳化液]废水(管道)	weak soluble waste water (WSWW)
弱烧成微粒	light-fired particle
弱渗碳剂	milder carburizer
弱渗碳剂渗碳	(同"软渗碳")
弱渗碳气氛	slightly carburizing atmosphere
弱束缚电子	loosely bound electron
弱酸	weak acid
弱酸废水(管道)	weak acid waste water (WAWW)
弱酸浸出	weak acid leach
弱酸(性)介质	weak acid medium
弱酸性溶液	slightly acid solution, weakly acidic solution
弱酸性阳离子交换剂	weakly acidic cation exchanger
弱酸性阳离子交换树脂	weak-acid cation-exchange resin
弱线(X射线中的)	weak line
弱相互作用	slight [weak] interaction

弱氧化 slight oxidation
弱氧化性气氛 weakly oxidizing atmosphere

S s

撒布器　dispenser, spreader
撒发热剂　hot topping
撒(盖)粉(剂)　(防止金属液面氧化) dusting (powder)
撒灰装置　【耐】dusting device
撒焦器　coke booster
撒拉萨尔铝合金　(2.25Mg, 2.5Mn, <0.2Sb,余量 Al) Thalassal
撒料　【团】dribble
撒料机　spreader
洒扫水　【环】cleanup water
洒水　sprinkling, watering
洒水冷却装置　【金】dripping cooling plant
洒水器　sprinkler, rose
洒水(式)冷却　water-sprinkled cooling ◇ 外部～
洒水养护的混凝土　water cured concrete
萨顿镁合金表面黑色皮膜处理法　Sutton process
萨尔茨吉特鲕褐铁矿　salzgitter ore
萨尔瓦克泵叶铅青铜　(87Cu, 0.1Pb, 0.6P,余量 Sn) Salvak bronze
萨尔泽尔锌基轴承合金　(10Sn, 4Cu, 1Pb, 余量 Zn) Sulzer's alloy
萨克管状浇口　saxophone gate
萨克史密斯圆环[磁力测定]天平　Sucksmith's balance
萨克索尼亚锌基轴承合金　(5Sn, 6Cu, 3Pb, 0.2Al,余量 Zn) Saxonia metal
萨拉铝合金　thalassal
萨马洛依耐热耐蚀铁镍合金　Thermally
萨美诺尔铁素体耐热钢　(16—18Al, 2Mo, 0.3V,余量 Fe) Thermenol
萨默特轴承青铜　(17—30Pb, 0—5Sn, 余量 Cu) Sumet bronze
萨姆高强度铸造黄铜　(83Cu, 10Zn, 5Si, 1Mn, 1Al) Sambrass
萨尼特脱硫法　【钢】Saniter process
萨特科铅基轴承合金　(1—2.5Sn, 0.05—0.6Ca, 0—0.25Hg, 95.5—98Pb 及微量 Al、Mg、K、Li 等) Satco metal
萨瓦德-李型喷嘴　Savard-Lee injector
腮片散热器　gilled radiator
塞棒　【钢】stopper, column of sagger (耐火黏土的) ◇ 风动渣口～*,机械式～ mechanical stopper, 空冷～ air-cooled stopper, 自动～机 autopour
塞棒安装室　restoppering station
塞棒操纵的中间包　stoppered tundish
塞棒淬火　【金】plug quenching
塞棒动作齿条　stopper rack
塞棒干燥　stopper drying
塞棒干燥炉　stopper drying stove, stopper-rod drying oven
塞棒关严　dry shut-off
塞棒横臂[横梁]　cross arm
塞棒机构　sliding bar, locking device
塞棒(可调)式中间包　stopper controlled tundish
塞棒控制　stopper control
塞棒(-塞座)式钢包[铸钢桶]　stopper(-nozzle) ladle, stoppered ladle
塞棒升降器　lifting gear
塞棒试验　【压】drift test
塞棒试验机　【压】drifter
塞棒损坏漏钢　running stopper
塞棒台架　stopper table
塞棒提升设备　stopper lifting device
塞棒(铁)芯　stopper-rod ◇ 空冷～*,水冷～*
塞棒头　stopper head
塞棒推杆[推进器]　plug-rod pusher
塞棒中心钢棒　central steel rod
塞棒砖　stopper brick
塞棒装置　stopper-rod assembly
塞棒座砖　stopper runner
塞槽焊接　plug and slot welding
塞尺　feeler [clearance] gauge, examiner
塞德拉菲特耐蚀合金　(63Fe, 23Ni, 5Cu, 5Al, 4W) Sideraphite
塞垫　plug cushion

塞垫技术(爆炸成形用) plug cushion technique
塞缝集料 key aggregate
塞弗特铝用焊料(21Zn,73Sn,5Pb) Seifert's solder
塞格尔流动性螺旋样模 【冶】saeger spiral
塞格锥 Seger cone
塞规 plug [male, feeler] gauge ◇ 基准校对~*,界限[极限]~ limit plug gauge
塞焊 plug welding
塞焊焊缝 filled plug weld
塞孔 jack, consent, pin hole, plug socket ◇ 桥接[并联]~ bridging jack
塞孔触点 female contact
塞孔簧片(排) jack strip
塞拉卢明铸造铝合金(1—3Cu,1—2Si,0.3—1.5Fe,0.1—1.0Mg,0.05—0.3Nb,余量 Al) Ceralumin
塞拉斯加热炉 Selas heating furnace
塞莱克特龙变形镁合金(2—3Zn,1—4Cd,0—2Ca,余量 Mg) Selektron
塞勒吉锌基轴承合金(10Sn,1P,4Cu,余量 Zn) Salge metal
塞隆 sialon
塞隆粉 sialon powder
塞隆陶瓷 sialon ceramics
塞罗贝斯铋铅共晶[易熔]合金(44.5Pb,余量 Bi;熔点124℃) Cerrobase
塞罗本德铋锡镉易熔合金(50Bi,27Pb,13Sn,10Cd;熔点70℃) Cerrobend
塞罗洛伊易熔合金 Cerroloy
塞罗马格铁氧体 Cerromag
塞罗马特里克斯铋铅锡锑易熔合金(48Bi,28.5Pb,14.5Sn,9Sb;熔点102—227℃) Cerromatrix
塞罗特鲁铋锡共晶[易熔]合金(58Bi,42Sn;熔点138.5℃) Cerrotru
塞罗西尔易熔合金 Cerroseal
塞罗铋最低熔合金 Cerro
塞曼－玻林 X 射线聚焦照相法 Seeman-Bohlin method

塞曼－玻林型照相机 Seeman-Bohlin(-type) camera
塞曼－玻林型照相机 X 射线光学装置 X-ray optics of Seeman-Bohlin type camera
塞曼 X 射线结晶分析法 Zeeman(n) method
塞曼分离 【理】Zeeman(n) separation
塞曼效应 【理】Zeeman(n) effect
塞美－索威式焦炉 Semet-Solvay oven
塞门杜尔钴铁簧片合金(50Co,50Fe) Semendur
塞浦里提克铬铜耐蚀钢(约含15Cr,9Cu) Cypritic steel
塞绳 (jack, flexible) cord
塞头 chock plug, end cap, column of sagger(耐火黏土的),【钢】stopper plug [head, crown] ◇ 水冷~ water-cooled stopper
塞头机(带材卷筒的) wrapping machine
塞头栓[销] 【钢】stopper pin
塞头砖 stopper (crown),【耐】head ◇ 黏土~【冶】clay plug,球顶~*
塞维斯 D 轻载式巴比合金(65 或 75Sn,12 或 15Sb,10 或 18Pb,2 或 3Cu) service D babbitt
塞袖砖 stopper brick
塞子 plug, stopper, tap, spig(g)ot
噻吩甲酰三氟丙酮分离(锆铪分离) thenoyltrifluoroacetone (TTA) separation
赛白金 platinite
赛贝尔搅拌式萃取塔 Scheibel column
赛波特比色计 Saybolt chromometer
赛波特通用黏度(单位为秒) Saybolt universal viscosity
赛波特通用黏度计 Saybolt universal viscosimeter
赛波特重油黏度计 Saybolt-furol viscometer
赛达铝(锌)合金 cetal
赛尔卡铝合金 sylcum
赛金刚青铜(88Cu,10Al,2Si) diamond

bronze
赛金刚石合金　diamondite
赛克尔 L 镍铬钢　Circle L（例 Circle L13：13Cr，＜0.25C，0.75Mn，＜0.75Ni,0.4Mo）
赛洛克斯砷碱脱硫法　Thylox process
赛茹尔内热挤压法　Sejournet extrusion process
赛璐珞被覆电极　cellulose-covered electrode
三－2－乙基己基胺　tri-2-ethglhexgl amine
三－3,5,5－三甲基－己基胺　tri－(3,5,5－trimethylhexyl) amine
三胺基　triamine
三胺溶液　triamine solution
三八面体　trioctahedron
三班操作　three shift operation
三班工作［作业］制　three-shift (work day) system
三瓣式戽斗挖土机　orange-peel excavator
三半径椭圆　three-radius oval
三倍精度　【计】triple precision
三倍字长工作　【计】triple length working
三臂钢包炉　three-arm ladle furnace
三臂开卷机　【压】three-arm payoff reel
三臂无点承坯架　wedge-stilt
三臂卸卷机　【压】three-arm unloader
三变平衡　tervariant equilibrium
三表量规　3-dial gauge
三层板　triplex sheet
三层镀镍法　three layers nickel plating
三层钢板(犁铧用)　three-ply plate
三层钢锭　【钢】three-ply ingot
三层金属复合轴瓦合金　three layers bearing
三层金属轴承合金　trimetal
三层卷焊管　triple wall brazed tube
三层式（电解精炼）炉　【色】three-storied furnace
三层式洗涤分级机　three-deck washing classifier

三层(液)法铝精炼电解槽　three-layer aluminium electrolytic cell
三层液铝电解精炼　three-layer aluminium electrolytic refinement
三层液铝电解精炼法　three-layer (electrolytic) process ◇胡普斯～*
三岔斜辊辊道　skew-Y-table
三沉淀场式电除［收］尘器　【冶】three-field-type precipitator
三承三通　three bell tee
三重对称　triod symmetry
三重回收　triple withdrawal
三重回收区域精炼炉　triple withdrawal refiner
三重简并［退化］　triply degenarate
三重线态　triplet state
三重线相互作用　triplet interaction
三重轴　tertiary［three-fold］axis, triad (axis)
三次处理机　triple processor
三次镀镍　tri-nickel plating
三次对称轴　trial axis
三次函数［方程式,曲线］　cubic
三次回火　triple tempering
三次混合机　tertiary mixer
三次晶轴　tertiary axis
三次空气　tertiary air
三次拉拔的钢丝　three-draught wire
三次平移　tertiary translation
三次弯曲式除［破］鳞机　triple processor
三次渗碳体　tertiary cementite
三次收缩模　【铸】grand-master pattern
三次弯曲式除［破］鳞机　triple processor
三次谐波　third［triple-frequency］harmonic
三次轴　three-fold axis
三带加热炉　triple-fired furnace
三代的　tribasic
三岛高矫顽力永磁合金　Mishima alloy
三碘化钐{SmI$_3$}　samarium triiodide
三碘化砷　arsenic triiodide
三碘化铊{TlI$_3$}　thallic iodide

三碘化钛	titanium triiodide
三碘化物	triiodide
三碘化铟{InI$_3$}	indium triiodide
三点测定法（镀锌附着量的）	triple-spot test
三点分级	three-point step
三点加载法（弯曲试验的）	three-point loading
三点加载缺口弯曲试样	notch bend three point loading specimen
三点探(针)头	three-point probe head
三点弯曲(法)	three-point bending
三点弯曲试验	three-point bending test
三点悬置	three-point suspension
三点载荷弯曲试验	bending test under three point loading
三电极 CO 气体检测报警仪	CO gas detecting and alarming meter with three electrodes
三电极盐浴炉	three-electrode salt-bath furnace
三电技术改造	technical reformation of computer, instrumentation and electrical drive system
三电一体化	EIC integration
三电子键	three-electron bond
三丁基膦化氧（TBPO）	tributyl phosphine oxide
三丁基氧化锡	tributyltin oxide
三动压力机[冲床]	triple-action press
三度空间对称	three-dimensional symmetry
三度空间结构	three-dimensional structure
三度空间模型【理】	three-dimensional model
三度空间切削【机】	three-dimensional cutting, oblique cutting
三度空间运动	spatial motion
三度平衡	tervariant equilibrium
三度性	triaxiality
三段操作	three-stage operation
三段磁选	three-stage magnetic separation
三段破碎	three-stage crushing
三段破碎机	tertiary crusher
三段区域精炼炉	three-stage refiner
三段曲线矫直法【连铸】	three-piece of curve straightening method
三段烧结	three-stage sintering
三段式加热炉	three-zone fired furnace, triple-fired furnace
三段式连续加热炉	triple-fired reheating furnace
三段式链算机	three-pass grate
三段台车	three-piece pallet
三对角线矩阵算法	tridiagonal-matrix algorithm
三垛式炉台	three-pedestal base
三方晶系	trigonal (crystal) system
三方晶轴	trigonal axis
三方硫砷银矿	trechmannite
三方硫碳铅石	susannite
三方硫锡矿	berndtite
三方氯铜矿	paratacamite
三方硼砂	tincalconite
三方闪锌矿	matraite
三方水硼镁石	macallisterite
三方硒镍矿	makinenite
三方系结构	trigonal structure
三废	production waste(s), three major polluting wastes
三废综合利用产品产值	output value of three-waste comprehensive utilization
三分度圆测角仪	three-circle goniometer
三分之一标准砖	two-cut brick
三氟丙酮	trifluoroacetone
三氟醋酸盐[酯]	trifluoroacetate
三氟醋酸乙酯{CF$_3$COOC$_2$H$_5$}	ethyltrifluoroacetate
三氟化铋{BiF$_3$}	bismuth fluoride
三氟化钚{PuF$_3$}	plutonium trifluoride
三氟化钴	cobalt trifluoride
三氟化铈{CeF$_3$}	cerous fluoride
三氟化铊{TlF$_3$}	thallic fluoride

三氟化钛　titanium trifluoride
三氟化钨{WF₃}　tungsten trifluoride
三氟化物　trifluoride
三氟化铟{InF₃}　indium trifluoride
三氟氧化磷　(同"磷酰氟")
三氟氧化铌{NbOF₃}　niobium oxytrifluoride
三氟氧化物　oxytrifluoride
三氟乙酰丙酮{CF₃·(CH₃CO)₂CH₂}　trifluoro-acetylacetone
三钙(盐)　tricalcium
三甘醇{(HOCH₂CH₂OCH₂)₂}　triethylene-glycol, triglycol
三甘醇化二氯　triglycol dichloride
三鼓式余[废]热锅炉　three-drum waste heat boiler
三股分配斜槽　three-way distributing chute
三硅酸镁　magnesium trisilicate
三硅酸盐{2MO·3SiO₂}　trisilicate
三轨重力辊式运输机　three-rail gravity roller conveyer
三癸基膦化氧　tri-n-decyl phosphine oxide
三辊成形机　three-roll forming machine
三辊钢坯轧机　three-high billet mill
三辊机组　three-roll [3-roll] block
三辊矫直机　three-roll unbender
三辊可逆式机座　three-high reversing stand
三辊劳特式中厚钢板轧机　three-high Lauth plate mill
三辊联合穿轧机　three roll piercing and rolling combined tube mill
三辊式齿轮座　three-high pinion stand
三辊式初轧机　three-high blooming mill
三辊式初轧机组　three-high blooming train
三辊(式)穿孔机　three-roll piercer, three-roll piercing mill
三辊式粗轧　three-high roughing mill
三辊式粗轧机组　three-high roughing (mill) train
三辊式粗轧机　three-high roughing mill
三辊(式)钢板轧机　three-high plate mill
三辊(式)机座　【压】three-high (rolling) stand, three-high mill ◇ 跳式～"
三辊式精轧机组　three-high finishing train
三辊式精轧机座　three-high finishing stand
三辊式卷取机　three-roll-type coiler
三辊式开坯机　three-high cogging [blooming] mill
三辊式开坯机组　three-high cogging mill train
三辊式配置　【压】three-high arrangement
三辊式型钢轧机　three-high shape mill, three-high jobbing mill
三辊式轧管[辗轧]机　Assel mill [elongator]
三辊(式)轧机　three-high (rolling) mill, trio mill
三辊式轧机机架　three-high housing
三辊式轧机机座　three-high mill stand
三辊式中厚板轧机组　three-high plate mill train
三辊弯曲机　three-roll bender, three-roll bending machine
三辊万能式轧机　three-high universal mill
三辊斜轧机　three roll cross mill
三合土　tabia ◇ 轻石灰～"
三弧法(成品圆孔)　【压】three-plug method
三混煤气　dreigas
三机座轧机　three-stand mill
三极电(弧熔炼)炉　three-electrode furnace
三极管　triode ◇ 充气～gastriode
三极检波管　audion
三极一线排列电弧熔炼炉　three-electrode-in-line furnace
三极闸刀开关　three-pole knife
三极真空管　pliotron, triode valve
三级串联捻股机　triple tandem strander

三级反应 third order reaction
三级混合沉降器 three-stage mixer-settler
三级金属油扩散泵 three-stage metal pump
三级蒸馏 three-stage distillation
三甲胺{N(CH₃)₃} trimethylamine
三甲基苯 trimethyl-benzene
三甲基金属{M(CH₃)₃} trimethide
三甲基壬醇 trimethyl nonanol
三甲铵氢氧基{-N(CH₃)₃OH} trimethyl ammonium hydroxide group
三甲胂 trimethylarsine
三甲铊{Tl(CH₃)₃} thallium methide [methyl]
三价 trivalence, trivalency
三价锕系元素 trivalent actinide
三价二价铁的 ferriferous
三价钴的 cobaltic
三价基 triad
三价镓化合物 gallic compound
三价金 trivalent gold
三价金属 trivalent metal
三价磷的 phosphorous
三价钼的 molybdenic, molybdic (钼盐)
三价铌化合物 niobous [columbous] compound
三价镍(的) nickelic
三价钐化合物 samaric compound
三价铈化合物 cerous compound
三价铊的 thallic
三价态 tervalent state
三价钛 trivalent titanium
三价钛的 titanous
三价钽的 tantalous
三价锑的 antimonious, antimonous, stibious, stibnous
三价铁的 ferric
三价铁离子 ferric ion
三价元素[原子] triad
三价钇的 yttric
三尖棱型钢 tripod shape
三铰拱 three-hinged arch

三铰构架式桁架 barn truss
三脚架 tripod (leg)
三脚结构 tripod structure ◇ 扎帕塔式 ~*
三脚起重机 gin
三角 triangle, delta
三角测量 triangulation
三角钉 crowfoot
三角断面 triangular section
三角股钢丝绳 triangular strand wire rope
三角函数 trigonometric function
三角基座 tribrach
三角架 tripod, brandreth ◇ 伸缩~ extension tripod
三角精轧孔型(Y形轧机的) triangular finishing pass
三角联结 【电】trianglular configuration
三角裂口 chevroning
三角皮带 【机】V-drive [cogged, wedge] belt, V-belt
三角皮带传动 V-belt drive
三角皮带轮 V-pulley, V-belt [grooved] pulley
三角皮带用钢丝帘布 steel cord for V-belt
三角-三角接线(法) delta-delta connection
三角台 tripod, tribrach
三角屋架 collar roof
三角系点阵 trigonal lattice
三角系晶胞 trigonal cell
三角系晶体 trigonal crystal
三角系组织[结构] trigonal structure
三角芯股芯丝 triangle core wire
三角-星形连接(法) 【电】delta-star connection
三角型材[型钢] 【压】triangular section [shape], three square
三角形 triangle, delta ◇ 吉布斯~ Gibbs triangle, 秃尖~*
三角形对称 trigonal symmetry
三角形股(绳的) triangle strand

三角形接线 delta (connection) ◇ 开口~*
三角形接线法 delta connection
三角形图解 triangular diagram
三角学因数 trigonometrical factor
三阶段法 【冶】three-stage process
三金刚石整修工具 triple diamond dressing tool
三金属 trimetal
三金属带材 tri-metallic strip
三金属带轧制装置 arrangement for folling tri-metallic strip
三进制的 【数】ternary
三进制数位 【计】trit
三晶粒接点处破裂 triple-point cracking
三晶粒接点裂纹 triple-point crack
三晶形金属 trimorphous metal
三晶形元素 trimorphous element
三井湿式接触系统 Mitsui's wet contact system
三聚氰酰胺{$C_3H_3(NH_2)_3$} cyanuramide, molamine
三聚盐 triple salt
三聚乙醛{$(C_2H_4O)_3$} paraldehyde
三开砂箱 three-part flask
三开芯盒 three-piece core box
三孔滑车 deadeye
三孔拉瓦尔氧枪 three-apertured Laval lance
三棱钩头钉 bayonet shaped spike
三棱刮刀 three-cornered scraper, striking knife
三联的 triple
三联方坯结晶器 【连铸】triple-square multi-mould
三联(炼钢)[三炉联炼]法 triplex-process, triplexing, three-furnace process
三联熔炼 triplex melting
三料钟 【铁】three bell
三料钟装料[作业] three-bell operation
三菱吹炼炉 Mitsubishi converter
三菱法 Mitsubishi process

三菱连续熔炼-吹炼法 Mitsubishi continuous smelting and converting process
三菱贝氏体低合金高强度钢 MB (Mitsubishi bainite) steel
三菱铝铸铁 Alsiron
三硫化二钼{Mo_2S_3} molybdic sulphide, molybdenum hemitrisulphide
三硫化二铯{Cs_2S_3} cesium trisulphide
三硫化二砷 arsenic trisulphide
三硫化二铊{Tl_2S_3} thallic sulphide
三硫化二锑 antimonous sulphide
三硫化二物 sesquisulphide, hemitrisulphide
三硫化二铟{In_2S_3} indium trisulphide
三硫化钼{MoS_3} molybdenum trisulphide
三硫化钨{WS_3} tungsten trisulphide
三硫化物 trisulphide
三硫酸盐 trisulphate
三硫氧钨酸盐 oxytrisulfotungstate
三流连铸机 three strand machine
三卤化物 trihalide
三路布料斜槽 (同"三股分配斜槽")
三氯代乙烯系统表面精饰涂层法 trichlorethylene finishing system method (TFSM)
三氯硅烷 trichloro-silicane
三氯化钒 vanadium trichloride
三氯化锆{$ZrCl_3$} zirconium trichloride
三氯化合物 terchloride
三氯化镓{$GaCl_3$} gallium trichloride
三氯化铼{$ReCl_3$} rhenium trichloride
三氯化磷{PCl_3} phosphorous trichloride
三氯化铝{$AlCl_3$} alchlor, aluminium trichloride
三氯化钼{$MoCl_3$} molybdic chloride, molybdenum trichloride
三氯化铌{$NbCl_3$} niobium trichloride, niobous chloride
三氯化硼 boron trichloride
三氯化钐{$SmCl_3$} samarium trichloride
三氯化砷 arsenic trichloride
三氯化铈{$CeCl_3$} cerium trichloride, ce-

rous chloride
三氯化铊 {TlCl₃}　thallic chloride
三氯化钛 {TiCl₃}　titanium trichloride
三氯化钽 {TaCl₃}　tantalous chloride, tantalum trichloride
三氯化铁 {FeCl₃}　ferric [iron] chloride
三氯化铁催化剂　ferric chloride catalyst
三氯化钨 {WCl₃}　tungsten trichloride
三氯化物　trichloride
三氯化物还原　trichloride reduction
三氯化稀土 {RECl₃}　rare earth trichloride
三氯化氧钼 {(MoO)Cl₃}　molybdenyl trichloride
三氯化铟 {InCl₃}　indium trichloride
三氯化铀 {UCl₃}　uranium trichloride
三氯甲烷 {CHCl₃}　trichloromethane, chloroform ◇ 铜铁试剂～萃取法*
三氯甲锗烷 {GeHCl₃}　germanium chloroform
三氯羟氧钼 {[(MoO)(OH)]Cl₃}　molybdenum oxyhydroxytrichloride
三氯氧钒　vanadium oxytrichloride
三氯氧化磷　(同"磷酰氯")
三氯氧化铌 {NbOCl₃}　niobium oxytrichloride
三氯乙烷　trichloro-ethane
三氯乙烯 {C₂HCl₃}　trichlorethylene, triclene
三氯乙烯铸造法　【铸】X-process
三醚　triether
三七黄铜　(同"七〇黄铜")
三氢化镧　lanthanum hydride
三氢化砷　arsenous hydride
三氢锗基　germyl
三壬胺　trinonylamine
三刃刮刀　three-cornered scraper
三熔锭　triple-melted ingot
三软管式割把　three-hose (gas) cutter
三软管式熔切器　three-hose cutting burner
三色硫细菌属　thiophysa
三色式红外线水分计　three-colour infrared moisture meter
三生渗碳体　tertiary cementite
三室式链算机　【团】three-chamber type grate
三室式链算机循环　three-pass grate cycle
三输入端加法器　【计】three input adder
三水合物　trihydrate
三水合氧化铝　alumina trihydrate
三水胶铝矿　gibbsitogelite
三水菱镁矿　nesquechonite
三水铝矿 {Al(OH)₃ 或 Al₂O₃·3H₂O}　gibbsite
三水铝石　(同"水铝矿")
三水铝石型铝土矿　trihydrate bauxite, gibbsitic bauxite ◇ 含磷酸盐的～phosphatic gibbsitic bauxite
三水铝石型铝土矿溶出　trihydrate bauxite digestion
三水氧化铝　(同"氢氧化铝")
三态逻辑电路　【计】tri-state logic (TSL)
三碳酸双氧铀 {UO₂(CO₃)₃}　uranyl tricarbonate
三碳酸盐　tricarbonate
三碳酸铀酰 {UO₂(CO₃)₃}　uranyl tricarbonate (UTC)
三体装配式台车　three-piece pallet
三烃[烷]基　trialkyl
三烃基磺化氯　trialkylsulphonium chloride
三烃基磺化物　trialkylsulphonium compound
三烃基甲基　trialky lmethyl
三烃基膦化氧 {R₃PO}　(trialkyl) phosphine oxide
三烃基砷　trialkyl-arsine
三通阀　three-way valve
三通管　three-way pipe [connection, piece], T-tube, (pipe) tee, tee pipe (connector)
三通管接头　three-way connection, T-joint
三通换向旋塞　three-way reversing cock
三通式热风炉　three-pass (hot) stove, centre combustion stove

三通旋塞　three-way (stop) cock, 3-way stopper
三通辙叉　crotch frog
三通砖　deflecting block
三烷基胺{R₃N}　trialkyl amine
三维布置　three-dimensional array
三维场　three-dimensional field
三维点阵[晶格]　three-dimensional lattice, trigonal dimensional lattice
三维点阵结构　three-dimensional lattice structure
三维对称　three-dimensional symmetry
三维固体　three-dimensional solid
三维光栅　three-dimensional grating
三维结构　three-dimensional structure
三维空间　three-dimensional space
三维空间传热　three-dimensional heat flow
三维空间流　three-dimensional flow
三维模型　【理】three-dimensional model
三维凝固　three-dimensional solidification
三维凝固壳厚度分布　3-dimensional distribution solidifying shell thickness
三维切削　【机】three-dimensional cutting, oblique cutting
三维塑性变形模型　3 dimensional plasticity deformation model
三维弹塑性边界元法　3 dimensional elastoplastic boundary element method
三维物体　three-dimensional body
三维性　triaxiality
三维衍射图[花样]　three-dimensional diffraction pattern
三维液流　3-D fluid flow
三维有限元法　three dimensional finite element method
三维有限元理论　three-dimensional finite element theory
三维坐标系　three-dimensional coordinate system
三位阀　three-position valve
三温区扩散炉　three-zone furnace

三线补偿器　three-wire compensator
三线式棒材轧机　three-strand rod mill
三线式发电机　three-wire [Dobrowolsky] generator
三线式拉管机　triple tube drawbench
三线式型钢轧机　three-strand rod mill
三线相互作用　triplet interaction
三线制　three-wire system
三相　triphase, three-phase
三相变压器　three-phase transformer
三相[态]点（水的）　(water) triple point
三相电弧焊　three-phase (arc) welding ◇ 手工～*
三相电弧炉　three-phase arc furnace, Heroult (electric) arc furnace
三相电流　three-phase current
三相电炉　three-phase furnace ◇ 韦布～【冶】Webb furnace, 沃尔塔～【钢】Volta furnace
三相电路　three-phase circuit
三相电桥　three-phase bridge
三相电压　three-phase voltage
三相电源　three-phase supply
三相钢　three-phase steel
三相功率因数计　three-phase power factor meter
三相供电　three-phase supply
三相合金　three-phase alloy
三相(交流)电动机　three-phase (current) motor
三相交流发电机　three-phase alternator
三相平衡　three-phase equilibrium ◇ 第一类～*
三相区　three-phase field
三相曲线　triple curve
三相熔矿炉　three-phase ore-smelting furnace
三相四线制　three-phase four-wire system
三相同步感应电动机　three-phase synchronous induction motor
三相制[系]　three-phase system
三相状态　three-phase(d) condition

三向法　axonometry
三向刮路机　three-way drag
三向图　axonometric projection
三向弯管　three-way pipe
三向压力　triaxial pressure
三向压制　three-dimensional compaction
三向应力　triaxial stress
三硝基甲苯　trinitrotoluene(TNT)
三硝基甲烷 {(NO$_2$)$_3$CH}　trinitromethane, nitroform
三效蒸发器　triple-effect evaporator
三斜点阵[晶格]　triclinic [anorthic] lattice
三斜对称　triclinic symmetry
三斜晶胞　triclinic cell
三斜晶系　triclinic (system)
三斜磷锌矿　tarbuttite
三斜石 {BeMnSiO$_4$}　trimerite
三斜(系)晶体　triclinic crystal
三斜组织[三斜系结构]　triclinic structure
三芯电缆　triple(x) cable, three-core cable
三辛胺　trioctylamine, tri-n-octyl amine
三辛基䏲化氧 {(C$_8$H$_{17}$)$_3$PO}　tri-n-octylphosphine oxide
三心拱　basket handle arch
三型板(叠轧的)　prials, priles
三溴化铝 {AlBr$_3$}　aluminium bromide
三溴化钼 {MoBr$_3$}　molybdic bromide
三溴化铊 {TlBr$_3$}　thallic bromide
三溴化钽 {TaBr$_3$}　tantalous bromide, tantalum tribromide
三溴化物　tribromide
三溴化氧钼 {(MoO)Br$_3$}　molybdenyl tribromide
三溴化铟 {InBr$_3$}　ndium tribromide
三溴氧化磷　(同"磷酰溴")
三氧化二铋　bismuthous oxide
三氧化二钒　vanadium trioxide
三氧化二钆　(同"氧化钆")
三氧化二锆　zirconium sesquioxide
三氧化二铬　chromic oxide, chromium sesquioxide
三氧化二钴　cobaltic oxide
三氧化二镓　gallic oxide, gallium (sesqui) oxide
三氧化二铼　rhenium sesquioxide
三氧化二镧　lanthanum sesquioxide
三氧化二铝钝化法　aluminium oxide passivation
三氧化二锰　manganese sesquioxide
三氧化二钼　molybdenum sesquioxide
三氧化二铌　niobium sesquioxide, columbium sesquioxide
三氧化二镍　nickel sesquioxide
三氧化二钕　(同"氧化钕")
三氧化二镨　(同"氧化镨")
三氧化二铯　cesium trioxide
三氧化二钐　samarium sesquioxide
三氧化二砷　arsenous oxide, arsenic white, arsenous acid anhydride
三氧化二铈　cerium sesquioxide, cerous oxide
三氧化二铊　thallic oxide, thallium sesquioxide
三氧化二钛　titanium sesquioxide
三氧化二铽　terbium sesquioxide
三氧化二铁　ferric oxide, iron sesquioxide
三氧化二物　sesquioxide
三氧化二物相　【金】sesquioxide phase
三氧化二钇　yttria, yttrium oxide
三氧化二铟　indium trioxide [sesquioxide]
三氧化二铕　europium sesquioxide
三氧化钒 {V$_2$O$_3$}　vanadous oxide
三氧化铬　chromium trioxide
三氧化合物　trioxide, teroxide
三氧化铼 {ReO$_3$}　rhenium trioxide
三氧化硫 {SO$_3$}　sulphur trioxide
三氧化钼 {MoO$_3$}　molybdic oxide, molybdenum trioxide
三氧化砷　arsenic trioxide
三氧化钛 {TiO[O$_2$]; TiO$_3$}　titanium (tri)oxide [peroxide]
三氧化锑 {Sb$_2$O$_3$}　antimony trioxide

三氧化钨 {WO₃} tungstic oxide, tungsten trioxide, yellow tungsten oxide ◇ α～*, β[紫色]～*, γ～*
三氧化钨还原 reduction of tungstic oxide
三氧化物 trioxide
三氧化铱 iridium black
三氧化铀 {UO₃} uranic [orange] oxide, uranium trioxide
三摇臂式(分批)酸洗机 three-arm pickling machine
三乙基铝 triethyl aluminum
三乙基铊 (同"乙基铊")
三乙酸铝 aluminum triacetate
三异辛胺 tri-iso-octyl-amine(TIOA)
三翼形锭 winged ingot
三硬脂精 (同"硬脂精")
三油精 (同"甘油油酯")
三元磁性合金 ternary magnetic alloy
三元共晶(体) ternary eutectic
三元共晶反应 ternary eutectic reaction
三元共析体 ternary eutectoid
三元固溶体 ternary solid solution
三元过磷酸钙 {3CaSO₄·2H₃PO₄} triple superphosphate
三元合金 ternary [three-component, three-part] alloy
三元合金槽 tertiary alloy bath
三元合金钢 ternary [triple-alloy] steel
三元合金系 【金】ternary system
三元化合物 ternary compound
三元化合物半导体 ternary semiconductor
三元混合物 ternary mixture
三元铁酸钙 ternary-calciumferrite
三元锡镴[锡锑铅合金] (79Sn, 15Sb, 6Pb) triple pewter
三元系 three-component system, ternary (system) ◇ 假～pseudoternary system
三元系分离 separation of three component system
三元系平衡状态图[三组元系平衡相图] ternary equilibrium diagram

三元系区域精炼炉 three-component refiner
三元(相, 状态, 系统状态)图 three-component [triangular] diagram, ternary (constitutional, phase) diagram
三元相 【金】ternary phase
三元相关系 ternary phase relation
三元(相)平衡(图) 【金】ternary equilibria
三元渣 ternary slag
三元中间化合物 ternary intermediate compound
三元组 triad
三原子的 triatomic
三月桂胺 {N[(CH₂)₁₁CH₃]₃} trilaurylamine
三正辛胺 tri-n-octyl amine
三脂肪胺 {N[(CH₂)ₙCH₃]₃} tri-fatty amine
三脂肪胺萃取剂 {N[(CH₂)n CH₃]₃} tri-fatty amine RC-3749
三钟 【铁】three bell
三钟(式)炉顶 【铁】three-bell top ◇ 莫尔～装料装置*, 特施～装料系统*
三种产物回收 three-product withdrawal
三轴向成型[压制] triaxial compaction
三轴性 triaxiality
三轴压制 (同"三向压制")
三柱连续逆流离子交换 three-column continuous countercurrent ion-exchange
三柱塞泵 【机】three-plunger [triple-plunger] pump
三爪卡盘 three-jawed chuck
伞齿轮 bevel [mitre] gear ◇ 差动器侧面～ crown gear, 偏轴～ hypoid gear, 小～ bevel pinion, 直齿～ straight bevel gear
伞齿轮检查仪 bevel gear tester
伞骨钢丝 umbrella wire
伞形发散喷嘴 divergent nozzle of umbrella type
伞状型芯 【铸】umbrella core
散布 scattering, spreading

散布热 spreading heat
散度 divergence
散堆切屑 shovel(l)ing turnings
散发 emitting, emission
散放物 【环】emissions
散光计 astigmatometer
散焦相位衬度 out-of-focus phase contrast, contrast out of focus phase
散焦(作用) defocusing ◇ 偏转~*
散卷输送机 loop conveyor
散开 untwining
散粒 particulate
散粒料 loose material
散粒料层 bed of granular solids
散粒流态化 particulate fluidization
散料 bulk [trickled] material, bulk cargo, spillage
散料处理系统 bulk material handling system
散料漏斗 dripping hopper
散料皮带机 spillage conveyer
散料压实系统 packed system
散裂 spall(ing), spallation ◇ 抗~能力 spalling resistance, 耐~性 spalling property
散落 dripping, spillage
散落砂 【铸】spilled sand
散凝 deflocculating
散热 heat radiation [dissipation, elimination], radiating, cooling
散热介质 heat elminating medium
散热片 (radiation, cooling) fin, radiator
散热片坯料 fin stock
散热器 radiator, heat sink, cooler ◇ 对流式~ convector radiator, 肋片板式~*, 腮片~ gilled radiator, 凸缘式~ flanged radiator, 下流式单位~*
散热式型芯撑(螺旋式) radiator
散热水 cooling water
散热条件 heat dissipation conditions
散热翼片 cooling fin
散砂 loose sand

散射 scatter(ing), diffusing, diffuseness, diffusion ◇ 不相干电子~*, 布喇格~ Bragg scattering, 德尔布鲁克~ Delbruck scattering, 合作[协作]~*, 康普顿~ Compton scattering, 体积[整体]~ bulk scattering, 屋室[墙壁]~ room scattering, 异常~ anomalous scattering
散射本底分布 diffuse background distribution
散射层 scattering layer
散射的X射线 scattered X-rays
散射电势[位] scattering potential
散射电子 scattered [scattering] electron
散射电子能量分布 energy spread of scattered electrons
散射辐射 scattered radiation
散射幅 scattering amplitude
散射光 scattered light
散射光光弹性 scattered light photoelsticity
散射角 scattering angle
散射截面 scattering (cross) section, cross-section for scattering ◇ 瑞利~*
散射介质 scattering medium
散射能力[本领] scattering power
散射能量 scattered energy
散射碰撞 scattering collision
散射频率 scattering frequency
散射强度 【理】scattering strength, intensity of scattering
散射区 fringing field
散射烧成 scattering firing
散射声 diffused sound
散射束 scattered beam
散射束锥形角(波束的) beam angle (of scattering)
散射速率 rate of scattering
散射损失 scattering loss
散射系数 scattering [dissipation] coefficient
散射线 scattered rays, line of scatter
散射原子 scattering atom

散射振幅 scattering amplitude
散射值 scatter value
散射中心 scattering centre
散射浊度计 nephelometer
散失电流腐蚀 stray-current corrosion
散碎废金属 loose scrap
散逸 dissipation, dissemination
散贮 bulk storage
散装 (in) bulk
散装货输送机 bulk cargo conveyer
散装料 bulk cargo ◇ 转炉～仓*
散装密度 bulk [loose, apparent] density ◇ 粉末～*
散装耐火材料 unshaped refractory
散装水泥 bulk [loose] cement
散装物料密度计 bulk density meter
散装装船[装运] bulk shipment
霰石{$CaCO_3$} aragonite
桑普森锌基轴承合金 (85—88Zn, 4—10Cu, 2—8Al) Sampson metal
骚动 disturbing, disturbance, perturbation, agitation
骚动浓度法 (区域熔炼) 【色】 method of perturbing concentration
骚动松散流化床 agitated non-adherent particulate bed
扫除 cleaning, cleanup, removal, wipe out, sweep(ing), hogging
扫除模中型砂用刷 soft brush
扫动位错 sweeping dislocation
扫接触点 wiping contact
扫描 scan(ning), sweep, trace ◇ 接触～ contact scanning, 算术～【计】arithmetic scan
扫描电路 scanning [sweep] circuit
扫描电(子显微)镜 scanning electron microscope (SEM), sweep electron microscope
扫描电子显微镜成像 scanning electron image
扫描电子显微术 scanning electron microscopy

扫描法 scanning method
扫描感应器 scanning inductor
扫描基线 time base
扫描激光器 scan(ned-)laser
扫描记录仪 scanning recorder
扫描监测器 scanning monitor
扫描间歇流体分光计 scanning stop flow spectrometer
扫描控制 scan-control ◇ 边缘位置的～*
扫描面 sweeping plane
扫描器 scanner, scanning [tracing] device
扫描中断 【计】scanner interrupt
扫描区 scanning zone, sweep range
扫描射束 scanning beam
扫描试样支架 scanning specimen holder
扫描速度 scanning [sweep] speed, sweep velocity
扫描速率 scanning [sweep] rate
扫描隧道显微镜 scanning tunnel microscope
扫描图像 scanned image ◇ 声学～*
扫描选择器 【计】scanner selector
扫描元件 scan(ning) unit
扫描增益 swept gain
扫描振荡器 sweep oscillator, scanning generator
扫描装置 scann(ing) device [unit], sweep unit
扫选 scavenging (scvg)
扫选机 【选】scavenger (scav.), scavenger [aftertreatment, retreatment] cell
扫选精矿 scavenger concentrate
扫越式催化重结晶(法) sweep through catalysed recrystallization (STCR)
扫帚用钢丝 broom wire
瑟罗铜铝锰电阻合金 (85Cu, 2—5.5Al, 9.5—13Mn) Therlo
瑟莫式连续加热炉 Thermo type furnace
瑟斯顿高锌黄铜 (0.5Sn, 55Cu, 44.5Zn) Thurston's brass
瑟斯顿锡基轴承合金 (19Sb, 10Cu, 余量

瑟斯顿锌基[锌锡铜]合金(80Zn,14Sn,6Cu) Thurston's alloy
色笔 crayon ◇ 测温～ colour pencil
色层电泳 electrochromatophoresis
色层(分离) chromatographic separation ◇ 瓦特曼～滤纸 Whatman's paper
色层(分离)法 chromatography ◇ 化学吸附～*,吸附～*,纸上～ paper chromatography
色层分离介质 chromatographic medium
色层(分离)谱 chromatogram,chromatograph
色层钢板 pluramelt
色层谱仪 chromatograph
色调[辉]计 tintometer
色调鲜明图像 harsh image
色度计 colorimeter,chromometer
色度学 colorimetry,chromatometry
色分离[选] colour sorting
色金 coloured gold
色灵敏度 (同"感色灵敏度")
色谱 chromatogram,colour spectrum
色谱[层]分析 chromatographic analysis ◇ 上行～法*
色谱(分析)法 chromatography ◇ 薄层～*
色散 (chromatic) dispersion
色散度 dispersity,dispersiveness
色散分析 dispersion analysis
色散率[本领] dispersive power
色散器 disperser,dispersor
色散系数 coefficient of dispersion, abbe number
色示温度 colour temperature
色像差 chromatic aberrations
色(中)心 【理】colour centre, F centre
铯{Cs} cesium,caesium ◇ 含～合金*
铯矾 (同"硫酸铯铝")
铯合金 cesium alloy
铯基合金 cesium-base alloy
铯榴石{2Cs₂O·2Al₂O₃·9SiO₂·H₂O} pollucite, pollux
铯绿柱石 verobieffite, rosterite
铯锰星叶石 cesium kupletskite
铯硼铝铍矿 rhodizite
铯铷矾 (同"硫酸铝铷铯")
铯锑(合金) caesium-antimony
铯原子钟 caesium atomic clock
森达斯特硅铝铁合金薄板 (磁性材料; 10Si,5Al,余量Fe) Sendust sheet
森德贝格钢轨顶面余热淬火法 【压】Sandberg sorbitized process
森基热平衡图 【冶】Sankey diagram
森吉米尔带钢冷轧机 Sendzimir cold strip mill
森吉米尔冷轧机 Sendzimir cold-rolling mill
森吉米尔热镀锌法 (同"分解氨热镀锌法")
森吉米尔式轧机 (二十辊冷轧机) 【压】ZR (Sendzimir) mill
森吉米尔行星轧机 Sendzimir planetary mill
森科(海瓦克)高真空回转油泵 Cenco (Hyvac) pump
森珀姆恒磁导率合金(10.54Si,16.19Ni,余量Fe) Senperm
砂 sand,grit,shot ◇ 含黏土的～ argillaceous sand,劣级～ badly graded sand, 黏土似(含黏土多)的～ clayey [gummy] sand,瘦(型)～*
砂疤(铸件缺陷) 【铸】sandbuckle, sand scab
砂坝 【铁】sand dam ◇ 贝克～*
砂斑 sand patch
砂泵 sand pump
砂布 emery [abrasive, sand, glass] cloth, coated abrasive
砂槽 【铸】sandpit
砂尘捕集器(熄焦塔内的) grit arrestor
砂成分 sand(-stone) constituent
砂舂 【铸】sandrammer ◇ 长柄～ floor rammer, 短柄～*, 手～ hand [bench]

rammer, 平头~butt ram(mer)
砂处理机 sand cutter
砂处理设备 sand conditioner
砂床 【铸】sand bottom, casting bed,【铁】sand bed（铸铁的）
砂床铸生铁（同"砂模生铁"）
砂床铸铁 sow
砂带磨光 linishing
砂带抛光 belt polishing
砂挡铁墙（流槽的） sand stopping
砂底 sand bottom
砂钉 【铸】brad, steeple
砂斗 sand hopper
砂坊 check dam
砂分离器[分选机] sand separator
砂封 sand seal
砂隔渣板 【铁】sand stopping
砂钩 【铸】lifter
砂浆 【建】mortar, sand pulp ◇ 沥青~asphalt grout, 气硬性~air-setting mortar
砂浆搅拌机 【建】mortar mixer
砂浆接缝 mortar joint
砂金 gulch [alluvial, stream] gold, placer (gold)
砂金矿 placer [gravel] mine ◇ 细粒~flour gold
砂金石 aventurine
砂壳 【铸】sand skin
砂坑 【铸】sandpit
砂矿 placer (deposit)
砂矿采选 alluvial working
砂冷 cooling by embedding in sand
砂砾 gravel, grail
砂粒 grained sand, girt,【铸】sand grain ◇ 纯~*
砂粒度测定器 【铸】sieve shaker
砂粒间隙 sand porosity
砂粒细度值 grain fineness number (gfn)
砂滤器 sand filter
砂轮 abrasive wheel [disc], emery cutter [wheel, disc, stone], grinder, grinding wheel

砂轮机 grinder, abrader ◇ 悬挂式~swing-frame grinder
砂轮锯 abrasive disc cutter, abrasive cutoff saw
砂轮切断机 abrasive cutoff machine
砂轮切割 abrasive cutoff
砂轮切割片 abrasive disc cutter
砂轮清理法 abrasive cleaning
砂轮清理工作台 grinding bed
砂轮驱动电动机 grinding wheel drive motor
砂轮头 grinding (wheel) head
砂轮修整机组 【压】grinding-wheel conditioning unit
砂轮修整器 dresser ◇ 金刚石~diamond dresser
砂轮研磨清理法 abrasive cleaning
砂轮整形器 grinding wheel dresser
砂轮整修装置 grinding wheel truing device
砂轮自动平衡器 grinding wheel auto-balancer
砂模生铁 sand mould pig iron, sand-cast pig
砂模铸造金属 sand-cast metal
砂模铸造轧辊 【压】sand roll
砂磨 sanding, ashing
砂抹镀锌 sand galvanizing
砂泥分离 sand-slime separation
砂泥（渣） sand slime
砂黏土 hazel earth, sand clay
砂皮（铸件上的） burning-on
砂壤土 loam sand, sandy loam
砂筛（分机） sand screen [sieve]
砂石 sandstone, dinas ◇ 除~degritting
砂石厂 aggregate plant
砂石成分 sand(-stone) constituent
砂石配备厂 aggregate preparation plant
砂蚀 sand erosion
砂榫 【铸】centring cones
砂胎 【铸】close-over, cod
砂胎模 【铸】odd sides, sand match

砂锡　stream tin

砂锡矿　tin placer deposit, alluvial tin

砂箱　【铸】(moulding, foundery) flask, casting [mould(ing), sand] box ◇ 带定位销的～flask with pin holders, 带凸缘的～flask with flange, 带箱挡的～flask with sand rib, 分格～sectional flask, 滑脱式～slip flask, 铰链式～pop-off flask, 可拆式～snap [pop-off] flask, 拼合[装配式]～bolted moulding box, 异型～*, 组合式～*

砂箱导销　flask pins

砂箱底板　flask [moulding] plate, stamping [turnover] board

砂箱底板板垛　board stack

砂箱垫板　bottom board

砂箱定位[固定]销　flask [box] pin, fixed (moulding box) pin

砂箱夹具[卡子]　flask [mould] clamp, sand grip

砂箱填砂机　flask filler

砂箱造型　flask [box] moulding

砂箱铸造　flask casting

砂芯　【铸】(sand) core

砂芯黏合　core pasting

砂芯黏合膏　core paste

砂芯黏合剂　core-gum

砂芯黏结剂　core binder

砂芯呛孔(缺陷)　core blow

砂芯涂料　core blacking

砂型　【铸】sand mould ◇ 闭式[合好的]～closed sand mould, 表面烘干～flared mould, 表皮干燥～skin dried mould, 风干～air-dry sand mould, 明浇～*, 组芯～core-sand mould

砂型表观硬度　apparent mould hardness

砂型吊钩　gagger

砂型干燥炉　mould-drying oven

砂型和型芯制备法　◇ "西山"～Nishiyama process

砂型假箱　odd sides

砂型孔隙金属液渗透(黏砂)　abreuvage

砂型离心浇注　sand spun casting

砂型离心铸造法　sand spun process

砂型涂黑　blacking

砂型硬度　sand hardness ◇ 钢球式～计 autopunch

砂型硬度试验计　mould-hardness tester

砂型铸件　sand mould casting

砂型铸铁轧辊　grain roll

砂型铸造　sand casting, open (sand) casting

砂岩　sandstone, silt rock

砂眼　【铸】blowhole, sand hole, slag pin hole, porosity, void, push-up ◇ 小～dit

砂印(钢板表面缺陷)　【压】sandmark

砂浴　sand bath

砂浴回火　sand-bath tempering

砂纸　abrasive [carborundum, sand] paper, coated abrasive

砂质黏土　dauk, loam, lam

砂中浇铸取样　sand-cast sample

砂铸场[砂型铸造场]　sand casting bed

砂铸生铁　sand cast pig iron

砂铸试样　【铸】sand-cast sample

砂砖　bath brick

砂桩　sand pile

砂状氧化铝　sandy alumina

砂子空隙度　sand porosity

砂子黏结剂　【铸】sandbinders

杀虫剂　pesticide

杀菌剂　bactericide

杀蜱剂　【环保】acaricide

杀氰质　cyanicide

杀鼠剂　rodenticide

刹车　braking, brake ◇ 液压～cataract

刹车带　brake ribbon, black tape

刹车辊　braking roll

刹车块　(同"制动块")

刹车面　brake lining

刹车片　brake disc ◇ 内胀型全金属～*

刹车装置　brake assembly [apparatus, equipment]

刹闸　braking

刹闸减速　braking
沙坝　sandbank, dam
沙床铸铁工　【铁】stocktaker
沙德克铜基贵金属合金（1—10Au，余量Cu）　Shadke
沙赫残余应力测定法　Sach's method
纱包漆包线　【电】cotton-enamel covered wire
纱包线　【电】cotton covered wire
纱窗　screen window, mosquito screen
纱(滤)网　gauze
筛　sieve, screen(ing), sifter, strainer ◇ 闭路~closed-circuit screen, 大尺寸~oversize screen, 大孔~griddle, 封闭式~closed-type screen, 小号[细目]~undersize screen
筛板　sieve-plate, sieve disk, screen deck ◇ 细孔~fines deck
筛板萃取塔　perforated-plate extraction tower
筛板脉冲萃取塔[交换柱]　perforated-plate pulse column
筛板式气体洗涤器　sieve-plate gas scrubber
筛板寿命　screen deck life
筛板塔　sieve-plate [sieve-tray, perforated-plate] column, sieve-plate tower
筛板柱　sieve-plate column
筛蔽　【电】screening
筛算条　grizzly bar
筛除大块　scalping, oversize removal
筛除焦粉[煤粉]　breeze extraction
筛底布钢丝　wire cloth wire
筛底托盘　screen-bottomed tray
筛分　screening, screen separation [classification], sieving, sizing, grading ◇ 闭路~*, 物料自动~*
筛分操作　sizing operation
筛分厂　screening [sizing] plant
筛分分级　sieve classification
筛(分)分析（同"筛析"）◇ 煤~coal-sizing analysis

筛分工段　assoring room
筛分规范　sieving specifications
筛分机　screening machine, bolting mill, bolter ◇ 带式~【选】belt screen, 感应加热~*, 滚筒~【选】revolver, 焦炭~coke screen, 摇动式~shaking grate, 运输~*
筛分级配　screen size gradation
筛分矿石　screened ore
筛分累计百分率　cumulative screen analysis
筛分粒度[尺寸]　screen [sieve, mesh, separation] size
筛分粒度分布　screen size distribution
筛分粒(度)级　screening [sieve(-sized), mesh] fraction
筛分能力　screening capacity
筛分设备　screening equipment [facilities], sizing device
筛分数据　sieving data
筛分特征　screening [sizing] characteristic
筛分系列　screen cascade [line]
筛分效率　screening [sizing] efficiency
筛分型砂【铸】　riddled sand
筛分性能　size characteristic
筛分运输机　separator conveyer
筛分站　screening station
筛分指数　screen index
筛分装载机　loadascreen
筛辊　sizing roll
筛过料　sized feed
筛号　screen size [mesh], sieve [mesh] number, mesh gauge
筛后碎矿　feel
筛级　screen grading
筛径　screen [sieve] aperture
筛孔　(sieve) mesh, screen [mesh, sieve] opening, screen [sieve] aperture, screen hole
筛孔尺寸　mesh size
筛孔堵塞　screen blinding [blockage, clogging]
筛孔管　anti-priming pipe

筛孔塔[柱]　orifice column
筛框[筛子框架]　screen frame
筛目　sieve mesh [size], mesh
筛目规　mesh gauge
筛砂机　【铸】sand sieving machine
筛上粉粒　oversize particle
筛上粉末　oversize powder
筛上(料,物)　oversize (O.S.), oversize product [material], plus mesh [sieve],【耐】shorts
筛上烧结矿　oversize sinter
筛上物累积量曲线　cumulative weight oversize curve
筛上物溜槽　oversize chute
筛上物运输机　oversize conveyer
筛式干燥机　screen-type dryer
筛式给料机　screen feeder
筛式运输机　screen conveyer
筛条　grid bar, grating ◇ T字形～ T-shaped rod
筛网　screen mat [mesh, cloth, deck]
筛网(钢)丝　screen wire, wire cloth wire
筛网隔膜　sieve diaphragm
筛网过滤器　screen [mesh] filter, strainer, granular membrane
筛网开孔面积　open area
筛网漏勺　wire-screen ladle
筛网面积[筛子有效面积]　screening area
筛网铅黄铜　leaded screen wire brass
筛网寿命　screen deck life
筛网眼　cmesh aperture
筛析　screen(ing) [sieve, sieving] analysis, particle sizing, sieve classifi-cation
筛析表　sizing diagram
筛析结果　sieving result
筛析粒度范围　sieve size range
筛析[分]试验　screen [sieve, sieving(-assay)] test
筛洗选[分级]　settling classification
筛隙　screen aperture
筛下部分[粒级]　undersize fraction
筛下范围　subsieve range

筛下粉矿　ore screenings
筛下焦粉　coke screenings
筛下(料,物,产品)　undersize (U.S., u/s), screenings, screen passing, undersieves, minus sieve [mesh], through product, feel ◇ 菲舍尔～粒度分析仪 Fisher subsieve sizer
筛下煤　tripping coal
筛下烧结矿粉末　sinter screenings
筛下原矿粉　R.O.M. (run-of-mine) screenings
筛屑　screen tailings, trash
筛屑槽　breeze bin
筛序　numerical aperture (NA, N.A., n.a.)
筛选　screen classification, preparation [dressing] by screening,【选】settling operation ◇ 金属网～运输机 wire netting belt
筛选富集　enriching by screening
筛选机　screening [sieving] machine
筛选矿石　screened ore
筛眼　(同"筛孔")
筛用钢丝　screen wire
筛余　screen tailings, oversize,【耐】shorts
筛余粗料　reject
筛余碾碎物　comminution of screenings
筛子故障　screen cut
晒蓝图　blue print drawing
晒(蓝)图机　blue printing machine
晒台　deck roof
晒图纸　blue printing paper, heliographic paper
晒印　printing
山(脉)　mountain
山崩　landslide
山顶　hilltop, (hill)crest
山谷　valley
山脊　(mountain) ridge, dorsum (复数 dorsa)
山梨酸酯　sorbate
山墙　【建】gable (wall)

山墙端	gable end
山嵛酸	(同"二十二烷酸")
删去符	【计】erase character
珊瑚泥	coral mud
栅	grate,【半】gate ◇ 重型钢梁~grillage
栅板	grid tray
栅格	grid, grill(e), lattice
栅格棒	grid bar
栅格表面	grate surface
栅格喷砂清理	grid blasting
栅格筛	grizzly screen
栅格式(气体)洗涤塔	hurdle-type scrubber [washer], hurdle washer
栅格填充(物)(洗涤塔用)	hurdle packing, grid (lattice) packing
栅格填料洗涤塔	hurdle packed scrubber
栅极	【电】grid (electrode), grating
栅极 X 射线管	【理】grid X-ray tube
栅极材料	grid material
栅极电离室	grid ionization chamber
栅(极电)流	grid [gate] current
栅极电容器	grid capacitor [condenser]
栅极电阻	grid resistance
栅极电阻器	grid resistor
栅极回路	grid circuit
栅极检波	grid rectification
栅极控制	grid control
栅极控制管	grid-control tube
栅极控制整流器	grid-controlled rectifier
栅极控制装置	grid control unit
栅极特性(曲线)	grid characteristic
栅极抑制器[电阻]	grid suppressor
栅极-阴极电容	grid cathode capacity
栅控二极管	【计】gate diode
栅控辉光放电管	grid glow tube
栅漏	grid leak
栅漏电阻	grid-leak resistance
栅偏(电)压	(grid) bias
栅偏电阻	grid-bias resistance
栅筛	grizzly
栅筛盘	grizzly disc
栅条填充塔	grid (packed) tower
栅线间距	【理】grating space
栅压调节器	【电】grid voltage regulator
钐钴永磁材料	samarium-cobalt permanent-magnetic material
钐合金	samarium alloy
钐化合物	samaric compound
钐基合金	samarium-base alloy
钐添加合金	samarium addition
钐中毒	samarium poisoning
闪铋矿	bismuth blende
闪变	flicker
闪电	(flashing) lightning, bolt
闪光	flash (light), spark, bursting ◇ 发~*,防~用护目镜 flash goggles, 眩目~(电弧等的) eye flash
闪光灯	flash lamp [light], flashing light [signal]
闪光电焊机(板带材对焊用)	flash welder
闪光电弧焊	flash welding
闪光顶锻对焊	flash upset welding
闪光对焊	flash butt welding
闪光对焊焊缝	flash butt weld
闪光对焊机	flash (butt) welder, flash butt welding machine ◇ 米巴赫高效~*
闪光对焊机板夹头	flash welding (clamping) die
闪光对焊接头	resistance flash weld
闪光放电管	strobo
闪光飞溅	【焊】flash spatter
闪光光泽	bright [brilliant] luster
闪光焊	flash welding (FW)
闪光焊飞溅	【焊】flash spatter
闪光焊覆层	flash welding coat
闪光焊焊条夹持器	flash welding electrode assembly
闪光焊夹紧钳口	flash welding (clamping) die, flash welding electrode
闪光焊接	flash welding joint
闪光焊接法	【焊】flash welding method
闪光合金	flash alloy
闪光[继续]继电器	flashing relay

闪光间隙	flashing gap
闪光孔	flash vent, flare opening
闪光射线分析[照相]	flash radiography
闪光生铁(开炉炼出的)	【铁】blazed pig iron
闪光时间	flashing time [period], flash off time ◇ 手工焊～manual flashing time
闪光显示	blinking indication
闪光现象	phosphere, scintillation
闪光信号	flashing signal [light], flicker signal
闪光信号灯	signal lamp flicker, blinker light
闪光行程(对焊机的)	【焊】flashing travel
闪光仪	strobo(scope), flashometer
闪光照明	flash illumination
闪弧	flash over, flashing
闪弧挡板	flash barrier
闪弧电流	flash current
闪击距离	striking distance
闪亮的	micaceous
闪绿岩	greenstone, diorite
闪络	arc-over ◇ 防～环 arc ring
闪络电压	flash over voltage
闪络距离	flash over distance
闪煤	anthrinoid
闪燃	flash (burning)
闪(燃)点	flash point (f.pl)
闪热烧结	flash heating sintering
闪熔镀覆[镀层]	flash plating
闪熔收缩损失(闪光对焊的)	flashing loss
闪烧脱蜡(法)	flash dewax
闪视	blink
闪烁	flicker, scintillation, flare (up), blink
闪烁光谱仪[分光计]	scintillation spectrometer
闪烁计数管	scintillation-counter tube
闪烁计数器	scintillometer
闪烁计数器光谱计	scintillation-counter spectrometer
闪烁继电器	flicker relay
闪烁检测器	scintillation detector
闪烁晶体	scintillation crystal
闪烁警报灯	alarm lamp flicker
闪烁谱仪	scintillation spectrometer
闪烁器	flasher, flicker, scintillator ◇ 信号灯～signal lamp flicker
闪烁扫描器[闪烁仪]	scintillation scanner
闪烁射线照相术	scintillography
闪烁停止	flicker stop
闪烁显示	blinking indication
闪速	flashing speed
闪速焙烧	flash (suspension) roasting, shower roasting
闪速焙烧炉	flash roaster [calciner]
闪速吹炼	flash converting
闪速电炉	flash smelting furnace with furnace electrodes
闪速干燥	flash drying
闪速干燥器	flash drier
闪速烘干	flash baking
闪速加热器	flash heater
闪速炉床能率	flash furnace specific capacity
闪速炉法	flash furnace method
闪速熔炼	flash [suspension] smelting, smelting in suspension ◇ 铜～*,氧气～*
闪速熔炼法	flash smelting [melting] process ◇ 奥托昆普～Outokumpu process
闪速熔炼技术	flash smelting technique
闪速熔炼炉	flash (smelting) furnace
闪速熔炼炉锍	flash furnace matte
闪速熔炼炉渣	flash furnace slag
闪速熔炼试验	flash smelting test
闪速熔炼现象	flash smelting phenomena
闪速烧结	(同"快速烧结")
闪速蒸发器	flash type evaporator
闪速蒸馏	flash distillation
闪铜铅矿	alisonite
闪锌矿{ZnS}	(zinc) blende, false galena,

black jack
闪锌矿焙烧 blende roasting
闪锌矿焙烧炉 zinc blende roaster
闪锌矿型结构 zinc blende type structure
闪蒸 flash(ing) ◇ 二次~
闪蒸槽 flash tank
闪蒸滴定管 flash burette
闪蒸发系统 flashing system
闪蒸发液 flashing liquor
闪蒸交换器 flash exchanger
闪蒸速度 flashing speed
闪蒸塔 flash tower [column]
闪正煌岩 vogesite
扇风机 fan (blower), fanner, ventilating fan ◇ 径流式[离心式]~ radial flowfan, 炉顶~(除尘风机) roof(-cleaning) fan, 叶轮式~ paddle-wheel fan, 轴流式[螺旋桨式]~ propeller-type fan
扇面展开机理(微粒子反向磁化的) fanning mechanism
扇尾形 fan tail
扇形 sector ◇ 呈~展开 fanning
扇形齿轮 segment gear, toothed sector
扇形电缆 sector-shaped cable
扇形段(圆盘过滤机的) filter sector
扇形给料器 fan gate
扇形拱 segmental arch
扇形火焰 fan shaped flame
扇形块(卷取机的) arc segments
扇形体 segment, quad(rant)
扇形图 fan [sector, pie] diagram
扇形仪表 sector-pattern instrument
扇形闸门[板] sector gate, segment shutter
扇形砖 radial [circle, bullnose] brick ◇ 侧砌~ circle brick on edge
缮写员 table man
嬗变 【理】transmutation ◇ (原子)核~ nuclear transmutation
伤害 hurt, injury
伤痕 scar, flaw, injury, bruise ◇ 运输磕碰~ traffic mark

伤亡 casualty
伤纹探测灵敏度 flaw detection sensitivity
商标 trade [identification] mark, brand (br)
商号 trade name
商品 commodity, goods, merchandise, commercial [marketable] product
商品薄板 commercial light-gauge sheet, merchant sheet
商品薄钢板 merchant sheet
商品纯铝 (同"工业纯铝")
商品等级 market grade
商品锻钢(件) commercial forging steel
商品废钢铁[金属] 【冶】merchantable scrap
商品粉末 commercial powder
商品钢板 commercial sheet
商品钢材 merchant shapes
商品黄铜 market brass
商品级别 market size
商品级硫酸 merchant-grade sulfuric acid
商品金属 (同"工业金属")
商品精矿 commercial concentrate
商品类别 market size
商品铝 commercial aluminium
商品名称 trade name
商品铅 market lead
商品球团 【团】commercial pellet
商品燃料 commercial fuel
商品生铁 (同"工业生铁")
商品试样 sale sample
商品条钢 merchant (bar) iron
商品铜 commercial [merchant] copper
商品锡 commercial tin
商品锌(通指98%—99%粗锌锭) (zinc) spelter
商品阴极钴 marketable cathodic cobalt
商品砖 commercial brick
商品最低价格 floor price
商(数) quotient
商业规格 commercial specification
商业化 commercialization

商业性应用　commercial application [adoption]
商业仲裁法庭　【企】commercial arbitration tribunal
商用机器　commercial machine
熵　entropy ◇ 点缺陷~*, 混合~entropy of mixing, 激活[活化]~ activation entropy, 空位形成~*, 无序~ entropy of disorder, 稀释 entropy of dilution, 消向~*, 振动~entropy of vibration
熵变(化)　entropy change, change in entropy ◇ 熔化~*
熵单位　entropy unit (E.U.)
熵起伏[涨落]　entropy fluctuation
熵值　entropy value
上半部(木模或铸型的)　flask cope
上半型　mould top half, mould cope
上半型暗冒口　【铸】cope bob
上贝氏体　【金】upper [high] bainite
上标(符)　superscript
上部边界法　upper-bound method
上部边界趋近法　upper-bound approach technique
上部电极　top electrode
上部单烧嘴长坑均热炉　rectangle equi-flux heater with single upper burner
上部二次冷却段[上部喷淋(冷却)段]　【连铸】upper spray sections
上部钢结构　steel superstructure
上部构造　superstructure
上部加热　overhead firing
上部结构　top structure
上部框架　live frame
上部炉瘤　top crust
上部炉身(高炉的)　upper inwall [stack]
上部平衡(工作辊的)　【压】puffing-up
上部平台　top platform
上部无浇冒口的底铸型　【铸】close-top mould
上部悬料　top hanging
上部烟罩　tube hood
上测头(X射线测厚仪的)　upper detector
上层澄清液　【环】supernatant clarified liquor
上层隔板　upper separator
上层建筑　superstructure,【钢】superstructure of furnace
上层面　upper deck
上层清液　supernatant layer [liquid, liquor]
上层台　upper deck
上插棒连续自焙阳极电解槽　【色】vertical-stud soderberg cell, soederberg cell with vertical studs
上插(棒)阳极　vertical (stud, spike, pin, stub) anode
上插(导电)棒　vertical (contact) stud [pin, spike, stub]
上插阳极镁电解槽　【色】magnesium electrolytic cell with topmounted anodes
上承梁　【建】deck beam
上承(式)桥　deck (type) bridge
上承桁架　deck truss
上冲杆　top [upper] plunger, upper punch
上冲头　upper punch
上冲头压力　upper punch pressure
上出料仓式泵　bin-type pump with upper outlet
上出线式(连续拉丝机)卷筒　【压】overhead take-off block
上锤头　upper ram,【团】upper striker
上淬(法)　up-quenching
上大下小　big end up (BEU)
上大下小封底式锭模　big end up mould with closed bottom
上大下小钢锭　big end up ingot
上大下小钢锭模　big end up (BEU) mould, mould flared at top
上大下小结晶器　【钢】mould flared at top
上大下小开底式锭模　big end up mould with open bottom
上大下小塞底式锭模　big end up mould with plug bottom

上 shang

上挡板（轧件用）	overhead gauge
上刀滑架（剪切机的）	upper knife slide
上刀架	top knife block [carrier]
上刀梁	top knife beam
上刀片	top blade [knife], upper blade
上刀片滑块	top knife block [head]
上导洞法隧道	bar and sill method
上等煤	fancy coal
上底漆	first [printing] coat
上电极	upper [top] electrode
上电极臂（接触电焊机的）	top horn
上电子枪	upper gun
上分式双管系统（热水供暖的）	double-pipe dropping system
上风道	uptake shaft
上风口高度	upper tuyere level
上浮部分	float fraction
上浮(的)	floating
上浮速度	raising velocity
上浮速率	raising rate
上浮性	floatability
上工作辊	top working roll
上拱度	camber
上光轮[机]	glazer
上辊	top roll(er)
上辊不传动的二辊式轧机	jump mill
上辊大升程初轧机	high lift bloomer
上辊可换轧槽块（罗克莱特冷轧管机的）	top die
上辊平衡缸	top roll balance cylinder
上辊平衡装置	top roll balance arrangement ◇ 弹簧式~*,液压式~*
上辊倾翻装置	top roll tilting equipment
上辊缘	top of rollers
上黑	【铸】blackening
上横梁（机座、牌坊的）	【压】entablature, upper separator
上滑动刀架	top knife head
上回转台压榨机	tilting-head press
上活套极限的检测	【压】detecting of up loop limit
上夹送(给料)辊	【压】top pinch roll
(TPR)	
上加热段	upper heat zone
上加热式[上面加热]炉	top-fired furnace
上架式安装法	overhang
上剪切装置	top shear unit
上胶	rubberizing
上浇法	top gating
上矫直辊	top levelling roller
上接点	upper contact
上接轴（轧机的）	top spindle
上界解	【数】upper bound solution
上卷式	overwind
上均热段	upper soak zone
上跨火道	【焦】crossover flue
上蜡（镀锌钢丝的）	waxing
上联接轴（轧机的）	top spindle
上料车	charge car
上料次序	filling sequence
上料点	feed point,【团】charging station
上料斗车	【铁】charging box car
上料管	feeding tube
上料机	charging machine
上料口	feed inlet
上料皮带	charging belt
上料皮带机	charging conveyer
上料设备	charging equipment
上料系统	charging system ◇ 自动~*
上料小车	【铁】charging wagon
上料卸料车	feeder tripper
上料装置	charging device [gear]
上临界磁场	upper critical field
上临界点	upper critical point
上临界冷却速度	upper critical cooling velocity
上临界温度	upper critical temperature
上流交换柱	upstream column
上流作业	upflow operation
上炉腹线	【冶】upper bosh line
上煤线[轨道]	coaling track
上煤站	coaling station
上面出料	top discharge
上面装模	top level die-filling

上模 【压】upper [moving] die
上模板（压力机的） upper plate
上模冲 top plunger
上模冲压紧压力 top-punch hold-down pressure
上模型 pattern cope
上挠度 (height of) camber
上盘 hanging wall (HW, H.W.)
上喷水器（轧制带材的） top water sprays
上喷嘴组 top sprays
上坡 uphill, uprise
上坡焊 uphill welding
上漆 varnishing
上气道[管] gas up-take
上切式剪切机 (up-and-)down cut shears
上清液 overflow [clear] solution, clear liquid,【环】clarified [clear] effluent, decanted water
上清液槽 supernatant tank
上清液溢流 clear solution overflow
上屈服点 upper yield point
上屈服点应力 upper yield stress
上刃台 top knife block
上砂箱 【铸】top (moulding) box, top part, flask cope
上烧嘴加热炉 【冶】top-fired (soaking) pit ◇ 单侧~*, 对角~*
上升 rising, ascension, ascending, climb, lifting, uphill
上升部 【铸】flowoff
上升部分（特性曲线的） incremental portion
上升冲程液压[水压]机 hydraulic upstroke press
上升道 uptake
上升道挡板[调节板] uptake damper
上升道隔板 uptake partition
上升管 rising [ascension] pipe,【焦】standpipe
上升管阀 【焦】ascension pipe valve
上升管桥管 【焦】ascension [stand] pipe elbow
上升管桥管清扫机 stand pipe elbow cleaner
上升管清扫器 【焦】ascension pipe cleaner
上升机构 elevating gear
上升口 centre riser
上升力 lifting force
上升流 upcurrent, up-draught, upward flow
上升煤气流 ascending gas current
上升气流 upward-flowing gases, upstream
上升气流分选机 （同"管式同轴分选机"）
上升气体 uprising gas
上升试剂气体 rising reagent gas
上升水流分级机 【焦】rising-current classifier
上升速度 elevating [lifting] speed, raising [upward] velocity
上升速率 raising rate, rate of rise
上升特性（曲线） rising characteristic
上升温度 increased temperature
上升压力 upacting pressure
上升烟道 gas up-take, uptake shaft
上升烟道隔墙 uptake partition
上升烟道锅炉 up-take boiler
上升运动 lifting movement
上升周期（气流的） up-stream cycle
上升总管（液体用） rising main
上死点（发动机的） upper dead point (UDC)
上凸肩（锻模的）【压】top fuller
上凸缘板 upper flange plate
上推式液压压下装置 up-push hydraulic screwdown
上推系统 push-up system
上托 【计】pop-up
上弯 up-bending, turnup（轧件前端的）
上弯曲辊 【压】upper bending roll
上位机控制原理 host computer control principle
上卫板 top guard [guide]

上吸式单张板皮带运输机　top singling belt conveyer
上系梁　top tie beam
上下层窗空间　spandrel
上下供热的炉子　top and bottom fired furnace
上下固定机构　hold-down mechanism
上下卷筒　double block
上下文无关文法　【计】context-free grammer(CFG)
上下文有关文法　【计】context-sensitive grammer(CSG)
上下限　limiting sphere, bound
上陷型模　【压】top swage
上限　upper [superior] limit, upgrade ◇规定的~ set upper limit
上限尺寸　top size, high limit of size
上限估计法　upper-bound method
上限截止频率　upper cut-off frequency
上限粒度　top size
上线性极限（超声波的）【理】upper linearity limit
上箱　【铸】top (moulding) box, coupe, cope
上箱碎裂[胀裂]　【铸】cope spall
上向渗滤浸出　upward percolation
上向斜焊　uphill welding
上小下大敞口式锭模　big end down mould with open top
上小下大钢锭　big end down ingot
上小下大(钢)锭模　big end down (BED) mould, narrow-end-up mould, retractable [wide-bottom] ingot mould, mould flared at bottom
上小下大结晶器　【钢】mould flared at bottom
上小下大瓶口式锭模　big end down mould with bottle top
上楔形导向装置　top wedge guide
上型　【铸】(mould) cope, coupe, mould cover half, cover die
上型箱　【铸】cover die, top part [case]

上行程最高点（结晶器的）　top of upstroke
上行(冲)程　up-ward stroke, upstroke
上行冲程压力机　upstroke press
上行焊(从下往上施焊)　upward welding
上行交叉点（三元相图的）　ascending fork point
上行立焊　vertic al-upward welding
上行皮带(运输)机　rising conveyer, sloping belt
上行色层分析法　ascending chromatographic technique
上压板　upward acting platen, top board
上压力　upward pressure, underdraft, underdraught
上压模　top die
上压式造型机　（同"顶压式造型机"）
上溢　overflow
上翼缘（梁的）　top flange
上釉　enamel plating, glazing, enameling
上釉顶层　gloss topcoat
上釉工　glazer
上釉搪瓷　gloss enamel
上釉陶器　glazed earthenware
上釉外涂层　gloss topcoat
上域值　upper range value
上预热段　upper preheat zone
上预热块（火焰清理用）　upper preheat block
上渣　【铁】cinder-notch slag
上渣沟　【铁】cinder runner
上渣试样　flush sample
上轧槽　top pass
上轧辊　top [upper] roll ◇弹簧平衡~*
上轧辊平衡　top roll balance
上轧辊平衡机构[装置]　top roll balancing mechanism
上轧辊组合部件　top roll assembly
上涨（钢锭的）　bleeding, rising
上涨钢锭　rising ingot
上支承辊　top back-up roll, top backing up roll

上轴承座　top chock [chuck]
上铸(法)　(同"顶铸(法)")
上注　(同"顶注")
烧板　cathode deposit resolution
烧剥　flame chipping ◇ 氧乙炔焰～修整*
烧杯　beaker
烧成(砖的)　【耐】burning of brick ◇ 鼓风～(砖的) blast roasting, 炉中～ kiln roasting, 弱～微粒 light-fired particle, 匣钵～法 boxing in, 氧化焰～ oxidizing burning
烧成带　burning zone
烧成段(带式焙烧机的)　firing zone
烧成范围　【耐】firing range
烧成费用　firing cost
烧成工段　【耐】firing section
烧成过程　firing procedure
烧成货物[商品]　firing goods
烧成技术　firing technique
烧成裂纹　firing crack
烧成镁砖　fired magnesite brick
烧成耐渣砖　slag resistant burnt brick
烧成膨胀　firing expansion
烧成[后]强度　【耐】fire strength
烧成曲线　firing curve
烧成缺陷　firing defect [fault]
烧成设备　firing equipment [unit]
烧成试验　firing test
烧成收缩　firing shrinkage
烧成温度　firing temperature
烧成效果　firing effect
烧成效率　firing efficiency
烧成性　fire property
烧成循环　firing cycle
烧成颜色　fired colour
烧成样品　firing sample
烧成窑　burning kiln
烧成油浸合成镁白云石砖　burned impregnated synthetic magnesite dolomite brick
烧成制度　firing regime, burning schedule

烧成制品　burned product
烧成砖　fired [burnt, fritted] brick
烧成装置　firing system ◇ 蓄热式～*
烧除[掉]　burn(ing)-out, removal by burning ◇ 用过量氧焰～生铁表面石墨【焊】searing
烧除涂料　paint burning
烧穿　burn(ing)-through, drop-through, 【冶】(炉子的) breakout, eating thrown, 【铁】runout ◇ 炉衬～ breakthrough, 炉腹～【铁】bosh breakout, 全厚～【焊】melt-thru
烧穿孔　burning hole
烧穿炉衬　breakthrough
烧穿器　arc burner ◇ 铆钉孔～*
烧堆　bing, drop
烧干　bake
烧割　burning
烧割性　crackability
烧割嘴　burning tool
烧根(电杆的)　charring
烧过的黏土　calcined clay
烧焊　burn-in ◇ 端部～ boxing, 中心～焊缝 centre pour weld
烧化(钢锭皮)　【压】swealing
烧化量　【焊】flashing allowance
烧坏的风口　burnt tuyere
烧毁　burn(ing)-out, burn down [up], over-firing
烧火门　【冶】fire door
烧碱(同"氢氧化钠")　◇ 片状～ caustic in flake
烧碱车间　caustic plant
烧碱液　white liquor
烧减损失　burning loss
烧焦　charring, 【机】scorching(碾磨的)
烧焦面　crozzled surface
烧结　sintering, agglomeration, agglomerating, agglutination, fritt(er)ing, cementation, cementing, dead burning, 【钢】fusing in ◇ 不完全[夹生]～*, 初期～ incipient sintering, 单体～【粉】batch sintering,

烧 shao

单相［均相］～*，等静压火花～*，低温～low-sintering，对接～*，多层～*，多相［不均匀］～*，额外［同化］～现象*，放电（加压）［电火花］～*，感应加热～induction sintering，高温～*，共晶～eutectic sintering，过～*，混合燃料～【铁】mixed firing，活化～*，机上冷却～*，激光束～*，加压～*，浸没～immersion sintering，快速～*，矿石铺底～*，扩散～diffusion sintering，冷风～*，链箅机～grate sintering，炉底～burn-in，密闭～（的）close-burning，盘式～pan sintering，泡筏排列～bubble raft sintering，熔浴～liquid bath sintering，闪热［急速加热］～*，渗碳～*，双重［两次］～double sintering，水平条带～*，松散粉末～*，未～的 green，无液相～fritting，下吸［下抽］风～*，盐浴～salt bath sintering，液相～*，再～advanced sintering，直接电阻～*，中间～*，重力（堆积）～gravity sintering，装箱～pack-sintering

烧结白云石 sintered dolomite, clinkered dolomite, doloset

烧烧结棒 sintered bar

烧结保护气体的干燥 drying of sintering atmosphere

烧结杯 sinter pot,【团】pot-grate furnace ◇ 单批～*

烧结杯试验 pot grate test

烧结焙烧 sinter [agglomeration] roast

烧结边界 sintered boundary

烧结变形 sintering warpage

烧结饼 sinter [agglomerated] cake ◇ 成品～*

烧结玻璃（多孔底）漏斗 sintered glass funnel

烧结玻璃过滤器 sintered glass filter

烧结玻璃过滤坩埚 sintered [fritted] glass filtering crucible

烧结铂 sintered platinum

烧结不锈钢 sintered stainless steel

烧结不足的 undersintered

烧结材料 sintered material

烧结操作 sintering operation,【粉】burning operation

烧结层 sinter(ed) layer, sintering bed

烧结产品 sinterings

烧结厂 sinter(ing) plant [facilities], ore-sintering plant, agglomeration plant [facilities] ◇ 利废～recycling plant

烧结厂返矿 sinter plant fines

烧结厂配置 sinter plant layout, arrangement of sinter plant

烧结厂设计 sinter plant design

烧结车间 sinter plant, sintering shop, sintering furnace department

烧结衬里 sintered liner ◇ 预制～*

烧结成的 as-sintered

烧结成型 sinter molding

烧结程度 degree of sintering, extent of agglomeration

烧结抽风机 sinter exhauster [fan]

烧结抽风量 sintering draught requirement

烧结处理 sintering treatment ◇ 循环加热～*

烧结磁铁 sintered magnet ◇ OP 钴铁氧体～OP magnet, 维克托莱特～*

烧结磁性材料 sintered magnetic material

烧结磁性零件 sintered magnetic parts

烧结带 sinter(ing) zone [strand],【粉】fritting zone

烧结带前缘 flame front

烧结底料 sintering bed charge, grate-layer material

烧结电极 sintered electrode

烧结电接触器材 sintered (electric) contact material

烧结电流 sintering current

烧结电气零件 sintered electric parts

烧结锭 sintered ingot

烧结动力学 sintering kinetics ◇ 离子晶体～*

烧结锻造 powder hot forging, sinter forg-

烧结段　sintering area
烧结段风机　sintering zone fan
烧结(段)风箱　sintering windbox
烧结段烟囱　sintering zone stack
烧结多孔镍滤杯　sintered porous nickel cup
烧结多元碳化物　【粉】cemented multicarbide, cemented multiple carbide
烧结多元碳化物刀具　【粉】cemented multicarbide tool
烧结二次混料　[铁]rerolling
烧结法　sintering (process), sinter process, agglomeration method [technique, system], method of sintering ◇ 抽风~*, 格林纳瓦尔特式不连续~*, 间歇式[分批, 间断]~*, 冷压真空~*, 普通~*, 双层~*, 一次[单程]~*
烧结返矿[料]　sinter returns, sintering revert fines, sinter return fines
烧结粉末冶金材料　sintered metal powder material
烧结风量　sintering air requirement
烧结风流　sintering air (flow)
烧结氟化剂　sintered fluorinating agent
烧结刚玉　sintered corundum, alundum
烧结钢　sintered [cemented] steel, pseudosteel
烧结沟　sintering groove
烧结铬镁砖　burnt chrome-magnesite brick
烧结工　agglomerant
烧结工段　sintering area [section, shop], induration section
烧结工序　sintering circuit
烧结工艺　sintering technique, agglomeration technology [process] ◇ 富氧点火~*, 小球团~*
烧结工艺参数　sintering parameter
烧结沟　sintering groove
烧结构造　sintered structure
烧结骨架　sintered skeleton

烧结贵金属　sintered precious metal
烧结锅　sinter(ing) [packing] pot, sintering chamber ◇ 鼓风~blast roasting pot
烧结锅法　pot process
烧结过程　sinter(ing) [agglomeration, cementing, coking, induration] process
烧结过度　excessive sintering
烧结过滤器　sintered filter
烧结海绵金属　sintered sponge
烧结含油轴承合金　sintered metal powder oil impregnated alloy
烧结焊剂　sintered flux
烧结合金　sintered alloy ◇ 埃尔科奈特钨铜~*, 马洛里1000钨铜镍粉末~Mallory 1000
烧结合金钢　sintered alloy steel
烧结后处理　post-sintering treatment
烧结黄铜坯块　sintered brass compact
烧结黄铜制品　sintered brass product
烧结混合料　sinter feed mixture, sinter mix, sintering mix(ture)
烧结混合料层　sinter-mix bed
烧结混合料堆比重[松散密度]　sinter mix bulk density
烧结活塞环　sintered piston ring
烧结活性　sintering activity
烧结机　sinter(ing) [agglomerating, induration] machine, sintering [agglomeration] unit ◇ 带式~*, 环式~*, 火花~*, 机上冷却式~*, 连续式~*, 盘式[间断式]~*, 移动炉箅~*, 圆盘~*
烧结机布料器　sinter machine feeding device, strand feeder
烧结机传动　sinter machine drive
烧结机导轨　sintering rail
烧结机返矿　sinter machine return fines
烧结机机尾　machine discharge
烧结机理　sintering mechanism
烧结机利用系数[床能率]　sintering machine specific capacity, productivity of sintering machine
烧结机排矿　strand discharge

烧 shao

烧结机日历作业率 【团】operating ratio
烧结机(上)脱硫强度 sintering machine desulphurization intensity
烧结机散料 【团】machine dripping
烧结机速度 strand speed
烧结机台车 sintering pallet
烧结机尾罩 sinter machine discharge end hood
烧结机械零件 sintered structural part
烧结机烟气 strand gas
烧结机(有效)面积 sinter strand area,【团】grate (bar) area
烧结机中心线 strand centerline
烧结技术 sintering technique ◇ 厚料层~*,冷压~*
烧结剂 agglutinant
烧结键 sinter bond
烧结节能点火器 low gas consumption sintering ignitor
烧结界面 sintered interface
烧结金 sintered gold
烧结金属 sintered [cemented, synthetic] metal, sinter-metal
烧结金属材料 metallic sintered material
烧结金属磁铁 sintered metal(lic) magnet
烧结金属磁芯 sintered metallic core
烧结金属粉末材料 sintered metal powder material
烧结金属粉末制件 sintered metal powder parts, powder metallurgy (PM) parts
烧结金属过滤器 sintered metallic filter
烧结金属基复合材料 sintered metal-matrix composite
烧结金属浸铝处理 dip calorizing of sinter-metal
烧结金属拉制 drawing of sinter metal
烧结金属离合器衬片 sintered metal clutch facing
烧结金属摩擦材料 sintered metal friction material
烧结金属抛光 buffing of sinter metal
烧结金属陶瓷制品 sinterings
烧结金属纤维毡 feltmetal
烧结金属学 ceramal(s), ceramet, cerametallics
烧结金属制品 sintered metal product
烧结金属轴承 sintered metal bearing
烧结金属着色 colouring of sinter metal
烧结颈 neck formation
烧结颈生长 【粉】neck growth
烧结壳 sinter skin
烧结控制(装置) sintering control
烧结块 sinter (block, cake), sintered briquette, sintering briquette [body], lump sinter, agglomerate, agglomerated cake ◇ 成品~*,热[高温]~ hot agglomerate,自熔性~*
烧结块称量漏斗 agglomerate weigh hopper
烧结块率 lump sinter rateio
烧结块溜槽(回转窑的) 【耐】clinker chute
烧结矿[体] sinter, sinter(ed) ore, (ore) agglomerate ◇ 大块~*,多组分~composite agglomerate,粉状~soft-dusty sinter,高还原度~highly reduced sinter,高碱度[高熔剂性]~*,合格~*,胡桃块~*,回转窑~lump,碱性~basic sinter,扩散型~*,冷~处理系统*,煤气~[块] gas sinter,欠烧[夹生]~*,熔剂性~*,熔融型~*,筛下~sinter screenings,试验~experimental sinter,酸性~acid sinter,豌豆粒~*,小球团~*,整粒~*
烧结矿槽 sinter bin
烧结矿层 sinter bed
烧结矿产量 sinter output [production, yield, make], sintering capacity
烧结矿产率 sinter rate [yield]
烧结矿成品率 (product) yield of sinter
烧结矿堆栈 sinter stockpile
烧结矿返矿 【铁】return fines
烧结矿粉尘 sinter dust
烧结矿粉化 sinter break-down

烧结矿供给线　sinter track
烧结矿合格率　ratio of good sinters
烧结矿化学成分　sinter chemistry
烧结矿化学成分控制　control of sinter chemistry
烧结矿给料装置　sinter feed
烧结矿碱度　sinter basicity
烧结矿(结构)形态　sinter morphology
烧结矿金属化(率)　metallization of sinter
烧结矿块[粒]度　sinter lump size
烧结矿矿物组成　mineralogy of sinter
烧结矿矿相　sinter morphology, mineral phases of sinter
烧结矿矿相[结构定量]分析　【团】quantification of sinter morphology
烧结(矿)冷却机　sinter cooler ◇ 蜂房式~*, 固定式~*, 环状抽风~*, 强制对流式~*, 竖式~*
烧结矿料层透气性　sinter-bed permeability
烧结矿品位　sinter grade
烧结矿破碎[碎裂]　sinter break-down
烧结矿破碎机　sinter breaker ◇ 四辊式~
烧结矿气孔率　sinter porosity
烧结矿强度　sinter resistance [strengrh]
烧结矿入炉比　【铁】sinter proportion [ratio], sinter consumption [content], percent sinter in burden
烧结矿筛分系统配置　sinter screening layout
烧结矿筛下返矿　return undersized sinter, sinter screenings
烧结矿烧透点　sinter burn-through
烧结矿生产　sinter production
烧结矿特性　sinter characteristics
烧结矿屑　sinter fines
烧结矿冶金性能　sinter metallurgical property
烧结矿用量[消耗(量)]　【铁】sinter consumption

烧结矿运送线　sinter conveyer line
烧结矿渣泡沫混凝土　agglomerate-foam concrete
烧结矿转鼓试验　sinter-drum test
烧结矿装车仓　sinter loading bin
烧结冷锻　sinter cold forging
烧结理论　theory of sintering
烧结利用系数　sinter productivity
烧结力　sintering force
烧结料　sintering feed, sinter burden, sinter feed mixture, sintered charge
烧结料层　sinter layer, sinter(-mix) bed, sintering bed charge
烧结料混合机　sinter mixer
烧结料生产方法　method of manufacturing sintered materials
烧结裂纹　【粉】sintering crack
烧结零件　sintered parts ◇ 多孔粉末~电解覆层法 etolizing
烧结流程图　【团】sintering flowsheet, induration scheme
烧结炉　sintering furnace [apparatus], welding furnace, 【团】induration furnace ◇ 传送带式~*, 多棒钟形~*, 辊道炉膛~*, 回转~*, 连续~*, 连续带式~*, 连续运送~*, 氢保护~*, 熔浴~*, 下移~*, 罩式~bell type furnace, 织带运送~*, 钟形~*
烧结炉算　sintering grate
烧结炉衬　sintered [roasted] lining
烧结炉床　fritted hearth
烧结炉底　sintered [fritted, fused] hearth bottom, burned bottom
烧结炉料　sintering charge
烧结铝产[制]品　sintered aluminium product
烧结铝法　SAP (sintered aluminum powder) process
烧结铝粉　sintered aluminium powder (S.A.P.)
烧结铝合金　sintered-aluminium alloy
烧结铝镍铁制品　sintered alnico product

烧 shao

烧结铝镍钴磁铁	◇阿尔尼科~*

烧结铝镍钴磁铁　◇阿尔尼科~*

烧结铝热剂（用于补焊空洞）　sinter thermit

烧结铝锡轴承　aluminium-tin sintered bearing

烧结镁砂　sintered magnesite, magnesite clinker, britmag

烧结密度　sintered density

烧结面积　sintering area, bed area,【团】grate (bar) area

烧结模型　sintering model

烧结摩擦材料　sintered friction material

烧结摩擦零件　sintered friction parts

烧结莫来石　sintered mullite

烧结耐高温材料　sintered high-temperature material

烧结耐磨材料　sintered wear-resistant material

烧结能力　sintering [agglomerating] capacity

烧结黏砂（缺陷）【铸】sand sintering [fritting]

烧结黏土道碴　burnt ballast

烧结镍　sintered nickel

烧结镍过滤杯　sintered nickel cup

烧结镍制品　sintered nickel product

烧结盘　sintering pan [disc] ◇格林纳瓦尔特式~ Greenawalt

烧结泡沫金属　sintered foamed metal

烧结膨胀　sintering swell [grow]

烧结坯　sintered blank

烧结坯块　（同"烧坯"）

烧结皮带通廊　sinter conveyer gallery

烧结铺底料　【团】grate-layer material

烧结期　sintering period

烧结气氛　sintering atmosphere ◇含锂~*

烧结气体转化器　gas converter in sintering

烧结强度　sinter strength

烧结翘曲　sintering warpage

烧结[粉冶]青铜(88.5Cu,10Sn)　sintered [compo] bronze ◇工业~制品*, 冷压~*, 吉内莱特无润滑~轴承合金*

烧结青铜轴承　compo bronze bearing ◇渗四氟乙烯~*

烧结轻金属　sintered light metal

烧结区　sinter(ing) zone

烧结熔剂　【铁】staflux

烧结蠕变　sintering creep

烧结砂块　burning sand

烧结设备　sinter plant, sintering equipment [apparatus, facilities, unit], agglomeration facilities, indurating equipment [unit]

烧结设备流程[系列]　【团】lineup of sintering equipment

烧结生产[实践]　sintering practice

烧结生产率　【团】productivity of sinter

烧结生产能力　sintering capacity

烧结(生产)线　sintering line ◇步进式分段抽风~*

烧结石灰衬里　fired lime liner

烧结石墨化轴承青铜　sintered bearing bronze

烧结石墨青铜　Durex

烧结石英　sintered quartz

烧结时辐射状收缩　radial shrinkage on sintering

烧结时间　sintering time

烧结室　sinter (ing) building, sintering chamber

烧结试验　sintering test [trial]

烧结试验程序　sintering testwork programme

烧结试验计划　sintering testwork program

烧结试验装置　sinter test rig ◇实验室~*

烧结试样　sintered specimen

烧结收得率　yield of sinter

烧结收缩　sintering shrinkage, shrinkage on sintering,【粉】thermal shrinkage

烧结输送系统　sinter (conveyer) system

烧结数据[指标]　sintering data

烧结速度　sintering speed [rate]

烧结损失 loss on sintering
烧结台[小]车 (sintering) pallet, fire grate car ◇ 循环~ circulating pallet
烧结台车起拱 suspending of pallet train
烧结台车体 pallet body
烧结碳钢 【粉】sintered [cemented] carbon steel
烧结碳化钨 (同"碳化钨硬质合金") ◇ 多孔~*
烧结碳化钨刀具 cemented tungsten carbide tool
烧结碳化物 sintered [cemented] carbide
烧结碳化物成分 cemented carbide composition
烧结碳化物刀具 sintered-carbide tool
烧结碳化物拉模 sintered-carbide die
烧结体 sintered [sintering] body ◇ 多层[组合]~*
烧结条件 sintering condition
烧结铁 【粉】sintered [cemented] iron
烧结铁矿 sintered iron ore
烧结铁零件 sintered iron parts
烧结铁制品 sintered ferrous product
烧结铜 sintered copper
烧结温度 sintering [burn-through] temperature,【团】induration [glazing] temperature ◇ 起始~*
烧结温度范围 sintering range
烧结钨棒 sintered tungsten bar
烧结无氧铜 coalesced copper
烧结物 sinter
烧结系统 induration scheme ◇ 霍姆伯格~【团】Holmberg system, 链算机-回转窑~【团】grate-kiln system
烧结现象 sintering phenomenon
烧结箱 sinter box ◇ 保护气体~*, 偏析式~*
烧结性 sintering property [characteristic, tendency], agglomerating capacity, agglomerability
烧结性指数 agglomerating index
烧结玄母岩 sintered basalt

烧结(压)应力 sintering pressure
烧结氧化铝 sintered alumina ◇ 多孔~隔膜*, 辛特克斯~车刀 Sintex, Sintox
烧结氧化铝坩埚 sintered-alumina crucible
烧结氧化铝管 sintered-alumina tube
烧结氧化铍坩埚 sintered beryllia crucible
烧结氧化物磁铁 ceramic magnet
烧结因素 agglomerating agent
烧结硬度 sinter hardness
烧结硬铝 sintered duralumin
烧结硬质合金 sintered hard alloy, cemented carbide
烧结硬质合金材料 sintered hard metal material
烧结用风 sintering air
烧结用燃料 sintering fuel
烧结铀 sintered uranium
烧结元件 sintered component
烧结原理 fundamentals of sintering
烧结原料(粉矿)[烧结用粉矿] sintering feed [material]
烧结原料化学成分 sinter feed chemistry
烧结原料组分 sinter feed component
烧结造块 【团】agglomeration sintering
烧结长大 sintering grow
烧结罩 【团】retort
烧结指数 agglomerating index
烧结致密铜零件 dense parts of sintered copper
烧结制度 sintering schedule, induration scheme
烧结制品 sintered product [article], sintering product, sinterings
烧结质量 sintering quality
烧结中脱硫 sulphur removal in sintering
烧结钟罩 sinter bell (jar), bell jar
烧结终点 burn-through point (BTP), sinter burn-through, end of sintering
烧结终点控制 burn-through control
烧结周期 sintering cycle [period],【团】induration cycle

烧结轴承材料 sintered bearing material
烧结轴承金属[合金] sintered-bearing metal
烧结轴承青铜 sintered bearing bronze
烧结砖 clinker (brick), baked brick
烧结装置 sintering head
烧结状态 as-sintered
烧进 burn-in
烧尽 burn(ing)-off, burn(ing)-out, burn-up, incineration
烧尽的 burned-up
烧开(出)铁口 【铁】lancing of taphole
烧空炉法除石墨(焦炉用) scurfing
烧蓝 (同"发蓝处理") ◇ 钢的碱液～处理 chemag
烧裂 fire crack(ing), firing crack ◇ 轧辊表面～ fire crack in roll
烧炉用风机 stove burner fan
烧绿石 {CaNb$_2$O$_6$·NaF} pyrochlore
烧煤 coal firing ◇ 直接～焙烧*
烧煤气的回转窑 gas-fired rotary kiln
烧煤气的钎焊炉 gas-fired brazing hearth
烧明矾 burnt alum
烧坯 sintering briquette [compact, shape], sintered compact ◇ 复合～*
烧坯孔隙度 sintered porosity
烧坯密度 sintered density
烧瓶 flask, carboy, bottle ◇ 克杰尔达尔[长颈]～Kjeldahl flask, 克莱森～Claisen flask
烧熔(焊接边缘的) 【焊】flashing off ◇ 手工送进～manual flash-off
烧熔边缘 flash off
烧熔过程(对焊的) arcing process
烧熔速度 【焊】burn off rate
烧熔余量(边缘的) flashing allowance [distance]
烧伤 【焊】die burn
烧上 burning-in
烧失量 loss on ignition (LOI), loss in [of] weight on ignition
烧石膏 plaster of paris, passanite

烧蚀 ablation, erosion ◇ 电弧～arc erosion, 电极接触表面～(点焊的) tipburn, 炉顶～【冶】cave in, 枪身～barrel erosion
烧蚀[损]处 burnt place
烧损 burning [fire] loss, fire waste, loss (on ignition), overfire
烧损性加入物 【耐】burning-out admixture
烧炭 charking
烧透 burn(ing)-through
烧透带 【团】burn through area
烧透的 double-burned ◇ 未～underburnt
烧透点 burn-through point [temperature], 【团】burn through area
烧透点测定 burn-through measurement
烧透点测定计 burn-through meter
烧透点控制 burn-through control
烧透速度 burn through speed (BTS)
烧透砖 hard burned brick ◇ 优质～body brick
烧完 after-combustion
烧析 【粉】exudation, sweating
烧窑 kilning
烧窑操作 【耐】burning operation
烧页岩 burnt shale
烧液体燃料的 liquid-fired
烧硬 bake hardening (BK)
烧油点火器 oil-fired ignitor
烧油锻造(加热)炉 【压】oil forge
烧油加热 oil heating
烧油炉 (同"燃油炉")
烧油烧嘴 oil(-fired) burner
烧渣 cinder ◇ 黄铁矿～burnt ore, cinder
烧渣含量 cinder loading
烧渣磨碎机 cinder mill
烧舟 (combustion) boat ◇ 碳(质)～carbon boat
烧砖窑 brick kiln, Dutch kiln (荷兰式)
烧嘴 burner (gun, nozzle), nozzle ◇ 端部[窑头]～end burner, 辅助～pilot burner, 高能力[高效]连续狭缝式～装置*, 焊割两用～*, 回转式～swivelling burn-

er,火舌管～flare stack tips,空气雾化～ air atomising burner,炉顶～*,铆钉穿孔用～*,煤气氧气～*,喷枪式～gun-type burner,切割～*,直喷式～direct-type gun,轴向喷火式～*
烧嘴风流　burner air flow
烧嘴能力　burner capacity
烧嘴喷管　burner pipe
烧嘴前墙　front of burner
烧嘴型式　burner design
烧嘴砖　burner tile［brick］
勺斗挖泥机　dipper dredger
勺淋（氧化）（锡精炼的）　tossing
勺式加料器　scoop feeder ◇ 单向～*
勺样　【钢】spoon sample
勺嘴　ladle lip
少电元素　hypoelectronic element
少量　a small amount ◇ 很～nibble
少量冷加工（带钢的）　killing
少数载流子注入　injection of minority carriers
少锡焊料　poor solder
少烟雾锡铜焊条合金　low-fuming bronze
少油断路器　【电】oil-minimun breaker
赊购　credit（buying）
蛇管冷凝器　coil condenser
蛇管冷却　coil cooling
蛇管冷却器　serpentine cooler
蛇纹石{(Mg,Fe)$_6$Si$_4$O$_{10}$(OH)$_8$}　serpentine, taxoit ◇ 焙烧～furnaced serpentine,风化～weathered serpentine,硅酸盐型～矿*,含镍～矿 ser pentine nickel ore,交织结构～interlaced serpentine
蛇纹石矿物　serpentine mineral
蛇纹石矿样　serpentine sample
蛇型捻股机　snake type strander
蛇形边（冷轧带材缺陷）　snaky edge
蛇形弹簧联轴器　Bibby coupling
蛇形堆叠（焊管坯）　Christmas candy
蛇形管　coil（pipe），pipe coil, coiler, snake pipe ◇ 复式加热～multiple heating coil,加热～coil of heating,预热空气用～*

蛇形冷却管　cooling coil
蛇形蒸汽管　steam coil
蛇状电芯　snake core
舌比（挤压半空心型材的）　tongue ratio
舌部（半空心型材挤压模的）　tongue
舌槽接合　tongued-and-grooved joint
舌簧　【电】reed
舌簧继电器　reed relay
舌尖（轧件压折）　【压】backedges
舌门　flapper
舌片　striking blade
舌头（缺陷）　full strip
舌形模　【压】bridge port die ◇ 带异型切断器的～spider die,整铸～*
舌形耐火砖　tongue type refractory
舌形组合模　(bolted) bridge die
舌状弯曲试验　tongue-bend test
舍菲尔德覆银钢板　Sheffield plate
舍菲尔德碱性平炉法　【钢】S.P.B. steel-making practice
舍菲尔德平炉法　【钢】Sheffield process
舍菲尔德造型材料　Sheffield composition
舍佛纳尔德微扭转试验机　Chevenard microtorsion machine
舍夫勒组织转变图　Schaeffler's diagram
舍入　【数】round(-off), half adjust
舍入误差　【数】rounding［round-off］error
舍伍德直接炼钢法　Sherwood direct steel process
摄动分析　perturbation analysis
摄动能级　perturbed (energy) level
摄谱比较仪　spectrographic comparator
摄谱学［术］　spectrography
摄谱仪　spectrograph, spectrometer ◇ X射线～*,β射线～*,γ射线～*,凹面（绕射）光栅～*,法布里—珀罗干涉～*,反射式～*,红外光电光栅～quantometer,棱镜～prism spectrograph,透射式～*,弯晶～*,吸收～*,衍射［绕射］光栅～*,直示～*,自动多元素～*,自动准直～*
摄谱仪分辨率［能力］　resolution of spec-

trograph
摄氏 Celsius (Cel,Cels)
摄氏热单位 centigrade thermal unit (CTU)
摄氏热量单位 Celsius [centrigrade] heat unit (CHU,C.H.U.)
摄氏温标(℃) Celsius (thermometric scale), Celsius [centigrade] temperature scale, Celsius [centesimale, centigrade] scale, centigrade (Cent., centig.)
摄氏温度 centigrade (degree)
摄氏温度计 centigrade [Celcius(')] thermometer
摄像机 (tele)camera
摄像器 photo-adapter
摄影 photography, filming
摄影测量 photographic surveying
摄影记录器 photorecorder
摄影显微镜 photomicroscope
摄影学 photography
射波探测法 acoustic sounding
射程 range, throw, amplitude
射出 ejaculation, ejection, throw off
射电频率 radio frequency (RF)
射电频谱学 radiospectroscopy
射击 firing
射击前瞄准时间 dead time
射击位置 firing point
射流 jet(-flow), fluid, efflux ◇ 颤振～ dithering jet, 主～ power stream
射流薄膜隔离器 fluid diaphragm isolator
射流编码器 fluidic encoder
射流槽道分流块 fluid channel divider
射流淬火[淬硬] beam hardening
射流存储器 fluid memory (device)
射流阀 fluid valve ◇ 双稳～ bistable fluid valve
射流法 jet-process
射流放大器 fluid amplifier ◇ 微分～*, 引流式～*
射流分类器 fluid sorter
射流功率系统 fluid power system

射流焊接 flow soldering
射流"或"门 fluid OR gate
射流技术 fluidics ◇ 克兰菲尔德～Cranfield fluidics
射流记录设备 fluid memory device
射流键钮板 fluid keyboard
射流开关 fluid switch
射流控制装置 fluid control apparatus, fluid controlled device
射流连接器 fluidic connector
射流逻辑触发器 fluid logic trigger
射流逻辑装置 fluid logic device
射流脉冲发生器 fluid pulse generator
射流脉冲转换器 fluid pulse converter
射流喷嘴 jet injector
射流时间门 fluid time gate
射流伺服控制 fluidic servo control
射流速度 jet velocity
射流特性 jet characteristics
射流系统 fluid operated system
射流显示器 fluid display
射流信号发生器 fluid signal generator
射流旋流传递 fluid vortex transfer
射流学 fluidics
射流压力基准 fluid pressure reference
射流硬件 fluidic hardware
射流元件 fluidic element ◇ 多通路～*
射流振荡器 fluid oscillator
射流中心 core of jet
射流装置 fluidic device, fluidizing system ◇ 多稳～*, 双稳～bistable fluid device
射流阻抗 fluid impedance
射流组件 fluidic module
射频 radio frequency (RF)
射频变压器 radio-frequency transformer
射频场 radio-frequency field
射频磁控溅射沉积 radio-frequency magnetron sputtering deposition
射频等离子体 radio-frequency plasma
射频电阻焊 radio-frequency resistance welding
射频发生器 【电】radio-frequency signal

generator, radio-frequency alternator
射频放电探测器　radio-frequency discharge detector
射频分量　radio-frequency component
射频感应加热　r-f induction heating
射频感应炉　radio-frequency induction furnace
射频焊　radio-frequency welding
射频加热　radio-frequency (R.F.) heating
射频加热学[术]　radiothermics
射频交流发电机　radio-frequency alternator
射频探伤仪　radio-frequency crack detector
射频焰　radio-frequency torch
射频振荡器　radio-frequency oscillator [generator]
射频质谱仪　radio-frequency mass-spectrometer
射气　emanation
射束　beam ◇ 大开度～ beam of wide aperture, 单色[单一波长]～*, 滤清的 ～ filtrated beam
射束分裂器　beam splitter
射束功率　beam power
射束会聚　beam convergence
射束会聚角　beam convergence angle
射束监测器　beam monitor
射束阱　beam trap
射束径迹　【理】beam path
射束孔径　aperture of beam
射束控制　beam control
射束扩展[分散]　beam spread
射束扩展角　angle of beam spread
射束面积　beam area
射束收敛角　beam convergence angle
射束限制孔径　beam limiting aperture
射束形成装置　beam forming arrangement
射束轴　beam axis
射水沉桩　jetted pile
射水除尘器　water jet dust absorber

射体　missile
射钍　diothorium
射线　ray ◇ 不透～的 radiopaque, 大布喇格角～ high angle arcs, 防～混凝土*
射线测厚　thickness measurement with ray
射线出口　exit of radiation
射线穿透计　penetrometer
射线发光　radioluminescence
射线分部[体截]照相术　body section radiography
射线隔板　personnel barrier
射线管窗口　tube window
射线活动照相术　cine radiography
射线检验　radio examination, radioscopy
射线交叉[交射]照相术　cross-fire radiography
射线金相学　radiometallography
射线料线仪　【铁】stockray
射线偏斜　wobbulation
射线强度　ray intensity
射线清晰度　line sharpness
射线束　beam, bundle of rays ◇ 有限 ～*, 窄～ pencil
射线束出口　beam exit hole
射线束截面　beam cross-section
射线束准直　beam collimation
射线束准直仪[平行光管]　beam collimator
射线图　radiogram, radiograph
射线危害性　radiohazard
射线硬度　beam hardness
射线硬度测定仪　radiochrometer
射线源　radiation source, radiant ◇ 线状 ～ line source
射线照片　radiograph, radiotelegram
射线照片衬度　radiographic contrast
射线照射　irradiation ◇ 经～合金 irradiated alloy
射线照相当量系数　radiographic equivalence factor
射线照相分析　radiographic analysis
射线照相合格率[性]　radiographic

soundness
射线照相检查　radiographic inspection
射线照相检验　radiographic test
射线照相胶[软]片　radiographic film
射线照相(乳胶)黑度　radiographic density
射线照相(术)　radiography ◇ 电子感应加速器的～ betatron radiography, 分部[分层,剖面]～ sectional radiography, 高电压～*, 高速～*, 高温～ hot radiography, 接触显微～*, 静电影象～ xeroradiography, 热致发光～*, 双曝光～*, 微型～ miniature radiography, 自(动)～ autoradiography
射线照相术应用　radiographic application
射线照相特性　radiographic quality
射线照相源　radiographic source
射线照相装置　radiography equipment
射芯机　【铸】core shooter, core shooting machine
射压造型　【铸】injection moulding
射压造型机　injection moulding machine
社会环境　social environment
社会铁态平衡原理　principle for ferri-balance in social environment
社会总产值　gross social output value
设备　equipment(eqpt), device(dev.), facilities, apparatus(app.), appliance, installation(inst.,instl.), plant, unit ◇ 大吨位[重型]～*, 一套～ single unit
设备不可靠性　mechanical unreliability
设备布置　plant layout [arrangement]
设备部分子句　【计】environment clause
设备参数　parameter of apparatus
设备定额　installed rating
设备费　【企】cost of installation
设备分配　【计】facility assignment
设备负荷率　equipment loading ratio
设备互换[兼容]性　【计】equipment compatibility
设备结构材料　plant constructional material
设备故障[失效]　equipment failure
设备就绪或未就绪状态　【计】device ready/not-ready
设备控制　device [plant] control
设备控制系统　device control unit
设备利用率　plant [equipment] utilization rate, device availability, rolling rate
设备名　【计】device [implementor] name
设备配置　configuration, layout of equipment
设备平面布置　plant design
设备容量　plant [apparatus] capacity
设备(生产)能力　installation [apparatus, plant] capacity
设备维修工　serviceman
设备效率　equipment efficiency
设备选型　sizing of equipment
设备运转率　equipment operation ratio
设备作业率　plant availability coefficient
设定控制　set-up control
设定控制系统　set-up control system
设定值控制[调节,调整]　set point control (SPC), fixed set point control
设定值预调　setpoint presetting
设计　design(ing), engineering, plan, project, layout ◇ 按标准型式～的 modular, 经过考验的～ favour time-proved design, 专门[定货]～的 customed-designed
设计安全系数　design load factor
设计标准　design standard [criteria]
设计参数　design parameter [variable]
设计产量　designed [projected] output, design throughput, planned production rate, projected output
设计成本[费用]　projected cost
设计程序　project approach, design [loyout] procedure
设计的主要机械性能　basic mechanical design feature
设计方案　design proposal [scheme, concept, precept, consideration]
设计负载[荷载]　design load

设计改进[完善] design sophistication
设计工程师 design engineer
设计公式 design formula (des. form.)
设计惯例 design convention
设计规范 design specifications
设计规格 design specification
设计耗量 design consumption
设计荷载安全系数 design load factor
设计基础 design basis
设计计算 design calculation
设计碱度 【团】design basicity
设计进度 design schedule
设计力 rated force
设计能力 design(ed) [planned] capapcity, design throughput, planned production rate
设计年产量 rated annual capacity
设计期限 designed period
设计任务书 project designs
设计师[者,人员] designer, constructor, design staff
设计使用期限 design life
设计手册 design handbook [manual]
设计寿命 design life
设计书 design
设计数据 design data [figure]
设计速度 design speed
设计特点 design feature
设计特性 design characteristics
设计条件 design condition
设计图 design drawing [chart, diagram, figure], plan, layout
设计详图 detail of design
设计效率 design efficiency
设计性能 design performance [characteristics]
设计修改 design modification
设计压力 design pressure
设计依据 design basis [consideration]
设计应力 design stress
设计资料 design data
设计准则 design criteria

设计总负责人 chief designer
设计最高能力[最大生产能力] peak design capacity
设立 establishing, setting up, erection
设施 facilities, installation, service
设想 assumption, design concept [consideration]
设置 setting up, installing, institution
砷{As} arsenic, arsenium, ◇除[脱]~*, 含~合金, 马什试~法 Marsh test
砷白铁矿 lonchidite, kyrosite
砷钡铀矿{Ba(UO$_2$)$_2$(AsO$_4$)$_2$·n H$_2$O}(n=10—12) heinrichite
砷铋钴矿 cheleutite
砷铂矿{PtAs$_2$} sperrylite
砷粉{As$_2$O$_5$} arsenic powder
砷浮渣 【色】arsenic skimmings
砷钙锰矿 rhodoarsenian
砷钙钠锌石 zinc-lavendulan
砷钙铜矿 conichalcite, higginsite
砷钙铀矿{Ca(UO$_2$)As$_2$O$_8$·n H$_2$O}(n=8—12) uranospinite
砷钴矿{(Co, Ni)As$_2$} smaltine, smaltite, grey cobalt, tin white cobalt {CoAs$_2$}
砷钴铀矿{Co(UO$_2$)$_2$(AsO$_4$)$_2$·n H$_2$O} kirschheimerite
砷华{As$_2$O$_3$} arsenolite, arsenic bloom
砷化合物 arsenic compound
砷化镓{GaAs} gallium arsenide
砷化镓激光器 gallium-arsenide laser
砷化铝{AlAs} aluminium arsenide
砷化镍结构 nickel arsenide structure
砷化铅{Pb$_3$As$_2$} lead arsenide
砷化氢 arsenic hydride
砷化氢中毒 arsine poisoning
砷化三氢{AsH$_3$} arseniuretted hydrogen, arsine (gas)
砷化铁{FeAs} iron arsenide
砷化物 arsenide
砷化铟 indium arsenide
砷黄锑矿 arsenostibite
砷黄铁矿{FeAsS} arsenical pyrite, ar-

砷 senopyrite, mispickel ◇ 含金～ auriferous arsenopyrite
砷矿 red arsenic
砷矿物 arsenic mineral
砷锍 【色】speiss ◇ 焙烧～ roasted speiss
砷铝锰矿 synadelphite, allodelphite
砷铝铀矿 {HAl(UO$_2$)$_4$(As$_2$O$_5$)$_4$·16H$_2$O} paulite
砷氯铅矿 georgiadesite, finnemanite
砷锰矿 armangite
砷镍矿 chloanthite {NiAs$_2$}, white nickel {NiAs$_2$}, nickeline {NiAs}
砷镍石 xanthiosite
砷铅合金 (0.15As, 0.10Bi,余量 Pb；用作电缆外皮) arsenical lead
砷铅矿 {(PbCl)Pb$_4$As$_3$O$_{12}$} mimetite
砷铅铝矾 hidalgoite
砷酸 arsenic acid
砷酸铋矿 atelestite, rhagite
砷酸钙 calcium arsenate
砷酸汞 mercuric arsenate
砷酸钠 sodium arsenate
砷酸铅 {Pb$_3$(AsO$_4$)$_2$} lead arsenate
砷酸铁矿 {3FeO·As$_2$O$_5$·8H$_2$O} symplesite
砷酸铜 copper arsenate
砷酸锌 zinc arsenate
砷酸盐[酯] arsenate
砷锑浮渣 arsenic-antimony skimmings
砷锑矿 antimoniferous arsenic, arsenical antimony
砷铜 (<0.5%As) arsenical copper
砷铜矿 abichite
砷烟 arsenic fume
砷银矿 arsenical silver
砷铀铋矿 walpurgite
砷铀矿 {(UO$_2$)$_3$As$_2$O$_8$·12H$_2$O} troegerite
砷黝铜矿 {Cu$_8$As$_2$S$_7$} tennantite, giraudite
砷真空镀层 arsenic vacuum coating
申尼克疲劳试验机 Schenick machine
申请专利 patent application [claim], applying [application] for a patent

伸臂 cantilever, overhanging, semi-girder
伸长 elongation, prolongation, extension, spread-out, stretch ◇ 蠕变破断～*, 逐渐～ progress elongation
伸长斑点 (X射线照片的) elongated spot
伸长单畴 elongated single domain (ESD)
伸长单畴(微粒)磁铁 ESD (elongated single domain) magnet, ESD particle magnet
伸长计 extensometer, elongation meter, (wire resistance) strain gauge, ductilometer, ductilimeter, tensometer ◇ 胡根贝格尔～*, 镜式棱柱光学～*, 西尔～ Searle's extensometer
伸长计夹持标距 extensometer clip gauge
伸长晶粒 elongated grain
伸长率 elongation (el.), extensibility, percentage elongation [extension], percent(age of) elongation
伸长器 elongating mill, lengthener
伸长试验 elongation test
伸长速率 【压】rate of stretch
伸长弹性 elasticity of elongation
伸长系数 lengthening coefficient, coefficient of extension
伸出 stretch, extention, overhanging
伸出部分 outshoot, setoff, stick-out
伸出长度 (悬臂梁的) overhanging length
伸出梁 【建】cathead
伸出水面的 overhand
伸角式压力机 horn press
伸屈起重机 lazy jack
伸缩 expansion and contraction ◇ 可～的 telescoping
伸缩尺 extension rod
伸缩地板 telescoping floor
伸缩缝 expansion joint ◇ 无浆～ dry joint
伸缩管 expansion [telescopic] pipe ◇ U形～ expansion U-bend

伸缩架　expansion bracket ◇ 可拆卸～ collapsible stripper
伸缩接合　expansion and contraction joint, slip joint
伸缩螺栓　expansion bolt
伸缩膜盒[软管]　flexible bellows
伸缩器　expansion bend [piece]
伸缩三角架　extension tripod
伸缩式　collapsible, telescopic-type
伸缩式比例气压机　pantograph cutter
伸缩式[伸缩自由的]电极　retractable electrode
伸缩式流槽　extensible chute
伸缩式皮带助卷机　retractable belt wrapper
伸缩式起重机[吊车]　telehoist ◇ 均热炉用～*
伸缩式线盘卸料器　【压】collapsible stripping spider
伸缩式心轴　telescopic spindle
伸缩式运输机　retractable conveyor
伸缩式助卷机辊　retractable wrapper roll
伸缩台　telescopic table
伸缩套管　telescopic tube, telescope tube
伸缩梯　extension ladder
伸缩性　elasticity, flexibility
伸缩罩　flexible skirt, telescopic cover
伸缩支柱　telescopic support
伸缩轴　telescopic shaft
伸悬臂拱式大梁　（同"悬臂弓形架"）
伸延　stretching
伸展　spread, stretch, tension ◇ 可～的 ductile
伸展器　stretcher
伸展式C形吊钩装置　spreader C-hooks
伸展[拉伸]凸缘　stretch flange
伸展[张]弯曲　【压】stretch bending
伸展性[可伸展性]　expansibility
伸张法　stretching process
伸张压力机　stretch(ing) press
伸胀缝（钢轨的）　expansion opening
伸直　uprise, 【压】straight cast

深凹口（接触焊的）　excessive indentation
深表面层　deep case
深部焊接　deep weld(ing)
深采掘　deep cutting
深槽　quirk
深槽的　deep-slot
深槽式环冷机　【团】deep trough rotary type cooler, deep trough annular cooler
深槽效应　【电】deep-slot effect
深槽转子　deep bar rotor
深草黄色　deep straw-yellow colour, full straw colour
深层表面清理　severe gouging
深层淬硬性　throughout hardenability
深层切割　severe gouging
深层钻探　deep prospecting
深冲　【压】deep drawing, cup-drawing ◇ 双动[两步,两工序]～ double-action drawing, 液压～*
深冲板钢　deep-drawing sheet steel
深冲薄(钢)板　deep-[drawing stamping] sheet
深冲材料　deep-drawing material
深冲操作　deep-drawing operation
深冲法　deep-drawing process ◇ 福尔马落锤～ Formall process
深冲钢　deep-drawing steel, drawing quality steel ◇ 超[优质]～*, 低碳～*, 重型～压力机 heavy draw press
深冲钢板　deep-drawing steel plate
深冲工具　deep-drawing tool
深冲件耳子　ear of deep-drawn part
深冲模　cupping [blind] die ◇ 加热－冷却式～*
深冲试验　drawing test
深冲性(能)　deep-drawing property, deep drawability
深冲延伸系数　cupping (ductility) value
深冲用带材　deep-drawing strip
深冲(用)黄铜　deep-drawing brass
深冲(用)润滑剂　deep-drawing lubricant, lubricant for deep-drawing

深冲质量　(deep-)drawing quality
深穿　deep piercing
深吹　gone high
深吹炼熔池　deep blowing molten pool
深淬硬能力　capability to depth-harden
深地下水位　deep water table
深度测定[测量]　depth measurement
深度锤（测量海洋用）　dip weight
深度淬火[淬硬]　deep [depth] hardening
深度计[规]　depth gauge (DEGA), depth indicator, depthometer, foot gauge ◇钻探～boring gauge
深(度)浸蚀　deep etch(ing) ◇达什～液*
深度浸蚀试验　deep etch test
深度冷冻　deep freezing, cryogenic refrigeration
深度冷冻槽　deep freeze tank
深度冷冻处理　deep freeze treatment
深度冷冻器　deep freezer
深度冷冻设备　deep freezing unit
深度渗碳　deep carburizing
深(度)脱磷　deep dephosphorization
深(度)脱硫　deep desulphurization
深(度)脱碳　deep decarbonization [decarburization]
深度旋压　flow spinning
深度硬化[淬火]钢　deep hardening steel
深坩埚熔化　deep-mould melting
深坩埚式电弧炉　deep-crucible (type arc) furnace
深海电缆　deep-sea cable
深海测深器　bathometer
深焊　throat welding
深横裂缝　butt crack
深红银矿{$3Ag_2S \cdot Sb_2S_3$}　antimonial silver blende, dark red silver ore
深黄铀矿{$CaO \cdot 6UO_2 \cdot 11H_2O$}　becquerelite
深灰金刚石（切削工具）　carbonado
深基础　deep foundation
深焦深　【理】great depth of focus

深浸蚀槽　deep etching bath
深浸蚀法　【金】deep-etch method
深井泵　bore hole pump ◇往复式～*
深井处置系统　【环】deep-well disposal system
深井灌注　【环】deep-well injection
深井水轮[涡流]泵　deep well turbine pump
深坑　deep pitting
深孔镜　cystoscope
深孔窥视仪　cave borescope
深孔凿岩　borehole drilling ◇机械化～*
深拉法　（同"深冲法"）, cupping process ◇橡皮～*
深拉钢　（同"深冲钢"）
深拉钢熔炼　deep-drawing heat
深拉管　deep-drawing tube
深拉试验　cup-drawing test ◇埃里克森～*
深拉性能[能力]　（同"深冲性能"）
深拉压力机　draw(ing) press ◇活动台面～slide drawing press, 下滑座式～*
深拉(延)　（同"深冲"）, cupping
深拉延润滑剂　deep-drawing lubricant
深拉用黄铜片　eyelet brass
深冷处理　refrigeration treatment, 【金】subzero cooling [treatment]
深冷(淬火)急热(回火)处理　uphill quenching (treatment)
深冷温度　cryogenic temperature
深埋气泡　deep-seated blowhole
深内孔窥视仪　cave borescope
深潜容器　deep-diving vehicles
深潜水位　deep water table
深切槽　【机】heavy cut, deep slotting
深青岩　greenstone
深缺口试样　deep notch specimen
深熔　anatexis
深熔池　deep molten bath
深熔池熔炼　【色】deep bath smelting
深熔池熔炼法　deep bath smelting method
深熔焊　deep (penetration) welding, pene-

tration fusion welding
深熔焊缝 penetration weld
深熔焊条 deep penetration electrode
深熔角焊 deep-fillet welding
深渗碳 deep cementing
深室式环状炉 deep-chamber ring furnace
深室型自由沉降分级机 deep-pocket free settling classifier
深水测深器 deep-sounding apparatus
深透渗碳(法) (同"均匀渗碳")
深脱硫剂 【钢】strong desulphurizer
深挖 deep cutting, dig deep
深压延件壁部的波形 puckering
深延(成型)操作 【压】cupping operation
深延[拉]组织 overdrawn structure
深轧 deep piercing
深杂质能级 deep impurity level
深锥浓缩机 deep cone thickener
神经元 neuron
神经(元)网络 【计】neural net(work) ◇ 反向传播～*,人工～*
神经(元)网络控制器 neural network controller
神经(元)网络控制系统 neural network control system
神经(元)网络内模控制 neural network internal model control
审查 examination, viewing, audit
审查程序 【计】audit program
审查人 examiner
胂气(砷化六氢){AsH₃} arsine gas
渗出 bleeding, oozing
渗出能力(渗透液的) bleed back
渗出物 ooze, effusion
渗出液 diffusate, percolate
渗出作用 【金】bleed out
渗氮 (同"氮化") ◇ 弗洛～法*,高频感应～*,高温～*,辉光放电[电离法]～*,加压～*,假[无氮化剂]～ blank nitriding,局部[选择]～ selective nitriding,两段～*,湿式～ wet nitriding
渗氮钢 nitrided steel ◇ 快速～ rapid nitriding steel,尼特拉洛伊石墨化～*
渗氮钢表面韧性 case toughness of nitrided steel
渗氮炉 nitriding furnace ◇ 竖罐式～*
渗氮炉炉膛 nitriding furnace chamber
渗氮(耐磨)铸铁 (2.58Si,1.22Cr,0.16V, 0.24Mo,1.01Al,余量Fe) nitricastiron
渗氮箱 nitriding box
渗氮硬化 nitride [nitrogen] hardening ◇ 表面～法*
渗镀铜 copper cementation
渗风 air infiltration, infiltrating air
渗干时间(渗透液的) drain time
渗铬 【金】chromizing, chromising, inchrome, inchromizing, chromalloying, chromium impregnation ◇ 粉红相～ pink-phase chromizing,扩散～*,气体～ gas chromizing,
渗铬法 inchrome [inchrom(ierung)] process ◇ BDS表面～ BDS process,奥内拉表面～*
渗铬钢 chromized steel ◇ 固体～*
渗铬硬化的 chromium-hardened
渗汞孔隙率测定法 【粉】mercury porosimetry
渗汞孔隙率测定仪 【粉】mercury porosimeter
渗硅 【钢】siliconising, siliconizing, silicon impregnation
渗硅薄(钢)板 siliconized iron plate
渗硅法 siliconising process, silicon impregnation ◇ 埃克曼～ Eckman process
渗金属处理 metal cementation
渗金属法 metallic-cementation process
渗金属塑料 metallized plastics
渗浸流速 percolation flow rate
渗井 percolation pit
渗开(渗透液的) 【金】blotting
渗坑 percolation pit
渗硫 sulphurization ◇ 低温放电～真空炉*,库贝特低温～法 Coubet method
渗硫处理 sulphurizing

渗硫铁系含油轴承 ferroporit bearing
渗流 transfusion, interstifial flow, influent, seepage
渗漏 leakage, drip, seepage,【钢】badly bleeding（钢锭缺陷）◇ 渠道～损失 canal seepage loss, 水分～weepage, 找出的～位置 located leak
渗漏空气 leaked-in air
渗漏塞棒 【钢】leaky stopper
渗漏水 percolating water
渗铝 aluminizing, aluminising, alumetizing, aliting, alitization, alitizing, calorisation, calorising, calorization, calorizing ◇ 固体～*, 耐热～法【压】alumincoat, 喷镀～spray calorizing, 热浸～法*
渗铝层 aluminized coating
渗铝法 altierfen
渗铝钢 alumetized [alumetizing, calorised] steel ◇ 阿姆柯～*
渗铝渣口 【铁】aluminizing slag notch
渗滤 percolation, colation, infiltration, drip ◇ 下向～(浸出) downward percolation
渗滤池 diffusion cell
渗滤处理 percolation treatment
渗滤法 filtration percolation
渗滤浸出 percolation leaching,【色】percolation ◇ 上向～upward percolation
渗滤(浸出)槽 percolation tank
渗滤浸出器 percolator, diffuser [diffusor] (for percolation leaching)
渗滤(浸出)设备 【色】percolation equipment
渗滤浸出系统 percolation system ◇ 逆流～*
渗滤离子交换 percolation ion exchange
渗滤水 seepage water
渗滤速度 percolation rate
渗滤液 percolate
渗滤溢流速率 percolation overflow rate
渗硼 boronizing, boronization, boronising, boronisation, boriding
渗氢 hydrogen charging

渗氰 cyanate ◇ 干式～法*
渗染作用 【金】bleed out
渗入 penetrating, penetration, infiltration, inleakage, interfusion, leak-in
渗入率 inleakage rate
渗入物 infiltrate, infiltration
渗水 seepage of water, weepage
渗水沟管 weeper drains
渗水井 drainage [negative] well
渗水铸件 leaker
渗四氟乙烯烧结青铜轴承 bronze fluon bearing ◇ PTFE～*
渗碳 carburization, carburizing, carbonization, carbonizing, carbon penetration, (carburizing) cementation, impregnation with carbon, carbon pickup, acieration, Brinelling ◇ 包装～pack carburizing, 表面～*, 防～覆层*, 坩埚～crucible carburizing, 固体渗碳剂[碳质固体]～*, 管式炉～tube carburizing, 过～over-carburization, 活性～activated carburizing, 加氢～*, 假[伪]～*, 局部[选择]～selective carburizing, 均匀[深透, 全断面]～*, 离子～ion carbonization, 气体～*, 氰化物～*, 软[弱渗碳剂]～【金】mild carburizing, 深(度)～*, 修复～*, 盐浴[熔盐]～*, 液体～*, 预先～precarburization
渗碳保护 carburizing protection
渗碳表面 carburized surface
渗碳层 carburized layer ◇ 厚～*
渗碳层厚度 case depth
渗碳齿轮钢 carburized gear steel
渗碳处理 (carburizing) cementation, carburizing treatment
渗碳带 cemented zone
渗碳法 carburizing [cementation] process, hardening method, method of cementation ◇ 超碳量～*, 脆性边界表面～*, 高温～*, 液滴～*
渗碳粉 cementing powder
渗碳钢 carburized [carburizing, cementa-

tion,converted] steel ◇ 克庐伯型~*,珠光体~hyperpearlitic steel
渗碳过程 carburizing [cementing, cementation] process
渗碳盒 carburizing [cementing] pot
渗碳机 hardening machine
渗碳机理 mechanism of carburization [cementation]
渗碳剂 carburizer, carburizing (re)agent [compounds, material], recarbonizer, cementation agent ◇ 表面硬化~*,粉状~cementing powder,缓和~milder carburizer
渗碳加速剂 energizer
渗碳阶段 【金】carbonizing period
渗碳介质 carburizing medium
渗碳炉 carburizing [cementing, cementation] furnace, carburizer ◇ 表层~case-hardening furnace,管式~*,连续式气体~*,摇动炉底式~*,装箱[固体]~*
渗碳磨齿修形 carbonized gear grinding with relief
渗碳硼钢 carburized boron steel
渗碳期 carburizing cycle
渗碳气氛 carburizing atmosphere
渗碳气体 carburizing gas ◇ RX~*
渗碳区 cemented zone
渗碳烧结 carbusintering ◇ 煤气~gas carbusintering
渗碳设备 【金】carburizing machinery
渗碳深度公式 ◇ 哈里斯表层~*
渗碳碳(素)钢 carbon carburizing steel
渗碳体{Fe_3C} ferric carbide, tri-ferrous carbide, cementite (carbide), carbide of iron ◇ 残余~residual cementite,初生[一次]~primary cementite,次生[二次]~secondary cementite,过剩~excess cementite,离异~divorced cementite,球状~*,三生[三次]~tertiary cementite,网状~cementite network,先共晶~*,自由[游离]~free cementite

渗碳体浸蚀剂 carbide etchant
渗碳体聚集 coalescence of cementite
渗碳体颗粒 carbide particle
渗碳体网 cementite network
渗碳添加剂 carburizing addition
渗碳-脱碳反应 carburization-decarburization reaction
渗碳温度 carburizing temperature
渗碳细钢丝(制特殊针用) pin bar
渗碳箱 carburizing box [pot], case-hardening box, cementing box [pot]
渗碳效应 carburization effect
渗碳焰 (同"碳化焰")
渗碳液 carburizing liquid
渗碳硬化法 cementing process ◇ 钢固体~harveyizing
渗碳浴槽 carburizing [cementing] bath
渗碳轴承钢 carburized bearing steel
渗碳装置 【金】carburizing machinery
渗碳组织 carburized structure
渗碳作用 carburization effect, carburation
渗铜 copper cementation
渗铜钢 【铜】cupric (cemented) steel, cemented steel
渗铜碳钢 cemented carbon steel
渗铜铁 【粉】copper-infiltrated iron, cemented iron
渗透 permeation, infiltration, penetrance, penetration, seepage, osmosis, endosmosis ◇ 全浸~full dip infiltration
渗透不充分 inadequate penetration
渗透法 permeability method, infiltration process
渗透剂 penetrant ◇ 液(体)氧中安全的~Lox-safe penetrant
渗透介质 permeating medium
渗透控制 permeation control
渗透浓度 osmotic concentration
渗透前端 permeation front
渗透曲线 【金】penetration curve
渗透烧结 infiltration sintering
渗透深度 depth of penetration

渗透时间　penetration time
渗透试验　penetration test ◇ 标准~*
渗透水　percolating water
渗透探伤法　penetrant flaw detection
渗透系数　percolation [permeability] coefficient
渗透显示　penetration indication
渗透性　penetration, permeability, perviousness ◇ 绝对~*
渗透压(力)　osmotic pressure ◇ 胶体~*
渗透压力差　【环】osmotic pressure difference
渗透液　liquid penetrant, penetrating fluid
渗透液检验　penetrant inspection
渗透液检验法　penetrant fluid test
渗透液渗入屏幕　falling curtain of penetrant
渗透液体染色检验法　【理】dye-penetrant process
渗透着色探伤法　penetrant-dye method
渗透作用　osmose, osmosis
渗析　dialysis
渗析膜[器]　dialyzer, dialyser
渗锡处理　【金】stannizing
渗锌(扩散渗锌)　zinc impregnation, zincizing ◇ 扩散~炉 sherardising furnace, 气化~ vapour sherardizing
渗锌法　sherardising process
渗压仪　consolidometer
渗硬铬　hard chromizing
渗油　oil impregnate
渗油撒粉探伤法　oil powder method
渗油速率(多孔制品的)　rate of oil flow
渗渣性　slag penetration
声波　sound [sonic, acoustical] wave, sound oscillations
声波测距法　sound-ranging
声波冲击试验　acoustic impact test
声波定位仪[水下声波定位仪]　sonar
声(波)化学发光　sonochemiluminescence
声波检验　sonic testing
声波疲劳　acoustic(al) [sonic] fatigue
声波散射　acoustic scattering, scattering of sound waves
声波探测法　acoustic sounding
声波探伤　sonic testing, sonic flaw detection
声波通道　acoustic line
声波图　audiogram, audograph
声波学　sonography
声波折射　sound deflection
声不连续(性)　acoustic discontinuity
声传感器　sonic transducer
声存储器　【计】acoustic memory [storage]
声发射检验[试验]　acoustic emission test
声反射系数　acoustic reflection coefficient, acoustic reflectivity
声干扰　acoustic disturbance [jamming]
声共鸣[共振]　acoustic resonance
声化学发光　sonchemiluminescence
声级　acoustical level, sound level [stage]
声间断(性)　acoustic discontinuity
声浪(大型风机的)　surging
声纳　sonar (sound navigation and ranging), acoustic susceptance
声纳控渣指导操作系统　【钢】sonar slag control operational guiding system
声能　sound [acoustic] energy
声耦合子　【理】acoustic couplants
声频变压器　audio former
声频磁学(用于探矿)　audio frequency magnetics (AFMAG)
声频发生器　audio-frequency generator
声频放大器　audio-frequency amplifier
声频计　audio-frequency meter
声频疲劳(机翼的)　acoustic fatigue
声频谱计　acoustic spectrometer
声频信号　sonic [audio, acoustical] signal
声频增益　audio gain
声频振荡器　audio-frequency oscillator
声屏　【理】sound panel
声谱　sound [acoustic] spectrum
声谱学　sonography
声强(度)　sound intensity

声容　acoustic capacitance
声衰减常数　acoustical attenuation constant
声速(度)　sound [acoustic] velocity
声速法　sound velocity method
声速实验台　acoustical bench
声透射系数　acoustic transmission coefficient
声吸收系数　acoustic absorption coefficient, acoustical absorptivity
声线法　【理】ray acoustics
声响　sound, noise ◇ 噼啪~(电弧的)【电】sputter
声响火警系统　fire alarm sounding system
声响检验　aural test, acoustic test (锤敲)
声响(指示)器　squealer
声响探测器　aural detector
声像　sound [acoustic(al)] image
声学化渣仪　【钢】audiometer
声学匹配　acoustic(al) matching
声学全息术　acoustic holography
声学扫描图像　acoustically scanned image
声学试验　acoustic test
声学透镜　sound [acoustic] lens
声学应变仪　acoustic strain gauge
声音反射装置　sound baffle
声(音)输入装置　acoustic input device
声音应答装置　【电】audio response unit
声音终端　【电】audio terminal
声硬度　acoustic stiffness
声振荡　【电】sound oscillation
声振动　sound vibration
声致发光　sonoluminescence
声子　phonon
声子谱　phonon spectra
生白云石　crude [green, raw] dolomite
生白云石耐火材料　raw refractory dolomite
生产　production, producing, manufacture, making ◇ 大量[大批]~", 满负荷[全规模]~ full scale production, 在~中 in operation (i/opn)

生产残料　treatment tailings
生产残渣　mill tailings
生产槽阳极　commercial anode
生产厂　production plant, producer
生产厂价格指数　producer price indices
生产成本　production [operating, first] cost
生产程序　production program [routine], sequence of produciton
生产单元　production unit
生产定额　【企】job rates [quota]
生产方法　production process [method], manufacturing process
生产方式　operating methodology
生产废钢　process scrap
生产废料　production scrap, production waste (水、气、渣)
生产废料利用　salvaging
生产费　【企】running expense
生产费用　production [manufacturing, operational, working] cost
生产工艺　process technique, production process, productive technology, manufacturing practice
生产工艺学　process technology
生产故障　production trouble
生产管理　production control [management], plant supervision
生产规划　production plan(ning)
生产过程　productive process, course of produciton
生产过程检测仪表　process instrumentation
生产过程简况　outline of process
生产过程溶液　process liquor
生产过程说明　process description
生产过程中存料　in-process inventory
生产过程自动化　process automation
生产过剩　overproduction
生产基地　production basis [base]
生产计划　production schedule [program], operating plan

生产计划员　scheduler
生产记录　record of production, performance
生产监控室　productive supervision room
生产进度表　【企】production schedule
生产经验　operating [service] experience
生产控制　production control
生产控制化学分析　mill-control check analysis
生产控制中心　production control centre (PCC)
生产力　productivity, productive power [forces] ◇ 年～分解
生产量　productive capacity, throughput (capacity), quantity of production ◇ 以立方量度的～cubic contents
生产灵活性　production flexibility
生产流程　production [process] flow
生产流程图　process flow diagram, process flowsheet
生产率　productivity (rate), throughput rate, production, output (rate), yield ◇ 单位时间～【企】throughput rate, 每人每小时～output per man-hour, 相对～generic efficiency
生产目标　production target
生产能力　production (capacity, rate), throughput (capacity), (productive, working) capacity, productivity ◇ 补充[附加]～*, 设计最大～peak design capacity, 月～monthly capacity
生产能力利用率[系数]　capacity factor, capacity utilization rate
生产气体　process gas
生产情况　performance
生产情况分析仪　production analyzer
生产人员　operating personnel [force], process man
生产溶液　process [plant] solution
生产设备　production [operating, working, manufacturing] equipment, production plant [unit]

生产设施　operating facilities
生产时间　on stream time
生产事故　industrial accident
生产试验　production [factory, shop] test, pilot production
生产数据　operational data [detail]
生产数字　production figure
生产损失　production loss
生产维修　productive maintenance
生产尾管　production liners
生产尾矿　mill [treatment] tailings
生产效率　production [operational] efficiency
生产性程序　【计】production routine
生产冶金学　production [extraction, extractive] metallurgy
生产用电解槽　production-scale cell
生产用设备　【金】plant-scale equipment
生产用水　process water, production water supply
生产用水处理[净化]厂　【建】process water treatment plant
生产用压机　production press
生产用造球设备　production-scale pelleting system
生产运转[运行]　production run
生产指标　production figure [index], target, process index, operating data
生产指数　production index (Pi)
生产装置　production plant
生产(作业)线　production line
生尘性　dust-forming quality, dustiness
生尘芽孢杆菌　Bacillus pulvifaciens
生成　creation, formation, generation
生成程序　generating program, generator ◇ 编译程序的～compiler generator
生成的炉渣　resultant slag
生成底影　fogging
生成方式　mode of origin
生成符号　【计】created [generated] symbol
生成煤气　generated gas

生成热	heat of formation
生成热焓	enthalpy of formation
生成热数据	heat of formation data
生成水垢	scaling
生成温度	formation temperature
生成物	【化】resultant, product
生成误差	generated error
生成星状花纹（在纯锑表面）	starring
生成氧化皮	scaling
生成自由能	free energy of formation
生吹法	【铁】finery [bloomery] process
生吹炉	catalan (forge, furnace)
生带（未经烧结的）	【粉】green strip ◇ 轧制～的厚度 strip thickness
生杜拉铝	cast duralumin
生高岭土	raw kaolin(e)
生垢	scale formation, scaling
生核	nucleation
生糊块连续阳极	【色】continuous anode of green paste blocks
生化法	biochemical method
生化期	biochemical period
生化生态学	biochemical ecology
生化脱酚	【焦】biochemical dephenolization
生化需氧量	【环】biochemical oxygen demand (BOD)
生化元素	biochemical element
生混合料	green mixture, raw mix
生活垃圾	domestic [house] waste
生活设施	living conditions
生活污水	domestic sewage [waste, discharges], sanitary [household] sewage, sanitary waste effluent
生活污水排泄系统	sanitary drainage
生活用水	sanitary [potable] water
生焦端	【焦】green side
生金菌属	Metallogenium
生精矿	raw [green, unroasted] concentrate
生精矿料仓	green concentrate bin
生精矿熔炼	green concentrate smelting
生精矿装料反射炉	【色】green-feed reverberatory furnace
生矿（石）	raw [run-of-mine, unroasted] ore
生理化学	physiological chemistry
生料	raw charge [mix], unfired [moist] material, wet charge, green mixture
生料层透气性	green bed permeability
生料带	green mix zone
生料球	fresh pellet
生料组分	burden constituents
生硫化矿	green sulphide
生锍	【色】green matte
生铝	cast aluminium
生命体	biomass
生膜	cfilming
生黏土	craw [unburned] clay
生泡试验（检查漏气用）	bubble test
生坯	【粉】(pressed) green compact, green-pressing, green body ◇ 复合～
生坯电极	green electrode
生坯件	green ware
生坯抗剪强度试验	green shear strength test
生坯抗压强度	green compressive strength (GCS)
生坯孔隙度	green porosity
生坯块	green briquette
生坯强度	green strength
生坯(湿态)密度	green [pressed] density
生坯弹性后效	【粉】green spring
生坯性能	green properties
生坯直径	green diameter
生坯状态	green state
生片	raw film
生铅	bullion [work] lead
生球	green pellet [ball], wet pellet
生球爆裂	rupture of green pellet
生球成层长大	ball growth by layering
生球分布	distribution of green ball
生球干燥	ball drying
生球干燥段	green pellet drying section

生球聚结长大 ball growth by coalescence
生球粒度分布 ball size distribution
生球强度 strength of green ball
生球强度系数 ball strength factor
生球筛 seed (sizing) screen
生球碎裂 ball degradation
生球同心长大 ball growth by assimilation
生球(团) green [crude, raw, unfired] pellet, green [wet, unfired] ball ◇ 不合格～sub-quality ball, 干(燥)～*, 预干燥～predried ball, 预热[加温]～*, 造[制]～green balling, kneading
生球团层厚 green ball depth
生球团成形 green ball formation
生球团落下强度 green impact strength
生球团强度 green strength
生球团烧[固]结 green ball induration
生球团生产 green pellet [ball] production
生球团性能 green ball property
生球团制造[成形] green ball formation
生球团制作方式 green balling mode
生球性能 green ball property
生球长大 ball growth
生球长大机理 ball growth mechanism
生球长大区 ball growth region [zone]
生球长大速度[率] rate of pellet [ball] growth
生熔剂 raw flux
生砂 【铸】virgin sand, greensand
生烧结矿[料] 【团】green sinter
生石灰{CaO} calcium [burnt] lime, quicklime, (unslaked, live, calcined, primary) lime ◇ 天然形态～pebble lime
生丝微菌属 Hyphomicrobium
生态环境监测 ecologic environment monitoring
生态平衡 ecological balance, eco-system balance [equilibrium]
生态系统 ecological system
生态系统平衡 eco-system balance [equilibrium]
生态学 ecology

生碳糊 green carbon paste
生锑 crude antimony, antimony crude
生体反应 vital reaction
生铁 pig iron, pigging ◇ 奥氏体～*, 巴西特～法, 赤铁矿～*, 重炼～remelted iron, 粗晶粒～coarse-grained iron, 低硅～dry iron, 低磷～*, 钢性[低碳]～semi-steel, 高硅镜面～*, 高磷～high phosphorus iron, 工业[商品]～*, 共晶～*, 含锰～*, 合金～alloy iron [pig], 机铸～chill cast pig, 碱性～basic pig (iron), 焦炭～*, 锦～*, 精炼～*, 矿渣～part mine, cinder pig, 冷～*, 冷风～cold-blast pigiron, 粒化～*, 炼钢～conversion pig (iron), 木炭(炉)～*, 全矿～*, 热风～*, 砂模[砂床铸]～*, 闪光～*, 酸性～acid pig, 退火～annealing pig iron, 脱硫～*, 无烟煤[白煤]～anthracite pig, 细晶粒～*, 银白～*, 再制～*, 制造可锻铁的～malleable pig iron, 铸造～casting pig, 转炉用～【钢】converter iron
生铁标号 pig iron brand
生铁仓库 pig iron storage
生铁产量 pig iron output, iron make
生铁锭 iron ingot
生铁堆(置)场[生铁库] pig iron storage, pig storage yard
生铁废钢(炼钢)法 pig and scrap process (P&S), pig-iron scrap process, martin process (平炉)
生铁沸腾法 【钢】pig boiling process
生铁粉 pig iron powder ◇ 雾化～*
生铁含碳量 pig iron carbon content
生铁耗焦炭 (同"入炉焦比")
生铁耗燃料 (同"综合焦比")
生铁牌号 pig iron brand, type of iron
生铁合格率 ratio of good pit iron
生铁级别 pig iron grade
生铁继承性 heredity of pig iron
生铁块 pig
生铁矿石(炼钢)法 pig-iron ore process

(P&O) ◇ 坦纳感应炉～Tanna process
生铁炼钢法　pig process
生铁(炉)料　【钢】(pig) iron charge
生铁熔炼　iron smelting, ironmelting
生铁生产　iron manufacture
生铁生产率　pig iron productivity
生铁石墨泡(混铁炉铁水的)　iron spill
生铁水淬粒化(法)　granulation of pig iron
生铁水泥法　(同"巴塞回转窑铁矿处理法")
生铁消耗　pig iron consumption
生铁冶炼过程　iron melt
生铁增碳　pig up
生铁铸块　pig casting
生铁铸造　iron founding
生铁铸造业协会　Iron Casting Society (ICS)
生铁装运线　【运】pig-loading track
生铜　【色】pig copper
生团块　【团】green briquette [brick], unfired agglomerate
生雾　fogging
生物材料　biomaterial
生物槽浸　tank bioleaching
生物成矿　biomineralization
生物处理　【环】bioprocessing
生物处理法　biological process
生物催化剂　bio-catalyst
生物地球化学　biogeochemistry
生物法废物处理　【环】biological waste treatment
生物反应　bioreaction
生物反应产物　bioreaction product
生物反应器　bioreactor
生物腐蚀　biocorrosion, biological corrosion
生物工程　bioengineering
生物过程　biological process
生物过滤法　biofiltration process
生物化学　biochemistry
生物化学法　(同"生化法")
生物机器人　biorobot

生物化学提取　biochemical extraction
生物积聚　biological accumulation
生物技术　biotechnology
生物计算机　bionic computer
生物降解　biological degradation
生物接触　biocontact
生物浸出　bioleaching
生物浸出法[过程]　bioleaching process
生物浸出菌群　bioleaching population
生物浸出速率　bioleaching rate
生物聚合物　biopolymers
生物聚集[积]　bioaccumulation, biological accumulation
生物量　biomass
生物滤池[过滤器]　biofilter, biological filter
生物滤床[层]　bacteria bed
生物黏泥　biological slime
生物能(学)　bio-energetics
生物曝气　bio-aeration
生物器件　biocomponent
生物溶浸　bioleaching
生物湿法冶金　biohydrometallurgy
生物湿法冶金工艺[过程]　biohydrometallurgical process
生物提取　biological extraction
生物提取冶金　bio-extractive metallurgy
生物脱氮　biological denitrification ◇ 缺氧－好氧法～工艺(见1559页)
生物污垢　【环】biological fouling
生物污泥　【环】biological sludge
生物物理学　biophysics
生物吸附剂　biosorbent
生物显微镜　biological microscope
生物需氧量　【环】biological oxygen demand (BOD)
生物絮凝　biofloculation
生物氧化　biological oxidation, bio-oxidation
生物氧化过程　bio-oxidation process
生物氧化技术　bio-oxidation technique
生物增长　bioaugmentation

生物质 biomass
生小球粒 【团】green micropellet
生效 come into force [operation], become effective
生谐畸变 harmonic distortion
生锈 rust(ing), formation of rust, stain(ing), rustiness, patination ◇ 防止[抑制] ~ rust inhibition, 金属锭 ~ ingot staining
生锈钢锭模 【铸】rusty mould
生压坯 green briquette
生压坯冲击强度 【粉】green impact strength
生压坯直径 green diameter
生阳极(未焙烧坯块) raw [green] anode
生阳极糊 green paste
生阳极糊块 green paste block anode
生油气 olefiant gas
生长 growth, growing, germination ◇ 反向夹层 ~，滑移阶深处 ~ (晶体的)【理】growth in depth of glide steps
生长层(晶体的) 【理】growth layer
生长动力学 【理】growth kinetics
生长方向 growth direction
生长惯态 【理】growth habit
生长花样 【金】growth pattern
生长机理 growth mechanism
生长阶(晶体的) 【理】growth step ◇ 环状 ~ growth loop
生长结 【半】grown junction
生长界面 【理】growth interface
生长良好晶体 well-developed crystal
生长孪晶 【理】growth twins
生长螺旋[蜷线](晶面上的) 【理】growth spiral
生长器 grower
生长速度 growth velocity [speed]
生长速率 growth rate
生长条件 growth condition
生长物 grower, outgrowth
生长状态的 as-grown
生长阻力 【理】growth resistance

生支 branching
生重锈 heavy rusting
生铸件 green casting
升板法(施工) lift slab construction
升程 up-running,【压】lift (轧辊的)
升高 rise, ascension, raising, elevation
升格 upgrade
升汞{HgCl$_2$} mercuric chloride, sublimate
升华 sublimation, subliming vapourization without melting ◇ 氯化物 ~ (法) chloride-subimation
升华焙烧 【色】volatilization roast(ing)
升华产物 sublimation product
升华带 subliming zone
升华点[温度] sublimation point [temperature]
升华和气化比谱分析 comparison of sublimation and vaporization
升华皿 subliming pot
升华热 sublimation heat
升华物 sublimate
升华压力 sublimation pressure
升降 go up and down, fluctuation
升降摆动台(三辊式机座的) lifting table
升降车 lift truck ◇ 带卷 ~ 【压】coil jack
升降储放进料台 【压】magazine elevator feeder
升降挡板 adjustable end stop, disappearing end bumper
升降道 【钢】down-take
升降斗 elevator scoop
升降堆垛机 elevating piler
升降舵控制索 elevator cable
升降杆 lifting arm
升降杆送料炉 lift beam furnace
升降观察器 lifting eye
升降辊 lifting roller, depressing roll
升降辊道 【压】mill table, disappearing table (剪切机后的), depressing table (剪切机旁的), deplace table (剪切机前后的) ◇ 铰链式 ~
升降回转台 【压】lifting-turning table ◇

带卷~*
升降回转运输机 lift-and-turn transfer
升降回转装置 lift-and-turn device
升降机 elevator (machine), jack, lift(er), hoist, hoisting machine ◇ 电动~ electric elevator, 斗式~*, 货－客两用~ good-passenger lift, 链式~ chain elevator, 施工~ builder's lift, 塔式~ column elevator, 真空吸盘式~ vacuum cup crane
升降机导轨 cage guides
升降机构 hoisting mechanism
升降机井 elevator hoistway, lift shaft
升降机井道 well hole
升降机控制阀接头 hoist control vslve adapter
升降机位置指示器 cage position indicator
升降机械 hoisting machinery
升降机用索 elevator cable
升降卷扬机 lift winch
升降螺杆 elevating screw
升降桥 lifting bridge
升降式导辊 flipper roll
升降式感应线圈 hoist type induction coil
升降式倾翻机构 hoist tipper
升降台 lifting [elevating] platform, lifting table（三辊式机座的）, cage as-sembly（拉单晶装置的）◇ 带吸盘装置的板材~ cup lifter
升降(台)式炉 elevator furnace
升降行程 lifting stroke
升降圆筒 lifting cylinder
升降运输车（接送带卷的） coil car [buggy]
升降装置 lifting device [gear], flipper, riser
升降装置观察器 lifting eye
升坡 elevation
升气管 ascension pipe,【焦】standpipe
升速特性（曲线）【电】rising-speed characteristic
升温 heating up, warm up
升温变形 elevated temperature deformation (ETD)
升温变形法 ETD process
升温等温淬火 （同"分级等温淬火"）
升温期 （同"加热期"）
升温气相色层(分离)法 programmed temperature gas chromatography (PT-GC)
升温区 heating (up) zone
升温时间 heating up time
升温速度 heating up speed ◇ 预热段~*
升温形变法 ETD (elevated temperature deforming) process
升压 boost(ing), boost pressure, step-up
升压泵 booster pump
升压变压器 step-up transformer
升压充电 boost(ing) charge
升压鼓风机 booster blower
升压剂 【色】depressor
升压力 boost pressure (b.p.)
升压器 booster, step-up transformer
升压线圈 boosting coil
升液泵 lift pump
升液斗 lift pot
升液管 lift tube [pipe]
升液器 lift montejus ◇ 压气[蛋形]~ monte-jus, 压缩空气~*
绳 rope ◇ 马尼拉[白棕]~ Manil(l)a rope
绳槽卷筒 grooved drum
绳钩 rope hook
绳滑车 rope tackle block
绳轮 rope pulley [sheave, wheel], sheave ◇ 蜗形~ fusee
绳(式)测功器[绳闸] rope brake
绳式股芯 independent wire rope core
绳式股芯钢丝绳 independent wire rope core wire rope
绳索钢 wire-rope steel
绳索轮 wire-rope pulley
绳索式拉床 rope drawbench
绳索输送机 cable conveyer

绳套　becket loop ◇ 用铝箍压接~的方法 Talurit process
绳梯　rope ladder
绳状表面　ropy surface
省工　saving of labor
省力装置　labor-saving device
省料型芯　【铸】metal saver
省略的　curtate
省煤[省热]器　economizer (econ.) ◇ 低压~*
盛钢桶　(同"钢包")
盛海绵金属的坩埚　sponge crucible
盛料罐　charge can
盛锍桶　matte ladle
盛铁桶　(同"铁水罐")
盛桶(熔融金属用)　tapping ladle
盛屑篮　chip basket
盛锌桶　【色】zinc ladle
盛盐罐(锆铪蒸馏炉内的)　salt can
盛渣器　slag catcher
盛渣桶台　slag-pot stand
剩磁　【理】residual magnetism, remanency, remanent induction [magnetism] ◇ 表观~[剩余]电感*
剩磁感应　【理】remanent induction
剩磁激励　residual excitation
剩余　surplus, remainder, residue, remnant ◇ 重的~部分*
剩余奥氏体　(同"残余奥氏体")
剩余磁场　residual (magnetic) field
剩余磁场(检验)法　residual field method ◇ 湿式~wet residual method
剩余磁感(应)　residual induction, magnetic remanence
剩余磁化强度　residual [remanent] magnetization
剩余磁通量　residual flux
剩余磁通(量)密度　residual flux density
剩余电荷　residual charge
剩余电离　residual ionization
剩余电流　residual current, 【半】after-current

剩余电压　residual voltage
剩余电阻率　residual resistivity
剩余辐射　restrahlen, residual radiation
剩余高炉煤气　surplus blast-furnace gas
剩余(化合)价　residual valence [valency]
剩余键　residual bond
剩余离子　residual ion
剩余能量　excess energy
剩余偏差　off-set
剩余强度　residual intensity, 【铸】retained strength
剩余切损　high crop loss
剩余散射　residual scattering
剩余射线　【理】residual rays
剩余湿度　remaining humidity
剩余水分　excess moisture
剩余碳化物　residual carbide
剩余铁心损失　residual core loss
剩余位错　residual dislocation
剩余温度(砌体加热的)　residual temperature
剩余误差　residual error
剩余压力　residual [surplus] pressure, overpressure
剩余延性　remaining ductility
剩余氧压　oxygen overpressure
剩余应变　residual strain
剩余淤泥　excess sludge
剩余原料　surplus material
失败　fail(ing), failure, slip-up, bust
失败风险(率)　risk-of-failure
失败试样　【金】failed test piece
失步　desynchronizing, out of step
失步继电器　out of step relay
失常　abnormal, aberration, disorder, disruption, out-of-gear
失磁继电器　excitation-loss relay
失电子蜕变　betatopic change
失控(反应堆的)　【理】excursion
失控速度　run away speed
失宽　【压】width lose control
失蜡型壳　【铸】invested mould

失蜡造型 （同"熔模造型"）
失蜡铸齿法 ◇马普洛登~*
失蜡铸造 （同"熔模铸造"）
失灵 malfunction, abort, dysfunction
失配误差 mismatch error
失去光泽 staining, tarnish(ing)
失去光泽的金属（由于腐蚀） fogged metal
失去控制的效应 【冶】wild effect
失去平衡 out-of-balance, disequilibrium
失去外层电子的原子[裸原子] stripped atom
失去轴对称性 lack of axial symmetry
失散电流腐蚀 current-spray corrosion
失事 fatal accident, crash, breakage
失水率 rate of loss of water
失速 stall
失调 imbalance, maladjustment, disturbance, disaccomodation, disorder, disruption, off-set, out of order (OOO) ◇炉况~*, 张力~【冶】stall tension
失调度 under-shoot
失调角 error angle
失稳 unstability ◇局部~破坏 crippling
失效 lose effectiveness, become invalid, be no longer in force, abatement ◇使~ neutralization
失效保险 fail-safety
失效保险系统 【计】fail safe system
失效率 failure rate
失效预测 【计】failure prediction
失修 disrepair
失修的 in bad repair
失真 【电】distortion, deformation ◇桶形~*, 正~*
失真因数 distortion factor
失真影像 fault image
失真纵波 distorted longitudinal wave
失重 weight loss [reduction], loss in weight, agravity
失重法 weight-loss method, loss in weight technique ◇氢中~*

失重曲线 weight-loss curve
失重试验 loss in weight test
施蒂策尔贝格尔直接还原法 Stuerzelberger iron reduction process
施感电路 inducting circuit
施工 construction, build ◇迪威符~法*, 在~中 under construction (u.c.)
施工便道 construction detour
施工标准 working standard
施工布置图 【建】construction plan
施工场地 builder's yard
施工程序 construction procedure [operation, program]
施工道路 construction access road
施工缝 【建】construction joint
施工工程 construction work
施工规程[规范] 【建】construction specifications
施工计划 construction program
施工绞车 builder's winch
施工进度表 schedule of construction
施工连接 field joint
施工千斤顶 builder's jack
施工人员 builder, constructer
施工设备 【建】construction equipment
施工设计 construction [final, working] design
施工升降机 builder's lift
施工台架 builder's staging
施工图 construction [working] drawing ◇建筑~*
施工现金储备 【企】construction cash reserve
施工详图 construction detail, detail of construction
施工(窄轨)铁路 constructor's railroad
施工质量 construction quality
施工总则 【建】general conditions of construction
施工组织设计平面图 construction plan
施焊操作 welding operation
施焊程序 bead sequence

施焊工艺条件 welding data
施焊过大截面 overwelding
施焊金属 welded metal
施焊图 welding procedure drawing
施焊准备 weld preparation
施加 exert, applying, application, impress
施加的功 applied work
施加的力 superposed force
施加荷载 application of load
施加推力 applied thrust
施加应力 stress application
施拉姆浸蚀剂（铜合金的）【金】 Schramm's reagent
施赖弗叶式压滤机 Shriver filter
施利伦系统 Schlieren system
施罗姆伯格锌基轴承合金（1.10Sn, 3Cu, 余量 Zn；2.40Sn, 0.4Cu, 0.2Pb, 0.15Fe, 余量 Zn）Schromberg alloy
施米格尔斯卡斯效应（又称卡肯达尔效应） Smigelskas effect
施密特临界切应力定律 Schmid's critical shear stress law
施密特准数 Schmidt number
施纳特冲击试验 Schnadt test
施特劳斯晶间腐蚀试验 Strauss test
施图策尔伯格黄铁矿渣直接炼制铁水法 Sturzelberg process
施行 executing, administration
施釉机 glazing machine
施照喷射抛光法 illuminated jet polishing
施主[体] donor ◇ 双重～double donor, 填隙式～*
施主分子 donor molecule
施主结合能 donor binding energy
施主离子 donor ion
施主能带 donor band
施主能级 donor level
施主浓度 donor concentration ◇ 过剩～*
施主原子 【半】donor atom
施主杂质 【半】donor impurity
施主中心 donor center

湿拔的 wet drawn ◇ 光亮～*
湿饱和器 wet saturator
湿材料 wet stock
湿处理 wet treatment
湿淬火 wet quenching
湿存水 hygroscopic water
湿大气腐蚀 wet [damp] atmospheric corrosion
湿袋 【粉】wet bag
湿电池 wet cell
湿度 humidity, moisture content, (degree of) moisture, (degree of) wetness, dampness ◇ 德拜－谢乐环～最大值*，适宜～*，允许～moisture allowance
湿度百分数 percentage of moisture (p.c.m.)
湿度比[比湿度] humidity ratio
湿度测定（法） humidity measuring, hygroscopy, psychrometry
湿度恢复（量） moisture regain
湿度计 hygrometer, humidiometer, humidity gauge [meter], drimeter, moisture gauge [meter], psychrometer（干湿球式）◇ 阿斯曼～Assmann psychrometer, 巴林杰～Ballinger hygrometer, 吹风式干湿球～*, 毛发～hair hygrometer
湿度计的 hydroscopic, hygroscopic
湿度记录仪 humidity [moisture] recorder ◇ 鼓式[转鼓]～drum-hygrograph
湿度检定箱 hygrostat
湿度控制 humidity [moisture] control
湿度平衡 moisture equilibrium
湿度取样 moisture sampling
湿度试验 humidity test
湿度调节 moisture-conditioning
湿度调节器 humidistat
湿度图 humidity chart, hygrogram
湿度吸收试验 moisture absorption test
湿度箱（腐蚀试验用） humidity cabinet
湿法 wet process, aqueous method, wet method（磁粉检验）◇ 煤气～除尘【冶】wet gas cleaning

湿法处理　wet processing
湿法分级　wet classification
湿法分金法　wet process of parting
湿法分析　humid [wet] analysis, wet assay
湿法化学处理　wet chemical processing
湿法回转笼式洗气机　Theisen washer
湿法混合[和]　wet-mixing
湿法加热处理　hydrothermal treatment
湿法精(拉)拔(钢丝镀铜后的)【压】　liquor finish (drawing)
湿法净化[提纯]　wet purification
湿法净化系统　【焦】wet cleaning system
湿(法)拉拔[拉制, 拉伸]　wet drawing ◇ 光亮～ wet bright drawing
湿法拉丝　wet wire drawing
湿法炼铜　copper hydrometallurgy
湿法炼铜厂　copper hydro-metallurgical plant
湿法炼锌　zinc hydrometallurgy
湿法硫化处理　wet sulphidizing
湿法磨矿　wet grinding
湿法抛光　wet tumbling
湿法喷补　wet spraying
湿法破碎　wet crushing
湿法气体电滤器　wet Cottrell plant
湿法气体洗涤器　wet gas scrubber
湿法清理　wet blasting
湿法去铁鳞[清除氧化皮]　wet-scale disposal
湿法熔剂镀锌　wet galvanizing
湿法筛分　wet sieving
湿法收尘　wet dust collection
湿法涂搪瓷　wet process enameling
湿法物理处理　wet physical processing
湿法熄焦　wet quenching
湿法洗涤　wet scrubbing [cleaning, washing]
湿法洗涤器　wet cleaner
湿法洗洗气　[冶]wet gas cleaning
湿法洗气机　wet washer
湿法氧化　wet oxidation
湿法冶金　hydro-metallurgy, hydrometallurgical method, wet(-process) metallurgy ◇ 电～, 高温～, 高压～
湿法冶金处理　hydro-metallurgical treatment, wet metallurgical processing
湿法冶金分离　hydrometallurgical separation
湿法冶金设备　hydrometallurgical plant
湿法冶金试剂　hydrometallurgical reagent
湿法冶金提取　hydrometallurgical extraction
湿法铸件清砂滚筒　wet tumbler
湿粉研磨机　wet-powder grinder
湿浮渣　wet dross
湿海绵锆　wetted zirconium sponge
湿海绵金属　wet sponge
湿氦(气)　moist helium
湿灰[粉尘]　wetted dust
湿混合料　moist mix
湿基(成分, 分析)　wet basis (包括水分的成分)
湿精矿　wet concentrate
湿精矿熔炼　wet-concentrate smelting
湿精矿造块　agglomeration of moist concentrate
湿空气　wet [moisture-laden] air
湿拉　wet drawing
湿拉(拔)用复合润滑剂　wet-drawing compound
湿拉机　wet drawing machune ◇ 串列～
湿拉线材　wet drawn wire
湿粒料　wet pellet
湿量　moisture content ◇ 按～(计算) wet basis
湿料　moist material, moistened mix, wet charge, damp mass
湿料吨数　wet ton
湿料反射炉　【色】wet-charge reverberatory furnace
湿料熔炼　wet (charge) smelting
湿滤饼　wet cake
湿密度　wet density

湿面　wetted surface
湿磨　wet [damp] grinding, wet-milling
湿磨炉渣　wet ground slag
湿碾机　wet pan mill, mixing pan (mill) ◇ 刃型连续～edge runner wet mill
湿抛矿渣混凝土　foamed slag concrete
湿抛光　wet polishing
湿平整(轧制)　wet skin pass rolling
湿气　humidity, moisture, damp(ness), unstripped gas
湿气饱和的　moisture-laden
湿气泵　wet-air pump
湿气离解反应　moisture decomposition reaction
湿气喷射系统　moisture injection system
湿气释出率　moisture release rate
湿气体　wet gas
湿气氧化　humid oxidation
湿气指示器　moisture indicator
湿强度(造型材料的)　【铸】wet strength, green bond (strength)
湿氢(气)　wet hydrogen
湿球　wet pellet [ball], green pellet [ball]
湿球团落下强度　【团】green impact strength
湿球温度　wet bulb temperature
湿球温度计　wet-bulb thermometer
湿热　muggy, damp and hot ◇ 使抗～tropicalization
湿热处理　hydrothermal treatment
湿热带性能试验　tropicalization test
湿热养护法　hydrothermal method of curing
湿润　humidifying, humidification
湿润处理　humidity treatment
湿润剂　humectant, surface-active agent (酸洗添加剂)
湿润器　humidifier, humectant, damper
湿润试验(镀锡熔剂的)　spread test
湿润液　wetting liquid
湿润作用　humidification
湿砂　green sand

湿砂环状型芯　【铸】green-sand ring core
湿砂假型　【铸】green-sand match
湿砂型　【铸】green sand mould
湿砂型芯　【铸】green sand core
湿(砂)型铸造　green(sand) casting
湿砂造型　【铸】green (sand) moulding
湿砂铸型　【铸】green sand mould
湿筛(法)　wet screening [sieving]
湿生球　【团】wet green ball
湿式饱和器　wet saturator
湿式闭路磨矿　(同"闭路湿磨")
湿式除[收,集]尘器　wet deduster [precipitator, scrubber], wet dust collector, cottrell washer, wet-type dust catcher, wet-type dust-collecting equipment
湿式除灰煤气发生炉　wet-bottom gas producer
湿式磁选机　wet (magnetic) separator
湿式电除尘[电收尘,静电除尘,电滤]器　wet electric precipitation plant, wet electric cleaner, irrigated precipitator
湿式分离[收尘,磁选](法)　wet separation
湿式分离器　wet separator
湿式腐蚀加工　chemical machining
湿式滚筒清砂法　wet tumbling process
湿式回火　wet tempering
湿式给料机　wet feeder
湿式焦　coke wet quenching
湿式进[装]料　wet feed
湿式净化法　liquid-purification process
湿式连续磁场法　wet continuous field method
湿式轮碾机　wet pan
湿式磨矿机　wet pan mill
湿式碾磨　wet pan grinding
湿式平整轧制装置　wet skin-pass rolling equipment
湿式破碎机　wet crusher
湿式强磁选(法)　wet high-intensity magnetic separation (WHIMS)
湿式清理　wet tumbling

湿式清理滚筒 【铸】wet tumbling barrel
湿式球磨机 wet ball mill
湿式润滑剂(拉拔用) wet lubricant
湿式渗氮 wet nitriding
湿式剩余磁场法 wet residual method
湿式跳汰选 【选】hotching
湿式脱硫 【焦】wet desulphurization
湿式脱硫法(煤气的) 【焦】liquid-purification process
湿式吸尘机 wet suction fan
湿式洗涤器 wet scrubber ◇ 多段～，文丘里管～"
湿式洗涤器排灰[料] wet scrubber discharge
湿式旋风除[收]尘器 cyclone washer, wet cyclone, wet rotoclone collector
湿式选矿 wet concentration
湿式烟气净化装置 wet Cottrell plant
湿式圆筒冷却机 quench trommel
湿式真空泵 wet vacuum pump
湿试金 wet assay
湿碎 wet crushing
湿态 green state
湿态抗压强度(砂型、型芯的) green compressive strength (GCS)
湿态强度 green strength (GS)
湿态透气性[率] 【铸】green permeability
湿态性能 【铸】green properties
湿套 【粉】wet bag
湿体积 humid volume
湿洗 water washing
湿洗滚筒 wet rolling barrel
湿显示剂(渗透检验用) aqueous developer
湿显像[影]剂 wet developer
湿小球粒 green micropellet
湿型砂 wet moulding sand, green sand
湿型芯 green core
湿型芯制造法 green coremaking method
湿型铸造 green(sand) casting
湿选 wet [water] concentration, wet separation [treatment]

湿选矿泥[尾矿] 【选】washery slurry
湿压 wet pressing
湿压强度(生坯的) green (compression) strength
湿研矿渣 wet ground slag
湿焰 wet fire
湿养护(混凝土) wet [moist] curing
湿冶法 (同"水冶法")
湿渣 wet slag
湿蒸汽 wet [damp] steam
湿治 wet [water] curing
湿治室(混凝土养护用) fog room
湿重 green-weight (GW, g.w.)
湿着 moisten
湿着能力 wetting ability
十八烷 {$CH_3(CH_2)_{10}CH_3$} octadecane
十八烷酸 (同"硬脂酸")
十的补码 【计】ten's complement
十二层多膛焙烧炉 twelve-hearth roaster
十二醇 laurgl alcohol
十二辊的 twelve-high
十二进制数 duodecimal number
十二进制(数系) duodecimal number system
十二面体 dodecahedron
十二面体滑移 dodecahedral slip
十二面体平面 【金】dodecahedral plane
十二碳烯胺萃取剂 amine 9D-178
十二烷 {$C_{12}H_{36}$} dodecane
十二烷醇 dodecyl[lanry]alcohol
十二烷基 {$CH_3(CH_2)_{10}CH_2$} dodecyl, laurogl
十二烷基胺 laurgl amine
十二烷基磷酸 dodecylphosphoric acid
十二烷酸(同"月桂酸")
十二烷酰 lauroyl
十级连续分离萃取器 【色】ten-stage continuous separation extractor
十进计数管 decatron, dekatron
十进刻度 decade scaler
十进位 decade
十进位换算电路 decade scaler

十进(位)计数器 decade counter, decimal scaler
十进制 decimal system [base], decade
十进制编码数字 decimal coded digit
十进制计算机 decimal [decade] computer
十进制加法器 decade adder
十进制减法器 decade subtracter
十进制数 decimal number
十进制数制 decimal numbering system
十进制数字[数位] decimal digit
十进(制)天平 decimal balance
十进制向[到]二进制的转换 【数】decimal to binary conversion
十进制小数 decimal fraction
十进制运算 decimal arithmetic operation ◇ 浮点~*
十六进制 【数】hexadecimal [sexadecimal] notation
十六进制数 hexadecimal number [numeral]
十六进制数字[数位] hexadecimal [sexadecimal] digit
十六烷{$CH_3(CH_2)_{17}CH_3$} nonadecane
十六(烷)酸 (同"棕榈酸")
十六烷值 cetane number(C. No)
十七烷{$CH_3(CH_2)_{15}CH_2-$} heptadecane
十七烷基{$CH_3(CH_2)_{15}CH_2-$} heptadecyl
十七烷基磷酸 heptadecyl phosphoric acid
十七(烷)酸{$CH_3(CH_2)_{15}COOH$} heptadecamok[margaric]acid
十三醇{$CH_3(CH_2)_{11}CH_2OH$} tridecand(1)$_3$ tridecyl aclohol
十三烷 tridecane
十三烷基{$CH_3(CH_2)_{11}CH_2-$} tridecyl
十三(烷)酸{$C_{12}H_{25}\cdot COOH$} tridecanoic acid
十四烷 tetradecane
十四(烷)酸{$CH_3(CH_2)_{12}CO_2H$} tetradecylic[myristic]acid
十五烷{$CH_3(CH_2)_{13}CH_3$} pentadecane

十五(烷)酸{$C_{14}H_{29}COOH$} pentadecanoic acid
十一边[角]形 hendecagon
十一面体 hendecahedron
十一烷 undecane, hendecane
十一(烷)酸 ($C_{10}H_{21}COOH$) hendecanoic [undecylic] acid
十亿(10^9) milliard, billion (美,法)
十亿分率(十亿分之几) parts per billion (ppb)
十字板剪力试验 vane (shear) test
十字标线 cross hair
十字标线目镜 【金】bifilar eye-piece
十字测温技术 cross beam temperature measuring technology
十字顶锤 cross-pane hammer
十字方向 cross direction
十字镐 pick (hammer), hack iron
十字跟踪 【计】cross tracking
十字管 cross pipe
十字架 【铸】cross
十字尖头锤 cross-peen hammer
十字交叉(焊丝)焊缝 cross-wire weld
十字交叉线材焊机 cross-wire welding machine
十字交叉线材焊接 cross-wire welding
十字接头 cross joint [connector]
十字轮机构[马尔泰十字轮机构] Maltese cross
十字头 crosshead, spider (圆锥破碎机的), 【机】pinblock (万向联轴节的)
十字头导座 cross-head guides
十字头式万向接轴 cross joint type universal spindle
十字头销 gudgeon [cross-head] pin
十字线 cross wire, graticule
十字线片测量 diaphragm measurement
十字型四辊万能轧机 sack mill
十字形钢凿[錾] crosscut chisel
十字形辊模(拉丝用) turks head die
十字形辊模头(拉拔用) 【压】turk(s) head ◇ 普通~ plain turks head, 万能式

~universal turks-head, 组合式 ~ combination turks head

十字形焊接残余应力试验 cruciform test

十字形接头[连接] cruciform joint

十字形卷线轴 spider reel

十字形控制杆 cross control rod, cruciform (shaped) control rod

十字形试样 cruciform test specimen

十字形轴头 【机】pinblock

石 stone (st., stn.) ◇ 克赛~ coesite, 伊利~ illite

石板瓦 backer, ragstone

石板状断口 slaty fracture

石钵 chopper

石碴 quarry rubbish (采石场弃料), 【建】ballast

石碴混凝土 ballast concrete

石川岛中村炉外钢液处理法 ishikawajima-Nakamura process

石川石 ishikawaite

石膏 {CaSO$_4$·2H$_2$O} gyp(sum), gypse, mineral white, parget, plaster (stone), salt lime ◇ 含~的 gyps(e)ous, 无水[硬]~*, 雪花~ alabaster

石膏煅烧 gypsum calcination

石膏缓凝水泥 【建】gypsum-retarded cement

石膏混凝土 gypsum [plaster] concrete

石膏矿渣水泥 slag-sulphate cement

石膏模 【铸】plaster pattern [mould]

石膏模型(锻模、压模的) plaster master

石膏屋面板 【建】gypsum roof plank

石膏型 gypsum [plaster] mould

石膏型精密铸造法 plaster mould process

石膏型铸造法 plaster casting ◇ 卡帕科~ Capaco process

石膏质[状]的 gyps(e)ous

石工 mason (工人), masonry (工作)

石灰 lime, kalk ◇ 吹入~*, 纯 carbonate free lime, 煅烧~ burnt lime, 含5%熟石膏的~ selenitic lime, 含镁~ dolomitic lime, 含铁~ ferruginous lime, 加~ lime feed, 加~过量的 overlimed, 凯米多尔~ Kemidol, 苛性~ caustic lime, 上~ liming, 生~*, 死烧~ dead burnt lime, 涂~槽 lime coating tank, 用过的~ used lime, 沾~*

石灰焙烧 lime roasting

石灰捕集器 lime-trap

石灰槽 lime bunker [reservoir], 【焦】lime leg (蒸氨塔的)

石灰沉淀法 lime precipitation (process)

石灰衬里[材料] lime liner

石灰衬里的还原钢弹 lime-lined bomb

石灰池 bankre

石灰处理 liming, lime coating (钢丝的)

石灰处理槽 lime bath

石灰处理光亮钢丝 lime bright wire

石灰处理过的 limed

石灰处理光亮钢丝 lime bright wire

石灰底层填料(转炉的) lime padding

石灰冻结(炉缸的) 【铁】lime bum

石灰法 【冶】calcic process

石灰-矾土熔体 lime-alumina melts

石灰沸腾 【钢】lime boil

石灰粉 lime powder, powder(ed) lime ◇ 精制~ whiting

石灰粉末喷口 lime-powder injection tuyere

石灰坩埚 lime crucible

石灰膏 lime paste [putty]

石灰工业 lime industry

石灰硅石 lime dinas

石灰过剩(指炉渣) lime setting

石灰浆 lime mortar (l.m.), lime sludge [slurry], limewash ◇ 水泥~ cement lime mortar

石灰浆喷洒装置 lime-wash sprayer

石灰结合硅质耐火材料 lime-bonded silica refractory

石灰结合硅砖 lime dinas

石灰界限浓度(转炉内的) lime dam

石灰浸槽 lime coating tank

石灰苛化 lime causticization

石 shi

石灰料仓	lime bunker
石灰流槽	lime chute
石灰泥渣	slaked carbide
石灰溶解法	lime dissolution process
石灰乳	lime milk, slurried lime
石灰乳槽	lime water tank, lime still, liming tub [vat]
石灰乳调制器	liming apparatus
石灰砂浆	lime mortar
石灰砂粒砖	sand-lime brick
石灰烧结法	lime-sinter process
石灰烧结矿	【团】lime sinter
石灰石	chalk, limestone, lime rock, fluxing stone ◇ 纯～ straight limestone, 冷却～*, 沥青质～ bituminous limestone, 泥质～*
石灰石粗集料混凝土	limestone coarse aggregate concrete
石灰石分解	limestone decomposition
石灰石粉	limestone fines
石灰石熔剂	limestone flux
石灰石熔剂性球团	【团】limestone (fluxed) pellet
石灰石消耗量	【钢】lime-stone consumption
石灰竖窑	lime shaft kiln
石灰水	lime water, whitewash, milk lye ◇ 浸～ liming
石灰苏打法	lime-soda process
石灰苏打烧结法	lime-soda sinter process
石灰稳定的氧化锆	【耐】lime stabilized zirconia
石灰消[熟]化	lime slaking
石灰消化系统	lime hydration system
石灰效率	lime efficiency
石灰岩	chalkstone, limestone
石灰-氧化亚铁-氧化铁熔体	lime-ferrous oxide-ferric oxide melts
石灰窑	lime (burning) kiln, lime pit
石灰-萤石渣	【钢】lime-fluorspar slag
石灰渣	lime residue [slag]
石灰质	calc, calcium carbonate

石灰质材料	【建】limy material
石灰质的	calcareous (cal.)
石灰质矿	limy ore
石灰质耐火材料	lime refractories
石灰质熔剂	lime-based flux
石灰质铁矿石	calcareous ore
石灰柱	liming column
石块	stone, gobbet
石块间隙缝（砌体的）	abreuvoir
石块铺底	bottoming
石蜡	paraffin (wax), ceresin wax ◇ 浸渗～的 paraffin-impregnated, 涂～*
石蜡晶体	paraffin crystal ◇ 金刚石状～*
石蜡渗透探裂法	paraffin test
石蜡油	paraffinic oil, petrolatum
石料	aggregated rock, building stones ◇ 规格～ dimension stone
石料衡量器	aggremeter
石料基础石	ground stone
石榴石	【地】garnet ◇ 铁磁性～*
石榴石型化合物	garnet compound
石煤	bone (coal), stone coal
石棉	asbestos (asb.), asbestus, asbest, earth flax, mountain cork, salamander [rock] wool ◇ 白丝状～ amianthus, 包～金属 asbestos covered metal, 薄片～ flaked asbestos, 废～ asbestos lumber, 高铁～*
石棉板	asbestos board, sheet asbestos ◇ 硬～*
石棉包线	asbestos covered wire
石棉布	asbestos cloth [fabric]
石棉衬里	asbestos lining
石棉粗绳	asbestos twine
石棉带	asbestos tape
石棉垫	asbestos pad [jointing]
石棉垫片	asbestos gasket [packing]
石棉垫圈	asbestos washer
石棉管	asbestos pipe
石棉辊	asbestos roller
石棉夹（钢丝热镀锌用）	asbestos pads

[press]
石棉夹擦拭器　asbestos wiper
石棉夹心胶合板　asbestos-veneer plywood
石棉卷筒（钢丝热镀锌用）　asbestos reel
石棉绝缘[绝热]　asbestos insulation
石棉滤器　asbestos filter
石棉抹镀锌（钢丝的）　wiped galvanizing
石棉抹镀锌钢丝　wiped galvanized wire
石棉绒　asbestos wool [fibre], amiant(h)
石棉乳　asbestos milk
石棉纱　asbestos yarn
石棉绳　asbestos rope [braid, cord]
石棉水泥　asbest(os) cement, eternit
石棉水泥板　cement asbestos board (A.C.B.) ◇ 波纹~*
石棉水泥波形瓦　fibrotile
石棉水泥管　cement asbestos pipe, asbestos-cemet pipe
石棉填料　asbestos packing [jointing]
石棉瓦　asbestos tile [shingle]
石棉围裙　asbestos apron
石棉纤维　asbestos fibre, salamander wool
石棉纤维板　asbestos fibre sheet
石棉线　asbestos yarn [wire]
石棉屑　asbestos lumber
石棉纸　【建】asbestos paper
石棉纸板　asbestos card-board [millboard], compressed asbestos sheet
石棉砖　asbestos brick
石墨　graphite, mineral black, black lead ◇ 不含铀~ dead graphite, 短棒状~ chunky graphite, 含~的 graphitiferous, 含~轴承* , 含铀~ live graphite, 畸变~ degenerated graphite, 胶体~*, 精制~ washed graphite, 卡尔贝特不透性~*, 类~ quasi-graphite (QG), 粒状~ graphite granule, 片状~*, 人工~ electrographite, 烧空炉法除~（焦炉用）scurfing, 脱除~ degraphitization, 析出~ indigenous graphite, 游离[单体]~ free graphite, 原生[初生、一次]~*, 最纯~*

石墨板　graphite plate
石墨棒　graphite rod
石墨棒电阻熔炼炉　graphite rod melting furnace
石墨棒阳极　graphite-rod anode
石墨棒阴极　graphite-rod cathode
石墨饼　graphite cake
石墨捕集器　kish collector
石墨沉淀　【金】graphite precipitation
石墨衬里　graphite liner [lining]
石墨催化剂　graphite catalyst
石墨脆性　graphite [graphitic] embrittlement
石墨的　graphitic, graphitiferous, plumbaginous
石墨点(可锻铸铁的)　grey spots
石墨电极　graphite [carbon] electrode, black lead electrode ◇ DGT 溶液浸渍~*, 控氧化~*
石墨电极板　graphite electrode slab
石墨电极炉　graphite bar electric furnace, carbon bar furnace
石墨电解槽　graphite cell ◇ 整体~*
石墨电刷　graphite brush, electric graphitized brush ◇ 青铜~ bronze graphite brush
石墨电阻辐射加热炉　graphite resistor radiation furnace
石墨电阻(加热)元件　graphite resistance element
石墨电阻炉　graphite resistor furnace
石墨电阻(器)　graphite resistor
石墨端包　【铸】graphite ladle
石墨分布板（通氯气用）　graphite distributor
石墨分级机　graphite grading machine
石墨粉　graphite powder [dust, flour], powdered [ground] graphite, plumbagine
石墨敷粉　【铸】graphite blacking
石墨腐蚀　graphite corrosion
石墨盖　graphite cover
石墨坩埚　graphite crucible [pot, cup,

mould], carbon crucible, black lead crucible, plumbago crucible [pot]

石墨坩埚铸锭炉 graphite crucible casting furnace

石墨感受器 graphite susceptor

石墨钢 graphitic steel

石墨高压炉 【粉】graphite pressure furnace

石墨膏 【压】graphite paste, oildag

石墨共晶 graphite eutectic

石墨管 graphite tube [pipe] ◇ 拼合～电阻炉*

石墨管热压炉 graphite-tube hot-pressing furnace ◇ 竖式～*, 卧式 [平放]～*

石墨辊 graphite roller

石墨过滤器 graphite filter

石墨核 graphite nucleus

石墨滑油 oildag

石墨化 graphitization, graphitizing, greying（铸铁的）◇ 第二阶段～*

石墨化电极 【冶】graphitized electrode

石墨化反应 【钢】graphitization reaction

石墨化钢 graphitizable steel, hybrid metal

石墨化硅钢（1.25—1.5C, 0.8—1.2Si, 0.35—0.5Mn, 低 P、低 S）Graph-Sil

石墨化合金 graphitized alloy

石墨化基体 graphitized matrix

石墨化机理 mechanism of graphitization

石墨化剂 graphitizer

石墨化炉（生产电极用）graphitizing furnace

石墨化钼钢（低钼: 1.25—1.55C, 0.75—1.0Si, 0.35—0.6Mo, < 0.25Cr, 余量 Fe; 高钼: 1.35—1.55C, 0.85—1.2Si, 0.2—0.3Cr, 余量 Fe）Graph-Mo

石墨化能力[倾向性] graphitizability

石墨化青铜 graphitized bronze

石墨化倾向 tendency to graphitization

石墨化区域[范围] 【金】graphitization region

石墨化碳 graphitized carbon

石墨化碳黑 carbopack

石墨化退火 【金】graphitizing anneal(ing)

石墨化钨钢（1.45—1.6C, 0.55—0.85Si, 0.35—0.5Mn, 0.4—0.6Mo, 2.5—3.2W）GraphTung

石墨化阳极块 graphitized anode block

石墨化元素 graphitizing element

石墨化铸铁 graphitized cast-iron ◇ 部分～*

石墨化作用 graphitization, graphitizing

石墨环 graphite annulus

石墨－环氧树脂复合材料 graphite-epoxy composite material

石墨回收设施 【冶】graphite recovery plant

石墨混合物 graphite mixture

石墨畸变 graphite degeneration

石墨极电弧焊 graphite-arc welding

石墨加热器 graphite heater

石墨加热元件 graphite heating element

石墨(减摩)合金（68Pb, 17Sb, 15Sn）graphite alloy

石墨浆（铸模涂料） graphite wash, black (lead) wash

石墨浆喷涂器 black wash sprayer

石墨浆涂料 【钢】darmold

石墨浇口 【冶】graphite sprue

石墨聚集（铸件缺陷） kish lock

石墨颗粒 graphite particle

石墨块 graphite block ◇ 大型～ heavy graphite block

石墨粒 graphite granule

石墨瘤 graphite nodule

石墨流槽 【冶】graphite spout

石墨流道 【冶】graphite sprue

石墨－铝混合(炉衬打结)料 ◇ 格拉弗拉姆～ 【冶】Graphram

石墨密封（炉墙砖缝） carbon sealing

石墨模 graphite die

石墨耐火材料 plumbago refractory

石墨泡（混铁炉内铁水的） refining foam

石墨片 graphite flake [cake], flake(d)

graphite
石墨青铜 (50Cu,50石墨；或79Cu,10Zn,11石墨) graphite [graphitized] bronze
石墨青铜合金 copper-graphite-bronze alloy
石墨青铜轴承 graphite-containing bronze bearing ◇多孔~
石墨青铜轴承合金 (89Cu,10Sn,1C) oilite
石墨球 graphite nodule
石墨球压 spheroidization of graphite
石墨球化试验 【铸】graphite spheroidizing test
石墨容器 graphite container [vessel]
石墨润滑 graphite lubrication, black lead lubrication
石墨润滑剂 graphite [graphitic] lubricant, oildag
石墨润滑油 graphite(d) oil
石墨润滑脂 graphite grease
石墨塞头 graphite end
石墨生成 【焦】carbon build-up
石墨生物腐蚀软化 (铸铁管的) graphite softening
石墨熟料坩埚 graphite-grog crucible
石墨水 (拔丝润滑剂) aquadag
石墨水泥 graphite cement
石墨碳 graphite carbon
石墨-碳化硅耐火砖 graphite silicon carbide firebrick
石墨-碳化硅热[温差]电偶 graphite-silicon carbide thermocouple, graphite to silicon-carbide couple
石墨-碳化硅砖 graphite silicon carbide brick
石墨-碳化硼热电偶 graphite-boron carbide thermocouple
石墨套管 graphite sleeve
石墨通气器 graphite breather
石墨涂料 graphite paint,【铸】(graphite) blacking
石墨团 graphite nodule

石墨托盘 graphite tray
石墨窝 (铸铁缺陷) 【铸】blacking hole
石墨析出 【金】graphite precipitation
石墨洗浆 graphite wash
石墨纤维偶合剂 graphite fibre coupling agent
石墨纤维-环氧树脂复合材料 graphite fibre-epoxy composite
石墨相 graphite phase
石墨型铸造法 【铸】carbon mould process
石墨形碳 graphitic carbon
石墨阳极 graphite anode
石墨阳极篮 graphite anode basket
石墨阴极 graphite cathode
石墨油 graphite(d) oil
石墨圆片 graphite disc
石墨圆筒 graphite cylinder
石墨圆柱(体) graphite solid cylinder
石墨增强铝复合材料 graphite-reinforced aluminium composite
石墨渣 kish slag
石墨蒸馏罐 graphite retort
石墨脂 graphite grease
石墨制品 graphite product
石墨质耐火材料 plumbago (refractory)
石墨舟皿 graphite boat
石墨轴承 graphite bearing
石墨轴承润滑剂 graphite-bearing lubricant
石墨铸模 graphite mould, graphite casting die
石墨铸铁 graphite cast iron ◇片状~，蠕虫状[短粗]~ vermicular iron, 致密
石墨注勺 【铸】graphite ladle
石墨砖 graphite brick [block]
石墨状的 graphitoid
石墨组织 【金】graphitic structure
石脑油 naphtha ◇重质溶剂~ heavy solvent naphtha
石脑油渣 naphtha residue
石青 (同"蓝铜矿")

石拾　shi

石球式热风炉　pebble stove
石绒　asbestos, asbestus, amianthine
石蕊试纸　【化】litmus paper
石松子粉　【铸】lycopodium powder
石髓　(同"玉髓")
石炭酸　(见"酚")
石炭纪的　【地】carboniferous
石屑　gallet, grit, attle
石盐{NaCl}　halite, rock salt
石英{SiO$_2$}　quartz (qtz), rock crystal,【冶】silex ◇ 含~的 quartz-bearing, quartzy, 潜晶质[隐晶]~*, 熔结~*, 烧结~ sintered quartz, 似~的 quartzy, 最纯的~ spectrosil
石英板岩　quartz slate
石英棒　quartz bar [rod]
石英玻璃　quartz [silica, silex] glass, fused silica
石英玻璃观察孔　silica window
石英玻璃管[电解槽]　quartz glass cell
石英粉　finely ground quartz, silica powder [dust, flour]
石英坩埚　quartz crucible, silica crucible [pot] ◇ 透明~ translucent silica pot, 锥形底~ conical-bottomed silica pot
石英管　quartz tube [pipe], silica tube
石英光谱仪　quartz spectrograph
石英夹持器　quartz holder
石英晶体　quartz crystal
石英晶体单色器　quartz monochromator
石英晶体力轴[V石英轴]　V axis
石英晶体振荡器　quartz-crystal oscillator
石英绝缘子　quartz insulator
石英马弗炉膛　quartz muffle
石英皿　silica dish
石英枪(转炉用)　silica [flux] gun ◇ 加尔~【色】Garr gun
石英熔剂　silica flux
石英容器　silica vessel
石英砂　quartz [siliceous] sand, (high) silica sand, arcnaceous quartz
石英砂岩　quartz-sandstone

石英烧舟　quartz boat
石英丝静电计　quartz-fiber electrometer
石英纤维[棉]　quartz fiber
石英岩　quartzite, quartz rock, silexite ◇ 带状赤铁矿~*
石英岩的　quartzitic
石英圆筒　silica cylinder
石英振荡器　quartz oscillator
石英蒸馏罐　quartz retort
石英质脉石　siliceous gangue
石英钟　quartz(-crystal) clock
石英砖　quartz(ite) brick
石油　petroleum (oil), crude [mineral] oil ◇ 风化~ mineral tar
石油残渣　petroleum residue
石油(钢)管　oil country (side) tubular goods (OCTG)
石油管道　oil line pipe, petroleum pipeline
石油化学[化工]产品　petrochemicals
石油化学工业　petrochemical industry
石油焦(炭)　petroleum [oil] coke ◇ 活性~*
石油焦操作(高炉的)　P-C coke operation [performance]
石油沥青　(oil) asphalt, asphaltum ◇ 填缝~掺合料*, 氧化~*
石油馏出物　petroleum distillate
石油气　petroleum gas, oil-gas
石油溶剂　white spirit
石油设备　petroleum equipment
石油蒸馏管　still pipe
石油钻井用钢丝绳　petroleum well drilling wire rope
石油钻探管　oil drill pipe
石制品　rock product
石状渣　【冶】stony slag
石状黏土　leck
拾波器　adaptor
拾波线圈　pick-up coil
拾取电压　pick-up voltage
拾取钳　pick-up tongs (锻工用) ◇ 废料~ scrap-handling tongs

拾音器　pick-up, adaptor
拾振器　oscillation [vibration] pickup
时标　【计】time scale
时标电路　timing circuit
时标脉冲发生器　clock [timing] pulse generator
时标(信号)发生器[时标振荡器]　timing generator, time-mark(ing) generator
时段　time interval
时分　【计】time division
时分通道[信道]　time-derived channel
时号　time signal
时基　time base (T.B.)
时基范围　time-base range
时基扫描　time-base sweep ◇ 收缩~*
时基信号发生器[时基振荡器]　time-base generator
时机　opportunity, occasion
时计　clock, chronometer
时间　time, hour ◇ 格林尼治~*, 经过~考验的 time-tested, 随~变化的[与~有关的] time-dependent, 随~的变化 time-variation, 一段~ session, 与~无关机理 time independent mechanism, 与~相关机理 time dependent mechanism
时间比例　【计】time scale
时间-变形关系曲线　time-deformation curve
时间表　(time-)schedule, time card
时间常数　time constant
时间定额　【企】time rate
时间对数　logarithm of time
时间发送器　timer
时间范围　time range [frame]
时间分辨率[能力]　time resolution
时间分辨谱仪　time resolved spectrometer
时间关系　time dependence
时间(关系)图　time diagram
时间关系图表　time-dependence plot
时间极限　time limit
时间计数器　time counter
时间继电器　time relay, timing relay [unit]
时间间隔　time interval [span, piece]
时间间隔计　intervalometer
时间校正增益　time corrected gain
时间控制　timing control
时间控制继电器　control timer
时间利用系数　time utilization coefficient
时间零点　time zero
时间律　time law
时间落后　time lag
时间衰减　time decay
时间顺序　timing sequence
时间损失　loss of time, time penalty
时间调节的增益　time-corrected gain (TCG)
时间调节器　timing device
时间图像　【理】time pattern
时间推移法　time lapse technique
时间-温度-奥氏体化曲线　TTA (time-temperature-austenitization) curve
时间-温度-奥氏体化图　TTA diagram
时间-温度关系曲线　time-temperature curve
时间-温度-晶间腐蚀敏化图　time-temperature-sensitization diagram
时间-温度曲线　time-temperature profile
时间-温度-转变　【金】time temperature transformation (TTT, T-T-T)
时间-温度-转变曲线(等温转变曲线或S曲线)　【金】TTT (curve)
时间温度转变试验　TTT test
时间-温度-转变图　TTT diagram
时间-温度状况　time-temperature profile
时间响应　time response ◇ 阶跃输入~*
时间消耗　time-consuming
时间循环调节器　time-cycle controller
时间延迟　time delay
时间因素[因子]　time factor
时间元件　time element
时间周期　time length
时间坐标　time base
时期　period

时区 time zone
时隙 interval
时限 time limit
时限估计(量) interval estimate
时限误差 interval error
时效 ageing, aging, maturing ◇奥氏体~(处理)*,常温~ natural [cold] ageing,长期~*,二级[段]~ two-steps ageing,高温短时~*,过~*,合金~ alloy ageing,间断[分级]~ interrupted ageing,冷~ cold ageing,两段~*,炉中~ oven ageing,热浴淬火~ hot-bath quench ageing,人工~ artificial ageing,完全~ full aging,无~(的) non-ageing,延缓~ delayed ageing,自然~*
时效不锈钢 aged stainless steel
时效不足 under-ageing
时效脆性 embrittlement by aging
时效法[过程] ageing process
时效范围 ageing range
时效钢 ageing [aged] steel ◇奥氏体~ ausageing steel,无应变~*
时效合金 ageing alloy ◇非~ non-ageing alloy
时效合金粉末 aged alloy powder
时效机理 ageing mechanism, mechanism of ageing
时效裂纹 ageing crack
时效炉 ageing oven
时效强化 ageing strengthening
时效软化 age-softening
时效试验 ageing test
时效特性 ageing characteristic,【半】ageing bebaviour
时效温度范围 ageing range
时效稳定性 ageing stability
时效系数 ageing coefficient
时效现象 ageing phenomena
时效行为 ageing behavio(u)r
时效硬化 age [precipitation] hardening ◇CCF 含铁钴~型铜线*,高于室温的 ~ warm hardening,可~的 age harde-nable
时效硬化沉淀 age hardening precipitation
时效硬化感受性 age hardening response
时效硬化钢 age hardening steel
时效硬化合金 age hardening alloy
时效硬化合金钢 age hardened alloy steel
时效硬化区域[(温度)范围] age hardening range [region]
时效硬化特性[特征] age-hardening characteristic
时效硬化析出 age hardening precipitation
时效硬化元素 age hardening element
时效状态 aged condition
时效(状态)硬度 age(ing) [precipitation] hardness ◇沉淀~*
时效作用 ageing effect
时序 timing sequence, time-sequential routine (脉冲的)
时序控制 sequential control
时序逻辑元件 sequential logic element
时域 time-domain
时滞 time delay [lag]
时钟 clock ◇实时~ real time clock
时钟磁道 【计】clock track
时钟计数器 clock counter
时钟逻辑驱动器 【计】clock logic driver
时钟脉冲 clock pulse
时钟脉冲发生器 【计】gate [time-pulse] generator, clock pulse generator
时钟脉冲分配 time-impulse distribution
时钟脉冲分配器 time-pulse distributor
时钟脉冲振荡器 clock pulse oscillator
时钟频率 【电】clock frequency
时钟信号 clock signal
时钟中断 【计】clock interrupt
时轴 time base, time axis
食品公害(食品污染造成的) 【环】health harazards by food contamination
食盐 (同"氯化钠") ◇水银法~电解*
食盐氯化焙烧 salt roasting, roasting with salt
食盐氯化焙烧焙砂 salt-roast calcine

食盐氯化焙烧厂　salt-roasting mill
食盐氯化焙烧法　salt-roast-process
蚀斑　【冶】pitting
蚀边结构　margination texture
蚀度[作用]　【地】alteration
蚀穿　eating thrown
蚀掉　eating away
蚀洞　scoring
蚀刻　etch(ing) ◇ 电解～cautery, 阴离子真空～*
蚀刻用黄铜　etching brass
蚀坑　pit ◇ 人工～artificial pit
蚀裂　corrosion crack(ing) ◇ 硫化物～*
蚀去(炉衬)　eating away
蚀损　corrosion damage
蚀象　corrosion figure [pattern]
蚀阴沟硫杆菌(旧称聚硫杆菌)　thiobacillus concretivorus
实测强度　observed intensity
实存储器　【计】real storage
实底钢锭模　solid [closed] bottom mould
实地址(区)　【计】real address (area)
实电阻　real resistance
实腹拱　【建】solid-spandrel arch
实腹梁　【建】solid web girder, plain girder
实际标准　actual standard (act. std.)
实际产量　actual production [output], effective output
实际掺入体　real inclusion
实际尺寸　actual [natural, true] size, actual dimension
实际尺寸模型　【理】full [real] scale model
实际电极电位　actual electrode potential
实际电阻　true resistance
实际断裂应力　actual stress at fracture
实际分解电压　practical decomposition voltage
实际负载　actual load
实际(钢丝绳)破断拉力　【压】actual breaking force
实际工作压力　actual working pressure (awp)
实际功率　true [actual] power
实际鼓风时间　actual blowing time
实际关键字　【计】actual key
实际关系　true relationship
实际机械压力　actual mechanical pressure
实际加工[操作]应力　actual working stress
实际接触面积　true area of contact
实际晶粒度　actual grain size
实际晶体　real crystal
实际净重　actual net weight (a.n.wt.)
实际空间　real space
实际密度　actual density
实际浓度　actual concentration
实际破坏应力　actual stress at fracture
实际气体　real [actual] gas
实际生产能力　effective capacity
实际蚀坑　【金】actual pit
实际输出　effective output
实际速度　actual velocity (A.V.)
实际塑性　【耐】actual plasticity
实际酸度　actual acidity
实际提取率　actual extraction
实际效率　actual efficiency
实际烟囱高度　【环】actual stack height
实际应用　practical application
实际总损失　actual total loss (a.t.l.)
实例指导系统　case-based guiding system
实曲线　solid(-line) curve
实施　conduct, implement(ation)
实时　real [true, actual] time
实时并行操作　【计】real-time concurrency operations
实时操作　【计】true time operation
实时传感器　real time sensor
实时多程序操作系统　real time multiprogram operating system (RTMOS)
实时复合计算机　real-time computer complex (RTCC)
实时计算机　real time computer
实时控制系统　real-time control system

实时联机操作	real-time on-line operation
实时软件	real-time software
实时时钟	real time clock
实时输出	【计】real-time output
实时数据简化[整理]	【计】real-time data reduction
实时探测	real-time detection
实时通信处理	【计】real-time processing commuication
实时系统	【计】real-time system
实时专家系统	realtime expert system
实收率	extraction yield [rate], recovery efficiency, casting yield (铸件的)
实收率误差	yield error
实数运算	【计】real arithmetic
实体[物]	entity
实体波	body wave
实体[物]	entity
实体芯棒[心轴]	solid mandrel
实物测量	full scale measurement
实物尺寸	full size
实物大小研究	full scale investigation
实物模型	mock-up, 【理】full scale model
实物造型	reproduced model moulding
实物支付	payments in kind
实线	full line [curve], active line
实线黑度[密度]	actual line density
实像	real image
实心棒材	【压】solid bar
实心磁极	solid pole
实心导辊	solid supporting roller
实心导线	solid conductor
实心钢锭	solid steel ingot
实心钢辊	solid steel roll
实心件锻造	solid forging
实心矫直辊	solid levelling roller
实心轮胎	band tyre
实心坯	solid billet
实心皮带轮	solid belt pulley
实心托辊	solid supporting roller
实心橡胶滚圈	solid rubber tyre
实心型材	solid section [profile, bar]
实心轴	solid axis [shafting]
实心砖	solid brick
实型	【铸】full mould
实型芯	single-piece core
实型铸造	full form casting, full mould process casting
实型铸造法	full mould (casting) process, cavityless casting (欧洲术语)
实行	carry out, implement, effectuation
实验	experiment (expr), experimentation, test, trial run ◇ 德拉贡~*, 试验室规模~*
实验程序[方法]	empirical procedure
实验法	experimentation
实验工厂	experimental plant
实验化学式	empirical chemical formula
实验技术	experimental technique
实验浇注[铸件]	pilot casting
实验结果处理	handling of results
实验炉	experimental furnace
实验设备	trial plant
实验式	empiric(al) formula
实验室	laboratory (lab., lbr)
实验室干燥器	laboratory dryer
实验室规模	laboratory-scale, laboratory size magnitude
实验室技术人员	laboratory technician
实验室间误差	tolerance between laboratories
实验室模型	laboratory model
实验室烧结试验装置	laboratory sintering apparatus
实验室设备	laboratory equipment
实验室试验	laboratory test, bench-scale experiment
实验室用试样	laboratory sample
实验室装置	laboratory device
实验数据	laboratory data
实验误差	experimental error
实验型(的)	laboratory-scale
实验型回转窑	laboratory type kiln
实验型磨机	laboratory mill

实验性设施	prototype plant
实验窑	laboratory kiln ◇ 工业性～pilot kiln
实验仪表	laboratory instrument
实验证据	experimental evidence
实验值	experimental value
实验装置	test installation, experimental facility
实样模型	full [block] pattern
实用单位	practical unit
实用功能	utilized [applicable] function
实用性	practicability
实在溶液	actual [real] solution
实质的	substantive, intrinsic, material
实轴	real axis
实足尺寸	full size
识别	recognition, identification
识别指示器	【电】sentinel
史密斯铁铬铝电阻丝合金	(55Fe, 37.5Cr, 7.5Al) Smith's alloy
史前金属	prehistoric metal
矢高	arrow height, bilge
矢积	vector(ial) product
矢量	vector (quantity) ◇ 伯格斯～*, 平行柏氏～*
矢量差速计	vector velocimeter
矢量场	vector field
矢量乘法	vector multiplication
矢量积	vectorial product
矢量控制	victor control
矢量图	vector [arrow] diagram, vectogram
矢圈(轮)	girth gear
使用	use, employ, applying, appliance, application ◇ 未经～的 virgin
使用不当	misapplication
使用错误	misapplication
使用费	running cost
使用风口	blowing tuyere
使用腐蚀	service corrosion
使用负载	work(ing) [service] load
使用规程[规则]	【企】service regulations
使用价值	value of service, use value
使用经验	service experience
使用可焊性	overall weldability
使用可靠性	serviceability
使用控制台	【计】utility control console
使用灵活性	operational versatility
使用率	rate, utilization, service rating
使用面积	floorage, usable floor area
使用磨损	service wear
使用年限	lifetime
使用频率[次数]	frequency of use
使用期限	lifetime, (operating, service) life, period [term] of service, working service, durability ◇ 全部～entire life, 延长的～extended service life
使用强度	handle strength
使用试验	service test
使用寿命	service [operation] life, working life [service]
使用寿命试验	intermittent life test
使用说明	service instruction, operation sheet
使用说明书	operating instruction (manual)
使用特性	operational performances, operating characteristic
使用条件	service [running] conditions, conditions of use
使用温度	service temperature
使用稳定性	service stability
使用系数	coefficient of performance (C.O.P.)
使用细则	service manual
使用仪表	service instrument
始板[极]槽	starting sheet cell
始标	beginning marker
始点	starting [initial] point, starting-up (熔炼的)
始锭	starting-ingot
始发脉冲	【理】inceptive impulse
始极片	【色】starting sheet, cathode (starting) sheet ◇ 铜～copper starting

sheet,纯铜～.

始极片槽 stripping tank

始极片制备工段（电解的）【色】starting section

始极片种[母]板 starting sheet blank

始极丝（碘化物法用）starting filament [wire]

始料（区域熔炼的） starting charge ◇ 纯～法.

始凝点 cloud point

始轧断面 【压】initial (pass) section

始值 initial value

示波计 oscillometer

示波器 oscillograph, oscillometer, oscilloscope ◇ 布朗管[阴极射线管]～.,电流计～.,回线[环线]～.,双射束[双电子束]～.,同步～oscillosynchroscope,阴极[电子]射线～.,印字～.

示波器测试头 oscilloprobe

示波器记录 oscillographic record(ing)

示波器图像 【电】scope pattern

示波术 oscillography

示波图 oscillogram, oscillograph trace

示差温度计 differential thermometer

示度盘（轧机压下的）【压】index gear

示范工厂 demonstration plant

示范性试验 try-out

示功器 indicator

示功图 indicator [forced-distance] diagram

示功仪表 indicator device

示构分析 【数】rational [phase] analysis

示构式 【数】rational formula

示号器 annunciator (ANN)

示号线路 annunciating circuit

示例图 typical drawing

示扭器 torsion indicator

示频器 frequency indicator

示色 show colour

示数(的) numeral

示数器 numerascope, numeroscope

示温棒 【冶】thermoscopic bar

示温合金 thermoscopic alloy ◇ 坦帕尔～.,坦普赖特～.

示温漆[涂料] heat indicating paint, thermindex,【冶】tempilac, thermal paint

示温球[丸] 【冶】tempil pellets

示温熔锥比值 pyrometric cone equivalent (P.C.E.)

示温色笔 temperature-indicating [temperature-sensitive] crayon, tempilstiks

示温颜料 thermocolours

示温仪 temperature indicating instrument

示意流程图 schematic flow diagram

示意模型 schematic model

示意配置图 diagrammatic arrangement

示意图 diagrammatic sketch [chart, layout], outline drawing, rough drawing [draft], schematic diagram [drawing, model] ◇ 简单～.

示踪 trace(r), tracing

示踪材料 tracer material

示踪测定 tracer determination

示踪分析 tracer analysis

示踪技术 tracer technique

示踪剂[物] tracer (agent, material) ◇ 放射性同位素～.

示踪扩散系数 tracer diffusion coefficient

示踪离子 tracer ion

示踪气体 tracer gas, search-gas

示踪球团[团]tracer pellet

示踪碳 carbon tracer

示踪同位素 tracer isotope

示踪稀释法 tracer dilution method

示踪元素 tracer [indicator, label(l)ed] element

示踪原子 tracer [tracing, label (l) ed, tagged] atom, isotopic tracer ◇ 含～的化合物 tracer compound

示踪原子法 tracer technique [method]

示踪原子法研究 tracer investigation

示踪原子扩散 tracer diffusion

世代[地] generation

世界专利索引 WORLD PATENTS IN-

DEX (WPI)
事故 accident (acc.), trouble, failure, casualty, emergency, eventuality ◇ 大~ major accident, 无~的 foolproof
事故保险 accident insurance
事故报警器 trouble alarm device
事故备用出钢槽 emergency launder
事故备用钢包 emergency ladle
事故备用系统 emergency stand-by system
事故出铁 【铁】emergency tapping
事故电源 emergency power
事故调查 trouble hunting
事故对策 emergency countermeasure
事故供电 emergency feeding
事故供电电池 battery emergency supply
事故集水池 emergency catch basin
事故继电器 emergency [fault] relay
事故剪切机 emergency shears
事故浇铸台 emergency casting stand
事故警报 disaster warning
事故率 rate of trouble
事故排放 【环】accidental discharge
事故切废 emergency cutting scrap
事故烧嘴 emergency burner
事故损坏 accident defect
事故停机 emergency stop
事故停浇塞棒 【钢】stopper plug
事故信号 emergency signal, warning
事故信号灯 emergency light
事故信号系统 alarm signal system
事故修理 emergency repair
事故用发电机 emergency (electricity) generator
事故用煤气 emergency gas
事故用水 emergency water
事故用水系统 emergency water system
事故预防 accident [disaster] prevention
事故致死 【环】accidental homicide
事故装置 emergency service
事件 event, incident, matter, occurrence
事件(发生)记录 log out

事前估计值 advance estimates
事务处理 【计】transaction
事务工作自动化 office automation
事先试验 pretest
事先退火 pre-annealing
势 force, tendency, potential
势差 potential difference (P.D.)
势场 potential field
势垒 【理】barrier (potential), potential barrier ◇ 科特雷耳~
势垒穿透 barrier penetration
势垒穿透性 potential barrier penetrability
势垒高度 barrier height
势垒宽度 barrier width
势垒理论 theory of obstacles
势垒效应 barrier effect [action]
势垒型电解液 barrier type electrolyte
势垒形状 【理】barrier shape
势能 potential (energy, head)
势能场 field of potential energy
势能峰 potential energy hill
势阱 【理】potential well [hole, trough]
嗜热硫杆菌 thiobacillus thermophilica
嗜热微生物 thermophilic microorganism
嗜热细菌 thermophilic bacteria
嗜酸铁氧化细菌 acidophilic iron-oxidizing bacteria
嗜酸细菌 acidophilic bacteria
嗜盐细菌 Halobacterium
噬硫杆菌 thiobacillus
噬硫杆菌氧化剂 thiobacillus thiooxidant
噬硫细菌 sulphur bacteria, thiobacteria
噬硫细菌铁氧化剂 thiobacillus ferrooxidant
噬硫氧化细菌 thiobacillus concretivorus bacteria
噬铁杆菌类 ferribacteriaceae
噬铁细菌 ferribacteriales, ferrobacillus
噬铁细菌硫氧化剂 ferrobacillus sulfooxidant
噬铁细菌氧化剂 ferrobacillus ferrooxidant

适当的 fit(ting), suitable, proper
适当曝光 correct exposure
适当温度操作 moderate-temperature process
适合 suit, fit, meet, adaptation, conformability, congruency
适合性 compatibility, fitness, suitability, versatility
适配部件 adapter unit ◇ 显示～
适配器 adapter ◇ 联线～【计】on-line adapter, 通道～【电】channel adapter
适销产品 marketable product
适宜 suitable, fit, appropriate, proper ◇ 最～成分 tailored composition
适宜范围(对人体的) comfort zone
适宜湿度[水分](型砂的)【铸】workable moisture
适应 adapt(ion), adaptation, accomodation, suit, fit ◇ 不～disaccomodation
适应设备 application ware
适应位错 【理】accommodation dislocation
适应系数 accommodation coefficient
适应性 adaptability, flexibility, applicability, suitability, versatility ◇ 操作～
适用 suit, apply to ◇ 使不～disable
适用标准 criterion of acceptability
适用性 usability, serviceability, acceptability, applicability
适者生存 survival of the fittest
释出 release
释出热 heat of evolution
释放 release, loosening, relief, trip, (电磁铁、继电器等的) deenergizing, deenergising
释放电压 release voltage
释放机构 relief mechanism, releasing device
释放器 releaser ◇ 双金属～bimetallic releaser
释放气体 release of gases
释放系统 release system
释放线圈 release coil

释热 heat [thermic] release, heat liberation
释热量 heat liberation ◇ 单位炉(子)体(积)～
释热速率 heat release rate
释热元件 fuel element, heat liberating devices
释热值 heat liberation value
释压阀 pressure relief valve
饰金 gilding ◇ 荷兰～
饰金金属 gilding metal
饰面 finishing, overcoating, facing,【建】dressing
饰面板 【建】facesheet, sheathing [shell] plate, veneer
饰面层 encasing
饰面的 faced
饰面砖 facing brick
饰物合金 jewelry alloy [metal]
饰物黄铜 latten alloy, Nu-gild
饰用金粉 venturine
市场 market
市场波动 demand fluctuation
市场产品 saleable product
市场调查[研究] market research [survey]
市场动态 market trend
市场分析 market analysis
市场经济 market economy
市场情况 market pattern
市场预测 market forcast
市政工程 public work, municipal engineering [work]
市政和工业废料 municipal and industrial refuse
室内变电(分)站 indoor substation
室内变压器 indoor transformer
室内除尘 room dedusting
室内大气腐蚀 indoor corrosion
室内电缆 house [inside] cable
室内土壤物理力学试验 soil physical mechanical laboratory testing

室内温度　indoor temperature
室内研究　laboratory study
室内照明　indoor lighting [illumination]
室内资料　in-house information
室式除尘器　chamber collector
室式干燥炉　chamber drying oven
室式干燥器[机]　chamber [cabinet, compartment] drier
室式环窑　transverse-arch kiln
室式炉　chamber [batch, compartment] furnace, chamber-oven, box-type furnace ◇ 通控制气氛的～curtain-type furnace
室式炉退火　batch annealing
室式轮窑　annular chamber kiln
室式退火镀锡板　batch type annealing tin plate
室式退火机组作业线　batch type annealing line
室式退火炉　batch annealing furnace
室式退火炉设备　batch type annealing plant
室式压滤机　chamber filter press
室式窑　chamber [compartment] kiln
室式装箱热处理炉　box batch type furnace
室外暴露(腐蚀)试验　outdoor-exposure test
室外变电所　outdoor substation
室外大气腐蚀　outdoor corrosion
室外电缆　outside cable
室外绝缘子　outdoor insulator
室外土壤力学试验　field soil mechanical test
室外温度　outside temperature
室外贮存　outdoor storage
室温　room temperature (R.T.)
室温变态　room-temperature modification
室温电导率　room-temperature conductivity
室温固压　room curing
室温固压黏结剂　room-temperature setting adhesive
室温碱洗液[机,装置]　room-temperature alkaline cleaner
室温强度　room-temperature strength
室温缺口韧性　room-temperature notch toughness
室温蠕变　room-temperature creep
室温时效[陈化]　room-temperature aging
室温弯曲　room-temperature bending
室温相　room-temperature phase
室温性能[性质]　room-temperature property
室状炉　batch type furnace
视比表面　apparent specific surface
视比重　(同"表观比重")
视差　(optical) parallax
视差因数[因子]　parallax factor
视场(显微镜的)　field of vision [view]
视场光阑　field diaphragm
视场深度　depth of field
视尺寸　apparent size
视度　visual degree
视角　visual angle, angle of viewing [vision]
视角范围　angular field
视接触角　apparent contact angle
视界　visibility
视距(测量)　stadia
视距乘常数　multiplication constant
视距镜　anallatic lens
视距仪　tachymeter
视觉　vision, visual sense, sight
视觉塑性法[理]visioplasticity method
视孔　eye hole
视孔盖　【铁】wicket, tuyere cap [wicket]
视孔砖　sight hole brick
视力　vision, sight
视(力)敏度　visual acuity
视能　apparent energy
视频　video (frequency), vision [image] frequency
视频发射机　video transmitter
视频技术　video(-based) technique

视频金相学　TV metallography
视频(控制)系统　vision system
视频显示　video display [presentation]
视频信号　videosignal
视频噪声　video noise
视频增益　【电】video gain
视气孔度　apparent porosity
视图　view
视网膜字符阅读器　【计】retina character reader (RCR)
视像管　vidicon
视效率　apparent efficiency
视野　visual field, field (of view), range of vision ◇ 角~ angular field
视应力　apparent stress
视域　field of vision, sight
视在表面　apparent surface
视在电阻　apparent resistance
视在功率　(同"表观功率")
视在孔隙率　apparent porosity ◇ 总~*
视在容积　apparent volume
视在容量[电容]　apparent capacity
试板　plate specimen ◇ 两边有裂纹的~ double edged cracked plate specimen
试棒　test bar [rod, stick] ◇ 带头的~ headed test bar, 端头车丝~ screwed test bar, 附铸~*, 校核用~ check bar, 端头座肩式(拉伸)~ (见"拉伸试棒")
试棒端头　test bar head
试棒横截面　cross-section of test bar
试棒弯曲试验　bar bend test
试车　test run [work], trial run (ning) [drive, operation], commissioning
试车期　start-up period, running-in (period), breaking in period
试淬(火)法测定相变温度　bracketing
试错法　trial-and-error method
试管　test tube
试管架　test tube stand
试焊　pilot joint
试焊焊缝　sample weld
试航　trial trip [run(ning)]

试剂　reagent ◇ 戴维斯~*, 未稀释~ undiluted reagent, 用~处理[加工] reagentizing
试剂处理[加工]　reagentizing
试剂分布　reagent distribution
试剂级品位　reagent grade
试剂空白试验　reagent blank
试剂气体　reagent gas
试剂消耗　reagent consumption, consumption of reactant
试件　test specimen [piece], sample piece
试接　pilot joint
试金　assay(ing), metallic assay ◇ 干式~(法) dry assay
试金吨砝码　assay ton weight
试金分析　assaying analysis, metallic assay
试金分析法　fire assay
试金坩埚　assay crucible, scorifier
试金炉　assay furnace
试金曲线　assay curve
试金石(丝绒状石英)　basanite, touchstone, lydianite
试金(实验)室　assay laboratory
试金天平　assay balance
试金物　assay
试块　check block [piece], briguette (标准的), 【冶】test block ◇ 基尔~ Keel block
试粒　test button
试炼　smelting trial
试炼炉次　blank heat
试料　sample material, assay
试料采样器　sampling thief
试料制备　sample preparation
试铝灵　aluminon
试镁灵　magneson
试镍剂　nickel reagent
试片　test plate
试铅(试金用)　test lead
试生产　trial operation ◇ 工业~阶段*
试生产作业线　pilot line
试钛灵　tiron
试探[试凑]法　(同"尝试法")

试铁灵 ferron, loretin

试铜灵 cupron, benzoinoxime

试铜铁灵 cupferron

试销合金 semi-commercial alloy

试行规范 tentative specification

试亚铁灵 ferroin, phenanthroline ion

试验 test(ing), experiment, trial, investigation, try-out ◇ 鲍曼~Bauman test, 布朗~*, 初步~rough test, 格雷-金【焦】Gray King assay, 经过严格的~high test, 林德~*, 罗伯逊法~*, 尼尔森~Nielson test, 小规模~scaled-down experiment

试验板 test plate [board]

试验报告 test [laboratory] report

试验编号 test number (T.N.)

试验表面 test surface

试验材料 test [experimental] material

试验场地 testing floor

试验厂 trial [experimental] plant

试验常数 experimental constant

试验车间 trial plant

试验程序 test routine [program], test [experimental] procedure

试验持续时间 test period

试验点 test point, 【金】data point (图表上的)

试验电解槽 experimental cell

试验方法 test(ing) method, test [experimental] procedure

试验符[代]号 testing symbol

试验高炉 experimental blast furnace (E.B.F.)

试验工作 test work

试验规范 test specifications

试验规模 experimental scale, pilot-scale

试验焊缝 test weld

试验荷载 test [trial] load

试验合金 experimental alloy

试验混合器 test mixer

试验机 test(ing) machine ◇ 带滚道的推力片式~grooved wash rigs, 磨损~*, 手动~*, 通径[塞棒]~drifter

试验机床 pilot machine

试验机夹头 grips of testing machine

试验技术 testing technique

试验记录单 test record sheet

试验阶段[时期] experimental stage

试验结果 test(ing) result

试验块 testing block ◇ 比较用~*

试验粒度 【选】testing size

试验炉 experimental furnace, test oven ◇ 中间工厂~pilot furnace

试验轮次 trial run(ning)

试验模型 pilot [experimental] model

试验膜 test film

试验盘 test board

试验平台 testing platform

试验器 tester, exerciser

试验气体组成 test gas composition

试验熔锥 test cone

试验筛 testing sieve

试验烧结矿 experimental sinter

试验设备 test(ing) equipment [apparatus, facility, assembly], trial plant [installation], experimental unit [rig], laboratory(-scale) plant

试验设计 experiment(al) design

试验室 (testing) laboratory, test room [house]

试验室尝试法 cut-and-try laboratory technique

试验室规模实验 laborator-scale experimentation

试验室设备 laboratory equipment [outfit]

试验室试验 bench scale experiment [test]

试验室研究 laboratory study [investigation]

试验室用炉 laboratory size furnace

试验室装置 laboratory installation

试验数据 experimental data, test data [figures]

试 shi

试验速度	trial speed
试验台	test bed [bench, board, desk, stand]
试验条件	test condition
试验统计的	test-statistic
试验统计量	test-statistics
试验误差	experimental error
试验误差法	trial-and-error procedure
试验吸收效率	experimental absorption efficiency
试验系列	test series
试验系数	experimental constant
试验系统	experimental arrangement, pilot system
试验线圈组（材料的）	test coil assembly
试验性工厂	pilot
试验性鼓风炉	experimental blast furnace (E.B.F.)
试验性还原	test reduction
试验性气体	probe gas
试验性熔炼	blank heat
试验旋塞	test [try] cock
试验研究	experimental investigation
试验应力	proof stress
试验样机	pilot machine
试验窑	laboratory type kiln
试验仪	tester
试验仪器	test apparatus
试验应力	proof stress
试验用单膛焙烧炉	single hearth test furnace
试验用电弧炉	laboratory-scale arc furnace
试验用反应器	test-reactor
试验员	tester
试验运行［运转］	experimental run
试验载荷	proof load
试验证明	evidence ◇ 经～有用的［经多次～的］well-tried
试验值	trial value
试验指标	test index, experimental data
试验中心	test(ing) centre

试验周期	test period
试验铸件	trial casting
试验铸块	cast test block
试验铸造车间	pilot foundry
试验转炉	experimental converter
试验桩记录仪	testing pile recorder
试验装置	test(ing) apparatus [facility, assembly, jig, installation, set], experimental apparatus [arrangement, plant], laboratory device, pilot machine
试样	(test, proof, laboratory) sample, (test) specimen, test piece [bar] ◇ 按比例配制的～（材料试验用）proportioning probe, 按比例取的～proportionated sample, 并合～composite sample, 部分～sample increment, 德拜－谢乐～*, 附铸～*, 每班～shift sample, 片状［薄片］【钢】napkin, 平均～average sample, 失败［未经受住试验的］～*, 四分～quarter sample
试样安置	specimen embedding
试样百分数	sample percentage
试样板	sample board
试样包埋	specimen embedding
试样标准偏差值	sample standard deviation
试样冲床	test piece punching machine
试样储存期限	sample storage life
试样电荷	charge specimen
试样锭	【钢】Keel block
试样端部	head of specimen
试样粉末（X射线照相的）	specimen powder
试样工	sampler
试样固定	specimen fixing
试样管	(test-)sample tube
试样畸变（电子光学的）	specimen distortion
试样几何形状	specimen geometry
试样夹	specimen grips [holder]
试样减分	sample division
试样截［剖］面	sample section

试样块 test block [piece], coupon
试样抛光机 sample polishing machine
试样平均值 sample average [median]
试样气门（气体的） sample port
试样切割器 sample cutter
试样热电偶（测量温度用） sample thermocouple
试样容器[罐] sample carrier
试样散射 specimen scattering
试样受辐照长度 irradiated length of specimen
试样算术平均值 sample arithmetic mean average
试样缩分 sample reduction
试样缩分器 riffler
试样缩分装置 sample conditioner
试样台（电子显微镜的） specimen stage
试样污染 specimen contamination
试样误调[未调准]【金】 missetting of specimen
试样旋转夹 rotating specimen holder
试样选取环 ring sampler
试样（衍射，绕射）环 specimen ring
试样支座振动 vibration of specimen holder
试样中间值 sample median
试样周转衍射用照相机 integrating camera
试样准备[制备] sample [specimen] preparation
试样准备间 sample-preparing department
试样钻屑【冶】 test drillings
试液 test solution
试液吸收带 drip flap
试用 (service) trial, try-out
试运行[转] test [pilot, experimental, trial, dummy] run, trial running [operation] ◇ 冷态～ cold-run trial
试运转费 start-up costs
试运转期间 running-in (period)
试纸 test [reagent, indicator] paper ◇ 姜黄～*

试制 advanced development, trial-manufacture
试制产品 trial product
试桩 test pile
铈{Ce} cerium ◇ 含～合金*
铈处理铸铁 cerium-treated cast iron
铈的高压形态 high pressure form of cerium
铈钙锆石 anderbergite
铈钙钛矿 {$CaTiO_3$, 含 Ce_2O_3 及 FeO} knopite
铈硅钙球墨铸铁 oz cast iron
铈硅磷灰石 britholite
铈硅铍钇矿 cergadolinite
铈硅石 cerite
铈合金 cerium alloy
铈黑帘石 bagrationite
铈基合金 cerium base alloy
铈镧钕镨合金（50Ce, 45La） mischmetal (1)
铈磷灰石 cerium apatite
铈热还原 cerio-thermic reduction
铈热还原剂 cerium-thermic reducer
铈烧绿石 ceriopyrochlore
铈钛铁矿 kalkowskite
铈添加合金 cerium addition
铈铁白云石 {$(Ca, Mg, Fe, Ce)CO_3$} cerium-ankerite, codazzite
铈铁氟化碳酸盐 {$(Ce, La)CO_3F$} bastinasite
铈铁（合金） ferrocerium
铈（同素异晶）的高压变态 high pressure modification of cerium
铈钍消[吸]气剂（电子管用；80Th, 20Ce） Ce-Th getter, ceto getter
铈钨华 cerotungstite
铈稀土 cerium mischmetal
铈钇矿 (fluss)yttrocerite
铈萤石 cerfluorite
铈铀铁钛矿 {$20FeO·8Fe_2O_3·4(RE)_2O_3·UO_2·74TiO_2$} ufertite
收板装置（镀锡机的） catcher ◇ 自动～

automatic catcher

收尘 dust collection [catching, arrest] ◇ 布袋～法 bag process, 干法～ dry dust collection, 静电～法 cottrell process

收尘程度 degree of dust precipitation

收尘袋 dust bag

收尘点 dust-collecting point

收尘器 dust-precipitator, (dust) collector, dust collecting unit, deduster, dust arrester [catcher, extractor, trap] ◇ 半闭路～*, 闭路[再循环]～*, 布袋[袋式]～*, 带振动过滤筛的～ vibrating screen deduster, 挡板式[百叶窗式]～ baffle type collector, 电沉积～*, 风力～ pneumatic deduster, 管式～*, 惯性～*, 阶式[分级]～ cascade-type deduster, 静电～*, 离心(式)～*, 鲁尔～ Luehr filter, 脉动～ pulsator deduster, 湿式～*, 水洗涤式～*, 弯管～ elbow separator, 旋涡～*, 重力～*

收尘设备 dust collection [arrestment] equipment ◇ 干式～[系统]

收尘室 dust (collecting) chamber, collecting chamber

收尘系统 dust collecting system

收尘效率 dust-catching efficiency

收尘装置 dust arrester installation, dust-separation equipment

收尘罩 dust hood

收得率 recovery, yield, recovery factor (矿石中有用组分的)

收得率损失 yield loss

收发话机 Voice transmitter-receiver

收发电路 transceiver circuit

收发报机 receiver-transmitter

收发键盘装置 【电】receive/send keyboard set (RSK)

收购价格 purchase price

收回 withdrawal, recovery, retrieval

收获率 yield (Y, yld)

收集 collecting, gather (ing), catching, containment, balling up (氧化皮)

收集槽 receiving tank

收集管线 gathering Line

收集辊道 【压】gathering table

收集孔 gathering hole

收集炉膛 (同"集砂炉膛")

收集盘 catch-plate, catch tray, collecting disc

收集器 accumulator, collector, divertor, receiver, assembler, gathere

收集器挡板 collector damper

收集栅 collecfor mesh

收集室 collecting chamber

收集效率 collection efficiency

收集(验收)方法(轧材的) take-up method

收孔(拉丝模的) battering

收口(空心锻件的) 【压】bottling, closingin

收口套接(管子的) spigot and faucet joint

收敛 converging, convergence, constriction

收敛部分 confractor

收敛冲击波 (同"会聚冲击波")

收敛法 【数】convergence method

收敛管道 constriction, converging clust

收敛级数 convergent series

收敛判剧 Convergence exponent

收敛角 convergence angle

收敛系统 Collective Systam

收敛项[子] Convergente

收敛形喷嘴 convergent nozzle

收敛指数 Convergence exponent

收料送料台 run-out-and-conveyor bed

收入帐户 【企】account of receipts

收湿的 hygroscopic

收湿性 hygroscopicity, water-absorbing quality

收缩 contracting, contraction, shrinkage, shrink-away, shrinking, collapse, constriction, gather(ing), retraction, slump (炉衬的) ◇ 拉瓦尔喷嘴型～ Laval constriction, 面积～【压】reduction in area, 无～

钢 non-shrinking steel
收缩变换　Shrinking transformation
收缩变形　contraction strain, shrinkage distortion
收缩程度　degree of shrinkage
收缩的γ相区　contracted gamma field, contracted γ
收缩点　shrink point
收缩定律　shrink(age) rule
收缩度　degree of shrinkage
收缩发裂　【金】check shatter crack
收缩缝　contraction [shrinkage] joint, shrink-off gap
收缩钢筋　shrinkage bar
收缩工序　【压】shrinking operation
收缩公差［容差,允许量］　shrinkage allowance, patternmaker's shrinkage
收缩-扩张［收敛发散形］喷嘴　(同"拉瓦尔喷嘴")
收缩焊接　shrink welding
收缩横断面　cross-sectional area of contraction
收缩畸变　shrinkage distortion
收缩孔　contraction [shrinkage] cavity, shrinkage [sink(ing)] hole
收缩孔隙［疏松］　shrinkage porosity
收缩量　amount of contraction [shrinkage], contraction
收缩裂缝［纹］　contraction [shrinkage, check] crack, shrinkage tear,【铸】pulls (铸件表面的)
收缩率　contraction ratio, shrinkage index [value], reduction,【团】degree of contraction
收缩模　contraction pattern ◇三次~*, 双重~*
收缩喷嘴　contracting nozzle
收缩器　contractor (contr.)
收缩前的膨胀　preshrinkage expansion
收缩趋势　shrinkage tendency
收缩圈［环］　shrink-ring
收缩时基扫描　contracted time-base sweep
收缩试验　shrinkage test
收缩撕裂　shrinkage tear
收缩损失　contraction loss
收缩特性　shrinkage characteristics
收缩条痕　contraction lines
收缩头　【钢】shrinker, head
收缩位错　contracted dislocation
收缩系数　contraction coefficient, shrinkage factor
收缩性　contracti(bi)lity
收缩应变　contraction [shrinkage] strain
收缩应力　contractional [shrinkage] stress
收缩余量　【铸】contraction allowance, allowance for contraction
收缩值表　shrink table
收缩指数　shrinkage index
收缩轴　contraction axis
收缩皱纹　shrinkage mark
收缩状态的卷筒　【压】collapsed mandrel
收缩作用　contraction
收线(钢丝的)　taking-up
收线架　take-up stand [frame]
收线卷筒　take-up block
收线设备　【压】taking-up equipment
收线装置　take-up
收益　【企】earnings, income, gains
收益电子　out-coming electron
收音机　radio [wireless] set,【电】receiver
收支平衡　【企】balance of payments
收支平衡帐目核算　balance-of-payments accounts
手扳压(力)机　(同"手动压力机")
手柄　hand shank [lever], arm, grip, handgrip, handhold, stick
手操纵　hand control (hc), manual manipulation
手册　handbook, manual, directory
手测(高炉料线的)　hand sounding
手铲　hand shovel
手车　(hand)cart
手持电极　prods

手 shou

手持焊接面罩　(welding) hand shield
手持送受话器　handset
手持小型装置　handset
手锤　hand hammer [rammer],【机】dresser
手锉　hand file
手电筒　electric torch, flashlight
手动操作的　manually operated (man. op), hand-operated
手动(操作)阀　hand(-operated) [manual] valve
手动操作开关　【电】hand-operated switch
手动的　manually operated (man.op), hand-operated
手动地址开关　manual address switch
手动定量进给阀　measuring valve
手动复位[重调]　hand reset
手动复位触点(常开)　manual reset contact (norm open)
手动焊接机　hand-held welder
手动焊钳　poke gun
手动焊钳点焊　poke welding
手动滑轮　lever block
手动夹具　【机】hand-operated jig
手动绞车　hand winch
手动卷扬机　hand hoist [winch]
手动控制　manual operation
手动控制流量指示器　flow indicator with hand controller
手动控制器　hand [manual] controller
手动控制系统　manual control system
手动喷雾器　hand sprayer
手动启动器　【电】hand starter
手动起重器[千斤顶]　hand jack
手动切刀[切割机]　hand-powered cutter
手动曲柄　hand crank
手动试验机　hand-power testing machine
手动弹簧压下装置　manual screw down with spring
手动调整　(同"手调")
手动压下螺丝　manually operated screw
手动压下装置　manually operated screwdown, hand screwdown gear
手动闸板　manually operated damper
手动装置　hand gear
手端包　【铸】hand ladle
手锻　smithing
手段　means, medium, measure, method, approach
手感热的　handwarm
手工安装　hand setting
手工操作　manual control (M/C), manual operation [manipulation], manhandle, operation by hand
手工操作焊接机　【焊】hand-operated welding machine
手工铲削清理　hand chipping
手工电弧堆焊　manual electric arc pile up welding
手工电弧焊　manual electric arc welding, electrode welding
手工电渣焊　manual electro-slag welding
手工动作　manhandle
手工割炬　hand cutting burner [torch]
手工焊电焊把　hand welding electrode holder
手工焊弧　manual arc
手工焊(接)　hand [manual] welding, manually welded joint ◇ 碳极电弧～
手工(焊接)焊缝　manual weld
手工焊接用保护气氛室　dry box for manual welding
手工焊炬　hand torch
手工焊闪光时间　manual flashing time
手工焊条　manual electrode
手工加工　handwork
手工拣选　(同"人工拣选")
手工浇注　hand ladling
手工矫正　hand dressing
手工紧固的　hand tight
手工紧固装配[手工拧接]　【机】handtight makeup
手工劳动　manual labor
手工拧接余隙　handtight stand off

手工嵌缝[敛缝,填隙] hand caulking
手工取样 hand sampling
手工三相电弧焊 twin-electrode welding
手工送进烧熔[焊]manual flash-off
手工涂油 manual greasing
手工造型法 【铸】hand mould process
手工制的 handmade (h.m.)
手焊工 manual welder
手机 handset
手拣富矿 rich hand-picked ore
手拣原矿 hand-picked crude ore
手锯 hand saw
手孔 handhole (H.H.)
手控 manual control
手控部分 hand-operated block
手控翻转装置 hand tilting [tipping] device
手控方式 【计】manual mode
手控平衡 manual balance (MB)
手控调节 manual regulation
手拉葫芦 chain block
手轮 hand wheel
手轮锁紧螺钉 wheel screw
手轮压下装置 hand wheel screwdown
手钳 pliers, hand vise [vice], hand clamps
手枪式高温计 【冶】pistol pyrometer
手勺取样试验 spoon test
手饰铜 gilding metal
手套 gloves ◇ 长[宽口大]~ gauntlet, gloves, 带指~ fingered gloves, 铬革长~ chrome leather gauntlet, 两指~*
手套(干燥)箱 glove box
手套式操作箱(真空设备等用的) glove box
手提式分光光度计 hand spectrophotometer
手提式设备 portable equipment
手提式硬度计 portable hardness tester ◇ 艾姆斯~*
手调 hand [manual] adjustment
手调闸门 manually adjusted gate
手推车 handcart, hand-operated carriage, wheel [hand] barrow, push(ing) car, barrow, dolly, lorry
手续 procedure (proc.), formalities, routine, process
手选 hand dressing [sorting], picking (out) ◇ 矸石~带【选】collecting band
手选矿石 screened ore
手选(矿石用两面)锤 scabbling hammer
手摇把[柄] hand crank
手摇的 hand driven
手摇干湿表 sling psychrometer
手摇绞盘 hand capstan
手摇钻 hand drill, brace
手摇钻床 hand drilling machine
手用工具 hand tool
手錾 hand chisel
手闸[手力制动器] hand brake
手闸控制 hand brake control
首次碾压 breakdown rolling
首批料 【冶】initial charge
首饰 jewel(le)ry ◇ 金银丝~filigree
首饰合金 jewellery alloy [metal]
首饰黄金 jewellery gold
首饰黄铜(一种含锡α黄铜；9—10Zn, 2Sn,余量Cu) jeweller's bronze
首饰抛光用红铁粉 jeweller's ronge
首数(对数的)【数】characteristic
首涂层 primary coat
守恒 conservation ◇ 不~凝固*, 非~运动
守恒定律 conservation laws
守恒凝固 conservative freezing
守恒运动 conservative motion
寿命 life(time), life-span, age, longevity, durability, duration, endurance, period of service, 【冶】campaign, length of life(炉衬的) ◇ 可能~*, 使用[工作]~*
寿命试验 life test
寿命周期 life cycle
售货机 vending [commercial] machine
受板台 catcher table
受补面(高炉喷补的) gunned face

受潮的	damped ◇ 未~ undamped
受电电缆	power receiving cable
受电开关	receive switch
受钉混凝土	nailable concrete
受话器	telephone receiver [earphone], receiver ◇ 热线式~ thermophone, 双耳~ biphone, 头戴~ head-piece
受火面层	fire face layer
受激电子	excited electron
受激离子	excited ion
受激能级	excited energy level
受激原子	excited atom
受激状态	excited state
受检材料	material under examination
受剪力钢筋	shearing bar
受控变量	controlled variable
受控掺杂	controlled doping
受控电弧	controlled arc
受控腐蚀	controlled etching
受控核聚变	controlled nuclear fusion
受控金属过渡焊接	controlled-transfer welding
受控孔隙度材料	【粉】controlled-porosity material
受控凝固	(同"定向凝固")
受控生长	controlled growth
受控氧化	controlled oxidation
受控元件	controlled member
受扩散控制的	diffusion-controlled
受扩散控制的生长	【金】diffusion controlled growth
受拉钢筋	tensioned wire
受拉连接	tension joint
受力钢筋	effective bar
受力构件	bearing carrier
受力状态	stressed state ◇ 非~ 腐蚀
受料[矿]仓	receiving bin
受料斗	receiving cone
受料格栅[台架]	receiving skid
受料隔栅	stationary grate
受料辊道	receiving roll table
受料[煤]坑	receiving pit
受料斗[漏斗]	【铁】receiving hopper
受料漏斗平台	reception hopper platform
受料台（炉子的）	【压】unscrambling bed
受料台格栅	unscrambling grid
受料运输机	receiving conveyor
受纳水流	【环】receiving stream
受纳水体	【环】receiving body of water
受内压管道	inner pressurized pipe
受迫振荡	forced oscillation
受迫振动	forced vibration [oscillation]
受热面积	hot area
受热器	heat receiver, thermoreceptor
受热碎裂[递降]	degradation on heating
受水面积	catchment area
受卸工艺	receiving unloading technology
受压(钢)筋	【建】compression reinforcement ◇ 配~ 的梁 double reinforced beam
受压构件	compression member
受压流体	pressure fluid
受压破坏	compression failure
受压纤维	compression fibre
受压诱发脆性－塑性转变	pressure-induced brittle-ductile transition
受压诱生相变	(同"压致相变")
受压蒸馏釜	pressurized still
受液槽	receiver tank
受抑全反射	frustrated total reflection (FTR)
受益	benefit
受益者负担原则	【环】he-who-benefit-sought-to-pay principle
受张[拉]力焊缝	tension weld
受主[体]	【半】acceptor
受主分子	acceptor molecule
受主结合能	acceptor binding energy
受主能带	acceptor band
受主能级	acceptor level
受主原子	acceptor atom
受主杂质	acceptor impurity
受主中心	acceptor centre
受阻沉降	【选】hindered falling [settling]

受阻沉降比　hindered settling ratio
受阻收缩(铸件的)　hindered contraction
瘦煤　carbonaceous [meagre] coal, black jack
瘦黏土　lean [weak] clay
瘦(型)砂　【铸】lean (moulding) sand, mild moulding sand
枢杆　hinged arm
枢机盖　hinged cover
枢铰　pivot hinge
枢接[枢轴活接头]　pivot joint
枢轴　pivot, abut, heel ◇ 球形～ball pivot
枢轴承　trunnion bearing
枢轴颈　pivot [vertical] journal, trunnion
枢轴臼　footstep
枢轴螺栓　pivot bolt
枢轴式皮带运输机　pivoted conveyor
梳刺　◇ 出现～finning
梳刀盘　chaser
梳形擦拭器　comb wiper
梳形件　comb
梳状裂纹(钢坯的)　reeds
殊余数　【计】modulo
输尘管　dust pipe
输出　output, outlet, export(ation)
输出变压器　output transformer
输出操纵工　run-out operator
输出侧　delivery side ◇ 轧机～*
输出成品皮带机　export product conveyer
输出程序　output program [routine]
输出电路　output circuit
输出电容　output capacitance
输出电压　output voltage, voltage output
输出额　output quantity
输出放大器　output amplifier
输出负载率　output loading factor
输出格式　【计】output format
输出工作队列[排队]　【计】output work queue
输出功率　【电】output power, (power, energy) output
输出管道　delivery pipeline
输出辊　run-out roller
输出辊道　【压】run-out [run-off, outlet, outgoing, exit] table, run-out [out-going, delivery, move-out] roller table, discharge roller path ◇ 钢坯～*, 冷床～*, 连铸坯～*, 炉internal～*
输出辊道(氧化)铁皮坑　run-out table scale pit
输出过程　output process
输出缓冲器　【计】output buffer
输出级　output stage
输出连接器　out connector
输出量　output (quantity)
输出媒体　【计】output medium
输出门　outgate
输出能力　output capacity
输出能量　energy output
输出排队[队列]　【计】output queue
输出喷嘴　delivery cone
输出起重机[吊车]　lay-off crane
输出器　follower ◇ 阴极～cathode follower
输出热函　output enthalpy
输出热量　delivered heat
输出设备　【计】output equipment [unit], outdevice
输出特性　output characteristic
输出通道　【计】output channel
输出线　output (line)
输出信号　output [outcoming] signal
输出信息　output information
输出压头(液压的)　delivery head
输出移送机(冷床的)　drag-off [pull-off] transfer
输出状态　【计】output state
输出阻抗　output impedance
输电　(electric) transmission
输电干线　electric mains
输电网　transmission network
输电系统　transmission system
输电线　power line [lead] ◇ 焊接用～welding power lead

输电线路　transmission line
输电效率　transport current efficiency
输电引线封接　lead seal
输煤机　coal transporter
输热管　heat transfer tube
输入　input, entry, entering, import(ation)
输入变压器　【电】input transformer
输入表　【计】input list
输入补偿电压　input offset voltage
输入参考值　【计】input reference
输入侧（轧机的）　【压】entering side
输[装]入程序　loading routine, loader, input program [routine]
输入称量辊道　scale approach table
输入储存台　entry ramp ◇ 带卷~
输入存储区　【计】input storage [block]
输入电解液　incoming electrolyte
输入电路　input circuit
输入端　input end, intake
输入放大器　【电】input amplifier
输入工作辊道　【压】ingoing main table
输入功率　【电】input (power)
输入管线　intake pipeline
输入辊道　【压】approach [run-in, entry, inlet] table, approach [feeding] roller table ◇ 机前~ingot receiving table
输入缓冲器　【计】input buffer
输入机[单元]　【计】input unit, reader ◇ 五单位~five track reader
输入寄存器　【计】input register
输入加载　【电】input loading
输入加载系数　input loading factor
输入键　【计】load key
输入块　【计】input block
输入量　input (quantity), inlet
输入门　in(-)gate, input gate
输入门电路　in-gate circuit
输入能量　intake
输入起重机[吊车]　lay-on crane
输入区　【计】input area [field]
输入热焓　input enthalpy
输入热量　incoming heat

输入设备　input device [equipment, unit]
输入/输出　input/output (I/O)
输入/输出操作　input/output operation
输入/输出处理机　【计】input/output processor (IOP)
输入/输出存储区　【计】input/output storage [area]
输入/输出打字机　【计】input/output typewriter
输入/输出(端)口　input/output port
输入/输出缓冲器　input/output buffer
输入/输出缓冲通道　【计】buffered input/output channel
输入/输出缓冲装置　【计】buffered input/output section
输入/输出奇偶中断　input/output parity interrupt
输入/输出寄存器　input/output register
输入/输出接口　input/output interface
输入/输出控制程序　【计】input/output control program (IOCP)
输入/输出控制器　input/output controller
输入/输出控制系统　input/output control system (IOCS)
输入/输出控制装置　input/output control unit
输入/输出媒体　input/output medium
输入/输出区　【计】input/output area
输入/输出设备　input/output device [equipment]
输入/输出设备处理器　input/output device handler
输入/输出系统　【计】input/output system
输入/输出信道[通道]　input/output channel
输入/输出语句　input/output statement
输入/输出指令　input/output instruction
输入/输出中断指示器　input/output interrupt indicator
输入/输出转接　input/output switching
输入/输出总线　input/output bus

shu 输叔舒

输入速度　speed of entering
输入数据　【计】input data
输入损失　input [entrance] loss
输入台　input desk
输入调节器　feed governor
输入温度　input temperature
输入文件　【计】input file
输入信息　【计】input information
输入延伸辊道　approach extension table
输入移送机（冷床的）　drag-on [pull-on] transfer
输入元件　input element, receiver
输入指令　【计】input instruction [order]
输入指令码　【计】input instruction code
输入装置　input device [equipment, unit]
输入状态　【计】input state
输入阻抗　【电】input impedance
输入作业流　【计】input (job) stream
输入作业排队　input work [job] queue
输水道　raceway, aqueduct
输水管道末端的压力水池　terminal reservoir
输送　delivering, convey(ing), transport(ation), transfer(ence)
输送泵　delivery [transfer] pump
输送带　conveyer [conveying] belt ◇ 水冷式～ water-cooled conveyer
输送带式炉　conveyer-type continuous furnace, belt conveyor furnace, travel(l)ing furnace
输送带移动方向　belt travel direction
输送斗[盘]　transfer container
输送法　mode of transportation
输送管　delivery pipe, pipeline
输送管道　transfer piping, conveying pipe, pipe conveyer
输送轨道　delivery track
输送辊　transportation roll
输送辊道　transfer table
输送机　conveyer (table), conveyor ◇ 板式～ apron conveyer, 槽式～*, 带式～*, 斗式～ elevator bucket, 翻板～ slate-type conveyer, 风动[风力]～*, 刮板～*, 辊道～ live-roller conveyer, 集料～ gathering conveyer, 架空式～ overhead conveyer, 宽带式～*, 缆[绳]索～ cable conveyer, 螺旋式～ feed auger, 万能～ all-round conveyer, 往复平移梁式～*, 箱式～ box conveyer, 液压～ hydraulic conveyer, 振动式～ vibratory conveyer, 重型～ heavy duty conveyer
输送机式干燥炉　conveyer drying oven
输送机式干燥器　conveyer-type drier
输送机拖运区段　drag conveyer section
输送机托辊　conveyer idler
输送机系统　conveyer system
输送机械　conveying machinery
输送机用塔式支柱　conveyer-support tower
输送机栈桥　conveyer bridge
输送量　delivery volume
输送能力　conveying capacity, deliverability
输送器　conveyer, conveyor, conveying device ◇ 链式～ chain conveyer, 压缩空气～ air slide conveyer
输送设备　transporter, handling facility, grass-hopper
输送速率　delivery rate
输送隧道　delivery tunnel
输送系统　conveying [conveyance, transport] system
输送线　transfer line, pipeline
输送效率　transport efficiency
输送装置　transporter
输氧(量)　oxygen input
输油泵　oil transfer pump, fuel delivery pump
输油管　oil pipeline
叔胺　tertiary amine ◇ 混合～ mixed tertiary amines
舒尔茨锌基轴承合金(91Zn, 6Cu, 3Al)　Schulz alloy
舒尔茨衍射仪反射组构测定法[X射线衍

射显微法] 【理】Schulz method
舒锐平炉　Schury open hearth furnace
疏电子的　electrophobic
疏干　unwater ◇ 钻井~【环】well dewatering
疏浚　dredging
疏浚机　dredge(r) ◇ 抓斗式~[船]clamshell dredge
疏浚用输送机　dredging conveyer
疏水胶体　hydrophobic colloid, hydrophobe
疏水井　drain well
疏水物　hydrophobe
疏水性　hydrophobicity
疏水性表面　hydrophobic surface
疏水性氢氧化铁膜　hydrophobic ferric hydroxide film
疏水性水泥　hydrophobic cement
疏松　looseness, weakness, 【钢】poriness（缺陷）
疏松部位（铸件的）　porous spot
疏松淀积层　friable deposit
疏松度　fraction void
疏松粉末　【粉】loose powder
疏松焊缝　porous weld
疏松灰　loose ashes
疏松炉结[瘤]　【冶】loose scaffold
疏松耦合　weak bond
疏松烧结　loose sintering
疏松铁矿　friable iron ore
疏松涂层　flock coating
疏松土　mellow soil
疏松物质　porous mass ◇ 非~non-porous mass
疏松型砂　fluffing moulding sand
疏松性　looseness
疏松锈层　loose rust
疏松压制　【粉】loose compaction
疏松氧化层　loosened oxide
疏松氧化皮　loose scale
疏液胶体　lyophobe, lyophobic colliod
书形空心砖（带凹凸边的）　book tile

熟白云石　magnefer, stabilized dolomite
熟化　curing, slaking（石灰的）
熟化池（石灰的）　slaking tank
熟化处理皮带机　【团】curing conveyer
熟化剂　curing agent
熟化时间　【团】curing time
熟化试验　slaking test
熟化性（质）　slaking property
熟黄铜　wrought brass
熟练程度　qualification
熟练工（人）[劳力]　skilled worker [help], master
熟练人员　well-trained crew
熟练性　practicability
熟料　agglomerated material, clinker（水泥的）,【耐】chamotte, precalcined clay, grog ◇ 黏土~burned fire-clay
熟料比　【铁】agglomeration rate [ratio], percentage of agglomerate
熟料捣打料　【耐】grog rammed mass
熟料过筛[分级]　【耐】grading of grog
熟料结圈　clinker ring
熟料耐火材料　grog refractory
熟料耐火泥　grog fireclay mortar
熟料耐火砖　grogged fire-bricks
熟料坯　briquette
熟料砂　【耐】compo, chamotte sand
熟料蒸馏罐（炼锌用）　grog retort
熟料砖　dobie, adobe, chamotte brick
熟球　fired pellet
熟石膏　plaster (of paris) ◇ 含5%~的石灰　selenitic lime
熟石灰　slaked [drowned, hydrated] lime, lime hydrate
熟石灰供给装置　lime hydrate feeding device
熟石灰加料斗　s-lime (slaked lime) hopper
熟石灰加料器　s-lime (slaked lime) feeder
熟石灰库　hydrated lime storage
熟石灰乳[液]　slaked lime milk water
熟石灰乳化器　s-lime repulper, slaked lime

repulper	
熟铁	wrought iron [metal], dug [knobbled, puddle] steel
熟铁吹炼炉	bloomery (furnace), catalan (furnace)
熟铁搅炼炉	knobbling furnace
熟铁渣（搅炼炉的）	hearth cinder
熟渣	matured slag
鼠笼式电动机	squirrel cage motor
鼠笼式粉碎机	rotating disintegrator
鼠笼式磨碎机	squirrel cage mill
鼠笼型感应电动机	induction motor with caged rotor
鼠笼型转子	squirrel-cage rotor
鼠尾(线)【铸】	rat tail ◇（铸型）严重～ (sand) buckle
术语	term(inology), nomenclature, technical terms
树痕（薄板的）	trees
树胶	(natural, vegetable) gum ◇ 阿拉伯～,含～的 gummy
树胶磁铁	ferrogum
树胶制的	gummy
树胶状的	gum-like, gummy
树枝石【采】	branched dendrite
树枝状粉粒【粉】	dendritic particle
树枝状粉末	dendritic [arborescent] powder
树枝状锆	zirconium dendrite
树枝状骨架【金】	dendritic network
树枝状结构	dendritic structure
树枝状结晶	dendritic crystal [crystallization, freezing], treeing, branched dendrite
树枝状晶粒	dendritic grain
树枝状晶体	(同"枝晶")
树枝状晶体簇	cluster of dendrites
树枝状晶体二次晶轴	subsidiary arms of dendrite
树枝状晶轴	arms of dendrite
树枝状巨晶（铸锭结构缺陷）	ingotism
树枝状凝固	dendritic freezing
树枝状偏析	dendritic segregation
树枝状铅	lead tree
树枝状钽	tantalum dendrite
树枝状突出物（电镀时阴极的）	treeing, trees
树枝状图案[图样]	dendritic pattern
树枝状网【金】	dendritic network
树枝状组织	(同"枝晶组织")
树脂	resin,【压】rosin ◇ 交联～ cross-linked resin, 洗提～ eluted resin, 铸塑～ cast plastic
树脂层	resin bed
树脂的	resinous
树脂覆膜砂【铸】	resin coated sand
树脂基复合物	resin matrix composite
树脂基碳纤维复合物	resin matrix carbon fibre composite
树脂浆	resin slurry
树脂胶合的	gummed
树脂交联度	cross-linkage of resin
树脂结合[黏结]剂	resin binder
树脂结合镁质白云石砖	resin-bonded magnesite-dolomite brick
树脂粒	resin particle [bead]
树脂黏结磁铁	resin-bonded magnet
树脂配合体活度	resin-ligand activity
树脂亲和力	resin affinity
树脂酸	resin acid
树脂酸钠	sodium resinate
树脂酸盐	resinate
树脂体	resinite
树脂涂层	resin coating
树脂网格	resin lattice
树脂相	resin phase
树脂载量[负载]	resin loading
树脂支承	resin support
树脂制品	resin
树脂质（煤岩）	resinite
树脂中毒（离子交换过程的）	resin poisoning
树脂中氰毒	thiocyanate poisoning of resin
树脂柱	resin column
树脂族	resinophore group

树脂羰基铁粉　polyiron
树桩　stub
束带　girding, lacing
束发散度　beam divergence
束缚　binding ◇ 弱～电子*
束缚电荷　bound charge
束缚电子　bound [fixed] electron
束缚激子态　bound exciton state
束缚空穴　bound hole
束缚能　bound [binding] energy
束缚原子　【半】bound atom
束射功率管　beam power tube
束射管　beam tube
束射四极管　beam tetrode
束砖　bonding brick
竖管　standpipe
竖管式热压炉　vertical-tube hot-pressing furnace
竖罐　vertical [upright] retort
竖罐炼锌　【色】zinc vertical retorting
竖罐炼锌厂　vertical retort zinc smelter
竖罐(炼锌蒸馏)炉　zinc vertical retort furnace
竖罐熔炼　vertical retort smelting
竖罐生产率　vertical retort specific capacity
竖罐式渗氮炉　vertical retort nitriding furnace
竖罐蒸馏　【色】vertical retorting, vertical retort distillation
竖罐(蒸馏)法　vertical retort method ◇ 连续式～*
竖罐蒸馏炼锌法　zinc vertical-retort process, vertical (retort) process
竖罐蒸馏炉　vertical retort [distillation] furnace
竖焊　vertical (position) welding ◇ 两侧～*
竖焊缝　vertical-down weld
竖接　vertical joint
竖井排水　drainage by vertical [shaft] well

竖井墙（热风炉燃烧室的）　well wall
竖井提升用钢丝绳　wire rope for shaft winding
竖炉　shaft furnace [kiln], shaft-type furnace [stove], vertical [high] furnace, vertical(-shaft) kiln ◇ 矮[低身]～*, 焙烧～roasting shaft furnace, 间接加热[外热式]～indirect heated shaft, 煤氧～*, 熔炼～*, 熔融还原～*, 瑞典式～*, 水冷～*, 圆形～*, 中等炉身～*
竖炉焙烧　shaft roasting
竖炉焙烧白云石　shaft-kiln dolomite
竖炉焙烧系统（球团矿的）　shaft-furnace roasting system
竖炉顶部装料口　top opening
竖炉法　【团】shaft-furnace process ◇ 米德兰德－罗斯～*
竖炉还原　shaft reduction
竖炉炉渣　shaft-furnace slag
竖炉氯化　shaft chlorination
竖炉球团　【团】shaft furnace pellet
竖炉球团法　shaft pelletizing
竖炉外壳　【冶】stack shell
竖炉(直接制取)海绵铁法　shaft furnace making sponge iron ◇ 诺尔斯克－斯塔尔～Norsk-staal process, 普罗费～Purofer process
竖毛(现象)（过剩磁化引起的）　furring
竖砌层　【建】upright course
竖砌砖　brick laid on edge, row-lock
竖砌砖层　course on end
竖式吹炉　【色】upright converter
竖式电炉　electric shaft furnace
竖式煅烧炉　vertical calciner
竖式干燥窑　vertical drier
竖式还原炉　vertical reduction furnace
竖式混合器　shaft mixer
竖式冷却器[机]　shaft(-type) cooler
竖式离心脱水器　【铁】Carpenter centrifuge
竖式连续蒸馏罐　continuous vertical retort

竖式炉熔炼 【冶】blast smelting
竖式氯化炉 shaft-type chlorinator
竖式球团冷却机 shaft-type pellet cooler
竖式三相电极炉 vertical three-phase electrode furnace
竖式烧结矿冷却机 shaft-type sinter cooler
竖式石墨管热压炉 vertical graphite-tube hot-pressing furnace
竖式室 vertical chamber
竖式洗涤器 vertical scrubber
竖式下移烧结炉 vertical lowering furnace
竖(式)窑 shaft [up-draft, vertical (-shaft)] kiln
竖式预热器 shaft preheater
竖式圆柱填料塔 vertical cylindrical packed tower
竖式蒸馏釜 vertical [upright] still
竖式蒸馏罐 upright retort
竖式转炉 vertical converter ◇ "大瀑布" ~*
竖筒磨矿机 【团】vertical mill
竖向发散(度)引起的反射增宽 broadening of reflection by vertical divergence
竖向箍筋 vertical stirrup
竖向荷载 vertical load
竖向可调节的 vertically adjustable
竖向偏析 vertical segregation
竖向调整 vertical adjustment
竖向往复运动 vertically reciprocation
竖向位移 vertical displacement
竖向稳定 vertical stability
竖斜面 talus
竖直 uprighting, end-up
竖直扫 vertical scanning [sweep]
竖轴 vertical axis
竖砖层 brick soldier course
竖砖拱 brick on end soldier arch
竖着 endways, endwise
数 number (No., Num., num.) ◇ 雷诺~ Reynold number, 努塞尔~ Nusselt number

数不清的 myriad
数传机 data set
数据 data (单数 datum), record, information ◇ 无用~garbage, 无用~总和 gibberish total, 已得~findings
数据安全[保密] 【计】data security
数据保护 【计】data protection
数据报文交换机 data message switch
数据变换器 data converter [reducer]
数据表 data sheet [table]
数据部分 【计】data division
数据采集 【计】data acquisition
数据参考书 data book
数据操作 【计】data manipulation
数据操作语言 data manipulation language (DML)
数据常数 data constant
数据储存单元 【计】data location
数据处理 【计】data processing [handling], processing of data ◇ 成批~batch data processing
数据处理机 data processing machine, data processor, datatron
数据处理设备 data processing equipment [apparatus]
数据传感器 data pick-up ◇ 角度~angle probe
数据传输[送] data transmission
数据传输系统 data communication system (DCS)
数据传送率 【计】data transfer rate
数据传送装置 data transmitting device
数据存储(器) data storage
数据存取 【计】data access
数据代码 【计】data code
数据单位 data unit
数据单元 【计】data cell [unit, location]
数据点(图表上的) 【金】data point
数据分层 【计】data hierarchy
数据复制 copy [replica] of data
数据管理 【计】data management
数据管理程序 data management program

数 shu

数据缓冲器 【计】data buffer
数据换算器 【计】data reducer
数据基 data base
数据集 【计】data set
数据记录打字机 data logging typewriter
数据记录器 data recorder [logger]
数据记事 【计】data logging
数据检索 data retrieval
数据简化系统 data reduction system
数据交换[转接] data switching
数据交换系统 data exchange system
数据精简[简化] data compaction [reduction]
数据控制块 data control block (DCB)
数据控制器 recording controller
数据库 data base [bank] ◇ 分布式～技术*
数据库管理系统 database management system (DBMS)
数据库数据模型 database data model
数据库系统 data base system
数据块 data block, block data
数据扩充块 data extent block (DEB)
数据累加器 data accumulator
数据类型 data type
数据链 data chaining
数据链路 data link
数据流程图 data flow diagram
数据码转换 datacode conversion
数据媒体[介] (同"数据载体")
数据描述 data description
数据区 data areq
数据识别 data recognition
数据设计 data design
数据收集 data collection [gathering]
数据收集过程 data gathering process
数据收集系统 data collection [gathering] system
数据收集站 data collection station
数据输出装置 data output device
数据通道 data channel [path]
数据通信 data communication
数据通信监督程序 data communication monitor
数据通信线(链)路 data link, tie line, data communicatian line
数据通信[讯]系统 data communication system (DCS)
数据通信站 data communication station
数据通信终端 data communication terminal
数据文件 data file
数据显示模件 data display module
数据项 data item
数据信息转接系统 data message switching system
数据延迟记录器 data delay recorder
数据有效性 data validity
数据元 data element
数据源 data source
数据阅读器 data reader
数据载体 data carrier [medium]
数据栈 data stack
数据整理 data preparation [reduction], interpretation
数据帧 data frame
数据转换 data conversion
数据转换实用程序 data conversion utility
数据转录 data transcription
数据字 data word
数据总线 data bus
数据组 data set [array]
数据组程序 data bank program
数控车床 【机】numerically controlled lathe
数控机床 numerical controlled machine tool
数控线切割 digital control wire-electrode cutting
数理逻辑 【数】mathematical logic
数理统计(学) mathematical statistics
数理语言学 mathematical linguistics
数量 quantity (qty), quantum, amount, magnitude, number

数量级	order of magnitude
数模	(同"数字模拟")
数–模变换器	(同"数字–模拟转换器")
数位	digit
数学逼近	mathematical approximation
数学表	mathematical table
数学处理	mathematical treatment
数学分析	mathematical analysis
数学函数库	mathematical function library
数学近似式	mathematical approximation
数学校验	mathematical check
数学理论	mathematical theory
数学模量	mathematical modul [modulus]
数学模型	mathematical model
数学模型计算	mathematical-model calculation
数学期望(值)	mathematical expectation
数学算符	mathematical operator
数学语言学	mathematical linguistics
数域说明符	numeric field descriptor
数值	(numerical) value, figure, magnitude
数值比较	numeric comparision
数值部分	mantissa, numerical part
数值传热学	numerical heat transfer
数值范围	number range
数值分析	numerical analysis
数值积分	numerical integration
数值(计算)法	numerical method
数值孔[口]径	numerical aperture (NA, n.a.)
数值控制	【计】numerical control
数值[字]模型	numerical model
数值因子	numerical factor
数值字	【计】numerical word
数字	figure, digit ◇ 换~档【电】figures shift, 用~表示 figure
数字 pH 计	digital pH-meter
数字比较	numeric comparision
数字编码	【计】numeric coding
数字编码声音	【计】digit-coded voice
数字变换器	digitalizer
数字表示法	digital representation
数字测尘仪	【环】digital dust measuring apparatus
数字常数	numeric constant
数字乘法器	digital multiplier
数字程序自动控制	programmed digital automatic control, prodac control
数字除法器	digital divider
数字代码	【计】digital [numeric] code
数字电路	digit(al) circuit
数字电压表[伏特计]	digital voltmeter
数字发生器	number generator ◇ 人工~ *
数字仿真	numerical simulation
数字分类	digital sorting
数字符号显示发生器	【电】digit-symbol display generator
数字[码]管	【计】Nixie light
数字过程控制	digital process control
数字化	digitization, numeralization
数字化装置	digitalizer
数字计数器	digit counter
数字计算电路	digital computing circuit
数字计算机	digital computer [machine]
数字计算机程序编制	digital computer programming (DCP)
数字加法器	digital adder
数字减法器	digital subtracter
数字–交流(电压)变换器	digital to a.c. converter
数字开关	digital switch (DSW)
数字控制	【计】numerical control (NC), digital control
数字控制系统	digital [numerical] control system
数字控制自动车床	【机】numerically controlled lathe
数字控制自动轧辊车床	N/C (numerical control) roll lathe
数字滤波	digital filtering
数字脉冲电路	digital pulse circuit
数字门电路	digital gate circuit

数字模拟　numerical simulation
数字－模拟转换器　【计】digital(-to)-analog (D/A) converter [transducer]
数字盘　dial
数字时间序列分析　【计】digital time series analysis
数字式仪表　digital instrument
数字速度传感器　digital velocity transducer
数字速度控制室　digital speed control cubicle
数字通信[讯]系统　digital communication system (DCS)
数字图像　【电】digital image
数字万用表　digital multimeter
数字网络(体系)结构　【计】digital network architecture (DNA)
数字位置指示器　digital position indication
数字系数　numerical coefficient
数字系统量化误差　digital system quantizing error
数字显示　【计】digital display [indication]
数字(显示)钟　digital clock
数字信号　digital signal
数字信号传送总线　digit transfer bus [trunk]
数字信号周期　digit period [time]
数字信息　digital information
数字指示管　digitron
数字指示器　digital indicator
数字转换器　quantizer
数字资料　digital [numerical] data
数字自动化　digital automation [automatization]
数字自动装置　digital automation [automatization]
数字自记器　digital recorder
数字自应用技术　digital adaptive technique
数字[值]字符　numeric character
数字组件检测器　digital module checker

数组段　array segment
数组说明　array declaration
数组元素　array element
数组元素后继函数　array element successor function
刷　brush ◇ 排[涂料]~【铸】blacking brush, 润湿模腔边缘用~water brush
刷尘器　dust scrubber
刷镀(镀锌)　brush plating ◇ 达利克~*
刷镀电极(局部电镀用)　tampon
刷镀用阳极刷　doctor
刷光机　brushing machine
刷辊　brush roll
刷浆　wash
刷净[掉]　scrape out
刷漆　painting, varnishing (刷清漆), japanning (对金属表面)
刷墙粉　【建】calsomine, kalsomine
刷砂笔　【铸】banister brush
刷式冷却液调合器　brush type coolant dispenser
刷式抛光轮　brush wheel
刷水(起模前的)　swabbing
刷涂层　brushing coating
刷涂料(在铸型表面上)　【铸】swabbing
刷握杆　【电】brush holder (arm)
刷洗槽　scrubbing tank
刷洗干燥机　scrubbing and drying unit
刷洗工段　scrubber zone
刷洗机　brush scrubber (machine), scrubbing unit
刷形触头　brush contact
刷用钢丝　brush (handle) wire
衰变　decay, disintegration ◇ α~*, 逆β~*
衰变产物　decay [disintegration] product, product of breakdown
衰变常数[恒量]　decay constant
衰变降级试验　reduction-disintegration test
衰变链　decay [desintegration] chain
衰变期　decay period

衰变速率　decay rate, rate of disintegration ◇ 绝对~*, 特征~*
衰变系数　decay coefficient
衰变因数　decay factor
衰耗　attenuation
衰耗器　attenuator
衰减　attenuation, damping, decay, weakening, weaking, degeneration, fading,【半】build down ◇ 不~波 maintained waves, 无~*, 圆柱状~*
衰减波　decaying [decadent] wave
衰减测量计　attenuation gauge
衰减常数　attenuation constant
衰减电平　【电】rejection level
衰减电阻　damping resistance
衰减定律　decay law
衰减对称　attenuation symmetry
衰减法（探伤）　damping method
衰减恒量　attenuation constant
衰减畸变　attenuation distortion
衰减控制　damping control
衰减量　decrement
衰减[耗]率　attenuation ratio
衰减能力　damping capacity
衰减期　decay period
衰减器　attenuator
衰减曲线　decay(ing) curve
衰减全反射　attenuated total reflection (ATR)
衰减时间　【电】decay time, down slope time（电流的）
衰减试验　damping test
衰减系数　attenuation coefficient [factor], damping coefficient [ratio], decay factor
衰减振荡　（同"阻尼振荡"）
衰减振动　（同"阻尼振动"）
衰减值　damped quantity
衰竭蠕变　【金】exhaustion creep
衰落　fading, downgrade
甩出杆　【压】take-off [throw-off] arm
甩动[尾]（镀锡薄钢板的）　whip(ping)
甩(活)套机构(围盘的)　flipper
甩击（轧件尾端的）　whipping
甩套器　【压】kicker
甩尾（活套的）　【压】back end whip
甩现机　kick-off
甩油环　splash [oil] ring, slinger
甩直板（锯齿冷床的）　straightening plate
甩子　swage hammer, loose tool（锻造工具）◇ 锻工用~ smithing snap
闩入式结构　locked-in construction
栓固辙叉　bolted rigid frog
栓轴　stud shaft
霜白表面　frosted finish
霜白处理（表面的）　frost
霜（冻）线　frost line
双-2-乙基己基磷酸　D2EHPA (di-2-ethylhexyl phosphoric acid)
双-2-乙基己基亚磷[膦]酸　D2EHPINA (di-2-ethylhexyl phosphinic acid)
双-2-乙基己基癸二酸　（同"S-辛基油"）
双-2-乙基己基酞酸酯　（同"辛基油"）
双1-异丁基-3.5-二甲基己基胺　bis (1-isobutyl-3.5-dimethylhexyl) amine
双C形吊钩（带卷用）　double C-hook
双U形对接焊　double-U butt [groove] welding
双U形坡口　【焊】double-U groove
双U形坡口对接焊缝　double-U butt weld
双U形坡口焊缝　double-U groove weld
双V形安全[防护]阀　double-V-type goggle valve
双V字形坡口　（同"X形坡口"）
双V形坡口对接焊缝　double-V butt weld
双凹透镜　concavo-concave [biconcave] lens
双半波检波　double-wave detection
双半径椭圆　double radius oval
双棒浇注装置　double-stopper arrange-

双杯状断裂 【压】double-cup fracture
双倍标准宽耐火砖 【耐】double standard
双倍长数 double-length number
双倍精度量 double-precision quantity
双倍精度数 double-precision number
双倍时间 doubling time
双倍试件－双倍轭铁法 【理】double-bar-and-yoke method
双倍收缩率 double contraction
双倍字长 【计】double length
双倍作用 doubling effect
双笔记录器 double-pen recorder
双壁漏斗 double-wall funnel
双臂杠杆 double-armed lever
双臂曲轴 double-throw crank shaft
双臂信号 double signal,【运】home and starting signal
双臂压力机 double-arm[double-sided] press
双边卷边对焊接头 double-flanged butt weld
双边卷边对接端焊焊缝 edge-flange weld
双变量[变数]平衡 bivariant equilibrium
双变数系 bivariant system
双标线目镜 (同"十字标线目镜")
双波长分光光度法 dual wavelength spectrophotometry
双参数目标函数 two-parameter objective function
双槽板 diglyph
双槽出钢平炉 bifurcated furnace
双槽出钢熔炼 split heat
双侧的 double-sided
双层 double ply (dp), bilayer, double-deck (桥面或承面)
双层扁股钢丝绳 double flattened strand wire rope
双层扁平产品 double-layer flat product
双层布料 double layer
双层底炉 double-hearth furnace
双层电动推料炉 double-deck electric push furnace
双(层)叠板 【压】doubles
双层镀铬[铬镀层] duplex chromium
双层放灰阀 double acting dust valve
双层分流式氧枪 double-deck separate-flow oxygen lance
双层晶体元件 bimorph cell
双层卷焊(钢)管 brazed double-wall steel tube, double wall brazed tube
双层缝焊机 double seam welder
双层结构 double structure
双层卷筒 double block
双层铠装电缆 double-armoured cable
双层镴焊钢管 bundyweld steel tubing
双层镴焊管法 bundyweld process
双层冷硬铸造轧辊 double-pour chill roll
双层炉 two-storied [double-deck] furnace, two-deck oven
双层炉壁 double furnace wall
双层麻口铸铁轧辊 double-pour grain roll
双层(密封放灰)阀 【团】double seal dust valve
双层砌砖 double-bricking
双层桥 double-deck(ed) bridge, double level bridge
双层清洗 diphase cleaning
双层人造丝包覆(的) double rayon covered (D.R.C.)
双层筛 double-deck screen
双层烧结法 double-layer sintering
双层烧结钟罩炉[双层钟罩] double-walled bell jar
双层水口 (同"巴格纳尔－贝瑟尔水口")
双层丝包(绝缘)的 double silk covered (D.S.C.)
双层涂层[涂覆] dual [duplex] coating
双层围盘 【压】double-deck repeater
双层细晶粒轧辊 double-pour grain roll
双层药皮焊条 double coated electrode
双层轧辊 sleeved roll
双层轧制 pair(ing)

双层罩式［内罩］炉　double-muffle [duo-muffle] furnace
双层纸包装（的）　double paper covered (D.P.C.)
双层铸铁轧辊　double-pour cast iron roll
双层铸造轧辊　double-pour roll
双层锥形放灰阀　double cone dump valve
双叉排料口　twin outlet discharge
双车道　double lane
双车道道路　double track
双衬板对接（锻焊的）　double-glut butt joint
双程泵　（同"双动泵"）
双程内反射元件　double-pass internal reflection element
双齿轮　double gear
双齿条式推钢机　double-rack type pusher
双齿条推床　double-rack manipulator ◇ 带翻钢钩的～ double-rack manipulator with fingers
双冲杆压模　double-punch die
双冲头冲床［压］ double puching machine
双重焙烧　double roasting
双重萃取　double extraction
双重氯化法　Floe process
双重电镀（物品）　duplex electroplate
双重非线性　double non-linearity
双重沸点物系　double boiling system
双重集管　double header ◇ 水力冲除氧化皮的～*
双重记录【计】dual recording
双重交叉滑移【理】double cross-slip
双重结构　double structure
双重晶粒度　duplex grain size
双重精炼方式（RH＋KIP）（KH-KIP）double refining manner
双重拉伸(脆断)试验　double tension test
双重冷却壁　double cooling stave
双重门　double door
双重配筋混凝土梁　double reinforced beam
双重绕组　duplex winding

双重熔点物系　double melting system
双重烧结　double sintering
双重设备　duplex equipment
双重施主　double donor
双重收缩【铸】double shrinkage
双重收缩模(型)【铸】double contraction [shrink] pattern, master pattern
双重退化［简并］　doubly degenarate
双重退火　double annealing, duplex anneal
双重弯晶照相机　double-curved crystal camera
双重系统　duplex system
双重线　doublet, duplet ◇ α～ α-doublet, $K\alpha_1$ 与 $K\alpha_2$ 密～*
双重线部分的分辨【理】resolution of double component
双重线成分（X射线的）　double component
双重线间隔　double interval
双重线圈灯丝　double coil filament
双重行星辊式轧机　double planetary mill, platzer-planetary mill ◇ 克虏伯～*
双重压力　dual-pressure
双重压制　double compression
双重折射　double refraction
双出铁场高炉　two-casthouse blast-furnace
双出铁口高炉　two taphole furnace
双出铁口装置　two iron-notch installation
双串平炉【钢】tandem furnace
双床电炉炼钢[铁]法　◇ 艾伯特德西～ Albert de Sy process
双床平炉【钢】dual [twin] hearth furnace
双锤式锻锤【压】double-ram hammer
双锤式高速锤【钢】two-ram machine
双磁场无芯感应炉　double magnetic field coreless induction furnace
双醋酸盐[酯]　diacetate
双带式铸连机　twin belt [chain] caster ◇ 哈彻莱特～*
双带式铸铁机　（同"双链式铸铁机"）
双档齿轮　two-speed gear

双刀的 【电】double-pole
双导向防偏辊 double steering roll
双道结构（空气加热器的） two-pass design
双底 double bottom (D.B.)
双地址 【计】double address, two-address
双地址指令 double instruction
双点电焊机 duplex spot welder
双点焊 duplex spot welding
双电层 electric double layer
双电层静电特性 electrostatic character of double layer
双电场电除尘器 dual field precipitator
双电动机传动 dual-motor drive
双电动机式卷扬机 two-motor winch
双电极 bielectrode
双电极电位测定 bielectrode potentiometric estimation
双电极焊接 twin-electrode welding
双电枢电动机 double-armature motor
双电枢电动机传动装置 double-armature drive
双电源供电（的） dual-feed
双电子束示波器 double-beam [dualchannel] oscilloscope
双锭跟踪轧制 semi-tandem rolling
双锭推钢机 double ingot pusher
双锭轧制 double ingot rolling, tandem rolling
双动 double-action
双动泵 double acting pump
双动冲床 （同"双冲头冲床"）
双动锤 double acting hammer
双动（锻压）成形（法） double-action forming
双动[程]活塞泵 double acting piston pump
双动剪切机 【压】down-and-up cut unit
双动桨叶式搅拌机 double-motion raddle mixer
双动深冲 double-action drawing
双动（式）压力机 double-action press
双动压制 （同"双效压制"）
双动液压千斤顶[水力起重器] opposed hydraulic jack
双动蒸汽锤 double acting steam hammer
双斗称量车 double hopper scale car
双端弗兰克－里德（位错）源 【理】double-ended Frank-Read source
双端活套拉辊 end-dual loop puller
双端源 double-ended source
双断触[接]点 double-break contact
双断路开关 double-break switch
双对数坐标图 double logarithmic diagram, log-log plot
双耳受话器 biphone
双二辊式平整机 【压】unit-temper mill
双二辊式轧机 double duo mill ◇ 道拉斯～ Dowlais mill
双二极管 duodiode
双翻斗车 double skip
双翻斗卷扬机 double-skip hoist
双反射 bireflection, double bounce
双沸点物系 double boiling system
双分道岔 double turnout
双分子反应 bimolecular reaction
双峰谐振曲线 double-humped resonance curve
双缝重写头 【计】dual-gap rewrite head
双覆层 dual [duplex] coating
双坩埚系统 double crucible system
双杆导向装置 two-bar guide
双杆推钢机 double-arm pusher
双缸 double barrel
双缸泵 duplex [twin] pump
双高保护渣（高碱性和高玻璃化）【连铸】dual high mould powder (mould powder with high basicity and high glass property)
双格式磨机 two compartment mill
双工位造型机 twin moulding machine
双功能的 bifunctional
双供料系统 【团】duplicate feed system
双钩起重机[吊车] twin hook crane

双钩环	double shackle
双股电缆	paired cable
双股扭绞	double-strand twisting
双股扭绞钢丝束	twin-twisted wire
双股绕组	bifilar winding
双股性	bifilarity
双拐曲(柄)轴	two-throw crankshaft
双管式热交换器	double-pipe heat-exchanger
双管循环真空脱气法	(同"循环真空脱气法")
双罐(乙炔)发生器	duplex generator
双罐渣车	twin-pot cinder car
双光束光度系统	double-beam photometric system
双硅酸钙{CaO·SiO$_2$}	calcium bisilicate
双轨	double track
双辊薄带连铸工艺	strip casting technology of twin-roll machine
双辊薄带连铸机	twin-roll CC for thin strip
双辊导轨	double-roller guide
双辊缝焊	double rolls seam welding
双辊环	cross collar
双辊连铸	twin-drum continuous casting, twin roll casting, twin-roll CC
双辊连铸机	twin-roll caster
双辊链	double-roller chain
双辊破碎机	double crusher
双辊(式)薄带连铸	thin strip continuous casting with double roller
双辊压力机	double roll press
双辊研磨机	end runner mill
双滚筒	twin drum
双滚筒卷取装置	double take-up
双滚轴链	double-roller chain
双锅式镀锡机组	double-sweep tenning unit
双焊缝连接	double joint
双行铆(接)	double riveting
双行铆钉连接	double-riveted joint
双合矿石	binary ore
双合透镜	doublet
双弧电焊机	twin-arc welding set
双弧法(成品圆孔)	【压】two plug method
双弧焊(接)	dual-arc welding
双滑移	double [duplex] slip, double glide
双环己基亚硝酸胺	dichan
双换能器超声波检测	double-transducer ultrasonic test
双换向器	double commutator
双回收回路	【色】double recovery circuit
双活塞爆炸压力机	double-piston explosive press
双活套坑装置	double-looping pit
双机架平整和二次冷轧机	two-stand [twin-stand] temper and D.C.R. (double cold rolling) mill
双机架平整机组	twin stand temper mill
双机架压力机	double-sided press
双机能的	bifunctional
双机系统	【计】dual system
双机座	double stand
双机座串列式轧机	two-stand tandem mill
双机座轧机	double stand rolling mill, two-stand mill
双迹示波器	double trace scope
双极	double-pole (dp), dipole
双极磁场	bipolar field
双极磁场开关	double-pole field switch
双极电极	bipolar electrode
双极电解槽	bipolar cell
双极集成电路	bipolar integrated circuit
双极晶体管	【电】bipolar transistor
双极开关	double-pole switch
双极性	bipolarity
双极性的	ambipolar, bipolar
双集气管	double collecting main
双级排烟风机	double-stage fume exhaust fan
双计算机	duplex computer
双夹送辊	double pinch roll

双 shuang

双夹送辊组　dual pinch roll unit
双尖辙叉　【运】double pointed frog
双碱度烧结矿　double [different] basicity sinter
双剪切机剪切作业线　double shear line
双键　double bond
双交叉限幅燃烧控制　dual-crossing limiting-amplitude combustion control, double cross limiting range combustion control
双浇（钢锭缺陷）　double teeming
双铰拱　two-hinged arch
双脚高架起重机　full gantry crane
双脚泥芯撑　【铸】double-head chaplet
双角风口　（同"螺旋风口"）
双角铁砧　two-beak iron
双接触点（电流双接触点，A点）　A-spot
双接触法制硫酸车间　double contact acid plant
双节点固溶曲线　【金】binodal line
双节点曲线（相图的）　binodal curve
双金属　bimetal, dual [duplex, composite] metal ◇ 电触头~contact bi-metal, 高温用~*, 恒温装置用~thermostatic bimetal
双金属板　bimetallic strip, bimetal sheet ◇ 两层或三层~overlay clad plate
双金属棒材　composite(-metal) rod
双金属包覆板　inlay clad plate
双金属材料　bimetallic material
双金属带　bimetallic strip
双金属带锯　bimetal bandsaw
双金属导线　bimetallic conductor
双金属电极　bimetallic electrode
双金属电流滴定的　【化】biamperemetric
双金属电流滴定法　dead-stop method
双金属锻钢工作辊　【压】forged bimetallic steel work roll
双金属断路装置　thermal trip
双金属腐蚀　bimetallic corrosion
双金属复合钢板　plymetal
双金属还原法（钠镁还原制锆铪法）　bimetallic reduction (technique)
双金属极间接作用电弧焊接　double electrode-arc welding
双金属及多层板材轧制　sandwich rolling
双金属及多层板材轧制法　sandwich rolling process
双金属挤压　coextrusion
双金属界面　bimetallic interface
双金属侵蚀　couple corrosion
双金属离合器盘　bimetallic clutch disc
双金属坯块　bimetal compact
双金属片　thermometal, bimetallic strip
双金属片继电器　bimetallic strip relay
双金属片压力[真空]计　bimetallic strip gauge
双金属释放器　bimetallic releaser
双金属温度计　bimetal thermometer
双金属温度调节[控制]器　bimetallic temperature regulator, bimetal thermoregulator, bimetallic thermostat
双金属线[丝]　bimetal [composite] wire, bimetallic conductor
双金属元素　bimetallic element
双金属制动片[闸盘]　bimetallic brake disc
双金属制品　bimetallic product [article]
双金属轴承　bimetallic bearing
双金属铸件　bimetal [composite] casting
双金属铸造　compound casting ◇ 格鲁兹~法 Grusz process
双进口风机　double inlet fan
双晶　bicrystal, (crystal) twin, twin(ned) [compound] crystal, 【金】macle ◇ 半体~hemitrope, 变形~deformation twin, 轮式~cyclical twin, 纽曼变形~*, 退火~annealing twin
双晶X射线分光[光谱]计　double crystal X-ray spectrometer
双晶变形　twin deformation
双晶带　twin(ning) band
双晶分光[光谱]计　double crystal spectrometer
双晶固溶体　solid solution with twinning

双晶滑移面	twin gliding plane
双晶面	twin(ning) plane
双晶摄谱仪	double crystal spectrograph
双晶石{HNaBeSi$_3$O$_8$}	eudidymite
双晶矢量	【金】twinning vector
双晶体(红锌及黄铜的)	pericon
双晶体X射线测角仪	double crystal X-ray goniometer
双晶体界面	bicrystal interface
双晶物质	dimorphous substance
双晶锡石	visor tin
双晶型金属	【金】dimorphous metal
双晶型元素	dimorphous element
双晶轴	twinning axis
双精度量	double-precision quantity
双精度数	double-precision number
双井式(焙烧)窑	double-stack kiln
双镜式辐射高温计	two-mirror-type radiation pyrometer
双聚光镜	double condenser lens
双聚焦	double focusing
双聚焦摄谱仪	double-focusing spectrograph
双卷层薄板试验机	double loop-sheet testing machine
双卷开卷机支座	double-headed coil stand
双卷位开卷机	double coil holder arrangement
双壳电弧炉	SKF double furnace
双壳炉	【钢】twin shell furnace
双空位	double [coupled] vacancy, bivacancy, divacancy
双空位结合能	binding energy of divacancies
双空位迁移	【理】divacancies migration
双孔阀	double goggle valve
双孔和无孔检测	【计】double-punch and blankcolumn detection
双孔型C形吊钩	double eye type C-hook
双控制极	double gate
双口矿槽	twin outlet bin
双口排料	twin outlet discharge
双馈变频调速技术	double-feeding frequency conversion governor technology
双扩散	double [doppel] diffusion
双拉门	◇同开~biparting door
双缆索道	bicable ropeway
双棱锥(体)	dipyramid
双离子束法	dual ion beam system
双粒度分别装料	two-size separate charging
双联(的)	duplex
双联泵	double [twin] pump
双联法生产的钢	duplex steel
双联火道	hairpin flue, 【焦】twinflue
双联火道复热焦炉	twinflue compound coke oven
双联(炼钢)法	duplex steelmaking, duplex(ing)(process) ◇塔尔伯特~Talbot duplex process
双联炉	duplex furnace
双联排气总管	double off-take main
双联熔炼	double melting
双联式加热炉	duplicate reheating furnace
双连的	doubly-connected
双连控制台	【电】duplex console
双链式拉拔机	dual-chain [double-chain] draw bench
双链式铸铁机	double-strand pig machine
双梁起重机	two-girder crane
双梁切割机	double portal cutting machine
双量子跃迁	double-quantum transition
双料车	【铁】double skip
双料斗卷扬机	double-track skip hoist
双料钟	【铁】double(-charging) bell
双料钟炉顶	double bell top
双料钟系统	two-bell system
双列比利时式轧机	double Belgian mill
双列滚珠轴承	double-row ball bearing ◇自动对位~*
双列推爪式炉用推钢机	double-dog type furnace pusher
双列直插式封装	【电】dual-in-line package (DIP)

双 shuang

双流喷嘴　dual flow nozzle
双流式冷凝器　two-pass condenser
双流体雾化　【粉】two-fluid [twin-fluid] atomization
双流氧枪　double flow oxygen lance
双炉壳直流电弧炉　twin-hearth DC electric arc furnace
双路开关　two-way switch
双路绕组　two-circuit winding
双路通信　two-way communication
双路拖运机　double-strand drag conveyer
双路旋塞　two-way stopcock
双路运输机　double-strand conveyer
双履带活块循环式薄板坯连铸机　twin block chain caster (TBCC)
双滤器　double filter
双轮滑车　double block
双轮胎　dual tyre
双轮小车　two-wheel trolley
双螺旋泵　twin-screw pump
双螺旋(桨)的　twin-screw
双螺旋灯丝　double helical heater, coiled coil
双螺旋分级机　double-spiral classifier
双螺旋混合机　double-worm [twin-shaft] mixer
双螺旋给[加]料机　double-screw feeder
双脉冲记录　【计】double-pulse recording
双镁合金板　Magclad
双门脉冲　double gate
双锰矿　kurnakite
双密封油管　tubing double seal (TDS)
双面 J 形[K 形]坡口对接焊缝　double-J butt weld
双面 J 形坡口　【焊】double-J groove
双面 J 形坡口焊　double-J groove welding, open-double-J butt weld
双面 J 形坡口焊缝　double-J tee butt weld
双面 J 形坡口接头　double-J joint
双面 U 形坡口焊　open-double-U groove welding
双面包覆(金属)　duoclad

双面包锡双金属轧制耐蚀铝板　◇津纳尔～Zinnal
双面差厚电镀锡薄钢板　differential(ly) coated (electrolytic) tinplate
双面差厚镀覆[涂镀]　differential plating [coating]
双面等厚镀层的电镀锡薄钢板　straight electrolytic plate
双面点焊　direct (spot) welding
双面镀锡薄钢板　dual-coat plate
双面锻锤　double-faced hammer
双面钢筋[双配筋]　double reinforcement
双面焊(接)　both sides welding, welding by both sides
双面焊缝连接　double joint
双面加热炉　top and bottom fired furnace
双面间断填角焊缝　double intermittent weld fillet
双面进料(的)　dual-feed
双面冷床　double sided bed, double cooling bed [bank]
双面立焊　two-operator vertical welding
双面连续角焊缝　double continuous fillet weld
双面模板　【建】double-faced [double-sided] pattern plate,【铸】match plate [board]
双面模板模　【铸】match-plate pattern
双面模板造型　match-plate moulding
双面坡　【建】double pitch
双面坡的　double pitched (D.P.)
双面坡口对接焊　open-double-bevel butt welding
双面坡口[铲边]焊缝　double-groove weld ◇ K 形～double-bevel weld
双面坡口加工　【焊】double-groove preparation
双面双头同时焊接焊缝　double-head weld
双面涂(感光)乳剂的胶片　double-emulsion film, double coated film, sandwich film

双面推床　double manipulator
双面弯曲侧弯成型（W成型）　dual-sided incline-curling forming process, W forming process
双面斜切　double bevel
双面型板　【铸】double sided pattern plate, match [built-up] plate
双模材机组（线材轧制）　twin module block (TMB)
双模冲压模　double-punch die
双目观察　【金】binocular observation
双目镜　binocular
双能带模型　two band model
双偶极间相互作用　【理】dipole-dipole interaction
双排(钉)铆接的　double riveted (d.r.)
双排风口　two-row tuyere
双排加热炉　double-reheating furnace
双排煤气点火器　two-row gas ignitor
双排三辊式轧机（钢管冷轧机）　double-set three roller mill
双排推钢机　double-arm pusher
双排液压式推钢机　double-row hydraulic-type pusher
双盘式自滑型牵引轮　double self-fleeting type capstan
双片刮板　double-bladed scraper
双平衡状态图　double equilibrium state diagram
双坡屋顶　double-pitch roof
双曝光射线照相术　double-exposure radiography
双歧状态　bifurcation
双气轮胎　dual pneumatic tyre
双铅钢线韧化处理　double lead patenting
双钳口筒式卷取机（炉用）　dual-slot mandrel type coiler
双枪示波器　two-gun oscilloscope
双巯丙氨酸　cystine
双区电收尘器　two stage precipitator
双曲柄　double crank
双曲柄压力机　double-crank press

双曲晶体　doubly bent [curved] crystal, crystal of double curvature
双曲面　【数】doubly curved surface, hyperboloid
双曲面暗场聚光镜　dark field bispheric condenser
双曲面齿轮　hyperboloidal [hypoid] gear
双曲面矫直辊　【压】hyperboloid straightening roll
双曲面柱　hyperbolic cylinder
双曲线　hyperbola, hyperbolic curve
双曲线辊矫直机　concave roll straightener
双曲线函数　hyperbolic function
双曲折连接　Z-strand
双曲轴压机　duplex crank press
双取向硅钢薄板　two-directional silicon steel, double oriented silicon steel ◇库贝克斯～Cubex, "四方"～Four-square
双绕无感线圈　bifilar coil
双绕组转子　double-wound rotor
双热电偶　double-thermocouples
双刃剪切机　double-cut shears
双刃切头剪　double-cut cropping shears
双熔　duplex melting
双熔点物系　double melting system
双熔锭　double-melted ingot
双溶剂萃取　double-solvent extraction
双软管式熔切器　two hose cutting burner
双塞棒钢包[铸钢桶,钢水罐]　two-stopper [twin-stopper, double-stoppered] ladle
双三角接线　double-delta connection
双三通旋塞　double three-way cock
双色比色法　bicolorimetric method
双色比色计　bicolorimeter
双色高温计　two-colour pyrometer
双纱包的　【电】double-cotton covered (D.C.C.)
双扇形阀　double quadrant valve
双射束示波器　double-beam oscilloscope
双砷硫铅矿　rathite, wiltshireite
双十进制的　double-decadic
双室(式)炉　double chamber furnace, du-

plicate [twin-chambered] furnace, two compartment furnace
双室式喷浆枪　double chamber gun
双室有芯感应炉　double-chamber channel induction furnace
双收线装置　twin spooler
双手用大锤　sledge [two-handed] hammer
双鼠笼转子　double-deck rotor, double squirrel cage rotor
双四极管　duo-tetrode
双速齿轮　two-speed gear
双速电动机　two-speed motor
双算符[算子]　【计】two-operator
双态条件（逻辑的）　bifurcation
双态元件　【计】binary element
双碳弧焊　twin carbon arc welding
双碳弧钎焊　twin carbon arc brazing
双碳极电弧　twin carbon arc
双碳素极(间接作用)电弧焊接　double carbon-arc welding
双探测器　twin probe, dual search unit
双探测装置　dual search unit
双探针技术　double-probe technique
双探针系统　double-probe system
双膛炉　double hearth furnace (DHF)
双填角焊缝　double-fillet weld
双通道控制器　【计】dual channel controller
双通的　bilateral
双通旋塞　two-way stopcock
双筒干燥炉　twin-drum dryer
双筒观察　【金】binocular observation
双筒混合机　twin cylinder mixer, twin-shell blender [mixer]
双筒卷扬机　double-drum hoist [winch]
双筒泥炮　double barrel mud gun
双筒显微镜　binocular [double] microscope
双投触点　double-throw contact
双投隔离开关　double-throw isolating switch
双投开关　double-throw [change-over] switch
双投影镜　double projector lens
双头扳手　double-head [double-end(ed)] wrench
双头触点　split contact
双头钢轨　bullhead [double-head] rail
双头割炬　double head burner [blowpipe] ◇坡口加工用～.
双头滚筒　twin drum
双头机车　double-ender
双头开卷机　【压】twin-head pay-off reel
双头开口扳手　open-end spanner of double type
双头拉丝卷筒　double-drawing capstan ◇无滑动～.
双头螺栓　(threaded) stud, 【机】brad
双头螺栓连接　studding
双头螺栓拧紧装置　stud driving equipment
双头通电磁化法　prod method
双头同时焊接焊缝　double-head weld
双头造型机　【铸】twin moulding machine
双凸透镜　biconvex [convexo-convex] lens
双腿式起重机　bipod
双拖动(装置)　dual drive
双驼峰砂　【铸】camelback (sand), one-screen
双瓦(型)制动器[双瓦(型)闸]　dual shoe-type brake, double-block brake
双弯道放大器　double leg elbow amplifier
双弯晶单色器　double (curved-crystal) monochromator
双弯曲线　ogee curve
双弯头[管]　double bend
双围盘轧制的　double repeated
双位　【计】dibit
双位夹具　two-station fixture
双位卷取机　duplicate recoiler
双位调节器　on-off controller
双位(置)控制　two-step [on-off] control
双纹锉　double-cut [crosscut] file

双稳射流阀 bistable fluid valve
双稳射流装置 bistable fluid device
双稳态触发器线路 bistable trigger circuit
双稳态电路 two-state circuit
双稳态多谐振荡器 bistable multivibrator, flip flop multivibrator
双吸口通风机 double-suction ventilator
双烯烃 diolefin
双纤维结构 duplex fiber texture
双线 twin-strand, double track(道路)
双线阀 dualine valve
双线供料系统 twin feed system
双线加工作业线 two-strand line
双线缆[双胶线] twin wire
双线螺旋 bifilar helix
双线皮带机通廊 double conveyer gallery
双线圈继电器 double-coiled [double-wound] relay
双线绕变压器 transformer double-wound
双线绕组 bifilar winding
双线式拉拔[拉丝]机 double-rod drawbench
双线(式)轧机 double-strand [two-strand] mill
双线示波器 bifilar oscillograph
双线推出移送机 【压】double-run pull-off transfer
双线退火酸洗作业线 two-strand anneal and pickle line
双线无感线圈 bifilar winding
双线线路 double line
双线线图 double re-entrant winding
双线性 bifilarity, bilinearity
双线悬挂 bifilar suspension
双线移送机 double-strand drag conveyer
双线轧制 two-strand rolling
双相奥氏体－铁素体不锈钢 duplex austenitic-ferritic stainless steel
双相不锈钢 duplex [two-phase] stainless steel
双相钢 two-phase [dual-phase] steel ◇ 高强度～钢丝*,热轧低碳～盘条*

双相合金(两相合金) deplex alloy
双相黄铜 (见"α-β(型)黄铜") ◇ 加铅～*
双相清洗 diphase cleaning
双相流 two-phase flow
双相整流 biphase rectification
双相整流器 biphase rectifies
双相状态(合金) two-phase(d) condition
双相组织 【金】duplex structure
双镶嵌式换能器 twin mosaic transducer
双像 double image
双向操作 bidirectional operation
双向尝试[试错]法 double-trial-and-error method
双向成型 【粉】two-direction compacting
双向打击锤锤头 【压】opposing ram
双向电路 bilateral circuit
双向硅开关(元件) silicon symmetrical switch (SSS)
双向计数器 bidirectional [reversible] counter, forward backward counter
双向继电器 bidirectional [duodirectional] relay
双向刻度 centre-zero scale
双向刻度仪表 zero centre meter
双向扩散 【半】bilateral diffusion
双(向)亮合器 double clutch
双向泥芯撑 【铸】double-head chaplet
双向配筋的钢筋混凝土 twoway reinforced concrete
双向送料爪 stationary dogs
双向通话设备 two-way telephone equipment
双向弯曲面 【数】doubly curved surface
双向线路 two-way circuit
双向信道 【电】duplex channel, two-way channel
双向压力压机 dual-pressure press
双向压力预成形机 dual-pressure preformer
双向压缩捣实法 【铸】double-compression method of ramming

双向压制 double-action [two-direction] pressing, double-action [two-direction] compacting, compaction by double action
双向影线 cross hatching
双向折弯(板材的) 【压】dog leg
双向止推轴承 double-thrust bearing
双向砖格子蓄热室 【冶】duplicate checkerwork regenerator unit
双向转换开关 two-way (reversing) switch
双向作用的 bilateral
双效 double-action
双效压制[压塑] double-action compacting [pressing, compression], compaction by double action
双效蒸发器 double effect evaporator
双斜晶体 double-oblique crystal
双斜面[K形]搭接坡口 【焊】double-bevel butt groove
双屑压球 【钢】biscrap pressed ball
双芯电缆 two-core cable, twin cable
双芯焊条 twinned electrode
双芯屏蔽电缆 two-conductor shielded cable
双星形接线 double star connection, double-way connection
双形孔型 dual-shape pass
双悬臂门式起重机 double cantilever gantry crane
双悬臂起重机 double-cantilever crane
双悬臂桥 double-ended cantilever bridge
双悬臂切割机 double cantilever cutting machine
双选通脉冲 double gate
双循环乙醚萃取法 dual-cycle ether extraction process
双压电晶片 bimorph
双压电元件 bimorph cell
双压痕法 double impression method
双压开关 dual pressure switch
双压力循环 dual-pressure cycle
双焰割炬[焊枪,燃烧器] two flame [headed] burner, fish tail burner
双焰式吹管 twin-flame torch
双氧钚(根) plutonyl
双氧镎(根) neptunyl
双氧水 hydrogen peroxide solution, oxydol ◇ 强～*
双氧铀(根) uranyl
双氧铀-磷酸三丁酯络合物 uranyl-TBP (tri-butyl phosphate) complex
双叶螺栓 butterfly bolt
双叶线 【数】double folium
双液淬火 double quench(ing)
双液电解槽 double fluid cell
双引出工艺设备 【压】equipment of dual-leading out process
双原子分子 diatomic molecule
双圆弧椭圆孔型 double arc ellipse pass
双圆角砖 double bull-nose brick
双圆筒造球 two-drum balling
双渣操作法 【冶】two-slag practice
双渣(法) 【钢】double slag
双渣留渣法 【钢】double slag and slag-remaining process
双闸板排矿[卸料] double door discharge
双闸门 double lock
双胀缩头[双胀缩卷筒式]开卷机 【压】double expanding head uncoiler, double spread head payoff reel
双折 duplicate
双折射 double refraction, birefraction
双折射晶体 birefringent [birefringence] crystal
双折射透明方解石 Iceland spar
双折射应力 birefringence stress
双支点轧辊 fully supported rolls
双钟斗装料装置[双钟双料斗装置] 【铁】double bell and hopper arrangement
双钟装料机构 【铁】double bell charging mechanism
双轴晶体 biaxial crystal
双轴(螺旋)搅拌[混合]机 double-shaft pug mill, double shaft mixer ◇ 槽型～*

双轴取向	biaxial orientation
双轴式搅拌机	twin-shaft mixer
双轴式轮碾[碾磨]机	fret mill, multi-mull mixer
双轴向负荷	biaxial loading
双轴应力	biaxial stress
双轴张力	biaxial tension
双肘杆压机	duplex toggle press
双柱联称法	double-cylinder continuous measurement method
双柱气割机	double portal cutting machine
双柱式	queen post, distyle
双贮斗装料机	double hopper
双转换器超声波检测	double-transducer ultrasonic test
双转双吸法制硫酸车间	DC/DA sulphuric acid plant
双锥离合器	double cone clutch
双锥(式)混合机	double cone-type blender [mixer]
双锥式混合制粒机	twin-cone mixer-granulator
双锥式卷取机	【压】double cone coiler
双锥型矿槽	double-conical type hopper
双足辊	【连铸】double feet roll
双组分炉料	two-component bruden
双嘴割炬	two-tip torch
双嘴手勺	two-lip hand ladle
双作用压模	double-action die
水	water ◇ 含～材料 hydrous material, 加～(量)*, 抗～的 hydrostable
水坝	dam, pen ◇ 闸门式～ curtain dam
水白铅矿	hydrocerussite
水白云石	hydro-dolomite
水斑铀矿{2UO$_2$·7H$_2$O}	lanthinite
水钡铀云母{Ba(UO$_2$)$_4$(PO$_4$)$_2$(OH)$_4$·8H$_2$O}	bergenite
水泵	water pump (wp) ◇ 高扬程～ high lift pump
水泵房[站]	pump room, (water) pump house, pump(ing) compartment, 【建】pumping plant
水泵机组	pump assembly
水变锆石	oerstedite
水变阻器	water rheostat
水标尺	water gauge
水表	water gauge (W.G.), water meter
水玻璃	(同"硅酸钠")
水玻璃二氧化碳硬化砂法	【铸】carbon dioxide process
水玻璃耐火水泥	water-glass refractory cement
水玻璃黏结保温帽	【钢】tiger top
水玻璃砂	water glass sand
水不溶性的	water-insoluble
水仓	water chamber
水槽	(water) trough, water tank [cell, bosh, bath]
水草酸钙石	whewellite
水测高温计	hydropyrometer
水产业	aquatic [marine] products industry
水产资源	【环】living aquatic resources
水沉降处理树脂	wet-settled resin
水成成团的	aquiferous
水成黏土	sedimentary clay
水成岩	aqueous rock
水澄清	water settling
水池淬渣法	【冶】bank expanding process
水赤铁矿{2Fe$_2$O$_3$·H$_2$O}	hydro-haematite, turgite
水冲除的氧化皮(进入地坑)	flushed scale
水冲斜槽	wet sluicing
水冲桩	jetted pile
水冲钻探	wash boring
水处理	water treatment [handling, dressing] ◇ 革兰氏阴性～ Gram-negative, 生产用～厂*
水处理房	water treatment house
水处理坑	water treatment pit
水处理装置	water handling [treatment] plant
水锤	water hammer

水锤式成形 water-hammer(-type) forming
水萃取的 water-extracted
水萃液 aqueous extract
水淬 water hardening [quench(ing)], quenching in water,【铁】(炉渣的) granulation, granulating ◇ 炉渣~(法)*, 喷水~*
水淬槽 water-quench tank,【铁】granulating tank
水淬池 【冶】cinder granulating tank
水淬钢 water-hardened steel
水淬工具钢 water-hardening tool steel
水淬(火)的 【金】quenched in water (Qw), water-quenched (W.Q.), quenched
水淬坑 【金】water quench pit
水淬裂纹 water crack
水淬流槽 【铁】granulating [granulation] launder
水淬炉渣 (water) granulated slag
水淬射流 【铁】granulating spray
水淬水温 granulation water temperature
水淬物料 bead material
水淬系统 【团】granulating system
水淬液 aqueous quenchant
水淬硬 water quenching
水淬用水 【铁】granulation water
水淬渣 slag beading
水单硫铁矿 hydrotroilite
水胆矾 {$CuSO_4 \cdot 3Cu(OH)_2$} brochantite, warringtonite
水当量 water equivalent
水道 (water) channel, waterway, water course, gullet, gout ◇ 开挖的~ canalized waterway
水道学[测量术] hydrography
水道整治工程 channel regulation works
水的化学处理 chemical treatment of water
水滴捕集器 spray catcher
水底电缆 submarine cable
水底混凝土 subaqueous concrete
水底隧道 subaqueous tunnel
水底微生物群落 benthic microbail community
水碲锌矿 zemannite
水电比拟法 electro-hydrodynamic method
水电解槽[池] water electrolyzer
水电站 hydroelectric (generating, power) station, water-power station [plant], hydraulic power plant
水电阻(器) water resistor
水法 aqueous method
水法冶金 (同"湿法冶金")
水矾土 diaspore clay
水钒钙铀矿 {$CaO \cdot 2UO_3 \cdot V_2O_5 \cdot 8H_2O$} tjuiamunite
水钒矿 vanoxite
水钒钠石 barnesite
水钒石 aloite
水钒铁矿 fervanite
水钒铜矿 volborthite, usbekite, uzbekite
水钒铀矿 ferghanite, ferganite
水分 moisture (content), water content, degree of moisture ◇ 不含~的 moisture-free, 除去鼓风中~ blast dehydration, 非结合~ mobile moisture, 含~的 moisture-bearing, 适宜~*, 中子测~*, 装炉~*
水分饱和的 moisture-laden
水分测定仪 (型砂的) moisture teller
水分分解反应 moisture decomposition reaction
水分分泌 weepage
水分含量 moisture content [level]
水分(含量)试样 moisture sample
水分集中 moisture concentration
水分控制 moisture control ◇ 电阻式~法
水分快速测定仪 (型砂的) moisture teller
水分冷凝 moisture condensation
水分离器[汽水分离器] water separator
水分喷射系统 【冶】moisture injection

system
水分迁移 moisture migration
水分取样 moisture sampling
水分渗漏 weepage
水分调节剂[器] moisture controller
水分析出 moisture evolution
水分吸收 moisture pick-up
水分再吸收 reabsorption of moisture
水分指示器 moisture indicator
水封 water seal [block, closing, lute, check], hydraulic seal
水封槽 water seal trough, water sealed tank
水封阀 water-sealed valve
水封挤压 extrusion into water
水封器 liquid packing
水封式除尘器 【铁】water-sealed flue dust pocket
水封式储气柜 water-sealed gasholder
水封退火炉 water-sealed annealing furnace
水氟钙钇矾 chukhrovite
水氟铝钙石 yaroslavite
水氟碳钙钍铈矿 thorbastnaesite
水腐蚀 aqueous corrosion
水钙镁铀石[水硅钙镁铀矿] $\{(Ca,Mg)_2 \cdot (UO_3)_2 \cdot (SiO_2)_5 \cdot nH_2O\}$ ursilite
水锆石 $\{8ZrO_2 \cdot 6SiO_2 \cdot 5H_2O\}$ orvillite
水工建筑物 hydraulic structure
水工学[技术] hydrotechnics
水沟 water course, gutterway ◇ 狭底~ canch
水垢 incrustant, incrustation, scale (deposit), scaly deposit ◇ 含砂~ gritty scale, 生成[形成]~ scaling, incrust
水垢净化器 scaler
水钴矿 $\{2Co_2O_3 \cdot CuO \cdot nH_2O\}$ heterogenite
水钴铜矿 trieuite
水管 water pipe [tube, carrier, conduit], aqueduct
水管冷却器 water-tube type cooler ◇ 立式~.

水管桥 water conduit bridge, aqueduct
水管式锅炉 water-tube boiler
水硅钒锌镍矿 kurumsakite
水硅钙铀矿 ranquilite
水硅铝钛铈矿 karnasurite
水硅铍石 $\{Be_3SiO_4(OH)_2 \cdot H_2O\}$ beryllite
水硅铅铀矿 orlite
水硅钛铈矿 vudyavrite
水硅铜铀矿 cuprosklodowskite
水硅钍铀矿 enalite
水硅铀钍铅矿 nicolayite
水滚筒 wet tumbler
水合 (同"水化")
水合反应性 hydration reactivity
水合分子数 hydration number
水合氟化铝 $\{AlF_3 \cdot 3H_2O\}$ hydrated aluminium fluoride
水合结晶 crystal(line) hydrate
水合金属氧化物 hydrated metal oxide
水合抗衡离子 hydrated counter ion
水合离子 aquated ion
水合硫酸盐 hydrated sulphate
水合能力[水合性] hydratability
水合氢离子 hydronium [hydroxonium, oxonium] ion
水合氢氧化铝 algeldrate
水合球粒 hydrated pellet
水合热 hydration heat, heat of hydration
水合三氧化铀 uranium trioxide hydrate
水合设施 hydration facilities
水合水分 hydrate moisture
水合碳酸镁 hydrocarbonate of magnesia
水合碳酸锌 hydrocarbonate of zinc
水合碳酸盐 hydrocarbonate
水合物 hydrate
水合物电离反应 hydrate ionization reaction
水合物活化反应 hydrate activation reaction
水合霞石 nepheline hydrate
水合盐 hydrated salt, salt hydrate

水合氧化铪 {HfO$_4$·2H$_2$O} hydrous oxide of hafnium
水合氧化铝 {Al$_2$O$_3$·3H$_2$O} hydrated alumina
水合氧化铁 hydrated ferric oxide
水合氧化物 hydrated [hydrous] oxide
水合氧化物滤饼 hydrous oxide cake
水合值 hydration value [number]
水鹤头 【运】crane head
水滑石 hydrotalcite
水化 hydration, aquation ◇ 完全～ 水泥*
水化程度 degree of hydration
水化低氧化物 hydroprotoxide
水化二氧化硅 hydrated silica
水化硅酸钙 hydrated calcium silicate
水化矿物 hydrated mineral
水化铝酸钙 hydrated calcium aluminate
水化器 hydrotor, liming apparatus（石灰熟化用）
水化倾向 tendency to hydrate
水化水[结合水] water of hydration
水化作用 hydration, aquation
水灰比(例)(混凝土的) water-cement ratio
水灰比高的混凝土 wet concrete
水回收设备 water saver equipment
水击作用 water hammer(ing)
水钾铀矾 zippeite
水胶 glue, gelatin(e)
水解 hydrolysis (hyd.), hydrolization, hydrolyzing, aquolysis, hydrolytic decomposition ◇ 分段～ graded hydrolysis, 优先～ selective hydrolysis
水解产物 hydrolysis product, hydrolysate
水解沉淀 hydrolytic precipitation
水解(程)度 degree of hydrolysis
水解反应 hydrolysis reaction
水解高压釜 hydrolysis autoclave
水解菱镁矿 {4MgO·3CO$_2$·4H$_2$O} hydromagnesite
水解平衡 hydrolysis equilibrium
水解器 hydrolyzer
水解洗提 hydrolytic stripping
水解质 hydrolyte
水解作用 hydrolytic action, hydrolysis
水界 hydrosphere
水介质 aqueous medium
水浸出 water leach(ing), leaching with water
水浸出液 water-leach liquor
水浸法（探伤用） immersion method
水浸耦合阻抗法 water-coupled impedance method
水晶 {SiO$_2$} quartz crystal, rock crystal [quartzite]
水井套管 water well casing
水井钻管 water well boring tube
水静压头 water lift
水静压制 hydrostatic pressing
水净化 water purifying [treatment, dressing] ◇ 生产用～厂*
水净化装置 water clarifier
水口 【钢】(stopper) nozzle（塞棒用），【铸】down-spout ◇ 巴格纳尔－贝瑟尔（专利）[串联,双层]～*, 浮集式(下)～ collector nozzle, 复合～ composite nozzle, 滑动[滑阀式]～*, 浸入式～*, 无漩涡～*, 自流式～*, 组合～ bicomponent nozzle
水口堵塞[结瘤] nozzle blocking [blockage, fouling] nozzle blocking
水口孔（钢包的） nozzle bore
水口耐火材料 nozzle refractory
水口凝滴[凝钢] nozzle drips
水口塞棒装置 nozzle-stopper equipment
水口托板 【连铸】tube holder
水口闸板 【连铸】nozzle gate
水口张角 submerged entry nozzle angle
水口砖 nozzle (brick) ◇ 多孔～*, 黏土～ clay nozzle
水口砖孔 pot-hole
水口座（钢包的） nozzle pocket
水口座砖 nozzle pocket brick, nozzle seat-

ing block, pocket block nozzle [pouring] shroud
水库供水量　reservoir yield
水冷　water cooling
水冷坝式隔渣墙　water-cooled bridge wall
水冷板[壁]　【铁】water-cooled plate
水冷槽（轧件的）　quench bath
水冷穿孔顶头　water-cooled piercing plug ◇ 内外~ *
水冷带式输送机　water-cooled conveyer
水冷底板　water-cooled base, water-cooled bottom plate
水冷底片暗盒　water-cooled film holder
水冷电极　water-cooled electrode (bar), cold electrode
水冷电极环　water-cooled electrode collar
水冷电极夹持器　water-cooled electrode clamp [holder]
水冷电极尖　water-cooled electrode tip
水冷电极头　water-cooled electrode head
水冷电接头　water-cooled contact
水冷顶板　water-cooled head plate
水冷锭模　water-cooled mould ◇ 容克式~ Junker's mould
水冷锭模电弧炉　cold mould arc furnace
水冷分隔器　water-cooled spacer
水冷风口　water-cooled tuyere
水冷复合电极　water-cooled complex electrode
水冷高频引线　water-cooled high frequency lead
水冷坩埚　cold-crucible, water-cooled crucible, cold hearth ◇ 自耗电极~电弧熔炼 *
水冷坩埚感应炉　cold-crucible induction furnace
水冷拱脚[座]　water-cooled skewback
水冷管道镜　water-cooled borescope
水冷焊炬　water-cooled welding torch
水冷滑道（炉内的）　wet [water-cooled] skid
水冷环管　cooling water circle pipe ◇ 高炉~ *
水冷黄铜环　water-cooled brass collar
水冷黄铜接头　water-cooled brass connection
水冷夹钳　water-cooled clamp
水冷接头　water-cooled joint
水冷坑　【压】water (quench) pit
水冷空心阳极　hollow water cooled anode
水冷拉丝卷筒　water-cooled capstan
水冷冷凝器　water-cooled condenser
水冷裂纹　water crack
水冷流槽　water-cooled launder
水冷炉箅　water grate
水冷炉壁　water-cooled furnace wall
水冷炉壁真空炉　cold wall vacuum furnace
水冷炉壁真空炉设备　cold-wall vacuum-furnace equipment
水冷炉底　water-cooled base
水冷炉盖　water-cooled cover
水冷炉壳　water-cooled shell, water-cooled furnace body
水冷炉栅　water-cooled grating
水冷门拱　chill arch
水冷密封　water-cooled seal
水冷密封盖　water-cooled gland
水冷模　water-cooled die
水冷内孔窥视仪　water-cooled borescope
水冷耙　【钢】water-cooled rake
水冷盘条　water-hardened wire rod
水冷前床　water-cooled forehearth
水冷切割　cutting with water quench
水冷却池　water-cooling pond
水冷(却)器　water cooler ◇ 大气~ *
水冷燃烧器　water cooled burner
水冷韧化处理　water toughening
水冷塞棒芯　【钢】water-cooled stopper rod
水冷塞头[浇口棒]　water-cooled stopper
水冷蛇[旋]管　water-cooled coil
水冷式电动机　water-cooled motor
水冷式化铁炉　water-cooled cupola
水冷式结晶器　【连铸】water-cooled mould

水 shui

水冷式螺旋运输机　water-cooled screw conveyor
水冷式输送带　water-cooled conveyer
水冷式引燃管　water-cooled ignitron
水冷竖炉　water-cooled shaft furnace
水冷塔　water-cooling tower
水冷调节　cooling water regulation
水冷套　water-cooling jacket, water-cooled shell
水冷铜电极顶杆　water-cooled copper electrode ram
水冷铜坩埚　water-cooled copper crucible [hearth, mould]
水冷铜坩埚熔化台　(真空铸锭炉的) water-cooled copper melting platform
水冷铜管坩埚　water-cooled copper tube crucible
水冷铜管原线圈　water-cooled copper-tube primary
水冷铜极靴　water-cooled copper shoe
水冷铜模　water-cooled copper mould
水冷退火　water annealing
水冷温度指示器　water-cooling temperature indicator
水冷钨尖电极　water-cooled tungsten-tipped rod
水冷系统　water-cooling system ◇ 无回收[直流式]～*
水冷烟道　(卡多尔转炉的)【钢】water-cooled offtake
水冷延伸部分　water-cooled extension
水冷(氧气)喷枪　water-cooled lance
水冷阴极　water-cooled cathode
水冷再冷凝器　water-cooled aftercondenser
水冷闸板式热风阀　water-cooled gate-type hot-blast valve
水冷罩　water-cooled hood
水冷真空管　water-cooled tube
水冷轴　water-cooled shaft
水冷铸件(冷却渣口、风口、金属口构件) tymp
水冷铸型　【铸】water-jacketed mould
水沥青铀矿 $\{x UO_2 \cdot y UO_3 \cdot n H_2O\}$　hydropitchblende
水力　waterpower, hydraulic power
水力测功器　hydraulic dynamometer ◇ 闸式～*
水力冲击　hydraulic impact
水力冲击作用　water hammer
水力冲矿机　hydraulic giant
水力冲填(土)坝　hydraulic-fill dam
水力冲填法　hydraulic fill method
水力出坯机构　(同"液压出坯装置")
水力除鳞机　【压】hydraulic descaler
水力除鳞喷嘴　descaling jet, water-descaling sprayer
水力除鳞喷嘴双集管[水力冲除氧化皮的双重集管]　double descaling header
水力除鳞系统　hydraulic descaling system
水力除鳞装置　water descaler, water descaling unit
水力除芯机　【铸】hydraulic core knockout machine
水力穿孔压力机　hydraulic piercing press
水力导向焊条顺序夹持多点电焊机　hydromatic welder
水力顶杆　hydraulic ram
水力定型机　hydraulic calibrating press
水力发电厂[站]　(同"水电站")
水力分级机　hydraulic classifier, lavodune apparatus ◇ 槽形～*, 流槽式干扰沉降～*, 自由沉降～*
水力分离器　hydraulic separator, hydroseparator
水力分离[分选]增稠器　hydrator-thickener
水力分析　hydraulic analysis
水力工程学　hydrotechnics
水力混汞捕汞器　hydraulic trap
水力活塞　hydraulic ram
水力卷扬机　hydraulic hoist
水力扩管机　【压】hydraulic expander
水力喷砂清理　【铸】sand-water [hydro-

	sand] blasting, sand-water cleaning
水力起重机	water crane
水力起重器	hydraulic jack
水力清理	hydraulic fettling
水力清模装置[工段]	mould hydraulic cleaning plant
水力清砂	【铸】hydraulic blast, hydroblast(ing), stream jet blasting
水力输送	hydraulic transport, fluming
水力调整缸	(同"液压调节缸")
水力提升	hydraulic lift(ing)
水力挖方[挖掘]	hydraulic excavation
水力型芯打出机	【铸】hydro-core-knock-out (machine)
水力蓄压器式水压机	water-accumulator power press
水力蓄压器压力传动	water-accumulator drive
水力蓄压装置	(同"水压蓄能设备")
水力旋流器	hydro(cy)clone, wet cyclone, solid liquid cyclone
水力旋流器分级	hydroclone classification
水力旋流器组	hydrocyclone group
水力旋流淘析器	hydraulic cyclone elutriator
水力学	hydraulics
水力学半径	hydraulic radius
水力压紧	liquid packing
水力运输机	hydraulic conveyer
水力增压器	hydraulic intensifier
水力闸	hydraulic brake
水力闸门	hydraulic gate
水力直径	hydraulic diameter
水力柱塞	hydraulic ram
水力铸件清理装置	hydraulic casting-cleaning plant
水力资源	waterpower resources
水量表旋塞	water-gauge cock
水量不足	deficient in water
水量平衡	water balance
水量平衡负差额	【环】negative water balance
水量平衡正差额	【环】positive water balance
水磷钙钍石	brockite
水磷铝铜石	zapatalite
水磷铝钇石	koivinite, koiwinite
水磷铅铀矿	$\{Pb(UO_2)_2(PO_4)_2 \cdot 2H_2O\}$ przhevalskite, prjevalskite
水磷铈矿	rhabdophane
水磷钇矿	$\{(Y)PO_4 \cdot 2H_2O\}$ churchite
水磷铀钙矿	$\{(Ca, U, Ce)PO_4 \cdot H_2O\}$ ningyoite
水磷铀矿	$\{Ca(UO_2)_2P_2O_8 \cdot 12H_2O\}$ uranospathite
水磷铀铅矿	$\{(PbO)_2(UO_3)_2 \cdot P_2O_4 \cdot 5H_2O\}$ dumontite
水磷铀钍矿	kivuite
水淋电极技术	technology of water sprayed electrode
水淋式空调设备	humidifying and air conditioning equipment
水淋(式)冷凝器	drip condenser
水菱钙镁铀矿	$\{CaMgUO_2(CO_3)_2 \cdot 12H_2O\}$ swartzite
水菱镁钙石	rabbitite
水菱铈矿	$\{(RE)_2O_3 \cdot 3CO_2 \cdot 4H_2O\}$ calkinsite
水菱钇矿	$\{CaY_3(OH)_3(CO_3)_4 \cdot 3H_2O\}$ tengerite
水菱铀矿	$\{UO_3 \cdot CO_2 \cdot n\ H_2O\}$ studite, diderichite
水硫砷铁石	zykaite
水硫酸铝石	$\{Al_2O_3 \cdot 3SO_3 \cdot 16H_2O\}$ alunogen
水硫酸铜	brochantite
水硫铀矿	(同"铀钙矾")
水馏分	aqueous distillate
水流	(aqueous) stream, hydraulic flow, fluent
水流开关	water-flow switch
水流量	water rate [flow]
水流量测量单位(1秒100升)	module
水流量继电器	water flow relay

水流喷射泵[器]	water-jet injector
水流循环	circulation of water
水龙带	hose (line)
水龙头	stopcock, bib (cock)
水路循环	water circuit
水铝氟石 {CaF$_2$·2Al(FOH)$_3$·H$_2$O}	prosopite
水铝铬石	knipovichite
水铝矿 {α-Al$_2$O$_3$·3H$_2$O}	hydrargillite
水铝石	empholite, diaspore, diasporite
水铝石耐火材料	diaspore [gibbsite] refractory
水铝石黏土	diaspore (-bearing) clay
水铝英石	allophanite
水铝铀云母 {Ca(UO$_2$)$_2$P$_2$O$_8$·12H$_2$O}	uranospathite
水氯镁石 {MgCl$_2$·6H$_2$O}	bischofite
水氯铅矿	fiedlerite
水氯铜矿	eriochalcite, antofagastite
水轮泵	(water) turbine pump ◇ 深井～*
水落斗	【建】gutter spout funnel
水落管	【建】waterspout, down-spout (D.S.), gullet
水煤浆	coal-water slurry (CWS)
水煤气	water-gas ◇ 增碳～ carburetted water gas
水煤气搭焊钢管法	【压】water-gas lap-weld process
水煤气发生炉	water-gas generator [set]
水煤气反应	water-gas reaction
水煤气管	water-gas pipe
水煤气火焰	water-gas flame
水煤气型两段炉	two-stage-gas reactor
水煤气焰焊(接)	water-gas welding
水煤气用焦炭	water-gas coke
水镁矾 {MgSO$_4$·H$_2$O}	kieserite
水镁石 {MgO·H$_2$O}	brucite
水镁铁矾	franquanite
水锰矾	mallardite
水锰矿 {Mn$_2$O$_3$·H$_2$O}	manganite, prismatic manganese ore, grey oxide of manganese
水密式仪器仪表	water-tight instrument
水密性混凝土	watertight concrete
水面降落	drawdown
水磨石	rubbed concrete, terrezzo, waterstone
水模实验	hydraulic model experiment
水模型	water model
水膜收尘器	water-membrane scrubber
水幕	water curtain [screen]
水幕冷却	water-curtain cooling, water floor cooling
水钼铁矿 {Fe$_2$O$_3$·3MoO$_3$·8H$_2$O}	ferrimolybdite
水钠铀石 {Na$_2$(UO$_2$)$_2$P$_2$O$_8$·12H$_2$O}	sodium uranospinite
水囊	water pocket [cell]
水泥	cement ◇ 粗～ cement grit, 低析水性～ low-water-loss cement, 矾土～*, 封气黏胶～ air tack cement, 高菱镁～*, 含铁波特兰～*, 缓凝～ retarded cement, 快凝～*, 快硬～*, 矿渣硫酸盐～ slag-sulphate cenment, 慢凝～ slow setting cement, 耐硫酸盐～*, 死烧白云石～*, 索雷尔镁质～ sorel cement, 细磨～ fine ground cement, 硬[无水]石膏～ anhydrite cement, 用～加固 consolidation grouting
水泥安定性试验	test for soundness
水泥拌合机	cement mixer
水泥测针	cement needle
水泥厂	cement plant
水泥成团	balling up of cement
水泥缝	cement joint
水泥敷面	cement dressing
水泥覆层	cement coating
水泥－骨料比率（混凝土的）	【建】cement-aggregate ratio
水泥固结球团	cement bound pellet
水泥管	cement pipe
水泥灌浆	cement grouting
水泥缓凝剂	cement retarder

水泥回转窑　cement (rotary) kiln
水泥混凝土　cement concrete
水泥活性　activity of cement
水泥浆　cement mortar (cem.m.), grout
水泥浆沫[浮]　bleeding cement
水泥浆喷枪　cement gun
水泥接缝　cement joint
水泥结碎石(路)　concrete-bound macadam
水泥量与骨料孔隙比率(混凝土的)【建】cement-space ratio
水泥抹面　cement plastering
水泥黏合砖　cementitious brick
水泥黏结[合]剂　cement binder [bond]
水泥黏结团块(法)　cement briquette
水泥凝固测针　cement needle
水泥喷枪　concrete-gun, cement jet
水泥砂　cement sand,【铸】cement bonded sand
水泥砂浆拌合机　cement mixer
水泥砂浆填料　【建】cement grout filler
水泥砂造型　cement (sand) moulding ◇ 戈德尔~法 Godel process
水泥烧块　【铸】(cement) clinker
水泥石灰浆　cement lime mortar
水泥试验机　cement test machine
水泥熟料[烧块]　(cement) clinker ◇ 细磨~ ground cement clinker
水泥刷面　cement rendering
水泥榫接合　cement joggle joint
水泥筒仓　cement (storage) silo
水泥涂层　cement coating
水泥稳定(法)　cement stabilization
水泥系数　【建】cement factor
水泥纤维板　cement fibrolite plate
水泥型块　cement block
水泥压团　balling up of cement
水泥窑　cement kiln
水泥用矿渣　cement slag
水泥罩面　cement finish [covering]
水泥重量投配器　cement weighing hopper
水泥砖　cement brick ◇ 泡沫~ cementitious brick
水镍铁矾　hornessite
水凝固　hydraulic set,【连铸】wash(ing) water solidification (喷水凝固)
水凝剂　hydraulic binder
水凝胶　aquogel, hydrogel
水排放和蒸发系统　【环】DREW (drainage-and-evaporation-of-water) system
水泡状的　bullate
水平摆锻锤头　horizontal (forming) shoes
水平错排管束　horizonally staggered tube bundle
水平带式输送机　horizontal belt conveyer
水平导板　level guide
水平导向辊(轧机的)　billy roll
水平电磁浇注　horizontal electromagnetic casting (HEMC)
水平锭料(区域熔炼的)　horizontal ingot
水平发散喷嘴扩散泵　horizontal divergent-nozzle pump
水平发散引起的反射增宽　broadening of reflection by horizontal divergence
水平方向力　horizontal force
水平分布　horizontal distribution
水平分量[力]　horizontal component
水平分配火道　horizontal distribution flue
水平格栅[篦条筛,炉箅]　horizontal grate
水平隔膜电解槽　horizontal-diaphragm cell
水平固定位置　horizontal fixed position
水平管(管式热风炉的)　lying pipe
水平管式炉　horizontal tube furnace
水平罐蒸馏炼锌　(同"平罐炼锌")
水平罐蒸馏炉　horizontal retort (distillation) furnace
水平辊机座　【压】horizontal roll stand
水平滚筒　horizontal drum
水平焊缝　horizontal weld
水平合力　horizontal resultant
水平滑座式热锯　【压】horizontal sliding-frame hot saw

水 shui

水平环槽感应电炉　horizontal ring furnace
水平火道　【焦】collecting flue
水平机架　horizontal stand
水平极限　horizontal limit
水平剪切[剪力]　horizontal shear (HS, h.s.)
水平浇铸　horizontal casting
水平浇铸机　horizontal casting machine
水平开裂　horizontal split
水平坑道口　adit opening
水平拉晶技术　【半】horizontal pulling technique
水平力　horizontal force
水平连铸　horizontal continuous casting ◇雅凯~法*
水平连铸机　horizontal continuous caster ◇圆坯~round billet HCC
水平连铸圆管坯　horizontal continuous casting round billet
水平链箅式冷却器　horizontal grate cooler
水平链箅式预热器　horizontal grate preheater
水平裂纹　horizontal crack
水平面　horizontal (plane), water level
水平面调节器　regulator of level
水平偏析　horizontal segregation
水平偏转电路的自动频率控制电路　synchro-lock
水平偏转最大长度（超声波的）　horizontal limit
水平剖[断]面　horizontal section
水平起重机　luffing crane
水平区域精炼　horizontal zone refining
水平区域熔炼　horizontal zone melting
水平散度[发散]　horizontal divergence
水平烧结　horizontal sintering
水平射束宽度　horizontal beam width
水平式反应器　horizontal reactor
水平式焦炉　slot-type oven
水平式运输筛　horizontal conveyer screen
水平式轧边机　【压】horizontal edger

水平速度　horizontal velocity
水平输送筛　horizontal conveyer screen
水平碳化室　【焦】horizontal chamber
水平填角焊　horizontal fillet weld(ing)
水平条带烧结　【粉】horizontal sintering of strip
水平投影　horizontal projection
水平位错列　dislocations of horizontal rows
水平线　level, horizon(tal), horizontal line
水平线性(偏转)范围　horizontal linearity range
水平巷道掘进　drifting
水平旋转轴离心铸造　(同"全离心铸造")
水平压力　horizontal pressure
水平压力机　【耐】level press
水平烟道　horizontal [stack] flue
水平烟道窑　horizontal-flue oven
水平移动[位移]　horizontal displacement,【理】level shift
水平移动带材备用量　horizontal strip storage
水平移动炉箅条　horizontal travelling grate
水平仪　level meter
水平轧辊　【压】horizontal roll
水平轧辊机座　horizontal roll stand
水平照明　horizontal illumination
水平舟区域精炼[提纯]　【半】horizontal-boat zone refining
水平柱塞压铸机　(同"卧式柱塞压铸机")
水平贮仓　horizontal bunker
水平转动焊接　horizontally-rolled-position welding
水－气分界面　water-air boundary
水气提取　whizzing
水铅铀矿{$Na_2O \cdot CaO \cdot PbO \cdot 8UO_3 \cdot 6H_2O$}　clarkeite
水枪　water jet, squirt gun
水墙冷却装置　waterwall cooling element

水羟钾铀矾 {(UO$_3$)$_2$SO$_3$·nH$_2$O} zippeite
水羟磷铝石 {3Al$_2$O$_3$·2P$_2$O$_5$·18H$_2$O} vashegyite
水羟铝矾 zaherite
水羟锰矿 vernadite
水渠 water channel, trench
水圈 hydrosphere
水热法 hydrothermal process
水融 aqueous fusion
水溶硅酸盐 water soluble silicate
水溶剂 aqueous solvent, hydro-solvent
水溶胶 hydrosol
水溶物含量 water soluble content
水溶型芯 water-soluble core
水溶性[率] water solubility
水溶性硫 water soluble sulphur (W.S.S.)
水溶液 water solution, aqueous solution (aq. sol.), solution in water
水溶液萃取[提取] aqueous extraction
水溶液电积(法) electrodeposition from aqueous solution
水溶液电解 aqueous electrolysis, electrolysis from aqueous solution
水溶液腐蚀 aqueous corrosion
水溶液浸出 aqueous leach
水溶液洗提剂 aqueous strip
水溶液系统 aqueous system
水溶液氧化 aqueous oxidation
水溶液氧化浸出 oxidizing aqueous leach
水容量 water capacity
水乳化油 water-emulsifiable oil
水乳化着色渗透剂检查法 【理】water-emulsifiable dye-penetrant process
水入电石式乙炔发生器 (同"注水式乙炔发生器")
水软化 water softening, demineralization, mitigation
水软化剂 water softener
水软化设备 water-demineralization plant
水软化装置 water-softening plant
水润滑轴承 water lubricated bearing
水润滑作用(挤压模面砖的) water lubrication
水色标准 【环】colour standard of water
水砂抛光处理 【铸】wet blasting
水-砂清理 hydro-sand blasting
水上打桩机 floating pile driver, pontoon pile driving plant
水上起重机 (同"船式起重机")
水射流 water jet
水射流技术 water jet technique
水射流切割 waterjets cutting
水砷镁铀矿 novacekite
水砷镍矿 {Ni$_3$(AsO$_4$)$_2$·8H$_2$O} nickel green
水砷锌矿 adamite
水砷铀矿 {Fe$_2$(UO$_2$)$_2$(AsO$_4$)$_2$·8H$_2$O} kahlerite
水深测量器 bathometer
水声测位仪[探测器] (同"声纳")
水生产率 water production rate (WPR)
水生黄杆菌 Flavobacterium aguatile
水生皱折[摺] watering wrinkle
水生物沉积 fouling
水铈铀磷钙石 {(U, Ca, RE)$_3$(PO$_4$)$_4$·6H$_2$O} lermontovite
水碎槽(炉渣的) water granulator
水碎熔剂 water-shorted flux
水碎渣 sla(c)king slag
水塔 water tower, balance tank
水钛锆矿 {3ZrO$_2$·2TiO$_2$·2H$_2$O} oliveiraite
水钛铌矿 gerasimovskite
水钛铌钇锑矿 scheteligite
水碳钙镁铀矿 rabbittite
水碳镧铈矿 calkinsite
水碳钇矿 yttrite
水碳钇石 lokkaite
水碳钇铀矿 bijvoetite
水碳镍矿 hellyerite
水碳酸钙铀矿 {UO$_2$·6UO$_3$·2CO$_2$·3CaO·12H$_2$O} wyartite
水碳酸钠铀矿 {Na$_2$CaUO$_2$(CO$_3$)$_3$·6H$_2$O}

水 shui

andersonite
水碳铀矿 {6UO$_3$·5CO$_2$·8H$_2$O} sharpite
水套 water jacket
水套冷凝器 water-jacketed condenser
水套冷却 jacket (type) cooling
水套(冷却)金属引燃管 water-jacketed metal ignitron
水套冷却器 water jacket cooler
水套冷却室 water-jacketed chamber
水套冷却铜坩埚 water-jacket(ed) copper crucible
水套炉 water-jacket furnace
水套炉墙 jacket(ed) wall
水套模 【铸】water-jacketed mould
水套散热损失 jacket losses
水套式气体发生装置 water-jacketed gasifier
水套水 jacket water
水套型芯 【铸】jacket core
水铁矾 schmollnitzite, szomolnokite
水铁矿 ferrihydrite
水铜矾 vernadskite
水头 (water) head
水钍石 hydrothorite
水位 water level, altitude ◇ 基准～datum level
水位表旋塞 water-gauge cock
水位玻璃管 water-gauge glass, gauge glass (锅炉用)
水位差 water head
水位差损失 head loss
水位尺 water [foot] gauge
水位传感器 level sensor
水位计 water [tank] gauge ◇ 放射性～
水位检测装置 water-level detecting device
水位控制[调节] water-level control
水位仪(河水用) fluviograph
水位指示器 water-level indicator, dipstick
水文测量(学) hydrometry
水文地理学 hydrography, hydrology
水文地质 hydrological geology
水文地质学 geohydrology, hydrogeology
水文气象学 hydrometeorology
水文条件 hydrological condition
水文图[学] hydrography
水稳定的 moisture-proof
水污染 【环】water contamination [pollution], aquatic pollution
水污染物 【环】aquatic pollutant
水雾 water mist, spray
水雾化(法) water atomization
水析分级法 elutriation method
水析器 wet elutriator
水吸附 water adsorption
水吸收 water uptake
水洗 water washing [scrubbing]
水洗涤式收[集]尘器 water washer type dust collector
水洗机 water cleaner, rinsing machine
水洗塔[器] water scrubber
水洗性渗透剂 water-washable penetrant
水洗性荧光渗透探伤法 【理】water-washable fluorescent penetrant inspection
水洗性着色渗透剂探伤法 【理】water-washable dye-penetrant process
水下(爆炸)成形 underwater forming
水下腐蚀 underwater corrosion
水下灌筑混凝土 subaqueous concreting
水下焊接 underwater welding
水下焊炬 underwater torch
水下气割炬 underwater gas cutter
水下切割 underwater cutting
水下切割烧嘴 underwater cutting burner
水下声波定位仪 (同"声纳")
水下试验 underwater test
水下用白色(巴比)合金 underwater white metal
水下用电焊条 underwater electrode
水下远距离操作 underwater standoff operation
水下铸造法 (同"水中铸造法")
水线腐蚀 water-line corrosion

水相 water [aqueous] phase
水相残液 aqueous raffinate
水相残液流 aqueous raffinate stream
水相产物（萃取的） aqueous product
水相出口 aqueous outlet
水相电解质 aqueous electrolyte
水相废液 waste aqueous phase
水相入口 aqueous inlet
水相堰 aqueous weir
水相堰板 aqueous weir guard
水相氧化 aqueous oxidation
水箱 tank (Tk, Tnk), water [box, jacket, tank, block], reservoir
水消耗量 【冶】water rate
水锌矾 {$ZnSO_4 \cdot H_2O$} gunningite
水锌矿 hydrocincite {$3ZnCO_3 \cdot 2H_2O$}, hydrozincite {$7ZnO \cdot 3CO_2 \cdot 4H_2O$}, zinc bloom {$ZnCO_3 \cdot 2Zn(OH)_2$}
水锌锰矿 hydroheterolite, wolftonite
水锈 incrustant, incrustation, scale (deposit), scaly deposit
水选 water concentration, water [wet] separation
水循环 water circulation
水循环泵 circulating-water pump
水循环泵电动机 water recirculation pump motor
水压 water pressure
水压泵 water pressure pump, hydraulic pump
水压锤 hydrohammer
水压锻造 hydraulic forging
水压防漏装置 liquid packing
水压缸 （同"液压缸"）
水压机 （同"液压机"）, water press ◇ 巴塞式上下双动型~*, 锻造~*, 管端扩口~ tube belling press, 开杆式~*, 快动双效~*, 汽动~ steam hydraulic press, 全~ all hydraulic press, 上升冲程~*, 水力蓄压器式~*, 四柱式~*, 下压式~*, 重型~ heavy hydraulic press
水压机锤 hydrohamme

水压机缸 ram cylinder
水压机构 （同"液压机构"）
水压机滑动横梁 press-head
水压机活塞 hydraulic ram
水压机压板 ram platen
水压机主缸 main press cylinder
水压均衡器 hydraulic pressure equalizer
水压开关 hydraulic pressure switch
水压冷室压铸机 【铸】hydropress cold-chamber diecasting machine
水压逆止阀 hydraulic back-pressure valve
水压起重机 water lift
水压上推系统 （同"液压上推系统"）
水压试验 hydraulic (pressure) test, hydrostatic [water] test
水压试验机 hydrostatic testing machine ◇ 管材~*
水压调节器 water pressure regulator, hydrostate
水压头 hydraulic head
水压蓄能设备 water-accumulator installation
水压总管 hydraulic main
水淹地区 flood land
水杨酸 {$HOC_6H_4CO_2H$} solicylic acid
水杨酸铋铈 bismuthi-cerii salicylas
水杨酸络合物 salicylic acid complex
水杨酸盐[酯] {OHC_6H_4COOM} salicylate
水养护 water curing
水冶 （同"湿法冶金"）◇ 浮选~设备*
水冶法 【色】hydro-metallurgical method
水冶和火冶联合法 combination of hydrometallurgy and pyrometallurgy
水冶精矿 hydrometallurgical concentrate
水翼[叶] hydrofoil
水银 {Hg} （同"汞"）
水银法(食盐)电解 【环】mercury process electrolysis
水银铬化 merchromizing
水银鼓泡瓶[器] mercury bubbler
水银继电器 mercury relay

水银开关 mercury contact, mercoid (switch)

水银密封 mercury seal

水银模(精密)铸造 mercast ◇ 冻结[冷冻]~法*

水银农药 【环】mercuric pesticides

水银气压计 mercurial [mercury] barometer

水银试验 (黄铜的) mercury test

水银温度计 mercurial [mercury] thermometer

水银压力表[计] mercury (pressure) gauge, mercury manometer

水银浴 mercury bath

水银真空计 mercurical vacuum gauge

水银整流器 (同"汞弧整流器")

水银中毒 mercurialism

水印 water stain

水硬度 water hardness

水硬度计 hydrotimeter

水硬(化) hydraulic set

水硬率 hydraulic index [modulus]

水硬石灰 hydraulic [water] lime

水硬水泥 hydraulic [water] cement

水硬性胶结 hydraulic bond

水硬性胶结物 hydraulic binder

水硬性浇灌耐火材料砌块 castable refractory block

水硬性耐火泥 hydraulic refractory mortar

水硬性耐火水泥 hydraulic refractory cement

水硬性泥浆 【建】hydraulic setting mortar

水硬性黏结剂 hydrated binding agent

水铀矾 {(UO$_3$)$_2$SO$_3$·nH$_2$O} zippeite, unranbloom

水铀矿 janthinite, ianthinite

水铀铜矿 (同"绿铀矿")

水域 waters, water area ◇ 共有~shared waters

水浴 water-bath, bain marie

水浴除尘器 wet dust collector

水源 water supply, source of water

水源地带 stream source area

水源接头 water connection

水云母 hydromica ◇ 伊利~illite

水运费 waterage, freight cost

水载排出物 【环】waterborne effluent

水载污染物 【环】waterborne pollutant

水在油中弥散 water-in-oil dispersion

水渣 water granulated slag, pumicestone slag, 【铁】granulated (blast-furnace) slag ◇ 制~贮槽【铁】water treatment pit

水渣车 【冶】slag buggy

水渣池 【团】granulating pit

水渣混凝土 foamed slag concrete

水渣坑 【铁】cinder granulation pit

水闸门 water gate, wicket

水针铁矿 hydrogoethite

水蒸馏器 water distiller

水蒸气 water vapour, steam

水蒸气保护电弧焊 water vapour arc welding

水蒸汽传递 water vapour transmission (WVT)

水蒸气渗透比 water vapour permeance

水蒸气渗透性 water vapour permeability

水蒸气压 water vapour pressure

水蒸气张力 aqueous tension

水蒸气传递速度 rate of water vapour transmission (WVT)

水质 water quality ◇ 饮用水~标准*

水质处理 【环】water conditioning

水质处理系统 water treatment system

水质处理用药剂 water conditioning chemicals

水质处理站 water treatment station

水质污染 water contamination [pollution]

水质污染防止[控制]法 water pollution control law

水蛭石 culsageeite, jefferisite

水中波程 water path

水中淬火 water hardening [quench(ing)], quenching in water

水中淬火的 quenched in water (Q$_w$)

水中方体[块]试验 cube in water test
水中方体[块]试验法 cube-in-water method
水中放电成形法 hydrospark forming process
水中稳定的 hydrostable
水中铸造法 【铸】SAC (subaquatic casting) process
水柱 water column, cascade
水柱高度 water head
水柱压力计 water column manometer
水柱铀矿{5UO$_3$·9.5H$_2$O; 3UO$_3$·7H$_2$O} paraschoepite
水状的 hydrous
水状馏分 watery distillate
水准管 level [bubble] tube
水准管轴测量 bubble axis
水准(基)点 bench mark (B.M.), datum mark, point of reference
水准器 balance [water, spirit] level
水准调整 level adjustment
水准效应 level(l)ing effect
水准仪 level (gauge), balance level, level(l)ing instrument, air (bubble) level (气泡式) ◇ Y形[活镜]~ Y-level, wye level, 框架[框形]~ frame level, 气泡[酒精]~ spirit level
水准轴 bubble axis
瞬变过程 transient (process)
瞬变过程分析器 transient analyzer
瞬变热流法 transient heat-flow method
瞬变时间 transient [transition, ringing] time
瞬变特性(曲线) transient characteristic
瞬变温度 transient temperature
瞬变响应 transient response
瞬动开关 【电】snap switch (SS), instanton switch
瞬发中子 【理】prompt neutron
瞬间[瞬时]磁化 flash magnetization
瞬间负载[瞬时负荷] momentary load
瞬间加热 sudden heating

瞬间蠕变 transient creep
瞬流变 transient flow
瞬蠕变曲线 transient-creep curve
瞬时比热 【理】instantaneous specific heat
瞬时变形 temporary set
瞬时测量 instantaneous measurement
瞬时冲击负荷 transient impact load
瞬时冲头能量(高速成形时的) instantaneous punch energy
瞬时磁导率 instantaneous permeability
瞬时磁化力 instantaneous magnetizing force
瞬时[瞬间]点焊 shot welding
瞬时点焊机 shot welder
瞬时电流峰值 momentary current peak value
瞬时短路 instantaneous short-circuit
瞬时断续接电 inching
瞬时断续接通的按钮 inching button
瞬时荷载 transient [passing] loading
瞬时恢复(应变等的) instantaneous recovery
瞬时加热 instantaneous [transient] heating
瞬时接触 momentary contact
瞬时料坯能量(高速成形时的) 【压】instantaneous billet energy
瞬时磨蚀速率 instantaneous erosion rate
瞬时偏差 transient deviation
瞬时屏蔽 flash barrier
瞬时破裂 instantaneous collapse
瞬时汽化干燥器 flash drier
瞬时强度 instantaneous strength
瞬时热电流 thermal short-time current
瞬时热膨胀系数 instantaneous coefficient of thermal expansion
瞬时数据传送率 【计】instantaneous data transfer rate
瞬时速度-瞬间载荷定理 【理】instant speed-instant load principle
瞬时塑性流变 instantaneous plastic flow
瞬时误差[错误] transient error

瞬时系数　instantaneous coefficient
瞬时响应　transient [split-second] response
瞬时应变　【理】instantaneous strain
瞬时应力　instantaneous stress
瞬时载荷　instantaneous [transient] load
瞬时值　instantaneous value
瞬时中子　prompt [instantaneous] neutron
瞬时轴(线)　instantaneous axis
瞬时状态　transient behaviour
瞬态　transient state, transition condition
瞬态操作特性　instant operating characteristic
瞬态电压　transient voltage
瞬态热流　transient flow of heat
瞬态时间常数　transient time constant
瞬态一维模型　one dimensional model in transient regime
顺岸码头　quay
顺磁磁化率[顺磁性系数]　paramagnetic susceptibility
顺磁共振[谐振]　paramagnetic resonance
顺磁合金　paramagnetic alloy
顺磁居里温度　【理】Curie paramagnetic temperature
顺磁式氧气分析器　paramagnetic oxygen (gas) analyzer
顺磁体　paramagnetic body
顺磁型电子分析器　◇贝克曼~*
顺磁性　paramagnetic characteristic [property], paramagnetism
顺磁性材料　paramagnetic material, paramagnet
顺磁性金属　paramagnetic metal
顺磁性居里点　paramagnetic Curie point
顺磁张[松]弛　paramagnetic relaxation
顺磁质　【理】paramagnet
顺次(冲压)成形　progressive forming
顺次的　serial
顺萃　forward extraction
顺料前流萃取级数　forward extraction stage

顺列论　syntax
顺流操作[作业]　concurrent operation
顺流萃取　co-current extraction
顺流干燥　co-current drying
顺流换向器回转炉　◇德布兰科尔~*
顺流混合器　concurrent flow mixer
顺流加热　concurrent heating [firing]
顺流浸出　concurrent [co-current] leaching
顺流倾析洗涤　co-current decantation
顺流式焙烧　【团】concurrent firing
顺流式干燥机　parallel flow dryer
顺流式回转窑　parallel flow rotary kiln
顺流式连续加热炉　parallel-flow heating furnace
顺流式炉　one-way furnace
顺捻(钢丝绳的)　【压】lang's lay
顺捻钢丝绳　(同"同向捻钢丝绳")
顺砌[砖]　【建】stretcher
顺(砌)砖层　【建】stretching course
顺时针(方向)旋转　clockwise rotation
顺时针方向　clockwise (ckw), right-handwise
顺式立构聚合物　【化】isotactic polymer
顺手焊接法　forehand technique
顺铣　【铁】climb milling [cutting]
顺行(炉况)　【铁】smooth operation, smoothworking, normal practice ◇不~ aberration, 高炉~*, 炉况[炉子]~*
顺序　sequence, rank, order
顺序变化的　gradual
顺序操作　sequential operation
顺序淬火　progressive hardening [quenching]
顺序点弧装置(多点焊用)　pressure-sequencing device
顺序感应加热淬火　progressive induction hardening
顺序号　order number (Ord. No.), running number
顺序寄存器　【计】sequence register
顺序渐进　progressive procession

顺序浸蚀	sequence etching
顺序控制	sequential [sequence] control
顺序取样	sequential (multiple) sampling
顺序旋转火焰加热淬火	progressive spinning flame hardening
顺序蒸馏	trap-to-trap distillation
顺轧端	【压】down-mill end
说明	explanation, illustration (illus.), show, instruction (instn.), specification, clarification, comment, interpretation
说明书	instruction (book), specification (spec.), manual, description leaf, directions ◇ 运行~【计】run book
说明性操作	【计】declarative operation
说明语句	【计】declarative statement
斯蒂尔焦炉	Carl Still coke oven
斯蒂尔美特烧结机械零件	Steelmet
斯蒂尔耐蚀铜锡合金	Steel metal
斯蒂费尔穿孔轧制法	Stiefel roll process
斯蒂费尔-曼内斯曼穿孔机	Stiefel-Mannesmann piercer
斯蒂费尔盘式穿孔法	Stiefel disc piercing process
斯蒂费尔盘式穿孔机	Stiefel disc piercer
斯蒂费尔式自动轧管机	Stiefel mill
斯蒂费尔锥辊式穿孔机	Stiefel-cone piercer
斯蒂费尔自动轧管法	Stiefel process
斯蒂芬-波尔茨曼定律	【理】Stefan-Boltzmann's law
斯蒂芬森锡铜锌铁合金（31Sn, 19Cu, 19Zn, 31Fe）	Stephenson's alloy
斯蒂瓦特铸造铝合金	Stewart alloy
斯凯夫热挤压法	Scaife process
斯科特(炼汞)瓦片炉	Scott furnace
斯科特容量计（测量粉末散装密度）	Scott volumeter
斯科特西直接冶炼法（黄铁矿的）	Scortecci process
斯克雷龙铝(基)合金（12Zn, 3Cu, 0.1Li, 0.6Mn, 0.5Si, 0.4Fe, 余量 Al）	Scleron
斯克雷坦铝青铜（90—94Cu, 5—9Al, 1.5Mg, 0.5P）	Scretan
斯库菲尔德-格拉斯速浸高温计	Schofield-Grace immersion pyrometer
斯库普粉末喷镀金属法	Schoop process
斯里兰卡天然石墨	Ceylon graphite
斯利德克斯镍银合金	Slidex alloy
斯利卡铅锡软焊料（66Sn, 余量 Pb）	Slicker Solder
斯利克旋转模锻轧机	Slick mill
斯密特低阻抗汞断流器	Schmitt's low-resistance cut-off
斯莫里铁水氢化物脱硫法	Smalley process
斯内兹柯式风动拔棒机	Snezhko air-operated puller
斯诺克峰	【金】Snoek peak
斯诺克效应	【金】Snoek effect
斯佩克粉末比表面测定仪	Spekker absorptiometer
斯佩里铅基轴承合金（35Sn, 15Sb, 余量 Pb）	Sperry's metal
斯皮德克斯镍银[银银, 铜镍锌合金]（5—33Ni, 50—70Cu, 13—35Zn）	Spedex
斯皮雷克型粉汞矿焙烧炉	Spirek furnace
斯氏体（铁磷共晶体）	phosphide eutectic, steadite
斯塔拉尼姆耐蚀铝镁合金（7Mg, 0.5Sb, 余量 Al）	Stalanium
斯塔纳姆高锡重载轴承合金（89Sn, 7.5Sb, 3.5Cu）	Stannum
斯塔桑诺直接还原法	Stassono direct reduction process
斯泰布赖特耐蚀可锻镍铬钢	Staybrite
斯太尔摩盘条轧制散卷[松卷]冷却法	Stelmor process
斯太尔摩(散卷)冷却	Stel(co)mor(gan) cooling
斯太尔摩四线散卷冷却作业线	4 strand Stermore line
斯坦尼欧尔高锡耐蚀合金（0.33—1Cu, 0.7—2.4Pb, 少量 Fe 及/或 Ni, 余量 Sn）	Stanniol

斯坦托尔锰钢（0.09C,1.6Mn,0.25Si） Stentor steel

斯特德脆性（低碳钢的） Stead's brittleness

斯特德浸蚀剂（铁基合金和铸钢用） Stead's reagent

斯特克尔冷轧机 Steckel cold mill

斯特克尔轧机（热轧带材用） Steckel mill

斯特拉杰克－尤地回转窑－电炉组合直接还原法 【铁】Strategic-Udy process

斯特拉克斯超高强度钢 Strux

斯特莱特（硬质）合金 （同"钴铬钨合金"）

斯特劳斯浸蚀剂（奥氏体钢和不锈钢用）【金】Strauss reagent

斯特雷福特燃气脱硫法 【焦】Stretford process

斯特里特 4 号铅锑轴承合金（10－15Sb,余量 Pb） Street's No.4 alloy

斯特利特耐蚀合金（54.5Cu,27Ni,16.5Zn,1.7Fe + Sn + Pb,0.2Mn） Sterlite

斯特林电弧炉炼锌法 Sterling process

斯特林高强度黄铜（66.2Cu,33.2Zn,0.6Fe,0.02Pb） Stirling metal

斯特林货币金（合金）（68.5Cu,17.88Ni,0.5－0.75Fe） Sterling gold

斯特林炼锌电弧炉 Sterling furnace

斯特林铝合金焊料（15Zn,11Al,8Pb,2.5Cu,1.2Sb,62.3Sn） Sterling's aluminium solder

斯特林铅黄铜（66Cu,33Zn,余量 Pb） Sterling brass

斯特林铜镍锌合金（68.5Cu,17.9Ni,12.8Zn,0.8Pb） Sterlin

斯特林（英币）银（92.5Ag,余量 Cu） Sterling silver

斯特罗含铁锰六O黄铜（60Cu,38.12Zn,1.5Fe,余量 Mn） Sterro metal

斯特耶铝基压铸合金（89Al,11Cu,约 0.1Ti） Stay alloy

斯通离心铸造用青铜（11－12Sn,0－1.5Zn,0.1－0.3P,余量 Cu） Stone's bronze

斯图迪钴铬钨合金（焊条） Stoody

斯图塔尔形变铝合金（97.7Al,1Mg,1.3Mn） Studal

斯托迪特钨钼硬质合金钢 Stoadite

斯托克斯定律 Stokes' law

斯托克斯公式（自由沉降公式） Stokes formula

斯托克斯凸轮式压机 Stokes press

斯托克斯压片机 Stokes tablet machine

斯托克斯压制机 Stokes briquetting press

斯托克斯直径 Stokes diameter

斯托克斯肘杆压片机 Stokes toggle-type tablet machine

斯托拉回转转炉直接还原法 Stora process

斯威塔洛伊耐蚀高镍合金钢 Sweetalloy（Sweetalloy 20：36Ni,18Cr,0.5Mn,0.3C,余量 Fe）

斯威特兰叶式压滤机 Sweetland filter [press]

撕裂 tear,tearing(-out),splitting fracture

撕裂断口 tear fracture

撕裂抗力 resistance to tearing-off

撕裂扩展 tear propagation

撕裂强度 tear(ing)[peel]strength,resistance to tearing-off

撕裂强度－屈服强度比 tear-strength/yield ratio

撕裂试验 tear test ◇ 落锤～*

撕裂型应力强度因子 tearing mode stress intensity factor

私人投资 private investment

私营公司 private corporation

司机室 driver's cage,operator cabin,(operators) cab

司机室控制 cab control

司米洛司基夹杂检测仪 Smialowski apparatus

丝 fiber,fibre,ply（几股钢丝）◇ 杜美

丝包的　silk-covered
丝包线　silk-covered wire
丝堵　pipe plug,【机】stopper plug
丝杆（车床的）　lead-screw drive
丝杠　threaded spindle, lead [guide] screw
丝杠导槽　lead-screw guide
丝杠轴　threaded spindle
丝光[状]断口　silky fracture
丝极　filament ◇ U 字形～*
丝极长度　filament length
丝极电积物（碘化物热离解法的）　filament deposit
丝极电源（碘化物法的）　filament supply
丝极电渣焊　electroslag welding with wire electrode
丝极温度　filament temperature
丝极引线　filament lead
丝扣（同"螺纹"）
丝扣保护环　thread protector
丝硫细菌属　thiothrix
丝煤[炭]　fusain, fusite
丝网（金属丝网）　wire mesh
丝网填料　gauze packing
丝质体　fusinite
丝状腐蚀　filiform [channel(l)ing] corrosion
丝状晶体　filament crystal
丝状体　filament
丝锥　【机】(screw)tap
锶硅钛铈矿　strontio-chevkinite
锶磷灰石{(Ca,Sr)$_4$[Ca(OH,F)][(P,As)O$_4$]$_3$}　fermorite
锶铈磷灰石　belovite
锶添加合金　strontium addition
锶铁钛矿　crichtonite
锶铁氧体　strontian ferrite
死焙烧　【色】dead burning, ultimate roasting
死点　dead center [centre], dead point
死端　dead end
死风口　blind tuyere

死灰　perish, dying embers
死角（炉内的）　dead volume
死金属区（挤压时的）　dead-metal (zone)
死[用过的]浸渍酸（毛面酸洗的）　dead dipping acid
死扣（钢丝绳的）　coil buckling, kink
死连接　dead joint
死料　dead mass
死料柱　【铁】pillaring
死区　blind spot [area], dead zone [band, space, spot], shadow (region), deadmetal (zone)（挤压的）, dead volume（炉内的）,【色】channels（炼铅炉内的）
死区调节器　dead zone regulator
死烧　dead burning [roast(ing)], sweet roast(ing)
死烧白云石　【耐】dead burned dolomite, magnefer
死烧白云石水泥　cement of dead-burned dolomite
死烧材料　fully fired material
死烧精矿[死焙烧矿]　dead-roasted concentrate
死烧镁砂[菱镁矿]　dead burnt magnesite
死烧石灰　dead burnt lime
死烧氧化镁　dead burned magnesia
死酸（酸洗中的）　killing pickle
死锁　【计】deadlock
死铁　【铁】dead man, ladle heel ◇ 高炉～bear, 炉底～old-horse
死铁层　salamander, fixed bed material（炉底材料）
死铁穿透（砌体内的）　salamander penetration
死停法　【化】dead-stop method
死弯（钢丝绳的）　dog leg
死亡率　death [fatality] rate
死亡事故　fatal accident
死相　【冶】dead phase
死循环　【计】endless loop
四氨络合物[四胺]　tetramine
四瓣式戽斗挖土机　orange-peel excavator

四边形　quad(rangle), tetragon ◇ 小～构件 quarrel
四变量[四度]平衡　quadrivariant equilibrium
四层电接触器材　four layer contact material
四(层)叠板(热叠轧的)　【压】fours
四成分电解质　(同"四元电解质")
四重式多辊矫直机　four high roller leveller
四重[次]轴　four fold axis
四次对称轴　tetrad axis, four fold axis of symmetry
四次方程　quartic equation
四次破碎　quaternary crushing
四次筛分　quaternary screening
四氮化三硅{Si_3N_4}　silicon nitride
四氮化三钍　(同"氮化钍")
四氮化三铀{U_3N_4}　uranium nitride
四等分　quartering, quadrate
四地址(制)　【计】quadruple [four] address
四碘化锆{ZrI_4}　zirconium tetraiodide
四碘化铪{HfI_4}　hafnium tetraiodide
四碘化钨{WI_4}　tungsten tetraiodide
四碘化物　tetraiodide
四碘化锗{GeI_4}　germanium tetraiodide
四点加载　four point loading
四点弯曲(法)　four point bending
四电场电除尘器　four field precipitator
四度简并态　four fold degenerate state
四端电路　quadripole
四端网络　four terminal network, quadripole ◇ 桥式～ X-quadripole
四端网络组成的线路　circuit network
四垛式炉台　four pedestal [stack] base
四方点阵[晶格]　tetragonal lattice
四方对称　tetragonal symmetry
四方畸变　tetragonal distortion
四方晶胞　tetragonal cell
四方晶系　tetragonal (system)
四方晶轴　tetragonal axis

四方硫砷铜矿　luzonite
"四方"双取向硅钢薄板　Four-square
四方钛铅矿　macedonite
四方铁钨矿{$FeWO_4$}　reinite
四方系晶体　tetragonal crystal, crystal of tetragonal symmetry
四方纤铁矿　akaganeite
四方相　tetragonal phase
四方形结构　tetragonal structure
四方性　【金】tetragonality
四分铲[锹]　【选】quartering shovel
四分(取样)法　quater dividing method, quartering (Qr), quartation, inquartation ◇ 堆锥～ cone quartering, 锥形～ coning and quartering
四分面体类　tetartohedral class
四分式下喷焦炉　4-divided underjet oven
四分试样　quarter sample
四分位直径　【数】quartile diameter
"四分一"铜银合金(日本产; 51—86Cu, 0.08—0.12Au, 余量 Ag)　shibu-ich
四分仪　quadrant
四分之三标准砖　three-quarter brick
四分之三硅酸渣(炼铅的)　three-quarter slag
四分之三硬(美国合金材料处理记号)　three-quarter hard
四分之三硬退火　three-quarter hard annealing
四分之三硬线材(铝材)　three-quarter-hard wire
四分之一　quarter (Qt, qt, qtr, quar.), one-fourth, one-quarter
四分之一(波长晶)片　quarter wave plate
四分之一硅酸渣(炼铅的)　(siliceous) quarter slag
四分之一硬(美国合金材料处理记号)　quarter hard
四分之一硬退火　quarter-hard annealing
四分之一最高硬度冷轧薄(钢)板　quarter hard temper (sheet)
四分轴瓦　【机】four part bearing shell

四分砖 quarter bat
四氟化锆挥发 sublimation of zirconium tetrafluoride
四氟化硅{SiF$_4$} silicon tetrafluoride
四氟化铪{HfF$_4$} hafnium fluoride
四氟化铈{CeF$_4$} ceric fluoride
四氟化碳[四氟(代)甲烷]{CF$_4$} carbon tetrafluoride, tetrafluoromethane
四氟化钍{ThF$_4$} thorium tetrafluoride [fluoride] ◇钙还原~法*
四氟化物 tetrafluoride
四氟化铀{UF$_4$} green salt, uranium tetrafluoride, uranous fluoride ◇工业品位~*,流态化床~半工业试验设备*
四氟化铀氧化制六氟化铀法 Fluorox process
四氟化铀与镁的混合物 green salt plus magnesium blend
四氟氧化钨{WOF$_4$} tungsten oxyfluoride
四辊精轧机 four high finishing mill
四辊可逆式初轧机 4-high reversing roughing mill
四辊可逆式带材冷轧机 four high reversing cold strip mill
四辊可逆式机座 four high reversing stand
四辊可逆式冷轧机 four high reversing cold mill
四辊可逆式炉卷轧机 （同"斯特克尔轧机"）
四辊拉坯机座【连铸】four roll set
四辊可逆式冷轧机 four high reversing cold mill
四辊冷轧机 four high cold mill ◇工作辊横移式~*,西门斯小~Simons mill
四辊连续式带材热轧机 four high continuous hot strip mill
四辊连续式冷轧机 four high tandem cold mill
四辊式粗轧机座 four high rougher (stand)
四辊式机座【压】four high stand, four high mill (stand)
四辊式烧结矿破碎机 quadroll sinter crusher
四辊(式)轧机 four high (rolling) mill, quarto mill, four high roll ◇可逆式~*,支承辊传动的~*
四辊(式)轧机组 quarto train
四辊式装置 four high set up
四辊万能轧制 4-high universal rolling
四辊轧机轧制厚板 quarto plate
四辊中板可逆轧机 four high reversal plate mill
四环大角差布料【铁】4-ring distributing burden with large angle-difference
四机座连续式带材冷轧机 four stand tandem cold strip mill
四基聚合物 quadripolgrmer
四机座连续式轧机 four stand tandem mill
四极 quadripole, quadrupole, four poles
四极管 tetrode, quadrode, dynatron ◇电子注[束射]~beam tetrode
四极矩 quadrupole moment
四极相互作用 quadrupole interaction
四极质谱仪 quadrupole mass spectrometer
四极子 quadrupole
四级变速齿轮 four stages change over gears
四级反应 fourth order reaction
四级混合沉降器 four stage mixer settler
四级洗提 four stage stripping
四级蒸汽喷射器系统 four stage steam ejector system
四甲苯{C$_{10}$H$_{14}$} tetramethyl-benzene
四甲基苯酚{C$_{10}$H$_{14}$O} tetramethylphenol
四价 tetravalence, tetravalency, quadrivalence, quadrivalency
四甲基吡啶{C$_9$H$_{13}$N} tetramethylpyridine
四价锕系元素 tetravalent actinide
四价金属 quadrivalent metal

四价卤化物	tetravalent halide
四价镍	tetravalent nickel
四价铈	ceric cerium
四价铈化合物	ceric compound
四价钛的	titanic
四价锡化合物	stannic compound
四价氧化合物	oxonium compound
四价元素	quadrivalent [tetravalent] element
四价锗化合物	germanic compound
四价正离子	tetrapositive ion
四碱的	quadribasic
四角形	（同"四边形"）
四立柱式	【铁】four column pillars
四联微球菌	micrococcus tetragenus
四列圆锥滚柱轴承	four row tapered roller bearing
四硫化钼{MoS$_2$[S$_2$]}	molybdenum tetrasulphide
四硫化物	tetrasulphide
四流连铸机	four strand continuous casting machine
四六黄铜	Muntz brass [metal]
四卤化物	tetrahalide
四氯硅烷	tetrachloro-silicane
四氯化苯	benzene tetrachloride(BTC)
四氯化二铊{TlCl·TlCl$_3$}	thallosic chloride
四氯化锆{ZrCl$_4$}	zirconium tetrachloride
四氯化锆-磷酰氯络合物	zirconium tetrachloride phosphorus oxychloride complex
四氯化锆还原	reduction of zirconium tetrachloride
四氯化锆蒸气	zirconium tetrachloride vapour
四氯化硅{SiCl$_4$}	silicon tetrachloride
四氯化硅氢还原法	hydrogen reduction of silicon tetrachloride
四氯化硅锌还原法	zinc reduction of silicon tetrachloride
四氯化铪晶体	hafnium tetrachloride crystal
四氯化铪蒸气	hafnium tetrachloride vapour
四氯化铼{ReCl$_4$}	rhenium tetrachloride
四氯化钼{MoCl$_4$}	molybdenum tetrachloride
四氯化铌{NbCl$_4$}	niobium tetrachloride
四氯化钛{TiCl$_4$}	titanium tetrachloride
四氯化钛运送泵	titanium tetrachloride pump
四氯化碳{CCl$_4$}	carbon tetrachloride (CTC) ◇ 阿索丁~ asordin
四氯化钍{ThCl$_4$}	thorium tetrachloride
四氯化钍生产槽	thorium tetrachloride production cell
四氯化钨{WCl$_4$}	tungsten tetrachloride
四氯化物	tetrachloride ◇ 固态~ solid tetrachloride; 吸湿性~
四氯化物净化	tetrachloride purification
四氯化物料罐	tetrachloride (charge) can
四氯化物蒸气	tetrachloride vapour
四氯化物装料	tetrachloride charge
四氯化铀{UCl$_4$}	uranous chloride, uranium tetrachloride
四氯化锗{GeCl$_4$}	germanium tetrachloride, germanic chloride
四氯乙烯{Cl$_2$C:CCl$_2$}	tetrachloroethylene
四醚	tetraether
四面顶锤	【粉】tetrahedral anvil
四面立方点阵[晶格]	tetrahedral cubic lattice
四面体	tetrahedron, tetrahedroid
四面体间隙	tetrahedral interstice
四面体结构	tetrahedral structure
四面体离子	tetrahedral ion
四面体座[位置]	tetrahedral site
四配价的	quadricovalent
四硼酸钠{Na$_2$B$_4$O$_7$}	sodium borate, borax glass
四偏心式振动机构	vibratory mechanism with 4 eccentric axies
四片铆接式料钟漏斗	four piece hopper

四片组合式结晶器 【连铸】four plate mould
四氢化苯{C_6H_{10}} tetrahydrobenzene
四氢化萘 tetrahydronaphthalene, tetrahydronaphthaline, tetralin
四氢铝酸盐 tetrahydro-aluminate
四氢锑基 stibonium
四氢氧化钨{$W(OH)_4$} tungsten tetrahydroxide
四氢氧化物 tetrahydroxide
四球式润滑油润滑性(能)评定机 four ball machine
四塞棒中间包 【钢】four stoppered tundish
四扇形块式卷筒 four section mandrel, four segment type mandrel
四舍五入 【数】round(-off)
四栓孔鱼尾板 4 bolt splice bar
四水合酒石酸钾钠{$KNaC_4H_4O_6 \cdot 4H_2O$} Rochelle salt
四水合硝酸钍{$Th(NO_3)_4 \cdot 4H_2O$} thorium nitrate tetrahydrate
四水镁矾 starkeyite
四水锰矾 ilesite
四水锌矾 boyleite
四羰基钴 cobalt tetracarbonyl
四羰基镍{$Ni(CO)_4$} nickel tetracarbonyl
四通阀 four way valve, four port connection valve
四通管 four way pipe, crossbar
四通旋塞[开关] four way cock
四位字节 【计】nibble, four bits
四线链式运输机 four strand chain conveyer
四线坯料分配器 four line billet switch
四线切分轧制 four-time(s) slit rolling
四线上甩套圆盘 【压】four way loop open top trough
四线式轧机(线材、盘条的) four strand mill
四线推出移送机 four run pull off transfer
四线制[线路] 【电】four wire system
四相(共存)点 quadruple [quadriple] point
四相平衡 quaternary equilibrium ◇第四类～*
四相(平衡)曲线 quadruple curve
四硝基苯胺(起爆用) tetranitroaniline (TNA)
四斜柱高炉钢结构 four poster structure
四芯电缆[(导)线] quad, quadded cable
四心桃尖拱 four centered arch ◇内外～【建】ogee arch
四溴化锆 zirconium tetrabromide
四溴化钼{$MoBr_4$} molybdenum tetrabromide
四溴化钛 titanium tetrabromide
四溴化物 tetrabromide
四溴甲烷 tetrabromomethane
四溴乙烷 tetrabromoethane (T.B.E.)
四溴乙烷选矿法 T.B.E. (tetrabromoethane) process
四氧化二铌{Nb_2O_4} niobium [columbium] tetroxide
四氧化二铷{Rb_2O_4} rubidium peroxide
四氧化二铯{Cs_2O_4} cesium peroxide
四氧化三镍{$NiO \cdot Ni_2O_3$} nickelous-nickelic oxide
四氧化三铅 lead orthoplumbate, lead tetroxide, red lead
四氧化三铊{$Tl_2O \cdot Tl_2O_3$} thallosic oxide
四氧化三铁{Fe_3O_4} ferroferric [ferrosoferric, ferriferrous] oxide, magnetic [black] iron oxide, black of iron
四氧化铯{$Cs_2[O_4]$} cesium tetroxide
四氧化物 quadroxide, tetroxide
四氧化铀{$UO_4, UO_2[O_2]$} uranium peroxide [tetroxide]
四摇臂式(分批)酸洗机 【压】four arm pickling machine, four arm (batch) pickler
四叶式交叉 【运】quarterfoil [cover-leaf] crossing
四乙基硅酸盐 tetraethylsilicate

四乙基金属	tetraethide
四乙(基)铅 $\{Pb(C_2H_5)_4\}$	lead tetraethyl, tetraethyl lead
四乙锗 $\{Ge(C_2H_5)_4\}$	germanium tetraethyl
四异丙醇盐	tetraisopropoxide
四元电解质	quaternary electrolyte, four component electrolyte
四元共晶合金(13.1Sn,49.5Bi,27.3Pb,10.1Cd;熔点70℃)	quarternary eutectic alloy
四元过量自由能	quaternary excess free-energy
四元合金	qua(r)ternary alloy, four component [part] alloy ◇阿戈-弗洛~*
四元(合金)[四组分]钢	qua(r)ternary steel
四元平衡图	quarternary equilibrium diagram
四元取代的	tetrasubstituted
四元系	quarternary system
四元相图	【金】quaternary diagram
四原子的	tetraatomic
四轧辊式矫直机	four high roller leveller
四张迭轧(薄板的)	roll fours
四锗氧烷	tetragermoxane
四周包焊	contour welding
四周打壳	outside crust breaking
四周气升搅拌器	edge-lift agitator
四轴式回转剪切机	4 arbor type rotary shears
四柱式水压机	four post hydraulic press
四柱悬挂式高炉	four post blast furnace
四爪锚	grapnel
伺服槽	service tank
伺服测量箱	servo measuring box
伺服电动机	servo(motor), actuating [pilot, pony, slave] motor ◇液压~ pencil motor
伺服电路	servo circuit
伺服阀	servo-valve, pilot valve
伺服罐	service tank
伺服机	servo
伺服机构	servo-gear, servomechanism, servounit
伺服控制	servo(-actuated) control
伺服控制机构	servo-control mechanism
伺服模拟计算机	servo-analog computer
伺服升降机	servolifter
伺服拖动(装置)	servo drive
伺服系统	servosystem
伺服系统动力传动装置	servodyne
似导体	quasi-conductor
似钢的	steely
似胶(状)的	gel-like
似金属相	metalloid phase
似晶石 $\{Be_2SiO_4\}$	phenacite
似晶质	crystalloid
似矿物	mineralloid, gel mineral
似铅的	leady
似石英的	quartzy
似锑的	antimonylike
似铜的	coppery, cupreous
似锌的	zincky, zincous
似液体	quasi-liquid
似银的	silvery
似渣	slaggy
似直线应力图	quasi-rectilinear stress diagram
松棒	reeling
松弛	relaxation, loosening, slack ◇预屈服[屈服限以下]~*
松弛度	slackness, looseness
松弛频率	relaxation frequency
松弛时间	relaxation time
松弛试样	【压】relaxation test piece
松弛衰减[内耗]	relaxation damping
松弛速率	relaxation rate
松弛损失	relaxation loss
松弛应力	relaxed stress
松弛振荡	【理】relaxation oscillations
松弛值	relaxation value
松村氏硬度计	Matsumura's hardness tester

松叠轧制	loose pack rolling
松动(样模)	【铸】rap
松动型芯	core relieving
松粉	【粉】loose powder
松节油	turpentine
松结合	weak binding
松紧衡重块	stretching weight
松紧调整器	slack adjuster
松卷	open coil, paying-off
松卷机	coil opening machine, delivery reel
松卷台	【压】expanded coil table
松卷退火	open coil annealing
松卷退火法(带材的)	open coil annealing process
松卷退火炉	open coil annealing furnace
松卷退火装置	open coil annealing plant
松卷装置	【压】pay-off
松开	loosening, unclamping, unclasping
松开的带卷	loose [expanded, opened] coil
松框式芯盒	【铸】collapsible core box
松模	【铸】rapping
松模杆	【铸】rapping bar [iron]
松模工具	rapper
松模装置	【铸】rapping device
松木板衬里	pine plate lining
松耦合[联轴节]	loose coupling
松配合	loose fit
松散材料	discrete material
松散床[层]	loose [expanded] bed
松散粉粒	fluffy particle
松散粉末烧结	loose powder sintering
松散钢丝绳	non-preformed wire rope
松散金属切屑	hand shovel turnings
松散料	loose material, loose-packed charge
松散流(态)化床	particulate fluidized bed ◇ 骚动~*
松散氯化物	fluffy [light] chloride
松散密度	aerated density, raw density (型砂的)
松散水泥	loose cement
松散体积	loose volume
松散物料	bulk material
松散型砂	【铸】aeration of moulding sand
松散性	looseness, fluffiness, friability
松散锈层	loose rust
松砂	loose sand, sand cutting, aeration of moulding sand
松砂机	sand cutter [aerator], sand-aerating apparatus, 【铸】aerator, desintegrator, disintegrator, fluffer ◇ 带式~*
松烧结块	soft sinter
松碎器	smasher
松体积	bulk (bk)
松土机	scarifier, fluffer
松(芯)棒机	mandrel bar loosening mill
松型(防压裂)	【铸】easing
松枝印痕(带钢的)	pine-tree marking
松酯胶	ester gum
松脂锡石	rosin tin
松装比重	loose specific weight
松装粉末	【粉】loosely packed powder
松装金属粉末熔焊法	bulk weld process
松装密度	apparent [bulk, loose] density ◇ 粉末~*
松装密度值	bulking value
松装烧结	loose sintering
松装体积	bulk [apparent] volume
松装重量	【粉】loading weight
送电	electric [power] transmission
送锭车	ingot buggy [bogie, chariot], transfer buggy [bogie]
送锭车锭座	ingot [chair, pot], bucket
送锭车翻斗	ingot pot
送风	(air) blowing-in, air blast (supply), air-flow, blow on, blow (ing), air input [charge], 【铁】on-blast (正在送风) ◇ 开始~*
送风吹炼	converting with air
送风端(回转炉的)	lancing end
送风管	air supply duct, blower [wind] tube, 【铁】blast supply ◇ 短铸铁~【铁】penstock
送风管道	delivery pipeline
送风机	blower, air feeder ◇ 离心~fan

blower,螺旋浆式~propeller-fan,引吸式~induced blower,助燃~combustion air fan
送风阶段 【铁】scavenging period
送风量 air input
送风期 on-blast（热风炉）,blast period（热风炉）,blowing [scavenging] period, on air
送风强度 blast intensity
送风设备 blowing equipment
送风时率 stack time efficiency
送风调节 forced-draft control
送风系统 【铁】blast system
送话器 transmitter,microphone
送进 feed(-in)
送进辊 feed roll(er),strip-feeding device
送进机构 feeding apparatus
送进机座 push mill
送进控制杆 feed control lever
送进坯 【压】feed
送进[送料]压力 【压】forward pressure
送进运动 feed motion
送卷装置 【压】coil handling apparatus
送卡箱 【计】(card) input magazine
送冷风 cold air blast,cold-blast inlet
送料 feeding
送料板 【化】feed plate
送料泵 feeding pump
送料槽 feed tank
送料管 conveying pipe
送料机 feeder,feeding device ◇盘式~*
送料机构 feed mechanism,pushing device
送料机嘴 feeder nose
送料孔型 swabbing pass
送料斜槽 feeder spout
送料爪（拖运机的） ducking [disappearing] dogs
送料装置 feeding apparatus [equipment]
送气 air-feed,air-in
送气[水]阀 induction valve
送气管 air pipe,induction line

送气期 change on gas
送氢泵 hydrogen blower
送水管 induction pipe
送丝 wire feed (WF)
送丝机 【焊】electrode feeding machine
送丝速度 【焊】WF (wire feed) speed
送丝装置 wire-drive unit
送酸器 acid feeder
送芯小车 【铸】core truck
送液管 induction pipe [line]
宋尼申电焊钢管法 Soennichsen process
搜索 search,scanning,hunting
苏必尔湖型铁矿石 Lake Superior type iron ore
苏长石 norite
苏打 （同"碳酸钠"）◇大~（同"硫代硫酸钠"）,轻~light ash,天然结晶~*,小~（同"碳酸氢钠"）
苏打粉 soda-ash,calcined soda ◇苛性~*
苏打粉焙烧炉 ash roaster
苏打粉除硫法 【铁】soda-ash process
苏打(粉)处理 soda-ash treatment
苏打锍[冰铜] soda matte
苏打溶液 soda solution
苏打石灰烧结法 soda lime-sinter process
苏打渣 soda slag
苏勒锌白铜（31.5Ni,25.5Zn,40.4Cu,2.6Pb） Suhler-white copper
苏帕门杜尔软磁合金（49Co,2V,余量Fe） Supermendur
苏维内尔单面或双面覆铜钢板 Su Veneer
苏西尼铝锰铜合金(系)（1—8Mn,1.5—4.5Cu,0.5—1.5Zn,余量Al） Susini
苏珀洛伊管装焊料合金（超硬表面层堆焊用；30Cr,8Co,8Mo,5W,0.2C,0.05B,余量Fe） Superloy
苏珀萨姆高温合金 supertherm
苏珀斯通高强度耐蚀铝青铜 Superston (Superston-40：11—14Mn,7—9Al,2—4Fe,1.5—5Ni,余量Cu)

苏珀希特钼合金电阻丝[钼基粉末电阻合金] Superheat
苏西尼铝合金 susini
素瓷（搪瓷涂料） bisque
素混凝土 plain concrete
素烧 biscuiting, bisque firing
素烧的 unglazed
素烧黏土填料 【耐】keramzite
素土夯实 packed soil
素质钢（不加废钢炼出） virgin steel
速爆炸药 high explosive
速比 speed [velocity] ratio
速动开关 quick-action switch, snap switch
速冻(的) quick freezing (Q.F., qf)
速度 velocity, speed
速度边界层 velocity boundary layer
速度不均匀(性) velocity discontinuity, wow and flutter
速度层 velocity layer
速度场 velocity field ◇ 动力学允许的～
速度[率]常数 velocity [rate] constant
速度范围 speed range, velocity interval
速度过程 【化】rate process
速度极限控制器 speed limit controller (SLC)
速度计 speedometer, speed meter [gauge], velocimeter, velocity meter ◇ 激光多普勒～
速度监视器 speed monitor
速度控制 speed control, rate-controlling
速度敏感性（变形的）【压】velocity sensitivity
速度曲线 speed [velocity, rate] curve
速度梯度 velocity gradient
速度调节器 speed regulator [adjuster]
速度调整 speed adjustment
速度系数[损耗率] coefficient of velocity
速度限制 rate limitation
速度限制阶段（反应的） rate-determining step
速度效应 speed effect

速度形成压力 velocity pressure
速度修正温度 velocity-modified temperature
速度遥控装置 remote speed control
速度因数 velocity factor
速度增长[增加速度] speed gain
速度锥 speed cone
速度自动调节器 automatic speed regulator (ASR)
速断 quick-break, quick release
速浸(式)高温计 quick-immersion pyrometer ◇ 斯库菲尔德-格拉斯～
速浸式热电偶 quick-immersion thermocouple
速率 rate, speed, velocity
速率定律 rate law
速率范围 range of speed
速率计 rate meter, speedometer, speed counter
速率控制 rate-control(ling)
速率控制法[控制过程] rate controlling process
速率控制因素（反应的） rate-controlling factor
速率曲线 rate curve
速率现象 rate phenomena
速率限制器 rate limiter, speed limiting device
速率(信号)发生器 rate generator
速率主控法[过程] rate determining process
速滤剂 accelerator
速凝处理 rapid solidification
速凝(的) quick freezing, rapid hardening
速凝粉末 rapidly solidified powder
速凝先凝物 rapid solidified precursor
速燃(的) quick burning [firing]
速热 rapid heating
速矢端线[速端曲线]【数】hodograph
速示（仪表指针的） dead-beat
速示仪表 dead beat instrument
速释 quick release

速位差[速度头] velocity head
速止反应 short-stopped reaction
塑变 flow
塑变组织 flow structure
塑-脆转折临界温度 Tce critical temperature for the ductile/brittle transition
塑度计 plastometer, plastigraph ◇ 摆式锤～pendulum plastometer
塑化剂 plastifier, plasticizing [workability] agent
塑化聚氯乙烯 plasticized polyvinyl chloride
塑解剂 peptizer
塑料 plastics, plastic material, plastomer ◇ 喷镀金属[渗金属]的～ metallized plastics, 塞里～(次乙酰塑料) Celite
塑料薄膜复型 tape replica
塑料层流板(带钢冷却用) plastic lamella
塑料覆层带材 plastic-coated strip
塑料覆面辊 plastic-covered roller
塑料覆面模 plastic-faced die
塑料复型 【金】plastic(s) replica
塑料管 plastic pipe [tube]
塑料管道 plastic conduit
塑料合金(两种以上合成树脂的聚合物) plastics alloy
塑料挤压机 plastic extruder
塑料-金属粉末制品 plastics-metal powder product
塑料金属喷镀 plastic plating
塑料模 plastic die
塑料黏结剂 plastic binder
塑料溶胶 plastisol
塑料容器 plastic container
塑料涂层钢板 plastic-coated steel sheet
塑料网 plastic wire mesh
塑料印相检验法 faxfilm process
塑料用工具钢 tool steel for plastics
塑料造型 plastic moulding
塑料制品 plastic product
塑料轴承 plastic bearing
塑料轴瓦 【机】plastic bearing shell

塑料铸型 plastic mould
塑流前缘 plastic front
塑像用青铜(75—94Cu, 3—10Sn, 1—6Pb, 1—19Zn, <0.3P, <0.7Ni) statuary bronze
塑型 moulding ◇ 分步～ fractional moulding
塑型模 moulding die
塑性 plasticity, ductility, plastic property [behaviour] ◇ 微观～microplasticity, 无～断裂[破坏] non-ductile fracture
塑性变形 plastic deformation [flow, strain], offset strain ◇ 基克-定律 Kick's law, 临界～*, 三维～模型*
塑性(变形)范围 plastic range [region], range of plasticity
塑性变形过程磁化曲线 magnetization curve under plastic deformation
塑性变形机理 plastic flow mechanism
塑性变形记录仪[范性变形图描记器] plastograph
塑性变形抗力 【压】plastic strength
塑性变形率 index of plastic deformation
塑性变形区 zone of plastic deformation, plastically deforming area
塑性变形性 plastic deformability
塑性变形阻力 plastic resistance
塑性变形组织 flow structure
塑性波 【压】plastic wave
塑性不稳定性 plastic instability
塑性材料 plastic material
塑性测定法 plastometry
塑性层 【焦】plastic zone
塑性成型 plastic making
塑性断裂[断口] plastic fracture ◇ 晶界～*
塑性粉末 plastic powder
塑性粉末挤压 plasticized-powder extrusion
塑性高铅轴承青铜(63—67Cu, 26—30Pb, 5Sn, 0—1Ni, 0—1Zn) plastic bronze
塑性高锡青铜轴承合金 plastic metal

bearing alloy
塑性功 plastic work done
塑性固体 plastic solid
塑性混凝土 wet [workable, quaking] concrete
塑性极限 plastic limit
塑性计 plastometer, plasticimeter ◇ 摆式~ pendulum plastometer, 吉塞勒~ Gieseler plastometer, 凸轮式~【压】cam plastometer
塑性计检验（金属的） plastometer test
塑性加工 plastic working ◇ 低温[温热]~*
塑性阶段 plastic stage
塑性介质 【压】yielding medium
塑性金属陶瓷复合材料 plasticmetal-ceramic composite
塑性理论 plastic theory ◇ 按~设计 plastic design
塑性(力)学 plasticity
塑性量度[测量] 【压】measure of ductility
塑性流变[屈服] plastic yield(ing) ◇ 裂纹顶端~*
塑性流变抗力 resistance to plastic flow
塑性流变量 amount of plastic flow
塑性流动 plastic flow
塑性流动前缘 plastic front
塑性模数[模量] modulus of plasticity
塑性耐火材料 plastic refractory
塑性耐火黏土 plastic fireclay
塑性泥浆 【耐】plastic paste
塑性黏土 plastic clay
塑性黏土碾磨机 plastic clay grinding mill
塑性凝胶 plastigel, plastogel
塑性凝胶模 plastigel mould
塑性扭曲 plastic twisting
塑性破坏 plastic failure, ductile fracture
塑性破裂 plastic rupture
塑性铅（用于修补铸件缺陷） plastic lead
塑性切变增量 increment of plastic shears
塑性青铜 plastic bronze ◇ 艾杰克斯~*
塑性区应力-应变关系 plastic stress-strain relation
塑性区(域)[范围] range of plasticity, plastic region, plastic zone（冷轧的）
塑性试验 plasticity test
塑性收缩 plastic constriction
塑性松弛 plastic relaxation
塑性体 plastomer
塑性条件 plasticity condition ◇ 冯米塞斯~ Von Mises criterion
塑性弯曲 plastic bending
塑性温度范围 plastic temperature range
塑性协调区 region of plastic accommodation
塑性形变机理 （同"范性形变机理"）
塑性应变 plastic strain
塑性应变比（板材的） plastic strain ratio
塑性值[指数] plasticity index (PI)
塑性状态 plastic state [stage]
塑制耐火材料 castable refractory
塑状焊接 plastic welding
酸 acid ◇ 废[用过的]~ spent acid, 脱~ acid stripping
酸泵 acid pump
酸比重计 acidometer, acidimeter
酸不足的 acid deficient
酸槽 acid(ic) bath [tank]
酸槽浓度 bath concentration
酸产物 acid product
酸常数 acid constant
酸处理 acid treatment (a.t.)
酸萃取 acid extraction
酸蛋 (acid, receiving) egg
酸度 acid value (A.V.), (degree of) acidity
酸度标准测定法 standard acid test
酸度计 （同"pH计"）
酸度指数 acid index
酸额 acid capacity
酸法 acid process [system]
酸废料 acid waste product
酸分解 decomposition with acid
酸腐蚀 acid corrosion

酸酐　acid anhydride
酸根[基]　acid radical [group]
酸含量　acid content
酸耗(量)　acid-consumption
酸化　acidation, acidification, acidulation ◇ 过度~ overacidification
酸化机理　acid mechanism
酸化剂[器]　acidulant, acidifier
酸碱测定法　acid-base determination
酸碱催化作用　acid-base catalysis
酸碱度　pH value, potential of hydrogen (pH)
酸碱度记录器　pH recorder ◇ 带警报的~ pH recorder with alarm (pHRA)
酸碱度控制器　pH controller (pHC)
酸碱度调节器　pH-regulator
酸碱度指示器　pH indicator (pHI)
酸碱平衡　acid-base equilibrium [balance]
酸碱指示剂　pH indicator, acid-base indicator
酸焦油　【焦】acid tar (oil)
酸结合剂　acid binding agent
酸解　acidolysis, acid hydrolysis
酸浸　acid leach(ing) [dip], pickle ◇ 常压~*, 高压釜[压煮器]~*, 光亮~ brightening dip
酸浸出　(同"酸性浸出")
酸浸出类精矿　acid leach type concentrate
酸浸处理　acid leach treatment
酸浸工段　acid leaching section
酸浸回路　acid leach circuit
酸浸检验　pickle test
酸浸流程(图)　acid leaching scheme
酸浸时滞性试验 (镀锡薄钢板的)　pickle lag
酸浸蚀　acid etch(ing), mordanting
酸浸树脂交换法　◇ 埃赛尔~*
酸浸提取　acid leaching extraction
酸浸系统　acid leach circuit
酸浸液　acid leaching liquors, dip
酸浸(渍)法　pickling process
酸可溶性　acid solubility

酸类　acids
酸类处理整面法(混凝土用)　acid treated finish
酸离子　acid ion
酸量测定分析　acidimetric analysis
酸量滴定法　【化】acidimetry
酸-卤素电解质　acid-halogen electrolyte
酸浓度　acid concentration [strength]
酸浓缩器　acid concentrator
酸气　sour gas
酸侵蚀　acid attack
酸溶解　acid dissolution
酸溶解度　acid solubility
酸溶铝　acid-soluble aluminium
酸溶水合物　acid-soluble hydrate
酸溶锌率　acid soluble zinc ratio
酸溶性脉石　acid-soluble gangue
酸溶元素　acid-soluble element
酸蚀　pickle
酸式氟化铵{NH_4HF_2}　acid ammonium fluoride
酸式氟化钾{KHF_2}　potassium acid fluoride
酸式氟化钠{$NaHF_2$}　sodium acid fluoride
酸式磷酸钠　sodium acid phosphate
酸式磷酸锶　acid strontium phosphate
酸式硫酸盐　acidic sulphate, bisulphate, bisulfate, disulphate, disulfate
酸式盐　acid salt
酸式乙基磷酸铪酰　hafnyl ethyl acid phosphate
酸水洗涤　acid rensing
酸塔　acid tower
酸雾　acid mist [fume, fog]
酸雾捕集器　mist trap
酸误差　acid error
酸洗　acid wash, dipping, mordanting, 【压】pickle, pickling, acid cleaning ◇ 初~ first [black] pickling, 呆液~ dead pickling, 电解~ anode pickling, 二次~ double pickling, 分批~*, 固定桶[槽]式~ stationary pickling, 光亮~ bright pickling, 黑

[粗]~ black pickling, 搅动 ~ agitator pickling, 经~的 bitten into, 静态~*, 浪击式~*, 连续(式)~*, 去~泥 desmutting, 塔式~ tower pickling, 梯流式~ cascade pickling, 未~斑点 unpickled spot, 稀~ dilute acid wash, 循环~(系统) circulating pickling

酸洗凹坑[麻点] pickle pitting

酸洗斑(点) pickle [pickling] patch, pickling smudge

酸洗薄板 pickled sheet (metal), white finished sheet

酸洗比色试验 acid wash test

酸洗-涂油的 pickled and oiled (P&O)

酸洗不足 【压】underpickling

酸洗材料通过量 throughput of pickled material

酸洗残渣 smut

酸洗槽 pickling tank [cell, vat], (acid) pickling bath, descaling [acidic] bath

酸洗槽里衬 pickling-tank lining

酸洗槽溶液 pickling tank solution

酸洗车间 pickling department

酸洗车间废酸 spent pickling-plant liquor

酸洗池 pickling cell

酸洗除鳞槽 descaling bath

酸洗处理 pickling treatment

酸洗疵点[蚀斑,污斑] pickle stain

酸洗脆性 pickle [acid, pickling] brittleness, acid [pickling] embrittlement

酸洗单馏粗苯 washed once-run benzole

酸洗电解理论 electrolytic theory of pickling

酸洗段 pickling zone

酸洗法 pickle [pickling] process

酸洗反应速率 pickling reaction rate

酸洗废液 spent pickling-plant liquor, spent pickling solution

酸洗腐蚀 bite

酸洗附加[阻蚀]剂 pickling inhibitor

酸洗钢板 pickled plate

酸洗工段 pickle house, pickling section [aisle, bay, zone]

酸洗钩 pickling hook

酸洗过程 pickling [pickle] process

酸洗(划)痕 pickle house scratch

酸洗缓蚀剂 restrainer

酸洗活化剂 pickling activator

酸洗机 【压】pickling machine ◇ 三摇臂式分批~*, 四摇臂式(分批)[周期式四摇臂]~*, 塔式~ tower pickler, 推拉式~ pull pickler, 摇臂式(分批)~*, 柱塞式~*

酸洗机组[(作业)线] pickling line (P.L)

酸洗剂 pickling agent, mordant

酸洗间 pickle house, pickling plant

酸洗间划痕 pickle house scratch

酸洗截面 pickling section

酸洗介质 pickling medium

酸洗净化 etch cleaning

酸洗跨 pickling bay

酸洗篮[筐] dipping basket, pickling cratle

酸洗-冷轧联合机组 continuous pickling and continuous cold rolling mill (CDCM)

酸洗轮 pickling wheel

酸洗麻面 pitted surface

酸洗镁锭 acid pickled magnesium ingot

酸洗抛光 【金】etch polish ◇ 光亮~[清整] bright dipped finish

酸洗泡 pickling blister

酸洗清洗喷射槽 pickle rinse spray tank

酸洗缺陷 pickling defect

酸洗热轧板卷 pickled hot rolled coil

酸洗设备 pickler, pickling plant [installation, machinery]

酸洗试验 pickling test

酸洗树脂 acid eluted resin

酸洗损失 pickling loss, loss on acid washing

酸洗添加剂 pickling addition

酸洗桶 pickling vat, acid wash drum

酸洗烟雾 pickling fume

酸洗液 pickle liquor [acid], pickler, pickling liquor [fluid, solution], dip, acid wash

solution ◇废~回收*
酸洗栅架 pickling rack
酸洗周期 pickling cycle
酸洗装置 pickling unit, pickler, acid dip pickler (沉浸式) ◇滚筒[转鼓]式~ drum-type pickler, 连续式带材~*, 脉动式~*
酸洗(作业)线 【压】pickling line (P.L)
酸性 acidity, acidic property, acidness ◇过度~superacidity, 微~的 subacid
酸性残渣 acid residue
酸性衬里 acid lining
酸性萃取剂 acidic extractant
酸性底吹转炉炼钢法 Bessemer process
酸性电弧炉钢 acid electric arc furnace steel
酸性电解液[质] acid eletrolyte, acidic bath
酸性电炉 acid electric furnace
酸性电炉钢 acid electric steel
酸性电炉炼钢法 acid electric process [practice]
酸性反应 acid reaction
酸性废水 【环】acid waste water
酸性腐蚀 sour corrosion
酸性钢 acid steel
酸性化铁炉 acidic cupola
酸性环境 acid environment
酸性还原作用 acid reduction
酸性回路 acid(ic) circuit
酸性焦炭 acid coke
酸性介质 acid(ic) medium
酸性金属 acid metal
酸(性)浸出 acid leach(ing) ◇流态化床~*
酸性浸出槽 acid leach(ing) tank
酸(性)浸出法 acid leach(ing) process [method]
酸性浸出剂 acid lixiviant
酸性浸出阶段 acid leaching stage
酸性浸出空气搅拌槽 acid pachuca
酸性浸出设备 acid leach plant

酸(性)浸出液 acid leach liquor
酸性矿物 acid mineral
酸性离解 acidic dissociation
酸性炼钢法 acid (steelmaking) process
酸性磷酸盐 superphosphate
酸性炉 acid furnace
酸性炉衬 acid lining
酸性炉料 acid burden
酸性炉膛[床] acid hearth
酸性炉渣 (同"酸性渣")
酸性铝酸盐 bialuminate
酸性脉石 acid(ic) gangue
酸性母液 【色】acid pregnant liquor
酸性钼酸盐 bimolybdate
酸性耐火材料 acid refractory
酸性耐火砖 acid (fire) brick, acid refractory brick
酸性黏土 acid clay
酸性浓缩 acid thickening
酸性平炉 acid open hearth (A.O.H.)
酸性平炉[马丁炉]钢 acid open-hearth steel
酸性气体 acid(ic) [sour] gas
酸性侵蚀渣 【钢】damaging acid slag
酸性球团 acid [oxidized] pellet
酸性熔剂 acid flux
酸性熔体 acid melt
酸性溶剂[溶媒] acid solvent
酸性溶液 acid(ic) solution
酸性溶液电解法 acid eletrolyte process
酸性烧结矿 acid sinter
酸性砷酸盐 biarsenate
酸性生铁 acid pig
酸性试验 acid test
酸性树脂 acid resin
酸性水 acid(ic) water
酸性碳酸盐离子 bicarbonate ion
酸性铁 acid iron
酸性土(壤) acid soil
酸性物含量 acidic content
酸性物(料) acid material, acids
酸性洗提液 acidic eluant

酸性系统	acid(ic) circuit
酸性效应	acidity effect
酸性蓄电池	acid accumulator
酸性烟尘	acid smoke
酸性岩	acid(ic) rock
酸性氧化物	acid(ic) oxide
酸性溢流	【色】acid overflow
酸性油	acid(-soluble) oil
酸性有机磷化合物	acid organophosphorus compound
酸性造渣成分	acid slag component
酸性渣	acid [siliceous] slag, long slag (炼锡的) ◇低铁～*,造～*
酸性渣操作	【铁】acid operation
酸性渣冶炼	acidic slag smelting, working with an acid slag
酸性直接电弧炉	acid direct-arc electric furnace
酸性直接电弧炉法[冶炼过程]	acid direct-arc electric furnace process
酸性转炉	(acid) Bessemer converter, acid (lined) converter, silica brick-lined converter, converter of acid lining
酸性转炉钢	Bessemer acid steel (B.A.S.), (acid) Bessemer steel, acid converter steel
酸性转炉精炼	Bessemer converter refining
酸性转炉铁	Bessemer pig (iron), acid (converter, Bessemer) pig iron
酸性转炉用铁矿	acid Bessemer ore
酸性转炉铸铁	acid Bessemer cast iron
酸性组分	acid constituents
酸液	acid liquor
酸液比重计	acidometer, acidimeter
酸液(浸洗)槽	acid (dip) tank
酸乙醚逆流萃取法	countercurrent acid ether process
酸雨	acid rain
酸再生站	acid regeneration plant
酸渣	acid sludge
酸蒸汽	acid vapour
酸值	acid value (A.V.), acid number
酸指数	acid exponent
酸贮槽	acid storage tank
酸组分	acid constituent
算法	algorithm ◇马尔可夫～*
算法逼近	algorithmic approach
算法程序	【计】algorithm routine
算法收敛	algorithm convergence
算法语言	algorithmic language (ALGOL)
算符	【数】operator
算式	formula, equation
算术表达式	arithmetic expression
算术乘积	arithmetic product
算术和	arithmetic sum
算术级数	arithmetical progression
算术校验	arithmetic cheque
算术平均值	arithmetic(al) mean [average]
算术扫描	【计】arithmetic scan
算术误差码	【计】arithmetic error code
算术移位	arithmetic shift
算术与逻辑运算部件	arithmetic and logical unit (ALU)
算术元素	arithmetic element
算术运算	arithmetic operation ◇二进制～*
算术运算符	arithmetic operator
算术指令	【计】arithmetic instruction
随从操作器	slave manipulator
随动	follow-up, servo (drive)
随动冲模	follow die
随动磁头	tracing [tractor] head
随动电动机	slave [follow-up] motor
随动电位计	follow up potentiometer
随动阀	follow [servo] valve
随动辊	【压】loose roll
随动机构	follower, servomechanism, detector
随动控制	【电】follow up control
随动系统	following up system, servosystem, servomechanism
随动线缆机构(煤气柜的)	follow-up ca-

ble mechanism	
随动装置	follow up device, servo, tracer
随后机械加工	subsequent machining
随后加热（焊接的）	subsequent heating
随机编码	【计】hat
随机波动	random fluctuation
随机磁极	【理】fugitive magnetic pole
随机存取	【计】random [direct] access
随机存取存储器	【计】random access memory (RAM), random access storage ◇ 可换式～*
随机存取分类程序	【计】random access sort
随机度	degree of randomness
随机故障	random failure
随机过程	stochastic process
随机化	randomization
随机试验	random test
随机数	random number [digit]
随机误差	random error
随机样品	random sample
随机移动	random walk
随机自适应控制	stochastic adaptive control
随炉冷却	furnace cool(ing), cooling in furnace
随时间变化	time-variation, variation with time
随时间变化的	time-dependent
随时间变化的增益	time variable again
随挖随填	cut-and-fill, cut and cover
随温度而变的	temperature-dependent
随意过程	spontaneous process
随意计划轧制	schedule-free rolling
随意取向	chaotic orientation
碎边（剪下的）	clippings
碎边剪边机	chopping shears
碎边剪切	cropping cut
碎边剪（切机）	scrap chopper ◇ 飞剪式～flying shear cutter
碎成粉	【粉】powdering
碎电极	crushed electrode, electrode scrap

碎断	spall fracture, cataclasm
碎废钢	shred(ded) scrap
碎废阳极残头	crushed scrap anode butt
碎钢粉	crushed steel
碎硅砖	crushed silica brick
碎化（晶粒的）	fragmentation ◇ 莫特～参数*
碎集料	crushed aggregate
碎焦	coke breeze [braize, dross], breeze, low-mesh [small (-sized), fine] coke, gleeds, char（低温碳化形成的）
碎焦槽	coke breeze bin
碎焦回收漏斗（料车坑的）	【铁】coke dust recovery chute
碎焦漏斗	coke breeze hopper
碎焦升降机[卷扬装置]	coke breeze hoist
碎解	disintegration
碎块	fines breeze
碎块金属	prill
碎矿车	crusher car
碎矿车间	ore-breaking plant
碎矿机	crusher, breaker
碎矿机颊板	cheek plate
碎矿间	【选】crushing room
碎矿设备	crushing plant [appliance]
碎裂	splintering, splintery [spall] fracture, craze (cracking), disintegration, degradation, 【金】puffing, fragmentation（晶粒的）◇ 抗[防]～antidegradation
碎裂程度	cleavage step
碎裂度[率]	disintegration degree
碎裂耐火材料	shuffs
碎裂趋势	tendency to crack(ing)
碎裂树脂	broken resin
碎裂指数	breakdown index, 【团】degradation [disintegration] index
碎裂作用	cataclasis, fragmentation, disruptive action
碎鳞	loosened oxide
碎鳞机	【压】descaling mill ◇ 二辊式～*
碎炉渣	crushed slag
碎煤	rice coal, conny

碎煤刀钢（采泥煤用） milling steel
碎煤机 coal crusher [breaker]
碎磨 comminution
碎木胶合板 chipboard
碎耐火砖 bat
碎片 fragment, chip, shive(ring), segment
碎片体（煤岩） micrinite
碎铅 scrap lead
碎切屑 crushed turnings
碎球率 【团】chip index
碎球（团） return chat(s), pellet fines
碎散 crumbling
碎砂机 sand cutter
碎烧结矿 sinter fines, broken sinter（粉碎的）
碎石 spall, broken [crushed, bray] stone, debris, gallet, debris, macadam ◇ 过筛的 ～ hoggin, 未筛分 [统货] ～ crusher-run stone
碎石碴 chip ballast
碎石厂 (rock-)crushing plant
碎石堆 scree, stockpile（养路用）◇ 山脚 ～ talus
碎石机 stoner, rock crusher [breaker], knapping machine, knapper, granulator
碎石路 crushed stone macadam, macadam [metal] road ◇ 沥青盖层 ～ coated macadam, 沥青灌 ～ 面 asphalt-grouted surfacing
碎石铺路 macadamized road
碎石铺路法 macadamization
碎石选分设备 chip rejector
碎铁 broken iron ◇ 铸造 ～【铸】foundery scrap
碎铁锤 drop weight
碎铁堆 baling of scrap
碎铁机 pig [drop] breaker, iron crusher, vertical drop machine
碎铁落锤 【冶】falling tup
碎土机 pulverizer ◇ 圆盘式 ～ disc cultivator
碎无烟煤（未筛分的） culm coal
碎锡矿 cased tin
碎锡矿渣 loob
碎屑 fragment, bits, chips, fines, muck ◇ 不含 ～ 的 fines free
碎屑仓 slack bin
碎屑机 chip breaker
碎屑钛铁矿 menaccanite
碎屑箱 chip box
碎渣 broken [disintegrating] slag, slag chipping
碎渣车 【冶】slag buggy
碎渣机 slag crusher [breaker]
碎渣壳器 bridge breaker
碎渣块（铺路用） slag ballast
碎砖 crushed [broken] brick, brick rubble ◇ 充填用 ～ 块 filling brick
碎砖片 brick fragment
隧道 【运】tunnel ◇（地下）电缆 ～ cable tunnel [subway], 开挖 ～ tunneling, 冷却 ～ cooling tunnel, 明挖 ～ open-cut tunnel, 上导洞法 ～ bar and sill method, 输送 ～ delivery tunnel
隧道长度 tunneling distance
隧道衬砌 lining of tunnel
隧道导洞 pilot tunnel
隧道底坑法 drift method
隧道冻结施工法 freezing method of tunneling
隧道工程 【建】tunneling
隧道管 tunneltron
隧(道贯)穿 【半】tunneling
隧道护拱 【建】umbrella arch
隧道结 tunnel(ing) junction
隧道两端挖方 approach cutting
隧道平巷顶支撑板 astel
隧道式干燥窑 tunnel dryer, tunnel drying oven
隧道式感应加热中间包 【连铸】channel-tundish with induction heating
隧道式烘(干)炉 drying tunnel, tunnel-type baker
隧道式连续干燥器 continuous tunnel dri-

隧道(式)炉 car [continuous] tunnel furnace, tunnel (type) furnace, channel oven
隧道式燃烧器 tunnel burner
隧道式退火炉 tunnel-type annealing furnace, tunnel-type furnace for annealing
隧道效应 【半】tunneling, tunnel effect
隧道效应长度 tunneling distance
隧道效应电流 tunneling current
隧道效应概率 tunneling probability
隧道窑 (car) tunnel kiln, channel oven, tunnel (type) furnace ◇ 车底式～car-type tunnel kiln, 大型～large tunnel kiln, 小车～car tunnel kiln
隧道窑车 tunnel kiln car
隧道窑还原(法) tunnel kiln reduction
隧道窑烧成 tunnel kiln firing
遂硼镁石[遂安石] suanite
燧石{SiO$_2$} flint, chert, fire stone ◇ 含铁～ferruginous flint
燧石板岩 lydianite
燧石玻璃 flint glass
燧石耐火黏土 flint fire clay
燧石黏土 flint clay
燧石黏土砖 flint brick
损害 harm, damage, impair, injure
损害赔偿 【环】compensation for damages
损耗 loss, waste, attrition, breakage, dissipation
损坏 damage, damaging, break(down), injure, casualty, impairment, destruction
损坏[伤]率 【金】damage ratio, spoilage
损坏试验 damaging test
损坏[伤]效应 damage effect
损漏容许限度 leak tolerance
损伤 harm, damage, damaging, injure, impair(ment), hurt, failure ◇ 未～的 unimpaired
损伤分析 destructive analysis
损伤曲线 damage curve
损伤线(疲劳特性) 【金】damage line
损失 loss, wastage ◇ 其他[未计入的]～ unaccounted losses
损失费用 failure costs
损失角 loss angle
损失时间 lost time
榫 tenon ◇ 带一口模 lock die
榫槽 gain, mortise
榫搭接 joggled lap joint
榫钉 dowel
榫钉连接 tenon dowel joint
榫接 joggle (joint)
榫接机 joggling machine
梭动式进料 shuttle-type feed
梭式板[带]形运输机 shuttle apron
梭式布料器 reciprocal feeder, feeder shuttle, reciprocating belt feeder, reciprocating conveyer, 【团】shuttle car belt, shuttle distributor [conveyer]
梭式给料机 reciprocal feeder
梭式矿车 shuttle car
梭式皮带布料器 reciprocating belt feeder
梭式皮带(运输)机 shuttle belt conveyer, reversible shuttle conveyer, shuttlecar [conveyer] belt
梭式小车 shuttle carriage
梭式窑 shuttle kiln
梭式运输机 shuttle conveyer
梭式装料器 shuttle feeder
羧化物 carboxylates
羧基 【化】carboxyl (group)
羧基化反应能力 carboxyreactivity
羧甲基纤维素 carboxymethyl cellulose (CMC)
羧酸萃取剂 carboxylic extractant
羧酸树脂 carboxylic(acid) resin
羧酸盐 carboxylate
羧酸阳离子交换剂 carboxylic type [acid] cation exchanger
羧酸阳离子交换树脂 carboxylic cation exchange, resin ◇ 216～Zeo-Karb 216, 226～Zeo-Karb 226, 杜利特 CS-100～Duolite CS-100, 卢泰特 C～Lewatit C, 沃法泰特 C～Wofatit C, 珀缪泰特 H-70

~Permutit H-70

羧酸阳离子树脂 carboxylic cation resin

缩尺 reduced scale,【铸】contraction [shrink(age), patternmaker's, moulder's] rule

缩顶(沸腾钢锭的) top hat

缩短 shorten, curtail, cutting-down, shrinking, shrinkage

缩短的风口 shortened tuyere

缩短法 short-cut method

缩短率(试件的) contraction

缩短型麦氏真空计 shortened McLeod gauge

缩多酸 polyacid

缩放仪 pantograph, eidograph

缩分 cutting-down

缩分法(试样的)【金】short-cut method

缩分取样 curtailed sampling

缩分试样 subsample

缩管【钢】(shrinkage) pipe, tube ◇ 消除~pipe elimination

缩管防止剂【冶】anti-piping compound

缩号(拉丝时的) sucking

缩合 condensation

缩合产物 condensation product

缩合反应 condensation reaction

缩合树脂 condensation resin

缩回 retraction

缩集气团 condensed atmosphere

缩减 reduction, run-down, decrement, diminution ◇ 面积~【压】reduction in area

缩减规模 down-scale

缩减因数 reduction factor

缩颈 neck(ing)-down, necking (effect), constriction ◇ 拉伸~necking in tension, 易割~【铸】break-off notch, 真空密封~*, 无~变形 neckfree deformation

缩颈锭【冶】notched ingot

缩颈断裂(拉伸时的)【金】necking-down

缩颈管 constricted tube

缩聚合(作用) condensation polymerization

缩聚物[缩合聚合物] condensation polymer

缩孔 contraction cavity, shrink(ing) hole, shrinkage (cavity, pipe, void), sunk spot, clowhole(美),【冶】cavitation, void, ◇ 表面浅注型~*, 敞开型[一次]~primary pipe, 分散~*, 集中性~gross shrinkage, 挤压~*, 晶间[显微]~micro pipe, 开口[外部]~*, 无~的*, 有~钢 piped steel, 有~金属(钢锭或铸件)【铸】pipe metal, 早期~*, 轴线~*

缩孔分层(带钢的) pipe lamination

缩孔焊合 filling in of scores

缩孔接缝 pipe seam

缩孔偏析 pipe segregation

缩孔损失【钢】pipe losses

缩孔尾[下]端(钢锭的) piped end

缩孔形成【钢】shrink-away, shrinking

缩口冲模 reducing die

缩口(短)管 converging tube

缩口接头 constricted-end joint

缩裂 casting [shrinkage] crack,【冶】contraction crack

缩松 (shrinkage) porosity

缩头锭(沸腾钢缺陷) receding metal

缩图 contracted drawing, minimizing chart

缩注【铸】blink

缩微胶片 microfilm, microfiche

缩陷【铸】shrinkage depression

缩小 reducing ◇ 按(某种)比例~[减少] scale down

缩小尺寸 size reduction

缩小的γ区【金】contracted γ

缩小运算【金】erosion

缩写 abbreviations (abbr.)

缩腰 waisting

缩展器 (同"压缩扩展器")

索拜珠光体 sorbitic pearlite

索查突舌(卡片的) tab

索铲 pull shovel

索车 cable car
索带状态 【团】funicular state
索道 cableway, tram rail, funicular, ropeway ◇ 高架～cable telpher, 架空～cableway, 双缆～bicable ropeway
索斗挖掘机 dragline excavator
索夫林金合金（91.7Au, 8.3Cu） Sovereign gold
索格利萃取 Soxhlet extraction
索格利萃取器 Soxhlet extractor [apparatus]
索环 (cord) grommet, grummet
索具 tackle, rigging
索缆拖曳 cable trailing
索勒缝隙（用于消除射线会聚或发散） Soller slit
索勒聚焦[平行]缝隙系统 focusing Soller slits system
索雷尔电炉炼铁法 Sorel process
索雷尔(镁质)水泥 Sorel cement
索雷尔锌基合金（1Cu, 1Fe, 余量 Zn） Sorel's alloy
索利特高度光亮镜用合金（4.1Zn, 64.6Cu, 31.3Sn） Sollit's alloy
索连状态 【团】funicular state
索卢米尼姆铝焊料（55Sn, 33Zn, 11Al, 1Cu） Soluminium
索罗铸轧法 【冶】Soro process
索诺雷超声波探伤仪 Sonoray
索赔 claim (indemnity), demand compensation
索森－罗登格渣处理法（用于钢液脱磷） Soisson-Rodange process
索氏体 【金】sorbite ◇ 回火～*, 一次[原生]～primary sorbite
索氏体淬火 sorbite quench
索氏体化 sorbitizing ◇ 钢轨顶面～法
索氏体显微组织 sorbite microstructure
索氏体铸铁 sorbitic cast iron
索氏体组织 sorbitic structure
索条 lacing
索条绞线 rope-lay conductor

索维尔定碳图（碳钢的） Sauveur's diagram
索维尔浸蚀剂（钢铁的）【金】Sauveur's reagent
索维尔溢流铸锭法 【钢】Sauveur overflow method
索眼 grommet, grummet
索引 index（复数 indices）, indexing, subscript
索引号 index number
索引图 key-drawing, key plan
索引文件 index file
索状表面 ropy surface
锁定 locking, lockout ◇ 铃木～*
锁定机构 lock(ing) gear [mechanism]
锁定继电器 lock-on [lock-up] relay
锁定脉冲 lock(ing) pulse, lockout impulse
锁定销 stop pin
锁定应力 locking stress
锁合 locking, closure
锁合横杆 locking cross bar
锁合装置 lock
锁环 locking [check, closing, clamping] ring
锁匠 locksmith
锁紧板 locking plate
锁紧垫圈 【机】lock [check] washer
锁紧环 clamping collar [ring], stop(per) [binding, chuck] ring
锁紧键（轮箍的） locking key
锁紧螺钉 lock [stop(per)] screw ◇ 手轮～wheel screw
锁紧螺母 lock [cap, check, jam, retainer] nut
锁紧圈 strengthening ring
锁紧螺栓 check [lock, catch] bolt
锁紧销 catch [steady] pin
锁紧装置 lock device, back set,【机】fixing device
锁口丝 bag tie wire
锁扣装置 locking device, locker
锁块 clamping piece

锁气装置　gas lock system
锁上　locking-up
锁丝钢丝绳　locked-wire rope
锁条　locking bar
锁头（钢丝绳的）　tapered end
锁销　【团】lock(ing) pin, cotterel

锁住　lock-in, latching, pinning
锁砖　key [neck, centre] brick
所得　【企】income, earnings
所属图纸　appertaining drawing
所有者权益　owner's equities
所在地　location, seat, site, occurrence

T t

他激 separate [independent] excitation
他形的 alltriomorphic
铊{Tl} thallium ◇ 含一价和三价~的 thallosic, 亚[一价]~的 thallous
铊的(正铊的) thallic
铊矾 {Tl$_2$SO$_4$·Al$_2$(SO$_4$)$_3$·24H$_2$O 或 TlAl(SO$_4$)$_2$·12H$_2$O} thallous alum
铊浮渣 thallium dross
铊合金 thallium alloy
铊化钠 {NaTl} sodium thallide
铊化物 thallide
铊基合金 thallium-base alloy
铊添加合金 thallium addition
铊氧硫光电管 thalofide photocell
铊渣 thallium dross
铊中毒 thallotoxicosis
塌料 avalanche, slip
塌陷 collapse, subsidence
塌箱 【铸】crush, sand crushing, drop (off), drop-out, downslide, sag ◇ 铸型~ mould crush
塌芯 【铸】sag
塌腰 warpage,【团】downward bowing (台车的)
塔板 tower [column] plate, dish, plate (蒸馏塔的), disk, disc ◇ 不起反应的~ physical plate
塔板效率 【化】plate efficiency
塔布碳化钨耐磨焊料 (碳化钨60,钢40) Tube Borium
塔齿轮 stepped gear
塔萃取 column extraction
塔顶 column top
塔顶废物 top discard
塔顶回流 top reflux
塔顶馏出物 overhead (product)
塔尔伯特[平炉]连续炼钢法 【钢】Talbot process
塔尔伯特双联炼钢法 【钢】Talbot duplex process
塔尔伯特液心(钢锭)轧制法 【压】Talbot (ingot) process
塔尔米假金(86—90Cu,9—12Zn,0—1Sn) Talmi gold
塔菲尔常数 Tafel constant
塔菲尔公式(电解过程的) Tafel equation
塔菲尔图(电解过程的) Tafel plot
塔夫诺尔绝缘环 Tufnol insulating ring
塔夫-斯塔夫铝青铜(8—14Al,2—4Fe,1Zn,0.5Mn,余量Cu) Tuf-stuf
塔格列费里电弧炉 【冶】Tagliaferri furnace
塔吉克石 tadzhikite
塔架 【电】pylon, tower
塔架式炉顶 tower top
塔架式砌炉机 【钢】reline tower
塔科马电解制铁法 Tacoma process
塔淋浸出 tower leaching
塔楼 turret
塔轮 cone [stepped] pulley, stepcone, cone gear
塔曼管状坩埚 Tammann tube
塔曼石墨电阻加热炉[塔曼管式电阻炉] Tammann furnace
塔姆能级 Tamm (energy) level
塔姆塔姆锡青铜(78Cu,22Sn) Tamtam
塔姆铁钛合金(15—21Ti,3.5—8C,余量Fe) Tam alloy
塔盘 tray (蒸馏塔盘) ◇ 基特尔~【焦】Kittel plate
塔式齿轮 cluster gear
塔式氟化器 fluorination tower reactor
塔式干燥机 vertical drier
塔式干燥炉 tower-type oven
塔式活套装置 【压】tower-type looper
塔式绞盘 cone capstan
塔式净化器 tower purifier
塔式[形]拉丝卷筒 (stepped wire) drawing cone, stepped drawing cone
塔式冷却 tower cooling
塔式冷却机 vertical-type cooler

塔式连续退火炉　tower-type continuous (annealing) furnace, multiple-strand annealing furnace
塔式连铸设备　tower-type plant
塔式炉(薄板带连续退火用)　tower-type furnace
塔式起重机[吊车]　tower [column(-jib)] crane
塔式升降机　column elevator
塔式酸洗　tower pickling
塔式酸洗机　tower pickle(r)
塔式陶瓷拉丝卷筒　【压】ceramic drawing cones
塔式旋臂起重机　rotary tower crane
塔式蒸发　tower evaporation
塔特莫钼工具钢　Tatmo steel
塔效率　column efficiency
塔形　【压】telescoping
塔形车削检验(钢材的)　【金】step cutting test
塔形钢卷(卷取缺陷)　telescoped coil
塔形(皮带)传动轮　drive cone
塔形切削检验(发纹检验)　step-down test
塔形(铸造)试样　steep bar
塔总高度　overall column height
踏板　footstep, 【机】treadle ◇ 旋转~开关 rotating paddle switch
踏板传动装置　pedal gear
踏板锤　treadle hammer
踏板垫　pedal pad
踏板轴　treadle shaft
踏步式基础　【建】offset footing
踏脚板　footstep
踏勘　exploratory survey, reconnaissance
踏面　【铁】seating face(料钟及料斗的接触面), 【压】tread(轮箍的)
胎具　mould, match
胎模　【铸】pattern match
胎型　bobbin
苔纹铜　moss copper
苔状晶粒　mossy grain

抬箱跑火　【铸】bleeder
抬芯　(铸造缺陷) floating core
台　platform, table, desk, post, skid, stage, stand, trestle
台板　bed plate, platen
台板压力　platen force
台车　【团】pallet (car), machine pallet ◇ 行走~ moving pallet
台车车轮　pallet roller
台车[更换台车用]吊车　pallet removal crane
台车风箱间T形滑道密封　pallet wind-box tee-base seal
台车(风箱间)密封　pallet-windbox seal
台车横[大]梁　pallet cross-member, transverse beam of pallet
台车间隙　pallet gapping
台车间隙自动补偿系统　automatic pallet take-up system
台车框架　pallet frame
台车拦板　pallet side plate
台车炉算面积　pallet grate area
台车跑偏　meander of pallet
台车碰撞　pallet-to pallet impact
台车清理　pallet scrubbing
台车清理器[清理器,刮刀]　pallet cleaner
台车式烘炉　car type oven
台车式浇包　buggy ladle
台车式炉　bogie furnace
台车式热处理炉　car-type heat treating furnace
台车式烧结机　pallet-type sintering machine
台车式万能装卸机　platform truck
台车式型芯炉　car-type core oven
台车枢轴　pallet pivot
台车体　pallet body [frame]
台车调节[补偿]系统　pallet take-up system
台车下温度　【团】undergrate temperature
台车卸料器　pallet tripper
台车中段铸件　pallet center casting

台秤　platform（weighing）scale, platform [table] balance, platform weighing machine, scale [weighing] platform, bench [table-type] scale, weighbridge（车辆用）
台基拉晶法（同"基座拉晶技术"）
台架　rack, bench, skid bank [bed], saddle piece,【压】bank
台阶高度　shoulder height, height of steps
台阶式浇注　cascade teeming
台阶式生长　terracing growth
台阶式挖[采]掘　bench excavation, benching ◇坑道~*
台阶形结构　terraced structure
台面　mesa, table top, deck
台面腐蚀　mesa etching
台面式晶体管　mesa transistor
台钳　bench clamp, vise
台式测微计　stage micrometer
台式称量机　platform weighing machine
台式吹芯机　【铸】bench blower
台式点焊机　bench type spot-welder
台式钢锭秤　table-type scale
台式计算机　desk [table] computer
台式曲柄冲床[压力机]　bench press
台式试验仪　table apparatus
台式屋顶　deck roof
台式震实机　bench jolter
台式钻床　bench drilling machine
台砧　bench anvil, little beak iron
台座　bed box, pedestal
台座起重机　abutment crane
台座式点焊机　pedestal spot welder
泰安炸药　pentaerythrite tetranitrate （P.E.T.N.）
泰尔贝克煤气燃烧器（热风炉用）　Terbeck gas burner
泰勒标准筛　Tyler sieve
泰勒标准筛序　Tyler（standard screen）series
泰勒带钢冷轧机　Taylor mill
泰勒点阵[晶格]　Taylor lattice
泰勒－怀特高速钢热处理法　Taylor-White process
泰勒拉丝法　Tayler process
泰勒位错（刃型）　Taylor dislocation
泰勒位错理论　theory of Taylor
泰雷铝硅合金　Telectal alloy
泰曼高锰钢丝　Timang
泰塞利锌基压铸合金（8.7Al, 3.5Cu, 0.3Si, 余量Zn）　Tyseley alloy
泰塞利装饰用锌合金（87Zn, 8.6Al, 3.6Cu, 0.5Si）　Tyseley metal
泰森式气体洗涤机　Theisen disintegrator, high speed disintegrator
泰森式洗气机　Theisen washer
泰特奈特钛钨硬质合金（加少量 Mo_2C）　Titanit
泰因通锌电解法（用高电流密度）　Tainton method
钛　{Ti} titanium ◇ α~ alpha-titanium, 碘化物法~*, 感应炉熔炼的~*, 高纯~ high purity titanium, 工业~*, 海绵~*, 试~灵 tiron
钛白　titanium white, titanium dioxide
钛板　titanium plate [sheet]
钛泵　titanium（getter）pump
钛衬里[内衬]　titanium lining
钛赤铁矿　haplotypite, basanomelan
钛磁赤铁矿　titanmaghemite
钛磁铁矿　titaniferous magnetite, titanomagnetic ore, titanmagnetite
钛氮化{渗氮}　nitriding of titanium
钛的（四价钛的）　titanic
钛碲矿　winstanleyite
钛电极　titanium electrode
钛电解槽　titanium electrolytic cell
钛锭　titanium ingot
钛氟化钾{K_2TiF_6}　potassium titanium fluoride
钛钙型焊条　lime-titania type electrode
钛钢　titanium steel ◇蒂塔诺尔~*
钛－锆－钼（合金）　titanium-zirconium-molybdenum（TZM）
钛锆钍矿[石]　zerkelite {(Ca, Fe)O·2

(Zr, Ti, Th)O₂}, zirconolite, zirkelite {(Ce,Fe,Ca)O·2(Zr,Ti,Th)O₂}

钛锆钍铀矿 blakeite

钛铬铁矿 titanoarmalcolite

钛钴镍铝合金磁铁 ◇ 新提科纳尔~*

钛硅合金 titanium-silicon

钛硅钠泥矿 pyrhite

钛硅铁(合金) ferrosilico-titanium

钛合金 titanium alloy ◇ α-β~*,超 α 型 ~*,单相~*,稳定 β 型~*,中间~*

钛合金 α'相 α-prime

钛褐钇铌矿 {RE(Nb,Ti,Ta)O₄} risoerite

钛黑云母 wodanite

钛化 (低碳钢表面的) titanizing

钛黄 titan yellow

钛辉石 titanaugite

钛基合金 titanium-base alloy ◇ 海莱特 65 高蠕变强度~*

钛基合金材料 titanium-base material

钛基阳极 titanium substrate anode

钛精矿 titanium concentrate ◇ 浮选高压浸出~*

钛矿床 titanium deposit

钛矿物 titanium mineral

钛冷轧合金 titanium cold rolled alloy ◇ β 型~*

钛榴石 schorlomite

钛铝合金 titanium-aluminium alloy ◇ MST~*

钛铝锆合金 ◇ 马洛里-沙顿~*

钛镁铁矿 kennedyite

钛镁系瓷 magnesium titanate system ceramics

钛母合金 (同"中间钛合金")

钛铌钙铈矿 {8[(Ce,La,Na,Ca,Sr)(Ti,Nb)O₃]} loparite

钛铌钽矿 {Ti,Nb,Ta,Fe)O₂} strueverite

钛铌铀矿 {Y,Er,Ce,U,Fe)(Ti,Nb)₂O₆} blomstrandinite

钛镍黄 titanium yellow

钛铈钙矿 ivoeringite

钛铍合金 titanium-beryllium

钛青铜 (53—59Cu,37—46Zn,少量 Mn、Al、Si、Sn、Mg、Fe,余量 Ti) titanium bronze

钛生产 production of titanium

钛实收率[产出量] titanium yield

钛丝 titanium wire

钛酸 titanic acid

钛酸钡 barium titanate

钛酸钡半导体 semiconductor barium titanate

钛酸铋 bismuth titanate

钛酸钙 {CaO·TiO₂} calcium titanate

钛酸钙瓷 calcium titanate ceramics

钛酸锆酸镧铅 lanthanumdoped lead zirconate-lead titanate

钛酸根 titanate radical

钛酸镧 lanthanium titanate

钛酸铝 aluminium titanate

钛酸镁 {MgO·TiO₂} magnesium titanate

钛酸锰 {MnO·TiO₂} manganese titanate

钛酸钠 {Na₂TiO₃} sodium titanate

钛酸铍 {BeO·TiO₂} beryllium titanate

钛酸铅 lead titanate

钛酸锶系统陶瓷 strontium titanate system ceramics

钛酸盐[酯] titanate

钛碳铁(合金) ferrocarbon titanium

钛钽铌铀矿 {(Nb,Ta)₂O₅(Ti,U,Th,Si)O₂} blomstrandine

钛锑烧绿石 titanantimonpyrochlore

钛添加合金 titanium addition

钛条 titanium bar ◇ 发夹形~ titanium hairpin

钛铁 (中间合金; 25—42Ti, 0.5—8Al, 4—20Si) ferrotitanium

钛铁矿 {FeTiO₃} titaniferous iron ore, ilmenite chrichtonite, gregorite, menaccanite

钛铁矿型焊条 ilmenite type electrode

钛铁砂 iserine, menakanite

钛铁霞辉石 jacupirangite

钛铁铀矿 {(Ti,U)O₂·UO₃(Pb,Fe)O·

Fe_2O_3} ferutite

钛铜 （中间合金；80－90Ti,10－20Cu） titanium copper

钛铜锌合金 ◇ 蒂塔纳洛伊~Titanaloy

钛钍矿 thorutite

钛微合金钢 microalloyed steel with Ti

钛稳定钢 titanium-stabilized steel

钛钨硬质合金 diatitanit ◇ 泰特奈特~"

钛锡合金 titanium-tin alloy

钛稀金矿 cobeite,kobeite

钛线 titanium wire

钛锌钠矿 murataite

钛型焊条 rutile(-type) electrode

钛型药皮 【焊】rutile coating

钛盐 titanium salt

钛氧基{TiO=} titanyl

钛液滴 titanium droplet

钛钇钍矿{(Y,Th,U,Ce){Ti,W}$_4$O$_{11}$} yttrocrasite,yttrokrasit

钛钇铀矿{(Fe,Y,U)(Ti,Sn)$_3$O$_8$} delorenzite

钛铀矿{U,Ca,Fe,Y,Th}$_3$·Ti$_5$O$_{16}$} brannerite

钛载体 titanium carrier

钛渣 titanium slag

钛铸铁 titanium cast iron

钛装甲板 titanium armo(u)r

钛族 titanium family

钛族元素 titanium family element

酞花青（染料） phthalocyanin(e)

酞酸胺 ammonium phthalate

酞酸丁酯 butyl phthalate

酞酸铪 hafnium phthalate

酞酸氢钾[邻苯二甲酸氢钾] potassium acid phthalate (KAP)

酞酸戊酯 amyl phthalate amoil

酞酸盐{C$_6$H$_4$(COOM)} phthalate

酞酸盐淀出物 phthalate-precipitated material

酞酸盐淀出氧化物 phthalate-precipitated oxide

酞酸乙酯 ethl phthalate

酞酸酯{C$_6$H$_4$(COOM)} phthalate(ester)

太空 space

太空采矿 space mining

太空科学 space science

太空时代 space age

太空时代材料 space age material

太空学 spatiography

太空站 space station

太空站时代 space station era

太(拉) trillion

太平门 emergency exit [door], fire escape (F.E.)

太平梯 emergency staircase, escape stair

太阳能 solar energy

太阳(能)电池 solar battery [cell], solaode ◇ 光生伏打~"

太阳能辐射区域精炼 【冶】zone-refining by solar radiation

太阳能炉 solar furnace

太阳能区域精炼 zone refining by solar

太阳能区域精炼炉 solar zone refiner

太阳能区域熔炼炉 solar zone furnace

坍方 collapse, landslide, rock slide, soil slip

坍方防御建筑物 avalanche baffle

坍方防御廊 avalanche gallery

坍落 slump ◇ 无~混凝土 no-slump concrete

坍落度试验（混凝土的） slump test

坍坡 landslide

坍塌 slump, fall down, collapse

坍陷 caving

摊堆煅烧 calcination in heaps

摊平（炉料至炉中）【冶】setting off

摊铺机 paver ◇ 混凝土~", 沥青~asphalt-spreader

弹簧 spring ◇ 叠板~bow type spring, 支承~bearing spring, 装~shock mounting

弹簧安全阀 spring safety valve

弹簧扁钢 spring flat

弹簧标记冲子 spring centre punch

弹簧插座 cushion socket

弹簧承载杆 【机】spring-loaded rod	弹簧扣　latch catch, snap hook
弹簧秤　spring balance [scale]	弹簧模具　floating die (assembly)
弹簧触点　spring contact	弹簧模台　floating die table
弹簧锤　spring hammer ◇ 不跳击～dead-stroke hammer	弹簧模压机　floating die press, dual-pressure press
弹簧挡　spring catch	弹簧模预压机　dual-pressure preformer
弹簧挡板　spring cushioned stop	弹簧模座　floating base
弹簧垫　spring pad [damper]	弹簧平衡导板　【压】guard balanced by a spring
弹簧垫圈　spring washer	
弹簧垫圈用钢丝　wire for spring washer	弹簧平衡吊挂卫板　spring balanced guard
弹簧定心冲子　spring centre punch	弹簧平衡上轧辊　spring balanced top roll
弹簧端板　spring-load dead-plate	弹簧平衡式接轴托架　spring-loaded spindle carrier
弹簧(浮沉)模　spring-floated die, spring(-loaded) floating die	
	弹簧平衡装置　spring balance device
弹簧钢　spring steel ◇ 带槽～grooved spring steel, 西克罗马硅钼～*	弹簧气动夹(电极的)　spring-pneumatic clamp
弹簧钢板　steel spring plate	弹簧青铜　spring bronze
弹簧钢丝　(steel) spring wire ◇ 阀用～valve spring wire, 克立奥忒赫超级～Cryotech, 油回火～oil tempered wire	弹簧塞棒操纵装置(钢包的)　spring lock
	弹簧式平衡　spring balance ◇ 轧辊的～spring roll balance
弹簧箍　spring band	弹簧式上辊平衡装置　top roll spring balance arrangement
弹簧固定式结晶器　spring mounted mould	
	弹簧(式)压力计　spring pressure gauge, spring manometer
弹簧刮刀　spring-held scraper	
弹簧合金　spring alloy ◇ MP35N 超级～*, 等弹性～*, 库米亚尔含铝铜镍～*	弹簧丝　spring wire ◇ 汽车阀门～(铬钒弹簧丝)*
弹簧划线冲子　spring centre punch	弹簧锁　spring lock
弹簧缓冲器　spring buffer [bumper]	弹簧探棒(高炉的)　spring-loaded rod
弹簧黄铜(冷轧的)　spring brass	弹簧调节器　spring-(loaded) governor
弹簧回火　spring temper	弹簧托架　spring bracket
弹簧机构　spring mechanism	弹簧油回火　【金】blazing off
弹簧夹　spring clamp [clip], pinchcock clamp	弹簧(滚动)轴承[弹簧座]　spring bearing
	弹簧装置　spring mechanism
弹簧加压密封　spring-loaded seal	弹回　rebound, spring(ing)
弹簧(加载)式拱脚斜石块　【建】spring-loaded skewback	弹开　bounce
	弹力　elastic force
弹簧减震器　spring damper [absorber]	弹黏(性)体系　elasto-viscous system
弹簧减震式结晶器振动装置　【连铸】low error mold oscillator with stroke adjustment and spring damping	弹射硬化　peen hardening
	弹塑性变形　plastoelastic deformation
	弹塑性力学　plasto-elasticity
弹簧卡盘　spring [split] chuck	弹塑性有限元法　elastic-plastic finite element method

弹跳	bounce, cushioning, spring(ing) ◇ 机座~*
弹跳接触	bounce contact
弹跳硬度	rebound hardness
弹性	elasticity, elastic property, springiness ◇ 超~*,去~钢丝*
弹性变形	elastic deformation [strain], temporary set ◇ 辊系~模型*,轧机牌坊的~*
弹性变形补偿系统	elastic deformation compensation system
弹性变形区[范围]	range of proportionality
弹性波	elastic wave
弹性材料	elastic [resilient] material
弹性参数	elastic parameter
弹性残存变形	elastic drift
弹性掺入体	elastic inclusion
弹性常数	elastic constant
弹性衬垫	elastic washer
弹性斥力	elastic repulsion
弹性顶尖	movable centre
弹性定律	law of elasticity
弹性(动)力学	elastodynamics
弹性断裂	elastic break-down
弹性断裂力学	elastic fracture mechanics
弹性对称	elastic symmetry
弹性反冲	elastic recoil
弹性范围	elastic range
弹性刚度	elastic stiffness
弹性各向同性体	elastically isotropic body
弹性各向异性	elastic anisotropy
弹性各向异性晶体	elastically anisotropic crystal
弹性固定	elastic fixing
弹性固体	elastic solid ◇ 胡克~Hookian solid
弹性合金	elastic alloy
弹性横向各向同性	transverse isotropy of elasticity
弹性后效	elastic aftereffect [lag, spring-back, drift], post-elastic behaviour, residual elasticity, spring-back ◇ 生坯~【粉】green spring
弹性恢复(变形的)	elastic restitution
弹性回复	elastic recovery [come-back], spring-back
弹性回复区(冷轧的)	elastic recovery zone
弹性回弹(能)	elastic resilience
弹性回跳	rebound elasticity
弹性基体	elastic matrix
弹性畸变	elastic distorsion
弹性极限	elastic(ity) limit (E.L.)
弹性介质	elastic medium
弹性劲度	elastic stiffness
弹性晶粒	elastic grain
弹性静力学	elastostatics
弹性理论	theory of elasticity, elastic theory
弹性力学	elasticity mechanics
弹性沥青	dopplerite, dopplerite
弹性联轴器[节]	elastic [flexible, resilient] coupling
弹性连续区	elastic continuum
弹性连续体	elastic continuum
弹性梁	elastic beam
弹性流体	elastic fluid
弹性流体动力学的	elastohydrodynamics
弹性模量[模数]	elastic(ity) modulus ◇ 表观~*,等效~*,体积~bulk modulus,通体~*,杨氏~*
弹性模量效应	modulus effect
弹性能	elastic energy
弹性膨胀	elastic expansion [dilatation]
弹性碰撞	elastic collision
弹性碰撞能量转移	energy transfer in elastic collision
弹性疲劳	elastic fatigue
弹性平衡	elastic equilibrium
弹性平衡方程	equation of elastic equilibrium
弹性破坏	elastic failure [break-down]
弹性强度	elastic strength

弹性切变　elastic shear
弹性区　elastic region
弹性屈服　elastic yield
弹性圈[环]　snap ring
弹性散射　elastic scattering
弹性散射截面　elastic-scattering cross-seciton
弹性伸长　elastic elongation
弹性石英　elastic quartz
弹性时间效应　elastic time effect
弹性收缩　elastic contraction [constrain]
弹性松弛　elastic relaxation
弹性-塑性断裂力学　elastic-plastic fracture mechanics
弹性塑性体　elastoplastic body
弹性体　elastic body, elastomer
弹性体积收缩　elastic volumetric contraction
弹性弯晶　elastically bent crystal
弹性弯曲　elastic bending
弹性位错　elastic dislocation ◇ 强度无限小的～*
弹性位移传播　propagation of elastic displacement
弹性系数　elastic coefficient, coefficient of elasticity, elastic(ity) modulus
弹性纤维　elastic fiber, spandex
弹性相互作用　elastic interaction
弹性楔　elastic wedge
弹性行为　elastic behaviour
弹性压扁（轧辊的）　elastic flattening
弹性压曲[弹性纵向弯曲]　elastic buckling
弹性压缩[压力]　elastic compression
弹性压缩区（冷轧的）　elastic compression zone
弹性延伸　elastic extension
弹性应变　elastic strain
弹性应变场　elastic strain field
弹性应变能　elastic strain energy
弹性应力　elastic stress [tension]
弹性应力应变曲线　elastic stress-strain curve
弹性约束　elastic constrain
弹性振动　elastic vibration
弹性支座　elastic support, yielding seat
弹性值　value of elasticity
弹性滞后　elastic hysteresis [lag]
弹性轴承　elastic bearing, elastically supported bearing
弹性撞击　elastic impact
弹性状态　elastic state, spring temper（有色金属的）
坦查洛伊铝锌铸造合金（8Zn, 0.8Cu, 0.4Mg, 余量 Al）　Tenzaloy
坦德姆合金（6Sn, 17Sb, 余量 Pb）　tandem metal
坦德姆锡青铜（78Cu, 22Sn）　tandem metal
坦噶洛陶瓷（刀具）　tungalox
坦纳感应炉生铁矿石炼钢法　【钢】Tanna process
坦帕尔示温合金　Tempil alloy
坦帕洛伊耐蚀铜镍合金（89—96Cu, 3—5Ni, 0.8—1Si, 0—4.7Al）　Tempaloy
坦皮赖克示温漆　Tempilac
坦普赖特示温合金（铅锡铋合金或铅锡镉合金）　Temperite alloy
坦赛莱特高强度耐蚀铸造黄铜（64Cu, 29.5Zn, 3Al, 2.5Mn, 1Fe）　Tensilite
坦提龙高硅耐酸耐热铸铁（0.7—1.2C, 14—15Si, 2—2.5Mn, 0.05—0.1P, 0.05—0.15S）　Tantiron
坦托尔钽镍铬合金工具钢　Tantal tool alloy
钽{Ta}　tantalum ◇ 亚[三价]～的 tantalous, 枝晶[树枝状]～tantalum dendrite
钽棒　tantalum rod
钽铋矿　bismutotantalite
钽衬里　tantalum lining
钽的（五价钽的）　tantalic
钽粉　tantalum powder
钽氟化钾　（同"氟钽酸钾"）
钽钙矿　rynersonite

钽 碳　tan

钽锆钇矿{(Y,Ca,Ce,U,Th)(Nb,Ta,Ti)$_2$O$_6$}　loranskite
钽隔板　tantalum spacer
钽钩　tantalum hook
钽管　tantalum tube
钽合金　tantalum alloy, tantaloy
钽化合物　tantalum compound ◇ 五价～ tantalic compound
钽基合金　tantalum-base alloy
钽夹　tantalum hook
钽加热元件　tantalum (heating) element
钽钾盐　tantalum potassium salt
钽矿床　tantalum deposit
钽粒　tantalum roundel
钽铝石　simpsonite, calogerasite
钽锰矿　manganotantalite
钽铌分离法　columbium-tantalum separation process
钽铌合金　tantalum-niobium alloy
钽铌矿　columbotantalite ore
钽铌酸盐　tanto-niobate
钽铌酞铀矿　guimaraesite
钽铌铁　ferrotantalum-niobium
钽铌铁合金　ferrocolumbium-tantalum
钽铌铁矿　ildefonsite
钽铌钇矿　khlopinite
钽镍铬合金工具钢 ◇ 坦托尔～Tantal tool alloy
钽烧绿石　haddamite
钽丝　tantalum wire
钽酸　tantalic acid
钽酸锂　lithium tantalate
钽酸钠{x Na$_2$O·y Ta$_2$O$_5$}　sodium tantaiate
钽酸盐{x M$_2$O·y Ta$_2$O$_5$}　tantalate ◇ 碱金属～alkali tantalate
钽钛硬质合金　tantalum-carbide titanium-carbide cobalt alloy
钽钛铀矿　djalmaite
钽锑矿　stibiotantalite
钽添加合金　tantalum addition
钽条　tantalum rod

钽铁　ferrotantalum
钽铁金红石{Ti, Nb, Ta, Fe) O$_2$}　strueverite
钽铁矿{(Fe, Mn)(Nb, Ta)$_2$O$_6$}　tantalite (ore), tantaline
钽土　soumite
钽钨合金　tantalum-tungsten alloy
钽锡矿　thoreaulite, thorolite
钽锡石　tantalian-cassiterite
钽稀金矿　tanteuxenite
钽盐　tantalum salt
钽钇矿{(Y, Fe, U, Ca)(Ta, Nb) O$_4$}　yttrotantalite, yttrotantal
钽钇易解石　tantalaeschynite-(Y)
钽易解石　tantalaeschynite
钽阴极　tantalum cathode
钽铀矿　uranotantalite
钽整流器　tantalum rectifier
钽(质热)反射器　tantalum reflector
碳{C}　carbon ◇ 不含～的 carbon-free, 覆～处理*, 富～区 carbonrich area, 胶体～colloidal carbon, 结合～bound carbon, 内含～internal carbon, 溶解～【冶】dissolved carbon, 外加～external carbon, 无～钢*, 无气～gas-free carbon, 有效[平衡]～available carbon
碳板　carbon plate [slab]
碳棒　carbon rod
碳棒电炉　carbon bar furnace
碳钡矿{BaCO$_3$}　witherite
碳倍数　carbon multiple
碳比(纯净煤中的)【焦】carbon ratio
碳铋矿　agnesite
碳丙铁　boydenite, austenite
碳尘　carbon dust
碳沉积　carbon deposition [distribution]
碳衬　【冶】carbon lining
碳处理　carbon treatment
碳传感器　【电】carbon pickup
碳单纤维　carbon monofilament
碳氮共渗　【金】nitrocarburizing, carbonitriding ◇ 气体～gas carbonitriding, 液体

~liquid carbonitriding
碳氮共渗硬化法 nicarbing process
碳氮化锆{ZrC-ZrN} zirconium carbonitride[cyanonitride]
碳氮化钛{TiC-TiN} titanium carbonitride
碳氮化钛涂层 titanium carbonitride coating
碳氮化钽{TaC-TaN} tantalum carbonitride
碳氮化物 carbon-nitride, cyanonitride
碳氮化物涂层 carbon-nitride coating
碳氮化铀 uranium carbonitride
碳氮钛矿 cochranite
碳当量 carbon equivalent (CE) ◇ 测~用高温计*, 流动性~*
碳底(炉底)分批热处理炉 car-bottom batch-type furnace
碳电池 carbon cell
碳电弧 【冶】carbon arc
碳电弧焊头 carbon arc-welding head
碳电极 carbon[charcoal] electrode, carbon rod ◇ 镀[披]铂~*
碳电极夹头[把持器] 【冶】carbon-electrode holder
碳堆调压器 carbon-pile (voltage) regulator
碳分布 carbon distribution
碳分子筛 molecular sieve carbon[coke]
碳粉 carbon powder[dust], powdered carbon
碳粉电阻(器) carbon-dust resistance
碳氟化合物 fluorocarbon, chempro
碳覆层 carbon coating
碳复合耐火材料 carbon-bearing refractory
碳复型 carbon replica
碳复型技术[制作方法] carbon replica technique
碳钙铋矿[碳铋钙石] beyerite
碳钙镁铀矿{CaMgUO$_2$(CO$_3$)$_3$·12H$_2$O} swartzite

碳钙铈石 (calcioancylite)
碳钙铀矿 zellerite
碳钢 carbon steel (c.s.) ◇ 阿维斯塔~*, 可淬硬~*, 马氏体类~*, 渗铜~*
碳钢锭 carbon steel ingot
碳钢轧辊 【压】carbon steel roll, straight carbon roll
碳钢铸件 carbon steel casting
碳锆锶矿 weloganite
碳铬合金钢 ◇ 杜罗伊德~(表面堆焊材料) Duroid
碳骼[架] 【耐】carbon skeleton
碳管电阻(加热)炉 graphite-tube resistance furnace
碳管(短路加热)炉 carbon(-tube) short-circuiting furnace, graphite-tube shortcircuit furnace, carbon tube furnace ◇ 氢气保护~*
碳管真空炉 carbon tube vacuum furnace
碳硅棒 globar
碳硅棒电阻(加热)炉 globar(-heated) furnace, globar resistance furnace
碳硅棒电阻加热元件 globar resistor element
碳硅棒发热[加热]元件 globar (heating) element, silit heating element
碳硅棒管式炉 globar tube furnace
碳硅比(生铁的) carbon-silicon ratio
碳硅钙石{Ca$_5$[SiO$_4$]$_2$[CO$_3$]} spurrite
碳硅钙钇石 caysichite
碳硅石{SiC} moissanite
碳硅铈钙石 kainosite
碳硅钛钕钠石 tundrite-(Nd)
碳硅钛铈钠石 tundrite
碳含量 carbon content ◇ 当量~*
碳含量计 carbometer
碳含量试验 carbon test
碳黑 (hydro)carbon[jet] black, black(ing)[deposited, soot] carbon, lampblack, conductex ◇ G.P.F.通用~G.P.F.(carbon) black, 槽法~*, 盘阀

碳 tan

~disc black,气~(同"气黑"),润滑剂~*,无~火焰 sootless flame,无尘~free flowing black
碳黑沉积物 carbon-black deposition
碳黑生成(气体渗碳时的) 【金】sooting
碳黑涂料 blacking carbon
碳糊 carbon(aceous) paste
碳糊车间 carbon paste plant
碳糊制备 carbon paste preparation
碳弧 【冶】carbon arc
碳弧表面切割(清理) carbon arc gouging
碳弧焊(接) carbon-arc welding (CAW) ◇间接~*,气体保护~*
碳弧焊接法 carbon arc process, carbon-electrode process
碳弧焊(接)焊缝 carbon arc weld
碳弧焊炬 carbon arc torch
碳弧气刨 carbon arc air gouging
碳弧焊头 carbon arc-welding head
碳弧切割 carbon arc cutting (CAC)
碳弧(硬)钎焊 carbon arc brazing
碳化 carbonizing, carbonisation, carbonization, carbonation,【化】carburisation, carburising, carburization, carburizing ◇半[局部]~ partial carbonization,坩埚~ crucible carburizing,高温~*,活性~activated carburizing,间歇~*,可~的 carbonizable,连续~*,流态化床~*,预先~ precarburization
碳化斑 carbon stain
碳化钚 plutonium carbide
碳化二钼{Mo_2C} molybdenum carbide
碳化二钨 ditungsten carbide
碳化钒 vanadium carbide
碳化腐蚀 (同"留碳腐蚀")
碳化钙{CaC_2} calcium carbide, acetylene lime
碳化钙料筐 carbide basket
碳化钙团块[压块] carbide cake
碳化锆{ZrC} zirconium carbide
碳化铬 chromic carbide {Cr_3C_2}, chromium carbide {CrC_3, CrC_4}

碳化铬拉模 chrome carbide die
碳化硅{SiC} silicon-carbide, carborundum, silicide of carbon, silicized carbon, silit(电阻材料),【钢】(增硅脱氧用) carbo-sil, ferrocarbo ◇氮化硅黏结~*,结晶~*,克里斯托隆人造~(研磨用) Crystolon,无定形~*,氧化物黏结~*
碳化硅棒 silit rod
碳化硅炽热棒 globar
碳化硅电炉 carborundum furnace
碳化硅电阻棒 silicon carbide resistance rod, carbonsilicide rod
碳化硅发热体 silit heating element
碳化硅非线性电阻 thyrite (resistor)
碳化硅辐射管 silicon carbide radiant tube
碳化硅坩埚 silicon carbide sagger
碳化硅高级耐火材料 ◇里弗雷克斯~ Refrex,西尔弗拉克斯~ Silfrax
碳化硅管 carborundum tube
碳化硅加热管 silicon carbide heating tube
碳化硅加热元件 silicon carbide heating element, carborundum heating element
碳化硅结块 【冶】carborundum accretion
碳化硅晶须 SiC crystal whisker
碳化硅耐火材料 silicon carbide refractory, carborundum refractory, refrax ◇硅结合的~*,卡波弗拉克斯~*,黏土结合~*
碳化硅纤维(隔热材料) silicon carbide fibre, fibrox
碳化硅增强体 silicon carbide reinforcement
碳化硅蒸馏罐 silicon carbide retort
碳化硅砖 silicon carbide brick, carborundum [SiC] brick
碳化硅转化涂层 silicon carbide conversion coating
碳化铪{HfC} hafnium carbide
碳化砂砖 carbonified sand-lime brick
碳化剂 carbonizer, carburetant, carburizer
碳化镧{LaC_2} lanthanum carbide
碳化锂{Li_2C_2} lithium carbide

碳化炉 retort ◇ 立式~【焦】vertical retort, 卧式~ horizontal retort, 移动算~*

碳化铝{Al₄C₃} aluminium carbide

碳化锰 manganese carbide

碳化钼 molybdenum carbide

碳化铌{NbC} niobium [columbium] carbide

碳化硼[碳化四硼]{B₄C} boron carbide, Norbide

碳化硼包铝复合板 ◇ 博瑞~*

碳化硼控制棒 boron carbide control bar

碳化硼铝 Boral

碳化铍{Be₂C} beryllium carbide

碳化期 carburizing cycle

碳化气氛 carburizing atmosphere

碳化球团 【团】carbonized pellet

碳化热 heat of carbonization

碳化三锰{Mn₃C} manganese carbide

碳化三铁{Fe₃C} tri-ferrous carbide, iron carbide

碳化铈{CeC₂} cerium carbide

碳化室 【焦】coking chamber, retort, carbonizer, oven ◇ 热砂~ hot sand carbonizer, 水平~ horizontal chamber

碳化室顶石墨 roof carbon

碳化室高度 chamber height

碳化塔 carbonators

碳化钛{TiC} titanium carbide

碳化钛粉末 titanium carbide powder ◇ WZ~烧结合金*

碳化钛基硬质合金 titanium carbide-base alloy

碳化钛金属陶瓷 titanium-carbide cermet

碳化钛涂层 titanium carbide coating

碳化钛型(药皮)焊条 titanium carbide electrode

碳化钛硬质合金 titanium carbide (alloy) ◇ 钴结~*, 海梅特~Hinet

碳化钽{TaC, Ta₂C} tantalum carbide ◇ 拉梅特~*

碳化钽刀具合金 tantalum tool alloy

碳化钽粉末 tantalum carbide powder

碳化铁{Fe₃C} ferrous carbide, carbide of iron ◇ 黑格[χ]~*, 溶性~ soluble iron carbide

碳化铁合金 iron carbide alloy

碳化铁体{Fe₃C} cementite (carbide)

碳化钍{ThC₂} thorium carbide

碳化温度 carburizing temperature

碳化钨(硬质合金) tungsten carbide (TC), wolfram carbide ◇ 阿列奈特~系列 Allenite, 卡勃洛伊~carboloy metal, 科佩尔梅特~合金 Copelmet, 烧结~*, 塔布~耐磨焊料*, 维迪阿~切削刀具 Widia cutting tool

碳化钨粉末 tungsten carbide powder

碳化钨-钴刀头 tungsten carbide-cobalt tool tip

碳化钨金属陶瓷 tungsten-carbide cermet

碳化钨磨球 tungsten carbide ball

碳化钨嵌芯式模子 tungsten carbide insert-type die

碳化钨压[拉]模 tungsten carbide die

碳化钨硬质合金(95.6W, 3.9C) cemented tungsten carbide, diamondite, carballoy ◇ 伐斯科洛依-雷曼~ Vascoloy-Ramet, 钴结~*, 铁结~*

碳化钨轧辊 tungsten carbide roll

碳化钨制品 tungsten carbide composition

碳化物 carbide, carburet, carbonide (金属碳化物) ◇ ε~*, 成串状~ stringer carbide, 多元[复合]~*, 富铬~ chromium-rich carbide, 共晶~ carbide of eutectic, 锯齿形~ saw-tooth carbide, 卡帕~*, 烧结~*, 生成~的元素【钢】carbide former, 网状~ carbide network, 先共析~ proeutectoid carbide, 形成~的合金元素 stabilizer, 一次[初生]~ primary carbide, 针状~ acicular carbide, 铸造~ cast carbide

碳化物边界 carbide boundary

碳化物层 carbide layer

碳化物沉淀 【金】carbide precipitate [precipitation]

碳化物沉淀区[范围] carbide precipitation range
碳化物刀具 carbide tool
碳化物分布 distribution of carbides
碳化物分解速率 【金】breakdown rate of carbide
碳化物分析 carbide analysis
碳化物粉末 carbide powder [dust], pulverized carbide
碳化物粉末混合物 carbide powder mixture
碳化物坩埚 carbide crucible
碳化物合金 carbide alloy
碳化物基金属陶瓷 carbide-base cermet
碳化物加热炉 carbide furnace
碳化物金属陶瓷 carbide cermet
碳化物浸蚀 carbide etch
碳化物晶须强化金属 carbide whisker reinforced metal
碳化物颗粒分布 carbide particle distribution
碳化物块 【粉】carbide ingot
碳化物离析 carbides isolation
碳化物氯化 carbide chlorination
碳化物弥散性[作用] dispersion of carbides
碳化物耐火材料 carbide refractory
碳化物－黏结剂混合物 carbide-binder mixture
碳化物偏析 【金】carbide segregation
碳化物片 【金】carbide platelets
碳化物强化铬基合金 carbide-strengthened chromium alloy
碳化物强化合金 carbide strengthened alloy
碳化物球化 carbide spheroidization
碳化物球化退火 carbide-spheroidization annealing
碳化物曲线(S曲线图上的) carbide line
碳化物热还原法 carbide reduction process
碳化物熔渣 【色】carbide sludge

碳化物熔渣坑 【焊】carbide sludge pit
碳化物烧结 cementing of carbides
碳化物退火(高速钢的) carbide annealing
碳化物网 carbide network
碳化物稳定剂 carbide stabilizer
碳化物稳定能力 carbide-retaining power ◇ 铸铁的～*
碳化物稳定元素 carbide stabilizing element
碳化物析出 carbide precipitation
碳化物析出物 【金】carbide precipitate
碳化物相 carbide phase [constituent]
碳化物型金属陶瓷 carbide-type cermet
碳化物形[生]成元素 carbide forming element, carbide former
碳化物形态 carbide morphology
碳化物形态学 morphology of carbides
碳化物渣 carbide slag
碳化物贮斗 carbide hopper
碳化物装炉箱 carbide tray
碳化物组分 carbide constituent [ingredient]
碳化压力 【焦】carbonization pressure
碳化焰 carbonizing [carburizing] flame
碳化钇{YC$_2$} yttrium carbide
碳化铀 uranium carbide
碳化作用 carbonification, carbonization, carbonisation, carbonation
碳还原 carbon-reduction, reduction by [with] carbon ◇ 电热～*
碳还原钨粉 carbon-reduced tungsten powder
碳基黏合剂 carbon-base binder
碳极 carbon electrode ◇ 电弧焊用～carbon arc electrode
碳极电池 carbon block cell
碳极电焊 carbon-electrode welding
碳极电弧 carbon arc
碳极电弧焊 carbon [graphite] arc welding ◇ 惰性气体(保护)～*, 气体保护～*

碳极电弧焊接法 （同"碳弧焊接法"）
碳极电弧手工焊 manual carbon arc welding
碳极端陷口 electrode crater
碳极挤压［压力］机 carbon-electrode press, carbon extrusion press
碳尖电极［碳极尖］ carbon (electrode) tip
碳浆法 carbon in pulp (CIP)
碳浸法 carbon in leach (CIL)
碳精 carbon, graphite
碳精板 carbon plate
碳精块 carbon block
碳块衬里 carbonblock lining ◇ 出铁槽［浇口］~*
碳块炉底 carbon bottom
碳扩散 carbon diffusion
碳镧石 lanthanite
碳砾 carbon gravel
碳粒 carbon granule, granular carbon
碳粒电阻炉 cryptol [granular-resistor] furnace
碳粒(短路加热)炉 graphite short-circuit furnace, kryptol furnace
碳粒发热体电炉 Arsem furnace
碳粒砂 【铸】carbon sand
碳量不足的还原 reduction with a deficiency of carbon
碳量测定 determination of carbon
碳量控制 carbon control
碳量梯度 carbon gradient
碳镁磷灰石 bialite
碳膜电阻(器) carbon-film [deposited-carbon] resistor
碳膜法 carbon film technique
碳浓度 carbon concentration
碳钕石 lanthanite-(Nd)
碳屏 carbon screen
碳迁移 carbon migration
碳青铜 (75.47Cu, 14.57Pb, 9.72Sn, 0.1C) carbon bronze
碳氢比 C－H (carbon-hydrogen) ratio
碳氢化合物 （同"烃"）◇ 不挥发性~*,

裂化~ cracked hydrocarbon
碳氢化合物类 hydrocarbons
碳氢化合物喷吹 hydrocarbon injection
碳氢化合物溶剂 hydrocarbon solvent
碳氢化合物溶液 hydrocarbon solution
碳氢化合物稀释剂 hydrocarbon diluent
碳氢氧焰切割 oxyhydrocarbon cutting
碳热法炼铝 carbothermic smelting of aluminum
碳热法炼镁厂 carbothermic magnesium plant
碳热还原 carbothermic [carbon-thermal] reduction
碳(热)还原法［碳热法］ carbon reduction process [technique], carbothermic [carbothermal] method [process]
碳热还原反应 carbothermic (reduction) reaction
碳溶解性［度］ carbon solubility
碳烧舟 carbon boat
碳势 carbon potential
碳铈钙钡石 ewaldite
碳铈镁石 sahamalite
碳铈钠石 carbocernaite
碳铈石 lanthanite-(Ce)
碳刷 carbon brush
碳水化合物 carbohydrate
碳锶矿 strontianite
碳丝 carbon filament
碳丝灯 carbon-filament lamp
碳素沉积 carbon deposition
碳素衬里［内衬］ carbon lining
碳素捣结料 【耐】carbon rammed mass
碳素电极 carbon electrode [pole]
碳素电阻体 carbon resistor block
碳素钢 carbon [ordinary] steel, plain (carbon) steel ◇ 普通~*,渗碳~*
碳素钢锭 carbon steel ingot
碳素格子 （氯化炉的） carbon resistor block
碳素铬铁 carbon ferrochrome
碳素工具钢 carbon [unalloyed] tool steel

碳 tan

◇ 银亮抛光~*
碳素结构钢 carbon constructional steel ◇ 优质~*
碳素晶格 carbon lattice
碳素炉底 carbon bottom ◇ 尤卡~*
碳素锰铁 carbon ferromanganese
碳素耐火砖 carbon refractory block
碳素黏结剂 carbon cement[binder]
碳素溶液 carbon solution
碳素涂料 foundery [wet] blacking
碳素阳极 carbon anode
碳素制品 【耐】carbon product
碳素铸钢 carbon cast steel
碳酸铵{$(NH_4)_2CO_3$} ammonium carbonate
碳酸铵浸出 ammonium carbonate leaching
碳酸铵亚铜 cuprous-ammonium carbonate
碳酸胺 amine carbonate
碳酸饱和 【代】carbonation
碳酸钡{$BaCO_3$} barium carbonate
碳酸钡矿 witherite
碳酸铋 bismuth carbonate, waltherite
碳酸钚 plutonium carbonate
碳酸镝{$Dy_2(CO_3)_3$} dysprosium carbonate
碳酸铥{$Tu_2(CO_3)_3$} thulium carbonate
碳酸二丁胺 dibutylamine carbonate
碳酸钆{$Gd_2(CO_3)_3$} gadolinium carbonate
碳酸钙{$CaCO_3$} calcium carbonate
碳酸酐 carbonic (acid) anhydride, barbon dioxide
碳酸钴{$CoCO_3$} cobalt carbonate
碳酸化固结【团】carbonate bonding
碳酸化器 carbonator
碳酸化曲线 carbonation curve
碳酸化塔 carbonating [carbonation] tower [column]
碳酸环己胺 cyclohexylamine carbonate
碳酸钾{K_2CO_3} potassium carbonate, potash ◇ 粗~potash black-ash
碳酸钪{$Sc_2(CO_3)_3$} scandium carbonate
碳酸锂{Li_2CO_3} lithium carbonate
碳酸镧{$La_2(CO_3)_3$} lanthanum carbonate
碳酸镭{$RaCO_3$} radium carbonate
碳酸镁{$MgCO_3$} magnesium carbonate
碳酸镁钙 magnesium calcium carbonate
碳酸镁铬矿{$6MgO·Cr_2O_3·CO_2·12H_2O$} stichtite
碳酸镁铁矿{$6MgO·Fe_2O_3·CO_2·12H_2O$} pyroaurite
碳酸钠{Na_2CO_3} sodium carbonate, soda (salt), washing soda ◇ 工业[商品]~*,加~熔炼*
碳酸钠反应 soda-ash reaction
碳酸钠含量 sodium carbobate inventory
碳酸钠浸出 sodium [alkali] carbonate leaching, soda leaching ◇ 高压釜~法*
碳酸钠熔融法 sodium carbonate fusion method
碳酸钠熔融(体) sodium carbobate fusion
碳酸钠洗提 sodium carbobate strip
碳酸镍{$NiCO_3$} nickel carbonate
碳酸钕{$Nd_2(CO_3)_3$} neodymium carbonate
碳酸镨{$Pr_2(CO_3)_3$} praseodymium carbonate
碳酸气 carbonic acid gas
碳酸铅{$PbCO_3$} lead carbonate
碳酸氢铵{$(NH_4)HCO_3$} ammonium bicarbonate
碳酸氢钙 calcium bicarbonate
碳酸氢钾{$KHCO_3$} potassium bicarbonate, saleratus
碳酸氢镁 magnesium bicarbonate
碳酸氢钠{$NaHCO_3$} sodium hydrogen carbonate, sodium bicarbonate, baking soda
碳酸氢铷{$RbHCO_3$} rubidium bicarbonate
碳酸氢铯{$CsHCO_3$} cesium bicarbonate
碳酸氢盐{$MHCO_3$} acid carbonate, bicar-

bonate
碳酸氢盐离子 bicarbonate ion
碳酸铷 {Rb_2CO_3} rubidium carbonate
碳酸钐 {$Sm_2(CO_3)_3$} samaric carbonate
碳酸铈 {$Ce_2(CO_3)_3$} cerous carbonate
碳酸铯 {Cs_2CO_3} cesium carbonate
碳酸锶 {$SrCO_3$} strontium carbonate
碳酸锶矿 strontianite
碳酸锶铈矿 {$(Ce, La)_4(Sr, Ca)_3CO_7(OH)_4 \cdot 3H_2O$} ancylite
碳酸铊 thallium [thallous] carbonate
碳酸铽 {$Tb_2(CO_3)_3$} terbium carbonate
碳酸铁钙复盐 iron calcium carbonate
碳酸铜 copper carbonate, mineral green
碳酸钍 {$Th(CO_3)_2$} thorium carbonate
碳酸锌 {$ZnCO_3$} zinc carbonate
碳酸亚铁 {$FeCO_3$} ferrous carbonate
碳酸盐 carbonate (carb.) ◇ 煅烧～ calcined carbonate
碳酸盐法 carbonation
碳酸盐高压浸出 carbonate autoclaving
碳酸盐浸出 carbonate leach(ing) ◇ 碱金属～*
碳酸盐浸出法 carbonate leaching process
碳酸盐浸出类精矿 carbonate leach type concentrate
碳酸盐浸出液 carbonate leach liquor
碳酸盐离解热力学 thermodynamics of carbonate dissociation
碳酸盐黏结球团 carbonate-bonded pellet
碳酸盐黏结团块(法) carbonate-bonded briquette
碳酸盐熔剂 carbonate flux
碳酸盐溶解 carbonate dissolution
碳酸盐溶液 carbonate solution ◇ 减压～脱硫法*
碳酸盐容量 carbonate capacity
碳酸盐-碳酸氢盐浸出 carbonate-bicarbonate leaching
碳酸盐-碳酸氢盐溶解 carbonate-bicarbonate dissolution
碳酸盐铀矿石 carbonate uranium ore
碳酸氧铋 bismuthyl carbonate
碳酸氧锆 {$(ZrO)CO_3$} zirconyl carbonate
碳酸钇 {$Y_2(CO_3)_3$} yttrium carbonate
碳酸镱 {$Yb_2(CO_3)_3$} ytterbium carbonate
碳酸铀配离子 uranium carbonate complexion
碳损耗 carbon loss
碳-碳复合物 carbon-carbon composite, C/C composite
碳-碳化硅热电偶 carbon-silicon carbide thermocouples
碳梯度 carbon gradient
碳铁镁铈石 sahamalite
碳铁烧结矿 carbon-iron agglomerate
碳铜钙铀矿 {$Ca_2CuU(CO_3)_5 \cdot 6H_2O$} voglite
碳铜铅钙石 schuilingite
碳团簇 carbon cluster
碳脱氧金属 carbon-deoxidized metal
碳吸附 carbon adsorption
碳吸热气化反应 endothermic gasification of carbon (EGC)
碳系离子交换剂 carbonaceous ion exchanger
碳纤维 carbon filament [fibre]
碳芯线 【钢】carbon core wire
碳锌比 carbon-zinc ratio
碳锌电池 carbon-zinc battery (CZB)
碳-氧反应 carbon-oxygen reaction
碳氧化 carbon oxidation
碳氧化期 【钢】carbon [boiling] period, carbon blow (转炉的)
碳氧化速率 rate of carbon oxidation
碳-氧平衡 carbon-oxygen equilibrium
碳钇锶石 donnayite
碳铀钙石 {$Ca_2(UO_2) \cdot (CO_3)_3 \cdot 10H_2O$} uranothallite
碳铀矿 joliotite
碳原子 carbon atom ◇ 结点间[填隙]～扩散*
碳源 carbon source
碳质变阻器 carbon rheostat

碳质沉积　carbonaceous deposit [sediment]
碳质打结炉底　carbon hearth bottom
碳质电极电弧焊　carbon-electrode arc welding
碳质电阻(器)　carbon resistance [resistor]
碳质复合耐火材料　carbon composite refractory ◇ 含钛~*
碳质坩埚　carbon crucible
碳质膏　carbonaceous cement
碳质固体渗碳　(同"固体渗碳剂渗碳")
碳质糊　carbonaceous cement
碳质化合物　carbonaceous compound
碳质还原剂　carbonaceous reducing agent [material]
碳质浇口砂　carbonaceous runner sand
碳质炉床　carbon hearth
碳质炉底　carbon hearth (bottom)
碳质耐火材料　carbon refractory ◇ 白云石~*, 无烟煤~*
碳质耐火材料侧墙环　【铁】carbon refractory sidewall annulus
碳质耐火堵泥　carbonaceous brasque
碳质泥料　carbon loam
碳质泥套泥料　【铁】carbon plastic
碳质黏合剂　carbon-base binder
碳质黏土　carbonaceous clay, bast
碳质炮泥[封泥]　(出铁口的) carbonaceous taphole clay
碳质气氛　carbonaceous atmosphere
碳质燃料　carbonaceous fuel
碳质烧舟　carbon boat
碳质物料　carbonaceous mass
碳质页岩　carbon shale
碳质炸药　carbonite
碳砖　【铁】carbon brick, 【耐】carbon product ◇ 波纹[波形]~*, 大块~【铁】carbon block, 热压~-陶瓷杯技术*, 尤卡~*
碳砖衬里[炉衬]　carbonblock lining
碳砖砌风口带　carbon brick breast wall
碳转变　【金】carbon change
碳阻棒　carbon resistor rod
碳阻(电)炉[碳质电阻炉]　carbon resistance [resistor] furnace, graphite resistor furnace ◇ 贝利~*, 霍斯金~ Hoskin's furnace
碳阻辐射加热炉　graphite resistor radiation furnace
碳阻(加热)元件　carbon resistance element
碳阻燃烧炉　carbon combustion furnace
碳作用(对砌体或发热体)　carbon effect
探棒　sonde
探槽　【地】ditch, trench
探槽取样【采】trench sampling
探测　detecting, detection, search, exploring, (exploratory) survey, sounding
探测裂缝生长用位移计　displacement gauge for crack growth detector
探测灵敏度　detectivity
探测脉冲　sound(ing) [direct] impulse
探测能力　detectivity
探测器　detector, detection instrument, locator, probe, search unit, sonde, prod (磁力探伤仪的) ◇ 带式~ tape probe, 防爆式~*, 缝隙式~*, 福斯特~ Foerster probe, 霍尔~ 测头*, 角度~ angle probe, 快速~ fast detector, 气动式~ air-operated detector
探测器缝隙　detector slit
探测器[探针]线圈　probe coil ◇ 袖珍~ hand probe coil
探测器[探针]线圈间距　probe coil clearance
探测[探漏]气体　probe [tracer] gas, search-gas
探测[探针]数据　probe data
探测试验(检漏用)　probe test
探(测)头　probe, detector, search unit, detecting [sensing] head, feeler, exploring block (探伤仪的)
探测线圈　search coil

探测元件 detecting element
探测装置 search unit, exploring block
探查 exploration, search
探尺 examiner,【铁】(测量料线用) stock [sounding, gauge, test(ing), trial] rod, sounder
探尺记录图 【铁】stock rod record
探尺卷扬机 【铁】stock rod winch, stock-line winch
探尺孔 【铁】try hole
探尺控制机构 test rod mechanism
探井[坑] exploratory well [shaft], test [bore] pit
探孔 handhole
探矿仪 mine locator
探矿者 mineralizer, prospector
探料尺 【铁】(同"探尺")
探(料)尺装置 stock (line) indicator
探料设备 【铁】sounding device
探漏器 leak tester [detector] ◇ 电火花线圈~*
探伤 flaw [defect, crack] detection, flaw inspection ◇ X射线~*, γ射线~gamma-ray test, 超声波~*, 反射式~法 reflection method, 斜射束~法 angle beam method, 在线~*
探伤灵敏度 flaw detection sensitivity
探伤器 flaw [crack] detector, scanner
探伤术 defectoscopy
探伤仪 defectograph, defectoscope, fault indicator [finder], hole detector (光电式) ◇ 电感[涡流]式~ probolog, 经~仔细检查的 scanned, 同位素~ isoscope
探索 search(ing), exploring, exploration, probing
探索性试验 exploratory experiment [test]
探索(性)研究 exploratory work [research]
探头式焊接[缝]缺陷探测仪 multiprobe type weld flaw monitor
探头线圈 surface probe coil

探头靴托 probe shoe
探针 probe, sonde, sounder, feeler (pin), (touch) needle ◇ 测温~ thermo probe, 吸气[取样]~ sampling probe
探针法 probe [sonde] method
探针间距 probe spacing
探针微量分析仪 probe microanalyzer
炭 charcoal ◇ 活性[吸收性]~*
炭笔 charcoal pencil, (charcoal) crayon
炭层过滤器 carbon filter
炭粉 carbon powder, powdered carbon ◇ 涂~ blackening
羰汞基荧光黄钠盐 mercurochrome
羰基法 carbonyl process ◇ 超细[胶态]~粉末*, 因科压力~*
羰基法粉末压(坯)块 carbonyl compact
羰基法金属 carbonyl metal
羰基法镍粉 carbonyl nickel powder
羰基法铁粉 carbonyl iron powder
羰基铬 chromium carbonyl
羰基钴{Co$_2$(CO)$_8$, Co(CO)$_3$} cobalt carbonyl
羰基化合物 carbonyl compound
羰基(化物)分解 carbonyl decomposition
羰基金属 metal carbonyl
羰基精炼[制] carbonyl refining
羰基络合物 carbonyl complex
羰基络合物形成金属 carbonyl-former
羰基钼 molybdenum carbonyl
羰基镍{Ni(CO)$_4$} nickel carbonyl, carbonyl nickel ◇ 蒙德~精炼法*
羰基镍涂层 carbonyl nickel coating
羰基镍蒸气 nickel carbonyl vapour
羰基铁{Fe(CO)$_5$} carbonyl iron, iron carbonyl
羰基铁分解 decomposition of iron carbonyl
羰基铁粉(热解纯铁粉) (ferro) carbonyl powder ◇ 西鲁弗尔~成形铁心 Sirufer
羰基铁粉粒 carbonyl iron particle
羰基物 carbonyl
羰基物挥发器 carbonyl volatilizer

镗床　boring machine [mill]
镗杆　【机】boring bar, cutter spindle
镗孔　bore
镗孔内壁检验器　bore wall tester
镗磨　honing ◇ 液体磨料～liquid honing
镗磨孔　honed bore
镗屑　borings ◇ 经分选的～selected borings
镗钻模孔　jig boring
汤道　【钢】gate runner
汤道砖　(同"流钢砖")
汤硅钇石　tombarthite
汤卡宝石合金　(35Cu, 28Ni, 7Sn, 7Pb, 7Fe, 7Zn, 7-8Sb) Tonca's alloy
汤姆逊电动势　Thomson electromotive force, Thomson emf
汤姆逊法(接触电阻对焊)　【焊】Thomson process
汤姆逊热电效应　(同"同质热电效应")
汤姆逊系数　Thomson coefficient
搪瓷　enamel plating, (porcelain) enamel ◇ 黑板用～blackboard enamel, 烘烤～baking enamel, 去除～de-enameling, 湿法涂～wet process enameling
搪瓷层　enamelled coating
搪瓷钢　glass-lined steel
搪瓷钢板　enamelled iron, enamelled pressed steel ◇ 脱碳～*
搪瓷钢带　enamell(ed) strip
搪瓷器皿　enamel-ware ◇ 单涂层～one-coat ware
搪瓷器皿用钢板　enamel-ware sheet
搪瓷用(薄)钢板　porcelain enamel(l)ing sheet, enamel sheet
搪瓷用低碳钢　porcelain enamel(l)ing iron
搪孔直径　bore diameter
搪磨　honing ◇ 气喷磨料～vapour honing
搪泥堵铁耙　【铁】checker, chequer, spade
膛式焙烧炉　hearth roaster
膛式干燥窑　hearth drier ◇ 机械搅动～rabbled-hearth drier
膛式炉炼铅法　ore-hearth process
唐南薄膜学说　Donnan membrane theory
唐斯电解槽(钠电解用)　Downs cell
糖浆水(铸型面涂料)　molasses water
糖шт[浆](黏结剂)　molasses
糖碳　sugar charcoal
糖碳粉　sugar carbon powder
躺滴法　【冶】sessile drop method
躺焊　fire cracker welding
淌度　(同"迁移率")
烫金(的)　gilt, gilding
烫模铸件　dummy casting
烫型浇注　【铸】idle pouring
逃脱过程　break away process
逃脱力　break away force
淘金盘　concentrating [gold] pan, abacus (复数 abaci)
淘矿机　vanner, vanning machine
淘汰盘　【选】table (classifier), buddle ◇ 摇动式～pendulum table
淘汰盘精选　table concentration
淘析　elutriating, elutriation
淘析法　elutriation method
淘析(法)分析　elutriation analysis, analysis by elutriation
淘析器　elutriator, 【选】sand washer ◇ 多管式～multi-tube elutriator, 空气～*, 水力旋流～*
淘析设备　elutriation apparatus
淘析装置　elutriating apparatus
淘洗　elutriating, elutriation, levigation
淘洗器　washing vessel
淘选　elutriating ◇ 干(法)～dry elutriation
陶瓷　ceram(ics), potter ◇ 坦噶洛～(刀具) tungalox
陶瓷杯　【铁】ceramic cup
陶瓷材料[陶瓷性物料, 陶瓷质物料]　ceramic material ◇ 耐高温～*
陶瓷刀具　ceramic (cutting) tool ◇ 德古西特～*

陶瓷粉末　ceramic powder
陶瓷粉末压制　ceramic powder compaction
陶瓷覆层风口　【铁】ceramic coated tuyere
陶瓷覆面模　ceramic-faced die
陶瓷复合钢管　ceramic-clad steel tube ◇ 自蔓延~*
陶瓷坩埚　ceramic [earthenware] crucible
陶瓷工业　ceramic industry
陶瓷过滤介质　ceramic filter medium
陶瓷过滤器　ceramic filter
陶瓷核燃料　【理】ceramic (nuclear) fuel
陶瓷合金　ceramal ◇ 金属~ ceramic metal
陶瓷基复合材料　ceramic matrix composite (CMC)
陶瓷基体　ceramic matrix
陶瓷结合　ceramic bond
陶瓷介电材料　ceramic dielectric material
陶瓷金属　ceramic metal, ceramal, cermet, cerametallics
陶瓷绝缘材料　ceramic insulating material, crolite
陶瓷绝缘子　ceramic [porcelain] insulator
陶瓷颗粒　ceramic(s) particle
陶瓷(拉)模　ceramic die
陶瓷炉衬　ceramic furnace lining
陶瓷马赛克　ceramic mosaic
陶瓷耐火材料炉缸　ceramic hearth
陶瓷黏结(剂)　ceramic bond
陶瓷切削刀具　ceramic cutting tool ◇ 米克罗利特氧化铝微粒~Milrolit
陶瓷燃烧器　ceramic burner
陶瓷染料　ceramic colorant
陶瓷热处理　firing
陶瓷熔剂　ceramic flux
陶瓷容器　earthware tank
陶瓷套管　ceramic bush
陶瓷涂(盖)层　ceramic coating
陶瓷涂料　【耐】ceramic coating [paint]
陶瓷托辊　ceramic supporting roller
陶瓷纤维　ceramic fibre ◇ 铝硅~*
陶瓷相　【冶】ceramic phase
陶瓷型　【铸】ceramic mould ◇ 肖氏~(铸造)法 Show process, 可溶性~芯*
陶瓷型铸造[铸件]　ceramic (mould) casting
陶瓷学[术]　ceramics
陶瓷冶金　cermet
陶瓷预成形坯(件)　ceramic preform
陶瓷造型　【铸】ceramic moulding
陶瓷罩　potted ceramic case
陶瓷制品　ceramic ◇ 金属~*
陶瓷贮槽[池槽]　ceramic tank
陶瓷砖　ceramic brick, tile
陶瓷着色剂　ceramic colorant
陶结块　keramzite
陶锦砖　ceramic mosaic
陶粒　ceramsite, haycite ◇ 全~混凝土 all haydite concrete
陶粒骨料混凝土　【建】hydite aggregated concrete
陶粒混凝土　【建】ceramsite [(sand-)haydite] concrete
陶鲁斯铸造铜合金(系)　Taurus bronze
陶皿　earthenware bowl
陶盆蒸汽浴　steam bath with earthenware bowls
陶器　earthenware, pottery, stoneware
陶器管　earthenware pipe
陶(器)盆　earthenware bowl
陶器烧制　pottery firing
陶器蛇管　earthenware coil
陶土 {(Ca, Mg) O·SiO$_2$·(Al, Fe)$_2$O$_3$} bentonite, earthenware [porcelain] clay, argil, pot clay (制坩埚用)
陶土管道　earthenware conduit
陶土贮槽　earthware tank
陶土砖换热器　tile recuperator
陶土状的　clay-like
陶渣(磨碎耐火材料)　grog
陶质耐蚀耐热镍基合金 ◇ 哈斯特洛伊~ceramic Hastelloy
套壁　jacket(ed) wall

套层蒸馏器　jacketed still
套杆　loop bar
套箍接头　girth joint
套管　casing (pipe, tube), bush(ing), socket (pipe, tube), telescopic pipe, casing, capsule, sheath, well, mould tube (结晶器的) ◇ API 标准~*, 勃特雷斯型双密封~*, 电阻焊~*, 涂油脂的~ greased sleeve
套管材料　sheathing material
套管接合　faucet joint
套管接头　telescope joint, junction of sleeves
套管冷凝器　double-pipe condenser
套管连接(管端的)　telescope joint
套管烧嘴[套管形喷嘴]　shell burner
套管伸缩轴　extension shaft
套管式换热器　shell-and-tube heat exchanger
套管式冷却器　shell-and-tube cooler
套管式喷流换热器　collar spraying exchanger
套管轴　extension [telescopic] shaft, quill
套管座板　thimble-batt
套规　socket gauge
套环　nave collar, sleeve ring
套环轴承　collar bearing
套接　bell socket, bell and spigot joint ◇ 管~*
套接管　socket pipe
套接接头　bell and plain end joint
套节　hub
套炉　blind roaster
套模　cover die,【粉】bag
套圈　ferrule
套筛　sieve set
套式加热[冷却]　jacketing
套筒　jacket, sleeve, bushing, muff(le), nave box, thimble,【钢】barrel (钢包塞棒的)
套筒扳手　box spanner [key, wrench], socket wrench [key], cap key

套筒处置设备　sleeve handling equipment
套筒接合　socket [spigot] joint, bell and spigot joint
套筒联轴器[节]　sleeve [box, muff] coupling, coupling sleeve
套筒连接　muff joint
套筒螺母　box nut
套筒式电压互感器　bushing potential transformer
套筒支架　telescopic support
套筒轴承　bush [sleeve] bearing
套铣管　fishing-bowl pipe
套箱(无箱浇注用)　mould jacket
套爪　collet
套爪夹头　collet chuck
套砖　【耐】sleeve brick
套装辊　shell-type roll(er)
套锥式卷筒开卷机　overhung mandrel payoff reel
特巴德烧结耐热合金(以 TiC 为主要成分, CrC 小于 10%)　Turbide
特巴迪尤姆船用铸造锰青铜(50Cu, 44Zn, 1Fe, 2Ni, 1.75Mn, 0.5Sn)　Turbadium
特薄板　【压】very thin plate ◇ 热轧~*
特比斯顿高强度铸造锰青铜(56—61Cu, 33—40Zn, 0.2—2.5Al, 0.2—2Mn, 0.5—2Fe, 0—15Sn)　Turbiston
特别标志　special indication (S.I., s.i.)
特别费　specific cost
特别检验　special inspection
特别快车　express train
特别提款权　special drawing rights (SDRs)
特别提款权分配额　allocations of special drawing rights
特别注明　special designation (SD, s.d.)
特超级硬铝合金　extra-super-Duralumin (ESD)
特超声(速)的　hypersonic
特纯材料　ultrapure material
特大焊缝　oversize weld
特大型浓缩机　superthickener

特点　(special) feature, characteristic, habit, peculiarity
特丁醇{(CH$_3$)$_3$COH}　tert-butyl alcohol
特丁基{CH$_3$C(CH$_3$)$_2$-}　tert-butyl
特定程序故障　【计】program-sensitive fault
特定粉末　specific powder
特定规格钢锭　specification ingot
特尔卡曼铜锰合金(85Cu,12Mn,3Ni)　Telcuman (alloy)
特尔康铜电热合金(44—46Ni,56—54Cu)　Telconst(antan)
特尔柯西尔低膨胀合金(54Fe,29Ni,17Co,用作灯泡引线)　Telecoseal
特尔梅耶尔铝硅轴承青铜(5—10Al,2.75Si,少量Fe,余量Cu)　Telmejer
特尔史密斯破碎机(偏旋式)　Telsmith crusher
特富矿块　prill
特富矿体　specimen ore
特高铅黄铜(63Cu,3.5Zn,2.5Pb)　extra-high leaded brass
特高速感光无屏蔽胶片　extra-fast no-screen film
特高压润滑剂　extreme pressure lubricant
特高烟囱　skyscraper
特号钢丝(制绳用,抗拉强度1.67—1.82GPa)　special improved plough steel wire
特号钢丝绳　plough steel wire rope
特号铅淬火冷拉钢丝(制绳用,1.37—1.52GPa)　special improved patented steel wire
特厚板　super-thick steel plate, heavy plate
特厚板轧机　super-heavy plate mill, special heavy plate mill
特怀曼综合团矿直接炼钢法　Twyman process
特级耐火材料　superrefractory
特级平光(电镀薄板的)　extra smooth
特级无线电用镍铁合金　super radiometal
特技淬火(用于防淬裂)　tricky quenching

特宽腰型材　extra-wide webs shape
特宽翼缘　very broad flange
特拉巴克锡镍合金(87.5Sn,5Sb,2Bi,余量Ni;镍银代用品)　Trabuk
特拉甘廷芯砂黏接剂　Tragantine
特莱伊细碲粉　Telloy
特郎斯瓦尔轧管机(三辊式)　Transval tube mill
特朗普误差曲线　Tromp error curve
特劳特文硫杆菌　thiobacillus trautweinii
特劳伍德线材直接电流加热法　Trauwood process
特勒法(炼铝烟气干式控制法)　Teller process
特勒克塔尔铝硅合金(13Si,余量Al)　Telectal alloy
特雷迪姆铅碲合金(<0.1Te)　Teledium
特里普尔H镍铬钼耐热钢　Triple H
特里普尔高速钢(0.9C,0.4Mn,3.5—4Cr,2.5Mo,2.5V,3.5—4W)　Triple steel
特亮抛光(板材的)　(planish) extra-bright
特林蒂尼表面光洁度测量仪　Trentini surface tester
特罗达洛伊铍青铜(1. 2.6Co,0.4Be,余量Cu; 2. 0.4Cr,0.1Be,余量Cu)　Trodaloy
特罗模莱特磁铁　Tromolite (magnet)
特罗佩纳斯(侧吹)转炉　【钢】Tropenas (converter)
特米特锡基轴承合金(73.5—74Pb,14.5Sb,5.75Sn,2.5—3C,2Cd,1As)　Termite
特莫弗莱克斯二元电阻合金　Thermoflex
特内伦铬锰氮不锈钢(<0.1C,18Cr,14.5Mn,0.4N)　Tenelon
特尼平炉　【钢】Terni furnace
特纽阿尔铸造铝合金(9.2—10.8Cu,1—1.5Fe,0.15—0.35Mg,余量Al)　Tenual
特平板　dead flat sheet

特软钢(含＜0.1C)　extra-soft steel
特软钢丝绳　special flexible wire rope
特软回火薄钢板　dead-soft temper (sheet)
特瑞-诺雅低温回火法　Terre-Noire process
特萨照相物镜　Tessar
特施三钟式炉顶装料系统(炉料布向中心)　Tesch type top charging system
特殊(安全)保护用品　special safety protection article
特殊部位砖衬　【冶】zoned lining
特殊[种]材料　special(ity) material
特殊处理钢材　special treatment steel (STS)
特殊大型型材[钢]　special heavy section(s)
特殊电性能钢　steel with special electrical properties
特殊锻钢　special forged steel
特殊(断面)钢材　special rolling-mill section
特殊粉末　specific powder
特殊钢　special steel, special treatment steel (STS), specials
特殊钢厂　special steel plant
特殊钢线棒材精轧　special steel rod and bar finishing
特殊检验　extraordinary inspection
特殊件　special piece
特殊铝青铜　Arms bronze
特殊耐火材料　special refractory
特殊膨胀性能金属　metal with special expansion properties
特殊青铜　specific bronze
特殊清扫装置　special clearance device
特殊取向　special orientation
特殊取向的重叠位错　superposed dislocations of special orientations
特殊热伸长钢　steel with special extention
特殊设备　speciality equipment
特殊碳化物　special carbide

特殊铜合金　special copper alloy
特殊凸度轧辊　special crown roll
特殊相对论　special theory of relativity
特殊性能　special property
特殊指示　special indication
特殊质量非合金钢　unalloyed special steel
特殊质量合金钢　alloyed special steel
特殊铸造合金　special casting alloy
特殊字符　【计】special character
特斯卡尔A铝钎焊合金　Thesscal A
特斯拉线圈[感应圈]　Tesla coil
特斯拉线圈试验　Tesla coil test
特塔里姆铅锡焊料(33Sn,66Pb)　Tertiarium
特弯特短钢筋　very short and bent reinforced bar
特戊基{$CH_3CH_2C(CH_3)_2-$}　tert-amyl, tert-pentyl
特细粒度　extraordinary fineness
特效塑性耐火砖　superduty plastic fire brick
特写图　close-up view
特性　character(istics), property, behaviour, characteristic property [feature], specificity
特性方程(式)　characteristic equation
特性辐射纯度　purity of characteristic radiation
特性函数　characteristic function
特性记述　characterization
特性黏度　inherent [intrinsic] viscosity
特性曲线　characteristic (curve), operating line, response
特性曲线族　family of characteristic curves, characteristic family
特性失真　【电】characteristic distortion
特性试验　characteristic test
特性数据　characteristic data
特性温度　characteristic temperature
特性要素图　characteristic diagram
特性资料　characteristic data
特性阻抗　characteristic [natural]

impedance
特许权费　royalty ◇ 直接投资费用和～*
特许(证)领有者　licencee, licensee
特异面　singular surface
特异型砖　【耐】extra-complex shape
特硬钢　glass-hard steel
特硬铝硅青铜(88Cu, 10Al, 2Si)　diamond bronze
特硬面轧辊　special chill roll
特硬烧成砖　very hard fired brick
特优钢　extra-fine steel
特优级[质量]的　extra best best (EBB)
特征　characteristic (feature), feature, property, nature
特征 X 射线　characteristic X-ray
特征 X 射线谱　characteristic X-ray spectrum
特征伯格斯矢量　characteristic Burgers vector
特征法　method of characteristics
特征辐射(X-射线的)　characteristic radiation
特征光谱　characteristic spectrum
特征函数　characteristic function, eigenfunction
特征卡片　aspect card
特征频率　characteristic frequency
特征谱线　characteristic spectral line
特征曲线　indicatrix
特征衰变速率　characteristic decay rate
特征位　【计】tag, flag (bit)
特征位错　【理】characteristic dislocation
特征温度　characteristic temperature ◇ 德拜～*
特征型　【理】characteristic mode
特征应变图样　characteristic strain pattern
特征[性]值　characteristic value
特制薄锡层镀锡薄钢板　special coke tinplate
特制算条　special make-up bar
特制的　purpose made (p.m.), tailor-made
特制厚锡层镀锡薄钢板　special charcoal tinplate
特制品　specials, speciality
特制烧嘴　special burner
特种棒钢　special bar quality (SBQ)
特种测量器　special measuring device
特种磁性钢　steel with special magnetic properties
特种发动机合金　◇ 罗杰斯～*
特种分级淬火(同时进行喷丸硬化处理)　special marquench
特种分离器　special separator
特种钢丝绳　special wire rope
特种工具钢　special tool steel
特种合金　special alloy
特种合金钢　special alloy steel
特种化学性能钢　steel with special chemical properties
特种化学性能合金　alloy with special chemical properties
特种黄铜　special brass
特种角钢　special type angle
特种铝基混合稀土合金(11 混合稀土, 2Si, 1.5Cu, 1.25Ni, 1Mn, 0.3Cr, 0.02Ti, 余量 Al; 能耐高温)　S.A.M. alloy, special aluminium mischmetal(loy)
特种膨胀性能合金　alloy with special expansion properies
特种青铜　special bronze
特种软钢(< 0.08C, < 0.05Si, 0.2—0.4Mn, < 0.05P, < 0.05S)　special soft steel
特种筛　special type screen
特种品名合金　special named alloy
特种声学性能合金　alloy with special acoustic properties
特种生铁　special pig
特种物理性能合金　alloy with special physical properties
特种盐基泥浆　special-base mortar

特种轧机　speciality mill
特种轧制　special rolling
特种铸铁　special (cast) iron
铽合金　terbium alloy
铽基合金　terbium-base alloy
铽添加合金　terbium addition
铽组金属　terbium metal
滕冈姆耐蚀黄铜(81-86Cu，＜3Al，＜2Ni，＜1Si，余量 Zn)　Tungum alloy
腾格林瓦合金　Tungelinvar
梯度　gradient (gdnt，grad.) ◇ 大~ heavy gradient
梯度变化曲线　gradient diagram
梯度传感器　gradient probe
梯度法　【数】gradient method
梯度分布　【半】graded distribution
梯度基区　【半】graded base
梯度冷凝　differential condensation
梯度(末端)淬火(法)　【金】gradient quenching
梯度涂层　gradient coating
梯度涂层材料　gradient coating material
梯段反应　staircase reaction
梯段检查(金属试样的)　step-down test
梯恩梯　trinitrotoluene (TNT)
梯级　stair(step), step
梯级(逐位)控制　cascade control
梯流浮选法　【选】cascade process
梯流式布置(酸洗槽的)　cascade
梯流式酸洗　cascade pickling
梯流系统　(同"串联系统")
梯式脚手架　ladder scaffold
梯式挖掘机　ladder excavator
梯台架　ladder scaffold
梯坦铝合金　titanal
梯温加热　taper heating
梯温炉　Rosenhain furnace
梯型钢材[断面]　trapezoidal section
梯形桁架　parallel chord truse
梯形孔型　trapezoidal pass
梯形溜槽　stair-type chute
梯状的　ladderlike

剔出废石　discard
剔除　rejecting
踢板(门脚护板)　【建】kick plate
踢脚板　foot plate, base board, mopboard
锑{Sb}　antimony, antimonium, stibium ◇ 爆炸 ~ *，电(解) ~ *，镀 ~ antimony plating, 高~炉渣 slag high in autimony, 含~的 anti monial, antimon(i)ous, 含~合金 *，精(炼)[星(纹)] ~ *，镜 ~ regulus mirror, 熔融~molten antimony, 三价[亚] ~ 的 *，生 ~ *，似 ~ 的 antimony-like, 阴极 ~ cathode antimony, 正[五价] ~ 的 antimonic, stibial
锑钯矿{Pd₃Sb}　stibiopalladinite
锑白(三氧化锑,商品名)　antimony white
锑焙砂　antimony calcine
锑焙烧炉　antimony roaster
锑玻璃　antimony glass
锑辰砂　red antimony sulphide {2Sb₂S₃·Sb₂O₃}, antimony vermillion {Sb₂S₃·Sb₂O₃}
锑的　antimonial, stibic, stibnic
锑碲铋矿　zodite
锑电极　antimony electrode
锑浮渣　antimonial dross, antimony skimmings
锑钙矾　peretaite
锑钙石{2CaO·Sb₂O₄}　romeite, schneebergite
锑汞矿　shahovite
锑合金　antimony [antimonial] alloy
锑红　antimony red
锑华{Sb₂O₃}　antimony bloom, white antimony, valentinite
锑化铬锰　chromium-manganese-antimonide
锑化合物　antimony compound
锑化镓　gallium antimonide
锑化物　antimonide, stibide, stibnide
锑化铟　indium antimonide
锑黄渣　antimonial speiss
锑基合金　antimony base alloy

锑金属锭　star metal
锑精矿　antimony concentrate
锑镜　regulus mirror
锑块　antimony slab [regulus], regulus antimony
锑矿(石)　antimony ore
锑矿床　antimony (ore) deposit
锑矿物　antimony mineral
锑硫镍矿　nickeliferous gray antimony, ullmannite
锑撒渣　antimony skimmings
锑铅合金　antimony-lead alloy, antimonial lead ◇ 雷古拉斯～*
锑铅银矿　fizelyite
锑青铜(7—8Sb,1.5—2.5Ni,余量 Cu)　antimony bronze
锑艳合金　antimon cesium
锑烧结块　antimony sinter
锑酸汞矿　ammiolite
锑酸钾　potassium antimonate
锑酸钠　sodium antimonate
锑酸铅(黄)　lead antimonate, antimony yellow
锑酸盐　antimoniate, antimonate, stibiate, stibnate
锑钛钙矿{5CaO·2TiO$_2$·3Sb$_2$O$_3$}　lewisite
锑钛铁矿{6FeO·5TiO$_2$·Sb$_2$O$_5$}　derbylite
锑添加合金　antimony addition
锑铁合金　antimony-iron alloy ◇ 雷奥米尔～*
锑铁矿　tripuhyite
锑铜合金　antimony-copoer alloy ◇ 维纳斯～*
锑铜矿　horsfordite
锑鎓　stibonium
锑锡焊料[药](38Sn,60Pb,2Sb)　antimonial tin solder
锑锡焊条　antimonial tin solder
锑锡矿　stistaite
锑线石　holtite
锑型点阵[晶格]　antimony lattice
锑烟(含锑烟雾)　antimony fume

锑冶金　antimony metallurgy
锑银矿{Ag$_3$Sb}　dyscrasite
锑渣　antimonial dross
锑中毒　antimony poisoning, stibialism
锑朱砂{Sb$_2$S$_3$·Sb$_2$O$_3$}　antimony vermillion
提波尔表面活性剂[阴离子去垢剂]　Teepol
提成　draw a percentage ◇ 折旧～*
提出　putting forward, representation
提纯　purification, purifying, refinement, refining, rectifying, depuration ◇ 定向～*,分批～ batch purification, 浮region～*,干法～ dry purification, 化学～ chemical refining, 湿法～ wet purification, 未～的 unpurified, 一次～ primary purification, 蒸馏～*
提纯比　purification ratio
提纯处理　refining treatment
提纯法　method of purification
提纯机　purifying machine
提纯剂　purifying agent, purificant
提纯器　purifier, refiner ◇ 往返互换～ reciprocating refiner
提纯柱　decontaminating column
提纯装置　purifying plant
提高　raise, enhancement, increasement, rise, upgrading
提高等级[品位]　up-grading, grading up
提供　offer, furnishing
提汞法　process of mercury extraction
提钩　lifter
提(货)单　bill of lading (B/L) ◇ 甲板装载～on deck B/L, 已装船～on board bill of lading
提金器(混汞的)　amalgamator
提炼　【色】extract, extraction ◇ 未～的 unrefined, 冶金～*
提料筋条[肋板]　lifter bar
提料叶片　lifting blade
提锍率　matte-fall
提门钩[焦]　lifting hook

提尼科西尔铜锌镍合金（42Cu,41Zn,16Ni,1Pb） Tinicosil (alloy)

提镍 nickel extraction ◇ 电解法～*,鹰桥盐酸选择浸出～法 Falconbridge process

提浓 concentrating

提前 advance, bring forward, lead

提前警报 【环】advance warning

提前开启(阀的) advanced opening

提取 extract (ing), extraction (ext., extn), draw, abstract(ion), win（从矿石中提取金属）◇ 不可～的 inextractable, 部分～ partial extraction, 从矿石中～金属 depletion, 电解～ electrolytic extraction, electowinning 分批～ batchwise extraction, 可～的*, 熔盐～ fused salt extraction, 水溶液～ aqueous extraction

提取大修理基金 【企】allowance for overhaul fund

提取的 extractive

提取-涤气塔 extraction-scrub column

提取反应 extraction reaction

提取方法 method of extraction

提取剂 【色】extractant

提取率 extraction rate [coefficient, yield], (rate of) extraction

提取器[设备] extractor (Ext.) ◇ 撞击式焦油～*

提取塔 extraction tower [column]

提取物 extractive

提取效率 extraction efficiency [coefficient]

提取[炼]冶金(学) extraction [extractive] metallurgy

提取折旧基金 【企】depreciation allowance

提取蒸馏 extraction [extractive] distillation

提升 hoist(ing), lift(ing), raising, elevating, advance

提升板(夹板锤的) lifting board

提升泵 lift pump

提升程序 hoisting sequence

提升带(摩擦锤的) lifter belt

提升堆垛台 elevating piler

提升吨位 hoisting tonnage

提升钢丝绳 elevator [lifting] rope ◇ 起重臂[挺杆]～ boom hoist cable

提升缸 lift cylinder

提升高度 lifting [hoisting] height

提升工序 hoisting sequence

提升挂钩 lifting hook

提升管 lift pipe [leg]

提升罐 lift pot

提升滑车 hoisting tackle, hoist block

提升滑轮 hoisting sheave

提升机 elevator (machine), hoisting machine, lifting unit, winding engine ◇ 带式～ band [belt] elevator, 单斗～ skip, 电动～ electric hoist, 斗式～*, 多斗～*, 翻斗～ 【耐】skip elevator, 风动～ pneumatic elevator, 桨轮[叶片]式～ paddle wheel elevator, 链斗～*, 螺旋～ screw elevator, 倾斜式～ inclined elevator, 心轴式～*, 液压～ hydraulic lift(er), 柱塞～*

提升机构 lifting [hoisting] mechanism, elevating gear

提升机卷筒 hoisting drum

提升机械 hoisting machinery

提升机戽斗轮 【选】basket wheel

提升架 elevator frame, elevating cradle

提升绞筒 winding drum (machine)

提升井 【采】hoisting shaft

提升筐架 elevating cradle

提升力 raising force

提升料罐 【铁】hoisting bucket

提升能力 elevating [hoisting] capacity, lifting power

提升皮带 belt elevator

提升器 lifting mechanism, lifter ◇ 摩擦～*

提升器轴 【机】lifter shaft

提升钳 hoisting tongs

提升设备　hoist(er), hoisting equipment
提升速度　elevating [lifting, hoisting] speed
提升索　lift(ing) cable
提升台　elevating [lifting] platform
提升系统　hoisting system
提升限制器　lift stop
提升线圈式感应(电)炉　lift-coil induction furnace
提升卸卷机　elevating stripper
提升液压缸　lift cylinder
提升装料台[分料机](炉用)　elevating [elevator] depiler
提升装置　elevating rig, hoisting unit [gear] ◇ 液压～．
提铜　【色】copper extraction
提锌　zinc extraction
提盐器　salt box
提要　summary (Sum.), abstract, brief, synopsis
提银机　silver recovery unit
提银炉　(同"灰吹炉")
提余液　raffinate
题目数据　【计】problem data
体波　body wave
体电阻　bulk resistance
体对角线　body diagonal
体积　volume (vol.), cubic content [capacity], solid volume
体积百分数　volume-percent (vol.pct), percent by volume
体积比　volume ratio [fraction], bulk factor (粉末压型前后的), volume to volume (v/v) (浓度)
体积变化　volume(tric) change, change in volume
体积测量　volume [cubic] measure, cubing
体积磁致伸缩　【理】bulk magnetostriction
体积单元　volume element
体积电离度　volume ionization density
体积度　specific volume (s.v.)

体积分配器　bulk distributor
体积分数　volume fraction
体积分析　volumetric analysis
体积干燥　volume drying
体积基准比表面　specific surface on volume base
体积计　volume meter, volumeter, volum(en)ometer
体积可变性　variability of volume
体积可压缩性　volume compressibility
体积扩散　volume [bulk] diffusion
体积扩散蠕变　volume diffusion creep
体积扩散烧结　sintering by volume diffusion
体积扩散系数　volume diffusion coefficient
体积量度　volume [cubic] measure
体积流动速率　rate of volume flow
体积流量　volume flow
体积流量计　volumetric flowmeter
体积模量[模数]　volume(tric) [bulk] modulus
体积摩尔的　molar
体积摩尔浓度　molar concentration, molarity
体积黏度　volume [bulk] viscosity
体积浓度　volume concentration, concentration by volume
体积配料(法)　batching [proportioning] by volume
体积膨胀　(同"体膨胀")
体积平衡　volumetric equilibrium [balance]
体积平均直径　volume mean diameter
体积散射　bulk scattering
体积收缩　volume(tric) contraction, volume shrinkage, contraction of volume, reduction in volume
体积收缩率　reduction in volume
体(积)弹性　volume [bulk] elasticity
体积弹性模量[模数]　【金】bulk modulus, volume(tric) modulus of elasticity

体积稳定性　volume stability
体积系数　volume factor
体积性质　bulk property
体积压缩模量　【金】modulus of cubic compressibility
体积应变　volume(tric)[cubic] strain
体积应力　volumetric stress
体积增加　increase in volume
体积重量　bulk factor, bulk density
体积装料法　volume filling
体积自由能　【金】volume free energy
体冷速度(循环淬火剂的)　cooling-volume velocity
体力劳动　muscular labour
体灵敏探测器　volume detector
体膨胀　cubic(al) dilatation[expansion], volume(tric) expansion
体膨胀系数　coefficient of cubical expansion (cub. exp.), cubical expansion coefficient, coefficient of volume expansion
体视角　stereo angle
体视试样夹　stereoscopic specimen holder
体视图　stereogram
体视显微镜　stereomicroscope, stereoscopic(al) microscope
体视显微术　stereoscopic(al) microscopy
体视显微照相[照片]　stereoscopic(al) micrograph, stereomicrograph
体视显微组织[微观结构]　stereometric microstructure
体视像　stereoscopic(al) image
体视照相术　stereoscopic photography
体系　system, syntax
体心的　body centred, volume-centered
体心点阵[晶格]　volume-centered lattice, I lattice, centre lattice
体心立方(晶格)　body centered cubic (BCC, bcc), body centred cube
体心立方变型　body centred cubic modification
体心立方的　cubic-centered
体心立方点阵[晶格]　【金】body-centered cubic lattice (b.c.c.l.), space-centered cubic lattice, body centred cube (space) lattice
体心立方合金　body centred cubic alloy
体心立方结构　body centred cubic structure[configuration]
体心立方结构相　【金】body centred cubic phase
体心立方金属(晶体)　BCC (body-centred-cubic) metal
体心立方晶胞　body centred cubic cell
体心立方晶格组织　(同"β组织")
体心立方晶系　body centred cubic lattice system
体心立方晶型　body centred cubic form[modification]
体心立方(晶型)铁素体[体心铁素体]　body centred ferrite
体心立方组态　body centred cubic configuration
体心四方点阵[晶格]　【金】BCT (body centred tetragonal) lattice, tetragonal body-centred lattice
体心四方结构　【金】body centred tetragonal structure
体心四方晶型[变型]　body centred tetragonal modification
体心位置　【金】space-centered[body-centered] position
体心斜方点阵[晶格]　body centred orthorhombic lattice
体心正方晶格　【金】BCT (body centred tetragonal) lattice
体应力　body stress
体制　system (of organization), structure, frame(work)
替代固溶体　(同"代位式固溶体")
替代式扩散　substitutional diffusion
替代式原子　substitutional atom
替代型缺陷　substitutional imperfection
替换　replace, displacement, interchange
替换机架　alternate housing

替换物	replacement alternatives
替续器	relay
剃齿法	shaving method
剃齿工序	shaving operation
剃齿机	【机】gear-shaving machine
剃刀片钢带	razor-blade strip
剃毛刺	shaving
天车	(overhead travelling) crane
天车工	craneman
天窗	trap-door, abatjour, dormer, skylight, top light
天电干扰	atmospheric interference
天顶距	zenith distance (ZD)
天顶螺栓(机车的)	tie [anchor, truss] bolt
天沟	crown ditch, drain gutter
天沟侧板	cant board
天花板	ceiling (board), platfond, plancier
天花板灯线盒	ceiling rose
天井	atrium, raise, raiserockhole (采矿的)
天蓝石	berkeyite, lazulite, tyrolite
天轮	head pulley [sheave]
天棚灯	ceiling lamp
天棚照明	ceiling [dome] illumination
天平	balance ◇ 杠杆～beam balance, 刻度盘～dial balance, 莫氏～Mohr's balance, 萨克史密斯圆环～˙, 十进(制)～decimal balance, 试金[分析]～assay balance
天平臂	balance arm
天平测定	balance measurement
天平梁	balance beam, crossbeam
天平盘	scale
天平托盘	balance pan
天平游码	balance rider
天平游码钩	balance rider hook
天平指针	balance pointer [indicator]
天桥	overline [platform, foot, monkey] bridge, overpass
天青石{$SrSO_4$}	zolestin, celestine, celestite
天然冰晶石	natural cryolite
天然铂	native platinum
天然材料	natural material
天然辰砂{HgS}	natural vermillion
天然磁石{Fe_3O_4}	loadstone, lodestone
天然磁石矿	lode ore
天然磁铁	native [natural] magnet
天然粗糙度	natural roughness
天然地下水位	natural ground-water level
天然碲化银{Ag_2Te}	hessite
天然碲铁	telluric (native) iron
天然锇(80Os,10Ir,5Rh)	osmite
天然放射性	natural radioactivity
天然放射性本底	natural radiation background
天然粉末	【粉】natural powder
天然汞	native mercury
天然光卤石	natural carnallite
天然合金	natural alloy
天然合金铁	natural alloy iron
天然混合集料(未经筛分的)	all-in aggregate
天然焦(炭)	carbonite, burnt [dandered] coal
天然胶	natural gum
天然结晶苏打{$Na_2CO_3 \cdot 10H_2O$}	natron
天然金	native gold ◇ 高银～(＞20Ag) Electrum
天然金刚砂	boart, bort
天然金属	native metal
天然金铑合金(≤40Rh,余量Au)	rhodium-gold
天然晶体	natural crystal
天然块金	nugget
天然矿石	natural ore
天然硫砷化铂	cooperite
天然铝氧石	native argil
天然氯化亚汞	hornquick silver
天然绿柱石晶体	natural beryl crystal
天然磨料	natural abrasives
天然磨石	grinding stone, grindstone
天然黏结剂型砂	【铸】naturally bonded

moulding sand
天然黏土　natural clay
天然镍铁合金(见于陨石中)　nickel-iron, kamacite
天然浓缩铀　uranium of natural enrichment
天然坡度　depositional gradient
天然铺底料　【团】natural hearth layer
天然气　natural gas ◇ 裂化～cracked natural gas,重整[转化]～reformed natural gas
天然气保护气氛　natural gas atmosphere
天然气-空气预混合烧嘴　natural gas-air premix burner
天然气喷吹　natural gas injection
天然气烧嘴　natural gas burner
天然铅丹{Pb_3O_4}　minium
天然燃料　natural fuel
天然熔剂　natural flux
天然砷　native arsenic
天然石墨　native [natural] graphite ◇ 斯里兰卡～Ceylon graphite
天然石墨粉　natural graphite powder
天然水　natural water
天然水腐蚀　natural water corrosion
天然水泥岩　natural cement rock
天然铁　native iron ◇ 木化石中的～sideroferrite
天然铁镍合金　(25Ni,余量 Fe) taenite
天然稳定元素　natural stable element
天然形态生石灰　pebble lime
天然盐　mineral salt
天然氧化膜　naturally occurring oxide film
天然氧化铀{$UO_2 \cdot UO_3, U_3O_8$}　uraninite
天然银　native silver
天然铀　natural [normal] uranium
天然铀-石墨反应堆　natural uranium-graphite reactor
天然元素　natural [native] element
天然造球特性　【团】natural balling characteristics
天体化学　cosmochemistry

天文台　observatory
天文钟　chronometer
天线　antenna, aerial ◇ 环形～塔 loop tower
天线方向调整器　goniometer
天线辐射　aerial radiation
天线角开度　angular aperture
天线系统　aerial
天线阵　trap
天轴　line shaft
添改　interpolation
添加　adding, addition, adjunction, affix, dope
添加比　percent addition, addition level
添加材料　filler material
添加合金　process(ing) alloy
添加合金元素　alloy(ing) addition
添加剂　additive (agent), addition (agent), added material, affix, dope, improver ◇ 佩弗洛～*,佩格洛～*,修正[调节]性～*
添加剂槽　addition bin
添加剂称量料斗　miscellaneous weigh hopper
添加剂分布　distribution of additions
添加剂给料机　additive feeder
添加剂浓度　additive concentration
添加剂设施　additive facilities
添加剂致密化　sophisticated densification
添加金属　additive metal, filler material
添加矿石　ore addition,【钢】feed ore（熔炼过程的）
添加量[比]　feed rate, addition level, rate of addition
添加料　added [adding, addition] material
添加率　percent addition
添加微量合金元素　(同"微合金化")
添加物　additive, improver, supplement, dope
添加元素　additional element
添加皂土　bentonite addition
添料器　filling vessel

添煤机	stoker
填背砂	backing sand
填补料	daubing
填补桩	filling pile
填充	pack(ag)ing, filling, stuffing ◇ 布里渊区～*, 拉希格～瓷圈*
填充标记	filling mark
填充材料	packing [filling] material
填充层	packed bed, packing layer
填充床	packed bed
填充萃取[提取]塔	packed extractor, packed extraction column
填充阀	fill valve
填充反应塔	packed reaction tower
填充干燥剂	filling drying agent
填充高度	packed [fill] height
填充焊道	filler pass [bead]
填充焊丝	filling [additional] wire, welding rod
填充剂	filler, stuffing bulking agent
填充金属	【焊】filler metal [material], added [deposited] metal, welding filler
填充金属试样	filler metal test specimen
填充金属送进机构	filler metal feed
填充冷却塔	packed cooling tower
填充料	stopping
填充率	fill(ing) ratio [factor], percentage fill, degree of fill, material loading
填充密度	packed [packing] density
填充坯锭法（挤钨管用）	filled-billet method
填充砌体	backfill(ing)
填充氢化物	interstitial hydride
填充圈	Lessing ring
填充砂	【铸】backing sand
填充数	【理】occupation number
填充[料]塔	packed tower [column], filled tower [column]
填充塔内形成沟流	【色】channeling in column
填充物	filler, filling, packer, adjustage
填充系数	fill factor, block coefficient
填充性能[特性]（油漆的）	filling property
填充阳离子	interstitial cation
填充液	packing liquid
填充因数	fill factor, packing index
填充阴离子	interstitial anion
填充(用)型砂	【铸】filler [backing] sand
填充蒸馏塔	packed distillation column
填充状态	filled [occupied] state
填洞	cavity fill
填方	fill ◇ 借土～borrow fill
填方数量	bank measure
填缝	caulking, joint filling
填缝料	joint sealing material, joint filler, choker
填缝石油沥青掺合料	blended asphalt joint filler
填缝小砖	【建】glut
填高	banking
填焊	sealing [caulk] welding ◇ 切槽～焊缝 filled slot weld
填角焊	fillet welding ◇ 交错断续～*, 立向～*, 水平～*, 凸面～convex fillet welding
填角焊缝	fillet weld, horizontal-vertical (fillet) weld, back bead ◇ T形[丁字接头]～ T-fillet weld, 侧面～ side fillet weld, 搭接～ lap fillet weld, 单面～焊接头 single-filled weld, 等边对称～ equal leg fillet weld, 双面间断～*, 凸形～ convex fillet weld, 正常～*
填孔光学检查仪（拉丝模的）	profiloscope
填块	packing block
填料	filler, filling (material, mass), packing (material), packaging, gasket, loading [jointing] material, padding, stuff, wadding ◇ 加～（在燃料或油内）dopping, 炉底～ bottom stuff, 无～塔 void column
填料板	packing [fill(er)] plate
填料棒	filler rod
填料层	packing layer

填料盖密封的供汽集管(锅炉的)　gland supply manifold
填料管座　filling socket
填料函　gland [stuffing] box
填料环　insertion ring
填料介质　packing medium
填料金属　filler metal
填料-聚氯乙烯片　fills-polyvinyl chloride sheets
填料受热端(回热旋转空气预热器的)　hot end tier
填料洗涤塔　packed tower scrubber
填料箱[盒]　packing [stuffing] box
填料压盖　packing gland
填料压盖衬套　packing bush
填料柱　packed [filled] column
填零　【计】zero fill, zeroize
填满　filling up, packaging
填满程度(能级的)　population
填满(电子)壳层　【理】completed (electron) shell
填密环　gasket ring, packing
填平　filling and leveling up
填腔　cavity fill
填圈　insertion ring
填入　filling in
填塞　stuffing, packing, packaging, filling, tamping, ca(u)lking
填塞料　stuffing, wad(ding), patching material
填塞砖　【建】closure
填塞桩　chock pile
填砂　packing sand ◇ 砂箱~机【铸】flask filler
填砂框　【铸】filling [sand] frame
填石　drop-fill rock, enrockment
填石坝　rock-fill dam
填实　tamping, ca(u)lking
填实管柱(混凝土的)　filled pipe column
填土　banket(te), earth embankment, earth-fill
填土机　back filler, pushfiller

填挖平衡的坡度　【运】balanced grade
填隙　gap filling, ca(u)lking
填隙焊缝　ca(u)lk(ing) weld
填隙合金　caulking metal
填隙-空位偶　Frenkel [interstitial-vacancy] pair
填隙离子　interstitial ion
填隙料　ca(u)lker, gap filler
填隙片　filling piece, shim
填隙(式)固溶体　interstitial solid solution
填隙式固溶元素极少的　extra-low-interstitial
填隙式合金　interstitial alloy
填隙式化合物　interstitial (type) compound
填隙式施主　【半】interstitial donor
填隙式(位错)割阶　【理】interstitial jog
填隙式位错环　【理】interstitial loop
填隙式杂质迁移[徙动]　【理】migration of interstitial impurities
填隙速度　interstitial velocity
填隙碳原子扩散　(同"结点间碳原子扩散")
填隙相　【金】interstitial phase
填隙型缺陷(结点间的)　interstitial imperfection
填隙原子　interstitial atom
填隙原子团　interstitial cluster
填隙砖　gap block
填絮　wad
填油灰　filling colour
填质　【地】matrix
填筑　reclamation
填筑地区[面积]　【建】reclaimed area
填筑机　【建】reclaimer
挑出(式)脚手架　outrigger [bracket] scaffold
挑杆式万能装卸机　pole truck
挑杆式装卸机　ram truck
挑台　【建】cantilever platform
挑选　choose, choice, select, pick
挑选称量　random weighing

挑选物　option
挑轴　tappet shaft
挑檐　【建】cornice
条　strip, band, slug, stick, tie
条板状　lath
条棒式分级运输机　bar conveyer
条材　mill bar, bar (steel rolled) stock ◇ 冷轧～cold-finished bar
条材输送起重机　bar crane
条带　stripe, band, striae, bands of secondary slip
条带磷铅石　sabalite
条带状成分　lithotype
条带状烟煤　banded bituminous coal
条锭铜　wirebar copper
条钢　bar [merchant] steel, bar [rod, section] iron, (steel) bar ◇ 成盘～coiled bar, 矩形～rectangular bar, 冷拔～cold-drawn bar, 冷轧～", 商品～merchant (bar) iron
条钢轧机　【压】merchant (-bar) mill ◇ 大型～heavy merchant mill
条钢轧机机组　merchant mill train, bar iron rolling train
条格筛　rod screen
条痕　streak, striation, tramlines (薄钢板的) ◇ 表面黏结～"
条痕板　【地】streak plate
条件编译　【计】conditional compilation
条件观测　conditioned observation
条件屈服强度　offset yield strength
条件屈服应力　constrained yield stress, offset yield (stress)
条件熵　conditional entropy
条件停机指令　【计】conditional [optional] stop instruction
条件语句　【计】conditional statement
条件转移　【计】conditional branch [jump, transfer]
条件转移指令　【计】conditional branch [jump, transfer] instruction
条金　bar gold

条晶体　fringe crystal
条款　clause, article, provision, stipulation
条理　orderliness, method ◇ 有～的 methodic(al)
条例　regulations, rules
条片(钢板缺陷)　sliver
条筛　bar screen [grit], slitbar screen
条式打印机　bar printer
条铁　bar iron
条纹　streak, fringe, striation, stripe, 【地】stria ◇ 不均匀应变～", 弗雷斯尼尔～Fresnel fringes, 纪尼埃－普雷斯顿～", 莫阿～"
条纹的　streaky
条纹缺陷肉眼检验　macro streak flaw test
条纹图样　【理】fringe pattern, stripe
条纹状[有条纹]的　streaked
条线图　bar chart [graph]
条形坯块　【粉】cored bar
条形砖　【耐】lath brick, beam, pups, soaps
条状电极　strip electrode
条状断口　slaty fracture
条状焊料　【焊】bar solder
条状夹杂物　inclusion line
条状结构　banded structure
条状试样　strip specimen
条状铁素体　ferrite lath
条状组织　slaty structure
调磁合金　magnetic shunt alloy
调磁器　magnetic shunt
调定温度　setting temperature
调风门　flow balance damper
调风闸门　damper
调幅　amplitude modulation (AM)
调幅器　(amplitude) modulator
调光圈(照相的)　diaphragming
调光装置　dimmer
调辊器　roll adjusting device
调好的火焰　balanced flame
调和方法　【压】harmonic mean
调和分析　【数】Fourier [harmonic] analysis

调和空气　tempering air
调和水量　amount of tempering water
调和中项[平均值]　【理】harmonic(al) mean
调和　tempering ◇ 没～好的 untempering
调剂料仓　surge bin
调浆槽　conditioner cell, surge tank
调焦　focusing
调节　regulating, regulation, adjustment, control, conditioning, setting, trim ◇ 人工～ hand regulation
调节板　damper, offset block（高度的）
调节比　turndown ratio
调节槽　regulating [conditioning] tank
调节齿轮　adjusting gear
调节挡板　regulating damper ◇ 空气流量～*
调节灯光变阻器　dimmer
调节电路　regulating circuit
调节电阻　adjusting resistance
调节阀　adjusting [control] valve
调节风门　air damper, louver-damper
调节风门板　damper plate
调节杆　regulating rod [stem], adjustable [governor] lever
调节缸　adjusting cylinder
调节拱　adjustable arch
调节鼓风　conditioned blast
调节环　adjustment ring
调节剂　regulating [conditioning] agent, conditioner,【选】modifier
调节加水　trim moisture addition
调节开关　bypass cock
调节炉渣　slag working
调节孪晶　accommodation twin
调节轮　adjustable pulley
调节螺钉　regulating [regulator, adjusting] screw
调节配件　regulating fitting
调节期　conditioning period
调节器　regulator, controller, adjuster, governor, conditioner, actuator ◇ 非线性[具有死区的]～ dead-zone regulator, 恒流～*, 无(定)向～ astatic governor, 无静差～ astatic regulator, 限流～*, 锥形～ cone governer
调节器控制阀　controller pilot
调节区　conditioning zone
调节室　conditioning chamber
调节送风(沿风口的)　controlled air distribution
调节弹簧　adjusting spring
调节系数　accommodation coefficient
调节系统　control [regulating] system, system of regulation
调节楔　adjusting key
调节性添加剂　【冶】corrective addition
调节仪表　monitoring instrument
调节因素　regulating factor
调节用变压器　【电】governor
调节滞后　control lag
调节砖　【焦】sliding brick [damper], distributor
调节装置　regulator, regulating [control] apparatus, adjusting device [gear], actuating device
调节作用　control action
调宽压力机　【压】width adjust pressure machine
调宽(压下)量　edging reduction
调宽轧制　edging rolling
调理段　conditioning section
调理室　conditioning chamber
调料槽　conditioner
调料设备　conditioning equipment
调零　zero set(ting)
调浓器　density controller, salinometer（电导式）
调配　allotment
调偏标准　offset standard
调频　frequency modulation (FM)
调频接收机　F.M. (frequency modulation) receiver
调频器　frequency regulator, tuner

| 调频声波速(探伤用) F.M. (frequency modulation) beam
| 调频-调幅 frequency modulation (FM-AM)
| 调频系统 frequency modulation system
| 调漆油 paint oil
| 调气器 register
| 调热间隙 hot gap
| 调热器 heat regulator
| 调湿 humidify(ing), moisten, (pre)wetting, damping ◇ 空气～设备*
| 调湿干燥 controlled humidity drying
| 调湿混合料 moistened mix
| 调湿液体 moistening liquid
| 调湿圆筒混合机 【团】wetting drum
| 调试 commissioning, debugging, troubleshoot
| 调试程序 debugging program [routine]
| 调试程序包 【计】debugging package
| 调试辅助程序 【计】debugging aids
| 调试宏指令 【计】debug macroinstruction
| 调试时间 development time [macro]
| 调试语句 【计】debugging statement
| 调速 speed regulation [governing, adjustment, control] ◇ 变频～*
| 调速板 speed control plate
| 调速管 klystron
| 调速器 (speed) governor, speed regulator [adjuster] ◇ 电子自动～electronic governor, 风扇～fan governor
| 调速星轮 retarding sprocket
| 调位 positional adjustment, positioning
| 调位螺栓 positioning bolt
| 调温 temperature adjustment, thermoregulation ◇ 预先～preset temperature
| 调温段(炉子的) heating (up) zone
| 调温风机 tempering (air) fan
| 调温风流[空气] temper air, tempering air flow
| 调温风门 tempering air damper
| 调温器 temperature regulating device, thermosistor

调温蛇管[旋管] tempering coil
调温速度[率] rate of temperature change
调相 phase modulation ◇ 重复～记录*
调谐 tuning, resonating, syntonization, syntony, syntonizing
调谐变压器 resonance [tuned] transformer
调谐电容器 tuning capacitor
调谐共振 tuning syntony
调谐器[设备] tuner, tuning unit
调谐线圈 tuning coil
调谐旋钮 selector, tuning knob
调谐指示管 tuning eye
调心滚珠轴承 (同"自动定位滚珠轴承")
调压 pressure adjustment, throttle
调压变压器 regulating [variable-ratio] transtormer
调压阀 pressure regulating valve
调压器 voltage regulator, pressure regulator ◇ 碳堆～carbon-pile regulator
调压式多辊矫直机 pressure regulating roller leveller
调压式刮料板 【团】cut-off levelling plate with feed pressure control
调压自耦变压器 regulating autotransformer
调焰烧嘴 variable-flame burner
调液厚层器 absorptiometer
调匀电解液 【金】level(l)ing solution
调渣 working slag
调整 adjusting, control, regulating, regulation, conditioning, debugging, dressing, governing, setting, trim(ming), tune-up, 【计】justification ◇ 人工～hand setting
调整X射线光阑 【理】blocking operation
调整板 adjusting plate
调整槽 conditioning vessel
调整点 set point
调整垫圈 【机】adjusting washer
调整阀 regulating valve
调整杆 adjusting rod

调整范围	turndown range
调整工	adjuster, setter, trimmer, fettler（轧机的）
调整柜	regulating cabinet
调整环	adjusting ring [collar]
调整环冲子	【压】locating center punch
调整活套	【压】loop control
调整机构	adjustment gear, control mechanism
调整剂	conditioning agent, modifying addition, 【金】rectifying agent
调整夹	adjustable clamp
调整计划	replanning
调整键	adjusting key
调整搅拌器	correction agitator
调整孔	access (ACS)
调整轮	stretching pulley
调整螺钉[螺丝]	set [governing] screw, adjust-screw, forcing off screw
调整螺帽[螺母]	adjusting [rating] nut
调整螺栓	adjust(ing) [set] bolt
调整偏差	off-set
调整配料	mixture adjustment
调整片垫圈	tab washer
调整器	adjuster
调整曲线	adjusted curve
调整圈	adjusting ring
调整溶剂	level(l)ing solvent
调整设备	control equipment
调整生产	turndown of production
调整系统	setting system, system of regulation
调整箱	regulating cabinet
调整楔	adjusting [tightening] wedge
调整旋塞	control cock
调整压下装置	roll-gap setting
调整液	correction liquor, make up solution
调整员	adjuster
调整圆弧	adjusting arc
调整渣	conditioned slag
调整轧辊位置	roll setting [setup]
调整针	adjusting needle
调整装置	adjusting device, adjustment gear
调制	modulating, modulation (Mod), conditioning ◇ 交叉～ cross modulation, 振幅～ amplitude modulation
调制放大器	modulated amplifier
调制分析	modulation analysis
调制混合料	conditioned mix
调制结构	modulated structure
调制解调器	modem, modulator demodulator
调制旁带（光谱的）	modulation sidebands
调制频率	modulation frequency
调制器	modulator, keyer
调制设备	conditioning equipment
调制性	modularity
调质奥氏体钢	modified austenitic steel
调质处理	quenching-and-tempering, hardening with subsequent drawing
调质度（镀锡薄钢板的）	temper
调质钢	hardened [quenched] and tempered steel, tough hardening steel
调质高强度钢	heat treated high strength steel
调质剂	modifying agent, improver
调质砂	【金】tempering sand
调质水	【金】tempering water
调质轧制	skin-pass
调质组织	【金】thermal refined structure
调中控制	centering control ◇ 钢流自动～
调准	adjusting, aligning, tune-up ◇ 未～ missetting
调准标记	adjustment mark
调准线	match line
调准针	adjusting needle
调准装置	adjuster, co-algnment
跳板	access [gang, diving] board, drawboard, catwalk, foot plank
跳动	pulsating, jitter, bounce, jumping, dancing（如仪表指针的）
跳动辊	dancer roll

跳动辊滑架　dancer roll slide
跳动接触　bounce contact
跳动偏摆　beat
跳动频率　frequency of jumping
跳动筛　jumping screen
跳焊　skip [stitch] welding ◇ 分段~*
跳焊法　skip procedure
跳弧[火]电压　spark-over [arcing] voltage
跳火　flash over, arcing ◇ 逆~【焊】back flashover
跳开　tripping off, bounce
跳迁　jumping
跳式三辊机座　【压】jumping three-high stand
跳汰床吸附塔[离子交换柱]　(同"脉动吸附塔")
跳汰法[跳汰选矿]　jigging
跳汰机　jig(ger), jigging screen ◇ 脉动~ pulsator (jig)
跳汰机富选[湿式跳汰选](铅矿)　【选】hotching
跳汰机筛下室　hutch
跳汰筛　【选】jigging screen, washbox bed-plate
跳线　【电】jumper (wire)
跳越距离　skip distance
跳越式切割　skip cutting
跳越指令　skip instruction
跳跃　jump(ing), 【计】skip (进位)
跳跃滑移　jerky glide
跳跃块焊接　skip block welding
跳跃运动(传导电子的)　hopping motion
跳闸　【电】trip(ing), out-of-gear
跳闸电路　trip circuit
跳闸线圈　tripping coil
跳闸指示器　trip indicator
贴标签机　label(l)ing machine, label(l)er
贴箔　foliation
贴胶　rubberizing
贴角焊　fillet welding ◇ 纵向~*
贴角缝焊脚　leg of fillet

贴角接头　fillet joint
贴金　gilding ◇ 钢件表面~法 Damascening
贴面瓷砖　furring tile
贴皮　【铸】lagging
铁{Fe}　iron, ferrum, ferro ◇ γ~ gamma iron, δ~ delta ferrite [iron], 阿姆柯~*, 奥斯蒙~ Osmund iron, 包镍~ nickel-clad iron, 除[脱]~ deferrization, 纯~ pure iron, 低[去]氢~ hydrogen-purified iron, 电解~*, 多孔~*, 光谱纯~(>99.999%Fe) puron, 含~粉尘【铁】blue dust, 含锰~ manganous iron, 号外[等外,不合格]~*, 合金~ alloy iron, 夹渣~ slag iron, 金属~ metallic iron, 耐酸~*, 凝-线~*, 渗铜~*, 天然~ native iron, 托马斯~ Thomas (pig) iron, 外冷~【铸】external chill, 维氏体~ Wuestite-iron, 无[不含]~的 iron-free, 再制~ synthetic pig iron
铁白云石{(CA, Fe, Mg)CO$_3$}　ferrodolomite, ankerite
铁斑[疵]点　iron spot
铁板覆铅　spot-homogen
铁板钛矿{Fe$_2$TiO$_5$}　pseudobrookite
铁棒　iron bar ◇ 连续铸造~法【铸】Flocast
铁表面镀覆铅锡合金法　spot homogen process
铁柄杆菌　◇ 盖氏~ Gallionella
铁铂母合金　ferroplatinum
铁测定　iron determination
铁车屑　iron turning
铁沉淀(相)　iron precipitation
铁沉淀槽　iron precipitating tank
铁磁畴　ferromagnetic domain, spontaneous magnetization domain
铁磁畴理论　domain theory of ferromagnetism
铁磁粉末　ferromagnetic powder
铁磁粉显示剂(磁力探伤用)　powder developer

铁磁粉悬浮液显示剂（磁力探伤用） wet-powder developer
铁磁共振[谐振] ferromagnetic [ferrimagnetic] resonance, ferroresonance
铁磁共振的 ferroresonant
铁磁计 ferrometer
铁磁结构 ferromagnetic structure
铁磁谱仪 iron magnetic spectrometer
铁磁体 ferromagnet(ic)
铁磁物质 【理】ferromagnetic substance [material]
铁磁性 ferromagnetism, ferrimagnetism
铁磁性薄膜 ferromagnetic film
铁磁(性)材料 【金】ferrimagnetic material
铁磁(性)合金 ferromagnetic alloy ◇ 费里马格～ferrimag
铁磁性金属 ferromagnetic metal
铁磁(性)晶体 ferromagnetic crystal
铁磁性居里点 ferromagnetic Curie point
铁磁性矿物 ferromagnetic mineral
铁磁性临界点 ferromagnetic critical point
铁磁性镍 【理】ferromagnetic nickel
铁磁性石榴石 ferrimagnetic garnet, ferrogarnet
铁磁学 ferromagnetics, ferromagnetism
铁磁学量子理论 quantum theory of ferro-magnetism
铁磁异常 ferromagnetic anomaly
铁磁质 ferromagnetics
铁锉屑 iron filings
铁丹 【化】rouge, colcother ◇ 抛光～polishing rouge
铁道 railroad, railway ◇ 地下～*，环行～ circuit railroad，市内（地下）～metropolitan railway，窄轨～*
铁道岔尖[辙尖] railroad point
铁道车站站长 【运】station master
铁道结构用钢 railway structural steel
铁的 ferric, siderous
铁电 ferroelectricity
铁电材料 ferroelectric material
铁电畴 ferroelectric domain
铁电极电解槽（钠电解用） Kastner cell
铁电晶体 ferroelectric crystal
铁电膜 ferroelectric film
铁电陶瓷 ferroelectric ceramics
铁电特性组织 Perovskite structure
铁电体 【理】ferroelectrics
铁电学[性] ferroelectricity
铁钉 iron nail, piton ◇ 冷～【铸】chill nail，平头大～holdfast
铁锭 iron ingot, pig iron
铁豆 【铸】cold shot, shot(ted) metal, shot defect（表面缺陷）
铁盾 iron shield
铁多晶体 iron polycrystal
铁多晶型(现象) iron polymorphism
铁矾 ferric [iron, Roman] alum
铁矾土 {$Al_2O_3 \cdot 2H_2O$}（red）bauxite, clayey earth
铁粉 ferrous [iron] powder, irons, powdered iron ◇ DPG 转盘雾化～*，包[镀]铜～*，纯～straight iron powder，电解～*，过磨～*，浸渍～*，粒化～granulated iron powder，曼内斯曼[雾化]～*，破碎～crushed irons，氢还原～*，瑞典～Swedish iron powder，羰基～*，脱碳～*，辛特罗帕克加铜～Sintropac，液碎[雾化]～*，制～法～*
铁粉尘 iron dust
铁粉焊条 iron-powder electrode
铁粉记录图 ferrograph
铁粉切割(加铁粉切割) iron powder cutting
铁粉切割法[加铁粉氧乙炔切割法] iron-powder process
铁粉涂层[涂料，药皮] iron powder coating
铁粉芯 (iron-)dust core
铁粉氧切法 oxweld cutting process
铁粉药皮焊条 iron powder coating electrode
铁氟化钾{K_3FeF_6} potassium ferric fluo-

ride
铁氟化物　ferri-fluoride
铁钙维氏体　calciferous wiistite
铁坩埚　iron crucible
铁坩埚炉　iron pot furnace
铁淦氧　(同"铁氧体")
铁淦氧磁物　(同"铁磁体")
铁橄榄石{Fe$_2$SiO$_4$}　fayalite
铁橄榄石型炉渣　fayalite-type slag
铁锆合金　ferrozirconium
铁格筛　grizzly
铁铬矾　redingtonite
铁铬合金　ferrochrome
铁铬铝电阻合金　◇ 阿尔克雷斯～*,阿尔克罗姆～*,法克拉洛伊～*,雷迪欧姆～*
铁铬铝电阻丝合金　◇ 费罗派尔～*,梅格派尔～Megapyr,史密斯～*
铁铬铝合金　◇ 费克拉伊尔～*
铁铬铝系电热丝　阿卢迪罗姆～ Aludirome
铁铬铝系高电阻合金　◇ 坎塔尔～*
铁铬耐热合金　◇ 派罗卡斯特～*
铁铬镍耐热合金　◇ 阿尔雷～*
铁铬系不锈钢　◇ 米希姆～*
铁工厂　iron works (IW, I.Wks)
铁钩　cramp iron, cleek
铁沟　iron runner ◇ 清理～*,移动[可换]～ replaceable trough,主～ main runner, sow (channel)
铁沟残铁[残留物](高炉的)　runners, runner scrap
铁沟耐火材料　runner refractory
铁沟凝铁　sow
铁沟取样　【冶】trench sampling
铁钴磁性合金　permendur
铁钴钒合金材料　Supermendur
铁钴合金　iron cobalt alloy ◇ 高导磁率～*
铁钴矿　wairauite
铁钴钼合金　◇ 548～*
铁钴系高磁导率合金　◇ 帕明杜尔～*

铁钴永磁合金　iron-cobalt permanent magnetic alloy
铁管　iron pipe (IP)
铁硅合金　◇ 布福卡斯特～Buffokast
铁硅基高强度钢　Fe-Si-base high tensile strength steel
铁硅钪矿　bazzite
铁硅铝磁(性)合金　Sendust, alsifer
铁－硅熔体　iron-silicon melt
铁硅酸盐　ferrosilicate
铁－硅组分图　◇ 莫勒～Maurer's diagram
铁棍　wrenching iron
铁含量　iron content
铁含量测定　iron determination
铁焊料　iron solder
铁焊条　ferrous electrode ◇ 涂石棉和助熔剂的～电弧焊 quasi-arc
铁耗【电】iron [core] loss
铁合金　ferro [iron] alloy ◇ 巴丁脱氧～*,电热～车间*,复杂～complexferroalloy,含镍～*,块状～briquette ferroalloy,弥散硬化～*,无碳～carbon-free ferroalloy
铁合金厂　ferroalloy works
铁合金粉末　ferroalloy [iron-base] powder
铁合金工业[生产]　ferroalloy industry
铁合金炉　ferroalloy furnace
铁合金熔炼　【冶】ferroalloy smelting
铁合金熔炼车间　【铁】ferroalloy smelting shop
铁合金熔炼(电)炉　electric ferroalloy smelting furnace ◇ 米格式～*
铁合金熔炼法　ferroalloy smelting process
铁合金元素　ferroalloying element
铁合金轴承　iron-base bearing
铁黑　black of iron
铁红(红色氧化铁)　iron (oxide) red
铁护框　iron shield
铁华[三氯化铁]　iron flower
铁化合物　iron compound
铁簧继电器　ferreed

铁 tie

铁火花检验	iron spark test
铁基	iron base
铁基合金	ferrous [iron(-base)] alloy, ferrous (base) metal ◇ α～alpha iron alloy, γ～gamma iron alloy, 恩杜罗耐蚀～*, 高温强度[耐高温]～*, 雷西斯塔～*
铁基晶体	matrix crystal of iron
铁基液相合金	iron-base liquid alloy
铁基轧辊	iron-base roll
铁基轴承合金	iron-base bearing alloy
铁甲	iron shield
铁架	brandreth
铁尖晶石{FeAl₂O₄}	hercynite, ferrospinel
铁碱式硫回收法	ferrox sulphur recovery process
铁匠锻锤(手锻用)	blacksmith forging
铁匠业	(black)smithery
铁焦	【焦】iron coke, ferrocoke
铁焦比	iron-coke ratio,【铁】melting ratio
铁焦团矿(块)	ferrocoke agglomerate
铁结壳(炉瘤)	【冶】iron skull
铁结碳化钨硬质合金	iron-cemented tungsten carbide
铁金红石	nigrin(e)
铁堇青石	iron cordierite, ferrocordierite
铁晶格	iron lattice
铁晶须	iron whiskers [filament]
铁精矿	iron ore concentrate ◇ 含硼～*
铁精矿烧结[造块]	agglomeration of iron ore concentrates
铁菌	iron-consuming becteria
铁铠装	iron shield
铁康铜	iron constantan (I.C.)
铁-康铜热电偶	I.C. (thermo)couple
铁壳镁砖	metal cased magnesite brick
铁壳砖	armoured [metal-(en)cased] brick ◇ 加筋～ferroclad brick
铁壳砖后墙	【冶】metal-cased back wall
铁口	(同"出铁口")
铁口保护架	dog-house
铁口出渣	front slagging
铁口凝铁圈	dog collar
铁口喷吹	blowing on tap hole
铁口钻	taphole drill
铁块破碎机	falling tup machine
铁矿	iron ore, iron mine ◇ 脆[疏松]～friable iron ore, 富[精]选～beneficiated iron ore, 高品位～high grade iron ore, 含铜～cuprous iron ore, 含有机矿物的红～clinton ore
铁矿床	【地】iron ore deposit
铁矿粉	iron-ore fines
铁矿料中退火	ore annealing
铁矿泥(浆)	【选】iron-ore slurry
铁矿球团	iron-ore pellet, pelletized iron ore ◇ 冷固结～*
铁矿球团厂	iron-ore pellet(izing) plant
铁矿球团法	iron-ore pelletizing
铁矿生球团	【铁】cold-bound iron-ore pellet
铁矿石	iron ore, ironstone ◇ 焙烧～burnt mine, 低磷～*, 高铝～*, 硅质脉石的～siliceous ore, 含锰[富锰]～manganiferous iron ore, 含钛～*, 红土型～*, 基律纳型～Kiruna type iron ore, 沥青质～*, 石灰质～calcareous ore
铁矿石磁化焙烧法	◇ 鲁奇～Lurgi process
铁矿石分选机	【选】iron-ore separator
铁矿石还原自动图示记录仪	stathmograph
铁矿石夹杂	iron-ore impurity
铁矿石精选[富集]	iron-ore concentration
铁矿石流态化还原	fluid iron ore reduction (FIOR)
铁矿石品位	iron content of ore, iron-ore grade
铁矿石评定	【铁】iron ore assessment
铁矿石评价	valuation of iron ore
铁矿石球团法原理	fundamentals of pelletizing of iron ore
铁矿石球团生产	iron-ore pellet production
铁矿石人造富矿	iron ore agglomerate

铁矿石熔融还原 iron ore smelting reduction	**铁菱锌矿** capnite, monheimite
铁矿石烧结[造块] iron ore sintering [agglomeration]	**铁硫磷铀矿** coconinoite
铁矿石烧结矿 iron ore sinter [agglomerate]	**铁炉瘤【冶】** iron skull
铁矿石团块 iron ore briquette	**铁路** railway (Rw, Ry), rail(road), track ◇ 标准轨距～ standard gauge railway, 施工[临时]～ constructor's railroad, 专用～ access railroad
铁矿石压块【团】 iron ore briquetting	**铁路编组场** railway marshalling yard
铁矿石预处理设备【团】 iron-ore pretreatment facilities	**铁路侧线** siding
铁矿石造块能力(设施)【团】 iron-ore agglomeration facilities	**铁路岔线【运】** railroad siding
铁矿石直接熔融还原 direct iron ore smelting reduction (DIOS)	**铁路车辆轴承黄铜**(65Cu, 5—10Sn, 5—30Pb) journal brass
铁矿石直接熔融还原法 direct iron ore smelting reduction process	**铁路车皮** rail(road) car ◇ 底卸式～
铁矿石制团[造球] iron ore pelletizing [briquetting]	**铁路车轴坯** railway axle
铁矿水泥 iron-ore cement	**铁路公路两用桥** double-deck(ed) bridge, railway and highway combined bridge
铁矿物 iron mineral	**铁路轨道** railtrack
铁矿岩 ferrolite	**铁路轨枕** railroad sleeper
铁类金属 ferrous metal	**铁路货运量** volume of railway freight
铁离子 iron ion ◇ 两价～ ferrous ion, 三价～ ferric ion	**铁路建设** railroad construction
铁锂云母 zinnwaldite	**铁路建筑(工程)** railroad construction
铁粒 iron shot, abrasive grit (铸件喷砂清理用) ◇ 高炉渣～ buckshot	**铁路交叉** railway crossing
铁料 iron burden [charge]	**铁路交货** delivery by rail
铁料系统 iron-bearing system	**铁路交货价格** free on rail (FOR)
铁磷共晶体 steadite	**铁路跨线桥** railroad underbridge
铁磷锂矿 ferrisicklerite	**铁路料仓** track hopper
铁磷锰矿 phosphoferrite	**铁路漏斗车** railroad hopper car
铁鳞 (同"氧化铁皮") ◇ 除～用供水(管道)【压】 scale flushing supply water (SFSW), 电化学除～法*, 锻造～*, 磨除～ abrasive descaling, 敲击～ scale knocking, 湿法去～ wet-scale disposal	**铁路平面调车** railway planar dispatch
	铁路水鹤 water crane
	铁路外运 rail loadout
	铁路网 railway network ◇ 工厂清理废钢的～ scrapworks trackage
铁鳞堆 cinder dump	**铁路线** line, trackage ◇ 厂内～ intraplant trackage, 工厂专用～ factory railway, 窄轨(距)～ narrow gauge track
铁鳞铁粉 Linz powder	
铁菱镁矿{MgFe(CO$_3$)} mesitite, breun(n)erite, mesitine	**铁路线路设计**(车间内的) track layout
	铁路卸车矿槽 railroad unloading pocket
铁菱锰矿 capillitite, ponite	**铁路卸车站** railroad car discharge station
	铁路与公路平交道 level crossing
	铁路运输 rail haulage, railway transportation

铁路枕木	railroad tie [sleeper]
铁路支线	spur road
铁路终点	railway terminal
铁路轴承	railroad bearing
铁路贮仓	railroad hopper
铁路(装车,装运)矿槽	railroad loading pocket, railway load-out bin
铁路装车设备	railroad loadout facilities
铁路装车站	railroad loading station
铁路自卸车	tipping railway car
铁铝合金	ferroaluminum, FeAl alloy ◇费尔~*
铁铝镍磁性合金	◇海尼卡~*
铁铝镍合金	iron aluminium nickel alloy
铁铝酸四钙	brown millerite
铁铝土	red bauxite, ferrallitic soil
铁铝氧石{$Al_2O_3 \cdot 2H_2O$}	bauxite
铁氯铅矿	hamatophanite
铁马	【铸】sweeping horse
铁帽型含金复合矿	goosan type-gold composite ores
铁镁硅酸盐	iron-magnesium silicate
铁镁辉石	violaite
铁镁矿物	sideromelane, ferromagnesian
铁镁明矾	shorsuite
铁镁质	fem, femic
铁锰钙辉石	urbanite
铁锰硅酸盐夹杂(物)	iron manganese silicate inclusions
铁锰合金	iron-manganese alloy
铁明矾{$Al_2Fe(SO_4)_2 \cdot 24H_2O$}	feather alum
铁钼钴永磁合金	◇莱马洛伊~*
铁钼合金	ferromolybdenum
铁铌合金	ferroniobium
铁铌钽碳化物	iron-columbium-tantalum carbide
铁铌钇矿	iron-rich samarskite, ishikawaite
铁泥(锌浸出的)	iron mud
铁腻子	beaumantage
铁镍磁性合金	◇西尼马克斯~*
铁镍低膨胀系数合金	◇纪尧姆~Guilaume alloy, 尼尔瓦~*
铁镍铬合金	iron-nickel-chromium ◇康涅尔~Conel
铁镍铬耐氧化合金	◇费龙~*
铁镍铬系耐蚀合金	◇阿罗开科~*
铁镍钴磁性合金	◇海尼柯~*
铁镍钴粉末冶金合金	◇布伦达洛伊32-12~Blendalloy 33-12
铁镍钴合金	teleoseal, fernico ◇埃尔科洛依~Elcolloy, 科瓦~*, 密封用~*
铁镍钴陶瓷封接合金	fernico ceramic sealing alloy
铁镍钴系永磁合金	iron-nickel-cobalt permanent magnetic alloy ◇雷科~Reco
铁镍合金	iron-nickel ◇安西斯特~*, 迪尔瓦~*, 杜美~丝*, 高导磁率~permalloy, 恒弹性(模量)~*, 可控热膨胀系数~*, 马坦普整磁用~Mutemp, 尼克洛伊耐蚀~*, 天然~*
铁镍合金粉	permalloy powder
铁镍恒范合金	◇尼尔瓦~*, 尼雷克斯~*
铁镍基软磁合金	◇康珀尼克~*
铁镍矿	awaruite
铁镍铝磁铁	iron-nickel-aluminium magnet
铁镍铝硅合金	◇阿尔尼西~*
铁镍铝钴(系)永磁合金	◇阿尔尼科~*, 奥斯特~oersted magnet
铁镍铝合金	calite
铁镍铝钛系永磁合金	◇尼帕马格~*
铁镍铝永磁合金	◇阿尔尼~*
铁镍锰高导磁率合金	◇梅格珀姆~*
铁镍钼导磁合金	molybdenum-permalloy
铁镍钼恒弹性合金	◇维布拉洛伊~*
铁镍齐	souesite
铁镍四元合金	◇阿夫蒂特~*
铁镍铜锰铬	mu-metal
铁镍透磁合金	Audiolloy
铁耙	iron rabble
铁泡石	iron froth
铁硼合金	ferroboron

铁硼烷　ferraborane
铁坯　balled iron ◇ 热压～块*
铁皮砖　ferroclip [metal-(en)cased, armoured, steel-clad] brick
铁屏蔽　iron shield
铁钎　wrenching iron, crooked chisel
铁铅锍[冰铜]【色】iron-lead matte
铁钳　hawkbill ◇ 大～grampus
铁橇　crowbar
铁撬棍　grab iron
铁青铜　ferrobronze
铁氰化钾{K₃[Fe(CN)₆]}　potassium ferricyanide, red prussiate of potash
铁氰化铁{Fe[Fe(CN)₆]}　ferric ferricyanide
铁氰化物{M₃[Fe(CN)₆]}　ferricyanide
铁氰化亚铁{Fe₃[Fe(CN)₆]₂}　ferrous ferricyanide
铁球　iron ball
铁热还原提取法　ferrothermic extraction
铁熔体　iron melt
铁砂　iron sand, cast iron shot
铁砂清理　rotoblasting
铁砂清理滚筒　rotoblast barrel
铁砂清理作业　rotoblast operation
铁砂箱【铸】iron flask
铁栅筛　bar screen ◇ 滚盘～disc-grizzly screen
铁闪锌矿{n ZnS·m FeS}　marmatite, newboldite
铁勺取样【冶】shovel sampling
铁砷浮渣【色】iron-arsenic dross
铁砷钴矿　spathiopyrite
铁砷铀云母{Fe₂(UO₂)₂(AsO₄)₂·8H₂O}　kahlerite
铁渗碳体平衡图　iron-cementite diagram
铁石墨平衡图　iron-graphite diagram
铁石墨轴承　iron-graphite bearing
铁铈合金　ferrocerium
铁收得率　iron yield
铁水　molten (pig) iron, iron melt, liquid iron, hot metal (H.M.), liquid metal (LM)
铁水保温分流布料器　liquid iron insulating flow-divided distributor
铁水槽【铁】iron trough
铁水车　hot metal car
铁水称量秤【铁】hot metal scale
铁水穿漏　runout, hot-metal breakout
铁水废钢法　hot-metal and scrap process
铁水分析　hot metal analysis
铁水供应站　hot metal station
铁水沟【铁】(iron) runner, (iron) trough, iron drain, hot metal runner, sow channel ◇ 移动式～*,铸铁场～平面图*
铁水沟维修　iron runner maintenance
铁水沟系统　iron runner system
铁水沟闸板　runner gate
铁水罐[包,桶]　(pig iron) ladle, iron ladle, hot metal ladle ◇ 敞口式[锥形]～*,出铁用～【冶】tap ladle,大～bull ladle,带流嘴的～labiate,混铁炉式～*,克灵式～Kling type ladle,梨形～Kling type ladle,鱼雷式～*,皮尤式～Pug-type ladle,运送～车*
铁水罐[包]车　iron-transfer ladle car
铁水罐车运输线　hot metal ladle car traffic
铁水罐衬修砌工段　hot metal ladle relining shop
铁水罐衬砖　ladle brick
铁水罐定位绞车　ladle-positioning winch
铁水罐耳轴　ladle trunnion
铁水罐翻转机　ladle tripper
铁水罐坑【铁】ladle well
铁水罐流铁槽　iron ladle spout
铁水罐流嘴　ladle lip
铁水罐砌衬修理　ladle rebricking
铁水罐停车场　ladle yard
铁水罐涂料【冶】ladle wash
铁水罐修理库　ladle-repair shop
铁水罐(运输)车　(hot metal) ladle truck, hot metal ladle and carriage, hot metal

(ladle) car, iron ladle car, buggy [transfer] ladle, jumbo
铁水罐准备场 ladle preparation station
铁水硅含量预报系统 predicting system for silicon content in molten iron
铁水(化学)成分 hot metal composition
铁水环流 circumferential molten iron flow, peripheral flow of molten iron
铁水加废钢冶炼法 hot-metal and scrap process
铁水浇注跨 【铁】hot-metal casting bay
铁水浇注台 hot metal pouring stand
铁水浇注温度 hot metal casting temperature
铁水静压力 ferrostatic pressure
铁水静压头 ferrostatic head
铁水粒化装置 iron granulation plant
铁水磷锰矿 baldanfite
铁水流体静压头 hydrostatic lift of iron
铁水炉渣分隔器 hot-metal and slag separator
铁水镁石 eisenbrucite
铁水喷粉脱硫 【钢】desulphurization of hot metal with powder injection
铁水烧蚀线(炉底的) iron penetration line
铁水深度(炉缸内的) depth of liquid iron
铁水渗透深度(对炉底砌体的) depth of iron penetration
铁水生产(量) 【铁】hot metal make
铁水试样 hot metal sample
铁水受注凹坑 hot metal receiving pit
铁水水淬粒化(法) granulation of pig iron
铁水脱硫 【钢】desulphurization of hot metal
铁水脱氧转炉炼钢法 killed Bessemer process
铁水预处理[脱硅] hot metal pretreatment, pretreatment of hot metal, pretreatment of liquid iron
铁水运输车 hot metal transfercar
铁水运输线 hot metal track

铁水支沟(铸床的) lateral channel
铁水主沟 taphole runner, sow channel, iron pool
铁丝 iron wire
铁丝盘 roll of wire
铁丝网 wire netting [meshes, entanglement]
铁丝芯骨 【铸】core wire
铁素体 ferrite ◇ α～alpha ferrite, 多角形～polygonal ferrite,, 含～的 ferritic, 块状～blocky ferrite, 片状～lamellar ferrite, 体心(立方晶型)～*, 条状～ferrite lath, 网状～ferrite network, 魏氏组织～*, 无碳～carbon-free ferrite, 先共析～*, 游离[自由]～*, 再结晶～*
铁素体不锈钢(<0.12C,<1Mn,<0.04P,<0.03S,<1Si, 14—18Cr) ferritic stainless steel ◇ C-布莱特超级～*, E-布赖特超级～*, 超纯～*, 低碳～*, 肖马克超级～*, 优质[高级]～*
铁素体促进剂 【金】ferritizer
铁素体带 ferrite banding [ghosts, streaks], line(s) of ferrite, ghost lines
铁素体范围 【金】ferritic range
铁素体富氧带 oxygen-rich area in ferrite
铁素体钢 ferritic steel
铁素体铬不锈钢 ferritic chromium stainless steel
铁素体鬼线 【金】ferrite [ferritic] ghost
铁素体合金 ferrite alloy, Alfer
铁素体合金钢 ferritic alloyed steel
铁素体化 ferritization, ferritizing ◇ 部分～part ferritization
铁素体化球墨铸铁 ferritised S G iron
铁素体化退火(铸铁的) ferritizing anneal
铁素体灰口铸铁 ferritic grey cast iron
铁素体基体 ferritic [α-Fe] matrix ◇ 纯[全]～*
铁素体晶格 ferrite lattice
铁素体晶粒度 ferrite grain size

铁素体晶粒界	ferrite grain boundaries
铁素体晶体	ferrite crystal
铁素体可锻铸铁	ferritic malleable (cast iron)
铁素体可锻铸铁件	ferritic malleable casting
铁素体马氏体组织	ferrito-martensite structure
铁素体耐热钢	◇ 杰索普 H40~*，萨美诺尔~*
铁素体强化元素	ferrite hardener
铁素体球墨铸铁	ferritic nodular cast iron
铁素体区	ferrite area, ferritic range
铁素体石墨共析(体)	ferrite-graphite eutectoid
铁素体条	ferrite lath
铁素体条纹	ferrite streaks
铁素体铁	ferritic iron
铁素体脱碳层深度	ferrite decarburized depth
铁素体网	ferrite net(work)
铁素体稳定化元素	ferrite stabilizer
铁素体显微组织	ferrite microstructure
铁素体形成元素	ferrite former, ferrite forming elememt
铁素体珠光体钢	hypopearlitic steel
铁素体珠光体基体	ferrite-pearlite matrix
铁素体铸铁	ferritic cast iron
铁素体组分	ferrite constituent
铁酸$\{HFeO_2(偏), H_3FeO_3\}$	ferrous acid
铁酸钡磁石	barium ferrite magnet
铁酸钡永久磁铁	◇ 英道克斯~ Indox
铁酸二钙$\{Ca_2Fe_2O_5\}$	dicalcium ferrite
铁酸钙$\{Ca(FeO_2)_2\}$	monocalcium ferrite
铁酸镁$(MgFe_2O_4, MgO \cdot Fe_2O_3)$	magnesioferrite, magnesium ferrite
铁酸钠	sodium ferrite
铁酸铜$\{CuO \cdot Fe_2O_3\}$	copper ferrite
铁酸锌$\{ZnO \cdot Fe_2O_3\}$	zinc ferrite
铁酸盐熔体	ferrite melt
铁燧岩	taconite, Lake Superior type iron ore
铁损	【电】iron [core] loss ◇ 低~材料 low coreless material，爱泼斯坦~测定装置 Epstein apparatus
铁损连续测量设备	continuous iron loss measuring equipment
铁索护栏	【运】cable guard rail
铁铊矿$\{7Ti_2O_3 \cdot Fe_2O_3\}$	avicennite
铁塔	iron tower [pagoda], mast ◇ 门形~gantry tower
铁钛合金	ferrotitanium ◇ 塔姆~*
铁钛矿	arizonite
铁-钛氧化物	iron-titanium oxide
铁弹性的	ferroelastic
铁钽锡石	ainalite
铁碳共晶	iron-carbon eutectic
铁碳合金	iron-carbon alloy [metal]
铁-碳化铁共析(体)	【金】iron-iron carbide eutectoid
铁-碳化铁平衡图	【金】iron-iron carbide diagram
铁碳化物	ferrous carbide
铁碳磷母合金	◇ 帕克特龙~*
铁碳马氏体	【金】iron-carbon martensite
铁碳硼烷	ferracarborane
铁碳平衡	carbon-iron balance
铁碳平衡[状态]图	iron-carbon (equilibrium, constitution) diagram
铁锑钙石$\{2CaO \cdot Sb_2O_4\}$	schneebergite
铁锑化合物	iron-antimony compound
铁锑酸钙石$\{2CaO \cdot Sb_2O_4\}$	schneebergite
铁添加合金	iron addition
铁条	iron bar
铁条打捆	【压】banding
铁挺(敲出尖楔工具)	drift punch
铁同质多晶型	【理】iron polymorphism
铁铜合金	iron-copper ◇ 超级多孔~*，纯~*，灰黄~*
铁铜混合粉末	◇ 辛特罗帕克~*
铁铜聚四氟乙烯轴承	iron-copper-fluon bearing
铁铜蓝	idaite
铁钍石	ferrothorite

tie 铁 1414

铁 tie

铁丸 (cast) iron shot, shot (iron), blasting shot [girt] ◇ 细流法制～shot ting
铁丸清理装置 shot blast plant
铁纹石 kamacite
铁钨合金 ferrotungsten
铁钨华 ferritungstite
铁硒合金 ferro-selenium
铁硒铜矿 eskebornite
铁锡合金 ferro-tin alloy
铁系烧结合金 steelmet
铁细菌 iron bacteria
铁细菌科 ferribacteriaceae
铁细菌目 ferribacteriales
铁箱试验 【焦】(iron) box test
铁销钉 iron pin
铁屑 iron chips [scurf, filings, dust]
铁屑集料(混凝土用) ferrolite
铁芯骨 【铸】iron core
铁芯铝制件热浸镀铝铸型法 ◇ 阿尔芬～*
铁心 【电】(iron) core ◇ E形～冲片 E-stamping, T形～冲片 T-stamping, 带绕～ tape-wound core, 电枢～ armature core, 剖切[C]～C (cut) core
铁心饱和 core saturation
铁心变压器 iron-core transformer
铁心材料 core material
铁心磁路 iron circuit
铁心磁性饱和 core saturation
铁心电感 core inductance
铁心扼流圈 iron-core reactor, iron-core choking coil
铁心感应 core induction
铁心感应(电)炉 cored(-type) induction furnace, ductor
铁心硅钢 electrical steel
铁心冷却电动机 core-cooled motor
铁心绕组 【电】cored winding
铁心损失[(损)耗] 【电】core loss ◇ 剩余～residual core loss
铁心损失比[率] specific core loss
铁心涂漆 core plating

铁心柱(变压器的) leg
铁锈{Fe_2O_3} rust, ferroxyl, cocoa powder
铁锈色砂 ferruginous sand
铁锈蚀检验(镀锌、镀锡或涂镀钢板的) ferroxyl test
铁锈蚀指示剂 ferroxyl indicator
铁须 iron filament
铁须生成 【团】fibrous iron formation, metallic-wire growth
铁烟囱 steel stack ◇ 缆绳拉紧的～ guyed steel stack
铁盐 ferric [iron] salt, molysite
铁研式抗裂试验(日本) Tekken type cracking test
铁氧化剂 ferrooxidant, iron-oxidizer
铁氧化物 ferriferous [ferous-ferric] oxide
铁氧化细菌 iron oxidizing bacteria ◇ 自养～*
铁氧体 ferrite ◇ 反尖晶石型～ inverse spinel ferrite, 费劳克斯普兰～*, 高温[热]～pyroferrite, 尖晶石型～spinel ferrite, 塞罗马格～ Cerromag, 硬磁性～ hard ferrite, 正尖晶石型～ normal spinel ferrite
铁氧体磁体 ferrite magnet
铁氧体磁铁粉 ferromagnetic oxide powder
铁氧体磁心 ferrite [oxide] core
铁氧体磁心存储器 ferrite core memory
铁氧体存储器 ferrite memory
铁氧体软磁材料 soft magnetic ferrites
铁氧体预烧料 presintering ferrites
铁氧系 iron-oxygen
铁液面花纹 play film, playing figure
铁银制品 iron-silver composition
铁英岩 itabirite
铁英岩精矿 itabirite concentrate
铁铀合金 ferrouranium
铁铀铜矾 gilpinite
铁铀云母{$Fe(UO_3)_2P_2O_8 \cdot 8H_2O$} bassetite
铁油灰 【建】iron putty

| 铁浴 iron bath
| 铁浴熔融还原法 iron bath smelting reduction process
| 铁浴式熔融还原炉 iron bath type smelting reduction furnace
| 铁陨石 siderolite, aerosiderite
| 铁渣 ferric [iron] cake, scruff, scum ◇出渣口~*,洗过的~ washed iron cake, 窑头~分离*
| 铁渣分离坑(铁水沟中的) skimming basin
| 铁-渣系 iron-slag system
| 铁渣再浆化槽 【色】iron-cake repulp tank
| 铁砧 (blacksmith) anvil ◇锻工~ smith's anvil, 尖嘴~ beak iron, 异型~ die block
| 铁砧锤头镜[平]面 anvil cinder plate
| 铁砧底座 anvil block
| 铁砧垫 anvil cushion
| 铁砧效应(硬度试验的) anvil effect
| 铁砧枕座 anvil cushion
| 铁砧自由锻 smithing operation
| 铁砧嘴 anvil beak
| 铁针 iron pin
| 铁置换 【色】cement with iron
| 铁制浮标 iron float
| 铁制品 iron make, ironwork, ironware
| 铁制熔锅 【色】iron melting pot
| 铁质高岭土 ferruginous kaolin(e)
| 铁质骨架 ferrous skeleton
| 铁质密致材料 ferrous dense material
| 铁质黏合[胶合]剂 iron cement
| 铁质渣 【铁】ferriferous slag
| 铁珠 iron ball [shot], shot iron
| 铁铸件 ferrous [iron] casting
| 铁(铸)型 iron mould
| 铁铸造 iron founding
| 铁族 【化】iron group
| 铁族金属 iron family metal
| 铁族元素 iron family element, iron-group element
| 铁钻屑 iron borings
| 听觉疲劳 auditory fatigue
| 听力损失 【环】hearing loss
| 听筒 receiver
| 听域测定仪 audiometer
| 听诊检验 stethoscopic test
| 烃 hydrocarbon
| 烃黑 hydrocarbon black
| 烃化合物 hydrocarbon compound
| 烃基{R} hydrocarbon radical, alkyl(radical)
| 烃基碱金属 alkyl alkali
| 烃基金属化合物 alkide
| 烃基铅 plumbane
| 烃基亚碲酸 tellurinic acid
| 烃类 hydrocarbons
| 烃类保护气氛 hydrocarbon atmosphere
| 烃类分布 hydrocarbon distribution
| 烃类分析 hydrocarbon analysis
| 烃类混合物 hydrocarbon mixture
| 烃类燃料 hydrocarbon fuel
| 烃类稀释剂 hydrocarbon diluent
| 烃溶剂 hydrocarbon solvent
| 烃溶液 hydrocarbon solution
| 烃氧基金属 alcoxide
| 烃氧基亚铊{TlOR} thallium alcoholate
| 廷曼焊料合金(66.6Sn,33.3Pb) Tinman's solder (alloy)
| 廷塞尔铅锌装饰合金(60Zn,余量Pb) zinc Tinsel
| 廷塞尔锡铅装饰合金 Tinsel
| 廷史密斯焊药(66Sn,34Cu) Tinsmith's solder
| 停产 shut-down, shutting down, stop production, close-down, closing down
| 停车 stop (page), shut-down, shutting down, halt, stall, power-off (发动机的)
| 停车按钮 stop button
| 停车板 stop plate
| 停车场 parking lot, stock of carriages
| 停车痕 stop mark
| 停车机构 stop device
| 停车区 parking area
| 停吹(转炉的) 【钢】turndown

停吹倾炉(转炉的)　final turndown
停吹碳(转炉的)　【钢】turndown carbon
停吹渣样　【钢】interrupted-blow (slag) sample
停电　power break-down, power failure
停电操作　cut-off operation
停电时间　power off-time
停顿　stop, halt, pause, hold-up, suspension, dwell, outage, 【计】quiescing
停顿时间　outage time
停风　【冶】blow out [down], off-blast, out-of-blast, shut-down, wind off, de-lay ◇ 计划~·【铁】scheduled delay, 炉子~ blow out furnace
停风闷火高炉　banked blast furnace
停风期[时间](高炉的)　off-blast period
停风信号(高炉的)　stand-by signal
停工　stop work, shut down, service interruption, out of service
停工率　downtime percentage
停工[产,机]**期**(间)　shut-down [idle, idling] period
停工[产,机]**时间**　stop [down, idle] time
停机　halt, closing down, stop, outage ◇ 完全~, 意外~【计】hang up
停机指令　【计】halt [stop] instruction
停留点　【金】point of arrest
停留时间　staying [standing, retention] time, 【铁】residence time (炉料的)
停留时间控制　retention time control
停炉　shut-down, breakdown, furnace shutdown, shutting down of kiln, blowing down [off], blowing out
停炉操作　【铁】blowing-out operation
停炉程序　(高炉的) downtime schedule
停炉炉型　【铁】blow out line
停炉期　shut-down period, 【钢】standing period, 【铁】off-blast period
停炉时间　furnace outage time, 【钢】standing period
停炉修砌　【冶】down for lining
停炉装料　shut-down loading (S.D.L.)

停-启程序　【计】terminator/initiator
停气操作　cut-off operation
停气阀　closing valve
停气点　cut-off point
停息-拉出连铸法(单炉浇注法)　pause-and-pull method of casting
停歇　standstill, stop, cease, close down
停歇空载时间　dwell idling time
停歇期间　idle period
停窑　shutting down of kiln
停业　out of service, close down
停止　stop (ping), stoppage, cease, cessation, halt, interruption, shutoff, outage, arrest (ment), discontinuous, dwelling, pause, standstill
停止按钮　stop button
停止单元　【计】stop element
停止杆(行程开关的)　knock-off level
停止工作　cut-off
停止机构　stop device
停止加料信号　【铁】"stop filling" signal
停止降碳(加脱氧剂)　【钢】spiking, stopping
停止拉碳　【钢】blocking of heat
停止时间　stop [off] time, interruption period
停止送风　【冶】out-of-blast ◇ 热风炉~【铁】shutting out
停止运转　shut-down
停止照明　lighting-off
停止指令　【计】stop instruction
停滞层　stagnant layer [film]
停滞的　stagnant, sluggish
停滞区　stagnant zone, stagnation region
停滞状态　stagnant condition
停注冷结　【钢】teeming arrest
停转　running down, stalling
挺杆　tappet, jib, gib arm (起重机的)
挺杆导承　tappet guide
挺杆滚轮　tappet roller
挺杆起重机　jib (boom) crane, gib [swing] crane ◇ 墙装~ wall jib crane,

旋转~ swinging jib crane
挺杆提升钢绳 boom hoist cable
通称值 nominal value
通带 band pass, passband, transmission band
通带宽度 band width
通道 passage (PASS.), pass (ageway), aisle, channel, gallery, walkway ◇ 砖格~*
通道程序 【计】channel program
通道地址字 【计】channel address word (CAW)
通道控制器 【计】channel controller
通道控制字 【计】channel control word
通道宽度 walk-way clearance
通道流量(传输率) channel capacity
通道命令字 channel command word (CCW)
通道偏析 channel segregation
通道适配器 【电】channel adapter
通电 energizing, power on
通电辊 power application roll
通电去除氧化皮法 dynamisator process
通电延迟 on delay
通-断 【电】on-off, break-make
通断开关 on-(and-)off switch
通断控制 on-off [two-step] control
通断时间 on-off time
通断调节器 on-off regulator
通分母 【数】reduction
通风 (air) ventilation, venting, (air) draught, draft, airing, aeration ◇ 强制~ blast draught
通风表 blast meter
通风不足 deficiency in draught
通风橱 (fume) hood
通风除尘 dust removal by ventilation
通风道 ventilation duct, air chimney
通风阀 vent(ilation) valve
通风风扇 draught fan
通风格栅 air grid
通风管 draught tube, vent pipe, air pipe [chimney]
通风管道 vent line, ventilating ducting
通风过度 overdraft
通风机 ventilator (vent.), (ventilating) fan, exhauster ◇ 车间用~ shop ventilator, 双吸口~*, 叶片式[风扇]~ fan ventilator
通风井 air well [pit] ◇ 房基~【建】dry area
通风开关 draught switch
通风坑道(隧道的) air heading
通风孔 air [draught, vent(ilation)] hole, (air) vent
通风路线 air course
通风门 ventilating door
通风面积(反射炉内的) draught area
通风面具(矿工用) aerophore
通风平衡系统 balanced system of ventilation
通风器 ventilator (vent.)
通风气流压力 draught head
通风式炉(自然式) wind furnace
通风室 air compartment
通风(竖)坑 down-cast
通风损耗 draft [windage] loss
通风系统 ventilation [ventilating] system ◇ 抽气式~*, 封闭式~*, 开式~*
通风系统布袋收尘器 ventilation baghouse
通风系统控制 ventilation system control
通风罩 ventilation [draught] hood
通过 passage (PASS.), passing, travel, traverse,【色】pass (区域熔炼的)
通过次数(区域熔炼的) 【冶】number of passes
通过次数与浓度关系曲线(区域熔炼的) pass-versus-concentration curve
通过端量规 【机】go gauge
通过率 percent of pass
通过能力 throughput (capacity), swallowing capacity (连铸坯的)
通过速率 throughput rate

通过物	through product
通氦	helium injection
通航水道	navigable water(way) [pass]
通弧	arc-through
通话连接	talking connection
通货	currency, current money ◇ 可兑换~*
通径试验	【压】drift test
通径试验机	drifter
通空气处理	【环】aerobic treatment
通廊	【建】traverse, vestibule
通量	【电】flux
通量反向	flux reversal
通量计	fluxmeter
通量密度	flux density
通量线	flux line
通路	access (ACS), passage (PASS.), passageway, path, approach, gangway
通氯石英管	silica chlorine tube
通频带	passband, transmission band
通气橱	vapour hood
通气道	gas flue
通气孔	air vent, vent-hole, breather, air drain, airway, 【铸】whistler
通气蜡线	vent wax
通气帽	abat-vent
通气芯	【铸】pencil core, puncture core (冒口的)
通气型芯	【铸】atmospheric core
通气针	【铸】vent wire
通融资金	finance
通体弹性模量	overall elastic modulus
通宵班	overnight shift
通信	communication, signalling ◇ 程序间~*
通信方式	communication mode
通信接口	【计】communication interface
通信结束(指令)	【计】sign off
通信控制装置	communication control unit
通信链路	【计】communication link
通信量	traffic
通信软件	【计】communication software
通信输入-输出控制系统	communication input/output control system (CIOCS)
通信系统	communication system
通信线路	telecommunication line
通信终端	communication terminal
通信转接	communication switching
通行能力(道路的)	traffic capacity
通讯	communication, correspondence ◇ 地对起重机~系统*
通讯电路	communication circuit
通夜灯	all-night lamp
通用变频器	general inverter
通用标准热电偶	working standard thermocouple
通用车皮	general utility truck
通用成形法	conventional forming method
通用程序	【计】general program
通用承重桩	【建】universal bearing pile
通用电动机	universal [general-purpose] motor
通用电解抛光液	universal electro-polishing solution
通用电气公司	General Electric Co. (G.E.C.)
通用电气公司型三级玻璃水银扩散泵	(美国) G.E.C. (General Electric Company) three-stage glass pump
通用电气公司重载钨铜镍合金(航空发动机曲轴用；90W, 4Cu, 6Ni)	G.E.C. heavy alloy
通用电气公司自动取样器	G.E.C. automatic sampler
通用方法	traditional approach
通用分类程序	【计】generalized sort program
通用分流器	【电】universal shunt
通用符号	conventional symbol
通用辅助操作	general utility functions
通用干燥装置	all-purpose drying unit
通用钢(重熔钢除外)	primary steel
通用钢包衬砖	universal ladle brick

通用高铜合金 common high brass
通用工程系统 general engineering system (GENESYS)
通用工具 general-utility tool
通用工艺流程图 【企】generalized flow-sheet
通用合金 general-purpose alloy
通用汇编程序 【计】general assembly program (GAP)
通用寄存器 general (purpose) register
通用寄存器地址 general register address
通用计算机 general purpose computer
通用卡车 general utility truck
通用例行程序 【计】general (purpose) routine
通用炉 versatile furnace
通用汽车公司（美） General Motors Corp. (GMC)
通用曲线 master curve
通用软件 【计】common software
通用赛波特黏度计秒数（黏度单位） Saybolt Universal Second (SUS)
通用商业语言（同"COBOL 语言"）
通用式车 carryall
通用双束型宽频带阴极射线示波器 duel beam type universal wide band cathode ray oscilloscope
通用物品 standard goods
通用显微镜 universal microscope
通用线性方程式 general linear equation
通用形状系数（波形因数） generalized shape factor
通用性 versatility, generality
通用仪表 general-purpose [all-purpose] instrument
通用语言 【计】general-purpose [all-purpose] language
通用黏度 ◇赛波特~*
通用照相机 universal camera
酮 ketone
酮醇{RCOCH$_2$OH} kero-alcohol
酮化作用 ketonization

酮肟 ketoxime
同步 synchronization (sync), synchronizing, synchronism, synchro ◇不~的【电】 free running, 使~ synchronizing
同步保存电路 synchro-lock
同步变流机 synchronous converter
同步操作 【计】synchronous operation
同步传动[同步机] 【电】synchro
同步错误 【计】timing error
同步道 【计】timing track
同步电动机 synchromotor, synchronous motor
同步电动调相机 dynamic condenser
同步电机 synchronous machine
同步电抗 synchronous reactance ◇纵轴~*
同步电抗器 synchronizing reactor
同步电容器 synchronous capacitor [condenser]
同步电钟 synchronous motor clock, synchroclock
同步发电机 synchro(nous) generator
同步发送机 synchro transmitter
同步焊接定时 synchronous weld timing
同步焊接时间继电器 synchronous weld timer
同步化感应电动机 synchronized induction motor
同步回旋加速器 synchro-cyclotron
同步机 synchronous machine
同步机构调整器 synchronizing mechanism adjuster
同步计 synchro(no)meter
同步计算机 synchronous computer
同步继电器 synchronizing [lock-on] relay
同步加[进]料器 synchron feeder
同步加速器 synchrotron ◇电子~ electron synchrotron
同步检验继电器 synchronizing checquerelay
同步控制[调整] sync(hronic) [synchronizing] control

同步(控制)变压器 synchrotrans
同步录音 【电】synchronous sound recording
同步脉冲 【电】sync [synchronization, clock] pulse
同步脉冲分配器 【计】timing pulse distributor
同步门电路[选择脉冲,选通脉冲] synchronous gate
同步耦合 synchro coupling, synchro-tie
同步破坏 desynchronizing
同步器 synchronizer ◇ 交流~autosyn
同步扫描 simultaneous scanning
同步时钟 【计】synchronous clock
同步示波器 synchro(no)scope, oscillosynchroscope
同步数据传送 【计】synchronous data transmission
同步速度 synchronous [synchronizing] speed
同步锁 synchro-lock
同步调相机 synchronous phase modifier, dynamic condenser
同步误差 synchronous [synchronization] error
同步系统 synchronous system
同步信号 【电】sync(hronizing) signal
同步旋转 synchronous revolution
同步旋转换流机 synchron rotary converter
同步轧制 symmetrical rolling
同步整流子 synchronous commutator
同步指示器 synchrometer, synchronizing [synchronism] indicator, synchronoscope
同步质谱仪 mass-synchrometer
同步转换 synchrotrans
同步转矩 synchronizing torque
同步装置 synchronizer, synchronizing device
同成分[熔点]化合物 congruent compound
同成分熔点(固液的) 【金】congruent (melting) point
同成分熔化(指金属间化合物) congruous [congruent(ly)] melting
同成分熔化物(固液的) congruently melting compound
同成分相变 congruent transformation
同成分转变点(相图的) indifferent point
同分异构 【理】isomerization
同分异构的 isomeric (isom.)
同分异构化热 heat of isomerization
同分异构体[物] isomer
同分异晶的 (同"同质异晶的")
同构 isomorph(ism)
同构的 isomorphic, isomorphous
同规格金属(多炉次的) 【铸】metal lot
同号刃型位错 edge dislocations of one sign
同号位错 similar dislocation, dislocations of the same signs
同化能力 assimilative capacity
同化烧结现象 (同"额外烧结现象")
同化阻力 assimilation resistance
同化(作用) assimilation ◇ 粒间~interassimilation
同极化合物 homopolar compound
同极键(合) homopolar linkage
同极键联 homopolar binding
同焦距的 parfocal
同结构的 isostructural
同晶型取代 isomorphous substitution
同晶型系 isomorphous system
同晶型(性) isomorphism
同晶型置换 isomorphous replacement
同晶型族 isomorphic groups
同晶形包体 isomorphous inclusion
同开双拉门 biparting door
同类原子 similar atom
同量异序元素 【化】isobar
同流 cocurrent flow
同流换热器[室] recuperator, recuperater ◇ 金属~metallic recuperator
同流换热塔 recuperator tower

同流换热系统	heat recuperation system
同流换热(作用)	(heat) recuperation
同流混合器	(同"顺流混合器")
同流加热	(同"顺流加热")
同流浸出	(同"顺流浸出")
"同"门	【计】match gate
同面位错阵列	【金】coplanar array of dislocations
同面性	coplanarity
同名极	【理】like poles
同喷	co-injection
同时沉积	codeposition
同时除去	co-removed
同时萃取	coextraction
同时读写	【计】writing while read
同时发生的	synchronous, concurring
同时放电	simultaneous discharge
同时滑移理论	theory of simultaneous slip
同时还原	simultaneous reduction, coreduction
同时回收	simultaneous withdrawal
同时计数电路	coincidence circuit
同时净化	simultaneous purification
同时率[系数]	simultaneity factor
同时输入输出	simultaneous input output
同时吸收	simultaneous absorption
同时氧化	simultaneous oxidation
同素异构金属	allotropic metal
同素异晶[形]	allotropy, allotropism
同素异晶型[异形类型]	allotropic form
同素异形变化	allotropic change [transformation]
同素异形变态	allotropic modification
同素异形体	allotropic substance, allotrope, allotropy
同素异形相	allotropic phase
同素异形性[现象]	allotropism, allotrophy
同态的	isomorphic
同调	coherence, coherency, coherent
同位	parity
同位变换吸收波长(点)	isosbestic point
同位标磁道组	【计】cylinder
同位素	isotope ◇ 偶 A[A 为偶数的]~*,奇 N[N 为奇数的]~*
同位素表	isotope chart
同位素测厚仪(轧件的)	【压】isotopic [nucleonic] thickness gauge
同位素成分	isotopic composition [constitution]
同位素分离	isotope separation
同位素分析	isotopic [isotope] analysis
同位素分析器	isotron
同位素丰度	isotopic [isotope] abundance
同位素混合物	isotopic mixture
同位素积聚点(机体内的)	hot spot
同位素交换	isotope exchange
同位素交换反应	isotope exchange reaction
同位素料位(指示)仪(高炉的)	nuclear ray stock gauge, nuclear burden-level gauge
同位素料线指示仪(高炉的)	nuclear stockline gauge
同位素气体分析(稀释法)	isotopic gas analysis
同位素示踪剂	isotopic tracer
同位素示踪剂测定[测量]	【理】isotope-tracer measurement
同位素示踪[指示剂]原子	tracer isotope atom
同位素探伤仪	isoscope
同位素吸收体	【理】isotope poison
同位素稀释	isotope dilution
同位素稀释法	isotopic dilution method
同位素稀释分析	isotope dilution analysis
同位素效应	isotope effect
同位素原子量	isotopic atomic weight (IAW), isotopic weight (I.W.)
同位素指示剂	isotopic indicator, tracer isotope ◇ 含~的化合物 tracer compound
同位素指示剂稀释法	【理】tracer dilution method

同位素质量　isotopic mass
同位素组　group of isotropy
同位素组成　isotopic composition
同位吸收波长(点)(光谱的)　isoabsorptive point
同系谱线　homologous line
同系温度　homologous temperature
同系物　homologue
同相　same-phase, in-phase, homophase, phase coincidence
同相分量　【理】in-phase component
同向捻　lang's lay
同向捻钢丝绳　【压】lang's lay wire rope ◇ 艾伯特~　Albert lay wire rope
同向铣削　【机】climb milling
同向右捻　【压】right-hand lang lay
同向左捻　【压】left-hand lang lay
同心波面　concentric front
同心电缆　concentric cable
同心钢丝绳　concentric wire rope
同心拱　【建】concentric arch
同心环　concentric ring
同心绞线　concentric-lay conductor
同心裂缝　concentric crack
同心炉口(转炉的)　【钢】concentric nose section, concentric nozzle
同心喷嘴　concentric nozzle
同心喷嘴气切[切割]器　concentric nozzle gas cutter, cutting burner with concentric nozzle
同心式扁平股钢丝绳　concentric flattened strand wire rope
同心套管喷射器　shrouded concentric injector
同心线圈　【电】concentrating coil, concentrically wound coil
同心性　concentricity
同心异径管节　concentric reducer (CR)
同心圆强度分布　【环】concentric intensity distribution
同心转炉　concentric converter
同型　homotype

同型的　isostructural
同型性　homotypy
同形　isomorph ◇ 准~性　morphotropism
同形晶体　isomorphous crystal
同行　colleague
同样情况　same case (SC, s.c.)
同一距离[期间]　identity distance
同一位置淬火法　【金】single-shot method
同一行程　identity distance
同一性　identity
同一周期　identity period
同源变质作用　allometamorphism
同质　homogenesis, homogeny
同质的　homogeneous
同质多晶现象　polytropism
同质多晶型物质　polymorphic substance
同质多晶型现象　polymorphism, pleomorphism
同质二形体　dimorphic
同质结　homojunction
同质热电效应　【理】(electrothermic) Thomson effect
同质体的　isomorphic
同质异构结构　【理】isomeric structure
同质异晶的　allomorphous
同质异晶(现象)　allomorphism, allomorph(y)
同质异能的　【理】isomeric
同质异能素　【理】isomer
同质异能素移位　【理】isomer shift
同质异象(结晶的)　heteromorphism
同质异形晶体　paramorph
同质异形物质　dimorphous substance
同轴电极　coaxial electrode
同轴电缆　coaxial [concentric] cable
同轴电容器　gang(ed) capacitor [condenser]
同轴电位器　gang potentiometer
同轴复合材料　coaxial composite
同轴控制　gang control
同轴流束喷射器　coaxial-streams injector
同轴热[温差]电偶元件　coaxial thermo-

couple element
同轴软电缆 coaxial flexible cable
同轴式喷枪 coaxial(-type) lance
同轴延迟电缆 coaxial delay cable
同轴衍射圆锥 coaxial diffraction cone
同轴圆筒黏度测定法 【理】coaxial-cylinder [concentric-cylinder] method
同轴圆筒黏度计 coaxial-cylinder viscometer
同轴圆柱体 coaxial cylinder
同轴中空锥族 family of coaxial hollow cones
同装(料) 【铁】mixed charging [filling]
同族元素合金(元素周期表的) column [row] alloy
铜{Cu} copper ◇ 凹[饱和]~*, 包[覆]~*, 扁~ flat copper, 不溶于~的 copper-insoluble, 沉淀[泥]~*, 沉积~*, 除[脱,去]~*, 纯[红]~ pure copper, 粗[泡]~*, 低品位[低级]~ low-grade copper, 电积~*, 电解~*, 镀铂~*, 镀[包]锡~*, 多晶~ polycrystalline copper, 二价~*, 废[杂]~ copper scrap, 高导电性~*, 海绵~*, 含~的 copper-bearing, copper-containing] coppery, cupreous, copperish, cupriferous, 含~合金*, 含硫~sulphur copper, 含氧~*, 黑~ black copper, 火法精炼~ fire refined copper, 块~ copper ingot, 炼~*, 炮~*, 熔析~*, 商品~*, 烧结~ sintered copper, 渗~ copper cementation, 似~的 coppery, cupreous, 提~ copper extraction, 退火[韧(化)]~ annealed copper, 脱[无]~溶液*, 无氧~ oxygen-free copper, 线锭~ wirebar copper, 阳极~ anode copper, 乙炔~ acetylide copper, 易切削~ free cutting copper, 阴极[电解纯]~*, 硬[冷加工]~ hard copper, 原生~ virgin copper, 再生~*, 造一期*, 针~*, 铸~ cast(ing) copper, 转炉~ Bessemer copper, 紫[工业纯]~ tough pitch (copper), 自然~ native copper

铜铵化合物 cuprammonium compound
铜铵络合物 copper ammine, cupric ammine complex
铜白钨矿{CaCuWO$_4$} cuproscheelite
铜斑 copper stain
铜板 copper plate, sheet copper, copper sheet (宽500mm, 厚0.075~4.5mm) ◇ 雕刻用~ engravers' copper, 罗坎含砷~(0.5As) Rocan copper, 制日用品用~ braziers' copper
铜板混汞法 【色】plate amalgamation
铜版 copper plate
铜棒 copper bar ◇ 扁~ flat bar copper
铜包覆层 copper cladding
铜包钢线 copper covered steel wire, copper-clad steel wire
铜包铝线 copper-clad aluminium conductor
铜包镍铁线 dumet wire
铜包皮 copper sheath
铜保护层 copper coating
铜背钨尖电极 copper-backed tungsten tip
铜铋合金 copper-bismuth alloy ◇ 纪尧姆~*
铜币(4Sn,1Zn,95Cu) copper coin
铜币合金 ounce metal
铜饼 copper cake
铜并联电解精炼系统 multiple [parallel] copper refining system
铜玻璃封接[焊封] copper-glass seal, copper-to-glass
铜铂合金 copper-platinum alloy ◇ 莫克~*
铜箔 copper foil, foil copper, clutch gold
铜箔叠层板 copper foil laminate
铜材 copper product ◇ 热轧~ hot rolled copper, 轧制~ rolled copper
铜层 copper layer
铜沉淀物 【色】copper precipitate
铜沉积 copper deposition
铜衬 pillow
铜-赤铜矿 copper-cuprite

铜 tong

铜串联电解精炼　series copper refining
铜吹炼　copper converting
铜吹炼车间　copper converting plant
铜吹炉　copper converter
铜磁黄铁矿　chalcopyrrohite
铜带　copper belt
铜带材　copper strip
铜带线圈　【电】bobbin coil
铜的　coppery, cupreous ◇ 正～cupric
铜碲汞矿　cu-coloradoite
铜碲合金　copper-tellunium alloy ◇ 库特恩～*
铜靛石{CuSO₄}　chalcocyanite
铜垫圈　copper washer
铜垫圈密封反应容器　copper-gasketed reaction vessel
铜电焊条　copper arc welding electrode
铜电极　copper electrode
铜电解　copper electrolysis
铜电解车间　copper tankhouse
铜电解精炼　copper electrolytic refining, copper electro-refining
铜电解精炼厂　copper electrolytic refinery
铜钉合金(64.4Cu, 18Sn, 10Zn, 7.6Pb) file alloy ◇ 沃格尔～Vogel's alloy
铜锭　copper ingot, ingot [cake] copper
铜镀层　copper coat(ing)
铜堆浸　copper dump leaching
铜矾{CuSO₄}　chalcocyanite
铜废料　waste copper, copper junk
铜分离　copper separation
铜粉　copper powder [filings], powdered copper ◇ 片状～flake copper, 氢析～法*, 阴极～压制烧结法*
铜粉厂　copper powder plant
铜粉洗涤　copper powder washing
铜粉压坯[压型]　copper-powder compact
铜浮渣　【色】copper dross (slag), copper scum ◇ 富[高]～copper-rich dross
铜坩埚　copper crucible [mould] ◇ 平底～flat copper hearth, 水冷～*, 水套冷却～*

铜钢　copper(-bearing) [copper-containing] steel ◇ 气～copper steel
铜锆合金　copper-zirconium alloy ◇ 阿姆泽克～Amzirc
铜镉合金　copper-cadmium alloy ◇ 架空电缆～*
铜镉渣(湿法冶炼的)　copper-cadmium residue
铜铬合金(0.5Cr, 余量 Cu)　chromium-copper
铜铬矿　macconnellite
铜汞合金[铜汞齐]　copper amalgam
铜钴矿　copper-cobalt ore
铜固溶强化金铜合金　copper-hardened gold
铜管　copper tube
铜管衬里风眼捣制转炉炉底　tube bottom
铜光泽　copper luster
铜硅焊条　coper-silicon welding rod
铜硅合金　copper-silicon alloy, cupro-silicon ◇ 赫尔克洛伊耐蚀～*, 西尔卡德尔耐蚀～*
铜硅镁铀矿　uranochalcite
铜硅锰合金　Everdur 雅各比～*
铜焊　braze welding, (copper, hard) brazing, braze (bonding), hard solder ◇ 电热～electric brazing
铜焊法[工艺]　brazing process, joint brazing procedure
铜焊合金　brazing alloy
铜焊剂　brazing agent, cubond
铜焊接的　brazed
铜焊料　brazing [copper] solder, brazing (filler) metal
铜焊料钎焊　copper bond
铜焊气氛　brazing atmosphere
铜焊(软)膏　brazing paste ◇ 库本德～(钢件炉焊用) Cubond
铜焊设备　brazing equipment
铜焊条　copper welding rod, copper arc welding electrode

铜焊头　copper bit
铜焊药　hard solder
铜耗　copper loss
铜合金　copper alloy, pinkus metal ◇ 946易切削高传导率～*,阿尔巴特拉～*,阿尔达里～Aldary,阿加索依德～*,安纳康达～Anaconda alloy,磁性～*,导电～*,科罗纽姆～*,里辛青～*,平基斯～Pinkus metal,希杜拉尔5～*,希杜拉克斯～*,约耳龙～*,铸造～*
铜合金废料　copper alloy scrap
铜合金钢　copper-alloy steel
铜合金添加剂焊条　bronze welding rod
铜合金显微组织腐蚀法 ◇ 罗顿-洛伦兹～*
铜黑精饰覆层(经阳极氧化处理得到)　electrojetal
铜华　copper bloom
铜化合物　copper compound
铜还原　copper reduction
铜辉铋矿　cuprobismutite
铜基合金　copper-base(d) alloy ◇ ERM～ERM alloy,巴塔尔布拉～*,基恩～*,理查森～*,马洛里～系 Mallory alloys,纳达～*,希杜拉尔～Hidural alloy
铜基合金粉末　copper-base powder
铜基合金基体　copper-base matrix
铜基合金浸渗剂　copper-base infiltrant
铜基合金摩擦材料　copper-base friction material
铜基合金铸件　copper-base casting
铜基体　copper matrix ◇ 多孔～*
铜基中间合金　copper master alloy
铜基轴承合金　copper-base bearing
铜加速乙酸-食盐溶液喷雾试验(铬镍镀层的)　copper-accelerated acetic acid-salt spray (CASS) test
铜结晶器　【连铸】copper mould
铜金　copper gold ◇ 比朗～*
铜金单晶体　copper-gold single crystal ◇ 长程有序～*

铜金合金　copper-gold alloy ◇ 面心立方～*,无序～*
铜金矿　cuproauride
铜金镍合金 ◇ 尼厄罗～Nioro
铜浸出　copper leaching
铜浸出电解再生法　Copper Leach electrolysis and regeneration (CLEAR)
铜浸焊　dip-braze
铜晶体　copper crystal
铜精矿　copper concentrate
铜精炼　【色】copper refining
铜精炼厂　copper refinery, copper refining plant
铜精炼厂阳极泥　copper refinery slimes
铜精炼炉　copper refining furnace, copper finery
铜-聚氟乙烯树脂轴承　copper-fluon bearing
铜-康铜　copper-constantan
铜-康铜热〔温差〕电偶　copper-constantan (thermo)couple
铜块　copper block [billet, cake]
铜矿　copper ore [mine] ◇ 自然～native copper ore
铜矿床　copper deposit
铜矿石核焙烧　kernel roasting
铜矿物　copper mineral
铜蓝{CuS}　covelline, covellite, indigo copper, bronze blue
铜冷却板〔壁〕【铁】copper stave, copper cooling plate
铜烙铁　soldering copper
铜离子　copper ion ◇ 二价～*,一价～*
铜离子浓度　concentration of copper ions
铜锂合金　copper-lithium alloy ◇ 库普拉利斯～(1－10Li) Cupralith
铜粒　copper granule [shot], shot copper
铜沥青铀矿　copper pitchore
铜磷合金　copper-phosphorus alloy
铜鳞　copper scale
铜菱锌矿　herrerite
铜菱铀矿{Ca₂CuU(CO₃)₅·6H₂O}　voglite

铜硫合金　copper-sulphur alloy
铜锍　【冶】copper matte (regulus) ◇ 高品位～*
铜锍沉积物　【冶】copper bottom
铜锍吹炉　【冶】converter for copper matte
铜铝焊　copper and aluminium welding
铜铝焊条　copper-aluminium welding rod
铜铝合金　copper-aluminium alloy, X alloy (3.5Cu, 1.25Fe, 0.6Mg, 0.6Ni, 0.6Si, 余量 Al) ◇ 阿伐莱特～*, 雷克尔～*, 雷西斯科～*, 阳极～*
铜铝矿　duramin
铜铝锰电阻合金　◇ 瑟罗～*
铜铝锰土　radbionite
铜铝镍合金　◇ 巴特里姆～*
铜铝锌合金　◇ 德瓦达～*
铜氯矾　connellite, coeruleofibrite
铜绿　copper green, (green) patina, verdigris ◇ 布满～patination
铜绿色　aerugo
铜绿色的　aeruginous
铜毛(锍中的)　capillary copper
铜冒气(铜在退火或焊接时出现)　gassing of copper
铜锰(电阻)合金(12Mn,<3Fi,余量 Cu)　copper-manganese alloy ◇ 雷西斯廷～*, 特尔卡曼～*
铜锰硅合金　◇ 阿戈菲尔～*
铜锰合金料　cupro-mangan(ese)
铜锰铝标准电阻合金　◇ 库马纳尔～*, 伊莎贝林～*
铜锰镍电阻合金(86Cu, 12Mn, 2Ni)　manganin alloy ◇ 康坦明～*, 欧玛尔～*
铜锰镍合金　copper-manganese-nickel alloy, cuniman ◇ 马尼克～*, 米纳尔法～*, 切伊斯 720～*
铜锰镍精密电阻合金　◇ 伊莎～*
铜锰青铜(58.5Cu, 39Zn, 1.4Fe, 1Sn, 0.1Mn)　copper manganese bronze
铜锰土　lampadite
铜模　copper mould ◇ 水冷～*

铜模底　copper mould base
铜膜　copper film
铜钼精矿　copper-molybdenum concentrate
铜钼矿　copper-molybdenum ore
铜泥(沉淀置换析出的)　copper sludge
铜镍电阻合金 ◇ 赫克努姆～*, 赫肯哈姆～*, 洛姆～*, 米德欧姆～*, 尼克林～*
铜镍高强度低合金钢　◇ 约洛依～*
铜镍高锍　nickel-copper bessemer matte
铜镍钴合金　◇ 鲍多英～*
铜镍钴永磁合金　◇ 库尼科～*, 帕米特～*
铜镍硅高强度合金　◇ 库尼西尔～*
铜镍硅合金　◇ 科森～*, 库普罗杜尔～*
铜镍焊条　copper-nickel welding rod
铜镍合金　copper-nickel (alloy), cupronickel (45—97.5Cu, 2.5—4.5Ni), constantan, Monel (metal) (26—30Cu, 65—75Ni, 少量 Fe, Mn) ◇ 仿银～imitation silvers, 费雷～*, 海绵～copper-nickel sponge, 科佩尔～*(类似康铜) Copel, 库尼亚尔特种～*, 库普龙～*(45Ni, 55Cu) cupron, 莱切森～*, 雷～*, 雷克尔～*, 米纳金特～*, 尼科林～*, 约科龙-库奈弗 30A～*
铜镍合金带　cupro-nickel strip
铜镍合金丝　◇ 康特拉～*
铜镍合金套　copper-nickel jacket (C.N.J.)
铜镍基合金　steamalloy
铜镍精矿　copper-nickel concentrate
铜镍库尼费 30 合金　◇ 约克郡 70/30～*
铜镍硫化矿　copper-nickel ore sulphide
铜镍锍　【冶】copper-nickel [nickel-copper] matte ◇ 国际镍公司～冶炼法*
铜镍锍转炉　copper-nickel converter
铜镍铝合金　◇ 打字机用～*, "饭高"～*

铜镍锰合金　◇库尼曼~*,尼克林~*
铜镍耐蚀合金　Super-nickel ◇安布拉克~*,奥达~*,尼克洛伊德~*,纽洛伊~*,帕里斯~*,西尔维林~*
铜镍铅轴承合金　◇凯尔梅特~*
铜镍铈用合金　◇托卡期~*
铜镍铁合金　◇巴特尼科英~*,库尼菲尔~*
铜镍铁锍　copper-nickel-iron matte
铜镍铁永磁合金　◇库尼菲~*
铜镍锡合金　◇艾多奈克~Adonic
铜镍锌焊剂合金　◇阿盖佐依德~*
铜镍锌焊料　platinoid solder
铜镍锌合金　copper-nickel-zinc alloy, German silver（52—80Cu, 5—35Ni, 10—35Zn,又称德银）, white copper（又称镍银、白铜）◇阿特赖特~aterite, 波托西~Potosi silver, 德国一条*, 弗吉尼亚~Virginia silver, 科罗拉多~*, 克拉克~*, 芒古斯~Mungoose metal, 梅科洛依~*, 梅勒霍特~*, 内华达~Nevada silver, 尼克林~*, 帕里西昂~*, 斯皮德克斯~*, 韦塞尔~*
铜镍锌耐蚀合金　◇安布罗斯~*, 马洛伊迪昂~*, 西尔沃尔~*
铜镍原子间距　copper-nickel distance
铜镍装饰合金　◇托卡斯~*, 西尔维罗伊德~*
铜泡石　tirote tyrolite
铜坯　copper billet ◇扁~copper slab
铜铍钴硅电导合金　◇马洛里100~Mallory 100
铜铍合金　copper-beryllium (alloy), beryllium copper ◇贝拉洛依~*, 比阿隆~*, 伯里尔科~*, 易切削~*
铜铍中间合金　◇比阿洛伊~（约含4Be）Bealloy
铜片[皮]　copper sheet
铜器　copper [bronze, brass] ware
铜钎焊　copper brazing ◇氢气氛~*
铜钎焊合金（16—25Cu, 80—10Ag, 4—38Zn, 0.5Cd）copper brazing alloy

铜钎焊钳　brazing tongs
铜钎接双层钢管　bundyweld tube
铜铅焊[料钎焊]　spelter brazing
铜铅合金　copper-lead alloy ◇米拉~*, 耐酸~acid lead
铜铅精矿　copper-lead concentrate
铜铅锍[冰铜]　copper-lead matte
铜铅镍青铜　copper leaded nickel bronze
铜铅青铜（70Cu, 30Pb；或65Cu, 35Pb）Cu-lead-ite ◇比里昂~合金*
铜铅容器合金　pot metal
铜铅铁矾　beaverite
铜铅锡合金　copper-lead-tin
铜铅霰石　schuilingite
铜铅系轴承合金　◇乌尔科尼~*
铜铅型耐磨合金　◇克拉默~*
铜铅轴承合金（60—75CU,余量Pb；有时含达5Ag, 4Sn, 4Mn, 2Ni, 2Sb）copper-lead bearings ◇艾伦~*
铜切屑　copper-turnings
铜熔炼　copper smelting
铜熔炼炉　copper smelter
铜溶金属　copper-soluble metal ◇低熔点~*
铜溶金属粉末　copper-soluble metal powder
铜闪速熔炼　copper flash smelting
铜砷铀云母　zeunerite
铜石墨电刷　copper-graphite brush
铜石墨合金　copper-graphite alloy
铜石墨制品　copper-graphite composition
铜石墨轴承　copper-graphite bearing
铜始极片　【色】copper starting sheet
铜水钴矿　schulzenite, mindingite
铜水绿矾　boothite
铜(水)套　copper jacket (c.j.), copper block
铜丝　copper wire ◇软拉~*
铜丝绳[缆]　copper rope
铜丝网　copper (wire) gauze
铜丝网接触垫　copper-braid contact pad
铜酸盐{M₂(CuO₂)}　cuprate

铜损(耗)　copper [ohmic] loss
铜钛铍合金　◇ CTB ~ *
铜钛银合金　◇ CTG ~ *
铜锑合金　copper-antimony alloy　◇ 维纽斯 ~ *
铜添加合金　copper addition
铜条　copper bar, bar copper　◇ 扁 ~ flat bar copper, 换向器 ~ commutator bar
铜铁粉　iron-copper powder　◇ 预先浸渍过的 ~ *
铜铁矾　ransomite
铜铁矿　delafossite
铜铁灵　cupferron
铜铁硫化物　copper-iron sulphide
铜－铁钎焊　copper-iron junction
铜铁试剂三氯甲烷萃取　【色】cupferron chloroform extraction
铜铁氧体　cu ferrite
铜钨合金　copper-tungsten
铜钨合金接触面　tungsten-copper contact
铜钨华　cuprotungstite
铜硒铁矿　eskebornite
铜锡钯　copper stannopalladinite
铜锡焊条　copper-tin welding rod
铜锡合金　copper-tin alloy, signal bronze　◇ 奥托 ~ *, 高镍 ~ *, 科西亚斯 ~ *, 莱茵 ~ Rhinemetal, 锣用 ~ *, 斯蒂尔耐蚀 ~ *, 银铃 ~ *, 约卡斯坦 ~ *
铜锡合金汞齐　copper-tin amalgam
铜锡合金涂覆层　tin-copper plating
铜锡锰系标准电阻丝合金　◇ W-306 ~ W306 alloy
铜锡铅锑耐蚀合金　◇ 雷兹 ~ *
铜锡铅轴承合金　◇ F.17 ~ *, 艾杰克斯 ~ *
铜锡锌合金　◇ G ~ *, 奥罗依德 ~ *, 奥姆鲁 ~ *, 利特尔 ~ *
铜锡锌铅轴承合金　◇ MH ~ *
铜锡锌三元合金　◇ 卡尔柯茨 ~ Kalchoids
铜线　copper wire　◇ 标准 ~ *, 裸 ~ bare copper wire
铜线锭(轧制线材用)　copper-wire-bar (ingot)　◇ 电解 ~ *
铜线锭精炼炉　copper wire-bar refining furnace
铜屑　copper filings
铜锌　copper-zinc　◇ 除 ~ 槽 *
铜锌焊料　copper-zinc solder
铜锌焊条　copper-zinc welding rod
铜锌焊药　copper zinc brazing mixture
铜锌合金　copper-zinc [pinchbeck] alloy　◇ 97 ~ *, 莱马夸恩德耐蚀 ~ *, 中国镜用 ~ *
铜锌基硬钎焊料　spelter brazing alloy
铜锌精矿　copper-zinc concentrate
铜锌矿　copper-zinc ore
铜锌硫化精矿　copper-zinc sulphide concentrate
铜锌镍电阻合金　◇ 普拉提诺依德 ~ *
铜锌镍电阻丝合金　◇ 弗里克 ~ *
铜锌镍合金　nickel-silver (50～70Cu, 13～35Zn, 5～33Ni, 又称"镍银")　◇ 阿尔芬尼德 ~ *, 奥尔兹莫洛伊 ~ *, 管工用 ~ *, 提尼科莱尔 ~ *, 维克托 ~ *
铜锌铅装饰合金　◇ 克里索桥克 ~ *
铜锌锡代金合金　◇ 曼海姆 ~ *
铜锌锡合金　ormolu, French gold　◇ 波廷 ~ Potin, 布里斯托尔 ~ *
铜心轧制法　【压】copper core process
铜锈　copper rust, aerugo, verdigris, patina
铜锈斑　copper stain
铜崖型转炉　Copper Cliff bath converter
铜盐　nantokite, nantoquita
铜阳极　copper anode　◇ 火法精炼 ~ *
铜阳极氧化处理　electrojetal
铜冶金(学)　copper metallurgy, metallurgy of copper
铜冶炼厂　copper smelter [smeltory], copper-smelting plant
铜业发展协会(英国)　Copper Development Association (C.D.A.)
铜银汞膏　cuproarquerite
铜银共晶合金　◇ 雷瓦尔 ~ Leval's alloy

铜银焊料合金	◇ 西尔福斯~*
铜银合金	Kufil (alloy) ◇ 比朗~*,莫塞特~*,"四分一"~*
铜银滤饼[渣]	copper-silver cake
铜硬钎焊料	(16—25Cu,80—10Ag,4—38Zn,0.5Cd) copper brazing alloy
铜铀矾	johannite
铜铀矿	$\{(Pb,Cu)_2O \cdot SO_3 \cdot H_2O\}$ caledonite
铜铀云母	chalcolite $\{Cu(UO_2)_2P_2O_4 \cdot 8H_2O\}$, torbernite $\{Cu(UO_2)_2P_2O_8 \cdot 12H_2O\}$, copper uranite $\{Cu(UO_2)_2Pb_2O_8 \cdot 8H_2O\}$
铜与钢[铜]的铝热焊	cadweld
铜渣	【色】copper dross [ash] ◇ 富[高]~ copper-rich dross
铜值	copper number [ratio]
铜制品	copper product [manufactures]
铜质的	copperish
铜质水冷扁水箱	hollow water cooled block of copper
铜质圆筒状阳极	hollow cylinder copper anode
铜中间合金	(20—31Mn,60—69Cu,20Ni) copper(-base) hardener
铜轴衬	axle brass
铜珠	copper shot
铜铸	casting in bronze
铜族元素	copper family element
铜最小含量	copper minimum content
桶	barrel (BL,brl), pail, tub, tank, 【冶】ladle (又称"包")
桶板	clapboard, stap, stave
桶泵	barrel pump
桶车	【冶】ladle car
桶衬	barrel liner, ladle lining
桶唇	ladle lip
桶到桶真空脱气法	ladle to ladle degassing
桶底虹吸池	【色】ladle well
桶壳	【冶】ladle casing [bowl]
桶口	bung, churn
桶瘤	【冶】ladle skull
桶内混合	ladle mixing
桶内加料	【冶】ladle addition
桶内结壳	【冶】ladle scull
桶内取样	【冶】ladle sample
桶内脱气法	(同"包内脱气法")
桶内脱氧	ladle deoxidation
桶身	【冶】ladle body
桶形畸变	barrel distortion
桶形曲率	barrel type curvature
桶形失真	barrel
桶形轧辊	barrel shaped roll
桶形轧辊穿孔机	barrel type roll piercing mill
桶样	【冶】ladle sample
桶样试验	ladle test
桶中激冷[降温]	【冶】ladle chill
桶装水泥	barrel of cement
桶状[形]烧结缺陷	barrel shape
捅出式落砂	【铸】push-out type shake-out
捅风口	【铁】reaming
捅风口[眼]机(转炉的)	tuyere puncher
筒仓	silo ◇ 水泥~ cement (storage) silo,细磨石灰石~ ground limestone silo
筒拱壳(体)	barrel vault shell
筒夹	collet chuck
筒锯锯切试样	trepan saw specimen
筒式干燥器	cylinder [drum] dryer
筒式过滤器	cartridge filter
筒式混铁炉	barrel mixer
筒式晶体单色反射器	barrel type reflector
筒式卷取机	drum reel, mandrel [drum-type] coiler ◇ 单钳口~*,双钳口~*
筒式旋转氧气炼钢炉	◇ 格雷夫~ Graef rotor
筒式选矿机	drum separator
筒式窑	drum-type kiln
筒型单色点聚焦器	barrel type point focusing monochromator
筒形涵洞	barrel culvert
筒形加热器	cartridge heater

筒形绕组　【电】cylindrical winding
筒形台式吹芯机　【铸】cartridge-type bench blower
统包合同　turn-key contract
统筹学(研究)　【数】operations research (OR)
统货碎石　crusher-run
统计波动[起伏]　statistical fluctuation
统计处理　statistical treatment
统计调查　statistical investigation
统计法　statistical method ◇ 费米-狄喇克~*
统计分布　statistical distribution
统计分析　statistical analysis ◇ 高级~程序语言*
统计分析法　method of statistical analysis ◇ 韦氏~*
统计估计　statistical estimation
统计过程控制　statistical process control (SPC)
统计过程控制系统　statistical process control system
统计计算机　statistical computer
统计(加)权　statistical weight
统计力学　statistical mechanics
统计量　statistic
统计论证　statistical justification
统计模式识别　statistical pattern recognition
统计平均数　statistical [median] average
统计评估　statistical estimation
统计热力学　statistical thermodynamics
统计热力学分析　statistico-thermodynamical analysis
统计设备　statistical aids
统计数字　statistics, statistical figures, census ◇ 标志性~*
统计物理学　statistical physics
统计误差　statistical error [discrepancy]
统计学　statistics
统计学特性　statistical property
统计直径　statistic diameter

统计质量控制[管理]　statistical quality control (SQC)
统计质量控制制度　statistical quality control system
统计中间数　median average
统一　unify, unite, unification, consolidation
统一数据处理　【计】integrated data processing (IDP)
统一性　unity
统制　governing, control
投标　tender, bid
投产　start of operation, start(ing)-up, commissioning, go into operation, starting
投产日期　commissioning [start-up] date
投出　throw out
投料　lowering of charge
投料机构(淬火的)　lowerator
投料量　inventory, material input
投料试车[生产]　trial run with load, commissioning test run
投配量(制药的)　dosage
投配器　batcher
投入产出表　【企】input/output table
投入产出模型　input-output model
投入运转　in operation
投射　projection, throwing ◇ 锥形~*, 白云石~机*
投影　projection
投影 X 射线图像　shadow X-ray image
投影法　projection method
投影放大仪　magnifying shape projector
投影[投射]极　projected pole
投影距离　projection distance
投影目镜　projection eyepiece
投影(平)面　projection plane
投影式布氏[维氏]硬度计　brivisor
投影透镜　projection [projector] lens
投影透镜的像转动　【理】image rotation of projector lens
投影透镜畸变　distortion of projector lens
投影透镜焦距　focal length of projector lens

投影图 projection drawing, sciagram ◇ 赤面～中心 centre of stereogram, 底面极射～*, 极射赤面～*

投影图法 axonometry

投影显微镜 projection microscope

投影显微镜成像 projection microscope image

投影显微射线照相术 projection microradiography

投影显微术 projection microscopy

投影像 shadow image

投影仪 projector

投影圆 projected circle

投影直径 projected diameter

投掷开关 throw(-over) switch

投资 investment ◇ 创办～*, 基本建设～*

投资额 anount of capital invested ◇ 核定～*

投资费(用) investment cost, capital cost [outlay]

投资分析 investment analysis

投资回收 returns on investment, capital recovery

投资总额 aggregate investment

头部 head(er), head end, top end (钢锭的), leading edge (轧件的)

头部切头(钢锭的) 【钢】topscrap

头部探测器 head end detector

头(部托)轮 head pulley [sheave], main wheel

头戴受话机 head-piece, head-telephone

头灯(矿工的) head lamp

头等(的) first-class, first grade

头馏分 overhead product [distillate], 【化】head (fraction)

头熔 first melt

头熔锭 first melt ingot

头熔渣锡 pillion

头酸 head acid

头尾废料 end-wastage

头尾链轮 head and tail sprockets

头尾斜边(待焊管材的) end bevelled

头尾圆边(管材的) end rounded

头尾直切正边(管材的) end squared

头渣 first (run) slag

透壁分气法 【压】atmolysis

透彻的 transparent, penetrating

透磁合金 permalloy, permeability alloy

透淬的 【金】hardened throughout

透度计灵敏度 penetrameter sensitivity

透光度[性] (同"透明度")

透光化线的 diactinic

透过 infiltration, transmission

透过性 permeability, perviousness

透焊 throat welding

透辉石 {Ca(Mg,Fe)(SiO$_3$)$_2$} diopside

透镜 (optical) lens ◇ 菲涅耳～ Fresnel lens, 会聚～ converging lens, 去像散～ anastigmat(ic) lens, 阴极[第一电子]～ cathode lens, 圆柱面～ cylindrical lens, 正～(聚焦的) positive lens, 静电～成像 charge image

透镜分辨率 lens efficiency

透镜孔 lenticular void

透镜套[座,装置] 【理】lens mounting

透镜系统数值孔径 numerical aperture of lens system

透镜像场 【理】lens field

透镜状成核 lenticular nucleation

透镜状分层布料(炉料的) 【铁】interlensing

透镜状型材 【压】lenticular section

透孔 punched [thru] hole

透锂长石 {LiAl(Si$_2$O$_5$)$_2$} petalite, castorite

透明 transparence, transparency ◇ 不～的*

透明安全片基(X射线胶片的) transparent safety base

透明玻璃聚焦屏 clear glass focusing screen

透明带 cellophane tape

透明度[性] transparence, transparency,

透 tou

transmittance, transmittancy
透明度测定仪　opacimeter
透明观察孔　transparent window
透明熔融石英　clear fused-quartz
透明熔融石英电解槽　clear fused-quartz cell
透明溶液　clear solution
透明石英　translucent [vitreous] silica
透明石英坩埚　translucent silica pot
透明石英管　transparent [vitreous] silica tube ◇ 罗曼～氯化炉*
透明石英熟料　vitreous silica grog
透明试样　transparent specimen
透明体　transparent [vitreous] body
透明图　transparency drawing
透明消失　devitrification
透明釉[珐琅]　transparent glaze ◇ 上～ vitreous enamelling
透明云母屏蔽片　transparent mica screen
透明真空箱　vitreous evacuated container
透明纸　cellophane [tracing] paper
透霓辉石　urbanite
透平泵　turbine pump, roturbo
透平发电机　(同"涡轮发电机")
透平鼓风机　turboblower, turbofan
透平(机)　turbine ◇ 抽气～ bleeder turbine, 单流式～ single flow machine
透平深井泵　turbine well pump
透平式排烟[吸气]机　turbo-exhauster
透平式压缩机　turbo-compressor
透平叶片用合金　jet alloy
透平制冷器[机]　turbine refrigerator
透气　aeration, permeation ◇ 不～的*
透气棒　permeability bar
透气炉箅　permeable grate
透气性[度,率]　(air, gas) permeability, vent(ing) quality (铸型的) ◇ 低～炉料 dense charge, 低潮～ trough permeability, 底层[垫底,铺底]料～【冶】bed porosity, 混合料燃结～*, 绝对～ absolute permeability, 料层[柱]～ bed permeability, 炉料～*, 硬化后～*, 最高[巅峰]～ peak permeability
透气性测定仪(泥芯的)　【铸】permmeter
透气性测定装置　air permeability apparatus
透气性测量　permeability measurement
透气性法(测量粉末比表面法)　air permeability method
透气性降低　loss of permeability
透气性控制　permeability control
透气性耐火材料　permeable refractories
透气性试验　permeability test
透气性值　permeability number
透气性指数　permeability index
透气砖　【钢】gas supply brick
透热　through heating, heat penetration
透热的　diatherm(an)ous, full hot
透热法　diathermy
透热计　diathermometer
透热深度　depth of heat penetration
透热性　diathermacy, diathermaneity
透熔焊接　melt-through welding ◇ 小～ cold running
透入能力　penetrativeness
透闪石{$CaMg_3(SiO_3)_4$}　tremolite
透射　(through) transmission, penetrance ◇ 异常～*
透射(X射线)照相　transmission photograph
透射比　transmittance
透射测厚仪(用γ射线)　penetron
透射点　transmission point
透射电子显微术[透射电镜观察]　transmission electron microscopy (TEM)
透射电(子显微)镜　transmittion electron microscope (TEM)
透射法　transmission method
透射辐射　hard radiation
透射光　transmitted light ◇ 暗视场～(线)法*
透射光强度　transmitted light intensity
透射(光线)观察法　transmission method of observation

透射光栅　transmission grating
透射技术　through-transmission techinque
透射率　transmittancy
透射强度　intensity in transmission
透射式电子微镜[透射电镜]　transmission eletron microscope (TEM), transmitting-type microscope
透射(式电子)显微镜观察　transmission microscope observation
透射式电子显微镜检验　transmission eletron microscope examination
透射式电子显微镜照片[照相]　transmission electron micrograph, TEM photograph
透射式摄谱仪　transmission-type spectrograph
透射式显微镜　transmitting-type microscope
透射图　【理】transmission pattern
透射系数　transmission coefficient [factor], transmittance, transmittancy ◇ 声～*
透射显微镜像　transmission microscopical image
透射线的　radiolucent
透射像　transmission image
透射衍射光栅　transmission diffraction grating
透射衍射线　transmitted diffracted line
透砷铅矿　schultenite
透深淬透性　throughout hardenability
透视石{H_2CuSiO_4}　dioptase
透视图　perspective view [drawing], perspective (persp.) ◇ 建筑～*
透水层　permeable stratum
透水性　water permeability
透析　dialysis
透液性　liquid-penetration
透硬钢　through-hardening steel
透硬能力　through-hardening capability
透紫的(回火色)　full purple
凸壁　spur

凸边(板坯、轧件的)　convex edge
凸边造币板　blank with rimmed edge
凸槽(闭口孔型的)　tongue
凸槽上轧辊(组成闭口孔型的)　tongue roll
凸出　protrusion, projection, overhanging
凸出部分　outshoot
凸的　convex ◇ 两面～lenticular
凸底箱形孔型　【压】convex box pass
凸点钢板　button plate
凸点焊接[凸焊接点]　projection-welded joint
凸肚墙　bulging wall
凸度(轧辊的)　(degree of) convexity, convex camber, crown ◇ 辊身～*, 轧辊～[辊型]调整*
凸度比率(焊件的)　【焊】convexity ratio
凸度和凹度　crown and concavity
凸度可变式轧辊(VC 轧辊)　variable crown roll
凸度控制(轧辊的)　crown control
凸耳　ledge, lug, 【焊】pimple
凸规划问题　convex programming problem
凸辊环　outer [positive] collar
凸焊　projection [relief] welding ◇ 筋状～ridge welding
凸焊道　【焊】convex bead
凸焊缝　【焊】convex [reinforced] seam
凸焊机　projection [press] welder, projection welding machine
凸焊用电极　(projection) welding die
凸极发电机　salient pole generator
凸肩　shoulder ◇ 下～*
凸角　lobe, convex angle
凸角板　lobe plate
凸块　lug, scab
凸棱(顺轧件)　fin
凸轮　cam (wheel) ◇ 齿～tinger cam, 膨胀[扩张]～expansion cam, 凸腹～convex glank cam, 心型～heart cam 支[偏置] offset cam, 直动～translation cam, 轴向[圆柱]～axial cam, 主～drive cam

凸 tou

凸轮操纵的 cam-operated
凸轮传动 cam drive
凸轮传动装置 cam gear
凸轮锤 cam hammer
凸轮导轨【团】cam rail
凸轮轨道 cam track
凸轮滚子 cam bowl
凸轮夯实机 cam-ram machine
凸轮环 cam ring
凸轮机构 cam mechanism, camshaft gear
凸轮接触 cam contact
凸轮控制压机 cam-controlled press
凸轮联轴器 shifting sleeve
凸轮盘 cam disc, edge cam
凸轮驱动出坯 cam-driven knock-out
凸轮式拉拔压力机 cam drawing press
凸轮(式)塑性计【压】cam plastometer
凸轮式限位开关 cam type limit switch
凸轮随动件 cam follower
凸轮凸角 cam lobe
凸轮推杆 cam carrier
凸轮箱 cam box
凸轮行程 cam throw
凸轮压(力)机 cam-controlled [cam-operated] press, cam type press ◇ 斯托克斯~Stokes press, 下滑座式~°
凸轮缘【机】crown
凸轮轴 cam-shaft, tappet shaft, axial cam
凸轮轴承 camshaft bearing
凸轮转换开关 cam switch
凸轮装置 cam gear
凸面 convex surface, convex edge (板坯、轧件的) ◇ 轻度~轧辊 full roll
凸面辊 crowned roller
凸面[鼓凸]加工 crowing
凸面坯块【粉】convex-shaped compact
凸面青铜压力衬垫 crowned bronze pressure pad
凸面(填)角焊 convex fillet welding
凸面轧辊【压】cambered [crowned] roll
凸模 male mould, terrace die
凸泡(带钢、钢板表面的) blister

凸片 lug
凸起(钢锭缺陷) protuberance
凸起部 lug boss ◇ 锻件表面~boss
凸起程度 (同"凸度")
凸起点(冷轧板表面的) high spot
凸起孔型【压】former
凸舌轧辊 tongue roll
凸台 bead, boss
凸透镜 convex lens [glass], positive lens, bull's eye
凸尾带钢 full strip
凸线辊型 convex camber, (roll) sweep, bow
凸向液体的界面 convex-toward-the-liquid interface
凸形 convex shape, crowning
凸形板【带】尾 convex camber
凸形辊身【压】convex barrel
凸形焊道【焊】convex bead
凸形焊缝 convex weld
凸形曲线 crest curve
凸形竖曲线 crest vertical curve
凸形(填)角焊缝 convex fillet weld
凸圆头 cheese head ◇ 有槽~螺钉 fillister head screw
凸缘 flange, lug, bump, ledge ◇ 带~的砂箱 flask with flange, 机械加工~machined flange, 去~ deflanging, 制作~flanging
凸缘安装 flange mounting
凸缘成形法【压】flange forming
凸缘对接 flanged butt joint
凸缘缝铆接 flanged seam riveting
凸缘钢 flange steel
凸缘管 flanged pipe
凸缘辊 flanged roller
凸缘焊缝 flanged seam
凸缘接合[连接] flange(d) joint
凸缘连接管 flanged (joint) pipe
凸缘螺母 flange(d) nut
凸缘密封 flange seal
凸缘配件 flanged fittings

凸缘式喷管　flanged nozzle
凸缘式散热器　flanged radiator
凸缘型钢　flanged section
凸缘轧辊　【压】collar roll
凸缘轧机(轧制粉末用)　flanged rolls
凸缘真空密封　flange vacuum seal
凸缘座　flange mounting
秃尖三角形　blunt corner triangle
突变　jumping, abrupt [sudden] change, mutation
突变点　discontinuity
突变度　degree of abruptness
突变性　mutability, discontinuity
突变株　mutant (strain)
突出　projection, protruding
突出部　setoff, bump, projection,【焊】pimple(凸焊的)
突出部分　ledge, sally, head
突出灯架　bracket
突出端　nose
突出炉内的风口　(同"长风口")
突出轮缘　collar rim
突出物[突起]　outshoot, outthrust, overhang, projection, eruption
突堤　jetty, mole, croy
突发性膨胀　【团】dramatic expansion
突杆　outrigger
突拱　【建】corbel arch
突破试验　breakthrough run
突起　bulge, bulging
突起高度　【钢】rising height
突起物　outrigger
突然变异　mutation, halmatogenesis
突然飞散　outburst
突然倾斜的矿　parachute mine (PM, P.M.)
突然析出(气体的)　outburst
突跳(指针的)　kick
突转弯头　sharp bend
图　figure (Fig.), chart (cht), diagram, drawing, picture, scheme, view ◇ 伯德~Bode diagram, 德拜~*, 吉雷特~*, 劳厄~*, 理查德~*, 塔菲尔~*
图案　pattern, design ◇ 画~【建】patterning
图案花纹压印法[工艺]　【压】imprinting process [technique]
图标　legend
图表　chart (cht), figure (Fig.), diagram (diag.), graph, plot, sheet, table ◇ 本恩~Bunn chart, 伯纳耳~Bernal chart, 格雷宁格~Greninger chart
图表计算器　tabular calculator
图带记录　strip-chart recording
图钉　drawing pin, thumbtack
图尔南黄铜(82.5Cu, 17.5Zn)　Tournay metal, Tournay's brass [alloy]
图画　drawing, picture,【电】frame
图集　atlas, collective drawings
图解　diagram (diag.), graph(ic), figure, scheme, illustration (illus., illut)
图解表示法　graphic(al) representation
图解法　graphic(al) method [solution, representation], diagram method
图解分析　graphic analysis
图解辅助法　graphical aids
图解计算法　graphics, graphic calculation
图解记录器　graphic recorder
图解设计法　graphical design [construction]
图解外推法　graphical extrapolation method
图卡浸蚀液(用于铝)　【金】Tucker's reagent
图康(显微)硬度　Tukon hardness
图康显微硬度计　Tukon tester
图朗－伦纳德银代用合金(86—88Sn, 14—12Cu)　Tourun-Leonard's alloy
图朗锡青铜(90Sn, 10Cu)　Tourun metal
图例　legend, conventional symbol
图示法　graphic(al) method, graphics, diagrammatic [schematic] representation
图示记录器　draught recorder
图示盘　graphic panel

图示仪器 graphic instrument
图算法 nomography
图书管理员 librarian
图书馆 library
图算法 nomography
图塔尼亚锡锑铜合金 （轴承：92.5Sn, 4.6Sb, 2.6Cu, 0.32Pb；家具：80Sn, 16Sb, 2.7 Cu, 1.3Zn；板材：90Sn, 2.7Cu, 6Pb, 1.3Zn） Tutania (metal)
图坦纳格镍银合金 （45Cu, 余量 Ni + Zn） Tutenag
图像 image, picture, graph, (re)presentation ◇ 二进制~数据*, 过度曝光的劳埃~ overexposed Laue film
图像处理 image [picture] processing
图像传播因数 pattern-propagation factor
图像存储法 【计】image storage method
图像[形]存取法 【计】graphic access method
图像发送器 video transmitter
图像放大器 image amplifier
图像分割 image segmentation
图像畸变[畸形] image fault, picture distortion
图像间隔[距离] image distance
图像亮度 image illumination
图像漂移 【理】image drift
图像频率 image [picture] frequency
图像平面 image plane
图像清晰度 image sharpness [definition], picture resolution
图像形成 image formation
图像照度 image illumination
图像质量 picture quality
图像转动 image rotation
图形 figure, graph, drawing, chart, pattern ◇ 利萨茹~【理】Lissajous pattern, 莫阿~*
图形识别 pattern recognition
图形数据处理 graphic data processing
图形显示(装置) graphical display (unit)
图形显示字符 【计】graphic character

图样 pattern, design, draft ◇ 考塞尔~*
图纸 drawing (sheet), blueprint
图纸记录仪器 chart-recording instrument
图纸目录 drawing list, table of contents for drawings
徒工 apprentice, helper
涂层 coat(ing), covering ◇ 薄~*, 被覆~ covering, 成品外部~ finishing layer, 导电~*, 多层~*, 晶质~耐久~ resistant coating, 涂掩饰~ masking-off, 增强~ reinforced coating, 阻止侵蚀的~*
涂层剥落 peeling
涂层薄板 coated sheet
涂层保护寿命[作用期限] protective life
涂层表面铬酸盐钝化处理 chromate coating treatment
涂层布袋收尘室系统 coated baghouse system
涂层刀片 coated-tips, 【粉】coated insert
涂层粉末 coating powder
涂层风口 coated tuyere
涂层汞合金 （同"胶泥汞合金"）
涂层厚度 coating thickness
涂层厚度(测量)仪 layer thickness meter
涂层厚度称量测定法 weight-of-coating test
涂层机 coater
涂层机排烟装置 coater fume exhaust
涂层黏附力 coating adhesion
涂层装置 plater
涂层组分 coating constituent
涂底 first [printing] coat, lining
涂底层(漆) priming
涂底漆钢板 preprimed sheet
涂镀 coating ◇ 保护层沉浸~法 dip pricess, 辊式~ roller coating, 浇流~ flow coating, 镜面光亮~ high lustre coating, 考克斯钢制零件除锈与~法 cox process
涂镀过程[工艺] coating process
涂镀强化剂 coating strengthener
涂镀设备[装置] coater, plater, coating unit

涂镀系统[作业线] coating line	涂料混合器 paint mixer
涂镀液 coating solution	涂料喷枪 paint-spraying pistol, blackwash sprayer
涂镀轧辊(防护层的) coating roll	
涂珐琅(低碳)钢板 (同"搪瓷钢板")	涂料起皮 【铸】blacking scab
涂敷粉粒 (同"包覆粉粒")	涂料气[黑]孔 【铸】blacking hole
涂敷铝 aluminium coat	涂料清除剂 paint remover
涂覆 coating, painting, application ◇ 流态化床～法*,再～处理*	涂料刷 【铸】blacking brush
	涂料桶 wash box
涂覆层 overlay	涂料组成(电焊条的) coating ingredient
涂覆规程 coating instruction	涂料作用 coating action
涂覆机 coating machine	涂铝钢 calorized [aluminized, alumetized] steel
涂覆金属玻璃板 metal-on-glass plate	
涂覆尼龙 nylon coating	涂模材料 adhering moulding material
涂覆药皮 【焊】flux coating	涂抹 daubing, smearing, painting, applying (膏脂的)
涂覆液供应设备 coating solution supply equipment	
涂覆油 coating oil	涂抹电镀 【金】sponge plating
涂汞锡合金 quicksilvering	涂抹焊药[料] pasting
涂黑[砂型涂黑] 【铸】blacking	涂抹料 coating mixture
涂黑处理法 black coating	涂抹装置(铸铁机铸模的) 【铁】swab
涂滑石粉 talcing	涂腻子 luting, putty
涂灰泥 parging, parget	涂漆 lacquer coating [finish], lacquering, paint coat, paint(ing), varnish coating, japanning ◇ 带材～作业线*
涂火酒漆 bodying up	
涂浆极板 grid plate	
涂焦油 tarring	涂漆薄钢板 lacquer, lacquer-coated steel, japanned sheet metal
涂胶 rubberizing, gumming, glu(e)ing	
涂胶铝箔 tenaplate	涂漆底 paint primer
涂胶泥 luting, putty	涂漆镀锡薄钢板 lacquer, lacquered plate
涂金 oil gilding	涂漆干燥炉 lacquer curing furnace
涂金属层板 plymetal	涂漆钢板 prepainted sheet
涂蜡 waxing	涂漆用滚刷 roller brush for painting
涂沥青 bituminous plastering	涂清漆 varnishing
涂沥青薄钢板 pitch-on metal	涂染 painting
涂料 coating (material, mixture), paint, daub(ing), moldwash, dressing,【耐】plaster ◇ 防黏～paint barrier, 含碳～*, 快干～quick drying paint, 清除～剂 paint remover, 示温～heat indicating paint, 吸声～acoustic paint, 洗涤型～wash primer	涂染背景 background colouration
	涂色 dyeing
	涂色标记[标志](铸锭的) colour coding
	涂石灰 liming, lime coating
	涂石灰槽 lime coating tank
	涂石蜡 paraffinization, paraffinize
	涂水银 quicksilvering
涂料层 paint coat	涂塑钢管 plastic-coated steel pipe
涂料辊 ink roll	涂碳粉 blackening ◇ 表面～*
涂料化合[混合]物 coating compound	涂搪瓷 enameling ◇ 干法～dry process

enameling
涂钍的　thoria-coated
涂钍钨电极　thoriated electrode
涂锡的　coated tin
涂橡胶　rubberize, rubberizing
涂型材料　【铸】facing material
涂掩饰涂层　【金】masking-off
涂氧化物灯丝　oxide coated filament
涂药焊丝　coated wire, flux covered wire
涂药焊条　(flux) coated electrode, covered [fluxed] electrode, coated rod
涂药焊条(电弧)焊接　covered electrode welding
涂药焊条电弧切割　covered electrode arc cutting
涂油　oiling
涂油白钢皮　fat liquoring
涂油操作(钢锭模的)　coating operation
涂油处理(线材的)　oiled finish
涂油辊　oiling roll(er) ◇法兰绒～"
涂油机　oiler, oiling machine ◇带钢～", 辊式～ oil roll machine, 静电～ electrostatic oiler
涂油热轧板卷　oiled hot rolled coil
涂油装置　oiling station
涂釉电阻　glazed resistance, cermet resistor
涂罩光漆　bodying up
土　soil, earth, terra ◇大孔性～loess
土坝　earth dam
土崩　landslide, soil slip
土层[体]　solum
土堤　earth bank [dike, embankment] ◇用吸泥船填成的～ barged in fill
土堤岸护墙[护面]　【建】chemise
土地　land, ground
土地沉陷　land subsidence
土地平整　【建】land leveling, grading
土地填筑　【环】landfill
土冻结深度　depth of freezing of earth
土方　【建】earth work, yardage
土方表　quantity sheet
土方工程　earthwork, ground work
土方工程量　earth quantity, volume of earthwork
土(方累)积曲线　【建】mass curve
土方平衡系数(收缩系数)　earthwork balance factor
土方修整　【建】grading
土高炉　【铁】native-style blast furnace
土工技术　geotechnique
土工建筑物　earthen structure
土工[土力]学　geotechnics
土罐炉(熔析生锑用)　【色】clay pot furnace
土夯　earth rammer
土黑铜矿{CuO}　melaconite
土焦　coke from primitive ovens
土块多的　cloddy
土粒分组　◇阿氏～ Atterberg's scale
土沥青　natural asphalt, maltha
土力学　soil mechanics
土磷锌铝矿　kehoeite
土硫铀矿{$SO_3 \cdot UO_3 \cdot H_2O$}　uraconite
土路　earthen road, packway
土铝矾　doughtyite
土木工程(学)　civil engineering
土木工程师　civil engineer (C.E.)
土木建筑　civil construction
土壤　soil ◇捣实～ packed soil, 化学(剂)稳定～", 挖出～ spoil, 用桩加固 palification
土壤层理　soil stratification
土壤沉降　soil settlement
土壤承载能力　soil bearing capacity
土壤承载试验　bearing test of soil
土壤触探仪　soil sounding device
土壤冻结法下沉基础　freezing method of sinking foundation
土壤分层图　boring log
土壤封面料　【环】soil sealant
土壤腐蚀　soil corrosion
土壤杆菌属　Agrobacterium
土壤化学处理　chemical treatment of soil

土壤结构 soil structure
土壤粒径分布试验 soil grain distribution test
土壤力学 soil mechanics
土壤水 【地】vadose [soil] water
土壤弹性均压系数 modulus of reaction of soil
土壤淘析器 soil elutriator
土壤退化 soil degradation
土砷铁矾 pitticite
土石膏 gypsite
土石流 【环】earth flow
土水铀矿 urgite, urhite
土酸(钒、铌、钽的五氧化物) earth acid
土酸性金属 earth acid metal
土酸性元素 earth acid element
土微菌属 Pedomicrobium
土压(测定)盒 soil pressure cell
土压力 【建】soil [earth] pressure ◇ 被动~*, 主动~*
土压力系数 coefficient of earth pressure
土制浮标 debiteuse
土砖 cob brick
土状赤铁矿 argillaceous hematite
土状断口 earthy fracture
土状石膏 gypsite
土状铁矿 earthy iron ore
土状杂质 earthy impurity
土族元素 earthy element, earths
土钻 ground auger
吐酒石 (同"酒石酸锑钾")
吐丝 loop laying
吐丝管 loop laying pipe [tube]
吐丝[线]机(高速线材轧机的) (loop) laying head [cone]
吐丝嘴 【压】wire nozzle
钍{Th} thorium ◇ 新~*
钍-230{^{230}Th} ionium
钍萃取[提取] thorium extraction
钍锭 thorium ingot
钍方铀矿 thoruraninite
钍锆贝塔石 zirconolite

钍合金 thorium alloy
钍黑稀土矿 thoromelanocerite
钍化物 thoride
钍基合金 thorium-base alloy
钍金红石 smirnovite, smirnowit
钍(金属)锭 thorium ingot
钍矿 thorium mine
钍矿床 thorium deposit
钍矿石 thorium ore
钍矿物 thorium mineral
钍络合物 thorium complex
钍钕混合物 thorium-neodymium mixture
钍铅[钍 D] (铅的同位素^{208}Pb, ThD) thorium lead
钍射气 thorium emanation, thoron
钍石{ThSiO$_4$} thorite, thoron stone
钍铈矿 euncrasite
钍铈消气合金(80Th, 20Ce) (电子管用) cero alloy
钍衰变链 thorium decay chain
钍钛矿 thorutite
钍钛铀矿 absite
钍添加合金 thorium additive alloy
钍钨矿 thorotungstite
钍钨线 thoriated-tungsten wire
钍系 thorium series [family]
钍乙醚 thorium ethyl oxide
钍铀矿 broeggerite, thoruraninite
钍铀滤饼 thorium-uranium cake
钍铀铅矿 aldanite
钍脂铅铀矿{(Pb, Th)UO$_3$·nH$_2$O} thorogummite
氡 thoron
湍动流态化床 turbulent fluidized bed
湍滑移 turbulent slip
湍流 turbulence, turbulent flow ◇ 液态金属~*, 防~冲击垫*
湍流边界 turbulent boundary
湍流淬火 turbulent hardening
湍流接触吸收器 turbulent contact absorber (T.C.A.)
湍流式焙烧炉 (同"旋风式焙烧炉")

湍流现象　turbulence phenomenon
湍型范性流变　turbulent plastic flow
团　group, cluster, lump
团聚　unite, rally, balling ◇ 反～deflocculating
团块　briquet(te), compact, agglomerate ◇ 格伦达尔法～Groendal briquette, 冷压～cold-pressed compact, 碳酸盐黏结～*, 综合[复合]～composite agglomerate
团块厂　briquetting [agglomeration] plant
团块固结方法　【固】process for hardening briquettes
团块混合物　briquette mixture
团块焦　coke briquette
团块料柱　briquette column
团块炉料　charge of briquettes, power-compacted charge
团块用煤　briquetting coal
团块状炸药爆炸成形　pellet-charge forming
团矿　briquetting, nodulizing, agglomerate, block ore, 【铁】briquetted ore, pelleted charge ◇ 板状～plate briquet, 含碳～*, 柱塞式～机[方～机]*, 装～pelleted charge, 综合[复合]～*
团粒　[团]aggregate, conglomerate
团球状共晶体　nodular eutectic
推板　pusher plate
推测的　tentative
推车　trolley
推车工　car pusher
推车轨　trolley guide
推车机　car pusher, 【钢】drag（铸锭车的）, 【耐】pusher, knock(-out) pin
推斥激发[励]　repulse excitation
推斥力　repulsion [repulsive, repelling] force
推斥启动电动机　repulsion start motor
推斥势(力场的)　【理】repulsive potential
推冲器　thruster
推出　push-off, pushing off, eject, detrusion

推出板　push-out plate
推出锤　ejector ram
推出缸　push-off cylinder
推出护板　pushing-off shield
推出机　pusher, 【压】ejector, push-off, kick-off (mechanism) ◇ 气动～airactuated stripper, 曲柄式～crank type pusher
推出机构　pullback mechanism, out punch, ejecting mechanism (水压机的)
推出机推料杆　push-off arm
推出式落砂　【铸】push-out type shake-out
推出装置　pushing-off device, lift-out attachment, knock down ◇ 带卷～*
推床　【压】manipulator, positioning device ◇ 夹辊式翻钢～*, 双面～double manipulator
推床齿条　【压】manipulator rack
推床导板　manipulator slide beam, side guard ◇ 出口～*, 轧机进口侧*
推床痕(轧材缺陷)　manipulator marks
推床活动导板　movable side guard
推床头部(导板)　manipulator head
推床推板　manipulator slide beam
推床推杆　manipulator arm
推导　derivation, deduction, fetch
推顶杆　【粉】penetrator ram
推顶力　ejection force
推顶器　ejector
推动　push (forward), promotion, actuating, impulse, motivation
推动力　motive [moving, driving] force, propelling force [power], impulsion
推断　deduction, infer
推杆　push rod, push(ing) [push-off] bar, pusher, ram, 【压】discharger, 【铸】stripping pins ◇ 出料～*
推杆传动装置　push rod actuator
推杆式顶出装置　pusher-type knockout
推杆式炉　pusher furnace
推杆速度(弯曲试验的)　ram speed
推杆行程　pusher stroke
推杆窑　pushed-bat kiln

推钢机 (billet, ingot) pusher, ejector, ram ◇ 齿条式～*,单排～ single pusher,杆式～ ram-type pusher,杠杆式～ lever pusher,炉用～ furnace pusher,摩擦式～ friction pusher,汽动～(活塞式) steam ram,双齿条式～*,双排[杆]～*,液压[水力]～ hydraulic ram,柱塞式～ plunger pusher

推钢机控制台 pusher control pulpit

推钢(机推)杆 pusher ram, peel [push(-out)] bar

推钢机行程 pusher stroke

推钢式板坯二次加热炉 pusher-type slab reheat furnace

推钢速度 【压】velocity of push, push rate

推荐流程 proposed flowsheet

推焦 【焦】(coke) pushing ◇ 加三～法 three-addition method

推焦[进]杆 (pushing) ram ◇ 尾部可折起的～ folded pusher ram

推焦杆头[靴子] pusher [ram] head, coke pusher shoe, pusher ram shoe

推焦机[器] coke pusher, pusher (machine), coke-pushing ram

推焦(机)侧 pusher side (P.S., p.s.), pusher end

推焦顺序 pushing schedule

推进剂(火箭用) propellant, propulser ◇ 固体～ grain

推进加料器 auger

推进力 impellent, propulsive force [thrust], driving power

推进器 impeller, impellor, propeller, propulser, mover

推进式喂丝装置 push-type wire feeder

推进式运送机 push(ing) conveyer

推卷机 【压】coiler kickoff, coil stripper (用于卷取机卸卷)

推开效应(挤压的) effect of ploughing

推拉设备 push-pull equipment

推拉式酸洗机 pull pickler

推拉式酸洗(带钢的) push-pull pickling

推理 reasoning

推力 thrust, propulsive force [thrust], push

推力测定 measurement of thrust

推力撑座 thrust block

推力负荷[载荷] thrust load(ing)

推力滚珠轴承 (同"止推滚珠轴承")

推力轴承 (同"止推轴承")

推料 stoking, dislodging, shove ◇ 自动～ automatic stoking

推料杆 push-off [charging] ram,【压】transfer arm ◇ 切头推出机～*

推料机 pusher, kick-out, lifter,【压】discharger, positioning device ◇ 电动气压～*,杆式～*,气动～ air cylinder pusher,卸料车式～ tripper stacker

推料机操纵工 pusher operator

推料机构 pushing device

推料机推杆(加热炉用) travel(l)ing bar

推料机小车 pusher carriage

推料器 stoker

推料式板坯二次加热炉 pusher-type slab reheat furnace

推料式钢坯加热炉 pusher-type billet heating furnace

推料式连续烧结炉 stoker-type continuous sintering furnace

推料式酸洗作业线 push-pickling line

推料[推送]式炉 pusher-type furnace

推料速率 stoking rate

推料叶片 pusher blade

推料装置[机构] pusher mechanism, knock down

推论 ratiocination, deduction, extrapolation, inference

推煤机 coal transporter

推盘式炉 pusher tray furnace, tray pusher furnace

推坯机构 【耐】knock(-out) pin

推起 boost

推敲 thrash(ing), deliberation

推入配合 sucking [push] fit

推送辊 push roll
推算 prediction
推算价值量 【企】imputation
推算蠕变强度 predicting creep strength
推算租金收入净额 imputed net rent
推土(用推土机) bulldozing
推土机 (bull)dozer, pushdozer, earthmover ◇ 刮板～rake dozer, 斜板～angledozer
推挽变压器 push-pull transformer
推下(运输机上的盘、卷) pushing off
推销商品 sales promotion, merchandising
推压 bulldozing
推压工作(挖土机的) racking
推移系统(钢锭模车的) beetle haulage system
推舟式炉 pusher furnace
腿部矫直机(型钢的) flange flattener
蜕变 decay, disintegration, breakdown, transmutation ◇ α～*, β～*
蜕变产物 (同"衰变产物")
蜕变定律 decay law
蜕变速率 (同"衰变速率")
蜕变系 transformation series
褪光 delustring, deading
褪光浸洗 matte dip, dead dipping
褪色 discolor, discoloration, fading
退出 withdrawal, bow out, quit, exit
退磁 (同"去磁")
退刀槽 recess
退格符 【计】backspace [space] charcter
退格键 【计】backspace key
退焊 back welding ◇ 分段～backstep welding
退化 degenerate, degeneracy, degeneration, degradation, catagenesis ◇ n倍～n-fold degenerate
退化方式 【理】degenerate mode
退化物质 【理】degenerate matter
退化系 degenerate system
退化(状)态 degenerate state [condition]
退回 return, back lash
退回重来 roll back
退火 annealing 【金】◇ 奥氏体(化温度)～austenite annealing, 不完全～*, 敞开～*, 成叠[堆垛]～pack annealing, 成卷[盘]～*, 初[第一次]～*, 磁场中～*, 带卷成批～*, 倒逆～*, 等时～isochronal annealing, 低温～lonnealing, 电炉～*, 电热～electric annealing, 堆叠～*, 惰性气氛～*, 发蓝～*, 非等温～anisothermal annealing, 分股～strand-annealing, 分批[室式炉]～batch annealing, 辐射管加热式～*, 改善加工性能的～*, 感应加热～induction annealing, 高温等温～法*, 工序间[中间]～*, 固溶～solution annealing, 光亮～*, 过度～overannealing, 黑～*, 阶段～step annealing, 浸酸～acid annealing, 局部～*, 可锻化～*, 空位集合体～*, 快速(加热)～*, 连续～continuous annealing, 两次～double annealing, 两段～twosteps annealing, 炉内～furnace annealing, 脉动～pulse annealing, 明焰[火焰直接]加热～flame annealing, 铅浴～lead-bath annealing, 双重～duplex annealing, 四分之一硬～*, 铁矿料中～*, 脱碳～*, 完全～*, 硝盐槽～saltpeter annealing, 消除应力～*, 选择～selective annealing, 盐浴～*, 预先[事先]～preannealing, 轧制道次间[中间]～*, 中温～*, 周期[连续等温]～*, 装箱～*, 自热～self-annealing
退火薄钢板 annealed sheet iron
退火不完全 annealing slack
退火操作 annealing practice
退火敞炉 annealing hearth
退火车间 annealing plant [department]
退火沉积 annealing deposit
退火重结晶 annealing recrystallization
退火除鳞作业线(带材的) annealing-descaling line
退火处理 annealing treatment ◇ 软化～*

退火脆性　annealing brittleness
退火带材[带钢]　annealed strip
退火电炉　electric annealing furnace ◇ 钟罩式~*
退火锻钢　annealed forged steel
退火钢　annealed steel
退火钢丝　annealed wire, stone (dead) wire
退火工段　annealing room [department]
退火工序　annealing operation
退火工艺　annealing practice
退火罐　【铸】saggar, sagger
退火过程　annealing process ◇ 流水作业线~*
退火焊波　annealing welding wave
退火焊缝[道]　annealing weld
退火黑薄板　annealed sheet iron
退火后抗张强度　annealed tensile strength
退火间　annealing room
退火件支架　【金】annealing rack
退火金属　annealed metal
退火坑　annealing pit
退火裂纹　fire crack(ing)
退火炉　annealing furnace [oven, kiln], annealer, leer (玻璃的), lehr (玻璃的) ◇ 车底式~*, 辊道炉膛~*, 机械燃煤~*, 密闭~*, 全纤维燃气双向运动~*, 水封~*, 驼峰输送带式~*, 箱式~*, 移动式~*, 有内罩的~ pot-annealing furnace, 罩式~*
退火炉跨　annealing span [bay]
退火炉冷却段(带材的)　cooling furnace
退火铝线　annealed aluminium wire
退火孪晶[孪生]带　annealing twin bands
退火黏结板　annealing sticker
退火盘　annealing tray
退火期　annealing period
退火色　annealing colour
退火设备　annealing facilities [installation]
退火生铁　annealing pig iron
退火时间　annealing time
退火室　annealing chamber

退火试样　annealed specimen
退火双[孪]晶　annealing twin
退火酸洗车间　annealing and pickling plant
退火酸洗机组[作业线]　annealing-pickling line ◇ 双线~*
退火酸洗作业　anneal-pickling operation
退火碳　annealing carbon
退火条件　annealing conditions
退火铜　annealed copper ◇ 国际~标准*
退火温度范围　annealing temperature range
退火温度与硬度关系曲线图　annealing temperature-hardness plot
退火线材　soft wire
退火箱　annealing can [pot], annealing box (板材的), 【铸】saggar, sagger
退火窑　annealing kiln
退火硬度　anneal hardness
退火浴槽　annealing bath
退火再结晶　recrystallization on annealing
退火罩　temper hood
退火支架　annealing rack
退火织构　annealing texture
退火钟罩　annealing bell
退火周期[制度]　annealing cycle
退火铸件　annealed casting
退火铸铁　annealed cast iron (ACI)
退火装置　annealer, annealing device ◇ 开卷~*
退火状态　annealing condition
退火状态硬度　anneal hardness
退火作业线　annealing line ◇ 带卷~*, 一次~*
退货　goods rejected, rejection
退极化剂　depolarizing agent, depolarizer
退敏(作用)　【金】desensitization
退耦　decoupling
退铅(不锈钢的)　【压】deleading
退缩　holdback, shrink back
退缩性　retrogression
退脱磁系数　demagnetization coefficient

吞拖托 tun—tuo

吞加整流器 tungar rectifier
拖 drag(ging), haul(ing)
拖板 【机】carriage, bogie
拖杯形转子 【电】drag-cup rotor
拖驳 double-trip, barge, tender
拖铲 dragscraper ◇ 缆索～cable drag scraper
拖铲挖土机 drag shovel
拖车 trailer (car) ◇ 工业用～industrial trailers, 挂钩～dog trailer, 平台～flat platform trailer
拖车式铸钢桶 trailer(-mounted) ladle
拖出 withdrawal, drag-over
拖动 driving ◇ 多～coordinated drive
拖钩 towing hook
拖挂车轮渡 ferry bridge
拖挂式载重车 coupled truck
拖拉铲运机 dragscraper
拖拉机 tractor ◇ 履带式～caterpillar tractor
拖拉机轮缘型钢 tractor tyre
拖拉机式电焊机 welding tractor
拖绳 towing [guide] rope
拖索 towing rope, towrope, jack chain
拖曳 drag(ging), haul(age)
拖曳电动机 dragging motor
拖曳电缆链 trailing cable chains
拖曳力 drag force, grabability
拖曳线 trailing lead
拖曳铸型 drag cast
拖运机 dragging device, drag-over unit, chain-and-ducking dog mechanism, handling [transfer, pull-over] gear, skid, transfer skid [table], 【压】drag, transfer ◇ 单路～*, 多钢绳～multirope skid gear, 链式～chain-type drag, 双路～*
拖运机部件 drag-over assembly
拖运机构 transfer mechanism
拖运机链条 drag chain
拖运绞盘 haul-off capstan
拖运缆绳 hauling cable
拖运式线盘移送机 drag-type coil conveyer
拖运小车 drag carriage ◇ 拨料～drag-on carriage, 堆料～drag-off carriage
拖运装置 haulage gear, transfer arrangement (横移轧件用的)
托板 supporting board, mounting, 【铸】backing plate
托板芯盒 combination core box
托宾海军黄铜(0.5—2.5Sn, 38—40Zn, <0.15Fe, <0.35Pb, 余量Cu) Tobin bronze
托宾青铜 Tobin bronze (Tob.brz), Tobin brass
托尔－马歇尔弯曲试验 Tour-Marshall test
托弗特镍铬铁电热合金(A型：80Ni, 20Cr; B型：65—75Ni, 16—23Cr, 余量Fe; C型：60Ni, 24Cr, 余量Fe) Tophet
托辊 support roller, supporting (trunnion) roller, roller-apron, idler, carrying roller (回转窑的), pulley (带式运输机的) ◇ 传动～back spin roll, 运输带的～apron roll
托辊系统(皮带运输机的) roller-apron system
托辊座 roller seat
托换基础 underpinning
托架 bracket (bkt, bkts), cradle, carrier, bearer, bogie, console, rest, stool
托架盖 pedestal cap
托卷辊 cradle roll
托卡斯铜镍装饰合金(35.6Cu, 28.6Ni, 余量为Fe、Al、Sn、Zn、Sb) Toucas (metal)
托科曲轴表面高频淬火法 Tocco (The Ohio Crankshaft CO.) hardening [process]
托利多钢刀 【钢】Toledo blade
托梁 rest beam, joist
托料辊(缠卷机的) carrier roll (up coil) ◇ 从动～*

托轮 ridging wheel, supporting trunnion roller, roller station（回转窑的）,【压】under-roller（筐篮式钢丝绳机的）
托马斯-吉尔克里斯特碱性炼钢法 Thomas-Gilchrist process
托马斯钢 Thomas steel
托马斯炼钢法 Thomas process
托马斯炉渣[碱性磷渣] (Thomas) phosphatic slag
托马斯铁 Thomas (pig) iron
托马斯转炉 【钢】Thomas converter [vessel]
托马斯转炉渣 Thomas slag
托模板 stamping board,【铸】turnover board
托姆铝合金 (10Zn,1.5Cu,2Mg,0-5Mn,余量 Al) Tom alloy
托盘 tray, underpan
托盘天平 table [counter] balance
托墙梁 breast-summer
托圈 ring,【铁】lintel girder [ring], deck ring, ring support ◇ 高炉～*,箱形断面～*
托圈板 mantle plate
托思锰还原氟化铝炼铝法 Toth process
托台 saddle
托运人 【企】shipper, consignor
托砖 【耐】bearing
托座 bracket,【建】angle-table
托座轴承 pedestal bearing
脱棒机 【压】stripper
脱苯（洗油的） 【焦】debenzolization, debenzolizing
脱苯沥青 benzol removed pitch
脱苯塔 benzole scrubber
脱苯油 debenzolized oil
脱苯装置[工段] debenzolizing plant
脱层 delaminating, delamination
脱成分腐蚀 dealloying
脱除 removal, elimination, deprivation
脱除粗苯初馏分 【焦】defronting
脱除粗苯初馏分蒸馏柱 defronting column

脱除锅垢 descaling
脱除率 removal efficiency
脱除石墨 degraphitization
脱除速率 rate of desorption
脱除锡层槽 detinning tank
脱磁系数 demagnetization coefficient
脱氮 denitrification, denitriding, nitrogen removal ◇ 生物～*
脱氮催化剂 denitrification catalyzer
脱氮反应器 denitrification reactor
脱氮硫杆菌 thiobacillus denitrificans
脱氮率 denitrification rate
脱锭 【钢】stripping
脱锭钢锭模 off-loading mould
脱锭机 stripper, ingot stripper (machine)
脱锭跨 stripping bay
脱锭起重机[吊车] (ingot) stripping crane, ingot drawing crane
脱锭钳 stripping tongs
脱锭装置 stripping device [mechanism]
脱芳族石油溶剂 dearomatized white spirit
脱方（轧件缺陷）【压】off-square(ness)
脱方度 【压】out-of-squareness
脱方公差 out-of-square tolerance
脱方轧件 diagonal stock
脱酚 【焦】dephenolization ◇ 粗苯萃取～法*,考伯斯蒸气循环～设备*
脱氟化氢 dehydrofluorination
脱氟（作用）defluorination
脱钙 decalcification, decalcify
脱镉塔 （同"除镉塔"）
脱铬 dechromization, dechromisation
脱汞作用 demercuration
脱钴 decobalt
脱管 tube reeling
脱管定径机 fine quality sizing (FQS)
脱管机 extracting mill
脱硅 desilication, desiliconization, desiliconisation, desiliconizing ◇ 高压釜[压煮器]～*

脱硅操作 【铁】desiliconizing operation ◇ 布瑞姆波~法*	**脱矿物质水** demineralized water
脱硅产物 desilication product	**脱蜡** dewaxing,【铸】burn(ing)-out ◇ 闪烧~(法) flash dewax
脱硅处理 【铁】desiliconizing treatment	**脱蜡炉**(蜡模造型后) burn-out furnace
脱硅吹炼 【铁】desiliconizing blow	**脱离** 【机】out-of-gear
脱硅过程 desilication	**脱离子器** deionizer
脱硅率 desilication yield	**脱离子水** deionized water
脱硅溶液 desiliconized solution	**脱磷** dephosphorization, dephosphorising, dephosphorizing, phosphor(us) removal ◇ 炉外~*
脱轨 derail, disorbit	
脱轨转辙器 derailing switch	**脱磷反应** dephosphorization reaction
脱焊管 seal-off tube	**脱磷精炼** phosphorus refining
脱合金成分腐蚀 dealloying	**脱磷平衡** dephosphorization equilibrium
脱灰 deliming	**脱磷生铁** dephosphorized pig iron
脱挥发份(作用) devolatilization	**脱磷速率** rate of dephosphorization
脱机 【计】off-line, off-lining	**脱硫** desulphuration, desulphurisation, desulphurising, desulphurization, desulphurizing, desulfation, desulphation, sulphur elimination, sulphur removal [expulsion], carrying-off the sulphur, ◇ 部分~*, 干式~法*, 连续~(法)*, 炉外~*, 珀罗克斯焦炉气催化氧化~法 Perox process, 气化~*, 强制~*, 萨尼特~法【钢】Saniter process, 赛洛克斯砷碱~法*, 湿式~*, 完全[充分]~*, 箱式[槽式]氧化铁~法【焦】oxide box, 伊玛特拉石灰粉~法 Imatra process, 重油直接~*
脱机处理 【计】off-line processing	
脱机存储器 off-line memory [storage]	
脱机方式 off-line mode	
脱机工作 off-line working	
脱机计算机 off line computer	
脱机批量[成批]处理系统 【计】off-line batch processing system	
脱机设备 off(-)line equipment [unit]	
脱机输出 【计】off-line output	
脱机系统 【计】off-line system	
脱焦油(作用) detarring	
脱介旋流器 scalping cyclone	
脱金 (同"除金")	
脱矩 parallelogram	
脱卷 【压】coil stripping	**脱硫焙烧** desulphurizing roasting
脱卷机 【压】coil stripper, coil stripping machine	**脱硫槽** sweetener bunker
	脱硫肠状菌属 Desulfotomaculum
脱开(轧辊) stripping	**脱硫程度** degree of desulphurization, extent of desulphuration
脱壳 shelling	
脱扣 trip(ping), release, drop-out, disconnection,【机】out-of-gear	**脱硫动力学** kinetics of desulphurization
	脱硫反应 desulphurization reaction
脱扣闭锁 trip lock	**脱硫粉剂** powdered desulphuring agent
脱扣机构 tripping mechanism [gear, device], release mechanism, trip gear	**脱硫富液** desulphurized rich solution
	脱硫弧菌 Vibrio desulfuricans
脱扣继电器 trip(ping) relay	**脱硫回路** desulphurization circuit
脱扣器 trip	**脱硫剂** desulphurizer, desulphurizing agent, sulphur remover
脱扣线圈 trip(ping) coil	
	脱硫率 degree of desulphurization, desul-

phurization ratio

脱硫能力 desulphurizing ability [power, capacity]

脱硫器 desulphurizer

脱硫曲线 【铁】desulphurization curve

脱硫(去磺)弧菌 desulfovibrio desulfurican

脱硫(去磺)弧菌属 desulfovibrio

脱硫熔剂 desulphurizing flux

脱硫设备 desulphurization plant

脱硫生铁 desulphurized pig iron

脱硫速度 rate of desulphurization, rate of sulphur expulsion

脱硫酸盐(作用) desulfation, desulphation

脱硫塔 thionizer

脱硫性 desulphurizing ability

脱硫渣 【钢】desulphurizing slag

脱硫装置 desulphur system ◇ 柯林式～*

脱硫作用 desulfation, desulphation, sulphur elimination

脱卤化氢 dehydrohalogenation

脱卤(作用) dehalogenation

脱铝(腐蚀)(铝青铜的) dealuminization, dealuminizing, de-aluminification

脱氯 dechloridizing, dechlorination

脱氯化氢 dehydrochlorination

脱氯剂 dechlorination agent

脱落 drop-out

脱落式芯盒 loose frame core box

脱镁 de-magging

脱锰 demanganization, demanganizing

脱醚槽 de-etherization tank

脱醚次液 de-etherized NOK liquor

脱模 extraction, mould release, pattern drawing, draw(ing), stripping

脱模操作 【钢】stripping operation [action]

脱模场[工段] stripper yard

脱模冲头 stripper punch

脱模法(钢锭的) method of stripping

脱模杆 【粉】stripper

脱模工具 extractor

脱模机 ingot stripper (machine), stripper, extractor (Ex., Ext.) ◇ 地上～*

脱模剂 antistick(ing) agent, die coating, 【铸】parting [separating] medium, release agent

脱模间 stripping room

脱模跨 stripping bay

脱模起重机[吊车] (同"脱锭起重机") ◇ 往复式～*, 移动式～*

脱模压力 ejection pressure

脱模用钢锭运输车 ingot transfercar for stripping

脱模装置 【粉】ejection mechanism ◇ 空气～*

脱萘塔 【焦】naphthalene scrubber

脱泥 desliming, desludging, slime-separation

脱泥分级机 desliming classifier

脱泥机 deslimer ◇ 虹吸～siphonsizer

脱泥矿石 deslimed ore

脱泥旋流器 desliming cyclone, cyclowash

脱泥锥(分级机) 【选】desliming cone

脱黏 decohesion

脱镍(作用) denickelefication ◇ 德麦勒沉淀脱镍法 De Merre Process

脱皮 flaking, peeling off

脱气 degasification, degasifying, degassing, gas removal, de-airing, 【冶】deaeration, scavenging (从熔融金属中除去溶解的气体), ◇ 包[桶]内～法*, 倒包～法*, 钢流～ stream degassing, 机内～*, 机外～*, 加助熔剂～ flux degassing, 连续～*, 预先～ predegassing, 真空提吸[(DH)提升]～法*

脱气槽 de-aeration vessel

脱气处理 degassing [outgassing] treatment

脱气钢 degasified steel

脱气挤泥机 【耐】de-airing auger

脱气剂 degasifier, degasifying [degassing] agent

脱气器[桶]　【钢】degasser ◇ 电弧～arc degasser
脱气熔剂　degassing flux
脱气室　de-airing chamber
脱气塔　degassing tower
脱气装置　degassing unit
脱铅塔　(同"除铅塔")
脱铅液　lead-free liquor
脱氢　dehydrogenation
脱氢处理　hydrogen relief treatment
脱氢能力　dehydrogenability
脱氰(作用)　decyanation
脱溶物　precipitate
脱色　decolorization, discoloration, decoloring, colour removal
脱色剂　decolorizing agent, decolourant
脱色作用　decolorization
脱砷　(同"除砷")
脱湿　dewetting, drying
脱湿剂　dewetting agent
脱湿器　moisture eliminator [separator], dehumidifier
脱水　dehydrating, dehydration, deliquefaction, dewatering, water removal, expulsion of water, deaquation, exsiccation
脱水槽　dehydration tank, dewatering tank [boot], drain sump, drainage bin
脱水传送带　dewatering conveyer
脱水带式运输机　drainage belt
脱水斗　dewatering cone
脱水段　【团】dehydration [preconditioning] zone
脱水段风机　【团】dehydration fan
脱水反应器　dehydration reactor
脱水房　dehydratic [dehydration] house
脱水工段　【团】dewatering section
脱水罐　drain sump
脱水光卤石　dehydrated carnallite
脱水机　dewaterer, hydroextractor ◇ 斗式～drag dewaterer, 刮板～scraper dewaterer, 离心～*, 旋转式～rotary dewaterer

脱水剂　dehydrant, dehydrating [dehydrogenation, dehydrolyzing] agent, dehydrater, dehydrator
脱水焦油　dehydrated tar
脱水精矿　dewatered concentrate
脱水矿石　dewatered ore
脱水离心机　dewatering centrifuge
脱水磷酸铵　ammonium dehydrate phosphate (a.d.p.)
脱水漏斗　hopper dewaterer
脱水滤饼　dehydrated cake
脱水滤池　dewatering filter
脱水螺旋运输机　dehydrating worm conveyer
脱水能力　dewaterability, water separation capability
脱水黏土　【铁】anhydrous paste
脱水浓缩机　dewatering thickener
脱水期[阶段](烧砖的)　【耐】water smoking period
脱水器　dehydrater, dehydrator, dewaterer, water separator [trap] ◇ 漏斗～hopper dewaterer
脱水球粒　dehydrated pellet
脱水曲线　dehydration curve
脱水筛　screen-type dryer, dewatering screen
脱水设备　dewatering equipment [facility]
脱水试验　dehydration test
脱水尾矿　dewatered tailings
脱水箱　dehydrating [dewatering] box
脱水性　dehydration property
脱水贮仓　drainage bunker
脱水锥　dewatering cone, cone dewaterer
脱水作用　dehydration, deaquation
脱酸　acid stripping
脱酸作用　deacidification
脱碳　carbon elimination [removal], decarburization, decarbonisation, decarburizing, decarburation, decarb(onization), decarbonizing, carbon drop ◇ 表面～层*, 氢氧～*

脱碳表面 decarburized surface
脱碳部分 【金】decarburized portion
脱碳层 decarburized layer [zone] ◇ 薄～*
脱碳带 decarbonation zone
脱碳法[过程] 【金】decarburizing process
脱碳反应 decarburizing [decarbonization] reaction
脱碳沸腾 【钢】carbon boil
脱碳钢 decarburized steel
脱碳厚度[深度] 【钢】decarburized [decarburization] depth
脱碳剂 decarbonizer, decarburizer, decarburizing agent
脱碳率 【钢】carbon-drop rate
脱碳模型 decarbonization model
脱碳泡面钢棒 aired bar
脱碳期 【钢】decarburizing cycle, carbon period
脱碳气氛 decarburizing atmosphere
脱碳气体 decarburizing gases
脱碳速率 decarbonization rate
脱碳搪瓷钢(板)(含碳量极低的钢板) decarburized enameling steel, zero carbon steel
脱碳铁粉 decarbonized iron powder
脱碳退火 decarburizing annealing ◇ 连续～(机组)作业线*
脱碳效应 decarburization [decarburizing] effect
脱碳铸铁粒 decarburized cast iron shot
脱铁 deferrization
脱铁槽 iron removal tank
脱铜 (同"除铜")
脱铜槽 【色】liberator cell
脱铜电解 copper stripping electrolysis
脱铜高压釜 copper stripping autoclave
脱铜溶液 decopperized [Cu-free] solution, depleted copper solution
脱尾(带材连轧的) tail-out
脱锡(锡青铜腐蚀现象) detinning, destannification

脱锡槽 detinning tank
脱锡法(锡层厚度测定法) stripping method
脱锡废铁 detinned iron scrap
脱锡装置 detinning apparatus
脱线处理 【计】off-line processing
脱线工作 off-line working
脱线系统 【计】off-line system
脱箱造型 flaskless moulding, removable flask mould(ing)
脱箱铸型 【铸】boxless mould
脱硝 denitrating, denitration ◇ 流(态)化床加热～*
脱硝反应 denitration reaction
脱硝锅 denitration pot
脱硝炉[器] denitrator
脱硝设备 denitration plant
脱硝细菌 denitrifying bacteria
脱锌 (同"除锌")
脱锌方法 dezincing method
脱锌过程[工艺,方法] dezincing process
脱锌率 dezincing degree
脱锌球团 dezinced pellet
脱锌物料 dezincified material
脱溴化氢 dehydrobromination
脱溴(作用) debromination
脱盐 desalination, desalinization, desalting
脱盐车间环境 desalination plant environments
脱盐剂 desalter
脱盐炉(钛锆等生产用) salt-removal furnace, salts separator
脱盐水 desalted [desalinated] water ◇ 完全～ fully desalted water
脱氧 de(s)oxidation, deoxidising, deoxidisation, deoxidization, deoxidizing, deoxygenation, oxygen removal,【钢】killing(使钢镇静) ◇ 包[桶]内～*,复合～法*,扩散～*,炉内初～[钢] furnace block,强制～*,全～钢*,碳～的 carbon-deoxidized,用铝～的金属 aluminium-deoxidized metal

脱氧不良钢　wild steel
脱氧产物　deoxidation product ◇二次～*
脱氧程度　degree of deoxidation
脱氧处理　【冶】deoxidation treatment
脱氧度试验(金属液的)　【铸】settling test
脱氧钢　deoxidized [killed, solid] steel ◇铝～*
脱氧钢锭　killed ingot
脱氧工艺　deoxidation technique
脱氧及晶粒细化中间合金　deoxidising and grain-refining master-alloy
脱氧剂　deoxidation reagent, de(s)oxidizer, de(s)oxidant, deoxidizing agent [addition], reducing agent [constituent], ◇钙锰硅～合金*
脱氧阶段　【钢】killing stage
脱氧能力　【冶】deoxidation power
脱氧平衡　deoxidation equilibrium
脱氧期　【冶】deoxidation period, 【钢】killing period
脱氧青铜　deoxidized bronze
脱氧熔剂　deoxidizing flux
脱氧熔炼　deoxidized heat
脱氧速率　rate of deoxidation
脱氧添加剂[物]　deoxidizing [finishing] addition
脱氧铜　deoxidized copper
脱氧温度　deoxidation temperature
脱氧效应　deoxidizing effect
脱氧型夹杂物　deoxidation-type inclusions
脱氧渣　deoxidizing slag
脱氧作用　deoxidizing effect, deoxidation
脱银　(同"除银")
脱渣　slag release
脱脂　degreasing ◇碱法～alkaline degreasing, 净化～过程*
脱脂槽　degreasing bath
脱脂带钢　degreased strip
脱脂段　cleaning section
脱脂剂　degreaser, degreasing agent [compound]

脱脂净化槽　cleaning tank
脱脂切屑　deoiled turnings
脱脂溶剂　solvent cleaner
脱脂设备　【压】degreasing plant
脱脂液　degreasing fluid
脱脂液面　cleaning level
脱脂装置　degreaser
脱脂作业线　degreasing line ◇清洗～*
脱字符　【计】caret
陀螺测试仪　gyrometer
陀螺测试仪型转速计　gyro-meter type tachometer
陀螺地平仪　gyrohorizen, gyro horizon
陀螺六分仪　gyro(Sextant)
陀螺动力学　gyrodynamics
陀螺感应[同步]罗盘　gyrosyn
陀螺[回转]瞄准器　gyrosight
陀螺罗盘　gyro-(compass), gyroscopic compass
陀螺倾斜[水平]仪　gyro-level
陀螺式芯撑　diabolo-type cast chaplet
陀螺系统　gyrosystem
陀螺(仪)　gyro(scope) ◇二自由度～rate gyroscope, 每速度～rate-of-turn gyroscope, 三自由度～free gyroscope, 振动～gyrotron
陀螺振子　gyrofron
驼峰辊道　hump table
驼峰链式运输机　hump chain conveyer
驼峰输送带式退火炉(不锈钢管用)　hump-back conveyer furnace
椭球形入体　ellipsoidal inclusion
椭球形掺入体　ellipsoidal inclusion
椭圆　oval, ellipse ◇成～形 ovalling, 类～型材 oval-like shape, 立～slug oval
椭圆板状粉末　oval plates powder
椭圆粗轧孔型　oval-shaped roughing pass
椭圆度[变形]　ovality
椭圆断面风口　oval-shaped tuyere
椭圆翻转装置　【压】oval turning device
椭圆-方孔型系统　【压】oval-square series [passes, sequence]

椭圆－方－椭圆孔型系统 oval-square-oval series
椭圆－方－椭圆孔型系统设计［轧制法］ oval-square-oval method
椭圆－方延伸孔型系统 oval-square breakdown sequence
椭圆钢 oval shape
椭圆钢丝 oval wire
椭圆格子砖 【钢】Moll checker
椭圆拱 elliptic(al) arch
椭圆股钢丝绳 oval strand wire rope
椭圆管 oval tube
椭圆－假圆孔型 oval-bastard round pass
椭圆尖头拱 elliptical pointed arch
椭圆矩形翅片管 elliptical rectangle fin pipe
椭圆孔型 oval pass [groove], oval ◇ 凹底～*, 成品前～ leading oval pass, 粗轧～pre-oval, 精轧～finishing oval pass, 立～off-round pass, 双圆弧～*
椭圆孔型外围盘 oval repeater
椭圆－立椭圆孔型系统 【压】oval-slug [oval-edge-oval] sequence
椭圆扭转导板 oval turner [twister]
椭圆体 ellipsoid, spheroid
椭圆头螺钉 oval head screw
椭圆－椭圆孔型系统 oval-oval series
椭圆－椭圆孔型系统设计［轧制法］ oval-oval-oval method

椭圆型材 oval shape
椭圆形 ovality, elliptic shape
椭圆形的 oval-shaped, elliptic(al)
椭圆形断面 elliptical section
椭圆形股 oval strand
椭圆形股钢丝绳 oval [elliptical] strand rope
椭圆形孔冲模板 oblong-punched plate
椭圆形连铸机 【钢】oval bow machine
椭圆形绳股 oval strand
椭圆形绳股钢丝绳 oval [elliptical] strand rope
椭圆形压勺 oval spoon
椭圆－圆孔型系统 oval-round sequence ◇ 用导板的～oval-round guide passes
椭圆－圆－椭圆孔型系统 oval-round-oval series
椭圆－圆－椭圆孔型系统设计［轧制法］ oval-round-oval method
椭圆轧槽 oval groove
拓扑(结构,学) topology
拓扑法 topological approach
拓扑密堆积[密排]结构 TCP (topologically close-packet) structure ◇ 过渡金属合金的～*
拓扑密排(结构)相 TCP phases
拓扑学模型 topological model
拓扑约束 topological constraint
拓扑约束 topological constraint

W w

挖槽 grooving, ploughing
挖槽机 groover,【建】channel(l)er
挖出料 borrow
挖出土壤 spoil
挖出物 dredging
挖方 excavation, cut ◇ 借土～ borrow cut, 隧道两端～ approach cutting, 引桥[引道,桥头]～ approach cutting
挖方工程 excavation
挖方和填方 cut-and-fill
挖沟机 ditch-and-trench excavator, ditcher, trench digger, side scraper ◇ 多斗～*
挖沟者[工人] ditcher
挖浇口铁片 【铸】gate cutter
挖掘 excavation, digging, dredging ◇ 台阶式～*
挖掘半径 digging radius
挖掘工 digger
挖掘机 excavator, excavating [digging] machine, digger, dredger, scraper ◇ 铲式～*, 斗轮～*, 索斗～* dragline excavator, 梯式～ ladder excavator, 柱坑～ posthole digger
挖空的空间 gob
挖孔板 cored slab
挖泥 dredge, dredging
挖泥槽(鼓风炉炼锌的) dredge tank
挖泥船 dredge(r), bagger, drag boat ◇ 袋匙式～*, 链斗式～ ladder dredge
挖泥斗(挖泥船的) dredge hopper
挖泥机 dredge(r),【建】bagger ◇ 柴油～ diesel dredge, 单斗[枸斗]～ dipper dredger, 混合～*, 轮式～ wheel dredger, 铣轮式～ cutter-head dredge, 抓斗式～*
挖砂 【铸】cutting-out, coping out
挖土 earth cutting, excavation,【建】cut ◇ 大规模～ bulk excavation
挖土工程 earth excavation
挖土滑运槽 excavating chute
挖土机 excavator, shovelling machine, earth mover ◇ 步行式～ walker excavator, 电动旋转式～*, 吊杆～ boom excavator, 反铲～*, 拉铲～ dragline, 链斗式～*, 履带式～*, 三瓣式[四瓣式]戽斗～ orange-peel excavator, 拖铲～ drag shovel, 正反铲～ convertible shovel
挖土机手 pitman, boom cat
蛙式打夯机 frog rammer
瓦格纳装饰用锡基空心铸造合金(10Sb, 3Zn, 1Cu, 1Bi, 余量 Sn) Wagner's alloy
瓦格纳金属铸造机 Wagner casting machine
瓦格纳浊度计 Wagner turbidimeter
瓦工镘 brick trowel
瓦赫尔锌基轴承合金(75Zn, 18Sn, 4.5Pb, 2.5Sb) Vaucher's alloy
瓦解 disintegration, disorganization
瓦科尔耐热玻璃 Vycor glass
瓦科尔(耐热玻璃)电解槽(熔盐电解用) Vycor cell
瓦科尔耐热玻璃管 Vycor tube
瓦科尔硼硅酸钠硬质玻璃 Vycor
瓦科尔熔池辐射高温计 Warchol pyrometer
瓦克－梅尔特(镍铬电热)合金(15—20Cr, 60—77.5Ni, 0—7Mo, 1—4Mn, 0.5—10.5Fe) Vac-Melt
瓦克岩 wacke
瓦兰水银扩散泵 Waran's pump
瓦里卷线机 【压】Vari-coil
瓦灵顿式钢丝绳 Warrington wire rope
瓦垄板 corrugated plate ◇ 齐洛伊锌基合金～*
瓦垄板辊压机 【压】corrugating [curving] machine
瓦垄板辊压作业线 corrugating line
瓦垄(板)机座 【压】corrugating stand
瓦垄板轧机 corrugating [corrugation] rolling mill, corrugator

瓦垄薄板　corrugated sheet ◇ 镀锌~*
瓦垄(薄)钢板　corrugated steel sheel, corrugated iron (c.i.), corrugated sheet steel [iron], undulated sheet iron, roofing iron
瓦垄辊(瓦垄面镇压器)　corrugated roller
瓦垄黑铁薄板　corrugated black sheet
瓦垄石棉板　corrugated asbestos plates
瓦垄石棉水泥屋面　【建】corrugated asbestos cement roofing
瓦垄形金属板　corrugated metal
瓦垄形金属薄板　corrugated sheet metal
瓦垄轧辊(轧制瓦垄板用)　corrugating roll
瓦曼压入式硬度计　Warman penetrascope
瓦纳纽姆耐蚀铸造铝合金(80Al, 14Zn, 5Cu, 0.75Fe, 0.25V)　vanalium
瓦尼特易焊锰钢　Vanity steel
瓦纽科夫联合鼓泡炉　Vanyukov combined bubbling furnace
瓦纽科夫熔炼法　Vanukov smelting process
瓦硼镁钙石　wardsmithite
瓦片式炉壳结构　【铁】shingle shell construction
瓦片填充塔　tile-packed column
瓦时计　watt-hour meter
瓦斯　gas ◇ 矿井~damp
瓦斯爆炸　gas shot [explosion]
瓦斯灰量　【铁】dust rate
瓦斯继电器　gas relay
瓦斯检测继电器　gas detector relay
瓦斯煤　fiery [bottle, gas-making, gas-producer] coal
瓦斯帕洛伊变形镍基耐热合金(19Cr, 14Co, 4Mo, 3Ti, 1.3Al, 1Fe, 0.1C, 微量 B+Zr, 余量 Ni)　Waspalloy
瓦特表[计]　wattmeter ◇ 高低档~high low wattmeter, 累计~ totalizing wattmeter
瓦特传感器　watt transmitter
瓦特光亮镀镍溶液　watt solution
瓦特曼色层分离滤纸　Whatman's paper

瓦铜矿　tile ore
瓦屋面　tile roof ◇ 联锁~*
瓦檐饰　antaefixae, cheneau
瓦闸　shoe [block] brake
歪扭　(a)skew
歪扭变形　warping
歪斜　obliqueness, obliquity, skewness
歪斜度　【压】out-of-squareness
外半径　outside radius (OR), external [outer] radius
外保温帽　outer hot top
外边　overside (O.S.), fringe
外边界　outer edge
外表检查　visual examination
外表面　external surface [face]
外表特征　physical appearance
外部标号　external label
外部操作　auxiliary operation
外部测量　external measurement
外部尺寸　external dimension
外部处理机　peripheral processor
外部传送　peripheral transfer
外部存储程序　externally stored program
外部存储器　external memory [storage]
外部调用　【计】external reference
外部堆栈　【计】outside stockpile
外部符号　【计】external symbol
外部符号字典　【计】external symbol dictionary (ESD)
外部焊缝　outside seam
外部函数　external function
外部加热介质　external heating medium
外部接口适配器　【计】peripheral interface adapter (PIA)
外部隔[绝]热材料　insulating back-up material
外部苛化　external [outside] causticizaiton
外部冷却介质　external cooling medium
外部冷却器　external cooler, 【铁】external chill
外部冷却水管　【铁】external cooling passage

外部料场[贮矿场] outside stockpile
外部排料压滤机 open-discharge filter press
外部喷水冷却 external spray cooling
外部缺陷 external [surface] defect
外部热交换介质 external heat exchange medium
外部热损失 external heat loss
外部润滑 external lubrication
外部洒水冷却 shower external cooling
外部设备 external device [equipment, unit], peripheral (equipment)
外部设备操作数 external device operand
外部设备接口通道 peripheral interface channel
外部设备控制 【计】external device control
外部设备数据流 【计】external device data flow
外部设备通信 【计】external device communication
外部设备指令 【计】external device instruction
外部设备中断 external device interrupt
外部水分 exteraneous moisture
外部水冷风口带 external water-cooled tuyere belt
外部缩孔 【钢】exterior [major] shrinkage
外部形状 exterior shape
外部旋流转换器 external vortex transformer
外部循环空气混合阀 mixing flap for outside-recirculated air
外部引用 【计】external reference
外部运算 【计】external arithmetic
外部振捣器 external [form] vibrator
外部中断 【计】external interrupt
外部中断状态 external interrupt sfatus
外部子程序 【计】external subroutine
外层 outer layer [skin]
外层电子 outer(-shell) electron ◇失去~的原子 stripped atom

外层电子排列[组态] outer electron configuration
外层钢板壁 outer steel plate wall
外层钢丝(钢丝绳的) cover [crown] wire
外层火焰 outer [envelope] flame
外层支承辊(十二辊和二十辊轧机的) caster roll
外插法 extrapolation (method)
外差的[法] heterodyne
外差电路 heterodyne circuit
外差振荡器 heterodyne (oscillator)
外衬 outer lining, outside liner
外承轮轨 easer rail
外齿式联轴节 outer toothed coupling
外传动辊式地下卷取机 surface-driven expanding type downcoiler
外传力法预应力 prestress without bond
外电路 external circuit
外电阻 external resistance (ER)
外镀层 (同"外涂层")
外二次线圈 out secondary (O.S.)
外翻(突缘) neck-out
外赋传导率 extrinsic conductivity
外感应器 OD heating coil
外功 external work
外观检查[检验] visual test, outer inspection
外观体积 apparent solid volume
外观图 appearance view, outside drawing
外光电效应 photoemissive effect, external photoeffect
外国公司 foreign company [corporation], alien corporation
外国证券 【企】foreign securities
外裹焦粉的 coke-coated
外裹煤粉圆筒机 coal coating drum
外焊缝 outside weld
外弧半径 external radius
外弧电炉 electric furnace with arc external to bath
外环箍 【机】outer rim

外环油封	【机】outer ring seal
外汇风险	exchange risk
外汇市场	【企】foreign exchange market
外汇稳定基金	exchange stabilization fund
外混合	external mixing
外极发电机	out-pole generator
外加场	applied field
外加电压	applied [impressed] voltage
外加负载	applied load
外加功	applied work
外加厚	external-upset (EU)
外加厚油管	external-upset tubing
外加还原剂	external reactant
外加缓凝剂	set-retarding admixture
外加剂	external reactant, admixture
外加力	applied force
外加燃料纯氧炼钢法[工艺]	oxygen-fuel steelmaking operation
外加热线圈	OD heating coil
外加碳	external carbon
外加推力	applied thrust
外加应力	applied stress
外浇口	【铸】pouring cup [basin], basin ◇ 池形～runner basin, 盘形～pouring disc
外角	quoin
外角墁刀	【铸】outside corner slick
外接圆	circumscribing circle
外界还原剂	outside reducing agent
外界面	outer boundary
外界条件	external condition
外界温度	(同"环境温度")
外界压力	ambient pressure
外静态特性曲线	external static characteristic
外径	outside diameter (OD), external diameter, outer diameter
外径(量)规	external [snap, horseshoe] gauge
外径千分尺[测微计]	outside micrometer
外卷边	beaded edge, stretch flanging
外卡规[尺]	outside cal(l)iper, horseshoe gauge
外卡钳	calipers
外科工具用钢	surgical steel
外壳	shell, hull, (outer) skin, encasing, enclosure, envelope, housing, jacket, sheathing, outer casing ◇ 软～bladder
外壳壁	shell wall
外壳材料	sheathing material, canning material (释热元件的)
外壳分离	【连铸】separation of skin
外壳高度(转炉的)	height of shell
外壳接地电路	hull return circuit
外壳结构	shell construction
外壳可抽出式混凝土桩	peerless pile
外壳破裂	shell rupture
外壳硬化	skin solidification
外壳占有电子	electron [shell] occupancy
外壳直径	diameter of shell
外廓尺寸	overall dimension
外来电子	out-coming electron
外来非金属夹杂物	【冶】exogenous non-metallic inclusion
外来夹杂	【钢】foreign inclusion
外来熟料	foreign grog
外来物质	foreign material [matter, substance], extraneous material
外来原子	foreign [stranger] atom
外来原子与位错间流体静压力相互作用	hydrostatic interaction between foreign atoms and dislocations
外来杂质	foreign [exogenous] impurities
外雷宾德尔效应(有关金属强度的)	external Rehbinder effect
外冷凝器	external [outer] condenser
外冷却套	externally cooled jacket
外冷铁	【铸】external chill
外力	external [outside, applied, superposed] force
外力溶解	heterolysis
外力图面积	area of force
外流气流	out-flowing gas stream
外露部分(焊条)	free length
外露岩石	day stone

外螺纹　male [external] thread
外螺纹梳刀　outside chaser
外螺纹锥度卡规　external-thread taper caliper
外貌　(visual) appearance, habit
外面焊缝　outside weld
外模　encasing, external mold
外膜　coat
外摩擦　external friction
外摩擦系数　coefficient of external friction
外能　external energy
外能级　outer (energy) level
外啮合　external gearing [toothing]
外排　【环】outfall
外排废水达标率　compliance with waste water discharge limitation
外排油孔　【机】outer drain
外皮　outer skin, facing, crust, sheath, braid (电缆的)
外皮层(钢锭的)　skin zone
外皮偏析　【钢】skin [rim] segregate
外墙　outer [exposed] wall
外切圆　circumscribing circle
外燃式热风炉　【铁】external-combustion (hot) stove ◇迪德～·, 马琴～M-P hot stove
外燃室　【铁】external [separate] combustion chamber
外热器　external heater
外热式竖炉　indirect heated shaft
外森贝格底片　Weissenberg film
外森贝格测角仪　Weissenberg goniometer
外森贝格型移动底片测角仪　Weissenberg(-type) moving film goniometer
外森贝格照相法　【理】Weissenberg method
外森贝格照相机　Weissenberg camera
外蛇管　external [outer] coil
外伸臂　overhanging arm
外伸炉(燃烧室)　extension furnace
外伸曲柄　overhung [side] crank
外伸燃烧室　external furnace

外伸式蒸汽锤　overhanging-type steam hammer
外伸轴承　outside bearing
外视图　appearance [external] view
外收缩制动带　external contracting band
外水口　【连铸】outer nozzle
外送运输机　outlet [run-out] conveyor
外胎　cover tyre
外套　jacket, shell, coat
外套围裙　wrapover apron
外通孔　accessible porosity
外凸弧(钢锭模边)　camber
外涂层　external [outside] coating, outer coat, topcoat
外推法　extrapolation (method)
外推距离　extrapolation distance
外围电子　peripheral electron
外围控制器　【计】peripheral control
外围设备　peripheral (equipment)
外围支援计算机　peripheral support computer
外斜斜度(炉身的)　【铁】outward batter
外形　appearance, (external) form, contour, configuration, outline, profile, 【压】boundary (轧槽孔型的)
外形草图　outline sketch
外形尺寸　overall dimension (o.a.d.), overall size, external dimension
外形偏差　deviation from contour
外形缺陷　shape defect
外形轧制　【压】contour rolling
外压(力)　external pressure
外延层　epitaxial layer
外延淀积　epitaxial deposition
外延硅　epitaxial silicon
外延结　【半】epitaxial junction
外延扩散法　epitaxial diffused method
外延气相生长　epitaxial vapour growth
外延生长　epitaxial growth, epitaxy
外延生长基底　epitaxial substrate
外延生长结　epitaxially grown junction
外延生长膜　epitaxial film

外延位错 epitaxial dislocation
外逸电子 outgoing electron, exoelectron
外溢 overtop
外应变 external strain
外应力 external stress
外圆角 bullnose, bull's nose
外圆角光子 （同"外角曼刀"）
外圆磨床 【机】cylindrical grinder
外圆磨削 【机】cylindrical [external, OD] grinding
外源凝固(铸件的) exogenous freezing
外缘[沿] outer edge ◇ 翻~成形法【压】flange forming
外运堆栈 stockpiling area for shipment
外在体积 exterior volume
外债 outstanding loan
外罩 outer cover, housing
外指示剂 external [outside] indicator
外置[伸]轴承 outboard [outborne, outer, outside] bearing
外周 circumference
外装的 out-board
外子程序 【计】external subroutine
外阻(力) external resistance (ER)
外座圈 outer race
豌豆粒烧结矿 "pea" sinter
弯板机 plate bending machine, sheet bending machine (薄板用), bending rolls ◇ 切线~tangent bender, 卧式~*
弯棒式搅拌器 bent rod type stirrer
弯边 crimp, crimping (大直径直缝焊管的), bosse, crease ◇ 扩孔~【压】burring
弯边板材 flanged plate
弯边锤 creasing [seam] hammer
弯边工序 【压】flanging operation
弯边机 edging [joggling] machine, beader (板材的)
弯边压力机 flanger, flanging machine [press], joggling press, folding and seaming press ◇ 钢丝~wiring press
弯边装置 edge former, beader
弯柄扳手 cranked spanner

弯成U形 U-ing
弯成O[圆]形 O-ing
弯成弓形 bowing
弯成钩形 hooking
弯道 bend, curve, cam track
弯度 bending(ing) deflection, flexure ◇ 预留~*
弯度指示计 deflection indicator
弯钢机 bulldozer
弯钢筋 bar bending
弯钢筋工具 bending iron
弯拱 camber arch, hog(ging)
弯钩钢筋 【建】hooked bar, bar with hooked ends
弯管 bent pipe [tube], (pipe) bend, elbow (pipe), knee,【铁】swan neck ◇ S形~swan neck, goose-neck, 风口小~【铁】bootleg
弯管分离器 elbow separator
弯管机 pipe bender, pipe [tube] bending machine
弯管收[集]尘器 elbow separator
弯管加工 bent tubing
弯管用合金(低熔点) bend metal [alloy]
弯轨 curved rail
弯轨机 rail bender, rail bending [cambering] machine
弯轨压力机 rail bending press
弯辊 roll bending
弯辊机 roll bending machine
弯辊系统 roll bending system
弯辊装置 bending up roll device (BURD), roll bending equipment
弯合试验(厚钢板180°) book test
弯角砧(金属制品用) dresser
弯结晶体 kinked crystal
弯筋表 bending list
弯晶 bent [curved] crystal
弯晶单色器 bent [curved] crystal monochromator, curved monochromator crystal ◇ 磨光聚焦~*, 双~*
弯晶单色器照相机 curved crystal mono-

chromator camera
弯晶分光[光谱]计 bent [curved] crystal spectrometer
弯晶摄谱仪 curved-crystal spectrograph
弯晶照相机 curved crystal camera ◇ 双重～*
弯矩图面积 bending moment area
弯力 bending force
弯梁 curved [camber] beam
弯裂[弯曲裂纹] bending crack
弯扭校直(型材的) detwisting
弯扭校直机 detwister
弯坯设备 【连铸】strand bending device
弯起钢筋 (同"斜钢筋")
弯曲 bend, bending (flexure), curve, curvature, bow(ing), flexion, flexure ◇ 连续～点阵*,向外～(边缘) neck-out,易～的 flexible
弯曲半径 bend(ing) [bevelling] radius
弯曲成型工序(板、带材的) forming operation
弯曲成形 bending forming ◇ 定心～*
弯曲成形模[工具] bending form(er)
弯曲处(曲线的) knee
弯曲垂度[变位] bending(ing) deflection
弯曲次数 bend number
弯曲度 flexibility ◇ 绝对～absolute deflection
弯曲断裂 bending failure [rupture]
弯曲断裂模量[系数] modulus of rupture in bending
弯曲-反弯曲试验 test by bending and unbending
弯曲负载 bending load
弯曲钢筋 bent (up) bar
弯曲工具 bender, flector
弯曲工作台 bending horse
弯曲固定装置 bending fixture
弯曲刮料板 【团】curved plow plate
弯曲管 curved pipe
弯曲辊 bending roller
弯曲过度 overbending

弯曲机 bender, bending [cambering] machine ◇ 轨梁～beam-and-rail bender,辊式～*
弯曲机工 bender
弯曲机夹头 bending head
弯曲夹具 bending jig
弯曲角 bend(ing) angle, angularity
弯曲晶体 (同"弯晶")
弯曲抗力 bending resistance
弯曲孔型 bending pass
弯曲力 bending force
弯(曲力)矩 bending moment (b.m.), moment of flexure 等效～*
弯曲轮辐(整轧车轮的) coning
弯曲面 bend plane
弯曲模 bending die ◇ 风动～air bend die
弯曲模槽(模具的) snaker
弯曲模量[模数] bending [flexural] modulus
弯曲模膛 bender(锻造的), breakdown die
弯曲内裂 internal bending crack
弯曲疲劳(钢丝绳的) bending [flexural] fatigue
弯曲疲劳强度 bending fatigue resistance
弯曲疲劳试验 bending fatigue test, repeated bend test ◇ 旋转～*
弯曲疲劳试验机 fatigue bending machine
弯曲疲劳试样 fatigue [endurance] bending test specimen
弯曲(疲劳)寿命 reverse bending failure life (RBFL), flex(ing) [flexible] life
弯曲器 bending apparatus ◇ 钢筋～bar bender
弯曲钳口 bending jaw
弯曲强度 bend strength
弯曲屈服点 【压】bending yield point
弯曲韧性 bend toughness
弯曲蠕变试验 bending creep test
弯曲-伸直试验 bending and unbending test
弯曲矢度 camber

弯曲试验 bend(ing) test, bend over test ◇ 奥地利~*，闭合~*，反复~*，交变缺口~*，康默莱尔~*，三点载荷~*，试棒~ bar bend test, 托尔-马歇尔~ Tour-Marshall test, 正面导向~*，纵向~*

弯曲试验机 bend [flex] tester, machine for bending test ◇ 往复~*

弯曲试验试样 bending test piece

弯曲试验台 bending trestle

弯曲试验装置 bending jig

弯曲试样 bending test piece

弯曲塑性 bend(ing) ductility

弯曲弹性 elasticity of bending [flexure], flexibility

弯曲位错 bent [curved] dislocation

弯曲芯棒[心轴] bending mandrel

弯曲型芯 snake core

弯曲性 bendability

弯曲性能 bending property

弯曲性试验 pliability test

弯曲压力机 bending press ◇ U形~*

弯曲岩盐晶体 curved-rocksalt crystal ◇ 圆柱形~*

弯曲样板 bending form(er)

弯曲样板直径 bending former diameter

弯曲摇杆 curved rocker

弯曲叶片 inclined [camber] blade

弯曲阴极 bent cathode

弯曲应变 bending [transverse] strain

弯曲应力 bending stress

弯曲应力强度 intensity of bending stress

弯曲用锤 paring hammer

弯曲轧制法 （同"蝶形轧制法"）

弯曲振动 bending vibration

弯曲支承辊组 bending backup roller set

弯曲轴线 axis of bending

弯曲装置 bender, bending device [apparatus] ◇ 母线~*

弯曲装置垫片 bending device gasket

弯－伸试验 bending and unbending test

弯头 elbow (pipe), (knee) bend, 【铁】bootleg ◇ 45°~*, 90°[直角]~*

弯头扳手 bent [crank] spanner, bent wrench

弯头搭接 set lap joint

弯头接合 elbow [toggle] joint

弯头螺钉用含铅黄铜（含 1—1.5Pb） clinching screw wire

弯腿台（焊接工字钢的） flange turning table

弯斜（坯料或板材的） cobble

弯心（弯曲试验用） pin

弯压模 bending die ◇ 复式~*

弯液面 liquid [water] meniscus

弯圆边压力机 circular flanging press

弯月面 (liquid) meniscus, meniscus level （钢水的）

弯月面流 meniscus flow

弯月形金属液面 【冶】meniscus

弯折 fold, fluting, kink

弯折点 break(ing) point

弯折法孔型设计（角钢的） flat and edge design

弯折辊（板、带材的） flexing roll

弯折机（钢筋的） crimper, bar folder

弯折应力（成 180°角） folding stress

弯直辊 debending [deflecting, deflector] roll

弯制型钢 joist webs

弯皱 crimp

弯嘴龙头 bib(cock)

剜边剪 side clipping shears

顽磁 【理】magnetic retentivity [remanence], remanency

顽磁性 (magnetic) retentivity

顽辉[火]石 $\{(Mg, Fe)SiO_3\}$ enstatite

顽金（混汞法难回收的） refractory gold

烷撑 alkylene

烷基{R} alkyl radical (AlK.), alkyl

烷基氨基硅烷 alkyl aminosilane

烷基胺（烷基取代的）{RN} alkyl(substituted)amine

烷基胺萃取剂 alkylamine extractant

烷基次膦酸 {$R_2 \cdot PO(OH)_2$} alkyl phosphinic acid
烷基甲酸 {$RHCO_2$} alkyl formate
烷基碱金属 alkali alkyl
烷基金属 metal alkyl
烷基磷酸 {$R \cdot PO(OH)_3$} alkylphophoric acid
烷基膦酸 {$R \cdot PO(OH)_2$} alkylphosphonic acid
烷基铝 aluminum alkyl
烷基硫酸 {RSO_4H} alkyl sulphuric acid
烷基脲 alkyl urea
烷基酰胺 alkyl-amide
烷基锌 zinc alkyl
烷基有机磷化合物 alkyl organophosphorus compound
烷烃 poraffin
烷氧基锆 {$Zr(OR)_4$} zirconium alkoxide
烷氧基铪 {$Hf(OR)_4$} hafnium alkoxide
完成 completion, finish, accomplish, fulfil, round
完成反应 complete reaction
完工温度(热加工的) finishing temperature
完工直径 finishing diameter
完好程度 soundness
完好晶体 well-defined crystal
完好率 availability
完美晶体 perfect crystal
完全奥氏体化 complete austenitizing
完全焙烧 complete [dead, ultimate] roasting, thorough burning
完全长程有序 perfect long-range order
完全程度 degree of completion
完全淬火[硬] full hardening
完全淬火成马氏体钢的最大硬度 maximum martensitic hardness of steel
完全淬透性 throughout hardenability
完全淬硬的 【金】hardened throughout
完全单色的 perfectly monochromatic
完全冻结 complete freezing
完全短路 dead short(-circuit)

完全反应 complete reaction
完全分离 clean separation
完全浮选法 【选】all-flotation
完全固溶体 (同"无限固溶体")
完全焊透 complete [good] penetration
完全合金化粉末 completely alloyed powder
完全互溶性 【金】complete miscibility
完全还原 complete reduction
完全挥发 full flashing
完全混合 complete [perfect] mixing
完全混合过程 complete mixing process
完全混合流 complete mixing flow
完全混合曝气系统 completely mixed aeration system
完全混溶性 【金】complete miscibility
完全冷淬 dead-cold chlling
完全冷却烧结矿 【选】illy cooled sinter
完全凝固 complete freezing
完全扭曲 complete twist
完全偏析 【金】complete segregation
完全破坏 eventual failure
完全气化 complete gassification
完全燃烧 complete [overall, perfect] combustion, completeness of combustion, thorough burning
完全热处理 full heat treatment
完全熔合[熔化] complete fusion
完全熔化的 clear-melted
完全熔透 【焊】good penetration
完全软化 complete softening
完全时效 full aging
完全水化水泥 completely hydrated cement
完全塑性 perfect plasticity
完全塑性金属 perfectly plastic metal
完全塑性体 perfectly plastic solid
完全酸洗薄板 full pickled sheet
完全弹性 perfect elasticity
完全弹性的 perfectly elastic
完全停机 【计】(drop-)dead halt
完全退火 complete [dead(-full), dead-

soft, full, true] annealing
完全退火低碳钢(＜0.15C) dead-soft steel
完全脱硫 complete disulphurization
完全脱水冰晶石 fully dehydrated cryolite
完全稳定状态 fully stabilized condition
完全无序 【理】complete disorder
完全性 completeness, integrity
完全氧化 complete oxidation
完全氧化混合物 fully oxidized mixture
完全氧化活性污泥法 【环】complete oxidation activated sludge process
完全氧化球 fully oxidized pellet
完全硬化组织 【金】completely hardened structure
完全有序 【理】complete ordering
完全有序(化)相 completely ordered phase
完全有序结构 perfectly ordered structure
完全再结晶 complete recrystallization
完全再生 full regeneration, highly efficient regeneration
完全真空 perfect vacuum
完全自动的 full automatic
完善 perfect, integrity
完整 perfection, roundness
完整材料 【理】perfect [good] material
完整程度 degree of completion
完整程序 【计】complete routine
完整点阵[晶格] perfect lattice
完整度 degree of perfection
完整晶体 perfect [well-defined] crystal
完整位错 perfect dislocation
完整性 perfection, integrity
完整油膜润滑 full film lubrication
碗模(焊管用) welding bell
碗形磁钢[铁] bowl-shaped magnet
碗形填料 【机】cup-type packing
碗状炉床(电炉的) bowl hearth
晚班 night [afternoon, back] shift
万分之一(含碳) 【钢】point
万能扳手 universal screw-key

万能表 【电】universal meter
万能补偿器 universal compensator
万能材料试验机 universal testing machine ◇ 奥尔森[杠杆]式~*
万能插孔 consent
万能断面控制 universal profile control
万能缝[滚]焊机 universal seam welder
万能[通用]钢板 universal steel plate
万能工作台 universal table
万能滚焊头 universal electrode wheel head
万能机械手 universal manipulator
万能剪切机 multipurpose [shearing machine, shears]
万能胶 universal glue
万能接头 universal contacf
万能卡盘[夹头] universal chuck
万能可逆式粗轧机 universal reversing roughing mill
万能孔型 universal groove
万能拉伸试验机 universal tensile testing machine
万能起重机 universal crane
万能强度试验机 universal strength tester
万能式扁坯初轧机 universal slabbing mill
万能式粗轧机 universal roughing mill
万能式钢梁轧机 universal beam mill
万能式轨梁轧机 universal structural mill
万能式精轧机座 universal finishing stand
万能式十字形辊模头 universal turkshead
万能式轧机机座 【压】universal mill stand
万能式中厚板轧机 universal plate mill
万能试验机(万能材料试验机) universal testing machine
万能输送机 all-round conveyer
万能凸度轧机 universal crown mill
万能推床 【压】universal manipulator
万能脱模起重机 【钢】universal stripper crane
万能挖泥机 universal dredger
万能弯管机 universal bender

万能铣床 universal miller
万能显微复型印制法（铃木式） Sump method, Suzuki's universal micro-printing method
万能型钢轧机 universal section mill
万能行星式轧机 【压】universal planetary mill
万能仪（表） multipurpose [all-purpose general-purpose, universal] instrument
万能运输机 all-round transporter
万能载物台显微镜 universal stage microscope
万能轧机 universal mill ◇ 平-立辊~*, 十字型四辊~ sack mill
万能轧制 universal rolling
万能照相机 universal camera
万能装卸车 【机】fork lift ◇ 带卷~ coil car [buggy]
万能装卸机 power truck, universal crane ◇ 叉式~*, 地行~ floor truck, 龙门式~*, 台车式~ platform truck, 抓斗式~ grab truck
万能装置 multipurpose plant
万能（自动）装卸机 straddle carrier
万向吊环 shackle hook
万向接头 universal joint, joint-coupling, gimbal, knuckle
万向接轴 universal (joint) spindle, universal shaft ◇ 十字头式~*
万向接轴扁头 coupling half, spindle tongue
万向节[头] universal [cardan] joint
万向联轴节 universal (joint) coupling, universal spindle coupling, star coupling, 【机】cardan universal joint
万向支架 gimbals
万亿（= 10^{12}） billion（英,德）, trillion（美、法）
万用（电）表 multimeter, avometer, universal meter ◇ 数字~ digital multimeter
万有引力 gravity, gravitation
万元产值能耗 energy consumption per RMB 10 thousand output value
汪纳高温计 Wanner's pyrometer
汪纳光测高温计 Wanner optical pyrometer
王水 aqua regia (aq. reg.), nitro-muriatic [chloroazotic] acid
王水溶解 aqua-regia dissolution
王子（锡锑）合金（15—25Sb, 84.75Sn） Prince's alloy
王笏黄铜 sceptre brass
网 mesh, net(ting), strainer, 【冶】mapping ◇ 乌里弗~【理】Wulff's net
网疤 【冶】veining
网带式炉 (wire) mesh belt furnace
网带式退火炉 netted belt-conveyor furnace
网钢丝 netting wire
网格 lattice, net, mesh, grid, grill(e)
网格法 grid method ◇ 应变测量~*
网格运动 mesh moving
网格运动法 method of mesh moving
网格状枝晶 【金】cellular dendrite
网格组织 cancellation
网环形接线 mesh connection
网际协议 internet protocol
网路 network, grid
网路电压 supply voltage
网络 network, mesh(work), graph ◇ 分布式~*, 集中式~*, 四端~组成的线路 circuit network
网络电压 mesh voltage
网络分析 network analysis
网络模拟 【计】network analog
网络拓扑图 【计】network topology
网络系统 network system ◇ 过程计算机~*
网络信息中心 network information center
网络型专家系统 【计】expert system based on artificial network
网络运行中心 metwork operation center
网络终端装置 【计】network terminating

unit (NTU)
网络状亚晶界结构 veining (structure) ◇ α~α-veining
网(脉凸)疤 【冶】veining, mapping
网膜读出器 【计】retina character reader
网目 mesh, screen, sieve number, reticulation
网目尺寸 mesh size
网(目)筛 mesh sieve
网屏 screen
网勺 wire-screen ladle
网式过滤器 (同"筛网过滤器")
网式运输机(镀锌用) spangle conveyer
网纹 overlapping curve, cob-webbing, 【钢】crazing, wove mesh (电镀锌板缺陷) ◇ 绒毛状~*
网纹板 floor plate
网纹钢 checkered [riffled] iron
网纹钢板 checker(ed) plate (C.PL.), checker(ed) sheet, checker(ed) steel plate, steel checker(ed) plate, riffled (steel) sheet ◇ 菱形~*
网纹钢板轧机 【压】checker (plate) mill
网纹钢板轧制 【压】checker plate rolling
网纹轧辊 【压】knurled roll
网形反馈装置 web feeding device
网形接线 mesh connection
网眼 mesh
网眼薄钢板 expanded sheet metal
网眼钢板[网形钢板, 网形铁] 【建】expanded metal (xpm)
网眼钢皮(抹灰用) perforated sheet lath
网眼密度 reticular density ◇ 最大~平面*
网眼状结构 areolar structure
网眼状位错 【金】cellular metwork of dislocations
网印 wire mark, 【钢】crazing
网状包丝药皮焊条 braided electrode
网状法 【理】cellular method
网状反应 【金】cellular reaction
网状钢板 checkered sheet

网状钢筋 steel mesh reinforcement
网状构造 cellular structure
网状结构[组织] net (work) [framework, reticulated] structure, reticulation, 【金】knitted[reticular] structure, reseau
网状裂纹 resillage
网状排列 netlike arrangement
网状屈氏体 troostite metwork
网状渗碳体 cementite network
网状碳化物 carbide network, net [reticulated] carbide
网状填充环 gauze rings
网状铁素体 【金】ferrite net (work)
网状物 network, mesh, reticulation
网状线 cross hatching
网状线圈 honeycomb(ed) coil
网状组织形成元素 network former
网状组织抑制元素 network modifier
往返互换提纯器 reciprocating refiner
往返运输 shuttle traffic
往复板式给料机 reciprocating plate feeder
往复动载试验机 【金】alternating impact machine
往复反应 reciprocal reaction
往复杆 reciprocating lever, 【机】balance beam
往复刮板运输机 reciprocating flight conveyor
往复焊接电极 reciprocating welding electrode
往复加热器(区域熔炼的) reciprocating heater
往复平移梁式输送机 reciprocating-beam type transfer
往复曲折变形[应变] crippling strain
往复曲折应力 crippling stress
往复燃烧 reverse combustion
往复式泵 displacement [reciprocating] pump
往复式飞剪 reciprocating type flying shears

往复式鼓风机　reciprocating blower
往复式刮刀[燕翅杆]　reciprocating cutter bar, reciprocating scraper
往复式锯　reciprocating (type) saw, shuttle saw, sliding (frame) saw
往复式孔板萃取器　reciprocating plate extractor [column]
往复式深井泵　deep well reciprocating pump
往复式脱模(起重)机　【钢】push-pull stripper crane
往复式运输机　reciprocating conveyer
往复式轧机　reciprocating rolling mill
往复式装船机　shuttling shiploader
往复弯曲试验机　forward and backward bending tester
往复运动　advance and return movement, back and forth motion [movement], reciprocal [reciprocating, jigging, to-and-fro] motion, reciprocation
往复运动结晶器　【连铸】reciprocated mould ◇ 具有负滑脱的～reciprocated mould operating with negative strip
往复运动循环(连铸结晶器的)　reciprocation cycle
往复折曲　crippling
往复振动式结晶器　oscillating mould
往复振实[摇实]容积　reciprocal tap volume
望板　【建】skin plate, roof boarding
威贝格直接还原法　Wiberg process
威恩含铅黄铜(28—35Zn, 2—2.3Ni, 0.5—1Pb, 0—0.5Fe, 62—68Cu)　Winn bronze
威尔顿管式炉　Wilton still
威尔弗莱型摇床　Wilfley [shaking] table
威尔科恒温器合金　Wilco alloy
威尔米尔共晶型铝硅合金(含13.5Si)　Wilmil
威尔浦式焦炉　Wilputte oven
威尔逊云雾室　fog chamber, Wilson cloud chamber

威克斯淤浆溶剂萃取法　waxco process
威廉条材连铸法　William's (continuous) process
威帕拉镍铬钢　Wipla
微胞　micell(a)e
微变形晶体　lightly deformed crystal
微标度　micro-scale
微波　microwave, hyper frequency wave, ripple
微波波长　microwave wavelength
微波测距仪　tellurometer
微波电路　microwave circuit
微波辐射计　microwave radiometer
微波干涉仪　microwave interferometer
微波光谱学　microwave spectrosopy
微波激射(器)　maser (microwave amplification by stimulated emission of radiation)
微波技术　microwave technique
微波继电器　microwave relay ◇ 方向比较式～*
微波鉴频器　microwave discriminator
微波区　microwave region
微波全息术　microwave holography
微波湿度计　microwave moisture meter
微补强对接焊　slightly reinforced butt welding
微操作　【计】micro-operation
微称量　microweighing
微程序　【计】microprogram ◇ 可编～的microprogrammable, 直接控制～*
微程序寻址【计】microprogram addressing
微程序控制【计】microprogram control
微程序设计　microprogramming, microcoding
微程序语言　microprogramming language, firmware
微程序只读存储器　microm
微处理机　microprocessor, microprocessing unit, microcomputer
微磁学　micromagnetics
微存储器　【计】microstorage
微代码　【计】microcode

微电池 microcell	微粉磁铁 lodox ◇ 盖卡洛伊～Gecalloy
微电机 micro-motor, miniature motor	微粉磨机 micronizer, micron mill, micropulverizer ◇ 喷射式～jet-O-Mizer
微电子电路 microelectronic circuit	微粉球磨机 micro ball-mill
微电子束分析 electron microbeam analysis	微粉末磁铁 lodox
微电子束探示器数据 electron microbeam probe data	微辐射计 microradiometer
微电子学[技术] microelectronics	微伏计 microvoltmeter
微动 inching, jogging	微伏(特)(10^{-6}伏特) microvolt
微动传动装置 【压】inching drive device	微观 microscopy
微动度盘 slow motion dial	微观变形 microdeformation
微动继电器 inching relay	微观残余应力 (同"海恩应力")
微动开关 microswitch	微观断口 microfracture surface
微动螺钉 micrometer screw	微观断口金相学 microfractography
微动摩擦磨蚀[微动腐蚀] fretting corrosion	微观对称要素 micro-symmetry element, microscopic symmetry element
微动装置 vernier arrangement	微观法 【理】micromethod
微断裂 microcrack, microseparation	微观反应 microreaction
微多相催化作用 microheterogeneous catalysis	微观分析 microscopical analysis, microanalysis
微分测量 【电】differential measurement	微观观察 microscopic observation
微分磁导率 differential permeability	微观过程 microprocess
微分(的) 【数】differential	微观机构[机理] micromechanism
微分电路 differential circuit, peaker, differentiator	微观检查[检验] micro-examination
	微观结构变化 microstructural change
微分法 differential method	微观结构成分 microconstituent
微分反应器 differential reactor	微观金相学 microscopic metallography
微分方程 differential equation	微观力学 micromechanics
微分放大器 differential amplifier	微观裂纹 microscopic crack
微分解 【数】differential solution	微观磨片 【金】microslice
微分介电常数[微分电容率] differential dielectric constant	微观偏析 microsegregation
	微观强度 【金】microstrength
微分能量分布 differential energy distribution	微观塑性 microplasticity
	微观形变 microdeformation
微分器 differentiator	微观岩相组分 microlithotype
微分器比较器(射流技术的) differentiator comparator	微观应力 micro-stress, microscopic stress
	微观状态 microstate
微分曲线 differential curve	微管检波器 capillary detector
微分射流放大器 differential fluid amplifier	微光偏振测量 twilight polarization measurement
微分示值读数 differential readout	微光束法 microbeam method [technique]
微分(形)式 differential form	微光速 microbeam
	微含量 trace content

| 微 wei

微焊接　microwelding
微合金锻钢　micro-alloy forged steel, microalloying forging steel
微合金工艺　microalloy technology
微合金化　【金】microalloy
微合金(化)钢　microalloy steel ◇ 非调质~*, 钛~*
微合金结　【半】microalloy junction
微合金结构钢　micro-alloy structural steel
微合金耐磨钢　microalloy wear-resisting steel
微合金元素　micro-alloying element
微滑移　microslip
微划痕硬度试验计　microcharacter
微化石　microfossil
微机　microcomputer
微机静态控制　minicomputer static control system
微机控制系统　computer control system ◇ 集散型~*
微机巡检　cycle inspection by computer
微积分学　calc(ulus)
微夹杂物　microinclusions
微碱性的　alkalescent
微截面检验器　micro cross-section detector
微结晶学　microcrystallography
微晶　microcrystal(line), minicrystal, (micro)crystallite, microlite ◇ 纳米~ nanocrystal
微晶玻璃　nucleated glass, neoceramic glass, sitall
微晶玻璃复合材料　glass ceramic composite
微晶高岭石 {(OH)$_2$Al$_2$[Si$_2$O$_5$]$_2$·nH$_2$O}　montmorillonite
微晶结构　micro-crystalline structure, microstructure
微晶粒　microcrystallite, micromeritics
微晶粒度引起的增宽　broadening due to small crystal size
微晶粒合金　micro-grain alloy

微晶粒状的　microgranular, micromeritic
微晶砷铜矿　algodonite
微晶质　microcrystalline
微镜惰煤　vitrinertite
微镜煤　vitrite
微矩阵法　micro-matrix approach
微聚焦(X射线)管　microfocus tube
微刻度　micro-scale
微空洞　microvoid
微孔　microporosity, millipore, microvoid, pinhead blister
微孔洞聚集　microvoid coalescence
微孔分气法　【压】atmolysis
微孔分气仪　atmolyzer
微孔团　pore cluster
微孔性[率]　microporosity
微孔性的　microporous
微拉拔[伸]　【压】soft-drawn
微粒　particle, micron, corpuscle
微粒X射线胶片　fine grain(ed) X-ray film
微粒磁铁　fine particle magnet
微粒发射　particle [corpuscular] emission
微粒非金属夹杂　【冶】slag clouds
微粒辐射　particle [corpuscular] radiation
微粒空气分级器　infrasizer
微粒污染　pollution by particulates
微粒照相乳胶　fine grain(ed) photographic emulsion
微粒子流量[通量]　corpuscular flux
微量　trace (tr.), trace amount, microscale, grain
微量测定　microdetermination
微量萃取　tracer-scale extraction
微量滴定管　microburette
微量电流计　micro-galvanometer
微量法　【理】micromethod
微量放射性　trace-level activity
微量分析[化验]　【化】microanalysis
微量分析器[仪]　microanalyzer
微量分析试剂　【化】microanalytical reagent

微量分析天平	micro-analytical balance
微量汞中毒	micromercurialism
微量光度测量	microphotometering
微量光度计	microphotometer ◇ 记录式～*，自记式～*
微量光度学[测量术]	microphotometry
微量化学	microchemistry
微量化学分析	microchemical analysis
微量化学仪器	microchemical apparatus
微量浸蚀[酸浸]	microetching
微量区域精炼	micro-scale zone-refining
微量天平	micro-balance
微量添加剂[物]【冶】	microadding
微量位移	microdisplacement
微量雾化【理】	microatomization
微量养分[营养元素]	micronutrient
微量冶金	micro-metallurgy
微量元素	trace [minor] element, microelement
微量杂质	trace (of) impurity
微量重金属	trace heavy metal
微裂	craze, craze crack(ing), checking, microfissure
微裂缝	crevice, microfissure
微裂纹	fine [flake] crack, hair (line) crack, micro-flaw, microcrack, microseparation,【金】checkmark,【铸】check ◇ 产生～microcracking
微裂纹铬镀层	microcracked chromium
微孪晶	microtwinning
微孪晶染[缀]饰	microtwin decoration
微码	microcode
微米波	micron wave
微米级厚度控制系统	micro-level AGC system
微命令【计】	micro-order, microcommand
微模射流逻辑	modular fluid logic
微黏滞性【理】	microviscosity
微凝胶过程	microgel process
微气孔	pinhead blister, micro pores (矿石的)
微球菌属	Micrococcus
微球(体)粒	microsphere
微区[微量]不均匀性	micro heterogeneity, microinhomogeneity
微区偏析【金】	minor segregation
微区破裂	microcrack(ing)
微扰动敏感特性(组织、结构的)	perturbation-sensitive property
微扰能级	perturbed (energy) level
微热量计	microcalorimeter
微熔颗粒	slightly fused granule
微蠕变	micro-creep
微弱焙烧	soft burning
微闪光	microflash
微商【数】	derivative
微射流	microjet
微射束	microbeam
微射束法	microbeam method
微射线自动照相	microautoradiograph
微生物	microbe, microorganism
微生物处理	bioprocessing, microbial processing
微生物代谢物	microbial metabolite
微生物地球化学	microbial geochemistry
微生物腐蚀	microbial [bacterial, microbiological] corrosion
微生物工艺	microbiological process
微生物回收金属	microbial metal recovery
微生物技术	biotechnology, microbiological technology
微生物金属回收工艺	microbial metal recovery
微生物浸出	microbiological leaching
微生物浸出法[过程]	bioleaching process
微生物浸出菌群	bioleaching population
微生物浸出速率	bioleaching rate
微生物控制【环】	microbiological control
微生物量【环】	microbial biomass
微生物胚原形质	microorganism germ plasma
微生物区系[群落]	microflora
微生物生长	microbial growth
微生物污染损害	damage by living organ-

isms
微生物吸附 microbial adsorption
微生物学 microbiology
微生物氧化 bio-oxidation
微生物氧化过程 bio-oxidation process
微生物氧化技术 bio-oxidation technique
微生物冶金学 microbial metallurgy
微生物预处理 microbial pretreatment
微生物造成的损害 damage by living organisms
微疏松 microporosity
微丝 fiber, fibre
微酸性的 subacid
微缩孔 microporosity, microshrinkage
微碳汽车板 trace carbon automobile steel plate
微探头[针] microprobe ◇ 螺旋式扫描～*
微调 trimming, inching, readjustment
微调变阻器 vernier rheostat
微调电容器 trimmer (capacitor)
微调电阻器 trimming resistor
微调聚焦 vernier focusing
微调螺钉[螺丝] micrometer screw, fine setting screw
微调装置 inching device, vernier arrangement
微温差电偶 microcell
微温的 lukewarm
微细(划痕,孔隙)电镀本领 microthrowing power
微细夹杂物 microinclusions
微细颗粒 fine particle, subparticle
微细弥散状态 finely dispersed state
微细研磨粉 micropowder
微纤维 microfiber
微咸水 【环】brackish water
微小缺陷 minute defect
微小差别(钢材试样强度的) nuance
微型保险丝 micro-fuse
微型操纵器[机械手] micromanipulator
微型操纵器与显微镜联合装置 micrugy

微型刀片 microknife ◇ 阿科～*
微型电动机 micro-motor, miniature motor, subfractional horsepower motor (1/20 马力以下)
微型电路 microcircuit
微型电子式控制器 miniature electronic type controller
微型高温计 pyromike
微型焊机 microminiature welder
微(型)计算机 microcomputer, pico-computer
微型结构 microstructure
微型开关 microswitch
微型内孔窥视仪 microborescope
微型喷嘴 microjet
微型射线照相术 miniature radiography
微型试样[样品] 【金】microsample, microspecimen
微型真空泵 minipump
微型组件 (micro)module
微压痕 microindent ◇ 埃贝巴赫～硬度计 Eberbach, 比尔鲍姆～硬度计*, 伯格斯曼～硬度计 Bergsman
微压痕硬度试验仪 micro penetration tester
微压计 micromanometer, microbarograph, differential gauge [manometer], micropressure gauge
微压记录器 microbarograph
微隐晶(的) microcryptocrystalline
微应变 microstrain ◇ 屈服前～*
微应变测量仪 microstrainer
微应变区 microstrain region
微应变压缩 microstrain compression
微应力 micro-stress
微应力计 microstress gauge
微硬度 microhardness ◇ 压入法测～*
微张力控制 minimal [low] tension control
微胀合金 invar
微真空的 microvac
微诊断 【计】microdiagnosis

微震造型机 shockless jolting machine	韦斯常数 【理】Weiss constant
微振磨损试验机 fretting apparatus	韦斯磁畴 Weiss domain
微指令 【计】microinstruction, microorder, microcommand	韦斯蒂科镍铬铁耐热合金(55—60Ni, 15—18Cr,余量 Fe) Westeeco
微中断 【计】microinterrupt	韦斯顿标准电池 Weston standard cell
危害 harm, endanger, detriment, damage, menace, 【环】hazard	韦斯顿电池 cadmium[Weston] cell
	韦斯顿光电管 Weston photronic cell
危害评价 【环】hazard assessment[evaluation]	韦斯近似法 (同"分子场近似法")
	韦斯特法尔比重秤 Westphal balance
危害线 【金】damage line	韦斯特铝焊料(75Zn, 20Al,余量 Cu) Wuest's solder
危险 danger, hazard, risk	
危险标志 hazard index	韦斯汀电弧焊接法(MIG 法的一种) Westing arc process
危险断面 dangerous section	
危险区 hazard zone	韦斯汀豪斯镍铜热磁补偿合金 Westinghouse alloy
危险温度 dangerous temperature	
危险系数 danger coefficient	违反 violation, infringement
煨弯(锻工操作) off-setting	桅杆 mast ◇ 起货～derrick, 重～gin pole
韦伯炼铁法 Weber process	
韦伯特炼钢合金剂(5—7Ti,其余 Al) Webbite	桅杆顶灯 top light
	桅杆式起重机[桅式吊机] mast crane
韦布里奇三联结晶器连铸机 Webridge continuous casting machine	桅式转臂起重机 derrick crane
	围板(保护机械用) brattice
韦布三相电炉 【冶】Webb furnace	围焊 weld all around
韦尔康高强度钢 Welcon	围护沟(基础的) perimeter trench
韦尔曼倾动平炉 Wellman tilting furnace	围护结构 exterior-protected construction
韦尔齐费尔有效价值常数 Wertziffer's value constant	围篱 hedge
	围炉平台 【铁】circular platform
韦尔什银铝牙科合金(50Al, 50Ag) Welch's alloy	围盘 【压】(mechanical) repeater ◇ 侧导式～*,出口～escapement repeater,方形孔型用～square repeater,管式～looping pipe,上甩套的～break-out repeater,双～轧制的 double repeated,双层～double-deck repeater,双线～double-strand repeater,椭圆孔型用～oval repeater
韦尔斯巴赫发火合金(70Ce 及其他稀土,余量 Fe) Welsbach's alloy	
韦勒疲劳试验 Woehler fatigue test	
韦纳伊单晶生长[拉单晶]法 Verneuil crystal growing technique	
韦奇型机械搅拌多膛焙烧炉 Wedge (mechanical multihearth) roaster	
	围盘槽 repeater trough
韦塞尔德银[铜镍锌合金](19—32Ni, 12—17Zn, 0—2Ag,余量 Cu) Wessel('s) alloy, Wessel silver	围盘管 looping pipe
	围盘活套槽 looping trough
	围盘开顶槽 open(top) trough
韦氏硼镁石 wightmanite	围盘甩(活)套机构 flipper
韦氏统计分析法 Weibull's method of statistical analysis	围盘轧机 guide mill
	围盘轧制 【压】repeat(-rolling)
	围盘轧制的 repeated

围盘转送　repeating
围绕　embrace, enclose, enclosure, gird
围绕铸核的点焊区　corona
围岩　wall rock, deads
围堰　cofferdam
围堰板桩　cofferdam piling
围堰底座　coffered foundation
唯能说　【理】energetics
帷　curtain
维阿布拉耐蚀铝黄铜(76Cu, 22Zn, 2Al)　Vialbra
维伯格海绵铁生产法　Wieberg process
维伯竖炉制取海绵铁法　【铁】Wiber-Soederfors process
维布拉洛伊铁镍钼恒弹性合金(50Fe, 40Ni, 9Mo)　Vibralloy
维持　maintain, keep, preserve, hold
维持费　【企】cost of maintenance [upkeep]
维德曼-弗兰茨定律　【理】Wiedemann-Franz's law [rule], law of Widemann and Franz
维德曼效应(磁致伸缩效应)　Wiedemann effect
维迪阿硬质合金(德国产)　Widia metal
维迪阿硬质合金[碳化钨]切削刀具　Widia cutting tool
维尔辛格特里克斯辊模拉丝机　Vercingetrix drawing machine
维格纳效应　Wigner effect
维弧电极　keep-alive electrode
维护　maintenance (MAIN., Maint.), maintaining, safeguarding, attendance, service, upkeep ◇ 可～性 maintainability
维护不当　maloperation
维护程序　【计】maintenance program
维护措施[设施]　maintenance prevention (MP)
维护费　maintenance cost, cost of upkeep
维护工段　maintenance workshop
维护规程　maintenance instruction
维护孔　watch window

维护控制板　maintenance control panel
维护人员　attendant, attending personnel
维卡洛铁钴钒永磁合金(36—62Co, 30—52Fe, 6—16V)　Vicalloy (magnet)
维卡仪(水泥稠度试验用)　Vicat apparatus
维卡针　Vicat needle
维克洛耐热镍铬合金钢(64Ni, 15—20Cr, 1C, 1Mn 0.5—1Si, 余量 Fe)　Vikro
维克托莱特烧结磁铁[钴铁氧体]($30Fe_2O_3$, $44Fe_3O_4$, $26Co_2O_3$)　Vectolite
维克托配件青铜(58.5Cu, 39Zn, 1.5Al, 1Fe, 0.05V)　Victor bronze
维克托铜锌镍合金(50Cu, 35Zn, 15Ni, 有时含<0.1Al, <0.3Fe)　Victor metal
维拉里(磁致弹性)效应　Villari effect
维莱拉和贝茵淬硬钢奥氏体晶粒度显示法　【金】Villela and Bain's method
维莱拉浸蚀剂　【金】Villela's reagent
维里莱特耐蚀合金(1—2.5Cu, 0—1.5Cr, 0.3—1.5Ni, 0—0.5Mn, 0—0.5Mg, 0—0.8Fe, 0—0.4Si, 余量 Al)　Verilite
维梁(底梁、系梁)　【建】collar
维林瓦尔镍铁钴钒合金　Velinvar
维硫铋铅银矿　vikingite
维硫锑铊矿　weissbergite
维梅特钨钛硬质合金　Wi(e)met
维纳斯锑铜合金(50Sb, 50Cu)　Venus regulus
维铌钙矿　vigezzite
维涅托帕涂聚氯乙烯钢板　Vynitop
维纽斯铜锑合金(50Cu, 50Sb)　regulus of Venus
维氏金刚石棱锥体硬度　Vickers diamond (pyramid) hardness
维氏棱锥压头硬度计　Vickers pyramid hardness machine
维氏体　Wuestite
维氏体生成阶段　Wuestite formation stage
维氏体铁　Wuestite-iron

维氏体铁相　Wuestite-iron phase
维氏微硬度计　micro Vickers
维氏硬度　Vickers-hardness（HV），diamond pyramid hardness（DPH，dph）
维氏硬度标　Vickers hardness scale
维氏硬度测定　Vickers pyramid hardness determination
维氏硬度单位　Vickers unit
维氏硬度计　Vickers, Vickers（hardness）tester
维氏硬度金刚石棱锥体压头　【金】Vickers diamond pyramid
维氏硬度试验　Vickers（hardness）test, diamond pyramid hardness test(ing)
维氏硬度试验机　【金】diamond pyramid hardness machine
维氏硬度值　vickers hardness number（VHN），Vickers hardness figure, Vickers number, Vickers pyramid number（VPN），diamond pyramid hardness number（HD）
维（数）　【数】demension
维索夫型风口　tuyere remoteness
维塔尔形变铝合金（1.15Zn，0.9Si，1Cu，余量 Al）　Vital
维塔留姆钴钼铬合金（62-65Co，27-35Cr，5Al，5Mo）　Vitallium
维塔（留姆钴钼铬）合金粉　Vitallium powder
维特恩超低碳不锈钢冶炼法　Witten's process
维特恩穿孔挤压法　【压】Witten's process
维瓦尔形变铝合金（≤98Al，0.6—1Mg，0.5—0.8Si，0—0.5Mn）　Vival
维瓦铝基合金　vival
维维安镍铜合金（50.09Ni，48.49Cu，0.82Fe，0.3Si，余量 Al）　Vivian's copper
维修　maintenance, maintaining, service ◇免～的【企】maintenance-free, 可[易]～性　maintenability, maintainability
维修保养　upkeep

维修部　maintenance service
维修车间　maintenance workshop
维修费　operating expenses, maintenance cost, upkeep
维修工　maintenance worker, repairman, maintainer
维修工程　maintenance engineering
维修工具　maintenance tool
维修工作　maintenance work
维修管理　maintenance management
维修规程　service manual
维修架　maintenance frame
维修进度表　maintenance schedule
维修频率　frequency of maintenance
维修（平）台　maintenance [service] platform
维修人员　maintenance personnel
维修设备　maintenance equipment
维修停产时间　maintenance downtime
维修用起重机　maintenance crane
维修诊断　maintenance diagnosing
维修组[班]　maintenance crew
维也纳金属黏结用汞齐合金（86Cu，14Hg）　Vienna metallic-cement amalgam
苇管状裂痕[裂纹]　reed（钢板或钢坯缺陷）
委托　consignment, trust, entrustment
伟震　megaseism
伪铂（马丁诺镍铜锌电阻合金）　martino alloy
伪操作　【计】pseudo-operation
伪沉淀　（同"假沉淀"）
伪电位法　pseudo-potential method
伪二元系　（同"假二元系"）
伪复型（制备）法　pseudoreplica
伪各向同性的　【金】quasi-isotropic
伪激活　pseudoactivation
伪激活过程　pseudoactivation process
伪晶　（同"假晶"）
伪热激活　pseudo-heat activation
伪形　pseudomorph
伪指令　【计】pseudo-instruction, quasi-in-

struction
尾部　tail (end), butt end (成卷带材的)
尾部滚筒　tail drum
尾部可折起的推焦杆　folded pusher ram
尾部送料压力机　breech loading press
尾锤　tail hammer
尾顶尖(车床的)　tail [back] centre
尾端　trailing end [edge], tail [back] end
尾端件　end piece
尾杆导架　tail rod guide
尾管　liner, tail pipe (排气尾管)
尾架　footstock, tailstock
尾矿　(ore) tailing, tail, reject, trash, garde (锡矿石选矿的),【采】refuse ore ◇ 生产～*, 选矿厂[场]～*
尾矿坝　tailing(s) dam, dike
尾矿场　tailing dump, tailingspile
尾矿池　tailing pond
尾矿池倾析液　tailings pond decant
尾矿处理　tailings disposal
尾矿堆　tailing(s) pile [dump], discard pile
尾矿堆置　impounding, impoundment
尾矿分段取样器　section tailings sampler
尾矿滤饼　tailing cake
尾矿浓缩池　tailing thickener tank
尾矿浓缩机　tailing thickener ◇ 沉箱式～*
尾矿取样　tailing sampling
尾矿试样　tailing sample
尾矿提升机　tailing elevator
尾矿溢流堰(跳汰机的)　tail board
尾料(带卷或盘条的)　remaining convolution
尾馏分　residual [tail] fraction
尾轮　lowering sprocket, tail pulley [drum] ◇ 皮带(输送)机～conveyer tail drum
尾排出槽　tailing launder
尾气　end [tail] gas
尾绳　tail rope, return cable (电耙的)
尾数　【数】mantissa
尾水头　draught head

尾随辊　tailing roll
尾随位错　trailing dislocation
尾销　end pin
尾卸卡车[尾卸式自动倾卸车]　rear-dump [end-dump] truck, end(-discharging) tip-per
尾液　raffinate, tail washings
尾印　tail marks
尾渣　slag tails
尾轴　tail shaft, trailing axle
尾轴承　tail bearing
尾轴颈　tail journal
尾砖　tailing block
尾锥　tail cone
纬度　latitude ◇ 等～点*
纬度圈　latitude circle
纬度线　latitude line
纬线(网筛的)　weft wire
未饱和的　unsaturated, nonsaturated
未饱和合金　unsaturated alloy
未焙烧精矿　(同"生精矿")
未焙烧矿石　unroasted ore
未焙烧料　unfired material
未焙烧球团矿　unfired [fresh] pellet
未变形的　undeformed, undistorted
未测试的　untested
未掺杂的　virgin
未掺杂[污染]废钢铁【钢】　contaminant-free scrap
未敞露标记(磁粉检验)　not-open indication
未车螺纹[未车丝]管　threadless pipe (TP)
未衬砌的　unlined
未充电　without charge (W.C., w.c.)
未充满　【压】underfill(ing) (孔型未充满),【铸】lean
未充满[孔型]道次　【压】underfilled pass
未充满孔型的断面　unfilled section
未除油带钢　non-degreased strip
未处理的　untreated, nudressed
未处理的炉顶煤气　total top gas

未穿通孔　unfair hole
未穿透　nonpenetration
未磁化状态　unmagnetized condition
未淬硬的　unhardened
未淬硬钢　nonhardening steel
未淬硬心部(零件的)　unhardened core
未打光的　【铸】raw
未带电的　nonelectrified
未捣实混凝土　【建】unrammed concrete
未倒角连接　unchamfered joint
未点燃的　unignited
未电离化合物　unionized compound
未定系数法　method of undetermined coefficients
未镀层的　uncoated
未镀层的铜结晶器　【连铸】unplated copper mould
未镀锡的　untinned
未镀锌的　ungalvanized
未煅烧焦炭　uncalcined coke
未对准　malalignment, mismatch, noncoincidence, poor match(指模具), misalignment(指中心线)
未对准中心　disalignment
未发表[未出版]的　not published (NP)
未发现的　not detected (n.d.)
未反应混合料　unreacted mix
未反应矿石　unreacted ore
未反应炉料　【冶】unreacted charge
未防护的　unprotected
未分辨峰值　unresolved peak
未分等级的　not graded (n.g.)
未分级的　unclassified (uncl.), unassorted, unscreened, unsorted
未分解的　uncomposed
未分类的　not graded (n.g.), unsorted
未分选的　unassorted
未富选的　【选】raw
未干扰"0"输出　undisturbed zero output
未干扰"1"输出　undisturbed one output
未固结的　unconsolidated
未光整冷轧　【压】non-skin pass

未规定的　not specified (ns, n.s.)
未规定条件的产品　【企】off-test product
未过滤的　unfiltered, unstrained, unscreened
未过筛的　unscreened, unsized
未焊合　poor fusion
未焊接的　unwelded
未焊透　lack of penetration
未焊透焊缝　shallow weld
未夯实土吸水能力　field moisture equivalent
未烘焙电极[焊条]　unbaked electrode
未滑移区(域)　unslipped area [region]
未化合的　uncombined
未还原球团　【团】unreduced pellet
未还原氧化物颗粒　unreduced oxide particle
未回火马氏体　untempered martensite
未混合的　unmixing
未机械加工的　unmachined
未畸变点阵　undistorted lattice
未畸变面　undistorted plane
未激发原子　【理】nonexcited atom
未激励的　unexcited
未计入损失　unaccounted losses
未加工产品　unwrought product
未加工的　undressed, coarse, dampy, green, raw, unmachined(未机械加工的)
未加工晶体　unworked crystal
未检出的　not detected (n.d.)
未校正(不正确)　out-of-true
未校准的　uncollimated
未结合的　unbound, uncombined
未结晶的　uncrystallized
未结束[未精加工]的　unfinished
未精炼的　unrefined
未精选的铅矿石　bonze
未精整锻件　platter
未精制的　unpurified
未净化气体　rough gas
未净化溶液　【化】crude solution
未净化烟气　unpurified gas

未来学 futurology	未烧透球团 【团】underfired pellet
未冷却的 uncooled	未烧透团块 【团】unfired agglomerate
未离解化合物 undissociated compound	未烧压块 【团】unfired briquette
未离子化 unionization	未渗[浸]透 nonpenetration
未利用的 not available (NA)	未失真的 undistorted
未满弧坑 【焊】unfilled crater	未试验的 untested
未满能级 unfilled (energy) level, unoccupied (energy) level	未受潮的 undamped
未满状态 unoccupied state	未受激原子 【理】nonexcited atom
未密封的 nonsealing	未酸洗斑点 unpickled spot
未浓缩铀 unenriched uranium	未损伤的 unimpaired
未配准 out-of-true	未提纯的 unpurified
未平衡结构 unbalanced construction	未提炼的 unrefined
未屏蔽的 unscreened	未填满(电子)壳层 incomplete electron shell, vacant shell
未破碎的 unbroken (unbr.)	未填满坡口 incompletely filled groove
未曝光胶片 raw [unexposed] film	未调准 missetting
未曝露[曝光]的 unexposed	未涂覆的 uncoated
未清理的 【铸】raw	未脱脂带钢 non-degreased strip
未清理铸件 undressed casting	未完成的 unfinished
未清洗砂 roughing sand	未污染的 （同"无污染的"）
未屈服状态 unyielded condition	未稀释试剂 undiluted reagent
未取向的 undirected	未削弱的 unimpaired
未燃尽[燃烧]的 unburned	未选矿石 crude [undressed] ore, green-ore
未燃碳 unburned carbon	
未熔的 nonfusible	未压紧 malcompression
未熔合 lack of fusion	未氧化的 unoxidized
未熔化的 unfused	未应变晶格 strain-free lattice
未熔化渣 unfluxed slag	未应变晶体 unstrained crystal
未熔炉料 unmelted charge	未硬化的 unhardened
未熔透 【焊】nonpenetration	未硬化钢 Armco-stabilized steel
未软化水 raw water	未用过的金属 （同"初级金属"）
未筛分炉料 unsized burden material	未游离的 unionized
未筛(分)碎石 crusher-run (stone)	未约化的 unreduced
未筛选矿石 【采】unscreened ore	未运行的 off-duty
未上釉的 unglazed	未轧完品 unfinished section
未烧成干燥黏土制品 white-hard	未轧完品卷取机 【压】cobble baller
未烧成[透]状态 underfired state	未沾污的 virgin
未烧结的 unsintered, green	未占位置 vacant position, 【理】open position
未烧(结)球团 【团】unfired pellet [ball]	
未烧黏土 unburned clay	未照准的 uncollimated
未烧透 underfiring, insufficient firing	未遮蔽的 unscreened
未烧透的 underburnt	未整粒的 unsized

未整粒炉料　unsized burden material
未知框　【计】black box
未知数　unknown (unkn)
未知损失　unknown loss
未铸满废铸件　short-run casting
未注满(铸件的)　【铸】poured short
未注明日期的　undated
未装料[药]　without charge (W.C.)
未装满重　short weight
胃八叠球菌　Sarcina ventriculi
喂板机(单张镀锡机组的)　sheet pickup feeder
喂垛装置　pile feeding device
喂钢侧　【压】feeder side
喂料　feed(ing), tracking, threading (轧制的) ◇ 重新~[压]rethreading
喂料工序(带材或焊管坯的)　threading operation
喂料机[器]　feeder
喂料漏斗　feed hopper
喂料系统　feeding system
喂料装置　【压】drawing-in device
喂入角(坯料的)　【压】feed angle
喂入孔型(轧件的)　【压】forward journey
喂入线材　inlet wire
喂丝　wire feed (WF)
喂丝机　wire feeder, wire-feeding machine, wire-feed mechanism ◇ 推进式~ push-type wire feeder
喂线技术　【钢】wire-feeding technique ◇ 钢包~*
喂线增碳　【钢】wire-feeding carbonization
魏氏组织　Widmannstaetten structure [pattern]
魏氏组织铁素体　Widmannstaetten ferrite
魏斯近似法　(同"分子场近似法")
位　place, location, post, position, potential, 【计】order, bit, 【数】digit
位差　potential difference (P.D., p.d.)
位场　potential field
位半操作符【计】bit string operator
位[比特]传送速率　bit transfer rate

位串行　bit serial, serial bit
位错　line defect, 【金】dislocation ◇ Z字形~zigzag dislocation, 被绊住的~stuck dislocation, 伯格斯~Burgers dislocation, 不滑动~ sessile dislocation, 带电~ charged dislocation, 带状[成对全]~zonal dislocation, 单位强度~*, 低能量~*, 弗兰克~Frank dislocation, 负刃型~*, 割切~cutting dislocation, 混合型~mixed type dislocation, 晶界~boundary dislocation, 巨~large dislocation, 可动~mobile dislocation, 离解~*, 领先[先导]~*, 螺型~*, 挠性[可弯]~flexible dislocation, 佩尔斯-纳巴罗~*, 适应~*, 泰勒~*, 同号~*, 网眼状~*, 沃特拉~Volterra dislocation, 肖克利~*, 压力诱发~*, 已长入~grown-in dislocation, 异号~*, 正刃型~*, 缀饰~decorated dislocation, 左螺旋型~left-hand dislocation
位错剥裂应力　break away stress of dislocation
位错崩　avalanches of dislocation
位错壁　dislocation wall, wall of dislocation ◇ 不完全~*, 刃型~*
位错边界　dislocation boundary
位错边缘　dislocation edge
位错缠结　dislocation tangle
位错缠结模型　dislocation tangle model
位错超点阵　superlattice of dislocation
位错成核[核化]　dislocation nucleation
位错重新排列　dislocation rearrangement
位错传播[扩展]　propagation of dislocation
位错错配　misfit dislocation
位错单位长度　unit length of dislocation
位错点阵[晶格]力　lattice force on dislocation
位错叠合　dislocation multiplication
位错动力学　dislocation dynamics
位错段　dislocation segment
位错断裂应力　break away stress of dislo-

cation
位错堆积　piling of dislocation
位错反应　dislocation reaction ◇ 洛莫~*
位错分布　dislocation distribution
位错分解　decomposition [dissociation] of dislocation
位错分裂[裂解]　splitting of dislocation
位错符号　sign of dislocation
位错俘获　trapping of dislocation
位错割阶　dislocation jog ◇ 空位式~【金】vacancy jog,填隙式~interstitialjog
位错割阶的形成　jog formation in dislocation
位错固定　pinning of dislocation
位错惯态　dislocation habit
位错合金效应　dislocation alloying effect
位错滑移　dislocation glide
位错环[圈]　dislocation loop [ring]
位错机理　dislocation mechanism
位错畸变　dislocation distortion
位错间距　spacing of dislocation
位错交割　【理】crossing of dislocation
位错交割过程　intersection process
位错交截　dislocation intersection
位错节[结]　dislocation node ◇ 析出相锁住的~*
位错节弯曲　bowing of dislocation segment
位错结构　structure of dislocation
位错抗断强度　breaking strength of dislocation
位错空洞　【金】holes in dislocation
位错宽度　width of dislocation
位错扩散　dislocation diffusion
位错理论　dislocation theory ◇ 滑移~*,泰勒~theory of Taylor
位错列　row of dislocation ◇ 水平~*
位错裂纹　dislocation crack, cavity dislocation
位错林　dislocation forest
位错露头　end of dislocation

位错马氏体　dislocation martensite
位错锚固(钉扎)　anchoring of dislocation
位错猛烈增多[激烈增殖]　mushrooming of dislocation
位错密度　dislocation density [concentration] ◇ 活动~*
位错模型　dislocation model
位错能(量)　dislocation energy
位错扭曲[扭折]　dislocation kink
位错偶极子　dislocation dipole
位错排列　dislocation arrangement
位错排列稳定度　stability of dislocation array
位错攀移[上升运动]　dislocation climb(ing) ◇ 莫特~模型*
位错攀移力　climb force on dislocation
位错攀移蠕变　dislocation climb creep
位错气团　dislocation atmosphere
位错气团凝聚　condensation of dislocation atmospheres
位错迁移　dislocation migration
位错迁移率　dislocation mobility
位错强度　strength of dislocation
位错侵蚀[腐蚀]坑　dislocation etch pit
位错侵蚀[腐蚀]坑图　dislocation etch pit pattern
位错缺陷　dislocation defect
位错溶度　dislocation solubility
位错柔性　dislocation flexibility
位错蠕变　dislocation creep
位错塞积[积聚]　dislocation pile(-up)
位错塞积群　dislocation pile-up group
位错栅　hedge of dislocation
位错上沉淀物成核　precipitate nucleation on dislocation
位错生长机理　dislocation growth mechanism
位错释出　release of dislocaiton
位错收缩　dislocation constriction, contraction of dislocation
位错受阻　hindering of dislocation
位错衰减[内耗]　dislocation damping

位错速度[速率] dislocation velocity [speed]
位错锁定 dislocation lock(ing), pinning of dislocation
位错通路 passage of dislocation
位错头 dislocation head
位错图样 【金】pattern of dislocation
位错脱离(障碍物) break away of dislocation
位错网(络) dislocation network
位错线 dislocation line ◇ 带正电的~ carrying positive charge dislocation line, 可弯~*
位错线交截 intersection of dislocation line
位错线张力 tension of dislocation line
位错相对论效应 dislocation relativistic effect
位错相交 crossing of dislocations
位错形成 dislocation formation
位错形状 form of dislocation
位错性质 nature of dislocation
位错亚结构 dislocation substructure
位错湮没[消除] annihilation of dislocation
位错要素 element of dislocation
位错抑止 trapping of dislocation
位错应变场 dislocation strain field
位错应力场作用范围 field of dislocation
位错与固溶间隙原子间的相互作用 dislocation interaction with dissolved interstitials
位错源 dislocation source
位错运动[移动] dislocation movement [moving, migration]
位错再排列 dislocation rearrangement
位错增殖机理 ◇ 弗兰克-里德~*
位错障碍 obstruction of dislocation
位错振荡 oscillation of dislocation
位错振动 dislocation vibration
位错阵列 dislocation array ◇ 刃型~*, 同面~*
位错挣脱 break away of dislocation

位错质量 dislocation mass
位错滞后运动 hysteretic motion of dislocation
位错中心 centre [kernel] of dislocation
位错缀饰 decoration of dislocations
位错阻塞 blocking of dislocation
位错组态 dislocation configuration
位错作用范围 field of dislocation
位行 bit string
位阱 【理】potential hole [trough, well]
位距 【计】distance
位垒 (同"势垒")
位垒贯穿本领 【理】potential barrier penetrability
位脉冲 【计】digit pulse
位能 potential energy [head]
位能谷区 furrowed field of potential energy
位平行 【计】bit parallel
位速率[速度] 【计】bit rate
位向变化 (同"取向变化")
位向量 【计】bit vector
位向无序(现象) orientation(al) disorder
位向消失 disorientation
位向效应[作用] orientation effect
位形积分 configuration integral
位移 displacement, shift(ing), drift, off-set ◇ 畴[界]壁~*
位移场 displacement field
位移传感器 displacement pick-up ◇ 感应式~*
位移分量 component of displacement
位移峰值 displacement spike
位移机构 displacement mechanism
位移计 displacement meter [gauge] ◇ 探测裂缝生长用~*
位移角 angle of shift
位移校准器 displacement corrector
位移空位 displacement vacancy
位移能 displacement energy
位移矢量 displacement vector
位移式转变 displacive transformation

位移体积 displaced volume
位移原子数最大值 displacement spike
位移增量 【理】increment of displacement
位置 position (pos.), location, place, site, situation, post ◇ 超过～setover
位置报警器 position alarmer
位置变量 【计】locator variable
位置标识符 【计】location identifier
位置不正 【计】misregistration
位置测定器 position measuring device, chorograph
位置传感器 position sensor [transmitter, transducer]
位置发送器 position transmitter
位置跟踪 position tracking
位置控制 position control
位置控制[跟踪]系统 position control system
位置模拟发送器 analog position transmitter
位置排列 space occupancy
位置调整 positional adjustment
位置无序(现象) positional disorder
位置指示器 position indicator
位置转换器官 position transducer
位置自动控制 automatic position control
位阻系数 steric factor
位阻效应 steric effect
位组合 【计】bit combination
位组合格式 【计】bit pattern
卫板 【压】stripping [stripper] guide ◇ 吊挂[平衡]～*
卫生工程(学) sanitary engineering
卫生管道装置 plumbing installation
卫生规程 sanitary regulations
卫生设备 sanitation (sanit.), sanitary equipment
卫星 satellite ◇ 人造～*, 小型科学～*
卫星城镇 satellite town
卫星处理机 【计】satellite processor
卫星导航计算机 【计】satellite navigation computer

卫星计算机 【计】satellite computer
卫星通信 【计】satellite communication
温变系数 thermal severity number (TSN)
温变形(不锈钢丝的) warm drawing
温标 temperature scale ◇ 华氏～*, 开[凯]氏～*, 兰氏～*, 摄氏～*
温差 temperature difference [differential, drop], difference in temperature
温差传感[传送]器 diff-temperature transmitter
温差磁补偿合金(<0.2C, <0.4Si, <0.1Mn, 28.5－31.5Ni, 余量 Fe) thermoperm alloy ◇ 克莱马克斯～*
温差电池 thermoelectric cell, thermobattery, thermogenerator
温差电池腐蚀 thermogalvanic corrosion
温差电动势 thermal electromotive force, thermoelectromotive force
温差电堆 thermoelectric generator, thermopile
温差电法 thermoelectric method
温差电冷却[致冷] thermoelectric cooling
温差电流 thermoelectric current, thermocurrent
温差电能变换[发电, 转移] thermoelectric energy conversion
温差电偶 (同"热电偶") ◇ 碱金属～ base metal couple
温差电势 thermoelectric voltage
温差电势率 thermoelectric power
温差电效应 thermoelectrical effect
温差电序 (同"热电序")
温差发电器 thermoelectric generator
温差偏转率 thermal deflection rate
温差应力 temperature stress
温差元件 thermopile
温带降雨林 temperate rain forest
温德洛伊耐蚀耐磨铜锰镍合金(20Mn, 60Cu, 20Ni) Wyndaaloy
温度 temperature (temp.) ◇ 费米～*, 环境[外界, 周围]～*, 居里～*, 兰氏

~*,奈耳~*,适当~ moderate temperature,与~无关的 temperature-independent,与~有关的(随~而变的) temperature-dependent

温度摆动 swing in temperature
温度保护装置 temperature protective device
温度变化 temperature change [variation], variation [shift] in temperature, thermal change,【理】temperature oscillation
温度变化过程 temperature history
温度变化速度 rate of temperature change
温度变化引起的尺寸变化 thermal growth
温度变换器 temperature converter
温度表 thermometer, thermograph
温度波动 temperature fluctuation [variation], swing in temperature
温度补偿 temperature compensation
温度补偿导线 temperature compensation lead
温度补偿合金 temperature compensation alloy
温度参数 temperature parameter
温度测量 temperature measurement
温度测量装置 temperature-measuring device
温度测试探针 temperatur7e probe ◇ 装料[炉]~*
温度差 ("同温差")
温度场 temperature field
温度传感器 temperature transducer [transmitter, probe, pickup], heat meter
温度-电流曲线 temperature-current curve
温度读数 temperature reading
温度度数 degree of temperature
温度反应 temperature response, thermotonus
温度范围 temperature range [region, interval, envelope, level]

温度范围宽的馏分 wide-boiling cut
温度分布 temperature distribution
温度分布曲线 temperature distribution curve
温度分布图 temperature pattern [profile]
温度分界层 temperature boundary layer
温度峰值 thermal peak [spike]
温度感测元件 temperature sensor
温度(钢)筋 temperature reinforcement
温度关系图表 temperature-dependence plot
温度函数 function of temperature
温度和湿度指数 temperature and humidity index (THI)
温度恒定 constancy of temperature, steady temperature
温度换能器 temperature transducer
温度换算 temperature inversion
温度换算表 temperature conversion table
温度基(准)点 temperature reference point
温度极限 temperature limit
温度计 temperature meter (TM), temperature gauge, thermometer, thermograph, heat indicator ◇ 阿斯曼吸引式~*,贝克曼~ Beckmann thermometer, 比色~ 2-color thermometer, 表面~ adrometer, 玻璃管~ glass thermometer, 部分浸没(式)~*,超高温~ hyperthermometer, 充液(体)~*,传声~ thermophone, 度盘式~ dial-type thermometer, 高精度比色红外光纤~*,接触[接点]~ contact thermometer, 酒精~ alcohol thermometer, 列氏~*,膨胀~*,气压~*,全浸~*,熔丝式~*,摄氏[百分]~ centigrade thermometer, 示差~*,双金属~ bimetal thermometer, 压差~ manometric thermometer, 遥测~*,液体~*,自记录式~*
温度计毛细管 thermometer stem
温度计时滞后 thermometric lag
温度计套 thermometer pocket

温度计用流体 thermometric fluid
温度记录控制器 temperature recorder controller ◇ 锻造加热炉～forge master
温度记录器[装置] temperature recorder, thermograph ◇ 自动式～thermometro graph
温度记录[自记]器粉末 thermographic powder
温度继电器 temperature [thermal] relay
温度间隔值 amount of temperature interval
温度间距 temperature interval
温度检测器 temperature detector
温度降(低)[下降] temperature drop [fall, reduction, decrease]
温度校正 temperature correction
温度校准电位计 temperature calibration potentiometer
温度均衡 temperature equalization
温度开关 temperature switch
温度控制 temperature control
温度控制开关 thermostatic switch
温度控制器 temperature controller, thermoregulator
温度控制装置 attemperator
温度漫散射 temperature diffuse scattering
温度敏感金属 temperature-sensitive metal
温度敏感性[灵敏度] temperature sensitivity
温度浓度曲线图 T-X diagram
温度膨胀系数 temperature expansion coefficient
温度漂移 temperature drift
温度平衡 temperature balance [equilibrium, equalization]
温度坡差曲线 thermal gradient diagram
温度曲线 thermal curve, temperature [heat] pattern, thermograph
温度容限 temperature tolerance
温度色 temperature colour

温度熵图 temperature-entropy diagram
温度上限 upper temperature limit
温度伸缩缝 temperature expansion joint
温度生长(尺寸变化) physical growth
温度升高 temperature rise [increase]
温度湿度计[记录器] thermohydrograph ◇ 气压～*
温度湿度增高条件下试验 tropicalization test
温度时间曲线 temperature-time curve
温度时间转变 temperature-time transformation
温度损失 temperature loss
温度探测器 temperature probe
温度梯度 temperature gradient (temp. grad.), temperature slope
温度梯度炉 gradient furnace
温度梯度区域精炼 temperature-gradient zone refining
温度梯度区域熔炼 temperature-gradient zone melting (TGZM)
温度调节[调整] temperature regulation [control, adjustment], thermoregulation
温度调节继电器 temperature regulating relay
温度调节器 temperature [heat] regulator, thermoregulator, thermoswitch, attemperator ◇ 双金属～*
温度调节装置 temperature regulating device
温度调节作用 attemperation
温度头 temperature head
温度误差 temperature error
温度系数 temperature coefficient
温度限制 temperature limitation
温度相关系数 temperature-dependent constant
温度响应 temperature response
温度效应 temperature effect
温度循环[周期] temperature cycle
温度压力曲线 temperature-pressure curve
温度遥测器 millscope

温度因数[因素]	temperature factor ◇ 德拜(-瓦勒)～*
温度振荡	【理】temperature oscillation
温度指示记录器	temperature indicated recorder (TIR)
温度指示控制器	temperature indicating controller (TIC)
温度指示器	temperature indicator (TI)
温度指示仪表	temperature indicating instrument
温度滞后	temperature hysteresis
温度质量曲线	thermogravimetric curve
温度周期变化	thermal cycling
温度状况	heat pattern
温度状况控制	heat pattern control
温度状况控制系统	heat pattern control system
温度自动记录器[仪]	automatic temperature recorder, thermograph
温度自动控制系统	automatic temperature control system
温度自动调节器	automatic temperature controller [regulator], thermostat
温度自记曲线	thermogram
温锻	warm forging
温和化净化(炼焦用煤的)	temperate purification
温挤(压)	warm extrusion
温加工	warm working
温克勒流化床(不连续流化床)	Winkler fluidized bed
温克勒煤炭气化法	Winkler gasification process
温拉拔法(钢丝的)	warm drawing
温谱图	thermogram
温热塑性加工	(同"低温塑性加工")
温熵图[解]	tephigram
温升	temperature rise
温升极限	temperature rise limit
温升试验	temperature test
温石棉{$H_4Mg_3Si_2O_9$}	chrysotile
温石棉毡	chrysotile felt
温室效应	【环】greenhouse effect
温斯科英巴比合金[低锡铅基轴承合金]	(5Sn, 9 或 15Sb, 80—86Pb, 0.5Cu) Wings Coin babbitt
温梯区域熔炼	(同"温度梯度区域熔炼")
温压	warm-press(ing)
温轧	warm rolling
文件	document, file, papers ◇ 成块～ blocked file, 提供～documentation
文件保护	【计】file protection
文件保密	file security
文件编排系统	【计】filing system
文件编址	【计】file addressing
文件编制	documentation
文件变动性	【计】volatility of file
文件操作	【计】file event
文件重建过程	【计】file reconstruction procedure
文件处理	【计】file processing
文件传送	file [document] transportation
文件分类机	【计】document sorter
文件管理	【计】file management
文件活动率	file activity ratio
文件集[组]	file set
文件集成	【计】file composition
文件间隔	【计】file gap
文件检索	file [document] retrieval
文件结束	【计】end-of-file (EOF)
文件结束标志	【计】end-of-file mark
文件结束码	【计】end-of-file code
文件结束指示符[器]	end-of-file indicator
文件卷盘	【计】file reel
文件类型	file type
文件目录	file directory [catalog]
文件识别	【计】file identification
文件说明[描述]表	file specification
文件维护	【计】file maintenance
文件阅读器	file [document] reader
文件转换	【计】file conversion
文件装填密度	【计】file packing density
文件组	file group [set]

文件组织 【计】file organization
文丘里多管涤气器 bank of Venturi (scrubber) tubes
文丘里[氏]管 Venturi (pipe, tube), ventury ◇锥形槽低压~*
文丘里管喉口 Venturi throat
文丘里管湿式洗涤器 Venturi wet scrubber
文丘里管洗涤器[文丘里管除尘器,文丘里涤气器,文氏管洗涤器,文丘里管洗涤塔] Venturi scrubber ◇串联调径~*
文丘里管洗气机[文丘里喷雾管] Venturi washer
文丘里管斜度 【铁】Venturi batter
文丘里接触器 Venturi contactor
文丘里流量计 Venturi(meter)
文丘里煤气净化系统 【冶】Venturi gas-cleaning system
文丘里式风口 Venturi-type tuyere
文丘里缩喉管 Venturi throat constriction
文石{$CaCO_3$} aragonite
文氏管 Venturi tube
文献检索 literature search
文献目录 bibliography
文摘服务(机构) abstracting service
文字读出装置 character reader ◇光学~*
纹理 grain, wein, streak, texture
纹理组织 veining structure
稳定 stabilization, equilibria, anchoring (指燃烧室中的火焰)
稳定β型钛合金 stable beta titanium alloy
稳定奥氏体 stable austenite
稳定白云石 stabilized dolomite
稳定白云石烧块 stabilized [stable] dolomite clinker
稳定板 quiescence plate
稳定变态 stable modification
稳定程度 degree of stability
稳定处理的预应力钢绳 stabilized strand
稳定电弧 stable [steady] arc

稳定电子组态 stable electronic configuration
稳定电流 standing current
稳定电位 stable potential
稳定度 degree of stability ◇尼奎斯特~准则[稳定判据]*
稳定反应器[堆] stabilizing reactor
稳定风流 constant air flow
稳定负荷[负载,载荷] steady load ◇不~fluctuating load
稳定合金 stable alloy
稳定滑移带 persistent slip band
稳定化 stabilization
稳定化处理 stabilization (treatment), stabilizing (treatment), stabilising ◇奥氏体~*
稳定化处理预应力钢丝 stabilized wire
稳定(化)钢 stabilized steel ◇阿姆柯~*,铝~*
稳定化合物 stable compound
稳定(化)热处理 stabilizing (heat) treatment
稳定化涂层 stabilizing coating
稳定(化)退火 stabilizing [stabilising] annealing
稳定化元素 stabilizing element
稳定火焰 steady flame
稳定极限 stability limit
稳定挤压(过程) stationary extrusion
稳定挤压压力 steady extrusion pressure
稳定剂 stabilizer, stabilizing agent ◇α相~alpha-stabilizer
稳定晶核 【金】stable nucleus
稳定抗蠕变钛合金 stable creep-resistant titanium alloy
稳定零点(仪器的) steady zero
稳定流(动) steady [constant, permanent] flow
稳定六方(晶系)氢化物 stable hexagonal hydride
稳定炉况[操作,冶炼进程] stabilization of furnace operation, steady operation

稳定络合物　stable complex
稳定平衡　stable [true] equilibrium
稳定期　stationary phase
稳定器　stabilizer, regulator, governor
稳定区域[范围]　stability range
稳定燃烧　smooth combustion,【铁】pulsation-free combustion（热风炉的）
稳定速率　steady rate
稳定同位素　stable isotope
稳定相　stable phase
稳定效应　stabilizing effect
稳定形态　stable form
稳定性　stability, stabilization, steadiness, constancy, sturdiness ◇ 绝对～absolute stability, 使用～service stability
稳定性白云石耐火材料　stabilized dolomite refractory
稳定性[度]试验　stability test
稳定性系数　stability coefficient
稳定性药皮　【焊】stabilizing coating
稳定焰　stable flame
稳定氧化膜　stable oxide film
稳定氧化物　stable oxide
稳定因数（焦炭的）　stability factor
稳定应力　steady stress
稳定元素　stable element, noble element（电解时的）
稳定[态]运动　【理】stationary motion
稳定装置　monitor
稳定状态　stable [stationary] state, stabilized condition, invariant equilibrium
稳定作用　stabilization, stabilizing effect, maturing, poising action
稳弧剂[装置]　arc stabilizer
稳流　equilibrium [steady] flow
稳流灯　barretter
稳流电阻　steady [ballast] resistance
稳流管　regulator tube
稳流器　current stabilizer [regulator],【电】dynamic reactor
稳态　steady [stationary] state
稳态超导体　stabilized superconductor

稳态电流　steady state current
稳态分布　steady state distribution
稳态功率输入　steady energy input
稳态加热　stationary heating
稳态扩散　steady state diffusion
稳态流　steady (state) flow
稳态浓度　steady state concentration
稳态热损失　steady state heat loss
稳态蠕变　steady state creep, secondary creep, second stage of creep, K-flow
稳态条件　steady state condition
稳态温度　steady state temperature
稳土剂　earth stabilizer
稳压槽　steady head tank
稳压二极管　voltage-regulator diode, Zener diode
稳压管　stabilivolt, regulator tube
稳压器　voltage stabilizer [regulator], potentiostat, manostat
稳焰器　flame stabilizer
紊流　turbulence, turbulent flow
紊流度　turbulence of stream
紊流模型　turbulence model
紊流强度　intensity of turbulence, turbulence level
紊流现象　turbulence phenomenon
紊流抑制器　turbulence suppressor
紊流运动　stirring motion
紊乱　disorder, confusion
紊乱切屑　tangled turnings
嗡鸣火焰　singing flame
瓮浸出　vat leaching
蜗杆　worm (screw), perpetual [endless] screw, hob ◇ 连接～connecting worm
蜗杆挤压机　screw extruder
蜗杆加料器　worm [screw] feed
蜗杆千斤顶　worm jack
蜗杆轴　worm shaft
蜗轮传动装置　worm gear(ing)
蜗轮减速机　worm gear, worm-gear speed reducer
蜗牛线　【数】cochleoid

蜗形管 volute chamber, worm pipe
蜗形绳轮 fusee, fuzee
涡电流 eddy current (EC)
涡动 eddy(ing) [whirling] motion, vortex (motion),【钢】swirling（钢液的）
涡流 eddy current (EC), vortex(ing), tubulence, erratic [cross, Foucault] current, eddy(ing) flow, swirl(ing)（煤气、空气的）
涡流测厚计 Isometric
涡流超声检验法 eddy-sonic method
涡流法金属丝检验仪 wiretester
涡流法圆柱形零件检查仪 ◇ 马格纳特斯特~【机】Magnatest
涡流分离器[分选器,选矿机] whirlpool separator
涡流腐蚀检验 eddy-current corrosion test
涡流检验（表面裂纹的） eddy-current inspection [test]
涡流控制闸 eddy control brake (ECB)
涡流流量计 swirl flowmeter
涡流黏度 eddy viscosity
涡流黏滞性 eddy viscosity
涡流式二次冷凝器 cyclone-type aftercondenser
涡流式合金分检仪 cyclograph
涡流式探伤仪 probolog
涡流损耗[损失] eddy-current loss
涡流探伤 eddy current test(ing) ◇ 智能化~仪*
涡流无损探伤 eddy-current non-destructive test
涡流引起的误差 hysteresis error
涡流运动 vortex [eddy(ing)] motion
涡流制动器[涡流闸] eddy-current brake [retarder]
涡流作用 swirling action
涡轮 impeller, impellor, snail
涡轮泵 turbine pump, turbopump
涡轮发电机 turbine generator, turbogenerator
涡轮风机[扇] turbo-fan

涡轮机 turbomachine ◇ 单流式~single flow machine, 蒸汽两次中间过热式~*, 中间过热式~reheat machine
涡轮搅拌机 turbine agitator
涡轮式混合机 turbo-type mixer
涡轮式(离心)干燥机 turbine dryer
涡轮式装置 turbine-type unit
涡轮叶片 turbine blade ◇ 迪斯卡洛伊~用耐热合金*
涡轮叶片超声波检验 turbine blade inspection by ultrasonics
涡轮叶片锻造 forging of turbine blade
涡轮增压器 turbosupercharger, turbocharger
涡轮增压器叶片 turbosupercharger bucket
涡形分离器[分选机,选矿机] snail separator
涡形管 scroll
涡形轮 snail
涡形选矿机 snail separator
涡旋分离换热装置 vortex separator-heat exchanger (VSHE)
涡旋效应 vortex effect
窝模 snap, cupping tools
窝头阀 double cone dump valve
卧管 【铁】lying pipe
卧管式余[废]热锅炉 horizontal tube waste-heat boiler
卧管式热压炉 horizontal tube hot-pressing furnace
卧模（地坑造型的） 【铸】bed in, bedding-in
卧式冲床[冲压机] 【压】horizontal punching machine
卧式吹炉 barrel converter
卧式单次拉丝机 single horizontal block
卧式单带卷车 horizontal single coil car
卧式电弧炉 electric arc horizontal furnace
卧式锻造机 horizontal forging machine, impactor, impacter, greenbat machine（热顶锻型）

卧式多级离心泵	horizontal multi-stage centrifugal pump
卧式分批热处理炉	horizontal batch furnace
卧式感应加热炉	horizontal induction furnace
卧式高压釜	horizontal autoclave ◇ 搅拌～*
卧式管状炉	horizontal tubular furnace
卧式滚筒	horizontal drum
卧式烘砂炉	horizontal sand-drying oven
卧式回转高压釜	horizontal rotating autoclave
卧式回转窑	horizontal rotary kiln
卧式火管型余热锅炉	horizontal fire-tube-type waste-heat boiler
卧式机架	horizontal stand
卧式挤压机	horizontal extruder
卧式碱洗	horizontal type alkaline cleaning
卧式净化装置	horizontal cleaner
卧式卷取机	【压】horizontal reel
卧式卷线筒	【压】horizontal block
卧式离心机	horizontal centrifuge
卧式炉	horizontal furnace
卧式炉还原	horizontal furnace reduction
卧式螺旋搅拌进料还原	horizontal screw-agitated feed reduction
卧式盘条卷取机	horizontal wire rod reel
卧式三柱塞型液压泵	horizontal triplex plunger type hydraulic pump
卧式石墨管热压炉	horizontal graphite-tube hot-pressing furnace
卧式碳化炉	horizontal retort
卧式弯板机	horizontal plate-bending machine
卧式线材卷取机	horizontal wire rod reel
卧式轧边机	horizontal edger
卧式柱塞压铸机	horizontal plunger die-casting machine
卧式转炉	horizontal converter,【色】barrel (type) converter
握柄滑轮	lever block
握裹力	bondability ◇ 混凝土和钢筋的～*
握紧器	holding device
握力计	dynamograph
肟	oxime
沃德－伦纳德式发电机－电动机组（带飞轮）	Ward-Leonard set
沃德－伦纳德式发电机－电动机组拖动（装置）	Ward-Leonard drive
沃恩白色装饰合金(73Sb,10Sn,7Ni,7Bi,3Co)	Warne's metal
沃恩银代用合金	Warne's alloy
沃尔坎含硅轴承青铜(1Si,少量 Ni 及 Fe)	Vulcan bronze
沃尔坎耐蚀铜合金(81Cu,11Al,0.7Cr,1.5Ni,4.4Fe,1Si,0.4Sn)	Vulcan metal
沃尔克型圆盘铸锭机	Walker casting wheel
沃尔塔三相电炉	【钢】Volta furnace
沃尔维特青铜轴承合金(91Cu,9Sn)	Volvit
沃尔兹回转窑烟压法	Waelz method
沃尔兹法烟化回转窑	Waelz kiln
沃尔兹回转窑烟化法	Waelz (fuming) process, Waelz method
沃法泰特 C 羧酸阳离子交换树脂	Wofatit C
沃法泰特 KS 磺酚阳离子交换树脂	Wofatit KS
沃法泰特 M 弱碱性阴离子交换树脂	Wofatit M
沃法泰特 P 磺酚阳离子交换树脂	Wofatit P
沃格尔铜钉合金	Vogel's alloy
沃格米特超硬质合金(93.5W,4.5C,2Fe)	Volomit
沃克拉型一步炼铜法	Worcra process
沃拉斯顿法铂丝	Wollaston wire
沃拉斯顿粉冶制铂法	【粉】Wollaston process
沃拉斯顿细丝拔制法	【压】Wollaston

process
沃林顿线规 Warrington wire gauge (W.W.G.)
沃姆-保尔电炉 Vom-Baur furnace
沃思特镍铬钼不锈钢(24Ni,20Cr,3Mo, 3.25Si,1.75Cu,余量 Fe) Worthite
沃特拉位错 Volterra dislocation ◇ 简单~ *
沃威尔(粗金)电解精炼法 Wohlwill process[method]
钨{W} tungsten, wolfram(ium),【冶】wortle(工厂中旧称)
钨靶[对阴极] tungsten target
钨棒 (同"钨条")
钨铋矿{Bi$_2$O$_3$·WO$_3$} russellite
钨垂 tungsten weight
钨磁钢 tungsten magnet steel
钨当量 tungsten equivalent
钨的 tungstic
钨电弧 tungsten arc
钨(电)极 tungsten[wolfram] electrode ◇ 涂[掺]钍~ thoriated electrode
钨电极电弧炉熔炼 tungsten-electrode arc melting
钨电极尖 tungsten tip
钨电阻加热元件 Stratit element
钨钒钢 ◇ 伐斯科~ *
钨废料 tungsten scrap
钨粉 tungsten powder ◇ 库里几~成形法 Coolidge's method,电积[电解沉积,电极沉积]~ *,刚还原的~ as-reduced tungsten powder,碳还原~ *
钨辐射 tungsten radiation
钨辐射X射线光谱图 X-ray spectrogram of tungsten radiation
钨钢 tungsten[wolfram] steel ◇ 克鲁司~ Kerus,石墨化~ *
钨钢拉丝模板 wortle
钨高速钢 tungsten high-speed steel
钨铬钒工具钢 tungsten-chromium-vanadium tool steel
钨铬钢 tungsten-chrome steel
钨铬工具钢 tungsten chromium tool steel
钨铬钴合金 stellite
钨钴合金(75—95W,余量 Co) tungsten-cobalt(alloy)
钨合金 tungsten alloy ◇ RHC宇宙空间用~ *,高密度~ *
钨华{WO$_3$·H$_2$O} tungstite, wolfram ocher
钨黄铜(60Cu, 22-34Zn, 2—4W, 0.1—14Ni,0—0.1Sn,0—2.8Al,微量 Mn) tungsten[wo-lfram] brass
钨基合金 heavy[tungsten-base] alloy
钨基合金电极 tungsten-base electorde
钨极电弧 tungsten arc ◇ 气体保护~点焊 *
钨极电弧焊 tungsten-arc welding ◇ 惰性气体[惰气]保护~ *,可控~ *,气体保护~ *
钨极电弧炉 tungsten electrode arc furnace
钨极电弧切割 tungsten-arc cutting
钨极惰气保护焊 inert-gas shielded tungsten arc welding
钨极氩弧焊接 argon tungsten-arc welding
钨夹 tungsten clip
钨加热元件 tungsten[wolfram] heating element
钨尖电极 tungsten-tipped electrode ◇ 水冷~ *,铜背~ *
钨尖电极电弧炉 tungsten-tipped-electrode arc furnace
钨矿 tungsten[wolfram] ore
钨矿床 tungsten deposit
钨矿物 tungsten mineral
钨铼合金 tungsten-rhenium alloy
钨粒 tungsten particle
钨锰矿{MnWO$_4$} huebnerite
钨锰铁矿 (同"黑钨矿")
钨锰铁矿氯化 chlorination of wolframite
钨钼合金 tungsten-molybdenum alloy, moly-B(metal)
钨钼热电偶 tungsten-molybdenum ther-

wu 钨

mocouple
钨镍合金（＜10Ni 或 10—25Ni，余量 W） tungsten nickel
钨盘 tungsten disc
钨坯块 tungsten briquette
钨铅矿 {PbWO$_4$} stolzite
钨青铜（90—95Cu，0—3Sn，2—10W） tungsten [wolfram] bronze ◇ 碱金属～*
钨砂 tungsten ore
钨烧结 tungsten sintering ◇ 镍活化～ nickel-activated sintering of tungsten
钨-石墨热电偶 tungsten-graphite thermocouple
钨丝 tungsten filament [wire]，wolfram filament ◇ U 字形～*，不垂坠的～ non-sag wire，单晶～*，敷［加］钍～*，库里几制～法 Coolidge process，拉～机*，螺线［螺旋］～*，再结晶～*
钨丝灯 tungsten filament lamp, osram lamp, osram Lamp
钨丝拉制机（同"拉钨丝机"）
钨酸 {H$_2$WO$_4$} tungstic [wolframic] acid ◇ 无碱金属～*
钨酸铵 {(NH$_4$)$_2$WO$_4$} ammonium tungstate
钨酸钡 barium tungstate
钨酸钙 {CaWO$_4$} calcium tungstate [wolframate]
钨酸钙还原 reduction of calcium tungstate
钨酸钙矿 scheelite
钨酸镉 cadmium tungstate
钨酸根 tungstate [wolframate] radical
钨酸糊 tungstic acid paste
钨酸钾 {K$_2$WO$_4$} potassium tungstate [wolframate]
钨酸锂 {Li$_2$WO$_4$} lithium tungstate
钨酸镁 magnesium tungstate
钨酸钠 {Na$_2$WO$_4$·2H$_2$O} sodium tungstate [wolframate]
钨酸钠还原 reduction of sodium tungstate

钨酸钠熔融体 sodium tungstate fusion
钨酸铅 lead tungstate [wolframate]
钨酸锶 {SrWO$_4$} strontium tungstate
钨酸铜 {CuWO$_4$} copper tungstate
钨酸盐 {M$_2$WO$_4$} tungstate, wolframate ◇ 熔融～电解*
钨酸银 {Ag$_2$WO$_4$} silver tungstate
钨钛碳化物 {TiC-WC} tungsten-titanium carbide
钨钛硬质合金 tungsten-carbide titanium-carbid cobalt alloy ◇ 普罗利特～*，维梅特～Wi(e)met
钨锑贝塔石 scheteligite
钨锑烧绿石 scheteligite
钨添加合金 tungsten addition
钨条 tungsten bar [rod] ◇ 粉冶～*
钨条旋锻机 machine for swaging tungsten bar
钨铁（中间合金；75—85W，低 C，低 Si，低 P） ferrotungsten, tungsten iron
钨铁块 button
钨铁矿 {FeWO$_4$} ferberite
钨铜电触头合金 tungsten-copper contact metal
钨铜电接触器材 tungsten-copper contacts, tungsten-copper contact material
钨铜复合物 tungsten-copper composite
钨铜合金（中间合金；10—15W 或 40—50W） tungsten copper, tungsten-copper alloy ◇ 埃尔科涅特～（焊条用）Elconite
钨铜合金覆面 tungsten-copper facing
钨铜镍电接触器材 tungsten-copper-nickel contacts
钨铜镍合金 tungsten-copper-nickel alloy ◇ 通用电气公司重载～*
钨铜镍制品 tungsten-copper-nickel composition
钨铜制品 tungsten-copper composition
钨钍矿 thorotungstite, yttrotungstite
钨污染（电弧熔化时的） tungsten contamination

钨系高速工具钢　tungsten series high speed tool steel
钨系合金　tungalloy
钨锌矿　sanmartinite
钨氩整流器　tungar rectifier
钨阳极　tungsten anode ◇ 圆盘形～tungsten disc anode
钨铱热电偶　tungsten-iridium thermocouple
钨阴极　tungsten cathode
钨阴影溅射处理　tungsten shadow casting ◇ 电子显微镜复型的～*
钨银电触头合金　tungsten-silver contact alloy [metal]
钨银电接触器材　tungsten-silver contact material
钨银合金　tungsten-silven alloy ◇ 西尔滕～*
钨－铀玻璃密封　tungsten to uranium glass seal
钨质电接触器材　tungsten contacts
钨中间电极　tungsten target
乌顿布格矿　uytenbogaardtite
乌尔科尼铜铅系轴承合金(65Cu,35Sb)　Ulcony metal
乌尔科铅基轴承合金(1—2Ba,0.5—1Ca,余量 Pb)　Ulco metal
乌尔马尔高强度高韧性铝镁合金(10Mg,1Si,0.5Mn,余量 Al)　Ulmal
乌里弗－布喇格定律　Wulff-Bragg's law
乌里弗网　【理】Wulff's net
乌钠铌钛石　vuonnemite, wuonnemite
乌尼杜尔铝锌镁合金　Unidur
乌氏硅热还原 U_3O_8 法　Voos method
圬工　masonry ◇ 琢石～ashlar masonry
圬工坝　【建】masonry dam
圬工构造(学)　masonry construction
污斑　stain, blotting,【压】dirt pit (钢板缺陷)
污点　stain, spot, smirch, smotch, blotting, smudge ◇ 有～的 spotted
污电解液　foul electrolyte

污垢　dirt, fouling
污垢排出器　dirt excluder
污痕　smudge
污泥　(sewage) sludge, mud ◇ 矿质[无机]～mineral sludge, 下水道～【环】sewage sludge, 消化～digested sludge
污泥处理[处置]　sludge disposal [treatment]
污泥分级消化　stage digestion of sludge
污泥浓缩器　sludge concentrator
污泥消化池　sludge digester
污泥淤积　accumulation of mud
污气　foul gas
污染　contamination, pollution, impurity ◇ 串料～*, 大气[空气]～*, 带入～*, 防～*, 空气中铅～*, 去～*, 无[未]～的*
污染测量仪(放射性的)　contamination meter
污染的　contaminated (contam.), contaminative, polluted
污染防止条令　pollution prevention ordinance
污染防治措施　antipollution measure
污染防治技术　pollution prevention (abatement) technique
污染防治设施　anti-pollution facility
污染负荷　pollution load
污染监测仪　contamination monitor
污染控制　contamination [pollution] control
污染控制设施　pollution control facilities
污染量　contaminant capacity
污染排放　dirty discharge
污染危害　contamination hazard
污染物　pollutant, pollution matter, contaminant ◇ 气态～gaseous pollutant, 潜在～latent pollutant, 水载～waterborne pollutant
污染物参数　pollutant parameter ◇ 关键～*
污染物单位负荷量　pollutant load per unit

污染物量	contaminant capacity
污染物质	pollutant, contaminant, contaminating material ◇ 溶解～dissolved contaminant
污染物综合排放合格率	qualified rate of all polutants discharging
污染系数	contamination factor
污染性产业	pollution-causing industry
污染源	contaminant [pollution] source, source of contamination, polluter
污染源实施标准	source performance standard
"污染者负担"原则	"polluter pays" principle (ppp)
污染指数	【环】pollution index
污水	sewage, drainage, contaminated [foul, polluted, waste] water, (aqueous) effluent
污水泵	sewage [sump] pump ◇ 舱底～ bilge pump
污水沉淀池	detention tank
污水池	【环】lagoon, cesspit
污水处理	【环】sewage disposal [treatment] ◇ 灌溉用～*
污水处理厂[场]	sewage disposal [treatment, purification] plant
污水处置	effluent disposal
污水分析	sewage analysis
污水干管	main [trunk] sewer
污水工程系统	sewerage system
污水沟	foul water sewer
污水管	sewer pipe, cesspipe
污水管道[总管]	sewage conduit
污水井	dumb well
污水净化(法)	sewage purification, clarification of sewage
污水净化三级过程	A-B-C process
污水净化需氯量	chlorine demand of sewage
污水净化学会(英国)	Institute of Sewage Purification (I.S.P.)
污水坑	cesspit
污水氯化	sewage chlorination
污水滤渣的掩埋	burial of sewage screenigs
污水排放	sewage discharge ◇ 未处理～ discharge of untreated effluent
污水排放速度	bleed rate
污水渗坑	【建】sink
污水稀释	effluent dilution
污水系统	sewerage ◇ 工厂生产～*
污水需氯量	chlorine demand of sewage
污水滞流沉淀池	detention tank
污物	sewage, dirt, muck
污阳极液	foul anolyte
污液	foul solution
污液泵	contaminanted liquor pump
污浊	dirty, blurring
屋顶	roof, housetop ◇ (平)台式～deck roof, 半圆形～compass roof, 防热[泻水假]～cricket, 盖～roofing, 球形～bulbous dome, 人字～*, 小跨度～*
屋顶板	roof-slab, shingle
屋顶窗	dormant window, dormer
屋顶电除尘器(转炉的)	roof electrostatic scrubber
屋顶高跨比	roof pitch ◇ 1/4 ～ one-fourth pitch
屋顶排水沟	valley
屋顶(倾)斜角	angle of roof
屋顶洗涤器	roof scrubber
屋顶洗涤装置	roof scrubbing installation
屋顶斜度	inclination of roof
屋架	roof truss ◇ 贝式弓形～Belfast roof truss, 叠层～lamella truss
屋架高跨相等的屋面坡度	full pitch
屋架间抗风剪力撑	wind brac(ing)
屋架下弦[屋花梁(桁)]	bottom chord of roof truss
屋面	roofing, roof (covering) ◇ 防水帆布～canvas decking, 铺～roofing, 瓦垄石棉水泥～*
屋面板	roof sheathing [boarding] ◇ 槽形～channel roof slab, 石膏～gypsum

roof plank	
屋面薄钢板	roofing sheet [iron]
屋面薄钢板的搭接	sticker patches
屋面材料	roofing, roofage ◇ 不凝气~*, 卷铺~ roll roofing
屋面衬板	sarking boards
屋面钉	roofing nail
屋面构造	roof construction
屋面坡度	roof pitch, slope of roof ◇ $33\frac{1}{2}°$~ third pitch, 屋架高跨相等的~ full pitch
屋前空地	frontage
屋室(墙壁)散射	room scattering
屋瓦	roof tile
无摆差仪表	dead beat instrument
无斑的	stainless
无斑点的	spotless, speckless
无包套轧制	bare rolling
无孢细菌	non-spore bacteria
无保护层材料	unprotected material
无保护电弧焊	unshielded arc welding
无保护气焊接	no gas welding
无背衬焊接法	non-backing process
无焙烧造块	(同"冷固结造块")
无铋铅	bismuth free lead
无变量的	non-variant
无变形钢	non-shrinking steel
无变形晶格	strain-free lattice
无变形切割	strain-free cutting
无变压器的	transless, transformerless
无标号公用块	【计】blank common block
无波动风温	straight-line blast temperature
无操作指令	no operation instruction
无槽轧制	grooveless rolling
无侧限压缩试验	unconfined compression test
无差拍(不摆)	dead bent
无差调整	floating control
无尘操作[处理]	dust-free handling
无尘的	dust-free, dustless
无尘碳黑	free flowing black
无沉淀(物)带[区](晶界的)	precititation [precipitate] free zone
无沉淀物排出水	【环】sediment-free effluent
无沉陷的	unyielding
无衬炉身	liningless stack
无衬铸钢罐	unlined cast steel pot
无触点传感器	contactless pickup
无触点元件	【电】non-contacting member
无窗厂房	black out plant
无窗墙	blank [blind, dead] wall
无疵表面	sound surface
无疵瑕	faultless
无磁铝合金	nonmagnetic aluminum alloy
无磁模具钢	non-magnetic steel
无磁性奥氏体铸铁	(10Ni, 5Mn, 余量 Fe) No-mag
无磁性材料	(同"非磁性材料")
无磁性钢	(同"非磁性钢")
无磁性耐热耐蚀钢	◇ 阿瑟~*
无磁性铜镍合金	nonmagnetic copper-nickel alloy
无磁性制品	non-magnetic product
无磁性铸铁	non-magnetic cast iron
无氮的	nitrogen-free
无氮化剂渗氮	(同"假渗氮")
无氮混合气吹炼法	【钢】mixed blast process
无底坩埚	potette, boot ◇ 圆筒形~*
无底钢轨(旧式)	edge rail
无底结晶器[钢锭模]	open-ended mould
无底座式模锻锤	(同"对击锻锤")
无电回路	dead circuit
无电极测量	electrode measurement
无电解液电镀	plating without electrolysis
无电压继电器	no-voltage relay
无电压释放(器)	no-voltage release
无电压释放开关	no-volt release switch
无顶头拔制(管材)	【压】(empty) sinking, sink drawing
无锭熔炼车间	ingot free melting shop
无锭轧机	direct rolling mill

无锭轧制　molten condition rolling, rolling from molten condition
无定位向　random orientation
无定向的　astatic,【理】omnidirectional
无定向电流计　astatic galvanometer
无定向控制　astatic control
无定向取向　chaotic orientation
无定向调节　floating control
无定向调节器　astatic governor [controller]
无定形　amorphism
无定形层　amorphous layer
无定形范性　amorphous plasticity
无定形粉末　amorphous powder
无定形固体　amorphous solid
无定形硅　amorphous silicon
无定形硅石[二氧化硅]　amorphous silica [quartzite]
无定形基质　structureless matrix
无定形硫　amorphous sulphur
无定形区　amorphous region
无定形石墨　amorphous graphite
无定形碳　amorphous [agraphite] carbon
无定形碳板　amorphous carbon plate
无定形碳电极　amorphous carbon electrode
无定形碳化硅　amorphous carborundum
无定形碳块　amorphous carbon block
无定形体　amorphous body
无定形物质　amorphous substance [material], non-crystalline substance
无定形现象　amorphism
无定形氧化铝　amorphous alumina, amorphous aluminium oxide
无定形状态　amorphous state [condition]
无毒的　non-toxic
无镀层斑点　uncoated spot
无镀层管　black pipe
无反应(的)　reactionless
无方向性结合　【理】nondirectional bond
无防护设施的　unprotected
无放射性的　nonradioactive, inactive

无废工艺　waste-free [wasteless] process
无沸腾熔炼　【钢】dead melting
无缝覆铝管件　seamless Alclad pipe and tube
无缝钢管　seamless steel pipe [tube], seamless pipe [tube], weldless tube ◇ 薄壁~*,不锈钢~*,大直径~*
无缝钢管桩　seamless steel pipe pile
无缝管　seamless pipe [tube], weldless tube ◇ 挤压~*,拉制~weldless drawn pipe,冷拔[拉]~*
无缝管坯　seamless bloom
无缝管延伸机　Diescher mill
无缝管轧机　seamless-tube rolling mill ◇ 连续式~*,皮尔格式~*,芯棒式~mandrel mill,周期式~*
无缝焊接　solderless joint
无缝环轧制　seamless ring rolling
无缝结构　jointless structure
无缝炉衬　seamless lining
无缝圆管　seamless round tube
无缝轴承　cutless bearing
无辐射跃迁[转变]　nonradiative [radiationless, Auger] transition
无盖地面铸造　open cast
无盖货车　gondola car
无干扰　【电】unjamming
无干扰运行　trouble-free operation
无坩埚区域熔炼　crucible-free zone-melting
无坩埚区域熔炼法　crucibleless zone melting method
无坩埚区域熔炼炉　non-crucible zone-melting furnace
无坩埚真空熔炼　【冶】crucibleless vacuum melting
无感电路　non-inductive circuit
无感电阻　non-inductive resistance
无感负荷　non-inductive load
无感绕法　curtis [noninductive] winding
无感绕组　non-inductive winding
无感线圈　non-inductive coil ◇ 双绕~*

无钢筋的 【建】unreinforced	无光光洁度 （同"毛面光洁度"）
无隔板离心机 （同"空心式离心机"）	无光黑漆[柏林无光黑漆] Berlin black
无隔膜电解池 diaphragmless cell	无光(火)焰 opaque [non-luminous] flame
无隔焰罩炉 unmuffled type furnace	无光浸蚀 mat etching
无功补偿 【电】reactive compensation	无光精整（同"毛面精整"）
无功部分[分量] reactive [idle, wattless, imaginary] component	无光泽表面 tarnish
	无光泽箔材 matte foil ◇ 一面～
无功电度表 wattless component watt-hour meter, var-hour meter	无光泽镀铬 matte chromium plating
	无光泽断口 lusterless fracture
无功电流 reactive [idle] current	无光泽断口熔渣 clouded slag
无功电起伏 reactive electric fluctuation	无光泽面 matte surface, frosting, frosted face
无功电压 reactive voltage	
无功伏安 volt-ampere reactive (VAR, var)	无光泽酸洗 【金】dull pickle
	无规混合(混匀) random blending
无功伏安小时 var-hour	无规力 random force
无功负载 reactive load	无规律变化 irregular variation
无功功率 reactive [wattless, imaginary] power, reactance capacity	无规律分布 random distribution
	无规起伏[涨落] random fluctuation
无功功率补偿 reactive power compensation	无规取向 random orientation
	无规取向合金 random orientation alloy
无功功率计 varmeter, wattless [reactive] power meter	无规散布 random scatter
	无规试验 random test
无功功率控制 reactive power control	无规试样 random sample
无功功率调节器 regulator for var	无规填充(床)层 randomly packed bed
无功功率因数表 reactive factor meter	无规性 randomness
无功时间 idle period	无规移动 random walk
无功线圈 idle coil	无规运动 random motion
无辜赔偿责任 【环】absolute liability	无规则碰撞 random collision
无钴高镍电解液 cobalt-free high nickel electrolyte	无轨矿车 trolley car
	无轨运输 free-wheeled transportation, trackless haulage
无股钢丝绳 nonstranded rope	
无故障操作 trouble-free [failure-free] operation	无轨装料机 （同"汽车式装料机"）
	无过失(赔偿)责任 【环】liability without fault
无固定顶盖连续式窑 archless continous kiln	
	无铪锆 hafnium free zirconium
无关标记[显示] nonrelevant indication	无害的 non-deleterious, harmless
无关"与"门 【计】don't care gate	无焊的 solderless
无惯性的 inertialess	无焊缝 weldless
无光薄板 dull-finish(ed) sheet	无焊缝料斗 【铁】one-piece hopper
无光玻璃 etched glass	无焊缝料钟 【铁】one-piece bell
无光电镀 dull plating	无胡克定律现象 （同"非胡克定律现象"）
无光镀锡薄钢板 dull plate	

无弧的　non-arcing
无滑动单次拉丝机　non-slip bull block
无滑动多次[级]拉丝机　multiple nonslip wire drawing bench, accumulation type wiredrawing machine, non-slip wire-drawing machine, accumulator multidraft machine
无滑动拉伸机　non-slip drawing machine
无滑动双头拉丝卷筒　non-slip double-drawing capstan
无滑动蓄丝[积线]式(多次)拉丝机 【压】non-slip cumulative type wire-drawing machine
无滑动蓄丝式九卷筒拉丝机　【压】non-slip cumulative type 9-block wire-drawing machine
无滑移区　no-slip region
无化学活性[反应]渣　nonreactive slag
无灰干燥　dry ash-free (d.a.f.)
无灰基(煤炭分析)　ash-free basis
无灰焦炭　ash-free coke
无灰滤纸　ashless filter-paper
无灰燃料　ash-free fuel
无灰物质[物料,泥料]　ash-free matter
无挥发性　non-volatility
无挥发性残渣　non-volatile residue
无回收焦炉　non-recovery coke oven
无回收水冷系统　nonrecovery water-cooling system
无活塞气压蓄力器　piston-less pneumatic accumulator
无活性渣　【冶】nonreactive slag
无火花的　non-arcing, sparkless
无机萃取　inorganic extraction ◇ 胺溶液 ~*
无机肥料　inorganic [mineral] fertilizer
无机化合物　inorganic [mineral] compound
无机化学　inorganic chemistry
无机灰尘　inorganic dust
无机架机座　【压】housingless stand
无机胶体　inorganic colloid
无机溶剂　inorganic solvent
无机试[药,添加]剂　inorganic agent
无机树脂　inorganic [mineral] resin
无机酸　inorganic [mineral] acid
无机酸净化　purification of inorganic acid
无机涂层[涂料]　inorganic [mineral] coating
无机污泥　mineral sludge
无机物　inorganic substance [matter]
无机吸附剂　inorganic adsorbent
无机絮凝剂　inorganic flocculant
无机盐　mineral [inorganic] salt
无机盐除锈剂　inorganic salt rust remover
无机阳离子交换剂　inorganic cation exchanger
无机阳离子吸附介质　inorganic cation-adsorption medium
无机营养　autotrophy, inorganic nutrients
无机营养生物　autotrophs
无机源　inorganic source
无畸变热处理　distortion-free heat treatment
无极测量　electrode measurement
无极化合物　homopolar compound
无极键　homopolar bond
无极键联　homopolar binding
无极晶体　atomic [covalent, homopolar] crystal
无极链式炉箅　endless chain grate
无极绳　endless cable
无级变速机构　stepless speed change mechanism
无级变速调整器　positive infinitely variable adjuster
无级传动机构　continuously variable gear
无价的　non-valent
无间隙接头焊接法　【焊】closed joint method
无间隙连接　close(d) joint
无间隙原子薄钢板[无晶隙薄钢板]　interstitial free sheet
无间隙[晶隙]原子钢　IF (interstitial-

free) steel ◇ 超低碳~*
无检修作业期　maintenance free period
无碱玻璃纤维　non-basic glass fibre
无碱金属钨酸　alkali-free tungstic acid
无碱物料　alkali-free material
无键晶体　homopolar crystal
无浆伸缩缝　dry joint
无铰拱　hingeless arch
无接触搅拌　non-contact stirring
无接触凝固　non-contact solidification
无接触式传感器　non-contacting pickup
无接触输送　non-contact transport
无接触转速计　contactless tachometer
无接箍管道　integral-joint tubing
无接头纤维编织皮带　endless fabric type belt
无节钢筋　plain bar [reinforcement]
无结构基质　structureless matrix
无结构凝胶体(煤岩)　collinite
无结果的　unproductive
无筋混凝土　plain concrete
无进位加　【计】false add
无晶间腐蚀钢　steel free from intergranular corrosion
无颈颗粒　【粉】neckless like particle
无静差调节器　astatic regulator
无静差调整　floating control
无静差调整法　【理】floating control mode
无开度圆盘剪切机[无间隙圆盘剪]【压】throatless rotary shearing machine
无抗电阻　nonreactive resistance
无空气的喷砂清理　airless blast cleaning
无空气溶液　air-free solution
无空窝燃烧(鼓风炉的)　【色】non-raceway burning
无孔粉粒　non-porous particle
无孔铬镀层　pore-free chromium
无孔构造　pore-free structure
无孔碳衬里 ◇ 卡尔贝特~的设备 Karbate lined plant
无孔隙的　imporous, non-porous
无孔隙膜　continuous film
无孔性　imporosity, non-porosity
无孔制品　pore-free product
无孔轴承　non-porous bearing
无孔转鼓式离心机　solid bowl centrifuge
无控波动　uncontrolled fluctuations
无控流动　uncontrolled flow
无宽展连续轧制　straight-away rolling
无矿沸腾　oreless boil
无亏损的　loss-free
无扩散合作运动　【金】diffusionless cooperative movement
无扩散转变　【金】diffusionless [athermal] transformation
无棱角砂　buckshot sand
无离子水　deionized water
无力火焰　lazy flame
无力作用时间　force [pressure] off time
无联营关系外国人　【企】unaffiliated foreigner
无量纲　(同"无因次")
无量纲变量　nondimensional variable
无量纲数　dimensionless value
无量纲系数　nondimensional coefficient
无料钟炉顶(高炉的)　bell-less top ◇ 并罐~*,串罐~*
无料钟顶高炉　blast furnace with bell-less top
无裂缝沉积　crack-free deposit
无裂纹铬镀层　crack-free chromium
无磷的　phosphorus-free, phosphorusless
无磷酸盐的　phosphate-free
无零点标度仪表　set-up-scale meter
无零点[零位]刻度(盘)　suppressed-zero [set-up] scale
无零点压力计　suppressed zero pressure gauge
无零点仪表　suppressed-zero (instrument, meter)
无硫残渣　sulphur-free residue
无硫腐蚀　sweet corrosion
无硫气体　sulphur-free [sweet] gas
无硫酸盐的硝酸钍　sulphate-free thorium

nitrate
无硫酸盐原料　sulphate-free material
无漏损的　leak-tight
无铝锌皂石　zincsilite
无氯的　chlorine-free
无螺纹栓　blank bolt
无毛边挤锻模　extrusion-forging die
无毛刺坯件　developed blank
无模锻造　flat die forging
无模拉丝法　dieless wire drawing
无模铸造[浇注]　mouldless casting
无摩擦穿过带　frictionless treading
无钼钢　molybdenum-free steel
无钠产物　sodium-free product
无内聚性　incoherence, incoherency, incohesion
无能隙超导体　gapless superconductor
无泥芯铸造　coreless casting
无黏结剂挤压(粉末挤压)　extrusion without binder
无黏结剂球团　pellet without binding agent
无黏结剂压团(法)　binderless briquetting
无黏结力预应力　prestress without bond
无镍不锈钢　nickelless stainless steel
无扭精轧机(线材的)　no-twist [twist-free] finishing mill
无扭精轧机组　no-twist finishing block
无扭精轧机座　no-twist finished stand
无扭(线材)轧机　no-twist [twist-free, block] mill
无扭轧制　no-twist [twist-free] rolling
无扭转拉丝　【压】torsion free wiredrawing, torsionless (wire)drawing
无牌坊的　housing-free
无牌坊机座　【压】housingless stand
无牌坊轧机　no-stand rolling mill
无膨润土球团　pellet without bentonite addition
无偏跟踪控制　tracking control without error
无偏析锭料　segregation-free ingot

无偏析合金　nonsegregation alloy
无偏析合金钢　non-segregated [segregation-less] alloy steel
无平衡装置机架　simple housing
无屏蔽的　unshielded
无屏蔽胶片　no-screen film ◇ 高速感光～ fast no-screen film,特高速感光～*,中速～*
无屏蔽曝光　no-screen exposure
无坡口连接　unchamfered joint
无气粉末　gas-free powder
无气金属　gas-free metal
无气泡钢　blister free steel, not blistering steel
无气喷漆机　airless painting spray machine
无气碳　gas-free carbon
无铅包电缆　non-lead-covered
无铅的　unleaded, nonleaded
无铅黄铜　nonleaded brass
无铅汽油　unleaded gasoline
无铅氧化锌　lead-free zinc oxide
无铅液体　lead-free liquor
无切口的　cutless
无切削成形　【压】chipless shaping
无切屑加工　chipless machining
无氢焊条　hydrogen-free electrode
无氢焦炭　hydrogen-free coke
无取向硅钢(薄)板　non-oriented silicon steel ◇ 冷轧～*,热轧～*
无取向合金　random orientation alloy
无取向膜　non-oriented film
无缺点的　spotless
无缺陷管理法　flawless management method
无缺陷焊缝　flawless [sound, zero-defect] weld
无缺陷金属　sound metal
无缺陷连铸坯　continuous cast slab free of defects
无缺陷料(木材)　clear-stuff
无缺陷型材　【压】defect-free section
无热的　athermal

无人观测气球 【环】kitoon, kytoon
无人值班的 non-attended, unattended
无熔剂保护熔融金属 naked molten metal
无熔剂法(生产锰铁) flux free method
无熔丝断路[开关]器 no fuse breaker (NFB), fuse free breaker (FFB), non-fuse breaker
无溶解力的 insolvent (insolv.)
无乳化剂轧制 dry rolling
无噻吩苯 thiophene free benzene
无色氨基亚铜 colourless cuprous ammine
无色光 colourless light
无色菌科 achromatiaceae
无色透明镜片 clear lens
无砂浆砌砖 dry-brick (building)
无商业价值 no commercial value (n.c.v.)
无砷浮渣 【色】non-arsenical dross
无伸缩性 non-elasticity
无声链 silent [laminated] chain
无声运行 silent running
无盛料器区域精炼 container-free zone refining, zone refining without a container
无时效钢 non-ageing steel
无时效性低碳钢 ◇ 伊泽特～*
无事故的 foolproof
无事实根据的 ungrounded
无收缩钢 non-shrinking steel
无束缚电子 nonbonding [unbound] electron
无束缚状态 unbound state
无数的 innumerable, countless, myriad, myri(a), trillion
无衰减 zero-decrement
无衰减的 undamped
无衰减振荡 undamped oscillations
无水氨 anhydrous ammonia ◇ 裂化～*
无水氟化氢过热器 A.H.F. superheater
无水光卤石 anhydrous carnallite
无水硅酸盐 anhydrous silicate
无水钾锰矾 manganolangbeinite
无水酒精[乙醇] absolute (ethyl) alcohol

无水冷炉底滑管 dry skid
无水冷却技术(加热炉的) cooling-free technique
无水硫酸铝{$Al_2(SO_4)_3$} anhydrous aluminium sulphate
无水卤化物 anhydrous halide
无水氯化铝{$AlCl_3$} anhydrous aluminium chloride
无水氯化镁{$MgCl_2$} anhydrous magnesium chloride
无水氯化镁电解炼镁法 I.G. process
无水氯化氢 anhydrous hydrogen chloride
无水氯化物 anhydrous chloride
无水镁盐 anhydrous magnesium salt
无水钠镁矾 vanthoffite
无水炮泥 【铁】waterless taphole mix
无水溶剂 anhydrous solvent
无水溶剂萃取 anhydrous liquid extraction
无水溶剂冶金 lyometallurgy
无水石膏{$CaSO_4$} (gypsum) anhydrite, cube spar
无水石膏水泥 anhydrite cement
无水石油 dry oil
无水酸 anhydrous acid
无水碳酸钠{Na_2CO_3} anhydrous sodium carbonate
无水无矿物质基(煤炭分析) dry mineral matter free (basis) (d.m.m.f.)
无水氧化铝 anhydrous alumina, anhydrous aluminium oxide
无塑性区 no-plastic zone ◇ 轧材～*
无塑性粉末 non-plastic powder
无塑性破坏[断裂] non-ductile fracture
无酸除鳞 【压】acidless descaling
无损测定法 nondestructive evaluation method
无损测量 nondestructive measuring
无损读出 nondestructive read
无损耗的 loss less, loss-free
无损化学分析 nondestructive chemical analysis
无损检验[探伤] non(-)destructive in-

spection [testing, examination] [test(ing)], testing without destruction
无损喷砂　nonerosive [seed] blasting
无损探伤法　nondestructive flaw-detecting method
无缩颈变形　neck-free deformation
无缩孔的　free of shrinkholes,【冶】pipeless
无缩孔钢　non-piping steel
无坍落混凝土　【建】no-slump concrete
无弹跳冲击　dead stroke
无碳奥氏体　carbon-free austenite
无碳表层　carbon-free surface layer
无碳不锈钢　carbon-free stainless steel
无碳产物　carbon-free product
无碳钢　carbon-free steel
无碳合金　carbon-free alloy
无碳合金钢　carbon-free alloy steel
无碳黑火焰　sootless flame
无碳化钨的硬质合金　tungsten-carbide-free hard metal
无碳结构组分　carbon-free constituent
无碳熔渣　【冶】carbon-free slag
无碳酸盐炉料　carbonate free burden
无碳铁合金　carbon-free ferroalloy
无碳铁素体　carbon-free ferrite
无碳铀　carbon-free uranium
无填料焙烧　fillerless roasting
无填料喷洗塔　spray-type unpacked scrubber, unpacked spray tower
无填料烧结　fillerless sintering
无填料塔　void column
无条件转移　【计】unconditional transfer [jump, branch]
无条件(最)优化法　(同"绝对最优化法")
无条理　incoherence, incoherency
无跳动燃烧　pulsation-free combustion
无铁硫酸盐　iron-free sulfate
无铁溶液　iron-free solution
无铜铝基合金　copper-free aluminium-base alloy

无铜溶液　(同"脱铜溶液")
无头螺钉[螺丝]　grub [headless] screw
无头轧制　endless rolling
无凸面焊缝　flush weld
无凸模拉深　punchless drawing
无凸缘轮箍　blind tyre
无涂层钢　non-coated steel
无涂料焊丝　bare wire
无维变数　nondimensional [dimensionless] variable
无尾工艺　tailing-free [tailingless] process
无尾损装置控制系统　【压】control system for non-tail-end-loss arrangement
无位错晶体　dislocation-free crystal
无钨硬质合金　tungsten-free cemented carbide
无污垢[污泥]的　non-fouling
无污染(的)　pollution-free, free from contamination, uncontaminated
无污染工业　【环】non-polluting industry
无污染工艺　pollution-free process
无析出(物)带[区](晶界的)　precipitation [precipitate] free zone
无吸收性模子　non-absorbent mould
无锡巴比合金　tin-free bearing metal
无锡高强度青铜　Mallory metal
无锡青铜　(同"铅青铜")
无锡轴承合金　tin-free bearing metal
无隙沉积物[覆层]　pore-free deposit
无隙氧化亚铁团块　non-porous ferrous metal briquette
无细料混凝土　【建】no-fines concrete
无瑕疵(的)　flawless, spotless, sound, speckless, stainless
无限　infinity, limitless
无限大平板模型　infinite slab model
无限公司　【企】company of unlimited liability
无限固溶体　all proportional solid solution
无限互溶性　unlimited mutual solubility,【金】complete miscibility
无限滑移量　unlimited amount of slip

无限冷硬轧辊 【压】indefinite chill roll
无限量滑移 unlimited slip
无限调速器 infinite governor
无限稀释 infinite dilution
无限小强度 infinitesimal strength
无限小位错 infinitesimal dislocation
无限循环 【计】endless loop
无限制变形 unrestricted change of shape
无限制的 unrestricted, unlimited, unbounded, unconfined
无线操作式起重机 wireless type crane
无线电报 radiogram, radiotelegram
无线电报机[术] radiotelegraph, aerograph
无线电操纵 radio control, telemotion
无线电测量仪器 radio-instruments
无线电传送的 radioed
无线电传真 radiovision, facsimile radio
无线电传真术 radio-photography
无线电传真照片 radio-photograph
无线电电路 electronic [radio] circuit
无线电定位 radiolocation, radio position finding
无线电定位器 radiolocator
无线电发送机 radiotransmitter
无线电方向测定仪 【电】goniometer
无线电放大器 radio amplifier
无线电干扰 radio interference ◇ 不产生～的 radioquiet, 不引起～的 radiop roof
无线电工程[技术] radio engineering
无线电广播 radio broadcast, telediffusion
无线电广播者 blaster
无线电话 walkie-talkie, radio(tele)phone
无线电控制 radio control
无线电联络指挥系统 radio paging system
无线电路 radio-circuit
无线电频率 radio frequency (RF)
无线电频率电阻焊 (同"射频电阻焊")
无线电摄影[传真照相] radiophoto
无线电设备 radio equipment, radio [wireless] set

无线电台 radio station [set]
无线电探测[定位]装置 radar
无线电通信[通讯] radio communication, telecommunication
无线电信号 radio-signal
无线电遥测 radiotelemetering
无线电遥控 radiotelecontrol, wireless remote control
无线电用[镍铁]高磁导率合金(50Ni,50Fe) radiometal
无线电自动控制 radio autocontrol
无箱造型 【铸】flaskless moulding, removable flask mould(ing)
无箱铸型 【铸】boxless mould
无向调节器 astatic governor
无向量轴 scalar axis
无向性孔隙 【粉】isotropic porosity
无效果的 inoperative
无效率的 inefficient
无效蠕变[滑移] sterile creep
无效时间 ineffective [inactive, lost] time
无效时间损失 dead-time loss
无效试验 blank experiment
无斜度锻件[锻造] no-draft [zero-draft] forging
无泄漏 non-leakage
无泄漏的 leakless, no-leak
无屑加工 chipless machining
无芯棒拔制(管材) sinking, sink drawing
无芯[心]的 non-centered, coreless
无芯感应电炉 coreless(-type) induction (electric) furnace, coreless furnace
无芯高频感应(电)炉 coreless high-frequency induction furnace, high frequency coreless induction furnace ◇ 埃弗科－诺思拉普～*
无芯头拉伸 【压】hollow sinking
无心磨削[研磨] centreless grinding
无心研磨机 centreless grinding machine
无型锤锻工艺 smithing technique
无型锻造 hammer forging
无型锻造锤 fore hammer

无锈的	rust-free
无蓄力器多次拉丝机	nonaccumulator multidraft machine
无序	disorder, disorganization
无序点阵	disordered lattice
无序度	degree of randomness
无序固溶体	disordered [random] solid solution ◇ 置换型~*
无序固溶体晶体	disordered solid solution crystal
无序合金	disordered [non-ordered, random] alloy
无序化	disordering
无序(化)相	disordered phase
无序化影响[作用]	disordering effect
无序结构	disordered structure
无序排列	random arrangement
无序区	【金】disordered region
无序取向	disordered orientation
无序散射	disorder scattering
无序熵	entropy of disorder
无序铜金合金	disordered copper-gold
无序线	disordus
无序性	randomness
无序-有序转变	【金】disorder-order transformation [transitions]
无序轧制多品种生产	disorder rolling of multiple varieties
无序状态	disordered [random] state
无漩涡水口	【连铸】nonswirl nozzle ◇ 定径式~*
无选择取样	random sampling
无压成形(法)	pressureless compacting, shaping without pressing
无压杆挤压	ramless extruding
无压焊接	non-pressure welding
无压(力)渗透[浸渍](法)	pressureless infiltration
无压烧结	pressureless sintering
无压塑型	pressureless compacting
无压缩空气喷雾装置	compressed air-free spraying device
无压下通过	dumming
无压油(油蒸气真空泵用油)	Apiezon oil
无压作用时间	force [pressure] off time
无烟	smokelessness
无烟火药	smokeless powder
无烟煤	anthracite (coal), anthracitic [hard, kilkenny, smokeless] coal ◇ 半~ carbonaceous coal, 过滤用~ Anthrafilt, 栗级~*, 碎~(未筛分的) culm coal, 煅制~ thermoanthracite
无烟煤粉	anthracite fines [duff]
无烟煤介质过滤器	anthrafilt filter
无烟煤末(未筛分的)	culm coal
无烟煤生铁	anthracite pig
无烟煤碳质耐火材料	anthracite-coal-base carbon refractory
无烟燃料	smokeless fuel
无烟燃烧室	smokeless furnace
无烟装炉	【焦】smokeless charging
无焰燃烧	flameless combustion, smoulder
无阳极电子枪	work-accelerated gun ◇ 区域提纯用~*
无氧电解质	oxygen-free electrolyte
无氧粉末	oxygen-free powder
无氧高导电性铜	(同"高导电性无氧铜")
无氧化	non-oxidation
无氧化加热	scale-free heating (钢的)◇ DX~用保护气体 DX gas
无氧化加热炉	scale-free heating furnace
无氧化浇注	【钢】non-oxidation casting
无氧化快速加热炉	non-oxidizing high speed heating furnace
无氧化炉	non-oxidized furnace, non-oxidizing annealing furnace
无氧化皮淬火	scale-free hardening
无氧化气氛	non-oxidizing atmosphere
无氧化气体	non-oxidizing gas
无氧化热处理炉	non-oxidizing heat-treatment furnace
无氧化退火炉	non-oxidized furnace, non-oxidizing annealing furnace

无氧化物的 oxide-free
无氧化预热炉 non-oxidizing preheating furnace
无氧化氯化物 oxide-free chloride
无氧钠 oxygen-free sodium
无氧培养器 anaerobic culture apparatus
无氧气氛 oxygen-free [anaerobic] atmosphere
无氧熔剂 oxygen-free flux
无氧铜 oxygen-free copper ◇ 阿姆克龙含铬～合金*,阿姆萨尔弗～(合金) Amsulf copper,阿姆特尔含碲～(合金)*,高导电性～*,含硅～*,烧结～*
无氧铜生产法 coalesced copper process
无药(皮)焊条 (同"光焊条")
无药皮焊丝 (同"光焊丝")
无液电镀 plating without electrolysis
无液气压计 aneroid (barometer)
无液相烧结 fritting,【粉】sintering in the absence of a liquid
无意曝光 accidental exposure
无翼缘主动轮 blind driver
无因次 zero dimension
无因次数 dimensionless [nondimensional] number
无因次系数 dimensionless [nondimensional] coefficient
无因次(形)式 dimensionless form
无阴影区 unshaded area
无应变的 unstrained
无应变粉末 strain-free powder
无应变时效钢 non-strain ag(e)ing steel
无应力的 unstressed
无应力区 stressless zone
无应力线圈 stress-free coil
无影照明 shadowless [indirect] lighting
无用板坯 dummy slab
无用风口 blind tuyere
无用数据 hash, garbage, nonsignificant data
无用数据总和 hash [gibberish] total
无用信息 【电】hash, garbage

无用字符 【计】ignore character
无铀的 uranium-free, U-free
无源传感器 passive transducer
无源元件 passive element
无约束变形 unrestricted change of shape
无约束的 unconfined
无杂质半导体 pure semiconductor
无杂质的 free from contamination
无载抽头切换开关[无载分接头切换装置] off-load tap-changer
无载电流时间 current off-time
无载继电器 no-load relay
无载释放(器) no-load release
无载损失 no-load [idling] loss
无载行速 no-load speed
无载运行 no-load operation [running], unloaded running
无载运转时间 idle running time
无噪声的 noise-free, noiseless
无皂土球团 pellet without bentonite addition
无增感屏 X 射线胶片 【金】non-screen X-ray film
无渣操作法 slagless [slag-free] operation
无渣感应熔炼 slagless induction melting
无渣金属 slag-free [slagless] metal
无渣炼钢 slagless steelmaking
无张力 no pull
无张力轧制 tension free rolling
无照电流 dark current
无砧座锤锤头 【压】opposing ram
无砧座(模)锻锤 impactor, impacter
无针孔材料 pinhole-free material
无振荡(的) dead-beat
无止境 infinity
无中间扩散层的覆层 alloy-free coating
无中心的 centreless
无钟炉顶 (同"无料钟炉顶")
无钟炉顶布料器 bell-less top distributor
无钟炉顶操作 bell-less top operation
无钟炉顶装料 bell-less top charging
无钟装料 bell-less charging

无珠光体钢	pearlite free structural (PFS) steel
无专利[专有]权	non-exclusive right
无转让权	non-transferable right
无锥度风口	straight-type tuyere
无自感线圈	【电】curtis winding
无阻沉积	【选】unhindered sedimentation
无阻沉降	【选】unhindered settling
无阻尼振荡	【理】undamped oscillation
无作用期间	inaction period
五氨络物	pentammine
五倍的	quinary
五倍子酸	gallic acid
五层钢锭	five ply ingot
五单位码	【计】five level [unit] code
五单位输入机	【计】five track reader
五段式连续加热炉	five zone heating furnace
五氟化铌{NbF$_5$}	niobium [columbium] pentafluoride
五氟化钽{TaF$_5$}	tantalic [tantalum] fluoride, tantalum pentafluoride
五氟化物	pentafluoride
五氟一氧络铌酸钾	(同"氟氧铌酸钾")
五辊式轧机	five roller mill
五机架串列(冷)轧机	five stand tandem (cold) mill
五极(电子)管	pentode
五级萃取	five stage extraction
五价	quinquevalency, pentavalency
五价的	pentavalent, quinquevalent
五价碘的	iodic
五价铌化合物	niobic [columbic] compound
五价钽化合物	tantalic compound
五价锑的	antimonic, stibial
五价钨的	tungstic
五角钢材[型材]	pentagonal section
五金	metal
五金工人	metallist
五金器皿	hardware
五金器皿精饰抛光	hardware finish
五进制的	【数】quinary
五硫化二磷{P$_2$S$_5$}	phosphorus pentasulphide
五硫化二钼{Mo$_2$S$_5$}	molybdenum pentasulphide
五硫化二锑{Sb$_2$S$_5$}	antimony pentasulphide
五硫化物	pentasulphide
五氯化铼{ReCl$_5$}	rhenium pentachloride
五氯化磷{PCl$_5$}	phosphorous pentachloride
五氯化磷合四氯化锆{2ZrCl$_4$·PCl$_5$}	zirconium tetrachloride addition compound with phosphorus
五氯化钼{MoCl$_5$}	molybdenum pentachloride
五氯化铌{NbCl$_5$}	niobium [columbium] pentachloride
五氯化镤{PaCl$_5$}	protactinium pentachloride
五氯化砷{AsCl$_5$}	arsenic pentachloride
五氯化钽{TaCl$_5$}	tantalic chloride, tantalum pentachloride
五氯化锑{SbCl$_5$}	antimony pentachloride
五氯化钨{WCl$_5$}	tungsten pentachloride
五氯化物	pentachloride
五氯化铀{UCl$_5$}	uranium pentachloride
五氯氢氧化钼{2MoCl$_2$·Mo(OH)Cl}	molybdenum hydroxy-pentachloride
五氯氢氧化物	hydroxypentachloride
五醚	pentaether
五面体	pentahedron
五栅管	pentagrid tube, heptode
五水(合)硫酸铜{CuSO$_4$·5H$_2$O}	(同"胆矾"), cupric sulfate pentahydrate
五水合物	pentahydrate
五水硼镁矿	halurgite
五羰基化物	pentacarbonyl
五羰基铁{Fe(CO)$_5$}	iron pentacarbonyl
五相平衡	quinary equilibrium ◇ 第五类 ~*, 第一类 ~*
五心柱变压器	five legged transformer

五溴化钽{TaBr$_5$} tantalum pentabromide, tantalic bromide
五溴化钨{WBr$_5$} tungsten pentabromide
五溴化物 pentabromide
五氧化二钒 vanadium pentoxide, vanadic oxide, red cake
五氧化二钒腐蚀 corrosion by vanadium pentoxide
五氧化二磷 phosphorus pentoxide
五氧化二铌 niobic [columbic] anhydride, niobium [columbium] pentoxide
五氧化二镤 protactinium pentoxide
五氧化二砷 arsenic oxide
五氧化二铊 thallic peroxide
五氧化二钽 tantalic oxide, tantalum pentoxide
五氧化二锑 antimony pentoxide
五氧化二钨 tungsten pentoxide
五氧化物 pentoxide
五元的 【金】quinary
五元合金 quinary alloy
五元合金钢 quinary steel
五元素(指钢中杂质元素 C, Si, Mn, P, S) five elements
五原子的 pentatomic
伍德易熔[低熔点]合金(50Bi, 12.5Sn, 25Pb, 12.5Cd; 熔点 70~72℃) Wood's alloy[metal]
伍兹钢 wootz (steel)
戊醇{C$_5$H$_{11}$OH} amyl alcohol(am. alc), n-pentanol
戊基油 Amoil(酞酸戊酯) ◇ S-~ Amoil-S(癸二酸戊酯)
戊酸{C$_2$H$_5$CH$_2$COOH$_2$} Valeric acid
戊烷{C$_5$H$_{12}$} Pentane
戊酰{CH$_3$(CH$_2$)$_3$CO-} valeryl
雾 fog, mist
雾淬 fog quenching
雾滴分离器 mist separator
雾化 atomizing, atomization, atomising, atomisation ◇ 溶解气体~*
雾化法 atomisation (process), atomization

◇ RZ 铁粉~*, 西梅塔格铁粉~ Simetag process, 转盘~*
雾化粉粒 atomized particle
雾化粉末 atomized powder
雾化干燥 flash drying
雾化干燥器 atomizing drier
雾化金属粉末 atomized metal powder
雾化器 atomizer, micromizer, pulverizer, disperser
雾化铅粉 atomized lead
雾化燃料 atomized fuel
雾化燃烧器 atomizer [atomizing] burner
雾化热 heat of atomization
雾化润滑 atomized lubrication
雾化设备 atomization plant, atomizing equipment [unit]
雾化生铁粉 atomized pig iron powder
雾化室 atomisation [spray] chamber
雾化试验(法) atomizer test
雾化铁粉 liquid-disintegrated powder, Mannesmann iron powder (用曼内斯曼法制得的) ◇ 内塞~生产法 Naeser process
雾化筒 atomizing cup
雾化锡粉 atomized tin
雾化锌粉 atomized zinc dust
雾化蒸汽 atomizing steam
雾化装置 atomisation plant
雾化锥 atomizer cone
雾沫捕集[分离]器 entrainment separator [trap]
雾沫塔 entrainment tower
雾室 fog chamber [room]
雾室(腐蚀)试验 fog test
雾室露点分析器 fog chamber dew point analyser
雾翳 fog ◇ 两色~ dichroic fog, 曝光致~(底片的) light fog, 显像~ development fog, 许可~值 tolerable fog value
雾状喷砂清理 vapour blast(ing)
物镜 object glass, objective (lens) ◇ 去像散~*

物镜测微计 object micrometer	物理吸着 physical sorption
物镜光阑[孔径] objective aperture	物理吸附(作用) physical adsorption, physisorption
物镜台 objective table	物理现象 physical phenomenon
物镜物理孔径 physical objective aperture	物理性能 physical character(istic) [property]
物镜遮光器 【金】flag	
物镜变化 physical change	物理性能钢 physical steel
物理变量 physical variable	物理性能检验 examination of physical properties
物理参数 physical parameter, physico variable	
物理测量[性能测定] physical measurement	物理性质 physical property [appearance, behaviour]
物理常数 physical constant	物理学家 physicist (phy.)
物理沉[淀]积 physical deposition	物理学应力 【理】physical stress
物理沉[淀]积法 physical deposition process	物理冶金(学) physical metallurgy, physico-metallurgy ◇ 过程～*, 应用～*
物理动力学 physical kinetics	物理因数 physical factor
物理法富集 enrichment by physical processes	物理状态 physical state [condition]
物理方法 physical process [method]	物料 material (Mtl, mat., matl), matter ◇ 单一～ individual material, 料仓中～分层【冶】bin segregation
物理过程 physical process	
物理化学 physical chemistry (phy. chem.), physico-chemistry	
物理化学参数 physico-chemical parameter	物料参数 parameter of material
	物料化学成分 material analysis
物理化学流体力学 physico-chemical hydrodynamics	物料检测器 material detector
	物料流 material flow
物理化学因数[因素] physico-chemical factor	物料流程图 material flow diagram
	物料流动机理 mechanism of material flow
物理检验试样 physical testing sample	物料流连续分析器 on-stream analyzer
物理结构 physical construction	物料平衡 material [matter] balance, burden balance (高炉的)
物理论证 physical argument	
物理气相淀积[被覆] physical vapour deposition	物料平衡表 balance sheet of materials
	物料平衡计算 burden balance calculation
物理情况 physical situation	物料输送设备 material handling equipment
物理缺陷 physical imperfection	
物理生长 physical growth	物料水分[含水量] material moisture content
物理数据 physical data	
物理损失 physical loss	物料损耗 material breakage
物理特性 physical behaviour [character(istic)]	物料通过时间 time of throughput
	物料通过(数)量 throughput (capacity), thruput
物理条件 physical condition	
物理稳定性 physical stability	物料性质 mass behaviour
	物料运输 material transport(ing) ◇ 厂

内~*
物料运输[搬运]机构　material transport mechanism
物料(运输)线　material track
物料装卸起重机　material handling crane
物料自动筛分　automatic stock screening
物态变化　change of state
物态方程　equation of state ◇ 范德瓦尔斯~*
物体　substance, body, matter (mat.), object
物相分离　isolation of phase
物相分析　phase analysis
物相检查　phase detection
物相鉴定　phase identification
物像　object image
物业　utility service(s)
物质　matter (mat.), mass, material, substance
物质波　material waves
物质不灭定律　【理】law of conservation of matter
物质传递[传输]　mass [matter] transport, mass [material] transfer
物质传递机理　mass-transfer mechanism
物质的量浓度　mass concentration [density, enrichment]
物质迁移　material transport
物质迁移机制【理】　mechanism of material transport
物质平衡　mass [material] balance
物质移动(区域熔炼的)　matter travel

物资储备　material reserve
误操作　misoperation,【计】bust
误测　false measurement
误查[检]　【计】false drop
误差　error, deviation, inaccuracy, discrepancy, imprecision ◇ 高斯~函数*, 有~的 inaccurate
误差百分率　percentage error
误差大小[量值]　magnitude of error
误差范围　error range [band, margin]
误差放大器　error amplifier
误差分析　error analysis
误差极限[限度]　limit of error, error margin
误差率　error rate [index], abuse coefficient
误差面积　error area
误差曲线　error [deviation] curve ◇ 特朗普~ Tromp error curve
误差修正系统　error-correction system
误差因素　error factor
误差原因　source of error
误差源　source of error
误差值　magnitude of error
误差指数　error index
误动作　malfunction
误读　misreading
误码率　【计】(bit) error rate
误算　counting loss, miscount
误显示[误示度]　false indication
误用　abuse, misuse

X x

析出 separating out, deposition, freezing out, precipitation, segregation ◇ 不连续～*, 从溶液中～ throw out of solution, 可～的 precipitable
析出电位 deposition potential
析出动力学 kinetics of precipitation
析出方式 deposition pattern
析出金属量 quantity of deposited metal
析出气体 liberated gas, liberation of gas
析出区[范围] precipitation range
析出热处理 precipitation heat treatment
析出石墨 indigenous graphite
析出速率 rate of desorption
析出物 precipitate, deposition ◇ 无～带*
析出物集合体 precipitate agglomerates
析出相 【金】precipitate(d) phase
析出相晶格 【金】precipitate lattice
析出相锁住的位错结 precipitate-locked dislocation node
析出效率 efficiency of deposition
析出行为 precipitating behaviour
析出硬化型耐热合金 ◇ 因科内尔 X～ Inconel "X"
析出硬化型热作模具钢（PH 钢；$2Cr_3Mo_2NiVSi$） precipitation hardened hot die steel
析出作用 precipitating action
析钢仪 steelscope, styloscope
析氢腐蚀 hydrogen-evolution corrosion
析取 extraction, disjunction, scorifying ◇ 炉渣的～ scorifying of cinder
析像能力 resolution (capabiliity)
析氧阳极 anode evolving oxygen
析银法 【色】(in)quartation
西巴恩晶体埃 Siegbahn Angstroem
西班牙石英质磁铁矿 marbella
西贝克电动势 Seebeck electromotive force, Seebeck emf
西贝克古典热电效应 Seebeck effect
西贝克系数 Seebeck coefficient
西博德法（干式脱硫） 【焦】Seaboard process
西布利铝锌合金（67Al, 33Zn） Sibley alloy
西尔波德银粉 Silpowder
西尔布拉洛伊低温钎焊合金 Silbralloy
西尔夫六 O 黄铜焊料[西尔夫青铜]（59Cu, 37.5—38.5Zn, 0.5—2.5Sn, 0—1.75Ni, 0—1Pb, ＜0.8Fe） Silfbronze
西尔福斯铜银焊料合金（15Ag, 5P, 余量 Cu） Silfos
西尔弗拉克斯碳化硅高级耐火材料 Silfrax
西尔弗拉姆耐热合金（30Cr, 1Ni, 余量 Fe） Silfram
西尔弗莱克斯镀锌法 Silflex process
西尔弗莱特银合金 Silverite
西尔金色耐蚀钎焊合金（铜和铜合金用） Silbraze
西尔卡德尔耐蚀铜硅合金（2.2Si, 0.5—0.7Mn, 余量 Cu） Silcurdur
西尔卡洛伊黄铜 Silcalloy
西尔卡姆高强度铝合金（9Si, 7.5Cu, 1.4Ni, 0.5Mn, 余量 Al） Sylcum
西尔卡兹锆铁合金（3—5Zr, 余量 Fe） Silcaz
西尔卡兹硅钙钛中间合金（35—40Si, 10Ca, 10Ti, 7Al, 4Zn, 余量 Fe） Silcaz
西尔马纳尔银锰铝永磁合金（87Ag, 8.5Mn, 4.5Al） Silmanal
西尔梅雷克铝硅耐蚀合金（1Si, 0.6Mg + Mn, 余量 Al） Simelec
西尔莫硅钼钢（＜0.15C, 0.5—2Si, 0.45—0.65Mo, 0.5Mn） Silmo
西尔尼克硅镍青铜（1.8Ni, 0.6Si, 余量 Cu） Silnic bronze
西尔伸长计 Searle's extensometer
西尔式钢丝绳 Seale wire rope
西尔坦低合金高强度钢（0.4C, 0.7—0.9Mn, 0.2—0.3Si, 余量 Fe） Sil-Ten

steel
西尔填充丝式钢丝绳　Seale filler wire rope
西尔瓦克斯(硅钛钒)锆铁合金(35—40Si, 10Ti, 10V, 6Zr, 0.5B, 余量 Fe)　Silvax
西尔瓦灵顿混合式钢丝绳　Seale Warrington wire rope
西尔瓦密封用铁镍钴合金　Sealvar
西尔瓦奈特金碲合金[(Au, Ag)Te$_2$]　Sylvanite
西尔维尔锰黄铜(68—73Cu, 7—12Mn, 12—16Zn, 0—6.5Ni, 0.5Pb, 2Fe, 0.2Al)　Silvel
西尔维林铜镍耐蚀合金(72—80Cu, 16—17Ni, 1—8Zn, 1—3Sn, 1—2Co, 1—1.5Fe)　Silverine
西尔维罗伊德铜镍锌装饰合金(48Cu, 26Ni, 25Zn, 1Pb)　Silveroid
西尔维罗伊德铜镍装饰合金(54Cu, 45Ni, 1Mn)　Silveroid
西尔沃尔铜镍锌耐蚀合金(62Cu, 18.5Ni, 19.2Zn, 0.3Pb)　Silvore
西尔滕钨银合金(用于火箭喷嘴; 11Ag, 余量 W)　Sil-Tung
西格里式煤气切断阀　【铁】Sigri-type isolation valve
西格马利姆铝合金(3.8Cu, 0.8Si, 0.7Mn, 余量 Al)　Sigmalium
西格蒙德金属电阻合金　Sigmund
西格示温熔锥　Seger cone
西格锥当量　Seger-cone equivalent (S.C.E.)
西卡尔硅铝合金(中间合金; 50—55Si, 22—29Al, 2—4Ti, 1Ca, <0.2C, <0.2Mn, 余量 Fe)　Sical
西克里坦铝青铜(5—9Al, 1.5Mg, 0.5P, 余量 Cu)　Secretan
西克罗马尔硅铬铝耐酸钢(<24Cr, <3.5Al, 1Si, 少量 Mo)　Sicromal steel
西克罗马硅铬钼弹簧钢(0.15C, 0.5Mn, 1.15—1.65Si, 0.45—0.65Mo)　Sicrome

西克罗莫硅铬钼系耐蚀耐热合金钢(<0.15C, 0.5—2Si, 0.75—10Cr, 0.45—1.1Mo, 余量 Fe)　Sicromo
西拉尔高硅铸铁(6Si, 3C, 0.7Mn, 0.3P, 0.1S, 余量 Fe)　Silal
西拉尔铝基合金(1.25Mg, 0.5Si, 0.8Mn, 0.3Ti, 余量 Al)　Silal
西拉方特硅铝合金(9—13Si, 0.3—0.6Mn, 0.2—0.4Mg, 余量 Al)　Silafont
西拉镍钴钛铁合金　hila
西莱尔含硅铸铁(5—6Si)　Silel cast iron
西兰克银锑合金(92—94.5Ag, 4—4.5Sb, 1—3Cd, <2.5Zn)　Silanca
西里乌斯耐蚀耐热合金钢(0.25C, 16Ni, 17Cr, 3W, 12Co, 2Ti, 余量 Fe)　Sirius
西里西亚锌蒸馏炉　Silesian furnace
西利科尼特电阻体(27.2C, 63.9Si, 3.82O, 5.14 其它)　Siliconit
西利科尼特炉　Siliconit furnace
西利曼铝青铜(86.5Cu, 9.5Al, 4Fe)　silliman bronze
西鲁弗尔羰基铁粉成形铁心　Sirufer
西马纳尔硅锰铝铁合金(20Si, 20Mn, 20Al, 余量 Fe)　Simanal
西梅塔格铁粉雾化法　Simetag process
西梅特预浸电解法(炼铜)　Cymet (cyprus metallurgical) process
西门塞特耐火材料　Siemensite
西门式破碎机　Symons crusher
西门斯公式(表示熔点与压力的关系)　Simons formula
西门斯小四辊冷轧机　Simons mill
西门锌基轴承合金(48Zn, 47Cd, 5Sb)　Siemen's alloy
西门子-马丁炉　Siemens-Martin furnace
西门子-马丁式电炉　Siemens-Martin electric furnace
西门子发生炉煤气　Siemens gas
西门子炉　Siemens-type furnace
西门子蓄热式平炉　Siemens regenerative open-hearth furnace

西蒙斯型(圆锥)破碎机 Symons crusher
西米勒含锡黄铜(9.5Zn,7Sn,余量 Cu; 10Zn,0.5Sn,余量 Cu) Similor
西米塔尔斯可锻镍银[镍铜锌合金](18Ni) Scimitars
西米特铅基轴承合金(75—76Pb,3—4Sn, 15—17Sb, 2Ni, 0.6—1.5Cd, 0.3—0.4Cu,0.5As,0.3P) Thermit (alloy)
西摩赖特耐蚀铜镍锌合金(64Cu,18Ni, 18Zn) Seymourite
西姆盖尔挤压铝合金(0.5Si,0.5Mg,余量 Al) Simgal
西纳索尔溶剂(用于失蜡造型) Synasol
西尼马克斯铁镍磁性合金(铁心材料; 43Ni,3Si,余量 Fe) 【铸】Sinimax
"西山"常温自硬砂造型法["西山"砂型和型芯制备法] N (Nishiyama) process
"西山"关系(马氏体转变的) Nishiyama relationship, Nishiyama's relation
西瓦含砷α黄铜(含0.04As的七三黄铜) Seva
西韦茨定律 【金】Sieverts' law
西维尔梅特银钨触头合金 Silvelmet
西乌林制海绵铁法 Sieurin process
西屋X射线厚度计 Westinghouse thickness gauge
西屋镍铜热磁补偿合金 Westinghouse alloy
西屋喷气机合金高温高转速试验 【冶】Westinghouse jet metal test
西屋式换接电极尖 Westinghouse transition tip
硒{Se} selenium ◇ 含～的 seleniferous, 加～钢 selenium steel
硒钯矿 allpalladium
硒铋化物 selenobismuthite
硒铋矿 frenzlite, gaunajuatite
硒不锈钢 selenium stainless steel
硒碲矿 hondurasite
硒钒剂 seleniovanadium
硒粉 selenium powder
硒鼓复印 xerography

硒光电池 selenium cell
硒光电管[元件] selenium photocell
硒化铵{(NH$_4$)$_2$Se} ammonium selenide
硒化法 【金】selenizing
硒化钙{CaSe} calcium selenide
硒化镉 cadmium selenide
硒化钾{K$_2$Se} potassium selenide
硒化钠{Na$_2$Se} sodium selenide
硒化铅 lead selenide
硒化砷 arsenic selenide
硒化物 selenide
硒化物型夹杂 selenide-type inclusions
硒金银矿 fischesserite
硒硫钴矿 musenite
硒铅矿{PbSe} clausthalite
硒砷硫磺 jeromite
硒酸铵{(NH$_4$)$_2$SeO$_4$} ammonium selenate
硒酸钙{CaSeO$_4$} calcium selenate
硒酸镓{Ga$_2$(SeO$_4$)$_3$} gallium selenate
硒酸钾{K$_2$SeO$_4$} potassium selenate
硒酸钠{Na$_2$SeO$_4$} sodium selenate
硒酸铷{Rb$_2$SeO$_4$} rubidium selenate
硒酸铯{Cs$_2$SeO$_4$} cesium selenate
硒酸盐[酯] selenate
硒铊银铜矿{(Cu,Tl,Ag)$_2$Se} crookesite
硒铁(中间合金;52Se,0.9C) ferroselenium
硒铁矿 achavalite
硒铜矿{Cu$_2$Se} berzelianite
硒铜失蜡合金(0.1—0.5Se,余量 Cu) selenium-copper alloy
硒锌矿 zinc selenide
硒银矿{(Ag,Pb)Se} naumannite
硒整流器 selenium rectifier
硒中毒 selenosis
锡{SeH$_3$} selenonium
矽肺病 pneumoconiosis, silicosis
矽钢片 (同"硅钢片")
矽卡岩矿 skarn
吸 suction, attracting, absorbing
吸氨器 ammonia absorber

吸苯油　benzole absorbing oil
吸潮　water-absorbing, moisture absorption
吸潮器　(air-)breather
吸尘管　dust pipe
吸尘器[机]　vacuum cleaner [sweeper], aspirator,【冶】(dust) catcher ◇ 湿式~ wet suction fan
吸持磁铁　holding [locking] magnet
吸持电路　holding [sustain] circuit
吸持线圈　holding(-on) coil
吸出　suction, extraction, scavenging
吸出管　suction pipe
吸氮　nitrogen absorption [pick-up]
吸电子的　electrophilic
吸掉　blotting, removal by suction
吸放氢过程　hydrogen absorption and desorption process
吸放氢(过程)动力学　kinetics of hydrogen absorption and desorption
吸风　air draught, (air) inflow, indraft, indraught, suction air
吸风机　suction blower, induced-draught fan
吸风口　suction opening
吸风总管　suction main
吸风烧结　down-draft sintering
吸附　adsorbing, adsorption ◇ 活化~ activated adsorption, 界面间~ interfacial adsorption
吸附表面膜层　adsorbed surface film
吸附层　adsorbed [adsorption] layer
吸附沉淀　adsorptive [adsorption] precipitation
吸附等温线　adsorption isotherm
吸附电势[位]　adsorption potential
吸附动力学　adsorption dynamics [kinetics]
吸附度　adsorptivity
吸附反应　adsorption reaction
吸附方程　adsorption equation ◇ 吉布斯 ~*, 弗洛因德里赫~*
吸附分离　adsorption separation, fractionation by adsorption
吸附过滤　adsorption filtration
吸附机理　adsorption mechanism
吸附剂　adsorbent, adsorption [adsorbing] substance, sorbent
吸附解吸过程　adsorption-desorption process
吸附离子　adsorbed ion
吸附力　adsorption force [affinity], adsorptive power
吸附流　adsorption current
吸附率　adsorption rate
吸附膜　adsorption film
吸附能　adsorption energy
吸附能力　adsorptivity
吸附平衡　sorption equilibrium
吸附气膜　adsorbed gas film
吸附气体　adsorbed gas
吸附曲线　adsorption curve
吸附热　adsorption heat
吸附色层(分离)法　adsorption chromatography
吸附设备　adsorption plant
吸附室　adsorption chamber
吸附树脂　occluded resin
吸附水　absorption water [moisture], adsorbed [occluded] water
吸附速率　adsorption rate
吸附塔　adsorption column ◇ 脉动[跳汰床]~*, 纤维素~ cellulose column
吸附碳　adsorption carbon
吸附提取　sorption-extraction
吸附物(被吸附的物质)　adsorbate, adsorption substance ◇ 洗去~(解吸) adsorption stripping
吸附系数　adsorption coefficient
吸附现象　absorption phenomenon
吸附型缓蚀[阻化]剂　adsorption-type inhibitor
吸附性　adsorptivity, adsorbability
吸附选择性　selectivity in adsorption
吸附有害离子(离子交换中的)　poison ◇

非永久性~*，轻度~*，永久性~*
吸附值[指数] adsorptive value
吸附柱 adsorption column
吸附装置 adsorption plant
吸附作用 adsorption, adsorbing
吸管 suction hose[pipe], tail pipe(泵吸管), pipet(te)
吸管式比重计 syringe hydrometer
吸光玻璃 absorption glass
吸光光度法 absorptiometry, absorption photometry
吸力 suction, attraction (force), suck
吸力表 suction[draught] gauge
吸力运输机 suction conveyer
吸量管 measuring pipet(te)
吸硫 sulphur absorption
吸留 【金】occlude, occlusion
吸留气体 occluded[occlusion] gas
吸滤漏斗 straining[suction] funnel
吸滤瓶 suction bottle, filter flask
吸滤器 suction[nutsch] filter
吸墨性 absorbency, ink holdout
吸能反应 endoe(ne)rgic reaction
吸能过程 endoergic process
吸泥泵 dredge[mud] pump
吸泥船 hydraulic suction dredger ◇ 用~填成的土堤 barged in fill
吸盘(电磁式) suction cup (垛板用), chuck ◇ 带~装置的板材升降台【压】cup lifter
吸盘式板材分[卸]垛机 【压】suction-cup lifting device
吸盘式板材升降台 cup lifter
吸气 suction (air), aspiration, indraft, indraught, occlusion, gas absorption
吸气点 suction point
吸气机 ◇ 透平式~turbo-exhauster
吸气能力 gas-absorption capacity
吸气歧管 suction[induction] mainfold
吸气器 aspirator, inhaler
吸气软管 suction hose
吸气探针 sampling probe, sniffer

吸气效应 gettering effect
吸气作用 gas absorption
吸氢 hydrogen absorption[pick-up]
吸氢过程动力学 kinetics of hydrogen absorption
吸取 absorbing, suction ◇ 边界层~*
吸去[开] blotting
吸热 heat pickup[absorption]
吸热变化 endothermal change, endothermic change[conversion]
吸热带 zone of heat absorption
吸热的 endothermal, endothermic
吸热反应 endothermal[endoergic] reaction, heat absorbing reaction
吸热分解 endothermic decomposition
吸热峰 absorption peak
吸热副反应 endothermic auxiliary reaction
吸热过程 endothermic[endoergic] process
吸热化合物 endothermic compound
吸热还原 endothermic reduction
吸热还原反应 endothermic reducing reaction
吸热基气氛 endothermic base atmosphere
吸热剂 endothermic compound, heat absorbent
吸热量 heat pickup
吸热能力 heat absorption capacity
吸热器 heat[thermal] absorber
吸热设备 heat sink
吸热(式)气氛 endothermic atmosphere (光亮退火用) ◇ RX~*
吸热特性 endothermic character
吸热型气体 endogas, endothermic gas
吸热型气体发生设备 endogas unit
吸热性气体发生炉 endothermic gas generator
吸热转化 endothermic conversion
吸入 suction, aspiration, indraft, indraught, sucking up, drawing-in
吸入阀 suction valve

吸入高度(泵的) draw(ing) lift ◇ 净~*

吸入管 suction line, induction pipe, snore (泵的)

吸入管道[吸收管孔] suction passage

吸入空气 suction air, snifting

吸入孔 suction opening [port]

吸入口 suction inlet

吸入量 intake

吸入器 inspirator, inhaler

吸入强度 intensity of draught

吸入区 suction zone

吸入物 indraft, indraught

吸入旋塞 suction cock

吸入罩 suction hood

吸色高温计 colour-extinction pyrometer

吸声材料 acoustic(al) absorbent, damping [sound-absorbing] material

吸声涂料[油漆] acoustic [antinoise] paint

吸声系数 sound absorption factor

吸升高度 suction lift

吸湿 moisture absorption, imbibition

吸湿崩解 perish

吸湿剂[吸湿性材料,吸湿性物质] hydroscopic material [substance]

吸湿湿度 hydroscopic moisture

吸湿性 (同"吸水性")

吸湿性散放物 【环】hydroscopic emissions

吸湿性四氯化物 hygroscopic tetrachloride

吸收 absorbing, (ab)sorption, suck up, soak up, pick-up, capture, merge,【金】occlude(吸收气体) ◇ 不~的 nonabsorbent, 反射光完全~*, 康普顿~ Compton absorption

吸收本领 absorbing power [ability], absorptive power, absorptance, absorption property

吸收泵(真空用) sorption pump

吸收表面 absorption surface

吸收材料[物质] absorbing material [matter]

吸收测量学 absorptiometry

吸收常数 absorption constant

吸收池[匣] absorption cell

吸收冲击功 absorb striking energy

吸收单分子层 absorbed monolayer

吸收电流 absorption [soak] current

吸收(定)律 absorption law

吸收断面峰值 peak absorption cross section

吸收法 【理】absorption method

吸收方程 absorption equation

吸收辐射剂量 absorbed radiation dose

吸收辐射(能) absorption radiation

吸收高温计 absorption pyrometer

吸收管 absorption tube

吸收(光,光谱,谱)带 absorption band

吸收(光,频)谱 absorption spectrum ◇ 差示~*,导数~(图)*

吸收光谱法[学] absorption spectroscopy [spectrometry]

吸收光谱分析 absorption spectral analysis

吸收光谱函数关系(图) derivative absorption spectrum

吸收光谱计[分光计,分析仪] absorption spectrometer

吸收过滤器 absorbent filter

吸收(极)限 absorption limit

吸收剂 absorbate, absorbent, absorber, absorbing material, sorbent

吸收剂层[吸收床] absorbent bed

吸收剂量 absorbed dose ◇ 积分[总,累积]~*

吸收计 absorptiometer, absorption meter (液体的)

吸收截面 absorption corss-section

吸收介质 absorbing medium ◇ 非~*

吸收控制杆(中子的) absorber [absorbing] control rod

吸收离子 absorbed ion

吸收量 absorbability, absorption capacity, pick-up

吸收率 absorption rate [ratio, coefficient], absorptivity, absorbing ability, absorbance

吸收滤光片 absorption filter

吸收滤光器[镜] absorption light filter

吸收滤色器 absorption color filter

吸收能力 absorption capacity [power, property], absorbing ability [capacity], absorptive capacity [power], sorptive capacity, absorbability, absorbency, absorptance ◇ 低～材料*, 高～材料*

吸收能量 absorbed [absorption] energy, absorbed power

吸收能量材料 【理】dissipative material

吸收频率 absorption frequency

吸收器 absorbent, absorber

吸收区 suction zone

吸收曲线 absorption curve

吸收热 absorbed [endothermic] heat, heat of absorption

吸收色层(分离)法 absorption chromatography

吸收摄谱仪 absorption spectrograph

吸收设备(气体的) absorption plant

吸收时间(气体的) clean-up time

吸收试验 absorption test

吸收水分 absorbed moisture

吸收速率 absorption rate

吸收损失 absorption loss

吸收塔 absorbing tower [column], absorption tower [column]

吸收体 absorber, absorbing material

吸收突变 absorption jump

吸收温度 absorption temperature

吸收误差 absorption error

吸收系数 absorbance, absorption coefficient [factor, index, ratio], absorptivity ◇ 本生～*, 康普顿～*

吸收线 absorption line

吸收效率 absorption efficiency

吸收性(能) absorptivity, absorption property, absorbability, absorbing ability

吸收性炭 absorbent carbon [charcoal]

吸收液 absorption [absorbing] liquid

吸收移液管 absorption pipette

吸收因素[因数] absorption factor

吸收跃变 absorption jump

吸收质 absorbate

吸收中子材料 neutron-absorbing material

吸收中子杂质 neutron-absorbing impurity

吸收柱 absorption [absorbing] column

吸收装置 absorption plant [apparatus, installation]

吸收作用 absorption effect [function]

吸水 water uptake [absorption]

吸水的 hydroscopic, hygroscopic, water-absorbing

吸水口格网 suction basket

吸水量(渗透液或乳化液的) water tolerance

吸水龙头 suction cock

吸水率(性) water absorption

吸水软管 suction hose

吸水特性 water absorption characteristic

吸水性 hygroscopy, hydroscopicity, hygroscopicity, hygroscopic nature [property], water absorption, water-absorbing quality

吸酸的 acid absorbing

吸碳 【冶】carbon pickup

吸氧 oxygen absorption

吸氧腐蚀 oxygen-absorption [oxygen-consumption] corrosion

吸氧剂 oxygen absorbent

吸氧器 oxygen breathing apparatus

吸液管法 pipette method

吸液管架 pipette stand

吸移管 pipette ◇ 滴液～ drop(ping) pipette

吸音材料 (同"吸声材料")

吸音的 sound-absorbing

吸音灰膏 acoustic(al) plaster

吸音剂 sound absorber

吸音器　sound absorber
吸音贴砖　【建】acoustolith tile
吸音系数　acoustical absorption coefficient (AAC)
吸引　attraction, draw, fetch
吸引比　entrainment ratio
吸引结(位错的)　attractive junction
吸引库仑电势[电位]　attraction Coulomb potential
吸引力　attraction force, traction
吸引喷射器　sucking injector
吸引升力　suction lift
吸引压力　suction pressure
吸引压头　suction head ◇ 净正~*
吸着　sorption ◇ 液相~(法) liquid-phase sorption
吸着平衡　sorption equilibrium
吸着气体　retained gas
吸着树脂　occluded resin
吸着水　hygroscopic [absorbed, occluded] water
吸着物　sorbate
吸着作用　sorption
锡{Sn}　tin ◇ α[灰]~ tin pest, grey tin, β~ beta tin, 奥克潘~*, 薄片[片状]~ flake tin, 标准~ standard tin, 衬~的 tin-lined, 除~ detin(ning), 纯~ pure tin, 电解~ electrolytic tin, 废~ tin refuse, 粉状~ powdery tin, 富~渣 hardhead, 工业纯~*, 含~的 stanniferous, 含~残渣*, 化~电炉 electric tin furnace, 化学纯~ chempure tin, 粒状~ granulated tin, 商品~ commercial tin, 涂~的 coated tin, 脱~*, 液态~ molten tin, 羽状~ feathered tin, 原生~ primary tin, 再生~ secondary tin
锡巴比合金(锡轴承合金)　tin bearing alloy
锡巴比合金1(91Sn, 4.5Sb, 4.5Cu)　tin babbitt alloy 1
锡钯矿　stannopalladinite
锡板　sheet tin

锡棒　tin bar
锡薄板　tin metal sheet
锡铋汞合金　◇ 穆西利特殊型~*
锡铋合金　tin-bismuth alloy ◇ 刘易斯~ Lewis's alloy
锡病　tin disease [pest], sick tin, (tin) plague
锡铂钯矿　atokite
锡箔　tin foil [leaf] ◇ 电容器用~*
锡箔制造机械　tin foil machinery
锡残渣　tin skimmings ◇ 粉状~*
锡层测厚仪　tin coating thickness gauge
锡产出率　tin yield
锡的　tinny, stannic ◇ 正[四价]~ stannic
锡滴　droplet of tin
锡锭　tin slab, pig [bar, block] tin
锡镀层　tinning, tinned coating, plated tin
锡发汗[锡"反常"偏析](青铜铸件上的)　tin exudation
锡粉　tin powder, powdered tin, tin filings ◇ 雾化~ atomized tin, 柱状[杆状]~ sprill tin
锡浮渣　tin dross [scum]
锡覆盖层　coated tin
锡钢片　tin plate
锡镉青铜　◇ 高导电率~*
锡汞合金　tin amalgam
锡锅　tin pot
锡焊　soldering
锡焊膏　tinol
锡焊管　soldered tube
锡焊料　【焊】quick solder, solder metal
锡焊液　killed spirits
锡汗　tin sweat
锡合金　tin alloy ◇ 阿什贝利~*, 硬~*
锡胡须切变强度　shear strength of tin whiskers
锡花(镀锌板的)　tin flower
锡化铌　columbium stannide
锡化物　stannide
锡黄铜　tin (-bearing) [one-ton] brass ◇ 杰克逊~*

锡灰(镀锡槽的) tin ash
锡基巴比合金 tin(-base) babbit alloy [metal], tin-base white metal, tin Babbitts (89Sn, 7.5Sb, 3.5Cu) ◇ 阿达曼特～adamant metal
锡基白合金 tin-base white metal
锡基白金属轴承合金 ◇ 帕森～*
锡基合金 tin-base alloy, Kamash alloy (12.5Cu, 1.2Pb, 余为Sn) ◇ 克勒～*, 米诺法餐具～, 莫塔洛粒状～Motaloy, 吕登沙伊特～*, 尼克林～*
锡基餐具合金 ◇ 银色～*
锡基空心铸造合金 ◇ 瓦格纳装饰用～*
锡基锡锑铜合金(即巴比合金) tin-based tin-antimony-copper alloy
锡基压铸合金 tin die-casting alloy
锡基轴承合金 tin(-base) babbit alloy [metal], tin(-base) bearing alloy [metal] ◇ 阿达曼特～*, "大和"～Yamato metal, 蒂尼特～Tinite, 哈诺瓦～*, 赫斯曼～*, 霍伊特～*, 卡尔马什～*, 赖利～*, 雷格尔～*, 理查德～*, 纳特基～*, 帕森～*, 齐恩～*, 瑟斯顿～*, 泽马～*
锡基装饰合金 ◇ 卡马施～*, 凯泽津～*
锡金属正四方体晶型 metallic tetragonal form of tin
锡精矿熔炼 tin concentrate smelting
锡精炼 tin refining
锡精炼厂 tin refinery, tin-refining plant
锡精炼车间 tin-refining plant
锡颗粒化 graining of tin
锡块 bar [pig, block] tin
锡矿 tin ore, wheal ◇ 废～tin ore refuse, 碎～cased tin, 圆柱～cylindrite, 碎～渣 loob
锡矿床 tin ore deposit
锡矿物 tin mineral
锡粒 granulated tin, tin shot
锡磷青铜 tin phosphorus bronze ◇ 尼达拔制用～*
锡磷青铜带 tin phosphorus bronze band
锡瘤(板材边的) list edge
锡铝合金 tin-aluminium alloy ◇ 布邦～*
锡鸣[嘶] tin cry
锡镍镀层 tin-nickel coating
锡镍合金(66.66Sn, 33.34Ni) tin-nickel alloy ◇ 特拉巴克～*
锡诺莫合金 stannum
锡坯 tin slab
锡皮线 tinned wire
锡片 tin metal sheet
锡钎焊 tin soldering
锡钎焊[锡焊料]合金(63Sn, 37Pb) tin soldering alloy ◇ P～*
锡铅60-40焊料[药] tin-lead 60-40 solder
锡铅宝石装饰合金 ◇ 法伦～*
锡铅铋易熔合金 Malott metal
锡铅镀层 tin-lead plating
锡铅焊料 tin-lead solder ◇ 电工用～*, 管工用～*
锡铅合金[锡镴] tin-lead alloy ◇ 板状～plate pewter, 法国～*, 克利谢～*, 莱伊～*, 英国～*
锡铅软焊料 tinsmith solder
锡铅锑合金 ◇ 博罗托～Boroto
锡铅锑轴承合金 ◇ 赫洛特～Hulot's alloy
锡铅装饰合金 ◇ 廷塞尔～*
锡青铜(20Sn, 余量Cu) tin bronze ◇ 艾昂尼尔～*, 加铅～leaded tin bronze, 耐酸～*, 珀金～*, 塔姆塔姆～*, 坦德姆～*, 图朗～*, 尤恰蒂尼斯～*
锡热析 tin sweat
锡熔炼厂 【色】tin-smelting plant
锡熔渣 tin skimmings
锡软钎料 softtin
锡砂 stream tin
锡石{SnO_2} tin-stone, cassiterite ◇ 黑色～black tin

锡石精矿　crop tin
锡酸　stannic acid
锡酸盐　stannate
锡钽铁矿　tintantalite
锡锑铋铜合金　Tutania alloy ◇ 板状~*
锡锑焊料　tin-antimony solder ◇ 奎因~ Queen's metal
锡锑合金　tin-antimony alloy ◇ 梅特~ (95Sn,5Sb) Meter,王子~*,银色~*
锡锑铅合金[白镴]　pewter ◇ 三元~*
锡锑铜合金　◇ 霍伊特~*,图塔尼亚~*
锡锑铜轴承合金　◇ 帕森-莫塔~*
锡锑铜装饰合金　◇ 不列颠~*,雅各比~*
锡锑系轴承合金　◇ 阿尔及尔~*
锡添加合金　tin addition
锡条　tin bar
锡铁钽矿　ixiollite,ixionolite
锡铜焊条合金　◇ 焊接烟雾少的~low-fuming bronze
锡铜合金　tin-copper alloy ◇ 密斯特里~ mystery,轴瓦衬用~*
锡铜锑(减摩轴承)合金　◇ 夏尔皮~*
锡铜锌铁合金　◇ 斯蒂芬森~*
锡铜轴承合金　◇ 法里~*,金斯顿~*
锡瘟[疫]　(同"锡病")
锡铜轴套　多孔烧结~*
锡污(镀锡薄)板　scruffy plate
锡屑　tin filings
锡锌合金　tin-zinc alloy ◇ 电镀~板材 tin-zinc electroplate
锡锌混汞合金　◇ 辛格~ Singer's amalgam
锡锌青铜(7—10Sn,2—5Zn,0—5Pb,余量 Cu)　gun metal
锡盐$\{SnCl_2, SnCl_2 \cdot 2H_2O\}$　tin salt
锡阳极　tin anode
锡铟50-50接封合金　tin indium 50-50 alloy
锡银95-50软焊料[钎焊]膏　tin-silver 95-50 soft solder paste

锡银焊料[药]　tin-silver solder
锡银钎焊合金(95Sn,5Ag)　tin-silver solder
锡渣　【色】scruff ◇ 粉状~powdery-tin skimming,高硅~*
锡渣精矿　tin slag concentrate
锡轴承合金　tin bearing alloy
牺牲阳极(电化学保护用)　sacrificial anode
牺牲阳极保护作用　sacrificial protective action
牺牲阳极腐蚀　sacrificial corrosion
牺牲阳极腐蚀防护　sacrificial (corrosion) protection
稀薄固溶体　dilute solid solution
稀氟氢酸过热器　D.H.F. superheater
稀化　rare faction
稀灰浆　lean mortar
稀碱浸出　dilute alkali leaching
稀矿浆　dilute [thin] pulp
稀泥浆　thin sludge ◇ 中性~*
稀缺材料　critical material
稀缺有色金属　【色】scarce nonferrous metal
稀溶液　dilute [weak] solution
稀散金属　rare scattering metal, dissipated metal
稀散金属合金　rare scattering metal alloy
稀释　diluting, dilution, thinning, attenuation, desaturation, liquefying, thin up (矿渣、炉渣的), cutback,【化】fluxing ◇ 加铜~法*
稀释比[率]　dilution ratio
稀释槽　diluting tank [trap]
稀释产品　【焦】cutback product
稀释产物　cutback
稀释定律　dilution law
稀释法　dilution method
稀释剂　diluent, diluting medium, thinner, thinning agent,【色】carrier (溶剂萃取的) ◇ 芳族~aromatic diluent,料层[床层]~*

稀释浸出 dilute leach	稀土磷铀矿 $\{U,Ca,RE\}_3(PO_4)_4 \cdot 6H_2O\}$ lermontovite
稀释空气鼓风机 dilution air blower	
稀释沥青 (同"轻制沥青")	稀土硫酸盐 (同"硫酸稀土")
稀释浓度 dilute concentration	稀土铝合金化 rare earth aluminium alloying
稀释热 dilution heat	
稀释溶液 diluted solution	稀土氯化物 rare earth chloride
稀释熵 dilution entropy	稀土铌铀锆石 $\{ZrSiO_4 + UO_3\}$ naegite
稀释相型燃料反应堆 dilute-phase-type reactor	稀土蠕墨铸铁 rare-earth vermes shape graphite cast iron
稀释效应 diluting effect	稀土锶磷灰石 saamite
稀释液 rarefaction	稀土硝酸盐 rare earth nitrate
稀释因数[因子] dilution factor	稀土氧化物 $\{(RE)_2O_3\}$ rare earth oxide
稀疏(波) rarefaction (wave)	稀土硬磁合金 rare earth hard magnetic alloy
稀疏矩阵 【计】sparse matrix	
稀酸浸出 dilute acid leaching	稀土元素 rare earths (R.E., REs), rare earth element (REE), lanthanide series
稀酸浸出操作 dilute acid leach run	
稀酸洗 dilute acid wash	稀土元素的钇组 yttria group of rare earths
稀酸液槽 dilute acid bath	
稀土草酸盐 (同"草酸稀土")	稀土元素氧化物类 rare-earth oxides (re-os)
稀土处理 rare earth treatment	
稀土钢 rare earth steel	稀土族金属 rare earths
稀土锆石 rebeirite, naegite	稀相 dilute phase
稀土钴合金 rare-earths-cobalt	稀相焙烧 dilute phase roasting
稀土钴永磁体 rare earthcobalt permanent magnet	稀油集中润滑系统 centralized oil lubricating system
稀土合金芯线 rare earth alloy cored wire	稀油集中压力润滑系统 centralized pressure-oil system
稀土混合物 rare earth mixture, lucium	
稀土金属 (rare) earth metal	稀油润滑 oil lubrication
稀土(金属)合金 (intra)rare earth alloy, REM alloy ◇(含铈)混合~ mischmetal (l), 特种铝基混合~	稀油润滑管路 oil lubricating piping
	稀油润滑系统 oil lubricating system
	稀油雾化润滑装置 oil mist lubrication unit
稀土金属化合物 rare earth compound	
稀土金属混合物 Di(不包括Ce) didymium	稀油雾化系统 oil mist system
	稀油循环润滑系统 circulating oil system
稀土(金属)矿物 rare earth mineral	稀油自动压力润滑 automatic oil-pressure lubrication
稀土金属冶金 rare earth metallurgy	
稀土金属中间合金 rare earth metal master alloy	稀有分散金属 (同"稀散金属")
	稀有贵金属 rare precious metal
稀土精矿 rare earth concentrate	稀有碱土金属 rare alkaline earth metal
稀土离子 rare earth ion	稀有金属 rare [less-common, minor, newer, scarce, uncommon] metal
稀土磷酸盐 $\{REPO_4\}$ rare earth phosphate	
	稀有金属碘化物 rare metal iodide

稀有金属氟化物	rare metal fluoride
稀有金属工业	rare metal industry
稀有金属合金	rare metal alloy
稀有金属矿物	mineral of rare metal
稀有金属矿石	rare metal ore
稀有金属氯化物	rare metal chloride
稀有金属提取	rare metal extraction
稀有金属温差电偶	rare-metal couple
稀有金属污染	rare metal pollution
稀有金属盐类	rare metal salt
稀有金属氧化物	rare metal oxide
稀有金属冶金	metallurgy of rare metal
稀有气体	rare [noble] gas
稀有气体化合物	rare gas compound
稀有轻金属	rare light metal
稀有元素	rare [less-common] element
稀有元素化学	rare element chemistry
稀有元素矿物	rare element mineral
稀渣	【冶】highly fluid slag
希杜拉 5 铜合金	(2Ni, 0.5Si, 余量 Cu) Hidural 5
希杜拉尔铜基合金	Hidural alloy
希杜拉克斯铜合金 [多元铝青铜]	(8.5—10.5Al, 0—5.5Ni, 1.5—6Fe, 0—6Mn, 余量 Cu; 2—4 Al, 1—3Fe, 12—16Ni, 余量 Cu) hidurax alloy
希杜米纽姆耐蚀硬铝合金	Hiduminium (alloy) (Hiduminium RR50; 0.8—2.0Cu, 0.8—1.75Ni, 0.05—0.2Mg, 0.8—1.4Fe, 1.5—2.8Ti, 余量 Al)
希夫黄铜焊料合金	(60Cu, 0.25Si, 余量 Zn) Sifbronze
希金斯半连续离子交换柱	Higgins column
希科尔铬钼不锈钢	Hicore
希罗克斯电阻合金	(6—10Al, 3—9Cr, 0—4Mn, 少量 Zr、B, 余量 Fe) Hirox
希默快速渗碳法	Shimer process
希·斯皮德·伊特硬化剂	【钢】Hi-speed-it
希斯温离心球磨机	Hyswing ball mill
希坦索高电导率青铜	(99.2—98.2Cu, 0.8 或 1Cd, 或 0.5—1.8Sn) Hitenso
熄弧	arc quenching, blow (out) ◇ 磁力~ arc magnetism
熄弧器	arc extinguisher, spark box [catcher], spark condensing chamber
熄弧室	spark condensing chamber
熄弧用阻尼(螺管)线圈	arc damper
熄弧罩	spark catcher
熄焦	【焦】coke quenching ◇ 干(式)~*, 湿法~wet quenching
熄焦车	quenching [coke] car ◇ 底翻式~*, 倾翻式~*
熄焦机	coke quenching machine
熄焦时间	quenching time [period]
熄焦水	coke quenching water
熄焦塔	quenching tower
熄焦贮水槽	quench tank
熄灭	quench (ing), lighting-off, extinguishment, extinction, black out, decay, 【焦】slake (焦炭的)
熄灭电压	extinction voltage
烯丙基	{CH$_2$ = CHCH$_2$ - } allyl (group)
烯醇	enol
烯醇式[型]	enol-form
烯醇盐	enolate
烯化	alkylene
席式供热系统	cable mat heating system
习用成形工艺	(同"一般成形工艺")
习用淬火油	(同"普通淬火油")
铣床	【机】shaper, milling machine ◇ 靠模~ die profiler, 制模型用~ pattern milling machine
铣刀	【机】milling cutter [tool], fraise ◇ 刻模[冲模切槽用]~ die sinking cutter, 异型~ router
铣刀杆	cutter spindle
铣刀钢	milling steel
铣工	【机】mill operator
铣轮式挖泥机	cutter-head dredge
铣头机	end facer, end facing machine
铣削	milling ◇ 化学~ chemical milling, 同向~【机】climb milling
铣削等级	milling-grade

铣削机	milling machine
铣削性	milling quality
洗氨器	ammonia scrubber
洗氨塔	[焦]ammonia washer
洗苯塔	[焦]benzol washer
洗苯油	[焦]benzole absorbing [wash] oil
洗槽	tank-washer, washtrough
洗车沟	car washing canal
洗尘车间	air-washing plant
洗尘器	dust scrubber
洗尘系统	◇ 液体 ~ liquid dust-suppression system
洗出(洗提)(离子交换柱的)	elution
洗出回路	eluant circuit
洗出溶液	wash solution
洗出液	eluate
洗涤	wash(ing), scrub(bing), flushing, rinsing, cleaning ◇ 逆流~*
洗涤变数	washing variable
洗涤操作[工序]	scrubbing operation
洗涤槽	wash(ing) [scrubber, rinsing] tank, wash [flushing] box, rinse [swill] bath, rinse vat
洗涤槽进料	washer feed
洗涤槽下料筒	washer boot
洗涤槽溢流	wash overflow
洗涤除尘	cleaning dust
洗涤方法	cleaning means
洗涤废水	washes
洗涤分级机	◇ 三层式~*
洗涤干燥机	scrubbing and drying machine [unit]
洗涤干燥作业线	scrubbing and drying line
洗涤工段	rinsing [scrubber] zone, scrubbing station
洗涤过滤机	washing filter
洗涤机	washer, scrubbing unit, rinsing machine
洗涤挤干辊	cleaning wring roll
洗涤剂	washing agent, cleaning means, strippant, detergent
洗涤阶段	washing stage
洗涤介质	scrubbing medium
洗涤冷凝器	scrubber condenser
洗涤冷却器	scrubber cooler
洗涤浓缩	wash thickening
洗涤浓缩机	washing thickener ◇ 层式~ tray wash thickener
洗涤瓶	washer bottle
洗涤器	washer, washing apparatus [vessel], scrubber, scrubbing unit ◇ 变径式~*, 错流核晶~*, 挡板式~【选】baffle scrubber, 辅助[备用]~【环】backup scrubber, 管状~ tubular washer, 滚筒式~【化】tumbling scrubber, 机尾~*, 焦炭~ coke scrubber, 径流式~ radial flow scrubber, 盘式~ tray scrubber, 喷射~ jet scrubber, 锐孔~*, 圆筒~ drum scrubber
洗涤器废液	scrubber effluent
洗涤器刷辊	scrubber brush roll
洗涤溶液	scrubbing solution
洗涤设备	washer, scrubbing plant (气体的)
洗涤式过滤器	scrubber [scrubbing] filter
洗涤水	wash(ing) [scrubber, rinse, rinsing] water
洗涤水处理	scrubbing water disposal
洗涤水浓度	wash concentration
洗涤水循环	scrubber water recycling
洗涤酸	washing acid
洗涤塔	wash(ing) tower [column], (wet) washer, scrubber, scrubbing column, tower scrubber [washer] ◇ 多段~*, 苛性碱~*, 泡罩~ bubble cap washer, 栅格式~*, 填料~ packed tower scrubber, 文丘里管~ Venturi scrubber, 折流板~*
洗涤塔给液泵	scrubber feed pump
洗涤桶	washtub, wash box
洗涤筒(钢丝用)	scouring barrel
洗涤物	washes, washings
洗涤系统	washing system [circuit]

洗涤效率　washing efficiency
洗涤型底漆［涂料］　wash primer
洗涤液　scrubber solution, scrubbing liquid [liquor], wash(ing) liquid, wash liquor, cleaning mixture
洗涤用空气　rinse air
洗涤渣　washed residue
洗涤装置　wash mill ◇ 空气～*
洗涤作业线　rinsing [scrubbing] line
洗锅(第二镀锡锅)　wash pot
洗净　washup, wash(ing)-out, rinse, depuration ◇ 非离子～剂 non-ionic detergent
洗净树脂　eluted resin
洗矿　hutch, washup, washed ore ◇ 斜面～(槽,床) buddle
洗矿槽　【选】hutch, trough washer
洗矿厂　【选】ore-washing plant
洗矿机　(ore, log) washer, washing apparatus ◇ 圆筒～*
洗矿泥水循环　washer-water circuit
洗矿水　wash water
洗矿水澄清［净化］　water settling
洗矿台洗矿　table concentration
洗矿筒　washer drum ◇ 重介质～*
洗炉　furnace purging, accretion removing practice, prepurging, flushing (用渣),【钢】wash heat(ing), washing,【铁】slug
洗炉金属　wash metal
洗炉料　【铁】Dutch pill
洗滤　filter wash(ing)
洗滤机　washing filter
洗滤器　filter washer
洗煤　coal washing [dressing], washed coal
洗煤厂　(coal) washery, coal washing plant
洗煤机　(coal) washer ◇ 槽式～launder washer
洗萘塔　【焦】naphthalene scrubber
洗铌部分［工段］　【色】columbium-stripping section
洗瓶　wash bottle

洗气　gas washing ◇ 干法～【冶】dry gas cleaning
洗气车间　gas washing plant
洗气机　gas-washer ◇ 干式～dry washer, 回转式～*, 离心～cyclone gaswasher, 泰森式［湿法回转笼式］～Theisen washer, 文丘里管～Venturi washer
洗气器　gas-washer ◇ 旋流～cyclone gaswasher
洗气温度　washed-gas temperature
洗去　washing off
洗去吸附物　adsorption stripping
洗砂机　sand washer
洗石机　washing apparatus ◇ 转筒～【耐】washer drum
洗刷干燥机组　brush scrubber
洗水　wash(ing) [scouring] water
洗钽部分［工段］　tantalum-stripping section
洗提(离子交换柱的)　strip(ping), elution, back wash(ing) ◇ 分别［优先］～differential stripping, 煤油～*, 四级～four stage stripping, 选择(性)［优先］～*
洗提部分［工段］　stripping section
洗提反应　stripping reaction
洗提分析　elution analysis
洗提分析技术　elution analysis technique
洗提回路［工序］　eluant circuit
洗提级数　stripping stage
洗提剂　stripper, stripping [eluting] agent, eluent, back washing agent ◇ 水溶液～aqueous strip
洗提甲基异丁酮　barren methyl isobutyl ketone
洗提器　stripper, elutriator, back wash extractor
洗提曲线(萃取的)　eluate [elution] curve
洗提溶液　strip(ping) solution
洗提设备　stripping apparatus
洗提树脂　eluted resin
洗提水溶液　aqueous strip(ping) solution

洗提塔	stripping tower, scrubbing column
洗提系统	elution system
洗提液	eluate, stripping liquid, strip (liquor), eluant
洗提液收集	collection of eluate
洗提装置	elution system
洗筒	washer drum
洗箱	tank-washer,【选】box
洗选	washing, dressing [preparation] by washing ◇ 可～性试验【焦】washability test
洗选厂	washing plant, washery
(洗)净粉矿	washed fines
洗选机	washer ◇ 旋流式～ cyclone washer
洗选矿石	washed ore
洗选黏土	washed clay
洗选强化剂	builders
洗选设备	washing plant
洗液	wash (solution), washings, decantate, decanted solution
洗液槽	wash water tank
洗液沟	wash water channel
洗油	wash oil ◇ 减压～脱苯设备*, 脂族～*
洗油变稠	wash oil thickening
洗油再生	wash oil regeneration
洗油再生器	oil regenerator
洗油蒸馏釜	wash oil still
洗渣	washery slag
洗渣法	slag washing process
洗渣熔化炉	wash-heating furnace
徙动	migrate
系	system, family, series ◇ 巴尔末～*, 赖曼～*, 帕芬德～*
系杆	tie bar, tie-rod, brace
系级[阶,序]	order of system
系结	fastening down
系梁	tie beam, collar
系列	series, bank, set (family), train
系列电流(电解槽的)	potline current
系列制品	systems
系留气球	kytoon
系绳铁角	cleat, cleet
系属组织	lineage structure
系数	coefficient (coef., coeff.), factor, constant, ratio, modulus ◇ 泊松～*, 豪斯纳～*, 霍尔～ Hall coefficient, 佩尔蒂埃～*, 汤姆逊～ Thomson coefficient, 西贝克～ Seebeck coefficient
系数乘法器	coefficient multiplier
系统	system, regime, series ◇ 施利伦～ Schlieren system, 有～的 methodic(al)
系统不确定度	systematic uncertainty
系统参数	system parameter
系统阐述	formulation
系统常数	system constant
系统程序	system program
系统程序员	system programmer
系统颠簸	thrash(ing), churning
系统对称性	system symmetry
系统仿真[模拟]	system simulation
系统分析	system analysis
系统改进时间	system improvement time
系统隔离继电器	system separative relay
系统工程	system engineering
系统工程理论	system engineering theory
系统工程师	system engineer
系统管理	system management
系统合成	system synthesis
系统化	systematization
系统校验	system check
系统接口	system interface
系统接口设计	system interface design
系统科学	system science
系统可靠性	【计】system reliability
系统控制块	system control block
系统控制面板	system control panel
系统理论	system theory
系统利用率	system utilization
系统模型	system model
系统内的	intrasystem
系统偏差	system deviation
系统任务	system task

系统软件	system software
系统设计	system design
系统失效	thrash(ing)
系统识别	system identification
系统试验	system test
系统输入装置	【计】system input device [unit]
系统通信	system communication
系统误差	system(atic) error
系统外产量	non-sector output
系统形成	system generation
系统性能监视器	system performance monitor
系统压力警报器	system pressure alarm
系统研究	systematic investigation, system study
系统优化	system optimization
系统诊断程序	system diagnostics
系统中断	system interrupt
系统装入程序	system loader
系统资源	system resource
系统综合	system synthesis
隙	gap, slot, porthole
隙磁阻(空气隙的)	gap reluctance
隙规	gap gauge
隙宽	gap length
隙密度	gap density
隙透法(测定蒸汽压力)	effusion method
细棒材	【压】rod
细胞学	cytology
细胞质	cellular material
细胞状晶体	【金】cellular crystal
细胞状枝晶	【金】cellular dendrite
细保险丝	micro-fuse
细部[节]	detail
细部图	detail drawing
细槽	stria
细长度	slenderness
细长颗粒[质点]	slender particle
细尘	fine dust
细齿	serration
细冲头	bit punch
细度	(degree of) fineness
细度模数	fineness [size] modulus
细分级	precise fractionation,【选】close sizing (按粒度)
细分散性黏土	finely dispersed clay
细粉	(powder) fines, fine powder, burgy ◇ 不含~的 fines free, 角状~ angular fines
细粉尘[细尘颗粒]	fine dust particle
细粉磁铁	fine (iron) powder magnet
细粉料	fines
细粉煤	finely pulverized coal
细粉末	low-density powder
细粉砂	【铸】fine silt
细缝	【铸】check
细钙粉	calcium fines
细杆	pin
细钢丝	small-gauge wire, fine wire (多次拉拔的)
细股	yarn
细硅线石{$Al_2O_3 \cdot SiO_2$}	fibrolite
细滑移	fine slip ◇ 结构化的~ structurized fine slip
细滑移带	fine slip band
细滑移线	fine slip line
细化(晶粒的)	refinement
细化的心部组织	refined core structure
细化剂	refiner
细焦点	fine focus
细节检查	detailed examination
细金属喷射过渡	fine spray metal transfer
细金属丝	fiber, fibre
细晶低碳钢	plastalloy
细晶锭	fine grained ingot
细晶粒	fine grain (f.g.), fine grain size ◇ 奥氏体~ fine austenite grain
细晶粒化(断口的)	fine granulation
细晶(粒)断口	fine grained [granular] fracture, even fracture
细晶粒钢	fine grained steel, grain refining steel
细晶粒合金	fine grained alloy

细晶粒合金轧辊	alloy grain roll
细晶(粒)结构[组织]	fine grain(ed)[crystalline] structure, fine grained texture
细晶(粒)金属	fine grained metal
细晶(粒)生铁	close-grained [fine-grained] pig iron
细晶粒铸铁	fine grained iron
细晶石{NaCaTa$_2$O$_6$(OH)}	microlite
细晶体	fine crystal, crystallite
细晶种	fine seed
细晶状物质	fine crystalline material
细颈瓶	ampoule
细聚焦管	fine focus tube
细聚焦调节	fine focus(s)ing control
细菌	bacterium(复数 bacteria) ◇ 反硝化[脱硝]~ denitrifying bacteria, 革兰氏阴性~", 耗铁~", 噬硫~ sulphur bacteria, 铁氧化~"
细菌焙烧	bacterial roasting
细菌堆浸	bacterial heap [dump] leaching
细菌分解	bacteria decomposition
细菌辅助浮选	bacteria-aided flotation
细菌腐蚀	bacterial corrosion
细菌光学密度	bacterial optical density (B.O.D.)
细菌活性	bacterial activity
细菌浸出	bacteria leach(ing), bioleaching
细菌门	Bacteriophyta
细菌培养基	agar(-agar)
细菌培养液	nutrient solution
细菌群体	bacteria population
细菌学	bacteriology
细菌氧化厂[设备]	bacterial oxidation plant
细菌氧化(法)	bacteria(l) oxidation
细菌冶金	bacteria(l) metallurgy
细菌作用	bacterial action
细颗粒	fine grain
细颗粒黏土	fine (grained) clay
细孔	fine pore
细孔层	fine pore layer
细孔筛	fine meshed sieve
细孔筛板	fines deck
细拉丝机	fine wire drawing machine
细砾石	bird's eye gravel
细粒	particulate, granule, meal, 【铸】blasting shot ◇ 清理~【铸】blasting shot, 小~ granula, granule
细粒部分	fine fraction [component]
细粒产物	fine product
细粒赤铁矿	fine grained hematite
细粒磁铁精矿	fine magnetite concentrate
细粒度	fine granulation
细粒返料	revert fines
细粒粉	【粉】fine powder
细粒粉末	small particle size powder
细粒浮渣	fine dross, dross fines
细粒含铁废料	fine waste material
细粒化	fine granulation, sliming
细粒混合料	fine mix
细粒级	fine particle size
细粒结晶	crystal fines
细粒金	mustard gold
细粒晶种	fine seed
细粒砂	【铸】fine grained sand
细粒砂金矿	flour gold
细粒筛分	【选】fine sizing
细粒塑性高级耐火黏土(型砂结合剂)	silklay
细粒淘分	infrasizing
细粒物料	fine material
细粒物料团块	fine particle aggregate
细粒效应	small-size effect
细粒选粒	fine sizing
细粒盐	fine grained salt
细粒状的	finely granular
细粒组分	fine component
细粒组织	fine grained structure, sappy structure
细料	smalls
细裂纹	fine flaws, crazing, worming, hair check
细硫砷铅矿	grato nite

细流法制铁丸　shotting
细滤机　polishing filter
细马氏体　【金】hardenite
细煤　duff
细磨　fine grinding, levigation ◇ 经~的 ground-down
细磨粉状产品　ground product
细磨硅岩粉　ground ganister
细磨矿粉　ground ore
细磨耐火材料　ground refractory material ◇ 两次过筛的~*
细磨耐火黏土泥浆　ground fireclay mortar
细磨熔剂　ground flux
细磨石灰石筒仓　ground limestone silo
细磨石墨　ground graphite
细磨水泥　fine ground cement
细磨水泥熟料　ground cement clinker
细末　fine breeze, dead smalls
细目筛　undersize screen
细目文件　detail [transaction] file
细盘条(线径 5.39—9.45mm)　light rod
细喷淋　drizzle
细片状珠光体　fine lamellar pearlite
细球形体　fine sphere
细散颗粒　finely divided particle
细散状态　fine state of subdivision
细砂布　polishing cloth
细砂质磨石　buhr
细筛　fine meshed sieve, fine screen, lawn, fine mesh(ed) (细筛过的), 【选】fine sizing
细石墨　fine graphite
细丝　filament, thread(let) ◇ 沃拉斯顿~拔剑法*
细丝拔制法　◇ 沃拉斯顿~*
细丝钢丝绳　fine wire rope
细丝工　filigree
细丝技术　tenuous wire technique
细丝拉拔　【压】fine drawing
细丝拉拔机　fine wire drawing machine
细丝湿拉拔机　fine wire wet drawing machine
细丝状的　filamentous
细丝做的　filaceous
细碎　fine crushing, comminution
细碎白云石　finely ground dolomite
细碎焦粉[末]　finely crushed coke breeze
细碎矿　fine crushed ore
细碎黏弹性复合材料　particulate viscoelastic composite material
细碎破碎机　fine crusher
细碎圆锥　fine cone
细碎圆锥破碎机　fine cone crusher
细条状　stringlet
细条状硫化物(夹杂)　stringer sulphide
细调　fine adjustment [control, regulation], minute adjustment
细微表面裂纹　minute surface crack
细微雾化　microatomization
细纹　microgroove ◇ 表面~(搪瓷件的) crizzling
细纹压模　shallow relief die
细瑕疵[伤痕]　fine flaw
细纤维状的　fine fibrous
细线　filament
细销　hairpin
细小泡疤　【冶】pinhead blister
细屑　fines
细屑切削　light cut
细型芯　slender core
细亚黏土　fine sand loam
细氧化铝粉(抛光用)　abradum
细则　detailed rules and regulations, manual
细针状结晶　fine needles
细直径(线材的)　light gauge
细珠光体　fine pearlite
细桩　buttress shafts
匣钵　【耐】saggar, sagger
匣钵烧成法　boxing in
匣钵黏土　sagger clay
霞石{(Na,K)AlSiO$_4$}　nepheline, nephelite
霞石精矿　nepheline concentrate

辖域	【数】scope
狭板	batten
狭边粗木锯	whip saw
狭长地带	slip, corridor
狭底水沟	canch
狭缝	slit
狭缝装置	slit arrangement
狭缝准直	slit collimation
狭馏分	【化】clean cut
狭窄 γ 相区	narrowed gamma field
瑕疵	flaw, bug, defect, unsound spot, blemish (金属表面的) ◇ 出~ flawing, 无~(的)*
下凹床身	gap bed
下凹锻模	swage
下凹形焊缝	concave weld
下半型	【铸】bottom half mould, mould bottom half, drag half of mould, (mould) drag, nowel
下半型暗冒口	【铸】drag bob
下贝茵[贝氏]体	【金】lower bainite
下标	subscript, suffix
下部板贮存滑道	bottom sheet storage skid
下部大墙(热风炉的)	lower-ring wall
下部点火	bottom priming
下部电接头	lower contact
下部基础	foot bed
下部加热	underfiring
下部加热元件	lower zone heating element
下部间隙	under-clearance
下部结构	substructure, infrastructure ◇ 炉段~*
下部进料	underfeed
下部控制界限	lower control limit
下部框架	stationary frame
下部料钟	【铁】bottom bell
下部炉缸	【铁】crucible hearth
下部炉身	【铁】lower inwall [stack]
下部燃烧的	underfired
下部试样	lower sample
下部悬料	【铁】bottom hanging

下部烟罩	plate hood
下侧	underside, downside
下层	lower layer, underlayer, understratum
下层漆	undercoat
下沉	sinking, drop, sag, subsidence
下沉面积	area of subsidence
下沉性	settling quality
下承梁	through beam [girder]
下承桥	through bridge
下冲	under-shoot, underswing
下冲杆	bottom plunger [punch], lower plunger [punch]
下冲头压力	lower punch pressure
下抽风烧结	(同"下吸风烧结")
下出套的活套挑	drop looper
下出套的气动活套挑	air-operated drop looper
下传动压力机	bottom drive press
下传动轧边机[立辊轧机]	underdriven vertical edger
下锤头	【压】lower striker, lower ram (无砧座锻锤的)
下垂带材	flapping strip
下大上小的(锭模)	small end-up (SEU)
下刀梁	bottom knife beam
下刀片	bottom knife, lower [bottom] blade (剪切机的)
下刀片滑块[下滑动刀架]	bottom knife head
下刀刃	bed knife
下刀轴	bottom cutter spindle
下导板	bottom guide
下导管	downcomer [downtake] pipe
下导轨	return strand [track]
下导卫装置	bottom stripper
下道工序	downstream process, downstream processing step
下电极臂	【焊】lower [bottom] arm, bottom horn
下电子枪	lower bun
下动压板	downward platen

下 xia

下段拦板 【团】lower sidewall section
下风井 downcast (DC)
下割烧嘴 undercutting nozzle ◇ 振动式～*
下工作辊 bottom work roll
下辊 lower [bottom] roll
下辊导向挡板 bottom roll deflector
下辊可换轧槽块（罗克莱特冷轧管机的） bottom die
下辊弯曲调整装置 bottom bend adjusting equipment
下辊轧制线调整 bottom roll pass line adjusting
下横梁 lower separator, bottom end rail ◇ 机座～bottom-mill separator
下滑板 【钢】slider, sliding gate plate
下滑轮 bottom block
下滑座式深拉压力机 bottom slide drawing press
下滑座式凸轮压力机 bottom slide cam press
下夹送辊 bottom pinch roll
下加热段 lower heat zone
下加热式炉 bottom fired furnace, under-fired furnace
下降 descending, drop(ping), lowering, fall(ing), decreasing, sink, 【建】drawdown ◇ 很快～dowse
下降道拱砖 downtake arch ◇ $1\frac{1}{2}$ 长～*
下降高度 lowering distance
下降管(煤气的) 【铁】downcomer, downtake
下降管放灰闸板 downcomer damper
下降函数 decreasing function
下降火道[焰道] 【焦】down-flow flue
下降炉料 【冶】descending charge [stock]
下降炉料柱 【冶】descending charge column
下降速度 lowering speed, falling velocity, descent speed
下降速度特性（曲线） 【电】dropping-speed characteristic
下降特性(曲线) dropping [falling, negative] characteristic
下脚料 reverts, revert material, remnant
下界限法 lower bound method
下卷式(的) underwind
下均热段 lower soak zone
下空转夹送辊 bottom idle pinch roll
下(联)接轴 bottom spindle
下料 blanking, punching out, baiting
下料不顺 【铁】irregular stock movement, sticking
下料工具 blanking tool
下料机 notching press ◇ 冷锯～*
下料加快 【铁】fast driving
下料量(炉料的) burden yield
下料溜槽 discharge duct
下料时间 stock-descent time
下料指示器 distributing indicator
下临界磁场 【理】lower critical field
下临界点(相图的) lower critical point
下临界共(混)熔温度 【金】lower consolute temperature
下临界区[范围] 【金】close-to-critical range
下临界温度 lower critical temperature
下流 downflow, downstream
下流操作 downflow operation
下流交换柱 downstream column
下流式单位散热器 downward discharge unit heater
下流塔 downflow tower
下流洗涤 downstream wash
下流洗液 downstream wash solution
下炉腹线 【铁】lower bosh line
下炉缸(高炉的) metallic reservoir, iron receiver
下炉膛 lower hearth
下落 drop, falling
下落断层 downcast (DC, D.C.)
下落芯 【铸】drop [wing] core
下锚 anchoring

下模　lower [female, counter] die, anvil swage ◇ 穿孔机~【压】bed
下模冲　(同"下冲杆")
下排孔型(三辊式轧机的)　bottom passes
下排烟式炉　downdraught furnace
下喷煤气管道　【焦】under-jet gas duct
下喷(式)焦炉　underjet (coke) oven ◇ 复热~*, 四分式~*
下喷水器　bottom water sprayer
下坡(度)　descending grade, downgrade
下坡焊　downhill (welding)
下坡焊位置　downward position
下气道　downcomer, down-take
下潜浇注　【钢】under-pouring
下切杠杆式剪切机　【压】upcut lever shears
下切剪切机　up-cut shears
下切式热剪　down-and-up cut hot shears
下倾　declination
下倾位置上焊接　downhill welding
下屈服点　lower yield point
下屈服应力　lower yield stress
下燃烧器[喷嘴]式炉　underburner-type oven
下砂箱　【铸】bottom (moulding) box, flask drag, drag (flask), nowel
下山　downward slope
下水道　sanitary sewer, cloaca
下水道工程　sewerage
下水道污泥　【环】sewage sludge ◇ 厌氧~*
下水干道　main sewer line
下水管　downcomer pipe [tube], sewer (pipe) ◇ S形~存水弯 S-trap
下水管道系统　sewerage system
下水口　collector nozzle
下死点(压力机压头的)　bottom dead centre (BDC)
下探测器　lower detector
下调　turndown
下凸肩(锻模的)　bottom fuller
下弯　turndown ◇ 轧件~*

下弯曲辊　lower bending roll
下围墙　lower-ring wall
下位　inferiority
下卫板　bottom guard
下吸风烧结　downward suction in sintering
下吸式单板皮带运输机　bottom singling belt conveyer
下陷型模　【压】bottom swage
下陷压痕　sinking indentation
下限　lower [inferior] limit
下限值　lower range value, lower limit
下向抽风　downdraft, downdraught (suction)
下向火焰　downward directed flame
下向渗滤(浸出)　downward percolation
下向凿岩机　sinker
下泄物　spigot product
下芯　【铸】core-setting, coring up
下芯工　core-setter
下芯骨　rodding
下芯机　core-setter
下型顶部浇口　top gate
下型模　anvil swage
下型箱　【铸】drag, nowel
下型芯用样板　【铸】core-setting gauge
下行程　【冶】downstroke
下行冲程　descent stroke, stroke down, downstroke
下行段　【团】return strand
下行轨　【团】return rail
下行立焊　vertical-downward welding
下行列车　down train
下修整工作辊　dressed bottom work roll
下悬式搬运车　over-the-load carrier
下压板　downward acting platen
下压力　overdraft
下压式水压机　hydraulic down-stroke press
下压式造型机　【铸】bottom squeeze moulding machine
下移烧结炉　lowering furnace ◇ 竖式

下移速度　downward velocity
下溢　underflow
下引辊　down leading roll
下游　downstream
下预热段　lower preheat zone
下预热块　lower preheat block
下渣　【铁】roughing slag,【钢】slag carry-over
下渣槽［沟］　【铁】skimming trough, roughing runner
下轧槽　lower［bottom］pass
下轧辊　bottom roll
下轧辊组合部件　bottom roll assembly
下支承辊　bottom backing up roll
下轴承座　bottom chock［chuck］
下铸　（同"底铸"）
下注　（同"底注"）
下注扁锭　【钢】bottom poured slab ingot
下注底板　【钢】bottom pouring plate
下注钢　bottom run steel
夏尔皮锡铜锑（减摩轴承）合金（83Sn, 11.5Cu, 5.5Sb）　Charpy's alloy
夏氏U形缺口试样冲击试验　Charpy U notch test
夏氏V形缺口　Charpy vee notch
夏氏V形缺口试棒　Charpy V-notch bar
夏氏V形缺口试样冲击动能　Charpy V-notch impact energy
夏氏V形缺口试样冲击试验　Charpy V notch test
夏氏冲击(动能)　Charpy impact
夏氏冲击韧性试件　Charpy test piece
夏氏冲击试验　Charpy（impact）test ◇预破裂～precracked charpy impact test
夏氏冲击试验机　Charpy impact testing machine, resilience testing machine
夏氏缺口　Charpy notch
夏氏钥匙形缺口　Charpy keyhole notch
夏氏钥匙形缺口(冲击)试样　Charpy key hole specimen
夏氏钥孔形缺口冲击试验　key-hole Charpy test
掀板（叠轧薄板的）　parting（of sheet pack）,opening
掀板机　opening machine
掀动挡板(卷取机的)　flap gate
氙壳电子　xenon core electrons
氙(气)灯　xenon lamp
先导位错　（同"领先位错"）
先断后合触点　break before make contact
先共晶奥氏体　proeutectic austenite
先共晶渗碳体　proeutectic cementite
先共析渗碳体　proeutectoid cementite
先共析碳化物　proeutectoid carbide
先共析体　proeutectoid
先共析铁素体　proeutectoid［free］ferrite
先共析组分　【金】proeutectoid constituent
先合后断触点　make-before-break contact
先进后出　【计】first-in last-out（FILO）
先进先出　【计】first-in first-out（FIFO）
先决条件　prerequisite, preconditon
先驱［先行］核　precurser
先头工序　upflow operation
先行进位　【计】carry lookahead
先行进位加法器　【计】anticipated carry adder
先行控制　【计】advanced control, look ahead control
先张法（预应力）混凝土　pretensioned concrete
先张法预应力　pretensioned prestressing
先张钢丝　pretensioned wire
先装焦炭(装料)法　coke-first charging
"仙"牌镍铜铁录音钢丝合金　Sen alloy
仙台硬质合金(中间合金；5—80W＋Ta, 2—80Mo, 5—50Cr, 少量 Fe、Ni、V、Mn）　Sendalloy
鲜樱红热(温度)　bright cherry red heat
纤钡锂石　bapholite
纤铋铀矿｛$Bi_2O_3 \cdot 2UO_3 \cdot 3H_2O$｝　uranospherite
纤发菌属　Leptothrix
纤铬绿矾　scherospathite

纤磷铝石{$3Al_2O_3 \cdot 2P_2O_5 \cdot 18H_2O$} vashegyite
纤磷铅铀矿{$Pb(UO_2)_2(PO_4)_2 \cdot 2H_2O$} przhevalskite, prjevalskite
纤锰锌矿 erythrozincite
纤丝 filament, fibril
纤碳铀矿{$UO_2 \cdot CO_3$} rutherfordite, diderichite
纤铁矿 lepidocrocite
纤铁钠闪石 blue asbestos
纤维 fiber, fibre, staple, filament ◇ 由~组成的 fibroid
纤维拔[推]出 fibre pull-out
纤维拔[推]出试验 fibre pull-out test
纤维板 fibreboard ◇ 木~ beaver board, 水泥~ cement fibrolite plate
纤维编织 fibrage ◇ 重型无接头~皮带*
纤维玻璃膜(挤压润滑剂) fibreglass veil
纤维材料 fibrous material
纤维层 fibre layer
纤维方向 direction of fibre
纤维覆盖层 fibre coating
纤维复合材料 fibre [fibrous] composite, fibre composite material [hybrid]
纤维管 fibre pipe
纤维管沥青 fibre pipe pitch
纤维光学 【理】fibre optics
纤维辊 fibre roller
纤维过滤除尘器 fabric dust collector
纤维过滤器 fabric filter
纤维化 fibrillation
纤维灰浆 staff
纤维混合材料 fibre composite hybrid
纤维胶 viscose
纤维胶木 fabroil
纤维结构 fibrous structure
纤维金属 fibre metal
纤维绝缘 fibre insulation
纤维拉长黏度测定法 (同"黏度纤维测定法")
纤维磷酸铝石{$3Al_2O_3 \cdot 2P_2O_5 \cdot 18H_2O$} vashegyite
纤维品 fabrics
纤维强化[增强] fibre reinforcing [strengthening]
纤维强化[增强]材料 fibre reinforced [strengthened] material
纤维强化[增强]复合材料 fibre reinforced [strengthened] composite ◇ 单~*
纤维强化[增强]合金 fibre strengthened alloy, filament reinforced metal
纤维强化[增强]金属 fibre reinforced [strengthened] metal, filament reinforced metal
纤维取向 fibre orientation
纤维蛇纹石{$H_4Mg_3Si_2O_9$} chrysotile
纤维伸长(率) fibre elongation
纤维(绳)芯(钢丝绳的) fibre centers [core]
纤维素{$(C_6H_{10}O_5)_{11}$} cellulose
纤维素覆层 cellulose coating
纤维素漆 cellulose lacquer
纤维素涂层 cellulose coating
纤维素吸附塔 cellulose column
纤维弹性的 fibro elastic
纤维涂层 fibre coating
纤维锌矿{ZnS} wurtzite
纤维锌矿型结构 wurtzite type structure
纤维性 fibring
纤维性混凝土 fibrous concrete
纤维冶金学 fibre metallurgy
纤维应力 fibre stress
纤维硬纸板 fiber, fibre
纤维预成形坯(件) fibre [fibrous] preform
纤维预成形坯(件)渗透 fibre preform infiltration
纤维增强[强化]塑料 fibre reinforced plastics
纤维增强体 fibre [fabric, filament] reinforcement
纤维织构 fibre texture

纤维织构照相	fibre texture photograph
纤维织品	cloth
纤维质的	fibrous
纤维质煤	board coal
纤维轴	fibre axis
纤维状断口	fibre [fibrous] fracture
纤维状断裂	fibrous break [fracture]
纤维状粉末	fibrous powder
纤维状构造	bacillar structure
纤维状硅酸盐	fibrous silicate
纤维状结构	filamentary [nerve] structure
纤维状结晶	【冶】whisker
纤维状金属铁生成	【团】fibrous iron formation
纤维状晶体	filament [fringe] crystal
纤维状离子的	fibre ionic
纤维状石灰岩	fibrous limestone
纤维状延性断口[断裂]	【压】ductile fibrous fracture
纤维(状)组织	fibre [fibrous] structure, fibration, fibre texture, fibrillation
纤维组织铸铁[纤维状铁]	fibrous iron
纤锌矿	buergerite, buergerita
纤锌锰矿	woodruffite
咸水	salt [saline] water ◇ 微～【环】brackish water
衔接器	adapter ◇ 联线～【计】on-line adapter
衔铁	armature (iron), anchor, keeper, reed
衔铁电压	armature voltage
闲频信号	idler
闲置能力	withdrawn capacity
闲置设备	idle unit
闲置时间	idle [stand-by] time
闲置寿命	shelf life
弦	string, 【建】chord, 【数】hypotenuse
弦板	chord plate
弦杆	chord (member)
弦模量(应力-应变曲线的)	chord modulus
嫌气性的	anaerobic
显谱皿	【化】developing dish
显气孔	macro porosity
显热	sensible [sensitive] heat
显色反应	colour [chromogenic] reaction
显色时间	developing time
显示	display, indicating, indication, (re)presentation, show, exhibit, discovery
显示表	indicating meter
显示表板	indicator board
显示表盘	indicating panel
显示部件	display unit
显示传送机	【电】indicating transmitter
显示度盘	indicator dial
显示方式	【电】display mode
显示管	display tube
显示回路	display circuit
显示剂	indicator ◇ 溶剂型～solvent developer, 湿～*
显示刻度	display scale
显示控制器	【计】display control
显示灵敏度	display sensitivity
显示器	indicator (IND., indic.), display (device), scope, visigraph ◇ 字母 数字 -图象-*
显示器[剂]法	indicator method
显示适配部件	【计】display adapter unit
显示数据分析	【计】display data analysis
显示数据询问器	【计】video-data interrogator
显示图	indicator [develop] diagram
显示文件	【计】display file
显示误差	indication error
显示线	【计】display line
显示仪表	indicating instrument, indicator device
显示荧光屏	indicator screen
显示映象管	【电】indicator tube
显示装置	indicating device, 【计】display unit [device]
显示字符发生器	【计】display character generator
显微测[计]量	micrometering

显微层间裂纹　microscopic interlaminar crack
显微纯洁度　【冶】micocleanness
显微电影摄影术　micro-cinematography
显微断面　microsection
显微法　【理】micromethod
显微分光光度计　microspectrophotometer
显微分聚[凝]　microsegregation
显微分离　microseparation
显微分析　microscopical analysis
显微分析器　microanalyzer ◇ 电子探针～
显微腐蚀　microcorrosion
显微高温计　micropyrometer
显微观察方法　microscopic means
显微光度曲线　microphotometer curve
显微光密度测量术　microdensitometry
显微光(密)度计　microdensitomer
显微光谱分析仪　microanalyser
显微技术　microtechnique ◇ 热离子发射～
显微检验　micrography
显微检验用试样　microtest piece
显微结构[构造]　(同"显微组织")
显微结构成分　microconstituent
显微金相学　microscopic metallography
显微浸蚀　micrographical etching, microetching
显微镜　microscope (mic., micros.) ◇ 阿斯卡尼亚～*，暗光阑～*，布氏～*，测量～ measuring microscope，反射式～*，飞点扫描[快速计数]～*，高温～*，格里诺～ Greenough microscope，激光～ laser microscope，摄影～ photomicroscope，生物～ biological microscope，双筒～ binocular microscope，通用～ universal microscope，投影～*，透射式～*，相衬～*，荧光～*，油浸[浸没]式～*，远距离～*，制造工具用～*
显微镜玻璃载片　microscope slide
显微镜成像　microscopic imaging
显微镜灯　microscope lamp
显微镜法　microscopical method
显微镜分辨率　resolution of microscope, resolving power
显微镜观察　microscope [microscopic] observation ◇ 发射式～*
显微镜观察的　microscope-viewed
显微镜计数　microscopic [microscope] count(ing)
显微镜计数法　microscope count method
显微镜检查[检验]　micro-examination, microscopic(al) examination
显微镜检查法　microscopy
显微镜粒度测定(法)　microscopic sizing
显微镜磨片(检验用)　microscopic section
显微镜目镜　microscope eyepiece
显微镜物镜　microscope objective
显微镜像　microscopic(al) image
显微镜研究　microscopical study ◇ 断口～术 fractography
显微镜有效放大倍数　useful magnification of microscope
显微镜载片　microscope slide
显微镜照明器　microscope illuminator
显微镜照相[照片]　micrograph, photomicrograph
显微径迹照相法　fission track etching method (FTEM)
显微孔隙(缺陷)　【铸】micro cavity
显微裂纹　microscopic crack
显微磨片　microsection, microslice
显微疲劳裂纹　【金】microscopic fatigue crack
显微强度　【金】microstrength
显微屈服点　microyield point
显微射线学[照相术]　microradiography
显微射线照相　micro-radiograph
显微试样　【金】microtest piece
显微缩孔　micro pipe, microshrinkage
显微探针分析　microprobe analysis
显微图形放大装置　【理】megalograph
显微维氏硬度计　micro Vickers
显微效应　microeffect

显微学[术] microscopy
显微压痕硬度 micro penetration hardness
显微衍射法 microdiffraction method
显微隐晶质 microaphanite
显微影[图]像 microscopic picture
显微硬度 microhardness ◇ 努氏[努普]~*,压入法测~*
显微硬度测定 microhardness testing
显微硬度法 microhardness method
显微硬度划痕 microcut
显微硬度计[试验仪] microhardness tester ◇ 肯特隆~*,图康~ Tukon tester
显微硬度压痕 microhardness indentation
显微硬度值 microhardness value
显微照片[照相] micrograph, microphoto (graph), microphotogram, photomicrogram ◇ 暗视场~*,明(视)场~*
显微照相底片 microfiche
显微照相机 photomicroscope, microscope camera
显微照相检验 micrographic examination
显微照相术 microphotography, photomicrography, micrography
显微照相图 microphotogram
显微照相研究 micrographic(al) investigation
显微照相装置 photomicrographic apparatus
显微组分 【金】microconstituent,【焦】maceral(煤岩的)
显微组织 microscopic structure, microstructure ◇ 奥氏体~*,贝氏体~*,次~metastructure
显微组织变化 change in microstructure
显微组织分析仪 microstructure analizer
显微组织检验 microstructural examination
显微(组织)图 micrograph
显相皿 developing dish
显像 display, video picture, developed image, developing, development

显像管 display [picture, image] tube, teletron ◇ 电子~kinescope
显像管控制器 cathode ray tube controller
显像管显示(器) cathod ray tube display
显像过度 overdevelopment
显像密度计[测密术] densitometer
显像雾翳 development fog
显像荧光摄影术 kinefluorography
显影 developing, development
显影不足 under-developing
显影[像]粉 development powder, toner
显影过度 overdeveloping
显影[像]剂 developer ◇ 阿米多~*
显影剂膜破裂 cracking of developer coating
显影时间 developer [developing, development] time
显影条件 developing condition
显影像 developed image
显影[像]装置 developing unit
显著的 notable, marked, remarkable
显著特性 prominent characteristic
显著性检定 【数】significance test
显字管 【计】charactron
显踪原子 tagged atom
藓状晶粒 mossy grain
现场 site, field, working place, spot
现场安装螺栓 field bolt
现场淬火 field quenching
现场调查 field investigation
现场分析[化验] in-situ analysis
现场灌[浇]筑混凝土 concrete in situ, in-situ concrete
现场焊接 field [site] welding
现场机器人 field robot
现场架设的贮槽 field elected tank
现场浇筑[捣](的) 【建】cast-in-place, cast in situ, pour-in-place
现场浇筑混凝土 【建】in-situ concrete
现场搅拌混凝土 【建】job mixed concrete
现场连接 field joint
现场培训 on-site training

现场人控型控制器	local manual controller
现场施工	site work
现场试验	field test(ing) [trial], site [in-situ] test, on-site trial, on-the-spot experiment
现场土壤力学试验	field soil mechanical test
现场修理	spot repair
现场研究	field investigation, work place study
现场养护的	job-cured
现场制作场	on-site plant
现场装配	field assembling [connection]
现成配料	ready-made mixture
现代化	modernization, modernizing, update, updating
现代化的	modern, up-to-date
现代化设备	sophisticated equipment, state of the art facility
现代化轧机	present day mill
现代冶金学	advanced metallurgy
现付	【企】cash payment
现浇混凝土	【建】cast-in-place [cast-in-situ] concrete
现浇式钢筋混凝土结构	monolithic reinforced concrete structure
现金储备	【企】cash reserve ◇ 施工~*
现金流动	cash flow
现金帐	cash account
现金支付	cash payment
现款[金]	cash ◇ 付~cash payment
现款[金]流量	【企】cash flow
现象	phenomenon, event ◇ 莱登弗罗斯特~*
现行标准	actual standard (act. std.), current standard
现行标准试样	working standard sample
现行美元计算数字	【企】current dollar estimates
现行指令寄存器	【计】current-instruction register
现行最佳实用控制技术	【环】best practicable control technology currently available (BPTCA)
现役高炉	current BF
现用文件	【计】active file
现有能力	existing capacity
现有设备	existing plant [equipment]
现值	present worth [value]
现抓取法取样	grab sampling
腺病毒	【环】adenovirus
陷波电路	trap circuit
陷波器	(wave) trap
陷进	gin
陷阱	trap
陷阱理论	trap theory
陷阱能级(半导体)	trapping level
陷口	swallow ◇ 碳极端~electrode crater
陷入	sink into, slump
陷窝(钢板缺陷)	dimples, dimpling
限电压短路过流继电器	voltage restrained short circuit overcurrent relay
限定	delimit
限动杆	arresting lever
限动器闸	bridle brake
限动芯棒	【压】retained-mandrel
限动芯棒迪舍尔轧管机	restrained mandrel diescher
限动芯棒连轧管机	retained mandrel (pipe) mill, multi-stand pipe mill (MPM)
限动芯棒轧制	retained mandrel rolling
限度	limit(ation), boundary, measure, range ◇ 阿氏~*
限额	quota, limit
限幅电路	clip(ping) [slicer, limiter] circuit
限幅器	【电】(amplitude) limiter, clipper ◇ 可调~adjustable limiter
限幅[流]指示器	limit indicator
限界氧化	【金】marginal oxidation
限量泵	metering pump
限量模锻	confined [trap] die forging
限流电抗器	current limiting reactor

限流电阻电路　economy circuit
限流电阻器　currentlimiting resistor
限流继电器　current limiting relay
限流调节器　current limiting regulator
限时淬火　【金】time quenching
限时继电器　time lag (ged) relay, time-limit relay
限速器　rate limiter, (speed) governor
限位环　spacing ring
限位开关　limit switch ◇ 凸轮式～cam type limit switch,旋转式～rotating limit switch,油-水密封～*
限位器　【粉】fork
限位[限制]器杆　【冶】restrictor rod
限位销　banking pin
限位转矩电动机　limited torque motor
限压燃烧　limiting-pressure combustion
限载电动机　load limiting motor
限制　restriction, limitation, restraint, confining, bound
限制尺寸　limiting dimensions
限制因素　limiting factor
限制(打击)行程螺母　stroke limiting nut
限制角焊抗裂试验　restrained fillet cracking test (R.f.C.T.)
限制宽展　restrained [restricted, suppressed] spread(ing)
限制器　limiter, restrictor, chopper, clipper, catch, eliminator (行程的) ◇ 电流～current limiter,视频～video limiter
限制式喷嘴　confined type nozzle
线　line, thread, strand, string, wire ◇ 比诺达尔～*,哈特曼～[滑移～]*,考塞尔～【理】Kossel lines,吕德斯～*,纽曼～【金】Neumann lines,渥拉斯顿～Wallastan wire
线棒材轧机　wire rod and bar mill
线爆成形　forming with an initiating wire
线材　wire (rod), rod (直径大于 5 毫米的) ◇ 半硬～*,超公差～*,打包用～binder,复合～composite [clad] wire,弧边轧扁～flattened wire,挤压～extruded wire,进入[喂入]～inlet wire,冷拔镀锡～drawn tinned wire,冷拉～cold-drawn wire,湿拉～wet drawn wire,四分之三硬～*,有纵裂纹的～cuppy wire,制铆钉用～rivet wire
线材包装　wire wrapping
线材成形机　【压】wire forming machine
线材打扁　wire flattening
线材废料　wire scrap
线材复绕机　【压】re-spooling machine
线材规格表　【压】wire gauge table
线材焊接　wire welding ◇ 十字交叉～*
线材号数　wire gauge
线材剪切机　wire shears
线材矫直机　【压】wire straightener, wire-straightening machine
线材进给装置　wire-feeding device ◇ 张拉式～*
线材卷　rod coil ◇ 断头盘条拉拔的～*,足重～full catchweight coil
线材卷取机　【压】coil winder, wire reel ◇ 加勒特式～*,卧式～*,伊登堡式～*
线材卷取机机体　tub
线材卷取装置　reeling facility
线材孔型　【压】(wire-)rod pass
线材拉拔装置　wire-drawing frame
线材坯　wirebar
线材清净作业线　wire-cleaning line
线材试验机　【金】wire testing machine
线材试样　wire specimen
线材送进辊　wire-feed roll
线材送进装置　wire-feeder
线材酸洗设备　wire pickling machinery
线材退火　strand-annealing
线材退火装置　wire annealer, wire annealing machine
线材弯曲机　wire bending machine
线材压扁　wire flattening
线材压扁机　wire flattening mill
线材延伸率　elongation of wire
线材轧机　【压】(wire-)rod [wire] mill ◇ 半连续式～*, 高速～*,活套式～*,

(交替二辊)横列式[比利时式]～*,连续式～*,无扭～*

线材轧机组 wire-rod mill train, rod mill rolling train

线材轧制 (wire) rod rolling

线材辗头机 wire pointing machine

线材直接电流加热法 ◇ 特劳伍德～ Trauwood process

线担 【电】cross arm

线电压 line volt(age)

线锭 wirebar

线锭精炼炉 wire bar refining furnace

线锭炉(铜的) wirebar furnace

线锭炉炉渣 wirebar slag

线锭铜 wirebar copper

线度 dimension

线断面重心 line-profile centroid

线分辨能力 line resolution ◇ 粉末法衍射图样的～*

线腐蚀 line corrosion

线光谱 line spectrum

线光源 line source

线规 wire gauge (W.G.), wire gauging equipment, 【压】rod pass ◇ 伯明翰～*, 布朗-夏普～*, 美国～*, 沃林顿～*, 英国～*

线规板 wire gauge plate

线轨应力迹 stress trajectory

线焊 line welding

线号 wire size

线夹 wire clip, fastener, cleat, 【电】(cable) clamp, connector

线夹钳间距 electrode opening

线架 【压】coil holder, swift

线接触钢丝绳 linear contact lay wire rope

线径测量装置(接触型) wire gauging equipment

线径规 wire gauge

线聚焦单色器 line-focusing monochromator

线聚焦辐射 line-focused radiation

线距 wire pitch

线锯 scroll saw

线卷 (wire) coil, wire in coils, boundle

线卷包装机 wire brushing machine

线卷回转台 coil turnaround

线卷紧卷[压紧]装置 coil compressor

线卷卷紧法 coil compacting method

线卷捆扎机 coil compactor

线卷支持器 coil holder

线捆 wire coil ◇ 重～*

线捆包装机 coil wrapping machine

线联"或"门电路 wired OR

线联"与"门电路 wired AND circuit

线路 circuit, line, path ◇ 跨～的 overline

线路安装系统图 wiring layout

线路编号 route number

线路变压器 line transformer

线路布置 track layout

线路电压 line [supply] voltage

线路断路器 line circuit-breaker ◇ 直流～ DC circuit breaker

线路工 lineman, wire man

线路回路 【电】line loop

线路交叉 transposition, crossing

线路接触器 line contactor

线路开关 line circuit-breaker, line switching

线路控制程序 【计】line control routine

线路损耗 line loss

线路图 circuit [wiring, cording, connection] diagram, wiring scheme

线路选择器 line selector

线路压降补偿器 line-drop compensator

线路噪声电平 【电】circuit noise level

线路转接[交换] circuit [line] switching

线路状态 line status

线密度 line(ar) density

线内计算机 on-line computer

线能量 line energy, 【焊】heat input

线排料回转真空过滤机 rotary vacuum string discharge filter

线盘 (wire) coil, disc spool, 【电】drum

线盘包装机 wire wrapper

线　xian

线盘捆扎　【压】coil strapping
线盘捆扎机　wire-tying machine
线盘冷却运输机　coil cooling conveyer
线盘箱[盒]　【压】wire reel magazine
线盘卸料器　【压】stripping spider ◇ 伸缩式~*
线盘卸下机　【压】wire coil stripping machine
线盘移送机　coil conveyer ◇ 拖运式~*
线膨胀　【理】linear expansion [swelling, stretch, dilatation]
线坯　wire rod
线频感应加热　line frequency induction heating
线平均直径　linear mean diameter
线谱　line spectrum
线切砖　wire-cut brick
线圈　【电】coil, winding ◇ 毕特~【理】Bitter coil, 加热~coil of heating, 铜带绕的~bobbin coil, 原边[一次]~primary coil, 自持~restraining coil
线圈磁化(作用)　【理】coil magnetization
线圈磁化法　coil method
线圈电阻　coil resistance
线圈架　bobbin
线圈间距　coil spacing, annular coil clearance（环形的）
线圈绕组　coil winding
线圈试验　coil test ◇ 特斯拉~*
线圈匝数　【电】turns
线缺陷　line(ar) defect, line imperfections
线(热)膨胀系数　linear (thermal) expansion coefficient
线绕变阻器　【电】wire rheostat
线绕转子　【电】(coil) wound rotor
线栅　wire grating
线上的(作业线上的)　on-stream
线生长速度(晶体的)　velocity of linear growth
线式打印机　wire printer
线式点火器　linear ignitor
线收缩　linear shrinkage ◇ 基普~试验*

线束(轨)迹　beam trace [path]
线速度　linear speed [velocity] ◇ 流态化~ space rate
线弹性断裂力学　linear elastic fracture mechanics
线弹性理论　linear elasticity theory
线头　thrum, stub
线条图(统计图表)　bar chart schedule
线图　diagram, (line) graph, plot ◇ 波尔贝克斯~*, 串接[升压]~boosting coil, 尼奎斯特~Nyquist diagram
线外计算机　off line computer
线网过滤器　wire mesh filter
线网焊接机　（同"钢丝网焊接机"）
线位错　line dislocation
线位移　line displacement [shift]
线位移感应式传感器　Nultrax
线显示发生器　【计】line display generator
线型分析　line-shape analysis
线型搅拌器　linear (type) stirrer
线型烧嘴　line burner
线形　line form
线性　linearity
线性变化　linear change [variation]
线性变形　linear deformation
线性补偿　linear compensation
线性部分法则(关于蠕变的)　line fraction rule
线性残余膨胀　【耐】linear after expansion
线性残余收缩　【耐】linear after contraction
线性程序设计　linear programming
线性电动机　linear motor
线性电荷密度　linear charge density
线性电势扫描法　linear potential sweep
线性电位计[器]　linear potentiometer
线性定律　linear law
线性对称展宽　symmetrical line widening
线性方程　【数】linear equation
线性放大(率)　【理】linear magnification [amplification]
线性放大器　linear amplifier

线性分布负载　line-distributed load
线性分析法　【金】lineal analysis
线性感应电动机　linear induction motor
线性关系　linear relationship
线性关系区[范围]　range of linearity
线性规划　linear programming (LP), linear optimization method
线性过滤器　linear filter
线性函数　linear function
线性极化技术　linear polarization technique
线性极限　linearity limit
线性加积分控制　(同"比例积分控制")
线性加速器　linear accelerator
线性距离　linear distance [separation]
线性控制[调节, 调整]　linear(ity) [proportional] control
线性扩展[展宽]　line widening
线性拉伸压力机　linear stretch press
线性冷却收缩　contraction in length on cooling
线性冷弯成型　linear contouring operation
线性离子　linear ion
线性弥散　linear dispersion
线性内插法　linear interpolation
线性能量转移　linear energy transfer (LET)
线性排列　line(ar) array
线性膨胀　(同"线膨胀")
线性偏振光　【理】linearly polarized light
线性平衡线　linear equilibrium line
线性区　【数】range of linearity
线性散射　linear scattering
线性扫描伏安法　linear scanning voltammetry
线性色散　linear dispersion
线性收缩　linear shrinkage ◇ 冷却～*
线性收缩系数　coefficient of linear shrinkage
线性损伤定律　linear damage law ◇ 迈因纳～*
线性吸收系数　linear absorption coefficient
线性系数　linear coefficient
线性压缩应变　linear compressive strain
线性硬化　linear hardening
线性元件　linear element
线性张力[拉伸]　【压】linear stretch
线性长大定律　【金】linear growth law
线性指数　line index
线性装置　【计】linear unit
线选存储器　linear selection storage
线移动　line shift
线应变　linear strain
线张力　line tension
线胀系数　(同"线膨胀系数")
线轴　bobbin, reel, spool(er), 【电】drum
线轴式开卷机　disc-type decoiler
线轴式拉丝卷筒　spooler block
线状(光)谱　line spectrum
线状光谱图　【理】line pattern
线状夹杂物　inclusion line
线状夹渣　slag stringer
线状晶体生长　filamentary crystal growth
线状链　linear array
线状(射线)源[线源]　line source
线状通道(位错的)　filamentary region
相　phase (ph.) ◇ 格里姆-佐默菲尔德～*, 青特耳～*, 休姆-罗瑟里～ Hume-Rothery phase
相比(萃取的)　phase ratio
相变　(phase) transformation, phase transition, metallurgical phase change ◇ α～ alpha transformation, 第一级[类]～*, 缓发～*, 扩散(型)～*, 同成分～*, 压致[受压诱生]～*
相变奥氏体　transformed austenite
相变产物　transformation product
相变迟滞　sluggishness of transformation
相变脆性　transformation embrittlement
相变点　transition point, 【金】change point, arrest
相变动力学　【理】kinetics of phase transformation

相变反应　phase change reaction
相变范围　phase transformation range
相变感生塑性钢（0.3C，9Cr，8Ni，4Mo，2Mn，2Si，余量 Fe）　transformation induced plasticity (TRIP) steel
相变机理　mechanism of phase transformation
相变加载法　transformation stressing
相变潜热　latent heat of phase change
相变热　heat of transformation
相变塑性　transformation plasticity
相变退火　【金】transformation annealing
相变温度　phase change temperature, temperature of phase change, transformation temperature ◇ 试淬（火）法测定～ bracketing
相变温度热处理法　【金】hump process
相变应变　transformation strain
相变应力　transformation stress
相变硬化　transformation hardening
相变诱导塑性　transformation induced plasticity (TRIP)
相变滞后　hysteresis of transformation
相不稳定性　phase instability
相参　（同"相干"）
相沉淀　phase precititation
相衬法　phase-contrast method
相衬观察　phase-contrast observation
相衬聚光镜　phase-contrast condenser
相衬显微镜　phase-contrast microscope
相衬显微术　phase-contrast microscopy
相衬显微照片[照相]　【金】phase-contrast micrograph
相衬象[相差衬映象]　phase-contrast image
相称温度　homologous temperature
相成分　phase composition
相萃取　extraction of phases
相当的　equivalent, correspondant, tantamount
相等　equality, equation, coincidence, congruency

相电流　phase current
相电压　phase(-to-phase) voltage
相电阻　phase resistance
相对编码　【计】relative coding
相对编址　【计】relative addressing
相对表面活度　relative surface activity
相对侧　opposite side
相对程序　relative [relocatable] program
相对尺寸　relative dimension [size, magnitude]
相对稠度　relative consistency
相对当量[等效值]　relative equivalent
相对导磁率　relative permeability
相对反射强度　relative reflection intensity
相对光谱[频谱]响应　relative spectral response
相对黑度　relative blackness
相对挥发度　relative volatility
相对活度　relative activity
相对价效应[作用]　relative valence effect
相对介电常数　(relative) permittivity, relative dielectric constant
相对可萃度　relative extractability
相对亮度　relative brightness
相对灵敏度　relative sensitivity
相对论　relativity (theory), theory of relativity ◇ 特殊～*
相对论效应　relativistic effect ◇ 位错～*
相对论行为　relativistic behaviour
相对论运动　relativistic motion
相对敏感性　relative sensitivity
相对摩尔自由能　relative molal free energy
相对黏度　relative viscosity
相对膨胀率　relative degree of swelling
相对疲劳强度　relative fatigue strength
相对强度　relative intensity
相对强度比(率)　relative intensity ratio
相对取向[方位]　relative orientation
相对溶解度　relative solubility
相对生产率[有效利用系数]　generic effi-

ciency	
相对湿度	relative humidity (RH, R.H.)
◇ 全年平均～*	
相对湿度示差	relative humidity differential
相对酸度	relative acidity
相对透光度	relative transmittance
相对透气性	relative permeability
相对误差	relative [proportional, fractional] error
相对下沉系数	coefficient of relative settlement
相对相(位)	relative phase
相对效率	relative eiifficiency
相对形态学	relative morphology
相对压缩性	relative compressibility
相对延伸	relative elongation
相对延伸率	relative amount of elongation
相对原子价效应	relative valency effect
相对运动	relative movement [motion]
相对值	relative value [magnitude]
相反的	contrary, opposite, reverse, inverse, invert
相反极	opposite [reciprocal] pole
相反溶质	opposite-type solute
相反物	counter
相反状况	counter condition
相分布	phase distribution
相分解	phase decomposition
相分离器	phase separator
相分析	phase analysis
相符化合物	congruent compound
相干	cohere
相干边界	coherent boundary
相干发射	coherent emission
相干辐射	coherent radiation
相干干涉	coherent interference
相干光	coherent light
相干晶核	【金】coherent nucleus
相干距离	coherence distance
相干强度	coherent intensity
相干散射	coherent scattering
相干相	【金】coherency (phase), coherent
相干效应	【理】cohere(nt) effect
相干性	coherency, coherence
相干应变	coherency strain
相干振荡[动]	coherent oscillation
相干状态	coherent state
相共振	phase resonance
相关	correlation, cohere, relevance
相关法	correlation method
相关方程	correlation equation
相关分析	correlation analysis
相关观察	dependent observation
相关函数	correlation function
相关技术	corelation technique
相关器	correlator
相关图	correlogram, correlatograph
相关微分曲线	correlation-derived curve
相关系	phase relation
相关系数	correlation [related] coefficient
◇ 复～*	
相关性	dependence, relativity, relevance, coherence, correlation
相关仪	correlator
相关因子	correlation factor
相互比较	intercomparison
相互对照表	cross reference list
相互反应	interreaction
相互干扰	mutual interference
相互关联	interlock
相互关系	correlations, interrelation(ship), interface, interplay
相互贯穿	interpenetration
相互贯穿点阵	interpenetrating lattices
相互检验	cross-checking
相互交叉	intercross
相互扩散	mutual diffusion, interdiffusion
相互扩散系数	interdiffusion coefficient
相互连接	interconnection
相互排斥	mutual repulsion
相互取向关系(共轭相的)	mutual orientation relationship
相互渗透	interpenetration

相 xiang

相互调制　intermodulation
相互吸引(力)　attractive interaction, interattraction
相互依存[依赖]关系　interdependence
相互引力　mutual attraction
相互制约　mutual constraint
相互转换　interconversion
相互作用　(mutual) interaction, interreaction, coactions, interplay, liaison, mutual effect, cross-coupling ◇ 中等强度～*
相互作用机理　mechanism of interaction
相互作用系数　interactive coefficient
相混合物　phase mixture
相机[照相机]　camera ◇ 平板～*
相畸变　phase distortion
相计算法　phase computation (PHACOMP)
相际反应　phase boundary reaction
相继滑移　consecutive slipping
相加定律　additivity law
相加性　additivity
相间变压器　【电】interphase transformer
相间的　interphase,【金】phase-to-phase
相间结合(力)　interphase bond
相间作用　phase interaction
相检定　phase detection
相鉴定　phase identification
相交　intersecting, interception, transposition, traversing
相交二重轴　intersecting diads
相交滑移面　intersecting slip plane
相交平面　intersecting plane
相交轴　concurrent axes
相结构　phase structure
相界　phase boundary, line of demarcation ◇ α 相～alpha phase boundary, γ 相～gamma phase boundary
相界测定　phase boundary determination
相界层　separation layer
相界面反应　phase boundary reaction
相界线　phase boundary line
相联处理机　associative processor
相联存储器　content addressable memory (CAM), associative memory [storage], associative pushdown memory
相联关键字　associative key
相联寄存器　【计】associative register
相联语言　associative language
相连续性　phase continuity
相邻防护涂层　adjacent protective coat
相邻设备　adjacent accomodation
相邻原子[质点]　【金】neighbo(u)r ◇ 等距离～*
相律　【金】phase rule ◇ 吉布斯～Gibbs phase rule
相敏检波器　【电】phase-sensitive rectifier
相配　match
相偏析　phase segregation
相频　phase frequency
相平衡　phase equilibrium
相(平衡)图　phase (equilibrium) diagram
相平衡状态[条件]　phase equilibrium conditions
相(平)面　【金】phase plane
相切　【数】contact, tangency
相区　phase field ◇ 拉弗斯～Laves phase field
相区域[相空间,相宇]　phase space
相绕组　phase winding
相容的　compatible
相容条件　conditions of compatibility
相容性　compatibility, consistence, consistency ◇ 化学～*
相似　similarity ◇ 不～dissimilarity
相似参数　similarity parameter
相似的　similar
相似定理[准则]　similarity principle
相似定律　law of similarity ◇ 巴尔巴～*
相似法　similarity [similitude, analogue] method
相似(理)论　theory of similarity
相似物　homologue
相似系数　similarity coefficient

相似性 similarity
相态 【金】phase state
相同条件 identical condition
相图固相线 phase diagram solidus boundaries
相图液相线 phase diagram liquidus boundaries
相歪扭 phase distortion
相位 phase ◇ 阳极～anodic phase,有～差的 dephased,整体～bulk phase
相位超前 phase lead,leading in phase
相位对比观察 phase-contrast observation
相位计 phase meter
相位角 phase angle
相位控制设备 phase control device
相(位灵)敏系统[装置] 【电】phase sensitive system
相位平衡器 phase equalizer
相位调整 phasing
相位调整器 phase shifter
相位调制 【电】phase modulation
相位同步 phase synchronism
相位旋转指示器 phase rotation indicator
相位一致 【电】phase coincidence
相(位)移 phase shift ◇ 90°～分量 quadrature component
相位移后的 dephased
相位滞后 phase lag
相稳定性 phase stability
相析出 phase precipitation [separation]
相向动作锤头 【压】opposed striker
相消失法 disappearing-phase method
相谐振 phase resonance
相移热量调节器(焊接电流的) phase shift heat controller
相应温锥号[测温锥] 【耐】pyrometric cone equivalent
相应原理 correspondence principle
相转变 phase transition
相转变自由能 free energy of transformation
相组成 phase composition

镶板 wall panel,veneer
镶板法崩裂性试验 【耐】panel spalling test
镶边 edging,fringe ◇ 金属带～implate
镶块(压铸机的) biscuit bloch
镶木 veneer wood
镶嵌件 inserts
镶嵌金刚石的制品 diamond-impregnated compositions
镶嵌(式模板)框 cliche frame
镶嵌式型芯(压铸用) knock-out core
镶嵌造型 insert moulding
镶墙边砖 closer
镶入(物) inlay
镶套过盈量 【压】inset shrink range
镶条 wedge adjusted slide
镶牙合金(5—12Ag,4—10Cu,余量 Au) dental gold
镶样机 mounting press
镶铸的 cast-in
镶装模 insert die
镶装叶片 inserted blade
香蕉形插头 banana plug [pin]
香蕉形插座 banana jack
香农板(炉腹用立式冷却板) 【铁】Shannon plate
箱 tank,box,chest,case,cabinet,container,cupboard,enclosure,magazine,receiver
箱挡[带] 【铸】flask [cross] bar ◇ 支撑型砂用～【铸】sand edge
箱涵 box culvert
箱夹 mould closer
箱卡 mould [flask] clamp
箱框 【铸】upset frame
箱内(式)退火 (同"密闭退火")
箱内退火电炉 electric box annealer
箱圈 【铸】raising
箱式淬火 【金】pot quenching
箱式干燥器 chamber dryer
箱式基础 coffered foundation
箱式冷却器 box cooler
箱式炉 (同"室式炉") ◇ 煤气加热～

箱式喷流换热器　box spraying exchanger
箱式输送机　box conveyer
箱式退火炉　box annealing furnace ◇ 辐射管加热～*
箱式压滤机　box [chamber] filter press, box pressure filter
箱式氧化铁(脱硫)法　【焦】oxide box
箱式浴槽　box type bath
箱外壳　cashing
箱形沉箱　box caisson
箱形成型模　box forming die
箱形电解槽　box cell
箱形断面托圈(转炉的)　【钢】box section ring
箱形涵洞　box culvert
箱形挤压型材　【压】extruded box
箱形孔型　【压】box pass [groove] ◇ 闭口式～*，开口～ open box pass，凸底～ convex box pass
箱形孔型系统　box pass sequence
箱形孔型系统轧制法　box pass method
箱形框架结构　box frame(d) construction
箱形联轴器　box coupling
箱形梁　box beam ◇ 多腹板～*
箱形天线　box antenna [loop]
箱形喂料器　box feeder
箱形小车(带式烧结机用)　box pallet
箱形窑　box kiln
箱形柱　box column
箱形桩接头　box pile joint
箱铸法　box casting
箱装退火的薄钢板　box annealed sheet
乡村大气中耐腐蚀试验　rural atmosphere test
详图　detail drawing [chart], detail (Det., det.)
详细检查　detailed examination
详细流程图　detail chart
详细设计　detail design, design details
详细数据[资料]　particulars
想象　imaging
响裂　clinks

响音高温计　noise thermometer
响应　response
响应度[性]　responsiveness, responsibility, responsivity
响应函数　【理】response function
响应器　【理】response device
响应曲线　response (curve) ◇ N 次循环的～*
响应时间　【理】response time
响应特性(曲线)　response characteristic
响应因数　【理】response factor
响应滞后(仪表的)　【理】response lag
项　item, 【数】term
项大小　【计】item size
项目　item, article, clause, project ◇ 按～前进【计】item advance
项目块　entry block
项目设计　item design
项目一览表　itemized schedule
橡浆　latex (复数 latices)
橡胶　rubber ◇ 布纳～ buna, 海帕伦～ Hypalon rubber, 加固～保护层(管道的) national coating
橡胶薄板　gum sheet
橡胶衬板　rubber liner [lining]
橡胶衬里　rubber lining [coating]
橡胶衬里钢槽　rubber-lined steel tank
橡胶代用品　rubber substitute
橡胶垫　rubber backing
橡胶垫圈　rubber washer [ring]
橡胶覆面　rubber cover [coating]
橡胶覆面挤干辊　rubber drying roll, squeegee roll, squeeze
橡胶[皮]覆面辊　rubber roll, rubber-covered roller
橡胶辊　gum roll
橡胶绝缘　rubber insulation
橡胶绝缘的(电缆)　cab-tyre sheathed (C.T.S.)
橡胶硫化作用　vulcanization
橡胶轮胎地面移动式装料机　rubber-tyred floor-type mobile-charging machine

橡胶密封圈	grommet, grummet
橡胶模冲压	rubber compression ◇ 格林~成形法*
橡胶黏着力试验	adhesion test
橡胶片	sheet rubber
橡胶圈	rubber [gum] ring
橡胶套管	gum sleeve
橡胶涂层	rubber covering
橡胶硬化器	vulcanizer
橡皮包套压制	【粉】rubber-bag pressing
橡皮衬垫盖	rubber gasketed lid
橡皮衬套	【机】rubber bush
橡皮冲头[阳模]	【压】rubber plug
橡皮带	rubber bett(ing)
橡皮袋	rubber bag
橡皮垫[填料]	rubber packing
橡皮垫圈	rubber washer [gasket]
橡皮垫片	rubber gasket
橡皮垫圈密封	rubber-ring seal
橡皮隔膜泵	rubber diaphragm pump
橡皮管	rubber tubing ◇ 可伸缩~ flexible rubber, 盘旋~*
橡皮辊磨床	rubber roll grinder
橡皮环	rubber ring
橡皮缓冲器	rubber buffer
橡皮胶合剂	rubber cement
橡皮浇口棒	【铸】rubber gate stick
橡皮绝缘	rubber insulation (RI)
橡皮绝缘软电缆	cab-tyre cable
橡皮绝缘软线	cab-tyre cord
橡皮密封	rubber seal ◇ 可伸缩~ flexible rubber seal
橡皮模成形	rubber pressing（冲压成形）, rubber (stretch) forming（张拉成形）
橡皮(模)冲床	【压】rubber(-bladder) press ◇ 单动~*
橡皮模(液压)成形法	rubber forming process ◇ 格林~*, 惠龙~*
橡皮模造型	【铸】contour moulding
橡皮膜	rubber membrane ◇ 液压~成形法*
橡皮膜压压实造型机	【铸】diaphragm squeeze machine
橡皮囊	rubber container
橡皮软管	rubber hose
橡皮塞	rubber stopper [plug, bung]
橡皮伸缩管	rubber bellows
橡皮深拉延法	【压】rubber-bladder process
橡皮手套	rubber gloves ◇ 长筒~*, 接电极~*
橡皮套	rubber jacket, boot
橡皮阴模反冲压法	marforming
橡皮直浇口(模拔上的)	rubber gate stick
橡皮铸型	rubber mould
像差	【金】(optical, chromatic) aberration ◇ 彗形~ coma aberration, 球面~ spherical aberration
像差焦散线	aberration caustics
像差调整	asrigmation control
像差源	aberrent source
像场边缘清晰度	【理】marginal sharpness
像场弯曲(显微镜的)	curvature of field
像点	picture [image] point, picture element
像力	image force
像散计	astigmatometer
像散校正装置	astigmator
像散[散光]镜	astigmatoscope
像散器[装置]	astigmatizer
像散透镜	astigmatic lens
像散性(现象)	astigmatism
像素	picture element
像位错	【理】image dislocation
向场透镜	field lens, field glasses
向红效应(增色)	bathochromic effect
向后散射	back scattering
向后运行	astern running
向量	(同"矢量")
向量变量	【数】vector variable
向量产生[生成]	【计】vector generation
向列液晶	nematic liquid crystal
向列(状)态相	【金】nematic phase

向内扩散	indiffusion
向内散射	scattering-in
向气性	aerotropism
向前道次(可逆机座的)	forward pass, odd numbered pass
向热	【铁】working [run] hot
向上动的压板	upward acting platen
向上堆积铸型铸造法	◇ 齐布林~Zueblin process
向上立焊	upward welding in vertical position
向上立焊焊缝	upward vertical weld, vertical-up weld
向上流动	upward flow
向上流动的气体	upward-flowing gas
向上翘曲	upwarping
向上渗滤	upward percolation
向上通风	up-draft, up-draught
向上液流	upstream
向上跃迁	upward transition
向上阻力(流态化床的)	upward drag
向外扩散	outward diffusion
向外迁移离子	outgoing ion
向外弯曲(边缘)	neck-out
向下火焰	downward flame
向下立焊焊缝	downward vertical weld, vertical-down weld
向下流动	downward flow
向下流动操作	downflow operation
向下液流	downstream
向下跃迁	downward transition
向心过滤器	outside-in filter
向心力	centripetal force
向心配合(价)体	ligand
向心球轴承	radial [annular] ball bearing
向心铸造	centripetal casting
向氧性	oxytropism, aerotropism
向右对齐	【计】right justify
向右旋转的	right-hand
向紫(增色)效应	【理】hypsochromic effect
象限	quarter (Qt, qtr, quar.), quad(rant)
象限静电计	quadrant electrometer
象限仪	quadrant
象征	emblem mark, symbolize, signify
象征常数	【计】figurative constant
削	cut, chipping, clipping
削边	chamfered edge
削边搭接	chamfered-edge lap joint
削边机	edging machine
削扁尖凿	cape chisel
削方	squaring
削尖	pointing, tapering
削平补强处理	【焊】flush finish
削平补强焊缝	flush weld
削平补强焊接	flush joint
削枕机	adzing machine
硝铵炸药	ammonium nitrate blasting agent (ANBA), ammonia dynamite
硝胺	nitr(o)amine
硝饼	niter cake ◇ 用~熔解 fluxing with nitre cake
硝化	nitrating, nitration, nitrifying ◇ 反~denitration, 离子氮~动力学*
硝化甘油(炸药)	$\{(O_2NO)_3C_3H_5\}$ nitroglycerine (nitro.)
硝基铂酸根	nitroplatinate
硝基氟处理法	nitrofluor process
硝基化合物	nitro-compound
硝石	$\{KNO_3\}$ nitrokalite, nitrate of potash, niter, nitre, saltpeter, saltpetre ◇ 钠[智利]~*
硝酸钡	barium nitrate, nitrobarite
硝酸钚	plutonium nitrate
硝酸处理	nitric acid treatment
硝酸镝	$\{Dy(NO_3)_3\}$ dysprosium nitrate
硝酸铥	$\{Tu(NO_3)_3\}$ thulium nitrate
硝酸铒	$\{Er(NO_3)_3\}$ erbium nitrate
硝酸钆	$\{Gd(NO_3)_3\}$ gadolinium nitrate
硝酸钙	$\{Ca(NO_3)_2\}$ calcium nitrate, nitrate of lime
硝酸甘油	monobel, nitroglycerin, grisounite
硝酸汞	$\{Hg(NO_3)_2 \cdot H_2O\}$ mercuric nitrate

硝酸铪{Hf(NO$_3$)$_4$}　hafnium nitrate
硝酸钬{Ho(NO$_3$)$_3$}　holmium nitrate
硝酸镓{Ga(NO$_3$)$_3$}　gallium nitrate
硝酸钾{KNO$_3$}　potassium nitrate, nitrate of potash
硝酸钪{Sc(NO$_3$)$_3$}　scandium nitrate
硝酸镧{La(NO$_3$)$_3$}　lanthanum nitrate
硝酸硫酸混合的电镀液　ackey
硝酸铝{Al(NO$_3$)$_3$}　aluminium nitrate
硝酸镁{Mg(NO$_3$)$_2$}　magnesium nitrate
硝酸镎　neptunium nitrate
硝酸钠{NaNO$_3$}　sodium nitrate [niter], Chile saltpeter [nitre]
硝酸钠熔盐处理　(同"熔融硝酸钠处理")
硝酸钕{Nd(NO$_3$)$_3$}　neodymium nitrate
硝酸钕镨{Di(NO$_3$)$_3$}　didymium nitrate
硝酸镨{Pr(NO$_3$)$_3$}　praseodymium nitrate
硝酸溶解　nitric acid dissolution
硝酸铷{RbNO$_3$}　rubidium nitrate
硝酸铯{CsNO$_3$}　cesium nitrate
硝酸钐{Sm(NO$_3$)$_3$}　samaric nitrate
硝酸铈{Ce(NO$_3$)$_3$}　cerium nitrate
硝酸铈镁　cerium magnesium nitrates
硝酸试验　【金】nitric acid test
硝酸锶{Sr(NO$_3$)$_2$}　strontium nitrate
硝酸双氧铀[硝酸铀酰]{UO$_2$(NO$_3$)$_2$}　uranyl nitrate (UN)
硝酸水溶液淬火　nitric acid quenching
硝酸铊{Tl(NO$_3$)$_3$}　thallic nitrate
硝酸铽{Tb(NO$_3$)$_3$}　terbium nitrate
硝酸铁{Fe(NO$_3$)$_3$}　ferric nitrate
硝酸铜　copper nitrate
硝酸钍{Th(NO$_3$)$_4$}　thorium nitrate ◇灯罩级～*
硝酸析银法　【色】(in)quartation
硝酸稀土　rare earth nitrate
硝酸纤维素载膜　cellulose nitrate support film
硝酸亚汞{HgNO$_3$·H$_2$O}　mercurous nitrate
硝酸亚铈钾{K$_2$[Ce(NO$_3$)$_4$]}　potassium cerous nitrate
硝酸亚铈钠{Na$_3$[Ce(NO$_3$)$_4$]}　sodium cerous nitrate
硝酸亚铁{Fe(NO$_3$)$_2$}　ferrous nitrate
硝酸亚铜　cuprous nitrate
硝酸盐[酯]　nitrate (nit.) ◇含氧～oxynitrate
硝酸盐离子　nitrate ion
硝酸盐溶液　nitrate solution
硝酸盐蚀裂　nitrate cracking
硝酸氧锆{ZrO(NO$_3$)$_2$}　zirconyl nitrate
硝酸氧铪{HfO(NO$_3$)$_2$}　hafnyl nitrate
硝酸氧化钪{(Sc$_2$O)(NO$_3$)$_4$}　scandium oxynitrate
硝酸氧钛{TiO(NO$_3$)$_2$}　titanyl nitrate
硝酸钇{Y(NO$_3$)$_3$}　yttrium nitrate
硝酸镱{Yb(NO$_3$)$_3$}　ytterbium nitrate
硝酸铟{In(NO$_3$)$_3$}　indium nitrate
硝酸银　silver nitrate
硝酸铀　uranium nitrate
硝酸铕{Eu(NO$_3$)$_3$}　europium nitrate
硝盐槽退火　saltpeter annealing
销钉　dowel, (male) pin ◇接合～bayonet
销钉棒材　pin bar
销钉传动　pin gearing
销钉扩管试验　【压】pin expansion test
销钉连接　dowel joint, pin seal
销键　pin key
销接头　cotter [pin] joint
销联接　pin coupling
销路　market
销路好的　marketable
销式顶推装置　pin knockout
销售　sell, market(ing) ◇可～产品 saleable product
销售经理[销售部主任]　manager of sales
销售情况　market pattern
销售商品　merchandising
销售市场行情　market conditions
销套　pin bush
销形连接[锁紧]　bayonet joint
销针　spike

销轴 wrist, bead
消除 elimination, removal, clear up, wipe off, deletion
消除脆性退火(结构钢的) water toughening
消除电离(作用) deionization
消除电路 cancel circuit
消除故障[差错] debugging
消除剂 remover, killer
消除空位的退火 annealing out of vacancies
消除冷作[加工]硬化效应 removal of work-hardening effect
消除冷作硬化 release of work hardening
消除内应力 relief of internal stress
消除内应力退火 relief annealing
消除器 suppressor, eraser, eliminator
消除翘曲【压】iron out
消除缩管 pipe elimination
消除烟雾(法) abatement of smoke
消除氧化皮 descaling
消除应变退火炉 strain-relief furnace
消除应力【压】release of stresses, stress relieving
消除应力处理 stress-relieving treatment
消除应力断裂 (同"再加热断裂")
消除应力回火 stress-relief tempering
消除应力裂纹 stress-relief crack(ing)
消除应力热处理 stress-relief heat treatment
消除应力退火 stress-relief annealing, recovery(冷轧后的)
消除应力退火炉 stress-relief [stress-relieving] furnace
消磁 demagnetizing, degaussing
消电离电势[位] deionization potential
消电离空气自动断路器 deion air circuit-breaker
消毒 disinfection, antiseptisis, decontamination (decon.)
消毒水 detoxicated water
消毒蒸锅 autoclave

消防 fire fighting [control, protection]
消防安全系统 flame safeguard system
消防车 fire fighter truck
消防队 fire brigade, fire fighting forces [crew]
消防规则 fire fighting rules
消防龙头(户外式) 【建】FH-O, fire hydrant (outdoor-type)
消防龙头(室内式) 【建】FH-I, fire hydrant (indoor-type)
消防龙头系统 hydrant system
消防器具 fire extinguisher
消防人员 fireman, fire fighter
消防软管[水带] fire hose
消防设备 fire fighting equipment, fire control unit
消防栓 fire plug (f.p.)
消防系统 fire fighting system
消防用水 fire fighting water
消防云梯 extension ladder
消费者呆[坏]账 consumer bad debts
消光 extinction, deaden, absorbance ◇ 一次[初级]~ primary extinction
消光法 photo-extinction method
消光角 extinction angle
消光距离(电子显微镜的) extinction distance
消光轮廓 extinction contour
消光系数 extinction coefficient
消光效应 extinction effect
消耗 consuming, consumption, depletion
消耗的热量 heat consuming
消耗电极焊(接) consumable-electrode welding ◇ 惰性气体(保护)~·
消耗功率 consumed power, power intake
消耗量 consumption ◇ 满负荷[满载]~ full load need
消耗量指示器 consumption indicator
消耗料[矿,煤]堆 live storage pile
消耗能量 wasted energy
消耗品 consumable(s)
消耗指标 consumption targets

消耗重量　consumed weight ◇ 锻造～consumed weight
消耗装置　consumer
消和槽　slaking tank
消和试验　slaking test
消和性(质)　slaking property
消和作用　slaking effect
消弧　arc extinction [extinguishing, quenching]
消弧触[接]点　spark extinguisher contact ◇ 辅助～arcing contact
消弧螺线管[螺管线圈]　arc blow compensator
消弧室　spark catcher
消化　digesting, digestion, assimilation, slaking ◇ 污泥分级～*
消化槽　【环】digester chamber
消化器[装置]　digester, slaker
消化设施　hydration facilities
消化石灰　slaked lime
消化污泥　digested sludge
消化药剂　digestive, digester
消火车　【焦】(同"熄焦车")
消火器　fire apparatus [exinguisher]
消火时间　【焦】(同"熄焦时间")
消火栓　fire hydrant [cock]
消极的　negative
消零　【计】zero elimination [suppression]
消灭　eliminating, elimination, abolishing, extinction, annihilation
消沫剂　defoamer [defoaming] agent
消能　energy dissipation ◇ 沟中～槛 ditch check
消泡　forth breakage
消泡器　forth breaker [destroyer], antifoam ◇ 冲击～impact froth breaker
消偏振(作用)　depolarization
消偏振镜　depolarizer
消气　gettering
消气硅　gettered silicon
消气合金　getter(ing) alloy ◇ 钍铈～*
消气剂　getter (material) ◇ 非蒸散型～*, 凯梅特钡镁合金～Kemet
消气剂溅射　getter sputtering
消气剂离子泵　【理】getter-ion pump
消气剂喷涂　getter sputtering
消气箱[柜,容器]　gettering container
消气性能　gettering property
消气液体　gettering liquid
消气元素　getter element
消气作用(真空管内的)　getter(ing) effect [action]
消球差镜　aplanat
消球差物镜　aplanatic object glass, aplanatic lens
消去法　【数】elimination method
消融　ablation
消散　dissipation, evaporation
消色差　achromatism, achromatization
消色差度　degree of achromatism, achromaticity
消色差目镜　achromatic eyepiece
消色差透镜　achromat, achromatic lens
消色差物镜　achromatic objective
消色差性　achromatism
消砂　【铸】blasting shot
消声　noise elimination, damping, deadening
消声器　silencer, muffler, snubber, suppressor, 【理】buffer
消失　disappearing, annihilation, distinction, evaporation ◇ 易～性 fugitiveness
消失螺纹量规　run-out gauge
消石灰　hydrated [killed, slaked] lime, lime hydrate
消退(性)　retrogression
消息缓冲　【计】message buffer
消熄器　extinguisher
消相法　disappearing-phase method
消向熵　entropy of disorientation
消焰器[装置]　flame trap
消音　silencing of noise, deaden, noise reduction
消音器　silencer, sound damper, muffler ◇

废气～exhaust gas silencer,共振～resonant silencer,进风～suction silencer
消音装置　silencing unit
消隐　blanking, black out
消震能力　shock-absorbing capacity
小坝　【铁】level weir ◇ 撇渣器～dam
小白点(钢材缺陷)　flakelet
小坂炼铅法　Kosaka lead smelting process
小板坯(镀锡薄钢板的)　coke bar
小半径曲线　sharp(-radius) curve
小棒形状　【金】rodlet
小剥裂处　multiple spall
小薄片　flakelet
小槽　fuller, sulculus
小产量车间　small-tonnage plant
小车　bogie, buggy, dolly, larry, lorry, trolley, wagon, wheel barrow
小车返回机构　carriage return mechanism
小车滑轮组　trolley block
小车浇铸　buggy casting
小车隧道窑　car tunnel kiln
小齿轮　pinion (gear) ◇ 灯笼式～lantern pinion
小齿轮线坯　pinion wire
小齿轮箱　pinion stand
小齿轮轴　pinion shaft
小尺寸效应　small-size effect
小尺寸异型钢材　shaped bar
小道钉　spike nail
小滴　droplet, dripping
小滴法　droplet method
小滴冷凝　weeping-out
小电车　electric industrial truck
小电流电弧　low current [amperage] arc
小电流焊接　cold running
小断面　light section
小断面铸件　thin-section casting
小吨位设备　small-tonnage plant
小范围屈服　【金】small-scale yielding
小方块　blockage, 【半】dice
小缝　tiny gaps
小服务程序　servlet

小盖　【铁】small bell
小格　【团】leg
小格(撒料)漏斗　fall out hopper
小功率电动机(0.735千瓦以下)　fractional horse power motor
小功率电炉　low-powered furnace
小功率电路　dry circuit
小功率机械　light-duty machine
小公差　close tolerance
小沟　fuller, minor groove
小规模　small-scale, experimental scale
小规模集成(化)[集成电路]　【米】small scale integration (SSI)
小规模生产[制造]　small-scale production, small-lot manufacture
小规模试验　pilot test, scaled-down experiment
小轨道　【运】bady track
小号筛　undersize screen
小厚度(板材的)　light gauge
小厚度纵剪作业线　light slitter line
小换向装置　tumbler [tumbling] gear
小计　minor total, subtotal
小间距取样　close sampling
小件铸造　miniature casting
小焦炭块　coke nuts
小浇包[浇注桶]　pony ladle
小角不对称间界　small-angle unsymmetrical boundary
小角度晶界　small-angle boundary
小角度入口锥模　small-angle die
小角(度)散射　small-angle scattering
小角对称倾侧间界　small-angle symmetrical tilt boundary
小角间界网络　network of small-angle boundary
小角晶界　low angle boundary
小角区域　low-angle region
小角衍射线对[偶]　【理】low-angle pair of diffraciton arcs
小角(衍射)照相机　low angle camera
小截面钢材　【压】light material

小晶体	tiny crystal
小颗粒	granula, granule
小刻面断口	facet fracture
小孔	eye, micropore ◇ 打~ eyeleting
小孔测量	diaphragm measurement
小孔切割器(带卡规的)	blow pipe with small hole cutting attachment
小口径	small calibre (SC, S. C.), small-bore
小口径管	fine tubing
小跨度屋盖	【建】cottage roof
小块废钢	fine [small-sized] scrap
小块焦(炭)	nut [egg] coke
小块料	(dead) smalls
小块煤	nut coal
小块石灰	small-size lime
小矿槽	small bin, roll feeder surge bin, surge hopper, raw mix hopper, 【团】mixed material hopper
小棱柱剥落试验	small prism spalling test
小砾石	pea gravel
小粒	granula, granule, micropellet
小粒焦	small-(sized) coke
小粒炉料	small-sized burden
小粒烧结矿	small size(d) sinter
小梁	【建】joist
小量拉伸	shallow draught(ing)
小量生产	short-run production
小(料)钟	【铁】small [upper] bell
小瘤	nodule, tubercule
小瘤状[形]腐蚀	tubercular corrosion, tubeculation
小漏(钢)	【钢】dribble
小密封条	【铸】bady dike
小面	minor face, facet
小面化晶体	【金】faceted crystal
小面积屈服	【金】small-scale yielding
小皿	【色】capsule
小脑模型	cerebellum model
小泡的	vesicular
小批量锻造	short-run forging
小批生产	【企】small-scale [short-scale] production
小平面	facet
小平台	footpath, berm
小起重机	donkey crane
小球	globule, 【团】microball, micropellet, semipellet, seed (pellet) ◇ 造~*
小球菌属	micrococcus
小球团	micropellet, semipellet
小球团法	micro-pelletizing
小球(团)烧结法[工艺]	MPS process
小球团烧结(矿)	【铁】hybrid pelletized sinter (HPS), mini-pelletized sinter (MPS) ◇ 全精矿~*
小球(团)烧结工艺	【团】MPS process
小容量电缆	low-capacity cable
小容量转炉	small vessel
小伞齿轮	bevel [cone] pinion
小时报表	hourly report
小时产量	output per hour, hourly gain in production
小时换气次数	air change per hour
小时(生产)效率[能力]	hourly capacity [efficiency]
小时最大用水量	maximum hourly consumption
小事故	minor accident
小室	cell, cubicle, culdy, cabinet (cab.), booth, chamber
小四边形构件	quarrel
小苏打	(同"碳酸氢钠")
小铁片(用于调节空气进口断面)	finger plate
小头(钢锭的)	【压】butt end
小透熔焊接	cold running
小细粒	granula, granule
"小心加矿石"温度范围	【冶】"ore with caution" range
小型焙烧罐	mini-pot
小型布氏硬度计	bady brinell
小型材轧机产品	bar mill products
小型车辆	dilly
小型初轧机	bady bloomer

小 xiao

小型电弧炉　laboratory-scale arc furnace
小型电解槽　small(-scale) cell
小型电解器　bench scale dissolver
小型电容器　midget capacitor [condenser]
小型电子管　midget [bantam] tube
小型电子束熔炼　laboratory-scale electron beam melting
小型钉　【铸】sprills
小型反应器　small vessel
小型废钢[铁]捆　bustling
小型干燥器　laboratory dryer
小型钢　figured bar iron
小型钢材　small [light] shape
小型钢材剪切机　bar shears
小型钢材轧机　bar iron rolling mill
小型钢铁厂　mini steel plant
小型工厂　minimill, miniworks, miniplant, small-scale [small-tonnage] plant
小(型)化铁[冲天]炉　small [baby] cupola, cupolette
小型混凝土拌合机　【建】half-bag mixer
小型或中型型钢轧机　jobbing mill
小型计算机　minicomputer
小型减速机　packaged reducer
小型焦炉　small scale coke oven
小型搅拌机　pony mixer ◇ 连续式～*
小型晶体　minicrystal
小型开口锭　small sized open head ingot
小型冷轧机　mini cold mill
小型量规　light gauge
小型坯连铸拉出　billet withdrawal
小型牵引机　tug
小型千斤顶　midget jack
小型热离解设备(碘化物法)　laboratory-scale deposition unit
小型溶解器　bench scale dissolver
小型设备　laboratory(-scale) plant, mini-plant
小型试验　small-scale test
小型试验设备　small-scale laboratory equipment
小型手动穿孔机　portable hand punch

小型水(力发)电站　small hydro-electric plant, micro-hydraulic station
小型型钢　small [light(er)] section, merchant bar, bar (steel rolled) stock
小型型钢卷取机　【压】thin-stock reel ◇ 加勒特式～Garret reel
小型型钢[型材]轧机　【压】small [light] section mill, jobbing mill
小型型钢轧机组　small-section mill train
小型圆角光子　【铸】egg sleeker
小型轧材　merchant bar
小型轧机　【压】bar (rolling) mill, merchant (bar) mill ◇ 摩根式～Morgan mill
小型轧机操作[轧钢]工　tongsman
小型轧机连续化　tandem rolling of small section mill
小型轧机用坯　bar mill feed
小型轧机中间机座　pony
小型真空泵　minipump
小型铸件　small [miniature] casting
小型铸造间　portable foundry
小型转鼓　mini-tumbler
小型转炉　small vessel
小型转筒式干燥机　packaged rotary drum dryer
小型装置　small-scale plant ◇ 手持～handset
小修　【企】minor maintenance [repair], minor [light] overhaul, current [temporary] repair, maintenance work, running maintenance [repair]
小修进度表　maintenance schedule
小修小补(道路的)　dribbing
小压下量　light reduction [draft]
小压下量道次　【压】light pass
小压下量轧制　saddening (初轧头道的), knobbling (为除去氧化皮)
小压下量轧制机座　dummy stand
小烟道　【焦】sole [bus] flue
小烟道炉算砖　【焦】sole flue port brick
小样取样　increment sampling

小异型钢　figured bar iron
小异型砖　small shape
小余量铸造　close tolerance casting
小圆锥齿轮　bevel pinion
小渣口[铁]monkey
小张镀镄[铅锡合金]薄钢板（约500×700mm）　short terne(plate)
小直径超薄壁　small-sized ultra-light-wall
小直径黄铜坯　brass wire bolt
小直径圆搭板点焊　button welding
小直径圆盖板点焊接头　button (spot) weld
小钟杆平球架　bell bearing
小钟料斗　small bell hopper
小钟平衡杆　small bell beam
小钟下料(高炉的)　small bell dump
小轴(杆)　staff
小柱(如栏杆柱)　colonnette
小组进位　【计】group carry
小砝码　set of weights
肖克利位错　Shockley's dislocation
肖马克超级铁素体不锈钢（0.003C, 0.15Si, 0.04Mn, 30Cr, 2Mo, 0.007N, 余量Fe) Shomac
肖式显微硬度试验计　microsclerometer
肖氏(回跳)硬度计　(Shore) scleroscope, Shore hardness tester
肖氏(回跳)硬度试验　Shore scleroscope hardness test, sleroscope test, Shore [drop, rebound] hardness test
肖氏陶瓷型(铸造)法　Shaw process
肖氏硬度　scleroscope hardness (Sc.H, scler.), Shore [drop, rebound, repulsion] hardness
肖氏硬度值　Shore hardness figure [number]
肖塔氧-乙炔焰表面快速淬火法　Shorter process
肖特基缺陷　Schottky defect
哮喘病　asthma
啸声　whistle ◇ 间断性～surging
效果　effect (eff.), effectiveness, result, impression
效力　potence, effect, efficacy
效率　productiveness, productivity, efficiency (eff., effic.), effectiveness
效率差[无效率]的　inefficient
效率量度[测定]　measure of effectiveness
效率曲线　efficiency curve
效率试验　efficiency test
效率试验机　efficiency testing machine
效率损失[降低]　loss of efficiency
效率提高　increase in efficiency
效益　beneficial result, benefit, achievements ◇ 经济～economic benefit
效应　effect (eff.), action, influence ◇ 埃廷豪森～*, 爱因斯坦-德哈斯～*, 奥罗万～【理】Orowan effect, 巴尼特～*, 鲍辛格～*, 贝可勒尔～*, 波特温-勒夏忒列～*, 德哈斯-范阿尔芬～*, 菲舍尔～【理】Fisher effect, 霍尔～Hall effect, 霍普金森～*, 贾奎斯～Jaques effect, 卡肯达尔～*, 科特雷耳～*, 克尔～Kerr effect, 克雷默～*, 雷宾德尔～Rehbinder effect, 理查森～*, 铃木～*, 罗斯科～*, 迈斯纳～【理】Meissner effect, 莫特-纳巴罗～*, 穆斯堡尔～Moessbauer Effect, 内雷宾德尔～*, 能斯脱～【理】Nernst effect, 逆维德曼～*, 佩尔蒂埃～*, 皮奥伯特～*, 热电放射[爱迪生]～Edison effect, 塞曼～*, 施米格尔斯卡斯～*, 斯诺克～*, 外雷宾德尔～*, 维德曼～*, 维格纳～*, 维拉里～*, 杨-泰勒～*, 约飞～Yoffe effect, 约瑟夫森～*
效用　effectiveness, efficacy, utility (ut.), usefulness, avail
楔　wedge, peg
楔固　choke
楔焊　wedge bonding
楔击缺口冲击试验　notch wedge impact
楔键　wedge [taper] key
楔角　【机】angle of wedge [taper]
楔模滚锻[横轧]　transverse wedge rolling

楔入 wedging
楔式的 wedge-like
楔体(土压)理论 wedge theory ◇ 库仑～*
楔调节装置 wedge adjusting device
楔调压力机 wedge press
楔调整器 wedge regulator
楔型空穴 wedge type void
楔形 wedge, cuneate, cuneatus, dovetail form
楔形安全臼(轧机的) wedge-type breaking piece
楔形板材 tapered plate
楔形薄板 tapered sheet
楔形扁材轧机 taper mill
楔形承坯架 wedge-stilt
楔形触点 wedge contact
楔形电解槽 electrolytic wedge tank
楔形断面(带钢的) wedge section
楔形拱 cuneatic arch
楔形夹头(拉伸试验用) templin grip [chuck]
楔形件试验 wedge test
楔形浇口 wedge gate,【铸】knife gate
楔形结晶器(薄板坯连铸用) wedgy mould
楔形进料螺旋压力机 screw wedge press
楔形晶体 cumeat
楔形拉延压杯试验 wedge draw cupping test
楔形面 wedge shaped face
楔形曝光 wedged exposure
楔形前端(送轧坯料的) nosed
楔形石 quoin
楔形试样 wedge(-shaped) specimen
楔形丝筛面 wedge-wire deck
楔形榫槽 dovetailed slot
楔形条钢 key bar
楔形调整滑块 wedge adjusted slide
楔形铜块 wedged cake
楔形位错 wedge dislocation
楔形物 end wedge, glut

楔形油膜 oil wedge
楔形轧件 wedge bar
楔形制动器[楔形闸] wedge [key-operated] brake
楔形砖 wedge [tapered, skew(back), arch] brick, bevel end brick, end wedge ◇ $1\frac{1}{2}$ 宽～bonder wedge,单侧～side feather,横向侧切～side skew,两侧～*,砌拱用～end arch
楔形座 wedge bed
楔轧 taper rolling
楔住 choke, jam, wedging
楔状扇形块 wedge segment
歇班的 off-duty
蝎尾型结构 ◇ 扎帕塔式～*
协变式 【数】covariant
协变性[协方差] covariance
协萃剂 synergist
协合特性[性质](萃取的) synergistic behaviour
协合增强(萃取的) synergistic enhancement
协合增强系数 synergistic enhancement factor
协合最佳的 synergetic, synergic
协合作用 synergism, synergistic effect, synergy
协会 association (Assn, assoc.), society, institute, institution
协聚合物 copolymer
协调 coordination, matching, harmonize, concert ◇ 不～maladjustment
协调规划模型 coordination model ◇ 二维层次～*
协调滑移 【理】cooperative slip
协同程序 【计】coroutine
协同萃取 synergic solvent extraction
协同的 synergetic, synergic
协作 coordination
协作作用 (同"合作作用")
携带 carry-over, bring ◇ 可～性 portability

携带式布氏硬度测定仪　telebrineller
携带式高温计　hand pyrometer
携带式焊枪　portable welding gun
携带式烘炉　knock down salamander
携带式回跳硬度计　duroscope, duroskope
携带渣(量)　slag carry-over
斜T形接合　inclined tee joint
斜板推土机　angle dozer
斜铋钯矿　froodite
斜壁沟　canch
斜边　hypotenuse, bevel edge, bevel (焊管坯的) ◇ 焊管坯～成形轧辊 scarfing roll
斜边焊管坯　bevelled edge skelp
斜边头尾　bevelled ends
斜边窄带材　skelp
斜槽　bevelled [skewed] slot, chute (work), spout, sloping platform (承接带卷的)
斜槽料仓　inclined zonal bunker
斜槽溜浇混凝土　【建】chuting concrete
斜槽闸门　chute gate
斜槽装料系统　chuting system
斜侧面滚动导轮　bevelled wheel
斜长岩　anorthosite
斜撑　diagonal bracing [bar, strut], brace, batter brace (桁架的), outrigger, 【建】crippling
斜齿轮　helical [spiral, bevel, twisted] gear, bevel wheel
斜齿轮传动　bevel pinion drive
斜吹氧气转炉　(同"卡尔多转炉")
斜吹氧气转炉炼钢法　(同"卡尔多炼钢法")
斜导板　angular guide
斜导架打桩机　batter leader pile driver
斜底料仓　inclined bottom bunker
斜底式炉　(longitudinal) sloping hearth furnace, roll-down furnace
斜垫圈　bevel washer
斜垫(自位)轴承　tilting bearing
斜顶　ramp roof

斜度　inclination, obliqueness, obliquity, (amount of) taper, tilt, slope, angularity, batter, steepness, slope (孔型侧壁的), leave (锻模的),【建】baking (道路的) ◇ 定～规 batter rule
斜度调整　slope control
斜度设计　draughting
斜度仪　slope meter
斜端砖　end-skew
斜方对称　orthorhombic symmetry
斜方辉铅铋矿 $\{Pb_2Bi_2S_5\}$　cosalite
斜方角闪石 $\{(Fe, Mg)_4Si_4O_{12}\}$　authophyllite
斜方晶胞　orthorhombic cell
斜方晶的　orthorhombic (ortho.), trimetric
斜方点阵[晶格]　(ortho)rhombic lattice
斜方(晶)结构　orthorhombic structure
斜方晶体　orthorhombic crystal
斜方晶系　(ortho)rhombic rhombic system
斜方蓝辉铜矿　anilite
斜方锰矿　ramsdellite
斜方排列[堆积]　orthorhombic packing
斜方羟砷锰矿　arsenoclasite
斜方砷钴矿　safflorite
斜方砷镍矿 $\{NiAs_2\}$　rammelabergite, white nickel
斜方砷铁矿　loellingite
斜方砷铜矿　paxite
斜方钛铀矿　orthobrannerite
斜方形面　rhombic face
斜方形型材[断面]　rhomboidal section
斜方锥　orthorhombic pyramid
斜风口　angle (flow) tuyere
斜杆　diagonal rod
斜钢筋　diagonal bar [reinforcement]
斜锆矿 $\{ZrO_2\}$　brazilite
斜锆石 $\{ZrO_2\}$　baddeleyite
斜锆石砾(斜锆石＋锆石英) $\{ZrO_2 + ZrSiO_4\}$　zirkite
斜锆石砾矿　zirkite ore

斜 xie

斜鼓形混凝土搅拌机　tilting drum concrete mixer
斜管压力计　inclined [-tube] manometer
斜硅钙铀矿　lambertite ◇ β~ *
斜硅镁石{Mg₉(SiO₄)₄(OH,F)₂}　clinohumite
斜硅铜矿　shattuckite
斜辊　skew (table) roll, cross [web] roll
斜辊道(工作台) tapered roller table, skew table
斜辊横矫直机　【压】two-roll straightening machine
斜辊矫直机　cross roll straightener, cross-roll straightening machine, straightener with cross rolls ◇ 旋转~ rotary straightener
斜焊　bevel welding
斜焊电焊机　deck welder
斜焊缝　inclined weld
斜焊接梁　tapered beam
斜红磷铁矿　metastrengite
斜后墙　inclined [sloping] back wall
斜滑道(炉旁的)　slide-down chute
斜激波　oblique shock (wave)
斜极电炉　electric furnace with inclined electrode
斜钾铁矾　yavapaiite
斜键　taper key
斜交(叉) oblique crossing, shew
斜交齿轮　skew gear
斜(交)拱　skew arch
斜交激震波面　oblique shock front
斜交角　skew angle
斜交角焊　oblique fillet welding
斜角　oblique angle, bevel (angle), inclination ◇ 拱脚砖~ angle of skew, 屋顶~ angle of roof
斜角规　bevel [miter] square, bevel protractor
斜角轨枕　bevelled rectangular sleeper sleeper
斜角轨枕　bevelled rectangular tie

斜角焊缝　bevel weld, oblique fillet welding
斜角立体投影　cabinet projection
斜角切割　bevel cutting
斜角系　oblique system
斜角砖　bevel brick
斜角坐标　oblique coordinates
斜接　bevel (led) [chamfered, oblique] joint, scarf (ing), miter [mitre] (45°接合)
斜接T形接头　oblque T joint
斜接焊接　mitre welding
斜接口[面]　【钢】vee, scaef
斜截角　bevel angle
斜截[剖]面　oblique [taper] section, oblique profile
斜截式　slope-intercept form
斜截锥　truncated cone
斜井用钢丝绳　wire rope for inclined plane
斜距条件[状况]　slant-range condition
斜靠模(回转锻造机的)　taper templet
斜口环密封　mitre ring seal
斜口剪切机　inclined throat shears
斜口接合法　【建】scarfing method, scarf joint method
斜(口)接头[斜口连接,斜接接头]　skew [scarf, chamfered] joint
斜跨度　skew span
斜拉杆式起重机　stiff leg derrick
斜梁　sloping [tapered] beam
斜裂纹　oblique crack
斜磷钙铁矿　tamanite
斜磷铅铀矿{(PbO)₂·UO₃·P₂O₅·H₂O}　parsonite
斜磷锌矿　spencerite
斜炉底　sloping hearth
斜炉箅　sloping grate
斜率　gradient, ascent, slope
斜率曲线　slope curve
斜率调整　slope control
斜面　oblique [inclined] plane, obliquity, bevel (face), angular [skew] surface, in-

clination, cant, slope（嵌接的）
斜面板　cant board, skewback
斜面锤　sloping hammer
斜面垫板　【运】canted tie plate
斜面断口　angular fracture
斜面滚圈　tapered tyre
斜面焊接　scarf welding
斜面焊接接头　scarfweld
斜面镜　incline mirror
斜面孔（铁砧的）　pitched hole
斜面台　bench board
斜面洗矿（床、槽）　buddle
斜面砖　bevelled brick
斜钠锆石｛Na$_2$O·ZrO$_2$·6SiO$_2$·3H$_2$O｝elpidite
斜配孔型轧制法　diagonal (flange) method
斜片百叶窗　abatjour
斜平面　inclined plane
斜坡　(downward) slope, descent, inclination, gradient, ramp, shelving
斜坡道　inclined track, skid transfer, grade of slope, slope ramp
斜坡排水　batter drainage
斜砌（砖）　【建】skew
斜桥　skew [askew, inclined] bridge,【铁】skip bridge, skip (hoist) incline
斜桥卷扬机　inclined hoist
斜桥上料机（高炉的）　hoist bridge [incline]
斜桥装料机运行速度　【铁】bridge travel (l)ing speed
斜切　bevel shearing, chamfering, oblique cut, angle cutting（管、棒材头部的）
斜切刀片　inclined cutting blade
斜切角　chamfer angle
斜切面　bevel [oblique] cut
斜刃切削　【机】oblique cutting, three dimensional cutting
斜入射　angular [oblique] incidence
斜三通　inclined tee joint
斜伞齿轮　skew bevel gear

斜射束探伤法　angle beam method
斜水沟　batter drainage
斜锁板　wedge
斜台　ramp
斜台架　sloping skid
斜钽锰矿　alvarolite
斜膛模（板材用）　wedge-shaped die
斜条格构　【建】lattice
斜铁镁铈矿　sahamalite
斜筒式混凝土拌合机　tilting drum concrete mixer
斜头平焊接　butt welded with chamfered ends
斜顽辉石｛Mg$_2$Si$_2$O$_6$｝clinoenstatite
斜钨铅矿｛PbWO$_4$｝raspite
斜下　decline
斜线对接焊接　scarf welding
斜线区　shaded area
斜削　splay, bevel
斜楔调整（轧辊位置的）　wedge adjustment
斜楔调整装置（压下量的）　wedge adjusting equipment
斜楔轧制试验　wedge rolling test
斜烟道　【压】inclined flue
斜轧　skew [diagonal] rolling ◇直腿钢～法
斜轧穿孔　rotary [roll] piercing, tube cross piercing
斜轧穿孔法　piercing mill method, Mannesmann process
斜轧穿孔机　Mannesmann (piercing) mill, cone mill
斜轧机　skew [slant] mill ◇二辊式～*，三辊～*
斜轧扩径　rotary expansion
斜轧扩径机　plug expander
斜轧式扩管机　rotary tube expanding machine
斜轧延伸（管材的）　rotary elongation
斜轧延伸机　rotary elongating pipe mill
斜张力　taper tension

斜支管	sloping branch
斜支柱	outrigger, raking strut
斜置钢筋	（同"斜钢筋"）
斜置孔型	diagonal pass
斜置孔型设计	diagonal (pass) design
斜置孔型系统	diagonal system
斜置孔型轧制	diagonal type rolling
斜置梁形孔型	diagonal-beam pass
斜置轧辊	cross roll
斜轴面	clinopinacoid
斜砖	skew brick
斜桩	batter pile
斜桩群	batter pile cluster
斜锥	oblique cone
斜座起重机	angle crane
胁变分量	strain component
谐波	【电】harmonic (wave)
谐波电流发生	generation of harmonic current
谐波发生[振荡]器	harmonic oscillator [generator]
谐波分量	harmonic component
谐波分析	harmonic [frequency] analysis
谐波分析器	harmonic [frequency] analyzer
谐波畸变[失真]	harmonic distortion
谐波级[阶]	harmonic order
谐波滤波[滤除]器	harmonic filter
谐波吸收滤波器	harmonic absorbing filter
谐函数	harmonic function, harmonics
谐和振动	harmonic vibration
谐量	【理】harmonic quantity
谐振	resonance, resonant [harmonic] vibration, resonance [harmonic] oscillation, syntony
谐振变压器	resonance [resonant] transformer
谐振电路	resonance [resonant] circuit
谐振电压	resonance voltage
谐振法	syntonization, resonance method
谐振范围	resonance range
谐振峰	resonance peak
谐振回路	resonant tanic [circuit, tank]
谐振频率	resonance [resonant, harmonic] frequency
谐振频率法	resonant frequency method
谐振器	resonator, cavity
谐振曲线形状	resonance shape
谐振试验	resonance test
谐振条件	resonance condition
谐振线	resonance line
写关键字	【计】write key
写脉冲	【计】write pulse
写入	write in, read in ◇ 允许～write enable
写(入)保护	【计】write protection
写入封锁	【计】write lockout
写(入)允许	【计】write enable
写时间	write time
写头	write [writing] head
写信号	write enable
卸车机	extractor unit ◇ 运行漏斗式～[卸船机]*
卸车线(铁路的)	dumping track
卸出辊道	kick-off table
卸除机	stripper ◇ 液压～hydraulic stripper
卸船机	ship unloader
卸垛(叠板的)	destacking
卸垛机	unpiler, depiling equipment, pack take-off device
卸放槽	drainage chute
卸辊高度	roll dismantling height
卸荷	outloading, unload
卸灰阀	dust [dump, unloading] valve
卸货处[卸车站,卸车地点]	tipping point
卸货起重机	unloading crane
卸货栈桥	unloading bridge
卸件装置	【机】shedder
卸卷(卷取机的)	coil stripping
卸卷臂杆	discharge arm
卸卷车	coil stripping carriage
卸卷机	coil stripping machine, coil strip-

per [pusher, unloader], ejecting gear ◇ 三臂～ three-arm unloader, 提升～ elevating stripper
卸卷机构(卷取机的) stripper [kick-off] mechanism
卸卷机机头 stripper head
卸卷器组件 stripper assembly
卸卷台架 coil unloading skid
卸卷托板 stripper plate ◇ 液压～*
卸卷小车 coil stripper car
卸开 stripping
卸矿槽 【团】discharge hopper
卸矿点 dump point ◇ 带式机～*
卸矿量 discharge rate
卸矿台 bridge
卸矿栈桥 ore (-handling) [unloading-stocking] bridge
卸矿站 【团】discharge station
卸料 unload(ing), outloading, discharge, discharging, dump
卸料[矿]仓 outloading bunker, bin dischargor
卸料槽 bin discharger
卸料侧 discharge side
卸料侧板(皮带机的) wing tripper
卸料场 dumping site
卸料[矿]车 tripper car ◇ 自动～*
卸料车式推料机 tripper stacker
卸料点 unloading point
卸料吊杆 unloader boom
卸料斗 discharge box
卸料端 【团】discharge side
卸料翻斗(热轧带卷的) discharge cradle
卸料翻转机 upender
卸料刮刀 unloader knife ◇ 皮带机～belt plow
卸料辊道 discharging roller table
卸料辊道的辊子 discharge roller
卸料滑道 unloading skid
卸料机 unloader, discharging machine, extractor unit, 【压】kick-off mechanism ◇ 斗式～ bucket unloader, 休利特电动～*
卸料角 angle of discharge
卸料坑 discharge [drawing] pit
卸料孔 discharge door
卸料口 discharge port [outlet, gate]
卸料流槽 discharge launder
卸料漏斗[斗仓] unloader hopper
卸料皮带机[带卸料小车的皮带机] tripper conveyer
卸料平台(用抛掷法) tipping stage
卸料坡道(炉旁的) discharge slope
卸料起重机 unloading crane
卸料器 discharge aid, tripper ◇ 带式～ belt tripper
卸料时间 discharge time
卸料台 unloading table, discharging platform
卸料台架 discharge skid
卸料箱 discharge box
卸料悬臂 unloader boom
卸料运输机 discharge conveyer
卸料闸门 discharge gate
卸料栈桥 unloading(-stocking) bridge
卸料站 unloading point, discharge terminal
卸料装备[塔,架] unloading rig
卸料装置 discharger, discharging [dumping, emptying] device, drawing [relief] mechanism, tripper ◇ 储仓～ bin discharger
卸煤坑 discharge pit
卸煤栈桥 unloading gantry, 【焦】coal bridge
卸下 discharge, outloading
卸线 【压】stripping
卸线钩[器] coil stripper, coil stripping machine
卸线卷机 wire coil stripping machine
卸载 unload(ing), outloading, off-load, loading out, uncharge
卸载活门 discharge valve
卸载机 unloader, unloading machine
卸载机械 unloading machinery

卸载皮带	tripper belt
卸载运输机	loading-out conveyer
卸载站	unloading station
卸渣炉算	dump plate
泄出	lapaxis, spill
泄放沟	drain passage
泄放机构	bleeder mechanism
泄放孔	bleed hole, escape orifice
泄放器	bleeder
泄漏	leaking, leakage, outleakage,【环】spilling, spillage ◇ 接头～*，无～的 leakless，易～性 leakiness
泄漏场	leakage field
泄漏功率	leakage power
泄漏检验	leak test ◇ 经～的 leak-tested
泄漏量	leakage rate, spillage
泄漏区[面积]	leaky area
泄漏水	leakage water
泄气阀	snuffle valve
泄水斗	drainage bin
泄水沟	drain ditch, catch-drain
泄水管	(water) drain pipe
泄水箱	drain box
泄水旋塞	draw-off cock
泄压	pressure relief, decompression
泄压阀	pressure relief valve
泄氧动力学	kinetics of oxygen evolution
泄液漏斗	draining funnel
泻利盐	(同"含水硫酸镁矿")
泻落运动[状态]	【团】cascading action
泻水假屋顶	【建】cricket
谢才公式(用于计算水流速度)	Chezy formula
谢拉德薄板连续电镀锌[铜，黄铜]法	Sherrite process
谢勒方程	Scherrer's equation
谢里特－高尔顿加压浸出镍钴铜粉法【色】	Sherritt-Gordon process
谢帕德铝阳极氧化处理法	Shepherd process
谢泼德断口淬透检验	【金】Sheppard P-F test
榍石{CaO·TiO$_2$·SiO$_2$}	titanite, aspidelite
芯板	【铸】core plate
芯棒	mandrel (bar, rod), plug, core rod [pin], cored bar, insert ◇ 穿孔～ piercing mandrel，浮动[游动]～ floating core rod，固定～*，拼合～ split core rod，球形～ ball mandrel，软[可变形]～ deformable mandrel，弯曲～【压】bending mandrel，沿～弯曲(板坯的) tangent bending，圆柱形～*
芯棒抽出机	【压】mandrel stripper ◇ 链式～ chain stripper
芯棒抽出机构	stripper mechanism
芯棒杆	mandrel [thrust] bar
芯棒钢	mandrel steel
芯棒划痕(冷拔管缺陷)	plug line
芯棒回送系统	mandrel bar return system
芯棒挤压法	mandrel extrusion method
芯棒控制装置	【压】mandrel manipulator
芯棒拉拔	plug drawing
芯棒坯	mandrel block
芯棒式无缝管轧机	【压】mandrel mill
芯棒涂油	core dressing
芯棒圆柱形部分	【压】plug bearing
芯棒轧管[轧制]	plug [mandrel] rolling
芯棒辗轧(管材的)	plugging (operation)
芯棒支承板	core-support plate
芯棒支座	bar steadier
芯棒转换装置	plugbar change-over unit
芯棒锥头部分	【压】plug cone
芯棒座	mandrel holder
芯饼	biscuit,【铸】cake (core)
芯撑	chaplet ◇ U 形钢丝～【铸】jammer，多孔铁皮(箱式)～*，双面型～ stud chaplet，陀螺[铸铁滚柱]式～*
芯垫(托板)	core cradle ◇ 烘干用～ core drier
芯锻	【压】core forging
芯杆(弯曲试验用)	(core) pin
芯钢丝	core wire
芯骨	【铸】core bar [rod, iron, grid] ◇ 管状～*，铁丝～ core wire

芯骨架　core skeleton
芯骨金属　core metal
芯盒　【铸】(core) box ◇ 对分式～split core box,多腔式～multiple core box,可拆式～*,普通框式～plain frame core box,倾出式～turnout core box,倾转式～tilting box,松框～collapsible core box,托板～*,脱落式～loose frame core box
芯盒翻转机　core drawer
芯盒内腔　core cavity
芯盒排气塞　core box vent
芯料　core material
芯片　【铸】cameron core ◇ 挡渣～choke,滤渣型～cup strainer core,易割冒口～knock-off core
芯腔　【铸】core cavity
芯塞　【压】plug
芯砂混合物　【铸】core sand mixture
芯砂黏结剂　【铸】core sand binder, core compound ◇ 特拉甘廷～Tragantine
芯数　number of cores
芯铁　【铸】core metal [iron, bar, grid]
芯头　【铸】core-print, core marker ◇ 水平型～horizontal core print,定向～*,加大～augmented core print,开口式～open core print
芯头间隙　block print clearance
芯线　core wire ◇ 稀土合金～*
芯型　core pattern
芯型砂　core sand
芯制板　core strickle
芯子粉　core powder
芯座　core seat [marker]
锌{Zn}　zinc ◇ 包～*,不合格[等外品]～off-grade zinc,除[脱,去]～*,粗～crude zinc,代替～的能力*,电解～*,镀～*,防蚀～anode zinc,富～壳*,高纯(度)～high purity zinc,工业用轧制～*,含～的 zinciferous, zincky, zincous, zinc bearing, 含～合金*, 加～*, 精炼～*, 冷轧硬化～hardened rolled zinc, 粒状～*, 熔析～liquated zinc, 似～的 zincky, zincous, 阳极～anode zinc, 液体～liquid zinc, 阴极～cathode zinc, 硬～*
锌氨络合物　zinc ammine complex ◇ 高价～*
锌白(粉){ZnO}　zinc [Chinese] white, white
锌白铅矿　iglesiasite
锌白铜(50—70Cu,13—35Zn,5—33Ni)　nickel-silver, copper-nickel-zinc alloy, argentan, German silver ◇ 阿尔帕卡～*,帕克顿～Packtong,帕克方～Pakfong, Packfong, 苏勒～*
锌板　zinc plate [sheet], sheet zinc
锌板厚度规　zinc gauge
锌版术　zincography
锌伴生金属　associate of zinc
锌半电池　zinc couple [half-cell]
锌棒　zinc rod
锌包层　zinc covering
锌饱和　zincification
锌刨屑　zinc shavings
锌钡白　lithopone
锌焙砂　【色】zinc calcine
锌冰铜　(同"锌锍")
锌箔　zinc foil
锌材规格　zinc gauge (Z.G.)
锌层厚度的电磁波测定　electromagnetic testing for zinc coating
锌尘浸出　leach of zinc fume
锌沉积　zinc deposition
锌沉积物　zinc deposit
锌赤铁矾　zincobotryogen
锌萃取法　zine extracting process ◇ 贝克～Baker process
锌单晶体　zinc single crystal
锌当量　zinc equivalent
锌的　zincous, zincky
锌电积阴阳极制备　zinc electrowinning cathode and anode preparation
锌电解　zinc electrolyzing ◇ 高电流密度[泰因通]～法 Tainton method

锌 xin

锌电解法　electrolytic zinc process
锌电解设备[车间]　zinc electrolyzing plant
锌电偶　zinc couple [half-cell]
锌锭　zinc slab [pig]
锌镀层　galvanizing coat,zinc coat(ing) ◇ 含铁~*,溶除~镀着量测定 stripping test
锌镀层扩散退火处理　galvannealing
锌矾{ZnSO$_4$·7H$_2$O}　zinc vitriol, zincosite, zinkosite
锌粉　zinc dust [ash],【粉】zinc powder ◇ 冷凝~*,雾化~atomized zinc dust
锌粉沉淀(法)　zinc-dust precipitation
锌粉法　zinc-dust process
锌粉还原　zinc powder reduction
锌粉加料器　zinc-dust feeder
锌粉净化　zinc-dust purification
锌粉气化热镀法　vapour sherardizing
锌粉热镀[扩散渗镀]　sherardising, sherardizing
锌粉蒸馏　zinc dust distillation
锌粉置换(沉淀)法　zinc-dust cementation process
锌浮渣　zinc scum,【色】zinc dross
锌腐蚀　zincification
锌镉电镀　zinc-cadmium plating
锌镉共晶合金　◇ 卡津~*
锌汞合金[锌汞齐]　zinc amalgam ◇ 博特杰~Bottger's amalgam
锌钴锍[冰铜]　zinc cobalt matte
锌硅玻璃　zinc-silicate glass
锌焊料[药]　spelter solder ◇ 硬~hard spelter
锌焊料合金　spelter soldering alloy
锌合金　zinc alloy ◇ 冲压用~*,减摩金属用~*,卡克塞特~*,莱德尔~*,压铸用~*,轧制~*
锌褐锰矿　moth
锌黑　zinc black
锌黑辰砂　leviglianite,guadalcazarite
锌黑锰矿　hetairite,wetherilite

锌糊　zinc mush ◇ 灰色~grey zinc mush
锌花(镀锌薄板的)　spangle ◇ 规则~*
锌花抑制装置　spangle suppressing equipment
锌华　zinc flowers(天然碱式碳酸锌矿),samples(锌蒸馏罐的)
锌华凝结器　【色】devanture
锌黄　zinc yellow
锌黄锡矿　custerite
锌灰　zinc ash(gray)
锌灰漆　zinc gray
锌挥发　zinc volatilization
锌回收　zinc recovery
锌回收炉　zinc-recovering furnace
锌基合金　zinc-base alloy ◇ A.C.41A~*,杜拉克~*,减摩金属用~*,齐洛伊锻造用~*,索雷尔~*,扎姆~Zam metal,轧制加铜硬化~*
锌基家具合金　◇ 比迪里~*
锌基铝铜焊料　Mouray solder
锌基耐摩轴承合金　◇ 芬顿~*
锌基凝壳铸造合金(4.75Al,0.25Cu,余量Zn; 5.5Al,余量Zn)　zinc-base slush casting alloy
锌基韧性合金(压铸件用; 含5.25—5.75Al; 杂质含量不大于: 0.1Cu, 0.1Fe, 0.005Cd, 0.005Sn, 0.007Pb)　unbreakable metal
锌基压印模合金　zinc-base stamping die alloy
锌基压铸合金　zinc(-base) die casting alloy(0.1—3.5Cu, 3.5—4.5Al, 0.02—0.1Mg, 0.1Fe, 0.007Pb, 0.005Sn,余量Zn), zinc-base alloy for die casting, reversed brass(90—92Zn, 7—8Cu, Pb+Fe<3) ◇ A.G.40~*,杜拉克~*,方坦-莫罗~*,马扎克~*,齐马尔~*,泰塞利~*,扎马克~*
锌基压铸合金铸件　zinc-base die casting
锌基压铸件机械抛光法　fadgenising
锌基轴承合金(4—10Cu, 2—8Al,余量Zn)　zinc-base bearing alloys [metal] ◇ 埃

尔哈特~*,芬顿~*,格里柯~*,格利维尔~*,哈密尔顿~*,吉曼尼阿~*,克虏伯~Krupp bearing alloy,莱德布尔~*,皮罗特~*,萨尔泽尔~*,萨克索尼亚~*,塞勒吉~*,桑普森~*,施罗姆伯格~*,舒尔茨~*,瓦赫尔~*,西门~*

锌尖晶石{ZnAl$_2$O$_4$} zinc spinel, gahnite
锌金属薄板 zinc metal sheet
锌金属研究学会(美) Zinc Metal Research Istitute (ZMRI)
锌精矿 zinc concentrate ◇ 白云石型~*
锌精炼 zinc refining
锌精炼厂 zinc refiner(y), zinc refining plant
锌精炼炉 zinc-refining furnace
锌精馏塔 zinc-refining column, zinc rectification column
锌精选尾矿 zinc cleaner tailings
锌壳 zinc crust, cadmia
锌壳处理 treatment of zinc crust
锌壳熔析锅 【冶】kettle for liquating zinc crust, zinc-crust liquating apparatus
锌壳蒸馏 【冶】distillation of zinc crust
锌壳蒸馏罐 zinc-crust distillation retort
锌孔雀石 cuprozincite, rosasite
锌块 (zinc) spelter
锌矿 zinc ore
锌矿焙烧厂[车间] zinc ore-roasting plant
锌矿床 zinc deposit
锌矿泥 zinc sludge
锌矿物 zinc mineral
锌蓝粉 zinc (blue) powder
锌冷凝器 zinc condenser
锌粒 zinc granule [granula], granulated zinc ◇ 制~zinc beading
锌粒化 zinc beading
锌菱锰矿 zincorhodochrosite
锌榴石 genthelvite
锌硫磷 phoxim baythion
锌硫锡铅矿 pufahlite
锌瘤 list edge (板材边缘上的),【铁】philosopher's stone

锌铳 【冶】zinc matte
锌铝合金 zinc-aluminium alloy ◇ E-~E-metal,阿卢明~allumen,齐斯康~*
锌铝铜合金 ◇ 凯姆勒~*
锌氯砷钠矿 zinc-lavendulan
锌绿 zinc green
锌绿铁矿 zinc-rockbridgeite
锌镁合金 zinc magnesium alloy ◇ 镀锌~*
锌镁胆矾 comstockite, zinc magnesium chalcanthite
锌镁矾 mooreite
锌蒙脱石 sauconite
锌锰橄榄石 roepperite
锌锰辉石 fowlerite, fowlerine
锌锰矿 hetaerolite
锌锰普通辉石 jeffersonite
锌锰土 tunnerite
锌明矾 {6ZnO·3Al$_2$O$_3$·2SO$_3$·18H$_2$O} zinc-aluminite
锌钠合金(98Zn,余量 Na;脱氧剂) sodium-zinc
锌泥 zinc sludge
锌镍合金 admiro
锌喷镀 zinc spraying
锌贫化 zinc depletion
锌钎焊合金 spelter soldering alloy
锌-铅界面 zinc-lead interface
锌铅矿矿石 zinc-lead ore
锌铅锡合金 calamine
锌蔷薇辉石 fowlerite
锌羟锗铁矿 zinc stottite
锌青铜 zinc bronze
锌日光榴石 genthelvite
锌熔炼炉 zinc smelter
锌熔析(精炼)炉 zinc liquation furnace
锌乳石{ZnO·4ZnS} voltzite
锌水包 【冶】zinc ladle
锌(丝)箱 zinc box
锌酸{H$_2$ZnO$_2$} zincic acid
锌酸钴 cobalt green

锌酸盐处理(铝合金的)	zincate treatment
锌添加合金	zinc addition
锌铁橄榄石	stirlingite
锌铁合金	zinc iron alloy
锌铁黄长石	justite
锌铁尖晶石{(Zn,Fe,Mn){Fe,Mn}$_2$O$_4$}	franklinite
锌铁磷酸盐涂层(钢的)	anchorite
锌铁铅青铜	◇ 方坦－莫罗～*
锌铁羟磷铁矿	zinc-rockbridgeite
锌铁氧体	zinc ferrite
锌铜焊料[合金]	spelter (solder)
锌铜合金	platine, muntzmetal
锌铜铝矾	glaucocerinite
锌铜铝合金	◇ 柯赛特～*,比迪里～*
锌钨合金	zinc tungstate alloy
锌雾	zinc fume
锌锡黄铁矿	ballesterosite
锌锡铜合金	◇ 瑟斯顿～*
锌锡轴承合金	Fenton (bearing) metal
锌芯	zinc core ◇ 可熔～*
锌烟尘	zinc powder
锌烟尘中毒病	【铸】brass founder's ague
锌烟雾	zinc fume
锌阳极	zinc anode
锌阳极板	zinc anode plate (ZAP)
锌氧粉{ZnO}	zinc white
锌冶金(学)	metallurgy of zinc
锌业发展协会(英国)	Zinc Development Association (ZDA)
锌叶绿矾	zincocopiapite
锌液	liquid zinc
锌液表面覆盖层(镀锌用)	galvanizing blanket
锌钇矿	murataite
锌银合金	zinc-silver alloy
锌黝铜矿	copper blende, fahlerz zinc
锌浴槽	zinc bath
锌云母	hendricksite
锌渣	cadmia, hard zinc (熔锌槽内的锌铁合金) ◇ 炉墙上沉淀的～*
锌蒸馏	【色】zinc distillation
锌蒸馏法	zinc distilling process
锌蒸馏罐	zinc (distillation) retort
锌蒸馏炉	zinc distillation furnace ◇ 西里西亚～Silesian furnace
锌蒸气	zinc vapour
锌置换防蚀保护	sacrificial (corrosion) protection
锌质炉瘤	cadmia
锌铸件	zinc casting
辛达尔变性铝合金(0.5Cr,0.1Zn,0.3Mg,余量 Al)	Cindal
辛氟碳钙铈矿	synchysite
辛格磷化法	Singer process
辛格锡锌混汞合金	Singer's amalgam
辛基油(油蒸气真空泵用)	octoil, di-2-ethyl hexyl phthalate
辛科马克斯永磁合金	Sincomax alloy
辛普雷克斯低碳(低硫)铬铁	simplex ferro-chromium
辛普雷克斯桩	【建】simplex pile
辛普森型混合器	Sympson type mixer
辛特克斯烧结氧化铝车刀	Sintex
辛特雷克斯电解铁粉(>99.0Fe,<0.03Mn,<0.02C,<0.02S,<0.015P,<0.01Si,痕量 Ni、Cr、Cu)	Sintrex
辛特罗帕克烧加铜铁粉[铁铜混合粉末]	Sintropac
辛托克斯烧结氧化铝车刀	Sintox
新 KS 磁钢(6Al,18Ni,35Cu,8Ti,余量 Fe;25Ni,12Al,3Ti,余量 Fe)	new KS magnet steel
新拌混凝土	green concrete
新棒	clean stub
新材料	advanced material
新采矿石	fresh ore
新产品试制费	funds for trial manufacture of new product
新陈代谢作用	metabolism
新导电棒	clean stub
新工艺设备	mint processing equipment
新技术[事物]	innovation

新建工厂　green field plant
新浇混凝土　green concrete
新晶核　new nucleus
新晶核的产生　production of new nucleus
新晶核形成　formation of new nucleus
新磷酸三丁酯萃取法　【色】new TBP (tributyl-phosphate) process
新炉衬　fresh lining
新配造型材料　virgin material
新配制的溶液　freshly prepared liquor
新喷雾焙烧技术　new spray-roasting technique
新日铁(日本钢铁公司)　Nippon Steel Corporation (NSC)
新三水氧化铝　nordstrandite
新砂　【铸】new [virgin] sand
新生晶粒　new-born grain
新生氢　nascent hydrogen
新生态　nascent state
新生(态)的　nascent
新生态氢　hydrogen in statu nascendi
新生碳　nascent carbon
新室温相　new room-temperature phase
新试铜灵　neocuproin
新酸储存池　fresh storage tank
新酸配料容器　fresh acid dosing vessel
新提科纳尔(钛钴镍铝合金)磁铁(35Co, 14Ni, 7Al, 5Ti, 余量 Fe)　new Ticonal magnet
新钍(新钍-Ⅰ：MsTh1, 镭同位素^{228}Ra; 新钍-Ⅱ：MsTh2, 锕同位素^{228}Ac)　mesothorium
新钍残渣　mesothorium residue
新污染源实施标准　【环】new source performance standard
新鲜进料　fresh feed
新鲜空气　fresh [live] air
新鲜空气管道　fresh air duct
新鲜空气入口　fresh air inlet
新鲜原料　fresh charge [feed]
新鲜蒸汽　live steam
新鲜装料　fresh charge

新兴产业　emerging industry
新型硫杆菌　thiobacillus novellus
新型砂　【铸】virgin sand
新有机相　fresh organic phase
新月型液面　water meniscus
新月形疲劳痕　fatigue crescents
新渣　fresh slag
新蒸汽加热器　live-steam heater
新蒸汽喷射管　live-steam sparge pipe
新蒸汽蛇管　open-steam coils
新制粉末　virgin powder
心部淬透性　core hardenability
心部回火装置　tempcore installation
心部晶粒细化处理　core refining
心部晶体　cored crystal
心部裂纹　heart check
心部强度　core strength
心部缺陷　core defect
心部硬度　【金】core hardness
心部组织　core structure ◇ 细化的~*
心墙　【建】core wall
心射切面投影[心射图法]　gnomonic projection
心射切面投影面　gnomonic plane
心射(切面投影)图　gnomonogram
心形凸轮　heart cam
心轴　arbor, mandrel, spindle, mandril, (core) axle, shaft centre ◇ 带齿~ toothed spindle, 固定~*, 可拆钟形~*, 扩孔锻造用~ expanding bar, 球端~ centre pin, 球形~ ball mandrel, 辗轧[锻]用~【压】becking bar
心轴锻造　mandrel forging
心轴钢　mandrel steel
心轴式提升机　spindle-type elevating machine
心轴座　becking stand, mandrel holder
信贷　credit ◇ 安排的~偿还*
信道　【电】channel
信管　fuse (tube), exploder
信号　signal, semaphore, annunciation
信号板　back plate [panel]

信号比 signal ratio ◇ "1"半选~
信号标[量] 【电】semaphore
信号标准化 【电】signal normalization
信号传送 signal transmission, signalling
信号灯 signal lamp (S.L.), alarm [call(ing), pilot, tell-tale] lamp, signal [emergency, indicating] light, semaphore
信号灯板 signal lamp board
信号灯标识 signal lamp designation
信号灯闪烁器 signal lamp flicker
信号电流 signal current
信号电平 【计】signal level
信号电平开关 level switch (LS)
信号发生器 signal generator
信号发送器 flag, sender unit
信号机 signalling device, annunciator, semaphore, teleseme
信号控制箱 signal control box
信号铃 signal bell
信号盘 annunciator board
信号器 signalizer, annunciator (ANN), signal indicator, signalling device, ringer ◇ 高声~
信号器插孔 annunciator jack
信号栅极 signal grid
信号设备 signalling equipment
信号时钟 signal clock
信号示踪[故障探测]器 signal tracer
信号说明 signal instruction
信号塔 (signal) beacon
信号梯[陡]度 signal gradient
信号提取 signal extraction
信号箱 signal(ling) box
信号消失 black out
信号压力计 alarm manometer
信号整形 【电】signal normalization [shaping]
信号指示器 signal indicator
信号滞后 signal lag
信号转换器 signal converter
信号装置 signal(ling) device, signalling, signal(l)er

信频射流振荡器 multi-frequency fluid oscillator
信息 information, message, news, intelligence ◇ 构成~的一个单位 log on, 无用~【计】hash, 遗失~drop-out
信息处理程序 message processing program
信息处理机 processor
信息处理语言V IPL (information processing language)-V
信息传输 【计】information fransmission
信息存储和检索 information storage and retrieval
信息存储(器) information storage
信息反馈系统 information feedback system
信息管理系统 information management system (IMS)
信息技术 information technology
信息技术策略 information technique stategy
信息检索 information retrieval
信息交换 【计】information interchange
信息结束符 EOM (end of message)
信息(科)学 informatics, information science
信息控制程序 message control program
信息编码装置 coding device
信息块传送结束符 end of transmission block
信息链路 information link
信息量 traffic
信息流控制 flow control
信息论 information theory
信息发送器[信息源] information generator
信息识别符 label
信息通报 information circular (IC)
信息通道 information channel, highway
信息吞吐[传输]率 【计】rate of information throughput (RIT)
信息网络 information network

信息位　information bit, message digit
信息系统　information system
信息语言　information language
信息中心　information center (IC)
信息转换器　transcriber
信息组　【计】block, byte, field
信息组长度　【计】field length
"信箱"区　【计】mail box
星 J 钴铬钨合金（45—55Co, 30—55Cr, 12—17W）　star J metal
星阀加料器　star valve feeder
星号　asterisk, star
星轮　sprocket
星轮式给料器　pocket feeder
星轮中心线　sprocket centres
星芒　asterism ◇ 劳厄斑点的～asterism of laue spots
星芒铅基轴承合金（1.7—19Sb, 9—10.5Sn, 1Cu, 余量 Pb）　star alloy
星球中元素分布量　stellar abundance
星式给料机[给料器,加料机,加料器]　rotary-vane feeder, (rotary) star feeder
星铁　mill star
星(纹)锑　(同"精锑")
星型发动机　radial engine
星形阀[给料器]　star valve
星形结构　【计】star configuration
星形连接　star(-type) connection, Y-connection, wye
星形轮　【机】star (wheel), spider
星形轮提取器　star wheel extractor
星形-三角形接线　star-delta connection
星形-三角形启动控制　star-delta control
星形-三角形启动器　star-delta starter
星形手柄[轮]　star handle
星形网络　【计】star network
星形线（电收尘器用）　star-wire
星叶石　astrophylite
星状断口　star [rosette] fracture
星状裂纹　star-like crack
星状物　asterisk
型　model, pattern, type,【铸】mo(u)ld

型板　template (temp.), shaping plate,【铸】plate pattern ◇ 假～【铸】match board, 双面～*
型材　section (Sec., sec.), bar section, section material, profile, profile ◇ 大型～*, 复杂～*, 弧边形～Gothic section, 挤压结构(钢)～*, 空心～hollow section, 冷轧～cold rolled section, 六角～hexagonal section, 轻型～*, 实心～*, 特宽腰～extra-wide webs shape, 透镜[扁平]状～lenticular section, 无缺陷～defect-free section
型材成形轧辊　former
型材件　shaped piece [objects]
型材精整　shapes finishing
型材拉伸矫正机　section stretcher, section stretching machine
型材冷弯轧制　cold-formed section
型材弯曲　buckle
型材弯曲机　profile bender
型锤　swage [sorting] hammer
型的下半部　【铸】drag half of mould
型钉　【铸】foundery nail
型锻　【压】swaging, swaged forging
型锻锤　swage
型锻法　swaging process
型锻模　swage (die)
型钢　【压】section steel [iron], profile(d) steel [iron], shape (steel), rolled section steel, steel section [bar, shape], merchant [commercial] steel, fashioned [bar] iron, bar [shape] ◇ H～H-beam, 简单断面～simple shape, 冷弯～formed section, 凸缘～flanged section, 小型～*, 形状复杂～complex shape, 沿～股边施焊焊缝 toe weld, 英国标准～*, 轧制～rolled section steel
型钢断面　sectional shape
型钢堆垛机　bar piler
型钢翻转机　bar stock turnover device
型钢分选机组　bar rolled stock sorting unit, shape-rolled stock sorting unit

型钢剪切机 joist shears
型钢[型材]矫直机 section [shape] straightening machine, section [bar] straightener, shapes gagger ◇ 辊式~*
型钢矫直台(齿条式) straightening rack
型钢矫直压力机 bull press
型钢结构 profiled steel structure
型钢拉拔机 bar bench
型钢坯 shape slab
型钢切割机 shape cutting machine
型钢弯曲机 section [profile] iron bending machine
型钢轧辊 shaped roll
型钢[型材]轧机 section mill, shape (rolling) mill, bar and shape mill ◇ 活套式~ looping merchant mill, 三线式~ three-strand rod mill, 万能~*, 周期断面~ reinforcing bar mill
型钢轧机成型机架 strand mill
型钢[型材]轧制 section rolling, rolling of sectional iron
型夹 die clamp
型焦 【焦】moulded coal [coke], form(ed) coke ◇ 连续炼~法, 铸造~ foundry formed coke
型焦法[工艺] formed coke process, process for formed coke
型壳 shell ◇ 失蜡~【铸】invested mould
型框 【铸】moulding flask
型面涂浆 【铸】washing
型模 gang mould
型内孕育[变质]处理 【铸】moulding inoculation
型坯锻造 【粉】preform forging
型腔 mould [die] cavity, 【压】impression
型砂 moulding [foundery] sand, moulding mixture, sand (mixture), plasticine ◇ 半肥[中强黏力, 半油脂]~*, 掺合~*, 多角~ angular-grained sand, 二氧化碳-水玻璃~*, 肥[强黏力]~*, 干燥~ dry moulding sand, 高流动性[自重流动]~ free flowing sand, 化学剂黏结

~*, 空气 硬化~ air-setting sand, 落砂后保留在铸件上的~ loose sand, 贫~ weak sand, 瘦~ mild moulding sand, 疏松~*, 填充用~ filler sand, 新~ virgin sand, 液态~ fluid(ized) sand, 已混~ sand blend
型砂拌合 sand cutting
型砂杯状试验 ◇ 底特律~ Detroit cup test
型砂仓 sand hopper
型砂钉 moulder's brad
型砂翻新器 【铸】revivifier
型砂粉碎 break(ing) up of sand
型砂干燥度电测仪 electric hydrocel
型砂干燥炉 sand-drying oven
型砂烘干板 sand drying plate
型砂回性 sand tempering [maturing]
型砂混合机 sand mixer
型砂混合物 (moulding) sand mixuture
型砂混炼机 puddle mill
型砂挤压机 squeezer
型砂控制 sand control
型砂溃散 break(ing) up of sand
型砂粒度测定仪 ◇ 安氏~ Andreasen pipette
型砂流动性 sand flowability
型砂耐久性 durability of moulding sand
型砂黏结剂 (foundery) sand binder
型砂配方 sand formulation
型砂配制 sand preparation
型砂配制[制备]工段 sand-conditioning plant
型砂起模性 liftability
型砂强度 sand bond [strength]
型砂强度测定仪[试验机] sand strength testing apparatus
型砂强度降低 weaking of moulding sand
型砂热稳定性[耐急冷急热性, 耐火度] refractoriness of sand
型砂韧性指数 sand toughness number (Stn)
型砂筛分机 sand riddle

型砂筛子 sand sifter
型砂烧结 sand sintering [burning]
型砂湿度 sand humidity
型砂试验 sand test
型砂寿命[使用期限] life [durability] of (moulding) sand
型砂水分控制器 mouldability controller
型砂水分快速测定仪 moisture teller
型砂松散性 sand friability
型砂塌砂 spalling-off
型砂添加剂 (foundery) sand additives
型砂调匀 sand tempering
型砂压实 compacting of sand
型砂抑制剂 foundery sand inhibitor
型砂硬度 sand hardness
型砂再生 reclamation of moulding sand
型砂震实机 foundery jolter
型砂铸造 sand casting
型式 type, model, pattern
型胎 former ◇ 炉顶砌砖用~*
型铁 mould pig iron
型箱 【铸】casting box, mould(ing) box [flask], flask
型箱底板 flask plate
型箱用钉 moulding pin
型芯 【铸】core, heart ◇ 安放~*, 扁平~ cake core, 插入~ insert core, 打(掉)~(core) knock-out, core shake-out, 二氧化碳快干(处理的)~ CO₂ core, 干燥[烘干]~ baked core, 化学硬化~ chemical-set core, 活动~*, 简化(造型用)~*, 金属~ inserts, 可拆~*, 可熔~*, 空气硬化[冷硬]~ air-set core, 黏土~ clay [loam] core, 拼合~ sectional die, 平衡[悬臂]~ balanced core, 嵌入式永久~ (压铸用) loosecore, 清理~用夹具 rubbing fixture, 热盒~ hot box core, 蛇状[弯曲]~ snake core, 省料[减薄金属的]~ metal saver, 湿砂形状~*, 松动~*, 通气~ atmospheric core, 下~用样板 core-setting gauge, 镶嵌式~*, 悬装~ suspended core, 一次~(永久铸型) ex-pendable core, 有~铸型 cored foundry mould, 预埋~ kiss core, 黏~用夹具 core-pasting fixture, 制造~用松散料 opener, 铸型~ foundery core, 组合~*
型芯材料 core material
型芯车床 core(-turning) lathe
型芯撑 chaplet, jammer ◇ 散热式~(螺旋式) radiator
型芯撑钉 chaplet nail
型芯吹制 core blowing
型芯打出机 core knockout ◇ 水力~ hydro-core-knock-out
型芯垫片 core splash
型芯堵头 core plug
型芯飞边缺肉 【铸】core fin
型芯干燥 core drying
型芯干燥炉 foundery [core-drying] stove
型芯搁架 core cradle
型芯工 core-maker
型芯骨(架) core skeleton [reinforcement, crab]
型芯刮板 core strickle
型芯盒 core box [magazine]
型芯盒充气孔 blow hole
型芯烘(干)板 core(-drying) plate, drying plate
型芯烘干炉 core baking oven, core drier
型芯烘干器 core carrier
型芯机 core machine
型芯记号 core mark
型芯夹具 core jig
型芯加油 core oiling
型芯检修夹具 core rubbing jig
型芯胶合 core pasting
型芯框架 core frame
型芯溃散性 core collapsibility
型芯落砂 core shake-out
型芯密度 core density
型芯耐火性[抗热折断能力] core refractiveness
型芯黏结剂 core binder ◇ 伊迪阿林~ Idealine

型芯黏砂　burning-on into core
型芯排气(孔)　core ventilation
型芯砂破碎机　core breaker
型芯填料　core filler
型芯通气孔　core vent [hole]
型芯透气性　core density
型芯涂料　core dressing [cover, wash]
型芯涂料喷枪　core sprayer
型芯位移　core shift
型芯下沉　core sag
型芯压板　core clamp
型芯研磨　core grinding
型芯样板　core template
型芯硬度　core hardness
型芯震实机　core jolter
型芯制造机　core-making machine
型芯轴　core barrel
型芯组装　core-setting
型芯座　core-print
型穴　depression
型铸　casting into moulds ◇ 一次～(件) dead mould casting
形变　deformation ◇ 升温～法*
形变不锈钢　wrought stainless steel
形变测定器　deformeter
形变带　deformation band, bands of deformation, Lueders lines ◇ 哈特曼～*
形变方式　mode of deformation
形变钢　wrought steel
形变功　work of deformation, work done in deformation
形变合金　wrought alloy
形变机理　deformation mechanism
形变加工软化　deformation work softening
形变抗力　deformational resistance
形变铝合金　wrought aluminium alloy ◇ 75S～*, 邦杜尔～*, 里弗莱克塔尔～*, 斯图塔尔～*, 维塔尔～*, 维瓦尔～*
形变孪晶　deformation [mechanical] twin
形变耐热合金　wrought heat-resisting alloy
形变强化　mechanical hardening
形变轻合金　wrought light alloy
形变热处理　thermo-mechanical treatment (TMT), ausform(ing), ausworking, skin ausrolling ◇ 奥氏体～*, 磁场～*
形变热处理钢丝　ausformed steel wire
形变热控制技术　thermomechanical control process (TMCP)
形变温度　temperature of deformation
形变线　deformation lines
形变仪　extensometer
形变硬铝合金　aluminium duralumin alloy
形变轴　deformation axis
形变状态稳定性　stability of deformed state
形成　formation (for.), forming, yielding, development (如结晶)
形成电压　formation voltage
形成颈缩[形成局部收缩]　necking-down
形成硫化物　sulphidize
形核点　nucleation point
形核动力学　nucleation kinetics
形核方式　pattern of nucleation
形核功　work of nucleation
形核机理　nucleation mechanism
形核剂　nucleation additive [agent]
形核阶段　nucleation period
形核能　energy for nucleation
形核区　nucleation zone
形核时间　time of nucleation
形核(速)率　nucleation rate
形空心砖　book tile
形式地址　【计】formal address
形数比　aspect ratio
形态　morphology, form, shape, habit(us)
形态对称　morphological symmetry
形态晶体学　morphological crystallography
形态类型(钢中夹杂的)　morphological typing, typing morphological
形态学　morphology, topography ◇ X 射

线衍射金属表面~*
形态研究 morphological investigation [research]
形态转变 mode transformation
形象 image, picture, figure
形象化 imagery, in images
形心轴线 centroid axis
形状 form, shape, appearance, fashion ◇ 高斯~*
形状不规则的 odd in shape
形状不正确的焊点(熔核) misshaped nugget
形状测量技术 shape measurement technique
形状分辨能力 shape resolution
形状复杂(冷弯)型钢 complex shape
形状各向异性 shape anisotropy
形状函数 shape function
形状回复 shape recovery
形状回复率 degree of shape recovery
形状记忆 shape memory
形状记忆合金 SME alloy, shape memory alloy (SMA)
形状记忆效应 shape memory effect (SME) ◇ 合金的~ shape memory effects in alloy
形状精确度 accuracy of shape
形状控制 profile control
形状偏差 deviation from shape
形状缺陷 shape defect
形状适位(性) shape accommodation
形状弹性 elasticity of form
形状系数[因数,因子] form [shape] factor
形状效应 shape effect
行波 travel(l)ing [running, constant] wave
行车桥(移动式高架起重机的) bridge of overhead travelling
行程 stroke, travel, course, path, range, trip ◇ 限制~螺母*,有限~滑块 stroke limiting slide

行程不足 under-shoot
行(程)差 progressive [run] error
行程传动装置 stroke drive
行程缸 travel(l)ing cylinder
行程轮 travel(l)ing wheel
行程速度 speed of travel
行程限制[限位]器 stroke limiter, safety stop ◇ 顶杆~*
行程小车(吊车上的) trolley
行程指示器 stroke indicator
行程止点(结晶器振动机构的) top of stroke
行进 process, motion, advance
行桥斗轮式取料机 wheel-on-bridge relaimer
行情走势 market trend
行声波 travel(l)ing sound wave
行驶范围 travel(l)ing range
行驶力矩 running torque
行为 behaviour, action
行线 gauge line
行星齿轮 planet(ary) [satellite, epicyclic] gear
行星齿轮减速机 planet-gear speed reducer
行星电子 planetary electron
行星式钢球旋锻机 planetary ball swager
行星式钢丝绳捻股机 planetary strander, planetary stranding machine
行星式减速机 sun-and-planet gear
行星式搅拌器 planetary compulsory mixer, planet stirrer
行星式冷却机 planetary cooler
行星式冷轧管机 planetary tube cold-rolling mill
行星式球磨机 planetary ball mill
行星式热轧机 planetary hot mill
行星式压下装置 planetary screwdown
行星(式)轧机 planetary (rolling) mill, PL mill ◇ 大同式单辊~*,广濑~Hirose's rolling mill,克虏伯-普拉策~*,森吉米尔~*,双重~*,万能~*

行星轧制　planetary rolling
行政办公楼　administration building
行政措施　administrative measure
行政费用　management charges
行政薪金和津贴　executive salaries and bonuses
行走起重机[吊车]　moving crane
行走台车　moving pallet
性能　performance, property, nature, behaviour
性能价格比　cost [price] performance
性能评定　【企】merit rating
性能评价[估价]　performance evaluation
性能曲线　performance [characteristic] curve
性能试验　performance test
性能说明书　performance specification
性能特征　performance characteristic
性能图　performance chart
性能系数　coefficient of performance (C.O.P.)
性能限度　performance limitations
性能指标　performance figure [index]
性能周期性　periodicity of property
性能周期性复现[重复]　periodic repetition of property
性质　property (prop., Ppty), quality, nature, character (Char.)
性质上的　qualitative
雄黄{As_2S_2}　realgar, red arsenic
雄榫　tongue, tenon
雄榫斜肩　gain
休伯斯发火[打火石]合金(85Ce,余量Fe)　Hubers' alloy
休风　standstill, halt, vacancy wind, stopped blast, shutting out,【铁】damping-down, delay, shut-down, wind off, blowing-down ◇ 倒流～*,计划～【铁】scheduled delay
休风率　【铁】downtime (percentage)
休风期　shut-down [standing] period
休风时间　【铁】down [idle, lost] time
休风图表　【铁】downtime schedule
休利特电动卸料机　Hulett electric unloader
休眠细胞　resting cell
休姆－罗瑟里电子化合物　Hume-Rothery compounds
休姆－罗瑟里定则　Hume-Rothery's rule
休姆－罗瑟里相　Hume-Rothery phase
休斯勒强铁磁性铜锰合金　Heusler's (magnetic) alloy
休斯铅基轴承合金(76Pb,14Sn,10Sb)　Hughes' metal
休息室　rest [recreation] room, lounge
休伊晶间腐蚀试验　Huey test
休伊特精密[硬巴比]合金(89Sn,7.5Sb,3.5Cu)　Hewitt's fine alloy
休伊特铅锑轴承合金(10－15Sb,2Sn,余量Pb)　Hewitt's bearing alloy
休止　cessation
休止角　angle of rest [repose]
修边　shaving
修边冲模　ripper die
修边冲头　【压】trimming punch
修边工序　shaving operation
修边模　trimmer [trimming, shaving] die
修补　mend(ing), (re)patching, repair, healing up (缺陷的修补), doctoring (用局部沉积金属法修补电镀层) ◇ 零星～(道路的) dribbing
修补材料　patching material
修补浇铸　casting-on
修补炉衬　【冶】fettling, patchwork, repatching, daubing
修补门　【铸】fettling hole
修车棚　car repair shed
修道工具　track tools
修订　revise (rev.)
修复渗碳　restoration cementation
修改　revise, amend, alter, modify, modification
修改带　【计】change tape
修合工序　matching operation

修剪 trimming ◇ 按尺寸～ trimming to size
修理 repair, mend, overhaul, revamp, make up ◇ 大～*, 日常～ current repair
修理表面缺陷(对锭、坯) deseaming
修理部 maintenance service
修理厂 repair shop
修理车间 repair [service, jobbing] shop
修理车间修理 workshop repair
修理队 repair crew
修理工 repairman, mender,【焊】dresser
修理工场 jobbing shop
修理工作 repair [jobbing] work
修理炉口内衬 【冶】nose reline
修理台架 repair stand
修理(延误)时间 repair (delay) time
修理用人孔 drop manhole (DMH)
修理站 service station
修炉 【冶】furnace repair
修炉费用 furnace repair cost
修炉口 【铸】fettling hole
修路工具 track tools
修磨机 conditioning machine
修配间 machine shop ◇ 机修厂～repair workshop
修平刀 【铸】sleeker, slicker, trowel
修坡口 【焊】veeing
修砌车(炉用) 【钢】reline car
修圩 impounding, impoundment
修芯腻料 【铸】core cream
修型时间(用压勺) 【铸】trowel hour
修匀 smoothing
修整 dressing, trimming, shaving, (re)conditioning, chip (ping), round-off, scarf, reclamation (废品的),【压】finishing, scalping (轧坯的) ◇ 经～的边 trimmed edge
修整车床 trimming lathe
修整冲孔 drifting
修整冲头 【压】shearing punch
修整锤 chipping hammer
修整锭料(区域熔炼的) cropping ingot

修整方法(毛刺等的) shaving technique
修整工段(锭、坯的) conditioning department [floor, yard, site], dressing yard
修整工序 shaving operation
修整机 finisher, trimming machine, scalper
修整机床 scalping machine
修整浇铸(缺陷的) casting-on
修整跨 scalping bay
修整炉坡 【冶】resurface
修整模 shaving die
修整平面锤 dead flat hammer
修整台(锭、坯的) conditioning bed
修整铸件锤 chasing hammer
修正 revise (rev.), revision, amend(ment), correction (corr.), updating
修正辐射 modified radiation
修正含量 correction content
修正系数 correction factor, coefficient of correction
修正项 corrective [correction] term
修正性添加剂 【冶】corrective addition
修正值 corrected value, correction
锈 rust ◇ 生重～ heavy rusting, 有～的 patinous
锈斑 rusty spot ◇ 有～的 stained
锈层 dross ◇ 白色～*, 疏松[松散]～ loose rust
锈点 rusty spot, splash of rust (钢板酸洗的)
锈痕 dross, iron mold,【冶】pitting
锈化 【压】rusting
锈接(铸铁件的) rust joint
锈膜 tarnish film
锈色[锈层覆盖]的 rusty
锈蚀 rust (iness), corrosion, stain (ing), tarnish (ing) ◇ 电解～ electrostaining, 金属锭～ ingot staining, 抗～(的) resistant to tarnishing
锈蚀薄膜 rust film
锈蚀材料火焰除锈[清理] flame cleaning of rusty material

锈蚀钢锭模 【铸】rusty mould
锈蚀倾向 tendency to rust
锈蚀形成 formation of rust
锈蚀抑制剂 rust inhibitor
锈蚀作用 action of rust
锈印 【压】rust mark
袖接 sleeve joint
袖珍 pH 值测定计 pocket pH-meter
袖珍带盘 【计】pocket-size reel
袖珍剂量计 pocket dosimeter
袖珍探测器线圈 hand probe coil
袖砖 【耐】sleeve (brick), rod cover
袖砖接头 junction of sleeves
袖砖压制机 sleeve press
溴{Br} bromine ◇ 液体~ liquid bromine
溴处理 brominate, bromination
溴化 bromination ◇ 阳极~（作用）anodic bromination
溴化铵 ammonium bromide
溴化钡 barium bromide
溴化镝{DyBr$_3$} dysprosium bromide
溴化钆{GdBr$_3$} gadolinium bromide
溴化钙 calcium bromide
溴化锆{ZrBr$_4$} zirconium bromide
溴化镉 cadmium bromide
溴化汞 mercuric bromide
溴化钴 cobaltous bromide
溴化钾 potassium bromide
溴化钪{ScBr$_3$} scandium bromide
溴化镧{LaBr$_3$} lanthanum bromide
溴化镭{RaBr$_2$} radium bromide
溴化锂{LiBr} lithium bromide
溴化锂制冷机 lithium bromide refrigerator
溴化镁 magnesium bromide
溴化锰 manganous bromide
溴化钼{MoBr$_2$, MoBr$_3$, MoBr$_4$} molybdenum bromide
溴化钠 sodium bromide
溴化钕{NdBr$_3$} neodymium bromide
溴化镨{PrBr$_3$} praseodymium bromide
溴化氢 hydrogen bromide ◇ 脱~ dehydrobromination
溴化铷{RbBr} rubidium bromide
溴化铯{CsBr} cesium bromide
溴化钐{SmBr$_3$} samaric bromide
溴化锶 strontium bromide
溴化铊 thallium bromide
溴化钽{TaBr$_3$, TaBr$_5$} tantalum bromide
溴化钛 titanium bromide
溴化铽{TbBr$_3$} terbium bromide
溴化铁 ferric bromide
溴化铜 copper [cupric] bromide
溴化钍 thorium, bromide
溴化钨 tungsten bromide
溴化物 bromide
溴化硒 selenium bromide
溴化锡 stannic bromide
溴化锌 zinc bromide
溴化亚汞 mercurous bromide
溴化亚铜 cuprous bromide
溴化氧铋 bismuthyl bromide
溴化氧钼{(MoO)Br} molybdenyl bromide
溴化钇{YBr$_3$} yttrium bromide
溴化镱{YbBr$_3$} ytterbium bromide
溴化铟{InBr$_3$} indium bromide
溴化银 silver bromide
溴化银光电管[元件] silver bromide photocell
溴化银晶体 silver bromide crystal
溴化银颗粒 silver bromide grain
溴化油 brominated [bromized] oil
溴化作用 bromination
溴角银矿 bromchlorargyrite
溴氰化提金银法 bromocyanide process
溴酸钡 barium bromate
溴酸钆{Gd(BrO$_3$)$_3$} gadolinium bromate
溴酸钾 potassium bromate
溴酸镧{La(BrO$_3$)$_3$} lanthanum bromate
溴酸镁 magnesium bromate
溴酸钠 sodium bromate
溴酸钕{Nd(BrO$_3$)$_3$} neodymium bromate
溴酸镨{Pr$_2$(BrO$_3$)$_3$} praseodymium bro-

mate
溴酸铷 {RbBrO₃} rubidium bromate
溴酸钐 {Sm(BrO₃)₃} samaric bromate
溴酸盐 bromate
溴酸银 silver bromate
溴铜矿 bromatacamite
溴氧化锆 {ZrOBr₂} zirconyl bromide
溴氧化镧 {LaOBr} lanthanum oxybromide
溴氧化钼 {MoOBr₂, (MoO₂)Br₂} molybdenum oxybromide
溴氧化钨 {WOBr₄} tungsten oxybromide
溴氧化物 oxybromide
溴氧化铟 {InOBr} indium oxybromide
溴铀酸盐 bromouranate
需氯量 chlorine demand
需气微生物 aerobes
需求波动 demand fluctuations
需热量 （同"热需要量"）
需氧菌 aerobe, aerobic bacteria
需氧量 【环】oxygen demand (OD)
需氧微生物 aerobe
需要 need, requirement, demand ◇ 根据～ on demand (OD, o.d.)
需要功率[动力] required [consumed] power, power requirement [intake]
需要(鼓)风量 blast requirement
需要量 requirement, quam, demand, amount of needs
需要温度 target temperature
需用功率 power demand
虚变形 virtual deformation
虚电荷 virtual charge
虚功 virtual work
虚功原理 principle of virtual work
虚构 fabricate, fiction, make up
虚构的 ungrounded
虚光源 virtual source
虚焊点 faulty soldered joint
虚焊接头 dry [rosin] joint
虚假的 false, untrue
虚假脉冲 ghost pulses
虚假信号 ghost [spurious] signal

虚零点(仪器的) false zero
虚漏 virtual leak, hang up (真空检漏的)
虚拟剥层法 fictitious stripping layer method
虚拟测厚仪(冷连轧机用) virtual gauge meter
虚拟存储器 【计】virtual memory
虚拟打孔法 fictitious drilling hole method
虚拟机 virtual machine
虚拟计算机 virtual computer
虚拟作业(运筹学的) dummy activity
虚设风箱 【团】false windbox
虚设物 dummy
虚设线圈 dummy coil
虚设阴极(电镀溶液处理用) dummy cathode
虚数部分 imaginary component [part]
虚线 dotted [dash(ed), sotty, broken] line
虚线图样[X射线照片] spotty pattern
虚像 virtual [false] image, mythical image (显微硬度的)
虚移动 virtual movement
虚影组织 phantom structure
虚轴 dummy [false] shaft, free axle, imaginary axis, loose shaft
须晶[须状晶体] whisker crystal, hair like crystal
须晶强化金属 whisker-reinforced metal, metal with grown-in whiskers
须晶强化铝 whisker-reinforced aluminium
徐变 creep ◇ 混凝土～*
许可 permit, allow, permission, allowance, consent, licence
许可雾霭值 tolerable fog value
许可证 licence, license, warrant, 【环】permit(废物排放的) ◇ 持～人【环】permittee
许可值 permitted level
许用应力 safe [admissible, allowable, working] stress

蓄电池 battery(Btry,Bty), storage[secondary] battery, accumulator(ACC, ac, acc), accumulator[secondary] cell, battery booster(充电器的) ◇ 备用～ backing battery, 镉镍～*, 碱性～*, 酸性～ acid accumulator
蓄电池槽 accumulator container
蓄电池车 electromobile
蓄电池充电 battery charge
蓄电池充电升压器 battery charging booster
蓄电池底座 battery stand
蓄电池点焊机 battery spot welding(machine)
蓄电池垫板 battery stand
蓄电池供电设备 battery power supply equipment
蓄电池合金(90Pb,9.2Sn,0.8Sb) accumulator metal
蓄电池极板 accumulator plate
蓄电池极板栅 accumulator grid
蓄电池接线夹 battery clip
蓄电池绝缘子 accumulator insulator
蓄电池连接片 cell connector
蓄电池驱动 accumulator drive
蓄电池式焊机 storage battery welding machine
蓄电池酸 battery acid
蓄电池添加剂 battery additive
蓄电池箱 battery cupboard, accumulator box[container, tank]
蓄电池支架 battery stand
蓄电量(电池的) charge capacity
蓄电室 power storage room(P.S.R.)
蓄积 storing, accumulation
蓄力器 accumulator(ACC) ◇ 气水～*, 气压～*, 轧辊平衡装置～*, 重锤式～*
蓄能 energy storage
蓄能(电阻)焊接 stored energy welding, energy storage welding
蓄能焊机 stored energy welder ◇ 静电～*
蓄能器 accumulator
蓄能容量(压力机或锻锤的) energy storage capacity
蓄热 stored heat, heat retaining, accumulation of heat ◇ 非～式炉*, 直流～(法)*
蓄热带[区] 【冶】thermal reserve zone
蓄热法 regeneration ◇ 逆流[回流]～*
蓄热法原理 【钢】regenerative principle
蓄热能力[容量] regenerative capacity, heat storage[retaining] capacity
蓄热器 heat accumulator[reservoir], recuperater, regenerator, thermal storage
蓄热器填料 regenerator filling[packing]
蓄热式二通热风炉 (同"考贝式热风炉")
蓄热(式)坩埚炉 regenerative[regeneration] crucible furnace
蓄热(式)焦炉 regenerative oven ◇ 联合交错～*
蓄热式均热炉 recuperative soaking pit ◇ 阿姆柯～ Armco soaking pit
蓄热式连续焙烤炉 continuous regenerative baking furnace
蓄热式炉 regeneration[regenerating, regenerative, recovery] furnace
蓄热式热风炉 【铁】regenerative(hot blast) stove
蓄热式热回收 regenerative heat recovery
蓄热式烧成装置 【耐】regenerative firing system
蓄热式窑 regenerator kiln
蓄热室 regenerator(chamber), recuperater, regenerative chamber[device], checker chamber ◇ 多室～*, 空气～ air chamber, 两通水平式～*, 砖格子～*
蓄热室底部 checker floor
蓄热室拱顶 checker chamber arch
蓄热室观察孔 checker wicket
蓄热室假墙 checker false wall
蓄热室砌砖 checkered brickwork

蓄热室前墙　checker front wall
蓄热室桥墙　checker bridge wall
蓄热室寿命　regenerator life
蓄热室烟道　【冶】regenerative flue
蓄热室主墙　【焦】regenerator piller wall
蓄热室砖　checker brick
蓄热循环［周期］　regenerative [regeneration] cycle
蓄热装置　【冶】regenerative device
蓄势器　(同"蓄力器")
蓄水　impounding, impoundment, store water
蓄水池　【环】impoundment bassin [lake]
蓄丝式(多次)拉丝机　【压】cumulative type wire-drawing machine
蓄丝式连续拉丝机　【压】cumulative type continuous wire-drawing machine
蓄套塔　looping tower
蓄压器　(同"蓄力器")◇空气-水力~*,液压风动~*
序号　serial number, order number (Ord. No.)
序列　order, rank, sequence
序列发生器　【计】sequencer
序数　ordinal (number)
絮结　flocculating
絮凝　flocculating, flocculation ◇澄清~器 clarifloccultor,反~*
絮凝层　floc bed ◇膨胀~dilated flocbed
絮凝池　flocculation basin
絮凝剂　flocculant (floc.), flocculator, flocculating [flocculation] (re)agent, sedimentation aid ◇无机~inorganic flocculant
絮凝搅拌器　flocculator
絮凝率［系数］　flocculation ratio
絮凝能　flocculation energy
絮凝室(浓缩机的)　flocculating chamber
絮凝体【物】　floc(culent)
絮凝相　phase of flocculation
絮凝性污泥　flocculent sludge
悬摆式黏度计　pendulum viscometer

悬臂　cantilever, bracket, suspension arm, stick-out (电极悬臂)
悬臂堆料机　boom stacker
悬臂弓形架　【建】cantilever arched girder
悬臂辊　overhung [open-end] roll
悬臂辊式冷弯成形轧机　overhung cold roll forming machine
悬臂辊式轧机　overhang roll type mill
悬臂结构　cantilever structure [design]
悬臂距离［开度］(焊机的)　【焊】throat [arm, horn] spacing, throat gap
悬臂跨度　cantilever span
悬臂梁　overhanging [cantilever] beam, outrigger, beam with one overhanging end, cantilever (疲劳试验的)
悬臂平台　【建】cantilever platform
悬臂铺料机　boom stacker
悬臂起重机台架　cantilever(ed) gantry
悬臂升降钢绳　boom hoist cable
悬臂式挡土墙　cantilever retaining wall
悬臂式堆料机　wing stacker
悬臂式锻锤　【压】open side hammer
悬臂式脚手架走道　cantilever(ed) gantry
悬臂式楼梯　bracketed stairs
悬臂式皮带助卷机　overhung type belt wrapper
悬臂(式)起重机[吊车]　cantilever [overhang, bracket, arm, console, jib] crane ◇墙上~wall jib crane
悬臂式人行道　overhanging footway, cantilevered foot path (桥梁的)
悬臂式沿墙移动起重机　wall bracket travel(l)ing crane
悬臂式轧辊　overhung roll
悬臂式胀缩卷筒　【压】canti-lever expand mandrel
悬臂托架开度(滚焊机或点焊机的)　throat opening
悬臂挖掘机　boom excavator
悬臂型芯　【铸】balanced core
悬臂罩　cantilever hood
悬臂装料杆　【冶】peel

悬锤 plumb
悬垂式加热炉 catenary type oven
悬垂物 overhang, pendle
悬垂线 catenary, catenarian
悬垂锥式开卷机 overhang cone-type pay-off reel
悬滴法 pendant drop method
悬吊 suspension, overhang
悬吊槽式运输机 suspended tray conveyer
悬吊[挂]磁铁 suspended magnet
悬吊电磁铁 suspended electromagnet
悬吊式炉顶旋架 roof suspension swing frame
悬吊轴承 (drop-)hanger bearing
悬吊装置 floater
悬浮 suspension, floating ◇ 易～的 floatable
悬浮焙烧 suspension roasting
悬浮焙烧炉 suspension roaster
悬浮分离法 floatation separation method
悬浮固体(物质) 【环】suspended solids (SS)
悬浮灰 suspended ash
悬浮剂 deflocculating [suspending] agent, deflocculator ◇ 黏土～*
悬浮浇注法 【钢】suspension casting process
悬浮结晶法 levitation crystallization method
悬浮介质 suspending medium
悬浮颗粒 suspended particle
悬浮矿尘 【采】aerial dust
悬浮粒级 suspended fraction
悬浮流 suspension flow
悬浮炉(直接还原用) 【铁】shower furnace
悬浮气化 suspension gasification
悬浮区域电子轰击法 floating zone electron bombardment technique
悬浮区域精炼[净化] 【色】floating zone refining
悬浮区域熔炼 floating zone melting (F.Z.M.), levitation zone melting ◇ 电子束～*
悬浮区域熔炼法 floating zone melting (method)
悬浮区域熔炼技术 floating zone technique
悬浮熔炼 suspension [levitation] smelting, smelting in suspension ◇ 因科～法
悬浮熔炼炉 levitation furnace
悬浮室 suspension chamber
悬浮体 suspension, suspended substance
悬浮体[物]沉淀 sedimentation of suspension
悬浮微粒 aerosol
悬浮微粒层 【环】aerosol layer
悬浮物 suspended material [matter]
悬浮物质 floating substance, suspended matter
悬浮性 floatability
悬浮液 suspending fluid, suspension, dispersion ◇ 稠～ thick dispersion, 粗粒～*, 重～*
悬浮铸造 suspension casting
悬浮状焙烧 flash (suspension) roasting
悬浮状气化装置 suspension gasifier ◇ 旋风器型～*
悬浮(状)态 suspended [suspension] state
悬拱 【建】hanging [suspended] arch
悬钩 suspension hook
悬挂 hanging, suspending
悬挂导板 【压】clearer
悬挂电缆的吊线 catenary, catenarian
悬挂钢板弹簧 suspended leaf spring
悬挂钢带 【冶】carrying band
悬挂料仓 overhead bin
悬挂炉顶 (同"吊挂式炉顶")
悬挂螺旋弹簧 suspension spiral spring
悬挂平拱 flat suspended arch
悬挂式导辊 flipper roll
悬挂式导卫板 flipper
悬挂式点焊机 pinch welder
悬挂式焊条夹持器 suspension-type elec-

trode holder
悬挂式话筒 suspension microphone
悬挂式浇包 trolley ladle
悬挂式脚手架 suspended scaffolding
悬挂式矿槽[仓] 【铁】suspension-type of bin
悬挂式砂轮[研磨]机 swing-frame grinder
悬挂式输送钢轨 trolley conveyer rail
悬挂式运输机 trolley conveyer
悬挂弹簧钢 suspension spring steel
悬挂线夹 suspension clamp
悬挂轴 overhung shaft
悬胶(体) suspensoid, suspension colloid
悬空微尘 aerosol
悬缆线 messenger wire, cable messenger
悬链 catenary, catenarian, braced chain
悬链拱 catenary arch
悬链式炉 suspension [overhead] conveying furnace
悬料 【冶】arching,【铁】hanging (of charge), hang(ing)-up, suspending burden, suspend, bridging, swell(ing) ◇ 上部～ top hanging
悬料现象 【冶】hang-ups phenomenon
悬料因数 【铁】hanging factor
悬墙 curtain wall
悬圈式电流计 suspended coil galvanometer
悬熔设备 levitating [drip] melting apparatus
悬式绝缘子 suspension insulator
悬索 catenary, catenarian, span wire
悬索道 blondin, runway ◇ 重级～ heavy duty runway
悬索桥 cable cantilever bridge, suspension bridge
悬索式加热炉 catenary reheating furnace
悬台 【建】balcony
悬挑 overhanging
悬置移动液压缸 travel(1)ing cylinder with suspension

悬钟式阀 【铁】mushroom(-type) valve
悬轴式浓缩机 suspension-shaft thickner
悬装型芯 【铸】suspended core
旋臂 swing arm
旋臂起重机 slewing [swing, turning, whirley] crane, rotary bridge ◇ 电动～*, 塔式～ rotary tower crane
旋臂式转柱起重机 pillar jib crane
旋冲钻 churn drill
旋出 back out
旋[镟]床 (turning) lathe ◇ 自动～*
旋磁效应 【理】gyromagnetic effect
旋打振筛机 Ro-tap sieve shaker
旋动反射轴 rotary reflection axis
旋锻 (rotary) swaging, swage, swage (forging)
旋锻锤 rotating [swaging] hammer
旋锻粉末冶金钨条 【粉】swaged powder metallurgy tungsten rod
旋锻机 (rotary) swaging machine, (rotary) swager, rotary forging machine ◇ 钨条～ 行星式钢球～*
旋锻(金属)条 swage bar, swaged rod
旋锻模 swage die
旋锻模板 【压】swage block
旋锻钼条 swaged molybdenum bar
旋锻用感应加热线圈 swaging coil
旋阀 cock (valve), stopcock
旋风 cyclone
旋风除尘[集尘,收尘]器 cyclone (dust) collector [separator], (dedusting) cyclone, centrifugal collector, cyclone settler, cyclone dust extractor, whirler-type dust catcher, whirler, rototctone ◇ ac 管～*, 长锥体～ long cone cyclone, 对流～*, 干式～*, 湿式～*
旋风除尘器组 cyclone bank
旋风分级机(超微粒多管型) cyclosizer
旋风分离器 air separator
旋风器型悬浮状气化装置 cyclone-type suspension gasifier
旋风式焙烧炉 turbulent layer roasting

furnace
旋风式煅烧系统　cyclonic calcining system
旋风式预还原炉　cyclone prereducer
旋风(式)转炉[吹炼炉]　cyclone converting furnace (CCF)
旋杆　swing arm
旋管　coil (pipe), pipe coil, spiral coil (螺状)
旋管冷却　coil cooling
旋管式冷凝器　coiled [worm] condenser
旋光　rotation
旋光度[性]　optical activity, rotation
旋回破碎机　gyratory (breaker, crusher)
旋回球磨机　gyratory ball-mill
旋桨式给[加]料器　rotary-paddle feeder
旋离　whizzing
旋流除尘　cyclonage
旋流除尘[集尘,收尘]器　(同"旋风除尘器")
旋流点火　cyclone firing
旋流分级机　cyclone classifier
旋流分级器　vortrap
旋流分离器[分选机]　cyclone separator [settler] ◇ 低压～*
旋流器　cyclone (cy.), rotoclone, swirler, gas flow rotator ◇ 摆线式～*, 除尘～*, 供料自身作介质的～ autogenous cyclone, 脱泥～*
旋流器风选[旋风器气力分选]　mechanical air separation
旋流器组　cyclone bank
旋流式喷枪　swirl-type lance
旋流式喷射器[喷嘴]　swirl injector [jet]
旋流式燃烧器　cyclone [vortex] burner
旋流式洗选机　cyclone washer
旋流式氧－煤喷枪　swirl-type oxygen-coal lance
旋流洗气器　cyclone gaswasher
旋磨粉末　eddy-milled powder [particle], vortex ground powder
旋钮　knob

旋绕　convolution, wind around
旋塞　cock, stopcock ◇ 放沫～ scum cock, 放气[放出]～ release cock, 联结～ coupling cock, 吸入～ suction cock, 直通～ straight cock
旋塞扳手　cock spanner
旋枢栅门　swinging gate
旋梯　caracole, circular newel stairs (环柱的) ◇ 圆盘～*
旋涡　swirl, vortex
旋涡层　turbulent layer
旋涡出灰　cyclone discharge
旋涡除尘[集尘,收尘]器　(同"旋风除尘[集尘,收尘]器")
旋涡底流　【色】cyclone underflow
旋涡分离　cyclone separation
旋涡计　swirlmeter
旋涡滤渣浇口　【铸】swirl gate
旋涡磨机　jet mill [pulverizer], vortex mill
旋涡喷枪　swirl injector
旋涡破碎　vortex crushing
旋涡熔炼　【色】cyclone smelting
旋涡熔炼法　cyclone furnace process, cyclone (smelting) method
旋涡(熔炼)炉　cyclone furnace ◇ 电热～*
旋涡熔炼室　cyclone smelting chamber
旋涡式火法熔炼法　cyclonic pyrometallurgical process
旋涡式浇注系统　whirl [spinner] gate
旋涡式喷嘴　swirler
旋涡收尘器出灰　cyclone discharge
旋涡速度　whirling speed
旋涡研磨　eddy milling
旋涡研磨机　【粉】eddy mill
旋涡运动　vortical [stirring] motion
旋压　spinning, flow turn(ing) ◇ 变薄～*, 反(向)～ backward spinning, 冷～ cold spinning, 流塑[深度]～ flow spinning, 模具～法*, 能量受控～法*, 强力～(减厚) power spinning, 压弯～法*, 液力～成型法 hydrospinning

旋压操作[工序]	die spinning operation ◇ 封头～dishing operation
旋压锻造	spin forging
旋压机	spinner, spinning machine ◇ 自动～*
旋压机床	spinning lathe
旋压技术[工艺]	die spinning technique
旋压速度【压】	spinning speed
旋叶给料器	rotary-vane feeder
旋轧	flow turn(ing)
旋制混凝土	spun concrete
旋转	revolving, revolution, gyration, rotary motion, rotation
旋转 X 射线谱	rotation(al) X-ray spectrum
旋转薄膜接触器(用于提取铀)	rotafilm contactor
旋转本征函数	rotational eigenfunction
旋转臂	swivel arm
旋转变流机【焊】	slip-pole [rotary, rotating] converter
旋转变压器	rotating [rotary] transformer
旋转布料器	rotary distributor, distributor gear,【铁】revolving distributing device, revolving distributor ◇ 布朗式～Brown distributor
旋转布料器炉顶【铁】	revolving [McKee] top
旋转槽	revolving pot
旋转冲头【压】	turret punch
旋转窗【建】	pivoted window ◇ 中心支承～centre pivoted window
旋转锤	revolving hammer
旋转磁场	revolving [rotating] magnetic field, rotating field ◇ 圆形～*
旋转磁化强度	rotary magnetization
旋转淬火	rotary [rolling] quenching, hardening by spinning, spin hardening
旋转导板	rotating guide
旋转底盘式炉	revolving tray oven
旋转电弧焊	rotating arc welding
旋转电极	rotary [rotating] electrode
旋转电极法	rotating electrode process
旋转锻打机	(同"旋锻机")
旋转锻细【压】	swaging down
旋转锻细法	swaging process [method]
旋转锻造【压】	rotary forging
旋转锻造压模[头]	swaging snap
旋转锻造延伸【压】	swaging operation
旋转锻造用感应加热线圈	swaging coil
旋转对称	rotational symmetry
旋转阀	rotary valve
旋转阀外壳	rotary valve casing
旋转反演	rotation-inversion
旋转方向	direction [sense] of rotation
旋转粉碎机	rotating disintegrator
旋转风挡	swivel damper
旋转钢丝绳	rotating wire rope
旋转缸	swivel [slewing] cylinder
旋转格筛	rotating grizzly
旋转工作台	revolving table
旋转供油(装置)	rotary oil supply
旋转鼓	going barrel
旋转光制(法)	gyrofinishing
旋转焊接	spin welding
旋转弧	arc of rotation
旋转弧形取样器	rotary-arc sampler
旋转混合机	rotary blender
旋转活塞鼓风机	rotary piston blower
旋转机构	turning gear, slewing mechanism
旋转给料阀	rotary feeder valve
旋转给料器	rotary feeder
旋转夹紧装置	turnover jig
旋转加料管	rotating feedpipe
旋转浇制混凝土	spun concrete
旋转浇铸台	rotary casting table
旋转浇注辊	rotary casting roll
旋转铰接	pivot hinge
旋转接合[接头]	swivel joint
旋转晶体法	rotating crystal method
旋转精加工	gyrofinishing
旋转开关	rotary switch
旋转拉伸弯曲(管子的)	rotary draw

bending
旋转冷却器　【冶】rotary cooler
旋转力矩　moment of rotation, turning moment
旋转梁式疲劳(试验)机　【金】rotating beam fatigue (testing) machine
旋转料斗　【铁】revolving hopper [chute]
旋转漏斗　slewing hopper
旋转炉底　revolving hearth
旋转炉炼钢法　rotary converter process
旋转螺栓　sling [shackle] bolt
旋转模锻　【压】circular forging ◇斯利克~轧机　Slick mill
旋转模座　rotating die holder
旋转能力　slewability
旋转喷头煤气洗涤塔　revolving-spray tower
旋转喷雾洗涤[喷洗]器　rotor-spray [revolving-spray] washer
旋转器　revolver, rotator, gyrator, spinning device
旋转气门[气闸]　butterfly (damper), swivel damper
旋转切割　rotary cutting
旋转熔池　【冶】rotating-bath
旋转扫描　swivel scan
旋转扫描法　rotating scanner method
旋转筛　rotary [gyratory] screen
旋转设计　rotable design
旋转式电铲　electric revolving shovel
旋转式吊包　【铸】radial ladle
旋转式锻造机　swager
旋转式翻车机　rotary car dumper
旋转式干燥器　revolving drier
旋转式钢管矫直机　rotary tube straightener
旋转式刮刀[燕翅杆]　rotary scraper, rotary cutter bar
旋转式(弧)焊机　rotary welding machine
旋转式焊接用变比机　motor-driven welding machine
旋转式夹模器　rotary die head

旋转式浸煮器　rotary digester
旋转式拉模盒　【压】rotary die box
旋转(式)炉顶　swinging [swing-type] roof
旋转式弥散器(粉末物料的)　rotating disperser
旋转式黏度计　rotational viscometer
旋转(式)起重机　revolving [rotary] crane
旋转式球团炉　【团】rotating nodulizing kiln
旋转式熔炉(搪瓷用)　rotary smelter
旋转式生物接触器　rotating biological contactor
旋转式凸轮驱动压片机　rotary-type cam-driven tableting
旋转式脱水机　rotary dewaterer, spin-drier
旋转式限位开关　rotating limit switch
旋转式压机　rotary press
旋转式圆筒造球机　【团】revolving balling drum
旋转式造型机　【铸】turnover moulding machine
旋转式装料机　rotary charger
旋转试验法　rotating test method
旋转速度[速率]　rotational speed, speed [rate] of rotation
旋转踏板开关　rotating paddle switch
旋转挺杆起重机　swinging jib crane
旋转头式压坯机　dial(-feed) press
旋转托架　gudgeon
旋转弯曲　rotational bending
旋转弯曲疲劳试验　bend rotating fatigue test, rotating-bending fatigue test
旋转弯曲疲劳试验机　rotating bending fatigue machine
旋转线圈　rotating [moving] coil
旋转斜辊矫直机　rotary straightener
旋转斜盘　swash plate
旋转卸料台(鼓风炉的)　rotating discharge table
旋转芯棒　rotating plug

旋转型搅拌器 rotating (type) stirrer
旋转悬臂梁式(疲劳)试验机 rotating cantiliver beam type machine
旋转压模台 rotating die table
旋转压片机 rotary tablet(t)ing press
旋转压线模(捻异形股绳用) revolving die
旋转压榨机 rotary squeezer
旋转阳极 rotating [spinning] anode
旋转阳极炉 rotating anode furnace
旋转氧枪 【钢】rotary oxygen lance
旋转阴极 rotating cathode
旋转圆盘 rotating disc [disk]
旋转圆盘萃取器 rotating-disc extractor
旋转圆试棒电位降腐蚀探测法 rotogellerative detection of corrosion
旋转圆筒混合机 rotating tumbling-barrel-type mixer
旋转圆柱法 rotating cylinder method
旋转圆柱体 rotating cylinder
旋转圆锥 rotating cone
旋转运动 rotary motion, rotational movement
旋转造型 【铸】turnover moulding
旋转振动器 rotating vibrator
旋转振实装置 Ro-tap fixture
旋转中心 centre of rotation
旋转轴 rotating [pivoted, oscillating] axle, rotation [revolution, spinning, slewing] axis
旋转轴承 swivel-bearing
旋转装置 rotating device
旋转钻机 rotary drill
旋转钻探机 rotary rig
玄武土[玄砂石] wacke
玄武岩 basalt ◇ 熔融~fused basalt, 熔铸~*, 中粒~anamesite
选别 discrimination
选购设备 optional equipment
选矿 ore [mineral] dressing, mineral separation [processing], ore-processing, ore concentration, (ore-) beneficiation, dress(ing) ◇ 蒂坦~法*, 干式~dry cleaning, 机械~*, 静电~*, 重力~*
选矿[选别]比 separation coefficient
选矿厂 (ore-) beneficiation [ore-dressing, concentration, preconcentrate, preparation, separating] plant, beneficiating facilities, ore improvement plant, concentrating mill, concentrator, dressing-works
选矿厂矿泥 milling slime
选矿厂[场]尾矿 mill tailings
选矿方法 mineral dressing method, beneficiating process [method]
选矿工 millman
选矿工段 concentrating section, concentration area
选矿工作者 dresser
选矿规程 concentration criterion
选矿过程 beneficiating process
选矿回收率 ore dressing recovery percentage
选矿机 concentrator, (ore) dresser, preparator ◇ 闭路循环~*, 槽式~*, 电晕式~*, 管式同轴~*, 螺旋~*, 筒式~drum separator, 涡形~snail separator
选矿机械 dressing machine, beneficiation machinery
选矿原理 mineral dressing principle
选矿中间产物 chats
选煤 coal dressing [separation]
选煤厂 coal preparation plant
选通 gating, strobe
选通电路 【计】gate [gating] circuit
选通脉冲 gate (pulse), strobe (pulse), gating (im)pulse ◇ 发出~strobe
选通脉冲发生器 gate pulse generator (gpg), switching pulse generator
选通脉冲照明 strobe illumination
选线继电器 selection relay
选样环 ring sampler
选择 selection (Se., sel.), choice, option
选择布线法 discretionary wiring method

选择吹炼(法)　selective converting
选择萃取　selective extraction
选择萃取剂　selective extractant
选择淬火　selective hardening [quenching]
选择度　selectance
选择法　(同"尝试法")
选择法则　selection rule
选择反射　selective reflection
选择方案　option
选择粉碎法　◇伯斯特兰~*
选择腐蚀　selective [extractive] corrosion, selective [attack],【金】differentiate etching ◇镍合金~denickelefication
选择富集　selective beneficiation
选择感应加热淬火　selective induction hardening
选择还原　selective [preferential] reduction
选择回火　selective tempering
选择校验　selection check
选择结晶　selective crystallization
选择浸蚀　selective etching
选择开关　selective [option] switch
选择控制器　selection control
选择冷凝法　vapour rectification process
选择连接法　discretionary wiring method
选择破碎　selective crushing
选择器　selector, chooser, designator
选择氰化　selective cyaniding
选择散射　selective scattering
选择渗氮　selective nitriding
选择渗碳　selective carburizing
选择铁浸出　selective iron leaching
选择停机　optional stop
选择停机指令　optional stop instruction
选择退火　selective annealing
选择吸收器　selective absorber
选择系数　selective coefficient, selectance
选择线　selection wire,【计】select lines
选择效应[作用]　selection [selective] effect
选择斜度(模锻用)　matching draught

选择性[能力]　selectivity
选择性焙烧　selective roasting
选择性沉淀　selective precipitation
选择性浮选　selective flotation
选择性[选择溶剂]共沸蒸馏　selective azeotropic distillation
选择性过滤器　selective filter
选择性回收　selective recovery
选择性氯化　selective chlorination
选择(性)亲(合)力　selective affinity
选择性熔炼　selective smelting
选择性溶剂　selective [preferential] solvent
选择性溶解　selective dissolution
选择性渗透的　permselective
选择性试验　selective test
选择(性)吸收　selective absorption ◇非~　neutral absorption
选择(性)洗提　selective stripping [elution]
选择性系数　selectivity coefficient [factor]
选择性再结晶　selective recrystallization
选择氧化法　method of selective oxidation
选址　site selection,【计】location
眩目闪光　eye flash
削波电路　clip(ping) circuit
削弱　slacking, weakness, impair ◇未~的　unimpaired
靴筒(钢锭缺陷)　bootleg, box hat, stove pipes ◇穿~*
薛定谔波动方程(式)　Schroedinger's wave equation
学报　bulletin (Bul., Bull.), (academic) journal
学会　society (Soc.), institute, institution, academy, association
学会会员　academician (A)
学会纪要　memoir
学科间研究　interdisciplinary study
学术会议　academic meeting [conferences]
学术机构　academic organization [institution]

学术团体	society (S)
学术演讲	disquisition
学说	theory, doctrine
学习程序	【计】Learning program
学习控制系统	【计】Learning control system
学习系统	learning system
学院	institute, institution, academy (A)
"学振"还原试验法	【团】Gakushin method, Gakushin reduction test
雪崩	avalanche ◇ 离子~【理】avalanche
雪崩击穿	avalanche breakdown
雪茄式合绳机	(同"管式合绳机")
雪茄式冷却器	【铁】cigar cooler
雪茄式捻股机	tubular type strander
雪松木油(显微镜用)	cedar(-wood) oil
血红色温度	blood red heat
血锈(钢件的)	blood
熏烧	smoulder
熏涂(钢锭模的)	reek(ing)
熏烟转筒记录器	kymograph
熏蒸法	fumigation
循环	circulation (circ.), circle, (re)cycle, loop, 【数】recursion ◇ 卡诺～Carnot cycle, 容汉斯－罗西～*
循环泵	(re)circulating [recycle] pump
循环比	(re)cycle ratio
循环变动的季数	【企】quarters for cyclical dominance
循环变动支配的月数	【企】months of cyclical dominance (MCD)
循环操作	cycling, 【计】loop operation
循环常数	cyclic constant
循环池	recycling tank
循环抽风	recycle draft
循环床	circulating bed
循环磁化(作用)	【理】circular [cyclic] magnetization
循环磁化条件	cyclically magnetized condition
循环次数	number of cycles, cycle life (耐火材料热稳定性指标), 【计】cycle index
循环淬火	circulation quenching
循环存储器	【计】circulating [cyclic] memory, cycle [cyclic, loop] storage
循环带火焰温度	【铁】raceway flame temperature
循环电解	cyclic electrolysis
循环风机	recirculating [recirculation] blower, (re)circulating fan
循环伏安法	cyclic voltammetry
循环复位	【计】cycle reset
循环负荷	circulating load
循环干湿法	【建】cyclic wetting and drying
循环干燥机	ring drier
循环管	circulator
循环管道[管路, 管线]	circulating pipe [line], circulation [recycling] pipe line
循环过程	cyclic process
循环恒温器	circulation thermostat
循环回流	circulating reflux
循环回路图	circular chart
循环混合机[器]	circulating mixer
循环给矿机	circular feeder
循环计时电势法	cyclic chronopotentiometry
循环计数器	cycle counter
循环加载	cyclic loading
循环加热材料	cycled material
循环加热烧结处理	【粉】TZ sintering treatment
循环焦炉	recirculation coke oven
循环结束	【计】loop termination
循环进位	【计】end-around carry
循环浸出	recycled leach
循环孔	recirculation opening
循环控制	cycle [circuit] control
循环口	recirculation opening
循环冷却器	recirculation cooler
循环冷却系统	circulation cooling system
循环流动	(re)circulation flow
循环流动系统	recirculating flow system
循环流化床	circulating fluid bed, recircu-

lating fluidized bed
循环母液　recycled liquor
循环喷射冷却风扇　recirculation jet cooling fan
循环铺板　circulating pallet
循环铺底料　recirculating hearth layer
循环曝气槽　circulating aeration tank
循环器　(re)circulator
循环气喷射冷却器　recirculation gas jet cooler
循环气体　circulating [recycled] gas
循环铅(量)　circulated lead
循环区(风嘴前焦炭燃烧空窝)　raceway
循环区渣　【铁】raceway slag
循环取样　round sampling
循环热烟气　【团】hot recuperation gas
循环溶液　cycling solution, recycled liquor
循环冗余(码)校验　【计】cyclic redundancy check (CRC)
循环润滑　circulating [circulatory] lubrication, circulation oiling ◇ 稀油～系统 circulating oil system
循环扇风机　recirculating fan
循环烧结台车　circulating pallet
循环时间　cycle time [length]
循环式破碎　cycle crushing
循环式直接炼钢法　cyclosteel process
循环收尘器　closed-circuit deduster
循环寿命　cycle life
循环数　number of cycles, 【理】number of reversals (应力的)
循环水　recirculated water (RW), circulating [circulation, reclaimed, recycles] water
循环水泵　circulating-water pump
循环水槽　recirculation tank
循环水冷却池　water-cooling pond
循环水站　water recirculating station
循环速度[速率,流量]　circulating [circulation] rate
循环酸　recirculating acid
循环酸洗(系统)　circulating pickling
循环算法　【计】round-robin algrothm
循环索　endless cable
循环条件蠕变性能　creep property of cyclic condition
循环脱气　recirculating degassing (RD)
循环脱气设备　recirculating degasser
循环网链　spangle conveyer
循环位移　cyclic shift, 【计】end-around shift
循环系统　recirculation [circulating, recycle, recycling] system
循环效率　circulation [cycle] efficiency
循环性应力张弛　cycle dependent stress relaxation
循环压制　【粉】cyclic pressing [compacting]
循环烟气袋滤室　circulating fume bag house
循环液　circulating liquid
循环移位　【计】circular [ring, cyclic] shift
循环阴极液　recycled catholyte
循环油缸　circulating oil cylinder
循环运动　cycle motion
循环运输器　endless (belt) conveyer
循环真空脱气(法)　【钢】closed-circuit vacuum degassing, circulation degassing process, circulation by gas lift degassing, R-H (Ruhrstahl-Hausen) process ◇ 磁感～*,双管[喷气]～*
循环执行　【计】looping execution
循环真空脱气装置(R.H.法)　circulation vacuum degassing system
循环周期　cycle time
循环装置　recirculator
循环总量　circulation flow
询价　inquiry
询问　enquire, inquire, inquiry, interrogate, 【计】polling ◇ 显示数据～器*
询问与通信系统　inquiry and communication system
询问与用户显示器　inquiry and subscriber display

询问终端显示器　inquiry terminal display
询问字符　【计】enquiry character (ENQ)
寻向偶极子　director
寻找　seek, search, finding, location, hunting
寻址　addressing
驯化作用　acclimation
巡道工　【运】track walker [man]
巡回检测器　data logger, cycle checking device
巡检　cycle inspection
巡游电子模型(磁性现象的)　itinerant electron model
训练　train(ing) ◇ 在职 ~ on-the-job training
训练操作人员　training operator
训练时间　training time
逊原子　subatom
迅速的　rapid, speedy, prompt (ppt)
迅速动作的　fast acting
迅速冷却(的)　cooled quickly (Cq)
迅速燃烧　deflagrate
迅速增长　mushrooming

Y y

压 press, push (down), squeeze
压凹操作 dishing operation
压板 clamp, platen, gag, hold-down,【铸】clamp plate, squeezer [squeezing] board (造型机的) ◇ 气动~*, 上[向上动的]~ upward acting platen
压板间距 daylight
压板压头(造型机用) squeeze head
压棒装置(钢包的) lifting gear
压包机 bundler
压薄点焊 mash spot welding ◇ 交叉焊条式~ mash welding
压薄缝[滚]焊 mash (seam) welding
压杯试验 cupping test ◇ 楔形拉延~*
压币机 coining machinery
压边 hold-down
压边滚焊[点焊]连接 mash-welded joint
压边焊接焊缝 mesh(ed) weld
压边浇 【铸】lap gate, lip casting
压边(内)浇口 【铸】connor gate [runner], kiss (gate) ◇ 开~ kissing
压边圈 clamping [hold-down] ring
压扁 flatten(ing), press flat, battering, lamination
压扁锤 peening [enlarging] hammer
压扁轧辊 flattened roll
压扁锻造 flattening forging
压扁机 flaking [flating] mill ◇ 线材[钢丝]~*
压扁机架 flattening stand
压扁模槽 flattener
压扁试验 crushing test, flattening test (管材的) ◇ 密合~*
压扁丝 flattened wire
压波浪弯(钢丝织网前的) crimping
压波纹机 folding [creasing] machine
压槽锤 fuller
压槽锤击 fullering
压差 differential pressure (dp), pressure difference [drop]
压差传感[传送,发送]器 diff-pressure transmitter, differential pressure transmitter
压差计 differential pressure [draft] gauge ◇ 皮托~(测流速用) Pitometer
压差温度计 manometric thermometer
压成炉料 power-compacted charge
压出机 extruder
压床 press (machine) ◇ 爆炸~ explosive press
压低辊 knock down roll
压垫 pressing disc, pressure pad
压电 piezoelectricity
压电变换器 piezoelectric transducer [sender]
压电材料 piezoelectric material
压电传感器 piezoelectric pickup [sensor]
压电厚度计 piezoelectric thickness gauge
压电换能器 piezoelectric transducer
压电晶体 piezo-crystal, piezoelectric crystal
压电(晶体)常数 piezoelectric constant
压电石英 piezoquartz
压电陶瓷 piezoelectric ceramics
压电系数 piezoelectric coefficient [modulus]
压电现象 piezoelectric phenomenon
压电效应 piezo-effect, piezoelectric effect
压电谐[共]振器 piezoelectric resonator
压电学 piezoelectricity, piezoelectrics
压电应变计[仪] piezoelectric strain gauge
压电振荡器 piezoelectric oscillator [generator]
压电轴(晶体的) piezoelectric axis
压电阻 piezoresistance
压顶梁 【建】capping beam
压顶砖 【建】coping brick
压锻 press (forging)
压锻成型 press forming
压锻机 squeezer, press

压粉铁芯 dust core ◇费罗卡特~Ferrocart	压痕试验 indentation test,【理】penetration test ◇圆锥形~*

压粉铁芯 dust core ◇ 费罗卡特~Ferrocart
压盖操作(钢锭的) capping practice
压盖(沸腾)钢 capped steel
压盖填密料 【机】gland packing
压杆 pressing stem, compression member,【压】pressure stem [ram, bar]
压汞法 mercury intrusion method
压管试验 crushing test
压光 rolling, press polish
压光辊 felt wrapped roll
压辊 drag [press, hold-on] roll
压舍钢锭(美) stuck ingot
压焊 pressure [roller, push] welding, welding with pressure, bonding ◇自热[熔]~*
压焊吹管 pressure torch
压焊机 press welder
压焊接头 pressure welded junction
压焊行程(对接电阻焊的) upset travel
压痕 impress(ion), indent(ation), indentation cup(硬度试验的), imprint, compression [handling] mark, dint,【压】dinge ◇多次[重复]~repeated indentation, 球形~*, 双~法*
压痕测量放大镜 hardness measuring magnifier
压痕法(测试硬度) indentation [indenter, pressing-in] method
压痕荷载 indentation load
压痕计硬度 penetrameter hardness
压痕棱锥体面积 pyramidal area of impression
压痕面积 impression area, area of indentation
压痕球面积 spherical area of indentation
压痕深度 depth of indentation [immersion]
压痕深度标度盘 indentation depth dial indicator
压痕深度量规 indentation depth gauge
压痕深度指示器 imprint depth indicator
压痕试验 indentation test,【理】penetration test ◇圆锥形~*
压痕硬度 indentation hardness [resistance], impression [pressure] hardness ◇锥形压头静态~*
压痕硬度计(直读式) indentometer
压痕硬度试验 indentation [impression] hardness test(ing), indentation test
压痕硬度试验机 indentation machine
压痕硬度值 indentation hardness number
压花 knurl(ing), coining, emboss(ing), ragging, riffling, stamp
压花板 embossed plate
压花机 embosser, embossing machine
压花模 embossing [coining] die
压花纹 【压】knurling, embossing
压花纹机 embossing press
压花阳模 embossing punch
压环 chuck ring, pressure disc
压火料(封炉的) 【铁】blanket
压机 (同"压力机")
压机底板 compression plate
压机构造[结构] press arrangement
压机机座 press bed
压机头 press-head
压机自动润滑 automatic press lubrication
压挤 compress, extrusion ◇鳄式~机 crocodile squeezer
压挤渗透 squeeze filtration
压挤渗透法[工艺] squeeze filtration process
压挤渗透复合材料 squeeze-infiltrated composite
压挤柱状物 extruded column
压挤铸造 squeeze casting
压挤铸造法[工艺] squeeze casting process
压尖 pointing, slendering
压尖机 【压】(push) pointer, bar pointer ◇电动~ power pointer, 钢丝~ wire pointer, 重型机动~*
压肩接头 joggled lap joint

压浆法　mud-jack method
压接面(焊前的)　pressure contact area
压紧　compacting, clamping, compress tightly, pinch, hold-down ◇ 水力～liquid packing, 未～malcompression
压紧垫圈　joint washer
压紧缸(旋压成形机的)　hold-down cylinder
压紧构件　holding-down member
压紧辊　hold-down roller, friction roll,【压】sensing roller(拉丝机的) ◇ 带钢～(抛光机的) break roll
压紧环　clamping [hold-down] ring
压紧机构　hold-down mechanism
压紧件　holding piece
压紧力　compacting force [pressure]
压紧梁　hold-down beam
压紧螺栓　pressure bolt
压紧器　compactor, collet(压模的)
压紧系数　compacting factor
压紧装置　hold(ing)-down gear, hold-down(gag), gag, clamping device, collet, compression arrangement(试验机的) ◇ 带～的剪断机 squeezer shears, 线卷～*
压浸辊　dunking roller
压具　hold-down, tamp
压块　hold-down, fag(g)oting, briquetting, briquette, pelleted charge ◇ 格伦达尔法～Groendal briquette, 未烧[冷法]～*
压块厂　briquetting plant
压块废钢铁　【冶】fag(g)oting scrap
压块废品　rejected compact
压块机　fag(g)oting press, bundler, briquetting machine ◇ 对辊～roll press, 金属屑[切屑]～*
压块炉料　powder-compacted charge
压块密度　【粉】compact density
压块-烧结双循环　double pressing and sintering cycle
压溃点　squeezing point
压溃力　【铸】collapsing force
压溃强度　collapsing strength
压溃试验　crushing test
压溃性(型砂的)　collapsibility
压溃载荷　breaking load
压溃值　【团】compression rupture value
压力　pressure(pres., press.), tension, compression, compressive force, press power ◇ 轻微～light pressure, 有效～fugacity
压力板　pressure plate
压力泵　pressure [force, forcing] pump ◇ 电动～*
压力闭合(阀门的)　positive closing
压力(变化)循环　pressure cycle
压力表　(同"压力计")
压力表接头　manometer connector
压力波持续时间(爆炸冲压的)　pressure-wave duration
压力波动　pressure fluctuation [surge]
压力波速度　pressure-wave velocity
压力补偿器　pressure equalizer
压力不正常　pressure off-time
压力不足　underpressure
压力槽　pressure [head] tank
压力测量[测定]　pressure measurement [survey], piezometry(流体)
压力差　(同"压差")
压力超载值　overload pressure
压力抽气　forced draught
压力穿孔机　【压】press piercing mill (P.P.M.)
压力穿轧法　press piercing method
压力传动装置(接触焊机的)　【焊】electrode-pressure system
压力传感[传送]器　pressure transducer [cell, sensor, transmitter, pickup], load cell, pressductor
压力传感器系统　load cell system
压力传感元件　(同"压敏元件")
压力淬火　press(ure) quenching
压力带过滤器　pressure belt filter
压力单位　unit of pressure
压力锻造　press forging ◇ 重～*

压力发送器　pressure transducer
压力阀　pressure valve, retainer
压力放大器　pressure multiplier
压力分布　pressure distribution
压力峰值　pressure peak
压力风扇　pressure fan
压力缸(成形机的)　squeezing cylinder
压力鼓风　forced air blast
压力管塞　manometer tube gland
压力罐　elevated tank, pressure bomb
压力灌浆法　【建】pressure grouting
压力辊　【粉】pressure roll
压力过滤机　(同"压滤机")
压力焊焊缝　pressure weld
压力荷载　compressive load
压力化学　piezochemistry
压(力)机　press, compacting press (粉末的) ◇ C 型机架~ gap (frame) press, O 形~ O-ing press, 爆炸~ explosive press, 杯突~【压】cupping press, 波纹~ crimping press, 冲料[落料]~*, 电磁~*, 电动~*, 多工位~*, 多柱~*, 二重双动~*, 钢管扩展~ tube expanding press, 高速~ high speed press, 拱式~ arch-type press, 管式~ pipe press, 辊式~ roll press, 后开式~*, 霍华德~*, 加护罩~ hooded press, 矫正~*, 脚踏~*, 考芬哈尔~ couffinhal press, 可倾式~ inclinable press, 空气~ air-pressure mill, 快速~*, 框架(结构)式~*, 拉槽(孔)~【压】broaching press, 联合式~*, 模座侧送料~*, 摩擦~ friction(al) press, 喷射~ ejecting press, 偏心(式)~*, 前送料~*, 切断~ cutting-out press, 曲轴(式)~*, 热等静(压)~*, 上行冲程~ upstroke press, 伸角式~ horn press, 手动[手板]~*, 双臂~*, 双辊~*, 双肘杆~ duplex toggle press, 水平~【耐】level press, 台式曲柄~ bench press, 弹簧模~ dual-pressure press, 尾部送料~*, 卧式~ horizontal press, 下滑座式凸轮~*, 液动压~ hydrodynamic press, 张力曲柄连杆式~ tension knuckle press, 肘杆式~*, 柱式~ column press, 抓斗送料~ gripper feed press, 自动送料~*
压力机操纵台　press control desk
压力机吨位　press tonnage
压力机工作台[压机台]　press table
压力机管状结构　【压】tubular press
压力机框架　press-frame
压力机能力　press capacity [tonnage]
压力机设计[构造]　press design
压力机压板　platen
压力机压力与行程关系曲线图　pressure-distance curve
压力机压制　press compacting
压力机阴模　press die
压力机张拉立柱　press tension column
压力机主冲头　【压】main press ram
压力机柱塞[冲杆]　press plunger
压力极限[范围]　pressure limit
压力急变　pressure shock
压力给[送]料槽　pressure-feed tank
压力计　pressure (mano)meter [gauge, indicator], manometer (测流体压力) ◇ U 形~ U-tube manometer 薄膜~*, 布登~ Bourdon gauge, 测微~ micromanometer, 差动[差示]~*, 电离~ ionization gauge, 多管~*, 放射性电离~*, 风箱式~ bellows manometer, 隔膜式~*, 虹吸~ siphon gauge, 记录式~*, 接触式~ contact manometer, 麦克利德[麦氏]~*, 毛细管~ capillary manometer, 锰白铜丝~*, 膜盒~*, 皮托~ Pitot pressure gauge, 热敏电阻~ thermistor gauge, 双金属片~*, 弹簧(式)~*, 斜管~ inclined manometer, 遥感[远距离感应]~*, 液柱~*
压力计管　manometer [pressure] tube
压力计用液体　manometric fluid
压力记录器　pressure recorder, manograph
压力加工　plastic working, press work, shaping ◇ 冷~作业*
压力监测器　pressure monitor

| 压力降 differential pressure (dp), pressure drop, draught loss
| 压力降-流量图 pressure drop-flow diagram
| 压力浇注 pressure pouring ◇ 可控～*
| 压力矫直机 press [gag] straightening machine, straightening press, gag straightener [press]
| 压力接合 compression bonding
| 压力进料 pressure feed
| 压力浸出 pressure leach ◇ 高温～*
| 压力剧变 pressure jump
| 压力开关[继电器] pressure switch (PS)
| 压力孔隙比曲线 pressure-void ratio curve
| 压力控制 pressure control
| 压力控制阀 pressure controlling valve (PCV)
| 压力控制器 pressure controller [monitor]
| 压力控制式点焊机 pressure controlled spot-welding machine
| 压力猛增 pressure surge
| 压力密封 compression sealing
| 压力-浓度曲线图 P-X diagram
| 压力-浓度投影图 P-X projection
| 压力喷浆面层 gunite covering
| 压力喷浆砌衬 gunite lining
| 压力喷射流 pressure jet
| 压力喷嘴 delivery cone, drive nozzle
| 压力喷嘴燃烧器 pressure jet burner
| 压力平衡 pressure equilibrium
| 压力气氛 pressure [pressurized] atmosphere
| 压力强度 (同"压强")
| 压力曲线 pressure curve
| 压力容器 pressure vessel [container] ◇ 核反应堆～*
| 压力容器钢 pressure vessel steel
| 压力容器钢板 pressure vessel plate
| 压力容器焊缝 pressure-tight seam
| 压力润滑 forced [force-feed, pressure] lubrication ◇ 集中～*, 稀油自动～*, 自动干油和稀油～系统*

压力上限 upper pressure limit
压力烧结 pressure sintering
压力升高系数 coefficient of increase of pressure
压力释放装置 pressure release device
压力试验 pressure test
压力水 pressure water
压力水池 pressure tank ◇ 输水管道末端的～terminal reservoir
压力水箱 elevated water tank
压力损失 pressure [draught] loss, loss of pressure
压力梯度 pressure [barometric] gradient
压力-体积-温度曲线图 P-V-T diagram
压力调节[调整] pressure control [adjustment]
压力调节阀 pressure regulating valve
压力调节器 pressure regulator [controller, governor] ◇ 阿斯卡尼亚～Askania regulator, 炉顶煤气～*
压力调节装置 pressure regulation unit
压力调宽机 sizing press
压力调直机 straightening press
压力突[跃]变 pressure jump, jump in pressure
压力突降 sudden drop in pressure
压力涂覆 press coating
压力-温度-成分曲线图 P-T-X diagram
压力稳定仪 compression standardizing box
压力雾化喷枪 pressure atomising lance
压力下降 loss of pressure
压力箱 pressure tank (PT), forbay
压力效应 pressure effect
压力-行程关系曲线图 pressure-distance curve
压力因次 pressure dimension
压力诱发位错 pressure-induced dislocation
压力造型 【铸】compression moulding

压力造型机　mould(ing) press
压力增大　pressure build-up
压力真空计[表]　pressure vacuum gauge
压力指示控制器　pressure indication controller (PIC)
压力指示器　pressure indicator (PI)
压力中心　center of pressure (CP)
压力铸造　(同"压铸")
压力铸造仪表设备　die-casting instrumentation
压力铸造用润滑剂　die-casting lubricant
压力转换　pressure commutation
压力锥印(坯块缺陷)　【粉】pressure cone
压力自动调节器　automatic pressure controller
压力自平衡式补偿器　【铁】pressure self-balance compensator
压力作用　press effect
压料板　pressure plate
压裂点　squeezing point
压裂负载　crushing load
压路机　(road, pavement) roller, road drag, road level(l)ing machine ◇ 滚筒式~drum roller, 振动~vibratory roll
压滤　filter pressing, pressure filtration
压滤饼　(filter) press cake
压滤布　filter press cloth
压滤法　forced filtration method, filter press technique
压滤机[器]　pressure filter, filter press ◇ 板框式~*, 伯特型圆筒~burt filters, 凯雷型~Kelley filter press, 框式~frame filter press, 梅耶尔~*, 密闭~closed filter press, 室式~*, 外部排料~*, 箱式~*, 叶(片)式~*
压滤机调浆槽　filter press surge tank
压滤机框板　frame plate
压滤机组　battery of presses
压滤箱　box filter press
压轮机　wheel-boxing press
压毛刺辊　bar masher
压铆机　(squeeze) riveter

压密机　densifying rolls
压敏电阻　piezo-resistance
压敏电阻件　piezo-resistor, varistor, varister
压敏管　pressure sensing tube
压敏黏结剂　pressure sensitive adhesive, contact adhesive
压敏元件　pressure responsive element, pressure cell
压敏柱销　【压】pressure sensitive pins
压模　press(ing) die [mould], compression die [mould], moulding [forming] die, die-press ◇ 衬碳化物[硬质合金]的~carbide-lined drawing die, 固定式~【机】fixed mould, 双冲杆[双冲]~double-punch die, 双作用~double-action die
压模安装　die setting
压模闭锁装置　【压】die-locking mechanism
压模材料　die material
压模衬片　die lining
压模衬套[筒]　die barrel
压模成型　moulding in dies
压模造型　diaphragm moulding
压模抽真空　evacuation of die
压模打磨　die dressing
压模定位器　mould positioner
压模附件　die accessories
压模工作面　die (inter)face
压模构件　die member
压模构造　die construction
压模固定　die setting
压模合金　die alloy
压模滑架　die yoke
压模机　molding press, moulding machine
压模面样板　die-face template
压模磨损　die wear
压模摩擦　die friction
压模内衬　die liner
压模抛光机　die polishing machine
压模嵌入块　cavity insert
压模润滑剂　die lubricant

压模设计	die design
压模台板	die platen
压模套管	die sleeve
压模元件	die segment
压模制模法	hobbing
压模装料(用粉末)	die-filling, die loading
压模装置	die arrangement [assembly] ◇ 连续压制的~*
压配合(公盈压配合)	【机】interference [force, press] fit
压坯	briquet (te), pressed compact [shape],【粉】(未经烧结的)(pressed) green compact, green-pressing ◇ 复合~*,组合~composite compact
压坯(坯块压制)	compacting, compaction ◇ 离心~*
压坯冲击强度	【粉】green impact strength
压坯冲头	【粉】compacting punch
压坯杆	compacting ram
压坯机	briquette press ◇ 快动机械~*, 旋转头式~dial(-feed) press
压坯孔隙度	green porosity
压坯密度	【粉】pressed density
压坯强度	【粉】green strength
压坯试样	compact specimen
压坯性能	【粉】green properties
压坯运搬试验	【粉】rattler test
压坯直径	【粉】green [compact] diameter
压片	pressing disc
压片机	tablet-compression machine, tableting [pill] press ◇ 标准机械~*, 斯托克斯~Stokes tablet machine, 旋转[转台]~*, 自动~*
压平	flatten, gagging, smashing, iron down, dress,【压】mushroom (成蘑菇状)
压平锤	enlarging hammer
压平机[器]	【压】flatter
压平隆起	knobbling
压气泵	gas compression pump
压气混凝土浇灌机	pneumatic concrete placer
压气机	compressor, air engine, gas booster ◇ 真空泵抽空~*
压气室	compressor house
压气软管	air hose
压气设备	gas booster
压气升液器	monte-jus
压强	(intensity of) pressure, tension
压强计	manometer, pressure gage, piezometer ◇ 电离~ionization gauge, 真空~prani gauge
压曲强度	buckling strength
压曲蠕变	buckling creep
压曲稳定性	buckling stabliity
压曲应变	【压】buckling strain
压曲应力	buckling stress
压屈	buckling, lateral deflection ◇ 可控~*, 蠕变~creep buckling
压屈极限	buckling limit
压屈临界载荷	buckling load
压屈试验	buckling test
压热(硫化)锅	autoclave press
压热器	pressurized equipment, autoclave
压入	press-in
压入法测(显)微硬度	microhardness indentation
压入法测硬度	hardness indentation
压入抗力(压头的)	indentation resistance, resistance to indentation
压入能力	imbedability, embedability
压入配合	press fit
压入式硬度计	penetrascope ◇ 瓦曼~Warman penetrascope
压入试验	【理】penetration test
压入污物	rolled-in dirt
压入氧化皮	trickle scale
压入应力	indentation stress
压勺修型时间	trowel hour
压伸器	(同"压缩扩展器")
压实	compacting, compaction, compress, ramming, densification ◇ 振动~vibration compaction
压实板	【铸】squeezing plate [table], squeezer plate

压实阀　squeezing valve
压实粉末　【粉】compacted powder
压实活塞　【铸】squeeze piston
压实机　compacting press, compactor ◇ 金属粉末~[压力机] powder metal press
压实机构　densification mechanism
压实机械　compacting machinery
压实力　compacting force
压实率　degree of compacting
压实密度　packing density
压实设备　compacting plant
压实(式)造型机　【铸】squeeze moulding machine ◇ 顶箱~*, 橡皮膜压~*, 液压~*
压实式制芯机　【铸】squeeze-type coremaking machine
压实体积　packing volume
压实土　【建】compacted soil
压实系数　compacting factor, coefficient of consolidation
压实性　packing characteristic(s)
压实造型机承梁　squeezer yoke
压实装置　densification mechanism
压实作用　compaction, compacting action, consolidation, densification
压送泵　forcing pump ◇ 煤气~ gas compression pump
压送管　forcing pipe
压送辊　【压】nip roll
压塑　compact(ing), compaction, (pressure) moulding ◇ 单效~*, 双效~*
压塑过程　compacting process
压塑型　pressure moulding
压塑性　compactibility, briquettability
压塑性试验　compactibility test
压塑压力　compaction pressure
压碎　crush(ing)
压碎的废钢铁　【铁】fragmented scrap
压碎工序　crushing operation
压碎机　crusher, crushing engine
压碎抗力　resistance to crushing

压碎强度　crushing strength ◇ 低温~*
压碎切屑　crushed turnings
压碎系数　crushability factor
压碎应力　crushing stress
压碎硬度　degree of hardness for crushing
压碎装置　crushing device
压缩　compression, compressing, reduction, compaction, narrowing, contraction ◇ 不完全~ malcompression, 经~的 reduced
压缩比　compression ratio (c.r.), reduction [contraction] ratio, rolling rate [reduction], coefficient of compressibility
压缩变形　compression (deformation), compressive strain, compressive load deformation
压缩变形抗力　resistance to compression
压缩波　compressional wave
压缩残余应力　compressive residual stress
压缩操作　squeezing operation
压缩测定弹簧　compression-measuring spring
压缩成形　compression forming
压缩冲程　compression stroke
压缩带　compression [reduction] zone
压缩废钢　pressed scrap
压缩负载　compression [compressive] load
压缩负载变形　compressive load deformation
压缩环　pressure ring
压缩机　compressor, compression engine, densener ◇ 空气冷却~*, 两级活塞式~*, 螺杆~ screw compressor, 气体喷射[喷气]~*, 透平式~ turbo-compressor
压缩机室　compressor house
压缩机站　compressor station [plant]
压缩计　compressometer
压缩空气　compressed-air, pressed [pressure] air
压缩空气冲压机　compressed air ram
压缩空气捣打装置　hammer impact machine
压缩空气(锻)锤　(同"风动锻锤")

压缩空气阀　compressed air valve ◇ 圆锥形~*
压缩空气分配　compressed air distribution
压缩空气鼓风机　compressed air blower
压缩空气管　compressed air pipe
压缩空气管道[管线]　compressed air line, compressed-air piping, airline pipe
压缩空气罐　compressed air cylinder
压缩空气过滤器　compressed air filter
压缩空气减压站　compressed air reducing station
压缩空气开挖隧道法　compressed-air method of tunneling
压缩空气喷雾法　compressed-air atomization
压缩空气瓶　compressed-air flask [bottle]
压缩空气容器　compressed air container
压缩空气软管　compressed air hose
压缩空气设备　compressed-air [pneumatic] plant
压缩空气升液器　pressure-air montejus
压缩空气式研磨机　air-pressure mill
压缩空气输送器　air slide conveyer
压缩空气系统　compressed air system
压缩空气蓄罐(水压机的)　air bottle
压缩空气振打机构　compressed air shaking mechanism
压缩扩展器　【电】compandor, compressor-expandor
压缩力　compressive force, force of compression, draught pressure
压缩量　draught, draft, amount of draught [reduction] ◇ 每道~【压】draught per hole
压缩率　percent(age) reduction, intensity of compression, compression ratio ◇ 每个模槽~(拉模的)【压】reduction per die
压缩孪晶　compression twin
压缩模　reducing [reduction] die ◇ 两次~*
压缩模量[模数]　compression modulus, modulus of compression [pressing] ◇ 体积(各向)~*
压缩碾压　【运】breakdown rolling
压缩扭折　compression kinking
压缩疲劳试验　compression fatigue test, repeated compression test
压缩破断　compression failure
压缩破裂　compression fracture
压缩器　compressor, reducer
压缩气体　compressed gas
压缩气体锻锤　compressed gas machine
压缩强度　compression [reduction] strength, intensity of compression
压缩区(域)　compressive region
压缩曲线　compression curve
压缩屈服点　compressive yield point
压缩屈服强度　compressive yield strength
压缩热　compression heat
压缩蠕变　compression [compressive] creep
压缩蠕变试验　compression creep test
压缩绳股　compressed strand
压缩试验　compression [compressive] test ◇ 侧限~*
压缩试验机　compression tester, compression testing machine
压缩速率　【压】reduction rate
压缩塑性流变　compressive plastic flow
压缩弹簧　compression spring
压缩弹性　elasticity of compression
压缩弹性极限　elastic limit under compression (E.L.C.), compressive elastic limit
压缩弹性模数　compressive modulus
压缩弯曲　compression bending
压缩系数　(coefficient of) compressibility
压缩纤维状组织　compression fibre structure
压缩线　compression line
压缩性　compressibility, coercibility,【耐】compacting properties ◇ 高~粉末*
压缩应变　compression [compressive] strain

压缩应力　compression [compressive] stress, stress in compression

压缩应力强度　intensity of compressive stress

压缩应力试验机　compression stress tester

压缩应力-应变图　compression stress-deformation [stress-strain] diagram

压缩永久变形　compression set

压缩载荷　compressive load ◇ 界面～bearing load

压缩载荷下使用　compression loading application

压缩轧制织构　compression rolling texture

压缩值测定弹簧　compression-measuring spring

压缩指数　compression index

压缩制冷　compression refrigeration

压缩周期　compressing cycle

压缩轴线　compression axis

压条　patand

压铁　clamp iron,【铸】mould [foundry, pouring] weight, clamp plate ◇ 加～*

压铁机　【铸】weight setter

压头　pressure head, press-head, squeeze head, top board,【机】measuring head,【金】(硬度试验用) indenter, indentor, impresso, penetrator ◇ 测微硬度～microindenter, 金刚石圆锥体～*, 球形～*, 造型机的～squeeze head

压头槽　head tank, headbox

压头常数(硬度试验机的)　indenter constant

压头加压力　ram pressing capacity

压头加压行程　ram pressing stroke

压头流量仪　head flow type meter

压头损失　head loss, loss in head

压头行程　ram stroke

压涂法　【焊】extrusion method

压团　briquetting, barbecuing ◇ 水泥～balling up of cement, 无黏结剂～(法)*

压团机　【团】balling press ◇ 柱塞式～plunger press

压团模　packing die

压瓦楞　【压】corrugation

压弯机　【压】bending press, bulldozer ◇ 车轮轮辋～dishing press

压弯模　bending die

压弯[旋压]法(封头的)　dishing process

压位差　pressure head

压纹　【压】emboss(ing)

压纹辊　graining roll

压纹机　("压花机")

压纹模　embossing die

压纹阳模　embossing punch

压下　【压】reduction, cogging ◇ 板坯的水平～slabbing action, 侧～indirect edging draght, 垂直～*, 二次[再]～double reduction, 冷轧～*, 轧制侧向～indirect rolling action

压下百分率　reduction percent ◇ 冷压～*

压下表　draught gauge

压下补偿　draught compensation

压下操纵工　screw operator

压下程序　draught stage

压下传动装置　screwdown drive

压下垫块(模具的)　pressure block

压下负荷表　load meter

压下缸　screwdown cylinder

压下规程[制度]　reduction [rolling, draughting] schedule

压下[压缩]辊　【连铸】reduction rolls

压下机构调整　screwdown setting

压下机构电动机　screwdown motor

压下控制　screwdown control

压下量　【压】(gauge) reduction, (amount of) draught, draughting ◇ 超高～轧制 hollow drawing, 大～轧制*, 带～的夹辊【连铸】withdrawal and reducing rolls, 道次～reduction in pass, 高度～reduction in height, 厚度～reduction in thickness, 金属（累计）总～*, 绝对～absolute draught, 每道～*, 平整～调节*, 宽调～edging reduction, 小～轧制*, 一道～

single draught
压下率 【压】degree of reduction [strain], relative draught, percent(age) reduction, percentage of reduction
压下螺母 screw box
压下螺丝 (roll-)adjusting [press(ure), forcing] screw, housing screw [pin]
压下螺丝操纵工 screw operator
压下螺丝位置发送器 screw-setting transducer
压下螺丝下部测压头 screw load cell
压下螺丝转动杆 screw key
压下(螺丝)装置 screwdown arragement
压下时间 screwdown time
压下调整螺丝 housing adjusting screw
压下系数 coefficient of reduction [draught]
压下系统 screwdown system, press down system, 【压】reduction system ◇ 轧机~*
压下指示盘[压下装置刻度盘] draught (indicator) dial
压下指示器 screwdown indicator
压下装置[机构] holding-down device, screwdown (device, gear, mechanism, structure) ◇ 程序调整的~ preset screwdown, 电动~*, 机械辅助~*, 进料辊~ feed rolls screwdown, 上推式液压~*, 手动~*, 调整~ roll-gap setting, 行星式~ planetary screwdown, 轧机~*
压下装置自动程序控制 automatic preset screwdown
压下装置自动控制 automatic screwdown control
压线模(捻股或合绳机的) die
压线模座 die box
压线瓦 stranding die
压芯电缆 pressed-core cable
压型 compaction, press mould ◇ 分批装模~法*, 熔模铸造的~ die mould, 自动~ automatic tamping
压型机 mould(ing) [forming] press, tamping machine
压型夹 die clamp
压型加热器(压铸用) die heater
压型模 die [compression] mould
压型排气孔 die vent hole
压型设备 tamping plant
压型涂料 die dressing
压型维修工段 die maintenance area
压檐梁 capping beam
压延 rolling, drawdown, recycle flattening
压延边缘 running edge
压延产品 rolled product
压延车间 rolling plant
压延淬火 rolled hardening
压延轧辊 reduction roll
压印 coining, stamping, impression, emboss, imprinting ◇ 闭式模~ closeddie coining, 可~的*, 立体~ full coining, 平面~ flat coining
压印操作[作业] relief work
压印冲头 coining punch
压印法 imprinting method ◇ 图案花纹~[工艺]*
压印机 coining press [mill], embossing [striking, marking] press ◇ 硬币~ coining machinery
压印模 coining [stamping, calking] die, matrix
压印模成形 impression die forming
压应力 (同"压缩应力")
压油润滑(法) forced lubrication
压余 【压】remainder, discard, heel, butt(-end)(挤压的)
压余顶出装置 discard-ejecting means
压余分离剪 【压】discard separator
压轧 nip ◇ 初次~ initial breakdown
压轧机架 【压】reduction stand
压榨(法) press, squeezing, compressing, expression
压榨机 squeezer, press(er) ◇ 旋转~ rotary squeezer, 摇头[上回转台]~ tilting-

head press
压折 lap, pinch,【压】fold
压直辊 debending [deflecting, deflector] roll
压纸板 pressboard, presspahn
压致相变 pressure-induced phase change
压制 pressing, compressing, compression, compacting, compaction, moulding ◇ 爆炸~*,常温~*,磁场中~*,单向~*,低温~*,二向[两面]~*,分步~*,高温~*,连续~*,两次~法*,流体~法*,疏松~【粉】loose compaction,双效[双动]~*,橡皮包套~*,振动~*,自动循环~*
压制棒材[坯] pressed bar
压制不足 underpressing
压制操作 pressing operation
压制磁铁 pressed magnet
压制电极 rolled electrode
压制方法 【粉】compacting method
压制方向 direction of pressing
压制粉末(磁)芯 pressed powder core
压制钢件 pressed steel
压制高度 【耐】pressing height
压制工 press operator
压制毂 pressed-out hub
压制过程 pressing [compacting] process
压制焊条 pressed electrode
压制机 【团】(briquetting) press ◇ 辊式[对辊]~*,斯托克斯~*
压制机构 compressing mechanism
压制机械 pressing machinery
压制焦 (同"型焦")
压制力 pressing force
压制裂纹 pressing [compacting] crack
压制毛刺 pressing fin
压制密度 pressing density
压制模具 compacting tool set
压制品 stampings ◇ 包[复]钢层~clad-steel laminate
压制坡莫合金粉 pressed permalloy powder

压制缺陷 pressing defect
压制润滑剂 pressing lubricant ◇ 挥发性~*
压制烧结弧熔法 PSM (pressing-sintering-melting) process
压制烧结熔化机 pressing-sintering-melting machine
压制烧结熔炼设备 pressing-sintering-melting unit
压制烧结制品 moulded and sintered product
压制速度 pressing speed
压制条件 pressing [compacting] condition
压制位置 pressing position
压制温度 pressing [compacting] temperature
压制性 briquettability, compactibility
压制循环 press cycle
压制压力 pressing [compaction, briquetting] pressure ◇ 单位~*
压制阴模(法) hubbing
压制硬化 rolled hardening
压制砖 pressed brick
压重 【铸】mould [pouring] weight
压煮处理 autoclaving
压煮器 (同"高压釜")
压铸[压力铸造] die-cast(ing), pressure (die-) casting, compression [squeeze] casting ◇ 充氧~*
压铸车间 die-casting shop
压铸成型 moulding in dies
压铸法 die-casting process, pressure casting [pouring] process, squeeze casting process ◇ 德斯科一次有效型芯~Desco process,高频振荡~vibrocast,真空~*
压铸工 die caster
压铸工程师学会(美国) Society of Die-Casting Engineers (SDCE)
压铸硅铝合金 ◇ A.13~*
压铸合金 die-cast(ing) alloy, alloy for die casting ◇ 电铸板用铅基~*,多莱尔铜

基~*,锌基~*

压铸机 die caster,(pressure) die-casting machine ◇ 低压~*,冷室~*,立式柱塞[冷压室]~*,气压式~*,热室式~*,热压室[浸没式鹅颈管]~*,水平[卧式]柱塞~*

压铸机锁型曲肘 die-locking toggle

压铸件 pressure (die-)casting,die casting

压铸件尺寸长大(时效后的) die-casting growth

压铸铝合金(3.5Cu,5Si,余量 Al) aluminium die-cast(ing) alloy,die-casting aluminium ◇ 360~*,伯马尔~ Birmal alloy,雷尼克斯~*

压铸铝基合金 (同"铝基压铸合金")

压铸模 compression [injection] mould, pressure casting die,die-casting die

压铸模具钢 die-casting die steel

压铸锌基合金 (同"锌基压铸合金")

压铸型 (die-casting) die,die cast mould

压铸压力 die-casting pressure

压铸(用)锌合金 zinc alloy for die casting (ZAC)

压铸轴承合金 die casting metal

压注缸(压铸机的) injection [shot] cylinder

压砖机 brick press ◇ 冲击式~ stamping press,杠杆~ lever [toggle] press,滑动成型~*,回转式~ revolver press,偏心轴~*,转动台式~*,转盘~ turntable press

压砖机厂 machine press plant

压砖煤 briquetting coal

压装齿轮[齿圈] pinion rings

压装机 assembling press

鸭嘴笔 drawing pen

芽孢 spore

芽孢八叠球菌属 Sporosarcina

芽孢杆菌属 Bacillus

芽孢弧菌属 Sporovibrio

牙板夹头(拉拔机的) gripper

牙痕(轧材硬伤) 【压】dog marks

牙科合金 dental alloy ◇ 蒂科尼姆~*,克娄勾~*,韦尔什银铝~*

牙科合金粉末 dental alloy powder

牙科黄铜[假金](Cu:Zn=2:1) wiegold

牙科耐蚀铸造合金 ◇ 卢诺里乌姆~*

牙科用汞齐合金(66.6—67.8Hg,26.10—28.2Sn,4.6—5.1Cu,0.2—1.7Zn) dental amalgam

牙科用钴铬铸造合金 ◇ 尼拉纽姆~*

牙轮钻头 roller bit,tri-cone rotary drill bit

牙嵌离合器 claw [dog,jaw] clutch

牙嵌联轴器 dog coupling

雅尔坦锰硅铜低合金钢(0.25C,1.5Mn,025Si,0.4Cu) Jalten

雅各比铅基轴承合金(85Pb,5Sn,10Sb;以及62Pb,27Sn,10Sb) Jacobl's alloy

雅各比熔铸制品 Jakobit

雅各比铜硅锰合金(94.9Cu,4Si,1.1Mn) Jacobl's alloy

雅各比锡锑铜装饰合金(85Sn,10Sb,5Cu) Jacobl's alloy

雅凯电解抛光法 Jacquet polishing technique

雅凯水平连铸法 【钢】Jacquet continuous ingot casting process

雅硫铜矿 yarrowit

哑点 dead spot [point]

哑铃形导线 (同"8形导线")

亚冰晶石 (同"锥冰晶石")

亚丙基[CH$_3$CHCH$_2$-] propylene

亚不稳定性 metainstability

亚层 subshell

亚碲酸 tellurous acid

亚碲酸钾{K$_2$TeO$_3$} potassium tellurite

亚碲酸钠{Na$_2$TeO$_3$} sodium tellurite

亚碲酸盐{M$_2$TeO$_3$} tellurite

亚碘酸盐 iodite

亚点阵 sub-lattice

亚锇的 osmious

亚钒的 vanadous

亚钒酸盐{M$_2$V$_4$O$_9$,M$_2$V$_2$O$_5$} vanadite

亚镉中子	subcadmium neutron
亚铬酸镍	nickel chromite
亚铬酸盐 {MCrO₂ 或 M₃[Cr(OH)₆]}	chromite
亚汞化合物	mercurous compound
亚共晶合金	hypoeutectic alloy
亚共晶铁碳合金	hypoeutectic iron-carbon alloy
亚共晶铸铁	hypoeutectic cast iron
亚共晶组织	【金】hypoeutectic structure
亚共析钢	hypoeutectoid steel, hyposteel
亚共析合金	hypoeutectoid alloy
亚共析组织	【金】hypoeutectoid structure
亚固相线	sub-solidus
亚甲键	methylene bond
亚甲桥	methylene bridge
亚结构	substructure
亚结构强化	substructural strengthening
亚金属的	submetallic
亚金酸盐	aurite
亚晶格	sublattice
亚晶界	sub-grain boundary, sub-network, sub-boundary ◇ 晶粒~*
亚晶界图样	pattern of sub-boundary
亚晶界组分	subboundary constituent
亚晶界组织	subboundary structure
亚晶粒	sub-grain
亚晶粒大小	sub-grain size
亚晶粒生长	sub-grain growth
亚晶(粒)形成	sub-grain formation
亚晶粒组织	sub-grain structure
亚晶态的	subcrystalline
亚晶体	subcrystal
亚壳层	subshell
亚铼酸盐 {M₂ReO₃}	rhenite
亚临界奥氏体	subcritical austenite
亚临界区[范围]	(同"下临界区")
亚临界退火	subcritical annealing
亚临界温度淬火	hardening at subcritical temperature
亚硫酸钾	potassium sulphite
亚硫酸钠	sodium sulphite
亚硫酸氢铵 {(NH₄)HSO₃}	ammonium bisulphite
亚硫酸氢钠	sodium bisulphite
亚硫酸氢铷 {RbHSO₃}	rubidium bisulfite
亚硫酸氢盐	bisulfite, bisulphite
亚硫酸氢盐浸出	bisulphite leaching
亚硫酸锶 {SrSO₃}	strontium sulphite
亚硫酸盐[酯]	sulphite, sulfite
亚麻仁油(型芯油料)	linseed oil
亚麻子状矿石	flaxseed ore
亚锰酸	manganous acid
亚锰酸盐	manganite
亚钼的	molybdous
亚铌的	niobous, columbous
亚黏土	【耐】loam
亚凝固温度	subfreezing temperature
亚铅酸	plumbous acid
亚铅酸盐	plumbite
亚砂土	loam sand
亚筛范围	subsieve range
亚筛分析	subsieve analysis
亚筛粉粒	subsieve size particle
亚筛粉末(小于 44 微米)	subsieve fraction, subsieve (size) powder
亚筛粒度范围	subsieve size range
亚筛粒度分析仪	subsieve size apparatus
亚钐的	samarous
亚砷酸	arsenous acid
亚砷酸酐	arsenous acid anhydride
亚砷酸钠	sodium arsenite
亚砷酸铜	copper arsenite
亚砷酸盐[酯]	arsenite
亚声(波)的	infrasonic
亚声波冷却	infrasonic cooling
亚铈	cerous cerium
亚铊的	thallous
亚钛的	titanous
亚钽的	tantalous
亚锑的	(同"三价锑的")
亚锑酸 {偏 HSbO₂,正 H₃SbO₃,焦 H₄Sb₂O₅}	antimonious acid
亚锑酸盐	antimonite

亚 ya

亚铁　ferrous [divalent] iron ◇ 试~灵*
亚铁化合物　ferrous compound, ferrocompound
亚铁还原滴定计　【化】ferrometer
亚铁离子　ferrous ion
亚铁氰化锆{Zr[Fe(CN)$_6$]}　ferrocyanide of zirconium
亚铁氰化铪{Hf[Fe(CN)$_6$]}　hafnium ferrocyanide
亚铁氰化钾{K$_4$[Fe(CN)$_6$]}　potassium ferrocyanide
亚铁氰化钠{Na$_4$[Fe(CN)$_6$]}　sodium ferrocyanide
亚铁氰化铁{Fe$_4$[Fe(CN)$_6$]$_3$}　ferric ferrocyanide
亚铁氰化物　ferrocyanide
亚铁氰化物沉淀　ferrocyanide precipitation
亚铁氰酸{H$_4$[Fe(CN)$_6$]}　ferrocyanic acid
亚铁氰酸锌粉　antwerp blue
亚铁溶液　ferrous solution
亚铁酸钡　barium ferrite
亚铁酸盐　perferrite
亚铁锌镀层（钢铁的）　protectorite
亚铁正铁化合物　ferroferric compound
亚铜氨络合物　cuprous ammine complex
亚铜化合物　cuprous compound, cuprocompound
亚铜容量　cuprous capacity
亚微颗粒　subparticle
亚微孔隙　submicroscopic porosity
亚微粒尘粒　【环】submicron-sized dust particle
亚微裂纹　submicroscopic crack
亚微米(级)体系　submicron system
亚微细粒　submicron-sized particulate, submicro
亚微型难熔分散颗粒　(同"难熔分散亚微颗粒")
亚稳奥氏体　【金】metastable austenite
亚稳定结构状态　metastable structural condition
亚稳(定)能级　metastable (energy) level
亚稳定系统　metastable system
亚稳定性　metastability
亚稳(定)状态　metastable state
亚稳定状态图　metastable diagram
亚稳固溶体　metastable solid solution
亚稳(晶,原子)核　metastable nucleus
亚稳平衡　metastable equilibrium
亚稳曲线　spinodal (curve)
亚稳热处理　intercritical heat treatment
亚稳态分解　spinodal decomposition
亚稳态原子　metastable atom
亚稳系　metastable system
亚稳线　spinodal line
亚稳相　metastable phase
亚稳型氧化铝　intermediate alumina
亚硒酸　selenous acid
亚硒酸钙{CaSeO$_3$}　calcium selenite
亚硒酸钾{K$_2$SeO$_3$}　potassium selenite
亚硒酸钠{Na$_2$SeO$_3$}　sodium selenite
亚硒酸盐[酯]　selenite
亚锡的　stannous
亚锡酸盐　stannite
亚细微粒　submicron solids
亚显微质点　submicroscopic particle
亚硝基-β-萘酚　nitroso-β-naphthol
亚硝酸钾{KNO$_2$}　potassium nitrite
亚硝酸钠{NaNO$_2$}　sodium nitrite
亚硝酸钠-硝酸钠浴槽　nitrite-nitrate salt bath
亚硝酸铯{CsNO$_2$}　cesium nitrite
亚硝酸锶{Sr(NO$_2$)$_2$}　strontium nitrite
亚硝酸盐[酯]　nitrite
亚硝酰(基){NO=}　nitrosyl
亚氧钒根　vanadylous
亚音频的　infrasonic
亚铀的　uranous
亚原子　subatom
亚锗的　germanous
亚锗酸盐{M$_2$GeO$_2$}　germanite
亚正铁化合物　ferroferric compound

亚洲开发银行　Asian Development Bank (ADB)
亚珠光体钢　hypopearlitic steel
亚组织　lineage structure
氩{A 或 Ar}　argon ◇ 吹～清扫＊, 焊接级[焊接用]～welding-grade argon
氩保护气氛　argon atomsphere ◇ 高纯度～＊
氩电弧炉　argon arc furnace
氩弧　argon arc
氩弧焊(接)[氩气保护电弧焊]　argon arc welding ◇ 金属极～＊, 钨极～＊, 自动～argonaut welding
氩弧焊机　argon arc welding machine
氩弧焊炬[喷枪]　argon arc torch
氩弧切割　argon arc cutting
氩弧熔化[炼]　argon arc melting
氩壳电子　argon core electrons
氩离子化鉴定器　argon ionization detector
氩离子激光(器)　argon ion laser
氩气　argon gas ◇ 钢流～保护【钢】impact method
氩气保护冷却室　argon cooling chamber
氩气氛　argon atmosphere
氩气管　argon tube
氩(气)搅拌熔体　argon-stirred melt
氩气净化　argon purification
氩气喷吹　argon injection
氩气瓶　argon gas bomb
氩气引入管　argon lead
氩－氧精炼　argon-oxygen refining
氩氧喷吹　argon-oxygen blowing
氩－氧脱碳　【钢】argon-oxygen decarburization[decarburizing] (AOD)
氩－氧脱碳法　AOD process
氩氧(脱碳)感应炉　argon-oxygen decarburization induction furnace (AODIF)
氩－氧脱碳精炼法　AOD refinement
氩－氧脱碳[精炼]炉　AOD furnace
烟　fume, smoke ◇ 带～气体 fume laden gas
烟尘　smoke dust ◇ 带走的～carry-over dust, 碱性～basic smoke, 酸性～acid smoke
烟尘比电阻　dust resistivity
烟尘捕集　fume arrestment
烟尘捕集器　dust arrester
烟尘捕集装置　fume arrestment plant
烟尘沉积　dust[smoke] deposit(ion)
烟尘沉降室　dust-settling compartment, dust chamber
烟尘出口　dust outlet
烟尘处理　dust handling
烟尘废料　dust wastes
烟尘分离　dust separation
烟尘分离设备　dust-separating appliance
烟尘回收　【冶】dust recovery
烟尘粒子[微粒]　smoke particle
烟尘量　dust loading
烟尘凝结体　【环】lithometeors
烟尘排出量　【钢】flue dust output
烟尘收集　fume containment
烟尘收集与处理装置　dust handling plant
烟尘损失　dust loss
烟囱　chimney (chy), chimney shaft[neck], (smoke) stack, gas evacuating flue ◇ 防[耐]酸～acid-proof chimney, 高炉横～furnace bridge, 集中排烟～＊, 紧急事故～emergency stack, 炉压调节～＊, 排放～bleed off stack, 燃烧废气的～flambeau, 特高～skyscraper
烟囱尺寸　chimney size
烟囱抽力　chimney[stack] draught
烟囱抽气罩　chimney aspirator
烟囱筏基　chimney raft
烟囱阀　chimney valve
烟囱泛水　【建】chimney flashing
烟囱废气　shimney[stack] gas
烟囱废气脱硫　stack-gas desulphurization
烟囱盖　chimney hood
烟囱高度　stack height
烟囱管　funnel pipe
烟囱滑阀　chimney slide valve
烟囱灰　chimney soot

烟 yan

烟囱冒烟　chimney emission
烟囱帽　chimney cap
烟囱排放量　stack emission
烟囱排放损失　loss on stack
烟囱排放物　【环】stack effluents
烟囱排放物监测仪　stack effluent monitor
烟囱排烟　stack discharge, chimney emission
烟囱清灰口　floss hole
烟囱身　chimney shaft
烟囱式冷却塔　chimney cooler
烟囱体　chimney stack
烟囱吸力　stack pull
烟囱效应　chimney effect
烟囱闸板　chimney damper
烟囱罩　stack cap, bonnet
烟囱阻力　stack friction
烟囱作用(电炉电极的)　【钢】chimneying
烟囱座基　chimney base
烟道　flue (duct), chimney flue [hole, intake, neck], gas flue [duct], smoke duct [flue], tunnel ◇ Z形[曲折]~ zigzag flue, 大~ windmain, 房式~ chamber flue, 废气燃烧~ flare (stack), 横~ cross flue, 活动~ movable flue, 旁通[支]~ bypass flue, 气球形~*, 小~【焦】bus flue, 砖格~ checker flue
烟道沉尘室　flue dust pocket
烟道抽力调节器　stack draught regulator
烟道废气　waste flue gas
烟道废气风扇　flue gas fan
烟道隔板　furnace bridge
烟道管(过热器的)　flue tube
烟道灰　flue dust
烟道灰尘排出量　【冶】flue dust make
烟道孔　flue hole [opening]
烟道口底部　port slope
烟道炉　flue furnace
烟道炉灰　flue dust
烟道耐火拱顶　flue bridge
烟道气　flue [effluent] gas
烟道气测定器　flue gas tester

烟道气分析　flue gas analysis
烟道气平衡　flue gas balance
烟道清灰口　floss hole
烟道清理　flue cleaning
烟道损失　flue [stack] loss
烟道碳黑　impingement black
烟道通风　stack draught
烟道温度　stack temperature
烟道系统　【冶】flue system
烟道渣　flue cinder
烟道闸板　(smoke) flue damper, flue shutter
烟道阻力　duct friction
烟管　smoke pipe
烟害　smoke nuisance, damage by fume
烟黑　smoke [soot, gas, jet] black
烟喉　gorge
烟化　fuming (fum.)
烟化法　fuming process ◇ 伯齐利厄斯回转窑~*, 炉渣~*, 沃尔兹回转窑~*
烟化炉　fuming furnace
烟化能力　fuming capacity
烟化速率　fuming rate
烟灰　soot, flyash
烟灰浓度　ash concentration
烟火　firework
烟火制造术　pyrotechnics
烟煤　bituminous [gas, soft] coal ◇ 高级~ gas coal, 炼焦~ byerlyte, 条带状~*, 中等挥发分~*
烟煤炉　bituminous coal furnace
烟气　flue gas, fume, smoke, fume laden gas, 【环】gaseous emissions ◇ 副产~ by-product fume
烟气成分　flue gas analysis
烟气出口　【钢】fume outlet
烟气除尘器　gas cleaner
烟气除尘设备　gas cleaning equipment [installation]
烟气倒流　puffing
烟气阀管接头(空气预热的)　fume outlet
烟气分析　stack-gas [flue-gas, smoke]

烟气腐蚀　flue gas corrosion
烟气含氧量测定　flue gas oxygen measurement
烟气净化　fume [gas] cleaning
烟气净化设备　fume cleaning equipment, gas cleaning equipment [installation]
烟气控制[处理]　smoke control
烟气量　gas volume
烟气流　fume flow, gaseous flux
烟气流量　fume flow
烟气密度计[测量仪]　flue density meter
烟气气化冷却器　vapour cooler
烟气清洗　fume cleaning
烟气入口　access of gas
烟气收集系统(转炉的)　fume collecting chimney
烟气抬升高度　plume height
烟气脱硫　flue-gas desulphurization
烟气温度　flue (gas) temperature
烟气洗涤　fume scrubbing
烟气洗涤器　smoke washer
烟气洗涤水　scrubber water
烟气洗涤塔　gas wash(ing) tower
烟气洗涤液　scrubber solution
烟气系统　gas system
烟气余热回收　off-gas heat recovery
烟气中氧含量测定　【冶】flue gas oxygen measurement
烟色黄玉　smoking topaz
烟水晶　smoky quartz
烟速率　fuming rate
烟炱　soot (black)
烟筒　funnel
烟雾　fume, fuming, smoke, mist ◇ 副产~by-product fume, 含硅~silica fume, 含钴~*, 消除~(法) abatement of smoke
烟雾层　【环】aerosol layer
烟雾抽引　fume extraction
烟雾气氛　hazy atmosphere
烟雾洗涤塔　fume scrubber
烟熏法　fumigation

烟罩　(fume) hood, draught [exhaust, furnace] hood, (smoke) helmet ◇ 敞口~open hood, 活动~*, 密闭~closed hood, 上部~tube hood
淹没　submergence, flooding
湮没　annihilation, black out ◇ 反射光完全~*, 位错~*
湮没反应　annihilation reaction
湮没辐射　annihilation radiation
湮没现象　annihilation
盐　salt ◇ 沉出~粒 salting up, 成~*, 罗谢尔~*, 用~处理 salination, 子[A] alite
盐饼{Na$_2$SO$_4$·10H$_2$O}　salt-cake
盐饼炉　salt-cake furnace
盐槽钎焊　salt soldering
盐沉清器　salt settler
盐萃取　salt extraction
盐度　【环】salinity
盐分　salt content, saline matter
盐釜　【化】salt furnace
盐湖　salt lake
盐护板(如钨酸钙)　salt screen
盐化　salify
盐混合物　salt mixture
盐类共晶　salt eutectic
盐量计　salinometer
盐屏[挡板]　salt screen
盐溶液腐蚀　brine corrosion
盐水　brine (water), saline water, salt brine [solution], 【环】brackish water (中等程度的)
盐水处理　salination
盐水腐蚀　brine [salt-water] corrosion ◇ 耐~性*
盐水浸出　brine leaching
盐水浸出剂[盐水溶剂]　brine lixiviant
盐水冷却(法)　brine refrigeration
盐水冷却管　【机】brine pipe
盐水冷却器　brine cooler
盐水冷却系统　brine refrigeration system
盐水喷淋试验(腐蚀试验)　saltwater

spray test
盐水试验　brine test
盐水循环泵　brine recirculation pump
盐酸〖HCl〗　chlorhydric [hydrochloric] acid, muriatic acid (旧名) ◇ 耐～合金*
盐酸化的　muriatic
盐酸回收工艺　hydrochloric acid regeneration process
盐酸回收装置　hydrochloric acid recovery plant
盐酸浸出　hydrochloric acid leach(ing), leaching with hydrochloric acid
盐酸-硫氰酸溶液　hydrochloric-thiocyanic acid solution
盐酸溶液(钎焊的)　spirit of salt
盐酸洗提　hydrochloric acid elution
盐酸贮槽室　hydrochloric acid tank room
盐雾(腐蚀试验用)　salt spray [fog, mist] test, salt spray corrosion test
盐雾腐蚀　salt spray corrosion
盐雾(腐蚀)试验　salt spray [fog, mist] test, salt spray corrosion test
盐雾腐蚀试验法　salt spray method
盐雾腐蚀试验箱　salt spray box [chamber]
盐雾气氛　salt spray atmosphere
盐析点　saltation point
盐析剂　salting (out) agent
盐析速度　saltation velocity
盐析蒸发器　salting out evaporator
盐相　salt phase
盐液　salting liquid
盐液密度计　salinometer
盐浴　salt bath
盐浴槽　salt bath furnace [pot], chemical bath ◇ 等温淬火用带式～*,浸没电极式～*
盐浴除鳞　salt bath descaling
盐浴淬火[盐淬]　salt bath quenching, molten [fused] salt quenching, brine quenching, salt hardening

盐浴淬火炉　salt bath hardening furnace
盐浴剂　salt bath medium
盐浴加热　salt bath heating
盐浴浸渍钎焊　salt bath dip brazing
盐浴炉　salt bath furnace [pot] ◇ 充气～渗氮[氮化],电热(式)～*,六极～*,内加热式～*
盐浴热处理　molten salt heat treatment
盐浴软氮化　tufftride
盐浴烧结　salt bath sintering
盐浴渗铬　salt bath chromizing
盐浴渗碳　carburizing by molten salts
盐浴退火　salt bath annealing, liquid annealing
盐浴退火槽[炉]　salt bath furnace
盐浴温度　salt temperature
盐渍土　salty soil
严格按照尺寸　trueness to gauge
严格锻造公差　tighter forging tolerances
严格检查[验]　close check, tightened inspection
严格控制　rigid [strict] control
严格试验　severe test ◇ 经过～的 high test
严酷气氛(腐蚀的)　severe atmosphere
严密　tightness
严重差错　gross error
严重(程度)　severity
严重粉尘损失　heavy dust loss
严重腐蚀　heavy corrosion
严重故障　heavy fault
严重过烧的　hard burned
严重偏析　macrosegregation
严重鼠尾(铸件缺陷)　(sand) buckle
檐槽　【建】gullet
檐沟　【建】drain [eaves] gutter, eaves board
檐口滴水条　【建】chantlate
檐墙　shadow wall
檐砖　【建】coping brick
研钵　mortar
研究　study, research, investigation (inv.),

survey ◇ 科学~*
研究班[会] seminar
研究报告 research report, memoir
研究部门 research department
研究范围 field of research
研究方法 research method [technique]
研究工作 research work
研究规划阶段 research planning stage
研究结果 findings
研究人员 research man
研究室 research department, facilities, cubicle
研究试验 research trial
研究试验室 research laboratory
研究所[院] (research) institute, institution
研究用反应堆 research reactor
研磨 grinding, abrasion, lapping, dressing, milling, snagging (去除浇口、飞翅等),【压】bedding in (拉模的) ◇ 过度~*, 化学~ chemical milling, 间歇[分批]~ batch grinding, 精细~ thorough grinding, 无心~*
研磨表面 grinding surface
研磨操作(工序) grinding operation
研磨长度 【机】grinding length
研磨方式 grinding mode [regime]
研磨费用 grinding cost
研磨粉 abrasive powder [dust], grinding powder ◇ 微细~ micropowder, 氧化铁~ crocus
研磨膏 grinding paste ◇ 金刚石~ diamond paste
研磨工段 grinding section
研磨工序 grinding stage
研磨光洁度 【机】grinding finish
研磨过度 overgrinding
研磨混汞器 grinding amalgamator
研磨混合机 putty-chaser-type mixer ◇ 连续~*
研磨机 grinder, (grinding) mill, lapper, lapping machine ◇ 皮带~ belt lapper, 轻便~ portable grinder, 刃型连续~*, 湿粉~ wet-powder grinder, 双辊~ end runner mill, 无心~*, 悬挂式~ swing-frame grinder, 旋涡~(粉) eddy mill, 压缩空气[气压]式~ air-pressure mill, 振动(式)~*
研磨剂 grinding materail, abradant
研磨间 grinding chamber
研磨介质[材料] grinding medium
研磨介质填充率 media precentage of mill volume
研磨精加工 【机】grinding finish
研磨精整 abrasive finishing
研磨冷却液 【机】grinding fluid
研磨冷却油 grinding oil
研磨力 abrasive power
研磨裂纹 grinding crack
研磨轮 abrasive wheel
研磨面 grinding face, abrasive surface
研磨盘 bucking board (试样的) ◇ 固定式~ fixed abrasive lap
研磨-抛光机 grinding-and-polishing machine
研磨砂带 abrasive belt
研磨烧伤 grinding burn
研磨设备 grinding equipment [facilities]
研磨特性 grinding characteristics
研磨体 grinding element
研磨头 grinding head, abrasive points
研磨系统 grinding system
研磨屑 grinding dust
研磨用钢[铁,金属]丸 abrasive shot
研磨(用)液体 grinding fluid, milling liquid
研磨轧辊 grinding roll
研磨纸 【金】abrasive paper ◇ 金属氧化物~ crocus paper
研磨作业线 grinding line
研碎 trituration
研讨会 symposium
研制 [advanced] development
研制工作 development work

研制设备 development plant
岩崩 rock slide, rockfall
岩层 rock stratification, stratum, terrain
岩洞 grotto
岩洞建筑 hypogee
岩颈 neck
岩脉 dike
岩溶 karst
岩石 rock
岩石的 rocky (rky)
岩石露头[外露岩石] day stone, outcrop
岩石煤 slate coal
岩石圈 lithosphere
岩石学 petrology
岩石压力 rock pressure (R.P.)
岩相成分[组成] macerals composition
岩相分析 petrographical analysis [examination], maceral [rock-facies] analysis
岩相检验 petrographic examination
岩相显微镜 petro-graphic microscope
岩相学 petrography (petrog.), lithology
岩相学的 petrographical (petrog.)
岩相学家 petrographer (petrog.)
岩相组分 petrographic constituent, maceral component, lithotype ◇ 微观～ microlithotype
岩芯 【地】core ◇ 取～钻头 coring bit
岩芯管 core barrel
岩芯记录 drill record, drill-log
岩芯钻 core drill
岩心钻头 core drill bit, coring [jack] bit ◇ 金刚石[镶有金刚石的]～*
岩性地层分析 lithostratigraphic analysis
岩盐{NaCl} rock [mineral] salt, halite
岩盐(晶体)单色器 rocksalt monochromator
岩盐型晶体 rock-salt type crystal
岩状磷钙土 rock phosphate
延长 extention, prolongation, elongation, lengthen
延长部分 extension
延长导线(热电偶的) extension lead wires
延长时间 extended period
延长线 extension wire
延长型带式烧结机 extended sinter machine
延迟 delay(ing), lag, retard(ation)
延迟电路 delay circuit
延迟断裂(高强度钢的) delayed fracture [failure], retardation of fracture
延迟反应 deferred [slow] reaction
延迟回波(信号) delay(ed) echo
延迟计时器 delay timer
延迟结晶 delayed crystallization
延迟门(脉冲) delayed gate
延迟能力 moderating power
延迟破裂 delayed cracking
延迟屈服(现象) delayed yield(ing)
延迟扫描 delayed sweep
延迟时基扫描 delayed time-base sweep
延迟时间 delay time, time of lag, 【企】detention period
延迟式自动增益控制 delayed automatic gain control
延迟弹性 【冶】delayed elasticity
延迟线 【电】delay line
延迟线存储器 delay line memory [storage]
延迟形变 delayed deformation
延迟选通脉冲 delayed gate
延迟元件 delay element [component, unit]
延迟作用 retarded action
延胡索酸{(:CHCO₂H)₂} fumaric acid
延缓 delay, inhibition
延缓能力 moderating power
延缓期 inhibition period
延缓时效 delayed aging
延缓作用 delayed action, inhibition [inhibitor] effect
延期 prolongation, delay, postpone
延期迟延(疲劳裂纹的) delayed retardation

延伸	extension, elongation, stretch(ing),【压】drawdown, rolling-out ◇ 渐进～ progress elongation
延伸度[性]	extensibility, extension
延伸辊道	extension [additional] roller table ◇ 机后辅助～ back auxiliary table
延伸计[仪]	extension meter, extensometer, elongation meter ◇ 激光～ laser extensometer
延伸孔型	【压】elongation [coggingdown] pass, break(ing) down pass
延伸孔型系统	breakdown sequence
延伸控制	elongation control
延伸量	extensive quantity ◇ 每道次～
延伸裂纹	expansion crack
延伸率	elongation (percentage, value), coefficient of extension [elongation], percentage elongation [extension], specific [unit] elongation ◇ 断裂～, 拉伸～ tensile extension, 临界～ critical elongation
延伸器(平罐蒸馏炼锌的)	prolong
延伸误差	【计】propagated error
延伸系数	elongation factor, coefficient of elongation, lengthening coefficient
延伸芯头[座]	【铸】tail core print
延伸性	expandability, extensive properly
延伸轧槽	drawing
延伸轧机	【压】elongating mill, elongator
延伸值	elongation value
延时	delay(ing), time delay [lag], retardation
延时 Petri 网	timed Petri nets
延时继电器	delay(ed) relay (DR), time delay [lag(ged)] relay
延时开关	(time) delay switch
延时释放	time release
延时元件	time element
延时整定	timing
延性	ductility, tensility ◇ 有～的 ductile
延性杯突试验机	cup test machine
延性材料	ductile material
延性-脆性转变	ductile brittle transition
延性断口[断裂面]	ductile fracture surface ◇ 纤维状～
延性断裂[裂纹]	ductile crack
延性断裂扩展	ductile crack propagation
延性极限	ductility limit
延性计	ductilometer, ductilimeter
延性晶粒[晶体]	ductile crystal
延性开裂	ductile cleavage
延性磨蚀特性	ductile erosion behaviour
延性偏析	【金】ductile segregation
延性破断	ductile failure
延性区(脆性断口的)	thumb nail
延性试验	ductility test ◇ 奥尔森～
延性试验机(板材的)	ductility (testing) machine
延性铁	ductile iron ◇ 贝氏体～ bainite ductile iron
延性铁冶炼设备系统	◇ IRSID～
延性涂[镀]层	ductile coating
延性增加原理	【压】principle of increasing ductility
延性铸铁	Ductalloy, ductile cast iron
延性转变	ductility transition
延性转变温度	ductility transition temperature
延续时间	duration, space of time, perdurability
延展阶段(金属的)	ductile stage
延展性	malleability, ductility
延滞期	lag phase
颜料	pigment ◇ 打底～ body pigment
颜色	colo(u)r, tinting
颜色测流速法	colour-velocity method
颜色的浓淡	tint
颜色偶合剂	colour coupler
颜色温度	colour temperature
颜色显示	show colour
沿海工业地区	littoral industrial area
沿横坐标	X-direction
沿晶体扩散	short circuit diffusion
沿径斥力	radial repulsion

沿径分量　radial component
沿棱焊缝　(同"根部焊缝")
沿位错线的管中扩散　pipe diffusion
沿线平均直径　linear mean diameter
掩蔽　masking(-off), blanket, hide, screen, shelter ◇ 放射线微粒～室 fallout shelter
掩蔽晶体　protected crystal
掩蔽扩散　masked diffusion
掩盖　covering ◇ 用膜～filming
掩码　【计】mask
掩埋　burial ◇ 污水滤渣的～*
掩模夹　mask holder
掩模原版　master reticle
掩模原图　mask artwork
掩膜　mask
掩饰处理　【金】masking
眼镜阀　(double) goggle valve ◇ 热胀式～*
眼镜形闸板　goggle plate
眼螺栓　eyebolt
眼圈接合　eye joint
眼(圈)螺母　eye nut
衍射　diffraction ◇ 计数器～计法*, 晶体[晶格]～*, 锐边～*
衍射斑点　diffraction spot [mottle, mottling] ◇ 晶粒度～*
衍射测微器　eriometer
衍射分析　diffraction analysis
衍射(分析)法　diffraction method ◇ 布喇格 X 射线～Bragg method
衍射分析相鉴定法　【金】identification by diffraction analysis
衍射峰[最大值]　【理】diffraction peak [maximum]
衍射峰轮廓　diffraction maximum profile
衍射辐射　diffracted radiation
衍射管　diffraction tube
衍射光谱　diffraction spectrum
衍射光谱计　diffraction spectrometer
衍射光栅　diffraction grating ◇ 刻线～*
衍射光栅间距　slit separation

衍射光栅摄谱仪　diffraction-grating spectrograph
衍射光束能量　diffracted-beam energy
衍射光束圆锥　cone of diffracted beam
衍射花样　(同"衍射图") ◇ 斑点～*, 背反射～*, 标定粉末法－指数用图解法*, 回摆晶体(X 射线)～*, 劳厄～*
衍射花样记录　diffraction pattern registration, pattern recording
衍射花样线　pattern lines
衍射环　diffraction ring ◇ 粉末～*, 试样～specimen ring
衍射级　order of diffraction
衍射角　diffraction angle
衍射结构分析　diffraction analysis
衍射掠射角　glancing angle of diffration
衍射面极点　pole of diffracting plane
衍射(平)面　diffracting plane
衍射强度　diffracted intensity
衍射区域[范围]　diffraction region
衍射散射　diffraction scattering
衍射术　diffractometry
衍射束　diffracted beam ◇ 聚焦～*, 零次[零级]～*
衍射束偏向　diffracted beam deviation
衍射条件　diffraction conditions ◇ 布喇格－偏差[偏离]*
衍射条纹　diffraction fringe ◇ 弗雷斯内尔～Fresnel fringes
衍射透镜　diffraction lens
衍射图　diffraction pattern ◇ 结晶～crystallogram, 周转～*
衍射图像　diffraction image
衍射图像视读仪(X 射线的)　film reading instrument
衍射显微镜　diffraction microscope ◇ 兰氏 X 射线～法 Lang's method
衍射线　diffracted rays, diffraction arcs 低布喇格角～*, 高布喇格角～*
衍射线轮廓(X 射线的)　diffraction line profile ◇ 德拜－谢乐～*, 非对称～*
衍射线偶[对]　pair of diffraction arcs

衍射线条　diffraction line
衍射线位置　diffraction arc position
衍射线圆锥　cone of diffracted rays
衍射线增宽　diffraction line broadening
衍射仪[计]　diffraction instrument, diffractometer ◇ 盖革计数器~*
衍射仪反射织构测定法　◇ 舒尔茨~ Schulz method
衍射用管　tube for diffraction work
衍射圆　diffraction circle
衍射圆锥　diffraction cone ◇ 布喇格~*,同轴~*
衍射照相　diffraction photogram
衍射照相机　diffraction camera
衍射照相术　diffraction radiography, diffractography
衍射指数　index of diffraction
衍射最强点轮廓　diffraction maximum profile
衍射作用　diffraction effect
演算　calculation, calculus
演绎　deduction, inference, fetch
堰(坝)　dam, weir
堰管　weir tube ◇ 高度可调节的~*
燕翅杆(混合机内的)　rotating bar,【团】paddle (shaft) ◇ 固定式~stationary cutter bar, 往复式~*
燕尾(槽)　dovetail (groove)
燕尾形导轨　dovetail guide
燕尾榫接头　dovetail joint
厌气菌[(微)生物]　anaerobe
厌氧处理　【环】anaerobic treatment
厌氧微生物腐蚀　microbiological anaerobic corrosion
厌氧细菌　anaerobic bacteria
厌氧下水道污泥　anaerobic sewage sludge
厌氧性梭状芽孢杆菌属　Clostridium
厌氧性消化装置　anaerobic digester
焰道　flue ◇ U字形~hairpin flue
焰锋　flame front [head]
焰锋速度　flame front speed
焰焊　torch welding

焰弧　flaming arc
焰火　firework
焰炬淬火　torch hardening
焰炬加热断焊　torch brazing
焰炬加热软化处理　flame softening
焰炬检验　flame torch test
焰炬切割场　flame cutting yard
焰炬压力　【焊】torch pressure
焰帘　flame curtain
焰煤　flame coal
焰色反应　flame reaction
焰舌　flame tail
焰心　flame heart [core, kernel], luminous core,【焊】flame core
验电器【电】electroscope, galvanoscope
验定吨(短吨为29.1667克, 长吨为32.67克)　assay ton (A.T.)
验定炉　assay furnace
验方角规[角尺]　try square
验后清洗(穿透检验的)　post-cleaning
验色管　chromoscope
验收　acceptance (inspection, check), control reception
验收标准　acceptance standard
验收单　acceptance certificate, receipt
验收钢印　【压】acceptance stamp
验收(合格)试验　acceptable test
验收(合格)质量标准　acceptable quality level
验收检验　reception test
验收取样　acceptance sampling
验收试验　approval [proof, reception, official] test
验收数　acceptance number
验收员　inspector, acceptor
验收证明书　acceptance certificate
验算　checking calculation, checkout
验证　proof, verification
赝单晶　pseudosingle crystal
赝晶　pseudomorph
赝形晶体　pseudomorphic crystal
杨氏弹性模数　Young's modulus of elastic-

杨氏模数 Young's modulus ◇ 比～*
杨－泰勒效应 【理】Jahn-Teller effect
扬尘 dust nuisance
扬程损失 head loss
扬格伯格法(瑞典电高炉炼铁法) 【铁】Ljungberg process
扬料板 lifting blade, lifter (bar),【团】internal lifter, lifting flight
扬起 rise
扬散 diffusing
扬砂泵 sludger
扬声器 (loud)speaker,【电】reproducer ◇ 高低音～duo-cone speaker
扬水率 pumpage rate
扬析(流化技术的) elutriation
扬唧 pumping
羊齿植物叶状晶体 fernlike [fern-leaf] crystal
羊脚(路)碾 sheepfoot roller
羊毛脂(拉拔润滑用) wool fat [grease], degras, lanolin
羊皮覆面辊 sheep skin roll
阳电 (同"正电")
阳电溶胶 positive sol
阳电子辐射体 positron emitter
阳极 anode, positive (pole, electrode) ◇ 靶可换～*, 板式～slab anode, 焙烧～baked anode, 残(余)～*, 打结～bulk anode, 大型～full size anode, 带套～bagged anode, 对开～split anode, 多层板式～multiple slab anode, 惰性～inert anode, 废～*, 辅助～booster anode, 隔膜(包裹式)～*, 挂耳式～coped-lug type anode, 管式～tube anode, 加速～acceleration anode, 螺栓固定～bolt on anode, 耐腐蚀～*, 人造～*, 析氧～*, 圆形～circular anode, 再生～secondary anode, 铸造～cast anode, 自蚀～corrosion piece
阳极靶 anode [plate] target
阳极靶盘(旋转阳极的) target disc
阳极靶至胶片间距 target-to-film spacing
阳极斑点 anode spot
阳极板 anode plate [sheet], positive plate
阳极棒 anode rod [stub],【色】(contact) spike
阳极棒孔 【色】(anode) pinhole
阳极包覆 anodic cladding
阳极保护 anode [anodic] protection, anodic control
阳极保护管 anode protection tube
阳极表面 anode surface
阳极部分 anode portion
阳极材料 anode material [stock]
阳极残头 anode remnants [butt, crop, stub, top] ◇ 碎废～crushed scrap anode butt
阳极操作 anode servicing
阳极层 anode layer
阳极产品 anodic product
阳极超电压[过电压] anode-overvoltage, anodic overvoltage [overpotential]
阳极沉淀 anodic precipitate
阳极成分 anode composition
阳极池 anode pool
阳极尺寸 anode dimension
阳极初次产物 primary anode product
阳极处理 anodic treatment, anodization
阳极处理法 anode (treating) process, anodic process ◇ 本戈硬铝～Bengough process
阳极处理用装置 anodizing plant
阳极传输 anodic transfer
阳极纯度 anode purity
阳极大梁 【色】anode centre beam
阳极袋 anode bag
阳极导板 anode guide
阳极导体 anode conductor
阳极底掌 anode bottom
阳极碘化 anodic iodination
阳极电池(组) anode battery
阳极电导 anode conductance
阳极电镀 anodization
阳极电解液 anolyte, anode [anodic, an-

odizing] solution, anode liquor
阳极电解液层　anolyte layer
阳极电抗器　anode reactor
阳极电流　anode-current
阳极电流密度　anode (current) density, anodic current density ◇额定~*
阳极电流效率　anodic (current, Faraday) efficiency
阳极电抛光　anode brightening
阳极电桥　anode bridge
阳极电位　anode [anodic] potential ◇可控~氧化滴定*
阳极电位降　anode (potential) fall
阳极电压　anode voltage
阳极电压降　anode (voltage, potential) drop
阳极电压降区域[范围]　anode drop region
阳极电源接头　anode [positive] power connection
阳极电源引线　anode power lead
阳极淀积　anode deposit, anodic deposition
阳极吊杆(预焙阳极的)　anode rod
阳极顶部　anode top
阳极定位　anode positioning
阳极镀层　anode coating, anode [anodic] finish
阳极钝化(处理)　anodic passivation
阳极钝化金属　【金】anodically passivated metal
阳极钝性[态]　anodic passivity
阳极发射　anode emission
阳极法　anode [anodic] process
阳极反应　anode [plate] reaction
阳极反应机理　anodic reaction mechanism
阳极防护(屏)　anode shield
阳极防蚀法　anodization
阳极废液　spent anolyte
阳极分析　anode analysis
阳极氟化　anodic fluorination
阳极腐蚀　anode corrosion [attack]
阳极腐蚀效率　anode corrosion efficiency

阳极负载　anode load
阳极格(电解槽的)　anode kettle
阳极工组　anode crew
阳极挂耳　anode lug
阳极过电压　anode-overvoltage, anodic overvoltage [overpotential]
阳极过热　target overheating
阳极海绵　anode sponge
阳极耗量　anode consumption
阳极合金　anode alloy
阳极糊　anode paste [mix] ◇连续自焙~*
阳极糊比电阻　anode paste resistivity
阳极化　anodizing, anodising, anodization, anodic treatment ◇本戈-斯图尔特轻金属~处理法*,铬酸~处理*,厚层~处理 thick anodizing
阳极化镀层　anodized coating
阳极环　anode ring
阳极缓蚀剂　anodic inhibitor
阳极黄铜　anode brass ◇普拉斯特~*
阳极辉点　anode spot
阳极回路　anode loop
阳极汇流排　anode busbar
阳极活度[性]　anode [anodic] activity
阳极极化　anodic polarization
阳极极化曲线　anodic polarization curve
阳极极化行为　anodic polarization behaviour
阳极计时电位测定法　anodic chronopotentiometry
阳极加工　fabrication of anodes
阳极检波　(同"阳极整流")
阳极溅射(处理)　anode sputtering
阳极浇铸模　anode casting mould
阳极接头　positive contact
阳极接线头　anode connection
阳极结构　anode construction ◇普通~*
阳极金属　anode [anodic] metal
"阳极-金属滴液"电子束炉　"anode-drop" furnace
阳极浸入深度　immersion depth of anode

阳 yang

阳极浸蚀 anode pickling
阳极聚合(作用) anodic polymerization
阳极孔径 anode aperture
阳极控制 anodic control
阳极块 anode block
阳极筐[篮] anode basket
阳极框架 anode frame [superstructure, carrier]
阳极扩散流 anodic diffusion current
阳极梁 anode beam
阳极炉 【色】anode furnace ◇ 旋转～
阳极炉炉渣 anode slag
阳极卤化作用 anodic halogenation
阳极氯化(作用) anodic chlorination
阳极面积 anode [anodic] area
阳极膜 anode film
阳极膜片 anode aperture
阳极母线 anode bus(bar), positive (bus-)bar
阳极泥 (anode) slime, anode sludge [mud], electrolyte [electrolytic] slime, anodic precipitate ◇ 沉积～ deposited slime, 海绵状～ slime sponge
阳极泥产出率 【色】yield of slime
阳极泥处理 (anode-)slime treatment, anode sludge treatment
阳极泥覆盖层 anode-slime blanket
阳极泥率 anode slime ratio
阳极镍 anode nickel
阳极抛光 anode [anodic] finish
阳极坯 green anode
阳极片 anode strip
阳极屏(蔽) anode shield, anodic shielding
阳极屏栅 anode-screening grid
阳极气体室 anodic gas chamber
阳极侵蚀 anodic etching
阳极清洗 anode [anodic] cleaning ◇ 马森内尔～法*
阳极区 anode portion [space], anodic area [zone]
阳极去极化剂 anodic depolarizer
阳极去油 anode [anodic] cleaning

阳极熔化炉 anode smelting furnace
阳极溶出伏安法 anodic stripping voltammetric method
阳极溶解 anodic dissolution, anode [anodic] solution ◇ 镀层～法 anodic stripping
阳极射束 anode stream
阳极射线 anode [positive] rays
阳极射线(电子)管 canal ray tube
阳极室 anode chamber [compartment, space]
阳极寿命 anode life
阳极输出器 anode follower
阳极刷(刷镀用) doctor
阳极碳 anode carbon
阳极碳块 anode block
阳极套 anode jacket
阳极特性 anode characteristic
阳极铜 anode copper
阳极铜铝合金 anodic copper-aluminium alloy
阳极涂层[涂料] anode [anodic] coating
阳极退火箱 anode annealing box
阳极脱脂 anode [anodic] cleaning
阳极尾杆 anode tail bar
阳极污染 target contamination
阳极吸附(作用) anodic adsorption
阳极相位 anodic phase
阳极箱 anode box
阳极消耗 anode consumption
阳极效率 anode efficiency
阳极效应 anode effect
阳极效应次数[系数] frequency of anode effect
阳极效应的发生 initiation of anode effect
阳极锌 anode zinc
阳极行为 anodic behaviour
阳极溴化(作用) anodic bromination
阳极旋动的 X 射线管 rotating-anode tube
阳极压制机 anode press
阳极氧化(处理) anodizing, anodization, anodising, anode [anodic] oxidation, an-

yang 阳　　　1612

odic (oxidation) treatment,【冶】passivating ◇ 吊篮式～basket anodizing,光亮～bright anodizing,滚筒式～barrel anodizing,经～的保护层 anodized coating,经～的铝 anodized aluminium,冷～*,连续～continuous anodizing,铜的～electrojetal,硬～*

阳极氧化处理槽　anodizing tank
阳极氧化处理层　anodized layer
阳极氧化处理电解液　anodizing electrolyte [solution]
阳极氧化处理用溶液　anodizing liquid
阳极氧化处理装置　anodizing plant
阳极氧化法　anodic oxidation process, aluminite process(轻金属的) ◇ 铝～*
阳极氧化膜　anodic oxide film
阳极氧化涂饰　anode [anodic] finish
阳极氧化着色处理　colour anodizing
阳极液　anolyte, anode liquor ◇ 含酸～*,碱性～*,污～foul anolyte
阳极液成分　anolyte composition
阳极液隔膜　anolyte membrane
阳极液配制[补给]槽　anolyte make-up tank
阳极液室　anolyte compartment
阳极液酸度　anolyte acidity
阳极液阳离子浓度　anolyte cation concentration
阳极液溢流　anolyte overflow
阳极液贮槽　anolyte (storage) tank
阳极抑制剂　anodic inhibitor
阳极-阴极面积比率　【电】anode-to-cathode ratio
阳极杂质　anode [anodic] impurity
阳极杂质特性　behaviour of anode impurity
阳极爪头　anode joint
阳极罩　anode cage [cap, hood]
阳极整流　anode(-bend) rectification
阳极支架[支柱]　anode support
阳极制备　anode preparation, preparation of anode

阳极制造　fabrication of anode
阳极质量　anode quality
阳极周期　anode period
阳极铸模　anode mould
阳极铸造　anode casting
阳极铸造工段　anode casting section
阳极铸造机　anode casting machine
阳极铸造炉　anode casting furnace
阳极装置　anode assembly
阳极组成　anode composition
阳极组分　anodic constituent
阳离子　cation, kation, basic ion, positively charged ion, positive [basic] ion ◇ 除去～(作用) decationizing,络～cationic complex
阳离子冲洗　cation rinse
阳离子导电率　cationic conductance
阳离子导体　cationic conductor
阳离子点阵位置[晶格结点]　cation lattice position
阳离子电泳沉积　cataphoretic deposition
阳离子电泳镀层　cataphoretic coating
阳离子隔膜　cation membrane
阳离子活度　cationoid activity
阳离子激活的　cation-active
阳离子极化　cation polarization
阳离子极化电位　cation polarization potential
阳离子交换　cation exchange
阳离子交换槽　cation cell
阳离子交换过程　cation exchange process
阳离子交换过滤器　cation exchange filter
阳离子交换回收　recovery by cation exchange
阳离子交换剂　cation exchanger, cation exchange material, cationite ◇ 磺化聚苯乙烯[聚苯乙烯磺酸型]～*,强酸性～*,弱酸性～*,羧酸～*,无机～*,液体～*
阳离子交换介质　cation exchange medium
阳离子交换膜　cation exchange membrane
阳离子交换能力　cation exchange ability

阳离子交换器　cation exchanger
阳离子交换设备　cation exchange unit
阳离子交换树脂　cation (exchange) resin ◇ 磺酚～*，有机～*
阳离子交换树脂选择性　cation resin selectivity
阳离子聚合电解质　cationic polyelectrolyte
阳离子空位　cation(ic) vacancy
阳离子空[缺]位位置　vacant cation site
阳离子络合物　cationic complex
阳离子浓度　cation concentration
阳离子去垢剂　cationic detergent
阳离子群药剂　【选】basic group reagent
阳离子树脂交换　cation resin exchange
阳离子树脂交换能力　cation resin capacity
阳离子树脂交换柱　cation (exchange) column, cation resin column
阳离子吸附　cation adsorption ◇ 无机～介质*
阳离子型离子交换　cationic type ion exchange
阳离子增亮剂　cationic brightener
阳模　positive [male] mould, male [movable] die, puncheon, formpiston, plunger ◇ 成形～【压】forming punch
阳模锻出肋条的锻件　male beaded forging
阳模座　stem holder
阳起石 $\{Ca_2(Mg, Fe)_5 \cdot Si_8O_{22}(OH)_2\}$　actinolite, actinote
阳台　【建】balcony
阳性基　positive group [radical]
阳性溶胶　positive sol
阳性元素　positive element
阳压模　positive mould
阳质子　proton
氧{O}　oxygen (Oxy.) ◇ 充～[用～处理]*，大量生产的[中纯度]～tonnage oxygen, 对～灵敏[敏感]的【金】oxygen-

sensitive, 供～oxygen supply, 含～的 oxygen-bearing, oxygen-containing, oxygenic, 用～饱和 oxygenating
氧-α铁固溶体　【金】oxyferrite
氧-γ铁固溶体　【金】oxyaustenite
氧苯吹管　oxy-benzene torch
氧苯焰　oxybenz flame
氧铋基　bismuthyl
氧差腐蚀(金属表面的)　aeration cell corrosion, differential aeration corrosion
氧-城市煤气切割　oxy-citygas cutting
氧处理　【冶】oxygenation
氧传递表面　oxygen-transfer surface
氧传输　oxygen transfer
氧弹量热计　oxygen-bomb calorimeter
氧的　oxygenic, oxygenous
氧等离子体切割　plasma oxygen cutting
氧碲基　telluryl
氧-丁烷焰　oxybutane flame
氧钒基　vanadyl
氧钒矿　doloresite
氧分析器　oxygen analyzer
氧分压　oxygen partial pressure (OPP)
氧腐蚀　oxygen-type corrosion
氧锆基$\{ZrO_2^+\}$　zirconyl
氧割喷粉　【焊】powder injection
氧钴根　cobaltyl
氧过电压　oxygen overvoltage
氧含量　oxygen content [level] ◇ 烟气中～测定*
氧焊的　oxywelded
氧焊炬阀　oxygen torch valve
氧弧　oxyarc
氧弧割炬[喷枪]　oxyarc [arc-oxygen] torch
氧弧切割　oxyarc cutting
氧弧切割电极　oxyarc cutting electrode
氧弧烧除铆钉　oxygen-arc derivetting
氧化　oxidation (Ox., oxid.), oxidization, oxidizing, oxidating, oxydation, burning (金属的) ◇ X射线作用下～X-ray oxidation, 催化去～*, 大气[空气]～atmo-

spheric oxidation, 电解 ~ electrooxidation, 防 ~ 剂*, 加压 ~ pressure oxidation, 抗[耐]~的*, 可[易]~的*, 抛物线 ~ *, 气相 ~ *, 弱 ~ slight oxidation, 受控 ~ controlled oxidation, 水溶液[水相]~*, 细菌 ~（法)*, 阳极 ~（处理)*, 抑制[阻止]~ oxidation inhibition, 用空气 ~ oxidation by air, air burning, 中止 ~【钢】blocked heat, 自发[自行]~*

氧化锕 actinium oxide
氧化奥氏体 【金】oxyaustenite
氧化钯 palladium (mon)oxide
氧化薄膜 film of oxide
氧化薄膜复型 oxide film replica
氧化钡{BaO} barium oxide, baria, baryta ◇ 煅烧 ~ calcined baryta
氧化钡砖 baryta brick
氧化焙烧 oxidizing roasting, air roasting, roasting in air ◇ 半~*, 部分 ~ *, 全脱硫 ~ sweet roast(ing), 蒸馏 ~ *
氧化焙烧炉 oxidizing roaster
氧化铋{$Bi_2O_3 \cdot Bi_2O_4$, Bi_2O_5} bismuth oxide
氧化表面 oxidized surface
氧化铂 platinum oxide
氧化钚 plutonium oxide
氧化残渣 oxidation residue
氧化槽 oxidizing tank
氧化层 oxide layer ◇ 疏松的 ~ loosened oxide
氧化产物 oxidation product
氧化程度 degree of oxidation
氧化重整 oxidation reforming ◇ 部分 ~ *
氧化处理 oxidizing [oxidation] treatment ◇ 布伦诺克斯发黑 ~ *, 杰塔尔－法 Jetal
氧化促进剂 oxidation promotor [accelerator]
氧化催化剂 oxidation [oxidative] catalyst, oxydization catalyzer

氧化带 oxidation [oxidizing] zone
氧化氮{NO} nitrogen oxide（通常指一氧化氮）, nitric oxide
氧化氮分离器 nitric oxide separator
氧化锝 technetium oxide
氧化镝{Dy_2O_3} dysprosium oxide, dysprosia
氧化碲 tellurium oxide
氧化电极 oxidizing electrode
氧化电位 oxidation potential
氧化铥{Tu_2O_3} thulium oxide, thulia
氧化动力学 oxidation kinetics
氧化度 oxidability, oxidizability
氧化锇 osmium oxide
氧化铒{Er_2O_3} erbium oxide, erbia
氧化发黑处理(钢的) black oxide finish [treatment] ◇ 表面 ~ *
氧化法 oxidation [oxidizing] process
氧化法测晶粒度 oxidation grain size
氧化法除锌 dezincing by oxidation
氧化钒{V_2O, VO, V_2O_3, VO_2, V_2O_5} vanadium oxide
氧化钒腐蚀 corrosion by vanadium pentoxide
氧化反应 oxidation [oxidizing] reaction
氧化钫 francium oxide
氧化防护 oxidation protection
氧化沸腾 【钢】oxidizing boil
氧化腐蚀 oxidation(al) etching
氧化钆{Gd_2O_3} gadolinium (sesqui)oxide, gadolinia
氧化钙{CaO} calcium oxide, calcia, (quick)lime ◇ 纯 ~ *
氧化钙坩埚 lime crucible
氧化高钴{Co_2O_3} cobaltic oxide
氧化高压釜 oxidation autoclave
氧化锆{ZrO_2} zirconium oxide [anhydride], zirconia ◇ 石灰稳定的 ~ *
氧化锆测氧仪 zirconium oxide oxygen measuring meter
氧化锆管加热炉 zirconia tube furnace
氧化锆涂层 zirconia coating

氧化锆砖　zirconia brick
氧化镉　cadmium oxide
氧化铬{Cr_2O_3}　chromium [chrome, chromic] oxide
氧化铬鳞皮(不锈钢的)　chromium oxide scale
氧化铬耐火砖　(同"铬砖")
氧化铬-氧化镁耐火砖　(同"铬镁砖")
氧化汞{HgO}　mercuric oxide
氧化钴{CoO}　cobaltous [cobalt] oxide
氧化硅　silicon oxide ◇ 胶态～ colloidal silica
氧化硅耐火砖　silica firebrick
氧化硅-氧化铝型杂质　silica-alumina-type impurity
氧化过程　oxidation [oxidative] process
氧化铪　hafnium oxide ◇ 水合～*
氧化铪氯化　chlorination of hafnium oxide
氧化化合物　oxygenated compound
氧化还原　oxidoreduction, oxidation-reduction, redox
氧化还原焙烧　oxidizing-reducing roasting
氧化还原滴定　redox [oxidation-reduction] titration
氧化还原电池　oxidation-reduction cell
氧化还原电位　redox [oxidation-reduction] potential
氧化还原法　redox [oxidation-reduction] process, oxidoreduction
氧化还原反应　redox [oxidation-reduction] reaction
氧化还原过程　redox process
氧化还原曲线　redox diagram
氧化还原系统　redox [oxidation-reduction] system
氧化还原循环　oxidation-reduction cycle
氧化还原指示剂　redox indicator
氧化还原作用　oxidation-reduction, redox
氧化挥发焙烧　oxidizing volatilization roasting
氧化钬{Ho_2O_3}　holmium oxide, holmia
氧化剂　oxidizer (Ox., ox.), oxidant, oxidation agent, oxygenant, oxidizing agent [material] ◇ 富～混合物 oxidant-rich mixture
氧化剂冷却的　oxidizer-cooled
氧化夹杂印相法　【钢】oxide printing
氧化钾{K_2O}　potassium oxide
氧化金　gold oxide
氧化浸出　oxidizing leach, oxidative leaching, leaching under oxidizing conditions ◇ 水溶液～*, 直接～*
氧化精炼　oxidizing refining, oxidation softening [improving] (粗铅的)
氧化精炼除锌法　dezincing by oxidation
氧化锔　curium oxide
氧化钪{Sc_2O_3}　scandium oxide
氧化矿　oxidized [oxide-bearing] ore ◇ 贫～*
氧化矿还原　reduction of oxide ore
氧化矿物　oxidized mineral
氧化铼　rhenium oxide
氧化蓝边(板材退火的)　blued edge
氧化镧{La_2O_3}　lanthanum oxide, lanthana
氧化离子　oxidizing ion
氧化锂{Li_2O}　lithium oxide, lithia
氧化沥青　(同"吹制沥青")
氧化力　oxidizing power
氧化裂片合金　fissia
氧化硫的细菌　sulphide-oxidizing bacteria
氧化硫杆菌　thiobacillus thiooxidans
氧化硫化矿　oxidizing sulphide ore
氧化硫铁杆菌　ferrobacillus sulfooxidans
氧化巯　sulphoxonium
氧化炉　oxidizing [oxidation] furnace
氧化镥{Lu_2O_3}　lutecium oxide, lutecia
氧化铝{Al_2O_3}　aluminium oxide, alumina, alumine ◇ α型～*, γ型～*, 等外级[不合格]～ off-grade alumina, 淀粉状～ starchy alumina, 煅烧～ calcined alumina, 高安息角～*, 工业～ commercial alumina, 固体～ solid alumina, 过渡型～*, 哈达斯～膜处理法 Hardas pro-

cess,硬质～膜处理法 alumilite method, 活性～ activated alumina,胶态～ colloidal alumina,结晶～ crystal alumina,可提取～ extractable alumina,良好再结晶～",良好再结晶～",面粉状～ floury alumina,泡沫～ foamed alumina,平板状～ tabular alumina,熔融［液态］～ molten [fused] alumina,砂状～ sandy alumina,烧结～ sintered alumina,亚稳［中间］型～ intermediate alumina,一水～",游离～ free alumina

氧化铝保护管 alumina protection [guard] tube

氧化铝层 alumina layer

氧化铝厂 alumina plant [producer, refinery], bauxite refining plant ◇ 拜耳法～ Bayer plant

氧化铝煅烧车间[设备] alumina-calcination plant

氧化铝分类 classification of aluminas

氧化铝粉 alumina [alundum] powder, powdered alumina ◇ 细～（抛光用）abradum

氧化铝粉尘 alumina dust

氧化铝钙 galumin

氧化铝干燥剂 alumina dryer

氧化铝工业 alumina industry

氧化铝管 alumina [alundum] tube

氧化铝管马弗炉 alundum tube muffle furnace

氧化铝结疤 alumina scale

氧化铝绝缘 alumina insulation

氧化铝磨料 adamite

氧化铝耐火砖 alumina firebrick ◇ 中级～"

氧化铝凝胶 alumina gel

氧化铝浓度 alumina concentration

氧化铝球 alumina ball

氧化铝水合物 {$Al_2O_3 \cdot 3H_2O$ 或 $Al_2O_3 \cdot H_2O$} alumina hydrate, hydrate of aluminium oxide

氧化铝涂层 alumina coat

氧化铝-氧化硅耐火砖 （同"硅铝砖"）

氧化铝制品 alumina product

氧化铝质耐火材料 alumina refractory

氧化铝贮仓 alumina silo

氧化铝贮罐 alumina container

氧化铝砖 alumina brick ◇ 熔铸～ fuse cast alumina

氧化率 【化】rate of burning

氧化麻点 【压】scale mark

氧化镅 americium oxide

氧化镁 {MgO} magnesium oxide, magnesia ◇ 苛性～ caustic magnesia,死烧～ dead burned magnesia

氧化镁粉 magnesia powder

氧化镁坩埚 magnesia crucible

氧化镁绝缘涂层 magnesium oxide insulated coat (MIC)

氧化镁乳剂 milk of magnesia

氧化镁添加剂 magnesia addition

氧化锰 manganese oxide ◇ 铅色～"

氧化膜 oxide film [skin], oxidation [tarnish] film ◇ M.B.V.铝～生成法", 除去表面～ detarnish,带色薄金属～电沉积法 electro-colour process,晶间～",热处理～ heat treating film

氧化膜生成能力 film forming capacity

氧化膜保护 protection by oxide films

氧化膜复型检验法 oxide replica technique

氧化膜破裂腐蚀 break away corrosion

氧化膜色 heat tine, hot tinting

氧化膜形成 oxide film formation

氧化钼 molybdenum oxide, molybdena

氧化镎 neptunium oxide

氧化钠 {Na_2O} sodium oxide, natron

氧化能 energy by oxidation

氧化能力 oxidizing ability, oxidability

氧化铌 niobium [columbium] oxide

氧化镍 {NiO} nickel(ous) oxide

氧化钕 {Nd_2O_3} neodymium (sesqui) oxide, neodymia

氧化钕镨 didymium oxide, didymia

氧 yang

氧化铍{BeO}　beryllium oxide, beryllia, berillia
氧化铍阀板　beryllia valve plate
氧化铍阀座　beryllia valve seat
氧化铍坩埚　beryllia crucible ◇ 烧结～*
氧化铍管　beryllia tubing
氧化铍耐火材料　beryllia refractory
氧化铍陶瓷　beryllia ceramics
氧化皮　oxide scale [skin], roll scale, firecoat, skull (钢锭表面的), mill cinder (轧制时形成的) ◇ 不生～的 non-scaling, 残余～层, 冲洗～*, 初次～*, 除～液 descaling solution, 打～锤 descaling hammer, 大块～收集箱 butt box, 干法排除～ dry-scale disposal, 花纹～*, 抗～化合物*, 磨除～ abrasive descaling, 黏附牢固的～ tight scale, 嵌入表面的～*, 清除～用沟[槽] scale flume, 去[消除]～*, 生成～ scaling, 湿法清除～ wet-scale disposal, 疏松的～ loose scale, 水冲除的～*, 通电去除～法*, 无～的 free from scale, 一次～*, 正火[常化]～*
氧化皮疤(钢锭的)　cinder patch
氧化皮沉淀池[槽]　scale settling tank ◇ 用抓斗清理的～[压] grab bucket sump
氧化皮沉积池　scale sump
氧化皮冲除箱　descaling box
氧化皮冲洗沟　flushing flume, channel
氧化皮处理系统　scale removal [handling] system
氧化皮堆　cinder dump
氧化皮覆盖面　scale-coated surface
氧化皮沟道排除系统　scale-sluice system
氧化皮壳(钢锭的)　scale jacket
氧化皮坑　scale pit (SP)
氧化皮排除系统　scale removal [handling] system
氧化皮清除机　scale breaker, descaler
氧化皮清除炉(板材的)　descaling furnace
氧化皮清理炬　descaling torch
氧化皮收集槽[沟]　scale flume
氧化皮收集器　scale trap
氧化皮收集斜槽　scaled-deflector chute
氧化皮损失[损耗]　【压】scale [scaling] loss
氧化皮形成　【压】scale formation
氧化镨{Pr₂O₃}　praseodymium sesquioxide [peroxide], praseodymia
氧化期　【冶】oxidation [oxidizing] period
氧化起鳞　scaling ◇ 耐～能力 resistance to scaling
氧化起鳞速率　scaling rate
氧化气氛　oxidative [oxidizing] atmosphere ◇ 钢的～加热*
氧化气氛炉　oxidizing furnace
氧化气体　oxidizing gas
氧化铅{PbO}　(yellow) lead oxide, yellow lead, litharge, litarge, lead monoxide ◇ 含铁～ iron minium
氧化铅渣　litharge slag
氧化倾向大的金属　oxygen hungry metal
氧化球团　【团】acid pellet ◇ 固结[焙烧]～ hardened oxide pellet
氧化球团竖炉　oxide pellet shaft furnace
氧化区　(同"氧化带")
氧化热　oxidation heat, heat of oxidation
氧化熔剂　oxidizing flux
氧化熔炼　oxidizing smelting [melting, fusion]
氧化溶解　oxidic solubility
氧化铷{Rb₂O}　rubidium oxide
氧化色　oxidation tint, heat colour ◇ 发蓝～ blued
氧化色检验　checking by blu(e)ing
氧化铯{Cs₂O}　cesium oxide
氧化钐{Sm₂O₃}　samarium oxide, samaria
氧化烧损　iron loss due to scale formation
氧化石油沥青(贝尔勒法生产的)　byerlyte
氧化铈{CeO₂}　ceria
氧化室　oxidation chamber
氧化锶{SrO}　strontium oxide, strontia
氧化水解反应　oxydrolysis
氧化水解高压釜　oxydrolysis autoclave

氧化水解回路[系统] oxydrolysis circuit
氧化速度[速率] oxidation speed [rate]
氧化损失 oxidation(al) [oxidizing, oxidic] loss
氧化铊 {Tl$_2$O, Tl$_2$O$_3$} thallium oxide
氧化塔 oxidation column
氧化态 oxidation state
氧化钛 titanium oxide
氧化钛药皮焊条 rutile(-type) electrode
氧化钽 {TaO$_2$, Ta$_2$O$_5$} tantalum oxide
氧化铽 {Tb$_2$O$_3$} terbium (sesqui)oxide, terbia
氧化锑 {Sb$_2$O$_3$} antimony oxide [bloom]
氧化条件 oxidized [oxidizing] condition
氧化铁 iron [ferric] oxide ◇ 蓝~残渣 (约50%铁) blue billy, 泥土状~ earthy iron oxide
氧化铁薄膜覆层 sull-coating
氧化铁残渣 iron oxide residue
氧化铁杆菌 ferrobacillus ferrooxidans
氧化铁还原 iron oxides reduction
氧化铁还原速度 iron oxides reduction speed
氧化铁夹杂(物) iron oxide inclusion
氧化铁矿石烧结(法) agglomeration of iron oxide ore
氧化铁硫杆菌 thiobacillus ferrooxidans
氧化铁抛光粉 【金】rouge
氧化铁皮 (iron) scale, iron oxide scale, rolling [air, fire, mill] scale ◇ 不结~的 resistant to scaling, 不结~钢 scale-resisting steel, 冲~水泵 scale pusher water pump, 打落~ scale knocking, 复合~形成*, 含砂~ gritty scale, 厚~ heavy scale, 清除~ removal scale
氧化铁皮斑点 kisser
氧化铁皮坑 scale pit (SP), cinder pit
氧化铁皮排除沟 sluiceway
氧化铁皮敲打锤 scale [scaling] hammer
氧化铁皮清除机[器](锭、坯的) descaling machine, (de)scaler
氧化铁皮添加料 roll-scale additions
氧化铁皮细孔 scale pore
氧化铁皮形成 (oxide) scale formation
氧化铁皮压入 rolled-in scale
氧化铁皮印痕 scale mark
氧化铁素体 【金】oxyferrite
氧化铁型电焊条 iron oxide type electrode
氧化铁型药皮 【焊】iron oxide coating
氧化铁研磨粉 crocus
氧化铜 copper [cupric] oxide, aerugo
氧化铜电池 cupron cell
氧化铜皮 copper scale
氧化铜渣 copper oxide slag
氧化铜整流器 (copper-)oxide rectifier, rector
氧化钍 {ThO$_2$} thorium oxide, thoria ◇ 钙还原~法*, 加~ thoriate
氧化钍白炽灯 Nernst lamp
氧化钍电阻炉 thoria resistor furnace
氧化钍基电阻 thoria-base resistor
氧化钍弥散镍 thoria dispersed nickel, TD nickel
氧化钍耐火材料 thoria refractory
氧化钍强化镍 thoriastrengthened nickel
氧化脱锌 dezincing by oxidation
氧化稳定性 oxidation stability
氧化钨 tungsten oxide, tungstic acid anhydride ◇ 褐色~*, 黄色~*
氧化物 oxide (compound), oxidate ◇ 低价~ suboxide, 含~的 oxidiferous, 含~矿石*, 活性~ active oxide, 夹杂~【冶】included oxide, 加入的~ input oxide, 泥质~ earth oxide, 片状~*, 涂~灯丝 oxide coated filament, 无[不含]~的 oxide-free, 游离~ free oxide
氧化物斑点 oxide patch, oxide speck (金属内的)
氧化物半导体 oxide semiconductor
氧化物薄膜 thin oxide coating
氧化物残渣 oxide residue
氧化物层 oxide layer
氧化物层剥裂 break away of oxide layer
氧化物衬里 oxide liner

氧化物磁铁　oxide magnet
氧化物电解　oxide electrolysis
氧化物电阻　oxide resistor
氧化物电阻炉　oxide resistor furnace, electric furnace with oxide resistor
氧化物煅烧　calcination of oxides
氧化物粉末　oxide powder, powdered oxide
氧化物浮渣(铅精炼的)　oxide dross
氧化物高温超导体系　high temperature oxide superconductor system
氧化物(核)燃料　oxide (nuclear) fuel
氧化物还原　oxide reduction
氧化物混合物　oxide mixture
氧化物基金属陶瓷　oxide-base cermet
氧化物夹杂　oxide inclusions
氧化物键　oxide bond [bridging]
氧化物－金属型金属陶瓷　oxide-metal type cermet
氧化物晶体　oxide crystal
氧化物矿物　oxide mineral
氧化物扩散　diffusion of oxide
氧化物粒度　oxide particle size
氧化物连接　oxide bond
氧化物炉瘤[结块]　oxide accretion
氧化物炉渣　oxide slag
氧化物氯化　chlorination of oxides
氧化物－氯化物转化法　oxide-chloride conversion process
氧化物氯氢化　hydrochlorination of oxides
氧化物弥散强化　oxide-dispersion strengthening
氧化物弥散强化材料　oxide dispersion strengthened material
氧化物弥散强化合金　oxide-dispersion strengthened alloy, OD (oxide-dispersed) alloy
氧化物弥散强化金属　oxide-dispersion strengthened alloy, OD (oxide-dispersed) alloy
氧化物膜　oxide film ◇ 绝缘～insulating oxide film

氧化物耐火材料　oxide refractories
氧化物黏结碳化硅　oxide-bonded silicon carbide
氧化物氢氟化　hydrofluorination of oxides
氧化物陶瓷　oxide ceramics
氧化物添加剂　oxide addition
氧化物涂层　oxide coating
氧化物纤维　oxide-fiber
氧化物相　oxide phase
氧化物相集合体　oxide phase assembly
氧化物型夹杂物　oxide type inclusions
氧化行为　oxidation behaviour
氧化物烟尘　oxide flue dust
氧化物烟气　oxide gas
氧化物阴极　oxide cathode
氧化物杂质　oxide impurity
氧化物蒸馏　oxide distillation
氧化物装料　oxide charge
氧化硒　selenium oxide
氧化锡　tin oxide [ash] {SnO, SnO$_2$}, stannic oxide {SnO$_2$} ◇ 金属～浮渣[镀锡 槽内形成的～] scruff
氧化稀土　(同"稀土氧化物")
氧化锌{ZnO}　zinc oxide, zincite ◇ 活性～active zinc oxide, 未经加工的～tutty, 无铅～lead-free zinc oxide
氧化锌薄膜　zinc-oxide film
氧化锌焙砂　zinc-oxide calcine
氧化锌粉　dust of zinc oxide
氧化性　oxidability, oxidizability, oxidizing property ◇ 可～oxidizability
氧化性能　oxidizable nature, oxidizing character, oxidation behaviour
氧化性气氛　oxidizing atmosphere
氧化性球团(矿)　oxidized pellet
氧化性渣　oxidic slag
氧化性质　oxidizing property
氧化溴　bromine oxide
氧化压力　oxidizing pressure
氧化亚铂　platinous oxide
氧化亚氮{N$_2$O}　nitrous oxide
氧化亚钒{V$_2$O$_3$}　vanadous oxide

氧化亚汞 {Hg_2O} mercurous oxide
氧化亚钴 {CoO} cobaltous oxide
氧化亚铊 {Tl_2O} thallous oxide, thallium monoxide
氧化亚铁 {FeO} ferrous oxide, iron protoxide ◇ 无隙~团块
氧化亚铁含量 ferrous iron value
氧化亚铁人造矿体 Wuestite
氧化亚铜 {Cu_2O} cuprous oxide, copper suboxide, red oxide of copper
氧化亚铜光电管[元件] cuprous oxide photocell
氧化亚锡 {SnO} stannous oxide, tin protoxide
氧化亚银 argentous oxide
氧化盐 oxidized [oxidizing] salt
氧化焰 oxidizing flame
氧化焰烧成 [耐]oxidizing burning
氧化钇 {Y_2O_3} yttria, yttrium oxide
氧化镱 {Yb_2O_3} ytterbia, ytterbium oxide
氧化铟 {In_2O_3} indium oxide
氧化银 silver oxide
氧化铀 uranium oxide ◇ 高价~ higher uranium oxide
氧化铀坩埚 urania crucible
氧化铕 {Eu_2O_3} europium oxide, europia
氧化渣 oxidizing slag
氧化锗 {GeO, GeO_2} germanium oxide
氧化蒸馏 oxidation distillation
氧化正亚铁 （同"四氧化三铁"）
氧化柱 oxidation column
氧化状态 oxidative state
氧化作用 oxidation (action, effect), oxidizing action, oxydation, oxidization
氧荒酸 xanthic [xanthogenic] acid
氧基醇 {$RCOCH_2OH$} keto-alcohol
氧基化合物 oxycompound
氧晶格 oxygen lattice
氧炬切割 lance cutting
氧利用率 oxygen efficiency

氧量计 oxymeter
氧料比 oxygen-charge ratio
氧磷灰石 {$10CaO·3P_2O_5$} voelckerite
氧硫铋矿 bolivite
氧流 oxygen flow, [冶]oxygen blast
氧矛 oxygen lance
氧矛把柄 【焊】oxygen lance holder
氧矛切割 oxygen lancing, oxygen lance cutting ◇ 加填料~ packed (tube) lancing
氧煤炼铁 coal injection with oxygen blast in ironmaking
氧煤气焰 oxycoal-gas flame
氧煤枪 【铁】oxy-gen-coal lance, coal-oxygen gun
氧煤燃烧器（高炉用） oxy-coal burner
氧钼根 molybdyl
氧钼基 {$MoO-, MoO_2=, MoO\equiv$} molybdenyl
氧浓差电池 differential aeration cell, oxygen concentration cell
氧浓差腐蚀 differential oxygenation corrosion, oxygen concentration corrosion
氧平衡（炸药的） oxygen balance (OB)
氧气 (gaseous) oxygen, oxygen gas ◇ 切割用~ cutting oxygen
氧气表面切割 oxygen gouging [machining]
氧气丙烷焰 oxypropane flame
氧气丙烷焰焊接 oxypropane welding
氧气丙烷焰切割 oxy-propane cutting
氧气侧吹转炉 oxygen side blown converter
氧气厂 oxygen installation
氧气车间 oxygen making plant
氧气－城市煤气切割 oxy-town-gas [oxy-city-gas] cutting
氧气－城市煤气烧嘴 oxy-town gas burners
氧气冲击速度 impact velocity of oxygen
氧气吹炼 oxygen blowing
氧气吹炼的钢 oxygen steel

氧气底吹炼铅法 Queneau-Schuhmann-Lurgi process
氧气底吹炼铅反应器 QSL reactor
氧气底吹转炉 oxygen bottom blown converter
氧气电池 oxygen [aeration] cell
氧气电弧切割 arcoxygen cutting
氧气顶吹 【钢】oxygen-top blowing
氧气顶吹炼钢工艺 top-blowing technique
氧气顶吹-斜吹转炉炼钢法 LD-Kaldo process
氧气顶吹转炉 BOF (Basic Oxygen Furnace), BOP (Basic Oxygen Process) converter, LD (Linz-Donawitz) converter [furnace, vessel], oxygen top-blown converter ◇ 碱性～*, 炉口对称型～ symmetric LD furnace, 罗托弗特高速旋转～法 Rotovert process, 喷石灰粉～*
氧气顶吹转炉车间 LD [BOF, BOP] plant
氧气顶吹转炉炼钢法 L-D (Linz-Donawitz) process
氧气发生器 oxygen generator
氧气阀 oxygen valve
氧气氛 oxygen atmosphere
氧气分解(作用) oxygenolysis
氧气分析器 oxygen gas analyzer ◇ 顺磁式～*
氧气风口 【钢】oxygen-tuyere
氧气腐蚀 corrosion by oxygen
氧气钢 oxygen steel
氧气割炬 oxygen cutting torch
氧气供入速度 【冶】rate of oxygen input
氧气鼓风 blast oxygen
氧气管道 oxygen (pipe) line
氧气呼吸器 oxygen breathing apparatus
氧气火焰(表面)切削加工 oxygen machining
氧气(火焰)切割机 oxygen cutting machine ◇ 平行四边形～oxygraph
氧气记录仪 oxygen recorder
氧气碱性转炉炼钢法 (同"碱性氧气转炉炼钢法")
氧气精整器 flame scarfer
氧气空气混合物 【冶】oxygen-air mixture
氧气库 oxygen store
氧气炼钢(法) oxygen steelmaking (OSM), oxygen-steel process
氧气炼钢旋转炉 rotating oxygen-blown steelmaking vessel
氧气流 oxygen stream
氧气流冲击 oxygen impingement
氧气流冲击区 impact area of jet
氧气流量计 oxygen-flow indicator
氧气煤油切割 oxy-kerosene cutting
氧气泡 oxygen bubble
氧气喷粉管(喷石灰粉) oxygen powder lance
氧气喷管 【铁】oxygen nozzle
氧气喷枪 【钢】oxygen lance [jet] ◇ 水冷～water-cooled lance
氧气喷嘴 【钢】oxygen jet [orifice], 【铁】oxygen nozzle
氧气平吹旋转转炉 Rotor
氧气平吹旋转转炉炼钢法 Rotor process
氧气瓶 oxygen cylinder [tank, bottle], (gas) bomb
氧气瓶阀 oxygen cylinder valve
氧气歧管 【焊】oxygen manifold
氧气切割 oxygen cutting (OC), oxycutting, oxygen machining, flame cutting, gas cutting, lancing
氧气切割阀 cutting valve
氧气切割法 oxygen cutting process
氧气切割工 oxygen cutting operator
氧气切割流 cutting-oxygen stream [jet]
氧气切割面 oxygen-cut surface
氧气切割喷嘴 cutting nozzle
氧气切割器[烧把] oxygen cutter
氧气切割设备 oxygen cutting equipment
氧气燃料精炼 oxygen-fuel refining
氧气燃料燃烧器 oxy-fuel burners
氧气燃料熔炼 oxy-fuel smelting
氧气燃气比率 oxygen-fuel gas ratio,

氧气熔剂切割 flux (injection) cutting, flux oxygen cutting
氧气熔炼 oxygen smelting
氧气软管 oxygen hose
氧气闪速熔炼 【色】oxygen flash smelting
氧气天然气烧嘴 oxy-natural gas burner
氧气天然气焰 oxy-natural gas flame
氧气天然气焰切割 oxy-natural gas cutting
氧气稳态平衡 steady state oxygen balance
氧气消耗量(通过氧枪吹入的) 【钢】rate of lancing
氧气压力 【冶】oxygen pressure
氧气压力计 oxygen manometer
氧气压力调节器 oxygen pressure regulator
氧气-乙炔气比率 oxygen-acetylene ratio
氧气转炉 【钢】oxygen(-blown) converter
氧气转炉钢(顶吹的) oxygen converter steel
氧气转炉高磷生铁块状石灰炼钢法 L.D.K. process
氧气转炉炼钢 oxygen converter steelmaking
氧气转炉炼钢厂[车间] oxygen converter(steel) plant
氧气转炉炼钢法 oxygen-converter process (OCP), oxygen steelmaking process, oxygen-blown process
氧气转炉内高磷生铁块状石灰炼钢法 ◇ LDK~L.D.K. process
氧气转炉烟气干法净化技术 dry cleaning technology for converter flue gas
氧枪 oxygen (core) lance, 【钢】lance ◇ 单孔拉瓦尔~*，单流道双流~*，煤粉保护底吹~*，三孔拉瓦尔~*，双层分流式~*，双流~*
氧枪除渣法 spear slagging
氧枪导轨 lance guide
氧枪吊车 lance handling crane
氧枪高度[距离] 【钢】lance height [distance]
氧枪滑架 oxygen lance carriage
氧枪搅拌平衡 lance bubbling equilibrium (LBE)
氧枪搅拌平衡复合吹炼法 BOF-LBE process
氧枪喷头 oxygen lance head, lance-tip ◇ 4孔~ four nozzles oxygen lance
氧枪喷头至金属熔池距离 lance-tip metal distance
氧枪枪头 lance nozzle
氧枪提升机构 lance hoist
氧切 burning ◇ 铁粉~法 oxweld cutting process
氧去极化腐蚀 oxygen-absorption [oxygen-consumption, oxygen-reduction] corrosion
氧炔焊 oxyacetylene welding
氧炔切割器 oxyacetylene cutter
氧炔焰 oxyacetylene flame ◇ 加熔剂~焊接*
氧炔焰(加热)表面淬火 autogenous hardening
氧炔焰硬钎焊 gas flame brazing
氧-燃料反射炉 oxy-fuel reverberatory
氧燃料火焰加热表面淬火 oxy-fuel flame surface hardening
氧燃气火焰切割 oxy-fuel gas cutting
氧熔剂表面清理 powder deseaming
氧熔剂表面缺陷烧除器 powder deseaming burner
氧熔剂穿孔 powder lancing
氧熔剂割嘴(喷)孔 cutting-oxygen (jet) orifice, cutting oxygen nozzle bore
氧熔剂火焰清理 powder scarfing [washing]
氧熔剂烧除器 powder washing burner
氧熔剂切割 flux oxygen cutting, oxy-flux [metal-powder] cutting, chemical flux cutting, powder lancing [cut]

氧熔剂切割法（高合金钢的） powder cutting process
氧熔剂切割器 powder cutting burner
氧熔剂烧割 powder burning
氧溶解 oxygen dissolution
氧探针 oxygen probe
氧锑根(基) antimonyl
氧调节记录器 oxygen controller recorder
氧鎓 oxonium
氧鎓化合物 oxonium compound
氧鎓离子 oxonium ion
氧鎓型 oxonium form
氧鎓盐 oxonium salt
氧污染 oxygen contamination
氧硒基 selenyl
氧硒矿 selenolite
氧吸附 oxygen adsorption
氧吸收 oxygen uptake [absorption]
氧效率 oxygen efficiency
氧压计 oxygen manometer
氧压浸出 oxygen pressure leaching
氧氩侧吹转炉炼钢法（联合碳化物公司的） Union Carbide process
氧焰切割 oxy-fuel cutting ◇带金属粉末的～ metal-powder cutting, 移动式～机小车 secator
氧焰清理(焊缝的) oxygen deseaming ◇喷铁粉～ powder washing
氧焰清理机 flame planer
氧液化(石油)气切割 oxy-L.P. gas cutting
氧乙炔 oxyacetylene
氧乙炔割炬 oxyacetylene cutting torch
氧乙炔焊(接) oxyacetylene welding (OAW)
氧乙炔焊缝 oxyacetylene weld
氧乙炔焊炬 oxyacetylene (welding) torch, oxyacetylene blowpipe
氧乙炔混合气 【焊】oxyacetylene mixture
氧乙炔(火)焰 oxyacetylene flame ◇高温～*
氧乙炔火焰清理 oxyacetylene scarfing
氧乙炔火焰清理机 oxyacetylene scarfing machine
氧乙炔气 【焊】oxyacetylene gas
氧乙炔气压焊[加压气焊] oxyacetylene pressure welding
氧乙炔钎焊 oxyacetylene brazing
氧乙炔切割设备 oxyacetylene cutting equipment
氧乙炔焰表面淬火 oxyacetylene surface hardening ◇多佩尔杜罗～法 Doppelduro process
氧乙炔焰表面切割 oxyacetylene (flame) gouging
氧乙炔焰加热 oxyacetylene heating
氧乙炔焰切割 oxyacetylene cutting
氧乙炔焰切割的切口 oxyacetylene cut
氧乙炔焰切割机 oxyacetylene cutting machine
氧乙炔焰烧剥修整 【焊】oxyacetylene deseaming
氧乙炔焰中心区 acetylene feather
氧乙炔钻孔 oxyacetylene boring
氧载体 carrier of oxygen
氧值 oxygen value
仰俯式堆料机 luffing stacker
仰俯式装船机 luff-shiploader
仰拱 【建】invert(ed) [inflected] arch
仰拱底 【建】bottom of invert
仰拱结构 【建】invert arch construction
仰焊 overhead (position) welding, uphand [inverted] welding
仰焊焊缝 overhead weld
仰焊位置 overhead (welding) position
仰焊用焊条 overhead electrode
养护 maintenance (mtce), curing (混凝土的) ◇高湿度～室*, 加速～的(混凝土) rapid-curing, 交替～ alternating curing, 铺湿砂～混凝土 wet sand cure of concrete, 现场～的 job-cured, 逾期～ deferred maintenance
养护覆盖 【建】curing mats
养护工 maintainer

养护剂 【建】curing agent [compound]	腰带扭转台 web twisting table

养护剂 【建】curing agent [compound]
养护温度 curing temperature
养护(周)期 curing period [cycle]
养路机 maintainer
样板 template, templet, shaping [sample] plate, master (plate), (control) gauge former ◇ 按～加工 finish(ing) to templet [gauge], 按～手工切削 【机】guided manual cutting, 车削轧辊用～ roll-turning template, 大～【机】macrotemplate, 混凝土振动～*, 下型芯用～*, 型芯～【铸】core template
样板规 shape gauge
样机 sample [test] machine, prototype (machine), model (machine)
样机(试制)工厂 prototype plant
样件 sample piece
样模 sampling mold
样品 (proof, test) sample, specimen (sp., spec.), prototype
样品材料 specimen material
样品尺寸 sample size
样品夹 sample [specimen] holder
样品间[室] sample [specimen] chamber
样品瓶 sample bulb
样品屏 specimen screen
样品试验 sample [specimen] test
样品台调节装置 specimen stage controls
样品头 specimen head
样品研磨机 sample grinder
样品有限尺寸引起的增宽 broadening due to finite specimen size
样值 【计】sample (value)
腰板端部焊机 web end welder
腰板活套装置系统(焊接型材的) web looper system
腰板矫直机(型材用) web leveller
腰边镦厚机 web edge upsetter
腰部厚度(工字钢的) web thickness
腰带 waistband, belt, girdle
腰带夹送辊(焊接工字钢的) web pinch roll

腰带扭转台 web twisting table
腰拱 rider arch
腰鼓炉 rotary smelting furnace
腰裂(初轧坯缺陷) 【压】waisting
腰预镦粗机(焊接型材的) web up-setter
摇把 cranking bar, handgrip, handhold, starting crank
摇摆 swing, rocking [wobbling] motion, rocking
摇摆机构 【机】wabbler (mechanism)
摇摆式冷轧管机 rockright mill
摇摆运输机 swinging [shaking] conveyer
摇摆周期 time of swing
摇臂 rocking arm, swing arm [bracket], rocker (arm, lever)
摇臂式(分批)酸洗机 arm [rocker-type] pickling machine
摇臂式点焊机 rocker-arm spot welder
摇臂式焊钳 rocker gun
摇臂轴 【机】balance beam
摇臂钻床 radial drilling machine, radial drill
摇表 megger, megameter, tramegger
摇床 table (classifier, concentrator), shaking [pendulum] table, wabbler ◇ 活底～ car deck, 精选～ concentrating table, 碰撞式[振动]～ percussion table, 威尔弗莱型～ Wilfley table
摇床处理 table treatment
摇床精选 table concentration
摇床尾矿 【选】table tailings
摇床选矿 tabling (tabl.), table work, rocking
摇动 shaking, swinging, rocking (motion), wobbling motion, jolt
摇动接头 rocker joint
摇动炉底加热炉 shaker hearth furnace
摇动炉底式渗碳炉 shaker-hearth type of carburizing furnace
摇动[摇筛]器 shaker, shaking machine
摇动筛 shaking screen [grizzly, sieve,

grate], rocking screen
摇动式电弧炉　rocking (arc) furnace
摇动式筛分机　shaking grate
摇动式淘汰盘　pendulum table
摇动装置　shaking device [apparatus]
摇杆　rocking bar [lever], swinging lever, rocker, control crank ◇ 弯曲[曲线]~*
摇杆臂　rocker arm
摇杆辊子　persuader roll
摇杆式飞剪　rocker-type flying shears
摇杆式焊钳　rocker gun
摇杆推料加热炉　rocker-bar (heating) furnace
摇杆轴承　rocker bearing
摇架　cradle
摇筐　dumping cradle
摇框　bracket
摇篮　cradle ◇ 工字轮~*
摇离接合钩　swing-out engaging claw
摇炉　converter
摇溶(现象)　thixotropy
摇溶沉淀　thixotropic precipitate
摇溶胶　thixotrope
摇溶性　(同"触变性")
摇筛　shaking [swinging] sieve
摇筛式接触器　swinging sieve contactor
摇筛式离子交换接触器　swinging sieve ion-exchange contactor
摇实密度　【粉】tap density
摇实密度杯　【粉】tap density cup
摇实体积　packed [packing] volume,【粉】tap volume
摇实重量　tap weight
摇台　working cradle
摇头皮带　oscillating feeder
摇头印刷[压榨]机　tilting-head press
摇振筛　Ro-tap sieve shaker
摇座　rocker bearing,【建】balance beam
遥测　remote measurement [metering, sensing], telemetering, telemetry
遥测安培计　teleammeter

遥测电压表[伏特计]　televoltmeter
遥测读数　distant reading (dr)
遥测读数压力计　distant reading manometer
遥测读数仪　remote-reading gauge
遥测技术　telemetering, telemetry
遥测计　telegauge, telemeter ◇ 自记式~telerecorder
遥测温度计　distance thermometer, distant (reading) thermometer, telethermometer
遥测温度自动记录器　telethermograph
遥测系统　remote-metering system
遥测信号　remote signal
遥测仪　telemeter, remote sensing instrument
遥测仪表　distant-action instrument
遥测转速计　teletachometer
遥测装置　telemetering gear
遥读转速计　distant reading tachometer
遥感　remote sensing
遥感压力计　remote induction manometer
遥控　remote control (R.C.), distance [distant] control, telecontrol, remote monitor (ing) [manipulation], teleautomatics
遥控板[屏]　remote-control panel
遥控泵　remote-controlled pump
遥控操作器[机械手]　remote(-control) manipulator, magic hand
遥控处理[运搬]　remote handling
遥控传感器　remote pickup
遥控电动机　telemotor
遥控阀　remote(-controlled) valve
遥控高速爆炸成形　【压】standoff high-velocity operation
遥控机　remote operated machine
遥控记录　distant recording
遥控记录仪表　remote indicating instrument
遥控开关　remote-control switch, teleswitch
遥控力学[机械学]　telautomatics, teleme-

chanics
遥控喷补　remote gunning
遥控器　robot handler, magic hand, remote controller
遥控设备　robot, remote control equipment
遥控系统　remote-control system
遥控信号　remote signal
遥控站　remote (control) station
遥控制备　remote fabrication
遥控装置　remote control device [gear]
遥控作用　remote action
遥示　remote indication
遥示器　remote indicator
遥示仪表　remote indicating instrument
遥源信息　remote information
遥远的　remote
遥远读出　remote sensing
窑　kiln, furnace ◇ 立波尔～Lepol system [furnace], 间歇式小车～envelope kiln, 有下料提升机的～elevator kiln
窑车　furnace car, [耐]kiln car
窑车底　car deck
窑车台面　[耐]car top
窑衬　kiln liner [lining], [冶]lining
窑衬耐火砖[材料]　kiln-wall refractory
窑抽力　kiln draught
窑抽力调节器　kiln damper
窑底　kiln floor
窑顶　crown
窑顶拱锁　kiln crown
窑盖　kiln hood
窑拱　kiln arch
窑烘干的　kiln-dried (KD)
窑壳　kiln shell
窑况　kiln performance [behaviour]
窑况失常　trouble in furnace condition
窑炉看火孔　kiln eye
窑门　kiln door
窑内烘干(铸型的)　kiln drying, kilning
窑内空间　free kiln space
窑内气流　furnace air flow
窑气　kiln gas

窑腔　kiln interior
窑头　(rotary-) kiln discharge, discharge (side, end), exit end of kiln, kiln hood (回转窑的)
窑头段壳体　[团]discharge end shell
窑头分选[铁渣分离]　[团]kiln discharge separation
窑头烧嘴　end burner
窑头烧嘴风机　kiln burner fan
窑头小炮(清除窑内结圈)　machine gun
窑头罩　[团]discharge hood
窑头罩观察孔　firing hood viewport
窑尾　feed [charge, loading] end, feed [charging] side
窑尾烟气　kiln exit gas
窑尾罩　feed hood
窑温状况　kiln temperature profile
窑效率　kiln efficiency
窑用砂　setting sand
窑用涂料　[耐]ceramic paint
窑用支架砖　kiln furniture
窑运转　kiln run
咬边　[焊]undercut
咬缝管　cased tube, close joint tube
咬合砌体[砖]　bonded brickwork
咬合试验(镀锌板的)　lock seam test
咬口接头　saddle joint
咬口模　lock die
咬入　bite, nip(-up) ◇ 轧辊～轧件
咬入表面　[压]gripping surface
咬入弧水平方向投影长度　(同"接触弧长投影")
咬入角　bite [nip, gripping] angle, angle of bite [nip], entering angle, angle of entry [rolling]
咬入速度　[压]bite speed
咬入条件　[压]bite condition
咬送辊　[压]nip roll ◇ 拉紧～drag pinch roll
咬住　nip-up, seizing, stick(-slip), jam
舀取期　scooping-out period
药包　cartridge, explosive charge

药剂　drug, reagent
药剂槽　reagent tank
药剂分布　reagent distribution
药剂溶解器　reagent dissolver
药皮(焊条的)　coating, sheathing ◇ 焊条~　electrode coating, 厚~焊条＊, 造气~＊
药皮成分(电焊条的)　coating ingredient
药皮电焊条　covered welding electrode ◇ 粉状碳化物~＊
药皮焊线　covered rod
药筒　cartridge
药芯焊丝电弧焊　flux cored (arc) welding
药芯焊条[丝]　cored [composite] electrode
药芯焊条保护焊接　innershield welding
要求数量　requisible amount
要求磨的级别　【选】milling-grade
要求值　desired value
要求(最终)成分　【冶】required (final) composition
要素　essential factor, (key) element
耶尔低锡黄铜(7.5—8Zn, 0.5—1.5Sn, 1Pb,余量Cu)　Yale brass
耶尔低锡青铜(89—91.5Cu, 7.5—8Zn, 0.5—1.5Sn)　Yale bronze
野外道路　exposed [rural] road
野外试验　field test(ing) [trial]
"野"相(矿热炉生产的)　wild phase
冶金不稳定性　metallurgical instability
冶金测量车　metallurgical measuring wagon [automobil]
冶金测试技术　metallurgical testing technique
冶金产品　metallurgical product
冶金产品分析　metallurgical product analysis
冶金长度　metallurgical length
冶金处理　metallurgical treatment
冶金传输现象　metallurgical transport phenomena
冶金粗(金属)料　metallurgical crudes
冶金单元过程[操作]　metallurgical unit process
冶金的　metallurgical (Met., met.)
冶金电解　metallurgical electrolysis
冶金反应　metallurgical reaction
冶金反应工程学　metallurgical reaction engineering
冶金粉尘造块　agglomeration of metallurgical dust
冶金(工)厂　metallurgical works [plant] ◇ 半联合~＊
冶金工厂废气　metallurgical waste gas
冶金工程　metallurgical engineering
冶金工程师　metallurgical engineer, engineer of metallurgy (E. Met.)
冶金工业　metallurgical industry
冶金工业部　Ministry of Metallurgical Industry
冶金工艺学　process metallurgy
冶金过程[方法]　metallurgical process
冶金化学　metallurgical chemistry
冶金机械　metallurgical machinery
冶金计算　metallurgical calculation
冶金焦(产,成焦)率　metallurgy coke ratio, (blast) furnace coke yield
冶金焦(炭)　metallurgical [smelter, furnace, metallurgy, skip] coke
冶金焦炭质耐火材料　metallurgical-coke-base carbon refractory
冶金接合　metallurgical bond
冶金炉　metallurgical furnace
冶金炉设备　furnace equipment
冶金炉渣　metallurgical slag
冶金煤　furnace coal
冶金平衡表　metallurgical balance sheet (M.B.S.)
冶金缺陷　metallurgical defect [imperfection]
冶金燃料　metallurgical [furnace] fuel
冶金热处理　metallurgic heat treatment
冶金热化学　metallurgical thermochemistry

冶金熔体　metallurgical melt
冶金设备　metallurgical equipment
冶金试验室　metallurgical laboratory
冶金述评　metallurgical review
冶金特性参数　metallurgical parameter
冶金提炼　metallurgical extraction
冶金添加剂　metallurgical addition agent
冶金文摘　Metallurgical Abstracts (Met. Abstra.)
冶金稳定性　metallurgical stability
冶金物理化学　physical chemistry in metallurgy
冶金系统工程　metallurgical systems engineering
冶金现象　metallurgical phenomena
冶金性能　metallurgical property
冶金(学)　metallurgy (Met., met.) ◇ 电解～ electrowinning, 电热～*, 汞齐～ amalgam metallurgy, 火法～*, 湿法～*, 细菌～ bacteria metallurgy, 应用～ adaptive metallurgy
冶金学家[冶金工作者]　metallurgist (met., metl)*
冶金学家协会(英国)　Institute of Metallurgists (IM)
冶金烟尘　metallurgical fume
冶金烟气　metallurgical smoke[gas]
冶金研究　metallurgy research
冶金氧枪　metallurgical oxygen lance
冶金(用)化铁[冲天]炉　metallurgical blast cupola
冶金用煤　metallurgical coal
冶金准则　metallurgical criteria
冶金组分　metallurgical constituent
冶炼　smelting ◇ 不能～的 unsmeltable, 供～用的矿石 shipping ore, 开始～ on-stream, 强化～【铁】sharp working, 酸性渣～ acidic slag smelting
冶炼操作　smelting operation, furnace practice
冶炼厂　smelter (y), smelting plant [works], metal production plant, metallurgical plant
冶炼车间　smelting room
冶炼费用　cost of smelting
冶炼工　smelter, furnace operator [tender]
冶炼工业　smelting industry
冶炼工助手　melter's mate
冶炼过程[方法]　smelting process
冶炼技术　smelting technique
冶炼进程　【钢】working ◇ 不稳定～*, 高炉～困难*, 炉内～ furnace drive [run], 稳定～*
冶炼炉　smelting furnace ◇ 高真空～*
冶炼强度　smelting intensity,【铁】rate of driving
冶炼强度指标(高炉的)　driving index
冶炼强度指数　index of combustion intensity
冶炼设备　smelting equipment
冶炼时间(一炉的)　heat time, duration [length] of heat
冶炼特性　metallurical property
冶炼[冶金]增碳　metallurgical carbonization
冶炼周期　tap-to-tap (cycle, period)
冶炼专家系统　【铁】smelting expert system
页片状的　sheet-like, lamellar
页式打印机　page printer
页式印刷机　page printer
页式阅读机　page reader
页岩　shale (sh.), shaly, shiver, slate, bind ◇ 烧～ burnt shale
页岩焦油　shale tar (pitch)
页岩水泥　slate cement
页岩质煤　bone coal
页岩(质)黏土　slaty clay
业务　business, transaction, service, professional work
业务中断　service interruption
业主收入　【企】proprietor' income
叶碲铋矿　wehrlite, pilsenite
叶碲矿　nagyagite, black tellurium

叶沸石 $\{H_4Ca_4Si_2O_{11}F_2\}$	zeophyllite
叶蜡石 $\{H_2Al_2Si_4O_{22}\}$	pyrophyllite
叶蜡石盖	pyrophyllite lid
叶轮	impeller, impellor, vane ◇ 叶片后弯~*, 重型~ high duty impeller
叶轮泵	impeller [vane] pump
叶轮泵唧能力	impeller pumping capacity
叶轮式粉磨机	impeller-type pulverizer
叶轮式格子塔盘	【焦】turbogrids plate
叶轮式混合机	(同"桨叶式混合机")
叶轮式给料机	vane feeder
叶轮式排气机	rotary impeller exhauster
叶轮式破碎机	impeller breaker
叶轮式曝气装置	【环】impeller aerator
叶轮式扇风机	paddle-wheel fan
叶轮水表	vane water meter
叶轮轴	paddle shaft
叶片	blade, vane, paddle, lobe ◇ 装置~ blading
叶片泵	vane pump ◇ 联动~ combination vane pump
叶片后弯叶轮	impeller with backward curved blades
叶片(式)过滤机	leaf (type) filter
叶片式混砂机	【铸】pug-mill (mixer), pugmill type mixer, kneading machine [mill], paddle mixer
叶片式搅拌器	blade type agitator
叶片式卷取机(炉用)	paddle type coiler
叶片式破碎机	blade crusher
叶片式提升机	paddle wheel elevator
叶片式通风机	fan ventilator
叶(片)式压滤机	pressure-leaf filter ◇ 凯利~ Kelly filter, 施赖弗~ Shriver filter, 斯威特兰~*
叶片式真空过滤机	vacuum leaf filter ◇ 穆尔~ Moore filter
叶片状构造	bladed structure
叶羟硅钙石 $\{H_4Ca_4Si_2O_{11}F_2\}$	zeophyllite
叶栅	cascade, blading
叶蛇纹石 $\{H_4(Mg,Fe)_3 \cdot Si_2O_9\}$	antigorite
叶状赤铁矿 $\{Fe_2O_3\}$	flag ore

曳锭器	(ingot) retractor
曳锭熔化	retractable-ingot melting
曳锭装置[机构]	ingot-retracting mechanism
曳光器	tracer
曳力系数	drag coefficient
曳力效应	【理】drag effect
曳引绞车	hauling winch
曳引绳	towline
夜班	(over)night shift [gang], dog shift, night-turn
夜光漆	luminous paint
液胺离子交换	amine liquid ion exchange
液盎司(衡量)	fluid ounce
液层	liquid layer
液池	liquid pool
液氮淬火	【金】nitrogen quenching
液滴	(liquid) drop, drip, droplet, globule
液滴捕集器	drop catcher, droplet seperator
液滴尺寸	drop size
液滴腐蚀	drop corrosion
液滴模型(原子核的)	liquid drop model
液滴渗碳法	drop feed carburization
液电效应	electrohydraulic effect
液动的	liquid-operated
液动压焊接	hydrodynamic welding
液动压(压)力机	hydrodynamic press
液动压造型机	hydrodynamic moulding press
液封	liquid [fluid] seal
液封淬火炉	sealed quench furnace
液封卸料(装置)	liquid-sealed discharge
液固萃取	liquid-solid extraction
液固分离	liquid-solid separation
液固色谱	liquid-solid chromatograph
液固吸附	liquid-solid adsorption
液固吸附富集(法)	concentration by liquid-solid adsorption
液固(相)界面	liquid-solid interface ◇ 原子跃过~的频率*
液氦	liquid helium

| 液化 liquefying, liquefaction, liquation, liquidation, liquidize, fluidify ◇ 可～的 |
| 液化点 liquefaction point |
| 液化空气 liquefied air |
| 液化煤 liquified coal |
| 液化器 liquidator(liq.), liquefier |
| 液化气体 liquid gas |
| 液化潜热 latent heat of liquefaction |
| 液化热 heat of liquefaction |
| 液化石油气 liquefied petroleum gas (LPG) |
| 液化天然气 liquefied natural gas(LNG) |
| 液化温度 liquefaction temperature |
| 液化乙炔气瓶 liquid-acetylene vessel ◇ 两片式～用钢板* |
| 液化作用 liquefaction |
| 液胶 sol |
| 液接电势 （见"液体接界电势"） |
| 液浸变形 【冶】liquostriction |
| 液浸镀覆 immersion plating |
| 液晶 liquid crystal ◇ 向列～* |
| 液晶显示器 【理】liquid-crystal display (LCD) |
| 液晶状态 【金】mesomorphic state |
| 液夸特(衡量) liquid quart |
| 液力－机械制动器 hydraulic-mechanical brake |
| 液力反压阀 hydraulic back-pressure valve |
| 液力举升 hydraulic lift(ing) |
| 液力联轴器 fluid coupling |
| 液力膜 hydrodynamic film |
| 液力旋压成型法 hydrospinning |
| 液力制动器 water [hydraulic] brake |
| 液料(溶剂萃取的) 【色】aqueous feed |
| 液流 (liquor) stream, fluid flow ◇ 向下～downstream |
| 液流冲击 hydraulic impact |
| 液流流量调节器 【冶】fluid flow regulator |
| 液流控制 fluid flow control |
| 液流目视指示器 sight flow indicator |
| 液流学 rheology |
| 液密性(铸件的) hydraulic soundness |

| 液面 (liquid, solution) level, liquid surface ◇ 基准～datum level |
| 液面测量计 liquidometer |
| 液面传感器 (liquid) level sensor |
| 液面传感指示器 level-sensing device |
| 液面计 level [tank] gauge, liquidometer, liquid level indicator ◇ γ射线～γ-ray level meter, 放射性～* |
| 液面监控器 level monitor |
| 液面控制电极 level control electrode |
| 液面控制(器) (liquid) level control ◇ 浮标～* |
| 液面控制装置 level(l)ing device |
| 液面流 meniscus flow |
| 液面流控制 meniscus flow control |
| 液面调节器 (liquid-) level controller [governor], regulator of level |
| 液面调节装置 level regulating device |
| 液面线 solution line |
| 液面指示警报器 level indicating alarm (LIA) |
| 液面指示器 level gauge (LG), level indicator ◇ 带接触变送器的连续～continuous level indicators with contact transmitter |
| 液膜 liquid film ◇ 冷却～cooling film |
| 液膜润滑 fluid film lubrication |
| 液汽平衡 liquid-vapour equilibrium |
| 液氢温度 liquid hydrogen temperature |
| 液碎[液态粉碎] liquid disintegration ◇ 转盘式～(法) |
| 液碎铁粉 liquid-disintegrated powder |
| 液碎铸铁 liquid-disintegrated cast iron |
| 液态 liquid state |
| 液态冰晶石 molten cryolite |
| 液态不混溶区[范围] 【金】liquid-immiscibility region |
| 液态产品收得率 liquid yield |
| 液态出渣炉 slag-tap [slag-drip] furnace |
| 液态除渣(法) slag drip |
| 液态淬火玻璃质合金 【金】liquid-quenched glassy alloy |

液态氮生产装置	liquid nitrogen plant
液态点	liquidus point
液态废钢脱铜	removal of copper from molten scrap
液态废料处理	liquid waste processing
液态废物	【环】liquid waste
液态分离	liquid separation
液态镉	liquid cadmium
液态鼓风反射炉	liquid state reverberatory smelting furnace
液态鼓风反射炉熔炼	liquid state reverberatory smelting
液态-固态范围[区域]	【金】liquid-solid region
液态硅酸盐	liquid silicate
液态合金	liquid alloy
液态互溶区	【金】liquid miscibility gap
液态互溶性	liquid miscibility
液态火焰加热淬火(法)	liquid flame hardening
液态挤压钢	liquid compressed steel
液态甲烷气	liquid methane gas (LMG)
液态焦	fluid coke
液态焦化	fluid coking
液态金属	liquid [hot] metal
液态金属腐蚀	liquid metal corrosion
液态金属结构	structure of liquid metal
液态金属料	liquid metal charge
液态金属渗透	liquid metal infiltration
液态金属湍流	【铸】metal turbulence
液态晶体相	【金】nematic phase
液态空气	(同"液体空气")
液态沥青	liquid pitch
液态流动性测验	castability test
液态流动性指数	coefficient of liquidity
液态流动渣	fluid cinder
液态流体	liquid fluid
液态炉渣	liquid slag
液态铝	molten aluminium
液态铝珠	liquid aluminium globule
液态模锻	forge casting
液态钠运送泵	sodium pump
液态熔剂	molten [liquid] flux
液态熔剂法(炼铅)	liquid-flux process
液态熔剂覆盖层	liquid flux cover
液态思维	【企】liquid type thinking
液态收缩	liquid contraction [shrinkage]
液态铁	molten [liquid] iron
液态完全互溶(性)	complete liquid miscibility
液态锡	molten tin
液态线	liquidus
液态型砂	fluid(ized) sand
液态压缩	liquid compression
液态氧	liquid oxygen (LOX, lox)
液态氧化铝	molten alumina
液态氧化渣	【冶】hot oxidizing slag
液态元素	liquid element
液态沼气	liquid methane gas (LMG)
液体	liquid (liq., lq), liquor, (liquid) fluid
液体氨	liquid ammonia
液体比重测定法	hydrometry, areometry
液体比重秤	hydrostatic balance
液体比重计	hydrometer, areometer
液体比重计法	hydrometer method
液体变阻器	liquid resistor [rheostat]
液体差压计	fluid differential pressure gauge
液体产物	liquid product, product liquid
液体冲击清理	liquid impact blasting
液体冲蚀	liquid impingement erosion
液体冲头	fluid [flexible] punch
液体冲压	liquid forging, fluid form
液体除尘系统	【冶】liquid dust-suppression system
液体传热	liquid heat transfer
液体萃取	liquid extraction
液体萃取提纯	purification by liquid extraction
液体淬火法	【金】liquid quenching method
液体单位晶格模型	【理】lattice cell model of liquid
液体氮	liquid nitrogen (LN)
液体氮化	(同"液体渗氮")

液体电极	liquid electrode
液体电解质	liquid electrolyte
液体分离	liquid separation
液体分离器	liquid trap
液体粉碎器	liquid disintegrator
液体腐蚀	liquid [fluid, wet] corrosion
液体汞齐	liquid amalgam
液体滚铣	liquid hobbing
液体环式泵	liquid ring pump
液体混合物	liquid mixture
液体接界电势[位]	liquid junction potential
液体结构	liquid structure
液体介质	liquid medium
液体介质中扩散渗铬	liquid chromizing
液体金属	liquid metal (LM), hot metal (H.M.)
液体金属表面熔渣(浇桶中的)	sullage
液体金属传送	liquid-metal transfer
液体－金属萃取	liquid-metal extraction
液体－金属系	liquid-metal system
液体金属锻造	liquid metal forging
液体金属粉碎	liquid metal pulverization
液体金属腐蚀	liquid metal corrosion
液体金属冷却快速增殖反应堆【理】	liquid metal cooling fast breeder reactor
液体金属喷雾塔	liquid-metal spray column
液体金属燃料反应堆	liquid metal fuel reactor (LMFR)
液体金属雾化(法)	atomisation of liquid metal
液体金属阴极	liquid metal cathode
液体金属载热剂	heat transfer metal
液体静压头	head pressure
液体净化塔	liquid-purification column
液体空气	liquid air ◇ 在～中淬火的 quenched in liquid air (Qla)
液体－空气静液挤压	fluid to air extrusion
液体空气冷却捕集器	liquid air trap
液体空气中淬火(的)	quenched in liquid air (Qla)
液体冷却	liquid cooling
液体冷却剂	liquid coolant
液体离子交换	liquid ion exchange
液体离子交换法(溶剂萃取法)	liquid ion exchange process
液体离子交换剂	liquid ion-exchange agent
液体离子交换溶剂	liquid ion exchange solvent
液体离子交换树脂	liquid resin
液体连接桥	liquid bridge
液体量度[量法]	liquid measure
液体流量	liquid [liquor] flow, liquid throughput
液体流量计	liquid (flow) meter, liquor [fluid] flow meter
液体流量控制	fluid flow control
液体炉渣	liquid slag
液体氯	liquid chlorine
液体密度	fluid density
液体模	flexible die
液体磨料抛光[镗磨]	liquid honing
液体摩擦	liquid friction
液体摩擦轴承	fluid friction bearing, oil flooded bearing, flood lubricated bearing, film lubrication bearing ◇ 摩戈伊尔～ Morgoil bearing
液体钼精矿[液体辉钼矿](辉钼矿蒸馏ающего发法)	liquid molybdenum concentrate
液体黏度[性]	liquid [fluid] viscosity
液体黏度计	liquid [fluid] viscosimeter
液体黏合剂	liquid cement
液体黏合理论	liquid cement theory
液体黏结剂	liquid-containing binder
液体培养基	liquid [fluid] nutrient medium
液体喷气燃料	liquid propellant (LP)
液体喷砂(处理,清理)	liquid blasting
液体喷射	liquid [fluid] jet, spouting of liquid
液体喷嘴	liquid jet

液体-气体界面　liquid-vapour interface
液体-气体系　liquid-gas system
液体铅　molten lead
液体氰化　liquid cyaniding
液体区域精炼　liquid zoning
液体取样装置　fluid sampling apparatus
液体燃料　liquid fuel, fuel oil (F.O.), oil-fuel (OF) ◇ 烧～的 liquid-fired
液体燃料火焰　liquid-fuel flame
液体燃料燃烧器　liquid fuel burner
液体润滑　liquid [fluid] lubrication
液体润滑剂　liquid lubricant
液体润滑轴承　fluid lubricated bearing
液体上升总管　rising main
液体色谱(法)　liquid chromatography
液体射流　fluid jet
液体渗氮　【金】liquid [bath] nitriding ◇ 查普曼～法 Chapmanizing, 加压～*
液体渗[增]碳　liquid carburizing [carburization], bath carburizing
液体渗碳氮化法[液体碳氮共渗]　liquid carbonitriding
液体渗碳剂　liquid carburizer, liquid carburizing material ◇ 表面碳用～【金】perlition
液体渗碳渗氮剂　◇ 杜菲利特～*
液体渗透剂　liquid penetrant
液体渗透检验(法)　penetrant fluid test, liquid penetration test
液体渗透试验设备　liquid-penetrant test equipment
液体渗透性　permeability for liquids
液体石油膏　paroline
液体试剂　liquid reagent
液体试样　liquor sample
液体四氯化物　liquid tetrachloride
液体速度　liquid velocity
液体调节滑件　liquid regulating slider
液体通过量　liquid throughput
液体温度计　liquid-filled thermometer, liquid-in-glass thermometer (玻璃球式)
液体雾化(法)　liquid atomization ◇ 转盘式～*

液体吸附　adsorption of liquids
液体吸附物　liquified adsorbate
液体洗尘系统　(同"液体除尘系统")
液体锌　liquid zinc
液体溴　liquid bromine
液体压缩　liquid compression
液体阳离子交换剂　liquid cation exchanger
液体氧　liquid oxygen
液体氧化剂　liquid oxidant
液体氧中安全的渗透剂　Lox-safe penetrant
液体-液体系　liquid-liquid system
液体阴极　fluidised cathode
液体阴离子交换剂　liquid anion-exchanger
液体增碳　liquid [bath] carburizing
液体置换法　liquid displacement method
液体中的固溶体　solutions of solids in liquids
液体中的液溶体　solutions of liquids in liquids
液体中子吸收体　fluid poison
液体撞蚀　(同"液体冲蚀")
液体状态　liquid state
液位测量仪　liquid level gauge
液位传感器　liquid level sensor, level transmitter
液位传送器　level transmitter
液位计　level meter, liquidometer ◇ 浮子式～ float type level gauge
液位开关　level switch
液位指示计[器]　liquid level gauge [indicator], indicating liquid level gauge
液位指示控制器　level indicating controller ◇ 带警报的～ level indicator controller with alarm
液析　【冶】liquation
液下导线辊　sinking roller
液限　liquid limit
液线定碳　【钢】carbon control by thermal

arrest

液相 liquid phase [phantom], liquidoid, solution phase
液相比(例) liquid fraction
液相萃取 liquid-phase extraction
液相成分 liquid composition
液相分配剂 liquid partitioning agent
液相工艺 liquid-phase process
液相还原 liquidoid reduction
液相急冷 (同"薄膜状急冷")
液相键 melting bond
液相溅射法 liquid-phase sputtering
液相扩散 liquid-phase diffusion
液相面 liquidus surface [face]
液相浓度 liquid-phase concentration
液相强化蠕变 liquid enhanced creep
液相区[范围]【金】liquid range
液相色谱仪 liquid chromatograph
液相烧结 liquid(-phase) sintering,【粉】sintering in the presence of a liquid
液相生成 liquid-phase formation
液相生长 liquid growth
液相外延生长 rheotaxial growth, liquid phase epitaxial growth
液相吸着(法) liquid-phase sorption
液(相)线 liquid line, liquidus (curve, line)
液(相)线烧结 liquidus sintering
液(相)线温度 liquidus temperature
液相形成剂 liquid-phase-forming material
液相穴 liquid pool [core], crater
液相氧化 liquid-phase oxidation
液相重力 liquid gravity
液相自由能曲线 liquid-phase free energy curve
液芯 liquid core
液芯顶弯 【连铸】liquid center bending
液芯(钢锭)轧制法 ◇塔尔伯特~
液芯轧制 liquid squeeze
液芯轧制钢锭 liquid squeezed ingot
液压板卷翻转机 【压】hydraulic downender
液压泵 hydraulic pump ◇卧式三柱塞型~

液压变矩器 hydraulic torque converter
液压表 liquid pressure gauge
液压箔材 hydrofoil
液压操作楔 hydraulically operated wedge
液压操作压下装置 hydraulic operated screwdown
液压测力[功]计 hydraulic dynamometer
液压拆卸机 hydraulic stripper
液压成形[型] hydroforming, fluid form ◇爆炸~
液压成形[型]法 hydroforming (process) ◇惠斯勒~
液压齿轮传动【机】oilgear drive
液压初轧方坯剪切机 hydraulic bloom shearing machine
液压出坯装置【粉】hydraulic knock-out mechanism
液压穿孔压力机 hydraulic piercing press
液压传动 hydraulic drive [transmission], fluidrive ◇闭路~系统
液压传动活套挑[压]hydraulic looper
液压传动机构[装置] hydraulic gear [actuator], fluid gear
液压传动系统 oilgear system
液压锤 hydraulic hammer
液压单独拖动(装置) self-contained pump drive
液压电动机 (oil) hydraulic motor, hydromotor ◇柱塞式~piston motor
液压顶杆 hydraulic ram
液压定心机(轧管用) hydraulic centring [centre] machine
液压动力 hydraulic power
液压动力中心 hydraulic centre
液压锻造 hydraulic [hydrostatic] forging
液压堆垛机 hydraulic stacker
液压阀 hydraulic valve
液压翻转机 hydraulic tilter
液压放大器 hydraulic amplifier
液压封闭器 hydraulic gate
液压风动蓄压器 hydropneumatic accu-

液 ye

液压缸　hydraulic cylinder ◇ 悬置移动～*
液压(缸操作的)卸卷托板　hydraulic cylinder operated stripper-plate
液压供水[油]管线　hydraulic supply line
液压管　hydraulic pipe
液压辊缝控制　hydraulic roll gap control
液压焊管法(大口径管的)　hydraulic weld process
液压焊枪　hydraulic welding gun
液压横剪机　hydraulic crosscut shears
液压横移装置　hydraulic traversing device
液压换挡[切换]机构　hydraulic shifter
液压换向阀　hydraulic change-over valve
液压回动装置　hydraulic reversing gear
液压回路图　hydraulic circuit diagram
液压活塞　hydraulic piston [ram]
液压机　hydraulic press [machine], hydrostatic press, fluid actuated press, hydropress (也见"水压机")
液压机构　hydraulic gear [mechanism]
液压挤压　fluid (pressure) extruding
液压挤压机　hydraulic extrusion press
液压夹紧装置　hydraulic clamp (device)
液压加载预应力轧机　hydraulically-loaded pre-stressed rolling mill
液压剪切机[剪床]　hydraulic shears, hydraulic shearing machine, hydrocut-shears
液压剪切作业线　hydraulic shearing line
液压减震器　hydraulic bumper [buffer]
液压绞盘　hydraulic capstan
液压介质　pressure medium
液压开关　hydraulic pressure switch, hydraulic selector
液压开口机　【铁】hydraulic rotary drill
液压控制　hydraulic control
液压控制器　hydraulic type controller
液压拉拔机　hydraulic drawbench
液压拉伸矫直　hydraulic flattening
液压拉伸矫直机　hydraulic stretcher
液压拉伸压缩疲劳试验机　pulsator

液压离合变速器　fluid coupling speed variator
液压离合器　hydraulic clutch
液压联轴节[器]　hydraulic coupling, hydrocoupling
液压料钟卷扬机　hydraulic(al) bell hoist
液压流体　hydraulic [power] fluid ◇ 防火用～*
液压密封　hydraulic seal
液压密封剂[胶,层]　hydraulic sealant
液压模塑[模压]机　hydraulic moulding press
液压能　hydraulic energy
液压牌坊嵌入件　hydraulic housing insert
液压配件　hydraulic fittings
液压膨胀试验　hydraulic bulge test
液压平衡　hydraulic balance
液压平衡系统　hydraulic balancing system
液压平衡轴　hydraulic (ally) balanced spindle
液压平衡装置　hydraulic balance device
液压千斤顶　hydraulic jack
液压倾卸机　hydraulic tilter
液压清砂(法)　【铸】hydraulic fettling
液压刹车　cataract
液压上推系统　hydraulic push-up system
液压上推装置　hydraulic push-up equipment
液压深冲　fluid form deep drawing
液压升降机[起重器]　hydraulic jack ◇ 带～小车(更换转炉炉底用) truck with hydraulic jack
液压式单排推钢机　single-row hydraulic-type pusher
液压式(放)渣口堵塞机　hydraulic slag stopper
液压式上辊平衡装置　top roll hydraulic balance arrangement
液压试验　hydraulic (pressure) test
液压试验装置　water test unit
液压输送　hydraulic transport
液压输送机　hydraulic conveyer

液压伺服电动机	hydraulic servomotor, pencil motor
液压损失	hydraulic slip
液压提升	hydraulic lift(ing)
液压提升堆垛机	hydraulic lift piler
液压提升机	hydraulic lift(er)
液压提升系统	hydraulic lifting system
液压提升装置	hydraulic lifting device
液压调节缸	hydraulic adjusting cylinder
液压调节机构	hydraulic adjusting mechanism
液压调整系统	hydraulic setting system
液压头	hydraulic head
液压推钢机	【压】hydraulic ram
液压推进杆	hydraulic thruster arm
液压推进装置	hydraulic push system
液压弯管装置	hydraulic pipe bending device
液压挖掘机	hydraulic excavator
液压位移缸	hydraulic displacing cylinder
液压系统	hydraulic system, hydraulics ◇闭路~*,成组传动~*
液压系统地下室	hydraulic cellar
液压系统回路	hydraulic circuit diagram
液压系统压力	fluid pressure
液压箱(取样器的)	tilting box
液压橡皮膜成型法	(同"液压成型法")
液压楔(压下装置的)	hydraulic wedge
液压卸除机	hydraulic stripper
液压行程传动装置	hydraulic travelling drive
液压蓄力[势,能]器	hydraulic accumulator
液压旋转钻机	hydraulic rotary drill
液压压紧装置	hydraulic hold-down
液压压实造型机	【铸】hydraulic squeeze machine
液压压下控制	hydraulic screwdown control
液压压下系统	hydraulic reduction system
液压压下装置	hydraulic screwdown
液压液体[油]	hydraulic fluid
液压圆锥破碎机	hydro-cone crusher
液压造型机	hydraulic moulding press [machine]
液压渣口塞棒	hydraulic slag stopper
液压轧机	hydraulic mill
液压胀形轧辊	hydraulic elastic bulging roll
液压振动	hydraulic oscillation
液压制动机	cataract
液压制动器	hydraulic [liquid] brake
液压中心	hydraulic centre
液压肘杆式压力机	hydraulic toggle press
液压柱塞	hydraulic ram ◇复谐式~泵*
液压转盘[台]	【连铸】hydraulic tilter
液压装置	hydraulic device [equipment, unit]
液压自动厚度控制	hydraulic automatic gauge control (HAGC)
液压自动厚度控制系统	HAGC system
液压总管	hydraulic main
液氧	liquid oxygen (lox)
液氧活门	oxygen valve
液氧库[贮罐]	liquid oxygen storage
液氧箱	oxygen tank
液氧中安全的渗透剂	Lox-safe penetrant
液液萃取[提取]	liquid-liquid extraction ◇单循环~*
液液萃取分离	separation by liquid-liquid extraction
液液萃取回收	recovery by liquid-liquid extraction
液液萃取混合器	liquid-liquid extraction mixer
液液萃取技术	liquid-liquid technique
液液萃取设备	【色】liquid-liquid contact equipment
液液交换	liquid-liquid exchange
液液界面	liquid-liquid interface
液液静液挤压	fluid to fluid extrusion, differential pressure extrusion
液液色谱	liquid-liquid chromatography

液浴　liquid bath
液浴炉　liquid (bath) furnace
液柱　liquid [fluid] column
液柱压力计　liquid (column) manometer
液状　liquidness
液状分散　liquid-like dispersion
液状晶体　(同"液晶")
一般成形工艺　conventional forming technique
一般(冲压)成形法　conventional forming method
一般费用　general expenses, oncost
一般概率分布　【数】generalized probability distributions
一般工程　general engineering
一般厚锡层镀锡薄钢板(平均锡层重量为1.1—2.3kg/基准箱)　ordinary charcoal tinplate
一般化学分析　wet analysis
一般金属　common metal
一般扩散定律　【理】general diffusion law
一般品位铁矿　conventional-grade iron ore
一般气孔(矿石的)　macro pore
一般线性规划问题　general linear programming problem
一般研磨　(同"普通研磨")
一般用途　general-purpose
一般原理　general principle
一般质量　ordinary quality
一般铸锭法　direct teeming
一步法　one-step method
一步混合　one-stage blending
一步炼钢法　(同"直接炼钢法")
一步熔炼　direct smelting
一步熔融还原法　single-stage smelting reduction process
一步式成型　one step forming
一步液态还原法　【铁】one step liquid reduction process
一长制　【企】one-man management
一次X射线束　primary X-ray beam
一次奥氏体　primary austenite

一次成形　single(-operation) forming
一次充填　one filling
一次重熔　【钢】once-melted
一次抽查取样[检验]　single sampling
一次萃取法　single-extraction process
一次淬火　primary quenching
一次代位固熔体　(同"置换型一次固熔体")
一次点火器　primary ignition furnace
一次电池　primary [galvanic] cell, one-shot battery
一次电子　primary electron
一次煅烧白云石　single-burned dolomite
一次对位　【焦】one-spot
一次反应　primary reaction
一次风管　primary air main
一次风机　primary air fan ◇预热烧嘴～*
一次风口　primary nozzle
一次固溶体　primary solid solution
一次光谱系数　coefficient of primary spectrum
一次滑移　primary slip
一次混合机　primary mixer
一次混料室　primary mixing building
一次活套　【压】primary loop
一次激发能级(与最小能级紧邻)　next-to-the-smallest (energy) level
一次给料机　primary feeder
一次加料　one filling
一次加热　single heat
一次加热轧成　【压】roll in one heat
一次搅拌的干拌物(混凝土等)　dry batch
一次结晶　primary crystallization
一次晶轴　principal axis
一次颗粒　【粉】primary particle
一次空气　primary air, main (combustion) air
一次拉拔　single draught, one holed
一次拉伸　single-pass drawing
一次拉丝机　single-hole wire-drawing machine

一次拉碳 【钢】one-go	一次文丘里管　first stage Venturi
一次冷床　primary cooler	一次雾化　primary atomization
一次冷镦机　single-stroke header	一次细筛　first fine screen
一次冷凝器　primary condenser	一次线圈　primary coil [winding]
一次冷却区　【连铸】first (cooling) zone	一次消光　primary extinction
一次冷轧钢板　【压】single-reduced plate	一次谐波　first [fundamental] harmonic
一次离子化原子　singly ionized atom	一次型芯(永久铸型)　expendable core
一次料斗　primary hopper	一次型铸(件)　dead mould casting
一次锍　coarse metal	一次形式　line form
一次模(型)　【铸】consumable [expended, lost, one-off] pattern	一次压制　first pressing, single-pressing
	一次压制法　single-press process
一次凝固壳(大气冒口的)　primary crust	一次压制与烧结坯　【粉】single pressed and sintered blank
一次浓缩机　primary thickener	
一次喷嘴　primary nozzle [lance]	一次衍射束　first order diffracted beam
一次破碎　primary [preliminary] crushing	一次氧化皮(炉内形成的)　furnace scale
一次气孔　【钢】primary blowhole	一次仪表　primary instrument
一次球磨机　primary ball mill	一次硬[强]化　primary hardening
一次燃料　primary fuel	一次用量　dose
一次燃烧空气　primary combustion air	一次再结晶织构　primary recrystallization texture
一次(初级)绕组　primary winding	
一次熔化　【钢】once-melted	一次造球　primary pelletization
一次熔炼　【冶】heat	一次造球机　primary pelletizer
一次熔模　【铸】disposable pattern	一次增亮剂　primary brightener
一次筛(分)　primary screen	一次轴　monad [one-fold] axis
一次烧结　first sintering	一次(铸)型　【铸】temporary [dispensable, expendable] mould
一次烧结处理　single-sinter treatment	
一次烧结法　single-pass sintering process	一次自磨　primary autogenous grinding
一次(初始)射线　primary rays	一次走刀　one-pass [single-pass] operation
一次渗碳体　primary cementite	一打(12件)　dozen (doz., dz)
一次石墨　(同"原生石墨")	一代磷酸锶{Sr(H$_2$PO$_4$)$_2$}　primary strontium phosphate
一次使用的　one-shot	
一次缩孔　primary pipe	一氮化铌{NbN}　niobium [columbium] nitride
一次索氏体　primary sorbite	
一次碳化物　primary carbide	一氮化钛　titanium nitride
一次提纯　primary purification	一氮化钽{TaN}　tantalum nitride
一次通过(区域熔炼)　【色】single pass	一氮化物　mononitride
一次通过的(编程序)　【计】one-shot	一氮化铀　uranium mononitride
一次通过分布(区域熔炼的)　【色】single-pass distribution	一道工序　(同"一次完成操作")
	一道压下量　single draught
一次通过区域熔炼　single-pass zone-melting	一等厚锡层镀锡薄钢板　premier charcoal tinplate
一次退火作业线　primary annealing line	一地址(码)　【计】one-address (code)

一碘化物　monoiodide
一碘化铟{InI}　indium monoiodide
一叠(钢板)　batch
一定尺寸晶体　crystal of finite size
一度结构　one-degree structure
一度空间的　【理】one-dimensional
一端搬运　end hauling
一段分级　one-pass classification
一段过滤器　primary filter
一段还原　single-stage reduction
一段混合　one-stage blending
一段浸出　【色】single(-stage) leaching
一段冷却(带式烧结机的)　first stage cooling zone
一段冷却(式)风机　primary cooling supply fan, first stage cooling fan
一段磨矿机　【选】primary mill
一段破碎　single-stage crushing
一段破碎机　single crusher
一段熔融还原法　single-stage smelting reduction process
一段渗氮[氮化]　single-stage nitriding
一段时间　session
一段式炉　single-fired reheating furnace
一段酸浸出　single-stage acid leaching
一对多　【计】one-to-many
一对一翻译　one-for-one [binary] translation
一对一翻译程序　【计】one-to-one translator
一对一汇编程序　【计】one-to-one assembler
一氟二氯化铊{TlFCl₂}　thallic fluodichloride
一氟二氯化物　fluodichloride
一氟化合物　monofluoride
一贯质量管理系统　throughout quality management system
一硅化二铜{Cu₂Si}　copper selecide
一火成材　【压】roll in one heat, rolling without reheat ◇ 连铸坯~
一火钢　single shear steel

一级(的)　first grade [order]
一级(薄钢)板　【压】prime sheet, primes
一级变量　【计】level-one variable
一级萃取　single-stage extraction
一级存储器　single level memory
一级代码　【计】one-level code
一级地址　【计】first level address, direct [one-level] address
一级电池　galvanic element
一级反应　【化】first order reaction
一级分离器　first stage separator
一级分批萃取　one-stage batch extraction
一级复膜[复型]　single-stage replica
一级钢材　【压】prime product
一级近似　first approximation
一级跃迁　first order transition
一级再生萃取器　single-stage regeneration extractor
一级子程序　【计】first order subroutine
一加一地址　【计】one-plus-one address
一甲基　monomethyl
一价　【化】univalence, univalency, monovalence, monovalency
一价汞化合物　mercurous compound
一价金　monovalent gold
一价金属　univalent [monovalent] metal
一价离子　monovalent ion
一价铊的　thallous
一价铜化合物　cuprous compound
一价铜离子　single-charge copper ion
一价盐　monovalent salt
一价元素　monad
一碱价的　monobasic
一阶　【数】first order
一阶惯性　first order lag
一阶跃迁　first order transition
一卷　a reel, tier
一捆　a bundle, truss
一览　general survey, bird's-eye view
一览表　general list (GL), list, table, catalogue, schedule ◇ 项目~ itemized schedule

一列式混合沉降器	in-line mixer-settler
一硫二氧化钼{MoO$_2$S}	molybdenum dioxysulphide
一硫二氧化物	dioxysulphide
一硫化钡	barium monosulphide
一硫化二铟{In$_2$S}	indium monosulphide
一硫化汞	cinnabar
一硫化锰{MnS}	manganous sulphide
一硫化铁	iron monosulfide
一硫化物	monosulphide
一硫族化合物	monochalcogenides
一炉	batch,【冶】heat
一炉(次)金属	heat of metal
一炉钢	【钢】heat of steel ◇ 混合冶炼中的～ master heat
一炉钢的化学成分	heat chemistry
一氯二溴化铊{TlClBr$_2$}	thallium chlorodibromide
一氯化铊{TlCl}	thallous chloride
一氯化物	monochloride
一氯化氧钼{(MoO)Cl}	molybdenyl chloride
一氯化铟{InCl}	indium monochloride
一氯氧化铈{CeOCl}	cerium oxychloride
一面无光泽箔材	matte one-side foil
一面压制	single-action compression
一目运算	monadic [unary] operation
一排料仓	bin line
一盘(盘条)	a reel, tier
一批	batch, lot
一批产品[一批料量]	lot size
一批料	【铁】round
一氢磷酸双氧铀[一氢磷酸铀酰]{UO$_2$HPO$_4$}	uranyl monohydrogen phosphate
一束	a bunch, a bob, a taft, pack, truss
一水合三氧化铀{UO$_3$·H$_2$O}	uranium trioxide monohydrate
一水合[化]物	monohydrate
一水合氧化铁	ferric oxide monohydrate
一水铝石型铝土矿	monohydrate bauxite (ore)
一水软铝石{α-Al$_2$O$_3$·H$_2$O}	(monohydrate) boehmite
一水软铝石型铝土矿	boehmitic bauxite
一水碳酸钠{Na$_2$CO$_3$·H$_2$O}	monohydrate of sodium carbonate
一水五氰基络高钴盐	pentacyanomonoaquocobalt(Ⅲ)ate
一水五氰基络钴盐	pentacyanomonoaquocobalt(Ⅱ)ate
一水氧化铝{Al$_2$O$_3$·H$_2$O}	monohydrate alumina, alumina monohydrate
一水硬铝石{Al$_2$O$_3$·H$_2$O}	diaspore, diasporite
一水硬铝石型铝土矿	diasporic bauxite
一顺一丁砌(砖)法	quarter bond
一碳化铌{NbC}	niobium carbide
一碳化钽	tantalum monocarbide
一碳化物	monocarbide
一碳化铀{UC}	uranium monocarbide
一套设备	a set of equipment, single unit
一体化管理	integrated management
一体化生产	integrated manufacturing
一体化生产线	integrated production line
一体化系统	integrated system
一维布置	one-dimensional array
一维磁气体动力学	one-dimensional magnetogasdynamics
一维光栅	one-dimensional optical grating
一维近似法	one-dimensional approximation
一维点阵[晶格]	one-dimensional lattice
一维模型	one-dimensional model
一维衍射图[花样]	one-dimensional diffraction pattern
一系列试验	run
一线六极电炉	six-electrode-in-line furnace
一线三极电炉	three-electrode-in-line furnace
一型多铸法	【铸】pattern grouping
一溴二氯化铊{TlBrCl$_2$}	thallium bromodichloride

一溴化物 monobromide
一溴化铟{InBr} indium monobromide
一氧化钡{BaO} barium monoxide
一氧化氮{NO} nitric oxide
一氧化碲 tellurium monoxide
一氧化二氮{N$_2$O} nitrous oxide, nitrogen monoxide
一氧化二铊{Tl$_2$O} thallous oxide, thallium monoxide
一氧化二铜{Cu$_2$O} cuprous oxide
一氧化钒 hypovanadous oxide
一氧化锆{ZrO} zirconium monoxide
一氧化汞{HgO} mercuric oxide
一氧化钴 cobalt black
一氧化硅{SiO} silicon monoxide
一氧化铪{HfO} hafnium monoxide
一氧化铪基 hafnyl
一氧化镓{GaO} gallium monoxide
一氧化硫 sulfur monoxide
一氧化锰{MnO} manganous oxide
一氧化锰-硅熔体 manganous oxide-silicon melts
一氧化钼{MoO} molybdenum monoxide, molybdous oxide
一氧化铌{NbO} niobium [columbium] monoxide
一氧化硼{BO} boron monoxide
一氧化铅{PbO} yellow lead, lead (mon) oxide [litharge]
一氧化铯{Cs$_2$O} cesium monoxide
一氧化铊 thallium (mon)oxide
一氧化钛{TiO} titanium monoxide
一氧化碳{CO} carbon monoxide
一氧化碳分[裂]解 carbon monoxide disintegration
一氧化碳还原 【铁】reduction by CO
一氧化碳还原焰道 CO flue
一氧化碳探测器 carbon monoxide detector
一氧化碳析出速率(转炉的) 【钢】rate of evolution of CO
一氧化碳焰 blue flame

一氧化碳中毒 carbon monoxide poisoning
一氧化物 monooxide
一氧化锡{SnO} stannous oxide
一氧化锗{GeO} germanium monoxide, germanous oxide
一元碳化物粉末 single carbide powder
一元系 【数】unitary system
一元运算 【计】unary [monadic] operation
一致 coincidence, uniform, conformability, conformity, congruency
一致的 consistent, consonant, compatible
一致化合物 【金】congruent compound
一致性 consistence, consistency, compatibility, identity, uniformity, unity ◇ 远程计算系统的～错误*
一砖半厚墙 brick and a haft wall
医疗补助费 【环】medical allowance
医用材料 medical material
医原性疾病 iatrogenic disease
铱铂合金 irid(i)oplatinum
铱的(四价的) iridic
铱锇 osirita
铱锇(铂族元素天然)合金(17—45Os,余量 Ir) iridosmine
铱锇矿 iridosmene
铱锇钌矿 X cabri
铱铬矿 irite
铱合金 iridium alloy
铱黑 iridium black
铱基合金 iridium-base alloy
铱基轴承合金(15.75Sn, 1.25Cu,余量 Zn; 22Sn,1Cu,余量 Zn) iridium bearing alloy [metal]
铱金 iridic gold, iraurite
铱丝 iridium wire
铱添加合金 iridium addition
依次火焰加热淬火 progressive flame hardening
依次蒸馏 trap-to-trap distillation
依存关系 dependance
依据标志 reference mark
依据轴 reference axis

依考特普硬度试验计	Equotip tester
依诺帕克铸铁孕育剂	Inopac
依瓦尼姆铝合金	Ivanium
伊登堡式线材卷取机	Edenborn coiler [reel], laying reel
伊迪阿林型芯黏结剂	【铸】Idealine
伊丁石[MgO·Fe$_2$O$_3$·3SiO$_2$·4H$_2$O]	iddingsite
伊尔格纳可变电压直流发电机组	Ilgner set
伊尔牌铅基耐磨合金(15Sb, 6Sn, 1Ni, 1.5Cd, 余量 Pb)	Eel brand antifriction metal
伊盖杜尔铝合金	igedur
伊格塔洛依钨钴硬质合金(82—88W, 3—5Co, 5.2—5.8C, 0—2Fe)	Igatalloy
伊拉耐蚀耐热合金钢	Era
伊拉耐蚀耐热锰钢	Era manganese steel
伊利格扩散渗硅法	【金】Ihrig method [process]
伊利水云母[伊利石]	illite
伊留姆耐热耐蚀镍合金(21—24Cr, 3—8Cu, 4—6Mo, 0—8Fe, 1—2W, 0—1.5Mn, 0—1Si, 余量 Ni)	Illium (alloy)
伊卢米奈特铝片	illuminite
伊玛迪姆高强度耐蚀黄铜(4—6Al, 0.5—3Mn, 1—2Fe, 55—70Cu, 余量 Zn)	Immadium
伊玛特拉石灰粉脱硫法	【钢】Imatra process
伊纳留姆铝合金(1.7Cd, 1.2Mg, 0.5Si, 余量 Al)	Inalium
伊诺格扎让镍铬不锈钢(13Ni, 13Cr, 0.07C, 余量 Fe)	Inoxargent
伊莎贝林 NCM 精密电阻合金(20Ni, 10Mn, 余量 Cu)	Isabellin NCM
伊莎贝林铜锰铝标准电阻用合金(13Mn, 3Al, 余量 Cu)	Isabellin
伊莎铜锰镍精密电阻合金(Isa50：12Mn, 5Ni, 余量 Cu)	Isa
伊万欧姆镍铬电阻合金(75Ni, 20Cr, 2.5Cu, 2.5Al)	Evanohm
伊万斯带钢轧机	Evans mill
伊星强磁性体模型	【理】Ising model
伊泽弗洛银焊料(50Ag, 18Cd, 16.5Zn, 15.5Cu)	easy-flo
伊泽特无时效性低碳钢(0.55Mn, 0.1C, 0.07N, 0.05Al, 0.04Si, 余量 Fe)	Izett steel
遗传本质(金属的)	inheritance
遗传工程	genetic engineering
遗传控制	genetic manipulation
遗传系统	genetic system
遗传(性)	heredity
遗传学	genetics
遗传学优化程序	genetic optimizer
遗留误差	【计】inherited error
遗弃废物	waste discharge
遗失信息	drop-out
移槽起重机[吊车]	spout crane
移车台	traversing crane
移出	shift out
移带器	belt shifter
移锭器	retracter ◇ 齿轮~*
移动	shift(ing), movement, moving, motion, migration, displacement, transference, travel, walk, journey (原子迁移) ◇ 可~性 portability, 奈特~【理】Knight shift
移动板(辊道的)	adjustable guard
移动算碳化炉	travel(l)ing grate retort
移动槽(翻钢槽)	shifting chute
移动侧板(辊道的)	adjustable guard
移动场	moving field
移动床	moving bed
移动磁场	travelling magnetic field
移动挡板(定尺剪切的)	movable [mechanical] gauge
移动挡板滑架	gauge carriage
移动挡板横臂(锯机的)	stopper head
移动导板	removable guide
移动底片测角仪(用 X 射线)	moving-film goniometer ◇ 外森贝格型~*

移动定尺挡板 measuring head	移动式惰性气体保护附件 【焊】trailing shield
移动盖 slip cover	移动式发电站 portable power station
移动感应圈 travel(l)ing induction coil	移动式翻钢机 travel(l)ing-down tilter
移动缸 shifting cylinder	移动式高架起重机 overhead travelling crane
移动格算机 travel(l)ing grate type furnace	移动式刮料机 travel(l)ing scraper
移动轨道 travel(l)ing rail	移动式辊道 travel(l)ing roller table
移动滑板 movable sliding plate	移动式焊机 portable welding machine
移动滑车 running block	移动式流嘴(出铁沟的) swing spout
移动加热器 moving heater	移动式龙门起重机 travel(l)ing gantry crane
移动检查台 transfer inspection bed	移动式炉 portable furnace
移动脚手架(法国式) French scaffold	移动式炉底 moving floor
移动晶界 moving boundary	移动式马弗炉 travel(l)ing-muffle furnace
移动锯 travel(l)ing saw	移动式平台 【冶】movable platform
移动链算碳化炉 moving chain-grate retort	移动式铺[堆]料机 travel(l)ing stacker
移动料仓 batch truck	移动(式)起重机 travel(l)ing [mobile] crane, jenny, crab derrick ◇ 单电动机 ~*, 电动[电力]~*, 复式~*, 高架~ transfer gantry
移动溜槽 shifting chute	
移动炉算 moving [travel(l)ing] grate	
移动炉算烧结机 travel(l)ing grate sintering unit	
移动炉算式干燥机 travel(l)ing grate type dryer	移动式切头剪 portable cropping shears
	移动式取料机 travel(l)ing reclaimer
移动耙料机 travel(l)ing plough	移动式热电偶 travel(l)ing thermocouple
移动取样器 moving sampler	移动式设备 portable equipment, mobile unit
移动溶剂法 travel(l)ing solvent method	
移动式摆臂堆料机 travel(l)ing slewing-boom stacker	移动式提升装置 mobile hoist unit
	移动式铁水沟 rocking [separate, tilting] runner
移动式摆动升降台 travel(l)ing tilting table	
	移动式退火炉 mobile annealing furnace
移动式棒条筛 travel(l)ing-bar grizzly	移动式脱模起重机[天车] travel(l)ing stripper crane
移动式变电所 portable substation	
移动式布料器 travel(l)ing charging machine	移动式氧割机小车 secator
	移动式装料漏斗 travel(l)ing (loading) hopper
移动式称量机 mobile weighing machine	
移动式大型起重机 goliath crane	移动式装料箱 mobile box charger
移动式带卷准备车 movable coil preparatory truck	移动速度 travel speed, migration rate [velocity]
移动式点焊机 portable spot welder	移动台 travel(l)ing platform
移动式电动切砖机 portable electrical saw	移动铁沟 【冶】replaceable trough
移动式定尺挡板杠杆 measure stopper arm	移动熄焦装置 moving coke quenching auxiliary

移动相　moving phase
移动小车　travel(l)ing car, traversing crane（烧结厂的）
移动杂质　migrating impurity
移动载荷　shifting load
移动支臂式取料机　travel(l)ing boom reclaimer
移动装置　shifting device, shifter
移轨器　rail slewer
移去器　remover
移送车　transfer car ◇ 带卷～*
移送杆　【压】transfer arm
移送机　transfer (bed, gear, skid, table), skid, handling [pull-over] gear, chain-and-ducking dog mechanism, drag (-over unit), dragging device ◇ 拨爪～*dog transfer, 齿条式～*conveyer rack, 单线～*, 多钢绳～*multirope skid gear, 钢丝绳～*rope transfer, 钩爪式～*dog-bar type conveyor, 冷床～*cooling-bed transfer, 链式～*, 输出～*, 双路～*double-strand drag conveyer, 双线推出～*, 四线推出～*
移送机构　transfer mechanism
移送机链条　drag chain
移送机推杆　transfer pusher
移送跨　transfer bay
移送升降机　transfer lifter
移送台　transfer table
移送台架　【压】transfer bank
移送装置　transfer arrangement
移挖作填　cut-and-fill
移位　shift, transposing, replace
移位操作　shifting (function),【铁】off-site operation
移位寄存器　【计】shift register
移位原子　displaced atom
移位指令　【计】shift instruction
移相变压器　phase-shifting transformer
移相电路　(phase-)shift circuit
移相器　phase shifter, phaser, phase-shifting device ◇ 自动脉冲～*

移相装置　phase changer
移项[置]　transposition
移行的　travel(l)ing
移液管　pipet(te) ◇ 量液～measuring pipet(te)
移植　transplanting, implantation, subculturing
移植技术　subculturing technique
仪表　meter, apparatus (app.), instrument, ga(u)ge ◇ 机内～*, 面板用～surface type meter, 嵌入式～flush type instrument
仪表板[盘]　instrument board [panel], (dash)board, gauge [fascia] board, console
仪表惯性　instrument lag
仪表回路　instrument loop
仪表机械工　instrument mechanic
仪表技术　instrument technique [technology]
仪表技术员　instrument technician
仪表记录　print
仪表架　instrument [gauge] stand
仪表鉴定　instrument identification
仪表空气发生器　instrument air generator
仪表面板　instrument panel
仪表屏　meter panel
仪表室　instrument house, instrumentation room
仪表[器]误差　instrumental error [aberration]
仪表修理车间　instrument workshop
仪表讯号电缆　instrumentation signal cable
仪表用变压器　instrument transformer
仪表用电分支线路　appliance branch circuit
仪表滞后　instrument lag
仪表装置　instrumentation [metering] equipment, metering device
仪器　instrument (instr.), instrumentation, apparatus, appliance, aid

仪器不稳定性	instrumental instability
仪器不正确操作	mishandling
仪器分辨率[清晰度]	instrumental resolution
仪器分析	instrument analysis
仪器校准	instrument calibration
仪器灵敏度	instrumental sensitivity, gauge factor
仪器配备[使用]	instrumentation
仪器维修	instrument maintenance
仪器响应时间	instrument response time
已得数据	findings
已废的	obsolete
已赋量语句	【计】parameter statement
已加工轧材	【压】finished rolled stock
已搅拌混凝土	ready-mix concrete
已漏气的	gassy
已染色的	coloured
已完成铸型	complete mould
已污染[掺杂]废钢铁	contaminated scrap
已长入位错	【理】grown-in dislocation
已知范围	prescribed limit
已知数	known number, datum
已知值	given value
已贮料仓	bunkerage
乙丙橡胶	ethylene-propylene terpolymer (EPT)
乙二磺酸{$HSO_3·CH_2·CH_2·SO_3H$}	ethanedisulfonic [ethionic] acid
乙基硅酸盐	ethyl silicate
乙基铊{$Tl(C_2H_5)_3$}	thallium ethide [ethyl]
乙基锌{$Zn(C_2H_5)_2$}	zinc ethyl
乙基锗{$Ge(C_2H_5)_2, Ge(C_2H_5)_4$}	germanium ethide
乙醚{$C_2H_5OC_2H_5$}	ether, ethylether ◇ 硫氰酸[HSCN]-~溶液*
乙醚萃取	【色】(diethyl-)ether extraction ◇ 双循环~法*
乙醚萃取法	ether process ◇ 旧式~*
乙醚萃取剂	ether extractant
乙醚萃取器	ether extractor
乙醚萃液	【色】ether extract
乙醚净化法	ether purification process
乙醚相	ether phase
乙炔	acetylene (ACET), ethyne ◇ 空气-~焊接*
乙炔灯阀	acetylene torch valve
乙炔发生器	acetylene [carbide] generator ◇ 低产量~*, 低压~*, 滴水式~water feed generator, 电石入水式~*, 干式~*, 高产量~*, 高压(式)~*, 固定式~*, 接触式~*, 浸渍式~*, 排代式~*, 排水式~*, 双罐~duplex generator, 中压~*, 注水式[水入电石式](~*)
乙炔干燥器	acetylene drying device
乙炔焊	acetylene welding
乙炔焊枪	acetylene burber
乙炔缓蚀剂	acetylenic corrosion inhibitor
乙炔-空气焰	acetylene-air flame
乙炔瓶[罐]	acetylene cylinder
乙炔气	acetylene gas
乙炔气管道	acetylene (pipe) line
乙炔气焊机	acetylene welding set
乙炔软管	acetylene hose
乙炔石	(同"碳化钙")
乙炔(碳, 烟)黑	acetylene smoke [black]
乙炔铜	acetylide copper
乙炔焰割炬[切割器]	acetylene [oxyacetylene] cutter, acetylene cutting torch
乙炔焰炬	acetylene torch
乙炔焰炬阀	acetylene torch valve
乙炔银	silver acetylide
乙炔再装填站	【焊】recharging plant
乙炔渣滓	acetylene smudge
乙炔站发生器间[房]	【焊】acetylene generating room
乙酸钡	barium acetate
乙酸钙	calcium acetate
乙酸钴	cobalt acetate
乙酸钾	potassium acetate
乙酸卡必醇	carbitol acetate
乙酸镧{$La(C_2H_3O_2)_3$}	lanthanum acetate

乙酸铝　aluminum acetate
乙酸镁　magnesium acetate
乙酸锰　manganese acetate
乙酸钠　sodium acetate
乙酸镍　nickel acetate
乙酸钕 {Nd(C₂H₃O₂)₃}　neodymium acetate
乙酸铅 {Pb(C₂H₃O₂)₂·3H₂O}　lead acetate, sugar of lead
乙酸铅试纸　lead acetate paper
乙酸溶纤剂　【化】cellosolve acetate
乙酸溶液　acetate solution
乙酸铯 {CsC₂H₃O₂}　cesium acetate
乙酸双氧铀 [乙酸铀酰] {UO₂(C₂H₃O₂)₂}　uranyl acetate
乙酸锶 {Sr(C₂H₃O₂)₂}　strontium acetate
乙酸铁　ferric acetate
乙酸铜　copper acetate
乙酸纤维胶片　acetate film
乙酸锌　zinc acetate
乙酸亚汞　mercurous acetate
乙酸亚砷酸盐　acetoarsenite
乙酸(亚)铊 {TlC₂H₃O₂}　thallium acetate
乙酸亚铁溶液　iron liquor
乙酸盐 {CH₃COOM}　acetate
乙酸银　silver acetate
乙烷二磺酸 {HSO₃·CH₂·CH₂·SO₃H}　ethanedisulfonic acid
乙戊基·乙辛基胺萃取剂　amine 21F81
乙烯基塑料覆面薄钢板　vinyl-coated sheet
乙烯基涂层电缆　vinyl-coated cable
乙烯树脂　vinyl resin, Vinylite, Forenvar ◇ 阿尔瓦～Alvar
乙烯树脂涂层钢板　vinyl coated steel plate
乙烯塑料溶胶　vinyl plastisol
乙酰苯 {CH₃COC₆H₅}　acetophenone
乙酰胆碱　acetyl choline (ACh)
乙锗烷　digermane
乙字钢　(同"Z形钢")
乙字钢孔型　【压】zee-bar pass

乙字梁　Z-beam
钇贝塔石　yttrobetafite, yttrotitan-pyrochlore
钇的(三价钇的)　yttric
钇氟钛硅矿　yftisite
钇硅磷灰矿　britholite-(Y)
钇合金　yttrium alloy
钇褐帘石　muromontite, allanite-(Y)
钇(褐)榴石　yttergarnet
钇黑稀土矿　yttromelanocerite
钇基超导材料　Y-base(d) superconducting material
钇基合金　yttrium-base alloy
钇磷灰石　yttrocalcite
钇铝石　yttroalumite
钇铝石[柘]榴石　yttrium aluminium garnet (YAG)
钇铝石榴石激光器　YAG laser
钇锰榴石　emildine, emilite
钇铌钛铀矿　yttrobetafite
钇铌钽铁矿　yttro-columbo-tantalite
钇铌[钽]铁矿 {(Fe,Mn,Y,U)(Nb,Ta)O₄}　yttrocolumbite
钇铌铁矿　yttroniobite
钇铅铀矿　yttrogummite
钇球墨铸铁　yttrium nodular iron
钇铈镧石　keihauite, yttrotitanite
钇钛烧绿石　yttrobetafite, yttrotitan-pyrochlore
钇钽矿　loranskite {(Y,Ca,Ce,U,Th)(Nb,Ta,Ti)₂O₆}, yttrotantalite {(Y,Fe,U,Ca)(Ta,Nb)O₄}
钇钽烧绿石　yttromicrolite
钇钽铁矿 {(Y,Fe,U,Ca)(Ta,Nb)O₄}　yttroniobite, yttrotantal, yttrotantalite
钇添加合金　yttrium addition
钇铁石榴石　yttrium iron garnet
钇铁氧体　yttrium ferrite
钇土　yttrium earths
钇土金属　yttrium earth metal
钇钨华　thorotungstite, yttrotungstite
钇细晶石　yttromicrolite

钇易解石{(RE,Ca,U)(Nb,Ti)$_2$O$_6$} priorite,aeschynite-(Y)
钇萤石{(Ca,Y)Fe$_{2-3}$} yttrofluoride,fluorite-(Y),yttrocalcite
钇铀矿{(U,Th,Pb)O$_2$ + Y$_2$O$_3$} nivenite,cleveite
钇(铀)烧绿石 obruchevite, yttropyrochlore
钇族稀土 yttrium earths [group]
钇族稀土金属 yttrium earth metal
艺术铸件 art casting
抑菌剂 bacteriostat
抑零式仪表 suppressed-zero (instrument)
抑泡剂 foam inhibitor
抑止剂 inhibitor
抑制 inhibition, suppression, depression, holdback, damping, reject, restrain
抑制层 prevent coating
抑制电平 【电】rejection level
抑制反应 inhibited reaction
抑制腐蚀 corrosion inhibition
抑制剂 inhibitor, depressant, depressor, depressing [inhibiting] agent, retardant, preventer (浮选用) ◇ 阳极~ anodic inhibitor, 阴极~ cathodic inhibitor, 有机~ organic inhibitor
抑制膜 inhibitive film
抑制期 inhibistion period
抑制器 suppressor, depressor, killer ◇ 直流(分量)~ DC suppressor unit
抑制栅(极) suppressor, gauze
抑制生锈 rust inhibition
抑制紊流中间包 turbulence-suppressing tundish
抑制作用 (同"阻止作用")
易剥落敏感性 【压】susceptibility to spalling
易剥膜[胶片] flaking film
易爆炸的 explosive
易焙烧矿石 free burning ore
易变的 unsteady, instable, volatile
易变辉石{(Ca,Mg)(Mg,Fe)Si$_2$O$_6$} pigeonite
易变率 degree of uncertainty
易变耐磨蚀性 variable corrosion resistance
易变态 labile state
易变形钢 easily deformable steel
易变载荷 mobile load
易操纵性 handiness
易潮解的 deliquescent
易沉降的 free settling
易除垢性 cleanability
易磁化方向 easy direction of magnetization
易读性 readabity
易锻造黄铜(59Cu,39Zn,2Pb) forging brass
易风化的 fflorescent (efflor.)
易腐蚀的 (同"可腐蚀的")
易腐蚀路径 【企】path of easy corrosion
易割冒口 necked-down [washburn] riser
易割冒口颈缩芯片 【铸】wafer core
易割冒口(芯)片 knock-off [neck-down] core, washburn riser core
易割片[冒口易割片] 【铸】washburn core
易割缩颈 【铸】break-off notch
易汞齐化金 free-milling gold
易焊位置焊接 position welding
易滑移 easy glide
易滑移面 plane of easy slip
易滑移区 easy glide region
易挥发渗透剂 highly volatile penetrant
易挥发性 fugitiveness
易挥发组分(树脂的) light-volatile component
易挤压金属 easely-extrudable metal
易解石{(RE,Fe,Th)(Nb,Ti)$_{22}$O$_6$,Ce$_2$O$_3$·ThO$_2$·TiO$_2$·(Nb,Ta)$_2$O$_5$} (a) eschynite
易浸蚀(结构)组分 rapid etching constituent
易净化性 cleanability
易炼焦煤 (同"高黏结性煤")

易裂性 fissility, fragility
易流动粉末 free flowing powder
易流动渣 freely flowing slag, free running slag
易破裂的 cracky
易切削【钢】 free machining
易切削不锈钢 free cutting stainless steel (SSF4：＜0.14C,＜0.75Si,＜1Mn,＜0.06P,＜0.15—0.25S,16—18Cr 及 Al、Cu、Mo 等)
易切(削)钢 free-cutting [free-machining, automatic] steel, fast machine steel ◇ USS 弗雷马克斯 15～*,USS 卡里洛依 FC～*,半镇静～*,含硫～*,莱德洛伊含铅
易切削合金 free cutting [machining] alloy
易(切)削黄铜 (58Cu, 40Zn, 2Pb) machinable [free-cutting, turning] brass ◇ 莱德赖特含铅～*
易切削金属材料 free cutting metallic material
易切削磷青铜 free cutting phosphor bronze
易切削轻金属 free cutting light metal
易切削软钢 soft free-cutting [free-machining] steel
易切削铜 free cutting copper
易切削铜铍合金 (2Be, 0.3Co, 少量 Pb, 余量 Cu) free cutting Be-Cu alloy
易切削性夹杂 free cutting inclusion
易切削铸造铅锰青铜 (61Cu, 0.75Sn, 0.25Mn, 0.75Al, 1.0Fe, 0.72Pb, 余量 Zn) leaded manganese bronze
易燃材料 inflammable material
易燃辰砂【朱砂,硫化汞矿】 inflammable cinnabar(ite)
易燃的 combustible, (in)flammable, free burning
易燃锆粉 pyrophoric zirconium powder
易燃合金 boiler plug alloy
易燃钠膜(钠还原法) pyrophoric sodium film
易燃气体 inflammable gas
易燃性 inflammability
易热裂度 crackability
易熔成分 low-melting constituent
易熔焊料 quick solder ◇ 高铋～ bismuth solder
易熔合金 fusible [low-melting(-point)] alloy, eutectic [slush] metal ◇ 阿戈－邦德～ Argo-Bond alloy, 铋锡铅镉～*, 布兰特～*, 达塞特～*, 非共晶～*, 格思里～ Guthrie's alloy, 镉～*, 骨科用～ anatomical alloy, 里希腾伯格～*, 罗斯～*, 牛顿铈铅锡～*, 塞罗洛伊～ Cerroloy, 塞罗西尔～Cerroseal, 伍德～*
易熔合金模 fusible alloy mould
易熔混合胶(制铸模用) plasticarve
易熔夹杂 secondary inclusions
易熔金属 fusible metal
易熔炉渣 fusible [low-melting-point] slag
易熔模型 【铸】fusible pattern
易熔黏土 vitrifiable clay
易熔铅合金 fusible lead alloy
易熔塞 【焊】fusible plug
易熔体结构 eutectic structure
易熔性 fusibility, fusibleness, eutexia
易熔质 【金】eutectic
易溶(解)的 freely soluble
易失存储 volatile memory [storage]
易碎材料 (同"脆性材料")
易碎粉粒 fluffy particle
易碎晶格 brittle lattice
易碎氯化物 fluffy chloride
易碎性 brittlement, fragility, frangibility
易损部分(炉衬的) vulnerable area
易损耗元素的损失 preferential elemental loss
易损件 wear part, consumable(s)
易损性 vulnerability
易弯曲的 flexible
易维修性 (同"可维修性")
易位 metathesis

易显现性	visualizability
易消失性	fugitiveness
易泄漏性	leakiness
易悬浮的	floatable
易选矿石	free milling ore
易氧化的	(同"可氧化的")
易运动方向	direction of easy motion
易折断的	breakable
易着色的	colourable
逸出	escape, emitting, effusion
逸出电子	outgoing [runaway] electron
逸出阀门	escape valve
逸出气体	emergent [evolved, exit] gas
逸出蒸汽	exit vapour
逸度[性]	fugacity
逸散	fugitive emission
逸散气体	fugitive gas
逸散热	dissipated heat
"疫病"降解（金属互化物特性）	"pest" degradation
意大利硅铝合金	italsil
意大利国家标准	Unificazione Nazionale Italiano (UNI)
意大利专利	Italian Patent (It. P.)
意外事故	unforeseen event, contingency
意外损耗	incidental dissipation
意外停机	【计】hang up
意外物料	tramp material
忆形	shape memory
忆形合金	(同"形状记忆合金")
忆形效应	(同"形状记忆效应")
溢出	overflow, (over) spill, flowoff, run-off, runout, pouring off, spillage（钢水溢出）◇ 阶码~*
溢出管	downflow spout
溢出检查	【计】overflow check
溢出检查指示器	overflow-check indicator
溢出口	【钢】outflow opening
溢出位	【计】overflow position
溢出物	overspill
溢出液体	overflowing liquid
溢出渣	run-off slag
溢洪道	(flood) spillway
溢口	flowoff,【色】pouring nozzle
溢流	overflow (O/F, ovfl.), overrun(ning), overspill, effluence, flooding,【焊】lap ◇ 焙砂~*, 澄清[(上)清液] ~*, 贫~*, 酸性~【色】acid overflow
溢流坝	overfall dam, spillway (dam)
溢流板	overflow plate
溢流泵	overflow pump
溢流壁	overflow wall
溢流槽	overflow chute [gutter, launder, tank, trough], overflow vessel, discharge overhead trough（冷却水的）◇ 沉淀器~*
溢流澄清度	overflow clarity
溢流淬火	flush quenching
溢流挡板	overflow baffle
溢流道	overflow dam
溢流阀	overflow [surplus, reducing] valve
溢流沟	overflow gutter
溢流管	overflow pipe [tube], runback
溢流管线	over-flow pipe line
溢流警报[信号器]	overflow alarm
溢流孔	overflow hole
溢流口	overflow port [hole, gate], flowoff,【铸】outgate, run-off
溢流流量计	weir gauge
溢流冒口	【铸】pop-off, flow-off
溢流面[线]	overflow level (OL)
溢流浓度	overflow concentration
溢流盘式涤气器	flooded disc scrubber
溢流渠	bypass
溢流溶液	overflow solution
溢流润滑	flood lubrication
溢流式球磨机	overflow-type ball mill
溢流式再磨球磨机	overflow regrind ball mill
溢流室	overflow chamber
溢流速率	overflow rate
溢流桶	【连铸】overflow ladle
溢流循环槽	overflow circulating tank
溢流堰	overflow(ing) weir [edge], weir

◇ 真空(溢流层)式～ aerated weir
溢流液 overflowing [effluent] liquid
溢流原理 overflow principle
溢流渣 flushing cinder
溢流指示器 overflow indicator
溢流铸锭法 ◇ 索维尔～
溢流装置 overflow device, overflow mechanism (机械压力机的)
溢流嘴 【冶】overflow lip
溢水孔板 decanting weir
溢水口 flowoff, gap, spillway
溢渣 flushing, boilings (钢水的)
溢渣口 slag lip
译码 decoding, interpretation, translating, decipher
译码操作 【计】decoded operation
译码器 decoder, decipherer, translator, function table ◇ 操作～ operation decoder
译码员 decoder, decipherer
译员 interpreter (口译), translator (笔译)
异丙苯{C_9H_{12}} isopropyl benzene
异步操作[工作] asynchronous operation [working]
异步传输 asynchronous transmission
异步电动机 asynchronous motor
异步电机 induction machine [dynamo]
异步电抗 asynchronous reactance
异步发电机 asynchronous [induction] generator
异步分时多路方式 asynchronous time-division multiplexing (ATDM)
异步计算机 asynchronous computer
异步交叉轧制 asymmetric and cross rolling
异步控制 asynchronous control
异步冷轧 asymmetrical cold rolling
异步启动 asynchronous starting
异步驱动回路 asynchronous drive circuit
异步时分多路方式 asynchronous time-division multiplexing

异步调相机 asynchronous condenser
异步通信 asynchronous communication
异步通信接口适配器 asynchronous communication interface adapter (ACIA)
异步信号发送 asynchronous signaling
异步轧机 asynchronous rolling mill
异常 unusual, abnormal, anomaly
异常报告 【计】exception report(ing)
异常电流 abnormal current
异常价 cryptovalence
异常晶粒长大 (同"反常晶粒长大")
异常侵蚀 abnormal erosion
异常散射 anomalous scattering
异常条件 【计】exceptional condition
异常透射 anomalous transmission
异常性 abnormality, anomalism
异成分 heterogeneity
异成分转变 incongruent transformation
异点 dissimilarity
异丁(烯)橡胶 butyl rubber
异丁(烯)橡胶墙角护条 butyl rubber beading
异分同晶(现象) allomerism
异分同晶的 allmeric
异分同晶质 allomer
异分子聚合(作用) copolymerization
异分子聚合物 copolymer
异构重整 【化】isoforming
异构化(作用) isomerization
异构体[物] 【理】isomer
异号位错 【理】dislocations of opposite signs, unlike dislocation
异化作用 【化】dissimilation
异极点阵 heteropolar lattice
异极键 heteropolar binding [bond, linkage]
异极矿{$Zn_2(OH)_2SiO_3, Zn_2O \cdot SiO_3 \cdot H_2O$} calamine, hemimorphite ◇ 硅质～ siliceous calamine
异极矿黄铜 calamine brass
异极性 heteropolarity
异己(丑)酮[异己酮-2] hexon(e) ◇ 萃

后～ effluent hexone
异己酮萃取 hexon(e) extraction
异己酮萃取法 hexon(e) process
异己酮－硫(代)氰酸盐分离法 hexone-thiocyanate separation process
异己酮－硫(代)氰酸盐萃取法 hexone-thiocyanate process
异己酮－硫(代)氰酸盐萃取系统 hexon(e)-thiocyanate extraction system
异金属夹杂 foreign metal
异径管接头 increaser
异径弯头 reducing elbow
异类原子 dissimilar [foreign] atom
异硫氰酸盐 isothiocyanate
"异"门 【计】(symmetric) difference gate, exjunction gate
异名极 opposite [reciprocal] pole
异酞酸二甲酯 dimethylisophthalate (DMI)
异态的 hetermorphous
异相 outphase
异型棒钢 deformed bar
异型材轧机 shape mill
异型产品 specials
异型初轧坯 shaped bloom
异型大砖 shaped block
异型带材[带钢] 【压】section strip
异型断面 shaped cross section [profile]
异型方坯 shaped bloom
异型钢 shape (iron), fashioned [profile(d)] iron, figured steel ◇ 小～ figured bar iron
异型钢材 shaped profile, special (rolling-mill) section, special rolled-steel bar, profiled bar, section of shaped steel, special-shaped steel ◇ 连接板用～(angle) splice bar, 小尺寸～*
异型钢材定尺切割 section dividing
异型钢材轧辊 profiled roll
异型钢锭 shaped ingot
异型钢管 shaped tube, profiled steel tube ◇ 高频焊接～*
异型钢丝 shaped [section, profiled] wire
异型管(材) (special) section tube, shaped tube, mechanical tube (美)
异型管轧机 tubular mill
异型[非标准]厚板 sketch plate
异型角钢 special-shaped angle steel ◇ 经济断面～*
异型接头 compromise joint
异型耐火材料 shaped refractory
异型耐火砖 quarl(e)
异型坯 bloom [shaped] blank ◇ 大～*, 清理炉底用～ cleanout slab, 轧制工字梁用的～ beam blank
异型砂箱 specially shaped moulding box
异型铁砧 die block
异型铣刀 router
异型型材 shaped section
异型轧材 【压】groove-rolled bar
异型制品 fashion part, formed part
异型轴 profile shaft
异型铸造[铸件] shaped [mould] casting
异型[形]砖 shaped [fashioned] brick, special brick shapes, 【耐】shape, specials
异形(火焰)切割 shape(-flame) cutting
异形机架辊 profiled breast roll
异形件 shaped piece [objects]
异形(件堆)焊 shape welding
异形孔型 forming pass, section groove
异形拉(丝)模 profile die, shape drawing die
异形零件 fashion part, formed part
异形模 intricate shape die, shaped die
异形模压成形 contour forming
异形轮廓气割机[火焰切割机] 【焊】flame profiling machine
异形切割机 shape [profile] cutting machine
异形探测器 shaped probe
异形凸轮 contour cam
异形(凸缘)孔型 flange pass
异形压板 shaped pressure squeeze board
异形足辊 special-shaped foot roller

异性石 {(Na,Ca,Fe)₆Zr(OH,Cl)(SiO₃)₆} eudialyte, eudyalite
异序同晶(现象) eutropy
异序元素 【化】isobar, heterotope
异议 objection ◇ 有～的 objectionable
异质材料 dissimilar material
异质材料连接 joining of dissimilar materials
异质衬底 foreign substrate
异质的 heterogeneous
异质热电效应 Seebeck effect
异质熔化 incongruent melting
异质同晶的 allmeric
异质同晶(现象) allomerism
异质外延 heteroepitaxy
异种金属 dissimilar [heterogeneous] metal
异种金属焊接 dissimilar metal welding
异种金属接触腐蚀 dissimilar metal corrosion
异种晶体 foreign crystal
异族溶解 heterolysis
翼(板) vane, wing
翼橡角钢 boom angle
翼管式热交换器 fin tube type heat exchanger
翼墙 wing [swing, monkey] wall
翼型风机 foiled fan
翼型弯曲叶片式风机 foiled incline blade type fan
翼型叶片 airfoil blade
翼形锭 winged ingot
翼形螺钉 thumb [winged, eared] screw
翼形螺母 thumb [wign(ed)] nut
翼缘 flange ◇ 蝶式[展开式]～flared out flange, 开口式～*
翼缘板 chord plate
翼缘厚度(工字钢的) flange thickness
翼缘加板工字型钢柱 H-column with cover
翼缘宽度(工字钢的) flange width
翼缘强化[增强] flange strengthening

茵斯皮雷欣转炉 INSPIRATION converter
因阿铅合金 inalium
因次 dimension ◇ 有～的 dimensional
因次分析 dimensional analysis
因次分析法 【理】dimensional method
因次理论 theory of dimensions
因达洛伊铟银焊料合金(90In,10Ag) Indalloy
因果关系 cause-effect [causal] relationship, Causality, Causation
因科800镍铬铁高温合金 Incoloy 800
因科高压羰化法[压力羰基(炼镍)法](国际镍公司专利) Inco (International Nickel Company) pressure carbonyl process, IPC process
因科内尔713LC镍铬超级铸造合金 (0.06C, 12Cr, 1.5Co, 4.5Mo, 0.6Ti, 6Al, 0.3Fe, 2Nb+Ta, 余量Ni) Inconel 713 LC
因科内尔X析出硬化型耐热合金 Inconel "X"
因科内尔镍铬耐热耐蚀钢 Inconel steel
因科内尔镍铬铁耐热耐蚀合金[镍合金] (80Ni, 14Cr, 6Fe) Inconel (alloy)
因科内尔镍合金料罐 Inconel (charge) can
因科镍(国际镍公司生产的) Inco (International Nickel Company) nickel
因科镍铬不锈钢(30Ni, 20Cr, 1.5Mn, 1Si, 0.1C, 余量Fe) Incoloy
因科镍铬耐热合金 Inco chrome nickel
因科悬浮熔炼法 【金】Inco (International Nickel Company) process
因数 coefficient, factor, facient ◇ H～(美)*, g～*, 德拜-瓦勒～*
因素 factor, element ◇ 人的～ humam factor
因特网 internet
因瓦低膨胀(系数)合金 Invar low expansion alloy
因瓦恒范镍钢 (同"不膨胀钢")

因瓦效应　Invar effect
因子　factor,【数】divisor
殷钢　(同"不膨胀钢")
音　(同"声")◇隔～acoustic insulation
音程误差　interval error
音量控制阀　volume control flap
音速　(同"声速")
音响材料　acoustic material
音响反射率　acoustic reflection coefficient
音响警报[报警设备]　audible alarm
音响试验　sound test
音响效果　acoustics
音响泄漏指示计　audible leak indicator
音响信号　audible signal [indication], acoustical [sonic] signal
音响仪(混凝土测定用)　sonoscope
音响指示　audible indication
阴暗　dark, dullness, cloudiness
阴挡层光电池　blocking layer cell
阴电荷　(同"负电荷")
阴沟　(under)drain, (foul water) sewer, cloaca, culvert
阴沟管模板　dod
阴极　cathode (electrode), negative (neg.), negative pole [electrode]◇附加～*,轰击[预热]～bombarding cathode,角～angle cathode,笼形～basket cathode,铆吊环～【色】cathode with riveted loops,弯曲[L形]～bent cathode,钟形～bell type cathode
阴极靶　target (cathode)
阴极板　negative plate
阴极棒　cathode bar
阴极包覆　cathodic cladding
阴极剥落物　crop of cathodes
阴极剥片次数[频率]　frequency of stripping cathodes
阴极保护　cathode [cathodic] protection
阴极表面　cathode surface
阴极部分　cathode portion
阴极材料　cathode material
阴极槽衬　cathode lining

阴极槽壳　cathode shell
阴极层　cathodic layer
阴极插入孔　cathode aperture
阴极产出率　cathode yield
阴极产物　cathodic product
阴极产物接受器　【色】cathode product receiver
阴极场致发光　cathodoluminescence, cathode luminescence
阴极长度(碘化物法的)　filament length
阴极超电压[过电压]　cathodic overvoltage
阴极沉积　cathode [cathodic] precipitation, cathodic deposition
阴极沉积过程　【色】cathode run
阴极沉积物　cathode deposit
阴极沉积周期　cathode depositing period
阴极池　cathode pool
阴极传输　cathode transfer
阴极袋　cathode bag
阴极导电棒　cathode collector bar
阴极导体　cathode conductor
阴极灯丝　cathode filament
阴极底　cathode bottom
阴极电解浸蚀　cathodic etching
阴极电解液　(同"阴极液")
阴极电流　cathode-current
阴极电流密度　cathodic (current) density, cathode-current density
阴极电流效率　cathode (current) efficiency, cathodic efficiency
阴极电容　cathode capacitance
阴极电势[位]　cathode [noble] potential
阴极电位调节器　cathode potential regulator
阴极电压　cathodic voltage
阴极电压降　cathode (potential) drop, cathode fall, cathodic voltage drop
阴极电压降范围[区域]　cathode drop region
阴极电源接头　cathode [negative] power connection

阴极电源引线	cathode power lead
阴极吊环	cathode loop
阴极镀层	cathodic coating
阴极断裂	cathode breakage
阴极堆	cathode stack
阴极发光	cathode light [luminescence]
阴极发射	cathode emission
阴极反应	cathode [cathodic] reaction
阴极防护	cathodic protection
阴极防护剂	cathodic protector
阴极分析	cathode analysis
阴极腐蚀	cathode corrosion, cathodic corrosion [attack]
阴极镉	cathode cadmium
阴极隔膜	cathode diaphragm
阴极隔膜袋	cathode bag
阴极跟随器	cathode follower
阴极工作时间	age of cathodes
阴极钴	cathodic cobalt
阴极过程	cathode process
阴极挂耳	【色】cathode lug
阴极挂钩[阴极夹]	cathode hook
阴极管	cathode tube
阴极辊	cathode roll
阴极环	cathode ring
阴极还原	cathodic reduction
阴极缓蚀剂	cathodic inhibitor
阴极辉点	cathode [hot] spot
阴极辉光	cathode glow [light]
阴极回路	cathode loop
阴极汇流排	cathode busbar
阴极激发光	(同"阴极场致发光")
阴极极化	cathode [cathodic] polarization
阴极极化电位	cathode polarization potential
阴极极化法	cathodic polarization method
阴极溅射(处理)	cathode [cathodic] sputtering
阴极接头	negative contact
阴极结构	cathode structure [construction]
阴极金属	cathode metal
阴极浸蚀	cathodic etching
阴极聚焦装置	cathode focusing structure, focusing assembly of cathode
阴极孔	cathode aperture
阴极控制	cathodic control
阴极块	cathode block
阴极流	cathode flame
阴极炉	cathode furnace
阴极铝	cathode [cathodic] aluminium
阴极面	cathode face
阴极面积	cathode area
阴极膜	cathode film
阴极母线	cathode bus (bar), negative (bus-)bar
阴极内衬	cathode lining
阴极镍	cathode nickel
阴极耦合多谐振荡器	cathode-coupled multivibrator
阴极片	【色】cathode (starting) sheet
阴极气体	cathode gas
阴极清洗	cathode [direct-current] cleaning
阴极区	cathode portion [space]
阴极去油	cathode cleaning
阴极圈	cathode loop
阴极韧铜	tough cathode copper
阴极熔(化)炉	cathode melting furnace
阴极栅	cathode grid
阴极射线	cathode rays (CR)
阴极射线电流	cathode ray current
阴极射线管	cathode ray tube (CRT), electron ray tube, electron-beam tube ◇长余辉～*
阴极射线管控制器	cathode ray tube controller
阴极射线管示波器	cathode-ray [Braun] tube oscillograph ◇通用双束型宽频带
阴极射线管显示(器)	cathod ray tube display [indicator]
阴极射线炉	cathode ray furnace
阴极射线示波器	cathode ray oscillograph

[oscilloscope]
阴极射(线)束 cathode (-ray) beam [stream]
阴极室 cathode chamber [compartment, department, space]
阴极试样 cathode sample
阴极输出器 cathode follower (CF)
阴极束靶 cathode-beam target
阴极酸洗 cathode [cathodic] pickling
阴极碳块 cathode block
阴极特性 filament characteristic
阴极锑 cathode antimony
阴极铜 cathode copper, tough cathode
阴极铜粉压制烧结法 【色】coalesced copper process
阴极透镜 cathode lens
阴极涂层[涂料] cathode [cathodic] coating
阴极拖车 【色】cathode trailer
阴极脱脂 cathode cleaning
阴极温度(碘化物热离解法的) filament temperature
阴极物质 cathode mass
阴极效率 cathode efficiency
阴极锌 cathode zinc
阴极修理间 【色】cathode repair shop
阴极-(阳极)靶距离[间距] cathode-to-target distance [spacing]
阴极-阳极间距离(电子管的) cathode-to-anode spacing
阴极液 catholyte, cathode liquor [liquid], cathodic solution ◇ 返回 ~ recycled catholyte, 废[负]~ *
阴极液成分 catholyte composition
阴极液隔膜 catholyte memebrane
阴极液室 catholyte compartment
阴极液贮槽 catholyte (storage) tank
阴极液组成 catholyte composition
阴极抑制剂 cathodic inhibitor
阴极引线 cathode [filament] lead
阴极支柱 cathode support
阴极制备 preparation of cathodes

阴极种板 cathode blank
阴极铸造机 cathode-casting machine
阴极转换 cathode transfer
阴极装置 cathode assembly
阴离子 anion, negative ion ◇ 含氧~ *, 引入~作用 anation
阴离子半透膜 anion-semipermeable membrane
阴离子表面活性剂 anionic surface-active agent, anionics
阴离子冲洗 anion rinse
阴离子导电率 anionic conductance
阴离子浮选法 anionic flotation
阴离子隔膜 anion membrane
阴离子极性可逆电极 anion-reversible electrode
阴离子交换 anion-exchange
阴离子交换槽 anion cell
阴离子交换过程 anion-exchange process
阴离子交换回收 recovery by anion exchange
阴离子交换剂 anion-exchanger, anionite ◇ 液体~ *
阴离子交换介质 anion-exchange medium
阴离子交换膜 anion-exchange membrane
阴离子交换能力 anion-exchange ability
阴离子交换树脂 anion-exchange resin ◇ HGR 磺化聚苯乙烯 ~ Nalcite HGR, 多孔~ decolorite, 强碱性~ *, 弱碱性~ *, 有机~ *
阴离子交换树脂选择性 anion-resin selectivity
阴离子可逆电极 anion-reversible electrode
阴离子空位 anion(ic) vacancy
阴离子亏损 anion defect
阴离子络合物 anionic complex
阴离子迁移数 anion transference number
阴离子去垢剂 anionic [anionique] detergent ◇ 提波尔~ Teepol
阴离子渗透膜 anion-permeable membrane

阴离子树脂交换　anion-resin exchange
阴离子树脂交换能力　anion-resin capacity
阴离子树脂交换柱　anion-exchange [anion-resin] column
阴离子团　anion radical
阴离子吸附　anion-adsorption
阴离子真空蚀刻　cathodic vacuum etching
阴离子助凝剂　anion coagulant aid
阴螺纹　female screw
阴面(锭、坯的)　cold side
阴模　female [lower, bed] die, female [negative] mould, matrix
阴模锻出肋条的锻件　female beaded forging
阴模工作区长度　bearing length (of die)
阴模合金　die alloy
阴模模座　matrix holder
阴模入口角　included die angle
阴模压力【压】die pressure
阴性元素　negative element
阴压模　negative mould
阴阳极间距离　anode-cathode distance [spacing]
阴阳极间隙　cathode-anode gap
阴-阳离子交换树脂　cation-anion resin
阴影　shadow, shade, umbra, cloud
阴影电子显微镜像　shadow electron image
阴影电子显微照片[照相]　shadow electron micrograph
阴影复膜[复型]　shadowed replica
阴影溅射处理　shadow casting
阴影溅射处理复型　shadow cast replica
阴影(溅射)法　shadow method
阴影(溅射)角　shadow angle
阴影区　shaded area, shadow zone, umbra
阴影图像电子显微镜观察　shadowgraphic electron microscope observation
阴影图像电子显微术　shadowgraphic electron microscopy
阴影显微术　shadow microscopy
阴影线　hatch(ures)

阴影照相　shadow photograph, shadowgraph
阴影照相术　shadow photography
铟铵矾　(同"硫酸铟铵")
铟合金　indium alloy
铟基合金　indium-base alloy
铟钾矾 $\{K_2SO_4 \cdot In_2(SO_4)_3 \cdot 24H_2O$ 或 $KIn(SO_4)_2 \cdot 12H_2O\}$　potassium indium alum
铟钠矾 $\{Na_2SO_4 \cdot In_2(SO_4)_3 \cdot 24H_2O$ 或 $NaIn(SO_4)_2 \cdot 12H_2O\}$ sodium indium alum
铟铷矾　rubidium indium alum
铟铯矾　(同"硫酸铟铯")
铟锑化合物　indium-antimony compound
铟添加合金　indium addition
铟锡氧化物　indium tin oxide
铟银焊料合金　◇因达洛伊～*
银{Ag}　silver (sil. silv.) ◇包～硬币 Billon, 标准～*, 除[脱]～*, 纯～*, 德～*, 副产～by-product silver, 高～含量的*, 海绵状～sponge silver, 含锑～antimonial silver, 科罗拉多～[铜镍锌合金]*, 内华达～Nevada silver, 熔铸～fused silver, 斯特林～*, 天然～native silver, 硝酸析～法【色】inquartation, 英国标准～*
银钯合金　silver-palladium alloy ◇阿尔巴～Alba alloy
银白色　silvery colour
银白色金属　silvery-white metal
银白生铁(断口呈银白色；5—17Si, 0.5—2Mn, 0.3P, 0.05S)　silver(y) pig iron
银钡锰矿　argentomelane
银币合金　coin silver
银箔　silver foil [paper]
银沉积物　silver deposit
银垫片[圈]　silver gasket
银电解槽　electrolytic silver cell
银锭　silver bullion [ingot] ◇含金～dore silver
银镀层　silver deposit, silvering
银锻　bodkin

银 yin

银粉 aluminium powder ◇ 西尔波德~Silpowder
银复合钢 silver ply steel
银镉锡钎焊合金 silver cadmium tin alloy
银镉轴承合金(97.6Cd,0.5Ag,1.9Cu) silver cadmium alloy
银汞膏[齐,合金] silver amalgam, arquerite,argental
银汞硅土 lithodeon
银焊 silver-alloy brazing,silver soldering
银焊料[焊条](Ag-Cu-Zr合金) silver solder ◇ 雷迪弗洛~*,麦特尔~Mattlsolda,伊泽弗洛~*
银焊料合金(10—80Ag,52—16Cu,38—4Zn,0.5Cd) silver soldering alloy ◇ 迪帕洛伊~Dimpalloy
银行 bank ◇ 代理~correspondent bank
银合金 silver alloy, billon ◇ 波托西~Potosi silver,仿~imitation silver,弗吉尼亚~Virginia silver
银灰色 metallic-grey
银回收 silver recovery
银基合金 silver-base alloy
银激活的 silver-activated
银金矿 electrum,gironite
银精炼法 silver refining ◇ 巴尔巴赫卧式电极电解~*
银矿 silver ore,silver mine
银矿床 silver deposit
银矿物 silver mineral
银矿物型合金 ◇ 阿格莱特~Arguerite alloy
银亮钢(含碳0.95—1.25,硫、磷极低) silver steel,bohler
银亮钢棒 bright bar
银亮钢丝 silver steel wire
银亮合金 ◇ 法伦~*
银亮磨光钢丝 bright-ground
银亮抛光碳素工具钢 bright polished carbon tool steel
银铃铜锡合金(41.5Cu,58.5Sn) silver bell alloy

银铝合金 aerdentalloy
银毛矿 owyheeite
银锰铝永磁[磁性]合金 ◇ 西尔马纳尔~*
银膜 silverskin,silver deposit(感光板的)
银幕 wall screen
银钼合金 silver-molybdenum
银钠盐 lechedor
银镍电接触器材 silver-nickel contacts
银镍合金 silver-nickel ◇ 巴扎尔~*
银器钢 silver steel
银钎焊 silver brazing
银钎焊合金(高熔点类为含10—20Ag的六O黄铜;低熔点类含银较高,除Cu、Zn外尚含<18 Cd) silver soldering[brazing] alloy ◇ 迪帕洛伊~Dimpalloy
银钎焊接 silver-brazed joint
银钎料 silver solder,silver-brazing alloy
银铅 argentalium,polytelite
银铅焊料[钎焊合金,焊药](97.5Pb,1.5Ag,1Sn) silver-lead solder ◇ 科姆索尔~(掺有少量锡)Comsol
银色光泽 silvering
银色金属 argentine
银色裂纹 【金】silver crack
银色漆 aluminium paint
银色青铜(67.5Cu,18Mn,1.25Al,0.25Si,余量Zn) silver bronze
银色锡基餐具合金(2—5Sb,0.5Cu,余量Sn) metal argentine
银色锡锑合金(85Sn,15Sb) argentine metal
银砷铜矿 argentodomeykite
银石墨电刷 silver-graphite brush
银丝 silver wire
银-碳化钨制品 silver-tungsten carbide
银锑合金 silver-antimony alloy ◇ 西兰克~*
银添加合金 silver addition
银条 silver bar
银铜合金 silver-copper alloy ◇ 阿姆西尔~*

银铜合金特殊时效硬化	Mitsche's effect
银微晶砷铜矿	argentoalgodonite
银钨电触头合金（20Ag，80W）	silver-tungsten ◇ 西维尔梅特～Silvelmet
银钨电接触器材	silver-tungsten contact material
银钨双金属带	silver-tungsten bimetallic band
银锡合金汞剂	silver-tin amalgam
银锌壳（铅精炼的）	(silver-)zinc crust
银锌壳蒸馏	distillation of zinc crust
银锌壳蒸馏罐	zinc-crust distillation retort
银锌铅壳（铅精炼的）	silver-zinc-lead crust
银星石	（同"潜晶磷酸铝石"）
银－氧化镉制品［复合物］	silver cadmium oxide
银冶金学	silver metallurgy
银液滴定（法）	argentimetry
银影密度高［厚］	intense
银云母	cat's silver
银制的	silvery
银朱	sulphide of mercury
饮用水	drinking [potable] water
饮用水水质标准	water quality standard for drinking water
引爆	igniting, priming, detonating ◇ 装药～成形 cord-charge forming
引爆电极	ignitor electrode
引爆法	ignition method
引爆混合剂	ignition mixture
引爆剂	booster, flashing composition ◇ 碘～*, 化学～chemical booster
引爆检测器	priming detector
引爆丝（液电成形用）	initiating wire
引爆温度	ignition temperature
引爆温度控制	ignition temperature control
引爆装置	igniter, ignitor
引槽	（同"引水渠"）
引出	draw forth, drawing off, extraction, eduction, exhaustion, diversion
引出板	【焊】run-off plate
引出槽	lander
引出端	leading-out end [terminal], outgoing terminal, exit
引出端控制	exit control
引出辊	drawing-off roller
引出帽	boot
引出热量	delivered heat
引出溶液	outgoing solution
引出线	leading [lead-out] wire, (output) lead, outgoing line, outlet
引带剂（钢丝拉拔的）	carrier
引导	guide, lead(ing), pilot, guidance, introduction
引导板	diverting flap
引导程序	【计】bootstrap (routine)
引导存储器	【计】bootstrap memeory
引导带	【计】pilot tape
引导记录	leader record, home record
引导输入程序	bootstrap input program
引导装入程序	bootstrap loader, bootstrap loading routine
引锭	dummy ingot
引锭杆	【连铸】dummy [starter, starting] bar, ingot starting stub ◇ 重上～restrand, 刚柔性～*, 可挠～flexible dummy bar
引锭杆摆动台	dummy bar tilter
引锭杆存放处	dummy bar storage
引锭杆导向器	dummy bar threader
引锭杆的插入	introduction of dummy bar
引锭杆底端	dummy bar bottom
引锭(杆接)头	dummy bar head
引锭(杆)坑	dummy bar pit
引锭(杆)链	dummy bar chain
引锭杆链运输机	dummy bar chain conveyer
引锭杆头	head of dummy bar
引锭杆脱扣	dummy bar disconnection
引锭坯	【连铸】dummy slab
引锭头	【连铸】stopping and withdrawing head, starter head（连续铸铜用）

引发　initiation
引发剂　initiator ◇ 化学～ chemical booster
引股(钢丝绳合绳时的)　threading-up
引弧　(arc) striking ◇ 接触法～*, 熔化式～*
引弧板　run-on plate ◇ 焊～ tab weld
引弧板焊接机(UOE焊管生产用)　tab welder
引弧点　firing point
引弧电位　striking potential
引弧端(焊条的)　striking end
引火柴　firewood, kindling
引火合金　sparking [pyrophoric] alloy
引火空气　pilot air
引火料　【冶】priming mixture
引火品质　pyrophoric quality
引火烧嘴用气体混合器　gas mixer for pilot burner
引火性质　pyrophoric property
引火装置　【冶】lighter
引进　introduction, import
引晶技术　seeding
引力　attraction (force), gravitation, gravitational force ◇ 范德瓦尔斯～*
引力场　gravitational [attraction] field
引力场源　gravitational-field source
引料杆　threading bar
引料台　threading table
引流沟　【环】diversion ditch
引流渠　【环】diversion channel
引流式射流放大器　induction fluid amplifier
引流元件(射流技术的)　induction amplifier
引起　lead (up) to, cause, arouse, bring to, induce
引起结构[组织]变化的　structurizing
引起乳化　emulsion-causing
引起注意中断　【计】attention interruption
引起注意装置　【计】attention device
引桥　approach bridge, (bridge) approach

引桥[道]挖方　approach cutting
引擎　engine
引擎盖　bonnet
引燃　ignition, flaming, inflame, detonation ◇ 不易～的 nonignitable, 自动～ autogenous ignition
引燃电极　igniter, ignitor
引燃电压　ignition voltage
引燃法　ignition method
引燃管　ignition rectifier, ignitron (tube), trigatron ◇ 气冷式～ air-cooled ignitron, 水冷式～ water-cooled ignitron, 水套冷却金属～*
引燃合金　ignition alloy
引燃火舌　pilot flame
引燃丝　ignition wire
引燃性　inflammability
引燃性能　ignition behavior
引入　induction, inlet, indraft, indraught, lead into, draw into, 【计】call
引入导管　inlet pipe
引入导线　lead-in wire
引入电缆　leading-in cable
引入端　leading-in end [terminal]
引入管　inlet tube
引入管道　inlet ductwork
引入管线　inlet line, intake pipeline
引入辊　draw(ing-in) roller
引入喇叭口　inlet spigot
引入量　intake
引入水　inlet water
引入线　incoming line (inc), lead-in, leading-in wire
引入线盘　leading-in panel
引入阴离子作用　anation
引入支线　inlet branch
引水　【环】water diversion
引水渠　channel of approach
引文　quotation, quoted passage ◇ 在同一～中 in the same cited
引文未列　no connection reported (nc rptd)

引吸喷射器 lifting injector
引吸式送风机 induced blower
引下线(避雷针的) down conductor
引线 lead (wire), outlet, leg wire, connection, threading-up (钢丝绳捻股时的) ◇ 爆炸~detonating fuse
引线盒 【电】pull box
引言 introduction (intr.), foreword
引语 quotation, citation
引证 quote, quotation, cite, adduction
隐蔽干扰 masking interference
隐蔽工程 concealed work
隐蔽棱边[晶棱] hidden edge
隐蔽缺陷 hidden defects
隐蔽式供暖 concealed heating
隐藏接缝 concealed joint
隐弧焊管机 submerged-arc weld mill
隐钾锰矿 cryptomelane, kalipslomelane
隐钾价 cryptovalence
隐晶 crypto-crystal
隐晶石英 cryptocrystalline quartz
隐模 【压】cavity of die
隐气孔率 closed porosity
隐丝(光学测温计的) disappearing filament
隐丝式高温计 disappearing filament pyrometer
隐丝式光学高温计 disappearing-filament optical pyrometer ◇ 巴伯~*
隐循环表 【计】DO-implied list
印度标准 Indian Standards (IS)
印度标准学会 Indian Standards Institution (ISI)
印度地质采矿冶金学会 Geological Mining and Metallurgical Society of India (G.M.M.S.I.)
印度金属学会 India Institute of Metals (I.I.M.)
印度矿产与五金贸易公司 Minerals and Metals Trading Corporation of India (MMTC)
印痕 impression, print, imprint, mark ◇ 废边~*
印痕对角线 diagonal of impression
印痕法 imprinting method
印痕制取法 model(l)ing
印花机 printing machine ◇ 带材表面涂层~strip printer
印记 impression, signet
印码电报机 recorder
印模 die (plate), stamp
印刷 printing
印刷电路 printed circuit
印刷电路板 printed (circuit) board ◇ 多重~multilayer board
印刷电路底板 copper foil laminate
印刷合金 printing alloy, type alloy [metal]
印刷机 printing machine [press] ◇ 摇头~tilting-head press, 页式~page printer
印刷品 printed matter
印刷术 printing ◇ 静电~xerography
印刷速度 printer speed
印图 impression
印纹辊 graining roll
印相 print ◇ 氧化夹杂~法【钢】oxide printing, 油墨直接~法(低倍检验用) ink print, 直接~(从底片) direct print, 接触~法【金】contact printing
印相机 printer
印像 printing
印像复型 【金】impression replica
印像辊 ink roll
印压机 platen press
印油 marking-out fluid, stamp-pad ink
印章 seal, stamp ◇ 检查员~inspector's stamp
印字机 inker, inkwriter ◇ 12倍补偿点式~*
印字示波器 ink-writing oscillograph
英安岩 dacite
英币银 ◇ 斯特林~*
英尺磅秒单位制 foot-pound-second system (FPS)

英道克斯铁酸钡永久磁铁　Indox
英迪斯科高压釜球团法　Indesco process
英帝国冶炼有限公司熔炼铅锌法　Imprial smelting process（ISP）
英帝国冶炼有限公司熔炼铅锌法专利　Imperial Smelting Patent（I.S.P.）
英国薄钢板、箍钢带标准量规　British sheet and hoop iron standard gauge（B.G.）
英国标准　British Standard（BS, Br. Std.）
英国标准（技术）规范　British Standard Specification（B.S.S.）, B.S. Specifications
英国标准加仑（=4.546升）　imperial gallon
英国标准铅字合金（2.5—4.0Sn, 2.5—3.0Sb, 余为Pb）　electrotype metal
英国标准筛　British Standard Sieve（B.S.S.）
英国标准筛规　British standard screen scale
英国标准线规　British standard wire gauge（B.s.w.g.）, British Standard Gauge（B.S.G.）, Imperial wire gauge（ISWG）
英国标准型钢　British standard section
英国标准学会　British Standards Institution（BSI）
英国标准银（纯度92.5Ag）　London standard silver
英国材料协会　British Institute of Materials（B.I.M.）
英国常衡制　avoirdupois
英国法定标准线规　Legal standard wire gauge
英国钢铁联合会　British Iron and Steel Federation（BISF）
英国钢铁协会　British Iron and Steel Institute（BISI）
英国钢铁研究协会　British Iron and Steel Research Association（B.I.S.R.A.）
英国个体经营钢厂主协会　British Independent Steel Producers Association（BISPA）
英国工程标准协会　British Engineering Standards Association（BESA）
英国工程用钢规范　En specifications
英国焊接学会　British Institute of Welding（BIW）
英国焊接研究协会　British Welding Research Association（B.W.R.A.）
英国胶　British gum
英国金属协会　British Institute of Metals（B.I.M.）
英国路易斯特毒气解毒药（二硫基丙醇）　British antilewisite（BAL）
英国镁砂（烧结镁砂）　britmag
英国耐火材料研究协会　British Refractories Research Association（BRRA）
英（国）式砌合　English bond
英国陶瓷学会　British Ceramic Society（BCS）
英国陶瓷研究协会　British Ceramic Research Association（BCRA）
英国透气性单位　【团】British Permeability Unit（B.P.U.）
英国锡铅合金［锡镴］（80Sn, 20Pb）　English pewter
英国线规　Imperial wire gauge
英国新标准　New British Standard（NBS）
英国硬质合金（制造业）协会　British Hard Metal Association（BHMA）
英国有色金属研究协会　British Nonferrous Metals Research Association（B.N.F.M.R.A.）
英国有色金属冶炼协会　British Non-Ferrous Metals Federation（B.N.F.M.F.）
英国铸铁研究协会　British Cast Iron Research Association（B.C.I.R.A.）
英国铸铁业协会　British Ironfounders' Association（BIA）
英国铸造工作者学会　Institute of British Foundrymen（IBF）

英国专利 British Patent (BP, Brit. pat.), English Patent (E.P.)
英加克莱德不锈复合钢 Ingaclad steel
英帕尔科铝基合金 Impalco alloy
英特乌班 27 号硬巴比合金 Interurban No. 27
鹰桥盐酸选择浸出提镍法 Falconbridge process
应变 strain(ing) ◇ 表观～ apparent strain, 不可恢复的[非弹性部分]～ unrecovered strain, 定速～试验装置 Strain pacer, 非平面～ antiplane strain, 恒定法～*, 屈服前～ preyield strain, 瞬时～*, 整体～ bulk strain, 支承～ bearing strain
应变比 strain ratio
应变测量 strain-gauging strain measurement
应变测量网格法 grid method for strain measurement
应变测量仪 strain-measuring instrument
应变测量装置 strain-measuring equipment
应变场 strain field
应变程度 degree of strain
应变弛豫 strain relaxation
应变传感器 strain transducer ◇ 电容～*, 拉式～ strain transducer
应变电阻合金 strain resistance alloy
应变电阻丝 gauge line
应变范围 strain range
应变分量 strain component
应变分析 strain analysis
应变感生沉淀[析出] strain-induced precipitation
应变感生有序化 strain-induced ordering
应变感生转变[相变] strain-induced transformation
应变各向异性 strain anisotropy
应变回复结晶 strain-relief crystallization
应变回火(处理) strain temper
应变孔 strain bore
应变裂纹 strain crack

应变灵敏度系数 gauge factor
应变率敏感材料 strain-rate-sensitive material
应变敏感性 strain sensitivity
应变模型图 strain pattern
应变能 strain energy
应变能(计算)法 strain energy method
应变能密度 density of strain energy
应变强度因子 strain intensity factor
应变强化 strain strengthening
应变-时间数据 strain-time data
应变时效 【冶】strain age(ing)
应变时效脆性 strain age embrittlement
应变时效钢 strain aged steel
应变时效硬化 strain age hardening
应变时效(状态)硬度 strain age hardness
应变速度 speed of straining
应变速度分量 strain-rate component
应变速度[速率]敏感(性)指数 【金】coefficient of strain rate sensitivity, strain-rate sensitivity index
应变速率 strain rate
应变速率关系 strain-rate dependence
应变梯度 strain gradient
应变图(形,样) strain figure [pattern] ◇ 定性～*, 特征～*
应变退火 strain-anneal(ing)
应变退火法 strain anneal(ing) method
应变退火晶体长大 strain-anneal crystal growth
应变退火生长的单晶 strain-anneal grown single crystal
应变椭圆 strain ellipses
应变线 strain [Lueders] line ◇ 等塑性～*, 吕德斯～ Lueders strain
应变仪[计] strain-measuring instrument, strain meter [gauge], strainometer ◇ 电感式～*, 电容式～*, 干涉～*, 记数式～*, 焦恩松～ CEJ strain gauge, 扭簧式～*, 声学～*, 约翰逊机械～*, 粘贴式电阻～*
应变仪箔片 foil strain gauge

应变仪指示器　strain-gauge indicator
应变应力比例定律　law of proportionality of strain to stress
应变硬度　strain hardness
应变硬化　strain-hardening ◇ 莫特金属～理论 theory of Mott
应变硬化金属　strain-hardening metal
应变硬化模数　modulus of strain hardening
应变硬化强度　strain-hardening strength
应变硬化区[范围]　strain-hardening range
应变硬化系数　strain-hardening coefficient
应变硬化性　strain hardenability
应变硬化性能　strain-hardened property
应变硬化指数　strain-hardening exponent
应变增量　strain increament
应变张弛　strain relaxation
应变张量　strain tensor
应变振幅　strain amplitude
应变轴　axis of strain
应变状态　strained condition
应变总能　total work of deformation
应变组织　strained structure
应答时间　answering [response] time
应答仪器　【理】response device
应得份额　quotient
应急按钮　【电】emergency [intervention] button
应急备用设备　on-premise standby equipment
应急措施　(同"紧急措施")
应急阀[活门]　emergency valve
应急费　【企】contingency
应急供水　emergency water supply
应急焦炭　emergency coke
应急开关　emergency [intervention] switch
应急燃烧　emergency combustion
应急设备　emergency set
应急维修　emergency maintenance
应急装置　emergency service ◇ 临时～ doctor
应力　stress, tension ◇ 表观[视]～ apparent stress, 附着[黏附]～ adhesive stress, 海恩[织构，微观残余]～*, 活化[激活]～ activation stress, 孪生～ twinning stress, 佩尔斯－纳巴罗～*, 施加～ stress application, 瞬时～*, 无～区*, 线轧～迹 stress trajectory, 消除～*, 最低～*
应力比　stress ratio
应力波　stress wave
应力波动[起伏]　stress fluctuation
应力波切割　stress-wave cutting
应力不连续线　line of stress discontinuity
应力不足的　understressed
应力测量　stress measurement
应力层　【金】stressed layer
应力场　stress field
应力弛豫　(同"应力张弛")
应力定时变化疲劳试验　interval test
应力冻结光弹性　stress-freezing photo-elasticity
应力断裂　stress fracture
应力断裂关系数据　stress-rupture data
应力断裂强度　stress-rupture strength
应力断裂曲线　stress-rupture curve
应力断裂特性　stress-rupture property
应力范围　stress range
应力分布　stress distribution
应力分布涂层检验法　stress coating
应力分量　stress component
应力分析　stress analysis
应力幅(度)　stress amplitude
应力符号变换　【压】reversal of stress
应力腐蚀　stress corrosion ◇ 抗～合金*
应力腐蚀穿晶断裂　transgranular stress corrosion cracking
应力腐蚀断口[断裂]　stress corrosion fracture
应力腐蚀断裂敏感性　stress corrosion cracking sensitivity
应力腐蚀机理　mechanism of stress corro-

应力腐蚀开裂　season cracking
应力腐蚀裂纹[断裂]　stress corrosion cracking
应力腐蚀裂纹扩展　stress corrosion crack propagation
应力腐蚀破裂机理　mechanism of stress corrosion cracking
应力腐蚀寿命　stress corrosion life
应力感生[诱致]扩散　stress-induced diffusion
应力感生有序化　stress-induced ordering
应力关系　stress dependence
应力轨迹　stress trajectory
应力函数　stress function
应力回火　（同"加载回火"）
应力极限　stress limit
应力极限范围　limiting range of stress
应力集中　stress concentration
应力集中部位[集中体]　stress raiser
应力集中点　focal point of stress
应力集中器　stress concentrator
应力集中系数[因数]　stress concentration factor
应力集中效应　stress concentration effect, edge effect
应力计　stress(o)meter, taseometer, stress detector ◇ 玻璃插入式～ glass insert stressmeter
应力加速腐蚀　stress-accelerated corrosion
应力检测板形控制系统　Stressometer flatness control system
应力交变[交替,更迭]　stress alternation
应力局部集中　localized stress concentration
应力可变分量　variable component of stress
应力类型　kind of stressing
应力连续性　continuity of stress
应力裂纹　stress crack
应力面　stress surface
应力平衡　stress equalization

应力破断试验　stress-rupture test
应力破坏试验机　stress-rupture testing machine
应力强度　stress intensity, intensity of stress ◇ 裂纹尖端～*
应力强度因子　stress intensity factor ◇ 界限[门槛]～幅度*,撕裂型～*,张开型～*
应力强化扩散　stress enhanced diffusion
应力区　stress zone ◇ 赫茨～*
应力屈服下降　stress yield drop
应力时效　stress-ageing
应力释放　stress-release
应力双折射　【理】stress birefringence
应力水平　level of stress
应力松弛　stress-release, relaxation of stress
应力-松弛曲线　stress-relaxation curve
应力梯度　stress gradient
应力调节　stress adjustment
应力图　stress diagram [sheet]
应力涂层　stress coating
应力椭圆　stress ellipses
应力稳定性　stress stability
应力消除　stress relief(ing) [equalization]
应力循环　cycle of stress
应力循环比　cycle ratio
应力循环变化　cyclic(al) variation of stress
应力循环次数　number of cycles of stress
应力-循环次数关系曲线　S-N (stress number) curve ◇ 残存 $P\%$ 的～*
应力-循环次数图　S-N diagram, stress-number of cycle diagram
应力循环频率　frequency of stress cycle
应力循环曲线　stress cycle curve
应力循环图　stress cycle diagram
应力研究　stress research ◇ X射线法～*
应力引起的溶质[溶解原子]扩散　stress-induced solute diffusion
应力应变促发形核　strain-and stress-as-

应力应变关系	stress-strain relation
应力应变回线	stress-strain loop
应力应变抛物线	stress-strain parabola
应力应变曲线	stress-strain curve ◇ 抛物线型~*
应力应变数据	stress-strain data
应力应变图	stress-strain [stress-deformation] diagram
应力应变性能	stress-strain property
应力应变正比区域	proportional region
应力增量	increment of stress
应力张弛	stress relaxation
应力张量	stress tensor
应力振幅	stress amplitude
应力周期变化	cyclic(al) variation of stress, stress cycling
应力轴	axis of stress
应力状态	stressed state, stress condition ◇ 高度之间~【压】high triaxiality, 在~下 on load
应力作用点	origin of stress
应用	applying, use, application, utilization
应用程序	application [utility] program
应用程序组[包]	application package
应用地质学	applied geology
应用范围	range [field] of application
应用粉末冶金	applied powder metallurgy
应用化学	applied chemistry (App. chem.)
应用力学	applied mechanics
应用热力学	applied thermodynamics
应用数学	applied mathematics
应用物理冶金学	applied physical metallurgy
应用研究	applied research, application study
应用冶金学	adaptive metallurgy
萤石$\{CaF_2\}$	fluor(ite), calcium fluoride, fluorspar
萤石矿床	fluorite deposit
萤石型结构	【金】calcium fluoride structure, fluorite type structure
营利	seek profits ◇ 非~组织机构【企】nonprofit institutions
营养的[物]	nutrient
营养源	source of nutrient
营业税	sale [business] tax
营运费	operation cost
营造	building operation
荧光	fluorescence, photoluminescence ◇ 本底~*, 发~率*
荧光 X 射线	fluorescence [fluorescent] X-rays
荧光 X 射线测厚仪	fluorescence X-ray (thickness) gauge
荧光 X 射线分析	fluorescent X-ray analysis
荧光 X 射线分析器	fluorescence X-ray analyser
荧光测定	fluorimetric determination
荧光测定法	fluorimetry
荧光产额	fluorescence yield
荧光磁粉检验	fluorescent magnetic particle inspection
荧光磁力探伤	fluorescent magnetic inspection
荧光磁性粒子探伤法	【理】fluorescent magnetic particle method
荧光淬灭	quenching of fluorescence
荧光灯	fluorescent lamp
荧光法	fluorescence method
荧光分光计	fluorescence spectrometer, spectrofluorimeter
荧光分析	fluorescence [fluorescent] analysis
荧光分析仪	fluorescence analyser
荧光粉	fluorescent powder [dye]
荧光辐射	fluorescence [fluorescent] radiation
荧光汞弧灯	fluorescent mercury arc lamp
荧光管	fluorescent tube
荧光光度计	fluorophotometer
荧光光谱	fluorescence spectrum

荧光光谱分析[测定法] spectrofluorimetry
荧光光谱学 fluorescence spectroscopy ◇ X 射线~*
荧光辉度 flourescent brilliance
荧光剂 fluorescer
荧光计 fluorometer
荧光检查仪 fluoroscope
荧光检验 fluorescent penetrant inspection, fluoroscope test, fluoroscopy ◇ γ 射线~*
荧光检验灯 fluorescent inspection lamp
荧光镜 fluorescope, fluoroscope, cryptoscope
荧光镜检测[透视] fluoroscopic viewing
荧光粒子检验 fluorescence particle inspection
荧光裂纹探测术 glo-crack
荧光屏 fluorescent [fluoroscopic] screen, bezel, besel ◇ 粉末~ powder screen
荧光屏效率 screen efficiency
荧光屏元件 baffling element
荧光染料 fluorescent dye
荧光射线分析 fluorescent ray analysis
荧光渗透剂 fluorescent penetrant
荧光渗透探伤 flourescent penetration inspection ◇ 水洗性~法*
荧光试验【理】fluorescent test
荧光探伤 fluorescent inspection
荧光探伤法 fluoroscopy ◇ 后乳化~*, 马格纳罗~ Magnalo process, 齐格罗油浸~*, 热消~*
荧光探伤试验【理】fluorescent test
荧光特性[征]波长 characteristic fluorescent wavelength
荧光透穿检验 fluorescent penetrant inspection
荧光物质【理】fluorescent material
荧光熄灭 fluorescence quenching
荧光显微镜 fluorescence microscope
荧光显微术[法] fluorescence microscopy
荧光性 fluorescence

荧光学 fluoroscopy, fluoroscopy
荧光液检裂[探伤]法 hyglo
荧光液渗透检验(探伤) fluid penetrant (test)
荧光液体渗透剂 fluorescent liquid penetrant
荧光印痕器 fluoroprint
荧光增倍管 image amplifier
荧光照相术 photofluorography, fluorography
荧光油加压试验(检漏) pressure dye test
荧石 (同"萤石")
赢利性 earning capacity
盈[赢]利 profit, gain, earnings
盈余 surplus, profit
影片 film, cine photos
影线(图纸的) hachure
影响 influence, affect
影响范围 domain of influence
影响线 line of influence
影像 (shadow) image ◇ A-(阴极射线管)扫描~ A-scan presentation, 粗(溴化银晶)粒~ coarse-grained image, 模糊~ blurred image
影像电子显微镜 shadow microscope
影像光电增强器 image (photoelectronic) intensifier
影像韧度 image tenacity
影像信号频率 image frequency
影像质量 image quality
影印 facsimile, photoprinting
影印法 photolithography
影锥角 shadow angle
硬 hard, stiff, tough ◇ 半~*
硬 X 射线 hard X-rays
硬 X 射线机 hard X-ray machine
硬暗盒 rigid cassette
硬疤 hard spot
硬巴比合金 ◇ 休伊特~*, 英特乌班 27 号~ Interurban No. 27
硬拔管 hard drawn tube
硬币 coin(age), hard currency ◇ 包金

[银]~ Billon,粉末冶金法制~*,制~材料 coin(age) material
硬币合金 coinage metal
硬币生产工艺 mint processes
硬币铜(4Sn,1Zn,95Cu) copper coin
硬币压印机 coining machinery
硬币压制机械 coining press mechanism
硬表堆焊 hard facing
硬表面 hardsurface
硬玻璃 hard glass ◇派列克斯~*
硬铂 hard platinum
硬超导材料 hard superconducting material
硬超导体 hard superconductor
硬衬垫 hard liner
硬稠混凝土 stiff concrete
硬磁材料 hard magnetic material, magnetically hard material
硬磁钢 magnetically hard steel
硬磁性 magnetic hardness
硬磁性材料 retentive material
硬磁(性)合金 hard magnetic alloy, magnetically hard alloy
硬磁性铁氧体 hard ferrite
硬脆 brinelling,dryness
硬带材 hard strip
硬底片 hard negative
硬点 hard spot
硬镀层 hard coating
硬度 (degree of) hardness,【压】temper (冷轧后的) ◇巴科尔[巴氏]~ Barcol hardness,布氏~*,淬火~ as-quenched hardness,等~曲线 isohardness curve,干(燥状)态~(如砂型) dry hardness,钢潜在最大~*,赫伯特摆式[赫氏]~*,宏观[粗视]~ macrohardness,碱性~ alkaline hardness,距离~*,绝对~*,路氏~*,落球回跳~*,洛氏~*,梅氏~*,莫氏~*,耐磨~ abrasion hardness,努普[努氏]~*,切削~ cutting hardness,射线~ beam hardness,声~ acoustic stiffness,时效(状态)~ age(ing) hardness,图康(显微)~*,退火(状态)~ anneal hardness,维氏[金刚石棱锥体压头]~*,肖氏(回跳)~*,铸(造状)态[铸件]~*,自然[原有]~ natural hardness
硬度变化 variation in hardness ◇不同深度的~曲线 hardness-depth curve
硬度标度 hardness scale
硬度测定 hardness determination [measurement],determination of hardness
硬度测量放大镜 hardness measuring magnifier
硬度等级 hardness level
硬度分布曲线 hardness distribution curve ◇U形~*
硬度各向异性 hardness anisotropy
硬度换算 hardness conversion
硬度换算表 hardness conversion table
硬度脊面压痕 ridging indentation
硬度计[仪] hardness meter [tester], hardometer, hardness testing instrument ◇艾弗里布氏~ Avery Brinell tester,波尔迪轻便型~ Poldi,迪奥斯考普~(携带式) Duoskop,迪特~ Dietert tester,弗思~ Firth hardometer,米克罗~ Mikrotester,手提式~*,松村氏~*,投影式布氏(维氏)~ brivisor,维式棱锥压头~*,压入式~ penetrascope
硬度检验 inspection for hardness
硬度精密测定仪 metallometer
硬度试验 hardness test ◇摆式~*,德夫利~ Devries test,富普尔~ Foeppl test,互压痕~*,基尔施~ Kirsch test
硬度试验机 hardness tester (HT),hardness testing machine ◇巴伦坦~*,贾格~*,轻便~*,依考特普~ Equotip tester
硬度试验器(用维氏或布氏压头) diatestor ◇锉式~ Hardnester
硬度梯度 hardness gradient
硬度系数 coefficient of hardness
硬度压痕 hardness impression [indenta-

硬度与温度（关系）曲线　hardness-temperature plot
硬度增高　increase in hardness
硬度值　hardness number [value, figure, index]
硬度指数　【焦】hardness factor
硬粉末　hard powder
硬辐射　hard radiation
硬钢 (0.4—0.5C, 0.15—0.25Si, 0.5—0.7Mn, <0.05P 和 S)　hard [high] steel
硬钢丝绳　coarse-wire rope
硬铬　hard chromium ◇ 电镀~（法）durionising, 镀~*, 渗~ hard chromizing
硬铬镀层　hard chromium
硬硅钙钍矿　freyalite
硬焊　braze weld(ing), hard soldering ◇ 箔材~ foil brazing
硬焊料 (60—68Ag, 20—30Cu, 7—13Zn)　brazing [hard, strong] solder, brazing (filler) metal ◇ 含铅~ leady spelter
硬焊料合金　hard soldering alloy
硬焊料钎焊的　brazed on
硬焊料钎焊缝　brazed seam
硬焊设备　brazing equipment
硬合金　hard alloy ◇ 超导电性~*
硬盒　rigid cassette
硬厚纸板　card-board
硬化　hardening, hard setting, stiffen, solidification, induration, 【铸】cure ◇ 锤击~【压】over-peening, 电火花加热［火花放电］~*, 费希尔-哈特-普里(FHP)~*, 滚压~ hard rolling, 过早~ premature hardening, 可~的 hardenable, 可使金属或合金~的元素 hardenable element, 扩散反应~*, 拉床拉拔［机加工］~ bench hardening, 冷却~ hardening by cooling, 冷作~*, 弥散~*, 喷丸~（处理）ball peening, 氰化~*, 全~钢 fully hardened steel, 全部~ through-hardening, 在空气中~的 hardened in air (Ha)
滞后~ after hardening
硬化表面层　hardened case
硬化表皮［外壳］【钢】solid outer skin
硬化仓　hardening bin
硬化层　hardened layer
硬化层深度　depth of hardening
硬化层深度-断口晶粒度淬透性试验法　penetration-fracture method
硬化成分　hardener
硬化法　hardening method
硬化钢　quenched steel
硬化后透气性　（同"干透气性"）
硬化回火处理　drawing treatment
硬化机　hardening machine, hardener
硬化机理　hardening mechanism
硬化剂　hardener, hardening agent [compound], rigidity agent ◇ 弗洛~*, 希·斯皮德·伊特~【钢】Hi-speed-it
硬化冷轧机　temper mill
硬化铝合金　hardening aluminum alloy
硬化能力　hardening capacity, capacity for hardening, ability to harden
硬化黏土　clunch
硬化深度　hardening depth
硬化时间　【铸】curing time
硬化时效　hardness ageing
硬化水　petrifying water
硬化速率　rate of hardening
硬化特性　hardening characteristics
硬化系数　hardening coefficient
硬化橡胶　rigidified [vulcanized] rubber
硬化效果［效应］　hardening effect
硬化锌合金　binding metal
硬化性能　ability to harden
硬化性增强硼合金　【钢】needling agent
硬化压力衬垫　hardened pressure pad
硬化元素　hardening element
硬化源　source of hardening
硬化指数（水泥的）　cementation index
硬化纸板　fiber, fibre
硬灰石　ragstone
硬击穿　【半】hard breakdown

硬级(美国形变铜合金处理记号)　hard
硬件　【计】hardware ◇ 核心~hard core
硬件程序包　【计】hardware package
硬件资源的分时分配　【计】time sharing allocation of hardware resources
硬焦炭　hard [strong] coke
硬焦油沥青　asphalt-tar pitch
硬结氧化物　rock oxide
硬金属　rigid metal
硬金云母　pholidolite
硬浸焊　dip brazing
硬拷贝　【计】hard copy
硬壳式机身[结构]　monocoque
硬块　hard lump
硬框　strong frame
硬拉拔　【压】hard drawing
硬拉钢丝　hard drawn steel wire
硬拉金属丝[硬拉线]　hard drawn wire (H.D.W.)
硬拉铜丝　hard drawn copper wire
硬粒的(磨粉,磨料)　hard grained
硬沥青　hard pitch, gilsonite
硬沥青水浆　pitch-water slurry (PWS)
硬裂　hard cracking
硬铝（2—4.5Cu, 0.3—1.2Mn, 0.3—1.2Si, 0.3—1.2Fe, 0.3—1.2Mg, 余量 Al）　dural, duralumin (alloy), duraluminium (alloy) ◇ SD 高强度~*, 阿尔德雷无铜~*, 包~dural alclad, 超高强度~*, 日本~Nippon duralumin, 烧结~sintered duralumin
硬铝板　duralumin sheet
硬铝粉　duralumin powder
硬铝管　duralumin pipe
硬铝坯块　duralumin compact
硬铝(型)合金　duralumin type alloy ◇ E含锌~*, F含锌~*, 阿尔杜拉尔包铝~Aldural alloy, 阿尔克拉德纯铝覆面的~Alclad, 特超级~*, 杜希米组姆耐蚀~*, 形变~*
硬绿泥石{H$_2$(Fe, Mg, Mn)AlSiO$_7$}　chloritoid, phyllite

硬煤　hard [strong] coal
硬锰矿　psilomelance
硬面堆焊　hard surfacing
硬面堆焊材料　hard surfacing material
硬面堆焊层　hard facing deposit
硬面堆焊(用)焊条　hard surfacing [facing] electrode
硬面堆焊用熔剂　hard facing flux
硬面堆焊用硬质合金　hard face alloy
硬面钢轧辊　steel chilled roll
硬面轧辊　chilled roll
硬模　【铸】matrix
硬模式　hard mode
硬模生铁　chill-cast pig iron
硬模铸造　【铸】chill cast, chilling, metal mold casting
硬膜铝　hard filmed aluminium
硬木　hard wood
硬黏土　leck, bind
硬黏土页岩　irestone
硬捻钢丝绳　hard laid wire rope
硬镍铸铁（4—4.5Ni, 1.5Cr）　Ni-hard cast iron
硬硼钙石{Ca$_2$B$_8$O$_{11}$·5H$_2$O}　colemanite
硬钎焊　(solder) brazing, braze weld(ing), hard brazing [soldering] ◇ 保护~*, 吹管~*, 电阻~*, 感应电热~induction brazing, 炉中~hearth brazing, 气焰[氧炔焰]~gas (flame) brazing, 碳弧~carbon arc brazing
硬钎焊焊条　brazing rod
硬钎焊合金　brazing alloy, hard soldering alloy
硬钎焊机　brazing machine
硬钎焊剂　brazing agent
硬钎(焊)料　brazing alloy ◇ 含钯~*
硬钎焊炉　brazing furnace
硬钎焊气氛　brazing atmosphere
硬钎焊青铜（45Zn, 3—5Sn, 余量 Cu）　spelter bronze
硬钎焊熔剂　braze welding flux
硬钎焊态　as-brazed

硬钎焊性 brazability	硬纤维芯（钢丝绳的） hard fibre core
硬钎接合 brazed joint	硬线 high-carbon wire rod
硬铅(含锑铅) antimonial [regulus, hard] lead, lead-antimony alloy	硬橡胶 hard rubber, ebonite
	硬橡胶衬 hard rubber lining
硬铅浮渣 【色】hard lead dross	硬橡皮 vulcanite
硬铅合金(84Pb,1—12Sb) hard lead alloy	硬锌(镀锌用熔锌槽的) hard zinc
	硬锌焊料 hard spelter
硬铅炉 antimonial-lead furnace	硬型 【铸】gravity die
硬铅阳极 antimonial lead anode	硬型[性]铸造 gravity die-casting
硬青铜 （见"钟铜"）	硬性成分(射线的) hard component
硬熔 【钢】hard melt	"硬性"电子管 hard tube
硬砂岩 greywacke, blaize	硬性金属 hardmetal
硬伤(钢锭缺陷) dog marks, bruising	硬性联轴节 fast coupling
硬烧白云石 shrunk dolomite	硬性射线 hard rays
硬烧的 hard [dead] burned, hard burnt	硬性状态 hard mode
硬烧结矿[块] hard sinter	硬岩层 【地】hard formation
硬烧耐火制品 hard burned refractory ware	硬岩盘 【地】hardpan
	硬阳极氧化处理(法) hard anodizing ◇ 铝~*
硬烧石灰 hard burned lime	
硬烧砖 hard burned brick	硬玉 jadeite
硬设备 【计】hardware	硬原子 hard atom
硬绳 coarse laid wire rope	硬渣 grit, scar
硬石 ragstone, adamant	硬振动模式 hard mode
硬石膏 （同"无水石膏"）	硬脂酸汞 mercuric stearate
硬石棉板 cement asbestos board	硬脂酸锂 lithium stearate
硬铈钍石 freyalite	硬脂酸铝 aluminium stearate
硬水 hard water	硬脂酸镁 magnesium stearate
硬水铝矿 diaspore	硬脂酸钠 sodium stearate
硬水铝石 （同"一水硬铝石"）	硬脂酸铅 lead stearate
硬塑料制砖模 【耐】clot mould	硬脂酸铁 ferric stearate
硬铁 hard iron	硬脂酸锌 $\{Zn(C_{17}H_{35}CO_2)_2\}$ zinc stearate
硬铜 hard copper	
硬头(锡锑铜合金) hardhead, tin-rich scale	硬脂酸盐 $\{C_{17}H_{35}CO_2M\}$ stearate
	硬纸板 hard board
硬土层 【地】hardpan	硬质[性] solidness
硬外层可锻铸铁喷丸处理 permabrasive	硬质巴比合金(90Sn,8Sb,余量 Cu) hardhead
硬外特性焊接电源 （同"恒电压焊接源"）	
	硬质表面钝化铝 hard alumite
硬钨合金 ◇ 埃尔沃太特~(<30W) Elwotite	硬质玻璃 ◇ 派列克斯~
	硬质纯巴氏合金(65—75Sn,10—18Pb, 12—15Sb,2—3Cu) hard genuine babbitt, Majestic babbitt, service D babbitt
硬锡合金(99.6Sn,0.4Cu) hard tin (alloy)	
	硬质焊敷层 hard-facing

硬质合金 carbide (alloy), hard carbide [alloy, metal], sintered-carbide ◇ TaC-TiC-Co~,埃马里特~Elmarit,贝泽热压~法 Baeza method,衬~的拉模[压模] carbide-lined drawing die,多元碳化物~",钢结~",高熔点~ refractory hard metal,钴(结碳化)钛~",卡塔尼特碳化物~",康姆斯托克热压~法 Comstock process,肯纳~Kennametal,肯塔纽姆~",耐高温~",烧结~cemented carbide,斯特莱特~",碳化钨~",维迪阿~",钨钛[WC-TiC-Co]~",无碳化钨的~",仙台~",伊洛塔洛依铬钴~",硬面堆焊用~ hard face alloy,凿岩机~衬片 rock drill insert,铸态~ cast carbide

硬质合金产品 hard metal product
硬质合金刀具 carbide tool, hard metal tool, hard alloy cutter, cemented carbide cutting tool
硬质合金粉末 hard alloy powder, cemented carbide powder
硬质合金钢 hard alloy steel ◇ 斯托迪特钨钼~Stoadite
硬质合金工具 hard metal tool, carbide tool ◇ 镶嵌有金刚石的~ diamond-impregnated hard metal tool
硬质合金工业 hard carbide [metal] industry
硬质合金化合物 hard metal compound
硬质合金挤压 extrusion of hard metal
硬质合金拉模 (sintered-)carbide die
硬质合金零件 cemented carbide parts
硬质合金模具 carbide die arrangement
硬质合金生产[制造] manufacture of hard metals
硬质合金体[制品]生产 production of hard-metal bodies
硬质合金涂层 hard coating
硬质合金制品 hard metal article [composition]
硬质合金组合轧辊 carbide shell roll

硬质黏土 flint [stone-like] clay
硬质黏土熟料 flint [hard] clay chamotte
硬质硼硅玻璃 hard borosilicate glass
硬质润滑涂料 solid lubricant coating
硬质碳化物 hard carbide
硬质物料 mechanically resistant material
硬质氧化铝膜处理法 alumilite method ◇ 哈达斯~Hardas process
硬状态(铝合金材的)【色】hard temper
硬状态铝板 【色】hard temper sheet
映像 image, imagery, imaging,【数】map (ping)
映像分辨能力 image definition
佣金 commission ◇ 拿~的代理商 commission representative
壅流 back (wash) water
涌进 influx
涌流 inrush current, flashy flow
涌塞现象 bottleneck
涌水速度 water production rate (WPR)
涌渣风口 【铁】sloppy tuyere
永磁材料 permanent [hard] magnet(ic) material ◇ 费劳克斯鸠尔~Ferroxdure (钡铁氧体)
永磁材料时效 ageing of permanent magnets
永磁电机 magneto, permanent magnet machine
永磁动圈式仪表 permanent magnet moving-coil type instrument
永磁发电机 magneto(-generator)
永磁合金 permanent magnet alloy ◇ K.S.铁钴镍钛~",比斯曼诺尔~",海马克斯~Hymax alloy,莱马洛伊(铁钼钴)~",维卡洛铁钴钒~",辛科马克斯~Sincomax alloy
永磁式仪表 permanent magnet instrument [meter]
永磁(体)钢 permanent magnet steel
永磁透镜 permanent magnetic lens
永磁性 permanent magnetism
永磁性质 permanent magnetic property

永磁转子自同步机 magnesyn
永电体 electret
永冻层 ever-frozen layer
永冻土(层) permanently [ever] frozen soil, permafrost
永恒运动 perpetual motion
永久变形 permanent deformation [distortion, set, strain], permanent change of form, (off-set) strain
永久变形测定法 【压】offset method
永久磁化 permanent magnetization
永(久)磁铁[永磁体] permanent magnet (PM, P.M.) ◇ KS~ KS magnet, 科鲁马克斯~*, 模压~*
永久垫板 permanent backing
永久电荷 permanent charge
永久接合 permanent joint
永久联轴节 permanent coupling
永久母板 permanent blank
永久凝固 permanent set
永久偶极键 permanent dipole bond
永久膨胀 permanent expansion
永久伸长 permanent elongation [extension], persisting elongation, permanent stretch (钢丝绳的)
永久收缩 permanent contraction
永久线性变化 permanent linear change
永久线性膨胀 permanent linear expansion
永久型铸造 【铸】permanent mo(u)ld casting
永久性 permanence, permanency
永久(性)存储(器) 【计】permanent memory [storage]
永久(性)建筑 permanent construction
永久性炉衬 [冶]permanent lining
永久性吸附有害离子[永久中毒](离子交换中的) permanent poison
永久压力 permanent compression
永久阴极电解法 permanent cathode electrolysis
永久应变 permanent strain
永久硬度 permanent hardness
永久硬水 permanent hard water
永久铸型 【铸】long-life mould
永偶极键 permanent dipole bond
用电量 power [energy] requirement, power demand
用废槽液 aged bath
用工具加工 tool work
用管取样 pipe sampling
用过的材料 spent material
用过的电解液 depleted electrolyte
用过的核燃料 depleted material
用过的型砂 【铸】used sand
用过的油 waste oil
用过量氧焰预热生铁[烧除生铁表面石墨] 【焊】searing
用过物质 depleted material
用户 user, consumer
用户代号 【计】user number
用户电度表 house service meter, consumer's kilowattmeter
用户话机 substation
用户接点 consumption point
用户状态 【计】user mode
用碱熔解[助熔] fluxing with alkali
用具 appliance, furniture, tackle
用量 dosage
用水浸出 leaching with water
用水泥加固 consolidation grouting
用图表示 figure
用途 use, usage, application
用完[尽]的 used-up
用盐处理 salination
用研磨带磨光 abrasive belt grinding
用研磨带抛光 abrasive belt polishing
用氧饱和 oxygenate
用氧处理 (同"充氧")
烱[放热] exergy
优等铅淬火钢丝(制绳用；抗拉强度1.24—1.39GPa) best patented steel wire
优化 optimization ◇ 多目标~模型*
优化工作 optimizing work

优 you

优化控制	optimizing [optimalizing] control
优先部分还原	selective partial reduction
优先沉淀	preferential [selective] precipitation
优先处理	priority processing
优先吹炼(法)	selective converting
优先萃取	preferential [selective] extraction
优先萃取剂	selective extractant
优先浮选	preferential [differential, selective] flotation
优先富选	selective beneficiation
优先还原	preferential [selective] reduction
优先挥发	preferential [selective] volatilization
优先回收	selective recovery
优先结晶	selective freezing
优先硫化	preferential sulphidization
优先硫酸化	preferential sulphation, selective sulphating
优先氯化	preferential [selective] chlorination
优先凝固	selective freezing
优先亲和力	selective affinity
优先(权,级,数)	priority
优先溶解	selective dissolution [solution]
优先水解	selective hydrolysis
优先析出[沉积]	preferential deposition [precipitation]
优先吸附	preferential [selective] adsorption
优先洗提	preferential [differential, selective] strip(ping), selective elution
优先絮凝	selective flocculation
优先氧化	preferential [selective] oxidation
优先氧化法	selective oxidation method
优先再结晶	selective recrystallization
优先增溶	preferential solubilization
优先蒸发	selective evaporation
优选成核(现象)	(同"择优成核")
优选(法)	optimization
优选法研究	operations research (OR)
优选腐蚀	(同"择优浸蚀")
优选滑移	preferential slip
优裕培养	enrichment culture
优裕培养基	enriched medium
优越性能	high performance
优值	figure of merit
优质	high quality (H.Q.), prime-quality (pq), good-quality
优质板	【压】primes
优质板垛箱	prime piling box
优质薄板	prime sheet ◇ 镜面光亮~*
优质材料	perfect [good, honest] material
优质产品	high grade product
优质产品大量生产	【企】quality-quantity production
优质低合金废料	high grade low alloy scrap
优质锭	sound ingot
优质锻件	quality forging
优质非合金钢	unalloyed quality steel
优质废钢	low residual scrap
优质钢	high quality [grade] steel, quality steel ◇ D 型~*, L 型~*, 航空[飞机]用~*, 冷冲压~*
优质钢板	premium sheet
优质钢比	quality steel ratio
优质钢材	prime product
优质(高级)铸铁	high test cast iron
优质高炉炉料	【铸】high grade blast furnace burden
优质焊缝	flawless [sound] weld
优质合金	high quality alloy
优质合金钢	alloyed quality steel
优质黄铜	high brass
优质灰口铁	high quality grey iron
优质结构钢	high quality structural steel
优质金属	high test metal, sound metal
优质精铜	best selected copper
优质精轧机	premium quality finishing

(PQF)
优质冷拔圆钢　drawing quality
优质冷轧板　cold-rolled primes
优质煤　high rank coal
优质镁铝锰合金　peraluman
优质耐火材料　superduty refractory
优质耐蚀不锈钢　super-corrosion-resistant stainless steel
优质黏土　high grade clay
优质燃料　high grade fuel, premium fuel
优质石灰石　high grade stone
优质商品冷轧薄板　cold-rolled commercial quality sheet
优质烧结矿　high quality sinter
优质烧透砖　body brick
优质深冲钢　(同"超深冲钢")
优质生铁　high duty pig iron
优质水泥　high grade cement
优质碳素钢　quality carbon steel
优质碳素结构钢　carbon constructional quality steel
优质铁精矿还原球团生产法　AGAP process
优质铁素体不锈钢　super ferrite stainless steel
优质轴承钢　bearing quality steel
优质铸件　quality [premium, sound] casting
优质铸铁　high quality [grade] cast iron
尤迪莱特镉镍电镀液　Udylite solution
尤迪梅特 520 沉淀硬化镍基耐热合金　Udimet 520
尤迪梅特镍基耐热合金（19—20Cr, 18—19Co, 4.2—4.3Mo, 2.9—3.0Ti, 2—3Al, 0.07—0.15 C, 0.006—0.008B, 余量 Ni）　Udimet alloy
尤蒂洛伊镍铬铁耐蚀合金（29Ni, 20Cr, 3Cu, 1.75Mo, 1Si, <0.07C, 余量 Fe）　Utiloy
尤耳明铝合金　ulminium
尤耳特拉铝合金　ultralumin
尤基电炉热还原法　Udy process

尤卡碳素炉底　【冶】UCAR (Union Carbide Corporation) carbon bottom
尤卡碳砖　UCAR (Union Carbide Corporation) carbon brick
尤雷卡 Rz5 镁锆铸造合金（4.5Zn, 1.25 稀土, 0.6Zr, 余量 Mg）　Eureka Rz5
尤雷卡高电阻铜镍合金（60Cu, 40Ni; 热电偶合金）　Eureka
尤马尔铝合金　ulmal
尤尼科拉姆单向柱状晶粒磁铁　Unicolumn magnet
尤尼洛伊铬镍合金钢（12Cr, 0.5Ni, 0.1C, 余量 Fe）　Uniloy
尤尼欧思铅基轴承合金（1.5Mg, 0.2Ca, 余量 Pb）　Union metal
尤尼滕普 1753 镍基耐热合金（16Cr, 9.5Fe, 8W, 7Co, 3Ti, 2Al, 1.5Mo, 0.24C, 0.1Si, 0.05Mn, 微量 B+Zr, 余量 Ni）　Unitemp 1753
尤尼滕普 212 耐热合金钢（25Ni, 16Cr, 4Ti, 0.5Nb, 0.15Al, 0.15Si, 0.08C, 0.06B, O.05Zr, 0.03Mn, 余量 Fe）　Unitemp 212
尤恰蒂尼斯铁水降硫法　Uchatius process
尤恰蒂尼斯锡青铜（92Cu, 8Sn）　Uchatius bronze
尤塔洛伊耐热镍铬钢（35Ni, 12Cr, <0.2C, 余量 Fe）　Utaloy
尤特克劳德共晶焊条（53.12Cu, 37.53Zn, 9.23Ni, 0.11Si, Mn、Fe 痕量）　Eutecrod
铀{U}　uranium ◇ β ~ *, γ ~ *, 超 ~ 元素 *, 工业品位 ~ *, 含 ~ 的 uraniferous, uranous（含四价铀的）, 烧结 ~ sintered uranium, 天然 ~ *, 未浓缩 ~ unenriched uranium, 无[不含]~ 的 uranium-free, 无碳 ~ carbon-free uranium
铀-233{^{233}U}　uranium-233
铀 X1{UX1, ^{234}Th}　uranium X1
铀 X2{UX2, ^{234}Pa}　uranium X2, brevium
铀Ⅰ{^{238}U}　uranium Ⅰ
铀Ⅱ{^{234}U}　uranium Ⅱ

铀铵磷石 {NH$_4$(UO$_2$)PO$_4$·3H$_2$O} uramphite
铀棒 uranium bar
铀的(六价铀的) uranic
铀电解槽 uranium electrolysis cell
铀(反应)堆 uranium pile [reactor]
铀矾 uranopilite
铀方钍矿 uranthorianite
铀钙矾 {CaO·8UO$_3$·2SO$_3$·25H$_2$O} uranopilite, medjidite
铀钙铌水石 {Ca, Fe, UO$_2$}O·Nb$_2$O$_5$·2H$_2$O} ellsworthite
铀钙石 {Ca$_2$(UO$_2$)·(CO$_3$)$_3$·10H$_2$O} liebigite, uranothallite
铀钙铜矿 uranochalcite
铀钢 uranium steel
铀合金 uranium alloy
铀黑 uranium black
铀后元素 transuranic element
铀华 uranbloom
铀基合金 uranium-base alloy
铀晶体 uranium crystal
铀精制法 uranium refining process
铀块 uranium button
铀矿 uranium mine
铀矿床 uranium ore deposit
铀矿精炼法 uranium ore refining process
◇流态化床~*
铀矿浓缩物 uranium ore concentrate
铀矿石 uranium ore
铀矿物 uranium mineral
铀磷灰石 uran-apatite
铀络合物 uranium complex
铀煤页岩 kolm
铀铌铁矿 uranniobite
铀铌钇矿 uransamarskite
铀铅沥青 carburan
铀区域精炼 zone-refining of uranium
铀锐钛矿 uranoanatase
铀烧绿石 uranium pyrochlore, uranpyrochlore
铀石 {U(SiO$_{44}$)$_{1-x}$(OH)$_{4x}$} coffinite

铀酸 {H$_2$UO$_4$} uranic acid
铀酸铵 {(NH$_4$)$_2$UO$_4$} ammonium uranate
铀酸钙 {CaUO$_4$} calcium uranate
铀酸钠 {Na$_2$UO$_4$} sodium uranate
铀酸双氧铀[铀酸铀酰] {UO$_2$UO$_4$} uranyl uranate
铀酸盐 uranate
铀钽铌矿 {(U,Ca)(Ta,Ni)O$_4$} hatchettolite
铀碳钙石 {Ca$_2$(UO$_2$)·(CO$_3$)$_3$·10H$_2$O} uranothallite
铀添加合金 uranium additive alloy
铀铁 ferrouranium
铀铜矾 johannite, uranvitriol
铀钍矿 {(U,Th)O$_2$·SiO$_2$} uranothorite
铀钍脂铅铀矿 uranothorogummite
铀系 uranium series [family], uranides
铀系元素 uranides
铀细晶石 uranmicrolite
铀酰 {UO$_2^{++}$} uranyl
铀酰离子 uranyl ion
铀酰氯 {UO$_2$Cl$_2$} uranyl chloride
铀酰络离子 uranyl ion complex
铀酰络阴离子 anionic uranyl complex
铀阳极电解法 uranium-anode electrolytic process
铀冶金 uranium metallurgy
铀易解石 uranoaeschynite
铀源铅 urano-lead
铀云母类 {Ca(UO$_2$)$_2$P$_2$O$_8$·8H$_2$O} uranite
铀族 uranium series
油 oil ◇奥克特~*，不透~的 oil-tight，带[多]~的 oily，废[用过的]~ waste oil
油斑 grease marks, oil staining (热处理零件的)
油板[片] oiling plate
油保持性 oil retention
油杯 oil cup, oiler, lubricator
油杯润滑 cascade oiling
油泵 oil pump, lubricating press ◇偏心缸回转~*，直接~传动 direct oil pump

油比重计 oil hydrometer
油槽 oil groove [sink], oil bath [tank]
油槽车 tank car [truck], tanker, oil carrier
油槽[池]润滑 oil bath lubrication
油层套管 oil string casing
油层尾管(接于套管下的) production liners
油沉淀器 oil sump
油池泵 sump pump
油出口 oil outlet
油船 tanker, tankship
油淬钢 oil hardened [hardening] steel
油淬回火炉 oil-quenching and tempering furnace
油淬(火)[油急冷(处理)] oil quench(ing), quenching in oil, oil-hardening ◇ 霍斯福尔～铅回火法*
油淬(火)的 oil-quenched (O.Q.), oil-hardened (OH), quenched in oil (Qo), hardened in oil (Ho, ho)
油淬火(性能)检验 quench oil test
油地毡 linoleum
油垫(指润滑油垫) oiling pad
油动泵 oil-driven pump
油断路器[油开关] 【电】oil circuit breaker (O.C.B.), oil breaker [switch]
油对油换热器 oil to oil heat exchanger
油发黑处理 【金】oil blackening
油分离器 oil separator [eliminator]
油分离器接受器 oil separator receiver
油封 oil-seal
油封的 oil-tight
油封环 oil-seal ring
油封夹紧装置 clipper oil seal
油刮子 oil skimmer ◇ 带式～*
油管 oil pipe [tube] ◇ 不加厚～non-upset tubing
油罐 oil tank, oil-can
油锅辊(薄板挂防腐涂层用) grease-pot roller

油耗 oil consumption
油盒 【机】cellar
油环(润滑油环) oil(ing) ring
油环润滑 ring lubrication [oiling]
油环(润滑)轴承 ring-lubrication [ring-oiling] bearing
油灰 【建】putty, slush, badigeon, filling colour ◇ 用～接合 luting
油灰粉 putty-powder
油灰腐蚀 (oil) ash corrosion
油回火 oil tempering
油回火弹簧钢丝 oil tempered wire
油回转泵(真空用) oil rotary pump
油焦 oil coke
油焦置换比 【铁】oil-to-coke [oil-per-coke] replacement ratio
油结块 caking of oil
油浸 immersion
油浸变压器 oil-immersed transformer
油浸电抗器 oil-immersed reactor
油浸电缆 oil-impregnated [oil-filled] cable
油浸电容器 oil condenser
油浸镀铅锡合金的钢板 oil finished terneplate
油浸法 immersion method [technique]
油浸法显微术 immersion microscopy
油浸法显微镜像 immersion microscopic image
油浸法显微照片 【金】immersion micrograph
油浸式变阻器 immersed rheostat
油浸式显微镜 immersion microscope
油浸探伤法 【金】oil penetrant process ◇ 帕特克斯～*
油浸物镜 immersion objective
油浸用油 immersion oil
油浸纸介电容器 oil filled paper condenser
油浸自动带式过滤器 oil-immersed automatic band filter
油浸自冷 oil-immersed natural cooling
油井管 oil well pipe, oil-well tubing, oil

country tubular goods (OCTG)
油井灌浆水泥 oil-well grouting cement
油井用钢丝绳 wire rope for oil well
油孔 oil hole
油库 oil depot, dome
油扩散泵唧系统 oil diffusion pumping system
油扩散(真空)泵 oil diffusion pump ◇ 分馏～*,三级金属～ three-stages metal pump,增压[辅助]～*
油类比重计 acrometer
油类燃料 oil-type fuel
油冷的 oil-cooled
油冷却器 oil cooler
油冷却系统 oil cooling system
油裂化器 oil cracker
油流量开关 oil flow switch
油流目视指示器 sight flow indicator
油流速度 rate of oil flow
油镏金 oil gilding
油路 oil circuit
油毛毡 (asphalt) felt, malthoid, bitumen sheet
油毛毡衬 sarking felt
油门操纵杆 throttle lever
油门旋塞 throttling cock
油膜 oil film
油膜润滑 fluid film lubrication ◇ 界面～*,完整～*
油膜轴承 film lubrication bearing, flood lubricated bearing, oil film [flooded] bearing, Morgoil bearing
油膜轴承合金(铜铅轴承合金) kelmet
油膜轴承轧辊 oil film roll
油墨辊 ink roll
油墨直接印相法 ink print
油母质 kerogen
油内冷却的 cooled in oil (Co)
油泥 oil sludge
油腻子 oil loam
油黏度测定计 fluid meter
油旁路阀 oil by-pass valve

油喷射器 oil ejector
油喷射(真空)泵 oil ejector pump, oil-jet type of pump
油漆 (oil) paint, (oil) varnish, lacquer ◇ 快干～ quick drying paint,吸声～ acoustic paint
油漆层 paint coat, varnish coating
油漆打底 paint base
油漆和清漆涂层保护 protection by paints and lacquers
油漆喷枪 paint-spraying pistol
油漆涂底 clear cole
油气 oil gas ◇ 生[含]～ olefiant gas
油气化 oil gasufucation
油气混合烧嘴[燃烧器] combination gas-oil burner
油气焦油 oil gas tar
油气润滑 oil-air lubrication
油燃料 oilfuel (OF)
油热媒传热 heat transfer by oil-carrier
油容积控制系统 oil volume control system
油砂(油脂黏结型砂) oil sand (O.S.)
油砂芯 【铸】oil (sand) core
油石 oil stone, whetstone, abrasive stick, emery brick
油水分离器 oil and water separator,【焦】decanter
油-水密封限位开关 oil and water tight limit switch
油田钢管 oil countryside tubular goods
油退火炉 oil annealing furnace ◇ 单垛～*
油位 oil level
油位指示器 oil level indicator
油温 oil temperature
油污 oily soil
油污染的废钢铁[金属] oily scrap
油雾 oil fog [mist]
油雾除尘器 oil mist dust collector
油雾发生器 mist generator
油雾供应 oil mist supply

油雾化	oil atomization
油雾化系统	oil mist system
油雾加油器	mist oiler
油雾排除系统	oil mist exhausting system
油雾喷射器	oil atomizer [sprayer]
油雾润滑(带材的)	(oil-)fog [oil-mist] lubrication
油雾润滑器	oil-mist lubricator
油雾润滑装置	oil mist lubrication unit
油熄弧	【电】oil blast
油箱	tank, oil box, fuel tank [cell], reservoir,【电】breather (变压器的)
油箱底排油泵	bilge pump
油箱油位警报器	tank oil level alarm
油箱油温警报器	tank oil temperature alarm
油消耗量	oil consumption
油楔	oil wedge
油芯	oil-core
油芯加油	wick oiling
油性	oiliness
油性黏土	unctuous clay
油旋转泵	(同"油回转泵")
油循环系统	oil circulation system
油压泵	oil-hydraulic pump
油压表	oil gauge [manometer]
油压传动	hydraulic transmission
油压传动机构	oil gear
油压传动系统	oilgear system
油压电动机	oil hydraulic motor
油压阀	oil brake
油压缸	oil hydraulic cylinder
油压缓冲器	oil shock absorber, oil buffer
油压回路	oil hydraulic circuit
油压机	oil(-hydraulic) press ◇ 快动~*, 直接驱动~*
油压减震器	oil shock absorber, oleo-gear
油压千斤顶	oil jack
油压系统	oil-hydraulic system
油压型控制器	oil-hydraulic type controller
油压压紧装置	oil gag
油压制动器[油压闸]	oil brake
油页岩	bituminous [oil] shale
油浴	oil bath
油浴回火	oil tempering
油浴加热	oil-bath heating
油浴炉	oil bath furnace ◇ 电热~*
油浴润滑	submerged [bath] lubrication
油在水中弥散	oil-in-water dispersion
油渣生成	【焦】sludge formation
油毡	asphalt felt, linoleum (lino.)
油毡覆(盖)面层	felt carpet
油站(润滑油站)	oil station
油真空泵	oil vacuum pump
油枕	(oil) conservator,【电】expansion tank
油蒸气真空泵	oil-vapour pump
油脂	grease ◇ 涂[加]~greasing
油脂杯夹持器	Stauffer clamp
油脂量调节器	grease volume regulator
油脂密封	grease seal
油脂溶剂	grease solvent
油脂润滑	greasing
油脂润滑剂	grease lubricant
油脂润滑系统	grease lubricating system
油脂质	lubricity
油脂黏结型砂	oil sand
油质混合物	oily mixture
油质涂料	oil paint (O.P.)
油中淬火	quenching in oil
油中淬火的	【金】oil-hardened
油中回火的	tempered in oil (Tpo)
油盅	lubricator
油渍	grease marks, oil stain
游标	vernier, movable-scale, slider, slipper
游标尺调整(轧辊的)	vernier adjustment
游标度标	vernier dial, slow motion dial
游标高度尺	vernier height gauge
游标卡尺	caliper (vernier), slide calliper [gauge]
游标刻度盘	vernier [slide-rule] dial
游标千分尺	vernier micrometer
游尺	vernier, movable-scale

游动	play, walk
游动弯曲辊（CBS 轧机的）	floating bend roll
游动顶头	floating plug
游动芯棒	floating mandrel [plug]
游动芯棒[顶头]拔制（管材）	floating plug drawing
游滑轮	loose pulley
游离氨	free [unbound] ammonia
游离氨蒸柱	free still
游离的	free, unbound(ed), uncombined
游离二氧化硅	free silica
游离氟化铝	free aluminium fluoride
游离灰分	free ash
游离碱	free soda
游离碱度	free alkalinity
游离碱浓度	free soda concentration
游离金属	free metal
游离近似度	【理】freedom number
游离晶体	free crystal
游离苛性碱浓度	free caustic concentration
游离硫酸盐浓度	free sulphate concentration
游离氯	free chlorine
游离能态	free energy state
游离氰化物	free cyanide
游离渗碳体	free cementite ◇ 聚集的～*
游离石墨	free graphite
游离水	gravity water
游离水分	free water [moisture]
游离酸	free acid
游离酸含量	free acid content
游离酸浓度	free acid concentration
游离碳	free [uncombined] carbon
游离碳含量百分率	【焦】carbon ratio
游离铁素体	free ferrite
游离铁素体(结构)组分	free ferrite constituent
游离碳原子含量	free carbon atom content
游离亚硫酸	free sulphurous acid
游离氧化钙	free calcium oxide
游离氧化铝	free alumina
游离氧化物	free oxide
游离轴	free axle
游离状态	free state [condition]
游码	rider, jockey
游丝	hair spring
游隙	play, backlash, clearance space
有疤表面	【钢】scabby surface
有疤铸件	scabbed casting
有槽导轨	grooved rail
有槽螺母	slotted nut
有槽凸圆头螺钉	fillister head screw
有槽轧辊	grooved [shaped, profiled] roll
有衬坩埚	lined crucible
有翅的	finned
有刺钢丝制造机	barbed wire machine
有底坩埚	closed-ended crucible ◇ 圆筒形～*
有电零件	live part
有毒的	poisonous (pois.)
有毒金属	toxic metal
有毒气体	noxious gas
有毒液流	toxic stream
有毒元素	toxic element
有毒蒸气	toxic vapour
有缝管	seam tube
有感线圈	inductive coil
有功电压	active voltage
有功分量	resistive [active] component
有功负载	resistive load
有功功率	active [real] power
有功损耗	active loss
有箍轮	tired wheel
有关部门	department concerned
有关事实	relevant facts
有关因数	【计】pertinency factor
有关主管机关	competent authority
有害	harmful, detrimental, nuisance
有害成分	objectionable constituent, injurious ingredient ◇ 炉料[配料]～*

有害大气污染物	hazardous air pollutant
有害废物	【环】hazardous [harmful] waste
有害辐射剂量测定	health measurement
有害化合物	【环】hazardous compound
有害空间	idle space
有害排放物[有害物质排放量]	harmful ejecta
有害气体	harmful [noxious] gas
有害缺陷	injurious defect
有害物质	【环】hazardous [detrimental, harmful] substance
有害氧化	harmful oxidation
有害因素	【环】adverse factor
有害影响	adverse [detrimental] effect
有害元素	objectionable element
有害杂质	harmful [detrimental, inimical, troublesome] impurity
有害中子吸收	neutron poisoning
有害中子吸收体	poison
有害组分	objectionable constituent
有害组分落地浓度	harmful component ground level concentration
有害作用	detrimental effect, ill-effect
有核的	nuclear
有环轴颈	collar journal
有机氨肥	ammoniate
有机半导体	organic semiconductor
有机玻璃	organic glass, ◇帕斯派克斯介电～Perspex, 普莱克希耐热～Plexiglas(s)
有机玻璃观察孔	perspex window
有机超导材料	organic superconducting material
有机萃取剂	organic extractant
有机萃取浸出	organic-extraction leach
有机萃取系统[回路]	organic-extraction circuit
有机氮	organonitrogen
有机氮化合物	organonitrogen compound
有机电解质	organic bath
有机废物	【环】organic waste, debris
有机覆[包]层	organic clad
有机硅	organosilicon(e)
有机硅烷	organosilane
有机过渡金属化学	organotransition-metal chemistry
有机焊条药皮	organic coating
有机化合物	organic compound
有机化学	organic chemistry (org. chem.)
有机环境	organic environments
有机还原剂	organic reducing agent
有机缓蚀[抑制]剂	organic inhibitor
有机磺酸盐	organic sulphonate
有机胶体	organic colloid
有机金属反应	organometallic reaction
有机金属化合物	metalorganic compound, organometallic compound [reagents], pentamethide
有机金属聚合物	organometallic polymers
有机金属络合物	organo-metallic complex
有机金属形态	organometallic state
有机晶体	organic crystal
有机矿物	organic mineral
有机离子	organic ion
有机锂化合物	organo-lithium compound
有机磷	organophosphorus ◇达派克斯～Dapex process
有机磷萃取剂	organophosphorus extractant [extractor], organophosphorus extracting agent
有机磷化合物	organic phosphorus compound, organophosphorus compound ◇酸性～*
有机磷缓蚀剂	organic phosphorus inhibitor
有机磷络合物	organophosphorus complex
有机磷试剂	organophosphorus reagent
有机磷酸	organophosphorus acid
有机磷酸萃取	extraction by organophosphorus acid
有机硫	organic sulphur
有机铝化合物	organo-aluminum compound

有机镁化合物　organo-magnesium compound
有机膜　organi film
有机摩擦材料　organic-type friction material
有机黏结剂　organic binder, organic binding agent
有机铅化合物　organo-lead compound
有机溶剂　organic solvent
有机(溶剂)萃取　organic (solvent) extraction
有机溶液　organic solution [liquid]
有机润滑剂　organic lubricant
有机砷化合物　organoarsenium compound
有机试剂[药剂]　organic agent
有机水银中毒　organic mercury poisoning
有机酸　organic acid
有机碳总量　total organic carbon (TOC)
有机锑化合物　organo-antimony compound
有机添加剂　organic addition, organic additive agent
有机涂层　organic coating [clad] ◇临时～*
有机涂层钢板　polymer-coated [organically coated] steel sheet
有机涂层型材　organic clad formed section
有机物被覆[带有机物药皮的]条　organic coated electrode
有机物(质)　organic matter [material, substance], organics, organism
有机锡化合物　organo-tin compound
有机稀释剂　organic diluent,【色】carrier (溶剂萃取的)
有机相　organic phase ◇新～fresh organic phase
有机相溢流　organic effluent
有机絮凝剂　organic flocculant
有机阳离子交换树脂　organic cation exchange resin
有机液体　organic liquid [fluid]
有机阴离子交换树脂　organic anion exchange resin
有机杂质　organic impurity
有机准金属化合物　organometalloidal compound
有极分子　(同"极性分子")
有极化合物　heteropolar compound
有极键　heteropolar binding [bond]
有极晶体　heteropolar crystal
有极性　heteropolarity
有价成分[组分]　valuable constituent
有价金属　economic metal
有价矿物　valuable mineral
有价元素　valuable element
有价值金属　valuable metal
有价组分回收　recovery of values
有角的　angular
有节的　nodated
有孔的　meshed
有孔件挤压成型　mouth-piece pressing compacting
有孔黏土　keramzite
有肋的　finned
有理分析　【数】rational analysis
有理公式　rational formula
有理数　【数】rational number
有理性　rationality
有理指数　【数】rational indices
有理指数定律　law of rational indices
有力的　dynamic
有料反应器　charged reaction vessel
有模造型　【铸】pattern moulding
有泡的　(同"鼓泡的")
有氢氯化(法)　chlorination in presence of hydrogen
有缺陷铸件　defective casting
有色玻璃　coloured [stained] glass
有色金属　non-ferrous metal ◇稀缺～*
有色金属材料　non-ferrous material
有色金属锭　non-ferrous ingot
有色金属废料　non-ferrous waste
有色金属工业　non-ferrous metal industry
有色金属焊条　non-ferrous electrode

有色(金属)合金　non-ferrous (metal) alloy

有色金属加工润滑剂　non-ferrous metal working lubricant

有色金属浸渗剂　non-ferrous infiltrant

有色金属矿　non-ferrous metal ore

有色金属矿床　non-ferrous metal deposit

有色金属熔化[炼]炉　non-ferrous melting furnace, melting furnace for non-ferrous metal

有色金属提取　extraction of nonferrous metal

有色金属提取冶金　non-ferrous extractive metallurgy

有色金属冶金(学)　non-ferrous metallurgy, metallurgy of non-ferrous metals

有色金属冶炼　non-ferrous smelting

有色金属冶炼厂　non-ferrou metal smelting works

有色金属轧材　【压】rolled non-ferrous metal, non-ferrous mill product

有色金属轧制　non-ferrous rolling

有色金属轧制车间　non-ferrous rolling plant

有色金属制品　non-ferrous metal product, non-ferrous article

有色金属铸件[铸造]　non-ferrous casting

有色(金属)铸造业协会(美国)　Non-Ferrous Founders' Society (NFFS)

有色轻金属　light non-ferrous metal

有色冶金球团法　【团】non-ferrous metallurgical pelletizing

有色冶金原理　principle of non-ferrous metallurgy

有色重金属　heavy non-ferrous metal

有头螺钉　cap screw

有系统[条理,秩序]的　methodic(al)

有限差分法　finite difference method

有限长锭料(区域熔炼的)　finite ingot

有限固溶度　partial solid solubility

有限固溶体　limited solid solution

有限互溶度[性]　limited mutual solubility, partial miscibility

有限精度数　【计】finite precision number

有限宽度源(辐射源)　source of finite width

有限冷硬轧辊　definite chill roll

有限溶解度　limited solubility

有限(射线)束(探伤法的)　bound beam

有限行程滑块　stroke limiting slide

有限元程序　finite element program

有限元法　【数】finite element method ◇三维～*

有限(责任)公司　company limited (co. ltd.), company of limited liability

有线电视　cable television

有向凝固　directional freezing

有向性　anisotropic nature, anisotropy

有向性常数　anisotropy constant

有向性的　anisotropic

有效靶面积(X射线管的)　effective target area

有效变形　effective deformation [strain]

有效表面(积)　available [active] surface

有效表面能　effective surface energy

有效补缩冒口　active feeder

有效层　active layer

有效层深　effective case-depth

有效长度　effective length, 【团】rolling length

有效成对相互作用　effective pairwise interaction

有效程度　level of efficiency

有效冲击能量　net energy of blow

有效抽风面积　【团】active windbox area

有效出力　available [effective] output

有效传输速度　effective transmission speed

有效磁场　effective field

有效磁导率　effective permeability

有效磁通程长度　effective flux path length

有效萃取　efficient extraction

有效带宽　【电】effective handwidth

有效地址	effective address ◇操作数~*
有效电功率	effective electrical power
有效电流密度	effective current density
有效电路磁导率	effective circuit permeability
有效电势[位]	effective potential
有效电压	useful voltage
有效电阻	effective [active] resistance
有效电阻率	effective resistivity
有效度	validity
有效断面	effective section
有效堆存能力	live storage capacity
有效钝化剂	actual passivating agent
有效范围[距离]	effective range
有效放大倍数	useful magnification ◇显微镜~*
有效分布系数	effective distribution coefficient
有效分离尺寸	effective separating size
有效分离系数	effective separation coefficient
有效分选粒度	effective separating size
有效风箱面积	【团】active windbox area
有效俘获截面	effective capture cross-section
有效负载[负荷]	active [real] load, payload
有效高度	effective height [depth],【铁】working hight
有效时间	effective [available] time,【计】operational use time
有效功率	effective [active, real, useful] power, available output, useful efficiency
有效鼓风	working [workable] blast ◇最低~*
有效焊接厚度	effective throat thickness
有效核半径	effective nuclear radius
有效化合价	active valence [valency]
有效挥发度	effective volatility
有效激磁[激发]功率	RMS exciting power
有效剂	active agent
有效碱(性物)	available base
有效截面	effective cross section, clear opening (管、孔道的)
有效截面试验	【金】clear cross test
有效空间[间隙]	real space
有效孔径	effective aperture
有效孔隙(度)	active [effective, efficient] porosity
有效跨度	effective span
有效冷却面	active cooling surface
有效离子半径	effective ionic radius
有效离子电荷	effective ionic charge, effective charge of ions
有效离子直径	effective ionic duameter
有效利用(率)	efficient utilization
有效量子能量	effective quantum energy
有效裂纹长度	effective crack-length
有效流动应力	effective flow stress
有效炉床面积	effective hearth area
有效炉底面积	active furnace area
有效炉算面积	active [open] grate area
有效率	virtual rating
有效面	active surface
有效面积	effective [active, useful] area, strand area (带式机的), bed area
有效能	available energy
有效能力	effective capacity
有效坡度	effective gradient
有效期间	term of validity
有效牵引力[功率]	effective tractive power
有效切应力	effective shear stress
有效区	coverage
有效热参数	【理】heat availability parameter
有效热量	available [useful] heat
有效溶剂	active solvent
有效容积	active [working] volume, displacement, (高炉的) effective inner [working] volume, available [useful] volume

有效容积利用系数 effective-volume utilization factor, coefficient of utilization of useful capacity
有效容积与炉缸面积比(高炉的) working volume-to-hearth area ratio
有效容量 useful [available] capacity
有效容量混匀能力(混匀料仓的) blending capacity
有效散射截面 effective scattering cross-section
有效筛分 effective screening
有效伸长 effective elongation
有效渗碳层深 effective case-depth
有效渗透深度 effective depth of penetration
有效生产能力 available capacity
有效石灰 available lime
有效寿命 useful life
有效输出量 available [effective] output
有效数(字) significant figure
有效数据传输率 【计】effective data transfer rate
有效双(倍)字 【计】effective double-word
有效态密度 effective density of states
有效弹性模量 effective elastic modulus
有效碳 available carbon
有效外伸长度(焊接机的) throat capacity
有效位 【数】significant digit [bit] ◇ 最大～*
有效温度 effective temperature
有效吸收容积 active absoption volume
有效洗提液 effective eluant
有效系数 useful efficiency, coefficient of efficiency
有效线路 active line
有效线圈 active coil
有效效率 effective efficiency
有效性 validity, availability
有效性检查 【计】validity check
有效性能 efficient performance
有效虚拟地址 effective virtual address

有效压力 effective pressure, fugacity
有效压头 available head
有效应力集中系数 effective stress concentration factor (Kf)
有效原子半径 effective atomic radius
有效原子序(数) effective atomic number
有效载荷 useful [live, pay(ing)] load
有效载重 net load
有效直径 effective diameter
有效值 effective [virtual] value
有效指令 【计】effective instruction
有效指数 availability index
有效质量 effective [active, chemical] mass
有效重量 active weight
有效贮存量 live storage capacity
有效状态密度 effective density of states
有效自由能 available free energy
有效字 【计】effective word
有效字节 【计】effective byte
有效作用 useful effect
有芯感应电炉 cored induction furnace
有芯铸件 cored casting
有型芯铸型 【铸】cored foundry mould
有锈的 patinous
有序参数 【理】order parameter
有序(程)度 degree [amount] of order
有序畴 ordering domain
有序点阵[晶格] ordered lattice ◇ Fe₃Al型～【金】Fe₃Al type
有序分布 ordered distribution
有序固溶体 ordered solid solution
有序合金 ordered alloy
有序合金多泡结构 foam structure in ordered alloy
有序化 ordering ◇ 合金～alloy ordering
有序化过程中对称性变化 【金】change of symmetry on ordering
有序化能 ordering energy
有序化强[硬]化 order hardening
有序化强化状态 order-strengthened temper

有序化曲线　ordering curve ◇平衡状态下～*
有序化现象的准化学原理　quasi-chemical theory of ordering phenomena
有序(化)相　ordered phase ◇完全～*
有序结构[组织]　ordered structure
有序金属间化合物　ordered intermetallic compound
有序金属间化合物高温合金　high-temperature ordered intermetallic alloy
有序金属间化合物合金　ordered intermetallic alloy
有序能级　ordered energy level
有序排列　ordered [regular] arrangement, ordered array [orientation]
有序排列纤维　properly oriented fibres
有序破坏　destruction of order
有序区域[范围]　ordered region
有序搜索　【计】ordered search
有序搜索算法　【计】ordered search algorithm
有序取向　ordered orientation
有序态　ordered state
有序－无序(转变)　order-disorder
有序－无序现象　order-disorder phenomenon
有序－无序转变　order-disorder change [transition, transformation] ◇合金～*
有序－无序转变点　order-disorder transition point
有序－无序转变温度　order-disorder transformation temperature
有序性　orderliness
有选(择的)还原　preferential reduction
有烟火焰　smoky fire [flame]
有眼螺栓　eyebolt
有焰炉　air [open-flame] furnace
有氧腐蚀　aerobic corrosion
有用废料[品,物]　utility refuse [waste], disposable waste
有用矿石　valuable ore
有用矿物　valuable mineral, ore [useful] material, pay dirt
有用面积　useful area
有用能　available energy
有用性　availability
有用压头　available head
有源传感[换能]器　active transducer
有源电路　active [alive] circuit
有源元件(射流技术的)　active element
有载萃取剂　loaded extractant
有载抽头变换器　on-load tap changer
有载抽头变换装置　on-load tap changing transformer
有载溶剂　loaded solvent
有质动力　pondero-motive force
铕{Eu}　europium
铕合金　europium alloy
铕基合金　europium-base alloy
铕添加合金　europium addition
黝方石{$3Na_2Al_2Si_2O_8 \cdot Na_2SO_4$}　nosean(e), noselite, nosin, nositer
黝锰矿{MnO_2}　polianite
黝铜矿{$4Cu_2S \cdot Sb_2S_3$}　tetrahedrite, fahlore, gray [grey] copper ore ◇含锑～*,含银～*
黝铜矿精矿　tetrahedrite concentrate
黝锡矿{$Cu_2S \cdot FeS \cdot SnS_2$}　stannite
右侧装置　right-hand unit
右焊[向焊接]法　rightward technique, backward welding, back hand method
右捻(钢丝绳的)　right lay, Z-lay ◇交叉～*,同向～*
右捻钢丝绳　right-hand lay wire rope, Z-lay wire rope
右倾传动(转炉的)　right-side drive
右视图　right view [elevation]
右手定则　【电】thumb [right-hand] rule
右向焊　right-hand welding
右向张力卷取机　right hand tension reel
右旋　right-hand rotation ◇向～转的 right-hand
右旋螺纹心轴　right-hand threaded spindle

右旋螺型位错　right-hand dislocation
右旋螺旋　right-handed screw
右旋螺旋轴　right handed screw axis
右旋糖　(同"葡萄糖")
右旋位错　right-hand dislocation
釉面陶器　glazed earthenware
诱导反应　induced reaction
诱导期　induction period, inhibition period (氧化铝生产的)
诱导式抽风炉　induced-draught furnace
诱导物　【化】inductor, inducer
诱导状态　【理】reduced state
诱发　inducing
诱发故障　induced failure
诱发循环　induced circulation
诱固　occasion
诱引通风　induced draft (i.d.)
迂(回)路　detour (road)
迂回密封套　labyrinth gland
淤积泥层　warp
淤泥　sludge, underflow product
淤泥堵塞[堆积]　mud accumulation
淤泥质沉淀　slimy precipitate
淤塞　silting-up
淤渣层　slime blanket
淤渣液　sludge liquor
于仁－佩林法(生产铬铁)　Ugine-Perrin method
于仁－塞儒尔内玻璃润滑钢材挤压法　【压】Ugine-Sejourne method [process]
于仁玻璃润滑钢材挤压法　【压】Ugine extruding [extrusion] process
余摆线　trochoid
余摆线型齿轮泵　trochoid pump
余差　increment
余地　margin
余额　【企】remnant, remaining sum
余辉(荧光屏的)　afterglow, persistence, decay
余辉屏(蔽板)　afterglow screen
余量　allowance ◇ 小～铸造*
余料　clout, oddments, offscourings, biscuit (压铸的)
余燃　residual combustion
余热　used [excess, waste] heat, afterheat ◇ 冷却～cooling heat,排烟～*
余热锅炉　waste [exhaust] heat boiler ◇ 辐射式～*,三鼓式～*,卧管式～*
余热回收　waste heat recovery, heat loss recovery ◇ 烟气～off-gas heat recovery
余热利用　waste heat utilization [recovery], heat salvage, heat loss recovery, salvaging
余热损失　waste heat loss
余热箱　waste heat box
余热烟道　waste heat flue
余数　remainder
余碳　extra carbon
余隙　clearance (space), (free) play, idle space ◇ 手工拧接～Handtight stand off
余隙值　stand off value
余项　remainder
余压发电设备(高炉的)　TRT (top recovery turbine) equipment
余渣　remaining slag
余震　【地】after quake, after-shock
逾常试验　exaggerated test
逾期养护　deferred maintenance
逾限变形　threshold deformation
逾限应力　【压】overhead stressing, supertension
逾限张力　overhead tension
鱼　fish ◇ 畸形～【环】malformed fish
鱼翅式热交换器　(同"鳍式热交换器")
鱼腹式梁　fish bellied beam
鱼骨形抗裂试验　fish bone cracking test
鱼口状焊缝　fish mouth weld
鱼口状接合　fish mouth joint
鱼口状裂口　【压】fish mouthing
鱼雷车　torpedo car
鱼雷式混铁车　fleet of torpedo cars
鱼雷式铁水(罐,包)车　torpeds, torpedo ladle car
鱼雷式铁水罐　torpedo ladle

鱼鳞板　flap shutter, clincher boarding
鱼鳞状断口　fish scale fracture
鱼卵石　oolite
鱼尾(轧件的)　fish tail (end) ◇ 热轧件~*
鱼尾板(钢轨连接用)　fish (tail) plate, fish plate bar, joint bar, (angle) splice bar, continuous rail joints ◇ 角型~*, 四栓孔~4-bolt splice bar
鱼尾板钢材　rail-joint bar
鱼尾板螺栓　fish bolt
鱼尾板型钢　(angle) splice bar
鱼尾板轧机　fish plate mill
鱼尾板(轧制)孔型　fish plate pass
鱼尾(端部)　fish tail
鱼尾式喷嘴(煤气燃烧器的)　fish tail burner, fish top
鱼尾状长尖角(带材的)　horns
鱼腥藻属　Anabaena
鱼眼石　xylochlore
鱼眼状裂纹(焊接白点)　fish eyes
鱼眼状微裂纹　halo
鱼油(型芯油用)　fish oil
鱼子状　oolitic
隅　corner
隅撑　bracket, angle brace
隅石　【建】quoin
雨点喷水器　shower-box
雨量计　rain gauge, pluviometer
雨淋(式)浇口　【铸】shower [pop, pencil] gate, Roncery runner, pencil runner
雨密度　rain density
雨水沟　【建】drain ditch (DD)
雨水井　catch-basin
雨水排泄管　rain water sewer
雨污水合流系统　storm-sewage system
雨污水合流下水道　combined sewer
与温度无关的系数　temperature-independent constant
与温度有关的　temperature-dependent
与(作用)循环有关的应力张弛　cycle dependent stress relaxation

宇航材料与加工工程师协会(美国)　Society of Aerospace Material & process engineers (SAMPE)
宇航材料与加工工程促进协会　Society for the Advancement of Materials & Process Engineering (SAMPE)
宇航合金　aerospace alloy
宇航站　space station
宇航站时代　space station era
宇宙　universe, cosmos
宇宙导航　space navigation
宇宙飞行器　spacecraft, space vehicle
宇宙飞行用金属　space metal
宇宙辐射　cosmic [space] radiation
宇宙化学　cosmochemistry
宇宙科学　space science
宇宙空间　aerospace, space ◇ RHC~用钨合金*
宇宙射电噪声计　riometer
宇宙(射)线　cosmic rays [radiation]
宇宙中元素丰度　cosmic abundance
语法错误　【计】syntactic [syntax] error
语法分析　syntactic [syntax] analysis
语法分析程序　syntax analyzer
语法规则　【计】syntax rule
语法图　【计】syntax chart [diagram]
语法制导的编译程序　【计】syntax-directed compiler
语句　【计】statement ◇ 参数[已赋量]~*
语言　language ◇ 公式翻译程序[FORTRAN]~*, 面向人的~*, 算法~(ALGOL)*
语言翻译　language translation
语言翻译程序　【计】language translator
语言转换程序　【计】language conversion program
羽痕(带材的)　feather (edge)
羽毛状结晶物质　feathery crystalline material
羽毛状晶体　【金】feather crystal
羽毛状组织　feathery structure

羽状断口(钢脆断的) chevron
羽状铅基轴承合金 (同"星芒铅基轴承合金")
羽状物 feathers
羽状锡 feathered tin
玉髓{SiO₂} chalcedony ◇ 粉红色~ pink chalcedony
愈创木(自润滑)轴承 lignum vitae bearing
浴 bath, dipping (冷却锭模)
浴槽 bath ◇ 分批(装料)式~ batch bath, 箱式~ box type bath
浴槽炉 tank furnace
浴槽循环 circulation of bath
浴炉 bath [periodical] furnace, pot-annealing furnace (板材或线材退火用) ◇ 连续式电热~.
浴炉[槽]加热 liquid-bath heating
浴深度 depth of bath
裕度 tolerance, abundance, margin
预拌混凝土 ready-mix(ed) concrete
预报 forecast, prediction
预报器 predictor
预备 preparation, making-ready
预备阶段 pre-stage
预备精炼炉 active (hot metal) mixer
预备位置 ready position
预焙电极 prebaked electrode
预焙电极厂 prebaked carbon plant
预焙电解槽 prebaked cell
预焙烧 preliminary [preparatory] roast(ing), preroasting
预焙烧炉 preroasting furnace
预焙烧烧结矿(熔剂性烧结矿) precalcined sinter
预焙石灰 precalcined lime
预焙碳板 prebaked carbon slab
预焙碳素车间 prebaked carbon plant
预焙阳极 【色】prebaked anode ◇ 不连续~*, 连续~*
预焙阳极电解槽 prebaked anode (type) cell, pot with prebaked anodes ◇ 彼施 涅型~*, 敞开式~*, 多~*, 非连续~*
预焙阳极块 prebaked anode block
预焙阳极铝电解槽 prebaked cell for aluminum-reduction
预焙阴极块 prebaked cathode block
预泵 backing [holding] pump
预变形 predeformation, scragging
预变形钢 prestressing steel
预变形器(钢丝绳的) preformer
预变形轧辊(锻压机的) maxirolling
预测 prediction, prognostication (PROG), estimation
预测控制 predictive control
预测系统 prediction system
预沉淀 (同"预析出")
预成型 preliminary shaping, preshaping, preforming (金属粉末的) ◇ 双向压力~机*
预成型钢丝绳 preformed wire rope
预成型毛坯 preform
预澄清池 preclarification tank
预充液阀(水压机的) prefill valve
预抽压力 fore pressure
预抽真空 forvacuum, backing pressure [space]
预抽真空泵 forvacuum pump, vacuum booster pump, forepump ◇ 机械~ mechanical forepump,
预抽真空管道阀 fore line valve
预抽(真空)时间 roughing time
预抽真空室 preevacuated chamber
预储存 【计】prestore
预处理 pretreatment, preliminary [first] treatment, pre-process, precondition
预处理程序 【计】preprocessor
预处理矿石 pretreated ore
预处理作业线 pretreatment line
预穿[冲]孔【压】prepiercing
预吹【冶】foreblow
预吹刷(炉子的) prepurging
预磁化 premagnetization
预淬火 prequench ◇ 表面~(钢筋的)

Tempcore
预点火　preignition
预电解　preelectrolysis
预定　preset, predetermine, reservation ◇ 按～程序轧制 preset,按～程序装料(高炉的) preset sequence filling
预定范围　preset range
预定荷载　predetermined load
预定料位　【冶】preset level
预定强度等级　predetermined strength level
预定取向　planned orientation
预定时间　preset time
预定时间日程表　scheduled timing
预定数值　predetermined value
预定水平　predetermined level
预定维修　scheduled maintenance ◇ 非～时间
预定温度　preset temperature
预定形状　predetermined shape
预定值　preset [predetermined] level
预定字　【计】reserved word
预镀薄板　precoated sheet
预锻　blocker forging, dummying
预锻模　rougher, blocker, blocking impression
预煅烧　precalcination
预煅烧炉　precalciner
预堆边焊　buttering
预镦粗机　pre-upsetter ◇ 腰～*
预反变形焊接　shrink welding
预防措施[办法]　preventive [precautionary] measure, precaution(s), potential trouble measures, provision
预防费用　prevention costs
预防剂　preventive
预防维护　maintenance service
预防维修　preventive maintenance (PM), prevention [predictive] maintenance, maintenance service
预防(性)的　preventive
预放电　pre-sparking, pre-arcing, pre-burning
预分析　pre-analysis
预粉碎　precomminution
预覆金属　precoated metal
预干燥球团[生球]　【团】predried ball
预鼓风风口　foreblow hole
预规格化　【计】prenormalize
预过滤　prefiltration
预焊机　tack welder
预合金粉末　prealloy powder
预合金化　prealloying
预还原　prereduction ◇ 炉料～
预还原处理　reducing pre-treatment
预还原炉　prereducing [prereduction] furnace
预还原炉料　pre-reduced burden [material]
预还原率　pre-reduction rate
预还原球团(矿)　pre-reduced pellet
预还原烧结矿[造块]　(pre-)reduced agglomerate
预还原团块　pre-reduced briquette
预混粉末　premixed powder
预混合料　premixed material
预混合煤气烧嘴　premix gas burner
预混合气体　premix gas
预混合燃气系统　premix gas system
预混机[炉,器]　premixer
预混匀　【铁】pre-blending
预混匀系统　【冶】preblending system
预计值　expected value
预加工　pre-processing
预加工程序　【计】preprocessor
预加应力　prestressing ◇ 弗雷西奈～法*
预加载(荷)[预负载]　preload, initial loading, prestrain
预浇注　precasting
预金属化　premetallization
预浸出　pre-leaching
预浸渍　preimpregnation
预浸渍铜铁粉　preinfiletrated iron-copper

powder
预浸渍 preimpregnation
预浸渍铜铁粉 preinfiltrated iron-copper powder
预精加工 【压】prefinishing
预精炼 prerefining, preliminary refining
预精炼金属 prerefined metal
预精炼炉操作 【钢】active mixer practice
预精炼期[阶段] 【色】prerefining period
预精炼装置 prerefining vessel
预精轧 prefinishing
预精轧机 prefinishing [pony-roughing] mill
预精轧机组 prefinishing mill train [group]
预精轧孔型 leader pass
预精整 【压】prefinishing
预净化气体 roughly cleaned gas
预均化 【铁】pre-homogenization
预可行性研究(投资前的) preinvestment study
预扩散方法 【半】prediffused technique
预拉(拔) predrawing, preliminary drawing
预拉钢丝 pretensioned wire
预拉伸(钢丝绳的) prestressing, pretensioning
预(冷)凝器 precondenser
预冷器(煤气的) 【铁】precooler
预冷却(洗涤)塔 precooling (wash) tower
预炼混铁炉 active (hot metal) mixer
预留混凝土块孔(接头用) block joint
预留浇注跨 future teeming bay
预留孔堵块 block outs
预留曲度(铸型的) bewel, camber
预留弯度 【铸】allowance for camber, counter-camber
预留砖孔(接头用) block joint
预氯化区 preliminary chlorination zone
预滤器 prefilter
预埋工程(管道或电线的) carcase work

预埋芯 superimposed core
预埋型芯 【铸】kiss core
预磨 pregrinding
预磨光装置 pre-lap unit
预磨阶段 pregrinding stage
预凝(固) presolidification, 【建】pre-setting
预拧接头机 coupling starter
预浓缩液泵 preconcentrated liquor pump
预喷(吹) preinjection
预喷工艺 preinjection process
预破裂能 precrack energy
预破裂试样 precracking specimen
预期断裂区 fracture expection zone
预期吸收效率 predicted absorption efficiency
预汽化器 pre evaporator
预清洗 precleaning
预屈服松弛 【金】preyield relaxation
预燃(光谱分析的) pre-arcing, pre-burning, pre-sparking
预燃时间 prearc period
预燃室 precombustion [stilling] chamber
预热 preheat(ing), preliminary [initial] heating, reheat, hot conditioning (浮选前矿浆的) ◇ 二次[再]～re-preheat,自身～【铁】self-preheating
预热带[区] preheat(ing) [precalcining] zone, preheat section
预热段 preheat section
预热段除尘器 preheat dust collector
预热段废气 preheat section exhaust
预热(段)风机 preheat fan
预热段风箱 preheat windbox
预热段/鼓风干燥段风机 【团】preheat/up-draft drying supply fan
预热段旁通管 preheat-bypass
预热段升温速度 heating up speed during preheat stage
预热方法 preheating method, expedient of preheating
预热鼓风 blast heating

预 yu

预热后焊接　welding with preheating
预热后切割　cutting after preheating
预热火焰道　preheating flame hole
预热(火)焰　preheating flame
预热机　preheater ◇带式～*
预热加压焊接　hot pressure welding
预热加压时间　preheat(ing) pressure time
预热空气　(pre)heated air
预热空气用蛇管　coil for preheating air
预热口(铸型的)　heating gate
预热炉　preheat(ing) [mill] furnace, preheater ◇无氧化～*
预热炉风扇　preheating furnace fan
预热煤料　preheated coal
预热煤装炉　【焦】charging of preheated coal
预热期[阶段]　preheating period
预热器　preheater, heat booster, fore warmer ◇高压蒸汽套管～*, 管式～tubular preheater, 空气[鼓风]～*, 料液～*, 竖式～shaft preheater
预热(器)效率　preheater efficiency
预热气体　preheating gas
预热球团　preheated ball
预热球团层　preheat pellet bed
预热烧嘴[燃烧器]　preheat burner ◇冲动式～*
预热烧嘴一次风机　【冶】preheat burner primary air fan
预热生球　preheated ball, prewarmed green ball
预热生铁　pig iron preheating ◇用过量氧焰～【焊】searing
预热时间　preheat(ing) time
预热式(贮)铁水炉　preheated forehearth
预热室　chamber for preheating, stilling chamber
预热温度　preheat(ing) temperature
预热循环　preheat cycle
预热压力　preheating pressure [force]
预热氧　preheating oxygen
预热阴极　bombarding cathode

预热余量　preheating allowance
预热站　preheating station
预热蒸发器　preheating evaporator
预热制度　preheating regime
预熔共晶　prefused eutectic
预熔炼　presmelting
预熔期　preliminary running-in period
预熔型连铸保护渣　premelted mold powder, premelting mold powder for continuous casting
预软化剂[软化器]　pre-softener
预润湿　prewetting
预筛分设备　pre-sizing facilities
预闪蒸柱　preflash tower
预烧　prefiring, fore fire, burn-in
预烧结　presinter(ing), first sintering ◇邦克-希尔～法*
预烧结棒　presintered bar
预烧结处理　presintering treatment
预烧结温度　presintering temperature
预烧结自耗电极　presintered consumable electrode
预烧坯　presintered compact
预烧砖　prefired brick, preburned tile
预设定控制　preset control
预设定器(轧机的)　pre-setting mechanism
预渗铁粉　prefiltron iron powder
预时效　preaging
预时效处理　preaging treatment
预示　prognostication (PROG)
预试打支撑桩[预试托换基础]　pretest underpinning
预塑性变形　prior plastic deformation
预算　【企】budget, costings
预填充　initial filling
预填骨料　【建】prepacked aggregate
预调　pre-setting
预调行程　preset stroke
预涂层钢　precoated steel
预涂底漆　prepriming
预涂底漆钢板　preprimed sheet

预涂覆[涂层] precoating ◇干式~【压】 dry precoating
预涂漆 prepainting
预涂漆钢板 prepainted sheet
预涂熔剂 prefluxing ◇钢丝~处理【金】 wire prefluxing
预脱硫 preliminary elimination of sulphur
预脱水带 predraining zone
预弯(焊件的)【焊】prespringing
预弯辊 camber(ing) roll
预弯机 pre-bending machine
预析出[脱溶] pre-precipitation, preliminary precipitation
预析出区 pre-precipitation zone
预洗涤 prewashing, precleaning
预(先)焙烧 preroasting
预先焙烧[结块]的 【冶】preburned
预先变形钢丝绳 preformed rope
预先除气 predegassing
预先处理 (同"预处理")
预先锤击硬化(处理) prepeening
预先氯化件扩散渗铬 pink-phase chromizing
预先堆边焊的接头 buttered joint
预先富集 preconcentration
预先干燥 predry
预先干燥机 predryer
预先还原 【冶】first reduction, prereduction
预先混合[搅拌] premix(ing)
预先火法精炼 preliminary fire refining
预先检验 pretest
预先阶段 pre-stage
预先浸渍过的铜铁粉 【粉】preinfiltrated iron-copper powder
预先警报 (同"提前警报")
预先拉伸 prestretching
预先氯化 (同"初步氯化")
预先破碎 preliminary crushing
预先确定的 preestablished
预先热处理 conditioning heat treatment
预先熔化 premelting
预先筛分 prescreening
预先烧结的 【冶】preburned
预先渗碳[碳化] precarburization
预先试验批料(砖) dummy run
预先调温 preset temperature
预先退火 pre-annealing
预先脱气 predegassing
预先细磨 pregrinding
预先造球 pre-pelletization, pre-granulation, pre-balling
预先钻孔的管坯 predrilled billet
预形变 prestrain
预形变材料流变应力 flow stress in pre-strained material
预形坯 【粉】predetermined shape
预选 pre-selection, preconcentration
预选厂 preconcentrate plant
预选废钢 【冶】preselected scrap
预选精矿 preconcentrate
预压 precompaction, preload
预压机 preformer, preforming press ◇弹簧模~*
预压[预型]坯 precompaction, preformed compact
预压坯块 prepressing, pre-pressings
预压时间(电阻焊的) squeeze time
预压弹簧[浮沉]模 pre-pressing-die-float
预压制 prepressing
预氧化 preoxidation
预阴影溅射处理复型 preshadowed replica
预应变 prestrain, scragging
预应力 prestress ◇弗雷西奈~法*,内表层~处理*,无黏结力~*,先张法~*,有黏结力~prestress with bond
预应力衬套(挤压筒的) prestressed liner
预应力成形法 【压】prestressed [creep] forming
预应力钢筋 prestressed reinforcement, steel tendon ◇混凝土~*
预应力(钢筋)混凝土 prestressed concrete (PC) ◇长线法~*

预应力钢丝　compressor [reinforcement] wire ◇ 稳定化处理～*
预应力钢丝束　steel tendon
预应力混凝土(结构)用刻痕钢丝　indented [deformed] pre-stressed concrete steel wire
预应力混凝土用钢丝　prestressed concrete wire
预应力机架　prestressed [preloaded] stand,【建】prestressed mill housing
预应力拉杆　prestressed tie rod
预应力梁　prestressed beam
预应力损失　loss of prestress
预应力轧机　【压】prestressed rolling mill ◇ 液压加载～*
预硬化反应[作用]　prehardening reaction
预硬化团块　prehardened briquette
预约时间　【计】session
预约字　【计】reserved word
预轧材　first shape
预轧道次　previous pass
预轧机　pony rougher
预轧孔型　【压】preceding [former, roughing] pass
预真空　fore vacuum
预真空泵　fore [backing, holding] pump
预蒸发器　pre evaporator
预蒸馏　predistillation
预整定装置　pre-setting apparatus
预置　【计】presetting, initializing
预制　【建】precasting, prefabrication
预制厂(构件的)　factory for prefabrication
预制衬里　preformed liner
预制电极　preelectrode
预制钢结构　fabricated steel construction
预制钢结构的机架　machine housing of facbricated steel construction
预制结构　prefabricated construction
预制构件[部分构造]　section(al) construction
预制(构件)场　【建】casting yard
预制(构件)床　【建】casting bed
预制合金锭料　pre-alloyed ingot
预制合金粉末　pre-alloyed powder
预制黄铜粉末　pre-alloyed brass powder
预制件　building block, prefab
预制块　pre cast block, prefabricated section
预制矿　pretreated ore
预制粒　pre-granulation
预制粒精矿　pre-granulated [pre-pelletized] concentrate
预制裂缝试样　preflawed specimen
预制耐火混凝土　prefabricated refractory concrete
预制坯(件)　pretreated blank
预制坯锻造　【粉】preform forging
预制坯密度　preform density
预制气氛　prepared atmosphere
预制墙板　prefabricated panel
预制墙板式房屋　panel-type house
预制烧结衬里　preformed sintered liner
预制水泥空心型块　cement block
预制铜镍合金粉末　pre-alloyed cupronickel powder
预制预应力梁　precast prestressed beam
预中和系统　【铁】preblending system
预装料(炉子的)　【冶】initial filling
预装料[装粉]压机　【粉】prefilling press
阈能　threshold energy
阈频率　threshold frequency
阈效应　threshold effect
阈应力　threshold stress
阈值设置[调定](材料试验的)　threshold setting
元　【数】dimension, member
元胞　elementary cell
元汇编程序　【计】meta assembler
元件　element (el.), component, cell, part, organ, member, unit ◇ 霍尔～*
元件误差　element [component] error
元件组　bank of cells
元明粉{$Na_2SO_4 \cdot 10H_2O$}　Glauber's salt

元素 element (el.), elementary substance ◇ B族～", 伴生～ accompanying element, 成酸～ acid-forming element, 次要～ minor element, 第八族～ eight-group element, 基底～ background element, 夹入[偶存,残存]～【钢】tramp element, 具有三种晶型的～ trimorphous element, 两晶型～ dimorphous element, 时效硬化～ age hardening element, 酸溶～ acid-soluble element, 添加～ additional element

元素半导体 element semiconductor
元素表 list of elements
元素定性分析 qualitative elementary analysis
元素分布量 ◇ 星球中～ stellar abundance, 宇宙中～ cosmic abundance
元素分析 elementary analysis, analysis for individual elements
元素粉末 elemental powder
元素氟 elemental fluorine
元素(光谱)线 【化】element line
元素合金 mischmetal
元素物质 elementary substance
元素周期表 periodic table (of elements)
元素周期系 periodic system
元素状态 elemental form
元素状态杂质 elemental impurity
元素组成[成分] elemental [elementary] composition
元素组分 elemental ingredient
元阳模 【压】hob
元语言公式 【计】meta-linguistic formula
原X射线束 primary X-ray beam
原奥氏体 preexisting austenite
原边线圈 primary coil
原标准电阻温度计 primary standard resistance thermometer
原材料 raw [starting] material, raw [original, rough] stock
原材料单位消耗 unit raw material consumption
原磁场 self-magnetic field

原地 in situ
原地沉淀析出 in-situ precipitation
原地浸出 【色】place [spot, in-situ] leaching, leaching in place [situ]
原地冷却 【团】in-situ cooling
原地(土壤)含水当量 field moisture equivalent
原地细菌浸出 bacterial in-situ leaching
原地转变 【金】in-situ transformation
原碲酸 orthotelluric acid
原碲酸盐 orthotellurate
原点 base point (BP), origin
原点阵 (同"原始晶格")
原电池 galvanic battery [element, cell], primary battery [element, cell], electric(al) cell
原电池组 primary battery
原电流分布(电极表面的) primary current distribution
原电子 primary electron
原动机 (prime) mover, prime motor
原动力 motive force [power], moving force, motivity
原钒酸 $\{H_3VO_4\}$ ortho-vanadic acid
原钒酸盐 ortho-vanadate
原废水 【环】raw waste water
原粉 【粉】initial powder
原辐射 original radiation
原钢 (同"粗钢")
原锆酸 $\{H_4ZrO_4\}$ ortho-zirconic acid
原光束发散度 primary beam divergence
原规模的 full scale
原硅酸 $\{H_4SiO_4$ 或 $Si(OH)_4\}$ ortho-silicic acid
原甲酸 $\{HC(OH)_3\}$ ortho-formic acid
原甲酸酯 orthoformate
原价 prime [first] cost, initial cost [value], self-cost
原焦 raw coke, run of oven coke
原金属 (同"初级金属")
原矿仓 crude-ore bin
原矿场 raw ore stockyard

原矿浆 raw pulp
原矿浆混合器(槽) raw pulp mixer
原矿浆温度 original pulp temperature
原矿浸出 raw ore leach
原矿块 ore bloom
原矿矿浆 raw ore slurry
原矿取样 【选】head sampling
原矿取样器 head sampler
原矿(石)(未选的) raw [crude, original, pit-run, undressed] ore, green-ore, run of mine (r.o.m.), mine run (m.r.), crudes ◇ 露天矿采出的~ run-of-pit ore, 手拣~ hand-picked crude ore
原矿试样 【选】head sample
原矿直接熔炼 direct ore smelting
原来的 original, former
原理 principle, (scientific) fundamentals, theorem, theory ◇ 阿基米德~ Archimedes principle, 范托夫~*, 勒夏特列~*, 容汉斯~*
原理图 schematic [basic, skeleton] diagram, diagrammatic layout
原料 raw [crude, basic, rough, starting] material, (feed) stock, original feed [stock], raw charge [feed], initial substance
原料搬运 raw material handling
原料仓库[堆置场] raw material storage
原料槽[贮仓] raw material bin [bunker, hopper], primary bunker, feed stock tank
原料场 stock yard
原料场吊车 scrap yard crane
原料处理 raw material processing [handling], material [stock] handling
原料处理设备 material handling equipment
原料处理系统 material handling system
原料分析[化学成分] raw material analysis
原料干燥机[窑] raw stock drier
原料工段 charge materials yard
原料供给线 feed line

原料化合物 starting compound
原料化学成分 feed analysis
原料混匀 bed blending
原料混匀设施 blending [bedding] facilities
原料截取 reclaiming
原料金属 feed metal
原料进厂铁路线 incoming raw-material track
原料进料系统 raw material intake system
原料精选 raw material beneficiation
原料颗粒 feed particle
原料跨 raw material bay
原料粒度 size of feed
原料配比 feed proportioning
原料气体 feed [unstripped] gas
原料输送管线 feed line
原料特性 burden property
原料条件 feed condition
原料系统 feed circuit
原料消耗 raw material consumption
原料选择 feed stock selection
原料与产品价格指数 【企】input/output price indices
原料预处理装置 raw material pre-treatment arrangement
原料预中和系统 【冶】preblending system
原料运输 material handling
原料运输[皮带]机 raw material conveyer
原料中和设备[设施] blending [bedding] facilities
原料中和系统 bed blending system, bedding system
原料贮存设备 stocking facilities
原料转运站 raw material transfer station
原料状况 raw material situation
原料准备 raw material preparation [processing, handling], feed preparation
原料准备流程 route of preparation
原料组成[成分] feed composition
原硫酸 ortho-sulphuric acid
原硫酸盐 ortho-sulphate

原铝	primary [virgin] aluminium
原铝土矿	raw bauxite
原煤	raw [rough, bank, altogether, duff, duft, run-of-mine] coal, mine run (m.r.) ◇入选～feed coal
原煤仓	raw coal silo
原煤高炉	raw-coal blast furnace
原煤气	crude gas
原模型	master mould ◇母模型的～
原硼酸{H_3BO_3}	ortho-boric acid
原坯件(锻造用)	part blank
原器	prototype
原砂	roughing sand
原砂透气性	【铸】base permeability
原射线	primary rays
原射线束	original [primary] beam
原射线束宽度	primary beam breadth
原砷酸{H_3AsO_4}	ortho-arsenic acid
原砷酸盐	orthoarsenate
原生放射性同位素	radioactive parent isotope
原生夹杂物	(同"固有夹杂物")
原生金属	primary [virgin] metal
原生孔隙	primary porosity
原生矿	primary ore
原生矿床	primary (ore) deposit
原生矿泥(浮选的)	primary slime
原生矿物	primary mineral
原生沥青铀矿	primary uraninite
原生锍[冰铜]	primary matte
原生铝锭	primary aluminium pig
原生煤气	primary gas
原(生)镁	primary magnesium
原生黏土	primary clay
原生铅	primary lead
原生屈氏体	primary troostite
原生缺陷	primary imperfection
原生石墨	primary [indigenous] graphite
原生索氏体	primary sorbite
原生铜	virgin copper
原生锡	primary tin
原生氧化膜	naturally occurring oxide film
原生质	(proto)plasm
原始奥氏体	original austenite
原始奥氏体晶界	original austenite grain boundaries
原始奥氏体晶粒	original [prior] austenite grain
原始标计长度(试样的)	original gauge length
原始标准试样	primary standard sample
原始材料	original [starting] material, initial substance
原始产品	primary product
原始成本	original [initial, first] cost
原始带	【计】grandfather tape
原始废料[废石,尾矿,切头]	primary shale
原始粉末	【粉】initial powder
原始辐射	primary radiation
原始合金	virgin alloy ◇具有析出物的～primary alloy with precipitations
原始厚度	ingoing gauge
原始结构	original [prototype] structure
原始晶格	【理】original [initial, primitive] lattice
原始晶粒	original grain [crystal]
原始晶体	parent crystal
原始晶种	original seed
原始颗粒	original particle
原始离子	parent ion
原始密度	initial density
原始模型	master mould
原始能量	primary [initial] energy
原始浓度	initial concentration
原始强度	initial strength
原始切头	primary shale
原始[生]缺陷(晶格的)	primary imperfections
原始溶液	base solution
原始溶液成分[组成]	initial solution composition
原始试样	original [bulk] sample
原始数据	preliminary [initial, raw] data

原始水分　initial moisture
原始酸度　initial acidity
原始碳　initial carbon content
原始体积　original volume
原始尾矿　【选】primary shale
原始物质　original [initial] substance
原始误差　initial error
原始形态　original form
原始氧　primary oxygen
原始状态　original [initial] state
原始资料　original material
原始组分　original constituent
原始组织　【金】original [primary, prior] structure
原始组织破坏(指铸造组织)　primary breakdown
原束发散度　primary beam divergence
原水　raw [crude] water
原酸　ortho acid
原态印相　nature print
原铁水　base iron
原头(铆钉的)　primary head
原委　all the details, circumstance
原钨酸　ortho-tungstic acid
原钨酸盐　ortho-tungstate
原物　orginal ◇ 与～一样大小的　full scale
原线圈　primary (coil, winding)
原型　prototype, (crude) model, primary form, protomodel
原型机　prototype (machine)
原样金属　bare metal
原液　raw liquor, 【色】aqueous feet
原油　crude [mother] oil
原有夹杂　(同"内在夹杂")
原有间隙　initial gap
原有炉衬　parent lining
原有磨损　initial wear
原有能力　existing capacity
原有位置　initial position
原有硬度　natural hardness
原有杂质　inherent impurity

原(有)重量　original weight
原则　principle (prin., princ.), fundamentals
原则流程　impractical flowsheet
原渣秤　raw cinder weigher
原轧辊(未热处理的)　green roll
原著　original (orig.)
原子　atom ◇ 打出的～(从晶格中) knock(ed)-on atom, 多电子～many electron atom, 分离的[被破坏的]～destroyed atom, 孤立～isolated atom, 激活～activated atom, 失去外层电子的～(裸原子) stripped atom, 杂质[外来, 局外]～stranger atom
原子X-射线机　atomic X-ray machine
原子百分数[率]　atom per cent (at.%), atomic percent(age)
原子半径　atomic radius
原子爆炸　atomic blast [explosion]
原子比　atomic ratio
原子参数　atomic parameter
原子层　layer of atoms
原子层堆垛　stacking of atom layers
原子层堆积　【理】layer packing
原子场　atomic field
原子重叠　overlapping of atoms
原子重排列　atomic rearrangement
原子磁化率　atomic susceptibility
原子磁矩　atomic magnetic moment
原子丛聚硬化　cluster hardening
原子大小[尺寸]　atomic dimensions [size]
原子大小程度[数量级]　atomic size magnitude
原子弹　atom(ic) bomb, A-bomb ◇ 防～掩蔽室 atomic (bomb-proof) shelter
原子当量化合物　equiatomic compound ◇ CrB型～*
原子点阵[晶格]　atomic lattice
原子电池　atomic battery [cell]
原子电离　atomic ionization
原子动力　atomic power

原子反应堆 atomic reactor [pile, furnace] ◇装配式~*
原子分布 atom distribution
原子分数 atom(ic) fraction
原子辐射 atomic radiation
原子辐射系数 atomic coefficient of emission
原子符号 atomic symbol
原子复型 atomic replica
原子工艺学 atomics
原子光谱分析 atomic spectrum analysis
原子过程 atomic process
原子含量百分数 atom per cent
原子焊(合) atomic welding ◇电弧~电极*
原子行列 line of atoms
原子核 【理】nucleus(复数 nuclei), atomic nucleus [kernel, core]
原子核半径 【理】nuclear radius
原子核堆 nuclear pile
原子核反应 nuclear reaction
原子核结构 atomic nuclear structure
原子核力 【理】nuclear force
原子核裂变 atomic fission
原子核区 nuclear field
原子核燃料 nuclear fuel
原子核嬗变 (同"核嬗变")
原子核实 【理】nuclear frame
原子核显微术 nucleus microscopy
原子激发 atomic excitation
原子集合体[集聚] atomic aggregate, aggregate of atoms
原子级尺寸 atomic dimensions
原子几何排列 【理】geometric arrangement of atoms
原子价 (atomic) valency, valence, adicity, atomicity
原子价力 【理】valence force
原子间干涉 【理】interatomic interference
原子间键合力 interatomic bonding force
原子间距[隔] interatomic distance, (inter)atomic spacing
原子间力 interatomic force
原子间力定律 law of the interatomic forces
原子间力曲线 interatomic force curve
原子间黏合力 interatomic bonding force
原子间引力 interatomic attraction
原子键(合) atom [interatomic] bond, (inter)atomic bonding [binding, linkage]
原子键合强度 atomic bond strength
原子结构 atom(ic) [atomistic] structure ◇玻尔~理论*,离散的~*
原子结合强度 atomic bond strength
原子晶体 atomic [covalent] crystal
原子壳层空位 shell vacacy
原子扩散 atomic diffusion [dispersion]
原子粒子 atomic particle
原子力 atomic force
原子量 atomic weight (a.w.)
原子量单位 atomic weight unit (awu)
原子列 atom row
原子论 atomic theory, atomology, atomism, atomistics
原子弥散 atomic dispersion
原子密度 atomic density, density of atoms, atom population
原子密排序列 close-packed rows of atoms
原子面 atomic plane, plane of atoms
原子模型 atom(ic) model
原子内的 intra-atomic, intratomic
原子内力 intra-atomic force
原子能 atomic power (A.P.), A-power, atomic [nuclear] energy
原子能工程 nuclear engineering
原子能工业用纯石墨 atomically pure graphite
原子能管理局(英国) Atomic Energy Authority (A.E.A)
原子能级 atomic energy level
原子能监察委员会(英国、加拿大) Atomic Energy Control Board (A.E.C.B.)
原子能委员会(美国) Atomic Energy

Commission (A.E.C)
原子能研究所(英国) Atomic Energy Institute (A.E.I.)
原子能研究中心(英国) Atomic Energy Research Establishment (A.E.R.E.)
原子能冶金 atomic energy metallurgy
原子浓度 atomic concentration
原子排 atom row
原子排列 atomic arrangement [array, configuration, packing]
原子配对[偶] 【理】pairing of atoms
原子碰撞 atomic collision
原子偏聚 clustering
原子平面 atomic plane
原子谱线 atom line
原子迁移 atomic migration ◇ 晶体中～机理*
原子迁移率 atomic mobility
原子氢 atomic hydrogen ◇ 用～还原 reduction by atomic hydrogen
原子氢电弧 atomic hydrogen arc
原子氢电弧焊 atomic arc welding
原子氢焊电极 atomic hydrogen-welding electrode
原子氢焊(接) atomic-hydrogen welding (AHW)
原子氢焊接管 atomic hydrogen welded tube
原子氢焊接机[装置] atomic-hydrogen welding apparatus, atomic-hydrogen welder
原子氢焰 atomic hydrogen torch
原子取代反应 atomic displacement reaction
原子燃料 atomic [nuclear] fuel
原子热 atomic heat (at.ht)
原子热激发 thermal excitation of atoms
原子热容 atomic heat capacity
原子热振动 thermal vibration of atoms
原子散射 atomic scattering
原子数 atomicity
原子碳 atomic carbon

原子体积 atomic volume
原子图像 atom picture
原子团 【化】atomic group, group of atoms, elementide, radical
原子蜕变 atomic disintegration
原子网 atomic net
原子位移 discomposition ◇ 静型～*
原子位置 atomic position, atom site
原子物理学 atomic physics
原子吸收 atomic absorption (AA)
原子吸收分光光度法 atomic absorption spectrophotometry
原子吸收光谱(测定)法 atomic absorption spectrography [spectrometry, spectroscopy] (AAS)
原子吸收光谱仪 atomic absorption spectrometer [spectroscope] (AAS)
原子吸收系数 atomic absorption coefficient
原子性 atomicity
原子序数 atomic number (At.No.), charge number ◇ 低～元素 low-Z element
原子学说 (同"原子论")
原子引力 atomic attraction
原子荧光光谱(分析)法 atomic fluorescence spectrometry
原子有序定律 law of atomic ordering
原子有序化 atomic ordering
原子跃过液－固相界面的频率 【理】jump frequency of atom across a liquid-solid interface
原子增殖[再生,转换]炉 atomic converter
原子折射 atomic refraction
原子振动 atomic vibration [oscillation]
原子振动频率 frequency of atomic vibration
原子直径 atomic diameter
原子质点 atomic particle
原子质量单位(法定单位,≈1.6605655× 10^{-27}kg) atomic mass unit (u)

原子钟　atomic clock ◇ 铯～caesium atomic clock
原子组态　atomic configuration
原子最密排列方向　line of closest atomic packing
圆棒电极磁性探伤法　prod method
圆棒模　billet mould
圆棒(试样)抗裂试验　round bar cracking test
圆边　round edge
圆边扁钢　【压】round-edged flat
圆边击平锤　round set hammer
圆边精整　rounding
圆边轮圈　round edged tyre
圆齿齿轮　knuckle gear
圆冲压坯　【色】circle
圆窗　bull's eye, roundel
圆搭板点焊　disc depression welding
圆底　round(ed) bottom
圆底槽　round-bottomed vessel
圆点　round dot
圆钉　wire nail
圆顶　circular domical vaul, (top, onion) dome
圆顶窑(地下式石灰窑)　dome kiln
圆顶砖　bullhead
圆锭　round ingot
圆锭～圆棒挤压　round-to-round extruding
圆度盘指示器　dial gauge
圆盖　dome
圆钢　rounds, round steel (bar, stock), round bar (iron), round section, smooth bar, bar round section, bar steel ◇ 导卫轧制～guide rounds, 经表面修整［车削］的～surface-conditioned rounds, 热轧～*
圆钢翻转机　apparatus for turning rounds
圆钢矫直机　round straightener
圆钢坯　cylindrical bloom
圆钢丝绳　circular rope
圆钢轧件　round steel bar
圆钢轧制　round rolling
圆根焊缝　beaded joint
圆鼓　drum (Dr.)
圆股钢丝绳　round strand wire rope
圆规　compasses, calipers
圆辊布料器［给矿机］　rotating roll [drum] feeder, roll(-type) feeder, feeding drum
圆辊布料器给料槽　roll feeder surge bin
圆辊布料器矿槽　(raw mix) roll feeder hopper
圆辊布料器转速控制　roll feeder speed control
圆滚线　【数】cycloid
圆滚线拱　cycloidal arch
圆夯　【建】circular rammer
圆弧插补　circular interpolation
圆(弧)拱　bull's eye arch, circular [skene] arch
圆弧面　【铸】hollows
圆弧形齿面　【机】barreled tooth
圆环　(circular) ring,【数】annulus
圆环电弧焊　cyc-arc welding
圆环断开表面张力测定法　anchor-ring method
圆环密封　O-ring seal
圆环筛　ring grizzly
圆环试样　ring-shaped specimen
圆环压缩　ring compression
圆键　round key
圆角　fillet, filleted corner ◇ 车成～radiusing
圆角半径　rounding [corner] radius
圆角方材(一般用作锻件)　round-cornered square
圆角方钢　quarter octagon steel
圆角蜡料　【铸】fillet wax
圆角镘刀[光子]　【铸】round sleeker ◇ 小型～egg sleeker
圆角皮条　【铸】fillet leather
圆角条　【铸】fillet
圆角样板　radius [fillet] gauge

圆截面　circular cross-section
圆锯　circular [annular] saw, trepan ◇ 摆动(式)~(机)*
圆孔型(成品前的)　round former
圆口钳　round (mouth) tongs
圆括号　parenthesis (复数 parentheses)
圆粒　roundel
圆量规(线材的)　circular mill gauge
圆螺母　circular nut
圆满　roundness
圆密尔(直径为密尔的金属丝面积单位, 1密尔=0.0254mm)　cir(cular) mil
圆盘　disc, disk, 【耐】plaque ◇ 进料~ feeding disc
圆盘布料器　feeding disc
圆盘刀　cutting disc
圆盘刀片　circular knife
圆盘刀片心轴[剪刀杆]　knife arbor
圆盘辊　spool roll
圆盘给料机[给矿机, 给料器]　(rotary) table feeder, disc feeder, (rotary) feeder table, rotating plate ◇ 铺底料~ hearth layer feeder table
圆盘剪旁的带卷台　slitter ramp
圆盘剪(切机)　circular [disc, circle, slitting] shears, rotary (disk) shears, rotary cutter ◇ 差速~*, 多刀~*, 金属板材~*, 切边~ rotary (side) trimmer, 无开度[间隙]~*
圆盘剪切机刀片　circular shear blade
圆盘剪纵切作业线　rotary-slitting line
圆盘剪作业线　rotary-shear line
圆盘搅拌机　circular pan mixer
圆盘锯　circular [slitting] saw ◇ 纵切~ slitting mill
圆盘开关　wafer switch
圆盘离合器　disc [plate] clutch
圆盘联轴器　disc coupling
圆盘切割　rotary cutting
圆盘切割机　circular cutting machine
圆盘绕组　disc winding
圆盘烧结机　round sintering machine

圆盘式避雷器　disc arrester
圆盘式变阻器　dial-type rheostat
圆盘(式)过滤机　disc-type filter ◇ 蒸汽~ steam disc filter, 八~ eight-disc filter
圆盘式混合机　rotating-pan mixer
圆盘(式)切边剪　rotary (side) trimming shears, circular blade side trimming shears
圆盘式取样器　fan plate sampler
圆盘式碎土机　disc cultivator
圆盘式轧碎机　disc crusher
圆盘式纵剪　slitter, slitting shears
圆盘形钨阳极　tungsten disc anode
圆盘形阳极　disc anode
圆盘形轧辊　piercer disc
圆盘旋梯　circular geometrical stair
圆盘造球　disc pelletizing [balling]
圆盘造球法[过程]　disc balling process
圆盘造球方式 [团]disc balling mode
圆盘造球机　rotary disk type pelletizer, disc balling machine, disc [pan] pelletizer, pelletizing [pelletising, rotating, granulating] disc, granulating pan ◇ 两段~ two-step disc
圆盘造球机系统　disc balling system
圆盘造球机组　balling disc bank
圆盘造球力学　mechanics of balling on disc
圆盘真空过滤机　disc filter ◇ 搅拌~ Agidisc filter
圆盘制动器[圆盘闸]　disc brake
圆盘制粒机　pelletizing disc
圆盘状的　dish-shaped
圆坯　round billet
圆坯的近终形高速连铸　continuous casting in high speed for near net shape of round billet
圆坯水平连铸机　round billet HCC
圆偏振光　【理】circularly polarized light
圆片　disk, disc
圆片颗粒　round plate particle
圆片离合器　plate clutch
圆瓶窑　bottle oven

圆切口搭接	circular slotted lap joint

圆穹顶　turtle-back arch ◇ 环状～*
圆丘(曲线顶点)　hump, dome
圆球度　degree of sphericity
圆缺孔板[测流孔]　segmental orifice
圆石　boulder, roundstone
圆试棒　test rod
圆试样　round specimen
圆竖井　【采】circular shaft
圆丝扣　round thread
圆铁钉　wire nail
圆筒　cylinder (cl), drum (Dr.), barrel
圆筒薄壳　cylindrical shell
圆筒掺和机　blunger
圆筒粉碎机　rotary disintegrator
圆筒干燥机[器]　cylinder [cylindrical, drum, roller] drier, rotary dryer, drying cylinder, rotating drum type drier, drier drum
圆筒过滤机　rotary filter
圆筒环　cylindrical ring
圆筒回转窑　cylindrical rotary kiln
圆筒混合　barrel mixing
圆筒混合机　drum (-type) [cylinder, trommel] mixer, mixing [conditioner] drum, rotary drum mixer ◇ 调湿～wetting drum, 二次～reroll(ing) drum, 倾斜～tilted cylinder mixer, 旋转～*, 直立～end-over-end mixer
圆筒混合造球[制粒]机　mix and re-roll drum, mixing reroll drum, drum pelletizer ◇ 强力～*
圆筒加料器　drum feeder
圆筒接头　girth joint
圆筒冷却机　cooling drum
圆筒碾磨机　cylinder mill
圆筒筛　cylindrical [trommel] screen, rotating [drum] sieve
圆筒筛给料机　cylindrical screen feeder
圆筒式充气装置　roll aeration device
圆筒式反射器　barrel type reflector
圆筒式磨机　tumbling mill

圆筒水冷机[湿式圆筒冷却机]　quench trommel
圆筒填充率[装料量]　drum loading
圆筒卧式转炉　PS converter
圆筒洗涤器　drum scrubber
圆筒洗矿机　drum washer, scrubbing drum
圆筒型除尘器　drum-type deduster
圆筒形粉末照相机　cylindrical powder camera
圆筒形坩埚　cylindrical crucible
圆筒形回转炉　revolving cylindrical furnace
圆筒形胶片(X射线衍射用)　cylindrical film
圆筒(形)炉　cylindrical furnace, drum-type furnace
圆筒形模　cylindrical die
圆筒形无底坩埚　cylindrical open-ended crucible
圆筒形有底坩埚　cylindrical closed-ended crucible
圆筒形蒸罐　cylindrical rotor vessel
圆筒形轴承　cylindrical bearing
圆筒形转炉　cylindrical rotor vessel ◇ 简单～*
圆筒造球　【团】drum balling
圆筒造球方式　drum balling mode
圆筒造球过程　drum balling process
圆筒造球机　drum pelletizer, balling [pelletizing, pelletising, reroll(ing), granulating, granulation, nodulising] drum ◇ 多锥形～multiple-cone durm, 旋转式～*
圆筒造球机给料　balling drum feed
圆筒造球机循环线　balling drum circuit
圆筒造球系统　drum balling system
圆筒真空过滤机　rotary vacuum filter
圆筒制粒机　drum pelletizer, pelletizing [gradulating, nodulizing]
圆筒桩　【建】cylindrical pile
圆筒状的　cylindric(al)
圆头　rounded end

圆头锤	ball (face) hammer, fuller hammer
圆头矫平锤	rounded flatter
圆头螺钉	round-head [cheese-head] screw
圆头螺栓	round-headed [cheese-head] bolt
圆头铆钉	cup [snaphead] rivet
圆图	circle [pie] diagram, circular graph
圆图记录	round-chart recording
圆屋顶	【建】(onion) dome, cupola
圆心	centre of circle
圆型空穴	round type void
圆形	roundness
圆形槽口抗裂试验	circular-groove crack test
圆形场地	circus
圆形底	rounded bottom
圆形断面	round section
圆形反射炉	circular reverberatory furnace
圆形钢轨	(同"环形钢轨")
圆形回转萃取塔	rotary annular column
圆形焦点	circular focus
圆形均热炉	circular (soaking) pit
圆形孔型	round pass
圆形铝阴极	aluminium circular cathode
圆形坯	round billet [bloom] ◇ 镦锻用~件【压】biscuit
圆形设备	circus
圆形竖炉	vertical cylindrical furnace, annular kiln,【团】circular shaft furnace
圆形图	circular graph
圆形图表	circular chart
圆形图表电位计	circular chart potentiometer
圆形物	round, roundel
圆形橡皮隔膜	circular rubber diaphragm
圆形型材[钢材]轧机	【压】mill for rolling circular shapes
圆形旋转磁场	【理】circular rotating field
圆形阳极	circular [round] anode
圆形闸门	circular gate
圆形铸锭机	【色】casting wheel
圆穴形电子束熔炼	【冶】button melter
圆窑	circular [round] kiln
圆翼管	gilled pipe
圆凿	gouge
圆周	circle, circumference (of circle), periphery ◇ 沿~方向 circumferential direction
圆周变形[应变]	circumferential strain
圆周槽口	circumferential notch
圆周齿节	circumferential pitch
圆周分布	peripheral distribution
圆周焊缝	circumferential seam ◇ 端顶~(压力容器的) head seam
圆周切割	circular [circle] cutting
圆周切线应力	circumferential stress
圆周切向线荷载	circumferential line load
圆周(取样)检验(锻件的)	【压】circumferential test
圆周速度	circumferential speed [velocity], peripheral speed [velocity], periphery speed
圆周线焊机	circular seam welder
圆周应力	circumferential [hoop] stress
圆周运动	circular motion
圆轴	circular shaft
圆柱	circular column, cylinder (cl)
圆柱半径度	【建】module
圆柱部分(转炉本体的)	【钢】belly portion
圆柱带圈	parallel
圆柱辊	cylindrical roller
圆柱辊颈轧辊	straight neck roll
圆柱键	cylindrical key
圆柱面	cylinder surface [face]
圆柱面透镜	cylindrical lens
圆柱器(超声波检验用)	cylindricator
圆柱设计	column design
圆柱体	solid cylinder (铸制的)
圆柱体(试件抗压)试验	cylinder test
圆柱筒壳	circular cylindrical shell
圆柱锡矿	cylindrite
圆柱形槽	cylindrical vessel

圆柱形沉降槽　cylindrical settler
圆柱形电子束　cylindrical beam
圆柱形反射器　cylindrical reflector
圆柱形晶体　cylindrical crystal
圆柱形桥墩　cylindrical pier
圆柱形试样　cylindrical specimen
圆柱形束　cylindrical beam
圆柱形弯曲岩盐晶体　cylindrical curved-rocksalt crystal
圆柱形芯棒[顶杆,顶头](拉拔用)　straight [parallel] plug
圆柱形铸铁冷却器　cast iron cigar cooler
圆柱轴颈　cylindrical journal
圆柱桩　cylinderical pile
圆柱状衰减　cylindrical attenuation
圆锥　(circular) cone ◇ 艾伦式分级～ Allen cone
圆锥澄清器　conical settler
圆锥齿轮　bevel [cone, mitre] gear ◇ 小～ bevel pinion
圆锥齿轮传动辊道　bevel gear roller table
圆锥齿轮检测仪　bevel gear tester
圆锥冲头杯突试验　conical cup test
圆锥度　conicity
圆锥法　cone test
圆锥分级机　cone classifier ◇ 带隔板的～ cone-baffle classifier
圆锥辊　tapered roll
圆锥辊传动[变速]装置　cone roll shifter
圆锥辊颈轧辊　taper neck roll
圆锥滚柱轴承　tapered roller bearing ◇ 四列～*
圆锥螺栓　(同"锥形螺栓")
圆锥破碎机　(rotary) cone crusher, conical [spindle] breaker, gyratory [breaker, crusher] ◇ 粗碎～ coarse cone crusher, 短头～ S.H. (short-head) cone, 二次～ secondary cone crusher, 细碎～ fine cone crusher, 液压～ hydro-cone crusher
圆锥球磨机　conical (ball) mill ◇ 哈丁～*
圆锥式开卷机　【压】cone-type payoff reel

圆锥式球团机　【团】cone pelletizer
圆锥四分法　cone and quartering
圆锥体　conicalness ◇ 截头～ truncated cone
圆锥头螺栓　coneheaded bolt
圆锥喂料机　【耐】conical feeder
圆锥销　conical [taper(ed)] pin
圆锥形涤气器[煤气洗涤机]　circular-wedge scrubber
圆锥形分选机　separating cone
圆锥形壳　conical shell
圆锥形锚塞(预应力钢筋混凝土用)　【建】conical plug
圆锥形磨矿机　cone mill
圆锥形浓缩机　cone thickener
圆锥形压痕　cone imprint
圆锥形压痕试验　cone penetration test
圆锥形压头硬度试验　cone thrust test
圆锥形转筒筛　conical trommel
圆锥(压头)压痕硬度试验　cone indentation test
圆锥造球机　cone pelletizer, balling [rotating] cone
圆紫铜棒　round copper bar
圆嘴夹钳(锻工用)　curved-lip tongs
源　source ◇ 弗兰克-里德～*
源程序　【计】source [subject] program, source routine
源程序模块　【计】source module
源代码　【计】Source code
源地址　【计】source address
源机器　source machine
源计算机　source computer [machine]
源记录　【计】source recording
源强度　source intensity
源数据　source data
源语言　【计】source [original] language
缘(边缘)　edge, fringe, brink
缘饰　【建】curb, edging
远测　remote indication
远场　far field
远程成批处理　【计】remote batch (pro-

远程处理 【计】teleprocessing, remote processing
远程存取 【计】remote access
远程风口 【铁】tuyere remoteness
远程供应的煤气 piped gas
远程集线器 【计】remote concentrator
远程计算机 remote computer
远程计算系统的错误检查 remote computing system error detection
远程计算系统的一致性错误 remote computing system consistency error
远程计算系统的执行错误 remote computing system execution error
远程计算系统语言 remote computing system language
远程继电器 distant relay
远程控制 remote [long-range] control
远程切变 far reaching shear
远程数据处理 remote data processing
远程数据终端 【计】remote data terminal
远程探询 【计】remote polling
远程信息 remote information
远程询问 【计】remote inquiry
远程氧设定调节 remote oxygen setpoint adjusting (ROSA)
远程诊断 【计】remote diagnostic
远程终端辅助设备 remote terminal support
远程(终端)设备 【计】remote device
远程作业输入 remote job entry (RJE) ◇会话式~*
远地 remote site
远动学 teleautomatics, telemechanics
远端 far end
远岸钻探 off-shore boring
远景 long-range perspective, prospect, future, outlook
远景规划 long-range planning, far seeing plan
远距操作 remote manipulation
远距电子枪 distant gun

远距离 distant range (DR)
远距离操纵阀 remote valve
远距离操纵机 remote operated machine
远距离操纵器 robot handler, teleoperator
远距离操作 remote(-controlled) operation
远距离操作仪表[指示仪器] distant-action instrument
远距离测量 remote measurement, telemeasurement
远距离传感器 remote pickup [transmitter]
远距离传送测量仪 remote-transmitting gauge
远距离读数 remote [distant] reading
远距离感应压力计 remote induction manometer
远距离高速爆炸冲压成形 (同"遥控高速爆炸成形")
远距离观察系统 remote viewing system
远距离记录 distant recording
远距离监测 remote monitor(ing)
远距离监视[观察] distant surveillance
远距离接收 distant reception
远距离控制 (同"遥控")
远距离控制[测量]仪表 telegauge
远距离控制制备 remote fabrication
远距离喷煤 【铁】long distance pulverized coal injection process
远距离摄影 telephotography
远距离显微镜 remote microscope
远距离运输的气体 long-range gas
远距离指示器 remote indicator, selsyn
远距辙光信号 【运】distant switch signal
远期汇票 time draught
远位检查系统 remote inspection system
远洋航船 ocean-going vessel
院士 academician
院长 president (Pr.)
约德式连续焊管机 Yoder pipe-and-tube mill
约飞效应 Yoff'e effect

约翰森贫铁矿还原法　Johansen's process
约翰式单色器　Johann-type monochromator
约翰式反射器　Johann-type reflector
约翰式聚焦　Johann(-type) focusing
约翰式聚焦摄谱仪　Johann-type focusing spectrograph
约翰逊低阻抗捕汞器　Johanson's low-resistance trap
约翰逊机械应变仪　Johanson's strain gauge
约翰逊－梅尔方程式　Johansson-Mehl equation
约翰逊式单色器　Johansson-type monochromator
约翰逊式反射器　Johansson-type reflector
约翰逊式聚焦　Johansson(-type) focusing
约翰逊式聚焦摄谱仪　Johansson-type focusing spectrograph
约翰逊轴承黄铜(90Cu,9.5Zn,0.5Sn)　Johanson's bronze
约化　reduction, simplification ◇ 未～的 unreduced
约化波数　reduced wave number
约化法　【数】method of reduction
约化曲线　reduced curve
约化型　reduced form
约简　【数】reduction (rdn)
约简方程　reduced equation
约卡尔布罗铝黄铜(76Cu,2Al,余量Zn)　Yorcalbro
约卡尔尼克铝镍青铜(91Cu,7Al,2Ni)　Yorcalnic
约卡斯坦铜锡合金(88Cu,12Sn)　Yorcastan
约科龙－库奈弗30A铜镍合金(30Ni,2Fe,2Mn,余量Cu)　Yorcoron-Kunifer 30A
约科龙铜合金(30Ni,2Fe,2Mn,余量Cu)　Yorcoron
约克郡70/30铜镍库尼费30合金(30Ni,0.8Mn,0.7Fe,余量Cu)　Yorkshire 70/30 cupro-nickel-Kunifer 30 alloy
约硫砷铅矿　jordanite
约洛依铜镍高强度低合金钢(0.08C,0.9Cu,2Ni,余量Fe)　Yoloy
约瑟夫森效应　【理】Josephson effect
约束　restrain, restraint, bind, bound, constraint, restriction
约束系数(冲压机械的)　constraint factor
约束下焊接试验　restrained weld test
约维诺特杯突试验　Jovignot test
越标　overshoot
越程[距]　skip distance
越野式轧机　cross-country (rolling) mill, zigzag mill
跃变性　discontinuity
跃迁　transition, jump ◇ λ型～*,俄歇[无辐射]～Auger transition
跃迁层　transition layer
跃迁概[几]率　transition probability
钥匙合金(80Cu,10Sn,5Pb,2Zn)　key alloy
钥孔形冲击试样　key-hole specimen
钥孔形缺口(冲击试验的)　key-hole notch ◇ 夏氏～*
月辉(黑色金属的)　moon-shining
月结表　【企】monthly schedule
月球基地　lunar base
月球细尘　lunar fine dust
月生产能力　monthly capacity
月牙桁架　crescent truss
月牙键　semi-circular key
月牙面(连续铸钢的)　meniscus level
月牙销　woodruff key
阅读率[速度]　【计】read(ing) rate
阅读器[机]　reader ◇ 曲线【计】～curve follower,数据～【计】data reader,页式～page reader
云母　mica
云母板　micarex ◇ 层合～micanite
云母玻璃　micalex
云母布　mica cloth
云母带　mica tape

云母的 micaceous	陨铜硫铬矿 gentnerite
云母电容器 mica capacitor [condenser]	允许 permit, allow, permission, 【计】enable
云母粉 mica powder [flour]	
云母海绿砂岩 gaize	允许不平衡度 allowable unequalization degree
云母滑石 {$H_2Mg_3Si_4O_{12}, 3MgO \cdot 4SiO_2 \cdot H_2O$} mica talc	允许负荷[负载] permissible load, load capacity ◇ 轴承～bearing capacity
云母晶体 mica crystal	
云母滤渣片 【铸】mica strainer	允许公差 allowable [permissible, admissible] tolerance
云母片 mica sheet [plate], sheet mica	
云母片岩 mica(ceous) schist	允许极限 allowable limit
云母屏蔽片 mica screen ◇ 透明～transparent mica screen	允许剂量 tolerance
	允许浓度 allowable concentration
云母铜矿 chalcophyllite, tamarite	允许蠕变速率 permissible creep rate
云母铀矿 {$Ca(UO_2)_2P_2O_8 \cdot 8H_2O$} uranite	允许湿度 moisture allowance
云母状赤铁矿 micaceous hematite	允许水平 permitted level
云室 【理】cloud chamber	允许误差 permissible error [variation]
云梯 scaling ladder ◇ 消防～extension ladder	允许写入 【计】write enable
	允许信号 enabling signal, signal enabling
云雾 cloud ◇ 呈～状 cloudiness	允许应力 allowable [permissible] stress
云状非金属夹杂 slag clouds	运搬夹钳 carrying tongs
云状花纹熔渣 【冶】clouded slag	运筹学 【数】operations research (O.R.), operational research
匀称的 symmetric(al)	
匀度系数 uniformity coefficient	运锭卡车 ingot transporting truck
匀速给料 moderate feed	运动 motion, movement, moving
匀质化 homogenization	运动不明显性 movement unsharpness
匀质化晶粒 homogenized crystal	运动场 athletic [moving] field
匀质混凝土 homogeneous concrete	运动方向 direction [sense] of motion
匀质结构 uniform structure	运动链系 kinematic chain
匀质性 uniformity	运动螺型位错 moving screw dislocation
陨铬石 ureyite, cosmochlore	运动黏度[性] kinematic viscosity
陨碱铜硫镍铁 djerfischerite	运动位错 moving dislocation
陨磷铁矿 schreibersite	运动位错产生的缺陷 【金】defect generation by moving dislocations
陨磷铁镍 shepardite	
陨磷铁镍矿 dyslytite	运动学 kinematics
陨硫铬铁 daubreelite	运动学相似 kinematic similarity
陨硫铁 troilite	运动轧件自动测量记录仪 instagraph ◇ 电子式～electronic instagraph
陨氯铁 lawrencite	
陨石 meteor	运费 freight (charges, cost), carriage, fare, transportation expenses, transport charges
陨铁 meteoric [cosmic] iron, siderite	
陨铁镍 chamasite, kamacite	
陨铁石 siderolite	运费率 freight rate
陨铁镍 chamasite	运河 canal

运河床 canal bed
运货舱位 freight space
运货车 camion, waggon
运距 haul distance ◇ 平均~average haul
运矿车 ore transfer car, ore wagon
运矿船 ore ship, ore-carrier
运料车 dumper, transfercar,【耐】pallet truck ◇ 电动~",分批~batch truck,倾卸式~",自行式~transfer buggy
运输 transport (Tp), carriage, conveyance, transportation, haulage (厂内的) ◇ 车间之间~",短途[近距离]~",用轮带~belting
运输包子 carrying ladle
运输车 carriage, delivery car, haulage vehicle, transfercar, wagon ◇ 单侧卸载~one-side transfercar,两侧卸载~both side transfercar,升降~",渣屑和废物~refuse truck,自推进~"
运输车辆 haulage [transport] vehicle ◇ 地面~"
运输车支架 carriage frame
运输秤 conveyer scale
运输带 conveyer [travelling] belt ◇ 钢丝网~wire mesh belt,钢质~steel conveyer belt,焦炭~coke supply belt,浸没式~【选】immersed belt,桥式~conveyer gantry
运输带托辊 apron roll
运输方式 mode of transportation
运输费 (同"运费")
运输高度 conveying height
运输工具 hauling unit, means of transport
运输辊 transport roll(er)
运输辊道 carry-over [processing, trailer] table ◇ 中间~"
运输过程中搅和(拌) mixed in transit
运输机 conveyer (conv.), conveyor, conveyer table, carrier ◇ 鞍式~",摆动式~",板带式~slat conveyer,板式~",算条[格栅式]~transfer grid,步进梁式~",车式冷却~",传送~transfer conveyer,磁力~magnetic conveyer,带式~",单轨~monorail conveyer,地沟~trench conveyer,地行式~",斗式~bucket conveyer,返回~",非连续式~",分类~sorting conveyer,风力~air conveyer,钩式~",刮板~",辊式~roller conveyer,横向~",环带~",环行~circus,回转式~rotary conveyer,机动~powered conveyer,机械化~mechanized conveyer,架空~aerial transporter,减速~decelerating conveyer,阶式~cascade conveyer,缆索式[缆车]~telpher conveyer,雷德勒型连续流~Redler conveyer,链板~",链式~",履带式~caterpillar conveyer,螺旋~",盘式[槽式]~",皮带~",平板~crocodile,气升~gas lift conveyer,倾斜盘式~",全封闭式~",筛式~screen conveyer,伸缩式~retractable conveyer,升降回转~",双路~",水力~hydraulic conveyer,梭式~",驼峰链式~hump chain conveyer,万能~all-round transporter,网式~",往复式~",吸力~suction conveyer,悬吊槽式~",振动~",中间辊式~",重力~",转移~carry-over conveyer
运输机构 transport mechanism
运输机系统 conveyer system
运输机械 conveying [transport] machinery
运输机栈桥 conveyer bridge
运输距离 conveying distance
运输磕碰伤痕 traffic mark
运输冷床 (同"机动冷床")
运输链 conveying chain
运输量 (amount of) traffic, freight volume
运输能力 conveying capacity
运输皮带 conveyer-belting
运输起重机 transfer crane
运输气体 transport gas
运输桥 conveying bridge

运输筛分机	conveyer [conveyance] screen ◇ 水平式～*
运输设备	conveying [load-carrying, transportation] equipment, transport(ation) facilities,
运输速度	conveying speed
运输条件	traffic condition
运输桶	carrying ladle
运输蜗杆	conveying worm
运输系统	conveying [conveyance] system ◇ 分支～*
运输小车	transport carrie, travel(l)ing bogie ◇ 钢瓶～cylinder trolley
运输效率	conveying efficiency
运输站	conveying station
运输支线	bypass conveying system
运输装载机	payloader
运输装置	conveying device [appliance, arrangement], transport mechanism, tong (带卷的)
运送	transport, shipping, conveyance, delivery, handling
运送板垛的吊具	pack [sheet] carrier
运送拌合混凝土	(同"车拌混凝土")
运送车	transfer cart ◇ 带卷～*, 熔化坩埚装置～*
运送车绞盘	buggy winching
运送带	travel(l)ing [moving] belt ◇ 淬火作业线～quench conveyor, 进料～feed conveyer
运送管	conveying pipe
运送机	transveyer ◇ 出料～outfeed conveyer
运送设备	load-carrying equipment
运送时间	transit time
运送铁水罐[包]车	iron-transfer ladle car
运送装置	transport
运算部件	arithmetic unit
运算地址	operation [arithmetic] address
运算电路	computing circuit
运算对象	operand
运算放大器	operational amplifier
运算符号	operational sign [symbol]
运算寄存器	arithmetic register
运算控制器	operation control
运算控制系统	computing control system
运算逻辑部件	arithmetic logic unit
运算器	arithmetic and logical unit, arithmetic unit [organ, section]
运算软件	operational software
运算时间	operating time
运算数	operand, operation number
运算因数	operation(al) factor
运算子	【数】operator
运土铲土机	earth-moving scraper
运土机(械)	dirt [earth] mover
运土设备	earth-moving equipment
运行	run, working, operation ◇ 满负荷[满载]～【机】full load run
运行成本	running cost
运行工程学	human engineering
运行机构	running gear
(运行)记录	log
运行阶段	【计】run phase
运行力矩	running torque
运行漏斗式卸船[车]机	travel(l)ing-hopper unloader
运行磨损	service wear
运行说明书	【计】run book
运行特性(曲线)	running characteristic
运行稳定	uniformity of operation
运用	utilization, application, usage
运用场所	infield
运油船	oil tanker, dirty ship
运载工具	【运】vehicle
运渣车	slag transfercar [truck, wagon]
运渣罐[桶]	slag truck ladle
运渣装置[机械]	slag-conveying machinery
运砖手推车	hackbarrow
运转	run(ning), operation, working ◇ 不能[难以]～的 unworkable, 投入～in operation, 在～中 in operation
运转电动机	operating motor

运转费用　operating expenses, working expenditure, running cost
运转负荷　operating load
运转规程　【企】service regulations
运转能力　running ability
运转期　running term
运转时间　running [machine] time
运转试验　running [actual] test ◇ 作过长时间~的 time-tested
运转速度　operating [running] speed
运转停止　interruption of service
晕流　corona current
晕圈　halo
晕影　halation
孕镶金刚石　impregnated diamond
孕镶金刚石工具[刀具,刃具]　diamond-impregnated tool
孕镶金刚石岩心钻头　diamond-impregnated core drill bit

孕镶金刚石制品　diamond-impregnated compositions
孕育　inoculation, incubation ◇ 使~【冶】inoculating
孕育处理　inoculation (treatment), modification ◇ 包中~*, 加铈~的铸铁*, 即刻~*, 型内~ moulding inoculation, 铸铁~*
孕育处理法　process of modification
孕育剂　inoculant ◇ 氮－稀土复合~ N-RE multi-inoculants, 依诺帕克铸铁~ Inopac
孕育期　incubation period, 【理】induction period ◇ 腐蚀~*, 加载后应变~*, 蠕变中的~*
孕育时间　incubation time
孕育铸铁　inoculated [inoculation] cast iron, mechanite metal, meehanite

Z z

匝比　【电】turn ratio, ratio of winding
砸裂　shattering
砸碎锤　granulating hammer
砸碎的废钢铁　drop-broken scrap
砸碎机　granulator
杂白钙沸石　cerinite
杂斑模纹（镀锡薄钢板的）　【压】mottle ◇ 有～的镀锡薄钢板 mottled plate
杂波　noise wave, spurious response
杂费　overhead expenses, oncost, extras, miscellaneous fee [expenses]
杂费开支　【企】overhead charges
杂酚油－沥青混合物　creosote-pitch mixture
杂锆石{$ZrO_2 + ZrSiO_4$}　zirkite
杂铬酸盐　heterochromate
杂工　shiftman,【企】odd man
杂钴华砷铁矾　yellow earthy cobalt
杂硅钙铅铀矿　nenadkevite
杂化　hybridization
杂化轨函数　hybridized orbital, hybrid
杂环构造　【化】heterocyclic structure
杂聚合(作用)　hetero-polymerization
杂孔雀石　musorin
杂蓝辉镍矿　kallilite
杂(类物)料　miscellaneous material
杂料称量料斗　miscellaneous weigh hopper
杂料回炉灰铸铁　ferrosteel
杂磷锌矿　hibbenite
杂菱镁白云石　konite
杂硫铅锌矿　youngite
杂铝英磷铝石{$3Al_2O_3 \cdot SiO_2 \cdot nH_2O$}　schroetterite
杂乱脉冲干扰　【电】hash, random pulse jamming
杂乱排绕　【钢】bad cast
杂乱数据[信号]　hash
杂铌矿　wiilite
杂拼　hybridization
杂散场　stray field
杂散磁通密度　stray flux density
杂散电流　stray current
杂散电流腐蚀　stray-current [curre-spray] corrosion
杂散辐射　stray [spurious] radiation
杂散辐射能　stray radiant energy
杂散光发射　stray-light emission
杂散影像　spurious image
杂色　mottling, parti-colour
杂色的　mottled, heterochromatic
杂色光　heterogeneous light
杂砂岩　graywacke, greywacke
杂石　variegated rocks, gob（填筑用）
杂酸　heteroacid
杂钛铁金红石　kalkowskite
杂碳铀钍矿　thucholite
杂铁锰尖晶石　garividite, verdenburgite
杂铁锰锌矿　kaliphite
杂铜　copper scrap, scrap copper
杂铜铁硫锌矿　lupikkite
杂钍硅铀铅矿　pilbarite
杂硒铜铅汞矿　zorgite
杂项费用　overhead [miscellaneous] expenses
杂项服务　【企】miscellaneous services
杂项开支　overhead cost ◇ 厂内～factory overhead
杂原子　heteroatom
杂原子的　heteroatomic
杂质　impurity (substance), foreign substance [material, matter], inclusion, admixture, contaminant, heterogeneity ◇ 伴生～*, 负型[N型]～*, 固有[内在]～*, 含～的 impure, 含氧～*, 难除[有害]～ troublesome impurity, 去～*, 填隙式～迁移[徙动]*, 无～的*, 移动[迁移]～migrating impurity, 主要～*, 自熔[自行造渣]～*
杂质半导体　impurity [extrinsic] semiconductor

杂质补偿度　degree of impurity compensation
杂质带　impurity band
杂质带电导　impurity-band conduction
杂质分布　distribution of impurities
杂质辐射　impurity radiation
杂质光谱　impurity spectrum
杂质光谱线　【化】impurity line
杂质含量　foreign matter content, impurity content [level], ballast content（煤的）
杂质含量百分率　【半】imperfection level
杂质积聚　accumulation of impurities
杂质激活能　impurity activation energy
杂质极限[限度]　impurity limitation, limit of impurities (l.o.i.)
杂质金属　contaminating metal
杂质扩散　impurities diffusion
杂质扩散系数　impurity diffusion coefficient
杂质离子　impurity [foreign] ion
杂质粒子[粉粒]　foreign particle
杂质量　contaminant capacity
杂质煤　attrital coal
杂质浓度　impurity concentration
杂质迁移率　【理】impurity mobility
杂质散射参数　【理】impurity scattering parameter
杂质添加剂　impurity additions
杂质污染　impurity contamination
杂质线　【化】impurity line
杂质相　【金】impurity phase
杂质循环量　circulating load of impurities
杂质元素　impurity [foreign] element
杂质原子　impurity [foreign, stranger] atom
杂质原子气团　impurity atmosphere
杂质原子与位错间化学相互作用　chemical interaction between foreign atoms and dislocations
杂质原子与位错间的流体静压力相互作用　(同"外来原子与位错间的流体静压力相互作用")

杂质源　impurity source
杂质状态　impurity state
杂质自扩散系数　impurity self-diffusion coefficient
灾害　calamity, pest,【环】hazard
灾难性故障　catastrophic failure
灾难性膨胀　(同"恶性膨胀")
载波　carrier wave
载波电话　carrier-phone
载波继电器　carrier relay ◇ 方向比较～*
载波距离继电器　carrier distance relay
载波频率　carrier frequency
载波线路　carrier line
载波信道[电路]　carrier channel
载荷　load(ing) ◇ 恒定～法 constant-load method
载荷-变形曲线　load-deformation curve
载荷-变形图　load-deformation diagram
载荷范围　loading range
载荷分布　load distribution
载荷-拉伸变形图　load-extension diagram
载荷能力　load-carrying ability
载荷溶剂　loaded solvent
载荷树脂　loaded resin
载荷树脂排出管　loaded resin offtake
载荷系数　load factor, loading coefficient
载荷-延伸率曲线　load-elongation curve
载荷子扩散　carrier diffusion
载金属炭　loaded carbon
载金炭　gold bearing carbon
载量　loading
载料列车　charging-buggy train
载流流体[液体]　carrier fluid
载流轴　current-carrying shaft
载流轴承衬套　(同"带电轴承衬套")
载流子　current carrier ◇ 少数～注入*
载流子浓度　carrier concentration
载流子迁移率(半导体的)　carrier mobility
载流子输送　【半】carrier transport

载模板 【铸】backing board [plate]	再稠化 redensification
载模体(等静压制用) mould carrier	再除尘器 reduster
载膜 support films, film carrier	再触发[点火] restrike, restriking
载片 slide	再处理 retreatment, reprocessing, re-run
载频 carrier frequency	再处理车间[再加工工厂] reprocessing plant
载气(真空)泵 gas ballast pump	
载热体[介质] 【理】heat carrying agent, heating agency	再处理粉尘 reprocessed dust
	再磁化 remagnetizing
载入方式 【计】load mode	再次冲压操作 second pressing operation
载色剂 vehicle	再(次)电解 re-electrolysis, secondary electrolysis
载体 carrier (material), bearer, supporter ◇ 数据~【计】data carrier	
	再次拉拔 【压】redraw(ing)
载体沉淀 carrier precipitation	再次送风 【铁】reblow
载体触媒[催化]剂 supported catalyst	再次选分 【选】reclamation
载体电解质 carrier electrolyte	再萃取 【色】re-extract(ion)
载体化合物 【化】carrier compound	再萃塔 re-extraction column
载体矿浆 carrier pulp	再萃液 re-extract liquor
载体扩散 carrier diffusion	再淬火的 quenched again (Q_2, Qa)
载体离子 carrier ion	再存入 【计】restore
载体气体 carrier gas	再打结(炉衬) 【钢】reramming
载体溶液 【冶】carrier solution	再点火 restrike, reignition
载物台(显微镜的) objective table, (object) stage	再点燃电压 reignition [restriking] voltage
载物台测微计 stage micrometer	再定义 redefining
载物台架 object stage	再度分解 secondary decomposition
载重板车 dray	再煅烧 【耐】reburning
载重车 bogie ◇ 拖挂式~coupled truck	再翻转 re-tilting
载重吨位 deadweight capacity (DWT, dwt)	再沸腾 【钢】reboil
	再分布 redistribution
载重钢丝绳 load [sling] rope	再分级[类] re-classification
载重链 load chain	再分类辊道 reassorting table
载重量 load [carrying] capacity, deadweight (船只的)	再浮选机 aftertreatment [retreatment] cell
	再腐蚀 【金】reetch
载重汽车 autotruck, lorry ◇ 带拖车的~trailer truck	再焊 rewelding
	再化合 recombination
再焙烧 【冶】reburning	再还原钼 re-reduced molybdenum
再沉淀 reprecipitation	再还原钼粉 re-reduced molybdenum powder
再称量 reweighing	
再成型 reshaping	再挥发 resublimation
再充电 recharge (R/C)	再辉点 【金】recalescence point
再充氦 helium backfill	再回火 retempering, redraw(ing)
再充气站 【焊】recharging plant	

再回火的	tempered again
再挤压	re-extrusion
再计[核]算	recalculation
再加工	re-working, reprocessing, retreat
再加硫再增磷低碳钢	resulphurized rephosphorized lowcarbon steel
再加热	reheating, saddening
再加热断裂	reheat cracking, stress relief cracking
再(加)热炉	reheater, reheating [mill] furnace
再加热特性	reheat behaviour
再浆化	repulp(ing)
再浆化槽	repulp tank, repulper ◇ 滤饼～ cake repulper
再浆化铅泥浆泵	repulped lead slurry pump
再结晶	recrystallization, secondary crystallization, recrystallizing ◇ 奥氏体～*, 二次～的抑制*, 基体～*, 加工～*, 就地～*, 抗～性*, 退火～*, 一次～*, 自生～*
再结晶程度	degree of recrystallization
再结晶多边形化理论	polygonization theory of recrystallization
再结晶钢	reacting steel
再结晶核心	recrystallization nuclei
再结晶结构[组织]	recrystallized [recrystallised] structure
再结晶晶粒	recrystallized grain
再结晶晶粒度	recrystallized grain size
再结晶控制轧制	recrystallizing controlled rolling
再结晶孪晶	recrystallization twin
再结晶区(域)	recrystallization zone [region], recrystallized zone
再结晶热处理	recrystallizing heat treatment
再结晶铁素体	recrystallized ferrite
再结晶图	recrystallization diagram
再结晶退火	recrystallization anneal(ing), recrystallizing anneal, process annealing
再结晶温度	recrystallization temperature
再结晶钨丝	recrystallized tungsten wire
再结晶性质	recrystallization behaviour
再结晶织构	recrystalline [recrystallization] texture
再结晶组织	recrystallized structure, recrystallzation texture
再结晶作用	recrystallization
再漫出	re-leach(ing)
再漫蚀	【金】reetch
再漫渍	reimpregnation
再精加工	refinishing
再精炼	re-refining, secondary refining
再精制	refinishing, repurify
再净化	repurification
再聚焦光束	(同"二次聚焦射束")
再拉道次	【压】redrawing pass
再拉伸[深]	redrawing ◇ 反向～ reverse redrawing, 直接～*
再冷凝器	after-condenser ◇ 水冷～*
再冷轧	double cold reduction
再冷装置	recooling plant
再利用	reuse
再炼铬铁	foundery ferrochrome
再炼炉渣	charge slag
再硫化	resulfurized
再氯化	rechlorination
再弥散	redispersion
再磨	regrinding (regr.)
再磨粉矿	reground fines
再磨机	regrind mill
再磨精矿	reground concentrate
再磨设备	regrinding equipment
再磨循环[流程]	regrind circuit
再黏合剂	rebinder
再凝固	resolidification
再排列	rearrangement
再排序	【计】restart sorting
再抛光	repolish
再起弧电压	(同"再点燃电压")
再启动	restart
再启动点	restart point

再清洗槽	reclearing tank
再取向	reorientation
再燃烧器	after-burner
再绕机	【压】re-spooling machine
再热槽[熔池]	reheating bath
再热初轧方坯	reheat bloom
再热器	reheater
再热试验	reheating test
再热压成型	hot re-compaction
再熔	【冶】remelt(ing), refusion ◇ 快速～ fast remelt
再熔坩埚	remelt crucible
再熔合金	secondary [remelted] alloy
再熔化法	【冶】remelt(ing) process
再熔炼	resmelting, melting down ◇ 二次～【钢】double melting
再熔炼费用	cost of remelting
再熔炉	remelting furnace
再熔铁	remelted iron
再溶解	re-dissolution, redissolve, resolution
再筛分	rescreening
再烧结	resintering, second [advanced] sintering
再烧结周期	resintering cycle
再深拉[再拉延]压力机	【压】redrawing press
再渗碳	recarburization, recarburisation, recarburise
再渗碳温度	recarburization temperature
再生	recover, recovery, reproduction, regeneration, reclaiming, 【计】rewrite ◇ 彻底～ starvation regeneration, 煤气～(法) gas reforming, 完全～ full regeneration
再生程序	【计】reproducer
再生磁道	【电】regenerative track
再生萃取器	regeneration extractor
再生淬火	regenerative quenching
再生存储器	【计】regenerative memory [storage]
再生电路	regenerative circuit
再生钢	secondary steel
再生工段	regenerative section
再生合金	secondary alloy
再生黄铜(63.5—88Cu)	yellow ingot metal
再生活性焦炭	regenerative active coke
再生剂	regenerant, reclaiming agent
再生剂用量(离子交换的)	regeneration level
再生金属	secondary metal ◇ 二次熔炼的～*
再生浸出溶液	regenerated leach solution
再生硫酸	reclaimed sulfuric acid
再生锍[冰铜]	secondary matte
再生铝	secondary aluminium
再生率	reproducibility
再生期	regeneration period
再生器	reproducer, regenerator, actifier
再生铅	secondary lead
再生酸	recovered [restored, reclaimed] acid
再生铜	secondary [reclaimed] copper
再生锡	secondary tin
再生现象	【电】regeneration
再生相	【金】second [minor] phase
再生相粒子	second phase particle
再生效率	regeneration efficiency
再生循环	regeneration cycle
再生阳极	secondary anode
再生原料	secondary raw material, reusable material
再生装置	reclaiming [regenerating] unit, 【冶】reclaiming machine
再升华	resublimation, resublime
再时效	【金】reageing
再碳化	recarbonization
再碳酸化	recarbonation
再碳酸化贫液	recarbonated barren solution
再提纯	repurify
再提取	【色】re-extract(ion)
再调(成矿)浆	(同"再浆化")
再调浆器	repulper

再调湿	【团】rewetting
再涂覆处理	replating
再退火	【金】reanneal
再析出	reprecipitation
再吸附(作用)	readsorption
再吸收	reabsorption
再吸收作用	resorption
再稀释	redilution
再显装置	【计】transcribor
再现	reappear, reproducing, playback, representation
再现性	repeatability, 【理】reproducibility
再现装置	reproducer
再选尾矿	rewash discard
再循环	recirculation (recirc.), recycling
再循环供暖机组	drawn-through heater
再循环管道	recirculation line
再循环孔[口]	recirculation opening
再循环料	recycled material
再循环气体	recycle gas
再循环收尘器	closed-circuit deduster
再循环水	recycled water
再循环系统	recycling system ◇ 闭环式～
再循环装置	recirculator ◇ 废气～
再压	recompression, repressing, second pressing [compacting], reshaping
再压操作	【粉】repress operation
再压下	double reduction
再压压力	recompression pressure
再压制	recompacting, re-compaction
再氧化	re-oxidizing, reoxidation
再氧化反应器	re-oxidation reactor
再氧化机理	reoxidation mechanism
再氧化锌	re-oxidized zinc
再引弧电压	resisting voltage (R.V.)
再硬化	rehardening
再用	reusing ◇ 可～的 reusable
再用废料	recirculating scrap
再预热	re-preheat
再运转	re-run
再增碳	【钢】recarburization, recarburizing, recarburisation, recarburising
再增碳剂	recarburizing agent, recarburizer
再轧	rerolling
再轧钢材(用小型轧机轧废旧钢材而得)	rerolled steel ◇ 旧轨～ rail steel products
再轧机	rolling mill
再轧坯	rerolling feed
再蒸发器	revaporizer
再蒸馏	redistillation
再蒸馏钙	redistilled calcium
再蒸馏锅	reboiler
再正火	renormalization
再植被	【环】revegetation
再植被稳定(法)	revegetative stabilization
再致密化	redensification
再制	reforming, reproduction
再制浆	reslurrifying
再制(生)铁	refined [synthetic] pig iron
再铸造	recast(ing)
再装料	recharge (R/c)
再组合车轮	retyred wheel
再钻	rdrlg (redrilling)
在岗培训	on-site training
在辊时间	time in rolls
在坑时间(均热炉的)	pit time
在前[先]	priority
在现场	in situ
在线30通道超声波探伤	【压】30 passages line supersonic flaw detection
在线操作	on-line operation
在线测径	【压】diameter measuring on line
在线常化	【压】on line normalizing
在线超声波检验	on-line ultrasonic testing
在线磁力探伤	on-line magnetic defect inspection
在线淬火	on-line hardening
在线带钢[坯]生产	on-line strip production (ISP)
在线带钢[坯]生产线	ISP line
在线多元素化学分析	on-line multiple element chemical analysis
在线分析	on-line analysis

在线监控　on-line monitoring
在线检验　on-line inspection
在线检验[测]系统　on-line inspection system
在线控冷工艺　on-line CCT
在线控制冷却　on-line controlled cooling
在线冷却　on-line cooling
在线螺旋轧制　on-line screw rolling
在线磨辊　on-line roll grinding (ORG)
在线磨辊机　on-line roll grinder
在线热处理　【金】on-line heat treatment
在线热处理钢轨　on-line heat treatment of rails
在线试验　on-line test
在线数据库　on-line data bases
在线探伤　【压】line flaw detection
在线无损检验[测]　on-line non-destructive inspection
在线轧制　in-line rolling
在线铸轧　(同"连续铸轧")
在职训练　on-the-job [in-service] training
在制品　in-process material, semi-product
暂磁性质　soft magnetic property
暂存带　【计】scratch tape
暂设房屋　temporary building
暂设工程　temporary construction
暂时保护　temporary protection
暂时磁铁　temporary [soft] magnet
暂时存储　volatile storage
暂时存储器[暂存器]　【计】temporary memory [storage], working storage
暂时黏结剂　temporary binder
暂时文件　【计】temporary file
暂时硬度(水的)　temporary hardness
暂(时状)态　(同"瞬态")
暂态电抗　transient reactance
暂停　intermission, suspend
暂行标准　tentative standard
暂行(技术)规程　tentative specification
暂硬水　temporary hard-water
錾钢含碳量　chisel temper
錾具(钢)韧度　chisel temper

錾具用钢(0.9C 或 3Ni, 0.4C)　chisel steel
錾平　chipping
錾子　chisel ◇ 开槽~【机】grooving chisel
赞塔尔铝青铜(81～90Cu, 8—11Al, 0—4Fe, 0—4Ni, 0—1Zn)　Xantal (alloy)
脏的　dirty, filthy, foul
脏物(金属表面的)　soil, dirt, foul
脏物沉淀池　dirt pocket
凿　chisel, straight bit ◇ 削扁[岬扁]尖~ cape chisel
凿槽　gouge
凿沟　riffling
凿沟机　【建】channel(l)er, channeling machine
凿井　cable-tool well
凿井工　sinker, shaftman
凿井机　miser
凿具用合金钢　alloy chisel steel
凿孔　gouge, perforating
凿平　chipping
凿平锤　chipping hammer
凿死　calking
凿头　point tool
凿岩　【采】boring, drilling
凿岩车　【采】dolly, jamb, drill rig
凿岩工　driller
凿岩机　【采】drill [perforating] press, rock [hammer] drill ◇ 手持式~jack hammer, 下向~sinker
凿岩钎杆用中空钢　hollow rock drill steel
凿岩台车　【采】bogie, jumbo
凿用工具钢　chisel tool steel
凿子　chisel
藻井(天花板的凹格)　caisson (ceiling)
藻类　alga (复数 algae)
藻质体(煤岩)　alginite
早期变形　initial fail
早期低强水泥　low-early-strength cement
早期警报系统　【环】early warning system
早期疲劳损伤　incipient fatigue damage
早期破坏　initial fail, premature failure

早期强度　early strength
早期缩孔　【钢】incipient shrinkage
早强混凝土　early strength concrete
早强剂　early strength agent [admixture]
早强水泥　early strength cement, rapid-setting cement
早熔　premature fusion
噪扰　noise, spurious response
噪声　noise, buzz ◇ 环境～ambient noise, 宽音域～ broad band noise, 无 ～ 的 noise-free, 有～的 noisy
噪声电平[噪声级]　noise level ◇ 线路～*
噪声电压　noise [hum] voltage
噪声发生器　noise generator
噪声公害　noise pollution
噪声计[噪声电平测试器]　noise meter ◇ 简易～*
噪声控制　【环】noise control
噪声容限　【环】noise margin
噪声探测仪　riometer
噪声系数　noise coefficient [factor, figure]
噪声消除　【环】noise elimination
噪声消除器　【电】noise killer [canceller]
噪声源　noise source
噪声自动限制器　automatic noise limiter
噪音　(同"噪声")
噪音病　acoustic trauma
噪音判据曲线　【环】noise criteria curve
噪音伤害　【环】damage by noise pollution
造币　coinage ◇ 凸边～板*
造币板冲裁　blanking of planchets
造币复合(金属)材料　coinage composite
造币坯板　coin blank
造币用设备　mint processing equipment
造船(钢)板　ship [hull] plate
造船用钢　shipbuilding steel
造堆　【团】building of pile ◇ 分条小堆～法 windrow method, 人字形分层～法 【团】chevron method
造堆机(矿石混匀用)　bedding stacker
造堆上料机　stack loader

造堆速度　【团】stacking rate
造价　cost of construction [building, manufacture], erected capital cost
造价分析　【建】analysis of prices
造价影响因素　【企】cost factor
造价预算(建筑的)　account valuation
造景　【环】landscaping
造孔　pore-creating, pore-forming
造孔剂[材料]　pore-creating material, pore-forming material [agent, substance]
造块　agglomeration, conglomeration ◇ 粉矿～*, 冷固结[无焙烧]～*, 冷黏结～法*, 烧结～*, 冶金[钢铁厂]粉尘～*
造块厂　agglomerating [agglomeration] plant
造块程度　extent of agglomeration
造块法　agglomeration technique [process, method] ◇ 钢铁厂废料～*
造块过程　agglomeration process
造块和团矿学会(美国)　Institute of Briquetting and Agglomeration (IBA)
造块技术　agglomeration technique
造块阶段　agglomeration step
造块精矿　【团】agglomerated concentrate
造块设备　agglomerating device [machine], agglomeration facilities [unit]
造块性　agglomerability
造粒机[器]　【团】nodulizer, Pelletizer ◇ 盘式～pan nodulizer, 转盘～*
造粒性能　balling behaviour
造林　【环】afforestation
造锍　【环】formation of matte
造锍法　matte-making method
造锍反射炉　reverberatory matting furnace
造锍熔炼　matte smelting ◇ 电炉～*
造锍熔炼炉　matting furnace
造气药皮　【焊】volatile coating, gas producing coating
造球　pelletization, pelletizing, pellet formation, green pellet production, green ball formation [production], (green) balling,

造 zao

granulation, granulating, nodulizing ◇ 单圆筒～ single-drum balling, 间歇[分批]～*, 难～矿石*, 双圆筒～ two-drum balling, 预先～*, 圆盘～*, 直接～用原料 direct pellet feed
造球参数 pelletization parameter
造球操作[作业] balling operation
造球度 degree of balling
造球段 pelletizing [pellet-forming, balling] section
造球段长度(圆筒机的) rolling length
造球法 pelletizing [balling, nodulizing] process, pelletising procedure, pelletizing method
造球方式 (green) balling mode ◇ 闭路～*
造球工 balling operator [attendant]
造球工段 pelletizing [pellet-forming] section, balling section [area, floor]
造球过程 pelletizing [nodulizing, balling] process
造球混合料 pelletized [balling] mix, balling (feed) material, granulated material, pelletable mixture
造球机 pelletizer, pelletiser, pelletizing mixer [unit], balling device [machine], [unit], granulating machine, granulator ◇ 多锥式～*, 离心转动型～*, 盘式～*, 圆锥～*
造球机理 mechanism of ball formation
造球机械 【团】balling machinery
造球技术 balling technique
造球理论[机理] balling theory
造球粒度 pelletizing size, balling fineness
造球难易程度 ease of balling
造球能力 ability to ball
造球盘 pelletizing disc, balling disc [pan], granulating pan, flying saucer
造球喷水(器) balling spray
造球设备 pelletizing [pelletising] equipment, balling equipment [facilities, machinery, plant, unit] ◇ 大型～*, 多系列

～*
造球时间 balling time
造球室 pelletizer house, pelletizing building, balling building [plant] agglomerating [agglomeration] plant
造球试验 balling test
造球水分 balling water [moisture]
造球速度 balling speed ◇ 临界～*
造球特性 pelletizing characteristic (s) [behavio(u)r] ◇ 天然～*
造球团坯 green balling
造球系列 balling circuit [line]
造球系统 pelletizing line [circuit], balling [granulating] system
造球细度 balling fineness
造球效果 balling result
造球性 pelletizing characteristic (s), balling tendency, ease of balling, 【铁】ballability (矿料的)
造球性能 balling behaviour, ability to ball
造球旋转盘 granulating turning table
造球循环 balling circuit [loop]
造球圆筒 pelletizing drum
造球原料 balling feed (material), granulated material
造球状况 pelletizing behavio(u)r
造生球团 【团】green balling, kneading (铁矿粉的)
造酸性渣 【冶】acid slagging practice
造铜期 【色】copper [finish] blow, copper-forming period, blister stage
造铜期工作函数 finish blow work function
造小球 micro-pelletizing, microball(ing), pre-pelletisation, pre-granulation
造小球混合料 micro-pelletized mix (ture), balled mix
造小球效果 micro-pelletising efficiency
造型 mo(u)ld(ing) ◇ 敞箱～ open sand mould(ing), 吹二氧化碳气硬化精密～法 CO_2 gas process, 吹砂～ blow moulding, 地坑～*, 干砂～ dry (sand) mould-

ing,工作台～bench mould,活块～*,活砂[活芯]～drawback,机器～machine moulding,假型板[双面模板]～match-plate moulding,静液压～hydrostatic moulding,两模～*,轮廓[橡皮模]～contour moulding,膜压～*,黏土～clay moulding,喷砂～blowing,熔模[失蜡]～*,砂箱～box moulding,射压～*,湿砂～*,实物[复制模]～*,手工～法hand mould process,水泥砂～*,镶嵌～insert moulding,压力～compression moulding,有模～pattern moulding,组芯～core moulding

造型材料 moulding material,plasticine ◇ 舍菲尔德～*,新配～virgin material

造型材料强度减弱 weaking of moulding sand

造型铲 moulder's peel [shovel],moulding spade

造型地面 moulding floor

造型粉 moulding powder

造型工 moulder ◇ 工作台～bench moulder

造型工段 moulding floor [hall]

造型工工作台 moulder's bench

造型工具 moulder's tool

造型工手槌[木槌,软槌] moulder's mallet

造型工序 mould operation

造型工用锤 moulder's hammer

造型刮板(黏土造型用) strickle board, moulding scraper

造型焊 shape welding

造型混合料 moulding mixture

造型机 moulding machine,moulder ◇ 爆炸～*,成形压实～*,电磁式～*,电动～*,顶[上]压式～*,定心～*,翻箱式～*,夯实～*,滑板输送式～*,机动～*,铰接翻转式～*,两向加压～*,漏模～*,膜压式薄壳～*,气动～*,双工位[双头]～*,微震[有减震装置的震实式]～*,下[底]压式～*,旋转式～*,压实式～*,液动压～*,液压～*,震实(式)～*,转台式～*

造型机翻转台 rock-over table

造型间 moulding hall

造型紧实力 moulding force (MF)

造型紧实压力 moulding pressure (MP)

造型黏土 bonding clay,bonderise,moulding [foundery,casting] loam

造型平板 mould(ing) [follow] board

造型筛 moulder's riddle

造型台 mould(ing) table,moulder,banker

造型铁锹 moulder's peel [shovel],moulding spade

造型斜度 mould taper

造型压力机 mould(ing) press

造型用钉 moulding pin,core iron

造型用定位销 moulding pin

造型用刷 water brush

造形 form,shaping

造渣 slagging,slag-making,slag-working,slag forming [formation],building of slag,flux(ing) ◇ 扒渣井～【钢】change of slag

造渣法 slagging practice,slag forming

造渣反应 slagging reaction

造渣过量 overslagging

造渣后期 gone high

造渣剂 slagging [slag-forming,slag-making] material,slagging [fluxing] medium,slag-forming element

造渣率 slag yield [fall]

造渣能力 slag(ging) ability,slaggability

造渣期 slagging period,slag-forming stage [period],【色】slag blow（硫吹炼的）

造渣期工作函数 slag blow work function

造渣区 slagging area

造渣试验 slagging test

造渣损失 loss by slagging

造渣添加剂 slag-forming [slag-making] addition

造渣温度 slag-making temperature,formation temperature of slag

造渣物料[物质] slag-forming material [substances], slagging [slag-making] material

造渣性能 slaggability, slagging characteristics

造渣组分 slag-forming [flux, shielding] constituent, slag-forming ingredient

造渣作业 slagging operation

造渣作用 slagging action, fluxing effect

造终渣 【冶】final slag formation

皂粉(润滑)拉拔 dry soap drawing

皂盒(拉丝机的) soap box

皂化 saponification (sapon.)

皂化剂 saponifying agent, saponifier

皂化值 saponification value (sap. val.)

皂化作用 saponification

皂碱液 soap solution

皂膜流量计 soap-film flowmeter

皂泡试验 soap bubble test

皂石 soap-stone, saponite {$2MgO \cdot 3SiO_2 \cdot nH_2O$}, zebedassite {$5MgO \cdot Al_2O_3 \cdot 6SiO_2 \cdot 4H_2O$}

皂土 bentonite, soapy clay

皂土黏合剂 bentonite binder

皂土添加比[量] bentonite/ore ratio

灶式炉 oven [box] type furnace

灶室干燥炉 cabinet drier

责任 liability, responsibility, duty ◇ 无过失～*

择优成核 【金】preferential nucleation

择优反射 selective reflection

择优极化方向 direction of preferential polarization

择优浸蚀 preferential etching

择优取向 preferred direction [orientation] ◇ 德拜环上～最大强度值*

择优取向(X射线)衍射花样 preferred orientation pattern

择优取向X射线照相 preferred orientation X-ray photograph

择优取向合金 preferred orientation alloy

择优散射 preferential scattering

择优生长 preferential growth

泽德伯格式大型电解槽 large Soederberg cell

泽尔科铝焊料(15Al, 2Cu, 余量Zn) Zelco

泽雷纳间接碳弧焊 Zerener welding

泽马锡基轴承合金(11Sb, 5.5Cu, 余量Sn) Zemma's bearing metal

"泽塔" 【理】zero energy thermonuclear assembly (Z.E.T.A.)

增补 enlargement

增产 increase production

增产节约 increase production and practise economy

增稠 thickening, densification, dewater

增稠剂 thickener, thickening agent

增稠面积 thickening area

增稠器 thickener ◇ 水力分离[分选]～ hydrator-thickener

增稠区 thickening area

增脆剂 embrittling agent

增大 magnifying, amplifying, enlargement, accretion

增电子反应 electronation reaction

增电子剂 electronating agent

增幅 amplification

增感 sensibilization

增感[光]屏 【电】intensifying screen ◇ 无～X射线胶片

增感作用 sensibilization

增光剂 sensitizer

增厚 build(ing) up

增辉 unblanking, intensifying

增加 increase (inc.), raise, add, growing, multiplication

增加电子(作用) electronation

增加量 incremental quantity, augmentation

增加生产[处理, 通过]量 increased throughput

增加速度 speed gain

增加物 accretion

增加载荷蠕变 【理】incremental creep
增进 improvement
增菌液 inoculum(复数 inocula)
增宽 broadening ◇ 波长展开度引起的~*,反射~*,辐射源有限宽度引起的~*,微晶粒度引起的~*,样品有限尺寸引起的~*
增量 increment, gain, pick-up,【计】augmenter, augmentor
增量成形胎具(板件的) incremental former
增量磁导率 incremental permeability
增量磁化[起磁]力 【理】incremental magnetizing force
增量磁化率 incremental susceptibility
增量磁滞[滞后]回线 【理】incremental hysteresis loop
增量磁滞[滞后]损失 【理】incremental hysteresis loss
增量电感 incremental inductance
增量电感磁导率 【理】incremental inductance permeability
增量段 incremental portion
增量峰值磁导率 【理】incremental peak permeability
增量感应 【电】incremental induciton
增量计算机 incremental computer
增量精简(数据)法 【计】incremental compaction
增量模型 【电】increment model
增量内禀[本征]磁导率 incremental intrinsic permeability
增量(偏移)磁通-电流回线 incremental (biased) flux-current loop
增量铁心损失 【电】incremental core loss
增量涡流损失 incremental eddy-current loss
增量显示 【计】incremental display
增量阻抗磁导率 incremental impedance permeability
增亮槽浴 brightening bath
增亮剂 brightening agent, brightener ◇

二次~*,阳离子~ cationic brightener,主要[一次]~ primary brightener
增磷 【冶】phosphorization, phosphorisation
增硫 【冶】resulfurization
增密 densification
增密粉末 densified powder
增密设备(氯化物处理用) 【色】densifier
增摩磨料 friction augmenting abrasives
增能 energization
增浓 densification
增浓还原(高压优先还原法) densification reduction
增频效应 【理】hypsochromic effect
增强 strengthen, enhancement, intensification, reinforcement, up-grading
增强板(焊缝的) reinforcement[reinforcing] plate
增强倍数 intensification factor
增强部分(焊缝的) reinforcement metal
增强衬板 reinforcing pad
增强光谱 enhanced spectrum
增强合金 【钢】toughener
增强剂[体,物] strengthener, reinforcement, intensifying agent,【钢】intensifier, toughener
增强剂淬火 intensifier hardening
增强颗粒 reinforcing particle
增强器 intensifier, booster
增强塑料 reinforced plastics ◇ 玻璃纤维~*,纤维~*,珠状~*
增强涂层 reinforced coating
增强相(矿热炉生产) 【冶】wild phase
增强型(指金属氧化物半导体晶体管) enhancement mode
增热 heat gain, gain of heat
增溶化(作用) solubilization
增设电路 extension circuit
增湿 humidify(ing), wetting
增湿鼓风 【铁】humidified blast
增湿剂 humidifier, humidizer
增湿器 humidifier,【铁】sprinkler ◇ 空气

~air humidifier
增湿设备　humidifying equipment
增湿室　moisture chamber
增湿塔　humidifying [conditioning] tower
增湿作用　humidification
增速　speed-up, speed increase,【压】zoom（连轧钢带的）
增速轧制　zoom rolling
增速装置　speeder
增塑剂　plasticizer, plasticizing [workability, fluidizing] agent
增塑指数　plasticity index
增碳　carburization, carburizing, carburisation, carburising, carbonization, carbonisation, carbon pickup, fill up carbon ◇ 达比熔池~法 Darby process, 防~覆层 anticement, 固体~*, 加生铁~ pigging (back, up), pig back, 喂线~*, 冶炼[冶金]~*, 液体~*, 再[二次]~*
增碳剂　carburant, carburetant, recarbonizer ◇ 复用~ repeating compound
增碳期　【钢】carbonizing period
增碳器　carburet(t)or
增碳水煤气　carburetted water gas
增碳添加剂　carburizing addition
增温器　heat booster
增压　pressurizing, supercharging, pressure boost [build-up]
增压泵　booster pump, inflator ◇ 玻璃油扩散真空~*, 管线~ line booster pump
增压处理　pressurization
增压风机　booster fan
增压器[机]　supercharger, booster, pressurizer, augmenter, augmentor
增压设备　pressurized equipment
增压速率(真空系统的)　rate of rise
增压调节器　boost control
增压系数　coefficient of increase of pressure
增压液体　pressurized fluid
增压油扩散真空泵　booster oil diffusion pump

增氧　oxygenation, aeration ◇ 鼓风~ oxygenation of blast
增益　gain ◇ 随时间可变的~ time variable gain, 指向性~ directional gain
增益界限[容限(伺服系统的), 余量(反馈系统的)]　gain margin
增益控制[调节]　gain control
增益系数　gain coefficient [factor]
增援处理机　【计】attached support processor
增载蠕变　【理】incremental creep
增载蠕变试验　incremental creep experiment
增长　increase, rise, growing, growth, build-up
增长时间　rise [building-up] time
增长速率　rate of rise
增长压力　upacting pressure
增殖反应堆　breeder (reactor) ◇ 液体金属冷却快速~*
增殖率　reproducibility
增殖系数(中子的)　multiplication factor
增殖性核燃料　fuel and fertile material
增殖性物质　【理】fertile materials
增值　added value
增值产品　value-added product
增值税　value added tax (VAT), added-value tax
增重　weight gain, dynamiting
甑式焙烧炉　【色】retort calcinating oven
甑式炉　retort oven ◇ 断续[周期]作用~*
扎　binding, tying
扎带　【电】binding
扎袋用丝　bag tie wire
扎紧的带卷　strapped coil
扎铝磷铜矿　zapatalite
扎马克锌基压铸合金(3.5—4.5Al, 2.5—3.5Cu, 0—0.1Fe, 0—0.5Mg, <0.005Cd, <0.005Sn, 余量Zn)　Zamak (alloy)
扎姆锌基合金　Zam metal

zha 扎渣

扎帕塔式三脚结构(深水钻井船的) Zapata tripod structure
扎帕塔式蝎尾型结构(钻井台架) Zapata scorpion
扎线 lashing wire, binding band (电枢的)
渣 residue, sediment, slag, refuse ◇ 初熔[新,热干]～ fresh slag, 除～ cake blow, 含～的 cindery, 含炭沫～ kish slag, 弃～场 slag pit, 易流动～*
渣比 【铁】slag ratio
渣饼 slag cake, (slag) pancake, cake [blob] of slag
渣饼控制法 slag pancake method
渣饼试验 【冶】pancake test
渣槽 slag pool [box]
渣槽平台[渣沟台] 【铁】cinder runner platform
渣层 slag layer [blanket] ◇ 大厚度～ thick slag
渣层厚度 slag depth
渣场 slag yard
渣场运输机 slag heap conveyer, stacking trailing conveyer
渣车 slag car [wagon], cinder car
渣车罐[桶] slag truck ladle
渣池 slag pond [basin, pool, bath]
渣处理 slag disposal ◇ 索森-罗登格～法*
渣处理场 slag yard
渣滴炉 slag-drip furnace
渣底 slag fill
渣堆 slag pile [muck, dump], (cinder) dump, wastedump
渣粉 slag powder, powdered slag
渣封 slag-sealing
渣风口 slag tuyere
渣浮选精矿 slag concentrate
渣覆电极 slag covered electrode
渣覆盖层 slag blanket
渣钢线 slag-metal
渣沟 slag [cinder] runner, 【铁】(slag) trough, cinder fall (旧名) ◇ 上～ cinder runner
渣沟挡板 cinder runner gate
渣沟流嘴 cinder spout
渣沟取样 trench sampling
渣沟系统 【冶】cinder runner system
渣罐[包] slag ladle [pot], cinder ladle [pot]
渣罐车 slag car [buggy], slag ladle car, slag ladle and carriage, transfer ladle, 【铁】thimble slag car ◇ 电动倾翻～*, 机动倾翻～*
渣罐车备用停车线 slag tapping standby track
渣罐吊车 slag-pot crane
渣罐喷浆装置 slag ladle spraying installation
渣罐清理 slag-pot washing
渣罐台 slag-pot stand
渣罐调整绞车 ladle-positioning winch
渣罐运输车 slag ladle transfercar, slag-pot transfercar, slag pot transport truck
渣罐运输机 slag ladle road transporter
渣罐运输线 【铁】cinder track
渣罐装入量 slag-pot weight
渣锅 slag pot
渣厚测量 slag thickness measurement
渣厚测量系统 slag thickness measuring system
渣化 slagging, scorifying, slag-making, slagging effect (废石的) ◇ 可～的 【冶】fluxible, 耐火材料～*
渣化表面 slagged surface
渣化法 scorification
渣化炉底 【钢】slagging bottom
渣化皿 scorifier
渣化能力 fluxing power
渣-金属比 slag-metal ratio
渣-金属(分)界面 slag-metal interface [surface]
渣-金属分离 slag-metal separation
渣-金属耦合反应 coupled slag-metal reaction

渣 zha

渣金(属)平衡　slag-metal equilibrium
渣金属平衡实验　slag-metal equilibrium experiment
渣金属乳化物　slag-metal emulsion
渣坎[挡]　【冶】slag [clinker] dam,【钢】slag plate
渣壳　(slag) crust, skull, scull ◇ 包[桶]底生成的～formation of skull, 防结～炉衬 skull resistant lining, 碎～器 bridge breaker, 真空～熔炼*
渣壳[皮]可分离性　【钢】removability of slag
渣壳块　crust block
渣壳内浇铸　skull casting
渣壳破碎工具(钢包用)　skull breaking tool
渣壳破碎机　skull cracker
渣壳熔炼　skull melting
渣壳熔炼炉　skull melting furnace
渣壳生成　formation of skull
渣坑　slag pocket [pit], cinder [hunch] pit, roughing hole
渣坑除渣电铲　slag-pit shovel
渣孔　slag eye
渣口　slag [flushing] hole, slag (notch) aperture, peepee, monkey ◇ 堵～botting, 风动开～*, 渗铝～*, 小～【铁】monkey
渣口法兰　【铁】cooler holder
渣口工　【铁】slagger, cindersnapper,【团】teazer
渣口(冷却)大套　【铁】slag notch cooler, (cinder) cooler, cooler holder
渣口冷却器　【铁】monkey cooler, jumbo
渣口冷却套　【铁】cinder cooler, monkey jacket
渣口塞　【铁】slag [cinder] notch stopper, slag bott, bod, bot, bolt
渣口塞杆　stopping bar, taphole plug stick
渣口塞杆操纵机构　【铁】bott operating mechanism
渣口渗铝工艺　【铁】slag notch aluminizing process
渣口水箱　【铁】monkey cooler [jacket]
渣口小套　【铁】(cinder) monkey, slag (notch) tuyere
渣口中套　【铁】intermediate cooler
渣块　slag lump [block], lump slag,【冶】crust block, slag patch (锭内缺陷)
渣粒　slag globule [particle, shot]
渣粒化池　(同"水淬池")
渣量　slag quantity [volume, bulk], amount [quantity] of slag ◇ 单位～【铁】slag ratio
渣量过多　overslagging
渣量影响(对炉况的)　【铁】slag volume effect
渣料　【冶】slag charge
渣瘤　slag build-up [nodule], manganese nodules
渣流　slag flow, dross-run
渣流道　slag runner
渣棉　slag cotton [wool], cinder wool, silicate cotton
渣面　slag level [surface], top of slag
渣模　slag mould
渣幕　slag screen
渣凝集　build up of skull
渣黏度　viscosity of slag
渣盘　slag pan, cinder ladle
渣皮　slag skin [skull]
渣皮凝壳式炉　skull furnace
渣铅　slag lead
渣塞杆　【钢】bot(t) stick
渣蚀区　slagging area
渣蚀作用　slagging action
渣损失　slag loss
渣铁比　【铁】slag ratio, slag volume per ton of iron
渣桶　(同"渣罐")
渣尾　slag tails
渣温　slag temperature
渣锡　slag tin
渣洗作用　slagging effect

渣线 slag level [line]
渣线范围[区域] slag line region
渣线砌块 flux line block
渣相 【冶】slag [ceramic] phase
渣相固溶体 solid solution of slag component
渣相连接 【团】bonding by slag
渣箱 slag [mud] box
渣箱热泼工艺(转炉渣的) 【钢】slag box hot splash process
渣屑和废物运输车 refuse truck
渣型 slag pattern
渣眼 sand hole [blister, inclusion]
渣样 slag specimen ◇ 停吹~
渣液保护浇铸 fluid mould casting
渣印法 【钢】slag-print process
渣浴 slag bath
渣中废钢 slag scrap
渣砖 cinder brick
渣状的 drossy, slaggy, scoriform
渣状金属 drossy metal
渣滓 【冶】scobs
轧疤 【压】backedge, fin
轧板机 plate mill ◇ 二辊式~
轧边 edge finish, edging, edge rolling [milling] (或厚板侧面的)
轧边工序 edge-rolling [edge-upsetting] operation
轧边辊 edger roll (E.R.), edging roll
轧边机 edger [edging] mill, (rolling) edger ◇ 独立的~ detached edger, 附设的~ attached edger, 水平式~ horizontal edger, 与主机座紧配的~ close-coupled edger, 下传动~
轧边机座 edger mill
轧边立辊 vertical edger [edging] roll
轧边输入辊道 edge approach table
轧扁 flattening, mushroom, beating
轧扁并纵切线材 flattened and slit wire
轧扁机 flattening mill
轧波纹 【压】corrugation
轧材 【压】rolled metal [stock, product], mill product [bar] ◇ 底架~ chassis sections, 短尺[等外]~ off-gauge material, 环形~ annular shape, 小型~ merchant bar, 已加工~ finished rolled stock, 异型~ groove-rolled bar
轧材和冷拔产品 wrought product
轧材切割机 machine for parting-off rolled sections
轧材无塑性区[无塑性部分,刚性区刚性部分] no-plastic zone in rolled material
轧槽 groove, pass ◇ 闭口~, 立轧~ edging groove, 上辊可换~块;下辊可换~块;延伸~ drawing, 周期断面[轧制钢筋的]~ deforming groove
轧槽边界[极限] limitation of groove
轧槽侧壁斜度 taper of [on] groove
轧槽侧边斜角 groove angle
轧槽(道次)顺序 succession of passes
轧槽截面形状 opening of groove
轧槽极限 limitation of groove
轧槽宽度 width of groove
轧槽宽展 spreading of groove
轧槽轮廓 pass contour, contour [boundary] of groove
轧槽内圆角 groove fillets
轧槽设计 groove design, grooving
轧槽深度 depth of groove
轧槽寿命 groove life
轧槽数目 groove number
轧槽速度 pass line speed
轧槽外形 boundary of groove
轧槽形状 form of groove
轧槽圆角半径 groove radius
轧槽中线(孔型的) axis of groove
轧槽中心线 centre line of groove
轧出侧张力卷取机 delivering tension reel
轧出速度 delivery speed
轧锻 【压】roll [gap-mill] forging
轧锻机 forge rolling machine
轧废 misroll
轧钢 steel rolling
轧钢厂 (steel, rolling) mill

轧钢车间　rolling plant
轧钢车间厂房　rolling plant building
轧钢车间辅助设备　rolling mill auxiliaries, mill ancillaries
轧钢车间主电室　engine-room of mills
轧钢工　(mill) roller, millman, rollerman, mill operator ◇ 粗轧机座～rougher, 机后～(活套轧机的) catcher
轧钢工长　head [boss] roller
轧钢工段　mill department
轧钢工作者　rollerman
轧钢机　(rolling) mill
轧钢机吊车　steel mill crane
轧钢机列　roll train
轧钢机组　rolling mill complex
轧钢接板　joint bar
轧钢皮　mill (roll) scale
轧钢屑　mill (furnace) cinder
轧钢制度　mill duty
轧管　tube rolling ◇ 迪舍尔(式轧机)～法*, 福伦～法*, 罗克莱特往复摆动式～法*, 专业化一厂*, 自动～法*
轧管机　pipe [tube, tubular] mill, tube-rolling mill ◇ CAM～*, 阿塞尔～[三辊式轧管机*, 三辊式辗轧机]*, 多机架～*, 冷～*, 特郎斯瓦尔～*, 周期式～rotary forging mill, 自动芯棒～*
轧管机机座　pipe-mill rolling stand
轧管机械　pipe-mill machinery
轧管机组　tube-rolling train
轧光　【压】planish(ing)
轧光辊(板材的)　planishing roll
轧光辊压下装置　planishing roll screw-down
轧光机　planishing mill
轧光装置　planishing device
轧辊　【压】(mill) roll, cylinder ◇ 安置～[调整～位置] roll setting [setup], 凹面～concave form of roll, 半硬面[细晶粒]合金～alloy grain oll, 车削～roll turning, 成套～set of rolls, 抽出～roll withdrawal, 对～的压力(金属对轧辊的压力) rolling pressure, 辅助～helper roll, 光面[平整]～smooth roll, 光制辊颈～necked roll, 辊身表面压嵌着氧化皮的～banded roll, 阶梯～step roll, 卡尔梅斯～*, 刻痕～ragged roll, 空心～hollow roll, 冷硬轧槽铸造～*, 磨光～【电】ground roll, 全加工～*, 双层铸造～*, 双支点～fully supported roll, 桶形～barrel shaped roll, 凸面～*, 涂镀～*, 悬臂式～overhung roll, 有槽～grooved roll, 支承～backing up roll, 锥形～cone-shaped roll, 组合式[双层]～sleeved roll, 作用于～的力矩 rolling [mill] torque
轧辊凹度　concave form of roll
轧辊剥落　spalling of roll
轧辊保护板　roll fender
轧辊备品总数　roll inventory
轧辊表面裂缝[辊身掉角]　fracture of roll
轧辊表面烧裂　fire crack in roll
轧辊表面温度检测仪　roll surface pyrometer
轧辊表面状况　roll surface condition
轧辊部件　roll assembly
轧辊测压计　roll force meter
轧辊车床　roll turning machine, roll lathe ◇ 电子控制仿形～*, 数字控制自动～*, 自动仿形～*
轧辊车工　roll turner
轧辊车间　roll shop
轧辊车间设备　roll shop equipment
轧辊车间轴承座拆卸装置　chock remover in roll shop
轧辊车削　roll turning
轧辊车削加工车间　roll-turning shop
轧辊车削样板　roll-turning template
轧辊重车[磨]　redressing of roll
轧辊重车系数　redressing coefficient of rolls
轧辊抽出装置　roll withdrawing device
轧辊串移　roll shift
轧辊淬火　【金】roll quenching
轧辊打滑　roll slip

轧辊导卫装置	furniture, roll fittings
轧辊电热器[炉]	electric roll heater
轧辊端头	roll end
轧辊锻压机	roll forging machine
轧辊堆放架	holster
轧辊反弯	negative roll bending
轧辊放置台架	roll rack
轧辊负荷测量装置	roll load measuring device
轧辊附件(导卫板)	roll arrangement
轧辊刚性	roll stiffness
轧辊钢	roll steel
轧辊工作表面	rolling face
轧辊工作开(口)度	(同"轧辊有效开度")
轧辊辊颈	roll neck [journal]
轧辊辊口处的摩擦	roll-bite friction
轧辊辊身	roll barrel, roll(er) body
轧辊(辊身)表面	roll face
轧辊辊身直径	roll (body) diameter
轧辊辊套	roll sleeve ◇ 组合式~sleeve
轧辊辊型	roll profile [crown(ing)]
轧辊辊型设计	roll contouring
轧辊弧度	roll crown
轧辊机座	stand of roll
轧辊给定间隙	preset gap, pre-set roll gap
轧辊加工	roll dressing
轧辊架	roll-cage
轧辊间	roll shop building
轧辊间隙	clearance between rolls
轧辊浇铸	roll casting
轧辊矫直法	roll straightening
轧辊接触弧	rolling arc of contact
轧辊精密磨床	precision roll grinding machine
轧辊开度不变轧机	constant-gap mill
轧辊开度测量仪	gaugemeter
轧辊开孔型	grooving of roll
轧辊开(口)度	roll gap, (roll, mill) opening, clearance between rolls ◇ 自整角机式~指示器*
轧辊刻网纹用钨工具钢	(1.2—1.4C, 5—8W, 0—1Cr, 0—0.5V) Riffel steel
轧辊刻纹	riffling
轧辊孔型	roll(er) pass, roll groove
轧辊孔型零位线	roll parting line
轧辊孔型设计	roll pass design [schedule], rolling mill roll design, grooving of roll
轧辊冷却	roll cooling
轧辊冷却剂喷射装置	roll coolant spraying device
轧辊冷却液	roll coolant
轧辊冷却(液)系统	roll coolant system
轧辊连接套筒	roll engaging sleeve
轧辊毛化	roll surface roughing
轧辊梅花头	roll wobbler
轧辊磨床	roll grinder, roll grinding machine
轧辊磨损	roll wear [abrasion]
轧辊磨削	roll dressing
轧辊磨制工	roll dresser
轧辊挠度	roll deflection [bending]
轧辊扭矩	roll torque
轧辊抛光机	roll polisher
轧辊配置	roll arrangement [assembly]
轧辊喷砂强化	mill roll etching
轧辊偏心度	roll eccentricity
轧辊平衡	roll balance
轧辊平衡锤	roll-balancing counterweight
轧辊平衡装置	roll-balance gear
轧辊平衡装置系统	roll balance system
轧辊平衡装置蓄力器	roll balance accumulator
轧辊强度	roll strength
轧辊清洗装置	roll cleaning device
轧辊缺陷	roll defect
轧辊设计	design of roll
轧辊升程	roll lift [stroke]
轧辊寿命	roll life [campaign]
轧辊速度	speed of roll
轧辊锁紧装置	roll locking
轧辊台架	holster
轧辊弹簧式平衡	spring roll balance

轧辊弹跳　roll springing
轧辊弹性压扁　roll flattening
轧辊提升夹钳　roll lifting tongs
轧辊调定开(口)度　preset gap, pre-set roll gap
轧辊调整　roll adjustment
轧辊调整机构[装置]　roll-adjusting gears [device], roll-separating mechanism
轧辊凸度　roll crown(ing), crown ◇ 加工～用凸轮 cambering cam
轧辊凸度[辊型]调整　crown adjustment
轧辊凸度控制系统　roll crown control system
轧辊凸度磨削装置　cambering device
轧辊无效开(口)度　passive roll gap
轧辊弯辊装置　roll bending equipment
轧辊弯曲　roll bending
轧辊压下装置　roller press-down apparatus, roll-positioning device
轧辊压制[压实](粉末的)　roll-compacting, compacting by rolling
轧辊研磨　roll grinding
轧辊咬入弧[辊口]的摩擦　roll-bite friction
轧辊咬入轧件　roll bite, biting
轧辊液压平衡系统　hydraulic roll-balance system
轧辊有效开(口)度　active roll gap
轧辊与磨轮间中心距　centre distance between roll and grinding wheel
轧辊预热器　roll preheating device
轧辊圆周速度[线速度]　velocity of roll periphery
轧辊运输夹钳　roll tongs
轧辊运送车　roll transfer [handling] car
轧辊在线修磨　roll on-line grinding
轧辊轧槽　roll groove
轧辊找平　roll alignment
轧辊罩[轴承架]　roll-cage
轧辊正压力　normal roll pressure
轧辊直径有效使用范围(总车削量)　roll dimensional life

轧辊轴承　roll bearing ◇ 带冷却水管的～cooling tube roll bearing
轧辊轴承部分清洗装置　roll chock washing machine
轧辊轴承座　roll carriage [chock]
轧辊轴承座导板　chock slide
轧辊轴承座夹[压]紧机构　roll chock clamping mechanism
轧辊轴承座压板　keeper plate
轧辊轴线　roll axis
轧辊轴线偏斜　crossing of rolls
轧辊轴向调整　lateral adjustment of rolls
轧辊轴心　roll center
轧辊主颈轴承　roll neck bearing
轧辊锥角　roll taper
轧辊作用力　roll force
轧过　passing
轧焊　roller welding
轧痕　roll marks [pick-up]
轧后厚度　delivery [exit, outgoing] thickness, delivery stock height, outgoing gauge
轧机　rolling mill [unit], mill, rolls, reduction unit ◇ 1-2-3 式十二辊～, M.K.W 多用途～, Y 型[考克斯]～*, 摆式～*, 不可逆八辊～E-MKW mill, 大型～heavy mill, 迪舍尔～*, 多线式～multistrand mill, 二辊式～*, 浮动式～*, 高速～*, 格雷式～*, 开口式～open-top mill, 凯斯勒～Kessler mill, 可逆式～*, 劳特式～*, 连续式～*, 罗克莱特～*, 洛德式～*, 曼内斯曼式～*, 皮尔格～*, 普通结构～conventional mill, 七辊冷～Y-mill, 三辊式～*, 森吉米尔式～(二十辊冷轧机)*, 双机座～*, 双线(式)～*, 斯特克尔～*, 四辊式～*, 凸缘～*, 往复式～*, 无锭～direct rolling mill, 小型(钢材)～*, 悬臂辊式～*, 越野式[之字形]～*, 轧辊开度不变[恒定辊缝]～constant-gap mill, 摆振式～oscillatory mill, 振动式～vibratory rolling mill, 中间～intermediate mill, 周期式～*

zha 轧

轧机布置	mill layout [setup]
轧机(部件的)摩擦	mill friction
轧机操纵工	rolling mill operator, mill supervisor
轧机操纵室[控制台]	mill pulpit
轧机操作人员	mill personnel
轧机产量	rolling mill yield
轧机出口侧推床导板	back side guards
轧机传动装置[减速机]	mill drive, rolling mill drive (apparatus)
轧机导卫板	rolling mill guides
轧机电动机	rolling mill motor [engine], stand motor
轧机电气设备	electricity of rolling mill
轧机吊索工具	mill tackle
轧机辅助[附属]设备	【压】mill auxiliaries, colleagues of mill
轧机负荷	mill load
轧机工长	rolling mill foreman
轧机工作故障	mill delays
轧机工作台	rolling platform
轧机功率	mill [stand] power
轧机轨座[地脚板]	mill shoe
轧机辊道	mill table ◇主轴集体传动式~*
轧机后工作辊道	back [rear] mill table
轧机机架	roll housing ◇闭口式~*
轧机(机)列[机组]	mill [roll] train
轧机机座	(rolling) mill stand, roll (mill) stand
轧机机座换辊侧	roll change side
轧机机座进出口水平导向辊	billy roll
轧机(机座)弹跳[弹性变形]	mill spring (ing)
轧机接轴	mill spindle
轧机进口侧操纵台	ingoing control post
轧机进口侧推床导板	entry side guards
轧机进料侧	roller's side
轧机进料段	mill entry section
轧机跨	mill span [bay, aisle]
轧机跨照明	mill yard lighting
轧机联接轴	mill spindle
轧机模数(即机架刚度)	mill modulus
轧机逆转时间	reversal time
轧机牌坊	mill post [housing]
轧机牌坊的弹性变形	【压】elastic displacement of mill housing
轧机牌坊轨座	housing base
轧机牌坊立柱应力	post stress
轧机牌坊设计	mill housing design
轧机牌坊水平支脚	shoe
轧机前后工作辊道	front and back mill tables
轧机入口温度	mill entry temperature
轧机设备总布置	mill general layout
轧机生产率[能力]	rolling mill yield, rolling rate, mill production (output) rate, mill productivity
轧机输出侧	delivery [outgoing] side of rolls
轧机输出辊道	mill delivery [run-out] table
轧机输入辊道	mill approach table
轧机甩带	【压】unthreading of mill
轧机调速	mill pacing
轧机调整	mill setting [setup]
轧机压下螺丝	mill screw
轧机压下螺丝装置	screwdown arrangement
轧机压下系统	rolling mill press down system
轧机压下装置	rolling mill screwdown
轧机仪表	instrumentation of mill
轧机用大功率直流传动装置	large direct-current rolling mill driver
轧机轧辊冷却系统	mill roll cooling system
轧机中心线	rolling mill axis, axis of mill
轧机主传动电机	main mill drive motor
轧机主机列线	rolling mill roll line
轧机主要技术数据[性能]	mill data
轧机装置	rolling mill assembly
轧尖	sharpening, pointing, tagging
轧尖机	pointing rolling machine

轧件 【压】rolled piece [material], rolling stock [metal], mill [rolled] product, mill bar, stock, feed ◇ 运动~自动测量记录仪 instagraph

轧件拨出装置 bar throw off gear
轧件缠辊 collar(ing)
轧件缠住(卷取机的)卷筒 collar(ing)
轧件存贮装置 strip-storage device
轧件带张力轧制 rolling with (stock) tension
轧件导卫装置 strip-guiding apparatus
轧件高度[厚度] height of rolled material
轧件高宽比 stock's aspect ratio
轧件宽度 breadth of rolled material
轧件前端 front of piece
轧件前端[头部]分层 crocodile, crocodiling
轧件上弯 overdraft
轧件下弯 underdraft, underdraught
轧件运动指示器 material detector
轧件轧前厚度 initial stock height
轧臼(中碎圆锥破碎机的) dish
轧坯 stock material, strip plate, 【粉】rolled compact ◇ 大截面~ large section, 中间~ workpiece
轧前板坯 incoming slab
轧前厚度 incoming [ingoing, entry] thickness, ingoing gauge
轧入 roll bite
轧入侧操作工 entry operator
轧入侧带卷(存放)鞍座 entry coil storage saddle
轧入侧带卷尺寸 entry coil dimention
轧入侧带卷小车 entry coil car
轧入侧开卷机 entry reel
轧入侧切头清除辊道 entry crop kick-off table
轧入侧张力卷取机 entry tension reel
轧入角 angle of bite [nip]
轧入空气(轧制粉末时的) rolled-in air
轧入碎铁皮 rolled-in scrap
轧入氧化皮 rolled-in scale

轧缩辊 【连铸】reduction roll
轧铜厂 copper mill
轧铜机 brass mill machine
轧屑 cinder
轧屑车 cinder car
轧屑坑 cinder pit
轧屑磨碎机 cinder mill
轧压 roll compacting
轧压坯块 rolled compact
轧压成型 (同"轧辊压制")
轧制 roll(ing), roll down, milling, reduction, drawdown ◇ 阿姆斯特朗双多属~法 Armstrong process, 包壳~ sheath rolling, 表面加热~ skin ausrolling, 成卷~ coil rolling, 大辊径差~*, 大压下量~*, 单块~ one-piece rolling, 单线~ one-strand rolling, 等断面~ parallel rolling, 低速~ idling, 蝶形[弯曲]~法*, 多线[条]~ multistrand rolling, 返回~ roll on return pass, 负偏差~*, 借导卫板进行~ roll by guide, 控制~*, 宽展~*, 连铸坯热芯~*, 平辊~ flat, 齐整~*, 轻压[小压下量]~*, 热辊~ hot groove rolling, 双锭~ double ingot rolling, 双线~ two-strand rolling, 铜心法*, 无包套~ bare rolling, 无头~ endless rolling, 无张力~ tension free rolling, 箱形[矩-方]孔型系统~法 box pass method, 斜配孔型~法*, 用导卫板的圆材~法 guide round mothod, 在线~ on-line rolling, 轧件带张力~*, 周期断面~*

轧制班组 rolling (mill) crew
轧制板材 rolled plate, rolled sheet material ◇ 杰特-麦克哈格-威廉斯~反转极点图求作法*
轧制板坯 rolling slab
轧制包覆(法) roll cladding, clading by rolling
轧制薄板 rolled sheet metal
轧制边(板带材的) rolled [mill, running, band] edge

轧制扁坯　rolling slab
轧制表面光洁度　mill finish
轧制操作　operation of rolling
轧制槽钢　rolled steel channel
轧制策略　rolling strategy
轧制产品　rolled product
轧制产品质量　rolled product quality
轧制长度　mill length
轧制程序　rolling program
轧制（程序）表　(roll) pass schedule, rolling schedule
轧制程序项目　rolling program entry
轧制带材厚度指示仪　readout
轧制带钢用扁钢　sheet slab
轧制道次　(rolling, run) pass, set of passes ◇ 第一 [开坯] ～ first pass
轧制道次间退火　between pass annealing
轧制道次数　number of passes
轧制的　rolled, reduced, roll-compacted (粉末轧制的)
轧制发热　rolling heat
轧制发纹　rolled flaw
轧制方向　rolling direction (RD)
轧制飞边　roller fin
轧制分离力　roll separating force
轧制粉带　rolled powder strip, powder-rolled strip
轧制粉带卷　coiled green strip
轧制粉带密度　strip density
轧制粉坯　rolled powder
轧制粉坯烧结　sintering of rolled powder
轧制负荷　rolling load
轧制钢板　rolled plate, rolled sheet material
轧制钢材　rolled steel (R.S., r.s.), rolled section [iron], rolling section
轧制钢筋的孔型 [轧槽]　deforming groove
轧制钢梁　rolled steel beam
轧制工　mill operator
轧制工艺 [实践]　mill rolling practice, rolling mill practice

轧制工艺滑润剂　rolling lubricant
轧制工艺润滑－冷却液　rolling solution
轧制工字钢　rolled steel joist (R.S.J.)
轧制工字梁用异形坯　beam blank
轧制工作者　roller
轧制功率 [能力]　rolling power
轧制公差　rolling tolerance [margin], mill limit
轧制管材　rolled tube
轧制光洁度　mill finish
轧制规范　mill condition
轧制规范数据库　rolling standard data base
轧制过程　rolling process
轧制加工等温淬火处理　ausroll tempering
轧制加铜硬化锌基合金　copper-hardened rolled zinc
轧制角钢的蝶式孔型　butterfly angles pass
轧制节奏自学习模型　self-learning mathematical model of rolling rhythm
轧制金箔　rolled gold
轧制宽度　rolling width
轧制冷却乳液　roll coolant
轧制力　roll(ing) force (RF), draught pressure
轧制力测定　roll force measurement
轧制力矩　rolling [mill] torque, rolling moment
轧制力预报　prediction of rolling force
轧制裂纹　rolling crack
轧制流程图表　mill pacing time chart
轧制能耗　required power
轧制泡疤表面　process blister
轧制坯　rerolling feed
轧制坯件　【粉】rolled compact
轧制品　rolled product
轧制平面　rolling plane
轧制缺陷　rolling defect
轧制润滑系统　rolling oil system
轧制设备　rolling equipment, rolling mill e-

轧制生产切边[头]　rolling mill scrap
轧制生带的厚度　strip thickness
轧制时间　rolling [pass] time
轧制速度　rolling [mill] speed
轧制条材　rolled bar
轧制条痕　mill streaks
轧制铜材　rolled copper
轧制图表　rolling scheme [plan, program]
轧制温度　rolling temperature
轧制(温度)范围　rolling (temperature) region
轧制线(孔型的)　roll(ing) [pass] line ◇ 下辊~调整*
轧制线剪切机　mill shears
轧制锌　rolled zinc ◇ 工业用~*
轧制锌合金（0.75—1.25Cu, 0.007—0.2Mg, 0.05—0.15Pb, 0.015Fe, 0.005Cd, 余量 Zn）rolled zinc alloy
轧制型材　rolling sections
轧制型钢　rolled section steel
轧制形变热处理(过冷奥氏体的)　aus(ten)rolling
轧制压力　roll [draught] pressure, pressure of rolling ◇ 平均~ average roll pressure
轧制压缩比　ratio of rolling reduction
轧制压缩率　rolling draught
轧制氧化皮　mill roll scale, rolling (mill) scale
轧制样板　pass template
轧制用坯　rolling billet
轧制诱致磁各向异性　rolling-induced magnetic anisotropy
轧制余热淬火　mill hardening
轧制裕量　rolling margin
轧制圆钢　rolled rounds
轧制织构　rolling texture
轧制制度　rolling schedule [pattern], mill conditions ◇ 合理~*
轧制中心线　axis of rolling
轧制周期　rolling cycle [period]
轧制周期图表　mill pacing time chart
轧制专业用语　mill language
轧制装置　rolling [reduction] unit
轧制状态　as-rolled condition ◇ 冷轧钢带~的边 No.2 edge
轧制状态金属　as-rolled metal
铡刀式剪切机　guillotine, guillotine [frame, gate] shears ◇ 杠杆摆动式~*

闸　brake, gate, gating
闸板　damper, shutter, flashboard, 【连铸】blank ◇ 变向~ diversion damper
闸板机构　damper gear
闸板架　gate housing
闸板截门　gate-type shutoff valve
闸板开闭机构　damper gear
闸板式给料斗　gate feed hopper
闸板式冷风阀　(同"冷风滑阀")
闸板[闸阀]式取样器　flap type sampler
闸板卸料[排矿]　dam-and-gate discharge
闸带　check band, strap of brake
闸阀　gate [damper] valve, sluice (type) valve ◇ 转动~ gate turn valve
闸杆　brake bar [arm]
闸盒　switch box [case]
闸块　shoe
闸块托　brake block holder
闸框　damper frame
闸流管控制　【焊】thyratron control
闸流晶体管　thyristor
闸轮　brake drum [pulley, wheel]
闸轮联轴器　ratchet coupling
闸门　damper plate, flap, hatch, valve, gate ◇ 储箱[储仓]~ bunker gate, 料仓~*, 摩擦~ friction lock, 球形~ ball gate, 手调~*
闸门式滑阀　gate-type slide valve
闸门式煤气调节阀　gate-type gas-regulating valve
闸门式水坝　curtain dam
闸门[板]蒸汽截止阀　gate-type steam shutoff valve

闸门型(的) gate-type
闸盘 brake disc ◇ 双金属～ bimetallic brake disc
闸钳 brake tongs
闸式排灰阀 slide-type dust valve
闸式水力测功器 hydraulic brake
闸索 brake cable
闸瓦 (同"制动块")
闸瓦托 brake head
栅栏 fence, barrier, hedge,【建】catch-frame
炸药 explosive (ex.), explosive material, blasting powder ◇ D 型～ dunite, 高效[速爆]～ high explosive, 苦拔～ coopal powder, 泰安～*, 碳质[锯屑]～ carbonite, 硝铵～ ammonia dynamite
炸药包 explosive charge [package]
炸药开孔法 【钢】jet tapping
摘车钩 【运】out-of-gear
摘(炉)门机 (同"启炉门机")
摘录 extract, excerpt, fragment
摘去 pick-off
摘要 summary (Sum.), abstract (abs., abst.), brief, digest
窄板材 ribbon
窄边 narrow side
窄边调整(板坯的) narrow side adjustment
窄扁钢 flat(-bar) iron, strip bar
窄槽面 splined surface
窄搭缝焊接机 narrow lap welder
窄搭接 【焊】narrow lap
窄带材 【压】narrow strip, (light narrow) flat, ribbon
窄带材用围盘 strip repeater
窄带材轧机 narrow strip mill
窄带钢[钢带] 【压】ribbon steel [iron], strip [riffled] iron, baling strip (打包用) ◇ 打包～*, 热轧～ mill coil
窄带钢轧机 narrow strip mill
窄带卷(纵切后的) slit coil [form]
窄带隙半导体 narrow-bandgap semiconductors
窄法兰 beaded edge
窄轨机车 narrow gage locomotive, dinkey engine [locomotive] (运土、石用)
窄轨距铁路线 narrow gauge [steel] track, small-gauge track
窄轨铁路 narrow-gauge railway ◇ 施工[临时]～*
窄焊道(焊条不横摆) string(er) bead
窄焊道堆焊 string beading
窄焊道焊接 beaded joint
窄焊缝 narrow [bead(ing)] weld
窄厚扁钢 bar of flat
窄弧切割 (transferred) constricted arc cutting
窄火焰 narrow flame
窄间距多重谱线 【理】narrow multiplet, multiple of narrow separation
窄间隙单面焊 narrow gap one side welding
窄间隙焊接 narrow gap welding
窄口加热炉 【压】slot furnace
窄馏分 close-cut fraction ◇ 分成～*
窄炉喉[口]的 【冶】narrow-mouthed
窄脉冲 narrow pulse; bang
窄面鼓肚 narrow face bulgine
窄(频)带滤波器 narrow(-band) filter
窄射束 fine [narrow] beam
窄射线束 pencil
窄翼缘 narrow flange
准直 X 射线束 finely collimated X-ray beam
债券 bond, debenture
毡 felt ◇ 烧结金属纤维～ fettmetal
毡布 ◇ 擦光～ bob
毡层 carpet coat
毡垫(片) felt gasket
毡辊 felt roll(er)
詹金斯反复弯曲试验 Jenkins' bend test
詹姆斯离心铸造法(英国) James spun-cast process
粘辊(氧化皮的) 【压】roll banding, roll

coating（轧铝的）◇ 板材～gathering	
粘连铁块（铸铁机的）【铁】pig sticker	
粘贴 paste, stick, glue	
粘贴式电阻应变计 bonded (resistance) strain gauge	
粘型芯用夹具 【铸】core-pasting fixture	
粘住 stick	
沾染煤烟 （同"煤灰污染"）	
沾湿的表面 wetted surface	
沾石灰（拉拔前） lime finish [dip]	
沾污 pollution, contamination ◇ 未～的 virgin	
沾污离子 contaminating ions	
斩波电路 chopper circuit	
斩波器 【电】chopper, clipper, interrupter	
辗锻锤 stretching hammer	
辗锻用心轴 【压】becking bar	
辗压 spreading ◇ 穿孔毛坯在芯棒上～ saddling	
辗轧 【压】rolling off（管坯的）, becking（轮箍环的）, expansion ◇ 车轮辐板～辊 web roll, 车轮凸缘和踏面的～辊 tread roll, 滚筒～操作*	
辗轧机（管材的） elongator ◇ 阿塞尔～*	
辗轧角 【压】toe angle	
辗轧[锻]用心轴 becking bar	
展薄拉伸 ironing	
展痕（薄板的） spreader mark	
展开 developing, development, spreading, evolvement, scanning ◇ 呈扇形～fanning	
展开长度 developed [stretched] length	
展开法 expansion method	
展开式翼缘 flared out flanges	
展开图 develop diagram, expanded [stretch-out] view	
展开系数 expansion coefficient	
展开线 evolute	
展开性 expandability	
展宽 spreading, expanding ◇ 强制～forced spread, 自由[不受限制]～*	
展宽作用 spreading action	
展平锤 paning hammer	
展平压力 【压】flattening pressure	
展色料 vehicle	
展望 outlook, look ahead	
展性 ductility ◇ 莫里森～青铜*	
展性锆 ductile zirconium	
展性合金 ductile alloy	
展性金属 ductile [malleable] metal	
展性镍 malleable nickel	
展性试验 ductility test	
展性钨 ductile tungsten	
栈桥 trestle bridge, high line ◇ 跨线～gantry, 卸矿～*	
栈桥贮斗（矿石场的） high line hopper	
栈式作业控制 【计】stacked job control	
占地面积 site area, space requirement [occupancy], floor area（设备的）, floor space (requirement) ◇ 净～net site area	
占据[有]空间 occupied space	
占空系数 space factor, duty cycle	
占空因数 duty [fill] factor	
占线继电器 busy relay	
占用 occupation, appropriation	
占用时间 holding time	
占有电子 electron occupancy	
占有概率（能级的） occupation probability	
占有率 occupancy, occupation ratio	
占有能带 band occupancy, occupied band	
占有数 occupation number	
占有态 【理】occupied state	
战车 chariot	
战略材料[物资] strategic [defense] material	
战略元素 strategic element	
章程 regulations, rules	
章度（色度学的） saturation	
章节 article (Art.), chapters and sections	
张弛长度 relaxation length	
张弛过程 relaxation process	
张弛频率 relaxation frequency	
张弛时间 relaxation time	

张弛现象　relaxation phenomenon
张弛振动　【理】relaxation oscillation
张角　【理】angular aperture, flare angle
张紧杆　nutted rod
张紧辊　tension roll, (tension) bridle roll（活套的）◇ S形~组*
张紧辊装置　tension unit ◇ 进口段~*
张紧辊座　bridle roll seat
张紧机构　strainer
张紧件　tension member
张紧卷筒　drawing capstan
张紧轮　tension [stretching, tightening] pulley, regulating wheel
张紧器　tightener, strainer, tensioner, turnbuckle
张紧楔　tightening wedge
张紧装置　tension device, tensioning gear, tightener, take-up（皮带或链条的）, tension bridle（辊式）,【压】（带材的）bridling equipment, bridle unit ◇ 出口~*, 带材~*, 辊式~*, 重力式~gravity take-up unit
张紧座（带式抛光机的）　back stand
张卷成形　stretch-wrap forming
张开　opening, expanding, spread-out
张开型应力强度因子　opening mode stress intensity factor
张开状态卷筒　expanded mandrel
张拉　stretching
张拉成型法　(strech) wrap forming
张拉钢筋（用千斤顶）　jacking
张拉钢丝　tensioned wire
张拉辊矫直机　pinch roll leveller
张拉辊装置　pinch roll unit
张拉裂纹　【冶】pulling
张拉伸长　stretch elongation
张拉式线材进给装置　pull-type wire feeder
张拉细丝（预应力混凝土用）　stretching wire
张力　（同"拉力"）◇（轧件）带~轧制*, 受~焊缝 tension weld, 水蒸气~ aqueous tension

张力成形　stretch forming ◇ 安得逊~法 Androform process
张力垫　tension pad
张力惰轮　jockey [gallow] pulley
张力钢板矫直机　tension sheet straightener
张力辊　tension(ing) [jockey] roller, tension [strain, stretch] roll, jockey pulley, bridle, pullers（平整机的）◇ 出口~*
张力辊组　tension roller unit
张力计用辊　tensiometer roll
张力减径（管材的）　stretch reducing [reduction]
张力减径机　stretch reducer, tension [stretch] reducing mill ◇ 钢管[管材]~*
张力[拉]矫直机　(同"拉伸矫直机")
张力矫直系统　tension levelling system
张力接触器　tension contactor
张力接头　tension joint
张力卷取机　【压】tension reel (T.R.), pull reel, winder, pull-type recoiler ◇ 右向~*, 轧出侧~*, 轧入侧~*, 胀缩式~*
张力卷筒　tension reel
张力控制　tension control
张力控制系统　tension control system ◇ 带材厚度~*
张力轮　stretching pulley
张力疲劳试验　fatigue tension test, tensile fatigue test
张力平整　tension levelling
张力平整机　tension leveller
张力曲柄连杆式压力机　tension knuckle press
张力失调　【冶】stall tension
张力式拉拔[拉丝]机　pull-type drawbench
张力弹簧　tension spring
张力调节辊　dancer roll
张力调节器　tension-regular device

张力调整臂 【压】waffle arm
张力头(张力矫直机的) stretcher head
张力轧制 tension-rolling
张力自动调节器 automatic tension regulator
张量 tensor
张数计数器 sheet counter
张延 stretching
张应力裂纹 tension crack
长大晶体 grown crystal
长大速率 rate of growth
掌部革制棉手套 cotton leather-palm glove
掌部双层帆布手套 double palm canvas mittens
掌握 hold, control ◇ 可～性 handleability
涨落 fluctuation ◇ 热力学～理论*
涨圈 caulking [seal(ing), gasket] ring, gasket ring, expansion bend ◇ 活塞～bule
帐单 bill
帐号 account number
帐户结余 【企】account balance
帐面价值 【企】book value
胀大 expanding, swelling
胀管 【机】expand tube, swell(ing)
胀管机 pipe expanding machine
胀(管)口 expand
胀开心轴 【机】expanding mandrel
胀裂 bursting
胀破压力 bursting pressure
胀起(铸锭时的) 【钢】rising
胀砂 【冶】buckle
胀缩机构 expanding mechanism
胀缩间隙 play for expansion
胀缩卷筒(卷取机的) 【压】collapsible [expanding] drum, expand-collapse mandrel ◇ 悬臂式～*
胀缩卷筒式带材预卷机 expansible coil preparatory coiler
胀缩卷筒式卷取机 expanding [collapsible] drum coiler, collapsible winder

胀缩卷筒式开卷机 expanding-drum uncoiler
胀缩联轴器 expansion coupling
胀缩式 collapsible
胀缩式卷取机 collapsible reel
胀缩式张力卷取机 collapsible tension reel
胀缩芯轴式开卷机 mandrel-type decoiler
胀隙 expansion gap
胀箱(缺陷) 【铸】swell(ing)
胀形 bulging
胀形模 expanding die
胀形试验试样 【压】bulging test specimen
障碍 barrier, drawback, hold-up, obstacle, obstruction, impediment
障碍层 barrier layer
障碍覆盖层 barrier coating
障碍理论 theory of obstacles
障碍物 obstacle, impediment, dike, gorge
障碍指示器[灯] obstacle indicator
障风装置 abat-vent
招标 【企】invitation for bid ◇ 公开～competitive bidding
爪 claw, pawl, jaw, dog, hook
爪痕(轧材的) dog marks
爪式卡盘[爪夹盘] jaw chuck
爪式冷床 pawl-type cooling bed
爪式离合器 claw [jaw] clutch
爪式起重机 claw crane, crab
爪销 pawl pin
爪形扳手 jaw spanner
爪形联接器 jaw coupling
爪形[式]联轴节[器] claw [ratchet, Ortmann] coupling, shifting sleeve
找出的渗漏位置 located leak
找平 level(l)ing, alignment
找平器 screeder
找齐 alignment
找正 spotting
沼地 slump, hag
沼矿 (同"褐铁矿")
沼煤 boghead [moor] coal
沼锰土 groroilite

沼气 (同"甲烷")
沼铁矿{2Fe₂O₃·3H₂O} meadow [brown, marsh] ore, bog iron ore, limnite
沼泽 marsh
沼泽地 glade, quagmire, marsh land ◇ 潮间～intertidal marsh
照度 illuminance, illuminancy, illumination (intensity)
照度计 illumination meter, illuminometer, lightmeter, luxmeter ◇ 光电式～*
照度平衡 candle balance
照度曲线 illumination curve
照度图 illuminated diagram
照管人员 attending personnel
照管与保养 care and maintenance (C & M)
照例的 conventional
照明 lighting, lighten, illumination ◇ 定向～配件*, 建筑～*, 克勒～Koehler illumination, 停止～lighting-off
照明安装图 installation plan for illumination
照明布置[方案] illumination arrangement
照明灯 illuminating lamp, illuminator, headlamp, exciter lamp
照明灯具 lighting fixture
照明电力系统 lighting power system
照明电路 lighting circuit
照明电源[干线] lighting mains
照明度 illuminance, illuminancy, illumination (intensity),
照明放大镜 illuminated magnifier
照明工程 lighting [illumination] engineering
照明镜 illuminating mirror
照明幕 light curtain
照明配电盘 lighting distribution board
照明配件 lighting-fittings
照明器 illuminator, illuminant
照明气(体) lighting [illuminating] gas
照明强度 illumination intensity

照明设备 lighting [illumination] equipment, lighting installation, luminaire
照明透镜 illuminating lens
照明线路 lighting [illuminating] wiring
照明信号箱 lighting signal box
照明指示盘 illuminated indicator board
照明装置 illumination arrangement, illuminator
照片 photo(gram), photograph ◇ 劳厄～中心*
照片衬度[反差] photographic [picture] contrast
照片模糊[雾翳] photographic fog
照射 shining, raying, lighting, illuminating, (radioactive) bombardment, irradiation, exposure ◇ γ～*, 短时间强～acute exposure, 放射性 ～atomic irradiation, 未受～的 unexposed
照射剂量 radiation [exposure] dose
照射器 source of exposure
照射时间 irradiation time
照射损伤 irradiation damage
照相 filming, photogram, photograph
照相凹版 photogravure plate
照相底片(负片) photoplate, plate, photographic negative [film] ◇ 点染[中间色调]～*, 平色调～*
照相法 photographic method
照相法测出的强度 photographically measured intensity
照相法强度测定(用X射线) intensity measurement by photographic method
照相反转底板 reversal plate [film]
照相分辨率[能力] photographic resolution
照相感速[感光速率] photographic speed
照相高温测量 photographic thermometry
照相高温计 photographic pyrometer
照相光敏度[性] photographic sensitivity
照相机 camera ◇ 布雷德利(型)～*, 戴维-威尔逊～*, 带测角头的～goniometer camera, 德拜-谢乐～*, 德沃尔夫

(型)~*,等倾角~*,对称背反射聚焦~*,高温~*,固定胶片~*,纪尼埃~*,加摆晶体~*,聚焦~*,可动胶片~ moving-film camera,兰氏~*,劳厄~*,全景 ~ cyclograph,塞曼-玻林型~*,试样周转衍射用~integrating camera,外森贝格~*,弯晶~*,显微~ photomicroscope,小角(衍射)~ low angle camera,圆筒形粉末~*

照相机校准 camera calibration
照相机快门 camera shutter
照相机调准 camera alignment
照相记录法 photographic recording (method)
照相记录器 photorecorder
照相胶[软]片 photographic film, photoplate
照相胶片特性曲线 characteristic curve of photographic film
照相密度 photographic density
照相平版印刷法 photolithography
照相乳胶 photographic emulsion ◇ 粗粒~*
照相乳胶层 photographic emulsion layer
照相乳胶黑雾 fog of photographic emulsion
照相乳胶颗粒 emulsion grain
照相乳胶曝光时限 latitude of a photographic emulsion
照相术 photography ◇ 干射线~dry radiography,射线交叉[射]~*,射线体截~*
照相物镜 photographic lens ◇ 特萨~*
照相正片 photographic positive (film)
照相装置 camera assembly, set of films (用 X 射线的)
照准 collimating ◇ 未~的 uncollimated
照准器[仪] alidade, hairline
罩 cover(ing), shade, hood, casing, cap, cage, housing
罩盖堆放场 cover depositing area
罩盖法检漏试验 hood test
罩壳(罩式退火炉的) cover casing
罩面 top facing, mat coat
罩内压力 hood pressure
罩上 belling
罩式加热炉 bell type heating furnace
罩式炉 cap cover furnace, cover(-type)[bell-type] furnace ◇ 带辐射管的煤气加热 ~ gas-fired bell-type furnace with radiating tubes,辐射管加热~*,高温~*,轻便~*,双层~*,装有 U 型垂直辐射管的~ bell type furnace with U-type vertical radiant tubes,装有水平辐射管的~bell type furnace with horizontal radiant tubes
罩式炉退火 cover annealing
罩式热处理炉 bell batch type furnace
罩式烧结炉 bell type furnace
罩式升温精炼技术 process of hooding in temperature increase during refining
罩式退火电炉 electric bell annealer
罩式退火镀锡板 batch type annealing tin plate
罩式退火机组 bell type annealing line
罩式退火炉 cover [hood, bell] type annealing furnace, top hat annealing furnace ◇ 多垛~*,高效能纯氢保护气氛~*,全氢~*
罩式退火炉设备 batch type annealing plant
罩式退火炉组 battery of bell type annealing furnace
兆欧表 megameter, megohm-meter, megger, tramegger
兆欧表测试 megger test
兆位 megabit
召集 call together
遮板 shield
遮蔽 cover, screen, masking(-off), shadowing
遮蔽剂 masking agent
遮闭 black out
遮窗 jalousie

遮断	interruption, intercept
遮断功率	rupturing [breaking] capacity
遮断功率额定值	【电】interrupting capacity rating
遮风板	shield
遮光板	aperture plate, diaphragm, shield, shadow shield（遮阳光板）
遮光剂	opacifier
遮光漆	black out paint
遮光性	opacity
遮护板	baffle plate
遮帘	blind
遮热板	shield, insulation board
遮水板（船的）	splasher
遮阳	sunshade, abatjour
遮阳(光)板	sun breaker, shadow shield
遮阳幕[板]	ante-venna
遮雨板	dashboard
遮住	bury
折板机	sheet doubler, folder
折板结构	folded plate structure
折臂式高架起重机	folding jib gantry
折边	flanged [raised] edge, bosse, flanging, creasing, edgefold, lapel
折边锤	creasing hammer
折边工序	【压】flanging operation
折边[缘]机	folding [creasing, edging] machine
折边连接(接触焊的)	coach joint
折带式过滤机	folded belt drum filter
折叠	folding, wrinkle, collapse, 【钢】lap, 【压】package（薄板叠轧时的）, jointing, doubling, shut（缺陷）, pincher（条钢缺陷）◇ 波状～*, 防活套～looping
折叠法(叠板轧制)	doubling process
折叠机(薄板的)	doubling machine, doubler, folder ◇ 自动～automatic doubler
折叠裂纹	【压】fold crevice
折叠式	collapsible
折叠式导向台	folding guide table
折叠弯折试验	【压】folding [double-over] test
折叠式门	folding door
折叠线材	slivery wire
折叠应力	【压】folding stress
折断	break(ing) off, discontinuity, failure, fluting, fracture, scrape out
折翻式防护面罩	tilting helmet
折返式拉拔	zigzag drawing
折返式拉丝机	return draw bench
折光度	diopter
折光率	coefficient of refraction
折光指数	refraction [refractive] index
折合	convert into, amount to
折痕	lap, 【压】fold（坯料缺陷）◇ 表面有～的钢丝 slivery wire
折减坡度	【运】compensating [compensated] grade
折旧	【企】depreciation ◇ 提取～基金*
折旧费	depreciation charge [fund], cost of depreciation
折旧率	depreciation rate [factor]
折旧提成	allowance for depreciation
折旧系数	depreciation factor
折裂	【压】fold crack
折流板	【色】baffle
折流板洗涤塔	baffle (washing) tower
折曲(往复的)	crippling
折曲管道	zigzag duct
折射	refraction, refringence, refringency
折射本领	refractivity, refringence
折射定律	law of refraction
折射计[仪]	refractometer
折射角	refracted [refraction] angle
折射介质	refracting [refractive] medium
折射晶体	refracting crystal
折射率	refractive index (R.I.), refraction index, coefficient of refraction, refractivity
折射系数	refractive exponent, refractivity
折射线	refracted rays
折射指数	refractive exponent, refraction index
折式滤器	folded filter
折算	obversion

折算长度 reduced length
折算焦比 【铁】specific coke rate
折算系数 reduction factor
折算综合焦比 specific coke ratio equivalent
折弯 bend, joggling
折纹 cross breaks, fluting（缺陷）, coil breaks（带卷开卷的）
折线 broken [fold, polygonal] line, zigzag, abrupt curve,【铁】bend line（炉喉与炉身交线）
折向板 deflector plate
折叶 hinge
折叶门 hinged door
折印(薄板叠轧缺陷) pinch(er)
折缘 flanging
折缘机 folding [creasing] machine
折纸漏斗 folded filter
折衷方案【法】 trade-off
折皱 pinch, wrinkle, elephant skin（锻造缺陷）, jump（薄板缺陷）, pincher trees（带钢缺陷）
折皱变形(带卷边的) scuffing
折皱的 corrugated
辙叉 【运】frog, cross ◇ 栓固～ bolted rigid frog
锗{Ge} germanium ◇ 掺杂～*, 块状本征～*, 区域精炼～*
锗半导体 germanium semiconductor
锗掺铜 copper-doped germanium
锗的(四价锗的) germanic
锗二极管 germanium diode
锗钒酸铅 lead germanate-vanadite
锗光电管[池, 元件] germanium photocell
锗硅合金 germanium-silicon alloy ◇ 富锗的～*
锗基合金 germanium-base alloy
锗结 germanium junction
锗晶体 germanium crystal
锗矿床 germanium deposit
锗馏分 germanium fraction
锗片 germanium wafer

锗氢化作用 hydrogermanation
锗三极管 germanium triode
锗石 germanite
锗酸铋 bismuth germanium oxide
锗酸锂 lithium germanium oxide
锗酸钠{Na$_2$GeO$_3$} sodium germanate
锗酸铅 lead germanium oxide, lead germanate
锗酸盐 germanate
锗铜焊料 germanium-copper brazing alloy
锗丸 germanium pellet
锗铀钇矿石 polycrase, polycrasite
锗元件 germanium element
锗整流器 germanium rectifier
赭褐色 ochre brown colour
赭色 ocher, salmon, reddish brown, auburn
赭色赤铁矿{Fe$_2$O$_3$} ruddle
赭砂 ferruginous sand
赭石 ocher, ochre
赭石赤铁矿(黏土类赤铁矿) red ocher
赭土 iron minium
褶缝压力机【压】 folding and seaming press
褶皱【地】bend, fold(ing)
褶皱系数【粉】coefficient of regosity
褶皱形成 formation of wrinkles
褶皱作用【地】folding
柘榴石【地】garnet
蔗渣纤维板 bagasse fiberboard
珍珠石{Al$_2$Si$_2$O$_5$(OH)$_4$} nacrite
珍珠陶土{Al$_2$Si$_2$O$_5$(OH)$_4$} nacrite
珍珠岩 perlite
珍珠岩混凝土 perlite concrete
真半导体 true semiconductor
真磁化(强度)【理】true magnetization
真核生物 eucaryote
真化合物 true chemical compound
真灰分 true ash
真金属 true metal
真菌 fungus（复数 fungi）, alga（复数 algae）

zhen 真　1742

真菌学的 mycological
真空 vacuum (vac.), vacuo, underpressure ◇ 不漏～的 vacuum-tight, 抽～*, 抽成[产生]～ vacuum production, 低～ poor vacuum, 放～阀 vacuum relief valve, 高[完全]～ perfect vacuum, 极限～ highest vacuum, 绝对～ absolute vacuum, 预抽～*
真空 O 形环 O ring
真空安全阀 vacuum relief valve
真空保温瓶 (同"杜瓦瓶")
真空杯 vacuum cup
真空泵 vacuum pump [fan] ◇ 抽真空容积与～效率之比值 time constant, 单级玻璃油蒸气～*, 分馏～ fractionating pump, 干式～ dry vacuum pump, 汞～ mercury vacuum pump, 回转(式)～*, 离心式～*, 喷油[油喷射]～ oil-jet type of pump, 湿式～ wet vacuum pump, 小[微]型～ minipump, 油～*, 预～*, 载气～ gas ballast pump, 增压[辅助]油扩散～*, 自动斯普伦格尔～*, 自馏～*
真空泵抽空压气机 vacuum pump compressor
真空泵油 vacuum (pump) oil, pump oil, pumping fluid
真空滗析 vacuum decanting
真空表 vacuum meter ◇ 麦氏～ McLeod gauge
真空捕集器 vacuum trap
真空测辐射热计 vacuum bolometer
真空成形(法) 【压】vacuum forming
真空澄清器 vacuum clarifier
真空重熔合金 vacuum remelted alloy
真空抽气管 pump-out tubulation
真空除气 (同"真空脱气")
真空除锌 vacuum dezincing
真空除锌法 vacuum dezincing process
真空除锌器 vacuum dezincing vessel
真空除锌设备(铅精炼用) vacuum dezincing equipment [apparatus]
真空储蓄器 vacuum reservoir

真空处理 vacuum treatment ◇ ASEA-SKF 电弧热磁搅拌～法*, 杰罗模顶～法*, 连铸过程中钢水连续～*
真空处理钢 vacuum-treated steel
真空处理混凝土 vacuum-treated concrete
真空处理设备 vacuum treatment equipment ◇ DH～【钢】DH vacuum unit, RH～【钢】RH-equipment, 钢包[盛钢桶]～*
真空吹氧精炼 【钢】vacuum oxygen refining (VOR)
真空吹氧精炼法 VOR process
真空吹氧脱碳法 【钢】VOD (vacuum oxygen decarbonization) process ◇ 带喷粉的～*
真空淬火炉 vacuum quenching furnace
真空的 air-free, vacuous
真空等离子喷涂 vacuum plasma spray (ing)
真空垫 vacuum pad
真空电弧 vacuum arc
真空电弧重熔 vacuum arc remelting (VAR)
真空电弧炉 vacuum arc furnace ◇ 自耗电极～*
真空电弧炉熔炼 vacuum arc (furnace) melting
真空电弧熔炼[熔化]法 vacuum arc melting (process)
真空电接触器材 vacuum contacts
真空电离表 vacuum ionization gauge
真空电炉 【冶】vacuum electric furnace
真空电阻测辐射热计 vacuum bolometer
真空电阻炉 vacuum resistance furnace
真空淀积 vacuum deposition
真空镀层[膜] vacuum coating
真空镀覆 vacuum plating
真空镀铝钢板 Al-vapour-deposited steel sheet
真空度 vacuum (degree), vacuity, underpressure, subatmospheric pressure
真空多级蒸发器 vacuum multistage evap-

真空恶化　loss of vacuum
真空阀　vacuum [evacuation] valve
真空法　vacuum process ◇ 顶吹[LD]-～【钢】LD-vac process
真空放电　vacuum discharge
真空分离　vacuum separation
真空分离时间　vacuum separation time
真空分离装置　vacuum separation apparatus
真空封闭剂　vacuum paste
真空浮选机　vacuum cell
真空干碾机　vacuum pug mill
真空干燥　vacuum drying
真空干燥炉　vacuum drying oven
真空干燥器　vacuum drier [desiccator]
真空干燥器干燥　vacuum-desiccator drying
真空感应电炉　vacuum-induction furnace
真空感应精炼　vacuum induction refining
真空感应炉熔炼的钢　vacuum-induction melted steel
真空感应熔炼　induction vacuum melting (I.V.M.)
真空感应熔炼法　vacuum-induction melting (process), inductrovac process
真空感应脱气(用于搅拌钢水)　vacuum-induction degassing
真空钢包炉　vacuum ladle furnace (VLF)
真空高温计　suction pyrometer
真空高温显微镜　vacuum hot-stage microscope
真空工艺学　vacuum technology
真空管　vacuum pipe [tube, valve]
真空管道[线]　vacuum line ◇ 预抽～阀 fore line valve
真空管电压表　vacuum-tube voltmeter
真空管感应加热　vacuum-tube induction heating
真空管检波器　vacuum-tube detector
真空管振荡器　vacuum-tube oscillator [generator], electronic generator

真空罐　vacuum tank [container, vessel], evacuated vessel, autovac ◇ 丹尼索夫式出镁～*
真空光电管　vacuum phototube
真空光谱[分光]计　vacuum spectrometer
真空光谱学　vacuum spectroscopy
真空规　(同"真空计")
真空锅　vacuum kettle [pan]
真空过滤　vacuum filtration
真空过滤机　vacuum (type) filter ◇ 巴特斯多叶～*, 带式～ belt vacuum filter, 多尔型圆筒～ Dorrco filter, 鼓式～[奥利弗滤器]*, 滚筒式～*, 回转～*, 间歇式～*, 可倾式～*, 连续～*, 努奇框式～ Nutsch filter, 盘式～ vacuum pan filter, 叶片式～*, 圆盘～*
真空过滤浓缩机　vacuum filter-thickener
真空焊接　vacuum welding
真空烘箱　vacuum drying oven
真空弧熔钼　vacuum-arc melted molybdenum
真空还原　vacuum reduction ◇ 亨特～钛精炼法 Hunter process
真空回火炉　vacuum tempering furnace
真空混合器　vacuum mixer
真空集管[联管箱]　vacuum header
真空挤压　extrusion under vacuum
真空挤压球团　vacuum extruded pellet ◇ 不烧结～矿*
真空给料机　vacuum feeder
真空计　vacuum meter [gauge], vacu(um)ometer, vacustat ◇ 布登～*, 电离～*, 辐射式～ radiometer gauge, 机械形变～*, 绝对压力～*, 冷阴极～ cold-cathode gauge, 李式皮拉尼～*, 麦克利德[麦氏]～*, 努森～ Knudsen vacuum gauge, 彭宁～*, 皮拉尼～*, 气体放电～ gas-discharge gauge, 热导率～*, 热敏电阻～ thermistor gauge, 双金属片～*
真空计压力　vacuum gauge pressure, underpressure
真空记录器　vacuum recorder

真空加热 vacuum [vacuo] heating, vacuum furnacing
真空加热提炼 vacuum hot extraction
真空检漏器 vacuum leak detector
真空检验[检漏试验] vacuum testing
真空浇注 vacuum casting [pouring, teeming]
真空浇注法 【钢】vacuum casting process
真空浇铸设备 【钢】vacuum casting plant
真空搅拌机 de-airing mixer
真空搅土机 【耐】de-airing pug mill
真空接受器 vacuum receiver ◇ 滤液～*
真空接头 vacuum connection
真空结晶器 vacuum crystallizer
真空解除阀 vacuum relief valve
真空金属喷镀[金属喷涂,喷镀金属] vacuum metalling [metallizing]
真空紧密的 vacuum-tight
真空浸油 vacuum oil penetration ◇ 麻芯～*
真空浸油箱(钢丝绳麻芯的) vacuum oil immersion tank
真空浸渍[渗] vacuum impregnating [impregnation]
真空浸渍的 vacuum-impregnated
真空精炼 vacuum refining ◇ 磁搅弧热～炉*, 粗锌～过程*
真空精馏 vacuum rectification, rectification under vacuum
真空净化 vacuum purification [cleaning]
真空净化设备 vacuum cleaning equipment [installation]
真空空间 evacuated space
真空快速蒸发 vacuum flash vaporization
真空快速蒸发器 vacuum flash vaporizer
真空快速蒸发装置 vacuum flash unit
真空扩散焊 vacuum diffusion welding
真空冷焊 vacuum cold welding
真空冷阱[凝气瓣] vacuum (cold) trap
真空冷凝 vacuum condensation
真空冷凝器 vacuum condenser
真空冷却 vacuum cooling

真空连续结晶机 vacuum continuous crystallizer
真空练泥机 【耐】de-airing pug mill
真空量 amount of vacuum
真空漏失[泄] vacuum leak
真空炉 vacuum furnace ◇ 电子束～*, 热壁～*, 水冷炉壁～*, 碳管～*
真空炉加热 vacuum furnacing
真空炉容器 vacuum furnace container
真空密闭罐 vacuum-tight retort
真空密闭容器 vacuum-tight container
真空密闭室 vacuum-tight chamber
真空密闭水冷金属钟形罩(烧结炉) vacuum-tight water-cooled metal bell
真空密封 vacuum-tight, vacuum (tight) seal ◇ 凸缘～flange vacuum seal
真空密封成形 vacuum-tight forming
真空密封炉 vacuum-tight furnace
真空密封炉盖 vacuum-tight furnace cover
真空密封门 vacuum-tight door
真空密封缩颈 constriction for vacuum seal
真空密封[气密]性 vacuum tightness
真空模板(混凝土用) vacuum mat
真空模塑 vacuum moulding
真空模压力铸造法 (同"真空压铸法")
真空膜盒 aneroid chamber, aneroid (diaphragm) capsule
真空碾[挤]泥机 vacuum pug
真空浓缩 vacuum concentration
真空盘架干燥器 vacuum trap drier
真空喷丸[砂] vacuum blasting
真空瓶 vacuum flash, Dewar's bottle
真空启动 vacuum start
真空气氛 vacuum atmosphere
真空气密试验 vacuum gas test
真空钎焊 vacuum brazing
真空清洁机 vacuum cleaning plant
真空驱气 vacuum purge
真空驱气期 vacuum purge cycle
真空热处理 vacuum heat treatment
真空热电偶 vacuo-junction

真空热还原　vacuum-thermal reduction
真空热还原法　vacuum-thermal method
真空热精炼　vacuum-thermal refining
真空热压烧结　vacuum hot pressing sintering
真空熔化　vacuum-fusion
真空熔化[熔解]法　【冶】vacuum fusion method
真空熔化分析　vacuum-fusion analysis
真空熔化炉　vacuum fusion furnace
真空熔炼　vacuum smelting [melting] ◇无坩埚～*
真空熔炼厂　vacuum melting plant
真空熔炼的　melted in vacuum
真空熔炼法　vacuum melting method
真空熔炼分析　vacuum melting analysis
真空熔炼钢　vacuum-melted steel
真空熔炼钢液　vacuum(-melted) heat
真空熔炼合金　vacuum melted alloy
真空容器　vacuum [evacuated] vessel
真空润滑系统　vacuum lift system of lubrication
真空闪蒸(蒸馏及蒸发)　vacuum flashing
真空烧成　vacuum firing
真空烧结　vacuum sintering, sintering in vacuum ◇冷压～法
真空烧结炉　vacuum sintering furnace
真空设备　vacuum equipment [apparatus, plant], evacuated device
真空设备接头　vacuum connection
真空渗碳[碳化]　vacuum carburization ◇海斯～处理法 Hayes process
真空渗碳炉　vacuum-carburizing furnace
真空升华　vacuum sublimation
真空式溢流堰　aerated weir
真空室　vacuum chamber [case, space, degasser], evacuated chamber [space]
真空受液槽　filtrate vacuum receiver
真空水银扩散泵　mercury diffusion pump
真空塔　vacuum column
真空抬包　vacuum ladle
真空碳还原[脱氧]钢　vacuum carbon deoxidized steel
真空提纯　vacuum purification
真空提炼[提取]　vacuum extraction
真空提取器　vacuum extraction still
真空提吸脱气法　(同"提升真空脱气法")
真空退火　vacuum annealing
真空退火合金　vacuum annealed alloy
真空退火炉　vacuum annealing furnace
真空退火设备　vacuum annealing plant
真空脱气(法)　【钢】vacuum degassing [outgassing] ◇ ASA-SKF 钢色～系统*,包到包[桶到桶]～*,包内～ladle degassing,出钢～*,单管提升～*,电磁搅拌～*,电弧加热～*,芬克尔～装置【冶】Finkl system, 钢流～stream degassing,(双管)循环～*
真空脱气钢　vacuum-degassed steel
真空脱气罐　vacuum receiver
真空脱气坑　【钢】degassing pit
真空脱气炉　vacuum degassing furance
真空脱气设备　vacuum degasification apparatus, vacuum degassing plant
真空脱水　vacuum dehydrating
真空脱锌容器　V.D.Z.(vacuum dezincing) vessel
真空温度计　vacuum thermometer
真空吸尘器　vacuum cleaner
真空吸尘器用铝铜合金(10Cu,余量 Al)　vacuum cleaner alloy
真空吸尘装置　cleaning vacuum plant
真空吸盘　vacuum cup
真空吸盘垛板机　vacuum-operated sheet piler
真空吸盘升降台　vacuum cup lifter
真空吸盘式升降机　vacuum cup crane
真空吸水处理混凝土　vacuum concrete
真空吸铸　【铸】vacuum suction casting, vacuum casting process
真空系统　vacuum system
真空箱　vacuum(-tight) tank, vacuum case, evacuated container, autovac ◇炉

zhen 真

用～furnace vacuum tank,透明～*
真空消除阀　break-vac valve
真空循环处理　vacuum recirculation process (VCP)
真空循环脱气(法)　(同"循环真空脱气(法)")
真空压力阀　vacuum pressure valve
真空压力计　vacuum pressure gauge, vacuum manometer
真空压力铸造　vacuum die casting
真空压制　【粉】vacuum-pressing
真空压铸法　evacuated die-casting process
真空氧化精炼　【钢】vacuum oxygenrefining
真空-氧脱碳　vacuum-oxygen decarburization
真空冶金　vacuum metallurgy
真空冶炼　vacuum melting
真空叶片过滤机　(同"叶片式真空过滤机")
真空仪　vacuscope
真空溢流层式溢流堰　aerated weir
真空用合金　vacuum alloy
真空油膏　vacuum paste
真空预热　【电】vacuum preheating
真空运搬系统[装置]　vacuum handling system
真空再蒸馏　vacuum rerun
真空造型　vacuo-forming
真空增强器　vacuum intensifier
真空渣壳熔炼　【钢】vacuum skull melting
真空渣壳铸锭炉　vacuum skull casting furnace
真空轧机　vacuum rolling mill
真空轧制　vacuum rolling
真空闸阀　vacuum lock
真空罩　vacuum hood
真空蒸镀　vacuum vapour plating
真空蒸发　vacuum evaporation
真空蒸发淀积　vapour vacuum deposition
真空蒸发淀积法　vacuum vapour deposition method
真空蒸发锅　vacuum kettle
真空蒸发器　vacuum evaporator [kettle] ◇多效～*
真空蒸馏　vacuum distillation [distilling], distil under vacuum
真空蒸馏除锌法(炼铅用)　vacuum distillation process for dezincing, dezincing by vacuum distillation
真空蒸馏釜　vacuum still
真空蒸馏罐　vacuum retort
真空蒸馏精炼技术　vacuum distillation refining technique
真空蒸馏炉　vacuum retort furnace
真空蒸馏镁　vacuum-distilled magnesium
真空蒸馏设备　vacuum distillation apparatus [plant], vacuum distilling apparatus
真空蒸馏塔　vacuum tower [column]
真空正火的　normalized in vacuum (Nv)
真空脂　vacuum grease
真空指示器　vacuum indicator
真空制备的试样　vacuum-prepared sample
真空制动器[真空闸]　vacuum brake
真空铸锭　【冶】vacuum casting
真空铸锭炉　vacuum-casting furnace
真空铸罐　vacuum ladle
真空铸造　【铸】vacuum casting process
真空转换开关　vacuum switch
真空装置　(同"真空设备")
真空状态　vacuum state
真空自动浇注系统　automatic vacuum ladling system
真空自耗炉　【冶】vacuum consumable electrode furnace
真空自蒸发器　vacuum flash vaporizer
真孔隙[气孔]率　true porosity
真平衡　true equilibrium
真热容　true heat capacity
真溶(解)度　real solubility
真溶液　true [real] solution
真实变形[真(实)应变]　true strain
真实掺入体　real inclusion
真实电流密度　effective current density

真实断裂应变	true fracture strain
真实断裂应力	true fracture stress
真实还原性	intrinsic reducibility
真实价	true valency
真实晶格	real lattice
真实均匀[真匀]应变	true uniform strain
真(实)密度	true [real, full] density
真实气体	(同"实际气体")
真(实)应力	true stress
真实应力-应变曲线	true stress-strain curve
真实应力-真实应变行为	true stress-true strain behaviour
真实应力-真实应变曲线	true stress-true strain curve
真实应力图	true stress diagram
真数	antilog(arithm)
真体积	true volume
真温度	true temperature
真吸收系数	true absorption coefficient
真细菌纲	eubacteriae
真细菌类	eubacteria
真液体	true liquid
真值表	【计】truth table, Boolean operation table
砧面	anvil face
砧式摆锻机	anvil forging press
砧头	fast tool
砧凿	anvil chisel
砧座(锻锤的)	【机】anvil stand [block, base, cap]
砧座台[凸]肩	anvil fuller
砧座羊角	anvil horn
针	needle, pin ◇ 维卡~ Vicat needle
针布钢丝	card wire, wire for card clothing
针齿轮	lantern gear
针赤铁矿	rafisiderite, raphisiderite
针碲金矿	aurotellurite, white tellurium
针碲金银矿	goldschmidtite, graphic tellurium
针碲矿	blattevine, elasmore
针碲银矿	petzite
针独居石	cryptolite
针阀	needle valve
针钙镁铀矿	rabbittite
针硅钙铅矿	margarosanite
针黄铜矿	chalmersite
针碱钙石	uxporite
针碱铌石	juxporite
针孔	pinhole ◇ 夹渣~ *
针孔缝隙	pinhole leak
针孔炉底	【钢】pin-bottom
针孔目镜	pinhole eyepiece [ocular]
针孔缺陷	hole defect
针孔缺陷探伤仪(带材的)	pinhole detector ◇ 红外线~ *
针孔系统	pinhole system
针孔装置	pinhole arrangement [system]
针孔状缩孔	pinhole porosity
针孔准直	pinhole collimation
针磷铁矿	koninckite
针硫铋铝矿	aikinite
针硫铋铅矿 $\{3(Cu_2Pb)S \cdot Bi_2S_3\}$	acicular bismuth, aciculite
针(硫)镍矿 $\{NiS\}$	millerite, nickel blende
针硫铅铜矿	betekhtinite
针硫锑铅矿	falkmanite
针帽[头]	pin cap (PC)
针镁钼矿 $\{MgO \cdot MoO_3\}$	belonesite
针镁石	hanusite
针磨机	needle polishing [grinding] machine ◇ 模孔~ *
针青铜	needle bronze
针闪锌矿	marmatite
针式打印机	wire printer
针式热电偶	needle thermocouple
针碎机	spike mill
针铁矿 $\{Fe_2O_3 \cdot H_2O\}$	needle ironstone, goethite
针铁矿法	goethite process
针形阀	needle valve
针形引带杆	needle bar
针印(钢板酸洗缺陷)	pin mark
针(用黄)铜 $(62Cu, 38Zn)$	pin-metal, pin-

	wire
针状断口	needle fracture
针状粉粒	acicular particle, needle
针状粉末	needle [acicular] powder
针状结晶	needle, acicular crystal
针状晶簇	cluster of needles
针状晶体	needle-like [needle-shaped, acicular] crystal, (acicular) needle
针状颗粒	acicular particle
针状马氏体	【金】needle-type [acicular] martensite
针状莫来石	mullite needle
针状气孔	needle-shaped blowhole
针状球墨铸铁	acicular spheroidal graphite cast iron
针状屈氏体	acicular troostite
针状(石油)焦	needle coke
针状碳化物	acicular carbide
针状物	needle
针状析出(物)	【金】needle-like precipitate
针状相(析出的)	【金】needle-like phase
针状长大	spike growth
针状铸铁(贝茵体铸铁)	acicular (cast) iron
针状组分	acicular constituent
针状组织[结构]	acicular structure, needle
榛褐稀金矿	caryocerite
枕垫(轴承的)	pillow block
枕间道碴	【运】boxed in ballast
枕距规	【运】distance-gauge for sleeper
枕距护木	【运】bond timber
枕块	pillow block, bolster
枕木	cross-tie, sleeper, dormant
枕形畸变	pincushion distortion
枕形抗裂试验	pillow test
枕状团块	【团】pillow-shaped briquette
枕座	pillow (block)
枕座[垫,块]支架	pillow block frame
诊断	diagnosis
诊断程序	【计】diagnostic program [routine] ◇ 编译程序的~*
诊断控制程序	diagnostic control program (DCP)
诊断系统	diagnostic(s) system
震颤纹(拉拔缺陷)	chatter marks
震[振]打器	knocker, shaker ◇ 自动~*
震打装置	rapping apparatus
震旦石	uranoaeschynite
震动	shaking, shock, vibration, chatter, tremor
震动冲剪机	【压】impulse cutting machine
震动舂砂	【铸】jar ramming
震动除芯机	【铸】core vibrator
震动打箱落砂法(熔模铸造的)	【铸】knock-out
震动固结	consolidation by vibration
震动机	vibration machine
震动减低器	vibration damper
震动盘	impact disc
震动器	jolter, shaker
震动筛	vibratory screen ◇ 冲击式~impact screen
震动试验	shock-testing
震动速率	jolting rate
震动台	jolting table, jarring table(造型机的), vibrobench
震动填料[填筑]	jolt-packing
震动运输机	shaker conveyer
震动铸锭法	【钢】jolting [jarring] of ingot
震动状态	jogging
震动阻尼装置	vibration damper
震击机	jarring machine
震裂	shattering, shatter crack
震裂强度	shatter strength
震裂试验	shatter test
震凝现象	rheopexy
震实	(ram-)jolt ◇ 台式~机 bench jolter
震实密度杯	【粉】tap density cup
震实式翻转起模造型机	【铸】jolt roll-over pattern-draw moulding machine
震实式漏模造型机	【铸】jolt pattern-draw moulding machine
震实(式)造型机	【铸】dumping [jar, bumping] moulding machine, jar ram

震 zhen

(moulding) machine, jolt [joggling, jarring] machine, bumper ◇ 气动~*, 有减震装置的~(同"微震造型机")
震实式制芯机 【铸】core jarring machine
震实台 plain jolter
震实造型 【铸】jolt moulding
震压式造型机 【铸】combination jarring squeezing moulding machine, jolt (ramming) squeezer, jolt squeeze moulding machine
震源[中] earthquake center, epicenter
震筑衬里 jolt-packed liner
震筑器 jolter
振摆式轧机 oscillatory mill
振波探漏仪 leak vibroscope
振荡 oscillation (osc.), oscillating motion, generation ◇ 无~(的) dead-beat, 空腔[穴]~ cavity oscillations
振荡单晶 oscillating single crystal
振荡点 oscillation [surge] point
振荡电流 oscillating current
振荡电路 oscillatory [oscillating] circuit
振荡电路线圈 oscillating circuit coil
振荡方式[模式,形式] (同"振动方式")
振荡管 oscillator, oscillating tube
振荡频率 oscillation [oscillatory] frequency
振荡器 oscillator (OSC), vibrator, generator, ticker ◇ 差频~* 固定选通脉冲~ fixed gate generator, 射流~ fluid oscillator, 时钟脉冲~*, 阴极耦合多谐~*, 主控~ exciter
振荡燃烧 oscillating combustion, hugging
振荡调制 modulation of oscillations
振荡图 oscillogram
振荡现象 oscillating phenomenon
振荡振幅[幅度] oscillation amplitude
振荡值 oscillating quantity
振荡指示器 cymoscope
振荡周期 period of oscillation
振荡自动控制 automatic oscillation control

振捣 vibrating, bumping down (粉末的) ◇ 球头式~棒 bullet nosed vibrator
振捣混凝土 vibrated concrete
振捣器[机] vibrator, vibrating tamper ◇ 表面~*, 插入式~*, 电动~ electric vibrator, 附着式~*, 混凝土~*, 内部~*
振动 vibration (vib.), vibrating action, shaking, jitter, oscillating motion, oscillation ◇ 爱因斯坦~模型 Einstein model
振动X射线谱 oscillation X-ray spectrum
振动板 vibrating board [plate]
振动棒 vibrating tamper
振动比热 【理】vibrational specific heat
振动臂 vibrating [shaker] arm
振动布料器 【团】vibrator [vibratory] feeder
振动成型 vibratory compaction [moulding], vibration-assisted compaction
振动成穴试验装置 vibratory cavitation test device
振动成穴[空化]作用 vibratory cavitation
振动持续时间 period of vibration
振动冲击负载 vibratory shock load
振动传感器 vibration [oscillation] pickup, vibrating sensor
振动床 vibrated bed
振动次数 number of vibration
振动挡板 vibrating baffle
振动挡板式弥散器 vibrating baffle disperser
振动捣实器 (同"振捣器")
振动底炉 shocking hearth furnace
振动电弧堆焊 vibratory arc surfacing
振动电机 oscillation motor
振动电流计 vibration galvanometer
振动堆焊 vibration welding
振动方式[模式] 【理】vibration(al) [oscillation] mode, oscillatory mode (of motion), mode of vibration
振动负荷 oscillating load

振动格筛 vibrating [vibration] grizzly
振动公害 vibration hazard [nuisance]
振动管取样器 vibratory tube sampler
振动光谱 vibrational spectrum
振动光谱学 vibrational spectroscopy
振动辊 vibratory roll
振动滚轮 【粉】vibratory roller
振动过滤网式收尘器 vibrating screen deduster
振动夯击机(压型用) jolt-ramming machine
振动荷载 racking load
振动机构 vibrating mechanism ◇ 四偏心式~*
振动激发 shock excitation
振动给料机[给料器,给矿机,加料器](电磁振动式) vibrator(y) [vibrating] feeder, pulsafeeder ◇ 热(矿)~ hot vibro feeder
振动给料 vibratory feeding
振动给料板 vibrating feed-shoe
振动给料箱 vibrating feed-box
振动计 vibrograph, vibro-meter, vibration meter
振动架(跳汰机的) jigging frame
振动监控器 vibration monitor
振动角 angle of oscillation
振动结点 【理】vibration node
振动进料器 shaking feeder
振动空化试验装置 vibratory cavitation test device
振动离心机 vibrating centrifuge
振动料斗 vibrating hopper
振动落砂格栅 vibratory knockout grid
振动摩擦腐蚀 fretting corrosion
振动能 vibrational energy
振动碾轮 【粉】vibratory roller
振动盘 vibrating tray
振动盘反应器 vibrating tray reactor
振动盘还原(用氢还原) vibrating tray reduction
振动盘式给料机 vibrating pan feeder

振动疲劳 sonic fatigue
振动片式黏度计 vibrating-plate viscometer
振动频率 vibration(al) frequency, frequency of vibration
振动谱线 vibrational line
振动起伏 wave
振动器 vibrator, oscillator, shaking apparatus, oscillating guide (蛇形排放带 材用) ◇ 磁~ magnetic vibrator, 滚筒式~ tumbling shaker, 旋转~ rotating vibrator
振动器给料 vibrator feed
振动球磨 vibratory milling
振动球磨机 vibration(ball) mill, Vibratom
振动取样器 vibrating sampler
振动热容 vibrational heat capacity
振动筛 vibration [vibrating, oscillating, jigging] screen, vibro-screen, vibration [vibrating] grizzly, (screen, oscillating) riddler, shaking sieve, sieve shaker, jigger ◇ 棒条~ rod deck vibrating screen, 低头型~(低фpen) low-head screen, 机械~ power riddler, 杰伊雷克斯~ Gyrex screen, 冷矿~ cold vibro screen, 偏心~ gyratory screen, 热(矿)~ hot vibro screen, 自定中心式~ ripple flow vibrating screen
振动筛式给料机[加料器,布料器] vibratory screen (type) feeder, vibrating feeder with screen
振动伤害 【环】damage by vibration
振动熵 entropy of vibration
振动烧结 vibratory sintering
振动式槽底 vibrating bin bottom
振动式结晶器 oscillating mould
振动式离心机 oscillating centrifuge
振动式流槽 oscillating launder
振动式螺旋分离器 shaken helicoid
振动式螺旋分配器 vibration dosing worm
振动式输送机 vibratory [vibrating] con-

振镇 zhe

veyer
振动式下割烧嘴　oscillating undercutting nozzle
振动(式)研磨机　vibration [oscillating] mill
振动式轧机　vibratory rolling mill
振动试验　vibration [vibratory] test
振动试验机　vibration [vibratory] testing machine
振动台　vibrating [vibration] table, vibrostand, joggling table, jigging platform
振动探漏仪　vibroscope
振动套筛　【选】sieve shaker
振动图像分析(法)　vibration signature analysis
振动脱气　degasification by vibration
振动雾化(法)　vibratory atomization
振动吸收器　vibration absorber
振动线圈　oscillating [vibrating] coil
振动形变热处理　vibration TMT
振动形式　(同"振动方式")
振动压路机　vibratory roll
振动压制[压实]　vibration compaction, vibratory pressing [compaction]
振动摇床　【选】percussion table
振动液化　vibratory liquefaction, thixotropy
振动运输槽　jigging screen
振动运输机　vibrating [vibro, oscillating, jigging] conveyor
振动周期　period of vibration
振动铸型铸造法　vibrocast process
振动铸造[凝固铸件]　vibrational casting
振动桩　vibropile
振动装粉法　vibration-assisted filling
振动装置　shaking appliance; vibrator
振动状态　state of vibrating
振动锥体[圆锥]　vibratory cone
振动子　oscillator
振动作用　vibrating action
振幅　vibration [oscillation] amplitude, amplitude (amp), swing ◇ 反常～效应*
振幅衬度　amplitude contrast
振幅共振　amplitude resonance
振幅鉴别器　amplitude discriminator
振幅频率响应(特性)曲线　amplitude frequency response
振幅调制　【理】amplitude modulation
振幅吸收系数　amplitude absorption coefficient (AAC)
振幅自动控制　automatic amplitude control (AAC)
振浮压实法(地基的)　vibrofloatation
振痕　【连铸】oscillation mark
振铃　【电】ringing
振铃电键　ringing [calling] key
振铃试验　ringing test
振蚀　fretting corrosion
振实　jolt ramming ◇ 往复～容积*
振实密度　packed density, 【粉】tap density
振实密度仪　【粉】tapping apparatus
振实台　【铸】plain bumper
振实体积　packed volume, 【粉】tap volume
振实重量　tap weight
振子　vibrator, oscillator, ticker
振子传感[拾音]器　oscillator pickup
镇静(钢液)　kill, quieting ◇ 自～反应 auto-killing
镇静钢　killed [deoxidized, degasified, solid, piping] steel, fully killed [deoxidized, finished] steel, dead melted steel ◇ 铝～(见"铝脱氧钢"), 全～quiet [dead] steel
镇静钢锭　killed ingot
镇静钢熔炼　killed heat
镇静剂　killing agent
镇静期　killing period
镇静熔炼　dead melting
镇静时间　holding time
镇静室　stilling chamber
镇流电阻　ballast [steady] resistance
镇流电阻(器)　ballast resister, barretter
镇流管　ballast tube
镇流器　current stabilizer, dynamic reac-

镇流阻抗　ballast
镇重　dead man
镇重物　ballast
阵列处理机　array processor
阵列打印机　array printer
阵列计算机　array computer
阵列逻辑　array logic
阵列体系　array system
阵向[面]　front
蒸氨器　ammonia distiller
蒸氨柱[塔]　【焦】ammonia still
蒸发　evaporation (evap., evpn), evaporization, vapourization, vapourizing, transpiration, deaden (浮选过程的) ◇ 加热～部分＊, 可～性 evaporability, 自～溶液 blow off liquor
蒸发残留物　evaporation residue
蒸发成像仪　evaporograph
蒸发单位　evaporation unit (ev.u.)
蒸发点[温度]　vapourization point
蒸发淀积复型(制备)法　vapour-deposited replica
蒸发动力学[分子运动]理论　kinetic theory of evaporation
蒸发镀层[镀覆]　evaporation coating
蒸发法　evaporative process, evaporation
蒸发负荷　evaporation load
蒸发锅　evaporating pan [pot]
蒸发过滤机　evaporator filter
蒸发合金工艺　evaporated alloying technology
蒸发回路　boiling loop
蒸发计　evaporimeter, atmometer
蒸发结晶器　evaporating crystallizer, crystallizing evaporator
蒸发冷凝机理　evaporation-condensation mechanism
蒸发冷却　evaporative [sweat, transpiration] cooling ◇ 全部～法＊
蒸发冷却法　evaporation-cooling method
蒸发冷却塔　evaporative cooling tower
蒸发率　evaporative duty
蒸发皿　(evaporating) dish ◇ 有柄陶瓷～casserole
蒸发能力　evaporative capacity, capacity for evaporation
蒸发浓缩　evaporation concentration, graduation
蒸发盘　evaporating pan, boiler tray (蒸发器内的塔盘)
蒸发盘[蛇]管　evaporating coil
蒸发器　evaporator, vapourizer ◇ 多管～＊, 机械～＊, 阶式～[化] cascade (casc.), 浸没管式～＊, 双效～＊, 蒸汽加热～ steam evaporator
蒸发器盘[蛇]管　evaporator coil
蒸发(潜)热　vapourization heat, (latent) heat of evaporation
蒸发曲线　vapourization curve
蒸发热焓　enthalpy of evaporation
蒸发设备　evaporation equipment [plant], evaporating unit
蒸发室　vapourizer [vapourizing] chamber
蒸发室阀门　vapourizing chamber valve
蒸发水　evaporated water
蒸发速度　evaporation rate (e.r.)
蒸发损失　evaporation [vapourization] loss, loss by evaporation
蒸发效率　evaporative efficiency
蒸发性[度]　evaporativity
蒸发掩膜[遮掩]法　【电】evaporation mask method
蒸发照相(测定仪)　evaporograph ◇ 红外线～evaporograph
蒸发柱　flash tower
蒸罐　cucurbit ◇ 离解器～dissociator retort, 圆筒形～＊
蒸罐炉　rotort furnace ◇ 断续[周期]作用～＊, 硅铁～＊
蒸罐熔炼　retort smelting
蒸馏　distillation, distilling, stilling ◇ 常压～＊, 初步[预]～ predistillation, 低压～＊, 分批～＊, 高温～＊, 共沸～＊, 恒速

蒸 zheng

~*,火焰加热~ fire distillation,间接加热~*,间歇~*,可~性 distillability,连续~*,裂化~*,流态化床~*,闪速[急骤]~ flash distillation,顺序[依次]~*,真空~ distil under vacuum
蒸馏部 distillation division
蒸馏残余物[残渣] distillation [retort] residue, bottoms
蒸馏产物 distillation product
蒸馏厂 distillery
蒸馏车间 distilling plant
蒸馏带[区] distillation zone
蒸馏法 distillation (process, method)
蒸馏范围 distillation range
蒸馏分离 separation [fractionation] by distillation
蒸馏釜 distillation still, distilling tank [still], distiller, still kettle, cucurbit ◇ 管式~ pipe still,立式[干酪盒式]~【化】cheese box still,受压~ pressurized still,竖式~*,蒸汽加热~ steam-heated still
蒸馏管 distillation tube, still pipe (石油蒸馏管) ◇ 炼油设备用~*
蒸馏罐 distillation retort, retort (vessel) ◇ 不锈钢~*,管状~ tubular retort,还原~ reduction retort,金刚砂~ carborundum retort,镍铬钢~*,倾斜~*,石墨~ graphite retort,熟料~*,碳化硅~*,铸铁~*
蒸馏罐壁 retort wall
蒸馏罐底 retort bottom
蒸馏罐法兰盘[凸缘] retort flange
蒸馏罐冷凝器 retort condenser
蒸馏罐压力 retort pressure
蒸馏罐压制机 retort press
蒸馏罐蒸馏 retort distillation
蒸馏锅 distiller, column boiler, (pot) still
蒸馏海绵金属 distilled sponge
蒸馏海绵体 retort sponge
蒸馏后溶液 distilled solution
蒸馏级联 distillation cascade
蒸馏净化[提纯] distillation purification

蒸馏冷凝器 distiller condenser
蒸馏馏分 distillation fraction
蒸馏炉 distilling [distillation] furnace, retort oven ◇ 汞齐~*,海绵锆~*,炉底装料立式~*
蒸馏炉料 distillation charge
蒸馏瓶 distillation flask, cucurbit
蒸馏器 distiller, distillator, distillatory kettle, distillation vessel [kettle] ◇ 氨~ ammonia distiller,汽提~ stripping still,套层~ jacketed still
蒸馏气体 retort gas
蒸馏溶液 distilled solution
蒸馏设备 distilling apparatus [plant], distillation apparatus [equipment, plant, head], still head
蒸馏时间 distillation time
蒸馏试验 distillation test
蒸馏水 distilled water (D.W.)
蒸馏水洗涤 distilled water wash
蒸馏速率[速度] distillation rate (DR), rate of distillation
蒸馏损失 distillation loss
蒸馏塔 distillation tower [column], column (still), dephlegmator ◇ 奥氏~ Oldershaw column,板式~ plate tower,单柱~ one-column still,多层[层板]~*,二柱~ two-column still,净化~ purification column,泡罩~ bubble cap tower,填充~*
蒸馏塔板[盘] distilling [distillation] tray
蒸馏温度 distillation temperature
蒸馏锌 distilled [retort] zinc
蒸馏氧化焙烧 distillation-oxidation roasting
蒸馏周期 distillation cycle
蒸馏柱 (同"蒸馏塔") ◇ 脱除粗苯初馏分~ defronting column
蒸馏装置 distillation system, distillery
蒸木油(木材用) creosote
蒸浓 inspissation, graduation
蒸浓器 inspissator

蒸浓柱　evaporating column
蒸气　vapour
蒸气槽　vapour bath
蒸气产物喷射泵　distillation products jet pump
蒸气发生　vapour generation
蒸气分馏法　vapour rectification process
蒸气空间色层法[层析(法)]　vapour space chromatography
蒸气空气混合物　vapour-air mixture
蒸气煤气混合物　vapour-gas mixture
蒸气密度　vapour density (V.D., vd)
蒸气膜　vapour film
蒸气熔剂　vapour flux
蒸气室　vapour dome
蒸气脱脂　vapour degreasing
蒸气制氢法　◇ 莱恩～Lane process
蒸汽　steam, vapour (V, v, vap.) ◇ 不漏～的 vapourproo, 加热用～heating steam, 排出～discharge steam, 新鲜～live steam, 自蒸发～flashed steam
蒸汽保护电弧焊　vapour-shielded arc welding
蒸汽饱和气氛　steam-saturated atmosphere
蒸汽泵　vapour-steam pump ◇ 喷射～steam-jet pump
蒸汽表　steam table
蒸汽捕集器　vapour trap
蒸汽成分　vapour composition
蒸汽冲击腐蚀　steam impingement corrosion
蒸汽冲压[捣矿]机　steam stamp
蒸汽重整天然气　steam reformed natural gas
蒸汽出口　steam outlet [exit, port]
蒸汽除鳞　steam descaling
蒸汽除鳞喷嘴　steam-descaling sprayer
蒸汽处理　steam [vapour] treatment, vapour cure ◇ 安蒂沃奇～石膏型法 Antioch process
蒸汽锤　steam hammer ◇ 双动～*, 外伸式～*
蒸汽淬火　steam quenching
蒸汽吊车　(同"蒸汽起重机")
蒸汽动力　steam power
蒸汽发蓝处理　barffing, steam bluing
蒸汽发生器　steamer, steam generator
蒸汽房　steam house
蒸汽分离器　steam separator
蒸汽腐蚀　corrosion by steam
蒸汽腐蚀抑制剂　vapour corrosion inhibitor
蒸汽干燥　steam drying
蒸汽干燥器　steam drier [dryer], steam drying apparatus
蒸汽供暖　steam heating ◇ 干式回水～系统*, 重力式～*
蒸汽鼓风　【铁】humidified [steam] blast
蒸汽鼓风机　steam blower
蒸汽鼓泡搅拌式高压釜　steam-bubbling type autoclave
蒸汽管　vapour pipe
蒸汽管加热干燥机　steam-tube drier
蒸汽管路　steam-pipe line
蒸汽管束　steam-tube bundle
蒸汽管弯头　steam bend (SB)
蒸汽锅炉　steam boiler ◇ 电热～electric steamboiler
蒸汽过热器　steam superheater
蒸汽红黄铜(3Zn, 7Sn, 3Pb, 余量 Cu)　steam metal
蒸汽回火(高速钢的)　steam tempering
蒸汽回收　steam recovery
蒸汽汇集器　steam header
蒸汽混合物　vapour mixture
蒸汽活化木炭　steam-activated charcoal
蒸汽加热　steam heating
蒸汽加热炉　steam-pipe oven
蒸汽加热器　steam heater
蒸汽加热溶出器　steam digester
蒸汽加热蛇管　steam (heating) coil
蒸汽加热套　steam-jacket
蒸汽加热蒸发器　steam (-heated) evapo-

蒸汽加热蒸馏釜 steam-heated still
蒸汽加热助滤(法) steam-assisted filtering
蒸汽搅拌 steam stirring
蒸汽搅拌高压釜 steam-agitated autoclave
蒸汽进[放]入阀 steam-admission valve
蒸汽空间色层法 vapour space chromatography
蒸汽-空气的 air-steam
蒸汽空气加热器 steam air heater
蒸汽控制阀 steam-control valve
蒸汽扩散泵 vapour-steam pump
蒸汽冷凝法 vapour rectification process
蒸汽冷凝区 vapour condensation zone
蒸汽冷凝器 vapour condenser
蒸汽冷却器 hot steam cooler
蒸汽两次中间过热式涡轮机 【机】double resuperheat machine
蒸汽磷酸盐处理(表面的) steam phosphating
蒸汽流 vapour stream ◇ 自蒸发～ flashed stream
蒸汽流量 steam flow
蒸汽煤 steam coal
蒸汽灭菌法 steam sterilization
蒸汽膜 film of vapour
蒸汽泥炮 【铁】steam-operated mud gun
蒸汽凝结 devaporation
蒸汽排出[放泄]阀 steam-trap valve
蒸汽排出孔 steam port
蒸汽盘管 steam coil
蒸汽喷管 steam jet [nozzle]
蒸汽喷砂机[设备,装置] steam(-jet) sandblaster
蒸汽喷砂清理[清理] vapour blast(ing)
蒸汽喷砂清理法 vapourblast process
蒸汽喷射泵 steam ejector, steam-ejector pump, injector ◇ 多级～*
蒸汽喷射管 steam injection pipe
蒸汽喷射搅拌器 steam jet agitator
蒸汽喷射器 steam ejector [injector], steam-jet injector [atomizer] ◇ 四级～系统*
蒸汽喷射热 steam sparging
蒸汽喷射式燃烧器 steam-injector type burner
蒸汽喷嘴 steam jet [nozzle], steam-jet blower
蒸汽起重机 steam hoist [hauler], donkey crane
蒸汽气氛 steam atmosphere
蒸汽清洗 【环】vapour rinsing
蒸汽曲线 vapour curve
蒸汽驱动的 steam-operated
蒸汽热 steam heat
蒸汽热交换器 steam heat-exchanger
蒸汽射流 steam jet
蒸汽生产[形成] steam generation
蒸汽室 steam chest [header], dome (锅炉的)
蒸汽套 vapour blanket [jacket]
蒸汽调节阀 steam regulating valve
蒸汽调温蛇管 steam-heated tempering coil
蒸汽透平 steam turbine ◇ 中间过热式～reheat machine
蒸汽脱[去]脂装置 vapour degreaser
蒸汽雾化 steam atomization
蒸汽箱 steam chest
蒸汽消耗 steam consumption
蒸汽需要量 demand for steam
蒸汽压(力) vapour pressure [tension], steam pressure ◇ 巴博～定律*
蒸汽压曲线 vapour-pressure curve
蒸汽压图 vapour pressure chart
蒸汽-氧气鼓风 oxygen-steam blast
蒸汽养护室(混凝土用) steam-curing chamber
蒸汽-液压剪切机 steam hydraulic shears
蒸汽浴 steam-bath, vapour-bath ◇ 陶盆～*
蒸汽圆盘过滤机 steam disc filter

蒸汽云(烟囱上空的) steam plume
蒸汽增压装置 steam-raising equipment
蒸汽罩 steam hood
蒸汽蒸发 steam raising
蒸汽蒸发器 steam evaporator
蒸汽蒸馏 steam distillation
蒸汽组成 vapour composition
蒸锌炉冷凝器 【色】devanture
蒸煮 digestion, decoct
蒸煮槽 digester chamber
蒸煮器 boiler, boiling vessel, digester
蒸煮作业 boiling operation
争夺[争用] 【计】contention
整版 【计】justification, justifying
整边操作 safe-ending
整边模 trimmer
整变量(取整数值的变量) integer variable
整步 【电】synchronization, synchronizing ◇ 使~ synchronizing
整步系统 synchronous system
整常数 integer constant
整冲压轴承(非金属) fully molded type bearing
整锭场 dressing [conditioning] yard
整定 adjusting, setting ◇ 操作点~*
整定点预调 setpoint presetting
整锻 monobloc forging
整锻支承辊 solid forged back-up roll
整个的 overall, whole
整个焊缝熔透 complete joint penetration
整合的[相]【地】coherency, coherent
整件铸造 monoblock [one-piece] casting
整浇电缆管道 monolithic conduit
整截面试样 full section specimen
整径机 reeling machine [mill]
整块的 monolithic, monoblock
整块炉衬 monolithic lining
整块实体压模 single-piece solid die
整块型芯 single-piece core
整拉的 seamless
整理 arrange, reorganization, sort out, trimming, marshalling, processing, interpretation (数据的)
整理序列 【计】collating sequence
整粒 sizing ◇ 焦炭~ coke grain adjustment
整粒产品 correct sized product, 【团】closely sized product
整粒厂 sizing plant
整粒焦炭 closely graded coke
整粒矿石 sized ore
整粒炉料 【铁】closely-sized burden
整粒烧结矿 sized [screened] sinter, 【团】closely sized sinter
整粒系统 size stabilisation system
整粒作业 sizing operation
整流 【电】rectifying, rectification, commutation ◇ 阳极~*
整流比 rectifying ratio
整流不足 undercommutation
整流电抗器 commutating reactor
整流电流 rectified current
整流电路 rectification [rectifier] circuit ◇ 扼流圈输入式~*
整流堆 rectistack
整流二极管 rectifier diode
整流管 rectifier diode, rectifying tube [valve] ◇ 合金~ alloyed rectifier, 辉光放电~*
整流焊机 metal rectifier welding set
整流火花 commutation spark
整流极 commutating pole, interpole
整流接触[接点] rectifying contact
整流片 【电】commutator segment
整流器[机] rectifier (unit), commutator ◇ p-n 结~*, 干式~*, 硅二极管~*, 合金~ alloyed rectifier, 金属~ metallic [dry] rectifier, 晶体管~*, 桥式~ bridge rectifier, 热离子~ thermionic rectifier, 钨氩[吞加]~ tungar rectifier, 阻挡层~*
整流器式焊机 rectifier-type welding machine

整流器式焊接装置　rectifier welding set
整流系数　rectification factor, rectifying ratio
整流效率　rectifier efficiency, efficiency of rectification
整流效应　【理】valve effect
整流装置　rectifier plant [unit]
整流子　【电】collector, commutator
整流子电动机　commutator motor ◇ 分激～*
整流子环　commutator ring
整流作用　rectifying action
整炉顶构造　full roof construction
整模　【钢】mould preparation
整模场[间]　mould yard
整模型测量　full scale measurement
整盘磁带　magnetic tape reel
整坯场　dressing [conditioning] yard
整平机(混凝土用)　bump cutter machine
整坡曲线　grading curve
整齐排绕　【压】dead cast
整数　integer, integral number
整数部分　integer part
整数分剖　partition
整数规划(运筹学)　integer programming
整数值　integral value
整套　package
整套承包工程　turn-key project
整套电刷　brush set
整套锭模　mould set
整体　integer, bulk, monolith, one-piece, universe
整体擦除器　【计】bulk eraser
整体材料　monolith
整体车轮　solid [one-piece] wheel
整体沉降　bulk settling
整体沉降速率　bulk settling rate
整体沉箱结构　caisson monolith construction
整体冲头[阳模]　one-piece male punch
整体磁化率[系数]　bulk susceptibility
整体捣结炉缸　【铁】monolithic hearth

整体的　unsplit
整体电动机(与设备直接联成一体的)　integrated motor
整体锻钢辊　solid forged steel roll
整体锻件　solid forging
整体多件组合模(一种压模)　solid multiple-segment die
整体风箱　monolithic windbox
整体腐蚀　total corrosion
整体刚性配电板　integrally stiffened panel
整体[罐衬]钢包内衬　monolithic ladle lining
整体焊缝　full sized weld
整体焊接构架　one-piece welded frame
整体化　integration
整体环　integral ring
整体架　【压】one-piece frame
整体检验　bulk inspection, one hundred per cent inspection
整体浇铸轴承合金　integration metal
整体结构　one-piece construction, integral structure
整体结构用耐火材料[泥料]　material for monolithic construction
整体卷筒(非涨缩式)　solid drum
整体拉制[拉伸的]　solid-drawn
整体料斗　【铁】one-piece hopper
整体料钟　【铁】one-piece bell
整体炉衬　【冶】monolithic lining
整体炉衬材料　monolithic lining material
整体炉床[底]　hearth monolith
整体炉底(转炉的)　solid bottom
整体模　solid [one-piece] die, solid mold
整体模型　【铸】solid [one-piece, full, unsplit] pattern
整体耐火材料　monolithic [cast] refractory
整体耐火结构　monolithic refractory construction
整体耐火炉衬　Monolithic refracto
整体耐火面层　monolithic refractory surface

整体喷管[嘴]	one-piece nozzle
整体皮带轮	solid belt pulley
整体清除器	【计】bulk eraser
整体熔模铸造法	block mould process
整体散射	bulk scattering
整体砂箱	【铸】tight flask
整体烧结[浇铸]的	monolithic
整体石墨电解槽	monolithic graphite cell
整体石墨坩埚	monolithic graphite crucible
整体式	solid type
整体式淬火炉	integral quench furnace
整体式钢筋混凝土结构	monolithic reinforced concrete structure
整体式建筑[构造]	monolithic construction
整体式路缘	monolithic curb
整体塑性墙	monolithic plastic wall
整体托圈(转炉的)	【钢】integral ring
整体相位	bulk phase
整体芯棒[心轴]	solid mandrel
整体性质	bulk property, mass behaviour
整体压模	single-piece solid die
整体应变	bulk strain
整体永久衬	integral permanent lining
整体轧辊	solid roll
整体轴承	solid [integral, cutless] bearing
整体轴承合金	integration metal
整体铸件	monoblock [one-piece, single, solid] casting
整体铸造	integral [solid] casting
整体铸造的	moulded-on
整型	integer, 【铸】dressing
整形	shaping, trimming, restriking 【铸】coining ◇ 爆炸～explosive sizing
整形电路	shaping circuit
整形锻压	【压】restriking
整修工具	dressing [truing] tool ◇ 多金刚石[镶多粒金刚石的]～*,三金刚石[镶有三粒金刚石的]～*,镶一粒金刚石的～ single (point) diamond dressing tool
整修压机	trimming press
整轧车轮	solid rolled wheel, one-piece wheel
整轧车轮轧机	solid wheel rolling mill
整轧钢轮	wrought-steel wheel
整轧轮箍	solid rolled tyre
整轧轮心	solid rolled centre
整轧坯	solid billet
整闸器	brake adjuster
整直电流	rectified current
整轴承	bush bearing
整柱石	{K$_2$O·4CaO·4BeO·Al$_2$O$_3$·24SiO$_2$·H$_2$O} milarite, giufite
整铸的	cast-in block
整铸模	one-piece die
整铸舌形模	one-piece bridge die
整铸(双面)模板	cast plate
整铸[整体]阴模	【压】simple one-piece female die
正八面体	octahedron
正半(棱)锥体	positive hemipyramid
正比关系	straight-line dependence
正比计数器	proportional counter (PC)
正比计数器光谱计	proportional-counter spectrometer
正比(例)	direct ratio [proportion]
正比例的	directly proportional
正比区域(应力应变的)	【压】proportional region
正常白班	normal day shift
正常闭合[闭路]	normal close
正常磁导率	normal permeability
正常磁感应曲线	normal induction curve
正常磁化曲线	normal magnetization curve
正常磁滞[滞后]回线	normal hysteresis loop
正常磁滞[滞后]损失	normal hysteresis loss
正常电子能带	normal electron energy band
正常额定功率	normal rated power

正常额定值 【电】normal rating
正常负荷 【铁】regular burden
正常钢(球光体全部为片状结构) normal steel
正常工作制度 medium duty
正常焊缝 normal weld
正常化 normalizing, normalization
正常价 【化】normal valency
正常价化合物 normal valency compound
正常晶粒度金属 【金】metal of normal grain size
正常开路[断开] normal open
正常料 【铁】regular burden
正常炉况 【铁】regular working ◇ 高炉～
正常磨蚀抗力 normalized erosion resistance
正常能带 【半】normal band
正常能级 normal (energy) level
正常凝固(杂质)分布 normal freezing distribution
正常偏析 【金】normal segregation
正常生产[作业] normal practice
正常矢量 normal vector
正常水化水泥 normally hydrated cement
正常松装密度 normal settled bulk density
正常填角焊缝 flat (faced) fillet weld
正常透气性 normal permeability
正常条件 normal condition
正常弯曲试验(焊缝的) normal bend test
正常维修 normal maintenance
正常涡流损失 normal eddy-current loss
正常误差律 normal law of errors
正常相位 normal phase
正常压力 normal pressure (n.p.)
正常焰 balanced flame
正常硬度 normal hardness
正常运行时间 【计】up time
正常组织 normal structure
正长石 orthose {(K, Na)(AlSi$_3$O$_8$)}, orthoclase {KAlSi$_3$O$_8$}
正车 forward running

正齿 spur
正齿轮 spur wheel
正齿轮传动装置 spur gear drive, spur gearing
正齿轮减速机 spur-gear speed reducer, cylindrical reducer
正齿小齿轮 spur pinion
正催化剂 positive catalyst
正当理由 justification
正导线(热电偶的) positive leg
正碲的 telluric
正电 positive electricity ◇ 带～的溶胶 positively charged sol, 接～positive power connection
正电荷 positive charge
正电极的 positive terminal
正电接头 positive contact
正电势[位] (electro)positive potential
正电性 electropositivity
正电性金属 electropositive metal
正电性杂质 electropositive impurities
正电子 positive electron, positively charged electron, positron, anti-electron
正电子湮没[灭] positron annihilation
正电子湮没[灭]寿命 life of positron annihilation spectrum
正钒酸{H$_3$VO$_4$} ortho-vanadic acid
正反铲挖土机 convertible shovel
正反两面挤压 opposed extruding
正反射 regular reflection
正反锁口钢板桩 reverse-lock sheet piling bar
正反向比 front to rear[back] ratio
正反应 positive reaction
正方边的 square-edged
正方矾石{Al$_2$O$_3$·SO$_3$·9H$_2$O} aluminite
正方管 square tubing
正方加工 squaring
正方晶系 tetragonal (system), quadratic system
正方势[位]阱 square-well potential
正方形 square, quadrate

正复型 【金】positive replica [transparency]
正复型(制备)法 positive replica
正负 plus-minus
正负变换器 sign changer
正负峰间幅值 peak(-to)-peak value
正割(弹性)模数 secant modulus
正汞化合物 mercuric compound
正拱 right arch
正构化合物 normal compound
正钴的 cobaltous
正规方程 normal equation
正规方式 normal mode
正规分布 regular [normal] distribution
正规化 normalization, regulariation, standardization
正规化常数 normalization constant
正规溶液 regular solution
正硅酸钙 calcium orthosilicate
正硅酸铁 fayalite
正硅酸盐 orthosilicate
正硅钛铈矿 orthochevkinite
正焊(半导体材料的) face up bonding
正火 normalization, normalizing ◇ 布伦纳~法*，光亮~ bright normalizing, 两次~ double normalizing
正火处理 normalizing, homogenization treatment ◇ 高温~*
正火钢 normalized steel
正火机理 mechanism of normalizing
正火炉 normalizing furnace ◇ 带材连续式~*，控制气氛连续~*
正火氧化皮(薄钢板缺陷) normalizing scale
正火作业线 normalizing line
正基 positive group
正畸变 positive [pincushion] distortion
正极 (同"阳极")
正极性 positive [normal] polarity, 【焊】straight polarity (S.P.)
正挤压 forward extrusion
正价 positive valence

正尖晶石 positive spinel
正尖晶石型铁氧体 normal spinel ferrite
正交 orthogonality ◇ 非~系统 non-orthogonal system
正交磁场 cross field
正交磁场发电机 cross connected generator
正交磁化(强度) (同"垂直磁化(强度)")
正交电刷 quadrature brush
正交多项式分解 orthogonal polynomial decomposition
正交方向 cross direction
正交分量 quadrature component
正交各向异性层压复合材料 orthotropic laminate composite
正交功率(无功功率) quadrature power
正交互作用能 positive interaction energy
正交挤压 【压】cross extrusion
正交剪应力 orthogonal shear stress
正交晶胞 rhombic cell
正交力 normal force
正交流动 cross-flow
正交流动区域精炼炉[提纯器] 【冶】cross-flow zone refiner ◇ 端部加料~*，平行加料~*
正(交)六方晶轴 orthohexagonal crystal axes
正交设计 orthogonal design
正交试验 orthogonal experiment [test, design]
正交试验法 orthogonal method
正交系晶体 rhombic crystal
正交系统 orthogonal system
正交轴 quadrature axes
正接 【焊】straight polarity
正解法 direct method
正抗蚀剂 positive resist
正拉(伸内)应力 normal traction
正冷却速率曲线(合金热分析用) direct rate curve
正离子 (同"阳离子")

正离子发射　positive(-ion) emission
正磷酸镧{$LaPO_4$}　lanthanum orthophosphate
正磷酸铈{$CePO_4$}　cerous orthophosphate
正磷酸双氧铀[正磷酸铀酰]{$(UO_2)_3(PO_4)_2$}　uranyl orthophosphate
正磷酸锶{$Sr_3(PO_4)_2$}　strontium orthophosphate
正磷酸镱{$YbPO_4$}　ytterbium orthophosphate
正铝酸{H_3AlO_3}　ortho-aluminic acid
正逻辑　【计】positive logic
正面　front, face, 【焊】face side（焊缝的）
正面导向弯曲试验（钢管的）　face guided bend test
正面宽度　frontage
正面拉杆　positive tie
正面投影　orthographic projection
正面图　front view (FV), elevation
正面弯曲试验（焊缝朝外的）　face-bend (test)
正面弯曲试样　face-bend (test) specimen
正母线　positive bus-bar
正目镜　positive eyepiece
正镍(的)　nickelous
正配孔型　straight pass ◇ 梁形～straight beam pass
正膨胀　normal dilatation
正偏差　positive deviation, plus tolerance
正偏差轧制　【压】overgauge
正偏析　positive [normal] segregation
正片(的)　positive
正片透明度　positive transparency
正切　【数】tangency, tangent
正切方向　tangential direction
正切检流计　tangent galvanometer
正切近似法　tangential approximation
正氢氧化铁{$Fe(OH)_3$}　ortho-ferric hydroxide
正区　【数】plus zone
正曲率　positive curvature
正确曝光　correct exposure

正确性　correctness, exactness
正刃型位错　positive edge dislocation
正容差　positive allowance
正色的　orthochromatic
正射投影　orthographic projection
正射线　positive [anode] rays
正砷酸　arsenic acid
正失真　positive [pincushion] distortion
正石髓{SiO_2}　quartzine
正式试验　official test
正铈化合物　cerous compound
正视　front view (FV)
正视图　front elevation [view], elevation (elev.)
正手(气焊)法　【焊】forehand method
正数　positive number [value]
正四方体晶型　tetragonal form ◇ 锡金属～*
正酸　ortho acid
正铊的　thallic
正态分布　normal distribution
正态随机变量　normal random variable
正态随机数　【数】normal random number
正态(振荡)模式　normal mode
正钛酸盐　orthotitanate
正锑的　stibial
正调节　positive governing
正(铁)亚铁的　ferriferous
正铁氧体　orthoferrite
正铜的　cupric
正透镜　positive lens
正外延　regular epitaxy
正位错　positive dislocation
正温度系数　positive temperature coefficient (PTC)
正温度系数热敏电阻　posistor, positive temperature coefficient thermistor
正钨酸　ortho-tungstic acid
正吸引压头　positive suction head ◇ 净～*
正锡的　stannic
正弦波　sine wave, sinusoid

正弦(波)信号 sinusoidal signal, sinusoid
正弦波型磁结构 sinusoidal magnetic structure
正弦关系(式) sinusoidal relation
正弦规 sine bar
正弦函数 sine [sinusoidal] function
正弦检流计 sine galvanometer
正弦量[值] sinusoidal quantity
正弦曲线 sine curve, sinusoid
正弦曲线分量 harmonic component
正弦曲线运动 sinuous movement
正弦(式结晶器)振动 【连铸】sinusoidal mould oscillation
正弦式近似法 sinusoidal approximation
正弦振动 sinusoidal vibration
正像 positive image
正向 forward [normal] direction, positive
正向电阻 forward resistance
正向读出 【计】forward reading
正向挤压 direct [straight-forward] extrusion ◇ 非润滑～
正向挤压法 direct [forward] extrusion ◇ 不加润滑的～ direct unlubricated extrusion method
正向计数器 forward counter
正向-逆向联合挤压 backward and forward extruding
正向偏压 forward bias
正向散射 forward scattering
正向探测器[探头] normal probe
正(向)旋压 forward spinning
正型杂质 p-type impurity
正序电抗 positive-sequence reactance
正压 positive [superatmospheric] pressure
正压吹管 positive-pressure torch
正压电效应 direct piezo-electric effect
正压炉 positive-pressure furnace
正压煤气燃烧器 pressure-gas burner
正压排气机 positive-pressure exhauster
正压烧结 pressure sintering, sintering under pressure
正压缩 direct draft

正压通风 positive draught
正压头 positive head
正压下 direct draft
正压状态 barotropic state
正压作业 positive pressure operation
正盐 normal salt
正应变 normal strain
正应力 positive [normal, direct] stress
正余量 positive allowance
正在送风 【铁】on-blast
正则方程 normal [regular] equation
正则型 normal mode
正值 positive value
正置辊(辊道的) straight table rolls
正质子 proton
正轴面体 orthopinacoid
正砖格 straight checker
正子 anti-electron
正坐标 【数】normal co-ordinate
政府津贴 【企】government subsidy
挣裂 bursting
挣脱力 break away force
帧 【电】frame
帧扫描 vertical sweep, frame scan
证据 evidence, proof, testmony
证明 evidence, proof, justification, verification
证(明)书 certificate
证明有理 justification
证券 bond, bill
证实 authentication, demonstration, confirmation, identification, verification
证实卡 identification card
枝晶 dendrite (crystal), fir tree crystal, arborescent [tree-like, pine-tree] crystal ◇ 网格[蜂窝,细胞]状～*
枝晶臂 dendritic arm
枝晶带 dendritic zone
枝晶锆 zirconium dendrite
枝晶间腐蚀 interdendritic corrosion
枝晶间结构 interdendritic structure
枝晶间浸蚀 interdendritic attack

枝晶间孔隙[疏松] interdendritic porosity
枝晶间偏析 interdendritic segregation
枝晶偏析晶体 cored crystal
枝晶区 dendritic zone
枝晶钽 tantalum dendrite
枝晶长大 dendrite growth
枝晶轴 dendritic branch
枝晶组织 dendritic [pine-tree, arborescent] structure, fir tree structure
枝聚物 branched polymer
枝芯 【铸】core branch
枝型聚合物 branched polymer
枝形吊灯架 chandelier
枝状动胶菌 zoogloea ramigera
枝状结晶 【金】branched dendrite
枝状晶带 dendritic ribbon
枝状晶体 dentritic crystal
枝状裂纹 branched crack
枝状生长 dendrite [dendritic] growth
枝状生长的蹼状晶体 dendritic grown web crystal
支臂斗轮式堆取料机 wheel-on-bottom stacker/reclaimer
支臂斗轮式取料机 wheel-on-bottom reclaimer
支臂倾角 boom angle
支撑 support, strut, brace, 【建】distance bar
支撑板 shoe plate
支撑(构)件 【建】support member
支撑结构 structural support
支撑梁 supporting beam, brace summer
支撑螺栓 clamping bolt
支撑物 spur, stilt, upholder
支撑型砂用箱挡[箱带] sand edge
支撑砖 rider brick
支承 (fulcrum) bearing, supporting ◇ 刃型~blade bearing
支承鞍架 supporting saddle
支承板 bearing [support] plate, 【铸】backing plate, carrier blade (链式炉内运输机的)

支承算条 supporting grid
支承臂端 border of supporting arm
支承点 bearing point
支承垫圈 bearing disc
支承杆 supporting lever [rod], carrying arm, cramp bar, support column
支承格框 supporting grillage
支承拱的壁柱 respond
支承构架 supporting frame
支承辊 【压】backing [backup, dummy, support] roll, supporting roller, back(ing) up roll ◇ 外层~*, 弯曲~组*
支承辊传动的四辊式轧机 four high driven mill
支承辊辊套(组合式) backup roll sleeve ◇ 组合式~rim
支承辊换辊装置 backup roll changing rig, backup roll extractor
支承辊磨床 backup roll grinding machine
支承辊弯曲 back-up roll bending (BURB)
支承辊心轴(组合式) backup roll arbor
支承辊直径 backup roll diameter
支承辊轴承 backup (roll) bearing
支承辊轴承座[盒] backup (roll) chock
支承环 supporting [back-up] ring
支承脊橡梁 【建】dragon beam
支承件 backup piece, anchor
支承结构 supporting structure
支承块 backup block, bearing piece, rest pad
支承力 bearing force
支承梁 rest beam, (导卫装置的) rest bar, cramp
支承轮 supporting trunnion roller, weight bearing wheel
支承面 (bearing) surface, carrying plane
支承面积 bearing area
支承钼丝 molybdenum support wire
支承能力 bearing power
支承墙 supporting wall
支承强度 bearing strength

支承台	rest
支承筒	【冶】supporting cylinder, carrying cylinder（矿热电炉的）
支承凸缘	support lug, bearing flange
支承系统	backup [support] system
支承压力	bearing pressure
支承压力不可调整的辊式矫直机	backed up roller leveller without pressure regulation
支承压力可调整的辊式矫直机	backed up pressure regulating roller leveller
支承液体（区域熔炼的）	supporting liquid
支承应变	bearing strain
支承轧辊	【压】backing up roll ◇ 组合式～ sleeved back-up roll
支承轴承	backing [block, support(ing)] bearing
支承柱	support column
支承砖	support brick
支承座	fulcrum bearing
支持	holding, support, sustain, backing
支持电极	supporting electrode
支持辊辊轴	backup shaft
支持[承]架	supporting rack
支持系统	【计】support system
支出	expenses, outlay, outgo
支道	bypath
支点	fulcrum, pivot (point)
支墩坝	buttress dam
支反应	side reaction, by-reaction
支风管	tuyere stock
支管	branch line [pipe], side tube, bypass, pipe branch ◇ 送风～【铁】blast connection
支管道	subsidiary conduit
支管线	bypass line
支管装置	manifolding
支化（作用）	branching
支架	support (frame), (supporting) stand, holder (-up), holdfast, rack, rest, (bearing) carrier, bearing, backing, superstructure ◇ 带～的炉顶 scaffold top
支架炉焙烧	shelf burning
支架喷射器	stand sprayer
支架式料仓	【铁】suspension-type of bin
支脚	foot, stand bar
支局	substation
支靠式焊条电弧焊	touch welding
支链	branched chain
支链伯胺	primary branched amine
支链乙醇[酒精]	branch chain(ed) alcohol
支链仲胺	branched secondary amine
支溜槽	split chute
支流	branch, side stream, ramification
支流反应	side stream reaction
支流苛化	【色】side stream causticization
支路	branch (circuit), bypass
支脉（山脉的）	branch (range)
支配	control, dominating, governing, arrange
支喷管[嘴]	branch nozzle
支票	check, cheque, bill, 【企】draught, draft
支圈	【铁】mantle (ring), ring support, 【压】curb（锻造用）◇ 高炉～*, 炉腰～*
支枢	pivot
支枢托架	fulcrum bracket
支枢轴承	pivot bearing
支线	branch line, bypass
支线辊道	branch roller table
支烟道	bypass flue
支援系统	support system
支轴	fulcrum
支柱	pillar, support, brace, prop, strut, mast, post, backbone
支柱垫板	foot plate
支柱绝缘子	support insulator
支桩	bearing pile
支座	abutment (abut.), seat, pedestal, footstep, supporting seat, bearer, bearing, carrier, holder
支座大砖	seating block

知识产权	intellectual property
知识系统	knowledge-based system
知识型的	knowledge-based
脂肪酸	fatty acid ◇ 耐~的 fatty acid resistant
脂肪族化合物	aliphatic compound
脂垢坑(薄板或带钢的)	grease or dirt pit
脂光石	elaeolite, lythrodes
脂褐帘石	cerin(e)
脂环族的	alicyclic
脂铅轴矿	{(Pb, Th, Ca) UO$_3$·nH$_2$O} gummite
之字路程	Z-path
之字线	zigzag, back shunt
之字形管道	zigzag duct
之字形窑	zigzag kiln
之字形轧机	zigzag mill
织带运送烧结炉	mesh-belt conveyer furnace
织构	texture ◇ 变形~ deformation texture,低~钢 low-texture steel,戈斯~*
织构化材料	【金】textured material
织构(化)钢	textured steel
织构化金属	textured metal
织构应力	(同"海恩应力")
织构硬化	texture hardening
织皮机	armouring [braiding] machine
织网运输带	mesh belt
织物	cloth, fabric, textile
织物衬垫	fabric lining
织物酚醛塑胶	textolite
织物过滤除尘器	fabric dust collector
织物(过)滤器	fabric [cloth] filter
织造物	fabrics
职工(人数)	work force
职务	post, duties, job, function, office
职业	occupation, profession
职业病	occupational disease
职业照射	occupational exposure
职责	duty, obligation responsibility, liability
直拔的	【压】rack drawn
直臂桨式混合机	arm straight paddle mixer
直臂搅拌机	straight-arm stirrer
直边	straight edge [flange], square edge (焊管的)
直边窄带材	skelp
直槽式铸机	vertical slot caster
直齿齿条	spur rack
直齿伞齿轮	straight [common] bevel gear
直齿小齿轮	spur pinion
直齿圆柱齿轮	straight spur gear, straight-cut gear
直尺	ruler, rectilinear scale, straight edge [scale]
直吹管	【铁】blast [blow, belly] pipe
直吹式燃烧	direct-firing
直达车线路	through-traffic track
直达列车	through train
直读秤	direct-reading balance
直读光谱(分析)仪	direct-reading spectrograph, quantometer
直读式分光计	direct-reading spectrometer
直读式仪表	direct-reading instrument [meter]
直读式转速表	direct reading tachometer
直度	straightness
直方图	【数】histogram
直缝焊	straight welding
直缝焊管	butt welded pipe [tube], straight welded tubing ◇ 高频~技术*
直缝焊管机	straight seam pipe mill, butt weld pipe mill
直辐(皮)带轮	straight-armed pulley
直氟碳钙铈矿	synchisite
直股钢板桩	straight web piling bar
直观 X 射线照相术	direct-view X-ray technique
直观推断法	heuristics
直观显示部件	【计】visual display unit
直观性	visualizability

直观研究	full scale investigation
直规	ruler
直焊道	string bead
直火蒸发	direct-firing evaporation
直记(式)的	direct-recording
直尖尖顶锤	straight peen hammer
直浇口	down [running, pouring] gate, down runner, downgate sprue, downsprue, sprue hole ◇ 切除~sprue cutting
直浇口棒	sprue stick
直浇口井[压痕](防溅)	sprue base
直浇口窝	sprue base, cushion
直浇口延长部分	downgate extension
直浇口组装件	trumpet assembly
直角	right angle
直角边缘	square bevel
直角光子	【铸】angle sleeker
直角规	try square
直角回转带[直角挂轮皮带]	quarter turn belt, quarter-twist belt
直角溜槽	right-angle chute
直角排送皮带	half-crossed belt
直角弯头	elbow [quarter, normal, 1/4] bend
直角(形)杠杆	bell crank (lever), bent lever [crank]
直角坐标	【数】rectangular coordinates
直角坐标分量	Cartesian component
直角坐标图	diagram in rectangular coordinates, Cartesian scale diagram
直角坐标系	rectangular [Cartesian] coordinate system
直角坐标轴	rectangular axes
直接爆炸成形	direct explosive forming
直接编码	【计】direct coding
直接编制	【计】direct organization
直接布料	direct feed
直接测定[测量]	direct measurement
直接插入函数	【计】in-line function
直接插入子程序	【计】in-line subroutine
直接差分法	【数】direct difference method
直接沉淀法	direct precipitation process
直接成型	direct forming ◇ 电磁脉冲~(作用)
直接冲击(试验)	direct action impact (D.A.I.)
直接出钢	direct tapping
直接处理	immediate treatment
直接传动	direct drive (dd.) ◇ 电动机~direct motor drive
直接传动辊	direct-coupled roll
直接传动机器	direct-drive machine
直接传动式剪切机	direct-driven shears
直接串联电弧炉	direct series arc furnace
直接吹炼法	direct smelting in converter
直接萃取	direct extraction
直接淬火(渗碳余热的)	direct hardening [quenching]
直接淬火法	direct quenching method
直接淬火时效	direct quench aging
直接存储器存取	【计】direct memory access (DMA)
直接存取	【计】direct access ◇ 可拆装的~存储器
直接存取通道显示器	direct access channel display
直接带隙半导体	direct-gap semiconductor, direct band-gap semiconductor
直接地址	【计】direct [immediate] address
直接点燃	straight firing
直接电弧	direct arc
直接电弧加热	direct-arc heating
直接电弧加热炉	direct-arc heating furnace
直接电弧炉	direct-arc (electric) furnace ◇ 凯勒~【冶】Keller furnace, 炉底不导电式~*, 炉底导电~*
直接电弧熔化炉	direct-arc melting furnace
直接电弧熔炼法	direct-arc melting method
直接电弧熔铸	direct arc-cast
直接电化学(腐蚀试验)法	【金】direct electrochemical method

直接电解精炼　direct electrorefining
直接电热淬火法　direct electric process
直接电阻烧结　direct resistance sintering
直接定向辐射　head on radiation
直接定氧技术　direct oxygen determination technique
直接毒性　【环】direct toxicity
直接读数　direct reading
直接断弧断路器　【电】plain-break breaker
直接法　direct process [method]
直接反射　direct reflection
直接反应　direct reaction
直接访问存储器　【计】direct access storage device (DASD)
直接访问文件　【计】direct access file
直接粉末还原　direct-route powder reduction
直接辐射[照]　direct radiation
直接观测电子显微镜　【金】direct observation electron microscope
直接观察　direct [immediate] observation, direct viewing
直接荷载　direct load
直接合金化　direct alloying
直接弧熔铸锭　direct arc-cast (ingot)
直接还原　direct reduction (D.R.) ◇ HIB法～厂 HIB facilities, 卡林－多姆纳费特回转窑～及脱硫法*, 煤基～工艺*, 米德雷克斯法～厂*
直接还原法　direct reduction (process) ◇ ACAR[爱立斯·恰默斯公司造块]～*, R-N～*, SL～*, 阿姆柯～ Armco process, 贝格勒夫铁矿石～*, 反应罐～ retort process, 菲奥～*, 弗里曼～*, 格伦达尔铁矿石～*, 哈曼铁矿石～*, 赫斯加费尔铁矿石竖炉低温～*, 霍恩塞多段回转窑低温～ Hornsey process, 可控气氛回转窑～*, 莱基～ Leckie process, 连续流化床～ADIprocess, 马达拉斯～*, 马依尔－莫科尔～*, 莫尔斯竖炉～ Morse process, 穆索回转反应罐～ Musso process, 喷射熔炼炉～*, 施蒂策尔贝格尔～*, 斯塔桑诺～*, 斯特拉杰克－尤地回转窑－电炉组合～*, 斯托拉回转炉～ Stora process, 威贝格～*, 住友粉尘～*

直接还原(法)炼钢工艺流程　DRP-steelmaking flowsheet
直接还原钢　direct-process steel
直接还原回转窑　direct reduction kiln
直接还原机理　mechanism of direct reduction
直接还原可锻铸铁　direct-process malleable iron
直接还原炼钢厂　direct reduction-based steel mill
直接还原炼钢(法)　DR-based steelmaking
直接还原炉　direct reduction furnace [kiln] ◇ 赫氏～ Herreshof furnace
直接还原率[度]　percentage of direct reduction, ratio of direct reduction
直接还原铁　direct reduction [reduced] iron (DRI), DRI iron ◇ 块状～*
直接还原用炉料[原料]　direct reduction feed
直接回火　direct tempering
直接回流(换热)　【团】direct recoup
直接回热集流管　【团】direct recuperation header
直接火焰加热　direct-fire heating
直接挤压　(同"正向挤压")
直接给料　direct feed
直接记录　direct-recording
直接记录式电磁示波器　direct writing electromagnetic oscillograph
直接加热　direct heating [firing], straight firing
直接加热带卷退火炉　direct-fired coil furnace
直接加热电弧炉　direct electric arc furnace, direct-heating arc furnace
直接加热电阻炉　direct resistance furnace
直接加热法(工件通电流加热)　snead process

直接加热干燥机　direct-heat drier
直接加热炉　direct-heating furnace
直接加热热处理炉　direct-fired furnace
直接加热式烘干平台　direct-fired drying floor
直接加热窑　directly fired kiln
直接加压的热压室式压铸机　direct pressure hot-chamber machine
直接－间接加热干燥机　direct-indirect heating drier ◇ 转筒式～*
直接键合结构　direct-bonded structure
直接浇口　【铸】direct [drop] gate
直接浇铸　【钢】direct casting [pouring]
直接接触爆炸成形工艺(板件的)　direct contact process [technique]
直接接触净化　【环】direct-contact cleaning
直接结合　direct-bonding
直接结合碱性砖　direct bonded basic brick
直接结合镁铬砖　direct-bonded periclase-chrome brick
直接结合耐火材料　direct-bonded refractory
直接结合砖　direct-bonded brick
直接金属(直接由矿石炼得)　direct metal
直接浸出　straight leaching
直接经营成本　direct operating cost
直接经营设施　direct operational features
直接控制　direct [self-actuated] control
直接控制连接　direct control connection
直接控制微程序　direct control microprogram
直接冷却　direct cooling
直接冷却器　direct cooler
直接冷却水　【环】contact cooling water
直接冷硬[激冷]　direct chilling (DC)
直接冷硬[激冷]铸造　DC (direct chill) casting
直接联系[连接]的　direct-connected
直接联轴器[直接连接]　direct coupling
直接炼钢　direct [one-step] steel making

直接炼钢法　direct steel process ◇ 弗洛丁电炉～Flodin process, 舍伍德～*, 特怀曼综合团矿～Twyman process, 循环式～cyclo-steel process
直接炼铁　direct ironmaking ◇ 流态化庆～炉*
直接炼铁法　direct iron process (DIP) ◇ O.R.F. 移动式炉箅～*, 奥卡普～Or-carb process, 布歇回转窑～Roucher process, 带式烧结机电炉联合～*, 杜佩伊～Dupey process, 多姆纳费特固体燃料回转窑～Domnarfvet process 格尔特～Gurlt process, 霍恩塞－威斯三回转炉～*, 加鲁塞尔天然气感应电炉～*, 卡瓦诺活动炉箅～*, 凯普－布拉塞特～*
直接炼铜　direct smelting of copper
直接硫酸铵法　【焦】direct sulphate process
直接卤化　direct halogenation
直接氯化　direct chlorination
直接氯化设备　direct-chlorination unit
直接码　【计】direct code
直接目测法　【金】direct vision method
直接耦合(传动, 联轴器)　through coupling
直接耦合放大器　direct-coupled amplifier
直接耦合晶体管逻辑电路　direct-coupled transistor logic (D.C.T.L.)
直接排放　【环】direct discharge
直接喷燃器　direct fire burner
直接起[启]动　line start, direct-on starting
直接起运矿石　direct-shipping ore
直接气体还原　direct gaseous reduction
直接汽化　direct boiling
直接驱动油压机　direct-drive oil-hydraulic press
直接燃烧　direct firing
直接热源　direct heat source
直接热轧　hot direct rolling (HDR)
直接熔炼　direct smelting ◇ 原矿～direct

ore smelting
直接扫描 direct scanning
直接闪光焊 straight flash welding
直接烧煤焙烧 【团】direct coal firing
直接生产费用 direct operating cost
直接试验 on-line test, straightway testing
直接书写记录器[仪] direct-writing recorder
直接数字控制 direct digital control (D.D.C.)
直接酸浸 direct acid leaching
直接损失 direct [straight-forward] losses
直接通地 dead earth
直接通电 direct passage of current
直接通电加热淬火法 tension electric process
直接通风炉 straight-draft furnace
直接投资费用和特许权费 【企】fees and royalties from direct investment
直接显示器 【计】direct display
直接线束 direct beam
直接相减(指令) 【计】direct substract
直接询问 【计】direct access inquiry
直接寻址 【计】direct addressing
直接氧化 direct oxidation (D.O.)
直接氧化浸出 D.O. leaching
直接氧化试验 D.O. test
直接冶炼法 direct process ◇ 斯科特西～*
直接印相(从底片) direct print
直接应力疲劳试验机 direct stress fatigue machine
直接油泵传动 direct oil pump drive
直接跃迁 direct transition
直接再拉伸 direct redrawing
直接在线测定法 direct on-line measuring method
直接造球用原料 【团】direct pellet feed
直接造渣 【冶】immediate fluxing
直接轧制 direct rolling ◇ 粉末～*, 连铸坯～*
直接照明 direct lighting [illumination]

直(接蒸)馏 straight (run) distillation
直接蒸馏产物 product of straight distillation
直接蒸馏法 straight distillation process
直接蒸汽 open steam
直接蒸汽蛇管 open-steam coil
直接指令 【计】direct instruction
直接制氨法 direct ammonia process
直接助熔 【冶】immediate fluxing
直接转变 【理】direct transition
直接装料 direct charge [charging]
直结晶器 【连铸】straight mould ◇ 立式～连铸机*
直井焙烧炉 ◇ 赫伦施米特～*
直井炉 shaft-type furnace
直径 diameter (dia., diam.) ◇ 粗～(线材) heavy gauge, 马丁[定方等分]～ Martin diameter, 斯托克斯～ Stokes diameter, 细～(线材) light gauge
直距线 bee line
直孔型 straight pass ◇ 梁形～ straight beam pass
直立火道式焦炉 vertical-flue oven
直立式转炉 【钢】upright converter
直立位置 upright position
直立圆筒混合机 end-over-end mixer
直立支杆 upright
直链 straight [linear] chain
直链醇 straight chain alcohol
直列式冷却器 【团】straight cooler
直裂纹 vertical crack
直馏产物 product of straight distillation
直馏沥青 straight-run pitch [bitumen, asphalt]
直流 direct current (DC), constant [continuous] current, uniflow
直流饱和电抗器 direct-current saturable reactor
直流并激[分激, 并绕]电动机 DC shunt (-wound) motor
直流测定[测量] direct-current measurement

直流传导法(探伤) direct-current conduction method
直流传动(装置) DC-drive ◇ 轧机用大功率～"
直流磁场 direct magnetic field
直流磁导率 DC permeability
直流磁化(作用) direct-current magnetization
直流磁控制溅射沉积 DC magnetron sputtering deposition
直流磁力接触器 DC magnetic contactor
直流等离子炬 DC plasma torch
直流等离子体 direct-current plasma
直流等离子体喷射(法) direct-current plasma jet
直流电 direct current (dc, DC), unidirectional current
直流电磁场 DC electromagnetic field
直流电磁连铸 DC electromagnetic continuous casting
直流电磁铸造[浇注] DC electromagnetic casting
直流电动机 direct current motor (D.C.M.), DC motor, continuous current motor ◇ 强制通风式～"
直流电动机控制 direct-current motor control
直流电焊 DC welding
直流电焊机 DC welding machine
直流电耗 DC power consumption
直流电弧 direct-current arc ◇ 连续～电源
直流电弧焊 direct-current arc welding, eletronic arc welding
直流电弧炉 DC electric arc furnace, DC EAF
直流电极 DC(-type) electrode
直流电解清洗 direct-current cleaning
直流电路 DC circuit
直流电能 direct-current energy
直流电压表 direct-current voltmeter
直流电源 DC (power) supply, direct current main (d.c.m.)
直流(电源)断电 DC dump
直流电阻 direct-current resistance
直流发电机 DC (direct-current) generator, constant-current [continuous-current] generator ◇ 电动～motordynamo
直流反极性 direct-current reversed polarity (DCRP)
直流放大机 metadyne
直流放大器 【电】direct-current amplifier
直流分量抑制器 DC suppressor unit
直流辅助传动(装置) DC-auxiliary drive
直流辅助电动机 DC auxiliary motor ◇ 恒压～"
直流干线 direct-current main
直流钢包炉 DC ladle furnace
直流焊接 DC welding
直流弧焊机 DC arc welder
直流回路 DC circuit
直流开关设备 DC-switch gear
直流可控电抗器 direct-current controllable reactor
直流连铸 DC continuous casting
直流炼钢电弧炉技术 DC arc furnace steelmaking technology
直流排放流程(冷却水的) 【环】once-through scheme
直流排放系统 once-through system
直流平波扼流圈 DC-smoothing choke
直流绕组 DC winding
直流式水冷系统 (同"无回收水冷系统")
直流输电 DC transmission
直流无电容断续电弧 intermittent D-C noncapacitive arc
直流线路断路器 DC circuit breaker
直流蓄热(法) 【冶】downflow [straight] regeneration
直流抑制器 DC suppressor unit
直流正极性 direct-current straight polarity (D.C.S.P.)
直螺脚绝缘子 bracket insulator

直配孔型轧制法（钢梁的）	straight (flange) method
直喷式烧嘴	direct-type gun
直切管端	plain end
直切口	square end
直切（正边）头尾	squared ends
直取	reclaiming
直热式阴极	heater [direct-heated] cathode
直热窑	directly fired kiln
直熔锭	dingot, direct ingot
直熔锭法（铀的）	dingot process
直熔锭还原弹外壳	dingot shell
直熔锭还原反应	dingot bomb reaction
直熔锭还原钢弹	dingot bomb
直熔锭块	dingot regulus
直熔锭清理	dingot cleaning
直熔锭修整	dingot scalping
直熔金属锭	dingot metal
直熔矿石	direct smelting ore
直熔铀锭	uranium dingot, dingot uranium
直闪石{(Mg,Fe)SiO$_3$}	anthophyllite
直射脉冲	direct impulse
直射式喷嘴	direct-type gun
直射束	straight beam
直射影像（荧光镜像）	direct image
直升火焰	up-draught fire
直升烟道	offtake stack
直示摄谱（分析）仪	direct-reading spectrograph
直收率	direct recovery
直通阀	straight-through valve
直通馈电线圈	feed through coil
直通螺栓	through bolt
直通式加热炉	push-through furnace
直通式炉	continuously passing furnace
直通式迷宫（密封）	straight-through labyrinth
直通铁路线	straight-through track
直通线	through-traffic track
直通旋塞	straight cock
直筒溜槽	straight chute
直投影像	direct-shadow image
直头机（带材等用）	coil opener [peeler], pulling device, opener, unbender (unit) ◇带卷[带材]~*，电磁~*
直头机旋转角	opener swing angle
直头装置（开卷机的）	tail forming device
直腿钢斜轧法	diagonal straight flange method
直弯机	【压】opener
直线	straight [right] line ◇在一~上的 in(-)line
直线焙烧炉	straight-line furnace
直线尺寸	linear dimension
直线淬火（用于钎子钢）	straight-line hardening
直线风温	straight-line blast temperature
直线关系	linear relationship, straight-line dependence [relationship]
直线过程	streamline process
直线函数	straight-line function
直线焊缝	straight bead
直线焊缝焊接	line welding
直线滑槽联杆[直肘杆]	straight link
直线化	linearizing
直线浇铸机	straight-line casting machine
直线节距	linear pitch
直线拉拔	straight-line drawing
直线切割	straight-line cutting
直线切割导板	straight-line cutting guide
直线切割机	straight-line cutting machine
直线式拉丝机	【压】straight-line (wire-drawing) machine
直线速度[空气直线速度]（流态化焙烧的）	space rate
直线位错	straight dislocation
直线性	linearity
直线延长[伸]	linear extension
直线运动	linear movement [motion]
直线运动感应式传感器	Nultrax
直线运动式取样器	straight-path sampler
直压	vertical compression
直焰	up-draught fire

直焰式退火炉　direct flame-fired annealing furnace
直焰窑　up-draught kiln
直译　transliteration
直轧闭口孔型　tongue-and-groove pass
直轧成品孔型设计　straight design of finishing passes
直轴　straight axle
直砖格　straight checker
直装　direct charge [charging]
直锥　right cone
直嘴夹钳　straight-lip tongs
植被　【环】vegetative [ground] cover
植被图　vegetation map
植被稳定(法)　vegetative stabilization
植物油　vegetable oil
执行程序　executive program [routine]
执行错误　execution error ◇ 远程计算系统的～*
执行电动机　operating motor
执行机构　actuating [operating] mechanism, actuator, servo
执行计算机　object-computer
执行时间　execution time
执行通路[路径]　execution path
执行系统　executive system ◇ 多道程序～*
执行诊断系统　executive deagnostic system
执行周期　execution cycle
执行状态　executive [state] mode
执照　licence, license, certificate, permit
执照领有者　licencee, licensee
值　value (val.), magnitude ◇ 埃里克森～Erichsen number, 恩斯林～Enslin value
值班　on duty, attendance
值班等修时间　stand-by time
值班工长　shift foreman
值班工程师　shift engineer
值班钳工　shift fitter
值班工[员]　operator on duty, operator-in charge, watchman
值班室　control house [compartment]
值班主任　shiftman, shift supervisor
指标　index (复数 indices), indication, indicatrix, target, subscript
指标杆　calibration bar
指标量[图,线]　indicatrix
指标器　pointer
指导　guide, guidance, directing, governing, conduct
指定范围　assigning range (a.r.)
指定界限　delimit
指定配合法(混凝土的)　arbitrary proportion method
指挥　command, directing, conduct
指挥台　command tower [set]
指挥仪　director, directive
指挥与控制系统　command and control system
指挥中心　brain
指令　order, command, directive, instruction
指令表　instruction repertory [set, list], code repertory
指令存储器　instruction storage
指令存储区　instruction area
指令代码　instruction code
指令地址寄存器　instruction address register
指令读出　command read-out
指令格式　instruction format, order structure
指令寄存器　instruction [order] register
指令计数器　instruction [location, sequence] counter
指令校验指示器　instruction check indicator
指令结构　command [order] structure
指令控制　command control
指令控制程序　command control program
指令码　instruction [order] code
指令脉冲　command pulse

指令区　instruction area
指令顺序寄存器　sequence register
指令系统　instruction repertory [set]
指令修改　instruction modification
指令周期　instruction cycle
指令字　instruction word, coding line
指令字符　instruction character
指令组件[单元]　command unit
指南　guide, directory, manual, handbook, guidebook
指南针　compass
指示　indicating, indication, instruction (inst.), order
指示表盘　indicating panel
指示传感[发送]器　indicating transmitter
指示灯　indicating lamp [light], indicator [display] lamp, pilot lamp [light]
指示灯光　indicator light
指示电极　indicator electrode
指示电路　display circuit
指示度盘　indicator dial
指示杆　indicator rod
指示剂　indicator,【理】tracer agent ◇ pH(酸碱)~ pH indicator, 放射性同位素 ~ radioisotopic tracer
指示剂法　indicator method, tracer method（用放射性同位素）
指示剂离子　tracer ion
指示剂纸　indicator paper
指示计　indicating meter [gage]
指示计最大最小读数差　total indicator variation (tiv)
指示继电器　indicating relay
指示控制灯　indicating control lamp ◇ 可见[目视]~*
指示量　indicatrix
指示流量计　indicating flow meter (I.F.M.)
指示面板　indicator board
指示器　indicator (I.N.D., indic.), pointer, indicating [sighting] device
指示器标度　indicator scale

指示器法　indicator method
指示器刻度　indicator scale
指示器盘　director panel
指示器总读数　total indicator reading (T.I.R.)
指示溶液　【化】indicator solution ◇ 等氢离子[可调]~*
指示设备　indicating equipment, designating device
指示数字　designation number ◇ 大致一致的 ~ coincident indicators
指示台(辊道的)　pointer table (PT)
指示图　indicator diagram, indicatrix
指示误差　indication [index] error
指示线　indicatrix
指示效率　indicated efficiency
指示压力　indicated pressure ◇ 平均有效 ~*
指示仪表　indicating instrument, indicator device
指示荧光屏　indicator screen
指示映象管　【电】indicator tube
指示元素　indicator element
指示装置　indicating [indexing] device, tell-tale (设备正常工作的)
指示字　【计】pointer ◇ 当前行 ~ current line pointer
指数　index (复数 indices), index number, indexing, exponent ◇ W ~ W-index, 劳厄 ~ Laue indices, 罗加 ~【焦】Roga index, 梅氏 ~ *, 米勒 ~ *
指数测定(衍射的)　assignment of indices
指数定律　exponential law
指数方程(式)　exponential equation
指数函数　exponential function
指数寄存器　index register
指数曲线　exponential curve
指数生长期　exponential growth phase
指数速率　exponential rate
指数图　index diagram
指数误差　index error (I.E.)
指数吸收定律　exponential absorption law

指数形状　exponential shape
指数因子[数]　exponential factor
指数值　exponent(ial) quantity
指套试验　thimble test
指向角　direction angle
指向塔　lead tower
指向性　directivity, directive property
指向性增益　directional gain
指形触点　finger contact
指形(回流)冷凝管　cold finger (reflux) condenser
指印[纹]【压】finger mark
指印现象(烧结多孔材料的)　fingering
指针　pointer, indicator, (indicating) needle, (guide) finger, hand, counter arm (压下指示器的)
指针板　dial plate
指针偏转　needle deflcetion
指针式测量仪表　pointer gauge
指针式检流计　needle galvanometer
指针式仪表　pointer [needle, dial] instrument
指状算条　finger bar
指状浇口【铸】finger gate
止车轨　dead-stop rail
止车楔　scotch block
止挡棘爪　ratchet stop
止动板　check plate
止动柄　lock(ing) handle
止动杆　stop(ping) [throw-out] lever, stop rod
止动螺钉　stop(per) [check, fixing, abutment] screw
止动螺栓　clamping [catch] bolt, dogbolt
止动器　retainer, chock
止动弹簧　stop [retaining] spring
止动销　retention [catch] pin
止动装置　back set, arresting device
止回阀　check valve (CV), back (pressure) valve, retaining [non-return, one-way] valve ◇ 摆动阀瓣~ swing-check valve

止回阀孔衬圈　check valve hole liner
止裂转向曲线【金】crack arrest transition curve
止汽化(作用)　devaporation
止水带　water stop
止碳【钢】blocked heat, blocking (operation) ◇ 炉内~ furnace block
止碳硅铬铁(10—17Si, 55—64Cr, 4—6C)　blocking chrome
止推导轮　guide thrust roller
止推垫圈　thrust washer
止推辊　thrust [tappet] roller
止推滚珠轴承　ball thrust bearing, end thrust ball bearing
止推滑座　thrust block
止推环　thrust ring [washer]
止推肩环　thrust collar
止(推)螺栓　bolt with stop
止推面　thrust face
止推能力　thrust capacity
止推支承[座]　thrust support
止推轴承【机】thrust [block, axial, longitudinal] bearing, plummer block ◇ 对开径向~ cup-and-cone bearing, 环形~ collar (thrust) bearing, 立式~ step bearing, 钟杆~ bell bearing
止推轴承板　bearing disc
止推轴承定位环　thrust bearing holding ring
止推轴承箱　thrust bearing box
止推轴颈　(thrust, blocking) journal, heel
止推座　thrust block
止退钳　backstop tongs
止销　stop pin
只读存储器【计】read-only memory (ROM), read-only [noneraseable] storage ◇ 电可变~*, 可编程序~*, 控制~*, 微程序~ microm
纸板　board (bd), paperboard, pasteboard ◇ 硬厚~ card-board
纸板桶(装箱用)　cardboard drum
纸包装的　paper covered ◇ 单层~*

纸箔 【色】foil paper
纸带 tape, strip chart（记录仪器的），【计】paper tape
纸带穿孔 tape punch [perforating]
纸浆废液 sulphite lye, spent pulping liquor ◇ 亚硫酸盐～ sulphite waste liquor
纸介电容器 paper capacitor [condenser]
纸滤器 paper filter
纸上色层(分离,分析)法 paper chromatography
致癌物 carcinogen
致电离本领[能力] ionizing power
致电离粒子 ionizing particle
致黑测量(薄膜的) 【理】blackening measurement
致冷 refrigeration, cooling
致冷混合物 frigorific [cooling] mixture
致冷剂 refrigerant, cryogen
致冷面 refrigeration surface
致冷器 refrigerator, cryostat, freezer
致冷设备 refrigerating [chilling] unit
致冷盐水 refrigeration brine
致密白云石(回转炉焙烧的) dense (rotary-kiln) dolomite
致密焙烧 tight burning
致密表面 sound surface
致密层 dense [compact] layer
致密长石 felsite, felsyte
致密淀积物 dense deposit
致密粉末 dense powder
致密硅岩 【耐】gan(n)ister
致密焊缝 tight weld [seam] ◇ 坚固[承载]～tight-strong seam
致密化 densification,【粉】condensation ◇ 金属铸件变形～*, 再～redensification
致密化动力学 densification kinetics
致密化速率 densification rate
致密接头 tight joint
致密结构 close [compact] texture
致密结块 dense cake
致密介质 【理】dense medium

致密金属 dense metal
致密金属小块 dense button
致密金属氧化膜溅射处理 【金】metal shadowing
致密晶粒 compact-grain
致密晶粒组织 【金】close-grained [compact-grain] structure
致密零件 dense part
致密炉顶砖 low porosity roof brick
致密氯化物 dense chloride
致密滤纸 hard textured filter paper
致密膜 dense film
致密耐火砖 dense firebrick
致密青铜 dense bronze
致密熔渣 compact slag
致密蠕虫状石墨铸铁(拟球状石墨铸铁) compacted vermicular cast iron
致密石墨棒 low porosity graphite rod
致密石墨铸铁 compacted graphite iron
致密铁氧体 compact ferrite
致密涂[镀]层 dense coating, tight coat
致密物质 condensed material
致密系数 coefficient of compactness
致密性 compactness, soundness
致密制品 【粉】dense product
致密铸件 sound casting
致密状材料 material in solid bulk form
致密组织 compact structure
致命错误 fatal error
致模糊 fogging
致偏电极 deflecting electrode
致偏聚焦 (同"偏转聚焦")
致偏矢量 (同"偏转矢量")
致死(剂)量 lethal dose (LD), fatal dose
置"0"脉冲 【计】reset pulse
置"0"置"1" reset-set (R-S)
置"0"置"1"触发器 (同"RS触发器")
置换 displacement (disp., displ.), substitution, replacement, metathesis, permutation ◇ 用镍粉～【色】cement with nickel powder, 用铁～【色】cement with iron
置换比(喷吹燃料的) 【铁】replacement

ratio [rate, factor] ◇ 临界～*, 煤焦～*

置换槽 displacement tank
置换沉淀槽 cementation [precipitating] tank
置换(沉淀)法 【色】cementation process, method of cementation
置换沉淀反应 cementation reaction
置换出 cement-out
置换法镀层 replacement coating
置换反应 replacement [cementation, substitution] reaction
置换分离[析出] separation by displacement
置换(固溶体)式合金 substitutional alloy
置换机理 replacement mechanism
置换晶格位置 (同"代位晶格位置")
置换浓缩机 displacement thickener
置换碰撞 【化】replacement collision
置换气相色层(分离) gas displacement chromatography (G.D.C)
置换式扩散 substitutional diffusion
置换式原子 substitutional atom
置换式杂质 substitutional impurity
置换速率 replacement rate
置换型固溶体 (同"代位式固溶体")
置换型缺陷 substitutional imperfection
置换型无序固溶体 random substitutional solid solution
置换型一次固熔体 primary substitutional solid solution
置换型钇铁石榴石 substituted yttrium iron garnet
置换元素 (同"代位元素")
置换柱 【色】column precipitator
置位 【计】setting
置信界限[限度] confidence [fiducial] limit
置信区间 confidence interval
置信水平 confidence level
置信系数(统计分析的) confidence coefficient

制靶材料 target material
制备 preparation, fabrication, make up
制备方法 fabricating method, route of preparation
制备混合料 prepared mix
制备时间 preparation time
制币材料 coin(age) material
制表机 tabulator
制表系统 tabular system ◇ 面向～的语言
制表员 tabulator
制箔 foliation
制成表格 tabulating
制成车间 finishing work
制成品 manufactured goods
制成球团 ball up
制成钟形 belling
制钉厂 nailery
制钉钢丝 nail wire
制钉机 nail(-making) machine
制定 draughting, establishing, institution
制动 brake, braking, damping, stopping, retaining, arrest(ment) ◇ 磁力～(器) magnetic brake
制动材料 stopping material
制动掣子 brake latch [pawl]
制动衬片 brake lining [facing]
制动磁铁 brake [damping] magnet
制动带 brake band [strap], check band
制动电阻器 braking resistor
制动杆 brake bar [arm, staff], arresting lever
制动钢丝绳[制动索]用钢丝 brake cable wire
制动工 leverman
制动功率 brake [braking, stopping] power
制动辊 braking roll
制动盒 brake box [housing]
制动环 brake hoop, stop(per) [damping, locking] ring
制动棘爪 brake pawl

制动键[按钮] brake [locking] key
制动块 brake block [pads, shoe], clamp dog, shoe brake
制动联杆[机械式制动联动机构] brake linkage
制动轮 brake pulley [drum], braked wheel, headblock
制动面 brake lining
制动盘 brake disc
制动片 brake block, arrester ◇ 双金属～ bimetallic brake disc
制动平均压力 brake mean pressure (b.m.p.)
制动器 brake (gear), brakestaff, stopper, damper, arrester ◇ 差动～ differential brake, 超重[超载]～load brake, 带式～ band [strap] brake, 电动气压～*, 蜂鸣～buzzer stop, 杆式～ lever brake, 滑块～ blocking brake, 机械～mechanical brake, 脚踏～ foot brake, 块式～ block [shoe] brake, 快动气力～*, 链式～ chain brake, 内胀～*, 手力～ hand brake, 双瓦(型)～*, 涡流～ eddy-current retarder, 圆盘～ disc brake, 重型～ heavy duty brake, 锥形～ cone brake
制动钳 brake tongs
制动软管 brake hose
制动手柄 brake arm
制动索 brake cable
制动踏板 brake pedal
制动凸轮 brake cam
制动系统 brake assembly [system, staff]
制动销 stop [banking] pin
制动员 【运】train man
制动圆筒 brake drum
制动闸 damping [holding] brake
制动爪安装板 dog plate
制动转矩 braking [drag] torque
制动装置 brake gear [staff], arrester, arrestor, catch
制动作用 braking [inhibitor] effect
制度 system, institution, regime

制粉 powder process, 【铁】pulverized coal preparation
制粉设备 powder manufacturing apparatus
制复型(电子显微镜用) replicate
制钢(包括加工) steel manufacture
制锆车间 zirconium plant
制锆设备 zirconium plant equipment
制管 tubulation ◇ 埃尔哈特～法*
制管用铅黄铜 tube brass
制罐机(罐头盒的) can body making machine, body maker
制好的 ready-made
制好的风口 fabricated tuyere
制活砂块的挡块 【铸】false part
制剂 preparation
制尖 pointing
制冷 refrigeration ◇ 氨～厂 ammonia cooling plant
制冷机 refrigerator, refrigerating [cooling] machine ◇ 溴化锂～*
制冷系统 refrigerating system
制粒【团】 pelletizing, granulating, nodulizing
制粒焙烧 pellet roasting
制粒混合料 micro-pelletized mix(ture)
制粒机[器] pelletizer, granulator ◇ 干燥～dryer-pelletizer, 混合～ mixer-granulator, 圆筒～*
制粒粒度 pelletizing size
制粒性 balling tendency
制料坯 briquetting
制氯电解槽 chlorine cell
制轮楔 linch pin
制轮爪 jumper
制模 patternmaking, moulding ◇ 流态自硬砂～法*, 模压～法【压】cold hobbing, 切压～(法) hubbing
制模车间 pattern-shop, 【耐】moulding shop
制模尺 patternmaker's rule
制模工 patternmaker, 【压】die-maker

制模工段	【耐】mould-making department
制模工缩尺	【铸】patternmaker's shrinkage
制模工作	formwork
制模金属	pattern metal
制模型车床	patternmaker's lathe, model maker's lathe
制模型用铣床	pattern milling machine
制逆轮	star wheel
制片机	tablet-compression machine, tableting press
制品	product, goods, ware
制品拔出装置	production extractor
制瓶压力机	【压】bottle making press
制球机	(同"造球机")
制生球	(同"造生球团")
制绳车间	twisting shop
制刷用钢丝	brush wire
制水渣贮槽	【铁】water treatment pit
制酸厂	sulphuric acid manufacturer, acid plant ◇ 接触法～contact plant
制酸塔	acid tower
制榫机	dovetailing [morticing] machine, dovetailer
制钛	production of titanium
制铁粉法	powdered iron producing process ◇ DPG～*, NY100 生铁脱碳～NY 100 process, 费鲁姆～*, 赫加纳克斯～*, 坎格罗电解～Kangro process, 派伦～*, 塔科马电解～Tacoma process
制图	drawing, draft(ing), draught(ing), mapping, graphical plot ◇ 坐标～器 coordinatagraph
制图比例尺	draughting [plotting] scale
制图法	draughting
制图机	graphic plotter
制图术[质量]	draughts manship
制图学	graphics
制图仪	charting machine, graph plotter
制图仪器	draughting [drawing] instrument
制图员	draughtsman, drawer
制团	briquetting, conglomeration, agglomerating, barbecuing, kneading (铁矿粉的) ◇ 铁矿石～iron ore briquetting
制团机	(同"压坯机") ◇ 辊式[对辊]～*
制丸机	shot making machine
制箱木料	boxing
制芯	【铸】coremaking ◇ 冷芯盒～法 cold box process, 热(芯)盒～法*
制芯材料	【铸】core-making material
制芯工	core-maker
制芯(工)工作台	coremaker's bench
制芯机	core(-making) machine ◇ 翻台式～*, 压实式～*, 震实式～core jarring machine
制芯间[工段]	core-room
制芯油	core oil
制芯轴	core spindle
制锌粒	zinc beading
制氩设备	argon recovery plant
制氧	oxygen generating [making] ◇ 变压吸附～*
制氧车间	oxygen generating [making] plant
制氧机	oxygenerator
制样	specimen preparation
制约	restrict(ion), constraint, restraint
制造	making, manufacturing, producing ◇ 人工～handwork
制造产品	manufactured goods
制造厂	manufactory, manufacturer, manufacturing plant, producer, mill
制造厂标准	manufacturer's standard
制造厂商标	(同"工厂商标")
制造成本	manufacturing cost
制造(方)法	manufacturing method
制造工具用显微镜	toolmakers' microscope
制造工序	manufacturing process [operation]
制造工艺	manufacturing engineering [practice]

制造公差	manufacturing tolerance
制造缺陷	manufacturing defect
制造设备	manufacturing equipment
制造设计	fabrication design
制造业	manufacturing industry, manufacture
制造者	maker, manufacturer
制造状态(的)	as-fabricated
制毡	felting
制针钢丝	wire for needle products
制针管材	needle tubing
制针黄铜丝	pin wire brass
制针线材	needle wire
制振钢板	composite damping steel sheet, damping sheet steel
制止	restraint, check, stop, prevention
制止螺杆	check bolt
制砖	brick making ◇ 硬塑料～模 clot mould
制砖厂	brick making plant
制砖机	brick moulding [making] machine ◇ 带式～ auger brick machine
制砖黏土	brick clay
制砖土	adobe soil
制砖用润滑油	brick oil
制作模型	model(l)ing
制作凸缘	flanging
智利含硫粗铜棒	Chili bar
智利磨机	Chilian mill
智利硝石	(同"钠硝石")
智能	intelligence
智能报警	intelligent alarm
智能变送器	intelligent transmitter
智能电弧炉	intelligent arc furnace (IAF)
智能电弧炉控制器	IAF controller
智能化	intellectualization
智能化数据库	intellectualized database
智能化涡流探伤仪	intellectualized eddy detector
智能机器人	intelligent robot
智能科学	intelligence science
智能控制	intelligent control ◇ 混合～系统
智能模型	intelligence model
智能系统	intelligent system
智能型的	knowledge-based
智能预测系统	intelligent predicting system ◇ 高炉炉况实时～*
智能终端	【计】intelligent terminal
秩	【数】rank
稚吹	(同"欠吹")
质变(体)	modification of quality
质点	particle
质点浓度	particle concentration
质点速度	particle velocity
质点振动速度	sound particle velocity
质荷比	mass-to-charge ratio
质量	quality, 【理】mass ◇ 产品平均～*, 一般～ ordinary quality, 有效～ 【理】chemical mass
质量百分比	【理】mass percent
质量保证	quality assurance
质量保证系统	quality insurance system (QIS)
质量保证验收标准	quality assurance acceptance standards (QAAS)
质量比	mass ratio, ratio by mass
质量标准	quality criterion [standard, level]
质量波动	quality fluctuation
质量磁化率	【理】mass susceptibility
质量等级	quality grade
质量巅	【理】mass peak
质量分布	mass distribution
质量分离	mass separation
质量分数	【理】mass fraction
质量改进	improvement in quality
质量管理	quality control (QC) ◇ 全面～*, 一贯～系统*
质量惯性矩	【理】mass moment of inertia
质量规范[技术条件]	quality specification
质量监督	quality supervision
质量检查	quality inspection
质量检验	quality testing

质量鉴定	quality determination [rating]
质量鉴定试验	qualification test
质量亏损	【理】mass defect
质量流	【理】mass flow
质量流量厚度控制	【理】mass flow gage control
质量流量计	【理】mass flowmeter
质量流(量)控制器	mass-flow controller
质量流率[流速]	【理】mass flow rate
质量摩尔浓度(溶质的)	molality of sotute
质量能量关系式($E = mc^2$)	【理】mass/energy relationship
质量－能量转换公式	【理】mass-energy conversion formula
质量浓度	mass concentration
质量平衡	【理】mass balance
质量评定	【企】quality rating, grade estimation
质量评价	【企】quality evaluation, merit rating
质量认证制度	quality certification system
质量散射系数	mass scattering coefficient
质量守恒	【理】mass conservation
质量数	【理】mass number
质量水平[水准]	quality level
质量速度	【理】mass velocity
质量特性	quality charateristic
质量提高	improvement in quality
质量体系认证	quality system certification
质量体系认证中心	quality system certification center, certification center for quality system ◇ 中国冶金工业～*
质量体系审核认证	quality system certification audit
质量体系审核注册制度	audit registration system in quality system
质量吸收系数	mass absorption coefficient
质量系[因]数	【理】quality factor (QF), quality value, Q-value
质量效应	【理】mass effect
质量压力	【理】mass pressure
质量验收标准	acceptance quality level
质量因数	factor of quality, goodness
质量因数计	Q meter
质量证明书	【企】certification of quality
质量指标	quality index, performance figure
质量指数	qualitative index, quality figure, figure of merit, Q index (球团的)
质(量中)心	(同"重心")
质量中心轴线	【理】centroid axis
质量转移[传递]	【理】mass transfer
质量作用	【理】mass action [effect]
质量作用常数	mass action constant
质量作用定律	mass action law
质量作用效应	mass action effect
质能相当性	mass-energy equivalence
质能关系	◇ 爱因斯坦～*
质谱	mass-spectrum
质谱测定法	(同"质谱学") ◇ 化学电离～*
质谱分光计	mass-spectrometer
质谱分析	mass-spectrographic [mass-spectrometric] analysis
质谱分析法[术]	mass-spectrography, mass-spectrometry ◇ 分离同位素的～*
质谱摄影仪	【理】mass-spectrograph
质谱图	【理】mass-spectrogram
质谱学	mass-spectrometry, mass spectroscopy ◇ (电)火花源[电光源]～*
质谱仪	mass analyzer [spectrometer, spectrograph] ◇ 班布里奇－乔丹～*, 布利克尼[交叉场]～*, 登普斯特～*, 飞行时间～*, 离子探针～*, 尼尔～*, 四极～*, 同步 ～mass-synchromer
质谱仪测量	【理】mass-spectrometer measurement
质谱(仪)检漏器	mass-spectrometric [mass-spectrometer] leak detector
质谱最大值	【理】mass peak
质子	proton ◇ 给～溶剂 protogenic solvent
质子磁子	【理】proton magneton
质子惰性溶剂	aprot(on)ic solvent

质子分解	protonolysis
质子轰击	proton bombardment
质子回磁比	proton gyromagnetic ratio
质子亲和力	proton affinity
质子显微镜	proton microscope
质子窄束	proton pencil
质子照射	proton irradiation
滞后	lag(ging), delay, hysteresis, drag ◇ (测量)数值指示～measuring lag, 处理时间～process time lag, 电容～capacity lag, 机械～*
滞后变形	【理】hysteresis set
滞后电流	lagging current
滞后回线	【理】hysteresis loop ◇ 偏移～bias hysteresis loop
滞后回线损失	hysteresis (loop) loss
滞后角	angle of lag, hysteresis angle
滞后理论	later theories
滞后裂纹	delayed cracking ◇ 氢致～*
滞后破坏	delayed failure [fracture]
滞后曲线	【理】hysteresis curve
滞后时间	delay [dead] time
滞后系数	lag [hysteresis] coefficient
滞后现象	hysteresis (phenomena)
滞后效应	lagging [hysteresis] effect
滞后硬化	after hardening
滞后作用	delayed action, hysteresis (effect)
滞后误差	hysteresis error
滞留	retention ◇ 加压～时间*
滞流	viscous flow, misrun
滞流区(炉子、熔池的)	stagnation region
滞黏性质	viscous behaviour
滞塞	jam, stick-slip, choking
滞塞进料	choke feeding
滞塞速度	choking velocity
滞弹性	anelasticity, elastic hysteresis, delayed elasticity, viscoelasticity
滞弹性变形	anelastic deformation
滞弹性材料	【理】viscoilastic material
滞弹性弛豫	anelastic relaxation
滞弹性力学	viscoelasticity
滞弹性能	anelastic [viscoelastic] behaviour
滞弹性试验	anelastic experiments
滞弹性现象	anelasticity phenomenn
滞弹性效应	anelastic effect
治本修理	permanent repair
治洪	flood control
蛭石	{(OH)$_4$Mg$_6$Si$_8$O$_{20}$·8H$_2$O} vermiculite, roseite
蛭石混凝土	vermiculite concrete
蛭石砖	vermiculite brick
中凹锻件	middle
中班	afternoon [back, middle] shift
中板	medium [jobbing] plate, light gauge plate
中板车间	medium plate shop
中板可逆轧机	reversal plate mill ◇ 四辊～*
中板轧机	medium-plate mill, jobbing sheet(-rolling) mill, light plate mill
中倍[中等放大率]物镜	medium-power objective
中波	medium frequency (M.F., m.f., m-f)
中部	middle
中部打壳	【色】centre crust breaking
中部加热元件	middle zone heating element
中部内衬	middle inwalls
中部试样	middle sample
中纯度氧	tonnage oxygen
中等尺寸[大小]	intermediate [median] size, medium-size
中等电流密度	medium current density
中等电阻钢丝	best best wire (美国商品名)
中等粉末	medium powder
中等腐蚀性水域	【环】medium rotten water
中等负载	medium load [duty]
中等高温	moderately elevated temperature

中等工作制　medium duty
中等功率机(床)　medium duty machine
中等规格　midsize
中等规模　medium-size
中等厚度内衬　semithin wall-type inwalls
中等挥发分烟煤　medium-volatile (bituminous) coal
中等回火钢　medium-temper steel
中等角度对称间界　medium angle symmetrical boundary
中等角度对称倾侧间界　medium angle symmetrical tilt boundary
中等晶体　medium crystal
中等宽度带钢　medium-width steel strip
中等冷却速率　intermediate cooling rate
中等粒度的　medium-grained
中等粒级　intermediate fraction
中等炉身竖炉　medium-shaft type furnace
中等密度　intermediate density
中等耐火泥浆　intermediate heat duty mortar
中等耐火砖　intermediate duty fireclay brick
中等配筋率的　medium reinforced
中等强度　medium intensity, medium [moderate] strength
中等强度材料　medium-strength material
中等强度电流　medium current
中等强度合金　medium [intermediate] strength alloy
中等强度级　intermediate strength level
中等强度相互作用　moderate-strong interaction
中等热值热量　medium grade heat
中等容量炉　medium-size furnace
中等速度[速率]　medium [moderate] speed (m.s.), moderate velocity, intermediate speed
中等温度　intermediate temperature
中等以上(质量)的　average-to-good
中等硬度　medium [intermediate] hardness ◇ 冷拔～(管材)【压】half hard

中等硬度钢　medium-hard steel
中等硬度拉拔　medium drawing
中等中矿　medium middlings (M.M.)
中低碳锰铁　medium and low-carbon ferro-manganese
中点　middle (mid), median, midpoint
中毒　poisoning, intoxication ◇ 非永久性～nonpermanent poison
中毒树脂　poisoned resin
中毒症状　symptoms of poisoning
中度腐蚀　moderate corrosion
中段铸件(台车的)　【团】centre casting
中断　interrupt, suspension, break (off, away, up), discontinue, cessation, failing, lapse, pause, standstill
中断处理　interrupt processing [handling]
中断等待时间　interrupt latency
中断级　interrupt level
中断记录　interrupt logging
中断屏蔽　interrupt(ion) mask
中断请求　interrupt request
中断时间　interrupt [outage] time
中断系统　interrupt system
中断响应　interrupt response
中断向量　interrupt vector
中断优先权　【计】interrupt priority
中断源　【计】interrupt source
中高铼酸　meso-perrhenic acid
中管提升搅拌器　central lift agitator
中规模集成　medium scale integration (M.S.I.)
中规模集成电路　medium scale integrated circuit (M.S.I.C.)
中辊　【压】central [centre, middle] roll
中国白涂料(氧化锌)　chinese white
中国赤铜(3.73—4.15Au, 0.08—1.55Ag, 0.11Pb, 余量Cu)　Chinese Shaku-do bronze Shaku-do bronze
中国工商银行　National Industrial and Commercial Bank of China
中国机械工业质量体系认证中心　China Certification Center for Machine-building

Quality System
中国金属学会 Chinese Society for Metals (CSM)
中国镜铜[镜用铜锌合金] chinese speculum metal
中国科学技术协会 China Association for Science and Technology
中国科学院 Chinese Academy of Sciences, Academia Sinica
中国美术黄铜[工艺品用铅锡黄铜](70—75Cu, 10—15Zn, 1Sn, 10—15Pb) Chinese art metal
中国镍银[白铜](26—40Cu, 16—37Ni, 41—32Zn, 0—2.5Fe) Chinese nickel silver
中国青铜(75—80Cu, 余量 Sn) Chinese bronze, bellmetal (也见"钟铜")
中国桐油 chinese wood oil
中国冶金工业质量体系认证中心 China Metallurgical Industry Quality System Certification Center
中国银(一种镍黄铜; 50—70Cu, 10—30Zn, 10—20Ni) China silver (alloy)
中国质量管理协会 China Quality Control Association
中国质量体系认证机构国家认可委员会 China National Accreditation Council for Registrars (CNACR)
中和 【化】neutralizing, neutralization (neutr.), neutrality, 【铁】blending ◇ 过度～ over-neutralization, 矿石～*, 原料～*
中和比 【铁】blending ratio
中和槽 neutralization vessel, neutralizing tank, 【铁】blending tank ◇ 风力～[仓]
中和池 neutralisation basin ◇ 间断操作～*
中和点 neutral point (n.p.)
中和堆场 【铁】blending [bedding] field
中和反应 【化】neutralization reaction
中和(方)法 【选】averaging method, mode of averaging
中和(工)段 neutralization section ◇ 连续～
中和过的废水 neutralised waste water
中和剂 neutralizing [neutralization] agent, neutralizer
中和料场 【铁】blending yard, bed blending plant [system], bedding facilities, bedding pile [plant, system], homogenization plant
中和料堆 【铁】blending [bedded] pile
中和器 neutralizer, 【冶】reclaiming machine
中和热 neutralization heat
中和溶液 neutralized solution
中和试验 neutralization test
中和酸 disacidifying
中和效应 neutralizing effect
中和值 neutralization value [number]
中和轴 zero line
中和装置 neutralization plant
中和作用 neutralization
中合金钢 medium-alloy steel
中厚板 medium plate
中厚板标志(打印)台[辊道] plate marking table
中厚板堆垛机 plate piler
中厚板翻转机 plate turnorer
中厚板厚度 gauge of plate
中厚板剪切机 plate shears [cutter]
中厚板精整 【压】plate finishing
中厚板拉伸矫直机 plate stretcher
中厚板平整[矫直]机 【压】plate-straightening machine, plate leveller, plate-levelling machine
中厚板双边修边剪切机 double-sided plate trimming shears
中厚板轧机 (heavy and medium) plate mill ◇ 万能式～universal plate mill
中厚钢板 medium plate, plate steel [iron] ◇ 切边～*
中厚钢板轧制 plate rolling
中厚黄铜板 brass plate

中级的[中级品位] medium grade
中级耐火黏土砖 medium-duty fireclay brick
中级氧化铝(耐火)砖 medium-alumina (fire) brick
中级氧化铝耐火材料 medium-alumina refractory
中脊面(马氏体的) midrib plane
中脊线 midrib
中继 relaying, trunking, translation
中继长途线 trunk line
中继电缆 junction [trunk, (inter)connecting, coupling] cable
中继电路 junction [trunk, repeat] circuit
中继继电器 trunk [repeater] relay
中继线 junction line, trunk (line), link
中继站 relay (point)
中间贝氏体 【金】intermediate bainite
中间壁 mid wall
中间补炉 intermediate reline [relining], partial relining
中间部位 midposition
中间槽 drop box
中间层 intermediate (layer), buffer layer
中间层面 intermediate deck
中间层试样 middle sample
中间产品 intermediate [between] product, intermediates, midds, semis, 【选】middling(s)
中间产物 intermediary [between] product, intermediate product [material], secondary
中间产物排出口 intermittent drain
中间产物品位 【色】cascade grade
中间厂规模 pilot-plant scale
中间沉淀物 (同"中间析出物")
中间乘积 【计】intermediate product
中间程序 【计】interlude
中间齿轮传动机构 intermediate gearing
中间存储器 【计】intermediate memory, [storage]
中间带 neutral zone

中间带卷 reroll
中间代码 【计】intermediate code
中间道次 pony roughing pass
中间电极 intermediate electrode
中间镀层 intermediate coat(ing)
中间堆栈 intermediate stockpile
中间对流加热器 intermediate convector
中间发送器 【电】half time emitter
中间反应塔 intermediate reaction tower
中间富集 intermediate concentration
中间钢水包 intermediate ladle
中间钢丝 process wire
中间工厂(规模)研究 pilot-plant investigation [work]
中间工厂试验 (同"半工业试验")
中间工厂试验炉 pilot furnace
中间工序冲床 subpress
中间罐 surge tank
中间罐[包] 【连铸】tundish,【钢】(pouring) basket, pouring box, trough ◇ 回转式 ~ swivelling tundish, 可倾动式 ~ tiltable tundish, 六流 ~ sixway tundish, 塞棒操纵的~*, 四塞棒~*, 隧道式感应加热~*, 自控[自量]式~*
中间罐[包]保护渣 tundish powder
中间罐[包]衬砖 tundish lining brick
中间罐[包]等离子加热 plasma tundish heating
中间罐[包]底 tundish bottom
中间罐[包]放置空位 vacancy for tundish
中间罐[包]盖 tundish cover
中间罐[包]工作衬喷涂料 【连铸】spraying material for continuous casting tundish working lining
中间罐[包]换衬作业区 tundish relining area
中间罐[包]浇铸 【连铸】tundish casting [pouring],【钢】trough casting, basket pouring
中间罐[包]冷却区 tundish cooling area
中间罐[包]里衬 tundish lining
中间罐[包]倾翻装置 tundish turnover

中间罐[包]水口　tundish nozzle
中间罐[包]维修区　rehabilitation area of tundish
中间罐[包]小车　tundish car
中间罐[包]冶金　tundish metallurgy
中间罐[包]预热[烘烤]　tundish preheating
中间罐[包]预热[烘烤]站　tundish preheating station
中间罐[包]运送车　tundish carriage
中间罐[包]支架　tundish support
中间罐[包]准备作业区　tundish preparation area
中间辊　【压】intermediate roll ◇ 第一层 ～"
中间辊道　【压】intermediate table, delay table（缓延和冷却轧件用）
中间辊环　【压】inner collar
中间辊式运输机　intermediate roller conveyor
中间过程　sub-process
中间过热式涡轮机[蒸汽透平]　reheat machine
中间和顶层联合浇铸　【铸】combined intermediate-and-top pouring
中间合反射　intermediates
中间合金　intermediate [preliminary, master, process(ing), rich] alloy, hardener, tempering[key] metal, alloyage ◇ 脱氧及晶粒细化～"
中间合金法　intermediate alloy process
中间桁架　【建】intermediate truss
中间化合物　intermediate compound, intermediates
中间换流器　intermediate convector
中间回火　intermediate temper
中间机组　intermediate train
中间机座　【压】intermediate stand, interstand, run-down mill, pony-roughing mill（小型型钢轧机的）
中间寄存器　【计】distributor

中间继电器　intermediate [auxiliary] relay
中间加热　intermediate heating
中间加热器　interheater, intermediate heater
中间间隔[隔墙]　mid-feather
中间浇注槽　【冶】bakie, tundish
中间浇注桶　intermediate pouring vessel
中间结构　intermediate structure
中间介质　intermediate agent
中间金属　intermediate [intermetallic] metal
中间金属相微粒　intermetallic phase particle
中间精选　intermediate concentration
中间卷线筒　【压】intermediate block
中间开坯机座　【压】intermediate bloomer
中间矿槽　feed surge bin
中间浪（板材缺陷）　buckles
中间冷凝器　intercondenser
中间冷却器　intercooler, intermediate cooler
中间粒级　midsize
中间联结辊道　translating table
中间联轴节[联接器,管接头,耦合,耦联器]　intermediate coupling
中间料仓　transfer hopper, intermediate bunker
中间料槽　surge bin
中间溜槽　transfer chute
中间馏分　intermediate fraction, heart cut
中间炉　intermediate furnace
中间炉膛　middle hearth
中间轮　dead pulley
中间密度　intermediate density
中间内壁　intermediate inwalls
中间配电盘　intermediate distributing board
中间平台　intermediate platform [deck]
中间破碎　（同"中碎"）
中间区段　centre section
中间热处理　intermediate heat treatment
中间热交换器　intermediate heat exchang-

中间软化退火　intermediate softening
中间色调照相底片　half-tone negative
中间砂箱　micldle box, mtermediate flask
中间烧结　intermediate sintering
中间室　intermediate chamber
中间试验厂　(semi-) pilot [semiwork-scale] plant
中间试验厂规模　pilot-plant scale
中间试验厂(规模)研究　pilot-plant investigation [work]
中间试验厂阶段　pilot-plant stage
中间试验厂试验　(同"半工业试验")
中间试验设备　pilot-plant installation [unit]
中间试验性生产　pilot-plant production
中间四碘化物　intermediate tetraiodide
中间钛合金　titanium master [mother] alloy
中间套管　protector string
中间体　intermediary, intermediate (compound)
中间透镜　intermediate lens
中间图像　intermediate image
中间涂层　intermediate coat(ing)
中间退火　【压】intermediate [(inter-)process, interpass, interstage, commercial] annealing, between pass annealing, annealing in process, interannealing
中间退火操作[工序]　【压】interstage annealing operation
中间退火钢丝　interannealed [annealed-in-process] wire
中间未熔合(焊缝的)　lack of interrun fusion
中间未熔透(多层焊缝的)　lack of interpenetration
中间位置　midposition, centre [middle] position
中间析出物　【金】intermediate precipitate
中间细痕(脉)(马氏体的)　midrib
中间相　intermediate phase, interphase ◇富铜~*
中间型硫杆菌　thiobacillus intermedius
中间型氧化铝　intermediate alumina
中间形态　intermediary
中间氧化物相　intermediate oxide phase
中间液相　internal liquid phase
中间影像　intermediate image
中间预热器　intermediate pre-heater
中间运输辊道　【压】intermediate table
中间渣　【钢】intermediate slag ◇扒~*
中间轧辊　middle [intermediate, central, centre] roll, intermediate mill
中间轧机　intermediate mill
中间轧坯　workpiece
中间轧制　intermediate rolling
中间轧制道次[孔型]　intermediate pass
中间轧制机组　intermediate train
中间轴　intermediate shaft [axle], stud shaft
中间贮仓　intermediate bunker [bin, silo], transfer bin, positive throughflow bunker
中间砖砌体　intermediate brick-work
中间转变　intermediate transformation
中间状态　intermediate state
中间组　centre section
中介　mediate
中介齿轮　【机】idle(r) gear
中介面黑度　intervenient surface emissivity
中介面温度　intervenient surface temperature
中介物　intermediary, intervenient
中径(螺纹的)　pitch diameter
中肯半径　【理】critical radius
中肯散射　【理】critical scattering
中肯元件　critical element
中空电极　hollow electrode
中空锻造　hollow forging
中空钢　hollow (drill) steel, cored steel (凿岩机用; 0.7—0.8C) ◇凿岩钎杆用 ~*
中空挤压锭　reamed extrusion ingot

中 zhong

中空型材 hollow section
中跨 mid-span
中块(过筛)煤 middle-grade coal
中矿 middlings (mid.), midds ◇ 中等~*
中粒玄武岩 anamesite
中沥青 medium pitch
中磷生铁 medium phosphorus iron
中煤重量校正 middlings deduction
中锰钢 medium manganese steel
中黏结性煤 medium caking coal
中频 intermediate frequency (IF), medium frequency (MF, m.f.)
中频淬火 mid frequency induction hardening
中频带频率 mid-band frequency
中频电路 intermediate-frequency circuit
中频感应炉 medium-frequency induction furnace
中铅黄铜[中铅铜合金](65Cu,34Zn,1Pb) medium leaded brass
中强黏力型砂 (同"半肥型砂")
中青铜 medium bronze
中上等的 average-to-good
中式盐 normal salt
中枢 (central) pivot, centre pin
中枢点 hub
中速 intermediate speed
中速齿轮 intermediate gear
中速干燥(的) medium-drying
中速和高速铸造区[范围] 【铸】medium/fast range of casting speeds
中速无屏蔽胶片 medium-speed no-screen film
中碎 medium [intermediate] crushing
中碎机 intermediate crusher
中碳钢(0.4—0.5C, 0.15—0.25Si, 0.5—0.7Mn, <0.05P 和 S) medium steel (M.S.), hard steel, medium-carbon steel
中碳钢丝(0.6—0.8C) bullet wire
中碳结构钢(0.3—0.4C, 0.15—0.25Si, 0.4—0.6Mn, <0.05S, <0.05P) semi-hard steel
中碳珠光体锰钢 medium carbon pearlitic manganese steel
中碳铸钢 medium carbon cast steel
中碳轴承钢 medium-carbon bearing steel
中微子 【理】neutrino
中位数 【数】median
中温回火 【金】medium [average] tempering
中温加工(临界温度下的) hot cold work(ing), warm working
中温沥青 medium temperature pitch
中温炉 medium-temperature furnace, moderate oven
中温黏土砖 moderate heat duty fireclay brick
中温烧成石灰 medium-burned lime
中温烧成砖 【耐】medium-burned brick
中(温)烧耐火制品 medium-burned refractory ware
中温退火 medium(-temperature) annealing
中锡焊料 【焊】medium solder
中洗煤 medium coal
中线 center line (C.L.), mid-line (M.L.), mean line, median, roll parting line (轧辊孔型的)
中线直径 median diameter
中线桩 centre stake
中箱 mid part
中小型钢铁厂 mini-medium mill
中锌黄铜 (同"浅红黄铜")
中心 center, centre (ctr), heart, core
中心拌合厂 【建】central mixing plant
中心标线(目镜的) central hair
中心层线 central layer line
中心齿轮 sun gear
中心抽头 【电】central tap
中心出料式卷线机 laying reel
中心传动式浓缩机 centre shaft [post] type thickener ◇ 多层~ tray thickener
中心带 core

中心导体磁化(作用)	【理】central conductor magnetization
中心到端面的距离	center to end (C. to E.)
中心到面的距离	center to face (C. to F.)
中心电极	centre electrode
中心对称类	【金】centrosymmetric(al) class
中心分流砖	deflecting block
中心供热式均热炉	vertically fired pit
中心管道现象	【铁】chimneying
中心罐	centre pot
中心光线锥	central pencil
中心过吹	【铁】vigorous central gas flow
中心荷载	centric load
中心夹持(电极夹持器的)	【冶】centre gripping
中心加[装]焦	central coke charging, central charging [feeding] coke
中心加料	centre charging
中心监督板	centralized supervisory panel
中心间距	between centers (BC, b.c.)
中心件	centre piece
中心浇口	【铸】central [centre] runner, central gate
中心浇口砖	【钢】centre brick
中心截面	center section (C.S.)
中心进料孔	central well
中心距	centre to centre (C.C.), between centres, centre distance (c.d.), centre-to-centre distance
中心坑	centre-punch
中心孔隙(铸的)	central porosity
中心跨距(建筑物的)	central span
中心立轴	king bolt, kingpin
中心料柱	【铁】pillaring
中心裂纹	heart check, centre crack (坯锭缺陷), centre burst (锻造缺陷)
中心裂纹试样	centre cracked specimen
中心零点式[零位]仪表	zero centre meter, centre-zero instrument [gauge]
中心流钢[汤道]砖	【钢】distributor [spider, king] brick
中心冒口	centre riser
中心煤气流(高炉的)	central gas stream
中心排油孔	【机】centre drain
中心配电板	central panel
中心配料厂	【建】central proportioning plant
中心偏析	centerline [centreline] segregation
中心气流过大	【铁】chimneying
中心强度	core strength
中心清晰度	central sharpness
中心区(钢锭的)	core zone
中心曲柄	centre crank
中心缺口板材拉伸试样	centre notched sheet tension specimen
中心缺口试样	centrally notched specimen
中心燃烧式均热炉	bottom centre-fired pit
中心燃烧式热风炉	centre combustion stove
中心烧焊焊缝	centre pour weld
中心石	【建】choke [key] stone
中心试验室	central laboratory, testing centre, centralab
中心疏松	central looseness (钢锭缺陷), central unsoundness (铸坯等的), central [centre] porosity (铸锭缺陷), centreline weakness (铸锭缺陷)
中心缩管[孔](铸锭缺陷)	central pipe
中心汤道砖	【钢】king brick
中心通风道	central air intake
中心位置控制	【压】central position control
中心吸气管	central air intake
中心纤维股芯(钢丝绳的)	fibre main core
中心线	centreline, axis
中心销	centre [core] pin
中心液压站	hydraulic centre
中心原子	central atom

中心窄束	central pencil
中心支承旋转窗	centre pivoted window
中心致密度	centre soundness
中心轴	central shaft
中心轴承	centre bearing
中心注管	(同"中注管")
中心砖	【冶】star,【钢】centre brick
中心桩	【建】centre stake [peg]
中心装料	centre charging
中心装料法	method of centre charging
中心钻	centre bit
中型	medium-sized, middle-sized, midsize, medium duty
中型(电解)槽	medium cell
中型钢材	medium section
中型机器	medium duty machine
中型宽带材轧机	medium wide-strip mill
中型企业	medium industry, medium-sized industrial enterprise
中型箱	【铸】cheek
中型(型钢)轧机	medium section mill
中型轴承	middle bearing
中型铸件	medium(-size) casting
中性	neutrality
中性焙烧	neutral roasting
中性表面	neutral surface
中性萃取	neutral extraction
中性导体	neutral conductor
中性点	neutral point (n.p.), no(n)-slip point
中性点接地电阻器	neutral grounding resistor
中性电解液[质]	neutral electrolyte
中性电抗器	neutral reactor
中性电阻	neutral resistance
中性电阻盘	neutral resistor panel
中性反应	neutral reaction
中性反应器	neutral reactor
中性分子	neutral molecule
中性钢	neutral steel
中性化的	neutralized
中性化合物	neutral compound
中性还原作用	neutral reduction
中性基	neutral radical
中性角	neutral angle, angle of nonslip point
中性介质	neutral medium
中性金属	neutral metal
中性浸出	neutralizing leach, neutral leaching
中性浸出槽	neutral leaching tank
中性浸出工段	neutral leaching section
中性浸出阶段	neutral leaching stage
中性晶体	neutral crystal
中性粒子浸蚀	neutral particle etching
中性炉衬[材料,砌料]	neutral lining
中性炉气	neutral [non-oxidizing] atmosphere
中性炉渣	【冶】neutral slag
中性滤光镜[片]	neutral filter
中性螺旋(对称)轴	neutral screw axis
中性面	neutral plane, neutral surface (指表面)
中性耐火材料	neutral refractory (material)
中性耐火砖	neutral refractory brick
中性浓缩	neutral thickening
中性气氛	neutral atmosphere
中性气体	neutral [indifferent] gas
中性区	neutral zone [region]
中性熔剂	【冶】neutral flux
中性溶液	neutral solution [liquor]
中性试剂	neutral reagent
中性试纸	【化】neutral test paper
中性树脂	neutral resin
中性体	neutral body
中性吸收	neutral absorption
中性稀泥浆	neutralized thin sludge
中性洗液	neutral wash solution
中性纤维(金属弯曲时的)	neutral filament
中性线	neutral conductor [line]
中性焰	neutral flame
中性氧化	neutral oxidation

中性原子　neutral atom
中性渣　[冶]neutral slag
中性轴线　neutral axis
中修(炉子的)　intermediate reline [relining], partial relining
中旋窗　[建]centre-hung swivel window
中压泵　medium-lift pump
中压燃烧器　medium-pressure burner
中压乙炔发生器　medium-pressure acetylene generator
中央　middle (mid.), centre
中央保护气体站　central protection gas plant
中央操作盘　【电】central operation panel
中央处理机[处理部件]　【计】central processing unit (CPU), central processor
中央处理计算机系统　central process computer system
中央存储器　central memory [storage]
中央电话总局　central telephone office
中央调度室　central dispatching room
中央隔板　central partition
中央监视盘　central supervisary panel
中央控制单元　central control unit ◇ 参考数值～*
中央控制盘　【电】central control panel
中央控制站　central station
中央立柱(油罐的)　gin pole
中央排料　central discharge
中央气升搅拌器　central lift agitator
中央强制干油润滑系统　central forced feed grease lubrication system
中央切口试样　central notched specimen
中央润滑油系统　central oil lubrication systems
中央试验室　central laboratory
中央台　【电】central station
中央卸料　central discharge
中央直属企业　enterprises directly under central management
中央终端装置　【计】central terminal unit (CTU)

中央周边排矿[料]　central peripheral discharge
中央周边排矿式磨机　central peripheral discharge mill
中翼缘　medium flange
中硬钢　half-hard steel
中硬金属　half-hard
中硬冷拔线材　medium-hard-drawn wire
中硬沥青　medium-hard pitch
中渣　(同"中间渣")
中真空　medium vacuum
中值　mid-value, median
中止　discontinuation, suspension, hang up, intermission, interruption
中止氧化　(同"止碳")
中轴　centre shaft, mean axis
中珠光体　medium pearlite
中注管　[冶]funnel,[钢]central [centre] runner, centre pot, feed trumpet, fountain, guide tube, trumpet,【铸】riser gate
中注管集中浇注法　hen and chickens method
中注管砖　fountain brick,【钢】central [centre] runner brick, guide tube
中注模[型]　centre-run mould
中子　neutron ◇ 吸收～材料*
中子测水分　neutron source moisture control
中子测水仪　neutron moisture gauge
中子产额　neutron yield
中子产生[生成]　neutron production
中子场　neutron bath
中子成像　neutron imaging
中子-电子间相互作用　neutron-electron interaction
中子发射[辐射]体　neutron emitter ◇ 缓发～*
中子发生器　【理】neutron producer, accelerator for neutron production
中子辐照脆化　neutron irradiation embrittlement
中子辐照金属　【理】neutron-irradiated [n-

irradiated] metal
中子辐照损伤 neutron irradiation damage
中子俘获 【理】neutron capture
中子俘获截面 【理】(neutron-) capture cross-section
中子感生的 【理】neutron-induced
中子光学的 neutron-optical
中子轰击 【理】neutron bombardment
中子活化[激活] neutron activation
中子活化分析 neutron activation analysis
中子积分通量 integrated neutron flux
中子计数管 neutron counter tube
中子龄 neutron age ◇ 费米~Fermi age
中子浓度 neutron concentration
中子谱学 neutron spectroscopy
中子谱仪[分光计] neutron spectrometer
中子迁移[穿透]截面 neutron-transmission cross-section
中子散射截面 neutron-scattering cross-section
中子嬗变掺杂单晶硅 NTD (neutron transmutation dosing) monocrystal silicon
中子射线照片[照相] neutron radiograph
中子射线照相[检验]术 neutron radiography
中子水分[湿度]计 neutron moisture meter, neutron gauge
中子束 neutron beam
中子调节棒 【理】shim rod
中子通量 【理】neutron flux
中子通量密度 neutron flux density
中子透射 neutron transmission
中子吸收 【理】neutron absorption [capture] ◇ 复合~材料*,有害~*
中子吸收剂 neutron absorber
中子吸收剂管 poison tube
中子吸收截[断]面 【理】neutron (absorption) cross section ◇ 铪的 ~ hafnium cross section
中子吸收能力 neutron absorption capacity
中子吸收体 neutron absorber [poison] ◇

液体~fluid poison
中子吸收元素 neutron absorbing element
中子选择器 (neutron) chopper
中子衍射[绕射] neutron diffraction
中子衍射法 neutron diffraction technique
中子衍射法磁结构分析 magnetic structure analysis by neutron diffraction
中子衍射分析 neutron diffraction analysis
中子衍射图[花样] 【理】neutron diffraction pattern
中子衍射研究 【理】neutron diffraction investigation [study]
中子衍射仪 【理】neutron diffraction apparatus, neutron diffractmeter
中子衍射照片[照相] 【理】neutron diffraction photograph
中子引起的 【理】neutron-induced
中子浴 neutron bath
中子源 【理】neutron emitter [producer, source]
中子源水分控制 neutron source moisture control
中子质量 neutron mass
中子中毒 neutron poisoning
中子自旋 neutron spin
钟摆 (clock) pendulum ticker ◇
钟表黄铜(62Cu,36Zn,2Pb) clock brass
钟表弹簧[发条] clock spring ◇ 艾索弗雷克斯小型~Isoflex
钟表弹簧钢 watch spring steel
钟底料罐 【铁】hopper charging bucket
钟斗式设备 【铁】cup-and-cone
钟斗式装料装置 【铁】bell and hopper arrangement, cup-and-cone arrangement
钟杆 【铁】bell rod
钟杆止推轴承 bell bearing
钟壳黄铜合金(68Cu,32Zn) clock case alloy
钟口接头 bell and spigot joint
钟乳石 【地】stalactite, dropper
钟乳石状的 stalactic
钟式挡板 bell damper

钟铜(又名中国青铜、硬青铜、锡青铜、钟用青铜,含 20—25Sn,有时含少量 Zn,余量 Cu) Chinese [bell, hard] bronze, bell metal ◇ 卡拉坎~*

钟形 bell ◇ 制成~belling

钟形沉箱 bell caisson

钟形底料罐 【铁】drop-bottom bucket

钟形阀 bell shaped valve, cup valve

钟形加热炉(烧结用) bell heating furnace

钟形卡盘 bell [cup] chuck

钟形烧结炉 sinter(ing) jar, sinter bell, bell jar (equipment)

钟形铜炉罩(烧结炉的) copper furnace bell

钟形物 bell

钟形阴极 bell type cathode

钟(形)罩 bell jar ◇ 气体(容器)~gas (holder) bell, 烧结~bell jar, 双层烧结~炉*, 退火~annealing bell, 真空密闭水冷金属~*

钟罩式布料机构 bell type distributing gear

钟罩式炉 bell jar equipment

钟罩式退火电炉 electric bell annealer

钟罩式退火炉 bell-type annealing furnace ◇ 辐射管加热~*

钟罩式窑 truck chamber kiln, top-hat kiln

钟罩试验(漏气的) bell jar testing

钟罩型电解槽 bell jar cell

钟状绝缘子 bell shaped insulator

终拔前尺寸 common draw size, base size

终点 end point (e.p.), goal, terminal, termination

终点吹炼 end point blow

终点挡板 end stop

终(点,结)反应 end reaction

终点钢水温度 final steel temperature

终点开关 limit switch [stop]

终点控制 end-point control

终点料栈[终点站堆料场] terminal stockyard

终点速度 terminal velocity

终点碳 aim carbon content

终点位置 final position

终点[终了]温度 finish [outlet] temperature

终点栈房 terminal building

终点站 【运】terminal station, terminus

终端 terminal, end, terminating, dead end ◇ 成批处理~batch terminal

终端处理机 terminal processor

终端电压 terminal voltage

终端负载 terminal [terminate] load

终端盒 terminal box

终端交换器 【计】terminal interchange

终端接口处理机 terminal interface processor

终端绝缘子 terminal [end] insulator

终端控制元件 final control element

终端设备 【计】terminal device [equipment, unit], end instrument

终端套管 terminator

终端条件 terminal condition

终端位置 end [extreme] position

终端限位开关 end limit switch

终端线夹 terminal clamp

终端压力 end pressure

终端装置 termination

终锻 finish forging

终锻模膛 finish impression

终沸点 final boiling point (f.b.p.)

终还原 final reduction

终还原率 final reducibility [reduction (rate)]

终冷工段 final cooling zone

终磨 final grinding

终凝时间 final setting time

终速 final speed [velocity]

终渣 finishing slag

终渣生成 【冶】final slag formation

终渣形成层 zone of final slag formation

终轧尺寸 delivery gauge

终轧道次[孔型] final [last] pass

终轧前孔型 leading pass

终轧温度　finishing temperature (F.T.), finish rolling temperature, end-rolling temperature
终站　dead terminal
终止符号　terminating symbol
终止温度　temperature of completion
种板　【色】mother [starting] blank, stripping plate, platter ◇ 阴极～ cathode blank
种板材料　blank material
种板槽　starting sheet cell, stripping tank, stripper [starter] cell
种板槽阳极　stripper anode
重钢系元素　heavy atinide element
重钢系元素分离　heavy atinide element partitioning
重差法容积　gravimetric volume (g.v.)
重差高度计　gravimetric altimeter
重差计　gravimeter
重掺杂籽晶　heavily doped seed
重锤　weight
重锤平衡式接轴　weight-balanced spindle
重锤平衡式接轴托架　counterweighted balanced type spindle carrier
重锤平衡装置　counterweighted balance device
重锤式平衡　counterweight balance
重锤式上辊平衡装置　top roll counterweight balance arrangement
重锤(式)蓄力器[重荷蓄压器]（同"重力蓄力器"）◇ 平衡～*
重锤式蓄势器用配重　ballast for weight type accumulator
重锤头　heavy ram
重萃液　heavy extract
重大事故　heavy accident [fault]
重的剩余部分　heavy ends
重点　key [focal] point, priority
重点称量　random weighing
重点工程　major [key] project
重点钢铁企业　key iron and steel enterprise

重电子　barytron, heavy electron, penetron
重负荷　heavy load [duty]
重负荷操作　forced working
重负荷用油　e.p. (extreme pressure) oil
重负载接触器　heavy duty contacts
重盖　【钢】heavy cap
重铬酸电池　bichromate cell
重铬酸钾 $\{K_2Cr_2O_7\}$　potassium dichromate
重铬酸钼 $\{Mo(Cr_2O_7)_3\}$　molybdenum dichromate
重铬酸铷 $\{Rb_2Cr_2O_7\}$　rubidium bichromate
重铬酸铯　cesium dichromate
重铬酸盐　bichromate, dichromate
重铬酸盐表面处理（镁合金）　dichromate treatment
重工业　heavy [basic, large-scale] industry
重工业设备　heavy industrial equipment
重骨料　【建】heavy aggregate
重轨　heavy rail
重轨钢　heavy railway steel
重荷载　heavy burden
重合金　heavy alloy [metal], high density tungsten alloy
重混凝土　【建】heavy concrete
重级导轨（滑槽, 起重机梁, 吊车梁）　heavy duty runway
重级路面　heavy duty pavement
重级悬索道　heavy duty runway
重焦油　heavy tar
重介质　【选】heavy media (H.M.), dense medium [media]
重介质黏度　dense medium viscosity
重介质洗矿筒　dense-medium washing drum
重介质选矿[重介选]　heavy media separation (H.M.S.), dense-media separation (D.M.S.)（富选）
重介质选矿设备　float and sink apparatus
重介质选筛　heavy media screen
重金属　heavy metal (H.M.) ◇ 低熔点

~*, X-射线被~屏蔽【理】blocking
重金属溶液化　heavy metal solubilization
重晶石{$BaSO_4$}　bolognian, barite, baryte, heavy spar, cawk
重空穴　【半】heavy hole
重矿物　heavy mineral
重粒子　【理】Y-particles
重沥青　heavy asphalt
重力　gravity (gr.), force of gravity, gravitation, gravitational force ◇ 靠~流动　flow by gravity
重力测定的　gravimetric
重力场　gravitational [gravity] field
重力场源　gravitational-field source
重力沉降　gravitational settling
重力沉降槽[器]　gravitation settler
重力除尘器　gravitational precipitator ◇ 干式~*
重力传送辊　gravity roller
重力传送辊道　gravity roller carrier
重力(传送)辊式运输机　gravity roller conveyor
重力堆积烧结　gravity sintering
重力翻斗式运输机　gravity bucket conveyor
重力分级　gravity classifying
重力分离　gravity separation
重力分析　gravimetric analysis
重力分析测定(法)　gravimetric determination
重力(分析)[重力测定]法　gravimetric method, gravimetry
重力分选　gravity classifying [separation]
重力过滤器　gravity [gravitation] filter
重力焊　gravity type arc welding
重力滑槽　gravity chute
重力滑道[滑移]　gravitational slip
重力混合机　gravity mixer
重力给料　gravity feed
重力给料机[装置]　gravimetric [bleed] feeder
重力加速度　gravity acceleration

重力加载[料]　gravity loading
重力加载蓄能[势,压,力]器　gravity loaded accumulator
重力浇注铸造　gravity-pour casting
重力搅拌机　gravity mixer
重力流　gravity flow
重力流动(物料装卸的)　flow by gravity
重力落锤　gravity-drop hammer
重力能　gravitational energy
重力偏析　gravity segregation
重力平衡　gravity balance, gravitational equilibrium
重力破碎机　gravity crusher
重力烧结　gravity sintering
重力式电弧焊　gravity(-type) arc welding, gravity position welding
重力式结合墙　boned gravity wall
重力式屋顶通风装置　gravity roof-ventilator
重力式张紧装置　gravity take-up unit
重力式蒸汽供暖　steam heating by gravity
重力试验　gravity test
重力收尘器　【环】gravity dust separator
重力水　gravity [bulk] water
重力送料槽　gravity (feed) tank
重力梯度仪　(gravity) gradiometer
重力位置　【理】gravity position
重力蓄力[压]器　dead-weight [weight-loaded] accumulator
重力选矿　gravity dressing [separation, concentration]
重力选矿法　gravity method, gravity dressing
重力压差式给料装置　gravity-head feeder
重力压头[高差]　gravity head
重力仪　gravimeter
重力运输　gravitation transportation, gravity haulage
重力运输机　gravity conveyor, gravitation transporter
重力铸造　gravity casting ◇ 反~*
重力装料(法)　gravity filling [loading]

重力自动出料炉 gravity-discharge furnace
重力自流式混合沉降器 gravity-flow type of mixer-settler
重梁(基础用) bearing pile
重量(日常生活中用) weight (WT, Wgt)
重料车 loaded skip car
重馏分 heavy distillate [fraction]
重炉料 【冶】heavy burden
重模[摩尔]溶液 molal solution
重铌钽(铁)矿{Fe(Nb,Ta)$_2$O$_6$} mossite
重黏土(烧砖用) gault (clay)
重切屑 【机】heavy cut
重氢[氕]{H$_2$} heavy hydrogen (H.H.), deuterium
重氢原子 D atom
重圈 【地】barysphere
重溶剂 heavy solvent
重润滑油 heavy lubricant, heavy lubricating oil
重水 heavy water
重水反应堆 heavy water reactor
重钽铁矿{(Fe,Mn)(Ta,Nb)$_2$O$_6$} tapiolite
重碳氢化合物 heavy hydrocarbons
重铁钽矿 skogbolite
重同位素 heavy isotope
重钨合金 ◇ 肯纳提姆 W2～Kennertium W2
重物升降[转移]滑行装置 skid
重线捆 【压】heavy coil
重相(萃取的) heavier [dense] phase
重相出口 heavy (phase) out
重相入口 heavy (phase) in
重相上升的混合沉降器 mixer-settler with dense phase lifted
重锌锑矿 ordonezite
重心 centre of gravity (c.g.), centroid, centre of mass, barycenter
重心法 【金】centre of gravity method
重心位置 centroid [centre-of-gravity] position
重心压应力 centroid compressive stress
重型材料 heavy [gravity] material
重型锻件 heavy forging
重型废钢铁 heavy scrap
重型钢梁栅 grillage
重型工业设备 heavy industrial equipment
重型构架 heavy duty frame
重型机床 heavy machine tool, power tool
重型机动压尖机 heavy duty power pointer
重型机器 heavy duty machine
重型机械 heavy (duty) machinery
重型剪切机 heavy duty shears
重型剪切机作业线 heavy shear line
重型铺板 solid apron
重型起重机[吊车] heavy (duty) crane, slingcart
重型器材 heavy [gravity] material
重型设备 large-tonnage plant, high tonnage equipment
重型深冲压力机 heavy draw press
重型输送机 heavy duty conveyer
重型水压机 heavy hydraulic press
重型无接头纤维编织皮带 heavy duty endless fabric type belt
重型叶轮 high duty impeller
重型制动器 heavy duty brake
重型锥形制动轮 heavy duty taper brake wheel
重悬浮液 【选】heavy suspension, dense medium, thick dispersion
重悬浮液分选[富选,选矿] float sink separation, heavy media separation
重悬浮液富集 enriching by heavy suspension
重悬浮液选筛 heavy media screen
重悬浮液再生[回收] heavy medium regeneration
重选 (同"重力选矿")
重选精矿 gravity concentrate
重压道次 【压】severe pass

重压盖　【钢】heavy cap
重压力锻造　【压】heavy press forging
重要仪器　key instrument
重要组分　key component
重液　heavy liquid, heavy-fluid
重液出口　heavy liquid outlet
重液入口　heavy liquid inlet
重铀酸铵{(NH$_4$)$_2$U$_2$O$_7$}　ammonium diuranate (ADU)
重铀酸钠{Na$_2$U$_2$O$_7$}　sodium diuranate
重铀酸盐　diuranate
重油　heavy [black, bunker, furnace, dead] oil, marzut, masout, mazout
重油代用品　substitute for heavy oil
重油煤粉(混合浆)喷吹　【铁】oil-coal slurry injection
重油喷射速率　【冶】oil injection rate
重油喷射系统　【冶】oil injection system
重油烧嘴[喷嘴,燃烧器]　heavy oil burner, oil-fired burner [ignitor]
重油脱硫设备　【环】heavy oil desulfurization facility
重油直接脱硫　direct desulphurization of heavy oil
重有色金属　heavy non-ferrous metal
重有色金属合金　heavy metal alloy
重元素　heavy element
重元素萃取分离法　heavy element partitioning by extraction (H.E.P.Ex.)
重原子　heavy atom ◇ 晶粒结构的～测定法*
重载荷润滑脂　heavy duty lubricating grease
重载启动工作制度　heavy starting duty
重载轴承　heavy duty bearing
重轧机负载　severe rolling mill load
重质部分　【选】headings
重质黏土工业　heavy clay industry
重质燃料油　heavy fuel
重质溶剂石脑油　heavy solvent naphtha
重质烃类　heavy hydrocarbons
重子　【理】baryon, barion, heavy particle

仲裁　arbitration ◇ 商业～法庭*
仲裁法　arbitration law
仲裁分析[化验,检定]　arbitral [arbitrary, arbitration] analysis, umpire assay
仲裁试棒　arbitration bar
仲裁试验　arbitrary [arbitration] test
仲裁条款　arbitration clause
仲钨酸　paratungstic acid
仲钨酸铵　ammonium paratungstate
仲钨酸钠{5Na$_2$O·12WO$_3$·28H$_2$O}　sodium paratungstate
仲钨酸盐　paratungstate
仲钨酸盐晶体　paratungstate crystal
仲针铁矿法　para-goethite process
舟皿熔炼　【色】boat melting
周边　perimeter, periphery
周边传动式浓缩机　traction type thickener
周边淬火[淬硬]　contour hardening
周边(分布)不平衡　circumferential imbalance
周边(分布)平衡　circumferential balance
周边焊　circumferential welding ◇ 端部～boxing
周边焊接用夹具　circumferential welding fixture
周边加料　peripheral loading
周边空气　periphery air
周边拉伸[拉深]成形　tangent forming
周边料位　circumferential burden level
周边流　peripheral flow
周边排矿式磨机　peripheral discharge grinding mill ◇ 中央～*
周边排料[矿]　peripheral discharge
周边气流　peripheral gas stream
周边围堤　peripheral dyke
周边卸料碾磨机　rim discharge mill
周边氧化　peripheral oxidation
周长　circumference, perimeter
周节　circular pitch (C.P.), circumferential pitch
周节误差(齿轮的)　(circular) pitch error

周节仪	pitch gauge
周率	frequency, periodicity
周频率	cyclic [circular] frequency
周期	period, cycle, circle, revolution ◇ 不连续~过程*, 大~【计】major cycle, 非~的 dead-beat
周期变化	cycling, periodic change
周期表(元素的)	periodic table
周期表的族	group in periodic table
周期操作法	batch process(ing)
周期重复加载	cyclic stressing
周期次数	number of cycles
周期断面	die-rolled section
周期断面钢材	period section steel, deformed steel bar ◇ 复合~*
周期断面钢筋	deformed bar
周期断面型材轧机	die rolling mill
周期断面型钢	periodic section
周期断面型钢轧机	reinforcing bar mill
周期断面轧槽	deforming groove
周期断面轧制	periodic [die, deformed] rolling, gap-mill forging
周期法冷轧管	rocked pipe [tube]
周期反复电镀	periodic reverse plating
周期反向电流(电镀的)	periodic reverse current
周期反向(电流)电解	P.R.C. (periodical reverse current) electrolysis
周期估计(量)	interval estimate
周期过渡时间	intercycle time
周期函数	periodic function
周期计量器	cycle counter
周期加热	cyclic heating
周期检查	periodic [cyclic] check
周期减速电动机	cyclo-reduction motor
周期孔型	periodic(al) pass
周期量	periodic [harmonic] quantity
周期裂纹(挤压件的)	fir tree defect
周期律	periodic law
周(期)/秒	cycle per second (c.p.s.), periods per second (p/s)
周期挪用	【计】cycle stealing
周期排渣	【冶】intermittent flushing
周期清理	periodic cleaning
周期取样	intermittent sampling
周期蠕变	cyclic creep
周期烧结	cyclic sintering
周期式带钢轧机	Kessler mill
周期式冷轧管	cold pilgered pipe
周期式四摇臂酸洗机	(同"四摇臂式(分批)酸洗机")
周期式无缝管轧机	Pilger seamless-tube mill
周期式轧管机	rotary forging mill ◇ 皮尔格~*
周期式轧机	intermittent-acting [step-rolled] mill
周期数	number of cycles
周期酸洗装置	batch pickler ◇ 柱塞式~*
周期退火	cycle [cyclic, periodic] annealing
周期退火炉	periodic annealing furnace
周期误差	periodic [interval] error
周期系(元素的)	periodic system
周期性	periodicity, cyclicity, intermittence
周期性点阵[晶格]场	periodic lattice field
周期性负载[工作]	periodic duty
周期性加热	cyclical heating
周期性加载	cyclic loading
周期性检修	periodic repair, cycled recondition
周期性结构	periodic structure
周期性力场	periodic field of force
周期性生产	discontinuous running
周期(性)中断	cyclic interrupt
周期压制	【粉】cyclic pressing
周期应变疲劳	cyclic strain fatigue
周期应变诱发蠕变	cyclic strain-induced creep
周期运动	cycle [periodic] motion
周期轧制	periodic rolling
周期装料	periodic charge
周期作业加热炉	in-and-out (heating, re-

heating, type) furnace
周期作业炉 batch [discontinuous] furnace
周期作用蒸罐炉[甑式炉] 【色】intermittent retort
周圈焊 all-around weld
周圈环焊 contour welding
周围大气 environmental atmosphere
周围电子 peripheral electron
周围焊缝 around weld
周围角焊缝 fillet weld all round
周围介质 【金】surrounding medium
周围介质压力 environmental pressure
周围空气 ambient air, environmental atmosphere
周围气氛[介质]作用 environment effect
周围条件 circumferential condition
周围温度 (同"环境温度")
周围压力 ambient pressure
周向变形[应变] hoop strain
周向传热系数 peripheral heat transfer coefficient
周延(性) distribution
周转 turnaround
周转单晶 rotating single crystal
周转额 turnover
周转晶体X射线分光计 rotating-crystal X-ray spectrometer
周转晶体X射线照相[(衍射)]花样 rotating-crystal (X-ray) pattern
周转(晶体)法(X射线分析的) rotating crystal method, rotation method
周转晶体分析(法) (同"晶体分析(法)")
周转晶体衍射(法) rotating crystal diffraction
周转晶体照相机 rotating crystal camera
周转率 turnover [turnround] rate
周转时间 【计】turnaround [turn-round] time
周转衍射图 rotation photgraph
周转周期 cycle of turnover

周转资本 working capital
轴 shaft, arbor, axis (ax.), axle
轴比 axial ratio
轴不对称 lack of axial symmetry
轴测法 axonometry
轴衬 axle [shaft, spindle] bush(ing), bush(ing), bearing segment
轴衬[套]青铜 bush metal
轴承 bearing (br,), shaft bearing ◇ 层压~*, 端[臼形]~ dead abutment, 对开式~ two-part bearing, (多孔)含油~*, 钢背~*, 含石墨~*, 环形阶式~ collar step bearing, 夹布 胶木 ~ fabric bearing, 铜-聚氟乙烯树脂~ copper-fluon bearing, 铜石墨~*, 无缝~*, 斜垫自位~ tilting bearing, 液体摩擦~*, 圆筒形~ cylindrical bearing, 整冲压~*, 整体~*, 支承~ backing bearing, 锥形~*
轴承杯压入器 bearing cup inserter
轴承材料 bearing material
轴承衬 bearing liner
轴承衬垫 bearing backing
轴承衬套 bearing bush(ing) [insert] ◇ 载流[带电]~*
轴承垫片 bearing shim
轴承垫圈 bearing gasket
轴承电流 shaft current
轴承粉料 bearing type mix
轴承盖 bearing cap [cover]
轴承刚性 【机】bearing rigidity
轴承钢 bearing steel ◇ 低氧含量~*, 优质~*
轴承钢棒材 bearing steel bar
轴承钢管 bearing steel pipe, ball bearing tubing
轴承滚珠 bearing ball
轴承滚柱 bearing roller
轴承合金 bearing alloy [metal], antifriction metal, (铅基及锡基轴承合金) Babbitt (alloy), babbitt('s) metal ◇ F.3 镉镍型~*, 比里昂~*, 迪朗斯~*, 高铅~*, 吉纳科~*, 浇注~ cast-on white

metal,卡梅利亚~*,可换~ interchangeable metal,莱昂~*,连杆(孔)~ connecting rod metal,铝基~*,莫尔-琼斯~*,米诺福尔耐磨~*,石墨青铜[(多孔)含油]~*,铜基~ copper-base bearing,铜铅~*,铸造~ cast babbit metal

轴承环 supporting ring

轴承黄铜(60Cu,1.5Al,1Mn,1Fe,36.5Zn) bearing brass ◇曲柄~ crank brass,(铁路)车辆~*,约翰逊~*

轴承架 bearing carrier [pedestal]

轴承金属 bearing metal

轴承壳 bearing shell

轴承螺栓 bearing bolt

轴承面 bearing surface

轴承摩擦损失 bearing friction

轴承强度 bearing strength

轴承青铜(10—12Sn,少量P,0—20Pb,余量Cu) bearing bronze(B.Bz.) ◇ F.2~*,半塑性~*,道森~*,格兰内耐磨~*,哈林顿耐磨~*,科尼须耐磨~*,卢门锌基~*,镍锑铅~*,软巴比~*,萨默特~*,烧结~*,塑性高铅~*

轴承屈服强度 bearing yield strength

轴承套 cage

轴承特性 bearing performance

轴承体 bearing body

轴承凸缘 bearing flange

轴承箱 bearing box [housing]

轴承性能 bearing performance

轴承压力 bearing pressure

轴承应力 bearing stress

轴承用减摩合金 soft metal

轴承允许负荷 bearing capacity

轴承载荷 bearing load

轴承罩 bearing cage [lock]

轴承罩套 bearing lock sleeve

轴承枕垫 pillow block

轴承支架 bearing support

轴承支座 bearing pedestal

轴承铸铁 bearing cast iron

轴承转座 swivel seat with bearing

轴承装配夹具 bearing assembly jig

轴承阻力 bearing resistance

轴承座 bearing seat [box,bracket,block],chock,pillow,【压】(轧辊的)bearing chock,journal box,chuck ◇浮动~【机】floating chock,铸钢~ cast steel chock

轴承座拆卸装置 chock remover ◇轧辊车间~*

轴承座夹紧装置 chock clamp

轴承座圈 race(way)

轴承座圈拉出器 bearing race puller

轴抖动 whipping of shaft

轴端 shaft end

轴对称变形 axisymmetric deformation

轴对称拉伸 axissymmetric drawing

轴耳 trunnion

轴杆 axle,axostylus

轴护套 axle guard

轴环 (axle)collar,axle ring,ruff

轴架 pedestal,plummer block

轴尖合金 pivot alloy

轴尖式量规 point gauge

轴间角 interaxial angle

轴角(结晶的) axial angle

轴颈 (neck)journal,(shaft)neck,axle journal [neck] ◇有环~ collar journal

轴颈合金 journal metal

轴颈轴承 neck [journal] bearing

轴颈轴衬 journal-bearing bushing

轴流泵 【机】axial-flow pump

轴流式鼓风机 axial(flow)blower

轴流式燃气涡轮合金 ◇ 713C~*

轴流式(扇)风机 propeller-type fan,axial(flow)fan

轴密封环 simmer-ring

轴面 axial plane

轴面体 pinacoid,pinakoid

轴伸长节 shaft extension

轴式混合器 shaft mixer

轴台 plummer [pillow] block
轴套 shaft [spindle] sleeve, sleeve (pipe), bearing segment, bush
轴调节器 shaft governor
轴头 stub, spindle nose
轴头编码器 shaft encoder
轴头式铰链 pivot hinge
轴头装置（线卷收集用） boom attachment
轴瓦 bearing bush (ing) [shell], bush (ing), (bearing) backing ◇ 对分~*，三层金属复合~合金 three layers bearing
轴瓦衬用锡铜合金（90Sn, 10Cu） reverse(d) bronze
轴瓦黄铜 axle brass
轴系 shafting, set of axes
轴线 center line (C.L.), axis ◇ 辊身沿~垂直面折断*
轴线对称挤压 axisymmetric extrusion
轴线缩孔（钢锭的） centreline shrinkage
轴箱 axle [housing] box, axle housing
轴箱导轨 (axle) box guide
轴向场 axial field
轴向抽出（换辊） axial withdrawn
轴(向)对称(性) axial symmetry
轴向分布 axial distribution
轴向负荷 axial load ◇ 抗~能力 thrust capacity
轴向缸 axial-cylinder
轴向横断面分层摄影法（X射线的） axial transverse laminography
轴向滑动（轧辊的） endwise slip
轴向孔隙(率) axial porosity
轴向拉力 axial tension
轴向拉伸 axial draw
轴向力 axial force, thrust
轴向连续加热炉（单根的） axial continuous furnace
轴向喷火式烧嘴 axial fire type burner
轴向平面 axial plane
轴向平行性 axial parallelism
轴向剖面 【机】axial section

轴向倾斜辊 axial sloped roll
轴向扇形块 axial segment
轴向疏松（缺陷） axial sponginess
轴向调整 axial adjustment ◇ 轧辊~*
轴向推力 axial [end] thrust
轴向位移 endlong movement, axial displacement
轴向压力 axial compression [pressure]
轴向压缩挠曲 axial compression flexure
轴向延长[延伸] axial elongation [extension]
轴向移动 axial [endlong] movement
轴向应变 axial strain
轴向应力 axial stress
轴向余隙 axial stand off
轴向载荷 axial [thrust] load
轴向载荷疲劳试验机 【金】axial fatigue machine
轴向张力 axial tension, axial tensile force
轴向止推导轮 axial guide thrust roller
轴向轴承 axial [longitudinal] bearing
轴向柱塞泵 axial-plunger pump
轴销 axle pin
轴心荷载 centric load
轴心进线的卷线机 deadhead coiler
轴心疏松（铸锭的） centreline weakness
轴用钢 axle-steel
轴用耐酸密封 shaft acidpoof sealing
轴载重 axle load [weight]
轴枕 pillow
轴(支)座 axle bed
肘柄 【机】grip toggle
肘杆 knee lever, toggle link [rod]
肘杆式冲床 toggle (joint) press
肘杆式压力机 knuckle [toggle] joint press ◇ 液压~*
肘杆压机 toggle lever press, toggle (-action) press
肘杆压片机 toggle-type tablet machine ◇ 斯托克斯~*
肘管 ell, bend, elbow (pipe), kee, side leg
肘接 elbow joint

肘节　toggle (joint), wrist
肘节杆　toggle [angle] lever
皱层　rugosity
皱面　corrugated surface
皱缩工序　【压】shrinking operation
皱纹　wrinkle, crease, ruffle, corrugation, puckering, ripple,【钢】lap,【压】fold, cockles（薄钢板边缘的）◇ 带钢单向～*, 起～ wrinklinge [corrugation, crimping], 有～表皮（铸件缺陷）creasy surface
皱纹锭模壁　corrugated ingot mould walls
皱纹状变形（不锈钢板表面的）【压】ridging, roping
皱折　crimp, fold, lap
昼夜不停的　around-the-clock
昼夜操作　day-and-night service
昼夜产量　【企】daily production
昼夜需要量　daily requirement
骤冷　shock chilling [cooling], quenching
骤冷槽　quench tank
骤冷室　shock chamber
骤冷作用　shock chilling function
骤增　surge
珠滴　droplet, globule
珠光石　argentine
珠光体　【金】pearlite, pearlyte, perlite ◇ 层状～lamellar pearlite, 粗片状～*, 离异～ divorced pearlite, 粒状～*, 片状～钢退火 lamellar annealing, 球状～ nodular pearlite, 屈氏[极细]～ troostite pearlite, 索拜～ sorbitic pearlite, 无～钢*, 细片状～ fine lamellar pearlite
珠光体反应　pearlite reaction
珠光体范围　pearlite range
珠光体钢　pearlitic steel
珠光体合金　pearlite alloy
珠光体幻线[珠光体带]　pearlite ghost
珠光体灰口铁　pearlitic grey iron ◇ 高硅～*
珠光体灰口铸铁　pearlitic grey cast iron
珠光体基体　pearlitic matrix ◇ 纯[全]～*

珠光体集合体[珠光体团]　pearlite colony
珠光体结[球]　pearlite nodule
珠光体结构　pearlitic texture
珠光体晶界　pearlite grain boundaries
珠光体晶粒　pearlite grain
珠光体可锻铸铁　pearlitic malleable (cast) iron ◇ Z～*
珠光体区　pearlite area [range]
珠光体区域　pearlite region, pearlitic domain
珠光体渗碳钢　hyperpearlitic steel
珠光体生铁　pearlite [pearlitic] iron
珠光体生长　pearlite growth
珠光体退化　pearlite degeneracy
珠光体显微组织　pearlite microstructure
珠光体型渗碳体　pearlitic cementite
珠光体型铁素体（共析铁素体）　pearlitic ferrite
珠光体形态学　pearlite morphology
珠光体铸铁　pearlitic (cast) iron, Lanz's cast iron ◇ 高强度～perlit, 兰兹～*
珠光体组织　pearlitic structure
珠焊　bead(ing) welding ◇ 平板上～焊缝[道] bead on plate weld
珠饰端缘　【建】beaded end
珠泽铁　pearlite
珠状凝结　dropwise condensation
珠状增强塑料　bead reinforced plastics
朱厄尔高强度耐热铁合金　Jewell alloy
朱红色　vermillion, bright red
朱砂　（同"辰砂"）
逐步逼近[近似]法　method of successive approximation
逐步反应　step reaction
逐步分解　stepwise decomposition
逐步排除法　method of successive exclusion
逐步膨胀（液化气的）　successive work expansion
逐步退焊法　backstep welding
逐步弯曲式连铸机　progressive bending

逐步消元[排除]法 method of successive exclusion
逐层长大机理(生球的) layering mechanism
逐层装料 【团】charging of layers one by one
逐出 expulsion
逐次地 in series
逐次近似法 【数】convergence [relaxation] mehtod, method of successive approximation
逐点火焰清理 spot-scarf
逐段等时退火 【金】successive isochronical annealing
逐级等温淬火 progressive austempering
逐渐过时(设备的) obsolescence
逐渐膨胀 gradual expansion
逐渐伸长 progress elongation
逐时变化流 time-dependent flow
逐水作用 water expulsion
逐条列举 itemize
竹节钢(筋) knotted bar iron, bamboo steel, ribbed [corrugated] bar
竹筋 bamboo reinforcement
烛煤 candle [cannel] coal
烛状导电棒 candle lead
煮(沸,开) boiling
煮沸溶液 boiled solution
煮解 digesting, high temperature digestion, (hot) digestion
煮解槽 digester chamber
煮解器 digester
煮盐锅 【化】salt furnace
主变形 principal strain
主变压器 main transformer (M.T.)
主变阻器 master rheostat (M.R.H.)
主波 dominant wave, 【理】principal mode (波导的)
主厂房 main building ◇ 炼钢炉~ main furnace building
主程序 【计】main [master] program, main routine
主齿轮 master gear
主抽风机 main suction fan
主触点 main [operating] contact
主传动 main [master] drive ◇ 辊道~长轴 table lineshaft, 轧机~电机 main mill drive motor
主传动联轴器 main drive coupling
主传动轴 line shaft, final drive shaft, main driving axle
主锤(多锤水压机的) main ram
主次梁式结构 beam and girder construction
主从操纵器 master-slave manipulator
主从计算机系统 master-slave computer system
主存储器 【计】main (internal) memory, main storage
主导相(结晶的) 【金】leading phase
主底板 main base
主点(透镜的) principal point
主电极 main pole
主电路 main circuit
主电室 motor room [building] ◇ 轧钢车间~engine-room of mills
主电阻箱[电阻器间] main resistor house (M.R.H.)
主调度程序 【计】master schedule
主调度程序任务 master scheduler task
主动齿轮 drive [driving, power] gear
主动滑移系统 active slip system
主动机构磁力轮 tracing wheel
主动链 drive [driving] chain
主动轮 drive wheel [pulley], driving wheel [pulley], action [running] wheel ◇ 无翼缘~blind driver
主动土压力 【建】active earth pressure
主动小齿轮 driving [driver] pinion
主动轴 drive shaft [axle], driving shaft [spindle, axle], capstan [axle, jack, pinion] shaft, leading [live] axle
主动轴柄 driving crank

主读存储器　read mostly memory
主断路开关[断路器]　main circuit breaker (M.C.B.)
主阀　main [master, king] valve
主反应　main reaction
主反应堆[器]　primary reactor
主返矿[料](仓)　main returns bin
主方式　【计】master mode
主放大器　main amplifier
主风管　primary air main
主风机　main fan, primary air fan
主干电源　main supply
主杆　mother rod
主钢筋　main [principal] reinforcement
主拱　main [principal] arch,【钢】main roof
主钩(吊车的)　main hoist (M.H.)
主钩起重　main hoisting
主鼓[送]风机　【铁】main blower
主关键字　【计】major key
主观误差　subjective [conscious] error
主管部门　competent department, department in charge
主管机关　competent authorities, responsible institution
主管道　main line
主合金　master-alloy
主横梁(水压机的)　main-ram crosshead
主滑轮　head pulley
主回路　major loop
主回路切断开关　main circuit (cut-out) switch
主机　host [master, principal] machine,【计】host computer
主机柜[架]　【计】main frame
主机接口　【计】host interface
主极绕组　main pole winding
主继电器　master relay
主减速机　main gearbox
主件　main units
主焦点　primary [principal, meridional, prime] focus

主结构　【计】major structure
主筋　main reinforcement
主晶　host-crystal, oikocryst ◇ 瓣状晶粒 ～ major lobe
主晶格方向　principal lattice direction
主晶原子　host crystal atom
主卷扬　main hoist
主开关柜　main switch cabinet
主开关器　main circuit breaker
主开关站　main switchgear
主控　master control ◇ 总线～【计】bus master
主控程序　master control (program)
主控[令]开关　master switch
主控制系统　main control system (MCS)
主控站[台]　main [master] control station (MCS), master station
主控振荡器　master oscillator (MO), exciter
主控制屏　main panel
主控制器　master [main, principal] controller, main control gear (水压机的)
主控制室　main control room
主控制台　【计】master [main] console
主冷凝器　main condenser
主联轴节[器]　main [principal] coupling
主连杆　main [master] connecting rod, mother rod
主梁　【建】main [primary] beam
主量元素　prime element ◇ 非～ non-prime element
主量子数　principal quantum number
主令基准　master reference
主流　mainstream, main [mother] current
主路径　【计】main path
主螺杆　engaging screw
主螺栓　king bolt
主脉冲　main [master] pulse
主牌坊(轧机的)　main housing
主配电盘　main switchboard [panel], main switch cabinet
主配线板　main distributing frame

(M.D.F.)
主喷道(射流技术的)　active leg, aperture
主喷枪　primary lance
主喷嘴　primary injector
主偏析　major segregation
主平巷　entry
主平面　main plane
主汽包　drum
主牵引运输机(线盘的)　main drag conveyer
主切曲线　asymptotic curve
主切应变　principal shearing strain
主切应力　principal shearing stress
主驱动电动机　main drive motor
主任工程师　chief engineer
主任建筑师(驻工地的)　chief resident architect
主烧嘴[燃烧器]　main burner ◇ 回转窑～风机　kiln burner fan
主烧嘴助燃风机　combustion fan for main burner
主射流　power stream
主时钟　master clock [timer], main clock
主时钟频率　master clock frequency
主数据　【计】master data [record]
主态　【计】master mode
主题　subject, motif, argument
主体　(main) body, main [principal] part, trunk
主体电解液　background electrolyte
主体角　solid angle
主体金属　base metal
主体晶体原子　host crystal atom
主体泥芯　【铸】body core
主铁(水)沟　main runner, sow (channel)
主凸轮　master cam
主推力　【建】active earth pressure
主文件　【计】master file
主文件清单　master file inventory
主吸收限(X射线的)　main (X-ray) absorption edge
主系统　main system

主线　principal line
主销　kingpin, master pin
主芯骨　【铸】crab
主芯骨架　core crab
主选通脉冲　【电】main gate, main gating pulse
主烟道　main (chimney) flue, 【钢】principal offtake
主衍射线条(X射线的)　principal lines
主要部件　main units
主要材料　parent material
主要产品　primary [prime, main] product
主要成本　major cost(s)
主要成分　essential component, staple
主要反应　main [primary] reaction
主要费用　major costs
主要负载　major load
主要工艺流程[作业表]　master schedule
主要工作辊道(轧机的)　main table
主要金属　major metal
主要矿物　essential mineral
主要倾向　mainstream
主要缺陷　major defect
主要设备　essential equipment, workhorse
主要设施　main facilities
主要(受力)焊缝　principal weld
主要特性　prominent [main] characteristic
主要特征　principal characteristic, leading features
主要图解　predominance diagram
主要形式　【理】fundamental mode
主要仪器　key instrument
主要因素　major [primary] factor
主要元素　major element
主要原料　main feed
主要杂质　principal [chief, major] impurity, impurity of importance
主要增亮剂　primary brightener
主要组分　chief [key] component, main constituent
主液压缸　main cylinder
主应变　principal strain

主应力　principal [primary] stress
主语言系统　【计】host-language system
主元件　master element
主轧辊　tread roll, king roller
主轧机　main mill
主轧跨　mill yard
主站　【计】master station
主振荡器　driving [master, king] oscillator
主正应变　principal normal strain
主正应力　principal normal stress
主值　principal value
主旨　purport, substance, gist, motif
主轴　main shaft [spindle], (driving) spindle, (main) arbor, principal [main] axis, major axis (椭圆的)
主轴承　main [base] bearing
主轴集体传动式(轧机)辊道　lineshaft-type mill table
主轴颈　king journal, trunnion
主轴箱(机床的)　headstock
主柱塞(水压机、挤压机的)　main press ram
主助燃空气透平风机　main combustion air turbo-fan
主装料运输带　main charging belt
主族元素　main group element
主最大值　【理】principal maximum
柱　column (col.), pillar, post, beam (光学用) ◇ 欧拉～公式
柱底脚　column footing
柱顶　column top
柱沟　【建】stria
柱环　【建】collar
柱环节链　stud chain
柱基　plinth
柱基础　column foundation
柱架式结构(高炉的)　column bracket structure
柱间距　column interval
柱间距离固定比　【建】intercolumniation
柱间斜撑　bracings between columns
柱脚　shoe, pedestal

柱浸　column leaching
柱晶[柱状晶体]　columnar crystal, cylindrulite
柱晶界　cell boundary
柱晶石{$MgAl_2SiO_6$}　kornerupine
柱坑挖掘机　posthole digger
柱磷锶锂矿　palermoite
柱硫铋铅矿　ustarasite
柱硫锑铅银矿　freieslebenite, donacargyrite
柱流　piston flow
柱氯铅矿　daviesite
柱帽　bonnet,【建】haunch
柱钠铜矾{$CuSO_4 \cdot Na_2SO_4 \cdot 2H_2O$}　kroenkite
柱塞　plunger, forcer ◇ 合型～【铸】closing plunger
柱塞(棒)式钢(水)包[钢水罐]　Bessemer ladle
柱塞泵　plunger (type) pump ◇ 复谐式液压～*, 轴向～axial-plunger pump
柱塞导管　plunger guide
柱塞杆　plug [plunger] rod
柱塞横梁　plunger crosshead
柱塞式分批[周期]酸洗装置　plunger mast-type batch pickler
柱塞式泥炮　【铁】plunger type (clay) gun
柱塞式酸洗机　plunger type pickling machine
柱塞式酸洗设备　plunger type pickler
柱塞式团矿机　plunger type briquetting machine
柱塞式推钢机　plunger pusher
柱塞式推料机　stripper plunger
柱塞式压团机　plunger press
柱塞式液压电动机　piston motor
柱塞提升机　plunger elevator
柱塞(推进)式给料机　plunger feeder
柱塞转换开关　plunger switch
柱式高压釜　column autoclave
柱式提升机　column elevator
柱式压机　column [pillar] press

柱销测压仪 【压】pressure sensitive pins
柱铀矿 schoepite
柱支承炉顶 column-supported top
柱桩绝缘子 anchor insulator
柱状(晶粒) columnar shape
柱状萃取器 column extractor
柱状断口 columnar fracture
柱状粉末 【粉】sprills
(柱状)富矿体 ore shoot
柱状合金扩散 outdiffusion
柱状(结)晶层 layer of columnar crystals
柱状晶带 zone of columnar crystals
柱状晶钢锭 scorched ingot
柱状晶粒 columnar grain
柱状晶粒生长 columnar grain growth
柱状晶区 【金】columnar zone, zone of columnar crystals
柱状坯块 cylindrical compact
柱状铁素体 columnar ferrite
柱状图 bar graph
柱状锡粉 sprill tin
柱状衍射花样 columnar diffraction pattern
柱状枝晶 columnar dendrite
柱状组织 【金】columnar structure
柱子轮廓图 column outline
助沉(降)剂 settling [sedimentation] aid
助催化剂 promoter, promotor, cocatalyst
助沸剂 【钢】rimming agent
助焊剂 scaling powder
助聚剂 promoter, promotor
助卷机(带材的) wrapper ◇ 皮带~*
助卷(机)辊 wrapper roll (wr) ◇ 伸缩式~*
助卷摩擦 wrapping friction
助理 assistant
助理工程师 assistant engineer (A.E.)
助力器 booster, augmenter, augmentor
助滤剂 filter(ing) medium, filter aid ◇ 预涂~的过滤机 precoat filter
助滤器 filter aid
助凝剂 coagulant aid ◇ 非离子型~*, 阴离子~ anion coagulant aid
助燃风机 combustion fan, combustion air ventilator ◇ 点火烧嘴~*, 烧嘴~*
助燃鼓[送]风机 combustion air blower [fan]
助燃空气透平风机 combustion air turbo-fan
助热器 heat booster
助熔 fluxing ◇ 煤氧~*, 用碱~ fluxing with alkali
助熔合金 fluxing alloy
助熔糊 fluxing paste
助熔剂 (smelting) flux, fluxing agent [medium], fusing agent, agent of fusion, fluxed additions ◇ 加~脱气 flux degassing
助熔金属 flux metal
助熔炉渣 flux slag
助熔能力 【冶】fluxing power
助熔性 fluxibility
助熔作用 fluxing action [effect]
助手 assistant, helper, subworker, adjunct, mate
助推 boost(ing)
助推器 booster, boost motor
贮备 store up, stock
贮备溶液 stock solution
贮仓 storage bin [hopper, silo] ◇ 间格式~ organ-pipe bunker, 强制流通~*
贮仓出料装置 outloading feeder
贮藏池 storage pond
贮藏器容量 tankage
贮藏设备 storage facilities
贮藏室 cellar, storeroom
贮藏所 depository, depot, cascade
贮槽 storage [stock, accumulator, holding, reserve] tank, bin, silo, tank ◇ 工地[现场]架设的~ field elected tank, 间格式~ organ-pipe bin
贮尘室 dust pocket
贮存 store, stockpile, impounding, impoundment, 【环】containment (污水的)

◇ 分类～component storage
贮存槽　holding bath
贮存场　stock place
贮存池(赤泥的)　impoundment lake
贮存罐　storage pot
贮存锅　storage kettle [pot]
贮存滑道　storage skid
贮存跨　stocking [yard] bay
贮存料　bunkering
贮存能力(料场的)　stockpiling capacity
贮存器　conservator
贮存(容)量　storage capacity
贮存入库　warehousing
贮存设施　stocking arrangement
贮存时间　period of storage
贮存装置　stocking arrangement
贮锭跨　ingot storing bay
贮斗　bunker
贮放场　storage compound [pen]
贮罐　stock tank
贮灰槽　ash-storage tank
贮焦量　coke storage capacity
贮矿仓　ore(-storage) bunker
贮矿槽　storage silo, stockpile, 【铁】ore bin
贮矿场　raw ore stockyard, stock yard [dump], storage yard [area], 【采】ore-blending plant, 【铁】ore field
贮矿场卸料沟　【铁】ore trough
贮矿场装料地沟　【铁】ore-reclaim tunnel
贮矿能力　ore storage capacity
贮矿仓　ore silo
贮料仓　storage bunker
贮料辊道　magazine table
贮料量　holding capacity
贮料塔　accumulator (ACC)
贮能焊接　stored-energy welding
贮气槽[箱]　gas tank
贮气罐　gas tank [holder], air vessel, plenum chamber (压缩空气系统的)
贮气柜　gas tank, gasometer
贮气瓶　gasometer
贮气容器　air vessel

贮氢材料　hydrogen storage alloy [material]
贮氢电极合金　hydrogen storage electrode alloy
贮乳器青铜(20Ni, 8Zn, 4Pb, 4Sn, 余量 Cu)　dairy bronze
贮水槽　water-storage tank, holding tank
◇ 高位～balance tank
贮水池　reservoir, holding pond, pool
贮水器　cistern, water back
贮铁水罐　holding [receiving] ladle
贮铁水炉　【铸】casting shoe
贮液　stock solution
贮液杯　cistern
贮液槽　solution storage, storage tank
贮液池　pool
贮油箱　conservator
贮渣箱　slag tank
铸疤　chink(ing), scabby
铸包内衬　【冶】ladle liner
铸币　coinage
铸成整体的　cast-on
铸成最终尺寸的　cast-to-size
铸床　【铁】pig bed
铸锭　ingot casting [pouring, making], teeming, casting ingot
铸锭侧　pouring side
铸锭车　casting car [carriage, bogie], ladle barrow, teeming truck
铸锭车间　pouring hall
铸锭车浇桶　truck ladle
铸锭底板　【钢】bottom plate
铸锭定心机构　【钢】casting-centering mechanism
铸锭法　ingot casting method, teeming practice ◇ 哈梅特加压～【钢】Harmet process, 均质～*, 卡纳利斯 加铝热剂 ～【钢】Canaris method, 瀑布式 ～*, 索维尔溢流 ～*, 一般～direct teeming, 自动～automatic ladling
铸锭废钢　pit scrap
铸锭钢　ingot (cast) steel

zhu 铸　　　　　　　　　　　　　　　1808

铸锭工　pourer,【钢】ladleman
铸锭工段　casting [pouring, teeming] aisle, pouring side
铸锭机　casting machine, pig moulding machine ◇ 动模 ～ moving mould casting machine, 沃尔克型圆盘～Walker casting wheel, 圆形～【色】casting wheel
铸锭进程送进闸门　ingot feed lock
铸锭坑　casting [teeming] pit
铸锭跨　ingot casting bay, casting [teeming] aisle, pouring bay [aisle] ◇ 炼钢车间～*
铸锭炉　casting furnace ◇ 石墨坩埚～*
铸锭凝固　growing of ingot ◇ 大型～*
铸锭偏析　ingot segregation
铸锭起重机　ingot charging crane,【钢】teeming crane
铸锭设备　casting unit
铸锭台　teeming platform
铸锭样　【钢】pit sample
铸锭组织　【金】ingot structure
铸锻联合成型机　casting and forging machine
铸废品　misfit cast, off-cast
铸钢　steel casting (S.C.), cast steel (c.s.), steel founding, teeming ◇ 坩埚～ crucible-cast steel, 含镍～*, 冷硬～ hard cast steel, 连续～*, 碳素～ carbon cast steel
铸钢板　cast steel plate (C.S.P.)
铸钢产品　cast steel product
铸钢厂[车间]　steel foundry
铸钢锭　cast steel ingot
铸钢工　steel founder,【钢】pourer
铸钢罐　cast steel pot
铸钢横梁　cast steel separator
铸钢机架　cast steel housing
铸钢件　cast steel product, steel-casting
铸钢模　cast steel die, steel mould
铸钢平台　casting platform
铸钢铺板　cast steel apron
铸钢扇形件　cast steel segment

铸钢设备　casting equipment
铸钢丸（喷射加工用）　cast steel shot
铸钢轧辊　【压】cast steel roll
铸钢轴承座　cast steel chock
铸工　founder, foundery hand, founderyman
铸工车间　(同"翻砂间")
铸工尺　moulder's rule
铸管　cast pipe [tube] ◇ 离心～*
铸管件　pipe casting
铸罐（铁水罐车的）　ladle pot
铸罐倒罐工段　reladling station
铸罐浇铸法　ladle practice
铸罐座架　ladle support
铸焊　burning-in, cast joint, cast-welding ◇ 钢轨～接头*, 熔化～*
铸焊焊缝　poured weld
铸焊件　cast-weld assembly
铸焊结构　【机】cast-weld structure
铸合　【铸】draining
铸机　caster, casting [foundery] machine ◇ 直槽式～vertical slot caster
铸痂形成　【铸】scabbing
铸件　casting, cast product, foundery casting work, foundery goods ◇ CO2 型～ CO2 mould casting, 薄壁[小断面]～ thin-section casting, 大型～ heavy casting, 单个～*, 厚壁[大断面]～*, 夹杂物多的～ dirty casting, 离心～ centrifugal casting, 流态砂型～ fluid mould casting, 米蒂斯～*, 去掉浇铸系统[清过砂]的～ fettled casting, 缺肉[有缺陷]～*, 热处理～ heat treated casting, 双金属～ bimetal casting, 小型～ miniature casting, 修整—锤 chasing hammer, 有疤～ scabbed casting, 有棱条的～ ribbed casting, 有气孔～ blistered [blown] casting, 有缺陷～ faulty [defect (ive), spoiled] casting, 有芯～ cored casting
铸件报[致]废　rejection of casting
铸件表面涂料　foundery facing
铸件表皮[结壳]　skin of casting, skin of

cast section
铸件分析 cast analysis
铸件和锻件缺陷冷态修补法 ◇梅塔洛克～Metalock
铸件合格率 casting yield
铸件横向截面缩小 sag
铸件加强肋 bracket
铸件落砂工段 casting removal station
铸件内腔 core cavity
铸件清理 fettling
铸件清理后重量 fettled casting weight
铸件清理机 casting cleaning machine
铸件清理台 fettling bench
铸件清砂工段 casting removal station
铸件清砂(滚)筒 rattle barrel ◇湿法～wet tumbler
铸件清洗[洗涤]机 casting washing machine
铸件清整工 casting dresser
铸件缺陷 casting defect
铸件设计 casting design
铸件体 body of casting
铸件应力 casting stress
铸件硬度 cast(ing) hardness
铸件圆角成形用冷铁 radius chill
铸件质量 cast product quality
铸件质量和表面比 mass-surface ratio
铸件皱纹 cold-shut, casting lap
铸件最后抛光 chasing
铸坑 foundery [casting] pit, jacket, fosse
铸坑耐火材料 pouring pit refractory
铸坑用吊车 casting-pit [centre-casting] crane
铸口 casting nozzle,【钢】green hole
铸块 ingot (bar), butt ◇试验～cast test block
铸拉 cast-drawing
铸流 cast strand
铸流间距(多流连铸的) strand distance inner-strand spacing
铸铝 cast aluminium
铸铝合金 cast aluminium alloy

铸模 mo(u)ld, moulding die, casting mould ◇带浇口的～gated pattern, 熔融～*, 石墨～graphite mould
铸模表面刨平 searing
铸模复杂程度 die complexity
铸模干燥炉 foundery stove
铸模喷洒液槽 【铁】mould spray tank
铸模润滑 mould lubrication
铸模润滑间 mould lubricating station
铸模寿命 mould life
铸模涂料 mould wash, mould facing material
铸坯 casting blank [block], strand ◇扁～cast slab, (金属)包套～canned billet
铸坯表面温度 strand surface temperature
铸坯导架 【连铸】strand guide
铸坯底部 bottom of casting
铸坯弯曲机 bender
铸坯轧压 【连铸】strand reduction
铸皮 casting skin
铸青铜 cast bronze
铸入管 cast-in (pipe)
铸勺 casting ladle, spoon tool (造型用)
铸石 cast stone (c.s.)
铸石件 molten-rock casting
铸石砖 clinker brick (C.B.)
铸塑复型(制备)法 cast replica
铸塑树脂 cast resin [plastic]
铸态 as-cast condition
铸态 Fe$_3$Al 合金 as-cast Fe$_3$Al alloy
铸态表面精整 as-cast finish
铸态共晶碳化物 as-cast eutectic carbide
铸态金属 as-cast metal
铸态晶粒 as-cast grain
铸态球墨铸铁 as-cast nodular cast iron
铸态硬度 cast(ing) [as-cast] hardness
铸态硬质合金 cast carbide
铸态铸件 green casting
铸铁 cast iron (C.I.), casting [foundry] iron, pig ◇埃梅尔～*, 奥氏体～*, 复合～composite casting, 钢性[低碳]～gun iron, 高级～*, 工程[机器制造用]

zhu 铸　　　　　　　　　　　　　1810

~*,钴镍~*,海绵~ spongy cast iron,含镍白口硬~*,合金~*,黑心~【铁】blackheart,兰兹[珠光体]~ Lanz's cast iron,冷~ chill cast pig,冷硬~*,耐磨~*,耐热~*,耐蚀~*,破碎~ crushed cast iron,气缸~ cylinder iron,球墨~*,铈处理[加铈变质处理]~*,纤维组织~ fibrous iron,液碎~*,针状~*,致密石墨~*

铸铁安全日(轧机压下系统的) iron pad
铸铁变质[孕育]处理 modification of cast iron
铸铁表面(喷)渗铝法 metcolising, metcolizing
铸铁场 【铁】casthouse ◇ 环形~*
铸铁场平台 【铁】casting platform
铸铁场铁水沟平面图 casthouse iron runner layout
铸铁场作业 casthouse work
铸铁厂 iron foundry
铸铁厂废料 iron-foundry waste
铸铁导板 cast iron guide
铸铁的碳化物稳定能力 【铸】carbide-retaining power of iron
铸铁电极 cast iron electrode
铸铁电阻(器) cast iron resistor
铸铁锭 pig casting
铸铁阀 cast iron valve
铸铁钢锭模 【铸】cast iron mould
铸铁割炬 cast iron cutting burner
铸铁工 iron founder,【铁】pig-casting operator ◇ 出铁场[砂床]~【铁】stocktaker
铸铁管 cast iron pipe (C.I.P.)
铸铁滚柱式芯撑 (同"陀螺式芯撑")
铸铁焊接 cast iron welding
铸铁焊料 cast iron solder
铸铁焊料合金 castolin
铸铁机 pig (cast, moulding) machine, casting plant ◇ 双链[带]~*
铸铁机废铁 casting-machine scrap
铸铁机架 【压】iron stand, cast iron housing

铸铁机链带 pig string
铸铁机试样 pig-machine sample
铸铁机黏连铁块 pig sticker
铸铁机铸模 pig mould
铸铁件 iron casting ◇ 工业[商品]~*,合金~ alloy iron casting
铸铁金相(组织)图 ◇ 格赖纳-克林根施泰因~*
铸铁可锻化退火 malleablizing annealing
铸铁块 mould pig iron, casting pig
铸铁冷却板[立冷板] 【铁】cast iron cooling plate
铸铁冷却壁 【铁】cast iron stave
铸铁粒 cast iron shot ◇ 冷硬~ chilled shot,脱碳~*
铸铁铝热剂 cast iron thermit
铸铁煤气切断器 cast iron gas cutter
铸铁配件 cast iron fittings
铸铁喷铝法 metcolising
铸铁铺板(轧机周围的) cast iron apron
铸铁切屑 cast iron shavings
铸铁容器 cast iron vessel
铸铁砂床 【铁】sand bed
铸铁水套 cast iron water-jacket
铸铁塔 cast iron tower
铸铁桶 foundery ladle
铸铁桶叉架 【冶】ladle shank
铸铁桶摇把 ladle shank
铸铁用(铜镍系)焊条合金 (32.2Cu, 65.3Ni, 1.3Fe, 1.2Mn) soft-weld
铸铁(轧)辊 【压】cast iron roll ◇ 带槽~ grooved iron roll,光面冷硬~*,加镍~ nickel iron roll,可锻~*,冷硬钼镍镁~,砂型~ grain roll,双层~*
铸铁长大[生长](现象) cast iron growth
铸铁蒸馏罐 【色】cast iron retort
铸铁制品 cast iron ware, yetling
铸铁中的石墨形状 graphite pattern in cast iron
铸铁轴承座 cast iron chock
铸铁组织图 ◇ 莫勒~*

铸铜 cast(ing) copper
铸铜(车)间 brass foundry
铸铜电焊条 electric welding cast copper solder
铸铜合金 casting copper alloy
铸型 casting mould [pattern, form], (cast) mould, matrix ◇ 杯形~*, 底注~ bottom pour mould, 地坑~ floor mould, 叠箱~ multiple mould, 多腔(组合)~*, 佛德斯薄壳~法*, 盖箱地面~ covered floor mould, 干砂~ dry sand mould, 烘酥[过烘干]~ dead burned mould, 铰接式(对开)~ book mould, 金属[冷]~ chill mould, 局部干燥~ partially dried mould, 可换~ interchangeable mould, 离心~*, 两砂箱[两开箱]~ two-part mould, 螺旋形流动性试样~ cury fluidity mould, 轻捣[压]实~ soft-rammed mould, 倾动式~ tilt mould, 湿砂~ green sand mould, 无[脱]箱~ boxless mould, 一次~ dispensable mould, 已完成~ complete mould, 永久~ long-life mould, 有型芯~ cored foundry mould, 装配式~ built-up mould, 组芯~ core mould
铸型补助浇口 dozzle
铸型充满能力 mould filling ability
铸型非正弦式振动 non-sinusoidal mould oscillation
铸型符号 form symbol
铸型干燥炉 mould-drying oven
铸型烘干 mould drying
铸型检查 mould inspection
铸型落砂(机) mould knock-out
铸型跑火 bleeding of mould
铸型膨胀 mould dilatation
铸型筛 moulder's riddle
铸型塌箱 mould crush
铸型涂料[浆] moulding wash(ing) [ink], mould coating (material), mould dressing, adhering moulding material, foundery [wet] blacking, sand wash, smoke black
铸型弯折 buckle
铸型系数 (同"模型系数")
铸型下部 nowel, drag
铸型型芯 foundery core
铸型形状 shape of mould
铸型严重鼠尾 (sand)buckle
铸型硬度 mould hardness (M.H.)
铸型振动 mould oscillation
铸型组装 mould assembly
铸－压－轧 casting-pressing-rolling (CPR)
铸－压－轧工艺 CPR process
铸样勺 say ladle
铸造 cast(ing), found(e)ry, founding, mint (货币) ◇ 爆炸~ explosive casting, 低压~(法) low-pressure casting, 动模~(法)*, 冻结~ freeze casting, 杜维尔回转~法 Dourville process, 多型~*, 翻箱~ inversion casting, 反压~*, 干型~ dry sand casting, 霍尔－阿德林铝热法*, 加压~*, 金属型[硬型]~*, 壳型~*, 可~的 castable, 可~性 castability, 空心~ cast hollow, 离心~*, 立式~ upright casting, 模板法~ planchet casting, 模压~ casting by squeezing, 墨鱼骨模法*, 齐布林向上堆积铸型~法 Zueblin process, 熔模~*, 砂箱~ flask casting, 湿(砂)型~ green(sand) casting, 石膏型~*, 石墨型~*, 实型~*, 适于~的 capable of being cast, 水中[下]~法*, 无盖地面[敞开]~ open cast, 无泥芯~ coreless casting, 小件~ miniature casting, 有泥芯~ cored casting, 整体[按模, 成一体]~的*), 重力~*
铸造埃发杜尔硅青铜(3—4Si, 1Mn, 1Zn, 余量 Cu) cast Everdur
铸造巴比合金 cast babbit metal
铸造巴比合金轴承 babbitt metal cast bearing
铸造变形 casting strains
铸造部 casting division [shop, station], foundery department

zhu 铸　　　　　　　　　　　　　　1812

铸造材料　foundery material
铸造产品质量　cast product quality
铸造场　casting bay [bed]
铸造场地　foundery floor
铸造厂　foundry (fdry), commercial foundry, jobbing foundry
铸造车间　casting shop [department, house, room], found(e)ry, foundery department ◇ 机械化～ mechanized foundry, 专业性～ specialty foundry (美)
铸造车间设备　foundery machinery
铸造重皮　casting lap
铸造磁钢　cast steel magnet
铸造磁铁　cast magnet
铸造底板　casting plate
铸造电解铁　cast electrolytic iron
铸造杜拉铝　cast duralumin
铸造返[回收]料　foundery returns
铸造飞边　casting fin
铸造废钢　casting scrap
铸造废料　foundery waste, casting rejects
铸造废气　foundery effluent
铸造废[碎]铁　foundery scrap
铸造工程　foundery engineering
铸造工人　caster, foundry-man
铸造工作　foundery work
铸造工作者　founder
铸造过程　found(e)ry
铸造和压铸铝合金 ◇ 356～*
铸造合金　casting [foundery, as-cast] alloy ◇ H蒙乃尔～H Monel, Y～*, 吉尔科纳尔锌基～*, 空心～ slush-casting alloy, 兰加洛伊高镍～*, 耐高压～*, 瓦格纳装饰用锡基空～*
铸造合金钢　cast alloy steel (C.A.S.)
铸造黄色黄铜(38Zn, 1Sn, 1Pb, 余量Cu) cast yellow brass
铸造黄铜(75Cu, 24Zn, 1Pb)　cast(ing) brass ◇ 奥卡～*, 高铜～*
铸造活塞环　piston ring casting
铸造机　caster, casting [foundery] machine ◇ 低压～*, 轮带式～ wheel belt caster, 阳极～*, 阴极～*
铸造加压室　plenum chamber
铸造焦　foundery [cupola] coke
铸造接缝　【铸】cast seam
铸造结疤　casting lap
铸造金属　cast metal
铸造坑　founding [casting] pit
铸造空心轧辊　hollow cast roll
铸造跨间　casting bay
铸造裂纹　casting crack
铸造炉　casting [foundery] furnace, teeming furnace (铸造电炉)
铸造铝合金　cast aluminium alloy, aluminium casting alloy ◇ 214～*, 40E～*, A.355～*, F.132～*, N.A.～ N.A. alloy, N耐蚀～*, 麦卡达米特～*, 塞拉卢明～*, 斯蒂瓦特～Stewart alloy, 特纽阿尔～*, 瓦纳纽姆耐蚀～*
铸造毛刺　casting fin
铸造镁合金　cast magnesium alloy ◇ A.M.100A～*
铸造锰黄铜(59Cu, 0.75Sn, 0.75Pb, 37Zn, 1.25Fe, 0.75Al, 0.5Mn)　manganese cast brasses
铸造锰青铜(59Cu, 0.75Sn, 0.75Pb, 37Zn, 1.25Fe, 0.75Al, 0.5Mn)　manganese cast bronze ◇ 1号～*, 高强度～*, 特巴迪尤姆船用～*
铸造耐热合金　cast heat-resistant alloy
铸造镍基耐热合金 ◇ IN-100～*
铸造坯　casting block
铸造起重机　casting [caster, pouring(-side), foundery] crane
铸造铅字合金(54—70Pb, 10—20Sn, 20—28Sb, 少量Cu)　foundery type metal
铸造切头　casting rejects
铸造青铜(3—4Ni, 11.5—13Sn, 0.05—0.3P, 余量Cu)　cast bronze, P.N. bronze
铸造青铜轴承学会(美国)　Cast Bronze Bearing Institute (CBBI)
铸造缺陷　casting defect [fault, flaw]

铸造设备	casting equipment [unit]

铸造设备 casting equipment [unit]
铸造设备制造厂商协会 Foundry Equipment Manufacturers Association (FEMA)
铸造生产 foundery practice
铸造生铁 casting pig, foundery iron [pig]
铸造试块 cast test block
铸造缩尺 contraction [shrinkage] gauge
铸造碳化物 cast carbide
铸造特性 casting characteristic [property]
铸造铜硅锌合金 ◇ 艾杰克斯~*
铸造铜合金(88Cu,8Sn,4Zn) cast(ing) copper alloy, copper casting alloy ◇ 盎司~*,陶鲁斯~(系)*
铸造型焦 foundry formed coke
铸造性能 casting characteristic [property], castability, founding property ◇ 具有~的 capable of being cast
铸造阳极 cast anode
铸造业务 foundery work
铸造艺术品 art castings
铸造应力 casting stress
铸造硬铝 cast duralumin
铸造用冲天炉 foundery cupola
铸造用锭 foundery ingot
铸造用反射炉 foundery air furnace
铸造用铬铁 foundery ferrochrome
铸造用工具 cast tool
铸造用耐火材料 foundery refractory
铸造用熔剂 foundery flux
铸造用砂 foundery sand
铸造原状 as-cast state [condition]
铸造轴承合金 cast babbit metal
铸造装置 casting plant
铸造状态(未经加工) as-cast state [condition]
铸造状态硬度 cast(ing) [as-cast] hardness
铸造组织 【金】cast structure
铸造组织破坏 breakdown of as cast structure
铸轧 casting-rolling ◇ 连续[在线]~*,

索罗~法【冶】Soro process
铸-轧工艺 casting-rolling process
铸-轧生产线 casting-rolling line
铸钟青铜 Chinese bronze
铸字 typecasting
筑堤 banking
筑炉工 furnace builder
筑路焦油 road tar
住友粉尘直接还原法 Sumitomo dust reduction process, S.D.R. (Simitomo Direct Reduction) process
住友预还原法 Sumitomo pre-reduction method (SPM)
注册 register, registration,【计】log on
注册商标 registered trade mark
注尺寸草图 dimensioned sketch
注解 comment, note
注口 pouring gate [hole, spout], sprue, stopper nozzle,【色】pouring nozzle ◇ 组合~bicomponent nozzle
注口耐火材料 nozzle refractory
注口塞 spout plug
注块 【耐】castable
注蜡器 【铸】wax injector
注明日期 date ◇ 未~的 undated
注铅充填物 lead filler
注铅检测(锻模尺寸)【压】lead proof
注入 pouring-in, inpouring, injection, influx(ion), impregnation
注入泵 filler pump
注入高度(到钢包的) pour(ing) height
注入机 impregnating machine
注入井(废水的) injection well
注入孔 filling hole [aperture]
注入口 influx, handhole,【铸】filling opening
注入器 injector
注入效率 injection efficiency
注入型激光器 injection laser
注入装置 injection equipment
注塞 pour plug
注射剂 injectant

注射器 injector, inspirator
注释[解]行 【计】comment line
注水式乙炔发生器 【焊】water-to-carbide acetylene generator, water-to-carbide system
注铁场 【铁】casting yard
注铁场平台 ingot casting platform
注销 【计】log off [out]
注液漏斗 filling funnel
注意 take care (TC, tc), attention ◇ 引起~中断
注意键 【计】attention key
注意事项 precautions
注意信号 caution signal, 【计】attention
注油器 oiler, oil lubricator
注油枪 (grease) gun
注油嘴 oil nipple, lubricator fitting
驻波 standing [stationary] wave
驻点 point of arrest, 【理】arrest
驻极(电介)体 electret
抓斗 bucket (grab), grab, crab bucket, grapple(r), clamshell (蚌壳式抓土器) ◇ 贝诺托式~*
抓斗起重机[吊车] bucket [grab(bing), clamshell (-equipped)] crane, scraper bridge
抓斗取样器 bucket sampler
抓斗式料桶 clamshell(-type dump) bucket
抓斗式疏浚船[机] clamshell dredge(r)
抓斗式挖泥机 grapple [clamshell, grab] dredge(r)
抓斗式挖掘机 bucket excavator, clamshell (excavator, shovel)
抓斗式万能装卸机 grab truck
抓斗送料压力机 gripper feed press
抓斗小车 grab car
抓具 gripping apparatus, grab
抓牢 clutch, anchor-hold
抓取 grab
抓手(机械手的) tongs, (hand)grip
抓土机 ream grab

抓岩机 【采】bucket grab, grab (bing) crane, scraper bridge
抓扬机 grab, grapple ◇ 自动~[抓斗] automatic grab
抓住 gripping, nip-up, capture, grasp, grappling
抓爪 gripper, grabhook
抓砖机[器] brick grab, grapple bucket
专长 speciality
专家 specialist, expert
专家规则 expert rule
专家系统 expert system
专利 patent (Pat.) ◇ 申请~*
专利的 patented (Patd)
专利局(美国) Patent Office (Pat. Off.)
专利侵权 infringement of patent
专利权 patent right, patent (Pat.), monopoly ◇ 取得~的 patented (Patd), 无~non-exclusive right
专利权所有人 patentee
专利说明书 patent specification
专利文献 patent literature
专利证书 patent certificate
专利执照 patent certificate
专卖权 (right of) monopoly
专门的 special
专门定制的 tailor-made
专门技能[知识] know-how
专门名词[术语] terminology, technical terms, nomenclature
专门设计的 custom-designed
专题论文 disquisition, monograph
专题研究 monographic study
专线连接 【电】private-line arrangement
专性好气[需氧]细菌 obligate aerobic bacteria
专性嫌气[厌氧]细菌 obligate anaerobic bacteria
专性需氧微生物 obligate [obligatory] aerobes
专性厌氧微生物 obligate anaerobes
专性异养细菌 obligative heterotrophic

bacteria
专性自养生物 obligate autotrophs
专业 speciality, occupation, specialized subject
专业化 specialization, professionalization
专业化轧管厂 single-product tube mill
专业小词典 glossary
专业性铸造车间 specialty foundry (美)
专用材料 special(ity) material
专用车辆 special-purpose vehicle ◇ 内部～ internal wagon
专用程序 specific program [routine]
专用存储区 dedicated memory [storage]
专用工具 special tool, non-general purpose tool
专用工作服 special clothing
专用计算机 special [limited, single] purpose computer
专用件 special piece
专用路 accommodation road
专用设备 speciality equipment
专用铁路 access raiload ◇ 厂内～线 intraplant trackage, 工厂～线 factory railway, 工业生产～线 industrial track
专用图 appropriate chart
专用线路 individual line, 【计】tie line
专用信道 【电】dedicated channel
专用轧机 【压】special(i)ty rolling mill
专用砖 special-purpose brick
专用字符 【计】special character
专有权 patent rights, exlusive right ◇ 无～ non-exclusive right
专著 monograph
砖 brick (br, brk) ◇ $1\frac{1}{2}$ 长直形～*, $1\frac{1}{2}$ 宽直形～*, 暗丁［半块］～ blind header, 半生［灰色, 欠火］次～ grizzle (brick), 风干～ adobe, 经久耐用的～ long-lasting brick, 炉墙上的丁字～*, 书形空心～ book tile 铁皮［壳］～ armoured brick, 镶墙边～closer, 制～*, 抓～器 grapple bucket

砖薄壳 brick shell
砖保护的 brick protected (B.P.)
砖层 bricklayer, course ◇ 侧砌～ course on edge, 平砌～ course on flat, 竖砌～ course on end
砖衬 brick lining, brickwork, bricking, 【冶】lining ◇ 炉腹～ bosh lining, 特殊部位～*
砖挡墙 brick baffle
砖等级 grade of brick
砖顶砌筑面积 stacking area for bricked roofs
砖缝 brickwork joint
砖格孔道 checker opening [passage], opening of checker, checkerwork stack
砖格通道 checker opening [passage]
砖格烟道[气道, 孔] checker flue
砖格窑 box kiln
砖格支柱(热风炉的) checker supporting column
砖格(子) checkerwork grillage, 【钢】checker, chequer (蓄热室的), 【冶】spray box, checker (bearer) wall (高炉热风炉的) ◇ 编筐［考伯］式～*, 带筋～ ribbed checker
砖格子蓄热室[器] 【冶】brickwork regenerator
砖格子支柱 checker bearer
砖格子自由截面 【钢】flue opening
砖工锤 【耐】bricklayer's hammer
砖拱 brick arch
砖红色 brick red colour
砖红色凹铜 brick red set copper
砖夹杂(钢锭缺陷) brick inclusions
砖夹子 grapple bucket
砖架(砖干燥用) 【耐】rack for bricks
砖接缝 brickwork joint
砖磨损试验机 brick rattler
砖木混合结构 half-timber construction
砖坯 air (dried) brick, green [unfired] brick
砖铺垫层[基床] bedding of brick

砖	
砖砌钢包[盛钢桶]	brick ladle
砖砌冷凝器	brick condenser
砖砌炉衬	brick work lining
砖砌炉床	brick hearth
砖砌炉顶	masonry arch
砖砌热风总管	【铁】brick lined hot blast main
砖砌体	brickwork, brick setting ◇ 立砌 ~ soldier course, 清水 ~ fairfaced brickwork
砖墙	brick wall ◇ 炉腹 ~、(高炉的)bosh wall(s)
砖石工	mason
砖石构造	masonry construction
砖石结构	brick masonry structure
砖烟囱	masonry stack
砖窑	brick kiln
转靶	rotating target
转包	【钢】tilting ladle, lip-pour ladle
转臂起重机	bracket swing crane, jibcrane ◇ A 型 ~ A-derrick, 枪式 ~ derrick crane
转臂式混合机	revolving arm mixer
转变	change, converting, conversion, transform (tsfm), transformation, turn ◇ λ 型 ~ *, 非等温 ~ *, 连续冷却 ~ *
转变层	transition layer
转变产物	transition product
转变点	transformation [change, arrest(ation)] point, transition point (tr. pt) (金相的), transition temperature ◇ Acm ~ *, 同成分 ~ *
转变动力学	transformation kinetics
转变范围	transformation [transition] range
转变概率	transition probability
转变机理	transformation mechanism
转变阶段[时期]	transition stage
转变孪晶	transformation twin
转变起点	【金】onset of transformation
转变起始曲线	【金】curve of incipient transition
转变前奥氏体	【金】preexisting austenite

转	
转变潜热	latent heat of transformation
转变区域	transition region
转变群	transformation group
转变热	transition heat, heat of transformation
转变速度	velocity of transformation
转变速率	rate of transformation
转变特性	transformation characteristic
转变图	【金】transformation diagram
转变退火	【金】transformation annealing
转变温度	transformation [transition] temperature, transus (temperature)
转变温度范围	transition temperature range
转变线	【金】transus
转变应变	transformation strain
转变诱发[感生]塑性	【金】transformation induced plasticity
转变终了曲线	【金】curve of complete transition
转变自由能(指相转变)	free energy of transformation
转播	rebroadcast, relay
转差率	slip ratio
转储	【计】dump, memory transfer
转储校验	【计】dump check
转存(信息)	【计】unloading
转底炉	rotary (hearth) furnace
转底式烘干机	rotating disk drier
转底窑	rotary hearth kiln
转调	modulation
转动	rotary motion, rotation, turn (round), 【机】revolution
转动 360°(指转炉)	【冶】swivel round
转动 X 射线谱	rotation(al) X-ray spectrum
转动传感器	rotation sensor
转动电极	rotating [wheel] electrode
转动反射轴	rotoflection [rotation-reflection] axis
转动反演	rotation-inversion
转动反演轴	rotation-inversion axis, axis

转 zhuan

of rotary inversion
转动缸 swivel cylinder
转动惯量 moment of inertia, rotary inertia
转动滑移 rotational slip
转动机构 rotation gear, rotating mechanism
转动给料刮板 rotatable feeding shoe
转动给料盘(装煤车的) 【焦】turn table
转动夹持装置 rotary jig
转动力矩 turning moment, rotating torque
转动流槽 swivel launder
转动炉床 revolving hearth
转动螺旋形加热器 rotating spiral heater
转动配合 running fit
转动－平移 rotation-translation
转动(谱)线 rotational line
转动烧嘴 swivelling burner
转动式翻车机 rotary tipper
转动台式压砖机 rotating (table) press
转动体 rotator, rotor
转动圆筒 tumbling barrel
转动闸阀 gate turn valve
转动轴 rotary [rotation(al)] axis, rotating axle
转动铸条法 rotary strip casting process
转锻 【压】flop forging
转发继电器 repeater relay
转发器 translator, repeater
转钩 swivel hook
转鼓 (revolving, rotary, rotating, tumble) drum, trommel, tumbling barrel ◇ 焦炭试验～drum of coke test, 小型～mini-tumbler
转鼓炉 rotary drum furnace
转鼓强度 【团】tumbler strength, resistance to tumbling
转鼓强度指数 tumbler strength
转鼓清理 【铸】barrel cleaning
转鼓筛 revolving-drum screen
转鼓湿度记录器 drum-hygrograph
转鼓式端头飞剪 rotary drum type flying crop shears

转鼓式干燥机 drum dryer
转鼓式混合机 (同"转筒混合机")
转鼓式给料[供料,加料]器 (同"转筒给料机")
转鼓式浸出槽 drum-type leaching vat
转鼓式冷却器 drum cooler
转鼓式坯料分配器 drum-type billet switch
转鼓式酸洗装置 drum-type pickling machine
转鼓式造粒机 rotary drum granulator
转鼓试验 tumbler test (测定焦炭及烧结矿的强度), 【团】drum [rattler] test ◇ 米库姆～*
转鼓试验过的焦炭 tumbled coke
转鼓试验台 drum dynamometer
转鼓指数 tumbler index (T.I.), resistance to tumbling ◇ 高～球团*
转鼓指数标准 tumbler-index specification
转化 change, transform, inverting, inversion, converting, conversion ◇ 诺曼一氧化碳～*
转化点 inversion point
转化法 conversion process [method] ◇ 干法～*
转化范围 transformation range
转化过程 conversion [inversion] process
转化阶段 transformation stage
转化曲线 inversion curve
转化设备 conversion apparatus
转化天然气 (同"重整天然气")
转化涂层 conversion coating
转化温度 inversion temperature
转化效率 conversion efficiency
转环 swivel
转环滑车 swivel block
转换 change(-over), transform, converting, switching, inversion, commutation, transfer ◇ 可～的 switchable
转换比 conversion ratio
转换部件 change-over unit
转换程序 【计】conversion program, con-

zhuan 转

verter transducer
转换触点　transfer contact
转换电键　transfer key
转换电路　switching circuit
转换阀　change-over [crossover] valve
转换法　conversion method
转换法则　conversion rule
转换功能　change-over function
转换过程　inversion process
转换函数　【计】transfer function
转换机构　change-over [switching] mechanism
转换开关　change-over switch (C.O.S., c.o.s.), throw(-over) [interchanging] switch, changer, commutator, switch(er), inverter, tumbler ◇ 按钮式～push-button switch, 抽头～", 鼓形～drum [barrel] switch, 凸轮～cam switch
转换脉冲发生器　switching pulse generator
转换器　switch box, switchboard, translator,【计】converter, convertor
转换设备　change-over facilities, conversion equipment [apparatus]
转换时间　change-over [switching, conversion] time
转换台　change-over station
转换误差　change error
转换效率　conversion efficiency
转换信号　switchover signal
转换因子[因数]　conversion factor
转换站　switching station
转换装置　switching [conversion] equipment, change-over gear, changer
转换子程序　【计】conversion routine
转嫁　imputation
转角管塞　angle cock
转　接　change-over, throw-over, interchange, transition, adapter coupling
转接板　【电】pinboard
转接插头　【电】patchplug
转接机构　change-over mechanism

转接皮带机　connecting conveyer
转接器　adaptor, adapter
转节　swivel
转矩　torque, turning moment
转矩补偿器　torque compensator
转矩磁力计　【理】torsional [torque] magnetometer
转矩电动机　torque motor ◇ 动圈式～", 极化式～"
转矩计　torque (dynamo)meter
转矩角　angle of torque
转矩-扭转角关系曲线　torque-twist curve
转矩曲线　torque curve
转炉　converter (conv.), convertor, vessel ◇ 备用～spare vessel, 大型[大吨位]～large [mammoth] vessel, 底吹～", (顶底)复吹～", 对称～", 固定式～stationary converter, 虹吸式～siphon converter, 碱性氧气～", 降温～", 卡尔多～", 空气鼓风～air-blown converter, 冷料～", 梨形～pear-shaped vessel, 炉口对称～", 罗伯特～【钢】Robert converter, 面吹～", 皮尔斯-史密斯式～Pierce-Smith converter, 偏口～eccentric vessel, 倾动～", 竖式～", 酸性[贝塞麦]～", 同心～concentric converter, 托马斯～", 卧式～", 小型[小容量]～small vessel, 氧气顶吹～", 圆筒形～", 直立式～【钢】upright converter
转炉半钢炼钢工艺　converter semi-steel steelmaking technology
转炉补吹模型　reblowing model for BOF operation
转炉残渣　【钢】converter residue
转炉车间　【冶】converter plant [department, house, mill]
转炉尺寸　vessel size
转炉吹炼　【冶】converter blowing
转炉吹炼法　【冶】converter practice
转炉顶罩　vessel hood
转炉多炉连铸　multi-heat continuous cast-

ing with converter
转炉耳轴 【冶】converter trunnion
转炉风箱 converter air [blast, wind] box
转炉钢 【钢】converter steel
转炉高拉碳钢 tapped-on-carbon steel
转炉工 blower
转炉工段 vessel area
转炉工作空间 vessel working space
转炉供风系统 【冶】converter air delivery system
转炉硅铁 Bessemer ferrosilicon
转炉烘干燃烧器 converter drying burner
转炉溅渣护炉技术 furnace maintenance with slag splashing technique in BOF
转炉口 vessel opening
转炉跨(间) 【冶】converter aisle, 【钢】vessel bay
转炉冷料比 【钢】converter cold charging
转炉冷却器 vessel cooler
转炉炼钢 convertor steelmaking ◇ 卡尔多～车间*, 托马斯～厂 Thomas stool works
转炉炼钢法 converter (steelmaking) process ◇ 氧气顶吹～*
转炉锍[冰铜] 【色】converter [Bessemer] matte
转炉锍分流 converter matte pull
转炉炉衬 【冶】converter [vessel] lining ◇ 更换[修理]～vessel reline
转炉炉底 【冶】converter [vessel] bottom ◇ 捣制预焊风眼～spiked bottom, 可分离[拆除]的～【钢】removable plug, 铜管衬里风眼捣制～tube bottom
转炉炉底起重车(装卸用) 【钢】converter bottom jacking car
转炉炉壳[外壳] converter shell, vessel casing [shell]
转炉炉口 converter mouth ◇ 清理～*
转炉炉口凸缘[突出部] 【钢】shoulder of vessel
转炉炉料 converter charge
转炉炉气 converter gas ◇ 炼铜～*

转炉炉身 converter body
转炉(身)修理车 【钢】converter-repair [vessel-repair] car
转炉炉体更换车 【钢】converter vessel changing car
转炉炉体直径 vessel shell diameter
转炉炉型 【钢】shape of vessel
转炉炉嘴 vessel mouth (lip), nose end
转炉煤气回收 converter gas recovery
转炉平台 converter platform
转炉倾动力矩 converter tilting torque
转炉倾动机构 【钢】converter tilting mechanism
转炉熔剂 converter flux
转炉容量 【钢】vessel capacity
转炉散料流槽 converter chute
转炉散装料仓 converter additions bunker
转炉上半部 top half of vessel
转炉生产率 converter production efficiency
转炉添加料搬运[处理] converter additions handling
转炉铜 Bessemer copper
转炉托圈 【钢】(converter) trunnion ring
转炉托圈耳轴 converter ring trunnion
转炉脱磷 converter dephosphorization
转炉型的 converter-shaped
转炉型铁熔池 converter-type molter iron bath
转炉烟尘 converter dust
转炉烟罩 converter hood
转炉用矿石 converter ore
转炉用生铁 【钢】converter iron
转炉渣 converter [vessel] slag
转炉直径 vessel diameter
转炉自动换衬 automated convertor relining
转炉总容积 overall vessel volume
转炉座 converter cradle
转录器 【计】transcribor
转轮 rotating wheel, revolver, reel
转轮喷砂机(清理带材和线材用) whee-

labrator machine
转模(拉丝用) revolving die
转磨抛光 tumbling
转盘 turn(out) table, turnover gear, turner, turning arrangement, swivel plate
转盘过滤机 rotary disk filter, rotating disc filter
转盘式除尘器 rotating-disk deduster
转盘式干燥机 rotating disk drier
转盘(式)给料机[加料器]【冶】rotating plate, rotary disk
转盘式液碎[液体雾化](法) rotating disk type liquid disintegration
转盘式装煤车【焦】rotary table charging car
转盘雾化法 rotating disk method
转盘雾化粉末 rotating disk powder ◇ 德古萨~法 Degussa process
转盘雾化器 rotating disk atomizer
转盘压砖机【耐】turntable [rotary] press
转盘造粒机 rotary disk type pelletizer
转盘铸锭机 ◇ 克拉克型卧式~ Clark casting wheel
转让 assignment ◇ 无~权*
转让支付【企】transfer payments
转入 roll in, switch to
转入-转出【计】roll-in/roll-out
转数 revolution (rev.), rotation number, number of revolutions [turns]
转数表传感器 tacho-generator
转刷式清带器 rotary-brush cleaning device
转送辊道 shifting table
转送设备[装置] grass-hopper
转速 rotating [rotational] speed, speed of revolution
转速比 gear ratio (g.r.)
转速测量法 tachometry
转速计[转速表,转数计,转数表] tachometer, tachograph, tachoscope, r.p.m. meter, revolution counter ◇ 电感式~*, 飞球~flyball tachometer, 积分~*, 记时式~*, 静电~ capacitor tachometer, 脉冲~ impulse tachometer, 陀螺测试仪型~*, 无接触~*, 遥读~*
转胎 positioner
转台 turnout [swivel, revolving] table, turret
转台式造型机【铸】turntable moulding machine
转台压片机 (同"旋转压片机")
转态过程 polling
转体 swivel
转桶式混汞法【色】barrel amalgamation
转桶提金法 barrel process
转筒 rotating [rotary] drum, trommel
转筒干燥器 revolving [rotary] drier
转筒滚镀(小零件的) barrel plating
转筒混合机 rotating [revolving] drum mixer, tumbling mixer
转筒给料机 (rotating) drum feeder, feed [distributor] drum, overshot rotary feeder
转筒给料机外壳 rotary valve casing
转筒结晶器 drum crystallizer ◇ 带叶片的~ vaned drum crystallizer
转筒喷尖处理 tumblast operation
转筒喷砂(除鳞) rotoblast, tumblast
转筒喷涂法 barrelling
转筒曲线记录器 drum-chart recorder
转筒筛 cylindrical trommel screen, drum [revolving] screen, trommel ◇ (圆)锥形~ conical trommel
转筒式多级结晶器 rotating drum multistage crystallizer
转筒(式)干燥机[器] (同"圆筒干燥机") ◇ 内加热~*, 小型~*
转筒式混凝土搅拌机 rotary [revolving] drum concrete mixer
转筒式抛光 (同"滚筒抛光")
转筒式汽热干燥机 steam-heated rotary drier
转筒式直接-间接加热干燥机 direct-indirect heat cylindrical drier

转筒洗石机 【耐】washer drum
转筒形烧结块溶出器(氧化铝生产的) rotary digester for roasted material
转弯 turn bend, slew
转位工作台 index table
转线轨道 【运】cross over ◇ 复式～double crossover
转向 turning, diverting, change direction
转向柄 steering handle
转向车 bogie
转向齿轮 toothed sector
转向阀 switching [crossover] valve, deflector [diverting] flap
转向辊 deflecting roller ◇ 带卷～*
转向滑轮 deflecting pulley
转向架承梁 bogie bolster
转向架轮 bogie wheel
转向架式烘(干)炉 bogie type drying stove
转向流槽 deflecting chute
转向器 diverter, steering gear
转向系统 steering system
转向销 kingpin
转向支承架 bogie bolster
转向轴 steering shaft [axle]
转向装置 steering device [gear]
转焰炉 rotaflame furnace
转窑 ring kiln
转移 shift, transfer, transition, carry-over, 【计】branch, jump
转移表 【计】transfer table
转移操作 【计】jump [transfer] operation
转移跟踪程序 【计】branch tracer
转移面 【金】transfer surface
转移系数 transfer coefficient [ratio]
转移现象(液相中的) 【金】transport phenomena
转移向量 【计】transfer vector
转移效率 transfer efficiency ◇ 合金元素～*
转移影像热固定 thermal fixing of transferred image
转移运输机 carry-over conveyer
转移指令 【计】branch [jump, transfer] instruction
转移滞后 transfer lag
转运 transfer, conveying, transport, transshipment ◇ 抗～强度*
转运仓 transfer hopper
转运点 transfer point
转运皮带 reclaiming belt
转运起重机 transshipment crane
转运塔 transfer tower
转运站 transfer station [tower, post]
转运装置 drag-over skid
转载矿槽 transfer hopper
转折 bend, transition
转折点 breaking [turning] point, breakthrough (point), transition
转辙柄 setting lever
转辙联动装置 switchgear
转辙器(铁路的) 【运】switch, shunter ◇ 脱轨～derailing switch, 自动～automatic switch
转辙器轨枕 switch tie
转枕 swivel block
转振光谱 rotation vibration spectrum
转轴 revolution [moment] axis, main bearing, (rotation) shaft
转柱起重机 (turntable) pillar crane ◇ 旋臂式～pillar jib crane
转子 rotor, rotator, armature, spinning device(离心机的), impeller, impellor(水泵的) ◇ 深槽～deep bar rotor
转子包扎钢丝 armature binding wire
转子流量[速]计 rotameter (type flowmeter)
转子绕组 rotor winding
转子铁心 rotor core
转子叶片 rotor blades
桩 pile, pole, stake ◇ 打～*, 打过头的～overdriven pile, 加套～lag pile, 扩底～club-footed pile, 拉逊氏～Larrson pile, 球形扩脚～bulb pile, 细～buttress

shafts,辛普雷克斯~*,用~加固土壤 palification
桩承底脚 pile footing
桩承台梁[桩帽梁] pile cap(ping) beam
桩承载能力 pile capacity
桩的拼接 pile splice
桩箍 pile band [collar,ring]
桩基(群桩基础) pilotis
桩基础 pile foundation [footing]
桩尖(端) point of pile
桩接头 pile joint ◇ 箱形~ box pile joint
桩帽 pile cap [cover]
桩排架[桥台] pile bent
桩群 【建】pile cluster, group of piles
桩栓 fastening bolt
桩头 pile crown
桩头面积 area of pile head
桩位布置图 piling plan
桩靴 pile shoe
桩堰 pile weir
桩用钢材 piled steel
桩载能力 pile capacity
桩栅 pile stockade
桩组 pile cluster
装棒量 rod charge
装备 equipment, outfit, fitting out
装车场 loading area, brow
装车跨 loading bay
装车码头[站台] loading dock
装车皮带机 loading conveyer
装车设备 loading machinery
装船 shipment, loading on board ◇ 散装~ bulk shipment
装船机 shiploader
装船码头 loading pier ◇ 海上~*
装袋 bagging
装袋秤 bagging scale
装袋机 bagger, bag packer, bagging machine [apparatus]
装电极手套(自耗电弧炉构件) electrode charging glove
装锭机 【压】ingot charger
装订 bookbinding, stitching
装订钢丝 bookbinder wire
装废料(转炉的) scrap handling
装粉高度 fill height
装粉体积 fill volume
装粉[料]靴 powder feeder
装管 tubulation, tubulating
装璜 decoration
装货单 bill of loading, shipping order
装货单据 shipping documents
装货清单 loading list
装机容量 installed rating [capacity]
装甲 armo(u)r
装甲板 armour plate ◇ 热轧~*
装甲板轧机 armour-plate rolling mill
装甲玻璃 wire glass
装甲材料 armour material ◇ 车身~ body armour material
装甲的 steel-armo(u)red, ironclad
装甲钢 armour steel
装甲钢板 armoured plate
装焦 coke charge
装卷控制台 charging pulpit
装铠机 armouring machine
装矿漏斗 【冶】feeder pot
装矿码头 ore loading berth
装矿石量 charge of ore
装料 charging, charge, (material) loading, feed, burden, fill(ing) ◇ 分批~*,干式~ dry feed, 料斗[箱]~*, 炉顶[吊篮]~ 【冶】basket charging, 重力~(法) gravity filling, 逐层~*
装料板(模具的) 【粉】loading sheet
装料比 【冶】charge [charging] ratio
装料标准 【铁】charge criteria
装料不均匀 non-uniform charging
装料不足 undercharge (u.c.)
装料舱口 loading hatch
装料仓 loading bin [pocket], charging hopper
装料操作 【冶】charging practice
装料(操作)工 charging operator [hand],

装 zhuang

charger, feeder, filler
装料槽 charging tank, charging launder
装料侧 【冶】open side
装料侧辊面高度 roll height at charge side
装料铲 charging scoop
装料场(地) loading [charging] area
装料车 charging larry [lorry, car], furnace carriage
装料程序 charging program [schedule], filling sequence
装料迟延 charging delay
装料窗 feeding hole
装料单 charge sheet
装料导板 stock guide
装料吊车 loading [charging] crane
装料顶杆 charging bar
装料斗 charging funnel [hopper, scoop], charger pan, filling funnel, loading bin [hopper]
装料端 charge [charging, loading, entrance] end, charging side
装料杆 charging peel, loading arm [rod], peel (悬臂式)
装料高度 stock level, fill height
装料工段 loading plant
装料管 charge pipe, charging [filling] tube
装料罐 charge can, charging bucket
装料轨道 charging track
装料辊道 【压】charging roller table ◇ 炉用~*
装料过度[过多, 过负荷] overcharge(O.C.), overburden(ing), surcharge (s/c)
装料过满 overfill
装料滑槽 loading chute
装料机 charging [filling, stocking] machine, charging carriage, charger, feeder,【铁】filling engine ◇ 齿条式~*, 地行式~*, 固定~rigid charging machine, 横梁式~*, 还原弹~bomb filling machine, 架空式~*, 卡尔德龙~*, 料车式~*, 落地式~*, 汽车式[无轨]~*, 双贮斗 ~double hopper, 橡胶轮胎地面移动式~*, 旋转式~rotary charger
装料机构 charge [charging, fill] mechanism, feeder unit
装料机推杆[装料杆] charger [charging] peel
装料记录(本) 【冶】charge book
装料计数器 furnace filling counter
装料架 skid bed
装料间断 pause of charging
装料坑 loading pit
装料孔 charging opening [port, hole], feeding hole, loading aperture
装料控制台 charging pulpit
装料控制系统 charging controls
装料口 charge door [hole], charging door [hole, opening], feed port, filling [receiving] opening
装料跨 【钢】charging bay [aisle]
装料筐 discharge basket
装料粒度 charge particle size
装料量 forced filling rate, material loading
装料列车 charging-buggy train
装料溜槽 receiving chute
装料龙门起重机[吊车] 【冶】charging gantry crane
装料漏斗 feed hopper, filling funnel, feeder pot ◇ 移动式~*
装料率 filling ratio
装料门 charge [charging, loading] door
装料门槛 【冶】charging door sill
装料面 【冶】open side
装料皮带 charging [loading] belt
装料平台 charging deck [floor],【铁】filling place
装料期 loading period
装料器 filling vessel, loader, charger ◇ 梭式~shuttle feeder
装料桥式起重机 loading bridge
装料区 charging zone, loading space
装料设备 charging equipment [device, ap-

paratus, appliance, arrangement, facilities], loading equipment [machinery, plant], feeding installation, filling equipment, tipping cradle（可倾式炉的）◇摆动式~ tilting magazine

装料室 charging chamber, loading space
装料顺序 charging sequence
装料速度 loading speed
装料梭 feeder shuttle
装料台 charging platform [floor, deck, level, magazine], loading platform [floor, table, station], depiler, depiling magazine, ramp,【钢】charging stage ◇ 储存式~*,带卷~ coil loading skid, 提升~*
装料台架 charging rack [skid]
装料台前运输机 conveyer to loading tables
装料特性 character of charge
装料体积 charge [fill] volume
装料桶 charging ladle
装料推杆 charging ram
装料位置 charging [fill(ing)] position
装料温度 【冶】charge temperature
装料[炉]温度测试探针 【冶】charge-temperature probe
装料系统 charging system ◇ 斜槽~ chuting system
装料箱 charger box [pan],【钢】charging box
装料小车 charge car
装料斜槽 【冶】charge shute
装料斜桥 charge bridge
装料斜台 sloping ramp
装料-卸料机 charge-discharge machine
装料循环[周期] charging [filling] cycle ◇ 一个~【铁】round(s)
装料站 loading station
装料重量 charged weight
装料周期 【铁】filling cycle
装料装置 loading device, feeding device [arrangement], feeder ◇ 钟斗式~*
装料准备 charge preparation

装料勺 charging scoop
装炉 charge, charging, furnace loading,【铁】filling（开炉装料）◇ 碳化物~箱 carbide tray, 与集气主管断开的~【焦】off-main charging, 与集气主管接通的~【焦】on-main charging
装炉辊道 furnace charging table
装炉机 furnace charging conveyer ◇ 焊管坯~[装置]*
装炉量 heat
装炉(炉料)水分 moisture as charged
装炉烟气烧管 【焦】smoke ignition pipe
装轮机 wheel-bushing press
装满 filling-up ◇ 未~重量 short weight
装满程度 degree of packing [admission]
装煤车 【焦】(coal) charging car, larry car ◇ 转盘式~*
装煤车煤斗 larry bin
装煤孔 【焦】charging hole
装煤孔盖 lid
装煤孔座 charging hole seat
装模 die-filling, packing compact
装模台 filling bench
装配 assemblage, assembly, assembling, fit(ting), fitting up ◇ 工厂~ factory assembling, 手工紧固~*
装配扳手 fitting key
装配部件 fitting up
装配侧 built up edge
装配场 assembly floor
装配车间 assembling shop [department, plant], assembly floor, fitting [fitter's, erecting] shop, fitting department, rigger's shop
装配电极 electrode building
装配方法 assembly [fabricating] method
装配缝隙 fitting up gap
装配工 assembler, fitter, adjuster, erector, millwright
装配(工)厂 assembling plant [factory]
装配焊接 erection [field] weld(ing)
装配夹具[夹紧装置] assembly fixture

[jig]
装配键　fitting key
装配连接　erection joint
装配螺钉[螺丝]　fitting screw
装配螺栓　assembly [assembling, erection] bolt
装配模块　【计】load module
装配起重机[吊车](高炉用)　jib boom crane
装配器　assembler
装配切削　matching cut
装配式板状结晶器　【连铸】plate mounted mould
装配式房屋　fabricated building
装配式构造　articulated construction
装配式建筑　prefabricated construction
装配式结构　fabricated structure, prefabricated construction
装配式结晶器　【连铸】built-up mould
装配式砂箱　bolted moulding box
装配式型钢桩　built-up steel pile
装配式原子反应堆　package atomic reactor
装配式铸型　built-up mould
装配台　assembling stand, assembly table [floor], erecting bed, setting desk
装配图　assembly [erection] drawing, installation diagram [drawing]　◇ 部件～【机】grouping
装配系统　assembly system
装配线　assembly line
装配压力机　assembling press
装配轴　built-up shaft
装坯机　billet charger, billet loader (挤压的)
装瓶　bottling
装燃料　fuel charging
装燃料量　charge of fuel
装入　load, build in
装入程序　loader, load(ing) program
装入机　charging machine ◇ 精矿～*
装入孔　filling hole

装入口　【钢】filling opening
装入矿仓　bunkerage
装入料　【冶】charge [charging] material
装入式淬火　built-in quenching
装入箱内　boxing in
装上　fitting on
装饰　ornament, decoration, embellishing, garnish
装饰材料　【建】finishings
装饰镀[涂]层　decorative coating, finishing coat
装饰工作　ornamental work
装饰拱　blank arch
装饰合金　fancy alloy　◇ 镉金～cadmium gold, 铝金～*, 莫克～*, 沃恩白色～*
装饰黄铜(75Cu, 22Zn, 2Sn, 1Pb)　ornamental brass, latten alloy ◇ 奥雷德～*, 翡翠绿～*, 纽-～*
装饰黄铜箔　leaf brass
装饰精整　decorative finish
装饰品　ornament, setoff
装饰品造型　【铸】ornamental moulding
装饰青铜　trim [jewellery] bronze
装饰物　garnish, ornamental
装饰型材[钢材]　patterned section
装饰性镀铬　decorative chromium plating
装饰性涂镀　finishing coat
装饰用红金(75—50Au, 25—50Cu)　red gold
装饰用青铜合金(3.73—4.15Cu, 0.8—1.55Ag, 0.11Pb, 余量Cu)　Chinese Shaku-do bronze
装饰用镶铝胶合板　Plymax
装饰用锌合金　◇ 泰塞利～*
装饰用铸件[装饰品铸造]　ornamental casting
装套　encapsulation
装填　filling up
装填高度　filling height
装填工具　tamper
装填机　filling device
装填密度(炉料的)　closeness of packing

装填系数　fill ratio
装填站(乙炔的)　【焊】recharging plant
装箱　boxing (in)
装箱表面硬化　pack-hardening
装箱清单　packing list
装箱烧结　pack-sintering
装箱渗碳炉　pack-hardening furnace
装箱渗碳(硬化)　pack-carburizing, box hardening, pack-hardening
装箱退火　box [pot] annealing, coffin-annealing
装箱退火的　box annealed
装箱退火法(深冲钢板的)　thuriting
装卸吊车　charging and drawing crane
装卸费　handling cost
装卸机　loader-unloader, charge-discharge machine ◇ 叉式电动～ electric fork truck, 刮板式水泥～ cement hog, 挑甲式～*, 万能(自动)～*
装卸机械　handling machinery, loading and unloading machine
装卸劳力费用　cost of handling labor
装卸桥　handling bridge
装卸日[天,昼夜]　lay day
装卸设备　handling equipment [facilities, machinery]
装卸损耗　handling loss, breakage through handling (焦炭的)
装卸台　platform ◇ 带卷～*
装卸作业　handling operation
装窑　setting of kiln
装窑用具　kiln furniture
装药　【采】charging
装药不足　under charge (u.c., u/c)
装药工[器]　【采】charger
装药量　【采】charge
装药容量　charge capacity
装药引爆成形　cord-charge forming
装运　shipment, loading ◇ 分批～ installment shipment, 散装～ bulk shipment
装运机　autoloader ◇ 吊斗～ bucket loader

装运矿槽(铁路的)　load-out bin
装运清单　list of shipment
装运设施　load-out facilities
装运塔　dispatching tower
装运系统　load-out system
装运箱　tote box
装－运－卸机组　loader-hauler-dumper (LHD)
装载　loading (ldg.), shipping, freight
装载表面　loading surface
装载仓　loading hopper
装载槽　【采】charging spout
装载滑轨　loading skid
装载机　(shovel, mechanical) loader, forklift truck ◇ 铲式～ shovel loader, 高架～ overhead loader, 掘进[前端]～ front end loader, 履带式～ caterpillar loader, 轻型～ low loader
装载机铲斗　loading shovel
装载量　burden, loading capacity
装载密度　density of charge
装载容量　charge [heap] capacity
装置　device (dev.), installation (inst.), apparatus (app.), equipment, appliance, arranger, arrangement, gear, assembly, facilities, plant, outfit, rig(ging), unit ◇ 施利伦～*
装置图　【计】set-up diagram
装置叶片　blading
装砖　【耐】setting
撞出(从晶格中)　【理】knocked-on
撞锤　ram
撞锤击碎(拆炉衬用)　impact hammer demolition apparatus
撞杆导轨　ram guide
撞击　impact, ramming, strike, brunt, impingement, percussion, knock, whipping (轧件尾端的) ◇ 摆式～硬度 Pendulum hardness
撞击锤　impact hammer
撞击挡板(烟气除粗尘用)　impingement plate

撞击点　impact point
撞击痕迹　dint
撞击机构　knocking gear
撞击激发　【理】impact excitation
撞击角　angle of attack
撞击扩散渗镀　peen plating
撞击力　striking [hitting] force
撞击滤尘器　impinger
撞击铆钉机　percussion riveting machine
撞击伞　（同"碰撞伞"）
撞击时间　time of impact
撞击式风动开口机　【铁】percussion-type air drill
撞击式过滤机　impingement type filter
撞击式焦油提取器　【焦】impingement tar extractor
撞击式煤气洗涤装置　impingement scrubber
撞击式破碎机　impact breaker
撞击式洗涤装置　impingement scrubber
撞击速度　impact [striking] velocity
撞击损伤　knock-on damage
撞击图像　percussion [impact] figure
撞压机　percussion (power) press
撞针　firing pin, striker, hammer ◇ 金刚石～hammer diamond
状态　status, state, condition (cond.), constitution, behaviour (运转的)
状态变化　change of state
状态参数　state parameter
状态方程(式)　equation of state ◇ 普遍化～*
状态分析　state analysis
状态符号(铝材处理的)　temper designation
状态监控　condition monitoring
状态监控软件　condition monitoring software
状态码　condition code
状态密度　【理】state density
状态密度曲线　density of states curve
状态图　state [constitution(al)], phase, sta-ble, structural] diagram, 【金】metallurgical equilibrium diagram ◇ 复合～【金】double diagram
状态向量　state vector
状态字寄存器　【计】internal function register
锥　awl, cone
锥冰晶石{3NaF·3AlF$_3$}　chiolite
锥柄工具卸出斜铁　【机】centre key
锥底槽　cone bottom tank
锥底气体弥散搅拌器　cone-bottom gas-dispersion agitator
锥度　(degree of) taper, conical degree, conicity, gradient, leave (锻模的) ◇ 车～tapering, 带～的边　tapered edge
锥度规　taper gauge
锥度卡规　taper caliper
锥管螺纹　taper pipe thread
锥光偏振仪　conoscope
锥黑铜矿　paramelaconite
锥角　cone angle, angle of taper
锥孔模　conical die
锥氯铜铅矿　cumengeite
锥轮　cone [conical] pulley ◇ 带外工作表面的～male friction cone
锥面滚圈　tapered tyre
锥模　tapered die ◇ 放射型～radiused conical die
锥磨机　conical (ball) mill
锥铈锶矿　webyeite
锥锶铈矿　ansilite
锥体　cone, taper ◇ 钝金刚石～blunt diamond cone
锥体法(确定混凝土流动性)　cone method
锥体压痕　cone [conical] indentation
锥头钉　cone-headed nail
锥头螺钉　coneheaded bolt
锥纹石　kamacite
锥窝接合装置　cone-and-socket arrangement
锥窝接头　cone-and-socket joint

锥稀土矿　tritomite
锥削度　conicity
锥销　taper pin ◇ 螺尾~conical bolt
锥锌矿　matraite
锥形杯冲深试验　◇ 福井式~
锥形柄　conical grip
锥形槽低压喷管[文丘里管]　low-pressure Venturi with cone tank
锥形层　tapered bed
锥形差温加热　taper heating
锥形沉降[澄清]槽　cone settling tank
锥形衬套　tapered liner
锥形冲压　blocking
锥形冲子[穿孔器]　【压】conical punch
锥形床　conical [tapered] bed
锥形磁结构　conical magnetic structure
锥形底　cone(d) [conical] bottom
锥形底冷凝器　cone-bottom condenser
锥形底石英坩埚　conical-bottomed silica pot
锥形垫圈　taper washer
锥形顶头　【压】tapered plug
锥形堵塞　cut-off conical plug
锥形端头挤压筒　conical-ended container
锥形端头坯料　conical-ended billet
锥形端头套接(管子的)　tapered(-end) joint
锥形阀　conical [cone, miter] valve
锥形分离器[分选机]　cone separator
锥形钢体　conical steel body
锥形固定刀杆[心轴]　【机】conical stationary mandrel
锥形管　continuous taper tube
锥形辊穿孔机　cone type piercer ◇ 斯蒂费尔~Stiefel-cone piercer
锥形辊辊道　tapered roller table
锥形滚柱轴承　taper roller bearing
锥形回转筛　conical rotating screen
锥形混合机[器]　cone-type mixer [blender], conical mixer
锥形挤压型材　tapered extruded shape
锥形加料器　cone type feeder

锥形接套[接头](电极的)　taper nipple
锥形接触　conial contact
锥形截流塞　cut-off conical plug
锥形壳　conical shell
锥形孔　conical hole, bellmouth, flare opening
锥形孔管　faucet pipe
锥形矿仓[矿槽,料仓]　conical bin ◇ 对开式~split cone bin
锥形拉紧螺栓　wedge bolt
锥形离合器　cone clutch
锥形联轴器　cone coupling
锥形料斗　feed hopper of conical shape
锥形漏斗　pyramid hopper, Bunsen funnel
锥形螺栓　conical [taper(ed)] bolt
锥形锚塞(预应力钢筋混凝土用)　【建】conical plug
锥形模　taper die
锥形摩擦传动机构　cone-friction gear, friction bevel gear
锥形(皮带)轮　cone pulley
锥形破碎机　(同"圆锥破碎机")
锥形穹顶　conical vault
锥形球磨机　conical ball mill
锥形取样器　cone sampler
锥形入口段(冲压阴模的)　tapered lead-in
锥形烧杯　conical beaker
锥形(烧)瓶　conical flask
锥形试样试验　tapered-bar test
锥形四分法　coning and quartering
锥形弹簧　conical spring
锥形镗孔轴承　bearing with taper bore
锥形套筒　conical sleeve
锥形调节器　cone governer
锥形铁水罐　(同"敞口式铁水罐")
锥形投射[影]　cone-type projection
锥形头(带材开卷机的)　【压】cone
锥形凸度工作辊　tapered crown work roll
锥形钨导线　tapered tungsten lead
锥形向下收缩底(流态化床干燥炉的)　constriction plate

锥形芯棒[心轴]　tapered mandrel
锥形压气阀　compressed air-operated cone valve
锥形压头　conical indentor
锥形压头静态压痕硬度　static cone indentation hardness
锥形轧辊　【压】cone-shaped roll
锥形制动器[锥形闸]　cone[conic] brake
锥形制动轮　taper brake wheel
锥形轴　cone axle, diminished shaft
锥形轴承　conical[tapered] bearing
锥形轴端　tapered shaft end
锥形轴颈　conical[pointed] journal
锥形转筒筛　conical trommel
锥子　awl
追加记录　addition(al) record
追加矿石　feed ore addition
追溯　retrieval
追踪　tracking, tracing, monitoring
追踪能力　traceability
缀饰　decorating, decoration ◇ 微孪晶~ microtwin decoration
缀饰法（显示晶体缺陷用）　decoration method
缀饰位错　【理】decorated dislocation
准埃洛石{Al_2O_3·2SiO_2·2H_2O}　metahalloysite
准备　preparation (prepn), preparing, get ready, making-ready
准备出钢的炉次　ready-to-tap heat
准备方式　stand-by mode, route of preparation
准备(好)的　prepared (prepd)
准备时间　preparation time,【计】set-up time
准备使用状态(转炉的)　standing ready for use
准备状态(熔炼的)　renewed state
准备作业线　preparing line
准操作　【计】pseudo-operation
准脆性断口　quasi-brittle fracture
准单变性　pseudomonotropy

准导体　quasi-conductor
准等温淬火　modified austemper
准碘{At,即"砹"}　eka-iodine
准锇{Pu,即"钚"}　eka-osmium
准沸腾层　pseudoliquid layer
准固体　pseudosolid (body)
准固体构造　pseudosolid body formation
准规　mortice gauge
准轨铁路　full gauge railway
准硅{Ge,即"锗"}　eka-silicon
准合同　quasi-contract
准衡　criterion
准化学方法　quasi-chemical method
准化学原理　quasi-chemical theory ◇ 有序化现象的~*
准钬　eka-holmium
准解理　quasi-cleavage
准解理断口　quasi-cleavage fracture
准解理面　quasi-cleavage plane
准金属　metalloid ◇ 有机~化合物*
准金属合金　metalloid alloy
准金属相　metalloid phase
准金属原子　metalloid atom
准晶质的　【金】quasi-crystalline
准静态裂纹增长　quasi-static crack growth ◇ 金属~*
准据　criteria
准距　stadia
准颗粒　【团】quasi-particle
准铼{Np,即"镎"}　rhenium
准立方晶形　pseudomorphic cubic form
准连续的　quasi-continuous
准连续能级[带,区]　quasi-continuum of energy
准连续区域精炼[区熔提纯]　pseudo-continuous zone refining
准铝{Ga,即"镓"}　eka-aluminum
准锰{Tc,即"锝"}　eka manganese
准黏滞性流变　quasi-viscous flow
准黏滞性曲线　quasi-viscous curve
准黏滞性蠕变　quasi-viscous creep
准凝固温度　pinch-off temperature

准钕{Pm,即"钷"} eka-neodymium
准硼{Sc,即"钪"} eka-boron
准片状石墨铸铁 quasi-flake graphite cast iron
准平衡状态 quasi-equilibrium condition
准球状晶粒 quasi-spherical grain
准曲线 directrix curve
准确 accuracy
准确度 (degree of) accuracy
准确度级别 accuracy class
准确度控制系统 accuracy control system
准确性 accuracy, exactness
准铯{Fr,即"钫"} eka-cesium
准数 criterion, dimensionless number ◇ 施密特~ Schmidt number
准双曲面齿轮 hypoid gear
准塑性 pseudo-plasticity
准塑性体 pseudoplastic
准弹性的 quasi-elastic
准弹性力 quasi-elastic force
准钽{Pa,即"镤"} eka-tantalum
准同形性 morphotropism
准稳能级 quasi-stationary (energy) level
准线 alignment, alinement, matchmark (零件装配的)
准线测微计[目镜] filar micrometer
准线图 alignment chart
准相 【金】pseudophase
准液化层 pseudoliquid layer
准元素[待寻元素] eka-element
准则 criterion (复数 criteria)
准直 collimating, collimation ◇ 射线束~ beam collimation
准直缝隙 collimating slit
准直管 collimator, tube deaphragm
准直光管 collimater
准直光圈[孔径] collimating aperture
准直平行射束 collimate parallel beam
准直器[仪] collimator, collimater, collimation arrangement
准直射束 collimated [fine] beam
准直透镜 collimating lens

准直轴 collimator axis
准直锥体 collimating cone
准坐标 quasi coordinates
卓林研磨剂(适用于铝及其合金) Geolin
琢石 chipped [broad] stone, ashlar
琢石圬工 【建】ashlar masonry
啄印(薄板的) pick-up
着火 inflammation, ignition, kindling ◇ 不易~的", 自动~ auto-genous ignition
着火点[温度] firing point (F.P.), firing temperature (F.T.), ignition point (I.P.), fire [burning, flammability] point, kindling point [temperature]
着火粉末 【粉】pyrophoric powder
着火时间 firing time (F.T.)
着火性能 ignition behavior
着色 colouration, colouring, dyeing, tinting ◇ 回火~", 空气~法", 热~法", 烧结金属~", 易~的 colourable
着色处理 dyed finish
着色法探伤仪 impregnating crack detector
着色腐蚀 stain etching
着色浸蚀 colour etching
着色菌科 Chromatiaceae
着色菌属 Chromatium
着色抛光 colour buffing
着色渗透剂 dye penetrant ◇ 水乳化~检查法
着色渗透(剂)探伤[检验] 【理】dye-penetrant test
着色渗透(剂)探伤法 dye-check penetrant process ◇ 可见~", 水洗性 ~"
着色渗透检验 dye penetration test
着色探伤 liquid penetrant test, dye check
着色性 stainability, dyeing property
着色荧光探伤法 ◇ 马格纳罗~ Magnalo process
着重点 stress
灼减(量) loss (of weight) on ignition, igloss
灼减损失 loss on ignition, loss in weight

灼热 broil, glow, glowing heat, incandesence
灼热的 glowing, incandescent, full hot
灼烧 burning
灼烧试验 【耐】burning behaviour test
灼烧损失 ignition loss
浊点试验 cloud test
浊度测定（法） turbidimetry, nephelometry
浊度测量仪 turbidimetric apparatus
浊度法[计]测定 【粉】turbidimetric determination
浊度计 turbidimeter, turbidometer, nephelometer, scopometer ◇ 光电～opacimeter, 理查森～*, 瓦格纳～ Wagner turbidimeter
浊度计法 turbidimetric method
浊回水（管道） turbid return water（T.R.W.）
咨询 inquiry
资本回收 capital recovery
资本货物部门 capital goods industries
资本[金]流转 flow of capital
资本配比 capital gearing
资本收益率 capital-income ratio
资本消耗的补偿 【企】capital consumption allowances
资本盈余与亏损 【企】capital gains and losses
资本支出 capital expenditure [outlay]
资本值 capitalized cost
资产 capital (fund), assets, property ◇ 存量～ existed capital
资产负债率 assets-liability ratio
资格 qualification
资格证书 qualification certificate
资金 fund, capital ◇ 流动～*
资金流动 cash flow
资金流转报告 fundflow reprot
资金流转 flow of capital
资料 data, information (infm, info.), document, material, 【计】file
资料处理 processing of data
资料工具书 data book
资料检索 document retrieval ◇ 自动～系统*
资料清单 documentation list
资料通报 information circular (I.C.)
资料学 informatics
资用假说 working hypothesis
资用强度 working strength
资用物质 working substance
资用应力 working stress
资源 resource, inventory
资源保存[护] resource conservation
资源重复利用 recycling of resources
资源分配 resource allocation
资源分[共]享 【计】resource-sharing
资源管理 resource management
资源管理程序 【计】resource manager
资源耗竭的补偿 depletion allowance
紫边（光谱的） 【化】blued edge
紫硅铝镁石 yoderite
紫褐色 purple-brown, brown purple
紫胶 shellac
紫金（78Au, 22Al） violet gold
紫锂辉石 kunzite
紫硫螺菌属 thiospirillum
紫硫细菌 purple sulphur bacteria
紫铝辉石{LiAl(SiO$_3$)$_2$} kunzite
紫钼铀矿 nourite
紫色光焦点 violet focus
紫色三氧化钨 violet tungstic oxide
紫水晶{SiO2} amethyst
紫四环镍 abelsonite
紫苏辉长岩（超基性岩） norite
紫苏辉石{(FeMg)SiO$_3$} hypersthene
紫铜 red copper, tough pitch (copper)
紫铜带 strip [band] copper ◇ 电刷用～ brush copper
紫铜盘条 【压】copper wire rod, copper rolled wire
紫铜条材 strip copper

紫外光过滤器	black light filter
紫外-可见光比色监测器	ultraviolet-visible colorimetric monitor
紫外可见分光光度计	ultraviolet-visible spectrophotometer
紫外线[光]	ultraviolet rays [light]
紫外线测宽仪	ultraviolet width gauge
紫外(线)灯	ultraviolet [vitalight] lamp ◇ 黑玻璃~
紫外(线)定量分析	ultraviolet quantitative analysis
紫外(线)辐射	ultraviolet radiation
紫外(线)光度计	ultraviolet photometer
紫外(线)光谱[分光]学	ultraviolet spectroscopy
紫外线内孔探测镜	ultraviolet borescope
紫外线强度[紫外光强]	ultraviolet intensity
紫外(线)区	ultraviolet region [band]
紫外线探伤法	glo-crack
紫外(线)显微镜	ultraviolet microscope
紫外(线)显微镜观察	ultraviolet microscope observation
紫外(线)显微术	ultra-violet microscopy
紫外(线)显微照片	ultraviolet micrograph
紫外(线)显微照相术	ultraviolet photomicrography
紫外线消毒	【环】ultraviolet disinfection
紫外(线)影像	ultraviolet image
紫外线照矿灯	mineralight lamp
紫外线照明	ultraviolet lighting [illumination]
籽晶	seed [matted, inoculating] crystal, crystallon, 【半】seed ◇ 加~ seeding, 重掺杂~ heavily doped seed
籽晶夹	seed chuck
籽晶夹头	seed holder
籽晶料	seed charge
籽晶取向	seed orientation
子程序	【计】subprogram, subroutine ◇ 内[直接插入]~ in-line subroutine
子程序表	【计】 subroutine table
子程序库	【计】 subroutine library
子单元	sub-element
子弹合金(94Pb,6Sb)	bullet alloy
子公司	subsidiary company [corporation]
子任务	【计】subtask
子试样[样本]	subsample
子午(平)面	meridian plane
子午线	meridian
子系统	subsystem
子盐	alite
子样	【计】sample
子子程序	【计】sub-subroutine
子作业	【计】subjob
自保持触点	self-holding contact
自保持电路	self-holding circuit
自保护管(一种 X 射线管)	self-protected tube
自保护焊接	no gas welding
自饱和	self-saturation
自爆	spontaneous explosion
自备能源焊头	self-powered (welding) head
自焙	self-roasting
自焙电极	【冶】self-baking [self-sintering] electrode
自焙矿石	self-roasting ore
自焙碳块	self-baking carbon block
自焙碳块-陶瓷砌体复合炉衬	【铁】self-baking carbon brick compound ceramic bonding lining
自焙碳砖	【铁】self-baking carbon brick
自焙阳极	self-baking anode ◇ 连续~
自编程序计算机	【计】self-programming computer
自编译的编译程序	【计】self-compiling compiler
自编译语言	【计】self-compiling language
自变量[数]	independent variable, argument
自补偿	self-compensating
自补偿支承辊	self-compensatory back-up roll

自补码 【计】self-complementing code
自差接收法 autodyne [self-heterodyne] reception
自差式接收机 autodyne receiver
自衬 self lining ◇ 炉子～技术*
自撑杆[支架] self-supporting bracing
自成坩埚法 auto-crucible method
自成坩埚熔炼 auto-crucible melting
自成坩埚熔炼设备 auto-crucible melting apparatus
自成核沉淀[析出] 【金】self-nucleated precipitation
自成形 【粉】self-compaction
自承重硬壳[皮] 【钢】self-supporting solid skin
自持线圈 restraining coil
自充填的 【铸】self-packing
自出辊辊道 dead roller table
自猝灭计数管 self-quenched counter
自催化反应 self-catalyzed reaction
自催化效应 autocatalytic effect
自催化作用 【金】autocatalytic action
自淬硬 self-quenching ◇ 马谢特～钢*
自淬硬高碳模具钢(2.25C,10W,2Cr,2.5Mn,1Si) maxtack steel
自导纳 self-admittance
自定心冲头[穿孔器] (同"自动定心冲头")
自定中心(式振动)筛 ripple flow vibrating screen
自动 automation, self-action, self-motion
自动板厚控制 automatic gauge control (AGC)
自动板形控制 automatic profile control (APC)
自动包装机 automatic packing unit
自动报警设备 automatic alarm
自动报文交换 【计】automatic message switching
自动闭塞系统[装置] 【运】automatic block system
自动编码 automatic coding, autocoding

自动编码器 【计】compiler, autocoder
自动编码语言 automatic coding language
自动编排系统 automatic patching system, autopatch system
自动编索引 auto-index
自动编译程序 【计】Autopiler
自动变负荷 automatic load change
自动变换 automatic reversal
自动拨号装置 【电】automatic dialing unit (A.D.U.)
自动拨火器 self-poking arrangement
自动波束控制 automatic beam control (ABC)
自动操作 automatic operation [performance]
自动操作系统 robotized system
自动测量记录仪 ◇ 运动轧件～instagraph
自动长度控制 automatic length control
自动车(挂)钩 automatic coupling
自动沉淀析出 autoprecipitation
自动称量给料机[器] autoweighing feeder, weighing controller
自动称量漏斗 【冶】automatic weigh(ing) hopper
自动称量器 weightograph
自动称量系统 【冶】automatic weighing system ◇ 带卷～*
自动成型机 automatic moulding machine
自动程序监控器 【计】automonitor
自动程序控制 automatic program control
自动程序控制系统 automatic sequence control system
自动程序设计 automatic programming
自动程序调整 automatic preset
自动程序中断 【计】automatic program interrupt
自动秤 automatic scale [weigher], weightometer
自动冲锤打桩机 automatic ram pile driver
自动冲压工具 automatic pressing tool

自动重发[重复发送]系统	【电】automatic repetition system
自动重合闸	recloser
自动重合闸(油)开关	automatic reclosing circuit-breaker
自动重合闸装置	automatic reclosing device
自动重调(的)	self-reset
自动抽样	autoabstract
自动出料[坯]	automatic ejection ◇ 重力~炉
自动传送带型(热处理)炉	automatic conveyer-type furnace
自动催化(作用)	autocatalysis
自动催化反应	autocatalytic reaction
自动催化还原	autocatalytic reduction
自动淬火装置	automatic hardening installation
自动存储区	【计】automatic storage
自动打包机	automatic flexible strapping machine, automatic packing machine
自动打壳机	automatic crust breaker
自动打捆机	automatic bander
自动打印机	automatic stamper
自动带宽控制	automatic bandwidth control (ABC)
自动等静压制	【粉】mechanized isostatic pressing
自动滴定仪	automatic titrating apparatus
自动递钢(机座间的)	automatic catching
自动点焊	automatic spot welding
自动点焊机	stitch welding machine
自动点火	automatic firing, autoignition
自动电镀	automatic plating
自动电焊机	automatic welder
自动电(弧)焊	automatic arc welding ◇ 连续送[供]丝~*
自动电弧焊机	automatic arc welding machine ◇ 单头~*,多头~*,焊丝进给~*
自动电话机	automatic [dial] telephone
自动电话交换机	automatic (telephone) exchange
自动电话局	automatic central office
自动电流调节器	automatic current regulator (A.C.R.)
自动电压调节器	automatic voltage regulator (A.V.R.)
自动电子发射	autoelectronic emission
自动电子数据交换中心	automatic electronic dataswitching centre
自动定时器	autotimer
自动定位	automatic positioning
自动定位滚珠轴承	self-aligning ball bearing
自动定位滚柱轴承	self-aligning roller bearing
自动定位控制	automatic position control (A.P.C.)
自动定位控制设定监控器	APC setting monitor
自动定心冲头[穿孔器]	【压】bell centre punch, self-centreing punch
自动定心进口导板	self-centring entry guide
自动定序	【计】automatic sequencing
自动镀锡设备	【压】automatic tinning equipment
自动断路(器)	auto-cut-out, automatic cut out, automatic circuit breaker
自动堆料机	automatic piler ◇ 钢坯~billet unscrambler
自动堆垛起重机	automatic stacker crane
自动堆垛台(坯料的)	【压】unscrambler
自动对焊	automatic butt welding
自动对位双列滚珠轴承	double-seated in self aligning ball bearing
自动对心辊	self-aligning centring roll
自动对中[定心]	self centring ◇ 钢卷宽度~装置*,卷高~*
自动多元素摄谱仪	autrometer
自动二进制计算机	automatic binary computer (ABC)
自动发送-接收机	【电】automatic send/

receive set (A.S.R.)
自动翻译 【计】automatic translation
自动方式 automatic mode
自动防护器[装置] automatic safety device
自动仿形轧辊车床 automatic contouring roll lathe
自动放出渣 【冶】self-releasing slag
自动放射线照相 (同"自动线照相")
自动分解 autodecomposition
自动分类机[装置] automatic sorter [classifier]
自动分离渣 【冶】self-peeling [self-releasing] slag
自动分时答问 【计】automated question answering time sharing
自动分析 automatic analysis
自动分选机 automatic classifier ◇ 钢板厚度～*
自动风量控制 automatic air volume control
自动扶梯 escalator
自动复位[复原](的) self-reset
自动负载分配调节器 automatic load dispatch regulator
自动干油和稀油压力润滑系统 automatic pressure-grease and oil lubrication system
自动干油集中润滑系统 automatic centralized grease system, centralized grease automatic system
自动干油(润滑)站 automatic central grease station
自动高速等静压制 automatic high-speed isostatic pressing
自动给油器 self-oil feeder
自动跟踪控制 automatic following control
自动关闭 automatic shut-off
自动轨道车 trackmobile
自动辊式(冷弯)成型机 automatic roll-forming mill
自动过滤器 auto-strainer, automatic filter

自动焊 automatic welding ◇ CO_2 药芯焊丝横向～*,包丝焊丝明弧～fusarc welding,埋弧～*
自动焊焊缝 automatic weld
自动焊接焊丝 automatic (welding) wire
自动焊接机 automatic (arc) welding machine
自动焊钳(点焊用) stitch welder
自动衡量器 automatic scales
自动恒温器 self-acting thermostat
自动厚度控制 (同"厚度自动控制")
自动呼叫应答器 【电】automatic calling and answering equipment
自动呼叫装置 【电】automatic calling unit (A.C.U.)
自动画流程图程序 autochart
自动化 automation, automatization, robotization
自动化程度 automaticity
自动化工程设计 automated engineering design (AED)
自动化炉 automatic furnace
自动化体系[系统] automatic system, system of automation
自动还原 automatic reduction, self-reduction
自动换辊 automatic roll changing ◇ 工作辊～*
自动换辊装置 automatic roll changing rig
自动换向 automatic reversing ◇ 热风炉～*
自动恢复[回收] self-recovery, automatic recovery
自动恢复程序 【计】automatic recovery program
自动回答 【电】auto-answer
自动绘图 autodraft, automatic plotting
自动混合装置 automatic mixing plant
自动活化 auto-activation
自动活套控制 automatic loop control
自动火焰清理 automatic scarfing
自动机 robot, automat (复数 automata),

automation, automatic machine
自动机床用钢 （同"易切削钢"）
自动机构 automation
自动机理论 【计】automata theory
自动给料[矿]器 autofeeder
自动计量加料机 （同"自动称量给料器"）
自动计量器 automatic weigher
自动计时器 autotimer
自动计数 automatic counting
自动计算机 automatic computer
自动计算机装置 automatic computing equipment (A.C.E., a.c.e.)
自动记力计 dynamograph
自动记录 automatic recording [logging], self-recording, self-registering, tracing
自动记录称量器 weightograph
自动记录秤[天平] recording balance
自动记录带 tracing tape
自动记录电流计 recording galvanometer, automatic current recording meter
自动记录光谱计 recording spectrometer
自动记录控制[调节]器 recording controller
自(动)记(录)器 automatic recorder, self-recording unit (SRU, S.R.U.), self-recorder ◇ 笔式～ pen recorder, 数字～ digital recorder
自动记录式压力计 recording gauge
自动记录式真空计 recording vacuum gauge
自动记录图表 recording chart
自动记录仪表 automatic recording instrument, recording instrument [meter], grapher, graphic instrument
自动记录仪校准 recorder adjustment
自动记录用墨水 recording ink
自动记录照相机 photorecorder
自动记录装置 self-recording unit (S.R.U.)
自动夹紧爪 self-gripping jaws
自动加料 automatic stoking

自动加料装置[设备] automatic feeding device
自动加热 spontaneous heating
自动加速(作用) automatic acceleration, auto-acceleration, self-acceleration（过程的）
自动加载 self-loading, autoloading
自动驾驶仪 automatic pilot
自动监控 automatic monitoring
自动监控器程序 automonitor routine
自动监视装置 automatic supervising device
自动检测程序 【计】autotester
自动检验 self-check(ing), automatic gauging [checking]
自动减[降]速装置(开卷机的) automatic slow down device ◇ 入口～
自动减压阀 auto-relief valve
自动交换(机) 【计】automatic exchange
自动浇注 automatic ladling ◇ 真空～系统
自动浇注法(锡铅合金锭的) 【铸】castomatic process
自动搅拌装置 self-poking arrangement
自动校验 automatic check [checque], built-in check ◇ 内部～
自动校验系统 【计】automatic checqueout system
自动校验中断 【计】automatic checque interrupt
自动校正 automatic correction, autocorrection
自动校准 self calibration
自动接地检查仪 automatic earth tester
自动截止 auto-cut-out, automatic cut-off
自动进给装置 automatic infeed device
自动进料 automatic-feed, self-acting feed, self-feed
自动进料器 self-feeder
自动浸渗 spontaneous infiltration
自动晶体切片机 automatic crystal slicing machine

自动精压 automatic coining
自动净化式过滤器 self-cleaning filter
自动聚合 auto-polymerization
自动开关 【电】automatic switch, automatic circuit breaker
自动开口钻 【铁】automatic taphole drill
自动抗生作用 autoantibiosis
自动空气断路器 air breaker, automatic air circuit breaker
自动孔径控制 automatic aperture control (AAC)
自动控制 automatic control [regulation], autocontrol
自动控制电路 automatic control circuit
自动控制杆 automatic control rod
自动控制(工程)学 automatic control engineering
自动控制回路 automatic control loop
自动控制器[仪] automatic controller [regulator], automaton
自动宽度控制 automatic width control (AWC)
自动捆扎 automatic strapping
自动捆扎机 automatic bander ◇ 柔性带~*
自动捆扎装置(带卷的) automatic bonding unit
自动例行程序 【计】automatic routine
自动粒度分析 automatic particle-size analysis
自动力除尘器 self-powered dust-collector
自动连接器 automatic coupling
自动连续轧机 automated continuous mill
自动埋弧焊 automatic submerged arc welding
自动脉冲 autopulse
自动脉冲移相器 automatic pulse phase shifter
自动门 automatic door
自动密封料斗 self-sealing hopper
自动灭火 self-extinguishing
自动灭火装置 automatic fire sprinkler

自动排版 【计】automatic typesetting
自动排废料[石]装置 automatic refuse discharger
自动排料 automatic discharge
自动排料装置 automatic discharging device
自动抛光机 automatic buffing machine
自动配料 automatic proportioning
自动配料器 autoproportioner
自动喷水控制 automatic spray control
自动匹配场法 ◇ 哈特里-福克~*
自动偏压补偿 automatic bias compensation (ABC)
自动频率控制电路 automatic frequency control circuit ◇ 水平偏转电路的~synchro-lock
自动频率调节器 automatic frequency regulator
自动平衡 auto-balance (A.B.), automatic balance [balancing, equilibrium] ◇ 磨轮[砂轮]~器*
自动齐边控制 automatic side register control
自动启动的 self running
自动启动器[启动装置] autostarter, automatic starter
自动气割机 automatic gas cutting machine ◇ 龙门式~flame planer
自动气焊机 【焊】automatic gas-welding machine
自动气体分析器 automatic gas analyzer
自动切管机 automatic casing cutter
自动倾翻装置 automatic tipping device
自动清洗 automatic cleaning
自动取样器 automatic sampler ◇ 通用电气公司~(美国)*
自动燃烧控制 automatic combustion control (A.C.C.)
自动燃烧系统 autocombustion system
自动润滑 automatic lubrication
自动润滑机理 mechanism of self-lubrication

自动润滑给料机 self-oil feeder
自动润滑器 【机】automatic lubricator, self-lubricator
自动塞棒机 【钢】autopour
自动扫描 automatic scanning
自动色层分析[分离]法 autochromatography
自动刹车控制 automatic brake control (ABC)
自动扇形区域报警技术 auto segmental zone alarming technique
自动闪光时间 automatic flashing time
自动上料系统 【铁】automatic charging system
自动射束控制 automatic beam control (ABC)
自动射线照相 autoradiogram, radioautogram, radioautograph
自动射线照相技术 radioautograph technique
自动射线照相术 autoradiography, radioautography ◇高分辨率~*
自动设备 auto-plant, automatic equipment
自动设计技术 【计】automated design engineering
自动生产线 automatic production line
自动时序计算机 automatic sequence computer
自动式蠕变试验炉 automatic creeptest furnace
自动式温度记录器 (同"自记录式温度计")
自动示波器 automatic oscillograph
自动收板装置(镀锡机的) automatic catcher
自动收报机 ticker
自动售货机 vending machine
自动输出控制阀 automatic delivery control valve
自动数据处理 【计】automatic [automated] data processing (ADP)
自动数据处理系统 automatic data processing system (ADPS)
自动数据交换中心 automatic data-switching centre
自动数据媒体 automated data medium
自动数字输入–输出系统 automatic digital input/output system (ADIOS)
自动水位检测装置 automatic water-level detecting device
自动斯普伦格尔真空泵 automatic Sprengel pump
自动送锭车 self-driven [self-propelled] ingot buggy
自动送进烧熔 【焊】automatic flash-off
自动送料压力机 mechanical feed press, feed press
自动送坯装置(送进加热炉内) bundle buster
自动速度调节器 automatic speed regulator
自动索引 【计】auto-index
自动提取 automatic abstracting
自动调弧氩弧焊 aircomatic welding
自动调节 autocontrol, automatic regulation, self-regulation
自动调节焊枪 self-adjusting gun
自动调节器 automatic controller [regulator]
自动调节式反射板 【团】automatic shifting deflector plate
自动调节特性 self-regulating characteristic
自动调整 automatic regulation [setting], self-regulation, self calibration, self-alignment
自动调整托辊 self-aligning idler
自动调整压头 self-adjusting squeeze head
自动停车机构(钢绳机的) stop motion mechanism
自动停机 automatic stop, autostop
自动停止装置 auto-stopper ◇带尾~*
自动同步 synchro, autosynchronous, selsyn

自动同步闭合装置 automatic sychronous closing equipment	mill
自动同步传感器 selsyn transmitter	自动信号 automatic signal
自动同步机 【电】synchromotor, autosyn, synchrotransmitter	自动形状控制 automatic shape control (ASC)
自动同步式鼓风机控制系统 selsyn-type blower-control system	自动性 automaticity, automatism
	自动性能 automatic performance
自动图示记录仪 autographic apparatus	自动旋床[旋压机] automatic spinning lathe
自动推进皮带走行车 【铁】self propelled belt tripper	自动选废 automatic rejection
自动推进式打壳机 self-propelled crust breaker	自动学 automatics
	自动循环压制 automated cyclic compacting
自动推料 automatic stoking	自动压机 automatic press
自动脱扣 automatic trip [release]	自动压片机 automatic tableting press
自动脱扣机 tripper	自动压型 automatic tamping
自动脱氧(作用) 【钢】self-deoxidation	自动氩弧焊 argonaut welding
自动温度调节器 (同"温度自动调节器")	自动扬料臂系统 automatical lifting-arm system
自动文件卷名识别 【计】automatic volume recognition	自动阳离子交换设备 automatic cation exchange unit
自动稳定器[装置] automatic stabilizer	自动氧化 auto-oxidation, autoxidation
自动无功功率控制 automatic reactive power control	自动氧化剂 autoxidator
	自动摇摆链式清除器 automatic swinging chain cleaner
自动误差校正(法) 【计】automatic error correction	自动遥控 automatic remote control
自动下线坑 continuous coiler	自动硬度计 automatic hardness tester
自动下芯机 automatic coresetter	自动油润轴承 selfoiling bearing
自动线 automatic line	自动预设定控制 automatic preset control
自动卸货船 self-unloading vessel	自动预调 automatic presetting
自动卸货(卡)车(倾卸式) (automatic-) dump truck	自动运输秤 automatic conveyer scale
	自动再启动 automatic restart, autorestart
自动卸卷车 coil stripping carriage	自动增益控制 automatic gain control (A.G.C.) ◇ 延迟式~
自动卸矿车 automatic tripper car	自动轧管法 (automatic) plug mill process, plug rolling ◇ 斯蒂费尔~ Stiefel process
自动卸料 automatic dump [discharge], self-dump	
自动卸料车 automatic discharge wagon, self-discharging wagon, automatic tripper car	自动轧管机 plug (tube-rolling, pipe) mill, automatic [high] mill, piercer, automatic tube rolling mill ◇ 瑞典~Swedish mill
自动卸料装置 automatic discharge unit	
自动卸载 self-discharge, self-dump	
自动卸载机 self-unloader	自动轧管机轧制的 plug rolled
自动芯棒轧管机 automatic plug-rolling	自动轧机 automatic rolling mill ◇ 程序

控制~*

自动摘要 【计】automatic abstracting, autoabstract

自动遮断 automatic cut out

自动折叠机 automatic doubler

自动震打[摇动]器 automatic shaker

自动震打装置(电收尘器的) automatic mechanical rapping system, automatic rapping device

自动振动给料器 automatic shaking feeder

自动振幅控制 automatic amplitude control

自动振筛机 automatic (vibratory) sieve shaker, automatic sieving machine

自动制动[刹车]控制 automatic brake control (ABC)

自动中断 automatic interrupt

自动铸锭 automatic ladling

自动抓斗[抓扬机] automatic grab

自动转矩控制 automatic torque control

自动转辙器 【运】automatic switch

自动装焦 automatic coke charge

自动装料 automatic loading

自动装料车 auto-loader

自动装料系统 (同"自动上料系统")

自动装填 automatic filling, self-loading

自动装卸车 lift truck ◇ 带卷~ coil car [buggy]

自动装卸机 power truck, truck loader

自动装置 automatic machine [system, arrangement], automatics, auto-plant, automation, automat (复数 automata)

自动准直 autocollimation

自动准直目镜 autocollimating eyepiece

自动准直摄谱仪 autocollimating spectrograph

自动准直仪[光管] autocollimator

自动着火[引燃] autogenous ignition

自动资料检索系统 automatic document retrieval system

自动作用 automatism

自发变形 spontaneous deformation

自发磁化(强度) spontaneous magnetization

自发磁化畴 spontaneous magnetization domain

自发磁矩 spontaneous magnetic moment

自发磁致伸缩 spontaneous magnetostriction

自发反应 spontaneous reaction

自发分解 spontaneous decomposition

自发辐射 spontaneous radiation [emission]

自发复合 spontaneous recombination

自发过程 spontaneous process

自发极化 spontaneous polarization

自发晶体 diomorphic crystal

自发孔 diomorphic pore

自发生的 diomorphic

自发衰变 spontaneous decay

自发吸附现象 spontaneous adsorption

自发氧化 spontaneous oxidation

自发跃迁 spontaneous transition

自反馈式磁放大器 【电】amplistat

自返 self-reversal

自防护膜 self-healing film

自放电 self-discharge

自封炉门 【焦】self-sealing door

自干强度 air(-dried) strength

自感磁通量 magnetic flux of self-induction

自感系数 self-induction coefficient

自感(应) 【电】self-induction ◇ 无~线圈 curtis winding

自跟踪相关器 self-tracking correlator

自功率谱 autopower spectrum

自共变函数 autocovariance function

自焊 self-brazing

自耗电极 【冶】consumable electrode, consutrode ◇ 非~电炉 permanent electrode furnace, 预烧结~*

自耗电极成型 consumable-electrode-forming

自耗电极电弧焊　consumable electrode arc welding
自耗电极电弧炉材料　consel material
自耗电极电弧(炉)熔炼法　consumable electrode (arc) process, consumable arc-melting process [technique]
自耗电极电弧(熔化)炉[自耗(弧熔)炉]【冶】consumable arc-melting [electro-arc] furnace, consumable-electrode (type) arc furnace
自耗(电极)电弧熔炼　【冶】consumable(-electrode) arc-melting
自耗电极电弧熔铸装置　consumable electrode arc melting and casting assembly
自耗电极二次重熔法　consumable electrode double melting process
自耗电极焊接　consumable electrode welding
自耗电极熔炼　consumable (-electrode) melting
自耗电极熔炼的　consumably-melted
自耗电极熔炼炉　consumable electrode melting furnace
自耗电极水冷坩埚电弧熔炼　consumable-electrode cold-mold arc melting
自耗电极真空电弧炉　consumable electrode vacuum arc furnace
自耗电极真空电弧熔炼法　consumable electrode vacuum arc melting (CEVAM) process
自耗弧熔锭　consumable ingot, consumably arc-melted ingot
自耗弧熔炼　consumable electrode vacuum arc melting
自耗式吹氧钢管　consumable steel pipe lance
自耗钛电极　consumable titanium electrode
自耗阳极　consumable anode
自滑型牵引轮　selg-feeting type capstan ◇双盘式～
自还原　self-reduction, autoreduction

自还原动力学　kinetics of self-reduction
自还原动力学模型　self-reduction kinetic model
自还原机理[机制]　self-reduction mechanism
自还原性球团　self-reduced pellet
自回归　autoregression (AR)
自回火　self tempering
自活化[激活]　self-activation
自激电路　self-excited circuit
自激多谐振荡器　free running multivibrator
自激控制　self-actuated control
自激振荡[发生]器　self(-excited) oscillator
自给电池　local battery
自给料　self-feeding (S.F.)
自给企业(指设备自给)　self-contained plant
自给式结壳　self-feeding crust
自给油压机　self-contained press
自给籽晶　self-seeding
自记测微计　self-recording micrometer
自记差示热膨胀计　recording differential dilatometer
自记秤[称重仪]　weightograph
自记电流计　recording galvanometer
自记风速表　anemograph, anemometrograph
自记高度仪　altigraph
自记高温计　autographic [recording] pyrometer
自记(录式)温度计　thermometrograph, (self-) recording thermometer
自记式膨胀仪　autographic dilatometer
自记式微量光度计　self-recording microphotometer
自记式遥测计　telerecorder
自记压力表　recording pressure gauge
自记仪[自记式仪表]　data recorder ◇带式～
自记仪器转鼓　recording drum

自记转速器　recording tachometer
自加热　self-heating
自加速电子枪　self-accelerated gun
自加速度　【理】self-acceleration
自检　self-check(ing)
自校正(的)　【计】self-repairing
自结炉衬炉　self-contained furnace
自紧密的　【铸】self-tightening
自净能力　【环】self-purification capacity
自净式过滤器　self-cleaning filter
自净作用　self-purification
自纠错码　【计】self-correcting code
自具能(量)　self energy
自可逆性　self-reversal
自控[自量]式中间包　【冶】self-metering tundish
自扩散　self-diffusion, autodiffusion ◇ 表面～*, 晶界～*
自扩散激活能　activation energy for self-diffusion
自扩散系数　self-diffusion coefficient
自来水　city [main, running, tap] water
自冷变压器　self-cooled transformer ◇ 干式～*
自立式钢结构(高炉的)　self-supporting structure
自立式高炉　self-supporting-type blast-furnace
自裂　spontaneous cracking
自馏真空泵　self-fractionating pump
自流　flow by gravity
自流井钻管　artesian well tube
自流式水口　【冶】free running nozzle
自律系统　autonomous system
自蔓延　self-propagating, self-propagation
自蔓延高温合成(法)　self-propagating high-temperature synthesis (SHS)
自蔓延燃烧　self-propagating combustion
自蔓延陶瓷复合钢管　self-spreading ceramic-clad steel tube
自磨机　autogenous grinder, autogenous grinding mill ◇ 瀑落式～cascade mill
自磨作用　self-grinding action
自黏结　self-binding
自凝坩埚熔炼　arc skull melting
自凝液体　self-solidifying liquid
自凝液体树脂　solidifying liquid resin
自耦变压器　auto-transformer (a.-tr.), autoformer, self-adjusting transformer, transtat, variac, divisor ◇ 调压～*
自耦变压器式启动器　autostarter
自偏电子枪　self-biased gun
自偏压电路　autobias circuit
自平衡电桥　self-balancing bridge
自启动泵　self-priming pump
自启动装置　self-starting device
自启动阀　self-actuated type valve ◇ 差压～*
自洽(力)场　self-consistent field ◇ 哈特里～*
自清洗粗滤器　self-cleaning strainer
自去磁　self-demagnetization
自然比例　natural proportion
自然铋　native bismuth
自然陈化　natural ageing
自然衬里　self-lining
自然衬里梯级溜槽　stone box step type chute
自然抽风式炉　natural draft furnace
自然对流　natural convection (flow), free convection
自然对数　natural logarithm (In), Napierian logarithm
自然二-十进制[二进制编码的十进制]　【计】natural binary-coded decimal (NBCD)
自然粉末　【粉】natural powder
自然腐蚀　natural corrosion ◇ 点状～*
自然干燥法　natural seasoning, air drying
自然镉　cadmium
自然铬　chromium
自然汞　native mercury
自然共[谐]振　nature [natural] resonance
自然结合　natural bond

自然界　nature
自然金　rusty [native] gold
自然金属　native metal
自然金属块　prill
自然冷却　natural (draft) cooling
自然黏结剂型砂　【铸】naturally bonded moulding sand
自然镍　native nickel
自然频率　(同"固有频率")◇有阻尼～ damped natural frequency
自然品位　natural grade
自然坡度　depositional gradient
自然砷　native arsenic
自然砷铋　arsenolamprite
自然砷锑矿　allemontit(e)
自然时效　natural [spontaneous] ag(e)ing,【金】seasoning
自然时效钢　naturally aged steels
自然时效合金　natural ageing alloy
自然锑　native antimony
自然条件腐蚀试验　natural condition test
自然铁　native iron, sideroferrite
自然通风　natural draft [ventilation]
自然通风冷却　natural air [draft] cooling
自然通风炉　air furnace
自然铜　(native) copper
自然铜矿　native copper ore
自然脱水　static dewatering
自然斜度(模锻的)　natural draft
自然型　natural mode
自然循环　natural circulation
自然循环汽化冷却　(同"低压汽化冷却")
自然银　native silver
自然印相　nature print
自然硬度　natural hardness
自然硬度钢　natural steel
自然振动　natural vibration
自然振动频率试验　natural frequency vibration test
自然蒸发(不加热)　natural [spontaneous] evaporation

自然周期(振动的)　natural period
自然资源　natural resources
自燃　self-combustion, self-ignition, autoignition, spontaneous combustion [ignition]◇可～混合物*
自燃粉末　【粉】pyrophoric powder
自燃合金　pyrophoric alloy
自燃性　pyrophoricity
自燃(性)混合物　hypergolic [self-inflammable] mixture
自燃(着火)点[温度]　spontaneous ignition temperature (s.i.t.), self-ignition point, autoignition temperature
自热　autogenesis, spontaneous heating, self-heating
自热焙烧　autogenous roasting, self-roasting
自热钙粉还原法(铀的)　autothermic calcium process
自热回火　self tempering
自热熔炼　autogenous [pyritic] smelting
自热熔炼法(炼铜)　【色】pyritic process
自(热)退火　self-annealing, spontaneous annealing
自热脱硫作用　【色】pyritic action
自热[熔]压焊　autogenous pressure welding
自熔合金(Ni-Cr系合金,用于喷镀)　self-fluxing alloy
自熔合金喷镀　self-fluxing alloy spraying
自熔性混合矿石　self-fluxing ore mix
自熔性混合料　self-fluxed mixture, self-fluxing blend
自熔性矿石　self-fluxing ore
自熔性炉料　self-fluxing burden [charge]◇全～*
自熔性炉料操作(高炉)　【铁】self-fluxing operation [practice]
自熔性球团(矿)　(self-)fluxed [self-fluxing] pellet
自熔性烧结矿　self-fluxed [super-fluxing] (lump) sinter, self-fluxing agglomerate

[sinter], self-fluxing sintered ore,【团】lime sinter ◇ 超~*, 低品位~*
自熔性硬钎焊料 self-fluxing brazing alloy
自熔性渣 self-fluxed slag
自熔杂质 self-slagging impurity
自软化 self-softening
自润滑 self-lubrication, self-lubricating
自润滑材料 self-lubrication material
自润滑性能 self-lubricating property
自润滑轴承 self-lubricating [selfoiling, oilless] bearing, maintenance-free bearing
自烧结电极 self-sintering electrode
自烧结还原 self-agglomerating reduction
自射线照相 (同"自动射线照相")
自身缠绕试验(钢丝的) 【压】button test, long eye test
自身承重型高炉 self-supporting-type blast-furnace
自身淬硬 (同"自淬硬")
自身的 in-house
自身电极(试料的) self-electrode
自身回火热处理法 Tempcore
自身冷却的 self-cooled
自身预热 【铁】self-preheating
自生(自动生成) autogenesis
自生复合材料 composite in situ
自生再结晶 spontaneous recrystallization
自蚀(光谱自蚀) self-reversal
自蚀片[阳极] corrosion piece
自适应 self-adapting, autotuning
自适应反馈控制 adaptive feedback control
自适应过程控制 autoadaptive process control
自适应计算机 【计】self-adapting computer
自适应控制技术 adaptive control technique
自适应控制器 adaptive controller
自适应系统 adaptive system
自适应性 adaptability
自适应预报 (self-)adaptive prediction

自适应最优化 adaptive optimization
自锁 auto-lock, self-lock, lock-on, latching, self-holding
自锁按钮 【电】latching button
自锁触点 retaining [self-holding] contact
自锁电路 retaining [self-holding] circuit
自锁定 self-locking
自锁钢卷钳 self-closing coil tongs
自锁继电器 holding relay
自体凝集作用 auto-agglutination
自(体研)磨 autogenous grinding ◇ 二次~*, 一次~*
自调变压器 self-adjusting transformer
自调电弧 self-adjusting [self-regulating] arc
自调多孔轴承 self-aligning porous bearing
自调恒温器 self-acting thermostat
自调(节,整) self-adjustment, self-aligning
自调式电弧焊焊头 self-adjusting arc head
自调式焊枪 self-adjusting gun
自调式压头 self-adjusting squeeze head
自调托辊 self-aligning idler
自停装置 self-stopping device
自同步 self-clocking, self-synchronizing
自同步电动机 autosynchronous [self-synchronous] motor
自同步发送器 transmitting selsyn
自同步机 austosyn, selsyn, synchro ◇ 永磁转子~magnesyn
自同步接收机 receiving selsyn
自同步连续矫直拉矫机 【连铸】self synchronous and progressive straightening withdrawal straightener
自推进运输车 self-propelled carriage
自退火 self [spontaneous] annealing
自脱氧的 【钢】self-killing
自脱氧(作用) 【钢】self-deoxidation
自外延生长 【半】autoepitaxis
自维持反应 self-sustained reaction
自维持燃烧 self-sustained combustion
自稳定电弧 self-stabilizing arc

自吸泵　self-priming pump
自吸收　self-absorption
自相关　autocorrelation, self-correlation
自相关函数　autocorrelation function ◇ 二维～*
自相关器　autocorrelater
自消磁[自行退磁(作用)]　self-demagnetization
自协变[自协方差]函数　autocovariance function
自协场　(同"自洽场")
自卸车　dumper, dump car, tripper ◇ 铁路～ tipping railway car, 尾卸式～ end tipper
自卸吊车[起重机]　clamshell car
自卸吊斗　self-discharge container
自卸汽车　automatic [rear] dump truck, (end-) dump truck [car], dumper ◇ 底卸式～ bottom dump hauler
自卸箱[料框, 料罐]　dump bucket
自形晶体　diomorphic crystal
自形孔　diomorphic pore
自行车内胎管　bicycle inner tube
自行控制　self-actuated control
自行式打壳机　self-propelled crust breaker
自行式混凝土灌筑机　self-propelled concreting plant
自行式运料车　transfer buggy
自行小车　self-propelling car
自行氧化　spontaneous oxidation
自行造渣杂质　(同"自熔杂质")
自修复(的)　【计】self-repairing, self-heading
自修改程序　【计】self-modification program
自旋　spin(ning)
自旋波　spin wave
自旋磁共[谐]振　spin-magnetic resonance
自旋磁矩(电子的)　spin-magnetic moment
自旋点阵[晶格]　spin lattice
自旋点阵弛豫[晶格张弛]　【金】spin-lattice relaxation
自旋电极法　spinning electrode process
自旋电子　spinning electron
自旋方向　spin direction
自旋分裂　spin splitting
自旋-轨道分裂　spin-orbit splitting
自旋-轨道力　spin-orbit force
自旋-轨道散射　spin-orbit scattering
自旋-轨道相互作用　spin-orbit interaction
自旋互逆取向　opposite spin orientation
自旋间多重性　spin-spin multiplicity
自旋间相互作用　spin-spin interaction
自旋(间)耦合常数　spin-spin coupling constant
自旋角动量　spin angular momentum
自旋-晶格间相互作用　spin-lattice interaction
自旋量子数　spin quantum number
自旋旁带(光谱的)　spinning sidebands
自旋平行取向　parallel spin orientation
自旋取向　spin orientation ◇ 反～*
自旋双重线分离　spin doublet separation
自旋态　spin state
自旋运动　【理】spinning motion
自旋轴　spin(ning) axis
自学习　self-learning ◇ 轧制节奏～模型*
自寻最优控制器　self-optimizing controller
自压实　【粉】self-compaction
自养　autotrophy
自养生物　autotroph
自养铁氧化细菌　autotrophic iron-oxidizing bacteria
自养细菌　autotrophic bacteria
自硬　air setting, self-hardening
自硬法　【铸】cold setting process
自硬钢　self-hardening steel
自硬化本领　【金】self-hardening capacity
自硬(化)黏结剂　self-set [air-set, cold-setting] binder, air-bond ◇ 不烘焙～*

自硬(化型)砂	【铸】self-hardening sand
自硬性	self-hardening capacity [property]
自硬性型砂[混合物]	【铸】self-curing mixture
自硬铸型	self-hardening form
自用产品[产量]	captive tonnage
自由变量	【数】free variable
自由变形	unrestricted change of shape
自由表面	free surface
自由表面扩散	diffusion on free surface
自由表面能	free surface energy
自由波动	uncontrolled fluctuations
自由侧	free side
自由场源	free source
自由长度	free length, overhanging length (悬臂梁的)
自由沉降[沉积,沉淀](微粒的)	【选】free [unhindered] sedimentation, free [unhindered] settling
自由沉降比	free settling ratio
自由沉降槽式分级机	free settling tank classifier
自由沉降分级机	free falling classifier, unhindered-settling classifier ◇ 浅室型~*,深室型~*
自由沉降固体物质	free settling solids
自由沉降水力分级机	free settling hydraulic classifier
自由沉降速度	free falling velocity
自由成型模	free forming die
自由成形	free forming
自由锤锻工艺	smithing technique
自由导轴	free steering axle
自由电荷	free charge [electricity]
自由电子	free [unbound] electron
自由电子理论	free electron theory ◇ 德鲁德-洛伦茨~*
自由电子模型	free electron model
自由电子能级	free electron (energy) level
自由电子碰撞	free electron collision
自由电子气	【理】free electron gas
自由电子云	free electron cloud
自由度	degree of freedom [liberty], freedom, free dgree
自由度数	number of degree of freedom
自由端	free end
自由端支承	free end bearing
自由锻(造)	【压】free [air, hammer, open, smith] forging, open [flat] die forging, forge smithing ◇ 铁砧上~ smithing operation
自由锻造车间	hammer [forge] shop
自由锻造锤	fore hammer
自由对流传[换]热	free convection heat transfer
自由格式输入	free format input
自由辊	【压】loose roll
自由过滤面积	free filter area
自由滑轮	loose pulley
自由活套	free loop
自由基	free radical
自由价	free valence
自由降落	free fall
自由降落式喷嘴	free fall type nozzle
自由降落速度	free falling velocity
自由金	free gold
自由近似度(电子的)	freedom number
自由空间	free space
自由空气剂量(辐射的)	free air dose
自由宽展	free spread(ing)
自由扩散的	freely diffusible
自由梁	free beam
自由流动	free flow
自由流动温度(炉渣的)	free running temperature
自由路径选择	【计】free routing
自由落体	free falling body
自由面扩散	【金】diffusion on free surface
自由能	free energy ◇ 带较高~的相 higher energy phase,亥姆霍兹~*,活化~*,吉布斯~*
自由能变化[改变](量)	free energy change

自由能-成分曲线　free energy-composition curve
自由能面　free energy surface
自由能起伏[涨落]　free energy fluctuation
自由能曲线　free energy curve
自由能曲线图　free energy diagram
自由能势　free energy potential
自由能态　free energy state
自由能图　free energy chart
自由能位　free energy potential
自由膨胀(度)指数　【焦】free swelling index (FSI.)
自由膨胀率　free swelling ratio
自由迁移率　free mobility
自由亲和力　free affinity
自由氰化物　free cyanide
自由热焓　free enthalpy
自由射流　free jet
自由渗碳体　free cementite
自由生长晶体　free crystal
自由水分　free water
自由碳　graphitic carbon
自由碳原子含量　free carbon atom content
自由体　free body
自由铁素体　free ferrite
自由弯曲试验　【压】free bend test
自由弯曲试样　【压】free bend specimen
自由位错　free(d) dislocation
自由下落的　free falling
自由项　free term
自由行程　free path [travel, stroke]
自由悬挂活套(成卷带材的)　free hanging loop
自由压碎　free crushing
自由原子　free atom
自由源　free source
自由运动　free motion [movement]
自由载流子吸收　free carrier absorption
自由轧制　schedule-free [size-free] rolling
自由展宽　【压】unrestricted spread(ing)

自由振荡　【理】free oscillation [running]
自由振动　free vibration [oscillation]
自由轴　free axle
自由转向轴　free steering axle
自由状态　unbound state, free condition
自由字段　【计】free field
自愈膜　self-healing film
自诊断监控器　self diagnosing monitor
自镇静反应　【钢】auto-killing, self-killing
自蒸发　flash vaporization
自蒸发槽　flash tank
自蒸发矿浆　flashing slurry
自蒸发器　flash type evaporator, pressure reducing vessel, steam separator
自蒸发(溶)液　flashing [blow-off] liquor
自蒸发系统　flashing system
自蒸发蒸汽(流)　flashed stream
自整角机　(同"自同步机") ◇ 粗读数～coarse selsyn, 交流无触点～telegon, 精读数～fine selsyn
自整角机式轧辊开度指示器　selsyn(-type) roll-opening indicator
自整角机指示器　selsyn indicator
自重　dead load (d.l.), own weight
自重流动型砂　【铸】free flowing sand
自转　autorotation, spinning, revolve on its own axis
自组织　【计】self-organization, self-organizing
自组织模糊控制器　self-organizing fuzzy controller
字标　word mark
字长　【计】word length [size, capacity]
字处理系统　【计】word processing system
字段　【计】field
字段长度　field length
字段分隔[割]符　field separator
字段名　field name
字段位置　field location
字符　character
字符边界　character boundary
字符编码　【计】Character code

字符长度 【计】character size	字组长度 【计】block length
字符串 (character, alphabetic) string	棕腐质 ulmin(e)
字符串变量 【计】Character string variable	棕榈油回收系统 palm oil recovery system
字符发生器 【计】character generator	棕色硫酸 brown oil of vitriol (B.O.V.)
字符串传输 【计】Character serial transmission	棕色氧化钨 brown tungsten oxide
	踪迹 trace, track
字符赋值语句 【计】Character assingnment statement	综合成材率 overall finished products yield
	综合成材率(锭→材) compositive yield (from ingots to rolled products)
字符行 【计】character string	
字符集[组] 【计】character set	综合等负荷函数 comprehensive average load function
字符间距 【计】Character pitch	
字符识别 【计】character recognition	综合反应 overall reaction
字符式打印机 character-at-a-time printer	综合防治 integrated control,【环】comprehensive prevention and cure
字符图形 【计】Charater graphic	
字符显示器 【计】character-mode display	综合废水处理 【环】combined waste water treatment
字符阅读器[输入机] 【计】character reader ◇ 视网膜~	
	综合公差 total [composite] tolerance
字节 byte, syllable	综合鼓风 【铁】blast modification
字节操作(处理) 【计】byte manipulation	综合管理系统 【计】total management system
字节组 【计】gulp	
字节地址 【计】byte address	综合过程控制 【电】integrated process control (IPC)
字轮 character wheel, type drum, print wheel (鼓式打印机的)	
	综合焊条 stranded electrode, stranded welding wire
字码管 【计】charactron (tube)	
字模 typehead	综合还原反应 overall reduction reaction
字模合金 matrix alloy	综合技术经济指标 overall economics
字模黄铜 matrix brass	综合计划方案 overall project
字母 letter, character	综合价格换算系数 implicit price deflator
字母编码 【计】alphabetic coding	综合检修 general overhaul
字母编址 【计】alphabetic addressing	综合焦比 【铁】fuel consumption (coke ratio equivalent), overall coke ratio ◇ 折算~
字母(代)码 【计】alphabetic code	
字母数字-图象显示器 【计】alphameric-graphic display	
	综合开发 comprehensive [overall] development
字母数字字符组 alphanumeric character set	
	综合控制[治理] synthetical control
字母显示器 alphascope	综合利润率 composite interest rate
字母字符 alphabet(ic) character	综合利用 comprehensive utilization
字盘秤 dial scale	综合鳞皮 synthetic mill scale
字时间 【计】word time	综合流程图 general flowchart
字样 type face	综合模型 generalized model
字组 【计】block	综合溶剂萃取 integrated solvent extraction

综合特性　overall characteristics
综合图　complex chart
综合土木工程系统　integrated civil engineering system (ICES)
综合团矿　【团】composite agglomerate
综合污染　【环】combined pollution
综合误差　composite error
综合影响　combined influence
综合指数　composite index (number), aggregative index number
综合自动控制连续轧机　【压】IPC (integrated process control) mill
综晶(体)[综晶反应]　【金】syntectic
综晶平衡　syntectic equilibrium
综述　summarization, overview, survey
总安全系数　overall safety factor
总安装图　general assembly drawing (g.a.d.), general installation drawing
总本征函数　total eiganfunction
总变度(煤、焦的)　total variance
总变形　overall [total] deformation, total strain
总表　general list (GL)
总表面积　total surface area
总不清晰度　total unsharpness
总布置(图)　general arrangement (g.a.)
总产量　total output, gross [ultimate] production, overall yield
总产值　total value of out-put ◇ 工业~*, 社会~*
总场地面积　gross site area
总长度　overall length (LOA), total length
总车站　【运】union station
总沉积　overall deposition
总成本　total [overall, assembling] cost
总成分　bulk composition
总尺寸　overall dimension (o.a.d.), overall [full] size
总抽风管　suction main
总传热系数　total [overall] heat-transfer coefficient
总吹炼时间　【冶】total blowing time

总调度　chief dispatcher
总吨数(船的)　gross ton (GT)
总镦粗量(零件的)　total upset
总额　(total) sum, amount, gross, total
总发射率　total emissivity
总阀　master valve
总反应　overall [summary] reaction
总反应速度常数　total [overall] rate constant
总反应速率　overall reaction rate
总放大系数　overall amplification
总废气阀　main exhaust valve
总风管　blast main, main blast line
总负荷[载]　total load
总概[]率　total probability
总高度　overall [total] height, height overall
总工长　chief foreman
总工程师　chief engineer (C.E.)
总功率[动力]消耗　total power consumption
总共过去[经过]的时间　total elapsed time
总管　main (pipe), line pipe, trunk ◇ 集气~*
总含氨量　total ammonia
总荷载　gross load
总还原度[量]　total amount of reduction
总还原率　overall reduction
总回采率　ultimate recovery (ult. rec.)
总回收率　overall [gross] recovery, ultimate recovery (ult. rec.)
总集料皮带机　main gathering belt
总剂量　integral (absorbed) dose, accumulated dose
总计　totalizing, (grand) total, amount, gross
总计划　general plan
总加热面　total heating surface (t.h.s.)
总碱浓度　total soda concentration
总建筑基地面积　【建】gross site area
总建筑面积　【建】gross building [floors]

area, overall flooorage
总建筑师 chief architect
总降尘管 main duct
总交换能力 total exchange capacity
总角动量 total angular momentum
总截面 bulk cross-section
总节流[气]阀 main throttle valve
总结 summary (Sum.), summarization
总结焦周期 gross coking time
总经济师 【企】chief economic manager
总经理 【企】general manager
总经营成本 overall operating cost
总开关 master switch (m.s.), main switch
总开销 overhead
总孔隙度[气孔率] overall [total, general] porosity
总控钥匙 【计】turn-key
总控制计数器 total control counter
总控制盘 general control panel
总控制室 main control room
总跨度 total span
总会计师 【企】chief [general] accountant
总冷凝器 main condenser
总利用率 overall utilization
总灵敏度 overall sensitivity
总流程图 general flowchart
总流量 total flow (rate)
总落差 overall drop, gross head
总煤气道 common duct
总面积 total area, gross area (房屋建筑)
总能量 total energy
总排气阀 main exhaust valve
总排水管 main sewer
总平衡 overall balance
总平面布置 general arrangement [layout]
总平面布置图 general arrangement plan [drawing]
总平面设计 site planning
总平面图 general layout, master plan, site-plan
总气孔率 overall porosity

总强度 total intensity
总燃烧热 gross heat of combustion
总热传导系数 (同"总传热系数")
总(热)焓 total heat content
总热量 total heat
总热能 gross calorific power, total heat energy
总热平衡 total [overall] heat balance
总热效率 overall [gross] thermal efficiency
总热值 gross [overall] heating value, gross calorific value
总熔化时间 overall melting time
总溶解固体(量) 【环】total dissolved solids (T.D.S.)
总容差 total allowance
总容积 total volume, overall (vessel) volume
总容量 total capacity [capacitance]
总蠕变变形(量) total creep
总烧结透气性 overall sintering permeability
总烧熔量 【焊】total flash-off
总设计师 chief designer
总使用寿命 entire life
总视在孔隙率 apparent total porosity (A.T.P.)
总试样 bulk [gross] sample
总(收)得率 gross recovery
总收入[得] overall gain
总收缩量 gross shrinkage
总输出 total output
总数 total(ity), sum
总衰耗[减] overall [complete] attenuation
总水管 water main
总水头 gross head
总速度常数 (同"总反应速度常数")
总损失 total loss (t.l.)
总碳(量) total carbon (T.C.), overall carbon content
总体 total(ity), population, overall ◇ 反

向～ inverse population
总体背景 general background
总体布置 (同"总平面布置")
总体尺寸 overall size
总体腐蚀 total corrosion
总体工程 systems engineering
总体规划 general planning, overall [master] plan
总体规划[设计]阶段 general planning period
总体[容]积 overall volume
总体平均值 population mean
总体设计 general planning, overall [system] design
总调节阀 main governor valve
总铁心损失 total core loss
总透光度[透射比] total transmittance
总图 general arrangement (g.a.), general drawing [plan, view], overall view, assembly drawing
总图布置 general layout
总位差 total head (th), gross head
总污水管线 main sewer line
总吸收(量) total absorption
总吸收剂量 integral (absorbed) dose
总吸收系数 total absorption coefficient
总系统误差 total systematic error
总线 highway, bus, trunk
总线性收缩 linear total shrinkage
总线主控 【计】bus master
总效率 overall [gross] efficiency
总效应 gross effect
总悬浮固体(量) 【环】total suspended solids (TSS)
总压差 total differential pressure
总压力 overall [total] pressure
总压力降 main pressure drop
总压力损失 loss of total pressure (LTP)
总压头 total head (th)
总压下量 overall [total] reduction
总烟道 main flue, common stack [duct]
总延伸[伸长](量) total [general, over-all] elongation, total [general] extension
总延伸率 general elongation
总延伸系数 total coefficient of elongation
总扬程 gross head
总氧含量 total oxygen
总应变 total strain
总应变法 total strain method
总营业费 overall operating costs
总余量 total allowance
总载重量 deadweight capacity (d.w.c., D.W.T.)
总则 general (rules, provisions)
总增益 overall gain
总站 master station, 【运】union station
总长大(晶粒的) overall growth
总值 total [gross] value, grand total
总质量 total mass
总重(量) total weight (T.W.), gross weight (GWT)
总贮量(贮槽的) total tankage
总装配图 general assembly drawing (g.a.d.)
纵边剪切工序(板带材的) side trimming operation
纵波速度 longitudinal wave velocity
纵波探棒[探测器] longitudinal wave probe
纵磁场 longitudinal magnetic field
纵断面 vertical [longitudinal] section (l.s.)
纵缝焊机 longitudinal seam welder
纵缝弯曲试验 longitudinal-bead bend test
纵割锯 rip saw
纵隔板 longitudinal partition
纵拱式窑 longitudinal arch kiln
纵焊 longitudinal welding
纵焊缝 longitudinal weld
纵行 column (col.)
纵痕(薄板的) tramlines
纵横流动区域精炼炉 (同"正交流动区域精炼炉")
纵剪 slitting (剪切) ◇多刀圆盘剪～ ro-

tary gang slitting

纵剪带卷　slit coil

纵剪和横剪作业线　slitting and shearing line

纵剪和卷取作业线　slitting and coiling line

纵剪和切边作业线　slitting and trimming line

纵剪(机)[纵切机,纵切剪]【压】slitting machine, slitter, slitting cutter ◇ 带材~*,非传动[拉过]式~pull-type slitter, 金属板材~metal slitting cutter

纵剪机组[作业线]　slitting line [unit], slitting shear(ing) line ◇ 冷轧带钢~*, 热~, 小厚度~*

纵剪切边作业线　slitting line

纵剪圆盘剪刀片　slitter knife

纵接　longitudinal joint

纵进刀　length feed

纵联复式汽轮机　tandem compound machine

纵列式轧机　tandem mill

纵裂　split crack

纵裂纹　vertical [throat, longitudinal] crack, rod crack (钢材或钢丝的) ◇ 有~的线材 (见"线材")

纵切　length [longitudinal] cutting, slitting (对成卷带材,见"纵剪")

纵切多刀圆盘剪　rotary gang slitter

纵切工序　slitting operation

纵切圆盘刀心杆(带钢的)　slitting roll

纵切圆盘剪　slitter, slitting shears

纵切(圆盘)锯　slitting mill

纵视图　longitudinal view

纵弯强度　buckling strength

纵弯曲　buckling

纵向　lengthwise, endwise, longitudinal direction

纵向刨床　【机】planing machine

纵向变形　linear deformation

纵向撑杆　spreader

纵向磁场　longitudinal magnetic field

纵向磁场探测器　longitudinal field probe

纵向磁化　longitudinal magnetization

纵向挡墙　【连铸】longitudinal bulkhead

纵向发裂(钢材的)　roke

纵向分布　longitudinal distribution

纵向钢筋　longitudinal reinforcement

纵向钢丝束(预应力配筋结构)　longitudinal cable

纵向各向异性　longitudinal anisotropy

纵向焊接用夹具　longitudinal welding fixture

纵向划痕(拉拔或挤压的)　die line

纵向加热炉　end-fired furnace

纵向进给　length feed

纵向拉伸[纵拉]　longitudinal draw

纵向拉伸应力　longitudinal tensile stress

纵向拉条　longitudinal tie rod

纵向力　longitudinal force

纵向梁　longitudinal beam

纵向裂纹　longitudinal crack

纵向排列[配置]　end arrangement, end-to-end arrangement [setup]

纵向排列电解槽　end-to-end placed cells

纵向膨胀缝　longitudinal expansion joint (LEJ)

纵向强度　longitudinal (direction) strength

纵向切分[割]　(同"纵切")

纵向切口　cannelure

纵向倾斜炉床　longitudinal sloping hearth

纵向热传导　longitudinal thermal conduction

纵向弹性　longitudinal elasticity

纵向弹性模量　modulus of longitudinal elasticity

纵向贴角焊　longitudinal fillet weld

纵向弯曲试验　longitudinal bending test, buckling test

纵向弯曲应变　buckling strain

纵向位移　longitudinal displacement

纵向形状　longitudinal shape

纵向压弯　crippling

纵向延展性　longitudinal ductility
纵向应变　longitudinal strain
纵向运动　longitudinal motion, lengthwise movement
纵向振荡【动】【理】longitudinal oscillation [vibration]
纵轧【压】longitudinal [axial] rolling
纵轴(线)　fore and aft axis, longitudinal [vertical] axis
纵轴同步电抗　direct-axis synchronous reactance
纵坐标　(scale of) ordinate, Y-axis
纵坐标轴　axis of ordinate
走刀法　method of feeding
走刀机构　delivering gear
走道平台　passable platform
走行缸　travel(l)ing cylinder
走行轮　running [travel(l)ing] wheel
租用设备　leased facility
足尺　full size [scale]
足尺设计图　full size design
足尺试验　full scale test
足辊【连铸】foot-roller ◇ 异形～*
足辊装置　foot-roller unit
足重线材卷　full catchweight coil
族　family, group (grp), array, genus, population ◇ 周期表的～*
阻碍　blocking, hindering, holdback, resist, impediment
阻碍物　impediment
阻挡　stop, resist, obstruct
阻挡闭锁层(半导体的)　barrier (type) coating
阻挡层　barrier (layer), block(ing) layer
阻挡层光电池　barrage cell, block layer photocell
阻挡层光电管　barrier [block] layer photo cell
阻挡层光电效应　barrier layer photo effect
阻挡层效应　barrier effect
阻挡层整流器　barrier [blocking] layer rectifier
阻冻　antifreezing
阻冻剂　(同"防冻剂")
阻断闸板【连铸】shut-off gate
阻风门　choker, choke valve
阻浮剂　depressor
阻隔　diaphragming
阻垢　anticlogging
阻化剂　paralysant, paralyzant, inhibitor, retardant ◇ 接触～contact inhibitor, 吸附型～*
阻活剂　anti-activator
阻抗　impedance ◇ 特性[固有]～natural impedance
阻抗电桥　impedance bridge
阻抗电压　impedance voltage
阻抗分析　impedance analysis
阻抗(均方根)磁导率　impedance (rms) permeability
阻抗耦合【电】impedance coupling
阻抗匹配【电】impedance match(ing)
阻抗平面图　impedance plane diagram
阻抗平面显示技术　impedance planar display technique
阻抗转换器【电】impedance converter
阻力　resistance (resis.), resistance force, resistivity, drag ◇ 雷诺～公式*
阻力矩　resisting moment
阻力系数　drag coefficient, coefficient of drag (C.D.), coefficient of resistance
阻力效应【理】drag effect
阻落比　hindered settling ratio
阻纳【理】immittance
阻尼　damp(ing), dampening, weakening, attenuation ◇ 临界～dead-beat
阻尼比　damping ratio
阻尼波　damped wave
阻尼不足　underdamp
阻尼常数　damping constant
阻尼磁铁[体]　damping magnet
阻尼电路　damping [buffer, antihunting] circuit

阻尼电容	damping condenser
阻尼电阻	damping [buffer, despiking] resistance
阻尼法	damping method
阻尼峰	【理】damping peak
阻尼隔板	quiescence plate
阻尼环	damping ring
阻尼减振	damping vibration attenuation
◇干摩擦～装置	dry friction dampler
阻尼介质	【理】damping medium
阻尼力	damping force
阻尼器	damper, buffer, bumper, attenuator, suppressor
阻尼绕组	damper [amortisseur] winding
阻尼试验	damping test
阻尼特性	damping characteristic
阻尼调整[控制]	damping control
阻尼系数	damping coefficient
阻尼线圈	damping coil, damper, choking-winding
阻尼相互作用	damping interactions
阻尼延迟器	dashpot
阻尼因数[子]	damping factor
阻尼振荡	damped [dying] oscillation
阻尼振动	damped [damping] vibration
阻尼值	damped quantity
阻尼装置	damping [antihunting] device
阻尼自然频率	damped natural frequency
阻黏剂	antiplastering agent
阻凝剂	anti-coagulant, anti-coagulin
阻气阀[活门]	choke valve
阻燃剂	fire [flame] retardant ◇复合～
阻燃性	flame retardance, fire resistance
阻塞	choking, clogging, block(ing), blockage, stop(ping), pinning
阻塞点	choking point
阻蚀的	corrosion-inhibitive
阻蚀剂	corrosion inhibitor, stopping agent
阻止	stop(ping), stoppage, prevent, restrain, inhibit(ion), interrupt
阻止剂	inhibiting agent
阻止侵蚀的涂层	inhibit coating
阻止氧化	oxidation inhibition
阻止作用	inhibition, inhibiting action [effect], inhibition [inhibitor] effect
阻滞	retard
阻滞本领[能力]	retaining [stopping] power
阻滞挡板（偏光显微镜的）	retardation plate
阻滞效应	retardation effect
阻滞性气体	retained gas
阻滞作用	retardation, hindered action
组	group (grp), battery (Btry, Bty), crew, array, block, set, team
组成	forming, formation, compose, make up, composition, constitution, constituent
组成工形柱	built H-column
组成[组分]过冷	【金】constitutional supercooling
组成三角形	【金】composition triangle
组成物	【金】partial
组成物分力	constituent
组成相	constituent phase
组分	component, constituent, ingredient, 【金】partial
组分粉末	component powder
组分隔符	【计】group separator (G.S.)
组分图	constitution(al) diagram
组合	combination, association, assembly, composition, compose, grouping
组合板梁	flitch(ed) beam
组合保温帽	【钢】composite head
组合槽钢(拼接的)	built channel
组合齿轮	compound [built-up] gear
组合冲模	sectional die
组合带卷	composite [built-up] coil
组合锻压	combined forged
组合电池	assembled battery
组合焊条[丝]	composite electrode
组合环箍	built-up rim
组合件	assembling unit, (sub)assembly
组合结构	composite structure [construc-

组合拉模 segment die ◇ 辊式~ turn head die

组合梁(由不同材料组成的) composite [built-up, combination, compound] beam ◇ 键接~*

组合轮圈[缘] built-up rim

组合逻辑电路 【计】combinational logic circuit

组合面 built up edge

组合模 combination [assembling, collapsible, composite, compound, insert, nest, segment(al), split-segment, split(ting)] die, split mould ◇ 舌形[带切断器的,带芯棒的]~ (bolted) bridge die, 整体多件~*

组合模板 built-up plate, segmental pattern plate

组合模板框 【铸】cliche frame

组合模衬 split die liner

组合模冲 segmented punch

组合模孔 split die orifice

组合模模块 die segment

组合模型 sectional [built-up] pattern

组合排气 aggregate venting

组合坯料 composite billet

组合容器 two-part container

组合烧结体 (同"多层烧结体")

组合式 built-in (type), combined [set-up] type

组合式磁铁 composite magnet

组合式发动机 compound engine

组合式结晶器 【连铸】composite mould, four plate mould (四片组合)

组合式精密锻模 segmented precision-forging die

组合(式)量规 combination [built-up] gauge

组合(式)砂箱 built-up (moulding) box

组合式十字形辊模头 combination turks head

组合(式)轧辊 【压】sleeved roll ◇ 硬质合金~*

组合式轧辊辊套 sleeve

组合式支承辊辊套 rim

组合式支承轧辊 composite [sleeved] back-up roll

组合水口[注口] bicomponent nozzle

组合四辊式异型拉拔模 turks head die

组合头 【计】combined [combination] head

组合屋面 built-up roofing ◇ 沥青~*

组合型芯 【铸】insert core, core assembly ◇ 黏结的~用量具 pasting gauge

组合型芯盒 combination core box

组合压坯 composite compact ◇ 层状~ composite compact

组合轴 built-up shaft

组合轴承 composition [combination] bearing

组合(铸)型 【铸】composite mould ◇ 多腔~ multicavity mould

组件 assembly, subassembly, module (Mod) ◇ 炉子~ furnace components

组件检测器 module checker

组码 【计】group code

组态 configuration

组态能量 【理】configurational energy

组态软件 configuration software

组态相互作用 configuration interaction

组芯夹具 【铸】core assembly fixture [jig]

组芯砂型 【铸】core-sand mould

组芯造型 【铸】core moulding

组芯造型用砂 core moulding sand

组芯铸型 【铸】core mould

组元 component, constituent

组元活度 component activity

组元元素 component element

组长 headman, leading hand, chargehand, chargeman, gang foreman

组织 organization, organize, setup, texture, structure, entity ◇ ε~ epsilon structure, 佩罗夫斯基~ Perovskite structure, 全马氏体~*, 热处理后~*, 魏氏~*

中文	英文
组织变化	(同"结构变化")
组织粗度	coarseness of structure
组织界面	structural interface
组织缺陷	structural defect
组织特点	structural feature
组织形成	(同"结构形成")
组织性能	structure property
组织应力	structural stress
组织硬化	structural hardening
组织转变	structural transformation ◇ 舍夫勒~图 Schaeffler's diagram
组指示	【计】group-indicate, group indication
组装	assembly, assembling, packaging, framing
组装车间	assembling plant
组装端	built up end
组装夹具	(同"装配夹具")
组装图	assembly drawing
组装(作业)线	assembling [assembly] line
钻	drill, drilling, boring, borer
钻车	drill carriage,【采】bogie, dolly
钻床	driller, drill(ing) machine, drill press ◇ 手摇~*, 台式~*
钻杆	drill rod (D.R.), drill stem (D.S.), boring bar, drill pipe ◇ API管端内壁镦厚~*, 对焊~*
钻杆钢	jumper steel
钻管	drill [cashing] pipe, core barrel,【地】liner (lnr) ◇ 轻型~*, 自流井~ artesian well tube
钻机	drill, drilling machine ◇ 冲击式~*
钻机壳	drilling shell (DRSH)
钻架	drill tower [mounting, rig]
钻架塔	boring tower
钻(金刚石)拉模孔	die drilling
钻进	drilling (Drg, drlg)
钻井	bored well, well drilling ◇ 缆索~ cable drilling
钻井泥浆	drilling mud [fluid]
钻井剖面	drill record [column], drill-log
钻井疏干[排水]【环】	well dewatering
钻具	drill(ing) rig [tool] ◇ 哈斯特莱特~钢 Hastellite
钻具打捞器	grab iron, dart
钻开出铁口	drill tapping
钻孔	drilling, boring, piercing ◇ 氧乙炔~ oxyacetylene boring
钻孔定心(坯料的)	drill centring
钻孔分布板	drilled distribution plate
钻孔机	borer, auger, piercer, drilling machine, boring and mortising machine
钻孔试验	drill test
钻孔柱状图	drill-log, log sheet
钻模	drill plate [jig], jig
钻模钻孔	jig boring
钻深计	boring gauge
钻石	diamond, brillian
钻塔	boring tower
钻探	boring, misering ◇ 水冲~ wash boring, 远峰~【地】off-shore boring
钻探驳船	drilling scow
钻探操作	drill practice (DP)
钻探管	drill pipe
钻探机	drill(ing) rig, boring machine, miser
钻探机船	floating rigs
钻探记录	boring log
钻探坑	bore pit
钻探目的	drill purpose (D.P.)
钻探深度计	boring gauge
钻探用桨叶式钻头	boring blade
钻探柱状图	boring log
钻探钻头	boring chisel
钻套	drill [jig] bushing
钻铤	【地】drill collar
钻铤锁接头	drill collar sub
钻头	drill (dr.), drill(ing) [bore] bit, aiguille, straight bit (冲击式钻机用) ◇ 刮刀~ blade drag bit, 钻探用桨叶式~ boring blade
钻头钢	drill steel
钻头规	drill gauge
钻头卡头	chuck

钻头锁头接头　bit sub
钻头镶焊硬合金　Stoodite
钻头样板　drill template (DR.TP.)
钻头硬质合金镶片　rock drill insert
钻土器　earth borer
钻削　drilling, touring ◇ 可～性[能力]【机】drillability
钻屑　drillings, borings ◇ 分选～selected borings, 试样～【冶】test drillings
钻岩机　rock-boring machine ◇ 锤击式～plugger, 金刚石～diamond drill
钻岩钻头　rock bit
钻眼　drill (dr.)
钻柱　drill-stem
钻柱锁接头　drill-stem sub
钻子　awl
嘴　mouth, lip, snout (管子的), beak (铁砧的)
嘴子　nose, notch
最差状况　worst-case condition
最初还原　【冶】first reduction
最初结晶线　primary crystal line
最初晶格　primitive lattice
最纯石墨　finest grade of graphite
最纯石英　spectrosil
最大产量　maximum yield, ultimate output
最大程度[范围]　maximum extent
最大出力　ultimate output
最大传输转矩　maximum transmitted torque
最大传送率　【电】maximum transfer rate
最大磁导率　maximum (magnetic) permeability
最大磁化力　maximum magnetizing force
最大(磁)能积　maximum (magnetic) energy product
最大萃取率　maximum extraction
最大等待时间　【计】maximum latency
最大地表浓度地点　【环】maximum ground concentration site
最大地震烈度　maximum seismic intensity
最大峰值　maximum peak

最大负荷[最高负荷,最大荷载]　maximum [peak, ultimate] load
最大负荷操作　peak load operation
最大负荷电度表　maximum demand watt-hour meter
最大高度　maximum [peak] height
最大工作压力　maximum working pressure (M.W.P.)
最大功率　maximum [peak] power, ultimate output [capacity]
最大公约数　highest [greatest] common factor
最大含尘浓度　maximum dust concentration
最大含铬量　chromium maximum content
最大焊缝厚度　maximum throat depth
最大厚度(板材的)　maximum gauge
最大间距平面(晶体的)　planes of greatest spacing
最大剪切能理论　【压】maximum shear energy theory
最大接触角　maximum contact angle
最大结圈点　【团】point of maximum buildup
最大静电荷　saturation charge
最大开度(轧辊的)　maximum opening
最大抗拉强度　(同"极限抗拉强度")
最大孔径　absolute pore size
最大孔隙直径　maximum pore diameter
最大拉力载荷　maximum tensile load
最大励磁　ceiling excitation
最大粒度范围　particle stoppage
最大流动度　maximum fluidity
最大流量　peak discharge, maximum stream flow
最大密度　(同"极限密度")
最大磨蚀速率　maximum erosion rate
最大排量　peak discharge
最大泡压法　maximum bubble pressure method
最大膨胀度　maximum dilatation
最大偏差　maximum deviation [deflec-

最大偏析 maximum segregation
最大偏转角 maximum deflection angle
最大强度 maximum strength
最大强度法 （同"极限强度法"）
最大切[剪]应力 maximum shear stress
最大切应力理论 maximum shear-stress theory
最大容量[能力] maximum capacity (max. cap.), ultimate capacity
最大容许剂量（辐射的） maximum permissible dose
最大寿命 ultimate life
最大输出 maximum [ultimate] output
最大塑性功原理 maximum plastic work principle
最大网眼密度平面 【金】plane of greatest reticular density
最大限度 high [maximum] limit, maxima, maximum
最大压下量 【压】maximum reduction
最大延伸 ultimate elongation
最大延伸系数 maximum factor of elongation
最大应变 maximum strain
最大应力 maximum stress (m.s.)
最大有效[自由]面积 maximum free area
最大允许单位面积轧制力 maximum permissible specific rolling force
最大直径（线材的） maximum gauge
最大值 maximum (value), peak [greatest] value ◇ 布喇格～Bragg maximum
最大值曲线 maximum curve
最低低水位 lowest low water level (L.L.W.L.)
最低地下水 basal water
最低锻造比(极限) 【压】minimum limit of forging ratio
最低鼓风量 critical air blast
最低(化合)价 【化】minivalence
最低价格 ground floor price, rock bottom price ◇ 商品～floor price
最低(交变)应力 minimum stress
最低可获利品位 minimum payable grade
最低完好[作业]率 minimum availability
最低温度 minimum availability
最低有效鼓风 working minimum blast
最低(有效)位[最低位有效数字] 【数】least significant digit (L.S.D.)
最短弧 shortest arc
最短距离 bee line
最高产出率 maximum yield
最高点 acme, peak, crest, summit
最高风箱温度 peak windbox temperature
最高高水位 highest high water level (H.H.W.L.)
最高工作频率 【计】maximum operating frequency
最高火焰温度 peak flame temperature
最高价 【化】maximum valency [valence], maxivalence, absolute valency
最高阶干涉最大值 【理】highest order interference maximum
最高能级 topmost (energy) level
最高能量电子 highest energy electron
最高[大]浓度 maximum concentration
最高[大]容许浓度（矿尘的） maximum allowable concentration (M.A.C.)
最高烧成温度 【耐】peak firing temperature
最高升华点 maximum sublimation point
最高(数)位 【数】most significant digit, highest significant position
最高水位 maximum high-water, highest water level
最高[大]速度 maximum speed [velocity], top speed
最高透气性 peak permeability
最高完好[作业]率 maximum availability
最高温度 maximum [peak] temperature, temperature maximum (T.Max.), thermal peak
最高[大]压力 maximum [top, ultimate] pressure, pressure peak

最高硬度冷轧钢板　(full) hard temper
最高[大]有效位　most significant digit
最高有效位字符　【计】most significant character
最后产量[收获率]　final yield
最后产物　terminal [end] product
最后道次　final pass
最后反应　end reaction
最后焊层(多层焊缝的)　cap weld
最后焊道　final run, capping bead
最后荷重软化温度　final temperature of softening under load
最后合金料[添加剂]　【钢】finishing material
最后计划　final project
最后阶段(工序的)　final stage
最后精炼　final refining [purification]
最后净化　final purification
最后冷却　final cooling
最后滤饼　final (filter) cake
最后密度　final density
最后破坏　eventual failure
最后溶液　end solution
最后酸浓度　terminal acid concentration
最后添加剂　【钢】finishing material
最后析出[沉淀]相　final precipitates
最后洗液　tail washings
最后预热器　final preheater
最后中和槽　final neutrolization tank
最坏情况设计　【计】worst case design
最坏条件　worst-case condition
最坏噪声模式　worst case noise pattern
最佳编码　optimum [forced] coding
最佳程序　optimum [optimizing] program
最佳程序设计法　method of optimal programming
最佳范围　optimum range
最佳工作效率　optimum working efficiency (OWE)
最佳含量　desired content
最佳化　optimization, optimizing, optimisation ◇ 绝对[无条件]~法*

最佳可行控制技术　best available control technology
最佳[最适宜]控制　optimum [optimalizing, optimizing] control
最佳冷却条件　optimal cooling condition
最佳粒度范围　optimum size range
最佳灵敏度　optimum sensitivity
最佳磨矿粒度　【团】optimal grinding fineness
最佳取向　preferred orientation
最佳燃料比操作　optimum-fuel-rate operation
最佳烧结透气性　optimum sintering permeability
最佳实用控制技术　best practicable control technology
最佳寿命(炉衬的)　optimum life
最佳数值选定工作　optimizing work
最佳水分　optimum moisture content
最佳特性[性能]　optimum characteristics [performance]
最佳条件　optimum condition
最佳透气性　optimum permeability
最佳絮凝形状　optimum flocculation formation
最佳移[运]动速率　optimum travel rate
最佳值　optimal [optimum] value
最佳状态操作[最佳规范工作]　【钢】optimum operation
最佳组成(合金的)　tailored composition
最近结点间距(晶格的)　shortest interpoint distance
最近邻距离(晶体中的)　nearest neighbour distance
最近邻位置　nearest neighbour position
最近邻[相邻]原子　【理】nearest neighbour (atom) ◇ 第一~*
最近邻质点　【理】nearest neighbour
最可能值　most probale value
最快访问编码　minimal access coding
最快访问程序设计　【计】minimal access programming

最亮处[最精采处] high light(s)
最密排列[堆积] closest packing ◇ 原子~方向*
最内层电子 innermost electron
最上面焊层(多层焊的) cap weld, capping bead
最适宜成分 tailored composition
最下部 foot
最显著地位 foreground
最小 minimum (min.) ◇ 降至~minimizing
最小波长 minimum wavelength
最小电流 valley current
最小二乘法 least square (method), method of least [minimum] squares
最小二乘曲面拟合 polynomial least squares surface fitting
最小范围 minimum range (min. rn.)
最小方差控制 minimum variance control
最小缝隙 minimum clearance
最小厚度(板材的) minimum gauge
最小计数值[最小读数](计器的) least count
最小间隙[距离] minimum clearance
最小检漏率 minimum detectable leak rate
最小接触角 minimum contact angle
最小距离 minimum distance, minimum range (min. rn.)
最小颗粒 ultimate particle
最小流变速率 minimum rate of flow
最小流(态)化空隙度 minimum fluidized voidage
最小流态化速度 minimum fluidization velocity
最小速度 minimum velocity
最小铜含量 copper minimum content
最小应变 minimum strain
最小赢利[利润率]的 【企】marginal
最小有效位 (同"最低有效位")
最小值 minimum (min.), minimum [least] value
最小值曲线 minimum curve
最小自由能原理 principle of minimum free energy
最新技术 latest technology
最新型式 up-to-date type
最易磁化方向 direction of easiest magnetization
最易磁化轴 easiest magnetization axis
最优薄锡层镀锡薄钢板(平均锡层重量0.68~0.79kg/基准箱) best coke (grade) tin plate
最优参数 optimum parameter
最优程序设计法 method of optimal programming
最优厚锡层镀锡薄钢板(平均锡层重量大于1.4kg/基准箱) best charcoal tin plate
最优化 optimization ◇ 自适应~adaptive optimization
最优控制 optimum [optimalizing, optimizing] control
最优速度 optimum speed
最优值 optimum (value), optimal value
最终焙烧温度 final indurating temperature
最终产品 final [finished, end, resultant] product
最终产品粒度 final product size
最终产物 (同"最后产物")
最终成本 assembling cost
最终成分 final [end] composition, ultimate constituent, final analysis ◇ 要求~*
最终尺寸 finished dimension [size], final [finishing] size
最终除铁槽 final Fe-removal tank
最终处理场 【环】terminal treatment plant
最终磁选精矿 final magnetic concentrate
最终定径(焊管的) end sizing
最终断面 finished section
最终鼓风(量) final blast
最终固结[硬化] final induration
最终还原率 final reduction rate

最终加工(带材的)	final processing
最终接焊长度(对焊的)	final extension
最终金属成分	final metal analysis
最终精整	final finishing
最终净化气体	finally cleaned gas
最终矿浆温度	end pulp temperature
最终炉渣	final slag
最终滤渣[饼]	final (filter) cake
最终磨矿粒度	final grind
最终磨蚀速率	terminal erosion rate
最终抛光	【企】finishing polish
最终熔炼	【冶】final melting
最终溶液	final [end] solution
最终筛分	final screening [sizing]
最终烧成	final firing
最终烧结	【团】final sintering
最终设计	final [ultimate] design
最终收得率	ultimate yield
最终水分	final [resultant] moisture
最终退火	finish annealing
最终退火和绝缘涂层作业线	final annealing and insulation coating line
最终细磨	final fine grinding
最终形状的	net-shaped
最终需氧量	【环】ultimate oxygen demand (U.O.D.)
最终(元素)分析	final [ultimate] analysis
最终直径	finishing diameter
最终值	final [end] value
最终组织[结构]	final [ultimate] structure
左侧	left hand (l.h.), left side
左侧装置	left-hand unit
左螺旋型位错	left-hand dislocation
左捻(钢丝绳的)	【压】left lay, S-lay ◇ 交叉~*,同向~left-hand lang lay
左捻钢丝绳	left-hand lay wire rope, S-lay wire rope
左倾传动(转炉的)	left-side drive
左视图	left view
左手定则	【电】left-hand rule
左手[向]焊	left-hand welding, forward welding, forehand welding
左旋	left-hand rotation
左旋(对称)轴	left-handed screw axis
左旋螺纹心轴	left-hand threaded spindle
左右对形性	enantiomorphism
左右对映变形[态,种]	enantiomorphic variety
左右对映晶体	enantiomorphic crystals
左右对映像	enantiomorphism
左右对映形类	enantiomorphous class
佐伽克低熔点高电阻合金(64Cu,20Ni,余量 Zn)	Zodiac
佐赖特耐热镍铬合金钢(35Ni,15Cr,1.75Mn,0.5C,余量 Fe)	Zorite
做工粗糙的	rustic
作坊	work shop
作废的	spoiled, invalid
作品	works, workmanship
作图	plotting, construction
作图法	graphical construction ◇ 埃瓦尔德~Ewald's construction,孔西戴尔~*
作图法标定指数	graphical indexing
作业	work, job, operation
作业步任务	job step task
作业侧	work side
作业场地	working floor
作业处理	【计】job processing
作业调度程序	【计】job scheduler
作业定义	【计】job [operational] definition
作业分类[类别]	【计】job class
作业管理	【计】job management
作业规范	【理】operating mode
作业计划	operative [production] plan, schedule
作业结束	end of job
作业控制	operating control, job control
作业控制语言	【计】job control language (J.C.L.)
作业库	【计】job library
作业率	work [operating] rate, availability (coefficient) ◇ 最高~ maximum availability

作业面	plane of working
作业时间	on stream time
作业输出流	【计】job output stream
作业说明(书)	job description
作业线	operating [production] line
作业线能力	line capacity
作业线上处理[加工]周期	in-line treatment cycle
作业线上的	on-stream
作业线速	line speed
作业选择	【计】job selection
作业研究	operation(al) research
作业指标	performance figure
作用	action, effect, function, operation, react(ion) ◇ 不起~的 inactive, inoperative, 起~ react, 无~期间 inaction period
作用半径	action [working] radius, radius of action (R/A)
作用常数	action constant
作用点	action spot
作用电势[位]	【理】action potential
作用范围	action range, active zone, domain of influence
作用滑移面	operative glide plane
作用基	functional group
作用机构	actuating mechanism, actuation gear
作用角(腐蚀试验的)	angle of exposure
作用距离	operating distance [range]
作用力	acting [applied, apply] force, effort
作用量子	quantum of action
作用线	action line
作用压力	actuating pressure
作用应力	applied stress
作用域	【计】(action) scope
作用质量	active mass
坐标	coordinate
坐标变形试验(法)	photogrid
坐标存储器	【计】coordinate storage
坐标几何程序	coordinate geometry (COGO)
坐标式电位差计	coordinate type potentiometer
坐标数据	coordinate data
坐标镗床	【机】jig borer
坐标网	abac
坐标系	coordinate system, reference frame ◇ 直角[笛卡儿]~*
坐标原点	origin of coordinates, zero
坐标纸	coordinate paper
坐标制图器	coordinategraph
坐标轴	coordinate [reference] axis
坐料	【铁】settling of charge, slip(ping), gobbed-up (高炉炉缸故障) ◇ 人工~*
座鞍黄铜	saddlery brass
座板	bed (ding) [support, shoe, stay] plate,【压】riser block
座环	stand [socket] ring
座架	seat frame, saddle, chair
座圈	housing washer, race, ring
座谈会	symposium
座砖	well block,【钢】(nozzle) pocket brick

以非汉字开头的词条

1040 镍基磁性合金（72Ni,14Cu,3Mo,余量 Fe） alloy 1040

1060 铝合金（99.6Al,余量 Si,Fe,Cu,Mn,Mg,Zn 和 Ti） 1060 alloy

1100 变形铝合金（99Al,余量杂质） 1100 alloy

<111>晶向（结晶学的） <111> directions

$1\frac{1}{2}$长拱砖 $1\frac{1}{2}$ length arch

$1\frac{1}{2}$长下降道拱砖 $1\frac{1}{2}$ length downtake arch

$1\frac{1}{2}$长直形砖 $1\frac{1}{2}$ length brick

$1\frac{1}{2}$宽楔形砖 bonder wedge

$1\frac{1}{2}$宽直形砖 large bonder brick

12-2 镍锰马氏体时效钢（12.5Ni,2Mn,8Co,4Mo,0.2Ti,0.1Al,余量 Fe） twelve-two maraging steel

1-2-3-4 式廿辊轧机 1-2-3-4 mill

1-2-3 式十二辊轧机 1-2-3 mill

12 倍补偿点式印字机 12-fold compensation point printer

1,2 苯并咔唑{$C_{16}H_{11}N$} 1,2-phenyl naphthyl carbazole 12,-benzocarbazole

1,2-苯环氮杂蒽{$C_{17}H_{11}N$} anthraquinoline

1,2-苯环蒽{$C_{18}H_{12}$} 1,2-benzanthracene

$\frac{1}{2}$长拱脚砖 half-length skew

1-2 式六辊轧机 1-2 mill

138 铝基合金（10Cu,4Si,0.3Mg,余量 Al） 138 alloy

1,2-二胺基丙烷 （同"丙膦二胺"）

1,2-二羟基苯-3,5-二磺酸钠 tiron

1,2-二羟基蒽醌{$C_6H_8(CO_2)_2C_6H_2$(OH)$_2$} alizarin

1,2-二氢化苯{C_6H_8} 1,2-dihydro benzene

^{13}C 伴线 ^{13}C satellite

1,3-丁二烯{C_4H_6} 1,3-butadiene

13 铬不锈钢 13 chrome steel, 13%-chromium stainless steel

1,3-环己二烯（同"环己间二烯"）

14 开金（相当于 585/1000 纯度金） gold 14

1/4 块砖 quarter bat

1/4（屋架）高跨比 【建】one-fourth pitch

15-30-45N 载荷级洛氏硬度试验机 15-30-45N-scale Rockwell machine

18-8 不锈钢（18Cr,8Ni,余量 Fe） 18-8 stainless steel, eighteen-eight steel

18 铬不锈钢 18%-chromium stainless steel

18 开金（相当于 750/1000 纯度金） gold 18

18 开金铜合金 18K gold-copper alloy

1Cr18Ni9Ti 超薄壁旋压管 spinned 1Cr18Ni9Ti steel extra-light wall tube

"1"半选信号比 【计】one-to-partial-select ratio

1 号硬度冷轧薄板 hard temper sheet

1 号铸造锰青铜（58Cu,1Sn,0.25Mn,1.25Al,0.4Pb,余量 Zn） No.1 manganese bronze

1-甲基蒽{$C_{15}H_{12}$} 1-methylanthracene

1-甲基二苯醚[1-甲基氧芴] 1-methyldiphenylene oxide

1-甲基异喹啉{$C_{10}H_9N$} 1-methylisoquindine

"1"输出信 【计】one output signal

"1"态 【计】one state

214 铸造铝合金（3.8Mg,余量 Al） 214 alloy

215 磺酚阳离子交换树脂 Zeo-Karb 215

216 羧酸阳离子交换树脂 Zeo-Karb 216

22.5°弯头 1/16 bend, sixteenth bend

225 磺化聚苯乙烯阳离子交换树脂 Zeo-

Karb 225

226 羧酸阳离子交换树脂 Zeo-Karb 226

22 开黄金（22Au,13/4Ag,1/4Cu；总计24） yellow gold (alloy)

2,3-苯环-4氮芴 $\{C_{16}H_{11}N\}$ 2,3-benzo-4-Carbazole

2,3-二甲苯酚 $\{C_8H_{10}O\}$ 2,3-xylenol

2,3-二甲基吡啶 $\{C_7H_9N\}$ 2,3-dimethylphridine

2,4,6-三甲苯基[3,5-二甲苯甲基]（同"莱基"）

2,4,6-三甲苯氧基（同"莱氧基"）

2,4,6-三甲基吡啶 $\{C_8H_{11}N\}$ 2,4,6-trimethylpyridine

24S 超硬铝（4.1—4.3Cu,1.2—1.6Mg,0.6Mn,<0.2Si,<0.2Fe,余量 Al） 24S alloy

2,4-二甲代苯胺 $\{C_8H_{11}N\}$ 2,4-xylidine

2,6,8-三甲基喹啉 $\{C_{12}H_{13}N\}$ 2,6,8-trimethylauinoline

2,6-二甲基蒽 $\{C_{16}H_{24}\}$ 2,6-dimethyllanthracene

2,6-二甲基萘 $\{C_{12}H_{12}\}$ 2,6-dimethylnaphthalene

2907 多元超耐热合金（46Ni,25Co,19W,7.5Fe,2.5Ti） 2907 alloy

2-吡咯三氟丙酮 2-pyrroltrifluoroacetone

2号硬度冷轧薄板（同"半硬回火薄钢板"）

2-苯基吡啶 $\{C_{11}H_9N\}$ 2-phenylpyridine

2-甲基-4-乙基苯酚 $\{C_9H_{12}O\}$ 2-methyl-4-ethylphenol

2-甲基-5,6-苯并喹啉 1-methyl-5,6-benzoquinoline

2-甲基吖啶 $\{C_{14}H_{11}N\}$ 2-methylacridine

2-甲基丁烷 2-methyl-butane

2-甲基菲 $\{C_{15}H_{12}\}$ 2-methylphenanthene

2-甲基咔唑 $\{C_{13}H_{11}N\}$ methylcarbazole

2-甲基喹啉 $\{C_{10}H_9N\}$ 2-methylquinoline

2-甲基硫杂茚 $\{C_9H_8S\}$ 2-methylthionaphthane

2-糠酰丙酮 2-furoylacetone

2-糠酰三氟丙酮 2-furoyltrifluoroactone

2-苄基萘 2-benzylnaphthalene

2-羟基羧酸 2-hydroxycarboxylic acid

2-羟基芴 $\{C_{13}H_{10}O\}$ 2-hydroxyfluorene

2-羟基氧杂芴[2-羟基（二）苯醚] $\{C_{12}H_8O_2\}$ 2-hydroxybiphenylene oxide

2-噻吩甲酰丙酮 2-thenoylacetone

2-辛基磷酸 2-octylphosphoric acid

2-乙基-4甲基苯酚 $\{C_9H_{12}O\}$ 2-ethyl-4-methylphenol

2-乙基-n丁基溶纤剂 2-ethyl n-butyl eellosolve

2-乙基吡啶 $\{C_7H_9N\}$ 2-ethylpyridine

2-乙氧基乙醇（同"溶纤剂"）2-ethoxy-ethanlo,cellosolve

3124 超耐热合金（85Co,11.25Fe,3.75Ti） 3124 alloy

315 磺酚阳离子交换树脂 Zeo-Karb 315

33$\frac{1}{2}$°屋面坡度 third pitch

3,3'-甲基联苯 $\{C_{14}H_{14}\}$ 3,3'-dimethyldiphenyl

3,4-苯环芴 $\{C_{17}H_{12}\}$ 3,4-benzofluorene

2-乙基己基磷酸 2-ethylhexyl phosphoric acid

2-乙基己基磷酸酯 2-ethylhexyl acid phosphoric acid ester

356 铸造和压铸铝合金（7Si,0.3Mg,余量 Al） 356 alloy

3,5-二甲基吡啶 $\{C_7H_9N\}$ 3,5-dimethylpyridine

3,5-二甲替苯酚 $\{C_8H_{10}O\}$ 3,5-dimethylphenol

3,5-乙基苯酚 $\{C_{10}H_{14}O\}$ 3,5-ethylphenol

360 压铸铝合金（9.5Si,0.5Mg,余量 Al） 360 alloy

380 压铸铝合金（8.5Si,3.5Cu,余量 Al） 380 alloy

3S 耐蚀铝锰合金（1.5Mn,余量 Al） 3S alloy

3d层电子　3d electron

3-甲基芘{$C_{17}H_{12}$}　3-methylpyrene

3-甲基菲{$C_{15}H_{12}$}　3-methylphenanthrene

3-甲基芴{$C_{14}H_{12}$}　3-methylfluorene

3-甲基吲哚{C_9H_9N}　3-methylindole

3-乙基-5-甲基苯酚{$C_9H_{12}O$}　3-ethyl-5-methylphenol

3-乙基吡啶{C_7H_9N}　3-ethyl pyridine

40E铸造铝合金(5.5Zn,0.6Mg,0.5Cr,0.2Ti,余量Al)　40E alloy

446可控膨胀系数合金(27－30Cr,余量Fe)　446 alloy

4,5-苯环茚{$C_{13}H_{12}$}　4,5-benzindan

4,5-菲撑甲烷{$C_{15}H_{10}$}　4,5-phenanthrylenemethane

45°角切割　mitre cutting

45°角斜接　mitre joint

45°弯头　1/8 bend,eighth bend

4,6-二甲基喹啉{$C_{11}H_{11}N$}　4,6-dimethylquinoline

4-79钼坡莫合金(79Ni,4Mo,余量Fe)　Moly-permalloy 4-79

4号硬度冷轧薄板　skin-rolled temper sheet

4-甲基戊醇{$CH_3COC_4H_9$}　4-methylpentanol-[2]

4-甲基茚{$C_{10}H_{10}$}　4-methylindene

4-羟基茚满{$C_9H_{10}O$}　4-hydroxyhydrindine

548铁钴钼合金(15－25Mo,30Co,<1Mn,余量Fe)　548 alloy

5号硬度冷轧薄板　dead-soft temper (sheet)

713C轴流式燃气涡轮合金(73Ni,余量其他元素)　713C alloy

750铝基轴承合金(6.5Sn,1Cu,1Ni,余量Al)　750 alloy

75S形变铝合金(1.6Cu,2.5Mg,5.6Zn,0.3Cr,余量Al)　75S alloy

7,8-苯并喹啉{$C_{13}H_9N$}　7,8-benzoquinoline

7-异吲哚{C_7H_6N}　7-isoindole

7-羟基得豆酮{$C_8H_6O_2$}　7-hydroxycoumarone

8-羟基喹啉　oxine,8-hydroxy-quinoline

8形导线　figure eight wire

8字形淬火　figure 8 quenching

90度相移分量　quadrature component

90列卡片　【计】ninety column card

90°弯头　1/4 bend, normal bend

946易切削高传导率铜合金(99Cu,1Pb)　946 alloy

97铜锌合金(70Cu,30Zn,0.05Hg)　alloy 97

A_0转变(钢中渗碳体的)　A0 transformation

A.13压铸硅铝合金(12Si,余量Al)　A.13 alloy

A_1转变(钢的共析转变)　【金】A_1 transformation

A_2转变(铁的磁性转变)　【金】A_2 transformation

A_2转变温度区域磁性变化　【金】magnetic changes in A_2 temperature range

A.355铸造铝合金(1.4Cu,0.5Si,0.8Mg,0.8Ni,余量Al)　A.355 alloy

A.3A变形镁合金(3Al,余量Mg)　A.3A alloy

A3转变(δ铁γ铁转变)　【金】A_3 transformation

A4转变(γ铁δ铁转变)　A_4 transformation

A5法国货币合金(90Al,5Ag,5Cu)　A_5

A-B-C标度洛氏硬度机　【计】A-B-C-scale Rockwell machine

A.C.41A锌基合金(4Al,1Cu,0.04Mg,余量Zn)　A.C.41A alloy

ACAR直接还原法　【团】Allis-Chalmers Agglomeration-Reduction (ACAR) Process

ADR低膨胀系数铁镍合金　ADR alloy

A.G.40锌基压铸合金(4Al,0.04Mg,余量Zn)　A.G.40 alloy

A.M.100A 铸造镁合金(10Al,0.1Mn,余量 Mg) A.M. 100A alloy
A.M.F. 耐蚀合金(57Ni,余量其他) A.M.F. alloy
API 比重 API (American Petroleum Institute) gravity
API 标准钢管 API standard tubing
API 标准套管 API standard casing
API 长接箍套管 API casing with long coupling
API 管端内壁镦厚钻杆(管材) API internal upset drill pipe
API 管端外壁镦厚管材 API external upset tubing
API 管线用管材 API line pipe
API 锯齿形螺纹套管 API buttress thread casing
API 锯齿形螺纹无缝管 API seamless buttress thread casing
APL 语言 【计】a programming language (APL)
A-R 高强度钢(0.35—0.5C,1.5—2.0Mn,0.15—0.30Si) A-R steel
ASA 管螺纹 ASA pipe threads
ASEA-SKF 电弧热磁搅拌真空处理法【钢】ASEA-SKF process
ASEA-SKF 钢包真空脱气系统 ASEA-SKF ladle vacuum degassing system
ASTM 晶粒度值 ASTM grain size number
ASV 超低碳不锈钢冶炼法 ASV process
ATR 锆铜钼合金 ATR alloy (0.5Cu, 0.5Mo,余量 Zr)
AT 耐蚀镍合金(99Ni,0.25Cu,0.15Si, 0.4Fe,0.35Mn,0.15C,0.01S) nickel AT alloy
AX 溶液涂盐处理法(不锈钢冷拔、冷挤前的) paroxite AX process
Acm 转变点(渗碳体析出温度) Acm point
Ac 点(钢加热的临界点) Ac point
A 底心(布喇菲)点阵 A-centered (Bravais) lattice
A 类电位计(实验室用高精密度的) Group A potentiometer
A 类孔 A-pore
A 铝合金(铝镁硅合金) A alloy
A 镍铬铁耐热合金(19Cr, 35Ni, 0.35C, 0.5Mn,余量 Fe) A metal
A-扫描影像(阴极射线管的) A-scan presentation
A 为偶数的同位素 even-A isotope
A 为奇数的同位素 odd-A isotope
A 型转臂起重机 A-derrick
A 形桁架 A-truss
A 盐 alite
A"与"B"非"门 【计】A AND NOT B gate, A expect B gate, negative A-implies-B gate, subjunction gate
B.195 铝基合金(4.5Cu, 2.5Si,余量 Al) B.195 alloy
B.A.S.No.233 铝镍钴永磁合金 B.A.S.No.233
BCS 理论 (同"巴丁-库珀-施里弗超导理论")
BDS 表面渗铬法 BDS process
BET 法(测量比表面用) 【理】BET (Beauner-Emmett-Teller) method
BET 法比表面积 BET[B.E.T.] area
BH 曲线描绘仪 BH curve tracer
B-I 式高压炉顶【铁】Bailey-IHI top
B/M 复相组织 B/M duplex microstructure
B.N.F. 喷射检验(用于测电镀层厚度) B.N.F. jet test
BTG 镍铬钨合金(10Cr, 60Ni, 2—5W, 1Mo,1—3Mn) BTG alloy
B 底心(布喇菲)点阵 B-centred (Bravais) lattice
B(副)族元素(周期表中的) B subgroup element
B"或"A 非门 A implies B gate
B 类电位计(实验室用精密的) Group B potentiometer

B 扫描(试件剖视的)　B-scan
B"与"A 非门　【计】B AND NOT A gate, subjunction gate
CA-FA20 耐蚀合金钢(19—21Cr, 28—30Ni, 3.5Mo, 4—4.5Cu, <0.07C)　CA-FA 20
CA—MM 耐蚀镍铜系合金(67Ni, 30Cu, 1.4Fe, 0.1Si, 0.15C)　CA-MM
CAM 轧管机　convergent Assel mill (CAM)
CAZ 耐蚀铜合金(3—6Al, 2—6Ni, 0.6—1Si, 2—10Zn, 余量 Cu)　CAZ alloy
CA 铜铝镍硅耐蚀合金　CA alloy (CA-1: 3—6Al, 2—6Ni, 0.6—1Si, 余量 Cu; CA-3: 3—6 Al, 2—6Ni, 1—2Si, <2Zn, <0.3Ti, 余量 Cu; CA-4: 3—6Al, 2—10Ni, 1—2Si, <2Zn, <0.3Ti, 余量 Cu)
CCD 技术　charger coupled device technology
CCF 含铁钴时效硬化型铜线(0.5—1Co, 0.75—1.5Fe, 余量 Cu)　CCF wire
CGS 电磁单位制　CGS-EM (centimetre gramme second-electro-magnetic) system of units
C-I-L 公司脱氮工艺　C-I-L denitration process
C.M.469 耐热合金(60Cr, 14Fe, 25Mo, 0.03C)　C.M. alloy 469
CM 高强度导电铜(0.3—1Cd, <2Cr, 0.03—0.06Ag, <0.15Zn, 余量 Cu)　CM copper
C.N.R.M. 法还原指数(比利时)　C.N.R.M. (Centre National de Recherches Metallur-giques) index
C.N.R.M. 还原试验法(比利时)　C.N.R.M. test (method)
CO_2 保护电弧焊　(同"二氧化碳保护电弧焊")
CO_2 搅拌　CO_2-stirring
CO_2 流量调节器　gassing gauge
CO_2 型铸件　CO_2 mould casting
CO_2 药芯焊丝横向自动焊(用 Circomatic 装置的)　Circomatic welding
COBOL 语言　common business oriented language (COBOL)
COBO 法球团　【团】COBO-pellet
CO 平衡(高炉煤气的)　CO balance
CO 气体检测报警仪　co gas detecting and alarming meter　◇三电极~*
CSP 板坯连铸机　CSP slab caster
CSP 式轧机　CSP mill
CTB 铜钛铍合金(4Ti, 0.5Be, 0.5Co, 1Fe, 余量 Cu)　CTB (Cu-Ti-Be) alloy
CTG 铜钛银合金(4Ti, 3Ag, 1Zr, 余量 Cu)　CTG (Cu-Ti-Ag) alloy
CTS 抗裂试验　【焊】controlled thermal severity cracking test, CTS test
CVC 轧机　CVC (continuously variable crown) mill
CaO 基脱硫剂　CaO-based desulphurizer
Corex(法熔融还原)厂　Corex plant
Corex(法熔融还原)设备　Corex unit
Corex(熔融还原)法　Corex process
CrB 型原子当量化合物　CrB-type equiatomic compound
C-布莱特超级铁素体不锈钢(0.01C, 0.25Si, 0.02Mn, 29Cr, 4Mo, 余量 Fe)　C-Brite
C 底心(布喇菲)点阵　C-centered (Bravais) lattice
C 曲线　TTT diagram,【金】C curve
C 扫描(材料平视的)　C-scan
C-水泥石　Celite
C 铁心　C (cut) core
C 型机架压力机　gap (frame) press
C 形磁铁　C magnet
C 形点焊钳　C-type gun
C 形点焊用杠杆式夹钳　C-type spot-welding head
C 形(吊)钩　C(-type) hook　◇伸展式~装置*
C 形换辊钩　【压】C-hook (roll changer)
C 形夹具拘束抗裂试验　FISCO (type)

cracking test

D.A.L. 法　D.A.L. (Diffusion Alloys Ltd.) process

DC 电弧炉　DC electric arc furnace

DGT 溶液浸渍石墨电极　DGT solution impregnated graphite electrode

DHH 真空处理装置　DHH vacuum unit

DHH 真空提吸脱气法【钢】DHH vacuum degassing [treatment] process

D-H 提升[真空提吸]脱气法【钢】D-H (Dortmund-Hoerder) process, D-H-vacuum degassing

DH 真空脱气器　DH degasser

DIOS 法　direct iron ore smelting reduction process (DIOS)

D.L.M. 带式烧结机-电炉联合直接炼铁法　D.L.M. (Dwight-Lloyd-McWane) process

DL 型带式焙烧机　Dravo-Lurgi straight-grate induration strand, Dravo-Lurgi travelling grate (pelletizing machine)

DL 型带式机械结法　【团】Dwight-Lloyd (sintering) process

DL 型[D.L.]带式烧结机　【铁】Dwight-Lloyd sintering machine, Dwight-Lloyd (con-tinuous grate sinter) machine, DL type sinter machine, Dwight-Lloyd sinter strand, Dravo-Lurgi installation, D.L. machine

DNS 抗蠕变碳钼钢(用于过热器)　DNS

DPG 制铁粉法　【冶】DPG-Schleuder process

DPG 转盘雾化铁粉　DPG-rotating disc powder

DRC 煤基直接还原技术　【铁】DRC coal base direct reduction ironmaking technology

DS 抗蠕变铅合金　DS lead

DW 热浸镀用铅基合金(2.5Sn,2Sb,余量 Pb)　DW metal

DX 放热式气氛(金属热处理无氧化加热用)　DX atmosphere

DX 无氧化加热用保护气体　DX gas

D 壳型吹成法　【铸】D process

D 镍(含 4—5Mn)　D-nickel

D 镍锰合金(含 4-5Mn)　D-nickel

D 型触发器　D-flip flop

D 型优质钢　steel type D

D 型炸药　dunite

ERM 铜基合金　ERM alloy

ESD 磁铁　(同"伸长单畴磁铁")

EX-B 黄铜合金(77Cu,8Sn,15Pb)　EX-B metal

En 类钢(英国锻钢类工程用钢)　En steels

E-布赖特超级铁素体不锈钢(0.001C,0.25Si,0.01Mn,26Cr,1Mo,0.01Ni,余量 Fe)　E-Brite

E 层电子俘获　E-capture

E 含锌硬铝合金(2-3Cu,15-20Zn,0.25-0.5Mg,0.25-0.5Mn,0.2Si,余量 Al)　E alloy

E-锌铝合金　E-metal

E 形铁芯冲片　E-stamping

F.1260 镍铬耐热合金(25Cr,20Ni,余量 Fe)　F.1260 alloy

F.132 铸造铝合金(9.5Si,3.0Cu,1.0Mg,余量 Al)　F.132 alloy

F.17 铜锡铅轴承合金(10Sn,10Pb,80Cu)　F.17 alloy

F.23 高负荷铅基巴比合金(82.5Pb,13Sb,1Sn,1Ag,0.5Cu)　F.23 alloy

F.2 轴承青铜(80Cu,10Sn,10Pb)　F.2 bearing bronze

F.3 镉镍型轴承合金(1—1.5Ni,98.5Cd)　F.3 alloy

F.D.P. 不锈钢(含钛奥氏体不锈钢)　F.D.P. (Firths Decay Proof) stainless steel

FHP 硬化　【金】FHP hardening

FID 耐热合金(铜的复合材料)　FID alloy

FIOR 法　fluid iron ore redution (FIOR)

FORTRAN 编译系统　【计】FORTRAN compiler system

F.S.L. 低碳不锈钢(0.05C,18.5Cr,10Ni) F.S.L.

FTG 喷吹法(用裂化重油气) FTG process

Fe₃Al 型有序点阵[晶格]【金】Fe₃Al type

FeAl 合金 FeAl alloy

F 含锌硬铝合金(2—3Cu,0.25—0.5Mg,0.25—0.5Mn,15—20Zn,0.2Si,余量 Al) F alloy

F 吸收带 F-absorption band

F 心【理】colour centre

G.E.C. 公司型三级玻璃水银扩散泵 G.E.C. three-stage glass pump

G.E.C. 公司重载钨铜镍合金(航空发动机曲轴用;90W,4Cu,6Ni) G.E.C. heavy alloy

G.E.C. 公司自动取样器 GECO automatic sampler

GLAG 超导理论 GLAG theory of super-conductivity

GLX-w 低温可焊接半镇静钢(0.016C,0.18S,0.05Si,0.75Mn,0.009P,0.04Nb,余量 Fe) GLX-w steel

G.P.F. 通用碳黑 G.P.F. (carbon) black

G-P 区 (同"纪尼埃-普雷斯顿区") ◇ 有~的合金 G-P zone alloy

GS 金银触点合金(90Ag,10Au) GS (gold-silver) alloy

GW 式烧结盘 G.W. type sintering machine

G 铝合金(18Zn,2.5Cu,0.35Mn,0.2Fe,0.75Si,余量 Al) G alloy

G 砷铅巴比合金(83.5Pb,12.75Sb,3As,0.75Sn) arsenical lead G babbitt

G 铜锡锌合金(40Cu,50Sn,10Zn) G metal

H335 铬镍钴耐热钢(0.3C,0.6Si,1.5Mn,20Cr,25Ni,25Co,3Mo) H335 alloy

H439 铬镍钴耐热钢(0.4C,0.6Si,1.5Mn,20Cr,30Ni,5Mo,30Co,2Ta) H439 alloy

H-B 曲线 H-B curve

HC 轧机 HC (high crown) mill

HCR 磺化聚苯乙烯阳离子交换树脂 Nalcite HCR

HDR 磺化聚苯乙烯阳离子交换树脂 Nalcite HDR

HD 锻造用超硬铝合金 HD alloy

H-D 曲线 H and D (Hurter and Driffield) curve

HE 硅镁铝青铜 HE alloy

HGR 磺化聚苯乙烯阴离子交换树脂 Nalcite HGR

H.H. 铬镍合金(26Cr,12Ni,余量 Fe) H.H. alloy

HIB 法直接还原设备[厂](流态化法) HIB facilities

HI-B 高磁感晶粒取向硅钢 HI-B grain oriented silicon steel

H.I. 铬镍合金(15Ni,28Cr,余量 Fe) H.I. alloy

H.K. 铬镍合金(26Cr,30Ni,余量 Fe) H.K. alloy

HOB 法 hot-ore briquetting (HOB)

HOC 均质钢铸锭法 (同"均质铸锭法")

HPL 矫直机 high performance leveller (HPL)

HPR 轧机 HPR mill

HRC 粉末锻造法 HRC (Haller Research Center) process

HSCN-乙醚溶液 (同"硫氰酸-乙醚溶液")

HV 轧机 HV mill

HyL(直接还原)法 HyL process

H 带 H-band, hardenability-band

H 带钢淬透性规范 H band hardenability specifications

H 机架 horizontal stand

H 蒙乃尔铸造合金 H Monel

H 型钢 H section, H-beam

H 型屏蔽电缆 H-type cable

H-形梁 H-girder

H形切槽拘束破裂试验　H-slit restraint cracking test
H因数(淬火的)　H factor(美国)
I.G. 无水氯化镁电解炼镁法　I.G. process
IF钢　(同"无间隙原子钢")
IN-100 铸造镍基耐热合金(0.15C, 10.5Cr, 14Co, 3.0Mo, 4.8Ti, 5.4Al, 1.0V+B, 0.06 Zr, 余量Ni)　IN-100 alloy
IN-102 变形镍基耐热合金(15Cr, 2.9Nb, 2.9Mo, 3W, 7Fe, 0.06C, 0.5Al, 0.5Ti, 0.005 B, 0.03Zr, 0.02Mg, 余量Ni)　IN-102 alloy
INCO型闪速炉　INCO flash smelting furnace
IN钢(0.77Mn, 0.35Si, 0.11C, 0.069Al, 0.022N)　IN (Ishikawazima-Nakamura) steel
IRSID连续炼钢法　(同"法国钢铁研究院连续炼钢法")
IRSID(延性铁冶炼设备)系统　IRSID system
IR-UT炉外精炼技术　IR-UT (injection refining-up temperature) secondary refining technique
ISO标准V型缺口冲击试验　ISO V-notch impact test
J.A.E. 镍铜合金(70Ni, 30Cu)　J.A.E. alloy
J.A.M. 快速磷化法　【压】J.A.M. coating process
JK触发器　【计】JK flip flop
J钴铬钼耐热合金　J metal
J钴铬耐热合金(60Co, 23Cr, 6Mo, 2Ta, 1Mn, 2C)　J-alloy
J积分　J-integral
J形防震片　J-strap
J形坡口　【焊】(single) J-groove
J形坡口[J形槽焊]焊缝　J-groove weld
J形坡口加工　J-preparation
J形坡口连接　J-groove joint

J字接头焊接　jump welding
K42B耐热镍铬钴合金　K42B alloy
KK耐蚀铜镍合金　KK metal
KLS法　KLS (Kosaka lead smelting) process
KMC高强度铝青铜(7—13Al, 0.2—1.5Cr, 0.2—3Ni+Fe, 余量Cu)　KMC metal
K-M法(直接还原)　Kinglor-Metor process
K.R. 蒙乃尔合金(29Cu, 0.9Fe, 0.85Mn, 0.5Si, 0.005S, 余量Ni)　K.R. Monel
K.S. 高钴磁钢　K.S. steel
K-S关系　(同"库尔久莫夫-萨克斯关系")
KS磁钢(0.7—1.0C, 5—9W, 1.5—3Cr, 30—40Co, 0.3—0.8Mn)　KS magnet steel ◇新～*
KS高弹性耐海水腐蚀青铜(2Sn, 0.1Ni, 微量Pb, 余量Cu)　KS bronze
K.S. 铝活塞合金(12Si, 4.5Cu, 0.7Mg, 1.2Mn, 1.5Ni, 余量Al)　K.S. piston alloy
K.S. 铁钴镍钛永磁合金(42Fe, 30Co, 12Ni, 12Ti)　K.S. alloy
KS永久磁铁　KS magnet
KTB法　KTB (Kawasaki top oxygen blowing) process
KTB氧枪　KTB oxygen lance
Kα1与Kα2密双重[谱]线　close doublet of Kα1 and Kα2
Kα分量(辐射的)　Kα component
K层电子　K-layer
K电子　K-electron
K空间　k space
K蒙乃尔合金(66Ni, 29Cu, 5Al)　K Monel
K能级　K-level
K吸收边(沿)　K-absorption edge
K吸收限　K-absorption edge
K-系辐射　K-radiation
K形坡口　【焊】double-bevel groove

K形坡口T形焊(接) double-bevel T
K形坡口对接【焊】double-bevel butt joint
K形坡口对接焊缝 double-bevel butt weld
K形坡口焊 double-bevel groove welding
K形坡口加工【焊】double-bevel preparation
K形双面坡口焊缝 double-bevel weld
K因数(烧结金属的) K-factor
L.B.142高锡铅基轴承合金(10—20Sn,12.5—15Sb,63.5—75Pb,0.2—1.5Cu) L.B.142 alloy
LD-AC转炉 LD-AC converter
LD-CB复合吹炼【钢】LD-CB combined-blowing process
LDK氧气转炉内高磷生铁块状石灰炼钢法 L.D.K. process
LD-真空法(同"顶吹真空法")
LD转炉(同"氧气顶吹转炉")
L.D.转炉车间 L.D. plant
LGL轮式连铸机 LGL wheel caster
L.K.A.B.抗压试验(瑞典)【团】L.K.A.B. compression test
LL法 ladle to ladle degassing
LM法 ladle-to-mould degassing
LT(转炉废气回收)法[工艺] Lurgi/Thyssen process
LWS底吹氧气转炉炼钢法(法国的) LWS process
L能级 L level
L型优质钢 steel type L
L形梁 L-beam, ell-beam
L形阴极 bent cathode
M.A.R.M.200镍基超级铸造合金(0.15C, 10Co, 9Cr, 12.5W, 5Al, 2Ti, 0.05Zr, 0.015B,余量Ni) M.A.R.M.200 alloy
M.B.V.铝氧化膜生成法(用作精饰底层) M.B.V.(modified Bauer-vogel) process
MB钢 MB (Mitsubishi bainite) steel

M.C.102镍合金(20Cr, 6.5Nb, 6Mo, 2.5W,余量Ni) M.C.102 alloy
MC型回磷钢 steel type MC
M.G.铝镁合金(5Mg,余量Al; 7Mg,余量Al) M.G. alloy
MH铜锡锌铅轴承合金 MH alloy (MH No.1: 88Cu, 8—10Sn, 2—4Zn; MH No.2: 86Cu, 8.5Sn, 2Zn, 2.5Pb)
M.I.A.变形镁合金(1.2Mn, 0.09Ca,余量Mg) M.I.A. alloy
M.K.W多用途轧机(轧辊直径可变) M.K.W mill
MK(三岛、养冢)磁钢(<20Co, 15—40Ni, 7—15Al,余量Fe) MK magnet steel
MM镍铬合金(96Ni,4Cr) MM alloy
MP35N超级弹簧合金(含Ni、Co、Cr、Mo的多相合金) MP35N alloy
MR炼钢法【钢】MR process
MR型钢(一般用作全度锡制品) steel type MR
MSO铁镍系磁性合金(30—50Ni, 1—18Cr,余量Fe) MSO alloy
MST钛铝合金(3Al, 5Cr,余量Ti; 2Al, 3Fe,余量Ti) MST alloy
MS磁补偿[磁分路]合金 MS (magnetic shunt) alloy
MT17耐热镍铬钴多元合金(30Ni, 21Cr, 19Fe, 3Mo, 1.5Mn, 2.2W, 21Co, 1.6Ti, 0.5Si, 0.06C) MT 17 alloy
MTU(密执安工业大学)冷黏结球团法 MTU cold-bond process
MT(三岛、牧野)高矫顽力加铝磁钢(1.5—3C, 6—9Al,余量Fe) MT magnet steel
M.V.C.耐蚀铸造硅铝合金(89Al, 11Si) M.V.C. alloy
Mf点(马氏体转变完成点) Mf point
MgO-C砖 MgO-C brick
Ms点(马氏体转变开始点) Ms point
M能级 M (energy) level
M-系辐射 M-radiation
M型断面(高炉料线的) M-shaped con-

M 形料线(高炉的)　M-stockline
N.155 变形耐热合金(0.15C,0.5Si,1.5Mn,21Cr,20Ni,20Co,3Mo,3W,1Nb,0.15N2,余量 Fe)　N.155 alloy
N.A. 铸造铝合金　N.A. alloy
N(E)曲线　【金】N(E) curve
N.P.N. 高压鼓风碱性转炉法　【钢】N.P.N. process
NM 高强度镍青铜　NM bronze
NX 氮基放热式气氛(金属热处理用)　NX atmosphere
NY100 生铁脱碳制铁粉法　NY 100 process
N 次循环的疲劳强度　fatigue strength at N cycles
N 次循环的平均疲劳强度　median fatigue strength at N cycles
N 次循环的响应曲线　【理】response curve for N cycles
N 次循环(条件下)残存 p% 疲劳强度　fatigue strength for p percent survival at N cycles
N–甲酰吗啉　【焦】N-formylmorpholine
N 耐蚀铸造铝合金(6Cu,3Mn,余量 Al)　N alloy
N–能级　N (energy) level
N 为偶数的同位素　even-N isotope
N 为奇数的同位素　odd-N isotope
N 型半导体　N-type (negative-type) semiconductor
N 型杂质　(同"负型杂质")
N 型再渗氮高强度钢　steel type N
N–亚硝基苯胲铌　cupferrate of columbium
OBM 底吹氧气转炉炼钢法(德国)　OBM process
OCP 顶吹氧气和石灰粉的托马斯生铁转炉炼钢法　OCP (Oxyg′ene-Chauh Pulv′erisee) process
O.G. 法烟气回收过程(顶吹氧气转炉的)　【钢】O.G. (oxygen gas) process
O.G. 法烟气回收罩系统(氧气转炉用)【钢】O.G. hood system
O.L.P. 炼钢法　O.L.P. (oxygen lance powder) process
O,O′–联苯酚{$C_{12}H_{10}O_2$}　O,O′-diphenol
OP 钴铁氧体烧结磁铁　OP magnet
O.R.F. 高温火焰下还原矿石直接制取铁水法　O.R.F. (Ontario Research Founda-tion) jet smelter process
O.R.F. 移动式炉箅直接炼铁法　O.R.F. travel(l)ing grate process
Osprey(熔体雾化)法　Osprey process
Osprey(预压)成形法　Osprey forming process
Ostward 熟化(机制)　Ostward ripening
O 形[成型]机　O-(form)ing press
P2 覆铝纯铁板(真空管阳极材料)　P2 iron
PC 轧机　PC (pair cross) mill
P.E.10 镍基耐热合金　P.E.10 alloy
P.E.K. 镍基耐热合金　P.E.K. alloy
P.E. 变形镁合金(3.25Al,1.2Zr,余量 Mg)　P.E. alloy
P–F 淬透性试验法　【金】penetration-fracture method
P–F 曲线(淬火的)　P-F curve
PHC 管桩端板　PHC pipe pile plank in end
PID 控制器　PID controller
PLC 连铸控制系统　PLC continuous casting control system
PL 法　Phoenix-Lance process
P.M.G. 硅青铜(4Si,2Zn,2Fe,0.5Mn,余量 Cu)　P.M.G. alloy [metal]
PR 法[周期反向电流光亮电镀法]　PR method
PS 转炉　PS converter
PTFE 渗四氟乙烯烧结青铜轴承　PTFE impregnated sintered bronze bearing
P 锡钎焊合金(55.5Sn,41.1Pb,3.4Sb)　P tin alloy
P 型砷化镓　p-type gallium arsenide

P 型杂质　p-type impurity
Q-BOP 底吹氧气转炉炼钢法　quiet-basic [quick-basic] oxygen process (Q-BOP)
QEK 底吹氧转炉炼钢法　QEK process
QSL 法　QSL (Queneau-Schuhmann-Lurgi) process
QSL 法反应器　QSL reactor
Q 耐热镍铬合金　Q-alloy (Q-alloy A: 66—68Ni, 15—19Cr, 余量 Fe; Q-alloy B: 60Ni, 12Cr, 余量 Fe)
Q 值　Q-value
Q 值计　Q meter
Q 指数　quality index (QI)
RGY(金属)快速腐蚀试验法　RGYM (Rikagaku kenky ushyo yamamoto method), RGY me-thod
RHC 宇宙空间用钨合金　(4Re, 0.35Hf, 0.24C, 余量 W) tungsten-RHC
RH 多功能精炼　【钢】RH multifunction vacuum refining method
RH 法　RH (Ruhstahl-Hausen) process
RH 脱气　RH degassing
RH 脱碳　RH decarburization
RH 真空处理设备　RH-equipment
RH 真空脱气(法)　RH-vacuum degassing
RH(真空)脱气器　RH degasser
R-N(直接还原)法　R-N (direct reduction) process
RR 沉淀硬化型铝合金　RR alloy (RR50: 2.5Si, 1Cu, 1Fe, 0.9Ni, 0.2Ti, 余量 Al)
RS 触发器　R-S (reset-set) flip flop
RX 渗碳气体　RX gas
RX 吸热式气氛(金属热处理用)　RX atmosphere
RZ 法铁粉　RZ powder
RZ 铁粉雾化法　RZ (Roheisen Zunder) process
R 蒙乃尔合金 (含 0.25—0.06S)　R Monel
R 值　(同"塑性应变比")
S.590 钴铬镍基形变耐热合金(0.4C, 1.2Mn, 0.4Si, 20Co, 20Cr, 20Ni, 4Mo, 4W, 4Nb, 余量 Fe)　S.590 alloy
S.816 形变钴基耐热合金(0.4C, 1.2Mn, 0.4Si, 20Cr, 20Ni, 4Mo, 4W, 4Nb, 4Fe, 余量 Co)　S.816 alloy
SAE 钢号标准　SAE steel standard
SAR 强碱性阴离子交换树脂　Nalcite SAR
SDR 法　Sumitomo dust reduction (SDR)
SD 超硬铝[SD 高强度硬铝]　SD alloy, Super duralumin
S-H 高强度高硬度含钛共晶石墨铸铁　S-H cast iron
SLPM 电弧炉金属化球团熔炼法　【钢】SLPM process
SL-RN 金属化法　SL-RN metallization process
SL-RN 直接还原法　SL-RN reduction process
SLPM 电弧炉内金属球团连续加料熔炼法　【钢】SLPM process
SL 直接还原法　SL direct reduction process
SMZ 硅铁锰锆合金(中间合金; 60—65Si, 5—7Mn, 5—7Zr, 余量 Fe)　SMZ alloy
SM 耐蚀硅铜　(2Si, 0.6Te + Se, 0.04P, 余量 Cu)　SM copper
S-N 曲线(疲劳试验的)　S/N (stress/number) curve ◇残存 $P\%$ 的~
SOD 脆断试验　SOD test
SPM 法　Sumitomo pre-reduction method (SPM)
SiC 增强体　silicon carbide reinforcement
SiC 砖　SiC brick
S 曲线　TTT diagram, s-curve
S-辛基油[S-奥克特油](油蒸气真空泵用油)　$[C_8H_{16}(COOC_8H_{17})_2]$ di-2-ethyl hexyl sebacate, octoil(-s)
S 型弯管[钩]　goose-neck
S 形曲线　S-shaped curve, ogee curve
S 形弯管　swan neck
S 形下水管存水弯　S-trap

S形张紧辊组　S-shaped bridle roller unit
S形支柱冲床　swan-neck press
S重载铅基巴比合金（82.5Pb,15Sb,1Sn,1As,0.5Cu）　S metal
T-1易焊高强度钢　T-1 steel
TAF铁素体耐热合金钢（12Cr,0.18C,0.8Mo,0.2Nb,0.2V,0.04B,0.015N）　TAF steel
TBP己烷溶剂　TBP-hexane
TBP煤油溶剂　TBP-kerosene
T.D.镍　（同"氧化钍弥散镍"）
T.E.镍铬耐热合金（30Ni,20Cr,38.7Fe,4Mo,0.7Mn,4W,1.9Ta,0.1C,0.5Si）　T.E. alloy
TIG焊接　tungsten-arc inert-gas welding（TIG,Tig）
TK磁钢（川口氏磁钢）（18W,12Cr,3—5Mo,<0.5V,余量Fe）　Tk magnet steel
TNT　triton
TTA曲线　（同"时间-温度-奥氏体化曲线"）
TTT曲线　（同"时间-温度-转变曲线"）
TaC-TiC-Co硬质合金　（同"钽钛硬质合金"）
T接　tee-off
T型大梁　T-section girder
T形算[筛]条　T-shaped rod
T形材[T形截面]　tee section
T形触发器　【电】T-flip [toggle-flip] flop
T形对焊　T[tee] butt welding
T形对接焊缝　T[tee] butt weld
T形钢　T-section,T-steel,tee-iron ◇宽腰～high webbed tee iron
T形钢轨　tee rail
T形钢焊接技术（用带钢的）　T welding technique
T形钢梁　T-beam,flange beam
T形管　tee pipe,pipe tee
T形管接头　T-piece,tee
T形焊　T[tee] welding,jump welding
T形接头　T-junction,tee joint [junction],tee connector
T形结线法　T-connection
T形抗裂试验　T cracking test
T形连接　tee joint
T形连接件弯曲试验夹紧装置　T-bend jig
T形梁　T-bar,tee
T形流槽　T-shaped launder
T形双坡口对接焊缝　double-bevel tee butt weld
T形填角焊缝　T-fillet weld
T形铁心冲片　T-stamping
T形弯曲试验（测试焊接性能用）　T-bend [tee-bend] test
T形型钢　tee-profile
T形砖　【耐】T-piece
T形组合角钢　back to back angles
T字对接焊缝　double-J tee butt weld
T字钢　（同"T形钢"）
T字形钢材　T-section
T字形弯曲试样　【压】tee-bend specimen
UC轧机　universal crown mill
UHE电炉　（同"超高效率电炉"）
USS弗雷马克斯15易切削钢（≤0.2C,0.9—1.3Mn,0.1—0.3Si,0.06—0.12P,0.2—0.3S,余量Fe）　USS（United States Steel Co.）Fremax 15 steel
USS弗雷马克斯45易切削钢（0.4—0.5C,0.9—1.3Mn,<0.15Si,<0.04P,0.2—0.3S,余量Fe）　USS（United States Steel Co.）Fremax 45 steel
USS卡里洛依FC易切削钢（0.47—0.55C,0.95—1.3Mn,0.6—0.9Si,0.15—0.25Mo,0.06—0.10S,余量Fe）　USS（United States Steel Co.）carilloy FC steel
USS坦尼隆高锰高氮（奥氏体）不锈钢（18Cr,14.5Mn,0.4N,<0.1C,余量Fe）　USS（Uni-ted States Steel Co.）Tenelon steel
U形槽　breeches chute

U形成型压力机 【压】U-press	U字形钨丝 hairpin shaped tungsten wire
U形磁铁 U magnet	U字形焰道 hairpin flue
U形吊环 shackle	VC支承辊 VC back-up roll
U形钉 staple	V.D.E.法还原度指数 V.D.E. index
U形断面 U-section, U-profiles	VLN炼钢法 (同"极低含氮量炼钢法")
U形钢(材) U-steel, U-iron	V槽块 vee block
U形钢丝芯撑 jammer	V-机架 vertical stand
U形管 U-tube, U-pipe, hairpin	V石英轴 V axis
U形管压力计 U-tube manometer	V铁铬母合金(38—42Cr, 31—40Fe, 8—
U形焊缝 U-weld	11Mn, 14—16Si) V alloy
U形环[匝] U-loop	V形波程 vee path
U形活套 【压】U-loop	V形传动带 【机】V-drive belt
U形夹 clevis	V形带卷座 vee shaped coil rest
U形夹销 clevis pin	V形导轨 V-guide, vee-guide ◇ 棱柱
U形螺栓 U-bolt	[V形]~ V-shaped guide
U形螺栓夹紧器 U-clamp	V形断面 【压】V-section, 【铁】V-shaped
U形坡口焊缝 single-U groove weld	contour (料线的)
U形坡口连接 【焊】U-groove joint	V形钢材 V-section
U形坡口预加工 【焊】U-preparation	V形辊式运输机 V-type roller conveyor
U形曲线(淬火硬度的) U-shaped curve, hairpin curve	V形焊缝 V-weld ◇ 两圆形件[管件] 间~ flare-V weld
U形缺口试样冲击试验 ◇ 夏氏~ Charpy U notch test	V形混合器 vee-blender
U形伸缩管 expansion U-bend	V形接线 open delta, open-delta connection
U形试样(垂直抗拉)强度 U-strength ◇ 点焊的~	V形金属夹环(换向器的) metal V-ring
U形试样点焊拉伸试验 U-tensile test	V形口闸瓦 V block
U形弯曲压力机(管材的) U-bending press, U-ing press	V形料线(高炉的) 【铁】V-stockline
U形弯曲作业 【压】U-ing operation	V形皮带 (同"三角皮带")
U形弯头 return bend	V形皮带传动法 【焊】V-belt drive
U形型材 U-section, U-profiles	V形皮带清刮器 plough, plow
U形硬度分布曲线(圆钢淬火的) U-curve	V形坡口 V-groove, vee (groove)
U字钉 clevis	V形坡口连接 vee(d) joint
U字形点焊抗拉试件 U-tensile test specimen	V形缺口 V notch, vee notch ◇ 带~的 vee-notched, 夏氏~试棒*
U字形铪条 hairpin of hafnium	V形缺口(冲击)试验 V-notch test ◇ 国际标准化组织标准~*
U字形加热元件 hairpin (heating) element	V形缺口试样 vee-notched specimen ◇ 夏式~冲击动能*
U字形丝极(碘化物热离解设备) hairpin shaped filament	V形缺口夏氏冲击试样 V-notch charpy specimen
	V形云母夹环(换向器的) mica V-ring
	V形凿 bent

V形座　vee block
W-306 铜锡锰系标准电阻丝合金　W306 alloy
W5 镍硅合金(4Si,0.3Mn,余量 Ni)　W5 alloy
WBR 弱碱性阴离子交换树脂　Nalcite WBR
WC-TiC-Co 硬质合金　(同"钨钛硬质合金")
WZ 碳化钛粉末烧结合金　WZ alloy
W形孔型　W-pass
W形孔型设计　W-pass design
X-B 高蠕变强度合金(15Cr,35Ni,余量 Fe)　X-B alloy
X-Y 记录仪　X-Y type recorder
XY 坐标绘图仪　XY potter
X 分量　X-constituent
X 辐射　X-radiation
X 光　(同"X 射线")
X 光摄影　shadowgraph
X 截晶体　X-cut crystal
X 射线　X-rays, roentgen rays ◇ β射线激发的~*,不均匀~ heteroge-neous X-rays, 次级~ secondary X-rays, 单色~*, 多色~*, 均匀~ homogeneous X-rays
X 射线靶　X-ray target
X 射线半峰宽度　half-peak breadth of X-ray line
X 射线被重金属屏蔽　【理】blocking
X 射线比浊法　X-ray turbidimetry
X 射线病　X-ray injury
X 射线波长　X-ray wavelength
X 射线波长单位　X unit (XU, xu)
X 射线测定晶格参数　【金】X-ray lattice parameter measurement
X 射线测厚仪　X-ray thickness gauge, Measuray ◇ 非接触式~*, 西屋~*, 荧光~*
X 射线测角器　X-ray goniometer
X 射线出口[发射口]　X-ray posit
X 射线穿透硬度计　qualimeter
X 射线带材测宽仪　X-ray width gauge

X 射线单色器　X-ray monochromator
X 射线点阵参数　X-ray lattice parameter
X 射线电子探针分析　X-ray electron probe analysis
X 射线定量分析　X-ray quantitative analysis
X 射线定性分析　X-ray qualitative analysis
X 射线发光　X-ray [roentgen] luminescence
X 射线发射带　X-ray emission band
X 射线发射光谱分析[光谱学]　X-ray emission spectroscopy
X 射线发射谱　X-ray emission spectrum
X 射线发生器　X-ray generator ◇ 动靶~*, 可拆式~*
X 射线法　X-ray method
X 射线法研究　X-ray study
X 射线法应力研究　X-ray stress research
X 射线反射　X-ray reflection, reflection of X-rays
X 射线反射级　order in X-ray reflection
X 射线非接触式检测(测定带材厚度用)　X-ray gauging
X 射线分层摄影法　laminography
X 射线分光[光谱]计　X-ray spectrometer ◇ 双晶~*, 周转晶体~*
X 射线分析　X-ray [roentgen ray] analysis, X-raying ◇ 德拜-谢乐~*
X 射线分析仪　X-ray analyzer
X 射线粉末法衍射图[花样]　X-ray powder pattern
X 射线粉末法衍射数据[资料]集　X-ray powder data file
X 射线粉末法衍射仪　X-ray powder diffraction apparatus, X-ray powder diffracto-meter
X 射线粉末法衍射法　【理】X-ray powder method, Debye-Scherer (powder) method
X 射线粉末衍射线　powder line
X 射线辐射计　X-ray radiometer
X 射线干涉　X-ray interference
X 射线干涉测量(法)　X-ray interferome-

try
X射线干涉仪 X-ray interferometer
X射线固定底片测角仪 stationary-film goniometer
X射线管 X-ray [roentgen] tube ◇ 封闭式~*,高压~*,环形电磁型~*,阳极旋动的~ rotating-anode tube
X射线管靶 target in X-ray tube
X射线管壁(厚度差)测量仪 X-ray pipe-wall gauge
X射线管(防护)屏 【理】tube shield
X射线管固有滤波作用 【理】inherent filtration of X-ray tube
X射线管焦点 X-ray tube focus
X射线管聚焦面 tube focal area
X射线管冷阴极 cold cathode of X-ray tube
X射线管热阴极 hot cathode of X-ray tube
X射线管性能 performance of tube
X射线管阴极靶 cathode of X-ray tube
X射线管组件 tube assembly
X射线贯穿(深度) X-ray penetration
X射线光电效应 X-ray photoelectron effect
X射线光电子能谱分析 X-ray photoelectron energy spectrum analysis
X射线光电子能谱学[光谱(分析)法] X-ray photoelectron spectroscopy (XPS)
X射线光化学效应 X-ray photo-chemical effect
X射线光谱分析 X-ray spectroscopic [spectrum] analysis
X射线光谱学 X-ray spectroscopy
X射线光谱仪 X-ray spectrograph, X-ray spectroscopic equipment
X射线光学 【理】X-ray optics ◇ 布喇德雷型照相机~装置*,塞曼-玻林型照相机~装置*
X射线光子 X-ray photon
X射线厚度计 (同"X射线测厚仪")
X射线花样 (同"X射线衍射花样")

X射线花样衍射计记录 diffractometer registration of X-ray pattern
X射线回摆晶体法 oscillating crystal method
X射线机 X-ray machine [apparatus], X-ray generator equipment, roentgenoscope
X射线积分宽度 integral breadth of X-ray line
X射线激射器 xaser
X射线技术 X-ray technique ◇ 高温~*
X射线技术员 X-ray technician
X射线剂量计 X-ray quantometer
X射线计 radiation [roentgen] meter, roentgenometer
X射线检晶[晶体检测]器 X-ray crystallographer
X射线检验[检测,检查,探伤] X-ray inspection [test(ing), examination], X-ay (crack) detection, inspection by X-ray, radiographic testing, X-raying, radioscopy
X射线件 X-ray parts
X射线胶[软]片 X-ray film ◇ 粗粒~*,非增感~*,高速~*,屏蔽型~*,双面涂感光药品的~ sandwich film,微粒~*,无增感屏~*
X射线胶片光敏度 X-ray sensitivity of film
X射线胶片颗粒度 grainness of X-ray film
X射线胶片特性曲线 characteristic curve of X-ray film
X射线结构分析 X-ray structure analysis
X射线金相学 X-ray metallography, radiometallography
X射线晶体[结晶]分析 X-ray crystal analysis ◇ 赫尔-法 Hull method,塞曼~法*
X射线晶体回摆法 X-ray oscillating method
X射线晶体学 X-ray crystallography
X射线聚焦 X-rays focusing

X 射线粒度测定(法)　X-ray particle size measurement
X 射线累积强度　【理】integrated intensity of X-rays
X 射线粒度测定(法)　X-ray particle size measurement
X 射线连续光谱　X-ray continuous spectrum
X 射线量子　X-ray quantum
X 射线轮廓　X-ray line profile
X 射线偏差　X-ray deviation
X 射线屏蔽　【理】X-ray shield(ing)
X 射线谱　X-ray spectrum　◇旋转[转动]~*,振动~*
X 射线谱系　series in X-ray spectra
X 射线谱线　(同"X 射线衍射花样谱线")
X 射线曝光　X-ray exposure
X 射线强度　X-ray intensity, intensity of X-rays
X 射线强度计　intensitometer
X 射线区　X-ray region
X 射线乳胶　X-ray emulsion
X 射线入射斜角　【理】obliquity of incidence of X-rays
X 射线散射　X-ray scattering
X 射线(扫描)微量分析器　X-ray (scanning) microanalyzer
X 射线烧伤　X-ray burn
X 射线摄谱仪　X-ray spectrograph [spectrometer]
X 射线束　X-ray beam, beam [bundle] of X-rays　◇入射~incident X-ray beam, 窄准直~*
X 射线束发散度　divergence of X-ray beam
X 射线束轴(线)　X-ray beam axis
X 射线束准直　X-ray beam collimation
X 射线数据　X-ray data
X 射线损伤[伤害]　X-ray injury
X 射线探针微量分析仪　X-ray probe micro-analyzer

X 射线特性　X-ray quality
X 射线透明度　X-ray transparency
X 射线透视法　roentgenoscopy, X-ray fluoroscopy
X 射线透视机　roentgenoscope
X 射线透视检查　X-ray radiographic examination
X 射线透照图(焊件的)　exograph
X 射线图标定　indexing of X-ray photographs
X 射线图像　X-ray image
X 射线图　X-ray pattern　◇锐线~*
X 射线微量分析　X-ray micro-analysis (X.M.A)
X 射线微射束　【理】X-ray microbeam
X 射线微束法　X-ray micro-beam method
X 射线位置　line position
X 射线无损检验[探伤]　X-ray non-destructive testing
X 射线物理学　X-ray physics
X 射线吸收　X-ray absorption
X 射线吸收法(测定密度用)　【理】X-ray absorption method
X 射线吸收分析　X-ray absorption analysis
X 射线吸收系数　X-ray absorption coefficient [index]
X 射线锡层测厚仪　X-ray tin coating thickness gauge
X 射线显微分析　X-ray microanalysis
X 射线显微分析仪　X-ray microanalyzer (XMA)
X 射线显微镜　X-ray microscope
X 射线显微镜观察　X-ray microscope observation
X 射线显微术　X-ray microscopy　◇反射~*
X 射线显微照片[照相]　X-ray micrograph, micro-radiograph
X 射线显微照相术　X-ray micrography, microradiography
X 射线相　X-ray appearance

X射线小角散射　X-ray small angle scattering

X射线星芒　X-ray asterisms

X射线学　radiology, roentgenology, roentgenography

X射线研究　X-ray research [investigation]

X射线衍射[绕射]　X-ray diffraction

X射线衍射测量术　X-ray diffractometer

X射线衍射定量分析　quantitative X-ray diffraction analysis

X射线衍射法　X-ray diffraction method　◇伯格-巴瑞特~ Berg-Barrett method, 布喇格~ Bragg method, 德拜-谢乐~*, 劳厄~*

X射线衍射分析　X-ray diffraction analysis

X射线衍射花样　X-ray pattern　◇纯组元~*, 粉末晶体~*, 回摆晶体~*, 择优取向~*, 周转晶体~*

X射线衍射花样谱线　X-ray (pattern) line

X射线衍射检验　X-ray diffraction testing

X射线衍射金属表面形态学　【金】X-ray diffraction topography

X射线衍射谱线重心　centroid of X-ray diffraction line

X射线衍射强度　X.R.D (X-ray diffraction) intensity

X射线衍射束　diffracted X-ray beam

X射线衍射图　X-ray diffraction curve, X-ray diagram　◇反射~*, 粉末法~*

X射线衍射图像　X-ray diffraction image

X射线衍射显微镜　X-ray diffraction microscope

X射线衍射显微术　X-ray diffraction microscopy　◇舒尔茨~ Schulz method

X射线衍射线计数器记录　counter recording of X-ray diffraction

X射线衍射仪　X-ray diffraction instrument [equipment], X-ray diffractometer, 【金】retigraph　◇单晶体~*

X射线衍射应用　X-ray diffraction application

X射线衍射最大值　X-ray diffraction maximum

X射线仪　X-ray instrumentation

X射线仪效率[有效作用系数]　efficiency of X-ray apparatus

X射线应力测定法　X-ray stress measuring method, X-ray method of stress determination

X射线应力测量(残余应力测量)　X-ray stress measurement　◇轻便式~仪*

X射线应力分析　X-ray stress analysis

X射线荧光　X-ray fluorescence

X射线荧光分光计　X-ray fluorescence spectrometer (XRFS)

X射线荧光分析　X-ray fluorescence analysis, fluorescence X-ray analysis, nore-lco fluorescen analysis

X射线荧光(分析)法　X-ray fluorescence method, X-ray fluoroscopy

X射线荧光光谱分析[光谱学]　X-ray fluorescence spectroscopy

X射线硬度　X-ray hardness

X射线硬度测量计灵敏度　penetrameter sensitivity

X射线硬度计　qualimeter

X射线源　X-ray source

X射线窄束　X-ray pencil

X射线照片　X-ray photograph [picture, appearance], radiogram, roentgenogram, scotograph, skiagram, skigram, skigraph, shadowgraph　◇虚线~ spotty pattern

X射线照片处理[加工]　processing of X-ray film

X射线照射　X-ray irradiation, X-raying

X射线照射范围　X-ray coverage

X射线照射防护　X-ray protection

X射线照射氧化　X-ray oxidation

X射线照相　X-ray photogram [photograph, picture], roentgenography, scotography, skiagraphy, skiagraph　◇锐线~*,

透射～*

X 射线照相标定　indexing of X-ray photographs

X 射线照相的　roentgenographic

X 射线照相机　X-ray camera

X 射线照相胶片生雾　fogging of X-ray film

X 射线照相术[学]　X-ray radiography, X-radiography, X-ray photography, roentgenography ◇ 高温～*,直观～*

X 射线照相用管　tube for radiographic work

X 射线折射　X-ray refraction

X 射线周转晶体法　X-ray rotation method

X 射线主吸收限　main (X-ray) absorption edge

X 射线装置　X-ray equipment, X-ray set ◇ 储槽形～tank-type X-ray unit

X 射线作用下氧化　X-ray oxidation

X 向运动　X-motion

X 型镍粒　X shot nickel

X 形对接坡口　【焊】double-vee (butt) groove

X 形焊缝　X-weld, double-vee weld

X 形接头[连接]　X-joint

X 形坡口　double V groove ◇ 不对称～*

X 形坡口对接焊缝　double-V butt weld

X 形坡口焊缝　double-V groove weld

X 形坡口焊接　double-vee groove welding

X 轴方向　X-direction

X 轴分量　X-component

X 轴向波　X-wave

Y 截晶体　Y-cut crystal

Y 截石英探测装置　Y cut quartz search unit

Y 粒子　【理】Y-particles

Y 铝合金（2.5—4.5Cu, 1.8—2.3Ni, 1.2—1.7Mg,少量 Fe 与 Si,余量 Al）　aluminium Y alloy

Y 型三辊辊模　【压】Y type three-roll die

Y 型三辊辊模拉拔　Y type three-high roller die drawing process

Y 型三辊冷连轧机　Y-type three high mill

Y 型轧机　block type mill with three roll stands, Y-model mini-mill, Kocks mill, Y-mill

Y 形槽口抗裂试验　Y-slit crack test

Y 形管　Y-pipe

Y 形管接头　wye

Y 形件　Y-piece

Y 形连接　【电】Y-connection

Y 形试块(测定机械性能用)　Y block

Y 形水准仪　Y-level, wye level

Y 形支管　Y-branch

Y 铸造合金(4Cu,2Ni,1.5Mg,余量 Al)　Y alloy

ZRE 镁锌锆合金(ZRE1:3—6Zn,0.5—0.8Zr,余量 Mg)　ZRE alloy

Z 电位　zeta-potential

Z 铝基轴承合金(93Al,6.5Ni,0.5Ti)　Z alloy

Z 为奇数的同位素　odd-Z isotope

Z 形的[件]　zigzag (ZZZ)

Z 形(断面)钢板桩[Z 形板桩]　Z-piling section, zee-type piling, zee-type sheet pile, Z-(type) piling bar

Z 形钢　Z-bar, zed(s), zee bar, zees, Z-iron

Z 形钢材[Z 形断面]　Z-section

Z 形钢轨　zee-rail

Z 形(钢)梁　Z-beam

Z 形钢柱　zed bar column

Z 形连接　Z-strand

Z 形线　back shunt

Z 形行程　Z-path

Z 形烟道　zigzag flue

Z 硬镍合金　(同"杜拉镍合金")

Z 轴方向　Z-direction

Z 珠光体可锻铸铁(0.3—0.8 化合碳,2—2.6 石墨碳,1Si,0.75—1.25Mn)　Z metal

Z 字形位错　zigzag dislocation

ac 管旋风收尘器　bank of several cyclone

tubes
g 因数　g(-)factor, gyromagnetic ratio
n-n 结　【半】n-n junction
n-p-n 结　【半】n-p-n junction
n-p-n 结结构　formation of n-p-n junction
n 倍退化[简并]　n-fold degenerate
n 重简并能级　n-fold degenerate (energy) level
n 次[阶]对称　【数】n-fold symmetry
n 次对称轴　n-fold axis of symmetry
n 方向(p-n 结的)　【半】n-side
n 列矩阵　【数】n-column matrix
n 型电导率　n-type conductivity
n 行矩阵　【数】n-row(ed) matrix
pH 计　acidimeter, acidometer, pH acidimeter　◇ 数字～digital pH-meter
pH 指示剂[器]　pH indicator
pH 值　pH value, potential of hydrogen (pH)
pH 值控制器　pH controller (pHC)
pH 值调节器　pH-regulator
p-n 结(半导体)　p-n junction
p-n 结结构　formation of p-n junction
p-n 结整流器　p-n junction rectifier
p-n 界面　p-n interface
p-p 结　【半】p-p junction
p 方向(p-n 结的)　p-side
p 型半导体　p-type semi-conductor
p 型电导率　p-type conductivity
p 型杂质　p-type impurity
skhl 低合金结构钢(原苏联牌号; 0.4—0.8Cr, 0.3—0.7Ni, 0.3—0.5Cu)　skhl steel
Ⅰ形接头　square joint
Ⅰ形坡口焊缝　square groove weld
Ⅲ-Ⅴ族化合物半导体　Group Ⅲ-Ⅴ compound semiconductor
Ω 螺纹　Omega thread
α+β 黄铜　duplex brass
α+β 混合相合金　mixed alpha and beta alloy
α-β 钛合金　alpha-beta titanium alloy

α-β(型)黄铜　alpha-beta brass (39-43Zn, 余量 Cu, 又称双相黄铜), hot stamping brass (58Cu, 40.5Zn, 1.5Pb, 又称热压印黄铜)　◇ 德尔托伊德～(60Cu, 40Zn) Deltoid
α 变态　alpha modification
α 放射性　alpha (radio) activity
α 幅射　(同"α射线")
α(钢轨)回跳硬度计　alpha durometer
α 铬基和钼基耐热合金　α alloy
α 固溶体　α-solid solution　◇ 均匀～*, 氧-～oxyferrite
α 硅钙铀矿　α-uranotile
α 硅铝明(10—30Si, 余为 Al)　Alpax alpha
α 化　alphatizing
α 化铬钢　chrome alphatized steel
α 黄铜　α(alpha) brass (38Zn, 余量 Cu; 又称单相黄铜), Tombac alloy [metal] (3—30Zn, 0—8Sn, 0—0.3As, 余量 Cu; 又称顿巴克黄铜)　◇ 西瓦含砷～*
α-甲基萘{$C_{11}H_{10}$}　α-methylnaphthalene
α 壳型法　【铸】alpha process
α 粒子[质点]　alpha particle
α 粒子电离真空计　alphatron gauge
α 硫酸铀矿{$6UO_3·SO_3·16H_2O$}　alpha-uranopilite
α 马氏体(淬火碳钢的)　α-martensite, alpha martensite
α'马氏体(钛合金的)　α' martensite
α'马氏体组织　alpha prime
α-萘胺{$C_{10}H_9N$}　α-naphthylamine
α-萘酚{$C_{10}H_8O$}　α-naphthol
α 青铜　α-bronze, alpha bronze
α-氰化萘{$C_{11}H_7N$}　1-cyanonaphthalene
α 蠕变　α-creep
α 射线　α-radiation, alpha radiation
α 射线发射[幅射]体　alpha radiator, alpha (ray) emitter
α 双重线　α-doublet
α 钛　alpha-titanium
α 铁　α-iron　◇ 由→向 γ 铁的加热转变

change from α-to γ-iron on heating
α 铁促成元素(Al, Mo, W, Si, V 等) alpha forming element
α 铁固溶体 【金】α-iron solid solution
α 铁基合金 alpha iron alloy
α 铁基体 【金】α-Fe matrix
α 铁素体 【金】alpha ferrite
α 蜕[衰]变 【理】α-decay, alpha decay, α-disintegration
α 锡 grey tin, tin pest
α 相 alpha phase, alpha constituent
α'相 alpha prime phase
α 相变 alpha transformation
α 相合金 alpha alloy
α 相结构 【金】alpha structure
α 相区 alpha (phase) field, alpha range, ◇扩大~ expan-ded alpha field
α(相)三氧化钨 alpha phase tungsten oxide, α-tungstic oxide
α 相稳定剂 alpha-stabilizer
α 相稳定元素 alpha-stabilizing element
α 相相界 alpha phase boundary
α 型 alpha form
α 型氧化铝{α-Al$_2$O$_3$} alpha-alumina, alpha-aluminium oxide
β-ZnS 型结构 wurtzite type structure
β 变态 【理】beta modification
β 方石英 beta cristobalite
β 放射性 beta activity [radioactivity]
β 硅钙铀矿{CaU$_2$O$_3$Si$_2$O$_8$·6H$_2$O} β-uranotile, beta uranophane
β 硅铝明合金(12.5Si, 0.4Mg, 0.5Mn, 余量 Al) beta silumin
β 合金 beta alloy ◇不含化合物的~ compound-free beta alloy
β 褐钇铌矿 fergusonite-beta
β 化 betatizing
β 黄铜(36—45Zn, 余量 Cu) β brass, beta brass
β 黄铜基体 【金】β-brass matrix
β-甲基萘{C$_{11}$H$_{10}$} β-methylnaphthaleno
β-甲基吡啶{C$_6$H$_5$N} β-methylpyridine

β 粒子[质点] beta particle(s)
β 硫酸铀矿{6UO$_3$·SO$_3$·10H$_2$O} beta uranopilite
β 马氏体 【金】β-martensite
β-萘酚{C$_{10}$H$_8$O} β-naphthol
β 蠕变 β-creep
β 三氧化钨 β-tungstic oxide, violet [blue] tungstic oxide
β 射线[辐射] beta ray [radiation]
β 射线测厚仪[厚度计] beta thickness gauge, β-gauge
β 射线测量计(测量厚度、密度等) beta ray gauge
β 射线辐射体 beta ray emitter
β 射线光谱学 beta (ray) spectroscopy
β 射线激发的 X-射线 beta ray excited X-rays
β 射线摄谱仪 beta (ray) spectrograph
β 铁 β-iron, beta iron [ferrite]
β 蜕[衰]变 【理】β-decay, beta decay, β-disintegration
β 位的 【化】beta
β 锡 beta tin
β 相 beta (phase, constituent)
β'相 【金】beta prime phase
β 相处理 beta treatment
β 相合金 beta phase alloy
β 相化 betatizing
β 相区 beta (phase) field, beta range
β 相三氧化钨 beta phase tungsten oxide
β 相钛合金 beta titanium alloy
β 相稳定元素 beta stabilizing element
β 斜硅钙铀矿{CaU$_2$O$_3$Si$_2$O$_8$·6H$_2$O} beta uranotile
β 型 beta form
β 型钛冷轧合金 beta titanium cold rolled alloy
β-乙基萘{C$_{12}$H$_{12}$} β-ethylnaphthalene
β 铀(铀的同素异形体) beta uranium
β 照射 beta irradiation
β 组织 beta structure ◇残余~
γ 变态 【金】gamma modification

γ 放射性   gamma activity
γ 辐射敏感度   gamma sensitivity
γ 辐射源   gamma (ray) emitter
γ 固溶体   γ-solid solution
γ 硅铝明合金(12.5Si,0.4Mg,0.5Mn,余量 Al)   gamma silumin
γ 黄铜(含 60—68Zn)   gamma brass
γ 回线   【金】gamma loop
γ-甲基吡啶{C_6H_7N}   γ-methylpyridine
γ 料位计   γ-ray level meter
γ 圈   【金】gamma loop
γ 三氧化钨   γ-tungstic oxide
γ 射线[辐射]   gamma rays [radiation]
γ 射线板坯探测器   gamma-ray slab detector ◇加热炉用～*
γ 射线测厚仪[厚度计]   gamma (thickness) gauge, γ-ray thickness gauge, gamma-ray thickness recorder
γ 射线测量计(测量厚度、密度等)   gamma-ray gauge
γ 射线辐射[发射]体   gamma (ray) emitter, photon emitter
γ 射线光谱学   gamma(-ray) spectroscopy
γ 射线盒   gamma-ray capsule
γ 射线活化分析   gamma activation analysis
γ 射线检测器   γ-ray detector
γ 射线检验   gamma-ray examination, gamma-ray test
γ 射线金属探测器   gamma-ray metal detector
γ 射线－量子   gamma(-ray) quantum
γ 射线料线测量仪   γ-ray stock gauge
γ 射线灵敏度   gamma sensitivity
γ 射线密度计   γ-ray density meter
γ 射线能谱测定法   gamma-ray spectrometry
γ 射线屏(蔽)[防护屏]   gamma shield
γ 射线强度   gamma intensity
γ 射线区   gamma ray region
γ 射线伤害   gamma-ray injury
γ 射线摄谱仪   gamma(-ray) spectrograph

γ 射线探伤   gamma-ray test
γ 射线液面计   γ-ray level meter
γ 射线引起的电离   gamma-induced ionization
γ 射线荧光检验   gamma-ray fluoroscopy
γ 射线源   gamma-ray source
γ 射线照片[照相]   gammagraph, gamma radiograph
γ 射线照相术[学]   gamma (ray) photography, γ-ray radiography, gammagraphy
γ 衰变   gamma decay
γ 铁   【金】γ-iron, gamma iron ◇ 氧－～固溶体 oxyaustenite
γ 铁基合金   gamma iron alloy
γ 相   gamma phase
γ'相   gamma prime phase
γ 相变   gamma transformation
γ 相合金   gamma phase alloy
γ 相结构   gamma structure
γ 相区   gamma (-phase) field, austenitic area, gamma loop [range] ◇ 闭合[封闭]～*, 开放[扩大]的～*, 收缩的～*, 狭窄～ narrowed gamma field
γ 相三氧化钨   gamma phase tungstic oxide
γ 相稳定元素   gamma-stabilizing element
γ 相相界   gamma phase boundary
γ 型   gamma form
γ 型氧化铝{$γ-Al_2O_3$}   gamma alumina, gamma aluminium oxide
γ 铀(铀的同素异形体)   gamma uranium
γ 照射   gamma irradiation
γ 值   point gamma
δ 变态   【理】delta modification
δ 黄铜(55—60Cu,少量 Ni、Mn、Pb,余量 Zn)   δ (delta) brass, delta metal
δ 黄铜合金系   delta alloys
δ 粒子   knock-on
δ 青铜(54—56Cu,1—3Mn,1—2Pb,余量 Zn)   δ-bronze, delta bronze
δ 区   【金】delta range
δ 射线   delta rays

δ 铁 delta ferrite [iron]	η'相 【金】eta prime phase
δ 相 【金】delta phase	λ 型转变[跃迁] 【理】λ-type transition, lambda type transition
δ'相 delta prime phase	
δ 相区 delta(-phase) field	μ 光介子 photomuon
δ 型 delta form	μ 合金(75Ni,20Fe,5Cu) Mumetal
ε'相 epsilon prime phase	μ 介原子 mu-mesic atom
ε 结构 epsilon structure	μ 介子 mu meson, muon
ε 马氏体(铁锰合金的) ε-martensite, epsilon martensite	μ 介子的 muonic
	μ 介子束 muon beam
ε 碳化物{Fe$_{24}$C} ε-carbide, epsilon carbide	π 光介子 photopion
	π 介原子 pi-mesic atom
ε 铁 ε-iron	π 介子 π-meson, pi-meson, pion
ε 组织 epsilon structure	π 介子束 pion beam
ζ 电位 zeta-potential	σ 相 【金】sigma phase
ζ 相 【金】zeta phase	χ 碳化铁 (同"黑格碳化铁")
η 相 【金】eta phase	χ 相 chi phase

附录一

计量单位表

中华人民共和国法定计量单位

中华人民共和国的法定计量单位(以下简称法定单位)包括:
(1)国际单位制的基本单位(见表1);
(2)国际单位制的辅助单位(见表2);
(3)国际单位制中具有专门名称的导出单位(见表3);
(4)国家选定的非国际单位制单位(见表4);
(5)由以上单位构成的组合形式的单位;
(6)由词头和以上单位所构成的十进倍数和分数单位(词头见表5)、法定单位的定义、使用方法等,见国家计量局另行规定。

表1 国际单位制的基本单位

量的名称	单位名称	英文名	单位符号
长 度	米	meter	m
质 量	千克[公斤]	kilogram	kg
时 间	秒	second	s
电 流	安(培)	ampere	A
热力学温度	开(尔文)	kelvin	K
物质的量	摩(尔)	molar	mol
发光强度	坎(德拉)	candela	cd

表2 国际单位制的辅助单位

量的名称	单位名称	英文名	单位符号
平面角	弧度	radian	rad
立体角	球面度	sphericity	sr

表3 国际单位制中具有专门名称的导出单位

量的名称	单位名称	英文名	单位符号	其他表示式例
频率	赫(兹)	hertz	Hz	s^{-1}
力,重力	牛(顿)	newton	N	$kg \cdot m/s^2$
压力,压强,应力	帕(斯卡)	pascal	Pa	N/m^2
能量,功,热	焦(耳)	joule	J	$N \cdot m$
功率,辐射通量	瓦(特)	watt	W	J/s
电荷量	库(伦)	coulomb	C	$A \cdot s$
电位,电压,电动势	伏(特)	volt	V	W/A
电容	法(拉)	farad	F	C/V

续表3

量的名称	单位名称	英文名	单位符号	其他表示式例
电阻	欧(姆)	ohm	Ω	V/A
电导	西(门子)	siemens	S	A/V
磁通量	韦(伯)	weber	Wb	V·s
磁通量密度,磁感应强度	特(斯拉)	tesla	T	Wb/m^2
电感	亨(利)	henry	H	Wb/A
摄氏温度	摄氏度	celsius	℃	
光通量	流(明)	lumen	lm	cd·sr
光照度	勒(克斯)	lux	lx	lm/m^2
放射性活度	贝可(勒尔)	becquerel	Bq	s^{-1}
吸收剂量	戈(瑞)	gray	Gy	J/kg
剂量当量	希(沃特)	sievert	Sv	J/kg

表4 国家的非国际单位制单位

量的名称	单位名称	英文名	单位符号	换算关系和说明
时间	分 (小)时 天[日]	minute hour day	min h d	1 min = 60 s 1 h = 60 min = 3600 s 1 d = 24 h = 86400 s
平面角	(角)秒 (角)分 度	radian	(″) (′) (°)	1″ = (π/648000) rad① 1′ = 60″ = (π/10800) rad 1° = 60′ = (π/180) rad
旋转速度	转每分	rotation per min	r/min	1 r/min = (1/60) s^{-1}
长度	海里	mile	n mile	1 n mile = 1852 m②
速度	节	knot	kn	1 kn = 1 n mile/h = (1852/3600) m/s
质量	吨 原子质量单位	ton	t u	1 t = 10^3 kg 1 u ≈ 1.6605655 × 10^{-27} kg
体积	升	liter	L [l]	1 L = 1 dm^3 = 10^{-3} m^3
能	电子伏	electron volt	eV	1 eV ≈ 1.6021892 × 10^{-19} J
级差	分贝	decibel	dB	
线密度	特(克斯)	tex	tex	1 tex = 1 g/km

注:①π为圆周率;②"海里"和"节"只用于航程。

表5 用于构成十进倍数和分数单位的词头和符号

数值	词头名称	符号	英文词头	数值	词头名称	符号	英文词头
10^{24}	尧(它)	Y		10^{-1}	分	d	deci
10^{21}	泽(它)	Z		10^{-2}	厘	c	centi
10^{18}	艾(可萨),兆兆兆	E	exa	10^{-3}	毫	m	milli
10^{15}	拍(它),千兆兆	P	peta	10^{-6}	微	μ	micro
10^{12}	太(拉),京兆,兆兆	T	tera	10^{-9}	纳(诺),毫微	n	nano
10^{9}	吉(咖),京,千兆	G	giga	10^{-12}	皮(可),沙,微微	p	pico
10^{6}	兆	M	mega	10^{-15}	飞(母托),尘,变微微	f	femto
10^{3}	千	k	kilo	10^{-18}	阿(托),渺,微微微	a	atto
10^{2}	百	h	hecto	10^{-21}	仄(普托)	z	
10^{1}	十	da	deca	10^{-24}	幺(科托)	y	

注:1.周、月、年(年的符号为a),为一般常用时间单位。2.( )内的字,是在不致混淆的情况下,可以省略的字。3.[ ]内的字为前者的同义语。4.角度单位分秒的符号不处于数字后时,用括弧。5.升的符号中,小写字母l为备用符号。6.r为"转"的符号。7.人民生活和贸易中,质量习惯称为重量。8.公里为千米的俗称,符号为km。9. 10^4 称为万, 10^8 称为亿, 10^{12} 称为万亿,这类词的使用不受词头名称的影响,但不应与词头混淆。

表6 应淘汰的常用计量单位与法定单位对照及换算表

量的名称	应淘汰的常用计量单位 名称	符号	法定计量单位 名称	英文名	符号	换算关系
长度	公尺	M	米	meter	m	1 M = 1 m
	公寸		分米	decimeter	dm	1 公寸 = 1 dm
	公分		厘米	centimeter	cm	1 公分 = 1 cm
	公厘	m/m,MM,M/M	毫米	millimeter	mm	1 公厘 = 1 mm
	公丝					1 公丝 = 0.1 mm
	公微	μ, mμ, μM	微米	micron	μm	1 公微 = 1 μm
	米厘		厘米	centimeter	cm	1 米厘 = 1 cm
	丝米	dmm				1 dmm = 0.1 mm
	忽米	cmm				1 cmm = 0.01 mm
	毫微米	mμm	纳米	nanon	nm	1 mμm = 1 nm
		KM,KMS	千米[公里]	kilometer	km	1 KM = 1 km
	费密					1 费密 = 10^{-15} m
	埃	Å				1 Å = 10^{-10} m
	英尺	ft				1 ft = 0.3048 m
	英寸	in				1 in = 25.4 mm
	码	yd				1 yd = 0.9144 m

续表 6

量的名称	应淘汰的常用计量单位 名称	应淘汰的常用计量单位 符号	法定计量单位 名称	法定计量单位 英文名	法定计量单位 符号	换算关系
面积	平方 公亩 公顷 平方码 平方英尺 平方英寸 靶恩	M^2 a ha yd^2 ft^2 in^2 b	平方米	squaremeter	m^2	$1 M^2 = 1 m^2$ $1 a = 100 m^2$ $1 ha = 10^4 m^2$ $1 yd^2 = 0.836127 m^2$ $1 ft^2 = 0.092903 m^2$ $1 in^2 = 6.4516 m^2$ $1 b = 10^{-28} m^2$
体积、容积	公升,立升 立方 立方码 立方英尺 立方英寸 美加仑 英加仑	 c.c.,cc yd^3 ft^3 in^3 USgal UKgal	升 立方米 毫升	liter cubic meter milliliter	L[1] m^3 mL[ml]	$1 公[立]升 = 1 L$ $1 立方米 = 1 m^3$ $1 cc = 1 ml[ml]$ $1 yd^3 = 0.7646 m^3$ $1 ft^3 = 28.32 L$ $1 in^3 = 16.39 cm^3$ $1 USgal = 3.785 L$ $1 UKgal = 4.546 L$
时间		y,yr hr (′) (″),S,sec	年 (小)时 分 秒	year hour minute second	a h min s	
频率	周 千周 兆周	C KC,kc MC	赫兹 千赫 兆赫	hertz kilohertz megahertz	Hz kHz Mhz	$1 C = 1 Hz$ $1 KC = 1 kHz$ $1 MC = 1 MHz$
旋转速度		r.p.m.,rpm	转每分	rotation per minute	r/min	$1 rpm = 1 r/min$
加速度	米每秒平方		米每二次方秒	meter per sqm.	m/s^2	$1 米每秒平方 = 1 m/s^2$
质量	公吨 磅 英吨(长吨) 美吨(短吨) 盎司(常衡) 盎司(金、药衡) 米制克拉 格令	T KG,KGS,Kg lb ton sh ton oz oz CM gr gn	吨 千克 [公斤] k	ton kilogram	t kg	$1 T = 1 t$ $1 KG = 1 kg$ $1 lb = 453.592 g$ $1 ton = 1016 kg$ $1 sh ton = 907 kg$ $1 oz(常衡) = 28.3495 g$ $1 oz(金、药衡) = 31.1035 g$ $1 CM = 200 mg$ $1 gr = 64.7989 mg$

续表 6

量的名称	应淘汰的常用计量单位 名称	符号	法定计量单位 名称	英文名	符号	换算关系
温度	开氏度	°K	开(尔文)	kelvin	K	
	绝对度	°K	开(尔文)	kelvin	K	
	度	deg	摄氏度	degree	℃,K	
			开(尔文)	kelvin		
	华氏度	°F				1 °F = 0.555556 K
	列氏度	°R				1 °R = 1.25 ℃
力、重力	千克,公斤	kg	牛(顿)	newton	N	
	千克力,公斤力	kgf				1 kgf = 9.80665 N
	达因	dyn				1 dyn = 10^{-5} N
	磅力	lbf				1 lbf = 4.44822 N
压力、压强、应力	巴	bar,b	帕(斯卡)	pascal	Pa	1 bar = 0.1 MPa
	托	Torr				1 Torr = 133.322 Pa
	标准大气压	atm				1 atm = 101.325 Pa
	工程大气压	at,kgf/cm²				1 at = 98.0665 Pa
	毫米水柱	mmH$_2$O				1 mmH$_2$O = 9.80665 Pa
	毫米汞柱	mmHg				1 mmHg = 133.322 Pa
	磅力每平方英寸	psi,PSI				1 psi = 6.8947 kPa
	千克力每平方米	kgf/m²				1 kgf/m² = 9.80665 Pa
动力粘度	泊	P	帕(斯卡)秒	pascal per sec.	Pa·s	1 P = 0.1 Pa·s
	厘泊	cP			Pa·s	1 cP = 0.001 Pa·s
运动粘度	斯托克斯	St	二次方米每秒	square meter per sec.	m²/s	1 St = 10^{-4} m²/s
	厘斯	cSt				1 cSt = 10^{-6} m²/s
功、能、热	尔格	erg	焦(耳)	joule	J	1 erg = 10^{-7} J
	(国际蒸汽表)卡	cal				1 cal = 4.1868 J
	大卡	kcal				1 kcal = 4.1868 kJ
	千克力米	kgf·m	千瓦时	kilowatt per hour	kWh,J	1 kgf·m = 9.80665 J
	度(电)		焦(耳)			1 度 = 1 kWh = 3.6 mJ
功率	千克力米每分	kgf·m/min	瓦(特)	watt	w	1 kgf·m/min = 0.163444 W
	米制马力	ch,cv,ps				1 ch = 735.499 W
	英制马力	HP,hp				1 HP = 745.7 W
	伏安	VA				1 VA = 1 W
	乏	var				1 var = 1 W
电流		a,amp	安(培)	ampere	A	1 amp = 1 A

续表6

量的名称	应淘汰的常用计量单位 名称	应淘汰的常用计量单位 符号	法定计量单位 名称	法定计量单位 英文名	法定计量单位 符号	换算关系
电荷(量)			库(仑)	coulomb	C	
电位(电势)			伏(特)	volt	V	
电容	微微法	$\mu\mu F$	法(拉)	farad	F	$1\ \mu\mu F = 1\ pF$(皮法)
电阻			欧(姆)	ohm	Ω	
电导			西(门子)	siemens	S	
磁通量	麦克斯韦	Mx	韦(伯)	weber	Wb	$1\ Mx = 10^{-8}\ Wb$
磁感应强度	高斯	Gs	特(斯拉)	tesla	T	$1\ Gs = 10^{-4}\ T$
磁场强度	奥斯特 安匝每米	Oe	安培每米	ampere per meter	A/m	$10\ e = 79.5775\ A/m$ 1 安匝每米 = 1 A/m
磁通势	吉伯	Gb	安(培)	ampere	A	$1\ Gb = 0.795775\ A$
物质的量	克原子,克分子 克当量,克式量		摩(尔)	molar	mol	
发光强度	国际烛光	IK	坎(德拉)	candela	cd	$1\ IK = 1.019\ cd$
光照度	辐透	ph	勒(克斯)	lux	lx	$1\ ph = 10^4\ lx$
光亮度	尼特	nt	坎德拉每平方米	candela per square meter	cd/m²	$1\ nt = 1\ cd/m^2$
	熙提	sb				$1\ sb = 10^4\ cd/m^2$
放射性活度	居里	Ci	贝可(勒尔)	becquerel	Bq	$1\ Ci = 3.7 \times 10^{10}\ Bq$
吸收剂量	拉德	rad	戈(瑞)		Gy	$1\ rad = 10^{-2}\ Gy$
剂量当量	雷姆	rem	希(沃持)		Sv	$1\ rem = 10^{-2}\ Sv$
照射量	伦琴	R	库仑每千克	coulomb per kilogram	C/kd	$1\ R = 2.58 \times 10^{-4}\ C/kg$

附录二

化学元素表

原子序数	中文名（拼音）	元素符号	英文名	原子序数	中文名（拼音）	元素符号	英文名
1	氢(qing)	H	hydrogen	28	镍(nie)	Ni	nickel
2	氦(hai)	He	helium	29	铜(tong)	Cu	copper
3	锂(li)	Li	lithium	30	锌(xin)	Zn	zinc
4	铍(pi)	Be (Gl)	beryllium (glucinium)	31	镓(jia)	Ga	gallium
				32	锗(zhe)	Ge	germanium
5	硼(peng)	B	boron	33	砷(shen)	As	arsenic
6	碳(tan)	C	carbon	34	硒(xi)	Se	selenium
7	氮(dan)	N	nitrogen	35	溴(xiu)	Br	bromine
8	氧(yang)	O	oxygen	36	氪(ke)	Kr	krypton
9	氟(fu)	F	fluorine	37	铷(ru)	Rb	rubidium
10	氖(nai)	Ne	neon	38	锶(si)	Sr	strontium
11	钠(na)	Na	soldium	39	钇(yi)	Y(Yt)	yttrium
12	镁(mei)	Mg	magnesium	40	锆(gao)	Zr	zirconium
13	铝(lu)	Al	aluminium	41	铌(ni) (钶)(ke)	Nb	niobium (columbium)
14	硅(gui)	Si	silicon				
15	磷(lin)	P	phosphorus	42	钼(mu)	Mo	molybdenum
16	硫(liu)	S	sulphur	43	锝(de) (钨)(ma)	Tc (Ma)	technetium (masurium)
17	氯(lu)	Cl	chlorine				
18	氩(ya)	Ar(A)	argon	44	钌(liao)	Ru	ruthenium
19	钾(jia)	K	potassium	45	铑(lao)	Rh	rhodium
20	钙(gai)	Ca	calcium	46	钯(ba)	Pd	palladium
21	钪(kang)	Sc	scandium	47	银(yin)	Ag	silver
22	钛(tai)	Ti	titanium	48	镉(ge)	Cd	cadmium
23	钒(fan)	V	vanadium	49	铟(yin)	In	indium
24	铬(ge)	Cr	chromium	50	锡(xi)	Sn	tin
25	锰(meng)	Mn	manganese	51	锑(ti)	Sb	antimony
26	铁(tie)	Fe	iron	52	碲(di)	Te	tellurium
27	钴(gu)	Co	cobalt	53	碘(dian)	I(J)	iodine

续表

原子序数	中文名(拼音)	元素符号	英文名	原子序数	中文名(拼音)	元素符号	英文名
54	氙(xian)	Xe	xenon	82	铅(qian)	Pb	lead
55	铯(se)	Cs	caesium (cesium)	83	铋(bi)	Bi	bismuth
				84	钋(po)	Po	polonium
56	钡(bei)	Ba	barium	85	砹(ai)	At	astatine
57	镧(lan)	La	lanthanum	86	氡(dong)	Rn	randon
58	铈(shi)	Ce	cerium			(Nt)	(niton)
59	镨(pu)	Pr	praseodymium	87	钫(fang)	Fr	francium
60	钕(nu)	Nd	neodymium	88	镭(lei)	Ra	radium
61	钷(po)	Pm	promethium	89	锕(a)	Ac	actinium
	(铱)(yi)	Il	(illinium)	90	钍(tu)	Th	thorium
62	钐(shan)	Sm	samarium	91	镤(pu)	Pa	protactinium (protoactinium)
63	铕(you)	Eu	europium				
64	钆(ga)	Gd	gadolinium	92	铀(you)	U	uranium
65	铽(te)	Tb	terbium	93	镎(na)	Np	neptunium
66	镝(di)	Dy	dysprosium	94	钚(bu)	Pu	plutonium
67	钬(huo)	Ho	holmium	95	镅(mei)	Am	americium
68	铒(er)	Er	erbium	96	锔(ju)	Cm	curium
69	铥(diu)	Tm, Tu	thulium	97	锫(pei)	Bk	berkelium
70	镱(yi)	Yb	ytterbium	98	锎(kai)	Cf	californium
71	镥(lu)	Lu	lutecium	99	锿(ai)	Es	einsteinium
	(镏)(liu)	(Cp)	(Cassiopeium)		(钚)(ya)	An	(athenium)
72	铪(ha)	Hf	hafnium	100	镄(fei)	Fm	fermium
		(Ct)	(celtium)		(钲)(zheng)	(Ct)	(centurium)
73	钽(tan)	Ta	tantalum	101	钔(men)	Md	mendelevium
74	钨(wu)	W	tungsten (wolfram)	102	锘(nuo)	No	nobelium
				103	铹(lao)	Lw	lawrencium
75	铼(lai)	Re	rhenium	104	𬭊(lu)	Rf	rutherfordium (kurchatovium)
76	锇(e)	Os	osmium				
77	铱(yi)	Ir	iridium	105	𨱏(han)	Ha	hahnium
78	铂(bo)	Pt	platinum	106	𨧀(du)	Db	dubnium
79	金(jin)	Au	gold	107	𬭳(xi)	Sg	scaborgium
80	汞(gong)	Hg	mercury	108	𬭛(bo)	Bh	bohrium
81	铊(ta)	Tl	thallium	109	𬭶(hei)	Hs	hassium
				110	鿏(mai)	Mt	meltnerium

图书在版编目(CIP)数据

汉英冶金工业词典／明举新主编．—长沙：中南
大学出版社，2000
ISBN 7-81061-293-X

Ⅰ.汉… Ⅱ.明… Ⅲ.冶金工业—词典—汉、英
Ⅳ.TF-61

中国版本图书馆 CIP 数据核字（2000）第 75565 号

汉英冶金工业词典

明举新　主编

《汉英冶金工业词典》编审委员会　审定

□责任编辑	刘石年　习传仁
□出版发行	中南大学出版社
	社址：长沙市麓山南路　邮编：410083
	发行科电话：0731-8876770　传真：0731-8829482
	电子邮件：csucbs@public.cs.hn.cn
□经　　销	新华书店总店北京发行所
□印　　装	望城湘江印刷厂

□开本	787×1092 1/32 开	□印张 60.25	□字数 3137 千字
□版次	2001 年 2 月第 1 版	□2001 年 2 月第 1 次印刷	
□印数	0001-2000		
□书号	ISBN 7-81061-293-X/TF·011		
□定价	128.00 元		

图书出现印装问题，请与经销商调换

图书在版编目(CIP)数据

汉英冶金工业词典 / 阎承纶主编. —长沙：中南
大学出版社，2000.
ISBN 7-81061-293-X

Ⅰ.汉… Ⅱ.阎… Ⅲ.冶金工业—词典—汉、英
Ⅳ.TF-61

中国版本图书馆 CIP 数据核字 (2000) 第 75565 号

汉英冶金工业词典

阎承纶　主编
《汉英冶金工业词典》编审委员会　审定

□责任编辑　刘志本　方伟忠
□出版发行　中南大学出版社
　社址：长沙市麓山南路　邮编：410083
　发行部电话：0731-8870970　传真：0731-8829482
　电子邮件：caoeba@public.cs.hn.cn
□经　　销　新华书店总店北京发行所
□印　　刷　冕宁县泸沽印刷厂

□开本　787×1092 1/32 千　□印张 60.25　□字数 3137 千字
□版次　2001 年 2 月第 1 版　□2001 年 2 月第 1 次印刷
□印数　0001-2000
□书号　ISBN7-81061-293-X/TF-011
□定价　128.00 元

图书出现印装问题，请与经销部调换